THE OXFORD HA

COMPARATIVE CONSTITUTIONAL LAW

Contents

PART II IDEAS

PART III PROCESS

PART IV ARCHITECTURE

PART V MEANINGS/TEXTURES

PART VI INSTITUTIONS

PART VII RIGHTS

PART VIII OVERLAPPING RIGHTS

PART IX TRENDS

Notes on the Contributors

General Editors

Michel Rosenfeld is Justice Sydney L. Robins Professor of Human Rights and Director, Program on Global and Comparative Constitutional Theory, Benjamin N. Cardozo School of Law

András Sajó is Judge, European Court of Human Rights, Strasbourg and University Professor (on leave), Central European University, Budapest

Contributors

Robert Alexy is Professor of Public Law and Legal Philosophy, Christian Albrechts University, Kiel

Susanne Baer is Justice of the Federal Constitutional Court (Germany), Professor of Public Law and Gender Studies, Humboldt University Berlin and James W. Cook Global Law Professor, University of Michigan Law School

Aharon Barak is Professor of Law, Radzyner School of Law, Interdisciplinary Center (IDC), Herzliya, Israel

Eric Barendt is Emeritus Professor of Media Law, University College London

Sergio Bartole is Emeritus Professor of Constitutional Law, University of Trieste

Olivier Beaud is Professor of Public Law, University Panthéon-Assas (Paris II) and Director, Institut Michel Villey

Armin von Bogdandy is Director, Max Planck Institute for Comparative Public Law and International Law

Anthony W. Bradley is Emeritus Professor of Constitutional Law, Edinburgh University and Research Fellow, Institute of European and Comparative Law, Oxford University

Manuel José Cepeda Espinosa is Former President of the Colombian Constitutional Court and Director, Program on Public Policies, Constitutional Rights and Regulations, Universidad de los Andes, Law School, Bogotá

Wen-Chen Chang is Associate Professor, College of Law, National Taiwan University

Sujit Choudhry is Cecelia Goetz Professor of Law, New York University School of Law

D.M. Davis is Judge President, Competition Appeal Court of South Africa and Honorary Professor of Law, University of Cape Town

Erika de Wet is Co-Director, Institute for International and Comparative Law in Africa and Professor of International Law, University of Pretoria and Professor of International Constitutional Law, University of Amsterdam

David Dyzenhaus is Professor of Law and Philosophy, University of Toronto

K.D. Ewing is Professor of Public Law, King's College, London

Héctor Fix-Fierro is Senior Researcher, Instituto de Investigaciones Jurídicas, Universidad Nacional Autónoma de México (UNAM)

Günter Frankenberg is Professor of Public Law, Philosophy of Law and Comparative Law, Goethe-Universität Frankfurt

Stephen Gardbaum is MacArthur Foundation Professor of International Justice and Human Rights, UCLA School of Law

Roberto Gargarella is Professor of Constitutional Theory, CONICET/CMI, Argentina

Jeffrey Goldsworthy is Professor of Law, Monash University, Melbourne

Dieter Grimm is Professor of Law, Humboldt University Berlin and Yale Law School and Former Justice, Federal Constitutional Court of Germany

Daniel Halberstam is Eric Stein Collegiate Professor of Law, University of Michigan Law School

Gábor Halmai is Professor of Law and Director, Institute for Political and International Studies, ELTE Faculty of Social Sciences, Budapest

Yasuo Hasebe is Professor of Constitutional Law, University of Tokyo, School of Law

Gedion T. Hessebon is S.J.D. Candidate, Central European University, Legal Studies Department and Assistant Lecturer, Addis Ababa University, School of Law

Stephen Holmes is Walter E. Meyer Professor of Law, New York University School of Law

Vicki C. Jackson is Thurgood Marshall Professor of Constitutional Law, Harvard Law School, and formerly was Carmack Waterhouse Professor of Constitutional Law, Georgetown University Law Center

Gary Jeffrey Jacobsohn is H. Malcolm MacDonald Professor of Constitutional and Comparative Law, Department of Government, University of Texas at Austin

Martin Kaspar is Chief of Staff, City of Schwäbisch Hall, Germany

Michael Kavey is Associate-in-Law, Columbia Law School

János Kis is Professor of Political Science and Philosophy at Central European University, Budapest

Claude Klein is Professor Emeritus of Law, Hebrew University

Juliane Kokott is Advocate General, Court of Justice of the European Union

Hoi Kong is Assistant Professor, Faculty of Law, McGill University

Martin Krygier is Gordon Samuels Professor of Law, University of New South Wales and Adjunct Professor, Regulatory Institutions Network (RegNet), Australian National University

Roderick Alexander Macdonald is F.R. Scott Professor of Constitutional and Public Law, Faculty of Law, McGill University

Catharine A. MacKinnon is Elizabeth A. Long Professor of Law, University of Michigan, James Barr Ames Visiting Professor of Law (long term), Harvard Law School and Special Gender Adviser to the Prosecutor, International Criminal Court (The Hague)

Matthias Mahlmann is Professor of Law, Chair of Legal Theory, Legal Sociology and International Public Law, University of Zurich, Faculty of Law

Chibli Mallat is Presidential Professor and Professor of Middle Eastern Law and Politics at the University of Utah and EU Jean Monnet Professor of European Law at Saint Joseph's University, Beirut

Susanna Mancini is Professor of Law, Law School, University of Bologna and Adjunct Professor of Law, SAIS Johns Hopkins University BC

Jenny S. Martinez is Professor of Law and Justin M. Roach, Jr, Faculty Scholar, Stanford Law School

Juan E. Méndez is Visiting Professor, Washington College of Law and UN Special Rapporteur on Torture and Other Cruel, Inhuman or Degrading Treatment or Punishment

Frank I. Michelman is Robert Walmsley University Professor, Harvard University

Laurence Morel is Professor of Political Science, Université Lille 2 (CERAPS)

Jan-Werner Müller is Professor, Politics Department, Princeton University

Vlad Perju is Associate Professor, Boston College Law School

Richard H. Pildes is Sudler Family Professor of Constitutional Law, New York University School of Law

Cesare Pinelli is Professor of Constitutional Law, Università 'Sapienza', Rome

Ulrich K. Preuß is Professor Emeritus of Law and Politics, Freie Universität Berlin, and Hertie School of Governance, Berlin

Susan Rose-Ackerman is Henry R. Luce Professor of Jurisprudence (Law and Political Science), Yale University

Daniel Sabbagh is Senior Research Fellow at Sciences Po, Centre d'études et de recherches internationales (CERI)

Pedro Salazar-Ugarte is Senior Researcher, Instituto de Investigaciones Jurídicas, Universidad Nacional Autónoma de México (UNAM)

Judit Sándor is Professor, Faculty of Political Science, Legal Studies and Gender Studies, Central European University (CEU), Budapest and Founding Director of the Center for Ethics and Law in Biomedicine (CELAB)

Bernhard Schlink is Professor Emeritus of Public Law and Legal Philosophy, Humboldt University Berlin and Former Justice of the Constitutional Court of the State of Northrhine-Westfalia

Ayelet Shachar is Canada Research Chair in Citizenship and Multiculturalism, Professor of Law, Political Science, and Global Affairs, University of Toronto Faculty of Law

Reva B. Siegel is Nicholas deB. Katzenbach Professor of Law, Yale University

Cindy Skach is Professor of Comparative Government and Law, University of Oxford

Daniel Smilov is Associate Professor at the University of Sofia, Bulgaria and Programme Director of the Centre for Liberal Strategies, Sofia

Dean Spielmann is Judge of the European Court of Human Rights, Strasbourg

Alec Stone Sweet is Leitner Professor of Law, Politics, and International Studies, Yale Law School and Department of Political Science, Yale University

Li-ann Thio is Professor of Law, Faculty of Law, National University of Singapore

Arun Thiruvengadam is Assistant Professor, Faculty of Law, National University of Singapore and Visiting Fellow, the West Bengal National University of Juridical Sciences, Kolkata, India

Michel Troper is Professor Emeritus, University of Paris Ouest-Nanterre

Mark Tushnet is William Nelson Cromwell Professor of Law, Harvard Law School

Renáta Uitz is Professor and Chair of the Comparative Constitutional Law Program, Central European University, Legal Studies Department, Budapest

Richard Vogler is Senior Lecturer in Law, Sussex Law School

Neil Walker is Regius Professor of Public Law and the Law of Nature and Nations, University of Edinburgh

Jiunn-Rong Yeh is Distinguished Professor, College of Law, National Taiwan University

Kenji Yoshino is Chief Justice Earl Warren Professor of Constitutional Law, New York University School of Law

Peer Zumbansen is Professor of Law, Osgoode Hall Law School, York University

List of Abbreviations

ABA	American Bar Association
APA	Administrative Procedure Act (United States)
APP	anti-paternalistic principle
ASEAN	Association of Southeast Asian Nations
BVerfG	Bundesverfassungsgericht
BVerfGE	Bundesverfassungsgerichtsentscheidung
BVP	Bayerische Volkspartei (Germany)
CC	constitutional court
CCM	crime control model
CCP	Chinese Communist Party
CEDAW	Convention on the Elimination of All Forms of Discrimination against Women
CEELI	Central and Eastern European Law Initiative
CFI	Court of First Instance
CLS	Critical Legal Studies
CPSU	Communist Party of the Soviet Union
DDP	Deutsche Demokratische Partei (Germany)
DDR	demobilization, disarmament, and reintegration
DKP	Deutsche Kommunistische Partei (Germany)
DNVP	Deutschnational Volkspartei (Germany)
DPM	due process model
DVP	Deutsche Volkspartei (Germany)
ECHR	European Convention on Human Rights
ECJ	European Court of Justice
ECtHR	European Court of Human Rights
EPRDF	Ethiopian People's Revolutionary Democratic Front
EU	European Union
FCC	Federal Constitutional Court (Germany)
FSU	Finnish Seamen's Union
GATT	General Agreement on Tariffs and Trade
hESC	human embryonic stem cell
HDR	Human Development Report

HPAT	Homosexual Policy Assessment Team (United Kingdom)
HRA	Human Rights Act 1998 (United Kingdom)
HRC	Human Rights Council
IACHR	Inter-American Convention on Human Rights
ICA	initiative constitutional amendment (United States)
ICC	International Criminal Court
ICCPR	International Covenant on Civil and Political Rights
ICESCR	International Covenant on Economic, Social and Cultural Rights
ICITAP	International Criminal Investigative Training Assistance Program
ICJ	International Court of Justice
IDEA	Institute for Democracy and Electoral Assistance
ILC	International Law Commission
ILEA	International Law Enforcement Academies
ILO	International Labour Organization
ISAF	International Security Assistance Force
ITF	International Transport Workers' Federation
IVF	*in vitro* fertilization
KPD	Kommunistische Partei Deutschlands (Germany)
LGB	lesbian, gay, and bisexual
LLP	liberal legitimacy principle
MMP	mixed-member proportional
MP	Member of Parliament
NATO	North Atlantic Treaty Organization
NBAC	National Bioethics Advisory Commission (United States)
NCMP	Non-Constituency Member of Parliament (Singapore)
NIE	new institutional economics
NGO	non-governmental organization
NMP	Nominated Member of Parliament (Singapore)
NPD	National Democratic Party (Germany)
NSDAP	Nationalsozialistische Deutsche Arbeiterpartei (Germany)
OBC	Other Backward Class (India)
ODIHR	Office for Democratic Institutions and Human Rights
OIC	Organization of Islamic Conference
OIRA	Office of Information and Regulatory Affairs (United States)
OLC	Office of Legal Counsel (United States)
OPDAT	Office of Overseas Prosecutorial Development, Assistance and Training
OSCE	Organization for Security and Co-operation in Europe
PAP	People's Action Party (Singapore)

PIL	public interest litigation
PL	John Rawls, *Political Liberalism*
PR	proportional representation
PSN	principle of state neutrality
SACC	South African Constitutional Court
SC	Scheduled Caste (India)
SCC	Supreme Court of Canada
SDF	Self-Defence Forces (Japan)
SIAC	Special Immigration Appeals Commission (United Kingdom)
SPD	Sozialdemokratische Partei Deutschlands (Germany)
SRP	Socialist Reich Party (Germany)
ST	Scheduled Tribe (India)
TEU	Treaty on European Union
TFEU	Treaty on the Functioning of the European Union
TJ	John Rawls, *A Theory of Justice*
TRC	Truth and Reconciliation Commission
UDHR	Universal Declaration of Human Rights
UN	United Nations
UNGA	United Nations General Assembly
UNSC	United Nations Security Council
USPD	Unabhängige Sozialdemokratische Partei Deutschlands (Germany)
VCLT	Vienna Convention on the Law of Treaties
WTO	World Trade Organization

INTRODUCTION

MICHEL ROSENFELD AND
ANDRÁS SAJÓ

THE purpose of the present volume is to provide an overview of the current status of comparative constitutional law as a discipline and an accounting of fundamental constitutional developments, concepts, and debates as they emerge through the lenses of the said discipline. The field of comparative constitutional law has grown immensely over the past couple of decades. Once a minor and obscure adjunct to the field of domestic constitutional law, comparative constitutional law has now moved front and center. The prominence and visibility of the field, both among judges and scholars has grown exponentially, particularly in the last decade. Even in the United States, where domestic constitutional exceptionalism has traditionally held a firm grip, use of comparative constitutional materials has become the subject of a lively and much publicized controversy among various justices of the US Supreme Court.[1]

The rapid growth and expansion of the field was propelled by the transitions to constitutional democracy in Eastern and Central Europe after the fall of the Berlin Wall in 1989, followed by the making of many constitutions in the 1990s, including in South Africa and in many South American countries. Many of these new constitutions have 'imported' constitutional norms from abroad—the South African Constitution explicitly mandates that the country's Constitutional Court consider foreign law when interpreting the domestic Bill of Rights—and many of the considered foreign constitutions have explicitly refrained from incorporating some of the latter's provisions into their new constitution.[2]

Another important factor in the growth of comparative constitutional law is the 'internationalization' of constitutional law through implementation of the provisions of international

[1] See Rosenfeld, Chapter 1B. [2] See Halmai, Chapter 64.

covenants such as the European Convention on Human Rights. Though such covenants are not formally or technically constitutions, their provisions—particularly as interpreted by courts such as the European Court of Human Rights—are the functional equivalent of constitutional norms. Moreover, a veritable dialogue among judges has emerged as a consequence of this process of internationalization. Thus, for example, judges on the European Court of Human Rights often consider the national constitutional jurisprudence in the relevant field—for example, free speech—of states that are party to the Convention. Conversely, constitutional judges in the latter states frequently consult decisions of the European Court both for purposes of conforming the respective jurisprudences where feasible and of taking into account valuable judicial insight on the issue at hand.[3]

On the other hand, comparative constitutional law is a subfield of comparative law (and it rates a mere 35-page entry in the 1,400-page *Oxford Handbook of Comparative Law*). Comparative constitutional law, however, is in several respects a standout subfield that seems more subject to contest and controversy, both on methodological and ideological grounds, than other subfields. Traditionally, comparison in private law has been regarded as less problematic than in public law. Thus, whereas it seems fair to assume that there ought to be great convergence among industrialized democracies over the uses and functions of commercial contracts, that seems far from the case in constitutional law. Can a parliamentary democracy be compared to a presidential one? Or, a federal republic to a unitary one? Moreover, what about differences in ideology or national identity? Can constitutional rights deployed in a libertarian context be profitably compared to those at work in a social welfare context? Is it perilous to compare minority rights in a multi-ethnic state to those in its ethnically homogeneous counterparts?

These controversies add an important dimension to the field of comparative constitutional law and they contribute to carving out a distinct domain of inquiry that displays many links to constitutional law, public law in general, and comparative law while remaining distinct from the latter in several significant respects. Furthermore, the subject matter coming within the sweep of comparative constitutionalism has been analyzed from the various perspectives of many different disciplines beyond law, including political science, political theory, and philosophy. Representatives from all these disciplines are among the contributors to the present *Handbook* and they complement, supplement, and enrich the insights emanating from within the discipline of law.

In order to place the contributions to this volume in their proper context, this Introduction proceeds as follows. Section I provides a brief overview of the history of comparative constitutional law. Section II focuses on the uses and purposes of, and the challenges confronting, comparative constitutional law. Section III addresses preliminarily the key issue of transplantation of institutions and norms from one constitutional system to the next. Section IV discusses in summary fashion some of the most salient methodological issues that have an important bearing on work in comparative constitutional law. And, finally, Section V accounts for the structure and organization of the *Handbook* and briefly situates each of its nine parts in the context of the project as a whole.

I. The History of Comparative Constitutional Law

The jacket design of this *Handbook* reproduces 'The Ideal City', a renaissance painting attributed to Piero della Francesca. It represents a harmonious public space, perhaps with reference to Plato's plan of the lost Atlantis. It is a Utopia: no citizens, no mess. In contrast, in a competing

[3] See Spielmann, Chapter 59.

representation of the Ideal City, Fra Carnevale combined idealized Roman and Florentine buildings, again with balanced harmony, but featuring humans populating the space. It is considered an allegory of good government through planning. The ruler takes care of his subjects, and safeguards the composite elements of public order: religion, security, and recreation.

The plan of the city is its constitution. Physical structure and the structure of rules combine under a single master plan, appropriate for the community living together in the public space carved out pursuant to the governing plan. In fact, in Ancient Greece, when a new colony was established, the urban plan went hand in hand with the constitution: both followed the master plan of the mother-city (the metropolis). The physical and political plans of the city were intended to correspond to some (divine) truth or ideal harmony. The plan of the ideal city mirrors that of the ideal metropolis. Cities are not exactly alike, but all conform to a recognizable type. Do not constitutions similarly attempt to emulate the ideal constitution of the ideal metropolis of their time? Cannot comparative constitutionalism be enlisted in the quest to live up to an elusive *measure or standard*?

The conception of an ideal government can be useful for purposes of comparison with actual governments. Plato's ideal, however, was so unachievable that it did not invite comparison to contemporaneous actual Greek states. Aristotle, on the other hand, was concerned with actual government, and thus meticulously compared abstract forms of government with actual, *Real-existierende* states in order to find out how best to approximate the relevant ideals. At its beginnings, the science of government concentrated on thorough and exacting comparison: it is quite likely that Aristotle undertook to compile a collection of the constitutions of 158 Greek city states for such reason (albeit that only his analysis of the Athenian Constitution survives). Significantly, it was on the basis of this comparative material that Aristotle developed his theory of government in his *Politics*.

Notwithstanding the collapse of government and the vanishing of the corresponding political science in antiquity, and notwithstanding the subsequent prevalence of religion and custom in matters of government, the comparative tradition did reemerge with the advent of modern political thought. Notably, Machiavelli's precepts were based on observations grounded in contemporary and historical practices of government. Whereas normative considerations and even extended use of biblical interpretation were common in the formation of modern constitutionalism,[4] the political science of the modern era would be unthinkable without continued reference to a rich anecdotal tradition of comparative work on government practices. Montesquieu's empiricism in the *Spirit of the Laws* provides perhaps the most notorious example of historical comparison, continuing the tradition of using comparative materials to generate normative conclusions, in this case culminating in the establishment of the foundations of modern constitutionalism.

Comparative constitutional inquiry became particularly relevant in the aftermath of the revolutions in the United States and France. The Founding Fathers and the French revolutionaries had to invent a new organization of the state and they could rely only to a limited extent on pre-existing structures. The empirical evidence offered by comparison was both a source of inspiration and of legitimation. In the Federalist Papers, references to foreign experiences are made for justificatory purposes.[5] In France, the translation of a collection of US state constitutions became one of the most important intellectual sources of reformist and revolutionary

[4] See eg Thomas Hobbes, *Leviathan* (1651); John Locke, *Two Treatises of Government* (1689); on the early natural law tradition, see Hugo Grotius, *De iure belli ac pacis* (1625).

[5] See eg, Alexander Hamilton, John Jay, and James Madison, 'The Alleged Tendency of the New Plan to Elevate the Few at the Expense of the Many Considered in Connection with Representation', *The Federalist Papers*, no 57 (1788).

political thought,[6] and comparisons with the US and English arrangements were common in the debates of the National Constituent Assembly.[7] In the liberal constitution-making process of the early nineteenth century, comparison with the various French constitutions was standard procedure and Latin American constitution-making often relied on a consideration and comparative analysis of the US constitution.[8] In liberal constitutional theory comparison, in some cases supporting developmental theories continued to be relevant, as was the case with J.S. Mill's Representative Government in matters of election law.[9] Constant, Tocqueville, and Eötvös used constitutional comparison extensively,[10] and Bryce developed a more systematic approach marked by his distinction between rigid and flexible constitutions.[11] However, by and large, constitutional law became at this stage an independent though somewhat narrow subject, and increasingly its consolidation meant the abandonment of comparison.

Characteristically, in Germany before the consolidation of the Empire and of its public law system, comparison was an important source of scholarly and reformist inspiration.[12] In fact, the nineteenth-century German attempt to tame the administrative (*police*) state necessitated reliance on comparative public law, and the theoretical and practical elaboration of the constitutional theory of the *Rechtsstaat* was influenced by comparison and had a major impact in Europe through the translations of the concept. Hence, the interest in comparing administrative justice as a freedom enhancing control over the administration. Even Dicey's *Introduction to the Law of the Constitution*[13] ventured into comparative studies. Interestingly, Dicey's misunderstanding of the French system can be compared to the inspiring errors of Montesquieu regarding checks and balances in Britain, a century earlier.[14] With the establishment of positive constitutional law in the nineteenth century, international comparison lost much of its appeal and legal science and public law practices became increasingly self-referential, as if the existence of a national constitution would have made foreign law irrelevant. This was the age of the exegetes, whose task was not to provide creative solutions but to guide authoritatively and reliably the lawyers and administrators through the maze of an ever-increasing body of laws. It seems that the prevalence of legal positivism successfully devalued all sources of interest other than the text of the positive legal norm. There was little need for comparative inspiration in a legal world where the lawyer is interested in serving existing power rather than the freedom of citizens. Legal science became self-centered and oriented toward systematization and thus its methodological goals did not leave much space for comparison.[15]

[6] See Louis-Alexandre La Rochefoucauld d'Enville, *Constitutions des treize États-Unis de l'Amérique* (1783); Nicolas de Condorcet, *De l'influence de la révolution d'Amérique sur l'Europe* (1786).

[7] See François Mignet, *History of the French Revolution 1789–1814* (1824), ch 3.

[8] See Russell H. Fitzgibbon, 'The Process of Constitution Making in Latin America' (1960) 3 *Comparative Studies in Society and History* 1.

[9] See John Stuart Mill, *Considerations on Representative Government* (1861).

[10] See Henri-Benjamin Constant de Rebecque, *The Liberty of Ancients Compared with that of Moderns* (1816); Alexis de Tocqueville, *Democracy in America*, vol I (Henry Reeve trans, 1835); József Eötvös, *The Influence of the Nineteenth Century's Dominant Ideas on the State* (1851, 1854).

[11] See further Grimm, Chapter 4.

[12] On comparisons with English self-government see Freiherr vom Stein, *'Nassauer Denkschrift' (Über die zweckmäßige Bildung der obersten und der Provinzial-, Finanz- und Polizei-Behörden in der preußischen Monarchie)* (1807); Heinrich Rudolf Hermann Friedrich von Gneist, *Communalverfassung und Verwaltungsgerichte in England* (1871). See further Caroula Argyriadis-Kervegan, 'L'Administration locale entre nature et état dans la pensée allemande du XIXe siècle' (2006) 23 *Revue française d'histoire des idées politiques* 83.

[13] A.V. Dicey, *Law of the Constitution* (1885); see Krygier, Chapter 10.

[14] See Charles de Secondat, Baron de Montesquieu, *The Spirit of Laws* (Ann M. Cohler et al ed and trans, 1989).

[15] See von Bogdandy, Chapter 1A.

But even in this era dominated by positivism, the academic interest in comparison survived.[16] In this context, comparison of governments became a focus that was intended to satisfy intelligent curiosity, and partly to inspire change.[17] Georg Jellinek, a leading exponent of legal positivism, developed a theory of the universalism of human rights relying on a comparative methodology.[18] For his part, Adhémar Esmein, who also considered the state and its sovereignty a legal phenomenon, stressed the relevance of using some comparison in discussing French constitutional law.[19] Even Duguit, whose scholarship was to a considerable extent directed against Esmein, continued to include comparative treatises in his work.[20] For Duguit, the 'foreign' experience served as an additional social fact that he used to fight juridical metaphysics.[21] Édouard Lambert, on the other hand, instituted (parallel to Henri Capitant) a civil law-based comparative law in France and the first French comparative law institute in 1921. Moreover, Lambert's description of the US jurisprudence pertaining to labor may be considered a precursor of the treatment of foreign constitutional law as an element comparative law.[22] In short, whereas legal positivism may not have been particularly favorable to the comparative approach, the latter served the practical needs of public law reform and constitution-making.[23]

In spite of the existence of a comparative interest in academic constitutional law (exemplified by the first international conference in 1900 and by the establishment of the 'Société de legislation comparée' in Paris in 1869), modern comparative law (as a semi-autonomous discipline) originated in the efforts of private law experts. This might be related to international commercial interests and also to the desire to export national civil law codes. Such 'imperialism' was certainly present in the promotion of the German Civil Code. The theories of comparative law reflected considerations and concepts of private law, and constitutional law was often neglected in the comparative study of great legal systems. The low profile of constitutional law in comparative law may be due to the difficulties in finding universal elements in constitutional law. Nevertheless, already in the period between the two world wars, comparative constitutional law became established as a separate scholarly discipline first and foremost thanks to the scholarship of Boris Mirkine-Guetzevitch.[24] Steeped in the positivist tradition, the latter hoped that the emerging state of law would give expression to democracy in a legal language, and he wished in particular that the post-First World War constitutions would provide for their own protection by deploying judicial review. One can attribute to him the idea of the internationalization of constitutional law in the sense of applying the binding force of international law for purposes of strengthening the constitutions of nation-states.

[16] Ibid.

[17] See Frederic Austin Ogg, *The Governments of Europe* (1913), VIII.

[18] Georg Jellinek, *The Declaration of the Rights of Man and of Citizens: A Contribution to Modern Constitutional History* (1895).

[19] Adhémar Esmein, *Éléments de droit constitutionnel français et comparé* (1899). Esmein was also the founder of *Nouvelle revue historique du droit français et étranger*.

[20] See Léon Duguit, *Law in the Modern State* (Frida Laski and Harold Laksi trans, 1901).

[21] Ibid 69–72.

[22] See eg Édouard Lambert, *Le Gouvernement des juges et la lutte contre la législation sociale aux États-Unis. L'expérience américaine du contrôle judiciaire de la constitutionnalité des lois* (1921).

[23] See in particular the constitutional and public law reforms in Japan. Harald Hohmann, 'Modern Japanese Law: Legal History and Concept of Law, Public Law and Economic Law of Japan' (1996) 44 *American Journal of Comparative Law* 151.

[24] Boris Mirkine-Guetzevitch, *Les Constitutions de l'Europe nouvelle* (1928 with ten additional editions).

While issues pertaining to comparative constitutionalism continued to be the subject of discussion within political science as part of government studies,[25] comparison became more popular due to the coming of age of rationalized parliamentarianism, followed upon its collapse by the growth of dictatorship. To a significant degree, interest in comparative constitutionalism was the result of emigration. Constitutional lawyers and legal theoreticians, being forced out of countries under ruthless dictatorship were particularly concerned with the weakness of the liberal state and motivated to find a theoretical answer to the apparent success of totalitarian regimes. The emerging scholarship includes such classic writings at the intersection of comparative constitutional law and political science as Loewenfeld's articles on Militant Democracy[26] and Naumann's Behemoth[27] and Fraenkel's Dual State.[28] Clinton Rossiter's 1942 dissertation, *Constitutional Dictatorship: Crisis Government in the Modern Democracies*,[29] pertains to this group, though Rossiter was born in the United States and had no law degree.

Comparative constitutional law scholarship did not emerge as an academic discipline until after the Second World War.[30] In post-Second World War Europe comparative constitutional law was influenced by the East/West divide. Foreign constitutional systems were often studied as part of Soviet legal studies, and, respectively studies on Western bourgeois state law. Comparative law was understood as the study of foreign systems, with a heavy ideological accent.

Whereas he was still operating within political science, Carl J. Friedrich, a first class scholar of German constitutional law, gave rise to a paradigm shift, by concentrating on the constitutionalization of modern government and stressing the importance of judicial review.[31] Friedrich, while still concerned with power as the central issue for modern political science, used constitutional law comparatively.[32] By doing so and by also engaging in historical comparison, Friedrich led constitutional theory's move away from the then prevailing paradigm towards a value-oriented approach. Friedrich summarized the ensuing paradigm shift in the following terms: 'If constitutional law begins to ask what people actually do under a particular constitution, and not merely what battle of words they engage in for the settlement of conflicts among them, the constitutional lawyer becomes a political scientist (one hopes).'[33]

The shift towards a value-based approach is certainly rooted in the coming to power of totalitarian regimes. It resulted from the discontent with positivism in political science and law as the latter had proved intellectually impotent against totalitarianism. While not explicit, this normative commitment to constitutionalism remains influential in comparative constitutional law, even if this results in the neglect of the study of non-liberal regimes. The interest in

[25] Ogg (n 17); Herman Finer, in *The Theory and Practice of Modern Government* (1932) continued the tradition of comparing governments while adding a theoretical-constitutionalist dimension. This was a lasting tradition: the last reprint of Finer's 1949 revised edition was published in 1970.

[26] Karl Loewenstein, 'Militant Democracy and Fundamental Rights, I' (1937) 31 *American Political Science Review* 417.

[27] Franz Leopold Neumann, *Behemoth: The Structure and Practice of National Socialism, 1933–1944* (1944).

[28] Ernst Fraenkel, *The Dual State* (1941).

[29] Published in 1948.

[30] Günther Doeker-Mach, 'Comparative Constitutional Law: Reflections on the Past and Concerns about the Future' in Günther Doeker-Mach and Klaus A. Ziegert (eds), *Law, Legal Culture and Politics in the Twenty First Century* (2004), 337.

[31] Carl J. Friedrich, *Constitutional Government and Democracy: Theory and Practice in Europe and America* (1941); see also Carl J. Friedrich, *Constitutional Government and Politics* (1937).

[32] Though closer to political philosophy, Friedrich von Hayek's *The Constitution of Liberty* (1960) fits into this tradition.

[33] Friedrich, *Constitutional Government and Democracy* (n 31), 505.

comparison motivated by the shift to a value-based approach continued to sustain a comparative interest after the Second World War, as part of Cold War thinking, as liberal democracies defended their system in opposition to communist totalitarianism. The post-war period was characterized by an international human rights revolution, with various waves of state formation and democratization, coupled with increasing judicialization of constitutional law.[34] Such comparative interest drew further inspiration from the enhanced protection of fundamental rights that issued from the US Supreme Court starting at the beginning of the 1940s. This robust protection was inspired by a political desire to define the United States as a bulwark of freedom in the face of totalitarianism, the arch enemy in the Second World War and in the Cold War. As A.L. Goodhart wrote it in his Foreword to *Bernhard Schwartz's American Constitutional Law*, a book with comparative references, as it was written for an English audience:

> The English reader will be interested to find that some of the problems which are now being considered in the United States are also of immediate importance in Great Britain. The first is concerned with the maintenance of our civil liberties at a time of 'cold war'. To what extent, for example, should freedom of speech be accorded to those who advocate the forcible overthrow of the existing system of government? The second is concerned with the modern development of the administrative process.[35]

Although Schwartz's work is a standard constitutional law treatise, it is characteristic that as a source for the study of 'foreign' constitutional law, it was considered as possessing lasting importance as part of the political science literature.

It is particularly noteworthy that in the transition from comparative government studies to comparative constitutional *law* as an academic discipline within the ambit of legal scholarship the interest in the subject matter proved to be primarily ideological. Indeed, a principal intent was to boost liberal constitutionalism against totalitarianism, and the elaboration of this new field was more the result of dissatisfaction with the prevailing positivistic method in law and government scholarship than an attempt to carve out a discipline or subdiscipline within jurisprudence. Comparison was intended to highlight theoretical trends and the object of the comparison became primarily government practice as the source and consequence of public law.

The above phenomena occurred in an international context where the level of state interaction and interdependence contributed to the spreading of more intense and new forms of constitutionalism. These trends created new needs both within law and in government, and these related in particular to constitution-writing as a matter of borrowing and international cooperation. However, according to Mark Tushnet, it was only the transition to democracy beginning in 1989 that has created the field of comparative constitutional law, resulting from the practical needs of constitution-drafting and institution-building, which produced a critical mass of knowledge and experts.[36]

Furthermore, the preservation of comparative constitutional law as a separate discipline with full-fledged practical relevance requires constitutional adjudication oriented toward comparison. In this respect, the role of international courts, and suggested or mandated comparison as is the case in the Constitution of South Africa which recognizes foreign

[34] For an early path-breaking survey see Mauro Cappelletti, *Judicial Review in the Contemporary World* (1971). See further Ran Hirschl, *Towards Juristocracy: The Origins and Consequences of the New Constitutionalism* (2004).

[35] See Bernhard Schwartz, *American Constitutional Law* (1955), X. The book is full of comparative references, as it was written for an English audience.

[36] See Mark Tushnet, 'Comparative Constitutional Law' in Mathias Reimann and Reinhard Zimmermann (eds), *The Oxford Handbook of Comparative Law* (2006), 1228.

constitutional law as a legitimate source of constitutional decision-making, play a crucial role. Concurrent with changes in national constitutional law and its internationalization, comparative constitutional law gradually became a rather self-contained discipline with its own methodology. Beyond its descriptive concerns, the discipline is confronted with a fundamental ideological dilemma as the liberal quest for identity across borders clashes against the pursuit of differences among constitutional arrangements.

Comparative constitutional law as an academic discipline has been slowly and gradually integrated into legal education. In the United States, Thomas Franck wrote a path-breaking volume that responded to the experiences of decolonization and resulting state-building that intended to present the transplantation of Anglo-American constitutional law into the newly developing countries of Africa and Asia.[37] The book (presenting a good number of cases—and reflecting therefore the specificity of modern constitutional law, namely constitutional law as a matter for litigation) was based on the assumption that those nations have accepted these as 'the traffic rules of the economic-social-political road to modernization'. This was followed by more collections in the late 1970s.[38] In France, comparative constitutional law as an academic subject was only gradually accepted in the legal curricula, though it was present as a political science subject matter. Like in Germany, the increased interest in comparative constitutional law was originally accommodated within national constitutional law. With the increased juridicization of constitutional law, that is, with the recognition that constitutional problems can be solved increasingly with the adjudicative tools of the rule of law state, legal interest in comparison was increasingly accommodated within a stand-alone discipline.[39] Comparative constitutional law was often part of the very movement towards the juridicization of constitutional law, as in the case of France where the importance of constitutional adjudication was recognized through comparative studies, in particular thanks to the activities of Louis Favoreu and his collaborators.[40] The increased interest in case law resulted in a new emphasis on rights, while earlier scholarship was more concerned with structural issues of governance. The use of comparative method was well established in the German legal sphere but it has remained somewhat secondary in the prevailing theoretical study of the state which was not constitution-centred.[41] Systemic specialized textbooks are still rare and relatively recent.[42] The recognition of the practical importance of the comparative method is, once again, intimately related to the increased importance of comparison in constitutional adjudication. For German legal science this means a partial paradigm change in legal methodology: comparison is understood as a new (fifth) method of legal interpretation.[43]

While comparison became to varying degrees integrated into domestic constitutional law (in many countries, for the simple reason that their constitutional system became part of a supranational system with its own supranational constitutional law) and therefore it is

37 Thomas M. Franck, *Comparative Constitutional Process. Cases and Materials. Fundamental Rights in the Common Law Nations* (1968).

38 Walter Francis Murphy and Joseph Tannenhaus, *Comparative Constitutional Law: Texts and Commentaries* (1977) (strong emphasis on judicial policy making); Mauro Cappelletti and William Cohen, *Comparative Constitutional Law: Cases and Materials* (1979).

39 In Italy, Giuseppe De Vergottini had already published his *Diritto costituzionale comparato* in 1981 (7th edn, 2010).

40 *Cours constitutionnelles européennes et droits fondamentaux* (1982).

41 Georg Jellinek, Allgemeine Staatsrechtslehre (1905); for the reliance on comparataive material see eg Georg Jellinek, *Das Recht des modernen Staates* (1900).

42 See eg Bernd Wieser, *Vergleichendes Verfassungsrecht* (2005).

43 Peter Häberle, *Rechtsvergleichung im Kraftfeld des Verfassungsstaates: Methoden und Inhalte, Kleinstaaten und Entwicklungsländer* (1992).

inherently related to national constitutional law studies, it became an academic discipline in its own right, reflecting not only upon commonalities and differences in national systems, but it is also a reflection upon the interaction of national and supranational constitutional institutions. This current stage of the development and its dilemmas is the subject matter of the *Handbook*.

II. Comparative Constitutional Law: Uses, Purposes, and Challenges

1. Uses

One can discern four principal uses of comparative constitutional law. Two of these, uses of foreign constitutional materials in constitution-making—broadly understood as encompassing constitutional revision or amendment—and in constitutional interpretation are in the hands of actors or *participants* in the constitutional arena. The other two uses, providing descriptive accountings and elaborating normative assessments of participant dealings with comparative constitutional materials, in contrast, are primarily reserved for those who assume the role of *observers*, namely scholars in law and in other relevant disciplines. Examples abound of actual uses of constitutional materials originating in a jurisdiction other than that in which the actual users of such materials carry out official functions in relation to their own constitution. Thus, for example, various constitutions, including the Canadian Charter of Rights and Freedoms (Constitution Act of 1982, Pt I), have influenced constitution-making in South Africa, New Zealand, and Hong Kong and the Basic Law in Israel.[44] Similarly, such uses have also occurred in constitutional interpretation, and are even sometimes explicitly endorsed by constitutions themselves, as in the South African Constitution, which, as noted above, specifically empowers courts to consider foreign law when interpreting the Bill of Rights.[45] These uses, moreover, have spread to transnational settings, where their constitution-making and their constitutional interpretation dimensions have, on occasion, been combined.

A prime instance of this occurred when the European Court of Justice (ECJ), the EU's highest judicial body, began filling constitutional gaps at a time when the governing treaties of the transnational unit that is now the EU lacked any fundamental rights-related provisions. In its landmark 1974 *Nold* decision,[46] the ECJ stated that in order to safeguard fundamental rights in the context of EU-imposed regulation, it had to start from the *common constitutional traditions* of the member states. Accordingly, the ECJ 'cannot... allow measures which are incompatible with fundamental rights recognized and guaranteed by the constitutions of those States'.[47] What *Nold* launches is both a piecemeal ECJ-driven constitution-making project relating to fundamental rights and an interpretive agenda depending on constitutional sources extrinsic to the EU (or its treaty-based predecessors). Indeed, what the ECJ imposed on itself

[44] See Sujit Choudhry, 'Globalization in Search of Justification: Towards a Theory of Comparative Constitutional Interpretation' (1999) 74 *Indiana Law Journal* 819, 821–2.

[45] See Margaret A. Burnham, 'Cultivating a Seedling Charter: South Africa's Court Grows its Constitution' (1997) 3 *Michigan Journal of Race and Law* 29, 44 (concerning the use by the South African Constitutional Court of comparative jurisprudence as a means for South Africa to claim 'its place among the world's constitutional democracies'); and *State v Mhlugu*, 1995 (3) SALR 867, 917 (CC) (according to Justice Sachs, South Africa's constitutional jurisprudence must take its place 'as part of a global development of constitutionalism and human rights').

[46] *J. Nold KG v EC Commission* (Case 4/73): [1974] ECR 491 at 507, [1974] 2 CMLR 338 at 354.

[47] Ibid.

in *Nold* in relation to its interpretation of EU law, was both to refer to the national constitutions of the EU member states and to distill what was common to all of the latter.

In order for constitution-makers and interpreters to make cogent and optimal use of foreign constitutional materials that they either must, or wish to, consider, it is necessary for the latter to gain familiarity with them and to become able to gauge what usefulness any particular foreign referent may have in a given concrete decision-making instance. This is likely to require both an understanding of how a foreign constitutional norm figures in its own institutional setting and how it compares to seemingly similar norms in one's own and other pertinent constitutional systems. Constitution-makers and judges do make use of institutional models, structures, processes, arguments, and doctrines coming from beyond their own jurisdiction, and they need sufficient familiarity with those materials to justify such use to themselves and to the audiences to which they must remain responsive. Moreover, judges can sharpen their relative knowledge and appreciation of foreign materials through dialogues with constitutional judges from various countries,[48] and through reference to relevant examination, analysis, and comparative assessment of the said materials in the works of comparative constitutional law scholars.

The latter scholars approach the relevant material as observers, and they tackle it from either a descriptive or a prescriptive perspective. From a descriptive standpoint, the scholar examines systematically the comparative constitutional work that participants undertake, performing a number of tasks ranging from classification to critical assessment. For example, a scholar may distinguish between areas or subjects in relation to which much comparison occurs and those that give rise to minimal comparison. Or a scholar may be critical of existing comparisons in a particular area, let us say free speech, upon concluding that constitutional judges base comparisons on superficial similarities while ignoring less apparent but much more important differences. Normative or prescriptive scholarly work, on the other hand, concentrates on what the scholar deems desirable or feasible, depending on the latter's empirical, ideological, or discipline-based position. One may be convinced, for instance, that constitutions are deeply anchored in a particular tradition and that use of foreign material is therefore bound to betray the imperative to maintain the uniqueness of every constitutional system. Or, one may be persuaded that fundamental rights are ultimately universal and that countries with less developed constitutional jurisprudence should always seek to benefit from the experiences of their counterparts with far more developed such jurisprudence.

2. Purposes

The key concern in comparative law as it emerged in the civil law tradition in the late nineteenth and early twentieth century was to find the *fonds commun législatif*. This was the position of Capitant and Lambert in France,[49] and it fostered the training of foreign lawyers in the national tradition in the name of comparative law. There is an analogous trend in comparative constitutional law emerging from the works of those who posit its principal goal as distilling what is universal or common in all constitutional systems and traditions. Accordingly, comparative constitutional analysis is sometimes animated by a search for the universal on the basis of what can be empirically observed or of conformity to the ideal (liberal, constitutionalist) arrangement through adaptation of manifold particular settings in varying cultural and historical circumstances. This search for the universal goes back to the early comparative law

48 Anne-Marie Slaughter, *A New World Order* (2004).

49 See eg Édouard Lambert, *Étude de droit commun législatif, la fonction du droit civil comparé* (1903).

tradition exemplified by Anselm Feuerbach, the early nineteenth-century German scholar who is credited with founding the discipline of comparative criminal law.[50] Also important was the influence of comparative linguistics, pursued by the liberal constitutionalist Wilhelm von Humboldt,[51] which was aimed at generating a universal sense of language based on comparative language studies. This focus on universals is especially salient in comparative constitutional law endeavors to compare national solutions in terms of constitutionalism's search for a political ideal of ordered liberty. Moreover, the strong emphasis on the universality of human rights and the use of comparison in human rights adjudication which are intended to find a measure or standard of universally applicable norms point in the same direction. Some argue, for example, that there is a generally accepted virtually universal method of justification when it comes to circumscribing the scope of fundamental rights: that provided by the standard of proportionality,[52] though judges and scholars differ in their conceptions of this ubiquitous standard.[53] In this context, the study of the constitution of illiberal democracies[54] centers on the reasons for departure from the ideal model, and focuses on the extent to which non-liberal constitutional systems can sustain a well-functioning legal order. Significantly, the influence of the constitution on the legal system in liberal democracies goes well beyond formal institutional settings and definition of legal sources: constitutional values become embedded in the various branches of law and even in private relations.[55]

There is a lack of consensus concerning the proper goals of comparative analysis that is due to broader ideological disagreements about the nature and function of law in general, and of constitutional law in particular. At one end of the spectrum are those who, consistent with the above remarks on universalism, believe that the legal problems that confront all societies are essentially similar and that their solutions are fundamentally universal.[56] Specifically, some argue that basic principles of constitutional law are essentially the same throughout the world.[57] Accordingly, the principal goals of comparative analysis are to identify and highlight the common or universal principles and to determine how particular constitutional jurisprudences do, or may be made to, conform to those principles.

At the other end of the spectrum, are those who maintain that all legal problems are so tied to a society's particular history and culture that what is relevant in one constitutional context cannot be relevant, or at least similarly relevant, in another. This position is encapsulated in Montesquieu's observation that 'the political and civil laws of each nation...should be so appropriate to the people for whom they are made that it is very unlikely that the laws of one nation can suit another'.[58] If that were indeed the case, then the only legitimate task for comparative analysis would be to explain how each constitutional system conforms to the singular needs, aspirations, and mores of the particular polity for which it has been designed. Consequently, besides fostering a systematic understanding of how law varies according to the particulars of its socio-political environment, the principal goal of comparison—at least as

[50] See Gustav Radbruch, 'Anselme Feuerbach, precurseur du droit comparé', *Recueil Lambert*, vol I (1938).

[51] See Tilman Borsche, *Sprachanansichten. Der Begriff der menschlichen Rede in der Sprachphilosophie Wilhelm von Humboldts* (1981).

[52] See eg David Beatty, *The Ultimate Rule of Law* (2004).

[53] Compare the respective chapters in this volume by Bernhard Schlink (Chapter 33) and Aharon Barak (Chapter 34).

[54] See Thio, Chapter 5.

[55] On horizontal effects see Gardbaum, Chapter 7.

[56] See eg Konrad Zweigert and Hein Kötz, *Introduction to Comparative Law* (Tony Weir trans, 2nd edn, 1987), 36.

[57] See David M. Beatty, *Constitutional Law in Theory and Practice* (1995).

[58] See Montesquieu (n 14), 8.

far as participants are concerned—would be a negative one. Because no two polities are likely to share essentially similar circumstances, there ought to be a strong presumption against use or adaptation of constitutional norms originated beyond one's borders.

Between the two positions described above, there are various other ones. Some believe that the problems confronted by different societies are essentially the same,[59] but that the solutions are likely to be different, owing to varying circumstances that distinguish one society from the next.[60] Hence, the principal benefit of comparative work would stem from its ability to highlight specificities that tend to be taken for granted, and to enhance the knowledge and understanding of one's own system. For yet others, the function of comparative analysis is the development of an even more critical, reflexive analytical capacity.[61] Critical theorists have argued that comparative constitutional law has a colonizing and hegemonic edge, as it tends to project the gloss of a dominant constitutional culture, such as that of the United States or Germany, onto constitutional systems operating in former colonies and other developing polities.[62] Accordingly, both comparativist practitioners and observers work wittingly or unwittingly towards co-opting constitutional development in the latter settings. Consistent with this, moreover, the proper goal for comparative analysis would be the 'debunking' of the hegemonic tendencies spread throughout the discipline. This raises the question of whether the ideological biases attributed by certain critical scholars to comparative constitutional law stand out on their own or whether they are in the end no different than similar biases claimed to be operating in purely domestic fields of public and private law.[63]

3. Challenges

Some claim that comparative analysis, in general, and comparative constitutional analysis, in particular, confront special challenges that do not figure in purely domestic fields of law. Richard Posner thus asserts that for linguistic reasons alone many foreign legal systems are difficult to access. Added to that, in Posner's view, domestic judges and scholars cannot easily attain a sufficient familiarity with foreign legal systems and with the social, cultural, and institutional systems in which the latter are embedded to warrant any confidence in the accuracy or utility of actual comparisons.[64] Furthermore, for those with universalistic tendencies, comparative constitutional law should aim at harmonization and convergence, and search for application of common or functionally equivalent concepts and institutions. Consistent with this, the hope is to achieve common and shared solutions, contributing perhaps to some kind of democratic world order of Kantian world citizens. Writing from a comparative law perspective, Pierre Legrand has cast a particularly stringent criticism on such ambitions:

> rules and concepts alone actually tell one very little about a given legal system.... They may provide one with much information about what is apparently happening, but they indicate nothing about the deep structures of legal systems. Specifically, rules and concepts do little to

[59] See eg Mary Ann Glendon, 'Rights in Twentieth Century Constitutions' (1992) 59 *University of Chicago Law Review* 519, 535.

[60] See Mary Ann Glendon, *Comparative Legal Traditions* (2nd edn, 1994), 10.

[61] See Günther Frankenberg, 'Critical Comparisons: Re-thinking Comparative Law' (1985) 26 *Harvard International Law Journal* 411 and Peer Zumbansen, 'Comparative Law's Coming of Age? Twenty Years after Critical Comparisons' (2005) 6 *German Law Journal* 1073.

[62] See eg Gunther Frankenberg, 'Stranger than Paradise: Identity and Politics in Comparative Law' (1997) *Utah Law Review* 259, 262–3.

[63] See eg Roberto Unger, *The Critical Legal Studies Movement* (1983).

[64] See Richard A. Posner, 'Foreword: A Political Court' (2005) 119 *Harvard Law Review* 31, 84–9.

> disclose that legal systems are but the surface manifestation of legal cultures and, indeed, of culture tout court. In other words, they limit the observer to a 'thin description' and foreclose the possibility of the 'thick description' that the analyst ought to regard as desirable.[65]

For Legrand, habits and traditions ('*mentalité*') play a decisive and divergent role in the interpretation of common rules and concepts. Accordingly, all comparison involves translation, and the current trend to internationalization of constitutional law[66] and to stressing analogies and convergences vastly increases the likelihood of 'getting lost in translation'.

Another kind of challenge stems from instances in which domestic courts place an implausible interpretive gloss on foreign authorities, apparently for strategic purposes. This may occur in the course of constitutional adjudication in relatively new constitutional democracies, when courts seek to shield controversial and contestable decisions through reference to the constitutional jurisprudence of an established and respected constitutional democracy. For example, several decades ago, the Israeli Supreme Court made reference to American free speech doctrine to justify decisions inconsistent with those of US courts in similar cases.[67] As presumably strategic citation of precedents and authorities also occurs in purely domestic settings—both by advocates and by judges endeavoring to emphasize the soundness of their decisions—a key question is whether the challenge posed by strategic uses of legal authorities is markedly greater in the comparative context as opposed to that of its purely domestic counterpart. One possible answer is suggested by reference to the claim that citation of foreign authorities should be avoided because it is inevitably selective. That is the reason Justice Scalia reproached the US Supreme Court's majority opinion reference to European jurisprudence in *Lawrence v Texas*,[68] the case in which the Court held as unconstitutional the criminalization of homosexual sex among consenting adults. Justice Scalia complained that citation of European jurisprudence was selective and thus misleading as in other parts of the world, such as jurisdictions in Asia and South America, the criminalization at issue was deemed constitutional. But by citing these latter jurisdictions, Scalia appears to undermine his assertion that selective citation poses a threat. Actually, familiarity with foreign material allows both promotion and neutralization of selective citations. Arguably, the same can be said for strategic citation.

III. Constitutional Borrowing and Transplantation

Constitutional borrowing and transplantation of constitutional norms, structures, doctrines, and institutions is a fact of life regardless of ideological or theoretical objections to these practices. Furthermore, even those who vigorously object to transplantation in one context may find it entirely appropriate in another. For example, in rejecting the relevance of foreign constitutional experience in the context of adjudicating a dispute concerning the limits of the national government's powers under US federalism, Justice Scalia emphasized that 'comparative analysis [is] inappropriate to the task of interpreting a constitution though it [is,] of course, quite relevant to the task of writing one'.[69] Given the proliferation of new constitutions

[65] Pierre Legrand, 'European Legal Systems Are Not Converging' (1996) 45 *International and Comparative Law Quarterly* 52, 56.

[66] See Michel Rosenfeld, *The Identity of the Constitutional Subject* (2010), 246–7.

[67] See Gary Jacobsohn, *Apple of Gold* (1993), ch 6.

[68] 539 US 558 (2003).

[69] See *Printz v United States* 521 US 898, 921 n11 (1997).

since the end of the Second World War, it would indeed be odd if constitution-makers refrained altogether from looking to foreign constitutions in the course of designing their own. Moreover, as noted, contemporary constitutional adjudicators often consult and cite foreign authorities which inevitably leads to some measure of borrowing or transplantation.

Constitutional 'transplants' and influences are thus relevant and important subjects of comparative analysis. However, their evaluation is bound to depend on the particular take one has on the dynamic between similarities and differences across separate constitutional orders. One important variable is how one construes the nexus between constitutional norms and national identity. If the nexus is weak, then transplants may be relatively unproblematic. For example, in advocating implantation of Western-type private property rights and against constitutionalization of social rights in new constitutions for formerly socialist East European polities in transition to market economies, one commentator observes:

> It is often said that constitutions, as a form of higher law, must be compatible with the culture and mores of those whom they regulate. In one sense, however, the opposite is true. Constitutional provisions should be designed to work against precisely those aspects of a country's culture and tradition that are likely to produce harm through that country's ordinary political processes. There is a large difference between the risks of harm faced by a nation committed by culture and history to free markets, and the corresponding risks in a nation committed by culture and history to social security and general state protection.[70]

Some have argued that the link between a country's constitution and its national identity may vary greatly. Thus, Mark Tushnet has contrasted the Indian Constitution, which he characterizes as quite removed from the country's identity, to the US Constitution, which he claims expresses the national character.[71] Does this mean that a country like the United States should be less susceptible to constitutional transplants than one like India? Or does it simply suggest that countries are open to different kinds of transplants, depending on how closely their constitution is linked to their national character?

Constitutional influence or transplants can be either positive or negative. As Andrzej Rapaczynski specifies in the context of borrowing from the United States:

> By 'positive influence' I mean the adoption or transformation of a legal concept, doctrine, or institution modeled in whole or in part on an American original, where those responsible are aware of the American precedent and this awareness plays some part in their decision. An example is the adoption of the American type of federalism in Australia, or the influence of American First Amendment doctrines on the free speech jurisprudence of Israel.... By 'negative influence,' I mean a process in which an American model is known, considered, and rejected, or in which an American experience perceived as undesirable is used as an argument for not following the American example. Examples of this kind of influence are provided by the Indian decision not to include a due process clause in the Indian constitution, or the portrayal of judicial review as a reactionary American institution in preventing its establishment in France in the first half of the twentieth century....[72]

In any case, influences and transplants tend to reflect transformation rather than mere copying. For example, the Indian rejection of a due process clause stemmed from a considera-

[70] Cass R. Sunstein, 'On Property and Constitutionalism' in Michel Rosenfeld (ed), *Constitutionalism, Identity, Difference and Legitimacy: Theoretical Perspectives* (1994), 383, 398.

[71] See Mark V. Tushnet, 'The Possibilities of Comparative Constitutional Law' (1999) 108 *Yale Law Journal* 1225, 1270–1.

[72] Andrzej Rapaczynski, 'Bibliographical Essay: The Influence of US Constitutionalism Abroad' in Louis Henkin and Albert J. Rosenthal (eds), *Constitutionalism and Rights: The Influence of the US Constitution Abroad* (1990) 94, 96–7.

tion of the US experience in enshrining substantive property norms in the early twentieth century.[73] Although this interpretation of the Due Process Clause was repudiated in the United States in the 1930s,[74] the Indian framers, acting in the late 1940s, considered the US experience and specifically opted to exclude property due process rights from their new constitution to ensure against repeating the US *Lochner* experience.[75]

Perhaps the most daunting task confronting the comparativist is that of properly evaluating similarities and differences. Initial appearances may not prove accurate.[76] In part, as critical theorists have warned, comparativists may overestimate similarities for ideological reasons. Günther Frankenberg has criticized mainstream comparativists as 'Anglo-Eurocentric' paternalists prone to imposing Western hegemonic approaches on the subject and has characterized comparative law as 'a postmodern form of conquest executed through legal transplants and harmonization strategies'.[77] On the other hand, the comparativist may overemphasize differences and thus fail to focus on more relevant similarities. And the latter failure may either be due to a failure of interpretation because of an insufficient grasp of a foreign constitutional culture or to an ideological bias. For example, reliance on US exceptionalism[78] to refuse to adhere to nearly complete worldwide condemnation of use of the death penalty as punishment for murders committed by juveniles as dissenting justices in *Roper v Simmons*[79] did, is arguably proof of ideological blindness to a worldwide moral consensus.

Once grafted onto a different constitutional system, transplants can grow, evolve, or atrophy. Growth and evolution are customary within domestic constitutional systems and it is therefore unsurprising that an imported constitutional unit or complex should do likewise while adapting to the new soil into which it has been implanted. Atrophy, in contrast, may stem from a transplant being a mistake or mainly strategic with the importing polity having designs altogether different from those established in the exporting polity. A striking example of atrophy, that may have originally rested on mistaken identification and often later opportunistically appropriated for strategic purposes, is the nearly verbatim importation of US separation of powers and federalism by some Latin American countries. Strikingly, these transplants of a system devoted to a division and decentralization of powers to preserve 'checks and balances' have on many occasions been stirred toward virtual presidential dictatorship with full centralization of all powers.[80] In sum, constitutional transplants, both positive and negative, play a central role in constitutional design and deployment. A proper handle on the subject is therefore essential for both participants and observers engaging in comparative constitutional analysis.

[73] See *Lochner v New York* 198 US 45 (1905) (New York law limiting number of hours of work of bakery employees held to violate due process property rights of employers and employees).

[74] See *Nebbia v New York* 291 US 502 (1934) and *West Coast Hotel Co v Parrish* 300 US 379 (1937).

[75] See Soli J. Sorabjee, 'Equality in the United States and India' in Louis Henkin and Albert J. Rosenthal (eds), *Constitutionalism and Rights: The Influence of the United States Constitution Abroad* (1990), 94, 96–7.

[76] See Michel Rosenfeld, 'Justices at Work: An Introduction' (1997) 18 *Cardozo Law Review* 1609, 1609–10.

[77] Günther Frankenberg, 'Stranger than Paradise: Identity and Politics in Comparative Law' (1997) 1997 *Utah Law Review* 259, 262–3.

[78] See Rosenfeld, Chapter 1B.

[79] 543 US 551 (2005) (holding death penalty decreed for crime committed by juveniles to be unconstitutional).

[80] See Keith S. Rosenn, 'Federalism in the Americas in Comparative Perspective' (1994) 26 *University of Miami Inter-American Law Review* 1.

IV. Methodology

As the question of methodology is comprehensively and systematically addressed in this *Handbook*—Chapter 2 by Vicki Jackson is entirely devoted to the subject, and many others touch upon it in many different ways—our purpose here is quite limited. Indeed, there would be no need to address this subject here except for two specific reasons: methodological issues are both central and particularly controversial in comparative constitutional law; and, our organization of this *Handbook*, which will be explained in Section V below, makes proof at least implicitly of certain methodological assumptions and commitments which fit within an overall framework. Consistent with this, we will discuss very generally what is distinct about methodology in comparative constitutional law and provide some specific comments on various positions on methodology within the field that we hope will shed light on the contents and organization of the present volume.

There are factual and normative issues regarding methodology and though the two are conceptually distinct, they are often linked in practice. For example, if one is of the view that 'constitutional essentials'[81] ought to be the same across all constitutional systems, then one may be naturally inclined to treat apparent similarities and differences among various constitutional jurisprudences in ways that depart significantly from similar inquiries launched from the perspective that each constitution is exclusively *sui generis* and that it can only be understood in a purely contextual manner. With this in mind, it becomes apparent that a large number of methodological issues confronting comparative constitutional law are no different than those that confront domestic constitutional law. For instance, in the United States there is an ongoing controversy between originalists—those who believe that the Constitution should be interpreted consistently with the intent of, or the meaning it had for, the framers[82]—and those who maintain that the Constitution should be interpreted in terms of the needs of each successive generation within the democratic polity.[83] Originalists, therefore, will be more prone to concentrate on historical analysis and will therefore be confronted by the methodological issues associated with the latter. Non-originalists, in contrast, will be preoccupied with how best the Constitution can be adapted to fit the needs of the current generation, and the methodological hurdles they will face will therefore be more akin to those encountered in political science or sociology rather than to those found in history. In short, as these two examples illustrate, there is an extent to which methodological divergences within comparative constitutional law seem no different in kind than those present within domestic constitutional law.

On the other hand, the key methodological differences between the two aforementioned fields center on comparison itself. Is comparison feasible, cogent, or useful? What are its dangers or pitfalls? What special skills does it require? Moreover, methodological issues relating directly to comparison seem likely to be compounded when added to them are issues common to comparative and non-comparative analysis. For example, whatever methodological issues may be triggered by comparing constitutional interpretation in the United States and Germany, would they not have to be supplemented by those raised by the split between originalists and non-originalists alluded to above?

Comparison consists in sorting out and accounting for similarities and differences among units that figure as objects of comparison. What ought to count as a relevant similarity or

[81] We borrow this formulation from Rawls. See John Rawls, *A Theory of Justice* (1971), 354.

[82] See Norman Dorsen et al, *Comparative Constitutionalism: Cases and Materials* (2nd edn, 2010), 219–24 (summarizing the debate over US originalism).

[83] See eg Stephen Breyer, *Active Liberty: Interpreting Our Democratic Constitution* (2005).

difference and the import of such similarity or difference are at the root of the most vexing methodological issues. There are two extreme positions concerning similarities and differences which make comparison trivial or superfluous. At one end of the spectrum is the view that there are no relevant similarities among constitutions and constitutional systems: both are exhaustively and inescapably context-dependent and no two contexts are meaningfully alike. In that case, comparison may still be worthwhile for purposes of adding to the recording of diversity among human institutions and practices, but would seem completely incapable of contributing anything of value to legal practitioners or scholars. At the other end of the spectrum, in contrast, is the view that in spite of all apparent differences, all constitutions are or ought to be similar. They all confront the same problems and offer, or clearly should offer, the same solutions. Consistent with this, comparison would be purely nominal and bereft of any functional role. Debates within comparative constitutional law would be substantively equivalent to those within domestic constitutional law. For example, there would be no relevant difference between debating whether the constitutional jurisprudence of country A strikes a better balance than that of country B between free speech and protection against terrorism and a similar debate among judges on the constitutional court of country C who disagree among themselves along the same lines.

In between these two extremes, however, comparison seems bound to be meaningful and the framing of relevant similarities and differences as well the determination of the latter's import methodologically contestable. Much of the debate focuses on striking a proper balance between identity and difference. Thus, Ruti Teitel argues that comparative constitutional law functionalists tend to overemphasize identity at the expense of difference;[84] that critical legal studies scholars do the opposite;[85] and that a proper balance is most likely to be struck through a dialogical process involving judges and scholars.[86] It may well be that critical scholars fear that exaggeration of similarities can serve hegemonic purposes as Frankenberg claimed in the passage cited earlier.[87] And it may make it easier for functionalists if similarities were to abound.

Upon further reflection, however, neither of these two positions depends on overemphasis in order to remain coherent. A sophisticated functionalist need not gloss over difference in order fruitfully to compare constitutions in terms of functions. Indeed, constitutions can serve a range of functions and these can make use of, or relate to, different configurations of the interplay between identity and difference depending on the circumstances. It may be, for instance, that all constitutions need to afford some bundle of fundamental rights protection in order for the overall scheme that they set to remain in good working order. It may also be that in one constitutional setting greater emphasis on individual rights would be functionally optimal, whereas in another greater promotion of group rights would be. A good functionalist comparativist would have to identify the relevant similarities and differences and analogies and disanalogies, assess their functional import, and do so in terms of the distinct respective overall constitutional schemes involved. Similarly, a thorough critical theorist may be led to conclude that overemphasis of difference may be as effective a tool as overplay of similarities for purposes of invoking constitutional protections better to screen domination and hegemonic designs. The debate on 'Asian values' in the context of international human rights provides an apt illustration here.[88] The

[84] See Ruti Teitel, 'Comparative Constitutional Law in a Global Age' (2004) 117 *Harvard Law Review* 2570, 2576, 2581.

[85] Ibid 2582.

[86] Ibid 2595–6.

[87] See n 77.

[88] See eg Michael C. Davis, *Constitutionalism and Political Culture: The Debate over Human Rights and Asian Values* (1998) 11 *Harvard Human Rights Journal* 109.

claim made by proponents of Asian values was that the spreading of international human rights was a political attempt by Western powers to impose their world-view and hegemonic designs worldwide thus trampling on traditional Asian culture and values. However, since the proponents of these claims were closely associated with authoritarian regimes, one could plausibly claim that invocation of difference in this context was designed to evoke the pursuit of liberty and self-determination while in fact boosting a regime bent on the exact opposite.

There are, of course, many other conflicts that arise in comparing constitutions, such as the one that apparently sets function against identity. To the extent that constitutions are expressions of national identity, a mere functional approach to comparison would be misleading. But so would be an exclusively identitarian account. As Vicki Jackson suggests, it may be optimal to combine a functional and identity-based approach.[89] Be that as it may, whereas there may be room for reasonable disagreement concerning where to draw the line between functional and identitarian concerns, it seems plain that a sound methodology would require some integration of both.

Finally, it is also important to stress that, even assuming consensus on the function versus identity divide, not all comparisons are likely to be the same or to have identical purposes or uses. One may, for instance, assume that euthanasia raises similar kinds of constitutional issues across most Western democracies, but that federalism inevitably varies significantly from one setting to the next. Thus, it may be that comparative work on euthanasia in Canada, Germany, Switzerland, and the United States can safely assume that sufficiently similar conditions in terms of medical science, societal values, and relevant constitutional jurisprudence prevail, so as to make direct comparison and even borrowing easily justifiable.[90] In contrast, no similar comparison seems warranted concerning the respective federalisms adopted in those countries. The purposes and institutional arrangements of these structurally different federalisms differ sufficiently so as to raise substantial questions regarding direct comparison.[91] But even if direct comparison is unwarranted in the context of adjudication, it may still be useful in terms of constitutional design or of a political science assessment of the relation between various institutional arrangements and democracy. More generally, there seems to be a wide range of potentially useful and productive opportunities for comparison at varying levels of abstraction. These start at the concrete doctrinal level as envisioned by Armin von Bogdandy who refers to the construction of a European (Union) public law doctrine built upon common elements emerging from the respective national constitutional jurisprudences of the EU member states.[92] These opportunities extend, moreover, all the way to abstract theoretical inquiries concerning constitutional justice and its relation to delimitation of an optimal interplay between identity and difference.[93]

[89] See Jackson, Chapter 2.

[90] See eg *Washington v Glucksberg* 521 US 702 (1997) (in deciding that there was no US constitutional right to assisted suicide, the Supreme Court referred to several Western jurisdictions that had already judicially dealt with the issue).

[91] See eg *Printz v United States* 521 US 898 (1997) (Justice Scalia and Justice Breyer disagreeing on the relevance of delegation of implementation of federal regulation to local federated state authorities under German federalism for purposes of determining the constitutionality of similar delegation under US federalism).

[92] See von Bogdandy, Chapter 1B.

[93] See Gargarella, Chapter 16; Rosenfeld, Chapter 35; Jacobsohn, Chapter 36.

V. Structure and Organization of the *Handbook*

Consistent with the preceding observations regarding methodology, the structure and organization of this *Handbook* is informed by the ongoing dynamic generated through interaction and conflict among the following intersecting and overlapping sets of polarities: similarity and divergence; function and identity; (level of) abstraction and context; theory and application; and (constitutional) law, politics, and (philosophical) criteria of justice and legitimacy. As we have seen, there is widespread disagreement regarding the handling and implications of each of these sets of polarities, and undoubtedly the actual and plausible interactions among the latter are likely to be subject to even greater contestation. We proceed on the assumption that the polarities in question do matter and that interaction among them does, can, and in some cases should, occur. Overall, this dynamic provides some fixed points of reference (eg all comparison encounters axes of similarity and axes of difference) and many overlapping arenas of contestation (eg at what level of abstraction is a comparison of different federalisms warranted?). We seek to account for the latter dynamic as much as possible both within each part and among all parts of the *Handbook*. Moreover, we aim to link this complex and multifaceted dynamic that encompasses a multiplicity of competing views on comparison to the established pillars of constitutional law: structure, process, rights, and the rule of law. This design, we hope, will best highlight the potential for dialogue emanating from the various contributions made from within a wide array of perspectives originating in several scholarly disciplines and associated with the principal positions within the comparative constitutional law wars.

Specifically, the *Handbook* is divided into nine parts. Part I, entitled 'History, Methodology, and Typology', provides a systematic as well as a historical and contextual account of the principal subjects linked to methodology and to typology. The focus is on the content and context of comparison. The focus on methodology proper is apportioned between analysis in two actual constitutional regimes (Chapter 1) and a systematic account offering a critical appraisal of the principal contending positions (Chapter 2). Typologies are considered from a systemic viewpoint (Chapter 3) and are placed in context through a history of ideas of constitutional designs and conceptions of constitutionalism (Chapter 4). Moreover, as much comparative constitutional analysis relies predominantly on reference to the constitutional systems of Western democracies, this raises the question of whether much that is taken as universally applicable in terms of methodology or typology holds once one moves away from the customary frame of reference. To address this question, examinations of constitutionalism in illiberal polities (Chapter 5) as well as in polities with pervasive poverty (Chapter 6) are provided. Finally, constitutionalists, whether comparative or not, frequently tend to treat constitutional law as all pervasive. But that is most often not the case, and in some settings it is even less so than others. To put all this in perspective, one needs to take a close look into the place of constitutional law in the legal system (Chapter 7).

At once unifying and divisive, some key concepts pervade the constitutional domain. These key concepts are ubiquitous and inherently contested and this becomes magnified and intensified when constitutions are approached comparatively. Part II, 'Ideas', tackles the most important among these key concepts: constitutionalism (Chapter 8); constitution (Chapter 9); rule of law (Chapter 10); democracy (Chapter 11); the state (Chapter 12); rights and liberties as concepts (Chapter 13); the public/private divide (Chapter 14); state neutrality (Chapter 15); the constitution and justice (Chapter 16); sovereignty (Chapter 17); dignity and autonomy (Chapter 18); and gendered visions of the constitution (Chapter 19). No cogent account of constitutional law, let alone comparative constitutional law, can dispense with these concepts. They at once erect a conceptual framework, anchor a common vocabulary and grammar, and break into a multitude of warring conceptions. They are all meant to provide a common currency, but each can yield more than one currency that may qualify as a candidate to become the common one. Consistent with this, each of these concepts is tackled by an author who, while referring to the plurality of relevant interpretations at stake, carves out his or her own distinct conception of the concept under study.

Part III, 'Process', zeroes in on the dynamics inherent in, and projected by, the constitution. It deals both with the constitution as process and with the processes launched or molded by the constitution. Constitution-making most clearly casts the constitution as process (Chapter 20), but so do, at least in part, emergencies (Chapter 21) and secession (Chapter 23) in as much as they relate to the continuation, suspension, or cessation of the constitution as well as being susceptible of figuring as processes provided for, and regulated by, the constitution. There are also processes grounded in, and shaped by, the constitution. Chief among these are: war powers (Chapter 22); referenda (Chapter 24); and elections (Chapter 25).

Process goes hand in hand with structure, but we have named Part IV 'Architecture' to convey that constitutions need and endeavor to construct more than mere structures. Architecture requires conception, planning, designing, and giving expression to a particular objective in terms of designated functions and in conformity with a distinct aesthetic design. The architect needs to integrate structure, function, and aesthetics in a proportionate and harmonious manner. Reliance on the concept of architecture, moreover, facilitates comparison as one can focus on how different architectural designs accommodate similar functional needs and on how architecture can be used to accommodate different functions and uses. Focus on architecture also allows for fruitful inquiry into the relation of the part and the whole and on the structural conjunctions between parts and between the latter and the whole. Included are analyses of: horizontal structuring (Chapter 26); vertical structuring (Chapter 27); internal ordering of the unitary state (Chapter 28); presidentialism (Chapter 29); parliamentarism (Chapter 30); and the regulatory state (Chapter 31).

Constitutions are expressions of the visions and goals of the polity to which they are attached. They project the identity of the latter while at the same time acquiring and developing an identity of their own. Constitutions at once interpret (the needs and aspirations of those they are designed for) and must be interpreted (both in whole and in part). Constitutions are endowed with meaning and at the same time are meaning-endowing. They also acquire texture as they accumulate the imprints of historical deployment in a particular socio-political setting. Part V, 'Meanings/Textures', deals with these subjects which at once greatly benefit from, and afford sharper insights into, comparative analysis. Indeed, concentration on meanings and textures highlights the relationship between poles of identity and poles of difference, both within a constitutional culture and across several different ones. Meanings and textures are front and center in interpreting the constitution (Chapter 32). Moreover, a particularly propitious comparative window into meanings and textures emerges in the context of proportionality. As already mentioned, some have claimed that proportionality has become the common currency throughout the entire constitutional domain. Accordingly, proportionality should allow for a systematic staking out of all that which is essentially similar across constitutional systems as well and at the same time providing the necessary tools to determine the exact thrust and import of every difference that ought to count. Yet, there are sharp disagreements as to the meaning and scope of proportionality which have prompted us to include two contending views on the subject. Proportionality I (Chapter 33), presents a rather restrictive conception of the proper role of the proportionality standard, whereas Proportionality II (Chapter 34) adopts a much more expansive view of it. As constitutions produce meaning, this raises the question of whether each constitution can develop a distinct identity of its own which differs from that of other constitutions and from the other relevant extra-constitutional identities, such as national identity, within the polity within which the constitution in question is embedded (Chapter 35). Finally, constitutions can and do incorporate values and principles that yield determinate meanings and textures (Chapter 36).

Constitutional order depends on the presence and proper functioning of institutions that attend to maintenance of the requisite integrity of structures, processes, to vindication of fundamental rights, and to the safeguard of the rule of law. Part VI, 'Institutions', concentrates on some of the most important institutions and institutional issues relating to maintenance of an optimal constitutional order: insuring constitutional efficacy (Chapter 37); constitutional courts (Chapter 38); judicial independence (Chapter 39); the judiciary (Chapter 40); and political parties (Chapter 41).

The next two parts of the *Handbook* are devoted to fundamental rights under the constitution. The division into two parts is motivated by the recognition that some rights, such as liberty or equality, are better conceived as distinct self-enclosed units, whereas others, such as abortion, as involving an overlap among a number of distinct rights, including liberty, equality, and privacy. From a comparative standpoint, rights appear to occupy a privileged position as both similarities and differences, convergences and divergences, seem immediately apparent, and explanations for these often strike one as being readily available (though further inquiry may at times prove initial impressions misleading). It thus seems evident that all religiously pluralistic polities need deployment of a constitutional right to freedom of religion, and yet a canvassing of such polities reveals that the right in question comes in many significant variations ranging from strict secularism to the recognition of an official state religion. More generally, there seems to be a widespread need for a bundle of the same rights across constitutional cultures and a different treatment of these rights depending on the particulars of each of the constitutional cultures involved. Part VII, 'Rights', addresses: freedom of expression (Chapter 42); freedom of religion (Chapter 43); due process (Chapter 44); associative rights (Chapter 45); privacy (Chapter 46); equality (Chapter 47); citizenship (Chapter 48); social rights (Chapter 49); and rights in the economic life (Chapter 50). Part VIII, 'Overlapping Rights', in turn addresses: abortion (Chapter 51); rights based on sexual orientation (Chapter 52); group rights (Chapter 53); affirmative action (Chapter 54); and, rights arising out of bioethics (Chapter 55).

Part IX, 'Trends', culls together relatively new constitutional movements and tendencies and others that are nascent but seem poised in all likelihood to assume a greater role in the future. What unites all these trends is that they are jointly and severally altering and expanding the boundaries of constitutionalism and of constitutional regimes. Also, these trends suggest greater interrelation and interpenetration among different constitutional regimes operating along both vertical and horizontal axes. Whereas on the surface these trends may seem to pull towards greater common identity, upon further consideration they seem more likely to reorient the dynamic between identities and differences than to foster uniformity across ever vaster expanses. The specific subjects covered are: the internationalization of constitutional law (Chapter 56); the European Constitution (Chapter 57); the constitutionalization of public international law (Chapter 58); the jurisprudence of the European Court of Human Rights and its effects on the constitutional systems of Europe (Chapter 59); militant democracy (Chapter 60); constitutional transformation and transitional justice (Chapter 61); Islam and constitutional ordering (Chapter 62); constitutional borrowings and transplants (Chapter 63); and the use of comparative constitutional law in constitutional adjudication (Chapter 64).

PART I

HISTORY, METHODOLOGY, AND TYPOLOGY

CHAPTER 1

COMPARATIVE CONSTITUTIONAL LAW: A CONTESTED DOMAIN

*A. Comparative Constitutional Law: A Continental Perspective**

ARMIN VON BOGDANDY

Heidelberg

* An earlier and longer version was published in (2009) 7 *International Journal of Constitutional Law* 364; for critical appraisals see Michel Rosenfeld, 'The Role of Constitutional Scholarship in Comparative Perspective' (2009) 7 *International Journal of Constitutional Law* 362; Matthias Kumm, 'On the Past and Future of European Constitutional Scholarship' (2009) 7 *International Journal of Constitutional Law* 401; Robert C. Post, 'Constitutional Scholarship in the United States' (2009) 7 *International Journal of Constitutional Law* 416; Alexander Somek, 'The Indelible Science of Law' (2009) 7 *International Journal of Constitutional Law* 424; Giulio Napolitano, 'Sul futuro delle scienze del diritto pubblico: variazioni su una lezione tedesca in terra Americana' (2010) 1 *Rivista trimestrale di diritto pubblico* 1. This chapter presents the results of comparative research on constitutional scholarship, published in Armin von Bogdandy, Pedro Cruz Villalón, and Peter M. Huber (eds), *Handbuch Ius Publicum Europaeum* [*Handbook Ius Publicum Europaeum*], Vol I *Grundlagen und Grundzüge staatlichen Verfassungsrechts*, Vol II *Offene Staatlichkeit-Wissenschaft vom Verfassungsrecht* (Joseph K. Windsor trans, 2007, 2008), with contributions by Walter Pauly for Germany, Luc Heuschling and Olivier Jouanjan for France, Christos Pilafas for Greece, Adam Tomkins and Martin Loughlin for the United Kingdom, Maurizio Fioravanti and Mario Dogliani with Cesare Pinelli for Italy, Remco Nehmelman and Leonard Besselink for the Netherlands, Alexander Somek for Austria, Irena Lipowicz and Piotr Tuleja for Poland, Kjell Å Modéer for Sweden, Rainer J. Schweizer, Giovanni Biaggini, and Helen Keller for Switzerland, Mariano García-Pechuán and Manuel Medina Guerrero for Spain, and András Jakab and Gábor Halmai for Hungary. Special thanks to Lorand Bartels, Marc Jacob, Martin Loughlin, and Alec Walen.

I. Premises, Object, and Purposes

New dimensions open up for comparative constitutional scholarship due to European integration, not least because it shakes traditional ways of undertaking constitutional scholarship. One challenge is the project of creating a European research area, including the humanities, social sciences, and legal scholarship,[1] in order to foster research through new opportunities and increased competition, as it happened with the Single European Market. More contact and more confrontation imply more comparison, and the establishment of the new area leads to questioning established topics and methods, publication and career patterns, reputation hierarchies, and even identities. The overwhelmingly national organization of constitutional scholarship is coming under pressure.

A second challenge stems from the rapid development of the European legal area with ever more issues of constitutional importance, often tightly interlinked with international legal phenomena.[2] This undermines the established scholarship's usual focus on one single source: the national constitution. Whereas the constitution was formerly conceived as creating a normative universe, it is now increasingly understood as being but a part of a normative pluriverse, pushing towards comparison.

A third challenge is occasioned by leading US institutions which considerably participate in the formation of future academic leaders for the European research area. As varied as legal research is in these institutions, it almost always contrasts with the usual way of carrying out legal research in Europe.[3] In a globalized system of legal research, the sheer prestige of these institutions, but also the competition for winning the best minds and influence abroad, call for a stocktaking of constitutional scholarship in Europe.

In light of these challenges, this contribution will compare some elements of the development of constitutional scholarship in Europe. The emerging European constitutional scholarship as a form of comparative constitutional law scholarship cannot be understood without looking at the traditions of scholarship at the level of national constitutional law. In the continent, the decisive form of scholarship can be described as one of *doctrinal constructivism*. As the focus of the discipline, this is defining its roles and identity. Doctrinal constructivism represents a singular combination of theory and practice, and stresses the practical importance of constitutional scholarship in many European countries.

When Ernest Gellner asserts: 'The foundation of the modern social order is not the executioner, but the professor',[4] this statement appears particularly suited for legal scholarship. Although not everyone would agree with this categorical assertion of theory's superiority to practice, no one would deny that legal scholars have a key role in the legal order of the member states of the European Union. Legal scholarship not only describes from an external point of view, it also shapes from within. One can even recognize the identity of a public law system as being grounded in scholarship's conceptual creations, illustrations of which are the concepts of *Staatssouveränität* for Germany, *service public* for France, or parliamentary sovereignty for Britain. Legal scholarship develops and often even devises the fundamental concepts and structures, elucidates and legitimates the current law in light of general principles, inspires

[1] Presidency Conclusions, Barcelona European Council point 47 (15 and 16 March 2002); the Lisbon Treaty of 2007 Art 179 para 1 TFEU explicitly mandates the Union to create a 'European research area'.

[2] See Chapter 56.

[3] Patrick S. Atiyah and Robert S. Summers, *Form and Substance in Anglo-American Law: A Comparative Study of Legal Reasoning, Legal Theory, and Legal Institutions* (1987); see, for the American perspective, Stephen M. Feldman, *American Legal Thought from Premodernism to Postmodernism* (2000), 162, 187.

[4] Ernest Gellner, *Nations and Nationalism* (1983), 34.

and criticizes legal developments, and shapes the next generation of jurists. Many legal scholars, often on the basis of scholarly reputation, also act directly as legal practitioners: as legal experts, advisors, counsel, or, in consummation of an academic career, as judges. A thorough understanding of a legal order is hardly conceivable without a familiarity with its legal scholarship.

This analysis presents legal scholarship as a science, at least in the meaning of the German concept of *Wissenschaft*. Granted, the use of the label 'science' is problematic, especially regarding academic writing presenting the law construed as legal doctrine, for various reasons. Distinctions between truth and falsity here have only limited relevance; there is only rudimentary methodological reflection on how to construe doctrine; and the active participation of many legal scholars in legal practice hardly seems to represent scientific neutrality.[5] It is certainly arguable that doctrinal analysis—the main field of legal scholarship in Europe—forms a part of the (legal) practice rather than of the world of science. Tellingly, the terms *Verfassungsrecht*, *diritto costituzionale*, and constitutional law denote not only the object, the constitutional law in force, but also the corresponding scholarly discipline.

Nevertheless, this observation need not undermine the conception of legal scholarship as a science, a *Wissenschaft*: legal scholars are members of institutions within the 'scientific system', dedicating thought, lectures, and publications to systematic exposition of public law, in a professionalized scheme and 'unburdened' by the need to decide cases. So it comes as no surprise that legal scholarship is institutionalized at universities. Accordingly, it is covered by the constitutional guarantee of a *freedom of science* (*Wissenschaft*),[6] and not only by the more general freedom of speech. Indeed, historically, the law faculty has from the beginning been one of the basic elements of the (continental) European university. Accordingly, most continental constitutional scholars conceive constitutional scholarship as a science, but few as a *social* science. *Geisteswissenschaft* or the stand-alone term of *legal sciences* (the plural is due to the dualism of canon law and civil law) embodies the predominant understanding. This corresponds well with the importance of doctrinal constructivism.

An examination of legal scholarship should not limit itself to examining the research. In perhaps no other *Wissenschaft* are research and teaching so closely connected. The development of material for instruction constitutes one of the central tasks of research in legal science: across Europe, the leading treatises and textbooks receive significantly more scholarly attention than in most of the other academic disciplines.[7]

II. The Evolutionary Paths

A legal dispute necessarily relates back to the actions of a constitution-maker, a lawmaker, or a court. Although this backward-looking dimension is an inherent aspect of law and legal scholarship, many legal scholars seem nonetheless forgetful of their discipline's history. Comparative constitutional law scholarship cannot be understood without looking into the national

[5] See especially Niklas Luhmann, *Rechtssystem und Rechtsdogmatik* [*Legal System and Legal Doctrine*] (1974), 13. See also Chapter 2.

[6] The German Constitution contains a specific guarantee of *Wissenschaftsfreiheit*: Grundgesetz [GG] (Constitution) art 5, §3; similarly on the inclusion of legal scholarship (and theology): Charter of Fundamental Rights of the European Union, 18 December 2000 (C-364/01) 13; Christian Starck in Hermann von Mangoldt (ed), *GG Kommentar* [*Commentary to the GG*] (5th edn, 2005), Vol 1, art 5, §3, marginal note 354.

[7] For an ironic description of this genre see Somek (n *), 426ff. For the teaching of comparative constitutional law as an academic discipline see Chapter 1B.

histories of constitutional law scholarship. Seldom is a concept or doctrinal proposition traced back to its originator and its original context.[8] What seems to matter most is a concept's acceptance in current legal discourse. This masking of the course of development need not cause alarm: forward-looking problem-solving, based on established positions, is a hallmark of a self-confident science. But such a stance does not eliminate the prior evolution: the historicity of all cultural and social phenomena, their 'path dependency', has been acknowledged since Vico, Montesquieu, and Romanticism.

1. The 'Positivist Legal Method'

In the development of Europe's diverse systems of constitutional scholarship, one can distinguish between synchronous and asynchronous milestones. Certain milestones were reached simultaneously by most scholarly systems. This type includes especially those of the 'positivist legal method'. Other milestones signify similar substantial achievements with comparable consequences, but different legal orders reach them at different points in time. Examples include the scholarly developments triggered by the progression to liberal and democratic constitutions or by the establishment of a constitutional court, or by Europeanization.

Nonetheless (or perhaps therefore), the 'positivist legal method's' disciplinary approach still informs the research of most public law scholars in Europe; this holds true *cum grano salis* even in the United Kingdom. This approach aspires to provide a comprehensive survey of relevant legal material, to develop structuring legal concepts, and to arrange the material accordingly. At the same time, it needs to be noted that scholarship is not as it was 100 years ago but has evolved on account of critique and a changing context. For example, consequentialist reasoning and balancing of interests are far more important today. Without a doubt, the way a 'legal system' is understood has also changed; such understanding is of formative importance for the understanding of the subject matter of comparison in comparative constitutional law scholarship. Previously, a system tended to be crypto-idealistically understood as inherent in the law, whereas today systems are more often (and correctly) seen as construed instruments for the ordering and managing of the law. Similarly, the understanding of what a system can accomplish in the law in general and in legal practice in particular has changed, thereby reducing its role. This, though, does not diminish the system-orientation of scholarship as such. Given the problems of the concept of positivism and this transformed and reduced understanding, *doctrinal constructivism* might be a more suitable terminology. This development has happened, however, within the discipline as it was founded then. The defining elements are the quest for systematicity through the development of general concepts and structures and the perception of these as 'internal' and operative within the legal system.[9]

'Constitutional court positivism' (*Verfassungsgerichtspositivismus*)[10] leads the agenda of the 'positivist legal method' forward into a new era, characterized by constitutional courts' fundamental rights decisions and the attendant materialization and expansion of constitutional law. This approach is again taken over as granted in comparative constitutional law scholarship, and is reinforced by the judicial use of the comparative method.[11] This positivism systematizes

[8] In the United States the situation appears to differ as far a constitutional law is concerned due to the importance of originalism.

[9] For an outstanding explication to an American audience see Somek (n *), 431ff.

[10] On this term see Bernhard Schlink, 'Bemerkungen zum Stand der Methodendiskussion in der Verfassungsrechtswissenschaft' (1980) 19 *Der Staat* 73, 89–92.

[11] See Chapter 64.

constitutional jurisprudence and thereby upholds the original doctrinal agenda in times of balancing-happy constitutional courts.

The general, pan-European success of this agenda in the early twentieth century did not lead to total uniformity of academic practice; actually, the scope of implementation of the agenda is quite varied.[12]

The realization that the law should be grasped and handled not only as a set of given rules, but also as the object and result of societal conflict, did not bring about an abandonment of the systematic working mode, any more than did the discipline's increasing socio-technological dimension. This facet should not be underestimated in terms of its significance for the possibility of a common, Europe-wide scholarship of law. This working profile also distinguishes European legal science from its US-American counterpart, where the 'legal positivist' or 'doctrinal' approach has been largely abandoned, at least in leading institutions, because of the impact of so-called legal realism, but also due to ethical conceptions along the lines of Ronald Dworkin.[13] Although casuistry, 'case law', has become more important in Europe, nowhere does legal scholarship operate as though a 'case law'-orientation could ever replace a conceptual-doctrinal orientation. One can also formulate this as an ethical argument: fostering and maintaining systematic coherence undergirds the ideas of legal certainty, equality, and, thereby, justice. These broad issues might constitute the future agenda of comparative constitutional law scholarship.

2. Expansion I: Reality, Theory, and Great Narratives

Most manifestations of the positivistic agenda lead to a division of the normative from the empirical, a separation of the law from social reality. Many consider this division constitutive of the discipline's autonomy; it is even conceived as an ontological datum. However, some constitutional scholars worry that this division may leave them out of touch with reality and may prevent them from doing justice to the 'life' which law and legal scholarship are supposed to serve. Precisely for this reason, the positivistic project faced vehement criticism from the very beginning—with remarkable delay in Austria due to Kelsen's overwhelming influence. In response to the establishment of the positivistic agenda, the call for an integration of 'reality' and 'fundaments' into constitutional and public law studies rang out almost everywhere, albeit with significant variation in volume and pitch.

This disciplinary agenda to 'integrate reality' expands the discipline of constitutional law into other areas after its successful establishment. The expansion permits the discipline to reflect on its foundations and to exchange—and compete—with other disciplines which also strive to analyse and interpret social reality. Today, many continental scholars could subscribe to some bland and broad form of realism.[14] The expansion becomes more justifiable the less

[12] Strong evidence suggests that German scholarship has spun an exceptionally intricate web of autonomous doctrinal concepts, providing an exceptionally thick layer of constitutional doctrine—due in no small part to the German language's peculiarly high capacity for creation of new nouns and compound words. This comes with a price: abstraction and conceptual creativity tend to obscure original context, a particular problem of German scholarship as is especially apparent from an external point of view.

[13] A.W.B. Simpson, 'The Rise and Fall of the Legal Treatise: Legal Principles and the Forms of Legal Literature' (1981) 48 *University of Chicago Law Review* 632, 677–9; the distance becomes apparent to the German jurist in James R. Maxeiner, 'US "Methods Awareness" for German Jurists' in Bernhard Großfeld (ed), *Festschrift für Wolfgang Fikentscher* [*Collected Essays in Honour of Wolfgang Fikentscher*] (1998), 114, 117–20.

[14] As in the reconstruction by Hanoch Dagan, 'The Realist Conception of Law' (2007) 57 *University of Toronto Law Journal* 607, which can accommodate doctrinalism.

weight one ascribes to the positivistic distinction between law and fact: the more one understands law as part of the societal whole, the better one can use legal expertise as the basis both for assertions about societal reality and for opinions on its development.

In contrast to the success of the agenda of the 'positivist legal method', the 'integration of reality' and theoretical reflection fail to conjoin into a common disciplinary platform: here, as opposed to the doctrinal sphere, the relevant insights are often incommensurate.

3. Expansion II: Seizing the Crown

For the formation of comparative constitutional law and its science, the expansion of constitutional law and scholarship with the intention of enthroning it as the supreme discipline among the ranks of legal scholarship ('seizing the crown') is of decisive importance. Constitutional scholarship tries to develop constitutional law's formal supremacy into a towering substantive influence of constitutional arguments in legal discourse in general. The metaphor 'seizing the crown' comprises diverse lines of development in both the legal order and constitutional scholarship over the past 50 years: strengthening of fundamental and human rights, constitutional judicial review, constitutionalization of the legal order (ie, the orientation of the entire legal order towards constitutional principles), an accordant ethos among legal practitioners, the comprehension of constitutional principles as social values, and the perception of constitutional law as a vehicle for social integration.[15] Comparative constitutional law is often used to demonstrate that these phenomena are part of a global trend and therefore have the legitimacy of normalcy.

Granted, I argue this development not only from the perspective of constitutional law, but additionally from a German point of view. For some systems of constitutional academia, an ascent to supreme discipline is more wishful thinking than current praxis. The relevant phenomena appear at different points in time and with varying intensity. Nonetheless, such developments occur in most legal orders in Europe, at times with the aid of European law. In this sense, Article 4(2) of the Treaty on European Union as amended by the Treaty of Lisbon even grounds the member states' identities in the basic features of the national constitution.[16] If the premises of this assumption are sound, then the constitution forms the core of the identity of the national legal order, which necessarily means it plays a role well beyond its merely formal supremacy. Article 4(2) can also be seen as the expression of political consensus on such an understanding of constitutional law among all member states; such a view falls in line with the concept of 'seizing the crown'. To put it another way, if there can be a supreme discipline within legal scholarship at all, then in Europe the crown can only belong to constitutional law.

The basis of this expansion is made up of fundamental and human rights and constitutional judicial review: more conflict, more cases, more constitutional law. The more the constitutional law, the more the available matter for comparison. After the Second World War, European legal orders procedurally and substantively bolstered their fundamental rights, most importantly by way of judicial review of statutes. In some instances this took place directly and massively, as a reaction to authoritarian or even totalitarian experiences (Germany, Greece, Italy, Poland, Spain, or Hungary); in other instances, it was in the course of

[15] See Chapter 36.

[16] The provision states: 'The Union shall respect the equality of Member States before the Treaties as well as their national identities, inherent in their fundamental structures, political and constitutional, inclusive of regional and local self-government.'

strengthening the rule of law (France, the United Kingdom, the Netherlands, Sweden, or Switzerland).[17] These developments invite scholarly comparative law reflections. In certain constitutional orders, international law plays a crucial role in this latter line of development: in France, the Netherlands, Switzerland, and the United Kingdom, the rights in the European Convention on Human Rights (ECHR) provide the foundation for this development; this even includes Austria's legal tradition, which is sceptical of balancing. Ultimately, constitutional scholarship succeeds in appropriating these rights as its own subject matter, even, as in the United Kingdom, under the premise of separation of constitutional law and human rights.

The body of law that sets up the state's structure is distinct from fundamental rights, inter alia, in that the former is a closed set. Fundamental rights, by contrast, can become relevant in an unforeseeable number of conflict constellations, usually covered by statutes and other legal acts ranking below the constitution. This relevance triggers a constitutionalization of the legal order, which is to say, an orientation of the entire legal order towards paramount constitutional principles, which in turn leads to a corresponding pre-eminence for the science that deals with this material. In the process, constitutional law is elevated above the mere status of one subject matter among many. To the extent human rights stand above the national setting, they necessitate a comparative scholarly approach.

Constitutionalization is especially intensive where the legal order provides for constitutional judicial review of judicial decisions, of *cases*. Due to the possibility of individual applications against court decisions under Article 34 ECHR and the corresponding expanding jurisprudence of the European Court of Human Rights, the various developments are increasingly framed within the common legal framework of the ECHR. Such constitutionalization sometimes leads to significant conflict, as exemplified by the continuous struggle between the Spanish Constitutional Court and the Spanish Supreme Court.[18] Widely varying motives may underlie this struggle—from the self-interests of certain disciplines and institutions to divergent conceptualizations of order and justice.[19]

III. Europeanization within the European Legal Area

1. Diagnosis: Crisis and Opportunity

The opening of national legal orders to supra- and international law, especially the law of the European Union and perhaps also the ECHR, has triggered a process of change, not only in national constitutional law, but also in its scholarship. Many believe that national constitutional law has even entered a new era.

This change is, first of all, of a thematic nature: new provisions in national constitutional law, such as integration clauses, have attracted the attention of constitutional scholars, and

[17] Accordingly, this development constitutes an initial emphasis of comparative constitutional law. See Rudolf Bernhardt, 'Eigenheiten und Ziele der Rechtsvergleichung im öffentlichen Recht' ['Peculiarities and Objectives in Public Law'] (1964) 24 *Zeitschrift für ausländisches öffentliches Recht und Völkerrecht* 431; Christian Starck, *Constitutionalism, Universalism and Democracy—A Comparative Analysis* (1999); Constance Grewe and Hélène Ruiz-Fabri, *Droits constitutionnels européens* [*European Constitutional Law*] (1995), 140–90; but see Guiseppe De Vergottini, *Diritto costituzionale comparato* [*Comparative Constitutional Law*] (6th edn, 2004), 230 (arguing with a consistent focus on state structures and summarizing questions on fundamental rights in 20 pages).

[18] On this conflict: Guerrero in von Bogdandy, Villalón, and Huber (n *), Vol I, §11, para 37; for a similar problem in Poland, see Tuleja in von Bogdandy, Villalón, and Huber (n *), Vol I, §8 , paras 42–5, 57.

[19] See Chapter 16.

traditional teachings, for example on sovereignty or democracy, have been rethought in light of the challenges of European law.[20] The change is also structural, wherein lies its true nature: thus, the discipline frees itself from the exclusive linkage to a specific source of law, that is, the domestic constitution; it develops new perspectives; comparative law gains in importance; a European level for institutionalized scientific exchange, career, reputation, and publication unfolds; and a European area of constitutional scholarship appears on the horizon.

However, as definite as the existence of change may be, the diagnoses remain unsure as to what exactly is changing, what recommendations should be made, and how one should react; and the prognosis is unclear as to what gestalt will permit the discipline to restabilize within the European legal area. One can already observe changes in scholarly styles, distribution of attention, public and private institutions, the media, reputational dynamics, and career paths, and perhaps even changes in loyalties and scholarly, political, and social identities. One can state that the advent of a European legal area inspires innovative constitutional theories and strengthens interdisciplinarity.

Because, in principle, the law of the European Union has uniform effect in each member's constitutional order, one can expect here to observe the most advanced Europeanization in constitutional scholarship. In fact, constitutional scholarship everywhere is aware of this challenge, and Union law has been integrated everywhere as part of mandatory university coursework. Usually, Union law is not only offered in an introductory specialized class, but also integrated in the teaching of various bodies of law. It would be worthwhile to study whether this instruction in its present form fosters a European identity in the future bar.[21]

Many constitutional scholars were not satisfied with merely retracing the developments. Instead, constitutional scholarship provides a platform for many voices critical of Europeanization, calling for a slowing or redirecting of the process. This fulfils both the discipline's societal function of contemporary critic and its practical function of intervening in the law's course of development. Often, categories of constitutional law, such as sovereignty or democracy, provide terminological points of reference for public discourse on the implications of European integration. In some states, only constitutional law, prepared by scholarly articles, could ultimately enable the formation of political opposition, which otherwise could find no voice in the political establishment. In a pluralist democracy, this scholarly engagement confirms the public role of this body of scholarship, thereby strengthening its functional legitimacy.

The constitutional impact of the ECHR is quite different for two main reasons. First, some states derive much of their domestic fundamental rights protection from the ECHR's provisions, whereas in other countries the autonomous fundamental rights of the national constitution fulfil this role. Secondly, the legal status of the Convention varies under different national constitutions: the ECHR does not—in contrast to Union law—determine its own status in domestic law. As a consequence, its role in research and university instruction among the member states is quite heterogeneous.

For example, the ECHR has difficulty in finding its place in Germany along the spectrum of scholarly attention, and it stands at the periphery of the required legal curriculum. Here, though, Germany appears to be rather the exception that proves the rule: most domestic scholarship incorporates the ECHR in constitutional doctrine relating to national fundamental rights. And this holds true, a fortiori, when the ECHR's provisions substantively fulfil the role of constitutionally guaranteed fundamental rights: then academic study of the ECHR is

[20] See Chapters 16 and 11.

[21] See Chapter 35.

not reserved to international law scholarship but becomes one of the main objects of constitutional scholarship.

From the perspective of the European area of research and that of the European legal area, the question arises: have the rights of the ECHR, the jurisprudence that deals with them, whether in the European Court of Human Rights, the European Court of Justice, or national courts, and the relevant legal scholarship begun to form a lingua franca in the discourse on fundamental rights in the European legal area?[22] This, in turn, confronts domestic constitutional scholarship, wherever the ECHR does not yet have a leading role, with a crucial question: should it continue its specific path of conceptual, doctrinal, and terminological development, guarding its identity, or instead join the European convoy for purposes of European cohesion, not least in order to gain a voice? Because fundamental rights have such a central role, the answer to this question will have deep implications for each and every part of constitutional law and the legal order in general.

At least as varied as the respective role of the ECHR is the role of comparative law in the national systems of constitutional scholarship.[23] In German constitutional law after the Second World War, some of the most important works had recourse to the law of the United States.[24] Comparative law's minimal influence may also be partially due to the occasionally held conviction that Germany's constitutional law is the best in the world: if so, little can be learned from foreign law. It is no accident that only as late as 2005 was a German-language textbook on comparative constitutional law published (having been penned by an Austrian!).[25] A parallel situation unfolded in the United Kingdom, where both of the fundamental texts celebrate British constitutional law as the world's best: Bagehot with respect to the Constitution of the United States, and Dicey with French public law in mind. In Sweden, as well, right up to the threshold of European Union membership, constitutional scholarship remained under the spell of the national constitution.

In the early 1990s, the situation began to alter. The 'second phase' of German public law saw an increase in the importance of intra-European comparative constitutionalism. Comparative law also made gains in the United Kingdom, albeit with less of a European connection than an interest in English-speaking, common law countries. The Swedish accession to the European Union even led to an international reorientation of Swedish public law, both as to content, for instance a new emphasis on separation of powers, and as to formal aspects, such as an increase in English-language publications.

[22] See Chapters 38 and 59.

[23] See Chapter 64.

[24] Comparative public law appears most developed in Italy with numerous professors dedicated to this topic, see, as an outstanding example, Alessandro Pizzorusso, *Il patrimonio costituzionale europeo* [*The European Constitutional Heritage*] (2002). For Germany, see Léontin-Jean Constantinesco, *Rechtsvergleichung* [*Comparative Law*] (1971); Peter Häberle, *Europäische Rechtskultur* [*European Judiciary Culture*] (1997), 9–32; the online public access catalogue (OPAC) of the Max Planck Institute for Comparative Public Law and International Law includes catalogues of monographs and volumes under the notations 'Rvgl: IX Aa' to 'Rvgl: IX Ae'. See <http://www.mpil.de/inthome/ww/de/int/intranet/opac.cfm> (last accessed 22 March 2010). Bibliographic references for articles on comparative constitutional law are available in the articles catalogue under the notations 'Rvgl 2.1' to 'Rvgl 2.7', see <http://www.mpil.de/ww/en/pub/library/catalogues_databases/doc_of_articles/comp_law.cfm>. When searching with these notations, the 'Field to search' should be set to either 'Notation (books)' or 'Notation (articles)'. Otherwise, German comparative legal study focused mostly on the law of socialist states.

[25] Bernd Wieser, *Vergleichendes Verfassungsrecht* [*Comparative Constitutional Law*] (2005). This may also have much to do with the fact that other legal orders have a subject along the lines of comparative law, *droit comparé, diritto costituzionale comparato* etc, whereas the German term *Rechtsvergleichung* refers, rather, to an activity, ie, 'comparing', than to a separate subject matter, which militates against its disciplinary establishment with separate textbooks. See Harold Cooke Gutteridge, *Comparative Law* (1949), 17.

In most other states, comparative law has for a much longer period played an important role in national constitutional studies, counting as an essential part of proper constitutional scholarship. Comparative law has been constitutive of both Greek and Polish public law since the early nineteenth century, with an accordingly strong academic emphasis. France's new system of constitutional scholarship includes a constituent comparative law component, facilitating a distancing from the dominant tradition of thought which has emphasized administrative law.[26] Thus, an epoch of comparative law is dawning in the European legal area. This leads to the prognoses.

2. Prognosis: *Ius Publicum Europaeum* by Comparative Constitutional Law

The above diagnoses permit the prognosis that comparative constitutionalism in the European legal area will increase in importance—and will increase in importance as a standard component of scholarship rather than as a separate discipline. It is more difficult to predict whether this will bring about a common public law, a new form of *ius publicum europaeum*.

The prognosis that the European Union's constitutional orders will *not* meld into a unitary system appears safe; rather, each constitutional order will integrate European influences into its existing lines of development preserving its own respective gestalt, both formally and substantively. Yet this does not rule out a *ius publicum europaeum*. This will require, in accordance with the term's dual meaning, first, a common constitutional law and, secondly, an integrated scholarship.

Historically, the term *ius publicum europaeum* describes both a common system of scholarship and a body of law assembled from diverse components, in particular the law of the Holy Roman Empire, the rights of the Territories, and a set of norms that would now be conceived of as international and natural law. In this sense, definite parallels can be drawn with the current legal situation in the European legal area, suggesting that reference back to the old term may prove useful.[27] The European legal area emerges from multiple masses of law, conceptualized simultaneously as interwoven *and* independent. These include Union law, the ECHR, and the various corpora of national public law. Inasmuch, there already is a *ius publicum europaeum*.

The situation is different in academia. The historical *ius publicum europaeum* implied an integrated scholarly culture. In nineteenth-century Germany, one even finds a public law discipline without an underlying, solid foundation of constitutional law,[28] in many aspects similar to legal studies in nineteenth-century Poland.[29] Today's situation is almost the inverse.

[26] See Elisabeth Zoller, *Introduction to Public Law* (2008).

[27] The term *ius publicum europaeum* can rightfully be freed from its association with Carl Schmitt; cf eg Carl Schmitt, *Der Nomos der Erde im Völkerrecht des Jus Publicum Europaeum* [*The Nomos of the Earth in International Law of the Jus Publicum Europaeum*] (1950); Pier Paolo Portinaro, *La crisi dello* jus publicum europaeum: *Saggio su Carl Schmitt* [*The Crisis of the* Jus Publicum Europaeum: *An Essay on Carl Schmitt*] (1982). On the roots of the term cf eg Joachim Hagemeier, *Iuris publici Europaei* [*European Public Law*], Vol 1 *De trium Regnorum septentrionalium Daniae, Norwegiae et Sveciae statu* (1677), Vol 2 *De statu Galliae* (1678), Vol 3 *De statu Angliae, Scotiae et Hiberniae* (1678), Vol 4 *De statu Imperii Germanici* (1678), Vol 5 *De statu proviniciarum Belgicarum* (1679), Vol 6 *De statu Italiae* (1680), Vol 7 *De statu regnorum Hungariae et Bohemiae* (1680), Vol 8 *De statu regni Poloniae et imperii Moscovitici* (1680).

[28] On German state and public law, see generally Michael Stolleis, *Geschichte des öffentlichen Rechts in Deutschland* [*History of the Public Law in Germany*] (1992), 322–80.

[29] Lipowicz in von Bogdandy, Villalón, and Huber (n *), Vol 2, §34, paras 10–15.

Europe shares two solidified layers of public law, each with constitutional elements: the law of the European Union and the law of the Human Rights Convention. But no European constitutional scholarship has similarly solidified in parallel. The systems of constitutional scholarship in Europe are still a long way from any *common* constitutional scholarship. The differences reflect the diversity of national scholarly styles and cultures. This evidences the obvious fact that a *ius publicum europaeum*, in the sense of a solidified European context for discussion and reception, currently still exists only in fragments.

Should there be such an overarching scholarship at all? Against the backdrop of the discipline's self-conception, as varied as its given manifestations may be, the answer can hardly be anything but in the affirmative. Such progression is beneficial beyond the discipline's own interests: there is a close nexus between a well-developed constitutional scholarship and a strong democracy.

What might such a scholarly field look like? Very probably, the research landscape will be differentiated even further. Far from drying out, national constitutional scholarship on the various domestic constitutions would, rather, be enriched. It seems anything but certain that the area of research most promising for reputation and career will always be that of the *ius publicum europaeum*; one must be careful not to underestimate the resiliency of the national systems.

With respect to the discipline of a *ius publicum europaeum*, one can expect the knowledge of its scholars to be fragmentary and heterogeneous: no one will know the law and the scholarly output in the European legal area to any similar extent as in a national legal area. Yet, a *ius publicum europaeum* will require more than occasional 'irritation' (understood in terms of system theory) of national production. At the same time, the litmus test for a common European scholarship should not be the emergence of comprehensive doctrinal patterns. It appears to be quite possible to respond to the heterogeneity of the legal material with a strengthening of theoretical components, as shown by the US research landscape, which encompasses 51 different legal systems.[30] This could lead to stronger recourse to legal philosophers who are considered part of the common European heritage, from Aristotle and Hobbes to Habermas and MacCormick, but also to the formation of disparate and separate transnational scientific communities, engaging in specific discourses on legal theory. Yet, the strong doctrinal component of most scholarly traditions in Europe makes a general substitution of doctrine by theory unlikely. The mindset of a lawyer educated in the tradition of doctrinalism is very different to that of a lawyer taught to believe that doctrines are more or less an illusion. Accordingly, the various doctrines could evolve by thickening the comparative component. A European comparative doctrinal discourse can distil legal arguments that are of general use when construing constitutional law under the various constitutions. Of great importance along this path will be legal education; its Europeanization, in the sense of a *ius publicum europaeum*, is still in a very early stage.

Can such a project of a *ius publicum europaeum* as a 'thick' scholarly discourse succeed? The road ahead is long, and the journey will be arduous: the language issue, the immensity of the research and publication landscape, and the myriad aspects of the European economic and legal area come immediately to mind. Nonetheless, in less than a century the discipline of constitutional scholarship has advanced from the periphery of the academic court to a leading role, perhaps even to the position of supreme discipline. In light of this successful legacy, one

[30] For the pull towards an American-style constitutional law, see Bernhard Schlink, 'Abschied von der Dogmatik' ['The Demise of Doctrine'] (2006) 60 *Merkur* 1125; the American scholarship certainly provides a viable, even attractive alternative path, see Post (n *), 420ff.

may dare to make the prognosis: constitutional scholarship in the European legal area can successfully reposition itself, focused on, but not limited to, doctrinal constructivism with a strong comparative element. That comparison within the European legal area is likely to develop numerous specificities as its context is so distinctive, in particular compared to comparative constitutionalism on a global scale.[31]

Bibliography

Patrick S. Atiyah and Robert S. Summers, *Form and Substance in Anglo-American Law: A Comparative Study of Legal Reasoning, Legal Theory, and Legal Institutions* (1987)

Rudolf Bernhardt, 'Eigenheiten und Ziele der Rechtsvergleichung im öffentlichen Recht' ['Peculiarities and Objectives in Public Law'] (1964) 24 *Zeitschrift für ausländisches öffentliches Recht und Völkerrecht* 431

Armin von Bogdandy, 'The Past and Promise of Doctrinal Constructivism: A Strategy for Responding to the Challenges facing Constitutional Scholarship in Europe' (2009) 7 *International Journal of Constitutional Law* 364

Armin von Bogdandy, Pedro Cruz Villalón, and Peter M. Huber (eds), *Handbuch Ius Publicum Europaeum* [*Handbook Ius Publicum Europaeum*], Vol I *Grundlagen und Grundzüge staatlichen Verfassungsrechts*, Vol II *Offene Staatlichkeit—Wissenschaft vom Verfassungsrecht* (Joseph K. Windsor trans, 2007, 2008)

Léontin-Jean Constantinesco, *Rechtsvergleichung* [*Comparative Law*] (1971)

Harold Cooke Gutteridge, *Comparative Law* (1949)

Hanoch Dagan, 'The Realist Conception of Law' (2007) 57 *University of Toronto Law Journal* 607

Stephen M. Feldman, *American Legal Thought from Premodernism to Postmodernism* (2000)

Ernest Gellner, *Nations and Nationalism* (1983)

Constance Grewe and Hélène Ruiz-Fabri, *Droits constitutionnels européens* [*European Constitutional Law*] (1995)

Peter Häberle, *Europäische Rechtskultur* [*European Judiciary Culture*] (1997)

Matthias Kumm, 'On the Past and Future of European Constitutional Scholarship', (2009) 7 *International Journal of Constitutional Law* 401

James R. Maxeiner, 'US "Methods Awareness" for German Jurists' in Bernhard Großfeld (ed), *Festschrift für Wolfgang Fikentscher* [*Collected Essays in Honour of Wolfgang Fikentscher*] (1998)

Giulio Napolitano, 'Sul futuro delle scienze del diritto pubblico: variazioni su una lezione tedesca in terra Americana' (2010) 1 *Rivista trimestrale di diritto pubblico* 1

Alessandro Pizzorusso, *Il patrimonio costituzionale europeo* [*The European Constitutional Heritage*] (2002)

Pier Paolo Portinaro, *La crisi dello* jus publicum europaeum*: Saggio su Carl Schmitt* [*The Crisis of the* Jus Publicum Europaeum*: An Essay on Carl Schmitt*] (1982)

Robert C. Post, 'Constitutional scholarship in the United States' (2009) 7 *International Journal of Constitutional Law* 416

Michel Rosenfeld, 'The Role of Constitutional Scholarship in Comparative Perspective' (2009) 7 *International Journal of Constitutional Law* 362

[31] Michael Stolleis, *Concepts, Models and Traditions of a Comparative European Constitutional History* (forthcoming).

Bernhard Schlink, 'Abschied von der Dogmatik' ['The Demise of Doctrine'] (2006) 60 *Merkur* 1125

Bernhard Schlink, 'Bemerkungen zum Stand der Methodendiskussion in der Verfassungsrechtswissenschaft' (1980) 19 *Der Staat* 73

Carl Schmitt, *Der Nomos der Erde im Völkerrecht des Jus Publicum Europaeum* [*The Nomos of the Earth in International Law of the Jus Publicum Europaeum*] (1950)

Alexander Somek, 'The Indelible Science of Law' (2009) 7 *International Journal of Constitutional Law* 424

Christian Starck, *Constitutionalism, Universalism and Democracy—A Comparative Analysis* (1999)

Michael Stolleis, *Geschichte des öffentlichen Rechts in Deutschland* [*History of the Public Law in Germany*] (1992)

Guiseppe De Vergottini, *Diritto costituzionale comparato* [*Comparative Constitutional Law*] (6th edn, 2004)

Elisabeth Zoller, *Introduction to Public Law* (2008)

B. Comparative Constitutional Analysis in United States Adjudication and Scholarship

MICHEL ROSENFELD

New York

I. On the Uses of Comparative Constitutionalism: Comparing Observer and Participant Perspectives

Comparative constitutionalism, a branch—albeit a particularly fragile one—of comparative law, has increasingly affected domestic constitutional law because of a marked intensification of transnational crosscurrents. On the one hand, as constitutions are typically deeply embedded in national psyches and cultures making comparisons seem hazardous. For example, whereas it stands to reason that there be convergence on the subject of commercial contracts among industrialized democracies, unsurprisingly similarly phrased free speech provisions have resulted in widely diverging scopes of protection.[1] On the other hand, in spite of these difficulties, there has been an increasing *use* of comparative constitutional materials over the last couple of decades by both constitution-makers and constitutional adjudicators.[2] The United States, however, has long resisted this latter trend, both in the context of constitutional adjudication and in that of constitutional scholarship. This is undoubtedly due mainly to the country's strong strains of constitutional exclusivism and exceptionalism, and to widespread perceptions of the US Constitution and constitutional adjudication as superior and unique.[3]

More recently, the United States has apparently begun to change course, by opening up to foreign constitutional influences. Instances of reliance on foreign materials go back centuries,[4] but only recent references to foreign authorities by a closely divided US Supreme Court in cases involving highly contentious issues such as the death penalty[5] and the rights of homosexuals[6] have ignited a fierce debate among judges and constitutional scholars. Moreover, the debate in question has framed American perceptions concerning the proper role of comparative constitutionalism in the context of constitutional adjudication and scholarship.

There are obvious differences between the *uses* of comparative constitutional materials by adjudicators and the *study* of such materials by comparativists. The uses in question are often strategic, as an adjudicator may seek to enhance legitimacy by reference to a longer established constitutional jurisprudence, or to temper reaction to a controversial decision by presenting it as consistent with widely respected foreign doctrine.[7] The comparativist, in contrast, is supposed to examine, within the bounds of accepted standards of scholarship, whether and to what extent similar provisions in different constitutions provide a basis for fruitful comparison. In other words, there seems to be a sharp dichotomy between adjudicators who become *participants* in the spread of comparative constitutionalism (or in resistance to such spread)[8] and scholars meant to engage the subject as *observers*. Consistent with this dichotomy, scholars should be in a position to cast a critical glance at strategic judicial uses of comparative constitutional materials and to elaborate criteria for principled judicial recourse to them. For example, it seems appropriate for a constitutional

[1] See Frederick Schauer, 'Free Speech and the Cultural Contingency of Constitutional Categories' in Michel Rosenfeld (ed), *Constitutionalism, Identity and Difference and Legitimacy: Theoretical Perspectives* (1994), 353.

[2] See Sujit Choudhry, 'Globalization in Search of Justification: Towards a Theory of Comparative Constitutional Interpretation' (1999) 74 *Indiana Law Journal* 819, 821–22 (Canadian 1982 Constitution influenced drafting of Bill of Rights in South Africa, New Zealand, and Hong Kong); Margaret A. Burnham, 'Cultivating a Seedling Charter: South Africa Grows its Constitution' (1997) 3 *Michigan Journal of Race and Law* 29, 44 (detailing the South Africa Constitutional Court's uses of comparative constitutional jurisprudence).

[3] See Norman Dorsen et al, *Comparative Constitutionalism: Cases and Materials* (2nd edn, 2010), 6.

[4] Ibid.

[5] See eg *Roper v Simmons* 543 US 551 (2005).

[6] See *Lawrence v Texas* 539 US 558 (2003).

[7] See eg Gary J. Jacobsohn, *Apple of Gold: Constitutionalism in Israel and the United States* (1993), ch 6 (discussing the Israeli Supreme Court's use of American free speech doctrine to justify decisions inconsistent with those of US courts in similar cases).

[8] See eg the scathing criticism against citations to foreign sources by Justice Scalia in his dissenting opinions in *Roper* 543 US 551 and *Lawrence* 539 US 558. The latter dissent will be discussed at greater length below. See Section III.2. See also Chapter 64.

adjudicator dealing with the constitutional status of assisted suicide for the first time to look to countries with accumulated experience on the subject;[9] but not for a constitutional adjudicator to cast an illiberal constitutional decision in the rhetoric of borrowed liberal constitutional doctrine.[10]

Upon further scrutiny, the above-mentioned dichotomy between participant and observer does not hold neatly or consistently. Participants do use the material strategically, but observers do not approach it neutrally. Their observations are inevitably ideologically grounded, and just as the strategic choice of a given participant is conditioned by one of the many plausible objectives open to that participant, the observer's perception is filtered through one of the many available ideologies allowing for a cogent grasp of comparative constitutional material. Put differently, the task of the participant is circumscribed by a contestable goal whereas the insights of the observer are framed by the essential dictates of a contestable ideology.

Because the current American controversy over the propriety of citations to foreign authorities in the context of constitutional adjudication sharply divides both American judges[11] and American scholars,[12] it affords a privileged vantage point for critical examination of the dynamic between participants' strategic uses of comparative constitutional materials and observers' ideological grasp of it. Some judges believe that foreign materials are helpful; others, that their use is obfuscatory and illegitimate.[13] For their part, some scholars believe that functional similarities and parallels among distinct constitutional jurisprudences predominate; others, that contextual differences are far more important than structural or functional convergence.[14]

This American controversy is particularly revealing from the standpoint of assessing the proper role of comparative constitutionalism in constitutional adjudication and scholarship. Not only does this controversy afford a unique highly concentrated glimpse into the respective dynamics of participants and observers as well as into that between those two groups; but it also does so in the especially instructive setting provided by the common law system, in which American constitutional adjudication is embedded. Traditionally, the common law relies on accumulated judicial experience through consideration of precedents. Consequently, American judges within one state often consider decisions by judges from other states (which do not have precedential value in the first state) for their instructiveness and persuasiveness, thus engaging in a veritable comparative enterprise.[15]

[9] Cf *Washington v Glucksberg* 521 US 702 (1997) (US Supreme Court referred to experience in foreign jurisdictions in its first decision on constitutionality of assisted suicide).

[10] Cf Michel Rosenfeld and András Sajó, 'Spreading Liberal Constitutionalism: An Inquiry into the Fate of Free Speech Rights in New Democracies' in Sujit Choudhry (ed), *The Migration of Constitutional Ideas* (2006), 142 (discussing the Hungarian courts' use of foreign liberal constitutional doctrine to justify illiberal Hungarian decisions). See Chapter 5.

[11] See eg *Roper* 543 US 551 at 608 (Scalia J dissenting); *Lawrence* 539 US 558 at 598 (Scalia J dissenting).

[12] See eg Daniel A. Farber, 'The Supreme Court, the Law of Nations, and Citations of Foreign Law: The Lessons of History' (December 15, 2006) UC Berkeley Public Law Research Paper No 954359, available at <http://ssrn.com/abstract=954359>; Jeremy Waldron, 'Foreign Law and the Modern *Ius Gentium*' (2005) 119 *Harvard Law Review* 129.

[13] See 'The Relevance of Foreign Legal Materials in US Constitutional Cases: A Conversation Between Justice Antonin Scalia and Justice Stephen Breyer' (2005) 3 *International Journal of Constitutional Law* 519 (hereafter, 'A Conversation Between Scalia and Breyer').

[14] See Section II below for discussion of these respective positions.

[15] See eg *Van Daele v Vinci* 51 Ill 2d 389 (Supreme Court of Illinois 1972) (private law case in which the Illinois court cited cases from New Jersey, Florida, and Missouri).

To best frame this current American controversy and to best assess its implications for the use and study of comparative constitutionalism, Section II below provides a brief bird's eye view of the main current scholarly positions on the scope and limitations of legitimate comparative legal analysis in the field of constitutional law. Section III undertakes a critical analysis of the current American controversy over citations to foreign legal authorities in US constitutional adjudications. Finally, Section IV assesses the implications of the use and study of comparative constitutionalism in the context of current American conceptions of constitutional adjudication and scholarship.

II. The Scholarly Controversy over the Proper Uses and Scope of Comparative Constitutionalism

The debate among scholars concerning the legitimate scope of comparative work in constitutional law centers around three broadly defined positions. Proponents of the first of these maintain that both the problems of constitutional law and their solution are, or ought to be, essentially the same across the spectrum of full-fledged constitutional democracies.[16] Advocates of the second position agree that the problems of constitutional law are the same for all, but are convinced that the solutions to these problems are likely to differ from one constitutional polity to the next.[17] Finally, partisans of the third position assert that neither the constitutional problems nor their solutions are likely to be the same for different constitutional democracies.[18] The first position tends towards constitutional universalism, and turns to comparative constitutionalism to elucidate the proper standards and to spotlight deviations from the latter. The second position is poised to highlight differences and to place them in their proper context, thus shedding light on how different one constitutional system is from the next, and why such constitutional systems—including the comparativist's own system—differ from one another. The third position leads to the conclusion that comparisons are most likely to be ultimately arbitrary, and that the comparativists choices and analyses are bound to be driven above all by ideology. From the standpoint of the comparativist's own constitutional system, the first position offers a standard of identity that allows for determination of conformity with the prescriptions of constitutionalism.[19] The second position provides a standard of differentiation pointing to how and why one's own constitution is distinct. Finally, the third position affords the means to refer selectively to apparent similarities and differences among constitutional jurisprudences to imprint a particular ideological gloss upon the comparativist's own.

All three positions are at least in part persuasive, and a dynamic conception of the interplay among them provides a credible insight into the true potential of comparativism. It is reasonable to reject the highly implausible hypothesis that comparison in the realm of constitutional law is either altogether impossible, or that its findings are bound to be utterly irrelevant. It follows from this that any hypothesis concerning the utility and the potential of comparison in

[16] See David M. Beatty, *Constitutional Law in Theory and Practice* (1995).

[17] See Mary Ann Glendon, 'Rights in Twentieth-Century Constitutions' (1992) 59 *University of Chicago Law Review* 519, 532 and Mary Ann Glendon, *Comparative Legal Traditions* (2nd edn, 1994), 10.

[18] See Günther Frankenberg, 'Stanger than Paradise: Identity and Politics in Comparative Law' (1997) *Utah Law Review* 259, 262–3.

[19] See Chapter 35.

this field must recognize that there must be both identities and differences among systems. Moreover, it should become evident that the latter are relevant for purposes of comparison even if the exact relevance of particular identities or differences or concerning what ultimately ought to count as a relevant similarity or difference remains in dispute.

Whether or not comparativists necessarily are ideologically biased may be a more controversial matter, but that seems of little consequence for present purposes. Indeed, critical theorists regard not only comparative constitutionalism but also domestic law as ideological.[20] Therefore, the crucial divide is not between comparativists and scholars focused solely on domestic law, but between those who maintain that law, judges, and scholars cannot escape being ideologically biased and those who reject that position.

There may be, however, different types of ideological biases bearing on one's approach to law. There may be philosophical or political biases: one may be a Marxist or a free market champion, a social democrat or a conservative, and each of these biases seems bound to be reflected in its respective proponents' approach to law. Moreover, there is no reason to suspect that these biases will not equally affect the comparativist and the scholar exclusively devoted to domestic law. Nevertheless, there is one bias, the national[21] one, that does seemingly set the comparativist apart. Regardless of internal domestic ideological divisions, scholars, judges, politicians, and citizens within the same country may share a national bias that sets them apart from their counterparts in other countries. The American ideology and legal culture is thus different from the French, German, or Russian one, and the American scholar will most likely be unable to shed his national identity when dealing with foreign legal materials. This seemingly inevitable national bias may even be stronger when dealing with constitutional law, which is likely to be closer to the core of national identity than other fields, such as a commercial law.

The key question concerns the importance rather than the existence of this national bias. Whereas more extensive consideration of this question will be postponed until Section IV below, it should be emphasized from the outset that this bias is not as important as it may at first appear for two principal reasons. First, the national bias is one among many that spreads across borders and that may be equally relevant from the standpoint of the comparativist. For example, regardless of national biases, judges and scholars in many jurisdictions confronting the threat of international terrorism divide over whether, or to what extent, civil liberties should be curtailed to enhance security.[22] Secondly, once aware of the national bias, one can take steps to mitigate it even if one can never eradicate it. One can explore the political and cultural context in which foreign constitutional law is embedded, read the foreign country's domestic scholarship, enter into dialogue with foreign comparativists, domestic constitutional law scholars, etc. In short, the comparativist is like a person who needs to learn and use a foreign language to function in an alien land. The person in question will never dominate the foreign language as she does her native one or shed her non-native accent in her newly acquired language. Nevertheless, she will manage to be understood and will in turn be able to learn much about her hosts and their way of life.

[20] See eg Roberto Unger, 'The Critical Legal Studies Movement' (1983) 96 *Harvard Law Review* 561.

[21] I use 'national' here broadly to encompass a political collectivity that shares a common identity, thus potentially including transnational groupings such as the European Union or Western democracies.

[22] See eg Robin Toner, 'A Nation Challenged: The Terrorism Fight; Civil Liberty vs Security: Finding a Wartime Balance', *NY Times*, November 18, 2001; Linda Greenhouse, 'Post-9/11 Detainee Cases On Supreme Court Docket', *NY Times*, November 3, 2003.

III. The American Controversy over Citation of Foreign Authorities

The American controversy is primarily among judges, though it has generated a significant secondary literature among scholars, and primarily among those in American constitutional law.[23] The plight of the comparative scholar discussed in Section II above is, however, quite relevant to the current quarrel among American judges. If the comparativist scholar can be a veritable observer-translator, then the relationship between observer and participant, scholar and judge, would not be essentially different when dealing with foreign law from that when dealing with domestic law. This is particularly true in the United States where federal judges must be ready to deal with 51 different bodies of law (the federal one and that of each of the 50 states). On the other hand, if the comparativist scholar is hopelessly trapped in his own national ideology, then the observer/participant line blurs, translations become entirely unreliable, and judges' recourse to foreign materials seemingly completely arbitrary.

Turning to the actual controversy, it has arisen in cases dealing with highly divisive issues such as the death penalty for juveniles[24] or the mentally impaired[25] and the rights of homosexuals.[26] These issues divide American judges and the larger polity along moral, political, religious, ideological, and constitutional grounds. In what follows, I will focus exclusively on the controversy regarding the rights of homosexuals because they arise in the context of a particularly contested area of constitutional law, namely that pertaining to unenumerated rights. American judges and jurists have long divided over whether the protection of fundamental rights under the US Constitution ought to extend to unenumerated rights in general and to the rights of homosexuals in particular. This divide is in large measure ideological, reflecting deep differences concerning morals, politics, culture, and the nature and role of the US Constitution. Accordingly, the cases dealing with homosexual rights are particularly apt to reveal whether, and to what extent, the ideological wars over citations to foreign legal authorities in constitutional adjudication differ from the ideological wars over recognizing unenumerated constitutional rights.

1. The American Unenumerated Rights Tradition and the Dispute over Homosexual Constitutional Rights

American unenumerated rights derive principally from two clauses within the US Constitution. The first is the Ninth Amendment (1791) which provides that 'The enumeration in the Constitution of certain rights shall not be constructed to deny or disparage others retained by the people.' The second is the Due Process Clause of the Fourteenth Amendment (1868) which provides that no state 'shall deprive any person of life, liberty or property without due process of law'. The Fourteenth Amendment is a less obvious source of unenumerated rights than is the Ninth, as 'due process' may be understood in purely procedural terms. Nevertheless, in many decisions, the US Supreme Court has given a 'substantive' interpreta-

[23] See n 12. See also Robert Post, 'Constitutional Scholarship in the United States' (2009) 7 *International Journal of Constitutional Law* 417, 420–1 (noting that unlike in Europe, in the United States, constitutional scholars tend to react to adjudication rather than elaborating a systematic approach suited for adoption by adjudicators).

[24] *Roper* 543 US 551.

[25] *Atkins v Virginia* 536 US 304 (2002).

[26] *Lawrence* 539 US 558.

tion to due process, recognizing fundamental liberty, property, and privacy rights.[27] In its 1965 *Griswold* decision,[28] the US Supreme Court recognized an unenumerated constitutional right to privacy and held that it protected the right of married couples to use artificial contraception. The Court later extended that right to cover unmarried heterosexual individuals in *Eisenstadt*[29] and to afford protection to a woman's decision to obtain an abortion in *Roe v Wade*.[30] The Court has been divided over the legitimacy of recognizing an unenumerated constitutional right to privacy, and the various opinions filed in *Griswold* afford a representative glimpse of the various positions among the justices. In his majority opinion, Justice Douglas derived a general right of privacy from incidents of it found in individual provisions of the Bill of Rights; Justice Goldberg from the Ninth Amendment; and Justice Harlan from the Fourteenth Amendment's Due Process Clause. On the other hand, the dissenting justices refused to recognize either a general right to privacy or the legitimacy of unenumerated rights.[31]

It is in this context that in its 5–4 decision in *Bowers v Hardwick*[32] the Court refused to extend privacy protection to homosexual sex. Seizing on the Court's elaboration since *Griswold* of a jurisprudence that predicated recognition of unenumerated rights on whether they were deeply steeped in tradition and ranked as fundamental to the achievement of justice or 'ordered liberty',[33] the majority in *Bowers* held that homosexual sex was not entitled to constitutional protection. The majority concluded that there was no tradition of protection of homosexual intimacy in the United States and accordingly upheld the constitutionality of a state statute that criminalized homosexual sodomy, and provided for up to 20 years' imprisonment as punishment.[34]

Bowers was overruled 17 years later in the 2003, 6–3 decision in *Lawrence v Texas*.[35] As we shall see, in both *Bowers* and *Lawrence*, reference was made to foreign law. In *Bowers*, it caused little controversy; in *Lawrence*, very substantial controversy.

2. The Battle over Citations to Foreign Law in *Bowers* and *Lawrence*

The most vivid invocation of traditional reprobation of homosexuality in *Bowers*, relying significantly on foreign authorities, is found in Chief Justice Burger's concurring opinion. After referring to strong condemnation pursuant to Judeo-Christian morals and Roman law,[36] the Chief Justice cited Blackstone's eighteenth-century characterization of homosexuality under English law as 'the infamous crime against nature', an offense of 'deeper malignity' than rape, 'the very mention of which is a crime not fit to be named'.[37] In his opinion for the Court's

[27] See *Lochner v New York* 198 US 45 (1905) (constitutionalizing fundamental property and freedom of contract rights) and *Griswold v Connecticut* 381 US 479 (1965) (constitutionalizing a fundamental right to privacy). See also Chapter 44 on due process generally; see Chapter 46 on privacy more generally.

[28] *Griswold* 381 US 479.

[29] *Eisenstadt v Baird* 405 US 438 (1972).

[30] 410 US 113 (1973). See Chapter 51.

[31] In his dissenting opinion, Justice Black argued that the Ninth Amendment was intended to assure the states that the Federal Bill of Rights was not meant to supersede or prohibit state-granted rights, nor to allow for the recognition of additional federal rights: 381 US 479 at 520.

[32] 478 US 186 (1986).

[33] Ibid 191.

[34] Ibid 196.

[35] Ibid 196–7. On sexual orientation in constitutional law in general, see Chapter 52.

[36] Ibid 197.

[37] 478 US 186 at 197 (citing Blackstone, *Commentaries*, 215).

majority in *Lawrence*, Justice Kennedy found, as had the dissenters in *Bowers*, that homosexual intimacy among consenting adults formed part of a larger deeply embedded tradition whereby an individual's choice of a partner to share 'enduring bonds'[38] is a deeply private matter that must remain beyond the reach of the state. Moreover, in the course of his opinion Justice Kennedy cited foreign law for two distinct purposes. The first was in order to demonstrate that Chief Justice Burger's sweeping conclusions relying on the foreign authorities he invoked were one-sided and misleading.[39] The second purpose, which proved much more controversial, was to provide additional authority—not in the sense of binding precedent but in that of a better emerging tradition—for the Court's decision to afford constitutional protection to homosexual sex. In Justice Kennedy's words,

> The right the petitioners seek in this case has been accepted as an integral part of human freedom in many other countries. There has been no showing that in this country the governmental interest in circumscribing personal choice is somehow more legitimate or urgent.[40]

Specifically, Justice Kennedy referred to European norms through citations to decisions of the European Court of Human Rights.[41] This unleashed a vehement reaction leading to calls for Justice Kennedy's impeachment[42] and to proposals for legislation prohibiting federal judges from citing foreign legal authorities while adjudicating constitutional cases.[43] These developments stand in sharp contrast to the virtually complete lack of reaction to the fact that Chief Justice Burger cited foreign authorities in *Bowers*.

Within the Court itself, Justice Scalia's dissent in *Lawrence* proffered a scathing rebuke to Justice Kennedy's reliance on foreign authorities. First, Justice Scalia asserted that the '*Bowers* majority opinion *never* relied on values we share with other civilizations'.[44] Secondly, and more generally, Justice Scalia made clear that,

> The Court's discussion of…foreign views (ignoring of course, the many countries that have retained criminal prohibitions on sodomy) is therefore meaningless dicta. Dangerous dicta, however, since this *Court…should not impose foreign moods, fads or fashions on Americans.*[45]

In short, for Justice Scalia the common traditions Americans share with others (mainly Europeans to the extent that Judeo-Christian mores and Roman and English law are involved) are irrelevant from a constitutional standpoint—even though reference to tradition has played a crucial role in the elaboration of a jurisprudence of unenumerated rights. Furthermore, any reliance on foreign views in the course of elaborating constitutional norms is, for him, downright dangerous.

3. The Controversy over Foreign Authorities in a Broader Context

Why reference to foreign law and mores by justices in the majority of *Bowers* did not cause an uproar comparable to that occasioned by similar references by Justice Kennedy in *Lawrence*

[38] 539 US 558 at 567.

[39] Ibid 572–3.

[40] Ibid 577.

[41] Ibid 576.

[42] See eg Jane Lampman, 'Bringing the Case against Judges', *Christian Science Monitor* (April 13, 2005), available at <http://www.csmonitor.com/2005/0413/p15s02-usju.html>; Dana Milbank, 'And the Verdict on Justice Kennedy Is: Guilty', *Washington Post*, April 9, 2005, at A03.

[43] See eg HR Res 372, 110th Cong (2007); S Res 92, 109th Cong (2005).

[44] *Lawrence* 539 US 558 at 598.

[45] Ibid, emphasis added.

17 years later is an important question. The reasons for the remarkable shift between 1986 and 2003 may well be manifold but, for our purposes, two of them stand out above all others. The first is the global spread of constitutionalism and its effect on American constitutional identity; the second, the dramatic exacerbation of a long-standing split regarding America's national identity. These two reasons are closely intertwined, moreover, because American constitutional identity figures so prominently in the country's national identity.[46]

The year 1989 marks a major turning point in the worldwide spread of constitutionalism much as, two centuries earlier, 1789 saw the dawn of modern constitutionalism with the entry into force of the US Constitution. After the fall of the Berlin Wall in 1989, constitutionalism promptly spread throughout the formerly communist polities in Europe,[47] followed by rapid expansion into other politics throughout the world, including South Africa,[48] much of South America,[49] and many countries in other parts of the world.[50] This trend towards constitutional rule throughout the globe started after the Second World War when Germany and Japan turned into constitutional democracies, but it accelerated enormously after 1989. Furthermore, this trend not only brought constitutional democracy to an ever-increasing number of polities, but it also led to the proliferation of constitutional adjudication by courts extending to all corners of the world.

These developments had two salient consequences for American constitutionalism. They put an end to American constitutional hegemony and they yielded a rich and varied judicial constitutional jurisprudence available to be mined for various purposes involving either identification or differentiation between American and non-American approaches and results with respect to similar issues.

Concurrently with the spread of constitutionalism, and particularly after the United States became the only superpower upon the dissolution of the Soviet Union in the early 1990s, there was an intensification of the divide among the respective proponents of two opposing visions of America. The first of these is the exclusivist vision.[51] In the exclusivist view, the United States is a country with a unique destiny, exemplary values and ideals, and it serves as a model for the rest of the world. Under the second, universalist view, on the other hand, the United States is a diverse cosmopolitan nation which is as much influenced by trends and developments coming from abroad as the rest of the world is influenced by it.[52] The exclusivist view fosters a national identity focused on divergences; the universalist view, one centered on convergences. Furthermore, the divide over these views became much more contentious after George W. Bush became president, reaching its peak in 2003, the year *Lawrence* was decided, because of the rift over going to war in Iraq between the United States and many of its traditional European allies such as France and Germany.[53]

In their current incarnations, the exclusivist view is mainly held by political conservatives; the universalist, by progressives.[54] Moreover, for the exclusivists, the US Constitution must

[46] See Michel Rosenfeld, *The Identity of the Constitutional Subject: Selfhood, Citizenship, Culture and Community* (2010), 73, 160–2. See also Chapter 35.

[47] See Rett R. Ludwikowski, *Constitution-Making in the Region of Former Soviet Dominance* (1996).

[48] See Dorsen (n 3), 1–2.

[49] See Juan J. Linz and Alfred Stepan, *Problems of Democratic Transitions and Consolidation: Southern-Europe, South America, and Post-Communist Europe* (1996).

[50] See Dorsen (n 3), 2.

[51] Mark Tushnet, 'Referring to Foreign Law in Constitutional Interpretation: An Episode in the Culture Wars' (2006) 35 *University of Baltimore Law Review* 299, 310–11.

[52] Ibid.

[53] See 'France and Allies Rally against War', *BBC News*, March 5, 2003, available at <http://news.bbc.co.uk/go/fr/-z/hi/middle_east/2821145.stm>.

[54] See Tushnet (n 51), 310–11.

remain purely American and free from foreign influence or contamination.[55] For the universalist, in contrast, there is a convergence of norms and values, at least among advanced constitutional democracies, which makes constitutional cross-fertilization attractive and often useful.[56] The split between these two constitutional visions is sharp and seemingly irreconcilable.

It is understandable that the aforementioned rift is particularly acute in the context of spelling out the tradition associated with unenumerated rights. Indeed, that task requires reprocessing elements of national identity—core elements at that—for purposes of elaborating key aspects of constitutional identity. The convergence of political ideology, conceptions of national identity, constitutional philosophy, and inferences from the dramatic historical changes since 1989, goes a long way in explaining the differences concerning references to foreign authorities between *Bowers* and *Lawrence* as well as those within *Lawrence*. Largely because of this convergence, moreover, these differences are overdetermined.

What most obviously accounts for the different impact of references to foreign authorities in *Bowers* and *Lawrence* is the change in historical circumstances and its effects on American self-perception. *Bowers* was decided before the end of the Cold War and before the explosion and proliferation (at least within sight of the American legal and judicial community) of foreign constitutional adjudication. At the time of *Bowers*, the geopolitical order was based on the balance of the United States versus the Soviet Union, with Western Europe largely on the side of the former. At the time of *Lawrence*, the United States, as the lone superpower, stood at odds with much of Europe over, among other things, Iraq. In addition, in *Bowers*, justices whose constitutional conclusions were most compatible with conservative politics relied on foreign authorities, whereas in *Lawrence* it was the opposite—the majority judicial position was aligned with progressive politics. This is important since progressives, tending to be universalists, are much less likely to object to the use of foreign references as such. Finally, and this is greatly magnified in relation to defining tradition, *Bowers* refers mainly to ancient and historically distant foreign sources that emphasize religious morality at least as much as law. *Lawrence*, on the other hand, relies primarily on the contemporary jurisprudence of the European Court of Human Rights. Accordingly, *Bowers* can be viewed as asserting that America's deepest traditions have roots in religious, moral, and legal values that it shares with the broad Judeo-Christian vision as it emerged throughout the Western World. *Lawrence*, in contrast, can be portrayed as having bowed to foreign contemporary legal precedent. Moreover, although Justice Kennedy makes it clear that he regards European judicial decisions as evidence of the relevant tradition (above all to refute the *Bowers* Court's erroneous account of that tradition), to an exclusivist what *Lawrence* does may seem worse than simply following foreign precedent. It may be, in part, the functional equivalent of following foreign precedent, but it also uses the latter to define the relevant tradition. For that reason, for the exclusivist such use of foreign precedents not only subverts America's constitutional jurisprudence, but it also pollutes its self-perception at the level of national identity.

The clash between the majority and the dissent in *Lawrence* replicates the basic rift between *Lawrence* and *Bowers*, but it does so against an altered backdrop. The universalist, progressive majority looks to Europe to elaborate further the evolving tradition issuing from *Griswold*, and relies on decisions of the European Court of Human Rights, not as precedents, but as examples of successful progressive judicial resolutions of the very issue before the US Supreme

[55] 'A Conversation Between Scalia and Breyer' (n 13), 521, 525. One way to exclude present-day foreign influences systematically is by adhering, as Justice Scalia does, to originalism (ibid).

[56] Ibid 528–9.

Court. The exclusivist conservative minority, on the other hand, rejects the example of Europe, and insists upon confining the relevant tradition to that already present in the United States at the time of the founding. Within this setting, what seems most puzzling is Justice Scalia's flat denial that *Bowers* relied on any foreign values, let alone foreign legal authorities, and his characterization of the European jurisprudence cited by the Court's majority as the product of 'moods', 'fads', and 'fashions'.[57] Indeed, even from a most exclusivist standpoint, American exceptionalism does not call for rejection of the Judeo-Christian heritage but, on the contrary, for its adoption and its perfection.[58] For the same reason, it would seem sufficient for an exclusivist to reject European, or for that matter any other, jurisprudence on the conviction that it can neither be authoritative nor become part of any relevant tradition on which it would be legitimate to rely in the course of adjudicating unenumerated rights cases.

The above puzzle can be solved, however, if one considers that European jurisprudence stands for what is most enlightened and most advanced in modern constitutionalism, and what therefore ought to be ideally embraced by all constitutional democracies. This last conclusion is consistent with the universalist position and implicit in Justice Kennedy's majority opinion.[59] An exclusivist arguing against this universalist position cannot simply reject foreign authorities because they are foreign. What is needed instead, and Justice Scalia does exactly that, is both to challenge the uniqueness and exemplarity of the European jurisprudence and to trivialize its importance and aspirations to universality. This Justice Scalia seeks to accomplish by reminding the United States that many non-European countries continue to criminalize homosexual sex, and by belittling the potential attractiveness of the European jurisprudence by labeling it a 'fad' and a 'fashion'.

Exclusivists and universalists sketch out different conceptions of national identity and of constitutional identity, though in both cases the former is closely intertwined with the latter. This raises the question of whether it would be more accurate to speak in the plural of competing national and constitutional identities rather than in the singular. Moreover, if the answer were in the affirmative, then it would seem that at both the national level and the constitutional one a clash of identities would be more likely than would the consolidation of a commonly shared identity.

IV. The Implications for Comparative Constitutionalism of the American Controversy over Citations to Foreign Legal Authorities

The preceding analysis reveals that the US Supreme Court is divided concerning both the legitimacy and scope of unenumerated rights under the Constitution, and the propriety of referring to foreign legal authorities in the course of adjudicating American constitutional cases. Moreover, on the question of the rights of homosexuals, the divide on the Court is over what ought to count as a relevant similarity or identity, what as a relevant difference, and over clashing ideologies regarding the legitimate boundaries of civil liberties and of the state's constitutional powers to regulate private morality. What is particularly salient for our purposes, is

[57] See n 44.

[58] See generally Rogers M. Smith, *Civic Ideals: Conflicting Visions of Citizenship in US History* (1997).

[59] A less sweeping though consistent variant would be that Europe best exemplifies Western culture and tradition of which the United States is a part.

that the divisions involved seem no different whether one focuses on the clash over foreign authorities or on the purely domestic debate over which, if any, unenumerated rights ought to be constitutionally recognized, and to what extent. Moreover, whether the relevant ideological conflict is over the narrower issue concerning the proper canons of constitutional interpretation or the broader moral issue that pits liberal followers of John Stuart Mill against social conservatives, the domestic controversy and that over recourse to foreign materials mirror one another.

Once ideological conflict is regarded as inevitable concerning issues over which the broader polity is deeply divided, then the difference between participant and observer noted at the outset seems much less decisive than it might have at first. Neither participants nor observers can be truly neutral, and even if the former act in a purely strategic result-oriented way and the latter do not, it would still be the case that neither group could act in conformity with the dictates of uncontested or uncontestable norms.[60]

The American scholarly debate over the propriety and desirability of citations to foreign authorities in constitutional cases closely tracks that among judges.[61] This suggests again that ideological differences play a more important role than those between users and observers. Scholars, like judges, differ over the proper canons of constitutional interpretation as well as over whether the state ought to be entitled to intervene within the sphere of private morality.

The debate among American scholars and that among American judges centers around the same three principal issues: the possibility of doing competent comparative work; the utility of comparisons in the realm of constitutional law; and the legitimacy of relying on such comparisons in elaborating one's domestic constitutional jurisprudence. With respect to the first of these issues, scholars have to play a different role than judges. American judges are sufficiently familiar, and hence comfortable, with the jurisprudence of the various American states, but often lack any basic familiarity with foreign jurisprudences. They are accordingly reluctant to refer to the latter lest they misinterpret and misuse them.[62] Scholars, on the other hand, can thoroughly examine foreign jurisprudences and can place them in their proper context even if they cannot overcome their national bias. In addition, because of this, comparative scholars can help judges to remedy their lack of familiarity with foreign jurisprudences. Indeed, the more good comparative scholarship there is, the more both litigants and judges will be in a position to become prepared to gauge the similarities and differences between diverse jurisprudences.

On the question of the utility of comparing constitutional jurisprudences and on appropriate occasions for drawing lessons from foreign jurisprudences, scholars and judges divide along the same lines. Exclusivists stress the uniqueness of the US Constitution, and consequently conclude that foreign experiences could not be relevant. Universalists, in contrast, expect sufficient convergence between the leading jurisprudences as to be confident that foreign jurisprudences can provide useful frames of reference, and, in some instances, worthy

[60] This is not to say that there is no difference between knowingly acting purely strategically and without scruples for the sole purpose of gaining an advantage or imposing one's will and doing one's best to understand complex legal phenomena without being able to avoid adherence to contested or contestable norms. There is certainly a crucial difference between the two from the standpoint of social responsibility and professional ethics. Nevertheless, both remain normatively contestable, and subject to condemnation or repudiation by a significant proportion of those affected by them.

[61] Compare eg Richard Posner whose position is close to Justice Scalia, see Richard Posner, 'Foreword: A Political Court' (2005) 119 *Harvard Law Review* 31, 84–90, to Vicki Jackson who essentially shares Justice Kennedy's views, see Vicki C. Jackson, 'Constitutional Comparisons: Convergence, Resistance, Engagement' (2005) 119 *Harvard Law Review* 109.

[62] See Posner (n 61).

insights that may be of great value in the elaboration of novel areas of domestic jurisprudence.[63]

Even if one accepts the exclusivist thesis, it does not seem to follow that comparativism would have virtually nothing to contribute to constitutional adjudication. At an absolute minimum, comparisons in the fundamental rights area could reinforce understanding of the exclusivists' conception of these rights and sharpen the contours of their self-perception as exclusivists.[64] At a maximum, on the other hand, comparison could better legitimize exclusivism and highlight its virtues. In a similar vein, the Canadian Supreme Court has been very effective in its endorsement of a free speech jurisprudence that is self-consciously distinct from its US counterpart after having acutely analyzed the latter and found it wanting in relation to Canadian constitutional objectives.[65] This stands in sharp contrast to Justice Scalia's exclusivist response in the *Roper* case dealing with the death penalty for juveniles to Justice Kennedy's pointing out that only in the United States and in Somalia was the punishment in question still in force. Justice Scalia responded as he did in *Lawrence* by asserting that the US judiciary should not follow the latest 'trends' or 'fashions'.

The question of the legitimacy of comparison also divides exclusivists and universalists. This question, moreover, is greatly sharpened in the context of unenumerated rights, particularly as the latter are correlated to deep-seated traditions within the polity. The more narrowly a tradition is framed, and the less the evolution of that tradition is taken into account, the less it would seem that comparative analysis would be helpful, at least to the judge.[66] At the extreme, consistent with American originalism, which confines legitimate constitutional interpretation to discovery and implementation of the Framers' intent, comparativism is downright illegitimate, a position embraced by Justice Scalia.[67]

Universalists, in contrast, may well find foreign authorities and common traditions shared with foreign polities' legitimate interpretive resources in the elaboration of an unenumerated rights jurisprudence. The broader the framing of the tradition, and the more it is conceived as an evolving one, the greater it would seem that comparative considerations would be fruitful.

Since the 1960s, American originalists have mostly been politically conservative.[68] This may explain why there was no great uproar concerning the citation of foreign authorities, such as the Bible, in *Bowers*. On the other hand, in *Lawrence*, originalists and social and political conservatives were on the same side against the Court's decision and against the European pro-homosexual rights jurisprudence relied upon by Justice Kennedy.

One of the fiercest arguments against comparativism in the unenumerated rights area made by exclusivists—including Justice Scalia[69] as well as some scholars[70]—is to the effect that

[63] See eg *Washington v Glucksberg* 521 US 702 (1997).

[64] The same may not equally apply to the structural areas of a constitution as it may be difficult, eg, to draw useful comparisons for purposes of adjudication between a presidential system and a parliamentary one. See Chapters 29 and 30.

[65] See eg *R v Keegstra* [1990] 3 SCR 697 (Canadian Supreme Court).

[66] The scholar could still use comparison better to highlight the uniqueness of a domestic tradition.

[67] See 'A Conversation Between Scalia and Breyer' (n 13), 535–6. Strictly speaking, even for an originalist, comparativism may still be legitimate to the limited extent that the framers intended that American rights be understood by reference to foreign jurisprudences. Even in that case, legitimate reference would only extend to foreign authorities, as they existed at the time of the making of the US Constitution.

[68] This was not always the case. See *Lochner v New York* 198 US 45 (1905) (Holmes J dissenting) (using originalist argument to counter constitutional enshrinement of fundamental property and freedom of contract rights interpreted as barring social-welfare legislation).

[69] See 'A Conversation Between Scalia and Breyer' (n 13).

[70] See eg Posner (n 61), 88–9.

looking beyond the shores of the United States when inquiring about the relevant tradition at play is undemocratic. Specifically, the charge seems to boil down to the proposition that foreigners should not be given a vote concerning what ought to count as a deep moral conviction of the American citizenry. Those who, like Justice Scalia, make this charge seem to assume that the deepest moral convictions embedded in the polity's very fabric are, or ought to be, the exclusive product of the democratic processes within the country. If this assumption were warranted, then reliance on foreign authorities would be completely illegitimate, not because it might be useless or obfuscatory, but because it would open the door to a form of imperialism or colonialism coming from distant shores.

This argument from democracy seems paradoxical if one remembers that the appeal to unenumerated rights ordinarily occurs in the context of an attack against democratically enacted laws supported by the relevant majorities. Thus, the anti-sodomy laws at stake in *Bowers* and *Lawrence* were the products respectively of democratic majorities in Georgia and Texas. This suggests that the relevant traditions that lend support to an unenumerated right must lie somewhat deeper than the arena for ongoing majoritarian politics. Consistent with this, moreover, whether it is legitimate to consult foreign sources in the course of determining the proper present contours of a deeply rooted tradition depends primarily on whether or not that tradition is widely shared with others beyond the country's borders. Exclusivists and universalists simply disagree on whether American traditions are virtually completely *sui generis* or whether they overlap and share much with certain traditions prevalent in other polities.

Ultimately, the preceding inquiry reveals that comparativism in constitutional adjudication can play an important positive role. This is *because* there are enough similarities, differences, and ideological issues with respect to constitutional adjudication and constitutional scholarship, and *because* these are contested and contestable. Paradoxically, were similarities, differences, and ideological biases obvious and fixed, there would be less of a need for comparativism. In that case, the coordinates of the relevant universes would remain immutable, and each could largely focus on their well-delimited turf. However, because the interplay between identities and differences and the irruption of ideological bias are constantly in a state of flux, the relationship between one's turf and the broader universe of which it is a part must be constantly re-examined.

V. Conclusion

In the last analysis, the controversy between exclusivists and universalists reveals that both American national identity and constitutional identity are dynamic, conflictual, and multifaceted. Exclusivists and universalists, however, are ultimately dialectically linked as they represent two distinct competing facets of America's self-perception as a country of destiny called upon to set an example for the rest of the world.[71] For the exclusivists, the United States can only accomplish this by strictly adhering to what makes it different. For the universalists, on the other hand, overemphasis on such differences led the United States to lag before the most advanced constitutional democracies in certain respects, thus requiring that it catch up to them before it can legitimately reassert its leadership role. Overall, exclusivists and universalists provide two different means to the same end, but in the course of aiming at that end, they each seem to reinvigorate the very obstacle that the other seeks to overcome. Hence, the

[71] See generally Anders Stephanson, *Manifest Destiny: American Expansion and the Empire of Right* (1995).

vehemence among the two, and the significant contribution that the conflict among them makes to the contemporary delimitation of America's national and constitutional identity.

Consistent with this, universalists readily incorporate comparative constitutionalism in constitutional adjudication and scholarship to overcome perceived competitive disadvantages with a view to straightening the course to perfection to which they are committed as citizens in a country of destiny. Universalists are thus guided by a paradoxical amalgamation of universalism and exceptionalism. They look to foreign authorities, not simply to emulate them, but to incorporate them in their unique drive to perfection.

Exclusivists, in contrast, would ideally make no use of comparative constitutional material, with one minor qualification. To the extent that exclusivists are originalists, they would deem it proper to have recourse to comparative constitutional analysis for purposes of ascertaining the constitutional intent of the framers of the constitution. Thus, if the American Framers relied on English law in the context of constitutionalizing a right to 'due process of law',[72] then that would make it proper to refer to relevant English materials in existence at the time of the American framing, but not to any such materials generated subsequent to that framing. Ironically, in spite of the exclusivists' strong aversion to contemporary comparative constitutional materials, they have been forced to refer to them in order to undermine the universalists' positive reliance on the latter. For example, as already mentioned, Justice Scalia referred to the constitutional jurisprudence of non-European countries that refuse to afford protection to homosexual conduct in order to cast Justice Kennedy's reliance on European jurisprudence as purely arbitrary.[73] In sum, at present, both exclusivists and universalists integrate comparative constitutionalism in American constitutional analysis. The former do so negatively and concentrate on differences; the latter approach the task positively and seek to emphasize identities. Neither, however, seeks to blend foreign and domestic constitutionalism as they both in the end remain steadfast to American exceptionalism.

Bibliography

David M. Beatty, *Constitutional Law in Theory and Practice* (1995)

Sujit Choudhry, 'Globalization in Search of Justification: Towards a Theory of Comparative Constitutional Interpretation' (1999) 74 *Indiana Law Journal* 819

Norman Dorsen et al, *Comparative Constitutionalism: Cases and Materials* (2nd edn, 2010)

Daniel A. Farber, 'The Supreme Court, the Law of Nations, and Citations of Foreign Law: The Lessons of History' (December 15, 2006), UC Berkeley Public Law Research Paper No. 954359, available at <http://ssrn.com/abstract=954359>

Günther Frankenberg, 'Stanger than Paradise: Identity and Politics in Comparative Law' (1997) *Utah Law Review* 259

Mary Ann Glendon, 'Rights in Twentieth-Century Constitutions' (1992) 59 *University of Chicago Law Review* 519

Mary Ann Glendon, *Comparative Legal Traditions* (2nd edn, 1994)

Vicki C. Jackson, 'Constitutional Comparisons: Convergence, Resistance, Engagement' (2005) 119 *Harvard Law Review* 109

Richard Posner, 'Foreword: A Political Court' (2005) 119 *Harvard Law Review* 31

Robert Post, 'Constitutional Scholarship in the United States' (2009) 7 *International Journal of Constitutional Law* 417

[72] See US Constitution, Amendment 5 (1791).

[73] See above n 44.

Michel Rosenfeld, *The Identity of the Constitutional Subject: Selfhood, Citizenship, Culture and Community* (2010)

Michel Rosenfeld and András Sajó, 'Spreading Liberal Constitutionalism: An Inquiry into the Fate of Free Speech Rights in New Democracies' in Sujit Choudhry (ed), *The Migration of Constitutional Ideas* (2006)

'The Relevance of Foreign Legal Materials in US Constitutional Cases: A Conversation Between Justice Antonin Scalia and Justice Stephen Breyer' (2005) 3 *International Journal of Constitutional Law* 519

Mark Tushnet, 'Referring to Foreign Law in Constitutional Interpretation: An Episode in the Culture Wars' (2006) 35 *University of Baltimore Law Review* 299

Jeremy Waldron, 'Foreign Law and the Modern *Ius Gentium*' (2005) 119 *Harvard Law Review* 129

CHAPTER 2

COMPARATIVE CONSTITUTIONAL LAW: METHODOLOGIES

VICKI C. JACKSON

Harvard

Methodologies of constitutional comparison vary at least as much as, if not more than, do methodologies more generally in comparative law. Methods vary in what they aim to do and in who is engaged in comparisons, particularly if the comparative enterprise is defined broadly to include doctrine produced by courts, features of government (such as parliamentary vs presidential systems, more typically studied by comparative government than by constitutional law scholars), and the processes of constitution-making and adoption. The methodological categories have considerable overlap and a single work may include examples of multiple methodologies, for example classificatory work and functional analysis.

The primary practitioners of comparative constitutional law are scholars—not only legal scholars, but also social scientists or historians who bring distinct disciplinary perspectives to the analysis of law, legal institutions, and legal change. In addition to scholars, adjudicators—including judges of national supreme or constitutional courts—sometimes consult, and perhaps less frequently refer to, comparative constitutional law and government experience in other countries. Finally, 'constitutional legislators'—those charged with drafting of new constitutions or constitutional amendments—quite commonly engage in comparative constitutional examination. Although constitutional adjudicators and constitutional legislators often draw from the work of constitutional scholars, their context and goals at times frame distinctive methodological orientations. This chapter will briefly discuss the different communities of comparative constitutional analysis and will close by noting some methodological challenges of comparative constitutional analysis.

I. Comparative Constitutional Scholarship

The world of comparative constitutional scholars includes several broad classes of methodological approach, which this chapter describes as (1) classificatory, (2) historical, (3) normative, (4) functional, and (5) contextual. Each of these categories may overlap with others in scholarly practice. Moreover, within these categories, different techniques may be used, as diverse as detailed analysis of one or more foreign constitutions' development, or constitutional courts' doctrine, on a matter of domestic interest, to case studies of one or two countries across historical and/or doctrinal development, to explorations of judicial self-understanding of role, to overtly comparative case studies by country of particular issues, to large-N statistical analyses of particular phenomena. Some of these techniques may be associated with particular kinds of inquiries; for example, large-N works tend to ask causal, functional questions;[1] detailed case studies tend to have historic and/or contextual focuses; normative work may be pursued through a number of different techniques. I illustrate these points below.

1. Classificatory Work: 'Families', Regional, Emerging

Much work in comparative law generally has been concerned with the classification of different legal systems into what has sometimes been described as 'families' of law. In comparative constitutional law, a number of contemporary works have explored the significance of the different 'families' of constitutional law, notably the divide between civil and common law legal systems, and between 'centralized' or 'decentralized' constitutional review.[2] Allan-Randolph Brewer-Caraís, for example, has analyzed the logical, as well as empirical, differences and similarities between constitutional review in civil and common law countries and its 'hybrid' forms in South America, challenging conventional assumptions that common law and civil law countries will consistently differ along the same axis in how they structure judicial review.[3]

[1] The term 'large-N' is used to here to refer to studies with a large enough set of comparators and factors to be subject to quantitative, statistical analysis designed to test and explore correlations and associations. Widely described as a valuable tool to test hypotheses generated by qualitative research, such studies, it is claimed, can also reveal magnitudes of effects and interactions not revealed by other methods. See eg Michael Coppedge, 'Theory Building and Hypothesis Testing: Large- vs Small-N Research on Democratization', Paper prepared for presentation at the Annual Meeting of the Midwest Political Science Association, Chicago, Illinois, April 25–27, 2002, available at <http://www.nd.edu/~mcoppedg/crd/mpsacoppo2.pdf>. See also Joachim Blatter, 'Case Studies' in Lisa M. Given (ed), *The Sage Encyclopedia of Qualitative Research Methods* (2008), vol 1, 68–9 (suggesting, inter alia, that case studies are more likely to produce 'theoretical innovation', while large-N studies help 'control the empirical scope of new theoretical concepts'; that large-N studies tend to focus on causal claims, while case studies tend to be more descriptive or interpretive; and that large-N statistical studies are associated with establishing external validity, while case studies are more associated with constructing internal validity).

[2] Louis Favoreu, 'Constitutional Review in Europe' in Louis Henkin and Albert J. Rosenthal (eds), *Constitutionalism and Rights: The Influence of the United States Constitution Abroad* (1990), 38–62; Mauro Cappelletti, *The Judicial Process in Comparative Perspective* (1989).

[3] Allan-Randolph Brewer-Caraís, *Judicial Review in Comparative Law* (1989) and *Reflexiones Sobre el Constitutionalismo en América* (2001); see also Louis Favoreu, *Constitutional Courts* (2001).

More recent scholarship has examined convergences as well as differences between centralized constitutional review in specialized constitutional courts and judicial review in more general supreme courts.[4] There is considerable scholarly work classifying domestic constitutional regimes as 'monist' or 'dualist' for purposes of international law; increasingly, these categories are being recognized as inadequate descriptors of the far more complex array of relationships national constitutions take towards the role of international sources of law in the domestic order.[5]

'Area' studies also contribute to efforts at classification, or better understanding of possible classification, of constitutional systems.[6] A key question is whether there are distinctive features of constitutional development in a region, either because of conquest or colonial influences, common religious or cultural heritage, or other aspects of the geopolitical legal environment. Although area studies depend on the distinctiveness and cohesiveness of geographic association, some 'area' work might be thought of as deconstructing its own analytic foundation, for example by denying claims of certain distinctively Asian forms of constitutionalism, while remaining conscious of the question of the effect of the regional characteristics.[7] Some work focuses on other regional constitutional characteristics, as in studies of presidentialism in Latin America[8] or Africa,[9] or of the relationships between state, rulers, people, and religion in Arab or Muslim countries.[10]

A wide literature exists on whether Europe has a constitution, and what this means.[11] This literature, often abstract and conceptual, at times seems to lack a self-consciousness of the possibility of understanding the query as one of 'area studies'. The literature is not concerned so much with exploring what is distinctive about the European setting but rather with characterizing what that setting is; indeed, some of this literature suggests that the legal conceptual-

[4] Victor Ferreres Comella, *Constitutional Courts and Democratic Values: A European Perspective* (2010) and 'The European Model of Constitutional Review of Legislation: Toward Decentralization?' (2004) 2 *International Journal of Constitutional Law* 461.

[5] Melissa A. Waters, 'Creeping Monism: The Judicial Trend toward Interpretive Incorporation of Human Rights Treaties' (2007) 107 *Columbia Law Review* 628; Tom Ginsburg, 'Locking in Democracy: Constitutions, Commitment, and International Law' (2006) 38 *New York University Journal of International Law and Policy* 707.

[6] On Asia, see Andrew Harding, 'Comparative Public Law: Some Lessons from South East Asia' in Andrew Harding and Esin Oriicu (eds), *Comparative Law in the 21st Century* (2002); Tom Ginsburg, *Judicial Review in New Democracies: Constitutional Courts in Asian Cases* (2003); Tania Groppi (ed), *Asian Constitutionalism in Transition: A Comparative Perspective* (2008).

[7] Jiung-Ronn Yeh and Wen-Chen Chang, 'The Emergence of East Asia Constitutionalism: Features in Comparison', Asian Law Institute Working Paper Series No 006, 2009, available at <http://law.nus.edu.sg/asli/pdf/WPS006.pdf>.

[8] Juan J. Linz, 'The Perils of Presidentialism' (1990) 1 *Journal of Democracy* 51; Carlos Santiago Nino, 'Transition to Democracy, Corporatism and Presidentialism with Special Reference to Latin America' in Douglas Greenberg et al (eds), *Constitutionalism and Democracy: Transitions in the Contemporary World* (1993).

[9] H.W.O. Okoth-Ogendo, 'Constitutions Without Constitutionalism: Reflections on an African Political Paradox' in Greenberg (n 8). For a regionally focused study of approaches to religious freedom, see Makau wa Mutua, 'Limitations on Religious Rights: Problematizing Religious Freedom in the African Context' (1999) 5 *Buffalo Human Rights Law Review* 75.

[10] Nathan J. Brown, *Constitutions in a Nonconstitutional World: Arab Basic Laws and the Prospects for Accountable Government* (2002); Abdullahi Ahmed An-Naim, *African Constitutionalism and the Role of Islam* (2006).

[11] J.H.H. Weiler, *The Constitution of Europe* (1999); Neil MacCormick, *Questioning Sovereignty: Law, State and Nation in the European Commonwealth* (1999); Kalypso Nicolaïdis and Stephen Weatherill (eds), *Whose Europe? National Models and the Constitution of the European Union* (2003).

izations called forth in Europe may be of use more generally to the rest of the world.[12] Nonetheless, there is a sense in which much of the literature concerned with the question of whether and what kind of 'constitution' Europe has, or may have, could be seen as a classificatory form of area studies.

Other forms of classificatory studies, conducted largely by political scientists, focus on particular attributes of constitutional systems, for example the classification of presidential and parliamentary systems, or of electoral systems, or of federal or more consociational forms of organization.[13] Some classificatory studies identify new and emerging categories of constitutional systems or phenomena. The literature on European constitutionalism has some of these characteristics,[14] as does work identifying and analyzing such new developments as 'weak form' judicial review, or 'commonwealth constitutionalism'.[15] So, too, does the work, often done by those with training in political science, analyzing emerging typologies of organizing executive and legislative power,[16] or identifying other constitutional phenomena previously overlooked.[17]

In addition to comparative work focused on large structural issues, there is a considerable amount of comparative scholarship that explores emerging trends in doctrine and interpretive methodology. Consider here the work being done examining doctrine in different countries around the methodological approach of proportionality or balancing as compared with formalism, or originalism, as efforts to understand 'families' of interpretive approaches, rather than 'families' of overall systems.[18]

Finally, there are revisionist or cautionary forms of classificatory or emergent phenomena, comparative constitutional scholarship, such as on the entrenchment of investment regimes that limit the regulatory and fiscal capacities of domestic governments.[19] We might likewise

[12] Mattias Kumm, 'The Cosmopolitan Turn in Constitutionalism: On the Relationship between Constitutionalism in and beyond the State' in Jeffrey Dunoff and Joel Trachtman (eds), *Ruling the World?: International Law, Global Governance, Constitutionalism* (2009).

[13] Giovanni Sartori, *Comparative Constitutional Engineering: An Inquiry into Structures, Incentives and Outcomes* (1994); Arend Lijphart, 'Constitutional Design for Divided Societies' (2004) 15 *Journal of Democracy* 96; Donald L. Horowitz, *Ethnic Groups in Conflict* (2000) and 'Conciliatory Institutions and Constitutional Processes in Post-Conflict States' (2008) 49 *William and Mary Law Review* 1213; John McGarry and Brendan O'Leary, 'Iraq's Constitution of 2005: Liberal Consociation as Political Prescription' (2007) 5 *International Journal of Constitutional Law* 679.

[14] Pavlos Eleftheriadis, 'The Idea of a European Constitution' (2007) 27 *Oxford Journal of Legal Studies* 1; Neil Walker, 'Reframing EU Constitutionalism' in Dunoff and Trachtman (n 12).

[15] Mark V. Tushnet, 'Alternative Forms of Judicial Review' (2003) 101 *Michigan Law Review* 2781 and *Weak Courts, Strong Rights: Judicial Review and Social Welfare Rights in Comparative Constitutional Law* (2009); Stephen Gardbaum, 'The New Commonwealth Model of Constitutionalism' (2001) 49 *American Journal of Comparative Law* 707. See also Stephen Holmes and Cass Sunstein, 'The Politics of Constitutional Amendment in Eastern Europe' in Sanford Levinson (ed), *Responding to Imperfection: The Theory and Practice of Constitutional Amendment* (1995), 286.

[16] Cindy Skach, *Borrowing Constitutional Designs: Constitutional Law in Weimar Germany and the Fifth French Republic* (2005); Bruce Ackerman, 'The New Separation of Powers' (2000) 113 *Harvard Law Review* 633.

[17] David Fontana, 'Government in Opposition' (2009) 119 *Yale Law Journal* 548.

[18] David Beatty, *The Ultimate Rule of Law* (2004); David S. Law, 'Generic Constitutional Law' (2005) 89 *Minnesota Law Review* 652; Vicki C. Jackson and Jamal Greene, 'Constitutional Interpretation in Comparative Perspective: Comparing Judges or Courts?' in Tom Ginsburg and Rosalind Dixon (eds), *Research Handbook in Comparative Constitutional Law* (2011). On the theory of proportionality, see generally Robert Alexy, *A Theory of Constitutional Rights* (2009); see also Alec Stone Sweet and Jud Mathews, 'Proportionality Balancing and Global Constitutionalism' (2009) 47 *Columbia Journal of Transnational Law* 72.

[19] David Schneiderman, 'Comparative Constitutional Law in an Age of Economic Globalization' in Vicki C. Jackson and Mark Tushnet (eds), *Defining the Field of Comparative Constitutional Law* (2002).

include work on increased executive, vis-à-vis legislative, power resulting from national and international responses to terrorism and other global problems, as a challenge across many countries for constitutionalism, with a wide range of potential normative ramifications.[20]

So classificatory scholarship can be backward-looking in historical or intellectual ways; it can be concerned with defining a relatively stable framework for classification and analysis. In its more historical forms focused on colonial relationships, it can also be concerned with identifying a normatively doubtful legal basis for constitutional phenomena, in order to explain existing circumstances or lay a foundation for change.[21] Yet classificatory scholarship can also be forward-looking, concerned with identifying and analyzing new phenomena. Stable and emergent classification can coexist in the same work. And for some scholars, classificatory work is a predicate for their functional conclusions.

2. Historical Work and the Migration of Constitutional Ideas

Classificatory work is closely related to historical work. Historical work is concerned with understanding the development of constitutional law or constitutional systems over time. There may be both 'genetic' forms of connections between systems, based on the influence one has on the development of another,[22] and 'genealogical' forms of connection, where one (or more) constitutional system(s) grew out of another, typically in countries emerging out of colonial relationships.[23] Scholarly work may proceed by examining how two systems that originate in a common legal system, or one system that originates in another, develop over time in similar or different ways.[24] It may also examine how a legal concept that exists in one system influences or migrates to another, focusing not only on the path of ideas but also on how those ideas are transmitted, for example as through graduate study abroad.[25] Historical work concerned with the influence and movement of constitutional ideas across national boundaries often exhibits a degree of skepticism about strong claims of 'transplants' found in the more general comparative literature.[26] Another form in which this work on migration of ideas occurs is one that identifies the historical role of transnational legal influences on a single constitutional system.[27]

[20] Kim Lane Scheppele, 'Law in a Time of Emergency: States of Exception and the Temptations of 9/11' (2004) 6 *University of Pennsylvania Journal of Constitutional Law* 1001 and 'The Migration of Anti-Constitutional Ideas: The Post-9/11 Globalization of Public Law and the International State of Emergency' in Sujit Choudhry (ed), *The Migration of Constitutional Ideas* (2006); Eyal Benvenisti, 'Reclaiming Democracy: The Strategic Uses of Foreign and International Law by National Courts' (2008) 102 *American Journal of International Law* 241.

[21] Okoth-Ogendo (n 9), 65–84; Nino (n 8).

[22] See Louis Henkin, 'A New Birth of Constitutionalism: Genetic Influences and Genetic Defects' in Michel Rosenfeld (ed), *Constitutionalism, Identity, Difference, and Legitimacy: Theoretical Perspectives* (1994); Henkin and Rosenthal (n 2); Jonathan M. Miller, 'The Authority of a Foreign Talisman: A Study of US Constitutional Practice As Authority in Nineteenth Century Argentina and the Argentine Elite's Leap of Faith' (1997) 46 *American University Law Review* 1483.

[23] Sujit Choudhry, 'Globalization in Search of Justification: Toward a Theory of Comparative Constitutional Interpretation' (1999) 74 *Indiana Law Journal* 819.

[24] See eg Martha A. Field, 'The Differing Federalisms of Canada and the United States' (1992) 55 *Law and Contemporary Problems* 107.

[25] David S. Law and Wen-Chen Chang, 'The Limits of Transnational Judicial Dialogue' (2011) 86 *Washington Law Review* 523.

[26] Symposium, 'Constitutional Borrowing' (2003) 1(2) *International Journal of Constitutional Law*; Choudhry (n 20); cf Eivind Smith, 'Give and Take: Cross-Fertilisation of Concepts in Constitutional Law' in Jack Beatson and Takis Tridimas (eds), *New Directions in European Public Law* (1998).

[27] See eg Vicki C. Jackson, *Constitutional Engagement in a Transnational Era* (2010), 103–16.

An important development in this field is Choudhry's concept of 'migration' of constitutional ideas—an idea that represents a broader range of influences on a broader range of actors than much of the pre-existing literature reflected. Yet 'the migration of constitutional ideas across legal systems is rapidly emerging as one of the central features of contemporary constitutional practice',[28] with far more complex cross currents than reflected in early work on the influence of the US Constitution.[29] More recent literature, for example, tracks the German constitutional influence on India's 'basic structure' doctrine,[30] the relative influence of German and US constitutional ideas in newer constitutional systems,[31] or the changing relationships between international law, foreign constitutional law, and domestic constitutional development.[32]

A cautionary note is sounded by Mark Tushnet's argument that comparative study of constitutions reveals a degree of 'bricolage', that is, of more or less random adaptation of what is 'at hand' in ways that contribute to a certain eclecticism within individual constitutions that poses challenges to interpretive theories founded on the coherence of legal instruments.[33] Migration may appear random and adventitious, as is generally appreciated in the comparative law literature,[34] and may also reflect competitive efforts among the universities of the world for foreign students.

Historical or positive analysis of the development or operation of a particular constitutional system, or set of systems related by region or history, may be explored through a framework that seeks both to understand it internally and to make it accessible to readers from other legal systems.[35] Such works are either explicitly or implicitly comparative, engaged both in analytical description and translation of national contexts for readers from other systems; at the same time, these works usually rest on implicit, or draw explicit, normative and/or functional conclusions.

Although scholarship in this vein is not typically quantitative, the field of 'citation studies' does employ empirical methods to attempt to analyze the role or influence of foreign or international law in domestic constitutional decisions. Thus, quantitative studies have sought to focus on the behavior of particular national constitutional courts in referring to transnational sources of law, how often the court refers to foreign law as compared to international law, or on the influence of particular courts in the jurisprudence of other coun-

[28] Choudhry (n 20), 13.

[29] See Henkin and Rosenthal (n 2).

[30] Sudhir Krishnaswamy, *Democracy and Constitutionalism In India: A Study of the Basic Structure Doctrine* (2009), xxvi–xxvii.

[31] Law and Chang (n 25).

[32] Jackson (n 27), 255–79.

[33] Mark Tushnet, 'The Possibilities of Comparative Constitutional Law' (1999) 108 *Yale Law Journal* 1225.

[34] Alan Watson, 'Aspects of Reception of Law' (1996) 44 *American Journal of Comparative Law* 335, 339–41 (noting the 'chance' that students from several African countries studied in Scotland, leading to reliance on Scots law by jurists in those countries).

[35] See eg Donald P. Kommers, *The Constitutional Jurisprudence of the Federal Republic of German* (2nd edn, 1997); John Bell, *French Constitutional Law* (1992); Alec Stone, *The Birth of Judicial Politics in France* (1992); Mary Volcansek, *Constitutional Politics in Italy: The Constitutional Court* (2000); Kim Lane Scheppele, 'Guardian of the Constitution: Constitutional Court Presidents and the Struggle for the Rule of Law in Post-Soviet Europe' (2006) 154 *University of Pennsylvania Law Review* 1757; Heinz Klug, 'Constitution-Making, Democracy and the "Civilizing" of Unreconcilable Conflict: What Might we Learn from the South African Miracle?' (2007) 25 *Wisconsin International Law Journal* 269; Herman Schwartz, *The Struggle for Constitutional Justice in Post-Communist Europe* (2000).

tries.[36] As its most sophisticated practitioners recognize, such studies provide only a partial and potentially misleading guide to influence; courts may be influenced by ideas from foreign or international legal systems without acknowledging the debt by citation. Both 'silent dialogues'[37] and 'prudential silences'[38] may result in noncitation of foreign material of which judges were aware and which influenced decision. At the same time, citations to foreign or international law may be more 'decorative' or supplementary in character, not analytically significant in the underlying decision. Citation studies thus provide only a partial picture, as they suggest trends in the courts' willingness to manifest an awareness of comparative or international law.

3. Universalist Search for Just or Good Principles

An important, yet at the same time controversial, form of comparative analysis is the effort, in Donald Kommers' words, to discover through comparative study, 'principles of justice and political obligation that transcend the culture bound opinions and conventions of a particular political community'.[39] For a similar normative aspiration expressed by another constitutional scholar, consider A.E. Dick Howard's view that 'comparative studies can . . . nourish our search for principles of ordered liberty and for theories of a just society'.[40] This approach has been termed a 'universalist' approach to comparative constitutional study.[41]

Much comparative work—even work that is 'classificatory', 'historical', or 'functionalist'—is motivated by a search, implicit or explicit, for transcendent principles—of the good, or the just—in constitutional theory, institutions, and doctrine. There is a literature—in comparative government, in philosophy, and in political science—about theories of the good society, work that may be informed by knowledge of constitutional practices in various countries. Yet foreign legal sources in such work may be examined, not with a view to understanding their comparative setting, but rather with a view towards constructing a general theory, using various legal sources as examples to help to refine, and to clarify, the analytics of a general problem in democratic or political theory, for example the relationship of equality to legitimacy,[42] or of judicial review and democracy.[43]

[36] See C.L. Ostberg et al, 'Attitudes, Precedents and Cultural Change: Explaining the Citation of Foreign Precedents by the Supreme Court of Canada' (2001) 34 *Canadian Journal of Political Science* 377; Bijon Roy, 'An Empirical Survey of Foreign Jurisprudence and International Instruments in Charter Litigation' (2004) 62 *University of Toronto Faculty Law Review* 99; Devika Hovel and George Williams, 'A Tale of Two Systems: Use of International Law in Constitutional Interpretation in Australia and South Africa' (2005) 29 *Melbourne University Law Review* 95; Peter McCormick, 'The Supreme Court of Canada and American Citations, 1945–94: A Statistical Overview' (1997) 8 *Supreme Court Law Review (2d)* 527; Shannon Ishiyama Smithey, 'A Tool, Not a Master: The Use of Foreign Case Law in Canada and South Africa' (2001) 34 *Comparative Political Studies* 1192.

[37] Judith Resnik, 'Law's Migration: American Exceptionalism, Silent Dialogues, and Federalism's Multiple Ports of Entry' (2005) 115 *Yale Law Journal* 1564.

[38] Jackson (n 27), 192.

[39] Donald P. Kommers, 'The Value of Comparative Constitutional Law' (1976) 9 *John Marshall Journal of Practice and Procedure* 685.

[40] A.E. Dick Howard, 'A Traveler from an Antique Land: The Modern Renaissance of Comparative Constitutionalism' (2009) 50 *Virginia Journal of International Law* 3, 41.

[41] Choudhry (n 23).

[42] See eg Wojciech Sadurski, *Equality and Legitimacy* (2008), 93–146.

[43] See eg Jeremy Waldron, 'The Core of the Case Against Judicial Review' (2006) 115 *Yale Law Journal* 1346.

In other work on constitutional theory by those who identify themselves as constitutional scholars, there is more attention to comparative analysis as a central means of trying to answer important jurisprudential or philosophical questions. Recent examples would include Michel Rosenfeld's scholarship exploring 'essential jurisprudential characteristics of the respective conceptions of the rule of law in three different legal traditions[:]...the German conception of the Rechtsstaat;...the French notion of the Etat de droit; and...the Anglo-American common law based elaboration of the idea of "the rule of law"' to analyze the rule of law's role in legitimating constitutionalism in democracies,[44] or work by social scientists theorizing the relationship between constitutionalism and democratic politics based on selected comparative case studies.[45] Moreover, ideas drawn from comparative constitutional study about the nature of constitutionalism itself have begun to influence scholarly discourses in international law, international organization, and global legal studies, with volumes devoted to the possibilities for 'world constitutionalism'.[46]

In addition to large-scale theories about justice and the nature of constitutions and constitutionalism, there is a middle level of theorizing towards good or just principles that is an important strand in this literature, focused more on specific doctrine and specific institutions. Comparative analysis is deployed to criticize the implications of domestic constitutional doctrine for presumptively shared or universal norms of equality, or democracy, or human dignity. Such discussions are found on a wide range of issues, including the legitimate scope of punishment, defenses to defamation, criminal sedition, whether hateful speech can be prohibited or must be protected, the permissible scope of campaign finance laws,[47] or the constitutionality of actions that have the effect, but not the purpose, of harming disadvantaged groups.[48] An interesting body of literature explores comparative approaches to social rights, or horizontal effects of constitutional rights.[49] This work is typically characterized by doctrinal analyses. Scholars' exploration of the varying assumptions, and interpretive approaches, of comparator countries may serve self-reflective normative purpose—at once trying to understand other systems and identify improvements of one's own.

Comparative work in this vein can focus not only on reform in the sense of identifying normatively more attractive and justice-seeking approaches but also on what Kim Scheppele has aptly described as 'aversive precedent',[50] exploring in normative terms the role of comparative examples as the antithesis of what countries properly committed to shared or universal values (of democracy, limited government, or the like) should aspire to. This method may be

[44] Michel Rosenfeld, 'The Rule of Law and the Legitimacy of Constitutional Democracy' (2001) 74 *Southern California Law Review* 1307, 1309.

[45] Andrew Arato, *Civil Society, Constitution, and Legitimacy* (2000); Ulrich K. Preuss, *Constitutional Revolution: The Link Between Constitutionalism and Progress* (1995).

[46] Ronald MacDonald and Douglas Johnston (eds), *Towards World Constitutionalism: Issues in the Legal Ordering of the World Community* (2005); see also Dunoff and Trachtman (n 12).

[47] Mark Tushnet, *Weak Courts, Strong Rights: Judicial Review and Social Welfare Rights in Comparative Constitutional Law* (2009), 6–8.

[48] See eg Vicki C. Jackson, 'Review of Laws Having a Disparate Impact Based on Gender' in Mark V. Tushnet and Vikram David Amar (eds), *Global Perspectives on Constitutional Law* (2009), 130–45.

[49] See eg Helen Hershkoff, 'Transforming Legal Theory in the Light of Practice: The Judicial Application of Social and Economic Rights to Private Orderings' in Varun Gauri and Daniel M. Brinks (eds), *Courting Social Justice: Judicial Enforcement of Social and Economic Rights in the Developing World* (2008), 290; Daphne Barak-Erez and Aeyal Gross (eds), *Exploring Social Rights: Between Theory And Practice* (2007).

[50] See Kim Lane Scheppele, 'Aspirational and Aversive Constitutionalism: The Case for Studying Cross-Constitutional Influence through Negative Models' (2003) 1 *International Journal of Constitutional Law* 296.

contrasted, for example, with that of Choudhry's analysis of the negative impact of *Lochner* on Canadian constitution-making and constitutional law;[51] that approach is more positive and historical, than normative or reformist, even though some of the techniques of investigation—including close analysis of doctrinal development—may be similar.

As has been observed, universalist justice-seeking approaches to comparative constitutional law most typically, though not inevitably, entail comparative work on rights, often linked with literature on human rights.[52] By contrast, functionalist approaches, discussed below, are often deployed in analyzing structural issues, for instance different forms of federalism, or presidentialism, or voting structures. For this reason, universalist scholarship about rights has tended to bring together work on comparative constitutional law with work on international law and especially international human rights and humanitarian law. Yet the search for 'just principles' of human rights law may be no more theoretical or universalist than the search for 'good' principles of government design, even though the reasoning used in connection with the latter search usually, though not always, sounds more in methods of functional consequentialism.[53]

4. Functionalism and Consequentialism; Positive and Normative

Perhaps the dominant method of comparative analysis, in constitutional law, as in other fields of law, is functionalist.[54] The scholar may identify an institution that exists in multiple constitutional systems and explore its function(s); or the scholar may identify one or more functions performed by constitutions or constitutional institutions or doctrines in some societies,[55] and analyze whether in fact the constitutional institution or doctrine believed to perform a valid function does so, or may analyze whether and how that function is performed elsewhere. Sometimes the work is positive, concerned not with questions of normative superiority but, for example, with how different institutions may perform roughly equivalent roles, or how differences in institutional design may correspond with broader differences in political society or behavior. Sometimes the approach is more normative, as where the scholar seeks to identify what constitutional designs or doctrines are better suited to producing consequences that are normatively valuable.[56] Sometimes the scholar may consider whether consequences asserted to flow from some institution or doctrine, questioned in normative grounds, in fact lead to or avoid the consequences its defenders identify. The goals of functional comparison may be as

[51] See Sujit Choudhry, 'The Lochner Era and Comparative Constitutionalism' (2004) 2 *International Journal of Constitutional Law* 5.

[52] Tushnet (n 47); see also Ronald J. Krotoszynski, *The First Amendment in Cross-Cultural Perspective: A Comparative Legal Analysis of the Freedom of Speech* (2006), 6; Adrienne Stone, 'The Comparative Constitutional Law of Freedom of Expression' in Rosalind Dixon and Tom Ginsburg (eds), *Research Handbook in Comparative Constitutional Law* (2011).

[53] For a more deontological argument about institutional design, see Waldron (n 43), 1374–5.

[54] Tushnet (n 33); cf. Ralf Michaels, 'The Functional Method of Comparative Law' in Mathias Reimann and Reinhard Zimmermann (eds), *Oxford Handbook of Comparative Law* (2006), 339–82; David S. Law, 'Constitutions' in P. Cane and H.M. Kritzer (eds), *Oxford Handbook of Empirical Legal Research* (2010).

[55] See eg Beau Breslin, *From Words to Worlds: Exploring Constitutional Functionality* (2009); Walter F. Murphy, *Constitutional Democracy: Creating and Maintaining a Just Political Order* (2007).

[56] See eg Cass Sunstein, *Designing Democracy: What Constitutions Do* (2001). Normative value here might be defined by nonmaterial conceptions of justice and morality, or by a normative commitment to utilitarianism in its various forms.

normative and universalistically theory-seeking as others described earlier, but the techniques used focus more on specific functional comparisons and questions of causation, rather than on the moral, principled appeal of comparative approaches.

Functional comparisons can be advanced through several techniques, including conceptual functionalism, detailed case studies, and large-N studies. *Conceptual functionalism* is a form of analysis that overlaps with the classificatory category: scholars hypothesize about why and how constitutional institutions or doctrines function as they do, and what categories or criteria capture and explain these functions, drawing examples from some discrete number of systems to conceptualize in ways that generate comparative insights or working hypotheses that can be tested through other methods. Thus, for example, Bruce Ackerman explained:

> My aim is to identify (a) one or another common problem confronting different 'constitutional courts,' and then follow up by specifying (b) different coping strategies these courts have adopted as they have tried to solve the problems. Once we have gained some clarity on these two issues, we may hope for a deeper insight into the comparative value of competing coping strategies.[57]

In this same article, Ackerman asked whether there 'are... patterns that repeat themselves in the successful establishment of written constitutions'.[58] This is a positive historical question, but with a functional orientation (and normative underpinning). Ackerman's technique is not quantitative, but a method of drawing insights about functional questions from comparative case studies, a form of 'concept thickening'.[59]

Some of the best work in comparative constitutional law is done in this vein. Consider Mark Tushnet's work, in which a constitutional institution—judicial review—is subjected to critical comparative analysis, both as to its value (in producing the positive consequences its proponents assert) and in terms of how it may in fact work differently depending on its legal status and other mechanisms available in different systems. Or consider Martin Shapiro's analysis, based in part on US experience, of the possible need to 'serv[e] the haves before beginning to serve the have nots' and of focusing on administrative law before constitutional law in countries with weak rule of law commitments as possible 'conditions for the success of constitutional courts' (as measured by courts' willingness to rule against governments),[60] or Ackerman's conceptual work on parliamentary and presidential forms of government.[61] Likewise Victor Ferres Comella compares centralized and decentralized constitutional review in functional terms and then, in a normative turn, makes recommendations for change in the

[57] Bruce Ackerman, 'The Rise of World Constitutionalism' (1997) 83 *Virginia Law Review* 771, 794. See also ibid:

> Much of the best comparative scholarship follows a similar method, first defining a common problem—for example, the protection of freedom of speech—and then considering different doctrinal solutions proposed by different courts, before passing a considered judgment on the best approaches.

[58] Ibid 775.

[59] Ran Hirschl, 'The Question of Case Selection in Comparative Constitutional Law' (2005) 53 *American Journal of Comparative Law* 125, 129–31.

[60] Martin Shapiro, 'Some Conditions for the Success of Constitutional Courts: Lessons from the US Experience' in Wojciech Sadurski (ed), *Constitutional Justice, East and West: Democratic Legitimacy and Constitutional Courts in Post-Communist Europe in a Comparative Perspective* (2002), 46–50.

[61] Ackerman (n 16).

way in which centralized review is conducted;[62] Gerald Neuman considers the functions of overlapping systems of constitutional and international human rights protections.[63]

Conceptual functionalism might also include economic or behavioral models of constitutional design, models that may be entirely theoretical, or derived from a single country, but that could, in theory, be tested against different comparative examples. This work may be concerned not only with the relationship between different constitutional designs and various forms of economic success, but also with the relationship between constitutional design and other goods more conventionally thought of as legal, such as protection of minority rights.[64]

Secondly, functional analyses may be reflected in *more detailed case studies* of how a constitutional institution or doctrine actually functions in two or more societies. They may differ only in degree from the more conceptual functionalism, which draws on case studies but of a more limited level of density. Scholars may be attempting to analyze the functional consequences, for good or bad, of a particular institution, as in studies of the effects of constitutional federalism in different countries in affecting social movements for equality of opportunities for women and minorities,[65] in managing ethnic conflict,[66] or to test more rigorously the positive association between an institution or doctrine and its purported positive, or negative, effects. Comparative functional inquiries may also examine the causal relationships between the operation or development of a legal institution, such as judicial review, and other conditions in the political system.[67]

The choice of comparators is relevant to the utility of the effort: comparator countries to be studied may be limited by the languages the scholar is familiar with, or the accessibility of the legal information. As Hirschl has suggested, comparator countries for case studies may be chosen using different techniques, for example those that are 'most similar' (except for the particular doctrine or institution at issue) or those that are 'most different' but seem to have a similar institution or doctrine. And, as Cheryl Saunders has suggested, even within the constraints of language and availability, there are standards of selection that ought to be applied with consistency.[68]

A benefit of the case study method in the comparative setting is the ability to explore how different features of the system may interact with and affect the operation of seemingly similar institutions or doctrines, that is, to see particular institutions or doctrines 'in action' in their own legal contexts. Kent Greenawalt proceeds on the assumption that US and Canadian free speech law is functionally comparable, and then analyzes the differences and relates them to differences in constitutional text and to differences in history.[69] Studies of US and European

[62] Ferreres Comella (n 4).

[63] Gerald L. Neuman, 'Human Rights and Constitutional Rights: Harmony and Dissonance' (2003) 55 *Stanford Law Review* 1863.

[64] For a recent review of developments in 'positive constitutional economics', see Stefan Voigt, 'Positive Constitutional Economics II: A Survey of Recent Developments' (2011) 146 *Public Choice* 205.

[65] Lee Ann Banaszak, *Why Movements Succeed or Fail* (1996); Vicki C. Jackson, 'Citizenships, Federalisms, and Gender' in Seyla Benhabib and Judith Resnik (eds), *Migrations and Mobilities* (2009), 439–86.

[66] See eg Horowitz (n 13); Donald L. Horowitz, 'Conciliatory Institutions and Constitutional Processes in Post-Conflict States' (2008) 49 *William and Mary Law Review* 1213; Arend Lijphart, 'Constitutional Design for Divided Societies' (2004) 15 *Journal of Democracy* 96.

[67] See eg Tom Ginsburg, *Judicial Review in New Democracies* (2003); Ran Hirschl, *Juristocracy* (2004); Ran Hirschl, *Constitutional Theocracy* (2010).

[68] Cheryl Saunders, 'The Use and Misuse of Comparative Constitutional Law' (2006) 13 *Indiana Journal of Global Legal Studies* 37.

[69] Kent Greenawalt, 'Free Speech in the United States and Canada' (1992) 55 *Law and Contemporary Problems* 5.

constitutionalism,[70] or in specific areas (such as free speech[71] or property law[72]) have drawn on comparative perspectives for purposes of both understanding US doctrine and sometimes arguing for its improvement. Even single-country case studies may contribute to functional understandings of constitutional law or institutions. While detailed case studies are able to explore a broader range of variables in a particular setting, the greater the detail, the smaller the number of comparable entities to validate results in the form of more general statements.[73]

Increasingly, scholarship has turned to the creation of what one might call structured comparative case studies, where scholars are asked to explain and analyze, on a country basis, a selected set of issues, so that the resulting volume provides a set of comparative perspectives on how seemingly similar issues are (or are not) addressed in different constitutional systems. Goldsworthy's volume on constitutional interpretation focuses on interpretive questions and the role of constitutional courts in six countries.[74] Useful two-country comparisons exist as well.[75] Baines and Rubio Marin's collection focuses on gender equality and related issues;[76] others focus on social welfare rights[77] or on doctrines addressing the horizontal implications of constitutional norms for private actors and private law.[78]

Thirdly, functional analysis is increasingly associated with *large-N studies* designed to reveal correlative or causal associations between some constitutional feature (institution or doctrine) and some other phenomena, desirable or undesirable. The literature on the effects of presidentialism vs parliamentary democracy is an example, albeit situated in the less 'law'- and more 'institution'-focused world of comparative government.[79] Elkins, Ginsburg, and Melton's work on constitutional longevity is exemplary of a more 'legally' oriented form of empirical, functional scholarship.[80] The authors compiled a database of constitutions around the world, developed criteria for defining longevity (eg what kinds of changes would be treated as a new constitution rather than as an amendment), and then analyzed, in some detail, what features of constitutions were associated with longevity. The authors were careful to note that longevity may or may not have normative value; but their work, as a positive matter, suggested that the longevity of constitutions was associated with the right degree of flexibility, the right degree of specificity, and the availability of judicial enforcement mechanisms; their study packs considerable normative work—assuming political stability of constitutions is a desideratum—into the framing of positive categories, and in the classification of the events studied. Similarly, Jennifer

[70] George Nolte (ed), *European and US Constitutionalism* (2005).

[71] Krotoszynski (n 52).

[72] Gregory S. Alexander, *The Global Debate Over Constitutional Property: Lessons for American Takings Jurisprudence* (2006).

[73] See Mark Tushnet, '"Country Studies" in Comparative Constitutional Law', Paper presented at the World Congress of Constitutional Law, International Association of Constitutional Law, Mexico City, Workshop No 17, 'How Comparative is Comparative Constitutional Law (9 December 2010).

[74] Jeffrey Goldsworthy (ed), *Interpreting Constitutions: A Comparative Study* (2006). Cf eg Brice Dickson (ed), *Judicial Activism in Common Law Supreme Courts* (2007).

[75] Sarah K. Harding, 'Comparative Reasoning and Judicial Review' (2003) 28 *Yale International Law Journal* 409; Jamal Greene, 'On the Origins of Originalism' (2009) 88 *Texas Law Review* 1.

[76] Beverly Baines and Ruth Rubio-Marin (eds), *The Gender of Constitutional Jurisprudence* (2004).

[77] Gauri and Brinks (n 49); Daphne Barak-Erez and Aeyal M. Gross (eds), *Exploring Social Rights: Between Theory and Practice* (2007).

[78] Dawn Oliver and Jörg Fedtke (eds), *Human Rights and the Private Sphere: A Comparative Analysis* (2007).

[79] See eg Linz (n 8).

[80] Zachary Elkins, Tom Ginsburg, and James Melton, *The Endurance of National Constitutions* (2009).

Widner's database of constitution-making processes, analyzed to explore relationships between process and outcomes, is another example of a relatively new form of quantitative scholarly work focused on comparative constitutionalism, that also contributes to understandings of the very different measures by which 'success' in constitution-making can be measured.[81]

Large-N studies of causal connections between constitutions and constitutional law and effects in society have rarely focused on doctrine and reasoning, perhaps in part because of the difficulty of reliable coding, in part because of the disciplinary assumptions (focused on results as outputs, fairly narrowly understood) of the political scientists who typically conduct large-N studies. Consider the various studies of the relationship, *vel non*, between various 'rights' protecting provisions in constitutions and respect for those rights 'on the ground'.[82] Large-N studies, however, may also be used not for functional purposes but for classificatory or historical ones, as in the spate of studies analyzing 'citations' to foreign or international law.[83] Also of note are efforts by economists to explore relationships between different forms of constitutional government and economic well-being.[84]

Although functionalism (both positive and normative) represents a dominant approach in comparative constitutional study, it has been subject to serious critique. A number of scholars have cautioned against the misleadingly homogenizing and obscuring perils of functionalism. It is all too easy, scholars such as Günter Frankenberg suggest, for a comparativist unconsciously to assume the categories of legal thought with which she is familiar, and thus to see foreign law only as either similar or different, without being able to grasp the conceptual or sociological foundations of other legal orders.[85] Professor Bomhoff, in a similar vein, has shown how doctrines with a similar name and seemingly similar function actually mean quite different things in a practice that is shaped by more particular contexts.[86]

5. Contextualism, Expressivism, and Self-Reflection

These critical cautions might be understood to argue for a form of contextualism in scholarly work. Public law, it has been argued, is particularly path dependent on initial institutional choices, and thus requires attention to particular systems operating in their own context.[87]

[81] Jennifer Widner, 'Constitution Writing in Post-Conflict Societies: An Overview' (2008) 49 *William and Mary Law Review* 1513.

[82] See generally Benedikt Goderis and Mila Versteeg, 'Human Rights Violations After 9/11 and the Role of Constitutional Constraints', Economics of Security Working Paper 11 (2009); Linda Camp Keith, C. Neal Tate, and Stephen C. Poe, 'Is the Law a Mere Parchment Barrier to Human Rights Abuse' (2009) 71 *Journal of Politics* 644; Steven C. Poe, C. Neal Tate, and Linda Camp Keith, 'Repression of the Human Right to Personal Integrity Revisited: A Global Crossnational Study Covering the Years 1976–1993' (1999) 43 *International Studies Quarterly* 291; Gerald Blasi and David Cingranelli, 'Do Constitutions and Institutions Help Protect Human Rights?' in David Cingranelli (ed), *Human Rights and Developing Countries* (1996), vol 4, 223; Christian A. Davenport, '"Constitutional Promises" and Repressive Reality: A Cross-National Time-Series Investigation of Why Political and Civil Liberties are Suppressed' (1996) 58 *Journal of Politics* 627.

[83] See n 36.

[84] See Voigt (n 64).

[85] Günter Frankenberg, 'Critical Comparisons: Re-Thinking Comparative Law' (1985) 26 *Harvard International Law Journal* 411.

[86] See Jacco Bomhoff, 'Balancing, the Global and the Local: Judicial Balancing as a Problematic Topic in Comparative (Constitutional) Law' (2008) 31 *Hastings International and Comparative Law Review* 555, 562; cf Pierre LeGrand, 'Issues in the Translatability of Law' in Sandra Bermann and Michael Wood (eds), *Nation, Language, and the Ethics of Translation* (2005), 30.

[87] John Bell, 'Comparing Public Law' in Andrew Hardy and Esin Orücü (eds), *Comparative Law in the 21st Century* (2002).

And much scholarly work can be understood as an effort to learn, from outsider perspectives, more about the particular context of one's own system, whether its functional 'packages' of features, or its particular socio-legal self-understandings or self-expressions.

Many studies of comparative constitutional law are concerned with questions of context and particularity. Without embracing the idea, advanced by some comparativists, about the necessary particularity of each legal system,[88] scholarship in this vein does emphasize either the ways in which particular institutional contexts may limit the ability to draw conclusions from the practices of other systems, or the expressive functions of constitutions or constitutional law within particular national contexts. Contextual approaches problematize the sense of 'false necessity' that may emerge from functional or universalist approaches. So, for example, Tushnet has suggested that even in the realm of understandings of rights, the particular national and institutional context matters to an understanding of constitutional doctrine. Thus, with regard to hate speech and libel, he suggests that institutional factors, including the decentralization of enforcement, may affect analysis of the desirable scope for constitutional protection even of hateful speech.[89] Such functional contextualism must be distinguished from more normative arguments about national identity, even though the latter may also assume empirical benefits, or harms, from particular national constitutional features.

Some contextually oriented scholarship seeks to elicit more intense understanding of how particular paradigmatic social or political concerns shape or are reflected in constitutional law. Gary Jacobsohn's work on constitutional identity perhaps epitomizes this school, which is necessarily associated with close analysis of particular countries, and particular institutions and doctrines.[90] Yet, as work on the role of politics in reshaping constitutional law suggests,[91] the content of a country's expressive identity may be complex and multi-stranded, and may shift over time;[92] Rosalind Dixon's work, among others, might be understood to raise cautions about the tendency of expressivist approaches to assume a fixed national identity.[93] Considering the plurality of understandings and interpretive possibilities within a single national constitutional culture may yield important degrees of nuance, complicating and perhaps defeating efforts to generalize from particular cases.

II. Courts

Courts' approaches to comparative methodology overlap considerably, though not entirely, with those of scholars. Some jurists argue for comparative constitutional consideration as a form of consequences-focused 'functionalism'.[94] For still others, consulting foreign law is an ordinary part of what it means to be a thoughtful jurist, especially in interpreting constitutional

[88] Cf. Pierre Legrand, 'The Impossibility of "Legal Transplants"' (1997) 4 *Maastricht Journal of European and Comparative Law* 111.

[89] Tushnet (n 47).

[90] Gary Jeffrey Jacobsohn, *Constitutional Identity* (2010), *The Wheel of Law: India's Secularism in Comparative Constitutional Context* (2005) and *Apple of Gold: Constitutionalism in Israel and the United States* (1994).

[91] See eg Reva Siegel, 'Constitutional Culture, Social Movement Conflict and Constitutional Change: The Case of the de facto ERA' (2006) 94 *California Law Review* 1323.

[92] See Resnik (n 37).

[93] See Rosalind Dixon, 'A Democratic Theory of Constitutional Comparison' (2008) 56 *American Journal of Comparative Law* 947.

[94] See eg *Printz v United States* 521 US 898, 976–8 (1997) (Breyer J dissenting).

provisions with a common genetic or genealogical root, but more generally, insofar as greater knowledge of other legal systems helps judges to strengthen their own.[95] Some constitutions themselves require interpretation in light of international law, which may invite comparative analysis of how other domestic courts have interpreted the same international provision.

1. Doctrinal Demands, Self-Reflection, and Expressive Comparisons

When facing an open issue, judges may benefit from knowledge that expands the range of interpretive options considered in implementing their own constitution. But there are also doctrinal demands that may require resort to foreign constitutional law, as when limitations clauses (such as Canada's) refer to government practices that can be justified in 'a free and democratic society' and thus contemplate resort to foreign practice. Judges' consideration of foreign or international sources can serve as a self-reflective check on constitutional judgment, as the national constitutional ethos is defined by comparison, positive and negative, with others.[96]

2. Scholars and Courts

In scholarly work, contextualism and expressivism may function as a prism for analyzing how a particular constitutional context or identity is developed in a particular country. Expressivism in judicial decisions may be somewhat different: scholars work to contribute to knowledge or understanding; judges give judgments, creating winners and losers. Part of the task of courts is to issue decisions that are likely to be complied with. For this and other reasons, courts may consider or be influenced by comparative constitutional law even when they do not openly refer to it.[97]

At least three factors are relevant to judicial decisions whether to engage in comparative analysis. The first is *the nature of the domestic issue*. Some constitutional issues arise within well-settled fields of domestic discourse, or may concern a distinctive and unusual constitutional text, such as the US Second Amendment. Secondly, the *nature of the transnational source* will affect its relevance. International law might have a particular salience in some cases, but sometimes comparative constitutional law might have more persuasive value than international law.[98] Thirdly, judges need to consider the *comparability of contexts*. On these issues, the courts are generally going to be dependent on the infrastructure of knowledge that scholars develop.

III. Constitutional Legislators

Constitutional legislators are, most fundamentally, persons having authority to propose a new constitution, which can then be ratified.[99] Considering comparative constitutional approaches is quite a common aspect of such constitution-making enterprises, as one sees in the drafting of both national and subnational constitutions. James Madison, an influential framer of the

[95] See Konrad Schiemann, 'A Response to The Judge as Comparatist' (2005) 80 *Tulane Law Review* 281, 297.

[96] See eg *Griswold v Connecticut* 381 US 479 (1965) (negative contrast with totalitarian governments); *Lawrence v Texas* 539 US 558 (2003) (positive comparison with Europe).

[97] See Olivier Duhamel de Lamothe, Member, Conseil Constitutionnel (Fr), 'Constitutional Court Judges' Roundtable' (2005) 3 *International Journal of Constitutional Law* 550.

[98] Jackson (n 27), 168–78.

[99] One may also conceive of those who may initiate or enact amendments to a constitution as constitutional legislators.

US Constitution, made himself conversant with foreign constitutions, both ancient and contemporary. Modern constitution-making often takes place under more or less explicit forms of international monitoring or supervision, with widespread consultation of experts.[100]

Although scholarly work in recent years has begun to focus more attention on legislators both as constitution-makers and as constitutional interpreters,[101] empirical work has not kept pace with theoretical developments. There are few studies of a comparative nature that explore how actual legislators, or members of constituent assemblies, behave and view their work. One leading scholar has suggested that foreign models or advice have little to contribute, given the dominance of local contexts in influencing conditions for successful constitution-making;[102] others offer cautious praise for foreign technical assistance and expertise, as compared to more active forms of intervention.[103] In some instances, it appears that foreign experts, bringing knowledge of their own constitutional systems, have been given key roles in the drafting process, in an effort both to harness expertise and to provide a form of legitimacy that only outsiders (of a particular sort) could do.[104]

A major scholarly effort is now focused on questions of institutional design in divided societies,[105] as the benefits of federalism, consociationalism, or other forms of recognition, accommodation, or power sharing are analyzed and modeled. Some of this scholarly work is intended to influence constitutional design decisions on the ground, though rarely do actual constitutional processes follow singular templates and models, instead displaying a 'mix and match' approach in which small differences in institutional design may yield large differences in outcomes. Scholarly work on normatively or functionally desirable constitutions sometimes gives insufficient attention to a consideration of actual "upstream" or "downstream" constraints on decision-makers.[106] For such knowledge to be usable by constitutional legislators, more study of the processes and political economy of constitutional change would be helpful to future decision-makers in being able better to link normative and functional goals with understandings of the political economy of constitutional change.

IV. Methodological Challenges

In concluding, this chapter addresses some of the special methodological challenges of comparative constitutional law, an issue that can only be addressed by understanding the goals of comparison.[107] A first goal is simply to develop a better intellectual understanding of one or

[100] See Laurel E. Miller (ed), *Framing the State in Times of Transition: Case Studies in Constitution Making* (2010).

[101] See eg Richard W. Bauman and Tsvi Kahana (eds), *The Least Examined Branch The Role of Legislatures in the Constitutional State* (2006); Jon Elster, 'Legislatures as Constiuent Assemblies' in Bauman and Kahana; Ruth Gavison, 'Legislatures and the Phases and Components of Constitutionalism' in Bauman and Kahana; Mark Tushnet, 'Interpretation in Legislatures and Courts: Incentives and Institutional Design' in Bauman and Kahana.

[102] Mark Tushnet, 'Some Skepticism About Normative Constitutional Advice' (2008) 49 *William and Mary Law Review* 1473.

[103] Miller (n 100).

[104] Ibid 616 (discussing Namibia).

[105] See Sujit Choudhry (ed), *Constitutional Design for Divided Societies: Integration or Accommodation?* (2008).

[106] For discussion of these constraints, see Jon Elster, 'Forces and Mechanisms in the Constitution-Making Process' (1995) 45 *Duke Law Journal* 364, 373–5.

[107] This section of the chapter, and one earlier paragraph, draw from my previously published article, Vicki C. Jackson, 'Methodological Challenges in Comparative Constitutional Law' (2010) 28 *Penn State International Law Review* 319.

more other systems. For this purpose, the challenges include time, the need to develop expertise, language barriers, and the need to understand the broader context—both legal and social—in which law operates. All these challenges are about the risks of error or oversimplification. However difficult it is to become *bilingual, bilegalism* is even harder to achieve. Not only is it necessary to understand foreign languages, or find reliable translations of foreign legal materials, but in order to understand one doctrine or institution of another legal system it is necessary to have at least some understanding of the broader canvas on which it exists.

Each of these risks raises another kind of challenge for scholars and that is the 'opportunity costs' of maintaining expertise in more than one system. What will scholars give up in order to develop this expertise? For judges, the opportunity costs might be framed differently: is there a risk of losing what Karl Llewellyn might have called a 'situation sense' about their own constitutional system if they spend considerable time developing expertise on others?[108]

A second goal for comparative constitutional study is to enhance capacity for self-reflection, to develop a better understanding of one's own system. In this regard, there are all of the challenges set out above, plus the following. While 'the unnoticed in our practices may become visible in the contrast with other cultural practices of law', which 'can help us to understand who we are', comparison alone 'cannot…tell us whether we should remain what we have been'.[109] Distinguishing 'true' from 'false' necessities is a distinct challenge.

A third purpose of comparative constitutional study goes beyond simple self-reflection and aims to develop an understanding of normatively preferable 'best practices'—whether from a 'universalist' perspective about rights or a more functional perspective about general political truths about well-designed constitutions.[110] There are at least three additional challenges in pursuing this goal. First, implicit is the need to identify a notion of the normative good, or of just results. Second, not only does this inquiry require a normative baseline of the good or just, it also depends on implicit notions of causality, that is, of the relationship between law and/or legal structures and good and/or just results in society; yet being able to make general statements of causal relations confronts the general problem of identifying relevant variables.[111] A related challenge is how to select cases for purposes of causal analysis in comparative constitutional law.[112]

A fourth goal may be to answer questions, asked by domestic constitutional doctrine or text, that are comparative in nature. For example, in Europe, the case law of the European Court of Justice resorts to the common constitutional traditions of the member states to help to protect fundamental rights.[113] One might think that the question of 'commonality' is a relatively simple empirical question. But determining what is common has a normative element as well. More relaxed standards for what counts as a common tradition may reduce the space for diversity and for localized democratic decision-making; more rigorous criteria for identifying the 'common tradition' will allow more space for diverse practices. So whether to adopt

[108] See Karl N. Llewellyn, 'Remarks on the Theory of Appellate Decision and the Rules or Canons About How Statutes Are To Be Construed' (1950) 3 *Vanderbilt Law Review* 395, 397–401.

[109] Paul W. Kahn, 'Comparative Constitutionalism in a New Key', (2003) 101 *Michigan Law Review* 2677, 2679.

[110] Kommers (n 39), 691–6.

[111] On the problems of 'omitted variables' in comparative constitutional analysis, see Tushnet (n 33).

[112] See Hirschl (n 59).

[113] Michel Rosenfeld, 'Comparing Constitutional Review by the European Court of Justice and the US Supreme Court' (2006) 4 *International Journal of Constitutional Law* 618.

a narrow or broad definition of commonality of constitutional tradition has important normative impacts in this context. Similarly, in applying the comparative inquiry about the practices of 'free and democratic' societies, translating from what is demonstrably justified in one free and democratic society to another may not be so easy a matter.[114]

Is there anything distinctive about the methodological challenges of constitutional comparisons as opposed to other kinds of legal comparisons? Limitations of time and resources, limitations of language and contextual understanding, are challenges that apply to any kind of comparative legal study; they can arise whether one is looking at contract law, tort law, or constitutional law in a comparative setting. Three other, possibly distinctive methodological challenges in comparative constitutional law are discussed below: the challenges posed by the complexity and path dependence of the historical context and the interdependence of constitutional provisions one on the other; the tendency in constitutional law and theory to conflate the normative and positive; and the expressivist aspects of constitutional law.

First, constitutions are made and then interpreted in complex and distinctive historical contexts; constitutional provisions are often interdependent, designed to create an overall system or balance, as in most federal systems. Comparisons on federalism issues are especially challenging because federal bargains are always historically contingent and arise out of particular deals struck by particular holders of power in society at one time.[115] But the degree to which these characteristics are distinctive to constitutional law is unclear. Substantive contract law's practical meaning, for example, may depend on the broader legal context, including the procedural rules for litigation, such as who pays attorney's fees, or the practical availability of lawyers or of other means of dispute avoidance or resolution. Nonetheless, the degree to which historic evolutions of particular public institutions influence public law,[116] of which constitutional law is a part, may differ (at least in degree) from analogous influences on other fields, such as contracts.

A second feature that might be considered distinctive is the tendency to conflate normative with positive claims about what is and is not constitutional. In constitutional systems such as the United States, where the Constitution is deeply entrenched and the system thus depends heavily on interpretation, there is a fairly strong tendency in both judicial opinions and scholarly literature to blend normative claims about what the Constitution should be understood to mean, and positive claims about what the courts are now doing or what the Constitution requires. This feature, while perhaps distinctive, may not be true for all constitutional systems, or even for all that depend strongly on interpretation; and there might be other areas of the law where this tendency to conflate also exists.

A third possibly distinctive feature that may affect comparative methodology is the expressivist role played by constitutions and constitutional law.[117] Constitutions serve as a form of public law that is particularly likely to be used to express, or help to constitute, or to influence, national identity. Constitutional preambles make this clear. Thus, Iraq's constitutional preamble asserts, 'We are the people of the land between two rivers, the homeland of the apostles and prophets,...pioneers of civilization...Upon our land the first law made by man was passed....'[118] This is a claim about who the people are. The preamble of the Constitution of

[114] That is to say, for example, that limitations on expression that may be 'demonstrably justified in a free and democratic society' with a history of Nazism may not be quite so readily 'demonstrably justified' in societies without that history.

[115] Jackson (n 27), 227–30.

[116] Bell (n 87).

[117] Tushnet (n 33).

[118] Permanent Constitution of the Republic of Iraq, Preamble, 2005.

China reads like a tract on national history and the accomplishments of a collective people.[119] The French Constitution announces its commitment to the declaration of rights of man and proclaims France an indivisible, secular, democratic, and social republic.[120] The German Basic Law asserts Germans' responsibilities before God and man.[121] The Irish Constitution invoked the 'Most Holy Trinity'.[122]

These are not claims about function and purpose; these are claims about identity and self-expression. The point here is the degree to which the expressive components of constitutions may complicate efforts to do comparative analysis, especially at the functional level. Whether a country sees religion as helping to constitute the state, or whether it sees government as instrumental to a specific social and economic vision, may be understood to influence both constitutional meaning and national identity. Correct, incorrect, better, best, functional, or not, is beside the point; the point from this perspective is that these are situated and embedded in layers of meaning of which the constitution is representative of deeper social and self understandings.

But should functionalism be seen as in some ways an opposite to expressivism? Good comparative analysis tries to reconcile rather than choose between them, though a *contextualized functionalism*. Contextualized functionalism requires a willingness to question whether functions, concepts, or doctrines that appear similar may in fact be quite different in different societies; an attention to how seemingly separate institutions or legal practices are connected to, and influenced by, others; and a commitment to be open to noticing how legal rules or doctrines may be affected by the identitarian or expressivist aspects of the constitution. It is in this vein that more important scholarly work in the future remains to be done, drawing on both qualitative and quantitative methods of analysis.

Bibliography

Bruce Ackerman, 'The Rise of World Constitutionalism' (1997) 83 *Virginia Law Review* 771

John Bell, 'Comparing Public Law' in Andrew Hardy and Esin Orücü (eds), *Comparative Law in the 21st Century* (2002)

Jacco Bomhoff, 'Balancing, the Global and the Local: Judicial Balancing as a Problematic Topic in Comparative (Constitutional) Law' (2008) 31 *Hastings International and Comparative Law Review* 555

Allan-Randolph Brewer-Caraís, *Judicial Review in Comparative Law* (1989)

Sujit Choudhry, 'Globalization in Search of Justification: Toward a Theory of Comparative Constitutional Interpretation' (1999) 74 *Indiana Law Journal* 819

Sujit Choudhry (ed), *The Migration of Constitutional Ideas* (2006)

Rosalind Dixon, 'A Democratic Theory of Constitutional Comparison' (2008) 56 *American Journal of Comparative Law* 947

Zachary Elkins, Tom Ginsburg, and James Melton, *The Endurance of National Constitutions* (2009)

Jon Elster, 'Forces and Mechanisms in the Constitution-Making Process' (1995) 45 *Duke Law Journal* 364

[119] See Xian Fa Preamble (1982) (People's Republic of China).

[120] 1958 Constitution, Art 1.

[121] Grundgesetz für die Bundesrepublik Deutschland (federal constitution), Preamble, May 23, 1949 (Federal Republic of Germany).

[122] Irish Constution, 1937.

Louis Favoreu, 'Constitutional Review in Europe' in Louis Henkin and Albert J. Rosenthal (eds), *Constitutionalism and Rights: The Influence of the United States Constitution Abroad* (1990)

Victor Ferreres Comella, *Constitutional Courts and Democratic Values: A European Perspective* (2009)

Stephen Gardbaum, 'The New Commonwealth Model of Constitutionalism' (2001) 49 *American Journal of Comparative Law* 707

Tom Ginsburg, *Judicial Review in New Democracies: Constitutional Courts in Asian Cases* (2003)

Jeffrey Goldsworthy (ed), *Interpreting Constitutions: A Comparative Study* (2006)

Ran Hirschl, 'The Question of Case Selection in Comparative Constitutional Law' (2005) 53 *American Journal of Comparative Law* 125

Stephen Holmes and Cass Sunstein, 'The Politics of Constitutional Amendment in Eastern Europe' in Sanford Levinson (ed), *Responding to Imperfection: The Theory and Practice of Constitutional Amendment* (1995)

Donald L. Horowitz, 'Conciliatory Institutions and Constitutional Processes in Post-Conflict States' (2008) 49 *William and Mary Law Review* 1213

Vicki C. Jackson, *Constitutional Engagement in a Transnational Era* (2010)

Vicki C. Jackson and Jamal Greene, 'Constitutional Interpretation in Comparative Perspective: Comparing Judges or Courts?' in Tom Ginsburg and Rosalind Dixon (eds), *Research Handbook in Comparative Constitutional Law* (2011)

Gary Jeffrey Jacobsohn, *Constitutional Identity* (2010)

Donald P. Kommers, 'The Value of Comparative Constitutional Law' (1976) 9 *John Marshall Journal of Practice and Procedure* 685

Mattias Kumm, 'The Cosmopolitan Turn in Constitutionalism: On the Relationship between Constitutionalism in and beyond the State' in Jeffrey Dunoff and Joel Trachtman (eds), *Ruling the World?: International Law, Global Governance, Constitutionalism* (2009)

David S. Law, 'Generic Constitutional Law' (2005) 89 *Minnesota Law Review* 652

Arend Lijphart, 'Constitutional Design for Divided Societies' (2004) 15 *Journal of Democracy* 96

Juan J. Linz, 'The Perils of Presidentialsim' (1990) 1 *Journal of Democracy* 51

Gerald L. Neuman, 'Human Rights and Constitutional Rights: Harmony and Dissonance' (2003) 55 *Stanford Law Review* 1863

H.W.O. Okoth-Ogendo, 'Constitutions Without Constitutionalism: Reflections on an African Political Paradox' in Douglas Greenberg et al (eds), *Constitutionalism and Democracy: Transitions in the Contemporary World* (1993)

Giovanni Sartori, *Comparative Constitutional Engineering: An Inquiry into Structures, Incentives and Outcomes* (1994)

Cheryl Saunders, 'The Use and Misuse of Comparative Constitutional Law' (2006) 13 *Indiana Journal of Global Legal Studies* 37

Kim Lane Scheppele, 'The Migration of Anti-Constitutional Ideas: The Post-9/11 Globalization of Public Law and the International State of Emergency' in Sujit Choudhry (ed), *The Migration of Constitutional Ideas* (2006)

Alec Stone, *The Birth of Judicial Politics in France* (1992)

Cass Sunstein, *Designing Democracy: What Constitutions Do* (2001)

Mark V. Tushnet, *Weak Courts, Strong Rights: Judicial Review and Social Welfare Rights in Comparative Constitutional Law* (2009)

Mark V. Tushnet, 'The Possibilities of Comparative Constitutional Law' (1999) 108 *Yale Law Journal* 1225

Stefan Voigt, 'Positive Constitutional Economics II: A Survey of Recent Developments' (2011) 146 *Public Choice* 205

Neil Walker, 'Reframing EU Constitutionalism' in Jeffrey Dunoff and Joel Trachtman (eds), *Ruling the World?: International Law, Global Governance, Constitutionalism* (2009)

Jiung-Ronn Yeh and Wen-chen Chang, 'The Emergence of East Asia Constitutionalism: Features in Comparison', Asian Law Institute Working Paper Series No 006, 2009, available at <http://law.nus.edu.sg/asli/pdf/WPS006.pdf>

CHAPTER 3

CARVING OUT TYPOLOGIES AND ACCOUNTING FOR DIFFERENCES ACROSS SYSTEMS: TOWARDS A METHODOLOGY OF TRANSNATIONAL CONSTITUTIONALISM

PEER ZUMBANSEN*

Toronto

I. Introduction: The Transnational Context of Comparative Constitutionalism

The purpose of this chapter is to outline and to assess the role of 'typologies' in comparative constitutional thought. At the outset, it is necessary to clarify whether we are to be concerned with a substantive comparison of constitutions as exercised—for example—by Aristotle in

* Canada Research Chair, Osgoode Hall Law School, York University, Toronto. I am grateful to Isabel Feichtner and Alexandra Kemmerer for insightful feedback and comments and to Elena Cohen for precious editorial work.

Politics, or with a formal one, which focuses on distinctions between written and unwritten, traditional and revolutionary constitutions and their complementing institutional orders, as has become routine in modern-day political and constitutional thought. Comparisons in both directions are available,[1] and it is against this background that we can here attempt to engage in a series of conceptual and theoretical reflections on the *exercise* and *practice* of comparative constitutional law. The aim of this undertaking is to scrutinize the possibility of carving out distinct forms, patterns, 'typologies' of constitutional design with view to identifying differences across systems.

While such effort is in order for a number of reasons that will be spelled out momentarily, at the same time it puts into question the conceptual framework that we are meant to apply and presuppose. This framework suggests that we can (still) readily distinguish between 'different systems', reach deep within them in order to assess and interpret recognizable differences in the design, practice, and culture of constitutional design. In fact, much suggests that the foundations on which we can base the identification and demarcation of distinct constitutional systems pertains more to historic than systematic evidence. In other words, we need to ask whether or not the increasing 'migration of constitutional ideas',[2] the phenomenon of 'judicial globalization',[3] and the impregnation of constitutional cultures through 'foreign' norms and principles,[4] while reflecting on a considerable degree of transformation, opening, and 'internationalization', still leaves the systematic structure intact.[5] Not unknown from the field of comparative law in general,[6] constitutional comparisons, too, are plagued by a great degree of methodological uncertainty and theoretical indeterminacy. But, while '[c]onstitutionalism is sweeping the world',[7] evidenced for example by 'at least 110 countries around the world' engaged in constitution writing or reform since 1990,[8] this evidence is itself extremely varied. Both causes and forms of constitutional change are anything but uniform and thus belie all claims regarding a worldwide and universal trend to a specific set of constitutional values or rights.[9] Rather, the intensity of constitutional creation, reform, and discourse around the world is illustrative of the complexity of this process. The search, thus, for an analytical architecture of typologies across these myriad

[1] Mauro Cappelletti and William Cohen, *Comparative Constitutional Law* (1979); Durga Das Basu, *Comparative Constitutional Law* (1984); Vicki C. Jackson and Mark Tushnet, *Comparative Constitutional Law* (2nd edn, 2006); Norman Dorsen, Michel Rosenfeld, András Sajó, and Susanne Baer, *Comparative Constitutionalism. Cases and Materials* (2nd edn, 2010), 36 ff.

[2] Sujit Choudhry (ed), *The Migration of Constitutional Ideas* (2006).

[3] Anne-Marie Slaughter, 'Judicial Globalization' (2000) 40 *Virginia Journal of International Law* 1103.

[4] Gérard V. La Forest, 'The Expanding Role of the Supreme Court of Canada in International Law Issues' (1996) 34 *Canadian Yearbook of International Law* 89; Louise Arbour and Fannie Lafontaine, 'Beyond Self-Congratulation: The Charter at 25 in an International Perspective' (2007) 45 *Osgoode Hall Law Journal* 239.

[5] But see Sujit Choudhry, 'Globalization in Search of Justification: Toward a Theory of Comparative Constitutional Interpretation' (1999) *Indiana Law Journal* 819, 941: 'A court's choice of interpretive methodology will affect more than the outcome of the particular case before it. It will also likely affect the broader constitutional culture of the interpreting court's jurisdiction.'

[6] Otto Kahn-Freund, 'Comparative Law as an Academic Subject', Inaugural lecture, University of Oxford, 12 May 1965; Otto Kahn-Freund, 'On Use and Misuse of Comparative Law' (1974) 37 *Modern Law Review* 1; Pierre Legrand, *Le droit comparé* (1999); Russell A. Miller, 'Introduction' in Abdullah Ahmed An-Naim, Michael J. Bazyler, Russell A. Miller, and Peter Yu, *Global Legal Traditions: Comparative Law in the Twenty-First Century* (2012).

[7] Susan H. Williams, 'Introduction: Comparative Constitutional Law, Gender Equality, and Constitutional Design' in Susan H. Williams (ed), *Constituting Equality. Gender Equality and Comparative Constitutional Law* (2009), 1.

[8] Ibid.

[9] See Chapter 36.

and continuously evolving constitutionalist cultures must reach deep into the constitutive elements of legal and political cultures, where the places, forms, and scopes of democracy continue to be 'unsolved riddles'.[10]

1. Methodological Orientation

In this chapter, I adopt the view that the above-described influences illustrate the difficulties of a comparative framework focusing on 'typologies' and 'differences across systems'. In light of the fundamentally changing environment of constitutionalism and constitutionalization, I suggest the adoption of an alternative perspective and argue for the need for a methodology of *transnational constitutionalism*. The importance here lies in the combination of *transnational* and *constitutionalism*, with each term taken to be hiding more than it is revealing. Importantly, the term 'transnational' does not merely signify the extension of—however institutionalized or formalized—normativity across borders, say, of nation-states or other jurisdictional confines. Instead, the term 'transnational' identifies an intricate connection of spatial and conceptual dimensions: in addressing, on the one hand, the demarcation of emerging and evolving spaces and, on the other, the construction of these spaces as artefacts for human activity, communication, and rationality, the term transnational is *conceptual*. To declare an activity transnational is not just the result of an empirical *observation*, say, of a border-crossing commercial transaction.[11] Instead, the term 'transnational' prompts a closer scrutiny of the definitional work that has gone into the description of the space *before* transnationalization. This line of questioning is of crucial importance as it reveals that the drawing of boundaries and the demarcation of 'spaces' is a conceptual undertaking.[12] Seen in this light, the imagery of 'constitutionalism beyond the state' is open for a conceptual inquiry as to the irreplaceable or alternative-less inscription of constitutionalism within the state.[13] To investigate the transnational nature of institutions or processes, in other words, is a methodological inquiry into the very structure of the language with which spaces of activity, regulation, or governance are constructed.

Thus, when speaking of transnational constitutionalism, we should not think of a normative order that emerges autonomously outside the confines of the nation-state and, as such, encompasses a distinct space of global governance with no relation to the world of states and the correlating measurements of law, namely national and international. Instead, transnational constitutionalism expresses the continuing evolution of constitutional principles, instruments, and doctrines as a particular form of legal evolution today. Transnational constitutionalism radically challenges but does not negate the distinction between the domestic and the international legal order. As suggested already in the 1950s by scholars in public and private law, the idea of 'transnational law' could aptly capture the emergence of norm creation and enforcement outside the confines of both private and public international law.[14] These propositions, which have over time resonated in different areas of law, predominantly in

[10] Susan Marks, *The Riddle of All Constitutions. International Law, Democracy, and the Critique of Ideology* (2000), 103, 146.

[11] Ross Cranston, 'Theorizing Transnational Commercial Law' (2007) 42 *Texas International Law Journal* 597.

[12] Richard Ford, 'Law's Territory (A History of Jurisdiction)' (1999) 97 *Michigan Law Review* 843; Yishai Blank, 'Localism in the Global Legal Order' (2006) 47 *Harvard International Law Journal* 263.

[13] Neil Walker, 'Taking Constitutionalism Beyond the State' (2008) 56 *Political Studies* 519, 523.

[14] Philip C. Jessup, *Transnational Law* (1956); Wolfgang G. Friedmann, 'Corporate Power, Government by Private Groups, and the Law' (1957) 57 *Columbia Law Review* 155.

commercial law and other subject areas of 'private' law,[15] have furthermore inspired a host of theoretical and conceptual work around legal pluralism,[16] human rights law,[17] and transnational legal theory.[18] Central to these approaches are two insights, one relating to the overwhelming evidence of norm creation which occurs outside the state's lawmaking apparatus,[19] the other connected to a particular understanding of law's relation to society. From this point of view, law is a particular form of societal communication, as such contributing to the overall totality of society, but not occupying a privileged or hierarchically superior vantage point. This approach, which is most closely associated with the systems theory account of society developed by the late German sociologist Niklas Luhmann, posits society as one 'without centre or apex'.[20] In such a society, the state represents a particular emblematic form of political organization the emergence (and fate) of which is historically embedded and thus contingent. That the centre (or, the top) of societies should be occupied by the state is—thus—both historically and geographically variable.

This has tremendous consequences for an understanding of law. While Western legal thought has over a considerable time span learned to associate law with the state,[21] it is by omission and a narrowing of one's gaze, that this nexus came to be universalized.[22] Today's interest in 'law and globalization'[23] should thus be seen as a welcome and most timely return to insights into the legal pluralist nature of law, which legal sociologists and anthropologists had already purported a long time ago.[24] Aiming for an understanding of society today through a legal lens, then, might not be the worst approach, as law can be seen as impressively reflecting the changing structure of society.[25] The crucial step, which can be made at this point, is to

[15] Berthold Goldman, 'Arbitrage International et droit commun des nations' (1956) *Revue de l'arbitrage* 115; Clive M. Schmitthoff, 'International Business Law: A New Law Merchant' (1961) 2 *Current Law and Social Problems* 129; Gralf-Peter Calliess and Peer Zumbansen, *Rough Consensus and Running Code: A Theory of Transnational Private Law* (2010).

[16] Gunther Teubner, '"Global Bukowina": Legal Pluralism in the World Society' in Gunther Teubner (ed), *Global Law Without A State* (1997); Sally Engle Merry, 'New Legal Realism and the Ethnography of Transnational Law' (2006) 31 *Law and Social Inquiry* 975; Paul Schiff Berman, 'The New Legal Pluralism' (2009) *Annual Review of Law and Social Sciences* 225.

[17] Craig M. Scott, '*Introduction to* Torture as Tort: *From Sudan to Canada to Somalia*' in Craig M. Scott (ed), *Torture as Tort* (2001); Harold Hongju Koh, 'Transnational Legal Process' (1996) 75 *Nebraska Law Review* 181.

[18] Craig M. Scott, '"Transnational Law" as Proto-Concept: Three Conceptions' (2009) 10 *German Law Journal* 859; Peer Zumbansen, 'Transnational Law, Evolving' in Jan Smits (ed), *Elgar Encyclopedia of Comparative Law* (2nd edn 2012).

[19] Sally Engle Merry, 'Legal Pluralism' (1988) 22 *Law and Society Review* 869; Marc Galanter, 'Farther Along' (1999) 33 *Law and Society Review* 1113.

[20] Niklas Luhmann, *Political Theory in the Welfare State* (John Bednarz trans, [1981] 1990).

[21] Max Weber, *On Law in Economy and Society*, orig in German *Wirtschaft und Gesellschaft* (Edward Shils and Max Rheinstein trans, Max Rheinstein ed, [1925] 2nd edn 1967).

[22] Andreas Fischer-Lescano and Gunther Teubner, 'Regime-Collisions: The Vain Search for Legal Unity in the Fragmentation of Global Law' (2004) 25 *Michigan Journal of International Law* 999; see already Adda B. Bozeman, *The Future of Law in a Multicultural World* (1971), ix, 'biased in favor of the assumption that differences between cultures and political systems are functions primarily of different modes of perceiving and evaluating reality'.

[23] An excellent overview is given by Paul Schiff Berman, 'From International Law to Law and Globalization' (2005) 43 *Columbia Journal of Transnational Law* 485.

[24] Eugen Ehrlich, *Fundamental Principles of the Sociology of Law*, orig in German *Grundlegung der Soziologie des Rechts* ([1913] 1962); Sally Falk Moore, 'Law and Social Change: The Semi-Autonomous Field as an Appropriate Subject of Study' (1973) 7 *Law and Society Review* 719; Harry W. Arthurs, *Without the Law: Administrative Justice and Legal Pluralism in Nineteenth Century England* (1988).

[25] Niklas Luhmann, *A Sociological Theory of Law* (1985).

perceive of society as one in which many communicative forms and rationalities come together, and thus as a society in which states are but historically and geographically identifiable emanations of political organization. This opens an important vista on the 'history', the 'histories', and the 'non-history' of the state,[26] while it allows us to conceive of society as 'world society'.[27] Understood in this vein, society becomes the backdrop and context for our iterations of law and, by consequence, for all ensuing attempts to engage in any form of comparative law. While it is true that 'constitutions are made and then interpreted in complex and distinctive historical contexts',[28] comparative law in a pluralistic world society[29] forms the larger context for any attempt to identify and isolate constitutional typologies.

But, here is the moment where we need to pause. This is required if only to take appropriate notice of the considerable anxieties that accompany today's assertions of a world society, of global governance, or global constitutionalism.[30] How have we arrived at this point? Much suggests, that—at least in the West—a pertinent obsession with the state lies at the root of the alluded-to globalization anxiety, an anxiety that might at least be partially abated through the insistence on constitutional comparisons. For, the very possibility of such comparison would allow a return, as it were, to known demarcations and confined realms of societal, political, and legal order.

Such realms are always in motion. A categorization of constitutional qualities and characteristics and the complementing mapping of their distribution *across time and space* must take into account the fact that historical and present-day depictions of this or that constitutional order are placed in a discursive field. In other words, rather than 'going out to see', comparative constitutionalism is confronted with and engaged in a discursive struggle of contentious statements about the political order at a given time. This has long preoccupied scholars of comparative political thought, an area which underlies and informs much of comparative constitutionalism today. At the centre of such work we find efforts to adequately identify, to interpret, and to label instantiations of 'change'. Bearing the problem of bias and viewpoint in mind, that we are likely only seeing what we set out to see,[31] any act of comparison continues to be haunted by grave doubts as to perception and method.[32] At the same time, the very dynamic of societal change itself seems to resist any comparative assessment, if not undertaken 'from within', that is on the grounds of a solid understanding of 'the times' and informed by an adequately sophisticated theory of society. Hence, the proximity of constitutional studies and historical political analysis, as illustrated by early 'comparativists' such as Montesquieu, Burke, or Tocqueville.[33]

[26] Florian F. Hoffmann, 'In Quite a State: Trials and Tribulations of an Old Concept in New Times' in Russell A. Miller and Rebecca Bratspies (eds), *Progress in International Law* (2008).

[27] Niklas Luhmann, 'The World Society as a Social System' (1982) 8 *International Journal of General Systems* 131; John W. Meyer, John Boli, George M. Thomas, and Francisco O. Ramirez, 'World Society and the Nation-State' (1997) 103 *American Journal of Sociology* 144.

[28] Vicki C. Jackson, 'Methodological Challenges in Comparative Constitutional Law' (2010) 28 *Penn State International Law Review* 319, 324.

[29] Michel Rosenfeld, 'Rethinking Constitutional Ordering in an Era of Legal and Ideological Pluralism' (2008) 6 *International Journal of Constitutional Law* 415.

[30] For a discussion of the 'four "i"s' (inappropriate, inconceivable, improbable, or illegitimate), see Walker (n 13), 520–5.

[31] Poignantly depicted by Jonathan Hill, 'Comparative Law, Law Reform and Legal Theory' (1989) 9 *Oxford Journal of Legal Studies* 101.

[32] Ralf Michaels, 'The Functional Method in Comparative Law' in Mathias Reimann and Reinhard Zimmermann (eds), *Oxford Handbook of Comparative Law* (2006).

[33] Alexis de Tocqueville, *Democracy in America* (H. Reeve trans, [1835] 2000).

While the attempt to discern architectural determinants, frameworks, and patterns of politico-constitutional organization is central to the comparative study of constitutional laws, the underlying motivations are highly divergent. While for some, the 'functional' comparison of working legal institutions and structures is at the forefront of the comparative enterprise, others pursue a discernibly more normative agenda.[34] And yet, the overlapping of political and constitutional analytical lenses can easily blur the lines between universalist and functionalist analysis,[35] and it is under our very eyes that the studied legal culture dissolves into a dizzying map of ambiguous assertions and directions. Yet, as we have learned, historical change does not reveal itself 'as such', offering itself for straightforward analysis and 'lesson-drawing': rather, the experience of 'progress' is one of a future coming upon us with accelerated velocity and unknown quality.[36]

Constitutions, we learn, fall with and rise from events of political tumult and overturn. 'Revolutions', then, can be read either to confirm the longest established, but not materialized freedoms or to bring about the death of those wrong forms of liberty existing at the time. 'The very idea of the fabrication of a new government', noted Edmund Burke in his *Reflections on the French Revolution*, 'is enough to fill us with disgust and horror. We wished at the period of the Revolution, and do now wish, to derive all we possess as an *inheritance from our forefathers*.'[37] In this context, Burke famously posits that:

> The institutions of policy, the goods of fortune, the gifts of Providence, are handed down, to us and from us, in the same course and order. Our political system is placed in just correspondence and symmetry with the order of the world, and with the mode of existence decreed to a permanent body composed of transitory parts; wherein, by the disposition of a stupendous wisdom, moulding together the great mysterious incorporation of the human race, the whole, at one time, is never old, or middle-aged, or young, but in a condition of unchangeable constancy, moves on through the varied tenour of perpetual decay, fall, renovation and progression.[38]

As noted by J.G.A. Pocock in his discussion of Burke, '[t]he history of ideas may legitimately, though not exclusively, be viewed as the history of the modes of explaining the world and its behaviour which have from time to time existed.'[39] In this context, Reinhart Koselleck remarked that the notion of revolution, which was first 'derived from the natural movement of the stars and thus introduced into the natural rhythm of history as a cyclical metaphor, henceforth attained an irreversible direction. It appears to unchain a yearned-for future while the nature of this future robs the present of materiality and actuality....'[40] 'To the extent that the past can be experienced only insofar as it contains an element of what is to come (and vice versa), the political existence of the state remains trapped within a temporal structure that can be understood as static mobility.'[41]

[34] David M. Beatty, *The Ultimate Rule of Law* (2004).

[35] Cappelletti and Cohen (n 1); Basu (n 1); Konrad Zweigert and Hein Kötz, *An Introduction to Comparative Law* (3rd edn, 1996).

[36] Reinhart Koselleck, 'Modernity and the Planes of Historicity' orig in German *Vergangene Zukunft der frühen Neuzeit* (1979), (1981) 10 *Economy and Society* 166, cited after Reinhart Koselleck, *Futures Past. On the Semantics of Historical Time* (Keith Tribe trans, 2004), 9ff, 22.

[37] Cited in J.G.A. Pocock, 'Burke and the Ancient Constitution: A Problem in the History of Ideas' (1989) *J.G.A. Pocock, Politics, Language & Time: Essays on Political Thought and History* 202, 205.

[38] Cited in ibid 211.

[39] Ibid 204–5.

[40] Koselleck (n 36), 23.

[41] Ibid 22.

This is an observation of crucial importance for the purpose of the task here at hand. As aptly presented by the historians of political ideas and semantics, the discursive context in which the depiction of the meaning of revolution occurs is but all-decisive. It is the eternal, immovable, inscrutable nature of the state as an all-encompassing entity and sphere, which appears to underlie and to inform the understanding of the revolution and of the political order which it brings into view. As the anchoring point for the liberties of those living within its confines, the state is indeed placed above the political order to which—in modern political parlance—it adheres. Whether or not the state can in fact predate and precede the very idea of a certain political order, becomes irrelevant in the moment in which the state is seen to become the personification of a long-standing, historically evolved political order. The state now becomes—because it arguably has been—the guardian of liberties, and as such the representation of the constitutional order.[42]

The state/constitutional order nexus would later become deeply steeped in a positivist depiction of the nature of the legal order itself.[43] Associated with the state, the constitutional order becomes a product emitted from and depending on the state.[44] From this perspective, comparative constitutionalism would thus be an exercise in comparing state legal orders with a particular focus on the regulation of fundamental liberties. A quest for typologies and 'differences across systems' seems to suggest the continuation of this precise inquiry. But, is it still adequate?

2. The Influence of Transnational Law on Comparative Constitutional Law

There is today prolific *evidence* of comparative constitutional studies 'in action', as courts around the world—with differing degrees of deference[45]—consider drawing on alternative, 'foreign' viewpoints in preparing and rendering their decisions.[46] This view of 'foreign' constitutional law as both a guidance to local decision-making and as a 'work of art'[47] has been the subject of significant development and change. The causes of such change, in turn, may be identified as mainly originating out of two core developments: one is the fundamental transformation of what we might want to call the reference space for comparative constitutional law. The renewed advent of globalization in the twentieth century[48] is marked by a far-reaching

[42] Pocock (n 37), 212.

[43] Dieter Grimm, 'Der Wandel der Staatsaufgaben und die Zukunft der Verfassung' in Dieter Grimm (ed), *Staatsaufgaben* (1996).

[44] Walker (n 13), 521: 'The invocation of the ideas and practices of constitutionalism involves a distinctive way of thinking about the world—an *epistemic horizon* and political imaginary that presupposes and refers to the particular form of the state.'

[45] Consider the 'controversy over citation', Dorsen et al (n 1), 6ff; see also the discussion of the 'living constitution' and the 'constitution as living tree' metaphors in Vicki C. Jackson, 'Constitutions as "Living Trees? Comparative Constitutional Law and Interpretive Metaphors' (2006) 75 *Fordham Law Review* 921, 941 ff.

[46] *Lawrence v Texas* 539 US 558 (2003); Ruti Teitel, 'Comparative Constitutional Law in a Global Age' (2004) 117 *Harvard Law Review* 2570; for a sceptical view see Christopher McCrudden, 'A Common Law of Human Rights? Transnational Judicial Conversations on Constitutional Rights' (2000) 20 *Oxford Journal of Legal Studies* 499. See also Chapter 64.

[47] Alexandra Kemmerer, 'Constitutional Law as Work of Art—Experts' Eyes: Judges of the World Examine the Constitution of Europe' (2003) 4 *German Law Journal* 859.

[48] Kevin H. O'Rourke and Jeffrey G. Williamson, *Globalization and History. The Evolution of a Nineteenth-Century Atlantic Economy* (1999); Jürgen Osterhammel and Niels P. Petersson, *Globalization: A Short History* (2004).

change in the position and status of states and sovereign political actors. The rise in importance of regional associations, such as the European Union from its beginnings in the post-Second World War context to its present form (and woes) at the beginning of the twenty-first century, echoes the complexity of transformation that—in an admittedly decentralizing direction—the former Soviet Union has undergone over the last 30 years or so.[49] The changes brought about for statehood since the Second World War, through decolonization and regionalization, reunification and emancipation[50] have drastically changed the anchoring and reference points for comparative constitutional studies: 'The transformation of statehood shatters the former unity of territory, power, and people, and challenges the constitution's ability comprehensively to encompass the political entity of the state.'[51] From the perspective, then, of the constitution's close association of the constitution and constitutionalism with the state, the prospects of comparative constitutional law seem to be tightly connected to the fate of comparative law in a globalized world, where the contours of statehood have become porous.[52] Arguably, the relevance of the concept of 'constitutionalism'—as opposed to 'constitution'—lies in its potential to build bridges between the constitutional law discourses within the nation-state and the investigations into legitimacy of global governance in the 'post-national constellation'.[53]

At the same time, the diminishing effect of constitutions on the global plane and the rise in importance of a rights- and entitlements-based concept of constitutionalism and constitutionalization for transnational human conduct give considerable cause of concern. The 'emergence of private authority in global governance'[54]—as expressed in areas such as trade agreements,[55] rating agencies,[56] product safety,[57] standardization,[58] or the *lex mercatoria*[59]—

[49] See András Sajó, *Limiting Government. An Introduction to Constitutionalism* (1999); Alexander Somek, 'Constitutionalization and the Common Good', Paper for the Cardozo-NYU I-CON Colloquium, February 2010, on file with author.

[50] Craig Scott and Peer Zumbansen, 'Foreword: Making a Case for Comparative Constitutionalism and Transnational Law' (2006) 46 *Osgoode Hall Law Journal* vii–xix; Rosenfeld (n 29); Timothy Brennan, 'Postcolonial Studies and Globalization Theory' in Revathi Krishnaswarmy and John C. Hawley (eds), *The Post-Colonial and the Global* (2008), 37ff, 39, highlighting the normative bias of modern globalization writing: 'The "now" is the new, and the new is rapturously and exuberantly embraced.'

[51] Petra Dobner, 'More Law, less Democracy? Democracy and Transnational Constitutionalism' in Petra Dobner and Martin Loughlin (eds), *The Twilight of Constitutionalism?* (2010), 141.

[52] David Kennedy, 'New Approaches to Comparative Law: Comparativism and International Governance' (1997) *Utah Law Review* 545; Christopher A. Whytock, 'Taking Causality Seriously in Comparative Constitutional Law: Insights from Comparative Politics and Comparative Political Economy' (2008) 41 *Loyola of Los Angeles Law Review* 629.

[53] Jürgen Habermas, *The Postnational Constellation* (2001); Jürgen Habermas, 'A Political Constitution for the Pluralist World Society?' in Jürgen Habermas (ed), *Between Naturalism and Religion. Philosophical Essays* (2008).

[54] R. Hall and T. Biersteker (eds), *The Emergence of Private Authority: Form of Private Authority and their Implications for International Governance* (2001).

[55] David Schneiderman, 'Investment Rules and the New Constitutionalism' (2000) 25 *Law and Social Inquiry* 757.

[56] Timothy J. Sinclair, 'Passing Judgment: Credit Rating Processes as Regulatory Mechanisms of Governance in the Emerging World Order' (1994) 1 *Review of International Political Economy* 133; Dieter Kerwer, 'Holding Global Regulators Accountable: The Case of Credit Rating Agencies' (2005) 18 *Governance* 453.

[57] Harm Schepel, *The Constitution of Private Governance. Product Standards in the Regulation of Integrating Markets* (2005).

[58] Nils Brunsson and Bengt Jacobsson, *A World of Standards* (2000).

[59] A. Claire Cutler, *Private Power and Global Authority: Transnational Merchant Law in the Global Economy* (2003).

constitutes a significant challenge for constitutional thought. These regulatory regimes in the transnational arena reflect, on the one hand, on a fundamentally changed role of the state in the exercise of 'public' governance,[60] the origins of which have to be seen, first, in a transformation of the inter-national context[61] and in the inner-state shift 'from government to governance'.[62] Secondly, these changes are associated with the emergence of norm-making processes, institutions of rule creation, implementation, and adjudication which scholars have not yet been able to re-categorize. Negotiating their allegedly 'autonomous' nature[63] 'without'[64] or 'beyond'[65] the state, legal scholars, political philosophers, and sociologists are equally faced with the following question:

> Is constitutional theory able to generalize the ideas it developed for the nation state and to re-specify them for today's problems? In other words, can we make the tradition of nation-state constitutionalism fruitful and redesign it in order to cope with phenomena of privatization and globalization?[66]

A present inquiry into the possibilities of 'carving out typologies' unfolds against the background of the two contexts of transformation—the international and the national one. That the field of comparative (constitutional) law, despite pertinent enterprises to scrutinize its methodological foundations,[67] still lacks satisfactory theoretization, has been remarked by scholars all around.[68] More importantly and substantively more fruitfully, scholars have highlighted the importance of a forceful engagement with the methodological challenges arising from any comparative legal project today.[69] This chapter embraces these insights and highlights, in particular, the importance of treating both terms—transnational and constitutionalism—as unknowns, as terms that need to be unfolded in order for us to gain a better understanding of their

[60] Armin von Bogdandy, Philipp Dann, and Matthias Goldmann, 'Developing the Publicness of Public International Law' (2008) 9 *German Law Journal* 1375.

[61] See eg Robert O. Keohane and Joseph S. Nye, 'Introduction' in Joseph S. Nye and John D. Donahue (eds), *Governance in a Globalizing World* (2000); Myres S. McDougal and W. Michael Reisman, 'The World Constitutive Process of Authoritative Decision' in Myres S. McDougal and W. Michael Reisman (eds), *International Law Essays* (1981); and John M. Hobson, *The State and International Relations* (2000).

[62] Mark Bevir, R.A.W. Rhodes, and Patrick Weller, 'Traditions of Governance: Interpreting the Changing Role of the Public Sector' (2003) 81 *Public Administration* 1; Alfred Aman Jr, 'Law, Markets and Democracy: A Role for Law in the Neo-Liberal State' (2007) 51 *New York Law School Review* 801; R.A.W. Rhodes, 'Waves of Governance' in David Levi-Faur (ed), *Oxford Handbook of Governance* (2012).

[63] Berthold Goldman, 'Frontières du droit et "lex mercatoria"' (1964) 13 *Archives de la philosophie de droit* 177; Klaus Peter Berger (ed), *The Practice of Transnational Law* (2001); for a critique see Thomas Schultz, 'Some Critical Comments on the Juridicity of Lex Mercatoria' (2008) X *Yearbook of Private International Law* 667; Peer Zumbansen, 'Piercing the Legal Veil: Commercial Arbitration and Transnational Law' (2002) 8 *European Law Journal* 400; Calliess and Zumbansen (n 15).

[64] Teubner (n 16).

[65] Ralf Michaels, 'The True New Lex Mercatoria: Law Beyond the State' (2007) 14 *Indiana Journal of Global Legal Studies* 447.

[66] Gunther Teubner, 'Fragmented Foundations: Societal Constitutionalism beyond the Nation State' in Dobner and Loughlin (n 51), 328.

[67] H. Patrick Glenn, 'Comparative Legal Families and Comparative Legal Traditions' in Reimann and Zimmermann (n 32), and Professor Glenn's groundbreaking textbook, soon to be published in its fifth edition.

[68] Ran Hirschl, 'The Question of Case Selection in Comparative Constitutional Law' (2005) 53 *American Journal of Comparative Law* 125.

[69] Miller (n 6), who draws on Patrick Glenn's concept of legal traditions to argue that 'the answer must be that legal tradition need not be the object of a comparative undertaking, but instead might be part of the inquiry to be made in better understanding the laws or legal institutions that eventually become the objects of comparison.'

traction today. Section II will provide a brief account of the changes in international relations and state sovereignty in the current era of globalization and argue for the emergence of 'transnational constitutionalism' as a methodological framework for comparative constitutional law, which incorporates the alluded-to transformation of the international and domestic contexts, in which we have been referring to the constitution. Section III further investigates the notion of constitutionalism and argues for the term's fusion of form and substance. In conclusion, Section IV exposes constitutionalism as an expression of law's exposure to conflicting regulatory and ordering rationalities.

II. Constitutionalism in World Society: Post-National, Post-Territory, Post-State?

Sociologists have long emphasized the need to conceive of society as a functionally differentiated, highly complex set of communications and processes.[70] In that context, states would count less as expressions of a territorially bounded, specifically peopled and governed space and, in turn, as natural reference points for (comparative) constitutional thought. Instead, the sociologist would see states with all of their characteristics as historically developed and particular instantiations of political power that can be found in different forms and shapes and at different places around the world and through time. While such time keeping has traditionally been seen to have begun in the seventeenth century with the creation of the 'Westphalian' order, it is the respective connotation of Westphalian statehood with ideas of law, rights, democracy, on the one hand, and with the concept of the constitution, on the other, which has given rise to a number of contestations. First, the nexus between the state and a particular form of political and legal rule has been rejected as inadequately excluding alternative forms of political/legal organization from view.[71] Secondly, the focus on the state as the decisive organizing entity gives undue primacy to the *political* form of societal organization, thereby turning a blind eye to the manifold forms of societal order.[72] Mirroring the constantly increasing level of differentiation in society as perceived against the contingent yet pertinent background of particular local contexts, there is a rapidly expanding space of functional differentiation beyond the confines of the nation-state. Security, the environment, financial organization, or work have attained the status of complex regulatory and organizational spaces, the institutional and normative scope of which it is no longer possible to grasp through concepts of the state or through the nineteenth-century distinction of 'state' and 'market'.[73] Thirdly, the focus on the Westphalian state as the prime entity of political organization has been accompanied by a connotation of sovereignty, which over time has become both decontextualized and ahistoricized. As a result, the present era of globalization is presented as an aberration, erosion, and transformation of state sovereignty due to the perceived increased interdependence among states. This depiction, however, rests on a very partial representation of the international history to this day, a history which has been marked by a distinctly uneven

[70] Niklas Luhmann, 'Globalization or World Society: How to Conceive of Modern Society?' (1997) 7 *International Review of Sociology* 67; Meyer et al (n 27).

[71] Ehrlich (n 24), 465ff; Merry (n 19); today: Teubner (n 66), 331.

[72] Merry (n 16).

[73] Helmut Willke, *Smart Governance. Governing the Global Knowledge Society* (2007), 53ff.

distribution of political and economic powers.[74] In turn, sovereignty, even when portrayed today as 'challenged' and 'transformed', for example by the rise in importance of non-state actors, claiming new subjectivity in international law[75] or driving constitutional rights creation in parts of Asia,[76] still tends to hide the underlying dynamics of inclusion and exclusion, the stark divide between 'core' and 'periphery'[77] and the persistent discrimination of the 'other'.[78]

Apart from a radically relativized status of the state from the point of view of a world society concept, human relations are being considered in an entirely new light as well. In the eyes of the legal and political philosopher, the 'civil society subject' (*bürgerliches Subjekt*) at the beginning of the modern constitutional era, which morphed into the subject of the twentieth-century 'mass society', has meanwhile been replaced by today's 'cosmopolitan subject', which is 'above all *smart*. It regards the world as resource for interesting projects.'[79] But, this leaves little room—or need—for the capacity to political judgment, if the 'historical *a priori* is not a communal space encompassed by the state, but functionally differentiated, transnational problem solving processes'.[80]

And the sociologists and philosophers of the risk society, which now spans the globe,[81] observe, that:

> Everybody, whether they want it or not, is shaped by the individualism and rationality of a single global culture which includes human rights culture as well as the culture of individualized suicide bombing. All cultural differences are now in the same society and of individualized persons who have to organize and reorganize, construct and reconstruct their ego and their personal and collective identity lifelong, and in order to do that they rely only on the (weak or strong) means of their own autonomy.... Yet, as 'free men' we are not looking with Sartre into the abyss of nothingness, but are acting against a dense and common background of relatively abstract, highly general and formal, thoroughly secular, nevertheless global knowledge that is implicit in the global social life-world. This is so simply because traditional identity formations no longer and nowhere are available without a permanently growing and changing variety of alternative offers, in Teheran as well as in New York, in the Alps of Switzerland as well as in the mountain regions of Afghanistan, Pakistan, or Tibet.[82]

[74] Antony Anghie, 'The Evolution of International Law: Colonial and Postcolonial Realities' (2006) 27 *Third World Quarterly* 739; B.S. Chimni, 'Third World Approaches to International Law: A Manifesto' (2006) 8 *International Community Law Review* 3.

[75] Philip Alston, 'The "Not-a-Cat Syndrome: Can the International Human Rights Regime Accommodate Non-State Actors?' in Philip Alston (ed), *Non-State Actors and Human Rights* (2005).

[76] Wen-Chen Chang, 'An Isolated Nation with Global-Minded Citizens: Bottom-Up Transnational Constitutionalism in Taiwan' (2009) 4 *National Taiwan University Law Review* 203, 222–30.

[77] Boaventura de Sousa Santos, 'The World Social Forum and the Global Left' (2008) 36 *Politics and Society* 247.

[78] Diane Otto, 'Lost in Translation: Re-scripting the Sexed Subjects of International Human Rights Law' in Anne Orford (ed), *International Law and its Others* (2006). On sovereignty more broadly see Chapter 17.

[79] Alexander Somek, 'Die Verfassung im Zeitalter ihrer transnationalen Reproduzierbarkeit. Gedanken zum Begriff der Konstitutionalisierung' in Claudio Franzius, Franz C. Mayer, and Jürgen Neyer (eds), *Strukturfragen der Europäischen Union* (2011), 141.

[80] Ibid 142.

[81] Ulrich Beck, *World at Risk*, orig in German *Weltrisikogesellschaft* (Ciaran Cronin trans, 2009).

[82] Hauke Brunkhorst, 'Constitutionalism and Democracy in the World Society' in Dobner and Loughlin (n 51), 186–7.

Comparative constitutional law scholars, hence, face a conundrum. Where they turn towards states in the international arena in order to depict particular types and forms of constitutional order, they find themselves in a 'new world'. Searching for institutional familiarity or, at least, complementarity, they are increasingly faced with the fluidity of the institutional and procedural frameworks that so far marked the anchor points for comparison, something which has been guiding the Canadian comparativist H. Patrick Glenn in his refutation of comparative studies that aim at circumscribing 'systems' through the association with static and fixed boundaries.[83] It also inspires the groundbreaking project of a transnational group of constitutional scholars in their efforts to explore the openness of 'global legal traditions'.[84] The changed transnational landscape, then, reflects a distinct transnationalization in the form of an emerging multilevel constitutional universe[85] pushing for an open-ended reconfiguration of constitutional and interpretative competences. A US court wishing to engage with the constitutional law of, say, France or Germany, will—despite a good understanding of the particular nature of constitutional review in both countries[86]—find itself confronted with the European Court of Human Rights' effect on what has long become a complex interplay of different levels of norm creation and compliance.[87]

Substantively, this altered landscape appears to elude claims of deliberation, reciprocity, and 'engagement' as risk management, 'hedging', and knowledge-driven assessments assume the dominant places in societal providence. Faced with this 'mismatch between societal complexities and the means and modes of governance',[88] the constitutionalist is prompted to reconsider her perspectives and options.[89] It is thus not surprising that comparative law scholars, in light of the porous confines of national constitutional orders, have been directing their view towards differently construed architectures of constitutional ordering. This is aptly reflected in the emergence of comparative *constitutionalism*,[90] present today, for instance, in vibrant discourses around the 'migration' of constitutional ideas[91] and 'transnational constitutionalism'.[92] Yet—despite the intensity of such endeavours—it still appears as if '[c]onstitutionalism is one of those concepts, evocative and persuasive in its connotations yet cloudy in its analytic and descriptive content, which at once enrich and confuse political discourse.'[93] Accordingly, an inquiry into the methodological foundations of comparative constitutional law cannot avoid a serious engagement with the notion of constitutionalism.

[83] H. Patrick Glenn, *Legal Traditions of the World: Sustainable Diversity in Law* ([2000] 2nd edn 2004).

[84] An-Naim et al (n 6).

[85] Christian Tomuschat, 'The Effects of the Judgments of the European Court of Human Rights According to the German Constitutional Court' (2010) 11 *German Law Journal* 513; Dorsen et al (n 1), 77ff ('The Transnational Constitution').

[86] Wolfgang Hoffmann-Riem, 'Two Hundred Years of *Marbury v Madison*: The Struggle for Judicial Review of Constitutional Questions in the United States and Europe' (2004) 5 *German Law Journal* 685.

[87] Tomuschat (n 85).

[88] Willke (n 73), 39.

[89] Abdullah Ahmed An-Na'im, *Islam and the Secular State. Negotiating the Future of Shari'a* (2008), 84ff (ch 3).

[90] Dorsen et al (n 1).

[91] Choudhry (n 2).

[92] Excellent: Dobner (n 51); and Walker (n 13), 525ff.

[93] Thomas C. Grey, 'Constitutionalism: An Analytic Framework' in J. Roland Pennock and John W. Chapman (eds), *Constitutionalism: NOMOS XX* (1979), 189.

The transnational transformation of international political sovereignty is characterized by the overlap and the intersection of historical associations of nineteenth-century governmental design and liberal political theory, on the one hand, and the insight into the tedious tension between legislative prerogatives and fundamental rights, on the other.[94] Constitutionalism unties the nexus between 'state' and 'constitution' by positing an inner connection between the form *and* substance of government.[95] In breaking down the complementary association between the state and the constitution, the concept of constitutionalism recreates opportunities to conceive of different foundations and ties of constitutional norms. Herein lies its great promise—and also its risk. Taking an optimistic view, constitutionalism can be seen as law's unveiling of its emancipatory potential: constitutionalism frees constitutional norm thinking from any given institutional framework and instead provides a space in which such a framework can or rather, must, first be designed. From a more sceptical vista, however, the accompanying notions of 'limiting' government tend to propel a normative assessment of the state's 'proper business' rather than merely demarcating the extent of its regulatory arm.[96] This focus on limiting, or placing constraints on, government powers, has arguably been part of what scholars have referred to as 'traditional constitutionalism'.[97]

1. Space

This limiting function of constitutional frameworks has, as we saw, been a crucial element in the evolution of politico-constitutional theorizing. It comes as little surprise, then, that a certain 'gist' is attributed to this history. Harking back to canonical texts of comparative legal theory, the underlying assumption of progress, often coupled with a strong plea *for* progress,[98] continues to have a strong impulse for the recognition and elaboration of border-crossing normativity. But, in the transnational context, this implication of normative progress—allegedly expressed, for example, (in the Western understanding) by the 'progress' in human rights law,[99] has tremendous consequences for a critique of emerging legal structures. In the heated discussion around an emerging 'global' legal order, two features in this context are particularly worthy of being highlighted. The first concerns the question of the connection between a *global* legal order and the *domestic* legal system. This question, then, turns on the degree of *autonomy* of one from the other. Arguably, claims of an emerging global legal order have been put forward precisely not only to illustrate the autonomy of global law from the (nation-)state,

[94] Bruce A. Ackerman, 'The Storrs Lectures: Discovering the Constitution' (1984) 93 *Yale Law Journal* 1013; Jürgen Habermas, 'On the Internal Relation between the Rule of Law and Democracy' (1995) 3 *European Journal of Philosophy* 12; Ronald Dworkin, 'Constitutionalism and Democracy' (1995) 3 *European Journal of Philosophy* 2; Sajó (n 49), xiv.

[95] Compare with Jeremy Waldron, 'Constitutionalism: A Skeptical View', New York University Public Law Legal Theory Research Paper No 10-87, 2010, available at <http://ssrn.com/abstract=1722771>, 13: 'Unlike, say, the Rule of Law, constitutionalism is not just a normative theory about the *forms* and *procedures* of governance. It is about controlling, limiting, and restraining the power of the state.'

[96] Ibid 17–18.

[97] Jiunn-Rong Yeh, 'The Emergence of Asian Constitutionalism: Features in Comparison' (2009) 4 *National Taiwan University Law Review* 39, 41. Professor Yeh has argued that this type of constitutionalism has been succeeded by 'transitional constitutionalism', marked by a high degree of dynamic change, future empowerment, and contingent constitutional arrangements, which are likely to be changed and adapted later. The last stage in this development he depicts as 'transnational constitutionalism', marked by the emergence of supranational constitutional frameworks (eg the EU), the tension between 'domestic' and 'transnational' constitutional norms, and the increasing institutional borrowing and judicial dialogue. Ibid 44.

[98] Zweigert and Kötz (n 35), 43ff.

[99] For a critique, see only Upendra Baxi, *The Future of Human Rights* (2002).

but in addition to underscore the distinct nature of the emerging body and system of norms.[100] The second strand in the cluster of arguments in favour of an emerging globality of law concerns the question of legitimacy. Here, again, the discussion has become considerably differentiated: while scholars in the context of assessing the prospects of public international law in the face of global terrorism, climate change, and unilateralism, argue for the increasing materiality of constitutionalist thinking outside the nation-state,[101] other scholars have been taking a closer look at the intersection between international law and political philosophy, scrutinizing the chances for a cosmopolitan legal order.[102] It is within the larger debate about cosmopolitanism, that some of the long-standing challenges of constituting a pluralistic, democratic political order become visible and open to scrutiny—from the perspectives of law, philosophy, and political science. What, on the one hand, differentiates but, on the other, also reconnects this strand of debate with the one focusing on global constitutionalism, is the distinct widening of the perspective from a predominantly legal inquiry towards one which places the constitution of a legal order within a comprehensive discussion of the legitimacy concerns of such an order.[103] Finally, a third strand in the context of assessing the challenges of a global legal order approaches the problem from a distinctly procedural angle. Arguing for the relevance of administrative law rules to further the legitimacy of global governance institutions, scholars in this field have been mobilizing the idea of a 'global administrative law'.[104] Over the span of a few years, this research has met with far-reaching attention, pressing for a further clarification and elaboration of central premises such as the comparative status of constitutional law concerns within the administrative governance orientation of the Global Administrative Law Project[105] or the prospects of the concept of the Rule of Law within the continuing debate around the institutional and normative pillars of global governance.[106]

This differentiation of the debate around an emerging global legal order is, as we have seen, intimately tied into questions of boundaries and legal or, regulatory 'spaces' (national/domestic vs 'global'), on the one hand, and questions of legitimacy, accountability, representation, on the other. This overlapping of inquiries into the status and nature of the evolving legal order has been contributing to a further approximation of legal theoretical discourse and parallel scholarly pursuits in disciplines such as geography, sociology, anthropology. These disciplines have been of crucial importance in illuminating and emphasizing the methodological complexity of global governance discourses and are central to a redefinition of constitutionalism,

[100] Gunther Teubner, 'The King's Many Bodies: The Self-Deconstruction of Law's Hierarchy' (1997) 31 *Law and Society Review* 763.

[101] Bruce A. Ackerman, 'The Rise of World Constitutionalism' (1997) 83 *Virginia Law Review* 771; see also the contributions to Ronald St John Macdonald and Douglas M. Johnston (eds), *Towards World Constitutionalism. Issues in the Legal Ordering of the World Community* (2005).

[102] Immanuel Kant, *To Perpetual Peace. A Philosophical Sketch* (Ted Humphrey trans, [1795] 2003); David Held, 'Cosmopolitanism' (2006) *Stanford Encyclopedia of Philosophy* (28 November), available at <http://plato.stanford.edu/entries/cosmopolitanism>; Daniele Archibugi, *The Global Commonwealth of Citizens. Toward Cosmopolitan Democracy* (2008).

[103] Brun-Otto Bryde, 'International Democratic Constitutionalism' in Macdonald and Johnston (n 101); Regina Kreide, 'The Ambivalence of Juridification. On Legitimate Governance in the International Context' (2009) 2 *Global Justice: Theory Practice Rhetoric* 18.

[104] Benedict Kingsbury, Nico Krisch, and Richard Stewart, 'The Emergence of Global Administrative Law' (2005) 68 *Law and Contemporary Problems* 15.

[105] Nico Krisch, 'Global Administrative Law and the Constitutional Ambition', LSE Law, Society and Economy Working Papers 10/2009, 2009, reprinted in Dobner and Loughlin (n 51), 245, available at <http://ssrn.com/abstract=1344788>.

[106] Benedict Kingsbury, 'The Concept of "Law" in Global Administrative Law' (2009) 20 *European Journal of International Law* 23. See Chapter 10.

as we will develop in greater detail in the concluding section. Meanwhile, they offer important echoes and re-instantiations of the type of questions raised by legal pluralists over the course of the twentieth century. Legal pluralism, arguably, has been concerned with critiquing the demarcation lines between 'official' and 'unofficial' rule systems, in other words with the identification and scrutinizing of the justifications offered to distinguish between law and 'non-law'.[107] In the context of analysing the nature of 'global law rules', the legal pluralists' interest in laying bare the political and ideological choices involved in differentiating spheres of rule-making proves to contribute a crucial perspective on the applied analytical lenses and methodological approaches.[108]

Against this background, it becomes questionable whether one may aptly characterize the above-mentioned approaches in studying global law as *spatial*.[109] This adjective would be justified to the degree that the metaphor of space continues to function as a helpful tool for the identification of constituted spheres of rule creation, enforcement, and political order. At the same time, it becomes less pervasive when applied in the context of an inquiry into the nature of evolving legal norms, which grow out of border-crossing, 'privatized', and transnational norm-making processes.[110] Space, then, ceases to demarcate an identifiable, confined realm, and instead points to the ambiguity and relative openness of reasons given for the constitution of space.

Despite a well-reasoned scepticism towards the metaphor of space in understanding the 'location' of global law, legal scholars have been insisting on the continued importance of making spatial metaphors part of the legal methodological calculus in order further to scrutinize the challenges—and shortcomings—of spatial representations of legal normativity.[111] From this perspective, references to space as well as to 'levels' of regulatory authority continue to be important in the context of global governance analysis, even where they are explicitly contested.[112] What should be retained, then, from this consideration of the significance of spatial metaphors in legal reasoning in the context of global governance, is the 'framing' nature of these metaphors in legal discourse. As impressively illustrated by the untiring inquiry into the promises and fallbacks of federalism, legal theory today can no longer confine itself to a juxtaposition of either-or choices, as between federalism or unity, regulatory competition or harmonization.[113] The crux of these order paradigms lies in their inconclusiveness: just as a system

[107] John Griffiths, 'What is Legal Pluralism?' (1986) 24 *Journal of Legal Pluralism and Unofficial Law* 1; Galanter (n 19).

[108] Paul Schiff Berman, 'Global Legal Pluralism' (2007) 80 *Southern California Law Review* 1155; Berman (n 16); Ralf Michaels, 'Global Legal Pluralism', Duke Public Law and Legal Theory Research Paper No 259, 2009, available at <http://papers.ssrn.com/sol3/papers.cfm?abstract_id=1430395>; Peer Zumbansen, 'Transnational Legal Pluralism' (2010) 1 *Transnational Legal Theory* 141, available at <http://ssrn.com/abstract=1542907>.

[109] Saskia Sassen, 'The Places and Spaces of the Global: An Expanded Analytic Terrain' in David Held and Anthony McGrew (eds), *Globalization Theory. Approaches and Controversies* (2007); Andreas Philippopoulos-Mihalopoulos, 'Spatial Justice: Law and the Geography of Withdrawal' (2010) 6 *International Journal of Law in Context* 201.

[110] Colin Scott, 'Regulatory Governance and the Challenge of Constitutionalism', EUI Working Papers, Robert Schuman Centre for Advanced Studies, Private Regulation Series-02, 2002, available at <http://ucd-ie.academia.edu/documents/0093/9406/RSCAS_2010_07.pdf>.

[111] Marc Amstutz and Vaios Karavas, 'Weltrecht: Ein Derridasches Monster' in Gralf-Peter Calliess, Andreas Fischer-Lescano, Dan Wielsch, and Peer Zumbansen (eds), *Soziologische Jurisprudenz. Liber Amicorum für Gunther Teubner zum 65. Geburtstag* (2009).

[112] William Twining, 'Diffusion and Globalization Discourse' (2006) 47 *Harvard International Law Journal* 507; Yishai Blank, 'Federalism, Subsidiarity, and the Role of Local Governments in an Age of Multilevel Governance' (2010) 37 *Fordham Urban Law Journal* 509.

[113] On federalism generally, see Chapter 27.

arguably resting either on principles of horizontal unity and equity or of hierarchical supremacy, a federalist system does not offer—on its own—answers to questions touching on the substance of the regulatory issue to be decided. Hence, whether or not a regulatory challenge is a matter of federalism, does not carry any weight for the resolution of the underlying substantive issue.[114] And yet, the existence or non-existence of a federal system (or, of a non-federalist one) has distinct consequences for the evolution and application of constitutional rules in a particular system,[115] which in turn is of relevance for the identification of comparative typologies.

2. Time

The *spatial* dimension of law, elaborated on in the previous section, is arguably complemented by a *temporal* one. This dimension begins to unfold when one takes into consideration the *transformation* of the legal systems under comparison. Stark expressions of such transformations become visible, of course, in cases of dramatic regime and system change, for example at times of 'transitional justice' or post-conflict regime-building.[116] The transformation of a legal system, in such instances, is embedded in and inseparable from a much more comprehensive change of the political, socio-economic, and even day-to-day system.[117] As such, a legal system's history is always part of and tied into a significantly more complex history of change (Sarat).

> The most salient feature of the post-colonial model is that both...the constitutional order and identity of the newly independent former-colony are elaborated in a dialectical process involving an ongoing struggle between absorption and rejection of the former colonizer's most salient relevant identities.[118]

The consideration of change *over time*, however, still needs to take into consideration the contested nature of what comes into view, what lies at the surface, and what is lurking in the background and underwood. As famously elaborated by Yerushalmi in his study of Jewish remembrance, a chronology of events is likely to be remembered as a chronology of experiences, the latter being both 'out of time' and yet embedded in a comprehensive narrative of collective identity.[119] The post-conflict context evokes, to be sure, a set of comprehensive and intricate demarcations concerning the nature and quality of 'things changed'. While post-conflict, retroactive, or transitional justice identifies perspectives on legal and political regime change following a fundamental breakdown, rupture, or decay of an existing order,[120] a wider perspective still would take into view the historical period in which the studied transformations occur. This certainly makes for an overwhelming panorama. Hence, the need to draw out the connections between the spatial and the temporal axis between which the present observations are being made. This 'reminder' of sorts, however, points to the considerable

[114] Susan Rose-Ackerman, 'Risk Taking and Reelection: Does Federalism Promote Innovation?' (1980) 9 *Journal of Legal Studies* 593.

[115] Kalypso Nicolaidis and Robert Howse (eds), *The Federal Vision. Legitimacy and Levels of Governance in the United States and the European Union* (2001).

[116] Inga Markovits, 'Selective Memory: How the Law Affects What We Remember and Forget from the Past: The Case of East Germany' (2001) 35 *Law and Society Review* 513.

[117] Ruti Teitel, *Transitional Justice* (2000). See also Chapter 61.

[118] Michel Rosenfeld, *The Identity of the Constitutional Subject* (2010), reproduced in part in Dorsen et al (n 1), 66–74, at 73.

[119] Yosef Hayim Yerushalmi, *Zakhor. Jewish History and Jewish Memory* (1982).

[120] See the contributions by Jennifer Llewellyn, Kirsten Anker, Rosemary Nagy, and Christian Joerges in Peer Zumbansen and Ruth Buchanan (eds), *Law in Transition. Rights, Development and Transitional Justice* (forthcoming 2012).

dilemma, which is underlying the task at hand. This dilemma results from the attempt to provide for a reasonable account of the evolution of political-constitutional structures, but there are non-negligible problems associated with such an undertaking.

3. Governance in Space and Time

Placing cases of state transformation, regime change, and transitional justice in a larger historical context, inevitably requires that we first clarify the location of a particular instance within the identified historical period (eg 'decolonization'), but moreover that we identify the boundaries of the period itself. To stay with the example of decolonization, historians have regularly called into question a straightforward, historic demarcation of both beginnings and ends of this 'period'.[121] This has to do, inter alia, with the immensely intricate and layered context in which such a demarcation would have to be made. Surely, the context of state formation and political emancipation in North Africa in the 1960s is a different one than that of the post-1989 political independence movements in Eastern Europe. In other words, such an exercise would first have to find convincing answers to questions such as: 'When did decolonization begin, when did it end—if it ever did?' Advances in comparative constitutional law point, however, to growing anxieties among scholars to suggest such answers. For example, comparative scholarship focusing on South East Asia, highlights the great diversity in 'post-colonial' development.[122] Similar problems of classification arise through the lens of legal transplants, which might be applied in order to trace the respective normative and institutional 'migrations' of legal instruments through time and space. Here, again, we see that the story is anything but straightforward.[123]

Yet another problem in the context of applying a 'governance' lens to the comparative study of constitutional cultures arises from the extreme volatility of normative regimes today. A governance view on these developments would at first glance reveal such volatility, in other words, the fragile balance between 'hard' and 'soft' institutions in the (re-)formation of a legal-political system, in the context of 'developing' nations.[124] It should not come as a surprise here that scholars engaging in the study of so-called 'new institutional economics'[125] would find this hybridity of the emerging 'economics of governance'[126] not too daunting, as it would only underline the ordinary tension between individual/collective societal activity, on the one hand, and state intervention/regulation, on the other. New institutional economics (NIE) scholars have been focusing on this tension with greater emphasis in constellations of 'lawlessness', arising, for example—but not only—in contexts of state transformation.[127] Rather than being attributions made in the context of post-conflict situations or fundamental regime change, NIE scholars' observations of lawlessness are also based on a normative assessment of 'state failure'. The latter is affirmed where the state falls short of providing the appropriate

[121] See eg Osterhammel and Petersson (n 48).

[122] Albert H.Y. Chen, 'Western Constitutionalism in Southeast Asia: Some Historical and Comparative Observations' (2010), available at <http://www.ssrn.com/abstract=1723658>.

[123] Choudhry (n 5).

[124] Telling: Oliver E. Williamson, *The Mechanisms of Governance* (1996), ch 6; see also Richard A. Posner, 'Creating a Legal Framework for Economic Development' (1998) 13 *The World Bank Research Observer* 1.

[125] For an insightful account, see Oliver E. Williamson, 'The New Institutional Economics: Taking Stock, Looking Ahead' (2000) 38 *Journal of Economic Literature* 595; see also Elinor Ostrom, 'Challenges and Growth: The Development of the Interdisciplinary Field of Institutional Analysis' (2007) 3 *Journal of Institutional Economics* 239, 242–3.

[126] Oliver E. Williamson, 'The Economics of Governance' (2005) 95 *American Economic Review* 1; for a discussion see Calliess and Zumbansen (n 16), ch 2, part III, C i. (113–19).

[127] Avinash K. Dixit, *Lawlessness and Economics. Alternative Modes of Governance* (2004).

regulatory framework for private activity; hence the NIE scholars' insistence on the need of 'private ordering'.[128] It is important to recognize that the analysis of lawlessness does not exhaust itself or grow out of studies of development contexts. Instead, the analysis unfolds very powerfully in the midst of mature and, as such, highly regulated nation-state environments, where the target of NIE scrutiny is the state's assertion of regulatory authority over what would allegedly be better left to the self-regulatory capabilities of private actors.[129] The assignment of law to set but the formal framework for societal self-regulation draws on legal sociological insights into the normative pluralism of complex societal settings,[130] but gives this analysis a conservative twist by drawing a line between the spheres of the 'state' and the 'market' and between the 'public' and the 'private', despite a longstanding refutation of such simplifying, and thus misleading, distinctions.[131]

This brief allusion to the themes of 'lawlessness' and 'private ordering' suggests an altogether ambiguous concept of the constitution, which is at work both in the context of developing states but also mature welfare states. Whereas the term constitution could refer to a—written or unwritten—text or set containing the ground rules of state conduct and civil rights, the struggle over the place of law in the evolution of political orders, then and now, suggests a much more comprehensive concept of the constitution. Such a concept becomes discernible from a political economy perspective, from which—since Adam Smith—the constitution has been referred to as the framework of state–market relations.[132] From that perspective, constitution captures the organization and normative ordering of a particular society. Where from the vantage point of the earlier depiction rendered by the NIE scholars, the constitution would refer to the rules and principles setting out the rights of both the state and the people living within it, a political economy perspective on the constitution would seek to capture all regulation and self-regulation to be part of the constitutional structure.

As a result, a historical periodization of constitutional phases in different parts of the world would face the choice of either having to assume at least a basic form of constitutional standards and ground rules, against which such changes could be measured, or giving up entirely on the idea of historical periodization for the purpose of comparative studies of constitutional developments in light of the complexity and particularity of each individual case.

III. The Form and Substance of Constitutionalism

But how, we must ask, can this complex background be encompassed and adopted by the notion of constitutionalism? This ambivalence is implied by constitutionalism's *fusion* of form and substance of government, and it is here that we can already recognize the vulnerability of

[128] Williamson (n 124); Williamson (n 126).

[129] See eg Gillian K. Hadfield and Eric Talley, 'On Public versus Private Provision of Corporate Law' (2006) 22 *Journal of Law, Economics and Organization* 414; Gillian Hadfield, 'The Public and the Private in the Provision of Law for Global Services' in Volkmar Gessner (ed), *Contractual Certainty in International Trade. Empirical Studies and Theoretical Debates on Institutional Support for Global Economic Exchanges* (2009).

[130] Ehrlich (n 24); Sally Falk Moore, *Law as Process* (1978); Arthurs (n 24); Griffiths (n 107); Merry (n 19).

[131] Robert L. Hale, 'Coercion and Distribution in a Supposedly Non-Coercive State' (1923) 38 *Political Science Quarterly* 470; Morris R. Cohen, 'Property and Sovereignty' (1927) 13 *Cornell Law Quarterly* 8.

[132] Adam Smith, *Wealth of Nations* ([1776] 1991); Karl Marx, *The Economic and Philosophic Manuscripts of 1844* (1988).

constitutional design to an usurpation by normative motivations, which are themselves removed from scrutiny, because they hide a qualitative dimension ('what should states do?'; 'what do we mean by state?') underneath an allegedly quantitative measurement in terms of the Lochnerian: '*Where* to draw the limits of state intervention?' In turn, this association of constitutionalism with the notion of 'limiting' government remains politically innocent and vulnerable for just about any inscription of what governments should or should not do; by reorienting what is really a normative decision about the goals of politics to the quantifiable measurements of state action, the fact that at the outset we were concerned with a normative question is effectively invisibilized.

But herein rests its great vulnerability, as constitutionalism—stripped of its institutional embodiment, on the one hand, and relatively defenceless in its reliance on its commitment to 'limiting government', on the other—is exposed to normative usurpation. Such usurpation can originate from just about any corner of society, perceived as functionally differentiated and structured by a—disharmonious—concert of different communicative rationalities. 'The administrative individualism of optimizing a rational conduct of life and the global moral missionary consciousness are two sides of the same coin.'[133] But, then again, the usurpation will not come from just any force of societal rationality, or simply originate out of functional differentiation without particular pulls and dynamics. In a knowledge society, marked by the ubiquitous presence of 'experts', practical judgment can tend to become clouded.[134] Meanwhile, certain 'rationalities', foremost the economic one, have become particularly influential and 'expansive'.[135] As has repeatedly been noted by sceptics of the 'new constitutionalism',[136] this has tremendous repercussions for the use of the concept to depict emerging forms of societal order on the transnational plane. In accordance with the ubiquitous triumph of economic rationality, myriad forms of private authority and empowerment, based on property rights and contractual freedom, have become the driving forces in a fast-expanding transnational space of market 'self-regulation'. It is here, at least from a Western perspective,[137] that the concept of constitutionalism merges with processes of 'constitutionalization'. In the grey zone between constitutionalism and constitutionalization, the former is above all associated with the erosion of institutionalized, accountable exercises of political authority, while the latter appears to capture the formative but disembedded driving forces of constitution-making. In this juxtaposition, constitutionalism still rings of the, if embattled and contested, glory of a constitutional promise, a text and its adversaries, while constitutionalization no more than ironicizes particular places of constitutional culture. In an evolving, transnational space, constitutionalization is the driver, wake-up call, and *désenchanteur* of a reliable constitutional culture.

In a multivocal and extremely fragmented and diversified universe of beliefs, traditions, and knowledge bodies, the constitutionalism which grows out of the constitutionalization of

[133] Somek (n 79), 145.

[134] Ibid.

[135] Gunther Teubner, 'Justice under Global Capitalism?' (2008) 1 *European Journal of Legal Studies* 1, available at <http://cadmus.eui.eu/dspace/bitstream/1814/10217/1/EJLS_2008_1_3_TEU_En.pdf>, 6.

[136] David Schneiderman, 'Transnational Legality and the Immobilization of Local Agency' (2006) 2 *Annual Review of Law and Social Sciences* 387; Cutler (n 59); see already Detlev F. Vagts, 'The Multinational Enterprise: A New Challenge for Transnational Law' (1969) 83 *Harvard Law Review* 739.

[137] Compare with Yeh (n 97), 47–9, stressing the 'thin understanding of liberal constitutionalism', whereby constitutional change in Asia in recent decades has—different to the transitional context in Eastern Europe—not been focused on market transformation, but on the simultaneous, non-oppositional development of liberal and social rights.

societal practices, has little in common with the world of 'comparative' constitutional law. Constitutionalization, in the transnational space, depicts the dynamic forces of constantly newly emerging functional and specialized fora of rule-making.[138] In this new environment, constitutionalism's central task to bring about a new fusion of form and substance of government, is always at risk of normative hijacking. In other words, by giving up the intricate tension within the constitution as both emancipating *and* limiting, the normative core of constitutionalism, so understood, can easily be oriented this way or that, through just about any dominant normative concept, the substance of which has never been subjected to a legitimizing process.[139]

And thus, it comes as no surprise that the intricate nature of this inner connection between form *and* substance of government must remain ambivalent. One way of addressing this situation has been to distinguish between constitutionalism and democracy.[140] The latter serves as both a yardstick for an assessment of the procedural and institutional safeguards of constitutionalism and a normative counter-position to the ambiguous openness of constitutionalism. But, how convincing is this move in light of the fact that the contours of democratic government have become elusive in a world society without world government?

IV. Societal Constitutionalism: Law's Troubled Relation to Society

Today, constitutional scholars must address questions of constitutional design, including the negotiation of political power and fundamental rights[141] against this background of a rapidly changed and changing regulatory environment. The general transformation of state sovereignty from 'above' must be seen in tandem with what the sociologist Saskia Sassen has coined the erosion of sovereignty from 'below', namely the alteration of formerly hierarchically conceived patterns of political and legal order through an increasing fusing of the state and market spheres of norm creation, implementation, and enforcement.[142] This bi- and multi-polar transformation of state functionality poses significant challenges for constitutional theories, which—as we have observed in Western legal thought—were largely developed against the background of a state-based system of political organization. As these societies are continuing to experiment with responsive, participatory, and substantively more open-ended forms of regulation, constitutional law becomes a crucial intersection forum for highly differentiated interests and demands from various sectors of society.[143]

[138] On point: Martin Loughlin, 'What is Constitutionalization?' in Dobner and Loughlin (n 51).

[139] Dobner (n 51); Alexander Somek, 'The Argument from Transnational Effects II: Establishing Transnational Democracy' (2010) 16 *European Law Journal* 375, depicting the unresolved nature of legitimacy in 'Global Administrative Law' as evidence for an assumed, but not scrutinized natural law basis of the project.

[140] Waldron (n 95), 40:

> Constitutions are not just about restraining and limiting power; they are about the empowerment of ordinary people in a democracy and allowing them to control the sources of law and harness the apparatus of government to their legitimate expectations. That is the democratic view of constitutions, but it is not the constitutionalist view.

[141] Carl Schmitt, *Constitutional Theory* (Jeffrey Seitzer trans, orig in German, [1928] 2008).

[142] Saskia Sassen, 'The State and Globalization' in Nye and Donahue (n 61).

[143] Karl-Heinz Ladeur, 'Risiko Sozialstaat. Expansion des Sozialstaats ohne verfassungsrechtliche Schranken' (2007) 46 *Der Staat* 61; Karl-Heinz Ladeur, 'Staat und Gesellschaft. Von der liberalen zur

But, the same dynamics which characterize and shape power relations, access, and accountability on the global level under the guise of constitutionalization[144] and 'good governance',[145] have their counterparts within domestic legal cultures—something that renders commitments to 'mutual respect' and 'trust' as core ingredients of an integrative constitutionalist culture[146] considerably aspirational.[147] With a view to the transformation of the state, depicted through notions such as the 'rule of law',[148] the 'social',[149] 'welfare',[150] or 'post-regulatory' state,[151] the realm of *constitutional* law has long begun to become unbounded. Especially in fast-capitalizing, Western nation-states, we can look back at a long history of crucial challenges to the regulatory nature of constitutional law. The history and experience of constitutional law in these societies is of greatest importance precisely because it provides for such a rich archive and mine of engagements with problems of inclusion and exclusion, access and redistribution, public and private power, which so markedly haunt global governance today.[152] Strikingly, however, hardly anything of this varied history, full of ambiguity, violence, frustration, and compromise,[153] finds its way into the global constitutional imagination. The assertion of, say, Global Administrative Law's 'constitutional modesty'[154] is hardly convincing. At the core we are concerned with the transfer of administrative law principles and concepts, which historically have evolved in the context of constitutional contestation, into a sphere, that would allegedly allow a separation of the procedural rules of political administration of highly diversified interests and power relations from underlying constitutional conflicts.[155]

postmodernen Gesellschaft' in Otto Depenheuer and Christoph Grabenwerter (eds), *Verfassungstheorie* (2010); Ernest A. Young, 'The Constitution outside the Constitution' (2007) 117 *Yale Law Journal* 408; and see already Niklas Luhmann, 'Verfassung als evolutionäre Errungenschaft' (1990) 9 *Rechtshistorisches Journal* 176.

[144] David Schneiderman, 'Realising Rights in an Era of Economic Globalisation: Discourse Theory, Investor Rights, and Broad-Based Black Economic Empowerment' in Wenhua Shan, Penelope Simons, and Dalvinder Singh (eds), *Redefining Sovereignty in International Economic Law* (2008).

[145] Kerry Rittich, 'Functionalism and Formalism: Their latest Incarnations in Contemporary Development and Governance Debates' (2005) 55 *University of Toronto Law Journal* 853.

[146] Dieter Grimm, 'Integration by Constitution' (2005) 3 *International Journal of Constitutional Law* 191; Walker (n 13), 531.

[147] Teubner (n 66), 341: 'one can only be amazed at the naivety of participatory romanticism'.

[148] Allan C. Hutchinson and Patrick Monahan (eds), *The Rule of Law: Ideal or Ideology* (1987).

[149] Michael Stolleis, 'Die Entstehung des Interventionsstaates und das öffentliche Recht' (1989) 11 *Zeitschrift für Neuere Rechtsgeschichte* 129.

[150] Francois Ewald, *L'Etat providence* (1986).

[151] Colin Scott, 'Regulation in the Age of Governance: The Rise of the Post Regulatory State' in Jacint Jordana and David Levi-Faur (eds), *The Politics of Regulation: Institutions and Regulatory Reforms for the Age of Governance* (2004).

[152] Nancy Fraser, *Scales of Justice. Reimagining Political Space in a Globalizing World* (2009); Partha Chatterjee, *The Politics of the Governed. Reflections on Popular Politics in Most of the World* (2004), 59ff; Rudolf Stichweh, *Inklusion und Exklusion. Studien zur Gesellschaftstheorie* (2005), 45ff; Niklas Luhmann, *Law as a Social System* (Klaus A. Ziegert trans, Fatima Kastner, David Schiff, Richard Nobles, and Rosamund Ziegert eds, 2004), ch 12; Walker (n 13), 540: 'a powerful continuing counterpoint'.

[153] Robert M. Cover, 'Nomos and Narrative' (1983) 97 *Harvard Law Review* 4; Philippe Nonet and Philip Selznick, *Law and Society in Transition. Toward Responsive Law* (1978); Daniel T. Rodgers, *Atlantic Crossings. Social Politics in a Progressive Age* (1998).

[154] Nico Krisch (n 105); for a critique see Somek (n 139) and Alexander Somek, 'Administration without Sovereignty' in Dobner and Loughlin (n 51), 267ff.

[155] For further elaboration see Kingsbury (n 106).

The fluidity of institutional structures in the emerging 'network society' suggests that constitutional law, based either on a text or emerging from historical common law practice, is best seen as a forum through which an endless number of linkages are constantly created, processed, changed, rejected, and affirmed, between law and politics. 'Constitution', then, becomes an anchoring point and reference perspective for the collision of existing and emerging legal semantics of society's self-governance. But, as such, the constitution is no longer a 'public law' text, emanating from state authority and sitting at the pinnacle of a pyramid of legal normativity. Instead, constitutions—written or unwritten—and constitutional law must facilitate the intersection of law and politics in a radically heterarchic, modern society.[156] As a consequence, the strict confines of the traditionally conceived subject matter of constitutional law itself have long begun to elude us.[157]

What does this mean, however, for the task undertaken by comparative constitutionalists? Comparative constitutional law has itself become fundamentally affected by a change in law's self-perception of its foundations, instruments, and institutions. Rather than with the 'laws' of, say, jurisdiction A and jurisdiction B, comparative lawyers, and notably comparative constitutional law scholars, find themselves confronted with a complex, multilayered, and hybrid structure of norms. Taking their cue from Zweigert and Kötz's instruction in functional comparisons,[158] such comparativists are today caught in a web of official and unofficial, 'hard' and 'soft' norms, that render a comparison of legal instruments and regulatory regimes much more challenging.[159] At the heart of comparing legal cultures now lies an unavoidably interdisciplinary study of legal and non-legal norms, routines, and social practices.[160] It is here, where the comparativist cannot fruitfully proceed without drawing on the insights from 'neighbouring' as well as complementing disciplines—both from outside and inside law. Through the interaction and engagement with political scientists, anthropologists, administrative law, and legal pluralism scholars, to mention only a few, comparative constitutionalists will be poised to draw a much more accentuated map of constitutional culture and change. It is here where we can catch a glimpse of what a turn towards an interdisciplinary understanding of functionalist comparisons might mean. Law's exposure to the myriad, conflicting rationalities and tendencies in a differentiating society throws law back upon itself. It must thus reflect on its own *constitution*. As legal doctrines, principles, and regulatory standards become crisscrossed, captured, alienated, and constantly turned on their head by economic, political, or religious contentions of efficiency, legitimacy, or truth, the very function of law becomes questionable. It becomes a constitutional question. One that is no longer answerable with reference to established patterns of hierarchy or authority, but in a radically open, undetermined way. Law's operation with the legal/illegal distinction is its existential self-assertion, its claim to take on board the pains of this world. It can only do so in its raw exposedness to competing regulatory rationalities, emerging from economics, politics, religion. Meanwhile, the constitutional 'subject' itself is too often constituted from within a known, unscrutinized, and closed context.[161]

[156] Luhmann (n 143); Luhmann (n 20).

[157] Waldron (n 95).

[158] Zweigert and Kötz (n 35), 34ff.

[159] See eg David C. Donald, 'Approaching Comparative Company Law' (2008) 14 *Fordham Journal of Corporate and Financial Law* 83.

[160] Glenn (n 83); Annelise Riles, 'Comparative Law and Socio-Legal Studies' in Reimann and Zimmermann (n 32); Peer Zumbansen, 'Comparative Law's Coming of Age? Twenty Years after "Critical Comparisons"' (2005) 6 *German Law Journal* 1073.

[161] Bruno Latour, *We Have Never Been Modern* (Catherine Porter trans, 1993).

Breaking these frames, the subject emerges as a fragile and vulnerable space of attribution, domination, and suffocation, one that can only be adequately studied in reaching beyond confines and treacherous 'inheritances'.[162] Comparative constitutional law, then, withers away as a field focusing on 'comparison', on 'constitutions', and on 'law', only to re-emerge as a critical enterprise in scrutinizing law's relation to a complex world society.

Bibliography

Abdullah Ahmed An-Naim, Michael J. Bazyler, Russell A. Miller, and Peter Yu, *Global Legal Traditions: Comparative Law in the Twenty-First Century* (2012)

Hauke Brunkhorst, 'Constitutionalism and Democracy in the World Society' in Petra Dobner and Martin Loughlin (eds), *The Twilight of Constitutionalism?* (2010)

Petra Dobner, 'More Law, Less Democracy? Democracy and Transnational Constitutionalism' in Petra Dobner and Martin Loughlin (eds), *The Twilight of Constitutionalism?* (2010)

Norman Dorsen, Michel Rosenfeld, András Sajó, and Susanne Baer, *Comparative Constitutionalism. Cases and Materials* (2nd edn, 2010)

Richard Ford, 'Law's Territory (A History of Jurisdiction)' (1999) 97 *Michigan Law Review* 843

Martin Loughlin, 'What is Constitutionalization?' in Petra Dobner and Martin Loughlin (eds), *The Twilight of Constitutionalism?* (2010)

Niklas Luhmann, 'Verfassung als evolutionäre Errungenschaft' (1989) 9 *Rechtshistorisches Journal* 176

Annelise Riles, 'Comparative Law and Socio-Legal Studies' in Mathias Reimann and Reinhard Zimmermann (eds), *Oxford Handbook of Comparative Law* (2006)

Michel Rosenfeld, 'Rethinking Constitutional Ordering in an Era of Legal and Ideological Pluralism' (2008) 6 *International Journal of Constitutional Law* 415

Saskia Sassen, 'The Places and Spaces of the Global: An Expanded Analytic Terrain' in David Held and Anthony McGrew (eds), *Globalization Theory. Approaches and Controversies* (2007)

Craig Scott and Peer Zumbansen, 'Foreword: Making a Case for Comparative Constitutionalism and Transnational Law' (2006) 46 *Osgoode Hall Law Journal* vii

Alexander Somek, 'Die Verfassung im Zeitalter ihrer transnationalen Reproduzierbarkeit. Gedanken zum Begriff der Konstitutionalisierung' in Claudio Franzius, Franz C. Mayer, and Jürgen Neyer (eds), *Strukturfragen der Europäischen Union* (2011)

Gunther Teubner, 'Fragmented Foundations: Societal Constitutionalism beyond the Nation State' in Petra Dobner and Martin Loughlin (eds), *The Twilight of Constitutionalism?* (2010)

Neil Walker, 'Taking Constitutionalism Beyond the State' (2008) 56 *Political Studies* 519

Peer Zumbansen, 'Transnational Legal Pluralism' (2010) 1 *Transnational Legal Theory* 141 (<http://ssrn.com/abstract=1542907>)

[162] Upendra Baxi, 'The Colonialist Heritage' in Pierre Legrand and Roderick Munday (eds), *Comparative Legal Studies: Traditions and Transitions* (2003).

CHAPTER 4

TYPES OF CONSTITUTIONS

DIETER GRIMM

Berlin

I. The Problem with Typologies

Typologies of constitutions are not at the centre of the rapidly growing literature on constitutionalism. If typological considerations appear at all, they form a by-product rather than the main concern of constitutional research. Moreover, the criteria for typifying constitutions vary from author to author. Although other criteria are easily conceivable, the question why some were chosen and others not remains mostly unanswered. But is this really surprising? The criteria according to which constitutions can be typified are innumerable. A choice has to be made and the choice is guided by the research interest that a scholar of constitutionalism pursues. Typologies are not ends in themselves. They help to answer other questions.

Someone who is interested in the legal and political relevance of constitutions may find a typology according to degrees of effectivity appropriate.[1] Someone who wants to understand the emergence of what has become 'constitutionalism' over time may distinguish between 'constitutionalism ancient and modern'.[2] For the purposes of comparative constitutionalism, a distinction on the basis of generic and particular or original and derivative constitutions comes to mind.[3] If the inquiry is into the 'subject of constitutional identity', one may distinguish constitutions according to the source of constituent power.[4] A scholar interested in the adaptation of constitutions to changing demands will emphasize the distinction between rigid and flexible constitutions.[5]

All these and many other typologies can be found in the legal literature. But law is not the only discipline interested in constitutions. A philosopher may distinguish between just and unjust constitutions,[6] a political scientist between integrative and disintegrative constitutions.[7] For economists, the emphasis will be on the choices that constitutions have made with regard to the economic system.[8] A scholar in religious studies will perhaps classify constitutions according to whether and how they refer to God or incorporate divine (natural) law. An art historian might be interested in the iconography and typography of constitutional documents.[9]

These examples suffice to show that a search for one typology of constitutions would be in vain. There are but various kinds of typologies and each draws its plausibility from the purpose of the research project in which it is embedded. This describes, at the same time, the risk of a chapter on types of constitutions that stands for itself. A choice is inevitable, yet not linked to a special topic the choice may seem more or less arbitrary. With this risk in mind, I will concentrate on two aspects that hopefully serve the objective of this volume. One is more systematic, the other more historical.

The first aspect concerns the constitution as law; to be more precise, a law with a special function and object, and the typological consequences that follow from its peculiarity. The second aspect concerns questions of content, namely the leading ideas, the governing principles, or regime-defining character, which influence the way constitutions try to fulfil their function. This attempt should not, however, be confused with a classification according to various institutional arrangements like monarchy or republic, federal or unitary system, parliamentarian or presidential government, unicameral or bicameral parliament, militant or acquiescent democracy etc. These are types of governmental systems established by constitutions rather than types of constitutions.

Neither is the difference between living and constant constitutions a suitable criterion to classify constitutions. David Strauss calls a living constitution 'one that evolves, changes over time, and adapts to new circumstances, without being formally amended'.[10] But this language is not quite accurate. The change he speaks of is not brought about by the constitution itself.

[1] Karl Loewenstein, *Political Power and the Governmental Process* (1957), 147ff; Brun-Otto Bryde, *Verfassungsentwicklung* (1982), 27ff.

[2] Charles Howard McIlwain, *Constitutionalism, Ancient and Modern* (3rd edn, 1966).

[3] Loewenstein (n 1), 140; David S. Law, 'Generic Constitutional Law' (2004–05) 89 *Minnesota Law Review* 652; Gary Jeffrey Jacobsohn, *Constitutional Identity* (2010), 112ff.

[4] Michel Rosenfeld, *The Identity of the Constitutional Subject* (2010), 149ff. See also Chapter 35.

[5] James Bryce, *Studies in History and Jurisprudence* (vol I, 1901), 124ff.

[6] John Rawls, *A Theory of Justice* (1971), 221ff.

[7] Hans Vorländer (ed), *Integration durch Verfassung* (2002).

[8] Thorsten Persson and Guido Tabellini, *The Economic Effects of Constitutions* (2003). Stefan Voigt and Hans-Jürgen Wagener (eds), *Constitutions, Markets and Law. Recent Experiences in Transition Economies* (2002).

[9] Horst Bredekamp, 'Politische Inkonographie des Grundgesetzes' in Michael Stolleis (ed), *Herzkammern der Republik* (2011), 9.

[10] David A. Strauss, *The Living Constitution* (2010), 1.

There is not one group of constitutions with an inherent force to evolve and another group that lacks this force. Rather, the change is a result of interpretation. 'Living' or 'static' are not qualities of constitutions but different ways of expounding constitutions. They characterize types of constitutional interpretation, not types of constitutions.

II. Identifying the Object

Typologies presuppose clarity about their object. So, what is a constitution? Or what is constitutionalism? There are, of course, many answers to this question as well. The complexity can, however, be reduced if one recognizes the fundamental difference between ancient and modern constitutionalism.[11] This chapter will deal only with modern constitutions as they emerged in the late eighteenth century from the American and the French Revolutions, were subsequently adopted in other countries, and, after many struggles and backlashes, had gained almost universal recognition by the end of the twentieth century. Yet, the characteristics of modern constitutions appear more clearly if compared to what was understood by 'constitution' or is seen as having functioned as 'constitution' before those revolutions. Both levels have to be taken into account in order to mark the difference: the semantic level as well as the level of realities.

The term 'constitution', or its equivalent in other languages, existed long before modern constitutions emerged.[12] But it designated a different object. Originally used to describe the state of the human body, it was soon applied to the body politic, yet not in a normative sense but as a description of the situation of a country as determined by a number of factors such as its geography, its climate, its population, its laws etc. In the eighteenth century, the meaning was often narrowed to the state of a country as determined by its basic legal structure. But still the notion 'constitution' was not identified with those laws. Rather, the term continued to describe the state of a country insofar as it was shaped by its basic laws. The basic laws themselves were not the 'constitution' of the country. 'Constitution' remained a descriptive, not a prescriptive, term.

If the term was used in a legal sense, it usually meant a certain type of laws, usually enacted by the Emperor, and often criminal codes, such as the *Constitutio Criminalis Carolina* of 1532 or the *Constitutio Criminalis Theresiana* of 1768, hence, laws that regulated individual, not governmental, behaviour. Certainly, laws the object of which was the exercise of public power did exist, even in the absolutist period; but they were not perceived as 'constitution'. They were called 'fundamental laws', 'governmental compact', and the like.[13] Some were relics of the medieval order in which the ruler had been submitted to a law that was believed to be of divine origin and therefore not at his disposition. Others had a contractual origin and emerged from negotiations between the monarch and influential groups in society, mostly the nobility.

It was characteristic of these laws that all of them presupposed the right of the ruler to rule. The fundamental laws only modified the right in this or that respect and, due to their contractual origins, only in favour of the privileged classes of society that were parties to the contract. They had neither constitutive force nor did they furnish a complete regulation of government.[14] Only after the emergence of the modern constitution were they retroactively called a

[11] McIlwain (n 2); Dieter Grimm, *Deutsche Verfassungsgeschichte* (3rd edn, 1995), 10ff.

[12] Heinz Mohnhaupt and Dieter Grimm, *Verfassung. Zur Geschichte des Begriffs von der Antike bis zur Gegenwart* (2nd edn, 2002); Italian translation: *Costituzione. Storia di un concetto dall'Antichitá a oggi* (2008).

[13] Rudolf Vierhaus (ed), *Herrschaftsverträge, Wahlkapitulationen, Fundamentalgesetze* (1997); André Lemaire, *Les Lois fondamentales de la Monarchie française* (1907).

[14] Grimm (n 11).

'constitution', first by the defenders of the old order who wanted to demonstrate that the country not only had a constitution but had a better one than the artificial product of a revolution, later by historians who got into the habit of describing the old political order in terms of a 'constitution'.

In England, which is often called the motherland of constitutionalism, things were slightly different.[15] Also in England, 'constitution' initially meant a formal law enacted by the King. With the growing participation of Lords and Commons in legislation, it was replaced by the term 'statute'. Cromwell's written document that constituted a republican government after the revolutionary break with the House of Stuart, and is often regarded as the first modern constitution, was not called a 'constitution', but an 'Instrument of Government'. Laws that concerned the organization of public authority were called a 'form of government'. But the term 'constitution' began to appear, mostly in the plural, as an equivalent to '*leges fundamentales*' or 'fundamental laws'.

After the Glorious Revolution in 1688, 'constitution' in the singular gained ground and meant the basic rules concerning the government. Yet, since the revolution restored the monarchy, albeit with a power shift towards Parliament, these rules did not gain constituent force. What was now called the 'British Constitution' shared with its continental equivalents the characteristic that it did not establish a new, but only modified an existing, public authority. A constituent power was, and to a large extent still is, absent in Britain. It was absorbed by the principle of parliamentary sovereignty. The rules forming the 'British Constitution', including the 'rights of Englishmen', were fundamental, but not supreme. The 'constitution' lacked supremacy.[16]

What, then, was new about the modern constitution? Apparently neither the name nor the capacity to bind the ruler with the force of law. The connection between the birth of modern constitutionalism and the two revolutions offers a clue. These revolutions differed from the many upheavals and revolts against rulers in history, including the Glorious Revolution, in that the revolutionary forces did not content themselves with replacing an oppressive ruler with another one. Rather, they set out to establish a new political system that differed fundamentally from the one they had accused of being unjust. In order to achieve this, they devised a plan of legitimate rule and endowed it with legal force before rulers were called to power and authorized to rule according to the legal framework.

In order for this to work, the constitution had to be distinguished from ordinary law. As an act that constituted legitimate public power in the first place, the constitution could not emanate from the ruler himself. It needed a different source. In both countries, this source was found in the people who had decided to form a polity and to whom the constituent power was ascribed.[17] The legitimating principle of the modern constitution was popular sovereignty instead of monarchical or parliamentarian sovereignty. But unlike the sovereign monarch or the sovereign parliament the people were incapable of ruling themselves. They needed repre-

[15] Besides Mohnhaupt and Grimm (n 12) see John W. Gough, *Fundamental Law in English Constitutional History* (1971); Gerald Stourzh, *Wege zur Grundrechtsdemokratie* (1989), 1ff, 75ff; Gerald Stourzh, *Fundamental Laws and Individual Rights in the 18th Century Constitution* (1984); Martin Loughlin, *The Idea of Public* Law (2003) and *Foundations of Public Law* (2010).

[16] Stourzh, *Fundamental Laws* (n 15); Martin Loughlin, 'Constituent Power Subverted: From English Constitutional Argument to British Constitutional Practice' in Martin Loughlin and Neil Walker (eds), *The Paradox of Constitutionalism. Constituent Power and Constitutional Form* (2007), 27.

[17] Loughlin and Walker (n 16); Egon Zweig, *Die Lehre vom Pouvoir constituant* (1909); Pasquale Pasquino, *Sieyes et l'invention de la constitution en France* (1998).

sentatives to govern in their name. Democratic government is government by mandate and as such stands in need of being organized.

In addition, the mandate was not conferred upon the representatives unconditionally. In contrast to the unlimited power of the British Parliament and the French King, the revolutionaries wanted to establish a limited government, limited in substance and limited in form. The first was a decision in favour of individual freedom that gained primacy over the *raison d'état* and found legal expression in catalogues of fundamental rights. The second followed from the conviction that freedom could best be secured if governmental power was not concentrated in one hand but distributed among various branches of government. The limits in scope and time as well as the separation of powers also required determination in the form of legal rules.

All this was by no means an original idea of the American and French revolutionaries. The idea that only the consent of the people could legitimize governmental power had older roots and gained widespread recognition when religion no longer served as the basis of the social order after the Reformation and gave rise to the construction of a social contract. The content of this contract varied over time and space. But more and more the conviction gained ground that the ruler's task was the protection of individual freedom. From the mid-eighteenth century, the treatises of natural law filled with growing catalogues of fundamental rights which the state was obliged to respect and to protect.

Although these theories contained all the ingredients that later appeared in the constitutions, they were not pushed forwards to the postulate of a constitution by the philosophers. For them, they functioned as a test of the legitimacy of the political system. A political system was deemed legitimate if it could be considered as if established by a consensus of the governed. With the sole exception of Emer de Vattel,[18] no author required a written document or a popular decision. The social contract served as a regulative idea. It was not considered to be the result of a real process of consensus building. Its authority was based on argumentation, not on enactment. No pre-revolutionary ruler had been willing to adopt it, and most rulers had explicitly rejected it. Natural law and positive law contradicted each other.

Only after the revolutionary break with traditional rule were these ideas able to become a blueprint for the establishment of the new order which filled the vacuum of legitimate public power that the successful revolutions had left behind. The ideas migrated from the world of intellectual discourse into the world of political action. Hence the important contribution of the American and French revolutionaries was to turn the ideas from philosophy into law. Only law had the capacity to detach the consensus as to the purpose and form of government from the historical moment and the actual participants and transfer it into a binding rule for the future, so that it no longer rested on the power of persuasion but on the power of a commitment.

There was, however, the problem that, after the collapse of the divinely inspired medieval legal order, all law had become the product of political will. Law was irreducibly positive law. Nothing else could be true for the law the function of which was to regulate the establishment and exercise of political power. This gave rise to the question how a law that emanated from the political process could at the same time bind this process.[19] The problem was solved by tak-

[18] Emer de Vattel, *Le droit des gens* (1758), vol 1.3, §27; ed M. P. Pradier-Fodéré, vol 1 (1863), 153.

[19] Regarding this basic problem of constitutionalism see eg Georg Jellinek, *Allgemeine Staatslehre* (repr of the 3rd edn, 1966), 337ff; Raymond Carré de Malberg, *Contribution à la Théorie générale de l'Etat* (vol II, 1922), 483ff; Carl Schmitt, *Verfassungslehre* (1928), 75ff; Loughlin and Walker (n 16); Ernst-Wolfgang Böckenförde, 'Die verfassungsgebende Gewalt des Volkes' in Ernst-Wolfgang Böckenförde, *Wissenschaft, Politik, Verfassungsgericht* (2011), 97.

ing up the old idea of a hierarchy of norms (divine and secular) and re-introducing it into positive law. This was done by a division of positive law into two different bodies: one that emanated from or was attributed to the people and bound the government, and one that emanated from government and bound the people. The first one regulated the production and application of the second. Law became reflexive.

This idea of a dualist democracy, as Bruce Ackerman calls it,[20] presupposed, however, that the first body of law took primacy over the second. The revolutionary thinkers had a clear notion of this consequence of constitution-making. The Americans expressed it in terms of 'paramount law' and deployed the distinction between master and servant or principal and agent, while Sieyes conceptualized it in the dichotomy of *pouvoir constituant* and *pouvoir constitué*, the former setting the terms for the latter.[21] Without this distinction and the ensuing distinction between constitutional law and ordinary law and the subordination of the latter to the former, constitutionalism would have been unable to fulfil its function.[22]

This legal framework was now called 'constitution'. Constitution thereby turned from a descriptive into a prescriptive notion. It differed from the older legal regulations of public authority in various respects. The most important one is that the constitution claims to *establish* legitimate government instead of only *modifying* the conditions for a pre-existing government that derives its legitimacy from sources other than the constitution. Moreover, it regulates the establishment and exercise of public power *systematically* and *comprehensively*. And it applies generally, not only in favour of some privileged groups. While every political entity had (or more precisely, was in) a constitution in the descriptive sense, a constitution in the prescriptive sense was a novelty that not every polity possessed.

Constitutionalism is therefore not identical with legalization of public power. Everyone who asserts that constitutionalism 'means little more than the limited state'[23] misses the point. It is a special and particularly ambitious form of legalization. There are, however, many ways to realize the project. Although the new instrument of legitimation and limitation of government was justified in universal terms by its founders, it had to be applied to a situation where political power was organized in the form of sovereign states with different traditions, conditions, and ideals. Therefore, it was realized in each state in a particular way. Constitutionalism originated in the form of national constitutions. For this reason, it seems more appropriate to describe it in functional rather than substantive terms.

These functional characteristics can now be summarized:[24]

[20] Bruce Ackerman, *We the People. Volume 1: Foundations* (1991), 3ff.

[21] James Madison, Alexander Hamilton, and John Jay, *Federalist Papers* (1788), no 78; Emanuel Sieyes, *Qu'est-ce que le Tiers Etat?* (1789).

[22] Gerald Stourzh, 'Vom Widerstandsrecht zur Verfassungsgerichtsbarkeit. Zum Problem der Verfassungswidrigkeit im 18. Jahrhundert' in Stourzh, *Wege zur Grundrechtsdemokratie* (n 15), 37; Rainer Wahl, 'Der Vorrang der Verfassung' in Rainer Wahl, *Verfassungsstaat, Europäisierung, Internationalisierung* (2003), 121.

[23] Cf Daniel S. Lev, 'Social Movements, Constitutionalism and Human Rights' in Douglas Greenberg et al (eds), *Constitutionalism and Democracy. Transitions in the Contemporary World* (1993), 38.

[24] Dieter Grimm, 'The Achievement of Constitutionalism and its Prospects in a Changed World' in Petra Dobner and Martin Loughlin, *The Twilight of Constitutionalism* (2010), 3. There are other attempts to describe the constitution, eg Louis Henkin, 'A New Birth of Constitutionalism: Genetic Influences and Genetic Defects' in Michel Rosenfeld (ed), *Constitutionalism, Identity, Difference and Legitimacy* (1994), 41ff; Joseph Raz, 'On the Authority and Interpretation of Constitutions: Some Preliminaries' in Larry Alexander (ed), *Constitutionalism. Philosophical Foundations* (1998), 153f.

(1) The constitution in the modern sense is a set of legal norms, not a philosophical construct. The norms emanate from a political decision rather than having their source in a pre-established truth.

(2) The purpose of these norms is to regulate the establishment and the exercise of public power as opposed to a mere modification of a pre-existing public power. Regulation implies limitation.

(3) The regulation is comprehensive in the sense that no pre- or extra-constitutional bearers of public power and no pre- or extra-constitutional means to exercise this power are recognized.

(4) Constitutional law is higher law. It enjoys primacy of all other laws and legal acts emanating from government. Acts incompatible with the constitution cannot claim legal validity.

(5) Constitutional law finds its origin with the people as the only legitimate source of power. The distinction between *pouvoir constituant* and *pouvoir constitué* is essential to the constitution.

If all these elements are present, we speak of the *achievement* of constitutionalism.[25] Constitutions with these characteristics rule out any absolute or arbitrary power of man over man. By submitting all government action to rules, a constitution makes the use of public power predictable and enables the governed to anticipate government behaviour vis-à-vis themselves and allows them to face government agents without fear. A constitution provides a consensual basis for persons and groups with different opinions and interests to resolve their disputes in a civilized manner and enables peaceful transition of power. Under favourable conditions the constitution can even contribute to the integration of society.

At the same time, it becomes clear that the achievement of constitutionalism rests on a number of preconditions, without which the constitution would not have emerged. The disappearance of these preconditions would not leave their functioning unaffected.[26] As a decision by a society on the purpose and form of its political unity, the constitution could not have emerged if questions of public order were not open to discussion. This facet was lacking wherever the public order was presumed to be given by God, for example in the Middle Ages. Under these circumstances, public authority had the duty to enforce the pre-established order, but had no right to change it or replace it by a different one.

Yet the medieval society did not have and could not have had a constitution for still another reason. It lacked an object capable of being regulated in the form of a constitution. No autonomous political sphere had yet developed and no public power specialized in governing a given territory existed. Only when, in an attempt to overcome the devastating religious wars and to pacify a rifted society, the princes started to concentrate the dispersed public powers in their hands, condensing them into a single, comprehensive public power and claiming the right to make law independent of the contested religious truth, did an object capable of being constitutionalized emerge. In continental Europe, this object was from the beginning in the sixteenth century perceived as the state, while in the Anglo-Saxon world it was long described as government and only in recent decades as the state.

[25] Grimm (n 24); Niklas Luhmann, 'Verfassung als evolutionäre Errungenschaft' (1990) 9 *Rechtshistorisches Journal* 176.

[26] Dieter Grimm, *Die Zukunft der Verfassung* (3rd edn, 2002), 31ff.

Historically, the emergence of the modern state, or its equivalent, was a necessary condition of the modern constitution. It was, however, not a sufficient condition. In order to fulfil its historic mission of pacifying a society divided by religious wars, the state claimed absolute power over society. Absolutism is the opposite of constitutionalism. Only when the mission had been fulfilled did absolute rule lose its plausibility. The demand for limited government based on the consent of the governed appeared as a further pre-condition for constitutionalism. The revolution was needed as a breakthrough for this idea, not as a pre-condition for the constitutions which followed.

The corollary of the gradual emergence of the modern state was the successive privatization of civil society. Public and private, still indistinguishable in the medieval world, became distinct spheres. The constitution did not question the concentration of public power in the hands of the state. Rather, it was this concentration that created the need for constitutionalism. The constitution's aim was to tame public power in the interest of individual freedom. The distinction between public and private was therefore constitutive for constitutionalism. If public power were in private hands the constitution could not fulfil its function. Conversely, if the state enjoyed the same freedom as private individuals it could not reach its aim.

Of equal importance is another borderline, that between outside and inside. As public power was organized in the form of states when the constitution emerged, the power of each state ended at its territorial borders. Beyond its borders there were other states with their public power. A constitution could fulfil its function only if the state held the monopoly of public power within its borders and was not submitted to any external power. Every submission to an external power would have meant a power that escaped the regulation of the constitution. The principle of territoriality was constitutive for the constitution.[27]

III. The Constitution as Law

The term 'achievement' should not be misunderstood as an ideal type of constitutionalism that in the real world can only be reached by way of approximation.[28] Constitutions that show all the characteristics of achievement did exist in history and do exist today. 'Achievement', however, also implies that there may be documents designated or understood as constitutions which lack some or most elements of a full-fledged constitutionalism. As a matter of fact, once invented the constitution could be instrumentalized for purposes other than the original ones, adopted only in part or even as a mere form. Nevertheless, achievement sets the standard for constitutionalism and just for this reason furnishes a basis for a typology.

1. The Legal Character of the Constitution

Written or unwritten—constitutions in the sense of achievement are enacted as law or even as 'hard law' as Van Alstyne insists, adding that 'nearly everything else depends on [this]'.[29] Enactment in the form of a law is nowadays the way in which new constitutions are set up everywhere, no matter who enacted them and which procedure preceded the enactment. Enactment

[27] Saskia Sassen, *Territory, Authority, Rights* (updated edn, 2008).

[28] Michel Rosenfeld 'What is a Constitution?' in Norman Dorsen et al (eds), *Comparative Constitutionalism* (2nd edn, 2010), 36.

[29] William W. Van Alstyne, 'The Idea of the Constitution as Hard Law' (1987) 37 *Journal of Legal Education* 174.

as law usually means that the constitution takes the form of a written document. When unwritten constitutions are mentioned, it is mostly in connection with the British Constitution. As a matter of fact, this Constitution consists to a large extent of conventions for which no authoritative textual source exists and which date back to the era of pre-modern constitutionalism.

But Eric Barendt reminds us that part of what is regarded as the British Constitution consists of statutes, some old like the Bill of Rights of 1689, some more recent like the Human Rights Act of 1998.[30] Barendt therefore introduces the distinction between *written* and *codified*. Most modern constitutions are indeed codified, that is, their norms are more or less coherently contained in a single document. But here again differences appear. Israel is often said to have no written constitution because the first Knesset, which was elected as a constituent assembly, did not discharge this task. Yet Israel has various Basic Laws that, according to a landmark decision of the Israeli Supreme Court, form the constitution of the country.[31] But they leave open many questions that usually find an answer in a constitution. The constitution is fragmentary.

Yet, here again, the differences seem to be gradual rather than principal. Austria has a codified constitution, but this constitution is surrounded by a number of additional constitutional laws that formally have a separate existence. In many countries, not all the rules pertaining to the organization and exercise of public power are contained in the codification. Some remain outside. In France, the category of *lois organiques* exists. It describes laws that rank between the constitution and ordinary laws, regulate a constitutional matter, and are provided for in the constitution and enacted in a special procedure.[32] Similar categories can be found in other countries (*ley organica, legge constituzionale, leis complementares*, etc).

However, sometimes the notion '*lois organiques*' is used for ordinary laws the content of which is of constitutional importance. In this sense, the notion corresponds with the distinction between the constitution in a *formal* and in a *substantive* sense.[33] The first one includes all norms that are part of the legal document called the 'constitution', regardless of whether they concern a matter of constitutional importance. The second includes norms which, although their object is constitutionally important, are not contained in the document called the 'constitution' but in a statute. In Germany, for instance, the election law is a constitutional law in the substantive, but not in the formal, sense.

These considerations show that the difference between written and unwritten constitutions should not be overestimated. For typological purposes the distinction between a modern legal (*prescriptive*) and a pre-modern non-legal (*descriptive*) constitution matters more. 'Law' and 'unwritten' are not mutually exclusive although the unwritten form of a 'constitution' is an indicator of a constitution in the older sense of the term, which could subsist along with the existence of laws that regulate government. Barendt himself admits this when he says that, under the British Constitution, it is difficult to determine whether government conduct is constitutional or not.[34]

Effective or ineffective—what seems much more important is that enactment in the form of a law does not guarantee legal effectivity. If today only a handful of the nearly 200 states in the

[30] Eric Barendt, *An Introduction to Constitutional Law* (1998), 26ff.

[31] *United Mizrahi Bank v Migdal Village* (1995), excerpts in English in (1997) 31 *Israel Law Review* 754.

[32] Francis Hamon and Michel Troper, *Droit constitutionnel* (31st edn, 2009), 41f.

[33] For the first time in Carl von Rotteck, *Lehrbuch des Vernunftrechts und der Staatswissenschaften* (1840), vol 2, 172ff; today common in German constitutional theory, see Bryde (n 1), 59.

[34] Barendt (n 30).

world are still without a constitution we may conclude that the constitution is universally accepted as a pattern of legitimation and organization of public power, but not that all constitutions matter.[35] Many remain on paper. They are often called *symbolic* constitutions.[36] In some cases, constitutions may be intended as mere window-dressing from the very beginning. In other cases they are suspended soon after enactment. Many are routinely disregarded when their norms enter into conflict with political plans or measures.

Karl Loewenstein therefore deems a typology based on the legal impact as most important. He distinguishes between normative, nominal, and semantic constitutions.[37] The decisive criterion is the degree to which the political reality conforms to the norms of the constitution. *Normative* constitutions are effective constitutions in the sense that the political process takes place within the constitutional framework and political actors usually comply with constitutional requirements. According to Loewenstein, a constitution in this sense depends on a socio-political environment where the value of constitutionalism has been internalized by both governors and governed.

In a *nominal* constitution, the constitutional norms find their limits in the given power structure, political as well as economical. The existing socio-economic conditions prevent the constitution from being applied faithfully, regardless of the interests of the power-holders. Insofar as a conflict between these structures and the norms appears, the norms will remain ineffective. According to Loewenstein, former colonies or feudal-agrarian societies are particularly prone to nominal constitutions. However, he concedes an educational function to constitutions of this type: they may aim at becoming normative constitutions.

Semantic constitutions are constitutions that are in line with the political reality, but only reflect this reality without imposing binding rules on it. Loewenstein tends to include all constitutions of dictatorial or totalitarian regimes in this category. Henkin portrays them as merely describing the existing system of government.[38] The term 'descriptive' is here not meant in the sense used to characterize pre-modern constitutionalism. It refers to a document that has been enacted in the form of a law, but without the intent to bind political behaviour. Others characterize this type of constitutions as 'instrumentalistic' or 'ritualistic'.[39]

[35] Fareed Zakaria, 'The Rise of Illiberal Democracy' (1977) 76 *Foreign Affairs* 22, and the interesting chart of Donald S. Lutz, *Principles of Constitutional Design* (2006), 4.

[36] Bryde (n 1), 27. 'Symbolic' is here understood as having no impact in the real world. It should be noted, however, that there is also an understanding of 'symbolic' as an additional, extra-legal effect that constitutions may develop when they succeed in symbolizing the aspirations, the unity of a polity, and thus contribute to the integration of societies. For a meaning of 'symbolic' in this sense see Dieter Grimm, 'Integration by Constitution' (2005) 3 *International Journal of Constitutional Law* 193; both meanings are used by Marcello Neves, *Symbolische Konstitutionalisierung* (1998), 79ff. For the US Constitution see Michael Kammen, *A Machine that Would Go of Itself. The Constitution in American Culture* (1986); Edward S. Corwin, 'The Constitution as Instrument and Symbol' (1936) 30 *American Political Science Review* 1071.

[37] Loewenstein (n 1), 147ff.

[38] Louis Henkin, 'A New Birth of Constitutionalism: Genetic Influences and Genetic Deficits' in Rosenfeld (n 24), 41. See also H.W.O. Okoth-Ogendo, 'Constitutions without Constitutionalism: Reflections on an African Political Paradox' in Douglas Greenberg et al (eds), *Constitutionalism and Democracy: Transitions in the Contemporary World* (1991), 65.

[39] 'Instrumentalistic' meaning that the constitution is exclusively used in the interest of the government or the power-holders, see Neves (n 36), 92f; 'ritualistic' meaning that the rules of the constitution are seemingly applied while the substantive processes take place elsewhere and are completed when the 'ritual' starts, see Bryde (n 1), 29ff.

2. Specialized in Regulating Public Power

Foundational or modifying—a constitution in the sense of 'achievement' is specialized in regulating the establishment and exercise of public power. 'Establishment' could be read as 'organization'. Understood in this way, the criterion would have little capacity to distinguish between various types of constitutions. There are constitutions in the modern sense that confine themselves to determining the organizational structure of a state, naming its organs, laying down their powers, regulating the relation among them, and prescribing the procedure they have to follow in discharging their tasks. The constitution of the second German Empire of 1871 and Australia's constitution are examples. But there is no constitution that refrains from regulating the organizational structure of the state.

'Establishment' as used here has a wider meaning. The constitution as an achievement is *foundational*. It constitutes a legitimate government rather than simply *modifying* a government that precedes the constitution and derives its legitimacy from elsewhere. Constitutions that follow a successful revolution are usually constitutive in this sense. But this does not mean that a revolutionary origin is a pre-condition of a full-fledged constitution. A new beginning, for instance after a lost war, can produce the same effect, as in Japan, Italy, and Germany after 1945. Radical shifts are also possible without a revolution, as in South Africa in 1994. The Swiss Constitution of 2000 owes its existence to the conviction that the constitution of 1874 no longer met the challenges of the twenty-first century.

Yet, although all constitutions regulate government, not all regulate its establishment. Still, a number of constitutions limit themselves to regulating the exercise of public power, not its creation. This was already the case shortly after modern constitutionalism emerged in the eighteenth century. As a matter of fact, once invented the modern constitution became immediately attractive outside the countries of origin. Constitutional movements emerged and requested constitutions without the ability to overthrow the existing political system and to establish a new one based on constitutional values. In that vein, a number of traditional rulers thought it wise to accommodate the popular wishes in order to prevent a revolutionary change.

Usually this meant the establishment of parliamentary representation based on elections by the people or its wealthy and educated classes. Often it also meant the introduction of a bill of rights. But it did not mean that the legitimation of public authority shifted from parliamentary sovereignty as in North America or from monarchical sovereignty as in France to popular sovereignty and thus to a system where the monarch no longer ruled by God's grace but by the people's grace. Hence, these constitutions, unilaterally granted by the ruler as they usually were, lacked the constitutive force of the prototypes. They merely modified the existing government, albeit in constitutional forms.

It was even possible that the rulers were not prepared to accept binding rules at all, but nevertheless found it advisable at least to purport that they ruled in accordance with a constitution. These constitutions can be understood as expressions of pseudo-constitutionalism. The history of the nineteenth century can be described as a struggle for constitutionalism in the sense of the achievement. It could well happen that a constitution that fell short of achievement developed into a full-fledged constitution over time, in the same way that full-fledged constitutions regressed to weaker forms of constitutionalism.

Formal and substantive—regulation always implies a certain degree of limitation. Unlimited government is the opposite of constitutionalism. Forms and degrees can vary. There are constitutions that confine themselves to formal and procedural limitations and constitutions that contain substantive limitations as well. The American Founding Fathers believed in the beginning that organizational and procedural rules would suffice to limit government and protect the citizens efficiently. The French revolutionaries found substantive limits so important that they enacted the Declaration of Rights even before the constitution was drafted. The US Bill of Rights was added to the Constitution four years later.

Both countries of origin were convinced that only a limitation in the form of separation of powers is compatible with the idea of a constitution. Article 16 of the French Declaration reads: 'Toute société dans laquelle la garantie des droits n'est pas assurée, ni la séparation des pouvoirs déterminée, n'a point de constitution.' As a matter of fact, the idea of limited government tends towards some separation. A total lack of separation is an indicator of deficient constitutionalism. But one can imagine rather weak borderlines between the various powers as compensated for by strictly competent and substantive limitations.

3. Comprehensive Regulation

This element has nothing to do with the question of how short or how detailed the establishment and exercise of public power is regulated. Likewise, it is not about gaps in a constitution. Sometimes gaps are the price that has to be paid for a constitution to be ratified. The requirement rather concerns the degree to which public power is submitted to law. We can speak of a full-fledged constitution only if all public authority is derived from the constitution and has to be exercised within the framework of the constitution. But the framework may leave ample room for politics. It only excludes extra-constitutional power-holders and unconstitutional ways and means of exercising the power.

This is by no means always guaranteed. All political systems where the right to rule precedes the constitution and is only modified by it cannot be comprehensive in this sense. Wherever a constitutional regulation is missing it will be the ruler who, by virtue of his pre-constitutional legitimation, is competent to act according to will. Constitutions of this type can be called semi-constitutionalism. They were and are frequent in number. All German constitutions of the nineteenth century were semi-constitutions in this sense. Not gained after a revolutionary break with traditional rule, they did not touch the pre-existing right of the ruler to rule. Rather, the traditional rulers agreed to limit their hitherto absolute power voluntarily by a constitution.

4. Supremacy

Higher or ordinary law—the constitution can fulfil its promise only if it enjoys supremacy. This means that all acts of public authority have to conform to the provisions of the constitution. Although the importance of supremacy was fully understood in constitutional theory from the beginning, constitutional practice hesitated long before following.[40] Such practice did not deprive the constitution of its quality as law. If a constitution completely lacks legal effect, the question of its supremacy does not arise. Supremacy presupposes the legal validity of the constitution. The question is not whether it is law, but whether it is higher law. If not, the functioning of the constitution will be severely hampered. Recognition or negation of the higher law quality of the constitution is therefore a typological difference of highest importance.

As to the extent of the loss, various degrees are possible. Lacking supremacy of constitutional law will usually not affect the organizational structure of government. The organs of the

[40] Wahl (n 22).

state are likely to exist in the form prescribed by the constitution. However, constitutions not only claim to regulate the organization, but also the exercise of public authority. It is this exercise that can legally evade the control of the constitution if constitutional law is not supreme. Here, again, different degrees are possible. In the past, most European constitutions were understood in a way that the bills of rights did not bind the legislature. This meant that their impact was reduced to a prohibition of infringements by the executive without a basis in law. The law itself was not submitted to fundamental rights.

In reaction to this weakness of fundamental rights in the nineteenth and even the twentieth century, a number of younger constitutions explicitly declared fundamental rights to be directly applicable law and to bind all branches of government, explicitly so in Article 1(3) of the German Basic Law. Canada in its Charter of Rights and Freedoms of 1982 does not mention the judiciary among the powers bound by fundamental rights and thus causes difficulties when it comes to applying the Charter in private law litigation.[41] A far-reaching provision is contained in the South African Constitution, according to section 8 of which the Bill of Rights 'applies to all law, and binds the legislature, the executive, the judiciary and all organs of state'. Under certain conditions, fundamental rights even bind natural and juristic persons.

In the Weimar Republic, the rule that the constitution could be amended by way of a two-thirds majority in favour of such legislative amendment, was interpreted such that every ordinary law passed with a two-thirds majority could set aside the constitution. A prior amendment was not regarded as necessary. Hence, the higher law quality was acknowledged, but the threshold could easily be transgressed. After the Second World War the Basic Law explicitly excluded this possibility in Article 79(1). Setting aside the constitution was even easier in states where the constitution ranked on the same level with ordinary law. In this case the rule applies that the more recent law supersedes the older law.

This attitude towards the higher law element of constitutions was facilitated by the formalist understanding that became dominant in the course of the nineteenth century in Europe and continues to prevail in a number of countries today. From a formalistic perspective, the special quality of constitutional law as opposed to ordinary law lies not in its function or importance, but exclusively in the requirement of a super-majority for amendments.[42] It was Carl Schmitt who tried to rectify this position. For him, the special quality of the constitution is not a consequence of the increased quorum for amendments. On the contrary, amendments are made more difficult because of the special quality of constitutional law.[43] It is the fundamental decision of a people as to the nature and form of its unity on which all further decisions are based, the law of the laws.

Rigid or flexible—as these observations show, there is a relation between the rank of constitutional law and the rules for constitutional amendment. If a constitution allows for amendments by way of ordinary legislation, that is, without requiring a super-majority, its quality as higher law is seriously hampered. The sense in requiring a super-majority is, inter alia, to furnish a consensus basis for political adversaries and a framework in which the political competition can take an orderly and peaceful route. If a simple majority can change this framework, the function of the constitution is put at risk. It becomes a tool in the hands of the majority and ceases effectively to protect the minority or the opposition.

[41] *Retail, Wholesale and Department Store Union v Dolphin Delivery Ltd* [1986] 2 SCR 573.

[42] Paul Laband, *Das Staatsrecht des Deutschen Reiches* (4th edn, 1901), vol 2, 34; Jellinek (n 19), 534.

[43] Schmitt (n 19), 18.

This is less so when a super-majority is required for a constitutional amendment. However, if the constitution endows parliament with an amendment power it is relatively easy for the main political actors to shape the constitution according to their needs. This is why many constitutions remove the amendment power from actors in the routine political business and entrust it to other organs, or require a referendum or prescribe a procedure other than the procedure for ordinary lawmaking.[44] The frequency of amendments depends to a large extent on the difficulty of the procedure.[45]

Some constitutions completely exclude certain provisions from abolition by way of amendment. The US Constitution exempts in Article V the equal suffrage of every state in the Senate from amendment without the consent of the affected state. In Italy and France, the republican form of the state is not subject to amendment. A far-reaching clause is contained in the German Basic Law. It is the post-war reaction to the experience that the democratic principle of the Weimar Constitution was abolished by democratic means after Hitler had taken power in 1933. Article 79(3) declares the principle of democracy, the rule of law, the principle of the social state, and the federal structure as well as the guarantee of human dignity as unalterable by amendment.

The same solution was introduced in India by a landmark decision of the Supreme Court without a textual basis in the constitution.[46] Behind this ruling one can discover Carl Schmitt's distinction between constitution and constitutional law.[47] According to Schmitt, the constitution is the decision of the constituent power, usually the people, about the nature and form of its polity. In Schmitt's view, this decision precedes the drafting of constitutional law and does not require or even allow a formal act. Constitutional law, in turn, concretizes the fundamental decision and may add to it provisions of a less fundamental character, even provisions of a non-constitutional character. As a consequence only constitutional law is open to amendment whereas the constitution can only be altered by the holder of the constituent power himself.

The rules on constitutional amendments vary greatly. Typologically one usually distinguishes rigid and flexible constitutions. Between these two poles many solutions are possible. The best-known example of a rigid constitution in this sense is the US Constitution (Art V). As a consequence formal amendments have been extremely rare in the United States.[48] On the other hand, the Japanese Constitution has never been amended although it is not rigid. Even more rigid than the US Constitution was the first French Constitution of 1791. A proposed amendment had to be voted on by three consecutive parliaments and affirmed by the fourth, which for that purpose was augmented by additional members. Since a parliamentary term was two years, an amendment could enter into force only seven years after the initiative (Title VII).

This inflexibility caused the early death of the constitution. Later constitutions made amendments easier; but the idea that the parliamentary assembly, which desires and votes for a constitutional amendment, should not have the final say, still characterizes a number of cur-

[44] See Chapter 24.

[45] Cf the statistical material in Donald S. Lutz, 'Toward a Theory of Constitutional Amendment' in Sanford Levinson (ed), *Responding to Imperfection. The Theory and Practice of Constitutional Amendment* (1995), 237.

[46] *Kesavananda Bharati v State of Kerala* [1973] Supp SCR 1. Cf Sudhir Krishnaswamy, *Democracy and Constitutionalism in India. A Study on the Basic Structure Doctrine* (2009).

[47] Schmitt (n 19), 20ff.

[48] Levinson (n 45).

rent constitutions. Often the consent of the next parliament is necessary so that an election lies between the preliminary and the final vote. This gives the sovereign an opportunity to express its will (eg Belgium, Denmark, the Netherlands). A number of countries allow constitutional amendments only by way of referendum (eg Ireland).

With or without judicial review—in spite of its higher rank, constitutional law is more vulnerable than ordinary law. While ordinary law emanates from the government and binds the people, constitutional law is attributed to the people and binds government. This fact entails a fundamental difference between the two types of law when it comes to enforcement. Law enforcement is one of the major tasks of government. If private persons violate the law the government has the duty as well as the coercive means to enforce the law. Since constitutional law binds the government, the addressee of the rules and the enforcer are here identical. This is one of the explanations for the rather small impact of constitutional law in the past and still today in many countries.

Many of the constitutions in the nineteenth century tried to solve the problem of non-compliance with the constitution by means of criminal law. Members of the government, but not the monarch, could be tried in court for an intentional violation of the constitution. In most countries special courts rather than the usual judiciary were competent to decide in cases of indictment of ministers. Since the procedural hurdles were usually very high and penal law principles required criminal intent, the number of cases in which members of government were eventually convicted remained small. Today criminal law is usually regarded as an inadequate means to solve this problem.

Only in the United States was constitutional law enforceable from the very beginning. But since the question whether the judiciary could declare acts of the legislature unconstitutional and therefore null and void had not been explicitly answered in the text of the constitution; it needed the landmark decision of the Supreme Court in *Marbury v Madison*, decided in 1803, and the acceptance of this decision in the United States to establish judicial review. This became a characteristic feature of American constitutionalism, although significant enforcement of fundamental rights only began in the twentieth century and the so-called counter-majoritarian difficulty still remains a concern in the political and legal discourse in the United States today.[49]

Still, the American solution remained singular for a very long time. Meanwhile, the judiciary in almost all common law countries and some civil law countries (eg Brazil, Japan, the Nordic countries) has the power to review laws, although some courts, such as the Japanese Supreme Court, make little use of it. But there were and still are other countries that explicitly prohibit judicial review, as with all French constitutions before the present constitution of 1958. At present, courts are prevented from reviewing the constitutionality of laws in the Netherlands and of federal laws (not cantonal laws) in Switzerland. In the United Kingdom the Civil Rights Act of 1998 allowed for judicial review but decisions are not binding on parliament. Likewise, Canada's Charter contains an override clause (section 33).

A new and very influential element in judicial review came with the Austrian Constitution of 1920. It established a specialized constitutional court with the exclusive power to review laws as to their constitutionality. A similar regime was adopted in Czechoslovakia. After the Second World War, this model entered the new constitutions of Italy and Germany—two of the defeated parties in the war (while the third, Japan, under strong American influence adopted the US model)—and countries with a dictatorial past which were determined to

[49] Alexander M. Bickel, *The Least Dangerous Branch* (1962). See also Chapter 40.

prevent a repetition of the experience. In this context the idea of an independent guardian of the constitution played an important role.[50]

Although first established in Austria (after an unsuccessful attempt in Germany during the revolution of 1848) judicial review by a specialized constitutional court is now widely known as the 'German Model'. The reason may be that the powers of the German court were far more numerous than those of the Austrian or the Italian court. In addition, the German court established itself as a very powerful court by developing a jurisprudence that gave high relevance to constitutional law, secured the court a strong backing in society, which, in turn, guaranteed an unusually high degree of compliance by the political branches of government.[51]

The last quarter of the twentieth century brought a breakthrough for constitutional adjudication.[52] It was no longer an exception but the rule. The movement is so strong that the Israeli Supreme Court felt entitled to interpret the Basic Law: Human Dignity and Liberty of 1992 as having opened the door to judicial review although the text did not explicitly say so. It argued that, today, adopting fundamental rights means adopting judicial review as well. 'The Twentieth century is the century of judicial review.'[53]

Although it is not generally true that constitutional adjudication is a necessary consequence of constitutionalism, as Hans Kelsen believed, or that constitutions whose rules cannot be invoked in court are not law, as Van Alstyne asserts,[54] history and contemporary experience show that in countries without a deeply rooted rule of law tradition constitutionalism is of little value in the absence of a special enforcement mechanism.[55] Especially when it comes to enforcing the primacy of constitutional law vis-à-vis politics, institutions matter. This does not mean that every newly established constitutional court is as influential as the German court. Just as there are weak constitutions, there are weak constitutional courts. Political attempts to discipline constitutional courts are numerous.[56] Yet, for typological purposes, the difference between constitutions with and without constitutional adjudication has become one of particular importance.

Inclusive or exclusive—without supremacy constitutional law has little relevance. But there is also an opposite danger. Constitutions can go too far in entrenching rules and thereby undermine the difference between constitutional and ordinary law from the opposite end of the spectrum. Everything that has been regulated in the constitution is no longer subject to

[50] See Chapter 39.

[51] David Robertson, *The Judge as Political Theorist. Contemporary Constitutional Review* (2010) calls the German Constitutional Court 'the most important of all', 11, and affirms that 'so important is this court that any synoptic discussion [of various courts] will depend on frequent mentions of the German approach', 79. See also Georg Vanberg, *The Politics of Constitutional Review in Germany* (2005), 17, 61; Donald P. Kommers, 'The Federal Constitutional Court in the German Political System' (1994) 26 *Comparative Political Studies* 470; Oliver W. Lembcke, *Hüter der Verfassung* (2007).

[52] C. Neal Tate and Torbjörn Vallinder, *The Global Expansion of Judicial Power* (1995); Jochen A. Frowein and Thilo Marauhn (eds), *Grundfragen der Verfassungsgerichtsbarkeit in Mittel- und Osteuropa* (1998); Tom Ginsburg, *Judicial Review in New Democracies. Constitutional Courts in Asian Cases* (2003); Victor Ferreres Comella, *Constitutional Courts* (2009); Alec Stone Sweet, *Governing with Judges* (2000).

[53] *United Mizrahi Bank* (n 31).

[54] Hans Kelsen, 'Wesen und Entwicklung der Staatsgerichtsbarkeit' in *Veröffentlichungen der Vereinigung der deutschen Staatsrechtslehrer* (1929), vol 5, 78ff; Van Alstyne (n 29), 180.

[55] Dieter Grimm, 'Constitutional Adjudication and Democracy' in Mads Adenas (ed), *Judicial Review in International Perspective, Liber Amicorum in Honour of Gordon Slynn* (2000), vol 2, 103.

[56] See eg the Russian case: Herbert Hausmaninger, 'Towards a "New" Russian Constitutional Court' (1995) 28 *Cornell International Law Journal* 349, and the Korean case: Ginsberg (n 52), 211ff.

political decision. Yet, the task of the constitution is not to make politics superfluous but to regulate the political process procedurally as well as substantively. It must leave room for political decisions and political change. The more detailed a constitution, the more difficult political change will be and the less elections will matter.

This explains the typological difference between exclusive and inclusive constitutions. Certainly, every constitution is to a certain extent exclusive. The democratic constitution excludes a system without participation of the people. A constitution with fundamental rights excludes a totalitarian system. 'Anything goes' is no constitutional maxim. Some constitutions even exclude certain options absolutely. They are not open to constitutional amendment. But this must be distinguished from constitutions that entrench the ideology or the programme of one political competitor so that all other competitors have no chance to realize their programme even after winning an election.

A certain inclusiveness as to ideologies and interests, political parties and their various programmes is therefore a precondition of a functioning constitution. If, on the contrary, the constituent power is used in order to entrench the political programme of the majority and thus exclude the programmes of competing political forces, an important benefit of constitutionalism, namely the possibility of peaceful change, is put at risk. The excluded parties are forced to use revolutionary means to realize their plans or to write a completely new constitution after coming to power.[57] This is not only a theoretical danger, but an often occurring experience, and not only in countries with a one-party system.[58]

5. Legitimating Principle

Truth or consensus—whether and to what extent a constitution is normative, nominal, or semantic in Loewenstein's terminology and whether it is comprehensive or allows extra-constitutional powers and extra-constitutional acts of public authority depends to a large extent on the principle on which the legitimacy of a political system is based. The decisive line runs between systems based on a supra-individual absolute truth, on the one hand, and systems that give primacy to individual autonomy, regard pluralism as legitimate, and base their legitimacy on consensus, on the other.

The absolute truth can be a religious truth, a value that is believed to be God-given. It can also be a secular truth, a vision of the perfect society, the final goal of all historical development. Whatever this absolute truth is, it always entails subordination of the constitution to the truth. The truth precedes the constitution and prevents it from being a comprehensive regulation of public power. The person or group of persons who embody or represent the truth, be it a priest or a group of clerics, be it a monarch or an avant-garde or a single political party that claims superior insight in the common best, remains above the constitution.

The legal impact of a constitution is limited by the absolute truth and the pre-constitutional right of the rulers who regard themselves as the embodiment or the guardian of the truth. Their mission is the enforcement of the truth. Any constitutional limitation in fulfilling this mission would be regarded as a betrayal of the truth. Law, constitutional law included, is reduced to an instrumental role. It regulates, limits, and guides the behaviour of the individuals and the inferior agents of the political system, not its leadership.

[57] Pasquale Pasquino, *Majority Rules in Constitutional Democracies* (forthcoming), 17, distinguishes between 'consensual constitutions' and 'coup de constitution'-constitutions.

[58] See Chapter 41.

If political systems based on an absolute truth adopt constitutions, which most of them do, be it for pragmatic or for opportunistic reasons, they usually lack those institutions that a full-fledged constitution contains in order to limit governmental power. They do not recognize the separation of powers. If the constitution provides for a division among various branches of government, the division is levelled by a uniform party that appears behind the facade of every branch and dodges the dividing lines. The same is true for the rule of law. It may serve as an instrument in the hands of the leaders, but they are not willing to submit themselves to law.

If constitutions of such political systems contain a bill of rights, as they also often do, it has a meaning that differs from the meaning fundamental rights have in full-fledged constitutions. The rights do not establish a sphere where, in principle, individual will prevails over governmental interests and limitations of the rights require a specific justification. Freedom of this kind would always imply the possibility of evading the requirements of the truth, to place individual above collective interests. Vis-à-vis the truth, freedom of speech, to use this example, would mean a right to express and propagate falsehood and cannot therefore be tolerated.

This shows at the same time why democracy or popular sovereignty is a necessary element of the achievement of constitutionalism, not just one way among others to establish constitutional rule. While the choice between a federal and a unitary system or between a one-cameral or a bi-cameral parliamentarianism can be made without the achievement of constitutionalism being affected, a legitimating principle other than democracy endangers the achievement. The legitimating principle, whatever it may be, will prevail over the constitutional guarantees and thus devaluate constitutionalism as such.

Reason or will—this distinction should not, however, be confused with the distinction between reason and will, justice, and legitimacy that is made by Paul Kahn and may sound similar at first glance.[59] The distinction between truth and consensus marks a difference between democratic and non-democratic constitutions, while Kahn's distinction is a distinction within democratic constitutionalism. Both elements are present in full-fledged democratic constitutions. They do not exclude each other, but they are in tension. For Kahn, 'the fundamental problem of constitutionalism is to negotiate the relationship between reason and will'.[60]

Depending on how this tension is resolved in a particular constitution, the constitutional order favours democracy over rights or vice versa.[61] This has a number of consequences. One of them is the different attitude towards universalistic claims. Another one is the role-perception of courts with constitutional jurisdiction. When a constitutional court speaks: 'Does it speak in the voice of the popular sovereign or in the voice of reason?'[62] In this distinction, Kahn finds an explanation for the differences between US and European constitutionalism. The US Supreme Court, according to Kahn, is primarily concerned with legitimacy, not justice, while the courts in Europe expand along the dimension of reason.

IV. Constitutions as Expressions of Political Ideas

Although inspired by theories of natural law, the modern constitution is positive law. It is the part of the law that regulates political decision-making. But this cannot save it from being a product of political will itself. As such, it is open to changing content. The content, in turn, is

[59] Paul Kahn, 'Comparative Constitutionalism in a New Key' (2003) 101 *Michigan Law Review* 2677.

[60] Ibid 2703.

[61] Here similarities appear to Bruce Ackerman's distinction between dualist democracy and rights foundationalism, cf Ackerman (n 20), vol 1, 7ff, 10ff.

[62] Kahn (n 59), 2703.

contingent on different conditions and different ideas of a just order. Competing ideas of justice may lead to different constitutions in different states or in one and the same state over time.[63] Social change may produce new challenges for constitutional law that provoke the enactment of new constitutions or the adaptation of old ones. In view of the fact that constitutionalism is now in its third century and has gained almost universal recognition it would be surprising if this had not led to different types of constitutions, according to the various principles to which they give legal expression. Since different principles can be combined or overlapping there is, however, little hope for clear-cut notions. The boundaries between the various types are fluid.

1. Liberal-Democratic Constitutions

Once again I start with the prototypes of modern constitutionalism. They can be characterized as liberal-democratic or democratic and rule of law-oriented (*rechtsstaatlich*). Both components had their roots in the theory of the social contract.[64] The idea of a social contract came to the fore when the transcendental legitimation of political power had been undermined by the Reformation of the sixteenth century. Yet, it did not come as a political postulate, but as an intellectual experiment. In search for a principle that could replace divine revelation as the legitimating ground for rulership, the contemporary philosophers placed themselves in a fictitious state of nature. In this state everyone was by definition equally free. The question, then, was what might cause reasonable people to leave this state and submit themselves to a government entitled to exercise power over them.

The answer was the fundamental insecurity of equal liberty in the absence of government. Entering into a state of rulership thus became a dictate of reason. Given everyone's equal freedom in the state of nature, this step presupposed a mutual agreement to form a government. Whatever the precise content of this agreement, the consent of the governed became the precondition of legitimate rule. The origin of government could be but democratic. The idea of an original contract raised the question under which conditions free individuals would be willing to form a government, or more precisely: which abandonment of natural freedom was deemed necessary in order to gain the security that was missing in the state of nature.

The answer to this question depended largely on the perception of a state without rule, and this perception was, in turn, influenced by the historical circumstances under which and for which the theory of the social contract was developed. In the period of the civil wars following the religious schism it might seem reasonable to exchange all natural liberties for the security of life, limb, and property that only an omnipotent ruler could guarantee. The monopoly of legitimated use of force was conceived and placed into the hands of a monarch who had the right to use it without limitation.

In this Hobbesian version only the original act of founding a body politic and establishing government was democratic. In a deeply rifted society with fundamental disagreement over absolute truths, the political system so established was not. The government had to be independent of societal consent and could not recognize any natural liberties without endangering its mission to re-establish internal peace. In its original version, the theory of a social contract justified the absolute state. A political system based on this theory was neither democratic nor liberal or *rechtsstaatlich*.

[63] See Chapter 16.

[64] John W. Gough, *The Social Contract* (2nd edn, 1957); Wolfgang Kersting, *Die politische Philosophie des Gesellschaftsvertrages* (1994). See Chapters 10 and 11.

However, the better the absolute ruler fulfilled his historical mission to restore internal peace, the less plausible was his claim to unlimited power. For Locke, writing 40 years after Hobbes, it seemed sufficient to relinquish the natural right to use force in order to defend one's rights, whereas all other liberties remained with the individual. The task of government could be reduced to protecting individual liberties against aggressors and perpetrators. This concept soon found support in the Kantian idea of the intrinsic value and autonomy of each individual that entitled him to self-determination, and the Smithian and physiocratic ideas that individual freedom and, as its consequence, an economy based on market mechanisms were a better guarantee of justice and welfare than feudal, corporate, and mercantile structures.

In this form, the theory became a guideline for revolutionary action in North America and France.[65] While in philosophy the social contract had been as fictitious as the state of nature, it now took the shape of a constitution understood no longer as a description of reality, but as distancing itself from reality and, instead, making normative demands on reality. Democracy was the legitimating principle of the state. The people not only held the constituent power. Democracy was also the principle for the organization of government. Those who governed received their mandate through the democratic act of popular election. The majority had the right to rule; but remained accountable to the electorate for the exercise of power.

The system was liberal insofar as majority rule did not apply absolutely. Rather, the natural rights were transformed into legal limitations of governmental power. Government did not lose the monopoly of legitimate force, but the purposes for which its power might be used were reduced to the protection of individual freedom and societal self-regulation in the form of market mechanisms and an analogy to market mechanisms in the political sphere where freedom of opinion and speech established a 'market place of ideas'[66] and different opinions and different interests could compete on the best way to pursue the common weal. Furthermore, the ruler was bound to rule by law and according to law.

The consequence was a transformation of the social order from duties to rights, or, as it has been famously described by Maine: from status to contract,[67] as well as a clear distinction between the spheres of state and society. The state no longer derived its legitimacy from the task of maintaining and enforcing a pre-established common weal against which no one could claim freedom. Rather, the state enjoyed freedom in fulfilling its task, while society was subject to bonds. Now the distribution of freedom and bonds changed. Free were the individuals and the limits of their freedom could be justified only in order to protect the freedom of others. Bound was government in order to prevent it from pursuing goals other than protecting individual freedom and societal self-regulation.

Yet, the system was also liberal in the sense that it favoured the propertied classes: indirectly, insofar as it placed special emphasis on the protection of property[68] (*'un droit inviolable et sacré'*, as Article 17 of the French Declaration put it) and its corollary, freedom of contract; and directly, insofar as only proprietors enjoyed the right to vote and could thus promote their interests through legislation. Being a pre-industrial concept, liberalism in this understanding was based on the assumption that, in a system where all feudal bonds had been dissolved and all were equally free, everyone had the chance to acquire property and become a voter.

[65] Bernard Bailyn, *The Ideological Origins of the American Revolution* (1967); B. Groethuysen, *La philosophie de la Révolution française* (1956).

[66] *Abrams v United States* 249 US 211 (1919), Justice Holmes dissenting.

[67] Henry Sumner Maine, *Ancient Law* (1861), chapter V, end.

[68] C.B. MacPherson, *The Political Theory of Possessive Individualism* (1962).

The institutional arrangement corresponded with the leading ideas. A key role was given to the law and together with it to the rule of law. Limitations of individual liberties required a basis in law. Laws were made by the representation of the citizens. The executive was bound by the law. An independent judiciary had the power to control whether the executive complied with the law. The separation of powers that corresponded to these functions diminished the risk of abuses of public power. The rule of law guaranteed that the democratically formed public will prevailed in executive action and at the same time that the liberal limitations of government were respected so that altogether 'a government of laws and not of men'[69] was established.

Although not foreseen by the framers of the early constitutions, the liberal-democratic type of constitutions sooner or later led to the emergence of political parties which competed with and fought against each other. It also led to the creation of interest groups which try to influence government behaviour from outside, while political parties are the driving forces within government. Consequently, liberal-democratic constitutions are always constitutions of pluralism. Pluralism of individual opinions and interests is accepted as legitimate, and the organized representation of similar opinions and interest is also accepted as legitimate. If one group were successful in suppressing pluralism, the constitution would cease to belong to the liberal-democratic type.

The internal differentiation between constitutions of this type depends on how the tension between the democratic and the liberal or rule of law component is dissolved. Systems without judicial review develop a tendency towards the democratic pole of the scale. If fundamental rights cannot be enforced, the will of the democratically elected branches of government prevails. The reverse conclusion that systems with judicial review tend towards the liberal pole would not be correct. Judicial review can be exercised with this or that tendency. Here Kahn's differentiation between reason and will takes effect.[70] It is a differentiation between liberty and democracy.

The distinction is also helpful to explain certain difference between the United States and Europe. While the United States leans more towards the democratic pole of the scale, the European states have developed an inclination towards the liberal or rule of law pole.[71] Certainly, there are European states such as the Netherlands whose constitution bars courts from checking the constitutionality of laws. But this prohibition has been undermined by the power of courts to review domestic laws as to their compatibility with the European Convention on Human Rights. These tendencies are, of course, to a large extent a matter of constitutional interpretation and of judicial activism or deference, but not only. They have roots in the constitutions themselves. Countries with the experience that democracy can fail are prepared to grant the judiciary more power than countries with an uninterrupted democratic record.

Moreover, the function of fundamental rights varied according to the circumstances. While the American colonists lived under English law, which was generally regarded as the most liberal law

[69] John Adams, *Thoughts on Government* (1776), Works, vol IV (1850), 106; Constitution of Massachusetts, Art 30; *Marbury v Madison* 1 Cranch 137 (1803).

[70] Kahn (n 59).

[71] What is here called *the* rule of law differs in meaning from system to system, see Richard Fallon, 'The Rule of Law as a Concept in Constitutional Discourse' (1997) 97 *Columbia Law Review* 1; Ulrich Scheuner, 'Die neuere Entwicklung des Rechtsstaats in Deutschland' in Ulrich Scheuner, *Staatstheorie und Staatsrecht* (1978), 185; Michel Troper, *Pour une théorie juridique de l'Etat* (1994); Michel Rosenfeld, 'The Rule of Law and the Legitimacy of Constitutional Democracy' (2001) 74 *California Law* Review 1307 (2001).

of the time, France had preserved the feudal system and exercised rigid control over the economy. These differences could not remain without impact on the revolutions in the two countries and consequently on the constitutions that emerged from the revolutions.[72] The revolutionary goal of the American colonists was external and political in nature. They fought for self-government after being treated unequally by the motherland, whereas the goal of the French revolutionaries was internal and social in nature. They wanted to liberalize the social and economic order, which, after many failed attempts to achieve this by reforms, presupposed a break with the political system.

This contextual difference found expression in the function of fundamental rights. Vis-à-vis an already liberal legal order, the US Bill of Rights could content itself with guaranteeing individual freedom against intrusion by the government including the legislature. This was the difference from England. Fundamental rights functioned as negative rights. In France, the Declaration was adopted in opposition to the existing legal order. This order had to be liberalized, and fundamental rights functioned as tasks and guidelines for the legislature in the complicated and long-lasting process of law reform. Before being able to function as negative rights they were positive rights. They had a programmatic function.

While the adoption of the US Constitution brought the revolutionary process to an end, the adoption of the French Constitution of 1791 set a revolutionary process in motion. It soon turned out that the constitution was not able to control this process. Rather, it became a victim of the process. With the expectations that the revolution had roused, every new wave of revolutionary activity carried the existing constitution away and replaced it by a new one. It was only Napoleon's rise to power that brought this process to a halt, albeit at the expense of the constitution. The various Napoleonic constitutions preserved the form of constitutional rule, but were not intended to limit the power of the ruler.

However, even when the monarchy was re-established in 1804 Napoleon did not touch upon the civil achievements of the revolution. An aristocracy was created, but the feudal order was not re-introduced. On the contrary, Napoleon consolidated the liberal order, and the most important instrument was the Civil Code which, other than the Constitution, remains in place today. A liberal private law regime coexisted with an authoritarian public law regime. Individual liberty was confined to the private sphere and found its field of activity in the economy while political liberties and participatory rights were curtailed. With the Napoleonic constitutions France departed from the liberal-democratic path.

2. Liberal Non-Democratic Constitutions

The rest of Europe became acquainted with constitutionalism through the Napoleonic conquests. Constitutions used to follow the French army. They served as an instrument to win over the population of the conquered territories where the desire for constitutions was greater than the power to gain them by one's own force. The constitutions enacted or demanded by Napoleon promised liberalizing reforms, economic freedom, elected representations of the people, and equal rights vis-à-vis the state. Although they marked progress compared to the traditional order, they did not live up to the standard set by the American and French Revolutions.

The possibility of semi-constitutions also guaranteed the survival of constitutionalism after the French hegemony in Europe had come to an end. The Napoleonic constitutions had con-

[72] Hannah Arendt, *On Revolution* (1963); Jürgen Habermas, 'Naturrecht und Revolution' in Habermas, *Theorie und Praxis* (1963), 57; Dieter Grimm, *Recht und Staat der bürgerlichen Gesellschaft* (1987), 192; Grimm (n 26), 67.

vinced many European monarchs that it was possible to adopt a constitution without adhering to the full programme of constitutionalism. As a consequence, many constitutions came into being that did not affect the princes' right to rule but required only some limitations on their hitherto absolute power. The loss of power was reconciled with the principle of monarchical sovereignty by a distinction between possession and exercise of public power that appeared for the first time in the restorative French Constitution of 1814. According to this Constitution, the monarch remained the exclusive holder of public power whereas on the level of its exercise he limited himself to the consent of parliament in certain matters.

The typological characteristic of these constitutions is the separation of the democratic and the liberal or rule of law component. Since the pre-democratic legitimation of the ruler remained uncontested, the constitutions were not enacted by a vote, popular or parliamentarian, but by a decision of the ruler, who 'granted' them to his people as the documents usually read. In a number of cases the text of the constitution was negotiated by the ruler and a representation of the people. But never were the people regarded as the origin or ultimate source of political power. On the other hand, although having freely decided to grant a constitution, the monarch was not entitled to repeal it unilaterally. Where this happened it was regarded as a breach of the constitution.

The constitutions were liberal insofar as they abolished the feudal system and the regulation of the economy or at least charged the state with the task of gradually altering the system. The recognition of fundamental rights was also liberal, albeit due to the origin of these constitutions not as human rights but as citizens' rights and, due to the non-democratic character of the constitution, sparing with political rights. Liberty was confined to the private sphere. The impact of these rights depended largely on the question whether they were endowed with derogatory effect vis-à-vis pre-constitutional law that was incompatible with the bill of rights. Most of them lacked this effect. Where they had derogatory effect the enforcement was weak as judicial review was usually regarded as incompatible with the monarchical principle.

The establishment of representations of the people was eventually liberal, usually based on census suffrage. In many cases, an unelected Upper House existed, designed to give the privileged classes of society additional political weight and to check the powers of the Lower House. Parliament always had a share in legislation and mostly the right to approve the budget, but rarely an influence on the formation of the cabinet. However, the executive was bound by the rule of law. The administration had to respect and enforce the statutes, and eventually the judiciary acquired the power to review the legality of administrative acts.

This type of constitution became the norm in Europe after 1815. The only democratic constitution that survived after that year was that of Norway. The leading constitution during the first, largely restorative, period was the French *Charte Constitutionnelle* of 1814. The greatest influence after 1830 is usually attributed to the Belgian Constitution of that year. This is true with regard to the formulation of the bill of rights and the organizational structure of the state. It is not true, however, with regard to the legitimating principle. The Belgian Constitution, the product of a successful revolution, was based on popular sovereignty for which most other European states were not yet prepared. The French Constitution of 1830, itself a product of a revolution, left the question open.

With reference to the discussion of a European Constitution, it has been suggested that there are two equally legitimate types of constitution, the democracy-oriented type and the rule of law-oriented type.[73] While it is true that these have coexisted in history, and to a certain extent still coexist today, it is, however, not the case that they are equally legitimate. While the

[73] Christoph Möllers, 'Verfassunggebende Gewalt—Verfassung—Konstitutionalisierung' in Armin von Bogdandy and Jürgen Bast (eds), *Europäisches Verfassungsrecht* (2nd edn, 2009), 227.

democracy-oriented type included the rule of law, the rule of law-oriented type excluded democracy. Because of this difference, the liberal constitution was commonly regarded as a deficient type of constitutionalism. The achievement of constitutionalism rests on a combination of both. Democracy alone cannot even secure that part of individual freedom on which democracy depends. Liberalism alone cannot guarantee that all citizens get a fair chance to articulate their opinions and interests in the political process.[74]

Much of the constitutional struggle in the nineteenth century and later was about full-fledged constitutions that recognized both components. Attempts to create them were undertaken almost everywhere in Europe in the revolutionary year of 1848. Democratic movements already went along with social demands of the so-called Fourth Estate, the class of manufacturing and industrial workers and peasants. The revolution failed in almost all countries, to a large extent because of the different revolutionary goals of the bourgeoisie and the working classes. However, a number of still absolutist monarchies were now turned into constitutional states. Yet far from being based on popular sovereignty, the constitutions were not constitutive in nature, but simply modified the pre-existing rule.

In this form, constitutionalism arrived in East Asia. Constitutions had been unheard of in this part of the world until the middle of the nineteenth century. But with the opening to the West in the 1860s, constitutionalism became a subject of interest. Japan adopted its first constitution in 1889. The Prussian Constitution of 1850 served as model.[74a] As with the Korean Constitution of 1899, it was based on the principle of monarchical sovereignty. The motivation for both constitutions can be found more in foreign policy considerations than in internal needs. As a consequence, different from the European model, the liberal elements of these constitutions remained largely on paper.

Where a constitution was still absent, the political system could not be called democratic. But this is not equally true for liberalism. The democratic and the liberal component have a different relationship with constitutionalism. It is difficult to conceive of democracy without a constitution. The reason is that in a democracy 'the people' is regarded as the sovereign, but cannot govern itself. This is true for both representative and plebiscitarian democracy. Even in a plebiscitarian democracy, the people have the decision-making power only in certain but not all matters. Because of the inevitable difference between those who govern and those who are governed, democracy is in need of being organized. This is what constitutions do.

The liberal component is less dependent on a constitution. The government can respect individual freedom and obey the rule of law without being constitutionally obliged to do so. The United Kingdom before the Civil Rights Act is an example. In Germany the rule of law had already emerged in the period of enlightened absolutism in the second half of the eighteenth century, independently of the American and French Revolutions. In the nineteenth century, the modernization of societies in the spirit of liberalism was not necessarily combined with constitutionalism. It could rely on the state's interest in a strong national economy. As the Napoleonic experience shows the liberalization of social and economic life could develop within an illiberal political environment. To a certain extent, private law can substitute for constitutional law.[75]

The difference between constitutional and non-constitutional liberalism lies not necessarily in the content of the law, but in the degree of the entrenchment. Self-limitations can be

[74] Frank Michelman, 'Law's Republic' (1988) 97 *Yale Law Journal* 1493; Jürgen Habermas, *Die Einbeziehung des Anderen* (1996) 154, 293.

[74a] Takii Kazuchiro, *The Meiji Constitution* (2007).

[75] Grimm, *Recht und Staat* (n 72) 192, 212.

reversed at any time. Laws can be repealed or amended. It is the constitution, provided that it enjoys supremacy, that furnishes the degree of durability and certainty that is desirable for such fundamental elements as freedom, equality, rule of law etc. Entrenchment functions as a barrier against attempts to abolish or reduce these guarantees. The full benefits of liberal democracy can only be obtained through a constitution.

3. Non-Liberal Democratic Constitutions

Just as it is possible that a constitution is liberal without being democratic, it is likewise conceivable that a constitution is democratic without being liberal. This seems possible in two quite different forms. One form is radical democracy. Here only the majority principle counts, and the constitution is confined to rules that regulate the decision-making process. Fundamental rights are regarded as anti-democratic because they stand in the way of majority decisions and by the same token constitutional review comes under the verdict of being anti-majoritarian. The rule of law is reduced to the obligation of the executive branch of government to implement the law. But the rule of law does not have any influence on the formation of the law.

Radical democracy was already on the agenda when the first constitutions emerged. In the debate of the French National Assembly on the Declaration of Rights 1789, the representative Crénière argued in a Rousseauean manner that there is but one fundamental right, namely the right of every citizen to participate in the formation of the general will.[76] In the early years of North American constitutionalism, the parliaments of the former colonies claimed for themselves the same sovereign power that the British parliament enjoyed and did not feel bound by the Bills of Rights they had only recently adopted. It needed the Philadelphia Convention to clarify that sovereignty belonged to the people, not the people's representatives.[77]

Radical democracies may seem particularly democratic. But they are not immune to majoritarian absolutism and they are threatened by an inherent tendency toward self-destruction. If the elected majority is omnipotent, it can use the majority vote to discriminate against the minority, tailor the rules of political competition in a way to prevent loss of power, restrict critical speech, and ultimately even abolish majority rule by a majority vote. This tendency remains latent as long as the system rests on a set of shared values which prevent the competitors from mutually regarding themselves as enemies and which function as non-legal limitation to majority decisions. When the moral basis erodes the constitution can, however, easily pervert.

For the latter, the Weimar Constitution of 1919 is often used as an example. And, indeed, what happened in 1933 in Germany was not a revolution against the democratic system but a self-destruction of democracy through democratic procedures. Afterwards no new National Socialist Constitution was adopted. Nazi rule was the opposite of constitutionalism. However, it would be incorrect to call the Weimar Constitution a constitution of the radically democratic type. It contained an elaborate bill of rights as well as a number of checks to parliamentary power and it provided for an, albeit rudimentary, constitutional court. Rather, it was a formalistic interpretation that regarded the events of 1933 as compatible with the Weimar Constitution.

[76] *Les déclarations des droits de l'homme de 1789. Textes réunis et présentés par Christine Faure* (1988), 127. Marat replied that without a limited power there would be no constitution, see 278, and Demeunier rejected the idea by calling it 'le système de Hobbes, rejeté de l'Europe entière', see 331.

[77] Gordon Wood, *The Creation of the American Republic 1776–1787* (2nd edn, 1998), 391ff.

One might expect all democratic constitutions without a bill of rights to belong to the radical democratic type. But this is not necessarily the case if democracy is not reduced to mere majority rule. Australia, for example, has deliberately renounced a bill of rights because it deemed individuals best served by ensuring to each an equal share in political power.[78] Nevertheless, Australia still accepts that the decision in favour of democracy implies the recognition of some unwritten fundamental rights, such as freedom of speech, without which democracy would lose its sense. Consequently, the Australian High Court declared a law null and void on the ground that it violated freedom of expression, which it regarded as being implied in the notion of democracy.[79] In this context, it is not without interest that all other states of the old Commonwealth (Great Britain, Canada, and New Zealand) have recently adopted bills of rights.

The second form of democratic non-liberal constitutionalism consists of constitutions that are based on the principle of popular sovereignty, but give little weight to the people's interests and opinions in the course of day-to-day politics. They put the emphasis on executive power and have low regard for the separation of powers and fundamental rights of the citizens. They often go along with a strong affiliation of the ruling elites with a religious creed and give special protection to the Church that represents and propagates this creed. The distinction between general laws and religious norms is low, the degree of accepted pluralism small.

This type of constitution played a big role in the Latin American countries after they had freed themselves from Spanish or Portuguese rule.[80] These two colonial powers themselves had deviated from the mainstream constitutionalism in Europe in 1820 when the struggle for independence in Latin America began. Since the constitutions were exclusive in the above-mentioned sense,[81] every power shift between the liberal and the restorative forces led to the abolition of the existing constitution and to the adoption of a new one. For the same reason, the frequent change of constitutions repeated itself in Latin America, although with a few exceptions: the third Chilean Constitution, for instance, was in force from 1833 to 1925.[82] Altogether, this continent saw more than one hundred constitutions in the nineteenth century alone and nor was constitutional stability reached during most of the twentieth century.

The vast majority of these constitutions are described as democratic in origin, but autocratic in practice, defending political elitism and moral perfectionism under the guidance of the Catholic Church.[83] In opposition to this type of constitution, some radical democratic constitutions were drafted, albeit with little success, and the same is true for liberal constitutions. Only Brazil differs to a certain extent from countries in the Spanish tradition.[84] All constitutions after the Imperial Constitution of 1824, with the exception of two dictatorial constitutions (1937 and 1967/69), were enacted by an elected constitutional assembly and contained growing catalogues of fundamental rights—the current one beating all records with its almost 150 rights.

[78] Harrison Moore, *The Constitution of the Australian Commonwealth* (1902), 329.

[79] *Australian Capital Television v Australia* (1992) 177 CLR 106.

[80] José M. Portillo Valdés, 'Constitución' in Javier Fernández Sebastián (ed), *Diccionario politico y social del mundo iberoamericano* (2009), vol I, 305; Jeremy Adelman, *Sovereignty and Revolution in the Iberian Atlantic* (2006); Jaime E. Rodriguez O., *The Independence of Spanish America* (1998), 192.

[81] 'Inclusive or exclusive', above at 113.

[82] D. Garcia Belaunde, F. Fernandez Segado, and R. Hernandez-Volle (eds), *Los sistemas constitucionales iberoamericanos* (1992).

[83] Roberto Gargarella, 'Towards a Typology of Latin American Constitutionalism' (2004) 39 *Latin American Research Review* 141.

[84] Paulo Bonavides and Paes de Andrade, *Historia Constitucional do Brasil* (8th edn, 2006).

Constitutions that look like liberal-democratic ones but tend to be democratic-non-liberal are quite frequent throughout the world. This is not to say, however, that the democratic component is well developed. As a matter of fact, it often finds itself in a rudimentary stage, although more advanced than the institutions of legal control and adjudication whose failure is often evident. This situation should, therefore, not be confused with that in the United States where the democratic component enjoys a certain prevalence over the rule of law component. This statement concerns a constitutional order which not only belongs clearly to the liberal-democratic type but also possesses highly developed institutions of legal control.

4. The Social or Welfare State Constitution

Liberalism fulfilled its promise only in part. While the productivity of a liberalized economy, and with it the wealth in society, increased considerably, the societal self-regulation did not result in a just order. The wealth was distributed unequally, and instead of the old feudal structures a division according to classes spread out in society. The liberal constitution, whether democratic or not, contributed to this development, although the text does not always reveal this. The bills of rights were formulated in universal terms and even when they protected only citizens they applied to all of them equally. Yet, this did not prevent the United States and other countries such as Brazil from upholding slavery; and it did not prevent any liberal state in the nineteenth century and thereafter from treating men and women unequally.

The more general problem was, however, that the equal rights applied to unequal conditions. All enjoyed freedom of property, but this freedom was useful for proprietors only. All enjoyed freedom of contract. No one could be compelled to conclude a contract that he deemed onerous or unjust. But for those whose only property was their capacity to work, there remained little choice but to accept any condition set by employers, landlords, etc. Thus, equal freedom, applied to unequal factual conditions, did not lead to a balance of interest but to exploitation. In the societal sphere that had been freed from state regulation, private suppression developed. Formal equality applied to situations of substantive inequality cements the status quo.[85]

This was the situation in many constitutional states, and it was aggravated by the Industrial Revolution. Political redress was less likely the more liberal the constitutions were. When it came to the right to vote the constitutions openly favoured bourgeois interests. The electoral system was based on census, and the census was even stricter with regard to eligibility. Thus, attempts to alleviate the situation of the working classes through legislation usually failed in the liberal parliaments. Disconnected from its original aim to secure justice, liberalism and its insistence on formal equality with the material pre-conditions of freedom left aside became doctrinal. A revision of liberal constitutionalism seemed necessary.

The year 1848 was a turning point in this respect. Marx and Engels published the Communist Manifesto. The French February Revolution was no longer a revolution of the middle classes against absolutism and feudalism as in 1789 or against the Bourbon restoration as in 1830, but a revolution of the working classes. The right to work was proclaimed. A new constitution, passed in November 1848 by a national convention emanating from general elections, promised in its preamble a more equitable distribution of burdens and advantages and in its bill of rights guaranteed free education, equality in labour relations, public work for the unemployed,

[85] See Chapter 47.

albeit no right to work, state aid for the sick and the elderly if they were unable to support themselves.

In spite of the short life of this constitution a new element was now on the constitutional agenda: the social. Put forward in reaction to the manifest deficits of liberalism, it came in two forms, a moderate and a radical one. In the first form, the social element was designed to complement, not to negate, the liberal element. The state should again assume responsibility for a just social order, guarantee a minimal standard of welfare, and prevent abuses of economic liberties. The constitutional devices were social and economic rights that the state had to implement. The second mode was anti-liberal and expected progress not from modifications, but from a replacement of liberalism. It ultimately led to socialist constitutions.

The route from the early attempts to infuse social elements into the constitutions to the realization of the project was long. In some countries nothing changed on the constitutional level. In others changes arrived late. The US Constitution is an example of the first alternative. After the Civil War, the Thirteenth and Fourteenth Amendments abolished slavery and guaranteed every person equal rights regardless of colour and race. But the Constitution did not react to the social problems of a rapidly industrializing society. The same is true for the European constitutions in the second half of the nineteenth century and for most constitutions in other parts of the world.

However, this did not necessarily mean that governments completely abstained from coping with the social problem. Although the French Constitution of 1848 was soon abolished, Napoleon III, the heir of the failed revolution, introduced a number of social programmes, but daily working hours did not fall below 12 and unions and strikes remained forbidden. Germany was the first country to introduce a comprehensive social security system in the 1880s that insured workers against illness, invalidity, and unemployment and provided old-age pensions. This shows that the welfare state, just like liberalism and the rule of law, does not depend on constitutional guarantees. These initiatives can be introduced on the legislative level.

Yet, even in the absence of explicit social provisions the constitutional setting is not irrelevant. Germany's backwardness in terms of constitutionalism facilitated its progressiveness in social matters.[86] The non-democratic monarchical state had never understood liberalism as an end in itself but as a means to promote economic growth. Likewise, it had never completely relinquished its responsibility for general welfare. Bismarck succeeded in getting support for his social security programme from a not fully liberal parliament whereas social measures were usually voted down in the parliaments of countries such as France.

The constitutional progressiveness of the United States, in turn, impeded measures of social policy for a certain time. While in Europe government measures that addressed the social problem could not be challenged in court, this was possible in the United States. The *Lochner* decision of 1905, which declared unconstitutional a law that limited the weekly working hours of labourers to 60, became characteristic for a whole period of dogmatic liberalism and stopped President Roosevelt's New Deal programme until he got the chance to appoint new justices to the Supreme Court who were willing to overrule *Lochner*.[87]

Since the United States never added social elements to their liberal-democratic constitution, the admissibility of social policy measures always remained a question of constitutional interpretation. In a number of other constitutional systems, the turn towards welfare state

[86] Grimm (n 72), 138.

[87] *Lochner v New York* 198 US 45 (1905); *West Coast Hotel v Parrish* 300 US 379 (1937).

constitutions gained momentum after the First World War. The Weimar Constitution of 1919 added social and economic rights and directives regarding the economic order to the classical liberties. Dignity appeared as a constitutional notion in the sense of a right to lead a dignified life, secured by entitlements to shelter, food, and clothing, and in a similar sense dignity was mentioned in the Irish Constitution of 1934. A comprehensive chapter on the economic and social order characterizes the Brazilian Constitution of 1934.

While Germany in its current constitution replaced the Weimar catalogue of social and economic rights by a general clause that Germany is a social state, many constitutions of former socialist countries and a number of post-colonial constitutions in countries with severe social differences, based on caste as in India or on race as in South Africa, contain chapters with social and economic rights or directives for legislation with the goal of creating equal conditions for the population. Affirmative action, a constant problem under the liberal US Constitution, is admitted and even prescribed in these countries. The guarantees of the classical liberties often contain notwithstanding clauses in favour of affirmative action. India's constitution is full of them; and the Brazilian Constitution of 1988 comprises a veritable social policy programme.[88]

Likewise, the social element is of great importance in the post-war constitutions of Japan (1946) and Korea (1949).[89] Both constitutions contain a right to work. According to Article 25, every Japanese citizen has the right to lead a life based on a minimum standard of health and culture. According to Article 34, all Korean citizens have the right to a dignified life. Both constitutions obligate the state to promote social welfare and social security. When these countries adopted those clauses they were under strong US influence, although it was not the US Constitution that could serve as a model in this respect. Japan and Korea constitutionalized Roosevelt's New Deal programme that had been implemented on the legislative level in the country of origin.

Just as a liberal-democratic constitution has to negotiate the relationship between democracy and liberty, social constitutions that attempt to correct the deficits of liberalism have to negotiate the relationship between liberty and equality. Constitutions belonging to this type can therefore be differentiated according to their preference for either liberty or equality. Generally speaking, countries with a discriminatory past (homemade as in India or externally imposed as in South Africa), which the constitution wants to overcome, tend to give considerable weight to equality. The same is true for countries without a strong liberal tradition and a culture not primarily based on values of individual autonomy as with the East Asian states.

On the contrary, countries in the Western tradition tend to subordinate equality to liberty. It is equal freedom that the various constitutions seek to achieve. Social and economic rights are primarily understood as guarantees of the material foundations of liberty. The social constitution thus breaks with a merely formal understanding of equality that prevailed under the liberal constitution, but in the interest of a deeper understanding and securing of liberty. Even in a constitution like the German one that does not contain social and economic rights, but the general principle of a social state, this principle is used to give the classical liberties a social content.[90]

[88] On affirmative action, see Chapter 54.

[89] Sung-Soo Kim and Hiroshi Nishihara, *Vom paternalistischen zum partnerschaftlichen Rechtsstaat* (2000), 25, 36.

[90] Dieter Grimm, 'The Protective Function of the State' in Georg Nolte (ed), *European and US Constitutionalism* (2005), 137.

The impact of the social component would be misunderstood if seen only as an addition of a new content layer to the constitution. It entails a structural change. Social and economic rights are a consequence of waning confidence in the self-regulation capacity of society. Social justice becomes again a concern of the state. As in the pre-liberal era, it is a goal that has to be actively pursued, but in a different way from the earlier period and not through illiberal means. Social and economic rights as a way to pursue this aim therefore differ considerably from classical liberties. These are primarily negative rights limiting the government. They are fulfilled through non-action. Social and economic rights, on the contrary, are positive rights the fulfilment of which requires state action.[91]

This has a double consequence. While there is only one way to comply with negative rights, namely to omit certain actions, there are various ways to fulfil positive rights. The government has a choice. Because of this difference negative rights correspond with entitlements of the rights holder, positive rights do not. Secondly, while the duty to omit certain actions does not create a scarcity problem, the duty to render services or distribute benefits does. For both reasons, social and economic rights are in need of legislative concretization and specification before they can entitle their beneficiaries and be enforced by courts.

This difference gave rise to the assumption that, despite their name, social and economic rights are not rights, but merely expressions of political intent without legal relevance. This is particularly, but not only, the case in common law systems where it seems difficult to conceive of a right without a corresponding remedy. However, it would be a mistake to assume that these rights are not justiciable at all. Courts in countries with positive rights may obligate the legislator to enact laws that give a concrete meaning to these rights and create entitlements for the individual on the legislative level. In some cases the obligation of the state to distribute benefits has even been derived directly from the constitution if laws were missing.[92]

Social and economic rights were a constitutional answer to the social problem that originated in the nineteenth century in the wake of industrialization. But this is no longer the only field where active state intervention in society takes place. Over time, the state again assumed comprehensive responsibility for the welfare and development of society. Government is, within the limits of its capacity, responsible for economic growth, infrastructural modernization, protection against the risks inherent in scientific and technological progress and its commercial use.

Not all of these tasks can be fulfilled by giving orders. The state is compelled to use indirect means like financial incentives to reach its aims. To the same extent that the state resorts to soft law instead of hard law it became dependent on the willingness of private actors to comply with demands. As a consequence, multilateral bargaining processes replace the traditional unilateral command. Private actors advance from societal forces that try to influence government decision to participants in decision-making. They gain an informal share in public power. The borderline between public and private is blurred.

All this is not without consequences for the constitution of welfare states. It finds expression in so-called third generation rights, such as the right to a healthy environment, clean air and water, etc. It is, however, difficult to individualize these collective goods and to formulate them in the language of rights. In many constitutions, therefore, they are not part of the bill of rights, but form a separate category, namely objectives of the state. As such, they claim binding force for government. Consequently, total neglect would amount to a violation of the consti-

[91] See Chapter 49.

[92] Superior Tribunal de Justiça of Brasil, SS 3751 of 20 April 2009; no 1.185.474-SC of 20 April 2010.

tution. But the measures to be taken in order to implement the objectives cannot be derived from the constitution. They are left to political will, according to the agenda of the ruling party and the financial capacity of the country.

Furthermore, the social type of constitution can no longer confine itself to limiting public power. It also adopts a programmatic function. Appellative and aspirational norms supplement the traditional prescriptive rules. The constitution expresses the values in which a society believes. They are not just solemn assertions, but they are understood as legally binding guidelines, for example for the interpretation of the bill of rights as section 9 of the South African Constitution requires. These constitutions are not limited to the sphere of the state, but formulate an overarching consensus for the political and the societal sphere. This goes along with more and more informal practices that replace or undermine the formal institutions and procedures. What is gained in range is lost in normativity.[93]

5. Socialist Constitutions

Socialist constitutions equal the type of constitutions discussed above in that they are also a reaction to the deficits of liberalism. They differ from these constitutions in that they break with liberalism altogether. Their attitude is not illiberal but anti-liberal. Karl Marx taught that fundamental rights are an instrument of exploitation and Ferdinand Lassalle extended this to constitutions in general: they conceal power structures, and power always prevails over law.[94] As a consequence, the limitations that are part of the liberal project are rejected: fundamental rights, separation of powers, rule of law, judicial review. If provisions are found in socialist constitutions that look like these limitations they usually have a different meaning and fulfil different functions. This can be explained by a look to the second element of modern constitutions, democracy. Are the socialist constitutions democratic?

The self-description of most socialist countries, past and present, says so: the People's Republic of China, the German Democratic Republic. In the constitutional texts this is usually explained by attributing all public power to the people. But this power is exercised in the form of a dictatorship, 'the People's Democratic Dictatorship' (Art 1 of the Chinese Constitution). Subject to this dictatorial power is not the people as such, but one class of the people, the 'working class' of workers and peasants. This class acts through an avant-garde, the Communist Party. The Communist Party is usually the only party. If other parties exist they are not competitors but cooperators.

The party exercises the power in accordance with the principle of democratic centralism, that is to say, top-down. The leadership, usually the politburo, is the avant-garde within the avant-garde. Its position is legitimized by superior insight in the ultimate aim of history and the true interest of the people. The legitimation principle is not consensus of the people, but an absolute truth. Consequently socialist constitutions are not constitutions of pluralism. If we find mechanisms that resemble democratic mechanisms in democratic constitutions, such as elections, they again have a different meaning and a different function.[95]

[93] Uwe Volkmann, 'Der Aufstieg der Verfassung. Beobachtungen zum grundlegenden Wandel des Verfassungsbegriffs' in Thomas Vesting and Stefan Korioth (eds), *Der Eigenwert des Verfassungsrechts* (2011), 23.

[94] Karl Marx, 'Zur Judenfrage' in Karl Marx and Friedrich Engels, *Werke* ([1843] 1970), vol I, 347; Ferdinand Lassalle, *Über Verfassungswesen* (1862 and 1907).

[95] See Chapter 25.

Since in socialist systems political power is legitimized by an absolute truth, everything that has been said about truth as legitimating principle applies to socialist constitutions. They are subordinated to this truth. Their function consists in serving this truth. This means that they cannot acquire primacy over governmental acts. A rule such as Article 5(1) of the Chinese Constitution must be read in light of the fact that the Communist Party is the sole authoritative interpreter of the Constitution and the laws. The Constitution rather assists the government in achieving the pre-existing purpose of political rule. Elections may offer a limited choice among candidates, but not among programmes or views of the common best.

The separation of powers does not acknowledge independency of state organs. It is a mere administrative utility principle, a division of labour, not of powers. The rule of law, understood as 'socialist legality', applies to the inferior agencies of the state, but does not bind the highest authorities.[96] Fundamental rights do not open spheres of self-determination of the individual. All rights are under the condition not to disrupt the truth. 'Disruption of the socialist system by any organization or individual is prohibited' (Art 1 of the Chinese Constitution).

Behind this perception lies the assumption that, with the abolition of capitalism, the antagonism between the individual and the state has disappeared. In the socialist system the interests of society and the interest of the individual are objectively in harmony, although not every member of society may subjectively be aware of this. In comparison with the objective situation, the subjective view of the individual deserves no legal protection. It can be disregarded and, if necessary, suppressed. The distinction between state and society, public and private is obsolete. The legal system is based on duties instead of rights. Fundamental rights no longer guarantee a private sphere free of state intervention, but guarantee the individual participation in the collective endeavour as well as the means necessary to render his or her service in the reproductive process of society.

Basically the same is true for constitutions in every political regime that legitimizes itself by an absolute truth. It is in particular true for theocratic regimes whose foundation is not a secular, but a divine, truth. The question is therefore whether it is justified to regard these constitutions as a type of constitutionalism. If the measure is what was called here the achievement of constitutionalism, all essential characteristics of constitutions are missing. The other types discussed may have been closer or farther away from the achievement, but they could all be accepted as species of the genus 'modern constitution'. Socialist constitutions are the anti-type to these.

V. A New Distinction: National and International Constitutions

The modern constitution is a particularly ambitious and a particularly successful means to submit public power to law. When it emerged, public power was in the hands of states. They held the monopoly of public power on their territory. As a matter of fact, only the concentration of the numerous dispersed powers that coexisted on a given territory made the constitution, understood as a law that comprehensively regulated the establishment and exercise of public power, possible. A polity where this concentration existed was regarded as a state. The constitutions were state or national constitutions. The modern state was the precondition of

[96] Gordon Chang, 'What Does the Rule of Law Mean in China?' (1999) 13 *China Law and Practice* 271; Randall Peerenboom, *China's Long March Toward Rule of Law* (2002).

the modern constitution. Earlier polities had laws and even fundamental laws that applied to power holders, but no constitution.

Beyond the state, no object capable of being constitutionalized existed. The only actors on the international scene were states. They were characterized by an attribute that no other entity had, namely sovereignty. Sovereignty meant that they held the supreme power within their territory and had no external powers above them. The law that regulated the relationship among sovereign states was international law. But because of the sovereignty of the states and the corresponding absence of an international public power, let alone an international legislation, legal bonds among states could only stem from voluntary agreements. International law was contractual law. It consisted of treaties. Treaties were not constitutions. In the absence of an international public power they could not be enforced if a party was in breach of a mutual agreement.

This situation lasted for almost 300 years, from the Westphalian Treaty of 1648 to the foundation of the United Nations after the Second World War in 1945. The United Nations differs from the many leagues and alliances that had existed before 1945, including the League of Nations, which had been founded after the First World War, in that the member states of the United Nations not only renounced the use of force in international relations (with the exception of self-defence), but that they transferred the power to enforce this commitment against aggressors, if necessary with military force, to the UN. After the founding of the United Nations no member state is as sovereign as states had been in the Westphalian order. There is now a public power above them.

In the meantime, other international organizations were created globally and regionally to which the member states transferred sovereign powers that are now exercised by these organization, potentially against the will of the member states. The most far-reaching organization of this type is, of course, the European Union. But other powerful international actors have also emerged: the European Council with the European Court of Human Rights; the International Criminal Court, whose legal basis is not a treaty but a legislative act of the UN Security Council and whose powers are not limited to signatory states; the World Trade Organization; to a certain extent also the International Monetary Fund, etc. In addition, public international law has brought forth a *ius cogens* that binds states independent of their consent. The borderline between inside and outside is blurred.

The erosion of traditional statehood that goes along with this development cannot leave the constitution unaffected.[97] If nation-states no longer hold the monopoly of public power, but share it with international organizations the national constitution looses the capacity of comprehensively legitimating and regulating all public power that claims validity within the national territory. The national constitution may still determine the transfer of powers to international organizations. But the use these organizations make of their powers is no longer subject to national constitutional law. The constitution is reduced to a partial order that regulates public power only insofar as it remains state power.

This gives rise to the question whether the decline of the national constitution can be compensated on the international level. After all, what is in need of being submitted to law is not the state, but public power, regardless of the entity through which it is exercised. The widely accepted answer to this question is constitutionalization. Unlike the making of a constitution, constitutionalization does not designate an act by which a constitution acquires legal force,

[97] Dieter Grimm, 'The Constitution in the Process of Denationalization' (2005) 12 *Constellations* 447. See also Chapter 56.

but a process that eventually leads to a constitution. The objects of this process are the treaties and charters of international organizations such as the United Nations, the European Union, the World Trade Organization, the various human rights pacts, sometimes public international law in general, and even self-organization and self-regulation processes of globally operating private actors,[98] all objects for which the term 'constitution' was not in use until recently.

If all this is correct, a new type of constitution is emerging: the international constitution as opposed to the national constitution. Whether or not it is indeed correct depends largely on the meaning of 'constitution'. If the term is understood in the sense of the achievement described earlier, the international world is relatively far from it. With the exception of the European Union, the international level still lacks an object capable of being constitutionalized in the sense of that achievement. International public power is fragmented; it lies in the hands of a few entities, most of which are specialized in exercising one singular function—such as regulation of commerce, protection of the environment, enforcement of human rights—and therefore endowed with one single public power, so far not integrated in a coherent system.

Undoubtedly, all these entities are submitted to law. But legalization and constitutionalization are not the same. Because of their legal nature the treaties, charters etc fulfil a number of functions that constitutions fulfil in states. However, they all lack the democratic element and are confined to the rule of law element of constitutionalism. In terms of the achievement of constitutionalism they lag quite far behind.[99] Yet, this was and is true for a number of national constitutions as well. For typological purposes it should not matter. Typologies help to distinguish between phenomena that are treated under the same name. This is their value also when it comes to national and international constitutionalism.

Bibliography

D. Garcia Belaunde, F. Fernandez Segado, and R. Hernandez-Volle (eds), *Los sistemas constitucionales iberoamericanos* (1992)

Roberto Gargarella, *Towards a Typology of Latin American Constitutionalism* (2004) 39 *Latin American Research Review* 141

Dieter Grimm, *Die Zukunft der Verfassung* (3rd edn, 2002)

Dieter Grimm, 'The Achievement of Constitutionalism and its Prospects in a Changed World' in Petra Dobner and Martin Loughlin, *The Twilight of Constitutionalism* (2010)

Louis Henkin, 'A New Birth of Constitutionalism: Genetic Influences and Genetic Defects' in Michel Rosenfeld (ed), *Constitutionalism, Identity, Difference and Legitimacy* (1994)

Paul Kahn, 'Comparative Constitutionalism in a New Key' (2003) 101 *Michigan Law Review* 2677

Karl Loewenstein, *Political Power and the Governmental Process* (1957)

[98] Among the rapidly growing literature see eg Dobner and Loughlin (n 24); Vicki C. Jackson, *Constitutional Engagement in a Transnational Era* (2010); Nico Krisch, *Beyond Constitutionalism* (2010); Jeffrey L. Dunoff and Joel P. Trachtman (eds), *Ruling the World? Constitutionalism, International Law and Global Governance* (2009); Jan Klabbers, Anne Peters, and Geir Ulfstein, *The Constutionalization of International Law* (2009); R. St J. Macdonald and D.M. Johnston (eds), *Towards World Constitutionalism* (2005).

[99] Grimm (n 24).

Heinz Mohnhaupt and Dieter Grimm, *Verfassung. Zur Geschichte des Begriffs von der Antike bis zur Gegenwart* (2nd edn, 2002)

Michel Rosenfeld, *The Identity of the Constitutional Subject* (2010)

Carl Schmitt, *Verfassungslehre* (1928). In English: *Constitutional Theory* (Jeffrey Seitzer ed and trans, 2008)

Uwe Volkmann, 'Der Aufstieg der Verfassung. Beobachtungen zum grundlegenden Wandel des Verfassungsbegriffs' in Thomas Vesting and Stefan Korioth (eds), *Der Eigenwert des Verfassungsrechts* (2011)

CHAPTER 5

CONSTITUTIONALISM IN ILLIBERAL POLITIES

LI-ANN THIO

Singapore

I. Illiberal Constitutionalism as a Category

1. The Range of Constitutionalisms: The Generic and the Particular

The idea of 'constitutionalism in illiberal polities' appears oxymoronic, insofar as constitutionalism is considered the antidote to tyranny, and illiberalism, its instrument.[1] Walker proposed the existence of a category of 'non-liberal constitutionalism';[2] to dismiss this as hostile to the constitutionalist enterprise is oversimplistic but unsurprising, as the dominant model of liberal constitutionalism is often treated as synonymous with constitutionalism itself.[3] This occludes pre-liberal versions of 'ancient' constitutionalism and extant non-liberal models.

Constitutionalism resists arbitrary power, whether located in despotic rule or imposed absolutist principle; descriptively and analytically, its content remains ambiguous. While every polity

[1] On constitutionalism more generally, see Chapter 8.

[2] Graham Walker, 'The Idea of Nonliberal Constitutionalism' in Ian Shapiro and Will Kymlicka (eds), *Ethnicity and Group Rights* (1997), 154, 169.

[3] Anti-liberal Carl Schmitt considered that constitutions were illiberal in nature, appreciating that state preservation sometimes requires suspending the legal order: *Constitutional Theory* (1928).

has a constitution, not all practise constitutionalism. Constitutions as foundational instruments publicly articulate a polity's political identity and normative architecture, its values and structural distribution of power, defining inter-institutional and government–citizen relations. In being objectified and independent of the political agencies creating it, constitutions provide norms for evaluating the legitimacy of political action. Constitutionalism is sited where 'national history, custom, religion, social values and assumptions about government meet positive law'.[4]

The primary objective of 'generic constitutionalism' is to regulate state power through rule of law commitments and institutions, simultaneously empowering and restraining government action. Given form and purpose, 'power is not free to be anything and everything at any time'.[5] Liberal constitutionalism is a particular expression of this broader phenomenon, associated with the separation of powers, democratic elections, and judicially enforceable rights. Purposively, both liberal and non-liberal constitutionalist forms regulate power through 'the legal limitation on government'.[6]

Many countries today are not liberal societies nor are liberal norms embraced without reservation. 'Illiberal' polities are 'varied and competing',[7] encompassing illiberal, pre-liberal, non-liberal, or semi-liberal societies, producing 'communitarian' or 'theocratic' forms of constitutionalism. Degrees of 'illiberalism' are measured against the features of liberal polities. The 'uniformity' of non-liberal theory consists of a few basic assumptions and most importantly, 'a common enemy'[8]—liberal constitutionalism. To interrogate the idea, features, and role of constitutionalism in illiberal polities, the concepts of constitutionalism and liberalism must be disentangled.

2. Liberal Constitutionalism and its Discontents

There is no singular liberalism, but many liberalisms.[9] No settled list of liberal values, rights, or interpretive methods exist, as 'liberalism is defined less by a set of fixed characteristics than by its struggle against illiberalism'.[10]

Put simply, liberal societies rest on two main pillars. First, the meta-liberal value of normative individualism, which prioritizes individual autonomy, secured through constitutional rights. Secondly, the 'neutral' state which does not espouse a shared conception of the good, with individuals free to pursue their own conceptions. Arguably, the liberal state is disinterested in its citizens' character. In contrast, illiberal societies prioritize community interests and actively promote a particular vision of communal life.

Aside from structural limits on power, Rosenfeld identifies two distinct features of 'modern constitutionalism'. First, 'the protection of fundamental rights';[11] Murphy further declares that

[4] Lawrence Ward Beer (ed), 'Introduction', *Constitutional Systems in Late Twentieth Century Asia* (1992), 2.

[5] Graham Walker, 'The Constitutional Good: Constitutionalism's Equivocal Moral Imperative' (1993) 26(1) *Polity* 91, 94.

[6] Charles Howard McIlwain, *Constitutionalism: Ancient and Modern* (1947), 21.

[7] Graham Walker, 'The New Mixed Constitution: A Response to Liberal Debility and Constitutional Deadlock in Europe' (1994) 26(3) *Polity* 503, 506.

[8] Stephen Holmes, *The Anatomy of Antiliberalism* (1993).

[9] Chandran Kykathas, 'Two Concepts of Liberalism' in João Carlos Espada et al (eds), *The Liberal Tradition in Focus* (2000).

[10] Michel Rosenfeld and András Sajó, 'Spreading Liberal Constitutionalism: An Inquiry into the Fate of Free Speech Rights in New Democracies' in Sujit Choudhry et al (eds), *The Migration of Constitutional Ideas* (2005), 142, 143.

[11] Michel Rosenfeld, 'Modern Constitutionalism as Interplay between Identity and Diversity: An Introduction' (1993) 14 *Cardozo Law Review* 497.

constitutionalism's central principle is 'respect for human worth and dignity',[12] which imposes substantive constraints even where government represents popular will. The legitimating standard derived from human dignity reflects what Katz considers the core of the 'basic Western notion of liberal democratic constitutionalism', reflecting the 'rationalist Enlightenment manner' in American and European constitutional thought.[13] Generic constitutionalism 'does not imply a comprehensive or overriding commitment to individual rights'.[14] Secondly, 'a levelling of status-based hierarchies' to establish the egalitarian premise that all persons carry 'an inherent capacity for moral choice, self-respect and dignity'. This denotes a shift from feudal subjecthood to citizenship, circumscribing 'the number of possible legitimate orderings of relevant identities and differences'.[15] Thus, liberal norms give rise to a court-centric rights-based constitutionalism.

'Modern' constitutionalism corrected traditional constitutionalism's defect: the absence of effective limits on power. Where the sole limits on governors in traditional settings were drawn from vague norms derived from traditions, custom, and natural law, compliance turned on the goodwill of political rulers, as the only external sanction for interfering with liberties or undermining public weal was revolution, consistent with Lockean and Confucian philosophies.

Two political developments transformed traditional constitutionalism: first, popular sovereignty became the fount of constitutional authority, limiting political absolutism. Secondly, as natural law became unfashionable and the divine right of kings withered, the shift to modern constitutionalism was marked by the state becoming secular and later, liberal, separating the public/political from the private/social. As Ghai observed, 'Constitutionalism, with its constituent concepts of the secularization, nationalization, separation and limitation of public powers emerged in Europe as part of bourgeois revolutions.'[16]

However, liberal precepts predicated on universalist principles of freedom and equality of all today lack self-evident status; liberal constitutionalism has been criticized for its conceptions of the self, polity, and secularity as organizing ideals, and the constraint-oriented liberal state's inability positively to address multiculturalism and development issues. First, liberal individualism flows from a reductive approach towards human knowledge and faith in Western rationalism, producing what communitarians consider a false view of the atomistic person as the source of value, who sees identity as self-constructed and revisable; instead, the individual participates in and owes allegiance to a given community.

Secondly, liberalism does profess a theory of what constitutes a just, proper order, scepticism towards the a priori or Rawlsian comprehensive doctrines notwithstanding. Communitarians, critical race scholars, and feminists have criticized liberal neutrality for its homogenizing universalism, covert exclusions, and coercive injustice in imposing partisan substantive values that displace its predecessors, determining which freedoms and values to tolerate and privilege. Liberal constitutionalism bears a close correlation with 'a conception of the good that embeds a form of market capitalism and laissez faire economics into the political and legal structures that are found in society';[17] it does not liberate but rather forms an autonomist, experimental

[12] Walter Murphy, 'Constitutions, Constitutionalism and Democracy' in Douglas Greenberg et al (eds), *Constitutionalism and Democracy: Transitions in the Contemporary World* (1993), 3. On human dignity and autonomy, see Chapter 18.

[13] Stanley Katz, 'Constitutionalism and Civil Society' (2000), available at <http://www.princeton.edu/~snkatz/papers/JeffersonLecture.pdf>.

[14] Beer (n 4), 14.

[15] Rosenfeld (n 11), 502, 508.

[16] Yash Ghai, 'The Theory of the State in the Third World and the Problem of Constitutionalism' (1990–91) 6 *Connecticut Journlal of International Law* 411, 413.

[17] David T. Butler Ritchie, 'The Confines of Modern Constitutionalism' (2004–5) 3 *Pierce Law Review* 1.

choice-oriented disposition in citizens, which is defective in valorizing choice over what is chosen; in such settings, non-liberal groups find themselves 'legally privatized and socially on the defensive'.[18] In a 'procedural republic',[19] public life is animated by rights-based liberal ethics which may spawn adversarial hyper-individualism, precipitate social decay, and preclude reasoned discussion and compromise over public issues.[20] Liberalism may lack the normative resources to sustain group solidarity and a viable political community. Given its focus on negative liberties, liberal constitutionalism is unable to implement social programmes proactively to address issues of poverty, development, and environmental degradation, at odds with the 'social constitutionalist' model associated with Latin American countries, fuelled by Marxist and *indigenismo* ideology.

Last, liberal neutrality struggles to accommodate popular desires to accord public status to an official religion or ethno-national identity, given its focus on individuals, rather than corporate identity.[21] Liberalism is resisted where seen as a competing universalist logic which thwarts loyalties to the divine or where the liberal constitutionalist goal to create a universal, rationalist human association espouses an anti-religious rather than anti-theocratic secularism which seeks to privatize and purge 'illiberal' religion from the public square; such 'hyper-liberalism' is as anti-constitutionalist as fascist rule.[22] Notably, constitutionalism *simpliciter* does not require 'moral or metaphysical scepticism'.[23] More moderate liberal visions recognize the legitimate role of religious convictions in public debate, subject to 'public reason', which some consider an appeal to subjective preferences. From the religionist's perspective, government indifference towards religion is tantamount to government promotion of 'religious relativism' such that state 'religious neutralism' operates as a 'civil religion'.[24] Liberal counter-arguments assert that liberalism's exclusions are less dangerous than those of authoritarian, paternalistic illiberalisms, claiming that liberalism's exclusions are less dangerous; liberalism has evolved and accommodates some forms of ethno-cultural diversity. Further, liberalism does not privatize morality; rather, liberal rights and values 'constitute a public morality';[25] and forms, rather than supplants, valuable communities.[26]

3. Anatomy of Constitutionalism in an Illiberal Polity

Unlike anti-constitutionalist regimes, illiberal polities do not lack limiting constitutive norms; constitutions in non-liberal polities may not primarily rely on individual rights but resort to methods such as federalism or separated powers to constrain public power. The state is expressly non-neutral, privileging a substantive vision of the good, informed by ethnicity, religion, or communal morality.[27]

[18] Graham Walker, 'The Mixed Constitution after Liberalism' (1996) 4 *Cardozo Journal of International and Comparative Law* 311, 320.

[19] Michael Sandel, 'The Political Theory of the Procedural Republic' in Gary C. Bryner and Noel B. Reynolds (eds), *Constitutionalism and Rights* (1987), 141.

[20] Mary Ann Glendon, *Rights Talk* (1991).

[21] See Chapter 43.

[22] Walker (n 2), 170–1.

[23] Ibid 176.

[24] Walker (n 18), 321–2.

[25] Stephen Macedo, 'The Constitution of Liberalism' in Stephen Macedo, *Liberal Virtues: Citizenship, Virtue and Community in Liberal Constitutionalism* (1990), 163, 169.

[26] Ibid 201.

[27] Walker (n 18), 315, 319.

4. Mixed Constitutionalism

The dominant position of the liberal-constitutionalist paradigm has been challenged by the existing variety of non-liberal and semi-liberal constitutions celebrating the community, sometimes against minority interests, as within Israel or American tribal societies.

All societies have a mix of liberal and illiberal practices, as 'the liberality of a culture is a matter of degree'. Given the absolutizing tendencies of both liberal and non-liberal principles such as individualism and nationalism, Walker proposed their reconciliation through a 'mixed constitution' which 'juxtaposes liberal and non-liberal principles (and institutions)' to moderate the absolutism of either side through acknowledging the 'defeasibility of all rival justice principles'.[28] Arguably, mixed constitutions which explicitly prefer non-liberal communal values are more respectful of difference than 'either wholesale liberalism or illiberalism',[29] as partial establishment supports some truth claims while tempering absolutist truth claims through respecting dissent and public truth-seeking. This vindicates the purpose of constitutionalism: to temper any form of absolutism, royal, liberal, or illiberal.

Breslin considers 'nonliberal or semi-liberal constitutions' as 'not wholly modern'[30] though they may best suit the political regime desired. Mixed constitutions, blending individual protection and communal values with counterbalancing institutions, are reflected in various post-Communist East European constitutions, as a moderating strategy. Nonetheless, he argues these are not 'objective' constitutions in that they do not exist independently of the empowering institutions, nor do they impose discernible limits on the sovereign. The German Basic Law is categorized as semi-liberal, being external to the German polity, and it is considered more objective than the governing charter of the unwritten Israeli Constitution.[31] The Israeli state sponsors a particular communitarianism founded on a vision of Jewish statehood the mission of which is promoting Jewish culture—embodied in the norms governing symbols and language; the Law of Return benefitting diaspora Jews; vesting state functions in religious bodies; and the absence of civil marriage—within a non-theocratic state with a secular judiciary. While the Israeli polity protects individual rights such as religious freedom, this is subordinate to Jewish unity, which legitimates restrictions on anti-Jewish speech or action; thus, communitarian priorities may 'suppress the liberal inclinations of its citizens'.[32] While non-Jews enjoy individual rights within a plural democracy where 'egalitarian norms are determined by a logic of pluralism' and 'cultural autonomy takes precedence over assimilation',[33] they are 'barred from meaningfully contributing to Israel's common good',[34] reflecting qualitative tiers of citizenship. Notably, constitutions committed to a secular liberal democracy may also deploy illiberal measures, such as restricting the associational rights of political parties advocating the introduction of Islamic law, which challenges Turkish *laïcité*.[35]

German rights clauses are classified as 'semi-liberal' in blending 'liberal declarations with undeniably communitarian ones'.[36] While individual rights and the inviolability of human

[28] Ibid 315, 318–19.

[29] Ibid 327.

[30] Beau Breslin, *The Communitarian Constitution* (2004), 183.

[31] Ibid 188.

[32] Ibid 186.

[33] Gary Jeffrey Jacobsohn, 'Alternative Pluralisms: Israel and American Constitutionalism in Comparative Perspective' (1989) 51(2) *Review of Politics* 159, 176.

[34] Breslin (n 30), 187.

[35] *Refah Partisi v Turkey* 42 ILM 560 (2003).

[36] Breslin (n 30), 186.

dignity comport with liberal individualism, the right of persons freely to develop their personality must not violate other rights or offend 'the constitutional order or the moral law'.[37] This 'critical nonliberal component' may temper 'the hyperindividualism tendencies of predominantly liberal regimes'.[38] The critical point is that non-liberal rights clauses in securing communal values ahead of liberal ones do not restrain majority will or limit government power as effectively as an individualist reading of a liberal right. The 'community-based component' in the form of duties owed to the state allows decision-makers to counterbalance individual entitlements against 'competing ideological values of possibly equal constitutional import',[39] derived from history or tradition, such as the German tradition of *Sozialstaat*, a blend of Christianity, liberalism, and socialism which considers citizen welfare paramount.[40] The West German Constitutional Court stated that the Basic Law rejects the notion of the 'isolated sovereign individual'; in adjudicating rights, the court seeks to relate 'the citizen to the community... without detracting from his individuality'.[41]

Further along the 'illiberal' end of the scale are rights preceded by a clause authorizing restrictions that the legislature considers 'necessary or expedient' on stipulated grounds, as in Malaysian and Singaporean free speech guarantees. The instrumental criterion of 'expediency' permits more state discretion than a substantive restraint which only legitimates limits 'necessary in a democratic society', after the European human rights model.

The relational dimension of identity, apart from autonomy, is particularly important in multicultural societies. These grapple with the distinct issue of whether and how a liberal polity, founded on political individualism, should 'tolerate' or accommodate illiberal groups defined by indigeneity, ethnicity, culture, or religion within the broader polity, and the capacity of constitutionalism to 'transform the unfathomable power of the ethnos into the responsible authority of the demos'.[42]

II. Illiberal Constitutionalisms: A Typology

1. Theocratic Constitutionalism

Insofar as religion is considered an illiberal force in the public realm, it challenges liberalism's 'rational and tolerant ethos';[43] conflict occurs where religious and secular liberal values compete to be the sole source of authority governing social relations.

Modern constitutionalism rejects non-secular authority; secular constitutionalism marks a shift from divine to human or popular sovereignty. The ideal of a liberal secular state operating upon a dichotomous ordering of the temporal/spiritual or public/private is alien to religions such as Islam where religion and politics are indivisible and only God is sovereign. While the equal treatment of religions by a constitutionally secular state is considered the best solution to religiously diverse societies, this alienates those wanting a religious basis to the

[37] Art 2(1), Grundgesetz, GG.

[38] Breslin (n 30), 184.

[39] Ibid 202.

[40] Ibid 200–1.

[41] BVerfGE 12 (7 July 1970).

[42] Ulrich Preuss, 'Constitutional Powermaking for the New Polity: Some Deliberations on the Relations between Constituent Power and the Constitution' (1993) 14 *Cardozo Law Review* 639, 660.

[43] Michael W. McConnell, 'Why is Religious Liberty the "First Freedom"' (2000) 21 *Cardozo Law Review* 1234, 1244.

constitutional order, and resentful of how liberal secularism marginalizes religion from public life. An aggressively anti-theistic secularism can operate like a theocratic republic in sacrificing pluralism to secure 'its transcendent goal of secular modernity'.[44]

In an increasingly re-enchanted world, religion is a powerful force in shaping constitutional orders. There exists a range of state–religion models, manifesting varying degrees of state separation, cooperation, and sponsorship of religion. These reside between two polar extremes: first, pure theocratic systems where supreme religious and political leadership is unified, such as the former Hindu Kingdom of Nepal or Saudi Arabia, where the Quran and Sunnah are the constitution;[45] secondly, strict separationist systems, as in France where religion is largely privatized. Where a constitution accords religion a public role, status, or otherwise privileges religion(s), which may be inegalitarian and illiberal, the challenge is to realize 'a functional governmental structure' where 'religious norms constitutionally balance with human rights and democratic norms.'[46] This is faced by all constitutions which refer to a religion as a source of national identity or law, establish religions, or permit public religious expression. An intermediate category of theocratic constitutionalism may be identified which defies both strict separation and union of religion and state; here, religious authority and political authority are formally separated and their officials operate within the constitutional framework, which must provide sufficient institutional checks and rights guarantees to prevent autocratic rule, religious or otherwise.

Constitutions address the status of religion(s) variously: they may simultaneously affirm popular sovereignty while recognizing an official religion(s) integral to 'the polity's national meta-narrative',[47] without precluding the coexistence of other religions. The Sri Lankan Constitution affirms the state's obligation to foster Buddhist doctrine while safeguarding other religions' rights.[48] The current Thai Constitution declares that the state 'shall patronise and protect Buddhism' as the majority religion, as well as other religions, and 'encourage the application of religious principles to create virtue and develop the quality of life'.[49] Drawing on religious values to articulate a common good is considered illiberal. Theocratic constitutions may designate religious law as *the* or *a* source of state law relevant to legislation and adjudication. Further, legislation inconsistent with religious law, like *syariah*, may be prohibited, as under Article 67 of the Maldivian Constitution.

Islamic constitutionalism is the most frequent type of theocratic constitutionalism examined, minimally involving the incorporation of Islamic principles within a constitutional scheme of limited powers, where the constitutional text identifies religious law—itself an internally diverse category—as a source of state law.[50] Jurists as interpreters of Islamic law continue their historic guardianship as 'a type of Fourth Branch to an Islamic constitutional government',[51] with constitutional provisions ranging from government duties to consult jurists in legislative or judicial processes, to according jurists final interpretive authority.

[44] Gunes Murat Tezcur, 'Constitutionalism, Judiciary and Democracy in Islamic Societies' (2007) 39(4) *Polity* 479, 493.

[45] Constitution of Saudi Arabia, Arts 1–8 (1992).

[46] Intisar Rabb, '"We the Jurists": Islamic Constitutionalism in Iraq' (2007–08) 10 *University of Pennsylvania Journal of Constitutional Law* 527, 555.

[47] Ran Hirschl, 'The Rise of Constitutional Theocracy' (2008) 49 *Harvard International Law Journal Online* 72.

[48] Constitution of Sri Lanka, Arts 3, 9, 10 (1978).

[49] Thai Constitution, sec 79 (2007).

[50] On Islam and the constitutional order, see Chapter 62.

[51] Rabb (n 46), 577.

In theocratic constitutional orders, political authority is not exclusively derived from a divine source, operating within a constitutional framework committed to secularism or some form of democratic process. Constitutions may resort to legal pluralism through institutionalizing religious authority to implement religious law, which may uneasily coexist with civil courts, clashing over issues of overlapping jurisdiction or judicial hierarchy and supervision.

Some reject the idea that religion may be a possible normative basis for constitutional orders. Hirschl considers the prospect of constitutional theocracy defective and dangerous, as religious affiliation transcends national bonds, rendering unavailable consociational or power-sharing mechanisms which mitigate chauvinistic ethno-nationalist impulses.[52] While to be respected, religion must be subordinated, with constitutional courts as the guardians of secularism, lest religious institutions supervise government activity. Constitutionalism cannot exist where transcendent concerns ground public decisions, as secularism insists 'on the possibility of a reason-based political society'.[53] The countervailing view is that all decision-making, based on religious or non-religious grounds such as perception and intuition, rests on someone's privileged insight, including a liberal state's assumption of neutrality between competing goods, which 'rests on untestable faith'.[54] Religion has been argued to be a rational discipline, as revelation is an evolving understanding of the moral universe, mediated through human interpretation.[55] Excluding religion from the liberal public sphere is an act of self-impoverishment, unfairly burdening religious citizens.

Liberal constitutionalism's commitment to equality is incompatible with a system where religious affiliation governs membership and capacity to participate in a polity, as where Maldivian non-Muslims cannot be citizens.[56] The danger is that members of the recognized religion may treat other religionists unequally. A concern with 'Islamic constitutionalism' is the perpetuation of historical *syariah*'s structure of religious discrimination, between men/women and superior believers/inferior non-believers, or *dhimmis*, who paid poll taxes in submission to Muslim sovereignty. The inability to accord full citizenship to all would perpetuate tensions in plural societies and constitute religious tyranny, not religiously grounded constitutionalist government.

The converse view admits the possibility that theocratic constitutionalism may be a 'normatively different'[57] but legitimate form of 'preferred values-based constitutionalism'.[58] The Iranian Constitution falls within this category, as it constitutes a religious state and organizes it through law. This provides some measure of direct accountability, as opposed to the Saudi Arabian polity whose powerful executive is 'circumscribed only by historical practices and Islamic ideas of governance',[59] a self-regulatory model.

The Iranian government is structured on the basis of separating the legislature, judiciary, and executive, supervised by the religious leadership.[60] Democratic elements exist: the people

[52] Ran Hirschl, 'The Theocratic Challenge to Constitution-Drafting in Post Conflict States' (2008) 49 *William and Mary Law Review* 1179, 1186.

[53] András Sajó, 'Constitutionalism and Secularism: The Need for Public Reason' (2009) 30 *Cardozo Law Review* 2401.

[54] Scott Idleman, 'The Role of Religious Values in Decision Making' (1993) 68 *Indiana Law Journal* 433, 446.

[55] Abdolkarim Soroush, *Reason, Freedom and Democracy in Islam: Essential Writings of Abdolkarim Souroush* (2000), 133, 144.

[56] Constitution of the Maldives, Art 9(d).

[57] Larry Cata-Becker, 'Theocratic Constitutionalism: An Introduction to a New Global Legal Ordering' (2009) 16 *Indiana Journal of Global Legal Studies* 101, 126.

[58] Ibid 131.

[59] Abdulaziz Al-Faad, 'Ornamental Constitutionalism: The Saudi Basic Law of Governance' (2005) 30 *Yale Journal of International Law* 375

[60] Constitution of Iran, Art 57.

elect the President and Islamic Consultative Assembly. Assembly deliberations are public. A qualified religious scholar heads the judiciary which dispenses Islamic justice and has in practice sustained clerical rule by upholding restrictive laws and suppressing dissent.[61] Jurists composing the Guardian Council review legislation for consistency with Islamic tenets.[62]

In post-Khomeini Iran, political and religious authority were de facto separated when the criteria for the Leader (*faqih*), the 'just and pious'[63] jurist who wields supreme authority, were broadened to include non-religious qualifications such as 'political and social perspicacity' and administrative competence; he is chosen by experts elected by the people. Thus, the polity seeks to realize Quranic justice and God's will under a religious guardianship which pursues a constitutionally mandated religious conception of the good; the government is tasked with cultivating value, securing political freedoms and a just economic system, and with strengthening universal Islamic brotherhood, for instance.[64] The exercise of constitutional rights such as association and assembly does not have to be detrimental to Islamic principles; the citizen's right to seek justice through judicial recourse is preserved.[65] The government must respect the human rights of recognized religious minorities, provided they do not conspire against the Islamic Republic.

Here, power is structured, not unbounded; this can produce a constitutional order whose 'internal logic' is rooted in 'theories of right and justice, permitting accountability and limiting discretion'.[66] Nonetheless, government by guardians possessing 'unique knowledge, wisdom and virtue'[67] in deeply religious societies, poses a perennial challenge to liberal democracies where judicial review operates as an external accountability check. The danger 'strong religion' poses to liberal constitutionalism is evident where religion seeks to govern social life contrary to human rights standards and where the insufficient separation of religion and state hampers competitive politics and pluralism.

Theocratic constitutionalism can rest on two different foundations of religious and liberal values. Such constitutions may contain justiciable fundamental rights, acknowledge popular sovereignty, and frame a national identity; the Egyptian Constitution constitutes an Arab nation and contains a 'constitutional Islamization' clause recognizing 'principles of the Islamic sharia' as the 'principal source of legislation'.[68] In such polities, the degree to which rights such as religious freedom and equality are enjoyed depends upon secular court jurisprudence. The Egyptian Constitutional Court acts as de facto interpreter of religious norms, having developed a creative interpretive technique which enables it to construe *syariah* law consistently with human rights, as part of the broader government objective of securing human welfare.[69] Judicial review, by providing authoritative interpretation and meaningful restraint on government power, advances rule of law values within illiberal polities.

Conversely, courts in polities with constitutional Islamization clauses may undermine constitutionalism, where secular judges import personal conceptions of religious law into constitutional interpretation, rendering individual rights nugatory and legitimating unequal treatment towards religious minorities. A case in point concerns how the explosive issue of

[61] Tezcur (n 44), 486.
[62] Constitution of Iran, Art 91.
[63] Ibid Art 5.
[64] Ibid Art 3.
[65] Ibid Arts 19–42.
[66] Cata-Becker (n 57), 155.
[67] Robert A. Dahl, *Democracy and its Critics* (1989), 52.
[68] Constitution of Egypt, Arts 1, 2, 3.
[69] Clark B. Lombardi and Nathan J. Brown, 'Do Constitutions Requiring Adherence to Shariah Threaten Human Rights? How Egypt's Constitutional Court Reconciles Islamic Law with the Liberal Rule of Law' (2005–06) 21 *American University International Law Review* 379.

apostasy of Muslims in Muslim-majority Malaysia is handled. The courts have treated religious conversions not as a function of voluntarist religious choice, but as a public order issue. In restrictively construing the scope of the recognized right to profess and practise religion, the High Court in *Lina Joy v Majlis Agama Islam Wilayah*[70] referenced Article 3, which identifies Islam as the Federation's religion, to underscore the government's duty to promote and defend Islam in recognizing its 'special position' as 'the main and dominant religion', and to emphasize qualifications to religious liberty. At inception, Malaysia was understood to be a secular nation;[71] the constitutional reference to Islam was meant to be ceremonial, not substantive; its judicial invocation was not to buttress liberal readings of the right to have or not have a religion, as some Islamic schools of thought allow; rather, it read religious freedom down, highlighting the Islamic community's concern towards losing a member. An affidavit from a formerly Muslim Malay woman who had become Christian was inadequate, as the court insisted that the issue was not governed by personal choice but by religious law, as unilateral conversion would precipitate chaos and confusion. She was directed to seek a declaration of apostasy from the *syariah* courts, which have never issued one to a living Malay; indeed, apostates may be preventively detained at religious rehabilitation centres, rendering the right to leave Islam under *syariah* law illusory. The court held that religious freedom did not contain the right to free conscience or religious choice, contrary to human rights standards, further asserting that the Malays could never leave Islam given the constitutional definition of a 'Malay' as a person 'who professes the religion of Islam, habitually speaks the Malay language, conforms to Malay custom'. This constitutional assignment of an apparently immutable religious identity, conflating ethnicity with religious affiliation, is oppressive and falls below the Rawlsian standard of 'decent nonliberal peoples'[72] in precluding exit from the nonliberal group. Islamic constitutionalism is not monolithic, as the interpretation of *syariah* law is a contested terrain, but this example illustrates a conflict with liberal constitutionalism.

Where religion as meta-ideology defines right and justice, apostasy may be viewed not as an exercised right to religious freedom, but as a grave political act. As a state founded on religious imperatives requires a community of believers for sustenance, losing a member diminishes the community and threatens public order, as apprehended by an Islamic polity. Religious freedoms for Muslims are not individual entitlements, but interests subject to Islamic requirements. Only non-Muslims have religious conversion rights, as the attenuated religious rights of Malays are subject to laws protecting the religious community.

2. Communitarian Constitutionalism: Cultural Imperatives, Developmentalist Priorities

Within liberal polities, socio-political organization is founded on the impersonal application of universal legal norms and democracy is associated primarily with rights. This leads to an asymmetric neglect of civic duties, responsibilities, and the common good which non-liberal communitarian polities prioritized. Where communitarian constitutionalism is practised, insiders esteem group interests like social harmony and national loyalty as co-equal if not pre-eminent, to autonomist values. The socially embedded rather than unencumbered self is the adopted vision where the community plays a role in forming personal identity and moral choice, with the state committed to equipping citizens to participate in self-rule.

[70] [2004] 2 MLJ 119 (High Court).

[71] Jospeh M. Fernando, *The Making of the Malayan Constitution* (2002).

[72] John Rawls, *The Law of Peoples: With the Idea of Public Reason Revisited* (2001), 61.

Courts tend to play a secondary rather than counterbalancing role to democratic processes in adjudicating rights; in rejecting rights-based liberalism, a more balanced approach favours a relational framework predicated on mutual responsibility which seeks to optimize interdependence, individual rights, and public good. Political, rather than legal, constitutionalist forms are relied on to secure accountability by achieving a balance of political power through consensus-seeking schemes of participatory democracy.

As the government determines collective interests, the constitutionalist quality of communitarian polities depends on whether institutional structures conduce to an authentic representation of community will in discussing internal communal values, beyond majoritarian or elite will. Breslin argues that communitarian constitutions exist 'only in premodern forms',[73] lacking strong accountability mechanisms and objectivity insofar as they defend internally derived political values and lack the self-conscious articulation of constitutional constraints.[74]

Communitarianism can too easily be invoked to promote statist values or constitutional authoritarianism, where the constitution is conceived as a tool of control, as associated with instrumentalist analysis of how communist parties utilize socialist constitutions to advance their agenda. To rein in its collectivizing impulse, community norms should realize some 'overarching values'[75] to allow some distance between the individual and the group; such polities should be pluralist to avoid perpetuating the exclusion of 'historically marginalised groups'.[76]

Prioritized collective interests may provide the justification for sustaining a 'strong state', where law facilitates effective government. The collective interest may be framed as protecting particularist communitarian cultures, often against the negative effects of Western liberal individualism; it may relate to promoting a national ideology or constitutional patriotism of sorts, in defining a diverse polity or constructing a nation by invoking common ideals or a shared future, in the absence of a historical nation.

The collective interest may be cast as an agenda for economic growth and development, requiring centralized state power able to maintain discipline and public order necessary to attract foreign investment and trade, which fuels economic take-off. This process is associated with the 'Asian values' model of law and development which economically successful East and South East Asian developmentalist states such as China, Singapore, and Malaysia, have articulated. This model, built on a thin rule of law which protects economic interests rather than political rights, posits that Western-style human rights and democracy be restricted until a certain level of development is attained as these are thought to flow sequentially rather than simultaneously through mutual reinforcement.[77] Developmentally oriented authoritarian rulers aloof from interest-group politics are better able to provide long-term stability by securing compliance with predictable rules.

Arguably, constitutionalism may facilitate economic reform and continued economic activity in rapidly developing societies by offering citizens and investors reliable transparency and consolidating democracy, which promotes orderly debate and informational flows essential for efficient markets.

Economic liberalization has in some cases given way to political liberalization, as in Japan, South Korea, and Taiwan where culture influences the workings of liberal constitutionalist imports. For example, South Korean courts, in choosing to declare legislation 'non-conformable' with the constitution rather than inconsistent and void, have manifested a 'Confucianist

[73] Breslin (n 30), 149.

[74] Ibid 181.

[75] Amitai Etizioni, 'A Moderate Communitarian Proposal' (1996) 24 *Political Theory* 159, 163.

[76] Will Kymlicka, *Liberalism, Community and Culture* (1989), 82–7.

[77] Amartya Sen, *Development as Freedom* (2000).

constitutionalism' in seeking to enter into dialogue with the President and Assembly to urge legal reform, rather than to act confrontationally. This reflects the mode of remonstrance by which scholars sought to check the Emperor, who wielded indivisible powers, when he acted contrary to *li* or ritual propriety.[78]

However, many Asian states with communitarian traditions are gradually liberalizing, while remaining committed to protecting a particular culture or religion. While constitutionalism is about constraining power, democracy is about accumulating power; 'elections and authoritarianism'[79] combined have produced a form of illiberal democracy which perpetuates the strong state. That 'decades of authoritarian governance in Africa...have yielded economic ruin, not development'[80] indicates that discipline and order alone do not produce economic growth; wise rulers, an anti-corruption culture, and 'Asian values', in the form of hard work, thrift, education, family—a kind of Protestant work ethic *sans* Western accent on individualism—are also required. This was the corrective to the egoism, dysfunctional families, and disrespect for public authority in the West.

Non-liberal religious and racially diverse polities like Malaysia and Singapore which inherited the British legacy of parliamentary democracy have drawn on culture, at least selectively, to construct a unifying national ideology. The brand of constitutionalism practised in Singapore is instructive in illustrating how rights, democracy, and national identity are addressed within non-liberal post-colonial constitutional orders driven by cultural imperatives and overriding economic priorities. The context is that of a strong, if not hegemonic, executive operating within a dominant party parliamentary system which has yet to experience political turnover, post-Independence; the dominant People's Action Party (PAP) is able to amend the supreme Constitution at will, as it commands more than the required two-thirds super-majority. Singapore's preferred ideological moorings are constructed by selective reference to traditional values and contained in a White Paper on 'shared values';[81] this is a form of 'soft constitutional law' which, while not legally binding, has some legal effect in defining the polity's character through hortatory norms, and appears to be reflected in judicial reasoning. Three points bear mention.

First, the communitarian bent of 'nation before community and society above self' is contrary to liberalism's commitment to limited government and maximized individual freedoms. The White Paper rejects the American distrust of concentrated powers, rooted in the Humean view that men are knaves. Instead, neo-Confucianist influences are evident in asserting the 'concept of government by honourable men (*junzi*)', who are duty-bound to act rightly for the people who trust and respect them, 'fits us better than the Western idea that a government should be given as limited powers as possible, and should always be treated with suspicion unless proven otherwise.' Within the context of an elective democracy, the Confucian idea of rule by a trustworthy, virtuous, educated elite bears resonance, distinct from liberal constitutionalism's preoccupation with external modes of accountability. This idea appears consistent with the heightened judicial valuation of the reputation of public men in political libel cases. Singaporean jurisprudence rejects the public figure doctrine and does not impute a heightened value to political speech; nor has free speech been fully theorized as serving democratic purposes through robust public debate. In balancing speech rights with reputational interests, two

[78] Tom Ginsburg, 'Confucian Constitutionalism? The Emergence of Constitutional Review in Korea and Taiwan' (2002) 27(4) *Law and Social Inquiry* 763, 780.

[79] Fareed Zakaria, *The Future of Freedom: Illiberal Democracy at Home and Abroad* (2003), 91.

[80] Kivutha Kibwana, 'Human Rights and/or Economic Development: Which Way Africa' in *Third World Legal Studies* (1993), 43.

[81] Cmd 1 of 1991.

things have been emphasized. First, the common interest in providing sufficient protection to 'sensitive and honourable men'[82] to ensure they are undeterred from seeking public office, where they may incur strong criticism. Secondly, the primacy of reputational interests; the High Court referenced Isocrates in underscoring the 'utmost importance' of character and an honourable name in inspiring trust and the ability to persuade one's listeners. If the plaintiffs, who held high ministerial office, were not publicly vindicated of libellous accusations, this would immensely damage 'their political reputation and moral authority as leaders'.[83] As defamation law presupposes an image of how people are relationally situated, the conceptualization and valuation of reputation affects the scope of free expression. The Singaporean approach seems consonant with the treatment of reputation as a form of honour, which is associated with a 'deference society' where individuals in a stratified setting are unequal; here, honour is not an individual attribute or attainment but flows from an ascribed social status.[84] Since it involves shared social perception, it is a public good; defamation law seeks to restore honour, which damages cannot comprehend. However, the award of onerous, punitive damages for political libel chills speech and discounts the value of political speech to democratic flourishing. Human dignity and the inviolability of personal honour outweighs liberal, free-speech conceptions, as embodied in US doctrine based on the marketplace of ideas and rational discourse.

Secondly, the value of 'consensus instead of contention' has manifested in the government's preferred brand of politics, the quality of democracy embodied in institution-making, and the role of the press. The idea of consensualist rather than adversarial politics is not unique to Singapore's brand of 'paternal democracy'—Indonesian President Sukarno rejected Western-style democracy in favour of a '*gotong royong* democracy', which advocates cooperation and mutual agreement in decision making. However, the question of the inclusiveness of this process cannot be ignored. The Singaporean Constitution was amended to reconfigure the electoral system from single-member constituencies to include Group Representation Constituencies in 1988, contested by teams of between three and six; one member must belong to a stipulated minority community. The ostensible object was to enshrine multiracialism through an ethnically-based legislative quota, although the scheme was subsequently amended to add local governance functions through managing town councils, each headed by an elected parliamentarian. This motive was to curb voter irresponsibility, expressed through casting anti-PAP protest votes, by inducing voter sobriety in selecting not a demagogue but an effective representative able to run a town estate. This would stabilize the political system and, not coincidentally, buttress PAP political dominance. Reminiscent of colonial tutelage schemes, the government argued that the opposition, which won six of 87 elective seats in the 2011 General Elections, should first learn how to run an estate, before aspiring to run the state.[85]

Additionally, two classes of unelected parliamentarians were created: the Non-Constituency (NCMP) and Nominated (NMP) Member of Parliament, both with diminished voting powers. The NCMP was uniquely designed to ensure a minimum number of parliamentary representatives not from the governing party.[86] Up to three NCMP seats would be provided to the top three

[82] Philip Lewis (ed), *Gatley on Libel and Slander* (8th edn, 1981), 206, quoted with approval in *Jetyaretnam v Lee Kuan Yew* (1992) 2 SLR 310 (Court of Appeal).

[83] *Lee Hsien Loong v Singapore Democracy Party* [2009] 1 SLR 642, 690.

[84] Robert Post, 'The Social Foundations of Defamation Law: Reputation and the Constitution' (1986) 74(3) *California Law Review* 691, 699–704.

[85] Li-ann Thio, 'The Right to Political Participation in Singapore: Tailor-Making a Westminster-Modelled Constitution to Fit the Imperatives of "Asian" Democracy' (2002) 6 *Singapore Journal of International Comparative Law* 181, 216–29.

[86] Constitution of Singapore, Art 39(1)(b).

losing opposition candidates, provided none won a seat outright. They would form the adversarial component of the House. Conversely, the NMP scheme would produce a source of 'constructive dissent', where nine individuals with no party-political affiliation and who were distinguished in their fields would be selected by a parliamentary committee to provide 'a range of independent and non-partisan' views. Their expertise would enhance parliamentary debates as the PAP has regularly affirmed, subtly undermining opposition politicians. Both schemes have been cast as the PAP-guided evolution of the political system as society matures and a more educated citizenry wants to debate national matters, while preserving good governance in the form of a government representing the varied interests in a plural society but able to act decisively.

In this managed democracy, parliamentary institutions fostering a wider range of views may promote consensus-seeking and minimize confrontation, particularly through co-opting politically unaligned voices. However, having alternative views does not translate into the crucial political check of an alternative government; in fact, these institutions may consolidate the political status quo of a 'strong state', as the constitutional provision of up to 18 unelected parliamentarians (and 84 elected seats) might sate the desire for oppositional politics. If so, the legislative within such 'electoral autocracies'[87] cannot effectively check an executive which controls an overwhelming majority of parliamentary seats.

In a democracy, the press wields tremendous power to influence public opinion without itself being accountable. The government's rejection of the press as the Fourth Estate or adversarial watchdog is also designed to mute contention, being a realistic posture against journalistic bias, sensationalism, and profit motive. The Singaporean government has issued informal guidelines instructing the press to report the news as a 'neutral medium'[88] rather than to advance political agendas. The executive urges a doctrine of responsible journalism, where the press acts as an instrument of nation-building rather than a check on political power, in explaining government policies in a consensus-building manner; criticisms must be constructive, not combative. The Court of Appeal has stated there is no room in Singapore for investigative journalism 'which carries with it a political agenda'.[89]

Thirdly, 'rights talk' has become almost synonymous with liberal constitutionalism, where judicial review restraints government by excluding appeals to collective goals or utilitarianism to justify limiting rights. This suggests a prioritization of interests which constitutional rights are supposed to secure, which is not reflected in Singaporean communitarian jurisprudence. Rather than immunizing individual entitlement from collective welfare claims, rights in non-liberal polities may be qualified where government intervention and the social meaning this expresses is consistent with the polity's character and priorities. While the shared values affirm the importance of 'regard and community support for the individual', the assertion that Asian societies like Singapore weigh group interests more heavily than individual ones tempers this. Thus, restricting individual due process, privacy, or equality rights in entrapment operations to curtail drug trafficking are justified by the social value of anti-drug-trafficking laws.[90] Property rights are not personal entitlements but have a 'public' dimension carrying social obligations; individual rights must give way to the public weal, effectuated by compulsory land acquisition laws with minimal compensation.[91]

[87] Fareed Zakaria, 'The Rise of Illiberal Democracy' (1997) 76 *Foreign Affairs* 23.

[88] K. Shanmugam (Home Affairs Minister), 'A Free Press for a Global Society', Columbia University, 4 November 2010.

[89] *Review Publishing Co Ltd v Lee Hsien Loong* [2010] 1 SLR 52 (Court of Appeal, Singapore).

[90] *Mohamed Emran bin Mohamed Ali v Public Prosecutor* [2008] 4 SLR 411.

[91] Li-ann Thio, 'Protecting Rights' in Li-ann Thio and Kevin Tan (eds), *The Evolution of a Revolution: 40 Years of the Singapore Constitution* (2009), 193, 200.

Rights are defeasible; 'public order', broadly construed, apparently trumps constitutional rights. Rights may be more usefully conceived structurally as 'channeling the kinds of reasons government can invoke when it acts in certain ways'.[92] Rights do not serve atomistic interests but realize common goods.

Preserving racial and religious harmony in multiracial and religiously diverse polities like Malaysia, Sri Lanka, and Singapore is an integral aspect of 'public order', a ground for restricting rights. Given the history of race riots in Peninsular Malaya and the position of the Chinese majority city-state of Singapore in a Malay-Muslim region, the 'especial sensitivity' of race and religion has domestic and geopolitical ramifications. The prospect of disrupting racial and religious harmony presents a bright line signalling the limits of free speech. Individuals making pejorative remarks against racial or religious minorities, particularly Malay-Muslims, have been successfully prosecuted under sedition laws for promoting feelings of ill-will or hostility between different races. Free speech is balanced against the interest of another's 'freedom from offence' and the broader public interest, considering the potential harm to one racial group and society at large. A commitment to pluralism obliges Singaporeans to refrain from acts which incite 'racial strife and violence';[93] thus, free speech is severely restricted where balanced against, or overwhelmed by, co-equal or prioritized communitarian concern in maintaining inter-religious peace and promoting the civic virtue of civility.

The fundamental imperative of 'racial harmony' stultifies public debate over sensitive issues, preventing a 'deep understandings, and cultural boundary-crossings as befitting a liberal conceptualization of "multiculturalism" '.[94] An individual-centric rights-oriented political culture is rejected in favour of a responsibilities- and public good-oriented discourse. While communitarian interests may legitimately define the contours of individual rights, without denuding them of content, the danger is that appeals to communitarianism guise the imposition of statist values in the name of expediency or efficiency. For example, a Singapore court justified a blanket ban rather than a proportionate targeted restriction on Jehovah's Witnesses' publications, because their beliefs oppose compulsory military service, as 'any order other ... would have been impossible to monitor administratively'.[95] This religious group had been deregistered under the Societies Act as their pacifist beliefs were considered 'prejudicial to public welfare and good order'. Rather than requiring the demonstration of a substantial risk to public order to justify restricting constitutional liberties, the court structured the balancing process in terms of ascertaining whether the right had a tendency to detract from the 'sovereignty, integrity and unity of Singapore'[96] which was extra-textually declared a paramount constitutional mandate. The court's statist orientation is also evident where, speaking in terms of rights limits, it conflated 'public order', which applies to general situations, with 'national security', which is reserved for exceptional situations relating to anti-subversion and emergency powers.[97] Liberty interests are insufficiently protected where appeals to 'public order' in the balancing process are determinative, such that the prospect of any meaningful restraint on power is remote, and that of non-constitutionalist government, clear and present.

[92] Richard Pildes, 'Why Rights are not Trumps: Social Meanings, Expressive Harms and Constitutionalism' (1998) 27 *Journal of Legal Studies* 725, 730–2.

[93] *PP v Koh Song Huat, Benjamin* [2005] SGDC 272.

[94] Chua Ben Huat, 'Political Culturalism, Representation and the People's Action Party of Singapore' (2007) *Democratization* 911, 917.

[95] *Colin Chan v PP* [1994] 3 SLR 662, 687C.

[96] Ibid 684.

[97] See Chapter 21.

III. Constitutions and Constitutionalism: The Possibility and Limits of Constitutionalism in Illiberal Polities

Human societies are shaped by unique sets of values and institutions which are expressed in a constitution as the fundamental law; functionally, constitutionalism is 'the ideal of establishing some form of effective and regularised restraint on the government',[98] through procedural or substantive limits. Constitutions may adopt non-liberal approaches towards empowering and restraining governments as constitutionalism, in securing 'the political conditions necessary to a relatively decent human life' is essentially 'not about individual rights but fettered power'.[99]

Liberal or modern constitutionalism which delineates state structures in 'distinctly rationalist terms' has been criticized for its inability to handle non-individualist societies or to engage in more honest discussions of the vision of good a state promotes, constricting 'our social and political possibilities'.[100] As Katz observed, forms of constitutionalism have been 'conceptualised and practised outside of the western democracies'; until the end of the Cold War, socialist constitutionalism was the dominant competing model. This has declined in importance outside China, Vietnam, and Cuba,[101] whose constitutions do not effectively constrain but place power at the Communist Party's disposal to service its constitutionally accorded leading role.[102] The dangers of nominal constitutionalism notwithstanding, the Third World seeks 'starkly alternative varieties of constitutionalism'.[103]

Reminiscent of Huntington's clash of civilizations thesis, theocratic and communitarian constitutionalism present alternative trajectories of constitutional orderings in non-liberal settings where cultural and religious identities or group moral solidarity is central to the polity's character. While the constitutional recognition of communal identity may be legitimating in the eyes of the governed in illiberal polities, care must be taken to impede their 'more worrisome expressions'[104] where governors seek to implement principles drawn from an exclusive ethno-religious or ideological regime in absolutist fashion. Non-liberal constitutionalism must not degenerate into becoming an anti-constitutionalist 'darling of fascists'.[105] This danger is apparent in certain types of communitarian societies where people with shared ends fulfil socially assigned roles derived from culture, religion, or totalizing ideology, as in caste-based, fascist, or communist systems. It also exists in post-colonial patrimonial states where developmentalist imperatives justify recentralizing state power through various mechanisms, which may be constitutionally specified, such as judicial ouster clauses or anti-subversion preventive detention laws which may be abused to quash political dissent. Such 'constitutional dictatorships' utilize constitutional forms to legitimate and effectuate their rule, to justify maximum state discretion while minimizing legal and political forms of accountability.[106]

[98] Carl Friedrich, *Constitutional Government and Democracy* (4th edn, 1968).

[99] Walker (n 2), 164.

[100] Butler Ritchie (n 17), 30–2.

[101] See n 14.

[102] Constitution of Vietnam, Art 4 (1992); Constitution of the People's Republic of China, Art 3 (1982); Constitution of Cuba, Art 5 (1992).

[103] See n 13.

[104] Walker (n 2), 155.

[105] Ibid 177.

[106] H.W.O. Okoth-Ogendo, 'Constitutions without Constitutionalism: Reflections on an African Political Paradox' in Douglas Greenberg et al (eds), *Constitutionalism and Democracy: Transitions in the Contemporary World* (1993), 73.

An exclusive focus on the dominant view of liberal constitutionalism which is closely aligned with the judicial enforcement of a binding 'higher' law, runs the risk of insularity oblivious to the varieties of legal culture and the possibilities of alternative constitutionalisms. Hahm, for example, in taking culture seriously, directs attention to the importance of civic virtue, not only institutions and rights, in the proper functioning of constitutionalism. He examines the role of '*li*', or ritual propriety, in Confucianist East Asian settings and argues that the state has a non-neutral interest in inculcating *li* not only through the political education of its citizens, but also in its constitutionalist application in disciplining rulers. Historically, this was buttressed by institutional mechanisms such as the constant surveillance of rulers by court historians who recorded what a king as a 'rites-bearer' during the Korean Choson dynasty said or did. The focus on internal forms of restraint is a reminder of the 'importance of the human dimension in political order'.[107]

Within illiberal polities, unusual routes towards democratization and constitutionalism in terms of regulated power, may also be observed from developments in intra-party democracy in China, even though the Community Chinese Party (CCP), in assuming total political power, would fall without the liberal understanding of party. While multi-partyism is rejected, developments within the party have ensured some measure of accountability and representation, a socialist rule of law distinct from Western-style democracy or the trichotomy of powers. The CCP has become more inclusive in opening membership to capitalists; in 2000, Jiang Zemin advocated the idea of *sange daibiao* ('three represents'), to ensure the CCP represented the entire nation. Downplaying the CCP's revolutionary nature as the workers' party, the CCP presents itself as faithfully representing the majority of Chinese people, the requirements of the most advanced forms of production, and the most advanced culture.[108]

A form of constitutionalism is evident in the creeping popular consciousness galvanizing the assertion of claims based on non-judicially enforceable rights in socialist constitutions. For example, citizens in Hanoi, Vietnam, joined in a popular outcry against an 'unconstitutional' police regulation allowing each citizen to register only one motorcycle, which was assailed as violating constitutional property rights. Through populist pressure with the aid of the media, the national assembly eventually supported the annulment of these rules. This notable vindication of individual rights did not threaten the political status quo; its focus on economic interests opened the space for a 'safe constitutionalism'.[109]

The self-restraint of virtuous rulers, intra-party democracy, and the populist path towards constitutionalism have inherent limitations, not least, the lack of effective legal remedies for constitutional violations. Communitarian and theocratic constitutional orders in their search for identity and authority may not sufficiently restrain abuses of public power or articulate a substantive articulation of the good and common life which is satisfactorily inclusive. Nonetheless, engaging these situations lends insight into the functions and possibilities of constitutions and how they frame politics in non-liberal polities; it tempers parochialism by cautioning against too easily considering one constitutional model inevitable, desirable, and generally transplantable, thereby contributing to the development of more pluralistic conceptions of constitutionalism in a postmodern and plural world.

[107] Chaihark Hahm, 'Constitutionalism, Confucian Civic Virtue and Ritual Propriety' in Daniel Bell and Chae-bong Hahm (eds), *Confucianism for the Modern World* (2003) 31, 35.

[108] He Baogang, 'Intra-party Democracy: A Revisionist Perspective from Below' in Kjeld Erik Brødsgaard and Yongnian Zheng (eds), *The Chinese Communist Party in Reform* (2006).

[109] Mark Sidel, *Law and Society in Vietnam: The Transition from Socialism in Comparative Perspective* (2008), 86.

Bibliography

Abdullahi Ahmed An-Na'im, *Islam and the Secular State: Negotiating the Future of Shari'a* (2008)

Talal Asad, *Formations of the Secular: Christianity, Islam, Modernity* (2003)

Larry Cata Backer, 'The Rule of Law, the Chinese Communist Party, and Ideological Campaigns: Sange Daibiao (the "Three Represents"), Socialist Rule of Law, and Modern Chinese Constitutionalism' (2006) 16 *Transnational Law and Contemporary Problems* 29

Daniel A. Bell, 'A Communitarian Critique of Liberalism' (2005) 27 *Analyse and Kritik* 215

Daniel A. Bell, *Beyond Liberal Democracy: Political Thinking for an East Asian Context* (2006)

Beau Breslin, *The Communitarian Constitution* (2004)

Nathan Brown, 'Islamic Constitutionalism in Theory and Practice' in Eugene Cortan and Adel Omar Sherif (eds), *Democracy, The Rule of Law and Islam* (1999)

Nathan Brown, *Constitutions in a Non-Constitutional World: Arab Basic Laws and the Prospects for Accountable Government* (2001)

Stephen L. Carter, *The Culture of Disbelief: How American Law and Politics Trivialises Religion* (1994)

Joseph Chan, 'Legitimacy, Unanimity and Perfectionism' (2000) 39(1) *Philosophy and Public Affairs* 5

Michael C. Davis, 'The Price of Rights: Constitutionalism and East Asia Economic Development' (1998) 20(2) *Human Rights Quarterly* 303

Gerald Doppelt, 'Illiberal Cultures and Group Rights: A Critique of Multiculturalism in Kymlicka, Taylor and Nussbaum' (2002) 12 *Journal of Contemporary Legal Issues* 661

Nenad Dimitrijevic, 'Ethno-Nationalized States of Eastern Europe: Is there a Constitutional Alternative?' (2002) 54(4) *Studies in East European Thought* 245

Michel Dowdle and Stéphanie Balme, *Building Constitutionalism in China* (2009)

Anver M. Emon, 'The Limits of Constitutionalism in the Muslim World: History and Identity in Islamic Law' in Sujit Choudhry (ed), *Constitutional Design for Divided Societies* (2008)

Izhak Englard, 'Law and Religion in Israel' (1987) 35(1) *American Journal of Comparative Law* 185

Kemal Faruki, *The Evolution of Islamic Constitutional Theory and Practice* (1971)

Noah Feldman, *The Fall and Rise of the Islamic State* (2008)

John Gillespie, 'Changing Concepts of Socialist Law in Vietnam' in John Gillespie and Penelope Nicholson (eds), *Asian Socialism & Legal Change: The Dynamics of Vietnamese and Chinese Reform* (2005)

Tom Ginsburg and Tamir Moustafa, *Rule by Law: The Politics of Courts in Authoritarian Regimes* (2008)

Raymond Guess, 'Liberalism and its Discontents' (2002) 30(3) *Political Theory* 320

Tracy E. Higgins, 'Why Feminists Can't (or Shouldn't Be) Liberals' (2004) 72 *Fordham Law Review* 1629

H.N. Hirsch, 'The Threnody of Liberalism: Constitutional Liberty and the Renewal of Community' (1986) 14 *Political Theory* 423

Ran Hirschl, *Constitutional Theocracy* (2010)

David S.J. Hollenbach, 'Contexts of the Political Role of Religion: Civil Society and Culture' (1993) 30 *San Diego Law Review* 877

Gary Jeffrey Jacobsohn, *Apple of Gold: Constitutionalism in Israel and the United States* (1994)

Gary Jeffrey Jacobsohn, 'Alternative Pluralisms: Israel and American Constitutionalism in Comparative Perspective' (1989) 51(2) *Review of Politics* 159

Herbert S. Klein, '"Social Constitutionalism" in Latin America: The Bolivian Experience of 1938' (1966) 22(3) *The Americas* 258

Donald P. Kommers, 'Liberty and Community in Constitutional Law: the Abortion Cases in Comparative Perspective' (1985) *Brigham Young University Law Review* 371

Will Kymlicka, 'Liberal Multiculturalism, Western Models, Global Trends and Asian Debates' in Will Kymlicka and Baogang He (eds), *Multiculturalism in Asia* (2005)

Will Kymlicka, *Multicultural Citizenship: A Liberal Theory of Minority Rights* (1995)

Stephen Macedo, 'The Constitution of Liberalism' in Stephen Macedo, *Liberal Virtues: Citizenship, Virtue and Community in Liberal Constitutionalism* (1990)

B.O. Nwabueze, *Constitutionalism in the Emergent States* (1973)

Joav Peled, 'Ethnic Democracy and the Legal Construction of Citizenship: Arab Citizens of the Jewish State' (1992) *American Political Science Review* 86

Randall Pereenboom (ed), *Asian Discourses of Rule of Law: Theories and Implementation of Rule of Law in Twelve Asian Countries, France and the US* (2004)

John Rawls, 'The Idea of Public Reason Revisited' (1997) 64 *University of Chicago Law Review* 765

Angela R. Riley, '(Tribal) Sovereignty and Illiberalism' (2007) 95 *California Law Review* 799

Glen O. Robinson, 'Communities' (1997) 83 *Virginia Law Review* 269

Mark D. Rosen, '"Illiberal" Societal Cultures, Liberalism and American Constitutionalism' (2002) 12 *Journal of Contemporary Legal Issues* 803

Michel Rosenfeld (ed), *Constitutionalism, Identity, Difference and Legitimacy: Theoretical Perspectives* (1994)

Michael Sandel, *Liberalism and the Limits of Justice* (1982)

William E. Scheuerman, 'Carl Schmitt's Critique of Liberal Constitutionalism' (1996) 58(2) *Review of Politics* 299

Benedict Sheehy, 'Singapore "Shared Values" and Law: Non East versus West Constitutional Hermeneutic' (2004) 34 *Hong Kong Law Journal* 67

Mark Sidel, 'Analytical Models for Understanding Constitutions and Constitutional Dialogue in Socialist Transitional States: Reinterpreting Constitutional Dialogue in Vietnam' (2006) 6 *Singapore Journal of International and Comparative Law* 42

Mark Sidel, *Law and Society in Vietnam: The Transition from Socialism in Comparative Perspective* (2008)

Mark Sidel, *The Constitution of Vietnam: A Contextual Analysis* (2009)

Richard C. Sinopoli, 'Liberalism and Contested Conceptions of the Good: The Limits of Neutrality' (1993) 55(3) *Polity* 644

Nomi Maya Stolzenberg, 'The Return of the Repressed: Illiberal Groups in a Liberal State' (2002) 12 *Journal of Contemporary Legal Issues* 897

Madhavi Sunder, 'Cultural Dissent' (2001) 54 *Stanford Law Review* 495

Cass R. Sunstein and Richard H. Thaler, 'Liberatarian Paternalism is Not an Oxymoron' (2003) 70(4) *University of Chicago Law Review* 1159

Charles Taylor, 'The Politics of Recognition' in Amy Gutmann (ed), *Multiculturalism: Examining the Politics of Recognition* (1994)

Charles Taylor, *A Secular Age* (2007)

Li-ann Thio, 'Apostasy and Religious Freedom: Constitutional Issues Arising from the Lina Joy Litigation' (2006) 2 *Malayan Law Journal* i

Li-ann Thio, 'Soft Constitutional Law in Non-Liberal Asian Constitutional Democracies' (2010) 8(4) *International Journal of Constitutional Law* 766

Li-ann Thio, 'Jurisdictional Imbroglio: Civil and Religious Courts, Turf Wars and Article 121(1A) of the Federal Constitution' in Andrew Harding and H.P. Lee (eds), *Constitutional Landmarks in Malaysia: The First 50 Years* (2007)

Li-ann Thio and Kevin Y.L. Tan (eds), *Evolution of a Revolution: 40 Years of the Singapore Constitution* (2009)
Neelan Truchelvam, 'Constitutionalism: South Asian Perspectives' in *Constitutionalism & Democracy: Transitions in the Contemporary World* (1993)
James Tully, *Strange Multiplicity: Constitutionalism in an Age of Diversity* (1995)
Graham Walker, 'The Idea of Nonliberal Constitutionalism' in Ian Shapiro and Will Kymlicka (eds), *Ethnicity and Group Rights* (1997)
Juinn-Rong Yeh and Wen-Chen Chang, 'The Emergence of East Asia Constitutionalism: Features in Comparison' (2011) 59(3) *American Journal of Comparative Law* 805
Fareed Zakaria, 'Islam, Democracy and Constitutional Liberalism' (2004) 119(1) *Political Science Quarterly* 1
Fareed Zakaria, *The Future of Freedom: Illiberal Democracy at Home and Abroad* (2003)
Fareed Zakaria, 'The Rise of Illiberal Democracies' (1997) 76 *Foreign Affairs* 22

CHAPTER 6

CONSTITUTIONALISM AND IMPOVERISHMENT: A COMPLEX DYNAMIC

ARUN THIRUVENGADAM AND GEDION T. HESSEBON*

Singapore and Budapest

I. Introduction

We live in times that are simultaneously marked by unrivaled opulence and extreme forms of suffering and deprivation. This has led the contemporary philosopher, Thomas Pogge, to fervently argue that the occurrence and persistence of global poverty is the great moral wrong and injustice of our time.[1]

* We thank Michael Dowdle, Varun Gauri, András Sajó, Ronojoy Sen, Mahendra P. Singh, Victor Ramraj, and Nick Robinson for constructive inputs and Timothy Liau for exemplary research assistance. The usual caveat applies.

[1] See Thomas Pogge, *World Poverty and Human Rights: Cosmopolitan Responsibilities and Reforms* (2002).

Combating impoverishment[2] has been the focus of several disciplines and fields, but has not attracted sufficient attention from scholars of constitutional and comparative constitutional law. We believe that this has happened for at least two reasons. The first arises from a tendency internal to constitutional law and scholarship, which has long treated social and economic rights—that seek to address the issues underlying impoverishment—as being outside the proper domain of constitutional law. A number of scholars have persuasively argued against this conventional wisdom and have demonstrated how and why socio-economic rights are properly within the realm of constitutional law and adjudication.[3]

Our contribution focuses on the second—and perhaps more fundamental—reason for the absence of issues of impoverishment on the horizon of constitutional scholarship. This arises from skepticism towards the idea that the discipline of constitutional law has anything to contribute to the project of eliminating impoverishment. In this view, a prerequisite for the practice of constitutionalism is a minimum level of economic, political, and social development, making issues of basic poverty lie beyond the pale of constitutional discourse. Advocates of such a form of 'sequencing'—who recommend focusing on economic development and institution-building before promoting democracy and freedom—have a long historical pedigree even within liberal thought. So, for instance, J.S. Mill's ideal of a liberalism that secured the conditions for the flourishing of individuality rested on having reached a degree of civilizational progress 'when mankind have become capable of being improved by free and equal discussion'.[4] After examining this view at some length in the first section of this chapter, we shift our focus to scholars who argue against such a view, by advocating for the simultaneous pursuit of constitutionalism and poverty eradication. They argue that a focus on impoverishment is essential because issues that underlie impoverishment are inextricably linked to other social problems emanating from inequality in general, asymmetric distribution of wealth and power, inadequate access to basic services and needs, and forms of institutional corruption. Most of these problems are in one form or the other very much the concern of mainstream constitutional discourse.

Our principal purpose, therefore, is to explore and ascertain the relevance and application of principles of constitutionalism for issues of impoverishment. We conclude from our survey that there is a deep connection between them, and seek to explore how constitutionalism can be—and has been—harnessed to eradicate impoverishment in meaningful ways. Through our case studies, we also seek to highlight precise ways in which the existence of deep and pervasive impoverishment poses real challenges for attaining the ideals of constitutionalism. We believe that a wider acknowledgment of this connection can lead to productive exchanges across more jurisdictions on ways in which poverty reduction can be accelerated through the use of constitutional institutions and principles.

[2] Although we use the terms 'impoverishment' and 'poverty' somewhat interchangeably, we bear in mind Upendra Baxi's powerful insight that the term 'poverty' has a passive connotation whereas using 'impoverishment' draws attention to the fact that poverty is not a natural state, and is often the result of dynamic processes adopted by governments and agencies at the national and international levels. Upendra Baxi, 'Introduction' in Upendra Baxi (ed), *Law and Poverty: Critical Essays* (1988), vi–viii.

[3] See Chapters 49 and 50. See generally Varun Gauri and Daniel Brinks, *Courting Social Justice: Judicial Enforcement of Socio-economic Rights in the Developing World* (2008). For analyses that move beyond the issue of adjudication of socio-economic rights, and address a broad range of issues affecting impoverishment, see Yash Ghai and Jill Cottrell, *The Millennium Declaration, Rights and Constitutions* (2011) and Henry Steiner, Philip Alston, and Ryan Goodman, *International Human Rights in Context* (2008), 263–370.

[4] J.S. Mill, 'On Liberty' in J.S. Mill, *Three Essays* (1975).

It is necessary to explain what we mean by the term 'constitutionalism'. The classic definitions of the term focus on ways by which political authority exercised through the agencies of the state are to be limited, constrained, and contained.[5] However, in the case of constitutions that were drafted more recently, and especially in countries that were grappling with problems of impoverishment, there was a keen awareness that states had to be empowered to undertake programs for the eradication of impoverishment and the crippling socio-economic conditions that accompany it.[6] In our conception of the term, constitutionalism aims at simultaneously constraining and facilitating the state in its attempts at advancing the negative and positive freedoms of its citizenry, which are the ultimate goals of constitutional institutions and principles.

II. Impoverishment and its Pervasiveness

Our understanding of 'poverty' and impoverishment' as used in this chapter is shaped by the capability approach, initially devised by Amartya Sen.[7] Sen developed the capability approach to draw contrasts between the utilitarians (who focus on individual happiness or pleasure) and mainstream economists (who assess a person's advantage in terms of his or her income, wealth, or resources), both of which, in Sen's view, inadequately capture the real-world impact of impoverishment. Sen's capability approach focuses, instead, on 'a person's capability to do things he or she has reason to value.'[8] Elsewhere, Sen has explained that 'What the capability perspective does in poverty analysis is to enhance the understanding of the nature and causes of poverty and deprivation.' This is achieved 'by shifting primary attention away from means (and one particular means that is usually given exclusive attention, viz, income) to ends that people have reason to pursue, and, correspondingly, to the freedoms to be able to satisfy these ends.'[9]

Poverty is a widespread phenomenon. Pogge cites statistics to show that nearly a quarter of the world's population—estimated at 6.8 billion at the time of writing—is living in life-threatening poverty. As he emphasizes in a recent work:

> 1020 million people are chronically undernourished; 884 million lack access to safe drinking water; 2,500 million lack access to improved sanitation; 2,000 million lack access to essential medicines; 924 million lack adequate shelter; 1,600 million lack electricity; 774 million adults

[5] See eg Carlos Nino, *The Constitution of Deliberative Democracy* (1996), concluding that 'everybody agrees that constitutionalism means something like "limited government"'.

[6] Uday Mehta argues that this is the principal difference between the making of the US and the Indian Constitutions. While the former, according to Mehta, focused exclusively on containing the state, the framers of the Indian Constitution also sought to

> imply an activist and capacious state, responsible for the eradication of poverty, undoing the stigmas of discrimination, building large industry, facilitating communication, fostering national unity, and, most broadly, creating conditions for the exercise of freedom.

Uday Mehta, 'Constitutionalism' in Pratap Bhanu Mehta (ed), *The Oxford Companion to Politics in India* (2010), 20.

[7] Sen's earliest reference to the 'capability approach' is in Amartya Sen, 'Equality of What?' in S. McMurrin (ed), *Tanner Lectures on Human Values*, vol 1 (1980). Later, Martha Nussbaum and Sen jointly edited *The Quality of Life* (1993) which developed this further. For a recent elaboration of Nussbaum's ideas on this issue, see generally, Martha Nussbaum, 'Capabilities as Fundamental Entitlements' in Bina Agarwal et al (eds), *Capabilities, Freedoms and Equality* (2007).

[8] Amartya Sen, *The Idea of Justice* (2009), 231.

[9] Amartya Sen, *Development as Freedom* (1999), 90.

> are illiterate; 218 million children are child labourers; . . . and about 18 million deaths annually, or nearly one-third of all human deaths, are due to poverty-related causes.[10]

Not surprisingly, the challenge of impoverishment is sharpest in the Global South. In many of these nations, there is a strong need to combat impoverishment at a domestic level. This is where notions of constitutionalism become relevant, especially for countries in Asia, Africa, and South America, which face the gravest levels of impoverishment.

III. The Imperatives of Development and Poverty Eradication: Skepticism about Constitutionalism and the Appeal of 'Developmental States'

Questions of addressing impoverishment are inextricably linked with issues relating to the appropriateness of societal goals and avenues to pursue them. Whether societal justice in relation to issues such as poverty elimination is better achieved by state intervention or by individuals acting for themselves has long been a focus of academic debate in social and political theory and in developmental economics.[11]

In the aftermath of the Second World War and the decolonization movement, several states across Asia and Africa experienced nationalist movements and leaders who promised to pursue socio-economic development and eradicate poverty. Yet, six decades later, relatively few of these states have succeeded. While several reasons have been identified, scholars of developmental studies have focused on the state of politics in many post-colonial nations—especially the politics of their systems of bureaucratic appointments—that resulted in discontinuity and uncertainty in their bureaucratic capacity, which in turn subverted the achievement of developmental goals.

More recently, especially in the second half of the twentieth century, the 'developmental states' in East Asia (including Japan, Korea, Taiwan, and Hong Kong) and South East Asia (Singapore, Malaysia, and more recently Indonesia and Thailand) have garnered attention for achieving spectacular growth, reducing or eliminating impoverishment, and building strong welfare systems. The term 'developmental state' was first used by Chalmers Johnson in the early 1980s to refer to the Japanese state.[12] Johnson identified some crucial features of the developmental state in Japan, the first of which was the intimacy of its relationship with the private sector, and the intensity of its involvement in the market. Another significant feature was the power, continuity, and autonomy of the elite bureaucracy.

In contrast with the failures of many postcolonial developing nations within Asia and Africa in achieving developmental goals, the Asian developmental states have been able to

> extract capital; generate and implement national plans; manipulate private access to scarce resources; coordinate the efforts of individual businesses; target specific industrial projects; resist political pressures from popular forces such as consumers and organized labour; insulate their domestic economies from extensive foreign capital penetration; and, most

[10] Thomas Pogge, 'Responses to the Critics' in Allison M. Jaggar (ed), *Thomas Pogge and His Critics* (2010), 177.

[11] See eg F.A. Hayek, *The Constitution of Liberty* (1960); John Rawls, *A Theory of Justice: Justice as Fairness* (1972); and Robert Nozick, *Anarchy, State and Utopia* (1974).

[12] Chalmers Johnson, *MITI and the Japanese Miracle* (1982).

> especially, carry through a sustained project of ever-improving productivity, technological sophistication and increased market share.[13]

The nature, scale, and speed of the transformation can be demonstrated by focusing on a single country: Singapore. In 1970, Singapore's per capita GDP was less than half that of the United Kingdom. Within three decades, this situation had transformed: in 1998, Singapore's GDP per capita was greater than that of the United Kingdom and was much closer to that of the United States. Looking at factors beyond income, the 1990 Human Development Report (HDR) notes that between 1960 and 1987, Singapore was one of the countries that made the 'fastest progress' towards increasing the average life expectation of its citizens.[14] Singapore also scores highly on other indices such as rates of adult literacy and home ownership, access to safe water, educational and health services, and basic goods, while simultaneously securing one of the lowest infant mortality rates in the world.

Nevertheless, it must be emphasized that these developmental states fare quite poorly on measures highlighted by most models of constitutional democracy. In general, nations in East and South East Asia have had a poor to middling record on issues of civil and political rights. In many of them, there has been a substantial concentration of political, ideological, and military power in the hands of the state. In several countries, this has been achieved or exacerbated by the continuity of a single, dominant political party. As a logical corollary, civil society and media have traditionally been weak (although this has changed in some, such as Taiwan and South Korea) and opportunities for public participation in crucial decisions are inhibited. The state adopts a highly interventionist role in most matters relating to individual autonomy and freedoms, and has avoided attempts at making it transparent and accountable. Several of these states have made extensive use of emergency powers and preventive detention laws to suppress opposition movements and assert the dominance of the ruling political parties.[15]

While a few of the developmental states in East and South East Asia have made strides towards constitutional democracy, some others have expressed great hostility towards such notions. Leaders such as Mahathir Mohammed in Malaysia and, perhaps more famously, Lee Kuan Yew in Singapore, have argued quite forcefully that their impressive achievements on economic development and poverty elimination have been secured by explicitly repudiating the standard norms, practices, and expectations of constitutional democracy. These leaders have argued for the virtues of 'development before democracy' and have espoused a strong, culturally based 'Asian Values'-approach to governance.[16] According to this view, freedoms and rights hamper economic growth and development. Such ideas justifying a 'soft authoritarian' state run against many of the axioms of constitutionalism because, as noted by scholars in the region, 'the ideas of separation of powers, limited government and fundamental rights appear to be cast to the wind'.[17]

[13] T.J. Pempel, 'The Developmental Regime in a Changing World Economy' in Meredith Woo-Cummings (ed), *The Developmental State* (1999), 139.

[14] Human Development Report (1990), 19–20.

[15] See Chapter 21.

[16] In his writings, Lee Kuan Yew has disputed the importance of a free and vibrant press for securing development or social harmony. See generally Lee Kuan Yew, *From Third World to First* (2000). Also see Fareed Zakaria, 'Culture is Destiny: A Conversation with Lee Kuan Yew' (1994) 73 *Foreign Affairs* 109.

[17] Kevin Tan, 'Economic Development and Prospects for Constitutionalism' in Anthony Chin and Alfred Choi (eds), *Law, Social Sciences and Public Policy* (1998). Also see Kevin Tan, 'Economic Development and Human Rights' in Joanne R. Bauer and Daniel A. Bell (eds), *The East Asian Challenge for Human Rights* (1999).

The notion of the developmental state is also witnessing a revival in the discourse of contemporary African states. More specifically, the dominant ruling parties in South Africa[18] and Ethiopia[19] have endorsed the developmental state paradigm as the model to emulate.

What has made such a stance salient is that China seems to be following suit—indeed, this is the argument of a leading China scholar, Randall Peerenboom, who uses the term 'East Asian model' to capture the experiences of some of the Asian developmental states that we have covered above. According to Peerenboom, the East Asian model consists of several stages.[20] In the early stages, there is 'an emphasis on economic growth, rather than civil and political rights' which results in 'a period of rapid economic growth occurring under authoritarian regimes.' This stage is also characterized by a pragmatic approach to economic reforms, along with simultaneous investment in human capital and institutions. As Peerenboom asserts, this model requires the postponement of democratization in the sense of freely contested multiple-party elections for the highest levels of political office until a relatively high level of wealth is attained. Relying on the cases of South Korea and Taiwan, Peerenboom asserts that as overall income levels in society rise, gradually authoritarianism will give way to constitutionalism and its institutions and principles, including the protection of civil and political rights. In Peerenboom's analysis, China and Vietnam are at the relatively early stages of this model, and are consequently less democratized. A considerable part of Peerenboom's argument relies on the strides that China has made in eradicating impoverishment, especially when compared to other developing nations. As Peerenboom notes, China has secured a stunning rise in wealth that has 'lifted over 150 million people out of poverty in less than a decade, and improved the quality of life of hundreds of millions more.'[21]

Peerenboom does concede, however, that there are genuine concerns about the numbers being impoverished as a result of state policies in China, including the plight of migrant workers and the effects on the availability of health services once the Chinese state withdrew its protective policies.[22] Moreover, Przeworski et al note that such spectacular successes are quite rare when viewed against a much larger set of cases.[23] Declaring categorically that they 'did not find a shred of evidence that democracy need be sacrificed on the altar of development', Przeworski et al provide reasons to doubt the viability of the East Asian model as a prescriptive formula for developing nations that are seeking to eradicate impoverishment.[24]

This discussion necessitates a reference to the 'law and development' movement which has more recently focused on 'rule of law' projects as a way of tackling problems of development in countries in the Global South.[25] The end of the Cold War witnessed a resurgence of the previously discredited idea that reforming the law and legal system was essential for bringing about social and economic progress. Consequently, there was a revival of large-scale projects involving huge sums of money: according to one analysis, the World Bank has supported 330

[18] Samantha and Susan Newman, 'The Developmental State and Post-Liberation South Africa' in Neeta Misra-Dextern and Judith February (eds), *Testing Democracy: Which Way Is South Africa Going?* (2010), 24.

[19] Brian Levy and Francis Fukuyama, 'Development Strategies Integrating Governance and Growth', Policy Research Working Paper 5196, World Bank, 2010, 14.

[20] Randall Peerenboom, *China Modernizes: Threat to the West or Model for the Rest?* (2007), 31–3.

[21] Ibid 129.

[22] According to Dorothy Solinger, regardless of the progress made towards diminishing poverty in recent years, China will continue to confront impoverishment for many years to come: 'A Question of Confidence: State Legitimacy and the New Urban Poor' in Peter Hays Gries and Stanley Rosen (eds), *Chinese Politics: State, Society, and the Market* (2010).

[23] Adam Przeworski et al, *Democracy and Development* (2000).

[24] Ibid 271.

[25] On the rule of law more generally, see Chapter 10.

rule of law projects in over a 100 countries between 1990 and 2006, spending about $3.8 billion since 1993.[26] The phase since the 1990s has been described as the 'new' law and development movement, to distinguish it from the 'original' movement, which lasted from the 1950s to the 1970s.[27]

These rule of law projects typically encompass a range of policy objectives and have included reforming public institutions, rewriting laws, upgrading the legal profession, and increasing legal access and advocacy. These in turn have covered a vast array of subjects including judicial reform, legislative strengthening, retraining prosecutors, police and prison reform, bolstering public defenders, introducing alternative dispute resolution, modernizing criminal laws, updating civil laws, introducing new commercial laws, strengthening bar associations, improving legal education, stimulating public interest law reforms, and many others.[28] It would seem, therefore, that the term 'rule of law' is perceived as a flexible concept which allows reformers to bring in both macro and micro elements that they believe would suit their overall purposes. There is by now a vast and sophisticated literature underlining the essentially indeterminate, amorphous, and contested nature of the concept of the 'rule of law'.[29]

Despite their scale, the achievements of these projects are not considered spectacular, even by their most ardent supporters. While many reasons for such failure have been identified, one line of criticism notes that meaningful legal reform requires not so much a focus upon foreign models or institutional goals, but 'close attention to, genuine respect for, and detailed knowledge of the conditions of the receiving society and its pre-existing mechanisms of social order.'[30]

The concept of the rule of law is generally regarded as one of the tenets of constitutionalism. However, the failure of rule of law projects does not suggest a failure of constitutional projects as a whole, because a commitment to constitutionalism requires taking the local context and legal culture seriously, while also enabling local voices to play a prominent role, which does not appear to have been the case in most such projects.

IV. The Symbiotic Relationship between Development and Freedom: Sen's Scholarly Work and Empirical Assessments

As seen in the previous section, the notion that development and constitutionalism are competing ideas has a fairly old pedigree. Responses to this notion, which emphasize the symbiotic rather than adversary relationship between these ideas, are also not new. Writing around

[26] Alvaro Santos, 'The Word Bank's Uses of the "Rule of Law" Promise in Economic Development' in David Trubek and Alvaro Santos (eds), *The New Law and Development: A Critical Appraisal* (2006), 253.

[27] See generally Carol M. Rose, 'The "New" Law and Development Movement in the Post-Cold War Era: A Vietnam Case Study' (1998) 32 *Law and Society Review* 93; and Amy Cohen, 'Thinking with Culture in Law and Development' (2009) 57 *Buffalo Law Review* 511.

[28] Thomas Carothers, *Aiding Democracy Abroad: The Learning Curve* (1999), 168.

[29] See generally, Randall Peerenboom, 'Varieties of Rule of Law' in Randall Peerenboom (ed), *Asian Discourses of Rule of Law* (2004), 1–55; Frank K. Upham, 'Mythmaking in the Rule of Law Orthodoxy' in Thomas Carothers (ed), *Promoting the Rule of Law Abroad: In Search of Knowledge* (2006).

[30] Upham (n 29), 101. Also see Kevin E. Davis and Michael J. Trebilcock, 'The Relationship between Law and Development: Optimists versus Skeptics' (2008) 56 *American Journal of Comparative Law* 895, 946.

the time that the 'Asian Values' discourse was beginning to be articulated in the early 1990s, the American scholar Louis Henkin argued that just as there cannot be any freedom or dignity without development, there could not, equally, be any authentic development without freedom.[31]

The work of Amartya Sen has powerfully built on this idea of the symbiotic relationship between development and freedom by developing it within the discipline of economics and relying on wide-ranging empirical studies.

In his 1981 book, *Poverty and Famines*, Sen made his famous claim about the role of democracies in preventing famines by showing, through detailed empirical analysis, that there has never been a famine in a functioning multi-party democracy. Sen based his argument on the political incentives generated by elections, multiparty politics, and investigative journalism. He argued that in non-democracies, political leaders do not have to suffer the consequences of their failure to prevent famines. By contrast, in democracies, leaders have political incentives to prevent situations that threaten to generate famines. Moreover, the processes of democracy—a free press and news media (which is unabashed in exposing embarrassing facts about governance) and strong opposition parties—provide vital information that enable governments to act decisively in a pre-emptive manner. This has led Sen to argue that 'a free press and an active political opposition constitute the best early-warning system a country threatened by famines can have.'[32]

As argued in Sen's classic work, *Development as Freedom*:

> Development requires the removal of major sources of unfreedom: poverty as well as tyranny, poor economic opportunity as well as systematic social deprivation, neglect of public facilities as well as intolerance or overactivity of repressive states.... In still other cases, the violations of freedom results directly from a denial of political and civil liberties by authoritarian regimes and from imposed restrictions on the freedom to participate in the social, political and economic life of the community.[33]

Sen argues that even affluent citizens living in authoritarian regimes are subject to impoverishment, and asserts that 'the significance of the instrumental role of political freedom as *means* to development does not in any way reduce the evaluative importance of freedom as an *end* of development.'[34] Sen contends that dismissing civil and political rights misses both their instrumental and constructive roles. As an example, he notes that Indian states (like Kerala) have achieved greater success in moderating population growth by using methods such as public education and discussion among women than comparable policies of coercion in China on the one-child policy have garnered. These normative arguments can be interpreted as making the case for a robust constitutional democracy that prioritizes social justice issues and moves towards eradicating impoverishment. While Sen acknowledges the importance of well-functioning institutions, he is careful to argue that 'democracy has to be judged not just by the institutions that formally exist but by the extent to which different voices from diverse sections of the people can actually be heard.'[35] We believe that this fits well with the more robust form of constitutionalism that is required to tackle issues of impoverishment at a fundamental level.

Is there empirical evidence to assess whether freedoms and rights do in fact hamper the achievement of economic growth and development?

[31] Louis Henkin, *The Age of Rights* (1990), 193. [32] Sen (n 9), 181.
[33] Ibid 3–4. [34] Ibid 37. [35] Sen (n 8), xiii.

For this chapter, we conducted a study of the ten poorest countries in the contemporary world, as ranked by the 2010 HDR.[36] These countries, ranked 169th to 160th in ascending order, are: Zimbabwe, Democratic Republic of Congo, Niger, Burundi, Mozambique, Guinea-Bissau, Chad, Liberia, Burkina Faso, and Mali. Some of these countries are landlocked, sparsely populated, and in arid localities. These and a host of related demographic, geographic, political, as well as external factors create some form of 'poverty trap.'[37] Debate regarding causes of extreme poverty in these nations has focused on whether external, as opposed to internal factors such as 'destiny' or 'policy', are to blame.[38] The state of constitutionalism in these countries has not received much attention as a factor that might have contributed to the prevalence of impoverishment.

From our perspective, it is significant that all these countries have had dismal records of constitutionalism. Recurrent coup d'états, civil wars, military and civilian authoritarian dictatorships, and one-party regimes have been the norm in these countries for the greater part of the second half of the twentieth century. Constitutions in these nations have been routinely abrogated and disregarded.[39] The cavalier attitude towards constitutionalism is best illustrated by the case of the Democratic Republic of Congo (the former Zaire) which experienced 21 legal instruments dubbed as constitutions during a 40-year period, under the kleptocratic autocracy of Mobutu Sese Seko.[40] While these facts do not necessarily imply that the absence of constitutionalism leads to poverty, they show that there is a significant correlation between governments which are not subject to constitutional restraint and arbitrariness, economic mismanagement, and corruption which in turn beget poverty.

This correlation between the virtual absence of constitutionalism and extreme poverty is extremely consistent. 'Poor people are much more likely to be ruled by dictators.'[41] Part of the reason why constitutionalism failed in these countries concerns their economic situation. Nevertheless, it seems that the lack of constitutionalism has also contributed to the economic disasters in these countries.

Studies also show that in low-income countries where there is ethnic diversity, dictatorial rule is extremely detrimental to the economy. Focusing on the experience of African countries, the economist Paul Collier argues that autocrats in poor, ethnically diverse African countries are forced to make dysfunctional choices in order to appease their ethnic bases.[42] He therefore argues that 'judged by economic performance, ethnically diverse societies need democracy more than those that are homogeneous'.[43] This is so because, although autocrats often claim to transcend ethnic divisions, in reality, at least in Africa, they have a narrow ethnic base which they try to strengthen through networks of patronage detrimental to the

[36] Human Development Report, 2010 Report Table 3—Inequality-adjusted Human Development Index, available at <http://hdr.undp.org/en/media/HDR_2010_EN_Table3_reprint.pdf>.

[37] Paul Collier, *The Bottom Billion: Why the Poorest Countries are Failing and What Can Be Done About It* (2007), 17–79.

[38] Paul Collier and Jan Willem Gunning, 'Why Has Africa Grown Slowly?' (1999) 13 *Journal of Economic Perspectives* 3.

[39] Benno J. Ndulu and Stephen A. O'Connell, 'Governance and Growth in Sub-Saharan Africa' (1999) 13 *Journal of Economic Perspectives* 47.

[40] André Mbata Betukumesu Mangu, 'The Road to Constitutionalism and Democracy in Post-colonial Africa: The Case of the Democratic Republic of Congo', Thesis, 1 January 2003, 477, available at <http://uir.unisa.ac.za/handle/10500/1761>.

[41] Przeworski et al (n 23), 269–70.

[42] Paul Collier, *Wars, Guns, and Votes* (2009), 64.

[43] Ibid 62.

national economy.[44] This observation is relevant for our analysis in the next section of this chapter, where we focus in greater detail on two nations that have had to tackle impoverishment against the backdrop of diverse, heterogeneous populations.

V. Country Case Studies: Ethiopia and India

Ethiopia and India are the second largest nations in their respective continents. We chose them primarily because of our own respective familiarity with these countries. Nevertheless, we believe that their contrasting experiences hold important lessons for those interested in exploring the connections between constitutionalism and impoverishment.

1. Ethiopia

Ethiopia's current constitution, adopted in 1995, sought to address persistent and endemic poverty by adopting some radical programs that were given constitutional sanction. As our analysis of the Ethiopian case will show, while constitutionalism offers promise for eradicating impoverishment (even if negatively, by demonstrating the perils of autocratic, non-constitutional government), the persistence of impoverishment also presents fundamental challenges for securing constitutionalism

Ethiopia is the second most populous nation in Africa, with a current population of 85.2 million. Its political history has been marked by long periods of monarchical rule, a brief period of foreign rule under the Italians (1936–41), the return of the monarchy (1941–74), rule by a military regime that had the backing of the Soviet Union (1974–91), and an embrace of constitutional government (1991–present) that is still incomplete and remains politically fragile. In large part because of its long history of feudalism and political instability, Ethiopia is one of the poorest countries in the world, and ranks 157th out of 169 countries in the 2010 UN Human Development Index.

Prior to the adoption of the current Constitution, Ethiopia had three different constitutions. Much of the political instability in the last five decades has been caused due to the recurrence of large-scale famines and attendant problems of acute poverty. The first written constitution of Ethiopia was adopted in 1931 which, like the 1955 Revised Constitution, enshrined an absolute monarchy. After the 1974 'Revolution' and rule through decrees by a 'Provisional Military Administration Council' (*Deurge*) that lasted for 13 years, a new constitution instituting a 'People's Democratic Republic' was adopted in 1987. This Constitution lasted only for four years and was replaced by a Transitional Charter adopted in 1991 when rebel forces triumphed over the military regime and took power. The Transitional Charter laid the foundations for the adoption of the current Constitution in 1995, called the Constitution of the Federal Democratic Republic of Ethiopia (FDRE Constitution).

The 1995 Constitution sought to provide the foundation for a federal democratic republic. It instituted a federal form of state with nine 'regional states' (most of which are formed on the basis of ethnicity), provided for a parliamentary form of government at the federal level, and included an extensive catalog of rights. There are, however, some unusual features of the Constitution. First among these is the state/public ownership of all land, which is provided for in Article 40(3) of the FDRE Constitution. Significantly, state ownership of all land and the prohibition of private ownership of land precede the current Constitution. When it assumed

[44] Ibid.

power in 1974, one of the first decrees issued by the Provisional Military Administration Council related to the nationalization of land. During the 1974 Ethiopian Revolution, Marxism was the dominant ideological outlook among the politically active sections of the population, most of whom were students. The Military Council, reflecting the ideological leanings of the political movement that ushered in the revolution, opted for state ownership of land by abolishing the feudal land-holding system set up by the *ancien regime*. The Ethiopian People's Revolutionary Democratic Front (EPRDF) is the political party that overthrew the military regime in 1991, and was the principal proponent of the current constitution. Its genesis lies in the student movement of the early 1970s because of which its political orientation is strongly to the left. The EPRDF argues that given the absence of a middle class and a large, autonomous, strong, and vibrant private sector, liberal democracy is not a feasible option for Ethiopia in the foreseeable future. Not surprisingly, therefore, the need for Article 40(3) has been defended by the EPRDF as justified and necessitated by the impoverishment and vulnerability of peasants.

This argument has been challenged by other Ethiopians, including most of the opposition parties, who contend that the need to ensure economic growth and food security makes it necessary to introduce private ownership of land. Advocates of this view note that unless farmers enjoy the security of tenure that only ownership can guarantee, they would be unable to make the investments needed to improve the productivity of the land.[45] Since the livelihood of more than 80 per cent of the population is based on land, and given the gravity of food insecurity in Ethiopia, the Constitution's position on land ownership is both crucial and controversial. The insistence of the Ethiopian state on maintaining state ownership of land is, however, unusual within the continent of Africa where many nations had similar land tenure systems.

Although the FDRE Constitution guarantees the enjoyment of civil and political rights, constitutional practice over the last decade has shown this to be illusory. Freedoms of expression, the press, association, and assembly are routinely violated.[46] The generous guarantees of constitutionalized socio-economic rights have proved to be irrelevant in the practice of Ethiopian constitutionalism, as has the provision guaranteeing the right to development. The promise of democratic governance embodied in the Constitution has yet to be realized after three largely uncompetitive elections and one competitive but controversial general election.[47] The elections held in 2005 were marred by post-election violence that led to the arrest and conviction of the leaders of the major opposition party coalition, human rights NGOs, and journalists on charges of treason and outrage against the Constitution.[48] Politically motivated arrests and charges of terrorism against members of certain ethnic groups occur at alarming rates.[49] The general picture is one where constitutionalism seems imperiled.

[45] Bereket Kebede, 'Land Tenure and Common Pool Resources in Rural Ethiopia: A Study Based on Fifteen Sites' (2002) 14 *African Development Review* 139.

[46] In the annual survey conducted by Freedom House, Ethiopia's status declined from 'Partly Free' to 'Not Free', *Freedom in the World: The Authoritarian Challenge to Democracy* (2011), 18. See also Lovise Aalen and Kjetil Tronvoll, 'The End of Democracy? Curtailing Political and Civil Rights in Ethiopia' (2009) 36 *Review of African Political Economy* 120, 193–207.

[47] See the Democracy index of the *Economist* where Ethiopia was previously classified as having a hybrid regime and is now reclassified as having an authoritarian regime. 'Democracy Index: Democracy in Retreat', Economist Intelligence Unit, p 18, available at <http://graphics.eiu.com/PDF/Democracy_Index_2010_web.pdf>.

[48] J. Abbink, 'Discomfiture of Democracy? The 2005 Election Crisis in Ethiopia and its Aftermath' (2006) 105/419 *African Affairs* 173, 192.

[49] Kjetil Tronvoll, 'Human Rights Violations in Federal Ethiopia: When Ethnic Identity is a Political Stigma' (2008) 15 *International Journal on Minority and Group Rights* 49.

The causal link between Ethiopia's poverty and the bleak state of its constitutionalism is difficult to determine with any certainty. However, given the fact that some African countries (including Benin, Mali, and Ghana) have managed to maintain a working constitutional democracy despite a high level of poverty, the misfortune of impoverishment in Ethiopia cannot be considered in and of itself as having doomed constitutionalism to failure.

The Ethiopian case also enables us to assess, in line with the 'developmental state' logic, whether the dismal state of constitutionalism might have given Ethiopia an advantage in bringing about economic growth. Looking at relevant comparators, it is clear that Ethiopia has not enjoyed an advantage over similarly situated African countries. Ethiopia's progress towards meeting the Millennium Development Goals has not been superior to that of Mali or Ghana, for instance.[50] These comparisons show that the exercise of power without constitutional restraints and democratic accountability does not necessarily give a state an edge in reducing poverty. If anything, it makes corruption, instability, and conflict more likely, thereby derailing prospects of development.[51]

Ethiopia's history also allows us to reflect upon the detrimental effect of unlimited and unaccountable power upon development. Development is more often than not possible only when violence is reduced. There is a clear causal link between human rights abuses, severe corruption, discrimination, and ethnic, religious, and regional competition and violent conflicts.[52] These factors are more likely to contribute to the eruption of violence in a state where the constitutional system has failed to curb abuse of power. The long civil wars that have immensely contributed to poverty in Ethiopia attest to this fact. Therefore, it seems safe to assert that, far from hampering development, constitutionalism could foster it by staving off violent conflicts. At least in the Ethiopian context, arguments in favor of benign authoritarian governments that are unconstrained by constitutional limits, while still advanced regularly, seem less and less convincing.

We have hitherto sought to use the Ethiopian case to provide support for our normative argument, relying on Sen's work, that constitutionalism is a potential ally for societies struggling with challenges of impoverishment. We must equally emphasize, however, that poverty makes it very difficult to realize the ideal of constitutionalism. In this regard, we can derive three important lessons from the Ethiopian experience. The first is that when citizens are economically impoverished, they are more vulnerable to pressures by the state than they would otherwise be. The poorer citizens are, and the more the state controls resources needed for survival, the easier it is for the state's relative economic might to be turned into an instrument of political repression. In Ethiopia, at any given time, at least a few million or so citizens suffer from food insecurity and are dependent on state programs for their survival. Since all land is state-owned and could be subject to redistribution, possessors of the land receive only a nominal compensation. This is particularly true in rural areas where the overwhelming majority of the population lives. In urban areas, the state is the main provider of employment, education, housing, and often the principal client for many key private businesses. All of these positions of the state as the sole landlord, as a major aid distributor, as provider of jobs, business, and social services on top of its coercive and regulatory powers enable it to wield enormous control

[50] Millennium Development Goals Report Card, 'Learning from Progress', Overseas Development Institute, Report, June 2010, 4, available at <http://www.odi.org.uk/resources/download/4908.pdf>.

[51] 'The World Development Report 2011: Conflict, Security, and Development', World Bank, 2011, available at <http://wdr2011.worldbank.org/fulltext>.

[52] Ibid.

over the lives of ordinary citizens.[53] The economic standing and might of the state in relation to its citizens is such that ordinary constitutional constraints in the form of a bill of rights and separation of powers seem to provide precious little restraint on the leviathan.

A second way in which the ideal of constitutionalism is undermined by poverty relates to the inability of people who are suffering under the weight of poverty, malnourishment, malaria, and illiteracy to assert their rights or sustain a meaningful degree of civic engagement. These conditions are hardly ideal for constitutionalism. In a situation where 39 per cent of the population lives on less than $1.25 per day and where 64 per cent of the population is illiterate,[54] few citizens are inclined to patronize newspapers or financially support civic associations. So, even if the Ethiopian state were to abide by constitutional limitations on power, the space for social and individual endeavor opened by these limitations might not be optimally utilized due to the constraints of poverty, illiteracy, and disease.

Ethiopia also provides evidence of a third way in which poverty impedes the attainment of constitutionalism. Since resources are scarce, and economic prospects in the private sector independent of the state are quite dim, a high premium is placed on gaining political power for the unique opportunity it affords to gain wealth. As Yash Ghai has noted, 'the combination of the dominance of ethnicity and the centrality of the state for accumulation leads to intense competition for the capture of the state.'[55] In a divided society where there is already competition between different ethnic groups, this intensifies the contention for power, and is hardly conducive to constitutionalism.[56]

2. India

India has been continuously engaged in a fascinating experiment with constitutional government since it gained independence from British colonial rule in 1947. Taking nearly three years, Indians drafted an indigenous constitution that contained many bold provisions, including the granting to all Indians (the majority of whom were illiterate and racked by desperate poverty) the right to universal adult suffrage. This flew in the face of liberal thought since the time of J.S. Mill, and resulted in Indians having the right to vote at a time when more developed countries continued to deny women and minorities this important right. The acceptance of universal adult franchise, along with the adoption of many other classic elements of liberal constitutionalism, committed India firmly to the path of democratic governance. In 2011, India completed 64 years of democratic constitutional rule, marred only by a brief period of internal emergency (1975–77). India has many of the hallmarks of a robust constitutional democracy: a vibrant political culture marked by the presence of diverse political parties, an assertive and free media which does not shirk from sharp criticism of governmental figures, independent constitutional institutions (including the Election Commission, the judiciary, and the office of the President) that act as real constraints on those holding executive and legislative power, and a vibrant and diverse group of civil society organizations that seek to promote important causes between elections. In the last two decades, India has gained

[53] For an extensive documentation of how the Ethiopian state uses the resources and services under its control for political repression, see 'Development without Freedom How Aid Underwrites Repression in Ethiopia', October 2010, Human Rights Watch, 34–66.

[54] See Ethiopia: Statistics, UNICEF, available at <http://www.unicef.org/infobycountry/ethiopia_statistics.html>.

[55] Yash Ghai, 'Chimera of Constitutionalism: State, Economy, and Society in Africa' in Swati Deva (ed), *Law and (In) Equalities- Contemporary Perspectives* (2010), 327.

[56] Claude Ake, *Democracy and Development in Africa* (1996), 129.

the focus of the world business community for the high rates of growth of its economy, leading to its being termed as an 'emerging superpower'. In a country that was under colonial rule for more than two centuries, has a recurring history of communal violence, deep-rooted social problems, and endemic poverty, this is a considerable achievement.

Scholars who have focused on the reasons for India's relative success as a constitutional democracy have identified a host of issues, some of which are specific to India.[57] A more general conclusion has relevance for our analysis of the Ethiopian case study. It has been asserted that India's success is a function of having accomplished, within the framework of a centralized state, a moderate accommodation of group demands (especially demands of ethnicity and some decentralization of power), which has ensured that its constitutional model of governance has endured and survived.[58] This insight ties in well with the third lesson that we drew from the Ethiopian case, of addressing the competition for scarce resources among ethnic groups in a polarized, heterogeneous society.

While the achievements of constitutional democracy in India are commendable, what is deeply troubling is the persistence of problems of impoverishment that have historically beset the nation, and at alarming rates. The 2010 HDR ranks India 119th among 162 countries. The report shows that much of India's population—which stands at 1.21 billion currently—continues to suffer from widespread illiteracy, avoidable morbidity, premature mortality, and deep-seated inequality of opportunity, and its rates for these factors are below even those of other South Asian nations. China, the only other country which is comparable in terms of population, ranks at 89th and has, as emphasized by Peerenboom, far more respectable figures for these categories. India is thus an example of a nation that has had reasonable success with establishing a constitutional democracy but has not been able to eradicate poverty substantially. One reason has been endemic political instability at both the federal and state levels of Indian politics that has resulted in what Khilnani describes as 'precarious governments dependent upon fragile and often obstructive coalitions'. Khilnani asserts that as a result of these developments, 'Indian democracy faces the absence of any mechanisms to bring together into a coherent form a representative political will, which speaks of a crisis of and in political representation.'[59]

The vacuum in Indian governance has led to attempts by other institutions to step in. One constitutional actor which has expressly used the interests of the poor as a justification for its actions is the Indian judiciary. The Indian judiciary is by design more powerful than regular courts in common law countries and has sought to expand its powers by acting in the name of the poor and marginalized sections of Indian society.[60] Starting in the late 1970s and early

[57] These include: the establishment of a relatively centralized state under British colonial rule and the introduction of proto-democratic institutions; the maturity and creativity exhibited by Indian nationalists who consolidated the gains of independence through sagacious political and constitutional choices; the genuine commitment to democracy displayed by India's founding Prime Minister, Nehru, who stayed in power for a significant period (1947–64); a well-functioning civil service; and a popular ruling party, the Indian National Congress, which led to political stability in the founding years. See generally Atul Kohli, 'Introduction' in Atul Kohli (ed), *The Success of India's Democracy* (2001).

[58] Kohli (n 57), 19.

[59] Sunil Khilnani, 'The Constitution and Individual Rights: A Comment on Dr Abhishek Singhvi's *India's Constitutions and Individual Rights: Diverse Perspectives*' (2009) 41 *George Washington International Law Review* 361.

[60] For details of the Indian judiciary's powers and a history of its functioning, see Burt Neuborne, 'The Supreme Court of India' (2003) 1 *International Journal of Constitutional Law* 476; Lavanya Rajamani and Arghya Sengupta, 'The Supreme Court' in Pratap Mehta and Nirja Jayal (eds), *The Oxford Companion to Politics in India* (2010), 80.

1980s, the judiciary began entertaining public interest litigation (PIL) that enabled the Court eventually to exercise a robust and all-encompassing form of judicial review which sought to provide access to justice to the most underprivileged sections of Indian society.[61] The judiciary's espousal of the rights of the poor and marginalized sections of Indian society in the initial phases of PIL suited the populist policies of the Indira Gandhi (1980–84) and Rajiv Gandhi (1984–89) governments. In a series of cases decided during the 1980s and early 1990s, the Supreme Court broke new ground by judicially creating rights to livelihood and housing, health and education for Indians and by issuing orders designed to implement these rights. What is striking about the conduct of the Court in many PIL cases is that it seeks to move away from an adversarial process to one where the parties work collaboratively to find workable solutions.[62]

In recent years, the Supreme Court has invoked its PIL jurisdiction to tackle enduring issues, most famously in the case of *PUCL v Union of India*, or the right to food case. The case arose when the petitioner organization, a civil rights group, approached the Supreme Court in 2001 arguing that the Indian government was failing to prevent famines and violating its constitutional duties. In a process lasting more than ten years, the Court has overseen the implementation of previously announced government programs, while also ordering new executive measures. It has done so by appointing an expert committee, and adding its imprimatur to the recommendations of the committee which, in turn, consulted government bodies, expert groups, and other institutions to evolve very specific measures and schemes. Gauri and Brinks have focused on this as well as similar decisions issued by courts in Brazil, Colombia, Indonesia, and South Africa to argue that there is a distinct but similar pattern in such judicial interventions. They contend that in these cases, courts are seeking to bring a measure of 'communicative rationality' to the process of governance, and are using their authority to structure a public forum of communication between various actors whereupon they compel implementation of policies to secure effective results for poor and marginalized sections in these societies.[63]

As detailed by Judge Dennis Davis in Chapter 49 of this volume, there are several objections to the adoption of such interventionist roles by judges, some of which carry great weight. The fact remains, however, that in at least some cases, judicial decisions have been able to have a discernible impact on the ground. The right to food case is a good example, because the actions of the Court over the last decade have both galvanized and provided support to civil society groups that have now started a campaign to have a federal law that guarantees food security.[64] Some scholars have argued that these moves by courts should be supported because in acting carefully and in coordination with a host of other constitutional actors, they are advancing the ideals of democracy and public reasoning that have the potential of producing enduring solutions to seemingly intractable social and economic problems.[65]

[61] Upendra Baxi, 'Taking Suffering Seriously: Social Action Litigation in the Supreme Court of India' (1985) 4 *Third World Legal Studies* 107. See generally A.K. Dias and Gita Welch (eds), *Justice for the Poor* (2009); Michael Anderson, *Access to Justice and Legal Process: Making Legal Institutions Respond to Poor People in LDCs* (2003).

[62] Jeremy Cooper, 'Poverty and Constitutional Justice: The Indian Experience' (1993) 44 *Mercer Law Review* 611.

[63] Varun Gauri and Daniel Brinks, 'Human Rights as Communicative Action', Paper presented at a conference on 'The Enforceable Right to Health?', Central University Budapest, June 2011 (unpublished, on file with authors).

[64] Harsh Mander, 'Ending Indifference: A Law to Exile Hunger?' (2011) 46(25) *Economic and Political Weekly* 45.

[65] Gauri and Brinks (n 63).

The high and persisting rates of poverty in India lead, as they do in Ethiopia and other nations in the Global South, to frequent calls for the adoption of more authoritarian forms of governance, which are, it is argued, more insulated from pressure groups. Dreze and Sen have countered this line of reasoning by noting that many of the problems relating to the poor in India have arisen because of the political marginalization of the underprivileged. As they astutely note, this problem cannot be solved 'by marginalizing them *even more* by further concentration of political power'. They have therefore argued for improving the existing arrangements for constitutional governance, by making them more participatory, accountable, and capable of delivering the real freedoms which are essential to eradicate impoverishment.[66]

VI. Conclusion

Our principal focus has been on examining broad constructs that have hampered the development of a robust discourse of constitutional scholarship on issues of poverty. Two recent works that are motivated by ideas similar to those we have emphasized, focus instead on grounded studies of micro issues that affect analyses of poverty issues.[67] Our hope is that mainstream constitutional scholars will be inspired to undertake close analysis of these and related issues in the future, given that eradicating impoverishment is one of the most pressing moral issues of our age.

Bibliography

Abhijit Banerjee and Esther Duflo, *Poor Economics: A Radical Rethinking of the Way to Fight Global Poverty* (2011)

Upendra Baxi, (ed), *Law and Poverty: Critical Essays* (1988)

Jeab Dreze and Amartya Sen, *Hunger and Public Action* (1989)

Yash Ghai, 'Chimera of Constitutionalism: State, Economy, and Society in Africa' in Swati Deva (ed), *Law and (In) Equalities—Contemporary Perspectives* (2010)

Uday Mehta, 'Constitutionalism' in Pratap Bhanu Mehta and Nirja Jayal (eds), *The Oxford Companion to Politics in India* (2010)

Randall Peerenboom, *China Modernizes: Threat to the West or Model for the Rest?* (2007)

Thomas Pogge, *World Poverty and Human Rights: Cosmopolitan Responsibilities and Reforms* (2002)

Amartya Sen, *Development as Freedom* (1999)

Amartya Sen, *Idea of Justice* (2009)

Amartya Sen, *Poverty and Famines* (1981)

Lucie E. White and Jeremy Perlman, *Stones of Hope: How African Activists Reclaim Human Rights to challenge Global Poverty* (2011)

Meredith Woo-Cummings (ed), *The Developmental State* (1999)

[66] For a comprehensive catalogue of their views on improving the practice of constitutional democracy in India, see the final chapter of Jeab Dreze and Amartya Sen, *India: Development and Participation* (2002), 347–79.

[67] Abhijit Banerjee and Esther Duflo, *Poor Economics: A Radical Rethinking of the Way to Fight Global Poverty* (2011); Lucie E. White and Jeremy Perlman, *Stones of Hope: How African Activists Reclaim Human Rights to Challenge Global Poverty* (2011).

CHAPTER 7

THE PLACE OF CONSTITUTIONAL LAW IN THE LEGAL SYSTEM

STEPHEN GARDBAUM

Los Angeles

If one takes a broad, panoramic perspective on comparative constitutional law, the now familiar narrative of the rise of world constitutionalism[1] suggests a fairly straightforward and uniform answer to the most general question of the place of constitutional law in a legal system, at least as a formal matter. So, too, the logically prior question of what constitutional law is. The 'post-war paradigm'[2] posits in its essential features, first, that constitutional law is the law codified in a country's written constitution, mostly establishing the ground rules of government and protecting certain basic or fundamental rights, and second, that this law sits at the apex of its legal system. It is the supreme law of the land, entrenched to reflect and preserve its primacy, and authoritatively interpreted and applied by a high court with the power to set aside conflicting non-constitutional law and legal acts. To be sure, there continue to be outliers from this dominant model as a whole and from one or other of its typical characteristics, none of which is strictly-speaking necessary, but in itself this is insufficient to undermine or complicate the straightforward answers.

Zooming in, however, on the theory and practice of constitutionalism in certain specific contexts and countries reveals that both questions have recently become interestingly more complex and the answers provided more nuanced and diverse. There has been fresh input that

[1] Bruce Ackerman, 'The Rise of World Constitutionalism' (1997) 83 *Virginia Law Review* 771. See also Chapter 8.

[2] Lorraine Weinrib, 'The Postwar Paradigm and American Exceptionalism' in Sujit Choudhry (ed), *The Migration of Constitutional Ideas* (2005).

enriches and transcends this standard, relatively formal and positivistic, conception of constitutional law and its place in a legal system. So, for example, what constitutional law is and the line between it and other law, what forms it can take and the judicial techniques it may employ, have been helpfully complicated by the development of theories of both the common law constitution and the statutory constitution in various English-speaking countries in recent years, including the 'big-c' constitution United States. Similarly, three quite different views of the general place of constitutional law in a legal system have been defended or described in different contexts, which when put together and contrasted with each other form a helpful spectrum running from political constitutionalism, to legal constitutionalism, and finally to what may be called 'total constitutionalism'.

Less globally, and perhaps also more familiarly, there are robust ongoing practical and scholarly debates about the place of constitutional law in certain specific areas of a country's legal system. Thus, the old question of the relative importance and centrality of constitutional law to issues of rights protection, on the one hand, and governmental structure, on the other, has been raised in a surprising variety of contexts and with interestingly different conclusions in recent years. The issue of the scope of constitutional law within the sphere of private conduct/private law has been a prominent one in recent bouts of constitution-making and judicial implementation, triggering much scholarly interest. Similarly, the debate about the role of constitutional law versus legislative politics in securing social and economic welfare has been enlivened and extended by recent experience, particularly in South Africa and Eastern Europe, and the scholarly attempt to digest it.

Overall, this increasingly rich literature suggests the importance of a genuinely comparative perspective that takes contextualized constitutional discourses seriously and results in distinct and broader conceptions of constitutional phenomena than provided by either purely domestic constitutional law or more abstract, philosophical reflection. Here, as elsewhere, focus on both sameness and difference, on paradigm and particularity, seems to offer the most useful and illuminating general methodology for the discipline.

I. What is Constitutional Law?

Taking a position on the general place of constitutional law in the legal system also involves, at least impliedly, taking a position on the place of ordinary or non-constitutional law. For it is the place of constitutional law in contrast with this latter that is mostly being considered.[3] Accordingly, it is necessary as a threshold matter to have a fairly clear sense of what constitutional law is and where the line between it and all other law falls. At the comparative level, several separate but overlapping discourses in recent years have rendered this question interestingly more complex and the resulting answer significantly less formal and uniform.

The traditional view is that constitutional law has a primary and a secondary meaning corresponding to the well-known two meanings of the related term 'constitution'. Thus, the first and primary meaning is 'big-c' constitutional law: the law contained in a written, codified constitution or plausibly inferred from it. Typically, although not necessarily, this law has the three characteristics referred to above of being supreme, entrenched, and enforced through

[3] In a few specific contexts, eg the impact of EU law on domestic constitutional rights, some courts and scholars have also addressed the issue of the relative place and position of constitutional law and international law within a national legal system.

the power of judicial review. Although contemporary constitutional law in this primary sense also has a typical content—establishing the relatively concrete ground rules of government and proclaiming a rather more abstract set of basic or fundamental rights—it is not the content or subject matter that determines its status as constitutional law. Indeed, there is no restriction on content. Any law that satisfies the formal criteria for becoming part of a big-c constitution qualifies.[4] Hence the possibility of a constitutional amendment prohibiting the manufacture, sale, or transportation of alcohol.

The second—and very much secondary—traditional meaning of constitutional law corresponds to the Aristotelian concept of a 'small-c constitution'. That is, constitutional law is the subpart of the aggregate body of rules, practices, and understandings determining the actual allocation of power in a polity (and the limits on it) that have formal legal status. Historically, this meaning of the term has mostly been limited to legal systems lacking a big-c constitution, such as the United Kingdom. Here, the more inclusive term 'the British Constitution', or just 'the Constitution', traditionally refers to the entire small-c constitution and 'constitutional law' the subset with common law or statutory status—the subset that is legally enforceable. But, in principle, this secondary meaning could also be employed in legal systems with big-c constitutions, and just as differences and even contradictions may arise between a system's big and small-c constitutions,[5] so too between a system's big and small-c constitutional law. Indeed, as we will see, this is in effect what has been posited by theorists of common law and statutory constitutionalism in the United States. Unlike the first meaning, small-c constitutional law is largely determined by subject matter and function. Laws concerning prohibition, for example, could not easily be part of constitutional law in this sense.

This conventional and fairly straightforward understanding of the line distinguishing constitutional and ordinary law has become a little more complicated recently as the result of at least four separate and mostly unrelated discourses taking place in a variety of different, particularized constitutional contexts. The first of these is the work of certain constitutional theorists in the United States just referred to who have challenged the traditional, exclusively big-c conception of constitutional law with its sharp line between the law contained (one way or another) in the venerable US Constitution and all other law. This challenge has taken the form of developing theories of both an unwritten, common law constitution,[6] focusing on the importance of precedent, conventions, extra-textual principles, and incremental styles of constitutional reasoning, and a supplementary statutory constitution of certain super-statutes, such as the Civil Rights Act of 1964, which are effectively entrenched and treated as higher law.[7]

The second is recent practice and theory in the United Kingdom. The practice is the enactment and subsequent evolution of the Human Rights Act of 1998, a statutory bill of rights which is sometimes recognized and referred to as a 'constitutional statute' in ways that

[4] Putting to one side the possibility of unconstitutional constitutional amendments.

[5] David S. Law, 'Constitutions' in Peter Cane and Herbert M. Kritzer (eds), *The Oxford Handbook of Empirical Legal Research* (2010).

[6] See Thomas C. Grey, 'Do We Have an Unwritten Constitution?' (1975) 27 *Stanford Law Review* 703; Henry P. Monaghan, 'Foreword: Constitutional Common Law' (1975) 89 *Harvard Law Review* 1; David A. Strauss, 'Common Law Constitutional Interpretation' (1996) 63 *University of Chicago Law Review* 877; Harry H. Wellington, 'Common Law Rules and Constitutional Double Standards: Some Notes on Adjudication' (1973) 83 *Yale Law Journal* 221.

[7] William N. Eskridge and John A. Ferejohn, 'Super-Statutes' (2001) 50 *Duke Law Journal* 1215; Bruce Ackerman, 'The Living Constitution' (2007) 120 *Harvard Law Review* 1738.

transcend the traditional small-c sense of the term and largely corresponds to the 'super-statute' meaning in the United States.[8] Some commentators have argued that even though it does not empower courts to invalidate inconsistent statutes, the Human Rights Act has ushered in a system of constitutional review of ordinary legislation and executive acts that in substance, if not form, is little different from that in the United States or Germany.[9] On the theory side and pre-dating the Human Rights Act, a robust theory of common law constitutionalism has been developed that also permits judges to review legislation and executive acts, here against rule of law principles such as due process and equality that are claimed to be an inherent part of the common law.[10] Here, constitutional limits applied by courts may help to determine the meaning and even the validity of a statute. Both developments provide examples of constitutionalization without a big-c constitution.

A somewhat different example of this phenomenon is provided by the recent rise of international constitutionalism as a leading approach to international law, primarily within Europe and especially Germany.[11] Although there are almost as many theories of international constitutionalism as theorists, the common core of the enterprise has been the attempt to co-opt the concepts and success of domestic constitutionalism and constitutional law at the international level. To the extent there is meaningful international constitutional law in various contexts, particularly that of the international human rights regime, this is also claimed to be mostly in the big-c sense—sharing its main characteristics as higher law—but without the big-c constitution. Within this account, international human rights treaties are in many ways perceived as international constitutional or super-statutes.

Finally, a theory of the 'total constitution' presented as an interpretation of modern German constitutional practice,[12] but which arguably could be applied to several other contemporary constitutional systems—including South Africa and certain Latin American countries—effectively erases the line between constitutional and non-constitutional law altogether. This is because a total constitution, one that answers or strongly influences virtually all legal and political conflicts in a society, tends to constitutionalize all law by requiring it to be not merely consistent with, but superseded by, the big-c constitution.

As a result of overlapping developments such as these, the dominant and relatively specific comparative paradigm is beginning to erode and there may be no single account of what constitutional law is to replace it, except perhaps at a significantly higher level of generality. So, in one direction, constitutional law is increasingly perceived as not limited either to written constitutions themselves or the legal systems that have one, but can also be found generally in statutory and common law forms. Accordingly, as the notions of a common law and statutory constitution have become more mainstream, it may soon be necessary to talk of a 'constitutional constitution' to distinguish this form from the other two. Most importantly, as a result the general understanding of what constitutional law is has begun to shift to stress the sub-

[8] See eg *Thoburn v Sunderland City Council* (2003) QB 151 (Sir John Laws LJ).

[9] Aileen Kavanagh, *Constitutional Review under the UK Human Rights Act* (2007), 416–21.

[10] See T.R.S. Allan, *Law, Liberty, and Justice: The Legal Foundations of British Constitutionalism* (1993); *Constitutional Justice: A Liberal Theory of the Rule of Law* (2001); Sir John Laws, 'Law and Democracy' (1995) *Public Law* 72–93; Sir John Laws 'The Constitution, Morals and Rights' (1996) *Public Law* 622–35.

[11] Jeffrey Dunoff and Joel Trachtman (eds), *Ruling the World? Constitutionalism, International Law and Global Government* (2009); Jan Klabbers, Anne Peters, and Geir Ulfstein, *The Constitutionalization of International Law* (2009).

[12] Mattias Kumm, 'Who is Afraid of the Total Constitution? Constitutional Rights as Principles and the Constitutionalization of Private Law' (2006) 7 *German Law Journal* 341.

stantive over the formal aspects. That is, regardless of precise source or status, constitutional law is functionally higher law that may be entrenched in several different legal and non-legal ways (and not only through a formal, super-majoritarian amendment process) and enforced by various techniques of constitutional review (and not only a formal judicial invalidation power). Subject matter is also more important than under the purely formal status approach of the traditional primary meaning, but also not sufficient as under the second, small-c meaning; rather there are higher law and perhaps also constitutional review implications of ascription. In other words, there is some merging of the two existing senses of constitutional law into a distinct and more general third sense that may be particularly important in comparative constitutional law. Within this third, more comprehensive sense, big-c constitutional law will be one important type of constitutional law but not the exclusive one, either across legal systems or within a particular one.

Constitutional law is also spreading in another direction, however, so that it does not necessarily presume a sphere of ordinary law at all but may be the only true norm-generating source in a legal system. This suggests perhaps a different, traditional separation of powers-defying division between higher and lower law, in which constitutional law alone performs the legislative function and all other law, including that enacted by the legislature, is essentially administrative in nature—executing, specifying, and applying the constitutional norms.

II. General Views on the Place of Constitutional Law

Taking this expanded, less formal conception of constitutional law into account, and looking comparatively at the theory and practice of constitutionalism in various particular contexts, there are currently three competing general accounts of the place of constitutional law in a legal system. These three accounts form a spectrum running from a non-existent to a comprehensive role for constitutional law.

The first position has come to be known as 'political constitutionalism' in the United Kingdom, where it has become a well-theorized and articulated response to the perceived trend towards its opposite, 'legal constitutionalism', in recent years.[13] The position itself, however, is a familiar one elsewhere, although increasingly more in theory than practice. In response to the general question of what type or number of moral/political/legal issues and conflicts in society should be resolved by constitutional law in either the big-c or newer, more comprehensive sense, the answer of political constitutionalism is essentially zero. All such conflicts should be resolved politically, through ordinary, non-constitutional laws made and executed by political actors who remain fully accountable for them to the electorate. More specifically, the constraints on legislatures in particular should be political and not judicially administered ones, with office holders held to account through political processes and in political institutions rather than legal ones.[14] Similarly, according to political constitutionalists, removing rights from democratic politics, as legal constitu-

[13] The two leading manifestos of political constitutionalism are Adam Tomkins, *Our Republican Constitution* (2005) and Richard Bellamy, *Political Constitutionalism: A Republican Defence of the Constitutionality of Democracy* (2007). Legal constitutionalism is well represented by the works cited in n 10.

[14] Graham Gee and Gregoire C.N. Webber, 'What is a Political Constitution?' (2010) 30 *Oxford Journal of Legal Studies* 273–299; Adam Tomkins, 'The Role of Courts in the Political Constitution' (2010) 20 *University of Toronto Law Journal* 1–22, 2.

tionalism typically does, is both an ineffective and illegitimate method of upholding and protecting them.[15] Although aiming to secure constitutionalism's traditional negative function of limiting political power, albeit by exclusively political rather than legal means, political constitutionalism also aspires to provide space for the more positive function of promoting constitutionalist values, such as individual autonomy and equal concern and respect.[16] As a normative theory with strong roots in republican conceptions of democracy, political constitutionalism is to be distinguished from empirical theories concerning the phenomena of formal constitutions and constitutional law that exist on paper but do not in fact determine any of the issues they purport to.

The binary opposite position of legal constitutionalism can take a number of particular forms, as the previous section clarifies. Indeed, to a significant extent, the development and refinement of political constitutionalism in the United Kingdom has been in response to the common law and statutory forms of legal constitutionalism—of constitutional law—that have evolved in both theory and practice in recent years. Nonetheless, of course, legal constitutionalism remains most familiar comparatively in its big-c, written constitution sense. Whatever form or forms it takes, however, legal constitutionalism's characteristic answer to the underlying general question is that constitutional law should (that is, its function is to) resolve *some* moral/political/legal issues and conflicts in society—typically those that might otherwise undermine or destabilize it—while leaving others to be resolved politically. Of course, justifying this answer and determining the precise boundary between the two has quite properly been a major focus of scholarly effort,[17] and important parts of the boundary question form the topic of the following section. But the basic idea that constitutional law both takes some issues off the political agenda and *leaves others on it*, has been central to its appeal in an era that has seen the rise of world constitutionalism alongside, and as part and parcel of, the rise of world democracy.

Although in its multiple guises and manifestations, the debate between political and legal constitutionalists often seems to suggest that these two options exhaust the terrain, the two answers they provide to the general question—constitutional law should resolve no moral/political/legal conflicts and some conflicts—appears to leave open the possibility of a third. That possibility has now been realized with the development of an interpretation of German constitutional practice that has been termed 'the total constitution'.[18] For, mirroring the total state, what is 'total' about the constitution in this position is that it essentially resolves—or strongly influences—virtually *all* moral, legal, and political conflicts in a society. Through an expansive interpretation of constitutional rights so that almost any governmental action triggers one or more, a broad conceptualization of the impact of constitutional law on private law, and a robust set of protective duties on the state, there are few issues on which the Basic Law is silent and so relatively little that is left to the free, unmediated play of political forces. Something like this conception of the enlarged place of constitutional law in a legal system and society is arguably also held at least in part elsewhere. Post-apartheid South Africa has a similar broad conception of constitutional rights and long list of protective duties, supple-

[15] Bellamy (n 13), 145–75; Jeremy Waldron, 'The Core of the Case against Judicial Review' (2006) 115 *Yale Law Journal* 1346.

[16] Bellamy (n 13).

[17] On constitutional law as a pre-commitment strategy, see Jon Elster, *Ulysses Unbound* (2000), and as an insurance policy for political losers, see Tom Ginsburg, *Judicial Review in New Democracies* (2003).

[18] Kumm (n 12). It should be noted that having coined this term, Kumm himself believes it is preferable to refer to 'complete constitutional justice'.

mented in its case by certain enforceable social and economic rights. Certain Latin American countries, such as Colombia and Argentina, whose constitutional courts have creatively filled legislative vacuums by directly enforcing constitutional rights against private actors,[19] may also be said to fit this model of total constitutionalism. Under it, constitutional law is not only supreme but comprehensive; it does not simply resolve a few potentially destabilizing issues or render certain more extreme or unreasonable policy options beyond the pale of permissible political choices, but specifies almost all outcomes. In this way, ordinary law and the political process that enacts and administers it loses its autonomous normative power and becomes in effect applied constitutional law.

These three positions—political, legal, and total constitutionalism—still do not quite fully occupy all possible territory, all possible positions on the general place of constitutional law versus ordinary law and politics in a legal system. Although the debate between political and legal constitutionalists tends to be conducted as if the choice is an either-or one, in reality most legal systems have elements of both even where one or the other is predominant.[20] Thus, a paradigmatically legal constitutionalist regime such as the United States still has swathes of putatively constitutional law that are typically politically rather than judicially enforced, such as separation of powers. Australia is perhaps the best example of a formally 'mixed regime', with a legal constitutionalist treatment of structural issues—federalism and, to a lesser extent, separation of powers—and a mostly political constitutionalist treatment of rights. But in addition to the prevalence of such formally or informally mixed regimes that apply one or other model to different substantive areas, there is also a separate and distinct model that attempts to blend political and legal constitutionalism across the board. This is variously known as 'the new Commonwealth model of constitutionalism' (based on where the model has taken hold), 'weak-form judicial review', 'the Parliamentary rights model', and 'the dialogue model' of judicial review.[21] At least according to some of its commentators, the distinctive feature of this new model is the attempt to incorporate both legal and political modes of accountability by combining some form of constitutional review by courts with a legislative power of the final word.

III. The Place of Constitutional Law in Specific Parts of the Legal System

The previous section discussed what might be thought of as macro-constitutionalism, differing views on the place of constitutional law in general. Is there a place for it at all and, if so, what should its general scope be compared to ordinary law and political accountability? In this section, I turn to micro-constitutionalism. What is and should be the role of constitutional law versus ordinary law and the political process that makes and executes it in certain specific and contested areas? In particular, those to be discussed are (1) rights protection and

[19] Willmai Rivera-Perez, 'International Human Rights Law and the Horizontal Effect of Constitutional Rights in Latin America', SJD dissertation, UCLA School of Law.

[20] See Bellamy (n 13); Tom R. Hickman, 'In Defence of the Legal Constitution' (2005) 55 *University of Toronto Law Journal* 981–1025, 1016; Gee and Webber (n 14).

[21] Stephen Gardbaum, 'The New Commonwealth Model of Constitutionalism' (2001) 49 *American Journal of Comparative Law* 707; Mark Tushnet, 'Alternative Forms of Judicial Review' (2003) 101 *Michigan Law Review*; Janet Hiebert, 'Parliamentary Bills of Rights: An Alternative Model?' (2006) 69 *Modern Law Review* 7; Tom Hickman, 'Constitutional Dialogue, Constitutional Theories and the Human Rights Act 1998' (2005) *Public Law* 306.

the structure of government; (2) private law and the conduct of private individuals; and (3) entitlements to state protection and socio-economic benefits.

Of course, the answers to these more micro or specific issues are relevant to, and in some cases determined by, the broader brushes of the macro positions discussed in the previous section. Thus, political constitutionalism's macro-no, as it were, implies negative answers to all three more micro-issues, and total constitutionalism's macro-yes the opposite. Indeed, it is the expansive answers given in precisely these three areas that underlie this interpretation of German constitutional practice. So in this sense, the debate here is conducted exclusively within the terrain of legal constitutionalism as a major part of the boundary issues determining the precise scope of constitutional law versus politics, the line between the 'some' issues to be decided by one and the other. Nonetheless, most of the scholarship on these three issues has been conducted at the micro-level, in that it has treated the three topics in a relatively self-contained and autonomous manner rather than as mostly implications of a general macro-constitutionalist position.

1. Rights versus Structure

The first more specific issue is whether, as a descriptive or normative matter, constitutional law has a greater or more essential role to play in matters of governmental structure or in matters of rights. Although the issue has not always been discussed explicitly in terms of these two alternatives, it has been a recurring one over the years in different contexts and there have been major paradigm shifts on it. Indeed, it has been argued that a new one is now taking place.

Prior to the end of the Second World War, constitutional law tended to focus on the ground rules of government, and democratic constitutions, in particular, on the essential framework of electoral politics. Rights were typically either not included at all or deemed non-justiciable. This focus on structure at least in part reflected the normative concerns about rights famously and influentially expressed by Hans Kelsen and institutionalized in his prototype European constitutional court in inter-war Austria.[22] Indeed, these concerns continued to dominate constitutional law in that country, which had no bill of rights until recent domestic incorporation of the European Convention on Human Rights, and still do in Australia.

By contrast, in the multiple waves of constitutionalization since 1945, the incorporation of a bill of rights into constitutional law—with its usual characteristics of supremacy, entrenchment, and judicial enforceability—has been a standard feature, one we now associate with a 'normal' state.[23] This is what has been referred to as the 'rights revolution'.[24] Indeed, it is not only that rights are now typically or presumptively present, as part of constitutional law, but their protection has come to be viewed as the central and primary function of constitutional law. From the post-Nazi Federal Republic of Germany, to post-communist states in Central and Eastern Europe, post-junta democracies in Latin America, and to post-apartheid South Africa, the entire post-war paradigm and rise of world constitutionalism is inexplicable apart from the central position that rights protection has assumed. This centrality is commonly given expression by the location of a bill of rights at the very beginning of modern constitutional texts, and is also manifested by the fact that it is specifically bills of rights that have been

[22] Hans Kelsen, 'La Garantie juridictionnelle de la constitution' (1928) 4 *Revue du Droit Public* 197.

[23] Sujit Choudhry, 'After the Rights Revolution: Bills of Rights in the Post-Conflict State' (2010) 6 *Annual Review of Law and Social Science* 301–22.

[24] Michael Ignatieff, *The Rights Revolution* (2000).

deemed to form statutory constitutions in countries like New Zealand and the United Kingdom. As one (skeptical) commentator puts it:

> Central to legal constitutionalism is the idea of constitutional rights. Constitutions do many other things beyond enshrining rights. But probably nothing has been so influential in driving constitutionalism along the path of legal rather than political thought than the emphasis on rights...[25]

This development in domestic constitutionalism parallels, and of course reflects the same zeitgeist as, the similar one over the same period at the international level with the rapid development of international human rights law.

The centrality of rights in contemporary constitutional law is also evidenced by the normative debate over constitutional or judicial review in that almost all arguments, both for and against, have focused exclusively on rights protection rather than issues of structure.[26] This is so even though it is widely acknowledged that as a historical matter, the need for a relatively neutral umpire to referee disputes among political institutions over vertical and horizontal allocations of government power—and particularly federalism—was an important factor in the rise of judicial review in the United States and elsewhere, and has continued to be in institutions such as the European Union.[27] In the United States, and notwithstanding this history, there is a well-known argument justifying this centrality in that issues of constitutional structure can safely be left to political constitutionalism while rights protection cannot.[28]

Within comparative constitutional law as a whole, however, it is possible that things may be turning full circle. For it has been argued that following the rise, we are now witnessing the decline of rights-based constitutionalism, at least in many contemporary post-conflict states, including Iraq, Bosnia, Kosovo, Sri Lanka, and Northern Ireland. In this context, structural issues concerning the allocation of power among rival ethnic or religious groups, and not bills of rights, have been at the heart of constitutional law and politics.[29]

2. Constitutional Law and the Private Sphere

The second more specific issue is the place of constitutional law within the sphere of non-governmental or non-public conduct and the (private) law that regulates it. Within comparative constitutional law this issue is generally known under the rubric of 'vertical' and 'horizontal effect'. These alternatives standardly refer to whether constitutional law regulates only the conduct of governmental actors in their dealings with private individuals (vertical) or also relations among private individuals (horizontal).

The traditional animating idea informing the vertical approach is the perceived desirability of a public-private division in the scope of constitutional law, leaving civil society and the private sphere free from the uniform and compulsory regime of constitutional regulation. The well-known justifications for this division lie in the values of autonomy, privacy, market

[25] Bellamy (n 13), 15.

[26] Recent work, on both sides of this debate, includes Richard Fallon, 'The Core of an Uneasy Case for Judicial Review' (2008) 121 *Harvard Law Review* 1693; Mattias Kumm, 'Institutionalizing Socratic Contestation: The Rationalist Human Rights Paradigm, Legitimate Authority and the Point of Judicial Review' (2007) 1 *European Journal of Legal Studies* 26; Bellamy (n 13); Waldron (n 15).

[27] Mauro Cappelletti, *Judicial Review in the Contemporary World* (1971).

[28] Herbert Wechsler, 'The Political Safeguards of Federalism: The Role of the States in the Composition of the National Government' (1954) 54 *Columbia Law Review* 543; Larry Kramer, 'Putting the Politics Back Into the Political Safeguards of Federalism' (2000) 100 *Columbia Law Review* 215.

[29] Choudhry (n 23).

efficiency, and federalism (where relevant). A constitution's most critical and distinctive function, according to this general view, is to provide law for the lawmaker not for the citizen, thereby filling what would otherwise be a serious gap in the rule of law.[30]

The general arguments for the opposite, horizontal approach express an equally well-known critique of the 'liberal' vertical position. First, to the extent the function of a constitution is viewed as expressing a society's most fundamental and important values, they should be understood to apply to all its members. Secondly, both the conceptual coherence of the public-private distinction and the practicality of applying it are questionable, especially given the widespread recent privatization of much governmental activity. Thirdly, constitutional rights and values are threatened at least as much by extremely powerful private actors and institutions as by governmental ones, yet the vertical approach automatically and unjustifiably privileges the autonomy and privacy of such citizen-threateners over that of their victims. Moreover, since the vertical position does not prevent private actors from being regulated by non-constitutional law, it is unclear why autonomy is especially or distinctively threatened by constitutional regulation.[31]

The issue of horizontal effect has sparked great interest among comparative constitutional law scholars in recent years. The reasons are, I think, twofold. First, it has become of enormous practical importance in the wake of the spectacular burst of constitution-making that has taken place around the world since 1989. Along with such other basic choices concerning the structure of constitutional rights as whether to include positive as well as negative rights, constitution drafters have had to decide whether, how, and to what extent private individuals are to be subject to new constitutional rights provisions. Secondly, the very range of situations with which these new constitutions have been designed to deal—from post apartheid and post-military junta to post communism—has challenged scholars to think anew about the nature and functions of constitutions. Are they merely law for the lawmakers or normative charters for reborn societies? Hobbesian social contracts between rulers and ruled, or Lockean ones among equal citizens? In this context, the issue of horizontal effect has been a central one, provoking fresh consideration of how constitutional law differs from other types and sources of law.

One of the major contributions that comparative constitutional law scholars have attempted to make to these real-world transformations has been to clarify the somewhat complex and confusing conceptual framework of the issue and to develop a coherent and user-friendly menu of options so that informed choices can be made. This became necessary because the simple and straightforward bifurcation between vertical and horizontal effect proved too crude to explain the different ways in which constitutional law can impact private actors or to capture the most common types of current constitutional practices. As only a little scratching beneath the surface soon reveals, the fact that under the vertical approach (where it applies) private individuals are not bound by constitutional law in no way entails that it does not govern their legal relations with one another,[32] and thereby determine what they can lawfully be authorized to do and which of their interests, choices, and actions may be protected by law. Rather, the traditional vertical position merely forecloses the most direct way in which a constitution might regulate private individuals, by imposing constitutional duties on them.[33]

[30] Richard S. Kay, 'The State Action Doctrine, the Public-Private Distinction, and the Independence of Constitutional Law' (1993) 10 *Constitutional Commentary* 329. On rule of law more generally, see Chapter 10.

[31] Erwin Chemerinsky, 'Rethinking State Action' (1985) 80 *Northwestern University Law Review* 503; Owen M. Fiss, 'Free Speech and Social Structure' (1986) 71 *Iowa Law Review* 1405.

[32] Harold W. Horowitz, 'The Misleading Search for "State Action" Under the Fourteenth Amendment' (1955) 30 *Southern California Law Review* 208, 210.

[33] Stephen Gardbaum, 'The "Horizontal Effect" of Constitutional Rights' (2003) 102 *Michigan Law Review* 387, 389.

Accordingly, in order to attain a richer understanding of the scope of constitutional law in any given system and to appreciate the actual/potential range of answers, it is necessary to supplement the most basic question of vertical or horizontal effect (are individuals as well as governmental actors bound by constitutional law?) with the following three additional ones. First, even with respect to governmental actors, do constitutional rights provisions bind all such actors or only some; and, if only some, which? In particular, do they bind the legislature and the courts? Secondly, does constitutional law apply to private law (and, in common law jurisdictions, to common law) as well as public law? Thirdly, does constitutional law apply to litigation between private individuals?

There is a range of answers to these supplementary questions in practice, with the consequence that the broader question of horizontal effect—the impact of constitutional law on private individuals—is not a simple yes or no issue but rather a matter of degree. Typical legal areas in which this impact occurs include defamation, invasion of privacy suits, and employer–employee law. So, for example, on the first, even though neither the German Basic Law nor the Canadian Charter imposes constitutional duties on private individuals, the Supreme Court of Canada (SCC) has held that Charter rights do not bind the country's courts.[34] By contrast, the German Federal Constitutional Court (FCC) has held that the rights in the Basic Law do bind the courts; indeed, the vast majority of successful constitutional complaints in Germany are against the lower courts. Under the statutory bills of rights enacted in the United Kingdom and both the Australian Capital Territory and state of Victoria, the rights are expressly stated not to bind the legislature, so as to maintain the essential core of parliamentary sovereignty—although the one enacted in New Zealand does—and in the United Kingdom and New Zealand, but not in the two Australian bills of rights, the rights also bind the courts.

On the second question, the issue of whether private law (and especially the Civil Code) is subject to the Basic Law was the cause of a major and prolonged debate in Germany before the FCC fixed its position in the landmark and influential *Lüth* decision of 1958.[35] The common law was held to be subject to Charter rights by the SCC in the case of *Dolphin Delivery* but, as we shall see shortly, not as fully or equally as private statute law. In South Africa, the common law is subject to both 'direct' (under section 8) and 'indirect' (under section 39) application of the Bill of Rights.[36] Both Australian jurisdictions have excluded the common law from being subject to their statutory bills of rights, and this issue has not yet been definitively resolved in the United Kingdom.

Finally, on the third question, because the Charter applies neither to private individuals nor the courts, the SCC also held in *Dolphin Delivery* that Charter rights do not apply to common law litigation between private individuals where the only official action is a court order.[37]

[34] Because s 32, the application clause, refers only to legislatures and 'government,' with the latter meaning the executive branch only. *Retail, Wholesale & Dep't Store Union v Dolphin Delivery Ltd* [1986] 2 SCR 573.

[35] BVerfGE 7, 198 (1958).

[36] Frank Michelman, 'On the Uses of Interpretive "Charity": Some Notes on Application, Avoidance, Equality and Objective Unconstitutionality from the 2007 Term of the Constitutional Court of South Africa' (2008) 1 *Constitutional Court Review* 1.

[37] At the same time, the SCC stated in *Dolphin Delivery* that Charter rights are not entirely irrelevant to such private litigation. Rather, 'the judiciary ought to apply and develop the principles of the common law in a manner consistent with the fundamental values enshrined in the Constitution': [1986] 2 SCR at 605. This distinction between the direct application of Charter *rights* and the general influence of Charter *values* in private, common law litigation has been maintained by the SCC ever since, and it elaborated on the practical significance of the distinction in *Hill v Toronto* [1995] 2 SCR 1130. Arguably, however, more recent cases in which courts have modified the common law in line with Charter values, such as *Grant v Torstar Corp* [2009] SCC 61 (creating a new defense in common law defamation actions of 'reasonable communication on matters of public interest'), have rendered the distinction a very fine one in practice.

By contrast, the major argument in the United Kingdom that the Human Rights Act does apply to such litigation stems from the inclusion of the courts among the 'public authorities' bound to act consistently with Convention rights. In South Africa, the Bill of Rights can apply directly to such suits, although it can also apply indirectly—as in Canada—by developing the common law in line with its 'spirit, purport and objects'.[38]

Moreover, those countries that impose constitutional duties on private actors also do so in different ways and to differing degrees. So, for example, in Ireland, the 'constitutional tort action' has been implied by the courts from a general textual duty on the state to protect and enforce the rights of individuals.[39] By contrast, in South Africa, horizontality is the express, if partial and complex, mandate of sections 8(2), 8(3), and 9(4) of the Constitution.[40] On degree, the constitutional courts of Argentina and Colombia have perhaps subjected private actors to constitutional rights most consistently and extensively.[41]

One principal scholarly achievement in this area has been the creation and refinement of a concept that describes an intermediate third position in between the polar positions of vertical and horizontal effect. Originating in the FCC's landmark *Lüth* decision, this concept is known in German as '*mittelbare Drittwirkung*' and more generally as 'indirect horizontal effect', as distinct from the 'direct' horizontal effect of the second polar position. In essence, this intermediate position is that although constitutional rights apply directly only to the government, they nonetheless have some degree of indirect application to private actors. More precisely, the distinction between direct and indirect horizontal effect is that between subjecting private *conduct* to constitutional rights on the one hand (direct), and subjecting private *laws* to constitutional rights on the other (indirect).[42] In other words, there are two different ways in which constitutional rights might regulate private actors, that is have horizontal effect: (1) directly, by governing their conduct; or (2) indirectly, by governing the private laws that structure their legal relations with each other and that they rely on or invoke in civil disputes. This second, indirect method of regulation limits what private actors may lawfully be empowered to do and which of their interests, preferences, and actions can be protected by law. Indirect horizontal effect has been further subdivided into stronger and weaker forms. The former means that private law is fully and equally subject to constitutional law; the latter that courts have a duty to take constitutional law into account in interpreting and developing private law.[43]

A second focus of comparative scholarship has been exploration of the connections between the structural issue of the scope of constitutional rights and the substantive issue of their content. Given that, as we have seen, indirect horizontal effect subjects (all or most) private law to constitutional rights scrutiny, in any country adopting this position—or, of course, direct horizontal effect—the actual consequences for private individuals turns wholly on the substance

[38] Michelman (n 36).

[39] Irish Constitution, Art 40.3.1 (1937); see eg *Meskell v Coras Iompair Eireann* [1973] IR 121.

[40] 'A provision of the Bill of Rights binds a natural or juristic person if, and to the extent that, it is applicable, taking account of the nature of the right and the nature of any duty imposed by the right': South African Constitution, s 8(2). Section 9(4) imposes a duty on private individuals not to discriminate against others on the same comprehensive set of grounds applicable to the state.

[41] See Rivera-Perez (n 19).

[42] Gardbaum (n 33); Mark Tushnet, 'The Issue of State Action/Horizontal Effect in Comparative Constitutional Law' (2003) *International Journal of Constitutional Law* 79–98; Halton Cheadle, 'Third Party Effect in the South African Constitution' in András Sajó and Renáta Uitz (eds), *The Constitution in Private Relations: Expanding Constitutionalism* (2005).

[43] Gavin Phillipson, 'The Human Rights Act, "Horizontal Effect" and the Common Law: A Bang or a Whimper?' (1999) 62 *Modern Law Review* 824; Gardbaum (n 33).

of those rights. So, for example, broad substantive constitutional equality or free speech norms (such as incorporating disparate impact or incidental burdens on speech) would result in much traditional contract, property, and tort law being unconstitutional or significantly altered to cohere with constitutional norms, and so have greater impact on individuals. Narrower substantive norms (such as prohibiting only intentional government discrimination or content-specific speech regulation) would not.[44] Indeed, this connection has led Tushnet to argue that the threshold 'state action' issue is conceptually equivalent to the issue of constitutional social and economic rights: the more extensive a commitment to social and economic rights, the more easily courts will lower barriers of scope; the greater the resistance to such substantive rights, the more courts will employ verticality as a threshold defense technique.[45]

Similarly, scholars have explored the subtle connections between jurisdictional, institutional, and procedural differences among certain highest courts—whether they are specialist constitutional or generalist courts, whether they have jurisdiction to interpret and apply private, common, or state/provincial law—and the operation of indirect horizontal effect in those countries.[46] Indeed, Kumm and Ferreres Comella have argued that given the particular constellation of these factors in Germany, there is effectively no practical difference between direct and indirect horizontal effect.[47] Particularly in countries with relatively little private law to interpret, however, as in certain Latin American jurisdictions where courts have stepped in to help to fill legislative vacuums, this is not the case.[48]

3. Constitutional Law and Positive Rights

A third important specific issue is the role of constitutional law versus ordinary law/politics in the bestowing of entitlements from the state. To what extent is and should constitutional law be confined to imposing duties of forbearance on (mostly) government action as contrasted with imposing affirmative obligations or duties of action? In other words, should there be constitutional entitlements or only political ones?

Modern constitutional law around the world contains two main types of such entitlements, or positive rights. The first is social and economic rights as, for example, the rights to education, health care, housing, social security, and work.[49] The second is protective rights, the right to protection or security from the state against certain types of action by fellow-citizens, such as violence and theft. Constitutions may and do contain both types of positive rights, one type but not the other, or neither.

As 'second generation' rights, social and economic constitutional rights are primarily the product of one of the two great modern bursts of constitution-making, the first after 1945 and the second after 1989. The 1947 Italian and the 1996 South African Constitutions are perhaps

[44] Gardbaum (n 33); Tushnet (n 42).

[45] Tushnet (n 42).

[46] Ibid; Mattias Kumm and Victor Ferreres Comella, 'What is So Special about Constitutional Rights in Private Litigation? A Comparative Analysis of the Function of State Action Requirements and Indirect Horizontal Effect' in Sajó and Uitz (n 42), 241–86; Michelman (n 36).

[47] Tushnet (n 42).

[48] Rivera-Perez (n 19).

[49] Not all social and economic rights are positive rights. Eg the right to choose an occupation and the right to educate one's child privately—where recognized by constitutional law—may (but need not) be exclusively negative in scope, requiring only governmental forbearance from prohibiting business entry and banning private schools.

paradigmatic in this regard. At the same time, however, overall the constitutions of the newly liberated countries of Central and Eastern Europe and South Africa, as well as those of developing nations, more consistently contain significant numbers of social and economic rights than either West European countries or common law jurisdictions.[50]

Whereas where granted, social and economic rights are typically expressly contained in a constitutional text, constitutional rights to protection are a little more evenly divided between text and judicial implication. So, for example, the constitutions of South Africa, Greece, Switzerland, and Ireland contain express rights to state protection.[51] Elsewhere, protective duties have been implied by the judiciary from certain textual rights that seem on their face negative. Thus, the best known and most important protective duties (*Schutzpflichten*) in Germany concern the right to life and freedom of expression. The FCC famously interpreted the former in the *First Abortion Case* to require the state to protect the lives of fetuses against such private actors as their mothers, presumptively through the criminal law.[52] The right to freedom of broadcasting was also interpreted by the FCC to require state regulation to ensure the protection of citizens' access to the full range of political opinions necessary for them to make informed decisions at elections.[53] Although admittedly an international court, the European Court of Human Rights has been particularly active in inferring protective duties—though not social and economic rights—from the seemingly negatively phrased civil and political rights contained in the European Convention.[54]

Unlike the case generally with negative constitutional rights, the practical impact of both types of positive constitutional rights is sometimes significantly reduced either by express statements that some or all such rights are not judicially enforceable or by judicial practice to similar effect. Starting with social and economic rights, the constitutions of Ireland, India, and Spain (in the latter case, apart from the right to education) expressly distinguish between rights proper and 'directive' or 'guiding principles' of social and economic policy that are intended to guide the legislature but are not cognizable by any court. Similarly, apart from the rights to primary education and to 'aid in distress', the Swiss Constitution contains a set of 'social goals' that is expressly declared to be non-justiciable.

Even where judicially enforceable, constitutional courts have generally been cautious about the scope of their review of social and economic rights and have tended to grant legislatures wide discretion at to the means of fulfilling their affirmative obligation. Accordingly, a reasonableness test has been the norm. In South Africa, this reasonableness standard—relative to available resources—is contained in the text as defining the positive obligations of the state with respect to most of its social and economic rights, and the constitutional court has as a result rejected the proposition that such rights entitle individuals to be provided with 'a minimum core'. As is well known, however, in the important cases of *Grootboom*[55] and *Treatment Action Campaign*,[56] the South African Constitutional Court (SACC) held that government

[50] Stephen Gardbaum, 'The Myth and the Reality of American Constitutional Exceptionalism' (2008) 107 *Michigan Law Review* 391.

[51] See eg South African Constitution, s 12(1): 'Everyone has the right to freedom and security of the person, which includes the right... to be free from all forms of violence from either public or private sources.'

[52] BVerfGE 39, 1 (1975).

[53] BVerfGE 12, 205 (1961).

[54] *X and Y v The Netherlands*, 91 ECtHR (Ser A) (1985); *Plattform 'Ärtze für das Leben'*, 139 ECtHR (Ser A) (1988).

[55] *Republic of South Africa v Grootboom*, 2002 (1) SA 46 (CC).

[56] *Minister of Health v Treatment Action Campaign*, 2002 (5) SA 721 (CC).

policies in the areas of housing for the desperately needy and combating mother-to-child transmission of HIV were unreasonable and thus unconstitutional. Moreover, in the latter case, the SACC ordered the government to change its restrictive policy on access to the drug Nevirapine. Both the Japanese and Korean supreme courts have subjected textual rights to minimum living standards to highly deferential reasonableness tests under which government programs were upheld, although both acknowledged that government failure to act at all to promote the constitutional objective would amount to an unconstitutional abuse of discretion.[57] The Italian Constitutional Court has also generally interpreted the many social and economic rights contained in the 1947 Constitution as imposing a reasonableness test on government policy in the relevant areas.[58] These differences have led Tushnet to classify social and economic rights into three types: (1) merely declaratory; (2) weak substantive rights; and (3) strong substantive rights.[59]

Similarly, the level of judicial scrutiny to which constitutional rights to protection are subject is typically lower—more deferential—than that afforded to negative rights within the same constitutional regime. Accordingly, protective rights generally grant to governments greater discretion in doing what they must do than negative ones grant in what they cannot. Constitutional rights are typically protected by a proportionality test under which the intensity of scrutiny varies, among other things, with the importance of the right in question. Even the relatively less important rights, though, are subject to the second, minimal impairment prong that provides additional protection above and beyond the first, rationality prong. Protective rights, however, are generally subject only to a form of reasonableness test, rather than the usual proportionality test. That is, courts typically ask only whether the state has reasonably fulfilled its positive duty, a usually lenient and deferential test that rarely results in findings of failure. The reasons for this more lenient test are the standard reasons for wariness about including positive rights in constitutions that we will briefly canvass in the next subsection: that in telling the elected branches of government what they must do, the judiciary lacks institutional expertise and assumes control of the public purse. In Germany, the FCC has not held that the government violated its protective duty with respect to the right to life and health in any case other than the two concerning abortion.[60]

Apart from descriptive work on particular countries, and here South Africa and the former Soviet-bloc nations have been the major subjects, more general or structural scholarship on positive constitutional rights has mostly focused on the following two issues. First, certain scholars have called into question the distinction between negative and positive rights, and others, while accepting the distinction in theory, have argued that the difference between them in practice is far smaller than assumed. Secondly, there has been a robust debate on whether constitutions should contain positive rights and to what extent, if any, socio-economic rights guarantees in particular make much difference in practice.

Although not the first to do so, Cass Sunstein has expressed skepticism towards the general distinction between negative and positive constitutional rights in that (1) 'most of the so-called negative rights require government assistance, not governmental abstinence', giving the examples of the creation and dependence of private property, freedom of contract, and criminal

[57] *Asahi v Japan*, 21 Minshū 5, 1043 (1967); *Livelihood Protection Standard Case*, 9-1 KCCR 543 (1997).

[58] Francisco Rubio Llorente, 'Constitutionalism in the "Integrated" States of Europe', NYU School of Law, Jean Monnet Center, Working Paper No 5/98, 1998.

[59] Mark Tushnet, *Weak Courts, Strong Rights* (2008).

[60] Gerald L. Neuman, '*Casey* in the Mirror: Abortion, Abuse and the Right to Protection in the United States and Germany' (2005) 43 *American Journal of Comparative Law* 273–314. On abortion more generally, see Chapter 51.

procedure rights on law and courts, and (2) '[a]ll constitutional rights [and not only positive ones] have budgetary implications; all constitutional rights cost money'.[61]

More specifically on practical differences between the two, David Currie pointed out that the effect of common general constitutional anti-discrimination provisions, such as the US equal protection clause, is to create 'conditional affirmative' duties of protection and provision of government services. '[I]f government undertakes to help A, it may have to help B as well.' That is, governmental omissions sometimes amount to unlawful discrimination. Moreover, given the practical impossibility of abandoning certain protective laws (such as the criminalization of murder and theft) and government welfare programs, the effect of such anti-discrimination provisions will often be the same as if there were an absolute affirmative constitutional duty to enact the laws or program.[62] Currie's point explains, for example, why in the United States, even absent a constitutional duty to protect the right to life of a fetus as exists in Germany, a finding that a fetus is a 'person' for constitutional purposes would probably entail in practice that the state must protect its life along with the other persons it chooses to protect. Failure to do so would likely amount to unconstitutional discrimination.

A second area that has attracted a good deal of scholarly attention is the issue of whether or not constitutions in general—and particularly the new constitutions of countries seeking to make the transition from centralized to market economies in Central and Eastern Europe—should include social and economic rights. Most of the arguments, for and against, have focused on pragmatic or instrumental concerns rather than theoretical, moral, or intrinsic ones. Arguments against such rights include that they either become meaningless promises and thereby threaten to undermine negative rights and the rule of law or are ruinously expensive for poorer countries,[63] and that they unduly interfere with the attempt to create market economies and hobble the creation of civil society.[64] More generally, it has been argued that pragmatic understanding of the operation of government and particularly the judicial system dooms any hopes that the recognition of positive rights will improve the lives of the intended beneficiaries.[65] A more general argument, although perhaps an increasingly naive one as the role of money in politics advances everywhere, is that given whom they benefit—typically the majority of citizens—the standard reasons for constitutionalizing rights rather than leaving them to the ordinary legal and political process do not obviously apply.

One argument for such rights is that court decisions on social rights can bolster elected politicians' ability to stand up to international financial institutions preaching 'market fundamentalism' and thereby enhance public support for democracy.[66] Another is that failure to include such rights would be viewed by the people as an attempt by the ruling elite to deprive citizens of their acquired rights and fatally undermine popular support for the new regime.[67]

[61] Cass R. Sunstein, 'Why Does the American Constitution Lack Social and Economic Guarantees' in Michael Ignatieff (ed), *American Exceptionalism and Human Rights* (2005). For a response to this argument, see Gardbaum (n 50), 445–6.

[62] David P. Currie, 'Positive and Negative Constitutional Rights' (1986) 53 *University of Chicago Law Review* 864.

[63] András Sajó, 'How the Rule of Law Killed Hungarian Welfare Reform' (1996) 5 *East European Constitutional Review* 31.

[64] Cass R. Sunstein, 'Against Positive Rights' (1993) 2 *Eastern European Constitutional Review* 35.

[65] Frank B. Cross, 'The Error of Positive Rights' (2001) 48 *UCLA Law Review* 857.

[66] Kim Lane Scheppele, 'Constitutional Courts in the Field of Power Politics: A Realpolitik Defense of Social Rights' (2004) 82 *Texas Law Review* 338.

[67] Wiktor Osiatynski, 'Social and Economic Rights in a New Constitution for Poland' in András Sajó (ed), *Western Rights? Post-Communist Application* (1996).

Whether and how positive rights in general and social and economic rights in particular are justiciable and enforceable has always been a major part of this issue.[68] Two developments in the past decade have enriched this aspect of the scholarly debate. First, both the fact that the SACC declared the final constitution's social and economic rights to be judicially enforceable and the manner in which it enforced two of them in the *Grootboom* and *Treatment Action Campaign* cases mentioned above had a substantial impact on this issue, even persuading some academic commentators partially to change their minds.[69] It has also provided fresh evidence and insights on the questions of whether and how social and economic constitutional rights make any real difference to the lives of the poor.[70] Secondly, the recent establishment and growth of what has variously been termed 'weak-form judicial review' and 'the new Commonwealth model of constitutionalism' has provided a new form of judicial review—in which the legislature has the legal power of the final word—that may be particularly appropriate for social and economic rights.[71]

Bibliography

T.R.S. Allan, *Constitutional Justice: A Liberal Theory of the Rule of Law* (2001)

T.R.S. Allan, *Law, Liberty, and Justice: The Legal Foundations of British Constitutionalism* (1993)

Richard Bellamy, *Political Constitutionalism: A Republican Defence of the Constitutionality of Democracy* (2007)

Jeffrey Dunoff and Joel Trachtman (eds), *Ruling the World? Constitutionalism, International Law and Global Government* (2009)

William N. Eskridge and John A. Ferejohn, 'Super-Statutes' (2001) 50 *Duke Law Journal* 1215

Stephen Gardbaum, 'The New Commonwealth Model of Constitutionalism' (2001) 49 *American Journal of Comparative Law* 707

Thomas C. Grey, 'Do We Have an Unwritten Constitution?' (1975) 27 *Stanford Law Review* 703

Aileen Kavanagh, *Constitutional Review under the UK Human Rights Act* (2009)

Mattias Kumm, 'Who is Afraid of the Total Constitution? Constitutional Rights as Principles and the Constitutionalization of Private Law' (2006) 7 *German Law Journal* 341

András Sajó and Renáta Uitz (eds), *The Constitution in Private Relations: Expanding Constitutionalism* (2005)

David A. Strauss, 'Common Law Constitutional Interpretation' (1996) 63 *University of Chicago Law Review* 877

Adam Tomkins, *Our Republican Constitution* (2005)

Mark Tushnet, *Weak Courts, Strong Rights* (2008)

Lorraine Weinrib, 'The Postwar Paradigm and American Exceptionalism' in Sujit Choudhry (ed), *The Migration of Constitutional Ideas* (2005)

[68] Matthew Craven, 'The Justiciability of Economic, Social and Cultural Rights' in Richard Burchill et al (eds), *Economic, Social and Cultural Rights: Their Implementation in United Kingdom Law* (1999); Martin Scheinin, 'Economic and Social Rights as Legal Rights' in Asbjorn Eide et al (eds), *Economic, Social and Cultural Rights: A Textbook* (2001).

[69] Cass R. Sunstein, 'Social and Economic Rights: Lessons From South Africa' in *Designing Democracy: What Constitutions Do* (2001).

[70] Dennis M. Davis, 'Socioeconomic Rights: Do they Deliver the Goods?' (2008) 6 *International Journal of Constitutional Law* 687–711.

[71] Mark Tushnet, 'Social Welfare Rights and the Forms of Judicial Review' (2004) 82 *Texas Law Review* 1895; Rosalind Dixon, 'Creating Dialogue About Socio-Economic Rights: Strong v Weak-Form Judicial Review Revisited' (2007) 5 *International Journal of Constitutional Law* 391.

PART II

IDEAS

CHAPTER 8

CONSTITUTIONS AND CONSTITUTIONALISM

STEPHEN HOLMES

New York

I. Introduction

Democratic theory conventionally defines a constitution as a 'higher law' that cannot be changed through normal lawmaking procedures in a popularly elected assembly.[1] Exceptional legal entrenchment is said to insulate constitutional rules from the majoritarian controls that purportedly govern ordinary legislation. In this way, a constitutional text strives to make fast the form of government (a presidential or parliamentary, a unitary or federal republic), the limits of government (inviolable rights and immunities), and the goals for which the

[1] Stephen Holmes, 'Precommitment and the Paradox of Democracy' in *Passions and Constraint: On the Theory of Liberal Democracy* (1995), 134–77.

government is empowered to act (to ensure domestic tranquility, provide for the common defense, and promote the general welfare).

With this rough understanding of a democratic constitution in mind, constitutional theorists routinely plunge into a heated debate over the counter-majoritarian dilemma, namely the question: Why would constantly renewed generations of voters remain committed to an inherited arrangement that was intentionally crafted to be difficult to change?[2]

The so-called counter-majoritarian dilemma, however, is both politically fraught and analytically confused. American liberals, for example, have an incurably schizophrenic attitude toward counter-majoritarian institutions. On the one hand, they favor rigid restraints on racially bigoted majorities but, on the other hand, they oppose rigid restraints on economically redistributive majorities. American conservatives are no more consistent. A theoretically coherent and nonpartisan approach to counter-majoritarian institutions is nowhere to be found.

The very idea of counter-majoritarianism suffers from a deeper flaw, moreover. The *lex majoris partis* is one of those decision rules that allow a population of human beings to make collective decisions for the first time. It may be a rational rule, but it is nevertheless a rule that is presupposed by, not produced by, collective choice, and that includes the choices attributed to an imaginary popular sovereign. Unless such a constitutive rule is already in place, the nation or the people cannot hammer out the kind of 'constitutive will' that could subsequently be thwarted or betrayed.

This consideration reveals the flaw in Jon Elster's much-discussed but abortive attempt to explain, by drawing an analogy between constitutional conventions and Ulysses ordering himself to be bound to the mast of his ship, how a democratic people could impose a constitution on itself.[3] That this eye-catching parable does little to illuminate the origins, survival, and function of democratic constitutions (by which democratic peoples purportedly bind themselves) is by now widely acknowledged, even by Elster himself.[4] The main defect of the analogy is that Ulysses operated as a coherent decision-maker, capable of issuing authoritative commands and being duly obeyed, prior to ordering his sailors to lash him to the mast. Only the acknowledged captain of a deferential crew, not a politically amorphous population operating without pre-established decision rules or a clearly demarcated boundary between members and nonmembers, could play such a constitutive role.

Unlike hundreds of thousands of independent villagers and subsistence farmers strewn across a lengthy Atlantic coastline, compact political elites have a pre-constitutional capacity to create, amend, interpret, and enforce constitutional rules that favor their real or imagined interests. But this does not necessarily mean that 'constitutionalization', as neo-progressives continue to urge, is 'driven primarily by political interests to insulate certain policy preferences from popular pressures'.[5]

Political, social, and economic elites have reasons to bind themselves that are related only incidentally to parrying majoritarian demands. This issue has been muddled in US historiography because the Contracts Clause was obviously inserted in the Constitution by creditors and their allies to resist the demands of debtors and tax delinquents.[6] But governments

[2] Lawrence Tribe, *American Constitutional Law* (2nd edn, 1988), 10.

[3] Jon Elster, *Ulysses and the Sirens: Studies in Rationality and Irrationality* (1984), 93–5.

[4] Jon Elster, *Ulysses Unbound: Studies in Rationality, Precommitment, and Constraints* (2000), 88–174.

[5] Ran Hirschl, *Towards Juristocracy: The Origins and Consequences of the New Constitutionalism* (2004), 213.

[6] Woody Holton, *Unruly Americans and the Origins of the Constitution* (2007).

routinely commit to repaying loans not only to resist the Sirens' songs of tax relief and paper money but also in a bid to become a Siren. By making credible commitments to pay back loans, a government can entice money, at relatively low interest rates, from the pockets of money-lenders in a way that unbound borrowers cannot easily do. The unlocking of foreign and domestic credit by governments that have established a reputation for creditworthiness is a good example of elite self-binding for the elite's own advantage. It suggests that the powerful can have a strong incentive to make their behavior predictable even in the absence of popular pressures. But this is only one example among many.

Historically, political, social, and economic elites have proved themselves willing to impose grueling discipline on their own membership, including years devoted to arduously honing uncommon physical, intellectual, and technical skills, to maintain their group's superior status over time. They have also accepted binding rules that facilitate the nonviolent resolution of intra-elite conflicts that, if not rapidly patched up, might risk opening the door to domestic insurrection or foreign conquest. And they have willingly offloaded time-consuming responsibilities in order to specialize on more lucrative tasks as well as to insulate themselves from annoying clientalistic demands.

But for constitutional theory, starting with ancient writings on the mixed regime, the most 'democratic' reason why elites have proved willing to impose limits on themselves is that such limits help to mobilize the voluntary cooperation of non-elites in the pursuit of the elite's most highly prized objectives, especially revenue extraction and victory in war, but also information gathering and the timely correction of potentially fatal errors of judgment. Even John Locke, that liberal saint, invoked *raison d'état* in his defense of constitutional restraints on power:

> that Prince, who shall be so wise and godlike as by established laws of liberty to secure protection and incouragement to the honest industry of Mankind, against the oppression of power and narrownesse of Party will quickly be too hard for his neighbours.[7]

No power-wielder is so powerful that he never requires voluntary cooperation from members of society weaker than himself. To obtain a sufficient 'supply' of men and money, enthroned kings once convened prominent taxpayers in parliaments and listened to their grievances. Today, even governments elected by universal suffrage spend more resources protecting the rights of citizens whose cooperation is essential to governance, such as investment-bank presidents, than they spend protecting the rights of citizens whose cooperation is worth little or nothing, such as homeless veterans. Full-fledged democracy has always been and will always remain more an aspiration than a reality; but genuinely democratic episodes occur when powerful actors discover, as they sometimes do, a palpable advantage in popular participation, government transparency, protections for minorities, and uncensored debate.

II. Realism and Idealism in Constitutional Theory

Those who disparage democratic constitutionalism as a well-meaning ideology do not mean to deny that constitutions are an observable reality. Polities have always been 'constituted' in the etymological sense of organized for collective defense and hierarchical domination. As

[7] John Locke, 'Second Treatise on Civil Government' in Peter Laslett (ed), *Two Treatises of Government* ([1689] 1965), sec 42, 340.

already suggested, dominant social groups have occasionally agreed to impose regularized restraints on their members in order to sustain, with a minimum of force, their group's privileges over time and to mobilize the cooperation of lower-status adult males for the sake of collective endeavors, especially war. Constitutionalism, by contrast, emerged only in the age of democratic revolutions, during the last three decades of the eighteenth century. It involved not any possible organization of political life but an ideal form of organization that subordinated political incumbents to a higher law that they were forbidden, in principle, unilaterally to change. Especially novel in the new conceptualization was the fiction that a republican constitution should not be revised by ordinary lawmaking procedures because it embodied the 'reflection and choice'[8] of the nation or the people.[9]

No constitution has ever lived up to the promise of democratic constitutionalism, aligning the interests of the rulers with the interests of the ruled. Nor has any constitution ever protected all citizens equally, without regard to the robust or tattered social networks within which different citizens were variously embedded. Idealists who imagine that really-existing constitutions could perform miracles of this sort have to explain how such morally just arrangements could possibly have emerged historically and why they would have survived. After all, powerless individuals with few allies are those who, by definition, are unable to impose their will on others, while the capacity to amass privileges and shift burdens onto others is exactly what characterizes social elites who are plugged into strong social networks.

Realism suggests that constitutional checks on political power emerged and survived, whenever they did, because they served, or appeared to serve, the interests of individuals associated with well-organized social forces. One of the best organized of all social forces, of course, is the government itself. If we want to examine constitutional limits with fresh eyes, therefore, a good place to start is with the advantages that governing elites might reap from accepting legal restraints on their freedom of action. The sustainability of constitutional restraints is difficult to understand if their primary purpose is to benefit the weak by disabling the strong.[10] On the other hand, if constitutions, for example, make it possible for powerful actors to cast off unprofitable or risk-laden or self-defeating forms of power and thereby make it easier for them to achieve their principal aims, the authority of constitutions, at least to those who inhabit and control the commanding heights of political power, is much easier to understand.

Some general remarks about rules will also prove helpful before we explore this theme in greater detail. What is true for renowned constitutional principles such as freedom of speech and the press is true for rules generally, namely that they can be enabling as well as disabling. A moment's thought about the rules of grammar will make this clear. The rules of grammar do not hinder but rather facilitate the ability to communicate, and that includes the ability to communicate surprising, unnerving, rude, unpopular, and even anti-constitutional ideas. It would obviously be inaccurate, therefore, to conceptualize such rules merely as don'ts, prohibitions, barriers, injunctions, no-trespass signs, or purely negative limitations on permissible behavior. True, the rules of grammar introduce certain rigidities into ordinary language. But rigidities, for a variety of reasons, can be prodigiously enabling.

Dissolving all rigidities would decrease rather than increase available options. For example, if human beings had no bones, they would be unable to walk. My initial, somewhat but not

[8] Alexander Hamilton, James Madison, and John Jay, *The Federalist Papers* (Clinton Rossiter ed, 1999), no 1, 27.

[9] See Chapter 20.

[10] As claimed by Giovanni Sartori, 'Constitutionalism: A Preliminary Discussion' (1962) 56(4) *American Political Science Review* 853.

entirely frivolous proposal, therefore, is that we analogize constitutional rules not to the incapacitating rope with which Ulysses had himself tightly bound to the mast to prevent him from yielding to an uncontrollable impulse, but to the facilitating grammar that enables human communication, to rules of a game that make it possible for players to compete, or perhaps even to the skeletons that facilitate nimble locomotion in vertebrates. But analogies with grammatical rules and animal skeletons are but the vaguest of gestures. Decision-making procedures, such as majority rule, bring us closer to where we want to be. They reveal how binding rules, rather than rendering fatal impulses inoperative in the manner of Ulysses' shackles, can facilitate cooperative action, provide access to hitherto unavailable possibilities, and even make an assemblage of individuals capable for the first time of collective choice.

We misunderstand the appeal of constitutional rigidities if we focus solely on the flexibilities they prevent while ignoring the flexibilities they simultaneously create. I want to begin, therefore, by looking at the emergence and institutionalization of enabling constraints in pre-democratic and pre-liberal societies where socio-economic hierarchy was embraced without embarrassment by ruling groups. This is not a detour. To explore the origins, survival, and function of 'primitive constitutions'[11] in societies where the rights of the weak were routinely trampled and their voices unheard, will help us to bring into focus the value of constitutional restraints from the viewpoint of ruling groups in liberal and democratic societies as well.

III. A Preliminary Example

Even when the ruled are too busy feeding their families to try to impose constitutional restraints upon their rulers, these rulers have found reasons of their own voluntarily to accept selective restraints on their power. Among modern monarchies, Machiavelli singles out France, where none of the kings who are 'born under such constitutions' (*nascono sotto tali constituzioni*) can 'break the brake that can correct him' (*rompere quel freno che gli può correggere*).[12] This is an extraordinarily interesting formulation. To concretize what Machiavelli means by a constitutional *freno* (brake) that can rectify the prince's mistakes and prevent him from making new ones, we should study Machiavelli's French disciple, Jean Bodin, arguably the greatest theorist of non-democratic constitutional restraints, that is, of constitutional restraints freely adopted by a powerful monarch with the aim of enhancing his power.

A work well known to the American Framers, *The Six Books of the Republic* (1576) contains a fascinating discussion of how constitutional restraints can help solve the principal–agent problem. The French king, Bodin observes, has an extremely difficult time learning what his provincial agents are doing in his name. He cannot easily solve this monitoring or oversight deficit bureaucratically, by assigning a second set of officials to keep tabs on the first. The solution chosen, observes Bodin, is parliamentary immunity, that is, an absolute limit to the king's discretionary power. Representatives in the Estates General have the right to complain loudly about the behavior of any of the king's agents, and to do so without any fear of punishment. Legally exempt from any liability for accusations leveled in the Estates General, representatives provide the king with information vital to his rule but which he would otherwise have no way of obtaining. Here is what occurs in the assembly, to whose members, while the body is in session, the royal power to punish does not extend:

[11] *The Federalist Papers* (n 8), no 18, 121.

[12] Niccolò Machiavelli, *Discourses on Livy* (Harvey Mansfield and Nathan Tarcov trans, 1996), 1.58, 116.

> there are heard and understood the just complaints and grievances of the poor subjects, which never otherwise come unto the prince's ears; there are discovered and laid open the robberies and extortions committed in the prince's name, whereof he knoweth nothing.[13]

A grant of immunity to those who lodge complaints against royal officials was expressly devised, in Bodin's account, to allow the principal to monitor his agents. Because the assembly's members could not be penalized for speaking freely, they could provide the king with vital intelligence about his own operatives that would otherwise remain hidden from him. A formally unlimited monarch embraced a proto separation-of-powers system in order to solve his principal–agent problem, that is, to unlock information he needed to enforce his will effectively. This institutional structure, while serving as a *freno* on the king's discretion in one sense, helped to correct his misapprehensions in another sense, allowing him to control his agents and ensuring that they operated in his interests rather than in their own interests while invoking his name.

Already in 1576, in other words, and in a monarchical system commonly (although inaccurately) called 'absolute', parliamentary immunity was described as a core principle of constitutional government, crafted explicitly to serve the interests of the powerful. It was a restraint on a powerful individual engineered to enhance his disposable power, by allowing the king to keep an eye on his agents and make sure that they were carrying out his instructions even when they operated in remote localities. A king allowed himself to be bound by this rule, or tied to this mast, because the exposés loosed by his self-limitation were palpably useful to his exercise of power. If he had insisted childishly on the crown's unconstrained prerogative to censure political speech, by contrast, the monarch would have been inadvertently helping his subordinates conceal secrets from himself.

This preliminary example, drawn from a pre-democratic constitution, suggests the political utility to the powerful of credible restraints on their own power. Bodin's explanation of parliamentary immunity (a narrowly tailored precursor to universal freedom of speech) implies that political elites can be brought to accept restrictions on their natural impulse to choke off irritating speech for the sake of expected benefits to themselves, even when there is no 'popular sovereign' to set the terms of the constitution or enforce its restrictions with the threat of insurrection. This example, therefore, provides anecdotal evidence for the hypothesis that constitutional restraints emerge and survive when they serve the interests not of all citizens equally but of those individuals whose lives are woven into a community's dominant social networks.

IV. Drill and Discipline

The original meaning of 'to constitute' is neither to constrain political power for the sake of individual liberty nor to force government to obey universal moral norms. What 'to constitute' signifies, in the first instance, is *to set up*. The word 'constitution', according to Diderot's *Encyclopédie*, 'signifie en general établissement de quelque chose'.[14] For the Latin writers of the classical age, to constitute (*constituere*) a republic meant to found and organize it for duration, prosperity, mutual assistance, common defense, and territorial aggrandizement. When he

[13] Jean Bodin, *The Six Books of a Commonweal* (Robert Knolles trans, 1962), bk 3, ch 7, 384.

[14] *Encyclopédie ou dictionnaire raisonné des sciences, des arts et des métiers* (1794), vol 4, 62.

referred to the republican *constitutio*,[15] Cicero meant the morphological structure and operating code of Rome's republican government, the system of major and minor magistracies, the scheduling and organization of elections and judicial trials, the citizens' right to appeal to a popular tribunal against penalties meted out by magistrates in peacetime, the interweaving of Senatorial deliberation, popular approval, and consular action, the legendary power-sharing agreement between the few and the many, and the policy of granting citizenship rights to conquered cities in exchange for military service. McIlwain identified Cicero's *haec constitutio* as the first recorded use of the word 'constitution' in the sense of a frame of government.[16] The Latin *constitutio* also implied an array of other connotations that remain pertinent to constitutional theory today. These include: making a pact or agreeing to act in concert, strengthening defenses in preparation for an enemy attack, fixing a future date for a group meeting, arranging to pay or repay an amount due, appointing someone to a position, and preparing a legal case or lodging an accusation before a tribunal.[17]

As these connotations suggest, *constitutio* broadly referred to an ordering that serves a purpose. Cicero brought this point home when he discussed the constitution of the human body, postulating that nature constituted human beings to walk upright so that they could see the sky and thereby have a chance to know the gods.[18] Rome itself was constituted, more by historical accident than by deliberate design, for military expansion and domination.

Another book well-known to the American Framers, Polybius's *Histories*, argues that Rome's military and political successes were due to its political institutions, that is, to 'the form of the state's constitution [*politeia*]'.[19] The entire Mediterranean world fell under Rome's sway because Rome was politically organized for domination. Polybius's association of constitutionalism with military success seems surprising to readers today only because we tend to think of a constitution as an instrument for controlling overbearing and self-dealing elites, not as an instrument for creating, consolidating, and increasing the power of a collectivity and enhancing the glory of its military commanders.[20] But the liberal-democratic view of constitutions is of recent coinage and provides little help in understanding why constitutions first emerged and historically endured.

The primary function of the ancient constitutions was not to limit preexisting power but to create power out of powerlessness. The legendary constitution-makers or Great Legislators of antiquity were worshipped as religious figures not because they protected minority rights but

[15] For Cicero's explicit reference to the *constitutio rei publicae*, see *De re publica*, in Cicero, *De re publica and De Legibus* (Clinton Walker Keyes trans, 1928), 2.21.37, 144–5; see also *De re publica*, 1.45.69, 104–5; 2.31.53, 162–3; 1.46.70, 104–7; and *De legibus*, 2.16.23, 398–9; 3.18.42, 508–9.

[16] Charles Howard McIlwain, *Constitutionalism Ancient and Modern* (1947), 25; see also Graham Maddox, 'A Note on the Meaning of "Constitution"' (1982) 76(4) *American Political Science Review* 805–9.

[17] Lewis and Short, *A Latin Dictionary* (1975), 437–8.

[18] Cicero, *De natura deorum* (H. Rackham trans, 1933), 2.56.140, 256–7. An analogy between anatomical constitutions and political constitutions was taken for granted in antiquity; even though a good constitution can prolong and improve the life of a community, the analogy implied, no constitution, however excellent, can prevent the ultimate onset of political decomposition any more than the healthiest regimen of exercise and diet can make a well-disciplined individual immortal.

[19] Polybius, *The Rise of the Roman Empire* (1979), I.1 41; VI.2, 302–3.

[20] According to Andrew Lintott,

> Polybius' association of Rome's phenomenal military success with the excellence of her constitution may surprise twentieth-century readers, but it was almost self-evident for a Greek intellectual from within the governing class of the period.

Andrew Lintott, *The Constitution of the Roman Republic* (1999), 1.

because they organized their communities for military defense and conquest. In its most primitive form, the challenge facing any perilously besieged collection of human beings was to turn a disorganized rabble into a fighting machine. Part of the answer, obvious to any student of ancient Rome's stunningly rapid imperial expansion, was relentless discipline and drill. Military hierarchies, alternative combat formations or orders of battle, principles of engagement and so forth include rules and roles of a primitive military constitution. One of the meanings associated with the Latin *constitutio*, in fact, was the way troops were deployed, stationed, drawn up, or set in battle formation. For example, 'Caesar stationed the legion' is 'Legionem Caesar…constituit'.[21] Machiavelli continued to use *constituire* in this sense.[22] A closely related usage survived into America's Founding period in references, for example, to the small professional army that the new federal government needed to repress insurrections and fight the Indians as 'a force *constituted* differently than the militia'.[23] The constitution of a fighting force included instructions for each soldier to maintain his place in the ranks as well as directives, drilled into troops to the point of automaticity, about how to reassemble quickly and reform a defensive perimeter after a line was broken and a massed formation was dispersed chaotically by a surprise attack.

Situated in an international environment inhabited by armed enemies and dubious allies, entire political communities had to be intelligently organized, or constituted, if they were to stay viable and flourish. Darwinian selection guaranteed that the early societies that managed to survive in the midst of marauding predators were those that had successfully subjected young males to rigorous military discipline. But it makes little sense to describe this discipline simply as a restriction on the freedom of those being subjected to its rigors. If they had not accepted the drill and discipline, as they presumably well knew, the inhabitants of such early societies would not have been free but, on the contrary, enslaved or dead. Loosed from all such restraints, early political societies would have quickly disintegrated under the hooves of better organized enemy forces.

The ancestors of the American Framers, the first settlers in the New World, understood this implicitly. They survived and flourished collectively, not individually. To them, individual freedom from all community obligations in the extreme libertarian sense would have meant the 'freedom' of the defenseless straggler to be scalped on the frontier. Later, after Independence, it would have meant the 'freedom' of the commercial seaman to be dragooned at musket-point into the Royal Navy. The hard experience of organizing collective self-defense in an unforgiving environment, therefore, predisposed eighteenth-century Americans to sympathize with the ancient idea of a constitution. The constitutions they created after 1776, including the federal Constitution of 1787, had many functions. But they were all meant to help struggling communities to maintain their boundaries, coherence, and resilience in a dangerous world.

The American Framers undoubtedly wished to design their new commonwealth for territorial expansion and annexation. The amply documented influence of Machiavelli's praise of Rome on their thinking should therefore also be reconsidered in this context. Machiavelli used *constituzione* exactly as Cicero had used *constitutio*, that is, to describe the institutional

[21] Caesar, *The Gallic War* (H.J. Edwards trans, 1917), 1.43, 68.

[22] Machiavelli (n 12), 1.14, 42.

[23] *The Federalist Papers* (n 8), no 28, 175, emphasis added; for an important 'constitutive' document in this sense, see *Baron von Steuben's Revolutionary War Drill Manual* (1985). This is a facsimile reprint of the 1794 edition.

set-up of a republic that was frequently at war. He compared and contrasted the constitutions (*constituzioni*) or forms of government of Athens, Sparta, and Rome, for example, to evaluate their relative military strengths and weaknesses.[24]

But Machiavelli's central contribution to the constitution-making project of the American Framers involved his own unrealizable or at least unrealized project for constitution-making in Italy. The constitutional solution that Machiavelli proposed for that humiliated land, where foreign superpowers conducted proxy wars, was basically a league among the Italian republics to fend off military domination of the peninsula by two great foreign monarchies, Spain and France. If the Italian city-republics did not successfully band together into a Union, Machiavelli reasoned, then those outsized neighboring monarchies would exploit conflicts among the Italian republics and thereby impose their will on the disunited and therefore defenseless mini-states. Only a robust Union among the republics, based on a sense of common destiny, could lead the Italian republics to pool their efforts and counteract the foreign superpowers' predictable strategy of divide and rule. The required sense of common nationhood could not thrive under a prince, he argued, but only if all Italy was organized as a republic—indeed as a republic of republics.

Machiavelli's proposed United Republics of Italy was ill-starred because Italy was not protected from the great European monarchies of his day by the Atlantic moat; and the various Italian republics were not drawn together by the alluring prospect of jointly seizing an immense and fertile continent from its essentially defenseless aboriginal occupants. Hamilton's and Madison's proposed Union was more luckily situated. All innovations duly noted, however, the United States was designed on Machiavelli's model to solve Machiavelli's problem, namely to prevent European monarchies of vastly superior power from using salami tactics to pick disunited republics off one at a time.

This Machiavellian perspective reminds us why so much of the *Federalist* is devoted to 'the safety of the people of America against dangers from FOREIGN force'.[25] As the revolutionary break with Great Britain drew near, the Continental Congress urged the colonies to enact written constitutions in order better to organize the coming military confrontation with British forces.[26] The drive for Union, a decade later, was led by the Framers and their allies in large part because they believed that 'weakness and divisions at home would invite dangers from abroad'.[27] Historically, the shortest-lived federations were those, such as the members of the Amphytonic league who, even in wartime, 'never acted in concert'.[28] Unless the states struggling to defend themselves under the loose federation designed by the Articles would accept a tighter Union, they would be unable, Madison warned, to escape 'the chains of Macedon'.[29] The semi-sovereign states must renounce a degree of autonomy for mutual assistance, to avoid being played off against each other and to create common front against foreigners. If they united their forces, in fact, the American republics might eventually 'soar to a dangerous greatness'.[30]

The authors of the *Federalist* chose to rally support for the proposed Constitution by emphasizing that a 'combination and union of wills, of arms and of resources' could provide the states with 'a formidable state of defense against foreign enemies'.[31] The sales pitch seems to have been persuasive. Common enemies dictate a common or collaborative defense, which implied,

[24] Machiavelli (n 12), 1.2, 13. [25] *The Federalist Papers* (n 8), no 4, 40.

[26] Willi Paul Adams, *The First American Constitutions* (new edn, 2001), 47–60.

[27] *The Federalist Papers* (n 8), no 5, 45.

[28] Ibid no 18, 119. [29] Ibid no 18, 120.

[30] Ibid no 11, 80. [31] Ibid no 5, 47.

at the time, that the state militias had to be placed 'under one plan of discipline'.[32] It is a small leap to consider the proposed Constitution itself as, among other things, a unified *plan of discipline* for coordinating otherwise militarily unimpressive states. For political elites within the states, the benefits of defensive and annexationist power apparently provided sufficient compensation for the cost of becoming small fish in a big pond.

V. The Paradox of Limited Power

The organization of political systems for military defense and offence has always been, and remains today, a major purpose of constitutional organization. But constitutions serve many other goals that are equally appealing to society's dominant forces without any particular regard to democracy or the rights of the weak.

The paradox that limited power can be more powerful than unlimited power probably provides the best explanation for why elites have sometimes, if not invariably, submitted themselves to constitutional restraints even when no popular movement or deadly urban riot has been looming on the horizon. The surprising contribution of self-restraint to the augmentation of power is what accounts, alongside the need for concert and cooperation in war, for the most notable successes that constitutions have enjoyed for more than two millennia. If limited power never produced greater power, constitutions would never have played the important role that they have so obviously played and continue to play in political life.

Social elites impose restraints upon themselves, when they do, to gain something they want, such as more security, more wealth, more territory, more cooperation, or more power. To pursue purposes of this sort, well-organized social groups can intentionally choose to impose new limits upon themselves, including limits that are subjectively experienced by individual group members as irritating fetters or burdens. This, for instance, is one way to make sense of the willingness of occupants of supreme executive power to submit periodically to the will of the electorate, that is, to a public tournament that they might possibly lose.[33]

Why would a powerful incumbent accept periodic elections rather than insisting upon life tenure? One reason is that life tenure gives the rivals of the incumbent, who want to remove him from office, a strong incentive to remove him from life. The brutally terminal methods that were used to impose term limits on several generations of 'life-tenured' Roman Emperors brings this point home. Periodic elections mitigate the frustration of the Outs by offering the hope that they will eventually join the Ins. The prospect (or certainty when constitutions limit elected leaders to one term only) of a potential end-point to the current ruler's incumbency reduces the felt need to eliminate him by violence; it will suffice to wait. The periodic chance to throw the rascals out may also allow for the periodic venting of popular discontent, protecting the dominant classes from a revolutionary explosion where elite heads are indiscriminately wedged onto the pointed ends of sticks.

Celebrated athletes, musicians, inventors, and other popular idols have invariably subjected themselves year after year to relentless physical and mental discipline to hone their skills and achieve a professional excellence unattainable by anyone who lounges about hedonistically, living day to day. In a fascinating passage on oligarchic constitutions,[34] Aristotle explains how

[32] Ibid no 4, 42. [33] See Chapter 25.

[34] I borrow this illuminating example from Elster (n 4, 93–4), who nevertheless insists that 'In politics, people never try to bind themselves, only to bind others' (ix).

political elites can impose similarly self-toughening and survival-enhancing regulations on themselves:

> The devices adopted in [these oligarchic] constitutions (ἐν ταις πολιτείας) for fobbing the masses off with sham rights are five in number. They relate to the assembly; the magistracies; the law courts; the possession of arms; and the practice of athletics. As regards the assembly, all alike are allowed to attend; but fines for non-attendance are either imposed on the rich alone, or imposed on the rich at a far higher rate. As regards the magistracies, those who possess a property qualification are not allowed to decline office on oath, but the poor are allowed to do so. As regards the law courts, the rich are fined for non-attendance, but the poor may absent themselves with impunity; or, alternatively, the rich are heavily fined and the poor are only fined lightly.

To sustain their caste's superiority over time, that is to say, the upper-caste framers of such rules impose a personally unpleasant but politically strengthening discipline on their own caste members while dispensing individually irresistible but collectively weakening exemptions to the lower classes. And Aristotle continues:

> In some states a different device is adopted in regard to attendance at the assembly and the law courts. All who have registered themselves may attend; those who fail to attend after registration are heavily fined. Here the attention is to stop men from registering, through fear of the fines that they may thus incur, and ultimately to stop them from attending the courts and assembly as a result of their failure to register. Similar measures are also employed in regard to the possession of arms and the practice of athletics. The poor are allowed not to have any arms, and the rich are fined for not having them. The poor are not fined if they absent themselves from physical training: the rich are; and so while the latter are induced to attend by the sanction of a fine, the former are left free to abstain in the absence of any deterrent.[35]

Rational members of an oligarchy can impose burdens (including hefty fines) on themselves while granting exemptions and immunities to commoners in order to maintain the dominance of their social caste over time. For the oligarchy in a Greek polis to think up and implement such a system, it must already be organized as a tight-knit corporate entity where obedience to leaders and the emotional-moral identification of caste members with each other can be taken for granted. Individuals within the oligarchic caste must willingly accept personal burdens in the present for the sake of future benefits that will accrue, in the future, to the oligarchic order understood as an entity that endures across generations. For their part, poorly organized commoners, unable to act in concert for temporally remote purposes, will accept the offered exemptions because the immediate benefits to individual commoners seem more salient than the long-term weakening of their already weak-knit group.

Aristotle disapproved of such one-sidedly oligarchic constitutions for various reasons, including the likelihood that commoners will not fight passionately for their city if the constitution gives them no political voice or honorable status in the city's life. This brings us back to what I previously called the most 'democratic' reason why elites have willingly imposed limits on themselves, namely to mobilize the cooperation of non-elites in the accomplishment of the elite's most pressing goals. With the military function of constitutions in mind, Aristotle therefore recommended the following: 'we must both pay the poor for attendance and fine the rich for non-attendance. On this plan, all would share in a common constitution.' Guaranteed a stake in the system, the urban poor will willingly fight against hostile cities, something they may not do if 'the constitution belongs to one side only'.[36]

[35] *The Politics of Aristotle* (Ernest Barker trans, 1968), 1297a, 186–7.

[36] Ibid 187.

The idea that a 'balanced' constitution of this sort could help social elites to manage dangerous class conflict by giving non-elites a palpable stake in the regime's successes was transmitted to modern constitution-makers by ancient theorists of the mixed constitution. Cicero, for example, argued that a constitution should grant 'freedom to the people in such a way as to ensure that the aristocracy shall have great influence and the opportunity to use it',[37] thereby denying that there was a zero-sum relation between popular rights and elite power. In response to the typical aristocratic complaint that the Tribunes of the Plebs have been granted too much power, Cicero responded that 'the power of the people…is sometimes milder in practice because there is a leader to control it'.[38] Viewed superficially, the Tribunes were hostile to Roman elites; but they also provided these elites with recognizable negotiating partners able to make and keep bargains between the rich and the poor. The Senatorial class was wise enough to restrain its own natural impulse to monopolize power, Cicero went on to argue, and, instead, acceded to the creation of the Tribunate, thereby sharing a modicum of power with the Plebs. By such remarkable self-restraint Rome's elite gained much more than it lost:

> consider the wisdom of our ancestors in this matter. When the Senate had granted this power to the plebeians, conflict ceased, rebellion was at an end, and a measure of compromise was discovered which made the more humble believe that they were accorded equality with the nobility; and such a compromise was the only salvation of the State.[39]

The classical idea of a mixed constitution provides an important clue to the origins and fate of constitutional democracy. In specific historical contexts, large numbers of citizens are granted participatory rights because their voluntary cooperation seems essential to achieving the strategic goals of ruling elites. If political dominant groups can see far enough ahead to impose burdens on their members for the sake of maintaining their privileges, they can also (with improved foresight) see the advantage of sharing power with commoners for the sake of gaining the cooperation they need in order to defend themselves as well as their privileges against the threat posed by hostile cities.

VI. Monarchical Constitutions

In non-republican systems, strategic constitutionalism will lead to forms of elite self-discipline entailing few participatory rights for non-elites. This brings us to Thomas Hobbes, who was neither a liberal nor a republican and who railed consistently against 'mixarchy', his denigrating term for a mixed constitution.[40] When he wrote of the 'constitution of sovereign power'[41] Hobbes meant, among other things, the way in which monarchies could and should be organized to enforce unquestioning obedience from a politically passive population. A brief look at monarchical constitutions, therefore, will bring us back to the thesis that constitutional restraints can be embraced by power-wielders for purposes of their own without any serious pressure from the people who, throughout most of history, have been in no position to threaten to withdraw cooperation needed by ruling elites.

A credible succession formula is an essential element in any monarchical constitution. This was already true for the medieval kingships from which Europe's early-modern monarchies emerged. The most important element in monarchical constitutions, commonly called the fundamental laws of the realm, was the order of succession, clarifying sequence and eligibility

[37] Cicero, *De legibus* (n 15), 3.17.38, 502–3. [38] Ibid 3.10.23, 484–5.
[39] Ibid 3.10.24, 487. [40] Thomas Hobbes, *Behemoth* (1990), 116.
[41] Thomas Hobbes, *Leviathan* (C.B. Macpherson ed, 1968), ch 18, 234.

of heirs to the throne and, ideally, specifying uniquely who will become king when the incumbent monarch expires. These rules of succession could privilege either sons or brothers (think of *Hamlet*), could exclude or include female heirs (think of *la loi Salique*), and so forth. That monarchical rules of succession were incomplete, not covering all cases—such as exhaustion of the male line—as well as ambiguous enough to embolden pretenders to the throne, goes without saying.

So why were such orders of succession widely viewed as binding, even in monarchical regimes where the king often claimed to be *legibus solutus*? The answer, which involves the shared desire of all powerful political forces to avoid a power vacuum or violent factional struggle for the throne (which might also expose the state to foreign invasion), tells us something important about voluntarily accepted constitutional constraints in modern democracies as well.

Orders of succession confirm the idea that every constitution is, in part, an emergency constitution.[42] The unexpected death of the king inevitably delivers a profound shock to the political system. It creates a crisis or emergency, throwing into question the political pecking order among courtiers and royal kinsmen that prevailed when the now-deceased monarch was still alive, thereby enflaming the ambitions of blood rivals.

Such an emergency can be managed most effectively by 'if-then' rules elaborated in advance and stockpiled in reserve, allowing the surviving courtiers, when the time comes, to 'discover' the dead king's true successor. These rules constitute the king's supernatural body, representing the 'perpetuity of the sovereign rights of the whole body politic'.[43] The king's 'immortal' body, codified in the order of succession, was engineered even to survive assassination and to help a deceased king's entourage to coordinate quickly on an heir to the throne. This will happen if the otherwise quarreling courtiers and blood relations share a desire to avoid settling the succession question by a resort to violence, which might expose the entire system to civil war and, as a consequence, to an external attack potentially devastating to all. Precomittment to specific rules of succession was meant not to guard an individual from weakness of the will, or uncontrollable impulse, but to guard a group against *the absence of any coherent will* and thus against deadlock, paralysis, regime meltdown, and a resort to perhaps spiraling violence to settle on an heir.[44]

A credible succession formula is not a restriction on the power of the head of state. It is eminently 'constitutional' but cannot be accurately described as a 'limitation on government by law'.[45] Rather, it is an outstanding example of strategic constitutionalism. It is an instrument by which political elites can coordinate quickly to install a new head of state before the last one's body grows cold. Such provisions are certainly not restrictions imposed on the powerful to protect the weak. Instead, they are scripts to help the powerful coordinate quickly on a pathway out of a crisis that they know will eventually come even though they cannot be sure when.

Containing a monarchical residue, presidential systems share with monarchies some of the challenges of avoiding chaos or maintaining continuity of government during an interregnum—challenges that parliamentary systems handle in a different way.[46] The Twenty-Fifth

[42] See Chapter 21.

[43] Ernst Kantorowicz, *The King's Two Bodies: A Study in Medieval Political Theology* (1957), 383.

[44] The utility of constitutional restraints for keeping elite conflicts within bounds supports Jeremy Waldron's criticism of the Ulysses analogy, namely that constitutionalism assumes not agreement but disagreement among the political decision-makers. Jeremy Waldron, *Law and Disagreement* (1999), 271.

[45] McIlwain (n 16), 22.

[46] See further Chapter 29 on presidentialism and Chapter 30 on parliamentarism.

Amendment to the US Constitution, in fact, can be understood as the US President's supernatural body, made not of flesh and blood but of protocols and rules. Introduced in 1965, in the wake of the Kennedy assassination (and ratified in 1967), the Twenty-Fifth Amendment was crafted to avoid a prolonged succession crisis, or power vacuum, in case the President, after an assassination attack or perhaps a stroke, survived in a vegetative state. The scenario by which a Vice President could step into the role of a disabled President was evidently not spelled out in the original Constitution with enough specificity to guide uncertain actors in an inherently stressful situation. By 1965, it had become clear that such a state of affairs could no longer be tolerated, not in the atomic age where split-second executive decision-making might be necessary at any time.

Section 4 of the Twenty-Fifth Amendment is an emergency protocol, detailing what to do and how to do it. It is definitely not a mere prohibition of undesirable action. It is not a restriction imposed on the powerful to protect the weak. Indeed, it is not any sort of manacle, check, barrier, or limit. Exactly like the succession formulas embedded in the Golden Bull of 1356 and other pre-democratic 'constitutions',[47] it is a script to help power-wielders coordinate quickly in a crisis.

If we think of constitutional rules as scripts, rather than ropes (and the US Constitution provides many other examples[48]), it is easier to understand why powerful actors, looking for protocols to facilitate rapid coordination, might be willing to incorporate them into their motivations as obligatory principles of conduct. They are not incapacitating but capacitating. They are not shackles making unwanted action impossible, but guidelines making wanted action feasible. Seen in this way, their 'binding power' becomes more commonsensical than mysterious.

VII. Cognitive Constitutionalism

One of the American Founders' basic assumptions was that the executive branch will, on balance, perform better if compelled to provide both Congress and the courts with plausible reasons for its actions. If a government stops being compelled to provide plausible reasons for its actions, it is very likely, in the relatively short term, to stop having plausible reasons for its actions. Liberating policy makers from the discipline of justification before independent tribunals routinely generates incoherent and self-defeating policies. This is just as true in oligarchies as in democracies.

Viewed from this perspective, America's eighteenth-century Constitution is based on three still-valid principles: all people, including political elites, are prone to error; all people, especially political elites, dislike admitting their blunders; and all people, especially political elites who are currently in opposition, relish disclosing the miscalculations and missteps of their bureaucratic or political rivals. The Constitution attempts to operationalize these principles, roughly speaking, by assigning the power to make mistakes to one branch and the power to correct these mistakes to the other two branches and to the public and the press. Its structural provisions, when combined with certain basic rights (such as freedom to examine the government and freedom of political dissent), set forth a series of second-order rules, that is, rules

[47] James Bryce, 'The German Constitution' in *The Holy Roman Empire* (1950), 225–47; *Encyclopédie ou dictionnaire raisonné des sciences, des arts et des métiers*, vol 4, 63.

[48] Provisions for filling vacancies in Congress, for executive vetoes and Congressional overrides, for admitting new states, for impeaching judges, for electing the President and Vice President if the Electoral College system fails and so forth.

specifying the process by which concrete decisions and first-order rules are to be made and revised. If America's eighteenth-century Constitution remains helpful in dealing with twenty-first-century problems it is largely because its second-order rules embody a distrust of false certainty and a commitment to procedures that facilitate the correction of mistakes and the improvement of performance over time.

Constitutions help to organize the process of decision-making to disfavor the unconsidered or impulsive judgments of incumbent politicians. If the constitution forces decision-makers to submit to an adversarial process of some sort, then their natural impetuosity, false certainty, tunnel vision, and rank prejudice can 'speedily give place to better information, and more deliberate reflection'.[49] We know in advance that 'the legislature will not be infallible' and that 'impressions of the moment may sometimes hurry it into measures which itself, on mature reflection, would condemn'.[50] One solution to this problem is to make sure that various institutionally independent members of the political elite examine the question being discussed from a variety of angles: 'The oftener the measure is brought under examination, the greater the diversity of the situations of those who are to examine it, the less must be the danger of those errors which flow from want of due deliberation.'[51]

That political power is a magnet for disinformation is also worth remembering. Shadowy groups with private agendas regularly feed lies and half-truths to power-wielders in the hopes of manipulating them into acting contrary to the interests of the rulers themselves. Judicial independence emerged and survived in part because professional judges, trained to sift truth from error, were valued for their ability to shield powerful politicians from manipulative disinformation. For this and other reasons, to be discussed in the next section, independent courts provide another illustration of strategic constitutionalism.[52] Insulated from the confirmation bias of executive officials keen on action, independent judges can strengthen the executive function by filtering out witness malice and other misleading falsehoods. That at least is Montesquieu's thesis. He argued that a king who acted as a judge, and thereby violated the constitutional separation of executive and judicial power, would easily become a plaything of malicious witnesses and other parties trying to steer public power into serving illicit private or factional purposes:

> The laws are the eye of the prince; by them he sees what would otherwise escape his observation. Should he attempt the function of a judge, he would not then labour for himself, but for impostors, whose aim is to deceive him.[53]

The echo here of Bodin's theory of parliamentary immunity is unmistakable. Confronted by no organized body capable of exercising critical judgment, free from fear of reprisal, unconstrained or unilateral power is much more likely to be duped by disinformation than a power that is compelled to submit to independent monitoring. The great literary mise-en-scène of this elementary constitutional truth is Shakespeare's *Othello*. When Othello was accused by Desdemona's father of seducing her with drugs, the false accusation was tested before an independent tribunal, the Council of Venice, which told the father that 'to vouch this is no proof',[54]

[49] *The Federalist Papers* (n 8), no 78, 468. [50] Ibid no 73, 442. [51] Ibid.

[52] See Chapter 39 on judicial independence as a constitutional virtue.

[53] Charles Secondat, Baron de Montesquieu, *The Spirit of the Laws* (Thomas Nugent trans, 1975), vol I, bk 6, ch 5, 79.

[54] To vouch this is no proof,
Without more wider and more overt test
Than these thin habits and poor likelihoods
Of modern seeming do prefer against him.
Othello, Act I, scene 3, lines 107–9.

eventually dismissing the charges after allowing Othello and Desdemona to tell their side of the story. But later, when Iago, speaking untruth to power, persuades Othello of Desdemona's infidelity, Othello does not say 'to vouch this is no proof'. He does not allow Desdemona to tell her side of the story, nor does he submit the case to an independent tribunal. He haughtily plays both *le juge et la partie*. As a result, Othello loses rather than gains autonomy. His refusal to submit himself to an institutional mechanism for the correction of errors, far from making him free, renders him completely rudderless. Othello's wrongful murder of his innocent wife is therefore a standing reminder of the vulnerability of political elites, when their powers are unilateral and unchecked, to manipulation by malicious purveyors of false information. Admittedly, being publicly corrected can sting the vanity of power-wielders. But such mighty individuals are likely to drive off cliffs if they disable the brakes that can correct them.

VIII. Insulation through Abdication

If we assume that the powerful never feel that they have enough power and that they are ceaselessly laboring to accumulate more, then voluntary abdications of power seem genuinely incomprehensible. But the mystery is dispelled, at least to some extent, if we start from the premise that power is not homogeneous and that some forms are much less attractive than others. No one is surprised that today's White House and Congress pay no attention to a child custody case, nor does anyone ask why politicians would 'cede power to judges' in such a context. Politicians cede this power because they do not want it and they do not want it because they have better things to do. Any sensible political ruler will want to delegate the donkey work. He will 'get off my case', that is to say, he will, once again, support the independence of the judiciary.

Abdications of judicial power can empower the government by insulating it not only from manipulative disinformation but from all manner of unwelcome chores and pressures. Delegations of power can be shrewdly strategic if they prevent organized interests from hounding officials into furthering factional ends. Shedding power is an appealing technique for fending off annoying supplicants and time-consuming petitions for redress of grievances. Focusing on their understudied deflecting or protective function can help us see constitutional 'limits' on power in a different light.

If the ruler pulls strings behind the curtains, people will notice where ultimate decision-making power lies, and, according to Montesquieu, the steps of the ruler's palace will resound 'with the litigious clamours of the several parties' hoping to influence upcoming decisions of the royal court. Keeping the judicial power in his own hands would reduce the king's power, on balance, because 'the courtiers by their importunity would always be able to extort his decisions'.[55] To avoid these pressures, a shrewd prince will respect the independence of judges from executive power, one of the keystones of any moderate constitution.[56] In a republic, too, the legislature can insulate itself from supplicants seeking favorable verdicts by genuinely renouncing all power to influence judges.[57]

The powerful, moreover, can often be persuaded to jettison powers that are likely to excite lasting hatred and resentment. To exercise judicial power is to create winners and losers. Winners may or may not feel appreciative; but losers almost certainly feel aggrieved. It is dangerous to wield judicial power because the powerful are eye-catching targets for the vengeance of those whom court decisions have really or supposedly harmed.

[55] Montesquieu (n 53), bk 6, ch 5, 78. [56] Ibid 77.
[57] *The Federalist Papers* (n 8), no 48, 307.

While a shrewd prince will forfeit powers that are resented, such as punishment, he will simultaneously retain powers that engender gratitude, such as the power to pardon. Montesquieu recognized the political benefits of separating the power to pardon from the power to condemn or acquit,[58] as did Machiavelli before him: 'Princes must make others responsible for imposing burdens, while handing out gracious gifts themselves.'[59] Loyalty and political support are excited by gifts that are totally undeserved, not by 'just' outcomes that seem legally compelled. The far-seeing ruler, for this reason too, will create a genuinely autonomous judicial body for whose actions the political branches receive neither credit nor blame. Independent tribunals will specialize in punishing malefactors and dispensing justice, while he, the prince, will retain for himself the discretionary power to issue pardons and confer other unjustifiable benefits, which presumably stir gratitude in, and secure political support from, the lucky beneficiaries who understand that they are receiving more than they rightly deserve.

And just as princes can empty their In Boxes and increase their most valuable capacities by deferring to independent courts, legislatures can protect themselves from a military coup by deferring to a semi-independent executive. Montesquieu justified the legislature's delegation of power to the executive on just these grounds: 'When once an army is established', he wrote, 'it ought not to depend immediately on the legislative, but on the executive, power.' One reason is that 'its business consist[s] more in action than in deliberation'. But that was not the most urgent consideration, from a republican point of view. Montesquieu's principal argument, instead, concerned the way in which civilian control of the military itself could be fatally weakened if the legislature tried to retain managerial control of the army:

> It is natural for mankind to set a higher value upon courage than timidity, on activity than prudence, on strength than counsel. Hence the army will ever despise a senate, and respect their own officers. They will naturally slight the orders sent them by a body of men whom they look upon as cowards, and therefore unworthy to command them. So that as soon as the troops depend entirely on the legislative body, it becomes a military government.[60]

Soldiers are naturally contemptuous of 'talking chambers'. Therefore, to help the legislature to avoid a military coup, a liberal constitution will place operational control of the army in the hands of someone whom military men are likely to salute and obey. This should be a single commander-in-chief who will nevertheless still operate under the eye of, and within guidelines set by, the legislature. The impeachment power should remain 'a bridle in the hands of the legislative body upon the executive servants of the government'.[61] But the chief executive must possess enough independent presence and prestige to command the respect of the troops. Not only the legislature's power, but its very survival as an independent political actor hinges on its willingness to abdicate power in this specific respect. Or so argues the most famous strategist (not only the most famous theorist) of the constitutional separation of powers.

IX. Joint Agency and Corruption

When Madison wrote that a good constitution should oblige the government 'to control itself',[62] he meant that it should prevent individual incumbents from yielding to the temptation to prefer their private interests to the interests of the government and thereby 'to betray

[58] Montesquieu (n 53), bk 6, ch 21, 92–3.

[59] Niccolò Machiavelli, *The Prince* (Harvey Mansfield trans, 1998), ch 19, 75.

[60] Montesquieu (n 53), bk 11, ch 6, 161.

[61] *The Federalist Papers* (n 8), no 65, 396.

[62] Ibid no 51, 319.

the solemn trust committed to them'.[63] This happened whenever office holders passed laws, created policies, or delivered judicial decisions in exchange for private payments from interested parties. The importance of this problem to the Framers is clear from the reference to 'bribery' in the Constitution's Impeachment Clause. Making bribery into an impeachable (as well as a prosecutable) offense was one way of discouraging incumbents from betraying their colleagues, if not their country, for a consideration.

Given the political context of the late eighteenth century, the greatest threat of bribery came from 'foreign gold'[64] or 'the desire in foreign powers to gain an improper ascendant in our councils'.[65] Hamilton, for example, explicitly contemplated the possibility that 'a few leading individuals in the Senate' could 'have prostituted their influence in that body as the mercenary instruments of foreign corruption'.[66] Serious precautions had to be taken because 'One of the weak sides of republics, among their numerous advantages, is that they afford too easy an inlet to foreign corruption.'[67]

The constitutional requirement that the President obtain the Senate's consent to treaties is meant to make it more difficult and costly for foreign powers to purchase treaties biased against US interests.[68] It eliminates the convenience of one-stop shopping for foreign purchasers of America's willing collaborators. Both Hamilton and Madison saw the anti-hijacking function of 'partial agency'[69] as essential to maintaining American autonomy in foreign affairs. They returned repeatedly to 'The security essentially intended by the Constitution against corruption and treachery in the formation of treaties'.[70] For instance, 'The JOINT AGENCY of the Chief Magistrate of the Union, and of two thirds of the members of a body selected by the collective wisdom of the legislatures of the several States, is designed to be the pledge for the fidelity of the national councils in this particular'.[71] The requirement of 'concurrent agency'[72] in treaty-making also obstructs bribery by making more difficult the air-tight secrecy that it requires.[73]

Members of the ruling elite normally exhibit an ingrained loyalty to the prominent network that provides them favors and protection. There is nevertheless 'a degree of depravity in mankind which requires a certain degree of circumspection and distrust',[74] and gives constitution-makers reason enough to anticipate worst-case scenarios.[75] These include defections from ruling circles and collusion between disgruntled and alienated members of the elite, on the one hand, and European diplomats and undercover agents, on the other. An 'ambitious' and 'avaricious' member of the political elite will occasionally 'make his own aggrandizement by the aid of a foreign power'.[76] When detailing 'many mortifying examples of the prevalency of foreign corruption in republican governments' and explaining how often enemy gold 'contributed to the ruin of the ancient commonwealths', Hamilton made clear that this threat had by no means disappeared, citing Holland as a recent example.[77]

Hamilton's insistence that the separation of powers can provide some protection against foreign corruption confirms once again the American Framers' commitment to strategic constitutionalism. Constitutional structures can be embraced by political elites, even in the absence of popular pressure, simply to protect the interests of the elite itself, in this case from rogue officials who might willingly betray their fellow office holders for that perennially irresistible piece of silver.[78]

[63] Ibid no 55, 341.
[64] Ibid no 55, 342.
[65] Ibid no 68, 411.
[66] Ibid no 66, 404.
[67] Ibid no 22, 145.
[68] Ibid no 75, 449–50.
[69] Ibid no 47, 299.
[70] Ibid no 66, 404.
[71] Ibid no 66, 404.
[72] Ibid no 67, 409.
[73] Ibid no 22, 145.
[74] Ibid no 55, 343.
[75] Ibid no 75, 450.
[76] Ibid no 75, 450.
[77] Ibid no 22, 145.
[78] Ibid no 22, 145.

X. Constitutionalism and Democracy

To argue that constitutions, as they function in practice, reflect and perpetuate asymmetries of power in society is not to obliterate all distinctions between autocratic and democratic political systems.[79] On the contrary, it is to say that constitutions are more or less democratic to the extent that power in the underlying society is distributed more or less widely and evenly. The way power is distributed in society can, in turn, be influenced at the margins by political institutions but, short of totalitarianism, will be shaped mostly by demographic, technological, cultural, economic, and other developments that operate relatively unconstrained by constitutional politics. In any case, when broad swaths of the population can credibly threaten to withdraw the voluntary cooperation indispensable to political and economic elites, the democratic implications of a constitution will wax. When, on the contrary, elites manage to liberate themselves from any need for the cooperation of most citizens (in oil-extraction economies, for instance, or when mass armies have been replaced by small volunteer professional forces operating push-button weapons), the democratic implications of the constitution under which they jointly live will wane. Historical inquiry strongly supports the hypothesis that the democratic effects of a single constitutional text will expand and contract in tandem with the extra-constitutional leverage of the citizens at large.

For a brief period at the end of the eighteenth century, the word 'constitution' shook off its association with the status quo and become a rallying cry for revolutionaries. Thomas Paine, for example, wrote at the time that 'The constitution of a country is not the act of its government, but of the people constituting its government.' It followed for Paine that 'A constitution is a thing antecedent to a government, and a government is only the creature of a constitution.'[80] The same distinction between the constituting people and the constituted government, implying against immemorial tradition that leaders in palaces would henceforth defer to subjects in cottages, was elaborated in France, around the same time, by the Abbé Sieyès. He described the government as a delegated authority or *le pouvoir constitué*, with no right to revise the rules of the game under which it was elected, and the people or the nation as *le pouvoir constituant* who promulgated those rules which the government had no right either to disobey or unilaterally to revise.[81]

True, even traditional theorists like William Blackstone admitted that political incumbents could be constitutionally punished for unconstitutional actions. For instance, Parliament had the right and duty to impeach the king's ministers whenever his 'prerogative is exerted in an unconstitutional manner'.[82] What Blackstone emphatically denied, however, was that an Act of Parliament itself could be either unconstitutional or constitutionally overturned. He could not accept, or perhaps even understand, what the revolutionary generation that followed him was zealously to allege, that there was a lawmaking authority *legally* higher than the lawmaking authority of the duly constituted legislature. In 1785, Blackstone's position was aggressively defended against the revolutionary constitutionalists of that decade by the British progressive, William Paley, who argued that 'An act of parliament in England can never be unconstitutional, in the strict and proper acceptation of the term.'[83]

79 On democracy more generally, see Chapter 11.
80 Thomas Paine, *Rights of Man* (1979), 93.
81 Abbé Sieyès, *Qu'est-ce que le tiers état* (1982), 67.
82 William Blackstone, *Commentaries on the Laws of England* (1979), vol I, ch 7, 244.
83 William Paley, *The Principles of Moral and Political Philosophy* (1867), 219–20.

The contrary and revolutionary concept, that legislative acts can be unconstitutional, has obscure origins, but one of its most important sources is Bolingbroke's *Dissertation upon Parties* (1733–34) which defined 'constitution' as a system for promoting the public good under which the community has voluntarily agreed to be governed.[84] The political authority of the people, for Bolingbroke, trumps the political authority of the government:

> constitution is the rule by which our princes ought to govern at all times; government is that by which they actually do govern at any particular time. One may remain immutable; the other may, and as human nature is constituted, must vary. One is the criterion by which we are to try the other; for surely we have a right to do so, since if we are to live in subjection to the government of our Kings, our Kings are to govern in subjection to the constitution; and the conformity or nonconformity of their government to it, prescribes the measure of our submission to them, according to the principles of the Revolution, and of our present settlement.[85]

If the government violates the constitution under which its subjects have agreed to be governed, then these subjects may legitimately withdraw their obedience and submission.

Most shocking was Bolingbroke's claim that statutes legally enacted by Parliament can sometimes be unconstitutional. He focused particular attention on the Septennial Act of 1716, by which the Parliament elected in 1715 unilaterally extended its term until 1722. This Act was unconstitutional in an elemental sense, according to Bolingbroke, because the Triennial Act of 1694, far from being just another statute, was a codification of the revolutionary settlement of 1688–89. Paine and other members of the revolutionary generation were to echo Bolingbroke's point here, singling out the unconstitutionality of the Septennial Act[86] when arguing for the superiority of revolutionary settlements over ordinary legislation. And of course they uniformly took issue with Blackstone, who had stubbornly argued that Parliament 'can change and create afresh even the constitution of the kingdom and of parliaments themselves; as was done by the act of union, and the several statutes for triennial and septennial elections.'[87]

This debate provides an essential backdrop for *Federalist* 53 where Madison famously explained American exceptionalism as rooted in the unique thinking about constitutions that developed in the colonies as they broke away from British control:

> The important distinction so well understood in America between a Constitution established by the people and unalterable by the government, and a law established by the government and alterable by the government, seems to have been little understood and less observed in any other country.[88]

A constitution unalterable by the government is a historically unprecedented departure, according to Madison, because previously: 'Wherever the supreme power of legislation has resided, has been supposed to reside also a full power to change the form of government.' And he continues:

> Even in Great Britain, where the principles of political and civil liberty have been most discussed, and where we hear most of the rights of the Constitution, it is maintained that the authority of the Parliament is transcendent and uncontrollable as well with regard to the Constitution as the ordinary objects of legislative provision.[89]

[84] Henry St John Bolingbroke, 'A Dissertation upon Parties' in David Armitage (ed), *Political Writings* (1997), letter 10, 88.

[85] Ibid.

[86] Thomas Paine, *Rights of Man* (1979), 95.

[87] Blackstone (n 82), vol I, ch 2, 156.

[88] *The Federalist Papers* (n 8), no 53, 328.

[89] Ibid.

To illustrate the principal difference between the traditional British and the new revolutionary concept of a constitution, in other words, Madison again invokes the Septennial Act of 1716, exactly like Bolingbroke decades before and Paine shortly thereafter.

Bolingbroke used the Septennial Act to exemplify unconstitutionality not because it violated private rights but because it overrode the right of the electorate to purge the House of Commons of those members who had succumbed to the allure of place, privilege, favoritism, and money handed out by the crown in exchange for legislative servility. Madison, like the other members of the revolutionary generation, was an heir to this outrage. Echoing the centrality which Bolingbroke attributed to 'the frequent returns of new elections',[90] Madison identified 'the restraint of frequent elections'[91] as the core institution of constitutional government: 'A dependence on the people is, no doubt, the primary control on the government.'[92] Indeed, Madison consistently wrote about 'free government, of which frequency of elections is the cornerstone',[93] placing the essence of constitutionalism not in the separation of powers but in fixed-calendar elections which political incumbents cannot safely, without risking ouster or overthrow, delay or suspend. Rulers who are 'created by our choice, dependent on our will'[94] have a strong incentive to act in the interest of the 'the great body of the people of the United States'.[95] That was the idea, or at least the hope.

Speaking of unrealistic hopes, the democratic constitutionalism of the revolutionary era aimed, by means of regular elections, to prevent 'the elevation of the few on the ruins of the many'.[96] With hindsight, of course, we can see that the success of democratic constitutionalism in this regard was occasional and erratic at best. What remains significant for constitutional theory is that the limited effectiveness of the restraint of frequent elections did not go unnoticed at the time. Even when arguing most forcefully that periodic elections, entrenched in the Constitution, could align the interests of legislators with the interests of citizens, Madison indirectly revealed his underlying doubts:

> the House of Representatives is so constituted as to support in the members an habitual recollection of their dependence on the people. Before the sentiments impressed on their minds by the mode of their elevation can be effaced by the exercise of power, they will be compelled to anticipate the moment when their power is to cease, when their exercise of it is to be reviewed, and when they must descend to the level from which they were raised; there forever to remain unless a faithful discharge of their trust shall have established their title to a renewal of it.[97]

Feelings of dependency on the people, elicited by periodic elections, can be effaced by the mere exercise of power! As Hamilton put the point, 'It is a misfortune incident to republican government, though in a less degree than to other governments, that those who administer it may forget their obligations to their constituents, and prove unfaithful to their important trust.'[98] Political experience had taught both Hamilton and Madison the inherent weakness

[90] Bolingbroke (n 84), letter 13, 125.

[91] *The Federalist Papers* (n 8), no 57, 350.

[92] Ibid no 51, 319.

[93] Ibid no 53, 329; the British have no 'Constitution', according to Madison, because Parliament, at the time, had the legal right to perpetuate itself beyond the term for which it was elected:

> The important distinction so well understood in America between a Constitution established by the people and unalterable by the government, and a law established by the government and alterable by the government, seems to have been little understood and less observed in any other country [outside the American states].

[94] Ibid no 25, 162.

[95] Ibid no 57, 349.

[96] Ibid no 57, 348.

[97] Ibid no 57, 350.

[98] Ibid no 62, 376–7.

of the electoral mechanism. But they learned the same lesson from their reading of Locke. Even when raised to high office by periodic elections, Locke had famously explained, public officials will 'come to have a distinct interest from the rest of the Community, contrary to the end of Society and Government'.[99] This is an arresting claim, and a central one to the entire liberal tradition.

Following Locke's suggestion, Madison agreed that holding power, however it was achieved, affects not only a person's opportunities but also his motivations. This political alchemy guarantees that the dominant or driving motives of power-wielders, even if elected and facing re-election, will deviate substantially from the leading motives of the rest of society. Even under the restraint of frequent elections, Hamilton would add, 'the representatives of the people' will be tempted to view themselves as 'superior to the people themselves'.[100]

Without contesting the republican principle that government must be based on the consent of the people,[101] Madison expressed strong doubts about the 'input' side of democracy. He understood perfectly well 'the vicious arts by which elections are too often carried'.[102] He also wrote about how men of factious tempers could 'obtain the suffrages' by 'intrigue' and 'corruption' or by playing on 'local prejudice'.[103] The American Framers knew nothing of political marketing or the application of advertising techniques to political campaigns. But they were perfectly aware that the will of the people does not always develop autonomously but is frequently shaped and manipulated by the dissemination of false rumors and other species of strategic disinformation. The chimerical accountability of the rulers to the ruled, moreover, even when frequent elections are constitutionally required, depends on the electorate's willingness and ability to gather information about the rival candidates and pay close attention. No constitution, however, can do much about the 'supineness' and 'ignorance' afflicting 'unwary and uninterested' voters.[104]

Asymmetry of information makes it difficult, if not impossible, for citizens to control politicians. If elected officials, once in office, can use administrative and other resources to misinform voters and keep them in the dark, then they, the incumbents, can successfully liberate themselves from the restraint of frequent elections, even without resort to vote-rigging and other more blatantly anti-democratic methods. The most common technique by which office holders have traditionally eluded accountability is probably the simplest: shameless lying. Because incumbents know things that the voters need to but do not know, periodic elections alone do not, as it turns out, allow citizens to hold politicians to account.

To supply this gaping defect in the electoral mechanism, as is well known, Madison offered a variety of 'auxiliary precautions',[105] all of which involve multiple delegates who will supposedly keep an eye on each other. To prevent office holders from misusing their delegated powers in secret and thereby escaping electoral reprisal, the constitution should give them the capacity and the motivation for mutual whistle-blowing as well as the capacity and motivation for mutual cooperation. These officials must play no role in each others' appointments or remuneration, but each must have an incentive to warn the electorate, between elections, when they spot rival politicians betraying the public trust.

As these passages suggest, the Framers advertised checks and balances as a republican version of *divide et impera*, this time designed to discourage corrupt self-dealing by public officials. Plural agency would ideally allow the electorate, which cannot make politics into a full-time job, to play various elected officials off against each other. Occupants of the various

[99] Locke (n 7), sec 143, 410. [100] *The Federalist Papers* (n 8), no 78, 466.
[101] Ibid no 22, 148. [102] Ibid no 10, 77. [103] Ibid no 10, 78.
[104] Ibid no 64, 389. [105] Ibid no 51, 319.

departments of government, including magistrates elected at the state level, could be constitutionally incentivized 'to sound the alarm to the people'[106] in case the occupants of rival branches begin to treat public resources as private assets. In such a system, periodic accountability to the electorate would be supplemented between elections by a form of peer review by rival delegates of the electorate.

It all sounds promising. But, at this point, the Framers' strategic constitutionalism met its Waterloo. Madison's constitutional engineering did not succeed in supplying the defect of periodic elections. His checks and balances proved unable, in the end, to align the interests of the government with the interests of the governed. The separation of powers could not even prevent 'a mercenary and perfidious combination of the several members of government'.[107] Members of formally separated branches had little trouble colluding in cloakrooms. Some democratic theorists argue that it was the rise of political majorities, able to dominate the legislative and executive branches simultaneously, that made the doctrine of checks and balances 'anachronistic' to the point that it 'just makes no sense'.[108] But, writing before the emergence of modern political parties, Madison was already fully conscious that 'the dispensation of appointments' could serve as a 'fund of corruption' providing the executive with a power of 'subduing the virtue' of Congress.[109] Such a purchase of legislative support by executive largesse, in fact, was exactly what Bolingbroke had had in mind when he spoke of the 'unconstitutional dependency'[110] of the House of Commons on royal patronage. Such theoretically disallowed but practically ubiquitous collusion was to make a mockery of the plural agency on which the dividing and ruling of the inattentive electorate were supposed to depend.

It is worth noting here that American Progressives, hostile to the anti-reform bias they ascribed to the US Constitution, were especially critical of the separation of powers. Not only did it insulate the rulers from the legitimate demands of the ruled, they argued. It also promoted rather than prevented corruption. They assumed, writing in an age of dizzying economic growth, that

> the Constitution, with its elaborate barriers to the exercise of effective governmental power, suited very well the aim of that group of flourishing big-business men who where to dominate politics in the latter part of the nineteenth century, giving to it the character of the age of the tycoon.[111]

Checks and balances, they argued, introduced so many easily captured veto points into the system that a status quo bias, beneficial to the rich, was inevitable. This diagnosis is ironic, given Madison's hope that the separation of powers would render corruption and state capture more difficult if not impossible. Contradictory as they are, both theories illustrate strategic constitutionalism. Madison valued the separation of powers as an instrument for discouraging corruption. The Progressives disparaged the separation of powers as a pliant tool of the corrupt. The latter analysis seems to have been vindicated by history. And it was not the only time that constitutional provisions introduced in a spirit of reform were turned inside out to serve the organized interests that they were meant to discipline and control.

[106] Ibid no 26, 168. [107] Ibid no 55, 342.

[108] Adam Przeworski, *Democracy and the Limits of Self-Government* (2010), 137.

[109] *The Federalist Papers* (n 8), no 55, 342.

[110] Bolingbroke (n 84), letter 13, 124–5.

[111] M.J.C. Vile, *Constitutionalism and the Separation of Powers* (1998), 290.

XI. Judicial Review

Blackstone employed the adjective 'unconstitutional' to refer to egregious transgressions of the public trust. Some transgressions could be so egregious, he admitted, that they justified a revolutionary response. But he did not dream of codifying this revolutionary response in a fundamental and paramount legal text. Much less did he suggest that laws passed by Parliament could be declared null and void by judges citing the higher law inscribed in such a super-text. Judicial review of legislation would have been wholly anomalous in the British context, 'for that were to set the judicial power above that of the legislature, which would be subversive of all government'.[112]

For reasons that remain somewhat obscure, prominent members of the revolutionary generation, at least in America, quickly became convinced that effective governance would be possible even if judges occasionally overturned the decisions of elected assemblymen. According to Hamilton, writing in 1788, 'whenever a particular statute contravenes the Constitution, it will be the duty of the judicial tribunals to adhere to the latter and disregard the former'.[113] He did not invent the idea of judicial review out of whole cloth, needless to say. Already in 1783, for example, James Iredell, who would later become an Associate Justice on the Supreme Court, had written of 'a Republic where the Law is superior to any or all the individuals, and the Constitution superior even to the Legislature, and of which the Judges are the guardians and protectors.'[114] And earlier precedents of contested relevance can also be exhumed from the archives. In any case, only a few years after the Constitution was ratified, Justice Marshall immortalized the claim that judicial remedies are available in the case of an unconstitutional act of the elected legislature. In a shrewd stroke of strategic constitutionalism, he overturned a law (the Judiciary Act of 1789) that had granted the Supreme Court a power that the Court did not want and could not safely wield.[115]

But what can we learn about constitutions and constitutionalism from the history of judicial review in the presumed land of its birth?

First, the vast majority of laws overturned by the US Supreme Court throughout its history have been state laws. This suggests that judicial review has advanced the purposes of the federal government more often than it has obstructed them. Really-existing judicial review, like the really-existing constitution to which it belongs, is perfectly capable of enhancing the power of the powerful. When evaluating the trompe l'oeil image of the Supreme Court as an adversary rather than ally of the powerful, as a result, the tactical uses of deception should therefore be kept in mind.

And which rights have the US Supreme Court more consistently protected: the rights of the weak or the rights of the strong? Before trying to answer this wholly rhetorical question, we need to examine, at a higher level of generality, the 'rights' that the Supreme Court is allegedly devoted to defending. Focused on strengthening the government, the American Framers famously considered and rejected the proposal to add a Bill of Rights to the Constitution.[116] They eventually agreed to do so only to head off anti-Federalist demands to reduce the powers

[112] Blackstone (n 82), vol I, ch 3, 90–1.

[113] *The Federalist Papers* (n 8), no 78, 467.

[114] James Iredell, 'Instructions to Chowan County Representatives' in Don Higginbotham (ed), *The Papers of James Iredell* ([September 1783] 1976), vol 2, 449; cf *Commonwealth v Caton* (1782), 8 Virginia (4 Call), 5; cf Hamilton's description five years later of federal judges as the 'guardians of the Constitution' (*The Federalist Papers* (n 8), no 78, 469).

[115] *Marbury v Madison* (1803), in John Marshall, *Writings* (2010), 229–52.

[116] Max Ferrand (ed), *The Records of the Federal Convention of 1787* (1966), vol 2, 588.

vested in the federal government by the proposed Constitution. Their initial reluctance is revealing.

Hamilton argued in *Federalist* 78 that it was the duty of federal courts to declare null and void all legislative acts contrary to the manifest tenor of the Constitution. He was no doubt thinking primarily of state laws, expecting that the federal bench would side with the other federal branches against what supporters of a strong national government viewed as the contumacy of the states.[117] But he did not imagine that the Supreme Court would overturn statutes, state or federal, based on the Justices' interpretation of airy moral platitudes. Indeed, he mocked the kind of splendid generalities later inscribed in the Bill of Rights as 'aphorisms' which 'would sound much better in a treatise of ethics than in a constitution of government' for the simple reason that they 'leave the utmost latitude for evasion', altogether depending for their binding power 'on public opinion' and 'on the general spirit of the people and of the government'. These latter forces, he wrote, provide 'the only solid basis of all our rights'.[118]

The formal enactment and informal nullification of the Fourteenth Amendment, in the decades after the Civil War, illustrate nicely the primacy of partisanship and power over ideal justice in constitution-making and especially in the constitutional interpretation of grand libertarian generalities. Power includes not only the power of social and economic elites, it should be said, but also the power of public opinion, now called popular constitutionalism, when enflamed by racism or revenge. When adopted, the Fourteenth Amendment was seen in the South as a blatant expression of victor's constitutionalism. The result of violent conquest, it soon became the legal face of military occupation.

No one can dispute the core of truth in this bitter perspective of the defeated South:

> What was politically essential was that the North's victory in the Civil War be rendered permanent, and the principles for which the war had been fought rendered secure so that the South, upon readmission to full participation in the Union, could not undo them.[119]

But the broad and expansive language of the Amendment opened up, as times changed, wide avenues for opportunistic reinterpretation. The 'amorphous, moralistic, rhetorical categories of liberty and equality' and 'the hazy "privileges and immunities" language'[120] of the Amendment invited judicial interpretations in line with shifting public and especially elite opinion.

After the withdrawal of Northern troops from the South in 1877, even half-hearted attempts to protect blacks from denigration, subjugation, and physical cruelty were effectively abandoned.[121] Finally, in *Plessy v Ferguson*,[122] the Supreme Court effectively nullified the Fourteenth Amendment as a higher law meant to protect black Americans. Revealing just how 'justice' can be constantly redefined in line with partisan politics and the interests of the powerful, this episode is typical not exceptional. Equal rights for black Americans in the South, to the extent that they were enforced, were enforced by Northern soldiers. When the troops withdrew, these rights were not worth the paper on which the Fourteenth Amendment had been printed. After the Northerners had grown weary and bored of punishing the South, the real Supremacy Clause of the post-Civil War Constitution reasserted itself, namely White Supremacy.

[117] *The Federalist Papers* (n 8), no 80, 474–5.
[118] Ibid no 84, 514.
[119] William E. Nelson, *The Fourteenth Amendment* (1988), 61.
[120] Ibid 52, 57.
[121] In *United States v Cruikshank* 92 US 542 (1876), the Court had already given a green light to KKK massacres of black Americans presumably because the public officials who organized the killings were not acting in their official capacity and were not dressed as state actors.
[122] *Plessy v Ferguson* 163 US 537 (1896).

In 1952, law clerk William Rehnquist wrote a defense of *Plessy*, arguing that 'in the long run it is the majority who will determine what the constitutional rights of the minority are'.[123] His motives may have been unsavory but his observation was essentially Hamiltonian. The only solid basis for the rights of black Americans resides in the general spirit of the people and the government. If this spirit is rotten with racial bigotry and *libido dominandi*, these rights will be violated with impunity.

As interpreted and applied, constitutions are never impartial. They never treat the powerful and the powerless in the same way. Nothing out of the ordinary happened, therefore, when, twisting the original meaning of the Fourteenth Amendment, 'the Court turned its back on the claims of blacks and opened its arms to those of corporations'.[124] Equal protection gave way to Corporate Supremacy alongside White Supremacy. Crudely speaking, the late nineteenth-century Supreme Court granted ample discretion to state legislatures whenever they hurt blacks but little discretion when they threatened to hurt businesses.

Through the history of the Supreme Court, it should be remembered, Justices have always been appointed by politically partisan Presidents and confirmed by politically partisan Senators. Why would judges who came to the Court by such a route be inclined to interpret vague libertarian generalities in a wholly non-partisan way? In the period under discussion, the amorphous right to 'liberty' guaranteed in the Fourteenth Amendment was opportunistically seized upon by American corporations and their allies to fight state attempts to regulate labor contracts in a way favorable to workers. The Supreme Court concurred, interpreting Fourteenth Amendment 'liberty' selectively to mean economic liberty, especially freedom of contract between consenting adults beyond the reach of state legislatures.[125] The Court thereby replaced the legislatures' judgment of what was reasonable with its own judgment of what was reasonable, which, in turn, happened to correspond to the economic interests of the Captains of Industry whom the Justices may or may not have admired.

XII. Conclusion

When studying *Plessy*, *Lochner*, and related cases, we should recall Aristotle's claim that 'the part of a state which wishes a constitution to continue must be stronger than the part which does not'.[126] Power in every known society is distributed unequally. Law, including constitutional law, necessarily reflects these asymmetries of power. When these asymmetries of power shift and rearrange themselves over time, laws, including constitutional laws, are amended or reinterpreted or enforced selectively in new ways. Far from being neutral and impartial, law is soaked through with partiality and favoritism.[127] This is just as true of constitutional law as of statutory law.

Constitutions emerge and survive because, with a little help from their judicial friends, they serve the perceived interests of the best organized and therefore most powerful social forces. When the powerful discover the advantages they can reap from making their own behavior predictable, they voluntarily submit to constitutional constraints. When non-elites gain leverage, one way or another, elites respond opportunistically by granting legal protections and

[123] Cass Sunstein, 'From Law Clerk to Chief Justice, He Has Slighted Rights: Rehnquist's 1952 Memo Sheds Light on Today's Court', *Los Angeles Times*, May 17, 2004.

[124] Peter Irons, *A People's History of the Supreme Court* (1999), 209.

[125] *Lochner v New York* 198 US 45 (1905).

[126] *The Politics of Aristotle* (n 35), 1296b, 185.

[127] Jean-Jacques Rousseau, 'Émile' in Jean-Jacques Rousseau, *Oeuvres complètes* (1969), vol IV, 524.

participatory rights in exchange for cooperation indispensable to elite projects. What we think of as democratic constitutions, as a result, emerge and survive as long as the best organized and therefore most powerful social forces find that they can promote their own interests most effectively by simultaneously promoting the interests of, and sharing political influence with, less powerful but not utterly powerless swaths of the population. That is the lesson taught by the ancient theorists of the mixed constitution. Their hypothesis was that constitutional restraints wax and wane, among other reasons, when non-elites gain and lose leverage over their social superiors. This ground-up approach to constitutionalism is superior to top-down normative approaches because it explains, as normative theorists cannot, why voters gradually lose the ability to control politicians when technological change, economic globalization and other dramatic developments reduce the observable dependency of the rich on the poor and the powerful on the weak.

Constitutional norms are 'binding' only when supported by organized interests. This is not a cynical observation. It is rather an instruction. If you wish a constitutional norm to govern the way politicians behave, you need to organize politically to give ruling groups an incentive to pay attention and accept restraints on their own discretion for their benefit and yours. No strategic constitutionalist would delegate such a daunting task to nine Justices presiding loftily in a marble hall.

Bibliography

Willi Paul Adams, *The First American Constitutions* (2001)

Ernest Barker, *The Politics of Aristotle* (1968)

William Blackstone, *Commentaries on the Laws of England*, vol I (1979)

Jean Bodin, *The Six Books of a Commonweal* (Robert Knolles trans, 1962)

Henry St John Bolingbroke, 'A Dissertation upon Parties' in David Armitage (ed), *Political Writings* (1997)

James Bryce, 'The German Constitution' in *The Holy Roman Empire* (1950)

Julius Caesar, *The Gallic War* (H.J. Edwards trans, 1917)

Marcus Tullius Cicero, *De natura deorum* (H. Rackham trans, 1933)

Marcus Tullius Cicero, *De officiis* (Walter Miller trans, 1913)

Marcus Tullius Cicero, *De re publica and De Legibus* (Clinton Walker Keyes trans, 1928)

Denis Diderot et al, 'Constitution' in *Encyclopédie ou dictionnaire raisonné des sciences, des arts et des métiers* (1794), vol 4

Jon Elster, *Ulysses and the Sirens: Studies in Rationality and Irrationality* (1984)

Jon Elster, *Ulysses Unbound: Studies in Rationality, Precommitment, and Constraints* (2000)

Max Ferrand (ed), *The Records of the Federal Convention of 1787* (1966)

Alexander Hamilton, James Madison, and John Jay, *The Federalist Papers* (Clinton Rossiter ed, 1999)

Don Higginbotham (ed), *The Papers of James Iredell* (1976)

Ran Hirschl, *Towards Juristocracy: The Origins and Consequences of the New Constitutionalism* (2004)

Thomas Hobbes, *Behemoth* (1990)

Thomas Hobbes, *Leviathan* (C.B. Macpherson ed, 1968)

Stephen Holmes, *Passions and Constraint: On the Theory of Liberal Democracy* (1995)

Woody Holton, *Unruly Americans and the Origins of the Constitution* (2007)

Peter Irons, *A People's History of the Supreme Court* (1999)

Ernst Kantorowicz, *The King's Two Bodies: A Study in Medieval Political Theology* (1957)

Andrew Lintott, *The Constitution of the Roman Republic* (1999)
John Locke, *Two Treatises of Government* (Peter Laslett ed, 1965)
Niccolò Machiavelli, *Discourses on Livy* (Harvey Mansfield and Nathan Tarcov trans, 1996)
Niccolò Machiavelli, *The Prince* (Harvey Mansfield trans, 1998)
John Marshall, *Writings* (2010)
Charles Howard McIlwain, *Constitutionalism Ancient and Modern* (1947)
Montesquieu, *The Spirit of the Laws* (Thomas Nugent trans, 1975)
William E. Nelson, *The Fourteenth Amendment* (1988)
Thomas Paine, *Rights of Man* (1979)
William Paley, *The Principles of Moral and Political Philosophy* (1867)
Polybius, *The Rise of the Roman Empire* (1979)
Adam Przeworski, *Democracy and the Limits of Self-Government* (2010)
Jean-Jacques Rousseau, *Émile* in *Oeuvres complètes*, vol 4 (1969)
Giovanni Sartori, 'Constitutionalism: A Preliminary Discussion' (1962) 56(4) *American Political Science Review* 853
Abbé Sieyès, *Qu'est-ce que le tiers état* (1982)
Lawrence Tribe, *American Constitutional Law* (2nd edn, 1988)
M.J.C. Vile, *Constitutionalism and the Separation of Powers* (1998)
Jeremy Waldron, *Law and Disagreement* (1999)

CHAPTER 9

CONSTITUTION

MARK TUSHNET

Cambridge, MA

DEFINITIONS of the term 'constitution' abound. According to Dicey, a constitution consists of 'all rules which directly or indirectly affect the distribution or the exercise of the sovereign power in the state', including 'all rules which define the members of the sovereign power, all rules which regulate the relation of such members to each other, or which determine the mode in which the sovereign power, or the members thereof, exercise their authority.'[1] For Cooley, a constitution is 'the body of rules and maxims in accordance with which the powers of sovereignty are habitually exercised'.[2] The *Oxford English Dictionary* defines the term as the 'mode in which a state is constituted or organized; especially, as to the location of the sovereign power' and as the 'system or body of fundamental principles according to which a nation, state or body politic is constituted and governed'.[3] Finally, the dictionary of the Académie Française offers, 'Ensemble des lois fondamentales, écrites ou coutumières, qui determinant la forme du gouvernement d'un pays et règlent les droits politiques des citoyens.'[4] These definitions, and

[1] Albert Venn Dicey, *Introduction to the Study of the Law of the Constitution* (1889), 22–3. On sovereignty more generally, see Chapter 17.

[2] Thomas M. Cooley, *The General Principles of Constitutional Law in the United States of America* (1898), 22.

[3] 'Constitution' in James A.H. Murray et al (eds), *The Oxford English Dictionary* (2nd edn, vol 3, 1989), defs 6 and 7.

[4] 'Constitution' in *Dictionnaire de l'Académie française* (8th edn, 2000), def II.2.

many others that could be assembled, refer to fundamental principles of sovereignty and authority. They attempt to be purely descriptive, reserving the term 'constitutionalism' or 'rule of law' for discussions of normative conditions for the appropriate exercise of sovereign power.

Definitions of the term *constitution* tend to circularity. Dicey's definition uses the term *sovereignty*. Tracing that term through the *Oxford English Dictionary*, we find it defined as 'supremacy in respect of power, domination, or rank; supreme dominion, authority, or rule'.[5] *Supreme* is defined in turn as 'highest in authority or rank; holding the highest place in authority, government, or power',[6] *authority* as 'power or right to enforce obedience; moral or legal supremacy; the right to command, or give an ultimate decision',[7] *right* as 'a legal, equitable, or moral entitlement',[8] and, finally, *entitle* as 'to give (a person or thing) a rightful claim'. Circularity of this sort is probably inevitable. Terms like *constitution* are more used than defined, and understanding them means knowing how they are used. The term *constitution* is used to identify fundamental institutional arrangements, mostly but not always dealing with the distribution of political power, that are more entrenched than is ordinary law. To understand the term, we have to see what people do when they describe something as fundamental, or entrenched, or as implicating political power.

Like all definitions, these rest upon some presuppositions, for example, that terms like *sovereignty* and *authority* are perspicuous. Attempting to make the terms used in the definitions precise rapidly gets into deep jurisprudential waters. Defining authority as a 'right to enforce obedience' immediately raises standard jurisprudential questions about the distinction between a power to enforce a command and a right to do so, or, perhaps equivalently, about the distinction between (mere) compliance and obedience. A complete understanding of how the term *constitution* functions in the discourse of constitutional law might require exploration of those and similar jurisprudential issues, and even an introduction to the subject will have to at least touch on those issues.

This chapter examines three topics that have persistently arisen in connection with discussions of constitutions as such: What is the relation between a constitution and a 'nation' or a 'people', understood as those who reside within the territory for which the constitution is a constitution (Section I)? What is the relation between written and unwritten principles of a constitution (Section II)? And, to what extent must constitutions and their constituent elements be more permanent than 'ordinary' legal rules, and by what mechanisms is the requisite degree of permanence maintained (Section III)?

I. Must a Constitution be Autochthonous?

The view that law, including constitutional law, resulted from a nation's 'spirit', itself the product of economics, geography, and path-dependent histories, emerged early in the development of comparative law as a subject of study. For Hegel, 'A constitution... is the work of centuries; it is the Idea, the consciousness of rationality so far as that consciousness is developed in a particular nation.'[9] Understood as a descriptive map of the relations of power that

[5] 'Sovereignty' in Murray et al (n 3), vol 16, def 2.

[6] 'Supreme' in ibid vol 17, def 2.a.

[7] 'Authority' in ibid vol 1, def 1.a.

[8] 'Right' in ibid vol 14, def 9.b.

[9] Georg Wilhelm Friedrich Hegel, *The Philosophy of Right* (trans T.M. Knox, 1967), 286–7, addition to 274.

regulate the exercise of public power, a constitution might be thought almost necessarily autochthonous, generated by arrays of power that inevitably differ from nation to nation. In 2010 Singapore's Constitution, in a descriptive sense, gave an important role to Minister Mentor Lee Kuan Yew, who occupied a position created by executive order for him alone; no other nation is likely to have such a position, and it may well disappear with Lee Kuan Yew's passing. Yet, to the extent that a nation's constitution has *some* stability, one might observe constitutional structures that have migrated across national boundaries.

1. Constitutions and the *Demos*

Another version of the idea that constitutions must be autochthonous, suggested for example by Hegel's reference to 'a particular nation', brings the idea of a constitution together with ideas of ethnonationalism. A nation's constitution, it might be said, constitutes the nation's people, in the sense that it ratifies—and perhaps ossifies—the identification of a *demos* (or, depending on the nation's self-understanding, an *ethnos*) with a state. France's commitment to *laïcité*, Israel's self-identification as a 'Jewish and democratic state' in its Declaration of Independence, and Kemalist secularism in Turkey are all versions of the idea that a nation's character qua nation is intrinsically connected to the idea that a nation has a constitution. The proposed Treaty for a Constitution for Europe elicited a substantial discussion of whether having a constitution presupposed the existence of a *demos* for which the Treaty would be a constitution, as have related discussions of the 'constitution' of the international community.[10]

One argument for the proposition that a constitution requires a *demos* rested on the conceptual point that a constitution must be created by a constituent power, which, so the argument goes, must preexist the exercise of the power to create a constitution. Constitutions might simultaneously presuppose and constitute a citizenry of some sort, though not necessarily an *ethnos*. Consider written constitutions: answering the question, Who may participate in the ratification process?, presupposes that there is some group for whom the constitution will be a constitution. At the same time, that group might not be tightly bound together before ratification; the decision to participate in ratification and to respect the outcome of the ratification process may tie groups together, at least provisionally. Indeed, constitution-writing at least, and perhaps reorganizing the descriptive constitution more generally, might occur only when the community for which the constitution is designed faces problems that might be characterized as putting into question the existence of a *demos*.

The conceptual connection between the existence of a *demos* (and even more, of an *ethnos*) and the descriptive constitution may be even weaker. In the basic, descriptive sense, the international community has a constitution even though it may not be a sovereign in the classic, state-oriented sense, because that community has organized methods of exercising whatever powers it has. Similarly, some—perhaps all—subnational entities have descriptive constitutions (and some have written constitutions), but not all subnational entities have a distinctive *demos*, being organized for mainly administrative purposes. Further, the connection between a descriptive constitution and an *ethnos* might not be as tight as the purely conceptual argument about constituent power suggests. Experience in some constitutional systems such as Canada and theorizing by Jürgen Habermas on constitutional patriotism suggest in contrast that a writ-

[10] Joseph H.H. Weiler, *The Constitution of Europe: 'Do the New Clothes Have an Emperor?' and Other Essays on European Integration* (1999); Jeffrey L. Dunoff and Joel P. Trachtman, *Ruling the World? Constitutionalism, International Law, and Global Governance* (2009).

ten constitution can provide an identity around which a nation can form.[11] Limited to entities that have sovereignty in the classic sense, a descriptive constitution may exist only with respect to a territorially defined nation-state, although one can imagine, perhaps only with a great deal of effort, a descriptive constitution for diasporic communities or the Islamic *umma*.

Further, written constitutions and even descriptive constitutions generally need not be the focal point for national identity. Ethnic origins and religious identities might be more fundamental to that, with the descriptive constitution playing a minor role. Even in the legal domain, one might think that the Civil Code in France serves to create that nation's *legal* identity much more than any of its constitutions has done.

2. Constitutional Borrowing

Scholars of general comparative law have examined the issue of autochthony under the heading of 'transplants' or 'borrowings'.[12] Measures of success for transplants are themselves contested. Some scholars believe that transplants are rarely successful because they tend to be incompatible with the 'spirit' of a nation's laws; others believe that transplants may succeed when they fulfill functional needs within a legal system whose specific resolution is a matter of indifference to those wielding power. That latter qualification suggests a view common in discussions of transplants—that however transplants work in private law fields, they work differently, and almost certainly less well, in constitutional law.

Most discussions of transplants deal with specific institutions and rules, and to that extent are predicated on the emplacement of the transplant into some *written* portion of a nation's constitution. Yet, constitutional ideas can be borrowed, and those ideas need not have a canonical verbal statement. No matter the form of the transplant, skepticism about the potential for success might be justified along these lines: a nation's constitution describes the way in which existing power relations regulate the exercise of government power. A transplant might disrupt those power relations, in which case power-holders will respond either by ignoring the transplant or by transforming it so that it maintains rather than alters existing power relations. In the latter situation the transplant's form remains but its substance has been hollowed out. Alternatively, the transplant might not have any effect on existing power relations. Then, however, the transplant would seem to have nothing to do with the nation's constitution in the descriptive sense. Finally, a transplant might reinforce power relations, for example by giving the most powerful in society the ability to exercise their power more effectively. Here the transplant is successful, but one might question whether the phenomenon should be described as a transplant rather than as an institutional innovation produced by a general search for more effective means of exercising power.

Assuming that we have a decent metric of success—perhaps something combining measures of persistence and effectiveness at achieving intended goals—some degree of skepticism about constitutional transplants does seem justified.[13] Constitutional ideas and structures might migrate,[14] but in the process they might well be transformed to conform to the local spirit of the laws. 'Proportionality' has been described as a 'universal rule of law',[15] and ideas of proportionality and even parallel doctrinal formulations of proportionality tests occur in

[11] See Jürgen Habermas, *Between Facts and Norms: Contributions to a Discourse Theory of Law and Democracy* (William Rehg trans, 1996). On constitutional identity, see Chapter 35.

[12] See also Chapter 64 on constitutional transplants, borrowing and migration.

[13] On constitutional efficacy, see Chapter 37.

[14] Sujit Choudhry (ed), *The Migration of Constitutional Ideas* (2006).

[15] David Beatty, *The Ultimate Rule of Law* (2004). See also Chapter 10.

several legal systems, but what they mean in each system appears to vary, at least to some extent, because of national traditions.[16]

At the same time there are enough examples of successful transplants to caution against overly strong assertions about the viability of constitutional transplants or borrowings. Miller has argued, for example, that the drafters of the Argentine Constitution of 1853 explicitly used the US Constitution as a model, down to the level of minute details.[17] He argues that the domestic constitution succeeded in achieving most of its drafters' aims, for at least a few generations, because the constitution gained legitimacy from its emulation of the widely admired US model. One might treat this is a version of an autochthonous constitution because domestic drafters chose the model to use in light of their goals and their understanding of how the adopted model would operate within the existing array of power. The example suggests that autochthony and borrowing, even extensive borrowing, are not necessarily incompatible.

Purely imposed constitutions present another variant. These constitutions may be imposed by a conquering nation on a defeated adversary. The post-1945 constitutions of Germany and Japan are typically offered as examples of successful imposed constitutions. An important feature of imposed constitutions is that the pre-imposition array of power has been massively disrupted, and those formerly holding power might be unable to reproduce to any significant extent their role in the constitution-as-power-map, which might explain these examples. Yet, even in these cases the degree of imposition, while quite substantial, can be overstated. The German Basic Law drew upon long-standing traditions of liberal constitutionalism in Germany, which had been suppressed during the National Socialist regime but which re-emerged after 1945.[18] The MacArthur-drafted Japanese Constitution of 1949 retained the position of Emperor in a concession to still-important power-holders, and the occupying forces allowed domestic legislators to devise the imposed document's translation into Japanese, giving the legislators at least a minor role in specifying the document's content.[19]

Constitutional transplants may well disrupt existing power relations without fully displacing them. They are in this sense an irritant to the descriptive constitution, and power-holders will respond to the disruption. Importantly, some of those with some power might find the disruption advantageous and the transplant a useful weapon in their ongoing efforts to transform the constitution-as-power-map, to expand their own power or limit their opponents'. Perhaps transplants are successful when they disrupt the existing array of power enough to provide openings for transformation, *and* also give some set of power-holders incentives to stabilize the transplant, perhaps adapted slightly, within a new descriptive constitution.

II. The Constitution's Boundaries

Until the late twentieth century, a recurrent topic for discussion was the distinction between a written constitution, for which the US Constitution of 1789 with its amendments was the paradigm, and an unwritten one, for which the constitution of the United Kingdom was the

[16] Jacco Bomhoff, 'Balancing, the Global and the Local: Judicial Balancing as a Problematic Topic in Comparative (Constitutional) Law' (2008) 31 *Hastings International and Comparative Law Review* 555; Moshe Cohen-Eliya and Iddo Porat, 'Proportionality and the Culture of Justification' (2010) 59 *American Journal of Comparative Law* 463. See also Chapters 33 and 34.

[17] Jonathan Miller, 'A Typology of Legal Transplants: Using Sociology, Legal History and Argentine Examples to Explain the Transplant Process' (2003) 51 *American Journal of Comparative Law* 839.

[18] For a collection illustrating the tradition, see Arthur J. Jacobson and Bernhard Schlink, *Weimar: A Jurisprudence of Crisis* (2000).

[19] Kyoko Inoue, *MacArthur's Japanese Constitution: A Linguistic and Cultural Study of its Making* (1991).

paradigm. The wave of constitution-making in the last half of the twentieth century substantially reduced the salience of that distinction in its usual form. Constitutions embodied in a single written document—which can incorporate both other documents by reference and amendments adopted by methods prescribed in the document itself and appended to or integrated within the document—or at least embodied in a well-defined set of a relatively small number of documents came to be seen as almost essential to identifying a nation as an actor on the international stage. Adopting such a constitution eased the path to recognition of statehood under developing norms of international law, such as the European Community Declaration on the 'Guidelines on the Recognition of New States in Eastern Europe and in the Soviet Union'. Because a constitution can provide a 'focal point for political cohesion' of a nation or of a people,[20] one might note here a tension between the idea that a constitution, written or not, is necessary for recognition of a state on the international scene, and the idea that a constitution, again, written or not, constitutes a nation in the ethno-nationalist sense, a tension arising from the distinction between state and nation upon which ethnonationalism rests. Further, constitutional review exercised by courts or court-like institutions, which spread throughout the world during the same period, seemed to require a foundation in a written constitution, although judicial decisions finding some constitutional amendments unconstitutional on substantive grounds seem defensible only if the courts are enforcing some unwritten 'preconstitutional' norm.[21]

By the beginning of the twenty-first century it could be plausibly contended that the United Kingdom, New Zealand, and Israel were the only nations in the world without written constitutions. And, it could be plausibly contended that Israel and New Zealand had constitutions that could be identified by 'stapling together'[22] a number of written documents such as the Basic Laws in Israel or fundamental statutes and executive directives in New Zealand,[23] or that the Human Rights Act 1998 completed the process of writing a British constitution by making it legally impossible to modify any of the other fundamental statutes by ordinary legislation, a topic addressed in more detail in the following section.

If the salience of the distinction between written and unwritten constitutions has diminished, the conceptual issues raised by that distinction remain important. The legal philosopher John Gardner described one such issue in asking, 'Can There be a Written Constitution?'[24] The question was of course a provocation, playing off the more common question, Can there be an unwritten constitution? Gardner drew on the positivist tradition in analytic legal philosophy, specifically H.L.A. Hart's argument that all law, including constitutional law, rested on a 'rule of recognition' that in the end could not be reduced to words. Rather, the ultimate rule of recognition could be found not in any document but only in the regular practices of officials orienting themselves to their actions with a specific cast of mind.

Frederick Schauer offered a striking example of why the ultimate rule of recognition cannot be written, or more precisely why the rule of recognition resides in social practices rather than in any written words.[25] Suppose one thought that the ultimate rule of recognition in the United

[20] Asem Khalil, 'From Constitution to Constitutionalism in Arab States: Beyond Paradox to Opportunity' (2010) 1 *Transnational Legal Theory* 421, 423.

[21] On unconstitutional amendments, see Kemal Gözler, *Judicial Review of Constitutional Amendments: A Comparative Study* (2008).

[22] John Gardner, 'Can There Be an Unwritten Constitution?', Oxford Legal Studies Research Paper No 17/2009.

[23] See Matthew Palmer, 'Using Constitutional Realism to Identify the Complete Constitution: Lessons From an Unwritten Constitution' (2006) 54 *American Journal of Comparative Law* 587.

[24] See Gardner (n 22).

[25] Frederick Schauer, 'Amending the Presuppositions of a Constitution' in Sanford Levinson (ed), *Responding to Imperfection: The Theory and Practice of Constitutional Amendment* (1995).

States was the written Constitution, which does declare its own supremacy over all other law. Then consider a scenario in which one person approaches another with two documents in hand: one labeled 'The Constitution of the United States', which contains a provision saying that whatever the person carrying it says, is the supreme law of the land, and the other a document labeled 'Law directing the transfer of all property to the bearer'. The person with the two documents demands that the other turn over all her property to him. She refuses, questioning whether the self-designated 'Constitution' is the real Constitution of the United States. The disagreement between the two parties will be resolved through law (as distinct from resolution through sheer physical power) by identifying other people in the society who are generally regarded as officials charged with enforcing and interpreting the law and finding out which document they treat as the US Constitution. Much in this account needs to be unpacked; for example, the qualification 'generally regarded as officials' is designed to deal with the problem that would arise were the person carrying the self-designated 'Constitution' to deny that someone whose opinion was sought, was indeed a public official. Still, the Hartian idea that the ultimate rule of recognition—and by inference the constitution—cannot be written seems plausible enough. One taking this view can even agree with the natural-law challenge to Hart, for on many accounts the natural law or the moral prescriptions that control the content of what can count as law (or as the ultimate rule of recognition) are themselves unwritten and perhaps cannot be written out in enough detail to cover all the contingencies to which the prescriptions will apply.

1. Constitutional Usages and Conventions

Gardner's argument applies high legal theory to constitutional law. Identifying unwritten constitutions, or unwritten portions of constitutions, raises questions on a lower level. The paradigmatic unwritten constitution—the classical British Constitution—consists of fundamental statutes such as Magna Carta, the 1689 Bill of Rights, the Acts of Union with Scotland and Ireland, and more than a handful of others, and, more important for present purposes, a group of practices generally referred to as constitutional *conventions*, or sometimes as *usages* (to avoid confusion with constituent assemblies).[26] All constitutions have conventions and usages within them. The principle of civilian control of the military is written nowhere in the US Constitution, there being no constitutional bar to an active-duty military officer serving as President and so commander-in-chief of the armed forces, yet it is as fundamental to the organization of the US government as is the rule that each state has two Senators. The United States may have a convention against secession as a result of the Civil War's outcome, and the Canadian Supreme Court, acting in a related context, identified constitutional conventions in that nation against unilateral secession *and* for a duty to negotiate the terms of secession in good faith when one or more provinces indicated by substantial majorities an interest in seceding.[27] The next section addresses whether and how fundamental statutes and usages can change.

Two preliminary questions arise in connection with usages and conventions: (1) how can we identify whether a practice is a convention rather than an empirical regularity that happens to exist but has no normative force and (2) how do constitutional conventions and usages

[26] Herbert W. Horwill, *The Usages of the American Constitution* (1925).

[27] *Reference re Secession of Quebec* [1998] 2 SCR 217; for a description of other constitutional conventions or usages in the contemporary US Constitution, see H. Jefferson Powell, *A Community Built on Words: The Constitution in History and Politics* (2002). On secession and self-determination, see Chapter 23.

arise (and, relatedly, how can we identify which statutes are so fundamental as to be part of the constitution)? For both questions the general account resembles Hart's account of the ultimate rule of recognition. We know that a convention is in place when officials generally comply with it without reflection, feel some obligation to explain their deviations from the ordinary practice by offering arguments invoking fundamental values such as the nation's preservation when under attack, and are likely to incur some substantial political cost when they do deviate from the ordinary practice. This account suggests that there might be fundamental statutes as well. Such statutes have characteristics similar to usages': officials rarely propose significant modifications to them, seek to justify such modifications by invoking equally or more fundamental values, and run significant political risks from merely proposing significant changes in the statutes. The statutes that are parts of the unwritten British Constitution almost all involve the political process, which Dicey's definition describes as 'the distribution or exercise of the sovereign power of the state'. Statutes that advance substantive policies such as civil rights, protection of the environment, and the like, might also be fundamental. As these observations suggest, there is no algorithm for identifying a constitutional convention or usage as distinct from a practice that is followed because it generally is convenient but whose observance is unaccompanied by any normative weight, or for identifying fundamental statutes as distinct from long-standing ones that happen to be functionally effective even in the face of substantial changes in their social context.

2. The Constitution 'Outside' the Constitution

In systems in which the written constitution dominates, these fundamental statutes might be described as 'The Constitution Outside the Constitution'.[28] Where courts exercise the power of constitutional review, fundamental statutes of this sort are different from the written constitution. No court will invalidate a later statute as 'unconstitutional' if a litigant contends that the later statute is inconsistent with a statute located in the constitution-outside-the-constitution, even if the reviewing court agrees that the later statute is indeed inconsistent with the earlier one. Fundamental statutes may have legal effects flowing from their 'fundamentality' nonetheless. Courts may construe later statutes to be consistent with the fundamental statutes, sometimes torturing or even departing from otherwise controlling methods of statutory interpretation.[29] They may construe later-enacted fundamental statutes to be implied repeals or modifications of earlier statutes, again even when doing so is contrary to otherwise controlling interpretive rules.

The constitution-outside-the-constitution consists in fundamental statutes. Cass Sunstein has identified another phenomenon, which he calls 'constitutive commitments'.[30] These commitments are the principles that underlie the statutes that make up the constitution-outside-the-constitution. Sunstein's concept clarifies the legal status of such statutes by making it easy to reject the view that mere amendments to them, such as ones that tinker with details or modify the statutes to make them more effective in achieving their goals (at least in the eyes of the amenders), are potentially unconstitutional. That view might be plausible were we to take

[28] Ernest A. Young, 'The Constitution Outside the Constitution' (2007) 117 *Yale Law Journal* 408.

[29] For a good example, see *R v Secretary of State, ex p Anufrijeva* [2003] UKHL 36, where Lord Steyn's comments can be read as suggesting that a statute could be 'construed' even against its plain meaning so as to make the statute consistent with fundamental law.

[30] Cass Sunstein, *The Second Bill of Rights: FDR's Unfinished Revolution and Why We Need It More Than Ever* (2004).

the constitution-outside-the-constitution to be on a par with the constitution itself, but it is implausible in principle. What remains unclear is whether a legislature could lawfully simply repeal a statute reflecting constitutive commitments, at least without acknowledging that it was engaging in a quasi-revolutionary transformation of the nation's constitution.[31]

All the ideas discussed in this section raise questions about the boundaries of the descriptive constitution. Carl Schmitt's identification of the 'state of exception', while directed at normative constitutionalism, suggests the possibility that the descriptive constitution can have no boundaries.[32] Schmitt argued that liberal constitutions were inevitably incomplete because they could never fully deal with what he called the 'state of exception', more recently denominated 'emergencies' threatening the life of the nation as identified by some important political actors. The conditions creating such emergencies could never be fully specified in advance, which meant, to Schmitt, that provisions in written liberal constitutions aimed at regulating the exercise of power in emergencies would always fall by the wayside—and this would be true even were some political actors to contend that the constitutional provisions actually dealt with the situation at hand, because other political actors could always pick out characteristics of that situation that made it different from the ones the constitution addressed. Schmitt argued that the only political actor well positioned to declare a state of exception was the executive, and he appears to have assumed that executives would always have strong incentives to do so when they found their major initiatives frustrated by political opposition. That is clearly wrong as a description of political reality, because executives might have reasons both moral and political for accepting constraints on their ability to pursue even major initiatives. Reframed as arguments about possibilities and probabilities, Schmitt's claims have found substantial support in worldwide experience. Though framed as a challenge to liberal constitutionalism, Schmitt's treatment of the state of exception applies to descriptive constitutions as well. The only difference is that, with respect to the descriptive constitution, the political actor claiming that a state of emergency exists is offering an institutional innovation to deal with the problem at hand, not 'violating' the descriptive constitution.

Some UK constitutional scholars have argued that that nation's constitution is political, in the sense that its provisions—including its protections of human rights—are only partially enforced by the courts but receive full enforcement through politics (or perhaps more precisely through civil society, which typically acts through politics).[33] The idea that there might be fundamental statutes and constitutive commitments that courts might not directly enforce even in systems with robust constitutional review suggests that at least portions of a nation's constitution must be political in the sense used by these scholars, and might support the conclusion that the distinction between a legal constitution and a political one can readily be overdrawn.

3. Operative and Sham Constitutions

As written constitutions became nearly universal, a distinction more closely connected to the idea of constitutionalism than to the idea of a constitution as such became more salient.[34]

[31] For a hint that it could not, see Bruce Ackerman, 'The Living Constitution' (2007) 120 *Harvard Law Review* 1737, 1753–4 n 38.

[32] Carl Schmitt, *The Concept of the Political* (George Schwab trans and ed, 2007).

[33] See Richard Bellamy, *Political Constitutionalism: A Republican Defence of the Constitutionality of Democracy* (2007); Adam Tompkins, *Our Republican Constitution* (2006).

[34] On constitutionalism more generally, see Chapter 8.

Normative constitutionalism provides the ground for distinguishing between a 'sham' constitution and an operative one.[35] Sham constitutions, of which the Soviet Constitution of 1937 is the paradigm, embody the normative values associated with constitutionalism in their texts but in operation fall dramatically short of actualizing those values, whereas operative ones actualize them to a reasonably high degree (though inevitably not perfectly). A descriptive constitution of course cannot be a sham in this sense, because the descriptive constitution simply is what it is. Some written constitutions reject normative constitutionalism on their face, for example by lodging all power in the hands of the chief executive or, as in the People's Republic of China, in the hands of the National People's Congress and its Standing Committee, 'under the leadership of the Communist Party'. Still, the distinction between sham and fully operative constitutions may highlight the fact that a constitution can be fully operative *and* inconsistent with normative constitutionalism. Further, some constitutions that seek to be constitutionalist as well can contain provisions that unintentionally obstruct the flourishing of constitutionalism. Typically these provisions give substantial power to the executive ('presidentialism') or deal with the exercise of power during ill-defined emergency situations, although Carl Schmitt argued that emergency powers necessarily conflict with constitutionalism.[36] Finally, sometimes descriptive constitutions contain elements that are not even intended to be fully actualized, at least in the short run. Such elements can be shams, but sometimes they identify national aspirations; examples might be the Directive Principles of Social (or State) Policy in the Irish and Indian Constitutions.

III. Constitutional Stability

Analytic clarity requires that the descriptive constitution be distinguishable from the ordinary law that happens to be in place at any one time. As the *Oxford English Dictionary* puts it, 'it is assumed or specifically provided that the *constitution* is more fundamental than any particular law, and contains the principles with which all legislation must be in harmony'.[37] The most obvious candidate for distinguishing between a constitution and ordinary law is that the constitution is more stable—is both less likely to change and more difficult to change—than ordinary law. Constitutions, it is thought, are more entrenched than are ordinary laws. So, for example, without additional argument one would not want to say that coalition governments were part of the entrenched British Constitution in 2010. Yet, the criterion of entrenchment may be difficult to apply. Should the dominance of social democratic parties in the Nordic countries for most of the second half of the twentieth century be treated as part of the descriptive constitution, even though those parties could have been displaced in a single election? During the same period corporatist bargaining between peak organizations of employers and workers mediated by state officials usually determined major social policies. Should corporatism be treated as part of the descriptive constitution? And, from the other direction, one can easily identify ordinary laws that have proven more stable than a nation's constitution, the French Civil Code being the most obvious example—a single statute that has persisted as one written constitution has replaced another.

[35] Walter Murphy, 'Constitutions, Constitutionalism, and Democracy' in Douglas Greenberg et al (eds), *Constitutionalism and Democracy: Transitions in the Contemporary World* (1993).

[36] See Schmitt n 32. See also Chapter 21 on states of emergency. On presidentialism, see Chapter 29.

[37] See n 3, comment on def 7.

1. Incentives for Stability

The analysis of the descriptive constitution must address two separate questions about stability: How are the fundamental arrangements embodied in the descriptive constitution maintained over time? and How are the mechanisms for maintaining them different from those that produce some degree of stability even in ordinary legislation? One potential answer lies in attention to the incentives political actors have: a practice may be sufficiently stable if political actors have reasonably strong incentives to restore the practice when one or a few actors deviate from it and as a result political actors have few incentives to try to alter the practice. Yet, sometimes ordinary law will have this characteristic. Politicians who propose to take away a widely distributed benefit will suffer political damage, yet only some such benefits—the general social safety net, for example—are plausible candidates for the label 'fundamental', whereas others, such as some tax deductions, are not, unless they can fairly be described as part of the general social safety net.

Perhaps we could supplement attention to incentives with attention to the *grounds* for deviating from existing practices. The ordinary law in place at any specific time is stable because those with the requisite degree of political power agree with that law, but it can be displaced if approval changes to disapproval, subject to a modest amount of inertia in the lawmaking process. Perhaps the descriptive constitution is stable enough when innovations are proposed for the purpose of achieving specific political outcomes because there are those who oppose the anticipated outcomes on the merits. Perhaps the descriptive constitution is less stable when innovations are proposed so as to restructure the descriptive constitution itself, and the reason may be that no one can be confident in predicting the innovation's results. Of course, the lack of confidence reduces the incentives anyone has to offer this type of change.

Separation-of-powers systems and judicial review exemplify mechanisms for producing stability in fundamental arrangements. In well-designed separation-of-powers systems, the members of different branches are selected by different processes, and for that reason are likely (it is thought) to seek to implement different policies. Each branch, personified, is alert to efforts by another branch to aggrandize itself because that kind of aggrandizement will interfere with the first one's ability to implement the policies it prefers. Judicial review stabilizes institutional arrangements more directly, when the courts enforce the bargains struck either in the written constitution or in long-standing usages. These mechanisms, and others with a similar structure, stabilize the descriptive constitution by creating institutions within which repeated interactions can occur, at some times advantaging one group, at others another. If political actors understand that though some have an advantage at the moment their advantage might disappear relatively soon and that current political disadvantages might be only temporary, everyone might choose to operate within a stable decision-making structure giving them some chance to succeed in the foreseeable future, especially because instability imposes its own costs on everyone's ability to achieve their desired policy goals.

Yet, a question bedevils this argument as well. Why should political actors operate within a status quo political structure that disadvantages them for the moment with respect to the policies they prefer if they have the power to replace that structure with another one that would allow them to implement their policies immediately? So, for example, in systems with judicial review why do political actors comply with court orders rather than defy them, or replace the sitting judges, or restructure the system of judicial review immediately? '[H]ow [do] political arrangements become "institutionalized"' in the relevant sense?'[38]

[38] Daryl Levinson, 'Parchment and Politics: The Positive Puzzle of Constitutional Commitment' (2011) 124 *Harvard Law Review* 657.

One possibility is that normative value attaches to status quo practices as such, sometimes described as 'the normative power of the actual'. One must describe this phenomenon with some care. Normative power must attach to status quo practices not merely because they promote (or impede) the adoption of substantive policies, and must be different from the efficiency associated with continuing to do things as they have been done and from the costs associated with devising and implementing a new way of doing things. Yet, it remains unclear why normative power would attach to the actual as such. Perhaps the status quo somehow places cognitive limits on those who would otherwise design institutional alternatives: they simply cannot imagine doing things much differently. Notably, scholars of comparative law, including constitutional law, often offer as a benefit of their study an expanded imagination for institutional design. A related point is that people gain experience in operating within the status quo institutions, and learning how to operate within newly created institutions is costly, perhaps more costly than the losses with respect to substantive policies that emerge from the status quo institutions.[39]

Drawing on the US experience, Bruce Ackerman has argued that fundamental institutional arrangements persist because they are adopted in periods of heightened public deliberation over constitutional fundamentals.[40] This argument may explain why constitutional arrangements have greater normative force than ordinary law, but it does not explain why constitutional arrangements are more firmly entrenched than ordinary law. When the 'constitutional moments' of heightened public deliberation have passed, the people acting in their quotidian way would have no reason, from their present point of view, to retain the institutions they chose earlier if they believe that those institutions are impeding their ability to adopt the policies they prefer. Perhaps more important here, Ackerman's argument might have some purchase in connection with some kinds of democratic constitutions and to normative constitutionalism, but it is obviously inapplicable to constitutions as such.

A final possibility invokes the argument about repeated interactions, this time on the institutional level. Consider a political actor disadvantaged by existing judicial mechanisms of constitutional review, such as long terms for judges. She might want to 'pack' the court with supporters. But, she might realize that her opponents might pack the court themselves were conditions to change, thereby making her institutional victory short-lived. The difficulty with this argument arises from the time-horizon over which political actors consider their prospects. It is one thing to accept an institutional arrangement that is currently producing undesired results, when those results can be changed within a few years through the status quo mechanisms, but another thing to accept institutional arrangements that systematically produce undesired results simply because new institutional arrangements might be displaced after what is likely to be a significant longer period. The logic here is straightforward: with respect to ordinary legislation produced by the status quo institutions, people are willing to wait a while to see if they can get what they want; but with respect to institutional arrangements people will 'take the money and run', that is, change the arrangements and get whatever they can from them as long as they persist.

2. Constitutional 'Regimes' and their Persistence

These and similar questions typically fall within the domain of political science and sociology, but constitutional law must advert to them. Focusing on the US experience, political scientist

[39] Ibid.

[40] Bruce Ackerman, *We the People: Transformations* (1991); for an application to constitutional development outside the United States, see Bruce Ackerman, *The Future of Liberal Revolution* (1992).

Stephen Skowronek has helpfully analyzed the existence of a succession of constitutional 'regimes'. These regimes consist of relatively stable institutional arrangements coupled with relatively deep programmatic commitments on the part of leading political actors, set within a relatively unchanging written constitution or within a relatively unchanging set of conventions and usages.[41] Suitably adapted to the political arrangements in other nations, Skowronek's approach seems a promising one for analyzing the distinction between a constitution and ordinary law. So, for example, one might speculate that the economic and social conditions of advanced democracies in the early twentieth century conduce to divided government or cohabitation in separation-of-powers systems and coalition governments in parliamentary ones. If so, one could treat coalition government as part of the British Constitution during the present time. Supporting that speculation would require insights and evidence drawn from empirical social science.

Generalized, Skowronek's insight is that political actors seek advantage by using the status quo constitutional arrangements—where the term refers to the descriptive constitution—to advance their ambitions and programmatic goals. If they succeed, they innovate institutionally, altering the descriptive constitution to stabilize and deepen their political support. Their opponents operated within the status quo arrangements, though, and they may resist the institutional innovations. Skowronek suggests that institutional innovation becomes more difficult the longer institutional arrangements are stable, as the beneficiaries of the status quo arrangements use the political power they have gained from those arrangements to impede change. Skowronek's insight could be applied to descriptive constitutions anywhere, including, notably, authoritarian constitutions that fall outside the concerns addressed by normative constitutionalism.

3. The Stability of Constitutional Usages and Conventions

Constitutional conventions and usages present a particular problem in this setting. Horwill describes several constitutional usages in the United States that have simply disappeared, and how they disappeared is worth note. At one time there was a convention that the US President would not travel outside the nation's territory, as exemplified by meetings the US President held with his Mexican counterpart on a bridge joining the two nations. After Thomas Jefferson decided to send his annual address to Congress in writing, believing that delivery in person had monarchical resonances, a convention developed that the US President would not address Congress in person. Woodrow Wilson 'defied' both conventions, presenting his address in person in 1913 and attending the peace conference in Versailles after the armistice ending the First World War. Wilson's actions shattered the conventions, which simply disappeared from the unwritten portion of the US Constitution thereafter. If a convention can be displaced so easily, why should it be treated as a convention rather than as a mere habitual practice? Here too incentives might matter: no political actor had a strong incentive to counter Wilson's deviation from the prior practices through some sort of political challenge to what Wilson did, so the custom or convention that Wilson breached disappeared.

Seen from another perspective, though, 'breaches' of conventions sometimes occur not because political actors do not oppose the deviation from prior practice but rather because they *do*, or more precisely because some political actors see the possibility of gaining advantage

[41] Stephen Skowronek, *The Politics Presidents Make: Leadership from John Adams to George Bush* (1993); for a now dated application of Skowronek's ideas to US constitutional law, see Mark Tushnet, *The New Constitutional Order* (2003).

by altering existing practices. They therefore contend that the practice they challenge has no normative force—is not a convention at all—but merely an ordinary practice that can be changed at will. Constitutional events in Australia in 1975 illustrate the point. On most accounts of Australia's constitutional conventions, the nation's prime minister—occupying a position not mentioned by name in Australia's written constitution—retained the position as long as he or she had the confidence of a majority in the lower house. In 1975 the Governor-General dismissed a prime minister who did have majority support in the lower house, citing governmental paralysis resulting from the prime minister's inability to get a budget adopted in the face of persistent opposition from the upper house.[42] Was this a breach of the constitution's conventions, as most commentators suggest, or action taken in novel circumstances not encompassed within the convention as previously understood? One can hear Schmittian themes in the background of these events.

The foregoing observations are brought into focus by studies measuring the 'lifespan' of constitutions.[43] The typical written constitution is in place for roughly two decades. Although these studies do not compare the lifespan of constitutions with that of ordinary legislation, it is hard to believe that the latter is much different from the former. Legislatures generally do not wipe the slate clean even after large electoral shifts—and when they do we tend to think that a constitutional revolution has occurred. Most ordinary laws, that is, are as stable as the descriptive constitution. The reason is clear. All the mechanisms that produce institutional stability with respect to the descriptive constitution are available with respect to ordinary legislation. Nor is it obvious why the mechanisms would be systematically stronger in connection with the constitution than with ordinary legislation. For example, why would we get greater stability across a wide range of institutional arrangements from the prospect of repeated interactions than we would get across a similarly wide range of ordinary legislation? The same question arises with respect to all the mechanisms that produce constitutional stability. Without an answer, we cannot distinguish, with respect to the entrenchment that is said to characterize the descriptive constitution, between it and the laws that happen to be in place at any specific moment.

IV. Conclusion

Distinctions pervade discussions of descriptive constitutions: between unwritten constitutions and those written in single documents, between constitutions codified in numerous written documents and those with important uncodified components 'outside' the codified constitution, between constitutions and fundamental statutes of near-constitutional stature and constitutive commitments on the one hand and ordinary laws on the other, between real and sham constitutions, between constitutions adopted by design and those that simply evolved, and more. Much important work is simply taxonomic, in trying to identify a specific descriptive constitution's characteristics. Yet, closely examined many of the distinctions are unstable: some ordinary laws are more stable than some constitutional provisions and even entire constitutions, for example. Even so, the classifying exercise can be important. Careful attention to the various categories regularly leads to anti-necessitarian conclusions: one can

[42] For an extended discussion, see George Winterton, *Parliament, the Executive, and the Governor-General: A Constitutional Analysis* (1983).

[43] Thomas Ginsburg, Zachary Elkins, and Thomas Melton, *The Endurance of National Constitutions* (2009).

find a counterexample for every characteristic said to be necessary for understanding descriptive constitutions. And such attention can be particularly valuable when it discloses a specific constitution's unexpected features. Examining those features then contributes to understanding the nation's constitution even if the concepts used to pick the out of the entire descriptive constitution might themselves dissolve when closely scrutinized.

Bibliography

Bruce Ackerman, *The Future of Liberal Revolution* (1992)

Bruce Ackerman, *We the People: Transformations* (1991)

David Beatty, *The Ultimate Rule of Law* (2004)

Richard Bellamy, *Political Constitutionalism: A Republican Defence of the Constitutionality of Democracy* (2007)

Jacco Bomhoff, 'Balancing, the Global and the Local: Judicial Balancing as a Problematic Topic in Comparative (Constitutional) Law' (2008) 31 *Hastings International and Comparative Law Review* 555

Sujit Choudhry (ed), *The Migration of Constitutional Ideas* (2006).

Moshe Cohen-Eliya and Iddo Porat, 'Proportionality and the Culture of Justification' (2010) 59 *American Journal of Comparative Law* 463

Thomas M. Cooley, *The General Principles of Constitutional Law in the United States of America* (1898)

Albert Venn Dicey, *Introduction to the Study of the Law of the Constitution* (1889)

Jeffrey L. Dunoff and Joel P. Trachtman, *Ruling the World? Constitutionalism, International Law, and Global Governance* (2009)

John Gardner, 'Can There Be an Unwritten Constitution?', Oxford Legal Studies Research Paper No 17/2009

Thomas Ginsburg, Zachary Elkins, and Thomas Melton, *The Endurance of National Constitutions* (2009)

Kemal Gözler, *Judicial Review of Constitutional Amendments: A Comparative Study* (2008)

Herbert W. Horwill, *The Usages of the American Constitution* (1925)

Kyoko Inoue, *MacArthur's Japanese Constitution: A Linguistic and Cultural Study of Its Making* (1991)

Arthur J. Jacobson and Bernhard Schlink, *Weimar: A Jurisprudence of Crisis* (2000)

Daryl Levinson, 'Parchment and Politics: The Positive Puzzle of Constitutional Commitment' (2011) 124 *Harvard Law Review* 657

Jonathan Miller, 'A Typology of Legal Transplants: Using Sociology, Legal History and Argentine Examples to Explain the Transplant Process' (2003) 51 *American Journal of Comparative Law* 839

Walter Murphy, 'Constitutions, Constitutionalism, and Democracy' in Douglas Greenberg et al (eds), *Constitutionalism and Democracy: Transitions in the Contemporary World* (1993)

Matthew Palmer, 'Using Constitutional Realism to Identify the Complete Constitution: Lessons From an Unwritten Constitution' (2006) 54 *American Journal of Comparative Law* 587

H. Jefferson Powell, *A Community Built on Words: The Constitution in History and Politics* (2002)

Reference re Secession of Quebec [1998] 2 SCR 217

Frederick Schauer, 'Amending the Presuppositions of a Constitution' in Sanford Levinson (ed), *Responding to Imperfection: The Theory and Practice of Constitutional Amendment* (1995)

Carl Schmitt, *The Concept of the Political* (George Schwab trans and ed, 2007)
Stephen Skowronek, *The Politics Presidents Make: Leadership from John Adams to George Bush* (1993)
Cass Sunstein, *The Second Bill of Rights: FDR's Unfinished Revolution and Why We Need It More Than Ever* (2004)
Adam Tompkins, *Our Republican Constitution* (2006)
Mark Tushnet, *The New Constitutional Order* (2003)
Joseph H.H. Weiler, *The Constitution of Europe: 'Do the New Clothes Have an Emperor?' and Other Essays on European Integration* (1999)
George Winterton, *Parliament, the Executive, and the Governor-General: A Constitutional Analysis* (1983)
Ernest A. Young, 'The Constitution Outside the Constitution' (2007) 117 *Yale Law Journal* 408

CHAPTER 10

RULE OF LAW

MARTIN KRYGIER

Sydney

I. Introduction

Rule of law is one of a number of overlapping ideas, including constitutionalism, due process, legality, justice, and sovereignty, that make claims for the proper character and role of law in well-ordered states and societies. Among these, 'rule of law' has in recent times come into its own. It is lauded by international agencies, pressed upon conflictual, post-conflict, and 'transitional' societies, and of course talked up by politicians and lawyers, particularly judges, all over the world. It is examined in political theory and jurisprudence, and also, though less often, has been subjected to sociological investigation. It used to be much criticized by Marxists and others on the Left, including by members of the Critical Legal Studies movement, but these criticisms are less audible today.

Beneficiary of such praise, called upon for so many purposes, examined in so many ways, deployed in so many domains, not only its virtues but also its meaning tend to swell in the telling. So underlabour needs to be done to clarify the concept, even though no amount of effort will clear away all doubts and differences among those who employ it. We can start with the phrase itself. Is it necessary for the rule of law that law rule? Is it sufficient?

Starting with necessity, it would be an odd rule of law without law. And so, one way a society could lack the rule of law is for its rule to be by means other than legal ones. In such a society, and of course I exaggerate to make the point, law would not be engaged in the exercise of power, which takes place without legal authorization, excuse, or form. This is the thought that underlies the old distinction between limited, even if authoritarian, government and tyranny. Thus Montesquieu, late in a long tradition, distinguished between monarchies, 'in which one alone governs, but by fixed and established laws', and 'despotic government [in which] one alone, without law and without rule, draws everything along by his will and his caprices'.[1] He favoured the former.

At the other extreme are societies where no one rules but many fight. Such is Hobbes's 'state of nature', 'solitary, poore, nasty, brutish and short'. Life in John Locke's natural state is less brutish, less solitary, and perhaps longer, but still inhabitants are minded to leave it, because

> *First*, there wants an *establish'd*, settled, known *Law*... *Secondly*,... there wants a *known and indifferent Judge*, with Authority to determine all differences according to the established Law [and] Thirdly,... there often wants *Power* to back and support the Sentence when right, and to *give* it due *Execution*.[2]

Remedy those three defects, and you have moved some way toward the rule of law. Similar reasoning applies to the anarchic 'failed states' common in the contemporary world. Again, and obviously, law does not rule in a failed state.

As to *rule*: whatever the character of the laws themselves and the will of political authorities to abide by and apply them, if law in a particular society is routinely trumped by, say, raw legally unauthorized exercise of power by gangsters, conmen, or more generally legally unauthorized power-wielders, it makes little sense to speak of the rule of law. Similarly, the political authority might speak through law and act within it, but no one listens because other authorities drown out what it says or make its pronouncements irrelevant to, or powerless against, ways life is lived and expected to be lived. Then it is not the law that rules, and so not the rule of law.

Thus, as long as we adopt a sufficiently flexible notion of 'rule', a necessary condition of the rule of law is that law must rule. Flexibility is important since, contrary to lawyers' conceits, law never rules in anything other than a socially mediated fashion.[3] This affects the character and extent of law's rule, and not always in ways that lawyers find easy to imagine. Law is no unmoved mover, self-starting and brooking no attenuation or modification or interpretation, on the way to those whom it seeks to rule. Even at its most ruly, which is in any case always a matter of degree, the rule of law is a qualified and variable thing, depending for its effectiveness on many social, legal, and political forces and agencies being 'in sync'.

Whatever the case with necessity, however, the mere existence and use of law are by themselves not sufficient for the rule of law. Common in the literature is a distinction between rule *of* and rule *by* law. In the second phrase, political power is exercised by legal means but key elements of the rule of law are lacking, two in particular. One is that governments not merely rule by law but are reliably and effectively constrained by it as well. In many states, law has been a very useful vehicle[4] (and at times equally useful camouflage) for authoritarian exercise of power. Where this is so, though rule might be by, it is not *of* law. Again, it must be stressed, we speak of differences of degree, not categorical distinctions of kind.

[1] Montesquieu, *The Spirit of the Laws* (Anne M. Cohler, Basia Miller, and Harold Stone eds and trans, 1989), bk 2, ch 1, 10.

[2] John Locke, *Two Treatises of Government* (Peter Laslett ed, 1963), 396.

[3] A point well made and graphically illustrated in Sally Falk Moore, 'Law and Social Change: The Semi Autonomous Social Field As An Appropriate Subject of Study' in Sally Falk Moore, *Law as Process* (1978), 54; see also Marc Galanter, 'Justice in Many Rooms: Courts, Private Ordering, and Indigenous Law' (1981) 19 *Journal of Legal Pluralism* 1.

[4] See Tom Ginsburg and Tamir Moustafa (eds), *Rule By Law. The Politics of Courts in Authoritarian Regimes* (2008).

Of course, this is always partly so. Much law serves as an instrument for the achievement of governmental administrative and regulatory goals in every modern state. Today's governments are not sporting umpires, simply enforcing inherited and rarely changing rules of a game made elsewhere and elsewhen. They are active in pursuing their own purposes, and make laws to serve them. However, where the state is framed and constrained by effective and independent legal institutions, professions, and traditions, and typically these days written, effectively binding and relatively fixed constitutions, we are a world away from a polity, such as the former Soviet Union, where regular legal constraint on the power of the Communist Party was for long periods not merely non-existent but unthinkable. Indeed, it was illegal given the 'leading role' constitutionally accorded the Party. So even though this polity was not lawless, since there was plenty of law about, its legal subordination to a supra-legal authority vitiated the feature that makes the rule of law distinctive and precious: constraint by law on the ways in which power can be exercised.

Secondly, though governments may rule by what they call law, this law might fail in some respects to be of a *character* that warrants use of the phrase, 'rule of law'. If the laws are secret, retrospective, contradictory, impossible to know, to understand, to perform, it has often been said, as we will see, they do not add up to the rule of law. Nor would they even if the government obeyed them.

If it is not enough for the rule of law that law should rule, what else is required? Conventional accounts usually start with what I have elsewhere called 'anatomical'[5] characterizations of the rule of law. That is to say, they stipulate elements of legal institutions, rules, and practices, and sometimes achievements, that are seen as adding up to the rule of law. I contrast such accounts with an expressly 'teleological' approach, which starts with reflection on immanent purposes and values of the rule of law, what it is for, and only then moves to spell out how such ends might be attained. That spelling out is likely to be more variable in content, and refer to many things besides legal institutions, than are familiar rule of law anatomies. All depends on what is needed in particular places and times which themselves vary, to achieve the ends of the rule of law. I begin here with some influential anatomies, and move on to teleology.

II. Anatomies of the Rule of Law

1. Institutions

Some writers, particularly lawyers, see the rule of law as inhering in particular features of legal institutions. Those who believe they have the rule of law often identify it with their own institutions; emulation is recommended for those benighted enough to lack them and envious enough of the rule of law to want them. The most influential account in English, that of the constitutional theorist Albert Dicey, is of the first sort; contemporary experiments in 'transitional' societies are often of the second kind.

According to Dicey, the rule of law depends on three characteristics of English law, lacking elsewhere. The first is a system of government which excludes 'the exercise by persons in authority of wide, arbitrary, or discretionary powers of constraint'.[6] The second is universal subjection to 'the ordinary law of the realm and amenable to the jurisdiction of the ordinary

[5] Martin Krygier, 'The Rule of Law. Legality, Teleology, Sociology' in Gianluigi Palombella and Neil Walker (eds), *Relocating the Rule of Law* (2009), 45.

[6] A.V. Dicey, *Introduction to the Study of the Law of the Constitution* (10th edn, 1959), 188.

tribunals'.[7] The third is a system whereby the 'general principles of the constitution' are developed as

> the result of judicial decisions determining the rights of private persons in particular cases brought before the courts; whereas under many foreign constitutions the security (such as it is) given to the rights of individuals results, or appears to result, from the general principles of the constitution.[8]

Each of these elements has a sting in its tail. Opposition to 'wide, arbitrary, or discretionary' powers implies that each adjective identifies dangers of the same order to the rule of law. However, whether wide or discretionary powers are incompatible with the rule of law depends on whether they inevitably bear some defect inconsistent with it; the most likely conjecture being that they allow or even promote arbitrariness. But must they? It is obvious that they could, if the powers were so wide that power-holders could do anything they wished in any way they chose, or discretion so untrammelled that, again, power was quite unconstrained and its manner of exercise able to be capricious and unpredictable. Dictatorships often frame their laws in such ways, and some imagined slippery slope in this direction appears to have underlain the fear of many opponents, among them Dicey, of the welfare state's expansion of governmental powers and discretions. However, it is not self-evident that discretion is of its nature illimitable or width unframeable, or either unreviewable or unaccountable.[9] Width and discretion might indeed be necessary for flexibility in many circumstances of governance, and for many legitimate ends. If they can be effectively framed and subjected to principles and to review, must one assume that they will involve arbitrariness,[10] which is the real foe of the rule of law? Eliding them all, however, does make it easier to oppose an active state.

Secondly, the notion that the rule of law depends on subjection of all to 'the ordinary law... [and] tribunals' rules out both continental public law and a great deal of public law in the Anglosphere as well. That is to rule out very many countries of the developed world.

Finally, it appears from Dicey that the rule of law is only consistent with 'common law constitutionalism', as it bubbles up from court decisions and not with a constitution derived from 'general principles', perhaps as set out in a written constitutional document. It is not clear that this accurately describes even the English Constitution of Dicey's time.[11] It certainly makes the rule of law rather a rare commodity today, rarer than is commonly imagined. Many people, after all, believe traces of it might be found even outside New Zealand, Israel, and pre-EU Britain, exemplary though these countries' unwritten constitutions might be. So if the concept of the rule of law is to lend itself to comparative use, rather than just to identify a peculiar even if apparently blessed eccentricity, Dicey will not be of much help.

The point is larger than one thinker. Institutions are products of particular histories and circumstances; the more detailed their specification, the more particular such products are likely to be. They often travel poorly. A lot that matters about the ways they work where they have grown—conventions, inherited understandings, shared but tacit knowledge among initiates and inheritors of local tradition—are not always easily identified, let alone packaged and

[7] Ibid 193. [8] Ibid 195–6.

[9] See Kenneth C. Davis, *Discretionary Justice* (1969), 216–17; Mortimer R. Kadish and Sanford H. Kadish, *Discretion to Disobey* (1973).

[10] For the distinction between 'the flexible and the arbitrary' as a key insight of the American Framers, see Stephen Holmes, 'In Case of Emergency: Misunderstanding Tradeoffs in the War on Terror' (2009) 97 *California Law Review* 301, 322.

[11] See Ivor Jennings, *The Law and the Constitution* (5th edn, 1933), 39–41.

shipped. They are easily overlooked and left behind. And a lot that matters where the institutions land is strange too, and not always supportive. To the extent that the rule of law is identified with just one way of doing things, therefore, it is unlikely to move very far or very well. If it does travel it will change, unless the indigenous recipients of its beneficence are overwhelmed or destroyed in the process, which, of course, has happened. That does not mean that the rule of law can only exist where it was born, however. For conceived as an ideal or cluster of ideals rather than a specific arrangement of particular institutions, routes to the rule of law might vary, without that rendering it unapproachable.

2. Rules

Legal philosophers tend to focus on more abstract features of legal orders than did Dicey. Particularly prominent have been certain formal characteristics of legal rules, which H.L.A. Hart called 'principles of legality',[12] and Lon Fuller describes as the 'internal morality of law'.[13] These features of the *character* of laws, rather than the substantive content of law are often equated with the rule of law. Fuller famously listed eight of them and others have further elaborated that list.[14] According to Fuller, the internal morality of law requires that it be expressed in general rules, rather than simply ad hoc pronouncements; publicly available to affected parties; prospective not retrospective; comprehensible; not contradictory; not requiring the impossible; not so changeable that they cannot provide guides to action; be administered in ways that conform to their terms. No legal system achieves perfection in any of these dimensions, nor is perfection a salutary ideal for a practical art. All depends on degree, and over-achievement is not necessarily superior achievement. However, a 'legal' system that does systematically poorly in any of these ways suffers degradation and degeneration in the *character* of its institutions and its output. The integrity of legal forms, captured in these eight 'principles of craftsmanship', according to Fuller, is denied by such laws, and with that denial, in extreme forms, so too the moral ground for obeying them. This, Fuller insists, is true quite apart from the substantive goals governments seek to achieve.

Two apparently simple assumptions underlie this and similar sorts of catalogue. One is that the rule of law, which involves law being a source of guidance to its subjects, depends upon people being able to know the law that applies to them when they are choosing how to act. The second is that these principles are necessary for people to be able to do so. Even if you accept these assumptions, what follows from them?

Legal positivist critics of Fuller accept the list and the assumptions but deny that there is anything intrinsically moral about his internal 'morality'. They are, they say, just principles of efficacy, necessary for the law to serve any purpose, but open equally to moral and immoral uses.[15] Though common, this is an odd argument. Tyrants often have good reason to conceal what they do from, among others, those to whom they do it. *Their* purposes may not rely on subjects' ability to know the provisions of the law, understand precisely what it prohibits and permits, plan their lives according to it, still less know what to do to avoid its sanctions or

[12] H.L.A. Hart, 'Problems of Philosophy of Law' in Paul Edwards (ed), *The Encyclopedia of Philosophy* (1967), vol 5, 274.

[13] Lon Fuller, *The Morality of Law* (1969).

[14] See Joseph Raz, 'The Rule of Law and Its Virtue' in Joseph Raz, *The Authority of Law* (1979), 210; Friedrich von Hayek, *The Constitution of Liberty* (1960), 149–50; Geoffrey Walker, *The Rule of Law: Foundations of Constitutional Democracy* (1988).

[15] See H.L.A. Hart's review of *The Morality of Law* in (1965) 78 *Harvard Law Review* 1286; Ronald Dworkin, 'The Elusive Morality of Law' (1965) 10 *Villanova Law Review* 634, Martin Golding, *Philosophy of Law* (1975), 49–50. And see Fuller's comments in his 'reply to critics' (n 13), 200ff.

object to abuses of it. It might be enough that they are terrified, knowing that whatever is done to them cannot be resisted, or that rulers have maximum flexibility and/or subjects maximum uncertainty. Evil regimes rarely will have reason to use laws that embody law's internal morality, at least when they do their worst.[16] Conversely, denial of Fuller's principles, often systematic, can help them to attain their purposes, and they have not been unaware of it.[17] Nor was Fuller.

This is a dramatic example of a more general point. Fuller insists on a distinction between 'managerial direction', a 'one-way projection of authority, originating with government and imposing itself upon the citizen',[18] and law properly so called, which depends upon *interaction* between law-giver and citizen. The manager wants jobs done at least cost to best effect; efficacy refers to the degree of success in achieving managerial goals. Elements of institutional character are subservient to such goals, and are therefore contingent; appropriate to, and only to, the extent to which they help in the achievement of centrally directed goals. If it would help achievement of such goals to keep things quiet, allow unfettered discretion to decision-makers, or change rules rapidly, there is no intrinsic managerial reason to object. Interaction has a different logic. For law to provide a reliable basis for reciprocal (not to mention mutually respectful) interaction between law-giver and legal subject, the trade for their obedience must be that the latter are able to predict and rely upon the routine ways in which power is exercised. Unlike managerial direction, interaction requires substantial adherence to the internal morality of law as a matter of principle, Fuller believes, not merely contingent and revisable practice.

And finally, this distinction between ways in which governments treat citizens in turn rests upon a less instrumental, more deontological, moral claim. It has to do with what Fuller calls 'the view of man implicit in legal morality'.[19] Here again the objection to deviation from the internal morality has in the first instance not to do with the external substantive purposes that might be pursued. Rather it concerns whether one treats persons with respect:

> Every departure from the principles of the law's inner morality is an affront to man's dignity as a responsible agent. To judge his actions by unpublished or retrospective laws, or to order him to do an act that is impossible, is to convey to him your *indifference* to his powers of self-determination.[20]

'Indifference' is a good word to use here, since it can span both intentional oppression or repression and well-meaning authoritarian direction. Even where the former is absent, there is a lot of the latter in modern societies, even those governed with the best of intentions and with a large measure of the rule of law. But there are also many elements that affirm and reaffirm human dignity: a high degree of the internal morality of law, defences in criminal law, provisions concerned with due process, publicity, rights, including rights of appeal, and so on.[21] These features are not all captured, however, by this list of formal features of the rules. They inhere in legal *procedures* characteristic of the rule of law. We move to these now.

[16] See Kristen Rundle, 'The Impossibility of an Exterminatory Legality: Law and the Holocaust' (2009) 59 *University of Toronto Law Journal* 65.

[17] See my 'Hart, Fuller and Law in Transitional Societies' in Peter Cane (ed), *The Hart–Fuller Debate in the Twenty-First Century* (2010), 107–34. The rest of this section draws on that article. See also Chapter 61 on constitutionalism and transitional justice.

[18] Fuller (n 13), 207.

[19] Ibid 162.

[20] Ibid 162–3, emphasis added.

[21] On human dignity and autonomy in modern constitutional orders, see Chapter 18.

3. Procedures

One reason why analytical legal philosophers commonly adopt such a thin and formal account of the rule of law as the preceding, is the fear that loading wide-ranging substantive ideals into the concept melts it into everything else we might like, and renders a separate and distinct concept otiose. As Raz expresses the point,

> if the rule of law is the rule of good law then to explain its nature is to propound a complete social philosophy. But if so the term lacks any useful function. We have no need to be converted to the rule of law just in order to discover that to believe in it is to believe that good should triumph.[22]

That seems to me a serious reason to be cautious about overly thickened substantive conceptions of it. However, there is arguably an important point between 'thin', purely formal accounts of the rule of law and those so 'thick' that they simply equate it with the good, the attainment of human rights, or the doing of justice.[23] That point has to do with values specifically associated with the operations of law. As we have seen, there are already values that underpin the selection of Fuller's eight characteristics of legal rules. But these are not the only values peculiarly (though not exclusively) relevant to legal orders.

Accounts of the rule of law of the Fullerian sort concentrate primarily on the *centrifugal* force of law, on the formal qualities of the messages legal institutions send out to citizens. However, law also draws citizens in, whether it is police picking them up on the street and delivering them to gaol, or when they come in to courts and other official institutions to do combat with other citizens or with the state. How the law treats them at such points, where other means of resolving differences have not prevailed and the stakes are therefore often high, is a particular concern of many legal traditions.

Whereas Dicey had a lot to say about relationships between this key aspect of law and the rule of law, legal philosophical treatments of the rule of law are rather light on in this respect. And yet, as Jeremy Waldron stresses, when ordinary citizens think of the rule of law, they are more likely to have this in mind than the formal quality of legal rules.[24] And in relation to this, as Neil MacCormick also emphasizes, 'law is an argumentative discipline'[25] and that is not through accident or misadventure. Nor is the argument left unstructured by the law. People with legal interests at stake need to be able to speak for those interests, whether they accuse or are accused. This requires a good deal of provision from legal orders, by way of procedures that require impartial third party hearings, defences, ability to speak, examine witnesses, present evidence, see evidence relied upon by the other side, and so on. As Waldron emphasizes:

> Argumentation (about what this or that provision means, or what the effect is of this array of precedents) is *business as usual* in law. We would be uneasy about counting a system that did not exhibit it and make routine provision for it as a legal system.... Courts, hearings and arguments—those aspects of law are not optional extras; they are integral parts of how law works; and they are indispensable to the package of law's respect for human agency. To say that we should value aspects of governance that promote the clarity and determinacy of rules for the sake of individual freedom, but not the opportunities for argumentation that a free and self-possessed individual is likely to demand, is to slice in half, to truncate, what the

[22] Raz (n 14), 211.

[23] Accounts of the rule of law are often distinguished according to the normative commitments they are asked to carry, in these terms. See eg Randall Peerenboom (ed), *Asian Discourses of Rule of Law* (2004).

[24] Jeremy Waldron, 'The Concept of Law and the Rule of Law' (2008) 43 *Georgia Law Review* 1, 22.

[25] Neil MacCormick, *Rhetoric and the Rule of Law* (2005), 14.

> Rule of Law rests upon: respect for the freedom and dignity of each person as an active intelligence.[26]

Respect for freedom and dignity are good things in general, of course, and there are many ways to manifest and deny them that have nothing to do with law. However, given that law is, in Fuller's words, an 'enterprise of subjecting human conduct to the governance of rules',[27] that enterprise is liable to impinge directly and even dramatically on these values. It is no accident, then, as Waldron stresses, that they are:

> in a deep and important sense associated foundationally with the idea of a legal system—that law is a mode of governing people that treats them with respect, as though they had a view of their own to present on the application of a given norm to their conduct or situation. Applying a norm to a human individual is not like deciding what to do about a rabid animal or a dilapidated house. It involves paying attention to a point of view and respecting the personality of the entity one is dealing.[28]

Both the unpredictability or unreliability of the exercise of power, and the inability to challenge it, are obnoxious for several of the same reasons as having one's own perspective silenced or ignored. For the rule of law is sought in opposition to *arbitrariness*, and that can come in many guises.

III. What's the Point?

According to Max Weber, 'Sociologically, the state cannot be defined in terms of its ends.... Ultimately, one can define the modern state sociologically only in terms of the specific *means* peculiar to it, as to every political association, namely, the use of physical force.'[29] Is Weber's general point applicable to the rule of law? Certainly, there has long been dispute between natural lawyers and legal positivists over whether the concept of law itself is to be understood in this way or rather is 'a concept like *hospital* rather than a concept like *state* (in Weber's sense)',[30] one that necessarily incorporates some reference to what it is for. Whatever the case with the concept of law, the *rule of law* is a more clearly compelling candidate for teleological understanding. The rule of law is not a natural entity, simply awaiting scientific description; it too needs to be understood in terms of what it is for. While such a purpose could in principle be value-neutral or even harmful, the rule of law is commonly thought valuable, an ideal for law. If we value that ideal we should seek to identify what might generate it. But without some principle of selection even if only tacit, we will not find a bunch of legal bits and pieces waiting 'out there' and neatly recognizable as the rule of law. As Rosenfeld has observed,

> Like the concepts of 'liberty' or 'equality,' the descriptive meaning of 'the rule of law' is dependent on the prescriptive meaning one ascribes to it; in the context of complex contemporary polities there likely will be vigorous disagreements concerning the relevant prescriptive standards at stake.[31]

[26] Waldron, 'The Rule of Law and the Importance of Procedure' in J. Fleming, *Getting to the Rule of Law* (2011).

[27] Fuller (n 13), 96.

[28] Waldron (n 26), 23–4.

[29] Max Weber, 'Politics as a Vocation' in Hans H. Gerth and C. Wright Mills (eds), *From Max Weber* (1948), 77–8.

[30] Jeremy Waldron, 'Legal and Political Philosophy' in Jules Coleman and Scott Shapiro (eds), *The Oxford Handbook of Jurisprudence and Philosophy of Law* (2002), 371.

[31] Michel Rosenfeld, 'The Rule of Law and the Legitimacy of Constitutional Democracy' (2001) 74 *Southern California Law Review* 1308–9.

This is evident, if implicit, even from the anatomical accounts we have just discussed. Thus Dicey did not merely choose three characteristics at random among the many that English law possesses. Rather, he believed them to be the specific sources of 'a trait of national character which is as noticeable as it is hard to portray'.[32] But what if he were wrong in that portrayal? Or, counterfactually, what should he have said if he could be persuaded that similar 'trait[s] of national character' could be found elsewhere with a completely different set of legal conventions, practices, and institutions? Would he deny that they had anything to do with the rule of law, or might he have to concede that he had misunderstood the sources of the rule of law, or at least been mistaken in suggesting that there were no other ways to the same end?

Similarly, there is nothing purpose-neutral or, indeed, value-neutral about Fuller's 'principles of legality' or MacCormick's and Waldron's stress on procedural requirements for the rule of law. The rule of law is a purposive and normative concept, not just a happenstance collection of legal-institutional characteristics. We might avoid many false steps were we to *start* by articulating the valued ends we associate with the rule of law, and only then move to speculate about how they might be approached. It is more common, however, to proceed the other way around.[33]

What is that valued state of affairs, which allows us to speak of the rule of law existing in a society? Here I would propose a distinction between external and immanent and values of the rule of law. Thus, according to the *World Justice Project*, the rule of law is 'the foundation for communities of opportunity and equity…the predicate for the eradication of poverty, violence, corruption, pandemics, and other threats to civil society'.[34] This extravagant list is of *external* consequences that flow, if they do, from the presence of the rule of law, rather than immanent ones, in the sense of this distinction. They are things we might value as elements in a good society, and presumably would still value, if we were handed them on a plate, whether or not we needed the rule of law to achieve them.

What ends are immanent in this sense? Here there is great room for argument, though we are not flying blind, since there are enduring themes in rule of law traditions. Even if my own specific proposal is rejected or augmented, however, I would urge the first point of this section: start with ends, so to speak, whatever you take them to be; do not jump too hastily to means.

One recurrent theme in rule of law traditions[35] is a contrast between the rule of law and *arbitrary* exercise of power. Institutionalizing ways of reducing arbitrary power is an immanent rule of law value, whatever else flows from it. The concept of arbitrariness is complex and insufficiently theorized. However, a good starting point is Philip Pettit's definition:

> An act is perpetrated on an arbitrary basis, we can say, if it is subject just to the *arbitrium*, the decision or judgement, of the agent; the agent was in a position to choose it or not choose it, at their pleasure.[36]

It is such unconstrained exercise of *arbitrium* that partisans of the rule of law have opposed and sought to eliminate. Unpredictable exercise of power is one way of treating its targets arbitrarily; another is its exercise, whether predictable or not, that takes no account of the perspectives of those whom it would affect.

[32] Dicey (n 6), 187.

[33] See Krygier (n 5), 45; Martin Krygier, 'Four Puzzles about the Rule of Law: Why, What, Where? And Who Cares?' in James Fleming (ed), *NOMOS L: Getting to the Rule of Law* (2011), 64.

[34] Rule of Law Index (2010), 1.

[35] See John Philip Reid, *Rule of Law* (2004).

[36] Philip Pettit, *Republicanism: A Theory of Freedom and Government* (1997), 55.

Why does arbitrariness matter? Because it tends ineluctably to: threaten the liberty of anyone subject to it; generate reasonable and enduring fear among them, even if arbitrary power happens *pro tem* not to be exercised in fearful ways, as long as it might be at any time; and deprive citizens of sources of reliable sources of expectations of, and coordination with, each other and with the state. And, as Fuller and Waldron have emphasized, it threatens the dignity of all who find themselves mere objects of power exercisable at the whim or caprice of another. These are four good reasons to value reduction of the possibility of arbitrary exercise of power.[37] To the extent that the rule of law can help to deliver such reductions, this is reason to value it. This is not, of course, merely a negative matter of removing evils, but can be expressed positively. A society in which law contributes to securing freedom, confidence, coordination, and dignity, is some great and positive distance from many available alternatives. There are other things we want from law, and many more things we might want in a good society, but ways of serving these values are goods immeasurably harder to attain without institutionalizing constraints on arbitrariness in the exercise of power.

There is nothing original or even lonely in nominating opposition to arbitrariness as a fundamental concern of the rule of law. However, taking the point seriously and starting with it has a number of implications that have not always been noted. The most important is that the utility of the anatomical accounts above depends on how adequately they capture what is necessary to secure this value. To the extent they do, they have aided us in identifying what the law needs to be like to serve the end of the rule of law. To the extent that they do not, however, it is not at all clear why we fix on them so, still less try to extend them to places where they might merely have parodic roles. The challenge for the rule of law is not primarily to emulate Dicey, Fuller, or Waldron, but to reduce the possibility of arbitrary exercise of power.

Taking this ambition seriously, moreover, may not only require different legal rules and practices from those we know, particularly in places we do not know, but also the recognition that many of the most significant sources, goods, and dangers to the rule of law are to be found in the wider society, not merely in or even near the obvious institutional centres of official law. There are numerous societies in which arbitrariness flows as much or more from extra-state exercises of power, sometimes aided by suborned official agencies, sometimes opposed to them. Sources of power are many, and possible constraints on it may come, or fail to come, from many domains of social life.

IV. Negative or Positive?

Many thinkers have combined a high regard for the rule of law with a negative view of it. This is only an apparent, verbal, paradox. For it is common to understand the rule of law as good less for what it creates than for what it might prevent. On this understanding, the rule of law is pre-eminently concerned to block the possibility of *unruly* power, to curb, restrain, and channel power's exercise.

This is not a new development. Thus the historian John Philip Reid emphasizes, of the English legal tradition imported to the United States, 'From time immemorial the legal heritage of Europe beyond the pale of Roman law had been law as restraint, not law as command.'[38] He quotes Bracton's revealing metaphor from the thirteenth century, of law as 'the bridle of power', by which a just king, as distinct from a 'tyrant', must 'temper his power'.[39] Again, Judith

[37] I discuss these four reasons more extensively in Krygier (n 33).

[38] Reid (n 35), 12.

[39] Henry de Bracton, *On the Laws and Customs of England*, vol 2, 305–6, quoted in Reid (n 35), 12.

Shklar, partisan of 'damage control',[40] as the first goal of political arrangements, insists that the prevention of evil, rather than a quest for the good, is the signal and precious virtue of the rule of law.

Whereas for Shklar the rule of law acts negatively to priceless effect, the legal philosopher Joseph Raz also construes its significance as negative, and though he praises it, the praise is relatively tepid (two cheers). He describes it as 'a purely negative value... merely designed to minimize the harms to freedom and dignity which the law might cause in its pursuit of its goals however laudable these might be.'[41] Shklar does not share Raz's lukewarm tone, and there are two mistakes here that she would be unlikely to make. First, the harms for which the rule of law is a suggested antidote are abuses of *power*, not merely of law. There are many ways in which power can be exercised, used, and abused, even by the state, without the intervention of law. The rule of law is intended to exclude all those other ways from the start. More is necessary, but that exclusion is no small matter where the dangers of arbitrary power are a concern. Secondly, what of all those power-holders outside the state, that might abuse power, though not through law? Constraining them *by* law is no small matter. Nevertheless, Shklar and Raz agree at least that the value of the rule of law lies in what it rules out rather than what it rules in; what it restrains and prevents, rather than what it generates and encourages to flourish.

A more complex way of characterizing the ambition to constrain and channel power by law that is simultaneously an instrument of power, is old in the English tradition of the rule of law. It was well described by Charles McIlwain,[42] and its rationale has recently been recovered and re-articulated by Gianluigi Palombella as central to the rule of law. According to this tradition, the point of the rule of law is 'to prevent the law from turning itself into a sheer tool of domination, a manageable servant to political monopoly and instrumentalism.'[43] It requires that, besides the laws that bend to the will of governments, ' "another" positive law should be available, which is located somehow outside the purview of the (legitimate) government, be it granted by the long standing tradition of the common law or by the creation of a 'constitutional' higher law protection, and so forth.'[44] The common law writers spoke of a *balance* between the sovereign's untrammelled right to pursue the ends of government (*gubernaculum*) and legal protection of the right (*jurisdictio*). The former must not overwhelm the latter, even if it is unlimited in its own sphere.

The solution was found in the common law, viewed not just as a moral limit but a binding legal one. Written and binding constitutions are more recent examples of such an ambition. In all these the ruler is constrained by something that is truly law but not his to rule, not able to be bent to his will. Such a conception, such a duality, Palombella argues, was missing, until the last century's spread of constitutions, from the continental European *Rechtsstaat*, which many, wrongly in his view, assimilate to the rule of law. Without this duality, a state may commit to Fuller's criteria of non-arbitrariness as its *form* of rule, without any overarching constraint that renders anything beyond its power. Its ultimate goals might have nothing to do with reduction of domination, fear, indignity, or confusion. They might simply amount to tidy, reliable, and controllable ways for officials to extend state power and transact matters of state. On

[40] Judith N. Shklar, 'The Liberalism of Fear' in Judith N. Shklar, *Political Thought and Political Thinkers* (1998), 24–5, 9; and see 'Political Theory and the Rule of Law', ibid 21.

[41] Raz (n 14), 228.

[42] Charles McIlwain, *Constitutionalism: Ancient and Modern* (revised edn, 1947).

[43] Gianluigi Palombella, 'The Rule of Law as an Institutional Ideal' in Gianluigi Palombella and L. Morlino (eds), *Rule of Law and Democracy: Internal and External Issues* (2010), 3, 4.

[44] Ibid 31.

Palombella's view, the rule of law goes further than this. It lawfully sets limits on even a sovereign's lawful powers.

Even in this version the stress is on constraint as the distinguishing feature of the rule of law. Not everyone agrees. One way to disagree is to say there is more to the rule of law than constraint on power. Another is to redescribe the significance of rule of law constraints themselves. Ronald Dworkin and Philip Selznick disagree in the first way; Stephen Holmes in the second.

Dworkin is sceptical of conventional 'rule book' conceptions of the rule of law, which insist that

> so far as is possible, the power of the state should never be exercised against individual citizens except in accordance with rules explicitly set out in a public rule book available to all... Those who have this conception of the rule of law do care about the content of the rules in the rule book, but they say that this is a matter of substantive justice, and that substantive justice is an independent ideal, in no sense part of the ideal of the rule of law.[45]

He, by contrast, regards the rule of law as an ideal and an eminently positive and substantive one, 'the ideal of the rule by an accurate public conception of individual rights'.[46] On this view, the rule of law is the rule, in 'law's empire', of Dworkin's theory of law.

Selznick has written more, and more variously, on the rule of law than Dworkin, and his views are more complex. On the one hand, he understands the appeal of the negative conception, and he has often emphasized its importance. Thus, he agrees with those political realists who stress the importance of legality as a restraint on, and see the rule of law as a precious protection against abuse of, power.[47] On the other hand, there is a 'larger promise of the rule of law', and this

> thicker, more positive vision speaks to more than abuse of power. It responds to values that can be *realized*, not merely protected, within a legal process. These include respect for the dignity, integrity, and moral equality of persons and groups. Thus understood, the rule of law enlarges horizons even as it conveys a message of restraint.[48]

This threatens to breach Raz's opposition to giving a concept so much work that it fails to do any useful job, but it need not. Selznick is particularly insightful about the dynamic pressures that a legal order will tend to generate, both when it fails to satisfy subjects' expectations as when it succeeds. Unusual among writers on the rule of law, Selznick was a distinguished sociologist, and in part his objection to a purely limited conception of legality is that:

> We cannot really separate the negative and positive aspects of the rule of law. Indeed it would be highly unsociological to try to do so, for we would then miss the moral and institutional dynamics which create demands for justice, and which induce rulers to accept accountability.... we should not reduce the rule of law to its most rudimentary forms.[49]

There is yet another sense in which the rule of law can be understood to be a *positive* achievement, one which does not deny that it is primarily a matter of constraints but interprets differently the significance of those very constraints. Thus, Stephen Holmes elaborates on the

[45] Ronald Dworkin, 'Political Judges and the Rule of Law' in Ronald Dworkin, *A Matter of Principle* (1985), 11.

[46] Ibid 11–12.

[47] *The Moral Commonwealth* (1992), 174.

[48] Philip Selznick, 'Legal Cultures and the Rule of Law' in Martin Krygier and Adam Czarnota (eds), *The Rule of Law after Communism* (1999), 26.

[49] Ibid 25–6.

empowering consequences of legal constraints, as elements of what he calls 'positive constitutionalism'. The 'paradoxical insight' of this tradition, that:

> constraints can be enabling, which is far from being a contradiction, lies at the heart of liberal constitutionalism.... By restricting the arbitrary powers of government officials, a liberal constitution can, under the right conditions, *increase* the state's capacity to focus on specific problems and mobilise collective resources for common purposes.[50]

As he goes on to show:

> constitutions not only limit power and prevent tyranny, they also construct power, guide it toward socially desirable ends, and prevent social chaos and private oppression, immobilism, unaccountability, instability, and the ignorance and stupidity of politicians. Constitutions are multifunctional. It is, therefore, a radical oversimplification to identify the constitutional function exclusively with the prevention of tyranny.[51]

On this second view, like an athlete who learns techniques and disciplines to marshal raw energy, so the power of a state to concentrate its powers where it should is enhanced by constraints which, among other things, deny it power to disperse them where it should not.

These are particularly important points in the context of contemporary anxieties about terrorism, and Holmes has applied his thought to that context. He argues that, so far from being a reason to discard the constraints of law, emergencies are precisely times when such pre-tested constraints are typically most needed. He is critical of the very common attempts by governments to 'release the shackles' of the rule of law in situations seen as emergencies—to rule without open, calculable rules, to dispense with safeguards of procedural fairness, suspend habeas corpus, diminish or discard the ordinary protections and contestatory opportunities traditionally associated with legal hearings. Such attempts pay no heed to the positive, enabling, competence-protecting role of the rule of law, and particularly to the dangers of panicked flailing about, over-inclusion, plain unaccountable incompetence, ignorance, and lack of exposure to tests of the reliability of information, that often attend the acts of power-wielders acting in secret and on the fly. To ignore this 'liberal paradox' is to ignore the powerful constructive significance of the rule of law.[52]

In making these arguments, Holmes speaks of constitutionalism as often as he does of the rule of law. Clearly he believes the arguments apply to both. More generally, it is clear that there is overlap both in the ends and means of constitutionalism and the rule of law, but they are not the same.[53] They are closer perhaps in ends than in means. Both seek to staunch possibilities of arbitrary power, but not every aspect of the rule of law is a constitutional matter, and not everything likely to be found, in a modern constitution at any rate, is part of the rule of law. Constitutions focus on states; they are central elements of public law. On the argument developed here, the rule of law has broader reach, since it deals not merely with acts of state but also with other sources of social power, and the law that affects them. This must include private law. On the other hand, constitutions typically say a good deal about the *content* of law, whereas many versions of the rule of law limit it more austerely to matters of form and procedure. And finally, constitutions primarily set *frameworks* for legally permissible government,

[50] Stephen Holmes, *Passions and Constraint: On the Theory of Liberal Democracy* (1997), xi. On enabling constraints in other contexts, see David Stark and Laszlo Bruszt, *Postsocialist Pathways* (1998). See also Martin Loughlin, *The Idea of Public Law* (2003) and Jon Elster, *Ulysses Unbound* (2000).

[51] Holmes (n 50), 6.

[52] Stephen Holmes, *The Matador's Cape: America's Reckless Response to Terror* (2007), 6. On states of emergency, see Chapter 21.

[53] On constitutionalism, see Chapter 8.

whereas the rule of law has a great deal to do with the *character* of laws. But if they are not identical they are inseparably conjoined. And both of them have crucial negative and positive contributions to make.

V. The Administrative State

One of the major developments of the twentieth century was the welfare state, and with it unprecedented expansion of state activity, even after neoliberal attempts to 'roll [it] back'. Much of this governmental activity has been increasingly directed to regulatory and distributive goals, which administrators, well supplied with open-ended legislative provisions, regulatory discretions, and particularized decisions to make, are mandated to achieve. Many writers have been concerned that however well meaning the motives of such activity, their pursuit exacts a high price, even if their goals are likely to be achieved, which many such critics also doubt. A significant part of the cost of the pursuit, it has often been alleged, is borne by the rule of law.[54]

Friedrich von Hayek had great influence here. He took the modern welfare state's 'instrumentalization' of law, purportedly in the interests of social justice, both to be the pursuit of a mirage, since social justice was a nonsense concept, and to threaten the end of the rule of law because of the style of law it generated. For him the notion that law must flexibly 'respond' to myriad social 'needs'—other than basic ones such as providing a clear framework of rules for individuals to guide their actions and interactions—emanates from a flawed social theory and presages a damaged polity. It pretends to a knowledge that no individuals but only markets, which aggregate more than anyone separately has, can possess. And the efficiency of those markets depends on clear, stable, general rules of the game, interpreted and enforced by independent arbiters, not on open-ended policy directives, increasingly vague and unspecific in their terms, and implemented by centrally determined goal-directed bureaucrats. Bad goals generate bad means, laws that do not guide, frameworks that keep being adjusted, prescriptions too vague and malleable to be followed, but altogether labile in the hands of their wielders.

Even by those who do not share Hayek's political or economic analysis have analysed changes in legal form in similar ways. Roberto Unger saw a flat contradiction between the transformations in the form of law generated by the welfare state, and the rule of law. For him, welfare state efforts to render law 'purposive' and responsive, engender 'policy-oriented discourse' that 'forces one to make explicit choices among values', the 'pursuit of procedural or substantive justice [that] requires rules be interpreted in terms of ideals that define the conception of justice', and an 'escalating use of open-ended standards and a swing toward purposive legal reasoning and procedural or substantive approaches to justice.' Together these trends 'repeatedly undermine the relative generality and the autonomy that distinguish the [autonomous] legal order from other kinds of law, and in the course of so doing they help discredit the political ideals represented by the rule of law.'[55] Eugene Kamenka and Alice Erh Soon Tay

[54] See eg Walker (n 14); F.A. Hayek, *Law, Legislation and Liberty* (vol 1, 1973; vol 2, 1974; vol 3, 1979); E. Kamenka and A.E.-S. Tay, 'Beyond Bourgeois Individualism—The Contemporary Crisis in Law and Legal Ideology' in E. Kamenka and R.S. Neale (eds), *Feudalism, Capitalism and Beyond* (1975). And from a different political perspective, see Brian Tamanaha, *Law as a Means to an End: Threat to the Rule of Law* (2006). More complex appraisals of such developments include Otto Kirchheimer, 'The *Rechtsstaat* as Magic Wall' in Otto Kirchheimer, *Politics, Law, and Social Change* (1969), 428; and Philippe Nonet and Philip Selznick, *Law and Society in Transition* (1979). On the regulatory state, see Chapter 31.

[55] Roberto Mangabeira Unger, *Law in Modern Society: Toward a Criticism of Social Theory* (1976), 195, 197.

offered a similar diagnosis to Unger's, but their evaluation was closer to Hayek's. They detected 'a crisis in the *form* of law, the result of its inability, on its existing form and principles, to accommodate the new content and role being demanded of it.'[56]

Lest such apprehensions all seem a thing of the pre-neoliberal past, Brian Tamanaha has recently argued that contemporary understandings of 'law as a means to an end' present a pervasive 'threat to the rule of law'. These anxieties have not died. Though these issues are too complex to deal with adequately here, there is one implication of this discussion which might be mentioned: it is impossible even to assess such apprehensions without more attention than is common to the *contexts*, including 'extra-legal' social contexts, in which they occur.

VI. Contexts and Conclusions

The historian E.P. Thompson, long time a Marxist and always a man of the Left, enraged erstwhile comrades with his encomium to the rule of law at the end of his, for this reason controversial, *Whigs and Hunters*.[57] Notwithstanding that his was a book about laws that he condemned, he concluded that 'the rule of law itself, the imposing of effective inhibitions upon power and the defence of the citizen from power's all-intrusive claims, seems to me to me an unqualified human good.'[58]

In insisting on the 'obvious point' that 'there is a difference between arbitrary power and the rule of law', it might be noted, Thompson starts with the *point* of the rule of law rather than with the particular institutional forms in which it might be found. Indeed, he noted that legal institutions were constantly being 'created...and bent' by 'a Whig oligarchy...in order to legitimise its own property and status'.[59] Still, that oligarchy could not do as it wished; its hands were often tied by the law it sought to exploit. How did Thompson show this? By describing the character of legal institutions and norms, or the experience of litigants, or internal legal balances? No. Rather, he called in aid facts such as that

> law was a definition of actual agrarian *practice*, as it has been pursued 'time out of mind'...'law' was deeply imbricated within the very basis of productive relations, which would have been inoperable without this law. And...this law, as definition or as rules (imperfectly enforceable through institutional forms) was endorsed by norms, tenaciously transmitted through the community.[60]

If it were possible to construct a scale of conditions for the rule of law, the eighteenth-century English legal order, as Thompson describes it, would score inordinately well, as Dicey already observed. Not everyone is so lucky. Legal orders differ greatly in the extent to which values, institutions, and practices that support the rule of law are strongly embedded, 'imbricated', and interwoven within them. Many are less strongly embedded in institutions, professions, legal and popular culture, and social structure.

Many Western legal orders are bearers of value, meaning, and tradition laid down and transmitted over centuries, and not only among lawyers. Prominent among the values deeply entrenched in these legal orders are rule of law values, and these values have exhibited considerable resilience and capacity to resist attempts to erode them. Perhaps that is why first-world

[56] Kamenka and Tay (n 54), 127.
[57] E.P. Thompson, *Whigs and Hunters. The Origin of the Black Act* (1977).
[58] Ibid 266.
[59] Ibid 260–1.
[60] Ibid 261.

legal and philosophical writing evinces so little concern with contexts. For many of the most difficult problems that might be found there have been taken care of, if not by them. They may well, of course, want to improve what they have, but since the underlying threats to legal effectiveness are to a considerable extent neutralized by law, they are often right to concentrate on legal institutions. That is not because they live in a different world, however, but because some universal problems have been dealt with in their part of it, and the character of the law counts there in ways it may not elsewhere.

In these circumstances of relative luxury, moreover, the options open to partisans of the rule of law are also more open than is sometimes acknowledged. Conservatives in rule of law rich countries, suspicious of any falling-off from some idealized version of it, often overreact to, say, injection of any substantive concerns into adjudication or discretionary authority in administration, indeed to any number of welfare state incursions on an idealized rule of Fuller-full-formal laws. These are interpreted as dangers to the existence of the rule of law as we know it, whereas they might be dangers only in circumstances where legality is already weak, and has no other resources with which to defend itself. Such reactions show little reflection on what the rule of law really depends upon, what it would be like to really threaten what they have of it, and what it would really mean to lack it. Radicals in the same societies, on the other hand, who treat some indeterminacy in appellate decision-making as testimony to fraudulence or at least to absence of the rule of law, exhibit a similar frivolousness about what it might really be to have to live without a good measure of it.[61]

Perspective is all; here as elsewhere. As Selznick again has argued:

> the very stability of the rule of law, where that has been achieved, makes possible a still broader vision and a higher aspiration. Without disparaging (to say nothing of trashing) our legal heritage, we may well ask whether it fully meets the community's needs.... So long as the system is basically secure, it is reasonable to accept some institutional risks in the interests of social justice.[62]

That suggests that not every potential source of threat to the rule of law will be equally salient in different legal orders: some will be much threatened, others less so, by the same things. It also suggests that different threats might require different defences. Not to mention that we might want to do more than ward off threats. Of course, the rule of law can be seriously threatened even where it appears to be in good shape. If we needed to recall it, the war on terror reminds us of that, as it does of the dangers of complacency in such circumstances. Yet there is still a lot to draw on, even there, which is unavailable in a tyranny, a failed state, illiberal democracy, and so on.

Rule of law promoters in transitional and post-conflict societies, by contrast, too often talk as though establishing the rule of law where it has not existed or is being shot to pieces, at times quite literally, is in principle the same sort of legalistic job requiring the same tools, if harder and more dangerous, as cultivating it where it has long grown and has deep roots, and where its presence is an often unreflected-upon ingredient of everyday life. A moment's comparative reflection on the extra-legal contexts of such ambitions make it hard to see why anyone would think that.

The conclusion is not that the rule of law can only thrive where it has thrived, and that where it has thrived it must continue to thrive. There is no compelling reason to support either

[61] I have particularly in mind Critical Legal Studies, a now dated movement but which has occasional echoes.

[62] Selznick (n 48), 464.

of these determinist prophecies.[63] On the other hand, the rule of law is so complex an achievement, dependent on so many factors in so many domains, that it is peculiarly miscast by lawyers' often solipsistic understandings and renditions. For as Amartya Sen has observed,

> Even when we consider development in a particular sphere, such as economic development or legal development, the instruments that are needed to enhance development in that circumscribed sphere may not be confined only to institutions and policies in that sphere.... If this sounds a little complex, I must point out that the complication relates, ultimately, to the interdependences of the world in which we live. I did not create that world, and any blame for it has to be addressed elsewhere.[64]

Bibliography

Thomas Carothers (ed), *Promoting the Rule of Law Abroad. In Search of Knowledge* (2006)
Albert Venn Dicey, *Introduction to the Study of the Law of the Constitution* (10th edn, 1959)
David Dyzenhaus (ed), *Recrafting the Rule of Law* (1999)
James Fleming (ed), *Getting to the Rule of Law* (2011)
Lon L. Fuller, *The Morality of Law* (1969)
Erik G. Jensen and Thomas C. Heller (eds), *Beyond Common Knowledge. Empirical Approaches to the Rule of Law* (2003)
Neil MacCormick, *Rhetoric and the Rule of Law* (2005)
José María Maravall and Adam Przeworski (eds), *Democracy and the Rule of Law* (2003)
Franz L. Neumann, *The Rule of Law* (1986)
Philippe Nonet and Philip Selznick, *Law and Society in Transition. Towards Responsive Law* (1978)
Gianluigi Palombella and Neil Walker (eds), *Relocating the Rule of Law* (2009)
Randall Peerenboom (ed), *Asian Discourses of the Rule of Law* (2004)
Judith N. Shklar, 'Political Theory and the Rule of Law' in Judith N. Shklar, *Political Thought and Political Thinkers* (1998)
Brian Z. Tamanaha, *On the Rule of Law. History, Politics, Theory* (2004)

[63] See Martin Krygier, 'Institutional Optimism, Social Pessimism, and the Rule of Law' in Krygier and Czarnota (n 48).

[64] Amartya Sen, 'What is the role of legal and judicial reform in the development process?', *World Bank Legal Conference* (2000), 10. Also see Brian Tamanaha, 'The Primacy of Society and the Failures of Law and Development: Decades of Refusal to Learn' (2011) 44 *Cornell International Law Journal* 209.

CHAPTER 11

DEMOCRACY

GÜNTER FRANKENBERG

Frankfurt

I. Histories

The conceptual histories of democracy span more than 2,500 years and refer to a variety of normative orders, institutional arrangements of political decision-making, social and economic structures, and basic values of a community. In bypassing pre-classical proto-democracies, as for instance in India and in Sumerian city-states, mainstream historiography generally traces the prehistory of popular (or self-) rule—very much like the development of other fundamental principles of modern limited, just, or lawful government—back to its initial circumstances in Greek city-states.[1] The concept of *dēmokratía*, a composite of *demos* (people) and *kratos* (power) or *kratein* (rule), denoted the rule of the people, respectively by the many, was developed in political philosophy (Plato, Aristotle) and practiced in the Greek, notably the Athenian, *pólis* characterized by membership (including only male citizens of age), autonomy, and equality before the law. If one keeps aloof from idyllic notions of the *pólis*[2]—and, incidentally, also from Cicero's idealizations of the Roman Republic—then classical philosophy and the *pólis* come into view as addressing the 'democratic question'[3] still relevant today despite

[1] David Held, *Models of Democracy* (3rd edn, 2006).

[2] Cornelius Castoriadis, 'The Greek *Polis* and the Creation of Democracy' in David Ames Curtis (ed), *Philosophy, Politics, Autonomy: Essays in Political Philosophy* (1991).

[3] Ulrich Rödel et al, *Die demokratische Frage* [*The Democratic Question*] (1989).

the differences of context and culture: How can societies govern themselves by establishing procedures and institutions for authoritative, participatory, egalitarian, and effective decision-making?

A different narrative reconstructs the English path to democracy by shifting the accent from membership and autonomy to sovereignty, representation, liberty, and, ultimately, equality as fundamental democratic values embodied in a peculiar institutional setting and constitutional framework.[4] Liberty is seen to be rooted in the restrictions on the power of the monarch originally laid down in the Magna Carta (1215) explicitly protecting certain rights of the king's subjects, notably freemen, and later displayed in a series of constitutional documents—the Petition of Right (1628), the Habeas Corpus Act (1679), and the Bill of Rights (1689)—as preconditions of a limited and lawful government that, in retrospect, was qualified as constitutional democracy.[5] The constitutional conflicts and civil wars of the seventeenth century focused on the concept and location of sovereign power and in the end led to a unique compromise that captures the gist of English constitutionalism and democracy: the formula of 'King-in-Parliament' symbolizes the reduction of both popular and monarchic/absolutist claims to power and established parliamentary sovereignty.[6] As a matter of consequence, the franchise and the struggles over its structure and scope took centre stage in English political history as well as constitutional and democratic theory and practice. The development towards representative democracy is mirrored by the gradual increase of the franchise and steps towards its uniformity, in particular when the so-called 'rotten boroughs', with a handful of voters electing a member of parliament, were eliminated by the Reform Acts of 1832 and 1867. With the gradual extension of the franchise Parliament became the dominant political actor, whereas the monarch was reduced to a largely ceremonial figurehead. Democracy developed as a constitutionalized regime of competition for power that, according to the optimistic vision, guaranteed the periodical exchange of the powers that be and representatives[7] and, according to the pessimistic perception, was reduced to competitive elitism[8] privileging expert government over popular sovereignty.[9]

It remains one of the mysteries of democracy that the term finally overcame the negative connotations it had been accompanied by for more than two thousand years and experienced a remarkable comeback when it gradually replaced the republic, a more moderate and prudent ideal and self-description,[10] under what are generally referred to as the conditions of modernity. Where the English concept of self-rule invoked tradition and reform and relied on conventions, the 'Great Democratic Revolutions' in the New England states and France at the end of the eighteenth century introduced democracy as a revolutionary neologism to capture the new way of imagining political reality and as a symbolic *dispositif* that crystallized around the agency of the individual as 'citizen' and/or the political existence of a social collective as 'people', 'nation', or 'state' as well as the values, objectives, structures, and ideologies of self-rule as the prototypical limited, legitimate, and effective government based on foundational

[4] On equality, see Chapter 47.

[5] A.V. Dicey, *An Introduction to the Study of the Law of the Constitution* ([1885] 1982); Shmuel Noah Eisenstadt, *Paradoxes of Democracy: Fragility, Continuity, and Change* (1999), chs 1 and 2.

[6] On parliamentarism, see further Chapter 30. On sovereignty, see Chapter 17.

[7] John Stuart Mill, 'Considerations on Representative Government' in H.B. Acton (ed), *Utilitarianism, Liberty, and Representative Government* (1951).

[8] See Max Weber, 'Politics as a Vocation' in Hans Heinrich Gerth and C. Wright Mills (eds), *From Max Weber* (1972) and Robert Michels, *Political Parties* (1962).

[9] Joseph Schumpeter, *Capitalism, Socialism and Democracy* (1942); Held (n 1), ch 5.

[10] Giovanni Sartori, *The Theory of Democracy Revisited* (1987), vol II, 287; Held (n 1), 29.

constitutional documents.[11] As distinct from the Greek *demos* gathered in the popular assembly, the people conveys a plurality, whereas its European equivalents—*peuple, populo, Volk*—denote a (fictitious) organic whole lending itself to holistic interpretations and translations and directing the focus on the problem of inclusion. Hence, since the revolutionary era, democracy has oscillated between individualist, collectivist, and organicist notions. Similarly, throughout history, democratic movements have agonized over what the power of the people should mean and how it could be exercised democratically. Today, models prevail that transform the fictive will of the people by elective procedures into regimes of (limited) majority rule on the basis of the representational transmission of power,[12] some representative regimes are complemented by forms of direct popular participation. And, consequently, the various narratives of democracy mirror until today the theoretical and practical-institutional attempts to limit majority rule in order to lend some credibility to the idea and ideology that minorities may become majority and vice versa—an interplay that qualifies democracy as legitimate popular self-rule.

II. Varieties of Constitutional Democracy

Democracy, an 'essentially contested concept',[13] has established itself—in conjunction with 'constitution', 'human rights', 'popular sovereignty', and 'republic'—as 'one of the major structures of ideological ambivalence'[14] within the pool of cultural representations of modernity. Ambivalence (of ideology/theory) and indeterminacy (of the semantics) have not prevented democracy from proliferating worldwide: it has come to be globally understood as designating the basic institutions and procedures of a polity shaping the form and mode of government. Due to its philosophical pedigree and the experience with non- and anti-democratic regimes—dictatorship and monarchy—democracy established its reputation as being better suited than any rival form of political will-formation and decision-making to reconcile the discordant elements of self-interest and common weal, wealth and poverty, class and community, liberty and equality.[15] Democracy's political career, however, produced a variety of institutional arrangements together with the accompanying ideologies. The following overview briefly discusses only the most influential specimens[16] from the perspective of constitutional law.

1. Direct Democracy

Direct democracy anchored in the ancient past, kept alive by republicanism in theory and social movements demanding participation in practice, appears as the counterpart of the *polis* and the closest approximation to genuine democracy. As far as it refers to the whole *demos*[17] present in the assembly, direct (or literal) democracy is characterized by a fairly homogenous social basis (*demos*) and a focus on the exercise of power through collective decision-making[18] within the social fabric of face-to-face relationships in small polities.[19] From a constitutional

[11] Robert R. Palmer, *Age of the Democratic Revolutions* (1959).
[12] Sartori (n 10), vol I, 28–35.
[13] W.B. Gallie, 'Essentially Contested Concepts' (1956) 56 *Proceedings of the Aristotelian Society* 167.
[14] Homi K. Bhabha, *Nation and Narration* (1990), 1.
[15] Robert Alan Dahl, *On Democracy* (2000).
[16] Held (n 1).
[17] Disregarding those not considered to be members.
[18] Sartori (n 10), vol II, 280–7.
[19] Held (n 1), 17.

point of view, it is remarkable that, due to the notion of the *polis* as a unitary entity not separated from civil society, no constitutional rights protected the citizens against interferences from the part of government. The only quasi-constitutional guarantee for citizens was originally based on their status as members of the (sovereign) assembly.

During the *longue durée* when the Greek *polis* and democracy fell into oblivion, their idea and ideology somehow survived and resurged under the guise of New England town-meetings, popular assemblies in Swiss cantons, revolutionary councils,[20] and more recent projects of direct democracy propagated by new social movements. Such modified replica of the *polis* or rather naive novelties were and are taken to prove the Rousseauvian point, in defense of 'assembly politics',[21] and widespread assessment that the possibility of direct democracy requiring super-activism on the part of its members is limited to the small-scale republics, communes, or city-states.

Under the conditions of the 'mature modernity', the classical project of autonomy that had been modified and propagated by republicanism[22] was rejuvenated for the purpose of regenerating democracy by opening up ossified political power structures and preventing civil desertion from the public sphere. Proposals for a 'strong'[23] or responsive democracy shifted the accent from the exercise of power to enhancing popular participation in politics: they advocated the introduction of referenda, popular legislative initiatives, and extended rights of political communication, thus reviving the ideal of assembly democracy. While some of these proposals seek to redress the deficits and pathologies of parliamentary representation, others such as the project of 'inclusive democracy' extend democracy beyond the limits of politics by including economic, social, and ecological decision-making.[24]

Feminist authors and movements focused their critique of established democratic regimes on the social conditions of domination and politics in patriarchal democracies,[25] the public–private distinction, and the Aristotelian notion of equality.[26] Therefore, their proposals to unsettle the male-dominated—direct democratic and parliamentary—tradition have a more transformative thrust.

2. Representative Democracy

Representative democracy is generally identified with liberal democracy,[27] in spite of the fact that the term covers a plurality of different institutional designs—parliamentary and presidential systems, constitutional monarchies, authoritarian-populist regimes, centralized and federal states, one- or two-chamber parliaments, etc—and a diversity of electoral systems. It is

[20] See Karl Marx, 'The Civil War in France' in Karl Marx and Frederick Engels, *Collected Works*, vol 22 (1986), 664.

[21] Jean-Jacques Rousseau, *The Social Contract* ([1762] 1968), 60–1.

[22] Philip Pettit, *Republicanism: A Theory of Freedom and Government* (1997).

[23] Benjamin R. Barber, *Strong Democracy: Participatory Politics for A New Age* (1984).

[24] Takis Fotopoulos, *The Multidimensional Crisis and Inclusive Democracy* (2005).

[25] Susan Moller Okin, *Women in Western Political Thought* (1980); Wendy Brown, *States of Injury: Power and Freedom in Late Modernity* (1995). For three classical statements see William Thompson, *Appeal of One-Half the Human Race, Women, against the Pretension of the Other Half, Men, to retain them in Political and thence Civil and Domestic Slavery* ([1825] 1983), Mary Wollstonecraft, *Vindication of the Rights of Women* ([1792] 1982), and John Stuart Mill, *The Subjection of Women* ([1869] 1980). See also Sheila Rowbotham, *Women, Resistance, and Revolution* (1972).

[26] Catherine Mackinnon, 'Feminism, Marxism, Method, and the State: Toward a Feminist Jurisprudence' (1983) 8 *Signs* 635. See also Chapter 19.

[27] Sartori (n 10), vol II, 383–98.

true, though, that most of them re-invent the community of fate underlying theories of direct democracy as a community of wills and interests and that, according to Marx's dictum, citizens represent themselves and need no longer to be represented. The representative model and the variations it allows owe their reputation as the only practical and freedom-preserving[28] transposition of self-rule into efficient political decision-making procedures in mass societies to both the assumed and real deficits of direct democracy and the blatant pathologies of and harms caused by autocratic regimes. Whether 'strictly a capitalist phenomenon'[29] or at least entertaining a problematic relationship with capitalism,[30] liberal democracy, despite critiques of political liberal theory[31] and the uneasiness concerning the justification of majority rule,[32] succeeded in transgressing the borders of the Western-capitalist hemisphere from where its ideology, rhetoric, and institutions proliferated globally and recently resurged, somewhat surprisingly, in Arabian countries presumed to be and remain strongholds of autocratic regimes.

Parliamentary democracy 'operating under a good constitution'[33] transfers everyday political decision-making from the sovereign self to the elected representatives and governors and appointed administrators who operate within a scheme of division of labor demarcating, more or less clearly, the functions of legislature, executive, and judiciary. Thus the 'self' of the project of self-rule is constitutionally fragmented and its power divided into competencies, which are then dispersed, pursuant to the logic of either separation (focusing on demarcation of functions to prevent abuse of power) or checks and balances (privileging cooperation and control of power), among different institutions and office holders. Within the framework of constitutional-liberal democracy self-rule is thus translated into law-rule according to the formula of a 'government of laws and not of men',[34] that is, the conjunction of the democratic sovereign with the rule of law (*Rechtsstaat, état de droit*).[35] Regimes of political representation transform the popular sovereign into (1) a *citizenry* invited, permitted, or only gently hampered to exercise its political freedoms by participating in public debates—euphemistically: the *plébiscite de tous les jours*[36]—and (2) an *electorate* that, under the terms of liberal ideology, by casting their vote produce a rough matrix for the politics thereafter to be freely pursued by the representatives in accordance with the dictates of their conscience protected by the ideology of the free mandate[37] or rather, realistically speaking, of their party's guidelines.

[28] See Walter Lippmann, *The Good Society* (1943); Bertrand Russell, *Authority and the Individual* (1949).

[29] C.B. Macpherson, *Democratic Theory: Essays in Retrieval* (1973).

[30] Adam Przeworski, *Democracy and the Market: Political and Economic Reforms in Eastern Europe and Latin America* (1992).

[31] eg Carol Pateman, *The Problem of Political Obligation: A Critique of Liberal Theory* (1985); Roberto Mangabeira Unger, *Knowledge and Politics* (1975); Macpherson (n 29).

[32] For an overview of the narratives of justification of majority rule, from Hobbes's *Leviathan* until today, accentuating fairness, respect, approximation of truth, preference intensity, legitimate authority, the prevention of anarchy and despotism etc, see only Jeremy Waldron, *The Dignity of Legislation* (1999) and Mathias Risse, 'Arguing for Majority Rule' (2004) 12 *Journal of Philosophy* 41.

[33] Cass Sunstein, *Designing Democracy: What Constitutions Do* (2001), 239.

[34] An Aristotelian idea reformulated by John Adams for the Constitution of Massachusetts, Part I, Art XXX (1780).

[35] On rule of law, see Chapter 10.

[36] Ernest Renan, *Qu'est-ce qu'une nation?* (1882).

[37] In his 'Speech to the Electors of Bristol' (1774) Edmund Burke humbly submitted the classical statement of this ideology: 'Parliament is not a *Congress* of Ambassadors from different and hostile interests,...but a deliberative Assembly of *one* Nation, with *one* Interest, that of the whole...'. Some constitutional documents explicitly provide for a free mandate (German Basic Law, Art 38; Austrian Federal Constitutional Law of 1929, Art 56) or prohibit 'instructions' to deputies (Swiss Constitution of 1999).

Liberal or representative democracy received much praise[38] for processing diverse political agendas, professionalizing politics, and concentrating expertise in parliamentary commissions and executive and administrative agencies to be controlled by parliaments and courts. The comments changed once it became apparent that parliaments and deputies were hardly able adequately to grasp and handle, in particular, the 'explosion of fact'[39] in industrial societies and the complex problems of steering the course of social-economic development and therefore had to rely on non transparent networks of experts operating beyond the horizon of democratic control. Nevertheless, parliamentarianism has proven superior to autocratic and centralized systems of government because of its capacity to correct political mistakes and damages[40] and of the systemic opportunities for periodic change and recall of incompetent office holders as well as its record of promoting prosperity, albeit selective, and peace.[41] These advantages become somewhat ambivalent once weighed against the corresponding drawbacks of representation, in particular the formation of oligarchies,[42] lobbyism, and corruption. A similar ambivalence taints both Tocqueville's observation that democracy inspires the people with the feelings and habits required for good government[43] and Lefort's interpretation of parliamentary democracy as shifting social controversy to the arenas of representation, thus deferring and civilizing conflicts and the passions they generate.[44] These diagnoses and interpretations are called into question by less favorable, sociologically informed assessments that attribute to the practice of indirect democracy political disaffection, alienation, and apathy on the part of the citizens as well as opportunism, careerism, and populist strategizing on the part of the political class, and come to the conclusion that many consolidated democracies are reduced to 'electoral' democracies.

3. Deliberative Democracy

Deliberative democracy, unlike direct or indirect democracy, does not designate a specific institutional arrangement but picks up, on the level of normative theory, liberal democracy's claim to legitimacy based on reasons—as distinct from a situationally contingent acceptance—and connects its key focus, not on a predetermined will but on the process of its formation, with participatory democracy's claim to popular participation.[45] Deliberation is introduced as a device for people to develop, discover, and articulate their proper interests, needs, and preferences through a process of discussion,[46] thus trying to solve the problem of 'enduring disagreement' and group polarization.[47] Privileging discourse transgresses the limits of 'adversary

[38] Sartori (n 10), vol II.

[39] Clifford Geertz, *Local Knowledge. Further Essays in Interpretive Anthropology* (3rd edn, 2000), 171.

[40] See already Alex de Tocqueville's praise for the advantages of democracy in *Democracy in America* ([1835/1840] 1968) and its differentiated discussion by Claus Offe, 'Political Disaffection as an Outcome of Institutional Practice' in Mariano Torcal and José R. Montero (eds), *Political Disaffection in Contemporary Democracies: Social Capital, Institutions, and Politics* (2006).

[41] Morton Halperin, Joe Siegele, and Michael Weinstein, *The Democracy Advantage: How Democracy Promotes Prosperity and Peace* (2004).

[42] By the permanent transfer of government to 'a small number of citizens elected by the rest': James Madison, *The Federalist Papers* ([1787/88] 1989), no 10.

[43] De Tocqueville (n 40).

[44] Claude Lefort, *L'invention démocratique* (1981).

[45] Bernard Manin, 'On Legitimacy and Deliberation' (1987) 15 *Political Theory* 338.

[46] Joshua Cohen, 'Deliberative Democracy and Democratic Legitimacy' in Alan Hamlin and Philip Pettit (eds), *The Good Polity* (1989); Jürgen Habermas, *Between Facts and Norms: Contributions to a Discourse Theory of Law and Democracy* (1998); Held (n 1), 231.

[47] Sunstein (n 33), 8.

democracy'[48] and may incidentally thwart the secular trend towards electoral democracy insofar as political decision-making relies on discursive procedures and popular consultation rather than voting.[49] Theories of deliberative democracy contain a republican element because they intend to reactivate the *citizens*, revitalize the public sphere, and structure their political institutions so that deliberation (or discourse) may become the decisive factor. They further contain an implicit or explicit constitutional project insofar as they call for a commitment to the pluralism of values and aims within a polity, require each member to recognize and respect the other members' deliberative capacity, and not only advance a theory of democratic legitimacy but also a theory of rights based on achieving the ideal of free and equal deliberation. Freedom implies that deliberation is (or should) not be bound by whatever external authority but only by the preconditions and results of the discursive procedures. Formal equality implies that anyone may put forth a proposal or criticize or support measures taken after deliberation and is complemented by the principle of substantive equality guaranteeing that no one be restrained by the distribution of power and resources or by norms counteracting the framework of free deliberation among equals. Freedom and equality are jointly to warrant that deliberation may reach its aim of a rationally motivated consensus.

Protagonists of discursive procedures[50] emphasize their rationality and openness to scientific knowledge, the approximation of impartiality, and the likelihood of moral correctness of decisions reached by deliberation as well as the greater emphasis placed upon settings and procedures of preference formation.[51] Critics charge the theory of discursive democracy with not addressing the problem of voting and the ideological bias in favor of liberal democracy. They argue that the deliberative project is based on unattainable conditions following highly abstract rules and therefore may work in theory whereas, due to its abstractness and moral absolutism, the project is bound to fail in practice because, very much like the theories of representative democracy, its normative maximalism negates the structures of inequality and domination in industrial societies and the constraints they place on actors willing to participate in public discourse.[52] Moreover, deliberation is likely to end not in consensus but disagreement, hence, for deciding the problem one has to turn back to majority rule again.

III. Dangers and Precautions

Democracy's triumph and global proliferation has left non-democratic regimes without strong arguments in support of their legitimacy and attractiveness.[53] Moreover, dynastic, fascist, state socialist, and military versions of political authoritarianism are wanting in attractive narratives of justification clearly on the retreat.[54] Theocratic regimes in the Islamic world have yet to prove their viability and efficiency over time; and dramatic uprisings of civil society challenge political authoritarianism in Tunisia, Egypt, and other Arabian countries. In the absence of convincing alternatives, democracy and majority rule[55] have consolidated their

[48] Jane J. Mansbridge, *Beyond Adversary Democracy* (1983).

[49] James S. Fishkin, *When the People Speak: Deliberative Democracy and Public Consultation* (2009).

[50] Risse (n 32); Held (n 1), ch 9.

[51] Claus Offe and Ulrich K. Preuß, 'Democratic Institutions and Moral Resources' in David Held (ed), *Political Theory Today* (1991).

[52] Amy Gutmann and Dennis Thompson, *Democracy and Disagreement* (1996); Iris Marion Young, *Inclusion and Democracy* (2000), 52–80.

[53] Amartya K. Sen, 'Democracy as a Universal Value' (1999) 10 *Journal of Democracy* 3.

[54] Offe (n 40), 46.

[55] Elaine Spitz, *Majority Rule* (1984); Dahl (n 15).

position as the primary form of government in the realm of politics, confirmed by constitutional documents, and in theoretical debates. Nevertheless, both consolidated and transitional democracies[56] are plagued by a number of endogenously and exogenously induced problems some of which qualify as dangers[57] that may lead to crises threatening their stability, performance, and output (social peace, prosperity) or even their legitimacy (acceptance, consensus).

1. Tyrannical Majorities

Tyrannical majorities have always been the quintessential fear accompanying, like a dark shadow, the development of democracy since ancient times until the rise of the liberal-democratic paradigm to ideological hegemony.[58] Participants in the long-standing debate concerning majoritarianism basically agree that permanent or structural majorities block the rules and procedures of competition and therefore discredit and delegitimize democracy. However, they agonize over (1) where to locate such majorities—on the political or societal level; (2) whether to qualify them numerically or politically by their capacity to outvote or dominate even numerical, yet non- or underrepresented majorities of society; and (3) how to prevent tyrannical majorities or control and remedy their effects. As regards the first question, it seems plausible within the context of democratic participation and decision-making to turn to the 'magistrates' and look for manifestations of majoritarian despotism within the regime of representative government.[59] This also answers, at least predetermines, the second question because both the rule of the many over the few and the rule of the few over the many come into view as potentially abusive forms of democratic power. Ever since Madison's authoritative statement that removing the causes of tyranny would imply abolishing liberty,[60] the discussion in democratic and constitutional theory has been preoccupied with controlling possibly hazardous effects of majority rule. While the discourse on ethical or behavioral antidotes, such as virtues, civil religion, and public spirit conducive to a democratic culture of 'accommodation' and self-restraint, flourished in the nineteenth century,[61] democratic theory and practice have since been more (and more importantly) concerned with developing a constitutional-legal design[62] that would guarantee the interplay between majority and minorities and thwart majoritarian despotism.

Some proposals, like James Madison's option for a federal structure of the Union or John Stuart Mill's argument privileging liberty over equality, failed squarely to address the problem of how to prevent the emergence of and then effectively control tyrannical elites. In general, however, the discourse on precautions against the majoritarian abuse of power[63] has relied on the following procedural, institutional, and substantive checks on majority rule and has rooted them in the constitutional framework.

[56] See Gavin Cawthra and Robin Luckham, *Governing Insecurity: Democratic Control of Military and Security Establishments in Transitional Democracies* (2003). On constitutionalism and transitional justice, see Chapter 61.

[57] Philippe C. Schmitter, 'Dangers and Dilemmas of Democracy' (1994) 5 *Journal of Democracy* 57.

[58] Held (n 1), ch 3.

[59] For a dualist conception see, however, John Stuart Mill, *On Liberty* (1859) (advocating protection also against 'the tyranny of the prevailing opinion and feeling') and de Tocqueville (n 40), vol I, ch XV.

[60] Madison (n 42), no 10.

[61] eg Alexander Hamilton, *The Federalist Papers* ([1787/88] 1989), no 85. For an influential rational-choice perspective see Jon Elster, *Strong Feelings: Emotion, Addiction, and Human Behavior* (1999).

[62] Sunstein (n 33).

[63] Pettit (n 22).

(1) The *dispersion of power* ranks high on the list of protective measures. Enhanced by social and party pluralism, dispersion of power may be institutionally ascertained by majority-controlling institutional arrangements, such as the decentralization of (federal) government and the division of functions and competencies by either allocating them, on the model of Montesquieu, to separated powers or by establishing a complex regime of US-style mutual checks and balances with its dysfunctional effects.

(2) The institutional arrangement of the political decision-making process were further connected with *rule of law constraints*—in particular the legal form of laws, constitutional procedures for lawmaking, independent courts, and the guarantee and use of Lockean rights 'to constrain or limit the [rulers] to act within a known and recognized constitutional structure of lawfulness'.[64]

(3) As another *counter-majoritarian condition*, those laws that are crucial for the majority–minority interplay were demanded to be removed from all-too-easy change and revision and instead require a qualified majority or even a constitutional amendment, a condition to be secured by judicial or constitutional review. Some authors have even advocated that majority rule be limited to reversible decisions; others favored constitutions with entrenched norms deemed to define the normative identity of the democratic polity and to enclose its most fundamental values and democratic procedures.[65]

(4) On a more practical note, there seems to be widespread agreement that constitutional democracy has to ensure the *contestability* of political decisions, measures, and proposals by opening up public arenas for debate, providing access to them, and requiring consideration of oppositional views. As contestability refers to the inclusiveness of majoritarian democracy, accountability is meant to ascertain its responsiveness.

(5) Since the democratic legitimacy of majority rule rests on the inherent possibility of minorities to become majority, representative-parliamentary regimes, most importantly, have to provide for the change of government. Hence, both periodical and fair (= free, equal, and general) *elections* are considered to be necessary conditions for the adequate representation of minorities and the (at least, potential) interplay of majorities and minorities.[66] Consequently, numerous measures to restrain or correct majoritarian despotism rely on extending the franchise by removing traditional qualifications of the right to vote—status, taxable income, race, gender, literacy, age, etc,[67] enhancing fair representation (proportional election laws, cumulative voting, re-designing electoral districts[68]), abolishing (feudal) structures of domination (secret voting, electoral duty, curbing parties' campaign funds), punishing electoral fraud and corruption, and promoting a high voter turnout.

[64] James Tully, 'Placing the Two Treatises' in Nicholas Philipson and Quentin Skinner (eds), *Political Discourse in Early Modern Britain* (1993), 261.

[65] The German Basic Law (1949) and the Namibian Constitution (1990) remove the guarantee of human dignity and the fundamental organizational principles (Basic Law, Art 79(3)) respectively the fundamental rights and freedoms (Namibian Constitution, Art 131) from repeal or amendment.

[66] On elections, see Chapter 25.

[67] Five amendments to the US Constitution (Arts XV, XIX, XXIV, and XXVI) mirror the persistent struggles concerning the extension of the franchise and the importance of change (Art XXII).

[68] The Seventeenth Amendment, a series of reapportionment laws and Supreme Court decisions point towards the repeated attempts to correct unfair representation. See Michel L. Balinsky and H. Peyton Young, *Fair Representation* (1982).

2. Political Extremism

As distinct from tyrannical majorities, politically extremist associations or parties are generally distinguished from the various brands of political radicalism by their aim to overthrow democracy from within or from without, if need be with violent means, by utilizing democratic procedures, institutions, and rules to gain popular support.[69] Rather than participating, however vigorously, in public debate and trying their luck in the struggle for power, which also implies accepting defeat, political extremists transgress the limits of competition for power and, once in power, discard the democratic method of persuasion (as 'bourgeois', 'capitalist', 'imperialist', 'corrupt', or whatever). They pursue a political agenda that, as a rule, is connected with claims to absolute truth or necessity to which they assert to have privileged access. Unlike other associations of civil society, however radical, they reject the theory of conflict underlying and justifying democracy based on horizontal relationships among citizens, which therefore requires their mutual recognition as equals and abstention from enemy rhetoric and violence.[70] In sharp contrast to the logic of democratic competition, political extremists operate on the basis of a Schmittian enemy/friend distinction and the corresponding normative grammar that allows for violent strategies, such as persecution and, if need be, killing of enemies, witch hunts, or ethnic purges. The spectrum of extremism ranges from Jacobin and anarchist groups in the nineteenth century to Leninist–Stalinist cadres and parties, fascist movements in the twentieth century, and more recently fundamentalist[71] organizations pursuing a political agenda in defense of religious or political orthodoxy or ethnic 'purity' against the modern heresies of secularism, liberalism, capitalism, or multiculturalism. Whereas they may propagate different political goals, they are united by the pursuit of some kind of normative absolutism justifying, in general, violation of the physical integrity of others.

Political extremism of whatever brand invokes the question how to deal with 'the enemies of freedom' (Abbé Sieyès). The discourse on precautions to be taken for the protection of democracy has focused on two basic options: tolerance or repression of extremism, each allowing for a plurality of institutional-legal concretizations. *Tolerance* characterizes the libertarian approach that mandates the abstention from establishing a protectionist regime and relies instead on strengthening democratic institutions and civil society.[72] The 'protection by promotion' strategy focuses on civic education, encouraging political participation, strengthening local government, enhancing constituency-building, and promoting pluralism.[73] Accordingly, extremist acts are treated like any other behavior and sanctioned—as duress, bodily injury, etc—according to the provisions of 'normal' criminal law, which implies that 'tolerant democracy', generally speaking, accepts anti-democratic views and methods as long as they stay within the bounds of non-violence. This strategy, however, becomes entangled in the almost hopeless venture to define 'violence'.

[69] On political parties and the constitution, see Chapter 41.

[70] Günter Frankenberg, 'Tocqueville's Question: The Role of a Constitution in the Process of Integration' (2000) 13 *Ratio Juris* 1; Rödel (n 3).

[71] For a definition of fundamentalism see Brenda E. Brasher, *Encyclopedia of Fundamentalism* (2001).

[72] Philippe C. Schmitter and Imco Brouwer, 'Conceptualizing, Researching, and Evaluating Democracy Promotion and Protection', EUI Working Paper SPS No 99/9 (Badia Fiesolana Florence).

[73] The Constitution of the Republic of South Africa (1996) provides for the funding of parties 'to enhance multi-party democracy' (s 9). In Germany, party funding is regulated by the Law Concerning the Political Parties that has been intermittently challenged on constitutional grounds. Similarly, the Constitution of Iraq (2005) accentuates the strengthening of civil society (Art 45).

Most—and in particular non-consolidated—democracies, however, shift the accent from promotion to *protection* and tend to draw the line more restrictively: one of the constitutional options could be to entrench the republican-democratic form of government.[74] Or else protection could be delegated to criminal law and there complementing the regular criminal offences and sanctions with a list of 'political crimes' penalizing political behavior and views, such as incitement to violence, defamation of the form of government or high-ranking office holders, etc[75] for the sake of the stability of the (democratic, republican, national, secular, or religious) political order. A different logic—namely the protection of minorities—dictates the sanctioning of hate speech and incitement to racism as criminal offences[76]—a logic that has to cope with drawing the line between 'actions' and 'words'.

3. States of Emergency

As a reaction to 'the totalitarian adventure'[77] and/or the defeat of democracy by authoritarian regimes,[78] numerous countries, from Germany to South Korea, from Spain to Namibia, tried to anticipate political crises and prepared against political dangers by integrating provisions regulating states of emergency, such as war, state of siege, catastrophes, political uprisings, etc.[79] The concepts range from the instruments and institutions of a *militant democracy*[80] to regimes of constitutional dictatorship.[81] While the latter generally provide for the temporary and partial suspension of the constitution, regimes of militancy tend to mask their exceptionalism behind the attire of normalcy: they provide for organizations and parties deemed dangerous to be outlawed, their organization dissolved, and their property confiscated; some also contain the forfeiture of political rights of individuals or severe restrictions on the freedoms of political communication. Short of destroying the constitutional fabric of a democratic polity, these precautionary provisions of risk aversion still insert explicit or implicit emergency clauses[82] in the constitutional text and normalize, in the name of security, situations and the vocabulary of political emergency.[83]

Constitutional self-protection, according to the logic of emergency or militancy, raises a number of tricky questions, notably (1) who or which institution is entitled to demarcate the

[74] The Constitution of the Republic of Italy (1948) divests even qualified majorities of the power to change the republican form of the state by constitutional amendment (Art 139). Art 79(3), the 'eternity clause' of the German Basic Law (1949), removes from regular constitutional revision the guarantee of human dignity and the fundamental organizational principles of government (democracy, republic, federalism, welfare state, and rule of law).

[75] eg Arthur J. Jacobson and Bernhard Schlink (eds), *Weimar: A Jurisprudence of Crisis* (2000).

[76] See Samuel Walker, *Hate Speech: The History of an American Controversy* (1994); Mari Matsuda et al, *Words that Wound: Critical Race Theory, Assaultive Speech, and the First Amendment* (1994).

[77] Lefort (n 44).

[78] For an empirical analysis of the transitions from authoritarian rule to democracy see Guillermo O'Donnell, Philippe C. Schmitter, and Laurence Whitehead (eds), *Transitions from Authoritarian Rule: Comparative Perspectives* (1991).

[79] On states of emergency, see further Chapter 21.

[80] Karl Loewenstein, 'Militant Democracy and Fundamental Rights' (1937) 31 *American Political Science Review* 417ff and 638ff; András Sajó (ed), *Militant Democracy* (2004). See also Chapter 60.

[81] Clinton Lawrence Rossiter, *Constitutional Dictatorship* (1948).

[82] 'Explicit' usually presupposes that the state of emergency has to be declared and its duration announced, whereas 'implicit' refers to the strategy of masking emergency measures as part of the set of regular provisions. For explicitness see Arts 352–60 of the Constitution of India (1949) or the more concise regulation in the Namibian Constitution, Art 26.

[83] Günter Frankenberg, *Normalizing the State of Exception—A Critique of Political Technology* (2010), ch I.

limits of the permissible, (2) how far can one go in protecting democracy without compromising democracy's fundamental legitimacy as self-rule and experimentalism, (3) what could be adequate rules for excluding organizations and individuals from the political process, and (4) what effect do emergency provisions have on the 'normal' constitution.[84] *Suspending* democratic experimentalism undoubtedly calls into question the normative claims and constitutional provisions of self-rule, pluralism, and free interplay among majorities and minorities. This strategy runs the risk of falling prey to the Schmittian romantic logic of the political as a combination of political existentialism plus preference for the state of emergency.[85]

Militancy may look less dictatorial but requires a democratic justification that, to be at least minimally plausible, has demonstrated how to rein in the excess tendency of this strategy to transform democratic experimentalism into a disciplinary regime privileging the political *juste milieu* and quietism. Basically three paradigms of justification appear to be available.

(1) The original (Cold War) institutionalization of and reasoning for militant democracy as a precautionary strategy against *all brands of political extremism* fail to pass the minimal plausibility-and-restraint threshold because the generalized idea of stabilizing order introduces a concept of abstract protection that does not even require a concrete danger. More importantly, this justification construes *anti-extremism* as a 'dangerous supplement'[86]—not assisting but always already permeating and undermining the 'normal' constitution.

(2) '*Negative republicanism*',[87] a narrower concept of militant democracy, changes the thrust from general anti-extremism to confronting, directly or indirectly, organized attempts to re-install a previous authoritarian or totalitarian regime, such as National-Socialism in Germany,[88] Fascism in Italy,[89] Francoism in Spain, apartheid in South Africa, or the Ba'ath party in Iraq.[90] Thus, militancy informs a *counter-constitution*

[84] For a discussion of these questions see the contributions of David Dyzenhaus, Otto Pfersmann, and Gregory Tardi in Sajó (n 80) and Gregory H. Fox and Georg Nolte, 'Intolerant Democracies' (1995) 36 *Harvard International Law Journal* 1.

[85] Frankenberg (n 83), ch IV.

[86] A concept borrowed from Jacques Derrida, *Of Grammatology* (1976).

[87] Peter Niesen, 'Anti-Extremism, Negative Republicanism, Civic Society: Three Paradigms for Banning Political Parties' (2002) 3 *German Law Journal* 7; Günter Frankenberg, 'The Learning Sovereign' in Sajó (n 80), 127; for the related concept of negative universalism see Klaus Günther, 'The Legacies of Injustice and Fear: A European Approach to Human Rights and their Effects on Political Culture' in Philip Alston (ed), *The EU and Human Rights* (1999), 117, 125.

[88] The German Basic Law, Art 21(2), may be read as a general anti-extremism clause—very much what the Federal Constitutional Court did in its two decisions outlawing the Sozialistische Reichspartei and the German Communist Party in the 1950s, 2 BVerfGE 1 (1952) and 5 BVerfGE 85 (1956). A narrower interpretation along the line of 'negative republicanism'—preventing the revival of Nazi ideology and the return of Nazis to power under whatever guise—played a crucial role, if ultimately to no avail, in the recent attempt to outlaw the neo-Nazi NPD and was also suggested in a recent decision of the Federal Constitutional Court (124 BVerfGE 300 [2009]).

[89] The Transitional Provisions to the Italian Constitution (1948) forbid 'to reorganize, under any form whatsoever, the dissolved Fascist party', restrict, if only for five years, 'the right to vote and eligibility of the leaders responsible for the Fascist Regime' (Art XII). Article XII keeps the members of the House of Savoy away from the ballot box and public offices and forbids the 'ex-kings, their consorts, and male descendants' access to the national territory.

[90] Constitution of Iraq, Art 7. Rather than directly addressing apartheid, like the Constitution of Namibia (Art 23), the South African Constitution (1996) pursues the path of an indirect negative republicanism by invoking in its preamble 'unity in our diversity', emphasizing 'non-racialism' as one of the founding provisions, and repeatedly stressing equality and non-discrimination on the ground of race.

specified by the national context in question and meant to prevent the resurrection of a defeated historical system of injustice and authoritarianism. Within this paradigm the perspective changes dramatically from stability of the system to the political-legal responsibility of a polity, deriving from and founded upon a specific historical experience, owed to victims and survivors.

(3) The *civil society* paradigm of militancy claims to secure the *agonistic democracy* by focusing on groups and associations that severely violate the most fundamental rules of conflict and democratic life-forms. This paradigm seriously increases the danger of generalization and has to deal with the indeterminacy of the very fundamental rules it seeks to defend.

4. Secrecy

Somewhat paradoxically, democracies rely, almost everywhere, on institutions which are not democratically structured and do not at all or only marginally operate according to democratic rules—in particular, military forces, the police, and intelligence agencies, in short: the security services. As a matter of fact, especially the activities of agents, informers, spies, and infiltrators as well as the methods of technical surveillance, sabotage, secret files and records, not to mention 'rendition', detention, and deportation, can hardly be accommodated with the constitutional grammar of democracy.[91] While military and police command-and-obey structures, despite the lack of deliberation and reasoning, may still be adapted, albeit rudimentarily, to an overall democratic design, secrecy of operations and the special claims of intelligence officials to legitimacy qua expertise reside beyond the democratic horizon. The latter is demarcated by the claim that decision-making and measures may not be left to the darkness of deals and resolutions of uncontrolled security 'powers that be' but, for the sake of accountability, have to be made accessible to public control.

The democratic farewell to arcane politics is directed against what Kant called the 'perfidiousness of shady politicians' and requires that the practices of deputies, governors, and administrative agencies pass the publicity test so as to be measured against constitutional provisions concretizing the public interest.[92] As a matter of consequence and of liberal ideology, deviations from the path of publicity and transparency have to remain the exception from the rule and call for a justification related to the specificity of the subject matter concerned or the deliberative process. Accordingly, parliamentary debates and in particular the adoption of laws have to be public, whereas the deliberation of parliamentary committees may, by way of exception, take place behind closed doors. Similarly, court trials, rulings, and reasons and also administrative decisions, as a rule, have to be made public; however, the public is closed out from the preceding deliberation. As distinct from parliaments, courts, and administrative agencies, security services operate partly (the police), to a great extent (the military), or systematically (intelligence agencies) behind the veil of secrecy. It would be naive and mean negating the functional modality of, particularly, the military forces and secret service agencies to call for, in the name of democracy, an end to their clandestine operations.

Nevertheless, constitutions do have to cope with adjusting secrecy to the political and normative claims of democratic regimes. Constitutional elites have indeed developed different strategies of dealing with the security complex.

[91] Concerning the practices, rationales, and dangers of security agencies see the impressive treatise by Laurence Lustgarten and Ian Leigh, *In From the Cold: National Security and Parliamentary Democracy* (1994).

[92] One of the most influential analyses of security, intelligence, and public interest has been provided by David Williams, *Not in the Public Interest* (1965).

(1) Silencing the issue of secrecy[93] and not mentioning the intelligence services[94] or camouflaging the discrepancy between publicity and secrecy behind the shield of executive privilege or a generalized national interest and relying on the logic of necessity lacks constitutional-democratic style and, moreover, invites public distrust.[95]

(2) A less modest but still minimalist strategic option, normatively speaking, grants the security services a legal mandate[96] or elevates the security services to the constitutional level, where their institutional existence is recognized, their commanders named, and their functions and powers laid down in general terms.[97]

(3) A more demanding option is illustrated by constitutional documents which integrate the security (particularly, intelligence) services, more or less explicitly, in emergency regimes and, at best, define its functions, demarcate its constitutional (or legal) mandate—self-defense against external threats, stability of the internal order, assistance in times of emergency and (natural) catastrophe, and averting the dangers and controlling risks of life in society[98]—and provide for principles of action and mechanisms of (parliamentary) control[99] to ascertain political accountability and public responsibility.[100] The strategy to bring democracy—or at least parliamentary commissions—back in was embraced by the German Federal Constitutional Court when it defined the armed forces as a 'parliament's army' and required that out-of-area operations be approved by the Federal Diet rather than left to (secret) considerations of the executive branch.[101] Similarly, the German Basic Law provided for the parliamentary control of secret service activity (Art 45d) to be concretized by secondary legislation, which inspired the scholarly proposal of a 'graded publicity'.[102] The South African Constitution demonstrates a somewhat stronger democratic spirit or wariness by affirming the security services' public responsibility and placing them under parliamentary control and civic monitoring. Egypt's Constitution of 1971, on the contrary, placed the decision concerning the state of emergency (Art 74), without any procedural or other qualifications, into the hands of the head of state (President) who also happened to be the military and police commander. No wonder then that the constitution had been suspended since 1981.

[93] The Constitution of the 'Honorable Government Junta' of Chile (1980) granted the Dictator-President Pinochet extensive emergency powers (Arts 24, 39–41) but did not mention the intelligence services.

[94] For a typification of intelligence services see Peter Gill, *Policing Politics: Security Intelligence and the Liberal Democratic State* (1994) who distinguishes domestic intelligence, political police, and an independent security state.

[95] A minimalist constitutional regime of the security services is illustrated by the US Constitution (1787).

[96] The legal mandate of the security establishment in Great Britain and other Westminster democracies is critically evaluated by Lustgarten and Leigh (n 91), 374–492.

[97] eg the Federal Constitution of Austria (1929/1994), Arts 78a–81; Constitution of Brazil (1988/1998), Arts 133–44 covering the military and the police forces.

[98] For a fairly elaborate constitutional treatment of the security services see the dispersed relevant provisions of the German Basic Law (1949). Concerning democratic control of the military and security establishments in transitional democracies see Cawthra and Luckham (n 56).

[99] As regards the control of intelligence services see Hans Born and Ian Leigh, *Making Intelligence Accountable: Legal Standards and Best Practice for Oversight of Intelligence Agencies* (2005).

[100] Regarding the legal and constitutional regimes of controlling the security establishment: Lustgarten and Leigh (n 91), 412–91. See also the detailed provisions of the South African Constitution (1996), ss 198–210.

[101] See decisions of the German Federal Constitutional Court 90 BVerfGE 286 (1994); 108 BVerfGE 34 (2003).

[102] The concept is basically meant to balance legitimate secrecy interests against the requirements of democratic publicity. See Christoph Gusy, 'Parlamentarische Kontrolle der Geheimdienste im demokratischen Rechtsstaat: Die Aufgabenverschiebung der Geheimdienste' in Norbert Röttgen and Heinrich Amadeus Wolff (eds), *Parlamentarische Kontrolle: Die Nachrichtendienste im demokratischen Rechtsstaat* (2008), 13, 22.

Whatever moderate advances may have been made on the road to controlling—not even democratizing the democratizeable aspects of—the security establishment, they have been compromised and some even rolled back, in many countries, during the last decades to the benefit of the war on terror.[103] On the one hand, ruling majorities in several countries have tried to bar representatives of the opposition from sitting in on hearings and/or having access to material concerning matters of national security or anti-terrorism. Thus, security concerns took precedence over parliamentary protection of minorities. On the other hand, the categorical imperative of the war on terror corresponds to the extension of emergency powers for the police, the creation of various forms of institutional and informational cooperation between the police and intelligence agencies—implying multiple, overlapping areas of competence, the establishment of interconnected informational networks and surveillance operations. Both trends testify to the emancipation of the security complex from public, parliamentary, and constitutional control. They also illustrate that the vocabulary of danger, fear, and apocalyptic scenarios is quite obviously more suited to stimulate the institutional imagination than is the sober rhetoric of democracy.

IV. Perspectives

Despite liberal democracy's ideological hegemony it would be rash to proclaim the end of democratic development. For, on the one hand, the dynamics of democratic *experimentalism* and, on the other, current *challenges* to democracy argue against any 'endism' whatsoever. The former has always undermined attempts to 'canonize' one or the other set of values or institutional arrangements as a kind of democratic orthodoxy and has kept the discourse open for transformative ideas and practices.

Today, democratic experimentalism thrives on internal critiques and projects that aim at improving different aspects of democratic regimes: *First*, the practitioners of democracy have barely begun to translate the reform proposals made by delibertarians[104] into preconditions of democratic participation, especially civic education programs and the enhancement of associationalism, and institutional-procedural provisions of deliberative, radical democracy, such as deliberative polls and referenda.

Secondly, participatory democracy has been advanced worldwide by numerous *e-democracy* programs.[105] Projects of 'digital democracy'[106] comprise various strategies that extend both direct democracy (e-voting, e-protest, e-activism, e-consultation etc) and indirect democracy (e-information, e-parliament, e-access to representatives and governmental agencies etc) to the cyberspace in order to facilitate bottom-up initiatives, representation, and top-down governance. As long as the democratic possibilities of information technology have yet to be exhausted and its risks to be fully assessed, the end of non-e- and e-democracy is not even by a long shot in sight. More importantly, practices of e-democracy have quite obviously bypassed such a risk assessment. Recent uprisings of oppositional movements and, much to the surprise of Anglo-European

[103] See only Antonio Vercher, *Terrorism in Europe: An International Comparative Analysis* (1992); Stephan Trüby et al (eds), *5 Codes: Architecture, Paranoia, and Risk in Times of Terror* (2006); Richard Jackson, *Writing the War on Terrorism: Language, Politics, and Counter-terrorism* (2005); Frankenberg (n 83), chs VI and VII.

[104] Held (n 1), 253.

[105] Benjamin R. Barber, 'Three Scenarios for the Future of Technology and Democracy' (1998) 113 *Political Science Quarterly* 573ff; Barry N. Hague and Brian D. Loader (eds), *Digital Democracy: Discourse and Decision Making in the Information Age* (1999); Elaine Ciulla Kamarck and Joseph S. Nye (eds), *Governance.com: Democracy in the Information Age* (2002).

[106] Kenneth L. Hacker and Jan van Dijk, *Digital Democracy: Issues of Theory and Practice* (2001).

political analysts, of the civil society in Iran and in countries of the Arab world were facilitated by the availability and popular use of e-democracy instruments and open social fora (Twitter, Facebook, collective blogs) where information could be deposited and spread immediately to mobilize and organize protest.[107] It appears to be both an irony of history and the cunning of electronic reason that the erstwhile decision of the Mubarak government to provide the people of Egypt with free access to the internet not only created a crucial condition for civil-societal networking and digital activism but also helped to dodge the mechanisms of censorship and, in the end, helped to overthrow the authoritarian regime.

Thirdly, the re-entry of *cosmopolitanism*, inspired by Kant's *Perpetual Peace* (1795), into the theoretical discourse is likely to stimulate further normative development. Two differently accentuated projects of normative political theory have recently become prominent both starting from what has been labeled 'the postnational constellation'[108] or, similarly, 'the post-Westphalian era'[109] in international relations. The project of *global democracy* features the geographic *extension* and organizational design of democracy. It presents the utopian vision not of a world government as a centralized form of global self-rule but a more flexible form of governance where the individual units are said or hoped to be committed to the participation of citizens' associations and the rule of law in the absence of a coercive power of last resort.[110] Such 'cosmopolitan' proposals aim at restructuring international institutions (in particular, the General Assembly of the United Nations, international criminal courts, World Trade Organization, International Monetary Fund, and World Bank) and organizations (United Nations, European Union) and at strengthening the associations of the global civil society. Whereas rendering interstate relations more democratic[111] and entrenching democratic values[112] on the transnational level have the dignity of certainly noble agendas, protagonists of geo-democracy, however, seem to be less concerned with institutional realism (the problem of fair representation and meaningful participation) and sensitivity to the ambivalences of global governance structures (the problem of tyranny and elitism). Therefore, global democracy should better be taken as a starting point for developing a novel institutional imagination and practices of digital activism (see e-democracy) rather than transferring the traditional concepts of 'demos', 'public', and 'parliament' to supra- and transnational levels.

The second variant of cosmopolitan democracy, while not opposing its geopolitical extension, does not place democracy in the theoretical context of governance but argues instead, following Hannah Arendt's concern for the other and every individual's right to have rights,[113] for a more *inclusive* democracy and the protection of weak social groups.[114] In a post-Westphalian

[107] For an overview see Heinrich Böll Foundation (ed), *People's Power—The Arab World in Revolt* (2011) 2 *Perspectives* (May). Concerning the future of despotism and the role of constitutional reforms: Günter Frankenberg, 'Restlaufzeit für Despoten. Anmerkungen zu den Verfassungsreformen in der arabischen Welt' (2011) 44 *Kritische Justiz* 124.

[108] Jürgen Habermas, *The Postnational Constellation* (2001).

[109] Richard Falk, 'Revisiting Westphalia: Discovering Post-Westphalia' (2002) 6 *Journal of Ethics* 311; Andrew Linklater, *The Transformation of Political Community* (1998), 179.

[110] Daniele Archibugi and David Held (eds), *Cosmopolitan Democracy: An Agenda for a New World Order* (1995); Held (n 1); Daniele Archibugi, *The Global Commonwealth of Citizens: Toward Cosmopolitan Democracy* (2008).

[111] Definitely more democratic than the interstate consultative mechanisms established by the Congress of Vienna or the model of NATO that some authors take as a starting point. See Archibugi and Held (n 110), 12.

[112] Deen K. Chatterjee (ed), *Democracy in a Global World: Human Rights and Political Participation in the 21st Century* (2008).

[113] See Hannah Arendt, *The Origins of Totalitarianism* (1951).

[114] Seyla Benhabib, *The Rights of Others. Aliens, Residents and Citizens* (2004); Seyla Benhabib et al, *Another Cosmopolitanism. Hospitality, Sovereignty and Democratic Iterations* (2006).

world, where state sovereignty has become an official hypocrisy, citizens, according to this brand of cosmopolitan theory, are committed to antithetical normative programs—universal human rights and a bounded notion of democracy. The normative conflict, we learn, can be mediated, though, by the concept of *agonistic cosmopolitanism* that severs the linkage between *demos* and *ethnos* and instead integrates universal cosmopolitan norms (respect, dignity, and hospitality) into democratic practice.[115] This variant of cosmopolitanism is both demanding and attractive as it plausibly assumes that (1) migration is a universal human condition that warrants the protection of (undocumented) aliens, migrants, and refugees, (2) emphasizes, in an almost Tocquevillean turn to democracy as a social phenomenon and not only a form of government, that democracy is a scheme of cooperation rather than a community of fate and therefore has to deal with everyday conflict and dissent, and (3) can be connected with the discourse on transnational citizenship.[116] There seems to be no need, though, to argue for a 'constitutional essentialism', because a democratic grammar—and practice—of conflict as outlined above will do. Moreover, Europe's importance as a paradigm case for the future of cosmopolitan democracy[117] should not be overstated.

Whereas its inherent experimentalism opens up democracy to changes from within, it has to deal, despite its hegemony, with challenges from without. On the one hand, democratic experimentalism is likely to be propelled by socio-economic and cultural development. Thus, the emergence of mega-cities challenges the concepts, institutions, and practices of local democracy. Local self-rule, always already undermined by tendencies to view localities as means of administrative governance rather than as democratic governments and institutions where actual politics takes place, is now threatened by processes of regional centralization and internationalization through global contestation.[118] Therefore local democracy has to be adapted to the diversity of small towns and global cities,[119] which means, to dramatically different, actually polarized contexts of local participation and decision-making under national and international legal regimes.

A different developmental problem is posed by emerging democracies. As their consolidation is neither safe nor predictably dictated by the logic of evolution or modernization there is always the danger to be reckoned with that they may deviate from the democratic path and be driven to (re-)turn to authoritarian rule.[120] Hence, unstable democracies put to the test the flexibility of democratic ideology and the adaptability of democratic institutions.

On the other hand, democracy has to meet challenges from the outside. Islamic states, though using the firm name of 'democracy' or 'republic', have advanced, during the last decade, a fundamental critique of Western-style, secular democratism and established theocratic governments.[121] While it is true that religion-based authoritarianism will yet have to prove its viability and competitive advantage over the 'second best' form of (democratic)

[115] A related, albeit different project, is pursued by Fred R. Dallmayr, *Achieving Our World: Toward a Global and Plural Democracy* (2001) also emphasizing the reinvigoration of democracy through the achievement of all or many countries based on viable cross-cultural self-other relations (transversality).

[116] Etienne Balibar, *We, the People of Europe? Reflections on Transnational Citizenship* (2004).

[117] Benhabib (n 114).

[118] Gerald E. Frug, *City Making: Building Communities without Building Walls* (1999); Yishai Blank, 'Localism in the New Global Legal Order' (2006) 47 *Harvard International Law Journal* 263.

[119] Saskia Sassen, *The Global City* (2nd edn, 2001); Gerald E. Frug and David J. Barron, *City Bound* (2008), 144.

[120] As is amply demonstrated by the project 'Transitions from Authoritarian Rule: Prospects for Democracy in Latin America and Southern Europe', established in early 1977, see O'Donnell, Schmitter, and Whitehead (n 78), with further references.

[121] On Islam and the constitutional order, see Chapter 62.

government, speaking of 'the failure of political Islam'[122] seems to be premature. Islamic 'democratic theocracies', whether mere facades of self-rule or hybrid versions of religious and democratic regimes, confront republican democracies with a problem their protagonists believed had been solved by modernization: modern democracies were and are widely assumed to have settled the precarious relationship between religion and politics[123] by abolishing any transcendent other—God, divine right, holy tradition etc—as a point of reference for the legitimation of political authority and power. It is further widely presumed that democracy succeeded in domesticating the historically divisive force of religions[124] by privatizing religious convictions and practices and separating organized politics (the state) from religious organizations (the churches). There can hardly be any serious doubt that in secularized societies religion has lost most of its power to authorize political decisions. Its primacy in politics and law is history. Constitutions have sealed this development by guaranteeing religious freedom and providing, more or less stringently, for the non-identification of the state with a confession or church.[125] However, a series of conflicts with religious connotations—concerning state-sanctioned school prayers, the headscarf (*hijab*) of Muslim schoolgirls and teachers, the slaughtering of animals according to Jewish or Muslim rites, anti-evolutionist movements in the United States, the prohibition of minarets in Switzerland, etc—intermittently disturb the social peace in secular societies and challenge the widespread conviction that religious freedom enjoys unquestionable constitutional protection. These controversies may not be symptoms of a 'return of religion' but indicate that the liberal-democratic rhetoric of preferences and interests, choice and voice, and beliefs as private attitudes very inadequately addresses the *condition humaine* in modern societies and people's 'ultimate concerns'.[126] A 'thin democracy'[127] might not be able, in times of crisis, both to protect civil societal pursuit of such concerns and to turn into democrats those who believe in a religion associated with heteronymous politics.

Bibliography

Daniele Archibugi and David Held (eds), *Cosmopolitan Democracy: An Agenda for a New World Order* (1995)

Etienne Balibar, *We, the People of Europe? Reflections on Transnational Citizenship* (2004)

Benjamin R. Barber, *Strong Democracy: Participatory Politics for A New Age* (1984)

Benjamin R. Barber, 'Three Scenarios for the Future of Technology and Democracy' (1998) 113 *Political Science Quarterly* 573

Seyla Benhabib et al, *Another Cosmopolitanism. Hospitality, Sovereignty and Democratic Iterations* (2006)

Wendy Brown, *States of Injury: Power and Freedom in Late Modernity* (1995)

[122] Olivier Roy, *The Failure of Political Islam* (1994).

[123] Marcel Gauchet, *La religion dans la démocratie. Parcours de la laïcité* (1998). On religion and the constitution, see also Chapter 43.

[124] Jay Sigler, *Minority Rights* (1983). See also José Casanova, *Public Religions in the Modern World* (1994) and Larry Diamond, Marc F. Plattner, and Philip J. Costopoulos (eds), *World Religions and Democracy* (2005).

[125] Modeled after the 'free exercise clause' and the 'establishment clause' of the First Amendment to the US Constitution.

[126] Paul J. Tillich, *Dynamics of Faith* (1957).

[127] As regards the difference between 'thick' and 'thin' democracy see Jean Bethke Elshtain, 'Religion and Democracy' (2007) 20 *Journal of Democracy* 5.

Deen K. Chatterjee (ed), *Democracy in a Global World: Human Rights and Political Participation in the 21st Century* (2008)
Robert Alan Dahl, *On Democracy* (2000)
Shmuel Noah Eisenstadt, *Paradoxes of Democracy: Fragility, Continuity, and Change* (1999)
James S. Fishkin, *When the People Speak: Deliberative Democracy and Public Consultation* (2009)
Marcel Gauchet, *La religion dans la démocratie. Parcours de la laïcité* (1998)
Jürgen Habermas, *Between Facts and Norms: Contributions to a Discourse Theory of Law and Democracy* (1998)
David Held, *Models of Democracy* (3rd edn, 2006)
Elaine Ciulla Kamarck and Joseph S. Nye (eds), *Governance.com: Democracy in the Information Age* (2002)
Claude Lefort, *L'invention démocratique* (1981)
C.B. Macpherson, *Democratic Theory: Essays in Retrieval* (1973)
Jane J. Mansbridge, *Beyond Adversary Democracy* (1983)
Ulrich Rödel et al, *Die demokratische Frage* [*The Democratic Question*] (1989)
Giovanni Sartori, *The Theory of Democracy Revisited*, 2 vols (1987)
Philippe C. Schmitter, 'Dangers and Dilemmas of Democracy' (1994) 5 *Journal of Democracy* 57
Joseph Schumpeter, *Capitalism, Socialism and Democracy* (1942)
Cass Sunstein, *Designing Democracy: What Constitutions Do* (2001)
Alexis de Tocqueville, *Democracy in America* ([1835/1840] 1968)
Iris Marion Young, *Inclusion and Democracy* (2000)

CHAPTER 12

CONCEPTIONS OF THE STATE

OLIVIER BEAUD*

Paris

I. Introduction

The very title of this chapter, inviting us to address 'conception*s* of the state' in comparative constitutional law, indicates the angle of approach: the aim is to examine the question of the state in the plural. And in assuming there to be more than one conception of the state, the editors clearly give us to understand that distinct constitutional traditions or cultures think of the state in different ways. Accordingly, the comparative outlook immediately introduces some form of '*relativization*' or differentiation, inviting law scholars to desist for a moment from thinking that their own legal systems and states are universal phenomena.

* Translated by Christopher Sutcliffe.

Yet it is striking that classical textbooks on comparative constitutional law are seemingly unaware of this feature of the comparative outlook.[1] For example, Giuseppe de Vergottini's classic—a *Standardwerk*—has a chapter on the concept of state as if it were a natural category of comparative constitutional law notwithstanding the observation that the state is not recognized in the United Kingdom.[2] Some recent studies, however, do break with this assumption that there is just one single conception. Élisabeth Zoller argues that public law, and so the state, too, is thought of differently in France and in the United Kingdom and the United States.[3] Similarly, in her recent textbook, Marie-Claire Ponthoreau writes that 'The legal concept behind the word "state" does not have the same consistency from one legal order to another'.[4] But ultimately, can we not be a little more radical in the treatment of our subject matter and consider that in constitutional law there are jurisprudential traditions in which the concept of state is not a central feature. Might we not venture even that in some countries *there simply is no conception of the state*?

Just think of England, which is so important for the understanding of modern constitutional law and of the satellite community of common law countries. Whereas the term *État* became established in seventeenth-century France, 'state' failed to find a foothold in England and has not done so since.[5] It will be objected that it is not because there is no word for something that there is no concept of. Yet it is precisely that there is a concept labelled 'state' which causes the problem when examining the English case. There is no idea of the state in England, remarks the writer of an important book on the subject.[6] This is what strikes foreign observers looking to give an account of English law. As Denis Baranger remarks, 'any talk of the state in Britain seems ... to raise certain problems'.[7] Likewise, those English jurists who have rubbed with continental and Roman legal science are alert to the strangeness of their own 'stateless' system.[8] One need only open Albert Dicey's textbook on British constitutional law[9] to see that it has no specific developments on the state.[10] And neither in theory nor in practice is the state at the heart of British publicists' thinking.[11] This observation is even more valid with respect to US legal literature. Whether one opens the most important textbooks of constitutional law (eg Lawrence Tribe, *American Constitutional Law*) or casebooks, the state plays a very limited

[1] In one dated but still valuable treatise, the state is presupposed in constitutional law with no possible variation in the meaning of the term being even contemplated: Manuel Garcia Pelayo, *Tratado de derecho constitucional comparado* ([1951] 7th edn, 1984), 101.

[2] Giuseppe de Vergottini, *Diritto costituzionale comparato* (1984), 80–1.

[3] Élisabeth Zoller, *Introduction au droit public* (2006), 121ff.

[4] Marie-Claire Ponthoreau, *Droit constitutionnel comparé* (2010), 315.

[5] H.C. Dowdall, 'The Word State' (1923) *Law Quarterly Review* 104–8.

[6] Kenneth Dyson, *The State Tradition in Western Europe* (1980), 41. The section title is 'England: an aberrant case', 36–45.

[7] Denis Baranger, *Ecrire la constitution non écrite. Une introduction au droit politique britannique* (2008), 245. Before him, Alessandro Passerin d'Entrèves perceptively made the same point noting that English lawyers preferred to speak of the Crown or of 'government', *La notion d'Etat* (French translation, 1969), 43–4.

[8] See Martin Loughlin, 'In Defence of Staatslehre' (2009) 48(1) *Der Staat* 1–28 and *Foundations of Public Law* (2010), pioneering and heterodox works in which he constantly returns to there being no state in the conceptual arsenal of common law jurists.

[9] A.V. Dicey, *Introduction to the Study of the Law of the Constitution* (1885).

[10] Which does not preclude Dicey from thinking of constitutional law as a branch of public law understood as the law of the state. This is paradoxical, notes Baranger (n 7), 255. Similarly in Ivor Jennings, *The Law and the Constitution* (1959) the most prominent twentieth-century British constitutionalist does not even include 'state' in the subject index let alone have a chapter on it.

[11] It suffices here to cite a contemporary British jurist Patrick Birkinshaw, *Grievances, Remedies and the State* (2nd edn, 1994), 9, cited by Baranger (n 7), 245.

part. Times have changed since a scholar such as Westel Willoughby sought to convert US jurists to the science of the state.

This lack of interest for the question of the state contrasts starkly with the theoretical over-investment to which the same concept has been subject in certain European countries and especially in Germany and France, but in others, too (Italy, Spain). Emblematically, in Germany it was even envisioned that a new discipline might be created by the name of *Allgemeine Staatslehre* (general theory of the state). This hesitancy in choosing between constitutional law and general theory of the state[12] for dealing with the state, is a field of study in itself.[13] It is worth recalling here as evidence that the question of the state is a central one for European constitutionalists.

As readers will have grasped, one of the aims of this chapter is to challenge the idea that the concept of the state is a central feature of constitutional law everywhere. Sociologists have stolen a march on jurists by questioning whether the state is a universal phenomenon. The argument here is that only continental European scholarship has come up with what can be judged a complete theory of the state. By comparison, Anglo-American constitutional law scholarship has a somewhat incomplete conception of the state. To demonstrate this, I shall rely not on the usual threesome invoked for defining the state (a government, a territory, a people), which presupposes a somewhat fictitious similarity among all states,[14] but on an examination of the relations of the state, first, with the concept of constitution, then with the concept of sovereignty, and finally with the concept of institution.[15] It is worth making one final point: this chapter lays no claim to being exhaustive; it is built on hunches and on some sparse evidence.

II. Two Distinct Ways of Viewing the Relationship between Constitution and State

For reasons to do with the subject matter of our inquiry and with space constraints, I shall not engage in any discussion of constitutional theory as to whether or not 'constitution' should be taken in the material or the formal sense. The purpose of my line of inquiry is more limited and is confined to underscoring the existence of two separate traditions: the continental, Roman, 'European' tradition that almost systematically associates the idea of constitution with that of state; and the common law tradition that tends to think of the one separately from the other.

1. The State as a Presupposition of the Constitution

The continental European tradition is distinctive in that it considers the concept of state itself as being presupposed by the concept of constitution. More often than not, the constitution is

[12] Carl Schmitt employs *Verfassungslehre* to disqualify the use of *Staatslehre*, just as Rudolf Smend adopts the term *Verfassungsrecht*. See the present author's detailed study of this point, 'Carl Schmitt, un juriste engagé', preface to Carl Schmitt, *Théorie de la Constitution* (*Verfassungslehre*) (Lilyane Deroche-Gurcel trans, French edn, 1993), esp 59ff.

[13] See for the Franco-German dialogue Christoph Schönberger, 'Der "Staat" ' der Allgemeinen Staatslehre: Anmerkungen zu einer eigenwilligen deutschen Disziplin im Vergleich mit Frankreich' in Olivier Beaud and Erk Volkmar Heyen (eds), *Une science juridique franco-allemande?* (1999), 111ff.

[14] This analytic definition is used above all in public international law and far less in constitutional law.

[15] See Olivier Beaud, *La Puissance de l'Etat* (1994) and Olivier Beaud 'La notion d'Etat' (1991) *Archives de philosophie du droit* 119.

defined by the (written) legal instrument that organizes and founds the state.[16] From this legal-regulatory conception flow two major consequences for understanding the constitution.

For one thing, it is perceived as being politically neutral. By this it is meant that the constitution is not necessarily devised to be liberal, to impose limits on power; it also purports to *organize* power. The constitution is the regulation of the state, that is, the legal arrangement by which the uppermost echelon of the state—its rulers—is organized and governed. This does not necessarily imply that power is limited, shared out, and controlled. The constitution can be thought of as ruling an authoritarian state, which is contrary to the most stringent requisites of constitutionalism. This accounts for the two sides of the constitution: it is at one and the same time an instrument that enables and an instrument that disables. Moreover, since the constitution is perceived as the 'articles of association' of the state, it is considered as binding on its addressees, the rulers and the ruled alike. It is thought of as a unilateral instrument, along the lines of the law of the state. Thus in several countries the constitution must be promulgated like any statute. In the instrument of promulgation it is stated that it must be performed like a 'law of the state'. Such an interpretation bars the road to another conception of the constitution that was current in the nineteenth century and that saw it as a sort of political contract, whether a constitutional pact or a federal pact.[17]

According to this tradition, then, the state has in some sense become a sort of second nature of modern constitutional law. It is a kind of unheeded element of this constitutional science that reappears immediately when the association between state and constitution becomes problematic. This is the case today with European construction, which has compelled constitutionalists to think again about the connection between the constitutional instrument and the political entity to which it pertains. If the constitution is the 'articles of association' of the state, for there to be such a European constitution there would either have to be a European state or the constitution would have to be dissociated from the state. Both solutions have been contemplated.[18]

2. A Constitution Thought of Without the State: The Rule of Law Imposes its Vision of a Simple 'Government' of Public Affairs

Alongside this European tradition, which is state-centred even in respect of the concept of constitution, however, stands the common law tradition that does not at all perceive the constitution as being intrinsically related to the state. Here the constitution is related to the idea of the rule of law, as transpires from reading Albert Dicey.[19] He conceives of the constitution as 'the security given under the English constitution to the rights of individuals'.[20] The concept of rule of law appears here as the great unwritten constitutional principle of English law. It implies three things: the principle of lawfulness, the equality of all citizens before law, and the judicial protection of rights.[21] Accordingly, constitutional law too is inspired by the maxim

[16] Adhémar Esmein, the founder of constitutional law as a discipline in France, wrote tersely: 'the constitution determines the form of the state and the form of the republic'. Raymond Carré de Malberg defined the constitution, further to German scholarship, as the 'articles of association of the state'.

[17] On the constitution as a pact, see the two major commentators Maurice Hauriou, *Précis de droit constitutionnel* (1923, 1929) and Carl Schmitt, *Verfassungslehre* (1928), ch 6.

[18] Based on the arguments in Dieter Grimm, *Braucht Europa eine Verfassung?* (1995), setting out the 'statist' terms of the debate.

[19] On the rule of law, also see Chapter 10.

[20] Cited by Ponthoreau (n 4), 322.

[21] Dicey (n 9) (10th edn, 1895), 148.

that 'remedies precede rights'[22] such that there is serious competition between the written constitution and the common law. One might somewhat provocatively claim, following Dicey, that there is no need for any specific constitutional law since the common law provides for everything. For a jurist from the continental European area, the relations between the two concepts (constitution and common law) remain a mystery.[23] Admittedly, one should not be too naive and mistake a part for the whole believing that constitutional law is exhausted with the rule of law. The rule of law does not extend to every domain. There is a whole sphere of 'governmentality' in English law that, thanks to what is left of the doctrine of prerogative or of Crown theory, escapes the control of the courts and even any political control. US law too has a sphere of power that is not controlled by the courts and which is even tending to grow dangerously.[24]

There arise a whole series of conceptual consequences from this sort of association made by Anglo-American jurisprudence between the rule of law and the constitution. The constitution is perceived as a set of legal rules by which the rights of individuals are safeguarded. Political power rests upon two pillars: the common law and the power of the courts. Dicey, once again, captured this primacy of the 'judicial State' in very clear terms: 'They [judges] rather than the government represent the august dignity of the State, or, in accordance with English terminology of the Crown'.[25] This is why the idea of judicial review becomes thinkable, including for a statute that supposedly emanates from the people when one is not stopped by the doctrine of parliamentary sovereignty. *Marbury v Madison* (1804), which is invariably cited to illustrate the birth of the control of constitutionality of laws, is a fine example of a common law procedure used to defend an individual right. Such pre-eminence granted to the rights of the individual assumes that it is admitted that the courts are third instances between the state and individuals; they are not fundamentally conceived as state institutions.[26]

The other obvious consequence is that the constitution is conceived also, or even primarily, as a charter of freedoms. This is a recent tendency, though. Initially in England, rights were protected by simple laws or by simple charters (such as the celebrated Magna Carta). In the United States, the Philadelphia Constitution admittedly contains a Bill of Rights, but its initial aim was not so much to protect human rights in general as to prevent the Union (the federation) from interfering excessively in the internal affairs of its member states.[27] However, since the Fourteenth Amendment introduced the Equal Protection Clause its massive use by the courts, combined with the equally massive use of the Due Process Clause has brought about a substantial upheaval in US constitutional law, which is mainly perceived as a law of freedoms within which the rights recognized by the Bill of Rights form the chapter headings of textbooks and casebooks. US constitutional jurists interested in institutional law pass for heterodox figures.[28]

[22] As is astutely noted by Zoller (n 3), 105.

[23] See the keen comments by Baranger (n 7), 255.

[24] Bruce Ackerman, *Decline and Fall of the American Republic* (2010).

[25] Dicey (n 9), 259–60. Cited by Baranger (n 7), 256.

[26] The state described here is a 'judicial State' (*Etat de justice*). Space is too short here to describe the convergence between the two traditions. In Europe, too, *Rechtsstaat* becomes *Justizstaat*.

[27] Jesse H. Choper, 'The Scope of National Power vis-à-vis the States: The Dispensability of Judicial Review' (1977) 186 *Yale Law Journal* 1613.

[28] One thinks here obviously of the work of Bruce Ackerman, whose historical and 'political science' orientation makes him a peculiar figure in the United States. Cass Sunstein and Mark Tushnet are other non-mainstream figures.

III. State, Sovereignty, and Federalism: Can the State be Thought of as Anything Other than the Unitary State?

Although the issue of sovereignty is examined in this volume by Michel Troper,[29] it shall nonetheless be addressed here for a very simple reason: when it is taken in the sense of sovereignty of the state (legal person) and not in the (democratic and organic) sense of sovereignty of the people,[30] it comes in a different way under the ideal-type contrast between the 'European' and 'non-European' conceptions.

On the one hand, there is a telltale sign in the Anglo-American tradition: in the *Oxford Handbook of Law and Politics*,[31] the word 'Sovereignty' is not to be found in the subject index. Jurists with an interest in sovereignty are exceptions in the jurisprudential landscape.[32] On the other hand, in countries of the Roman law tradition, the term 'sovereignty' is invariably found in equivalent dictionaries. In France, it is found in most dictionaries,[33] and at any rate in constitutional dictionaries,[34] as it is in Germany in the *Lexikon* on core concepts (Koselleck, Brunner, and Conze, *Staatslexikon*) or in Italy.[35] If the concept of sovereignty is central in the continental European tradition, it is because it is considered that it is and that it remains the criterion of the state. However, this question is quite simply not posed in Anglo-American constitutional scholarship. And so the concept of sovereignty illuminates the clear contrast between European doctrine, which gives precedence to state power that prizes sovereignty, and the Anglo-American doctrine, which is unaware of sovereignty or ignores it.

1. Sovereignty as a Criterion of the State and the Tropism of the Unitary State

In the European tradition, and by virtue of sovereignty, state power is held to be a power of dominance, even an irresistible power, such that the state may be defined as a 'unit for decision-making and action'.[36] Admittedly, this idea has been contested,[37] but it does still structure the way the state is perceived. Notably, it has a major effect on the way in which *forms of state* are accounted for. It long implied that just a single form might be described: the *unitary state*. Federalism came along to spoil this fine harmony and plunge jurists into terrible turmoil. A second form had to be invented, the federal state, which allowed greater autonomy—that could extended to constitutional and legislative autonomy—to 'infra-state' authorities referred to as 'federated entities'.[38]

Undoubtedly, the tropism of sovereignty leads the state to be perceived of principally as a unitary state. The unitary state has been defined as the one which 'legally appears to be that

[29] See Chapter 17.

[30] See Chapter 17 by Michel Troper on the various meanings of sovereignty.

[31] Keith E. Whittington, R. Daniel Kelemen, and Gregory A. Caldeira (eds), *Oxford Handbook of Law and Politics* (2008).

[32] A notable exception is Martin Loughlin, 'Ten Tenets of Sovereignty' in Neil Walker (ed), *Sovereignty in Transition* (2005), 55.

[33] *Dictionnaire de culture juridique* (2004).

[34] Olivier Duhamel and Yves Mény (eds), *Dictionnaire constitutionnel* (1992).

[35] Noberto Bobbio, Nicola Matteucci, and Gianfranco Pasquino (eds), *Dizionario di politica* (2004).

[36] The great Herman Heller might be cited here.

[37] Either by categorically denying the very idea of sovereignty, which was perceived of as metaphysical (Duguit, Kelsen) or by replacing it with the idea of public or state power (*Staatsgewalt*) (Jellinek).

[38] On federalism, see further Chapter 27.

whose Power lies in its founding, in its structure and in its exercise'.[39] It might be more judicious, though, to define it by the idea of centralization of political power.[40] By such a definition it can be taken that, in a unitary state, authorities other than the state are not entitled to exercise political power; they are *administrative* bodies. Such political centralization is reflected, legally, by the idea of 'the unity of law or of statute within the country (unity of legislation)'.[41] In France, which is the land of the unitary state *par excellence*, political centralization is reflected in the terms of the Constitution by the principle that the Republic is indivisible. This principle means that 'a single political power exercises sovereignty over the whole territory of the Republic, albeit that power may attribute certain competencies, including competencies differentiated by location, to other authorities, notably local authorities'.[42] This idea may be worded differently: statute law remains a monopoly of the central state.[43] This monopoly is narrowly interpreted. In 1991, the Conseil constitutionnel dismissed the idea that the Corsican Assembly might enjoy a sort of right to intervene in the legislative process even for bills concerning the region and considered that the mere reference in the act of the expression 'the Corsican people' was unconstitutional.[44] Political centralization, specific to the unitary state, does not preclude a degree of flexibility in managing administrative issues. It is equally at ease with administrative centralization as with administrative decentralization. France is the prime example of the doubly (politically and administratively) centralized state that has evolved towards a form of decentralized unitary state in the administrative sense of the word.

Some countries of Europe, notably Italy and Spain, are evolving from 'unitary' states into 'regional' states.[45] A form of political regionalism is thus developing that resembles federalism without being federalism. Let us take the case of Spain, whose 1978 Constitution recognizes the existence of a plurinational reality. It guarantees the 'right to self-government of the nationalities and regions' (Art 2). Two types of autonomous status are provided for by the Constitution that may be characterized as ordinary and special status. The Constitution also provides that historical nationalities (Catalonia, Euskadi, Galicia) may immediately accede to self-government by different channels. While the state retains all the attributes of sovereignty (foreign policy, defence, currency, Crown property, justice, criminal and commercial legislation), the regions have exclusive competence for town and country planning, tourism, health, agriculture, and so on. They have a wide autonomy, including legislative autonomy. But such entities cannot be considered sovereign and remain subject to the control of the law of the Spanish state. The institutional status of the self-governing communities remains largely ring-fenced by the state constitution.[46] It is therefore not at all surprising, in terms of positive constitutional law, that the Spanish Constitutional Court should have annulled in 2010 a large part of the organic law of 19 July 2006 reforming the Statute of Autonomy of Catalonia. Yes, the state statute passed by the Cortes had been approved by its Catalan people further to a referendum, pursuant to the procedure in force;[47] but that democratic approval was insufficient since, in the case in point, certain provisions of the Catalan statute purported to give the

[39] Georges Burdeau, *Traité de science politique. Vol II: L'Etat* (3rd edn, 1980), 368.

[40] See on this Maurice Hauriou, *Précis de droit administratif* (1911), 116.

[41] Ibid (11th edn, 1927), 44.

[42] Guy Carcassonne, *La constitution* (6th edn, 2004), 40 n 7.

[43] Article 34 of the French Constitution of the Fifth Republic states tersely: 'Parliament shall pass statutes' (*La loi est votée par le Parlement*).

[44] Conseil constitutionnel, no 91-290 DC, 9 May 1991 (Corsica).

[45] For a sound outline in French see Philippe Lauvaux, *Les grandes démocraties contemporaines* (3rd edn, 2004), 790ff, esp nn 271ff (Italy) and nn 297ff (Spain).

[46] See esp ibid, 994–5 n 298.

[47] Sentencia 31/2001 of 28 June 2010.

Autonomous Community the right to administer justice independently and autonomously, which was an encroachment on the competence of the Spanish state. Unsurprisingly the Constitutional Court also annulled other provisions for extending competencies, notably fiscal powers.

It is not wrong, therefore, to claim that the principle of sovereignty continues, despite all the tinkering with it, to govern most unitary states. Generally, the federal state appears to jurists steeped in a unitary state culture to be an abnormal state compared with the normal, unitary state.

2. Federalism is Perceived Differently in the Two Constitutional Traditions

If the state is thought of as being necessarily sovereign, it is not readily compatible with the federal structure. This contradiction is especially marked when dealing with the federal state, the description of which raises a serious problem for continental European jurists. State sovereignty is mainly manifested in the existence of an indivisible bundle of powers and competencies exercised by a single entity termed the state.[48] But federalism radically challenges this form of state sovereignty by dividing what is indivisible between two tiers of government, the federation and its member states. There arises from this a natural infirmity of the federal government that is dominated by the 'principle of incompleteness': 'a federal government is in essence incomplete'.[49] European scholarship has come up with several more or less radical solutions to overcome the antinomy between federalism and sovereignty. One is to abandon the criterion of sovereignty and consider that the federal state is a state that is itself made up of states, which is to accept that there are such things as non-sovereign states: federated states. Another solution contemplated is to consider that the federal state is merely a highly decentralized state, but this solution presents the drawback of denying that there is anything particular about federalism. In short, European thinking has enormous difficulty with the federal arrangement because European thinking is state-centred.

In contradistinction, thinkers with a common law constitutional culture have studied federalism rather pragmatically. They have treated it as a fact that thrusts itself upon them and have not wondered whether it had to be reconciled with state sovereignty, a category that is not central to their world of thought. A commentator such as Dicey has a whole chapter on the question of federalism without making an issue of the contradiction with sovereignty. He studies parliamentary sovereignty, the cardinal principle of his country's law, at length, but ignores it when he studies US or Swiss federalism. Or again, Kenneth Wheare, the most influential writer on federalism, deals with the issue without ever broaching the potential conflict with sovereignty.[50] US jurists reason differently because the basis of their thinking is not state sovereignty but the federal structure. From their standpoint, it is sovereignty that appears to be a legal absurdity.[51] Or when they study true federations, they evoke the existence of a 'double sovereignty' or a 'divided sovereignty'. This was the thesis of 'dual federalism' the Supreme

[48] Following Herbert Krüger, *Allgemeine Staatslehre* (1964), I have proposed naming this the 'principle of the state's omnicompetence'. See Olivier Beaud, *La puissance de l'Etat* (1994), 144.

[49] Élisabeth Zoller, 'Aspects internationaux du droit constitutionnel. Contribution à la théorie de la fédération d'Etats' (2003) 294 *Collected Courses of the Hague Academy* 119–20 n 129.

[50] 'By the federal principle, I mean the method of dividing powers so that the general and regional governments are each, *within a sphere, coordinate and independent*': Kenneth Wheare, *Federal Government* (4th edn, 1947), 10.

[51] 'Sovereignty, in the classic sense, has no meaning: divided as power is, the element of absoluteness which is essential to the concept of sovereignty is not present': Richard Leach, *American Federalism* (1970), 1.

Court was to invent after Justice Marshall[52] to try to find a compromise between the supporters of the Union and the supporters of the member states. One of the most famous expressions of this doctrine is found in the Supreme Court ruling:

> Our dual form of government has it perplexities, state and nation having different spheres of jurisdiction... but it must be kept in mind that we are one people, and the powers reserved to the states and those conferred on the nation are adapted to be exercised, whether independently or concurrently, to promote the general welfare material and moral.[53]

Such an argument is still taken up today, whether by the Supreme Court[54] or by the scholarly literature.[55] For their part, the proponents of 'national federalism' have resorted to the theory of the sovereignty of the people, which has proved the most economical way to overcome this obstacle.[56] This theory effectively construes federalism as a simple form of *separation of powers*. Accordingly the idea of federation, that is, of the Union, that lies at the heart of the Articles of the Confederation and of the 1787 Constitution, is relegated to the subordinate rank of 'auxiliary precaution'.[57] We have there, then, a dominant interpretation of federalism that considers it not as a political form, a form of state, but simply as a 'vertical' separation of powers.[58]

In a nutshell, whereas continental European doctrine endeavours to think of federalism in its various guises[59] through the form of the state, the federal state, common law jurists never refer to the federation as a 'state'. This is very striking for the United States where the term 'the Union' substitutes for an abstract concept and saves answering the question of principle (federalism versus statism). For me, it has to be concluded from this that a state-centred analysis is unsuitable for describing the specificities of federal government. Federal government 'seen from the inside... has nothing to do with a "state"'[60] with the result that it can be taken, not unparadoxically, that 'American federalism' allows us 'to think of federalism outside of the theory of the federal state'.[61] So Anglo-American legal scholars think of federalism without the theory of the federal state whereas continental European legal scholarship adapts (betrays?) its theory of state to make it compatible with federalism as a fact and to avoid the tropism of the unitary state.[62]

[52] For a very good recent description of such federalism see Robert Schütze, *From Dual Federalism to Cooperative Federalism* (2010).

[53] *Hoke v United States* 227 US 308 (1913). Cited by Edward S. Corwin, 'Constitution versus Constitutional Theory' in Edward S. Corwin (ed), *American Constitutional History Essays* (1964), 103.

[54] Justice Kennedy in *US Term Limits, Inc v Thornton* 514 US 779 (1995).

[55]

> Federalism as an American constitutional principle may be defined as the existence of two tiers of sovereignty in which each person is a citizen of the nation in respect of the powers and obligations of that government, but also a citizen of the state where he lives.

Theodore Lowi, 'Le fédéralisme 1787–1987' in Marie-France Toinet (ed), *Et la constitution créa l'Amérique* (1987), 104.

[56] Hit upon by James Wilson, this idea is the crux of *MacCulloch v Maryland*. See the excellent book by Samuel Beer, *To Make a Nation: The Rediscovery of American Federalism* (1993).

[57] Ibid ch 9.

[58] Here again Kenneth Wheare is quite representative of the mainstream as pointed out by Murray Forsyth, *Union of States* (1981), 2.

[59] This ideal-type describes European (German, Swiss), North American (United States, Canada), Central and South American (Mexico, Brazil) and even Australian federalism.

[60] Zoller (n 49) 61 n 21.

[61] Ibid 73 n 37.

[62] It is to escape this dead-end that I proposed thinking about the federation without resort to the theory of the state. See Olivier Beaud, *Théorie de la Fédération* (2nd edn, 2009). See also Christoph Schönberger, *Unionsbürger* (2005).

IV. The State as an Institution: Asymmetric Treatment

For a European constitutional law scholar, it goes without saying that the state is a personalized entity, separate from those who govern. This obvious point is reflected by the idea that the state is an artificial person. Thus the state is at one and the same time a political body and a juristic person. What is obvious here in Europe ceases to be so across the Channel or across the Atlantic. The absence of institutionalization of political power by Anglo-American scholarship confirms the argument proposed here that the concept of state is incomplete in the cultural area of what is called the common law.

1. Objectivization of Power by the State Conceived of as an Institutionalized Power (or Juristic Person)

In the European tradition, jurisprudence has inferred from this and other related facts that the state is to be distinguished from the sovereign, the 'rulers' and from the government.[63] The state, writes Georges Burdeau, is 'an institutionalized power'.[64] And so it is from the vantage point of the institution that we shall examine the state now considered as a juristic person, an abstract entity that is an artificial person.[65] Here the job is to think about the mediation between the sovereign (sovereignty) and the state, that is, to think about the objectivization of power.

It should next be emphasized that before being the subject of one or rather several legal theories, the state was first a practical challenge. Jurists had to invent a legal category, that of 'person' or 'body', to meet the circumstances of the time. The precursors of international law *had to* legally systematize interstate relations and overcome the diversity of forms of government of the different European states (absolute monarchy, constitutional monarchy).[66] It took two centuries, from Grotius to Vattel, for this construction of the legal personality of the state to be constructed in international law doctrine.[67] Constitutional law supplements international law by finding the way to think of making power perpetual and impersonal thanks to the concept of institution applied to the state.

2. Institutionalization or Perpetuation of Power

Historically, it was the practical challenge posed by the death of the sovereign that led jurists to invent solutions for institutionalizing power. French and English jurists turned to various legal fictions as a basis on which to perpetuate royal power. Thus the monarchic state brought about the first modern form of such institutionalization, as attested by Bossuet's celebrated apostrophe: 'You die, O Princes, but your state must be immortal'.[68] Accordingly, this neutralization of

[63] Loughlin, *Foundations* (n 8), 183ff.

[64] Georges Burdeau, *Traité de science politique*, vol II (1980).

[65] The theory of juridical personality of the state has occupied many jurists. It suffers from the absolutist image bequeathed by German scholarship that made the state an artificial person with subjective rights of domination over individuals. For a description of this Gerber–Laband doctrine see Olivier Jouanjan, *Une histoire de la pensée juridique allemande* (2004).

[66] Helmut Quaritsch, *Staat und Souveränität* (1970), 475.

[67] See on this the highly instructive argument by Emmanuelle Jouannet, *Emer de Vattel et l'émergence doctrinale du droit international classique* (1998).

[68] Policy derived from Holy Scripture itself, cited by Marcel Prélot and Jean Boulouis, *Institutions politiques et droit constitutionnel* (6th edn, 1975), 16.

political power was to be able to serve the monarchical and democratic causes alike, the nation substituting for the king as a timeless category.[69] But this institutionalization of power did not concern just the succession of rulers, sovereigns; it also affected the passing on of public offices and of public property. A judge authorized by the sovereign continues to hold office notwithstanding the death of the sovereign who personally invested him. The continuity of office (of public functions) is to be thought through; the continuity of property too. Property acquired or ceded by the state must remain so. Thus jurists were to invent distinctions between the state as owner and the rulers, between the republic as owner and the sovereign as administrator, and between office holder and office, inspired by the civil law distinction between the ownership of property and the enjoyment or use of it. The theory of the inalienability of public property is the fortunate corollary of the institutionalization of state power.

In declaring the state immortal, it is merely a matter of thinking of it as independent of its rulers' existence. From this standpoint, the theory of state is heir to Roman-canon law, for solutions already hit upon by canon lawyers for thinking of the Church as an institution have been simply transposed and adapted.[70]

3. The Impersonalization of Power: Rulers Represent the State

The institution-person does not have as its sole function to perpetuate power; it forms a decisive divide between the public person and the private person. This can be understood from the fundamental issue of the ascribing of deeds done by people, rulers, to a legal entity, a juristic person, the state.

Here we shall start out from a far-sighted observation by Alf Ross:

> certain acts that are in reality performed by definite individuals—and who else could perform an act—are spoken of as being performed not by the physical person in question, but by a subject called 'the State'. The act, one can also say, is attributed to 'the State'.[71]

It is striking to observe that even the most nominalist of jurists have been compelled to admit that, behind the deed done by an individual, the law has been bound to imagine a 'subject that one imagines as it were standing behind him'.[72] Whether they realize it or not they fall in with Thomas Hobbes, who plainly separates the republic (the state, the commonwealth) from the sovereign who is its representative, and to whom Hobbes ascribes a dual capacity: a 'political capacity' when he acts on behalf of the state and a 'natural capacity' when he acts for his own account, as a private individual. There results a split between the state and its rulers, and a duality of rulers who have a dual public (representative of the state) and private side (as a natural person). Thus through the institutionalization of power the great question of representation is played out. The state acts through its representatives. Before having a democratic meaning, whereby the rulers represent the ruled by virtue of a trust (Locke), representation has an eminently state or institutional meaning: rulers (like civil servants) represent the institution, the state. It is this objective dimension that Martin Loughlin describes when he says that sovereignty is 'authoritative'.[73]

[69] See esp Ralph Giesey, *Cérémonial et puissance souveraine. France VXe–XVIIe siècles* (1987), 85.

[70] The remarkable work by Ernst Kantorowicz, *The King's Two Bodies* (1957) is invariably cited, but this idea is commonplace in the history of law.

[71] Alf Ross, 'On the Concepts "State" and "State Organs" in Constitutional Law' (1961) 5 *Scandinavian Studies in Law* 115.

[72] Hans Kelsen, 'Droit et Etat du point de vue d'une théorie pure' (1936) *Annales de l'Institut de droit comparé de l'Université de Paris* 48.

[73] Loughlin (n 32).

Thus, as it is conceived in Europe, the theory of the state as an institution allows us to handle the continuity of power and the attribution of acts to a juristic person. It is the essential complement to the subjective theory of sovereignty.[74] Even so, one must be aware of the political danger of this doctrine when it is instrumentalized by the power in place. It can lead rulers to shelter behind the person of the state to escape their own responsibility for any negligence or wrongdoing on their part. The concept of the juristic person may thus be the screen behind which rulers hide and so endorse a denial of responsibility although responsibility is one of the fundamental concepts of modern constitutionalism.[75]

To conclude on this point, it is important to grasp the scope of this phenomenon of the impersonalization of power in the construction of the modern state: it exceeds the single field of constitutional law. It prohibits the 'assetization' of the state. Rulers are not the owners of their power; what is public is clearly separate from what is private. They hold competencies, legally, that they do not own.[76]

4. The Anglo-American Conception or the Non-Institutionalized State

It would be an exaggeration to claim that Anglo-American jurists are unfamiliar with the concept of the institutionalization of power. There are obviously fragments of it. English jurists too resorted to various legal fictions on which to found royal power, as is readily apparent from the Tudor metaphor of *The King's Two Bodies*,[77] so masterfully reconstructed by Ernst Kantorowicz. But here too jurists do not have the possibility of turning to the concept of state in cases where European jurists are able to do so. To prove this hypothesis, we shall settle for a single piece of evidence, which is resort to the concept of the Crown in English law.[78] One might also refer, in a broader domain than constitutional law, to the comparison Maitland makes between the English concept of 'trust' and Gierke's famous theory of the German corporation.

As might be expected, the legal concept of the Crown is not unequivocal and English jurists are still divided over its exact meaning.[79] The term may designate the holder of various prerogatives the characteristics of which are that they are not fully subject to the rule of law. The Crown has also gradually become the symbol of government. More materially, one might say that the word 'Crown' simply meant formerly the king (Anson) or nowadays the queen (Wade). The throng of uses of the Crown in public law has been commented on.[80] But the main point about this concept is that it apprehends the polity as a corporation, the English particularity of which is supposedly that it is here a 'corporation sole' and not a 'corporation aggregate'. What the non-English jurist needs to know of the Crown is that it allows 'a natural

[74] In a way, I am trying to tip into the theory of the institution what other commentators (here Loughlin and Baranger) pigeon-hole under sovereignty. But what matters in the end is that both theories relate to one theory, that of the state.

[75] On constitutionalism, see further Chapter 8.

[76] Here one cannot overemphasize the importance of the section Jellinek devotes to this issue as 'Die Rechstellung der Staatsorgane' in *Allgemeine Staatslehre* (1911), 560ff.

[77] See on this Kantorowicz (n 70), the reading of which is greatly facilitated by the erudite warnings in Giesey (n 69), 9ff.

[78] There are probably others.

[79] See Maurice Sunkin and Sebastian Payne, *The Nature of the Crown: A Legal and Political Analysis* (1999). My thanks to Denis Baranger for drawing my attention to this work which is central to the subject.

[80] Baranger (n 7), 204–14.

person [the king] to be depersonalized' or that it has made it possible to raise the royal person 'to a new rank: that of an institution of government'.[81] In many respects the concept of the Crown reminds the European jurist of the concept of the state in the sense of institutionalized power and yet it is not the equivalent of the state.

The dividing line with the European tradition lies in the fact that English law does not view the Crown as a juristic person capable of incorporating the polity.[82] As Kantorowicz writes, the 'concept of Crown' was not the artificial person, but 'a personification in its own right, which was not only above its members, but also divorced from them.'[83] The essential thing is, however, in the role of institutionalization played by the concept of the Crown in creating an indissociable whole with the monarch.[84] There is much common ground between the formation of legal personality in the history of European law and that of the Crown in the history of English law, but these similarities do not preclude us from remarking upon one major difference: unlike the legal person or institution, the concept of the Crown has never been used to characterize the state as a polity endowed with a legal nature. In other words, the complete incorporation of the polity has not been made possible by the doctrine of the Crown. There has been 'bodyfication' but not 'personification'. The upshot is that it can be said in the United Kingdom that 'the state is not personalized'.[85] A formula that one might equally well turn around by saying that, with respect to the European model of the complete state, the absence of personalization of power means there can be no talk of state in the United Kingdom.

The difficulty with this principle was raised by Maitland who observed that 'English lawyers... liked their persons to be real'.[86] The usually concrete view of the Crown, thought of as the monarch, or nowadays as the symbol of executive authority, thus proceeds from the 'traditional antipathy of English common lawyers towards abstract thinking'.[87] This turn of mind probably explains why English law has not adopted identical solutions to European public law with respect to the institutionalization of power: the attribution of a patrimony to the state, a clear dissociation between public management and private management, the gradual attribution of state responsibility for acts that are part of public administration etc.[88] We shall not dally here over the visible political consequences of this doctrine of the Crown, which are both contrary to the theory of the rule of law (with respect to immunity) and to republicanism. It is not this residue of monarchism that is worth attending to but the fact that such a doctrine attests to the difficulty, already pointed out, for English law to escape from the domination of the common law and a private law style of thinking.[89] Now, there is no possibility of constructing a theory of the state if one remains caught up in schemes that are the legacy of private law.

[81] These two formulas are borrowings from ch 4, 'Ce qu'il est advenu de la Couronne' in Baranger (n 7), 197 and 200.

[82] Martin Loughlin, 'The State, the Crown and the Law' in Sunkin and Payne (n 79), 55–6 (interpreting the history of English law and Kantorowicz, *The King's Two Bodies*).

[83] Kantorowicz (n 70), 382.

[84] Loughlin (n 82), 33.

[85] Baranger (n 7), 264.

[86] Frederic William Maitland, 'The Crown as Corporation' (1910) in Frederic William Maitland, *Collected Papers*, vol III (1911), 246.

[87] Loughlin (n 82), 59.

[88] See the developments by Martin Loughlin who shows the harmful consequences of over-use of the concept of the Crown.

[89] Loughlin (n 82), 76.

V. Conclusion

It would not be impossible to contemplate other examples to prove the difference in outlook between the state-centred doctrine of jurists from the Roman law family and the state-decentred doctrine of jurists from the common law family. The place of the courts might be indicative of another major difference: the courts are related to the state in the European tradition but, rather, to civil society in the common law tradition. One might also point out the differences in the way in which citizenship and nationality are thought of in the various cultural spaces. But the purpose of this chapter has been to show that political power is not perceived in the same way by constitutional law scholars. In other words, the question of whether to ascribe a central position to the concept of 'state' is indeed a question that divides the world of constitutional law.

Bibliography

For a very good bibliography, related to public law and state, see Martin Loughlin, *Foundations of Public Law* (2010), 468–510

Olivier Beaud, *La puissance de l'Etat* (1994)

Olivier Beaud, *Théorie de la Fédération* (2nd edn, 2009)

Samuel Beer, *To Make a Nation: The Rediscovery of American Federalism* (1993)

Ernst-Wolfgang Böckenförde, *Staat, Verfassung, Demokratie* (1991)

Kenneth Dyson, *The State Tradition in Western Europe: A Study of an Idea and Institution* (1980)

Hermann Heller, 'Staatslehre' in *Gesammelte Schriften*, vol 3 ([1934] 1971)

Erst Kantorowicz, *The King's Two Bodies: A Study in Mediaeval Political Theology* (1957)

Martin Loughlin, *Foundations of Public Law* (2010)

Martin Loughlin, 'In Defence of Staatslehre' (2009) 48 (1) *Der Staat* 1

Martin Loughlin, 'The State, the Crown and the Law' in Maurice Sunkin and Sebastian Payne (eds), *The Nature of the Crown: A Legal and Political Analysis* (1999)

Frederick Maitland, *Collected Papers*, vol III (1911)

Alexandre Passerin d'Entrèves, *The Notion of State: An Introduction to Political Theory* (1967)

Helmut Quaritsch, *Staat und Souveränität* (1970)

Alf Ross, 'On the Concepts "State" and "State Organs" in Constitutional Law' (1961) 5 *Scandinavian Studies in Law* 113

Carl Schmitt, *Theory of the Constitution* (Jeffrey Seitzer trans, [1928] 2008)

Maurice Sunkin and Sebastian Payne (eds), *The Nature of the Crown: A Legal and Political Analysis* (1999)

Michel Troper, *Pour une théorie juridique de l'État* (1994)

Élisabeth Zoller, *Introduction to Public Law: A Comparative Study* (2008)

CHAPTER 13

RIGHTS AND LIBERTIES AS CONCEPTS*

ROBERT ALEXY

Kiel

THE debate over rights and liberties—not unlike the debate over justice—is a never-ending discussion, reflecting normative, analytical, and institutional considerations. Questions respecting the rights and liberties that an individual can lay claim to are fundamental normative questions in every society. They represent major themes not only in the law, especially constitutional law, but also in practical philosophy, and they count as central points of political

* I should like to thank Stanley L. Paulson for suggestions and advice on matters of English style.

dispute, too. This fundamental normative character is connected with a high degree of complexity. With respect to liberties, Isaiah Berlin has spoken of 'more than two hundred senses of this protean word recorded by historians of ideas'.[1] Rights are no less complicated. To these analytical problems, one has to add, finally, the institutional dimension. As soon as rights and liberties are recorded in a constitution as constitutional rights and liberties that bind the legislature and are subject to constitutional review, questions respecting the democratic legitimation of constitutional adjudication arise.

Not losing track in this tangle of problems requires conceptual clarity. In the first section, I will present a brief analysis of the general structure of rights and liberties. The themes of Section II are the concepts of human and constitutional rights. Finally, Section III concerns the construction of constitutional rights, especially the connection between constitutional rights and proportionality.

I. Rights and Liberties in General

1. Will and Interest Theory

Ever since the nineteenth century, various versions of the will and interest theories have competed on the question of the most adequate explanation of the concept and nature of rights or, more precisely, of subjective rights.[2] Adherents of the will theory claim that an individual's having a right means that his will or his choice, his freedom, is recognized. With this, rights are closely connected with liberties. Proponents of the interest theory, by contrast, argue that it is essential for rights that they protect or promote the interests or the benefit, the well-being, of the holder of the right. This applies, for example, to social rights.

2. A Three-Stage Model of Rights

The division of the theories of rights into will theories and interest theories is, if they are interpreted as strict alternatives, unfortunate. Some norms conferring rights may aim at the recognition of freedom of the will, others may have the purpose of protecting and advancing interests, and still others may do both. The puzzles stemming from this, puzzles that have occupied so very many legal theorists for such a long time, can easily be avoided if one grounds the analysis of rights on the distinction among (1) reasons for rights, (2) rights as legal posi-

[1] Isaiah Berlin, *Four Essays on Liberty* (1969), 121.

[2] Proponents of the will theory in the nineteenth century are, eg, Friedrich Carl von Savigny, *System des heutigen Römischen Rechts*, vol 1 (1840), 7: 'the power to which an individual person is entitled: a realm ruled by his will' (translation by Robert Alexy), and John Austin, *Lectures on Jurisprudence or the Philosophy of Positive Law*, vol. 1 (5th edn, 1911), 398: 'Right;—the capacity or power of exacting from another or others acts or forbearances;—is nearest to a true definition.' Early exponents of the interest theory are Jeremy Bentham, *Of Laws in General* (H.L.A. Hart ed, 1970), 57: '*By favouring one party in point of interest the law gives another a right to* services', and Rudolf von Jhering, *Geist des römischen Rechts auf den verschiedenen Stufen seiner Entwicklung*, Part 3 (5th edn, 1906), 339: 'Rights are *legally protected interests*' (translation by Robert Alexy). More recently, H.L.A. Hart, 'Legal Rights' in H.L.A. Hart, *Essays on Bentham. Studies in Jurisprudence and Political Theory* (1982), 188, has defended a version of the will theory, whereas Neil MacCormick, 'Rights in Legislation' in P.M.S. Hacker and Joseph Raz (eds), *Law, Morality, and Society. Essays in Honour of H.L.A. Hart* (1977), 204–5, has argued for a version of the interest theory. These are, of course, simply two examples among many.

tions and relations, and (3) the enforceability of rights. This distinction leads to a three-stage model of rights.[3]

The first stage comprises reasons for rights. Each and every argument that can be put forward for establishing rights of whatsoever kind has its place at this first stage. This includes not only the recognition of freedom of the will and the protection and promotion of the interests of the holder of the right, that is to say, individual goods, but also collective goods. It is possible, for instance, to attempt to justify private property through the general economic effectiveness of an economy based on private ownership, that is, by reference to a collective good. To be sure, an exclusively collective justification of individual or subjective rights gives these rights a much weaker standing than a justification based exclusively or supplementarily on individual goods. But this does not suffice to exclude collective goods from the first stage of the three-stage model, for this model is no more than an analytical tool and has, as such, a formal character. It comprises all conceivable reasons for subjective rights. Whether they are good or bad reasons remains a matter of substantive normative argument.[4]

At the second stage rights as legal positions and relations are to be found. An example is the right of *a* as against *b* that *b* should not obstruct *a* in φ-ing, for instance the right a citizen has against the state, namely, that the state should not obstruct this citizen's freedom of speech.

Finally, the third stage comprises those legal positions that are related to the enforcement of legal rights, especially by bringing an action. This stage connects powers concerning enforcement with the positions and relations of the second stage.

All three stages are important for a theory of constitutional rights. The central elements, however, are the positions and relations at the second stage. They are what the reasons for rights located at the first stage intend to justify and they, again, are reasons for the enforceability to be found at the third stage. Their nature and their different kinds can be expounded by means of a system of basic legal positions and relations.

3. A System of Basic Legal Positions and Relations

The basis of the system of basic legal positions and relations is a threefold division into (1) rights to something, (2) liberties, and (3) powers. This division is linked both to Bentham's distinction between 'rights to services', 'liberties', and 'powers'[5] and to Bierling's distinction between 'legal claim' (*Rechtsanspruch*), 'simple legal permission' (*einfache*[*s*] *rechtliche*[*s*] *Dürfen*), and 'legal ability' (*rechtliche*[*s*] *Können*).[6]

(a) Rights to Something

Rights to something or claim rights are three-place relations of which the first element is the beneficiary or *holder* of a right (*a*), the second is the *addressee* of the right (*b*), and the third is the *subject matter* or object of the right (*S*).[7] This three-place relation can be expressed by '*R*'. The most general form of a statement of a right to something can thus be expressed by

[3] See on this Robert Alexy, *A Theory of Constitutional Rights* (Julian Rivers trans, [1985] 2002), 115–18.

[4] See on this Robert Alexy, 'Individual Rights and Collective Goods' in Carlos Nino (ed), *Rights* (1992), 170, 175–6, where the thesis is presented that a legal system that comprises no subjective rights established by individual reasons cannot be justified.

[5] Bentham (n 2), 57–8, 83–92, 119.

[6] Ernst Rudolf Bierling, *Zur Kritik der juristischen Grundbegriffe*, Part 2 (1883), 49–50.

[7] In *A Theory of Constitutional Rights* (n 3), 120, the subject matter or object is represented by '*G*'. This is due to the fact that a subject matter or an object in German is '*Gegenstand*'.

(1) *RabS*.

This scheme can give rise to a great variety of rights, depending on what *a*, *b*, and *S* stand for. When *a* refers to a natural person and *b* to the state and *S* to an omission, a classical liberal defensive right is expressed. If *S* represents a positive act of the state, a right to positive state action is at hand, for example a protective right or a social right. Many other problems of the theory of constitutional rights can be constructed as questions of what can be substituted for each of the three variables. If, for instance, one puts the question of whether natural persons can be substituted not only for *a*, the holder, but also for *b*, the addressee, the problem of the horizontal effect of constitutional rights is drawn up, and if, to give a further example, the questions is raised of whether not only individuals but also groups, for instance minorities of whatever kind, can be substituted for *a*, the problem of collective constitutional rights is at stake.

It is of great importance for the theory of rights that

(1) *RabS*

is logically equivalent to

(2) *ObaS*.

'*O*' in this formula is a three-place or relational form of the elementary deontic operator '*O*' which can be read as 'It is obligatory that ...'.[8] When (1) expresses

(3) *a* has a right against *b* that *b* grant *a* asylum,

(2) expresses

(4) *b* is vis-à-vis *a* obligated to grant *a* asylum.

(1) and (2) are what Wesley Newcomb Hohfeld terms 'right' and 'duty' qua 'jural correlatives'.[9] Jural correlatives are converse relations. For this reason, the sentence

(5) $RabS \leftrightarrow ObaS$

represents an analytical truth. This does not mean that every obligation or duty implies a right. The non-relational duty

(6) *ObS*

does not imply

(1) *RabS*.

[8] On more details see Alexy (n 3), 131–8.

[9] Wesley Newcomb Hohfeld, *Fundamental Legal Conceptions as Applied in Judicial Reasoning* (1919), 36.

But it does mean that rights imply duties. There cannot exist a right without a correlative duty.[10] This is of considerable systematic importance, for it connects the concept of a right with the concept of the 'ought'. Sentences that contain an 'ought' express—individual or general—norms. This leads to the further corollary that there cannot exist rights without norms.

(b) Liberties

One has to distinguish the general concept of liberty and the concept of legal liberty as a special case of general liberty. Liberties, in general, are three-place relations between a liberty-holder, a liberty-obstacle, and a liberty-object.[11] The paradigmatic cases of liberty-holders are natural persons. But it is also possible to talk about the liberties of associations. With respect to the liberty-object the most fundamental distinction is the difference between a choice of action and a single act. An example of a choice of action is the option of professing a certain religion or not. In this case one can speak of a negative liberty. An example of a single act as the object of liberty is the profession of a certain religion. In this case one can speak of a positive liberty.[12] Positive liberty stands at the centre of Kant's moral philosophy: 'The positive concept of freedom is that of the ability of pure reason to be of itself practical. But this is not possible except by the subjection of the maxim of every action to the condition of its qualifying as universal law.'[13] Herewith, positive liberty is defined as the liberty to do what is right or correct, and as not the liberty to do whatever one wishes to do. In the moral life of a person positive liberty can be of great importance. Making positive liberty the basis of the political system, however, has despotic consequences. For this reason, constitutional rights are essentially guarantees of negative liberties. Therefore, only negative liberties shall be considered here.

The liberty-obstacles, too, can be of very different kinds. Economic want and social pressure are examples. In these cases one can speak of economic and social 'unfreedom'. With a view to constitutional rights, legal liberty-obstacles are of special importance. Legal liberty-obstacles consist, first and foremost, of legal prohibitions and legal commands. If *a* is both free from legal prohibitions to express his opinion and free from legal commands to do so, no legal liberty-obstacles exist, and *a* is free to express his opinion. This implies an intrinsic relation between legal liberty and permission. If the expression of *a*'s opinion is neither prohibited nor required, *a* is both permitted to express his opinion and permitted not to do so. For this reason, legal liberty can be defined as the conjunction of the permission to perform an act and the permission to omit it.[14]

[10] Against the triadic construction of rights it might be objected that rights without addressees are possible. An example would be a right to medical aid in cases of serious sickness. This right could acquire the following structure: *RaS*. *RaS* represents what traditionally is designated as '*ius in rem*', in contrast with a '*ius in personam*'. It is, indeed, for reasons of simplicity often sufficient to speak of rights in the sense of relations between a legal subject and an object. If, however, there exists no duty of any addressee at all, in our case, for instance, no duty at all for those who are able to help, then talk about the existence of a right would make no sense. See on this Alexy (n 3), 121.

[11] Ibid 140.

[12] Ibid 140–2.

[13] Immanuel Kant, 'The Metaphysics of Morals' in Mary J. Gregor (ed and trans), *Immanuel Kant. Practical Philosophy* (1996), 375.

[14] If '*P*' is used to express a permission, '*S*' to express the subject matter or object of the permission, and '*L*' to express liberty as a normative modality, legal liberty can be defined as follows:

$$LS = PS \ \& \ P\neg S.$$

It is, of course, possible to transform this scheme into a scheme that expresses a legal relation:

$$LabS = PabS \ \& \ Pab\neg S$$

All constitutional rights that refer to actions of their holders, for instance exercise of religion, expression of opinion, and choice of profession, are liberties in the sense just defined. But if they were only such liberties, they would be poor liberties. A liberty as such does not imply a right to be unhindered in the realization of this freedom. Such a right is a right to something and is fundamentally different from a combination of permissions. In order to obtain a fully-fledged constitutional right the unprotected liberty must be protected by a substantively equivalent right against the state that the state should not prevent the liberty-holder from doing what he is constitutionally free to do.[15] This right against the state—which, again, has to be combined with a power to challenge infringements before the courts—is the core of constitutional rights. For this reason, rights to negative or positive actions on the part of the state, that is, rights to something, are the centre of the theory of constitutional rights. One might call this the 'centre thesis'.

(c) Powers

The centre thesis is true also with respect to powers. Legal powers or competences consist of the normative possibility to change the legal situation by means of a declaration that expresses the (actual or imputed) intention to bring about this change. An example is the power to acquire and to dispose of property. This power is an essential element of the constitutional guarantee of property.[16]

Legal competences are closely related to liberties. They 'add something to the freedom of action of the individual, that he does not have by nature'.[17] Any removal, limitation, or obstruction of powers or competences of an individual is an infringement of the individual's respective constitutional right. The central character of the right to something results from the fact that the decisive question in such cases is whether the right of the individual against the state to omit such infringements is violated. In what follows, therefore, the right to something as a right to either negative or positive action will be in the foreground of the discussion.

II. Constitutional and Human Rights

1. Constitutional Rights

All constitutional rights are rights, but not all rights are constitutional rights. This leads to the question of the specific character, the *differentia specifica*, of constitutional rights. This question concerns the concept and the nature of constitutional rights. Three concepts have to be distinguished: a formal, a procedural, and a substantial concept.

(see on this Alexy (n 3), 145). '*LabS*' is not the same as Hohfeld's 'privilege'. According to Hohfeld a privilege 'is the mere negation of a *duty*' (Hohfeld (n 9), 39). This means that Hohfeld's privilege is nothing else than *Pab¬S*, for *Pab¬S* is equivalent to ¬*OabS*, that is to say, the negation of the (relative) duty of doing *S* (Alexy (n 3), 134–6). For this reason, legal liberty necessarily comprises two privileges, one with a negated subject matter (¬*S*), and one with a non-negated subject matter (*S*).

[15] Alexy (n 3), 149.

[16] Ibid 156–8.

[17] Georg Jellinek, *System der subjektiven öffentlichen Rechte* (2nd edn, 1905), 47 (translation by Robert Alexy).

(a) Formal Concept

A formal concept of constitutional rights is employed if fundamental rights are defined as rights contained in a constitution, or in a certain part of it, for instance in a catalogue of constitutional rights, or as rights endowed by the constitution with special protection, for example a constitutional complaint brought before a constitutional court.[18] Concepts of this kind are useful in many cases. They do not suffice, however, where the question arises of whether a right recorded in a constitution is really a constitutional right and not, for instance, a competence of an instrument of state, or when the problem is posed of whether a right established outside a catalogue of constitutional rights is a constitutional right or not, or when a dispute comes up of whether a right not explicitly endowed with special protection requires such protection. Questions like these cannot be excluded from the beginning, and they cannot be answered on the basis of an exclusively formal concept.

(b) Procedural Concept

The procedural concept of constitutional rights focuses on the institutional problems connected with constitutional rights. Recording constitutional rights in a constitution and granting a court the power of judicial review with respect to all state authority is to limit the power of parliament. In this respect, constitutional rights are an expression of distrust in the democratic process. They are, at the same time, both the basis and the boundary of democracy. Corresponding to this, the procedural concept of constitutional rights holds that constitutional rights are rights which are so important that the decision to protect them cannot be left to simple parliamentary majorities.[19]

The procedural concept, indeed, points out an important feature of constitutional rights, but this concept, too, is not able to grasp the nature of constitutional rights. The reason for this is that the procedural concept, as such, is unable to provide for an answer to the question of which rights are so important that the decision about their protection cannot be left to simple parliamentary majorities. This can be elaborated only within the framework of a substantial concept of constitutional rights.

(c) Substantial Concept

Human rights are at the core of the substantial concept of constitutional rights. Constitutional rights are, as the formal and the procedural concept illustrate, positive, institutionalized rights, that is to say, positive law at the level of the constitution. But this does not suffice to explain their nature. Positivity is but one side of constitutional rights, namely, their real or factual side. Over and above this they also possess an ideal dimension. This might be termed the 'dual nature thesis'. The ideal dimension stems from their connection with human rights qua moral rights. Constitutional rights are rights that have been recorded in a constitution with the intention of transforming human rights into positive law—the intention, in other words, of positivizing human rights.[20] This intention is often an intention actually or subjectively held by the constitutional framers. And, over and above this, it is a claim necessarily raised by those who set down a catalogue of constitutional rights. This claim is a special case of the claim to

[18] Robert Alexy, 'Discourse Theory and Fundamental Rights' in Augustín José Menéndez and Erik Oddvar Eriksen (eds), *Arguing Fundamental Rights* (2006), 15–16.

[19] Alexy (n 3), 297.

[20] Alexy (n 18), 16–17.

correctness necessarily connected with law in general.[21] A catalogue of constitutional rights is correct if and only if it matches the requirements of human rights. All catalogues of constitutional rights, therefore, can be conceived as attempts to transform human rights into positive law. As with attempts generally, attempts to transform human rights into positive law can be successful to a greater or lesser extent. To this extent, the ideal dimension plays a critical role even after the transformation into positive law. This is of pivotal importance for the interpretation and application of constitutional rights. Their wording and the concrete original intent of the framers of the constitution by no means lose their importance. But wording and concrete original intent are relativized by the ideal intent directed to the realization of human rights. For this reason, the dual nature of constitutional rights necessarily requires a certain degree of judicial activism.

2. Human Rights

The dual nature thesis presupposes the existence of human rights. It might be objected that human rights qua moral rights do not exist. A reply to this objection requires an answer to two questions. The first concerns the problem of what it means to say that a human right qua moral rights exists, whereas the second concerns the problem of whether the conditions for the existence of moral rights can be fulfilled.

(a) The Concept of Human Rights

Human rights are, first, moral, second, universal, third, fundamental, and, fourth, abstract rights that, fifth, take priority over all other norms.[22] With respect to the problem of existence only the first of these five defining properties of human rights need be considered: their moral character. Rights, in general, exist if they are valid. The validity of human rights qua moral rights depends on their justifiability and on that alone. Human rights exist if and only if they are justifiable.

(b) The Justification of Human Rights

Theories about the justification of human rights can be classified in many ways. The most fundamental division is that into theories which generally deny the possibility of any justification of human rights and theories which claim that some kind of justification is possible. An example of the sceptic view is Alasdair MacIntyre's thesis that 'there are no such rights, and belief in them is one with belief in witches and in unicorns'.[23] The less or non-sceptic approaches can be divided in eight groups: first, religious, second, intuitionistic, third, consensual, fourth, sociobiological, fifth, utility maximizing or instrumentalistic, sixth, cultural, seventh, explicative, and, eighth, existential approaches. The first six approaches are confronted with serious difficulties.[24] The seventh, the explicative approach, however, is of special interest. This approach attempts to provide a foundation for human rights by making explicit what is necessarily implicit in human practice. Its starting point is the practice of asserting, asking, and arguing, that is to say, the practice of discourse. This practice presupposes rules of discourse that

[21] On the claim to correctness as connected with law in general see Robert Alexy, *The Argument from Injustice. A Reply to Legal Positivism* (Bonnie Litschewski Paulson and Stanley L. Paulson trans, [1992] 2002), 35–9.

[22] Alexy (n 18), 18.

[23] Alasdair MacIntyre, *After Virtue* (2nd edn, 1985), 69.

[24] Alexy (n 18), 19–21.

express the ideas of freedom and equality. Freedom and equality, in turn, are central elements of human rights.

This argument as such, however, does not suffice to justify human rights. Why should we take our discursive capabilities seriously? The answer can be given only within the framework of the eighth approach, the existential approach. We must take our discursive capabilities seriously if we want to take ourselves seriously as, to use an expression of Robert Brandom's, 'discursive creatures',[25] or, in classical terms, as reasonable beings. This is a decision about our identity. The explicative argument can be conceived as objective, the existential argument as subjective. The combination of both is the explicative-existential argument. The explicative-existential argument is objective as well as subjective. As an objective-subjective justification it offers, on the one hand, much less than pure objectivity, but it establishes, on the other, much more than pure subjectivity. Perhaps one can say that it provides enough objectivity to be qualified as a justification. If this is true, human rights exist.

III. The Construction of Constitutional Rights

The concept of constitutional rights depends not only on their general structure as rights and on their relationship to human rights but also on their construction. There are two fundamentally different constructions of constitutional rights: the rule construction and the principles construction.

1. Rules and Principles

The basis of both the rule and the principles construction is the norm-theoretic distinction between rules and principles.[26] Rules are norms that require something definitively. They are *definitive commands*. Their form of application is subsumption. If a rule is valid and applicable, it is definitively required that exactly what it demands be done. If this is done, the rule is complied with; if this is not done, the rule is not complied with. By contrast, principles are norms requiring that something be realized to the greatest extent possible, given the factual and legal possibilities at hand. Thus, principles are *optimization requirements*. As such, they are characterized by the fact that they can be satisfied to varying degrees, and that the appropriate degree of satisfaction depends not only on what is factually possible but also on what is legally possible. Rules aside, the legal possibilities are determined essentially by opposing principles. For this reason, principles, each taken alone, always comprise a merely prima facie requirement. The determination of the appropriate degree of satisfaction of one principle relative to the requirements of another principle is balancing. Thus, balancing is the specific form of the application of principles.

2. Proportionality

The struggle between the rule construction and the principles construction is far more than a discussion of a norm-theoretic problem. It is a debate about the nature of constitutional rights, which has far-reaching consequences for nearly all questions of the doctrine of constitutional rights. For this reason, it is a basic question of constitutionalism.

[25] Robert Brandom, *Articulating Reasons* (2000), 26.
[26] See Alexy (n 3), 47–9.

If the principles construction should prove to be correct, that is to say, if constitutional rights are to be conceived as optimization requirements, constitutional rights are necessarily connected with proportionality analysis.[27] The principle of proportionality, which in the last decades has received ever greater international recognition in the theory and practice of constitutional review,[28] consists of three sub-principles: the principles of suitability, of necessity, and of proportionality in the narrower sense. All three sub-principles—and this is the gist of the matter—express the idea of optimization. Principles qua optimization requirements require optimization relative both to what is factually possible and to what is legally possible.

The principles of suitability and necessity refer to optimization relative to the factual possibilities. The principle of suitability precludes the adoption of means that obstruct the realization of at least one principle without promoting any principle or goal for which it has been adopted. If a means M, adopted in order to promote the principle P_1, is not suitable for this purpose, but obstructs the realization of P_2, then there are no costs either to P_1 or P_2 if M is omitted, but there are costs to P_2 if M is adopted. Thus, P_1 and P_2, taken together, may be realized to a higher degree relative to what is factually possible, if M is abandoned. P_1 and P_2, when *taken together*, that is, as elements of a single system, proscribe the use of M. This shows that the principle of suitability is nothing other than an expression of the idea of Pareto-optimality. One position can be improved without detriment to the other.

The second sub-principle of the principle of proportionality, the principle of necessity, requires that of two means promoting P_1 that are, broadly speaking, equally suitable, the one that interferes less intensively with P_2 has to be chosen. If there exists a less intensively interfering and equally suitable means, one position can be improved at no cost to the other. Under this condition, P_1 and P_2, *taken together*, require that the less intensively interfering means be applied. This is, again, a case of Pareto-optimality.

In the debate about proportionality analysis the first two sub-principles, that is, optimization relative to the factual possibilities, is scarcely contested. This shows that even opponents of balancing do not completely dismiss the idea of optimization. The real difference begins where costs are unavoidable. Costs are unavoidable when principles collide. Then, according to the principles construction, balancing becomes necessary. Balancing is the subject of the third sub-principle of the principle of proportionality, the principle of proportionality in the narrower sense. This third sub-principle, that is, balancing, is the central issue of the proportionality debate.

3. The Rule Construction

The rule construction claims that balancing can be avoided in the application of constitutional rights without loss of rationality. This claim would be justified if the rule construction could propose an alternative to balancing that provides for a higher degree of rationality than balancing—or, at least, as high a degree.

One alternative suggests itself: interpretation. In Germany, Ernst Forsthoff insisted that the problems of the application of constitutional rights should be resolved by means of the traditional canons of interpretation.[29] These canons of interpretation comprise, above all, the word-

[27] On proportionality, see further Chapters 33 and 34.

[28] See eg David M. Beatty, *The Ultimate Rule of Law* (2004); Alec Stone Sweet and Jud Mathews, 'Proportionality Balancing and Global Constitutionalism' (2008) 47 *Columbia Journal of Transnational Law* 72–164.

[29] Ernst Forsthoff, *Rechtsstaat im Wandel. Verfassungsrechtliche Abhandlungen 1954–1973* (2nd edn, 1976), 173.

ing of the constitutional rights provisions, the intentions of those who framed the constitution, and the systematic context of the provision being interpreted. There are, indeed, numerous cases that can be resolved without any problem simply by appeal to wording, intent, or systematic context, that is to say, by subsumption or classification connected with interpretation, just as anywhere else in the law. Hearing the Rolling Stones in a library, for instance, is not an exercise of religious freedom even if someone believes that this kind of music is the highest source of inspiration. But as soon as the case becomes more complicated, the rule construction causes problems. Several constitutions guarantee freedom of religion without any limiting clause. If one takes the wording seriously and if a particular religious faith requires for religious reasons that apostates be killed, then this killing must be classified as a practice within one's religion. Naturally, adherents of the rule construction will not arrive at the result that killing required by a religious faith is allowed. But they have difficulties justifying this result. Not classifying the killing as a religious act would contradict the wording of the constitutional rights provision. For this reason, the rule construction has to explain why the religious act is a forbidden religious act. The intent of the framers of the constitution may be offered as a reason. What else, however, other than the protection of life and the religious freedom of the apostates should this argument refer to? If the argument refers to these rights, the protection of life and the religious freedom of the apostates, then the argument boils down to something ultimately based on balancing. The right to live together with the religious freedom of the apostates is given precedence over the religious freedom of those who want to kill the apostates for religious reasons. If the result of balancing were in all cases as clear as it is here, an elaborated theory of balancing might, indeed, be of some theoretical interest, but it would not have very much practical importance. But there are many cases in which the solution of collisions between constitutional rights as well as collisions between constitutional rights and collective goods are far more difficult. Here, the principles construction has the advantage of directly addressing the issue.

No less serious are the problems of the rule construction in cases in which constitutional rights are connected with a limiting clause. In Germany, a limiting clause, namely, that, 'These rights may only be interfered with on a statutory basis',[30] is attached to the right to life and to bodily integrity. If one follows the rule construction and takes these provisions literally, the limiting clause makes possible any interference with life and bodily integrity as long as the interference is based on a statute. One may attempt to avoid this by adding more rules, for instance, by applying a rule that forbids infringing on the core content of a constitutional right. Even here, however, the legislature remains completely free at every point beneath the threshold of the core content. Moreover, it is highly unlikely that the core content can be determined at all without resorting to balancing.[31]

A rule construction orientated towards wording, intent, and systematic context can be assigned to positivism. The rule construction, however, need not be positivistic. A non-positivistic alternative to balancing is proposed by Ronald Dworkin. According to Dworkin, striking a balance is a matter of 'asking whether the benefits of our policy outweigh its costs to us'.[32] This is a kind of economic calculation.[33] The application of the constitutional right is said to concern 'the very different question of what morality requires, even at the expense of our own

[30] See *Grundgesetz für die Bundesrepublik Deutschland* (German Basic Law), Art 2(2)(3).

[31] Alexy (n 3), 192–6.

[32] Ronald Dworkin, *Is Democracy Possible Here? Principles for a New Political Debate* (2006), 27.

[33] In this direction points also Carl Schmitt, 'Die Tyrannei der Werte' in *Säkularisation und Utopie. Ebracher Studien. Ernst Forsthoff zum 65. Geburtstag* (1967), 39.

interests'.[34] With this argument, Dworkin presupposes that there exists an intrinsic relation between balancing and interests, a relation that amounts to the thesis that each and every instance of balancing is a balancing of interests. This, however, must be contested. It is, indeed, possible to strike a balance in a conflict of interests. But this does not imply that balancing is possible only between interests and not between rights. The principles construction tries to show that balancing rights is possible. Still another point in Dworkin's argument has to be rejected. Dworkin conceives balancing and moral arguments as opposites. The reply to this is that balancing rights is a form of moral argument.

4. The Principles Construction

The principles construction attempts to resolve the problems of the rule construction by establishing a necessary connection between constitutional rights and balancing. Many authors have raised objections to this approach. The most serious objection is the irrationality objection. It has been prominently articulated by Jürgen Habermas and Bernhard Schlink. Habermas's central point is that there exist 'no rational standards' for balancing: 'Because there are no rational standards for this, weighing takes place either arbitrarily or unreflectively, according to customary standards and hierarchies.'[35] Where Habermas speaks about arbitrariness and unreflected customs, Schlink employs the concepts of subjectivity and decision: balancing is, 'in the final analysis, subjective and decisionistic'.[36]

The irrationality objection can be rejected if balancing can be established as a rational form of legal and moral argument. This is, indeed, the case. The basis of balancing is a rule that can be called the 'Law of Balancing'. This rule states:

> The greater the degree of non-satisfaction of, or detriment to, one principle, the greater must be the importance of satisfying the other.[37]

The Law of Balancing excludes, inter alia, an intensive interference with principle P_1 that is justified only by a low importance assigned to the satisfaction of the colliding principle P_2. Such a solution would not be an optimization of P_1 *together with* P_2.

The Law of Balancing is to be found, in different formulations, nearly everywhere in constitutional adjudication. It expresses a central feature of balancing and is of great practical importance. If one wishes to achieve a precise and complete analysis of the structure of balancing, the Law of Balancing has, however, to be elaborated further. The result of such a further elaboration is the Weight Formula.[38]

The Weight Formula defines the weight of a principle P_i in a concrete case, that is, the concrete weight of P_i relative to a colliding principle P_j ($W_{i,j}$), as the quotient of, first, the product of the intensity of the interference with P_i (I_i) and the abstract weight of P_i (W_i) and the degree of reliability of the empirical assumptions concerning what the measure in question means for

[34] Dworkin (n 32), 27.

[35] Jürgen Habermas, *Between Facts and Norms. Contributions to a Discourse Theory of Law and Democracy* (William Rehg trans, [1992] 1996), 259.

[36] Bernhard Schlink, 'Der Grundsatz der Verhältnismäßigkeit' in Peter Badura and Horst Dreier (eds), *Festschrift 50 Jahre Bundesverfassungsgericht*, vol 2 (2001), 461 (translation by Robert Alexy).

[37] Alexy (n 3), 102.

[38] Robert Alexy, 'On Balancing and Subsumption' (2003) 16 *Ratio Juris* 443–8; Robert Alexy, 'The Weight Formula' in Jerzy Stelmach, Bartosz Brożek, and Wojciech Załuski (eds) *Studies in the Philosophy of Law. Frontiers of the Economic Analysis of Law* (2007), 9–27.

the non-realization of P_i (R_i), and, second, the product of the corresponding values with respect to P_j, now related to the realization of P_j. It runs as follows:

$$W_{i,j} = \frac{I_i \cdot W_i \cdot R_i}{I_j \cdot W_j \cdot R_j}$$

Now to talk about quotients and products is sensible only in the presence of numbers. This is the problem of graduation. The question of graduation is a central problem of the theory of balancing, for balancing presupposes scales.[39] At exactly this point the distinction between continuous and discrete scales is of pivotal importance. Continuous scales run over an infinite number of points between, for instance, 0 and 1. The crude nature of law excludes their application. Discrete scales are defined by the fact that between their points no further points exist. Balancing can begin as soon as one has a scale with two values, say, light and serious. In constitutional law a triadic scale is often used, which works with the values light (*l*), moderate (*m*), and serious (*s*). There are various possibilities in representing these values by numbers.[40] If one chooses a geometric sequence like 2^0, 2^1, and 2^2, it becomes possible to represent the fact that the power of principles increases overproportionally with increasing intensity of interference. This is the basis of an answer to the reproach that principles theory leads to an unacceptable weakening of constitutional rights. If the concrete weight ($W_{i,j}$) of P_i is greater than 1, P_i precedes P_j, if it is smaller than 1, P_j precedes P_i. If, however, the concrete weight ($W_{i,j}$) is 1, a stalemate exists. In this case, it is both permitted to perform the measure in question and to omit it. This means that the state, especially the legislator, has discretion.[41] This is of utmost importance for a reply to the reproach that principles theory leads to an overconstitutionalization.[42]

The objection has been raised to the Weight Formula that it 'expresses the ideal of a precise, one might say mathematically precise, science',[43] and that this is 'a methodological chimera'.[44] This objection rests on a misconception of the role of the Weight Formula. Its purpose is not to reduce legal reasoning to calculation, but to grasp those elements that play a role in balancing and to see how these elements are connected. The numbers that have to be substituted for the variables represent propositions, for instance the proposition 'The interference with the freedom of expression is serious'. This proposition has to be justified in order to establish its claim to correctness and this can only be done by argument. In this way, the Weight Formula is intrinsically connected with legal discourse. It does not claim to substitute calculation for discourse, but attempts to lend to discourse a rational structure.

The abstract explanation of the principle of proportionality in the narrower sense shall be illustrated by means of a case. The case in question is a decision of the German Federal Constitutional Court that concerns the classic conflict between freedom of expression and

[39] See Aharon Barak, *The Judge in a Democracy* (2006), 166: 'One cannot balance without a scale'.

[40] On this issue see Alexy, 'The Weight Formula' (n 38), 20–3.

[41] Alexy (n 3), 408, 410–14.

[42] The discretion in case of stalemate can be termed 'structural discretion'. A second kind of discretion is epistemic discretion. Epistemic discretion is incorporated in the Weight Formula by means of R_i and R_j, the variables referring to the degree of reliability of the empirical assumptions on the basis of which judgments about the intensity of interferences rest. See on this ibid 414–25.

[43] Matthias Jestaedt, 'The Doctrine of Balancing—its Strengths and Weaknesses' in Matthias Klatt (ed), *Institutionalized Reason* (2012), 163.

[44] Ibid 165.

personality right.[45] A widely published satirical magazine, *Titanic*, described a paraplegic reserve officer who had successfully carried out his responsibilities, having been called to active duty, first as 'born Murderer' and in a later edition as a 'cripple'. The Düsseldorf Higher Regional Court of Appeal ruled against *Titanic* in an action brought by the officer and ordered the magazine to pay damages in the amount of DM 12,000. *Titanic* brought a constitutional complaint. The Federal Constitutional Court undertook 'case-specific balancing'[46] between freedom of expression of those associated with the magazine (P_1) and the officer's general personality right (P_2). To this end the intensity of interference with these rights was determined, and they were placed in relationship to each other. The judgment in damages was treated a 'lasting'[47] or *serious* (*s*) interference (I_1) with freedom of expression. If the Court had confined itself simply to qualifying the interference as serious, rational argument would be missing. This seems to be the picture of balancing that stands behind the irrationality objection. But the Court gives reasons for its assessment of the interference as serious. Its main argument is that awarding damages could affect the future willingness of those producing the magazine to carry out their work in the way they have done previously. To this it adds that if exaggerations and alienations were not allowed as stylistic devices, satirical magazines would have to give up their characteristic features.[48] This can be conceived as rational argumentation. In a next step the description 'born Murderer' was placed in the context of the satire published by *Titanic*. Here several persons had been described as having a surname at birth in a 'recognizably humorous' way, from 'puns to silliness'.[49] This excludes an 'isolated assessment' of the description 'born Murderer' by taking it 'literally'.[50] The interference with the personality right was thus treated as having a *moderate* (*m*), perhaps even a *light* or minor intensity (I_2). Even those who do not agree with this result must concede that this rating of the intensity of interference with P_2 is backed by reasonable arguments. More cannot be required in law. The two assessments of intensity completed the first part of the decision. In order to justify an award of damages, which is a serious (*s*) interference with the constitutional right to freedom of expression (P_1), the interference with the right to personality (P_2), which was supposed to be compensated for by damages, would have had to have been at least also serious (*s*). But according to the assessment of the Court, it was not. It was at best moderate (*m*), perhaps even merely light (*l*). This meant that the interference with the freedom of expression was, according to the Law of Balancing and, with it, the Weight Formula,[51] disproportional and, therefore, unconstitutional.

Matters, however, were different in that part of the case where the officer had been called a 'cripple'. According to the Court, this counted as 'serious harm to his personality right'.[52]

[45] Decisions of the Federal Constitutional Court, BVerfGE 86, 1. On freedom of expression more generally, see Chapter 42.

[46] BVerfGE 86, 1 (11).

[47] Ibid 1 (10).

[48] Ibid.

[49] Ibid 1 (11).

[50] Ibid 1 (12).

[51] It is of interest that the Court refers only to the intensity of interference on both sides (I_i, I_j). This makes sense of the assumption that the Court attributes the same abstract weight (W_i, W_j) to the freedom of expression (P_1) and the right to personality (P_2). Such silent graduations are to be observed in many cases. For the Weight Formula this means that W_i and W_j can be reduced. The same seems to apply to the degree of reliability of the empirical assumptions (R_i, R_j). This shows that the Weight Formula is an instrument that provides not only a description of what a court has explicitly presented but also a reconstruction of what it has implicitly assumed. In this respect, the Weight Formula can play not only a reconstructive but also a critical role.

[52] BVerfGE 86, 1 (13).

This assessment was justified by the fact that describing a severely disabled person in public as a 'cripple' is generally taken, these days, to be 'humiliating' and to express a 'lack of respect'.[53] Such public humiliation and lack of respect reaches and undermines the very dignity of the victim. The graduation of the intensity of interference is, in this way, again backed by reasons. And—this is a reply to Dworkin's separation of balancing and morality—these reasons are moral reasons. The result is stalemate. The serious (*s*) interference (I_1) with the freedom of expression (P_1) was countered by the great (*s*) importance (I_2) accorded to the protection of personality. Consequently, the Court came to the conclusion that it could see 'no flaw in the balancing to detriment of freedom of expression'[54] in the decision of the Düsseldorf Higher Regional Court of Appeal. *Titanic*'s constitutional complaint was thus only justified to the extent that it related to damages for the description 'born Murderer'. As far as the description 'cripple' was concerned, it was unjustified.

The *Titanic* decision shows that balancing is a test of whether an interference with a right is justified. This can be generalized. All constitutional rights are rights against unjustified infringements.[55] The most rational way of distinguishing justified and unjustified infringements is proportionality analysis. This leads to a necessary connection between constitutional rights and proportionality. The claim to correctness, necessarily connected with constitutional rights as with law in general, requires that the application of constitutional rights be as rational as possible. The highest possible degree of rationality can be achieved only by proportionality analysis. In this way, the claim to correctness establishes a necessary connection between constitutional rights and proportionality. This implies that proportionality is included in the very concept of constitutional rights.

Bibliography

Robert Alexy, *A Theory of Constitutional Rights* (Julian Rivers trans, [1985] 2002)

John Austin, *Lectures on Jurisprudence or the Philosophy of Positive Law*, vol 1 (5th edn, 1911)

Aharon Barak, *The Judge in a Democracy* (2006)

David M. Beatty, *The Ultimate Rule of Law* (2004)

Jeremy Bentham, *Of Laws in General* (H.L.A. Hart ed, 1970)

Isaiah Berlin, *Four Essays on Liberty* (1969)

Ronald Dworkin, *Is Democracy Possible Here? Principles for a New Political Debate* (2006)

Jürgen Habermas, *Between Facts and Norms. Contributions to a Discourse Theory of Law and Democracy* (William Rehg trans, [1992] 1996)

H.L.A. Hart, 'Legal Rights' in H.L.A. Hart, *Essays on Bentham. Studies in Jurisprudence and Political Theory* (1982)

Wesley Newcomb Hohfeld, *Fundamental Legal Conceptions as Applied in Judicial Reasoning* (1919)

Neil MacCormick, 'Rights in Legislation' in P.M.S. Hacker and Joseph Raz (eds), *Law, Morality, and Society. Essays in Honour of H.L.A. Hart* (1977)

Alec Stone Sweet and Jud Mathews, 'Proportionality Balancing and Global Constitutionalism' (2008) 47 *Columbia Journal of Transnational Law* 72

[53] Ibid.

[54] Ibid.

[55] See on this Mattias Kumm, 'Alexy's Theory of Constitutional Rights and the Problem of Judicial Review' in Matthias Klatt (ed), *Institutionalized Reason* (2012), 213–17.

CHAPTER 14

CONSTITUTIONS AND THE PUBLIC/PRIVATE DIVIDE

FRANK I. MICHELMAN

Cambridge, MA

LIKE an *ostinato* motif, the theme of public/private plays and replays in the constitutional law of many countries. Or does it? No doubt, as we shall see, the figuration recurs in countless doctrinal classifications in constitutional law. But is it truly all the same idea, each repetition the sign of one and the same fixture in constitutional-legal thought and discourse?

This chapter begins with a broad-brush survey of the doctrinal play of public/private in constitutional law. It then turns to the question of a public/private 'ghost' presiding from behind the scenes over all the public/private coding we meet on stage—shaping it, guiding it, imbuing it with point and purpose: some master spirit, then, whose sundry outcroppings in institutional design and doctrinal construction could be expected both to vary and to converge in interestingly describable and classifiable ways across instances of the legal forms and practices we label as 'constitutional'.[1]

[1] This chapter is mainly concerned with public/private divides at the doctrinal level in constitutional law. On institutional-design effects, see Frank I. Michelman, 'The Interplay of Constitutional and Ordinary

I. Public/Private (and Allied) Classifications in Constitutional-Legal Doctrine: A Brief Survey

1. Types of Laws

We start with two crosscutting divisions-in-kind among laws or bodies of law.

In Table 14.1, the two columns divide laws according to whether they are specially directed to the acts and relations of the state or government or rather are directed widely to acts and relations of persons and groups in society at large. The two rows divide laws according to whether they are or are not meant to control all other lawmaking, as fixed and enduring commitments of the regnant constitutional order. Note that our terminology is stipulative and may not exactly match variant local usages. Depending on the place and context, professional usage may sometimes class major regulatory legislation for the social sphere as 'public' law. Laws may be classed as 'constitutional' when they fall into any of cells I, II, or III. Cell IV includes what is often called the 'general' or 'background' or 'common' law (in civilian systems, it would be mainly the law of the Civil Code). The term 'ordinary law' will typically refer to laws in cell III as well those in cell IV.[2]

As the table shows, there is no necessitating logic of correlation across our two axes of differentiation of laws. Among a given system's laws undoubtedly directed to a governmental ('public') sphere of application, certainly some but likely not all will be classed as basic ('constitutional') in depth and force. Conversely, among a system's laws undoubtedly received as basic in depth and force, some will very likely reach beyond the governmental to the social

Table 14.1 Two Categorizations of Laws

		by sphere of application	
		'public law' specifically directed to state and government	*'private law' generally applicable across society*
by normative depth and force	*basic law fixed and controlling*	I. basic law for the state sphere	II. ? basic law for the social sphere ?
	ordinary law variable and controlled	III. ordinary law for the state sphere	IV. ordinary law for the social sphere

Jurisdiction' in Rosalind Dixon and Tom Ginsburg (eds), *Research Handbook in Comparative Constitutional Law* (2011), 278ff.

[2] I note here, and reserve for brief discussion later, the possibility that prevailing ideas in some countries would reject the Table 14.1 schema more or less in its entirety. See Section III.2 below.

sphere—possibly just a few[3] or possibly quite a few,[4] but the number almost certainly will not be none at all.[5]

Logical independence does not, however, equate to an absence of tendencies-in-practice toward correlation across our table's intersecting axes of division. To the contrary, cell II in our table—the space of so-called 'horizontal' application of basic-law guarantees—is seemingly everywhere felt to be an exceptionally contested and problematic space. Some greater or lesser pull towards evacuation of that space, leaving application of the basic laws more or less restricted to the state sector, is a commonplace expectation of constitutional lawyers around the globe.[6] The cause, however, plainly is not conceptual; it must rather be political: the greater or lesser prevalence in a society's decisive quarters of some combination of (1) a special commitment to freedom of choice of aims and activities by persons and groups in society, (2) a correlative reluctance to extend throughout society the same set of restraints we devise for the state viewed as the monopolist of lawful force, the sole power from the reach of whose command there is virtually no exit; and perhaps, along with those, (3) a belief in the superior ability of on-the-spot parliaments—as compared with rarely assembled constitutional framers—to work out contextually responsive, aptly fair, and freedom-optimizing solutions to societal conflicts, at least as long as the parliament acts under the effective control of good basic laws (a bill of rights). It seems it must always be some combination of such beliefs that will argue, more or less persuasively depending on the time and place, toward confinement of the application of basic laws to the state sector, leaving non-state operations to be controlled by the more concretized processes of occasional, ordinary lawmaking.[7]

2. Object Fields: Powers of Decision

We come, then, to public/private division not of laws but of object-fields. An object-field is a class of items (it might be actions, actors, powers, functions, purposes, concerns, 'spheres') on whose characterization as X or not-X depends the legal system's choice of which of two or more arguably applicable rules or doctrines to apply to a case. In any system that differentiates bodies of public and private *law* in the manner of Table 14.1's two columns, we must expect also to encounter public/private characterization in at least one object-field, simply because the system requires some way of delimiting the respective scopes of application of the two types of laws.

[3] In the United States, eg, extension of the Constitution's prohibition of slavery (US Constitution, Amendment 13) to legally optional private sector relationships registers as an exception from a general rule that only 'state' actors and actions are subject to control by constitutional requirements and prohibitions. See eg *Jones v Alfred H Mayer Co* 392 US 409, 438–9 (1968); *Civil Rights Cases* 109 US 3, 20–1 (1883).

[4] See eg South African Constitution, s 8(2) (providing for the binding effect of bill-of-rights guarantees on 'natural persons' to the extent appropriate in view of 'the nature of the right and ... any duty imposed by the right').

[5] See Stephen Gardbaum, 'The Myth and Reality of American Constitutional Exceptionalism' (2008) 107 *Michigan Law Review* 391, 431–44 (comparing results from 'state action' rules in the United States and Canada with results from the German doctrines of 'third party' and 'radiating' effect, and finding US results to approach those in Germany).

[6] See generally the papers collected in András Sajó and Renata Uitz (eds), *The Constitution in Private Relations* (2005).

[7] See Larry Alexander, 'The Public/Private Distinction and Constitutional Limits on Private Power' (1993) 10 *Constitutional Commentary* 361, 372, 374–7; Charles Fried, 'The New First Amendment Jurisprudence: A Threat to Liberty' (1992) 59 *University of Chicago Law Review* 225, 234–7.

Table 14.2 Public/Private Classifications of Powers of Decision ['→' = tends towards, argues for, in constitutional-legal doctrine.]

	decision power classed as		
	of the state	*not of the state*	
'verticality'	→ certainly controlled by both governmental ('public') and basic ('constitutional') law and	→ possibly shielded from basic law and	'state action' doctrines
official immunity vs. rule of law	possibly shielded from civil ('private') law	certainly controlled by civil ('private') law	

Table 14.2 depicts a doctrinal practice of public/private characterization on a field called 'powers of decision', but terms such as 'actor' and 'action' might have served as well.

Table 14.2 shows two possible lines of doctrinal consequence from characterization of a power as belonging or not to the state. First, state powers will almost certainly be subjected to control by whatever laws in a system are deemed basic, whereas non-state powers may be shielded from such control.[8] Secondly, doctrines of state or official immunity may shield state powers from some parts of the general civil ('private') law—say, of delict.[9] Both kinds of shielding doctrines may be contentious. Below, we will notice how such contention may solidify into wholesale resistance to the very idea of a differentiation, in constitutional-legal discourse, between 'state' and 'non-state' powers.[10] But of course contention in relation to the shielding doctrines may also work at retail, focusing on where and how to draw the lines dividing one or another field between public and private. Thus, we run into controversies over whether an act of one or another parastatal or 'hybrid' organization is to be classed as 'of the state' for purposes of subjecting that act to the full, formal control of a constitutional bill of rights, and whether conduct by a private sector organization of an assertedly 'inherently public' social operation should call into play basic-law principles whose application is nominally restricted to state deciders.[11]

[8] Extension of basic-law controls to non-state powers tends everywhere to be a matter of contention and possibly of uncertainty and confusion. See generally Sajó and Uitz (n 6); Stephen Gardbaum, 'The "Horizontal Effect" of Constitutional Rights' (2003) 102 *Michigan Law Review* 387ff.

[9] On doctrines of official immunity in relation to other public/private doctrines in constitutional law, see Christopher D. Stone, 'Corporate Vices and Corporate Virtues: Do Public/Private Distinctions Matter?' (1983) 130 *University of Pennsylvania Law Review* 1441ff.

[10] See Section II.4 below.

[11] For engagement in such controversies, including exemplary case decisions, see eg Daphne Barak-Erez, 'Civil Rights in the Privatized State: A Comparative View' (1999) 28 *Anglo-American Law Review* 503, 506–7 (approving preservation of public/private in constitutional law while calling for a 'functional' not 'formal' approach to drawing the lines); David A. Strauss, 'State Action After the Civil Rights Era' (1993) 10 *Constitutional Commentary* 409ff (proposing a relaxed application of constitutional guarantees to subdivisional state institutions, such as universities and municipalities, that operate in fields open to competition).

3. Object Fields: Matters to be Decided

In Table 14.2, above, public/private coding occurs on the field of decision-powers. In Table 14.3, by contrast, coding occurs on the field of matters at issue or at stake in a legal dispute. Table 14.2 looks at choices *between* public-constitutional and private-ordinary law as decisive for a given case, showing how characterization of a power as state or non-state may bear on such choices. Table 14.3, by contrast, looks at choices *within the body of public constitutional law*, showing how characterization of a dispute's bone of contention as predominantly public (social) or private (personal) can affect constitutional-legal conclusions regarding the state's regulatory competence and obligation.

Table 14.3 employs the term 'matters to be decided' quite sweepingly. The 'matter' might be a line of conduct or activity (say, a person's conduct of her intimate relationships),[12] or it might be control over a space or locale (eg a person's home), or over an item of belonging (eg of personal memorabilia), or information (eg a medical record).[13]

Much familiar constitutional law imposes limits on the permissible objectives of state coercion. Those limits often include a requirement that the state's objectives meet some threshold test of joint or collective concern to the public at large (thus, a 'public' purpose or use), so that an objective's failure to meet the test precludes its pursuit by coercive state powers of taxation, regulation, or expropriation.[14] As shown in column B of Table 14.3, such a negative 'ultra vires' conclusion can find doctrinal expression in terms of failure to meet a test of 'rational basis', 'legality', or 'principles of fundamental justice'.[15]

Column C represents a set of doctrines providing a special shield—typically expressed as a demand for an exceptionally urgent justification—against state control of individual and group pursuits classed as 'core' components of personal liberty (autonomy, privacy, dignity).

Table 14.3 Public/Private Classifications of Dominant Concerns in Matters to be Decided ['→' = tends towards, argues for, in constitutional-legal doctrine.]

	matter to be decided classed as	
A	*B*	*C*
intensely public (social) concern	***threshold general public concern***	***intensely private (personal) concern***
→ mandatory retention or assumption of control by state authorities	→ permissible exercise of (proportionate) state coercion	→ specially shielded against the state's coercive regulation or intrusion
anti-delegation doctrines	doctrines of ultra vires ('legality'), 'rational basis', 'fundamental justice'	doctrines of strongly guarded 'fundamental' rights of personality and dignity
	↕ ↕	↕ ↕
	'proportionate	justification'

[12] See Chapter 46. [13] See Chapter 46. [14] See Chapters 33 and 34, and Chapter 44.

[15] See eg *R v Malmo-Levine; R v Caine* [2003] 3 SCR 571 (Canada) paras 90, 96–9, 131, 135 (construing the phrase 'principles of fundamental justice' as used in the Canadian Charter of Rights and Freedoms, s 7).

These doctrines aim not at preventing the state from stepping into matters devoid of public import—that being the business of the column B ultra vires doctrines—but rather at blocking state intrusions into matters deemed intensely personal despite the assumed probity of the state's reasons for intruding.[16] In some systems, doctrinal material gives expression to this difference in motivations by prescribing a categorically stiffer test of justification for laws found to intrude into the core liberties of column C than for those questioned only on the ultra vires grounds of column B.[17] In others systems, the difference may be blurred by a blanket resort to a test of proportional justification for all coercive state measures.[18]

At the opposite end of the spectrum from column C lies column A. Where column C represents a strong constraint *against* state control, designation of a matter as intensely public or social, hence falling into column A (eg the conduct of public elections, primary and secondary education, street policing), may bring into play a directly contrary constraint on the state's relinquishment of control over that matter to non-state authorities.[19]

Of course, both of these policy-limiting doctrines, like the power-ownership doctrines of Table 14.2, are often politically contentious. Within countries, we can observe shifts over time of controversial matters from one space to another in apparent harness with changing political tides; for example, in the United States, a shift of the matter of domestic violence from

[16] See Frances Olsen, 'Constitutional Law: Feminist Critiques of the Public/Private Distinction' (1993) 10 *Constitutional Commentary* 319, 320 (taking note of the difference).

[17] See Chapters 33 and 34, and Chapter 44.

[18] See eg *Beit Sourik Village Council v Government of Israel*, HCJ 2056/04, paras 57–62 (Israel, 2004) (finding lack of proportionate justification for location of one stretch of Israel's 'separation fence' in the occupied territories, in view of grave disruptive effects on the lives and livelihoods of inhabitants, but without doubting either the probity of the state's objectives or the substantial serviceability to those objectives of the state's chosen path for the fence).

We should note a further ramification of the impulse to shield core personal freedoms from collective control. Regard for private freedom of choice appears to be a chief ground of reluctance to extend bill-of-rights controls 'horizontally' to cover acts and relations of ordinary citizens. To that concern, a standard rejoinder is an assurance that doctrines allowing for justification for prima facie bill-of-rights infringements (as by proportionality review) will dependably save most private actions from ultimate constitutional-legal liability. See eg Paul A. Brest, 'State Action and Liberal Theory: A Casenote on *Flagg Brothers v Brooks*' (1982) 130 *University of Pennsylvania Law Review* 1296, 1323–34.

[19] See eg three chapters in Jody Freeman and Martha Minow (eds), *Government by Contract: Outsourcing and American Democracy* (2009); Gillian E. Metzger, 'Private Delegations, Due Process, and the Duty to Supervise' in ibid 291–309; Paul R. Verkuil, 'Outsourcing and the Duty to Govern' in ibid 310–34; and Laura A. Dickinson, 'Public Values/Private Contract' in ibid 335–59; Jody Freeman, 'The Private Role in Public Governance' (2000) 75 *NYU Law Review* 543, 574–91.

Constitutional law provides a congeries of public/private-coded doctrines in response to the same basic impulse. These include the 'essential state function' branch of 'state action' doctrine, doctrines of direct and indirect horizontal application of bill-of-rights guarantees, doctrines imposing a 'protective function' on the state, and, arguably, the inclusion in constitutional law of positive socio-economic guarantees. For consideration of the distinctions and connections among these doctrinal types, see Freeman, above; Gardbaum (n 8); Dieter Grimm, 'The Protective Function of the State' in Georg Nolte (ed), *European and US Constitutionalism* (2005), 137ff; Mark Tushnet, 'State Action, Social Welfare Rights, and the Judicial Role: Some Comparative Observations' (2002) 3 *Chicago Journal of International Law* 435ff; Richard S. Kay, 'The State Action Doctrine, The Public–Private Distinction, and the Independence of Constitutional Law' (1993) 10 *Constitutional Commentary* 329, 330–2. For the purposes of this chapter, it suffices to note the functional overlaps among these doctrinal strategies for ensuring the effectuation of constitutional or 'public' values in the law.

Constitutional controls on outsourcing may also draw on separation-of-powers ideas concerning reservation of powers designated 'legislative' or 'executive' to appropriate branches of government. See eg Catherine M. Donnelly, *Delegation of Governmental Power to Private Parties: A Comparative Perspective* (2007), 117–63 (examining such doctrines in the United States, the European Union. and the United Kingdom).

presumptively off-limits to government (space C in Table 14.3) to presumptively a mandatory topic of regulation (space A).[20] Across countries, we observe synchronous disagreements over placement—for example, of the matter of early-stage abortion choice: today in Germany, that matter lies in space A, while in Canada it lies at a junction of spaces B and C.[21]

4. The Question of the 'Reality' of Public/Private

Our survey confirms what logic suggests: a legal system cannot institute a differentiation between 'public' and 'private' *laws* without also supplying some doctrine or doctrines of field-division by which the respective scopes of application of the two types can be ascertained. But must it, then, be one doctrine or may it be several, unified by nothing beyond mere verbiage? Is public/private, after all, a *real* distinction?

In US constitutional law, we find 'public/private' used to classify actors, functions, purposes, concerns, information, uses, spaces and belongings, activities and relationships, 'forums', 'figures', and more. But since each occurrence, each usage, is specific to some discrete context of dispute,[22] a question remains about a convergence of all of them on a unified, common core of meaning or reference. They might, after all, just be labels of convenience opportunistically plastered on sundry judgments made for sundry reasons on sundry topics. (Suppose we had one law for things 'high' and another for things 'low', and so we found the judges dividing the fields according to ordinary speech: high price (expensive), high temperature (warm), high voice (treble), high volume (loud), high dudgeon (angry), high purpose (noble), high-minded (pure).)

Our question here is not so much whether there *is* any common semantic essence that ties together all these usages of public/private, as whether we have any reason for presuming that there is or supposing that there might be. All we have in hand so far is a set of observations suggesting that the legal practice of one or another country can more or less manage with public/private verbiage to delimit, in sundry topical contexts, the fields and modes of application of constitutional law. We do not yet have a reason to suppose any deep, semantic unification of these sundry sorting practices across contexts or across countries.

What type of consideration could supply such a reason? How about detection of a common germ of public/private, ensconced from the start in the very thought of a legal constitution or constitutional law?[23]

II. The 'Ghost' Conjecture

1. 'Dualist' Constitutionalism

Lying just outside or at the limit of any possible practice of positive legal ordering—so we are advised by highly influential, jurisprudential teachings—there must always be found a soci-

[20] See eg Jeannie Suk, *At Home in the Law: How the Domestic Violence Revolution is Transforming Policy* (2009), 9–54; Reva B. Siegel, '"The Rule of Love": Wife-Beating as Prerogative and Privacy' (1996) 105 *Yale Law Journal* 2117ff.

[21] Relevant materials are collected in Vicki C. Jackson and Mark Tushnet, *Comparative Constitutional Law* (2nd edn, 2006), 74–136.

[22] Thus, classification of 'forums' and 'figures' as public or private occurs in US doctrine on constitutional protection of freedom of expression. See eg Laurence H. Tribe, *American Constitutional Law* (2nd edn, 1988), 873–86 (figures), 986–1009 (forums).

[23] See Section II.2 below.

ety's convergence on an implicit, unwritten rule for the formation of laws to control the further production of laws.[24] If so, then every possible practice of positive legal ordering may be said to have, in that sense, its constitution.[25] Of course, not every such practice purports to sort its total corpus of express 'positive' laws between the two layers of basic and subordinate, 'constitutional' and 'ordinary'.[26] But still many do, no doubt including most of those of chief interest to users of this volume. Let us use the term 'dualist' to designates the ones that do.[27]

By our definition, a system will be classed as dualist as long as it sustains any distinct component of relatively fixed, positive 'higher' law whose demands other law is required to heed, even if that component is quite narrowly drawn. Imagine, then, that the substantive content of a country's positive higher law consists of the single mandate that state functionaries shall not engage in intentional acts of race-based discrimination. If that requirement is held controlling on ordinary law and those engaged in making it, the system is dualist. Of course, the system also is dualist if the higher law prohibition on race-based discrimination is written in terms that control private-on-private as well as state-on-private discrimination.

2. Inspirations and Implications of Dualism

Our conjecture posits the fixture in, specifically, *dualist* constitutional thought of an abstract and formal idea—'ghost'—of a public/private divide on the field of legal operations. According to a standard view, here very loosely recounted, the dualist differentiation of constitutional from ordinary law takes shape historically in response to political demands for the simultaneous achievement of four effects. These demands compose a conjectural set of 'proto-liberal' inspirations (as we may call them) for the rise of dualist constitutionalism when and where it did arise, in Europe in the eighteenth century (although, of course, the proto-liberal antecedents go further back than that).[28] They are: *first*, a demand for effective imposition, on powers that form and roam in society, of peace- and order-keeping by means of the issuance of positive laws backed by sufficient force (a legally ordered society); which implies, *second*, for each self-standing territory or population, the concentration in a single institutional nexus (the

[24] See H.L.A. Hart, *The Concept of Law* (2nd edn, 1994), 106–8 ('ultimate rule of recognition'); Joseph Raz, 'On the Authority and Interpretation of Constitutions: Some Preliminaries' in Larry Alexander (ed), *Constitutionalism: Philosophical Foundations* (1998), 152, 161–2 ('rule of recognition').

[25] See Frank I. Michelman, 'What Do Constitutions Do That Statutes Don't (Legally Speaking)' in Richard W. Bauman and Tsvi Kahana (eds), *The Least Examined Branch: The Role of Legislatures in the Constitutional State* (2006), 273, 285–6.

[26] For a classic expression of an opposite 'one law' conception, see Albert Venn Dicey, *Introduction to the Study of the Law of the Constitution* (10th edn, 1959); Section III.2 below.

[27] What I am calling 'dualist' has been called 'almost definitional' for constitutional-legal regimes, see Kay (n 19), 338. See, however, for other significations of 'constitutional' as applied to law and legal systems, Chapters 8 and 9. My use here of the term 'dualist' chimes with Bruce Ackerman's use of 'dualist democracy' to mark out systems that provide for two distinct 'tracks' of lawmaking: a 'higher track' for constitutive lawmaking by the people and another, 'lower track' for subordinate lawmaking by the people's constituted government. See Bruce Ackerman, 'Constitutional Law, Constitutional Politics' (1989) 99 *Yale Law Journal* 453, 461–2.

[28] I have drawn this account, and the resultant conjecture, from writings of Dieter Grimm, but my crude renditions must not be blamed on him. See Dieter Grimm, 'The Constitution in the Process of Denationalization' (2005) 12 *Constellations* 447ff; Dieter Grimm, 'The Achievement of Constitutionalism and its Prospects in a Changed World' in Petra Dobner and Martin Laughlin (eds), *The Twilight of Constitutionalism?* (2010), 3ff. Kay (n 19) develops in a similar way the inescapability of a public/private divide in dualist constitutional law. Kay does not trace this inescapability to the conjectural proto-liberal inspirations for dualist constitutionalism as I do here, following Grimm; he places more weight on a felt need to limit the reach of constitutional law in order to avoid a total juridification of politics. See ibid 324, 339–41.

state) of these positive-legislating, order-keeping powers and functions; and so implies also, *third*, a vesting in that same institutional nexus of the sole, final disposition over deployments of coercive powers (state monopoly of lawful force); and then, finally and recursively, *fourth*, a demand for subjection of these state-concentrated powers—which themselves now appear as an imposing instance of powers forming and roaming—to positive legal controls: in other words, constitutional government, government under law.

It seems that always and already contained in such a play of political thought is the idea of a body of laws expressly designed for control of the state's exercise of its unique power to make and enforce further laws for the control of society. It seems, moreover, that these 'constitutional' laws for the lawmaking state to be under must necessarily be conceived as distinct from those other 'ordinary' laws of which the state itself is the uniquely commissioned maker. Already at that point—so runs the developing conjecture—*some* abstract and formal idea of a categorial divide on the field of legal operations is in play, instinct in the very concept, the very notion, of (dualist) constitutional law. The doctrinal play of public/private is thus conceptually instigated from the start by the most primitive modern (proto-liberal) inspirations of dualist constitutionalism.

No doubt an impulse of contemporary political preference must feed and bolster any such remote conceptual instigation. Who, today, would *wish for* (let alone easily conceive of) a complete merger of the laws controlling state governors with the laws the governors make? Only those, it seems, who feel totally certain that legal controls on society *ought*, as a matter of the highest policy, to match exactly, in every substantive respect, the controls imposed on rulership (so that, for example, parents handing out discipline to their children would be directly controlled by standards of procedural justice identical to those imposed on governments regulating society).[29] To any who retain the slightest doubt in that regard, a concentration of rulership powers in the state implies that there must be a space of activity left over which *is not* the exercise of rulership. There must be left over the space of the addressees of these powers—the space of 'society', populated by the ruled or the governed.

Thus:

> A system where the state enjoys the freedom of private persons would have as little a constitution as a system in which private persons may exercise public power [i.e., the power of rule]. If private persons gain a share in public power, the constitution can no longer fulfill its claim to regulate the establishment and exercise of public power comprehensively unless the private actors submit themselves to constitutional rules whereby they would lose their status as free members of society [i.e., as addressees of the state's exercise of its powers of rule].[30]

In sum, 'the concentration of all public power in the hands of the state' carries as its corollary 'the privatisation of society'.[31]

Ruling implies ruled. Government implies society. Concentration of powers of rule in a state nexus specialized to that work means that the addressees of rulership—society—compose a sphere of activity distinct and apart from that of the rulers or government, appropriately subject to a correspondingly different body of normative controls. The 'ghost'—the ineluctable primitive, maximally abstract notion of a public/private divide in the law—thus

[29] The example comes from Frances E. Olsen, 'The Family and the Market: A Study of Ideology and Legal Reform' (1983) 96 *Harvard Law Review* 1496, 1505–6. Compare Grant Gilmore, *The Ages of American Law* (1977), 110–11 ('In Hell, there will be nothing but law, and due process will be meticulously observed').

[30] Grimm, 'Achievement of Constitutionalism' (n 28), 12.

[31] Ibid.

appears to be a direct reflex of the division between governing and governed already contained in the very idea of dualist constitutionalism or of its supposed proto-liberal political inspirations.

Can we hazard some prediction about how this ghost might be expected to manifest its presence in the doctrinal part of a dualist-constitutional legal practice? So far, all we have is the idea of a binary coding of *laws* as meant-for-the-state and meant-for-society. But if we add the anticipation of a doctrinal process of making ascertainable the proper scopes of application of the two types of laws, assuring and delimiting a scope for each of them, then something more must follow. We must expect the emergence of a parallel practice of coding, as actually or properly 'of the state' or 'of society', of items in at least one, and very possibly more than one, of such object-fields as acts, actors, powers, affairs, functions, and concerns—quite consistently, it seems, with what our survey in Section I discloses.

3. Test Drive: Dualism Modified?

No doubt any constitutional-dualist legal system requires 'some way' to delimit the respective fields of application of constitutional and ordinary law.[32] But must that way necessarily be the way of public/private?

Consider a modified version of Table 14.1:

A system described in the terms of Table 14.1A would apparently extend the overriding mandates of the basic law to all matters coded 'religious', however public or private their venues might be. In precincts of society no less than in precincts of the state—in homes, families, markets, workplaces, clubs, and sanctuaries—any and all affairs deemed 'religious' would fall under regulation by applicable basic-law directives. Very possibly—although not necessarily; it would depend on what matters were found to be 'religious' in import, which in turn would partly depend on the substantive content and coverage of the basic-law texts in question—those overriding mandates could reach to matters of dress, diet, child-rearing, sex, artistic expression, trade, and so on without limit.

Just as a master partition of all laws between 'public' (for-the-state) and 'private' (for-society) instigates the rise of doctrine for the division of some object-field or fields between 'of the state' and 'of society' (Section I.2 above), so will a master partition of all laws between

Table 14.1A Two Categorizations of Laws

		by sphere of application	
		'religious law' directed to matters of religion	*'secular law' directed to any and all other matters*
by normative depth and force	*basic law fixed and controlling*	I. basic law for the religion sphere	II. ? basic law for the secular sphere ?
	ordinary law variable and controlled	III. ordinary law for the religion sphere	IV. ordinary law for the secular sphere

[32] Kay (n 19), 342.

'religious' (for-the-religion sphere) and 'secular' (for-the-secular sphere) be attended by its own, parallel doctrines of field-division. In a cultural setting where liberal political sensibilities retain some purchase, the results could possibly, in some degree, track those we would expect to find at work in the 'public/private' systems depicted by Table 14.1. (So, for example, the question of one's choice of a domestic partner might be coded 'secular'—and thus placed beyond the reach of basic-religious law—just because that question feels so intensely 'private'.) But it seems that any such congruence with liberal outcomes would be purely accidental, a contingency of local political preference. 'Public/private' coding is not expressly (as it were) built into Table 14.1A as it is into Table 14.1. Where Table 14.1 calls expressly for doctrinal codings of matters as 'state-or-not', Table 14.1A calls for codings of matters as 'religious-or-not'; and it seems the results could cut wildly across any plausible, liberalistic map of public/private divides. A real-world Table 14.1A system could thus be decidedly anti-liberal in character.

Yet such a system would also, apparently, be 'dualist' in structure. With its two rows dividing 'ordinary' from 'basic' law, Table 14.1A appears to posit both a workaday institutionalized process of ('ordinary') legislation and the subjection of that process to legal control by a relatively fixed and enduring body of 'basic' law. The two rows thus mark Table 14.1A as 'dualist' on its face. And yet the sort of system depicted by the table stands apparently far distant from any proto-liberal inspiration. If we may speak in the language of rough-hewn ideal-types, Table 14.1A models a 'constitutional theocracy', in contrast with the liberal 'constitutional democracy' represented by Table 14.1.[33]

The difference is marked by the labels on the respective tables' two columns. As we have already noticed, Table 14.1A's 'religious/secular' partition seems essentially non-correlated with Table 14.1's 'state/society' partition. And yet the two tables' rows are identically labeled. In what would seem to be the key respect of sustaining a differentiation of 'basic' from 'ordinary' law, Table 14.1A, like Table 14.1, is dualist on its face. The apparent easy imaginability of real-world practices corresponding to Table 14.1A[34] would thus seem to pose a strong challenge to our conjecture of a tight, generative bond between 'dualist' constitutionalism and public/private line-drawing in constitutional law.

That impression may fade, however, under closer inspection. The question is whether we will see, already implicit in Table 14.1A's differentiation of constitutional ('basic') from 'ordinary' law, a differentiation of 'law-for-the-state' from 'law-for-society'. But that is precisely what we will see, if we follow the conjectural account (Section II.2 above) of the genesis of dualist constitutionalism in a historically emergent, complex political demand for 'government under law'—the demand for a 'state' to legislate for an otherwise intolerably unruly 'society' (ordinary law), but to do so under the control of a law (basic) of which the state cannot, then, itself be the maker.

A reading of Table 14.1A through the lens of the 'ghost' conjecture thus discloses in the table a third, suppressed axis of differentiation, hiding (as it were) behind the overt differentiation of 'basic' from 'ordinary' law. The fully unfolded table then will be sixfold, not fourfold, constructed in a three-dimensional space on three orthogonally intersecting axes of differentiation: status of laws (basic/ordinary); topics of laws (religious/secular); and powers targeted by laws (of-the-state/of-society). Public/private doctrinal coding of powers can then be expected to ensue.

It is only (to repeat) through the lens of the conjecture that the third (state/society) dimension turns up in Table 14.1A. But why, it may be asked, must we read through that lens? Are we

[33] Ran Hirschl, *Constitutional Theocracy* (2011).

[34] See ibid 26–40 for real-world illustration of a range of approximations.

not free to read the table quite differently, to represent a scheme in which the notion of the 'religious' is so expansive, and the basic law's textual prescriptions are so substantively sweeping, that every possible social and personal question or issue is fully decidable by application of the basic law's religious directives, and no space is left for 'private' ordering?

The answer must be that we are not free to read the table in that way. In such a religiously totalizing scheme, the 'basic' law would be, in effect, the only law. But such a system—leaving no space for 'ordinary' lawmaking or for a 'state' to serve as the maker (thus collapsing the two rows of Tables 14.1 and 14.1A)—would not qualify as 'dualist' in the sense intended by the conjecture.[35] The conjecture—of the 'fixture [of public/private] in [specifically] dualist constitutional thought' (Section II.2 above)—is meant only for constructions that leave over some space where laws originating from a legally constituted 'state' (and not directly and conclusively from the very laws that constitute the state) can take hold and make a difference for 'society'.

As a matter of historical contingency, it might happen that exactly such a specification would cover most or all of the political formations observable on Earth at a given time. If such were found to be case today, then—according to the conjecture—that observation would go far to explain the seeming ubiquity of doctrinal public/private line-drawing in constitutional law the world over. Not only, then, would we have redeemed the 'ghost' conjecture from the challenge posed by the apparent easy imaginability of purely theocratic governance. We would have bolstered and enriched the conjecture, to the point of having it affirmatively suggest that the proto-liberal promptings to dualist constitutionalism might, in some epoch (say, ours), become so very widespread across the globe as to be more or less inescapable. The conjecture would then give us reason to peer hard at any constitutional regimes that might claim or appear to be purely theocratic in character, with the expectation of finding public/private divides cropping up in their constitutional-legal operations.

4. Test Drive: Resilience to Critique?

The conjecture works only as an abstraction. It tells us nothing about which object-fields (actors, function, concerns) will be targeted for line-drawing or about where or how the lines will be drawn. It is strong in confidence but thin in substance. However contentious, uncertain, or confusing the play of public/private may be or become in any country's politics and laws, that play will carry on—so runs the conjecture—until, if ever, we arrive at the moment of the erasure from that country's prevailing political sensibility of the proto-liberal impulse for state-centered ordering.[36]

As suggestive evidence, one might cite the history of a long-standing left-theoretical onslaught, and a more recent feminist-theoretical onslaught, against public/private divides in the law of the United States.

[35] It would be, in Hirschl's terms, a 'pure' and not a 'constitutional' theocracy. See ibid 7.

[36] The conjecture thus evades a possible objection that there is and can be no de-politicized space because there is no space from which relations and depredations of power are absent, and this truth holds regardless of the monistic or dualist structure of a legal system. See Catherine A. Mackinnon, *Toward a Feminist Theory of the State* (1989), 160–2. The proposition under examination here is not that of a morally sustainable divide between the 'political' and the (non-political) 'personal'. It is that of a divide between that which is 'state' (public) and that which is 'society' (private) with respect to certain issues of choice of law in a dualistically structured legal system. Repudiation of the political/personal divide says a lot about how and how not (morally) to draw the state/society line. It does not rebut the necessity of somehow drawing the lines, wherever legal-systemic dualism prevails.

The idea of the private has been a bone of left-versus-right contention over generations extending back (at least) to Karl Marx.[37] Still very much alive today is a set of legal-theoretic challenges launched nearly a century ago by writers of the school of American Legal Realism, more recently revived and extended by critical legal and feminist-legal scholarship.[38]

Four moments may be said to mark the Legal Realist–CLS assault on public/private in the law. At a moment of *setup* (as we may call it), writers easily demolish overdrawn portrayals, from the right, of 'the private' as a zone of personal self-sufficiency and autonomous self-direction, to be contrasted with the 'public' (ie the state) portrayed as a zone of dependency, subjection to external controls, and oppression-in-the-offing. At a moment of *relativization*, writers suggest an approximate functional equivalence between powers enjoyed by civil society players under private law supporting exclusive property rights and so-called 'sovereign' powers supposedly granted solely to the state,[39] and so also to an approximate equivalence between the threats to freedom respectively posed by those private-law-sanctioned powers and by the state's own direct actions;[40] all of this leading to pointed questions about why constitutional-legal restraints against oppression should not extend fully to acts of corporations and other players in the so-called 'private' sector. On top of which come demonstrations—call this the moment of *the deduction of the ubiquity of the state*—of the state's plain responsibility for the permissions and empowerments, no less than for the prohibitions and immunities, that its own lawmaking weaves into the overall fabric of the private law,[41] from which an inference is drawn that every case at law falls within the purview of a constitutional bill of rights no matter how strictly 'vertically' directed.[42]

These contentions have long been in wide circulation. Not only are they formidable, they enjoy today the assent of many, maybe most defenders of doctrinal public/private divides.[43] An alleged result of their acceptance—and here is the fourth moment of the left/feminist

[37] See Karl Marx, 'On the Jewish Question' in David McLellan (ed), *Karl Marx: Selected Writings* (1977), 39ff.

[38] For leading examples of the Critical Legal Studies (CLS) contribution, along with rebuttals, see the essays collected in 'Symposium: The Public-Private Distinction' (1982) 130 *University of Pennsylvania Law Review* 1289ff.

Important feminist-theoretic writing distinguishes the public/private divide with which this chapter is centrally concerned—ie, the grand divide between the spaces of the state and of society and the laws respectively applicable to them—and another construction, mainly internal to 'private' law, by which a relatively 'public' space of the market is divided from a relatively 'private' space of the family. See Olsen (n 29), 1501–2 and passim (also showing complex and powerful interactions between the two 'dichotomies'). Accordingly, we find within feminist-theoretic writing both a strain addressed to the family/market divide (decrying, eg, its relation to ideas of woman's separate sphere, see eg Olsen (n 16), 322–3), and a strain addressed to the state/society divide, largely coincident with the 'left' critique of the private summarized here.

[39] See eg Morris R. Cohen, 'The Basis of Contract' (1933) 46 *Harvard Law Review* 553ff; Morris R. Cohen, 'Property and Sovereignty' (1927) 13 *Cornell Law Quarterly* 8ff; Felix Cohen, 'Dialogue on Private Property' (1954) 9 *Rutgers Law Review* 357ff.

[40] See eg Robert L. Hale, 'Coercion and Distribution in a Supposedly Non-Coercive State' (1923) 38 *Political Science Quarterly* 470ff.

[41] See Wesley N. Hohfeld, 'Some Fundamental Legal Conceptions as Applied in Judicial Reasoning' (1913) 23 *Yale Law Journal* 16ff.

[42] See Johan van der Walt, 'Progressive Indirect Horizontal Application of the Bill of Rights: Towards a Co-operative Relation between Common-law and Constitutional Jurisprudence' (2001) 17 *South African Journal of Human Rights* 341ff ('the most consistent position to take would be that one can never take the…involvement of the state out of…private legal relations, be these relations founded on statutory private law or common-law private law').

Such claims are subjected to strong and sometimes quite subtle contestation. See eg Frank I. Goodman, 'Professor Brest on State Action and Liberal Theory, and a Postscript to Professor Stone' (1982) 130 *University of Pennsylvania Law Review* 1331ff.

[43] See eg Alexander (n 7), 361–8; Kay (n 19), 334–7.

assault on public/private doctrine—is the *stereotypification* (or call it the hyper-formalization) of public/private.[44] On all sides, confidence is lost in the both the rational determinacy and the material persuasive power of ever more routinized arguments pro and con the classification of this or that actor, power, function, concern, or whatever as public or as private, and so the whole business of classifying comes increasingly to be seen as mere cover for conclusions that can only have been reached on political or ideological grounds.

In the wake of such objections, constitutional-legal doctrines of public/private appear to many to lie more or less in shambles. Yet not only do spirited defenses of these doctrines continue to appear,[45] the doctrines show no sign of receding from their salient position in constitutional law—good news, one might say, for the ghost.

5. The Case of South Africa

The point holds not only for such entrenched market-liberal societies as the United States may be taken to represent, but also for constitutional orders distinctly identifiable as social-democratic[46] or 'post-liberal'.[47] A telling instance occurs in South Africa, where post-transition constitutional discourse and doctrine convey what is perhaps the dualist constitutional world's strongest stance of resistance to public/private divides in the law. Regarding South Africa's *dualism* there can be no question: the Constitution is declared 'the supreme law of the Republic' with which all (other) law must be 'consistent' in order to be 'valid'.[48] No less apparently pronounced, though, is the system's all-out push—no doubt as influenced in part by the Realist–CLS–feminist critiques of public/private—towards constitutionalization of the entire legal order.[49] The Bill of Rights 'applies to all law'; the rights the Bill entrenches 'bind' non-state actors; and the Bill directs South African courts at all times to construe statutes and develop private law doctrines in harmony with its 'spirit, purport, and objects'.[50] To top off all the rest, the South African Constitutional Court (SACC) has declared most emphatically that

> there are not two systems of law, each... operating in its own field with its own highest court.... There is only one system of law. It is shaped by the Constitution which is the supreme law, and all law... is subject to constitutional control.[51]

[44] Duncan Kennedy, 'The Stages of the Decline of the Public/Private Distinction' (1982) 130 *University of Pennsylvania Law Review* 1349ff; see Olsen (n 16), 324–5; Olsen (n 29), 1508–13.

[45] See eg John Harrison and Lillian BeVier, 'The State Action Principle and its Critics' (2010) *Virginia Law Review* 1767ff.

[46] See eg the German Basic Law, Art 28(1) ('The constitutional order in the Länder must conform to the principles of a republican, democratic and social state governed by the rule of law, within the meaning of this Basic Law').

[47] Karl Klare, 'Transformative Constitutionalism and Legal Culture' (1998) 14 *South African Journal of Human Rights* 146, 151–6 (detailing social-transformative commitments that distinguish South African constitutionalism from core-liberal comparators).

[48] South African Constitution, s 2.

[49] See eg Klare (n 47); Dennis M. Davis and Karl Klare, 'Transformative Constitutionalism and the Common and Customary Law' (2010) 26 *South African Journal of Human Rights* 403ff.

[50] South African Constitution, ss 8(1), 8(2), 39(2); see *Carmichele v Minister of Public Safety* [2001] ZACC 22; 2001 (4) SA 938 (CC), paras 33–9.

[51] *Pharmaceutical Manufacturers Association of South Africa: In re Ex Parte President of the Republic* [2000] ZACC 1; 2000 (2) SA 674 (CC), para 44. The SACC was responding, in part, to a jurisdictional turf-battle with South Africa's ordinary judiciary, but its declaration was plainly meant to convey a deeper message about the unity of South African law under the Constitution. See Frank I. Michelman, 'The Rule of Law, Legality, and the Supremacy of the Constitution' in Stuart Woolman, Theunis Roux and Michael Bishop (eds), *Constitutional Law of South Africa* (2008), vol I, ch 11 at 16–23, 36–8 (chapters separately paginated).

How, then, do we make sense of these simultaneous declarations of the Constitution's supreme-law status and of the unity of South African law? Over what law, then, is the Constitution's law supreme? Plainly, it is supreme over bodies of state-made ordinary law that cannot, then, themselves be constitutional law, and the system is in that sense 'dual' in structure. But the system also is detectably *dualist* in our further sense (Section II.2 above) of the persistence within it of a proto-liberal impulse to resist—to resist as a matter of value and of policy—a full merger in substance of the laws controlling governors with the laws controlling society.

No doubt, current South African jurisprudence is marked by its unrelenting demand for harmonization of the country's ordinary, private law with constitutional value-orderings. No doubt that demand covers, along with ordinary statute law, South Africa's extensive and frequently decisive body of common law. And yet—so says the SACC—common law development is to be guided by the common law's 'own paradigm'. How so? Because often, when the pre-constitutional common law's treatment of a problem is found to stand in need of some adaptation to the Constitution's value-orderings, a trained common lawyer will be able to perceive the possibility of several different doctrinal entry points for making the needed adjustment, any one of which might satisfy the Constitution and so preserve the unity (in that sense) of the entire law of South Africa. In such cases, the Constitution's law—as some might say—runs out before all the available, ordinary legal-doctrinal options are resolved. And the choice, then, among constitutionally satisfactory ordinary-legal resolutions, can still be shaped by considerations having to do with which choice would be most 'beneficial for the common law' when regarded as an identifiable, bounded component of South African law, organized internally by its own logic or 'paradigm'.[52] The SACC visibly and pointedly implements this view through discretionary exercise of its powers of docket control—typically, by refusing leave for direct access, or for direct appeal from trial-level decisions, before litigants have exhausted their ordinary-legal claims and contentions before the ordinary appellate judiciary.[53]

Thus does the 'ghost'—the proto-liberal impulse toward a division of public from private law—continue to haunt South Africa's decidedly post-liberal mind.

Views and practices in Germany, South Africa's predecessor and rival as a world leader towards horizontalism, appear to be quite similar.[54]

III. Comparison Functional and Taxonomic

1. Left–Right Scalar Cross-Country Comparison and the 'Relative Autonomy of Law'

The 'ghost' conjecture predicts an appearance of some sort of doctrinal public/private divide in every dualist constitutional legal practice. The prediction, however, is highly abstract and approximate. To say that at least one of the object-fields (from among actors, functions, and so on) must undergo 'state'/'society' sorting is to leave open everything else about where or how the lines will be drawn. This open-endedness in the conjecture suggests a possible mode of comparative study of the play of public/private in constitutional law.

[52] *Carmichele* (n 48), paras 55–6.
[53] See Michelman (n 51), 6 n 2.
[54] See Michelman (n 1).

We might make it a scalar study. Rather than a collection of dichotomous categorial partitions of various object-fields, we could take public/private to signify an ideological continuum along which various countries' summative locations can be plotted. For example, taking our cue from Section II.3 above, we could set up a scale running from a total privatization to a total 'public-ization'[55] of religion.[56] Section II.4 suggests a different possibility. Our scale could run from 'left' to 'right', from red to blue, from relatively collectivist-leaning to relatively individualist-leaning. Each country could be assigned a summative score or location along such a substantive-ideological, red-to-blue axis, but with the score compiled strictly and only from observations of about where and how that country's legal doctrines do and do not draw public/private lines across various object-fields.

Comparisons of this kind appear to be workable. If, for example, we look at the relevant deployments of public/private on the doctrinal levels of current South African and US constitutional-legal practice, we will find South Africa lying consistently to the red ('post-liberal') side of the United States. In South Africa but decidedly not in the United States:

- the Constitution obligates the state to protect persons against private violence;[57]
- group-vilifying private speech is a virtually mandatory public concern, for which state regulatory controls are not only permitted but invited;[58]
- the Constitution requires a continuing audit of the entire corpus of private law—extending, for example, to such matters as fair dealing and 'conscionability' in private-market contracting—for compatibility with the 'spirit, purport, and objects' of the guarantees in the bill of rights;[59]
- the Constitution expressly permits compulsory taking of land by the state for the sole purpose of equitably redistributing this resource;[60]
- the Constitution expressly provides protection for labor-union activity in private markets;[61]
- the Constitution obligates the state to exert maximum feasible effort toward fulfillment of everyone's basic material needs, by off-market means insofar as necessary;[62]

and so on, nor do there appear to be any counter instances. South Africa plainly lies more toward the red pole of the spectrum, the United States more toward the blue. We thus see how comparative arrays of cross-country (or cross-temporal) variations in legal doctrine might figure in larger historical, political, and cultural studies.

[55] The term 'public-ization' is owed to Jody Freeman, see her 'Extending Public Accountability Through Privatization: From Public Law to Publicization' in Michael Dowdle (ed), *On Public Accountability: Designs, Dilemmas and Experiences* (2006).

[56] As an example of such a study (only making the continuum a loop instead of a bipolar axis, in order to show how extremes of both privatization and publicization (or 'state-ification') of religion can impair religious freedom) see W. Cole Durham, 'Perspectives on Religious Liberty' in Johan D. van der Vyver and John Witte, Jr (eds), *Religious Human Rights in Global Perspective* (1996).

[57] Compare the South African Constitution, ss 7(2), 12(1(c) and *Carmichele* (n 50) with *DeShaney v Winnebago County* 489 US 189 (1989).

[58] Compare the South African Constitution, s 16(2)(c) with *RAV v St Paul* 505 US 377 (1992).

[59] Compare *Barkhuizen v Napier*, ZACC 5; 2007 (5) SA 323 (CC), paras 28–30 with *Flagg Bros v Brooks* 436 US 149 (1978).

[60] Compare the South African Constitution, s 25(4), (5) with *Hawaii Housing Authority v Midkiff* 467 US 229 (1984).

[61] See ibid s 23.

[62] Compare ibid ss 25(5), 26, 27, 28 with *DeShaney* (n 57).

But then how would these qualify as studies *in law*, as distinct from studies in society (history, politics, culture) that merely happen to use legal-doctrinal data-points as social indicators? Of what interest might such studies be to specifically *legal*-theoretic knowledge? In what way do we think a national society's specifically *legal* thought and discourse—as distinct from the rest of its political-cultural milieu—might affect its location on a political–cultural scale running from red to blue? To put the question in another form: How, if at all, might our plottings of these locations tie into the thesis of law's 'relative autonomy' vis-à-vis society—the thesis (put very crudely) of an alternating exchange of cause and effect between a distinguishably legal domain of thought and practice and other social domains such as politics and culture.[63] And what is there, then (if anything), within *specifically legal* thought and discourse, that could affect a country's summative location on a political–cultural scale running from red to blue?

To questions of that sort, our 'ghost' conjecture stands poised, in a way, with a response. It says that the red-to-blue location of a country's constitutional-legal practice is not necessarily or solely a matter of being at one point or another *along* the scale; it is, at least as interestingly, a matter of being *on* (and not off) the scale. In the view of the conjecture, the point to see is that both US and South African constitutionalism are very evidently *on* the scale, market-liberal though the one society's self-understanding may be and post-liberal the other's. The universality (such as it may be) of public/private lies not in any putative sameness of each country's relatively left or relatively right position on the scale, but rather in the fact that a very great many countries do, in fact and not accidentally, share the two characteristics that they sustain constitutional-dualist legal structures and they occupy a location somewhere along the scale of legal-doctrinal deployments of public/private—which is to say, their deployments of public/private are not *nil*.

Is the lesson, then, that not only must a body of constitutional law be found in every law-governed society (Section II.1 above), but that every body of constitutional law must occupy a location along a left–right scale of public/private line-drawing on various object fields? No law without a state, no state without constitutional law, no constitutional law without a location along the scale?

Our conjecture does not go so far. It says nothing against the possibility of a constitutional construction devoid of a lawmaking state, or against the idea that practices of law can still take shape within such radically anti-statist constructions. The conjecture rather would point out that such a state-denying construction could not ever be 'dualist', in the stipulated sense of sustaining a distinct body of law specially aimed at a state making laws for society. Allowing for the possibilities of anti-statist constitutional constructions, and of law-without-a-state, thus leaves untouched the conjecture of strong attractive forces binding dualist constitutionalism at one end to proto-liberal political impulses and, at the other end, to bodies of legal doctrine marked by public/private divides. We have not yet run into or thought of a case in which one of those three moments—proto-liberalism, dualist constitutionalism, public/private coding on some legal-doctrinal object-field—is plainly parted from the other two.

2. From 'Functional' to 'Taxonomic' Comparison: British Constitutionalism

Our putative left–right scalar comparison is of a type known to the trade as 'functional' or 'functionalist'. From a functional-comparative angle, we look for a conjectural common aim

[63] See eg Robert W. Gordon, 'Critical Legal Histories' (1984) 103 *Stanford Law Review* 103ff.

or compulsion to which the constitutional-legal practices of variously circumstanced countries might all be responding by their differing combinations of institutional and doctrinal devices.[64] The 'ghost' conjecture takes up a certain subset of device-variations, composed of doctrinal public/private and kindred divides as variously drawn in various systems in various ways on various object-fields. These may all, says the conjecture, be understood as outcomes of pressures to accommodate a persistent set of proto-liberal impulses, inscribed in legal-systemic dualist practice, to otherwise widely variant historical, material, cultural, and other societal circumstances.

Functional comparison of the doctrinal play of public/private thus would operate *within* the set of identifiably dualist legal systems. 'Taxonomic' comparison, by contrast, would operate *across* the boundary separating such systems from whatever other type or types we care to posit. Given a conjecture that the pull toward public/private coding is an accompaniment, specifically, of *dualist* constitutional thought and practice, we can look to see whether ostensibly non-dualist systems are, as we might predict, comparatively free of public/private fixations. If, perchance, we find to the contrary, we can ask whether that ostensibly non-dualist system might perhaps turn out, on a closer look, to be dualist (as it were) *malgré elle*.

In that spirit, having taken our glance at the impulse of South African constitutionalism to be simultaneously legal-dualist and legal-unitarian (Section II.5 above), we now take up the case of the United Kingdom with its proud tradition of legal unitarianism and common law constitutionalism, marked by historic resistance to continentalist differentiations of 'public' from 'private' law.[65] (We mean, of course, vintage Britain, Britain prior to the adoption, under pressure of treaty obligation, of a separated, basic-law layer in the form of the Human Rights Act 1998.[66]) The British case poses an important test for us, because Britain's modern history of political ideas has proto-liberal roots as sure and deep as any country's, and 'public/private' talk is—as we confirm just below—easily detectible in the doctrinal discourse of British common law constitutional practice. Where does Britain fit, taxonomically, in the view of the conjecture? Dualist or not?

On the vintage account, Britain is constitutional-unitarian, not dualist. On the one hand, all persons equally are bound by the common law. On the other hand, state officials are simply persons who happen, for a time, to be 'employed in the service of the state'. And so, correspondingly, 'the general principles of the constitution' are nothing but 'the result of... decisions determining the [common law] rights of private persons in particular cases brought before the courts.'[67] The results can be quite jarring to liberal-constitutional sensibilities—as when, for example, the common law libertarian principle that all conduct not prohibited to a person by law is permitted to him (in the absence of any applicable Act of Parliament) to defeat any possibility of a claim against the legal permissibility of telephone tapping by, or by the order of, the Home Secretary.[68]

[64] See eg Cheryl Saunders, 'Towards a Global Constitutional Gene Pool' (2009) 38 *National Taiwan University Law Review* 1ff; Mark Tushnet, 'The Possibilities of Comparative Constitutional Law' (1999) 108 *Yale Law Journal* 1225ff.

[65] See Dicey (n 26); J.W.F. Allison, *A Continental Distinction in the Common Law: A Historical and Comparative Perspective on English Public Law* (1996).

[66] See Geoffrey Marshall, 'The United Kingdom Human Rights Act, 1998' in Vicki C. Jackson and Mark Tushnet (eds), *Defining the Field of Comparative Constitutional Law* (2002), 107ff.

[67] Dicey (n 26), 193, 195.

[68] See *Malone v Metropolitan Police Commissioner* [1979] Ch 344. This case example and two more to follow are taken from Allison (n 65), 79–80.

Regarding such judgments, Professor Allison remarks that 'without a clear conception of the state administration, [jurists have] had no clear reason to distinguish the legal consequences of administrative disputes from those of private disputes.'[69] But the picture is not and cannot be so simple. It turns out that those 'rights of private persons' can be—and on the view of our conjecture they predictably will be—flexed this way or that depending on whether, indeed, the relevant persons are *private*; or, in other words, on whether one or another party to the case should happen (or not) to be acting as a part of the state service. Thus, we see cases such as *Air Canada v Secretary of State for Trade*,[70] where the judges construe a common law 'public interest/administration of justice' rule for document discovery by litigants to allow special consideration to a *Secretary of State's* plea for confidentiality of *ministerial* deliberations; or such as *Attorney-General v Jonathan Cape Ltd*,[71] where the judges develop common law protections against 'breach of confidence' in a special way for application to disclosures of Cabinet proceedings in the memoirs of a former minister. Evidently, Britain has not been immune to the dualist pull to produce a body of law that is specialized to the control of state-concentrated, ultimate powers of rule—which is where, after all, on the view of the conjecture, constitutional-legal dualism begins. And then the advent of the Human Rights Act, we might say, moves the story along the conjectural track

Bibliography

J.W.F. Allison, *A Continental Distinction in the Common Law: A Historical and Comparative Perspective on English Public Law* (1996)

Morris R. Cohen, 'Property and Sovereignty' (1927) 13 *Cornell Law Quarterly* 8

Daphne Barak-Erez, 'Civil Rights in the Privatized State: A Comparative View' (1999) 28 *Anglo-American Law Review* 503

Dennis M. Davis and Karl Klare, 'Transformative Constitutionalism and the Common and Customary Law' (2010) *South African Journal of Human Rights* 403

Albert Venn Dicey, *Introduction to the Study of the Law of the Constitution* (10th edn, 1959)

Catherine M. Donnelly, *Delegation of Governmental Power to Private Parties: A Comparative Perspective* (2007)

Jody Freeman, 'The Private Role in Public Governance' (2000) 75 *NYU Law Review* 543

Jody Freeman and Martha Minow (eds), *Government by Contract: Outsourcing and American Democracy* (2009)

Dieter Grimm, 'The Achievement of Constitutionalism and its Prospects in a Changed World' in Petra Dobner and Martin Laughlin (eds), *The Twilight of Constitutionalism?* (2010), 3ff

Dieter Grimm, 'The Constitution in the Process of Denationalization' (2005) 12 *Constellations* 447

Dieter Grimm, 'The Protective Function of the State' in Georg Nolte (ed), *European and US Constitutionalism* (2005), 137ff

Stephen Gardbaum, 'The "Horizontal Effect" of Constitutional Rights' (2003) 102 *Michigan Law Review* 387

Robert L. Hale, 'Coercion and Distribution in a Supposedly Non-Coercive State' (1923) 38 *Political Science Quarterly* 470

Rand Hirschl, *Constitutional Theocracy* (2011)

[69] Allison (n 65), 80.

[70] [1983] 2 AC 394.

[71] [1976] QB 752.

Catherine A. Mackinnon, *Toward a Feminist Theory of the State* (1989), ch 8
Karl Marx, 'On the Jewish Question' in David McLellan (ed), *Karl Marx: Selected Writings* (1977), 39ff
Frank I. Michelman, 'The Interplay of Constitutional and Ordinary Jurisdiction' in Rosalind Dixon and Tom Ginsburg (eds), *Comparative Constitutional Law* (2011)
Frances E. Olsen, 'The Family and the Market: A Study of Ideology and Legal Reform' (1983) 96 *Harvard Law Review* 1496
András Sajó and Renata Uitz (eds), *The Constitution in Private Relations* (2005)
'Symposium: The Public-Private Distinction' (1982) 130 *University of Pennsylvania Law Review* 1289–609
'Symposium on the State Action Doctrine' (1993) 10 *Constitutional Commentary* 309–442
Mark Tushnet, 'State Action, Social Welfare Rights, and the Judicial Role: Some Comparative Observations (2002) 3 *Chicago Journal of International Law* 435

CHAPTER 15

STATE NEUTRALITY

JÁNOS KIS

Budapest

THERE is a widespread agreement in modern democracies that a state should not force its citizens to lead lives they do not endorse themselves. It is also generally agreed that state acts should not be justified by appealing to the authority of religious books. This kind of agreement is often reflected in key constitutional provisions regarding, among others, freedom of religion and equality rights. Claims relating to the agreement in question are often reformulated as holding that state action should be neutral with respect to the ideals of the good life, or that the justification of state acts should be neutral with respect to basic beliefs. But does the use of the term 'neutral' add anything important to the original wording? Does it point to a common principle—a principle of state neutrality (PSN)—that unites such judgments? If it does, what normative work is PSN supposed to do? What is its basis? What are the things towards which it requires the acts of the relevant type to be neutral? Such questions call for a *theory of neutrality*.

The theory of neutrality has its natural home in the liberal tradition. Liberalism had a neutralist bent since its beginnings. But a systematic account of PSN was not laid out before the 1970s and 1980s when John Rawls and others restated the foundations of liberal theory.[1]

While particular neutrality judgments are widely accepted, the general conception of liberal neutrality elicited strong critical reactions. Some of the critiques took liberalism's commitment to neutrality as evidence that the liberal view of the individual, society, and politics is deeply flawed.[2] Others attacked liberal neutrality as reflecting a mistaken inter-

[1] See John Rawls, *A Theory of Justice* (rev edn, 1999); John Rawls, *Political Liberalism* (1993); Bruce Ackerman, *Social Justice in a Liberal State* (1980); Ronald Dworkin, *A Matter of Principle* (1985); Charles Larmore, *Patterns of Moral Complexity* (1987).

[2] See Michael Sandel, *Liberalism and the Limits of Justice* (1982); Alasdair MacIntyre, *After Virtue* (1985).

pretation of what liberalism really is about.[3] The debate subsided in the last decade or so, without settling, however, on a standard view. State neutrality remains a controversial idea. This chapter attempts to spell out its main tenets and to explain how they hang together. It examines the central objections, and explores revisions that may enhance the theory's defensibility.

I. Preliminaries

Neutrality is a distinctly political principle. Personal morality does not require its subjects (human individuals) to be neutral in the way political morality requires its subject to do (the state acting through public officials). It does not prohibit, for instance, our assisting others in carrying out their projects which we deem admirable while, at the same time, denying assistance to projects we do not value.

Neutrality is a relational attribute. Acts cannot be neutral *simpliciter*. When an act is neutral, it is neutral between different things, say, between X and Y. X and Y cannot stand for just anything. A principle requiring state acts to be neutral towards everything would be self-defeating. First, it would itself be a member of the class of things with regard to which states are required to be neutral. In order to satisfy PSN, a state would have to remain neutral between the claim that it is required to satisfy PSN and the opposite claim that it is not so required. That is incoherent.

Furthermore, neutrality is not the only principle that states must satisfy. Satisfying PSN must be consistent with satisfying the other principles. Therefore, PSN cannot apply to the latter. It cannot hold, for instance, that states ought to be neutral between the requirement of treating citizens as equals and the denial of this requirement.

Does PSN apply to everything else? That would not affect its consistency. But it would make it overbroad. PSN should be understood as a principle identifying *specific types of non-neutrality* as objectionable. The question is, then, under what conditions is non-neutrality morally objectionable.

A further question is related to the aspects of the relevant public acts on which PSN focuses. It may focus on the outcomes of state action or on its underlying reasons. An act is *outcome-neutral* between X and Y if it leaves the relative positions of X and Y unaffected. An act is *reason-neutral* between X and Y if the reasons for taking it rely on no evaluative ranking of X and Y. Outcome-neutrality is an implausible requirement. Many believe that a law that excludes openly gay people from military service is objectionably non-neutral. Suppose now that, as a response to the demand of neutrality towards the sexual orientation of servicemen, the ban is repealed. Very likely, the proportion between straight and gay servicemen will change as a consequence, so the legislative change would violate outcome-neutrality. This would count, however, in favor of the amendment, rather than against it.

An act can be required to be reason-neutral in two interesting ways: the requirement may apply to the reason actually proposed by the agent or to the best reason that could be provided for it under certain idealized conditions. We can speak, in the first case, about *neutrality of intent*, while in the second, about *justificatory neutrality*. Neutrality of intent means that a policy benefitting A more than B is not *in fact* justified by a judgment of comparative value about the basic beliefs or lifestyles of A and B. Justificatory neutrality means that a policy distributing advantages between A and B unequally could be provided with a plausible

[3] See William Galston, *Liberal Purposes* (1992); Stephen Macedo, *Liberal Virtues* (1992).

justification that does not rely on a judgment of comparative value about the basic beliefs or lifestyles of A and B.

The actual aim of particular legislators is often difficult to reconstruct, and there may be no unique way to combine the individual aims into a collective aim of the legislature. More importantly, the intent's failure to satisfy PSN need not compromise a law which lends itself to a plausible neutral justification. So the advocates of PSN tend to settle on justificatory neutrality.[4]

Sometimes, however, the actual intent matters on its own account. It matters, for example, when it is made explicit by the wording of the preamble to a law. In such cases, the intent may compromise the law even if its regulatory content could be given a non-objectionable justification. One way of dealing with such cases is for a court empowered to subject it to constitutional review not to strike down the law but to instruct the lower courts to disregard its preamble.

Finally, we should say something about the *theoretical status* of PSN. Some authors take PSN to be a foundational principle. According to Bruce Ackerman, for instance, the principles of justice result from conversations among citizens.[5] For the process of conversation to yield determinate and morally acceptable outcomes it must be constrained in a certain way: the permissible arguments must satisfy the condition of neutrality.[6] It is, thus, a fundamental commitment to neutrality that binds legitimate states to adopt a particular conception of equality, toleration, and individual rights. Ronald Dworkin, on the other hand, insists that neutrality properly understood is a derivative principle; it relies on the deeper principle that states should treat their citizens as equals.[7]

The foundationalist view is unappealing: it raises the suspicion that neutrality is based on ethical skepticism, that it is a principle for people with no convictions. And it deprives PSN of the conceptual tools for distinguishing between values towards which a state is permitted or even required to be non-neutral and those with which it is required to deal in a neutral manner.

This chapter will take it for granted that PSN is a derivative principle. It will assume that the main principle underlying PSN is the one according to which states should express equal concern and respect for each citizen both in the way they treat them and in the way they speak to them and about them. It will accept, furthermore, as a main factual assumption, that citizens of modern democracies are divided by deep, pervasive, and protracted disagreements. The disagreements are deep in the sense that they revolve around basic—religious, metaphysical, epistemological, ethical—beliefs and around general ideas on how to live well. Liberal neutrality as developed in the 1970s and 1980s argues from these main premises for a two-pronged PSN. First, state acts that discriminate between citizens on the ground of (controversial) value judgments regarding their 'conceptions of the good' are objectionably non-neutral. Secondly, a state act is objectionably non-neutral if its actual or possible justification appeals to reasons that some citizens cannot be expected to share.

[4] Will Kymlicka, 'Liberal Individualism and Liberal Neutrality' (1989) 99 *Ethics* 883.

[5] On the constitution and justice, see Chapter 16.

[6] Ackerman (n 1), 11. Charles Larmore, too, advocates making neutrality 'the primary ideal of liberalism' (Larmore (n 1), 46). But, not fully consistent with this proposal, he also suggests that, rather than taking their commitment to neutrality to be foundational, liberals should make sense of it in terms of a more basic principle of equal respect (ibid 59ff).

[7] Dworkin (n 1), 205.

Sections II and III discuss these two requirements. Section IV present the main objections leveled at liberal neutrality. Sections V and VI offer a revision of PSN in light of those objections. Section VII addresses the specific issue of religious neutrality.

II. Neutrality as Non-Discrimination

Advocates of liberal neutrality often identify the paradigm of objectionably non-neutral state action with the coercive imposition of valuable ways of life or coercive prevention of the pursuit of lifestyles that are worthless. But when they explain why trying to make people's lives better by coercive means is morally impermissible, they often appeal to a principle other than neutrality. Coercion is not a proper way to improve peoples' lives, Ronald Dworkin argues, because 'someone's life cannot be improved against his steady conviction that it has not been'.[8] What this argument objects to is forcing people to lead their lives in ways they do not endorse, and this is precisely what we understand by paternalism. At least on one occasion, though, Dworkin proposes a different account of PSN:

> People have the right not to suffer disadvantage in the distribution of social goods and opportunities, including disadvantage in the liberties permitted to them by the criminal law, just on the ground that their officials or fellow-citizens think that their opinions about the right way for them to lead their lives are ignoble or wrong.[9]

What makes a state act objectionably non-neutral, on this account, is that it disadvantages people only on the ground of a judgment about their ways of life. The disadvantage may, but need not, be inflicted by way of coercively restricting the options open to those people. So understood, the neutrality principle requires states not to favor or disfavor anyone on the ground of an official judgment about their conception of the good life.

This is a principle of non-discrimination, a principle outlawing discriminations of a special kind. In contrast, consider racial discrimination. Race is not a proper object of evaluative assessment. So when people are advantaged or disadvantaged by virtue of belonging to a social group constructed on the basis of real or alleged racial characteristics, the discrimination is either arbitrary, having no reason at all, or it is prejudice-based, having for its reason false value attributions. Advantaging or disadvantaging someone on the basis of her religious outlook, for instance, is different. A person's religious outlook submits to value judgments. Of course, those judgments may be prejudiced. But they need not be. PSN does not presuppose that the official judgment is prejudiced or that it is mistaken in some innocent way. Even if the disadvantaged person's conception of the good life is in fact worthless, disadvantaging him on the basis of a controversial official judgment is morally objectionable. What is wrong with it?

Let us see first what is wrong with paternalist state action. Paternalism is wrong because and when it usurps an individual's responsibility and right to be the one who decides what to make of her life. The wrong of non-neutral state action, as defined in the previous paragraph, is also related in some way to denying this right and responsibility, although in a more complicated manner. When everyone is allowed to lead their lives in their own light, the cost, for each individual, of reaching his aims is fixed as a function of the choices of others. My supreme goal may be that of erecting a huge temple in honor of my god. The more people are dedicated to the same goal, the less costly it will be for me to achieve it, and vice versa. If my religious

[8] Ronald Dworkin, *Sovereign Virtue* (2000), 283.

[9] Dworkin (n 1), 353.

community shrinks below a critical level, the costs become prohibitive. In general: as long as people are free to choose their lifestyles, plans, and projects, the costs of an individual's preferred pursuits vary with the choices of others. Suppose that the distribution of resources against which I and the other members of my society form our preferences is deeply unjust. Or suppose the formation of preferences is subject to coercion or manipulation. Then morality disapproves of the structure of preferences in my society and the resulting structure of the costs, for different individuals, of reaching their personal aims. Other things being equal, state intervention aiming to rectify the distribution of resources or to eliminate manipulation and coercion is, therefore, morally permissible. But state intervention aiming to encourage the pursuit of valuable projects or to discourage the pursuit of projects of low or negative value is morality tainted: it makes the structure of the costs of personal pursuits depart from what it would be if it were determined by autonomous choices adopted under the circumstances of justice. Suppose the government decides to co-fund the temple-building project on the ground that honoring that god is of utmost importance. In so doing, it lowers the cost of building the temple for those committed to this aim by making others not so motivated contribute as taxpayers. It either violates the requirement of treating individuals with appropriate respect for their right and responsibility to lead their lives in light of their own best judgment or it violates the requirement of treating individuals with equal concern for their flourishing, or both.

The scope of PSN is both wider and narrower than that of the anti-paternalist principle (APP). It is wider, since it applies to state acts that disadvantage certain individuals without coercively restricting their options. It is narrower since it is restricted to political communities as they act through their state, while the APP is a principle of both personal and political morality. As Dworkin puts it, '*no one* can improve another's life by forcing him to behave differently, against his will and his conviction.'[10] But we can improve, as private individuals, the lives of others by contributing to their projects, without being embarrassed by the possibility that assisting projects we deem admirable while not assisting projects in which we take no interest may affect, at least to some small degree, the relative costs of different pursuits.

III. Neutrality as Shared Reasons

The debate on liberal neutrality has been framed by John Rawls's seminal works, *A Theory of Justice* (*TJ*) and *Political Liberalism* (*PL*), even though the term itself does not appear at all in *TJ*, and crops up only occasionally in *PL*.

TJ argues for neutrality as non-discrimination. '[T]he principles of justice cover all persons with rational plans of life, whatever their content', it insists.[11] They regulate the distribution of the all-purpose 'social primary goods', leaving it to the individuals to form, revise, and pursue their particular life-plans, within the limits of their just share in those goods. 'Systems of ends are not ranked in value' by the principles of justice,[12] nor do these principles reflect any bias in favor of particular plans of life or conceptions of the good.[13] Hence PSN, as discussed in Section II, should not disadvantage anyone merely on the ground of a (controversial) value judgment about their conception of the good life. So understood, PSN requires states to be neutral among (controversial) conceptions of the good.

[10] Ronald Dworkin, 'Foundations of Liberal Equality' in Stephen Darwall (ed), *Equal Freedom* (1995), 304.

[11] Rawls, *A Theory of Justice* (n 1), 223.

[12] Ibid 17. [13] Ibid 222.

PL adds two important considerations to this. First, it distinguishes controversies dividing reasonable persons—persons seeking fair terms for their cooperation, conscious of their own fallibility, and taking seriously the arguments of the other side—from controversies where at least one of the parties is not reasonable in this sense, and it restricts the scope of neutrality as non-discrimination to conceptions of the good subject to *reasonable disagreement*. It also provides an open-ended list of the sources of 'reasonable disagreement' (it calls these the *burdens of judgment*): the evidence bearing on controversial cases is hard to evaluate; even if one agrees on the relevant considerations, one tends to disagree about their weight; our concepts in general and especially our moral concepts are vague and they are subject to hard cases, and so on.[14] Secondly, *PL* insists that justifying a state act by an appeal to reasons that are controversial among reasonable people is morally objectionable whether or not the act in question results in an unequal distribution of advantages. This is so because such justifications violate what we could call the liberal legitimacy principle (LLP). LLP holds that no one may be subjected to a political organization's coercive power without providing him with a justification that that organization has a right to monopolize such power. For a state to have legitimate monopoly of coercive power, it is not sufficient that it in fact has the right to monopolize coercive power. In other words, it is not sufficient that its claim to have such a right is true. It is also necessary that its claim can be justified to all its subjects, severally. The assumption of a pervasive fact of 'reasonable disagreement' poses a difficulty for LLP. Justifying the claim of legitimate monopoly of power to someone presupposes that the justification is provided in terms of reasons that they can be expected to share.[15] But if the reasons figuring in the justification are subject to intractable disagreement among reasonable persons, then they cannot be expected to be shared by everyone.

In order to resolve this difficulty, *PL* proposes to distinguish 'political conceptions' from 'comprehensive doctrines'. A doctrine is more or less comprehensive if it entails normative and factual assumptions regarding non-political matters: assumptions belonging to the domain of theology, metaphysics, epistemology, personal morality, ethics, and so on. A conception is narrowly political if it has for its subject the basic structure of society—roughly speaking, its coercive institutions.[16] Comprehensive doctrines tend to be subject to reasonable disagreement. The narrowly political reasons can be expected, however, to be beyond reasonable controversy. Therefore, justifications of state acts satisfy LLP if they are neutral towards the diversity of comprehensive doctrines. It must be given in narrowly political terms.

But if liberalism requires the state to be neutral in this way, how can the justification *of this requirement* succeed? Arguably, it must itself meet the standard which it sets for other justifications: it must be based on reasons all reasonable citizens can share. But, traditionally, liberalism is understood as a comprehensive doctrine, its political tenets relying on a particular conception of personal autonomy and of human flourishing. 'Comprehensive liberalism' is a controversial view, so it cannot provide the required justification. In order to avoid being 'just another sectarian doctrine', Rawls concludes, liberalism must apply PSN to itself. It must set aside the metaphysical, epistemological, ethical etc foundations of its own political principles and justify the latter by appealing to nothing else but 'ideas implicit in the public political culture of a democratic society'.[17] Restated as a narrowly political theory, liberalism will occupy a higher ground relative to the conflicting 'comprehensive doctrines', or so Rawls hopes. It does not compete with them. It rather enables a democratic citizenry to remain divided by controversial basic beliefs and ways of life, and yet to coexist in mutual respect.

14 Rawls, *Political Liberalism* (n 1), 56–7.

15 Ibid 243.

16 Ibid 10–11.

17 Ibid 8, 13ff.

Earlier I said that the truth of a conception that justifies the claim of monopoly of coercive power is *not sufficient* for that claim to command legitimacy. Rawls wants to say more. According to him, truth is not even necessary for legitimacy. Citizens may be skeptical about truth altogether and still agree 'political liberalism' as a set of principles which individuals seeking fair terms of cooperation can each accept. Thus, 'The political conception does without the concept of truth'.[18]

To take stock: treating citizens as equals involves, according to *PL*, a two-pronged PSN. The first prong outlaws discrimination based on judgments regarding the comparative worth of basic beliefs and ways of life on which reasonable citizens disagree. The second rules out justifications of claims of legitimate coercive power that rely on 'comprehensive views', failing to provide reasons that all citizens can be expected to share. The domains of the two prongs are disjunct. Neutrality as non-discrimination applies to the way the state *treats* its citizens. Neutrality as shared reasons applies to the way the state *speaks* to them and about them.

IV. Objections to Liberal Neutrality

Liberal neutrality provoked huge debates, the main criticisms coming from two corners: communitarian[19] and perfectionist.[20] For our present aims, it is not necessary to enter into the history of the controversy. It will suffice to reconstruct the main arguments that seem to call for a serious revision of PSN.

Consider first the core objection to neutrality as non-discrimination. To recall: the non-discrimination prong of PSN entails that political communities, acting through their states must not interfere with social interaction on the basis of controversial judgments regarding the comparative value of individual preferences. The argument underlying this conception tacitly assumes that the preferences themselves are fixed prior to social interaction: it is only the costs of their satisfaction that vary with changes in the patterns of the latter. But individuals do not form their conceptions of the good out of nothing: they draw on the cultural forms and practices available in their social environment. Changes in the patterns of interaction change the environment; changes in the environment do not involve changes in the costs of personal pursuits only: they give occasion to changes in the preferences themselves. And so it simply does not make sense to claim that an individual is disadvantaged by the state's action because, *prior to it*, he held preferences that the institutional agents judged not worthy of support. To be sure, if the change in preferences is induced coercively or by means of manipulation, the state's action can be correctly criticized on that account. But that criticism is not neutrality-based. If, on the other hand, the adjustment of preferences is left to the individuals' autonomous agency, it does not seem morally objectionable, for a democratically authorized government to divert collective resources for promoting valuable pursuits. To conclude, states are morally permitted to engage in action characterized and rejected by Rawls as perfectionist, that is, action aiming to promote 'human excellence in the various forms of culture'.[21]

[18] Ibid 94. [19] Sandel (n 2); MacIntyre (n 2).

[20] Vinit Haksar, *Equality, Liberty and Perfectionism* (1979); Joseph Raz, *The Morality of Freedom* (1986); George Sher, *Beyond Neutrality. Perfectionism and Politics* (1997).

[21] Rawls, *A Theory of Justice* (n 1), 22.

Let us turn now to neutrality as shared reasons. Rawls's proposal of a 'free-standing' political theory relies on the tacit assumption that reasonable persons whom the 'burdens of judgment' prevent from reaching agreement on matters of a comprehensive nature are nevertheless capable of reaching agreement on the political principles of justice. But the 'burdens of judgment' (insufficient evidence, conceptual vagueness etc) are not specifically related to comprehensive doctrines. If they give rise to passionate disagreements over non-political ideals, then they are likely to give rise to passionate disagreements over political principles, too.[22]

At first blush, it seems as if *PL* had an answer to this objection: the reasonable comprehensive doctrines allowed to flourish by the liberties characteristic of constitutional democracies, diverging as they should be as to their non-political content, converge on the same political principles, *PL* maintains. This is what Rawls famously calls the 'overlapping consensus'.[23] If the claim of overlapping consensus holds, then the 'burdens of judgment' are safe for 'political liberalism'. The pervasive fact of 'reasonable disagreement' leaves the domain of the political unaffected.

But the belief that the content of the political principles—as an object of general agreement—can be neatly separated from 'comprehensive' views—as objects of disagreement—seems to ignore the fact that the relevant political principles command something like a consensus only as long as they are formulated at a very high level of abstraction. It is not a mere historical accident that the basic principles of the great constitutions are drafted in abstract language. This is what allows citizens of the same as well as of successive generations to live under a shared constitution that each can regard as their own, notwithstanding their deep disagreements. But the consensus secured by abstract wording comes at a price. Abstract principles do not, in themselves, provide determinate answers to the question whether they are satisfied by specific institutional rules and procedures or in particular contexts. They need to be interpreted in light of that question, and the interpretation cannot proceed without involving further premises, not entailed by the abstract principles. It must show that the controversial reading is consistent with other normative commitments and factual beliefs one wants to uphold, commitments and beliefs that have their natural home in 'comprehensive doctrines'.[24]

As a consequence, the strategy to seek a higher ground for 'political liberalism', to raise it above the plurality of 'comprehensive conceptions', is doomed to fail. Liberals must not defend their theory as an impartial arbiter in the conflicts of the many 'sectarian doctrines' but rather as a controversial view that claims to be true.[25]

If so, then LLP and, together with it, neutrality as shared reasons must either be abandoned or revised.

V. Neutrality as Non-Discrimination Revisited

To reiterate, the objection to neutrality as non-discrimination holds that states can engage in creating valuable opportunities without discriminating between persons on the basis of a judgment concerning the relative value of their conceptions of the good life. This is because

[22] For a similar argument see Simon Caney, 'Liberal Neutrality, Reasonable Disagreement, and Justice' in Richard Bellamy and Martin Hollis (eds), *Pluralism and Liberal Neutrality* (1999), 22ff.

[23] Rawls, *Political Liberalism* (n 1), 39ff.

[24] eg the question whether a woman's right to control her own body entails a right to early abortion cannot be answered without taking sides on the moral status of the fetus. See Chapter 51.

[25] See Larry Alexander, 'Liberalism, Religion, and the Unity of Epistemology' (1993) 30 *San Diego Law Review* 763.

the conceptions of the good life themselves are responsive to changes in the social and cultural environment.

The non-discrimination prong of PSN as it was reconstructed in Section II entails that perfectionist state action is always morally impermissible. The objection implies that it is never impermissible, at least on the assumption that different individuals respond to new opportunities similarly, irrespective of the variations in their cultural background and personal capacities/dispositions.

Once that—rather implausible—assumption is dropped, the claim of a general permissibility of perfectionist state action loses its persuasiveness. If people with different cultural endowments etc are unequally responsive to new opportunities, then some will be advantaged on the ground of a judgment regarding preferences they are more likely to make their own than others. Neutrality as non-discrimination comes back, in a slightly modified form.

The perfectionist argument can be rescued, however. Its proponents may concede that state action aiming to promote particular lifestyles is objectionably non-neutral. But, then, they can add that perfectionist state action may be justified by a more abstract aim. Rather than aspiring to promote this or that particular way of life, or project, or goal, it may aspire to improve people's sense of the significance of the choices they face, and to facilitate more reflective choices (eg by making programs of ethics part of public education). Or it may aim at protecting and increasing the richness and complexity of the general cultural environment against the background of which the personal choices are made (eg by supporting the arts). If so, then even if it aims to forward 'human excellence in the various forms of culture', perfectionist state action is not objectionably non-neutral among particular conceptions of the good.

As restated in this form, the argument does not imply that perfectionist state action is *always permissible*. It upholds neutrality as non-discrimination, and condemns perfectionist state action whenever it is justified by the aim of promoting particular conceptions of the good. But it does imply that perfectionist state action is *not always impermissible*: it is consistent with neutrality as non-discrimination when a state act's justifying aim focuses on promoting deep and reflective choices taken against the background of a rich and complex cultural environment.[26]

However, even in this form, the argument raises hard questions. Consider the funding of the arts. Artistic genres and forms as such are not biased for or against particular conceptions of the good life: rather, they enrich the language and the models in terms of which people can form and reflect upon their own conceptions. True, only a minority of citizens—and mostly those with a better education and higher income—go to opera, visit exhibitions, or read novels. But they are not the only beneficiaries of the flourishing of artistic practices. 'High culture' is not separated by a Chinese wall from 'mass culture': it provides 'mass culture' with reference, style, tropes, and much else. So it indirectly benefits almost everyone.[27]

But the funding does not go to the arts in general. It is always extended to particular artistic ventures and given the limited amount of resources a community can divert to the arts, it necessarily involves choices. The argument discussed above suggests that the choice is not objectionably non-neutral if it is based on a judgment on the likelihood of competing artistic ventures to increase the richness and complexity of the general cultural environment. It is not

[26] For a similar claim, see Steven Wall, 'Neutralism for Perfectionists: The Case of Restricted State Neutrality' (2010) 120 *Ethics* 232. Wall, however, proposes a case for a limited neutrality principle that actually defends the APP rather than PSN. He says that coercing people to adopt a particular lifestyle undermines their sense of equal worth, and so even perfectionists must reject it. That is true, but it is not an argument in favor of a separate neutrality principle.

[27] Dworkin (n 1), 229.

clear, however, how this judgment would be separated from judgments on the content of the particular competing ventures. For instance, were we not to think that a new production of *Hamlet* is going to provide an original interpretation of the tragedy, one that links Shakespeare's text to the present in an innovative way, we would not believe that it has the potential to enrich the general cultural environment.

The interdependence between the judgment on the impact of a particular artistic venture on the general cultural environment and the judgment on its intrinsic value makes the distinction between perfectionist state action consistent with neutrality as non-discrimination and one incompatible with it open to reasonable disagreement. A funding decision that, for its advocates, is neutral towards the ranking of different artistic currents and traditions may raise the suspicion of objectionable non-neutrality in the eyes of its opponents.[28] This means, however, that neutrality as non-discrimination lacks criteria for deciding issues to which it purports to apply. It must be amended.

I suggest that we look at the concept of 'reasonable disagreement' with a fresh eye. Rawls identifies 'reasonable disagreement' with intractable disagreement among reasonable people. This characterization allows for two readings. It can be understood as applying only to controversies between persons who *in fact* treat their disputes in a reasonable manner. Or it can be understood as also covering controversies the parties to which may not actually be reasonable but would not be able to settle their disagreement even if they were. There is an important parallel between the two readings, and there are significant differences as well. They are similar in assuming that the parties lack the epistemic resources necessary for achieving reasoned consensus. But they make different assumptions regarding the way the parties respond to the insufficiency of epistemic resources.

The first reading takes the parties to be trying to make as good a case for their position as they can, other things being equal. The second allows for the possibility that some of the parties (or all of them) are reluctant to do so. Such reluctance is particularly onerous on the part of those who have the power to enforce a state act against the judgment and will of its opponents: it casts doubt on whether making and enforcing that act treats everyone with equal concern and respect.

Suppose advocates and opponents of a state act disagree on whether it satisfies PSN. Suppose their disagreement rests on a deeper disagreement on what neutrality, correctly interpreted, requires. Suppose, finally, that the two sides lack the epistemic resources necessary for resolving their disagreement, and consider a case when those responsible for defending the act make a good-faith attempt to track the correct interpretation and tailor the act to that interpretation. By hypothesis, they have no proof for their position, such that the opponents of the act, if reasonable, could not but accept it. But they give evidence that they take seriously the moral taint the act would incur if it violated PSN. This is the best they can do, under the circumstances, in order to make sure that the act satisfies the principle of equal concern and respect (to the extent that this depends on whether the act is neutral in the relevant sense). The act's opponents may think in good faith that it reflects a defective interpretation of what PSN requires. This is not a sufficient ground, though, for them to claim that the act expresses contempt for their (or for anyone else's) status and interests.

Consider, now, a case when those with a responsibility to defend the act disregard their duty to support it by a plausible enough conception of state neutrality. That is evidence that they do

[28] See Harry Brighouse, 'Neutrality, Publicity, and the State Funding of the Arts' (1995) 22 *Philosophy and Public Affairs* 35.

not take seriously the consequences of violating PSN. Thus, even if the opponents of the act cannot prove beyond controversy that it violates PSN correctly interpreted, the disregard for the duty to support the act by a plausible enough conception of state neutrality counts, decisively under the circumstances, against the act.

To sum up: a state act with an impact of redistributing advantages among people who pursue different conceptions of the good is permitted by PSN if the underlying value judgment refers to how the redistribution affects the overall cultural environment rather than particular cultural forms and practices belonging to it. On the other hand, whether the real basis of the act is such a holistic judgment or a judgment regarding particular cultural forms and practices may be a controversial matter, the parties to the disagreement lack the epistemic tools to resolve it. In such cases—in cases of reasonable disagreement—the belief of the critics that the act is objectionably non-neutral is not a sufficient ground for treating it as illegitimate if the advocates of the act make a good-faith attempt to justify their contrary belief, while the same judgment is a sufficient ground for treating it as illegitimate if those responsible for defending the act refuse to take their justificatory duty seriously.[29]

One might object: the question whether a state act reflects a serious *attempt* to satisfy the neutrality requirement is as open to 'reasonable disagreement' as the question whether it in fact *achieves* that aim, the only difference consisting in that the latter question divides defenders and critics of the act while the former emerge between different critics.

What a reasonable critic may see as an act issued from a good-faith—even if failed—attempt to satisfy the correct interpretation of PSN, other, no less reasonable critics may see to be an outright rejection of the very requirement of neutrality. So we need more refined tests capable of dealing with this further disagreement.

Here are two examples of such tests. The first asks whether a particular state act charged with violating neutrality as non-discrimination receives a justification that faces up to the moral gravity of the criticism. This test—call it the *adequacy test*—rests on the idea that citizens have a right of equal respect publicly to object to their state's acts and to receive an answer that takes their objections seriously. The adequacy test does not fail a state act for lacking knock-down proof of its neutrality; by hypothesis, no such proof is available. But it fails the act if those having the power to make and enforce it simply ignore their duty to meet objections of non-neutrality adequately, and not to dismiss them without due consideration. It also fails the act which, while being claimed in principle to satisfy neutrality as non-discrimination, appeals to specific judgments on the comparative value of competing pursuits (as when a government, while declaring its intention to support the arts with the neutral aim of maintaining a rich and complex cultural environment, takes at the same time the blasphemous character of certain artistic works as a reason to deny eligibility for support to those works).

A second test that I would call *the outcome test* asks whether a putatively neutral act is characterized by strong outcome bias. Its question does not rest on mistakenly taking outcome neutrality for a plausible neutrality principle.[30] It rather rests on the assumption that strong outcome bias is a reason for suspecting that the allegedly neutral justification of the controversial act is not forwarded in good faith. The outcome test fails an act that, while claiming

[29] This is a further reason why, as I mentioned in Section I, the early advocates of liberal neutrality were mistaken to think that the neutrality requirement applies only to the reasons that can possibly be marshaled in favor of it ('justificatory neutrality'), and never to the reasons actually appealed to ('neutrality of intent').

[30] For the implausibility of interpreting neutrality as neutrality of outcomes, see Section I.

neutrality towards competing views on how to live well, rigs the distribution of burdens and benefits against a particular view.[31]

VI. Neutrality as Shared Reasons Revisited

To recap, the pervasive fact of 'reasonable disagreement' raises a difficulty for LLP. The question is, how can a justification that is controversial among reasonable citizens appeal to each of them. Rawls proposes 'political liberalism' as a solution to this difficulty. This solution is not workable, however: the 'burdens of judgment' underlying the facts of 'reasonable disagreement' are not specific to 'comprehensive doctrines'. Members of modern, democratic societies tend to disagree on just about everything, including the political principles of justice, freedom, equality, and toleration. Thus, the shared reasons prong of PSN must either be abandoned or revised.

I suggest that we follow the strategy of revision explored in the previous section. Suppose the shared reasons available to citizens of a democratic republic are insufficient for allowing those with a responsibility to defend a state act to provide a compelling argument in terms of reasons their opponents can be expected to share. And suppose that these people take seriously their obligation to try to provide an argument in terms of such reasons. Then, the critics must understand the controversial act as resulting from a good-faith—even if unsuccessful—attempt to work from a conception of legitimacy that rests on reasons each citizen can be expected to share. In this case, given the fact of 'reasonable disagreement', they are not justified to see the act as denying equal respect to those who disagree with it. Suppose now that those with a responsibility to defend the act disregard their duty to provide everyone with reasons they can be expected to share. Then, again given the fact of reasonable disagreement, the critics are justified in suspecting that the act fails to treat with equal respect those who disagree with it.

LLP as amended requires political communities seriously *to try* to provide each citizen with reasons they can be expected to share; its verdict does not hinge on the success of the attempt. Non-neutrality in the shared reasons sense violates LLP, and is therefore morally objectionable, if and only if it reflects *a failure to make the requisite effort* to justify the controversial act in terms of reasons each citizen can be expected to share.[32]

However, the question whether a state act reflects a serious attempt to provide a justification each citizen can be expected to share is as open to 'reasonable disagreement' as the very content of the justification. So the distinction, as the previous section suggested in the

[31] Consider an individual in the grip of a terminal illness. Suppose she thinks that a life in debilitating pain and dependence undermines her dignity, and asks for medical assistance to discontinue it. And suppose the law makes voluntary euthanasia a punishable crime. The legislator says, however: euthanasia is an insult to God and to the order of nature, but this judgment does not figure among the reasons for its prohibition. We prohibit it because we have to take the interests of other terminally ill patients into consideration, too: those who think that by successfully resisting the temptation to precipitate death they will achieve their life's greatest victory or want to live on for some other reason. Permitting euthanasia would deliver them to the arbitrary will of their relatives, tired of assisting them or desirous to inherit their property. Such a reasoning is not entirely groundless. There is no legal regulation of end-of-life decisions that would maximally fit the interests of both types of terminally ill people. Any regulation must be suboptimal at least from the point of view of one of the two groups. But placing the whole burden of regulation on one of the groups—especially if its interests do not carry the sympathy of the legislator—raises the suspicion that the actual motivation for the act is not neutral between the conflicting decisions.

[32] See Ronald Dworkin, *Justice for Hedgehogs* (2011), 322.

context of a similar problem, needs more elaborate tests. Here are, again, two examples of such tests.

The first test was widely discussed in the debates about liberal neutrality; it is of an epistemic character. Call it the *accessibility test*. The accessibility test draws a line between two different ways a reason may be ineligible for being a shared reason. Sometimes a person cannot be expected to share a reason because it is inconsistent with her other views. She examines the proposed reason against the backdrop of the views she already holds, and ends up rejecting it as unsuitable for being integrated into the web of those views. When, on the other hand, a reason is inaccessible to her, such an examination cannot even begin. How, then, to make sense of this claim?

In a paper from the late 1980s, Thomas Nagel suggests that for a reason to be publicly accessible, 'it must be possible to present [it] to others . . . , so that once you have done so, they have what you have.'[33] In reply, Joseph Raz argues that the proposed criterion is too demanding: it rules out reliance even on everyday observations of fact. Suppose I am the only eyewitness to an accident, and I report to you what I have seen. Under certain conditions, you would take my report as the basis of your judgment on what happened. But you would not have what I have. My sensory perceptions and memories would not become yours.

Is it possible to resolve this difficulty by relaxing Nagel's criterion? Raz's answer is: no. Suppose you know that the accident could not have happened the way I described it, or you have your doubts about the reliability of the visual perception and memory of eyewitnesses in general. Then, you have reasons for not trusting my report. And yet you would agree that if my story were not grossly implausible, and if my memory were not distorted by hearsay and newspaper reports etc, then my report would be acceptable as evidence of what had happened. If you do not trust my report, you and I do not have shared beliefs concerning the accident. But my report is accessible to you since it would make perfect sense for you to rely on it if the requisite conditions obtained, and you and I agree on what those conditions are.

Unfortunately, relaxed in this way, the criterion becomes too weak, Raz goes on to argue. Certain types of reasons that Nagel would want to rule out as lacking public accessibility would pass it: 'Others may doubt whether the Centurion saw Jesus rise from his grave. But they agree that if he did, it is evidence . . . of the Resurrection.'[34] On the relaxed test, there seems to be no difference between the epistemic status of the Centurion's account of what he saw as an eyewitness to the miracle of Resurrection and my account of what I saw as an eyewitness to an accident.

The conclusion does not seem to follow, though. For a religious audience, the report on what the Centurion saw has a deeper meaning than that of evidence for an empirical fact. It involves them in the mystery of the existence of the supernatural. For people with a secular outlook, mystery is but an unresolved intellectual problem calling for further inquiry or explanation. For a religious person, the fact that mystery defies rational explanation is not a defect to be superseded but rather a gift of grace that allows one to be initiated into the presence of the divine in the world. The sense of awe accompanying the belief in religious facts such as the resurrection of Jesus is not a further belief people with a secular outlook do not hold true being able to agree, at the same time, that if it were true it would be evidence for the fact of resurrection or for other religious claims such as the one holding that Jesus was the son of God. Rather, it is a personal experience of encountering something greater than man, greater even

[33] Thomas Nagel, 'Moral Conflict and Political Legitimacy' (1987) 16 *Philosophy and Public Affairs* 215, 232.

[34] Joseph Raz, 'Facing Diversity: The Case for Epistemic Abstinence' (1990) 19 *Philosophy and Public Affairs* 3, 40.

than humanity.[35] And yet, it secures an exalted status to the underlying beliefs that radically distinguish them from ordinary secular beliefs and is experienced as a warranty to their truth. Beliefs of such exalted status are inaccessible to non-believers. If someone with a secular outlook found the eyewitness report of the Resurrection to be reliable, then he would take it as evidence not for an exalted fact but rather for an ordinary fact that calls for an explanation in terms of his ordinary beliefs. Justifying a legitimacy claim by reasons that are inaccessible to some people in this way amounts to denying equal respect to this people, and so it is failed by the accessibility test.

Does this mean that all religious reasons are inaccessible to non-believers? I will argue in Section VII that it does not: actually, religious reasons are likely to pass the accessibility test significantly more often than to be failed by it. But this does not mean that the accessibility test cannot be given consistent interpretation or that it is empty for some other reason. It means only that it is a test with relatively limited power.

The early advocates of liberal neutrality paid much less attention to the second test I want to consider now. This is regrettable since, as I will attempt to show in the next section, this test—I would call it the *recognition test*—is much more powerful than the accessibility test.

Here is how it goes: reasons for adopting and enforcing a state act sometimes make explicit or implicit reference to the social identity of the community in whose name the act is made and applied. When they do, and when the group identified in this way is less inclusive than the citizenry as a whole, then some citizens cannot but see themselves as being denied recognition as full members of the citizenry. The recognition test fails such reasons because people whose status is degraded in this way cannot accept the reasons in question without resigning their sense of full citizenship. Thus, the recognition test is indeed a test of neutrality as shared reasons. It is similar to the accessibility test in that it is a consequence of the requirement of equal respect. But it is dissimilar to that test in the way it is linked to equal respect. The accessibility test is linked to equal respect indirectly, through an assessment of the epistemic status of the controversial reasons. The recognition test is linked to it directly, through the examination of the scope of the group identified with 'we the people'.

It is not only reasons in the strict sense of the word that are proper objects of the recognition test. States may adopt group-specific symbols which are not provided as reasons for adopting and enforcing an official act but which submit themselves to the question whether their adoption is consistent with attributing full status to each and every citizen. Think of hanging the crucifix in classrooms of public schools or in courts of justice. There are good grounds to presume that the display of the crucifix conveys the message that the state belongs to the community of Christian believers and that, as a consequence, non-Christians and non-believers are at best marginal citizens. That presumption is open to rebuttal, but it marks the default option, and given the threat to the status as citizens for some, really strong reasons are needed for the rebuttal to succeed.

I conclude this section by a remark on the relationship between neutrality as non-discrimination and neutrality as shared reasons. I said, towards the end of Section III, that the two prongs of PSN have separate domains: the first applies to the way the state treats its subjects while the second applies to the way it speaks to them and about them. The discussion of the recognition test reveals, however, that although separate, the two prongs are closely related. Once we see that mere symbolic expressions fall within the scope of the recognition test, it is a small step to discover that discriminating between citizens on account of a judgment

[35] See Tim Crane, 'Mystery and Evidence', *The Opinionator: New York Times*, 5 September 2010, available at <http://opinionator.blogs.nytimes.com/2010/09/05/mystery-and-evidence/>.

about their basic beliefs or lifestyles may carry a symbolic message, one that is condemned by the recognition test. Acts that violate neutrality as non-discrimination may, by the same token, also violate neutrality as shared reasons by conveying the judgment that 'we'—the people in whose name the act is carried out—are not *like this*. Judgments that fail the recognition test may, in their turn, serve as a basis for distributing advantages and disadvantages in a way condemned by neutrality as non-discrimination.

VII. Religious Neutrality

The problem of the place of religion in a liberal state is at the heart of the conception of state neutrality.[36] PSN originally emerged as a response to this problem, in order to be gradually generalized throughout the history of constitutional debates and struggles in modern democracies. Even as it grew more and more general in scope, the way it handles religion remains a major test for its accuracy.

PSN would prove grossly inadequate if it rested on a bias for or against religion. Does this mean that it must treat all conflicts based on disagreements between people of religious versus secular outlooks in the same way as it treats conflicts based on disagreement between secular-minded people or on disagreement between religious people? It does not since the tests of neutrality may not be equally satisfied by reasons of religious and secular character.

Consider neutrality as shared reasons first, beginning with the accessibility test. There seems to be no secular counterpart to miracles and revelations. The special attitude towards mystical experience described in the previous section seems to be constitutive of the religious outlook and largely alien from the secular one. Thus, secular reasons are unlikely to be failed by the accessibility test, while it is not difficult to see how a religious reason may be failed by it.

This claim must be treated with caution. Religious reasons are not reducible to reports of mystical experience. Their body entails a large set of claims—ethical, moral, prudential, metaphysical, and empirical—that non-religious individuals are fully capable of assessing against their own background beliefs. Theologians often rely on nothing but 'natural' reasons, that is, reasons available to the ordinary human mind, unaided by divine revelation.[37]

Here is an example: 'Human persons are equal since God has created all of us to His own image.' Such propositions are not rendered inaccessible to non-believers in virtue of their religious connotation. Actually, much of the modern, secular moral theory emerged from translations of Judeo-Christian moral theology and from a critical engagement with it. So if it is the inaccessibility test that fails religious claims, then PSN does not disqualify religion-based reasons *as such*. Rather, it cuts across the domain of religious reasons, ruling out a relatively small part of them.

The recognition test seems to have more far-reaching implications. Religions are not exhausted by sets of beliefs. They typically constitute a community, setting apart insiders from outsiders. Religion tends to define social identity in a way secular belief systems do not. This difference has momentous consequences.[38]

To recall, the state speaks in the name of 'we the people'. Explicitly or implicitly, its pronouncements say something about who 'we the people' are. Respect for the equal status of citizens requires the state not to attribute to 'we the people' a social identity that is less inclusive

[36] On religion more generally, see Chapter 43.

[37] See Raz (n 34), 40.

[38] There are exceptions. Marxism in the early periods of its history was one.

than the citizenry as a whole. Imagine a law starting with this preamble: 'Whereas God has given the earth to humankind for common use'. The text of the preamble echoes a thesis of Christian theology. Combined with the implicit claim of speaking in the name of the people, it implies that 'we the people' are a community of Christian believers. It signals to non-Christians and non-believers that they are not full members.

There are, thus, serious grounds for assuming that neutrality as shared reasons fails religious reasons significantly more often than it fails secular reasons. It always judges as inappropriate a state acting to appeal to religious reasons, but it does not necessarily judge official appeals to controversial secular reasons to be inappropriate. It mandates the avoidance of religious language not because religious claims are false or otherwise problematic; it does so because of the social identity-related implications of its use by official state acts. According to Charles Taylor, to have a legislative clause: 'Whereas Kant said that the only thing good without limits is a good will', or 'Whereas Marx said that religion is the opium of the people', would be as improper as having a legislative clause appealing to some religious tenet.[39] But the appeal to the Kantian dictum would have no consequences for the social identity of 'we the people'. The Marxian clause would, since it identifies the community in the name of which the law speaks as opposed to religion. Anti-religious language is ruled out by neutrality as shared reasons on the same ground as is religious language, while secular language as such is not.

Those insisting that PSN is biased against religion because its shared reasons prong disqualifies them more often than it disqualifies secular reasons should consider how the non-discrimination prong deals with the difference between religious and secular reasons. If the shared reason prong expresses an anti-religious bias, then the non-discrimination prong is loaded by a reverse—anti-secularist—bias.

To explain: there are special cases when neutrality as non-discrimination allows privileged treatment to be given to people committed to basic beliefs or pursuing ways of life of a particular kind. The property of the beliefs or lifestyles that justifies privileged treatment in such cases is that they involve special obligations that may conflict with the obligation to obey the law. Consider a conscript committed to a religious creed that prohibits taking up arms. Neutrality permits granting an exemption to such a person, since the exception clause need not rely on a comparative judgment about his views on how one should live and the views held by others. It rather rests on the judgment that enforcing the law against a person's sincerely held ethical convictions is an affront to moral integrity—whether or not those convictions are correct.

To be sure, for the exemption to fit neutrality as non-discrimination, the class of the beneficiaries of the exception clause must coincide with the class of those whom the requirement to obey the law would implicate in a serious conflict of conscience. All sorts of radical pacifists, religious or not, face the same conflict when called up to serve in the army. Thus, narrowing the justification of the exception clause to holders of a religious system of belief would unjustly discriminate against pacifists with a secular outlook.[40]

No such discrimination is involved, however, by exemptions that honor the ritual code of certain religions. As an example, think of the permission given to Sikh men riding a motorcycle to wear their turban rather than a safety helmet. Such exemptions are individual to particular

[39] Charles Taylor, 'How to Define Secularism', Paper presented at the Colloquium on Legal, Political, and Social Philosophy, New York University School of Law, 11 November 2010, available at <http://www.law.nyu.edu/ecm_dlv3/groups/public/@nyu_law_website__academics__colloquia__legal_political_and_social_philosophy/documents/documents/ecm_pro_067143.pdf>.

[40] On when legal exemptions are and are not objectionably non-neutral, see Kwame Anthony Appiah, *The Ethics of Identity* (2003), 88–9.

religions; they have no application to people committed to some secular system of belief. This is because religions, unlike secular creeds, constitute nomic communities: they set conventional norms of conduct with which the faithful are expected to comply. Nomic communities regulate activities which may also be subject to legal regulation. Coincidences of the two codes—the religious and the political—tend to give rise to conflict of conscience similar to the one inflicted upon radical pacifists by military conscription. No such conflicts are likely to emerge for people with a secular outlook.

Thus, the exception is properly restricted to people belonging to certain religious groups: neutrality as non-discrimination endorses this rather than condemning it.[41]

In sum, if PSN deals with religion in a special manner, the special restrictions and exemptions are not due to bias but rather to the special characteristics of religion as a belief system and as a social institution.

Philosophers and legal scholars with a religious background insist that, on the contrary, PSN does not give appropriate consideration to the special character of religion. The requirement to bracket out religious reasons silences citizens whose views on matters of policy are motivated by faith and, by assuming that their concerns can be exhaustively rendered in secular terms, it trivializes their deepest convictions.[42]

Is this complaint against liberal neutrality well founded? It may ring, perhaps, persuasively when it is raised in France but not in the United States where, to put it bluntly, it is the kiss of death for a politician openly to confess to a lack of religious faith. But the question is not whether it is a fact about politics in contemporary liberal states that religious believers find themselves marginalized by it, but whether it is true about the principle of state neutrality that, properly understood, it implies such a marginalization. Clearly, PSN requires *the law* to use secular language. But, for the complaint to hold, it must be the case that PSN requires the public discourse *about* the law to use secular language, too. Does it entail such a requirement? Not necessarily, since not all participants of public deliberation speak in the name of 'we the people', and when they do not, their language does not determine the political status of those disagreeing with them nor is it subject to the requirement of state neutrality on some other ground.

When citizens participate in the informal processes of public deliberation, they speak in their own name, and so PSN does not bear on their discourse. Judges speaking in the court are at the opposite extreme, since they give authoritative interpretations of the law. Legislators are somewhere in between: while not speaking in their own name, rarely do they speak, as individual members of the legislature, in the name of the legislative body—and, therefore, the citizenry—as a whole. Their pronouncements contribute to public deliberation in a pluralistic society including many particular perspectives. Typically, they speak from one of the many perspectives of which the religious perspectives represent one legitimate family. So PSN leaves some latitude for legislators to give voice to religious reasons.[43] How wide is that latitude?

In *PL*, Rawls argues that the duty of civility binds citizens to explain their position to others in terms of public reason.[44] If that is true about ordinary citizens, it is doubly true about their representatives, especially when they speak in the legislature, as participants in the process of

[41] See Jeremy Waldron, 'One Law for All?' (2002) 59 *Washington and Lee Law Review* 3–34.

[42] See Stephen L. Carter, 'The Religiously Devout Judge' (1989) 64 *Notre Dame Law Review* 932; Michael W. McConnell, 'Religious Freedom at a Crossroads' (1992) 59 *University of Chicago Law Review* 115.

[43] Habermas insists that, nevertheless, religious discourse must be kept out even from legislative debates: the Speaker of the Parliament must have the power, he says, to delete from the protocols religious statements and justifications. It is unclear why this should be the case. See Jürgen Habermas, 'Religion in der Öffentlichkeit' in Jürgen Habermas, *Zwischen Naturalismus und Religion* (2005), 137.

[44] Rawls, *Political Liberalism* (n 1), 217 ff.

legislation. But Rawls also mentions two considerations that may override the presumption. In both cases, religious reasons are additive to the reasons presented in secular language. They may be added, according to Rawls, either as evidence of the sincerity of a religious legislator's commitment to a particular political position, or with the aim of giving strength to the political conception.[45]

One could cite further considerations. When the political argument seems to run out, religious ideas may be introduced into the debate in the hope of providing the non-religious party with fruitful metaphors that may help to unblock the controversy. Ironically, the non-religious side may also find an interest in making the religious background of the opponent's position explicit. They may want to show that that position is not implied by the underlying religious views: one can adopt a different political position without being compelled to give up those views.

To conclude, PSN—including neutrality as shared reasons—requires strict exclusion of religion from the language of the state's acts and their official justification; its requirements become less stringent when the speaker does not speak in the name of the state and, through it, the citizenry. Liberal neutrality, properly understood, has no impact on silencing people with deeply held religious beliefs.

To be sure, religious language is not part of the shared language of a pluralistic community, and it is appropriate to presume that representatives—unlike ordinary citizens—ought to stick to the shared language. Rawls invokes, in *PL*, the ideal of civility in support of such a presumption.

Bibliography

Bruce Ackerman, *Social Justice in a Liberal State* (1980)
Kwame Anthony Appiah, *The Ethics of Identity* (2003)
Robert Audi, *Religious Commitment and Secular Reason* (2000)
Richard Bellamy and Martin Hollis (eds), *Pluralism and Liberal Neutrality* (1999)
Ronald Dworkin, *A Matter of Principle* (1985), chs 8, 9, 11, 17
Ronald Dworkin, *Sovereign Virtue* (2000), chs 3, 6
Robert Goodin and Andrew Reeve (eds), *Liberal Neutrality* (1989)
Jürgen Habermas, *Zwischen Naturalismus und Religion* (2005)
Vinit Haksar, Equality, *Liberty and Perfectionism* (1979)
George Klosko and Steven Wall (eds), *Perfectionism and Neutrality. Essays in Liberal Theory* (2003)
Charles Larmore, *Patterns of Moral Complexity* (1987)
Steven Lecce, *Against Perfectionism. Defending Liberal Neutrality* (2008)
Alasdair MacIntyre, *After Virtue. A Study in Moral Theory* (1985)
Michael J. Perry, *The Political Morality of Liberal Democracy* (2010)
John Rawls, *A Theory of Justice* (1999)
John Rawls, *Political Liberalism* (1993)
Joseph Raz, *The Morality of Freedom* (1986)
Michael Sandel, *Liberalism and the Limits of Justice* (1982)
George Sher, *Beyond Neutrality. Perfectionism and Politics* (1997)
Steven Wall, *Liberalism, Perfectionism, and Restraint* (2006)

[45] Ibid 247, 251.

CHAPTER 16

THE CONSTITUTION AND JUSTICE

ROBERTO GARGARELLA

Buenos Aires

THIS chapter consists of three sections. In Section I, I examine a *procedural* approach to the constitution. According to the *procedural* reading, a just constitution has to be *neutral* among different views and establish a fair procedure through which rival parties seek approval from the people. In order to study the procedural approach, I shall seek support in John Rawls's *Theory of Justice*, where the constitution is examined as an exemplar of *imperfect procedural justice*. In Section II, I distinguish between two different interpretations of the procedural constitution, one related to libertarianism and the other to egalitarianism. These interpretations allow us to reflect on the neutral character of the procedural constitution. In Section III, I contrast the procedural approach with an alternative, republican understanding of the constitution. In order to illustrate the differences between these theories, I examine their conflicting views regarding whether a just constitution should incorporate, or not, a list of social rights in its Bill of Rights.

I. PROCEDURAL JUSTICE

1. Rawls, the Constitution, and (Imperfect) Procedural Justice

In his well-known book, *A Theory of Justice*, John Rawls presents the constitution as one of the main examples of what he calls *imperfect procedural justice*. So understood, the constitution comes to set up 'a form of fair rivalry for political office and authority'.[1] In order to understand

[1] John Rawls, *A Theory of Justice* (1971), 227.

what Rawls means by the idea of imperfect procedural justice, it is necessary to examine the three general ideas of procedural justice that are studied in *A Theory of Justice*.

The first idea refers to *perfect procedural justice*. Here, there is an independent criterion for deciding what is a fair outcome ('a criterion defined separately from and prior to the procedure which is to be followed'), and a procedure that guarantees that we get that outcome. An example of this case would be a procedure for dividing a cake where the one who slices the case picks last. In this case we have an independent criterion of justice (equal slices for all), and a procedure that is appropriate for reaching that outcome.

The second idea is the one of *imperfect procedural justice*. Here we also have, as in the first case, an independent criterion that allows us to define what is a fair outcome; but we do not have, as in the previous case, a procedure that ensures the desired outcome. An example that could illustrate this case is that of a criminal trial. In effect, here we know that we want to condemn only the guilty, but the procedure that we have created for dealing with these situations cannot guarantee us the desired outcome. In fact, as Rawls says, it seems impossible to design the legal rules so that they always lead to the correct result.

Finally, we have the case of *pure procedural justice*. In this situation, and contrary to what happened in the previous two, we do not have an independent criterion for the right result. What we do have is a fair procedure such that the outcome is likewise correct, provided that the procedure was properly followed. The example would be that of gambling, where we do have a procedure, but not a pre-defined fair outcome.

The constitution is, according to Rawls, an exemplary case of imperfect procedural justice.[2] This is so because

> there is no feasible political procedure which guarantees that the enacted legislation is just even though we have (let us suppose) a standard for just legislation.... The constitutional process, like a criminal trial (cannot guarantee) that only just and effective legislation is enacted.[3]

To favor the enactment of just legislation, the procedural constitution needs to be framed so that 'it is more likely than any other (arrangement) to result in a just and effective system of legislation'.[4] For such a purpose, it is crucial that the constitution guarantees *equal participation*. In his words, 'all citizens are to have an equal right to take part in, and to determine the outcome of, the constitutional process that establishes the laws with which they are to comply'.[5] The point is extremely important: if the state wants to exercise its coercive authority in a legitimate way, then the constitutional process has to preserve this equal representation to the degree that is feasible.[6]

Other crucial characteristics of the procedural constitution would be the following. First, and in order to satisfy the principle of equal participation, it is necessary but not sufficient that the charter guarantees periodic, free, and fair elections. In a proper constitutional regime, Rawls maintains, we should also find 'firm constitutional protections for certain liberties, particularly freedom of speech and assembly, and liberty to form political associations'.[7]

In addition, Rawls believes that the usual devices of constitutionalism (such as checks and balances, separation of powers, etc) can be consistent with the principle of equal liberty (although they certainly limit it), provided that 'the constraints introduced are likely over time to fall evenly upon all sectors of society'.[8] In every case, the idea is to ensure that 'those similarly

[2] Ibid 221.

[3] John Rawls, 'The Justification of Civil Disobedience' in John Rawls, *Collected Papers* (1999), 180.

[4] Rawls (n 1), 221. [5] Ibid.

[6] Ibid 222. [7] Ibid 222–3. [8] Ibid 224.

endowed and motivated... have roughly the same chance of attaining positions of political authority irrespective of their economic and social class.'[9] Rawls is well aware that the liberties in question lose much of their value whenever the rich (or, in general, the most advantaged) are allowed to use their privileges to bias the public debate in their own favor. Such an unfair situation may always occur, although it is more typical—according to Rawls—in societies that allow 'private ownership if the means of production, property and wealth' to be 'concentrated in a few hands, rather than widely distributed'.

Finally, Rawls establishes a strong connection between the political conception of justice and political liberalism. Liberalism helps us to understand what the *constitutional essentials* or essential features of the constitution must be. In Rawls's words, the essential features would be the following:

> the powers of the legislative, executive, and the judiciary, the limits and scope of majority rule, as well as the basic political and civil rights and liberties legislative majorities must respect, such as the right to vote and to participate in politics, freedom of thought and liberty of conscience, and also the protections of the rule of law.[10]

So organized, the political process becomes 'a just procedure for choosing between governments and for enacting just legislation',[11] or, in other words, a procedure through which 'rival parties seek the citizen's approval... against a background of freedom of thought and assembly in which the fair value of political liberty is assured.'[12]

Rawls's insistence on the procedural character of the constitution is intimately related to his rejection of an opposite alternative, namely that of having a constitution that expresses and enforces a comprehensive view of justice. For him, if we want to have a 'workable political conception of justice', the conception of justice embodied by the constitution must be able to 'gain the support of a diversity of comprehensive doctrines'. Political liberalism is not 'a view of the whole of life: it is not a (fully or partially) comprehensive doctrine'.[13]

[9] Ibid 225. In effect, the principle of equal liberty, which implies the notion 'one elector one vote', requires that 'each vote has approximately the same weight in determining the outcome of elections' (ibid 223). See further Chapter 6 on constitutionalism and impoverishment and Chapter 50 on economic rights.

[10] John Rawls, 'The Domain of the Political and Overlapping Consensus' in Rawls, *Collected Papers* (n 3), 481. In this way, the political conception of justice comes to provide a 'reasonable framework of principles and value for resolving questions' concerning the constitutional essentials. For that reason, diverse and opposite comprehensive doctrines are able to endorse the political conception, even though 'it may have little specific to say about innumerable economic and social uses that legislative bodies must regularly consider' (ibid).

[11] John Rawls, 'Distributive Justice' in Rawls, *Collected Papers* (n 3), 141.

[12] Ibid 227.

[13] John Rawls, 'The Idea of Public Reason Revisited' in Rawls, *Collected Papers* (n 3), 480. Rawls's rejection of the picture of a society dominated and organized by a comprehensive view was always present in the background of his reasoning and writings, but became almost an obsession in his later work, and particularly so since his *Political Liberalism* (1993). He himself clarified this point in one of the few interviews he conceded in those years. In his words:

> I'm concerned about the survival, historically, of constitutional democracy. I live in a country where 95 or 90 percent of the people profess to be religious, and maybe they are religious, though my experience of religion suggests that very few people are actually religious in more than a conventional sense. Still, religious faith is an important aspect of American culture and a fact of American political life. So the question is: in a constitutional democracy, how can religious and secular doctrines of all kinds get on together and cooperate in running a reasonably just and effective government? What assumptions would you have to make about religious and secular doctrines, and the political sphere, for these to work together?

John Rawls, '*Commonweal* Interview with John Rawls (1998)' in Rawls, *Collected Papers* (n 3), 616.

2. Justice and the Constitution: The Liberal View

In the present context of societies characterized by 'the fact of pluralism', liberals reject the use of the state's coercive powers in the name of any particular view. As the moral philosopher Michael Sandel has put it, liberals assume that '[since] people disagree about the best way to live, government should not affirm in law any particular vision of the good life. Instead, it should provide a framework of rights that respects individuals as free and independent beings, capable of choosing their own values and ends.' Liberals assert 'the priority of fair procedures over particular ends,' and this is why he refers to this view as 'the procedural republic'.[14]

In this procedural republic, the constitution is seen as fundamentally *neutral* in its content, which means that it is not committed to any particular comprehensive doctrine. This is to say, for liberals, the main mission of the constitution is to set a framework that is compatible with substantively different approaches.

Now, to state this does not mean to deny that the procedural view is premised on the defense of one particular value, namely individual autonomy. In any case, one needs to consider that the value of individual autonomy has the particular characteristic of being able to accommodate, in principle, all other different values and conceptions of the good. A constitution that consecrates the value of personal autonomy is, then, a constitution that is equally open to radically different projects, both at the personal and political level.

A central element of the struggle led by liberalism in defense of personal autonomy was its proclaimed distrust of the power of the state. The state came to represent the source of evil, the risk of oppression, the permanent threat that could violate the most sacred individual liberties. That which, over the course of long years, liberals had learned was the foremost threat to everyone's liberty originated there: in concentrated power, the state that controlled both budget and arms. This omnipotent state was the same one that had persecuted religious dissidents, the one that had expropriated, the one that had threatened property, freedoms of expression, and association. Hence, for many, the solution, when faced with such a risk, turned out to be the severe restriction of the state's powers; if a powerful state meant the risk of oppression, an absent state or one with its hands tied held the promise of liberty.[15]

The whole procedural constitutional can be read as an attempt to protect individual autonomy and limit the influence of the state. If we pay attention to the two main parts of the liberal constitution, we can see that it consists of a bill of rights, which is basically aimed at the protection of individuals' rights against perfectionist impulses; and a structure of 'checks and balances', which purports to establish strict controls over the different branches of power, against possible, foreseeable excesses. Let us explore the specific content of each of these sections in more detail.

(a) Bill of Rights

As the philosopher Jürgen Habermas has stated, in the liberal approach

> the status of citizens is defined primarily by negative rights against the state and other citizens. As bearers of these rights, citizens enjoy government protection as long as they pursue their private interests within the boundaries set by legal status, and this includes protections

[14] Michael J. Sandel, *Democracy's Discontent: America in Search of a Public Philosophy* (1996), 4; Michael J. Sandel, 'The Constitution of the Procedural Republic' (1997) 66 *Fordham Law Review* 1.

[15] Because of this, many liberals began to defend the idea that the public life of the community should be the simple and *spontaneous* result of what was agreed upon by its members by means of formal or informal contracts that they would celebrate amongst themselves.

> against government interventions that exceed statutory limits. Political rights have not only the same structure but also the same meaning as private rights that provide space within which legal subjects are free from external compulsion.[16]

A good example of this view of rights as barriers against the state can be found in the very origins of constitutionalism in the United States. At the time, important efforts were directed primarily at impeding the imposition of a particular religion by the central state over a socially and culturally heterogeneous population. Within this framework, the principal protagonists of North American life tended to coincide in defense of practicing tolerance toward religious diversity. While some, like the famous Roger Williams, defended the separation of Church and state as a form of protecting different faiths from the state's nefarious influence, others supported the freedom of religion clause because of their fear that the public power would impose, in the different states that made up the Union, a religion other than the one that predominated in each one of them. Finally, other politicians, like James Madison, encouraged the strict separation of Church and state, bearing in mind the mutual convenience of both authorities, and others still, like Jefferson, defined this separation as a means of protecting the state from persistent interference by the Church—only thereby, thought Jefferson, could the citizens be guaranteed a free choice between distinct political options.[17]

Organized in such a way, the section of rights, in the liberal constitution, comes to 'shield' individuals' lives from external, undue influences. The idea was—as Jefferson graphically stated—to build a 'wall of separation' that separated individuals from the state.[18] Granted, the image of a 'wall of separation' was primarily used to refer to the need for preventing the use of state coercion in religious matters. However, that image helps us to see the liberals' general approach to the issue of the coercive powers of the state. In the end, they wanted to build a 'wall of separation' that protected each person from the arbitrary imposition of *any* conception of the good.[19]

[16] Jürgen Habermas, *Between Facts and Norms: Contributions to a Discourse Theory on Law and Democracy* (1996), 269–70.

[17] The neutrality imposed on the state was entrenched in the US Constitution's First Amendment. It establishes that the Congress cannot dictate any law instituting a particular religion or prohibiting the free exercise of any particular religion. Although many liberals had initially resisted the incorporation of these types of amendments because they thought the state should not assume powers not directly delegated to it, the consecration of this guarantee began to symbolize the liberal commitment to the ideal of neutrality. On state neutrality more generally, see Chapter 15. On freedom of religion, see Chapter 43.

[18] In his words:

> Believing with you that religion is a matter which lies solely between man and his God, that he owes account to none other for his faith or his worship, that the legislative powers of government reach actions only, and not opinions, I contemplate with sovereign reverence that act of the whole American people which declared that their legislature should 'make no law respecting an establishment of religion, or prohibiting the free exercise thereof', therefore building a wall of separation between church and State. Adhering to its expression of the supreme will of the nation in behalf of the rights of conscience, I shall see with sincere satisfaction the progress of those sentiments which tend to restore to man all his natural rights, convinced he has no natural right in opposition to his social duties.

Letter to the Danbury Baptist Association, January 1, 1802, in Thomas Jefferson, *Political Writings* (1999), 397.

[19] In effect, the liberals' defense of religious neutrality implied a broader claim, one against any kind of state interventions against individuals' personal convictions. Individuals, they maintained, had to enjoy their 'privacy', a 'space' free from public interference. The 'private' sphere appeared, therefore, as a sacred and intangible area where each individual was the absolute sovereign. The idea was, then, to ensure the distinction and separation between this 'private' sphere, and the 'public' one: Charles E. Larmore, *Patterns of Moral Complexity* (1987), 198; Michael Walzer, 'Liberalism and the Art of Separation' (1984) 12 *Political Theory* 315. See further Chapter 14 on the public/private divide and Chapter 46 on privacy.

Individual rights function, therefore, like 'trump cards' by which to defy and defeat all collective claims.[20] Through the defense of individual rights, liberals asserted their basic assumption that each person was worthy of respect independently of the fact that the majority or dominant group rejected or disliked his or her own personal project. Each person had to count as an end in him or herself.

(b) Checks and Balances

The liberal system of checks and balances is mainly directed at preventing the abuses coming from an arbitrary executive authority. At the same time, this system of multiple controls reduces the threats posed by a too powerful Congress, such as the oppression of minority groups, or extreme state interventionism.

Madison explained and justified the creation of a system of checks and balances in *Federalist Papers* no 51, where he stated:

> the members of each department should be as little dependent as possible on those of the others, for the emoluments annexed to their offices. Were the executive magistrate, or the judges, not independent of the legislature in this particular, their independence in every other would be merely nominal. But the great security against a gradual concentration of the several powers in the same department, consists in giving to those who administer each department the necessary constitutional means and personal motives to resist encroachments of the others.

The system of checks and balances was thus based on the same goals and assumptions that supported the adoption of the Bill of Rights, namely individualism, self-interest, and the protection of personal choices. The logic that regulated the system was also the same that was present in the former case, this is to say, an *invisible hand* mechanism, which favored that selfish motives became transformed into actions that promoted the interests of society as a whole.[21]

Together with these initiatives, liberals tended to resist institutional arrangements that permitted or promoted the establishment of close bonds between representatives and their constituencies, based on the idea that these arrangements would render impartial decision-making impossible. This, they argued, was the case not only because of the difficulty presented to adequate reflection by the large numbers in the group, under such conditions, but also, mainly, because when subject to the demands of their electorates, representatives would put aside all concern for the general interest in order to focus on the demands of those who pressured them the most. The constant pressures of the electorate would come to directly impede the delegate's ability to change his opinion through conversation with the other delegates; in this way, representatives would turn into the 'mouthpieces' of their electorates. Hence, the preference for representative systems that rested fundamentally on the independent and isolated decisions of representatives. With this type of system—added Madison—'*it may well happen*

[20] Ronald Dworkin, *Taking Rights Seriously* (1977).

[21] In the same text, *The Federalist Papers*, no 51, Madison described the motivational basis of the whole system, which is also telling with regard to the liberal view. He wrote:

> Ambition must be made to counteract ambition. The interest of the man must be connected with the constitutional rights of the place. It may be a reflection on human nature, that such devices should be necessary to control the abuses of government. But what is government itself, but the greatest of all reflections on human nature? If men were angels, no government would be necessary. If angels were to govern men, neither external nor internal controls on government would be necessary. In framing a government which is to be administered by men over men, the great difficulty lies in this: you must first enable the government to control the governed; and in the next place oblige it to control itself.

that the public voice, pronounced by the representatives of the people, will be more consonant to the public good than if pronounced by the people themselves, convened for the purpose' (emphasis added).

Without a well-functioning representative system and without an appropriate system of checks and balances—liberals assumed—decisions became less than rational, or, as was often sustained in that period, less guided by reason than by passion. Moved by passion and other reprehensible impulses, minority or majority groups tended to become *factions*, that is to say (in accordance with the famous definition given by Madison in the *Federalist* no 10) groups that acted against the interests of the nation and the rights of individuals. The liberal constitution, in sum, appeared as a way to reintroduce rationality into politics, and to prevent politics being dominated by powerful groups as well.

II. Libertarianism and Egalitarianism on Substantive Justice

So far we have seen that one of the main virtues claimed by the procedural constitution resides on its neutral character. The fact is, however, that in spite of this claim, supposedly neutral procedures are frequently interpreted as being only or mainly compatible with very specific distributive outcomes. Neutral procedures appear, then, to be thick enough to contain particular distributive mandates.

Let us take, for instance, the case of the US Constitution, which is frequently read as a relevant example of what a procedural, neutral document is or should look like.[22] According to many authors, that Constitution is not a mere catalog of basic, empty rules. Rather, the Constitution is seen as containing particular directives about substantive justice, which would prevent certain distributive outcomes, while promoting certain others.

Many libertarians, for example, consider that the US Constitution is a good example of a well-designed constitution, which is defined as one that organizes the political order so as to 'channel the self-serving behavior of participants towards the common good in manner that comes as close as possible to that described for us by Adam Smith with respect to the economic order.'[23] For this view, the US constitutional system would be a successful attempt to use people's rational egoism for the sake of the individual rights and the nation's interests (which seemed to be under the threat of factions). Accordingly, most of the Founding Fathers, and James Madison in particular, appear, in this approach, as lucid precursors of the so-called public choice analysis. In Buchanan's words,

> When persons are modeled as self-interested in politics...the constitutional challenge becomes one of constructing and deigning framework institutions or rules that will, to the

[22] John Ely, *Democracy and Distrust* (1980). In effect, at the level of constitutional law, many have identified the US Constitution with such a procedural position. This was, eg, how the legal scholar John Ely approached the US Constitution. For Ely, there are no substantive values to be 'discovered within the four corners of the document'. Rather, it is the task of each generation to fill that space with new contents (ibid). The idea is then not

> to focus on whether this or that substantive value is unusually important or fundamental, but rather on whether the opportunity to participate either in the political process by which values are appropriately identified and accommodated, or in the accommodation those processes have reached, has been unduly constricted (ibid 77).

[23] James Buchanan, *The Economics of Politics* (1978), 17.

> maximum extent possible, limit the exercise of such interest in exploitative ways and direct such interest to furtherance of the general interest. It is not surprising therefore, to discover the roots of a public choice perspective...in the writings of the American Founders, and most notably in James Madison's contribution to *The Federalist Papers*.[24]

More significantly, libertarians consider that those origins reveal that the US Constitution embodies a very specific view of justice. As James Dorn has claimed, for Madison, 'justice meant the protection of property, broadly conceived, and it was the primary function of a just government to afford such protection'.[25] The main goal of the Constitution would have then been 'to protect persons and property and provide a structure of government that limited the potential for injustice, that is, for the taking of property without the consent of the rightful owner(s)'. The idea was to 'limit government and provide the maximum scope for individual freedom under the higher law of the Constitution'.[26] In sum, and according to this view, the US Constitution would include a particular view of (distributive) justice that would prevent the undue taking of property.

Of course, this is a debatable reading of the procedural constitution, in general, and a disputable reading of the US Constitution, in particular. In fact, one could reasonably challenge the libertarian presentation in its descriptive aspects, and claim that the libertarian view does not offer a plausible reconstruction of US constitutional history.[27] More significantly, one could also challenge the normative view that libertarians derive from this particular constitutional text and its history.

A good illustration of the latter can be found in the work of the legal scholar Ronald Dworkin. Dworkin interprets the US Constitution as embodying two fundamental values, namely those of freedom and equality. For him, the only plausible interpretation of the text is an egalitarian, moral reading, which demands that every person be treated with equal consideration and respect. This interpretation would be derived from the American constitutional text and practice, and would suggest specific responses for all significant hard cases. In Dworkin's words,

> The moral reading proposes that we all—judges, lawyers, citizens—interpret and apply these abstract clauses on the understanding that they invoke moral principles about political decency and justice....So when some novel or controversial constitutional issue arises—about whether, for instance, the First Amendment permits laws against pornography—people who form an opinion must decide how an abstract moral principle is best understood....The moral reading therefore brings political morality into the heart of constitutional law.[28]

For Dworkin, an appropriate interpretation of the main principles incorporated into the constitution forces on us relevant conclusions regarding many of the main debates of our public life, including issues about human rights, the role of religion in politics, questions about social justice, the distribution of economic wealth, and the character of the dominant decision-making process. Not surprisingly, Dworkin considers that the specific responses that

[24] James Buchanan, 'The Public Choice Perspective' (1983) 1 *Economia Delle schelte publliche* 7, 14; James Buchanan and Gordon Tullock, *The Calculus of Consent: Logical Foundations of Constitutional Democracy* (1998), 24–5.

[25] Ibid 65.

[26] James Dorn, 'Public Choice and the Constitution: A Madisonian Perspective' in James Gwartney and Richard Wagner (eds), *Public Choice and Constitutional Economics* (1988), 75.

[27] eg other legal scholars have read the same history and authors as embodying a commitment to deliberative democracy, or republicanism. See eg Cass Sunstein, 'Beyond the Republican Revival' (1988) 97 *Yale Law Journal* 1539; Frank Michelman, 'Law's Republic' (1988) 97 *Yale Law Journal* 1493.

[28] Ronald Dworkin, *Freedom's Law: The Moral Reading of the American Constitution* (1996).

derive from the abstract principles of the constitution are liberal-egalitarian in their nature and content. These principles allow him to challenge conservative approaches in matters of religion; resist contemporary criticisms on American tax and social policy; and also defy the politics of the so-called war on terror.[29]

At this point, it is not necessary that we solve the dispute between the libertarian and egalitarian readings of the constitution. This is an interpretative disagreement, which is the object of an ongoing and unfinished debate (John Ely, for example, challenges both readings from a more strictly procedural approach to the US Constitution).[30] It is sufficient to say, by now, that both approaches link the US, procedural Constitution, with a specific view of substantive justice, and that both are reasonable interpretations of the history, values, and practices that surround the Constitution. In other words, both positions come to challenge the idea that the procedural constitution is agnostic in terms of distributive justice. In the end, what this dispute does is to question the idea that the procedural constitution is compatible with the enforcement of almost any position in terms of justice.

III. The Republican Alternative

1. Against the Procedural Approach

Probably, one of the main reasons that makes it difficult for the procedural view of the constitution to stand as an undisputable neutral conception is the fact that, from the very beginning, it incorporates controversial assumptions regarding the individuals' moral character and moral dispositions, their main motivations, and their capacities for acting together. In effect, as we already know, the procedural view tends to take the fact that individuals are rational agents as given. It also assumes that individuals are mainly motivated by self-interest; that they are not particularly interested in participating in politics; or that they have difficulties with behaving rationally, when acting together in large assemblies.[31]

Not surprisingly, then, those who do not share such controversial assumptions tend to have a different approach to the constitution, and think about questions of institutional design in different terms: different subjects with different motivations require, in the end, a different constitutional machinery. One of the most interesting examples, in this respect, is the one represented by the republican alternative.

The republican alternative offers a different reading about the relationship between the constitution and justice. In this reading, the constitution does not appear as a procedural mechanism, open to all different conceptions of the good and ideas of distributive justice, but rather as an expression of a social compact that aims to work for the common good. More in particular, the republican constitution comes to promote, first, certain qualities of character and moral dispositions—a model of a virtuous citizen—and then, also, a certain specific view of social justice—an egalitarian order, capable of fostering a better communal life. Here, positive

[29] Ronald Dworkin, *Is Democracy Possible Here?* (2008).

[30] Ely (n 22), ch 3; Habermas (n 16), 261–86.

[31] As James Madison put it, in *The Federalist Papers*, no 55, 'all very numerous assemblies, of whatever character composed, passion never fails to wrest the sceptre from reason. Had every Athenian citizen been a Socrates, every Athenian assembly would still have been a mob.' These assumptions, eg, moved the Founding Fathers of the US Constitution to regard representative democracy not as a 'necessary evil' but rather as a first, desirable option. They also explain why they assumed that 'the public voice, pronounced by the representatives of the people, will be more consonant to the public good than if pronounced by the people themselves, convened for the purpose' (*The Federalist Papers*, no 10).

liberty or, in other contemporary views, liberty as non-domination, occupies the place that negative liberty occupies in the liberal model.[32]

The starting point of republican constitutional theory is a different conception of the person, which allows its proponents to object to the liberal picture of self-interested individuals, both from a descriptive and normative point of view. They reject the idea that self-interest constitutes the individuals' main motivation, and they also defy the proposal that says that the institutional system has to take self-interest as a given fact as the combustible that fuels the institutional system, and the main motivation that the institutional system promotes.

As a consequence of all these differences, republicans tend to challenge the procedural approach to the constitution, and also the idea of having a constitution that works as an open document, compatible with all possible character traits, conceptions of the good, or ideas of social justice. In contrast with such a view, most republicans maintain that the institutional system has to be organized for the common good. More specifically, they consider that the preservation of a self-governing republic requires the presence of active and committed citizens, who are identified with their fellow citizens and committed to their community.

The republican Constitution of Pennsylvania, 1776, which was written by the British radical Thomas Paine, provides us with an interesting example of how republicans could conceive of the constitution. Among other things, the Constitution asserted that all power 'derived from the people'; that all officers of government were 'their trustees and servants, and at all time accountable to them' (Art 4); and that the people had the right to 'assemble together, and to apply to the legislature for redress of grievances, by address, petition, or remonstrance' (Art 16). Profoundly republican, it declared 'a firm adherence to justice, moderation, temperance, industry, and frugality', virtues that, assumedly, were necessary to 'preserve the blessings of liberty, and keep a government free' (Art 14).

This different, republican understanding of the people's moral character and motivations went hand in hand with a different approach to a majoritarian democracy. In contrast with the profound distrust to mass meetings and collective bodies shown by liberals, most republicans saw massive assemblies as a source of wisdom. They claimed: 'the most respectable assemblies we have any knowledge of and the wisest, have been those, each of which consisted of several hundred members.' Some of them seemed to subscribe a general principle about the virtues of large collective bodies, to which the 'more numerous state assemblies and conventions have universally discovered more wisdom, and as much order, as the less numerous ones'.[33] Others defended the creation of large assemblies for instrumental reasons: 'the variety prevents combination, and the number excludes corruption', they argued.[34]

[32] Philip Pettit, *Republicanism: A Theory of Freedom and Government* (2000); Quentin Skinner, *Liberty Before Liberalism* (1998).

[33] Letter from the 'Federal Farmer' in Herbert Storing, *The Complete Anti-Federalist* (1981), vol 2, 284.

[34] Thomas Paine, *Pennsylvania Packet*, December 5, 1778. In Latin America, the radical liberal Ponciano Arriaga argued that 'legislation becomes wiser when the legislative assembly is more numerous'. 'It is not true', he asserted, contradicting the judgments of his opponents,

> that when we have more deputies we find less conscience and less patriotism among the elected. These difficulties we will have even if we restrict the numbers. However, experience teaches that the more dispersed and fragmented is the authority, the more public spirit and respect for the democratic institutions we find.... What happens is that many are still horrified with the people.... If we increase the number [of deputies] Congress will be filled by new and humbler men, who won't believe they are wise. Perhaps, then, everything will be better, because we will find more faith and stronger commitments [among the representatives].

Following the same line of thought, Ignacio Ramirez criticized the creation of small legislative bodies, arguing that they would be more easily corrupted: Francisco Zarco, *Historia del Congreso Constitucional de 1857* (1957). The Ecuadorian Juan Montalvo also believed that 'great social ideas' required 'the approval of a numerous and august body': Arturo Andrés Raoig, *El pensamiento social de Montalvo* (1984), 231–2.

Given their defense of majoritarianism and, thus, of the supreme authority of Congress, republicans tended to reject institutional arrangements that allowed other branches of power to interfere with the decisions of the legislature. More specifically, they challenged all those proposals that allowed the executive or the judiciary to obstruct the decisions of the majority. Instead of a system of checks and balances, republicans favored a system of *strict separation of powers* where no power had the right to interfere with the actions of the others. As Maurice Vile explained in his study on the first constitutional discussions in the United States: 'they [the radicals] all adhered to the doctrine of the separation of powers, and they all rejected, to a greater or a lesser degree, the concept of checks and balances.'[35]

In coherence with those principles, republicans advocated the expansion of certain specific rights, namely, those that appeared as a precondition to the government of the majorities. Remarkably, as an expression of their defense of self-governing communities, republicans were frequently behind the demands for more political rights. The fight for expanding the list of 'citizens', in fact, defined political radicalism since its origins.

In addition, republicans were also concerned with ensuring the people's subsistence and independence, which were seen as crucial preconditions for having a self-governing community. Some radicals argued against large-scale manufacturing and wage labor, assuming that it would foster the dependency of workers. They believed that 'the dependency of workers under industrial capitalism' would 'deprive[] workers of the independence of mind and judgement necessary to meaningful participation in self-government.'[36] Similarly, many of them defended a substantive revision of the status quo, proposing, for example, a far-reaching redistribution of land. Initiatives of the kind may be found, for example, in Thomas Paine or Thomas Jefferson's defense of 'agrarian republicanism', but also in those of many early constitutional thinkers, also linked to republicanism, all around Latin America.[37] This is why republicanism can be considered the main theoretical antecedent behind the present growth of (what we call) *social rights*.

In the next and final section of this chapter, I shall examine how libertarians and liberals have dealt with social rights. In particular, I shall explore what their ideas about the incorporation of social rights into the constitution were. This examination will allow us to have a better picture of the differences that exist among all these theories, regarding what a just constitution should look like.

[35] Maurice Vile, *Constitutionalism and the Separation of Powers* (1967), 133. The system of 'strict' separation seemed to have many virtues when compared to other alternatives. First, it was based on a mechanism that was clear, simple, and easy to understand. Through its implementation, everyone would know what branch of power was doing what. There would be no confusions. Secondly, the system of 'strict' separation helped to prevent an undesirable scenario: through its functioning, none of the different branches of power would feel the temptation to subtly begin to replace the others. In other words, when the institutional system allowed one of the branches to interfere with the actions of the others, then, it suddenly 'opened the door' to unacceptable encroachments. Each power would use each possible situation for taking the place of the others. Clearly, for people who assumed, as did republicans, that most public officers tended to behave selfishly, this possibility was obviously threatening. Thirdly, the system made clear that, in order to check the government, what was necessary was to ensure 'exogenous' or 'popular' controls. Finally, and most importantly, the system of 'strict' separation fenced the Congress against the intrusive actions of counter-majoritarian institutions: Alexander Bickel, *The Least Dangerous Branch* (1962). Particularly, it helped to strengthen the powers of the congress vis-à-vis a tradition of strong executives, namely, of strong royal governors. In the end, the republicans' defense of the system of 'strict' separation was, above all, a way of preserving the radical character of the republican government. See also Chapter 40.

[36] Sandel, *Democracy's Discontent* (n 14), 326.

[37] Roberto Gargarella, *The Legal Foundations of Inequality. Constitutionalism in the Americas, 1776–1860* (2010).

2. Social Rights

There is a sharp contrast between the level of disagreements that we find in theoretical discussions about social rights, and the present, daily life of social rights.

In actual practice, social rights have already been included in a majority of constitutions, and at the same time there has been an enormous growth and development of judicial activism in the area.[38]

As we know, social rights were first incorporated into a constitution in Weimar, 1919, but even earlier in Mexico, 1917.[39] The tendency towards the adoption of social rights was strongly reinvigorated after the Great Depression and the Second World War, which both strengthened the demand for a more active state. In the United States, Franklin Roosevelt promoted the adoption of a 'Second Bill of Rights' as a means to ensure 'the realization of freedom from want'—which, in Roosevelt's view, meant 'economic understanding which will secure to every nation everywhere a healthy peacetime life for its inhabitants.'[40] Meanwhile, in Europe, and soon after the war, Germany and Italy decided to include social clauses in their constitutions. During the 1970s, and in a second wave of democratization, Greece, Portugal, and Spain also incorporated social guarantees in their constitutions.

European constitutions have opted for these rights in different ways. The Portuguese Constitution, for example, is one of the most detailed, distinguishing between different categories of people in need, including the young, the elderly, the disabled, workers, and the unemployed. The constitutions of France, Italy, the Netherlands, Malta, or Spain are very expansive on the rights they secure, and the levels at which they should be granted. Meanwhile, the Constitution of Cyprus simply stipulates that individuals have a right to 'decent existence and social security', without going into further detail.[41]

In spite of all these practical developments, different theories of justice continue to present substantial disagreements regarding what the status of social rights should be; how these rights compare with first-generation rights (such as freedom of expression or the right of due process); whether they should be incorporated or not into constitutions; and whether and how these rights should be enforced.

In the previous section, for example, we examined the republican alternative approach, and recognized it as an important antecedent in the development of constitutional social rights—republicans, we said, were always supportive of the writing of more 'social' constitutions. However, other theories of justice tend to assume strongly different views on the topic. Libertarians, for instance, adopt a very critical view regarding social rights. For the philosopher Robert Nozick, the problem with social rights is that they 'treat objects as if they appeared from nowhere, out of nothing', ignoring thus the existence of property rights.[42] Many legal

[38] Varun Gauri and Daniel M. Brinks (eds), *Courting Social Justice* (2008); Roberto Gargarella, Pilar Domingo, and Theunis Roux (eds), *Courts and Social Transformation in New Democracies: An Institutional Voice for the Poor?* (2006); Mark Tushnet, *Weak Courts, Strong Rights* (2008).

[39] In Latin America, most constitutions followed the early Mexican example, and promptly began to grant long list of social rights in their constitutions. This is what happened in Brazil, with the 1937 Constitution; in Bolivia, 1938; Cuba, 1940; Ecuador, 1945; Argentina, 1949; and Costa Rica, also in 1949. This strong wave of social constitutionalism was continued and deepened at the end of the century, with a new series of constitutional reforms (ie in Bolivia and Ecuador, 2001), which strengthened these constitutions' commitment to social, economic, and cultural rights.

[40] Cass Sunstein, *The Second Bill of Rights* (2004), 2. However, the US Constitution has finally not incorporated social rights into its text.

[41] Gráinne de Búrca and Bruno de Witte, *Social Rights in Europe* (2005).

[42] Robert Nozick, *Anarchy, State and Utopia* (1974), 160.

scholars related to libertarian theory do not see reasons to commit a constitution to those kinds of provisions. For instance, in the United States, Judge Richard Posner has claimed that 'the Constitution is a charter of negative liberties; it tells the state to let people alone; it does not require the federal government or the state to provide services, even so elementary a service as maintaining law and order.'[43] Similarly, Judge Scalia has said that 'it is impossible to say that our constitution traditions mandate the legal imposition of even so basic a precept of distributive justice as providing food to the destitute';[44] and Judge Bork strongly rejected the possibility of 'finding' welfare rights in the (US) Constitution.[45]

For the liberal-procedural (and even for the liberal egalitarian) tradition, the issue of social rights seems more difficult to tackle. Rawls's approach to the topic—particularly as it was developed in his book *Political Liberalism*—may be illustrative of the difficulties found by liberalism in this respect. In *A Theory of Justice*, the question about social rights and the constitution was still not fully developed, although some of his views on this issue had already generated some controversy. Thus, for example, the legal philosopher Jeremy Waldron criticized the 'original position' that was presented and defended in the book, for not being able to accommodate a 'social minimum'. For Waldron, it was clear that 'an economic system without a social minimum is not a system that could possibly be agreed on in an original position: the strains of commitment rule it out as a possible subject for agreement.'[46]

In *Political Liberalism*—Rawls's second important book—the question of social rights was examined in more detail. In this book, Rawls concedes that a social minimum should be constitutionalized. However, and perhaps surprisingly, he also states that the constitution should deal differently with issues related to basic freedoms, and those related to social and economic questions. Rawls explicitly claims that the constitution has to provide constitutional protection to the basic freedoms, while denying it to the principles that govern social and economic inequalities, that is to say, to the difference principle and the principle of fair equality of opportunity. Rawls lists four reasons for justifying such a different treatment. The reasons are (1) that 'the two kinds of principles specify different roles for the basic structure'; (2) that it is 'more urgent to settle the essentials dealing with the basic freedoms'; (3) that it is 'far easier to tell whether those essentials are realized'; and (4v) that it is 'much easier to gain agreement about what the basic rights and liberties should be'.[47]

[43] Peter B. Edelman, 'The Next Century of Our Constitution: Rethinking our Duty to the Poor' (1988) 39 *Hastings Law Journal* 1, 23.

[44] Ibid 24.

[45] Robert Bork, 'The Impossibility of Finding Welfare Rights in the Constitution' (1979) 1979 *Washington University Law Quarterly* 695; but contrast these views with Frank Michelman, 'Poverty, Economic Equality, and the Equal Protection Clause' (1972) 1972 *Supreme Court Review* 41; Frank Michelman, 'In Pursuit of Constitutional Welfare Rights: One View of Rawls' Theory of Justice' (1973) 121 *University of Pennsylvania Law Review* 962; Frank Michelman, 'Possession vs Distribution in the Constitutional Idea of Property' (1987) 72 *Iowa Law Review* 1319; Frank Michelman, 'Democracy-Based Resistance to a Constitutional Right of Social Citizenship. A Comment on Forbath' (2001) 69 *Fordham Law Review* 1893.

[46] Jeremy Waldron, 'John Rawls and the Social Minimum' in Jeremy Waldron (ed), *Liberal Rights* (1993), 267. Soon after the apparition of *A Theory of Justice*, Norman Daniels published an important critique of Rawls's book, based on the types of inequalities that were there justified. For Daniels, this particular outcome was inconsistent with the very principles that were maintained in the book. More recently, Gerald Cohen has also presented a powerful criticism of the book, with a similar structure. For Cohen, *A Theory of Justice* tolerated inequalities that it was not supposed to tolerate, given the very principles that were defended in the book. See Norman Daniels, 'Equal Liberty and Unequal Worth of Liberty' in Norman Daniels (ed), *Reading Rawls: Critical Studies on Rawls'* A Theory of Justice (1975); Gerald Cohen, *Rescuing Justice and Equality* (2008).

[47] Rawls, *Political Liberalism* (n 13), 230.

None of these reasons seems, in principle, particularly attractive. In fact, all his claims may be true (it may actually be 'more urgent to settle the essentials dealing with the basic freedoms'; it may also be easier to 'tell whether those essentials are realized' or 'gain agreement about what the basic rights and liberties should be'), but even in that case it would not be clear why those facts would support denying constitutional protection to the principles related to social and economic inequalities altogether.[48] As Jeremy Waldron has put it, 'Rawls's theory is certainly not hostile to the idea of welfare provision', but principles requiring the constitutionalization of social rights 'do not feature among Rawls's... principles of justice as fairness—the principles that constitute his conception of justice.'[49]

In sum, an analysis of how different theories of justice deal with the issue of social rights can be particularly helpful for recognizing their different understanding about what it means to have a just constitution.

Bibliography

James Buchanan, *The Economics of Politics* (1978)

James Dorn, 'Public Choice and the Constitution: A Madisonian Perspective' in James Gwartney and Richard Wagner (eds), *Public Choice and Constitutional Economics* (1988)

Ronald Dworkin, *Freedom's Law: The Moral Reading of the American Constitution* (1996)

Ronald Dworkin, *Is Democracy Possible Here?* (2008)

Cécile Fabre, *Social Rights Under the Constitution* (2000)

Varun Gauri and Daniel M. Brinks (eds), *Courting Social Justice* (2008)

Jürgen Habermas, *Between Facts and Norms: Contributions to a Discourse Theory on Law and Democracy* (1996)

Frank Michelman, 'Law's Republic' (1988) 97 *Yale Law Journal* 1493

John Rawls, *A Theory of Justice* (1971)

John Rawls, *Collected Papers* (1999)

John Rawls, *Political Liberalism* (1993)

Michael J. Sandel, *Democracy's Discontent: America in Search of a Public Philosophy* (1996)

Cass Sunstein, *The Second Bill of Rights* (2004)

Maurice Vile, *Constitutionalism and the Separation of Powers* (1967)

[48] Cécile Fabre, *Social Rights Under the Constitution* (2000); Cécile Fabre, 'A Philosophical Argument for a Bill of Rights' (2000) 30 *British Journal of Political Science* 77; Michelman (n 45); Josep J. Moreso and José Luis Martí, 'La constitucionalización del principio de la diferencia' in Claudio Amor (ed), *Rawls Post-Rawls* (2006).

[49] Jeremy Waldron, 'Socioeconomic Rights and Theories of Justice', NYU School of Law, Public Law Research Paper No 10-79 (2010), 1.

CHAPTER 17

SOVEREIGNTY

MICHEL TROPER

Paris

THE idea that the state possesses and exercises a supreme and absolute power is central to constitutional law. It is almost impossible for anyone writing in the field to avoid discussing it, even if in some cases the discussion leads to denying that it is a meaningful concept. This is because theories of sovereignty have been a central part of constitutional discourse at least since Bodin defined it as 'the absolute and perpetual power of a commonwealth... that is the highest power of command'.[1] Several constitutions expressly refer to theories of sovereignty, proclaiming for instance that the Republic of X is a sovereign state,[2] or that sovereignty belongs to the people,[3] or that the state will accept limitations of its sovereignty in order to protect peace.[4] Even when the word is not to be found in the constitutional document, the concept is nevertheless used or some of the ideas it conveys are used by courts or scholars to justify legal rules and legal decisions. On the other hand, constitutional law itself has sometimes been defined as the set of rules organizing the state and regulating the powers of its organs. Obviously, this calls for a definition of the state and one of the key elements of such a definition has been for centuries precisely that the state is sovereign. Sovereignty has traditionally

[1] Jean Bodin, *Les Six Livres de la République* (6 vols, 1576), English trans *On Sovereignty. Four Chapters from The Six Books of the Commonwealth* (J.H. Franklin trans, 1992), bk I, ch 8.

[2] eg Constitution of Romania, Art 1: 'La Roumanie est un État national, souverain et indépendant, unitaire et indivisible'.

[3] eg French Constitution of 1958, 'Art 3: National sovereignty shall vest in the people, who shall exercise it through their representatives and by means of referendum'.

[4] eg Italian Constitution, 'Art 11: 'L'Italia... consente, in condizioni di parità con gli altri stati, alle limitazioni di sovranità necessarie ad un ordinamento che assicuri la pace e la giustizia fra le nazioni...'.

been considered an essential and distinctive characteristic of the state. Max Weber's famous definition of the state as 'an entity which claims a monopoly on the legitimate use of violence' has been shown to be based ultimately on the concept of sovereignty[5] and on the fact that an entity deprived of sovereignty could not qualify as a state.[6]

The concept has also played a central role for general jurisprudence, for instance in the following sentences: 'by some definitions, legal positivism is the view that legal rules are rules willed by a sovereign'; 'international law is the law produced by agreements between sovereigns and whose main addressees are sovereign states'; 'because public law is a system of rules regulating the relations between the State and its citizens it is defined a sphere of heteronomy, since these rules can be forced unilaterally by the sovereign State on citizens, in contrast with private law, which is viewed as a sphere of autonomy left by the sovereign to agreements between private subjects'.

However, none of these propositions has been universally accepted. Scholars disagree about every aspect of the theories of sovereignty: whether they were first devised with the creation of the modern state after the end of the Middle Ages or have medieval origins; whether every state is sovereign or one can conceive of a non sovereign state; whether sovereignty is indivisible; whether there is a sovereign in every state; whether in the contemporary world sovereignty is compatible with the fact that states are subject to international law, with the idea of the *Rechtsstaat*, the rule of law, or with fundamental rights. At least some of these disagreements reflect different ideological preferences. Others result from conceptual confusion and can be clarified. But first, two remarks are in order.

In the first place, many of the writings on sovereignty are ideologically laden in very diverse ways. They do not focus on the question of whether states are actually sovereign and what it means or whether there is a sovereign in every state and who that sovereign is in a particular state, but rather whether it is a good or a bad thing that states are or were sovereign at some period in history. Hobbes has argued that a sovereign authority is a necessary guarantor of peace and security within a society, but liberals have claimed that on the contrary an unchecked power is dangerous and asked 'whether we should not strive towards institutional control of the rulers by balancing their powers against other powers.'[7] The Westphalian system of international relations has been praised for bringing peace through equilibrium between sovereign states, while critics argue that peace can only result from the primacy of international law, which is incompatible with the sovereignty of national states.[8] In Europe, scholars and politicians are deeply divided on the merits of more integration and the theory of sovereignty plays an important part in the discussion: naturally, those who are in favor of strong nation-states claim that the states should retain their sovereignty; but this leaves several roads open to the partisans of European integration. They can argue either that the European Union leaves the nation state's sovereignty intact or conversely that the states should abandon their sovereignty (or that they have already lost it) in favor of the European Union, which would then become a super-state. They can also maintain that we can imagine a world without sovereignty altogether because, as Neil MacCormick famously wrote, sovereignty is not like

[5] Hans Kelsen, *Der soziologische und der juristische Staatsbegriff: Kritische Untersuchungen des Verhältnisses von Staat und Recht* (2nd edn, 1928).

[6] In Olivier Beaud's words 'whoever thinks of the state is constrained to think of sovereignty and vice versa': *Etat et souveraineté. Eléments pour une contribution à une théorie de l'Etat* (1989), 4.

[7] Karl Popper, *The Open Society and its Enemies* ([1945] 2002).

[8] Hans Kelsen, *Das Problem der Souveränität und die Theorie des Völkerrechts* ([1920] 2nd edn 1928). More recently, Neil MacCormick wrote that 'One of the main upshots of universal sovereign statehood was two disasters—world wars': 'Beyond the Sovereign State' (1993) 56(1) *Modern Law Review* 1.

property 'which can be given up only when another person gains it', but 'more like virginity, something that can be lost by one without another's gaining it',[9] and whose loss 'in apt circumstances can even be a matter for celebration'.[10] Liberals fear that theories of sovereignty can be used to justify authoritarianism[11] but democrats, even if they are committed to liberty, define democracy as the sovereignty of the people.[12]

Secondly, the word 'sovereign' is often used to denote the character of a state that is politically or economically truly independent as in the sentence 'few states in the world are large enough to be really sovereign'. In this sense, sovereignty is an empirical character and, provided we agree on the size of the territory or the army or the GNP that are required to be called sovereign, we can easily find which states are really sovereign. But in constitutional law we are dealing not with facts but with legal concepts. We may eventually be able to draw a legal classification of states, such that some states will not be qualified as sovereign, for example member states in a federal system, but this qualification will never depend on factual elements such as size or military might. Indeed, in the traditional conception of the state, be that of constitutional law or international law, Monaco is as much a sovereign state as France or the United States and the Charter of the United Nations speaks of the 'sovereign equality of all its members'.[13]

The question thus is only whether it is a valid concept, that is, whether it may help us to perform a meaningful analysis of constitutional law. But we can ask that question in two different ways, because 'sovereignty' can be used at two different levels. On the one hand, lawmakers or courts use it in the language of positive law and scholars in the language of legal theory when they talk about the state or about constitutional law. In the latter case it is a metaconcept. These two concepts are mutually independent. For instance, some scholars may argue that the state is not really sovereign or that one should get rid of the concept of sovereignty, because the state is subject to international law or because they find it to be incompatible with the rule of law. But these same scholars do not deny that constitutional documents, lawmakers, or courts use not only the word 'sovereignty', but also arguments drawn from the theory of sovereignty. This does not falsify their own theories. The two concepts belong not only to different levels but also to different kinds of discourse. The language of positive law is prescriptive not only in the sense that it is made of commands to perform certain actions, but also that it mandates certain modes of justification, which will be considered valid independently of their truth value. For instance, it may be that an argument drawn from a religious or a moral doctrine or from the theory that a collective will exists is a valid argument for some legal systems. Thus, the same scholar could assert that states are not really sovereign because they are subject to international law or that none of the political branches of government possess an absolute and unlimited power and at the same time describe the positive law of the country and write, without contradicting herself, that the constitutional rules or the doctrine of the courts are based on the principle of national sovereignty. Alternatively, we could find that, in some legal

[9] Neil MacCormick, *Questioning Sovereignty: Law, State, and Nation in the European Commonwealth (Law, State, and Practical Reason)* (1999), 126.

[10] MacCormick (n 8).

[11] See Harold Laski, 'Studies In The Problem of Sovereignty' in Paul Hirst (ed), *Collected Works of Harold Laski: Studies in the Problem of Sovereignty*, vol 1 ([1917] 1977) ('Is there not a tremendous danger in modern times that people will believe the legal sovereignty of a State to be identical with its moral sovereignty?').

[12] In the French Constitution of 1958, Art 1 states that France is a democratic republic, Art 2 reproduces Lincoln's definition of democracy as 'government of the people, by the people and for the people' and Art 3 proclaims that 'national sovereignty shall vest in the people'.

[13] Art 2(1).

systems, no mention is ever made of sovereignty, but that the state can nevertheless be usefully described as sovereign.

Ideally, we should conduct two separate inquiries. However, the task is complicated by the fact that at both levels, scholars as well as legal actors use the word 'sovereignty' with different meanings, so that it refers to multiple concepts.

We should therefore distinguish between these concepts, starting from an analysis by the most important French constitutional scholar of the past century, Raymond Carré de Malberg, who identified in the French language three meanings of the word sovereignty and therefore three concepts of sovereignty:

> In the original sense, the word 'sovereignty' refers to the supreme character of the State's power. In a second sense, it refers to the whole range of the powers included in the State's authority and it is therefore synonymous with that authority. Thirdly, it is used to characterize the position occupied within the State by the highest organ of the State's authority and in that sense, sovereignty is the same thing as the power of that organ.[14]

Carré de Malberg stresses that the French language is poor in that it contains only one word for the three concepts of sovereignty. The same could be said of English. However, the German language has three words, one for each of these senses. *Souveranität* corresponds to sovereignty in the first sense, that is, the supreme character of the state on the international as well as on the domestic level. *Staatsgewalt* is the power of the state in the second sense. *Herrschaft* is the power of domination by an organ. Carré de Malberg believed that these distinctions could help us to discover the 'true nature' of sovereignty.[15] Such a belief may be naive, but the distinction is nevertheless useful to clarify a few traditional puzzling questions.

One of these is whether it is possible to divide sovereignty. On the basis of Carré de Malberg's distinction, it is easy to see that sovereignty in the third sense, the quality of the highest organ of the state, is indeed indivisible, because, as soon as one divides it between several organs, none is the highest.[16] On the other hand, if sovereignty in the second sense is the range of powers that can be exercised by the state, it is perfectly divisible. It is even possible to divide them by their subject matter (the power to wage war, to control a currency, to render justice etc) as Pufendorf did with the *partes potentiales*,[17] or by the type of legal acts that are necessary to exercise them (like legislation, execution, and adjudication). Separation of powers is precisely a division of sovereignty in this sense.

In the same way, these distinctions help us to understand why some sentences that use the concept of sovereignty may seem to be incompatible or contradictory but are simultaneously true. Thus, at the time of Carré de Malberg, during the French Third Republic, it was possible to answer the question 'who is the sovereign', by any one of three sentences: 'the French state is the sovereign', 'the French Parliament is the sovereign', and 'legislation is a sovereign power'. In the first sentence, sovereignty refers to the supreme character of the state's power, which enables it to act on the international level and interfere with other sovereigns, or to dominate the Church or any other institution. In the second sentence, sovereignty is a quality of an organ of the state, and in the third sentence it is one of the powers that the state may exercise.

[14] Raymond Carré de Malberg, *Contribution à la Théorie générale de l'Etat; spécialement d'après les données fournies par le droit constitutionnel français* ([1920] 2003), vol I, 79.

[15] Ibid 86.

[16] However, several organs could exercise sovereignty jointly, see below.

[17] Samuel von Pufendorf, bk VIII, 'Où l'on traite des principales parties de la souveraineté' in *Le droit de la nature et des gens, ou systeme general des pricipes les plus importans de la morale, de la jurisprudence, et de la politique* (1706), Eng trans *Of the Law of Nature and Nations. Eight Books* (1703).

Carré de Malberg's distinction also helps to clarify an ongoing debate about the origin of the modern concept of sovereignty. Scholars who follow a long tradition attribute the theory of sovereignty to Jean Bodin and consider that sovereign of the state dates from the end of the religious wars and the birth of the absolute monarchy. But others argue that the concept of sovereignty is more ancient and can be traced to the Middle Ages.[18] However, while it is true that the idea of a supreme power existed and even that some authors found in the people the ultimate justification for the existence of such a supreme power, it is only in the seventeenth century that sovereignty was thought to include an unlimited range of powers and the capacity to legislate on every possible aspect of human life.[19] Following Carré de Malberg's method, we can examine at this point whether the three concepts are still necessary, at the two levels that we have distinguished, that is, both for scholars and for legal actors.

But before turning to this task, another remark seems to be in order. Carré de Malberg's distinction does not give sufficient account of some sentences that we find in constitutional documents as well as in the discourse of state authorities. Take for example, 'the sovereign is the people' or 'sovereignty belongs to the people'.[20] Such a sentence obviously does not mean that the French people *is* the state and effectively acts on an international level, or that it exercises a power of domination and certainly not that the people *is* a range of powers. In reality, they are used to justify other sentences: for example, in French legal discourse, 'sovereignty belongs to the people' was used during the Third Republic to justify 'Parliament is sovereign' or 'the law is sovereign'. It meant that Parliament exercised a sovereignty that was not its own, but that belonged to the people and was exercised *in the name of* the people, or that the law expressed the will of the sovereign people. In this context, when imputed to the people; the word 'sovereignty' is thus used in a fourth sense: it refers to the quality of a being in whose name sovereignty in the first three senses is exercised. The doctrine of sovereignty in this fourth sense is a principle of imputation. Depending on the type of justification that is necessary in a given system, the entity that is being called the sovereign in this fourth sense can be the people, the king, the nation, or even the state itself, as in the German legal doctrine of the nineteenth century. We can see that while sovereignty in the first and second sense are characters of the state, in the third and the fourth sense it is a character of some entity within the state.

I. Sovereignty of the State

When we say that the state is sovereign, we mean two things. First, that the state has the absolute power to make decisions on every aspect of human life, and, secondly, that it is independent of every other external power.

1. Internal Sovereignty of the State

From the beginning, the claim that the state is sovereign had two aspects: first that the state possesses and exercises a power that is its own, that it has not been empowered to exercise; secondly, that this power is unlimited. We should distinguish between these two aspects,

[18] eg Walter Ullman, *Principles of Government and Politics in the Middle Ages* (1961); Marcel David, *La souveraineté du people* (1996).

[19] Some authors who accept talk of a medieval sovereignty, still maintain that modern sovereignty is specific (Olivier Beaud, *La puissance de l'Etat* (1994), 33.

[20] French Constitution of 1958, Art 3.

because it is conceivable that some superior authority creates another and entrusts it with unlimited power, just as it is conceivable that some authority has not been created by another but is nevertheless limited by law. For instance, we know of constitutions which give parliaments unlimited and unchecked power, because under these constitutions there is no judicial review of legislation and we know of constitutionally created courts that put limits to the constituent power, although the constituent power has been created by another power, still superior.

However, these two aspects are closely linked within the framework of the theory that law is a product of the will.[21] This theory does not necessarily deny the existence of natural law, but stresses that only positive law is legally binding. This fundamental idea has two consequences. The first is the idea of the hierarchy of norms, and the second is the absence of any substantial limits to the power of the state.

Regarding the hierarchy of norms, obviously every sentence that looks like a command is not law. Only those that have been issued by some authority empowered to produce commands are law. But this empowering authority similarly has to be empowered by a still higher authority, and so on until we reach the ultimate level above which we cannot find a higher human authority. This highest authority has not been empowered by any legal rule, unlike all other authorities. Its powers are *suo jure*. They derive from its own nature.

On the other hand, since that authority is the ultimate lawmaker, it is necessarily unbound, *legibus solutus*. However, being unbound can have two different meanings. First, it can mean that the state is also unlimited in the functions that it can exercise and the fields that it can regulate.[22] In the terms of German scholars, the state has a *Kompetenz-Kompetenz*, the competency to determine its own competency. But, secondly, being unbound can also mean having the power to decide with complete discretion, but within a limited field and on a limited number of matters. The word 'sovereign' is used to convey both meanings. In the second sense, when one speaks for example in French of a 'sovereign court' or one says that a professor is sovereign when she grades her students, what that means is that the court's or the professor's decisions cannot be appealed. It is also in that sense that in a federal system member states are said to be sovereign or in the United States that Native American tribes are sovereign.[23]

This double meaning helps to explain the long debate in federal systems on the doctrine of dual sovereignty. If sovereignty means the unlimited capacity to determine one's own competency and to exercise an unlimited power in every possible field, then dual sovereignty is logically and practically impossible, since the federal state could take away the powers of the member states and the member states could take away the powers of the federal state. But if it means simply that each entity exercises discretionary power within its own jurisdiction, or that the Staatsgewalt is divided between the federal state and the member states, then it is both possible and actual.

Thus, if we take the words 'internal sovereignty' in the strict sense, obviously only the state as a whole, and in a federal system only the federal state, has the *Kompetenz-Kompetenz* and can be said to be sovereign.

[21] Beaud (n 19), 56 ff.

[22] 'Sovereignty, then, is not limited either in power, or in function, or in length of time': Bodin (n 1), bk I, ch 8.

[23] *US v Lara* 541 US 193 (2004); similarly, the European Court of Justice has claimed that 'European institutions [have been] endowed with sovereign rights, the exercise of which affects member states and also their citizen.' Judgment of the Court of 5 February 1963, *NV Algemene Transport- en Expeditie Onderneming van Gend & Loos v Netherlands Inland Revenue Administration.*

The theory of sovereignty was precisely devised after the religious wars in order to justify the claim that the state could decide on every subject matter, especially religious matters. This may be the reason why in the seventeenth century jurists chose a particular way of listing the state's powers. These powers or functions of the state, also called 'attributes of sovereignty', 'marks of sovereignty', or '*partes potentiales*' did not correspond to the modern functions or powers of government, legislation, execution, and adjudication. Nor were they a list of possible subject matter on which the state could act. Rather, they were a bizarre combination of the two typologies, the former formal, and the latter substantial. The list starts with the power of making laws. The first attribute of the sovereign prince therefore is the power to make law binding on all his subjects in general and on each in particular. But, to avoid any ambiguity, one must add that he does so without the consent of any superior, equal, or inferior being necessary. The other attributes include the powers to make war, to hear appeals from all courts, and to tax subjects, among others. Similarly, Pufendorf later distinguishes between the legislative power, the vindicative power, the judiciary power, the power of war and peace, the right of appointing magistrates, the right of levying taxes, and the right of examining doctrines.[24]

Jean-Jacques Rousseau would later criticize the theory of the attributes of sovereignty, but Bodin himself had already noted the strangeness of the list: all the other attributes and rights of sovereignty are included in this power of making and unmaking law, so that strictly speaking this is the unique attribute of sovereign power. It includes all other rights of sovereignty.[25] This is because all these other functions are being exercised either in the form of law or in a mode authorized by law. In any case, it is perfectly clear that there are no substantial limits to what the sovereign can do. For instance, his powers included religious matters. It was held in France that the Pope could not legislate for the French Church except with the consent and confirmation of the king, and that the king could exercise surveillance over religious orders and intervene in doctrinal matters.[26]

This is the reason why the typology of the state's functions was radically changed in the eighteenth century, with the new doctrine of the separation of powers. Instead of putting formal and substantial functions in a single list, the Enlightenment distinguished two or three main functions, legislative, executive, and judiciary, defined only formally in their relation to the law. Since there is general acceptance of the idea that there are no limits to what the state can do, there is no need for a list of the substantial functions of the state. Moreover, it was difficult to reconcile this list with the idea that sovereignty is indivisible.[27]

[24] Pufendorf (n 17), bk VII, ch IV. We find similar lists in many different works throughout the seventeenth century, eg Loyseau:

> faire loys, créer officiers, arbitrer la paix et la guerre, avoir le dernier ressort de la justice et forger monnoye. Lesquels sont du tout inséparables de la personne du souverain et tellement attachez à la souveraineté que quiconque en entreprend aucun, entreprend quant et quant la souveraineté est coulpable de lèze majesté…

Charles Loyseau, *Traité des seigneuries* (1908), quoted in Joel Cornette, *Le roi de guerre. Essai sur la souveraineté dans la France du grand siècle* (1994), 120.

[25] Bodin (n 1).

[26] See generally Dale K. Van Kley, *The Religious Origins of the French Revolution: From Calvin to the Civil Constitution, 1560–1791* (1996).

[27] Jean-Jacques Rousseau, *The Social Contract and Discourses by Jean-Jacques Rousseau* (G.D.H. Cole trans, 1923), ch II ('that sovereignty is indivisible'). Rousseau's main argument is that if the attributes of sovereignty were divided and distributed between several authorities, sovereignty would be destroyed, as none of them would be sovereign. See Robert Derathé, *Jean-Jacques Rousseau et la science politique de son temps* (1974).

The doctrine of the separation of powers, on the contrary, is perfectly compatible with it, because the three powers are not part of sovereignty. Only the legislative power is sovereign, as Kant, following Rousseau makes perfectly clear:

> Every State contains three authorities within it, that is, the general united will consists of three persons (trias politica): the sovereign authority (sovereignty) in the person of the legislator; the executive authority in the person of the ruler (in conformity to law) and the judicial authority (to award to each what is his in accordance with the law in the person of the judge.[28]

Sovereignty in this sense obviously also includes the power to regulate private law. In pre-revolutionary France, private law was regulated by custom, but jurists stressed that custom only has binding force 'by the sufferance and during the good pleasure of the sovereign prince, and so far as he is willing to authorize it'.[29] Thus, according to this doctrine of sovereignty, the power of the state is in effect without substantial limits. In the words of the German jurist Georg Meyer: 'a State must be in a condition to make whatsoever it chooses an object of its activity'.[30]

At this point, one could argue that this is only a self-description of the system, and that, in spite of what some lawyers say, the state is not really sovereign in these senses or that it may have been sovereign in the past but that it is now subject to substantive limitations, either because some of its traditional functions have been deregulated and left to private corporations or because it has become a *Rechtsstaat* and is subject to the constitution and an obligation to respect fundamental rights, and in the European Union because states have transferred a great number of important powers to European authorities.[31]

The first idea can be rapidly dismissed: if the state has left some of its functions to private enterprise, it is not in order to comply with a legal obligation (at least not an obligation under domestic law) but as a matter of policy, a policy that can always be reversed. We have thus no limitation.

As to a limitation by the constitution and fundamental rights, the argument misses the fact that the constitution is not above the state but is a law made by the state itself. While it is true that the constitution creates and imposes limitations, these limitations only bind state authorities and the branches of government, but it does not bind the state as a whole, because it can always change its constitution. Amending the constitution or changing it altogether may be difficult or unpractical, depending on the required procedure, but it is not forbidden.

The strongest argument of those who claim that internal sovereignty has been lost by the state focuses on European integration. The states, so the argument goes, have transferred many of their traditional sovereign powers to the European Union in many very important fields and are now incapable of exercising them. The argument has two branches: on the one

[28] Immanuel Kant, 'The Doctrine of Right' in *The Metaphysics of Morals* (Mary J. Gregor trans, 1996), §§45, 90–1. Similarly, Blackstone writes:

> Legislature as was before observed, is the greatest act of superiority that can be exercised by one being over another. Wherefore it is requisite to the very essence of Law, that it be made by the supreme power. Sovereignty and legislature are indeed convertible terms; one cannot subsist without the other.

William Blackstone, 'Of the Nature of Laws in General' in William Draper Lewis (ed), *Commentaries on the Laws of England: In Four Books*, vol 1 ([1765–69] 2007), Introduction, ss 2, 38.

[29] Bodin (n 1).

[30] Quoted by Charles Edward Merriam, *History of the Theory of Sovereignty Since Rousseau* (1972), 544.

[31] Luigi Ferrajoli, *La sovranità nel mondo moderno* (2nd edn, 1997), 33–4.

hand, that the state has lost the *Staatsgewalt*, because it has lost the power to make rules in every possible field; and on the other hand, that the hierarchy of norms has been modified as Acts of Parliament are no more supreme and even those powers that states may still exercise are now submitted to EU law.

As impressive as it may seem, the argument should nevertheless be examined at the two levels of legal language, that of positive law and that of legal scholarship. On the level of legal language, that of the constitutional texts and of the jurisprudence of the courts, we find that although, as we have seen, some constitutions mention that they accept 'limitations of sovereignty',[32] several among them still proclaim the principle of 'national sovereignty'. Because of these provisions, in several cases the treaties that organized the transference of powers to the European Union were referred before ratification to constitutional courts, in order to check whether the transference was compatible with the constitution, especially with the principle of national sovereignty. The case of the French Constitutional Council is particularly interesting. The Council used an ancient and important distinction in French public law between the essence and the exercise of sovereignty. It decided that a provision of a treaty would only be unconstitutional when it would bring about a transfer of the essence of sovereignty. For the Council, this can happen when some extremely important powers are transferred to a European authority, for example control of the currency, and when that authority is empowered to decide by a majority vote or by some procedure that could result in France being in a minority and constrained against its will. But even if the treaty is to be found incompatible with the constitution on this account, the constitution can still be amended in order to authorize the process of ratification. This has happened a few times, for example for the Maastricht Treaty or for the failed Constitutional Treaty of 2005. In that case, the principle of national sovereignty remained the same, because the text of Article 3 of the Constitution ('National sovereignty shall vest in the people, who shall exercise it through their representatives and by means of referendum') was not reformulated. This shows that in the language of the French Constitution and of the Council, the transfer of competences is not incompatible with the principle of national sovereignty but only with the 'essential conditions of the exercise of national sovereignty'. The essence of sovereignty has never been lost, because the powers themselves have not been transferred and can always be recovered by renegotiation, by denunciation of the treaties, or a new constitutional amendment. It may be that the latter solution would be a violation of EU law, but that would not make it invalid from the point of view of French law. Similarly, the German Federal Constitutional Court has decided that the European Union was not a federal state (*Bundesstaat*), but only a union of states (*Staatenbund*), so that while states may exercise jointly some powers they still retain their sovereignty.[33]

According to the second branch of the argument, some competences are exercised jointly by the states and the European Union. In those fields, in case of a conflict of norms, EU law prevails over domestic law. The prevalence of European Union law has been mandated both by the national constitutions and by EU law, that is, by the jurisprudence of the European Court of Justice[34] and lately by the Lisbon Treaty.[35] Constitutional courts have used comparable strategies to avoid abandoning national sovereignty. For example, the French courts had initially resisted the European Court of Justice by deciding that EU law may prevail over

[32] The Italian Constitution or the Preamble to the French Constitution of 1946.

[33] Judgment of 30 June 2009.

[34] Case 06/64 *Costa/ENEL*.

[35] Declaration No 17 attached to the Treaty.

statutes but not over norms of a constitutional level. Later, after the Lisbon Treaty made EU law prevail over national law including the constitution, the Constitutional Council developed an argumentation in two stages.[36]

First, the source of the obligation to apply EU law is to be found not in the treaties, but in the Constitution. Therefore, EU law prevails over the constitution to the extent that the constitution prescribes that EU law prevails over itself. It follows that the constitution could not, without contradiction, decide to submit to a European rule that would go against its own express provisions or the principles that shape the constitutional identity of France. Therefore, it has implicitly protected such provisions or principles and EU law cannot have primacy over them. Only the French constituent power could derogate those principles.[37]

Thus, the state is still the master of its own competencies. It may decide not to exercise or to delegate the exercise of some of them, but ultimately the rules by which they are exercised remain under its control. Nevertheless, this point is hotly debated and some scholars who deny that the state is sovereign stress that it is bound by international law.

2. External Sovereignty

(a) *External Sovereignty in Classical International Law*

For the classical doctrine of sovereignty, international sovereignty was just another aspect of internal sovereignty. A state was sovereign if it was not subject to any other power, whether internal or external. Even before the national kings constituted themselves as sovereigns with absolute power over their subjects, they had claimed to be independent from the Pope and the Emperor. Being sovereign never meant to be unbound by treaties. On the contrary, being bound by treaties to which he had consented meant that the sovereign was only bound by his own will. The capacity to make treaties and be bound by them was thus viewed not as a limitation but as an expression of sovereignty—Bodin places it among the attributes of sovereignty, as part of the power of making war and peace.

This is the reason why the system of international relations that was established after the Peace of Westphalia in 1648 was an order between sovereign states. Several consequences follow: first, that only sovereign states have the power to enter into international relations and that entities that do not have that power, such as member states in a federal system, are not sovereign states; today, some international organizations can make treaties but on the basis of the treaty that created them. Secondly, that because they are all sovereign, all states are legally equal; equality of the states is still the dominant principle of contemporary international law as it has been proclaimed by the Charter of the United Nations.[38] Thirdly, that states keep their internal sovereignty to the effect that they are free from an intervention by another state in

[36] Decision no 2004–496 DC, 10 June 2004, Loi pour la confiance dans l'économie numérique: Art 88(1) of the Constitution provides:

> The Republic shall participate in the European Communities and in the European Union constituted by States which have freely chosen, by virtue of the treaties that established them, to exercise some of their powers in common.

Thus, the transposition of a community directive into domestic law is a constitutional obligation.

[37] Decision no 2006–540 DC, 27 July 2006, Copyright and related rights in the Information Society: 'the transposition of a Directive cannot run counter to an rule or principle inherent to the constitutional identity of France, except when the constituting power consents thereto.' See also Chapter 35 on constitutional identity.

[38] Art 1(2).

their affairs and that their subjects are not the direct subjects of international law, but only of domestic law.

The question whether states keep their sovereignty although they are subject to international law is dependent on the position one takes on the issue of the relation between the domestic and the international legal systems. According to the dualist theory, the two systems are distinct and separate, so that the validity of the norms belonging to one system is not based on a norm belonging to the other and one norm or one action could be valid under one system and invalid under the other. According to the monist theory, domestic law and international law are not two distinct legal systems but form a unity. Most prominent among the authors who favor the monist theory is Hans Kelsen, who has argued that within this unity there are two sets of rules, the international legal order and the national legal order, which in his view is just another name for the state. In their mutual relation, international law prevails because 'by coming into legal existence, the State is subjected to preexisting international law'. It is international law that determines and delimits not only the so-called 'elements of the state', its territorial, personal, and substantial spheres of validity in relation to other states, but also 'the reason of validity of the national legal orders', because 'international law empowers the "fathers of the constitution" function as the first legislators of a State'.[39] International law does not usually place substantial limits on the constituent power, but this is not at all impossible and there have been cases where treaties have mandated constitutional amendments.

Kelsen's monist theory of the relation between domestic and international law is open to a number of objections. Most of his arguments are based on a specific conception of validity that allows him to beg the question, for instance the idea that international law determines the sphere of validity of the state. We can imagine an Act of the British Parliament mandating driving on the left in France. Is this Act valid? If valid means 'in accordance with a higher rule', then, obviously, the Act is not valid according to international law, but it is definitely valid according to domestic law, because there is a constitutional rule that empowers the British Parliament to produce general rules without any substantial limit to that power. Thus, Kelsen's thesis holds only if we agree with him that one action cannot be simultaneously valid and not valid, but this is a premise that he fails to prove. On the contrary, is quite possible that an action is valid under the rules of one system and invalid under the rules of another. This is precisely what happens, not only between law and morality, but also between two national legal systems. Kelsen's only counter-argument is that international law and national law form not two, but just one system, which is precisely what he needs to demonstrate and is not justified in using as a starting point.

The monist theory falls under another objection, one derived from a different theory of validity, one that Kelsen has himself used in other parts of his work, and which is equated with formal validity: a valid norm is one that has been produced by a competent authority according to the prescribed procedure and has not been nullified. Whenever there is no way to nullify a norm because there is no judicial review, then the norm produced by a competent authority is valid. An Act of the British Parliament that cannot be nullified by a British court on the ground that it is contrary to a constitutional rule or an international rule is valid and remains valid, even if there were an international court that could nullify it on the ground that it contradicts an international rule.

Thus, external sovereignty is not affected by international law and the state is only bound by its own will. However, the relation between international law and domestic law in the

[39] Hans Kelsen, *General Theory of Law and State* (1945), 350ff and 367.

contemporary world seems slightly different. Important changes have taken place both at the level of general international law and of regional, especially European, law.

(b) External Sovereignty in Contemporary International Law

First, scholars of international law have stressed that, after the horrors of the Second World War, states have agreed to relinquish part of their sovereignties as a means to protect peace. The most notable example of such renouncement is the UN Charter, which prohibits the use of force, once one of the main attributes of sovereignty and a monopoly of the state, except in a case of self-defense or for 'the common interest', that is, in accordance with the purpose of the organization.[40] Moreover, the Security Council itself has received the right to use force against states.[41]

Another important case is that of international criminal courts, such as the International Criminal Tribunal for the former Yugoslavia or the International Criminal Tribunal for Rwanda, both created by the Security Council of the United Nations and the International Criminal Court in the Treaty of Rome in 1998. These courts have the power to try citizens against the will of their own states.

But the most significant development has taken place in Europe with the European Union and the European Convention on Human Rights. In both cases, states may be bound by decisions to which they have not consented. What makes the change particularly striking is that EU law or the European Convention can be applied not only against the will of the state, but by the state's own courts.

All these developments are obviously of the greatest political significance. We can doubt, however, if they are as meaningful from the legal point of view and whether they constitute a real challenge for the theory of the international sovereignty of the state. First, these arguments are formulated at a metalinguistic level. The language of the treaties themselves and that of the courts are very different. Several of the treaties invoke the principle of sovereignty. Besides, Article 1(2) of the UN Charter, the Vienna Convention on the Law of Treaties explicitly mentions the principles 'of sovereign equality and independence of all States, of non-interference in the domestic affairs of States.'[42] We have seen how constitutional courts tend to safeguard the principle of national sovereignty by basing the supremacy of the law produced by international organizations not on the treaties but on the national constitutions and how they let the constituent power have the final word.

On the other hand, it must be noted that, even if treaties have limited the exercise of their powers by the states, this is only because the states themselves have signed and ratified them, on the basis of their sovereignty. The existence of these limits does not prove a loss, but rather a manifestation of sovereignty. Moreover, the limits last only as long as the states consent and

[40] The Preamble to the Charter of the United Nations proclaims 'that armed force shall not be used, save in the common interest', and Art 2(4) that

> All Members shall refrain in their international relations from the threat or use of force against the territorial integrity or political independence of any state, or in any other manner inconsistent with the Purposes of the United Nations.

[41] Ibid Art 42:

> Should the Security Council consider that measures provided for in Article 41 would be inadequate or have proved to be inadequate, it may take such action by air, sea, or land forces as may be necessary to maintain or restore international peace and security. Such action may include demonstrations, blockade, and other operations by air, sea, or land forces of Members of the United Nations.

[42] Ibid Preamble.

they can always denounce the treaties. True, denunciation is prohibited by the Vienna Convention, but the Vienna Convention only binds the states that have ratified it and one could easily argue that since the Convention could not possibly refer to itself but only to other treaties, a state could denounce the Vienna Convention. And, even if denunciation were considered a violation of international law, the act of denunciation could still be valid under domestic law.

II. Sovereignty in the State

1. The Existence of a Sovereign

This was Carré de Malberg's third concept of sovereignty, the quality of the highest organ in the state. Early positivists needed this concept for their definition of law: a legal rule was defined as a 'command laid down by a sovereign' and judge-made law or custom were law in that they were tacit commands of the sovereign.[43] The sovereign himself was defined as one whom the majority of society habitually obeys and who renders habitual obedience to no one. Moreover, they claimed that one such sovereign was to be found in every state.

H.L.A. Hart has famously criticized this definition of the sovereign on these two elements of the definition.[44] About the habit of obedience, Hart stresses that from 'the people habitually frequent the tavern on Saturday nights', we cannot infer that they ought to do so. Why then, if they habitually obey one man, should we say that they are under an obligation to obey him and that this man has the 'right' to lay down rules? It is not even true that there is always such a habit: if the sovereign dies, obviously no one is in the habit of obeying his successor. In fact, says Hart—and Kelsen too—we need such concepts as obligation or empowerment in order to distinguish the power of the sovereign from raw power.

The definition of the sovereign by the habit of obedience is undoubtedly extremely weak and Hart and Kelsen are certainly right when they point out that without such concepts we cannot tell why the sovereign's commands are *valid* rules. But they both seem to miss the crucial benefit of the theory of sovereignty. It is not a legal theory devised to answer the question of legitimacy of the supreme authority of the land, but it serves on the contrary to avoid that question altogether. While giving legitimacy to every authority in the state, it provides for the basis of validity of commands issued by subordinate officers. These officers cannot draw their power from their biological nature or their social prestige, but only from the fact that they have been empowered by the sovereign. It is this empowerment that justifies them to require obedience from the subjects. But what is the basis for the obligation to obey the sovereign? The answer is precisely this: because he is the sovereign. If one asks a further question, 'Why is he the sovereign?', the only possible answer is to refer to some political theory, the divine right of kings or the democratic theory. But these political theories are not necessary for the legal system or for the functioning of the state and the same sovereign could be equally justified by several competing theories. The legal questioning stops here.

In this respect, the function of the theory of sovereignty resembles closely the theory of the *Grundnorm*. It is not a starting but a final point to a series of questions about the validity of norms. If we understand that the theory performs such a function, the question we need to

[43] John Austin, *The Province of Jurisprudence Determined* (W. Rumble ed, [1832] 1995).

[44] H.L.A. Hart, *The Concept of Law* (1961), 50–60.

ask is not what makes the rules laid down by the sovereign valid, but simply whether it is true that in every state there is a sovereign organ, one who is not only habitually obeyed but who does not obey anyone or rather who is not subject to any legal limits.

This second element of Austin's definition also comes under Hart's critique.[45] Since Austin had in mind the British Parliament, Hart points out that there are many societies where the supreme legislative power is limited by a constitution. He concedes that in some cases the legislature operating a special procedure may be able to remove those limitations and therefore 'it is arguable that it may be identified with the sovereign incapable of legal limitations, which the theory requires'.[46] But, he also stresses that there are other cases where the constitution can only be amended by a special body or where the restrictions are altogether outside the scope of any amending power and Hart sees this as a difficulty for the theory.

However, this critique is strange. If a special authority can freely amend the constitution, that authority is able not only to remove limitations on the legislature, but also to impose fresh ones or, as Kelsen clearly saw, to adopt rules that are formally constitutional and that may have any substantial content. That authority is not limited by any substantial rules and should be identified with the sovereign, just as in the case described by Hart of a legislature able to change the constitution.

It is true that it must follow some procedural rules, but these procedural rules are only constitutive rules. They do not limit the power of the amending body, but define that body as the constituent power and the rules they enact as constitutional amendments. If a group of men vote and adopt an amendment to the constitutional document, this group is not an amending authority unless its members have been appointed in a certain way, and the rule they enact is not a constitutional amendment unless discussed in a certain way and adopted with the required majority. That group having thus complete discretion as to the substance of the amendment can be defined as the sovereign.

One must keep in mind that the sovereign, whether a legislator or a constituent power, need not be composed of one single authority. The author of a decision in the legal sense is the authority, whether composed of an individual, a group, or several groups, to whom the decision is jointly imputed and this is the case when the decision cannot be adopted without the consent of any single component, which nevertheless could not have decided alone. Thus, the British Parliament, although composed of the King, Commons, and Lords, is the sole author of statutes. The same is true for the constituent power: it is rarely composed of a single authority. For example, the procedure requires several steps: first, the legislature must vote for a bill, then another assembly will vote and adopt the bill with a super-majority. In that case, the constituent power is the complex authority composed of the legislature and the special assembly.

The fact that certain provisions of the constitution may not be amended does not really change the picture. Article 89 of the French Constitution of 1958 prohibits changing 'the republican form of government'.[47] Similarly, Article 69(3) of the German Basic Law prohibits affecting the most fundamental principles.[48] However, it has been suggested that these

[45] Ibid 65: 'the importance of the theory…lies in the claim that in every society where there is law there is a sovereign'.

[46] Ibid 72.

[47] Art 89: 'The republican form of government shall not be the object of any amendment'.

[48] Art 79(3): 'Amendments to this Basic Law affecting the division of the Federation into Länder, their participation on principle in the legislative process, or the principles laid down in Articles 1 and 20 shall be inadmissible.'

prohibitions could be easily lifted in two steps.[49] First, one could amend Article 89 of the French Constitution. Such an amendment would not in itself be a change in the republican form of government. It might reveal an intention to change it, but the possibility would still be there that no change finally occurs. Thus, the amendment would not fall clearly under the prohibition. Then, once the provision had been removed, a second amendment would change the republican form of government.

On the other hand, such prohibitions have no consequences unless another body has the power to decide that the amendment is unconstitutional and void. When there is no constitutional court, constitutional amendments cannot be reviewed. When there is a constitutional court, it is not clear that they have the power to review amendments. But in case they do claim to exercise it, as in India,[50] then we ought to examine whether these courts are an element of the constituent power. The answer depends on the theory of adjudication that is being used. If we think that adjudication is a mere application of a previous rule which the judge must discover but does not have the power to change, then the court cannot be considered to exercise discretion and *consent* to the amendment. But if we agree that the court cannot review amendments without interpreting and even creating the fundamental principles which the amending power must respect; that this process involves a very large margin of appreciation; and that the choices the court makes depend on the political, moral, or religious preferences of the judges, then we must analyze its role as one of consenting to constitutional amendments. The court then becomes a part of the constituent power, exactly as the House of Lords in the British Parliament of the eighteenth century. Sovereignty is not shared between the elements of the constituent power, but exercised jointly. That this is a joint exercise is more visible when the court strikes down a constitutional amendment. But it is no less real when it upholds it, exactly as the President of the United States as an element of the legislative power, both when he vetoes a law and when he consents to it.

The idea that sovereignty lies in the constituent power has repeatedly been used in Europe as an argument to justify judicial review of legislation against the theory that it is undemocratic. Some scholars have claimed that the constituent power, which, as a supreme authority, is the true representative of the sovereign people, can always overrule a decision of the court striking down a statute. When it does, it is an exercise of sovereignty. The same can be said when the constituent power does not amend the constitution in reaction to a decision by the court, because by this abstention it expresses tacit consent.[51]

Even more strikingly, some courts have used the theory that the constituent power is sovereign as an argument to justify a refusal to review constitutional amendments. For example, the French Constitutional Council decided in 1992 that 'the constituent power is sovereign; it has discretion to abrogate, modify or supplement any rule of constitutional rank in the form that it considers most appropriate.'[52] In Vedel's words, 'the constituent power being the supreme power in the State cannot be bound, even by itself'.[53]

Thus, courts do acknowledge the existence of a body that exercises an absolute power in the sense not only that it is unlimited and that its rules are binding on everyone, but also that

[49] Georges Vedel, *Manuel élémentaire de droit constitutionnel* ([1949] 2002), 117.

[50] In 1967, in *Golak Nath v The State of Punjab* and *Minerva Mills Ltd v Union of India*, in 1981.

[51] Georges Vedel, 'Schengen et Maastricht (A propos de la décision no 91-294 DC du Conseil constitutionnel du 25 juillet 1991)' (1992) *Revue Française de droit administratif* 173.

[52] eg the French Constitutional Council no 92-312 DC, 2 September 1992, 'Traité sur l'Union européenne; or the official commentary of décision no 2003-469 DC du 26 mars 2003' in *Cahiers du Conseil constitutionnel, no 15* (2003).

[53] Vedel (n 49), 117.

every rule and every legal decision is binding only because they have been derived from these rules or because their creation has been authorized by that body.

In some states, the power that is exercised by that supreme authority is its own. That was the case with the English Parliament or with the king in pre-revolutionary France. However, in the modern state, the sovereign authority, the organ of the state that renders habitual obedience to no one, exercises a power, legislative or constituent, which it does not claim to be its own but that of the 'real sovereign' whom it represents. This is the fourth function of the theories of sovereignty: justifying the actual exercise of power by the legislative or the constituent authorities by imputing their decisions to another being.

2. The Holder of Sovereignty in the State

One of the virtues of the hierarchy of norms is that it allows every norm-maker to contend that he is applying the will of another. That other is not necessarily a physical human being or a group of human beings. The French parliaments which resisted the king's laws in the eighteenth century asserted that they were applying his real will, of which he was not aware, or that they represented the immortal body of the king whose will they expressed against the will that had only been expressed by mistake by the mortal king.[54] Later the 'Parlements' pretended to represent the nation.

This episode shows the nature of the theory of representation that was used at the time, later confirmed by the French Revolution and still at work in contemporary constitutional law. Carré de Malberg has made clear that representation, according to this theory, is not a contract between two persons, one appointing the other as its representative and giving her a mandate to accomplish some action, then exercising some sort of control.[55] This is due to the fact that the represented has no existence preceding that of the representative. It only exists because it is represented and it is represented only because the constitution-makers contend that they act in its name. Many modern constitutions designate an entity as the holder of a sovereignty that the government merely exercises. Thus, by pretending to have received a delegation of power, it is the representative that creates the represented.[56]

We see here another use of the distinction between the essence and the exercise of sovereignty, solemnly proclaimed in the Declaration of the Rights of Man and of the Citizen of 1789 in its Article 3, 'the principle of all sovereignty resides essentially in the nation'. The theory has a double function, a negative function (the lawmaker is not the sovereign, but a mere representative) and a positive function (the rules he makes are binding because they express the will of the real sovereign). Article 6 of the Declaration of the Rights of Man and of the Citizen asserts that 'Law is the expression of the general will'. This sentence does not mean that in a society well ordained law should coincide with the general will, but that the justification of the law is that it is presumed to possess the inherent quality of expressing the general will. Thus, once the competent authority has made the law, no one may question it, but every citizen ought to obey it because he will then only obey the general will. In addition, when the law serves as a basis of every norm in the system, they all appear to be ultimately derived from the will of the sovereign. For instance, court decisions in Italy are rendered 'in the name of the Italian people'.

[54] Francesco Di Donato, *La rinascita dello Stato—Dal conflitto magistratura-politica alla civilizzazione statuale europea* (2010); Jacques Krynen, *L'état de justice: France, XIIIe–XXe siècle. Tome 1, L'idéologie de la magistrature ancienne* (2009), 268.

[55] Malberg (n 14), vol II, 199 ff.

[56] Lucien Jaume, *Le discours jacobin et la démocratie* (1989).

But whose will is the general will? Who is the real sovereign, the holder of the essence of sovereignty? In the German Empire, the state itself was the sovereign, in whose name the various organs acted. Modern constitutions name either the people or the nation. How does one chose between them?

According to a common presentation, members of constitutional conventions derive the provisions they favor from their political ideologies. The actual provisions of the constitution therefore reflect the relative strength of political groups and express the beliefs of the majority. The most progressive democrats would favor sovereignty of the people, the more conservative sovereignty of the nation. This is because the people is viewed as a reality, a group of citizens living in a country, whereas the nation is an abstract entity made up not only of citizens but also of the long-term general interests that may transcend the interests of citizens. Scholars who accept these views assume that several practical consequences follow from each of the two doctrines.

Three consequences are supposed to follow from the principle that the people are sovereign. Since it exists in the real world, citizens will only delegate those powers that, for practical reasons, they could not exercise by themselves. They will also exercise by themselves those powers that they do not delegate. Thus, there will be some form of direct democracy, with a popular referendum.[57] On the other hand, all members of the people have a right to participate in the exercise of sovereignty that is a right to vote, either in a referendum or to elect their representatives. Votes will be by universal suffrage. Thirdly, the representatives will carry an imperative mandate; voters will give them instructions and will have a right to recall them if the representatives have not acted according to those instructions.

The doctrine of national sovereignty is supposed to carry opposite consequences. The nation, being an abstract entity, cannot exercise sovereignty and must delegate it to representatives. The system will not be a democracy, but a representative government. Therefore, citizens have no personal right to vote. Participation in an election is a function that is entrusted to citizens by the nation, that is, by its representatives. That function need not be entrusted to all citizens, but only to those who are qualified or have an interest to exercise it well, either because they have received an education, or because they are wealthy, or because they are not dependent on other men. Finally, since voters are not the sovereign, representatives are not their delegates and they cannot be bound by an imperative mandate. The will expressed by the representatives cannot be compared to that of the sovereign, since the sovereign, being an abstraction, is incapable of having a will. The will expressed by the representatives is presumed to be the expression of the general will and this is an absolute presumption, which can never be rebutted.

This idea that provisions of a constitution are deduced *more geometrico* from a set of general principles is naive and flawed. It is easy to see from a few examples that national and popular sovereignty are not as strongly different as is usually assumed and that the choice between recognizing the nation or the people is not the consequence of ideological preferences but that they are *ex post* justifications for the distribution of powers.

We can see that some constitutions, for example the French Constitutions of 1793 and 1795, explicitly proclaim the principle of popular sovereignty, but nevertheless are very reluctant to introduce direct democracy and explicitly prohibit the imperative mandate. Individual members of the legislature are not representatives of the voters in their constituency, but the legislature as a whole represents the people and there is no possible recall.[58]

[57] On referendum, see Chapter 24.

[58] Michel Troper, *La séparation des pouvoirs et l'histoire constitutionnelle française* ([1973] 2010).

On the other hand, the idea that the people, unlike the nation, are not an abstract entity but a real being is also profoundly naive. In order for a group of men to be called 'a people', we need a rule to decide which individuals count as members of that people. Then, since all its members cannot possibly vote, there must be another rule to decide on the conditions (age, gender, mental capacity, residence…) that have to be met by citizens in order to vote. The people and the citizens are no more real than the nation. They are a legal category produced by the constitution.

The reason why the sovereign was called 'nation' in some constitutions and 'people' in others lies in the structure of the legislative power. Thus, in the first French Constitution, in 1789–91, the legislative power was attributed jointly to an elected legislature and to the king, who could veto the bills adopted by the legislature. Since the power they exercised was not their own, the writers of the Constitution had no choice but to consider that they expressed the general will and were both representatives of the sovereign.[59] The structure of the legislative power was that of a mixed government, where sovereignty is exercised jointly by the king and the people. With such a structure it was logically impossible to consider that the king is a representative of the people and exercises sovereignty with the people or that the people exercises his sovereignty, jointly with the king, yet is represented by him. The only solution was to declare that the sovereign is the nation, which is represented by the two elements of the legislative power.[60] This solution ceased to be logically necessary when the republic was established and the executive had no veto power. Later constitutions could then declare either that sovereignty belongs to the people or use the words 'nation' and 'people' as synonyms.

By proclaiming that the people are the sovereign, constitutions assert their democratic legitimacy. A great number of constitutional documents include such proclamations.[61] They do not serve a purely rhetorical purpose. Courts make abundant use of such provisions as important arguments. Thus, the French Constitution proclaims that 'National sovereignty shall vest in the people, who shall exercise it through their representatives and by means of referendum'. This formulation relates to the distinction between the essence and the exercise of sovereignty. For the Council, the system is democratic because the people is not merely the holder of the essence of sovereignty, but also exercises it by itself. There are two ways for the people to exercise their sovereignty: through representatives and by referendum. Democracy is thus alternately indirect or direct. And the Constitutional Council justifies its refusal to review laws adopted by referendum by stating they are the 'direct expression of national sovereignty'.[62]

The need to refer to the people as a holder of sovereignty explains some of the difficulties in the relations between the European Union and the national legal systems. Neither the treaties nor the European Court mention a European people. Apart from the fact that it is hard to conceive of a democracy without a *demos*, the absence of a European people makes it impossible to present decisions made by the European organs as the expression of a general will.[63] The only possible justification is that they express the general will of the national people.

[59] French Constitution of 1791, Title III, Art 2: 'The nation wherefrom all powers proceed can only exercise them by delegation. The French constitution is representative: the representatives are the legislature and the king.'

[60] Pierre Brunet, *Vouloir pour la nation. Le concept de représentation dans la théorie de l'Etat* (2004).

[61] eg Constitution of Portugal, Art 3; Russia, Art 3; Brazil, Art 1; Thailand (1997), Art 3, et al.

[62] Constitutional Council: Décision no 62-20 DC, 6 November 1962, Loi relative à l'élection du Président de la République au suffrage universel direct, adoptée par le référendum du 28 octobre 1962.

[63] Dieter Grimm, 'Does Europe Need a Constitution?' (1995) 1(3) *European Law Journal* 282.

Maintaining that these decisions, even when they prevail over domestic law, including the constitution, prevail in virtue of the national constitution can do this.[64]

III. Conclusion

The question whether the theory of sovereignty is valid must be answered in the affirmative for two different reasons, both connected to fundamental conceptions of constitutional theory.

First, we can see the task of constitutional theory as a general description of positive constitutional law. In that case, we find that an adequate description can be made, even in the contemporary world, using the various concepts of sovereignty: states do exist and they must still be defined with the help of these concepts; they are not legally bound by any external or internal rule, they have unlimited power to decide on the range of powers they intend to exercise; in every state, we find a supreme authority or group of authorities capable of producing the highest rules in the system, without being themselves subject to any rule and finally they produce these rules in the name of an entity supposed to be supreme and whose supremacy cannot be questioned.

But, these propositions can only be proved to be true by describing the actual behavior of some actors, especially national courts, and by checking whether they find that states are bound against their own will or that there is no supreme entity in whose name every power in the state is being exercised and how they justify their decisions. Constitutional theory then describes the law through an analysis of legal discourse and it is an empirical fact that actors use the language of sovereignty. We could even go as far as saying that, since in a system characterized by the hierarchy of norms, theories of sovereignty are, if not the only possible legal justifications for a number of decisions, certainly the most practical, then this type of discourse is the product of the system itself. And if sovereignty is a constitutive character of the state, then, it is not the law that is produced by the state, but the state that is produced by the law.

Bibliography

Guillaume Bacot, *Carré de Malberg et l'origine de la distinction entre souveraineté du peuple et souveraineté nationale* (1985)

Olivier Beaud, *La puissance de l'Etat* (1994)

Olivier Beaud, *Théorie de la Fédération* (2007)

Jean Bodin, *Les Six Livres de la République* (en 6 livres, 1576), English trans *On Sovereignty. Four Chapters from The Six Books of the Commonwealth* (J.H. Franklin trans, 1992)

Raymond Carré de Malberg, *Contribution à la Théorie générale de l'Etat; spécialement d'après les données fournies par le droit constitutionnel français* ([1920] 2003)

Agostino Carrino (ed), *Kelsen e il problema della sovranità* (1990)

Sabino Cassese, *La crisi dello stato* (2002)

Marcel David, *La souveraineté du peuple* (1996)

A. London Fell (ed), *Origins of Legislative Sovereignty and the Legislative State* (vols 1 and 2, 1983; vol 3, 1987)

Luigi Ferrajoli, *La sovranità nel mondo moderno* (2nd edn, 1997)

[64] Decision no 2006-540 DC (n 37).

Dieter Grimm, 'Comments on the German Constitutional Court's Decision on the Lisbon Treaty. Defending Sovereign Statehood against Transforming the European Union into a State' (2009) 5 *European Constitutional Law Review* 353
Dieter Grimm, *Souveränität. Herkunft und Zukunft eines Schlüsselbegriffs* (2009)
Hermann Heller, *Die Souveränität. Ein Beitrag zur Theorie des Staats-und Völkerrechts* (1920), in *Gesammelte Schriften*, vol 2 (1971)
Hent Kalmo and Quentin Skinner (eds), *Sovereignty in Fragments: The Past, Present, and Future of a Contested Concept* (2010)
Hans Kelsen, *Das Problem der Souveränität und die Theorie des Völkerrechts* ([1920] 2nd edn 1928)
Claude Klein, *Théorie et pratique du pouvoir constituant. Critique des discours sur le pouvoir constituant* (1996)
Hugo Krabbe, *The Modern Idea of the State* ([1922] 1980)
Paul Laband, *Le droit public de l'Empire allemand* (1900)
Harold Laski, *Foundations of Sovereignty* ([1921] 1968)
Neil MacCormick, 'Beyond the Sovereign State' (1993) 56(1) *Modern Law Review* 1
Neil MacCormick, *Questioning Sovereignty: Law, State, and Nation in the European Commonwealth (Law, State, and Practical Reason)* (1999)
Charles Edward Merriam, *History of the Theory of Sovereignty Since Rousseau* (1972)
Edmund Sears Morgan, *Inventing the People: The Rise of Popular Sovereignty in England and America* (1988)
Costantino Mortati, 'Principi Fondamentali' in Giueseppe Branca (ed), *Commentario della Costituzione italiana. Arts 1–12* (1975)
Gianluggi Palombella, *Costituzione e sovranità. Il senso della democrazia costituzionale* (1997)
Helmut Quaritsch, 'Souveränität: Entstehung und Entwickung des Begriffs' in *Frankreich und Deutschland von 13 Jh bis 1806* (1986)
Pierre Rosanvallon, *La démocratie inachevée. Histoire de la souveraineté du peuple en France* (2000)
Carl Schmitt, *Théologie politique* (Jean-Louis Schlegel trans, 1988)
Quentin Skinner, *The Foundations of Modern Political Thought* (1978)
Anne-Marie Slaughter, *A New World Order* (2004)
Susan Strange, *The Retreat of the State : The Diffusion of Power in the World Economy* (2nd edn, 1998)
Neil Walker (ed), *Sovereignty in Transition* (2003)

CHAPTER 18

HUMAN DIGNITY AND AUTONOMY IN MODERN CONSTITUTIONAL ORDERS

MATTHIAS MAHLMANN

Zurich

I. Human Dignity: Hopes and Doubt

The concept of human dignity is as difficult and loaded with substantial problems as it is central for the contemporary architecture of human rights. The latter role is evident: human dignity forms a foundational concept for the international legal order of human rights.[1] Many national legal orders incorporate it explicitly, in the post-war era often following the example set by the Universal Declaration of Human Rights.[2] Supranational international organizations like the European Union have recently done the same[3] as have regional systems for the protection of human rights, though sometimes in quite questionable terms.[4]

A further category of norms and instruments relevant for the legal positivation of human dignity are those whose scope is coextensive with central parts of what human dignity is about. Various international instruments, including the international humanitarian and the prospering international criminal law,[5] are aiming at protecting human dignity, mostly explicitly so through action against genocide,[6] crimes against humanity, torture,[7] war crimes, or patterns of discrimination.[8] On the level of constitutional norms and constitutional instruments, prohibitions on inhuman and degrading treatment, torture, or slavery are evident examples, as are prohibitions of discrimination on the grounds of ascribed race, ethnic origin, sex, religion and belief, disability, and—increasingly so—other characteristics such as sexual orientation.

In legal orders—national or international—without explicit foundation in the positive law, dignity nevertheless plays a sometimes even pivotal role: here it is included in the law through interpretation of other norms, more or less closely related to dignity, by case law.[9]

[1] Cf for some examples: UN Charter, Preamble; Universal Declaration of Human Rights, Preamble and Art 1; International Covenant on Civil and Political Rights, Preamble; and International Covenant on Economic, Social and Cultural Rights, Preamble, acknowledge a foundational role of dignity for human rights.

[2] Cf for examples from different continents: Finland: s 1; Germany: Art 1; Japan: Art 24; Portugal: Arts 1, 13, 26, 67, 206; Mexico: Art 3(c); South Africa: Art 10; Spain: Art 10; Switzerland: Art 7.

[3] Charter of Fundamental Rights of the European Union, Art 1. The European Court of Justice (ECJ) had already acknowledged human dignity as part of the fundamental rights, forming part of the general principles of the then European Community law, cf eg ECJ, Case C-377/98 *Netherlands v European Parliament*, para 70. See Matthias Mahlmann, '1789 Renewed? Prospects of the Protection of Human Rights in Europe' (2003) 11 *Cardozo Journal of International and Comparative Law* 903.

[4] The American Declaration of the Rights and Duties of Man, 1948: recitals, Preamble, Art XXIII; The American Convention on Human Rights, 1969, Arts 5(2), 6(2), 11; The African (Banjul) Charter on Human and Peoples' Rights, 1981: Preamble, Art 5; The Arab Charter on Human Rights 2004: Preamble, Arts 2.3, 3.3, 17, 20.1, 33.3, 40.1. Arts 2.3 or 3.3 are examples for questionable positivations.

[5] Rome Statue of the International Criminal Court, Arts 5–8.

[6] Convention on the Prevention and Punishment of the Crime of Genocide, 9 December 1948 (without an explicit reference to human dignity).

[7] Convention against Torture and Other Cruel, Inhuman or Degrading Treatment or Punishment, 10 December 1984 (dignity in preamble).

[8] International Convention on the Elimination of All Forms of Racial Discrimination, 21 December 1965 (dignity in preamble); Convention on the Elimination of All Forms of Discrimination against Women, 18 December 1979 (dignity in preamble); Convention on the Rights of Persons with Disabilities, 6 December 2006 (dignity in preamble).

[9] The European Convention on Human Rights does not contain a reference to human dignity, although such reference is included in additional protocols, cf Protocol 13 noting that 'the abolition of the death penalty is essential for the protection of this right and for the full recognition of the inherent dignity of all human beings'. The European Court of Human Rights (ECtHR) assigned dignity a pivotal role in the architecture of the Convention: *Pretty v United Kingdom*, App no 2346/02, para 65. The Court connects human dignity with Art 3 (para 52) and states that human autonomy is protected by Art 8 (para 61).

The central role of human dignity in the global culture of law is by no means self-evident. Human dignity as an ethical and political idea has very powerful history. As a legal concept, it had a rather slow career. It appeared late on the scene of modern constitutional law[10] before its inclusion in the UN Charter and the Universal Declaration of Human Rights sparked off further development.

And there is another point why the central role of human dignity may seem less evident than it sometimes appears: human dignity is not at all a fully trusted lodestar of the international human rights culture and its hard legal normative core in the multi-layered, manifold intertwined, differentiated, and heterogeneous systems of human rights protections through constitutions, sub- and quasi-constitutional human rights bills, supra- and international instruments.[11] For some, the light it sheds is not the light of judicial insight and normative progress, but the dubious, phosphorescent, seductive glow of a legal will-o'-the-wisp that leads one astray in the dangerous swamp of hidden ideologies, false essentialism, masked power, and self-righteous cultural and religious parochialism treacherously adorned in the splendid robe of universalism.

And there are reasons for this perspective: the reference to human dignity in legal instruments or court decisions is sometimes not at all in accordance with fundamental values like liberty, equality, and true concern for the worth of individual personality. In any event, it is heterogeneous and full of discord: in important legal matters, the law and courts may refer to human dignity but draw radically different conclusions of what that means for the issue at stake.

Human autonomy is habitually ranked as a central, perhaps even necessary, content of human dignity. This conceptual affiliation, however, nourishes doubts as well as seems to presuppose the idea of a reasonable, self-determining human subject that is for many since its inception profoundly and disdainfully biased by particularistic perspectives such as gender, ethnic background, cultural origin, or social status and rightly deconstructed in contemporary discourse.

On the other hand, is it really imaginable to do away with human dignity in modern law? After all, the quest for grasping the core of human dignity has accompanied human reflection since its beginnings, not necessarily as a term, but as the idea that human beings are invested with a particular worth commanding care and respect, for others and for their own proper selves. And its particular role in the international rights debates is not just a kittenish twist in a contingently unfolding normative narrative of the last century. To the contrary, its rise had to do with epochal shifts—the final dawn of the European empires, decolonization in political, ideological, and theoretical terms, the fall of patriarchies, the critique of dehumanizing ideologies such as racism, democratization, and the economic emancipation of wider parts of societies because powerful social movements claimed their due. And, not to be forgotten, its cruel and unwilling midwife at birth was nothing but the illumination of what its negation practically means provided by the crude light of the gas chambers and other atrocious offspring of a dire epoch.

The controversy around human dignity as a foundational concept for the law in general and constitutionalism in particular is thus no superficial affair. To find a way out of this maze, the

[10] For early references see Art 151 of the Weimar Constitution of Germany (1919) not establishing a subjective right but a principle of economic organization; see further the Preamble of the Constitution of Ireland of 1937. Christopher McCrudden, 'Human Dignity and Judicial Interpretation of Human Rights' (2008) 19 *European Journal of International Law* 664 lists other examples. Dignity, however, was included in the Constitution of Finland by amendment of 17 July 1995 before the Constitution of 1999 came into force. It was included in the Constitution of Portugal by amendment of 11 June 1951 before the Constitution of 1976 came into force. The Preamble of the Cuban Constitution of 1976 refers to human dignity, but not the Preamble of the Constitution of 1940, Art 20 which includes human dignity in a non-discrimination clause. The Constitution of Mexico of 1917, Art 3, did not contain a reference to dignity, the amendment of Art 3c dates from 1946. § 139 on the prohibition of the death penalty in the *Paulskirchenverfassung*, 28 March 1849 was based on the opinion of the drafters that the human dignity of criminals has to be respected, cf Jörg-Detlef Kühne, *Die Reichtsverfassung der Paulskirche* (2nd edn, 1998), 344.

[11] Cf Christopher McCrudden (n 10), 655.

following steps will be taken: First, problems of the method and theory of comparative legal perspectives will be discussed and the core issue to which they lead: the antinomy of practical universalism and theoretical relativism of human rights (Section II). Secondly, a few remarks will sketch some relevant aspects of the history of the idea of human dignity (Section III). Thirdly, the discussion will turn to the content of human dignity and its doctrinal unfolding as a legal concept (Sections IV and V). Finally, some tentative remarks will comment on the deeper cultural and political issues at stake (Section VI).

II. Dignity and the Antinomy of Human Rights

It is an interesting property of contemporary court practice of constitutional and particularly human rights adjudication to incorporate comparative perspectives: a new hermeneutical cross-border curiosity is the jurisprudential mark of the day. The methodological justification of this development is, however, far from clear.[12] One common ground for scholarly work is the interest in understanding the many paths of the law in different legal systems.[13] However, the concrete impact of such studies is problematic for judicial decision-making. For some, a functional approach seems appropriate that tries to describe and evaluate the answers of different legal systems to the common problems each legal system faces.[14] Others may aim to distil from the heterogeneous legal worlds the normative best, not least by studying unconvincing attempts,[15] perhaps pursuing a universalist stance, in general or limited to human rights with their apparent (though contested) universalist potential.[16] Other alternatives encompass a constructive dialogue of different legal systems[17] or pluralistic perspectives: from the latter point of view, legal concepts are irredeemably embedded in cultural and political contexts and expressions of the particular being or decisions of the community that creates the law.[18] The universalist credentials of a term such as 'dignity' may even be a functionally useful shell to give—contrary to appearance—cultural pluralism its due: the universalistic appearance permits particularistic conceptions to unfold, unrealized, perhaps, by actors like courts. From this perspective, comparative analysis serves to make this transparent and to criticize, deconstruct, and prevent naive uses of a legal concept such as dignity by legal actors.[19]

The central question behind these debates is the possibility of normative universalism, a position very much under strain in the contemporary debates. The main problems in this respect are not the variety of interpretations of shared legal concepts or the importance of

[12] Cf Vicki C. Jackson in Chapter 2 of this volume.

[13] Cf Konrad Zweigert and Hein Kötz, *An Introduction to Comparative Law* (3rd edn, 1996), 3; cf Norman Dorsen, Michel Rosenfeld, András Sajó, and Susanne Baer, *Comparative Constitutionalism* (2nd edn, 2010), 1.

[14] Zweigert and Kötz (n 13), 15ff.

[15] A famous example is the study of the US-American experience with the death penalty by the South African Constitutional Court (SACC), concluding that South Africa 'should not follow this route', *S v Makwanyane and Another* (CCT3/94) [1995] ZACC 3; 1995 (6) BCLR 665; 1995 (3) SA 391; [1996] 2 CHRLD 164; 1995 (2) SACR 1 (6 June 1995), para 56 (Chaskalson).

[16] Cf Dorsen et al (n 13), 3. Jürgen Habermas, 'Das Konzept der Menschenwürde und die realistische Utopie der Menschenrechte' (2010) 58 *Deutsche Zeitschrift für Philosophie* 343, 347: human dignity imports an egalitarian-universalist morality into law.

[17] Cf Ruti Teitel, 'Book Review: Comparative Constitutional Law in a Global Age' (2004) 117 *Harvard Law Review* 2570, 2586.

[18] These are common approaches; cf the taxonomy of Mark Tushnet, *Weak Courts, Strong Rights* (2009), 5ff, distinguishing functionalism and normative universalism, on the one hand, from contextualism and expressivism, on the other.

[19] This is the central point of McCrudden (n 10), 710.

context for the understanding of legal precepts. There are many different conceptions and understandings of fundamental legal concepts not only between but *within* various legal systems and cultures, as any dissenting court opinion illustrates. Human dignity is of course no exception in this respect. The interesting question is, however, whether all these conceptions are of equal normative plausibility—a question that the observable variety poses, not answers.

In addition, contexts certainly matter for what a legal concept in a particular legal system really means.[20] On the other hand, one should avoid the mystification of contexts: there is much to be said about the different contexts, say, of administering the death penalty in the United States or in South Africa.[21] At the core, however, everywhere a hard normative question is at stake: Can the taking of life for penological purposes be justified? Stressing contexts should not be used to cloud the core of these questions and their often painful normative and political implications.

The real question is thus whether any justification of certain understandings of normative concepts can be normatively relevant for other systems because any such justification is itself *intrinsically dependent* on the cultural, historical, and social background and thus not transferable to other legal orders.

For human rights, this question can be reformulated more precisely as the question of the possibility of a culturally non-relative justification of a *theory of fundamental rights*. Human rights and connected norms, like clauses of limitations are regularly specifically underdetermined by the positive law. Their text is opaque, open-textured, and abstract. A theory of fundamental rights fills the hermeneutical space opened by the abstract structure of human rights norms by providing those normative principles that guide their interpretation: it is an encompassing account of the structure and normative point of an order of fundamental rights and the particular normative positions it creates.[22] Such a theory of fundamental rights must be based on the positive law it serves to interpret. A fascist theory of fundamental rights is irreconcilable with the European Convention on Human Rights. Beyond such extreme cases, a theory of fundamental rights can, however, (and with hermeneutical necessity) not be determined in the last instance by positive human rights norms as the opaqueness and openness for different interpretations of these norms formed the reasons to have recourse to theoretical reflection in the first place. The content of a theory of fundamental rights cannot itself be determined by the normative material the content of which it serves to define.

There are now several reasons why it may seem doubtful that a non-relativist theory of fundamental rights is possible. Most importantly, perhaps, a universalist approach faces many challenges of normative epistemology. The critique of metaphysics through analytical non-cognitivism,[23] the element of avowal and decision in value statements in Max Weber's analysis,[24] the social and cultural genealogies of Critical Theory,[25] structuralism,[26] and post-modernity[27]

[20] This is correctly highlighted by Tushnet (n 18), 10ff.

[21] Cf eg David Garland, *A Peculiar Institution* (2010) on the US-American context.

[22] For some background see Matthias Mahlmann, 'Dictatorship of the Obscure? Values and the Secular Adjudication of Fundamental Rights' in András Sajó and Renata Uitz (eds), *Constitutional Topography: Values and Constitutions* (2010), 343ff; Matthias Mahlmann, *Elemente einer ethischen Grundrechtstheorie* (2008).

[23] eg see Rudolf Carnap, 'Überwindung der Metaphysik durch logische Analyse der Sprache' (1931) 2 *Erkenntnis* 219ff on moral concepts as pseudo-concepts or Alfred Jules Ayer, *Language, Truth and Logic* (1936).

[24] Cf eg Max Weber, 'Politik als Beruf' in *Max Weber Gesamtausgabe*, Bd 17 (1992), 99ff.

[25] Max Horkheimer and Theodor W. Adorno, *Die Dialektik der Aufklärung* (1969).

[26] Cf eg Michel Foucault, *Les mots et les choses. Une archéologie des sciences humaines* (1966); Michel Foucault, *L'archéologie du savoir* (1969).

[27] Jean-François Lyotard, *La condition postmoderne* (1983).

have rendered it profoundly doubtful that any universalist claim could be epistemologically justified. After all, which foundational argument does not become entangled in the maze of dogmatism, infinite justificatory regress, tautologies, or recourse to contingent traditions? For many, the only intellectually respectable position is therefore one or another form of relativism founding normative arguments in the last instance on cultural traditions, social semantics, discourse formations,[28] operations of social systems,[29] shifting narratives, or exchangeable final languages.[30]

There is a political point against universalism, too. Universalism smacks of paternalism, even cultural imperialism that raises serious problems not least in the context of multi-layered systems of human rights, because the universalist stance of one court, say an international court like the European Court of Human Rights, may unduly curtail the self-determination of a political community.

There is, however, a fundamental catch: the very architecture of international human rights law seems to imply the possibility of universalism. This is not just a functional universalism through factual interdependence in multilayered systems of human rights protection. It is an axiological universalism: the various national, supranational, and international human rights codes presuppose through their interconnection that not only irreconcilable norms collide, but that something common is secured and new common ground is gained in the process of adjudication. This was, after all, the core aspiration of the post-Second World War normative recalibration though the political practice of powers continued to remain remote from it. This assumption is the lifeblood as well of fundamental new beginnings of communities that want to re-join the better normative heritage of humanity after years of suppression and injustice—from post-war Germany to South Africa's post-apartheid constitutional resurrection.[31]

The antinomy of international human rights law is thus formulated: there is a practical universalism implied in the very architecture of modern human rights law; this universalism seems, however, theoretically indefensible and politically doubtful. This fundamental problem of all human rights is of particular importance for the idea of human dignity which since its inception has been at the heart of the whole human rights project.

A plausible approach to the solution of this problem cannot be outlined by abstract argument alone but presupposes a reconstruction of the content, the various conceptualizations of the concept human dignity, and some thoughts about their respective legitimacy. Methods and their substantial theoretical underpinnings are sometimes most clearly stated (and to a certain degree legitimized) by the practice of their application. This is what we turn to now, first in a historical perspective.

III. The Quest for Dignity

1. The Point and Perils of Historical Reflection

The reflection about the value status of human beings occupies a central place in the history of normative ideas. This complex and sometimes contradictory history is the background and base for the concrete incorporation of dignity in legal systems. It is therefore rightly not amiss in any

[28] Cf eg Foucault, *Les mots et les choses* (n 26); Foucault, *L'archéologie du savoir* (n 26).

[29] Niklas Luhmann, *Die Gesellschaft der Gesellschaft* (n 26).

[30] Richard Rorty, *Irony, Contingency, and Solidarity* (1989), 73ff.

[31] Cf on the constitutional aspirations of civilized nations SACC, *Makwanyane*, para 278 (Mahomed); Laurie W.H. Ackermann, 'Equality and the South African Constitution: The Role of Dignity' (2000) 63 *Zeitschrift für ausländisches öffentliches Recht und Völkerrecht* 537, 539.

serious treatment of the matter. Crucially important for gaining a somewhat fuller picture of the content of this history is to look not only at the development of ideas but also at the real history of social practice and struggles. This holds for the contemporary world, too. The most impressive manifestations of human dignity are certainly not found in books (great though some of them are) but in human lives—to be clear, not only or even predominantly so in the lives of the real or imagined heroes and heroines of politics, science, and art, but in the ordinary lives led around the corner that are unnoticed by history books and still embody what this term is about.

Equally significant is to search for manifestations not only where the term dignity and its many synonyms and circumscriptions are used but in other than linguistic forms of human expression as well. There is certainly much to be learned about human dignity from Sophocles' tragedies, Michelangelo's sculptures, or Goya's etchings. Some accounts of the historical development of the concept of human dignity overlook this and conflate recorded theoretical thought with the whole history of this complex normative idea. One detrimental consequence of this stance is that those predominantly non-European, non-Western cultures where such records do not exist (because they were not produced or because they were destroyed by conquerors, empire-building imperialists, and the like) do not even appear on the screen of historical recollections.

A second important point concerns the fallacy of concluding from the absence of a term like 'dignity' in a particular language the absence of the normative substrate in the minds of the people using that language. That this is in fact a fallacy seems to be a rather clear lesson of the contemporary theory of the relation of language and mind.[32] Mental representations of any sort (concepts etc) can be realized in a variety of ways without the need for a proper term for what is meant: a native English speaker may lack the word *Gemütlichkeit* without being devoid of the feeling that this term designates and the ability to express this subjective emotional state linguistically. This has some significance for a central issue at stake: one finds, not rarely, the opinion voiced that culture X lacks the idea of human rights in general or of human dignity in particular because language Y used in X lacks a special term for human rights or dignity.[33] This in itself is often not true but even if it were so, it is—given what has been said before about the relation of language and mind—of no interesting consequence for the substantial question at stake.

A third point concerns the distinction between what people think and express about the norms that are applicable to them and the norms that are in fact applicable to them. The fact that a person or a group of persons was or is of the opinion that human dignity is (or is not) a normative status its members enjoy, does not entail that they do (or do not) enjoy it. Thus a culture of fervent dignity-deniers may still possess what they deny.

Finally, it is worth noting that genealogy and justification are distinct things in normative argumentation. A consequence of this distinction is that even if a certain culture has a certain normative tradition, this does not mean that this tradition is justified only for this culture or even justified at all. It may be a good, a bad—or the usual case—a mixed tradition, including better and worse ideas. Historical genealogy of a normative concept thus does not avail one of the tasks for providing a justification for its understanding.[34]

[32] Cf Steven Pinker, *The Language Instinct* (1994), 55ff.

[33] eg former judge of the German Federal Constitutional Court, Paul Kirchhof at the Humboldt-Universität, Berlin in 2009, asserting—in the context of an argument for the Christian origins of human dignity—that the Turkish language is lacking a term for human dignity, cf *Der Tagesspiegel*, 23 April 2009; *Die Welt*, 23 April 2009.

[34] Genealogical reconstructions often show exclusionary tendencies. Cf the theses voiced by Ernst von Caemmerer, in Hans-Jürgen Papier and Detlef Merten (eds), *Handbuch der Grundrechte*, Bd VI/1 (2010), § 136, paras 104–112, that human rights are intrinsically connected to the Christian, and less so the Judean, tradition, but are alien to Islam.

2. Dignity in History: Some Tentative Observations

Looking at the history, paying due attention to these methodological parameters, one could make the following observations about the historical trajectory of the idea of dignity:[35]

The idea of what is today called human dignity concerns the intrinsic value status of human beings as human beings irrespective of other properties. As words in general, human dignity and its synonyms can be used to designate other designata, for example a relative position within a given, contingent social hierarchy.[36]

This idea is not bound to any particular culture or religion. One finds it in classical antique thought, for example in Greece[37] or China,[38] in the framework of polytheistic,[39] pantheistic,[40] different monotheistic[41] and secular, agnostic, or atheistic worldviews.[42] Undoubtedly, violations of human dignity were often defended within these frameworks. The point here is only that the basis for unfolding a concept of dignity is equally present in many cultural and religious contexts, long as the way may be.

The ascription of dignity demands respect and recognition as a creature with particular worth equally shared by every human being. A more precise statement with more clear-cut normative consequences of what this worth means is to regard human beings as *last-order purposes of human intentions and actions*. Human beings are regarded as *Selbstzwecke*, as ends-in-themselves, a term that can be derived from Kant's version of this thought—a *version*, not the *origin*, given other traditions, something to be underlined because the idea is sometimes attributed to Kant alone.[43] The normative consequence of this status is the protection of

[35] For more detail cf Mahlmann, *Elemente* (n 22), 97–173.

[36] Classic example for this is Cicero, *De inventione rhetorica*, II, 166. The distinction helps to evaluate the thesis that dignity is honour universalized by the Nazis, cf James Q. Whitman, 'Nazi "Honour" and New European "Dignity"' in Christian Joerges and Navraj S. Ghaleigh (eds), *Darker Legacies of Law in Europe* (2003), 243ff: the point of human dignity proper is that it is a value status intrinsic to any human being, the very point the ideology of racial honour denies—with lethal consequences for those devoid of this 'honour'. The idea of the universalization of the highest rank appears in a different context in Jeremy Waldron, 'Dignity and Rank' (2007) 48 *Archives européennes d'archéologie* 201.

[37] Cf Sophocles, *Antigone* (1997), lines 332ff, where the greatness of human beings is praised.

[38] Cf Mencius on human nature, James Legge (trans), *The Works of Mencius* (2nd edn, 1895), Bk 6, ch 6, 16, 17 on the nobility of human nature; cf Kwong-Ioi Shun, *Mencius and Early Chinese Thought* (1997), 136 ff.

[39] eg Sophocles (n 37).

[40] An important source for the reflection of the worth of humans is the Stoa. Cf the testimony about earlier Stoic thought in Cicero, *De officiis*, 1, 105.

[41] Both for Judaism and Christianity the idea of an image of god (*imago dei*) is of central importance, cf Gen 1, 26; 27. Similar ideas are found in other religious frameworks, cf eg for Islam, The Quran, Sure 2, 30 on human beings as 'representatives' or 'successors' of God.

[42] One of the central elements of Kant's ethics which is foundational for the modern theory of dignity is its principled secularity, cf Immanuel Kant, *Die Religion innerhalb der Grenzen der bloßen Vernunft*, Akademie Ausgabe, Bd VI, 3. One of the bedrock assumptions of John Rawls's ethics was that humans share an 'aristocracy of all', cf his reconstruction of this idea in Kant's work, John Rawls, *Lectures on the History of Moral Philosophy* (2000), 213, 306, developed in his later years within a non-religious framework, cf John Rawls, *On my Religion*, in John Rawls, *A Brief Inquiry into the Meaning of Sin and Faith: With 'On My Religion'* (2009).

[43] Cf Thomas Aquinas, *Summa Theologica*, II-II, q 64: human beings 'propter se ipsum existens'; John Locke, 'The Second Treatise' in *Two Treatises on Government*, ch II: 'Being furnished with like faculties, sharing all in one Community of Nature, there cannot be supposed any such Subordination among us, that may Authorize us to destroy one another, as if we were made for one another's uses' (emphasis in original).

the subject status of human beings, the ability to become authors of their lives and thus of their *autonomy*. The negative counterpart of this is the *prohibition of instrumentalization and objectification*. This denies the status of a subject to human beings by making them the instruments for the realization of ends beyond themselves.[44]

If human dignity is ascribed, its source can be transcendent or immanent. The dignity of religious ethics[45] and some particular ontologies[46] are examples of the former. The latter can lead to derivative accounts of human dignity which make the dignity of human beings dependent on some other immanent source, for example Hegel's conditioning human dignity on partaking in the *Sittlichkeit* of the state.[47] The immanent account for dignity can take a further step and base the ascription of dignity on nothing but the humaneness of humans: this is the path of modern humanism in its various Enlightenment or Post-Enlightenment forms.[48]

It is noteworthy that a strong current of dignity scepticism has accompanied these thoughts. The most radical critique is that there is no shared supreme worth of all human beings, either because all or a portion of humanity is sufficiently wretched and wicked or because worth is not connected to humanity as such but is relative to the performance of certain tasks in society.[49] Others argue that dignity as a normative concept suffers from severe weaknesses. Schopenhauer's catchphrase of dignity as the 'Shibbolet of all clue- and thoughtless moralists'[50] has therefore gained considerable popularity.

Given this scepticism, the problem of justification of the predication of dignity to humans gains some importance. The fundamentally different theories outlined about the sources of dignity—transcendent, immanent, derivative, original—entail different theories of justification of dignity. A transcendental conception bases the justification of the ascription to a transcendental legitimacy-conferring cause, prominently an act of grace by a divine force. The immanent derivative theories depend on the justification of the dignity-conferring entity central to such a theory—for example Hegel's theory of the state. The immanent original theories are most commonly based on particular properties of humans that legitimize the predication of dignity to human beings. These properties can be relevant for a transcendent theory as well, for example as the gifts of god. Interestingly, across cultures and times a limited set of properties has been used to legitimize the ascription of dignity. Prominent among them rank the capability to reason and think, moral orientation, self-determination, freedom of will and action and, in consequence, the ability for self-creation through culture.[51]

[44] Cf eg Immanuel Kant, *Grundlegung zur Metaphysik der Sitten, Akademie Ausgabe*, Bd IV, 434 and passim; Immanuel Kant, *Kritik der praktischen Vernunft, Akademie Ausgabe*, Bd V, 87, 131ff; Immanuel Kant, *Kritik der Urteilskraft, Akademie Ausgabe*, Bd V, 435.

[45] Cf n 41.

[46] Cf Martin Heidegger, *Über den Humanismus* (1999), 32 where the position of a human being is described as a 'Hirt des Seins' a 'shephard of being'. This particular 'ontical' position of humans is regarded to be the source of dignity and human worth.

[47] G.W.F. Hegel, *Grundlinien der Philosophie des Rechts* (1986), §258.

[48] The paradigmatic theory is Kant (n 44).

[49] For a classic example see Thomas Hobbes, *Leviathan*, ch 10. For a modern variant (human dignity and other human rights functional fiction of an autopoietic social system for the purpose of self-reproduction) see Niklas Luhmann, *Grundrechte als Institution* (1965); Luhmann (n 29), 1075ff.

[50] Arthur Schopenhauer, *Preisschrift über das Fundament der Moral* (1979), 64: 'Schiboleth aller rath- und gedankenlosen Moralisten'.

[51] Examples for other justifications include Avishai Margalit, *The Decent Society* (1996) (the ability of new beginnings); Ronald Dworkin, *Life's Dominion* (1994), 84 (investments in personal development); Ronald Dworkin, *Justice for Hedgehogs* (2011) (recognition of objective value of life); Jürgen Habermas, *Die Zukunft der menschlichen Natur* (2005), 62ff (reciprocal communicative recognition).

IV. The Content of Human Dignity as a Legal Concept

Human dignity as a legal concept fulfils various functions in constitutions, constitutional instruments, and international law: It serves as a normative protection of individuals. It constitutes objective law and an important part of the general principles of the law, not least as a guideline for the interpretation of other fundamental rights. It formulates principles for the structure of the state and other political, legally institutionalized, transnational orders. As with any other norms investigated from a comparative perspective, legal guarantees of human dignity differ considerably from each other both on the level of positive texts and judicial interpretation. These differences will first be surveyed in relation to some important systematic points (Section IV), then the normative merits of these different solutions will be considered (Section V).

1. The Scope of Dignity

(a) Elements of Concretization

Central elements of concretizations of human dignity prominent in the history of ideas across cultural, religious, and philosophical frontiers can be found in international jurisprudence as well. The preservation of certain *minimum standards of treatment of persons*, the *protection of the subject status of human individuals* implying the *guarantee of their autonomy*, and a *prohibition of their instrumentalization and objectification* rank prominently in various jurisdictions, as explicit arguments or implicit principles. These contents are spelled out in different forms. The two most important strategies, sometimes combined, are, as for other human rights, first abstract and more or less precise intentional delineations of the content of human dignity; secondly, the often only implicit unfolding of the content through case law on violations of dignity.

A rather straightforward abstract definition stems from the German Federal Constitutional Court. This definition is a standard reference point in comparative analysis of dignity jurisprudence, not least because of the prominent role of human dignity in the German Basic Law due to its historical background.[52] The position of the individual human being as the highest-order purpose of the law is the explicit central element of this jurisprudence, although only after years of jurisprudence on the matter.[53] The negative flipside is the prohibition on making a person the object and thus the means of state action, the so-called '*Objektformel*' (object-formula) of the court.[54]

[52] Cf eg Edward J. Eberle, *Dignity and Liberty* (2002); Lorraine E. Weinrib, 'The Charter in the International Context: Human Dignity as a Rights-Protecting Principle' (2004) 17 *National Journal of Constitutional Law* 325; Giovanni Bognetti, 'The Concept of Human Dignity in European and US Constitutionalism' in Georg Nolte (ed), *European and US Constitutionalism* (2003), 85.

[53] Its first decision on dignity refers to 'Erniedrigung, Brandmarkung, Ächtung' (humiliation, stigmatization, ostracism), BVerfGE 1, 97 (104). In the decision on the prohibition of the right extremist party SRP, the Court referred to the intrinsic worth of human beings irreconcilable with a totalitarian state, BVerfGE 2, 1 (12). In the decision on the ban of the communist party KPD, the Court stated that human dignity is the supreme value of the constitution, respecting a human being as a person that is concretely entitled to be a subject of a the political, democratic process, BVerfGE 5, 85 (204ff). The priority of the person over the order of the state is emphasized in BVerfGE 7, 198 (205). BVerfGE 45, 187 (227) formulated then programmatically: human beings are a 'Zweck an sich selbst'—a purpose in itself.

[54] Fully established by BVerfGE 27, 1 (6) and standing case law, despite some sceptical remarks in BVerfGE 30, 1 (25). The 'object-formula' is attributed to Günter Dürig, *Die Menschenauffassung des Grundgesetzes* (1952), 259, stating that the human being as conceptualized under the Basic Law was not the mere object of state power as under Nazi rule; Günter Dürig, 'Der Grundrechtssatz von der Menschenwürde' (1956) 81 *Archiv des Öffenlichen Rechts* 117, 127.

In addition, the duty to protect human beings against violations of the respect they are entitled to beyond cases of instrumentalization has also been underlined.[55] This formula has been applied—sometimes more, sometimes less convincingly—over the decades in many contexts, on procedural rights,[56] privacy,[57] limits of state surveillance,[58] criminal sanctions,[59] abortion,[60] or killing of third parties to protect the lives of others.[61]

Other concretizations, although adopting a similar path, stress the open-textured content of human dignity as the expression of an ungraspable essence of human beings, on the basis of respect for the uniqueness and individuality of the person and protection against objectification[62] or degradation[63] or focus more abstractly on the particular equal worth entitling human beings to respect and equal consideration underlining as well the importance of autonomy and self-determination.[64]

The second judicial strategy to get to grips with the content of human dignity is to give the content of dignity contours via cases where a violation of dignity is assumed without an abstract definition of what it is about. This approach is of particular importance for the delineation of the scope of the right even if the first approach is adopted because it helps to concretize this abstract content. Important areas where dignity plays a role revolve, first, around autonomous self-determination, secondly, the preservation of personal (bodily and psychic) integrity, thirdly, the violation and preservation of the equality of status rights, fourthly, the provision of material preconditions of human life, fifthly, the social expression of human worth, and sixthly, foundational principles of the structure of the state and of democracy. Prominent examples of the first group are issues of privacy and abortion;[65] for the second, prohibitions of torture and degrading, cruel, unusual, and inhuman treatment and punishment;[66] for the third, cases of discrimination;[67] for the fourth, dignity-based social rights;[68] for the fifth, matters of individual reputation[69] or

[55] BVerfG NJW 1993, 3190: flooding of prison cell with faeces is a violation of dignity. Cf in this context *Brown v Plata*, 563 US _ (2011): 'A prison that deprives prisoners of basic sustenance, including adequate medical care, is incompatible with the concept of human dignity and has no place in civilized society.'

[56] These were already relevant in early decisions preparing the mature jurisprudence BVerfGE 7, 53; 7, 275; 9, 89; or in criminal law BVerfGE 57, 250.

[57] BVerfGE 27, 1: as an early decision on data protection.

[58] BVerfGE 30, 1: declaring a constitutional amendment as reconcilable with dignity that limited access to secret service data to a parliamentary committee, with a sharp (and convincing) dissent, BVerfGE 30, 1 (39).

[59] BVerfGE 45, 187: life imprisonment only reconcilable with dignity if legally regulated possibility to regain freedom.

[60] BVerfGE 39, 1; 88, 203.

[61] BVerfGE 115, 118 on a law allowing for shooting down airplanes in the hands of terrorists to save others, declaring it unconstitutional.

[62] Swiss Federal Court BGE 127 I 6, 14ff. The prohibition of objectivation is underlined in the context of procedural rights, BGE 124 V 180, 181; BGE 127 I 6, 13ff; Hungarian Constitutional Court, Decision 23/1990, 31 October 1990, 3 (Sólyom concurring): humans not to be 'changed into tool or object'.

[63] eg SACC, *National Coalition for Gay and Lesbian Equality and Another v Minister of Justice and Others* (CCT11/98) [1998] ZACC 15; 1999 (1) SA 6; 1998 (12) BCLR 1517 (9 October 1998), para 28.

[64] Cf eg Supreme Court of Canada, *Law v Canada* [1999] 1 SCR 497, para 53.

[65] eg *Planned Parenthood of Southeastern Pennsylvania v Casey* 505 US 833, 846 (1992) and below.

[66] Cf eg *Public Committee Against Torture in Israel v The State of Israel*, 6 September 1999, paras 23–32: shaking, forced crouching on one's toes, cuffing in contorted positions, covering the head with a sack, long-term exposition to loud music, the (contorted) 'Shabach' position on a chair, deprivation of sleep to break a person without further reasoning what exactly makes the concrete acts violations of dignity. Cf Mordechai Kremnitzer and Re'em Segev, 'The Legality of Interrogational Torture: A Question of Proper Authorization or a substantial Moral Issue?' (2000) 34 *Israel Law Review* 509.

[67] eg European Commission on Human Rights, Report of 14 December 1973, *East African Asians v United Kingdom*, para 207.

[68] eg SACC, *Government of the Republic of South Africa and Others v Grootboom and Others* (CCT 11/00) [2000] ZACC 19; 2001 (1) SA 46; 2000 (11) BCLR 1169 (4 October 2000), para 44 and below.

[69] eg BVerfGE 30, 173 (194).

collective issues such as pornography,[70] prostitution,[71] or hate speech;[72] and for the sixth, decisions on rights-based constraints on the structures of states and democracy.[73]

An interesting example in this context is the role of dignity in US constitutional law.[74] It has been observed that dignity played an ambivalent role in US constitutional law: 'In one sense, the entire edifice of U.S. constitutional law is built on a vision of human dignity, as reflected in popular sovereignty, representative government and entrenched individual rights.'[75] On the other hand, violations of human dignity were legally buttressed or implicitly accepted, including accommodation of unequal voting rights, of slavery and segregation on the base of attributed race, the constitutional framing of US colonialism, or of eugenics.[76]

As far as the jurisprudence of the US Supreme Court is concerned, from the 1940s onwards, references to human dignity have played a significant, if not doctrinally, systematically clarified role.[77] The concept has been important for matters such as cruel and unusual punishment, the constitutionality of the death penalty, prisoners' rights and conditions of confinement, (body cavity) searches, taking of bodily fluid and other intrusions on bodily integrity, and procedural rights such as the privilege against self-incrimination or personal reputation.[78] It is noteworthy that constitutional arguments about such high-profile topics as the death penalty,[79] abortion,[80] or sexual self-determination[81] were prominently and contentiously in part based on human dignity.

Constitutional jurisprudence on these matters oscillates between more or less wide and precise determinations of which treatment is irreconcilable with human worth. Human dignity can coalesce with general personality rights or can be more narrowly circumscribed to

[70] eg SACC, *De Reuck v Director of Public Prosecution* (CCT 5/03) [2003] ZACC 19; 2004 (1) SA 406 (CC); 2003 (12) BCLR 1333 (CC) (15 October 2003), paras 61ff, para 63 referring to degradation and objectification of children through child pornography.

[71] eg *S v Jordan and Others* (CCT 31/01) [2002] ZACC 22; 2002 (6) SA 642; 2002 (11) BCLR 1117 (9 October 2002) (O'Regan and Sachs), para 74: no infringement in the dignity of prostitutes by criminalizing their activities because the violation of dignity actually lies in the 'commodification' of the human body.

[72] eg Supreme Court of Canada, *R v Keegstra* [1990] 3 SCR 697.

[73] Cf BVerfGE 2, 1 (SRP); 5, 85 (KPD).

[74] The federal Constitution does not contain a reference to human dignity. On the level of states, the Montana Constitution of 1972, Art II(4) provides that the 'dignity of the human being is inviolable'. In addition, there are a reference to dignity in the Louisiana Constitution, Art I(3) and the Illinois Constitution, Art 1(20). Only the Montana clause, it appears, had any and partly quite interesting legal effects, cf Vicki C. Jackson, 'Constitutional Dialogue and Human Dignity: States and Transnational Constitutional Discourse' (2004) 65 *Montana Law Review* 15.

[75] Gerald L. Neuman, 'Human Dignity in United States Constitutional Law' in Dieter Simon and Manfred Weiss (eds), *Zur Autnomie des Individuums, Liber Amicorum Spiros Simitis* (2000), 249, 251.

[76] Ibid 249, 252ff.

[77] As the first reference *In re Yamashita* 327 US 1, 29 (Murphy, dissenting):

> If we are ever to develop an orderly international community based upon a recognition of human dignity it is of the utmost importance that the necessary punishment of those guilty of atrocities be as free as possible from the ugly stigma of revenge and vindictiveness.

(On the question of punishment for war crimes of a Japanese General.)

[78] For an overview cf Neuman (n 75), 255ff, and Jordan J. Paust, 'Human Dignity as a Constitutional Right' (1984) 27 *Howard Law Journal* 145; William A. Parent, 'Constitutional Values and Human Dignity' in Michael J. Meyer and William A. Parent (eds), *The Constitution of Rights: Human Dignity and American Values* (1992), 47; Frederick Schauer, 'Speaking of Dignity' in ibid 178; Louis Henkin, 'Human Dignity and Constitutional Rights' in ibid 210; Maxine D. Goodman, 'Human Dignity in Supreme Court Constitutional Jurisprudence' (2006) 84 *Nebraska Law Review* 740ff.

[79] See below n 84.

[80] *Planned Parenthood of Southeastern Pennsylvania v Casey* 505 US 833, 846 (1992) and below.

[81] *Lawrence v Texas* 539 US 558, 567 (2003).

particularly qualified acts.[82] A central common function is to draw a baseline for what is impermissible treatment of individuals under any circumstances. A classical testing case, whether human beings are regarded as a worth at all, is the death penalty.[83] Consequently, human dignity plays a prominent role in determining its permissibility in four main aspects: as to the implicit denial of any human worth of the accused by execution,[84] the modes of execution,[85] including the death row phenomenon,[86] the violation of the continuing subject status of the convict,[87] and the implicit objectification and instrumentalization of the accused for penological purposes.[88] The death penalty has ceased to be a central political concern in many countries, given the momentum of the international abolitionist movement. Its great human drama serves, however, as a looking-glass to make more visible the critical role dignity can serve in human rights adjudication. It is interesting to observe that with the idea of intrinsic worth, protected status as a subject and purpose of action and the prohibition of instrumentalization and objectification arguments again play a decisive role that belongs to the core tenets associated with human dignity in historical and systematic perspectives. These elements are significant for other cases, too, for example life imprisonment,[89] legal protection of pre-natal life,[90] prostitution,[91] or child pornography.[92] Another testing case that has more recently gained prominence and raises similar concerns is torture, especially for the purpose of protection of third parties.[93]

The protection of human dignity encompasses not only respect of persons by public authorities and others but is also regarded as aiming to protect the sense of self-worth of an individual—another element already present in the history of ideas.[94]

[82] An example of a doctrinal path differentiating dignity from other personality rights is the course taken by the German Federal Constitutional Court which created through jurisdiction a general right to protection of the individual personality by reading Art 2(1) (personal liberty) in conjunction with Art 1 (dignity), allowing—unlike dignity—for limitations by all other rights, cf BVerfGE 54, 148 (153).

[83] Cf for a comparative overview Paolo Carroza, '"My Friend Is a Stranger": The Death Penalty and the Global *Ius Commune* of Human Rights' (2003) 81 *Texas Law Review* 1031.

[84] *Trop v Dulles* 356 US 84, 100 (1958) on the 'dignity of man' as the underlying concept of the 8th amendment:

> Death is truly an awesome punishment. The calculated killing of a human being by the State involves, by its very nature, a denial of the executed person's humanity.... In comparison to all other punishments today, then, the deliberate extinguishment of human life by the state is uniquely degrading to human dignity.

Furman v Georgia 408 US 238, 270ff, 290 (1972) (Brennan J concurring); SACC, *Makwanyane*, para 271 (Mahomed).

[85] Consequently, graphic descriptions of the realities of executions and the death row phenomenon play a significant role in jurisprudential arguments, cf eg Supreme Court of Canada, *Kindler v Canada* [1991] 2 SCR 779 (Lamer and Cory dissenting); SACC *Makwanyane*, paras 26ff (Chaskalson); 335 (Regan).

[86] *Furman v Georgia* 408 US 238, 288ff (1972) (Brennan concurring); SACC, *Makwanyane*, para 55 (Chaskalson).

[87] SACC, *Makwanyane*, para 251 (Madala): no individual beyond reformation.

[88] Cf SACC, *Makwanyane*, para 144 (Chaskalson); para 166 (Ackerman); paras 313, 316 (Mogkoro); Hungarian Constitutional Court, Decision 23/1990, 31 October 1990, 3. (Sólyom concurring): humans not to be 'changed into tool or object'. Note that the element of contempt for human worth displayed in the mode of execution does not necessarily imply an instrumentalization—the latter is an additional and separate aspect.

[89] The protection of the subject status was decisive in BVerfGE 45, 187.

[90] Cf eg Conseil Constitutionel, Decision 2001-446 DC, 27 June 2001: violation of dignity through 'reification de l'embryon humain'.

[91] eg *S v Jordan and Others* (n 71) (O'Regan and Sachs) para 74.

[92] SACC, *De Reuck v Director of Public Prosecution* (n 70), paras 61ff, 63.

[93] ECtHR, *Gäfgen*, App no 22978/05, 1 June 2010 (Grand Chamber), paras 87, 107.

[94] Cf SACC, *National Coalition for Gay and Lesbian Equality v Minister of Justice* (CCT10/99) [1999] ZACC 17; 2000 (2) SA 1; 2000 (1) BCLR 39 (2 December 1999) para 42 on the effect of discrimination of gays and lesbians:

An interesting aspect concerns the relation of individual and community. It has been underlined that respect for the dignity of a person does not imply disregard for importance of membership of a community.[95]

One means employed by courts to avoid an inflation of dignitarian claims is to demand a sufficiently qualified impact on the individual: An act has to touch upon central concerns of human existence to fall within the scope of protection of a right to dignity.[96]

Dignity is often regarded as unalienable. In legal terms, this can mean different things: that the content of the protection is not modified according to the actions of the bearer, that human beings are not only the necessary bearer of this right, but that this status is unforfeitable or that there are specific limits to any system of limitations. What is meant is hardly spelled out in jurisprudence and doctrine.[97]

(b) *The Cosmopolitan Framework*

Human dignity has appealed to many worldviews.[98] Consequently, courts tend to be reluctant to embark on any in-depth justification of their interpretation of human dignity wedding this concept to judicial authority to any specific approach. A recurrent element, however, is the attempt to embed a concrete interpretation in the international context and its consensual elements and thus to transcend a purely local perspective. It is noteworthy that the ideas of dignity are vindicated by other than the so-called Western cultures—with self-confidence and sometimes in politically central moments, as the example of South Africa shows, where dignity was claimed for the post-apartheid normative re-orientation as an intrinsic part of the African normative tradition and the value of *ubuntu*.[99]

(c) *Dignity as a Subjective Right*

An important question is whether human dignity is taken as a subjective right as in certain systems.[100] As to other conceptions, various alternatives have been formulated, including objective law[101]

> The denial of equal dignity and worth all too quickly and insidiously degenerates into a denial of humanity and leads to inhuman treatment by the rest of society in many other ways. This is deeply demeaning and frequently has the cruel effect of undermining the confidence and the sense of worth of lesbians and gays.

[95] BVerfGE 45, 187 (227).

[96] The German Federal Constitutional Court demands eg that the position of a subject is put into question 'in principle', BVerfGE 97, 209 (228). An example is the dismissal of the claim that the wrong spelling of a person's name may violate human dignity, German Federal Administrative Court BVerwGE 31, 236 (237). Examples like the spelling case are sometimes taken as illustrations of a dangerous expansion of dignity law. This, however, would only be the case if the claims were not only made but were successful due to structural properties of dignity guarantees.

[97] See the argument in death penalty cases, that someone who has committed certain crimes, has forfeited his right to dignity, cf the argument of the South African Attorney General in SACC, *Makwanyane*, para 136, taken to be fallacious by the court, ibid para 137. The same conclusion was reached by Brennan, in *Furman v Georgia* 408 US 238, 273 (Brennan J concurring): even the vilest criminal remains a human being.

[98] The drafting history of dignity guarantees is full of pluralistic influences, without clear dominant strands that are sometimes identified from Kant to Jacques Maritain, *The Rights of Man and Natural Law* (1944). Cf Johannes Morsink, *The Universal Declaration of Human Rights* (1999), Mary Ann Glendon, *A World Made New* (2002); Mahlmann, *Elemente* (n 22), 244ff.

[99] Cf Chaskalson, Langa, Mahomed, and Mogkoro, SACC, *Makwanyane*, paras 131, 223ff, 263, 300ff, at 313 with an explicit connection of the prohibition of instrumentalization with the discussed indigenous African tradition and *ubuntu*; paras 358ff, 374ff (Sachs).

[100] BVerfGE 1, 97 (104). BVerfGE 45, 187); SACC, *Dawood and Another v Minister of Home Affairs and Others; Shalabi and Another v Minister of Home Affairs and Others; Thomas and Another v Minister of Home Affairs and Others* (CCT35/99) [2000] ZACC 8; 2000 (3) SA 936; 2000 (8) BCLR 837 (7 June 2000), para 35.

[101] Cf Dürig, 'Der Grundrechtssatz von der Menschenwürde' (n 54) 119.

or principles of interpretation.[102] The matter is of practical significance because it may be decisive for the legal standing of individuals. If human dignity is not a subjective right, its invocation may be impossible or conditioned on its relevance for the interpretation of other rights.

(d) Personal Scope: The Bearer of the Right

If human dignity is regarded as a subjective right, humans are necessarily the bearers of this right. Constitutional dignity guarantees are commonly conceived as universal rights and not just as the rights of the citizens of the respective state. The same holds for supra- and international instruments. It is not, however, extended to legal persons like corporations as is done for other fundamental rights through transferral norms[103] or interpretation. Another question of ongoing discussions concerns the question whether dignity is to be extended to animals or even nature in general. Some constitutional law and cases exist in this respect.[104]

(e) Objective Element of the Law

Dignity can in addition to (or alternative to) its position as a subjective right be part of objective law.[105] Public authorities are in consequence bound by it, though individuals may not have the possibility to base complaints solely on this ground. This is not necessarily completely clarified by doctrine. An interesting example in this respect is the argument that the death penalty violates not only the subjective rights of the convict, but violates the dignity of those that administer and institutionalize it.[106]

In this objective respect, human dignity is sometimes interpreted not only as a protected legal interest of individuals but as a norm guaranteeing the integrity of the human species as such. It becomes the legal embodiment of a species ethics.[107] This has gained some practical significance in the framework of biotechnologies that may not violate the rights of any existing human individual but may endanger the given character of the human species.

(f) Horizontal Effect

As for any human right, the question arises for human dignity as well, whether at all and if so how it unfolds normative effects not only between the individual and the state but between

[102] For the United States, Neuman (n 75) sums up:

> There is no constitutional right to human dignity as such, no objective constitutional norm prohibiting all state action inconsistent with human dignity, and no mandate upon the state to ensure the realization of human dignity. Human dignity informs the interpretation of particular constitutional rights, including the general rights to equality and liberty.

See also sceptical remarks about dignity as subjective rights by David Feldman, 'Human Dignity as a Legal Value-Part I' (1999) *Public Law* 682.

[103] eg German Basic Law, Art 19(3).

[104] The Swiss Federal Court has applied the 'dignity of the creature' (Swiss Federal Constitution, Art 120(2)) in a leading case on research with primates restricting this research, although not out ruling it in principle. It held that there is a difference between the 'dignity of the creature' of Art 120(2) and human dignity of the Swiss Federal Constitution, Art 7, without clearly stating what this difference is, BGE 135 II 384, 403. In Israel, the Supreme Court has referred ambiguously to the dignity or honour (kavod) of animals (concretely alligators in the context of alligator wrestling) in *Let the Animals Live v Hamat Gader Recreation Enterprise*, LCA 1684/96, cf McCrudden (n 10). The Court did not refer to the Basic Law of Dignity and Freedom, but statutory law on animal protection (thanks to Dr Liat Levanon for clarification on the Hebrew text). In a later case, *'Noah'—The Israel Federation of Animal Protection Organizations v The Attorney General*, HCJ 9232/01, 11 August 2003, the Court did not refer to honour or dignity, but to the suffering of animals.

[105] Cf BVerfGE 39, 1; 88, 203.

[106] SACC, *Makwanyane*, para 314 (Mokgoro).

[107] The German Federal Constitutional Court has referred to the 'Würde des Menschen als Gattungswesen', to 'the dignity of a human being as a species-being', BVerfGE 87, 209 (228).

private parties as well. Some constitutions and legal instruments contain explicit horizontal regulations for the respective fundamental rights catalogue, although it is not always clear whether these general regulations also apply to human dignity.[108] A system—if it allows any horizontal effect—may restrict this to an indirect horizontal effect through the interpretation of other norms in light of fundamental rights.[109] Human dignity, however, is one of the fundamental rights where a direct horizontal effect is more often assumed than in the case of other human rights.[110] It is, for example, a widespread assumption that slavery is prohibited by human dignity without need for further positive law which implies such a direct horizontal effect.[111]

(g) Positive Duties and Rights; Procedural Elements

Fundamental rights are today often taken as the origin of positive duties. This is true for dignity guarantees as well which can be interpreted as the source of duties to protect the dignity of individuals.[112] This raises—apart from the standard questions about positive duties, especially prerogatives of the legislature—an important structural and apparently paradoxical problem: Can human dignity that is so closely associated with autonomy in fact be used to curtail autonomy? Differently put: Can the individual consent to relinquishing the protection of her dignity with legal effects? If this is denied, the conception of dignity at the base of this denial may seem paternalistic. There is some case law on this matter—much discussed are cases such as dwarf throwing,[113] peep shows,[114] or laserdromes.[115] Another more fundamental issue already mentioned is slavery. There is little doubt that dignity implies the prohibition to disclaim the fundamental liberty of a person by handing herself over into slavery. This is an interesting observation as it indicates that the question is not so much whether dignity can be protected at all against the will of the person whose dignity is at stake, but under which qualified circumstances it is justified to do so.

Human dignity gives rise in some legal orders not only to negative rights but to positive rights as well. The most important positive right is the right to the provision of a minimal standard of living.[116]

Guarantees of human dignity have distinct procedural dimensions. The subject status they guarantee is secured through procedural safeguards that give persons the possibility actively and effectively to pursue their rights and interests[117] or make them subjects in their working life.[118]

[108] Cf eg Constitution of South Africa, ss 8(2) and 8(3); Swiss Constitution, Art 35(3). On horizontal effect see Chapter 26.

[109] BVerfGE 7, 198.

[110] The Constitution of South Africa, s 9(4), enacts a direct horizontal effect of the prohibition of discrimination, which in turn is governed by human dignity, cf Ackermann (n 31), 538, 550ff. Direct horizontal effect seems to be implied in BVerfGE 24, 119 (144); 115, 118 (153).

[111] Dignity may not be explicitly mentioned, cf Art 4 ECHR, 13th Amendment of the US Constitution.

[112] Cf in the case of abortion BVerfGE 39, 1 (41); 88, 203 with rather wide-ranging conclusions.

[113] Conseil D'Etat, no 136727, 27 October 1995, *Commune de Morsang-sur-Orge v Société Fun Production et M Wackenheim*.

[114] German Federal Administrative Court, BVerwGE 64, 274 (278ff).

[115] ECJ, C-36/02 *Omega* (14 October 2004).

[116] The reference to social rights to human dignity is common, eg Universal Declaration of Human Rights, Art 23(3). For a right to the provision of minimum livelihood cf BVerfGE 45, 187 (228); 82, 60 (85); 125, 175 (222).

[117] Cf Swiss Federal Court BGE 124 V 180, 181; BGE 127 I 6, 13 ff; BVerfGE 7, 275 (279).

[118] BVerfGE 28, 314 (323).

(h) Beginning, Diachronical Continuity, and End

An important question to determine the beginning and end of human dignity is whether the existence of individual human life is a sufficient condition for the ascription of dignity or whether it is conditioned on qualified—for example self-conscious—forms of human life. These questions are connected with the problem, whether personhood is the reason for dignity and when personhood begins—with conception, nidation, sometimes in the pre-natal maturation process (eg sensitivity to pain, viability), at birth, or even later. Another issue concerns diachronically continuous personal identity and its impact for the protection of self-determination, for example as to a person's pre-dementia decisions for post-dementia issues.

Consequently and not surprisingly, given the ethical, political, and religious subtexts of these questions, there is particular variety in jurisprudence and doctrine. Of particular concern is the beginning of human life, either because life and dignity are regarded to be diachronically coextensive or because the existence of human life is at least a precondition for ascribing dignity at all (though it may be not or only ambiguously done in a particular jurisdiction). Courts have regarded conception[119] or at least nidation[120] as the beginning of protection of both life and dignity. Others have followed a different course, giving for example special weight to viability for any legally protected status of the pre-natal life[121] or suspended or deferred the answer as to life and dignity.[122] There is a further complication from the fact that the beginning of the normative protection through dignity can refer to dignity as a subjective right[123] or a tenet of objective law.[124]

A diachronically discontinuous conception of dignity has so far only reached the academic debate. The question when dignity ends, however, has occupied various courts: in some jurisdictions dignity defies death as it is protected post-mortem.[125]

[119] This is the tendency of BVerfGE 88, 203 (251) or of the dissent of Rupp-von Brünneck BVerfGE 39, 1 (80). The ECJ, C-34/10, *Brüstle v Greenpeace* (18 October 2011) ruled that any ovum after fertilization, any non-fertilized human ovum into which the the cell nucleus from a mature human cell has been transplanted, and any non-fertilized human ovum whose division and further development have been stimulated by parthenogenesis constitute a human embryo. This interpretation is derived from the need to protect human dignity, paras 32–34.

[120] Cf BVerfGE 39, 1(37).

[121] Cf *Roe v Wade* 410 US 113, 163 (1973); *Planned Parenthood of Southeastern Pennsylvania v Casey* 505 US 833, 846 (1992). The rights of the embryo/fetus are not explicitly constructed as related to dignity by the Court, the reasoning uses, however, central notions of what this term is about, cf eg 'the profound respect for the life of the unborn', *Planned Parenthood of Southeastern Pennsylvania v Casey* 505 US 833, 877 (1992). Cf *Stenberg v Carhart* 530 US 914 (2000); *Gonzales v Carhart* 550 US 124 (2007), stating that the Act under review 'expresses respect for the dignity of human life', without, however clarifying whether this was the constitutional stake for the Court as well.

[122] Cf ECtHR, *A, B and C v Ireland*, App no 25579, 16 December 2010, paras 233, 237: rights of unborn engaged, states enjoy a margin of appreciation as to the legal definition of the beginning of life. In *Vo v France*, App no 53924/00, 8 July 2004, para 84, the Court, however, stated:

> At best, it may be regarded as common ground between States that the embryo/foetus belongs to the human race. The potentiality of that being and its capacity to become a person—enjoying protection under the civil law, moreover, in many States, such as France, in the context of inheritance and gifts, and also in the United Kingdom...—require *protection in the name of dignity* (emphasis added).

[123] This seems to be implied in BVerfGE 88, 203, 210, 283, 306 as in the dissent in BVerfGE 39, 1, 79.

[124] In ECtHR, *Vo v France*, App no 53924/00, 8 July 2004, para 84, the reference must be to objective law as persons as necessary bearers of subjective rights are assumed not yet to exist. The state's interest in protecting the life of the fetus referred to by the US Supreme Court (n 121) appears also to refer to objective law, as it is the 'state's interest' that is of concern, not the interest of an individual.

[125] eg Germany, BVerfGE 30, 173, 194; BVerfG NJW 2001, 2957, 2959; Israel, *Frederika Shavit v Rishon Lezion Burial Society*, CA 6024/97, 6 July 1999, paras 4, 16, 20, 26 confirming earlier judgments, in particular *Jerusalem Community Jewish Burial Society v Kestenbaum*, CA 294/91. The case concerned the right to inscribe non-Hebrew letters and to use the Gregorian calendar in a Jewish cemetery. On the background see ibid Englard (dissenting), para 18: 'behind this dispute, forces are warring for the character of Judaism and the state of Israel'. The issue can thus be of more than individual concern.

2. Interference

The delineation of an interference is of particular relevance for a conception of human dignity that excludes justified limitations as there is no further step of determining a violation of dignity: interfering with dignity means violating it. Consequently, the discussion of interference can be quite loaded with substantive consideration that doctrinally may belong to another sphere. The scope of the right concerned is an obvious candidate in this respect

3. Limitations and Justification

One of the practically most important questions concerns the limitations of human dignity. Dignity can be protected absolutely, without allowing any such limitations. This approach can extend to the dignity provision as such,[126] or to particular elements of what is usually taken to be within its scope.[127] However, legal provisions on human dignity can also foresee or can be interpreted as containing limitations.[128] Then it has to be determined which weight human dignity has in relation to other rights and protected legal interests. This weight is regarded as quite considerable—only other values of high order can outweigh dignity concerns, not, for example, the expediency of daily politics.

Those systems that acknowledge limits to dignity can limit the limitations through residual guarantees of a core area, for example by protecting the 'essence' of the right or equivalent jurisprudence.[129] In any case, any limitation has to undergo (differently framed and named) tests that set limits to encroachments of the right and that deal at their core with matters of proportionality.

The question of limitations is not the least relevant in such contentious areas as abortion.[130] Here the particular case of conflicts of the dignity of one person with the dignity of another person may arise: if both the embryo and/or the fetus and the women are the bearers of dignity, and if in the case of abortion dignity concerns are taken to be relevant for both sides, such a conflict ensues. As far as pre-natal life is concerned—if it is regarded as the bearer of a subjective right or as an object of protection through dignity as objective law—a violation of this right is based on the ending of the pre-natal life through abortion.[131] As far as pregnant women are concerned, the recognition that the dignity of women and not only other, minor concerns are at stake has been of central legal importance. Crucial for this has been the insight that the fundamental status as subjects of their lives is put into question by certain restrictions on abortion.[132] The solution of this conflict is not obvious, but tends to be shaped by the kind of time-sensitive model of abortion that has become widely accepted in liberal constitutional states.[133] This is important to emphasize to prevent the misperception that ascribing dignity to

[126] The standard interpretation of the Basic Law, Art 1. Cf Philip Kunig, in V. Münch/Kunig (eds), *Grundgesetz-Kommentar* (5th edn, 2000), Art 1 paras 4ff; Wolfram Höfling in Michael Sachs (ed), *Grundgesetz Kommentar* (6th edn, 2011), Art 1 para 11; Horst Dreier in Horst Dreier (ed), *Grundgesetz Kommentar* (2nd edn, 2004), Art 1, paras 131ff.

[127] Cf ECtHR, *Gäfgen v Germany*, App no 22978/05, 1 June 2010 (Grand Chamber), paras 87, 107.

[128] See eg in *Public Committee Against Torture in Israel v The State of Israel*, 6 September 1999, para 23.

[129] Cf Swiss Constitution, Art 36(4) , though it remains to be clarified what limitations are possible under Swiss law.

[130] See Chapter 51.

[131] Cf BVerfGE 37, 1, 43; 88, 203, 255.

[132] Cf *Planned Parenthood of Southeastern Pennsylvania v Casey* 505 US 833, 851 (1992); BVerfGE 88, 203, 254, and—clearly pronounced—the dissent BVerfGE 88, 203, 340ff, 348 (Mahrenholz and Sommer dissenting).

[133] Cf Federal German Constitutional Court, BVerfGE 39, 1; 88, 203 allowing an abortion for reasons of life and health of the mother, cases such as rape and well-being thus establishing de facto freedom of the ultimate decision of the woman concerned in the first trimester, although with various procedural qualifications, not all convincing.

pre-natal life precludes due concern for the fundamental rights of women. It is noteworthy that the legal recourse to their dignity had for women in the framework of abortion a quite substantial emancipatory effect.[134]

For torture it has been argued but not taken up by the courts that the same constellation of colliding claims arises, especially in the case of torturing a kidnapper to disclose the whereabouts of her victim (or any of the much discussed ticking bomb scenarios).[135]

In any case, dignity as other human rights not only constitutes individual claims but restricts them as well. If dignity is taken to be absolute, the restriction is defined by any act of interference. Any exercise of any other right cannot go as far as to violate the dignity of another person.[136] If dignity is not taken to be absolute, weighing and balancing exercises including principles of proportionality (and their doctrinal functional equivalents) determine the respective reach of other rights.

4. Relation to Other Fundamental Rights and the Political Order

The delineation of the scope of different fundamental rights is a general problem that takes, in the case of dignity, a particular twist: as human dignity is often regarded as the foundation of all fundamental rights, one could conclude that it is implicitly at stake for any case.[137] One way to avoid this conclusion is to narrow the scope of the right or demand necessary qualification of an interference. Another solution is subsidiarity—dignity guarantees are only practically considered if no other fundamental right is violated.[138] A special case is the relation of dignity and equality: dignity is often regarded as fundamental for equality—it serves as a yardstick to calibrate constitutional equality guarantees, sometimes without explicit reference to the term.[139]

Dignity is traditionally regarded as a foundation of democracy and a normative yardstick for the structure of the state.[140]

[134] Cf the summary of the development in *Gonzales v Carhart* 550 US 124 (2007) Ginsburg (dissenting), 171 n 2; 183ff or in BVerfGE 88, 203, 340, 348 (Mahrenholz and Sommer dissenting).

[135] ECtHR, *Gäfgen*, App no 22978/05, 1 June 2010 (Grand Chamber), paras 87, 107. The argument could run like this: the state has a duty stemming from dignity to protect the victim of a kidnapper against instrumentalization; the kidnapper is turned into a means for the provision of information through torture.

[136] BVerfG NJW 2001, 2957, 2959.

[137] The problem is illustrated by the following passage (internal quotations omitted) from *Frederika Shavit v Rishon Lezion Burial Society*, CA 6024/97, 6 July 1999, para 9 (Barak concurring):

> From one point of view I assume that the value (or liberty) of freedom of religion is an aspect of human dignity, from the other point of view there is the value (or liberty) of freedom from religion, which is also an aspect of human dignity.... This is not the first time we have weighed different aspects of the same liberty.... Thus we also behaved when the right to one's good name (which is part of human dignity) clashed with the right to freedom of expression (which, in my view, is another aspect of human dignity).

[138] Cf Swiss Federal Court BGE 127 I 6, 14.

[139] For an example for the violation of the basic worth of a human being through discrimination *Brown v Board of Education* 347 US 483, 494 (1954).

[140] James Wilson formulated: 'Man, fearfully and wonderfully made, is the workmanship of his all perfect Creator: A State; useful and valuable as the contrivance is, is the inferior contrivance of man; and from his native dignity derives all its acquired importance', *Chisholm, Ex'r v Georgia* 2 US 419, 2 Dall 419, 455 (1793). Cf Supreme Court of Canada, *Kindler v Canada* [1991] 2 SCR 779 (Cory); SACC, *Makwanyane*, para 330 (Regan); BVerfGE 5, 85 (204).

V. Problems and Solutions

The preceding remarks have outlined some aspects of the heterogeneous world of contemporary dignity law. Now the next question arises: What are the merits of the various approaches outlined?

1. The Scope of Dignity

(a) Content and Legitimacy

Human dignity as a legal concept aims to protect the inherent, supreme, and inalienable worth of human beings. As was indicated in the historical observations, there is a striking tendency to connect a central normative concern (called dignity, something else, or being present as an implicit premise of an, on the surface, quite different looking argument) with the idea that human beings are ends-in-themselves, highest-order purposes of human motivation and correspondent action who therefore have the right that their status as an autonomous subject of their live is protected. This leads to a prohibition of instrumentalization, objectification, and reification and general demands for respect. These ideas play a crucial role in legal conceptions of human dignity as well, as courts regularly explicitly or implicitly refer to these principles as foundational principles.

This raises the question of the possible justification of these principles. Despite the shortcomings of some argumentations in the history of ideas and of contemporary debates, including Kant's,[141] such a justification does not seem impossible. A starting point is the anthropological fact that for human beings—pathological cases aside—the fulfilment of their individual lives is a natural end in itself. This worth of a human life to its possessor is not limited to a particular class of individuals with an elevated content of life.[142] On the contrary, no human life is worth more for its bearer than any other, an observation paving the way to a critique of all social arrangements that deny this worth, for example on the ground of racism, sexism, contempt for the economically and socially unfortunate, and the like. Applying the basic principle of justice to treat equal things equally, respect for the status of any human life as a purpose of equal worth is a universal right. Every human person is the justified last-order purpose of action, because human beings are, through their factual quest for happiness, a purpose in themselves. Universalization as a command of justice demands the ascription of this purpose-status to all.

As Pufendorf nicely formulated, human beings have a particularly fine sense of self-respect.[143] To protect this human need for respect is certainly justified purely because of a concern for the feelings of human beings. The fact of self-respect does not, however, answer the question, whether this attitude is justified because the self is in fact worthy of respect or whether the self-estimation of human beings is just a (pleasant) subjective illusion. This is an important and difficult question.

Still, if one looks at the existential properties of human life, the *Selbstzweckhaftigkeit* or being-an-end-in-oneself seems to be based on some good reasons. Human beings construct in one way or another a mental explanatory image of the world and have learned to accept its

[141] For a detailed review of Kant's theory cf Mahlmann, *Elemente* (n 22), 152ff.

[142] As Nietzsche thought: see Friedrich Nietzsche, 'Fünf Vorreden zu fünf ungeschriebenen Büchern' in Friedrich Nietzsche, *Kritische Studienausgabe* (1999), Bd I, 776.

[143] Samuel von Pufendorf, *De Officio Hominis* (1997), VII, §1.

sometimes challenging results as to the rather precarious position of human life in natural history. They appropriate aesthetically human existence with its many, not always pleasant, sides in art. They unfold the emotionally richly textured self of a transient being faced with its own mortality without guarantee that their pursuits will lead to happiness. They live these lives in the mode of self-reflective consciousness and self-determination under moral principles that motivate them sometimes to regard the well-being of others to be of greater importance than their own—an ability to benevolent self-transcendence that is the daily bread of care and affection. All this confers dignity to human life—at least from the (only available) human point of view.

Given these reasons for predicating dignity to human beings, dignity is not only legitimately ascribed to human beings, but rightly taken as unalienable: Because one cannot lose the existential human properties that play a decisive role for its foundation, one cannot lose the dignity that is their consequence.

(b) Dignity and Autonomy

Autonomy is a contested subject in the international discourse about dignity: autonomy is challenged as an antiquated idea because of the modern consciousness of the many influences on human self-determination, for example the subconscious sources of motives, wishes, and desires and their powerful sway over human choice and action or the social and cultural structures that limit the possibilities of action and colour profoundly what is aimed at in the first place. All of this is real enough but no reason to debunk the normative idea of autonomy. It is a misunderstanding of this concept to think it is irreconcilable with these perspectives. The reason is straightforward: it is a concept that does not presuppose that none of these influences exist, but merely that they are not all that counts, that there is an element of residual human self-determination the protection of which is consequently of crucial importance

(c) Dignity: Widely or Narrowly Defined?

Jurisprudential experience seems to teach that there are good reasons to differentiate a protection of human dignity as such from other personality rights, the enjoyment of particular liberties and equality, and thus to circumscribe its scope narrowly. This is best done by limiting the scope of the right to matters that pertain to the subject status of the individual as such and core matters of her worth: to force a women seriously to compromise her health for giving birth puts the subject status in question, to force someone to drive a victim of an accident to a hospital does not, though both are cases of instrumentalization. To imprison someone in an ugly cell is not a violation of dignity by a display of lack of respect for the aesthetic dimension of her life; to do so in cell regularly flooded by faeces, however, is. This aids avoiding an inflationary use of dignity deprived of any concrete contours and meaning.

(d) Subjective Right, Objective Law, Personal Scope

As human dignity is about the worth of individuals and their autonomy there are not reasons discernible not to understand it as a judicially enforceable subjective right. The limitation of dignity to natural human persons also appears to be quite plausible. Legal persons are not ends-in-themselves but creations for well-defined purposes. That dignity guarantees are of universal scope is well warranted—to limit the protection of this right, for example to the citizens of particular states, fails to grasp the core of its meaning.

Given its origin and mode of legitimation, dignity as a proper legal concept is best reserved for human beings. As practice shows, the expansion of dignitarian concerns leads to fussy legal concepts and carries with it the danger of weakening the protection of humans. As to animals and nature in general, this by no means indicates a lack of concern as there are other ways effectively to protect non-human organisms or the environment.

Human dignity is in a certain respect the expression of the normative self-confidence of every individual. Human dignity implies in addition the perception that humanity understood as the decisive set of properties shaped by the process of natural history making humans human is something worth protecting, treasuring, and respecting, too. A way to express this perception is to interpret the objective dimension of dignity guarantees as a legal element of species ethics. A concretization of this dimension worth thinking about may be the following: human dignity protects as objective law the set of properties resulting from natural history constitutive of the character of the human species against modification. Dignity is an individual trump of law, but a legal element of the justified self-preservation of the human species as well.

(e) Horizontal Effect, Positive Duties and Rights, Procedural Elements

The tendency to give dignity guarantees effects between private persons is well warranted. Given the constitutive importance and—in a proper doctrinal construction—the clearly circumscribed scope of a dignity guarantee, there is no reason to deny a direct horizontal effect. The not unusual acceptance of a prohibition of slavery directly on the ground of human dignity is an expression of the plausibility of this construction.

As for other human rights, positive duties, including duties to protect and procedural concretizations are to be taken as elements of the scope of a dignity guarantee. This does not necessarily lead to an unwarranted paternalism. Dignity protects autonomy and any protection of dignity against the will of the concerned person consequently needs very good reasons. The case of slavery, as mentioned above, illustrates that in principle there are such reasons: voluntary slavery is not acceptable under a modern human rights conception. To say that there are such duties does not imply that the reach of this duty should be interpreted excessively. Positive duties stemming from dignity guarantees only lead to what is properly called paternalism if they are interpreted paternalistically—which does and may happen (as a freedom may be interpreted quite illiberally) but not necessarily so.

Human dignity is a decisive argument for social rights: if humans are ends-in-themselves they are to be treated as such as to the available necessary material preconditions of a human life.

The procedural aspects of human dignity have been rightly underlined: one way to protect human dignity is to enable human beings to defend their autonomy themselves, in the courtroom and through social and political structures of more than feigned participation.

(f) Beginning, Diachronical Continuity, and End

There seems no plausible reason to dissociate dignity and human life. If there is human life, it has dignity. As to the beginning of human life, there is a good case for taking conception as the crucial moment as at least one genetically individualized human organism comes into existence.[144] It is crucial to rationalize debates to underline, that, as indicated above, this perception does not predetermine the solution of the problem of abortion. For this, competing rights have to be taken into account, most importantly the dignity of the mother. Therefore, ascribing dignity to pre-natal life does not entail the entry of new dark ages of reproductive instrumentalization of women.

[144] On the extensive debates on the matter, not least on the arguments from belonging to the human species, the continuity of human development from conception via birth to adulthood, the potentiality of pre-natal life and the identity of pre-natal life with the post-natal human being, see Mahlmann, *Elemente* (n 22), 293ff.

The legal status of pre-natal life is not only of concern for the question of abortion. It can be of importance for the protection of this phase of the existence of a human being against harm, including life and bodily integrity,[145] of increasing concern in the wake of new biotechnological possibilities.

There is no reason for a diachronically discontinuous conception of human dignity and autonomy. The human substrate of the right is the person in its physical and mental entirety, continuously existing in human life and thus the bearer of an uninterrupted personal right. There is equally no reason for post-mortem protection of human dignity as a subjective right. Such a right presupposes the existence of its bearer which ends with death. Legitimate concerns motivating the post mortem protection of dignity can be dealt with by other legal means, for example entitlements of descendants, relatives, partners, and the like and by the objective dimension of human dignity.

2. Interference, Limitations, and Justification

The possible modes of interference in dignity include beyond final, direct, legal, and sanctioned acts by public authorities other forms that violate the scope of the right, even if unintentional, indirect, factual, and devoid of sanctions. The sufficient gravity of the interfering act is best discussed on the level of the scope of the right.

The problem of the beginning of life and dignity has led already to the question of abortion, which is a core issue of the limitations of the right. Abortion can imply a constellation where claims of dignity collide: the right of the unborn human organism to become a full personality and the right of the mother to stay the subject of her life and not to be instrumentalized for giving birth. The abortion regimes, now common in many constitutional states that allow for abortion under certain conditions (as to danger to life and health of the women, because of the cause of pregnancy, eg in the case of rape or as to the life situation of the mother), taking into account temporal factors of maturation, draw the right conclusion from this insight.

There is no other comparable situation and in this sense dignity is absolute. It is perhaps worthwhile to underscore that torture and, more precisely, torture to save the lives of others in particular is not such a situation, despite arguments to the contrary. There are three central reasons for this: in real life (thought not in theoretical ticking bomb scenarios) it is always unclear whether or not the person tortured has the information she is supposed to disclose, and if so, whether she will disclose it and not lie. Secondly, torture is not only dehumanizing the tortured persons, but the torturer as well. Under the rule of law, torture would need a proper legal, institutional, and personal framework. To legally institutionalize barbarous acts is, however, unthinkable under a constitutional rule of law. Thirdly, given the ubiquitous reality of torture only an absolute ban is a suitable means against its practice.

3. Dignity, Other Fundamental Rights, and the Structure of the Body Politic

Dignity is foundational for human rights, but its scope is not coextensive, but in principle more narrowly circumscribed than rights to liberty and equality. One may accept (odd as it may seem) that someone enjoys certain liberties but deny her equal worth. A historical example of this is the liberty of privileged slaves. Not every violation of a liberty is, on the

[145] An example is ECtHR, *Vo v France*, App no 53924/00, 8 July 2004.

other hand, a violation of human dignity: there are good reasons to think that a prohibition to evaluate the quality of a wine in strong, vulgar terms is a violation of freedom of speech.[146] The permission to critique only without such strong, vulgar terms would, however, not be a violation of human dignity.

The relation of human dignity and equality is no different: the preservation of equality does not suffice to protect human dignity, as the case of a non-arbitrary or unbiased administration of the death penalty illustrates: this punishment, although administered perfectly equal, would still violate the dignity of the convicted. Not every unjustified unequal treatment is, on the other hand, necessarily a violation of human dignity.[147] The preservation of equality is a necessary, not a sufficient, condition of the preservation of dignity, a violation of dignity is a sufficient, not a necessary, condition of a violation of equality. Dignity is, however, for equality guarantees of particular importance: it spells out their substantial concerns. This is a prerequisite of their application as the demand of equality as such does not exclude uniform bad treatment, as the example of the death penalty shows. Only if there is a substantial notion attached to it, equality's point becomes clear.[148] This central notion is the intrinsic worth of human beings.

The idea of human dignity always had a distinct political side. It not only demands and forbids certain actions by the state but is a normative standard for the structure of the political order as such. It demands that human beings are the subjects of political life. The right to structures of participatory democracy with the legal infrastructure that it entails is one of its central consequences. The ethical and political point is clear: if human dignity is to be taken seriously, national and international structures of governance have to give human individuals—as far as possible on this scale and as mediated as it may be unavoidable—some meaningful share in the process of political self-determination.

VI. The Universalist Stance: Yet Another Particularism?

These remarks have tried to reconstruct some elements of human dignity as a legal concept from a comparative perspective, embedding the contemporary debates in the history of this idea—as a part of normative theory and as a part of the struggles of real life. The identified core tenets are by no way new and surprising: they are the core tenets of a liberal, egalitarian, and secular humanism. Their origin in secular reflection is important not because of disregard for the impressive contributions of religious beliefs to a culture of dignity, but because only such a justification fits in a methodologically necessarily secular science and can hope to win support across the borders of cultures and religious traditions.

This humanism takes a universalist stance without epistemological embarrassment, as, contrary to the assumptions of some theories mentioned above, there are quite plausible

[146] ECtHR, *Uj v Hungary*, App no 23954/10, 19 July 2011.

[147] Not to take into account periods of employment completed by an employee before reaching the age of 25 in calculating the notice period for dismissal can be regarded with convincing reasons to form discrimination on the ground of age, but hardly as a violation of human dignity, cf ECJ, C-555/07 *Seda Kücükdeveci v Swedex GmbH & Co KG*, para 57 (19 January 2010). An interpretation of equality and non-discrimination clauses as in *Law v Canada* [1999] 1 SCR 497 paras 52ff which constructs the equality guarantee to demand a violation of human dignity is in danger of interpreting the equality guarantee too narrowly or human dignity too broadly. Cf Supreme Court of Canada, *R v Kapp*, 2008 SCC 41, para 22.

[148] Cf Susanne Baer, 'Dignity, Liberty, Equality: A Fundamental Rights Triangle of Constitutionalism' (2009) 59 *University of Toronto Law Journal* 455.

reasons for such an orientation. As has been indicated in the remarks on the history of ideas, arguments from the (often wrongly reported) lack of explicit cultural traditions, from language or genealogy do not justify in principle relativist conclusions. Furthermore, it appears to be not very plausible that the elements of justification referred to are relative to one culture. The perception that life is an end in itself and something worth enjoying for people in Calcutta as much as in Cape Town or Anchorage appears rather plausible. That any of the particular properties of human beings that are the base of the ascription of dignity are limited to a certain class of people—say whites or men—has fortunately lost some of its century-proofed appeal, as the idea that the worth of a human being can be forfeited, for example by religious heresy. That the principle of equal treatment of equals is valid in London as in Beijing or Riyadh sounds likewise not very outlandish. In addition, there are quite interesting mentalistic approaches reconstructing the basis of human moral judgment, including precepts of justice or non-instrumentalization by means of the modern theory of the human mind that may offer a promising framework for a fallibilistic, non-foundational but universalist moral and legal epistemology.[149] Relativism is certainly not without theoretical alternative.

These remarks imply an answer to the problem of the antinomy of human rights: they show that the practical universalism of the modern human rights culture is theoretically actually well justified. Comparative analysis consequently has a normative point: it is an effective antidote against judicial parochialism, stirs judicial imaginativeness, and shields against the danger of overlooking convincing normative ideas that have been formulated elsewhere but to solve a similar problem. It can thus supply arguments for doctrinal developments if the positive laws leave room for it. If the respective positive law excludes certain conceptions that seem reasonable they may still be useful for critical assessments of the given legal framework and, finally, these conceptions may be helpful for the shaping of future developments of the law. Comparative research has thus rightly become a constitutive element convincing legal heuristics.

The thus in light of what can be regarded as usual standards of justification of any human rights content, justifiable ascription of dignity has to be fleshed out for concrete cases and new challenges, often with no immediately evident solutions, and no easy matter as for any other fundamental right.

The courts around the world have made some progress in this respect, for example as to discrimination, the death penalty, or personal autonomy. Accomplishments such as these may seem insignificant, but are—with an eye to the short history of human rights as legal instruments and the power of the forces pursuing ends other than the realization of the dignity of individuals—in fact quite considerable.

Human dignity tells a simple story: there are no human lives of greater or lesser worth, whether one of the many, or one of the few that somehow, legitimately or illegitimately, catch the admiring imagination of those to come. Dignity is the value of humans as humans, in this central respect one is like the others irrespective of personal properties and achievements. This idea is consequently the most profound critique of any bifurcation of humanity in guardians and toilers, masters and servants, deserving and undeserving, touchables and

[149] Cf Mahlmann, *Elemente* (n 22), 512ff; Matthias Mahlmann, *Rationalismus in der praktischen Theorie* (2nd edn, 1999); Matthias Mahlmann, 'Ethics, Law and the Challenge of Cognitive Science' (2007) 8 *German Law Journal* 577, 577; John Mikhail, *Elements of Moral Cognition* (2011); John Mikhail, 'Moral Grammar and Human Rights: Some Reflections on Cognitive Science and Enlightenment Rationalism' in Ryan Goodman, Derek Jinks, and Andrew K. Woods (eds), *Understanding Social Action, Promoting Human Rights* (forthcoming); Erica Roedder and Gilbert Harman, 'Linguistics and Moral Theory' in John Doris (ed), *The Moral Psychology Handbook* (2010), 273.

untouchables, gender that rules and gender that serves which has dominated much of human history and has been transfigured by thought, as in the magnificent beauty of Plato's prose or stripped naked to its unappealing core in the doctrines of racists, sexists, and their like.

Respect for dignity is not costless: dignity demands human solidarity not only in words but in deeds that understand the price to be paid for the enjoyment of humans' common bequest.

There are no grounds for any too magnificent hopes for human civilization, because all rosy fogs of illusion about the human lot have been dispersed by the crisp winds of past horrors and the uneasy hunch that humans will—again and again—have more of this in stock for each other. The taste of dignity is not the mawkish flavour of narcissistic human self-admiration and anthropocentrism, although this appears in the history and present as well, sometimes abundantly. The taste is—in the better and certainly in the great contributions—rather saturated with doubt and the uneasy consciousness of the uncanny depth of what makes up the core of the human self. But it still gives reasons to straighten the neck in an unbent existential pride that is able to look in the eyes of what may come.

To make human dignity a cornerstone of the modern architecture of human rights at the core of constitutionalism is therefore a well-advised move. There is no reason to downgrade it doctrinally, to reduce its importance in legal systems that protect it, or prevent its incorporations in those, where it plays no or only a limited role through interpretation, with due respect to the limits of this enterprise, or through further development of legal instruments.

The law often served and serves power and the interests of a few. A constitutionalism, national and beyond nations' borders, based on the dignity and autonomy of human beings, is part of a different conception of the law. Below the diaphanous folds of legal argument and thought, there is something to be detected that is not wedded to one religious or theoretical creed, but to a fundamental relation to human life: the conviction that care for humans has a point as the being that is at its centre is worth the effort of thought, hope, courage, and sometimes quite profound despair.

Bibliography

Laurie W.H. Ackermann, 'Equality and the South African Constitution: The Role of Dignity' (2000) 63 *Zeitschrift für ausländisches öffentliches Recht und Völkerrecht* 537

Thomas Aquinas, *Summa Theologica* (1933ff)

Paolo Carroza, '"My Friend Is a Stranger": The Death Penalty and the Global *Ius Commune* of Human Rights' (2003) 81 *Texas Law Review* 1031

Cicero, *De officiis* (2007)

Günter Dürig, *Die Menschenauffassung des Grundgesetzes* (1952)

Ronald Dworkin, *Life's Dominion* (1994)

Jürgen Habermas, 'Das Konzept der Menschenwürde und die realistische Utopie der Menschenrechte' (2010) 58 *Deutsche Zeitschrift für Philosophie* 343

Jürgen Habermas, *Die Zukunft der menschlichen Natur* (2005)

Louis Henkin, 'Human Dignity and Constitutional Rights' in Michael J. Meyer and William A. Parent (eds), *The Constitution of Rights: Human Dignity and American Values* (1992)

Mary Ann Glendon, *A World Made New* (2002)

Immanuel Kant, *Grundlegung zur Metaphysik der Sitten, Akademie Ausgabe*, Bd IV (1911)

Immanuel Kant, *Kritik der praktischen Vernunft, Akademie Ausgabe*, Bd V (1913)

Mordechai Kremnitzer and Re'em Segev, 'The Legality of Interrogational Torture: A Question of Proper Authorization or a Substantial Moral Issue?' (2000) 34 *Israel Law Review* 509

John Locke, 'The Second Treatise' in *Two Treatises on Government* (1991)

Matthias Mahlmann, 'Dictatorship of the Obscure? Values and the Secular Adjudication of Fundamental Rights' in András Sajó and Renata Uitz (ed), *Constitutional Topography: Values and Constitutions* (2010)

Matthias Mahlmann, *Elemente einer ethischen Grundrechtstheorie* (2008)

Matthias Mahlmann, 'Ethics, Law and the Challenge of Cognitive Science' (2007) 8 *German Law Journal* 577

Matthias Mahlmann, *Rationalismus in der praktischen Theorie* (2nd edn, 1999)

Avishai Margalit, *The Decent Society* (1996)

Christopher McCrudden, 'Human Dignity and Judicial Interpretation of Human Rights' (2008) 19 *European Journal of International Law* 664

John Mikhail, *Elements of Moral Cognition* (2011)

Johannes Morsink, *The Universal Declaration of Human Rights* (1999)

Gerald L. Neuman, 'Human Dignity in United States Constitutional Law' in Dieter Simon and Manfred Weiss (eds), *Zur Autonomie des Individuums, Liber Amicorum Spiros Simitis* (2000)

Jeremy Waldron, 'Dignity and Rank' (2007) 48 *Archives européennes d'archéologie* 201

James Q. Whitman, 'Nazi "Honour" and New European "Dignity"' in Christian Joerges and Navraj S. Ghaleigh (eds), *Darker Legacies of Law in Europe* (2003)

CHAPTER 19

GENDER IN CONSTITUTIONS

CATHARINE A. MACKINNON*

Ann Arbor & Cambridge, MA

CONSTITUTIONS found nations, define states, and ground and bind governments.[1] Largely absent from official constituting processes and decisive interpretations until recently—flags of democracy flying notwithstanding—have been the voices and concerns of women,[2] a group that comprises over half of most populations worldwide. Historically, constitutions have been almost exclusively man-made, and it shows.

Women and men are socially organized as such—into sexes—by cultures that attribute that designation and assignment to the biology of their sex. Gender is the social meaning of sex.[3]

* The resourceful and intrepid research assistance of Shauna Lani Shamas, Aisha Harris, the ever-amazing University of Michigan Law Library is gratefully acknowledged. Lisa Cardyn provided, in addition, astute conceptual help with the database and perceptive collegial comments, for which I am in her debt. Time to conceive this chapter was supported by the Diane Middlebrook and Carl Djerassi Visiting Professorship at the University of Cambridge Centre for Gender Studies, Lent Term, 2011.

[1] Other than as noted, the database created for this chapter is confined to written constitutions included in HeinOnline's World Constitutions Illustrated database, of which 198 country constitutions were considered, including one for the entity European Union. Of those, four jurisdictions—the Vatican, United Kingdom, Israel, and New Zealand—do not have textual constitutions, leaving 194, including the EU. In the 22 instances in which the most recent English language version of a constitution was unavailable, it was drawn from Albert P. Blaustein and Gisberg H. Flanz (eds), *Constitutions of the Countries of the World* (1971–2011), 20 vols plus supplements. The translations provided by these two sources were relied upon unless otherwise noted.

[2] Accounts and documentation of women's participation in recent constituting processes can be found in Alexandra Dobrowolsky and Vivien Hart (eds), *Women Making Constitutions: New Politics and Comparative Perspectives* (2003). For an analysis of women's participation, or attempts to participate, in constitutions historically, see Helen Irving, *Gender and the Constitution: Equity and Agency in Comparative Constitutional Design* (2008), 4–22.

[3] A definition of gender evoking much of its broad domain is provided by the United Nations Office of the Special Advisor on Gender Issues (OSAGI):

> Gender: refers to the social attributes and opportunities associated with being male and female and the relationships between women and men and girls and boys, as well as the relations between

Socially, the qualities ascribed to biological females are deemed feminine in gender; those thought biologically male are considered masculine in gender—thus ascribed to women and men as such respectively. Most individuals, regardless of biology, present a rich mix of both sets of traits, supporting a showing that the assertedly natural basis of these stereotyped social features is a pervasive ideology.[4] The sexes, paralleled by the genders attributed to each, are, with variation, documented unequal in status and treatment throughout the world and over time, with men assigned a superior social position of power and worth over women—often through the collaboration of official patterns of intervention or deference, affirmation or neglect—masculinity accorded preeminence over femininity and granted a higher rank and value.[5]

I. Analytical Framework

Gender is institutionalized in constitutions, along with most areas of social life, in ways great and small, textual and structural, blatant and subtle. Gendered language pervades constitutions, including in seemingly habitual use of the masculine generic, such as usage of 'his' or 'he' in reference to rights-bearers, impliedly equating citizenship with maleness. Some constitutions use gendered terms as the equivalent of every individual, as Armenia, which grants 'his or her' rights 51 times.[6] The Cambodian Constitution provides a range of specific rights to 'Khmer citizens of either sex',[7] raising the question of the effect of explicitly calling attention to sex at all. Provisions protecting women and men from enslavement[8] pose a similar question, although slavery can take sex-specific forms, as is seemingly recognized in constitutional provisions committed to women's freedom from prostitution, trafficking, and other forms of

> women and those between men. These attributes, opportunities and relationships are socially constructed and are learned through socialization processes. They are context/time-specific and changeable. Gender determines what is expected, allowed and valued in a women or a man in a given context. In most societies there are differences and inequalities between women and men in responsibilities assigned, activities undertaken, access to and control over resources, as well as decision-making opportunities. Gender is part of the broader socio-cultural context. Other important criteria for socio-cultural analysis include class, race, poverty level, ethnic group and age.

UN Women, OSAGI, Concepts and Definitions, available at <http://www.un.org/womenwatch/osagi/conceptsandefinitions.htm>. The latter attributes are normally understood as part of gender analysis through their intersections with it. Except where a distinction between the two is being discussed, the terms 'sex' and 'gender' will be used relatively interchangeably here, since constitutional law is a social discipline and sex inequality is a social, not biological, fact, much as 'race' is a biological construct that is pervasively used to designate an inequality that is social.

[4] See eg Anne Fausto-Sterling, *Myths of Gender: Biological Theories about Women and Men* (rev edn, 1992); Anne Fausto-Sterling, *Sexing the Body: Gender Politics and the Construction of Sexuality* (2000).

[5] For some current documentation of this incontrovertible proposition, see generally UN Department of Economic and Social Affairs, *The World's Women 2010: Trends and Statistics* (2010), available at <http://unstats.un.org/unsd/demographic/products/Worldswomen/WW2010pub.htm>; UN Development Programme, *Human Development Report 2010, The Real Wealth of Nations: Pathways to Human Development* (2010), available at <http://hdr.undp.org/en/reports/global/hdr2010/>, 76–7, 89–94, 156–60.

[6] See eg Constitution of the Republic of Armenia, Art 16, for just one illustration.

[7] Constitution of the Kingdom of Cambodia, Arts 34, 35, 36, 43, 50, 76.

[8] Contrast eg Constitution of the Commonwealth of the Bahamas, Preamble ('[N]o Man, Woman or Child shall ever be Slave or Bondsman to anyone'), with Constitution of Bosnia and Herzegovina, Art II(3)(c) (according '[a]ll persons within the territory of Bosnia and Herzegovina … [t]he right not to be held in slavery or servitude'); Constitution of the Republic of Serbia, Art 26(1) ('No person may be kept in slavery or servitude'); Constitution of the Republic of Seychelles, Art 17(1) ('Every person has the right not to be held in slavery or bondage').

sexual exploitation,[9] which, in turn, call sex-specific constitutional attention to a radically gender-skewed problem, the victims of which are, however, by no means confined to women.

Tacit gender-based language guarantees to all citizens 'fundamental freedoms and *the Rights of Man*', an Algerian constitutional reference to human rights that is common in the French tradition. It also refers to the national heritage as 'the common *patrimony* of all Algerians [masculine] and Algerians [feminine]'.[10] On the other end of the spectrum, in provisions with clear differential bite, Tonga's Constitution enforces primogeniture by distinguishing between male and female children in property succession.[11] Only male children ('son[s]') are mentioned in the elaborate and labyrinthine constitutional rules for succession to the throne of Brunei.[12] Here, not even a daughter of the most prized 'blood' is considered over her ever more distant male relatives. And the Constitution of Myanmar, having prohibited sex discrimination in civil service, comes right out and says that 'nothing in this Section shall prevent appointment of men to the positions that are suitable for men only'.[13]

Despite gendered language littering the surface of constitutions, with consequences great and small, few indications exist that the substance of gender inherent in the sex-unequal status and life chances of women have been considered in making conventional constitutional decisions, certainly not until the modern period, and not usually even then. Yet evidence and logic indicate that constituting choices, including those that have no gender on their face, can have powerful consequences for women as women, meaning women as a sex in the gendered sense. The observation that women may receive more recognition of rights from distant than near authorities[14] implies that more centralized and internationally receptive systems may advance their rights more decisively than do federated and local systems. Common law systems, which allow direct access to courts by individuals with lawyers and conceive law as open-ended and intrinsically responsive to changing social perceptions and realities as well as to individual circumstances, may be somewhat less elite and exclusionary, hence more amenable to gender equality, than civil law processes that favor legislation. Judicial supremacy allows appeals to principle over power, predominant in many legislatures, from which women have been effectively excluded in the past, although some scholars have argued that legislatures, as deliberative bodies, are more conducive to needed changes for women.[15] The division and scope of powers of each branch, including whether and with what reach legislatures are permitted to guarantee equality rights where inequality reigns, doubtless affects social outcomes for women and lower status men. These structural questions, along with whether presidential or parliamentary systems are more receptive to women's voices and interests, must be

[9] See eg Constitution of the Kingdom of Bhutan, Art 17 ('The State shall endeavour to take appropriate measures to eliminate all forms of discrimination and exploitation against women including trafficking, prostitution, abuse, violence, harassment and intimidation at work in both public and private spheres'); Iraqi Constitution, Art 37(3) ('Forced labor, slavery, slave trade, trafficking in women or children, and sex trade shall be prohibited').

[10] Constitution of the People's Democratic Republic of Algeria, Art 32 (emphasis added). However, this could as well be translated, as the Algerian mission to the UN does, to guarantee 'a common heritage of all Algerians, men and women'.

[11] Act of Constitution of Tonga, Arts 32, 111.

[12] Constitutional Matters II, Succession and Regency Proclamation, 1959, Art 5(1) (Brunei Darussalam).

[13] Constitution of the Republic of the Union of Myanmar (formerly Burma), Art 352.

[14] This is argued regarding international law in Catharine A. MacKinnon, 'Introduction: Women's Status, Men's States' in Catharine A. MacKinnon, *Are Women Human? And Other International Dialogues* (2007), 1–14.

[15] See eg Jennifer Nedelsky, 'Rethinking Constitutionalism through the Lens of the Gendered Division of Household Labour' in Beverley Baines, Daphne Barak-Erez, and Tsvi Kahana (eds), *Feminist Constitutionalism: Global Perspectives* (2012).

regarded as hypothesis-generating at present, calling for further inquiry into their impact on gender-based inequality.[16]

Each regime's concept of, and attitude toward, rights as such profoundly shapes the capacity of constitutions to be used to change gender-based inequality in law and society. Rights can be aspirational and open-ended or concrete and limited to specified areas, negative or positive, individual or collective. Sources of law and their ranking can be crucial. International law occupies varied places in national systems ranging from incorporation and deference to rejection in favor of the parochially domestic. The place and content of religion or customary law can be decisive, as family law is often governed by extra- or pre-legal systems, and women's lives are often confined to and by the family. Criminal law, defining gender crimes and accountability for them through a wide variety of constitutional rubrics, can also be shaped by religious, customary, international, or common law with major impact on women's equality, dignity, and personal security, all dimensions of their gender status. Demonstrably central is the approach adopted by each constitutional court to interpreting and implementing equality obligations.

The larger political context in which a constitution is framed and interpreted powerfully affects its utility for gender justice as well. Democracy may or may not improve women's situation, as illustrated by the collapse of women's electoral representation with the erosion of their social and economic rights across Central and Eastern Europe after the fall of communism,[17] although women's presence in a legislative body that itself has little power cannot be considered effective representation. (As with occupations, perhaps the less power a legislature has, the more women may be found in it.) The role of women's movements,[18] especially whether seen as indigenous or alien, influences constitutional developments as well, as shown by gains in many Latin American settings, including after authoritarianism.[19] Additional variables that appear to contribute to determining whether constitutions move toward gender equality include the quality, depth, and organization of civil society and the norms governing its relation to the state;[20] the effectiveness of addressing racism and social and economic rights; the

[16] A useful review of the literature on gender in the context of women's place in constitutional offices is Paula A. Monopoli, 'Gender and Constitutional Design' (2006) 115 *Yale Law Journal* 2643.

[17] See generally Denise M. Walsh, *Women's Rights in Democratizing States* (2011) (comparing Poland, Chile, and South Africa, and arguing that discourse legitimizing gender injustice prevails in most democratizing states).

[18] Although it does not focus upon constitutional law as such, the work of the Research Network on Gender Politics and the State (RNGS) is highly informative, some of it reported in Dorothy McBride Stetson and Amy G. Mazur (eds), *Comparative State Feminism* (1995), and Joyce Outshoorn and Johanna Kantola (eds), *Changing State Feminism: Just Debate and Gender Justice in the Public Sphere* (2007), investigating the effects of women's movements on women's state agencies, looking at policymaking processes, debates, and outcomes in 13 post-industrial Western countries over a 30-year period relying on a database comprising 'a unique source of cross-national, cross-sectoral, and longitudinal information on comparative gender policy issues'. RNGS, available at <http://libarts.wsu.edu/polisci/rngs/index.html>. See also UN, Department of Economic and Social Affairs, 'The Impact of Women's Participation and Leadership on Policy Outcomes: A Focus on Women's Policy Machineries', UN Doc EGM/EPWD/2005/EP.5 (December 12, 2005) (prepared by Amy Mazur), available at <http://www.un.org/womenwatch/daw/egm/eql-men/docs/EP.5_Mazur.pdf>.

[19] A sense is provided by Martha I. Morgan, 'Emancipatory Equality: Gender Jurisprudence under the Colombian Constitution' in Beverley Baines and Ruth Rubio-Marin (eds), *The Gender of Constitutional Jurisprudence*, (2005), 75–98, and Alda Facio, Rodrigo Jiménez Sandova, and Martha I. Morgan, 'Gender Equality and International Human Rights in Costa Rican Constitutional Jurisprudence' in ibid 99–121. Both factors are illuminatingly discussed in Amrita Basu, 'Gender and Governance: Concepts and Contexts' in Martha Nussbaum et al, *Essays on Gender and Governance* (2003), 20–58.

[20] A thorough analysis of this factor within the comparative constitutional setting of affirmative action, including a useful comparison of Germany with the United States, can be found in Ann Peters, *Women, Quotas, and Constitutions: A Comparative Study of American, German, EC, and International Law* (1999), 277–327.

systemic role of the military; and the conditions and recency of internal or external conflict among men. Media, from the contributions of a free press to the ravages of the pornography industry, powerfully control how and what people can know and think and feel, hence do, on gendered dimensions as well as others. Corruption—self-dealing of the powerful using resources that are unequally distributed (inter alia) on the basis of sex and gender—can undermine any legal guarantee, underlining the importance of knowing whether the rule of law is the rule, corruption the exception, or corruption is the rule.[21] Constitutions are regnant over these factors but also reflect their imprint.

If no scholarship yet considers all these determinants together in a consolidated field theory, considerable work has been done in a number of these discrete areas, some of it comparative, some in considerable depth in a single jurisdiction. The relation of constitutional provisions addressing gender and gendered realities to women's situations on the ground has thus not yet been established in a systematic way, although promising beginning attempts have been made.[22] Comparing measures of sex inequality[23] with relatively explicit constitutional provisions in the gendered domain discloses revealing patterns. Of the two countries with the highest international ranking for equality of the sexes, Norway has no equality provisions in its constitution and Australia has no formal written constitution at all, although both have documents that fill this approximate function. The next two countries with the highest sex equality in international rankings—the United States (although its high rate of sexual assault is not taken into account) and Ireland—have generic equality provisions that do not mention sex or gender textually. In contrast, many nations with the lowest equality rankings in the world have strongly worded provisions guaranteeing equality generally, sex equality specifically, gender equality, and equal rights between women and men concretely and with admirable particularity. Malawi has one of the most detailed constitutional provisions for equality of the sexes in the world, guaranteeing equal protection of the law, women 'the same rights as men in civil law',[24] invalidating laws that discriminate based on gender, requiring legislation be passed to eliminate discriminatory customs and practices including 'sexual abuse, harassment and violence' as well as discrimination at work and in property, guaranteeing full participation in all spheres of society, and requiring implementation of laws to address 'domestic violence, security of the person, lack of maternity benefits, economic exploitation and rights to property'.[25] Malawi rests at number 153 in sex inequality among the 169 nations ranked. In the Democratic Republic of the Congo—number 168 of 169 in sex inequality

[21] The World Bank's Worldwide Governance Indicators project offers a useful tool for evaluating indicia pertaining to the rule of law internationally. See eg <http://info.worldbank.org/governance/wgi/index.asp>.

[22] See Priscilla A. Lambert and Druscilla L. Scribner, 'A Politics of Difference versus a Politics of Equality: Do Constitutions Matter?' (2009) 41 *Comparative Politics* 337; Eileen McDonagh, 'Political Citizenship and Democratization: The Gender Paradox' (2002) 96 *American Political Science Review* 535. Grasp of legal factors could at times be more fully informed. See eg Priscilla Lambert and Druscilla Scribner, 'Gender Matters: A Case Study Analysis of Constitutional Provisions in Botswana and South Africa', Paper presented at the annual meeting of the American Political Science Association, Boston, MA, August 2008, (comparing Botswana with South Africa, misunderstanding substantive equality and failing to consider gender hierarchy), available at <http://citation.allacademic.com/meta/p_mla_apa_research_citation/2/7/9/5/4/pages279546/p279546-1.php>; Laura E. Lucas, 'Does Gender Specificity in Constitutions Matter?' (2009) 20 *Duke Journal of Comparative and International Law* 133 (comparing Canada with Colombia discussing 'women's protection'), available at <http://www.law.duke.edu/shell/cite.pl?20+Duke+J.+Comp.+&+Int%27l+L.+133+pdf>.

[23] This measure of inequality does not include reported or actual incidents of violence against women.

[24] Constitution of the Republic of Malawi, Art 24(1)(a).

[25] ibid Arts 24(2)(a), 13(a)(iii).

measures even without its astronomical incidence of rape in ongoing conflicts not reflected in that measure—the Constitution requires that 'the public powers see to the elimination of any form of discrimination concerning women' and 'take measures to struggle against all forms of violence made against women in public and in private life'.[26]

On this qualitative level at the extremes, the evidence approaches a constitutional paradox: attention to gender in a constitution may as much indicate a problem to be solved as provide a tool for its solution. Often the reasons for the gap between guarantee and reality—surely as extreme for gender as for the relation of constitutional law to any other social regularity—lie elsewhere than in constitutions. Norway has had a Gender Equality Act in force since 1979 that refers directly to its ratification of the international Convention on the Elimination of All Forms of Discrimination against Women (CEDAW) the same year.[27] The Norwegian women's movement has had notably strong working relationships with women in parliament and women's public policy agencies during this period as well, a factor found to powerfully potentiate gender egalitarian policy results.[28] Having expanded its statutory prohibitions on gender discrimination repeatedly, Norway's Human Rights Act 1999 incorporated CEDAW into domestic law, guaranteeing its precedence over other national legislation.[29] Australia too has signed CEDAW, enabling its federal government to enact strong domestic legislation to enforce nondiscrimination against women in the absence of a written constitution.[30]

Where statutory law is as or more effective on the ground below, and international law more supreme in the sky above the space that constitutions, were they present, would institutionally occupy, constitutional guarantees are less missed in their absence. Or perhaps constitutional guarantees are an expressive, even desperate, gesture in some situations, nonetheless providing a basis for potential mobilization as well as a signal flare of hope. International law in particular can supplement, supplant, or suffuse domestic law on gender questions,[31] challenging the degree to which constitutional law as such occupies a comparable place across states, even calling into question the analytic relevance of investigating the constitutional envelope altogether where gender-based issues are concerned. Whether constitutional provisions are a particularly meaningful unit of analysis or index to rights or their delivery on questions of gender remains to be established.

If a gendered perspective calls for deeper and more complex approaches to constitutions, many barriers obstruct connecting constitutions with lived outcomes in the gendered domain.

[26] Constitution of the Democratic Republic of the Congo, Art 14.

[27] Gender Equality Act (2005) (Norway), available at <http://www.regjeringen.no/en/doc/Laws/Acts/The-Act-relating-to-Gender-Equality-the-.html?id=454568>. The full text of the Convention is available at <http://www.un.org/womenwatch/daw/cedaw/cedaw.htm>.

[28] See Beatrice Halsaa, 'A Strategic Partnership for Women's Policies in Norway' in Geertje Lycklama à Nijeholt, Virginia Vargas, and Saskia Wieringa (eds), *Women's Movements and Public Policy in Europe, Latin America, and the Caribbean* (1998), 167–87.

[29] Gender Equality Act (2005) (Norway), available at <http://www.regjeringen.no/en/doc/Laws/Acts/The-Act-relating-to-Gender-Equality-the-.html?id=454568>; Human Rights Act (1999) (Norway), available at <http://www.ub.uio.no/ujur/ulovdata/lov-19990521-030-eng.pdf>.

[30] See Isabel Karpin and Karen O'Connell, 'Embedded Constitutionalism, the Australian Constitution, and the Rights of Women' in Baines and Rubio-Marin (n 19), 22–47.

[31] For an illuminating discussion, see Ruth Rubio-Marin and Martha I. Morgan, 'Constitutional Domestication of International Gender Norms: Categorizations, Illustrations, and Reflections from the Nearside of the Bridge' in Karen Knop (ed), *Gender and Human Rights* (2004), 113–52, analyzing the role of international gender norms in domestic constitutions in terms of assimilation, supplementation, and adaptation. For a statistical treatment of the relationship between the adoption of CEDAW and women's rights domestically in the domains of education, employment, and reproductive control, see Beth A. Simmons, *Mobilizing for Human Rights: International Law in Domestic Politics* (2009), 202–55.

Gender, and the inequality based on it, is so pervasive in law and life that positing any link risks overdetermination. Where constitutions are strong on sex equality and gender inequality in life is somewhat attenuated, even if only comparatively speaking, the potential for simultaneity bias is rife: the same forces that determine women's status relative to men in particular cultures and jurisdictions may control whether constitutional guarantees of sex equality are present and how robustly they are interpreted and enforced, clouding inference of constitutional causality. Many apparently causal factors operate with varying force in diverse settings. In some places, the power of a guarantee may derive less from its language than from its judicial interpretation. The strength of the Canadian Charter of Rights and Freedoms for women, for example, is due less to its terms, although they have merit, and more to its implementing equality theory, predicated on a substantive approach to sex inequality.[32] Constitutional language can be highly specific and extensive, as in Brazil, but a comparatively weak role for the judiciary can make it less potent.[33] International law can be creatively implemented in constitutions, as in India for instance,[34] providing crucial leverage for advancing women's rights on specific issues and support for local nongovernmental organizations. But corruption of various kinds can intervene to vitiate its effectiveness on the ground. Countries like Israel have a constitutionalistic norm and strong judicial discourse of sex equality with no written constitution.[35] Despite such challenges, comparative constitutional consideration of gender inequality has begun,[36] including unmasking the masculinity that discernibly animates the institutions men design, of which a constitution is an apex legal form in most contemporary national states. But at this stage, comparative analysis of gender in constitutions leans toward a descriptive, qualitative, and contextual understanding that is more art than science.

II. Application

The central gender question posed by comparative constitutional analysis is the impact of intervention at the constitutional level on gender hierarchy in life and law. The gendered features of constitutional regimes, in their relations to the social and legal contexts they reflect and shape, can be analyzed along four principled dimensions through which sex inequality is institutionalized, and along which it is being contested. The first concerns equality. It appears that the more a country addresses the substance of gender hierarchy in its equality jurisprudence, as opposed to taking the traditional sameness-difference approach to sex, the more it will promote gender equality through law. The second concerns relative freedom. For if gender equality is to be real, women's voice and choices need to be real, rather than their consent being presumed under conditions of coercion, which include law and socialization. The third involves the structural private. Arguably, the more issues conventionally regarded as private in the gendered domain are addressed as the public issues of sex discrimination that they are,

[32] See *Andrews v Law Society of British Columbia* [1989] 1 SCR 143 (Canada); see also *R v Kapp* [2008] 2 SCR 483 (Canada).

[33] Various sex-based rights are provided in the Constitution of the Federative Republic of Brazil at Arts 5, 7, 20, 143(21), 183, 189, 201.

[34] *Vishaka v State of Rajasthan*, AIR 1997 SC 3011.

[35] See eg HCJ 953/87 *Poraz v Municipality of Tel Aviv-Jaffa* [1988] IsrSC 42(2) 309; HCJ 4541/94 *Miller v Minister of Defense* [1995] IsrSC 49(4) 94; HCJ 453/94 *Women's Network v Minister of Transportation* [1994] IsrSC 48(5) 501; HCJ 1284/99 *Plonit v Chief of Staff* [1999] IsrSC 53(2) 62.

[36] Valuable contributions include Baines, Barak-Erez, and Kahana (n 15); Baines and Rubio-Marin (n 19); and Susan H. Williams (ed), *Constituting Equality: Gender Equality and Comparative Constitutional Law* (2009).

including through jurisdiction, the more gender inequality will be weakened as a structural factor. The fourth involves the political in the broadest sense. Morality, especially when cultural or religious, can be a guise for power-ordered relationships based on sex and gender, yet is frequently regarded as exempt from gender scrutiny. A gender perspective on constitutions exposes such realms to scrutiny. Often the four dimensions intersect and interact. For example, the family is considered structurally private and can be controlled by moral rules of religious or customary law, shaping realities of gender hierarchy that would trigger equality law (law that itself may either be constructed around difference or in opposition to dominance). These interconnections can make gendered issues doubly or even triply difficult to reach and remedy constitutionally.

1. Difference and Dominance

Gender is an inequality. A telling analytic dimension along which the constitutional treatment of gender can accordingly be traced—one readily susceptible to comparative study—concerns the faces and features of equality as a constitutional guarantee. Not all gender inequality will be found subject to constitutional equality guarantees. Even where such guarantees are not absent, they can be flaccid or deemed inapplicable to gendered areas of life. This principled dimension of analysis thus focuses upon the extent to which constitutional equality standards that do exist confront, deconstruct, and dismantle gender hierarchy or continue to permit, essentialize, and institutionalize it.

Constitutional remediation of the pervasively unequal status and treatment of women based on gender through equality guarantees has been slow, despite their facial promise. Understanding men as men in the legal context has been even slower. Possibly this is because considering women as particular and different and marked as 'the sex', men as generic and standard and universally human, unmarked by sex or gender specificity, has elevated men over women on the human scale, even as the consequences for men who fall below masculine gender standards are punishing. One constitutional index to this larger matter are the 12 constitutions that expressly stipulate that the use therein of exclusive sex-based terms, usually the masculine generic, means both sexes. Cyprus, for example, provides that 'words importing the masculine gender include females'.[37] That said, most constitutions contain equality guarantees that differentially bear upon the gendered domain. Whether equality is formal or substantive, abstract or concrete, general or specific, vertical or also horizontal, an overarching norm or a strictly legal claim,[38] its second-order attributes can decisively define how effective the guarantees prove to be.

Nearly 200 countries (including for this purpose the European Union as an entity and Vatican City) have written constitutions.[39] Of these, 184 guarantee gender equality in one or more of its various forms, although the reality of gender equality exists nowhere. Least common are general constitutional grants of abstract equality only, the text naked of specific grounds or groups, a pattern seen only in Indonesia, Kuwait, Latvia, Lebanon, Saudi Arabia, Singapore, United Arab Emirates, and the United States. States in the United States are

[37] Constitution of the Republic of Cyprus, Art 186 s 1(2). Cyprus finishes the sentence with 'and words in the singular include the plural and vice-versa'. One wonders if the 'vice-versa' also means that words importing the feminine gender include males.

[38] Kathleen M. Sullivan, 'Constitutionalizing Women's Equality' (2002) 90 *California Law Review* 735, lucidly analyzes some of these factors in terms of what may be better for women, but without real-world data or consideration of their intrinsically gendered character.

[39] The figures included in this paragraph were derived from the sources listed in n 1.

forbidden to 'deny to any person within its jurisdiction the equal protection of the laws'.[40] As a contrasting instance, Uruguay's still comparatively sparse equality commitment is more expansive: 'All persons are equal before the law, no other distinctions being recognized among them save those of talent and virtue'.[41] By distinction, 139 countries expressly provide for sex equality or nondiscrimination on the basis of sex, 71 of these recognizing both equality generally and sex equality specifically. The vast majority of constitutions thus textually guarantee equality of the sexes in some facially explicit form, prohibiting discrimination 'on grounds of' or 'on the basis of' sex, or according rights to all citizens 'regardless of' sex. States that guarantee equal rights to women and men by name, registering a more substantive vision of the people who possess the rights, are also substantial in number—114 constitutions from Afghanistan to Zimbabwe reflect this pattern—often with culturally specific variations that were clearly carefully considered. Of these, 20 provide for equality between males and females, or male and female persons, as in Canada's hard-fought, but so far unused, Section 28.[42] A perhaps surprising 66 expressly provide for gender equality, as in 'Lao citizens are all equal before the law irrespective of their gender'.[43]

Some gendered constitutional provisions are female protective in ways that may be intended to equalize against an unequal reality or may have the paternalistic purpose or effect of keeping women in a subordinate role. Examples of the former, as in the Central African Republic, may take special notice of violence against women.[44] Among the latter are incentives for motherhood and prohibitions on women working at night.[45] Ambiguously in this respect, some constitutions prescribe different pension requirements by sex[46] or require sex-segregation of incarcerated women.[47] Spouses, or husbands and wives, are granted equality in the family in numerous constitutions, among them some of the 29 countries in which marriage is confined to a man and a woman by constitutional fiat.[48] Most of these examples are found in Latin American constitutions that also possess equality provisions, the simple sex discrimination inherent in dictating

[40] US Constitution, Amendment 14, s 1.

[41] Constitution of the Oriental Republic of Uruguay, Art 8. Uruguay contains other provisions guaranteeing equality for women as well.

[42] Canadian Charter of Rights and Freedoms, s 28. For further discussion, see Penney Kome, *The Taking of Twenty-Eight: Women Challenge the Constitution* (1983). This figure does not include Bolivia, which has such a provision only for foreigners.

[43] Constitution of the Lao People's Democratic Republic, Art 35. Some constitutions provide for equality on the basis of 'gender identity', likely addressing issues presented by transgendered and transsexual persons. See Constitution of the Plurinational State of Bolivia, Art 14; Constitution of the Republic of Ecuador, Art 11(2).

[44] See eg Constitution of the Central African Republic, Art 6 ('The protection of the woman and of the child against violence and insecurity, exploitation and moral, intellectual and physical neglect, is an obligation of the State and the other public collectivities'). Similar provisions also appear outside of the protectionist context. See eg Constitution of the Kingdom of Bhutan, Art 8, para 5 ('A person shall not tolerate or participate in . . . abuse of women . . . and shall take necessary steps to prevent such acts'), Art 9, para 17 ('The State shall endeavour to take appropriate measures to eliminate all forms of discrimination and exploitation against women including trafficking, prostitution, abuse, violence, harassment and intimidation at work in both public and private spheres').

[45] See eg Constitution of Albania, Art 54; Political Constitution of Colombia, Art 53. For further discussion, see dimension four below.

[46] See eg Constitution of the Federative Republic of Brazil, Art 40, s 1(III)(a)(b).

[47] See eg ibid, Art 5, s XLVIII; Political Constitution of the United Mexican States, Art 18; Constitution of the Republic of Nicaragua, Art 39, para 2; Constitution of the Republic of Palau, Art IV, s 7; Constitution of the Republic of Seychelles, Art 18(13).

[48] See eg Constitution of the Republic of Belarus, Art 32; Constitution of the Republic of Honduras, Art 112; Constitution of the Republic of Lithuania, Art 38; Constitution of the Republic of Tajikistan, Art 33.

one's marital partner by sex apparently overlooked. Although they position women and men equally in a social institution on their face (particularly as against plural marriage, for instance), such provisions may, depending upon the circumstances, be considered equality-promoting or inequality-entrenching, even as their gendered nature is unambiguous.

Whatever the textual language, various equality theories are deployed by the judiciary in interpreting and applying gender terms. Demonstrably crucial is whether sex and gender are seen as a matter of sameness and difference, abstract and generic and symmetrical, as in the traditional Aristotelian model of likes alike, unlikes unalike,[49] or whether sex and gender are recognized as presenting a question of social domination and subordination, a substantive and asymmetrical hierarchy, as do some modern constitutional systems, notably Canada and South Africa.[50]

The standard Enlightenment question of whether gender should be addressed under general equality principles or through its particularity as to sex both derives from and serves to obscure the question of whether the standard for generic equality is defined in masculine terms—hence whether the content of sex-specific rules compound or counter gender hierarchy. The real issue here is not the constitutional language alone, but whether the equality standards applied to interpret it recognize and oppose substantive hierarchy, an approach that concrete sex-specific language may or may not accomplish or encourage. The related question of whether classifications by sex should be limited or prohibited, or whether the class women should be specifically protected, derives from and stands in for the same question of fundamental posture: Is sex a symmetrical abstraction, as in the traditional sameness/difference model, or is gender inequality seen as an artifact of an historical disadvantage that is asymmetrical and subject to rectification?

The gap between equality guarantees in constitutions and the unequal relative status of the sexes is striking in virtually all settings.[51] A look at the world's constitutions suggests little if any determinate relationship between a constitution addressing women's rights and their equality of status relative to men. There is much such language to look at. Austria requires governmental entities 'subscribe to the de facto equality of men and women';[52] 'Women in the People's Republic of China enjoy equal rights with men in all spheres of life';[53] 'Women and men are equal before the law' in the Dominican Republic[54] and in many other states. 'Women and men shall have the same rights and duties in all areas of family, political, economic, social and cultural life' in Timor Leste.[55] In Iran, 'All citizens of the country, both men and women, equally enjoy the protection of the law and enjoy all human, political, economic, social and cultural rights, in conformity with Islamic criteria.'[56] In Yemen, 'Women are the sisters of men. They have rights and duties, which are guaranteed and assigned by the Shari'ah and stipulated

[49] See Catharine A. MacKinnon, *Sex Equality* (2nd edn, 2007), 4–5.

[50] A lucid discussion of the South African concept of equality can be found in Kate O'Regan and Nick Friedman, 'Equality' in Tom Ginsburg and Rosalind Dixon (eds), *Comparative Constitutional Law* (2011), 473–503.

[51] One commentator on Arab state constitutions finds not so much a gap between guarantee and reality but a 'gap in the legal system which is further exaggerated by patriarchal practices': Nawal Ammar, 'Arab Women in their States' Constitutions' (2004) 4 *International Journal of Comparative Criminology* 196. She calls for a restructuring of constitutional guarantees to support empowerment of Arab women, the problem substantive equality is designed to address.

[52] Constitution of Austria, Art 7(2).

[53] Constitution of the People's Republic of China, Art 48.

[54] Constitution of the Dominican Republic, Art 39, para 4.

[55] Constitution of the Democratic Republic of Timor-Leste, s 17.

[56] Constitution of the Islamic Republic of Iran, Art 20.

by law'.[57] In their Preamble, the people of Zambia 'recognize the equal worth of men and women in their rights to participate, and freely determine and build a political, economic and social system of their own free choice.'[58] More affirmatively still, Syria 'guarantees women all opportunities enabling them to fully and effectively participate in the political, social, cultural, and economic life. The state removes the restrictions that prevent women's development and participation in building the socialist Arab society.'[59] These countries rank up and down the sex inequality scale with little to no discernible relation between equality of the sexes in life and the strength of constitutional language. This does not mean that recognizing women's rights in constitutions is not symbolically and/or practically important for advancing gender equality in any particular situation or overall. These examples may indicate more about the role and rule of law itself in the jurisdiction than anything else.

Where approaches to equality are most substantive—in that the substance of gender hierarchy is identified and addressed in the text—constitutional provisions may look like Colombia's Article 13 which, after providing for equality before the law and prohibiting discrimination 'on the basis of gender', states:

> The state will promote the conditions necessary in order that equality may be real and effective and will adopt measures in favor of groups which are discriminated against or marginalized. The state will especially protect those individuals who on account of their economic, physical, or mental condition are in obviously vulnerable circumstances and will sanction any abuse or ill-treatment perpetrated against them.[60]

As this language suggests, whether or not affirmatively acting to produce sex equality is distinguishable from prohibition of discrimination is (again) further derivative of whether the model of inequality is one of sameness and difference, in which case the distinction holds, or of hierarchy, specifically domination and subordination, in which case there is no such distinction. Failing to act to end subordination and enforcing subordination both maintain dominance and disadvantage, hence is simply discriminatory.

Paradigmatic on this issue is Article 3(2) of Germany's Basic Law: 'The State shall promote the actual implementation of equal rights for women and men and take steps to eliminate disadvantages that now exist.'[61] As applied, this clause aims at 'overcom[ing] men's traditional domination over women'.[62] The jurisprudence under this article understands that ending discrimination against women is not positive discrimination in their favor; it is equality, not discrimination at all. Article 3(3) states, 'No one may be disadvantaged or favored because of his sex'. Instead of using this provision to make impossible any steps toward real equality, as called for under Article 3(2), in what the Aristotelian approach would call neutrality, women are understood as socially substantively unequal to men, historically and currently, hence the two clauses do not conflict.[63] The Greek Constitution concisely adopts the asymmetrical equality

[57] Constitution of the Republic of Yemen, Art 31.

[58] Constitution of the Republic of Zambia, Preamble.

[59] Constitution of the Syrian Arab Republic, Art 45.

[60] For discussion of interpretations by the Constitutional Court of Colombia as a substantive equality provision, which nonetheless contains some denigrating essentializing elements, see Morgan (n 19), 86–91.

[61] Basic Law for the Federal Republic of Germany, Art 3(2).

[62] Blanca Rodriguez Ruiz and Ute Sacksofsky, 'Gender in the German Constitution' in Baines and Rubio-Marin (n 19), 149, 155.

[63] Because European Union law under the directives (specifically Council Directive 76/207/EEC, 1976 OJ L 39/40) has tended to be interpreted in Aristotelian terms, steps some Europeans would take, specifically Germans (Case C-450/93 *Kalanke v Freie Hansestadt Bremen* [1995] ECR 1-3051) or Swedes (Case C-407/98

principle: 'Adoption of positive measures for promoting equality between men and women does not constitute discrimination on grounds of sex. The State shall take measures for the elimination of inequalities actually existing, in particular to the detriment of women.'[64] As under the Canadian Charter of Rights and Freedoms, acts that eliminate the disadvantage of a disadvantaged group are treated as acts that are not unequal—not acts that are unequal but permissible, rather simply as steps toward equality.[65]

Where a substantive approach to gender inequality is largely used, as in Canada, South Africa, Germany, and Colombia, substantive issues of gender inequality that are not traditionally addressed by equality law on the ground that the sexes are 'different'—issues like reproductive rights[66] and sexual assault, as well as issues located in the outpost of the private, such as family (including divorce)—are all strongly affected by gender equality considerations and may be governed by sex equality guarantees. Canada provides the original template, although many areas that are resolved favorably to gender justice under the aegis of its approach may not be decided in equality terms technically. A substantive gender equality approach is at times taken without calling it that.[67] Some issues, like same-sex sexuality, that could be pursued on a gender basis under a substantive sex equality—indeed are suffused with sex and gender in substance—have also not been. Most constitutional courts have recognized sexual orientation as a separate and distinct ground for prohibition of discrimination, Canada again taking the lead.[68] So lesbian women receive same-sex equality rights as members of the gender neutral group 'homosexual' or 'gay', rather than as women, discriminated against because their gender—sexuality being a dimension of gender—is discriminatorily not seen to fit their sex. In the process of imperfectly implementing a substantive gender equality standard, use of the concept of 'dignity' has at times been used as a mediating gap-filler,[69] despite its tendency to be gendered unequal in itself.

International law, which has traditionally taken the mainstream essentialist approach to equality—at times attributing unequal realities produced by gender hierarchy to the inherent nature of women and men, considering them 'differences' or not—has become increasingly substantive in the last two decades, recognizing the basis in social hierarchy of the problem of gender inequality, in particular in the European and Latin American regional systems and some UN treaty bodies.[70] This development makes the extent to which international law is

Abrahamsson and Anderson v Fogelqvist [2000] ECR I-05539) instituting affirmative action to produce equality for women authorized by their domestic equality approach have been invalidated by the European Court of Justice as inequality for men. This is further illustrated in *Marschall*, where a savings clause allows individual male candidates to be selected (Case C-409/95 *Marschall v Land Nordrhein-Westfalen* [1997] ECR I-6363).

[64] Constitution of Greece, Art 116(2).

[65] *R v Kapp* [2008] 2 SCR 483(Canada).

[66] This is especially visible in Colombia. See Political Constitution of Colombia, Art 43 (guaranteeing pregnant women and new mothers 'the special assistance and protection of the State'); Art 53 (expressing the state's commitment providing 'special protection' for 'women' and 'motherhood'); Art 134 (constitutionalizing women's right to maternity leave).

[67] Canadian examples include *R v Lavallée* [1990] 1 SCR 852 (battering), and *Moge v Moge* [1992] 3 SCR 813 (support after divorce).

[68] See eg *Egan v Canada* [1985] 2 SCR 513; *Vriend v Alberta* [1998] 1 SCR 493; *M v H* [1999] 2 SCR 3. See also *Lawrence v Texas* 539 US 558 (2003).

[69] *M v H* [1999] 2 SCR 3 began this; *R v Kapp* [2008] 2 SCR 483 (Canada) recognized some of its drawbacks.

[70] In Europe, *MC v Bulgaria*, 15 ECtHR 627 (2003) (on rape), and *Opuz v Turkey*, ECtHR App no 33401/02, Judgment (2009) (on battering), are especially significant, with the Convention of Belém do Pará, Inter-American Convention on the Prevention, Punishment and Eradication of Violence against Women (Convention of Belém do Pará), Belém do Pará, June 6, 1994, 33 ILM 1534 (1994), as well as adjudications such as *Mejía v Peru*, Case 10.970, Inter-Am CtHR, Report No 5/96 (1996), and *González et al ('Cotton Field') v Mexico*, Inter-Am CtHR (Ser C) No 205 (2009).

embodied in domestic constitutions a significant factor in constitutional adjudications of gendered questions, a feature also illustrated by the relative positioning of CEDAW in cases in which a domestic constitutional provision is challenged.[71] Also as a result, reservations to CEDAW may show more about gender under the law in a given jurisdiction than does examination of constitutional provisions alone.[72]

2. Coercion and Consent

Women have not, in general, written constitutions or decided on constitutional matters. Men in power have written them: many long ago and as if women did not exist, as in the United States; some after wars, in the waging and ending of which women actively participated only marginally, if at all, as in Japan; many recently, by foreign experts, as in Central and Eastern Europe after communism, where it has been generally assumed that Western liberal models are an adequate template for rights with gendered dimensions. In recent times, women have had some voice in constitution-making, often after revolutions, but nowhere near half the clout in either constitutional design or constitutive decision-making. Accordingly, a second dimension of gender and its contestation arises with the assumption that women consent to being ruled under constitutions when they were not consulted on their terms.

In democratic systems—most contemporary constitutions are considered democratic instruments—all citizens are deemed to consent to their government, from which it derives its legitimacy. The CEDAW Committee's observation that '[s]ocieties in which women are excluded from public life and decision-making cannot be described as democratic'[73] applies in spades to their constitutions. The assumption that women agree to governmental structures and processes in the construction of which they did not participate and from which they were afforded no meaningful opportunity to dissent renders this consent illusory. The constitutive nature of constitutions, combined with the fact that women did not actively participate in framing them and in most instances were not permitted to vote to elect representatives under them until very recently, in addition to raising legitimacy problems, suggests that the structures of representation and traditional practices of elections may have built-in gender bias that can persist long after women, as a biological demographic group, are permitted to take part. For example, proportional voting schemes have been shown to elect more women than do single member majority/plurality systems,[74] yet women have virtually never been given the chance to choose between these systems, but rather have inherited whatever system men previously chose. Consent in any sense of affirmative agreement is more attributed than meaningful in such circumstances, relying more upon acquiescence than choice between open and equally available and consequential alternatives. The efficacy of women's political participation has also been crippled over generations by sex-based poverty and illiteracy, that is, by deprivation of economic and social rights because they are women. Improvements in education and suffrage have begun to address women's representation as a group, but the deeper structural issues of gender inequality, including those built into constitutional frameworks, remain.

[71] See eg *Botswana v Unity Dow*, 103 ILR 128 (Court of Appeals of Botswana, 1992).

[72] See Rebecca J. Cook, 'Reservations to the Convention on the Elimination of All Forms of Discrimination Against Women' (1990) 30 *Virginia Journal of International Law* 643.

[73] Committee on the Elimination of Discrimination against Women, General Recommendation No 23, UN Doc A/52/38/Rev.1 (1997), para 14.

[74] Lane Kenworthy and Melissa Malami, 'Gender Inequality in Political Representation: A Worldwide Comparative Analysis' (1999) 78 *Social Forces* 235; Andrew Reynolds, 'Women in the Legislatures and Executives of the World: Knocking at the Highest Glass Ceiling' (1999) 51 *World Politics* 547.

As of 2011, 22 countries have attempted to address the problem of women's lack of political representation in government by entrenching sex-based electoral quotas in their constitutions,[75] some, including Argentina[76] and France,[77] through a mix of constitutional and statutory provisions. Electoral quotas demonstrably improve women's representation in numbers in the affected elected branches,[78] promoting bringing their perspectives to all levels of government, including to constitutional questions. Most sex-based electoral quotas in constitutions refer explicitly to women but not to men.[79] Many Latin American countries impose a quota of at least 30 percent women in the covered positions, with the aim of achieving a critical mass.[80] On the constitutional equality concern, leading researchers Dahlerup and Freidenvall argue, with evidence, that quotas come closer to providing real equality of opportunity for women than equality of result, hence are supported by formal as well as substantive equality models. Most quota schemes do not reserve seats, hence would not be construed as reverse discrimination under the Aristotelian model.[81] The concern that quotas on party lists will divide the national community has also been argued to be misplaced.[82] But as often, particularly with women's issues, numbers do not tell the whole story. Quotas may give women greater political voice, as in India's local panchayats,[83] but can also be used to support the party in power where largely male parliamentarians nominate the women who will fill the women's quota, as in

[75] International Institute for Democracy and Electoral Assistance (Stockholm, Sweden), Global Database of Quotas for Women, available at <http://www.quotaproject.org>. As of the date of this writing, in a very fluid situation, 104 countries had legal gender quotas of some kind in their electoral systems. Ibid.

[76] See Ley de Cupos (Quota Laws) (Law 24.102). Dispute as to its constitutionality was settled by a larger constitutional reform in 1994, in which it was asserted that 'real equality of opportunity between men and women regarding access to elective and political party positions will be guaranteed by positive action in regulation of political parties and in the electoral code': Constitution of the Argentine Nation, Art 27.

[77] See Loi sur la parité (Parity Law) (Constitutional Law No 99-569), Art 3 (stating that 'statutes shall promote the equal access of women and men to elective offices and positions'), and Art 4 (directing that '[p]olitical parties shall contribute to the implementation of the principle [of parity] as provided by statute', subsequently clarified by Law No 2000-403 of June 6, 2000, Journal Officiel de la République Française (Official Gazette of France), June 7, 2000, at 8560, specifying the conditions under which it applies).

[78] See Drude Dahlerup and Lenita Freidenvall, 'Gender Quotas in Politics—A Constitutional Challenge' in Williams (n 36), 29–52.

[79] See eg Constitution of the Islamic Republic of Afghanistan, Art 84(3); Constitution of the People's Republic of Bangladesh, Art 65(3); Constitution of the Central African Republic, Art 74; Constitution of India, Art 243D(3).

[80] See Jacqueline Peschard, 'An Overview of Quota Systems in Latin America' in *The Implementation of Quotas: Latin American Experiences—Workshop Report, Lima Peru, February 23–24, 2003* (2003), 22, available at <http://www.idea.int/publications/wip/upload/peschard-Latin%20America-feb03.pdf>.

[81] Dahlerup and Freidenvall (n 78), 36. Most require equality on party lists, or in primaries. See ibid 40–4 (comparing quota systems of Argentina, Costa Rica, and France, which are legislated, and Rwanda, exemplifying the alternative of reserved seats for women, elected from among an all-female slate of candidates by an electoral college consisting of local councils and women's organizations). Crucially, the constitutional mandate that women occupy at least 30 percent of posts in decision-making organs did not become a ceiling. More than 30 percent of those elected in 2003 and 2008 were women—the actual figure being 56.3 percent, the highest in the world. Ibid 49. See also Susan H. Williams, 'Equality, Representation, and Challenge to Hierarchy: Justifying Electoral Quotas for Women' in Williams (n 36), 53–72.

[82] See Noelle Lenoir, 'The Representation of Women in Politics; From Quotas to Parity in Elections' (2001) 50 *International and Comparative Law Quarterly* 219.

[83] The 73rd and 74th Constitutional Amendment Acts 1992 in India reserved 33 percent of local election seats for women. Their impact is considered in Niraja Gopal Jayal, 'Gender and Decentralisation', Background paper commissioned by the United Nations Development Programme for Discussion Paper Series 1, Decentralisation in India: Challenges and Opportunities, 2000, 30; Asmita Resource Centre for Women, 'South India' in Yasmin Tambiah (ed), *Women and Governance in South Asia: Re-Imagining the State* (2002), 362.

Bangladesh at the national level.[84] Women may not represent women's interests, or always bring women's experiences to the fore in public conversations affecting them as such, and men may do so, although in governments, in which men have overwhelmingly predominated, they largely have not. Women's movement actors have frequently been found to represent women's interests, promoting women's political participation, particularly in policy processes and debates on sexual violence, enhancing policy outcomes across national settings.[85]

In conceptual parallel, a further example on the coercion/consent dimension of gender principle can be found in the laws of sexual assault. Under them, women are conventionally presumed to consent to acts imposed upon them under conditions of sex inequality, a form of coercion that not recognized by laws of sexual assault, which itself is frequently ringed with constitutional support for the rights of criminal defendants. Much as women are deemed to consent to the state in which they live, hence its entire constitutional framework, whether or not such consent was ever given or is meaningful, they are deemed to consent to sexual relations with men, despite undisputed conditions of gender inequality that frequently give them little real choice and can disempower them from effectively declining. The same dominant social and cultural gender norms widely animate the rules, including constitutional ones, that shape legal accountability for gender crimes.

Sex crimes have not historically been understood as gender-based at all, hence are not yet generally seen to raise principled gender questions on the constitutional plane. Developments in international law, particularly the law of war and international humanitarian law,[86] have increasingly grasped sex crimes as gendered, encouraging the complementary implementation of this concept in national constitutional orders. In the absence of this perspective, prohibitions on gender crime, for example sexual assault or domestic battering, are not typically constitutionally entrenched, while strong procedural rights of accused perpetrators of such crimes often are. Rights of accused victimizers that may be backed up by constitutions include due process rights—full answer and defense, right of confrontation, right to fair trial—the presumption of innocence, freedom of expression, and evidentiary concepts of relevance. In an exceptional constitutional balance yet to register on the realities in South Africa, the Constitutional Court has decisively recognized the rights of women to the enforcement of laws against gender-based violence, in one instance allowing a woman to sue the police and prosecutor for failing to comply with a legal duty to prevent a man, previously convicted of rape and on trial for further related offences, from harming her.[87] Elsewhere, the pattern is typically one of constitutional rights that are designed to be used primarily for those in circumstances in which men predominate (although of course the text does not say so) as against an absence of countervailing rights for those who are victimized based on their gender, predominantly women. These procedural rights are not considered gendered, despite operating to the systematic disadvantage of (mainly but not exclusively) women who are victimized by

[84] See Yasmin Tambiah, 'The Impact of Gender Inequality on Governance' in Nussbaum et al (n 19), 77.

[85] See S. Laurel Weldon, 'Beyond Bodies: Institutional Sources of Representation for Women in Democratic Policymaking' (2002) 64 *Journal of Politics* 1153; S. Laurel Weldon, *Protest, Policy, and the Problem of Violence Against Women: A Cross National Comparison* (2002) (addressing sexual violence policy outcomes in 36 countries).

[86] See eg Rome Statute of the International Criminal Court, July 17, 1998, 2187 UNTS 90, Art 7(1)(g)–(h) (enumerating as crimes against humanity, 'Rape, sexual slavery, enforced prostitution, forced pregnancy, enforced sterilization, or any other form of sexual violence of comparable gravity' and 'Persecution', respectively); Art 8(e)(vi) (establishing as war crimes 'rape, sexual slavery, enforced prostitution, forced pregnancy, as defined in article 7, paragraph 2(f), enforced sterilization, and any other form of sexual violence also constituting a serious violation of article 3 common to the four Geneva Conventions').

[87] *Carmichele v Minister of Safety and Security*, 2001 (4) SA 038 (CC).

gender crime, seldom providing either procedural or substantive rights needed by the victims of gender crimes. Constitutional law, through its rules and lack of rules, including its tacit one-sided entrenchment of rights for perpetrators but few to none for victims, thus effectively renders coercion consent, participating in widespread impunity for gender crime and contributing to the normalization of violence against women.

3. Public and Private

The distinction between public and private, a third principled dimension of gender under constitutional law, has many layers.[88] For purposes of comparing constitutions on a gendered plane, beyond being a feature of positive law, this distinction has a structural feature.[89] The public has traditionally been gendered masculine, conceived as superior and dominant and external, and thought associated with and appropriate for men. The private is gendered feminine, considered subordinate and inferior and internal compared with the public, and is associated with and considered the sphere for women. But it is in private where men are, by virtue of exemption from public intervention even as the public orders its relations, sovereign. The sphere called private has been extensively found to be a (perhaps the) crucible of gender inequality, notably of the patriarchal family, labor stratification and the feminization of poverty, denial of reproductive control, and male dominant stereotypical sexual practices and rape ringed with rape myths rationalized as love or culture.[90] Institutionally, public/private distinctions have functioned to justify limits on constitutional intervention, itself considered public, into settings imagined as private that are customarily ruled by gender hierarchy: the family, the marketplace, reproduction, and sexual relations. This is not to say that these sites are not constitutionally shaped. Rather, it is gender *equality* rules, suddenly considered public, that are often held inapt for them, even as the same constitutions may impose gender inequality in the same spheres without objections of intrusiveness.

One form the supposed bipolarity between public and private has taken is the standard distinction between horizontal and vertical rights in constitutions. In many constitutions, rights, including equality rights, are confined to the vertical, meaning they are guaranteed between the individual, regarded as private, and the state, regarded as public. In law, the line is frequently doctrinally guarded under some version of the rubric of 'state action', as illustrated by the United States and constitutions so patterned. In such systems, horizontal relations between people and other people—civil society is regarded as the private here—a key site of gender hierarchy, cannot be directly reached by constitutions, as they are, for example, in contemporary South Africa, where 'no person may unfairly discriminate directly or indirectly against anyone on one or more grounds, including...gender, sex...'.[91] Restricting assertable rights to a narrow concept of state action can render them especially superficial where gender, an inequality across society as well as between the government and the people, is concerned.

Federalism by design draws public/private jurisdictional lines to shield subnational units from intervention by external central authority. As a consequence, the more federated the

[88] For further discussion that includes a gendered dimension, see Frank Michelman in Chapter 14 of this volume. Professor Michelman's 'ghost' animating the public/private distinction, seen through the analysis of the present chapter, would be gendered male.

[89] A lucid summary of the philosophical foundations of this concept in this context, as it has been criticized from a gendered perspective, can be found in Martha Nussbaum, 'Gender and Governance: An Introduction' in Nussbaum et al (n 19), 5–15.

[90] See sources and analysis in MacKinnon (n 49), ch 7, 9.

[91] Constitution of the Republic of South Africa, s 9(4).

system is, the less reach constitutional gender equality guarantees may have. Federalism as a way of keeping women down and out further functions through a failure to see the gender dimensions of, for example, family law, due in substantial part to federal structures that have deemed the family, read private, unsusceptible to constitutional equality standards, read public. This framework remains despite the fact that family law disputes are typically resolved in courts and under laws, neither of which are actually private, often with systematically gender unequal results. Whole separate regimes for family law jurisdictionally permit implementation of legal systems ungoverned by equality rules to the systematic disadvantage of women as a sex.

Although the relation between devolved power and women's status has not been conclusively resolved empirically, locating power in smaller units does not seem to increase women's power in those units.[92] This hypothesis finds support, again, in the United States, where federalism as a constitutional interpretation has waxed and waned over time, recently being deployed at its zenith to invalidate the national anti-sex-discrimination Violence Against Women Act, passed because states' approaches to the named problem have been so demonstrably ineffectual.[93] A similar effect can be observed in the impact of international law, seen as the more centralized public system, on constitutional systems in national units, read as the smaller private ones.[94] Arguably, the weaker the public-private distinction, through the stronger embodiment of international gender equality norms in a constitutional structure, as in an exemplary manner in Costa Rica,[95] the more favorable constitutional developments will be to addressing gender crime and other violations that are shielded from accountability in what is euphemized as the private.

4. Morality and Politics

A fourth analytic dimension through which the role of gender in constitutional law can be analyzed revolves around a distinction between morality and power. In the sense used here,

[92] Some scholars have concluded that the subnational representation of women is not influenced by a state's degree of federalism. See Richard Vengroff, Zsolt Nyiri, and Melissa Fugiero, 'Electoral Systems and Gender Representation in Sub-National Legislatures: Is There a National-Sub-National Gender Gap?' (2003) 56 *Political Research Quarterly* 171. Discussions of the Australian setting can be found in Irving (n 2), 65–89, and Karpin and O'Connell, 'Speaking into a Silence' in Baines and Rubio-Marin (n 19), 22–47.

[93] See *United States v Morrison* 529 US 598 (2000); Catharine A. MacKinnon, 'Disputing Male Sovereignty: On *United States v Morrison*' (2001) 114 *Harvard Law Review* 135. The division of governmental authority among federal, state, and municipal levels was also used to partly explain Mexico's failure to respond effectively to the mass rape and murder of women in Ciudad Juárez, under international rubrics. See Committee on the Elimination of Discrimination against Women, 'Report on Mexico Produced by the Committee on the Elimination of Discrimination against Women under Article 8 of the Optional Protocol to the Convention, and Reply from the Government of Mexico', UN Doc CEDAW/C/2005/OP.8/MEXICO (January 27, 2005), available at <http://www.un.org/womenwatch/daw/cedaw/cedaw32/CEDAW-C-2005-OP.8-MEXICO-E.pdf>.

[94] For illumination, see Hilary Charlesworth and Christine Chinkin, *The Boundaries of International Law: A Feminist Analysis* (2000). The jurisdictional structure of international law draws its own public–private lines, notably between state sovereignty and transnational guarantees. But international law also cuts across many boundaries between public and private, for instance in the domains of human rights and humanitarian law, supporting social and economic rights, including those affecting gender status, regardless of sphere, and the gender-based rights of victims of intimate violence in recognized conflicts.

[95] The Constitutional Chamber of the Supreme Court has interpreted Art 7 of the Constitution as incorporating and granting supra-constitutional status to human rights conventions that Costa Rica has ratified, making them self-executing. A 1993 opinion held that human rights instruments 'have not only a value similar to the Constitution, but to the extent that they grant greater rights or guarantees to the people, they prevail over the Constitution'. Voto No 5759–93. See Facio, Sandova, and Morgan (n 19), 99.

morality concerns questions of value, judgments of right and wrong, good and evil, while power concerns questions of fact, distributions of status, rank, and social hierarchy that operate as the political domain. Gendered questions posed by culture and religion especially, often affecting issues of family and sexual relations, typically present themselves in constitutional discourse as matters of morality: culturally relative, value-based, open to differing judgments, demanding tolerance. As often with the dimensions discussed, these cultural or religious concepts—for instance, as applied to the law and policy of the family or sexual assault—may frequently serve as guises for gendered power differentials and their exercise, as evidenced by their deeply unequal gendered consequences. Again, the role of international law in the constitutional regime can be decisive in countering this tendency, as international law does not permit custom or religion to override human rights, including gender-based ones.

Customary law is often couched in and defended as enunciating moral or traditional values while at the same time elevating women over men in value or resources, constraining women's life chances in ways that reinforce their relative powerlessness or inferiority on the basis of their sex.[96] Constitutions may openly structure such questions outside their purview, as to some extent in India, where issues of family law are ceded largely (but not exclusively) to religions courts,[97] or in Zimbabwe, where customary law, with unequal proscriptions for women and men in families, sits side by side with equality in the Constitution, no priority constitutionally prescribed for either over the other.[98] A constitutional collision between gender equality norms on the one hand and traditional views of custom in family relations on the other is particularly visible where polygyny is permitted by customary law, 'creat[ing] a situation whereby all bar the husband/father are the losers'.[99] South Africa constitutionally recognizes cultural rights while disallowing them to limit the expression of other rights, seeking harmonization, relying on the resolution of this complex tension case by case.[100]

Frequently, even typically, discussions of constitutional rights that are gender-based in reality present themselves as moral when they are, in fact, political, obscuring the exercise of power behind a discourse of morality. Protectionist maternalist guarantees for certain classes of women in constitutions, including pregnant women or nursing mothers that likely derive from pro-natalist religious culture, could be considered moral laws in this sense, rather than failed equality laws.[101] These provisions often appear in the form of constitutional support for

[96] For discussion, with varying emphases, see eg Irving (n 2), 236–9; Jewel Amoah, 'Watch GRACE Grow: African Customary Law and Constitutional Law in the Equality Garden' in Baines, Barak-Erez, and Kahana (n 15); and Chuma Himonga, 'Constitutional Rights of Women under Customary Law in Southern Africa: Dominant Interventions and "Old Pathways"' in ibid.

[97] For one analysis and relevant citations, see Catharine A. MacKinnon, 'Sex Equality Under the Constitution of India: Problems, Prospects, and "Personal Laws"' in MacKinnon (n 14), 120–38.

[98] See Constitution of Zimbabwe, ss 23(3)(b), 89.

[99] Fareda Banda, 'Between a Rock and a Hard Place: Courts and Customary Law in Zimbabwe' in Andrew Bainham (ed), *The International Survey of Family Law* (2002), 471, 485. In a useful framework, Professor Fareda Banda identifies three constitutional models on the matter of sex equality and customary law: strong cultural relativism, as in Zimbabwe, allowing customary law to exist unfettered by equality provisions; weak cultural relativism, as in Tanzania, which recognizes both without elevating one over the other; and the universalist position, as in South Africa, making both customary law and a right to culture subject to equality standards. See Fareda Banda, *Women, Law, and Human Rights: An African Perspective* (2005), 34.

[100] Constitution of the Republic of South Africa, ss 30, 31.

[101] These laws are especially prevalent in the constitutions of Latin America. See eg Constitution of the Plurinational State of Bolivia, Art 45(V) ('Women have the right to safe maternity with an intercultural practice and vision; they shall enjoy the special assistance and protection of the State during pregnancy and birth and in the prenatal and postnatal periods') even as the criminalization of abortion, which endangers

protective labor laws, quite common in Latin America, or as clauses exempting women from compulsory military service or allowing women voluntary military service where it is compulsory for men.[102] Even Germany, ordinarily alert to gender-inegalitarian assumptions, provides in its constitution that while women aged 18–55 may be called upon for service in emergencies, they may '[u]nder no circumstances... be required to render service involving the use of arms'.[103] The civilian consequences of training only men in the use of weapons while women are officially disarmed, together with the discrimination against men entailed in requiring that only they risk injury and loss of life in military service, half of whom would not be in this dangerous position were the requirement gender neutral, appears to be unnoticed. Instead, morality is interwoven into the interpretation of constitutional rubrics as if gender equality is not involved, as is the case with substantive due process rubrics in the United States. One result is that issues such as abortion, for example, are customarily discussed and litigated as moral issues rather than as posing the sex inequality considerations that make it a gender question legally and socially.

One consequence of the absence of women's equal participation in framing constitutions and shaping constitutional interpretive traditions is that constitutions can institutionalize, without any need to mention gender, the power of men over women in the form of entrenched rights, appearing only to make gender neutral value choices. Combined with the absence of countervailing sex equality rights, the lack of gendered flags may make law appear free of gender bias—hence legitimate—when it is hardly gender neutral. The law of sexual assault typically illustrates. Interpreting freedom of speech or expression to support the pornography industry as a constitutional right in the face of uncontested evidence of its sex-unequal effects is a further contested example, ruled on for women's equality in Canada, for the pornographers in the United States.[104] The presentation of the issue as one of morality (is pornography good or evil?), then of a conflict of rights (speech or equality?) obscures the division of power between women and men under two layers of constitutional discourse, one that can be stacked against a gender equality resolution. When constitutional rights are extended without considering their substantive effect on gender inequality,[105] and socially embedded throughout society to reinforce male supremacy, constituting groups with power do not need to make gender visible on the face of a constitutional text or decision to establish and maintain hegemony through it.

pregnant women, often fatally, remains. Protective laws have even survived communism. See eg Constitution of the Republic of Cuba, Art 44 (guaranteeing 'to the working woman paid leave for maternity before and after childbirth'); see also Constitution of the Democratic Republic of the Congo, Art 128(10) (guaranteeing leave before and after childbirth without wage loss, rest periods during nursing, and job security to pregnant women).

[102] Brazil, for instance, exempts women from compulsory military service. See Constitution of the Federative Republic of Brazil, Art 143(21). Examples of protective laws for women at work include Political Constitution of the Republic of Costa Rica, Art 71 ('The laws shall provide special protection to women and minors in their work'); Political Constitution of Colombia, Art 43 (granting special assistance to and protection of women during pregnancy and after delivery, including food subsidies if needed, and especially when head of household); Constitution of the Republic of Moldova, Art 43(2) (extending state protection to 'working conditions for women and young people'); and Constitution of the Republic of El Salvador, further pairing women with children, Art 38 ('Unhealthy or dangerous work is prohibited for persons under eighteen years of age and for women').

[103] Basic Law, Art 12a(4) (Germany). Denmark provides 'every male person able to bear arms' shall contribute to that national defense under statutory rules. Constitutional Act of Denmark, s 81.

[104] Compare *American Booksellers Ass'n Inc v Hudnut*, 771 F2d 323 (7th Cir 1985), with *R v Butler* [1992] 1 SCR 452.

[105] For discussion of the meaning of substantive equality, see Catharine A. MacKinnon, 'Substantive Equality' (2011) 96 *Minnesota Law Review* 1.

Recognitions of the need to equalize the sexes on the basis of gender are as pervasive in constitutions as gender inequality is commonplace in social life. The reasons why, and the way forward, may be found transnationally, if anywhere.

Bibliography

Nawal Ammar, 'Arab Women in their States' Constitutions' (2004) 4 *International Journal of Comparative Criminology* 196

Beverley Baines, Daphne Barak-Erez, and Tsvi Kahana (eds), *Feminist Constitutionalism: Global Perspectives* (2012)

Beverley Baines and Ruth Rubio-Marin (eds), *The Gender of Constitutional Jurisprudence* (2005)

Alexandra Dobrowolsky and Vivien Hart (eds), *Women Making Constitutions: New Politics and Comparative Perspectives* (2003)

Helen Irving, *Gender and the Constitution: Equity and Agency in Comparative Constitutional Design* (2008)

Priscilla A. Lambert and Druscilla L. Scribner, 'A Politics of Difference versus a Politics of Equality: Do Constitutions Matter?' (2009) 41 *Comparative Politics* 337

Laura E. Lucas, 'Does Gender Specificity in Constitutions Matter?' (2009) 20 *Duke Journal of Comparative and International Law* 133

Dorothy McBride Stetson and Amy G. Mazur (eds), *Comparative State Feminism* (1995)

Eileen McDonagh, 'Political Citizenship and Democratization: The Gender Paradox' (2002) 96 *American Political Science Review* 535

Paula A. Monopoli, 'Gender and Constitutional Design' (2006) 115 *Yale Law Journal* 2643

Martha Nussbaum et al, *Essays on Gender and Governance* (2003)

Joyce Outshoorn and Johanna Kantola (eds), *Changing State Feminism: Just Debate and Gender Justice in the Public Sphere* (2007)

Ann Peters, *Women, Quotas, and Constitutions: A Comparative Study of American, German, EC, and International Law* (1999)

Ruth Rubio-Marin and Martha I. Morgan, 'Constitutional Domestication of International Gender Norms: Categorizations, Illustrations, and Reflections from the Nearside of the Bridge' in Karen Knop (ed), *Gender and Human Rights* (2004)

Druscilla Scribner and Priscilla A. Lambert, 'Constitutionalizing Difference: A Comparative Analysis of Gender Provisions in Botswana and South Africa' (2010) 6 *Politics & Gender* 37

Beth A. Simmons, *Mobilizing for Human Rights: International Law in Domestic Politics* (2009)

Denise M. Walsh, *Women's Rights in Democratizing States* (2011)

S. Laurel Weldon, *Protest, Policy, and the Problem of Violence Against Women: A Cross National Comparison* (2002)

Susan H. Williams (ed), *Constituting Equality: Gender Equality and Comparative Constitutional Law* (2009)

PART III

PROCESS

CHAPTER 20

CONSTITUTION-MAKING: PROCESS AND SUBSTANCE

CLAUDE KLEIN AND ANDRÁS SAJÓ

Jerusalem and Strasbourg

I. Introduction

It was part of the foundational myth of ancient constitutions that they were given by a wise man-legislator, like Lycurgus in the case of Sparta, worthy of hero worship by posterity. Though these ancient constitutions were often subject to fundamental changes, in principle they were supposed to be perpetual, as in the case of Sparta thanks to an oath taken by the people never to break with the system.

The future framers of modern constitutions were confronted with a tradition of immutable, tradition-sanctioned constitutions and, many among them, have gradually accepted the rationalistic approach of enlightenment: constitutions can be designed and perhaps even crafted, *more geometrico*. Both the American Framers and the French revolutionaries alike, thought that the model constitutions of ancient liberty were based on public participation, the legitimate authority of the people was at work behind the act of creation by wise man. People had to consent at least, if not deliberate.[1] However, even within this understanding a fundamental difficulty continued to haunt the founders:

> Is it not a little remarkable that in every case reported by ancient history, in which government has been established with deliberation and consent, the task of framing it has not been committed to an assembly of men, but has been performed by some individual citizen of preeminent wisdom and approved integrity.[2]

Making a constitution is not a matter of pure engineering design. Whatever the dictates of wisdom and prudence would be, the process of making and the resulting constitution are at the mercy of historical contingencies. Constitution-making is 'a pre-eminently political act'.[3] 'It is a decision-making process carried out by political actors, responsible for selecting, enforcing, implementing, and evaluating societal choices; and it is shaped by the socio-political order in which it takes place and, in turn, it strongly influences that order.'[4] The participants are aware that they are involved in 'higher law-making'[5] and this creates special expectations, roles, and rules. Constitution-makers may rise above ordinary attitudes of 'business as usual' and are capable of adapting non-parochial, long-term perspectives. The constitutional enthusiasm of the constitutional moment may have such impact, or it may not. The great pages of the history of constitution-making are full of human pettiness and, increasingly, institutional self-interest. Nevertheless, trial and error notwithstanding, through short-sightedness and egotism, certain regularities with normative consequences have emerged that characterize modern constitution-making.

Originally, it was not obvious that constitutions can be made by deliberate human choice and design. The idea of *making* (new) constitutions has become a fashionable activity only since the eighteenth century, at least in some countries like France, Germany, as well as in a few others. For example, France has known more than ten constitutions in 200 years. (The exact number is unclear since some constitutions are not considered by all historians and experts as valid).[6] While constitutions were designed to withstand time and change, only a few countries, in particular the US, have been able to stay with the same basic constitu-

[1] 'What degree of agency these reputed lawgivers might have in their respective establishments, or how far they might be clothed with the legitimate authority of the people, cannot in every instance be ascertained': James Madison, 'The Same Subject Continued, and the Incoherence of the Objections to the New Plan Explosed' (1788) *The Federalist Papers*, no 38.

[2] Ibid.

[3] Daniel Elazar, 'Constitution-Making: the Pre-eminently Political Act' in Keith G. Banting and Richard Simeon (eds), *Redesigning the State: The Politics of Constitutional Change in Industrial Nations* (1985), 232–48.

[4] Miriam Kornblith, 'The Politics of Constitution-Making: Constitutions and Democracy in Venezuela' (1991) 23 *Journal of Latin American Studies* 64, 61–89, referring to the classic political science positions of William H. Riker and Peter C. Ordeshook, *An Introduction to Positive Political Theory* (1973), 1–7.

[5] Bruce Ackerman, *We the People: Foundations* (1991), 266–94.

[6] One could argue that constitutional stability is the exception and not the rule, notwithstanding the pre-commitment principle that underlies all constitutions. Eg, Venezuela had 26 constitutions from its original Bolivarian one of 1811 until the current 1999 constitution. See further, Zachary Elkins, Tom Ginsburg, and James Melton, *The Endurance of National Constitutions* (2009).

tional document for over 200 years.[7] But such perpetuity might be misleading: while constitutions may formally remain the same, it is possible that through amendments the constitution becomes fundamentally different from the one which remains in formal existence, raising the issue of fundamental change of the constitution without making a formally new constitution.[8]

Making constitutions appears as a process that follows certain rules (and) or rites which have been progressively established. How do we make constitutions? Are there neatly distinct models of constitution-making? What are the grounds for choosing one or another model? What makes a constitution-making process legitimate?

The stability of the constitution remains a characteristic aspiration: drafters intend to set values and institutions for generations to come. How to achieve stability (how to protect the constitution including against fundamental changes that go against its essence) and how to grant sufficient flexibility by allowing reasonable accommodation to emerging changes.

This chapter considers the procedural and resulting legitimacy issues of constitution-making and fundamental constitutional amendment. (Fundamental amendments mean an essential change that would, in theory, require higher lawmaking in the sense that not only special procedural requirements are to be met (eg super-majority) but a special commitment, a conscious and specifically legitimated effort that the textual change makes a break with past fundamental values.) These procedures are partly related to the different historical scenarios and substantive (material) factors that give rise to e-constitutions.[9] We will consider only those political and economic factors which contribute to specific constitution-making features. In this regard, revolutions, regime change, and state-building are particularly relevant. In the case of revolutions there is a deliberate departure from, a rupture with, the existing constitution and the processes of legal and therefore legitimate change. This raises a fundamental issue of legitimacy: What gives the right (authority) to enact a new constitution? In this chapter we refer to the process that is not based on pre-existing rules of procedure as one of creation and the related constitution-making is called creation *ex nihilo* (see Chapter 45). In the case of regime change or reform the procedural modalities of the existing constitution might be observed.

The constitution is made by a pre-constitutional or extra-constitutional entity (power) and constitution-making includes the self-constitution of the power that creates it. In the situation of creating the constitution *ex nihilo* the constitution emerges from a legal void. *Ex nihilo* constitution-making can be revolutionary or state-creating (where there is no previous state

[7] The Norwegian Constitution is technically the 1814 Constitution though fundamentally amended over the decades and the Belgian Constitution formally dates from 1831. Austria has technically had the same constitution since 1920, since the first constitution was re-enacted in 1945, though with a great number of amendments: 75 between 1929 and 1999.

[8] See eg Bruce Ackerman's theory of higher order lawmaking. Ibid 266–94.

[9] Jon Elster has listed the following political and economic grounds for making a constitution: social and economic crisis, as in the making of the US Constitution of 1787 or the French Constitution of 1791; revolution, as in the making of the 1830 Charter in France or the French and German 1848 Constitutions; regime collapse, as in the making of the new constitutions in Southern Europe in the mid-1970s and in Eastern Europe in the early 1990s; fear of regime collapse, as in the making of the French Constitution of 1958, which was imposed by de Gaulle under the shadow of a military rebellion; defeat in war, as in Germany after the First and Second World Wars, or in Italy and Japan after the Second World War; reconstruction after war, as in France in 1946; the creation of a new state, as in Poland and Czechoslovakia after the First World War (or the Reconstruction of the South after the American Civil War); liberation from colonial rule, as in the United States after 1776 and in many third world countries after 1945: Jon Elster, 'Forces and Mechanisms in the Constitution Making Process' (1995) 45 *Duke Law Journal* 364.

whose constitution could have been considered and the constituent is pre-constitutional).[10] In the revolutionary version of *ex nihilo* constitution-making the constitution in force is disregarded, while in the nation-state-building version there is allegedly no previous constitution to be disregarded (although very often the secession (the declaration of independence) is also based on disregard of the applicable constitutional arrangement).[11]

In the transition model, the rules of creation are determined in the very constitution that is to be replaced.[12] Besides those two main models there are special situations where sovereign decisions do not rest fully with the constitution-makers, like in post-war and de-colonization situations where foreign powers or former colonial masters had considerable influence on the process and the content, and in post-conflict situations in which the international community is active.[13]

II. Constituent Power and the Legitimacy of Constitution-Making

In the European (continental) theory the process of constitution-making has traditionally been ascribed to a power defined as 'constituent power', mostly known through its French qualification '*pouvoir constituant*',[14] as opposed to *pouvoir constitué* (constituted power, for example the existing legislation). In this chapter we will deal only briefly with that important theoretical quasi-philosophical question: What is the constituent power? Is it a legal power?

A legal theory of 'constituent power' basically assumes that it is a legal power, which implies that the undoing power has a legal character. Olivier Beaud argues that before starting the (new) constituent process another constitution-making moment must be declared.[15] This

[10] The actual division is not so clear-cut. Post-colonial constitutions were created under the umbrella of the colonial power, or even by the colonial power. In the latter case in some instances the element of rupture disappears as the creation is carried out under the mandate of the constitution of the colonial power. This was clearly the case with Canada and the Austro-Hungarian monarchy in 1867, and to a much lesser extent with India beginning in 1946.

[11] The two versions are not always clearly distinguishable, while constitutional restoration brings a paradox. Here a self-proclaimed body, after having obtained power through force, declares the return to a previous constitution often submitting the act of return to a referendum. While the idea of restoration as a constitutional concept originates in the rule of Louis XVIII, the monarchy could not return to the pre-revolutionary status quo. There are, however, better contemporary examples of restoration. After free elections in 1990, Latvia's Parliament (the majority) declared independence and restored the 1922 Constitution. These measures were reaffirmed by a referendum a year later.

[12] See Michel Rosenfeld, *The Identity of the Constitutional Subject* (2010), 185–210.

[13] Making a constitution for the European Union presents special problems related to supranationalism. See Martin Loughlin and Neil Walker (eds), *The Paradox of Constitutionalism: Constituent Power and Constitutional Form* (2007), ch III, 209–338. Ulrich K. Preuss claims a *sui generis* situation: Ulrich K. Preuss, 'Is There a Constituent Power in the European Union' in Oliver Cayla and Pasquale Pasquino (eds), *Le pouvoir constituant et l'Europe* (2011), 75.

[14] The distinction is attributable to Abbé de Sieyès. The US doctrine would at times use the term 'framing power' as opposed to the 'amending power' stemming from the constitution. In the British tradition, it is common to use the literal translation 'constituent' power. Note that Albert V. Dicey in his *Introduction to the Study of the Law of the Constitution* (1965) describes quite coherently and accurately the constitutional process in 'written constitutions' but never refers to a 'constituent power', preferring to use the distinction between 'flexible' and 'rigid' constitutions. The German tradition, of course, knows the concept very well: it is rendered by the complex wording '*verfassungsgebende Gewalt*'. See further, Claude Klein, *Théorie et pratique du pouvoir constituant* (1996).

[15] Olivier Beaud, *La puissance de l'Etat* (1994).

approach is also heavily reliant on the Schmittian view, known as 'decisionist theory'.[16] The *pre-constituent* decisions include also the *de-constituent* decision, that is, the decision to abolish the former constitutional order and the decision to create a new one.[17] This 'de-constituent' phase of the entire process by which the pre- existing constitutional order is abolished is generally taken with solemnity, since the new regime wants to establish its new legitimacy with its new ideological direction. Beaud distinguishes between the decision of 'pre-constituent initiative' and the decision 'attributing the constituent power'.

In the cases where the decision is a 'de-constituent' decision, that is, when the former constitutional order is abolished, the decision itself is a revolutionary one, made by a primary constitution-maker, a *gouvernement de fait*.[18] The very first establishing or empowering norm that sets into motion the constitutional decoupling is very often a factual one.[19] The style would generally be that of 'ordinance' (eg, a decree or even proclamation of the provisional government) for the election of a constituent assembly, which supposes also the answer to the question: Who is entitled to elect and the method of the election (representation) to the Assembly? However, the primary constitution-maker has to take into consideration the existing structures (local or territorial) and constituencies that they trust. Moreover, the constitution-maker has to respect prevailing ideologies about the subject of the constitution and allow for participation of those whose input will make the constitution legitimate, efficient, and accepted. These matters might have decisive effects on the composition of the Assembly and hence on the outcome.

In the case of *ex nihilo* constitution-making, the first act consists in the (auto) determination of the entity that will constitute the constituents. This must be an act of self-affirmation by definition. This is, quite often, a matter of the decision of a small elite that relies on force and violence. Such self-constitution is revolutionary (and it is very often part of a social revolution). It is an act of denial of the previous regime (the existing constitutional setting); it is denied that the existing structures can determine who can decide who is included in the constituent people. The primary constituting body may itself undertake constitution-writing, as is the case with military juntas that proclaim the constitution (*pronunciamiento*). More often, the primary constituting body introduces an interim skeleton set of rules of government (including an interim skeleton constitution) and calls at the same time for another body to draft and eventually adopt a constitution. In the making of constitutions that satisfy the criteria of constitutionalism and/or democracy, the preferred (and successful) body is an elected (or at least delegated) constituent body, a constituent assembly.

Historically constituent assemblies were often delegates of existing territorial or other entities (as it was the case in 1789 in France, and in 1830 in Belgium where provincial governments were asked by the interim government to send delegates).

As always, the empirical processes on setting up the constituent body are odd mixtures: in 1789 the representatives were elected according to the (somewhat obscure) rules existing in the monarchy, but they then undertook an act of auto-proclamation to constitute themselves

[16] Roughly and concisely, 'decisionism' may be defined as an approach putting the decision-making process by a certain authority at the forefront of the legal analysis thus transcending the legalistic approach.

[17] Ibid 265.

[18] Those are governments without legal basis at their inception, but their power being effective over a period of time and a defined territory.

[19] The question of the lawful or legal character of that initiating step is of course well beyond the scope of this chapter on the process of constitution-making. German authors (mainly the famous Georg Jellinek) have used the following illuminating formula: '*Die Lehre von der normativen Kraft des Faktischen*' (the theory of normative force of the factual). See Andreas Anter (ed), *Die normative Kraft des faktischen: Das Staatsverständniss Georg Jellineks* (2004).

as representatives of the people (though elected by a tiny minority of the people living in France).

Resonating revolutionary democratic ideologies, modern democratic theories relate constituent power to the ultimate source of state power, namely to people.[20] According to Thomas Paine's well-known dictum: 'The constitution of a country is not the act of its government, but of the people constituting a government'.[21] But who is the people? Jennings had already stated (in another sense) that 'people cannot decide until somebody decides who are the people'.[22] It is well known that 95 percent of people living in America were excluded by pre-existing laws from participating in the ratification of the Constitution. The 'People', that is the constituency may change as part of the constitution-making, or perhaps it is the change in the composition of the constituency that drives and dictates the constitution-making. Thus, the French 'people' of 1945 was quite different from the 'people' in 1936 (when the last elections before the Second World War took place): for instance, in 1936 women still did not have the vote in France, whereas 'someone' (de Gaulle) decided in 1945 that women would have the vote. The same is true in regard to Germany (in 1918) and Italy (1946) with the extension of voting rights. Where constitution-making power in the substantive sense pertains to the nation it is possible that people who pertain to the nation on ethnic grounds will be selected and granted voting rights. In practical terms, this means that in the actual determination of the constituent assembly, nationality-based inclusion or exclusion by the initial decision-makers will be significant. The composition and even the form of representation of the peoples behind the constituent assembly might be decisive and are not necessarily subject to the original design. The tragedy of the partition of India in 1947 illustrates this dialectic.[23]

It is believed that the more participatory the constitution-making, the higher its legitimacy and acceptance. But popular participation is often absent or formal, and even where participation has created constitutional enthusiasm this may not result in lasting or widespread acceptance of the constitution, especially where high expectations of empowerment do not materialize. On the other hand, even an imposed constitution may gain acceptance and even legitimacy thanks to its conflict-reducing effects, and in particular if it provides a frame that provides affluence. Participation does not equal consent: acquiescence is the condition that most constitutions may aspire to in society. But for a theory of constitutionalism, it is not the democratic nature of the participation through constituent bodies and referenda that matters, but the lack of unilateral imposition. The principle of public participation in the drafting of the US Constitution was 'that the people should endow the government with a constitution and not vice versa'.[24]

The 'people' is not sufficiently structured to develop a constitution. Nor are empirical people very welcome by the actual constitution-making elite. Moreover, empirically, society is often divided about the constitution, many of them resisting it. Quite often those who oppose it are

[20] Some constitutions originate in interstate treaties. Though even here popular sovereignty might play a primary role in the theory of constituent power, constituent state consent continues to play a role. (See also the need of state ratification in making the US Constitution.) This is certainly an issue in the case of making a European Constitution.

[21] Thomas Paine, *Rights of Man* (1791), 53.

[22] Ivor Jennings, *The Approach to Self Government* (1956), 55.

[23] While the Muslim League under Jinnah asked for two constitution-making bodies, the British colonial authorities opted for one where were members were indirectly elected by the members of the Provisional Legislative Assemblies (a minority of them fully controlled by Muslims). Muslims were in the minority at the Constituent Assembly. Partition was the 'preferred' constitutional arrangement.

[24] Quoted in Hannah Arendt, *On Revolution* (1963), 144.

denied participation in the process. The British loyalists were de facto excluded from participation in the ratification of the US Constitution, or earlier in the process of calling for a state constitution. The standard solution to the problem of the participation of the people is one based on representation: a specifically designated body, elected by the majority will exercise the constitution-making power. This was the idea behind the formulation of Article 3 of the French Declaration: 'The principle of all sovereignty resides essentially in the nation'. People are replaced by the abstraction of the nation to avoid claims of being responsible to a specific electorate's whims. The nation (or even people) is only a point of location. The original word '*principe*' refers to source. To be a source of sovereignty is different from being the sovereign.[25]

In accordance with the concept of representation of this specifically elected body, a constituent assembly is deemed to have the authority and legitimacy to carry out the task (though for practical reasons it often works in small committees).

The understanding of constituent power has a fundamental impact on the constitution-making process. Competing concepts have emerged in the last 250 years as to the nature of this constituent power, with implications for the articulation of the will of the power. Certain practices became accepted as having greater or lesser legitimacy but the constitution-making process remains to some extent a matter of power contingency and these contingencies determine which elements of the toolkit of constitution-making apply.

The ambiguity of constitution-making power emerged most spectacularly in the making of the US Constitution. There is an ongoing debate concerning the democratic credentials of the US Constitution. Madison famously argued:

> the principle of representation was neither unknown to the ancients nor wholly overlooked in their political constitutions. The true distinction between these and the American governments, lies *in the total exclusion of the people, in their collective capacity*, from any share in the *latter*, and not in the *total exclusion of the representatives* of the people from the administration of the *former*. The distinction, however, thus qualified, must be admitted to leave a most advantageous superiority in favor of the United States.[26]

III. Launching Constitutions

Prima facie, a constitutional process is, in the formal sense, no different from any other norm productive process. Producing a constitution starts with an initial decision (known as the 'initiative'): Who decides the initiative and what does it mean? In this respect, some models are apparent. The process goes on with a decision on how to position the process vis-à-vis the existing structure (eg to amend the constitution, or to have a new one according to the existing formalities of constitution-making or disregard the existing patterns) followed by the choice (elections) for the deliberating body or the draft constitution-preparing body (the constituent assembly). The process includes also the working technique of that body (how are the articles of the future constitution prepared?). Lastly, the question of the final decision or approval appears: approval by the body itself or by a referendum (most likely nowadays) a veto right, a review right, a promulgation right, etc.

[25] See Keith M. Baker, 'Constitution' in Francois Furet and Mona Ozouf (eds), *A Critical Dictionary of the French Revolution* (Arthur Goldhammer trans, 1989), 484.

[26] James Madison, 'The Senate (Continued)' (1788) *The Federalist Papers*, no 63. Akhil Reed Amar, *America's Constitution* (2005), 14, argues that this position is not anti-democratic but 'a republican proceduralist pondering how best to structure lawmaking institutions'.

How does it start? Who gives the starting signal leading to a constitutional process, that, to the setting up of a (future) constitution? How is the signal delivered? This is a question of legitimacy: Is it the existing constitution or some other external source to give power and set the force and form of the change? Is the constitution made by a constituent power or by a constituted one?

1. Models of *Ex Nihilo* Creation

(a) *The Revolutionary Version*

The great revolutionary constitutions were established in total rupture with the former constitutional regime.[27] In most modern cases, if not in all, a process establishing a new constitution, starts from a decision to *do*, which, in our view, in turn starts from a decision to *undo*, the previous existing constitutional order. The foundational event of modern constitutionalism, the Philadelphia Convention[28] had already raised the intriguing question of the legality of the Convention in light of the Articles of the Confederation of 1777. The very convening of the convention may be considered as a 'de-constituent' step, on the verge of a legal revolution.[29]

In a legal (technical) sense undoing means that the rules of replacing the constitution are disregarded. Such disregard presupposes that the constitution considers itself (or its essence—see below on amendments) immutable or it requires a special process for it that is then disregarded.[30]

In revolutionary constitution-making, the disregard of the pre-existing constitution-making system means that the body making the new constitution has to constitute itself in this sense. In Locke's natural law right of revolution people retained their right to cancel the implied contract with the king. Following Locke only to some extent the American Declaration of Independence identified sovereignty of the people as the source of the emerging government. The state constitutions which were enacted after 1776 were written texts and were 'the self-conscious expression of a collective people speaking as the sovereign and giving direction to government…'.[31]

The French National Assembly (in 1789), that was convened for a different purpose, proclaimed itself as that constituent assembly. Beaud qualifies that decision as a kind of 'speech act'. Likewise, the Founding Fathers who had a limited mandate to amend the existing Articles of Confederation took upon themselves at least a drafting power and defined the final consti-

[27] Examples include the United States (both in 1776 and mainly in 1787), France in 1789 and during the entire revolutionary episode as well as the Soviet Russia vis-à-vis the czarist regime.

[28] See Max Farrand, *The Framing of the Constitution of the United States* (1937), and of course James Madison, *Notes of Debates in the Federal Convention of 1787* (1987).

[29] We may define a revolution in the legal sense as an amendment to the constitution, disregarding the rules of amendment. This was the case of the Articles of the Confederation.

[30] Such express provision is contained eg in Section 30 of the Constitution of the Argentine Nation:

> The Constitution may be totally or partially amended. The necessity of reform must be declared by Congress with the vote of at least two-thirds of the members; but it shall not be carried out except by an Assembly summoned to that effect.

Article 146 of the German Basic Law allows its demise under non-specific conditions:

> This Basic Law, which since the achievement of the unity and freedom of Germany applies to the entire German people, shall cease to apply on the day on which a constitution freely adopted by the German people takes effect.

[31] Christian G. Fritz, 'Recovering the Lost Worlds of America's Written Constitutions' (2005) 68 *Albany Law Review* 261. See further Gordon S. Wood, *The Creation of the American Republic 1776–1787* (1969).

tuent power in the ratification through the states in popular assemblies. At the convention that was called to create the constitution of the newly independent Belgium in 1830, which was fully aware of the creation rituals that had emerged during the French Revolution, the first sentence uttered was: 'The National Congress constitutes itself in the name of the Belgian people' (not 'nation'!) ('*Le congrès national s'installe au nom du peuple belge*').[32] It is equally telling that ten minutes after the convention was opened the debate concerned the urgency of ratifying the mandates, which was the first act of self-constitution: 'There must be something in existence before creating the standing order.'[33]

According to the democratic-popular theory of constituent power it is the people (perhaps in the exercise of ultimate popular sovereignty) that constitutes the body that determines the text of the constitution. In some instances additional ratification is required. But 'democratic choice is commonly supposed to be a form of popular sovereignty over political results. In any complex, polity, however, this supposition is at best metaphorical, as the large post-war literature on democratic theory suggests.'[34]

i. *The Idea of the Constituent Assembly*

While the French revolutionary approach to the idea of the constitution is often characterized as being fascinated with the constitution as if it were a pudding to be made following a recipe, the oath that constituted the constituent assembly from the delegates of the Third Estate by the end of June 1789 was certainly not premeditated.[35] In the Tennis Court Oath they directed themselves to 'fix [*restore*] the constitution of the realm, carry out regeneration of the public order and maintain the true principles of monarchy'. It took some time to understand that the traditional structure cannot be restored and regeneration means drafting a new constitution *ex nihilo*.

The typical expression of self-assertion at (revolutionary, ie, non-legal) constituent assemblies consists of a reference to the source of all power (people, nation, supreme being). In June 1789, the delegates placed themselves in a constitutional vacuum: the constituent power was perceived by Sieyès as a return to the state of nature. The only source and authority to rely upon, in the logic of Sieyès was the nation as the ultimate political entity. Only with the Declaration and the abolition of feudal privileges did the majority of the Assembly accept that they had to create a constitution. But the idea that they had to give legitimacy to themselves emerged from the very beginning when the Third Estate representatives met in Versailles: they reserved to themselves the right to approve the delegates' mandate.

In the workings of the French Constituent Assembly, trial and error resulted in certain normative expectations about the frames and principles a constituent assembly has to observe. The Constituent Assembly, while acting as an ordinary legislator, at a certain point came to the conclusion that it should cease to operate after the constitution was adopted. Moreover, following Robespierre's motion members of the assembly became ineligible. The emerging doctrine attributed a unique status of incompability to constituent assemblies, granting it a unique mission, including the seldom observed principle that they should not become involved in

[32] Emile Huyttens, *Discussions du Congrès national de Belgique*, vol 1 (1844), 100.

[33] Ibid 102. 'M. le baron de Stassart observe *qu'il faut être quelque chose* avant de faire le règlement'.

[34] Russell Hardin, *Liberalism, Constitutionalism, and Democracy* (2003), 152.

[35] Massachusetts in 1780 had already vindicated and practiced the right to have its own convention acting independently of government (including the elected legislature) to draft a constitution. (See Arendt (n 24), 301.) This model was known in Paris but not followed: the Assembly was a quasi-legislative body called up by the king.

ordinary legislation.[36] *Ex post facto* the involvement of the Assembly in legislation became problematic. The Constituent Assembly has a special popular mandate to make the constitution and other considerations of ordinary politics would undermine this sacred mission. In a way, additional functions result in the confusion of constituent and constituted power.

The original uncertainty in 1789 and the incredible social and political complexity of the Revolution made French constitution-making erratic. The drafting was time and again discontinued in order to solve more pressing political and legislative issues, because of political stalemate or simply because it took time to clarify various new concepts and their implications. In consequence, the drafting lasted more than two years and ended only because the unfortunate escape of the king to Varennes ended in a fiasco and he lost his ability to resist and could not but take the oath on the Constitution on September 14, 1791. The conclusion for the theory of constitution-making was that time limits should be set (limited mandate).

In the 1789–91 period, the powers of the constitution-makers changed continuously with major impacts on the rather irregular procedures. Procedural rules (rules of counting votes, rules on preparing drafts, standing orders) were improvised and even the circle of actors participating in the process changed, including major changes in the role of the king, who lost his veto power regarding the enactment of the constitution.

The use of constituent assemblies as an instrument of *ex nihilo* creation became a type of norm thanks to the authority of the French Revolution.[37] The authority of the French Revolution and the logic of generating power in a political vacuum made it natural after the 1830 Revolution in Belgium to call a National Congress to enact a constitution for the newly independent state.[38] This has to be understood in the context of the alternative that prevailed in early nineteenth-century constitutional monarchies. These constitutions were 'granted' like the granted charters in French constitutional history: this was the case of the two 'granted' Charters in 1815 and in 1830 (*chartes constitutionnelles 'octroyées'*).[39]

The reliance on the technique of the constituent assembly was more or less self-evident in the Latin American liberation/independence context. The use of formative constitution-making through specific constituent assemblies (with Simon Bolivar participating in several projects) created a kind of model or path dependence for future Latin American constitution-making.[40] (The tradition was particularly respected because, like in France, restrictive constitutions were often and typically promulgated as charters dictated by caudillos. These were simply approved by legislation.)

[36] For a contemporary application of the non-eligibility rule see the case of the Constituent Assembly of Colombia in 1991.

[37] Some of these assemblies were called congresses. For an overview see Darrel R. Reid and Patrick Fafard, *Constituent Assemblies: A Comparative Survey* (1991).

[38] Characteristic of the sentiments prevailing when a nation-state creates a revolutionary assembly, the Belgian constituents—with personal memories and affiliations with the French Revolution—considered their assembly an original one, being created by the Belgian nation in a time of trouble without any preliminary rules to rely on: Philippe Raxhon, 'Mémoire de la Révolution française de 1789 et Congrès national belge (1830–31)' (1996) 26 *Revue belge d'histoire contemporaine* 33, 51.

[39] Technically, the Belgian Constitution of 1831 originated in the rejection of a Dutch Constitution that was unilaterally imposed.

[40] Following the liberation wars led by Simon Bolívar, the Congress of Cúcuta was called up with specifically elected representatives. This convention promulgated the Constitution of Cúcuta (unifying various territories of the former Spanish Viceroyalty into the short-lived federation of Gran Colombia on August 30, 1821). The addition of the referendum to the constituent assembly process became increasingly attractive in Latin America too, at least from the 1990s (see, eg, Venezuela, with a strong emphasis on direct popular legitimation).

Beyond theoretical considerations, recourse to the constituent assembly was also dictated by technical constraints: it was nearly impossible in the nineteenth century to rely on plebiscites in large countries. No French constitution was submitted to referendum in 1789–92, in 1793–95, in 1848, or in 1871.[41] This was the basis of the French understanding of 'convention power' where there are no limits to the power of the assembly.

ii. Mixed Constitution-Making in Times of Mass Democracy (the Emergence of the Referendum)

A study of twentieth-century constitution-making indicates that the idea of constituent assemblies has been only partly retained. Here we review the making of a few continental constitutions which were theoretically innovative or politically influential.

Weimar. In the aftermath of defeat in the First World War—in the course of the German 'Revolution' of 1918—on November 9, 1918 the Republic was proclaimed, simply by a declaration of one of the leaders of the socialist party. This founding 'de-constituent' act—by which the old 'Kaiser' regime was abolished—had created a constitutional vacuum which necessitated a new constitution which necessitated a new process. A provisional government of *Volksbeauftragte* (delegates of the people) was established which in turn decided to elect a 'National Assembly', in order to adopt a new constitution for Germany. The elections were quickly organized: as early as January 19, 1919, with the first meeting taking place in Weimar on February 6, 1919. The Constitution of the Weimar Republic was adopted on August 11, 1919.[42] The Constitution was adopted without being presented to a popular referendum. Notwithstanding the special electoral process that satisfied in principle the requirement of popular authorization, the Constitution suffered from a deep lack of legitimacy due to the German defeat.[43]

Transition to the Fourth Republic in France. France emerged victorious from the Second World War in 1945, but the old institutions of the Third Republic had disappeared in 1940, at the moment of the collapse of France and the establishment of the Vichy regime. The theoretical problem was that of the status of the pre-existing structures. The official position of de Gaulle, the head of the provisional government of France, was that Vichy was *nul et non avenu*, that is, had never legally existed.[44] Thus the question was: How would the new institutions be installed or the old institutions reinstalled? The democratic answer was clear: the people itself should decide. Thus, on October 21, 1945, the French people were called to the polls and had to cast three different ballots: the first gave the people the right to decide whether they wanted to abolish the Third Republic initiating a new constitution. The answer was yes by a huge majority. The yes to the second ballot determined the process of writing the new constitution: it authorized a Constituent Assembly (with limited powers[45]) to be elected. The final say had been granted again to the people through a referendum (for the results see below).

[41] See, however, the plebiscite of 1851 to grant constitution-making powers to Louis Napoléon Bonaparte. See also the 1802 plebiscite making Napoléon into a consul for life, and the 1804 plebiscite on the French Empire.

[42] See Ernst Huber, *Deutsche Verfassungsgeschichte seit 1789*, vol 6 (1981), 5–23.

[43] On the various constitutional processes in Germany see Henning von Wedel, *Das Verfahren der demokratischen Verfassunggebung: Dargestellt am Beispiel Deutschlands 1848/49, 1919, 1948/49* (1976).

[44] A position that was hardly tenable: the 'Ordonnance portant rétablissement de la légalité républicaine' (August 9, 1944) declared that the Republic never ceased to exist and that all laws and regulations of the regime are void, but that voidness must be declared *expressis verbis*! In fact, a very small number of such laws with ideological content were formally declared void.

[45] If the people were to answer 'no' to the first question, the elected assembly would have become the legislative assembly in the constitutional framework of the (maintained) Third Republic.

Italy. A comparable process took place in Italy in 1946, though formally within the frame of the pre-existing constitutional setting of the monarchy. The process, however, was initiated in breach of the existing legal system by a decree of the executive,[46] based on an agreement that was reached during the war (*decreto Bonomi*). People were called to choose by referendum between republic and monarchy (12.7 million for the republic and 10.7 million for the monarchy). At the same time, they elected a constituent assembly which subsequently adopted the new constitution by the end of 1947 without referendum.

Democratization in Russia and Romania. Regime change including transition to democracy from totalitarianism (as in the case of Russia in 1993) is also centered on the body or authority that decides on the assembly that will have constituent power. In 1993 President Yeltsin, after receiving confirmation by referendum that expressed confidence in the President, handpicked an assembly to draft a new constitution. The Congress of the People's Deputies (the body with constituent powers) and its Supreme Soviet reserved for itself constitution-making powers relying on the provisions of the constitution in force. After a violent dissolution of the Supreme Soviet, Yeltsin submitted 'his' draft to an 'all-national vote' (a process established by presidential decree).

As in Russia in 1993, in Romania in 1989, following a violent transfer of power a self-proclaimed National Salvation Front Council set the rules of transition to a new constitution. It enacted laws for the election of a bicameral parliament which was called to act as a constituent assembly (sitting in joint session). The Constituent Assembly adopted the text of the constitution which was ratified by referendum at the end of 1991, two years after Ceausescu was summarily executed. The parliament continued to operate.

These variations indicate that the revolutionary element in the process is a matter of degree. The mandate of the constituent body may be self-imposed (France, 1789; America, 1787) or subject to popular authorization. Even where the process begins while the previous constitutional regime is in place (France, 1789; Italy, 1946; France, 1958) the popular or self-promotional mandate means that a rupture with the previous regime and a new source of constitution-making power and legitimacy emerges.

To sum up these developments, the problem of legitimacy of the *ex nihilo* creation—that is, when someone sets into motion an extra-legal process in denial of the existing forms—has attracted increased attention, at least at the beginning of the twentieth century, in order to make the act of creation more credible beyond reference to to the people or the nation. It is for this reason that the very departure from constitution-making rules and from the constitution in force was increasingly subjected to participatory affirmation, or even preliminary popular approval. In Italy, in 1946, the setting up of the constituent assembly was preceded by a referendum on the form of state; in Colombia there were referenda to authorize the President to rely on a constituent assembly.[47] In addition, indirect elements of external support may contribute to the legitimation, as was the case with the referendum initiated to prepare for the impeachment of Yeltsin for his constitution-making and other matters. International recognition of an interim government may have similar effects. Finally, with the increased popularity

[46] In the case of creating the Fifth Republic in France the process of undoing the regime in force for the sake of a new constitution was 'legalized' in the sense that as a first step the then ruling elite accepted the constitutional law of June 3, 1958 which provided for an amendment of the 1946 Constitution according to a new procedure, disregarding the original procedure.

[47] The 1991 constitutional changes in Colombia were adopted by a constituent assembly. This procedure was not foreseen in the Constitution of Colombia, but was called upon and legitimated in two prior referenda.

of the referendum, it has now evolved to corroborate popular support for the assembly, and indirectly for the whole process (beginning in France with the case of making the Constitution of the Fourth Republic).[48]

(b) Nation-State-Building Constitutions

i. State-Building as an Act of National Sovereignty

While the *ex nihilo* creation model assumes that constitution-making is formally defined by a rejection of a pre-existing process and a denial of the legitimacy of pre-existing institutional actors, the making of nation-state-building constitutions is not defined in terms of the denial of an available procedure and underlying authority. Many aspects of the self-constitution and self-referentialism that is so characteristic of revolutions are present here too. The distinction is sometimes purely academic. While revolutionary in substance, the making of the US Constitution in 1787 is also one of nation/state-building. By creating a more integrated government, 'the true objective of the American Constitution was not to limit power but to create more power, actually to establish and duly constitute an entirely new power center ... whose authority was to be exerted over a large, expanding territory.'[49]

As with the case of the original American states, newly created states need a constitution for purposes of self-assertion. The state must affirm itself by granting itself a structure of government. This was the task for Israel in 1948 after the Declaration of Independence, though the constitution-making had to remain unfinished. This was the task of the framing of the constitution for Belgium in 1830–31, of the new states created after the First World War (such as Poland in 1921 or Latvia in 1922[50]) or for Croatia in 1990. Newly formed post-colonial states faced the same problem in the late 1950s and early 1960s: they had to create a government structure.

Although the constitution-making process may rely on revolutionary popular acts of creation, substantively these are different from purely revolutionary constitutions. To the extent the state is based on ethnic homogeneity or the affirmation of a special nationality and its identity with the new state, the constitution will reflect nationalistic aspirations and the constituency (the people entitled to representation) might be ethnically limited.

ii. Constitution-Making as an International Effort

Constitution-making in the absence of full national sovereignty represents special features. Though this may seem an aberration in view of popular theories of constitution-making, it is actually a rather common occurrence in the history of constitution-making and has lasting implications on the constitution. The lack of *de iure* or at least *de facto* sovereignty has an important impact on this procedure.

For present purposes, it is useful to distinguish two main forms of constitution-making without sovereignty. A country may lose its sovereignty because of a war. The occupation forces may determine the process of the restoration of sovereignty, inter alia, by setting the terms of reference and procedure for the new constitution. In this regard the occupying power may not only be the undoer of the previous constitutional system (the power appointing a

[48] Of course, such complicated and staggered processes are not only the result of a need for legitimation; they also reflect political compromises and uncertainties where some of the groups agreeing to the process hope to increase power through the process by mobilization.

[49] Arendt (n 24), 152.

[50] After a war of independence a constituent assembly was called to enact a constitution for the country that had already received international (diplomatic and treaty) recognition of its sovereignty.

new constituent entity) but may also be involved in the actual drafting. This involvement may reach the level of imposition (constitutional *octroi*).[51] The drafting of the Japanese Constitution under the guidance of General MacArthur borders such *octroi*.[52] The German Basic Law of 1949 was created on an Allied initiative as part of the restoration of German state sovereignty, with the Allied forces insisting on certain substantive solutions (eg federalism). The particular features of (West) German constitution-making, including disregard of the then prevailing and established constitution-making wisdom related to constituent power and assembly process, are related to these circumstances. The Basic Law was adopted by a 'parliamentary council', a body of 65 representatives of the local parliaments (of the Länder) called up by the occupation forces. The three Western Military Governors authorized the Germans to draft their constitution in the 'Frankfurt Documents' of July 1, 1948. Hoping for unification with Germans in the Eastern sector, the Germans would have preferred an interim governance document. For this reason, notwithstanding strong American objections, they refused to have a convention and ratification by referendum and submitted to ratification by the local parliaments. It was thus not approved by the people.[53] The absence of a referendum is partly related to the distrust in the institution that originated in Hitler's successful use of the plebiscite with the same population.

Partly related to decolonization and increasingly due to the participation of the international community in the handling of post-conflict situations, an increasing number of contemporary constitutions are drafted under the aegis (or even authority) of international organizations[54] and, in peace processes, with the participation of foreign mediating powers. This is often carried out with de facto power of persuasion, as in the case of the Dayton Agreements which determined the Constitution of Bosnia-Herzegovina, turning it to some extent into an international institutional regime (with powers granted to international civil servants under the High Representative and a constitutional court composed of foreigners).

In the archetypal situation for such constitution-making, a specific territory, on the verge of independence, is about to adopt a constitution: this constitution being guided and inspired, sometimes imposed, by the international community. One very interesting example had already been furnished in 1947 by Resolution 181(II) of the General Assembly of the United Nations which recommended the establishment of two states in Palestine (one Jewish and one Arab). Article 10 of the resolution described the process leading to the adoption of democratic parliamentary constitutions (excluding thus a presidential regime) in both states and guaranteeing the principles of equality.

[51] Imposed constitutions have a long history, related to various forms of colonialism. The Constitution of 1908, imposed on Bosnia-Herzegovina within the frame of the Austro-Hungarian Empire was one of the most elaborate and progressive constitutional documents of its days.

[52] For the history of the constitution-making in Japan under occupation see Koseki Shoichi, *The Birth of Japan's Post War Constitution* (Ray A. Moore trans, 1997). See further Andrew Arato, *Constitution-Making under Occupation: The Politics of Imposed Revolution in Iraq* (2009), 2.

[53] See Inga Markovits, *Constitution Making After National Catastrophes: Germany in 1949 and 1990* (2008) 49 *William and Mary Law Review* 1307.

[54] Related to internationalization (integrated participation in international organizations), international organizations may play a participatory and certifying role in constitution-making which has implications for the formal structure of constitution-drafting. The Venice Commission of the Council of Europe was deeply involved in making the Romanian Constitution and the same Commission monitored the constitution-making in Hungary in 2011.

Similar steps were taken more recently by the United Nations in the case of states or territories such as Cambodia, East Timor, and even Afghanistan.[55] An interesting constitutional complication is who, and at which stage, can amend or alter such a constitution.[56]

2. Constitution-Making 'By the Rules'

There are instances where transition to the new constitutional regime is a relatively smooth one, in search of formal continuity, thus avoiding political turmoil and a crisis of legitimacy. Most often this takes the form of fundamental amendments but sometimes a new constitution is preferred for reasons of consistency or ideology. To the extent new constitutions can be created via amendment, this process is not reserved to the constituent power of the people. The Swiss or Venezuelan[57] solution is quite unusual: here, there can be a popular initiative for constitutional change, although subject to (some) control by the existing institutions. A number of constitutions (expressing reservations regarding populism) prohibit popular initiatives intended to amend the constitution, at the price of separating the constitution from the constituent power.

Even where the constitutional change is more ambitious, amounting fundamentally to regime change, we quite often witness a quasi-pathetic attempt to rely, *a minima*, that is, almost indirectly but nevertheless clearly, on the outgoing order, as if this reliance could add 'something' to the legitimacy of the new order. One should not underestimate 'the magic of constituent power'.[58] A certain quality is attributed to so-called 'constituent power' which means that if the magic current passes through the amending power, it suffices to render the entire process legal and legitimate, at least superficially, hence the efforts of numerous revolutionary leaders to show, despite even minimal credibility, that their seizure of power, followed by the establishment of a new constitution, has a basis in the existing constitutional chain. (See the adoption of new constitutions after free elections in the post-communist transition.) Quite often, reliance on the pre-existing amendment procedure is part of the compromise underlying the transfer of power.[59] It was for this reason that in Hungary the negotiated transition from communism was based on the fully amended constitution adopted as an amendment to the 1949 constitution by the still in place communist Parliament. The anti-communist opposition refused to accept a new constitution enacted by a non-democratically elected Parliament. Although after the free elections the fully amended text served the needs of the new democracy well, political mistrust had not permitted the making of a new constitution.[60] However, in other countries going through post-communist transition,

[55] For a case of extremely strong international impact see East Timor under a UN administration. See Rosenfeld (n 12), 206–7.

[56] See *Sejdic and Finci v Bosnia and Herzegovina*, ECtHR App nos 27996/06 and 34836/06, Judgment of 22 December 2009 (government claiming that it cannot change the internationally mandated constitution in order to grant passive voting rights to members of non-national ethnic groups. Only Bosnians, Serbs, and Croats were eligible but not the Roma and Jews).

[57] The initiative can come from 15 percent of the citizens registered in the Civil and Electoral Register; or by 30 percent of the members of the National Assembly or (from) the President of the Republic in the Council of Ministers: Venezuela Constitution, 1999, Art 341(1).

[58] To be published (2012) under the title 'La théorie du pouvoir constituant' in Michel Troper and Dominique Chagnollaud (eds), *Traité international de droit constitutionnel*, vol 3 (forthcoming 2012).

[59] South Africa may also be attached to the transitional model. Like the former communist countries, agreements were progressively reached in order to allow smooth transition, without any revolutionary rupture.

[60] Only after 2010 when a new super-majority emerged with a reference to the revolution in the ballot box did it venture into successful constitution-making.

freely elected parliaments (not created as constituent assemblies but with constitution-making powers under the old constitutions) enacted new constitutions.

Formal reliance on existing constitution-making or amending procedures is characteristic of what is called 'fraud to the constitution' which alleges smooth transition from democracy to an autocratic regime.[61] This was the case, for instance, with the Vichy order established through the law of July 10, 1940.[62] As a matter of fact, this was also the case with the transition from the Weimar Republic to the Nazi regime, starting with the empowering ('enabling') law of March 23, 1933. Should we not be consistent and admit that such fraud may work in the other direction (from autocratic to democratic) too? Consider the cases where passage was allowed from an autocratic regime to a new, modern liberal one: as well as the cases of Portugal and Spain (from quasi-fascist regimes to liberal regimes) there are also those of some of the former communist countries (eg, Poland where most of the fundamental changes were introduced into the old constitution *after* the free elections; which was followed by a delayed enactment of the new constitution by referendum).

IV. The Drafting Process

We now enter the reconstruction phase, or 're-constituent' phase. We have supposed that the former constitutional order has been abolished and that a new one is to be established. The process is similar to any legislative process where we must know who is in charge and how the task will been conducted.

Obviously, in our democratic times, seldom would a new constitution be drafted by a non-elected body.[63] The idea that a constitution should be approved by the people is now undisputed, even in regimes where the people is not really free to choose. The value of affirmation by plebiscite remains dubious. It may be assumed that today a new constitution would not be ratified or approved without the direct involvement of the people.[64] However, given the transformative nature of the process and the political vulnerabilities of the powers who had initial control over the process, contemporary exceptions are rather common, especially in the case of 'pacted' transfers of power (Czechoslovakia, 1991; Czech Republic, 1992: Slovakia, 1992; Bulgaria, 1991; Hungary, 2011).[65]

Determining the powers of the drafting body is crucial for the process. From the theoretical perspective, a constituent assembly representing the nation or people as the ultimate depository of constituent power should not have its powers restricted, except if one accepts the idea of a binding mandate. This was the original position of the French representatives in 1789 who

[61] See Georges Liet-Veaux's doctorate, *Essai d'une théorie juridique des révolutions* (1943) and his series of articles under the title '"La Fraude à la Constitution": Essai d'une analyse juridique des révolutions communautaires récentes Italie, Allemagne, France' (1943) *Revue du droit public* 116–51.

[62] A similar technique was used in making the French Constitution in 1958 though the doctrinal distance between the 1946 order and the 1958 order is much less important than between the Third Republic and the Vichy order.

[63] But this was the case for the Fifth French Republic, through the constitutional law of June 3, 1958. It was also, in part, the case of the German Basic Law, in 1949 (see below).

[64] This is the case, for instance, of the German Weimar Constitution in 1919, which was not submitted to a referendum. The same applies to the Austrian Constitution in 1920.

[65] See further Jon Elster, 'Constitution Making in Eastern Europe: Rebuilding the Boat in the Open Sea' (1993) 71 *Public Administration* 169–217. Of course, lack of referendum may originate from other circumstances as was the case with the Constitution of Croatia in 1990 which emerged in a unilateral secession.

tried to buy time by requesting authorization from their constituents. However, Siéyes's radical position that they represent the whole (indivisible) nation put an end to this approach.

Notwithstanding theory to the contrary, the power that put into motion the process often sets substantive and procedural criteria (eg a timeline) to the constitution-making body, for example in the edict that sets up the procedure. (See, for example, the mandate of the drafting council in 1958 in France or the constitutional orders of the Romanian Salvation Front in 1989–90.) Nevertheless, even in such circumstances the powers of the drafters—that is, the members of a constituent assembly—are not always clearly defined, in particular with regard to the necessity of a referendum[66] and there is a place for self-constituting autonomy, including the setting of procedure and the guiding principle. The Declaration of the Rights of Man and of the Citizen of 1789 remains a self-imposed reminder that was created by a constituent assembly for itself and for legislators for posterity.

A constitution-drafting plan starts with a first 'intellectual' draft, reflecting the desired political and constitutional orientation of the regime to be established. This might include so-called 'technicalities' (federalism or unitary regime, parliamentary or presidential regime ...) or even a new ideological direction. Individual vision may play a role here, too. Two quite different examples of such intellectual drafting will be presented: Kelsen's drafting in 1919 leading to the Austrian Constitution and de Gaulle's speech in Bayeux on June 16, 1946.

Hans Kelsen's contribution shows the power of original intellectual thinking. The idea of the inclusion of a centralized constitutional court into the design of the constitutional vision is to be attributed to Kelsen, although he considered himself merely the legal redactor of the guidance presented to him by Chancellor Karl Renner (also leader of the Socialist Party).[67] Renner presented the main political orientations—'soft' federalism, parliamentary system combined with an elected President of the State.[68]

A successful constitutional vision originating from politicians is not restricted to the glorious days of Athens. In recent French constitutional history, General de Gaulle's speech at Bayeux (June 16, 1946) had a lasting effect. It presented a complete scheme for a constitution which would respond to and cure the French disease of multipartyism and allow for a strong executive. Though it could not determine the outcome of the (second) constitutional referendum of 1946, which adopted a pure parliamentary model, it served as a blueprint for the Constitution of 1958.[69]

Notwithstanding the role of individuals and their ideas, the intellectual process of the drafting is submitted to the logic of working in committees.[70] Recent scholarship emphasizes the decisive importance of procedural rule-setting and group dynamics in decision-making. In this regard the openness of the process seems crucial (in the broad sense, ie, to what extent

[66] The experience of 1958 is rather peculiar in that respect: the draft was prepared by a non-elected body, defined as 'consultative' which had to prepare a draft around defined lines, but the referendum was mandatory. The French Constitutional Act of July 10, 1940 empowered 'the government under the authority and the signature of Maréchal Pétain' to promulgate a new constitution of France which should guarantee the 'Rights of Work, the Family and the Fatherland', adding that the Constitution would be ratified by the nation and applied by the created assemblies. On the validity issue see Klein (n 14), 72.

[67] See in Kelsen's biography by Rudolf A. Métall, *Hans Kelsen, Leben und Werk* (1969), 34–6.

[68] The preparation of the Weimar Constitution was also greatly influenced by a technical inspirer: it was Hugo Preuss (1860–1925), himself inspired by Max Weber and Robert Redslob.

[69] See François Luchaire and Didier Maus (eds), *Documents pour servir à l'histoire de l'élaboration de la Constitution du 4 octobre 1958 Tome IV. Comité national chargé de la publication des travaux préparatoires des institutions de la Vème République, La Documentation française, 1987–2002* (2002).

[70] See William N. Eskridge and John Ferejohn, 'Structuring Lawmaking to Reduce Cognitive Bias: A Critical View' (2002) 87 *Cornell Law Review* 620–2, 616–47.

public opinion and other legitimate and non-authorized actors may influence the drafting). At the Philadelphia Convention, great and successful efforts were taken to ensure secrecy of the debates; although the opposite model was found imperative in 1789 in Paris.[71] The drafts and debates of the National Constituent Assembly were published daily and commented on in endless pamphlets within hours. The debates were open and it seems that it was very fashionable at the time to be seen during the deliberations. Threats from the gallery and the street and the immediate reactions of public opinion played a remarkable role. The imperfections of the work in committees and the noise in the general debate that lost arguments contributed to inefficiency. Notwithstanding the inconveniences, in view of popular legitimation and increased demands for transparency the Assembly was considered an inspiring example, showing due respect for the great Revolution.[72] Later, democratic ideas kept the debates flowing and became the rule in constitution-making. Nonetheless, the situation prevailing in France at that time does not preclude principal drafters in other situations from taking fundamental decisions in private.[73]

V. The Process of Certification and Ratification of Constitutions

The last step in constitution-making is the certification of the constitution (ratification in US terminology) which in turn will allow its promulgation signaling its validity and its coming into force. What happens to the draft once it has been approved depends on the decision made before the assembly was elected unless the assembly itself decides to amend the rules. Often the constituent body claims to have powers to promulgate, although historically in monarchies at least royal assent was needed (this was a major issue in the making of the 1791 French Constitution, where the position of the king was changed under duress during the process). The prevailing contemporary finalizing act is consent by the people in the form of a referendum (see above).

Another question is that of the 'material' limitations imposed in certain cases on the drafters, that is, certain principles they should introduce and respect in the draft: which in turn will raise the question of the body in control of those principles and rules. In some cases the constitution needs certification, namely a declaration according to which the draft proposed is in conformity with the principles set up before the process began. In this regard, see the French constitutional law of July 10, 1940 and that of June 3, 1958: both cases were situations where the legitimacy of the process was doubtful. Technically the inclusion of guiding principles has the following meaning: the authority issuing the norm containing the guiding principles is 'higher' than that which will be submitted to those principles.

With the consolidation of the powers of constitutional courts, the formal judicial certification of the constitution before promulgation became a possibility (for additional judicial review of constitutional changes see below). The most famous example is that of the South

[71] See André Castaldo, *Les méthodes de travail de la constituante* (1989).

[72] Tocqueville, as a member of the 1848 constituent assembly, wrote in his *Souvenirs* how the Assembly was haunted by the shadow of the great Constituent of 1789 and of the second Assembly, the Convention (1792–95). An attempt was even made to dress similar to Robespierre! Alexis de Tocqueville, 'Souvenirs' in *Oeuvres*, vol III (2004), 811.

[73] One of the most spectacular examples of such closed deals comes from making the Spanish Constitution: Francisco Rubio Llorente, 'Writing of the Constitution of Spain' in Robert A. Goldwin and Art Kaufman (eds), *Constitution Makers on Constitution Making: The Experience of Eight Nations* (1988).

African Constitution. After the collapse of the apartheid system, a provisional constitution was adopted in 1994. This document prepared for the election of a constituent assembly: it provided for 34 principles to be observed and introduced in the new constitution, under the control of the South African Constitutional Court. In May 1996, the Court rejected the first draft of the constitution—it considered that the principles had not been fully respected.[74] A new draft was prepared and finally ratified by the Court; a process which was qualified as a 'certifying process'.[75] Other cases are slightly different, for example provisions may require certification by an external body (a high religious order in religious states, approval by a body of 'sages', etc (see Iran)). These external bodies are intended to be the guardians of the principles, a task which is elsewhere in the charge of the courts.

VI. Between Amendment and Constitutional Change: Protection of Unamendable Provisions

Official doctrine distinguishes somewhat pedantically between the framing power versus the amending power. In the present framework, we will not enter the convolutions of those discussions. Suffice it to say that the amending process has, by its very nature, certain repercussions on constitution-building. In this section we will discuss instances where amendment functions as fundamental change resulting in a substantively new constitution,[76] thereby raising fundamental issues of legitimacy. Further, we will discuss the substantive limitations to the amending process, including protection of the allegedly immutable provisions of the constitution.

The constitution is an instrument designed to solve the pre-commitment problem. At a down-to-earth political-sociological level it is intended to perpetuate a certain power arrangement (at least excluding certain groups from exercising dominant power: see the anti-aristocracy and anti-royal power provisions in the 1791 French Constitution or the Belgian Constitution of 1831, the anti-clerical provision in the 1917 Mexican Constitution etc, to the extremes of the Soviet constitutions which used to limit power to the Communist Party and in principle to 'toilers' only). As a foundational document the founders' ambition is to perpetuate a vision of social order, or at least its fundamental underlying values concerning government and nation. Jefferson's opinion that the dead should not govern the living and that every generation has the right to a new constitution based on necessity never carried the day. Nevertheless, early popular revolutionary theory and practice expressly recognized the people's right 'to reform, alter, or totally change'.[77]

[74] *Ex parte Chairperson of the Constitutional Assembly: in re Certification of the Constitution of the Republic of South Africa*, 1996 (4) SA 744 (CC); 1996 (10) BCLR 1253 (CC).

[75] The Court held on December 4, 1996 that most of the grounds for non-certification of the earlier constitutional text had clearly been eliminated in the amended constitutional text. *Certification of the Amended Text of the Constitution of the Republic of South Africa*, 1996 (CCT37/96) [1996] ZACC 24; 1997 (1) BCLR 1; 1997 (2) SA 97 (December 4, 1996). In 2011, the Hungarian Constitutional Court was confronted with the issue of the constitutionality of the new constitution in the absence of a certification power. The Court ruled that it had no authority to rule on the matter but most judges wrote concurring opinions expressing their criticism with regard to the process: Decision 61/2011 (VII.13) of the Constitutional Court of the Republic of Hungary.

[76] Certain constitution like the Russian one expressly differentiate between core provisions which are difficult to amend and others which are considered more technical and in need of constant revision and therefore subject to easy amendment.

[77] Massachusetts Constitutions of 1780, Declaration of Rights, Art VII. 'Alter and abolish' clauses became gradually accepted in the post-revolutionary period and 'recurrence' was quite common. 'Bypassing

It is not surprising that constitutions developed procedural and substantive solutions for their protection; currently practically all constitutions have such provisions.[78] Amendment and the making of new constitutions can be cumbersome. In modern constitutions the idea of non-amendable provisions became increasingly popular with the possibility that judicial control is applied to protect the constitution both in terms of procedure (related to judicial review of electoral and referenda results and of legislative procedure) and substance.

1. The Amending Process and its Meaning

From its inception, at the end of the eighteenth century, modern constitutional theory understood that provisions should be made allowing for revision or amendment of the constitution, since no human written norm could be considered as perpetual and since future generations should be able to deliver themselves from the yolk of those previous.[79] In a modern judicial formulation: 'A static system of laws is the worst tyranny that any Constitution can impose upon a country. An unamendable Constitution means that all reform and progress are at a standstill.'[80]

The amending process may be defined as a key to the constitution: it will allow the opening of the entire constitutional system and eventually its transformation or amendment. Thus the nature of the amending process gives the precise measure of the protection of the constitution and may induce collateral attempts to amend it. It reflects the understanding of popular sovereignty.

A standard approach is to apply the expectations of constitution-making to amendments. In this logic, amendments are to be carried out by specifically elected constituent assemblies, or at least submitted to referenda. Where referendum is the principal form of constitutional lawmaking, amendment is also by referendum, as in Switzerland.[81] The alternative is to grant amendment power to ordinary legislation but add super-majority requirements and special procedures for cooling down periods. Germany is an example of this approach which may offer very limited protection: in Slovakia, 60 percent of parliamentarians in a single chamber may pass constitutional amendments. In the Dutch-Norwegian system, parliament is entitled to make changes but under very strenuous political conditions, which make the populist political abuse of the process politically very costly or at least risky. The basic idea is that after a super-majority has adopted an amendment, the legislation has to be dissolved and the amendment has to be adopted by the newly elected parliament within a short period of time. According to the French Constitution of 1958, the initiative of revision is reserved to the executive and to parliament, while ratification is by referendum if it was initiated by parliament (the two chambers in identical terms). This opening up to popular will had more to do with de

procedures were founded on the people's sovereignty'. Constitutional conventions were even called in disregard of existing rules and such practice was legitimate and 'circumvention' was quite common at the state level. Fritz (n 31), 82ff. See also Art 28 of the French Declaration of the Rights of Man and of the Citizen (1793): a people has always the right to review, to reform, and to alter its constitution. One generation cannot subject to its law the future generations.

[78] Compare with the data of the Constitutional Design Group, which puts this figure at 94 percent. See <http://constitutionmaking.org/reports/constitutional_amendment.html>.

[79] Jefferson even considered that 'the earth belongs to the living' and thus rejected, in principle, the very idea of entrenchment clauses, ie, the idea of making it hard for future generations to amend the constitution. Condorcet had imagined a system in which each generation would ratify the constitution.

[80] *IC Golaknath v State of Punjab* (1967) 2 SCR 762; AIR 1967 SC 1643, at 918.

[81] Notwithstanding the fact that the mandatory referendum relies on the double majority system in a national popular referendum (majority of the people and majority of the cantons) the Swiss Constitution (federal like that of the United States) has very often been amended. Referenda seem not to provide much protection for the constitution.

Gaulle's mistrust of the Senate, and less to do with respect for popular sovereignty. Revisions initiated by the executive can be ratified by Congress (three-fifths of parliamentarians). The republican form of government cannot be subjected to revision.

The results concerning the stability of the constitution differ even though the concept of a 'difficult amending system' is not a scientific concept. The best known example of stability is, of course, that of the US Constitution with an initiative by a bicameral super-majority (or by a convention called by two-thirds of the states) and a ratification by three-quarters of states. In consequence, only 27 amendments have been adopted since 1787 (some of them repealed): compare this with the Federal Republic of Germany with 50 amendments in 60 years (the process being simple and requiring 'only' a majority of two-thirds in both houses). Countries like the United States with a 'difficult' system of amendment have in fact developed alternative, non-textual ways of introducing changes in the life of the constitution (in part, of course, through judicial review of legislation).

2. Substantive Limitations to the Amending Process

The basic idea here is that of protection of the constitution against attempts to amend its very essence according to the amending process but leading to another political regime.[82] In 1884 the French Constitution (which was at that time simply a series of constitutional laws) was amended to prohibit any future amendment which would abolish 'the republican form of the government'. At a period in French history when the restoration of monarchy was still seriously considered, the intention was clear: prohibiting it constitutionally. This was the beginning of a new period in comparative constitutional practice (and theory) which may be called the age of the 'eternity clauses'.[83] After the Second World War those clauses become more and more frequent: the German Basic Law had also introduced its famous Article 79(3) provision (human dignity, the separation of powers being immutable),[84] as a very clear reaction to and safeguard against fascist or other anti-democratic attempts legally to introduce anti-democratic amendments. The Portuguese democratic constitution of 1975 contains 35 such provisions. Some constitutional courts (Germany, Romania, and Austria)[85] are constitutionally authorized to review amendments. This is particularly relevant for the protection of immutable provisions.

[82] Cf Otto Pfersmann, 'De l'impossibilité du changement de sens de la constitution' in *L'esprit des institutions, l'équilibre des pouvoirs, Mélanges en l'honneur de Pierre Pactet* (2003), 353. See further Chapter 17 on sovereignty.

[83] The Constitution of Afghanistan 2004, Art 149 provides:

> (1) The provisions of adherence to the fundamentals of the sacred religion of Islam and the regime of the Islamic Republic cannot be amended. (2) The amendment of the fundamental rights of the people are permitted only in order to make them more effective. (3) Considering new experiences and requirements of the time, other contents of this Constitution can be amended by the proposal of the President or by the majority of the National Assembly in accordance with the provisions of Art. 67 and 146 of this constitution.

Secularism seems to be an immutable principle in the Turkish Constitution.

[84] As the provision only refers to other very broad articles, its meaning is not obvious. In *Klass* the German Federal Constitutional Court had to review an amendment to the inviolability of telecommunications provision of the Basic Law, enabling restrictions ordered by administrative bodies, instead of judicial authorization. The Court found (5:3) that this is not a breach of Art 79. The Turkish Constitutional Court took the opposite approach, ruling that rule of law is part of the republican form of state. The republican form of state cannot be amended, and that applies to its *characteristics* listed in the Constitution: Kemal Gözler, *Judicial Review of Constitutional Amendments: A Comparative Study* (2008), 46.

[85] The Romanian Constitutional Court regularly exercises a priori review of amendment initiatives. See further ibid 5–7.

Note also the debates around another form of limitations to the amending power: the so-called implied limitations, that is, those which are not expressed but derive from the very sense of the constitution which should not be abrogated from or amended under a formal process of amendment, in pure formal conformity with the amending process. In turn, this opens the debate on the judicial review of such proceedings. Inconsistency with other provisions might be an additional reason for such review. The protection of the constitution, or at least its core elements (like the republican form of government) poses a fundamental challenge to the idea of constituent power which was found in a sovereign source outside the constitution. After all, one could argue that the power was transferred but it did not extinguish the source of power. Even if one does not accept that the power to give entails the power to repeal (though the express authorization to change the constitution or even replace it corroborates that assumption), the very foundation of making the constitution rests on its extra-legal sources. The constitutionalist doctrine that goes back to Benjamin Constant, indicates that people's sovereign power was never full and did not include the destruction of the very fundamentals of its existence by authorizing despotism. Fundamental human rights cannot be disposed of, even by people.

The Supreme Court of India offers a practical application of this logic. It concluded that irrespective of express provisions of the Constitution of India to the contrary (which denied the power of the Court to review constitutional amendments), certain fundamental elements of the Constitution cannot be amended. The Supreme Court argued that it has an unwritten mandate to protect the basic structure of the Constitution against unconstitutional constitutional amendments. The Indian concept was followed in Pakistan and recently in Bangladesh.[86]

The Indian Supreme Court argued that:

> It was the common understanding that fundamental rights would remain in substance as they are and they would, not be amended out of existence. It seems also, to have been a common understanding that the fundamental features of the Constitution, namely, secularism, democracy and the freedom of the individual would always subsist in the welfare state. In view of the above reasons, a necessary implication arises that there are implied limitations on the power of Parliament that the expression 'amendment of this Constitution' has consequently a limited meaning in our Constitution and not the meaning suggested by the respondents.... [T]he appeal by the respondents to democratic principles and the necessity of having absolute amending power to prevent a revolution to buttress their contention is rather fruitless, because if their contention is accepted the very democratic principles, which they appeal to, would disappear and a revolution would also become a possibility.[87]

Indeed, revolution remains the ultimate form of constitution-making, pointing towards the non-legal dimension of constitutionalism.

Bibliography

Olivier Beaud, *La puissance de l'Etat* (1994)

Olivier Cayla and Pasquale Pasquino (eds), *Le pouvoir constituant et l'Europe* (2011)

Jon Elster, 'Intemporal Choice and Political Thought' in George Loewenstein and Jon Elster (eds), *Choice Over Time* (1992)

[86] *Fazlul Quder Chowdhury v Abdul Hague* [1963] PLD (SC) 486; *Anwar Hussain v Bangladesh* (the 8th Amendment case). The French Constitutional Council, the Supreme Court of Ireland, and earlier the Hungarian Constitutional Court rejected the legitimacy of such review.

[87] *His Holiness Kesavananda Bharati Sripadaglavaru v State of Kerala*, Supreme Court (India) (1973) Supp SCR.

Jon Elster and Rune Slagstad, *Constitutionalism and Democracy* (1988)
Claude Klein, *Théorie et pratique du pouvoir constituant* (1996)
Arnaud Le Pillouer, *Les pouvoirs non-constituants des assemblées constituantes, Essai sur le pouvoir instituant* (2005)
Martin Loughlin and Neil Walker (eds), *The Paradox of Constitutionalism: Constituent Power and Constitutional Form* (2007)
Michel Rosenfeld, *The Identity of the Constitutional Subject, Selfhood, Citizenship, Culture and Community* (2010)
Carl Schmitt, *Theory of the Constitution* (2008)
Michel Troper and Dominique Chagnollaud (eds), *Traité international de droit constitutionnel* (2012)

CHAPTER 21

STATES OF EMERGENCY

DAVID DYZENHAUS

Toronto

I. Introduction

States of emergency may play a unique role in constitutional practice and theory.[1] As we will see, a comparison of constitutional orders reveals that they have to choose between seeking to entrench in a written constitution, if they have one, rules about how the state may respond to an emergency and leaving such responses to be decided as and when an emergency occurs. Consider, for example, that the US Constitution contains only one clear constitutional prescription for emergencies: Article 1.9, 'The privilege of the Writ of Habeas Corpus shall not be suspended, unless when in Cases of Rebellion or Invasion the public Safety may require it.' In contrast, as we will see below, the German Constitution contains a detailed set of prescriptions for the federal authority's response to an emergency.

If the first choice is made, there has to be another choice between two models of emergency power: the 'executive model', which delegates to the executive the authority to decide on whether there is an emergency and how best to respond to the emergency; and the 'legislative model', which requires the legislature to design a legal regime that deals with both of these issues. Whichever is chosen, there has to be yet another choice about the extent to which judicial supervision is part of the emergency regime. Indeed, if judicial supervision is given a very large role, one might see emerging a third basic constitutional model for emergencies—the 'judicial model'. We will also see that the latter two choices have to be made even when a legal order does not have a constitutionally entrenched emergency regime, whether because there

[1] This chapter draws extensively on previous work. Specific references will be given below but my most comprehensive treatment is David Dyzenhaus, *The Constitution of Law: Legality in a Time of Emergency* (2006). See also David Dyzenhaus, 'L'état d'exception' in Michel Troper (ed), *Traité International de Droit Constitutionnel* (forthcoming).

is a minimal or no attempt within the written constitution to regulate emergencies or because the legal order has opted not to have a written constitution.

Of course, it does not follow from the fact that a legal order has no written constitution that it is not a constitutional order. Within the common law tradition arguments are made that the unwritten constitution is a source of principles for regulating emergencies. These principles are given expression by judges in the course of deciding particular cases, so that their main manifestation is in judicial decisions. Similar arguments can be made that the principles of a written constitution, often again as interpreted by judges, govern emergencies even if the constitution does not explicitly say this. It is even arguable that the very commitment to constitutionalism shapes the choice of model, so that the constitutional regulation of emergencies will take that shape whatever an actual written constitution says.

The premise of this argument is that all legal orders have one constitutional feature in common, no matter how much they differ in other respects. They are committed to a principle of legality, which in written constitutions will be given different kinds of concrete expression. But the content of that principle is not exhausted by such concrete expression since the principle has to be presupposed in order for these orders to be such—to be *legal* orders. It is this last argument that get us close to the point of seeing why states of emergency may play a unique role in constitutional practice and theory.

However, a full appreciation of this possible role for states of emergency to illuminate constitutionalism requires one more step.[2] We need to take into account the counter-argument that actual emergency practice in any constitutional order will reveal the limits of constitutionalism, even and more dramatically that such practice shows the emptiness of the liberal constitutional project, by which I mean the constitutional commitment to put in place the rule of law rather than the arbitrary rule of men.[3] In short, states of emergency might be thought to show the impossibility of constitutionalism. And thus an inquiry into what states of emergency reveal about constitutionalism cannot remain at the level of comparative design and practice; it has to engage with profound questions of legal and political theory.

Here the classic text remains John Locke's *Second Treatise of Government*.[4] Locke extolled the virtues of the rule of law—of the advantages to liberty of life under 'settled, standing' legislated rules common to all in contrast to 'the inconstant, uncertain, unknown, arbitrary will of another man'.[5] But he also insisted that in emergencies the government had to have a prerogative or legally unconstrained power to 'act according to discretion, for the publick good, without the prescription of the Law, and sometimes even against it'.[6]

Locke is thus responsible within the liberal tradition for the view that an emergency is ungovernable by the legal regime in place for regulating normal life since an effective response to an emergency may require that some state institutions respond quickly and effectively to threats either without legal authority or even against the law. Lockeans regard it as clear that neither the legislature nor the judiciary is capable of the swift, energetic action required to deal with an emergency, which leaves the executive by default as the authoritative body. However, they also suppose that that such a response can be on liberal terms since the executive should be guided by the supreme law of nature—the safety of the people.[7]

[2] On constitutionalism more generally, see Chapter 8.
[3] See Chapter 10 on rule of law.
[4] John Locke, *Second Treatise of Government* (1980).
[5] Ibid paras 22 and 137.
[6] Ibid para 160.
[7] Ibid chs XIII and XIV.

In the twentieth century, Locke's idea was radicalized by Carl Schmitt, in the opening line of *Political Theology*: 'Sovereign is he who decides on the state of exception'.[8] Schmitt also supposes that in abnormal times the sovereign is legally uncontrolled. But Schmitt's thought goes further. Not only is the sovereign legally uncontrolled in the state of emergency, he who *is* the sovereign is revealed in the answer to the question of who gets to decide *that* there is an emergency such that a declaration of a state of emergency is appropriate.

Schmitt's position presupposes that sovereignty is a pre-legal idea; the sovereign's authority is not ultimately constituted by law. It resides in a political, not a legal constitution. Closely bound up with Schmitt's claim about states of emergency is another claim about 'the political'.[9] According to Schmitt, the political is prior to law and its central distinction is between friend and enemy, so that the primary task of the sovereign is to make that distinction. It is in the moment of the emergency that the existential nature of the political is revealed. Since to make that distinction is to make a kind of existential decision, he who makes it has to be capable of acting in a decisive way, which for Schmitt, as for Locke, ruled out both the judiciary and parliament, leaving the executive as the only serious candidate.[10] But it follows for Schmitt that even when liberals recognize the problem that a state of emergency is a state of exception to regular norms and principles, they do not have the theoretical or practical resources to cope with that problem. The state of emergency is 'something incommensurable to John Locke's doctrine of the constitutional state'.[11]

Because of this incommensurability, Schmitt thought that liberal theorists and liberal states will and should reject the idea that a legally uncontrolled executive has authority not only to respond to an emergency, but also to decide that there is an emergency. Such a refusal, in his view, characterized the neo-Kantian legal theory elaborated by Hans Kelsen in the twentieth century. But the consequence of that refusal is that protections for individual liberty associated with the *Rechtsstaat* and the rule of law become ever more attenuated until the point where the rule of law is said to exist as long as the executive can claim that it has a valid or purely formal authorization for its actions.

Put differently, the liberal dream of the constitutional state in which public coercive judgments are made by a centralized legislature and put into laws of general application deteriorates inevitably into the nightmare of the administrative state, in which such judgments are made by the decision of particular officials at the point of application of the laws. But what is applied is neither the law nor something authentically public. Rather, we get an exercise of arbitrary power by a particular official legitimized by a legal theory evacuated of all liberal substance and thus reduced to an empty proceduralism: the rule of law is reduced to a regime of delegations of authority in which the constraints are purely formal.

It does not then matter much, even at all, to Schmitt whether liberals adopt the Kantian, principled stance that the rule of law can and should control politics even in times of great political stress or the more pragmatic, Lockean liberal stance that the liberal state has to respond in such times outside of the law. For the Kantians content themselves with law's form, permitting liberalism's enemies to capture politics from within, whereas the Lockeans give to liberalism's enemies the license to capture politics by using extra-legal methods.[12]

[8] Carl Schmitt, *Political Theology: Four Chapters on the Concept of Sovereignty* (2005), 5. See further Chapter 17.

[9] Carl Schmitt, *The Concept of the Political* (1976).

[10] Carl Schmitt, *Der Hüter der Verfassung* (1985).

[11] Schmitt (n 8), 13.

[12] Oren Gross pioneered contemporary interest in what he called the 'extra-legal measures model'; for his most recent discussion, see Oren Gross and Fionnuala Ní Aoláin, *Law in Times of Crisis: Emergency Powers in Theory and Practice* (2006), 110–72.

Schmitt is and has to be taken seriously because the claim that the executive is the real agent in responding to emergencies seems to have considerable support in legal and political experience. Usually, this claim is put on a practical basis—only the executive branch has the information and the capacity to act quickly and decisively in response to an emergency. But that practical basis is always combined by implication if not explicitly with a normative one. Here 'ought' seems to follow from 'is'. Since only the executive is capable of the kind of decision required to respond effectively to an emergency, the constitutional authority that inheres in every legal order to declare and react to the state of emergency belongs to the executive. At most, the legal order can inscribe in its constitution its recognition that the executive has the constitutional authority to decide both when there is an emergency and how to respond to it.

Consider, for example, Article 16 of the 1958 French Constitution, which has been described as one of the 'broadest grants of emergency powers to the executive in a modern constitution'.[13] Article 16 gives the President unilateral authority to declare an emergency

> when the institutions of the Republic, the independence of the Nation, the integrity of its territory or the fulfillment of its international commitments are under serious and immediate threat, and when the proper functioning of the constitutional public powers is interrupted.

The President decides both that there is an emergency and how to respond to it.

Article 16 does set out some conditions. It stipulates that the measures 'must stem from the desire to provide the constitutional public authorities, in the shortest possible time, with the means to carry out their duties' and it requires both that 'Parliament shall convene as of right' and that the National Assembly shall not be dissolved during the exercise of the emergency powers. In addition, the President has to consult the Constitutional Council with regard to the measures. Finally, a 2008 amendment requires the Constitutional Council to give its opinion after 60 days as to whether the emergency conditions persist. The President is not, however, bound to adopt the opinion of any other institution, though Article 68 permits Parliament to impeach the President for a 'breach of his duties patently incompatible with his continuing in office'. Thus the possibility exists of a formal legal sanction, likely triggered by the fact that other public institutions continue their operation and are given the opportunity to express public disagreement with the President. But there are no internal, enforceable checks on the President's authority.[14]

Consider also that Bruce Ackerman, a leading US constitutional theorist, argued in the wake of 9/11 that legal controls are impractical in a time of emergency, in part because judges always defer to the executive during such a time. As a result, he sketched an elaborate scheme of political safeguards to control the executive rather than legal ones. Yet Ackerman too succumbed to the pull of the rule of law by making it an essential component of his model for dealing with emergencies that these safeguards be either put into a written constitution or a statute, so that their observance would be reviewable by judges.[15]

[13] Jenny S. Martinez, 'Inherent Executive Power: A Comparative Perspective' (2005–06) 115 *Yale Law Journal* 2480, 2496. However, it has been invoked only once, by Charles de Gaulle, in 1961 during the Algeria crisis.

[14] Article 36 of the French Constitution sets out another model for dealing with emergencies, the 'state of siege'. The Council of Ministers, led by the President, has the authority to declare a state of siege for up to 12 days; any further extension has to be approved by the Parliament. The state of siege basically involves the transfer of powers ordinarily exercised by civilian authorities to the military but it is also regulated by legislation, which diminishes the extent of executive authority under it. See William Feldman, 'Theories of Emergency Powers: A Comparative Analysis of American Martial Law and the French State of Siege' (2005) 38 *Cornell International Law Journal* 1021, 1028–9.

[15] Bruce Ackerman, *Before the Next Attack: Preserving Civil Liberties in an Age of Terrorism* (2006).

In the next section, I will set out some further examples of constitutional design and also look at some examples of constitutional practice that will show the basis for the Schmittean view of states of emergency and their implications for constitutionalism. Indeed, it is important to note that the ramifications of this issue go far beyond states of emergency, a phenomenon of which lawyers and political scientists in the United States are well aware as they seek to deal with the way in which the office of the president and the executive in general seem increasingly free of constitutional and legal constraints.[16]

But, as we will see in Section III, the examples hardly tell unambiguously in favor of Schmitt. Indeed, they might serve to show that the constitutional choice is not between various institutions—the executive, the legislature and the judiciary—but between a vacuous or merely procedural account of legality and one that links procedure to substance. Moreover, the latter requires that all three powers work together in ensuring that responses to emergencies accord with constitutional principles.

II. Constitutional Design/Constitutional Practice

The constitutional design of models of emergency power is haunted by two historical experiences—in countries with written constitutions that of Article 48 of the Weimar Constitution and in common law countries that of martial law.

The doctrine of martial law proposes that the executive has an inherent constitutional authority to proclaim martial law when it deems there to be a public emergency, a proclamation that entitles the executive to act as it sees fit to respond to the emergency. The executive may, for example, deploy the military to deal with civil unrest and may authorize the military to try civilians in accordance with whatever procedures and penalties seem appropriate. In the nineteenth century, the threat of the imposition of martial law was an essential resource for the officials who maintained the British Empire, as they sought to defend imperial interests in the midst of an often very hostile local population. In invoking the threat, and on occasion martial law itself, the officials drew on examples from England's own earlier history when martial law facilitated the executive's suppression of internal challenge, and on very recent examples from Ireland, which though not technically a colony was treated in many ways as such.

[16] For a recent treatment, a companion essay to the book cited in the last note, see Bruce Ackerman, *The Decline and Fall of the American Republic* (2010). A full appreciation of this point can be found in recent work by Adrian Vermeule, who follows Schmitt in arguing that the executive is as a matter of fact uncontrollable by legal norms both when it comes to emergency decisions and the ordinary day-to-day decisions taken by the officials who staff the administrative state; Adrian Vermeule, 'Our Schmittian Administrative Law' (2008–09) 122 *Harvard Law Review* 1095. As he sees it, on Schmitt's view, liberals should not fear that the lack of legal constraint in emergency times will spill over into ordinary times; rather, there is a 'type of reverse spillover, from ordinary to extraordinary times' in any complex administrative state; ibid 1135. Moreover, taking his cue from Schmitt, Vermeule thinks it is normatively desirable that the US president be legally unconstrained when it comes to emergency decisions. See Eric A. Posner and Adrian Vermeule, *Terror in the Balance: Security, Liberty, and the Courts* (2007). But his reasons for thinking so is not that such lack of constraint enables the distinction between friend and enemy to be made in a way that will establish the substantive homogeneity of the people. Rather, he supposes that the kind of cost–benefit analysis associated with a laissez-faire picture of society argues for the efficiency of leaving such decisions to the President. And, it seems, the question of the extent to which the officials of the administrative state should have their legally uncontrolled powers is also to be settled on efficiency grounds. The difference between him and Schmitt is that Vermeule is confident that a highly individualistic society can sustain itself even in the face of existential threats, given that the kind of legally uncontrolled decision that has to be made to deal with such threats is a fact of life in ordinary times.

However, the claim that the executive has this power is puzzling since it suggests that there can be a valid use of law by the executive to do away with law's control over the executive.[17] Of course, those who regard martial law or something like it as inevitable in times of severe political stress want to justify it as only a temporary killing off of law—a suspension. They also say that the acts done under martial law are both lawful and in the long-term interests of legal order. On their view, martial law is not a complete absence of law, nor is it a special kind of law—a scheme of legal regulation. Rather, it is an absence of law prescribed by law under the concept of necessity: a legal black hole, but one created, perhaps even in some sense bounded by, law.

This puzzle is anathema to constitutionalism, which is why in the most famous work on the English constitution, A.V. Dicey claimed that common law constitutionalism does not know martial law, by which he meant an executive prerogative to act as it sees fit in times of emergency. 'Martial law', he said, 'in the proper sense of that term, in which it means the suspension of ordinary law and the temporary government of a country or parts of it by military tribunals, is unknown to the law of England.'[18] 'This', for Dicey, was 'unmistakable proof of the permanent supremacy of the law under our constitution.'[19]

However, in his magisterial work *Human Rights and the End of Empire: Britain and the Genesis of the European Convention*, A.W.B. Simpson says of Dicey's claim about martial law that it is 'grossly and perversely misleading' since under martial law 'precisely what happens is the suspension of ordinary law, followed by the government of the relevant area by the military'.[20] Moreover, Simpson argues that the fact that martial law is no longer invoked has to be understood not as a victory for the rule of law and for constitutionalism. For, the reason that it is no longer invoked is that in the twentieth century the parliaments of common law jurisdictions have simply provided the military and the security services with advance statutory authority to do whatever they would have claimed it necessary to do in the past under the cover of martial law.[21]

Simpson's claim is grist to Schmitt's mill. The puzzle that martial law presents is one only from the perspective of those like Dicey who think that there can be a meaningful legal regulation of emergencies, one in accordance with constitutional principles, whereas from Schmitt's perspective there is no puzzle, only an illustration of the fact that emergency measures are not amenable to such regulation.[22]

[17] See David Dyzenhaus, 'The Puzzle of Martial Law' (2009) 59 *University of Toronto Law Journal* 1.

[18] A.V. Dicey, *Introduction to the Study of the Law of the Constitution* (8th edn, 1924), 283–4.

[19] Ibid.

[20] A.W.B. Simpson, *Human Rights and the End of Empire: Britain and the Genesis of the European Convention* (2001), 60.

[21] Simpson, ibid 75–90, who chooses 1936 because of the comprehensive nature of the Palestine Martial Law (Defence) Order in Council of 26 September 1936, the making of which was authorized by the Defence of the Realm Acts, introduced during the First World War. Simpson remarks (86) that '[w]ith such a code in force who need martial law?' But his rhetorical question requires him to accept the correctness of the majority of the House of Lords' decision in *R v Halliday, ex p Zadig* [1917] AC 260, discussed below. Others would date the statutory introduction of martial law to the Defence of the Realm Acts, beginning in 1914. See Charles Townshend, *Making the Peace: Public Order and Public Security in Modern Britain* (1993).

[22] For Schmitt's view of martial law in this regard, see Carl Schmitt, *Die Diktatur: Von den Anfängen des modernen Souveränitätsgedankens bis zum proletarischen Klassenkampf* (5th edn, 1989), 174–6. Note that Schmitt had not at the time of publishing the first edition of this book (1922) given up entirely on the idea that there could be some legal regulation of an emergency. He still preserved in it a distinction between limited commissarial and unlimited sovereign dictatorship. But the logic of his own argument does not permit this distinction and he gave it up in late Weimar.

Of course, it might seem that Schmitt's perspective has rather too easy a time in a constitutional context in which there is a supreme legislature, which has the authority to delegate vast powers to the executive. But one has to recall that his theory of emergency powers was developed in the context of the Weimar Constitution, a written constitution that was drafted in a time of civil unrest and that explicitly sought to define the authority of the executive.[23]

The two crucial paragraphs of Article 48, the emergency powers provision, read as follows:

1. If a state [*Land*] does not fulfil the duties imposed on it by the Constitution of the Reich or by a law of the Reich, the President can ensure that these duties are performed with the help of armed force.
2. If the public safety and order of the German Reich is seriously disturbed or endangered, the President may take the measures necessary for the restoration of public safety and order, and may intervene if necessary with the help of armed force. To this end he may temporarily revoke in whole or in part the fundamental rights contained in Articles 114 [inviolability of personal liberty], 115 [inviolability of the home], 117 [privacy of mail, telegraph, and telephone], 118 [freedom of opinion and press], 123 [freedom of assembly], 124 [freedom of association], and 153 [inviolability of private property].

The exercise of these powers required the countersignature of the Cabinet; and the Cabinet, while appointed by the President, had to enjoy the confidence of the Parliament. But the President also had the power to dissolve the Parliament, a power limited only by the vague requirement that he could do this 'only once on the same ground'.[24] The President's power to dissolve the Parliament combined with his power to appoint the Cabinet meant that he could ensure a Cabinet which would give him the requisite countersignature and which did not have the confidence of the Parliament simply because there was for the time being no Parliament in existence.

On July 20, 1932, Field Marshall von Hindenburg, the President, issued a decree 'concerning the restoration of public safety and order in the area of the *Land* [state] of Prussia'.[25] This decree is a crucial moment in the breakdown of Germany's first experiment with democracy.

The decree was issued under the authority granted the President by Article 48. It declared the Chancellor of the Reich, Franz von Papen, to be the Commissioner for Prussia—the largest and most powerful of the German states—and gave him authority to take over its political machinery. It was issued at the behest of Papen's Cabinet and it formed an integral part of the strategy of the then Minister of Defence, General von Schleicher. The decree responded to the alleged inability and unwillingness of Prussia's government—a coalition in which the main socialist party, the Social Democratic Party, dominated—to deal with the state of political unrest and violence within Prussia. This coalition was the most important base of institutional resistance to the Nazi march to power and it was removed at the stroke of a pen.

The Prussian government considered armed resistance. But both because it seemed that such action would end in defeat and because, as social democrats, they were committed to

[23] I set out the story in more detail in David Dyzenhaus, 'Legal Theory in the Collapse of Weimar: Contemporary Lessons?' (1997) 91 *American Political Science Review* 121.

[24] Article 25 of the Weimar Constitution.

[25] For the full text, see the collection that contains the transcript of the case: *Preussen contra Reich vor dem Staatsgerichtshof: Stenogrammbericht der Verhandlungen vor dem Staatsgerichtshof in Leipzig vom 10. bis. 14 und vom 17. Oktober 1932* (1976), 481.

legality, they chose to challenge the constitutional validity of the decree before the *Staatsgerichtshof*—the court set up by the Weimar Constitution to resolve constitutional disputes between the Federal Government and the states.

The legal and political importance of this case was clear to Germans. Some of the most important public law theorists of the day, including Schmitt who with four other lawyers represented the federal government, argued before the court, turning the forensic debate into a battle of constitutional theories. In his argument, Schmitt did not contest the claim put by Prussia's lawyers that the court was the guardian of the Constitution. But he said that this guardianship role of the court was confined by its character as a court of law and thus it was guardian only in so far as the issue was one appropriate for a legal and judicial body. Since the issues were deeply political, and the President was the guardian of the Constitution in matters political, the question of constitutionality was for him to decide. That he had this role was for Schmitt made clear by the powers the President had in terms of Article 48 to decide the crucial questions of politics.[26] The court effectively upheld the decree in late October, by which time the Social Democratic Party was no longer an effective force. And so it might seem that, at least in the context of Weimar, Schmitt's general argument about emergency powers was vindicated.

The reaction to this experience in Germany after the war was a conscious attempt to refute, as it were, Schmitt by creating within the framework of Germany's Basic Law a 'constitution within a constitution'—a 'precise and comprehensive regulatory framework for emergency measures' that reflects, in Rainer Grote's words, 'a firm commitment to the preservation of the twin principles of democratic legitimacy and rule of law even in times of fundamental crisis.'[27] It thus constitutes 'an emphatic rejection of the model followed by the (in)famous Article 48(2) of the Constitution of Weimar, with its emphasis on broad emergency powers for the executive, including the power to suspend most political rights of citizens.'[28]

Since the German states retain police powers, the Basic Law distinguishes between internal and external emergencies, and thus leaves it up to the individual states to decide how to respond to internal emergencies. However, in the case of an internal emergency the federal authority may intervene when an emergency affects the territory of more than one state or when a state government either will not or cannot respond to the internal emergency.[29] While the decision that there is an emergency rests with the government of either the affected state or the federal government, the Federal Parliament retains its powers, including the power to order an end to government action; the government is not authorized to derogate from any of the fundamental rights guaranteed by the Constitution (including the right to strike); and judicial review is preserved of the measures taken for responding to the emergency.

In regard to external emergencies, the Basic Law distinguishes between the state of tension, the clear danger of an armed attack, and the state of defense, a directly imminent or actual attack. It is up to the Federal Parliament, with the consent of the Federal Council (the legislative body that represent the states at the federal level) to decide when a state of tension exists and it seems clear that it also will decide on the termination of the state. Moreover, the state of tension does not permit derogation from fundamental rights.

26 Ibid 466–9.

27 Rainer Grote, 'Regulating the State of Emergency—The German Example' (2003) 33 *Israel Yearbook on Human Rights* 151, 153–4. My summary of the German model relies heavily on the account in Grote.

28 Ibid 177.

29 There are three types of internal emergency: those caused by a natural disaster or a serious accident; by a threat to public safety or order; or by the imminent danger to the existence or the free democratic order of the federation or a state.

The Federal Parliament will ordinarily decide by two-thirds majority whether a state of defense exists. But if immediate action is required and the parliament either cannot convene in time or constitute a quorum, then a Joint Committee, composed of both the parliament and the Federal Council, decides again by two-thirds majority vote. In either case, the decision is subject to review by the Federal Constitutional Court, whose powers remain unrestricted. Finally, if an armed attack is in progress, and neither of the first two modes of declaring a state of defense is possible, the Federal President may make the declaration.

During a state of defense, the government has no special powers other than those delegated by the Federal Parliament. In this regard the Federal Parliament can decide to centralize powers radically in the hands of the federal government. But the most egregious interference with fundamental rights permitted is that the period of deprivation of liberty without judicial decision may be extended from one day to four days. Moreover, the right of access to the courts remains unaffected as does the right to a fair trial, all government action and parliamentary measures remain vulnerable to judicial review, and the jurisdiction of the Federal Constitutional Court remains unaffected. The Federal Parliament acting with consent of the Federal Council terminates the state of defense by simple majority.

However Grote also points to the possibility of what he terms 'supra-constitutional emergency law', based on the federal and state reaction to the Red Army activity of the 1970s.[30] He draws attention to the executive ban on detainees' contacts with the outside world including their lawyers, which was justified by supporters of the ban on the basis of the principle of necessity in the German Penal Code. The invocation of the principle of necessity in the context of public law leads, he says, to supra-constitutional emergency law, thus rendering the constitutional control meaningless because at its core is 'virtually unlimited flexibility and adaptability to changing circumstances'.[31] And in a paper about Germany's legal response after 9/11, Oliver Lepsius has expressed concern that the federal counter-terrorism law that came into effect on January 1, 2002 has important consequences for the protection of freedom, since it does encroach upon basic rights, and in general is evidence of a trend to make security a prior value to liberty, instead of the approach he deems proper of understanding security as part of a scheme of constitutionally protected liberties.[32]

While one should not exaggerate the extent to which Germany has moved towards a legal regime that subverts the official constitutional regime,[33] it is still significant that, as Grote points out, the regime does not seem to have excluded the possibility of such a move. Thus, there is a basis for the cynical or perhaps realist observation that Germany has not to this point been properly tested and that the experience of history shows that when the test comes, necessity will be invoked and the constitutional regime will be bypassed, perhaps as Lepsius might be taken to suggest, by enacting legislation that begins to put in place the executive model and that operates, as it were, under the constitutional radar of the entrenched bill of rights. And, as indicated, the same observation may seem to have an even stronger basis in the transition in common law jurisdictions from a martial law to a legislative model for dealing with emergencies.

[30] Grote (n 27), 173–7.

[31] Ibid 176.

[32] See Oliver Lepsius, 'The Relationship between Security and Civil Liberties in the Federal Republic of Germany After September 11', 2002, the American Institute for Contemporary German Studies, Johns Hopkins University, available at <http://webdoc.sub.gwdg.de/ebook/lf/2003/aicgs/publications/PDF/lepsiusenglish.pdf>, 10.

[33] See eg Kim Lane Scheppele, 'Other People's Patriot Acts: Europe's Response to September 11' (2004) 50 *Loyola Law Review* 89, 98–117.

However, a closer inspection of the experience of the United Kingdom might show that constitutional principles can have more of a grip on the control of states of emergency than is often thought to be the case, a grip that is exercised through the different institutions or powers co-operating within the structure of what can think of as a 'derogation model' for dealing with emergencies. Moreover, since this experience takes place in the absence of any written constitution, let alone an entrenched bill of rights, it has a particular salience in the debate about the viability of different constitutional models for the following reason. As we have seen, the transition from proclamations of martial law to legislative regulation of emergencies has been said to make little or no difference, since in a system of parliamentary supremacy, parliament can give and has given the executive all the powers it would have previously claimed under the title of martial law. If in that situation, constitutional principles of legality still operate, there are clear implications for systems like the French one in which the constitution seems to recognize something close to a Schmittean sovereign,[34] or the German one, where an elaborate system of explicit and entrenched controls seems vulnerable to being undermined by executive action or legislation or some combination, or the constitutional order of the United States, which has, as we have seen, only one provision that speaks directly to states of emergency. In particular, we will see that thrown into question is one of the most significant bits of evidence for the Schmittean view, namely, that judges tend to defer to the executive during the first stages of emergency rule and become willing to step in to impose the rule of law only during a second phase—a time when there is general agreement that the emergency is over.[35]

III. The Derogation Model

As I have indicated, the claim associated with the executive model that the executive is entitled to rely on extra-legal measures in a time of emergency has significant scholarly support, but will not generally be articulated by governments. Rather, the executive will nearly always say either that its authority to act as it sees fit is an inherent constitutional one or that the legislature has delegated such an authority to it. Consider that in the United States the post 9/11 Congressional Resolution—'The Authorization for Use of Military Force'[36]—empowering the President to 'use all necessary and appropriate force against those... he determines planned, authorized, committed, or aided the terrorist attacks... on September 11, 2001'[37] was argued by the Bush administration's lawyers to give the President legislative authority to act as he saw fit in the war on terror.

In claiming the mantle of legality, the executive answers to what I have called in other work the 'compulsion of legality'—the perceived necessity to have a legal authorization for state action because legally unauthorized action is widely considered illegitimate.[38] Put differently,

[34] Consider that when de Gaulle introduced Art 16 in 1961, France had not yet ratified the European Convention on Human Rights and constitutional review was more limited. Thus the invocation of Art 16 of the Constitution for the introduction of a measure such as an indefinite detention regulation would be subject to Art 15 of the European Convention on Human Rights. For reasons to do with the Constitutional Council's stance that international treaties are not automatically part of constitutional law, one could not seek review of the measure on the basis of the Convention. But if the Council were to accept jurisdiction, one could seek review on the basis of a constitutional doctrine such as proportionality. (I am grateful to Michel Troper for his answer to my question on this topic, of which the above is my summary.)

[35] Posner and Vermeule (n 16), 120–3.

[36] Authorization for Use of Military Force, Pub L No 107-40, 115 Stat 224 (2001).

[37] Ibid §2(a).

[38] See David Dyzenhaus, 'The "Organic Law" of Ex Parte Milligan' in Austin Sarat (ed), *Sovereignty, Emergency, Legality* (2010), 16.

compliance with legality is seen as a necessary if not sufficient condition for legitimate state action. But, as I have also recognized in that work, the compulsion of legality can set in motion two very different cycles of legality. In one virtuous cycle, the institutions of legal order cooperate in devising controls on public actors that ensure that their decisions comply with the principle of legality, understood as a substantive conception of the rule of law. In the other cycle, the content of legality is understood in an ever more formal or vacuous manner, resulting in the mere appearance or even the pretence of legality. Here, the compulsion of legality results in the subversion of constitutionalism.

However, as we will now see, as long as judges adopt the right interpretive approach and as long as the legal order undertakes appropriate experiments in institutional design, the virtuous cycle is enabled. And, while this claim might seem to be shakily dependent on two contingencies, it is important to recall that the Schmittean challenge to constitutionalism, one which has more than a toehold in both liberal theory and the practice of liberal democratic states, asserts the inevitability of the vacuous cycle, whatever the efforts of the judiciary and of other institutions. The story starts in what may seem like unpromising terrain—two dissenting judgments in the House of Lords during the world wars.

In the United Kingdom during the First and Second World Wars, the indefinite detention of individuals who were perceived to be risks to national security had to follow a procedure set out in regulations. Each decision was in principle subject to an appeal to an executive committee, whose chairman had to inform detainees of the grounds of their detentions, so that they could make a case to the committee for their release. The Home Secretary could decline to follow the advice of the committee, but had to report monthly to Parliament about the orders he had made and about whether he had declined to follow advice. The committee, however, lacked rule-of-law teeth.[39] Not only did it fail to require the real reasons for detentions from the intelligence branch, but in any case if it thought that someone had been wrongly detained, it could only advise the Home Secretary of its view.

When judges are required to pronounce on the legality of such a regime, they have three options. First, they can try to give the regime rule-of-law teeth. Secondly, they can say that the regime is legal without making the attempt, in which case they give the regime the imprimatur of the rule of law by equating that rule with rule by law. Finally, they might find that the regime is illegal because it is incompatible with constitutional principles of legality. The majority of the House of Lords in the First World War decision *Halliday*[40] and in the Second World War decision *Liversidge*[41] on the legality of the detention regime adopted the second option. They said that the demands of legality were satisfied by the detention regime and that such regimes were appropriate given the context of wartime emergency.

In contrast, Lord Shaw in his dissent in *Halliday* chose the option of invalidation. He started with the assumption that Parliament must be taken to intend that its delegates act in accordance with the rule of law, which meant that it had explicitly to authorize any departures from the rule of law. As Lord Shaw put it, the judicial stance should be that 'if Parliament had intended to make this colossal delegation of power it would have done so plainly and courageously and not under cover of words about regulations for safety and defence.'[42] For judges to allow the right to be abridged is to revolutionize the constitution, perhaps, more accurately to

[39] A.W.B. Brian Simpson, *In the Highest Degree Odious: Detention Without Trial in Wartime Britain* (1992).

[40] *Halliday* (n 21).

[41] *Liversidge v Anderson* [1942] AC 206.

[42] *Halliday* (n 21), 292–3.

undertake a counter-revolution. It amounts to what he called a 'constructive repeal of habeas corpus',[43] a repeal by the executive which is then ratified by judges. He would, he said, have come to his conclusion even thought the language of the statute 'had been much more plain and definite than it is'.[44] Since the Defence of the Realm Consolidation Act 1914 did not explicitly authorize a detention regulation, the regulation that brought the detention regime into play was invalid.

When civil servants put together the detention regime for the Second World War, they took note of Shaw's dissent and so ensured that the authorizing statute explicitly permitted the establishment of a detention regime by regulation. The government also responded to concerns raised in Parliament about the wording of the initial version of the detention regulation. It substituted 'reasonable cause to believe' when it came to the grounds for detention for the original proposal of 'if satisfied that'. It was on the basis of that substitution that Lord Atkin held in his famous dissent in *Liversidge* that a court was entitled to more than the government's say-so that an individual is a security risk, thus seeking, in line with the third option, to make the scheme into something better. The majority disagreed on the basis that it was inappropriate in wartime for judges to go beyond the mechanism explicitly put in place, the toothless review committee. Lord Atkin thus accused his fellow judges of being more executive-minded than the executive and of acceding to arguments that had not been put to a court since the days of the Star Chamber.[45]

Despite the fact that Lords Shaw and Atkin were in dissent, *Halliday* and *Liversidge* are plausibly understood as episodes in the virtuous cycle of legality. First, Lord Shaw's insistence in *Halliday* on what we would call today a 'clear statement rule', the rule that the legislature must expressly delegate authority to infringe fundamental rights, did have the result that the authorization to detain was put into the Defence of the Realm Act in the Second World War and was thus subject to parliamentary debate. That subjection meant that the question of the content of the regulation as well as the question whether there should be such a regulation came up for debate in Parliament, instead of being regarded as matters of executive discretion, given the delegation of vast powers to the executive to act as it sees fit in the stature. And, as we have seen, debate on the former question led to the substitution in wording.

Secondly, while Lord Atkin put rather too much emphasis on the substitution, he was entitled to infer from it and indeed from the very existence of the toothless executive committee that the legislature and the executive did think that some review of detention decisions was not only possible but also desirable. Indeed, it is worth noting that in the leading speech for the majority in *Liversidge*, Viscount Maugham said that if an appeal against the Home Secretary's decision 'had been thought proper, it would have been to a special tribunal with power to inquire privately into all the reasons for the Secretary's action, but without any obligation to communicate them to the person detained'.[46] He too therefore thought that review is possible, though not in the absence of institutional innovation.

And, to cut a long story short, precisely such an innovation was attempted when the UK Parliament responded to the adverse decision of the European Court of Human Rights in *Chahal*[47] by creating in the late 1990s the Special Immigration Appeals Commission (SIAC). Because the tribunal is staffed by people who have a combination of experience in security matters and adjudication, it has the expertise and the authority to review executive decisions

[43] Ibid 294. [44] Ibid 293.
[45] *Liversidge* (n 41), 244. [46] Ibid 220–2.
[47] *Chahal v United Kingdom* (1996) 23 EHRR 413.

made on national security grounds. It has access to all the information on which the executive bases its claims and may hold closed hearings when confidential information is in issue, in which it has the services of a special advocate to test the executive's case, although the special advocate is severely hampered by the fact that he or she may not communicate with the person subject to the decision on the basis of material presented in the closed hearings. Finally, it may issue its decisions in two parts—one closed and one public.

The first decision of the House of Lords after 9/11 did not, however, bode well for any effective judicial review of government emergency action. In *Secretary of State for the Home Department v Rehman*,[48] SIAC had rejected the government's argument that the question of what could constitute a threat to national security was a matter for the exclusive decision of the Secretary of State. But the House of Lords held, on separation of powers grounds, that it was for the executive to decide what is in the interests of national security and on the issue of the particular allegations against an individual that these must stand unless they can be shown to be absurd.[49]

However, things changed when the House of Lords pronounced on the Anti-terrorism, Crime and Security Act of 2001, the United Kingdom's reaction to 9/11. That statute put in place a system of indefinite detention for aliens who were suspected of being security risks but who could not, also the result of *Chahal*, be deported because of the risk of torture. It was accompanied by a derogation notice under Article 15 of the European Convention on Human Rights:

> 1. In time of war or other public emergency threatening the life of the nation any High Contracting Party may take measures derogating from its obligations under this Convention to the extent strictly required by the exigencies of the situation, provided that such measures are not inconsistent with its other obligations under international law.
> 2. No derogation from Article 2,[50] except in respect of deaths resulting from lawful acts of war, or from Articles 3,[51] 4 (paragraph 1)[52] and 7[53] shall be made under this provision.
> 3. Any High Contracting Party availing itself of this right of derogation shall keep the Secretary-General of the Council of Europe fully informed of the measures which it has taken and the reasons therefor. It shall also inform the Secretary-General of the Council of Europe when such measures have ceased to operate and the provisions of the Convention are again being fully executed.

The government had notified its intention to derogate from the Article 5 protection of liberty and section 30 of the Act gave SIAC exclusive jurisdiction in derogation matters. In *Belmarsh*,[54] the majority of the House of Lords found the derogation invalid and the system incompatible with the Human Rights Act (1998)[55] both because the system was disproportion-

48 [2002] 1 All ER 123.

49 See especially Lord Hoffmann's 'Postscript', 142.

50 Right to life.

51 Prohibition on torture.

52 Prohibition on slavery/servitude.

53 Convictions of only those criminal offences in existence at time of act.

54 *A v Secretary of State for the Home Department* [2005] AC 68, commonly known as *Belmarsh*, as it concerned the challenge by men held in indefinite detention in Belmarsh prison to the statutory provision which authorized their detention.

55 The Human Rights Act (1998) does not give judges the authority to invalidate a statute. All they may do is make a declaration of incompatibility.

ate since less intrusive measures had been devised for dealing with citizens who were deemed security risks and because in singling out aliens for detention it violated a right to equality—Article 14—which had not been derogated from. According to Lord Bingham's summary of the Attorney General's argument, the government submitted

> that as it was for Parliament and the executive to assess the threat facing the nation, so it was for those bodies and not the courts to judge the response necessary to protect the security of the public. These were matters of a political character calling for an exercise of political and not judicial judgment.[56]

In other words, the government adopted the typical stance of governments that claim emergency powers by presenting an argument with two limbs. First, it asserted that the question whether there is an emergency is so quintessentially a matter for political judgment that courts must submit to the government's and Parliament's assessment without any scrutiny of the basis of that assessment. Secondly, it claimed that since the question of the most appropriate response to the emergency is no less quintessentially a matter for political judgment, courts must also submit to the government and Parliament on that question, again without conducting any scrutiny of the justifications relied on. In effect, the government was arguing that these are non-justiciable questions: questions not appropriate for or capable of judicial resolution.

Lord Bingham's response to the Attorney General was that while Parliament, the executive, and the judges have 'different functions', 'the function of independent judges charged to interpret and apply the law is universally recognised as a cardinal feature of the modern democratic state, a cornerstone of the rule of law itself.' It was thus wrong to 'stigmatise judicial decision-making as in some way undemocratic'.[57]

It is significant that Lord Bingham did not find his ultimate ground in the Human Rights Act, but in the constitutional nature of the democratic state with its inherent commitment to the rule of law. Put differently, his understanding of the judicial role does not look to any particular statute, not even the Human Rights Act itself, as the basis for the judicial authority to review legislation and executive decisions for their compliance with human rights and the rule of law, since the legal order is assumed to be a constitutional one, and thus premised on judges having such authority.

Lord Rodger elaborated this point:

> If the provisions of section 30 of the 2001 Act are to have any real meaning, deference to the views of the Government and Parliament on the derogation cannot be taken too far. Due deference does not mean abasement before those views, even in matters relating to national security.... Moreover, by enacting section 30, Parliament, including the democratically elected House of Commons, gave SIAC and the appellate courts a specific mandate to perform that function—a function which the executive and the legislature cannot perform for themselves—in relation to the derogation. The legitimacy of the courts' scrutiny role cannot be in doubt.[58]

However, it is not that easy to claim this decision as a victory for the constitutional project and the virtuous cycle of legality for two reasons. First, the majority of the House of Lords were reluctant to scrutinize the government's claim that there was a public emergency of the sort described in Article 15 despite the fact that they admitted that there was reason to doubt the cogency of that claim.[59] However, they found shelter behind the fact that SIAC in coming

[56] *Belmarsh* (n 54), 110. [57] Ibid 113–14. [58] Ibid 158.

[59] Ibid Lord Bingham 104, Lord Scott 151, Lord Rodger 155.

to the decision that it should defer to the government's claim that there was an emergency had seen confidential material from the government in closed session. The Attorney General, however, had declined to ask the House of Lords to read the same material. Still the majority seemed to think that because SIAC had seen confidential material in closed session and come to a conclusion on its basis that the claim that there was an emergency must have been strengthened by that material.[60] And they thought this despite the fact that SIAC had expressly not relied on the confidential material in coming to its conclusion.

However, as we have seen Lord Rodger put it, 'Due deference does not mean abasement'. Even if a less strict standard of scrutiny is required for the question whether there is an emergency than for the question about how best to respond to it, the scrutiny has to be of the reasons if the reasons are to be given the stamp of approval of adequacy. To give, as one judge put it, the government the 'benefit of the doubt' at the same time as he expresses 'very grave doubt'[61] about the government's case seems peculiar, especially when the government chose not to allow the court to see evidence that might remove some of that doubt.[62]

My point here is not that the majority in *Belmarsh* were wrong to defer, but that they failed to require that a proper case for deference be made. And in failing so to require, they in effect conceded to Schmitt the first limb of his claim about states of emergency—that it is for the executive to decide when there is a state of emergency. Moreover, they concede that limb in a way that makes things worse from the perspective of the rule of law. They still, contra Schmitt, adopt the regulative assumption that all exercises of public power are legally constrained. But their understanding of constraint is so thin that it becomes merely formal, with the result that they claim that the declaration of the state of emergency has met the test of legality, even as they empty the test of serious content, which introduces a severe tension into their reasoning.

For even though Article 15 isolates the question of the existence of a public emergency from the question of the proportionality of the means to combat it, determination of the latter question necessarily involves consideration of the former. It is the fact of the emergency that justifies the derogating measures, and assessing their proportionality in meeting the emergency must necessarily involve consideration of the nature and level of the threat.

This of course does not answer the question of how judges are to go about this exercise. But, as I have argued elsewhere, it is well within the bounds of the legal imagination to design a system of parliamentary committees that could in closed session hear the executive's case for the existence of a public emergency that could then be made available to judges on review, in the same way as the material in the closed sessions before SIAC can be made available to judges.[63]

[60] Ibid 104–5.

[61] Ibid Lord Scott, 51.

[62] The majority also relied on decisions of the European Court of Human Rights that held that the Court should generally defer to a national government's determination that there is such an emergency; ibid 105. But such reliance fails to give proper effect to the gap some of the judges acknowledged between the situation in which the European Court defers to a decision by a government that has withstood challenges before that government's national courts and the situation in which the highest national court has to evaluate the government's challenge; ibid Lord Bingham, 112–13 and Lord Hope, 139. That is, a stricter standard is arguably appropriate in the latter situation and the application of such a standard there would make more sense of the application of the more relaxed standard in the first situation. See Tom R. Hickman, 'Between Human Rights and the Rule of Law: Indefinite Detention and the Derogation Model of Constitutionalism' (2005) 68 *Modern Law Review* 655.

[63] David Dyzenhaus, 'Deference, Security, and Human Rights' in Benjamin J. Goold and Liora Lazarus (eds), *Security and Human Rights* (2007) 125, 147ff.

The second reason why it is not that easy to claim the *Belmarsh* decision as a victory In addition for constitutionalism is that the government's response was the Prevention of Terrorism Act 2005, which introduced a system of control orders that applies to both citizens and aliens. There are derogating control orders, which impose obligations incompatible with the controlee's right to liberty under Article 5 of the European Convention, and which are made by a court. And there are non derogating control orders, considered not to limit Convention-protected rights, made by the Secretary of State and subject to judicial review.

There are grounds for supposing that this response to *Belmarsh* made things worse rather than better. For even the less severe, non-derogating control orders were experienced by those subject to them as just as or more debilitating than detention in Belmarsh prison, and because of the limit on communication between the special advocates and those subject to the control orders, it seemed that the services of the former in contesting the orders was close to useless, imposing what an English judge referred to as a 'thin veneer of legality' over substantive arbitrariness.[64]

However, as Adam Tomkins, a leading public lawyer, has argued, the record on control orders has not proved to be altogether dismal.[65] A series of judgments by national courts and the European Court of Human Rights on the implications of the protection in Article 6 of the right to a 'fair and public hearing within a reasonable time by an independent and impartial tribunal' has 'sharpened the courts' teeth in making aspects of judicial procedure in national security cases more robust'.[66] In addition, the same author argues that this augmentation of procedural protections is accompanied by a greater readiness on the part of reviewing bodies to entertain substantive challenges to security measures.[67]

One can, in my view, take the following lesson from this story. The insistence on a clear statement rule in *Halliday* makes sense only if it is followed by meaningful review of the executive decisions once properly authorized. Moreover, such insistence also makes possible such review, because it forces the executive to bring its activity within the scope of a deliberately and democratically designed statutory regime, one which has at least the potential of providing rule-of-law teeth. At least one can take that lesson, if the insistence does not inevitably result in a mere thin veneer of procedural legality, to which judges give their blessing.

This point can be reinforced by a quick analysis of *Hamdi v Rumsfeld*,[68] the first major post 9/11 decision of the US Supreme Court. A plurality of the Supreme Court (Justice O'Connor, joined by the Chief Justice, Justice Kennedy, and Justice Breyer), held that the Congressional resolution in reaction to 9/11 mentioned above—the Authorization for Use of Military Force—authorized the detention of enemy combatants, since detention of individuals for the duration of the conflict was 'so fundamental' and accepted an incident to war as to be an exercise of the 'necessary and appropriate force' Congress has authorized the President to use. The plurality also held that the detainees were entitled to contest their detention orders before an independent tribunal.[69] Finally, the plurality indicated that a military tribunal would be an appropriate forum for the contest to take place with its procedures determined in accordance with a

[64] *MB v Secretary of State for the Home Department* [2006] EWHC 1000 (Admin), [103].

[65] Adam Tomkins, 'National Security and the Role of the Court: A Changed Landscape?' (2010) 126 *Law Quarterly Review* 543. Note that these control orders are reviewed in the first instance not by SIAC but by an Administrative Court, which like SIAC, is entitled to see all the confidential material and has available to it a special advocate.

[66] Ibid 552.

[67] Ibid 552ff.

[68] 542 US 507, 518 (2004).

[69] Ibid 533.

cost–benefit calculation, that is, one which weighs security and rights considerations together; and that it would be appropriate for the detainee to have to rebut a presumption—established through the process of the initial military decision to detain—that he is an enemy combatant (the category developed by the Bush administration in order to wage its war on terror) .[70]

In his dissent in that case, Justice Scalia, joined by Justice Stevens, held that Hamdi, a US citizen held on US soil, was entitled to a writ of habeas corpus because the Congressional resolution did not explicitly suspend the writ as required by Article 1.9—the Suspension Clause of the Constitution. He supported this holding by a lengthy discussion of the common and constitutional law history of the writ.[71] In contrast, Justice Thomas in his dissent staked out a quasi-Schmittean position that the executive was justified in acting as it did as a matter of inherent authority and both constitutional and congressional authorization.[72] Justice Souter in a minority opinion, joined by Justice Ginsburg, concurred in the judgment of the plurality in order to give it practical effect, but did not agree that the Congressional resolution authorized detention and also expressed doubts about the kind of truncated due process that the plurality seemed to endorse.[73]

Lord Shaw's critique of the majority in *Halliday* applies, in my view, with equal force to the reasoning of the plurality in *Hamdi*, since the plurality also ratified a constructive repeal of habeas corpus. Moreover, the plurality can be said to have made things even worse by signaling to the executive and to Congress that, when it came the checking the legality of the detention of enemy combatants, the Court would be satisfied in the future with a rather minimal form of executive-devised due process, presided over by an executive-created, military tribunal.[74]

And as Justice Scalia's dissent and the minority's opinion illustrate, there were alternative paths open to the Court. It could, with Justice Scalia, have required of Congress that it suspend habeas corpus, or, with the minority, that Congress put in place a legislative scheme for detention of enemy combatants that prescribed procedures and substantive criteria in a way that reflected Congress's understanding of its obligation of fidelity to the Constitution. The second option would reflect Congress's understanding of a set of procedures and criteria that provided an adequate regime of legality, one to which the Court should, if the scheme were challenged, defer. Congress would have been required to devise a comprehensive regime for arrest and detention and probably, given the inevitability of some criminal trials, for prosecution as well.

The second option seems preferable because it approximates more what I referred to earlier as the derogation model. Consider, for example, Trevor Morrison's argument that when Congress suspends the writ of habeas corpus unlawful detentions are not converted into lawful ones.[75] His argument is specifically aimed at Justice Scalia's dissent, a model Morrison calls 'suspension-as-legalization'. On this model, suspension provides not only an 'affirmative grant of authority to detain, but also displaces any constitutional or other legal objection…that

[70] Ibid 538.

[71] Ibid 555–7 and 566–9.

[72] Ibid 579.

[73] Ibid 539–40.

[74] I trace the problematic way in which the Supreme Court's jurisprudence unfolded in Dyzenhaus (n 38). For an excellent analysis of the same process, see Jenny S. Martinez, 'Process and Substance in the "War on Terror"' (2008) 108 *Columbia Law Review* 1013.

[75] Trevor W. Morrison, 'Suspension and the Extra Judicial Constitution' (2007) 107 *Columbia Law Review* 1533.

might be raised against the detention.'[76] Suspension thus creates a 'lawless void, a legal black hole, in which the state acts unconstrained by law'.[77] This model, as Morrison has pointed out, has attracted the support of prominent academics, including David Shapiro, who argues that the 'practical reality' of emergencies requires that the executive be freed 'from the legal restraints on detention that would otherwise apply'.[78] For Shapiro, suspension amounts to legalization because otherwise executive actors might be 'deterred from engaging in the very activity needed, and contemplated, to deal with the crisis by an . . . understandable reluctance to violate their oaths to support the Constitution.'[79] Morrison, in contrast, argues that executive actors must always seek to uphold the Constitution.

Morrison's claim raises the question of how to understand the fact that legality is still preserved in some meaningful way, despite the suspension, and he seeks to answer the question through investigating reforms internal to the executive. This is a valuable line of inquiry, but one should, I think, be careful to avoid giving the basis for an inference that judicial review cannot or should not play a role. Here I take my cue from the English Habeas Corpus Suspension Acts—the historical backdrop against which Article 1.9 was drafted.[80]

Those Acts were what we can think of as primitive derogations from the constitutional morality of the legal order. They were *derogations* because they did not purport to change the constitutional order but only to provide a temporary immunity from its normal operation. (Indeed, as Dicey pointed out, all they sought to achieve was a temporary immunity from habeas corpus for people detained on a charge or on suspicion of high treason.)[81] They were derogations from *constitutional morality*, not constitutional rules, because, following Ronald Dworkin's distinction between principles and rules, the choice of derogation is evidence of the fact that the legal norm derogated from is recognized as a fundamental principle that cannot be overridden except at the cost of constitutional revolution. And they were *primitive* in three overlapping respects—formally, institutionally, and doctrinally, as I will now explain.

First, derogation differs from suspension formally in the following respects. It entrenches both a monitoring mechanism that goes beyond the legislature to international bodies[82] and rights from which there can be no derogation; it puts in place the test of strict necessity of the doctrine of proportionality that presupposes that the derogation itself as well as the derogating measures are subject to judicial review; rights must be explicitly derogated from, which means that all rights not explicitly derogated from are in force, as well as all non-derogable rights together with the government's other international obligations; finally, the principle of legality is left intact. As Tom Hickman has put it, the 'derogation model creates a space between fundamental rights and the rule of law. Whilst governments are permitted to step

[76] Ibid 1539.

[77] Ibid quoting from David Dyzenhaus, 'Schmitt v Dicey: Are States of Emergency Inside or Outside the Legal Order?' (2006) 27 *Cardozo Law Review* 2005, 2006.

[78] David L. Shapiro, 'Habeas Corpus, Suspension, and Detention: Another View' (2006) 82 *Notre Dame Law Review* 59, 86 and 89. As Morrison points out, Shapiro does not contemplate a total black hole, as at 90–5, he confines his argument to the issue of detention thus removing from its scope issues like treatment during detention; Morrison (n 75), 540. On my argument, Shapiro's qualification merely evidences the grip of the compulsion of legality.

[79] Shapiro (n 78), 89.

[80] See eg Paul D. Halliday, *Habeas Corpus from England to Empire* (2010), 253.

[81] Dicey (n 18), 224–6.

[82] For the ambiguous role of such bodies in monitoring emergencies, see Gross and Ní Aoláin (n 12), 304–25.

outside the human rights regime their action remains within the law and subject to judicial supervision.'[83]

Secondly, the institutional imagination of the time of the Habeas Corpus Acts did not include the sophisticated apparatus of the administrative state of the late twentieth century that makes possible hybrid bodies such as SIAC that combine executive and adjudicative expertise. Thirdly, the sophisticated version of the doctrine of proportionality in constitutional law and human rights law (both international and domestic) had not yet been developed, a doctrine that has the potential to promote a highly nuanced, transparent and context-sensitive evolution of ways to cater to both security and human rights concerns.[84]

It could thus be said that at least in the first and third respects the United States remains to some extent stuck in a time when an all-or-nothing approach to constitutional and human rights bolsters the sense among lawyers and other scholars that emergencies are not susceptible to constitutional control.[85] On the argument of this section, it could also be said that the adoption of the derogation model in the United States would render Article 1.9 redundant.

IV. Conclusion

As we have seen, constitutions deal with the topic of emergency powers in a wide variety of ways, ranging from silence to detailed attempts to establish the grip of constitutional principles on their exercise. But whatever mode they adopt, the questions raised by the topic go to the fundamentals of constitutionalism, namely, whether it is even possible to establish a meaningful constitutional control.

However, I have suggested that comparative experience issues in two conclusions. The first is firmly established and it is that a constitutional order and the governments that act within them must make the attempt to establish such control. They will respond to the compulsion of legality. The second conclusion is that it is possible for a virtuous rather than a vacuous cycle of legality to unfold as long as one sees that the challenge is not to decide on which institution or power should be the primary actor, but that the legislature, the executive and the judiciary have to participate together in a common constitutional project. In other words, we do not have to choose between a legislative, an executive, or a judicial model for dealing with emergencies. Rather, what we need is a normative framework for understanding how, in the light of experience, the grip of constitutional principles can be maintained. Here I suggested that the derogation model is fruitful.

The second conclusion is more tentative than the first, since this model is still being tested. But it has already shown sufficient resilience and capacity for innovative development to

[83] Hickman (n 62), 659. Tomkin's essay (n 65) may even provide support for the claim that the preservation of legality provides resources for judges to help to develop regimes more friendly to human rights. One also has to take into account the potential of international courts, a notable example being the judgment of the European Court of Justice (Grand Chamber) of 3 September 2008, Joined Cases C-402/05 P and C-415/05 P *Yassin Abdullah Kadi, Al Barakaat International Foundation v Council of the European Union, Commission of the European Communities, United Kingdom of Great Britain and Northern Ireland* (2008), available at <http://curia.europa.eu/jurisp/cgi-bin/form.pl?lang=EN&Submit=rechercher&numaff=C-402/05>. For discussion, see Kim Lane Scheppele, 'Global Security Law and the Challenge to Constitutionalism after 9/11' (2011) *Public Law* 353. See further Evan J. Criddle and Evan Fox-Decent, 'Human Rights, Emergencies, and the Rule of Law' under submission at the *European Journal of International Law*.

[84] See further Chapters 33 and 34 on proportionality.

[85] Naturally, that sense would then feed a claim that emergencies perhaps illustrate a more general phenomenon—the trend noted towards an accretion of constitutionally uncontrolled power to the executive even in normal times.

undermine the pessimism associated with the Schmittean claim that all attempts at meaningful constitutional control of emergencies are doomed to failure.

Bibliography

Bruce Ackerman, *Before the Next Attack: Preserving Civil Liberties in an Age of Terrorism* (2006)

Bruce Ackerman, *The Decline and Fall of the American Republic* (2010)

Evan J. Criddle and Evan Fox-Decent, 'Human Rights, Emergencies, and the Rule of Law' under submission at the *European Journal of International Law*

A.V. Dicey, *Introduction to the Study of the Law of the Constitution* (8th edn, 1924)

David Dyzenhaus, 'Deference, Security, and Human Rights' in Benjamin J. Goold and Liora Lazarus (eds), *Security and Human Rights* (2007)

David Dyzenhaus, 'Legal Theory in the Collapse of Weimar: Contemporary Lessons?' (1997) 91 *American Political Science Review* 121

David Dyzenhaus, 'L'état d'exception' in Michel Troper (ed), *Traité International de Droit Constitutionnel* (forthcoming)

David Dyzenhaus, 'Schmitt v Dicey: Are States of Emergency Inside or Outside the Legal Order?' (2006) 27 *Cardozo Law Review* 2005

David Dyzenhaus, *The Constitution of Law: Legality in a Time of Emergency* (2006)

David Dyzenhaus, 'The "Organic Law" of Ex Parte Milligan' in Austin Sarat (ed), *Sovereignty, Emergency, Legality* (2010)

David Dyzenhaus, 'The Puzzle of Martial Law' (2009) 59 *University of Toronto Law Journal* 1

William Feldman, 'Theories of Emergency Powers: A Comparative Analysis of American Martial Law and the French State of Siege' (2005) 38 *Cornell International Law Journal* 1021

Oren Gross and Fionnuala Ní Aoláin, *Law in Times of Crisis: Emergency Powers in Theory and Practice* (2006)

Rainer Grote, 'Regulating the State of Emergency—The German Example' (2003) 33 *Israel Yearbook on Human Rights* 151

Paul D. Halliday, *Habeas Corpus from England to Empire* (2010)

Tom R. Hickman, 'Between Human Rights and the Rule of Law: Indefinite Detention and the Derogation Model of Constitutionalism' (2005) 68 *Modern Law Review* 655

Oliver Lepsius, 'The Relationship between Security and Civil Liberties in the Federal Republic of Germany After September 11', 2002, the American Institute for Contemporary German Studies, Johns Hopkins University, available at <http://webdoc.sub.gwdg.de/ebook/lf/2003/aicgs/publications/PDF/lepsiusenglish.pdf>

John Locke, *Second Treatise of Government* (1980)

Jenny S. Martinez, 'Inherent Executive Power: A Comparative Perspective' (2005–06) 115 *Yale Law Journal* 2480

Jenny S. Martinez, 'Process and Substance in the "War on Terror"' (2008) 108 *Columbia Law Review* 1013

Trevor W. Morrison, 'Suspension and the Extrajudicial Constitution' (2007) 107 *Columbia Law Review* 1533

Eric A. Posner and Adrian Vermeule, *Terror in the Balance: Security, Liberty, and the Courts* (2007)

Preussen contra Reich vor dem Staatsgerichtshof: Stenogrammbericht der Verhandlungen vor dem Staatsgerichtshof in Leipzig vom 10. bis. 14 und vom 17. Oktober 1932 (1976)

Kim Lane Scheppele, 'Other People's Patriot Acts: Europe's Response to September 11' (2004) 50 *Loyola Law Review* 89

Kim Lane Scheppele, 'Global Security Law and the Challenge to Constitutionalism after 9/11' (2011) *Public Law* 353

David L. Shapiro, 'Habeas Corpus, Suspension, and Detention: Another View' (2006) 82 *Notre Dame Law Review* 59

Carl Schmitt, *The Concept of the Political* (1976)

Carl Schmitt, *Der Hüter der Verfassung* (1985)

Carl Schmitt, *Die Diktatur: Von den Anfängen des modernen Souveränitätsgedankens bis zum proletarischen Klassenkampf* (5th edn, 1989)

Carl Schmitt, *Political Theology: Four Chapters on the Concept of Sovereignty* (2005)

A.W.B. Simpson, *In the Highest Degree Odious: Detention Without Trial in Wartime Britain* (1992)

A.W.B. Simpson, *Human Rights and the End of Empire: Britain and the Genesis of the European Convention* (2001)

Adam Tomkins, 'National Security and the Role of the Court: A Changed Landscape?' (2010) 126 *Law Quarterly Review* 543

Charles Townshend, *Making the Peace: Public Order and Public Security in Modern Britain* (1993)

Adrian Vermeule, 'Our Schmittian Administrative Law' (2008–09) 122 *Harvard Law Review* 1095

CHAPTER 22

WAR POWERS

YASUO HASEBE

Tokyo

I. Introduction

An essential function of every state is to protect the lives and property of its citizens, but it is not a sole purpose for states to wage wars. When states go to war, their aim is often rather to protect their own constitutions or to change the form of government of their enemies. In Jean-Jacques Rousseau's understanding, 'The principle of life of the body politic and, so to speak, the heart of the state, is the social pact which, as soon as it is injured, causes the state instantly to die.'[1] States exist to protect their citizens, but to sustain their constitutions, they must have

[1] Jean-Jacques Rousseau, 'The State of War' in *The Social Contract and Other Later Political Writings* (Victor Gourevitch ed, 1997), 171.

the power to coerce their citizens to sacrifice their lives. As Rousseau observes, 'Man becomes a soldier only after having been a citizen'.[2]

In its war against the Allied Powers from 1941 to 1945, Japan fought to preserve its imperial, militaristic form of government. However, when continuing the war threatened its society with total devastation, Japan surrendered, accepting the necessity of transforming itself into a liberal democracy. As Rousseau argues, the ultimate object of armed attack is the enemy state's social pact, for 'that is all the essence of the state consists in. If the social pact could be severed with a single strike, straightway there would be no more war; and with that single strike the state would be killed, without a single man dying'.[3] To preserve the lives and property of the citizens, Rousseau suggests, the better course is sometimes to remove the social pact and kill the state. Some scholars argue that this is the course the East European countries took in discarding their communist forms of government to end the Cold War.[4]

Liberal democratic states wage war to maintain their basic form of government against attack, whether from states with different constitutional principles or terrorist organizations intent on destroying their integrity. Notwithstanding the demand of the UN Charter that all member states refrain from the threat or use of force against other states in their international relations (Art 2(4)), such threats and uses of military forces occur frequently. The question of how liberal democracies can restrain and control the use of force democratically is therefore an acute one in this non-ideal world. If a state undermines its form of government during a war by, say, irreversibly damaging its democratic political process, or by committing gross violations of human rights in the course of the war, it deforms its constitution and in effect loses the war. Notably, these eventualities do not present the same constitutional threat to non-liberal, non-democratic states in waging war; they have other principles to which they must adhere.

As a means of securing democratic control of the military, a number of liberal democratic states have come to require the authorization of their national parliaments in decisions to deploy military forces. Katja Ziegler observes that parliamentary consent for military deployments not amounting to a formalized state of war is required in Austria, the Czech Republic, Denmark, Germany, Hungary, Italy, the Netherlands, Norway, Spain, Sweden, and Turkey.[5] To this list we may with confidence add Japan,[6] Korea,[7] and France;[8] the situations in the United Kingdom and United States are less clear.[9]

In support of the necessity of parliamentary consent, Immanuel Kant argues that citizens

> must always be regarded as co-legislating members of states (not merely as means, but also as ends in themselves), and therefore give their free assent, through their representatives, not

[2] Ibid 166.

[3] Ibid 176. In other words, dissolving a regime can resolve even a 'supreme emergency' that the regime confronts. For more on supreme emergencies, see Michael Walzer, *Just and Unjust Wars* (4th edn, 2006), 251–68. On states of emergency, see Chapter 21.

[4] Philip Bobbitt, *The Shield of Achilles: War, Peace, and the Course of History* (2002), ch 4. This does not mean that the aim of 'regime change' in other states can be a moral or legal justification for waging war.

[5] Katja Ziegler, 'Executive Powers in Foreign Policy: The Decision to Dispatch the Military' in Katja Ziegler, Denis Baranger, and Anthony Bradley (eds), *Constitutionalism and the Role of Parliaments* (2007), 143. It makes little sense to require parliamentary consent only for formal declarations of war, since such declarations are quite rare. With regard to this point, see nn 37 and 62 below.

[6] See Section VI below.

[7] The Korean Constitution of 1987, Art 60(2).

[8] See Section IV.2 below.

[9] See Sections II.2 and III below.

> only to waging war in general but also to each particular declaration of war. Only under this limiting condition can a state direct them to serve in a way full of danger to them.[10]

The requirement of parliamentary consent for waging of war might furthermore be expected to have several beneficial effects. It should make decisions to go to war more difficult to take and, as a result, more prudent; as John Hart Ely recommends, 'it should take quite a number [of keys] to start a war'.[11] At the same time, parliamentary consent, once given, should accord more legitimacy to, and to consolidate popular support for, military operations, thereby increasing their effectiveness. Yet it is hard to say whether the requirement of parliamentary consent actually yields such benefits, if only because parliaments tend to be reluctant to take responsibility on such serious issues.[12]

An institution that states have employed to ensure the effectiveness of the parliamentary consent requirement in restraining the armed forces is military conscription.[13] Conscription provides the public with a strong incentive to avoid unnecessary wars, an attitude members of parliament might be expected to reflect. Conscription furthermore keeps military forces anchored in a given society, in contrast to standing armies, which tend to embrace interests different from those of citizens. However, conscription can have such beneficial effects only where democratic political processes function well. Moreover, in this age of highly technological warfare, the concept of conscription itself has come to seem obsolete.

Beyond relying on parliamentary consent and conscription systems, states have tended, since the Second World War, to constrain the use of military force by delegating judgments about its legitimacy and legality to international institutions such as the United Nations.[14] Military deployments have been conducted under the auspices of international institutions to resolve not only inter-state but also intra-state conflicts, with missions including peacekeeping, preventing genocide, and restoring democratic government. Member states of the European Union have increasingly coordinated their overseas humanitarian and peacekeeping operations. In addition, both German case law and Japanese parliamentary statutes explicitly refer to decisions of international institutions as part of the legal basis of foreign deployment.[15]

The tendency of states to defer to international organizations does not inherently increase democratic accountability. International society is a society of states, and its traditional mode of decision-making is not majority rule but consensus. Moreover, a significant number of its constituent members are not liberal democracies, and in any case, most international institutions are not democratically accountable to the citizens of their member countries.

Robert Dahl points out that

> from a democratic perspective, the challenge posed by internationalisation is to make sure that the costs to democracy are fully taken into account when decisions are shifted to international levels, and to strengthen the means for holding political and bureaucratic elites accountable for their decisions.

[10] Immanuel Kant, *The Metaphysics of Morals*, in Mary Gregor (trans and ed), *Practical Philosophy* (1996), 484 [A 345–346].

[11] John Hart Ely, *War and Responsibility: Constitutional Lessons of Vietnam and Its Aftermath* (1993), 4. With regard to Ely's view, see Section III.1 below.

[12] Ely's observation may shed light on the attitude of the US Congress. Ibid ch 3. See also the text accompanying nn 48 and 49 below.

[13] Michael Dorf, *No Litmus Test: Law versus Politics in the Twenty-First Century* (2006), 173.

[14] As the case of the Iraq War in 2003 shows, the United States is a salient exception on this point.

[15] See Sections V.2 and VI.2 below respectively.

Dahl continues, 'Whether and how these [aims] may be accomplished is, alas, far from clear.'[16] Dahl's conclusion is especially applicable to the use of armed force.[17]

This chapter offers a comparative survey of war-power arrangements in the United Kingdom, the United States, France, Germany, and Japan. The United Kingdom, the United States, and France, long-standing liberal democracies and permanent members of the UN Security Council, have been quite active in deploying military forces abroad. In contrast, Germany, and Japan are latecomers both as liberal democracies and as participants in international military operations. It should be noted that this chapter focuses mainly on powers of initiating armed conflicts, including that of deploying armed forces into actual or potential conflicts, but deals neither with conducting war nor ending it, nor with related treaty-making power.

II. United Kingdom

1. The Crown as the Sole Decision-Maker

The United Kingdom exemplifies the state in which war powers are vested solely in the executive. That the British Parliament has no formal role in the deployment of the armed forces makes the United Kingdom exceptional among contemporary democracies. However, there is latitude for doubting whether the United Kingdom and the United States differ in practice in this regard.[18]

In the case of the United Kingdom, one must distinguish carefully between matters of law and of convention. As a matter of law, the prerogative power to declare war or engage the armed forces in conflict rests solely with the government; the government can lawfully exercise 'without the authority of the Act of Parliament' any act 'done in virtue of [the] prerogative.'[19] Though prerogative powers are not immune from judicial review, the courts have not been prepared to review the decisions of the government on deployment of the armed forces.[20]

However, according to the Bill of Rights of 1689, 'the raising or keeping of a standing army within the Kingdom in time of peace, unless it be with consent of Parliament, is against law.' Thus, while the Royal Navy may be maintained without authorization by virtue of the prerogative, the authority of Parliament is required for the maintenance of the British Army, the Royal Air Force, and other land-based forces. In addition, as in other countries, Parliament holds power over the supplying of forces.[21] Consequently, the government cannot deploy the

[16] Robert Dahl, *On Democracy* (1998), 183.

[17] Charlotte Ku and Harold Jacobson, 'Toward a Mixed System of Democratic Accountability' in Charlotte Ku and Harold Jacobson (eds), *Democratic Accountability and the Use of Force in International Law* (2003), 349.

[18] See the text accompanying nn 46 and 47 below.

[19] Albert V. Dicey, *An Introduction to the Study of the Law of the Constitution* (10th edn, 1959), 425. Hamilton criticized this attribution to the Crown of the powers of 'the declaring of war' and 'the raising and regulating of fleets and armies', which powers under the US Constitution, he claimed, 'would appertain to the legislature', *The Federalist* (Terence Ball ed, 2003), 336–7 (no 69). See the citation accompanying n 32 below.

[20] *Council of Civil Service Unions v Minister of State for Civil Service* [1985] AC 374 (which held that the courts can review the manner of exercise of discretionary powers conferred by the prerogative). Cf *China Navigation Co Ltd v Attorney General* [1932] 2 KB 197; *Chandler v Director of Public Prosecutions* [1964] AC 763 (which held that the courts cannot question whether the Crown has wisely exercised its discretionary power regarding the disposition of the armed forces); Crown Proceedings Act 1947, s 11.

[21] Anthony W. Bradley and Keith D. Ewing, *Constitutional and Administrative Law* (14th edn, 2007), 260 and 343–4.

armed forces in large-scale operations for extended periods without the support of Parliament.

As a matter of convention, it has not been the practice of British governments to ask for parliamentary permission to deploy the armed forces. In 1982, the government sought no explicit authorization for the military engagement in the Falklands. The government furthermore did not seek parliamentary authorization for the engagement of the armed forces either in the conflict in Yugoslavia in 1999 or in Afghanistan in 2001.

However, before embarking on military intervention in Iraq in 2003, the government asked the House of Commons to approve the use of all necessary means, including military force, 'to ensure the disarmament of Iraq's weapons of mass destruction'.[22] While opinions differ on whether this precedent established a constitutional convention that parliamentary approval must be obtained before the use of military force,[23] it has been astutely observed that 'there are unlikely to be any circumstances in which a government could go to war without the [at least implicit] support of Parliament'.[24]

2. Prospects of Modernization

Against this background, the House of Lords Select Committee on the Constitution recommended in 2006 that 'there should be a parliamentary convention determining the role Parliament should play in making decisions to deploy force or forces outside the United Kingdom to war, intervention in an existing conflict or to environments where there is a risk that the forces will be engaged in conflict'.[25] The Committee maintained that the convention should pursue the following measures:

(1) The government should seek parliamentary approval (for example, in the House of Commons, by laying of a resolution) if it is proposing the deployment of British forces outside the United Kingdom into actual or potential conflict.

(2) In seeking approval, the government should indicate the deployment's objectives, its legal basis, likely duration and, in general terms, an estimate of its size.

(3) If, for reasons of emergency and security, such prior application is impossible, the government should provide retrospective information within 7 days of its commencement or as soon as it is feasible, at which point the process in (1) should be followed.

(4) The government, as a matter of course, should keep Parliament informed of the progress of such deployments and, if their nature or objectives alter significantly, should seek a renewal of the approval.[26]

The government's initial reaction to the report was less than enthusiastic. Its response concluded, the

> Government is not presently persuaded of the case for... establishing a new convention determining the role of Parliament in the deployment of the armed forces. The existing legal

[22] HC Deb vol 401, col 760, 18 March 2003.

[23] Colin Turpin and Adam Tomkins, *British Government and the Constitution* (7th edn, 2011), 192–3.

[24] House of Lords Select Committee on the Constitution, 15th Report, *Waging War: Parliament's Role and Responsibility*, vol I: Report (HL Paper 236-I, 2006), para 98.

[25] Ibid para 108.

[26] Ibid para 110.

> and constitutional convention is that it must be the Government which takes the decision in accordance with its own assessment of the position.[27]

However, in a Green Paper on constitutional reform published in July 2007,[28] the government under the premiership of Gordon Brown admitted that the current state of affairs was 'outdated' in a modern democracy, and proposed that 'the House of Commons develop a parliamentary convention that could be formalised by a resolution', which requires an approval of the House of Commons for the government to deploy the armed forces into armed conflict.[29]

III. The United States

1. Ambiguous Allocation of War Powers

In the United States, the Constitution vests in Congress the power 'To declare War, grant Letters of Marque and Reprisal, and make Rules concerning Captures on Land and Water' (Art 1, s 8(11)). It also makes the President the 'Commander in Chief of the Army and Navy of the United States, and of the Militia of the several States, when called into the actual Service of the United States' (Art 2, s 2(1)). While the Constitution clearly divides the power to wage war between Congress and the President, where exactly the division falls is ambiguous. The courts, reluctant to become entangled in the political questions surrounding military deployments, have not established reliable precedents.[30]

In this context, some pro-Congress scholars have argued that the power of Congress to declare war means that every deployment of the armed forces requires the prior authorization of Congress.[31] According to this argument, the Founders clearly intended to divorce the power to initiate war from the power to prosecute it, and hence, endorsed a limited commander-in-chief power. According to Alexander Hamilton,

> The President will have only occasional command of such part of the militia of the nation as by legislative provision may be called into the actual service of the Union.... [The President's commander-in-chief power] would amount to nothing more than the command and direction of the military and naval forces, as first general and admiral of the confederacy; while that of the British extends to the declaring of war and to the raising and regulating of fleets and armies; all which by the Constitution under consideration would appertain to the Legislature.[32]

[27] *Government Response to the House of Lords Constitution Committee's Report*, November 2006, Cm 6923.

[28] *The Governance of Britain*, July 2007, Cm 7170.

[29] Ibid 18–19. Neither the Constitutional Reform and Governance Bill, presented to Parliament in July 2009, nor the resulting Constitutional Reform and Governance Act 2010, contained provisions to regularise the involvement of Parliament in decisions on the deployment of armed forces in conflicts overseas.

[30] The Supreme Court explicitly rejects the claim that the President's military power as 'Commander in Chief of the Armed Forces' includes the power to take possession of private property in order to keep labour disputes from stopping production. See *Youngstown Sheet & Tube Co v Sawyer* ('*Steel Seizure Case*') 343 US 579 (1952). On the other hand, the Court seems to suggest that the non-delegation doctrine is especially weak with regard to the President's regulation of the sale of arms and munitions to foreign countries. See eg *United States v Curtiss-Wright Export Corp* 299 US 304 (1936).

[31] Ely (n 11), 67. Ely advocates reviving the non-delegation doctrine, which generally requires that 'important policy choices are to be made by Congress' (ibid 24). Compare n 70 below with regard to the German Federal Constitutional Court's implicit invocation of the 'essential matters' doctrine, which is a German version of the non-delegation doctrine.

[32] Hamilton (n 19), 336–7 (no 69).

James Madison explained that 'the executive is the branch of power most interested in war, and most prone to it. [The constitution] has accordingly with studied care, vested the question of war in the Legislature.'[33] While it would be unrealistic to exclude the President from decisions on going to war, it makes sense, according to this line of reasoning, 'to "clog" the road to combat by requiring the concurrence of a number of various points of view'; that is to say, '[i]t should take quite a number [of keys] to start a war.'[34] Including the House of Representatives in the decision process, in particular, invites a 'sober second thought', and given that the burdens of war fall disproportionately on ordinary people, the 'People's House' should have a say in any case in decisions to go to war.[35]

Yet there are weaknesses in this argument. First, it is unclear whether 'to declare war' should be equated with 'to commence war';[36] American history since the Founding is replete with cases in which the President sent armed forces abroad without the prior authorization of Congress. Congress has declared war only five times in all of American history.[37]

Moreover, the debates of the Constitutional Convention indicate that the Founders considered the executive to have 'the power to repel sudden attacks'.[38] To respond to an imminent threat or actual sudden attack is beyond the ability of a deliberative body composed of numerous members. In the *Prize Cases*,[39] the Court upheld President Lincoln's blockade of southern ports after the secession of the southern states. Justice Grier argues, in his opinion,

> If a war be made by invasion of a foreign nation, the President is not only authorised but bound to resist force by force. He does not initiate the war, but is bound to accept the challenge without waiting for any special legislative authority. And whether the hostile party be a foreign invader, or States organised in rebellion, it is none the less a war, although the declaration of it be 'unilateral'.

Furthermore, the Office of Legal Counsel (OLC) in the Department of Justice has consistently argued that while Congress has the power to 'declare war', the President has the power to initiate armed conflicts which, because of their anticipated 'nature, scope and duration', do not amount to 'war' in the constitutional sense without the authorization of Congress.[40] Even when the President seeks the authorization of Congress, according to OLC, the authorization need not be explicit or addressed to a specific conflict. Hence, OLC justified the planned invasion of Haiti

[33] 'Letter from James Madison to Thomas Jefferson, 2 April 1798, quoted in Ely (n 11), 4.

[34] Ely (n 11), 4.

[35] Ibid.

[36] Michael Ramsey, in his 'Textualism and War Power' (2002) 69 *University of Chicago Law Review* 1543, concludes that in the eighteen century, the phrase 'declare war' was understood to include an armed attack without a formal proclamation. War might be 'declared' either by word or action (ibid 1609–13). Hence, Congress's power to 'declare war' broadly encompasses the power to initiate war. However, even in this reading, uses of military force short of *wars*—the acts of a sovereign resolving its disputes by force—need not be authorized by Congress (ibid 1631–5).

[37] The five declared wars are the War of 1812, the Mexican–American War of 1846–48, the Spanish–American War of 1898, the First World War, and the Second World War. In all of these conflicts, war was declared after hostilities were underway. See Philip Bobbitt, 'War Powers: An Essay on John Hart Ely's *War and Responsibility: Constitutional Lessons of Vietnam and Its Aftermath*' (1994) 92 *Michigan Law Review* 1364, 1397.

[38] *The Debates in the Federal Convention of 1787 Which Framed the Constitution of the United States of America*, reported by James Madison (eds Gaillard Hunt and James Brownscott, 1920), 418. Thus, when President Jefferson sent the US Navy to Tripoli to defend US ships from Mediterranean pirates, Hamilton criticized the cautious attitude reflected in his annual message to Congress. According to Hamilton, 'when a foreign nation declares, or openly and avowedly makes war upon the United States... any declaration on the part of Congress is nugatory: it is at least unnecessary.' See 25 *The Papers of Alexander Hamilton* (Harold Syrett et al ed, 1977), 444, 455–7.

[39] 67 US (2 Black) 635 (1863).

[40] Walter Dellinger, 'Deployment of United States Armed Forces into Haiti', 27 September 1994, available at <http://www.justice.gov/olc/haiti.htm>.

not only on the basis that the deployment would not be a 'war', but also that implied authorization could be found in an appropriation bill. OLC also offered implicit authorization as a justification for the US intervention in Kosovo.[41] To require explicit prior authorization for each particular conflict is particularly unworkable in the world after 9/11, in which 'the cost of inaction can be extremely high'.[42] In authorizing the use of military force against Iraq in 2002, notably, Congress did not indicate when or for how long the President was authorized to use force.[43]

Even the arguments of some leading scholars in the pro-Congress camp suggest that, although Congressional authorization is necessary, it need not be explicit. Laurence Tribe argues, for example, that

> it seems apparent that Congress is given the power to declare war, for deciding whether the country should indeed go to war—and, by negative implication, that the President does not have the power affirmatively to make war (as opposed to defending the nation from a military assault) without consulting with and gaining the genuine approval of Congress.[44]

However, he supports this claim not on the basis of Congress's power to 'declare war', but rather on that of its power over the public purse.[45] In this argument, the Constitution does not presuppose the existence of armed forces in the first place. Rather, it assigns the decision to create them to Congress, vesting Congress with the power to 'raise and support Armies' and to 'provide and maintain a Navy' (Art 1, s 8 (12)(13)). The executive cannot make war if Congress does not supply armed forces. Thus, the power to make war 'resembles the power to incorporate a national bank; that is, it amounts to an implied means that must serve the powers that are enumerated and must be accomplished through the ordinary statutory processes that are specified by the text.'[46] Tribe's argument explains how appropriation statutes may work as authorizations of deployments of the armed forces by the executive. If this explanation is correct, then there is no great difference, finally, between the war powers of Congress and those of the British Parliament, notwithstanding Hamilton's assertion.[47]

If Congressional authorization may be implicit and not prior but subsequent to deployment of the armed forces, Congress faces a serious dilemma: it must choose between supporting military actions it is inclined to oppose, or to decline to fund them, cutting supplies and thereby endangering troops already in the field.[48]

[41] Randolph D. Moss, 'Authorisation for Continuing Hostilities in Kosovo', 19 December 2000, available at <http://justice.gov/olc/final.htm>; cf William Michael Treanor, 'The War Powers Outside the Courts' in Mark Tushnet (ed), *The Constitution in War Time* (2005), 145. Note that both of these cases took place after the War Powers Resolution was adopted.

[42] John Yoo, *The Powers of War and Peace* (2005), x.

[43] Authorization for Use of Military Force against Iraq Resolution of 2002, Pub L 107-243, 116 Stat 1498 (2002).

[44] Laurence Tribe, *American Constitutional Law*, vol 1 (3rd edn, 2000), 663.

[45] Ibid 664. Here Tribe draws on Philip Bobbitt's argument. See Bobbitt (n 37), 1388–92.

[46] Ibid 1365–6.

[47] See the citation accompanying n 32 above.

[48] In the Kosovo conflict, the House of Representative failed to pass a resolution authorizing air attack, but passed a bill funding the war just a week later. See Dorf (n 13), 172. As early as in 1829, William Rawle pointed out that

> as to a war [in which] the US might be involved by the conduct of the executive, without the participation of the legislature...no other restraint appears to exist, than that of withholding the supplies to carry it on.

Rawle observed that

> in England, the king is, in this respect, equally dependent on the parliament, and its history shows that this dependence is not always adequate to prevent unpopular wars.

William Rawle, *A View of the Constitution of the United States of America* (1829) (2nd edn, H. Jefferson Powell ed, 2009), 109–10.

2. War Powers Resolution

To resolve this dilemma, Congress passed the War Powers Resolution (50 USC §§1541–1548) in 1973, in the waning days of the Vietnam War, over President Nixon's veto. However, this effort by Congress to strengthen its hand in decisions to use military force is widely regarded as having failed. Despite the Resolution, Congress remains powerless to prevent the President from deploying the military in the first place, and remains reluctant to use its full power once troops are in the field.[49]

The War Powers Resolution requires the President 'in every possible instance' to consult with Congress before introducing US troops into hostilities, and after the deployment of forces, to consult regularly with Congress until the troops have been withdrawn. If there has been no declaration of war by Congress, the President is required to submit a report to Congress within 48 hours whenever troops are introduced into hostilities (§1543(a)).

Within 60 days of submitting this report, the President must terminate the use of armed forces, unless Congress (1) has declared war or enacted a specific authorization for the use of force, (2) has extended the 60-day period, or (3) is physically unable to comply as a result of an armed attack upon the United States. The 60-day period may be extended for not more than an additional 30 days if the President determines and certifies to Congress in writing that unavoidable military necessity respecting the safety of US armed forces requires the continued use of armed forces in the course of bringing about a prompt removal of the forces (§1544 (b)).

Moreover, at any time that the armed forces are engaged in hostilities outside the territory of the United States without a declaration of a war or specific statutory authorization, the President is obligated to remove the forces if so directed by a concurrent resolution (§1544(c)).

Provision §1544(c) is regarded by many scholars as unconstitutional in light of *INS v Chada*,[50] which requires that actions by Congress having 'the purpose and effect of altering the legal rights, duties and relations of persons, including... Executive Branch officials'[51] must be subjected to the possibility of presidential veto. Adoption of a concurrent resolution under §1544(c) would have the purpose and effect of altering the rights and duties of the President, but would not be subject to presidential veto.

Successive American Presidents have taken the position that the War Powers Resolution is an unconstitutional intrusion on the executive's war powers. While they have asked for congressional authorization of large-scale military actions such as the Gulf Wars, they have couched such requests in language of being 'consistent with' the War Powers Resolution rather than in compliance with it.[52] Thus, despite this effort of Congress to increase its role in America's use of military force, we may conclude that progress in the United States towards greater democratic accountability for military deployments is difficult to discern.[53]

[49] Ely (n 11), 48–54; Bobbitt (n 37), 1397; Tribe (n 44), 667–9; Dorf (n 13), 172. According to Ely, 'Ulysses tries... to tie himself to the mast in 1973, but the knots were loose, and he was soon back to his old ways of avoiding responsibility' ((n 11), 53).

[50] 462 US 919 (1983).

[51] 462 US at 952.

[52] Ernest Young, 'Taming the Most Dangerous Branch: The Scope and Accountability of Executive Power in the United States' in Paul Craig and Adam Tomkins (eds), *The Executive and Public Law: Power and Accountability in Comparative Perspective* (2006), 181–1.

[53] Michael Glennon, 'The United States: Democracy, Hegemony, and Accountability' in Ku and Jacobson (n 17), 344.

IV. France

1. The President, the Commander-in-Chief

While France's current Constitution of 1958 contains several articles on military affairs, these articles are formulated rather vaguely, and are apparently self-contradictory in some regards. The Constitution specifies that the President of the Republic is 'the commander–in-chief of the armed forces (*le chef des armées*)', and that he shall 'preside over the higher national defence councils and committees' (Art 15). On the other hand, Article 21 stipulates that the prime minister 'shall be responsible for national defence'.

The Constitution of 1958 seems to provide a relatively strong role for the President in the national defence in comparison to preceding republican constitutions. The Constitutional Act of 25 February 1875 of the Third Republic stipulates that 'the President of the Republic shall dispose the military forces' (Art 3), but that 'each act of the President shall be counter-signed by a minister' (Art 3). The Constitution of 27 October 1946, of the Fourth Republic, stipulates that the President shall preside over the higher national defence council and committee and hold the 'title of the commander-in-chief of the military forces' (Art 33), but that 'the prime minister [*le président du Conseil*] secures the direction of the military forces and co-ordinates the implementation of national defence' (Art 47(3)). In these regimes, either the prime minister or the Cabinet was viewed as being in charge of the national defence, and the role of the President was viewed as, to borrow the expression of Paul Bastid, no more than a 'symbolic vestige'.[54] Georges Vedel, furthermore, characterizes the presidential title of 'commander-in-chief' as 'purely honorific', maintaining that 'the real direction of national defence, in the time of peace as well as war, belongs to the prime minister, the ministers in charge of military departments, and the Cabinet.'[55] In the wake of the Vichy regime, no doubt, the power of the President, who was not directly responsible to the populace,[56] was an object of suspicion for the French political classes;[57] the President was supposed to have neither his own political or defence programme, nor the personal authority to direct the military forces.[58]

In the Fifth Republic, the situation changed dramatically. In response to the urgent circumstances of domestic political instability and decolonization wars abroad, the regime equipped the President with 'proper powers' (*pouvoirs propres*), including the power to nominate the prime minister (Art 8(1)), dissolve the National Assembly (Art 12), propose national referendums (Art 11), and take the measures required to respond to national emergencies (Art 16), as well as the authority to exercise these powers without the counter-signature of ministers. At least since the amendment of the Constitution in 1962, which introduced direct popular presidential elections, the President has been construed to have his own political programme, to direct the Cabinet when the presidential majority coincides with the parliamentary majority, and to use his constitutional powers to influence Cabinet policy when the two majorities do not coincide (*cohabitation*). This construal applies to the conduct of government in general,

[54] Quoted in François Frison-Roche, 'Art 15' in François Luchaire, Gérard Conac, and Xavier Prétot, *La constitution de la République française: Analyses et commentaires* (3rd edn, 2009), 508.

[55] Georges Vedel, *Droit constitutionnel* (1949), 516.

[56] In the Third and Fourth Republics, the President was elected by Parliament, united as a Congress. The direct election of the head of state in the Second Republic had left bad memories for the constitution-makers of later regimes.

[57] Frison-Roche (n 54), 509.

[58] Field-Marshal Mac-Mahon was an exception in this regard. The Second President of the Third Republic personally intervened in national politics with his official powers. Mac-Mahon was forced to resign in 1877 after a failed attempt to bring down the political opposition by dissolving the House of Deputies.

and encompasses the President's 'shared powers' (*pouvoirs partagés*), the execution of which require the counter-signature of the prime minister (and in some cases, other concerned ministers) (Art 19).

The 'shared powers' of the President include his powers as commander-in-chief of the armed forces. The President chairs the Council of Defence, which takes the most important decisions concerning national defence; the Council is composed of the prime minister, the ministers of defence and foreign affairs, other concerned ministers, the secretary-general of defence, the chiefs of the general staff, and the general director for armaments (*délégué général pour l'armement*).

However, with regard to decisions concerning the nuclear forces, the decree of 12 June 1996 stipulates that the chief of the general staff 'shall execute the order of engagement of nuclear forces, given by the President of the Republic, the commander-in-chief'. Thus, the decision to use nuclear force belongs exclusively to the President.

In other areas of national defence as well, even in the period of *cohabitation*, the prime minister, though supposedly 'responsible for national defence' (Art 21), generally refrains from any abridgment of the power of the presidency, which he may hope some day to enjoy himself. Thus, the President remains the principal decision-maker.[59]

2. Authorization by Parliament

In its original form, Article 35 of the current Constitution consisted of just one sentence (the current section 1), which stipulates that declarations of war must be authorized by Parliament. The principle that only Parliament may declare war has its origins in the revolutionary period;[60] the Constitution of 3 September 1791 specifies that the king is the 'commander-in-chief' (Art 1, Ch IV), but that 'war shall be decided only by a decree of the Legislative Corp' (Art 2(1), Ch III).

Subsequent constitutions, however, assign Parliament a lesser role. The Constitution of the Third Republic (the Constitutional Act of 17 July 1875) stipulates that 'The President of the Republic may not declare war without the prior assent of the two Houses of Parliament' (Art 9). The Constitution of 27 October 1946 prescribes that 'War may not be declared without a vote of the National Assembly and the prior assent of the Council of the Republic' (Art 7). These clauses specify only that declarations of war be authorized by Parliament; the power to declare war itself belonged to the executive. This remains the case in Article 35 of the current Constitution, which furthermore includes no requirement that parliamentary authorization be prior to the declaration of war.

Broadly interpreted, the principle of requiring parliamentary authorization of war might be understood to apply to every engagement in which military forces are committed. In practice, however, 'war' has been construed strictly to refer to 'war proper', excluding military actions against non-states or resulting from UN Security Council resolutions. Numerous deployments in sub-Saharan states to quell coups d'état have not been considered 'wars', because the French interventions were at the invitation of local governments. The French military action in the Gulf War was not regarded as a war between France and Iraq, but rather as a 'collective

[59] Frison-Roche (n 54), 520; see also Bernard Chantebout, 'Le président de la République, chef des armées' in *Mélanges Pierre Pactet* (2003), 574–7 and Francis Hamon and Michel Troper, *Droit constitutionnel* (32nd edn, 2011), 606.

[60] Frison-Roche, 'Art 35' in François Luchaire et al (n 54), 928–30.

security' operation authorized by a UN Security Council resolution; the President did convene Parliament to debate this engagement, but for the purpose of approving the government policy in accordance with the procedure stipulated in Article 49, rather than for the purpose of authorizing a declaration of war.[61] In the case of the Kosovo conflict in 1999, the government neither informed Parliament of the French engagement nor solicited a vote of confidence in support of its policy.

Hence, we may conclude that the difference between France and the United Kingdom, in regard to democratic accountability for military deployments, is not very great. Article 35 of the Constitution of 1958 does not in practice function to give Parliament control over the government's use of military force.[62]

In 1993 the Vedel Committee, commissioned to advise President Mitterrand on possible improvements to the Constitution, proposed that the following paragraph be added to Article 35:

> The Government shall notify Parliament of its every decision to have the armed forces intervene abroad, at latest eight days after the beginning of the said intervention. This notice shall be followed by a debate. If Parliament is out of session, Parliament shall reunite for this purpose.[63]

The President apparently found this proposal too constraining; the draft of the amendment proposed by then Prime Minister Bérégovoy read as follows:

> The government shall inform the competent committees of Parliament of its every decision to have the armed forces intervene abroad, at latest forty eight hours after the beginning of the said intervention. The government shall notify Parliament of the intervention, where the nature of the intervention justifies it. This notice shall be followed by a debate. If Parliament is out of session, Parliament shall reunite for this purpose.[64]

According to this proposal, parliamentary debate of military deployments abroad would not be organized automatically, but at the discretion of the government. Yet even this moderate change to the Constitution did not materialize at the time.

However, an amendment initiated by President Nicolas Sarkozy that is similar to that originally proposed by the Vedel Committee was adopted in 2008. The amendment adds three new sections to Article 35 that read,

> The government shall notify Parliament of its decision to have the armed forces intervene abroad, at the latest three days after the beginning of the said intervention. It shall detail the objectives of the said intervention. This notice may give rise to a debate, which shall not be followed by a vote.
>
> Where the said intervention shall exceed four months, the government shall submit the extension to Parliament for authorisation. It may ask the National Assembly to make the final decision.

[61] Ibid 936; Yves Boyer, Serge Sur, and Olivier Fleurence, 'France: Security Council legitimacy and executive primacy' in Ku and Jacobson (n 17), 294.

[62] Alexander Hamilton observed that even at the time of the founding of the US Constitution, formal declarations of war were increasingly rare (Hamilton (n 19), 117 (no 25)). They remain so, notwithstanding the Hague Convention III of 18 October 1907, which required that hostilities 'must not commence without previous and explicit warning, in the form either of a reasoned declaration of war or of an ultimatum with conditional declaration of war' (Art 1). As Michael Dorf points out, 'Modern military conflicts are too fluid, and arise too suddenly, for a declaration of war to serve any practical purpose' (Dorf (n 13), 172).

[63] Georges Vedel et al, *Propositions pour une révision de la Constitution* (1993), 59 and 94.

[64] Frison-Roche (n 60), 937.

If Parliament is out of session at the end of the four-month period, it shall express its decision at the beginning of the following session.

These provisions seem to establish less parliamentary constraint on executive control of the military than the US War Powers Resolution. While the amended Article 35 equips Parliament with new powers to constrain the government's deployment of military forces, however, the actual text of the amendment is weaker than that of the proposal of the Balladur Committee on which it was based, which reads, 'The government shall notify Parliament of its every decision to have the armed forces intervene abroad. Where the said intervention exceeds three months, the extension shall be authorised by an Act of Parliament.'[65]

3. Prohibition of Aggressive Wars

The Constitution of 3 September 1791 declared, in the spirit of the Revolution, 'The French nation renounces to undertake war for the purpose of making conquest, and shall never use force against free people' (Title VI). The same principle, expressed in the same formulation, was incorporated into the fourteenth paragraph of the preamble to the Constitution of 27 October 1946. This principle is therefore a component of the 'constitutional bloc' (*bloc de constitutionnalité*) under the Constitution of the Fifth Republic, though there has not yet been any decision by the Constitutional Council on this matter.

V. Germany

1. The Military under the Basic Law[66]

As originally promulgated, the German Basic Law of 1949 does not mention the existence of armed forces. While Article 26 declares that any acts 'tending to and undertaken with intent to disturb the peaceful relations between nations are unconstitutional', and 'shall be made a criminal offence', the Basic Law (in contrast to the post-war Constitution of Japan of 1946) does not contain an explicit prohibition against the establishment of armed forces.

In pursuit of membership for West Germany in the failed European Defence Community (EDC), the Adenauer government argued inter alia, first, that the federal authority over 'foreign affairs' conferred by Article 73(1) implies the power to legislate on 'military affairs'; secondly, that the provision of Article 4(3) on conscientious objection to military services presupposes the existence of armed forces; and thirdly, that Article 24 allows the federal government to become a party to a 'system of collective security'.

After the 1953 election gave the Adenauer government enough seats to amend the Basic Law, four constitutional amendments were adopted in 1954. The amendments added the power of 'defence' to the powers of the federation (Art 73(1)), empowered the Bundestag to declare 'a state of defence' (*Verteidigungsfall*) (Art 59a), and provided for the establishment of 'armed forces for defence purposes' (Art 87a). These amendments paved the way for West Germany to become a member of the North Atlantic Treaty Organization (NATO). In 1968,

[65] *Rapport du Comité de réflexion et de proposition sur la modernisation et le rééquilibrage des institutions de la Ve République: Une Ve République plus démocratique*, 62–3 (proposition 53e), available at <http://lesrapports.ladocumentationfrancaise.fr/BRP/074000697/0000.pdf>.

[66] See generally, Donald Kommers, *The Constitutional Jurisprudence of the Federal Republic of Germany* (2nd edn, 1997), 160–2; Georg Nolte, 'Germany: ensuring political legitimacy for the use of military forces by requiring constitutional accountability' in Ku and Jacobson (n 17), 231–53; Ziegler (n 5), 141–66.

Article 87a of the Basic Law was amended to include a new paragraph, which affirmed that apart from defence, 'the armed forces may be employed only to the extent expressly permitted by this Basic Law'.

2. The *Military Deployment* Case

Relative to other democratic countries, the Federal Constitutional Court plays a significant role in decisions regarding the deployment of armed forces abroad,[67] as the *Military Deployment* case of 1994 illustrates.

As a consequence of its historical experience in the first half of the twentieth century, Germany is a latecomer to international military deployments. Although successive federal governments through the late 1980s maintained that the Basic Law prohibited any use of the armed forces except for purposes of self-defence and within the area of the alliances covered by NATO and the WEU (Western European Union), Helmut Kohl's CDU-FDP government decided in the early 1990s to deploy military forces outside the NATO countries. In the *Military Deployment* case of 1994,[68] the question in dispute was that of the constitutionality of the deployment of German military units in NATO's monitoring of compliance with the UN embargo against Serbia, in enforcing the UN resolution establishing a 'no-fly-zone' over Bosnia and Herzegovina, and in the UN humanitarian mission in Somalia.

The Federal Constitutional Court ruled that both the UN and NATO treaties constitute systems of 'collective security' in the meaning of Article 24(2), and that the Bundestag's approval of these treaties under Article 59(2) embraces the implied authority to implement the terms of these agreements, including the deployment of German military forces. At the same time, the Court also held that under the Basic Law, the government was required in principle to seek the Bundestag's explicit approval prior to any deployment of the armed forces abroad, because under the Basic Law, the armed forces are conceived to be a 'parliamentary army' (*Parlamentsheer*).[69] Since the Basic Law does not require such approval explicitly, some commentators have suggested that the Court 'ventured into the field of judicial lawmaking'.[70] Nonetheless, the decision successfully 'transformed the debate on the use of German forces abroad from one centred on the question of "whether" into the question of "how"... and from a debate between elite and popular sentiment into a debate on democratic accountability'.[71] In compliance with the Court's ruling in this case, the SDP-Green Party government under

[67] There is no political question doctrine in Germany.

[68] 90 BVerfGE 286.

[69] Kommers (n 66), 162–4. The Court has referred to the German constitutional tradition at least since the Weimar Constitution of 1919, which required that war and peace should be declared by parliamentary statute (Art 45(2)).

[70] Nolte (n 66), 237. Some commentators argue that the Court might implicitly rely on the 'essential matters' doctrine (*Wesentlichkeitstheorie*), which requires parliamentary decisions when essential matters are affected (Nolte (n 66), 243–4; Memorandum by Katja Ziegler, 'The Model of a Parliamentary Army Under the German Constitution' in House of Lords Select Committee on the Constitution, 15th Report, *War Making Powers*, vol II: Evidence (HL Paper 236-II, 2006), 39–40; Ziegler (n 5), 158–60). Ziegler observes that

> The impact on the soldiers whose right to life and physical integrity may be interfered with by sending them into a war zone should be a sufficient reason alone to consider a decision about military deployment as crossing the threshold of an essential question (ibid 159).

[71] Nolte (n 66), 237.

Gerhard Schröder asked the parliament to authorize the deployment of the armed forces to intervene in the Kosovo crisis in 1998.[72]

3. The Parliamentary Participation Act

Parliament codified the requirements of the ruling by the Court that emerged from the 1994 case in the Parliamentary Participation Act of 18 March 2005. The Act stipulates the following:[73]

- First, in principle, any 'deployment of armed forces abroad' requires the consent of the Bundestag (s 1(2)), irrespective of the type of deployment and whether or not it is within a multilateral or collective security action. However, no consent is required for preparatory measures, planning, and humanitarian services and assistance of the army where weapons are carried solely for self-defence and the soldiers are not expected to become involved in armed action (s 2(2)).
- Secondly, under the standard procedure, the government submits an application with detailed information about the intended deployment (s 3(1)(2)). While the Bundestag may approve or reject the government's request, amendments to the request shall not be permissible (s 3(3)). Under the simplified procedure for minor involvements, consents are deemed to have been granted unless the Bundestag becomes active within seven days after being informed (s 4).
- Thirdly, in emergency situations and for the rescue of nationals abroad, consent may be given *ex post* (s 5).

As the Act comes into force, the Federal Constitutional Court should be freed of the burden of resolving the highly political questions of military deployments abroad, which often arouse significant controversy among the German populace.

VI. Japan[74]

1. Article 9 and the Self-Defence Forces

Informed by a modern history not dissimilar to that of Germany, Article 9 of the Constitution of Japan promulgated in 1946 states the following:

> (1) Aspiring sincerely to an international peace based on justice and order, the Japanese people forever renounce war as a sovereign right of the nation and the threat or use of force as means of settling international disputes.
>
> (2) In order to accomplish the aim of the preceding paragraph, land, sea, and air forces, as well as other war potential, will never be maintained. The right of belligerency of the state will not be recognised.

[72] Nolte observes that the

> long, earnest, and searching' debate preceding the parliamentary decision on this occasion worked as 'a catalyst for public opinion which, until then, had not envisaged German troops acting without UN Security Council authorisation (ibid 247).

[73] Cf Memorandum by Ziegler (n 70), 31–46. Ziegler's memorandum includes an English translation of the Parliamentary Participation Act (ibid 44–6), on which the following description draws.

[74] See generally, Akiho Shibata, 'Japan: Moderate Commitment within Legal Strictures' in Ku and Jacobson (n 17).

Despite the apparent purity of the pacifist tone of these clauses, the government of Japan has consistently maintained that they prohibit neither the use of military force for the purpose of self-defence, nor its maintenance of the armed forces necessary to achieve that purpose.[75] The armed forces of Japan are accordingly called the Self Defence Forces (SDF). In the authoritative opinions of the Cabinet Legislation Bureau (*Naikaku Hôsei Kyoku*), Article 9 restricts the SDF to the use of force only for the purpose of self-defence, and the meaning of 'self-defence' is limited strictly to individual, rather than collective, self-defence. Hence, the SDF may not be used for the defence of a foreign country, even if the security of that country is intimately related to that of Japan.

The Supreme Court of Japan has not yet touched on the constitutionality of the SDF, though it has ruled that the Japan–US Mutual Security Treaty is not unconstitutional, since Article 9 concerns only the kind of forces the Japanese government may maintain, whereas US forces stationed in Japan are under the command of the US government.[76] These prudent positions of the government and the court are broadly supported by the public, which still harbours strong pacifist sentiments as well as fears of foreign attack.

The Constitution includes no language concerning war powers.[77] The Self-Defence-Forces Act, however, stipulates that the prime minister is the commander-in-chief of the SDF (s 7), and that the prime minister may order the engagement of the SDF when an armed attack is clearly imminent and the necessity of the engagement is recognized (s 76(1)). However, the use of force must be authorized in advance by the Diet, except in cases in which there is no time to acquire it. Given the pacifist sentiments of the general public, it is unlikely that the government or prime minister would be accorded a free hand in commanding the SDF, even in the event of armed attack from abroad.

2. UN Peacekeeping Operations Act

Since the end of the Cold War, the government has cautiously begun to send the SDF abroad for purposes beyond the national self-defence. In 1992, the Diet enacted the UN Peacekeeping Operations Act, which authorized the SDF to participate in peacekeeping operations sanctioned by either the UN General Assembly or the UN Security Council. In principle, the prime minister must secure the Diet's approval for each deployment in advance when the operation potentially involves the use of force, as in operations to monitor ceasefires or to disarm conflicting parties (s 6(7)). The Act also permits the SDF to participate in humanitarian relief operations at the request of specific listed international organs, including the UN High Commissioner for Refugees, UNICEF, or the World Food Programme. However, the Act stipulates that the SDF may not use force on these missions beyond the use of small firearms for the self-defence of soldiers or persons under their guard (s 24), since the Constitution allows the use of force by military units of the SDF acting as such only for the purpose of Japan's national self-defence.

[75] Many constitutional scholars argue that the maintenance of the SDF is inconsistent with Art 9. This academic view runs counter to the essence of constitutionalism, which entails supporting the fair social cooperation of people embracing mutually inconsistent, even incommensurable worldviews. On this point, see my 'Constitutional Borrowing and Political Theory' (2003) 1 *International Journal of Constitutional Law* 242–3.

[76] *Sakata v Japan*, 13 Keishû 3225 (Sup Ct GB, 16 December 1959), *Sunakawa* case.

[77] Article 66(2) of the Constitution states, 'The prime minister and other cabinet members must be civilian'. This clause was inserted, during the deliberation of the draft constitution at the National Diet, at the request of the Far East Commission, which oversaw the governance of the US occupying forces in Japan. The Commission foresaw the possibility of Japan's rearmament, even under Art 9.

Because of this restriction, the deployment of the SDF to conflicts abroad is allowed only when ceasefire agreements have been reached between the conflicting parties, and the parties and other countries involved agree to the participation of the SDF. If such agreement is revoked, the government must withdraw the SDF (s 6(13)).

In addition to the UN Peacekeeping Operations Act, the Diet has enacted several pieces of legislation approving deployment of the SDF abroad on an ad hoc basis. This legislation enabled the SDF to participate in reconstruction operations in Iraq after the Gulf War, and to supply fuel to warships and other vessels engaged in anti-terrorist operations in the Indian Ocean after the 9/11 attacks. In these missions too, the SDF was restrained from using force, in compliance with the government's official policy. The reticence of the government to engage the SDF in overseas operations, and the close parliamentary oversight of such operations, is likely to continue for the foreseeable future, barring amendment of the Constitution.

VII. Conclusion

We may conclude that until the first few years of the twenty-first century, parliamentary control of war powers in the United Kingdom, the United States, and France did not work very effectively. These long-standing liberal democracies and permanent members of the UN Security Council have been quite active in deploying military forces abroad. Both the British and French Parliaments have played no effective role in the deployment of the armed forces. The US Congress has been powerless to prevent the President from deploying the military in the first place, and remains reluctant to use its full power once troops are in the field, despite the existence of the War Powers Resolution. While there are some moves towards the strengthening of parliamentary control in the United Kingdom and France, these efforts may encounter difficulties similar to those under the US War Powers Resolution.

On the other hand, in Germany, the Federal Constitutional Court has played a significant role to place the deployment of armed forces under the control of the Bundestag. And the Japanese government has maintained that the SDF may not be used for the defence of a foreign country. Dispatches of the SDF for purposes beyond the national self-defence are permitted only when the Diet approves them for the limited purposes designated by statutes, and their use of force is restrained by the government's official interpretation of the Constitution.

Both German case law and Japanese statutes explicitly refer to decisions of international institutions as part of the legal basis for deployment abroad, for missions including peacekeeping, preventing genocide, and restoring democratic government. However, the efficient solution of regional conflicts often demands timely military actions by ad hoc coalitions of willing and capable states that usually include the old liberal democracies, such as the United States, the United Kingdom, and France. As, for example, the cases of the Kosovo conflict and the Iraq War show, these states reveal, if not their scepticism, at least highly selective attitudes regarding the desirability of using force under the authority of international organizations. It remains to be seen if the lack of effective parliamentary control in these countries might bring about more insecurity rather than security in the world.

Bibliography

Philip Bobbitt, *The Shield of Achilles: War, Peace, and the Course of History* (2002)

John Hart Ely, *War and Responsibility: Constitutional Lessons of Vietnam and Its Aftermath* (1993)

House of Lords Select Committee on the Constitution, 15th Report, *War Making Powers*, vols I and II (HL Paper 236-I, II, 2006)
Charlotte Ku and Harold Jacobson (eds), *Democratic Accountability and the Use of Force in International Law* (2003)
Katja Ziegler, 'Executive Powers in Foreign Policy: The Decision to Dispatch the Military' in Katja Ziegler, Denis Baranger and Anthony Bradley (eds), *Constitutionalism and the Role of Parliaments* (2007)

CHAPTER 23

SECESSION AND SELF-DETERMINATION

SUSANNA MANCINI*

Bologna

I. Introduction: A Comprehensive Theory of Secession

Secession is at once the most revolutionary and the most institutionally conservative of political constructs. Its revolutionary character lies in its ultimate challenge to state sovereignty;[1] its conservative side, in the reinforcement of the virtues of the latter. This inherent duality is reflected in the legal regulation surrounding secession. With very limited exceptions, secession is prohibited both by international law as well as, albeit often implicitly, by the overwhelming majority of state constitutions. Nevertheless, a state born out of a successful secessionist project, is likely to be recognized both by international organizations and by the community of states. Often though, in that connection the term 'secession' is substituted by 'dissolution' (Yugoslavia) or 'voluntary disassociation' (Bangladesh, Eritrea, Czechoslovakia, the Soviet Union). Thus, it becomes apparent that legal regulation of secession tends to run counter and to dissimulate its revolutionary character, while legitimizing its conservative dimension, through state building in the context of a new sovereign entity.

State-building is also the primary focus of traditional definitions of secession by international law scholars, in terms of the creation of a new state upon territory previously forming

* Parts of Section III and Section IV of this chapter draw on my article 'Rethinking the Boundaries of Democratic Secession: Liberalism, Nationalism and the Right of Minorities to Self-Determination' (2008) 6 *International Journal of Constitutional Law* 553.

[1] On sovereignty, see Chapter 17.

part of an existing one.[2] Some scholars tailor this definition so narrowly as to only comprise the actual *event* of secession, while others, more broadly, view secession also as the *process* conducive to the creation of a new state. Irrespective of how broad the definition, however, according to these outcome-based approaches, secession does not challenge the very notions of statehood, citizenship, and sovereignty, but, quite to the contrary, it emphasizes their Westphalian conceptualization: the absolute monopoly of power residing in states, and the congruency of territory, state, people, and nation.

In this chapter, I adopt a comprehensive approach to secession, one that encompasses both its revolutionary and its institutionally conservative dimension. Secession can be viewed as one among other means of political separation within a multinational state, a 'possibility' inscribed within a state's political and constitutional discourse, without necessarily connoting the establishment of a new state. In this light, the analysis of secession logically fits within the broader discussion relating to minority rights and citizenship in multinational societies.[3] This approach has two major advantages. In the first place, it confers a higher degree of coherence to the overall discussion concerning secession. Under prevailing circumstances, secessionist movements operate in the context of multinational states inhabited by autochthonous, territorially concentrated minorities which share a national or quasi-national identity. Thus, secession is not an isolated phenomenon, but rather part of a broader dynamic between a state and its subnational communities. In this light, traditional territorially-based minority rights and the right to secession fall within the same overall category, as they raise analogous moral, political, and legal questions focused on the difficulties in reconciling political theories on citizenship and nationalism, self-determination and sovereignty. Analogously, in international law, the problems that arise in relation to minority protection have always been strictly intertwined with those regarding the right to statehood.

The second advantage of the comprehensive approach is that it construes secession as a flexible, multi-functional device, that can serve different purposes, depending on the context within which it operates. A paramount consideration in any secession-related discussion is that, irrespective of the nature of secessionists claims, secessions are not prima facie desirable, because they jeopardize world stability. However, demonizing secession, turning it into a constitutional taboo, often adds fuel to secessionist claims. On the other hand, if secession is constructed as one among the many rights and options offered to a state's subnational groups, chances are that it will lose much of its appeal. Secessionist claims are often loaded with emotions and passions, but, if secession is 'normalized', and subject to legal rules, if it is rationalized, it is likely to lose its evocative power, and thus to prompt secessionist movements to redirect their agenda towards less disruptive objectives. The other side of the coin is that the presence of a legal right to secession in a multinational state, by challenging the absoluteness of the principles of perpetuity and of territorial integrity, is likely to prompt the government to take nationalist claims, and minority rights, seriously. Ironically, thus, secession might constitute an important step in the pursuit of satisfactory forms of accommodation within, and not beyond, multinational states. But one should caution against uncritically assuming that *secession* is always a source of instability as that would be misleading. There are doubtless cases in which *existing state borders* are the actual source of instability.[4] If this is the case, to integrate secession within a state's constitutional and political discourse, might prove critical in ensuring

[2] Peter Radan, 'Secession: A Word in Search of a Meaning' in Aleksandar Pavković and Peter Radan (eds), *On the Way to Statehood: Secession and Globalisation* (2008), 18.

[3] On citizenship, see Chapter 48.

[4] Timothy William Waters, 'Boxing Pandora: Defining Borders in a Democratizing World', unpublished manuscript, 2011.

a peaceful secessionist process, and the building of a new state on democratic premises, all to the advantage of international, as well as domestic, stability.

A comprehensive theory of secession, unlike traditional, outcome-based approaches, requires a re-conceptualization of traditional concepts of statehood, sovereignty, and citizenship. By recognizing secession as one among various minority rights one squarely challenges the monopoly of state power, and the supremacy of state law, by assuming that sub-state entities posses a form of quiescent sovereignty, that might be activated under certain conditions. This stands against the traditional notion of perpetuity as a structural element of state constitutions and against sovereignty as strictly indivisible. In this respect, a comprehensive theory of secession, by calling for a voluntaristic (or con-federal) dimension in a state constitution, tends to blur the line between the realm of constitutional law and that of international law.

This chapter proceeds in three steps. I first briefly outline the principal theories that justify secession. Next, I analyze the evolution of secession in international law and in international practice, as a corollary of the right of all peoples to self-determination. Finally, in the last section, I turn to the relationship between secession and constitutionalism and ask whether the constitutionalization of the right to secede can, in particular context, be regarded as a constructive response to secessionist challenges and what its implications are for constitutional law.

II. Justifying Secession: Theoretical Views

There are two principal types of theories of the right to secede: Primary Right Theories and Remedial Right Theories. The latter construct the right to secession as a remedy for injustices, that is, as derivative upon the violation of other rights. The former theories, to the contrary, posit that a right unilaterally to secede exists per se, independently from the violation of other rights.

Primary Rights Theories are of two types: nationalist and democratic. Nationalistic theories of secession are built on the premise that there is a moral value in the *nation*, that is, in the fact of belonging to a, broadly speaking, 'culturally homogeneous' community. This basic assumption can, of course, be defended on different theoretical and ideological grounds. While nineteenth-century nationalists constructed nations as exclusionary organic communities, contemporary liberal nationalists, such as Margalit and Raz,[5] uphold versions of nationalism that include components of universalism and inclusivity. In this light, national groups are valuable because the self-worth and self-respect of individuals depends to a large extent upon their group membership. Hence, while liberal nationalism theories justify secessionist claims on the basis of the value that they attach to the collective autonomy of groups, they do not antagonize the liberal individualist approach: national groups are valued primarily because they powerfully contribute to the interests of individuals.

Nationalist theories of secession assume that the state is the optimal political form to preserve a national culture, and, by the same token, that states with strong national identities are more likely better to realize social justice within their borders.[6] This is coherent with John Stuart Mill's assumption that the commonalities among citizens are a fundamental condition for viable states, and that without a homogeneous polity, government would be coercive.[7]

[5] Joseph Raz and Avishai Margalit, 'National Self-Determination' (1990) 87 *Journal of Philosophy* 12.

[6] David Miller, *On Nationality* (1995).

[7] John Stuart Mill, *Considerations on Representative Government* ([1861] 1991).

Accordingly, for contemporary liberal nationalists, such as Michael Walzer, Michael Lund, and David Miller, nationalism does not constitute a threat to democracy, but is instead a condition for it, because it ensures the solidarity, trust, and shared sentiments and values among citizens that democracy requires.[8]

In light of nationalist theories, the legitimacy of secession depends on two conditions: the pre-existence of a 'nation', and the existence of a relationship between the latter and a given territory. This poses a first problem, in that various different groups might have equally legitimate claims on the same territory. Moreover, even if in principle all nations should be granted the right to their own state, in practice, to satisfy the aspirations of given nationalities through secession, necessarily implies the frustration of other nationalities.[9] If there are trapped minorities within the separatist subunit, granting secession to the latter on the basis of national self-determination provokes a clash between competing collective rights (that of the seceding group versus that of the trapped minorities) as well as between the collective and individual rights of, respectively, the seceding group and those individuals within it who are opposed to secession. Justifying the legitimacy of secession on nationalist theories could also encourage nation-building programs, with the aim of dismantling existing groups and/or preventing the formation of new ones.

Finally, if, as posited by Miller, secession is legitimate when the borders of a state and those of a nation do not overlap,[10] not only the break-up of multinational states would in principle be acceptable, but secession would be legitimate only if aimed at the formation of homogeneous states, but not of multinational ones. This ignores the natural fluidity of identities and the effects of globalization, in terms of infusing diversity into political communities,[11] and sets the premises for an exclusionary model of citizenship.

The second type of Primary Right Secession Theories can be defined as 'democratic' or 'choice' theories. Choice theorists, including Robert McGee, Christopher Wellman, Daniel Philpott, and Harry Beran, posit that freedom of association and democracy should, at least in principle, apply when drawing state borders and that the right to secession is derived from the individual right to voluntarily choose associations. Their emphasis is not on the *collective* autonomy of nations, but rather on the *individual* autonomy of groups' members. Individual autonomy is the fundamental value which ultimately justifies secessionist claims, because it constitutes the ground in which is rooted the right to associate politically, that is the basis of any legitimate government. Consensus is a prerequisite for the legitimacy of political authority, as democracy is based on popular consent and voluntary membership. Democratic governments make decisions binding on *all* citizens, irrespective of whether they approve or disapprove of them. Hence, for a state to be legitimate, citizens should at a minimum agree to be included and observe a core of common rules. If the individuals who form part of a group within a state no longer consent to the state's authority, they must be granted the right to secede. Autonomy and freedom of association confer, in fact, to all individuals the right to associate, but also that to withdraw from an association, including the political association *par excellence*, the state. It follows that, for choice theorists, the right to secede should be granted irrespective of a group's cultural or ethnic homogeneity, and even in the absence of a strong territorial claim by the separatist group. What really matters are a group's political abilities and its desire of its own state, that is, a group's will to associate in a political and independent unity.[12] Thus, there is a 'political-

[8] On democracy, see further Chapter 11.

[9] Ernest Gellner, *Nations and Nationalism* (1983).

[10] Miller (n 6), 112.

[11] Costanza Margiotta, *L'ultimo diritto. Profili storici e teorici della secessione* (2005).

[12] Christopher Heath Wellman, *A Theory of Secession: The Case for Political Self-determination* (2005), 168.

territorial' rather than a 'national' right to secession[13] that is legitimated by aggregated individual choices. To grant the right to secede only to nations, that is, to large culturally distinct groups, would not only collide with the principle of democracy, but also produce uncertainty, because cultural distinctness is often a matter of degree, making it difficult to draw clear-cut lines, and decide, for example, whether a group constitutes one or more nations.[14]

Choice theorists construct secession as a primary right. This does not mean, however, that it is an unqualified right. According to Harry Beran 'liberal political philosophy requires that secession be permitted if it is effectively desired by a territorially concentrated group within a state and is morally and practically possible.'[15] Hence, the right to secede should not be granted to groups that are not in the position of giving birth to viable states and that do not satisfy certain conditions.[16] For Christopher Wellman, to base the right to secede on an unqualified freedom of association is a 'recipe for anarchy'. States, in fact, must be territorially contiguous in order to perform their functions, and contiguity would not be possible if states could coerce only those who consent. In Wellman's view, thus, secession should be allowed only if it does not interfere with the production of essential political functions and does not jeopardize the remaining state from doing so. In other words, the territorial boundaries of existing states can be reconfigured according to the preferences of inhabitants only as long as this does not interrupt the benefits of political stability.[17]

Thus, choice theories are based in principle on universal values and universal rights, but, in practice, only apply to individuals and groups that are in a favorable situation. Political stability, territorial contiguity, and the overall practicability of secession prevent many (most?) groups from enjoying the democratic right to secession. Moreover, choice theorists posit that a political community is legitimate only if membership of is based a voluntary act of adhesion. It is very unlikely, however, that within a territorially clustered group *all* individuals would actually agree to secede. This means that a plebiscite in favor of secession would either force the non-secessionist individuals to leave their territory, or it would set the ground for an illegitimate political association, due to lack of consensus.[18] Thus, if consensus stands as the ultimate criterion of legitimacy for democracy, then the new (post-secession) frontiers may end up being just as undemocratic as the old ones were.

Another problem with choice theories is that they assume that populations are basically fixed entities, not subject to change,[19] which is not the case in today's globalized world. According to choice theories, a group of migrants could settle in a given territory and legitimately claim the right to secede and to establish its own state. This potential threat would likely prompt states characterized by large immigration flows to impede the formation of homogeneous territorially-concentrated groups,[20] and/or to prevent new minorities from becoming politically organized and economically autonomous.[21]

[13] David Copp, 'Democracy and Communal Self-Determination' in Robert McKim and Jeff McMahan (eds), *The Morality of Nationalism* (1997), 277ff.

[14] Harry Beran, 'A Liberal Theory of Secession' (1984) 32 *Political Studies* 21.

[15] Ibid 23.

[16] These include: being large enough to assume the responsibility of statehood, being able to guarantee the rights of trapped minorities, inhabiting a territory that will not form an enclave within the existing state, that is not culturally, economically, or military essential to the existing state, and that does not have a disproportionately high share of the economic resources of the existing state: Beran (n 14).

[17] Wellman (n 12), 34ff.

[18] Allen Buchanan, 'Theories of Secession' (1997) 26 *Philosophy and Public Affairs* 31.

[19] Allen Buchanan, 'The International Institutional Dimension of Secession' in Percy Blanchemains Lehning (ed), *Theories of Secession* (1998), 248.

[20] Margaret Moore, *The Ethics of Nationalism* (2001), 172.

[21] Buchanan (n 18), 52.

In the end, choice theories reproduce, at least in part, the flaws of national self-determination theories. In order to secede democratically, a group must express its will in a referendum or plebiscite.[22] Accordingly, in order to democratically address a secessionist dispute, the first step would consist in determining in which portion of the territory the referendum should be held and who would be accorded the right to vote.[23] With very limited exceptions, there is a complete overlap between the territorial unit and the historical tradition that links a given group to the territory. These two dimensions—tradition and territory—preexist consensus, as the territory can only be defined as the area that has been traditionally occupied by a group of people, which has the right to continue occupying it and, as a consequence, to express its will in the referendum regarding secession. If tradition preexists consensus, secession cannot be justified entirely on the basis of democracy, but must be bolstered by other, pre-democratic elements, such as the historical link between a group and the territory it inhabits. Groups that traditionally inhabit a clustered territory and that express a will to secede are, in the overwhelming majority of cases, ethnic or cultural minorities. Hence, in practice, in the overwhelming majority of cases, the right to secede ends up by being granted mainly on the basis of nationality.

Remedial Right Theories of Secession, unlike national self-determination and choice-theories, are built on the premise that secession is not a primary right of all peoples, but rather a remedial right that applies in a restricted number of cases, where certain conditions are met. Just cause theorists, such as Allen Buchanan[24] and Wayne Norman,[25] assume that a well-functioning, liberal democracy will provide for fair procedures for reaching collective decisions about government policy, and give every individual and every group the right of voice hence obviating any need for a primary right to secede. According to this view, secession should speak to the wrongs suffered by a group thus being justified only if some kind of injustice is present. Injustice can result from a past annexation to which the group has never consented (such as annexation of the Baltic states by the USSR), or from an unfair treatment by the government of the inhabitants of one of the polity's subunits: a lack of protection of their basic rights and security, a failure to safeguard the legitimate political and economic interests of their region, or a persistent discriminatory redistribution. Rainer Bauböck adds to the list of injustices that can justify secession violations of federal agreements and of distinctive collective rights.[26]

Remedial Right Theories also raise a number of problematic questions. The first is the difficulty in defining injustice. It might be hard, for example, to identify the boundary between 'economic exploitation' and a redistribution that penalizes certain subunits in acceptable fashion, because, even if the relevant state subunit is charged with bigger economic contributions than others, the ultimate advantages and drawbacks of unity seem more likely to reach a point of balance. Furthermore, one must take into account the advantages, not immediately quantifiable in money terms, that the state's component units enjoy by virtue of belonging to it: cultural life, international image and weight, broader labor market etc. The second, deeper question with remedial right theories, on the other hand, concerns their assumption that the

[22] On referendum generally, see Chapter 24.

[23] Margiotta (n 11), 232.

[24] Allen Buchanan, *Secession: The Legitimacy of Political Divorce From Fort Sumter to Lithuania and Quebec* (1991).

[25] Wayne Norman, *Negotiating Nationalism: Nation-Building, Federalism, and Secession in the Multinational State* (2006).

[26] Rainer Bauböck, 'Why Stay Together? A Pluralist Approach to Secession and Federation' in Will Kymlicka and Wayne Norman (eds), *Citizenship in Diverse Society* (2000), 366ff.

status quo is, in principle, fair. Existing borders, however, are not pre-given; they result from historical processes that can hardly be assumed as being necessarily just.

A variant of the Remedial Right Theory is the 'territorial interpretation' of secession offered by Lea Brilmayer. Brilmayer argues that the legitimacy of secession does not depend on certain characteristics that distinguish a given group from a state's majority. Secessionists must demonstrate that justice requires they be granted a right to a given territory:

> What matters is not that it is 'a people' who are seeking to be free. What matters is that this group—whether a homogeneous 'people' or not-has a right to a particular parcel of land, a right that was wrongfully taken from them by a powerful neighbor.[27]

This is, however, a very problematic argument. From a moral standpoint, one does not see how a historically-based claim should be superior to one based on nationality. It is true that there is nothing 'natural' and inherently just in today's state borders, but the same is true about past borders. How far can history go in providing a just cause for secession? Moreover, a territorial claim might be 'just' for the majority of the members of a given group, but unjust for minorities. In fact, the correspondence between 'the people at the time of the loss of independence' and 'the people now' may be attenuated by time. Many states unjustly deprived of sovereignty have been the victims of central government policies aimed at weakening their ethnic identity by transplanting 'colonizers' of different stock or from the dominant nation (as in the case of ethnic Russians in the Baltic states), who, in turn, became so rooted in the new territory as to become 'citizens' with full rights. Citizens of this type are problematic, however, as they are likely to remain sufficiently tied to their (formerly annexing) state of origin to militate against full independence of their new state of citizenship. In view of this, basing the legitimacy of secession on the existence of a 'just' territorial claim, is often likely to advantage ethnic majorities within sub-state units, and, thus, to lead to the same shortcomings present in both national self-determination and in choice theories of secession.

III. Secession and Self-Determination in International Law and in the International Practice

In international law, self-determination is 'the freedom for all peoples to decide their political, economic and social regime'. Hence, it is both a collective right of peoples autonomously to decide the course of their national life and to equally divide power, and a right of all individuals freely and fully to participate to the political process.[28] Moreover, self-determination combines elements of nationalism and of democracy:[29] peoples may invoke the right to self-determination either in order to *secede* from a state and give birth to a new one; or, in order to achieve other aims, such as to make internal coercion cease, to overturn the state government, or to establish autonomous regimes within the sub-state units.[30] International law,

[27] Lea Brilmayer, 'Commentaries on Lea Brilmayer, Secession and Self-Determination: A Territorial Interpretation: One Decade Later', Faculty Scholarship Series, Paper 2439, 2000, available at <http://digitalcommons.law.yale.edu/fss_papers/2439>.

[28] J.J. Paust, 'Self-Determination: A Definitional Focus' in *Self-Determination: National, Regional, and Global Dimension* (1980), 13.

[29] Patrick Thornberry, 'The Democratic or Internal Aspect of Self-Determination with Some Remarks on Federalism' in *Modern Law of Self-Determination* (1993), 105.

[30] Chen Lung-Chu, 'Self-Determination: An Important Dimension of the Demand for Freedom' (1981) 75 *Proceedings of the American Society of International Law* 89.

and the practice of the international community, have never provided coherent guidance to respond to the tensions between these different dimensions (collective/individual and democratic/nationalistic) of self-determination. In particular, neither international law nor international practice have ever produced an agreed-upon definition of the characteristics a 'people' should have to warrant the right to the 'external' or nationalistic dimension of self-determination, or, in other words, the right to secede.

'Self-determination' entered the international scene in the early twentieth century, with the advent of the First World War and the Bolshevik Revolution.[31] According to Lenin, self-determination was a general criterion for the liberation of oppressed peoples, which, in turn, should contribute to the success of the socialist revolution. In Lenin's view, however, the socialist cause always took priority over the principle of self-determination, which Lenin championed only strategically, insofar as it furthered class struggle.[32] US President Woodrow Wilson, on the other hand, viewed self-determination primarily as a corollary to popular sovereignty, and thus as the right of peoples freely to choose their government. Domestically, this translated into 'self-government'; externally, Wilson understood self-determination as the criterion best suited to govern territorial changes, and, in particular, the division of the Ottoman and Austro-Hungarian Empires. Wilson also advocated the use of self-determination as a guiding principle in settling colonial disputes, but thought that self-determination had to be reconciled with the interests of the colonial powers.[33]

The Wilsonian ideals prevailed in the post-First World War settlement, when the 'peoples' entitled to statehood were identified, at least in principle, in all national or ethnic communities. Wilson recognized the right of national/ethnic groups to form states on the territories they inhabited, without relying on existing borders, and explicitly rejected subordination of such groups' interests to territorial concerns.[34] In practice, however, the impossibility to found nation-states for all nationalities and to found ethnically homogeneous nation-states in the territories of former multiethnic empires, obliged the Allies to address the *nationality* problem also in terms of *minority* rights. This was done in drawing up the Covenant of the League of Nations and the treaties on minorities. The League system did not, however, provide a minimum standard of protection for all European minorities, since obligations were imposed only on the newly-independent states, and not on Allied and associated states and not even on Germany. In practice only the new states were obliged to limit their newly awarded sovereignty by accepting minority clauses imposed by the Great Powers, as a condition for recognition of their new boundaries. *Minority protection represented therefore a limitation of self-determination for the new states* and was connected to the rise of expansionist and irredentist nationalism.

The League of Nations was confronted directly with the issue of secession in the Åland Islands case. The Council of the League adopted the view that self-determination was not a *positive rule* under international law, and, that, in particular, 'national groups' did not have a right to unilateral secession.[35] The League did not, however, completely rule out the possibility

[31] Prior to that, the principle of self-determination had already emerged in the American Declaration of Independence of 1776 and in the French Revolution of 1789, as a key component of the principle according to which the government should be responsible to the people. See Antonio Cassese, *Self-Determination of Peoples: A Legal Reappraisal* (1999), 5ff.

[32] Ibid 18.

[33] Ibid 19.

[34] Hurst Hannum, 'Self-Determination, Yugoslavia, and Europe: Old Wine in New Bottles?' (1993) 3 *Transnational Law and Contemporary Problems* 57.

[35] Report of the International Committee of Jurists entrusted by the Council of the League of Nations with the task of giving an advisory opinion upon the legal aspects of the Aaland Islands question, League of Nations, Official Journal Special Supplement No 3, October 1920, 5.

of secession. The dispute, in fact, was settled by obliging Finland to increase the guarantees granted to the Islands. In the event that Finland refused to grant the Åland population such guarantees, the League would have supported the separation of the Islands from Finland.[36] Thus, the League, constructed self-determination as strictly intertwined with territorial autonomy and minority rights, and conceptualized secession as a de facto remedial right.

After the Second World War, a new universal and individualistic conception of human rights prevailed. In comparison with the post-First World War period, the minority problem was significantly less dramatic, thanks to the various transfers of populations that had occurred, and to the changing of international boundaries. Moreover, the atmosphere in Europe had changed. The fight for independence carried out by various national minorities had been a prominent factor in the First World War, which from its start, involved the rights of small nationalities, such as Serbia and Belgium. Thus, collective minority rights fell into disfavor, as they were seen as a threat to peace. Neither the UN Charter nor the Universal Declaration of Human Rights of 1948, explicitly protects the rights of minorities. The International Covenant on Civil and Political Rights (ICCPR) of 1966 contains in Article 27 a clause on minority protection that is very limited in scope and structured in strictly individual terms. The ICCPR, however, also contains Article 1, according to which, 'All peoples have the right of self-determination', by virtue of which they 'freely determine their political status and freely pursue their economic, social and cultural development'. The ICCPR does not contain a definition of these two categories. However, in the discussion which took place within the Commission for Human Rights, the majority of state delegates agreed that minority rights should not be interpreted as authorizing any group which inhabits a portion of a state territory to constitute communities capable of jeopardizing national unity or security.[37] Thus, minorities, regardless of their defining characteristics, lack a right to self-determination. However, the very fact that the states felt the need specifically to address this issue reveals that they were keenly aware of the tenuous basis for the different treatment of the two above-mentioned categories.

The Final Act of the Conference on Security and Cooperation in Europe of 1975 contains a similar dichotomy. On the one hand, it affirms the right of all peoples to self-determination in particularly wide terms, that encompass all of its dimensions, including the external and nationalistic ones. The Act does not define who the 'peoples' are, but since the state parties are exclusively European, the term cannot be taken to refer to 'colonial peoples'. Moreover, according to the Act, 'The participating States will respect the equal rights of peoples and their right to self-determination', which suggests that the 'peoples' may not necessary coincide with each state's constitutionally determined people. Given all this, the only possible category of European people to whom self-determination might apply are subnational ones, that is, national minorities. The Act, however, seems to exclude minorities from the right to self-determination, as it refers to the rights of peoples belonging to national minorities, in terms that are very close to those of Article 7 of the ICCPR. The Helsinki Act does not make any definitional attempt to clarify what features make minorities different from peoples and exclude them from the right to self-determination.

Thus, in the post-Second World War international law system, self-determination was constructed as a *right* of all peoples, which had not been the case in the League of Nations era. However, the ambiguity regarding its beneficiaries and the strong disfavor regarding secession

[36] Report by the Commission of Rapporteurs, League of Nations Council Doc B7 21/68/106, 1921.

[37] 16 UN ECOSOC, Supp 8, p 7, para 54, UN Doc E/2447, 1953. On socio-economic and economic rights, see Chapters 49 and 50.

that emerged in international practice, neutralized the potential of self-determination, turning it in little more than a chimera. The right to external self-determination was granted solely to 'peoples' under colonial rule who could not be defined in ethnic or national terms, but, rather in political and territorial ones, as the *political* majorities formed by the *multiethnic* peoples under colonial rule.[38] The latter were considered as a unity together with the territories which the colonial powers had delimited. This clashed with the individual dimension of self-determination, according to which each individual may decide to which polity s/he wants to belong to, as well as with the nationalistic dimension of self-determination, as the de-colonization process did not take into account the desires of ethnic or national groups. Many boundaries were changed under the aegis on the UN, without consulting the (individual and collective) peoples directly affected by such changes. Think, among many other cases, of Rwanda, Burundi, British Cameroon, the federation of Ethiopia and Eritrea, and Palestine.

For non-colonial 'peoples', the right of 'all peoples' to self-determination was conceived in 'domestic' terms, emphasizing its 'democratic' rather than its 'nationalistic' dimension. Conservative international principles prevailed over the right to secede: the ones barring intervention in the internal affairs of states, with its obvious corollary, the inviolability of frontiers; and the threat or use of force against their territorial integrity and political independence. States, thus, are supposed to meet the obligations associated with the right to self-determination of *all* peoples, of whatever size or nature, by safeguarding their linguistic, ethnic, and cultural heritage and guaranteeing both their enjoyment of fundamental rights and the possibility of access to government on an equal footing with the rest of the population. Such access to government is not shaped as a group right to political participation. The right to self-determination, rather, protects the individuals that compose the minority groups, which should not be excluded from political participation, for example by being denied the right to vote.[39] Only where such guarantees are absent or gravely limited can the right to self-determination become specified as the right to secede: that is, where a people is subjugated in violation of international law, it must be able to regain freedom by constituting itself as an independent and sovereign state.[40]

Between 1947 and 1991, secession occurred only in the case of Bangladesh, as international law viewed state boundaries as permanent features of the international state system and the practice of states and the United Nations prevented the 'external' or nationalistic dimension of the right to self-determination from going outside the boundaries of the colonial world. Moreover, even in the colonial context, territorial changes were contingent on assessments of appropriateness and acceptability by the 'great powers'. For example, the attempted secession of Katanga from the Congo was initially considered of merely internal relevance and hence coming under the principle of non-intervention on the postulate that the United Nations had the object of maintaining the territorial integrity and political independence of the Congo. With the danger of secession over, the Secretary-General declared that the UN 'has never accepted, does not accept, and... will never accept a principle of secession from a Member State'.[41] Similarly, the uprising of the Ibo minority in Biafra, coupled with an accusation of

[38] Margaret Moore, 'Introduction, The Self-Determination Principle and the Ethics of Secession' in Margaret Moore (ed), *National Self-Determination and Secession* (1998).

[39] Diane F. Orentlicher, 'International Responses to Separatist Claims: Are Democratic Principles Relevant?' in Steven Macedo and Allen Buchanan (eds), *Secession and Self-Determination* (2003), 19ff.

[40] Aurelio Cristescu, *The Right of Self-Determination. Historical and Current Development on the Basis of the United Nations Instruments*, UN Doc E/CN/4/Sub.2/404/rev.1, 1981, para 173.

[41] René Lemarchand, 'The Limits of Self-Determination: The Case of the Katanga Secession' (1962) 56 *American Political Science Review* 404.

genocide by the Nigerian government before the United Nations led to no international intervention, on the postulate—a cavil—that since no party had invoked the Security Council, such intervention would not be possible, as well as on the principle of the inviolability of the sovereign independence of member states. The United Nations did not even oppose the unilateral abolition by Ethiopia of the status of federated region awarded to Eritrea in 1952 based on a recommendation by the General Assembly or the military support that Addis Ababa was receiving from the USSR and Cuba.

A dramatic change occurred with the end of the Cold War, the break-up of the socialist federations, and the 'ethnic revival' that rapidly spread around the world. The emergence of democracy as a legal obligation of states now permits the international community to concern itself with both the procedure and substance of 'democratic' decisions concerning ethno-cultural groups. As a consequence, minority rights, self-determination, and secession have regained a central position in the international arena.

Post-1989 democratization has often exacerbated ethnic conflicts. If democracy is not understood simply as majority rule, cultural conflicts in democratic states must be resolved in a way that is either acceptable, or defensible in relation, to all citizens and groups. However, in many formerly authoritarian societies, democracy has been structured as 'majoritarianism with elections',[42] which turns into disadvantage for the losers. In the long run, constitutionalism-related principles and institutions, including the protection of fundamental rights, will possibly ameliorate the risks inherent in rapid democratization. These, however, are processes that require time, whereas the adoption of the 'majoritarianism with election' model has quickly spread in many multiethnic societies, where democracy without liberalism has often turned borders into a 'trap for the losers'.[43]

After a long period during which the borders of European states had remained strictly stable, the collapse of Yugoslavia and the USSR posed the problem of recognition of new states in dramatic terms. The European Union developed its 'Guidelines on the Recognition of New States in Eastern Europe and in the Soviet Union',[44] which stipulated that, inter alia, democracy, the rule of law, human rights, the rights of minorities, and a commitment to respect the inviolability of frontiers and to peaceful settlement of disputes were all necessary criteria for state recognition. The United States produces analogous policy documents. These guidelines never developed into binding international provisions. In particular, it should be noticed that the European system does not provide for universal standards of minority protection. West European states are free to protect or not to protect minorities, as long as they comply with the principle of non-discrimination. In France, for example, the Constitutional Council declared the European Charter of Regional Languages not consistent with the French Constitution because it confers 'specific rights to those speaking regional or minority languages within the territories in which such languages are spoken'.[45] Thus, one can say that the post-Cold War situation shows certain analogies with the post-First World War settlement, with the Great Powers imposing minority protection on newborn states in order to contain their expansionist and irredentist nationalism. Once again, m*inority protection has come to represent a limitation of self-determination for the new states* and has become connected with the preservation of regional stability.

On the other hand, the development of these additional and unorthodox criteria for state recognition, enriched and expanded the significance of self-determination and secession. During the whole of the nineteenth century and the first part of the twentieth, the 'great

[42] Waters (n 4). [43] Ibid. [44] To be found in (1992) 31 ILM 1486–7.

[45] Conseil Constitutionnel, Decision no 99-412 DC of 15 June 1999.

nations' were seen as the engines of historical development, while smaller, less-developed nations could progress only by abandoning their national character and permitting their assimilation into one of the great nations.[46] In the post-Cold War period, however, new states have been required, as a condition of recognition, to acknowledge and protect ethnic and national pluralism. This testifies to a more elastic conception of the rights of minority groups, because it postulates a close connection between freedom and equality, and without denying the primarily individual dimension of human rights, it recognizes the role that groups play in the formation and recognition of individual identity. This conception is reflected in the opinions rendered by the Arbitration Commission of the Conference on Yugoslavia ('Badinter Commission').[47] According to the Commission, by virtue of self-determination, 'each human entity might indicate his or her belonging to the community... of his or her choice'. This means that each individual can call upon the right to self-determination to choose the group to which she decides to belong. In the specific context of former Yugoslavia, this translated in the duty of the states concerned to accord to Serbs in Bosnia-Herzegovina and Croatia, if they so desired, the nationality of their choice (most likely, Serbian nationality). This seems to suggest that the Commission recognized the existence of a distinction between 'nationality' and 'citizenship' similar to that provided in the Treaty on European Union signed in Maastricht.[48] Moreover, the Badinter Commission placed much emphasis on the democracy of the process leading to independence, requiring that referenda be held as a condition for recognition.

The tendency to legitimize secession under certain procedural and substantive conditions has been confirmed in the more recent cases of Montenegro and Kosovo. In 2003, the Federal Republic of Yugoslavia converted into the State Union of Serbia and Montenegro. Despite its formal domestic nature, the conversion was strongly promoted by the EU. The Constitutional Charter was adopted following the procedure prescribed by the 1992 Constitution, without any formal break of constitutional continuity. Article 60 of the new Constitution contained a secession clause which provided that upon the expiry of a three-year period, a member state has the right to initiate the withdrawing procedure. Such a decision had to be made after a referendum had been held. The referendum was dependent on an Act on Referendum that had to be passed by a member state. Hence the member state controlled the organization of the referendum, but under the condition that recognized democratic standards were taken into account. In other words, it was agreed that one member state could unilaterally withdraw from the Union, following strict procedural rules. The European Union legitimized the new Constitution of 2003, and, later, the secessionist process of 2006. Under rules proposed by the European Union and approved by Montenegro's Parliament, a 55 percent majority was needed to mandate secession, in order to guarantee the participation of all groups, and particularly of the Serbian minority (30 percent of the population). Montenegro did not experience any difficulty in obtaining international recognition.

[46] Will Kymlicka, 'Introduction' in Will Kymlicka (ed), *The Rights of Minority Cultures* (1995).

[47] The Arbitration Commission of the Conference on Yugoslavia ('Badinter Commission') was set up by the EEC Council of Ministers on August 27, 1991 to provide the Conference on Yugoslavia with legal advice. The Commission has handed down 15 opinions on 'major legal questions' which have arisen from the split of the Socialist Federal Republic of Yugoslavia. The text of the first ten opinions of the Commission was published in the *European Journal of International Law*. Opinions 1 to 3 are reproduced in (1992) 3 *European Journal of International Law* 182ff; Opinions 4 to 10 are reproduced in (1993) 4 *European Journal of International Law* 74ff.

[48] Alain Pellet, 'The Opinions of the Badinter Arbitration Committee A Second Breath for the Self-Determination of Peoples' (1992) 3 *European Journal of International Law* 178.

Kosovo unilaterally declared its independence from the Republic of Serbia on February 17, 2008. For almost a decade, Kosovo had been administered by a UN provisional authority, the United Nations Mission in Kosovo (UNMIK).[49] Prior to 2008, the Kosovar representatives together with the Serbian leadership and UN and EU representatives, had tried to negotiated the future of Kosovo on several occasions, without ever reaching consensus. The 2008 declaration of independence affirms that it 'fully accepts' the UN Secretary-General special envoy's Kosovo Status Settlement. These include respect for the principle of democracy, the rule of law, and fundamental rights of individuals and minorities. The Kosovar representatives, thus, alongside their Montenegran counterparts, seemed to be aware that respect for democracy and minority protection can ensure a smoother secessionist process, and, thus, implicitly, to acknowledge the legitimacy of the involvement of the international community in the elaboration of the constitutional framework of the newborn state. The Kosovar unilateral declaration of independence was judged not in violation of international law by the International Court of Justice[50] which implicitly suggests the legitimacy of a democratic and 'gradual' secessionist process, heavily involving regional and/or international authorities.[51]

While some scholars fear that tolerating such a process will turn UN-led administrations into 'nothing but a road towards secession',[52] others justify the secession of Kosovo as a case of 'earner sovereignty'. Under the 'earner sovereignty' approach, a breakaway entity does not merit recognition as a new state immediately after its separation or quest to separate from its mother state. Instead, such an entity needs to earn its sovereignty, demonstrating that it is capable of functioning as an independent state, and that it would be a reliable sovereign partner for the international community of states.[53]

In any case, undeniably, the post-Cold War attitude towards secession suggests that international law and the practice of the international community is gradually moving towards the legitimization of the 'secessionist option', albeit only if it is compatible with democracy, and with a pluralistic understanding of citizenship, and if it is gives enough guarantees that it will not undermine geopolitical equilibria.

IV. Secession and the Constitution

'Secession' derives from the Latin verb *secedere*, which refers to the action of separating or moving away from something. In ancient Roman times, the word did not have a territorial connotation: individuals and groups could *secedere* from their community for a variety of reasons, including political ones, as in the secession of the Plebeians who went to the Sacred Mountain in 494 BC.

[49] See Interim Agreement for Peace and Self-Government in Kosovo, February 23, 1999, UN Doc S/1999/648 (June 7, 1999) ('Rambouillet Accords').

[50] *Accordance with international law of the unilateral declaration of independence in respect of Kosovo (Request for Advisory Opinion)*, Advisory Opinion ('*Kosovo Opinion*').

[51] A similar pattern was followed in the case of East Timor. In 1999, the East Timorese people voted in a UN-organized referendum to separate from Indonesia. Indonesia protested the referendum results and backed violent militias to attack and intimidate the East Timorese populations. The UN Security Council, in Resolution 1264, established a peacekeeping force, the International Force for East Timor, to safeguard East Timor. East Timor was then administered by the United Nations, with substantial support from other countries, until it became a sovereign state on May 20, 2002.

[52] International Court of Justice, CR 2009/24, 60 (*Zimmermann*).

[53] James R. Hooper and Paul R. Williams, 'Earned Sovereignty: The Political Dimension' (2003) 31 *Denver Journal of International Law and Policy* 355.

The conceptualization of secession as a *specific* kind of political action was developed in Johannes Althusius' *Politica* (1643). For Althusius, political order was rooted in social bonds and duties. Sovereignty resulted from the symbiotic relation among independent social orders, which delegate authority to a higher social unity. Althusius' construction was an embryonic modern federative polity, based on consent. Consent was not conceived by Althusius as requiring unanimity. Moreover, whereas social contract theorists, such as Hobbes, posit that once the sovereignty of individual wills is transferred to the sovereign office it cannot be recalled, in Althusius' *Politica* each social unit remains free legally to secede from the higher social unit to which it has delegated authority.[54]

It was only in connection with the American Civil War that secession acquired a clear territorial dimension and the modern discourse on secession was launched. This new discourse called into question the relationship between federal power and states' rights, the nature of the federal constitution, and the very notion of sovereignty. It resulted in a political demonization of secession,[55] and in its being construed as incompatible with constitutionalism.

The heritage of the American Civil War has deeply influenced the subsequent discussion surrounding secession. Liberal federations have been reluctant to enshrine a secession clause[56] in the Constitution, for a variety of reasons. One of these is the potential strategic use that can be made of it, either by the state or by its subunits. In periods of nation-building, the central government might use the secession clause as a blandishment to entice its subunits and/or other independents states that it aims as annexing. The secession clause may be a crucial tool in this process, because existing subunits and new states rely on it and accept the limitation of their sovereignty, given the assurance that they will be able to regain it. In other words, the central government uses the secession clause as an enticement to subunits or other independent states to accept annexation. The latter, as long as they can count on a future option to withdraw, are more amenable to transferring powers to the central government or to joining a federation. Once the central power has achieved its objectives and consolidated its power, however, the secession clause typically either disappears or becomes a dead letter. The 1931 Constitution of the Chinese Soviet Republic (a date when the Communist Party did not control the whole national territory) recognized 'the right of the national minorities to self-determination . . . going as far as the formation of an independent State for each of them', specifying that minorities 'may join the Union of Chinese Soviets or secede from it and form a sovereign State'. After the Communists consolidated their control over the mainland and subjugated neighboring territories such as Tibet, the secession clause found in their constitution disappeared. Consistent with that, Article 4 of the 1975 Constitution stated that 'The Chinese People's Republic is a unitary multinational State. The areas having regional autonomy are inalienable parts of the Republic.'[57] The charter of the Soviet Union had similarly constitutionalized the right of secession. Recognition of this right, in Lenin's opinion, in no way led to the 'formation of small States, but to the enlargement of the bigger ones—a phenomenon more advantageous for the masses and for the development of the economy.'[58] The Constitution of

[54] Donald W. Livingston, 'The Very Idea of Secession', *Symposium: Secession and Nationalism at the Millennium* (1998) 35 *Society* 38.

[55] Margiotta (n 11), 57.

[56] The 1983 Constitution of the Federation of St Kitts and Nevis, contains a provision on the 'Secession of Nevis' at Art 115, according to which 'If, by virtue of a law enacted by the Nevis Island Legislature under section 113(1), the island of Nevis ceases to be federated with the island of Saint Christopher, the provisions of schedule 3 shall forthwith have effect.'

[57] Lee C. Buchheit, *Secession: The Legitimacy of Self-Determination* (1978), 101–2.

[58] Vladimir. I. Lenin, *Prosvestcenie*, n 4, 5, 6, April–June 1914, quoted by Buchheit (n 57), 122.

Burma of 1974 also contained a secession clause, but no one had any illusions concerning it ever being put into actual use. Analogously, the guarantee of the right of secession in the Ethiopian Constitution of 1994 seems largely motivated by the desire to strengthen cohesion by dissuading the component subunits of the state from following the example of Eritrea.

The federation's subunits may also take advantage of the right to secede in order to seek gains having little to do with secession. For example, in the United States in the 1860s, in order to strengthen the constitutional position of the South,

> many statesmen advocated the extreme position of temporary separation from the North... A.H. Handy, [Secession] Commissioner from Mississippi, in urging the Governor of Maryland to take steps towards separation, defended his position on these grounds: 'Secession is not intended to break up the present government, but to perpetuate it... we go out for the purpose of getting further guarantees and security for our rights... our plan is for the Southern States to withdraw from the Union for the present, to allow amendments to the Constitution to be made, guaranteeing our just rights.[59]

The democracy and transparency of decision-making processes may be undermined when the right of secession is exploited by the most populous or richest subunits, taking advantage of their greater bargaining power to put forward non-negotiable demands in search of immediate gains instead of compromise solutions, to the detriment of the national interest. In such cases cooperation between the state's various component parts is replaced by forms of autonomous development, reducing the level of interdependence among the subunits.

Arguing against the constitutionalization of the right to secede on the basis of its potential strategic uses raises an important objection. The absence of a secession clause does not necessary prevent stronger subunits from achieving an excessively strong bargaining position, through the strategic use of the secessionist threat, simply because everyone is aware that secession can (and in most cases actually does) occur regardless of its legal legitimacy. Moreover, the legal impossibility to secede is more likely to turn the relationship between separatist subunits and the central government into a tug of war and encourage the use of violence. On the other hand, a clause which subjects secession to strict procedural conditions is likely to encourage subunits to cooperate and to compromise. Hence, secession need not play into the hands of richer or stronger subunits. To the contrary, as Daniel Weinstock puts it, a constitutional secession clause forces secessionists to make 'a cold and lucid cost/benefit analysis' of withdrawing versus remaining in the existing federation, that is, to consider seriously the legal obstacles that they must overcome before they can successfully secede.[60]

A more convincing objection to the constitutionalization of secession is that the latter might not provide a stable solution to ethnic conflict while actually worsening the situation of sub-minorities.[61] Most secessionist attempts are motivated by the will of subnational groups to form their own state. Subnational units, however, are almost never completely ethnically homogeneous: in Kosovo, for example, there are Serbian enclaves, in Quebec there are Anglophones and aboriginal minorities etc. In the event of a secession, trapped minorities are excluded from the body that confers legitimacy on the new state, and thus risk becoming 'second-class' citizens. For example, the Preamble to the Croatian Constitution of 1990 states that:

[59] Jesse T. Carpenter, *The South as a Conscious Minority* (1930), 167.

[60] Daniel Weinstock, 'Toward a Proceduralist Theory of Secession' (2000) 13 *Canadian Journal of Law and Jurisprudence* 262.

[61] Donald L. Horowitz, 'The Cracked Foundations of the Right to Secede' (2003) 14(2) *Journal of Democracy* 6.

> Proceeding from ... the inalienable, indivisible, nontransferable and inexpendable right of the Croatian nation to self-determination and state sovereignty, the Republic of Croatia is ... established as the national state of the Croatian people and a state of members of other nations and minorities who are its citizens.

In other words, Croatia is the state of a collective subject (the Croatian people) entitled to statehood, and of some individuals that do not belong to it.

One should caution, however, against uncritically assuming that *secession* is always harmful to trapped minorities, or, at least, that it is *more* harmful than intra-state autonomy. Secession empowers minorities to achieve the ultimate, but certainly not the only, means of political separation. Other modalities of political separation implemented to protect and promote subnational groups' rights might have similar, or worse, consequences on trapped minorities than does secession. Strong, territorially concentrated subnationalities are often granted a high degree of cultural and political autonomy, which confines the role of states to the setting of basic principles and excludes their interference in decision-making processes that are critical in the development of the national life of the minority. Quebec and Flanders are examples of highly homogeneous self-governing territorial subunits, where the strict application of linguistic territoriality, while undoubtedly effective in protecting the regional majority, results in systematic interference with the cultural and linguistic rights of the individuals and groups that do not belong to the dominant *ethnos*. In such cases, minority protection has been conceived in 'ethnocentric' rather than 'multicultural' terms, because it has encouraged minorities to separately develop their national lives and to overemphasize their diversity as against the rest of the state's population. In deeply divided federations, such as Belgium and Canada, but also in regional contexts (eg Catalonia and South Tyrol), the state subunits ironically end up reproducing in a reduced scale a French-style state exhibiting rigorous neutrality regarding group based differences. Trapped minorities such as Francophones in Flanders, end up being stuck in strictly monolingual subunits within their multinational states. It is true that *at the federal level* all languages and groups enjoy an equal status; *at the local level*, however, minorities are not only not protected, but not even legally defined as such. In other words, state protection does not apply to trapped minorities because the very 'multinational formula' rejects the notion of minority and promotes federal equality among all national groups. International protection does not apply to trapped minorities either, because, as the Human Rights Committee admitted in a case concerning the status of Anglophones in Quebec, 'the minorities referred to in article 27 [of the ICCPR] are minorities within ... a State, and not minorities within any province'.[62] In the event of secession, however, trapped minorities within a sub-state unit will be elevated to the status of national minorities within a sovereign state. This could give them more visibility, and set the premises for a wider recognition of their rights. This is particularly true in the European context, where, as pointed out in Section II, the recognition of emerging states has been conditioned upon, inter alia, the guarantee that minorities will be effectively protected in the newborn state. Moreover, 'balkanization' must be considered jointly with the European integration process: integrating into a super-constitutional entity with democratic features might counterbalance the birth of mono-national states as a consequence of secessions.

The most challenging objection to the constitutionalization of the right to secede, is that secession is incompatible with the very nature of the constitution, because it suggests that the

[62] United Nations Human Rights Committee, 47th session, Communications Nos 359/1989 and 385/1989, *John Ballantyne and Elizabeth Davidson, and Gordon McIntyre v Canada*, views adopted on March 31, 1993, (11.2).

sub-state units posses a form of 'quiescent' sovereignty, which runs counter the understanding of sovereignty as the monopoly of the state. A secession clause contributes to the perception that a constitution, in the language of secessionist South Carolina Senator John C. Calhoun, is a 'compact between' states rather than 'a Constitution over them'.[63] The idea that the constitution could be viewed as a compact was brought to bear in the United States in the 1860s by Lewis M. Stone, precisely in 'the hope of developing stronger *constitutional* arguments for secession'.[64] Stone, who represented Pickens County to the state convention that Alabama convened in 1861 to discuss secession, started from the fundamental premise of state sovereignty and derived

> two concepts of the nature of the union depending upon the character of the Constitution: the international-law concept and the business partnership concept. Under the first, the Constitution became a treaty, under the second, a compact; and in either case the right of secession was equally legitimate.[65]

The US Supreme Court rejected both doctrines in *Texas v White*, in 1869, insisting that the Constitution was ordained 'to form a more perfect Union. It is difficult to convey the idea of indissoluble unity more clearly than by these words. What can be indissoluble if a perpetual Union, made more perfect, is not?'[66] Thus, a state could not claim a right to withdraw from the Union:

> The act which consummated her admission into the Union was something more than a compact; it was the incorporation of a new member into the political body. And it was final. . . . There was no place for reconsideration or revocation, except through revolution or through consent of the States.

Over a century later, in 1998, the Canadian Supreme Court adopted a radically different approach in the advisory opinion it rendered concerning certain questions relating to the unilateral secession of Quebec from Canada.[67] 'The Constitution—according to the Canadian Supreme Court—is not a straitjacket'. Hence, 'the continued existence and operation of the Canadian constitutional order could not be indifferent to a clear expression of a clear majority of Quebeckers that they no longer wish to remain in Canada.'[68] The Canadian Court did not legitimize an unconditional unilateral right to secede. It did however affirm the legitimacy of a negotiated secession. According to the Court, a referendum unambiguously demonstrating the desire of a clear majority of Quebeckers to secede from Canada, would give rise to a reciprocal obligations of all parties of the Confederation to negotiate secession. Such negotiations should be conducted on the basis of the principles which constitute the core of the Canadian constitution: democracy, the rule of law, federalism, and respect for (trapped) minorities. Accordingly, considerable weight should be given to any expression by a clear majority of Quebeckers of a common desire to secede, but any ensuing requisite negotiations with a view to secession would depend on reconciliation of the rights and obligations of various principal affected parties: the federal government, Quebec, Canada's remaining provinces, and minority groups that would be significantly impacted by secession.

[63] See John C. Calhoun, *A Discourse on the Constitution and Government of the United States*, reprinted in John C. Calhoun, *The Papers of John C. Calhoun*, vol 28, 69, 82 (Clyde N. Wilson and Shirley B. Cook ed, 2003).

[64] Carpenter (n 59), 207.

[65] Ibid.

[66] *Texas v White* 74 US 700, 726 (1869).

[67] *Reference re Secession of Quebec* [1998] 2 SCR 217.

[68] Ibid 151.

Between 1869, when the US Supreme Court ruled out categorically the very possibility of secession, and 1998, when the Canadian Court legitimized a democratic secession process, the conceptualization of federalism and the actual implementation of federal models had changed dramatically. In an inversion of the historical tendency that saw federalism emerge from a process of unification, today the formula of political decentralization is mostly used to divide, that is, to contain centrifugal tendencies, by providing subnational groups a high degree of autonomy.[69] In sum, most federal constitutions today are not ordained to form 'a more perfect Union', but, rather, to loosen the ties to a union that has become unbearable to many. Thus, the idea that constitutions do not necessarily look to 'indestructible unions'[70] and that they may contain international (or confederal) elements seems to re-emerge in contemporary constitutionalism. In fact, comparative analysis shows that there is an increasing number of 'borderline constitutions ' that combine federal and confederal features. The most striking case is the Belgian Constitution,[71] which does not even contain a supremacy clause for federal sources of law. At the end of a long federalizing process, we find—lying at the core of the Belgian state and serving as the basis of its functioning at all levels—its two largest linguistic communities. The federal government must always decide by consensus. In the federal parliament, the agreement between the two linguistic groups is also always necessary, as each may block the legislative procedure in all 'sensitive' matters and veto constitutional reforms. At all levels and for all purposes, the federal system is based on a necessary consensus between Flemish and francophone Belgians. The structural risks of this system are legislative paralysis and political deadlock: after the general elections of December 2010, Belgium was not able to form a government for over 400 days, beating all world records. There are other instances of constitutions that contain 'special regimes' that come close to enshrining sovereign rights for certain minorities, including the 'override clause' in Canada[72] and the right of 'interposition' granted to the Finnish Åland archipelago.[73] These kinds of arrangements may be considered as a 'middle ground' between independence and integration and a way by which minorities may exercise their right to self-determination.[74] Sub-state entities, moreover, play an increasing role in regional organizations such as the EU and the Organization for Security and Co-operation in Europe.

[69] On federalism, see Chapter 27.

[70] *Texas v White* (n 66).

[71] Marc Uyttendaele, *Précis de droit constitutionnel belge. Regards sut un système institutionnel paradoxal* (2005).

[72] Article 33 of the Canadian Charter of Rights and Freedoms enables provincial and federal legislatures to override by ordinary majority the rights contained in the Charter for a renewable period of five years. Formally, this clause is applicable to all provinces. However, 'a constitutional convention seems to have arisen...that the override provision should not be used at all' either by the federal Parliament or by any of the provinces, with the exception of Quebec. The legislature of Quebec, two months after the enactment of the Charter, in response to adoption of the latter without its consent, passed Bill 62, which basically immunized it as far as possible against the constitutionalized Charter. This bill repealed and re-enacted all of the province's pre-Charter legislation with the addition of an override clause to each (the 'omnibus' feature) automatically added such a standard override clause into all new legislation, and 'gave the override clause a retroactive effect'. The Supreme Court later invalidated the retroactive effect but upheld the preemptive use of the override 'by interpreting Section 33 as containing only minimal formal requirement...and therefore as providing only very limited scope for judicial review of exercise under it': Stephen Gardbaum, 'The New Commonwealth Model of Constitutionalism' (2001) 49 *American Journal of Comparative Law* 707.

[73] State acts that relate to the principles governing real or business property in Åland and international treaties pertaining to matters within the competence of Åland shall not enter into force in the islands without the consent of the local assembly. Act on the Autonomy of Åland, §§28, 59 (1991/1144).

[74] Markku Suksi, 'Keeping the Lid on the Secession Kettle—A Review of Legal Interpretation Concerning Claims of Self-Determination by Minority Populations' (2005) 12 *International Journal of Minority and Group Rights* 195.

In contemporary constitutional systems, there is not necessarily a strict dichotomy between constitutional and confederal elements. Hence, constitutions survive with internal contradictions or, put differently, with elements that originate in the logic of both constitutional and international law. This may produce a certain degree of fluidity, which can actually be a precondition for the system's working, especially in deeply divided societies. After all, the EU's experience shows how problematic it is to draw a clear line between an international treaty and a federal constitution.[75] Analogously, domestic constitutions may 'import' confederal (international) elements that prove critical for their functioning. A secession clause may be one such element.

The Canadian Court upheld the right to secede combining elements of both national self-determination as well as of choice theories of secession, and adding a further element to the construction. The existence of a national community, that traditionally inhabits a clustered territory, and the rules of democracy (expressed in a referendum), in fact, are not sufficient alone to legitimize the right to secede, because secession must be negotiated according to substantive values. On the other hand, the Court clearly rejected remedial right theories of secession, as Quebec cannot claim to have been subject to past or present injustice.

The Court pointed to another important issue: the difference between the international right to self-determination and the constitutional right to secession. The Court correctly affirmed that the right to external self-determination was manifestly inapplicable to Quebec.[76] Secession, however, according to the Court, cannot only be governed by the international right to self-determination, which does not apply in non-colonial and democratic contexts. This does not exclude the role of the international community in secessionist processes. However, the international community, in order to decide the legitimacy of a given secession, must refer to domestic law. In the case of Canada, the legitimacy of secession springs from the negotiated character of secession, as well as from respect for substantive constitutional values. Hence, while it is true that secession is conceivable, even if it were conducted outside the constitutional framework, a breach of the latter would entail 'serious legal repercussions', both at the domestic political level, as well as at the international level.[77] On the other hand, the community of nations would be more likely to recognize a sovereign Quebec born of negotiations conducted in conformity with constitutional principles and values, also in the light of the emphasis placed on analogous principles and values by the most recent criteria developed in Europe on the recognition of new states.[78]

Finally, the Canadian Court's decision successfully strikes a balance between the political and legal dimensions of secession. The Court describes secession as 'a legal act as much as a political one',[79] limiting its role to the 'identification of the relevant aspects of the Constitution', while subjecting the 'political aspects of constitutional negotiations' 'only to political evaluations'.[80] However, the non-justiciability of the political aspects of secession 'would not deprive the surrounding constitutional framework of its binding status'.[81] In other words, constitutional

[75] Giuseppe Federico Mancini, 'The Making of a Constitution for Europe' (1989) 26 *Common Market Law Review* 595.

[76] *Reference re Secession of Quebec*, paras 135, 138. The Constitutional Court of Russia reached analogous conclusions in its Decision No 671 of 13 March 1992 concerning the independence of the Republic of Tatarstan.

[77] Ibid paras 102, 103.

[78] Ibid para 143.

[79] Ibid para 83.

[80] Ibid para 100.

[81] Ibid para 102.

law has an important role to play in secessionist disputes: without intruding in the political process, it can set the rules to channel an inevitably conflict-provoking process, often loaded with emotion and irrationality, to rules of democratic logic.

Bibliography

Harry Beran, 'A Liberal Theory of Secession' (1984) 32 *Political Studies* 21

Lea Brilmayer, 'Secession and Self-determination: A Territorial Interpretation' (1991) 16 *Yale University Journal of International Law* 177

Allen Buchanan, *Secession: The Legitimacy of Political Divorce From Fort Sumter to Lithuania and Quebec* (1991)

Lee C. Buchheit, *Secession-The Legitimacy of Self-Determination* (1978)

John C. Calhoun, *A Discourse on the Constitution and Government of the United States*, reprinted in John C. Calhoun, *The Papers of John C. Calhoun*, vol 28 (Clyde N. Wilson and Shirley B. Cook ed, 2003)

Antonio Cassese, *Self-Determination of Peoples: A Legal Reappraisal* (1999)

Don H. Doyle (ed), *Secession as an International Phenomenon: From America's Civil War to Contemporary Separatist Movements* (2011)

Michael Eisner, 'A Procedural Model for the Resolution of Secessionist Disputes' (1992) 33 *Harvard International Law Journal* 407

Thomas M. Franck, 'The Emerging Right to Democratic Governance' (1992) 86(1) *American Journal of International Law* 46

Marcelo G. Kohen (ed), *Secession: International Law Perspectives* (2006)

Will Kymlicka, 'Federalism and Secession: At Home and Abroad' (2000) 2 *Canadian Journal of Law and Jurisprudence* 207

Donald W. Livingston, 'The Very Idea of Secession', *Symposium: Secession and Nationalism at the Millennium* (1998) 35(5) *Society* 38

Susanna Mancini, 'Rethinking the Boundaries of Democratic Secession: Liberalism, Nationalism, and the Right of Minorities to Self-Determination' (2008) 6 *International Journal of Constitutional Law* 553

Avishai Margalit and Joseph Raz, 'National Self-Determination' (1990) 87(9) *Journal of Philosophy* 439

Margaret Moore (ed), *National Self-determination and Secession* (1998)

Wayne Norman, 'The Ethics of Secession as the Regulation of Secessionist Politics' in Margaret Moore (ed), *National Self-determination and Secession* (1998)

Daniel Philpott, 'In Defense of Self-Determination' (1995) 105(2) *Ethics* 352

Christian Tomuschat (ed), *Modern Law of Self-determination* (1993)

Daniel Weinstock, 'Toward a Proceduralist Theory of Secession' (2000) 13 *Canadian Journal of Law and Jurisprudence* 262

Christopher Heath Wellman, *A Theory of Secession: The Case for Political Self-determination* (2005)

CHAPTER 24

REFERENDUM

LAURENCE MOREL

Lille, France

THE referendum is a device of direct democracy by which the people are asked to vote directly on an issue or policy. It differs from an election, which is a vote to elect persons who will make decisions *on behalf of* the people, or a recall, by which citizens are given the opportunity to remove from office an elected representative.[1] Although this distinction between issue voting and person voting is apparently clear, it may be questioned, such as when the referendum is, formally or de facto, a vote of confidence or about the accession or permanence in power of a person. This is often the case in authoritarian regimes, but it also happens in democratic contexts (eg, the use of referendums by de Gaulle in France). Such referendums are often qualified as 'plebiscites', although the word, which goes back to ancient Rome, literally means 'a law enacted by the common people' (*plebis scitum*). Because a plebiscite is commonly regarded as highly manipulative, the term has a negative connotation. The term 'plebiscite' is sometimes extended to all government-initiated referendums, especially if ad hoc, insofar as they would automatically trigger a vote of confidence. But the word has also traditionally been used in a more neutral way, to refer to popular votes on sovereignty issues (eg, the so-called plebiscites

[1] On elections, see Chapter 25.

proposed by the League of Nations after the First World War to settle boundary disputes).[2] The word 'referendum' appeared much later, possibly in sixteenth-century Switzerland, to indicate the procedure by which delegates to cantonal assemblies submitted certain issues to their constituents for ratification (*ad referendum*). Here, I use the word in a general sense, which includes all types of popular votes bearing formally on an issue. I prefer the plural 'referendums' (as a Latin gerund *referendum* has no plural), although the form 'referenda' is equally accepted by most dictionaries.

The referendum is a classical issue in constitutional law and political science, but its importance in liberal democracies has increased a lot in the recent period. Both its provisions and regulations in constitutions or other legislative texts, and its effective practice, at the national, but most of all subnational level (eg, state or region), have greatly increased, albeit substantial country differences persist. Before considering these developments of the provisions and the practice of referendums, we will review in the first section what most prominent constitutionalists and democratic theorists have said about the referendum. We will then turn in the final section to the question of judicial control, which, following the general trend, has dramatically gained relevance in the specific case of referendums in the past two or three decades.

I. Theory of Referendums

Most theoretical accounts on referendums belong either to the constitutional debate or to democratic theory. What distinguishes the two debates in a rather precise way is the set of questions raised: while the classical, constitutional, debate questions the issue of the compatibility of the referendum with representative democracy and the extent and modalities of its use, the democratic debate rather focuses on the democratic quality of the referendum and whether its extension could help to improve the quality of contemporary democracies. We will analyse these two debates in succession.

1. The Constitutional Debate

The origins of the constitutional debate on the referendum are often indicated in the two contrasting theories of Rousseau and Montesquieu. While the former regarded popular legislation (or at least legislation ratified by the people) as the only valid form of legislation, the latter clearly stated that the people was competent only to choose its legislators, not to legislate. The actual debate, however, came later as a debate among advocates of representative democracy (the overwhelming majority of political thinkers) discussing whether the referendum could or could not constitute a supplement (not an alternative) to representation. Arguments on both sides mixed theoretical and practical considerations. According to the authors of the Federalist, who neither introduced provisions for referendums in the US Constitution nor submitted it for approval to the people, popular legislation would lead to incompetent decisions and endanger individual liberties through tyranny of the majority. 'Pure' representation was not seen as contradicting popular sovereignty since the people could choose its rulers and hold them accountable through re-election. On the opposite side, the Anti-Federalists believed that the principle of popular sovereignty required that the people should as far as possible govern itself and that no check should bear on popular majorities. A few years later, the French political

[2] On sovereignty more generally, see Chapter 17.

thinker and delegate of the Tiers-Etat Sieyès articulated a theory of representative government rooted in the concept of national sovereignty, which was more efficient than popular sovereignty in excluding the people—regarded as fully incompetent—from legislation, and inspired generations of French constitutionalists hostile to the referendum. Nonetheless, the principle of the constitutional referendum came about during the revolution, with the solemn declaration of the Convention that 'il ne peut y avoir de constitution que celle approuvée par le peuple'. The question of the referendum really emerged however one century or more later in the context of strong criticisms against representative government. In the United States, provisions for direct legislation were introduced in many states (especially in the West) under the influence of the Populists, who denounced the corruption of representatives, considered as a prey to the influence of special interests and party machines. In Europe, the debate started in England at the end of the nineteenth century with Dicey's claim that parliamentary absolutism and the dictature of parties were inconsistent with the 'doctrine which lies at the basis of English democracy, that the law depends at bottom for its enactment on the consent of the nation as represented by the electors.'[3] His proposal for a mandatory referendum on constitutional and sovereignty issues, which would serve as a popular check ('people's veto') on the House of Commons, was not adopted however.[4] The years following the war saw an intensification of this debate, especially in continental Europe. In Germany, while Schmitt asked for the replacement of parliamentarism with a plebiscitarian democracy, Kelsen did not believe that there could be any alternative to parliamentarism. Thus he advocated its reform 'in the direction of a new strengthening of the democratic element' (which he regarded as the essence of parliamentarism), beginning with the extension of the referendum and popular initiative.[5] In France, a whole issue of the *Annuaire de l'Institut International de Droit Public* was dedicated in 1931 to the referendum. In a famous article, Carré de Malberg rejected the thesis, personified at that time by Esmein, according to which the referendum would be incompatible with the principle of national sovereignty.[6] Parliamentary sovereignty (ie the monopolization of sovereignty by Parliament) was only a 'degenerescence' of national sovereignty, which only implication was the necessity of representation.[7] The people could very well represent the nation. In Carré de Malberg's view, the referendum was the logical outcome of representative government since the invention of which responded to the intent of making the people the source of the law. He recommended (vainly) popular initiatives to counterweight the 'absolute parliamentarism' of the French Third Republic.[8] His defence of the referendum was also inspired by the spreading of direct democracy in post-war European constitutions, about

[3] A.V. Dicey, *A Leap in the Dark* (2nd edn, 1911), 19.

[4] See also A.V. Dicey, 'Ought the Referendum to be Introduced into England?' (1890) 57 *Contemporary Review* 15 or A.V. Dicey, 'The Referendum and Its Critics' (1910) 212 *Quarterly Review* 538. In Dicey's view, the referendum was to replace the old check of the House of Lords (which he regarded as having lost legitimacy).

[5] Carl Schmitt, *The Crisis of Parliamentary Democracy* ([1926] 1985); Hans Kelsen, *Vom Wesen und Wert der Demokratie* (2nd edn, 1929), in particular chs III and IV. I mention here the original German text as ch IV on the reform of parliamentarism was not translated in the (very recent) English translation (to be found in Arthur J. Jacobson and Bernhard Schlink (eds), *Weimar. A Juridiction of Crisis* (2000)).

[6] Adhémar Esmein, *Eléments de droit constitutionnel français et comparé* (1906). In this book, Esmein was particularly worried about what he regarded as a general trend towards popular sovereignty in the institutions and practice of democracies.

[7] Raymond Carré de Malberg, *La loi, expression de la volonté générale* (1931).

[8] Raymond Carré de Malberg, 'Considérations théoriques sur la question de la combinaison du référendum avec le parlementarisme' (1931) 2 *Annuaire de l'Institut International de Droit Public* 272.

which Mirkine-Guetzévitch, in the next article, reported quite critically. The discussion of the Russian constitutionalist focused in particular on a new variety of referendums and popular initiatives aimed at solving conflicts between the executive and the legislative, which could lead to the dissolution of parliament or the revocation of the head of the state. Mirkine-Guetzévitch regarded this as contradictory with the trend toward a 'rationalization' of parliamentarism, by means of a strengthening of executives, which he welcomed as the great novelty of these constitutions.[9]

To a large extent this classical debate became obsolete after the Second World War, as the legitimacy of the referendum became undiscussed, regardless of the fact that the record of its practice in the inter-war period had scored far below the positive expectations of its proponents.[10] The theoretical arguments against the referendum had proved very weak indeed, since the election of representatives, through which the people can de facto influence legislation, is an inherent part of the theory of representative government (be it founded on popular or national sovereignty). On the other side, the practical arguments against the referendum could no longer justify its total exclusion in the context of 'victorious' democracy. The contemporary debate thus became among those advocating a very moderate, exceptional, use of the referendum, and those in favour of a more routinized practice. The former view, which has been far more common, is well illustrated by Friedrich, who wrote in the 1950 edition of *Constitutional Government and Democracy* that the referendum might constitute 'a genuine adjustment for modern constitutionalism', provided it is used only 'from time to time' and 'circumscribed by constitutional provisions guaranteeing a free choice to the electorate'.[11] The main issues at stake have been whether the referendum should deal only with constitutional matters or also ordinary legislation, whether it should be compulsory or facultative, and, in the latter case, work as a pure majoritarian device or as a tool for minorities. On the whole, a broad agreement seems to exist on the constitutional referendum, although the opposite view, that popular votes should be restricted to 'unimportant' issues, also has its advocates, and not everyone agrees that constitutional referendums should be compulsory, especially if they also include referendums on sovereignty issues.[12] A current discussion is about the recent increase of constitutional referendums in democracies, most remarkably in Europe. According to Tierney, this is a positive phenomenon by which constitutionalism will gradually be supplanted by republicanism (the ultimate power of the constitution being replaced with the ultimate power of the people). Although this author acknowledges that there is an important way in which these referendums may be criticized: more than any other referendum, they presuppose the existence of a *demos*, the very act of staging a constitutional referendum being 'both a declaration that a people exists and a definition of that people'.[13] Thus, the pluralist objection

[9] Boris Mirkine-Guetzevitch, 'Le référendum et le parlementarisme dans les nouvelles constitutions européennes' in *Annuaire de l'Institut International de Droit Public* (1931), vol II. The author had, however, expressed a rather different position one year earlier, in *Les Constitutions de l'Europe nouvelle* (1930), where he wrote that 'the referendum is the logical conclusion of the process of rationalization of parliamentarism' (ibid 28).

[10] For a balanced account of world practice of referendums until the end of the 1940s, see Carl J. Friedrich, *Constitutional Government and Democracy* ([1937] 1950), ch XXV: 'Direct Popular Action'.

[11] Ibid 571.

[12] Following Karl Loewenstein, *Political Power and the Government Process* (1957), the constitutional doctrine normally distinguishes between three types of constitutional referendums: on the approval of the constitution, on its revision, and on sovereignty issues (like the foundation of a new state or the transfer of powers from the state to sub-state units or a supranational order).

[13] Stephen Tierney, 'Constitutional Referendums: A Theoretical Enquiry' (2009) 72(3) *Modern Law Review* 360.

that referendums may act as homogenizing devices and harm minorities, especially in divided societies, is particularly applicable to that kind of referendum.[14] Although things can also be considered the other way round, by taking into consideration the positive impact of constitutional referendums when they take on a vital nation-building role. Both arguments have been discussed at length in the last decades with regard to referendums on European integration and the prospect of European-wide referendums. Is there something like a European people? Could such referendums help to bring about a *demos*? Or would they most likely act as constraining mechanisms by which an artificial people would be created *ex machina* to the detriment of the various European peoples? All these questions, which conflate on technical issues like the definition of the proper electorate, the majorities necessary for the adoption of the change, the legal consequences of the vote, or the possibility for the minority to opt out, evoke classical issues regarding referendums of self-determination or on territorial matters.[15]

2. Referendum and Democracy

While the constitutional debate is mainly about the possibility to combine direct and representative democracy, democratic theorists rather discuss the referendum as a possible way to improve the quality of democracies, which entails first of all the question of whether it is, or can be, a truly democratic device. From the beginning of the referendum practice, this has been a problematic issue and critics have often pretended that it was a form of government less democratic than representative democracy. Elected officials would be better at producing policies that accurately reflect the will of the majority, because they can aggregate preferences, while the referendum, as a device of *semi-direct* democracy, does not allow the collective elaboration of policies by the people (unlike citizens' assemblies). Because of this, legislation approved by referendum, unless it comes from parliament, would almost inevitably reflect minority views (those of its proponents). From a different point of view, it is also argued that referendums do not reflect the will of the majority on the question asked because of abstention, which is higher than at elections, and dramatically increases when their use becomes frequent; because voters often answer a different question, as typically occurs when they express a vote of confidence in the incumbents (the so-called 'plebiscitarian deviation'); or because they just follow party lines, or are easily manipulated by minorities with more intense views and organizational or financial superiority.[16] Conversely, a classical argument is that the referendum would lead to majority tyranny against minorities, because 'it knows nothing about compromise', as it gives only a choice between 'yes' and 'no'.[17] Those who believe so generally also doubt that referendums can generate more legitimate decisions and solve conflicts.

[14] In this context, Tierney explores the possibility of applying deliberative democracy as a model for constitutional referendums that might help to recover the constitutionalist tradition by supplying inclusion for all groups. On this, see also Simone Chambers, 'Constitutional Referendums and Democratic Deliberation' in Matthew Mendelsohn and Andrew Parkin (eds), *Citizens, Elites and Deliberation in Referendums Campaigns* (2001).

[15] A valuable contribution to this debate is the book by Andreas Auer and Jean-François Flauss (eds), *Le référendum européen: actes du colloque international de Strasbourg, 21–22 février 1997* (1997). See in particular the introduction by Auer and the chapters by Olivier Beaud, Brun-Otto Bryde, and Pierre Cot. On self-determination referendums, see the two chapters by Philip Goodhart and Vernon Bogdanor, 'Referendums and Separatism' in Austin Ranney (ed), *The Referendum Device: A Conference* (1981). On self-determination and secession more generally, see Chapter 23.

[16] On this see Giovanni Sartori, *The Theory of Democracy Revisited* (1987).

[17] Max Weber, 'Parliament and Government in Germany under a New Political Order' in Peter Lassman and Ronald Speirs (eds), *Weber. Political Writings* (5th edn, 2007), 225.

Rather, they would enhance divisions. This problem, mentioned above in the specific case of constitutional referendums, has recently received new attention by proponents of deliberative democracy, who recommend supplementing referendums with popular deliberative forums that would take place before the actual wording of the question or proposed legislation is formalized. A different approach regards the capacity of the referendum to produce policies *for* the people, that is, in the interest of the people. Together with majority tyranny, the most common criticism addressed to direct democracy, dating back to ancient authors, is indeed that ordinary people lack expertise to legislate. This was also a classical argument against elections, it should be noted, but referendums would be worse as the competence required to choose legislators would be inferior to that required for deciding policies directly.[18] Another shortcoming of referendums would be their structural bias against change, people being naturally conservative or tending to be so when they do not have firm preferences—which is often the case at referendums since most issues are complex.

These questions about the democratic quality of the referendum are of course central to the argument contrary to its development in democracies. Further, opponents to referendums emphasize their negative political consequences. Referendums would weaken representative government by undermining the role and responsibility of political parties and elected representatives, and, when used too frequently, generate voter fatigue and low electoral participation. Moreover, it is argued, popular initiatives would overload the political system by continually introducing new demands. Supporters of referendums, on the contrary, believe that representative democracy does not provide for accurate reflection of popular will and regard referendums as superior in this respect. They also insist on the positive political implications of referendums, such as the maximization of citizenry (by enhancing both participation and education); or the capacity of popular initiatives to be an alternative channel for raising issues and, as the example of Switzerland shows, for encouraging representatives to be more responsive and accommodative in the preparation of legislation (which would also result in creating a stronger attachment of the people to the political system). At the beginning of the twentieth century, Bryce, in his analysis of modern democracies, gives a rather complete account of all these arguments.[19] In the same year, the Italian law philosopher Rensi writes that direct democracy institutions, according to the Swiss or American model, are the only way to circumvent elite domination as brought to the fore by Mosca and Pareto.[20] After the Second World War, 'participationists' like Pateman, Macpherson, or more recently Barber,[21] will logically stand on the side of the referendum although regarding it as a poor substitute for 'pure' direct democracy (assembly democracy), which alone allows the collective elaboration and deliberation of policies (considered essential to achieve compromise and enlightened decisions). On the opposite front, 'elitists', or 'representationists', following Schumpeter and

[18] This was the famous assertion made by Montesquieu in *L'Esprit des lois*, to which the classical answer is that if the people is competent to choose its legislators, there is no reason why it should not be able to decide about policies. The French constitutionalist Léon Duguit even goes further as he believes the opposite is true, that is, ordinary people would be less competent to decide about legislators than about issues, for they would obey ideological considerations in the first case, not in the second (Léon Duguit, *Traîté de droit constitutionnel* (3rd edn, 1927).

[19] James Bryce, *Modern Democracies* (1921).

[20] Giuseppe Rensi, *La democrazia diretta* ([1902] 1995); Gaeteno Mosca, *The Ruling Class* ([orig in Italian 1884] 1939); Vilfredo Pareto, *The Rise and Fall of Elites: An Application of Theoretical Sociology* ([orig in Italian 1901] 1991).

[21] Carole Pateman, *Participation and Democratic Theory* (1970); C.B. Macpherson, *The Life and Time of Liberal Democracy* (1977); Benjamin R. Barber, *Strong Democracy. Participatory Politics for a New Age* ([1984] 2004).

Sartori,[22] believe that the essence of democracy lies in the right to elect representatives, not to influence policies, for which citizens are both unwilling (time constraint) and incompetent. This point has been strongly reasserted by Sartori in the context of the 'crisis of knowledge' which he sees as typical of complex societies despite the rise of educational levels. In this author's view, democracies suffer a 'participationist drift' which needs to be inverted. A somewhat more moderate stance, but still not very favourable to the referendum, is expressed by authors advocating a 'horizontal' diffusion of representative democracy to new political (eg, subnational) or non-political (eg, economic, social, private...) spheres, rather than a 'vertical' in-depth move toward more direct democracy.[23] For the time being, the prevailing orientation among democratic theorists is not very referendum-oriented since 'democrats' have also to a large extent abandoned it. Theories of democratic innovation, which have burgeoned in the last two decades as a response to party disaffection and rising expectations of post-modern citizens, prefer to supplement representative institutions with new arrangements or participatory mechanisms ensuring deliberation,[24] rather than with direct popular majoritarian decision-making. Similarly, proposals for a greater involvement of interests[25] (especially so-called 'excluded' or 'mute' interests[26]), or the democratization of supranational bodies and the establishment of a transnational democracy, hardly mention the referendum.[27] The position in favour of an increase of direct democracy is thus wholly marginal. Its main contemporary supporter is Budge, who advocates a move of liberal democracies towards direct democracy, intended as 'a regime in which the adult citizens as a whole debate and vote on the most important political decisions, and where their vote determines the action to be taken.'[28]

[22] Joseph Alois Schumpeter, *Capitalism, Socialism and Democracy* ([1942] 1994); Sartori (n 16).

[23] Often with a view that diffusion is the condition for representative democracy to work better in the 'classical' political sphere. See eg Harry Eckstein, who argued that the permanence of authoritarian patterns in social life was an obstacle to the full realization of democracy in a country (*Patterns of Authority: A Structural Basis for Political Enquiry* (1975)).

[24] 'Deliberationists' have taken over from 'participationists' in denouncing the poor performance of semi-direct democracy with regard to deliberation (see eg Jürgen Habermas, *Between Facts and Norms: Contributions to a Discourse Theory of Law and Democracy* ([1992] 1996)). However, following Robert Alan Dahl's early proposal of *minipopulus* (first in *After the Revolution* (1970), then, with a greater emphasis, in *Democracy and Its Critics* (1989)), James S. Fishkin has become the champion of a direct-deliberative democracy, that is, a democracy in which *deliberative polls* (assemblies of randomly selected citizens deliberating on policy issues) would turn around some classical obstacles to direct democracy such as the impossibility of meetings of all citizens or the problem of competence. More than 40 such deliberative polls have taken place all around the world up to now (see James S. Fishkin, *Democracy and Deliberation: New Directions for Democratic Reform* (1991); or 'Beyond Referendum Democracy' in Elliot Abrams (ed), *Democracy: How Direct? Views from the Founding Era and the Polling Era* (2002)).

[25] See eg Paul Q. Hirst, *Associative Democracy* (1993); or Philippe C. Schmitter, 'The Irony of Modern Democracy and the Viability of Efforts to Reform its Practice' in Eric Olin Wright (ed), *Associations and Democracy* (1995).

[26] See eg Iris Marion Young, *Inclusion and Democracy* (2000); or Robin Eckersley, *The Green State: Rethinking Democracy and Sovereignty* (2004). Progressively these theories of 'inclusive', or 'presence' democracy, have come to believe less and less in procedural democracy and to turn rather towards liberal solutions such as the constitutionalization of new rights (group rights, rights of nature...).

[27] See eg David Held, *Models of Democracy* (3rd edn, 2007); or John S. Drizek, 'Transnational Democracy' (1999) 7(1) *Journal of Political Philosophy* 30. In a sense these theories are the continuation of 'diffusion' theories (see above). However, it should be noted that Held includes transnational referendums (which should deal with cross-borders issues) in his proposal for a 'cosmopolitan' democracy. But, like proponents of inclusive democracy, his model increasingly relies on the constitutionalization of rights rather than on democratization.

[28] Ian Budge, *The New Challenge of Direct Democracy* (1996), 35. According to Budge, this move is made possible by the new opportunities of 'virtual' democracy (internet), which have reconciled participation and

II. Provisions for Referendums

1. Typologies

Democratic theorists, as was just seen, argue for or against the referendum by referring to their alleged democratic quality or political effects. But this has been until now to a large extent an endless and inconclusive debate since we know very little about the actual implications of referendums. This small advancement of knowledge on the referendum is due to the lack of empirical studies, but, above all, to the extreme variety of forms that it can take, which stands as a barrier against any generalization and formulation of an encompassing theory. Among the numerous modalities of the referendum that can be found in constitutional texts or practices, the *initiative* is considered to be the most important. Most typologies of referendums are indeed based on this criterion and distinguish between 'mandatory' (also termed 'compulsory' or 'obligatory') referendums, on one side, and 'optional' (or 'facultative') referendums, on the other side, with a distinction within the latter category between referendums initiated by institutional actors such as the executive, the legislative branch, or a parliamentary minority, and popular initiatives. Many authors use the word 'referendum' for mandatory referendums and optional referendums initiated from within institutions, while votes demanded by popular minorities are referred to as 'initiatives'. Others refer to the *formal object*, using 'referendum' for votes on existing legislation, either current ('abrogative' or 'resolutory' referendum) or pending ('suspensive' or 'deliberative' referendum) and 'initiative' for votes which are 'propositive', that is, dealing with proposals for future legislation (specifically or generally worded) or questions of principle. The *category of legislative act* it deals with (eg, ordinary legislation, constitutional reform, international treaty), the *subject* (eg, institutional, international, territorial, moral, economic...), the *legal consequences* of the vote (consultative—also termed advisory—or binding), are other frequent variables included in the typologies, creating numerous designations for the referendum.[29] In our sense, a good typology should focus on three basic variables, which measure the extent to which legislative power is shared with the people and/or the opposition. The first variable is the *initiative*, which applies only to optional referendums. But the fundamental divide is not as much between institutional and non-institutional initiative as between government and non-government initiative. Government-initiated referendums are decided either by the executive alone (prime minister or head of state), by the legislative alone, or, more frequently, by a common decision of the executive and the legislative. The common feature of these referendums is not to allow the people or the opposition to seize the legislative power. Non-government-initiated referendums are in the hands either of the opposition (parliamentary minority or, eg, a minority of regions in Italy or cantons in Switzerland), or of a popular minority. Mandatory referendums give maximum legislative power to the people (the popular vote being guaranteed, not

deliberation (by creating conditions of deliberation closing the face-to-face assembly) and reduced the cost of voting (electronic vote). This should not mean however the end of representative institutions. The only institution which would be substantially affected is parliament (reduced to an advisory role). Most importantly, parties would keep a very important role, the new regime being renamed by Budge 'party direct democracy'.

[29] An excellent list and analysis of the numerous modalities of the referendum can be found in the online report 'Referendums in Europe—An Analysis of the Legal Rules in European States' issued in 2005 by the European Commission for Democracy through Law (the so-called 'Venice Commission') of the Council of Europe, available at <http://www.venice.coe.int>. See also, by the same Commission, the replies by country to the questionnaires on these legal rules (2004).

depending on popular demand for it), but might nonetheless be classified behind propositive popular initiatives in this respect, since they can deal only with legislation originated in the institutions (generally pending legislation just approved by parliament). This introduces the second crucial variable, that is, the *author of the legislation* (in other words, the initiator of the legislation), which refers to the capacity of the initiator of the referendum to put a proposal of his own to the vote (thus again a variable which regards only optional referendums). This is a better criterion than the above-mentioned formal object of the referendum, since the referendum may be permitted on a law proposal, but not one formulated by its initiator, or a proposal requiring the previous assent of another actor (as in the case of the president-initiated referendum on constitutional revision in France, which can deal only with bills approved in first reading by parliament). Or the referendum may be restricted to pending legislation but nonetheless be in substance propositive, as when the parliament can submit to the people a law that it has just approved (a quite frequent case). The third variable regards the *scope* of the referendum. Here a first distinction must be between referendums on constitutional revisions, which deal essentially (although not exclusively) with institutional issues, and referendums on ordinary legislation. Within the latter category, one should then differentiate according to the subject: institutional, international (alliances, treaties...), territorial (secession, decolonization...), or other (eg economic, social, moral, environmental...), and take into account eventual restrictions within each field (such as when the referendum can only deal with a few predetermined institutional issues).[30]

2. Country Variations: Existence of Provisions

As of 2008, only 20 per cent of the 193 countries deemed independent by Freedom House had no provision at all for referendums at the national or subnational level.[31] These were mostly in Asia (eg, China and India), the Middle East, and Central America. As may be expected, 'free' countries (by Freedom House ranking) have more often provisions for referendums (only 13 per cent have no provisions of any kind at any level) than 'partially free' or 'not free' countries (24 per cent have no provisions for referendums). This is mostly due to provisions for subnational referendums, which are much more prevalent in free countries (55 per cent) than in the other countries (26 per cent).

Provisions for referendums have tended to increase in the past few decades, either in free or not-free countries. In the latter, this is partly due to new democracies, whose constitutions have often made more space for the referendum than those of 'old' democracies. Thus. for example. in Eastern and Central Europe, post-communist countries have introduced substantial provisions for referendums and popular initiatives at all territorial levels as part of their democratization process.[32] In Western Europe, the increase has more to do with provisions for subnational referendums (often including popular initiative), although some countries like France or Luxembourg

[30] I do not consider in this typology the distinction between legally binding and consultative referendums, which does not appear to be very discriminant in practice (on this see eg J.-M. Denquin, Référendums consultatifs (1996) 77 *Pouvoirs* 81).

[31] Statistics in this paragraph are drawn from IDEA (Institute for Democracy and Electoral Assistance: <http://www.idea.int>). This is, together with the Center for Research on Direct Democracy (<http://www.c2d.ch>), the most extensive database on referendum practice and regulations. Provisions for referendums are normally included in the Constitution but sometimes only appear in specific referendum Acts.

[32] See Andreas Auer and Michael Bützer (eds), *Direct Democracy: the Eastern and Central European Experiences* (2001).

have recently enlarged their constitutional provisions for nationwide referendums. It should be added that there has been a dramatic expansion in the last decades of the legislation regulating referendums, which has contributed to their stronger institutionalization (see previous section). At this time there is no comprehensive theory up regarding the factors responsible for the introduction and the extent of referendum provisions in democracies. According to Uleri, the fact that a few countries have extensive provisions and the great majority only restricted opportunities has to do with the existence or not of organized parties prior to full democratization (universal suffrage), since parties have historically been the main opponents to direct democracy.[33] In the first case, like England, parties have blocked demands for introducing the referendum (which arose precisely to counter their omnipotence); while in the second case, like Switzerland, referendum provisions, typically including the mandatory constitutional referendum and popular initiative, have made their way as a sort of logical next step after franchise.[34] This an interesting model, which also works quite well for the recent period, since the growing interest for referendums in mature democracies has been concomitant with party crisis.[35] However, there are important exceptions to this model, like France or Italy. In France, the Third Republic remained until the end hostile to any form of referendum, in a context of universal male suffrage and still very weak parties. This shows that not only are parties hostile to the referendum but the representative elite in general. What makes the difference ultimately if we compare France and England on one side, Switzerland and the US states on the other side, was the existence in these two latter countries of a rooted tradition of direct democracy able to compete ideologically with representative government. In Italy, the abrogative referendum was introduced in the 1946 constitution at the initiative of the strong Christian-Democrat party, which conceived it as a potential minority weapon in the event of an electoral victory of the communists. There are thus special conditions, in this case the presence of a strong anti-system party, in which governing parties might become favourable to substantial exceptions to representative democracy. On the other side, why they may accept limited exceptions (typically the introduction of the constitutional referendum) has had historically more to do with ideological considerations relating to the contractualist liberal myth and the belief in popular sovereignty, than with strategies of self-preservation.[36]

3. Country Variations: Types of Referendums

From a worldwide perspective, the IDEA dataset shows that at the national level, 'mandatory referendums' and 'optional referendums' (the latter category including citizens' initiatives on existing or pending legislation in IDEA classification) are much more prevalent (54 per cent and 60 per cent of all countries, respectively) than citizens' initiatives for future legislation

[33] On political parties and the constitution, see further Chapter 41.

[34] Piervincenzo Uleri, *Referendum e Democrazia. Una prospettiva comparata* (2003).

[35] On this point see Vernon Bogdanor, 'Western Europe' in David Butler and Austin Ranney (eds), *Referendums around the World. The Growing Use of Direct Democracy* (1994), 91–5.

[36] In Italy, the vote in 1970 of implementing legislation allowing the practice of the abrogative referendum was again promoted by the Christian-Democrats, this time on purely tactical and short-term grounds. The referendum was supposed to be a recourse against the law introducing divorce, which the Catholics were unable to defeat in parliament. On this see Laurence Morel, 'Referendums, Direct Democracy and Party Government in Liberal Democracies' (1998) 6(2) *European Review* 203; for a deeper analysis of the motivations behind the use of referendums by governments and parties, see also Laurence Morel, 'The Rise of Politically Obligatory Referendums. The 2005 French Referendum in Comparative Perspective' (2007) 30(5) *West European Politics* 1041.

(16 per cent). Twenty per cent of all countries have a popular initiative of one type or another, but only 15 per cent of not free or partially free countries (23 per cent of free countries). It is remarkable, however, that a device to challenge political authorities such as the popular initiative can be found in the constitutions of countries like the Russian Federation, the Asiatic republics of the former USSR, Togo, or Uganda—although it is never used. Table 24.1 (see next section) goes into deeper detail regarding a group of mature democracies (mostly Western democracies), by focusing on the three basic variables brought to the fore in Section II.1. It clearly shows country variations in the extent to which the people can participate in a direct way in the legislation. As for 2011, four countries (the Netherlands, Norway, the United Kingdom, and the United States) have no provisions at all for referendums, while six countries have only (Canada, Finland, Greece) or almost exclusively (France,[37] Iceland, Portugal) government-initiated referendums. Another group of six countries has mandatory referendums, which essentially deal with institutional/constitutional issues, but none of the varieties of non-government-initiated referendums (Australia, Iceland, Ireland, Israel, Japan, Portugal). Then comes a group of four countries with non-government-initiated referendums but no mandatory referendums: Luxembourg and Sweden, where a parliamentary minority can trigger a referendum on a constitutional revision, and Italy and New Zealand, which are a different case since popular minorities are entitled to call a referendum on almost every issue. Finally, five countries have both mandatory and non-government-initiated referendums: Austria and Spain, where these referendums are limited to constitutional revisions; Denmark, where a parliamentary minority may call a referendum on pending legislation; and Malta and Switzerland, where popular initiatives can deal with ordinary legislation.

These country variations in the provisions for direct legislation should not however be considered as a measure of the 'total' influence of the people on legislation, which depends on the whole range of opportunities for direct or indirect participation. First of all, provisions for subnational referendums should be taken into account, especially since both these provisions and the competences of subnational governments have increased in the last decades.[38] Direct participation in legislation is also fostered by mechanisms like the citizen's agenda initiative,[39] which has been introduced in many democracies and, recently, at the level of the European Union; or, more classically, by provisions for early elections, which give the people the opportunity to pronounce on a conflicting issue, and sometimes are part of the referendum process (eg in Denmark in the case of constitutional revision) or constitute a possible alternative to it (eg in Ireland in the case of referendums initiated by parliament). Other mechanisms, like the recall, must also to be taken into account since they allow the people to interfere in the government process and make elected officials highly dependent on their electors. Thus, popular influence on legislation is also determined by general factors such as the degree of accountability and responsiveness of representatives. Some authors also believe that proportional representation is an important way by which electors can influence legislation.[40] However,

[37] France introduced in 2008 a referendum by a combined parliamentary/popular/presidential initiative, but it still needs implementing legislation (see Table 24.1).

[38] The two phenomena being related since traditionally federal or highly decentralized countries tend to have more opportunities for subnational referendums than unitary countries, as the US case exemplarily shows. Germany is another case of a federal country with no provision for nationwide referendums but extensive provisions for referendums in a number of Länder.

[39] Whereby a number of citizens can submit a proposal that must be considered by the legislature but is not necessarily put to a vote of the electorate.

[40] This is a controversial issue, however, since the majoritarian system allows more direct influence on the choice of government.

coming back to referendums, their effective role in a political system cannot be fully assessed without referring to their actual practice (although the mere provision for referendum may result in influencing the legislators, as is clearly the case with the popular initiative in Switzerland).

III. Practice

1. History

A first glance to referendum practice must regard the history of the device. It is generally associated with three countries. On one side are Switzerland and the United States and, on the other, France. As mentioned above, in the first two, the practice of referendum has its roots in a tradition of direct democracy by popular assemblies at the local level (the American town meetings and the Swiss cantonal *Landsgemeinde*), dating back to the Middle Ages in the case of Switzerland. In the United States, the referendum experience was initiated with the submission of state constitutions to the people (the first case was the rejection of the Constitution of Massachusetts by the people in 1778) and the introduction in many states of the obligatory referendum on constitutional amendments proposed by the legislature. But it was never extended beyond the state level, either in the federal constitution or in practice. In Switzerland, the first major development of the referendum occurred at the cantonal level, under the impulse of the democratic Liberals in the 1830s, although early forms of referendums were found before this period (as mentioned above). At the time, it appeared as an acceptable substitute for the direct democracy assemblies, which had become impractical. In addition, the examples of the United States and France were very influential in promoting the constitutional referendum (the first nationwide referendum had actually been held in Switzerland in 1802 to approve the Napoleonic constitution). During these years, all cantonal constitutions, with the exception of Friburg, were approved through referendums, and provisions for popular initiatives, on constitutional or legislative matters, were introduced in many of them. The 1848 federal constitution was also submitted to the people in a majority of cantons, and included the obligatory referendum for amendments to the constitution as well as the constitutional popular initiative for total revision of the constitution. In both countries, a decisive extension of the referendum was achieved under the influence of political reform movements in the second half of the nineteenth century: the Democratic Movement in Switzerland (1860s) and the Progressive Movement in the United States (1890–1920). As a result of these movements, provisions for popular initiatives were enhanced in the Swiss federal constitution (1874: the initiative on laws within 90 days of their publication; 1891: the constitutional initiative for partial revisions) and introduced in many US states, especially in the west (more than 80 per cent of the 24 states that have today the popular initiative adopted it during the Progressive era). In the two countries, these movements drew support from popular dissatisfaction with representative democracy, with politicians being accused of corruption and of fostering the interests of only the richest sections of the population. France has a different story as it had no tradition of direct democracy. Nevertheless, its referendum experience started much as it did in the United States, with referendums on the revolutionary constitutions of 1793 and 1795, following the end of monarchic rule. Moreover, the 1793 constitution greatly advanced democratic principles by introducing universal male suffrage and a popular initiative on laws within 40 days of their adoption. This constitution was actually a great source of inspiration for Switzerland. Ultimately, however, it was never applied, and the only form of referendum that found its way into France was the constitutional referendum. Overall, France would soon take a different road with the plebiscitary use of the referendum by Napoleon I and Napoleon III, to some extent perpetuated by the presidential use of the referendum under the Fifth Republic.

2. Practice

Initially confined to a few 'mother' countries, the referendum has extended its practice all over the world in the twentieth century. As for the 1980–2008 period, it is possible to classify countries according to the intensity of their practice of nationwide referendums.[41] A preliminary observation should be that frequent use of the referendum is associated with the popular initiative and its practice on a wide range of issues (not strictly constitutional or of special importance). A first group of very frequent users (5 countries) includes Switzerland (246 referendums), with Italy (60), Liechtenstein (38), Ecuador (33), and Micronesia (31) far behind. All these countries have provisions for popular initiatives, which represent the bulk of the practice in Switzerland, Italy, and Lichtenstein. The second group consists of frequent users (4 countries), such as Ireland (21), with its practice of mandatory constitutional referendums, Palau (19), Colombia (19 since it became free in 1990), and Lithuania (18 referendums since independence), the latter two showing occasional use of the popular initiative. The third group, consisting of medium users (7–13 referendums), has 16 countries, among which are some occasional practitioners of the popular initiative (eg, Bolivia, Hungary, Slovakia, Slovenia, New Zealand) and a more frequent user (Uruguay). One should also mention here Australia, with its practice of mandatory constitutional referendums. Unlike the previous groups, this set of countries also includes not fully free countries (6), such as Egypt, Belarus, and Morocco. Non-free countries are more prevalent in the next two groups of occasional users (23 countries with 4–6 referendums) and rare users (71 countries with 1–3 referendums), which include only a small minority of free countries (and only 3 countries with some practice of the popular initiative: Venezuela, Latvia, and Macedonia). This suggests that the sporadic use of the referendum often has to do with the quest for popular acclamation of authoritarian policies. It should be added that it is often difficult in the case of non-democratic countries to assess whether a referendum has been mandatory, optional, or ad hoc. A prevalence of authoritarian regimes is not, however, found in the last group, consisting of non-users (70 countries), which has comparable proportions of free countries and partially free or not free countries. Among the most prominent non-users of the referendum are the United States, Germany, China, India, Japan, and Israel. The United States and Germany, however, have an intense practice of referendums, especially popular initiatives, at the state level, albeit with important differences from one state to another. Regarding subnational referendums, it should be noted that federal countries and decentralized countries actually have a major propensity for them (Switzerland being an exemplary case). It is also probably true, at least in democratic countries, that the decrease in territorial level (from nation to region or from state to city) will likely correlate with a higher number of referendums. From a dynamic perspective, a general trend towards an increase in the practice of referendums is clearly observable. The number of nationwide referendums between 1980 and 2008 (close to 900 referendums) is almost three times the number registered for 1950–79 (362 referendums). Moreover, the use of referendums dramatically increased during the 1980–2008 period. As a matter of fact, in the post-war

[41] The data in this paragraph is drawn from IDEA. It is much more difficult to assess the practice of subnational referendums, for which no exhaustive dataset exists.

period, there was a twofold increase in the use of referendums: in the 1970s and 1990s, when it more than doubled (compared with the previous decade). This does not mean that the referendum has become more frequent in every country or that the increase of its practice has had the same entity everywhere. For example, in Western democracies, the increase in referendum use, if we compare the 1940–69 period with the following period, has been much more marked in Switzerland, Italy, Ireland, and Australia than in other countries (Table 24.2). Nonetheless, the referendum has made its apparition in countries where it had never been practised before (United Kingdom and the Netherlands), or in a democratic context (Austria, Greece, Portugal, Spain), or where it had not been practised since 1940 (Finland, Luxembourg, Norway). Moreover, it has made a sort of comeback on stage in two countries where it seemed obsolete (Iceland and Malta). Only in Belgium, and to some extent in France, where a somewhat less intense but nonetheless recurrent practice has replaced Gaullist plebiscitarism, has it lost some ground. In Western Europe, much of the increase has had to do with the submission to the people of the different steps of European integration or of new, cross-cutting issues such as civil, nuclear, or so-called moral questions, like divorce or abortion. Clearly enough, from a world perspective, the increase in referendum use in the 1970s and 1990s also reflects the rise in the number of independent countries and the use of the referendum during the process of nation-building in these countries, as well as the spread of democratic regimes around the world.

IV. Judicial Review

1. The Juridicization of the Referendum

The referendum has not escaped the general trend of juridicization. As for the countries mentioned in Table 24.1, this is to some extent expressed in the number of ad hoc referendums, which is stable over the two periods considered (respectively 14 for each), although the number of referendums has increased (see Table 24.1).[42] It should be noted that the share of these referendums remains very modest (although almost half of the countries with a referendum experience since 1940 have had some), and that only a small minority of them has been decided by ad hoc governmental decrees (4 out of 28), in the particular context of transitions to democracy (eg the referendums on monarchy versus republic in Italy and Greece). All other ad hoc referendums were decided by specific laws regularly adopted by parliaments (eg the British and Norwegian referendums on EC membership). The juridicization of the referendum is clearly correlated with two other processes. First, the amount of legislation regulating referendums in order to ensure fair practice has substantially increased. It has become clear, indeed, that referendums, just as elections, can vary from being highly democratic to the exact opposite depending on the conditions surrounding their practice. Thus, implementing referendum legislation has flourished everywhere, and filled a void in some countries which had previously experienced referendums in the absence of such legislation (eg the United Kingdom, Canada, France…). In particular, regulations concerning campaigning, funding, and the vote have been introduced. Such regulations have tried to catch the specific nature of referendums compared to elections. For example, in many countries, funds or time on public television channels are shared between the 'yes' and the 'no' camps rather than between single

[42] Note that the second period is also longer.

Table 24.1 Provisions for (2011) and practice of (1940–2011) nationwide referendums in 25 consolidated democracies[1]

	1. INITIATOR OF REFERENDUM							2. AUTHOR OF PROPOSAL		3. SCOPE							4. PRACTICE		
	Is referendum optional or mandatory?							Can initiator be author?		Which issues can be put to referendum?[2]									
	Who can initiate optional referendum?																		
	optional						*mandatory*												
	gov initiated			non-gov initiated						*constit*	non-constitutional								
	exe+ leg	*leg*	*exe*	*mino (leg)*	*mino (subn)*	*mino (pop)*		*propo -sitive*	*non prop*		*instit*[3] *most*	*instit*[3] *few*	*internat*	*territ*	*other most*	*other few*	*1940 1969*	*1970 2011*	*Tot.*
	1.a	1.b	1.c	1.d	1.e	1.f	1.g	2.a	2.b	3.a	3.b	3.c	3.d	3.e	3.f	3.g			
Australia																			
1.			X						X	X								4	4
2.							X			X							8	14	22
		X						*X*			*X*		*X*	*X*	*X*			*1*	*1*
Austria																			
1.		X						X			X		X	X	X			1	1
2[4]				X					X	X									
3.[5]							X			X								1	1
Belgium																			
	X							*X*		*X*							*1*		*1*
Canada[6]																			
1.	X							X		X									
	X							*X*								*X*	*1*		*1*
	X								*X*	*X*								*1*	*1*
Denmark																			
1.				X					X		X		X	X	X		4		4
2.							X			X							1	1	2

(continued)

Table 24.1 Continued

	1. INITIATOR OF REFERENDUM							2. AUTHOR OF PROPOSAL		3. SCOPE							4. PRACTICE		
	Is referendum optional or mandatory?							Can initiator be author?		Which issues can be put to referendum?[2]									
	Who can initiate optional referendum?																		
	optional						*mandatory*												
	gov initiated			non-gov initiated						*constit*	non-constitutional								
	exe+ leg	*leg*	*exe*	*mino (leg)*	*mino (subn)*	*mino (pop)*		*propo -sitive*	*non prop*		*instit[3] most*	*instit[3] few*	*internat*	*territ*	*other most*	*other few*	*1940 1969*	*1970 2011*	*Tot.*
	1.a	1.b	1.c	1.d	1.e	1.f	1.g	2.a	2.b	3.a	3.b	3.c	3.d	3.e	3.f	3.g			
3.							X					X					3	2	5
4.[7]							X						X					5	5
	X							*X*					*X*					*1*	*1*
Finland																			
1.	X							X		X	X		X	X	X			1	1
France																			
1	X							X			X		X	X	X				
2.			X					X			X		X	X	X		4	4	8
3.[8]			X						X	X								1	1
4.							X			X									
5.1g 3e	*X*								*X*	*X*							*1*		*1*
							X			*X*							*2*		*2*
			X					*X*		*X*							*2*		*2*
Germany																			
Greece																			
1.	X							X			X		X	X	X				
2.	X							X							X				
			X					*X*		*X*								*1*	*1*
Iceland																			
1.			X						X		X		X	X	X			2	2
2.[9]							X									X			
	X							*X*		*X*							*1*		*1*
							X							X			1		1

	1.a	1.b	1.c	1.d	1.e	1.f	1.g	2.a	2.b	3.a	3.b	3.c	3.d	3.e	3.f	3.g	*1940 1969*	*1970 2011*	*Tot.*
Ireland																			
1.	X								X		X		X	X	X				
2.							X			X							3	29	32
Israel[10]																			
1.							X							X					
Italy[11]																			
1.				X					X	X								2	2
2.					X				X	X									
3.					X				X		X				X			2	2
4.						X			X	X									
5.						X			X		X				X			68	68
			X					*X*		*X*							*1*		*1*
	X							*X*					*X*					*1*	*1*
Japan																			
1.[12]							X			X									
Luxemburg																			
1.[13]	X	X	X					X			X		X	X	X			1	1
2.				X					X	X									
3.						X			X	X									
4.				X					X	X									
5.						X			X	X									
Malta																			
1.		X						X			X		X	X	X			2	2
2.						X			X		X								
3.[14]							X			X									
			X						*X*	*X*							*1*		*1*

(*continued*)

Table 24.1 Continued

	1. INITIATOR OF REFERENDUM							2. AUTHOR OF PROPOSAL		3. SCOPE							4. PRACTICE		
	Is referendum optional or mandatory?							Can initiator be author?		Which issues can be put to referendum?[2]									
	Who can initiate optional referendum?																		
	optional						mandatory												
	gov initiated			non-gov initiated						constit	non-constitutional								
	exe+ leg	leg	exe	mino (leg)	mino (subn)	mino (pop)		propo -sitive	non prop		most	instit[3] few	internat	territ	other most	few	1940 1969	1970 2011	Tot.
	1.a	1.b	1.c	1.d	1.e	1.f	1.g	2.a	2.b	3.a	3.b	3.c	3.d	3.e	3.f	3.g			
Netherlands[15]		*X*						*X*					*X*					*1*	*1*
N-Zealand																			
1.						X		X			X		X	X	X			4	4
2.		X						X				X					1	4	5
							X									X	9	6	15
	X							*X*								*X*	*4*	*1*	*5*
	X							*X*				*X*						*2*	*2*
Norway	*X*							*X*					*X*					*2*	*2*
Portugal																			
1.	X							X			X		X	X	X			2	2
2.			X					X			X		X	X	X				
3.							X					X						1	1
Spain																			
1.	X							X			X		X	X	X			2	2
2.[16]				X					X	X									
							X			X									
			X						*X*	*X*								*1*	*1*
							X			X								1	1
Sweden																			
1.		X						X			X		X	X	X		2	3	5
2.				X				X		X									

	1.a	1.b	1.c	1.d	1.e	1.f	1.g	2.a	2.b	3.a	3.b	3.c	3.d	3.e	3.f	3.g	*1940 1969*	*1970 2011*	*Tot.*
Switzerland																			
1.[17]		X						X		X							6	24	30
2.					X				X		X		X	X	X				
3.						X		X		X							21	124	145
4.						X			X		X		X	X	X		25	95	121
5.							X			X							33	92	125
6.							X						X					3	3
7.							X									X	2	9	11
U.K.	*X*								*X*				*X*					*2*	*2*
USA																			

1 This table is the product of my own elaboration. It shows constitutional or legal (specific referendum laws) provisions (columns 1 to 3) as well as the effective practice (column 4). Six countries (names in *italic*) have no provisions of any kind for nationwide referendums. Four of them have had referendums; however, all decided by ad hoc referendum laws. Other countries with provisions for referendums have had referendums not falling into any of these provisions (reported on the last lines), which have been held either under previous constitutional or legislative provisions, or through ad hoc laws or government decrees. Ad hoc referendums are reported in *italics*. Concerning these referendums, the first three questions refer to the 'actual' initiator, to whether the referendum was propositive or not, and to the issue on which it has dealt (the distinction between 'most' and 'few' issues making no sense here, referendums have been systematically mentioned in the column 'few'). Referendums held under authoritarian regimes are not reported (eg the Spanish or Greek referendums under the dictatures).

2 Provisions generally refer to the category of legislative act (especially constitutional or ordinary legislation) and/or the subject. We report both in this table. Most constitutional issues are institutional, although mere are exceptions, like in Switzerland, where the constitution includes a great variety of norms which belong in other countries to ordinary legislation. Referendums on European integration have been sometimes held under provisions for referendums on constitutional revisions (Austria and Ireland). In a particular field, provisions generally concern most issues or most issues of primary importance (typically, 'total revisions' of the constitution, or, in the field of ordinary legislation, 'questions of national importance'). In the case of non-constitutional issues and 'other ordinary legislation', they are however sometimes restricted to a few issues (eg electoral age in Denmark, regionalization in Portugal, or the status of the Church in Ireland).

3 Institutional issues not included in the constitution Israel, New Zealand and the United Kingdom have no proper constitutionnal text. In this case the category of non-constitutional issues includes all institutional issues.

4 Partial revision of the constitution.

5 Total revision of the constitution.

(*continued*)

6 Canada has no provision for nationwide referendums in its constitution. However it has a referendum law, adopted after the 1992 referendum, with the view that there should be a set of procedures in place in advance of a future referendum.

7 This referendum on delegation of powers to international authorities is mandatory only in case the text has been approved by a majority inferior to five-sixth in parliament.

8 France: 3 and 4 refer to the referendum on constitutional revision. The referendum is mandatory only when the revision has been initiated by parliament; it is optional (decided by the President of the Republic) when the revision has been initiated by the President of the Republic on proposal of the Prime Minister). Type 5 was introduced in 2005, for future treaties of accession of countries to the EC. However, since 2008, the parliament may decide by a majority of three-fifth to approve the treaty without a referendum. France has also introduced in 2008 a new initiative for the referendum on non-constitutional matters (types 1 and 2), by a combined parliamentary/popular/presidential decision. But it won't be in force before the approval of an implementing legislation.

9 Mandatory referendum for any modification of the status of the Church.

10 Israel has introduced provisions fpr a referendum on the restitution of an annexed territory in 2000 but only in 2010 has the law of implementation for this referendum been approved by the Knesset. The referendum is mandatory only in case the law deciding the restitution of a territory has been approved by a less than two-third majority.

11 1, 2, and 4 refer to referendums on constitutional amendments, which can be initiated however only if the amendment has been adopted by Parliament with a majority inferior to two-third. In 2001 the referendum was initiated by a parliamentary minority while in 2006 it was a combined minority initiative of parliament, regions and citizens (both referendums ranged in column 1d).

12 Only in 2010, the Japanese Diet has approved the implementing law enabling the holding of the constitutional referendum provided for in the Constitution since 1947.

13 Article 51 of the constitution (types 1, 2, 3) is extremely vague about the conditions of application of this referendum and still waiting a specific law defining such conditions. The prevailing interpretation up to now has been that the referendum is government initiated and can deal only with non-constitutional matters. Types 4 and 5 refer to a provision for a constitutional referendum introduced in 2003 (revision of article 114 of the Constitution). A revision of the Constitution which would introduce a popular legislative initiative is currently under discussion.

14 Only referendum mentioned in the constitution. The two other forms are only dealt with in a special 'Referenda Act'.

15 There are no provisions for nationwide referendums in the constitution of Netherlands. A 'Temporary Law on Referendums' introducing some forms of referendums has been introduced in 2002 but suspended in 2005. The 2005 referendum on the Treaty for a European Constitution was held on the basis of a different, ad hoc, law.

16 Like in Austria, the referendum is mandatory for the total revision (type 3) and initiated by a parliamentary minority for any partial revision adopted by parliament.

17 Counterproject to a popular initiative.

Table 24.2 Practice of nationwide referendums in 25 consolidated democracies by decade (1940–2011)[1]

	1940–49	1950–59	1960–69	1970–79	1980–89	1990–99	2000–11	1940–2011
Australia	5	1	2	11	6	2		27
Austria				1		1		2
Belgium		1						1
Canada	1					1		2
Denmark		2	6	3	1	3	2	17
Finland						1		1
France	4	1	4	1	1	1	2	14
Germany								0
Greece				1				1
Iceland	2						2	4
Ireland		1	2	5	4	10	10	32
Israel								0
Italy	1			3	12	32	26	74
Japan								0
Luxembourg							1	1
Malta			1				2	3
Netherlands							1	1
New Zealand	6	2	6	3	3	8	3	31
Norway				1		1		2
Portugal						2	1	3
Spain				2	1		1	4
Sweden		2			1	1	1	5
UK				1			1	2
USA								0
Total	19	10	21	32	29	63	51	225
Switzerland	17	45	26	86	62	88	113	437

1 Referendums held under authoritarian regimes are not reported (eg the Spanish or Greek referendums under the dictatures).

parties or groups. Concerning the vote, special conditions like qualified majorities or quorums of approval or participation have sometimes been introduced, as a way of protecting minorities against immoderate popular decisions. Rules pertaining to the issue, such as the unity of form, of content, or the unicity of the question asked, aimed at ensuring the best expression of popular will, or substantive limits like the respect of entrenched fundamental rights or higher rank legislation, are also widespread; or rules concerning the legal effects of referendums (eg consultative versus legally binding), their implementation (when they consist in a question of principle or a generally worded proposal), or the revision of popular decisions (parallelism of procedures versus right of parliament to reverse a decision taken by the people).[43] Although the amount of these regulations has increased, academic works or think tank reports on referendum monitoring suggest that a lot may still have to be done to ensure referendum best practices.[44] Moreover, it should be noted that substantial country differences persist: while some countries are rather under-regulated, the details of the referendum practice being almost completely left to the parliament (eg Finland, Luxembourg), other countries have extensive regulations (eg Italy, Switzerland). Another important difference concerns the extent to which these rules can be and are actually subject to judicial review, which is the second way by which the juridicization of referendums has increased in recent decades[45] (reflecting the general increase of judicial review).

2. Types of Judicial Review

What can be the object of judicial review, to whom must the request be addressed, by whom and when: all these questions have answers which vary greatly according to country.[46] Regarding the *object*, judicial review traditionally applies to the process (respect of rules pertaining to the initiation of the referendum, the campaign, the vote…) and, less frequently, to the issue, from a both formal and material point of view. The formal validity of the issue is generally appreciated with regard to the clarity and the unicity of the question or subject (eg the US states, Switzerland, or Italy), which increasingly appears as a minimal requirement of referendums.[47] The material validity of the issue is first of all a matter of whether it actually belongs to the field open to the referendum. But it can also regard the conformity of the referendum proposal to the status quo, in some determined areas, or, more commonly, to higher ranking legislation (Constitution, bill of rights…). This depends on whether the referendum is legislative or constitutional, but also on the ranking of referendum legislation in the hierarchy of norms. *Authorities* exercising judicial review are sometimes political bodies, like the Federal Assembly in Switzerland, but more often courts. In this case, there might be an admin-

[43] I mention here only the most common regulations surrounding referendum practice. A more complete overview of these regulations can be found in the above-mentioned Venice Commission reports.

[44] One might refer here to Ranney (n 15), ch 5 ('Regulating the Referendum'), or to the numerous IRI publications (Initiative and Referendum Institute) on the subject (to quote just one: ch 4 by Andreas Gross in Bruno Kaufman and M. Dane Waters (eds), *Direct Democracy in Europe. A Comprehensive Reference Guide to the Initiative and Referendum Process in Europe* (2004)).

[45] Marthe Fatin-Rouge Stéfanini speaks of a 'banalisation of judicial review of referendums' in the conclusion of her seminal comparative study on the subject (*Le contrôle du référendum par la justice constitutionnelle* (2004) (foreword by Louis Favoreu)).

[46] And to types of referendums: referendums on legislation approved by parliament actually need much less control than propositive popular initiatives. Similarly referendums on constitutional revisions are less subject to material judicial review than referendums on ordinary legislation.

[47] Fatin-Rouge Stéfanini (n 45), 167–95.

istrative court which checks the regularity of the process, and a judicial court—generally the constitutional court in countries which have one—in charge of reviewing the issue (eg Italy). The control might be automatic or compulsory (eg in France since 2008), or depend on seizure by some authorized actor. Thus, a crucial criteria to assess the extent of judicial review is *who may lodge an appeal.* There is a much variation in this respect: while in some countries any elector may initiate a recourse (eg Greece, Ireland, Italy, Switzerland), or any person directly concerned (the Netherlands), in other countries this capacity is restricted to political parties (eg Spain) or certain authorities, for example the President of the Republic or the Presidents of the Chambers (France until 1974). Finally, another important modality is the *moment* (before or after the vote). While a priori control seems logical, and is actually the rule for checking the formal regularity of referendums (eg the US states, with the exception of California, or Italy), things are not so clear regarding the material control of the issue (especially its conformity to higher ranking legislation), which is sometimes perceived as conflicting too much with popular sovereignty if a posteriori. This was indeed the reason why the French Constitutional Council declared itself incompetent when asked, after the referendum of November 1962 introducing the direct election of the President of the Republic, to decide about the admissibility of this referendum held under Article 11 of the Constitution (which in the event was only a question of knowing whether it was possible to revise the Constitution through this article). Yet, it appears that most countries that provide for a constitutional review of the issue have placed it a posteriori, actually after the promulgation of the referendum law: for example the United States and Switzerland (both at the sub-state level), which are actually the only two countries which really practise it, or Italy, Ireland, and Portugal (the two latter having also a priori control).[48]

3. Country Profiles

To a large extent, the importance of judicial review of referendums in a specific country reflects the general situation of judicial review in that country. Thus, countries with no or little judicial review, like Switzerland, Denmark, Ireland, New Zealand (or even Great Britain, Sweden, Finland, Greece, or Luxembourg, as much less frequent users of the referendum), have no judicial control, or only formal judicial control, that is, a control which is limited to checking the regularity of the process or the form of the issue.[49] Since 1999, however, it should be noted that Switzerland has introduced a material limitation to the popular constitutional initiative: according to Article 139(2) of the new federal Constitution, a popular initiative may be declared invalid by the Federal Assembly (a priori control) if it 'fails to comply with the requirements of consistency of form, and of subject matter', but also 'if it infringes mandatory provisions of international laws'.[50] This might be seen as a new protection for minorities, since

[48] One could also mention in this list of criteria surrounding judicial review the consultative or binding nature of this review, which is relevant, eg, in France (see ibid 147–52).

[49] Interestingly, in Great Britain there was an appeal to the courts in 2008 to oblige the Brown government to hold its promise to organize a referendum on the EU Constitution. The judicial review was granted but the appeal rejected, the judges declaring that only parliament was entitled to make a legal bid to force the referendum. It would of course have been surprising if the decision not to hold a referendum was in the competence of the judges when the decision to hold one was not (see ibid 136–7 for a discussion of the legal means to force political authorities to organize a referendum).

[50] Another requirement is the possibility of implementing the initiative in practice (see ibid 63). Differently, there is extensive material control at the subnational level: eg, cantonal initiatives are subject to a control of conformity to federal legislation.

it could appear that popular initiatives must not violate texts like the European Convention on Human Rights or the United Nations Pacte II. However, the decision to reject an initiative, it should be recorded, is in the hands of a political assembly, and not susceptible to litigation in the courts. Moreover, the limitation to 'mandatory' provisions drastically reduces the possibility of rejecting an initiative, as illustrated by the 'anti-minaret' initiative, which was declared admissible by the Federal Assembly in 2008 since the international human rights violated by this proposal (eg the freedom of religion according to Article 9 of the ECHR) were not part of the *jus cogens*, as defined by the 1969 Vienna Convention, that is, core human rights to which any state owes strict obedience.[51] Identically, another initiative potentially dangerous for minority rights (mandatory life incarceration for certain prisoners) had been declared admissible by the Federal Assembly in 2001 since it did not violate *jus cogens* (all the formal requirements being otherwise fulfilled). Actually, these two initiatives have been successively approved by the Swiss people, without any possibility of challenging them legally a posteriori. The only case of a rejection of a popular initiative by the Federal Assembly referring to a violation of *jus cogens* was in 1995 (the so-called 'anti-asylum initiative'), before the introduction of the new provision in the Constitution, which was to a large extent an adaptation of the right to this precedent.[52] The Federal Assembly regarded this initiative as contradicting the non-*refoulement* principle and thus the vote did not take place. Although the possibility of material control of a popular initiative remains thus very limited in Switzerland, it should be noted however that the Swiss Parliament is allowed to discuss popular initiatives before the actual vote takes place, and may formulate a counter-proposition (which it did not in the anti-minaret and incarceration cases) or simply a recommendation on how voters should decide on the issue (which it did extensively, against the proposal, in these two cases).

Conversely, countries with a stronger tradition of judicial control, like the United States, Australia, Italy, or Spain, or countries with a recent increase in judicial review, like France, have extensive possibilities for judicial review, including material control of issue.[53] As for the US states, material a posteriori control of the issue may regard the conformity of referendum legislation to state constitutions (statutory referendum laws), or to the federal constitution (constitutional revisions raising a federal constitutional issue).[54] US states are particularly active in this regard: in the five strongest initiative states (California, Oregon, Washington, Colorado, Arizona), 49.5 per cent of all voter-approved initiatives were challenged with a success rate (invalidation) of 45 per cent (corresponding to 22.25 per cent of all voter-approved initiatives) since the beginning of the 1970s.[55] The same-sex marriage case in California is a recent and still ongoing very illustrative example of the dialectic interplay between the people and the courts that can take place. In this particular case, the state courts first defeated the popular statutory legislation banning homosexual marriages, which was then reformulated as an initiative constitutional amendment (ICA) and voted again by the people, before being rejected a second time by the US Supreme Court. On the whole, it seems however that judicial

[51] See the 27 August 2008 report by the Federal Assembly: *Message 08.061 relatif à l'initiative populaire 'contre la construction des minarets'*, available at <http://www.admin.ch/ch/f/ff/2008/6923.pdf>.

[52] On this see Jean-François Flauss, 'Le contrôle de la validité internationale des initiatives populaires en Suisse' (1995) 23 *Revue française de droit constitutionnel* 625.

[53] For a definition and discussion of the distinction between 'formal', or 'extrinsic' control, and 'material', or 'intrinsic' control, see Fatin-Rouge Stéfanini (n 45), 207–12.

[54] See eg Julian N. Eule, 'Judicial Review of Direct Democracy' (1990) 7 *Yale Law Journal* 1503, for a discussion of judicial review of referendums in US states.

[55] Percentages calculated on the basis of the data provided by Kenneth P. Miller, *Direct Democracy and the Courts* (2009), 106.

review operates as a strong constraint on direct democracy only in states where the ICA does not exist, or when the issue put on the ICA raises a federal constitutional matter. In these two cases, the last word is with the courts. Otherwise, it is with the people. According to Miller, popular initiative has created in some states a hybrid constitutional system of 'popular constitutionalism', involving the people and the courts, and marinating the legislature.[56] Reforms aimed at moderating the power of both the people and the courts should thus be introduced. However, the system altogether works rather well, with the judicial system providing an efficient check to abuses of popular majorities on minority or individual rights. Thus Miller writes: 'a fair reading of the record suggests that direct democracy's most consequential impact on rights has been to limit the *expansion* of rights in a number of areas, including affirmative action, bilingual education, marriage, and certain areas of criminal law.' But, he adds, 'on balance, where direct democracy has threatened rights, the judicial power has effectively countered this threat'.[57]

Italy is another case of a strong activism of judicial review regarding both formal and material aspects of the abrogative minority referendum (Art 75 of the Italian Constitution). While the *Ufficio centrale per il referendum*, which emanates from the higher administrative court, focuses on procedural verifications, the Constitutional Court decides on the admissibility of the issue, with a clear tendency to increase over the years the restrictions on the use of the abrogative referendum (facilitated by the imprecision of Article 75 and its implementing legislation). Thus no less than 46 demands for abrogative referendums have been rejected by the Constitutional Court between 1971 and 2011, against a total of 68 abrogative referendums declared admissible and effectively held.[58] Formal motivations for rejecting referendums have been of two kinds, both relying on criteria established by the Court in its successive rulings. A first motivation has been the exclusion of constitutional laws from laws which can be the object of the abrogative referendum, asserted in the no 16 1978 ruling, which rejected the referendum on the Concordat. The second, very frequent motivation, has been the insufficient clarity or homogeneity of the question. The technical complexity of the abrogative referendum, which may ask for the cancellation of only small parts, or even commas, of a law, surely responds to the difficulty of promoters in fulfilling this requirement. Yet, there is no doubt that the Italian Court has progressively increased its demands on the matter, as in its 1987 ruling, when it justified the rejection of the referendum to abrogate some parts of the hunting legislation on the ground that it was impossible to understand the 'intrinsic aim of the abrogative act', or in its 1997 and 2000 rulings, when it mentioned the criteria of the 'capacity of the demand to reach its objective' and the 'reasonableness of the law'. This jurisprudence is regularly criticized for being arbitrary or politicized, or anti-referendum oriented, but it remains true that the Italian Court is also trying to guarantee the fair expression of popular will in the context of a very complex type of referendum. Material motivations for rejecting referendums have referred first to the subject limitations in Article 75 (eg the exclusion of tax laws or budget Acts). Again, this has been interpreted in a more and more restrictive way (see 1995 and 1997

[56] Ibid 13.

[57] Ibid 155. According to Christmann, as for California only, 14 popular initiatives have tried to restrict civil rights between 1990 and 2010 (and 10 in Switzerland during the same period) (Anna Christmann, 'Voters' Support for Judicial Review of Anti-Minority Initiatives. Survey Results from California and Switzerland', Paper prepared for presentation at the IPSA and ECPR Conference Sao Paulo, February 2011).

[58] It should be added that many abrogative initiatives have also been rejected by the *Ufficio centrale per il referendum*, which reviews the demand for referendum in the first place.

rulings). They have also referred to the legislative consequences of the abrogation, considered from multiple perspectives: thus, for example, the referendum on the Senate electoral law was rejected in 1991 because the abrogation would have had a legislative effect, that is, the referendum would have been de facto propositive; conversely, the Court rejected in 1995 and again in 1997 the referendums to eliminate the share of seats elected by proportional representation in the two Chambers on the ground that they would have created a legislative vacuum; it also regularly rejected referendums proposing to repeal standards the loss of which would result in rendering ineffective some parts of the Constitution, operating in that way a sort of control of constitutionality *ex ante*, which has sometimes been regarded as a way to protect individual rights (as in the case of the cancellation by the Court of the two referendums on work at home and patronage and social care in 2000, or on the law on assisted reproduction in 2005). It remains, however, that in theory a constitutional review a posteriori of a law abrogated by referendum is also possible, as recognized by the Court itself in its 1981 ruling, although it seems that it has until now preferred to exercise as far as possible such control a priori rather than to expose itself to the criticism of overturning the popular will.[59]

Finally, France is an interesting example of a country which was first characterized by low judicial review of referendums, but has moved recently towards much more demanding standards through the jurisprudence of the Constitutional Court and the constitutional reform of 2008. The rarity of referendums, however, makes it difficult to assess the exact scope of these changes. Until the 2000 referendum on the constitutional revision reducing the presidential mandate from seven to five years, the French Constitutional Council only accepted conducting control a posteriori of the voting process. Thus, in 1962, it refused to rule on the constitutionality of the law approved by the referendum held under Article 11 of the Constitution (see above), arguing that its role according to the Constitution was to control the parliament, not popular decisions, which are the 'direct expression of national sovereignty'.[60] On the other hand, the Council of State also interpreted its role in a very restrictive way which included only control of the decrees organizing the campaign. As a result, the only case that could have led to material control of the issue under Article 11 was the referendum on a treaty, which, according to Article 11, must not be contrary to the Constitution to take on this article (this was not necessary in the case of the Maastricht Treaty and the Treaty establishing a Constitution for Europe since the parliament had conducted the constitutional revisions made necessary by these treaties in the months before the referendums). However, it must be recognized that after Pompidou, the French presidents of the republic, who are the initiators of the referendum under Article 11, clearly took a position against the Gaullist use of this article to revise the constitution, which corresponded to a sort of self-control of constitutionality in the absence of control by the Court. Things changed substantially in 2000 with the 'jurisprudence Hauchemaille', by which the Constitutional Court acknowledged its competence to exercise a priori control over some preparatory acts to the referendum such as the presidential decree of convocation, which seemed to include the possibility of material control of the issue.[61] The latter, however, was clearly introduced by the 2008 constitutional reform, according to which the law proposals mentioned in Article 11 must obligatorily be subject to constitutional review before their submission to the referendum (Art 61 of the Constitution). Thus,

[59] On this see Fatin-Rouge Stéfanini (n 45), 125 and 224–30.

[60] A decision which has generated a lot of ambiguity about the status of referendum legislation, which could now appear above the Constitution, while on the other hand it was admitted that popular laws could be modified by a simple parliamentary law. On this see ibid 95–101.

[61] See ibid 157–66.

after having been criticized for giving full powers to the president of the Republic in calling a referendum, France is now a quite unique case of a country with constitutional review of the referendum which is not only a priori, but also mandatory.[62]

V. Concluding Remarks

> The progressive development of law is characterized by the fact that the same problems raised in the late eighteenth century as *philosophical* and ideological problems, appear nowadays as technical issues only. [Thus] in the twentieth century, the referendum follows the fate of the other institutions of constitutional law and moves from the doctrinal phase to the positive phase, with the result that the referendum is not anymore a theoretical issue.... In front of the free peoples lies not an abstract problem, but a practical problem: is the referendum a rational process, is freedom better or less ensured through it? Therefore we can and we must, in the twentieth century, consider the problem only as a pure *technical* issue.[63]

These comments by Mirkine-Guetzévitch written in 1931 have not lost their timeliness. Rather, they are probably more relevant today than they were on the eve of the fall of European democracies, which demonstrated that the people were not ready, either for direct or for representative democracy. Thus only today, in the context of mature democracies, has the referendum become a 'purely technical issue'. This does not mean, however, that the classical drawbacks of the referendum, such as the risk that popular decisions are incompetent, dangerous for liberties, or do not correctly reflect popular will, have disappeared. But, as Mirkine-Guetzévitch meant, these are now problems which can to a large extent be solved by technical adaptations of the device. In other words, the technic might today be enough to ensure the desired ends: democracy and liberty. This is of course where the law can be useful, and already is, as evidenced by the ongoing process of juridicization. Direct democracy, just as representative democracy, is happier with the help of constitutionalism.

Bibliography

Andreas Auer and Michael Bützer (eds), *Direct Democracy: the Eastern and Central European Experiences* (2001)

Andreas Auer and Jean-François Flauss (eds), *Le référendum européen: actes du colloque international de Strasbourg, 21–22 février 1997* (1997)

Virginia Beramendi, Andrew Ellis, Bruno Kaufman, Miriam Kornblith, and Larry LeDuc et al (eds), *Direct Democracy: The International IDEA Handbook* (2008)

Ian Budge, *The New Challenge of Direct Democracy* (1996)

David Butler and Austin Ranney (eds), *Referendums around the World. The Growing Use of Direct Democracy* (1994)

Raymond Carré de Malberg, 'Considérations théoriques sur la question de la combinaison du référendum avec le parlementarisme' (1931) 2 *Annuaire de l'Institut international de droit public* 272

[62] It is also generally accepted that referendum legislation could be subject to a control of conformity to international law (eg the European Convention on Human Rights), although this would be the competence of ordinary courts.

[63] Mirkine-Guetzevitch (n 9), 294–9 (my translation).

Simone Chambers, 'Constitutional Referendums and Democratic Deliberation' in Matthew Mendelsohn and Andrew Parkin (eds), *Citizens, Elites and Deliberation in Referendums Campaigns* (2001)

Thomas E. Cronin, *Direct Democracy. The Politics of Initiative, Referendum and Recall* (2nd edn, 1999)

A.V. Dicey, 'Ought the Referendum to be Introduced into England?' (1980) 57 *Contemporary Review* 15

A.V. Dicey, 'The Referendum and Its Critics' (1910) 212 *Quarterly Review* 538

European Commission for Democracy Through Law, 'Referendums in Europe—An Analysis of the Legal Rules in European States', 2005. Available at <http://www.venice.coe.int>

Marthe Fatin-Rouge Stéfanini, *Le contrôle du référendum par la justice constitutionnelle* (2004) (foreword by Louis Favoreu)

Bruno Kaufman and M. Dane Waters (eds), *Direct Democracy in Europe. A Comprehensive Reference Guide to the Initiative and Referendum Process in Europe* (2004)

Larry Leduc, *The Politics of Direct Democracy: Referenda in a Global Perspective* (2003)

Kenneth P. Miller, *Direct Democracy and the Courts* (2009)

Boris Mirkine-Guetzevitch, 'Le référendum et le parlementarisme dans les nouvelles constitutions européennes' in *Annuaire de l'Institut International de Droit Public* (1931), vol II

Laurence Morel, 'Referendums, Direct Democracy and Party Government in Liberal Democracies' (1998) 6(2) *European Review* 203

Laurence Morel, 'The Rise of Politically Obligatory Referendums. The 2005 French Referendum in Comparative Perspective' (2007) 30(5) *West European Politics* 1041

Austin Ranney (ed), *The Referendum Device: A Conference* (1981)

Piervincenzo Uleri, *Referendum e Democrazia. Una prospettiva comparata* (2003)

Stephen Tierney, 'Constitutional Referendums: A Theoretical Enquiry' (2009) 72(3) *Modern Law Review* 360

CHAPTER 25

ELECTIONS

RICHARD H. PILDES*

New York

I. Introduction

Legitimate elections are not sufficient to ensure democracy, but they are its most necessary condition. Regular and genuine elections remain the primary institutional mechanism through which rulers are made accountable to those in whose name they exercise political power. We can envision elections without democracy (indeed, we have plenty of experience of exactly that), but it is difficult to envision modern democracy without meaningful elections.

Yet if elections are central to democratic systems of governance, the precise ways in which elections and representative institutions are structured vary greatly across democratic countries. At a high level of generality, a consensus exists regarding the minimal conditions under which elections must take place to be legitimate, such as a broadly distributed suffrage among citizens, the right to speak freely about political matters, the right to form political associations, including political parties, and the right to run for office. But no broad consensus exists on the relationship between democracy, elections, and the forms that political structures must take for countries to be 'democratic'. Some democracies use first-past-the-post elections, others use proportional representation; some are parliamentary systems, others presi-

* For a great deal of help with research in the production of this chapter, I thank Lynn Eisenberg. I also thank Jeff Oakley for additional research assistance.

dential systems; some democracies view separated legislative and executive powers as central, others do not; some democracies have bicameral legislatures, others, unicameral. In addition, different democracies have dramatically different institutions for overseeing the electoral process and disputes concerning elections. Through constitution or statute, some countries expressly create various independent institutions to oversee and preserve the workings of the electoral process. Other countries leave these issues to be addressed by the ordinary institutions of government, whether courts or political institutions. In some countries, election districts are designed by sitting legislators; in other countries, by independent commissions.

Comparative assessment of democracy and elections can thus focus at any of many different levels. It can focus on questions of institutional design; some studies, for example, offer typologies that compare the design of democratic institutions, with an emphasis on questions such as the extent to which different systems permit simple majorities to authorize action or require broad consensus (across groups and interests) to do so.[1] Comparative studies can instead attempt to assess the policy consequences of different ways of organizing elections and institutions. Within political science, for example, a great deal of literature exists trying to assess the comparative performance of presidential versus parliamentary systems, particularly with respect to their stability or risk of lapsing into authoritarian rule. Other social scientists seek to explore how policy outcomes are affected by the particular design of democratic institutions—for example, whether the size of election districts affects the extent of political corruption or policies concerning economic growth.[2] Or comparative analysis can focus on the level of policy, such as by comparing legislatively adopted rules regarding matters such as who is eligible to vote, what preconditions to voting must be met, including voter registration issues, and the like.

This chapter will focus on comparative discussion of the issues surrounding elections that have tended to come before judicial institutions. Over the last generation, we have witnessed what I elsewhere have called 'the constitutionalization of democratic politics'.[3] Starting with the US Supreme Court's one-person, one-vote decisions in the 1960s, and accelerating greatly over the last 20 or so years, courts throughout the world have become more and more actively engaged in evaluating the design of democratic institutions and processes. Court decisions now routinely engage certain expressive aspects of democracy and elections, such as who should be understood to have the right to participate, and can also have significant instrumental consequences on the ways in which democracies function, such as when courts determine what kinds of regulations of election financing are constitutionally permissible. In addressing various constitutional challenges to the way legislative rules structure democratic participation and elections, courts struggle to reconcile protection of essential democratic rights; the need to permit popular experimentation with the forms of democracy; the risk of political insiders manipulating the ground rules of democracy for self-interested reasons; and the need to protect democracy against anti-democratic efforts that arise through the political process itself.

[1] Many of the classic works of this sort were written by Arend Lijphart, such as *Democracies: Patterns of Majoritarian and Consensus Government in Twentyh-One Countries* (1984).

[2] Torsten Persson and Guido Tabellini, *The Economic Effects of Constitutions* (2003). For another important book in this vein, see Timothy Besley, *Principled Agents? The Political Economy of Good Government* (2006).

[3] Richard Pildes, 'Foreword: The Constitutionalization of Democratic Politics' (2004) 118 *Harvard Law Review* 29.

II. The Right to Participate

Most modern democracies extend the suffrage broadly to all citizens of a certain age. The areas of limitations, and of differences across democracies, tend to center around the issues of age, mental capacity, citizenship, and the status of felons and ex-felons in the democratic process. In addition, democracies typically have voter-identification laws designed to ensure that only eligible voters actually vote; the conditions in these laws vary and have been the subject, in some countries, of court challenges.

1. Age

Age-based voting restrictions reflect the greatest consensus among democratic regimes. While almost every country limits the right to vote to individuals of at least 18 years of age,[4] even this is not universal. Brazil, for example, allows voters as young as 16 to cast a ballot,[5] while many countries in Asia including Japan, Taiwan, Singapore, and South Korea have a higher voting age—20 or 21.[6] The widespread practice of setting the voting age at 18 has itself become a focal point and a basis for coordination between countries. In 2004, for example, the United Kingdom's Electoral Commission considered a proposal to lower its voting age to 16, but decided to revisit the issue in the future; in making its determination, the committee noted that 'most countries have a minimum voting age of 18 and a pattern of harmonized voting and candidacy ages prevails across Europe and Commonwealth countries.'[7]

In federalist democracies, voting age can vary locally, raising special constitutional issues. In the United States, for example, eligibility to vote is primarily determined at the state level, with the federal government setting minimum protections. When Congress tried in 1970 to lower the voting age in all elections to 18, the Supreme Court held that Congress had the power to set the voting age only for national elections; as a result, the law was held unconstitutional with respect to state and local elections.[8] In response, Congress and the states passed the Twenty-Sixth Amendment to the Constitution, setting the maximum prerequisite age to vote at 18.[9] In Australia, the High Court found that section 41 of the Constitution, which states that 'No adult person who has or acquires a right to vote at elections for the more numerous House of the Parliament of a State shall, while the right continues, be prevented by any law of the Commonwealth from voting at elections for either House of the Parliament of the Commonwealth',[10] applied only to Australians over the age of 21, regardless of whether younger Australians were entitled to

[4] Louis Massicotte, Andre Blais, and Antoine Yoshinaka, *Establishing the Rules of the Game: Election Laws in Democracies* (2004), 17.

[5] Massicotte et al (n 4), 17. Other, less democratic countries that allow 16-year-olds to vote include Cuba and Nicaragua, while Iran allows 15-year-olds to vote. Greg Hurst, 'Ministers Contemplate Cut in Voting Age to 16', *The Times & Sunday Times*, 14 February 2003, available at <http://www.timesonline.co.uk/tol/news/politics/article876843.ece>.

[6] Massicotte et al (n 4), 17; The Electoral Commission, 'Voting Age Should Remain at 18 says the Electoral Commission', 2004, available at <http://www.electoralcommission.org.uk/news-and-media/news-releases/electoral-commission-media-centre/news-releases-reviews-and-research/voting-age-should-stay-at-18-says-the-electoral-commission>.

[7] Electoral Commission (n 6).

[8] *Oregon v Mitchell* 400 US 12 (1970).

[9] US Constitution, Amendment XXVI.

[10] Australian Constitution, s 41; *King v Jones* [1972] HCA 44.

vote in certain states.[11] As in the United States, Australian law was overhauled soon after this decision and the voting age was lowered to 18 for all Australians.

2. Mental Capacity

All democratic regimes, with the exception of Canada, Sweden, Ireland, Italy, and Austria,[12] restrict voting based on mental capacity. In the United States, voting restrictions based on mental capacity vary greatly from state to state; in some states individuals under court-imposed guardianship must affirmatively prove capacity to vote, while in other states the court must prove incapacity.[13] European countries similarly vary considerably in the way in which they restrict voting rights based on mental capacity. Recently, however, courts have become more involved in order to ensure more individualized determinations. Thus, in 2010 the Constitutional Court of the Czech Republic found that deprivation of voting due to mental incapacity had to be determined on an individualized, case-by-case basis and could not be based on a bright-line rule that applied to all persons judicially adjudicated to be mentally incapacitated; in applying its own rule, the Court found that 'the approach of the ordinary courts was disproportionate in virtually all cases'.[14] That same year, the European Court of Human Rights, invoking similar reasoning, found that while

> it should be for the legislature to decide as to what procedure should be tailored to assessing the fitness to vote of mentally disabled persons, ... the treatment as a single class of those with intellectual or mental disabilities is a questionable classification, and the curtailment of their rights must be subject to strict scrutiny.[15]

It is not just courts, however, pushing towards increased franchise for the mentally disabled. Recently, 147 countries signed the United Nations Convention on the Rights of Persons with Disabilities.[16] Article 29 of the Convention states that 'states should ensure that persons with disabilities can effectively and fully participate in political and public life on an equal basis with others ... including the right and opportunity for persons with disabilities to vote and be elected.'[17]

3. Citizenship and Residency

All democracies also limit voting in some way based on citizenship or residence.[18] Restrictions based on citizenship, even in an era in which globalization is undermining traditional conceptions of sovereignty, are justified expressively, as a way of defining membership in the political

[11] *King* (n 10).

[12] Massicotte et al (n 4), 27; Ladislav Vyhnánek, *Mental Disability and the Right to Vote in Europe: A Few Notes on the Recent Development* (2010), 1.

[13] For a description of the breadth and variety of US state law on mental capacity and voting, see Brescia, 'Modernizing State Voting Laws that Disenfranchise the Mentally Disabled with the Aid of Past Suffrage Movements' (2010) 54 *Saint Louis Law Review* 943, 947–8.

[14] Vyhnánek (n 12), 7.

[15] ECtHR, *Kiss v Hungary*, App No 38832/06, Judgment of 20 May 2010, para 13, available at <http://www.echr.coe.int/eng>. See also Vyhnánek (n 12), 7.

[16] Although 147 countries signed the Convention, only 99 countries went on to ratify the Convention. See UN 'Rights and Dignity of Persons with Disabilities', available at <http://www.un.org/disabilities/>.

[17] Vyhnánek (n 12), 6; United Nations (n 16).

[18] See Chapter 48 on citizenship.

community, and instrumentally, as a way of ensuring voters have the requisite 'stake in the electoral process and its outcomes'.[19] Yet this is an area in the midst of considerable flux.

While the vast majority of democratic countries, including the United States, limit voting to citizens, a significant expansion of non-citizen voting at the local level has occurred in recent years. The broadest example stems from the European Union. As a condition of membership in the European Union, each of the 27 member states must allow residents who are citizens of another member state to vote in local elections. In carrying out this directive, the member state must ensure that, 'The principle of equality and non-discrimination between national and community voters and candidates... [is] observed', including mandating voting for registered, non-citizen residents in areas where citizens themselves are compelled to vote.[20] In an effort to comply with this rule, countries had to change their local laws and, in some cases, their constitutions. In Germany, the Federal Constitutional Court had previously struck down local laws allowing non-citizen local voting on the grounds that citizenship was required under the German Constitution.[21] That position has been overridden now by the requirements of the European Union.

This distinction between local elections—which are meant to represent local needs—and national elections is a common feature of the relationship between citizenship and voting laws. In Ireland, British citizens are permitted to vote in legislative but not presidential elections.[22] Even in the United States, where debates about citizenship and immigration are increasingly fierce, localities are beginning to allow non-citizens to vote. Non-citizen residents may vote in school counsel elections in Chicago[23] and in local elections in six Maryland municipalities.[24] Allowing non-citizens to vote in local elections is not new in the United States—all but ten states allowed non-citizens to vote for at least some time period before and into the early parts of the twentieth century.[25] While the Supreme Court has affirmatively held that limiting the right to vote to citizens is constitutional,[26] it has never held the Constitution requires that voting *must* be restricted to citizens.

In addition to issues of citizenship, federalist systems, such as the United States and the European Union, face related issues concerning how to determine state and local residency for purposes of allocating the right to vote within the federal system. As noted, member states of the European Union may not disenfranchise residents who are citizens of other member

[19] Andre Blais, Louis Massicotte, and Antoine Yoshika, 'Deciding Who Has the Right to Vote: A Comparative Analysis of Election Laws' (2001) 20 *Electoral Studies* 41, 42 (citing Richard S. Katz, *Democracy and Elections* (1997), 216).

[20] Europa, 'Participating in Municipal Elections: The Right to Vote and to Stand as a Candidate', available at <http://europa.eu/legislation_summaries/justice_freedom_security/citizenship_of_the_union/l23026_en.htm>.

[21] Samuel Issacharoff, Pamela Karlan, and Richard Pildes, *The Law of Democracy: Legal Structure of the Political Process* (3rd edn, 2010), 56.

[22] Massicotte et al (n 4), 28.

[23] The Immigrant Voting Project, 'Immigrant Voting Rights in Chicago', available at <http://www.immigrantvoting.org/statescurrent/Chicago.html>. Similarly, New York City allowed non-citizens to vote in school board elections until 2003. Ron Hayduk, *Democracy for All; Restoring Immigrant Voting Rights in the United States* (2006), 5.

[24] The Maryland municipalities include: Takoma Park, Barnesville, Martin's Additions, Somerset, Garrett Park, and Chevy Chase section 3. The Immigrant Voting Project, 'Immigrant Voting Rights in Maryland', available at <http://www.immigrantvoting.org/statescurrent/maryland.html>; Hayduk (n 23), 5.

[25] The ten states that have never allowed non-citizen voting are: Alaska, Arizona, California, Hawaii, Iowa, Maine, Mississippi, New Mexico, Utah, and West Virginia. Hayduk (n 23), 19–20 (T 2.1).

[26] *Cabell v Chavez-Salido* 454 US 432 (1982).

states in local elections. According to the 2010 EU Citizenship Report, 'In 2009, residence-related issues formed the biggest proportion (38%) of all complaints regarding the functioning of the Single Market.'[27] In the United States, the Supreme Court has recognized the legitimate concern that states have in preventing fraud through the use of residency requirements. However, the Court struck down a Tennessee law requiring residence within the state for a year before voting, holding that while 'bona fide' residency requirements are constitutional, durational requirements are not.[28] This concern for residency is not limited to distinctions within federalism regimes, however. About 14 percent of countries require that naturalized citizens reside in the country for a minimum period (ranging from a few months to several years) before voting.[29]

Finally, countries differ in their treatment of local citizens residing in other countries. US citizens do not lose their right to vote in federal elections due to residency in another country.[30] In a study performed by Andre Blais, Louis Massicotte, and Antoine Yoshinaka, researchers found that 'more established democracies are less inclined to disenfranchise citizens residing abroad', noting that more than half of the former colonies of the United Kingdom do so, while the United Kingdom itself does not.[31]

4. Felons and Ex-Felons

Democracies around the world vary considerably in the degree to which convicted citizens maintain the right to vote. All prisoners retain their voting rights in Canada, the Czech Republic, Denmark, France, Germany, Israel, Japan, Kenya, the Netherlands, Norway, Peru, Poland, Romania, South Africa, Sweden, and Zimbabwe.[32] Germany[33] and South Africa go even further than this by placing a burden on the state to ensure that prisoners are given an opportunity to cast a ballot, rather than placing the burden of voter registration on the prisoner himself.[34] On the other end of the spectrum, many East European countries, as well as the United Kingdom and Spain, seek to limit voting to released offenders.[35] In some countries such as Belgium, Greece, Italy, and Luxembourg, the court may remove an offender's right to vote based on the length of a sentence or seriousness of a crime; in these countries, an offender may remain disenfranchised for a period of time after he or she has been released.[36] In the United States, where the issue is a matter of state law, practices vary widely across the states; some, such as Maine and Vermont, do not disenfranchise any felons, while other states, such as Kentucky, disenfranchise all convicted felons for life.

In the United States, the Supreme Court has concluded that the text of the Constitution itself permits states to disfranchise felons; this textual provision, in the Court's view,

[27] *EU Citizenship Report 2010: Dismantling the Obstacles to EU Citizens' Rights* (2010), 14.

[28] *Dunn v Blumstein* 405 US 350 (1972).

[29] Blais et al (n 19), 56.

[30] Overseas Citizens Voting Rights Act of 1975, 100 Stat 927.

[31] Massicotte et al (n 4), 32. Canada, a very established democratic country and former colony of the United Kingdom, allows its citizens to vote from abroad for a maximum of five years only.

[32] American Civil Liberties Union, *Out of Step with the World: An Analysis of Felony Disfranchisement in the US and Other Democracies* (2006), 6.

[33] Issacharoff, Karlan, and Pildes (n 21), 30, citing Nora V. Demleitner, 'Continuing Payment on One's Debt to Society: The German Model of Felon Disenfranchisement as an Alternative' (2000) 84 *Minnesota Law Review* 753.

[34] *August and Another v Electoral Commission and others* [1991] CCT 8/99.

[35] American Civil Liberties Union (n 32), 6.

[36] Ibid 6.

immunizes felon disfranchisement provisions, as long as they are not racially discriminatory, from the kind of judicial scrutiny the Supreme Court gives to other restrictions on the franchise.[37] Thus, the US Supreme Court does not require felon-disfranchisement laws in general to meet any kind of standard of proportionality. The Court has held that felon disfranchisement laws adopted for racially discriminatory reasons are unconstitutional.[38]

Outside the United States, however, many High Courts have struck down felon disenfranchisement laws on the grounds that they are disproportionate to the state's purposes and/or serve no justifiable penal purpose. In 2004, the European Court of Human Rights struck down blanket disenfranchisement in the United Kingdom because the law did not differentiate based on the nature of the offense and Parliament had not considered a more narrow law in an attempt to make the ban proportional, as the European Convention judged proportionality.[39] Similarly, the Supreme Court of South Africa held that the constitutionality of felon disenfranchisement, 'Comes down to whether there is a rational connection between the aim and the restriction' and rejected the argument that the need for the government to appear 'tough on crime' warranted the deprivation of voting rights to prisoners.[40] This focus on proportionality underscores a key difference between countries in which courts aggressively scrutinize felon disenfranchisement laws and countries, such as the United States, which consider such laws to have direct constitutional authorization.

In some countries, such as Israel and Canada, courts have gone beyond focusing on proportionality and rejected disenfranchisement entirely as being fundamentally at odds with a democratic society. In *Sauve v Canada*, the Court noted, 'Denial of the right to vote on the basis of attributed moral unworthiness is inconsistent with the respect for the dignity of every person that lies at the heart of Canadian democracy.'[41] The Israeli High Court agreed, holding that President Yitzhak Rabin's murderer could not be deprived of the right to vote because 'it is the foundation of the right to vote for the Knesset, from which democracy flows'.[42] Thus, many commentators have concluded that the United States is 'exceptional' in its lack of aggressive judicial scrutiny of felon disenfranchisement laws.[43]

5. Voter Identification Laws

Most countries require that voters present a valid identification document at the polling location. In a study of 63 democratic countries, the vast majority—47 countries—required all voters to present some form of identification before voting, while an additional five countries required that certain voters present valid identification.[44] These requirements, however, vary significantly. In some countries—and in some US states—only government-issued,

[37] 418 US 21, 54–5 (1976).

[38] *Hunter v Underwood* 421 US 222 (1985).

[39] *Hirst v United Kingdom (No 2)*, App no 74025/01, Judgment of 6 October 2005, para 79 ('there is no evidence that Parliament has ever sought to weigh the competing interests or to assess the proportionality of a blanket ban on the right of a convicted prisoner to vote').

[40] *National Institution of Crime Prevention and the Re-Integration of Offenders (NICRO), Erasmus and Schwagerl v Minister of Home Affairs* (2004) CCT 03/04 (holding that the legislature cannot deprive convicted prisoners of valuable rights that they retain in order to correct a public misconception as to its true attitude to crime and criminals).

[41] *Sauve v Canada* (Attorney General) [2002] 3 SCR 519, 550.

[42] *Hilla Alrai v Minister of the Interior* [1996] PD 50 (2)18.

[43] See Alec C. Ewald and Brandan Rottingham (eds), *Criminal Disenfranchisement in an International Perspective* (2009).

[44] Massicotte et al (n 4), 121.

photo-identification documents are accepted, while in other countries, such as Canada, Ireland, Sweden, and India, a wide variety of documents are accepted.[45]

In the United States and other countries that have not traditionally required voter identification,[46] the proposed enactment of voter identification laws has been criticized as an unnecessary and disproportionate method of counteracting potential fraud. In recent years, there has been increased litigation concerning these laws. All High Courts considering the issue have accepted that some limitations on accessibility to the polls may be necessary to meet legitimate government ends. Whether the court allows the implementation of voter identification laws specifically, depends significantly upon the value that the country places on eliminating fraud from the electoral system, as compared to the value it places on facilitating easy access to the polls.

In the United States, the Supreme Court recently concluded not only that combating voter fraud is a legitimate governmental end, but also that 'public confidence in the integrity of the electoral process has independent significance, because it encourages citizen participation in the democratic process' and that combating the mere appearance of fraud therefore is, standing alone, a legitimate governmental objective.[47] Likewise, the Supreme Court of Canada recently held that, while the right to vote must be given a liberal interpretation, some reasonable limitations are necessary, because 'the electoral rights guarantee meaningful participation, not unlimited participation'.[48]

In general, courts have rejected facial attacks on the constitutionality or legality of voter identification laws. In the United States, the Supreme Court's 2008 decision in *Crawford v Marion County Election Board*[49] rejected facial challenges to voter identification laws that do not require *payment* to obtain the identification. The Court noted that there was no evidence regarding just how many people would be affected by these identification requirements or any real evidence that seniors, poorer citizens, or students would have difficulty obtaining the requisite government-issued identification.[50] Likewise, the Canadian Court, faced with a similar voting law, held that 'Constitutional issues should be determined in the context of a concrete set of facts, not in the abstract or hypothetically'.[51] Unlike the US Supreme Court, however, the Canadian Court found that evidence of the likely effect of a voter identification law was not 'hypothetical' and 'a possible consequence is that some eligible citizens (though likely few in number, given the extensive measures Elections Canada has taken to facilitate voting) may be unable to cast a vote in future elections.'[52] Nevertheless, the Canadian Court, like the US Supreme Court, found that the government interest in preventing both actual fraud and the appearance of fraud outweighed these possible effects.

[45] For a comparison of various identification laws with the law at the center of the US Supreme Court case, *Crawford v Marion County Election Board* 553 US 181 (2008), see Frederic Charles Schaffer and Tova Andrea Wang, 'Is Everyone Else Doing It: Indiana's Voter Identification Law in International Perspective' (2009) 3 *Harvard Law and Policy Review* 397.

[46] In the United States, only three states—Florida, Georgia, and Florida—require photographic identification of all voters and will not allow voters without identification to vote after signing an affidavit; 24 states require some form of identification. Schaffer and Wang (n 45), 397. However, 37 states are presently considering implementing or altering voter identification laws. See Nhu-Y Ngo and Keesha Gaskins, Brennan Center for Justice, *Voter ID Legislation in the States* (2011).

[47] *Crawford v Marion County Election Board* 553 US 181, 197 (2008).

[48] *Henry v Canada* [2010] BCSC 610.

[49] *Crawford* (n 47).

[50] Ibid.

[51] *Henry* (n 48).

[52] Ibid.

The possible detrimental effect on voter turnout of certain forms of voter identification laws is particularly apparent in countries with large Muslim populations. In India, where the court weighs the government interest in preventing fraud much more highly than it does the individual right to vote, the Supreme Court rejected the argument that female Muslim voters be given special identification cards rather than show their faces in their pictures, in violation of their religious beliefs. The Court held, 'If you have such strong religious sentiments, and do not want to be seen by members of public, then do not go to vote. You cannot go with burqa to vote. It will create complications in identification of voters.'[53] Canada faced a similar problem in 2007, when Elections Canada, an independent, non-partisan agency responsible for running federal elections, allowed women in *burqas* to refrain from lifting their veils to vote; Parliament responded by introducing a bill to require that every voter's face be visible when voting. Ultimately, the issue was resolved through a compromise allowing Muslim women to affirm an oath of identity and eligibility.[54]

As noted in both the *Crawford* opinion in the United States and *Henry* opinion in Canada, it is difficult to determine what detrimental effect on voter turnout in practice, if any, more stringent identification requirements create. A study in Ireland, where the government-initiated new identification requirements in 2003, found that about 3 percent of registered voters did not have any of the required identification documents and that 1 percent of voters who went to a polling station were not permitted to cast a ballot because of missing identification.[55] As more countries and states implement voter identification laws, it is likely that this will remain an area of significant litigation and controversy.

III. Political Parties

Well-functioning political party systems are central to the legitimacy of modern democracies, given the need for intermediary entities that can effectively mobilize and organize citizen participation (as well as organize the processes of governance).[56] While older constitutions did not always reflect appreciation of this reality, modern constitutions do. Thus, before 1950 the right to form political parties tended not to exist in written constitutions; since then, however, 60 percent of the constitutions in effect in 2000 guarantee such a right.[57] Moreover, courts in many countries aggressively protect the perceived constitutional rights of political parties.[58]

The German Federal Constitutional Court, for example, has been aggressive in striking down regulations that limit a political party's access to the ballot. Finding that a 500-signature requirement for new parties interfered with open and fair political competition, the Court invalidated that barrier.[59] Similarly, the Court held unconstitutional, for lack of compelling

[53] Dhananjay Mahapatra, 'Life Veil for Voter ID, SC Tells Burqa-clad Women' (2010), *The Times of India*, available at <http://articles.timesofindia.indiatimes.com/2010-01-23/india/28147714_1_electoral-rolls-burqa-clad-women-veil>.

[54] Amber Maltibie, note, 'When the Veil and the Vote Collide: Enhancing Muslim Women's Rights Through Electoral Reform' (2010) 41 *McGeorge Law Review* 967, 991–2.

[55] Schaffer and Wang (n 45), 404–5.

[56] For a further discussion of political parties see Chapter 41.

[57] ConstitutionMaking.Org, Option Report—Political Parties (2008), 3, available at <http://www.constitutionmaking.org/files/political_parties.pdf>.

[58] For a fuller analysis of the comparative treatment of political parties under various constitutional regimes, see Richard H. Pildes, 'Political Parties and Constitutionalism' in Tom Ginsburg and Rosalind Dixon (eds), *Comparative Constitutional Law* (2011), 254.

[59] *Ballot Admission Case*, 3 BVerfGE 19 (1953).

justification, one state's requirement that a candidate nominated by local voters' groups secure a minimum number of signatures to appear on the ballot, while political parties did not face a similar obligation.[60] The Canadian Supreme Court has similarly invoked that country's constitution to protect the rights of regional or smaller political parties in the context of campaign-finance laws. In the landmark *Figeuroa* case,[61] the Canadian Supreme Court invalidated election laws that required a political party to nominate candidates in at least 50 election districts in order to be an officially registered party, with the various state-provided benefits, including election financing, that accompanied registered-party status. The government defended these provisions as designed to ensure that only parties reflecting large coalitions with broad geographic appeal could seek office. The Court held that these provisions violated the guarantee in the Canadian Charter of Rights and Freedoms of each citizen's right to play a meaningful role in the electoral process.

In many countries with proportional representation systems, minor parties have challenged electoral thresholds as violations of various constitutional provisions reflective of democratic principles, such as the right to vote. These challenges typically have failed, except in unusual contexts. Thus, the German Federal Constitutional Court, informed perhaps by Weimar's experience with a highly fragmented and paralyzed parliamentary system, has rejected several challenges to that system's 5 percent threshold; the Court has accepted a strong governmental interest in effective governance institutions.[62] The constitutional courts of the Czech Republic and Romania have similarly upheld challenges to their systems' 5 percent threshold for representation.[63] But in the exceptional context of the immediate aftermath of German reunification, the German court struck down 5 percent thresholds on the view that this threshold would suppress competition and representation from the former East Germany, given the nascent state of democracy in its initial importation into East Germany.[64]

In addressing the constitutional status and rights of political parties, courts have also had to wrestle with whether post-Second World War notions of 'militant' democracy justify states in banning or otherwise restricting parties that are thought to be antagonist to the fundamental principles of democratic regimes. Courts in countries including Germany, Spain, India, Turkey, and Israel, along with the regional European Court of Human Rights, have been forced to confront this question. The types of parties banned or otherwise restricted range from neo-Nazi and Communist parties in Germany, to religiously-based and Kurdish separatist parties in Turkey, and to ethnic parties in many constitutions in Asia, sub-Saharan Africa, post-communist Eastern Europe, and the nascent constitutions of Afghanistan and Iraq.[65]

The form of the restriction on impermissible parties varies. India, for example, does not ban parties, but its electoral code regulates 'corrupt practices', which include appeals to vote for or against candidates on the ground of religion, race, caste, community, or language, or the use of, or appeal, to religious symbols. The Indian High Court has permitted state electoral

[60] *Stoevesandt Case*, 12 BVerfGE 10, 25 (1960).

[61] *Figueroa v Canada (Attorney General)* [2003] 1 SCR 912.

[62] Donald P. Kommers, *The Constitutional Jurisprudence of the Federal Republic of Germany* (2nd edn, 1997), 87.

[63] See generally Wojciech Sadurski, *Rights Before Courts: A Study of Constitutional Courts in Postcommunist States of Central and Eastern Europe* (2005), 154–5.

[64] *National Unity Election Case*, 82 BVerfGE 322 (1990).

[65] Useful resources on these issues include Samuel Issacharoff, 'Fragile Democracies' (2007) 120 *Harvard Law Review* 1405–67; Gregory H. Fox & Georg Nolte, 'Intolerant Democracies' (1995) 36 *Harvard International Law Journal* 1–70; and Matthias Basedau, 'Ethnic Party Bans In Africa: A Research Agenda' (2007) 8 *German Law Journal* 617–34.

authorities to overturn election results when winning candidates have been found to violate these prohibitions.[66] In Israel, as a result of several back-and-forth exchanges between the Israeli Supreme Court and the parliament, the state denies 'anti-democratic' parties the right to seek elective office but does not ban them more broadly.[67]

When tested, these party restrictions have been upheld by many courts to date, even as the courts recognize the tension between these restrictions and the rights of democratic association and participation.[68] The most dramatic of these cases come from Turkey and involve the Refah Partisi (Welfare Party), a mass-based Islamic organization that at one time was the largest political party in the Turkish parliament. Yet the Turkish Constitutional Court found the Welfare Party to be 'anti-democratic' and in violation of the Turkish constitutional commitment to a democratic and secular state; the Court therefore ordered the dissolution of the party, the surrender of its assets to the state, the removal of four Refah members from parliament, and the banning of the party's leaders from elective office for five years.[69] When the Welfare Party turned to the European Court of Human Rights, that Court in turn upheld the Turkish courts on the ground that

> a State cannot be required to wait, before intervening, until a political party has seized power and begun to take concrete steps to implement a policy incompatible with the standards of the Convention and democracy, even though the danger of that policy for democracy is sufficiently established and imminent.[70]

Thus, constitutional courts in many countries permit restraints on 'extremist parties' that would clearly be unconstitutional within the First Amendment tradition of the United States.

Courts in at least some countries have also been aware of the 'inherent authoritarian' potential in democratic regimes: the risk that existing office holders will use their power to re-write election laws so as to insulate themselves in power.[71] In response, these courts have struck down such laws as violating various constitutional provisions. In addition, courts are beginning to struggle with the problems posed by one-party democracies, such as South Africa—democracies in which one political party is so dominant as to control electoral outcomes over many elections, even when the elections are fair and legitimate.[72]

IV. Campaign Finance

Legislative and regulatory approaches to campaign financing vary greatly across democracies. Even among common law countries with shared histories, the variations can be extreme; Australia, for example, has a laissez-faire system, with no restraints on the *sources* or *size* of campaign contributions or expenditures (other than disclosure requirements), while the

[66] See eg *Prabhoo v Shri Prabhakar Kasinath Kunte et al* [1995] SCALE 1 (upholding invalidation of the election of the mayor of Bombay).

[67] See Basic Law: The Knesset §7A (excluding anti-democratic parties from elections).

[68] See eg *Socialist Reich Party Case*, 2 BVerfGE 1 (1952).

[69] Turkish Constitutional Court, Decision no 1998/1, January 16, 1998.

[70] *Refah Partisi (The Welfare Party) and Others v Turkey*, App nos 41340/98, 41342/98, 41343/98, and 41344/98, Judgment of 13 February 2003 (Grand Chamber).

[71] See Richard H. Pildes, 'The Inherent Authoritarianism in Democratic Regimes' in András Sajó (ed), *Out of and Into Authoritarian Law* (2002).

[72] For the leading article on this subject, see Sujit Choudhry, '"He Had a Mandate": The South African Constitutional Court and the African National Congress in Dominant Party Democracy' (2009) 2 *Constitutional Court Review* 1.

United Kingdom imposes strict limitations on election spending, including limiting spending by third parties (actors other than candidates or parties) to a paltry £500. When democracies regulate election financing, they typically do so on the basis of one or more of three rationales: (1) preventing corruption or the appearance of corruption—the risk that legislators will trade political benefits, including votes, for large campaign contributions or expenditures; (2) promoting political equality—the view that citizens should not only have equal voting power, but some kind of equal opportunity to influence the electoral process; and (3) enhancing public confidence in the legitimacy of democracy. When democracies do regulate the election-financing system, different democracies rely on a range of different means of doing so: *contribution limits*, which cap the amounts that can be given to candidates or parties; *spending limits*, which limit how much candidates, parties, or third parties can spend; *public subsidies*, which involve public financing of parties, candidates, or campaigns; *free or discounted advertising time*, which is usually made available only to parties or candidates; and *disclosure requirements*, which require public disclosure of the sources of large contributions or expenditures.[73]

Just as varied as the policy approaches across democracies to these issues has been the response of courts to these measures. Two bases for challenges typically arise. The most common rests on the claim that these measures violate individual rights to liberty or to free expression (the source of these rights might be constitutional or common law). A secondary basis in some countries is the argument that particular measures have the purpose and effect of manipulating the democratic process, either by favoring particular actors and interests or by seeking to entrench the parties and office holders who currently control the legislative process.

In few areas of comparative constitutional law are the responses of courts more radically at odds with each other. Courts across democratic countries differ not on the application of generally shared legal principles, but on foundational questions in this area, such as what kinds of interests are even legitimate ones for governments to pursue in regulating the financing of elections. Some of these differences appear attributable to differences in the provisions of constitutional texts in different countries, but many of the divergences in judicial treatment appear more to reflect deeper politico-cultural differences about how democracy should best be understood. This section looks briefly at the ways several High Courts have addressed these issues, including the US Supreme Court, the High Court of Australia, the German Federal Constitutional Court, the Supreme Court of Canada, the Supreme Court of Japan, and the European Court of Human Rights.

For all these courts, the determinative factor in whether a regulation is found to be constitutional is the degree to which it relates to a legitimate government aim. Key differences exist, however, in the courts' conceptions of whether the government's objectives are deemed to be legitimate. The European Court of Human Rights, for example, has found that the government has a 'legitimate aim of securing equality between candidates'.[74] Likewise, the Supreme Court of Canada has recognized that, 'Limits on [independent] spending are essential to maintain an equilibrium in financial resources and to guarantee the fairness' of the electoral process.[75]

[73] For a discussion on the range of regulatory efforts as well as the factors affecting a country's choice of regulations, see Keith D. Ewing and Samuel Issacharoff (eds), *Party Funding and Campaign Financing in International Perspective* (2006), 6.

[74] *Bowman v Commonwealth* [1996] 26 EHRR 1.

[75] *Libman v Quebec* [1997] 3 SCR 569.

In the United States, in contrast, the Supreme Court has expressly rejected the idea that the government has a legitimate interest in eliminating financial inequalities between political parties or candidates. First articulated in the 1976 landmark case of *Buckley v Valeo*[76] and re-confirmed in the 2010 *Citizens United v FEC* decision,[77] this principle has led the US Supreme Court to 'reject[] the premise that the Government has an interest "in equalizing the relative ability of individuals and groups to influence the outcome of elections"'.[78] Similarly, the High Court of Australia, in the seminal case of *Australia Capital Television Pty Co v Commonwealth*,[79] rejected an Australian law (modeled after one in the United Kingdom) that banned paid broadcast advertising and granted political parties regulated free broadcast advertising; the government had argued that the law would reduce corruption by diminishing the role of large campaign contributions and would promote equality.[80] The similarities between the US and Australian courts is particularly striking because, while the text of the Constitution in the former includes a free speech guarantee written in absolutist terms (unlike the more expressly limited free speech provisions in the Canadian Charter), Australia has no explicit protection for freedom of speech in its Constitution. Nevertheless, Australia's High Court found that the constitutional commitment to representative government implied rights of political communication and that such rights were violated by these bans on paid broadcast political advertisements.

The Supreme Court of Canada and the European Court of Human Rights, however, have been more willing to permit government to pursue political equality and anti-corruption aims even when in tension with freedom of speech concerns. Thus, the Supreme Court of Canada has concluded that 'the principle of fairness presupposes that certain rights or freedoms can legitimately be restricted in the name of a healthy electoral democracy'.[81] Likewise, the European Court of Human Rights finds support for balancing free political speech with the goal of ensuring equality in elections in the text of the Article 10 of the Convention, which recognizes that freedom of speech 'may be subject to such formalities, conditions, restrictions or penalties as are prescribed by law and are necessary in a democratic society' among other legitimate limitations.[82] Thus, enormous differences across systems exist with regard to foundational questions concerning the relationship of political equality to free speech.[83]

A different concern about campaign-finance laws, addressed in the courts of some countries, is that sitting legislators will use this power to entrench themselves and their allies. Of course, it should be noted that the failure to adopt legislation in this area can also be a means of entrenching the status quo. After all, sitting legislators have been elected, by definition, under the existing legal framework, and changes in the status quo often create uncertainty as to how those changes will play out on the ground; thus, sitting legislators might be assumed presumptively to want to maintain the financing rules under which they were elected. But the temptation to ensure their own re-election prospects or the continuing dominance of their partisan control can also lead to the enactment of new laws designed to favor the legis-

[76] 424 US 1 (1976).

[77] 130 S Ct 876 (2010).

[78] Ibid 904.

[79] *Australia Capital Television Pty Co Ltd v Commonwealth* [1992] 177 CLR 106.

[80] For a fuller discussion of the Australian judicial cases, see Graeme Orr, Byran Mercurio, and George Williams, 'Australian Electoral Law: A Stocktake' (2003) 2 *Election Law Journal* 383, 384–5.

[81] *Libman* (n 75).

[82] *Bowman* (n 74).

[83] For a fuller survey of these cases, see Richard H. Hasen, 'Regulation of Campaign Finance' in Vikram Amar and Mark Tushnet (eds), *Global Perspectives on Constitutional Law* (2009).

lators' allies or punish their opponents. Thus far, few courts appear to have confronted this problem directly in the area of election financing. An intriguing 1999 decision from the Constitutional Court for the Republic of Korea, however, shows one judicial approach to this issue.[84]

The Korean government had enacted a statute banning political contributions by labor unions. The government justified the statute as of way of preventing the politicization of unions and of protecting union finances. The Korean court, however, held that this statute violated the Korean Constitution's guarantees of freedom of expression and association, because the statute singled out labor unions from among all 'social organizations' for this unique proscription. The court noted that in the modern era, 'Interest groups and political parties are indispensable elements of democratic opinion-making', and that 'individuals can realize their political identities through groups that synthesize, prioritize, and reconcile their various interests and desires.' Though the statute sought to define labor organizations as limited to improvement of working conditions through collective bargaining, the court concluded both that the statute interfered with political freedom, by not permitting unions to contribute to campaigns, and was also discriminatory, because it singled out labor unions for this prohibition; as the court put it, 'the role of social organizations in the people's political decision-making is equally applicable to labor unions'. One wonders how much this decision rests on substantive grounds of political freedom rather than on the discriminatory nature of singling out unions for special prohibitions. In the United States, for example, the courts have long accepted even-handed bans on union and corporate general treasury contributions to candidates and campaigns.

Similarly, different cultural understandings of democracy inform interpretations of textually similar free speech guarantees in other arenas involving the campaign process. Article 21 of the Japanese Constitution, for example, guarantees 'Freedom of assembly and association as well as speech, press and all other forms of expression'; in addition, it provides that 'No censorship shall be maintained, nor shall the secrecy of any means of communication be violated'.[85] Yet despite these provisions, the Japanese courts regularly uphold relatively severe (by comparison to the United States, at least) legal restrictions on election-related speech activity. In doing so, these courts defer to 'communal interests', such as the public welfare, that justify restrictions on individual freedoms[86] for the purpose of what is perceived to be protection of the fairness of the election system as a whole.[87]

In the well-known *Taniguchi Canvassing Case*, for example,[88] the Japanese Supreme Court upheld the Public Office Election Law's ban on candidates engaging in door-to-door canvassing for votes. The Court deferred to the legislative conclusion that canvassing could lead to bribery, 'voting for vested interests', or disturbing the voters' peace. The Supreme Court declared that broad restrictions on campaigns are constitutional even when they ban practices

[84] *Trade Unions' Political Contributions Case* [1999] 11-2 KCCR 555, 95 Hun-Ma 154. This discussion is based on a quoted summary of the decisions available at <http://english.ccourt.go.kr>.

[85] The translations of these provisions is taken from Ronald Krotoszynski, *The First Amendment in Cross-Cultural Perspective* (2006), 141, which also offers an excellent broader comparative perspective on first amendment issues more generally.

[86] Public Offices Election Law, Law No 100 of 1950. Article 138 states that 'No one shall conduct a door-to-door canvass with the intention of soliciting a vote for oneself or another person or to prevent the voter from voting for another person.'

[87] Krotoszynski (n 85), 154.

[88] *Taniguchi v Japan* [1967] 21 Keishū 9 1245, reprinted in Hiroshi Itoh and Lawrence W. Beer, *The Constitutional Case Law of Japan: Selected Supreme Court Decisions, 1961–70* (1978), 149.

that do not 'substantively violate the spirit of fair elections'.[89] The Election Law also prohibits newspapers and magazines from 'interfering' with free elections by providing 'information and comment' that 'might affect a specific candidate's elections chances'. The Supreme Court unanimously upheld this law against a convicted publisher's constitutional challenge (though the Court construed the law narrowly and exempted from its scope what the Court called 'truly fair information and comment').[90] With respect to modern technologies of communication, Japanese election law flatly bans candidate communications via email, websites, and social media are subject during the campaign period.[91]

V. Conclusion

One of the most striking developments over recent decades is the way courts around the world have moved from enforcing individual rights and principles of equality to policing the structures and processes of democracy itself. In areas ranging from the rights of political participation, the role of political parties, the financing of elections, the resolution of disputed elections, and the design of democratic institutions, courts have increasingly brought constitutional law to bear on the heart of the political process. This constitutionalization of democratic politics has great promise as well as great risk. Democracy is an ongoing process of self-correction and self-determination, as political communities struggle over defining the kinds of political processes that will generate widely accepted, legitimate forms of self-governance; the risk is that by constitutionalizing democratic politics, courts will wrongly freeze in place existing democratic arrangements and frustrate the power of political communities to determine for themselves how best to be perfect the democratic process. The promise is that courts will find ways to counter the inherent pathologies of democratic systems, through which political insiders attempt to entrench themselves more deeply in power, as well as ensuring that democratic systems remain open, inclusive, and competitive.

Bibliography

Keith D. Ewing and Samuel Issacharoff (eds), *Party Funding and Campaign Financing in International Perspective* (2006)

Gregory H. Fox and Georg Nolte, 'Intolerant Democracies' (1995) 36 *Harvard International Law Journal* 1

[89] Ibid 150. More recently, a concurring opinion by Justice Ito dismissed the previous reasons for upholding the law against constitutional challenge, finding 'the public welfare' insufficient to justify the restrictions on freedom of expression entailed by the canvassing ban. *Takatsu v Japan* [1981] 35 Keishū 5 at 568 reprinted in Itoh and Beer (n 88), 598. Nonetheless, Justice Ito ultimately would have upheld the ban, too, because of the 'wide discretion given to the legislature to make . . . rules' governing fair elections. Because, in his view, 'an election campaign . . . is not a context where all sorts of speeches can compete with each other with the minimum necessary restraints', he concluded the Japanese constitution did not require striking down the canvassing ban.

[90] *Nonaka v Japan* [1979] 33 Keishū 7 at 1074, reprinted in Lawrence W. Beer and Hiroshi Itoh, *The Constitutional Case Law of Japan, 1970 through 1990* (1996), 604.

[91] Takaaki Ohta, 'Fairness Versus Freedom: Constitutional Implications of Internet Electioneering for Japan' (2008) 11 *Social Science Japan Journal* 106. Reform proposals have been introduced and gained momentum with the unprecedented victory of the Democratic Party of Japan in the 2009 election, but have thus far failed: Matthew J. Wilson, 'E-Elections: Time for Japan to Embrace Online Campaigning' (2011) 4 *Stanford Tech Law Review* 1.

Samuel Issacharoff, Pamela Karlan, and Richard Pildes, *The Law of Democracy: Legal Structure of the Political Process* (3rd edn, 2010)

Donald P. Kommers, *The Constitutional Jurisprudence of the Federal Republic of Germany* (2nd edn, 1997)

Louis Massicotte, Andre Blais, and Antoine Yoshinaka, *Establishing the Rules of the Game: Election Laws in Democracies* (2004)

Richard H. Pildes, 'Foreword: The Constitutionalization of Democratic Politics' (2004) 118 *Harvard Law Review* 29

Richard H. Pildes, 'Political Parties and Constitutionalism' in Tom Ginsburg and Rosalind Dixon (eds), *Comparative Constitutional Law* (2011)

Wojciech Sadurski, *Rights Before Courts: A Study of Constitutional Courts in Postcommunist States of Central and Eastern Europe* (2005)

PART IV

ARCHITECTURE

CHAPTER 26

HORIZONTAL STRUCTURING

JENNY S. MARTINEZ

Stanford

I. Introduction

The term 'horizontal structuring' refers to the constitutional system for allocating power among government actors at the same geographic level of organization. The concept is referred to in some systems as 'separation of powers'.[1] Separation of powers is considered normatively desirable for several reasons, including: the idea that dividing power will inhibit government action and therefore tyranny; the idea that different types of government bodies are more or less competent at certain tasks; and the idea that certain allocations of authority will help ensure democratic legitimacy for government policies. Horizontal structuring should be distinguished from vertical structuring, which involves the division of authority between different organizational levels of government,[2] for example federal and state governments. Horizontal structuring, by contrast, involves the division of power between the executive, legislative, and judicial branches of one level of government.

Modern democracies do not all employ the same forms of horizontal structuring. For example, while presidential systems typically involve a sharp distinction between executive and legislative power, parliamentary systems do not. Indeed, constitutional systems range in a spectrum from those with strong separation of powers (eg the United States) to those with greater fusion of powers (eg the United Kingdom), with many falling somewhere in the middle. Some constitutions further subdivide power within a branch of government—for example by creating a bicameral legislature with an upper and lower house, or by creating both a president and a prime minister. This chapter explores the various forms of horizontal structuring employed in modern constitutional democracies, as well as debates about their relative advantages and disadvantages.

II. History

Western political theory usually traces the idea of constitutional separation of powers to the writings of Montesquieu, although it is also acknowledged that related ideas appear in the earlier writings of others.[3] One of the earliest antecedents to modern notions of separation of

[1] See generally M.J.C. Vile, *Constitutionalism and the Separation of Powers* (1967).

[2] On which, see Chapter 27 of this volume.

[3] See generally W.B. Gwyn, *The Meaning of the Separation of Powers: An Analysis of the Doctrine from Its Origin to the Adoption of the United States Constitution* (1965); M.J.C. Vile, *Constitutionalism and the Separation of Powers* (2nd edn, 1998); Sharon Krause, 'The Spirit of Separate Powers in Montesquieu' (2000) 62 *Review of Politics* 231.

powers is the concept of *mixed government*. The mixed government concept posits combining rule by the one (the monarch), the few (the aristocrats), and the many (the people).[4] Aristotle discussed the possibility of combining monarchy, oligarchy, and democracy, and Polybius and Cicero further popularized the idea of mixed government. These later writers suggested that the Roman Republic constituted a successful form of mixed government through its combination of monarchy (through the consuls), aristocracy (the senate), and the people (assemblies), each of which checked and balanced the other.[5] Theories of mixed government were widely discussed by European political theorists in the seventeenth century.

The constitutional struggles between the king and parliament in England in the seventeenth century gave rise to the related, but distinct, idea of a *functional* separation of powers, which is the core of the modern doctrine.[6] Functional separation of powers is the idea of dividing different government functions—for example, the function of generating new legal rules through legislation and the function of applying legislation to the facts of particular cases—among different government actors. This line of thinking was reflected in the writings of John Locke, who distinguished between the legislative and executive functions of government. In his 1689 *Second Treatise on Government*, Locke explained that because human frailty led men to 'grasp at power', it was dangerous 'for the same persons who have the power of making Laws, to have also in their hands the power to execute them.'[7] Locke argued that 'the legislative is the supreme power',[8] and suggested that 'in all moderated Monarchies and well-framed Governments' the 'legislative and executive power are in distinct hands.'[9]

Several statutes passed in the wake of the Glorious Revolution of 1688 reinforced the idea of a distinction between executive and legislative power in England, as well as the notion of judicial independence. The English Bill of Rights Act of 1689 established some of the central principles of Britain's constitutional monarchy by declaring that 'the pretended power of suspending the laws or the execution of laws by regal authority without consent of Parliament is illegal' and that parliamentary consent was required to raise revenue or maintain a standing army. The Act also sought to preserve the independence of Parliament and the courts by providing 'That election of members of Parliament ought to be free', and 'That jurors ought to be duly impanelled and returned, and jurors which pass upon men in trials for high treason ought to be freeholders.'[10] The 1701 Act of Settlement limited the king's ability to influence parliament, providing 'that no person who has an office or place of profit under the King, or receives a pension from the Crown, shall be capable of serving as a member of the House of Commons.' That Act also strengthened judicial independence by requiring that judges should remain in office during good behavior and could only be removed by parliament.[11]

[4] See Richard Bellamy, 'The Political Form of the Constitution: Separation of Powers, Rights and Representative Democracy' in Richard Bellamy (ed), *The Rule of Law and the Separation of Powers* (2005), 257–9.

[5] See Edward Rubin, 'Judicial Review and the Right to Resist' (2009) 97 *Georgetown Law Journal* 61, 68; Scott D. Gerber, 'The Court, the Constitution, and the History of Ideas' (2008) 61 *Vanderbilt Law Review* 1067, 1088–112.

[6] Gordon S. Wood, *The Creation of the American Republic 1776–1787* (2nd edn, 1998), 151; M. Elizabeth Magill, 'The Real Separation in Separation of Powers Law' (2000) 86 *Virginia Law Review* 1127, 1162–3.

[7] John Locke, *Two Treatises of Government* (Ian Shapiro ed, 2003), 164.

[8] Ibid 166.

[9] Ibid 171.

[10] An Act Declaring the Rights and Liberties of the Subject and Settling the Succession of the Crown (England, 1689), available at <http://www.britannia.com/history/docs/rights.html>.

[11] The Act of Settlement (England, 1701), available at <http://www.guardian.co.uk/uk/2000/dec/06/monarchy>.

It was against this backdrop that Montesquieu wrote his seminal book *The Spirit of the Laws*, published in 1748. Montesquieu explicated his theory of separation of powers through a discussion of the English system,[12] which he praised for being the one nation in the world 'that has for the direct end of its constitution political liberty'.[13] Many commentators have criticized Montesquieu for providing an inaccurate description of the English system, which involved a greater degree of fusion of power in practice than he acknowledged. But it is undoubtedly true that the British system and the developments of the Glorious Revolution provided Montesquieu with much of his inspiration.

Montesquieu's main contribution lay in his extended development of the *functional separation of powers*, though he also wove in earlier notions of *mixed government* and *checks and balances*.[14] Montesquieu described governments as falling into one of several categories: republican (either democratic or aristocratic), monarchical, and despotic. For Montesquieu, the various forms of republican and monarchical government each had their virtues, but despotism—the situation in which 'a single person directs everything by his own will and caprice'—was undesirable.[15] Despotic governments left their subjects in a state of poverty, insecurity, and fear. Stable republican governments and law-abiding monarchies, on the other hand, yielded conditions of liberty and prosperity. A central problem, however, was that these forms of government were not always stable, and without good management could collapse into despotism. Montesquieu believed that since 'Constant experience shows us that every man invested with power is apt to abuse it... [it is] necessary from the very nature of things that power should be a check to power.'[16] Accordingly, he argued that the powers of government should be divided among different persons or bodies, which would act as a check on each other. If powers were concentrated in one person or body, there would be no check on the exercise of power and this results in a swift descent into despotism.

Modern writers typically attribute the tripartite categorization of functional separation of powers into legislative, executive, and judicial power directly to Montesquieu, although the author himself broke things down slightly differently. 'In every government there are three sorts of power', he explained, 'the legislative; the executive in respect to things dependent on the law of nations; and the executive, in regard to matters that depend on the civil law.'[17] The first, the legislative power, consisted of the power to enact or amend laws. The second, the foreign affairs aspect of the executive power, included the power to make war or peace, send and receive ambassadors, establish public security, and protect against invasion. The third, 'the executive in regard to matters that depend on the civil law', consisted of punishing criminals (which he termed simply the 'executive power of the state') and resolving disputes that arise between individuals (which he termed 'the judiciary power').[18] It is worth noting the blurring of executive and judicial functions in Montesquieu's third category, particularly with regard to the function of professional judges (as opposed to lay juries, upon whom Montesquieu focused great praise).[19]

[12] Philip Resnick, 'Montesquieu Revisited, or the Mixed Constitution and the Separation of Powers in Canada' (1987) 20 *Canadian Journal of Political Science* 97, 99ff.

[13] Montesquieu, *The Spirit of Laws* (vol I, 1750), 215.

[14] See Bellamy (n 4), 261–3.

[15] Montesquieu (n 13), 11.

[16] Ibid 214.

[17] Ibid 215.

[18] Ibid 216.

[19] See Lawrence Claus, 'Montesquieu's Mistakes and the True Meaning of Separation' (2005) 25 *Oxford Journal of Legal Studies* 419, 423 (describing 'ongoing ambivalence about whether the professional judges who actually executed the law—applied it to the facts found by juries—were anything other than executive officers').

Montesquieu believed that 'When the legislative and executive powers are united in the same person, or in the same body of magistracy, there can be then no liberty', for in such a system tyrannical laws may be put in place and executed in a tyrannical matter.[20]

As for the judicial power, he advocated that judges in republics must strictly follow 'the letter of the law', an idea that proved particularly influential in France.[21]

Montesquieu's model acknowledged an inevitable overlap in powers and indeed demanded it in certain ways (as, eg, with the executive's veto power over legislation) as the mechanism by which the powers could check each other's actions. Nevertheless, Montesquieu believed that the core of each function should be retained by its designated branch, a somewhat essentialist idea for which he has been criticized.[22]

Even if the actual English system involved a greater fusion of power than Montesquieu might have thought desirable,[23] William Blackstone, directly assimilated Montesquieu's ideas into his influential *Commentaries on the Law of England*. Like Montesquieu, Blackstone tended to mingle the idea of a *functional* separation of powers with the idea of mixed government and its checks and balances. For instance, Blackstone explained, 'It is highly necessary for preserving the balance of the constitution, that the executive power should be a branch, though not the whole, of the legislature.'[24] Blackstone grounded his observations in the particular English experience of the struggle between king and parliament in the seventeenth century.[25]

Montesquieu's ideas were also particularly influential on the architects of the American[26] and French Revolutions. The French Declaration of the Rights of Man in 1789, for example, stated that 'A society where rights are not secured or the separation of powers established has no constitution at all',[27] and the American Continental Congress called him 'the immortal Montesquieu'.[28]

James Madison, writing in Federalist no 51,[29] explained that separation of powers was 'admitted on all hands to be essential to the preservation of liberty', and was to be achieved by 'contriving the interior structure of the government as that its several constituent parts may, by their mutual relations, be the means of keeping each other in their proper places.' Reflecting the views of the time about which branch would be most powerful, Madison wrote in Federalist no 51 that 'In republican government, the legislative authority necessarily predominates' and he suggested that 'the weakness of the executive may require... that it should be fortified'. Over the centuries, of course, it has become clear that the executive needs little fortification.

[20] Montesquieu (n 13), 216.

[21] Ibid 218; also see John Henry Merryman, 'The French Deviation' (1996) 44 *American Journal of Comparative Law* 109.

[22] Claus (n 19).

[23] See generally R.S. Crane, 'Montesquieu and British Thought' (1941) 49 *Journal of Political Economy* 592.

[24] William Blackstone, *Commentaries on the Laws of England* (vol I, 1st edn, 1765–69), 149.

[25] Ibid 149–50.

[26] See Wood (n 6), 159.

[27] 'Article 16 of the Declaration of the Rights of Man and the Citizen 1789' in S.E. Finer, V. Bogdanor, and B. Rudden, *Comparing Constitutions* (1995), 210.

[28] Wood (n 6), 152.

[29] *The Federalist Papers* are a famous series of essays (numbering 1–85) defending the proposed US Constitution. The complete series is available at <http://www.constitution.org/fed/federaoo.htm>.

It is important to recognize that separation of powers was never conceived as involving a perfect and hermetically sealed division of responsibility. For example, Madison, writing in Federalist no 47, anticipated some overlap in authority, noting that serious concerns arose primarily 'where the whole power of one department is exercised by the same hands which possess the whole power of another department'.

Madison urged that the appointment and maintenance in office of officials of each branch be kept as separate as possible, but suggested that:

> the great security against a gradual concentration of the several powers in the same department, consists in giving to those who administer each department the necessary constitutional means and personal motives to resist encroachments of the others.... Ambition must be made to counteract ambition.

Madison's ideas about how to protect against the undue influence of different factions of society through governmental structures are also significant, and represent the evolution of ideas of mixed government into a form suitable for a republican nation.[30]

Participants in the French Revolution were also influenced by Montesquieu, but they took quite different lessons from his writings. In France, a main project of the revolution was 'to protect the executive against judicial interference', which had been common in the *ancien régime* in which judges were 'centers of conservative power'.[31] Thus, in revolutionary France, rules were put in place ensuring that judges 'could not issue regulations, question the legality of administrative rules, orders or other executive action, examine the legality of the conduct of public officials or compel reluctant officials to perform their legal duties.'[32] As John Merryman wrote, 'The most powerful consequence of the French doctrine of separation of powers may have been to demean judges and the judicial function.'[33] Following Montesquieu's ideas of the judge as a mechanical applicator of law to facts, there emerged the idea that judges could not 'make rules applicable to future cases', nor could they 'question the validity or alter the meaning of legislation'.[34] As a consequence of these restrictions on the judiciary, there eventually emerged a separate system of administrative tribunals formally located within the executive branch, culminating in the Conseil d'État.

Not all constitutional systems, of course, claim to have been influenced by Montesquieu's model. Referring to Canada's mixed constitution, for example, one scholar explained that 'Canadians are not in the habit of looking to Montesquieu for an understanding of the nature of political institutions in their country', and that his work is generally deemed to have been more influential in France and the United States than Britain or former British colonies, which is undoubtedly true.[35] But in recent years, even Britain has moved towards greater separation of powers, for example with the removal of its highest appellate court from the House of Lords into an independent Supreme Court.[36] Moreover, the basic functional categories of executive, legislative, and judicial power remain analytically useful in examining how different constitutions divide government power. Emergent democracies in the past few decades have adopted a wide variety of structures, some of which draw inspiration from the American, French, or British models, and some of which combine them in new ways.

[30] Bellamy (n 4), 264–6. [31] See Merryman (n 21), 111.
[32] Ibid 111. [33] Ibid 116. [34] Ibid 111. [35] Resnick (n 12).
[36] David Pannick, QC, 'Farewell to the law lords', *The Times*, 30 July 2009.

III. Executive and Legislative Power

1. Presidential versus Parliamentary Systems: The Basic Distinction

Observers divide most constitutional systems into presidential (typified by the United States), parliamentary (typified by the United Kingdom), and semi-presidential (typified by France). In a presidential system, the chief executive (the president) is elected separately from the legislature. In a parliamentary system, the chief executive (the prime minister) and sometimes other executive officials (cabinet ministers) are chosen by—and in some systems may be drawn from—the membership of the legislature. In parliamentary systems, the prime minister typically may be removed during office by a no-confidence vote in the legislature, while in a presidential system the president's tenure in office does not depend on legislative support (absent the rare circumstances of impeachment for misconduct). The most obvious consequence of these differences in structure is that in a presidential system, the president is independent of the legislature, and indeed may be from a different political party than the majority of the legislature. In a parliamentary system, on the other hand, whichever party or coalition of parties controls the legislature also controls the executive branch (sometimes called 'the government'). Presidential systems thus exemplify a relatively high degree of separation between executive and legislative power, while parliamentary systems involve a greater fusion of executive and legislative authority. There are also hybrid systems, sometimes called 'semi-presidential' systems, that fall somewhere in between.

The next sections describe some prominent presidential and parliamentary constitutions, and their key attributes on matters such as: the procedures by which the head of government is selected and removed from office; the powers of the chief executive in proposing or vetoing legislation; the structure of the legislature and its areas of authority. This limited survey of systems is intended simply to highlight some of the key differences in how separation of powers is implemented.

(a) Presidential Systems

i. The United States: The Classic Presidential System

The United States has the quintessential presidential system, with the President and the legislature selected independent of one another. Article II of the US Constitution provides that 'the executive power shall be vested in the President of the United States of America'. The President is elected following a nationwide vote for that office on a fixed schedule through a mechanism known as the Electoral College. Because most states employ a winner-takes-all approach to allocating their electors' votes, it is possible for a candidate who won a majority or plurality of the nationwide popular vote to nevertheless lose in the Electoral College. This has happened in several elections, including the 2000 presidential election, prompting criticism of the Electoral College as antiquated and undemocratic.[37]

The 'legislative powers' of the federal government are vested in the Congress, which consists of the Senate and the House of Representatives.[38] Each house is given certain special responsibilities. Legislation is enacted by vote of a simple majority of each house followed by presentation to the President. The Congress can override a presidential veto by two-thirds

[37] See Akhil Reed Amar, 'Some Thoughts on the Electoral College: Past, Present, and Future' (2007) 33 *Ohio Northern University Law Review* 467.

[38] US Constitution, Art I, s 1.

vote of each house. The President may recommend legislation to the Congress, but the Congress is not obliged to act on his recommendations.[39]

ii. Latin American Countries: Troubled Presidentialism

Presidential systems predominate in Latin America, likely due to the hemispheric influence of the United States.[40] Countries in the region with presidential systems include Argentina, Bolivia, Brazil, Chile, Colombia, Costa Rica, Dominican Republic, Ecuador, El Salvador, Guatemala, Honduras, Mexico, Nicaragua, Panama, Paraguay, Peru, Uruguay, and Venezuela. Indeed, only Belize (a former British colony) and some of the Caribbean nations have parliamentary systems.

Until relatively recently, democracy had a troubled history in Latin America, which some scholars have attributed in part to flaws in the presidential model (combined, of course, with other social, political, and economic factors).[41] There are a variety of different theories for why this might be so, but a dominant one is the idea that when the president does not enjoy the support of a majority of the legislature (which can happen in presidential but not most parliamentary systems), the resulting paralysis can lead to frustration and eventually to constitutional breakdown. Others have noted that the presidential systems that have survived intact for long periods of time have mainly involved two-party systems, while multi-party presidential democracies have proven more prone to deadlock and breakdown.[42]

In addition to the basic fact of presidentialism, many scholars have examined the differences between presidential systems in Latin America and the United States in an attempt to discern any formal legal factors (as opposed to social factors) that might help explain why the US presidential system has remained stable and so many in Latin America have not. Scholars have noted that many Latin American constitutions in the mid to late-twentieth century provided for comparatively greater powers in the office of the presidency and reduced authority in the legislature and courts. For example, 'it was noted that many constitutions permitted the executive branch to introduce bills into congress, and in some countries, only the president could initiate legislation' on certain subjects. Moreover, 'In several nations, promulgation of executive-initiated laws was automatic if congress did not reject the measures.'[43] Many Latin American presidents had the power of 'line-item veto',[44] and greater independent authority to appoint federal and state officials. Finally, many Latin American constitutions included emergency provisions that entitled the executive to declare a state of siege or emergency.[45]

More recently, a greater number of Latin American countries have achieved democratic stability, but have not abandoned the presidential model, casting some doubt on the importance of presidentialism in their previous instability. Of course, only time will tell whether these regimes remain stable in the long run.

[39] US Constitution, Art II, s 3.

[40] Scot Mainwaring, 'Presidentialism in Latin America' (1990) 25 *Latin American Research Review* 157, 159.

[41] See generally Juan J. Linz and Arturo Valenzuela (eds), *The Failure of Presidential Democracy* (1994).

[42] Ibid 168.

[43] Mainwaring (n 40).

[44] The 'line-item veto', also known as the 'partial veto', is the power of an executive to nullify specific provisions of a bill without vetoing the entire legislative act.

[45] Mainwaring (n 40).

iii. Presidentialism in Eastern Europe and the Former Soviet Union: Renewed Promise or Renewed Threat?

Many constitutions adopted in the 1990s in newly independent states of the former Soviet Union follow a presidential model.[46] Indeed, according to one study, of the roughly 25 countries formed out of the former Soviet Union and Eastern Europe, 'only three—Hungary, the new Czech Republic, and Slovakia—have chosen pure parliamentarianism'.[47] While some have used the prevalence of presidentialism in the former Eastern bloc to suggest that presidentialism is alive and well in constitution-making,[48] it is worth noting that most of the former Soviet republics that adopted presidential systems—Azerbaijan, Kazakhstan, Kyrgyzstan, Tajikistan, Turkmenistan, and Uzbekistan, for example—rank very low on indices of functioning democracies.[49] Many East European countries that adopted parliamentary or semi-presidential regimes—Poland, Bulgaria, Croatia, and Romania, for example—rank comparatively higher in terms of having at least partially functional democracies.[50] One study suggested a strong division between Eastern Europe and the former Soviet states, suggesting that parliamentarianism has dominated in Eastern Europe, while presidentialism has dominated in the former Soviet republics.[51] Other scholars have argued that more of the former communist constitutions should be classified as 'semi-presidential', an argument discussed below in the section on semi-presidentialism.

iv. South Korea

South Korea is today considered a prominent example of a relatively well-functioning presidential system. After decades of authoritarian presidential regimes exercising emergency powers, South Korea successfully transitioned to become a stable democracy in the late 1980s and early 1990s. The current South Korean Constitution retains a presidential system, but this Sixth Republic constitution successfully broke the historic pattern of dictatorship in part because it 'strengthened the power of the National Assembly and considerably reduced the power of the executive'.[52]

Under the current constitution, the South Korean President is directly elected by popular vote and serves a single, five-year term.[53] There is a unicameral legislature called the National Assembly. The President also appoints a Prime Minister with the consent of the National Assembly. The Prime Minister 'shall assist the President and shall direct the Executive Ministries under order of the President'.[54] Members of the State Council are appointed by the President upon recommendation of the Prime Minister.[55]

[46] Gerald M. Easter, 'Preference for Presidentialism: Postcommunist Regime Change in Russia and the NIS' (1997) 49 *World Politics* 184.

[47] Alfred Stepan and Cindy Skach, 'Presidentialism and Parliamentarianism in Comparative Perspective' in Linz and Valenzuela (n 41), 119, 120.

[48] See Steven G. Calabresi, 'The Virtues of Presidential Government' (2001) 18 *Constitutional Commentary* 51, 52–3.

[49] See Easter (n 46), 190 (listing regime types); Economist Intelligence Unit, Democracy Index 2010, available at <http://graphics.eiu.com/PDF/Democracy_Index_2010_web.pdf>.

[50] See Economist Intelligence Unit (n 49).

[51] Easter (n 46), 187–9.

[52] Jenny Martinez, 'Inherent Executive Power: A Comparative Perspective' (2006) 115 *Yale Law Journal* 2480, 2502–3 (quoting Andrea Matles Savada and William Shaw (eds), *South Korea: A Country Study* (1992), 201–2, available at <http://countrystudies.us/south-korea>).

[53] Constitution of the Republic of South Korea, Arts 67, 70, available at <http://english.ccourt.go.kr/home/att_file/download/Constitution_of_the_Republic_of_Korea.pdf>.

[54] Constitution of the Republic of South Korea, Art 86.

[55] Ibid Art 87.

(b) Parliamentary Systems

i. United Kingdom: Westminster Model

The modern British system, sometimes called the Westminster model, is a parliamentary system with a relatively high degree of fusion of executive and legislative power. Indeed, at one point it was said that 'The efficient secret of the English Constitution may be described as the close union, the nearly complete fusion, of the executive and legislative powers.'[56] England has a bicameral legislature, consisting of the House of Commons and the House of Lords. Members of the House of Commons are popularly elected from single-member districts, while the House of Lords consists of life peers (appointed by the monarch on the recommendation of the Prime Minister), bishops, and elected hereditary peers. Although the House of Commons has a greater role in the legislative process, the House of Lords is considered an important check on the government.[57]

The political party (or coalition of parties) with a majority in the House of Commons selects a Prime Minister. Voters do not vote directly for the Prime Minister, but instead for their particular member of parliament. The Prime Minister and the Cabinet remain members of the legislature, and play a large role in setting the legislative program. The Prime Minister also exercises control over parliament because of his or her power to dissolve parliament and call for new elections.[58] Because the Prime Minister and legislative majority are drawn from the same party, there is less likelihood of deadlock and a greater chance that legislation will pass. It is worth noting, however, that 'While there is in practice a fusion of legislative and executive *powers*, there is in principle a distinction between the two *functions*', and the government cannot change statutory law without passing legislation through a parliament.[59] In other words, the Prime Minister cannot change the laws at his or her discretion; the formal legislative process must be observed.

ii. Constrained Parliamentarianism: The Examples of Germany and South Africa

(1) Germany

Many other countries with parliamentary systems differ somewhat from the Westminster model. The German system has been described, in contrast to the Westminster model, as 'constrained parliamentarianism'.[60] The German Constitution, or Basic Law, formally creates two executive officials, a President and a Federal Chancellor, but the President in practice serves a mostly symbolic, non-partisan role.[61] The Federal Chancellor is appointed and removable by the Bundestag, the lower house of parliament.[62] The 'constrained' part of German parliamentarianism comes in part from the limits on the power of the legislature to remove the Chancellor. The Bundestag cannot remove the Chancellor from office without appointing a successor.[63] This was designed to avoid the instability that had characterized German

[56] R.H.S. Crossman (introd), *The English Constitution* (1963), 65 (quoting Walter Bagehot) (quoted in Eric Barendt, 'Separation of Powers and Constitutional Government' in Bellamy (n 4), 275, 289).

[57] See 'Role and Work of the House of Lords FAQs', available at <http://www.parliament.uk/about/faqs/house-of-lords-faqs/role/>.

[58] Barendt (n 56), 289.

[59] Ibid 291 (citing *Case of Proclamations*, 12 Co Rep 74 (1611)).

[60] Bruce Ackerman, 'The New Separation of Powers' (2000) 113 *Harvard Law Review* 633, 670.

[61] Thomas Poguntke, 'A Presidentializing Party State? The Federal Republic of Germany' in Thomas Poguntke and Paul Webb (eds), *The Presidentialization of Politics* (2005), 63.

[62] German Basic Law, Arts 63, 67, available at <https://www.btg-bestellservice.de/pdf/80201000.pdf>.

[63] Ibid Art 67.

government under the Weimar regime. The legislature also cannot ordinarily be dissolved early, except following the failure of a confidence vote and even then only if a new Chancellor has not been elected.[64]

(2) South Africa

South Africa provides a different example of 'constrained parliamentarianism'. The constitution vests legislative power in a bicameral parliament consisting of a National Assembly and a National Council of Provinces.[65] Cabinet members, deputy ministers, or members of the national assembly may introduce bills, though certain types of financial bills must be introduced by the relevant cabinet minister.[66] Despite being termed a 'president', the South African President is actually selected by the parliament rather than by direct election,[67] with the result that the system is best classified as a form of parliamentary system. The President is both head of state and head of government.[68] He or she is selected by the National Assembly from among its members.[69] Unlike some parliamentary systems, however, South Africa constrains the ability of the legislature to remove an executive once in office; the President may be removed only by a two-thirds vote of the National Assembly on grounds of 'a serious violation of the Constitution or the law', 'serious misconduct', or 'inability to perform the functions of office'.[70]

(c) Hybrid or Semi-Presidential Systems

i. France

The French system is a hybrid, with aspects of both presidential and parliamentary models, and is sometimes called a 'semi-presidential' system. Under the 1958 Fifth Republic Constitution, the French President is elected by direct universal suffrage.[71] The President appoints a Prime Minister, who must enjoy the support of a majority of the parliament. Though the President is by far the stronger of the two offices, the President and Prime Minister to some degree share executive power. During periods of 'cohabitation', when the parliamentary majority is from a different party than the President, Prime Ministers have enjoyed greater control over domestic policymaking. To a lesser degree, Prime Ministers have also participated in foreign and defense policy.[72]

The French legislature consists of a bicameral parliament comprised of the National Assembly (elected by direct, universal suffrage), and the Senate (elected through an indirect, electoral college system).[73] The National Assembly represents the entire citizenry and the Senate represents France's territorial units. Power is split unequally between the two houses, with the National Assembly exercising much broader powers than the Senate. Most significantly, only the National Assembly may dissolve the government, either through a vote of no confidence or by refusing to endorse the government's program.[74] Ordinarily, legislation must pass both

[64] German Basic Law, Art 68. Nevertheless a dissolution based on an agreement of all parties was held constitutional by the Federal Constitutional Court.

[65] 1996 South African Constitution, s 42, available at <http://www.info.gov.za/documents/constitution/1996/index.htm>.

[66] Ibid s 73.

[67] See ibid s 86.

[68] Ibid s 83.

[69] Ibid s 86.

[70] Ibid s 89.

[71] David S. Bell, *Presidential Power in Fifth Republic France* (2000), 10.

[72] Andrew Knapp and Vincent Wright, *The Government and Politics of France* (4th edn, 2001), 115–19.

[73] French Constitution, Art 24, available at <http://www.assemblee-nationale.fr/english/8ab.asp>.

[74] Ibid Art 50.

houses in the same terms to become law. However, when the two houses cannot agree, the government can, with few exceptions, grant the National Assembly final say on the issue.[75]

ii. Other Semi-Presidential Systems

Some scholars argue that semi-presidentialism, rather than presidentialism or parliamentarianism, is the most popular model in recent constitutions.[76] Like the French system, these semi-presidential systems combine 'a popularly elected head of state with a head of government who is responsible to a popularly elected legislature.'[77] Cindy Skach argues that the constitutions of Belarus, Croatia, Poland, Romania, Russia, and Ukraine are best characterized as semi-presidential. However, the Russian Constitution defines the role of the President in substantially broader terms than other semi-presidential or even presidential systems. As a result, the Russian system is sometimes referred to as 'superpresidentialism.'[78] Skach notes that, in most of these systems, 'the power to preside over cabinet meetings and to direct national policy, is shared between these two executives', which can be problematic as 'such power sharing precludes a neat division or clear separation of powers, often leading to constitutional ambiguity.'[79] This issue is addressed in more detail in the next section.

(d) Normative Arguments about Parliamentary versus Presidential Systems

Parliamentary, presidential, and semi-presidential systems each have advantages and disadvantages. This section surveys the lively normative debate about whether one type of system is preferable to the other.

Beginning in the 1990s, the troubled history of democracy in Latin America led some political scientists, most notably Juan Linz, to suggest that presidential systems may be inherently unstable compared to parliamentary systems.[80] While it is difficult to untangle causation, these scholars noted that of the 93 countries that became independent between 1945 and 1979, all of those that remained continuously democratic between 1980 and 1989 were parliamentary systems, while none of the non-parliamentary systems remained continuously democratic.[81] Some of these observers hypothesized that when the president and the legislature in a presidential system are from different political parties or are otherwise unwilling to cooperate, the resulting deadlock can lead to frustration and ultimately collapse of the system as one actor seizes power. Linz thought this was particularly likely in presidential systems due to the combination of a propensity for political stalemate and the already inherent concentration of powers in the executive.[82]

Of course, a deadlock between the president and legislature does not inevitably lead to collapse of democracy. The president and the legislature may cooperate and compromise;

[75] Ibid Art 45.

[76] Cindy Skach, 'The 'Newest' Separation of Powers: Semipresidentialism' (2007) 5 *International Journal of Constitutional Law* 93.

[77] Ibid.

[78] Amy J. Weisman, 'Separation of Powers in Post-Communist Government: A Constitutional Case Study of the Russian Federation' (1994) 10 *American University Journal of International Law and Policy* 1365, 1372–3.

[79] Skach (n 76), 96.

[80] See Juan Linz, 'The Perils of Presidentialism' (Winter 1990) 1 *Journal of Democracy* 51, 52; Linz and Valenzuela (n 41), 4; Ackerman (n 60), 646.

[81] Giovanni Sartori, 'Neither Presidentialism nor Parliamentarianism' in Linz and Valenzuela (n 41), 106–7 (cited in Ackerman (n 60), 646).

[82] Linz and Valenzuela (n 41), 69–74.

perhaps achieving a solution that is better than the one that each might have imposed had they been able to act unilaterally. Bruce Ackerman labeled this the Madisonian hope, based on James Madison's optimism that the structure of American government would check faction and lead to good policy. Finally, a third possible outcome of deadlock between the president and the legislature is neither good governance nor outright collapse, but 'endless backbiting, mutual recrimination, and partisan deadlock'.[83]

Ackerman suggested that parliamentary governments will know that the legislation they pass can be undone if they lose the next election. By contrast, in presidential and semi-presidential systems, when the president actually enjoys the support of the legislature—what he described as a system of 'full authority'—the government has the power to entrench its policies into place for a longer period of time. This, he asserted, is because the government knows that even if it loses the legislature at the next election, it may retain the presidency or other offices. But paradoxically, he argued, politicians in this scenario will focus on policies that have large symbolic impact in order to further their chances in the next election rather than policies that will be truly effective in a middle range of time.[84]

Not everyone agrees that presidential systems are less stable. Political scientists Matthew Shugart and John Carey, for example, found 'no justification for the claim of Linz and others that presidentialism is inherently more prone to crises that lead to breakdown', noting numerous breakdowns of parliamentary systems, as well as the fact that in more recent years presidential systems in Latin America and elsewhere have achieved much greater stability. Donald Horowitz 'pointed out that in postcolonial Africa and Asia, the Westminster model of parliamentarism was the "institutional villain" behind a string of failed democracies, resurgent authoritarianisms, and unstable polities'.[85]

Steven Calabresi in his response to Ackerman contended that most of the countries writing constitutions in the 1980s and 1990s chose presidentialism over parliamentarianism. He contended that American-style presidentialism: better embodies democratic principles; promotes stability; provides the executive branch with more democratic legitimacy; allows for more robust judicial review; is more compatible with federalism; and better protects individual liberty.[86]

There seem to be comparatively fewer academic advocates for semi-presidentialism. This structure creates the opportunity for 'warring executives', and power-sharing within the executive can make it less clear to the public who is responsible for government policies. Cindy Skach, for example, suggested that 'even French constitutional scholars' admit that under their system 'it's difficult to know who makes the decisions, and things don't always work out that well'.[87] Semi-presidential systems are particularly problematic when, in a multiparty system, divided minority governments result, in which neither the party of the president nor of the prime minister enjoys a majority in the legislature. Thus, the success of such regimes depends in part on the party structure of a given country.[88]

There are so many variables in the construction of presidential, parliamentary, and semi-presidential systems that it is hard to say in the abstract that one is always superior. The success of parliamentary systems, for example, may depend in part on the mode of election. Electoral systems that employ varieties of proportional representation that allow many different

[83] Ackerman (n 60), 647.
[84] Ibid 650–3.
[85] Easter (n 46), 186.
[86] See Calabresi (n 48), 52–93.
[87] Skach (n 76), 98.
[88] Ibid 105.

political parties to gain seats in parliament often result in unstable coalition governments. In countries that use this sort of system, such as Italy, particular cabinets may remain in power for very short periods of time as coalitions form and collapse. Countries like Germany, on the other hand, that employ modified versions of proportional representation and/or set a minimum threshold of support before a minor party can gain seats, tend to produce more stable governments.[89]

In short, given the large number of successful and unsuccessful examples of both types of systems, it seems less than fruitful to claim that either presidentialism or parliamentarianism is suitable for all nations. Rather, the success of any given system depends on multiple variables including how the constitution implements the model and the history and social and economic qualities of the particular nation.

(e) *Judicial Review of Executive Appointments and Removal*

Occasionally, conflict between the executive and the legislature over the appointment and removal from office of executive officials has results in constitutional litigation, though constitutional courts have shown a preference for resolution of such conflicts through the political process. For example, at a time when the President and the majority of the national assembly in South Korea were from different parties, the assembly initially failed to vote on the president's choice for prime minister, and the president then installed his chosen candidate as acting prime minister. The constitutional court rejected a challenge brought by members of assembly from the majority party, with various justices noting that the members of the legislature who had brought the suit could have acted in their legislative capacity to resolve the matter through a legislative vote.[90] Similarly, the Russian constitutional court noted, in response to a conflict over then-President Boris Yeltsin's choice for Prime Minister, that the constitutional provision requiring dissolution of the legislature and new elections should the legislature reject a president's choice for prime minister three times was a mechanism for overcoming disagreements between the president and legislature through 'free elections', thus promoting the goal of a 'democratic, rule of law state'.[91]

In some countries, the judiciary may also play a role in resolving disputes involving the attempted impeachment and removal of officials by the legislature. For example, in a case concerning the attempted impeachment of South Korean President Roh Moo-Hyun, the Constitutional Court reinstated the president, finding that his alleged misconduct (eg in commenting favorably on one party in advance of elections, in violation of a constitutional provision prohibiting the president from engaging in electioneering) did not constitute violations of the fundamental constitutional rules sustaining democracy and therefore were not proper grounds for impeachment.[92]

In the United States, the President, Vice-President, and 'all civil officers of the United States', may be removed from office 'on impeachment for, and conviction of, treason, bribery, or other high crimes and misdemeanors'.[93] The House of Representatives has the

[89] Ackerman (n 60), 653–5.

[90] Competence Dispute Between the President of the Republic and Members of the National Assembly, Constitutional Court (Republic of Korea) 29 KCCG 583, 98 HunRa1, 15 July 1998.

[91] Russian Prime Ministerial Appointment Case, Constitutional Court (Russia), Decision 28-P of 11 December 1998.

[92] Impeachment of the President (Roh Moo-Hyun), Constitutional Court (Republic of Korea), Case 16-1KCCR 609 (2004).

[93] US Constitution, Art II, s 4.

power of 'impeachment'—that is, of bringing charges against a federal official,[94] while the Senate is given the power to 'try all impeachments', with a two-thirds vote required for impeachment.[95]

The Supreme Court has held that the propriety of the Senate's impeachment of a federal judge was a non-justiciable political question; while this case involved a judge rather than an executive branch official, the court's reasoning would seem equally applicable to cases involving legislative impeachment of executive officials.[96]

2. Beyond the Presidential versus Parliamentary Debate: Other Issues in the Structuring of Executive and Legislative Power

(a) Subdivision of Legislative Power

It is very common for systems to employ a bicameral, or two-house, legislature. The bicameral legislature has its origins in theories of mixed government, and was classically represented in the British Parliament with its House of Lords (representing the aristocracy) and House of Commons (representing the broader populace). Many have argued that the US Senate was originally conceived of as fulfilling a similar role in relation to the House of Representatives, although the absence of a hereditary aristocracy in the United States altered the underlying calculus.

In contemporary constitutions, federalism has replaced class structure as a justification for bicameralism. It is common for countries with a federal system of government involving a vertical separation of powers to reflect this in their bicameral federal legislatures.[97] Typical in this regard is the German system. The German legislature consists of the Bundestag, which is directly elected, and the Bundesrat, which represents the states (or *Länder*). While the Bundestag is more prominent, the Bundesrat must be involved when legislation is passed that requires the states to take certain actions or that involves revenue shared between the states and the federal government. In the United States, the Senate contains two members from each state, regardless of population, and is thus considered to in part represent the interests of the states. Other countries with bicameral legislatures in which one house is linked to regional subunits include South Africa (with its National Assembly and National Council of Provinces), Mexico (with its Senate and Chamber of Deputies), and India (with its House of the People and Council of States).

Even in some unitary states, such as France (with its National Assembly and Senate), bicameralism is employed, with the two houses designed to serve as checks on each other. In many systems, the members of the upper house are selected by a different mechanism than members of the lower house. Members of the French Senate, for example, are selected indirectly by regional officials and the members of the National Assembly.

At the same time, a great number of countries employ unicameral legislatures. Unicameral legislatures are considered to be more efficient. Both presidential and parliamentary countries may employ unicameral legislatures. Parliamentary systems with unicameral legislatures may be particularly efficient, but they are criticized by commentators for having insufficient checks and balances.

[94] Ibid Art I, s 2. [95] Ibid Art I, s 3.

[96] *Nixon v United States* 506 US 224 (1993). [97] Ackerman (n 60), 673.

(b) Subdivision of Executive Power

There are also a number of debates about the internal structuring of the executive branch, including whether it is desirable to have officials or departments within the executive branch independent of the chief executive—for example an independent attorney general, special independent prosecutors, or independent agencies.

In the United States, the contemporary debate at the federal level has centered around a school of theories concerning the 'unitary executive'—that is, the idea that the US President 'must be able to control the execution of all federal laws' through broad supervisory powers over inferior executive branch officials as well as the discretion to remove those officials from office.[98] As is typical in the United States, part of this debate concerns the original intent of the framers of the Constitution, with some arguing that the idea of the unitary executive is 'just plain myth' and 'a creation of the twentieth century, not the eighteenth',[99] and others asserting that the founding generation intended a strongly unitary executive.[100] Another dimension of the debate concerns the normative desirability of a strongly unitary executive branch.

These debates were spurred to prominence by a series of cases in the late 1980s in which the US Supreme Court held that statutes providing that certain executive branch officials could only be removed for 'good cause' did not violate the constitutional separation of powers.[101] The most notable case involved a statute allowing for the appointment of an 'independent counsel' to 'investigate and, if appropriate, prosecute certain high-ranking Government officials for violations of federal criminal laws', which the Court upheld in *Morrison v Olson*.[102] The 'independent counsel' was removable 'only by the personal action of the Attorney General, and only for good cause'.[103] While there was immediate academic controversy about whether the decision was correct, the issue became even more prominent in the late 1990s when independent counsel Kenneth Starr's investigation of President Bill Clinton's involvement in the failed Whitewater Development Corporation expanded into an investigation of Clinton's sexual relationship with White House intern Monica Lewinsky, which in turn led to efforts to impeach the President. This, many believed, fulfilled the fears that an unchecked and unaccountable prosecutor could wreak havoc on the system.[104]

At the same time, below the federal level, many states within the United States in fact insist on the separate election of prosecutors or state attorney generals. For example, as of 2002, 38 out of 50 states provided for separate election of the attorney general.[105]

As noted previously, countries with semi-presidential systems also subdivide executive power, as with the roles of the French President and Prime Minister. Russia, with its President and Chairman of the Government (ie, prime minister), seemingly employs a similar division

[98] Steven G. Calabresi and Saikrishna B. Prakash, 'The President's Power to Execute the Laws' (1994) 104 *Yale Law Journal* 541, 544; see also Steven G. Calabresi and Kevin H. Rhodes, 'The Structural Constitution: Unitary Executive, Plural Judiciary' (1992) 105 *Harvard Law Review* 1153.

[99] Lawrence Lessig and Cass R. Sunstein, 'The President and the Administration' (1994) 94 *Columbia Law Review* 1, 2.

[100] Calabresi and Prakash (n 98), 549.

[101] *Mistretta v United States* 488 US 361, 408–12 (1989); *Morrison v Olson* 487 US 654, 685–93 (1988).

[102] 487 US 654, 660 (1988).

[103] Ibid 686.

[104] Christopher S. Yoo, 'Symposium: Presidential Power in Historical Perspective: Reflections on Calabresi and Yoo's *The Unitary Executive*' (2010) 12 *University of Pennsylvania Journal of Constitutional Law* 241, 242.

[105] G. Alan Tarr, 'Interpreting the Separation of Powers in State Constitutions' (2003) 69 *New York University Annual Survey of American Law* 329, 338.

of executive power.[106] Portugal's 1976 Constitution established a semi-presidential system in the hope that maintaining two centers of executive power (a strong Prime Minister that could counterbalance an equally strong President) would protect against both an excessively strong executive and parliamentary instability.[107] While constitutional revisions in 1982 shifted this original structure more toward pure parliamentarism,[108] Portugal continues to divide executive power between a popularly elected president and a government dependent on the confidence of the legislature.[109] Still other countries have plural executives that defy easy categorization, such as the Swiss system, which employs a seven-member Federal Council.[110]

(c) Boundaries and Overlap between Legislative and Executive Power

i. Legislation versus Administrative Regulation

Because regulation in the contemporary world is so complex, most legal systems recognize that rules of conduct may be promulgated not only by the legislature through statues, but also through the executive branch and/or specialized administrative agencies in the form of regulations.

For example, the French Constitution explicitly recognizes that both the legislature and the executive will engage in lawmaking. The Constitution specifies that rules governing certain areas of law must be enacted through the legislature as statutes (*lois*), including those governing serious crimes, taxation, civil rights and liberties, and nationalization of private companies. In other areas—including protection of the environment, property, contracts, and employment law—the legislature is required to lay down at least the 'basic principles'.[111] Matters falling outside these areas may be regulated by the government through decrees (*règlements*). When the legislature enacts *lois* in areas that fall within the domain of *règlements* (as determined by the Conseil Consitutionnel), the policies may be amended by *règlements* after consultation with the Conseil d'État.[112] The government can also receive permission for a limited time to take measures in areas that are ordinarily covered by legislation through *ordonnances* issued in the Council of Ministers after consultation with the Conseil d'État.

In the United States, the US Supreme Court has held under the 'non-delegation' doctrine that the legislature cannot delegate the entire domain of policymaking to an executive branch agency, but must at least set out 'intelligible principles' to guide the agency's discretion.[113] The 'non-delegation' doctrine is mostly a theoretical constraint, however, since it has not been applied by the Supreme Court since the 1930s.[114] In contemporary times, if the doctrine remains alive at all, it survives as a canon of statutory interpretation.[115]

[106] Gordon B. Smith and Robert S. Sharlet, *Russia and its Constitution: Promise and Political Reality* (2008); Edward W. Walker, 'Politics of Blame and Presidential Powers in Russia's New Constitution' (1994) 3 *East European Constitutional Review* 116, 117.

[107] Eric Solsten (ed), *Porgtugal: A Country Study* (1993), available at <http://countrystudies.us/portugal/76.htm>.

[108] See David Corkill, 'The Political System and the Consolidation of Democracy in Portugal' (1993) 46 *Parliamentary Affairs* 517.

[109] Jose Antonio Cheibub, 'Presidentialism, Parliamentarism, and the Role of Opposition Parties: Making Presidential and Semi-presidential Constitutions Work' (2009) 87 *Texas Law Review* 1375, 1395–6.

[110] Arend Lijphart, *Patterns of Democracy* (1999), 119–20.

[111] See French Constitution, Art 34.

[112] Ibid Art 37.

[113] *Hampton v United States* 276 US 394, 401 (1928).

[114] See Erwin Chemerinsky, *Constitutional Law* (3rd edn, 2006), 327–31.

[115] See Cass R. Sunstein, 'Nondelegation Canons' (2000) 67 *University of Chicago Law Review* 315.

Recall that the British system, or Westminster model, involves a relatively high degree of fusion of executive and legislative power. It is therefore not surprising that:[116]

> In the United Kingdom and in self-governing Dominions and colonies it has long been the custom for the legislature to invest the executive with power to make regulations... the legal content of which it would be difficult to distinguish from legislation.

The amount of discretion given to the executive for promulgating regulations can be substantial. The Australian High Court, for instance, recognized that the separation of powers doctrine formed a part of the Australian Constitution and precluded the legislature from conferring legislative power on the executive. Nonetheless, it construed the phrase 'legislative power' in such a way that 'subordinate regulations, however wide the discretion under which they were made, could not be considered as an exercise of legislative power.' Consequently, the court concluded that 'a grant of regulative authority is not a delegation of [Parliament's] legislative power'—and so there is no separation of powers violation—even when the executive is given the authority 'to prescribe conduct and regulate rights and duties, however untrammeled the discretion.'[117] As a result, there is almost no limit on the extent to which the Australian Parliament may grant lawmaking authority to the executive.

The German Federal Constitutional Court has noted that, as an aspect of separation of powers, 'the legislature is obligated... to make all crucial decisions in fundamental normative areas, especially in those cases where basic rights become subject to governmental regulations.' Nevertheless, the court has allowed relatively broad delegations of authority to the executive branch in regulatory programs. For example, it rejected a challenge to the Atomic Energy Act, which it found was sufficiently precise to satisfy the legislature's constitutional obligation, concluding that it was 'within the legislature's discretion to use either undefined legal terms or precise terminology' and that it was permissible for the legislature to conclude that the executive should have the task of adjusting safety requirements based on current technological developments.[118]

ii. Conflicts between the Executive and the Legislature over Policy

Conflicts between the executive and the legislature over policy are often resolved through the political process, but sometimes courts are called up to intervene and resolve the dispute as a matter of constitutional law. In the case of *Youngstown Sheet & Tube Co v Sawyer*,[119] the US Supreme Court held invalid President Harry Truman's seizure of steel mills as not within his inherent executive authority and contrary to statute. In a famous passage, Justice Jackson, writing in concurrence, explained that presidential actions could be grouped into three categories. In the first, when he acts 'pursuant to an express or implied authorization of Congress, his authority is at its maximum, for it includes all that he possesses in his own right plus all that Congress can delegate.' In the second, when the president acts in 'absence of either a congressional grant or denial of authority', the president must rely on his own independent powers but there is a 'zone of twilight in which he and Congress may have concurrent authority' and the outcome depends on 'imperatives of events' rather than 'abstract theories of law'. Finally, in the third category, when the president 'takes measure incompatible with the

[116] Owen Dixon, 'The Separation of Powers in the Australian Constitution' (2008) 10 *Constitutional Law and Policy Review* 35, 38.

[117] Ibid 39.

[118] *Kalkar I Case*, Federal Constitutional Court (Germany), 48 BVerfGE 89 (1978).

[119] *Youngstown Sheet & Tube Co v Sawyer* 343 US 579 (1952).

expressed or implied will of Congress, his power is at its lowest ebb, for he can rely only upon his own constitutional powers minus any constitutional powers of Congress over the matter.' This framework has proven influential in separation of powers jurisprudence. When the US Supreme Court struck down the military commissions set up to try accused terrorists in *Hamdan v Rumsfeld*, it was because the Court concluded that the commissions set up by the administration of President George W. Bush fell into this third category and contravened legislation that limited the use of military commissions to situations that were consistent with the laws of war, including the Geneva Conventions.[120]

Courts, in general, seem particularly reluctant to interfere with the internal workings of legislatures. The Israeli Supreme Court, for example, has held that 'in general, questions of the day-to-day affairs of the legislature are not institutionally justiciable'[121] that 'only if it is claimed that the violation of rules regarding internal management harms the parliamentary fabric of life and the foundations of the structure of our constitutional system of government is it appropriate to decide the issue in court.'[122]

iii. Power over Foreign Affairs

Countries vary in their allocation of authority over foreign affairs to the executive and legislature. Montesquieu, the reader will recall, viewed foreign affairs powers as being executive in nature, but most modern systems divide these powers between the branches.

It is quite common for constitutions to require legislative approval of at least some, though often not all, international agreements. The French Constitution, for example, gives the president the power to 'negotiate and ratify treaties', but specifies that certain types of treaties 'may be ratified or approved only by virtue of an Act of Parliament', including

> Peace treaties, commercial treaties, treaties or agreements relating to international organization, those that commit the finances of the State, those that modify provisions which are matters for statute, those relating to the status of persons, and those that involve the cession, exchange or addition of territory.[123]

Similarly, the German Constitution requires that 'Treaties that regulate the political relations of the Federation or relate to subjects of federal legislation shall require the consent or participation, in the form of a federal law, of the bodies responsible in such a case for the enactment of federal law.'[124] South Korea requires legislative votes for treaties

> pertaining to mutual assistance or mutual security; treaties concerning important international organizations; treaties of friendship, trade and navigation; treaties pertaining to any restriction in sovereignty; peace treaties; treaties which will burden the State or people with an important financial obligation; or treaties related to legislative matters.[125]

In the United States, the President concludes treaties subject to the advice and consent of two-thirds of the Senate. Although alternative procedures are not mentioned in the Constitution,

[120] 548 US 557 (2006).

[121] Public Committee Against Torture, HCJ 769/02, Supreme Court (Israel) (2005) (citing HCJ 9070/00 *MK Livnat v The Chairman of the Constitution, Law, and Justice Committee*, 55(4) PD 800, 812; HCJ 9056/00 *MK Kleiner v The Chairman of the Knesset*, 55(4) PD 703, 708).

[122] Public Committee Against Torture, HCJ 769/02, Supreme Court (Israel) (2005) (citing HCJ 652/81 *MK Sarid v The Chairman of the Knesset*, 36(2) PD 197; HCJ 73/85 *'Kach' Knesset Faction v The Chairman of the Knesset*, 39(3) PD 141; HCJ 742/84 *Kahane v The Chairman of the Knesset*, 39(4) PD 85).

[123] French Constitution, Arts 52, 53.

[124] German Basic Law, Art 59.

[125] Constitution of the Republic of South Korea, Art 60.

in practice the United States enters into some international agreements by way of bicameral legislation (so-called congressional-executive agreements, which are common in the area of international trade) and the President also has the power to enter into sole executive agreements.[126]

Many systems also require legislative participation in the decision to engage in war. (See Chapter 22.) In this area formal constitutional requirements are not always adhered to in practice, and executives in many countries are prone to use force without *ex ante* legislative authorization. The US Constitution famously gives the Congress the power to declare war,[127] but presidents have not always sought congressional authorization in advance for their military actions. This is true in many other countries as well.[128]

In this regard it is not only the prevailing power sharing among the branches that counts but also a country's troubled history with military dictatorship. For example, the South Korean Constitution requires legislative approval not only for formal declarations of war, but also for any 'dispatch of armed forces to foreign states, or the stationing of alien forces in the territory of the Republic of Korea.'[129] Although the President is commander-in-chief, he operates 'under the conditions as prescribed by the Constitution and Act', and that 'The organization and formation of the Armed Forces' is determined by law.[130]

Many commentators consider some independent executive authority in these areas desirable,[131] for reasons originally expressed by Alexander Hamilton: 'Decision, activity, secrecy, and dispatch will generally characterise the proceedings of one man in a much more eminent degree than the proceedings of any greater number; and in proportion as the number is increased, these qualities will be diminished.'[132] Others contend that maintaining legislative control over powers of war and peace is essential to democracy, and have argued for various changes to increase the likelihood of legislative involvement.[133]

iv. Executive versus Legislative Control of Emergency Powers

Times of crisis strain the ordinary separation of powers framework. While there is no widely accepted definition of what constitutes an emergency,[134] Mark Tushnet provides a helpful starting point:[135]

> An 'emergency' occurs when there is general agreement that a nation or some part of it faces a sudden and unexpected rise in social costs, accompanied by a great deal of uncertainty about the length of time the high level of cost will persist.... 'Emergency powers' describes the expansion of governmental authority generally and the concomitant alteration in the

[126] See generally Oona Hathaway, 'Treaties End' (2008) 117 *Yale Law Journal* 1238.

[127] US Constitution, Art I, s 8.

[128] See Martinez (n 52), 2492–5.

[129] Constitution of the Republic of South Korea, Art 60(2).

[130] Constitution of the Republic of South Korea, Art 74.

[131] See eg John Yoo, *The Powers of War and Peace: the Constitution and Foreign Affairs* (2005).

[132] Hamilton, *The Federalist*, no 70 (n 29).

[133] See John Hart Ely, *War and Responsibility: Constitutional Lessons of Vietnam and Its Aftermath* (1995); Lori Fisler Damrosch, 'Constitutional Control over War Powers: A Common Core of Accountability in Democratic Societies?' (1995) 50 *University of Miami Law Review* 181.

[134] Note that some constitutions specifically delineate the criteria that must exist for the government to claim a state of emergency. See eg German Basic Law, Art 115a; Constitution of the Republic of South Korea, Art 76. This can be an important constraint on the exercise of emergency powers, particularly when coupled with an effective mechanism for reviewing the government's claim.

[135] Mark Tushnet, 'The Political Constitution of Emergency Powers: Parliamentary and Separation-of-Powers Regulation' (2008) 3 *International Journal of Law in Context* 275, 275–6.

> scope of individual liberty, and the transfer of important 'first instance' law-making authority from legislatures to executive officials, in emergencies.

The transfer of power to the executive results from the belief that, when a country is faced with an urgent threat, executive officials are 'better able than legislators to act quickly, in a co-ordinated response, on the basis of adequate information'.[136] But this efficacy comes at a price: the expansion of executive power through the invocation of emergency powers can result in human rights violations[137] or, in the extreme, breed dictatorship.[138] Some support broad, largely unchecked executive authority to assess the threat and adopt appropriate measures to protect national security. Others contend that the need to maintain robust checks and balances on executive power is most important during times of crisis, which 'provide the best test for our cherished values of liberty and freedom'.[139] Mark Tushnet calls this sort of check on the executive's exercise of emergency powers 'political control', and argues that—when effective—this type of control is preferable to 'legal control', which relies on the courts to determine whether a novel government practice violates a fundamental principle of law.[140] In response to Tushnet's contention, Adam Shinar argues that political controls are wholly ineffective in Israel, where a parliamentary system coupled with proportional representation from a party list ensures that 'members of parliament have a strong incentive to comply with party policy even if they object to it on a personal level'.[141] As a result, he contends, government policies and actions in the realm of national security are rarely checked by the Israeli legislature. At the same time, the Israeli Supreme Court has exercised vigorous review of measures including detention of suspected terrorists, interrogation methods, and targeted killings, though its interventions in these areas have drawn criticism as judicial activism.[142]

As this demonstrates, however desirable balancing emergency powers between the legislature and executive might be, formal divisions can readily break down when there is popular support for expansive, executive authority. (For a review of national answers to emergency see Chapter 21.) As in other areas of separation of powers theory, 'the practical effectiveness of formal divisions of power seems to depend a great deal on political context', and 'legislators are often quite willing to cede their powers'.[143] Of course, the courts may also be as a check on emergency powers, as discussed in the next section.

IV. The 'Least Dangerous Branch'? The Judiciary and Separation of Powers

This section addresses the issue of the relationship between the judicial power and the legislative and executive powers. There is wide agreement that judicial independence is desirable—that is, that judges engaged in the process of adjudication must be independent from direct political and financial influence. Judges should not decide cases based on bribes, threats, or

136 Ibid 275–6.

137 Ibid 276.

138 Martinez (n 52), 2506–7.

139 Adam Shinar, 'Constitutions in Crisis' (2008) 20 *Florida Journal of International Law* 116.

140 Tushnet (n 135), 277.

141 Shinar (n 139), 162.

142 See eg Public Committee Against Torture in Israel, Supreme Court (Israel) (2005); Mersel, 'Judicial Review of Counter-Terrorism Measures: The Israeli Model for the Role of the Judiciary during the Terror Era' (2005) 28 *NYU Journal of International Law and Politics* 67.

143 Martinez (n 52), 2510–11.

instructions from other government officials. But countries have chosen widely divergent structures to achieve this goal. Numerous questions arise in this context. What role should the legislature and executive play in the appointment and removal of judges? Should some or all judges be formally placed in their own separate branch of government or is it acceptable for some judges to reside formally within the executive branch? Should some or all judges have the power of judicial review—that is, the power to declare legislative or executive enactments invalid on the basis of constitutional or other higher law principles?

1. Judicial Independence and 'The Judicial Branch'?

While all modern democracies recognize the importance of judicial independence, the segregation of the judiciary into an entirely separate branch of government is not always considered necessary for this. For example, many systems allow for certain types of adjudication to be carried out within the executive branch. In France, administrative tribunals within the executive branch, culminating in the Conseil d'État, review the legality of public actions. The particular idea of separation of powers that was put in place during the French Revolution prohibits ordinary judges from exercising this type of power, and as a consequence these administrative tribunals are not considered courts proper, although they certainly engage in functions that would in most other countries be regarded as adjudication.[144]

Until recently, the highest appellate court in the United Kingdom was the Law Lords, made up of members of the House of Lords, the upper house of the legislature. In 2009, the appellate function was transferred to a new Supreme Court that is no longer formally a part of the legislature. Even under the previous system, however, the Law Lords functioned as an independent group, and lay peers did not participate in the functioning of the House of Lords as an appellate court. Still, the fact that the Law Lords could participate in legislative debates was considered problematic. The British decision to create a new, separate Supreme Court may be seen as an acknowledgement that the previous system was conceptually troublesome, even if it worked relatively well in practice. In addition, the United Kingdom maintains a significant functional separation of judicial powers at other levels of its court system. Judges 'may not sit in the House of Commons and they are protected from summary removal under the Act of Settlement [of] 1701.'[145]

The United States is considered to have a strongly independent federal judiciary. The 'judicial power' of the United States is vested 'in one supreme Court, and in such inferior Courts as the Congress may from time to time ordain and establish.'[146] The Congress has through legislation established federal trial courts and regional courts of appeal. Federal judges are nominated by the President and confirmed by the Senate in a process that is often contentious and politically charged. Once in office, however, they 'hold their Offices during good Behavior', and their compensation may not be reduced during their time in office.[147] However, federal judges may be removed by impeachment. State judges in many areas of the United States are popularly elected, a practice which some criticize as undermining their independence.

The jurisdiction of the federal courts is constitutionally and statutorily limited to certain types of cases, and there is a long-standing and unresolved debate among legal scholars about whether the Congress can use legislation to strip the federal courts of jurisdiction to hear

[144] See Merryman (n 21), 111.

[145] Barendt (n 56), 291.

[146] US Constitution, Art III, s 1.

[147] Ibid Art III, s 1.

certain types of cases (eg abortion cases).[148] A variety of decisions in the United States define the contours of judicial power and independence. In *Hayburn's Case*, for example, the members of the US Supreme Court rejected a statutory scheme whereby judicial decisions regarding pension benefits were subject to rejection by the Secretary of War. The Court found this executive control over judicial decisions to be 'radically inconsistent with the independence of that judicial power which is vested in the courts'.[149] Nevertheless, in practice a large amount of adjudication is carried out within executive branch administrative agencies by judges who do not enjoy the life-tenure protections of Article III. For instance, immigration courts, which fall under a department of the executive branch, received 391,829 cases and issued 232,212 decisions in 2009.[150] The Supreme Court has held that this is constitutionally permissible as long as the 'essential attributes' of judicial power are retained in Article III courts.[151]

The South Korean Constitution strongly emphasizes judicial independence. Judges 'shall rule independently according to their conscience and in conformity with the Constitution' and laws.[152] The Chief Justice of the Supreme Court is appointed by the President with the consent of the National Assembly, while other Supreme Court justices are appointed by the President on the recommendation of the Chief Justice and with the consent of the National Assembly. Lower court judges are appointed by the Chief Justice with the consent of the Conference of Supreme Court justices.[153] Justices serve fixed terms, and no judge may be removed except by impeachment or on conviction of a serious crime.[154]

An area deserving of additional study is the effect of lodging adjudicative bodies within the executive branch of government. A recent study of state-level administrative courts in Mexico found that states were roughly split in whether they placed administrative courts formally within the executive branch or formally within the judicial branch of government. Those administrative courts that were lodged in the judicial branch were found to rule against the government in a larger percentage of cases.[155] (See further Chapters 39 and 40.)

2. Judicial Review

The term 'judicial review' describes the power of courts to declare legislation or actions of the executive in violation of the constitution. The practice is often considered important to preserving constitutional structure and individual rights, but is also subject to criticism that it is in tension with democratic principles because it allows judges to countermand the will of elected legislators and executive officials.

The practice was established in the United States in the landmark case of *Marbury v Madison*.[156] Chief Justice Marshall, writing for the Court, explained that 'The government of the United States has been emphatically termed a government of laws, and not of men'.[157] And,

[148] See Richard H. Fallon, Jr, Daniel J. Meltzer, and David L. Shapiro (eds), *Hart & Wechsler's The Federal Courts and the Federal System* (6th edn, 2009), 275–83.

[149] *Hayburn's Case* 2 US 409 (1792).

[150] Executive Office for Immigration Review, *FY 2009 Statistical Yearbook* (March 2010), A1, available at <http://www.justice.gov/eoir/statspub/syb2000main.htm>.

[151] *Commodity Futures Trading Comm'n v Schor* 478 US 851 (quoting *Crowell* 285 US 22, 51 (1932)).

[152] Constitution of the Republic of South Korea, Art 103.

[153] Ibid Art 104.

[154] Ibid Arts 105, 106.

[155] See Ana Elena Fierro and Adriana Garcia, *Design Matters: The Case of Mexican Administrative Courts* (2010).

[156] *Marbury v Madison* 5 US 137 (1803).

[157] Ibid 163.

Marshall explained, 'it is emphatically the province and duty of the judicial department to say what the law is'.[158] A key characteristic of judicial review in the United States is that it is 'decentralized', meaning 'the jurisdiction to engage in constitutional interpretation is not limited to a single court'. Rather, 'it can be exercised by many courts, state and federal'.[159] Argentina, Australia, Canada, India, and Japan employ similar, decentralized systems of judicial review. South Africa's constitution, written in the wake of apartheid, significantly increases the power of the judiciary by instantiating a strong principle of judicial review to ensure protection of individual rights.[160] Judicial review extends even further in India, where the Supreme Court 'may review a constitutional amendment and strike it down if it undermines the basic structure of the Constitution.'[161] This is contrary to judicial review in its more ordinary conception, which presumes a constitutional amendment can override an unpopular court ruling.

Many European countries vest the power to review legislation for constitutionality in specialized bodies. This may be referred to as the 'centralized' model of judicial review.[162] (For details, see Chapter 38.)

Not all modern democracies allow judicial review. The United Kingdom continues to operate on the principle of parliamentary supremacy, and its courts lack the power to invalidate legislation on constitutional grounds. Pursuant to the Human Rights Act of 1998, however, British courts now engage in something that looks very much like judicial review when they apply the European Convention on Human Rights. But formally they are only entitled to declare legislation incompatible with the Convention, with the power to change the law still residing in parliament.

In an interesting recent development, the expanding authority of transnational treaties and courts, such as the European Court of Justice, is partially decentralizing the exercise of judicial review in some European countries with centralized systems. The Court's doctrines of 'direct effect' and supremacy of European Union law permit individuals to invoke provisions of international treaties against contrary provisions of national law in ordinary, domestic courts.[163] The willingness of some national courts to refer cases to the European Court of Justice, follow its jurisprudence, and abide by its decisions is leading these domestic courts to assert more judicial review-like functions, sometimes in the face of direct opposition from other branches of national government. A striking example of this occurred in Britain, where '[national] courts overturned the sacrosanct doctrine of parliamentary sovereignty and issued an injunction blocking the effect of a British law pending judicial review at the European level.'[164]

In Israel, the role of judicial review is still evolving. Due to political struggles, Israel's first Knesset (parliament) did not enact a constitution, instead 'instructing that the constitution be composed in piecemeal fashion of individual chapters, each constituting basic law.'[165] Originally, Basic Laws were not considered superior to other legislation, and the Israeli

[158] Ibid 177.

[159] Vicki C. Jackson and Mark Tushnet (eds), *Comparative Constitutional Law* (2nd edn, 2006), 465.

[160] Pius N. Langa, 'The Separation of Powers in the South African Constitution', *Symposium: A Delicate Balance: The Place of the Judiciary in a Constitutional Democracy* (2006), 4.

[161] S.P. Sathe, 'Judicial Activism: the Indian Experience' (2001) 6 *Washington University Journal of Law and Policy* 29, 88.

[162] Louis Favoreu, 'Constitutional Review in Europe' in Louis Henkin and Albert J. Rosenthal (eds), *Constitutionalism and Rights: The Influence of the United States on Constitutions Abroad* (1990).

[163] Anne-Marie Slaughter, 'Toward a Theory of Effective Supranational Adjudication' (1997) 107 *Yale Law Journal* 273, 291–92.

[164] Anne-Marie Slaughter, 'Judicial Globalization' (2000) 40 *Virginia Journal of International Law* 1103, 1105–6.

[165] Shinar (n 139), 147.

Supreme Court 'did not exercise judicial review over primary legislation'. This changed in 1995, when the Supreme Court 'held that the Basic Laws are normatively superior to Knesset legislation' and asserted its authority to strike down legislation that violated rights protected in the Basic Laws.[166] The Court has since taken a very active role in evaluating and invalidating actions of the Knesset as well as the executive, even in cases that involve security measures—an area previously considered beyond the reach of the courts.[167] However, this has generated a significant backlash against the Court. In response to the Court's activism, the legislature and executive are attempting to weaken the Court, particularly its power of judicial review. Moreover, recent public opinion polls evince a substantial decline in public confidence in the Court.[168] Consequently, the future potency of judicial review in Israel remains uncertain.

3. Jurisdiction and Justiciability

Given the overlap and competing ambition of the branches of government, it is of constitutional relevance how the apex courts handle the emerging conflicts in terms of jurisdiction and justiciability, which are only partly carved out by these supreme courts. Because every court in the United States has the power to declare statutes in violation of the Constitution, procedural rules place relatively stringent limits on the types of cases that federal courts can adjudicate. For instance, courts in the United States can only rule on constitutional challenges within the context of concrete cases or controversies. As the Supreme Court explained, the words 'cases and controversies' in Article III of the US Constitution 'define the role assigned to the judiciary in a tripartite allocation of power to assure that the federal courts will not intrude into areas committed to the other branches of government'.[169] These 'justiciability' doctrines are considered an aspect of separation of powers.

On the other hand, countries with specialized constitutional courts are likely to have more lenient gate-keeping procedures. In a decentralized system like the United States, procedural rules are often a means to avoid deciding major constitutional issues. In centralized systems such as those common to Europe, constitutional courts exist 'for the express purpose of *deciding* constitutional issues, not evading them'.[170] Consequently, the need to restrict access on procedural grounds is substantially less compelling.

(a) Advisory Opinions

Some constitutional systems allow the judiciary to offer advisory opinions about the constitutionality of measures before they have been enforced, or indeed limit such jurisdiction to abstract questions, as is the case with the French Constitutional Council.[171] In France, historically concerned with 'judicial excess that could only be controlled by rigorously protecting the executive and legislative powers of government from any form of judicial control',[172] this type of review may be the only politically palatable form, since *post hoc* judicial nullification conflicts with the long-standing preference for a restrained judiciary. However, the advisory

[166] Ibid 148.

[167] Ibid 150.

[168] Asher Arian et al, *Auditing Israeli Democracy: Democratic Values in Practice* (2010), available at <http://www.idi.org.il/sites/english/SectionArchive/Documents/Auditing_Israeli_Democracy_2010.pdf>.

[169] *Flast v Cohen* 392 US 83, 95 (1968).

[170] Herman Schwartz, 'The New East European Constitutional Courts' (1992) 13 *Michigan Journal of International Law* 741, 752–3.

[171] See Merryman (n 21), 117.

[172] Ibid 110.

process is initiated solely by legislators, leading some to criticize the process for being overtly political—forcing courts into the role of policy makers and consequently violating separation of powers. As Alec Stone Sweet argued,

> abstract review exists only to the extent that politicians seek to alter legislative outcomes, by having their policy choices ratified or the government's and parliamentary majority's choices watered down or vetoed. If politicians ceased to use referrals as political weapons, abstract review would disappear.[173]

Many countries with specialized constitutional courts similarly favor considering constitutional questions in relatively abstract terms, including Germany, Italy, and Spain.

The US federal courts, by contrast, are not allowed to render advisory opinions but can only decide live disputes involving individual claimants who will be affected by the outcome. The issue first arose in the early days of the country, when then-Secretary of State Thomas Jefferson sent the Supreme Court a list of questions related the meaning of various treaties and laws as they related to American neutrality in the war between England and France.[174] The Supreme Court declined to answer, however, explaining that the

> three departments of the government...being in certain respects checks upon each other, and our being judges of a court in the last resort, are considerations which afford strong arguments against the propriety of our extra-judicially deciding the questions alluded to.[175]

Closely related is the doctrine of 'standing', which the US Supreme Court has said is 'built on a single basic idea—the idea of separation of powers'.[176] Standing doctrine requires, among other things, that the plaintiff have suffered or be in immediate danger of an individual injury that is traceable to the defendant's conduct and that will be redressed by the court's decision.[177] The Court held, for example, that a 'citizen suit' provision of the Endangered Species Act allowing any person to sue for enforcement of the law was unconstitutional because of separation of powers, finding that citizens' desire to see endangered animals living in the wild was insufficient to give them standing to sue.[178]

Because the United States is a federal system, not all state level courts follow the same standing doctrine as federal courts. The Hawaiian Supreme Court, for example, decided to depart from the federal doctrine and allow citizens to have standing to enforce state environmental laws.[179] That court explained that its basic approach was 'that standing requirements should not be barriers to justice'. The court did note that:

> [the] judicial power to resolve public disputes in a system of government where there is a separation of powers should be limited to those questions capable of judicial resolution and presented in an adversary context. For 'prudential rules' of self-governance 'founded in concern about the proper and properly limited role of courts in a democratic society' are always of relevant concern.[180]

[173] Alec Stone Sweet, 'Abstract Constitutional Review and Policy Making in Western Europe' in Donald W. Jackson and C. Neal Tate (eds), *Comparative Judicial Review and Public Policy* (1992).

[174] See Chemerinsky (n 114).

[175] Quoted in Fallon, Jr et al (n 148), 52.

[176] *Allen v Wright* 468 US 737, 752 (1984); *Lujan v Defenders of Wildlife* 504 US 555 (1992).

[177] 468 US 737, 758–9.

[178] 504 US 555.

[179] *Citizens for Protection of North Kohala Coastline* 979 P2d 1120 (Hawaii 1999).

[180] *Life of the Land v Land Use Commission of State of Hawaii* 623 P2d 431 (1981).

Even given these constraints, however, the court found it appropriate to allow the various environmental challenges in those cases. Indeed, many state constitutions in the United States have long allowed state courts to render advisory opinions. The Massachusetts state constitution of 1780, for example, stated that 'Each branch of the legislature, as well as the governor . . . shall have authority to require the opinions of the justices of the supreme judicial court, upon important questions of law, and upon solemn occasions.'[181]

Across different constitutional systems, rules of standing vary from extremely restrictive to nearly unconstrained. In India, for example, the rules of standing are exceptionally liberal, to the point that they 'may be said to have ceased to present any real obstacle to the . . . litigant'.[182]

(b) *The Political Question Doctrine*

One of the most confusing doctrines in US law is the so-called 'political question doctrine', which rejects certain issues as beyond the institutional competence or proper authority of courts. The doctrine has its origins in *Marbury v Madison*, the very case that established judicial review, in which Chief Justice John Marshall explained that 'Questions, in their nature political, or which are by the constitution and laws, submitted to the executive can never be made in this court.'[183] Courts in the United States, of course, frequently decide highly politicized questions—such as the constitutional right to abortion, or the outcome of the 2000 presidential election. As the Court has explained, 'The doctrine of which we treat is one of "political questions", not one of "political cases".'[184] So when does the doctrine apply? In *Baker v Carr*, the Court provided a not entirely helpful list of circumstances reflecting the separation of powers concerns that underlie the doctrine:

> prominent on the surface of any case held to involve a political question is found a textually demonstrable constitutional commitment of the issue to a coordinate political department; or a lack of judicially discoverable and manageable standards for resolving it; or the impossibility of deciding without an initial policy determination of a kind clearly for nonjudicial discretion; or the impossibility of a court's undertaking independent resolution without expressing lack of the respect due coordinate branches of government; or an unusual need for unquestioning adherence to a political decision already made; or the potentiality of embarrassment from multifarious pronouncements by various departments on one question.[185]

At the opposite end of the spectrum, German law specifically rejects the notion of a political question doctrine as a bar to litigation. In dismissing the suggestion that such a doctrine exists in Germany, Professor Kommers wrote, 'All questions arising under the Basic Law are amenable to judicial resolution if properly initiated . . . includ[ing] the highly politicized field of foreign affairs.'[186] Nonetheless, the substantial deference the German judiciary affords the government in cases that concern foreign affairs might be said to result in a similar doctrine in

[181] Massachusetts Constitution, Part II, Chapter III, Art II. See also eg Rhode Island Constitution, Art X, §3 (requiring 'The judges of the supreme court [to] give their written opinion upon any question of law whenever requested by the governor or by either house of the general assembly'); see also Jonathan D. Persky, 'Note, "Ghosts that Slay": A Contemporary Look at State Advisory Opinions' (2005) 37 *Connecticut Law Review* 1155.

[182] Jamie Cassels, 'Judicial Activism and Public Interest Litigation in India: Attempting the Impossible?' (1989) 37 *American Journal of Comparative Law* 495, 498–9.

[183] 5 US 137, 163 (1803).

[184] *Baker v Carr* 369 US 186, 217 (1962).

[185] 369 US 186, 217 (1962).

[186] Donald P. Kommers, *The Constitutional Jurisprudence of the Federal Republic of Germany* (1989), 163.

practice, if not in theory.[187] As Thomas Franck argued, the doctrine is simply redefined, focusing 'not [on] *whether* but *how* judges decide'.[188] According to this argument, German courts achieve the same result as their US counterparts (generally deferring to the government's discretion in matters concerning foreign affairs and national security), but through different means.

The recent and contentious issue of targeted killings highlights the continued importance of justiciability doctrines. The legality of this technique was challenged in courts in both the United States and Israel. The Israeli Supreme Court, which explicitly rejected the idea that principles of standing or the political nature of the questions presented by a case should deter it from exercising review,[189] heard the case on its merits and decided that the government's ability to engage in targeted killings was constrained by various legal rules.[190] A quite similar case brought in the United States was dismissed on procedural grounds due to the plaintiff's lack of standing[191] and for violating the political question doctrine.[192]

V. Conclusion

One of the complexities of separation of powers jurisprudence is that the abstract distinctions between executive, legislative and judicial powers will very often be blurred in practice. As Richard Bellamy explains:

> When judges, for example, adjudicate on which rules do or do not apply in particular cases, they also often end up setting precedents that in effect constituted new rules. Similarly, officials frequently have to create rules in the course of implementing a given law that in turn come to take on a life of their own. Legislators, too, are inevitably concerned with how the laws they frame will be interpreted and applied to specific cases. Thus, each branch of government will find itself engaged in all three activities to one degree or another.[193]

As this chapter has shown, modern democracies employ a wide range of strategies to achieve the checks and balances that separation of powers is designed to foster. Measures that some countries deem essential to separation of powers are totally ignored by other countries, which rely on different structures or doctrines to achieve the same basic goals. As in so many areas of comparative constitutional law, there seems to be more than one effective way to do things.

Bibliography

Bruce Ackerman, 'The New Separation of Powers' (2000) 113 *Harvard Law Review* 664

Richard Bellamy (ed), *The Rule of Law and the Separation of Powers* (2005)

Steven G. Calabresi, 'The Virtues of Presidential Government' (2001) 18 *Constitutional Commentary* 51

[187] See generally Thomas M. Franck, *Political Questions/Judicial Answers: Does the Rule of Law apply to Foreign Affairs?* (1992).

[188] Ibid.

[189] Shinar (n 139), 149 (citing *Resler v Minister of Defense*, HCJ 910/86, Isr SC 42(2) 441, 462 (1986)).

[190] See *The Public Committee against Torture in Israel v The Government of Israel*, HCJ 769/02 (2005).

[191] *Al-Aulaqi v Obama* 2010 US Dist LEXIS 129601, 86 (DDC Dec 7, 2010).

[192] Ibid 121.

[193] Bellamy (n 4), 253, 256.

Gerald M. Easter, 'Preference for Presidentialism: Postcommunist Regime Change in Russia and the NIS' (1997) 49 *World Politics* 184

Thomas M. Franck, *Political Questions/Judicial Answers: Does the Rule of Law apply to Foreign Affairs?* (1992)

Juan J. Linz and Arturo Valenzuela (eds), *The Failure of Presidential Democracy* (1994)

Scot Mainwaring, 'Presidentialism in Latin America' (1990) 25 *Latin American Research Review* 157

Jenny Martinez, 'Inherent Executive Power: A Comparative Perspective' (2006) 115 *Yale Law Journal* 2480

John Henry Merryman, 'The French Deviation' (1996) 44 *American Journal of Comparative Law* 111

Montesquieu, *The Spirit of Laws* (1750)

Adam Shinar, 'Constitutions in Crisis' (2008) 20 *Florida Journal of International Law* 116

Cindy Skach, 'The "Newest" Separation of Powers: Semipresidentialism' (2007) 5 *International Journal of Constitutional Law* 93

M.J.C. Vile, *Constitutionalism and the Separation of Powers* (2nd edn, 1998)

CHAPTER 27

FEDERALISM: THEORY, POLICY, LAW

DANIEL HALBERSTAM*

Ann Arbor

* Thanks to Jenna Bednar, Roderick Hills, Donald Regan, and George Tsebelis for comments and discussions.

I. Introduction

Even France now values local government. Over the past 30 years, top-down appointment of regional prefects and local administrators has given way to regionally elected councils and a revision of Article 1 of the French Constitution, which proclaims that today the state's 'organization is decentralized'.[1] The British Parliament, too, has embraced local rule by devolving powers to Scotland, Wales, and Northern Ireland. And in China, decentralization has reached a point where some scholars speak of 'de facto federalism'.[2] A systematic study of the distribution of authority in 42 democracies found that over the past 50 years, regional authority grew in 29 countries, remained stable in 11, and declined in only two.[3] And various projections over the past half-century place over 50 percent of the world's landmass into federal systems in 1964,[4] 40 percent of the world population in federal systems in 1987,[5] and 50 percent (or up to 70 percent if we include China) of the world's population in federal systems by 2009.[6]

Just as subnational authority is on the rise, so, too, global governance is gaining ground. With the creation of the European Union, the birthplace of the nation-state has fostered an historic enterprise of governance beyond the state. The nation-states of Europe have also created the most ambitious and effective international human rights regime to date.[7] Efforts of transnational governance are taking shape in Africa, the Americas, and Asia.[8] Three-quarters of all states have joined the World Trade Organization with its compulsory jurisdiction over, and adjudication of, trade disputes.[9] The United Nations is more active than ever before in peacekeeping missions, resolutions, and direct actions against individuals.[10] And an International Criminal Court has been established to prosecute individuals for crimes against humanity, war crimes, and genocide.

From Belgium to India, traditional forms of federalism are generally understood to be constitutional arrangements. But the extent to which constitutional law serves as the foundation for some of the other arrangements is very much contested. France's devolution is tied to the constitution by only a thin thread, China's is a product of simple legislation formally reversible at will, and whether Britain's will be deemed constitutional only time can tell. On the global level, the very idea of applying constitutional language to governance beyond the state is still hotly debated and conceptually uncertain.[11]

This chapter focuses on federalism. But it presents the terrain of federalism to lay the foundation for understanding the constitutional significance of arrangements among multiple

[1] For a brief overview of French decentralization, see Martine Lombard and Gilles Dumont, *Droit Administratif* (6th edn, 2005), 89–91.

[2] See eg Yongnian Zheng, *De Facto Federalism in China: Reforms and Dynamics of Central-Local Relations* (2008); cf Gabriella Montinola, Yngyi Qian, and Barry R. Weingast, 'Federalism, Chinese Style: The Political Basis for Economic Success in China' (1995) 48(1) *World Politics* 50.

[3] Gary Marks, Liesbet Hoogh, and Arjan H. Schakel, *The Rise of Regional Authority* (2010), 52.

[4] William H. Riker, *Federalism: Origin, Operation, Significance* (1964), 1.

[5] Daniel J. Elazar, *Exploring Federalism* (1987).

[6] Jenna Bednar, *The Robust Federation* (2009), 2 n 1.

[7] See eg Alec Stone Sweet, *A Europe of Rights* (2008).

[8] See eg Louise Fawcett, 'Exploring Regional Domains: A Comparative History of Regionalism' (2007) 80 *International Affairs* 429.

[9] For a list of members, see <http://www.wto.org/english/thewto_e/whatis_e/tif_e/org6_e.htm>.

[10] The expansion in UN activity since the end of the Cold War is enormous. See generally Karen A. Mingst and Margaret P. Karns, *The United Nations in the 21st Century* (2007). For numbers, see eg <http://www.globalpolicy.org/home.html>.

[11] See eg the debate between Daniel Halberstam and Joseph Weiler in Gráinne de Búrca and J.H.H. Weiler (eds), *The Worlds of European Constitutionalism* (2011), 284–301.

levels of authority from private to global governance. As we shall see, even traditional federalism covers a broad set of legal arrangements. And the fact that federalism is generally understood to be a constitutional arrangement should not be taken to suggest that the role that constitutional law does or should play in federal systems is uncontested. To the contrary, for some, such as Proudhon, the idea of federalism even contains a hint of anarchy.[12]

The chapter proceeds in six sections. Section II critically examines the (relevance of) historical debates about defining federalism. Section III turns to arguments about the origins of federations. Section IV analyzes normative federalism theory and its applicability in legal disputes. Section V discusses the sustainability of federal systems. Section VI considers the consequences of federalism for various policy outputs. Section VII takes federalism beyond its traditional boundaries—first down to regional, local, and private governance, and then up into the global arena. A brief conclusion ends the chapter.

II. Federalism—Federation—Confederation

Federalism can be a charged and sometimes confusing word. A political rallying cry for decentralization in the United States, the F-word means more Brussels in Europe. Back when James Madison, Alexander Hamilton, and John Jay battled their opponents in pamphlets, both sides of the debate desperately sought the mantel of federalism to help their cause. And among academics, what is and what is not federalism has been embroiled in definitional squabbles that have been, at times, quite caustic[13] and, more often, of questionable significance.[14]

1. Capturing 'Federalism'

Part of the problem is an accident of history. Recall that at the birth of modern federalism in the United States, the Founders described their novel creation as 'in strictness neither a national nor a federal constitution; but a composition of both'.[15] As contemporary discussion and usage in the Federalist Papers suggested, the word '*federal*' at that time signified a distinctly international idea 'which regards the Union as a *confederacy* of sovereign states'.[16] Put another way, 'federal' was roughly synonymous with what we would generally call 'confederal' today.[17] The new American Republic was in this sense a hybrid system of governance that combined international with national modes of governance. For example, according to Madison's Federalist 39, the American Republic exemplified the 'federal' form in the mode of constitutional ratification (ie, assent via ratification convention in every state that joined the Union) and in the states' equal representation in the Senate.[18] But, again according to Madison, the new republic also had 'national' features, as for instance, the representation of the people 'in the same proportion, and on the same principle, as they are in the Legislature of a particular State'.[19] A similarly 'national' feature of the new government was that the central government's

[12] Pierre-Joseph Proudhon, *Du Principe federative* (1963).

[13] See eg William H. Riker, 'Federalism' in Fred Greenstein and Nelson Polsby (eds), 5 *Handbook of Political Science: Government Institutions and Processes* (1975), 98–9 (criticizing K.C. Wheare).

[14] See S. Rufus Davis, *The Federal Principle: A Journey Through Time in Quest of Meaning* (1978).

[15] James Madison, 'The Federalist no 39' in J.E. Cooke (ed), *The Federalist* (1961), 250, 257.

[16] Ibid 253.

[17] See Martin Diamond, 'What the Framers Meant by Federalism' in Robert Goldwin (ed), *A Nation of States* (1974), 25.

[18] Madison (n 15), 254–5.

[19] Ibid.

powers operated not merely 'on the political bodies composing the confederacy, in their political capacities' but directly on the individual citizen.[20]

In their campaign documents, the Founders deployed a strategy of imprecision. For instance, in a proper confederation of the type known at the time (or indeed since then), the mode of ratification within each signatory state would ordinarily rest with each signatory state's internal legal requirements. The US Constitution, by contrast, spelled out the mode of its own ratification within each state by demanding popular ratifying conventions that bypassed existing state government institutions. It was, after all, to be a product of 'We, the People' not the 'We, the States'. In this sense, even the purportedly 'federal' features of the US Constitution were far less 'federal' (ie in modern terms, far less 'confederal') than the Framers let on.

The most cunning imprecision of all, however, still influences how we think of the subject today. Call it the Federalists' strategic synecdoche. By presenting their distinctly hybrid form of governance in 'The Federalist' papers, the Founders appropriated for the whole of their new enterprise a term that only described part of the arrangement: 'federalism'. The 'national' bit was subtly dropped. The public relations campaign (and the quest to create the American republic) was a success. And so, today, 'federal' and 'federalism' are understood primarily in terms of the American hybrid form of governance as opposed to the older idea of federalism as confederation.

But that was not the end of conceptual controversy. In modern times, K.C. Wheare's influential work *Federal Government* promoted an American-centered understanding of the 'federal principle' as 'the method of dividing powers so that the general and regional governments are each, within a sphere, coordinate and independent.'[21] On Wheare's account, the United States, which exemplified the federal principle, was an 'association of states' in which federal and state governments are 'co-equally supreme within their sphere'.[22] But for all his focus on the United States, it was questionable whether Wheare understood American federalism properly, especially as it had developed over time. As critics were quick to point out,[23] Wheare neglected the cooperative elements of US federalism as well as the role of the Supremacy Clause. More important for present purposes, Wheare defined federalism so narrowly that it excluded Argentina, the Weimar Republic (and later the Federal Republic of Germany and many others), in which central and constituent government institutions were more closely intertwined than in Wheare's idealized conception of federalism in the United States.

What followed was a long battle of definition and redefinition—at least within English speaking scholarship—mostly to broaden the scope of 'federalism' beyond Wheare's particular (and mostly outdated) understanding of the American model. William Livingston, for example, suggested a sociological approach that focused not on 'legal and constitutional terminology' but on the 'economic, social, political, [and] cultural' forces necessary to sustain federal government.[24] Carl Friedrich, in turn, insisted on a strong conceptual link between federalism and constitutionalism, but viewed both not as fixed legal constructs but as dynamic 'processes' by which society continually organizes and reorganizes itself.[25] And just as Morton

[20] Ibid 255.
[21] K.C. Wheare, *Federal Government* (1946), 11.
[22] Ibid 2.
[23] William Anderson, 'Book Review' (1946) 40 *Publius* 995.
[24] William S. Livingston, *Federalism and Constitutional Change* (1956), 1.
[25] Carl J. Friedrich, *Trends of Federalism in Theory and Practice* (1968).

Grodzins famous 'marble cake' metaphor debunked the idea that US federalism involved mutually distinct spheres,[26] so Daniel Elazar's simple definition of federalism as a combination of 'self-rule plus shared rule' expanded the reach of 'federalism' and 'federalisms' well beyond the US model to describe such arrangements as Union, Federation, Confederation, Federacy, Associated Statehood, Condominium, and League.[27]

The most lasting definitional contribution, however, has come from William Riker. His was grounded in, and accompanied by, an approach to federalism studies that has dominated the political science literature ever since: causal analysis of actors engaged in rational political strategies within defined institutional settings.[28] Riker's classic definition held that

> A constitution is federal if (1) two levels of government rule the same land and people, (2) each level has at least one area of action in which it is autonomous, and (3) there is some guarantee (even though only a statement in the constitution) of the autonomy of each government in its own sphere.[29]

Mostly usable to this day,[30] Riker's definition should be taken as properly linked to a specific research project. It should not be taken to distract from the fact that in some federal systems, such as Brazil, the European Union, Germany, or India, more than two levels of government have constitutionally based claims to rule that can usefully be analyzed in terms of federalism as well. And it should not deflect attention away from a more modern conception of the distribution of powers (in the United States and around the world), which recognizes that jurisdiction and accompanying policy actions of the various levels are not distinct and autonomous from one another but compete and intermingle with one another.[31] Finally, Riker's definition should also not distract from the general importance in a federation of each level of government's organizational autonomy as distinct from any substantive jurisdiction over execution, adjudication, or promulgation of law and policy. An alternative definition that embraces all these features might take federalism to mean *the coexistence within a compound polity of multiple levels of government each with constitutionally grounded claims to some degree of organizational autonomy and jurisdictional authority*.[32]

2. The Territory of 'Federation'

One of the useful analytic insights to emerge from the definitional debates is the central importance to traditional federalism of territorial government, or what Ivo Duchacek long ago termed the 'territorial dimension of politics'.[33] Some scholars along the way have suggested a more abstract understanding of federalism that would include jurisdictions organized not along geographic but along functional lines. Most prominent in this regard, has been the work

[26] Morton Grodzins, *The America System: A View from the States* (1966).

[27] Elazar (n 5), 12, 33–79.

[28] For various theoretical expositions along these lines, see eg Bednar (n 6); Fritz W. Scharpf, *Games Real Actors Play* (1997); George Tsebelis, *Veto Players: How Political Institutions Work* (2002).

[29] Riker (n 4), 11.

[30] See eg Michael Filippov, Peter Ordeshook, and Olga Shvetsova, *Designing Federalism: A Theory of Self-Sustainable Federal Institutions* (2004), 5.

[31] See eg Robert Schütze, *From Dual to Cooperative Federalism: The Changing Structure of European Law* (2009).

[32] See Daniel Halberstam, 'Federalism and the Role of the Judiciary' in Keith E. Whittington, R. Daniel Kelemen, and Gregory A. Caldeira (eds), *The Oxford Handbook of Law and Politics* (2008), 142.

[33] Ivo Duchacek, *Comparative Federalism: The Territorial Dimension of Politics* (1970).

of Swiss economists Bruno Frey and Reiner Eichenberger, who advocate a system of functional overlapping competing jurisdictions (FOJCs).[34] Such jurisdictions would have governance authority over a single policy issue (such as education or religion) and not be organized along geographical boundaries.[35] Analogies between such functionally organized jurisdictions and federalism do indeed exist and can yield useful insights.[36] And yet, in common parlance as well as in the scholarly literature, there is still considerable force to Livingston's blunt statement that 'No government has ever been called federal that has been organized on any but the territorial basis.'[37]

In a less promising move, scholars such as Preston King,[38] Ronald Watts,[39] and Michael Burgess[40] have argued for distinguishing between federalism and federation along normative/institutional lines. King, for example, suggested that federalism is best thought of as an ideology, political philosophy, or normative concept as distinguished from the institutional manifestation of federalism in federation.[41] This, he thought, would help to focus debates about the political philosophy that underpins federal arrangements. But it is not clear that anyone was ever seriously confused by the use of 'federalism' to signify both normative theory and institutional practice. And so this particular distinction between federalism and federation has never taken root.

Somewhat more promising has been the effort to tease out the idea of a federation as only one particular kind of federal arrangement. Ronald Watts, for example, notes that

> Within the genus of federal political systems, federations represent a particular species in which neither the federal nor the constituent units of government are constitutionally subordinate to the other, i.e. each has sovereign powers derived from the constitution rather than another level of government, each is empowered to deal directly with its citizens in the exercise of its legislative, executive and taxing powers and each is directly elected by its citizens.[42]

Whether using the term 'federal system' or 'federalism' as the umbrella term, most scholars seem to take the basic point about genus versus species. An accepted distinction, then, exists between federalism as the general phenomenon (be it normative or institutional) and federation as a more specific institutional manifestation. To be sure, as we shall see, scholars still quibble about the precise institutional characteristics of a federation. But 'federation' lays the foundation for teasing out one particular institutional manifestation of federalism and distinguishing it from the others.

3. Beyond 'Confederation'

Among the species of federalism, the distinction between federation and confederation has long generated the most interest. The German-speaking literature on federalism has

[34] Bruno Frey and Reiner Eichenberger, *The New Democratic Federalism for Europe. Functional, Overlapping, and Competing Jurisdictions* (1999).

[35] Bruno Frey, 'Functional, Overlapping, Competing Jurisdictions: Redrawing the Geographic Borders of Administration' (2005) V *European Journal of Law Reform* 543.

[36] See Section VII below.

[37] Livingston (n 24), 2–3.

[38] Preston T. King, *Federalism and Federation* (1982).

[39] Ronald L. Watts, *Comparing Federal Systems* (1999).

[40] Michael Burgess, *Comparative Federalism: Theory and Practice* (2006).

[41] King (n 38), 20–1.

[42] Watts (n 39), 6–7.

been especially focused on this distinction, that is, between *Staatenbund* (confederation) and *Bundesstaat* (federation), as first Switzerland and then Germany moved from looser alliances to more closely knit forms of federalism. Because the 'state' as fundamental unity has loomed so large in the German legal tradition,[43] scholars (especially lawyers) have grappled hard with understanding the very possibility of federalism. Today, we witness a new variant of these debates as scholars, judges, politicians, and citizens argue about whether, for example, the European Union is a federal state, federation, confederation, or *sui generis* entity.[44]

All these definitional arguments, however, say more about the conceptual imagination or intellectual agenda of those arguing for one view over another than they do about the entity being discussed. At times, such inquiries focus on the rather elusive (and frequently unhelpful) idea of 'sovereignty', as in asking whether sovereignty ultimately resides at the central level (federation) or component state level (confederation).[45] They occasionally worry about whether the system as a whole qualifies as a 'state' (either under the definition of international law or on Weber's definition of the monopoly of the legitimate use of violence) before speaking of federation. Or they may turn to more concrete operational questions, such as (1) whether the central level of government has the authority to expand its powers without the unanimous consent of the component states,[46] (2) whether there is a direct electoral link between the citizen and the central level of government,[47] and (3) whether the central government can directly impose legal obligations on the individual as defining elements of a federation.[48] Reasonable arguments can be made for the significance of many of these operational characteristics in distinguishing between federations and confederations. But the choice of elements selected by the various definitions here, too, will usually depend mostly on the purpose of the academic study or political argument advanced.

When opting for one or more of these characteristics to distinguish federations from other federal arrangements, we are therefore well advised to heed Harold Greaves's early dictum that 'it is not always possible to draw clear and incontestable distinctions[;] ... alliance shades into league, league into confederation, confederation into federal state, federal state into unitary state.'[49] The Italian scholar and statesman Pellegrino Rossi made a similar point back in 1833 noting that in moving from federation to confederation he saw no bright lines but only 'degrees and nuances'.[50] Federalism, federation, and confederation may therefore be deployed one way or another as a matter of rhetoric for political gain. But for purposes of theoretical or empirical scholarship, it makes no sense to speak about the accuracy of one definition over another in the absence of a specific research project or theory regarding the causes, effects, or normative implications of the phenomenon being defined.

[43] See Christoph Möllers, *Staat als Argument* (2000).

[44] For a discussion of some conceptual difficulties, see eg Schütze (n 31).

[45] See eg Paul Laband, *Das Staatsrecht des Deutschen Reiches* (1911), 58.

[46] See eg Dieter Grimm, 'The Achievement of Constitutionalism and its Prospects in a Changing World' in Petra Dobner and Martin Loughlin (eds), *The Twilight of Constitutionalism?* (2010), 3; Georg Jellinek, *Allgemeine Staatslehre* (3rd edn, 1929), 770–1, 783.

[47] Filippov et al (n 30), 9.

[48] Bednar (n 6), 19.

[49] Harold Richard Goring Greaves, *Federal Union in Practice* (1940), 10.

[50] See Olivier Beaud, *Théorie de la Fédération* (2007), 83 n 3.

III. The Origins of Federal Systems

Koen Lenaerts and Alfred Stepan (writing separately in different fields),[51] distinguish between two principal ways in which federations come about. In the first, 'integrative' (Lenaerts) or 'coming together' (Stepan) federalism, independent states form a federation to reap the gains of unity while maintaining the individuality of their component parts. In the second, 'devolutionary' (Lenaerts) or 'holding together' (Stepan) federalism, a unitary state devolves power to component governments in an effort to appease political demands for decentralization or to pacify separatist movements while maintaining the unity of the overarching state.[52] By introducing this basic distinction, both Stepan and Lenaerts sought to counteract the normalization of the American experience in the study of federations. Stepan, in particular, took aim at Riker's exclusive focus on federalism as the coming together of independent sovereign states. Federations such as India, Spain, and Belgium, did not fit that model and yet they needed a home at the core of what we understand as federalism.

Especially with regard to integrative federations, scholars continue to debate what caused them. Riker boldly posited that such federations are created because politicians desire territorial expansion in the face of an external military threat or opportunity.[53] This 'primacy of the military motive'[54] as well as the original hypothesis that such threats or opportunities are always external, has come under severe attack.[55] Scholars soon noted that the threat could come equally from internal, as opposed to external, sources as in the case of Nigeria's attempt to control ethnic factions within the federation.[56] The origins of the European Union in an attempt of Franco-German reconciliation could be added as an example here as well. Others urged that federation reflects an ideological commitment of elites[57] or the social qualities of its people.[58] Reviewing the literature on the subject in light of the formation of a host of federations, Michael Burgess concludes that the theory about the necessary existence of a military threat is not very informative. 'Closer historical analysis' in his view 'demonstrate[s] that a complex amalgam of socioeconomic, historical and political variables were also present at the creation'.[59] Burgess ultimately pleads for a theory—we might call it an anti-theory—of federal formation: the theory of 'circumstantial causation'.[60] With regard to the various motives for federation, all of which are easily identifiable, he concludes that 'it remains very much a matter of conjecture as to how far we can prioritize among them'.[61]

[51] Koen Lenaerts, 'Constitutionalism and The Many Faces of Federalism' (1990) 38 *American Journal of Comparative Law* 205; Alfred Stepan, 'Federalism and Democracy: Beyond the US Model' (1999) 10(4) *Journal of Democracy* 19. In evidence of the remarkable disciplinary divide between law and political science, Lenaerts' pathbreaking article does not refer to William Riker's work at all. Stepan, in turn, reinvents the distinction that Lenaerts made nearly a decade earlier in the *American Journal of Comparative Law*.

[52] Stepan suggested a third category of somewhat lesser significance, that of 'putting together' federalism, where federalism is imposed on a group of states by an outside hegemon. The significance of this category in suggesting consequences for politics within the union should not be overlooked, even though it seems to figure in Stepan's taxonomy as somewhat of an afterthought.

[53] Riker (n 4), 12–13.

[54] Ibid 19.

[55] See eg Davis (n 14), 132 ('a mere truism'); King (n 38), 34 ('trivial'); Burgess (n 40), 97 ('at best exaggerated and at worst erroneous').

[56] Anthony H. Birch, 'Approaches to the Study of Federalism' (1966) XIV(I) *Political Studies* 32.

[57] See Michael Burgess, 'Federalism as Political Ideology' in Michael Burgess and Alain-G. Gagnon (eds), *Comparative Federalism and Federation* (1993), 102.

[58] See eg Livingston (n 24), 2; Maiken Umbach, *Federalism and Enlightenment in Germany, 1740–1806* (2000).

[59] Burgess (n 40), 101.

[60] Ibid 97.

[61] Ibid 81.

Later studies have tried to hone in more closely on what motivates the choice between federation and its alternatives in the formation of a new political union. Daniel Ziblatt, for instance, calls into question Riker's hypothesis that a federation derives from a failure of the expanding power to 'overawe' its neighbors in the unsuccessful attempt to achieve a greater, unitary state.[62] Ziblatt suggests, instead, that elites with expansive ambitions seize upon the capacity of each of its potential negotiating partners to govern their own internal affairs effectively. He argues for what we can call a supply-side theory of federalism. It holds that

> the most decisive factor in [the] moment of institutional creation is the preexisting supply of regional political institutions...with high levels of institutional capacity that can be used both to negotiate the terms of polity formation and to govern after the polity has been formed.[63]

Ziblatt, then, would turn the traditional theory of formation on its head: 'federalism was not a second-best strategy adopted when necessary. Instead, federalism emerged when possible, while it was unitary structures that were viewed as necessary.'[64]

Chad Rector's recent study approaches the comparison from the other end.[65] He asks why independent states seeking the benefits of union opt for federation as opposed to some form of looser, international alliance. Rector's argument is also radical. The principal reason for institutions of federalism, on his account, is not to enhance gains from cooperation but to impose costs for defection. He suggests that states which have less to lose from the potential breakdown of cooperation would prefer an international alliance whereas states with more to lose want federation. Accordingly, the principal purpose of federation is to 'contrive symmetry'[66] among the parties where none would otherwise exist. After investing in federation, everyone loses equally if the deal breaks down.

Despite several sophisticated contributions, debate about the origins of federations will clearly continue. No single accepted theory has taken the place of Riker's rash model. The more general theories tend to be vague or in the nature of anti-theories. The more specific theories need more proof. For example, Ziblatt's and Rector's studies provide the most nuanced current analyses of the choice between federation and the alternatives of a unitary state, on the one hand, and an international alliance, on the other. And yet, each suffers from obvious limitations (many of which the authors themselves acknowledge). Ziblatt, for example, creatively draws four comparisons from his two-system study by including a difference analysis among the component states of each (would be) federation. After reaching his conclusions, he adds a quick sketch of a broader comparison throughout Europe. This goes a long way to unsettle previous assumptions. But it will take more detailed work outside his two principal case studies to confirm his specific thesis. Rector's analysis, while comparing a good deal more systems than Ziblatt's, often includes judgments of self-restraint through investment that are uncomfortably close to the simple manifestation of dominance. So, for example, he argues that non-vulnerable states must and do invest more heavily in federal institutions as a way to post a credible bond in favor of cooperation with their more vulnerable partners.[67] At the same time, however, such relatively greater investment of strong states in the institutions of

[62] Daniel Ziblatt, *Structuring the State: The Formation of Italy and Germany and the Puzzle of Federalism* (2006).

[63] Ibid 144.

[64] Ibid 142.

[65] Chad Rector, *Federations: The Political Dynamics of Cooperation* (2009).

[66] eg ibid 15.

[67] Ibid 46.

federalism—say, Prussia's preeminence in the German Federation of 1871—may also reflect a hegemonic element within the federation that simply serves to benefit the stronger party.

Perhaps most important, however, we should be careful in this terrain before privileging too much any given moment of 'creation' or distinguishing too starkly between 'coming-together' (or 'integrative') federations and their opposites. Returning to Lenaerts and Stepan, for example, they seem to characterize a federal system based on a chosen moment of creation as falling into one or the other category for all time. But by privileging the moment of foundation to characterize the system as a whole in this way, they suggest that the founding dynamic of politics is the one that will persist and dominate the life of the federation. And yet, a system of governance—especially a long-lived one such as Switzerland, the United States, Germany, Canada, or Venezuela—may undergo successive periods of integration and devolution over time. Indeed, before any given system emerged as a holding-together federation in the first place (as in the case of, say, the modern-day United Kingdom), it most likely had come together at a much earlier point in time to form the unity from which power is now being devolved.

IV. Why Federalism?

The terrain of normative political theory on federalism is well worn. And yet all too often one still finds no more than a disparate collection of individual reasons for or against central or local authority without considering the analytic structure of federalism theory as a whole. This leads to blind spots. Some scholars, for example, thereby fail to appreciate the significant difference between federalism and decentralization or which of several potential values of federalism are at stake in any given decision.[68] As existing federal systems continue to struggle with maintaining a workable division of authority among their various levels of government, and as questions of the constitutional design gain renewed importance around the world, it is therefore useful to bear in mind a *general* (albeit brief) normative theory of federalism.[69]

US scholars and judges may shy away from using the term, but the key theoretical concept underlying a general theory of federalism is what Europeans call 'subsidiarity'.[70] To make it palatable to all, we shall simply call it here the 'federal power principle'. Regardless of name, the basic principle should be familiar to Americans. It animated the Virginia Plan, which James Madison drafted and Governor James Randolph introduced in Philadelphia to serve as the blueprint for the US Constitution. With striking similarity to the later European analogue

[68] See eg Malcolm M. Feely and Edward Rubin, *Federalism: Political Identity and Tragic Compromise* (2008).

[69] Although some scholars of federalism will include non-democratic federations within the scope of their study, eg Bednar (n 6), whereas others limit the scope of study to democratic federations, eg Filippov et al (n 30), 9. Elazar has suggested that all (true) federations are democracies. Elazar (n 5), 108–9. And although some insist that there is no necessary connection between federalism and democracy, it seems that most studies gain most of their insights from the study of democratic federations. So, too, here, the theory of federalism will derive largely from a background assumption of democratic federalism despite the fact that some arguments and insights may find application in non-democratic federalism as well.

[70] Derived from the Latin 'subsiduum', which referred to auxiliary troops of the Roman military, and related to the English 'subsidy', the term subsidiarity entered the modern lexicon of European federalism via the Catholic Church. For a very brief discussion, see eg Daniel Halberstam, 'Federal Powers and the Principle of Subsidiarity' in Vikram David Amar and Mark V. Tushnet (eds), *Global Perspectives on Constitutional Law* (2009). For a more extended analysis, see eg George A. Bermann, 'Taking Subsidiarity Seriously: Federalism in the European Community and the United States' (1994) 32 *Columbia Law Review* 331; Joseph Isensee, *Subsidiaritätsprinzip und Verfassungsrecht* (1968), 14–18.

of subsidiarity, the plan proposed that the central legislature be given the power 'to legislate in all cases to which the separate States are incompetent, or in which the harmony of the United States may be interrupted by the exercise of individual legislation.'[71] The Constitutional Convention voted in favor of the provision and used it as the basis for the more specific enumeration of powers found today in Article I, section 8 of the US Constitution. As it turns out, unpacking the Randolph plan, that is, unpacking subsidiarity, gets us all we need (or, more accurately, gives us all we can get) from a general normative theory of federalism.

1. The Benefits of Local Power

Subsidiarity begins with a presumption in favor of a multiplicity of local authorities. Ever since Rousseau argued in favor of small states over large ones, democratic theory and public choice literature have recognized important arguments in support of local over central authority.[72] Some arguments trade principally on size, others emphasize the multiplicity of local power, and yet others build on both. This terrain is for the most part all too well known. But it is nonetheless useful to sketch out briefly before we turn to arguments in favor of a single central authority.

(a) Voice

It is a staple of federalism literature that, all else being equal,[73] local government will better reflect citizen preferences if citizens with different preferences cluster within different jurisdictions.[74] Even if such clustering is slight (or non-existent at first) mobile citizens can move from one jurisdiction to another, thereby sorting themselves into the various jurisdictions that best satisfy their individual preferences.[75] Politicians at local levels will have greater incentives to respond to this diversity than will the politicians in a central government eager to form 'universalistic coalitions'.[76] And even in the absence of mobility or preference diversity, the smaller the jurisdiction, the greater the weight of an individual citizen's vote and the greater the individual citizen's access to, and control of, his or her representative.

(b) Community

Smaller jurisdictions are often said to foster and reflect a greater sense of community among its citizens than do larger jurisdictions.[77] One argument is that smaller jurisdictions increase

[71] Max Farrand (ed), *The Records of the Federal Convention of 1787* (1911), 20–1. The principle of subsidiarity, as articulated in the Catechism of the Catholic Church, provides:

> a community of higher order should not interfere in the internal life of a community of a lower order, depriving the latter of its functions, but rather should support it in case of need and help to co-ordinate its activity with the activities of the rest of society, always with a view to the common good.

Catechism of the Catholic Church, para 1883.

[72] Unless specifically stated otherwise, central and local are used throughout this chapter as generic opposites without referring to any particular level or institution of government.

[73] Of course, all else usually isn't, but this will be unpacked in Section III.2 below.

[74] See Michael W. McConnell, 'Review: Federalism: Evaluating the Founders' Design' (1987) 54 *University of Chicago Law Review* 1484, 1494. For the classic theorem, see Wallace E. Oates, *Fiscal Federalism* (1972), 54.

[75] Charles M. Tiebout, 'A Pure Theory of Local Expenditures' (1956) 64 *Journal of Political Economics* 416.

[76] See Roderick M. Hills, Jr, 'Compared to What? Tiebout and the Comparative Merits of Congress and the States in Constitutional Federalism' in William A. Fischel, *The Tiebout Model at Fifty* (2006), 239, 249–53.

[77] Cf eg Michael J. Sandel, *Democracy's Discontent* (1996), 347. Most of these arguments, too, can already be found in Rousseau's *Social Contract*.

the quality of democratic interaction and incline individuals more charitably toward their fellow citizens and to public engagement. The anti-federalists generally called this sentiment republican or civic 'virtue'.[78] Madison took the point and was therefore keen on maintaining states alongside the federal government in the new compound republic. De Tocqueville later would add that when coupled with larger jurisdictions, smaller jurisdictions serve as schools of democracy for citizens and representatives alike.[79] The deeper sense of community in smaller jurisdictions may have benefits for the enforcement and implementation of laws as well, as citizens will more likely follow the rules of a more closely knit community than of one that is large and diffuse.

Scholars have, of course, argued that many constituent states in federal systems are so large today that the argument based on size cannot carry much weight. Constituent units are too large to create the kind of deeply affective community envisioned by the anti-federalists of the eighteenth century. And yet, conclusions about the existence of thicker forms of political participation in smaller jurisdictions as compared to larger ones[80] are remarkably robust even when those smaller jurisdictions contain, say, up to a million citizens.[81] More broadly, regional affinities including language, religion, ethnicity, history, or morality indeed reflect commonalities within a component state that are not shared by the larger citizenship of the federal polity as a whole.[82]

(c) Expertise

Smaller jurisdictions can be more effective because local decision-makers have a better grasp of the relevant local facts than would actors at the central level of governance. This argument about information asymmetries, in particular, applies well beyond democratic settings and even well beyond federalism.[83] In the federalism literature, the classic example is the property tax, where local officials are likely better than national officials at valuation.[84] But the point can be extended to any other matter of local variation presumed to be within the better grasp of local officials. In the European Union, this basic idea is one of the driving forces behind issuing so-called 'directives'. Even after having decided on a certain policy goal at the central level of governance, a directive (at least in theory) leaves the implementation to local officials who can better tailor the appropriate measures to local conditions.[85]

(d) Risk

A multiplicity of jurisdictions helps to manage risk. This is only an indirect argument in favor of smaller units of government, as its main focus is on the multiplicity of jurisdictions. Spreading governance authority over multiple jurisdictions can increase resistance to bad rule and lower the cost of governance experiments more generally. For example, it should come as

[78] See Herbert J. Storing, *What the Anti-Federalists Were For: The Political Thought of the Opponents of the Constitution* (1981), 41–2, 73.

[79] Alexis de Tocqueville, *Democracy in America* (J.P. Mayer ed, 1988), 62–70.

[80] See Robert Dahl and Edward Tufte, *Size and Democracy* (1973).

[81] Eric J. Oliver, *Democracy in Suburbia* (2001). See also Sidney Verba, Kay Lehman Schlozman, and Henry E. Brady, *Voice and Equality: Civic Voluntarism in American Politics* (1994).

[82] See eg Daniel J. Elazar, *The American Mosaic* (1994); Tom Vandenbrande (ed), *Mobility in Europe* (2006), 26, available at <http://www.eurofound.europa.eu/pubdocs/2006/59/en/1/ef0659enpdf>.

[83] A related argument about informational asymmetries underlies the basic argument for the decentralized mechanism of allocating goods through the market. See George J. Stigler, 'The Economics of Information' (1961) 69 *Journal of Political Economics* 213.

[84] See eg Bednar (n 6), 29.

[85] See Sacha Prechal, *Directives in European Community Law* (1995), 3–5.

no surprise that the first move of fascist government in Germany was the elimination of federalism through '*Gleichschaltung*' of the *Länder*.[86] So, too, in Venezuela, federalism has recently come under attack as an obstacle to the move from democracy to a more authoritarian regime.[87] There can be, of course, no paper guarantee for the preservation of federalism (or constitutionalism or the rule of law). But the existence of multiple sites of authority within a system of governance is designed to protect against the ill effects of tyrannical elites seizing power over any one level or unit of government. Similarly, seeing how a politician first does in a component jurisdiction is often a good way of testing for, and assuring citizens (especially in fledgling democracies) of, the trustworthiness of potential leaders of the republic as a whole.[88]

Federalism helps to hedge our bets not only against tyrants, but also against the risk of bad policy. Better that Drachten and Ipswich try out the elimination of all road signs in an effort to increase traffic safety than that we run this experiment Europe-wide. Or that Oregon and the Netherlands experiment with physician-assisted suicide while the rest of us look on. And most important, if we really want experiments to take the federal polity tomorrow where it may not want to go today, we must give local governments the power to choose their own policy goals as well.[89] Thus, local experience with same-sex unions in the United States comes at a time when a majority of Americans is still firmly opposed to the practice and public opinion is slowly changing.[90] Justice Brandeis famously captured this phenomenon in saying that 'It is one of the happy incidents of the federal system that a single courageous state may, if its citizens choose, serve as a laboratory; and try novel social and economic experiments without risk to the rest of the country.'[91] A related, but sometimes less well recognized, argument is that by allowing a multiplicity of jurisdictions to try their own policy experiments, federalism can unsettle policies that have become entrenched at the central level of government due to inertia, capture, or corruption.[92] Here, too, the effects of bad (in)decision can be mitigated by unsettling the status quo through local action.[93] Sometimes local experiments with locally contained costs lead the nation by shining example. At other times, local experiments prod the nation into considered action by causing national irritation.

2. The Benefits of Central Power

The literature on the benefits of central power is vast as well. Here, too, modern arguments in public choice literature often echo theorists and statesmen of long ago. In any event, the arguments can be usefully grouped into the following three simple categories.

[86] See Daniel Halberstam, 'Of Power and Responsibility: The Political Morality of Federal Systems' (2004) 90 *Virginia Law Review* 731, 753.

[87] See eg Michael Penfold-Becerra, 'Federalism and Institutional Change in Venezuela' in Edward L. Gibson (ed), *Federalism and Democracy in Latin America* (2004), 198.

[88] See Roger B. Myerson, 'Federalism and Incentives for Success of Democracy' (2006) 1 *Quarterly Journal of Political Science* 3.

[89] Cf Michael C. Dorf and Charles F. Sabel, 'A Constitution of Democratic Experimentalism' (1998) 98 *Columbia Law Review* 267.

[90] Jeffrey M. Jones, 'Americans' Opposition to Gay Marriage Eases Slightly', Gallup, May 24, 2010, available at <http://www.gallup.com/poll/128291/americans-opposition-gay-marriage-eases-slightly.aspx>.

[91] *New Ice Co v Leibman* 285 US 262, 311 (Brandeis J dissenting).

[92] See eg Heather Gerken, 'Dissenting by Deciding' (2002) 57 *Stanford Law Review* 1745; Daniel Halberstam, 'The Foreign Affairs of Federal Systems: A National Perspective on the Benefits of State Participation' (2001) 46 *Villanova Law Review* 1015.

[93] See also Section V.1 below.

(a) Cost Savings

The basic point about economies of scale and scope needs little elaboration. Just as it can be cheaper to produce certain goods or services by consolidating production or supply, so, too, it can be cheaper to consolidate certain government activities in a central authority. In the European Union, for example, one argument in support of the creation of a common currency was the cost savings entailed by eliminating currency conversion in cross-border market transactions.[94] Similarly, American businesses operating nationwide often lobby for a single federal regulation that preempts state regulation as a way to save the cost of having to comply with 50 different local rules.[95] Greater policymaking resources at the central level may also mean that difficult policy problems are better solved at the central level of government than by experimentation throughout smaller constituent entities.[96] In law enforcement, too, scholars and officials have advanced scale efficiencies as supporting prerogatives of federal over state powers.[97] Others have argued that delegation of policymaking powers to a central agency saves costly ad hoc negotiations once overall policy goals have been set.[98]

These and similar transactions cost savings point in favor of establishing central power, although not all of them argue for displacing local authority at the same time. In some cases the existence of more cost-effective governance facilities at the center could simply function as resources that component units could tap into at their convenience. Where the center has greater policy-solving or crime-solving capacity, for instance, local governments might avail themselves of the central resource by choice. In other cases, however, such as a common currency, the cost savings derives from the singularity of the central government policy. In these cases, any savings necessarily depend on engagement of the central government and simultaneous disengagement of the component states.

(b) Inter-Jurisdictional Difficulties

The second category reflects problems that arise due not to size but to the multiplicity of local jurisdictions. And they arise not merely due to the increased costs of doing things many different times instead of once but because of difficulties of coordinating multiple jurisdictions. Call this category 'inter-jurisdictional difficulties'.

The most commonly cited inter-jurisdictional difficulty is an externality, which figures prominently in Wallace Oates's famous decentralization theorem.[99] Policy effects—whether negative or positive—that radiate beyond any given local jurisdiction can lead to regulatory mismatches for several related reasons. The jurisdiction externalizing effects on others may under-appreciate those effects because it does not feel them; it may value those effects differently even if it were to feel them; or it may be trapped in a multilateral prisoner's dilemma in which all jurisdictions feel each other's externalized effects and value them equally but cannot

[94] This argument is based on the broader Optimal Currency Area theory, attributed to Robert Mundell. See eg Ronald McKinnon, 'Mundell, the Euro, and Optimum Currency Areas' in Thomas J. Courchene (ed), *Money, Markets, and Mobility* (2002).

[95] Roderick M. Hills, Jr, 'Against Preemption: How Federalism Can Improve the National Legislative Process' (2007) 82(1) *NYU Law Review* 20.

[96] Ken Kollman, John H. Miller, and Scott E. Page, 'Decentralization and the Search for Policy Solutions' (2000) 16(1) *Journal of Law, Economics, and Organization* 102.

[97] Jamie S. Gorelick and Harry Litman, 'Prosecutorial Discretion and the Federalization Debate' (1995) 46 *Hastings Law Journal* 967.

[98] Andrew Moravcsik, 'Preferences and Power in the European Community: A Liberal Intergovernmentalist Approach' (1993) 31 *Journal of Common Market Studies* 473.

[99] Wallace E. Oates, *Fiscal Federalism* (1972), 54.

reliably coordinate their regulatory responses. And, indeed, externalities of one sort or another justify a good deal of central government power from certain forms of environmental regulation to central government support for roads or higher education.

But there are other consequences arising from the lack of coordinated policy strategies of multiple jurisdictions as well. Although many might be packed into the model of an externality, some collective action problems are best thought of as creating rather distinct kinds of inter-jurisdictional difficulties.

For example, scholars have long pointed to the twin aspects of Tiebout's famous sorting hypothesis.[100] Think of it as two sides to the coin of mobility: 'voter mobility' and 'object mobility'. On the one side is the mobility of the resident as 'voter' who moves from one jurisdiction to another in search of the proper mix of taxes and services. On the other side is the mobility of the resident as 'object' of regulation, say a manufacturing plant that can flee a costly regulatory regime. As long as the costs and benefits of a particular local regulation roughly fall on the same entity, Tiebout sorting can be a straightforward affair, happily leading to the proverbial race to the top. I move to a certain jurisdiction because of the packages of taxes and benefits I receive much as I buy a widget at a certain store for a price I like.

But as soon as the incidents of regulation fall heavily on one entity, say a manufacturer (and its workers), while the benefits fall on another or on citizens more generally, object mobility limits the exercise of public power. This is why, for example, redistributive policies are difficult to maintain at the level of local government, as the US Supreme Court recognized in upholding federal unemployment laws.[101] Indeed, component jurisdictions within federal systems have often found themselves in competition with one another for movable capital investments, leading to what some have called a race to the bottom.[102] Whether giving up on environmental standards, worker protection, or, ultimately, taxes, subunits within federal systems have frequently sought to outbid one another to attract mobile industry.[103]

The effects of this kind of inter-jurisdictional competition are hotly debated. Some scholars have challenged the race-to-the-bottom hypothesis by arguing that such competition is generally efficient. They claim that this kind of hustling merely reveals each jurisdiction's true preference for trading off tax revenue and other regulatory impositions for the jobs and the economic development the state expects incoming capital investments to provide.[104] Indeed, Barry Weingast maintains that the limitation of public power by virtue of component unit regulation of the economy and the (constitutionally enforced) mobility of the objects of economic regulation are key elements of the 'market preserving federalism' that has sustained economic growth in the West.[105] And yet, others find it is hard to see the value in moving a fixed number of jobs from Seattle to Chicago, as happened in the case of Boeing, in exchange for state and local tax breaks.[106] One component jurisdiction gains at the expense of another, while the federal system as a whole has lost public revenue and compromised its power of regulation.

[100] Tiebout (n 75).

[101] *Steward Machine Company v Davis* 301 US 548 (1937). Most policies, however, have (re)distributive effects, which makes the category of redistributive policies that should be shifted to the central level of government difficult to assess in the abstract.

[102] See eg Paul E. Peterson, *The Price of Federalism* (1995), 27–30, 108–28.

[103] See eg John D. Donahue, *Disunited States* (1997).

[104] Richard Revesz, 'Rehabilitating Interstate Competition: Rethinking The "Race-To-The-Bottom" Rationale For Federal Environmental Regulation' (1992) 67 *NYU Law Review* 1210.

[105] Barry R. Weingast, 'The Economic Role of Political Institutions: Market-Preserving Federalism and Economic Development' (1995) 11 *Journal of Law, Economics, & Organization* 1.

[106] Bednar (n 6), 37.

Whether this is a good or bad outcome mostly depends on one's theory of public choice and whether democratic government is seen as benign or malign. If one has reason to believe that democratic government is merely a self-interested affair by those in power, the analogy between jurisdictional competition and competition among widget manufacturers makes a good deal of sense. In that case, we should applaud the loss of regulatory and taxing power that federalism occasions. If, on the other hand, one has reason to believe that government policies reflect some broader common good, then we might be more worried about certain forms of inter-jurisdictional competition. On the benign view of democracy, allowing the central government (ie, a monopoly jurisdiction or at least one with what economists would call 'market power') to extract supra-competitive 'rents' from industry is not, in principle, objectionable. It all depends on the uses to which the government puts its gains from trade.

Even from a component state's perspective, it can often be vexingly difficult to sort through whether any particular limitation of public power through regulatory competition is ultimately beneficial or harmful. Put another way, it's hard to tell whether the race is to the bottom or the top. As Fritz Scharpf has explained in discussing the European Union, to understand whether a race is benign or malign, we must attend to a host of factors that affect local regulatory capacity as well as those that affect central regulatory capacity.[107] These can range from formal legal authority and institutional voting rules to whether regulatory standards are embedded in goods or services and the extent to which signaling can mobilize market actors who reward quality. Which way a race tends to run can therefore be judged only by looking at the particular dynamics of the sector in question.

Perhaps the only general conclusion we can draw is the following rather obvious principle. Call it the 'federal conservation of powers principle': unless a loss of component state authority is made up for by a gain in authority at the center, federalism institutionalizes a bias in favor of deregulation. And whether that bias is good or bad depends (once again) not on federalism, but on one's theory of democracy, regulation, and the market.

(c) Intra-Jurisdictional Difficulties

The final reason for moving politics from constituent units to the center is a failure of the political process within the component units of governance. Call this an 'intra-jurisdictional difficulty'. This reason is entirely absent from Wallace Oates's famous theorem on decentralization. Perhaps as a result, it receives less attention in the public choice literature on federalism even though this reason figured prominently in the Framers' argument.

An intra-jurisdictional difficulty focuses on the political process of a given jurisdiction. But it is not concerned with the failure to consider costs and benefits external to that jurisdiction. Instead, an intra-jurisdictional difficulty is the failure of the political process at the local level to take into account and respond properly to interests that are internal to the local jurisdiction itself. Even when the costs of failure are borne entirely by locally affected parties, shifting politics to the center can help to make politics—in particular, democratic politics—better.

This was Madison's well-known argument in Federalist 10. In small jurisdictions, representatives may win elections by 'vicious arts', become 'unduly attached' to local interests, and be swayed by a 'fe[w] distinct parties and interests' forming relatively consistent majorities.[108] All this, Madison argued, leads to the oppression of minorities. His answer was to enlarge the republic:

[107] Fritz Scharpf, *Governing in Europe: Effective and Democratic?* (1999), 84–120.

[108] James Madison, 'The Federalist No 10' in Cooke (n 15), 56, 61.

> Extend the sphere, and you take in a greater variety of parties and interests; you make it less probable that a majority of the whole will have a common motive to invade the rights of the other citizens; or if such a common motive exists, it will be more difficult for all who feel it to discover their own strength, and to act in unison with each other.[109]

In addition, 'where there is consciousness of unjust or dishonorable purposes, communication is always checked by distrust, in proportion to the number whose concurrence is necessary.'[110] Madison's idea, then, was safety in numbers. As for central power in a federation, this meant 'that the same advantage . . . in controlling the effects of faction . . . enjoyed by a large over a small republic . . . is enjoyed by the Union over the States composing it.'[111]

We see responses to such intra-jurisdictional difficulties in a variety of federal settings. Federal systems often protect certain basic rights at the central level of government—especially when fearing an invasion of rights by factions that form local majorities but remain national minorities. A classic response is, for example, the combination of the Bankruptcy Clause and the Contracts Clause in the US Constitution. Taken together, these provisions protected creditors against local levelers while lodging politics over debt relief squarely with the central government. The post-Civil War provisions granting Congress the power to protect civil rights were similarly enacted out of mistrust of state politics—in that case on matters of race. Indeed, state political dysfunction on race continued for so long in the United States that William Riker concluded his comparative study of federalism with the scathing lines: 'If in the United States one disapproves of racism, one should disapprove of federalism.'[112]

More generally, scholars of democratization have cautioned that decentralized power abets the persistence of subnational authoritarian practices, and complicates efforts to deepen democracy in federations that have made the formal transition to democracy at the federal level.[113] Perhaps the most dramatic provisions intended to protect against this kind of failure of local politics are those guaranteeing the republican or democratic character of constituent state governments. Rarely used in most federations, it can, however, be a powerful weapon of centralization in the hands of some. For example, a transplant of the Guarantee Clause has enabled the federal government of Argentina to take over state government functions repeatedly and for extended periods of time.[114]

3. Subsidiarity Redux: Instrumental or Intrinsic?

Recall the basic federal power principle: the center will assist the constituent units of government (only) in case of need and help to coordinate their activities with the rest of society with a view to the common good. Subsidiarity may be used, as it was in the Randolph plan, to sort out the distribution of powers when founding a federation. But no constituent assembly can specify with precision all the powers of the various levels of government necessary to sustain a functioning compound polity. And unless a polity governs by frequent constitutional revisions or

[109] Ibid 62.

[110] Ibid.

[111] Ibid.

[112] Riker (n 4), 155.

[113] See eg Edward L. Gibson, 'Boundary Control: Subnational Authoritarianism in Democratic Countries' (2005) 58 *World Politics* 101. Others argue that party system dynamics, rather than federal institutions, play a causal role in the persistence of authoritarian enclaves. See eg Alberto Diaz-Cayeros, 'Do Federal Institutions Matter? Rules and Political Practices in Regional Resource Allocation in Mexico' in Gibson (n 87).

[114] Gibson, 'Boundary Control' (n 113), 102.

referenda (as, say, in Switzerland), the various actors (including courts) must make due with interpreting existing power provisions to fit the problems of the day. This is where subsidiarity enters the life of the federation as an operative principle of constitutional law.

But subsidiarity is easier said than applied. How do we assess 'need' or 'the common good?' How do we decide (to use the Randolph formula) when component states are 'incompetent' or when the harmony of the union risks being 'interrupted'? Unpacking the federal power principle into its component claims in favor of local and central authority, as we have just done, provides a much better grasp on the structure of the various arguments hidden in the sleek opening formula. But it does not yet fill these arguments with content. That is because subsidiarity contains a further difficulty.

In addition to the complex empirical judgments involved in some of the arguments in favor of local or central authority, many of these arguments will raise questions of first principle that cannot be resolved absent politics. Take the rather simple sounding idea of externalities. How do we know when they should matter?[115] Every policy affects interests beyond its jurisdictional boundaries even if only because outsiders who know about the policy do not like it. Slavery in the American South had tangible economic effects in the North and elsewhere. It also offended the moral sensibilities of many northern Unionists. Capital punishment in Poland most likely would have a negligible economic impact outside its borders. It is restricted today as a condition of membership in the European Union because it offends stated European values. Gay marriage, physician-assisted suicide, and the use of medical marijuana have all made it onto the national agenda of politics in the United States in large part due to ideological objections voiced outside the jurisdictions in which these policies were instituted. Are such ideological externalities bona fide externalities? The Millean harm principle is of little help here, as it does not come with ready-made content.[116] After all, one jurisdiction's externality may be another's autonomy.

What is often overlooked is that this basic question bedevils most arguments in favor of central (or local) authority. Consider the simple case of transactions costs. They are worth reducing only, of course, if we have agreed on the goal we are trying to pursue. Otherwise, high transactions costs may indeed be a welcome safeguard against policies we dislike. Intra-jurisdictional difficulties, too, create harm only to the extent that we view the particular form of intra-jurisdictional politics we are trying to cure as problematic. When African-Americans are excluded from the franchise, the answer is easy. But whether felon disenfranchisement at the component state level compromises the local democratic process already generates little agreement in the United States.[117] Although we may be able to reason our way from universally accepted principles to a few conclusions, we will often need politics to get there. What Robert Dahl observed with regard to the question of how to determine the proper boundaries of a democratic polity applies with equal force here: 'Democratic ideas . . . do not yield a definitive answer. They presuppose that one has been somehow been supplied, by history and politics.'[118]

In trying to apply the federal power principle to concrete cases, it can therefore be useful to distinguish between two kinds of arguments. The first are instrumental arguments, which presuppose agreement on the goal or interest to be achieved. These arguments debate only which level of government will best get us there. The second kind are intrinsic arguments, which

[115] See Don Herzog, 'Externalities and Other Parasites' (2000) 67 *University of Chicago Law Review* 895.

[116] John Stuart Mill, *On Liberty* (1859) (Elizabeth Rappaport ed, 1978), 9.

[117] Cf Laurence H. Tribe, 'The Puzzling Persistence of Process-Based Constitutional Theories' (1980) 89 *Yale Law Journal* 1063.

[118] Robert A. Dahl, *Democracy and Its Critics* (1989), 209.

debate the very goals and interests. These arguments ask which level of government has the better claim to determine the goals and interests in the first place. This difference between instrumental and intrinsic arguments of federalism can often be confusing. And both kinds of argument can be in play at the same time. And yet, when applying subsidiarity, especially (but not only) in judicial settings, it can be useful to tease out which of these arguments is at stake.[119]

Take, for example, the European Union's subsidiarity clause, which sets forth an exclusively instrumental version of subsidiarity:

> Under the principle of subsidiarity...the Union shall act only if and in so far as the objectives of the proposed action cannot be sufficiently achieved by the Member States, either at central level or at regional and local level, but can rather, by reason of the scale or effects of the proposed action, be better achieved at Union level.[120]

This provision assumes that the Union has the authority to decide upon the goals of a given action by virtue of an enumerated power spelled out elsewhere in the treaty. Article 5 adds that the Union must now consider whether the member states can achieve this Union-determined goal equally well on their own. For example, in enacting a European-wide deposit guarantee scheme, the Union was to have considered whether exercising its legislative power under then Article 57 of the EC Treaty was necessary to achieve the goal of protecting depositors against loss.[121] The prior question whether the Union should have power to set goals in the area of financial services regulation had already been made by then-Article 57 EC. It may not be very hard in this case to decide that inter-jurisdictional difficulties would require Union legislation once the decision is taken that a baseline of deposit protection is needed throughout the Union. And so, applying subsidiarity might well be rather easy here.

Consider, by contrast, Canada's Peace Order and Good Government (POGG) Clause, which contains both substantive and instrumental elements of subsidiarity:

> It shall be lawful for the Queen, by and with the Advice and Consent of the Senate and House of Commons, to make Laws for the Peace, Order, and good Government of Canada, in relation to all Matters not coming within the Classes of Subjects by this Act assigned exclusively to the Legislatures of the Provinces.[122]

This residual clause in favor of central power is paired with a competing residual clause in favor of exclusive provincial power: 'In each Province the Legislature may exclusively make Laws in relation to...[g]enerally all Matters of a merely local or private Nature in the Province.'[123] In applying these clauses, we must ask not only which level of government can better achieve a set goal. We must also determine which level of government should have the power to set a particular policy goal in the first place.

A jumbled mix of unstated subsidiarity considerations seems to animate a host of judicial decisions interpreting various enumerations of powers. Nowhere has this been more apparent than in the United States. Here, the exceptional difficulty in amending the constitution has created tremendous hydraulic pressure on interpretation. And so, important shifts in interpretation are often accompanied by an implicit return to the federal power principle that animated the distribution of power among the federal government and the states in the first place. Justice Holmes's landmark decision upholding federal power to make a treaty protecting

[119] For further discussion of this idea, see Daniel Halberstam, 'Comparative Federalism and the Issue of Commandeering' in Kalypso Nicolaidis and Robert Howse (eds), The *Federal Vision* (2001).

[120] Treaty on European Union, Art 5.

[121] Case C-233/94 *Germany v Parliament and Council* [1997] ECR I-2405, paras 22–8.

[122] Constitution Act, 1982, s 91.

[123] Ibid s 92(16).

migratory birds, for example, appealed to subsidiarity by pointing out that 'the States individually are incompetent to act' and noting that the treaty furthered 'a national interest of very nearly the first magnitude... [that] can be protected only by national action in concert with that of another power.'[124] Justice Cardozo's opinion in *Steward Machine Company* upheld a national unemployment tax as necessary because states had 'held back through alarm lest in laying such a toll upon their industries, they would place themselves in a position of economic disadvantage as compared with neighbors or competitors.'[125] And Justice Stone noted for the Court in *United States v Darby* that 'interstate commerce should not be made the instrument of competition in the distribution of goods produced under substandard labor conditions, which competition is injurious to the commerce and to the state from and to which the commerce flows.'[126] More recently, Justice Stevens in *Gonzales v Raich* upheld federal preemption of California's medical marijuana laws as necessary to regulate (ie, suppress) the nationwide market in the drug.[127] Conversely, the Court struck down several pieces of federal legislation not because of a lack of connection to interstate commerce, but because the kind of connection to interstate commerce present in those cases would have allowed the federal government to regulate family law, education, and violent crime.[128] Many of these subsidiarity questions turn on conceptually simple but empirically complex questions about instrumental rationality. But other subsidiarity decisions turn on substantive claims about national interests and local prerogatives that cannot be solved absent moral argumentation and political contest. Recognizing (and acknowledging) which of these are at stake would allow courts, in particular, to understand better their own powers and limitations in sorting out the various claims.

V. Sustaining Federalism

Scholars have pointed out that the relation between federalism and democratic governance is far more complicated than the happy story of normative theory would suggest. Subsidiarity and high-minded normative theories of federalism are not enough to control the political avarice that can make federalism fail. Courts can help,[129] but they are only a (small) part of the story. A sustainable federation needs a system of institutions that can channel the ambitions of powerful actors to the benefit of the federation and its citizens. The point is as old and as simple as Madison's classic caution in the *Federalist Papers* that we will not be governed by angels, or even enlightened statesmen. As we might put it here (only somewhat tongue in cheek), politicians are not inherently apt to act with subsidiarity in mind. Madison's conclusion was clear: 'Ambition must be made to counteract ambition. The interest of the man must be connected with the constitutional rights of the place.'[130]

1. Incentive-Compatible Federalism

In the language of modern political science, federalism must be embedded in an 'incentive compatible' system that gives actors concrete political incentives to put their energies to

[124] *Missouri v Holland* 252 US 416, 433, 435 (1920).
[125] 301 US at 588.
[126] 312 US 100, 115 (1941).
[127] 545 US 1 (2005).
[128] *See United States v Lopez* 514 US 549 (1995) and *United States v Morrison* 529 US 598 (2000).
[129] See generally Halberstam (n 32).
[130] James Madison, 'The Federalist No 51', in Cooke (n 15), 349.

productive uses. To move beyond mere 'parchment barriers', federalism—along with any other constitutional arrangement—must channel political ambition to create a 'self-enforcing' system.[131] This involves politicians as well as all other actors within the system. As Rui de Figueiredo and Barry Weingast succinctly put it 'The general problem concerns how to structure the political game so that all the players—elected officials, the military, economic actors, and citizens—have incentives to respect the rules.'[132]

This is no easy task. Jenna Bednar, for example, has demonstrated that any one institutional arrangement for punishing what she terms shirking, encroachment, or burden-shifting in a federation is not enough.[133] A federation needs structural, popular, political, and judicial safeguards, each providing a different 'trigger mechanis[m]' to punish aberrant actors.[134] Safeguards must cover all the different kinds of transgressions, complement each other in the nature of the punishment they offer, and be a sufficiently redundant check for mistakes.[135] If we add to Bednar's theory an understanding that what counts as a transgression is itself the subject of intense debate, the matter becomes even more complicated. Other authors therefore push for a greater reliance on less structured 'populist safeguards of federalism'.[136]

2. The Role of Political Parties

The key challenge of designing a federal system seems to require giving political elites incentives to consider the interests of the federation as a whole. In this vein, Riker long ago stressed the significance of the political party system for the creation of vertical links across jurisdictions.[137] Such links may push uncomfortably toward unification as in the case of US Senators who, at times, controlled the fortunes of local politicians.[138] And yet, they may also reign in the central government when central government politicians must rely on the support of the local machine for their electoral success, as Larry Kramer has shown.[139] Jonathan Rodden has similarly pointed out how incentives of local politicians to act in the interests of the national party can be highly beneficial for the stability and efficiency of the union as a whole. Contrasting fiscal responsibility of political subunits in Germany and Australia with the fiscal profligacy on the part of constituent states in Brazil, he writes:

> German state officials, like those of Australia are embedded in a highly integrated national party system that shapes their career prospects. Protecting the value of a national party label

[131] See eg Rui J.P. de Figueiredo, Jr and Barry R. Weingast, 'Self-Enforcing Federalism' (2005) 21 *Journal of Law, Economics, & Organization* 103. Cf Filippov et al (n 30), 145 (defining an incentive-compatible institution). For discussions in legal scholarship, see Daryl J. Levinson, 'Parchment and Politics: The Positive Puzzle of Constitutional Commitment' (2011) *Harvard Law Review* 657; Ernest A. Young, 'Making Federalism Doctrine: Fidelity, Institutional Competence, and Compensating Adjustments' (2004) 46 *William and Mary Law Review* 1733; Mark Tushnet, *Taking the Constitution Away From the Courts* (1999), 123–6.

[132] Ibid.

[133] Bednar (n 6), 9.

[134] Ibid.

[135] See eg ibid 215–17.

[136] See Robert A. Mikos, 'The Populist Safeguards of Federalism' (2007) *Ohio State Law Journal* 1669; Larry D. Kramer, *The People Themselves Popular Constitutionalism and Judicial Review* (2004).

[137] Riker (n 4), 91–101. On political parties see further Chapter 41.

[138] William H. Riker, 'The Senate and American Federalism' (1955) 49 *American Political Science Review* 452.

[139] Larry D. Kramer, 'Putting the Politics Back into the Political Safeguards of Federalism' (2000) 100 *Columbia Law Review* 215; Larry D. Kramer, 'Understanding Federalism' (1991) 47 *Vanderbilt Law Review* 1485.

is generally not a priority for state-level officials in Brazil, providing few electoral incentives to avoid debt and bailout demands.[140]

Similarly, if local politicians had no realistic aspirations to higher office, the logic of collective action would suggest that few local jurisdictions would run costly policy experiments for the benefit of all.[141]

For politicians, then, this often means acting against the best interests of their most immediate electorate. As Mikhail Fillipov, Peter Ordeshook, and Olga Shvetsova put it, an important element of creating a self-sustaining federation is to make political elites '*imperfect agents* of those they represent and to motivate citizens to reward such imperfection'.[142] The most consistent finding in this regard is that an integrated party system must tie politicians not only to their immediate electorate, but to the political system (and hence the electorate) of the system as a whole. Voters, in turn, can similarly be drawn into this incentive structure if parties and party labels are effective at both national and regional levels of governance at once.[143]

VI. Does Federalism Deliver?

Does all this work? There are, of course, innumerable ways to ask this question. In the following, however, we shall concentrate on only two concrete considerations: policy stability and polity stability.

1. Policy Stability

One of the most persistent critiques in the literature stems from the understanding that federalism in one form or another constrains the central government and, thereby, the central (or, better, the general) body politic.[144] Given that powers in a federation are, in one way or another, distributed or shared among the central and component governments, the central government in a federation has more limited powers as compared to the government of a unitary state. With the exception of Venezuela,[145] the central legislature in a federation depends to varying degrees on the concurrence between a lower house and an upper chamber representing geographic units or component governments. This upper chamber, in turn, departs—again to varying degrees—from the principle of equal representation of citizens in favor of the principle of equal representation of territorial units. As a result, politics at the center do not reflect the equality of each individual's voice in the way that democratic theory often seems to demand. Indeed, in some federal systems, such as Brazil and the European Union, even the composition of the lower chamber departs significantly from the strict principle of equality of

[140] Jonathan A. Rodden, *Hamilton's Paradox: The Promise and Peril of Fiscal Federalism* (2006), 274.

[141] For an argument that subunit politicians have an insufficient incentive to take on the costs of a risky policy experiment, see Susan Rose-Ackerman, 'Risk Taking and Re-Election: Does Federalism Promote Innovation?' (1980) 9 *Journal of Legal Studies* 593. But see eg Roderick M. Hills, Jr, 'Federalism and Public Choice' in Daniel Farber and Anne Joseph O'Connell (eds), *Research Handbook on Public Choice and Public Law* (2010), 207, 222.

[142] Filippov et al (n 30), 40. See also eg ibid 169–76.

[143] See eg ibid 254.

[144] See Robert A. Dahl, 'Federalism and the Democratic Process' in J. Roland Pennock and John W. Chapman (eds), *NOMOS XXV: Liberal Democracy* (1983), 95.

[145] In 1999, Venezuela adopted a new constitution that abolished the Senate and instituted a unicameral legislature. See Penfold-Becerra (n 87), 217–19.

individuals in favor of boosting the representation of the smaller territorial component units of the federal system.[146] All these institutional features shape the decision-making at the central level of governance on matters ranging from ordinary legislation and the selection (and removal) of presidents, judges, and other officials to amending the constitutional framework itself.

(a) Demos-*Constraint and the Status Quo*

Alfred Stepan has called these institutional features of federalism '*demos* constraining'.[147] The principal observation regarding this constraint on the general *demos* has been that, as compared to a unitary state, the institutional structure of federalism creates a systematic policy bias in favor of the status quo. Concerns have focused in particular on the politics of redistribution. Recall that decentralization of redistributive decisions, say the provision of welfare, has the tendency to create a race to the bottom. Because subunits will fear becoming welfare magnets in the competition for mobile capital, each individual unit will have an interest in lowering welfare payments as compared to neighboring jurisdictions.[148] That is why in a federation redistributive measures should be moved to the central level of government. But as it turns out, here, too, redistributive policies face hurdles.

For instance, a broadly representative lower house with the backing of a popularly elected President may vote in favor of easing inequalities in wealth only to be foiled by a less broadly representative upper chamber upon whose consent the legislation also depends. Madison, of course, thought of federalism and bicameralism along with the separation of powers as just such bulwarks against the dangers of populism: 'a rage for paper money, for an abolition of debts, for an equal division of property, or for any other improper or wicked project, will be less apt to pervade the whole body of the Union, than a particular member of it.'[149] And, indeed, the phenomenon of federalism and bicameralism stalling redistributive reform[150] has replayed itself the world over. The status quo is maintained not by general preferences but by a 'structure-induced equilibrium', to use Kenneth Shepsle's term.[151] In the case of Brazil, for example, a small group of Senators representing only 9 percent of the population can block legislation, foiling broadly shared preferences to tackle economic inequality.[152] Comparative studies investigating this phenomenon across democratic systems have found a significant correlation between federalism and greater income inequality.[153]

[146] See Scott P. Mainwaring, *Rethinking Party Systems in the Third Wave of Democratization: The Case of Brazil* (1999); Jonathan Rodden, 'Strength in Numbers? Representation and Redistribution in the European Union' (2002) 3 *European Union Politics* 151. Malapportionment is, of course, not limited to federations. See eg David Samuels and Richard Snyder, 'The Value of a Vote: Malapportionment in Comparative Perspective' (2001) 31 *British Journal of Political Science* 651.

[147] Alfred Stepan, *Arguing Comparative Politics* (2001), 335–6.

[148] See Peterson (n 102), 1995.

[149] Madison (n 108), 65.

[150] Ian Shapiro, *The State of Democratic Theory* (2003), 109–10.

[151] Kenneth Shepsle, 'Institutional Arrangements and Equilibrium in Multidimentional Voting Models' (1979) 32 *American Journal of Political Science* 27. See also Kenneth Shepsle and Barry R. Weingast, 'Structure-Induced Equilibrium and Legislative Choice' (1981) 37 *Public Choice* 503.

[152] Stepan (n 147), 339. See also ibid 351.

[153] See eg Pablo Beramendi, 'Inequality and the Territorial Fragmentation of Solidarity' (2007) 61(4) *International Organization* 783; Vicki L. Birchfield and Markus M.L. Crepaz, 'The Impact of Constitutional Structures and Collective and Competitive Veto Points on Income Inequality in Industrialized Democracies' (1998) 34 *European Journal of Political Research* 175–200; Evelyne Huber, Charles Ragin, and John D. Stephens, 'Social Democracy, Christian Democracy, Constitutional Structure, and the Welfare State' (1993) 99 *American Journal of Sociology* 711.

To the extent we find an institutional bias against change at the center, however, it is not limited to the redistribution of wealth. Multiplying veto points favors the policy status quo across all political domains, including spending.[154] Structure-induced equilibria can limit the redistribution of wealth as well as new forms of central government regulation. Conversely, it can lead to overspending and overregulation by locking in spending and regulatory programs whenever change is subject to the agreement of multiple actors. Especially when change from the status quo depends on the concurrence of the federal government and the states, this can lead to the infamous 'joint decision trap'.[155]

One question that has largely eluded the federalism literature is the general normative evaluation of this dynamic in cases where it exists. Some amount of policy stability is, of course, necessary for people and economic actors to have projects, plans, and goals. At the same time, too much stability can perpetuate certain forms of domination. And so, as is often the case, much depends on ones normative priors to figure out how much policy stability is just right with regard to any given policy domain. Some scholars applaud federalism as a protective shield against overregulation and too much redistribution.[156] Others worry about a loss of regulatory power and the persistence or exacerbation of inequality of income.[157] As Daniel Treisman puts it, 'Entrenching the status quo may be desirable or undesirable, depending on what gets entrenched.'[158]

But there are far deeper problems with this picture about *demos*-constraint and the bias in favor of the status quo. First, it is not clear whether an authoritative *demos* constrained by federalism exists in any meaningful sense. Secondly, not all forms of federalism contain the same degree of bias in favor of the status quo. Indeed, some federal systems help to foster change and may even feature less of a status quo bias than unitary systems.

(b) *Which* Demos?

The assumption that a particular '*demos*' is being 'constrained' by the federal institutional architecture can be quite misleading. Take redistribution. The suggestion seems to be that the *demos* would have redistributed wealth in the absence of federalism. The people generally would have voted for redistribution, but the popular will is foiled by an unrepresentative upper chamber. Or so the argument goes. But we should not forget that the raw calculation of majority preferences within a given system does not necessarily indicate that an authoritative democratic will in favor of change is being foiled by a less authoritative democratic will blocking change. That would be giving in to the Schmittian fallacy.[159] After all, the political system under investigation may not (and, in an important sense, does not) exist in the absence of federalism and its 'constraining' political institutions.

The European Union, for example, might well be added to the roster of federations with an institutional bias against redistribution. And yet it would be odd to posit a pan-European *demos* that is being constrained in its desire to equalize wealth across Europe. Without the

[154] See generally Tsebelis (n 28).

[155] Fritz Scharpf, 'The Joint Decision Trap' (1988) 66 *Public Administration* 239.

[156] See Madison (n 108); Weingast (n 105).

[157] Scharpf (n 107); Stepan (n 147).

[158] See Daniel Treisman, *The Architecture of Government: Rethinking Political Decentralization* (2007), 208, 274.

[159] Recall that Carl Schmitt complained about Weimar parliamentarism as a constraint on the German *demos*, which he took to exist apart from the institutions of democratic governance. See eg Carl Schmitt, *Verfassungslehre* (1928), 235; Carl Schmitt, *Die Geistesgeschichtliche Lage des Heutigen Parlamentarismus* (5th edn, 1979).

Union, questions of redistribution between Germany and Greece, for example, would be discussed under the rubric of foreign aid. Income inequalities would be maintained all the same but no one would be talking about a stalled *demos*. In short, we should be careful not to use the idea of a '*demos*' as a mystical entity that we identify with only one or another of the institutions in a federation or with majority preferences and polls writ large. The positing of an actual '*demos*' that transcends the institutional architecture of the federation itself may be more imagined than real. In a federal system, the compound polity is all we ever have.

(c) What Constraint?

Federal systems need not increase constraints on policy action.[160] To be sure, bicameralism (along with the separation of powers) adds more veto points as compared to a unified parliamentary system. But just as not all unitary systems are created equal, not all institutional elements of federalism add barriers to change. Some may even counteract the status quo.

For example, Jonathan Rodden and Erik Wibbels have suggested that in terms of macroeconomic policy, the constraining effects of decentralization posited by Weingast and others are contingent on a host of features more specific than the brute fact of federalism itself.[161] Systems with weak national parties that rely on intergovernmental transfers, for example, tend to allow subunit politicians to compete among one another in ways that ultimately put pressure on the central government to run up the deficit. But where vertical party linkages exist and subunits have the capacity to, and are forced to, rely on their own revenue, subunit politicians seem to resist the temptation to spend beyond their means.

Important differences exist more generally in terms of federal architecture. Distinguish, for example, among three kinds of federal governing mechanisms. Call them 'joint rule', 'multiple rule', and 'separate rule'. 'Joint rule' is where the central government and the component states must both agree before making a change to the status quo. 'Multiple rule' is where both levels of government have the authority and resources to act on their own in the same policy area unless and until a conflict arises between two positively chosen policies. 'Separate rule' is the idea that each level separately governs mutually exclusive arenas of action. Multiple and separate rule line up closely with what are often called concurrent and exclusive powers (or competences).[162] But the idea of 'rule' as used here extends beyond the formal distribution of powers to include principles of preemption as well. A component state may, for example, enjoy concurrent powers with a central government over a given area but see its powers displaced as soon as the center acts. The idea of multiple rule presumes weaker preemption norms, favoring rule by multiple governments until more concrete conflicts develop. Multiple rule is also made stronger where a federation's upper house is independently elected, as in the United States today, as opposed to being composed of recallable emissaries of component state executives, as in Germany or the European Union.[163]

[160] See eg Treisman (n 158), 206.

[161] See Jonathan Rodden and Erik Wibbels, 'Beyond the Fiction of Federalism: Macroeconomic Management in Multitiered Systems' (2002) 54 *World Politics* 494; Erik Wibbels, *Federalism and the Market* (2005); Rodden (n 140).

[162] Although there is considerable overlap between the labels introduced in the text and the more traditional 'competitive', 'cooperative', and 'dual' federalism, the more traditional labels are often used without analytic precision. For example, it is often unclear whether 'cooperative' federalism (or the frequently invoked 'shared' rule) involves 'joint' or 'multiple' rule as used here. Also, the traditional labels characterize the general effect or character of federalism as opposed the specific underlying governance mechanism, which is important for our present discussion.

[163] See generally Halberstam (n 119), 213.

In areas of multiple rule, the institutions of federalism may counteract the status quo that results from policy inertia. This has been the central idea behind what is commonly called 'competitive federalism'.[164] When, for example, component states have the authority and capacity to make and implement policies on their own—subject only to central government preemption through positive law—states can prod the center into action. Component state officials (and political parties that form local majorities but national minorities) may adopt and implement policies as a way of competing with central government politicians and governing majorities for voters' affection. This adds an element of 'vertical competition' to governance in federal systems to the 'horizontal' competition among the component states.[165]

Multiple rule federalism can thereby push against the status quo especially where separation of powers and bicameralism have multiplied the number of veto players at the federal level of governance and slowed federal response to change. A slow federal government can now be moved to action by constituent state policies that irritate the federal system by altering the status quo. Even in such matters as foreign affairs, where the number of veto players at the national level is reduced by virtue of executive branch dominance, component states can push for change that would not otherwise occur. Component states can prod the center into action by engaging foreign governments and global corporations to bring pressure to bear on the central government to change, reconsider, or reaffirm through more deliberate action existing policies.[166]

Under multiple rule federalism, the multiplicity of actors at federal and component state levels does not create additional 'veto' points but instead adds more policy drivers. To be sure, at times component units thereby may impose what others will perceive to be negative externalities on other jurisdictions or actors within the system. For example, it is especially important in multiple rule settings to maintain fiscal responsibility for the actions that each level chooses to pursue. If the component level can take on financial obligations in the hopes of a central government bailout, for example, multiple rule can turn into a fiscal disaster.[167] But where bailout is not an option or component government officials are held partially accountable to the national electorate, multiple rule federalism becomes a viable option.[168]

Externalities created by multiple rule federalism can often be in the nature of a Socratic gadfly or beneficial irritant. Given sufficient mobilization and legal authority at the center, the center can always react by preempting, adopting, or even tolerating the individual state action. The multiplication of arenas for democratic decision-making and policy activity in such multiple rule federalism thus serves to create 'political disequilibria' that unsettle the status quo—especially one based on inaction.[169] Indeed, we can turn Shepsle's term on its head to suggest that multiple rule's political disequilibria are *structural disequilibria* because that the local median voter is unlikely to match up perfectly with the median voter of the system as a whole. To be sure, there are limits to this effect in that component units will still face the familiar fear of leading a charge in favor of redistribution or other costly investments in public goods.[170]

[164] See eg Geoffrey Brennan and James M. Buchanan, *The Power to Tax: Analytical Foundations of a Fiscal Constitution* (1980), 168–86.

[165] Albert Breton, *Competitive Governments: An Economic Theory of Politics and Public Finance* (1998), 184–90.

[166] See eg Halberstam (n 92).

[167] See eg Rodden (n 140).

[168] Ibid 270–5.

[169] Halberstam (n 86), 824.

[170] See Peterson (n 102); Shapiro (n 150), 109–10.

More generally, however, these political disequilibria can yield productive conflicts by forcing constructive engagement among the multiple authorities throughout the system.

2. Polity Stability

The greatest promise and challenge of federalism is to sustain the compound polity. This means preventing centripetal forces from collapsing the federal polity into a unitary entity, on the one hand, and centrifugal forces from exploding the polity into its separate parts, on the other. The first of these is the (sometimes bland) worry that federal systems will centralize authority over time. The second is the (often more acute) worry that federalism will exacerbate political cleavages that motivate secession, strife, and civil war. Incentive-compatible federalism seeks, of course, to address both.[171] Nonetheless, a separate debate has developed with respect to the management of divided societies, to which we shall turn briefly here.

(a) Fate Follows Formation?

Some scholars seek to derive lessons for the longevity of the Union from the history surrounding its formation. Leslie Goldstein, for instance, has suggested that federations 'formed in the crucible of revolt against imperial power will be more likely to have state resistance to central power'.[172] Such unions may be less stable than federations formed under other circumstances, as a comparison between the Dutch, American, Swiss, and European federations would seem to indicate. Friedman similarly suggests that unions 'precipitated by a war among its member states will be less likely to undergo overt member-state rejection of its authority'.[173] These explanations seem to draw on the political and cultural dispositions of actors whose self-understanding has been indelibly marked by the history of formation.[174]

A different kind of argument based on federal formation would be that a stable federation demands the continued presence of the original cause for union. For instance, federations formed to gain economies of scale in matters of military security may become unstable as the outside military threat (or opportunity) evaporates.[175] Riker, for example, maintained that the ejection of Singapore from the Federation of Malaysia was occasioned by the perception that Indonesia was no longer as threatening as it had once appeared.[176] Although Riker's specific argument regarding Malaysia has been discredited,[177] recent European experience may provide some support for a version of the more general suggestion. As calls for secession in Flanders, Walloon, Scotland, and the Basque region may indicate, separatist movements are likely to draw strength from the fact that the state from which they wish to secede is embedded in a larger union that would, in any event, provide security to everyone involved.

Arguments based on the continued presence of the causes for federation can seize upon other suggested causes of federation as well. In this vein, scholars have argued that where elite ideological commitment to federalism drove formation of the union, the loss of that commitment will imperil the longevity of the federation over time.[178] One could add to this other,

[171] See Section IV above.

[172] Leslie F. Goldstein, *Constituting Federal Sovereignty* (2001), 151.

[173] Ibid.

[174] A similar culturally based suggestion is that unions 'where obedience to the rule of law is more routinized in general will experience less resistance by member state officials to the rule of federation-level authorities.' Ibid.

[175] See Jonathan Lemco, *Political Stability in Federal Governments* (1991), 144.

[176] Riker (n 13), 30–1.

[177] See Burgess (n 40), 93.

[178] See Thomas M. Franck, *Why Federations Fail* (1968).

more speculative theories. For example, if Ziblatt is right that the choice between federation and unitary state depends on the supply side of constituent states' governance capacity, then the erosion of that capacity or the increased direct governance capacity of the center (as, say, in the United States) would allow for a renewed push for centralization.[179]

What's good for formation is good for dissolution—or so it seems. These theories look for the causes of endurance in the causes for federation. They posit a rather direct relationship between the purpose of federation and the endurance of a union. First-order reasons for federalism are translated into long-term cultural dispositions of all the actors of the system. Or first-order reasons for federalism drive the formation as well as the endurance of the union as actors continually re-evaluate whether those first-order reasons still apply. Either way, these views see federation as an outcome that actors independently choose based on their bird's eye perspective or historical experience of whether the values of federalism are (still) being served.

(b) Back to Politics

Incentive compatible federalism presumes, by contrast, that politicians are likely to act based on more immediate gain than on whether the values of federalism are ultimately served by their actions. For these theorists, the prescription to prevent secession and strife follows from the prescription for other areas: fuse the interests of individual actors with the interests of the polity as a whole. This means the maintenance of an integrated party system here, as well.

An integrated federal party system, however, does not spell consociationalism.[180] This point taps into a longstanding debate about whether federalism or consociationalism better promotes polity stability in divided societies.[181] The common argument against federalism is that territorially divided rule exacerbates regional separatism by giving institutional structure and governance capacity to destabilizing regional identities.[182] Scholars such as Lijphart present consociationalism as the cure. Others dismiss consociationalism as an independently workable solution. Pointing to the Netherlands, Israel, and Lebanon, for instance, Daniel Elazar has argued that consociationalism in the absence of territorialization, that is, without some form of federalism, is inherently unstable.[183] Some go one step further and reject the usefulness of consociationalism even as an element of federalism.[184] Based on the experience of Nigeria, Canada, and Malaysia, Donald Horowitz has argued that federalism lowers political stakes by diffusing decisions into multiple arenas, creates coalitions across ethnic divides within constituent states, and socializes citizens and politicians at the local level into conducting productive politics system-wide.[185] An important element in the latter calculus is that subnational federal units remain

[179] This is not Ziblatt's idea. It is a variant of an argument made by Justice Stevens in dissent in *Printz v United States* 521 US 898, 959 (Stevens J dissenting).

[180] Consociationalism brings together rival subgroups by including them in governing coalitions, granting the various groups mutual vetoes, ensuring proportional representation in elections, cabinets, civil service positions, and granting self-governance authority to segmented groups over such matters as education and culture. See Arend Lijphart, 'Consociation and Federation' (1979) 12 *Canadian Journal of Political Science* 499, 500.

[181] See Sujit Choudhry (ed), *Constitutional Design for Divided Societies: Integration or Accommodation* (2008).

[182] See Philip G. Roeder, 'Ethnofederalism and the Mismanagement of Conflicting Nationalisms' (2009) 19 *Regional and Federal Studies* 203, 217–19.

[183] Elazar (n 5), 23–4.

[184] Donald L. Horowitz, *A Democratic South Africa? Constitutional Engineering in a Divided Society* (1991), 221.

[185] Ibid 214–27. See also Treisman (n 158), 240–2.

heterogeneous even if they allow for a particular group to gain a majority in any given component state, and that an ethnic minority not be aggregated in a single state.[186]

An integrated party system may indeed help the federalism side of this debate. Dawn Brancati, for instance, has provided empirical support for the value to stability in divided societies of maintaining parties that operate beyond a single region.[187] As Sujit Choudhry points out, however, there are still many unanswered questions, from whether societies divided by language differ from those divided by religion to whether the management of natural resources located in a given region should occasion special rules.[188]

VII. Federalism All the Way?

How far can the model of federalism take us? The question has implications for liberal theory, public policy, and political practice writ large. Scholars have explored whether federalism can inform dispersing power further down within the constituent state or up into the realm of global governance. Although parts of this terrain are well trodden, it is a vast terrain that is still largely underexplored. Some quick thoughts will have to suffice here.

1. Federalism All the Way Down?

Federalism traditionally has focused on only two levels of government. And yet, some scholars have argued for recognizing the possibility of extending federalism further down into the state. From a normative perspective, this is consistent with a vision of liberal democratic federalism that sees 'the preservation of diverse, semi-autonomous forums' as allowing 'a citizen to become a member of several "issue publics", each responding to different aspects of a citizens interests or identities and each providing a manageable arena for individual political engagement.'[189]

There are three aspects to this potential extension of federalism, some obvious and others speculative. First, constitutional protections can be taken down to cities and regions, as they are, for example, in Brazil[190] and India.[191] In light of Tiebout's famous sorting hypothesis, running federalism down to cities is, of course, nothing fancy, but simply following first principles of basic theory. And yet, questions remain, such as whether all but the largest cities can engender sufficient loyalty to create effective political communities or whether they have sufficient capacity for governance to warrant hard constitutional autonomy guarantees.[192] Municipal autonomy may also backfire as it can weaken the component states and enable the center to gain more power than it otherwise could.[193]

[186] Henry Hale confirms the importance of dispersing a dominant ethnic group as a way of taming secessionist tendencies. See Henry Hale, 'Divided We Stand: Institutional Sources of Ethnofederal State Survival and Collapse' (2004) 56 *World Politics* 165. Even where the polity is not in immediate threat of breaking up, much is to be gained from drawing competitive election districts in the context of racially or ethnically polarized voting, see Ellen D. Katz, 'Reviving the Right to Vote' (2007) 68 *Ohio State Law Journal* 1163.

[187] Dawn Brancati, *Peace by Design: Managing Intrastate Conflict through Decentralization* (2009).

[188] See Sujit Choudhry, 'Federalism, Secession, and Devolution: From Classical to Post-Conflict Federalism' in Tom Ginsburg and Rosalind Dixon (eds), *Research Handbook on Comparative Constitutional Law* (2011).

[189] Halberstam (n 86), 823–4 (internal footnotes omitted).

[190] See Brazil Constitution, Arts 18 and 30.

[191] See India Constitution, Art 243B.

[192] For a sampling of some of these problems, see eg Jacob T. Levy, 'Federalism, Liberalism, and the Separation of Loyalties' (2007) 101(3) *American Political Science Review* 459.

[193] See J. Tyler Dickovick, 'Municipalization as Central Government Strategy: Central-Regional-Local Politics in Peru, Brazil, and South Africa' (2007) 37 *Publius* 1.

Secondly, we might recognize school districts, water districts, and other functionally defined jurisdictions as elements of federalism.[194] Heather Gerken would add such institutions as the jury as a domain for the exercise of circumscribed public power.[195] Here, too, normative federal theory fits these other forms of power dispersion quite naturally. And yet, the political phenomenon of functional federalism differs sufficiently from territorially based federalism to warrant some caution before drawing on more specific lessons gained from territorial federalism. For instance, territorial federalism draws its practical force from conducting a reasonably broad range of politics within any given jurisdiction. Single-issue districts, however, prevent the cross-issue tradeoffs and bargains that are essential to productive politics and peace throughout a (traditionally conceived) federal system.

Thirdly, following federalism all the way down suggests understanding many forms of private governance and perhaps even the autonomy rights of individuals as continuous with federal principles and federal design.[196] As a matter of constitutional practice, protected spheres of private governance may come in disguise. Some free speech doctrines, for example, show evidence of constitutionally protected self-governance rights of social institutions.[197] Political parties may be constitutionally protected, sometimes explicitly so.[198] The family, too, is a constitutionally protected institution of collective self-governance.[199] And even though traditional democratic theory tends to reject placing the individual on a continuum from small to large spheres of governance,[200] it is not entirely implausible to understand individual rights as constitutionally protected spheres of governance as well—especially where an individual makes decisions that affect others.

To be sure, the normative structure of federalism may quickly seem both empty and all-encompassing on this account. But that may not be the result of any mistake in applying federalism theory all the way down. It may, instead, reveal that federalism theory is just as thin and demands just as many off-stage substantive decisions when applied to the traditional realm of territorial federalism. Taking federalism all the way down to private governance, then, is quite possible. Its usefulness as an organizing concept just depends on what we seek to gain.

2. Federalism All the Way Up?

At least since Immanuel Kant's essay 'On Perpetual Peace',[201] liberal theory has toyed with the idea of world federation. More recently, an increase in the density and impact of global governance regimes has pushed the more general question to the fore: can federalism play a

[194] See Halberstam (n 86), 824.

[195] See Heather Gerken, 'Foreword: Federalism All the Way Down' (2010) 124 *Harvard Law Review* 6, 28–33.

[196] Many, of course, will not take federalism this far down See eg Gerken (n 195); Richard Schragger, 'Federalism All The Way Down', September 23, 2009, at <http://www.constitution2020.org/node/87>.

[197] See eg Robert Post, 'Informed Consent to Abortion: A First Amendment Analysis of Compelled Physician Speech' (2007) 12 *University of Illinois Law Review* 939; Daniel Halberstam, 'Commercial Speech, Professional Speech and the Constitutional Status of Social Institutions' (1999) 147 *University of Pennsylvania Law Review* 771.

[198] See Richard H. Pildes, 'Political Parties and Constitutionalism' in Tom Ginsburg and Rosalind Dixon (eds), *Comparative Constitutional Law* (2011), 254.

[199] See Roderick M. Hills, Jr, 'The Constitutional Rights of Private Governments' (2003) 78 *NYU Law Review* 144.

[200] See eg Dahl (n 118), 205.

[201] Immanuel Kant, 'Perpetual Peace: A Philosophical Sketch' in Hans S. Reiss (ed), *Kant: Political Writings* (2nd edn, 1991), 93.

useful role in how we should understand the relationship between global and domestic levels of governance?

Modern constitutional enthusiasts from Hans Kelsen to David Held have argued for global, hierarchically organized, multilevel rule.[202] These scholars and their fellow global travelers have tapped into certain conceptual and functional continuities between constitutional orders within and beyond the state.[203] One way or another, such cosmopolitan constitutionalists draw on functional and normative theories to suggest that the global level of governance is but another central authority to which the state—even the federal state—is now local.

Then there are the skeptics. In particular, a new group of sovereigntists insists on grounding all claims of legality in the constitutions of independent states.[204] This group of scholars denies any real claim of authority to international law. International law is presented as what emerges when states act based on self-interest. On this view, as Posner and Goldsmith put it, international law is '*endogenous* to state interests'.[205] International law may purport to prescribe particular conduct for a given state. But a state need not and will not follow that prescription unless it matches the state's independent rational calculus of self-interest. This is not offered as a general theory of law according to which no law has normative pull beyond that which matches self-interest or an independent moral evaluation. Instead, it is offered as a distinction between a state's domestic legal system, which has normative pull, and the realm of international law, which does not.

A third way to mine the continuities between federalism and global governance is to reimagine the role of constitutional law both within and beyond the (federal) state. This approach rejects the view that constitutional law is synonymous with a hierarchically ordered legal system. Instead, it recognizes that constitutional law can lead to a multiplicity of claims of authority without a single, final, legal authority, or to what Neil MacCormick first dubbed the idea of 'constitutional pluralism'.[206]

The pluralist approach opens up new vistas. As various writers forging this tradition have shown,[207] we can learn a good deal about global governance and perhaps even understand domestic constitutionalism better when considering that constitutionalism does not spell universal hierarchy and settlement. To be sure, there are grand discontinuities between federalism and global governance. Even if we agree that some form of international community exists, it stretches the imagination to think of the global community as a compound polity. And yet, for federalism, the idea of pluralism and the unsettled nature of legal authority among different levels of governance is a coming home of sorts. After all, the Federalists created a new

[202] See eg Jürgen Habermas, *The Divided West* (2006), 115; David Held, *Democracy and The Global Order* (1995); Hans Kelsen, *Reine Rechtslehre* (1934), 129–54; Hermann Mosler, 'The International Society as a Legal Community' (1974) 140 *Recueil des Cours* 11; Thomas Pogge, 'Cosmopolitanism and Sovereignty' (1992) 103 *Ethics* 48; Christian Tomuschat, 'International Law: Ensuring the Survival of Mankind on the Eve of A New Century' (1999) 281 *Recueil des Cours* 9.

[203] See eg Bardo Fassbender, 'The United Nations Charter as Constitution of the International Community' (1998) 36 *Columbia Journal of Transnational Law* 529; Ernst-Ulrich Petersmann, 'The WTO Constitution and Human Rights' (2000) 3 *Journal of International Economic Law* 19.

[204] See Peter J. Spiro, 'The New Sovereigntists' (2000) 79 *Foreign Affairs* 9.

[205] Jack L. Goldsmith and Eric A. Posner, *The Limits of International Law* (2005), 13.

[206] Neil MacCormick, *Questioning Sovereignty* (1999), 104.

[207] See eg Daniel Halberstam, 'Local, Global, and Plural Constitutionalism' in de Búrca and Weiler (n 11); Mattias Kumm, 'Democratic Constitutionalism Encounters International Law: Terms of Engagement' in Sujit Choudhry (ed), *The Migration of Constitutional Ideas* (2006), 256; Miguel P. Maduro, 'Contrapunctual Law' in Neil Walker (ed), *Sovereignty in Transition* (2003), 501; Neil Walker, 'The Idea of Constitutional Pluralism' (2002) 65(3) *Modern Law Review* 317.

hybrid that mixed international and domestic forms of governance. And they created a hybrid that sought to complicate the question of final authority beyond what was conceived of as possible at the time.

VIII. Conclusion

'The twentieth Century', Proudhon predicted, 'will open the age of federations, or else humanity will undergo another purgatory of a thousand years.'[208] How the destruction wrought in the twentieth century compares to purgatory is anyone's guess, but the age of federations has certainly come. Federalism as a normative ideal has captured the imagination of political theory, and federalism as a concrete institutional arrangement has proven useful and reasonably enduring around the world. So much so that the world seems headed for more federalism and more federation, not less. This chapter has provided a framework for how we should approach this development as a matter of theory, policy, and law.

Having sorted through competing definitions of federalism, and placed the endeavor of conceptual classification of federations and their historical origins into critical perspective, this chapter turned to articulating a succinct general normative theory of federalism. By elaborating on the idea of subsidiarity, termed here the 'federal power principle', the chapter teased out the various arguments in favor of local and central rule. Arguing in favor of the local under minimal conditions of diversity, we find familiar claims of greater democratic voice, solidarity, expertise, and risk management. Arguments in favor of central power can be usefully grouped into the three categories of cost savings, inter-jurisdictional difficulties, and intra-jurisdictional difficulties.

The succinct general theory allows us to see that there are two fundamentally distinct aspects of the federal power principle—the first regarding instrumental claims to rule and the second regarding intrinsic claims to rule. This, in turn, allows us better to understand political and judicial practice. It shows, for example, that in some jurisdictions, such as the United States, courts argue over subsidiarity without quite knowing it. And it shows that others—indeed most—fail to distinguish adequately between instrumental and intrinsic arguments. We may indeed need distinct procedures and forms of review to evaluate the various claims depending on which value of federalism we are intending to protect or which kind of claim a given actor intends to advance.

In practice, federalism has always been far more messy and dangerous than normative theory would suggest. At the same time, however, there seem to be basic answers within federalism to the two principal worries: policy stability and polity stability. Regarding the first, we have seen that federalism need not contain a pervasive structural bias in favor of the status quo. In contrast to 'joint rule' or 'separate rule' federalism, 'multiple rule' federalism may even lead to structure induced 'political disequilibria' that can be useful in unsettling an ill-considered or under-considered status quo. Regarding polity stability, the literature seems to suggest that an integrated party system can help to mitigate the centrifugal forces of accommodation so as to allow federalism to reap the best of both worlds of the proverbial unity and diversity of a federation.

The chapter concludes by suggesting that federalism might well go all the way from private to global governance, depending on the purpose for which we employ the model. Comparative studies of political incentives across a more strictly defined set of 'federations' may well yield

[208] Pierre-Joseph Proudhon, *The Principle of Federation* (Richard Vernon trans, 1979), 68–9.

certain insights that cannot be translated sensibly to a broader context. And yet, many structural principles of federalism seem to apply to a pluralist conception of multilevel governance from the global level all the way down. The anticipated discomfort that such a move may engender would not be new. After all, federalism shattered preconceived notions of hierarchy and settlement from the very start.

Bibliography

Jenna Bednar, *The Robust Federation* (2009)

Michael Burgess, *Comparative Federalism: Theory and Practice* (2006)

Sujit Choudhry and Nathan Hume, 'Federalism, Secession & Devolution: From Classical to Post Conflict Federalism' in Tom Ginsburg and Rosalind Dixon (eds), *Research Handbook on Comparative Constitutional Law* (2011)

Daniel Elazar, *Exploring Federalism* (1987)

Michael Filippov, Peter Ordeshook, and Olga Shvetsova, *Designing Federalism: A Theory of Self-Sustainable Federal Institutions* (2004)

Jürgen Habermas, 'Does the Constitutionalization of International Law Still Have a Chance' in *The Divided West* (2006)

Daniel Halberstam, 'Of Power and Responsibility: The Political Morality of Federal Systems' (2004) 90 *Virginia Law Review* 731

Roderick M. Hills, Jr., 'The Constitutional Rights of Private Governments' (2003) 78 *NYU Law Review* 144

Kalypso Nicolaidis and Robert Howse, *The Federal Vision: Legitimacy and Levels of Government in the United States and the European Union* (2001)

Wallace E. Oates, *Fiscal Federalism* (1972)

Paul E. Peterson, *The Price of Federalism* (1995)

William H. Riker, 'Federalism' in Fred Greenstein and Nelson Polsby (eds), 5 *Handbook of Political Science: Government Institutions and Processes* (1975)

Jonathan A. Rodden, *Hamilton's Paradox: The Promise and Peril of Fiscal Federalism* (2006)

Fritz W. Scharpf, 'The Joint-Decision Trap. Lessons From German Federalism and European Integration' (1988) 66(2) *Public Administration* 239

Robert Schütze, *From Dual to Cooperative Federalism: The Changing Structure of European Law* (2009)

Alfred Stepan, *Arguing Comparative Politics* (2001), 315

Charles M. Tiebout, 'A Pure Theory of Local Expenditures' (1956) 64 *Journal of Political Economy* 416

Daniel Treisman, *The Architecture of Government: Rethinking Political Decentralization* (2007)

CHAPTER 28

INTERNAL ORDERING IN THE UNITARY STATE

SERGIO BARTOLE

Trieste

I. Different Meanings of the Word 'State'

The word 'state' (as well as similar words in other languages: the German 'Staat', the French 'État', the Italian 'Stato', etc) has many meanings even in the legal language, which is generally technically accurate and unambiguous. As such, it allows for frequent misunderstandings. An important distinction of meaning deserves underlining in view of the focus of this chapter. On the one hand, the word 'state' is frequently used to refer to the free and independent association of a people in a territory under an organized and stable authority. On the other hand, however, the word 'state' can often be reserved to the central branches of that authority. In this latter case, the state is but one of the institutions which exercises public functions within the territory in question, coexisting with other organized entities which have their own designated responsibility for certain territorial or subject-limited areas. These other entities can be independent of the central state, and their governing bodies may either be directly elected by the people living in the territory concerned (or affected by the subject in question), or they may be branches of the central authorities which directly appoint their leadership and control their activity.

The distinction is evident in many European constitutions. According to Article 20 of the German Constitution, the Federal Republic of Germany is defined as 'a democratic and social federal state', and 'all state authority is derived from the people'. In this case, the state includes both the central organization of the power and the *Länder*, the member entities of the federal Republic. On the other hand, however, in Article 7, *state* and *Länder* are clearly distinguished: 'the entire school system shall be under the supervision of the state...private schools that serve as alternatives to state schools shall require the approval of the State and shall be subject to the laws of the Laender.' To take another example, Article 1 of the Belgian Constitution states that 'Belgium is a Federal State constituted of Communities and Regions', but Article 170 clearly separates 'taxes to the benefit of the State' and 'taxes to the benefit of Communities or Regions'.

This linguistic inconsistency is also present in the constitutions of states which are not organized along federal lines. On the basis of Article 1 of the Romanian Constitution, the Romanian state 'is a sovereign, unitary and indivisible National State'. This provision clearly refers to the overall organization of the Romanian people within its territory, but then Article 137 makes separate mention of 'the State budget...and the local budgets of communes, towns and counties'. This also occurs in the Irish Constitution, which refers to Ireland as a 'sovereign, independent, democratic state' in Article 1, but can be contrasted with Article 28, s 4.2, which does not refer to the overall Irish state when, in regarding the organization of the government, it provides that 'the Government shall be collectively responsible for the Departments of State administered by the members of the Government.' In Italy as well, the Constitution provides that the Constitutional Court shall pass judgment on conflicts arising 'from allocation of powers of the State and those allocated to State and regions' (Art 134), but state and regions, as well as municipalities, provinces, and metropolitan areas, are part of the Republic, and as such part of the overall legal order of the state (Art 114).

II. The Unitary State and the Nation

1. Civic and Ethnic Conceptions

As the Romanian Constitution demonstrates, the concept of the national unitary state uses the word 'state' according to the first meaning mentioned above: it refers to the association of a people under an organized authority within a territory which is supposed to be indivisible. Romania is not the only example of this model of state; indeed it has been adopted by many other European states. The cradle of the unitary state was France, whose history largely coincides with the history of the origins of the state itself. Alexis de Tocqueville contested the idea that the centralization of the power in France was the result of the Revolution alone, demonstrating that the work of the Revolution was anticipated by the centralization of power which had occurred within the monarchical central administration's assumption of control over the functioning of the fragmented feudal authorities which were spread in large numbers over the territory of France.[1]

[1] Alexis de Tocqueville, *L'ancien régime et la revolution*, II.

On the basis of this construction, the existence of a unitary state as one indivisible territory implied the creation of a central body to which the main public functions were entrusted: it was the establishment of an organization which we can call a 'state' in the second of the meanings previously mentioned. After the French Revolution, the source of all sovereignty was no longer the ruling dynasty but the nation: the people's will and the equality of human beings before the law was substituted for the God-given origins of monarchical legitimacy and of the social hierarchy.

During the nineteenth century, this development was voiced in two different ideologies affecting the terms themselves of the coexistence of a people within the frame of the state and the criteria to be used to identify the nation. On one hand, the nation was considered the association of the persons who shared the civic and constitutional values of a state (ie, the citizens of the state), and, on the other hand, the identification was based on the common ethnic and linguistic heritage of a people, if not the natural bonds of blood and territory which connected the interested persons. The first conception implies an open idea of the state, that is a commitment to common civic and constitutional values by persons who want to be included as citizens in the state's people. According to the second conception, the unitary state is the realization of the self-government of people identified by pre-existing cultural or natural bonds. To this kind of state is especially reserved the qualification of national state since European nations, identified on the basis of their ethnic and linguistic characteristics, gained their independence from the great, multinational Empires (the Austrian–Hungarian monarchy, the Russian and the Turkish Empires). The idea became increasingly attractive in Italy, Germany, and the Balkans in the second part of the nineteenth century, and the nation-state became the norm in all Europe after the First World War and had a new epiphany when the old member states of the Warsaw Pact and the Yugoslav Federal Republic substituted the nationalistic ideology for the old, communist one in shaping their new identity and adopting the new constitutions.

For instance, the preamble of the Croatian Constitution connects 'the inalienable and indivisible, non transferable and non-exhaustible right of the Croatian nation to self-determination and state sovereignty' to 'the millenary identity of the Croatian nation', and Article 4 of the Polish Constitution states that 'the supreme power in the Republic of Poland shall be vested in the Nation', whose 'identity, continuity and development' have their source in the 'cultural goods' to which the Republic shall provide conditions for equal access to all the people (Art 5).

2. National Minorities and their Territorial Relevance

The coincidence of the ethnic and linguistic identity of a state and the parallel characteristics of its people has never been complete. Therefore, with the advent of national states, the problem of protection of national minorities arose. The geographic boundaries of the new states necessarily also included autochthonous people who did not share the *ethnos* and the language of the nation which was in the majority in the state where they resided: they often identified themselves with the nation represented by another state (so-called kin-state). If the concession of citizenship was allowed on an ethnic and linguistic basis, the principles of the national state deprived these autochthonous people of the possibility of becoming citizens of their state of residence, or, if they obtained citizenship, they were discriminated against in the enjoyment of their rights and freedoms and failed to have their historical and cultural identity recognized and safeguarded.[2] The problem of the protection of national minorities

[2] On citizenship see Chapter 48.

has gained—during the twentieth century—an international dimension and it was unsuccessfully dealt with on a state-by-state basis by the peace treaties entered into after the First World War. The international institutions created after the Second World War (the United Nations, the Council of Europe, the Organization for Security and Co-operation in Europe) first tried to solve the problem through the recognition of universal human rights and fundamental freedoms, and—later—adopted general international instruments to provide the required protection, even if in some cases the solution to the problem was directly agreed by bilateral treaties between the state of residence of the minority concerned and the relevant kin-state.

However, international rules for the protection of national minorities, when implemented within the frame of the internal legal orders of the state, avoid discrimination of the state's citizens on an ethnic and linguistic basis, but do not eliminate the relevance of their difference from the members of the nation which is identified in the state itself. The Hungarian Constitution is an interesting exception as far as its Article XXIX states that the minorities living in the Republic of Hungary 'participate in the sovereign power of the people: they represent a constituent part of the State'. Minorities are a territorial presence with historical roots, and, as a consequence of their request for recognition of the right to self-determination, some states have agreed to allow self-government of ordinary institutions in the territorial areas in which the interested minorities live. This is the case of the Swedish-speaking community in the Åland Islands (Finland), of the Russian-speaking populace in Crimea (Ukraine), and the German- and, respectively, French-speaking people in the Regione Trentino-Alto Adige/Südtirol and in the Regione Valle d'Aosta/Vallée d'Aoste (Italy), where special territorial autonomies have been established in view of ensuring the extension of the protection of the rights of the linguistic and ethnic minorities to participate in the exercise of public functions. The same result is obtained in Spain through the institutions of the Autonomous Communities, for instance in Catalonia and the Basque country in coherence with the statement in Article 2 of the Constitution which recognizes the right of nationalities and regions to achieve self-government. This solution implies the permanence of those minorities within the concerned states and avoids the danger of tentative secession moves by those communities under the auspices of exercising the right of self-determination, which international law is not yet ready to recognize.[3]

Obviously, the territorial government which is created in this way interests not only the persons belonging to the minority but also all the people living in the area, even if they do not belong to the national minority whose protection is the main aim of autonomous self-government. Therefore, in Article 20 of the Framework Convention for the Protection of National Minorities, reference is made to national minorities which 'are in a minority nationally but form a majority within one area of the State', binding them to 'respect the national legislation and the rights of others, in particular those of persons belonging to the majority or to other national minorities.'[4]

The United Kingdom is an interesting case, where the policy of devolution has at the same time taken into consideration the historical, unitary sovereignty of the Parliament and self-government of domestic affairs in Scotland, Wales, and Northern Ireland by establishing different institutions with different modalities of devolution of the state's functions to those institutions.

[3] See Chapter 23.

[4] Explanatory report, subsection III.

III. The Organization of the State's Territory

1. Centralist Tendencies and the Prefects

The end of the previous paragraph touches upon aspects of internal organization of the state and its central authorities, which deserves to be dealt with taking into consideration the territorial dimension. Territory is an essential element of the state, and therefore one aspect of special interest in internal organization is the distribution of public functions across the territory, which can imply, on the one hand, the creation of bureaucratic structures at the centre and at the periphery of the state, or, on the other hand, the erection of autonomous territorial agencies according to the different historical traditions of the particular territories.[5] France is again an interesting model from which we can proceed in dealing with the problems of centralization or decentralization of power within a state: the analysis will also cover the state as the central structure of power and the state as the organization of all the people living in that state's territory.

After the French Revolution, since the 1791 Constitution, the territory of the French state—which was proclaimed indivisible—was divided into 83 departments.[6] Notwithstanding the tendency of the monarchy towards a growing centralization of decision-making, the feudal system involved the presence of many different agencies within the frame of the state's territory, which was heavily conditioned by the causal effects of the distribution of prerogatives by the king and the hereditary transfer of property, and which therefore did not completely ensure the unity of administration and implementation of the ideal of equality of all citizens. The purpose of the creation of the departments was a surgical reorganization of power at the local level to substitute a rational division of the national territory for the casual feudal arrangements with a view to ensuring uniformity of the state's territorial institutions and guaranteeing the equality of relations between the people and the ruling authorities across the state.[7] Until recent times, the fundamental governing text was the Law of 10 August 1871, which revised the innovations introduced after the fall of the feudal monarchy. The departments have been only one of the elements in a system of *territorial units*, whose task has been the adoption of decisions involving the operation of functions which can be better exercised at a local level. More recent constitutional developments have again opened the discussion about the coexistence of departments and other more autonomous agencies of local government. This discussion, with which France has been occupied since a legislative Act in 1831, provided for the election of deliberative bodies for the *communes*, even though the mayors were appointed by the state's authorities until the reform of 1884. However, the idea that the municipalities are administrative (ie, not political) authorities has prevailed in France and that opinion is still largely accepted today according to the view of Pierre Rosanvallon.[8]

In principle, the state's departmental organization was arranged according to the rule of *centralization*. In that regard, the decision-making power for all the territory of the state is held by the central administration which operates through territorial services, whose

[5] According to the distribution of the matter in this volume, which assigns the legislative and judicial powers to other chapters, this chapter will discuss the organization of the administrative functions only.

[6] Title II, Art 1.

[7] Francois Furet and Mona Ozouf, 'Départment' in *Dictionnaire critique de la Révolution Française* (1988).

[8] Pierre Rosanvallon, *Le modèle politique français* (2004), 369.

functions are the result of a *déconcentration* of central functions and constitute the competences of the state's local services. The hierarchical subordination of these services to central authorities was intended to guarantee the unity of the direction of public power. A heritage of this centralistic approach, which was connected to the existence of the departments, is the presence in the current French Constitution of a provision entrusting the representatives of the state in the territories to guarantee 'the national interests, the administrative supervision and the observance of the law'.[9]

The conception of the executive as the guarantor of the unity of the state required the presence of state offices in all parts of the state, even in the institutions of local government. The mandate of those offices was both to preserve the state's interests and to supervise the activities of local government agencies with a view to ensuring an absence of conflict with those interests. While the constitutional history of the United Kingdom is characterized by the progressive expansion of the democratic autonomy of local government institutions with the disappearance of sheriffs and justices of the peace appointed by central government, in France the post-revolutionary choice of entrusting the newly created prefects with the task of representing the executive across the territory of the state has been a constant feature of the state's organization, notwithstanding evident and frequent frictions with the system of local government. Also, after the recent revision of the Constitution, its Article 72 provides for the presence in every territorial community of the republic of a high-level civil servant representative of the state who 'shall be responsible for national interests, administrative supervision and the observance of the law'. The French prefect is a powerful institution when compared with other similar institutions (eg the Italian prefect) because all the territorial state offices depend on the prefect's intermediary role for implementation of guidelines and orders from various ministries or from the central agencies: therefore, it is endowed with general competence, while in other countries all branches of the state across the national territory report directly to their central superior offices.

The French example is followed, for instance, in Romania where according to Article 122 of the Constitution 'the Prefect is the representative of the Government at the local level and shall direct any decentralized public services of the Ministries and other central agencies in the territorial-administrative units.' In Germany, due to its federal organization, there are no permanent representatives of central government but the Federal government, which exercises oversight to ensure compliance of the *Länder* with federal laws, 'may send commissioners to the highest *Land* authorities and, with their consent or, where such consent is refused, with the consent of the Bundesrat, also to subordinate authorities.' In this regard, the execution of federal laws belongs to the competence of the *Länder* 'insofar as the Basic Law does not otherwise provide or permit'[10] and, even in these cases, federal functions can be delegated to the *Länder*. In Spain, a regionally unitary state, 'a delegate appointed by the Government shall direct State administration in the *territorial* area of each Autonomous Community and shall co-ordinate it, when necessary, with the Community's own administration.'[11] This arrangement probably follows the example of a similar provision in Italy's 1948 Constitution,[12] the abrogation of which by the constitutional reform of 2001 does not prevent the existence of representatives of the state in every region, who still coexist with the prefects acting on a provincial basis, while control and supervision of the functioning of local government is shared by state authorities and the regional governments. It is apparent

[9] Art 72. [10] German Constitution, Art 83.
[11] Spanish Constitution, Art 154. [12] 1948 Italian Constitution, Art 124.

that the management of unitary national interests is dealt with on a central basis in the United Kingdom where, notwithstanding devolution, Secretaries of State for Northern Ireland, Scotland, and Wales continue to exist: regular intergovernmental meetings provide coordination between the devolved administrations and the central agencies, especially through bilateral agreements.

2. The Autonomy of the Local Government: Examples of Constitutional Provisions

It can easily be seen that the principle of unity and uniformity of the state's public administration has been competing with the principle of territorial self-government, which means the right of local collectivities for management of their interests in a free and autonomous way. In France, besides the departments, there are municipalities, regions, and collectivities with a particular statute. All of them are freely self-governing entities entrusted with their own functions and resources whose decision-making bodies are elected by the people of that territory. This modality of administration, which is an evident manifestation of the principles of democracy and freedom, is called *decentralization* (especially in countries with a tradition of centralization) and implies the creation of entities which are distinct from the central and local organization of the state and which have a separate legal personality. Presently, the local entities constitute an intermediate level of separate autonomous authority between the state and the citizens.[13] *Decentralization* should give special emphasis to the local interests of the communities which are not supposed to coincide with the interests of the state and are not meant to be a mere territorial expression of them.

This model is very common in continental Europe, where it has found scientific elaboration since the nineteenth century. Especially in the German-speaking world, the recognition of local government entities was traditionally connected, on the one hand, to the theory of independence of territorial self-government elaborated by Gneist,[14] taking into account the experience of the voluntary (ie, without salary) service of local administrators in the United Kingdom, and, on the other hand, the extension of the organic theory elaborated by Gierke[15] to self-governing institutions, according to the principle that every organic community is able to create law and, therefore, to exercise powers of self-government.

The concept which inspires this model of organizing the exercise of administrative functions at the local level is local autonomy.[16] Local autonomy is a flexible concept. It can be defined as the right and effective capacity of local collectivities to rule and manage important areas of public interest within the frame of the law.[17] Therefore, the concept of local autonomy covers not only the legal and formal attribution of functions affecting local businesses but also

[13] While the original purpose of the model of the *déconcentration*, which was the basis for the creation of the departments, was instead the establishing of a direct link between the state's central administrative bodies and the citizens, in view of the implementation of national interests and legislation.

[14] Heinrich Rudolf Gneist, *Geschichte und heutige Gestalt der englischen Communal Verfassung und des Selfgovernment* (1866).

[15] Otto Friedrich von Gierke, *Das deutsche Genossenschaftsrecht* (1868).

[16] Its general relevance in Europe is confirmed by the European Charter of local autonomies adopted by the Council of Europe (Strasbourg, 15 October 1985). This document does not pretend to introduce a binding organizational uniformity across the different institutions of local government in Europe; rather, it elaborates principles which are supposed to be part and parcel of the common constitutional heritage of those countries.

[17] See Art 3 of the Charter.

the concrete and material (ie, financial) conditions of the exercise of those functions for the advantage to the people living in that territory. Undoubtedly, the interests dealt with by the local collectivities are connected with the national interests of the state and have clear public relevance. But they are primarily considered by the law as interests of the local collectivities and have to be promoted according to the choices and the will of the local electors.

Local autonomy does not require local collectivities' qualification as legal persons. However, in terms of their judicial standing, there is a need for the free exercise of their competences through effective judicial remedy. This was a consideration in the jurisprudence in England during the 1980s, in cases dealing with central/local conflicts concerning finance.[18]

Respect for local autonomy is not unconditionally constitutionalized but, in the twentieth century, it is frequently reflected in the presence of provisions concerning local government in the constitutions.[19] The differentiation between local interests and the interests of the central authorities of the state has been seen as requiring a constitutional guarantee of the independent existence and functioning of the institutions of local government against overwhelming measures taken by the central bodies of the state aimed at curtailing their powers or depriving them of resources which are necessary to their efficiency. An interesting and advanced example of this tendency of the modern constitution is offered, inter alia, by Article 28 of the German Constitution. According to which

> municipalities must be guaranteed the right to regulate all local affairs on their own responsibility, within the limits prescribed by the law.... The guarantee of self-government shall extend to the bases of financial autonomy; these bases shall include the right of municipalities to a source of tax revenues based upon economic ability and the right to establish the rates at which these sources shall be taxed.

In addition, Article 106 entrusts to the federal legislation the apportionment of tax revenues which are shared by different levels of government.

The competences of the local units are not explicitly listed in constitutions. They certainly deal with interests which are primarily considered by law as interests of the local collectivities and have to be promoted according to the choices of the local electors. However, on the basis of the principle of subsidiarity, municipalities are usually entrusted by the ordinary law with services affecting individual needs and interests of the persons belonging to the territorial communities (in the matters of health, primary education, social assistance, local transport, and so on).

In this context, the position of the United Kingdom is certainly uncharacteristic insofar as a constitutional guarantee of local government is missing. Therefore, for instance, the Parliament—even in situations of international engagements—could apparently abolish local government or deprive it of its main functions and of its resources. Historical developments point in the opposite direction, insofar as they evidence a progressive substitution of one local authority entrusted with all services in its area for the pre-existing ad hoc bodies for specific and sectional purposes. Certainly, the councils governing the local collectivities do not derive their legitimacy by Crown appointment, as happened historically with sheriffs and justices of the peace, but—since the introduction of the 1888 Local Government Act—from their election by the residents of the relevant local areas. For that reason, they cannot be seen as a territorial

[18] See *Nottinghamshire CC v Secretary of State for the Environment* [1986] AC 240 and *Hammersmith and Fulham v Secretary of State for Environment* (1990) 3 All ER 589: Ian Leigh, 'The New Local Government' in Jeffrey Jowell and Dawn Oliver (eds), *The Changing Constitution* (5th edn, 2004), 304.

[19] eg Czech Constitution, Arts 99–105; French Constitution, Arts 72–72-2; Irish Constitution, Art 28A; Romanian Constitution, Arts 119–22.

expression of a unitary national government. However, the absence of constitutional rules binding the national authorities does give these authorities some freedom of movement, as evidenced by the reforms adopted by Parliament at the end of the twentieth century. In principle, most of the local authorities are today single-tier authorities, but in some parts of rural England the two-tier model has been retained, notwithstanding the revisions of the 1972 Local Government Act.[20]

With these exceptions, which also include the special solutions adopted for London, this choice of simplification differentiates the United Kingdom[21] from other countries where the coexistence of different levels of local government is possible.[22] Moreover, the UK reform introduced other novelties into the organization of local government agencies providing for the delegation of functions to committees of councillors and for the possibility of establishing executive bodies directly elected by the people or appointed by the councils. Eventually the rigidity of the *ultra vires* principle was relaxed, thereby allowing the local councils to manage a greater part of the local interests according to their own requirements.

3. Regions with Legislative Powers in the Unitary States and other Regional Solutions

The legal and political doctrine clearly differentiates unitary states from federal states,[23] which are created by the union of pre-existing states and have a composite structure made up of the organizations of different state-like entities, which are historically and politically distinguished by their different processes of formation and consolidation of their constitutional identity.[24] Notwithstanding the presence of interesting historical events and doctrinal opinions which support the idea of identification of federal states and regional states resulting from a process of devolution,[25] the best solution is to avoid all too easy comparisons and adhere to the relevant provisions of the constitutions of the respective states. The establishment of a regional state is always the result of the restructuring of a unitary state in order to ensure the promotion and the management of specific territorial interests within its frame. It takes into

[20] Leigh (n 18), 307.

[21] But see eg Arts 163–4 of the Polish Constitution and Art 78 of Icelandic Constitution.

[22] See Art 72 of the French Constitution, providing for the existence of communes, departments, and regions; in Italy, see Art 114 enlisting municipalities, provinces, metropolitan areas, regions; in Hungary, see Art 41 mentioning the capital, the counties, the cities, the communities, and the districts.

[23] See Chapter 27 on federalism.

[24] The advent of a federation implies the unanimous adoption of a constitution by the participant states or other territorial entities entrusting some important functions (eg foreign policy, defence, finance, and markets) to a new organization, the central federal state.

[25] However, in some places, from the point of view of historical developments, there is no radical distinction between federalism and regionalism. Eg, the formation of the Belgian federal state followed an unusual path. The cultural and linguistic diversities of Belgium fostered in the second half of the twentieth century the creation of three (French, Flemish, and German) cultural communities (which were given a limited autonomy in cultural matters by the 1970 constitutional revision) and (by the revisions of 1980 and 1988–89) of three (Flemish, Walloon, and Brussels-Capital) regions, which were empowered with the relevant social and economic functions. These reforms were the basis for the final transformation of the previous unitary state into a federal state with a new constitutional revision in 1993 followed by the adoption of the entirely revised Constitution which entered into force in 1994. The Belgian constitutional developments affect the credibility of the traditional model of the process of the federal state's formation insofar as they apparently remind the different phenomenon of the devolution of the state's competences to local and regional authorities within the frame of a unitary state. See Francis Delpérée, *La Belgique, État fédéral?* (1972), 607.

consideration the exigencies of a decentralization of the power to reduce the impact of a previous centralized state organization (Italy), existing traditional territorial differences (Spain), or the promotion of an articulated system of economic and territorial planning (eg France, but with organizational solutions different from those adopted in other states).

The creation of an intermediate level of government between the central state and minor local governmental entities provided for by the constitutions both of Italy and Spain entailed the creation of the Regions and the Autonomous Communities, whose territorial borders were defined taking into account the traditional connections and the new economic and social needs of geographical areas larger than those of the municipalities. Therefore, they are entrusted with legislative and administrative competences in many fields transferred to them from the central, national level of the state. But both of their constitutions exclude the possibility of finding any similarity with the processes of formation of federal states and make a completely different choice: the Italian Constitution states that the Republic is 'one and indivisible', and therefore local autonomies are recognized and promoted by the state and are not a founder or a constituent part of the process of its formation.[26] The Regions—whose creation is provided for by Title 5 of the Second Part of the Constitution—are autonomous entities comparable to municipalities and provinces, although their competences do not depend on the ordinary law because they are explicitly listed in the Constitution, which affords them a specific guarantee enforceable before the Italian Constitutional Court. On the other hand, in Spain, according to Article 2 of the Constitution, 'the Constitution is based on the indissoluble unity of the Spanish Nation, the common and indivisible country of all the Spaniards.' But even if this statement did allow a federal solution (insofar as the second part of the same article declares that nationalities and regions are component parts of the Spanish nation), only the right of autonomy is recognized and guaranteed to them: therefore the constitutional position of specific nationalities and regions does not have a separate and independent legitimacy but is derived from the basic decision made by the Spanish Constitution. Obviously, it could be said that constitutional texts do not offer a conclusive basis for the elaboration of scientific doctrines. We have to look at the concrete functioning of both the constitutional systems and the relations of the Autonomous Communities and of the Regions, with the central bodies of the national state. In fact, taken from this point of view, elements supporting a similarity with federal states are extremely sparse.

For instance, both the Spanish Autonomous Communities and the Italian Regions have legislative powers with regard to minor matters. Those matters are given to them by way of exclusive competence; in addition, they have legislative powers subordinate to principles, bases, and guidelines established by state legislation. But, at least in Italy, they cannot legislate in matters covered by the key civil and criminal codes or by the civil, criminal, and administrative judicial procedure legislation and, according to the Italian Constitutional Court, the principle of subsidiarity can justify the substitution of the national legislator for the regional one in matters of national interest.[27] Moreover, neither the Spanish Autonomous Communities nor the Italian Regions have constituent powers because the Statutes of the Autonomous Communities (ie, their 'constitutional charters') have to be adopted by the central Parliament, and those of the Italian Regions, even if they are approved by the regional councils without the intervention of the Chamber of Deputies or the Senate of the Republic, have to be 'in compliance with the Italian Constitution', which determines their main bodies and entrusts to state legislation the laying down of the fundamental principles of the system of election for their

[26] Article 5: 'the Republic, one and indivisible, recognizes and promotes local autonomies'.

[27] Decision 303/2003.

executive and legislative assembly.[28] In both of the Constitutions, a provision similar to Article 79 of the German Constitution (stating the inadmissibility of amendments to the Basic Law affecting the division of the federation into *Länder*) is missing. Even if recognition and the guarantee of the right to autonomy is one of the fundamental principles in the Preliminary Title of the Constitutions of Spain and Italy, together with other basic principles, it is evident that in both states the national legislative power has greater flexibility and discretion in revising the Constitution in matters of organization of the autonomies than has the German legislator. Neither the Italian nor the Spanish Constitution requires the direct participation of the regional entities in the process of adoption of constitutional amendments. Taking into account these differences, the majority of legal doctrine distinguishes Spain and Italy from the federal states and classes them together (even if the Spanish communities have more power than—at least—the ordinary Italian Regions) in the above-mentioned special category of regional states.

In Italy, special constitutional laws were approved by the national parliament to adopt the statutes of five special Regions which have a differentiated autonomy—Sardinia, Sicily, Friuli Venezia Giulia, Trentino Alto Adige/Südtirol, and Valle d'Aosta/Vallee d'Aoste—in view of the economic and social aspects of the ethnic and linguistic peculiarities of those territories. These entities have greater legislative and administrative powers than the powers of the ordinary Regions. Therefore, they have the chance of managing matters which directly affect their social and economic development and of providing for the promotion and management of the specific identity of their ethnic and linguistic minorities. Italy can be defined as an asymmetric regional state.[29] However, the Italian Constitutional Court decided that the unity of the state requires that even these constitutional laws have to comply with the fundamental principles of the Constitution,[30] leaving to its own jurisprudence the identification of those principles on a case-by-case basis.

According to the Spanish Constitutional Court, 'autonomy makes reference to a limited power... autonomy is not sovereignty... in no case can the principle of autonomy be opposed to that of unity',[31] and recently the same judge stated that 'the Constitution recognizes only the Spanish Nation and the Unitarian sovereignty of the Spanish people'.[32] But Article 147(2) of the Constitution correctly underlines the importance of preliminary identification of individual communities, stating that the relevant statutes must contain both the name of the community which best corresponds to its historical identity and the delimitation of its territory. In fact, the Spanish Constitution does not list the communities to be instituted (as opposed to the Italian Constitution which does so in Article 131), and therefore the choice has to be made at the time of the institution of the specific community and the approval of the relevant statute. Again, the central state has a constituent task in the conformation of the system of autonomy.

The recent decision by the French constitutional legislator of providing for the institution of regions does not apparently have any connection with the Spanish and Italian model of the regional state. The French regions are not especially differentiated from the other territorial units of the Republic and do not have legislative powers: the new Article 72 of the French Constitution mentions them along with the communes, departments, units with a special statute, and overseas territories. The protection of the French Constitution only covers the

[28] Spanish Constitution, Arts 147–52 and Italian Constitution, Arts 117 and 121–3.

[29] Peter Pernthaler, *Der differenzierte Bundesstaat* (1992).

[30] See Decisions 6/1970 and 1146/1988.

[31] Decision STC 4/1981.

[32] Decision STC 31/2010.

existence of the regions and—in principle—their autonomy. Therefore, extension of their powers, the amount of their financial resources, and their interrelation with the state have to be decided by the Parliament; in the regions a representative of the state is entrusted with the functions of controlling their activity and ensuring respect for the national interest. Moreover, the territorial units are not organized hierarchically and there are no superior bodies charged with the task of controlling them. However, assistance with interpretation of this reform is offered by the previous case law of the French Constitutional Council, which recognized the power of the legislator to institute local self-governing entities not explicitly provided for by the Constitution (in this case, the Region of Corsica) on the conditions of respecting constitutional principles and rules, ensuring the exercise of self-government through free elections, and restraint from transferring to them powers concerning 'matters to be regulated by the parliamentary law', even where it is admissible to authorize the relevant regional bodies to ask the delegation of regulatory powers 'to adapt [the national rules] ... to specific circumstances'.[33]

After the adoption of the recent measures for devolution for Scotland, Wales, and Northern Ireland, the United Kingdom can also be distinguished from federal states, notwithstanding that these measures take into consideration the specific historical identities of the three countries. The United Kingdom does not have a written constitution, the concerned territorial entities are not involved in the amendments of the relevant rules, and the guarantee of the distribution of powers between the centre and the periphery is not ensured by a specific court. This means that the superiority of the Westminster Parliament is preserved.[34] But the devolution arrangements are different in each of the three countries. In Scotland, they are Westminster-based with a Scottish Parliament and government, which means that central government maintains control and oversight of the devolved powers and which also provides for a clear distribution of issues between the UK authorities and the Scottish governing bodies and for the establishment of a multi-layered democracy. In Wales a more restrained policy was adopted, granting secondary powers to the relevant institutions, and especially to its National Assembly. For Northern Ireland, a 'peace' solution for the conflict—which saw the majority of the population aiming at a union with Great Britain and a minority favouring unification with the rest of Ireland—was adopted at a midway point between a large degree of devolution and a preparatory move in view of a possible merging with the Irish Republic. The 1998 Belfast Agreement, while providing for the establishment of the relevant assembly and executive, consolidated the institutions for cooperation between the concerned parties (Great Britain, Republic of Ireland, and Northern Ireland) according to a trend which developed during the long process of negotiations to settle the conflict.

The creation of regions is envisaged for the remaining part of the United Kingdom, that is, England.[35] The idea is to establish elected assemblies for each of the eight regions into which England is divided. The implementation of the choice depends on the decision of the Secretary of State to call a referendum on the matter in view of evidence of a sufficient level of interest among the population of England. These assemblies will not have legislative powers but will focus on promoting economic and social developments, public services, and the protection of the regional environments, while taking into account the exigencies of geographical areas larger than those of the municipalities.

[33] Decisions 91-290 DC and 2001-454 DC.

[34] eg in the case of Scotland see *Whaley v Watson of Invergowrie*, 2000 SC 340.

[35] See the Government White Paper, *Your Region, Your Choice: Revitalising the English Regions* (Cm 5511, May 2002).

IV. The Organization of the Central Executive Branches of the State: The Role of the Parliament

The arrangements concerning the branches of the central state is a practical matter but it has a well-known constitutional dimension. Here we concentrate on the impact of such organization on the powers of the executive branch. The historical formation of unitary states is strictly connected with the growth of the power of the European monarchies. The example of France is again impressive: the progressive establishment of the unitary state resulted in concentration of power in the hands of the king, with particular emphasis on his executive functions and on the officials depending on him. These functions were retained by the new monarchical executives when, after the Revolution, they took up the heritage of the absolute monarchy, while they shared or renounced the legislative function in favour of a representative parliament. It was not only a technical arrangement, it also had a political relevance as far as it was justified by the idea that the unity of the state had to be preserved by the unity of power in the executive branch and through the central exercise of relevant functions. Dealing with the termination of the Revolution, Michel Troper has correctly underlined the peculiarity of the position and of the role of executive power after the Directorate (in the French Constitution of 1795).[36] This was the starting point of developments that interested all European countries. Frequently justified—from the perspective of European history—by the threat of or actuality of continental wars and by the complexities of the social question, the executives moved to occupy a central position in the internal ordering of the state, with a tendency to be identified with the unitary state.[37] Such developments have had, in some instances even in times of peace, perverse effects when they offered a basis for the epiphany of authoritarian and dictatorial changes of systems of the government with the progressive reduction of the role of parliament (eg Italy, Spain, and Germany). However, in other countries, commentators can also easily be found who criticize the growing enlargement of the executives notwithstanding the presence of an active elected parliament and the absence of really authoritarian regressions.

In principle, in modern and contemporary constitutions, the introduction of the separation of powers should have resulted in the submission of the executive bodies of the state to the legislative arm, but the executive did not easily accept being fully subordinated to the elected assemblies and having its functions limited to execution of the law: it always, and also successfully, aimed at managing political coordination and the administrative direction of all actions concerning the government of the country and management of the armies. First, this enlargement interested the constitutional monarchies and, later, the parliamentary governments with their increasing ruling role and separation of government—made up of political personnel—from the monarchy. In spite of the fact that, in light of democratic principles, the parliament, which is supposed to be the representative body of the unity of the nation, has been charged not only with the legislative function and also with exercising control and scrutiny of the government, the executive was seen as the main body responsible for the unity of the state and also as the operator of public administration and state-provided public services—which were often identified with the state, at least in the eyes of the general public.

But the continental constitutional practice in the field of the central branches of the state was especially based, even before the advent of parliamentary government, on attempts by the legislator to regulate and control the activities of the executive by the adoption of normative

[36] Michel Troper, *Terminer la Révolution* (2006), 180.

[37] Peter von Oertzen, *Die soziale Funktion des staatsrechtlichen Positivismus* (1974), 63–4.

Acts the application of which should be the task of the executive according to the political purposes of government. With the advent of the constitutional state, the competences of the central authorities are often listed in the constitution, and not only in the regional unitary states such as Spain,[38] Italy,[39] and, partially, Portugal,[40] but even in France with special regard to the parliament.[41]

The main obstacle to these developments, which required an expansion of the legislative shaping of the organization and functions of the executive, was the traditional recognition for it of a specific autonomy and self-sufficiency in creating and ruling its own branches which was strictly connected, at least before the advent of parliamentary government, with an interpretation of the principle of the separation of powers aimed at keeping the executive dependent on the authority of the monarchy and independent of parliament. If it is true that even in the Germany in the eighteenth and the nineteenth centuries, the existence of a preliminary law was required in view of administrative interference in the exercise of rights and freedoms, the above-mentioned difficulties in the field of the arrangements of the executive branches were explicitly overcome only when the dependence of the administrative organization on the legislative decisions of the parliament began to be stated in the constitutions. In the United Kingdom where, inter alia, the executive has always had the guide of parliamentary activities, in the absence of a written constitution the intervention of parliamentary statutes in shaping the departments of central government has emerged only in the twentieth century.

Constitutional provisions which entrust parliamentary laws with the task of organizing the offices and branches of the executive powers can be found in many European constitutions. For instance, in Spain Article 103 of the Constitution not only provides that 'the Public Administration serves the general interest with objectivity and acts in accordance with the principles of efficiency, hierarchy, decentralization, deconcentration and coordination, being fully subject to justice and the law', but also states the rule that 'the organs of the State Administration are created, directed and co-ordinated in accordance with the law'. According to Article 116 of the Constitution of Romania, 'Ministries shall be set up, organized, and function in accordance with the law... Autonomous administrative authorities may be established by an organic law.' In Italy, on the basis of Article 97 of the Constitution, 'public offices are organized according to the provisions of law, so as to ensure efficiency and the impartiality of administration.' Perhaps the Hungarian Constitution leaves more room for the self-regulation of the executive when it only states that 'the Ministries shall be listed in a special Act' (Art 17), even if it does not specifically list the matters falling within the competence of the legislator and of the regulations adopted by the executive. Such a distribution is present in the French Constitution but did not prevent a progressive enlargement of the parliamentary legislation's space by the case law of the Conseil Constitutionnel.[42]

Ministries and departments are normally the main constitutive branches of the executive. Their number usually matches the number of members of the Cabinet or Council of Ministers, which is chaired by the Premier and is the top executive's deliberative body. But we also have examples of countries where there are ministries or departments entrusted to the responsibility of ministers who are not members of the Cabinet (United Kingdom) or to Undersecretaries of State (recently in Italy). The distribution of the functions among these branches of the

[38] Spanish Constitution, Art 149. [39] Italian Constitution, Art 117.

[40] Portuguese Constitution, Arts 164 and 165. [41] French Constitution, Art 34.

[42] Decision of 30 July 1982.

executive is normally made on the basis of the homogeneity of the concerned fields of activity: they are supposed to work in coordination with the national agencies or corporations and the entities of local government which have concurring competences in the respective matters. Only the Premier has a power of general political coordination.[43]

Moreover, the constitutional experience offers examples of increasing relevance of the chiefs of the state's offices outside the presidential or semi-presidential regimes. This phenomenon is taken into consideration by some new constitutions. In Poland, Article 143 of the Constitution provides for the establishment of the Presidential Chancellery as 'the organ of assistance to the President of the Republic. The President of the Republic shall establish the statute of the Presidential Chancellery and shall appoint and dismiss its Chiefs', and in Croatia, for instance, the President shall appoint—in case of special necessity—advisory bodies to be assisted in the performance of his duties, while advisory, expert, and other tasks shall be normally performed by the Office of the President, whose organization and competence shall be regulated by law and internal rules.[44] The phenomenon is present even in the absence of constitutional provisions. For instance, the President of the French Republic avails himself of 800 people, who are organized on the basis of areas of activity (foreign affairs, culture, economic and social matters etc) which are in parallel with the branches of government.[45] The rules concerning this structure are adopted by the President directly.

V. The *Droit Administratif* and the Advent of the *Sozialer Rechtstaat*

The new social and economic demands of the twentieth century have called for an enlargement of the functions of the executive with important consequences for compliance with the principle of the rule of law.[46] The problem was taken into consideration by the legal doctrine as it occurred in the Germany of the Weimar Republic with the emergence of the idea of the *Sozialer Rechtstaat*, which implicitly expanded the state's functions in view of the implementation of social and economic principles and within the frame of compliance with the principle of the rule of law. But it was not easy to implement these doctrines. With the exception of the United Kingdom, continental European countries have seen, at least since the nineteenth century, the advent of a new special branch of law essentially devoted to regulating the activities of the executive. The starting point was the idea—especially elaborated in France by the administrative judges and by the scientific doctrines of legal scholars—that a particular legal nature should be accorded to the administrative acts of the executive, taking into consideration the typical characteristics of public agents and their management of public interests. These acts required specific rules and the submission of possible and relevant claims by the people affected to a special jurisdiction—administrative justice—which was intended to have exclusive knowledge to deal with conflicts between the state's administration and its citizens and which would be entrusted with the competence to resolve them in compliance with public interests. This was another product of the long story of the claimed independence and self-sufficiency of the executive, but—step by step—it moved far away from being an instrument

[43] In Germany, 'the Chancellor shall determine and be responsible for the general guidelines of policy': German Constitution, Art 65.

[44] Croatian Constitution, Art 106.

[45] Francis Hamon and Michel Troper, *Droit constitutionnel* (2005), 621–2.

[46] See Chapter 10.

of privilege for public officials and resulted in the transformation of the originally authoritarian profile of the administrative organization into a system attentive to the exigencies of protection of the rights and freedoms of the people.

According to its common law tradition, the United Kingdom followed a different approach in dealing with the same problems. The interpretation of the rule of law has been first and more directly connected with the protection of rights and freedoms, which is ensured by the 'ordinary' judiciary through its case law which is the direct source of law. Therefore, while the continental constitutional practice in the field of the central branches of the state was based, even before the advent of parliamentary government, on the attempt by the legislator to regulate and control the activities of the executive by the adoption of normative acts the application of which should be their task according to the political purposes of the government, the English model of rule of law evolved through the action of the courts. At the end of the nineteenth century, the late A.V. Dicey suggested that, while in France the acts of the public officers were submitted to a distinct system of administrative courts, the English law was based on the principles that every man, whatever his formal rank or position, shall be subject to the ordinary law and the jurisdiction of the ordinary tribunals.[47] However, in more recent times, even the English case law, legal doctrine, and legislation have opened the way for recognition of the peculiarity of the position of public authorities, whose functions have a discretional profile, which Dicey's theory denied. If the phenomenon was labelled 'Administrative State' only in the twentieth century, today opinion is generally shared that discretion is necessarily connected with the powers of choice of the public authorities and affects private persons who interrelate with the public administration. The rule of law is respected as far as the possible openness of the provisions of the law is balanced by their implementation through consensual regulations and by the procedural fairness of the executive's activities.

Both in continental Europe and in the United Kingdom, the development of a public industrial and commercial sector resulted in great innovation. The traditional administrative rules were not sufficient for public authorities dealing with the economic and social problems whose solutions were newly entrusted to the states. They were not adequately flexible and their usually strict application was a disadvantage in implementing rules that were to be complied with by the operators of the private economic sector. Everywhere, the administrative law has been revised to cope with the new exigencies of the state. These developments led to the creation of new structures which were to be autonomous with regard to the executive authorities and were frequently regulated by ad hoc amendments to the general legislation concerning private corporations. For instance, in France and Italy measures of nationalization were adopted with the establishment of new public institutions (in France *établissements publics nationaux*) and of entirely public or mixed public-private corporations (in Italy *società a partecipazione statale*), while their governing boards were appointed by the governments in view of ensuring the coherence of their activity with its general policies, even if they had the great freedom of choice and movement required by the exigencies of industrial and commercial management. Only with the advent of new European economic regulations was this tendency abandoned, but the heritage of the past is still present in some places after the claimed reduction of powers of the public authorities in the economic field to mere regulatory functions (eg in Italy). In the United Kingdom, the presence of independent regulatory and advisory bodies entrusted with the task of regulating public enterprises in some specific fields, coexisted with the executive bodies set up to manage nationalized enterprises since the advent

[47] Albert V. Dicey, *Introduction to the Study of the Law of the Constitution* (8th edn, 1915).

of the initial interventions of the state in the economy at the beginning of the twentieth century. With the expansion of the private market, the legislation has preserved their peculiar relevance to ensure the fair and correct provision of services and goods for the benefit of the general community.

VI. The Hierarchical Structure of the Executive: Civil Servants

The internal organization of the state's executive branches has been reformed not only in connection with the expansion of the *Sozialstaat*. The requisite of the hierarchical structure of the public administration which is present—for instance—in the previously quoted Article 103 of the Spanish Constitution, was in the past the common feature of the European unitary states. It was generally accepted that the organization of the executives could ensure the unity of the administrative activity of the state only through the establishment of different levels of bureaucratic structures held by officers, whose legal *status* was not regulated by private law but by specific legislation to ensure their neutrality, liability, and stability (eg by allowing dismissal only for misconduct).[48] The high position of the superior offices resulted in their power of commanding the inferior departments by the adoption of orders and guidelines which were supposed to take into consideration the state's unitary interests and produce their effects down the pyramid, to affect and bind the functioning of the inferior branches of the executive which were in direct contact with the practical application of the law. In this way, all levels of the administrative organization were supposed to be—through the personal dependence of their holders—under the controlling and supervisory functions of the state's bodies which were in charge of the unity of the executive and, therefore, of the unity of the state. The advent of new public entities in the field of the state's economic and social intervention broke the machinery of the hierarchical organization: they required autonomy of management and functioning outside the strictures of administrative law and implied substantial changes of the regulation of the concerned personnel's *status* which was deprived of the guarantee of stability, but had great freedom of movement.

Interesting developments have also affected the traditional performance of the state's administration. The administrative hierarchy has always implied, on the one hand, difficulties in keeping separate the political and the legal dimensions of the state's activities and has, especially in recent times, complicated, on the other hand, the relations between the technical and legal profiles of administrative actions. The neutrality of civil servants was endangered by the request from the top political bodies to have their commands complied with, while the dependence of the inferior offices of the public administration on the guidelines of the superior authorities reduced their capacity to cope with the growing exigencies of the technical requirements of practical administration. These problems were extensively dealt with in a constitution for the first time in Articles 128 to 131 of the Constitution of the Weimar Republic on the basis of the principle that the state's civil servants have to serve the entire community and not solely the interests of a political party. After the fall of the fascist dictatorship in Italy, its new constitution stated that the 'civil servants are exclusively at the service of the Nation',[49]

[48] On the constitutionalization of these concerns and the resulting need for neutrality, see below the Weimar experience.

[49] Italian Constitution of 1948, Art 98.

providing that 'public offices are organized according to the provisions of law, so as to ensure efficiency and the impartiality of administration. The regulations of the offices lay down the areas of competence, duties and responsibilities of their functionaries.'[50] A similar tendency is present in the recent Greek Constitution which was adopted after the advent of the democratic regime: 'civil servants shall be the executors of the will of the State and shall serve the people, owing allegiance to the Constitution and devotion to the Fatherland',[51] and in Spain the above-mentioned Article 103 introduces principles limiting—in the name of the objectivity, efficiency, and compliance with justice and law—the relevance of the hierarchical organization. Similar considerations appear in new post-totalitarian constitutions. For instance, in Bulgaria, the state's employees are required to be 'the executors of the nation's will and interests. In performance of their duty they shall be guided solely by the law and shall politically neutral',[52] and in Slovenia, the Constitution provides that 'duties and functions associated with the public administration shall be conducted independently and at all times pursuant to, and consistently with, this Constitution and the law.'[53] Consequently, the tendency of adopting solutions of delegating state functions to autonomous agencies, which are separated from the public administration branches, should be appreciated. One noteworthy point is the example of the English government of creating *quasi-governmental organizations* and *quasi-non-governmental organizations*, or entrusting the regional decentralized offices with 'general decisive authority on matters of their district' as has happened in Greece.[54] Another solution as regards regulation of the decision-making process itself, which frequently implies an emphasis on the administrative functions close to the interested people, is that, according to Article 105 of the Spanish Constitution, 'the law shall regulate the hearing of citizens directly, or through the organisations and associations recognized by law, in the process of drawing up the administrative provisions which affect them.'

Bibliography

Costantinos Bacoyannis, *Le principe constitutionnel de libre administration des collectivités territoriales* (1993)

Sergio Bartole, Roberto Bin, Giandomenico Falcon, and Rosanna Tosi, *Diritto regionale* (2003)

Francois Burdeau, *Histoire du droit administrative* (1995)

Albert V. Dicey, *Introduction to the Study of the Law of the Constitution* (8th edn, 1915)

Robert C. Fried, *The Italian Prefects: A Study in Administrative Politics* (1963)

Francis Hamon and Michel Troper, *Droit constitutionnel* (2005)

[50] Italian Constitution of 1948, Art 97.

[51] Art 103.

[52] Art 116.

[53] Art 120. Arts 195–7 of the recent Constitution of the Republic of South Africa (1996) provided a long list of the basic values and principles governing public administration and for the establishment of a Public Service Commission whose functions have to be exercised 'in the interest of the maintenance of effective and efficient public administration and a high standard of professional ethics in the public service.' The expression 'public service' refers to persons who are employees in the public administration according to terms and conditions regulated by national legislation. In the Nordic countries, safeguarding the public interests of the efficiency and the high professional standards of public administration is the main task of a particular organ which has recently also attracted the attention of other states, the Ombudsman: see Donald Cameron Rowat, *The Ombudsman: Citizens Defender* (1965).

[54] Art 101.

Olivier Jouanjan (ed), *Figures de l'État de droit* (2001)
Jeffrey Jowell and Dawn Oliver, *The Changing Constitution* (5th edn, 2004)
Hermann Mangoldt and Christian Starck, *Das Bonner Grundgesetz* (5th edn, 2005)
Jean-Pierre Massias, *Droit Constitutionnel des États d'Europe de l'Est* (2nd edn, 2008)
Machado Santiago Munoz, *Derecho de las Comunidades Autonomas*, vols I and II (2nd edn, 2006)
Peter Pernthaler, *Der differenzierte Bundesstaat* (1992)
Pierre Rosanvallon, *Le modèle politique français* (2004)
Markku Suksi, *Autonomy: Application and Implication* (1998)

CHAPTER 29

PRESIDENTIALISM

HÉCTOR FIX-FIERRO AND
PEDRO SALAZAR-UGARTE

Mexico City

I. Concepts

A presidential system is a form of government in a republican state. From this perspective, it is an alternative to monarchy. However, its historical origins and theoretical background are found in monarchical government. The idea that one and the same person holds the offices of head of state and head of government is akin to both presidential systems and traditional monarchies. Whenever these two roles are separated, the foundations are laid for either a constitutional monarchy or a parliamentary government. Thus, presidentialism as a form of government was born as an alternative to both monarchy (absolute or constitutional) and parliamentarism (republican or monarchical).

In terms of the historical evolution of the theory of forms of government, we can say that presidentialism takes on a republican dimension as opposed to a monarchy,[1] while within a

[1] Nicolò Machiavelli, *The Prince* ([1532] 1989).

republican order, it takes on a democratic dimension as opposed to an aristocracy.[2] Indeed, even though it incorporates some elements of a monocratic tradition, our definition of presidentialism is based on a broad concept of democracy, rather than on an idea of autocratic rule.[3]

To characterize presidentialism as a republican and democratic alternative implies the conceptual exclusion of other systems of government in which one person plays the role of head of state and head of government at the same time. Regimes such as sultanates,[4] military dictatorships, 'hereditary' presidential systems (eg Haiti under the Duvaliers, or, until recently, Egypt, Tunisia, Yemen, and Algeria), or executive monarchies (Saudi Arabia and Oman) cannot be considered presidential systems of government in the proper sense. We justify such exclusion on two theses that complement each other: (1) the presidential form of government is, broadly speaking, a subspecies of modern democracy (the latter being a subspecies of the republican form of state), that is, a system in which the head of government is periodically and institutionally renewed via popular election; and (2) presidentialism is an alternative to parliamentarism, the main difference between both democratic systems being that the separation of powers is one of the essential features of a presidential constitution.

Certainly, depending on the extent to which power tends not to be distributed but is concentrated in the hands of a unipersonal organ (the presidency or the executive power), presidentialism can easily lead to authoritarian deviations. By the same token, however, it can also easily respond to democratic expectations. This occurs, in the first place, because it enjoys a legal-rational legitimacy of its own,[5] and secondly, because such legitimacy finds its basis in popular elections. Clearly, not every source of legal-rational legitimacy and not every kind of election are democratic per se. However, in the case of presidentialism, both elements are generally linked to a democratic perspective. In comparison with traditional and charismatic sources of legitimacy, the source of presidential legitimacy is impersonal.[6] And in contrast with its autocratic alternatives, presidential legitimacy flows bottom-up as an expression of citizens' political autonomy.[7]

The source of legitimacy of presidential power lies, then, in a set of rules (laws and institutions) that broadly correspond to the forms of modern democracy. More precisely, these rules provide for the necessary, regular and periodic replacement of the head of the executive power through popular vote. The decision as to who will be elected president in a democratic setting depends on the outcome of an electoral process that must satisfy specific conditions: all the adult members of the community may participate peacefully and on an equal, non-discriminatory basis; every vote carries the same weight; and the vote of the majority determines the outcome of the election.[8] If these conditions are met, and furthermore, the political minorities who lost the election are given the possibility to participate and win in a future electoral round, then we may conclude that the election of the president has been fairly democratic.[9]

If, on the contrary, one or more of the conditions and rules described are ignored, and, if minorities are structurally excluded from exercising power, we must then conclude that the

[2] Charles Marie Secondat de Montesquieu, *The Spirit of the Laws* ([1748] 1989).

[3] Hans Kelsen, 'On the Essence and Value of Democracy' in Arthur Jacobson and Bernhard Schlink (eds), *Weimar: A Jurisprudence of Crisis* (2002). On democracy, see Chapter 11.

[4] Max Weber, *Wirtschaft und Gesellschaft. Grundriss der Verstehenden Soziologie* (1922); Juan Linz, 'Presidential or Parliamentary Democracy: Does It Makes a Difference?' in Juan Linz and Arturo Valenzuela (eds), *The Failure of Presidential Democracy* (1994).

[5] Weber (n 4).

[6] Norberto Bobbio, *Teoria Generale della Politica* (1999).

[7] Kelsen (n 3).

[8] Bobbio (n 6).

[9] Ibid; Robert Dahl, *Polyarchy: Participation and Opposition* (1972).

regime is presidential in nature, but only democratic in appearance. This is, for example, the case of presidential systems under the rule of a hegemonic party,[10] or of the authoritarian presidential governments of some Latin American (eg the regime of President Hugo Chávez in Venezuela) and African countries. In any case, presidentialism is characterized by the periodic renewal of the branches of power through presumably democratic processes. Whenever a political leader holds on to power for an indefinite time, even if he is called the President of the Nation (like Fidel Castro in Cuba), the system can no longer be considered presidential, but dictatorial. Presidentialism is therefore compatible with democratic governments, as well as with some instances of electoral authoritarian systems, but must not be mistaken for lifelong or hereditary autocracies.

Presidentialism stands on one of the conceptual and institutional pillars of liberal constitutionalism: the separation of powers. This pillar forms the basis for two other fundamental principles of modern constitutionalism: the principle of legality and the principle of impartiality. The former requires a separation between the main state functions while according priority to the legislative function over the executive and judicial functions. Impartiality, on the other hand, requires the separation of the organs authorized to carry out these state functions, taking particular care that the independence of the judicial branch vis-à-vis the other two branches of power is guaranteed. The priority given to the legislative function has a logical explanation: the executive and judicial functions presuppose the existence of general and abstract laws. The independence of the judiciary is explained by teleological arguments: effective compliance with the law is only possible if judges are independent from the political branches of government.[11] This relationship between state functions and the state organs that carry out these functions is crucial in defining presidential systems. Moreover, the manner in which executive and legislative branches are linked to and interact with each other is of particular relevance.

In order to understand the way in which these principles operate in presidentialism, it is important to consider how a presidential system differs from a parliamentary government. Two criteria will be mentioned here: first, the source of legitimacy of the legislative (parliament or congress) and executive (president) branches, and secondly, some of the substantive powers vested in them. In presidentialism, citizens directly elect the members of each of these branches, so both are institutionally and organically independent from the other. A government with dual legitimacy emerges[12] because each of the branches of power—the executive and the legislative—may claim their own independent source of legitimacy. Each one enjoys a considerable degree of political independence vis-à-vis the other: the legislature may not remove the government by a vote of no confidence, nor can the government dissolve the parliament and call for new elections. In consequence, a complex system of institutional checks and balances emerges,[13] which must operate for a fixed term without the possibility of anticipated citizen intervention (new elections).

The renewal of the presidency is provided for in the constitution and carried out at fixed intervals. Besides exceptional circumstances such as impeachment, death, resignation and the like, the president stays in office for a fixed period (generally between four and six years), with or without the possibility of being elected for more than one term. Re-election for a limited

[10] Giovanni Sartori, *Comparative Constitutional Engineering. An Inquiry into Structures, Incentives and Outcomes* (2nd edn, 1997).

[11] Charles McIlwain, *Constitutionalism: Ancient and Modern* (1940). See further Chapter 8.

[12] Linz (n 4).

[13] Montesquieu (n 2); Michel Troper, *La séparation des pouvoirs et l'histoire constitutionnelle française* (1973).

number of terms is possible, as in Angola, Argentina, Brazil, South Africa, and the United States, while it is absolutely prohibited in Mexico and Nicaragua.

The renewal of the legislature also follows fixed terms, which may, or may not, be concurrent with presidential elections. The terms of office of the members of the judiciary tend to be much longer (a career judiciary exists in most countries) and non-concurrent, for the sake of judicial independence, with the terms of office of the other branches of power.

Between parliamentarism and presidentialism other intermediate forms of government are possible (semi-presidentialism or semi-parliamentarism). They also observe democratic rules and recognize the principle of the separation of powers, but the relationship between the legislature and the executive adopts different modalities. If the legislative power is preeminent, the form of government is called semi-parliamentarism. If the executive power enjoys a privileged position, then we are speaking of semi-presidentialism. From among the different modalities that these intermediate forms of government may adopt, the design of coincident powers is especially favorable to a flexible and stable operation of the particular separation of powers. Mechanisms providing for shared responsibilities (eg joint appointment of cabinet members, or joint design and implementation of governmental programs) seem to be fairly common.

II. History and Evolution

Presidentialism as a form of government was born in the United States in 1787. The US model was later adopted and adapted by other newly independent countries, whether in nineteenth-century Latin America or twentieth-century Africa. Thus, it appears to be especially well suited to countries facing the complex tasks of independent nation-building and development. The emergence of authoritarian or dictatorial governments in most of these countries seems to be a frequent side effect of adopting a presidential constitution before a more democratic and balanced system can be established.

1. The Birthplace of Presidentialism: The United States of America (1787)

The presidential form of government was conceived by the 1787 Philadelphia Constitutional Convention.[14] Certainly, it was not born in the full and complete shape it has now, but the Founding Fathers defined the essential features that have marked its development in the United States and its diffusion and adoption, with numerous variations, in other regions of the world: the president is both the head of state and the head of government, and is elected for a fixed term that is independent from that of the legislature or national representative body.

The final design of the presidency in the Federal Constitution of the United States was the result of arduous debates and continuously revised solutions based on compromises. The Framers were sufficiently clear on the type of national government they wanted to establish, as well as the role the executive power would play in it: the president had to be independent from the legislature if he was to serve as the check and counterbalance of legislative power. However, unlike the ineffective executive power created by the states after the Declaration of Independence in 1776, the president had to possess legitimacy, energy, and a decision-making capacity of his

[14] Sydney M. Milkis and Michael Nelson, *The American Presidency. Origins and Development, 1776–2002* (4th edn, 2003); Sydney M. Milkis, 'History of the Presidency' in Michael Nelson (ed), *Guide to the Presidency*, vol 1 (3rd edn, 2002).

own. At the same time, it was necessary to prevent the president from becoming an oppressive, tyrannical power—as the British monarch and colonial governors had often behaved—or a demagogue who was subject to the demands and whims of the masses.

Nevertheless, at the opening of the Congress there was insufficient clarity on the specific nature and powers the institution was to assume. The so-called Virginia Plan (drafted by James Madison) was quite vague regarding the executive power. Thus, the delegates had to discuss whether the executive power was to be single or plural (single); whether the president could be re-elected or appointed for life (re-election with no limits, but not for life); whether he was to be appointed by the legislature or independently (election by a special body, the Electoral College); and whether his term of office should concur with the terms of office of the other powers (non-concurrent term). The delegates also had to resolve a number of other significant issues raised by the presidential institution: such as the requirements for holding office and the corresponding oath or affirmation; succession in case of resignation, disability, or removal; incompatibility with other offices; and even the president's compensation for rendering services. The name of the officer itself—the title of 'president' was usually assigned to the officer presiding over assembly or legislature sessions—was adopted without debate.

The Framers also defined the particular powers the president was to exercise:

- a veto power over legislation (which can be overridden by Congress);
- the role of commander-in-chief of the armed forces (but only Congress has power to declare war);
- the power to make treaties (with the advice and consent of the Senate), as well as the power to recognize foreign nations;
- the power to appoint ambassadors, officers of the United States, and judges (with Senate confirmation);
- the power to issue pardons;
- the power to inform Congress on the state of the Union and the power to recommend legislation;
- the power to call Congress to special sessions.

The enumeration of presidential powers in the constitutional text notwithstanding, its exercise in practice has been shaped by the personal character and political beliefs of the presidents themselves, as well as by the debates that constitutional life has posed over the course of time (eg the meaning and scope of the phrase 'he (the president) shall take Care that the Laws be faithfully executed'), and which have been the main motor of its evolution.

Shortly after the new Constitution went into force, two diverging conceptions of the role of the presidential institution and the scope of its powers arose: on one hand, the 'Hamiltonian' view of the president as the leader of a vigorous national government, vested with all the necessary powers, and even implicit ones; and on the other, the 'Jeffersonian' perspective, aimed at circumscribing and limiting the role of national governmental powers and, in particular, those of the president.[15] This latter vision triumphed with the election of Thomas Jefferson as president of the United States in 1800. It marked the beginning of a long cycle of growing dominance of Congress over the presidency that lasted throughout almost the entire nineteenth century.

[15] Raymond Tatalovich and Thomas S. Engeman, *The Presidency and Political Science. Two Hundred Years of Constitutional Debate* (2003).

Its lowest point was reached after the Civil War, with the attempt to impeach President Andrew Johnson (1865–69) and the enactment of the Tenure of Office Act, which prohibited the president from removing any Senate-ratified executive officer without the consent of the Senate. Significantly enough, in 1885 Woodrow Wilson—who would later be elected president (1913–21)—published his classic treatise on the constitutional system of the United States entitled *Congressional Government*. Certainly, many presidents of those times fought hard to restore the powers of the presidency and won many a victory over Congress.

The predominance of Congress notwithstanding, the exercise of presidential power itself underwent major transformations during the nineteenth century. Such transformations would set the stage for the new tasks the presidential institution would assume in the twentieth century. The most significant changes lie in the emergence of political parties as central and preeminent organizations in political processes, as well as in the growing connections and responsiveness of the president towards the demands and expectations of a dynamic, expanding citizenry.[16] Thus, US presidents arrived at the conviction that they—not the legislators who represented rather their district or state constituencies—were the true representatives of the nation. They felt obliged towards citizens' aspirations, and this belief led them to seek direct contact with them (the role of the press in this sense became crucial), including the possibility of directly appealing to the people when faced with situations of conflict with Congress or national emergencies. Presently, the consummate manifestation of those direct links between the president and citizens lies in the primaries for selecting presidential candidates (thus sidestepping the political parties) and the media-driven (and more recently internet-driven) election campaigns.

The enormous changes and dislocations that the United States witnessed over the last decades of the nineteenth century and first decades of the twentieth century—accelerated economic growth, urbanization, increasing presence and influence in the international arena—propelled the presidency towards the center of political action, and made it the vehicle of governmental activism geared towards the regulation of change, particularly economic change, as well as the arbitrator of conflicts between social groups and classes.

This new transformation finds perhaps its beginnings in the Theodore Roosevelt Administration (1901–09), during the so-called Progressive Era, but it picked up pace and reached its peak with President Franklin Delano Roosevelt's New Deal (1933–45) and President Lyndon B. Johnson's Great Society (1963–69). It has been accompanied not only by an extraordinary growth of the administrative apparatus of government, but also of the office of the president itself. In 1939, President F.D. Roosevelt established the Executive Office of the President based on a law passed by Congress. This office, which comprises several agencies placed under the immediate authority of the president, is designed to give him the tools he needs in order to start and carry out his projects and policies, as well as to control an ever-growing and increasingly complex administrative apparatus. As a result, the influence of the Executive Office of the President has expanded and grown, even under those presidents who came into office promising to reduce Big Government, to the point of it becoming a type of government within government, and even, as some authors put it, a fourth branch of government: the presidential branch.[17]

In the first decade of the twenty-first century, the president is still the most salient and powerful figure in the political life of the United States, and perhaps of the world. However, the increasing intricacies of society and of the interests that contemporary government must regulate make

[16] On political parties, see Chapter 41.

[17] James P. Pfiffner, *The Modern Presidency* (3rd edn, 2000).

bargaining, approving, and implementing domestic reforms, in a context of a persisting and insidious financial crisis, ever more difficult and painful. Even the international arena, which used to be where presidential power could be displayed most freely, is increasingly complex and obstacle-ridden. If the United States is truly in (relative) decline, this cannot fail to have an impact on the institution that has most contributed to the unfolding and consolidation of its status as a superpower: the presidency.

2. The First Expansion of Presidentialism: Latin America (Nineteenth Century)

Between 1809 and 1830, the territories that have come to be known collectively as Latin America attained their independence from the Spanish and Portuguese empires. The new nations adopted a republican form of government and, in particular, presidentialism, under the inspiration of the 1787 Federal Constitution of the United States. However, its adoption was not immediate, nor was it exempt from national nuances and variations. Moreover, at different times and for short periods, several Latin American states experimented with parliamentarism and parliamentarian formulas, particularly in the twentieth century (eg Chile 1891–1923, Uruguay 1934–42, Cuba 1940–52, and Brazil 1961–63). Latin American states introduced four models of government at the time of independence and in the immediately ensuing period.[18]

The first model is embodied in *monarchical projects* since monarchical ideas were popular in the early years after independence and even beyond. We can mention Henri Christophe in Haiti (1811–20) and the ephemeral Mexican Empire of General Agustin de Iturbide between 1822 and 1823 (a second attempt between 1864 and 1867, with Maximilian of Habsburg as the emperor, was also short-lived). Brazil remained an empire from 1822 to 1889 because Peter I, the heir to the Portuguese crown, proclaimed Brazilian independence and crowned himself emperor.

The second model adopted by the first Latin American constitutions was the *plural executive*. Its sources can be found in the ideas of Rousseau and the 1793 and 1795 French revolutionary constitutions, as well in the 'governing *juntas*' (*juntas gubernativas*) that sprung up with the Napoleonic invasion of Spain and the ensuing abdication of the Spanish kings in 1808. As examples of this model, we can cite the 1811 Constitution of Cundinamarca in the event that Ferdinand VII could not occupy the throne; the 1812 Constitution of Quito; the 1811 Constitution of Venezuela; and the 1814 Mexican Constitution, known as the Apatzingán Constitution. However, the flaws and drawbacks of this form of government soon surfaced and prompted it to be abandoned.

Thirdly, we cite the *presidency for life* as suggested and inspired by Simon Bolívar. In Bolívar's own words, referring to the Constitution of Bolivia:

> The president of the Republic is to our Constitution like the sun, which, firm in its center, gives life to the universe. This supreme authority must be perpetual; because in systems without hierarchies, more than in others, a fixed point is needed, around which the magistrates and citizens turn.... For Bolivia, this point is the president-for-life. On him our whole order is predicated, without having action because of this. His head has been cut, so that no one should be afraid of his intentions, and his hands have been tied, so that he does nobody harm.

Experimentation with this form of government was quite short-lived: no more than two years in Bolivia (1826–28) and seven weeks in Peru (1826).

[18] Salvador Valencia Carmona, *El poder ejecutivo latinoamericano* (1979).

Between 1821 and 1830 and based on the model of the US Constitution but incorporating some significant influences from Spanish constitutionalism, such as the countersignature of executive decrees and orders by ministers, the institution of the Council of State or government, or parliamentary interpellation (of which many survive to this day), the presidential system was finally adopted by almost all Latin American countries.[19]

The republican and presidential government of the United States enjoyed considerable prestige among the fathers of Latin American constitutions, who admired their northern neighbor not only for its political success, but also for its economic progress. Circulating copies and (bad) translations of the 1787 Constitution, as well of the *Federalist Papers*, were their main sources of knowledge about the US Constitution. However, active propaganda by US diplomats and agents also made a significant contribution. Joel Roberts Poinsett served as special agent or envoy to Argentina and Chile between 1810 and 1814, and to Mexico between 1822 and 1830; Stephen F. Austin, a US citizen who had moved to Spanish Texas to start a colony, arrived in Mexico in 1822, where he befriended several members of the First Constitutional Congress and drafted several projects that influenced the 1823 Constitutive Act of the Federation. The so-called Monroe Doctrine, proclaimed by US President James Monroe (1817–25) in 1823, not only rejected the intervention of European powers in the Americas, but also, by implication, their political systems.

The introduction of presidentialism did not result in a balance of powers nor in democracy, but in *caudillismo*. *Caudillos* were strong men—at first from the military, and later of civilian extraction—who dominated the political life of their respective countries for long periods (emblematical examples are the Perpetual Dictatorship of Jose Gaspar de Francia in Paraguay from 1816 to 1840, or the prolonged dictatorial government of Porfirio Díaz in Mexico from 1876 to 1910). These men strove to become the builders of their nations and the promoters of their social and economic development, but many of them became dictators, with paternalistic features to be sure, but dictators nevertheless (an inexhaustible motif of Latin American literature). From the presidency, they set out to mold constitutional institutions in their own image. As pointed out by several scholars, Latin American constitutional history became a study in biography. The period of *caudillos* extended to a good part of the nineteenth century (and in Mexico, to the first three decades of the twentieth century).

The factors leading to *caudillismo* are diverse and complex. On the one hand, despite the preeminence granted in many constitutional texts to the legislature, the strict separation of powers had the opposite effect, obstructing the control of Congress over the executive. The same enlightened argument that had served to entrench the autonomy of the parliament and deflect interference from the executive served the president equally well to evade any check the legislature may have wanted to wield against his powers.[20] On the other hand, a number of social and cultural factors favored, and indeed required, the concentration of power in the hands of the president of the republic: the survival of economic and social structures from colonial times; the absence of a capable and consolidated ruling class; permanent civil strife and the fight against foreign interference or invasions; the lingering presence of a scarcely integrated and backward society, and so on. As these factors gradually began to recede and state structures gained in strength, so did the *caudillos* slowly begin to abandon the political stage.

In the twentieth century, Latin American presidential constitutions evolved towards a regime of clear presidential dominance over the other branches of government. According to

[19] Jorge Carpizo, 'Essential Characteristics of the Presidential System and Influences for its Establishment in Latin America' (2007) 8 *Mexican Law Review* (Carmen Valderrama trans, online version only).

[20] Diego Valadés, *La parlamentarización de los sistemas presidenciales* (2nd edn, 2008).

Valencia (1979), the Latin American executive power displayed the following common features:

- a marked personal character of presidential power;
- some traces of parliamentarianism, in most cases of a purely formal nature (cabinet, ministerial countersignature);
- the constitutionally entrenched dominance of the presidency over the other two powers, as manifested in the president's broad powers to intervene in the legislative process (introducing legislative bills, the veto); to make appointments; to declare states of siege or emergency, a practice that, by virtue of its constitutional design, but also of its frequent use, amounted to 'constitutional dictatorship';[21]
- a vast administrative apparatus, including the management of state-owned companies and monopolies, at the president's disposal;
- presidential regulation and promotion of development, with wide-ranging powers of economic and social intervention.

While most Latin American constitutions of the time sought to impose a few checks on presidential power, such as the precise and explicit enumeration of presidential powers or a non re-election clause, these limitations did not prevent several presidents from instituting oligarchic and repressive dictatorships after a time (as seen with the Somozas in Nicaragua, Stroessner in Paraguay, and the Duvaliers in Haiti), nor did they stop the frequent occurrence of coups d'état that resulted in the establishment of military governments and dictatorships. In fact, in most Latin American countries, the armed forces came to play the role of a 'reserve power' that was called upon to restore 'order' whenever social conflict or the reformist policies of some presidents threatened to get out of hand, that is, the interests of the ruling elites. The Cold War also fostered frequent military interventions, backed by the US government, under the pretext of the fight against the spread of communism in the region.

In the 1980s, Latin American countries under military rule slowly began to reinstate their civilian governments. The end of the Cold War and the disrepute of military governments for the serious human rights violations committed under them opened up an advantageous opportunity for democracy that has lasted to this day.

None of the countries in the region has abandoned presidentialism. The introduction of constitutional mechanisms of parliamentarian origin (see below) is intended to foster more stable and smoother executive-legislative relations, but the ever-present presidential temptation to seize supreme power has not been eradicated, as witnessed by the persistent (and successful) attempts to sanction presidential re-election or by enacting new constitutions and constitutional amendments tailored to the political projects of a new generation of *caudillos*.

3. The Struggle against Colonialism and the Challenges of Development: Africa, the Middle East, and Asia (Twentieth Century)

At the end of the Second World War, the decolonization process in Africa, the Middle East, and Asia brought forth the establishment of new states and the re-emergence of old nations that had fallen under the dominion of Western powers. A new period of expansion of

[21] Diego Valadés, *La dictadura constitucional en América Latina* (1974).

presidentialism began. Suddenly, the newly independent nations were facing some of the challenges and dilemmas that Latin American countries had had to address in the early nineteenth century: both the complex task of nation-building and the urgent demands of economic and social development called for clear, decisive, and legitimate political leadership. Not surprisingly, most of these countries ended up adopting the presidential form of government, notwithstanding the fact that during their colonial periods they had received strong parliamentarian imprints from the European powers that had ruled their territories (France, Great Britain, Belgium, the Netherlands). It is true that in the years after their independence, the new states kept the parliamentarian legacy of their colonial masters, a legacy whose adoption had even been a condition for independence. But this state of affairs was short-lived.

A good example in Africa was Ghana, which became independent in 1957 and adopted the British system of government, even with Queen Elizabeth II as titular head of state. However, in 1960, a constitution establishing a unitary, presidential state was passed. Between 1960 and 1962, 13 African states proclaimed new constitutions or amended the existing ones for the purpose of replacing parliamentarism with presidentialism, following the model President Nkrumah had introduced in Ghana.[22] But like the Latin American experience, the new African presidential systems were soon transformed into personal autocracies, if not outright dictatorships, under the rule of a strong man who frequently proclaimed himself president-for-life. Coups d'état by the armed forces were also a frequent consequence of power struggles.

In many countries, presidential supremacy was reinforced by various factors unique to the region and the historical moment. There was a conscious movement in Africa towards the suppression of multipartyism, seen as a divisive factor that weakened the new nations, and subsequently towards the concentration of power in the hands of one party and, ultimately, of one man. The adoption of various versions of socialism, including Marxist socialism, also contributed to strengthening authoritarian rule.[23]

In the 1980s and particularly in the 1990s, African countries did not escape the transformations that swept over other regions of the world in response to economic and social crises, and to the democratic demands of civil society backed by world public opinion. Multiparty systems were restored and market reforms introduced. Reluctantly and under intense pressure from the people, many of the strong men either had to resign their positions or submit to the judgment of voters, who did not hesitate to send them packing, thus giving way to a new phenomenon: the 'retired African president'.[24] A visible, institutional consequence of these democratic changes has been the inclusion of presidential term limits in more than 30 African constitutions (but many others still do not provide for them).

Despite the evident moderation of presidential absolutism in post-authoritarian Africa, presidential supremacy persists.[25] The debate on the causes of such persistence oscillates between 'cultural' explanations, focused on the traditions and practices of African kingship, and 'rationalist' accounts, which point out that the pending tasks of national integration and socio-economic development, together with the lack of a liberal and parliamentarian background that can be traced back to the colonial era, still support the centrality of the state and

[22] William Tordoff, *Government and Politics in Africa* (3rd edn, 1997); H. Kwasi Prempeh, 'Presidential Power in Comparative Perspective: The Puzzling Persistence of Imperial Presidency in Post-Authoritarian Africa' (2008) 35 *Hastings Constitutional Law Quarterly* 761.

[23] Tordoff (n 22).

[24] Roger Southall and Henning Melber (eds), *Legacies of Power. Leadership Change and Former Presidents in African Politics* (2006), available at <http://www.hsrcpress.ac.za>.

[25] Muna Ndulo, 'Presidentialism in the Southern African States and Constitutional Restraint on Presidential Power' (2001) 26 *Vermont Law Review* 769; Prempeh (n 22).

of executive administration as vehicles for development. Undoubtedly, the still unfinished process of constitutional reform, particularly that pertaining to defining presidential powers and the relationship between the branches of government, also plays a significant role in maintaining alive the 'imperial presidency'.

The history and evolution of presidential systems in several Middle Eastern countries (such as Egypt, Syria, Iraq), as well as in Asia (the Philippines, Indonesia, South Korea), are not much different from the post-colonial experiences in Latin America and Africa. The names of Mubarak in Egypt, Hussein in Iraq, Marcos in the Philippines, and Suharto in Indonesia suffice to evoke long periods of individual, despotic, and corrupt rule, which finally yielded to the pressures and demands of citizens and of world opinion. These advances notwithstanding, they should be viewed as constitutional systems in transition, particularly due to the fragility of their party systems.

4. The Compromise between Past and Present: The Former Soviet Union and the ex-Socialist Countries after 1989

Finally, the 'third wave' of democracy in the late 1980s and early 1990s brought a fourth wave of presidential constitutions in most of the former Soviet republics after the dissolution of the Soviet Union in 1991.

We should recall that in the Soviet model of government, all power was placed in the hands of the Supreme Soviet as the highest body of people's representation. All other powers and functions derived from it and were subject to its control. In practice, however, the Politburo of the Communist Party of the Soviet Union (CPSU) and its secretary general had complete control of the State apparatus in their hands.

Mikhail Gorbachev's appointment as secretary general of the CPSU in 1985 marked the beginning of a reform process (known as *glasnost*, or openness, and *perestroika*, or restructuring), which, among others things, had the purpose of institutionalizing state functions by wresting them away from the monopoly the CPSU had over all public offices. Thus, between 1988 and 1990 Gorbachev prompted a series of amendments to the 1977 Brezhnev Constitution that were designed to establish a new executive power, the 'President of the Soviet Union', a position to which he was afterwards elected.

Prior to the attempted coup d'état that led to the dissolution of the Soviet Union in 1991, the constitutional amendments of March and December 1990 defined the president as an officer who was to be elected by direct popular vote (although not the first time) for a five-year term with the possibility of a second term. The president was both head of state and head of government, and he had the power to appoint a prime minister and a cabinet who were responsible to both him and the Congress of the People's Deputies.[26]

The 1993 Constitution of the Russian Federation established a strong presidency, resembling a semi-presidential constitution in certain aspects, but it ultimately entrenches presidential supremacy. The president of the Russian Federation is elected by popular vote for a period of six years, and he cannot hold this position for more than two consecutive terms. The president appoints the prime minister as head of government with the consent of the Duma (parliament), and when proposed by the prime minister, he appoints and dismisses the rest of the cabinet of ministers. In case the Duma casts a vote of no confidence in the government, the president may dismiss the government or, alternatively, dissolve the Duma and call for new elections.

[26] Manuel Becerra Ramírez, 'La presidencia soviética. Notas sobre los cambios en la Constitución soviética' (1991) XXIV(70) *Boletín Mexicano de Derecho Comparado* 67.

With the exception of the Baltic states of Lithuania, Latvia, and Estonia, the rest of the former Soviet republics in Europe and Central Asia (Armenia, Azerbaijan, Belarus, Georgia, Kazakhstan, Kyrgyzstan, Tajikistan, Turkmenistan, and Ukraine) have established presidential systems of government in which the president is both head of state and head of government, but under one of three basic modalities: first, the government is solely in the hands of the president; secondly, the president appoints a prime minister and a cabinet of ministers who are solely responsible towards him; and thirdly (as is the case in six of nine countries), the president appoints a prime minister and a cabinet that require the support of the national assembly, or must be nominated by the assembly.

However, in most of these republics, the lack of a democratic tradition and of an effective separation of powers has resulted in authoritarian and even dictatorial governments under the control of strong men who, in some cases, have held the presidency uninterruptedly since the dissolution of the Soviet Union. In this sense, we do not perceive any essential differences with respect to the trajectory of presidential systems in other regions of the world. For the same reason, a process towards a more democratic and balanced form of government may be expected in the future.

III. Debates

Even though we have described presidentialism as both a subspecies of modern democratic government and an alternative to parliamentarism, the debate remains as to whether, and to what extent, both institutional designs—presidentialism and democracy—are compatible with each other. In principle, presidentialism is related to those autocratic forms in which political power is concentrated at the summit of the pyramid of authority. If democracy evokes the ideal of a distribution of power legitimized from the bottom, then presidentialism would be incompatible with democracy. However, from our perspective, such incompatibility does not exist. Although the origins and trajectory of presidentialism are not necessarily democratic, and even if its institutional characteristics do encourage the concentration of power in the hands of the president, it is also true that, unlike other forms of monocratic government, presidentialism finds its legitimacy at the bottom of the pyramid of power by way of rules and legal institutions; it provides for the necessary and periodic renewal of political offices (the presidency in the first place); and it incorporates the principle of separation of powers, which is a legacy of political liberalism.

The elements we have just mentioned are, therefore, the main reason why presidentialism and democracy are compatible. Moreover, they display a tendency toward distributing and limiting power that moves presidentialism away from monocratic and autocratic forms of government. This is not to say that presidential systems may not be subject to decay; quite the opposite is true. They may more or less be easily turned into autocratic and absolutist systems, and consequently, into undemocratic and illiberal polities. As we have stated before, in such cases, we cannot speak of a presidential system in the proper sense, despite the fact that many political regimes will continue to apply this term to themselves (eg the 'hereditary' presidency or the 'presidency-for-life' that have existed in some Arab countries for several decades), and notwithstanding the fact that a democratic presidential government may have existed at the beginning of the process of decline. In our view, a presidential system ceases to exist because the institutional channels that allow for the periodic renewal of political legitimacy, including the separation of powers, no longer operate.

A second set of relevant issues are closely related to the one just discussed. Scholars of democracy have asked themselves whether a presidential system increases the risk of instability in democratic institutions and, consequently, of autocratic degradation.[27] This debate finds itself at the very core of the democratic paradigm, that is, it purports to determine which institutional elements, whether presidential or parliamentary, enable democratic consolidation or, on the contrary, increase the risk of authoritarian rule.

Critics of presidentialism point out that: (1) presidential regimes are more fragile than parliamentary systems in times of political crisis; (2) presidentialism tends toward immobility, especially in situations of 'divided government', that is, the president does not have the support of a majority in Congress; (3) presidents may easily deceive themselves regarding the meaning of their public mandate in an election based on 'the winner takes all' principle; and (4) presidentialism often favors conditions in which improvised characters with little political experience and even fewer democratic convictions manage to get elected as presidents.[28] Each of these statements needs to be considered separately.

The alleged weakness of presidential systems is mainly attributed to its inflexible terms of office. A fixed term of office for the president makes it more difficult to find institutional solutions to sudden political and economic crises. Thus, while presidential rule appears to enjoy considerable stability in comparison with the frequent turnover of prime ministers and cabinets in parliamentary systems, the truth is that it does not have the appropriate instruments successfully to face a political crisis. While parliamentary systems incorporate institutional mechanisms, such as votes of no confidence and anticipated elections, that offer an internal and democratic answer to a moment of political crisis, mechanisms that would allow for the anticipated renewal of the mandate or legitimacy of the government in exceptional circumstances are not available in presidential systems. Consequently, presidents are often compelled to declare a 'state of emergency' (witness the experience of many Latin American countries during most of the twentieth century), with all the risks and perils associated therewith, but they are just as often tempted to suspend or even terminate the democratic process through extra-institutional means. Impeachment and social unrest leading to the removal or resignation of the president before the end of his or her term has recently emerged as a possible outcome of political conflict in presidential systems (see below).

In our perspective, there is real cause for this concern. Certainly, the stability of a democratic system may be reinforced by institutional means geared towards a more flexible process of presidential succession or replacement (eg shorter terms of office, constitutional mechanisms for appointing temporary presidents, and the like). Nevertheless, parliamentarism seems definitely to have the upper hand in this respect.

The possibility of political paralysis in presidential systems is another recurring concern for scholars. Whereas parliamentary systems invariably operate on the basis of legislative majorities or coalitions that support the sitting government, in presidential systems so-called 'divided' or 'minority' governments are fairly common. A president who does not enjoy the support of a legislative majority to carry out his or her policies becomes politically and institutionally weakened as a result. In turn, governmental ineffectiveness, either because the president is politically unable to govern or because he or she chooses confrontation and conflict with the legislature, may endanger the stability of the system as a whole. For this reason, some

[27] Scott Mainwaring and Matthew Soberg Shugart, *Presidentialism and Democracy in Latin America* (1997); Linz and Valenzuela (n 4).

[28] Linz (n 4); Karl Loewenstein, 'The Presidency Outside the United States: A Study in Comparative Political Institutions' (1949) 11(3) *Journal of Politics* 447; Alfred Stepan and Cindy Skach, 'Presidentialism and Parliamentarism Compared' in Linz and Valenzuela (n 4); Scott Mainwaring, 'Presidentialism in Latin America: A Review Essay' (1990) 25(1) *Latin American Research Review* 157; Arend Lijphart, *Parliamentary versus Presidential Government* (1992). On parliamentarism, see also Chapter 30.

scholars support the introduction of mechanisms designed to guarantee a legislative majority to the party of the president ('majority clauses', 'legislative governability bonds').

Once again, the risks associated with divided or minority governments in presidential systems are a real cause for concern. Political immobility will most certainly convey a sense of a loss of legitimacy in the eyes of citizens. A perceived or real, systematic obstruction of his or her policies by the legislature may easily induce the president to explore potentially authoritarian alternatives.

The possibility that presidents come to view their election as a manifestation of citizens' consent detached from the mandate given to the legislature, and in effect losing sight of the relativity of political consensus, is nothing but yet another consequence of the two issues analyzed above. In fact, combined with fixed presidential terms of office, an election based on 'the winner takes all' principle may cause the winner to disregard the need to build alliances and coalitions with other political forces, even if the election was won by a narrow margin, a common occurrence in presidential systems. (A runoff election apparently addresses this problem, but it may only produce an 'artificial' majority in support of the winner, and not an absolute mandate.) The election of President Salvador Allende in Chile in 1970 is a good case in point. Allende received about 36 percent of the popular vote, and the Congress elected him as president only after Allende reached an agreement with the Christian Democratic Party. However, his left-wing political allies pressured Allende into behaving as if a majority of the Chilean people had actually chosen a Socialist transformation. Allende's decisions were the cause of tremendous political tensions, in the end resulted in the tragic coup d'état led by General Augusto Pinochet in September 1973.

The adverse effects of this institutional flaw of presidential systems are compounded if the person elected president lacks political experience, is not familiar with traditional party politics, displays features of an authoritarian personality, or intends to establish a charismatic leadership. Although such concerns have an institutional basis and are born of historical experience (see Fujimori in Peru or Chávez in Venezuela), the danger of political leadership turning into a kind of 'postmodern *caudillismo*'[29] that drags down all democratic institutions is not alien to parliamentary systems either (see Berlusconi in Italy). The problem of 'delegative democracy',[30] then, is latent in both forms of government.

A useful institutional element to take into consideration, to the extent that it is present in some presidential constitutions, is federalism.[31] Only a few of the existing presidential systems (the United States, some Latin American and African countries) have adopted a federal organization. Federalism implies a twofold separation of powers: a horizontal separation of the three traditional branches of power (the executive, legislative, and judicial branches), and a vertical separation between the various levels of government (commonly the national, state, or provincial, and local levels). In this context, federalism means that presidentialism, with all its flaws and virtues, is also reproduced at the level of the constitutive entities of the union: states or provinces elect governors and legislatures that follow the main features of the national presidential constitution. Thus, the federal organization may serve as an additional check to the power of the president of the republic, particularly if state governments are in the hands of a party other than the ruling party or parties at the national level. But these positive effects, reinforced by the liberal logic of the distribution of power, may be offset by adverse consequences, to the extent that national political leadership is weakened and instability becomes more likely.

[29] Michelangelo Bovero, *Contro il governo dei peggiori* (2000).

[30] Guillermo O'Donnell, 'Delegative Democracy' (1994) 5(1) *Journal of Democracy* 55.

[31] Linz (n 4). See further Chapter 27.

Aside from the discussion on the dangers posed to democracy by presidential systems in comparison to parliamentarism, another broad vein of the debate focuses on the relative merits or deficiencies of both systems in terms of democratic governability. A few aspects of this debate have already been examined in the previous paragraphs, but some others are worth adding here, because, according to some scholars, they provide arguments favoring presidentialism over parliamentarism. Paradoxically, or only apparently so, if parliamentarism seems to be more favorable to the consolidation of democratic government from a certain perspective, presidentialism may provide a better anchor for governability.[32] We may come to this conclusion by inverting the logic we used to analyze the rigidity of presidential mandates and cast a critical glance at the possibility of votes of no confidence and anticipated elections in parliamentary systems instead.

From this alternative vantage point, parliamentarism may generate conditions that are more favorable for political instability than presidentialism (Italy during the second half of the twentieth century is a good example in this respect). As we can see, the rigidity of presidential constitutions and the flexibility of parliamentary ones may both be viewed as factors that favor either the stability or instability, as the case may be, of a political system. The difference in judgment depends on the criterion applied in each case: democracy or governability. Thus, scholars apparently agree that parliamentarism can better secure democracy, but may lead to ungovernability. Presidentialism, by contrast, seems to be a better guarantor of a stable government, but tends to unsettle democratic institutions. Not surprisingly, and as a possible corollary of this consensus, the current debate no longer turns on the dilemma between parliamentarism and presidentialism. As far as presidentialism is concerned, scholars now prefer to examine the question of how to 'make presidentialism work' (or, at least, 'work better').[33]

In order to stabilize presidentialism and prevent it from becoming an autocratic regime, it is necessary to increase the governing capabilities of the executive branch without unbalancing the democratic institutions. There are two possibilities in this direction: either the president's ability to influence legislative work is strengthened, or the ability of the members of the legislature to influence the operation of the government is reinforced. In other words: the dilemma now lies between strengthening the executive and increasing the power of parliament.

The first possibility may be accomplished by a wide array of measures: by strengthening the president's veto power on legislation passed by the legislature; by giving preference to the legislative bills introduced into the legislature by the president (any such bill must be passed or rejected within a peremptory time); by giving the president more powers to issue decrees with legislative force, or, ultimately, by reserving the power of introducing legislative bills to the president. The first type of measure is reactive, the rest are proactive.[34] Conversely, the legislature can get involved in the appointment and removal of cabinet members; it can strengthen its powers to make the government accountable (periodic reports and appearances by cabinet members); or, more generally, its powers to shape public policy can be broadened.

Modulating these and similar alternatives define the more or less parliamentary character of presidentialism, and the more or less presidential character of parliamentarism, described as semi-presidentialism and semi-parliamentarism, respectively. In this context, other institutional

[32] Sartori (n 10).

[33] Jose Antonio Cheibub, *Presidentialism, Parliamentarism, and Democracy* (2007); Jose Antonio Cheibub, 'Presidentialism, Parliamentarism, and the Role of Opposition Parties: Making Presidential or Semi-presidential Constitutions Work' (2009) 87 *Texas Law Review* 1375; Andrew Ellis, J. Jesús Orozco Henríquez and Daniel Zovatto (eds), *Cómo hacer que funcione el sistema presidencial/Making Presidentialism Work* (2009).

[34] Matthew Soberg Shugart and John M. Carey, *Presidents and Assemblies* (1992).

factors, like party systems and electoral rules, may also play a relevant role. These are distinctive features of all democratic systems and they have a crucial impact on the governability of both presidential and parliamentary systems, as well as of their hybrid or intermediate forms.[35] It is a complex issue that has been the object of much discussion by political scientists, and for this reason we only make a passing reference to it.

Finally, in trying to assess the accomplishments and failures of the various models of political organization—in terms of the level of their democratic engagement, their degree of governability and stability, and so on—besides the institutional factors we have already cited, scholars draw attention to environmental and contextual factors,[36] such as the geographic dimension, the population and its associated variables, other economic and cultural factors, and so on. Since institutions operate within specific contexts, it is only reasonable to assess presidential systems within such contexts.

IV. Trends and Positions

We open this section by pointing out an intriguing trend in a considerable number of presidential systems from the 1990s onwards: the attempts to remove unpopular presidents, or presidents charged with corruption and other abuses, through impeachment proceedings before the legislature, as well as the fall of those presidents who saw themselves forced to leave office before the end of their terms as a consequence of popular and media pressure. This trend has been particularly visible in Latin America, if for no other reason than the prevalence of this form of government throughout the region. Between 1992 and 2005, no less than 12 Latin American presidents had to face impeachment proceedings, many of which were successful and resulted in their removal from office (eg Presidents Fernando Collor de Mello in Brazil in 1992 and Carlos Andrés Pérez in Venezuela in 1993), or else were not able to remain in office for their full term due to popular unrest (eg Argentinean President De la Rúa in 2001).[37] However, the presidents of several countries in other regions of the world, such as the Philippines, Russia, Madagascar, Nigeria, or South Korea, have also recently faced serious impeachment challenges.[38]

Interestingly and paradoxically enough, even in cases in which the president resigned or was removed from office, democracy did not break down and the crisis was somehow managed by peaceful and institutional means. Certainly, we may or may not qualify this trend as a new form of instability, but impeachment (and, to a certain extent, this is also true of street protests and media scrutiny) appears to be an effective check on executive power that is similar—a sort of functional equivalent—to, but more extreme than, a vote of no confidence in parliamentary systems.[39] In fact, the main discernible trend of recent decades may be called the 'parliamentarization' of presidential systems, that is, the abandonment of 'pure' presidentialism and the adoption of mechanisms of parliamentary origins for the purpose of making executive-legislative relations more stable, flexible, and collaborative.[40]

[35] Linz (n 4).

[36] Fred W. Riggs, 'Presidentialism vs Parliamentarism: Implications for Representativeness and Legitimacy' (1998) 18(3) *International Political Science Review* 253.

[37] Aníbal Pérez-Liñán, *Presidential Impeachment and the New Political Instability in Latin America* (2007); Kathryn Hochstetler, 'Rethinking Presidentialism: Challenges and Presidential Falls in South America' (2006) 38(4) *Comparative Politics* 401.

[38] Jody C. Baumgartner, 'Introduction: Comparative Presidential Impeachment' in Jody C. Baumgartner and Naoko Kada, *Checking Executive Power: Presidential Impeachment in Comparative Perspective* (2003).

[39] Ibid.

[40] Valadés (n 20).

A few authors propose the denomination of 'parliamentary-presidential system' (also called 'constrained parliamentarism') to describe systems in which institutions of both subspecies of republican democratic government are combined, giving form to either 'constrained' presidentialism or to 'constrained' parliamentarism.[41] In fact, there is also a reverse trend whenever institutions of a presidential origin are incorporated into parliamentary systems. In these cases, we refer to the 'presidentialization of parliamentarian systems' (eg Italy after 1994 or Israel, where the prime minister was directly elected by popular vote from 1992 until 2001).

The trend toward the parliamentarization of presidential systems implies that, despite the introduction of institutions and mechanisms of parliamentary control, the basic structure of the receiving presidential constitution is preserved. A more balanced interplay of the branches of government is intended, in turn, to foster greater stability in the constitutional system as a whole, without fully abandoning presidentialism. Typically, parliamentarization carries adjustments and changes in the following strategic areas: (1) the election of the head of government and the appointment of his or her cabinet; (2) the procedures for the exercise of power; (3) the term of office of the head of government; (4) the system of responsibilities; and (5) the relationship between chief of state and head of government. This reaffirms the idea that the separation of powers is a central element for characterizing presidential systems and their alternatives.

The trend towards parliamentarization implies broadening the legislature's capacity to control the executive. This, for example, becomes manifest by means of establishing rules that allow the parliament to confirm the appointment of cabinet members, or to issue a vote of no confidence vis-à-vis the government. These are not identical hypotheses. While confirmation (as provided for in the US Constitution) means that a person's appointment has been ratified because he or she complies with the legal and ethical requirements of the office, the vote of no confidence (eg provided for in the constitutions of Peru, Uruguay, Belarus, Georgia, the Russian Federation, and Ukraine) carries a kind of shared responsibility between the legislature and the appointed officers that is usually accompanied by legislative support to government programs and policies.[42] In the latter case, a relationship of shared political responsibility between the legislature and the government is established beyond mere parliamentary control.

With respect to African countries, most constitutions also tend towards a 'hybrid' or mixed model of institutional designs seeking a better balance of power. In Francophone and Lusophone Africa, this has been mainly accomplished by reinstating the prime minister. In Anglophone countries that have adopted a hybrid form, such as Zambia, Uganda, and Ghana, a nationally elected president typically rules with a cabinet of ministers, all (or at least a majority) of whom have been selected from among the members of the legislature.[43]

Another sphere in which the parliamentarization of presidential systems may be observed is in the operational dynamics of executive-legislative relations. It concerns, for example, the rules governing the attendance of members of the government in the legislative chambers. Such appearance is called for whenever the laws vests them with the power to attend or participate in parliamentary sessions; whenever they are obliged to be periodically present at those sessions, or whenever, by contrast, the legislature is the body empowered to compel their attendance.

The great majority of democratic presidential constitutions provide for the power of the legislature to call for the ministers to appear before it. In some systems, ministers have the

[41] Bruce Ackerman, 'The New Separation of Powers' (2000) 113(3) *Harvard Law Review* 634.

[42] Valadés (n 20). [43] Prempeh (n 22).

possibility of making use of the legislative rostrum (in Latin America, this is a possibility in Argentina, Brazil, Chile, Colombia, Costa Rica, Dominican Republic, Guatemala, Peru, and Venezuela). In others, they may appear only before legislative committees. In any case, the purpose is to transfer control over the executive to the legislative seat.

Some of these controls are *soft* (eg interpellation or parliamentary questions). Others are *hard* (this is the case of the vote of no confidence). Interpellations and questions represent a soft form of control that may be expressed in written form, or directly (orally) in the parliamentary seat. Their essential purpose is to keep open channels of communication, as well as information exchanges between the parliament and the government. The vote of no confidence is a hard type of control (widely instituted in Latin American constitutions: eg in Argentina, Colombia, Costa Rica, Ecuador, El Salvador, Guatemala, Panamá, Paraguay, Peru, Uruguay, and Venezuela) that translates into the censure of a minister or of the cabinet as a whole.

This latter hypothesis—the censure of the government by the legislature—may result in the removal of one or more ministers, or even the dismissal of the prime minister, but, in contrast to parliamentary systems, not of the president himself as the head of government. For the same reason, constitutions that give the president the power to dissolve the congress (eg as in Ecuador, Peru, Uruguay, Venezuela, and the Russian Federation) place in his or her hands an excessive power that may reinforce the authoritarian tendencies of presidentialism, especially where presidents continuously seek plebiscitary legitimacy.

Taking the dilemmas and debates described in the previous section into account and following the logic of democracy, we approve of parliamentary controls over the executive within a context of separation and balance of powers, and in contrast reject potentially authoritarian measures, such as the dissolution of the legislature by the president.

Another visible trend in recent decades has been the proliferation of constitutions establishing systems of government that can be categorized as 'semi-presidential'. According to one distinguished scholar,[44] semi-presidential constitutions today represent about a quarter of democratic systems in the world. In terms of 'parliamentarized' presidential systems, semi-presidential constitutions go a step further on the road towards full parliamentarism. Not surprisingly and beyond the definitional problems posed by this form of government, in practice many nominal semi-presidential constitutions operate as parliamentary systems (eg Finland or Portugal). The reason why constitution-makers do not simply adopt a full parliamentary system from the beginning is apparently the belief that a popularly elected president may serve as an adjudicator of political conflicts and ultimately a leader who is not subject to the whims of a majority and, therefore, an effective check on the power of parliament.[45]

Observing available models in comparative perspective, we find the 1958 French Constitution emblematic. It is an institutional arrangement that is not easy to categorize within the distinction between parliamentarism and presidentialism, since it operates with the dominance of one or the other model, depending on the specific political constellation. This ambiguity lies at the heart of the tensions among its creators—along with a strong undercurrent of presidentialist tendencies promoted by General de Gaulle—which were finally resolved by means of the following principles: (1) universal suffrage as the source of legitimacy for both the executive and legislative powers; (2) the separation of powers; and (3) the government's accountability to parliament. To these principles, the distinction between head of state

[44] Cheibub (n 33). [45] Ibid.

(president of the republic) and head of government (prime minister) was added. Thus were the foundations laid for a model that allows for periods in which the system emphasizes its presidentialist features (when the president's party has a majority in the legislature and, consequently, control over government), and periods in which the system operates under parliamentarian premises (in times of *cohabitation*, which Duverger defines as a 'state in which a president of the Republic coexists with a parliamentary majority of a different political orientation').[46]

This flexible scheme—which allows for alternations between a system with strong presidentialist features and another with parliamentary tendencies—is made possible by a constitutional design that combines elements of both forms of government, as well as concrete devices (such as the distinction between head of state and head of government; the incompatibility of exercising a parliamentary role in a cabinet position; the vote of no confidence over the government, and holding of legislative elections after the presidential election) that integrate the institutional elements with the political vicissitudes of the day. Under particular circumstances, the president and the prime minister find themselves in a situation of political rivalry that triggers the existing institutional checks, thus weakening the presidentialist features of the model; at other moments, the president may have a parliamentary majority effectively situating him above the head of government.

We have made reference to the 1958 French Constitution (including its later amendments) because it exemplifies a hybrid formula between presidentialism and parliamentarism that, under a flexible and dynamic design, has achieved a balanced combination of stability and governability. It embodies the tension that in practice can be observed between the parliamentary and the presidential poles. The dominance of one or the other depends on the particular correlation between the political forces of the day.

V. Comparative Perspective and Recapitulation

In previous sections we have presented a brief overview of presidentialism, its evolution and development, its problems and transformations. We now close this chapter with a broad summary and a few general conclusions.

In 1949, Professor Karl Loewenstein, in his classic essay on 'The Presidency Outside the United States', wrote the following:

> The economic and technological prestige of the United States is not equaled by the popularity of its form of government. In this period of hectic political reconstruction remarkably few among the nations seem inclined to follow the constitutional pattern commonly spoken of as presidentialism under the separation of powers. While its suitability for this country is conceded, the adoption of either this pattern as a whole, or of its most distinguishing feature, presidential leadership, is generally considered abroad to be at variance with the national environment. This is not surprising, in view of the fact that in the past the transplantation of the American model was likewise the exception and that in its primary area of adoption, Latin American it rarely if ever produced lasting political stability.[47]

In light of the constitutional developments of the following decades, Professor Loewenstein turned out to be both right and wrong. Wrong, because after the end of the Second World

[46] Maurice Duverger, 'A New Political System Model: Semi-presidential Government' (1980) 8 *European Journal of Political Research* 165; Maurice Duverger, *Bréviaire de la cohabitation* (1986); Valadés (n 20).

[47] Loewenstein (n 28).

War, a good number of newly independent countries, especially in Africa and Asia, adopted some form or another of presidentialism. A new wave of presidential constitutions also emerged after the collapse of the Soviet Union and its allies. Even in its 'primary area of adoption', some of the Latin American countries that had been experimenting with parliamentary mechanisms returned to the fold of the presidential form of government (in 1993, the Brazilian people voted to keep a republican and presidential form of government, rejecting both the monarchy and parliamentarism). So, at present, over 75 countries (most of them in Latin America and Africa) have a presidential system of government, and to these we should perhaps add a significant number of nations that have established a semi-presidential constitution.

But Professor Loewenstein was correct in the sense that some of the central features of American presidentialism, as adopted by other countries, 'are at variance with the national environment'. Undoubtedly, the history and development of the presidential system in the United States has been completely different from its evolution and functions in other regions of the world, where it has assumed particular modalities and variations that preclude speaking of a single, 'pure' model of presidential government.

Countries that have instituted a presidential system reveal great diversity in terms of territorial expanse, history and culture, levels of economic and political development etc, but all of them seem to share a common and deliberate reason for adopting presidentialism: the need to build strong and decisive political leadership, capable of guaranteeing the defense of national independence and sovereignty, and, at the same time, carry out the tasks of economic development and social integration. With this in mind, presidentialism appears to be better equipped than other systems of government for successfully facing these challenges.

However, the same capacities that make presidentialism attractive hide the ever-present temptation of presidential supremacy over the other branches of government, especially in countries lacking a democratic tradition and the means effectively to check presidential power. At the extreme, presidential supremacy may give way to dictatorial and corrupt governments, which increases the likelihood of coups d'état and violent regime changes. A recurring cycle of instability and authoritarian government ensues, until the prevailing political conditions make a democratic transformation both necessary and possible. Democratization, in turn, translates into changes and adjustments to the existing regime, not only for the purpose of an enhanced balance of powers but, more importantly, for the sake of a more stable, flexible, and cooperative system of government. A few instruments deemed suitable in this respect can be found in parliamentary systems, and their adoption by presidential constitutions ('parliamentarization of presidentialism') has even led to the creation of hybrid or mixed systems, such as semi-presidentialism.

The above considerations summarize, to a great extent, almost two centuries of experience in Latin America with presidentialism, and this experience can serve as a valuable reference point for countries in other regions that want to transform their presidential constitutions in a democratic direction. To be sure, Latin American countries have not solved many of the problems associated with their systems of government, but they have come a long way in the process of institutional reform.

Finally, we have said that presidentialism is compatible with democratic government, but we have equally asserted that their mutual relationship is fraught with considerable complexities and difficulties. Herein lies perhaps the source of relentless dynamism and the transformational capabilities of presidential government. And this is also the reason why this chapter can at most offer an incomplete snapshot of presidentialism in the contemporary world.

Bibliography

Bruce Ackerman, 'The New Separation of Powers' (2000) 113(3) *Harvard Law Review* 634

Jody C. Baumgartner, 'Introduction: Comparative Presidential Impeachment' in Jody C. Baumgartner and Naoko Kada, *Checking Executive Power: Presidential Impeachment in Comparative Perspective* (2003)

Manuel Becerra Ramírez, 'La presidencia soviética. Notas sobre los cambios en la Constitución soviética' (1991) XXIV(70) *Boletín Mexicano de Derecho Comparado* 67

Norberto Bobbio, *Teoria Generale della Politica* (1999)

Michelangelo Bovero, *Contro il governo dei peggiori* (2000)

Jorge Carpizo, *El presidencialismo mexicano* (1978)

Jorge Carpizo, 'Essential Characteristics of the Presidential System and Influences for its Establishment in Latin America' (2007) 8 *Mexican Law Review* (Carmen Valderrama trans, online version only)

Jose Antonio Cheibub, *Presidentialism, Parliamentarism, and Democracy* (2007)

Jose Antonio Cheibub, 'Presidentialism, Parliamentarism, and the Role of Opposition Parties: Making Presidential or Semi-presidential Constitutions Work' (2009) 87 *Texas Law Review* 1375

Tun-jen Cheng, 'Political Institutions and the Malaise of East Asian New Democracies' (2003) 3 *Journal of East Asian Studies* 1

Josep M. Colomer and Gabriel L. Negretto, 'Can Presidentialism Work Like Parliamentarism?' (2005) 40(1) *Government and Opposition* 60

Edward S. Corwin, *The President. Office and Powers, 1787–1948. History and Analysis of Practice and Opinion* (3rd edn, 1948)

Robert Dahl, *Polyarchy: Participation and Opposition* (1972)

Robert E. DiClerico, *The American President* (5th edn, 1999)

Maurice Duverger, 'A New Political System Model: Semi-presidential Government' (1980) 8 *European Journal of Political Research* 165

Maurice Duverger, *Bréviaire de la cohabitation* (1986)

Robert Elgie (ed), *Semi-presidentialism in Europe* (1999)

Andrew Ellis, J. Jesús Orozco Henríquez, and Daniel Zovatto (eds), *Cómo hacer que funcione el sistema presidencial/Making Presidentialism Work* (2009)

Kathryn Hochstetler, 'Rethinking Presidentialism: Challenges and Presidential Falls in South America' (2006) 38(4) *Comparative Politics* 401

Mark P. Jones, *Electoral Laws and the Survival of Presidential Democracies* (1995)

Hans Kelsen, 'On the Essence and Value of Democracy' in Arthur Jacobson and Bernhard Schlink (eds), *Weimar: A Jurisprudence of Crisis* (2002)

Arend Lijphart, *Parliamentary versus Presidential Government* (1992)

Juan Linz, 'Presidential or Parliamentary Democracy: Does It Makes a Difference?' in Juan Linz and Arturo Valenzuela (eds), *The Failure of Presidential Democracy* (1994)

Juan Linz and Arturo Valenzuela (eds), *The Failure of Presidential Democracy* (1994)

Karl Loewenstein, 'The Presidency Outside the United States: A Study in Comparative Political Institutions' (1949) 11(3) *Journal of Politics* 447

Nicolò Machiavelli, *The Prince* ([1532] 1989)

Scott Mainwaring, 'Presidentialism in Latin America: A Review Essay' (1990) 25(1) *Latin American Research Review* 157

Scott Mainwaring and Matthew Soberg Shugart, *Presidentialism and Democracy in Latin America* (1997)

Charles McIlwain, *Constitutionalism: Ancient and Modern* (1940)
Sydney M. Milkis, 'History of the Presidency' in Michael Nelson (ed), *Guide to the Presidency*, vol 1 (3rd edn, 2002)
Sydney M. Milkis and Michael Nelson, *The American Presidency. Origins and Development, 1776–2002* (4th edn, 2003)
Charles Marie Secondat de Montesquieu, *The Spirit of the Laws* ([1748] 1989)
Muna Ndulo, 'Presidentialism in the Southern African States and Constitutional Restraint on Presidential Power' (2001) 26 *Vermont Law Review* 769
Dieter Nohlen and Mario Fernández (eds), *Presidencialismo versus Parlamentarismo* (1991)
Guillermo O'Donnell, 'Delegative Democracy' (1994) 5(1) *Journal of Democracy* 55
Aníbal Pérez-Liñán, *Presidential Impeachment and the New Political Instability in Latin America* (2007)
James P. Pfiffner, *The Modern Presidency* (3rd edn, 2000)
H. Kwasi Prempeh, 'Presidential Power in Comparative Perspective: The Puzzling Persistence of Imperial Presidency in Post-Authoritarian Africa' (2008) 35 *Hastings Constitutional Law Quarterly* 761
Fred W. Riggs, 'Presidentialism vs Parliamentarism: Implications for Representativeness and Legitimacy' (1998) 18(3) *International Political Science Review* 253
Giovanni Sartori, *Comparative Constitutional Engineering. An Inquiry into Structures, Incentives and Outcomes* (2nd edn, 1997)
Matthew Soberg Shugart and John M. Carey, *Presidents and Assemblies* (1992)
Roger Southall and Henning Melber (eds), *Legacies of Power. Leadership Change and Former Presidents in African Politics* (2006), available at <http://www.hsrcpress.ac.za>
Alfred Stepan and Cindy Skach, 'Presidentialism and Parliamentarism Compared' in Juan Linz and Arturo Valenzuela (eds), *The Failure of Presidential Democracy* (1994)
Raymond Tatalovich and Thomas S. Engeman, *The Presidency and Political Science. Two Hundred Years of Constitutional Debate* (2003)
Michel Troper, *La séparation des pouvoirs et l'histoire constitutionnelle française* (1973)
Jeffrey K. Tulis, 'The Two Constitutional Presidencies' in Michael Nelson (ed), *The Presidency and the Political System* (6th edn, 2000)
Diego Valadés, *La dictadura constitucional en América Latina* (1974)
Diego Valadés, 'El presidencialismo latinoamericano en el siglo XIX' (1982) XV(44) *Boletín Mexicano de Derecho Comparado* 613
Diego Valadés, *El gobierno de gabinete* (2nd edn, 2005)
Diego Valadés, *La parlamentarización de los sistemas presidenciales* (2nd edn, 2008)
Salvador Valencia Carmona, *El poder ejecutivo latinoamericano* (1979)
Max Weber, *Wirtschaft und Gesellschaft. Grundriss der Verstehenden Soziologie* (1922)

CHAPTER 30

PARLIAMENTARISM

ANTHONY W. BRADLEY
AND CESARE PINELLI

Oxford and Rome

I. The British Origins

A classical statement of the model of parliamentarism as it had developed in the United Kingdom was given in 1858:

> It is a distinguishing characteristic of Parliamentary Government that it requires the powers belonging to the Crown to be exercised through Ministers, who are held responsible for the manner in which they are used... and who are considered entitled to hold their office only while they possess the confidence of Parliament, and more especially the House of Commons.[1]

The long history of parliament in the United Kingdom may be said to have begun in 1265, when representatives of the cities and boroughs in England were summoned to join the feudal

[1] Earl Grey, *Parliamentary Government* (1958).

nobles, bishops, and knights of the counties in a gathering derived from the *Curia Regis*.[2] By the sixteenth century, the bicameral structure of Parliament was already established, and the two chambers of Lords and Commons authorized taxation, appropriated revenue to the use of the Crown, made new laws (eg creating the Church of England when Henry VIII broke from the Pope), and expressed the grievances of the people. During the seventeenth century, the struggle between Crown and Parliament involved the execution of one king, a bitter civil war, a period of republican government under Cromwell, restoration of the monarchy, and the removal of another king in the Glorious Revolution of 1688–89. The Bill of Rights 1689 left executive power with the monarch, but imposed conditions upon exercise of that power to protect the interests of Parliament. Those conditions, and the emergence of the office of Prime Minister from 1723, required the king to ensure that his ministers were supported by the two Houses of Parliament, in particular by the House of Commons which had the exclusive privilege of funding the policies of the government that were conducted in the name of the monarch. The continuing development of responsible as well as representative government was affected by reform of the electoral system from 1832 and by evolution of the party system. It became a firm convention of the unwritten constitution that ministers of the Crown were chosen by the Prime Minister but must command the confidence of the elected House, failing which the Prime Minister must either resign or advise the monarch to dissolve Parliament to enable a general election to be held.

The essence of parliamentarism in modern constitutions is that executive power is exercised by the Prime Minister and other ministers, who have the confidence of the legislature; if this confidence is withdrawn, the Prime Minister loses authority to govern and must either advise the head of state (monarch or president) that a general election be held, or must resign so that a different government can be formed. In the latter event, if a different government can be formed that has the support of a majority in parliament it will enter into office; if not, a general election must be held. The British model of parliamentarism emphasizes that (1) ministers must be Members of Parliament (mainly in the elected house, although in Britain a few ministers may sit in the House of Lords and may be granted peerages for this purpose); (2) ministers must account to Parliament for their policies and decisions, and are thus ultimately accountable to the electorate.[3]

The general features of parliamentary government are found in many countries today, but variants from the British model are also found.

(1) In some countries, Members of Parliament (MPs) who become ministers are required to give up that membership; the constitution or other law may provide for the election or appointment of a substitute member, and (possibly) for the original member to return to Parliament when he or she ceases to be a minister.

(2) In Britain, the decision that a government has lost the confidence of the Commons does not require that a motion to this effect has been adopted; a similar result will follow if a government motion seeking the confidence of the House fails, and possibly if the government is defeated on other essential issues—for example on a budget resolution or on a bill that the government insists is essential to its programme. In other countries, the constitution may

[2] Raoul Van Caenegem, *An Historical Introduction to Western Constitutional Law* (1995), ch 5, outlines the growth of parliamentarism in the late medieval ages. And also see Kaare Strøm, Wolfgang C. Müller, and Torbjörn Bergman (eds), *Delegation and Accountability in Parliamentary Democracies* (2003), 6–13.

[3] For an extensive survey of British parliamentary government, see Vernon Bogdanor (ed), *The British Constitution in the Twentieth Century* (2003), in particular ch 4 (the cabinet system, by Anthony Seldon), ch 5 (the House of Commons, by Paul Seaward and Paul Silk), and ch 8 (ministerial responsibility, by Diana Woodhouse).

specify the form of decision required if the government is to be held to have lost the confidence of the assembly.

(3) In the United Kingdom, following the appointment of a new government, ministers may take up their duties at once and no decision in Parliament is needed to confirm that the government is supported by a majority; if that support is in doubt, an opportunity for a vote on the matter may be provided or will in any event arise in relation to the government's proposed programme. In other countries, a formal resolution in parliament may be required before a new government is confirmed in office.

(4) While in the United Kingdom a general election must be held after five years from the previous election, an earlier election may be held at a date chosen by the Prime Minister. Whenever an election is held, the new Parliament may serve for the full five years. In some countries where the constitution provides for a fixed-term parliament, it may also provide that an early election does not affect the regular cycle of elections, thus creating a strong disincentive to hold an early election.

Some other underlying points may be noted.

(A) Since the United Kingdom has no written constitution, the parliamentary system is founded upon 'constitutional conventions'—customary practices affecting government, Parliament, and the political parties that have developed during the history outlined above. Disputes as to whether a convention has been observed are in principle outside the jurisdiction of the courts. Where a constitution contains the essential rules of the parliamentary system, it may also specify the circumstances in which the ministers are deemed to have lost the confidence of the legislature, and also such matters as the procedure to be followed while a new government is formed. In these cases the supreme court or a constitutional court may have jurisdiction to decide disputes on these matters, but in practice the court may avoid deciding questions that are essentially political in character.

(B) For the same reason that there is no written constitution, the British model of parliamentarism is linked with the legal doctrine of parliamentary sovereignty: in its classical formulation, as expressed by Dicey, there are no legal limits upon the laws that may be enacted by Parliament and there is no judicial review of Acts of Parliament.[4] We must emphasize that there is no necessary connection between parliamentarism and parliamentary sovereignty. As mentioned in the previous paragraph, constitutions that are founded on parliamentarism often provide for judicial review of legislation and a special procedure for constitutional amendment.

(C) Under parliamentarism, the ministers who form the government are themselves able to exercise executive powers (whether acting in their own name or in the name of the head of state in whom powers are vested *de iure*) and are accountable to parliament for use of these powers. Thus, there is no formal separation between legislative and executive powers, a matter that is of some importance from the standpoint of constitutional theory. It does not, however, follow that the legislative and executive powers may be said to be 'fused', a claim that was central to Bagehot's analysis of the British constitution. Nor is it correct to regard the ministers who form the cabinet as being a committee of the legislature. One reason for this may be found in John Stuart Mill's emphasis on the practical significance of parliamentarism:

> There is a radical difference between controlling the business of government, and actually doing it.... It is one question, therefore, what a popular assembly should control, another what it should itself do.... Instead of the function of governing, for which it is radically unfit,

[4] A.V. Dicey, *The Law and the Constitution* (10th edn, E.C.S. Wade ed, 1959), ch 1. See also Jeffrey Goldsworthy, *The Sovereignty of Parliament: History and Philosophy* (1999) and Jeffrey Goldsworthy, *Parliamentary Sovereignty: Contemporary Debates* (2010).

> the proper office of a representative assembly is to watch and control the government; to throw the light of publicity on its acts...and, if the men who compose the government abuse their trust,...to expel them from office, and either expressly or virtually appoint their successors.[5]

We now turn to consider the question of whether aspects of parliamentarism are found in other constitutions.

II. Continental Europe's Original Version

While in the United Kingdom the parliamentary system was established and developed mainly through constitutional conventions, in other democratic countries in Europe it was based from the beginning on written constitutional provisions, albeit that these afforded only a general framework for the development of conventional relationships among governmental institutions. These relationships, together with parliamentary regulations, electoral laws, and the structure of the political system, play everywhere a major role in shaping the parliamentary model.

Before we address its main institutional mechanisms, it is worth recalling that in France, and in the rest of continental Europe, 'parliamentarism' was originally identified with democracy, being intended more as a principle of legitimacy for the exertion of public power than as a form of government. Such connection with democracy resulted from the reaction against absolutism. While under the *ancien régime* the monarch's legitimacy relied on the unchallenged tradition of the absolutist state, according to the revolutionary ideal of 1789 parliament's legitimacy derived from the people that it represented. But, although opposed to each other on the ground of their content, both these principles of legitimacy corresponded to an absolute conception of sovereignty: parliament was put at the top of the institutional machinery under the new democratic system, as the king had been under the *ancien régime*.

No other authority, be it the executive or the judiciary, could thus bind parliament, nor could any other act override legislation. Reflecting the political philosophy of the Enlightenment, the 1789 *Déclaration des droits de l'Homme et du Citoyen* presumed that legislation was per se aimed at pursuing the public good, both because it expressed the *volonté générale*, and because it was expected to consist of general and abstract rules. The authors of the *Déclaration*, as well as of the constitutional texts of the Revolution epoch, were driven by the presumption that legislation would ensure the best protection to citizens' rights, rather than by the suspicion that it might infringe them. Nor was the separation of powers, solemnly affirmed in Article 16 (stating that 'Any society in which the guarantee of rights is not secure or the separation of powers is not determined has no constitution at all'), interpreted in the sense that powers were put on an equal footing. Given the premise of parliamentary supremacy, judges were intended to act as '*bouches de la loi*', and the executive's functions were the same with respect to the parliamentary will.

The fact that, at that time, and throughout the nineteenth century, parliamentarism was understood to mean parliament's supremacy over the other powers, needs to be distinguished from developments in constitutional history. Under the German Empire, and to a certain extent under the Italian Kingdom and in France, the prevailing form of government was one of constitutional monarchy. It was grounded on the separation of powers between parliament

[5] John Stuart Mill, *Considerations on Representative Government* (1861), reprinted in John Stuart Mill, *On Liberty and Other Essays* (John Gray ed, 1991), 271, 282.

and the monarch, due to the compromise that the latter, heir to absolutism, was forced to accept with the former. In chairing the cabinet, and directing the whole government through a prime minister responding to his own will, the monarch was head of the executive. Parliament, in turn, would legislate on matters concerning liberty and property.

Exceptions to the separation of powers arose from the possibility of impeaching ministers for illegal acts, and this sometimes functioned as an indirect way of ascertaining whether the cabinet still had the confidence of the parliamentary majority. On the other hand, the monarch was entitled to participate in the legislative process through giving the royal assent, and, first and foremost, he had the power to dissolve the assembly at his discretion, namely whenever he reputed that the parliament was acting contrary to the state's interests. This institutional setting was intrinsically unstable, being strongly affected by conflicts concerning the very constitutional foundations of the state. In spite of their increasing popular legitimacy due to the progressive extension of the franchise, the assemblies were in fact threatened by the monarch's claim to represent the continuity of the state beyond the contingent parliamentary majorities.

It was only under the Third Republic in France (1875–1940) that a parliamentary system was established in continental Europe. Notwithstanding the Constitution's attempts to balance the assembly's power of designating the cabinet with the power of the president of the republic to dissolve the assembly whenever a parliamentary majority failed to be reached, in practice the power to dissolve was never exercised, with the consequence that the legislative branch gained an effective supremacy over the executive. A *tradition républicaine* recovering the ideals of 1789 was thus formed. However, given the scarce solidity of parliamentary majorities, governments were frequently forced to resign: it was as if democracy could flourish at the cost of a permanent instability in government. Parliamentarism, in the specific form of '*gouvernement d'assemblée*' practised under the Third Republic, thus revealed a gap between its democratic legitimacy and the capacity for decision-making that it sought to ensure. It was an extreme form of parliamentarism that has an unhappy record.[6]

III. How a Common Consent was Finally Reached on the Meaning of 'Parliamentarism'

At the same time, a different version of parliamentarism demonstrated that the system was not per se condemned to governmental instability. Depicted in terms of 'the close union, the nearly complete fusion, of the executive and legislative powers'[7], the British version was grounded on the relationship between those powers, namely the confidence that the executive received from the legislature, whichever might prevail over the other in the exertion of political power.

Once the old suspicion towards the executive was left behind, both constitutional scholarship and the political elites of European countries gave attention to the already consolidated, and allegedly successful, British version, albeit in the awareness that its conventional sources were due to specific historical circumstances. The issue of parliamentarism thus shifted from an ideological to a technical dimension, that consisted of discovering how the same result might be achieved in the absence of such circumstances. This is the reason why most European

[6] See eg M.J.C. Vile, *Constitutionalism and the Separation of Powers* (1967), 190–6, 256–62.

[7] Walter Bagehot, *The English Constitution* ([1867] 1983), 65–8.

constitutions enacted throughout the twentieth century not only provide that the government's staying in office depends on its maintaining the confidence of parliament, but also afford institutional devices and procedures, conceived as alternative means to the British conventions.

Such attempt to ensure stability for governmental action, already afforded in the Constitutions of Weimar (1919), Austria (1920), Czechoslovakia (1920), Poland (1921), and Spain (1931), was called '*rationalisation du régime parlementaire*' by Boris Mirkine-Guetzevitch[8]. But these constitutions were overwhelmed with the rise of the Nazi or of fascist regimes.

Parliamentarism as such was then under attack, on theoretical not less than on political grounds. According to Carl Schmitt, parliamentarism was connected with the nineteenth century's liberalism rather than with democracy,[9] since its claim to legitimacy consisted in truth-seeking through discussion and openness, which might however be pursued even by a small group of disinterested persons. Democracy, to the contrary, required 'an identity between law and the people's will',[10] presupposing the maintenance of national homogeneity at the expenses of the outsiders, and, on the other hand, the superiority of a dictator's acclamation over the secret ballot for electing the MPs. Contrary to those of Mirkine, Schmitt's assumptions went far beyond a technical criticism of parliamentarism, and anticipated in many respects the Nazi regime's ideology.

After the Second World War, the model of rationalized parliamentarism was again introduced in a series of European constitutions. It may consist inter alia in establishing a certain quota of MPs for the proposal of a no confidence vote and in delaying the parliamentary debate on such a proposal in order to avoid a sudden withdrawal of support for the government (eg the 1948 Italian Constitution), or, according to the German Basic Law (1949) and the Spanish Constitution (1978), in binding the supporters of such a motion to propose at the same time the election of a new premier on the basis of an alternative majority ('constructive motion of no confidence').

Furthermore, while maintaining the position of head of the state, be it the president of the republic or the monarch, these constitutions generally do not designate him or her as head of the executive. Accordingly, provided that a definite parliamentary majority exists, the powers of appointing the prime minister and of dissolving parliament are exercised only as a formal matter by the head of the state. These powers, apart from the case of constructive motion of no confidence, might acquire a substantial meaning only in the face of a government crisis the solution of which appears uncertain. The role of the head of the state in managing these situations is not merely discretionary. Being driven by the aim of restoring a parliamentary majority, it is essentially an arbitral rather than a political role. Even in this respect, European constitutions broadly follow the British model, in particular the transformation in the monarch's functions since the advent of the parliamentary system.

Contrary to the failures encountered in the first half of the twentieth century, in the last decades the model outlined above succeeded in reconciling governmental stability with democracy, with the exceptions of the Fourth French Republic and of Italy. That success depended to a large extent on the changed historical context, given the apprehension of the evils of totalitarianism and the democratic commitment of major national parties, together with electoral laws that corrected purely proportional representation with a view to enhancing competition for government among two main political parties or coalitions. Constitutional

[8] Boris Mirkine-Guetzévitch, *Les nouvelles tendances du droit constitutionnel* (1936).

[9] Carl Schmitt, *The Crisis of Parliamentary Democracy* ([1923] 1988), 34ff.

[10] Ibid 15.

provisions alone, as we have already seen, afford no more than the general framework of a certain form of government.

This account matches the conclusion reached by Armel Le Divellec:

> The 'family' of parliamentary regimes is diverse yet united. It brings together governments emanating from a democratically elected parliamentary majority, and unable to work except in accordance with it. Dissimilarities arise in relation to the law, which in most European countries differs from the British model.[11]

In other words, the fact that, 'In the British version of democracy we rely mainly upon an elected House of Parliament to check, control, and call to account those who exercise the executive power', and that 'The doctrine of ministerial responsibility is an essential feature of the arrangements which exist for these purposes',[12] is common to most European countries, with the difference that the rules capturing the substance of parliamentarism, together with the devices already mentioned that aim at ensuring governmental stability, are there generally provided for in constitutional texts.

Far more significant diversities lie outside the mechanisms of parliamentary government. Unlike the British model, most European constitutions are not only rigid, but have introduced judicial review of legislation, a federal or regional structure, and, frequently, a referendum, with the effect that the machinery of government and even the very functioning of democracy, appear more complex than in the United Kingdom. These elements were introduced with a view to limiting the possible tyranny of parliamentary majorities, and, at the same time, to guarding against the excesses of a purely representative democracy, which had revealed its fragility with the advent of totalitarian regimes. But they were not believed to counteract the already mentioned devices aimed at ensuring the good functioning of parliamentarism, and therefore at achieving with partially different means the same results of parliamentarism as in the United Kingdom.

Bruce Ackerman has labelled the continental model as 'constrained parliamentarism', and distinguished it from that of Westminster on the ground that 'no single institution is granted a monopoly over lawmaking power'.[13] The notion of 'constrained parliamentarism' presupposes that 'parliamentarism' is per se 'unconstrained', namely sovereign in the Diceyan sense. Such presumption leaves on one side the essential meaning of parliamentarism as the mechanism through which the executive is able to stay in office through the consent of a democratically elected parliamentary majority. As we have already seen (Section I above), this meaning of parliamentarism is not necessarily connected with parliamentary sovereignty, and it appears not only more respectful of the historical background. It also serves, as we will see, to distinguish the parliamentary system from other forms of government.

IV. The Waves of Democratization and the Worldwide Diffusion of the Parliamentary System

We must add that the recent waves of democratization have gradually engendered a worldwide expansion of parliamentarism. The new democratic states that followed the dissolution of European colonial empires, in particular those that achieved independence of British rule,

[11] Armel Le Divellec, 'The Westminster Model in Europe' in Katja S. Ziegler, Denis Baranger, and A.W. Bradley (eds), *Constitutionalism and the Role of Parliaments* (2007), 100.

[12] Colin Turpin, 'Ministerial Responsibility: Myth or Reality?' in Jeffrey Jowell and Dawn Oliver (eds), *The Changing Constitution* (2nd edn, 1989), 55. On the working of ministerial responsibility in Britain today, see Colin Turpin and Adam Tomkins, *British Government and the Constitution* (2007), ch 9.

[13] Bruce Ackerman, 'The New Separation of Powers' (2000) 113 *Harvard Law Review* 685.

whether before or after the Second World War (including Australia, Canada, New Zealand, and India, as well as states in Africa and the Caribbean) were mostly established through a written constitution that provided for the parliamentary form of government. A similar phenomenon occurred later in Eastern Europe with the collapse of Communism, and in South Africa with the end of apartheid.

Nonetheless, in Africa, in Asia, in Latin America, and even in Eastern Europe, a significant number of young democracies have adopted the semi-presidential or the presidential model.[14] Some of these should be classified as 'illiberal democracies', given the unchecked violations of fundamental rights that occur and the scarce respect for the rule of law. But the number of fully democratic regimes adopting semi-presidential or presidential systems suffices to demonstrate that democracy is no longer to be identified with parliamentarism, as was sustained even by Hans Kelsen, the most important theorist of democracy in continental Europe.[15] Rather than on the ground of their capability in ensuring democracy, these systems of government differ in terms of the relationship between public powers, and of their respective legitimacy.

V. Forms of Government and Separation of Powers

Contrary to parliamentarism, presidentialism is grounded on the separation between the legislative and the executive branches, each of which is occupied by a popularly elected authority. Accordingly, the executive's term of office is directly established by the constitution and the executive does not depend on the confidence of the legislature for staying in office. It is true that the legislature ('Congress' under the US Constitution) might remove the President by means of impeachment. But such possibility is very different from the power of a parliament to withdraw its confidence from a prime minister or from the whole government.

Conversely, the absence of a parliamentary majority to sustain the government in office does not mean that parliament is subject to dissolution. Given the separation, no impartial authority is needed to oversee the relationship between legislature and executive, and the president holds the office of head of the state together with that of chief of the executive; he or she has the power to appoint and dismiss ministers without the need for parliamentary approval (except that under the US Constitution, the appointment of key officials takes place with the advice and consent of the Senate). The presidential form of government differs therefore from the parliamentary, both because of the concurrent popular legitimacy of the legislative and executive branches, and because of the separation between them.

The semi-presidential model combines a popularly elected fixed-term president with a prime minister and a cabinet who are responsible to the legislature; this brings together the presidential system's type of legitimacy with the relationship among political institutions that characterizes the parliamentary system. This means that the term 'semi-presidential' fails to give an accurate account of the basis of the model, but despite scholarly criticism, it is still widely adopted due to the lack of consensus over an alternative formula.

In examining the costs and benefits of the parliamentary system vis-à-vis the presidential and the semi-presidential, attention should first be given to their respective basic structure. To the extent that it is grounded on a single popularly elected authority, the former tends not

[14] Sophia Moestrup, 'Semi-Presidentialism in Young Democracies. Help or Hindrance?' in Robert Elgie and Sophia Moestrup, *Semi-Presidentialism Outside Europe* (2007), 39ff.

[15] Hans Kelsen, *Vom Wesen und Wert der Demokratie* (1929), 85ff.

only to avoid conflict between political institutions, but also to concentrate power in the hands of one political authority, be it parliament or government. The opposite is true for the latter, given the concurrent popular legitimacy that characterizes these systems.

A caveat should, however, be added. 'Conflict' and 'concentration of power' are not necessarily an evil. Provided that it does not threaten the system's stability, conflict might ensure pluralism, thus enhancing democracy. And concentration of power might enhance the accountability of the rulers as well as the efficiency of the political process, and it should not be seen as paving the way to absolutism as far as the functions of non-majoritarian authorities, and of courts in particular, are respected. To some extent, then, both conflict and concentration of power are likely to pursue objectives that are compatible with constitutional democracy. The diverse objectives that these forms of government are respectively likely to achieve appear to be sufficiently balanced on normative grounds.

In discussing the merits and demerits of parliamentarism and presidentialism, James Bryce observed that the former is

> calculated to secure swiftness in decision and vigour in action, and enables the Cabinet to press through such legislation as it thinks needed, and to conduct both domestic administration and foreign policy with the confidence that its majority will support it against the attacks of the Opposition. To these merits there is to be added the concentration of Responsibility. For any faults committed the Legislature can blame the Cabinet, and the people can blame both the Cabinet and the majority.

On the other hand, presidentialism, 'by dividing power between several distinct authorities...provides more carefully than does the Parliamentary [system] against errors on the part either of Legislature or Executive, and retards the decision by the people of conflicts arising between them.'[16]

In descriptive terms, however, the above account gives only a preliminary idea of the costs and benefits of the diverse institutional models, and should be complemented with the analysis of their effective functioning, and of further structural features affecting contemporary democracies.

As for their functioning, conflicts arising from the concurrent popular legitimacy of the legislature and of government are differently managed according to various factors, among which are the structural differences between the presidential and semi-presidential systems, and the role of political parties. In the United States, given the separation of powers, the legislature is likely to paralyse the executive's political agenda to the extent that the party that does not occupy the White House may possess a majority in either or both houses of Congress. Nonetheless, party discipline in Congress may be sufficiently loose to give the President some chance of obtaining the support of single representatives from the party opposing his policy and thus limiting the existence of complete gridlock. Hence, it may be that an apparent political stalemate does not reach the point of threatening the system's stability.

Such a result is hardly imaginable in Europe, because of a traditionally far stricter party discipline in the assemblies. This is perhaps the most important reason why the presidential system has never been adopted there. Even the semi-presidential model's functioning usually resembles that of the parliamentary model, to the extent that previous agreements among parties and/or the country's tradition have created constitutional conventions that deprive the President of significant political power, in spite of his being popularly elected (see inter alia Austria, Portugal, and Finland). The same happens under the Fifth Republic in France,

[16] James Bryce, *Modern Democracies* (1921), 465ff.

whenever the presidential majority diverges from the parliamentary, thus bringing in a state of *cohabitation* between the two institutions. But where these majorities coincide, the President holds together the constitutional powers of head of the state with those of chief of the executive, resulting from his leading the parliamentary majority, with the effect that both the appointment and the dismissal of the Prime Minister are at his disposal. No higher concentration of political power is granted to a sole authority in the landscape of contemporary democracies, including those adopting the parliamentary model.

A wide concentration of power may also derive from unchecked resort to emergency powers by the elected president, as occurs frequently in Latin America irrespective of the formal adoption of a semi-presidential (Argentina) or of a presidential system (Brazil). That practice goes far beyond the need for remedying exceptional situations, tending to substitute presidential decrees for ordinary legislation and therefore extinguishing the role of parliament. Once again, an understanding of the functioning of the institutional machinery requires an examination of specific practices that goes beyond the distinction between forms of government.

Moreover, the territorial distribution of power in its various forms, in particular the unitary and the federal (or regional) systems, is also likely to have a crucial effect on that functioning. While the former presupposes a sole legislature within the state, and sometimes is even founded on a unitary administration, the latter enhances pluralism, and is likely to engender competition and conflict among diverse governmental authorities. Parliamentary systems, as well as other forms of government, correspond increasingly to federations, with important consequences for the national decision-making process, including the fact that a second chamber representing the regional components of the federal state is usually established (for the operation of parliamentary systems in such states, see the instances of Australia, Austria, Germany, India, and South Africa).

However, the traditional association of federalism with the ideal of divided government does not necessarily correspond to its functioning. Federal systems are inter alia differentiated according to whether powers among the federation and regional territories are strictly separated ('dual federalism'), or mostly shared ('cooperative federalism'). In countries adopting the cooperative system, the upper chamber is usually composed of regional representatives, with the effect that the majority may differ from that in the elected lower chamber. The political stalemate thus arising in Germany between the Bundestag and the Bundesrat led in 2006 to a major constitutional reform of the federal system.[17]

These references suffice to demonstrate that the territorial distribution of power is not less significant than the national form of government in ascertaining the degree to which power is concentrated or, by contrast, is subject to the coexistence of conflicting authorities. Following this criterion, the US system appears less concentrated than the German and the French, being founded on the presidential model and on dual federalism. The German system, combining a parliamentary model with cooperative federalism, appears more concentrated than the United States but less so than in France, that exhibits the greatest concentration of political power, since it combines a unitary state with the above-mentioned version of the semi-presidential model.

The above account is referred to the functioning of, and to the interplay between, political institutions. But, as already mentioned, concentration of power should not be seen as paving the way to absolutism as far as the functions of non-majoritarian authorities are respected.

[17] Fritz Scharpf, 'No Exit from the Joint Decision Trap? Can German Federalism Reform Itself?', EUI Working Papers, RSCAS No 2005/24, 2005, 8 ff, and Simone Burkhart, 'Reforming Federalism in Germany: Incremental Changes instead of the Big Deal' (2009) 39(2) *Publius* 341ff.

These authorities, namely courts, including constitutional courts wherever distinguished from the ordinary, and independent authorities, usually acting in the market field, are entrusted with the task of ensuring the fundamental rights of citizens, and more generally constitutional principles and rules that are believed to stand above the appreciation of parliamentary majorities. Hence derives the need for granting them independence from the political branches, which is commonly achieved in contemporary constitutional democracies irrespective of their forms of government.

In particular, the establishment of judicial review of legislation has deeply transformed the role of the judiciary, vis-à-vis its resilient definitions as a '*pouvoir en quelque façon nul*' (Montesquieu), or as 'the least dangerous branch' (Hamilton). As was already noticed in a general survey of constitutional justice in Western democracies, 'constitutional review proves to have become the irreplaceable counterweight to the supremacy of the majority principle.'[18] And the more recent waves of democratization (see Section IV above) were regularly complemented with the establishment of constitutional courts.

While taking account of the structural connection between the executive and the legislative power affecting parliamentarism (and to a great extent the semi-presidential system), and, on the other hand, the independence of the judiciary from the political branches, in our time the ultimate meaning of the separation of powers appears closer to that emerging from Henry de Bracton's distinction between *gubernaculum* and *iurisdictio*, or from the medieval dichotomy between *leges* and *iura*, than from Locke's and Montesquieu's celebrated theories.

VI. The Status of Member of Parliament

The rules concerning the status of the individual members of the national parliament include their rights, privileges, responsibilities, immunities, and obligations. These rules are fundamentally related to the existence of Parliament as an institution, whether it functions within a parliamentary, semi-presidential, or presidential system. However, reference to the status of members is justified here, because many aspects of that status have resulted from the historical development of parliamentary government.

In the United Kingdom, the history of Parliament and the common law are the basis for the bundle of rights, responsibilities, and immunities that are together referred to as 'parliamentary privilege'. Since the granting of special privileges to any group of individuals is often questioned today on grounds related to the equality of all persons, the existence of parliamentary privilege must be justified as being in the public interest. In 1999, a committee of both Houses at Westminster declared:

> Parliamentary privilege consists of the rights and immunities which the two Houses . . . and their members and officers possess to enable them to carry out their parliamentary business effectively. Without this protection members would be handicapped in performing their parliamentary duties, and the authority of Parliament itself in confronting the executive and as a forum for expressing the anxieties of citizens would be correspondingly diminished.[19]

In the United Kingdom, parliamentary privilege has never been the subject of comprehensive legislation. The essential privileges include some that inhere in the collective body

[18] Alexander von Brunneck, 'Constitutional Review and Legislation in Western Democracies' in Christine Landfried (ed), *Constitutional Review and Legislation. An International Comparison* (1988), 250.

[19] Report of Joint Committee on Parliamentary Privilege, HL Paper 43, HC 214 (1998–99), para 3.

(including the exclusive right of a house to regulate its own proceedings)[20] as well as privileges of the collective body which confer a direct benefit on the individual member, notably the absolute freedom of speech in parliamentary proceedings, that has long been protected by Article 9 of the Bill of Rights 1689.[21] Arising from that freedom of speech is the protection that MPs enjoy as individuals for what they say or do in the course of parliamentary proceedings against certain aspects of the criminal law and civil law that might otherwise restrict the freedom of speech in Parliament.[22] However, the exercise by MPs of their freedom of speech in Parliament is subject to the control that the House of Commons exercises over the conduct of debates. Moreover, British MPs enjoy no general immunity from the criminal law, whether relating to arrest, prosecution, trial, conviction, or penalty; and disqualification from the Commons follows upon certain sentences of imprisonment.[23] In 2010, the UK Supreme Court held that, since the ordinary criminal law applies fully to MPs, the making by them of false claims for parliamentary expenses is outside the area of parliamentary proceedings covered by privilege.[24] In Australia, where the parliamentary system is derived from that in the United Kingdom, the law of parliamentary privilege has been placed on a modern legal basis by statutory codification.[25]

In nearly all constitutions (particularly in Europe), there is provision for the status and privileges of MPs. These privileges vary greatly, but they often include both a statement of non-liability for what is said or done in the course of parliamentary debate (*l'irresponsabilité*) and also some form of individual immunity from the criminal process (*l'inviolabilité*), especially in respect of personal liberty.[26] One aim of such immunity may be to protect members from being harassed by politically motivated prosecutions, and it may not apply when a member is arrested *flagrante delicto*. It is generally limited to the period of a member's electoral mandate; often the immunity may be taken away by a resolution of the parliament or by a parliamentary body. Even with these limitations, the existence of immunity from criminal process raises issues of principle as to the application of the ordinary law to elected persons.[27] This immunity can be abused in a corrupt political system, and not all parliaments have effective rules requiring the disclosure of a member's financial interests.

[20] This right includes the power to maintain order and discipline within the House. Issues of human rights may arise when non-members of the House are penalized for contempt of Parliament, as in *Demicoli v Malta* (1991) 14 EHRR 47.

[21] Absolute privilege for speech during a debate was held by the European Court of Human Rights in *A v UK* (2003) 36 EHRR 917 to be compatible with human rights, the Court placing weight on the established practice in many European states. In the United Kingdom, the privilege does not extend to statements made outside Parliament. eg in public speeches or in media interviews. Cf *CGIL & Cofferati v Italy* (ECtHR, 24 February 2009).

[22] Protection is not only against civil liability for defamation, but also against criminal liability for such matters as obscenity, incitement to disaffection, and racial hatred.

[23] Disqualification results from being sentenced to prison for more than a year (Representation of the People Act 1981) and disqualification also results from conviction for electoral offences.

[24] *R v Chaytor* [2010] UKSC 52, [2011] 1 All ER 808.

[25] Parliamentary Privileges Act 1987 (Australia).

[26] See eg Austria (Constitution of 1920, Art 57); Belgium (Constitution of 1994, Arts 58, 59); Cyprus (Constitution of 1960, Art 83); Czech Republic (Constitution of 1992, Art 27); Denmark (Constitution of 1953, s 57); Finland (Constitution of 1999, ss 28, 30, 31); France (1958 Constitution, Art 26, as amended in 1995); Italy (Constitution of 1948, Art 68); Turkey (Constitution of 1982, Art 83). On parliamentary immunity in Turkey, see *Kart v Turkey* (ECtHR, 3 December 2009).

[27] On the application of the criminal law of bribery to elected representatives, see *US v Brewster* 408 US 501 (1972) and contrast (in India) *Rao v State* (1998) 1 SCJ 529.

A wide variation exists in the extent of the protection from civil liability for the making of statements that would otherwise be defamatory. As we have seen, in the United Kingdom this protection is limited to statements made in Parliament itself. In other countries the protection may extend to statements by an elected member that concern matters of current political significance, even though they are made outside the course of parliamentary debate. This extension in its scope enhances the risk that this protection may conflict with the fundamental rights of the victim of the damaging statements.[28]

Another constitutional guarantee that, in the public interest, is intended to preserve the personal freedom of MPs to decide how to exercise their parliamentary functions derives from Edmund Burke's celebrated doctrine that MPs are not delegates of a local or political or economic caucus but represent the whole nation.[29] This doctrine has sometimes been seen as going to the heart of a representative system, in justifying the making of decisions in parliament that are based on the will, or sovereignty, of the entire people, and in giving members protection against attempts by local or other sectional interests to dictate how they shall vote. In various forms it is found in very many constitutions. Thus in France, the *mandat impératif* is excluded; in Germany, members of the Bundestag must be 'representatives of the whole people, not bound by orders or instructions, and responsible only to their conscience'; in Greece, MPs 'enjoy unrestricted freedom of opinion and right to vote according to their conscience'; and in Italy, each MP 'represents the Nation and carries out his duties without constraint of mandate'.[30] It is difficult to reconcile these statements of principle with the constraints that arise from the system of political parties, the result of which is that a member will, except on rare issues that give rise to a question of personal conscience, be likely to support the position of the party on whose platform he or she was elected: and great pressure may be brought to bear on members by the party organization to vote as its leaders wish, especially on an issue upon which the continuance of the party in government may depend. However, one consequence of the principle is that members whose conduct in Parliament disappoints the expectations of their party or their electorate have constitutional protection against being removed from their seats during the period for which they were elected. These venerable rules are found in very many democracies, but it is arguable that their continuance today involves a wide degree of hypocrisy regarding the democratic process. It may be questioned whether they will preserve their significance and legitimacy in the future, as popular demands are made for securing the greater accountability of those involved in the political process. In some political systems, electors already have a right to recall their representative in some situations. In the United Kingdom, the coalition government formed in May 2010 undertook to legislate to introduce a power of recall, allowing a petition signed by 10 per cent of voters in a constituency to force a by-election where their member had been found to have engaged in 'serious wrongdoing'.

[28] As well as *CGIL & Cofferati v Italy* (above), see *De Jorio v Italy* (2005) 40 EHRR 42 and *Cordova v Italy (No 1)* (2005) 40 EHRR 43 (parliamentary immunity held to violate the right of access to the courts under Art 6(1), ECHR).

[29] In his *Speech to the Electors of Bristol* (1774) (reported in Philip Kurland and Ralph Lerner (eds), *The Founders' Constitution* (vol I, 1987), 447), Burke argued that while a representative ought to give great weight to the interests of his constituents, he owed it to them to exercise 'his unbiased opinion, his mature judgement, his enlightened conscience' in his parliamentary acts.

[30] In the respective constitutions see for France, Art 27; for Germany, Art 38(1); for Greece (Constitution of 1975), Art 60(1); for Italy, Art 67. And see eg Austria, Art 56(1) (no binding mandate); Bulgaria (Constitution of 1991), Art 67; Poland (Constitution of 1997), Art 104(1); Turkey, Art 80.

VII. Differences and Analogies within the Family of Parliamentary Systems

Parliament's functions are deeply affected not only by the adopted form of government, but also by differences emerging within each form, of which the following are the most significant with respect to parliamentarism.

1. Making and Unmaking Governments

In parliamentary systems, the parliament is rarely entrusted with the formal power of investing government with its functions. Once members of government are appointed by the head of the state, the confidence of the house is generally presumed to exist, except in the case of the Italian Constitution, according to which both the Chamber of Deputies and the Senate must approve the incoming cabinet in an investiture vote within ten days of its appointment.

Under the German Basic Law and the Spanish Constitution, the prime minister is elected from the elected house on the proposal of the head of the state, and he or she is then appointed by the latter together with the ministers. A further variation is afforded by the Japanese Constitution, which requires that the prime minister, after having been elected from the lower house and then appointed by the emperor, appoints, and may dismiss, the ministers. Finally, South Africa's Constitution provides that the republic's president, elected from the National Assembly, is head of the executive; members of the government are invested with their functions after being appointed by the president and 'are accountable collectively and individually to Parliament for the exercise of their powers and the performance of their functions' (s 92(2)).

These differences need to be taken into account in considering the nature of parliamentary government. As already mentioned, the British convention that cabinet ministers should be MPs is not generally adopted. Even among countries strongly influenced by the Westminster model, that rule is not absolutely followed: under the Indian Constitution, there is no bar to the appointment as minister of a person from outside the legislature, although he or she is bound to secure within six months a parliamentary seat by election or nomination. In many democratic countries, the two positions are merely compatible as a matter of law, although, given the importance of being a MP for ensuring the minister's accountability before the electorate, in practice ministers are usually chosen from among MPs. Finally, some constitutions (such as the Belgian, the French, and the Dutch) provide that, once appointed minister, the MP is bound to resign his parliamentary seat in order to ensure the separation of powers.

A further significant difference is that under parliamentarism disequilibrium may occur between the parliamentary majority's power to force the cabinet to resign and that of the prime minister to dissolve parliament. Given all these diverging features, scholars tend to give a minimal definition of parliamentary government, as consisting of that system 'in which the Prime Minister and his or her cabinet are accountable to any majority of the members of parliament and can be voted out of office by the latter.'[31] Once having entered into office, can members of a government be voted out by parliament? And, if so, what are the consequences of such a crisis? Within the family of parliamentary systems, there are many diverse answers to these two questions.

[31] Kaare Strøm, Wolfgang C. Müller, and Torbjörn Bergman, 'Parliamentary Democracy: Promise and Problems' in Strøm et al (n 2), 13.

Concerning the former matter, the accountability of the government to parliament is in general secured through motions that expressly deal with the issue of confidence or no confidence. According to a widely diffused convention, that is codified under the Italian Constitution (Art 94(4)), a government should not have to resign because of the rejection of a government bill.

Motions of no confidence, namely the motions put before a parliament by the opposition with the intent of defeating the government, and thus distinguished from the constructive motions of no confidence, differ significantly on procedural grounds according to national experience. These differences include the quota of MPs required for proposing such motions, the time limit applying to such motions, and the majorities requested for the motion to be approved. The stricter these requirements, the more counterproductive a motion of no confidence on trivial matters may appear to its proposer.

The individual accountability of ministers is also attained in many parliamentary systems through no confidence motions, be they provided for in the constitution or established by convention as in the United Kingdom. Ministers are responsible 'in the sense that they are answerable to Parliament for their departments. In this way individual ministerial responsibility describes a "chain of accountability". Officials answer to ministers, who answer to Parliament, which, in turn, answers to the electorate.' However, in the United Kingdom, 'attempts to challenge the credibility of a minister are seldom successful when the government in power enjoys a substantial majority in the House of Commons.'[32]. The same occurs in other systems where a minister is called to account before Parliament.

Motions of confidence may be proposed by the government with the aim of ensuring that it has the support of the majority for its complete programme, or for a single bill or policy. Rather than challenging the opposition, these motions are likely to prevent dissident members of the parliamentary majority from voting against the government. Article 49(3) of the French Constitution goes even further, stating that the government may make the passing of a bill an issue of the government's responsibility to the National Assembly, with the effect that the bill shall be considered adopted unless a resolution of no confidence is introduced within the next 24 hours and adopted. Such provision appears unique on the ground of legislative procedure: its effect is to replace the ordinary approval of a bill by parliament with a challenge to a vote of no confidence issued by government.

In principle, a government must resign whenever parliament approves a no confidence motion, or rejects a confidence motion. This duty is inherent in the accountability rule, and is common to the whole family of parliamentary systems. The only exception is when, as an alternative to resignation, the government has power (as in the United Kingdom) to order the dissolution of parliament and the holding of a general election. The resignation of the government will be followed by the formation of a new cabinet, if that proves possible. The rules that apply in such situations usually result from constitutional conventions, but they may be explicitly laid down in the constitution, as in Japan. The hypothesis of a new cabinet following a governmental crisis demonstrates that parliamentarism does not require that fresh elections be held whenever a government has lost its parliamentary majority resulting from earlier elections. Indeed, the opposite possibility is presupposed where there is provision for the constructive vote of no confidence, notwithstanding the fact that this interrupts the 'chain of accountability' between the government and the electorate.

Finally, significant differences within the family of parliamentary systems emerge with respect to the dissolution of parliament, both on the ground of its limits and of its functions.

[32] Peter Leyland, *The Constitution of the United Kingdom. A Contextual Analysis* (2007), 129.

Dissolution is in some systems excluded for one year after early elections (France, Spain) or in the first period after a general election (Norway, Russia), or admitted only in the event of a deadlock in cabinet formation and after the loss of a vote of confidence (Germany), or is limited by the strong disincentive that a new parliament would be elected only for the remainder of the dissolved parliament's term (Sweden). In the United Kingdom, the power to advise the monarch to dissolve Parliament is accepted to be a strategic instrument in the hands of the prime minister that he may wish to use to remain in power; there would have to be highly exceptional circumstances before the monarch would be justified in rejecting that advice. By contrast, in Italy the dissolution of parliament may be required to maintain a parliamentary majority, whenever this is unavailable in the current legislature; in this case the head of state acquires substantial powers, to the extent that an impartial authority is needed for the final decision that the current composition of parliament fails to produce a majority.

2. Legislative Function

Most students of parliamentarism have recently noticed the declining role of parliaments in the process of legislation, in spite of the traditional pre-eminence of legislation among the functions of parliament. Two indicators of this decline are not only the increasingly rare approval of bills that are not proposed by the government but initiated within parliament, but, first and foremost, the huge number of government bills that pass through parliament without being amended (except possibly when ministers have been persuaded to amend their own original proposals).

It is difficult to generalize about this situation, but there is no doubt that in many countries the role of parliament in practice is to give the stamp of formal approval to the government's proposals. Even in the United Kingdom, this often appears to be the role of the elected House of Commons, and it is left to the appointed House of Lords to examine in detail bills that have been approved by the Commons without any scrutiny. This is possible in part because no single party has a majority in the Lords and members of the House hold their places for life and are not subject to being re-elected. By this central paradox of parliamentarism, while the majority in the elected House of Commons has the primary duty of maintaining the government in power, this necessarily diminishes their ability to scrutinize the government's proposed legislation. Accordingly, in the United Kingdom, and in countries where the Westminster model applies, the government's bills often pass through the House of Commons without having been modified, but subject to the ability of the upper house (if there is one) to make the government think again. Elsewhere, however, including many European democracies, parliaments may play a more active role. These differences are not simply due to the governing party's dominance over the legislative process that generally exists in the Westminster model, by comparison with the reduced power of coalition governments. Further elements to be taken into account include the British executive's monopoly on introducing financial measures, and the limited opportunities to introduce legislation on their own initiative which backbench MPs at Westminster may exercise.

On the other hand, the fact that certain parliaments play some role in amending governmental bills appears significant to the extent that their function in lawmaking is believed to consist in making autonomous decisions. This assumption presupposes, in turn, that the power of parliament vis-à-vis that of government is likely to be assessed as if the two institutions were structurally separated one from the other. But this hypothesis corresponds to the presidential system, and applies wherever the legitimacy of the government is not dependent on maintaining the confidence of parliament. It was for that reason that, until the Lisbon

Treaty, the European Parliament's powers were likely to be limited by those of the European institutions. The possibility of an autonomous role for parliament is, to the contrary, impeded by the very dynamic of the parliamentary model, which is founded on a constant connection between parliament and government that requires a parliamentary majority for maintaining government in office.

Given this premise, the better the parliamentary model happens to function, the more parliament is reduced to that of a forum where the cabinet's decisions are only formally discussed and approved. The obvious question that arises is why the legislative procedure is even in that case still followed, notwithstanding the common awareness of its merely formal nature. On that basis, what is the role that parliament is likely to play?

It is worth recalling that, in a parliamentary system, the representative assembly alone is provided with the resource of democratic legitimacy, which it exercises not only by voting on issues of confidence, but also while carrying out its other functions, including legislation and deliberation on matters of national importance. Democratic legitimacy is exercised through a process of deliberation that necessarily includes the opposition parties, and at the same time takes place in public. Contrary to decision-making within a closed system of government, where the absence of openness reflects the need for internal cohesion, the functioning of parliament is driven by the principle of publicity exactly because it is entrusted to a democratically elected institution. A century and a half ago, John Stuart Mill captured these features of parliamentarism by affirming:

> I know not how a representative assembly can more usefully employ itself than in talk, when the subject of talk is the great interest of the country, and every sentence of it represents the opinion either of some important body of persons in the nation, or of an individual in whom such bodies have reposed their confidence.[33]

However, the fact that contemporary politics is strongly conditioned by the media, if not media-driven, affects deeply the meaning of political representation, and the principle of openness that characterizes parliamentary procedure. It is in this respect, rather than for the loss of a decision-making capacity, that the issue of parliament's decline should properly be addressed. In a media-driven scenario, the core of the public debate shifts from the adequacy of governmental policies to the prime minister's capability in persuading the people of his own political, if not private, virtues. The content of parliamentary debates is in turn anticipated, and distorted, through the lens of the media. The traditional view that the debates shed light on the executive's most important decisions, and determine the public's support for the contending political parties, is thus challenged.

According to political scientists, the increasing personalization of government due to the media, together with the increasing importance of foreign policy and the related expansion of the executive's action, drive towards a 'presidentialization of politics'.[34] The fact that political leaders seek an informal popular legitimacy for their own actions through media exposure affects parliamentarism in particular, since democratic legitimacy pertains to a collective body which is traditionally less at ease than the presidential model with the personal element. However, it does not follow that the mechanisms of presidentialism are likely to be inserted within the structure of parliamentarism, as the formula of presidentialization might induce

[33] John Stuart Mill, 'Considerations on Representative Government' (1861) in *Collected Works of John Stuart Mill* (vol 19, Jean O'Grady and John Robson ed, 1991), 353.

[34] See inter alia Thomas Poguntke and Paul Webb, *The Presidentialization of Politics. A Comparative Study of Modern Democracies* (2005).

one to believe. Given their informality, media circuits appear rather juxtaposed to the mechanisms of the diverse forms of government. Their effects amount, therefore, to a 'personalization of politics', namely to a phenomenon that was designed in these terms half a century ago,[35] although it has become since then increasingly important.

3. Controlling Functions

The dynamic of the parliamentary system conditions the exertion of parliament's controlling functions no less than its role in legislation. Given that a majority backs the government, control or oversight of administrative activities is less significant than it is within a presidential system.

Differences emerge, however, even here according to different countries, and to different mechanisms of control. In some parliamentary democracies, ministers use reports not to respond to control but to anticipate possible criticism by efficient propaganda to show their efficacy.[36] But this is not always the case.[37]

As for the power to authorize spending, one of parliament's oldest functions, the fact that this has become nominal in most countries depends not only on the rules governing the parliamentary system, but also on the lack of effective parliamentary control over the budget: this would require inter alia an effective committee system, sufficient time, and access to essential information on revenue and spending.[38] Nonetheless, in the United Kingdom, the Public Accounts Committee, operating in a less partisan way than most other parliamentary committees, and being supported by an independent authority (the National Audit Office), is believed to provide the House of Commons with 'some degree of control over government finance'.[39] Similarly, in India the independence of the Comptroller and Auditor-General is assured.[40]

As regards the scrutiny of foreign and defence policy, the Bundestag is constitutionally provided with more significant powers than those usually conferred on parliaments, including the requirement to consent to the deployment of the military. These features, stemming from the constitutional climate in Germany since the Second World War, have shaped the whole relationship with the government in the field, although the Federal Constitutional Court has affirmed that it is not the exemption from parliamentary decision-making in foreign affairs that needs to be justified, but parliament's involvement.[41]

Questions and interpellations addressed to ministers relate to further, although less effective, forms of parliamentary control over the executive. While the former are exhausted with the minister's answer, the latter demand a prompt response which in some parliaments is followed by a short debate and a vote on whether the government's response is deemed

[35] Albert Mabileau, 'La personnalisation du pouvoir dans les gouvernements démocratiques' (1960) 10 *Revue Française de Science Politique* 39ff, and Otto Kircheimer, 'The Transformation of the Western European Party Systems' in Joseph LaPalombara and Myron Weiner (eds), *Political Parties and Political Development* (1966), 177ff.

[36] Klaus von Beyme, *Parliamentary Democracy. Democratization, Destabilization, Reconsolidation, 1789–1999* (2000), 82.

[37] Turpin (n 12), 57ff.

[38] Joachim Wehner, 'Assessing the Power of the Purse: An Index of Legislative Budget Institutions' (2006) 54 *Political Studies* 767ff.

[39] Leyland (n 32), 110.

[40] Durga Das Basu, *Introduction to the Constitution of India* (20th edn, 1989), 187.

[41] References in Katja S. Ziegler, 'Executive Powers in Foreign Policy: The Decision to Dispatch the Military' in Ziegler, Baranger, and Bradley et al (n 11), 148ff.

acceptable. This technique is sometimes linked to a vote of no confidence or a censure motion, although it seldom reaches the point of dismissing government. Furthermore, the purposes of such inquiries frequently consist in the elected member's aim of drawing attention to a certain interest of his or her constituency. Given these premises, the introduction of television cameras in some parliaments has revitalized the culture of control by question and has enhanced transparency, but it is also exploited for propaganda purposes.[42]

In general, parliamentary control of the executive is perceived as being particularly needed given the great expansion in the importance of international relations, and in governmental activities connected with the adhesion to supranational organizations. An example of this may be seen in the efforts of European parliaments to recover in terms of the scrutiny of governmental action what they have lost in terms of decision-making at the EU level (the European 'democratic deficit').[43] These efforts were rewarded in 2009 with the Lisbon Treaty, that significantly enhances the role of national parliaments within the EU decision-making procedures. But the issue must be seen in light of a wider range of phenomena, those relating to the structural gap between the still national dimension of politics and the global or continental scale of markets, media, and technocratic agencies. In that domain, states may have a chance of playing an active role through their governments, rather than through representative assemblies. Inevitably, the latter are left on one side, and even their potential for providing a checking function appears modest.

VIII. Is Parliamentarism Declining?

These factors, together with those connected with the increasing mediatization and personalization of politics, are likely to deprive parliamentary deliberation progressively of its meaning. Hence there is emerging among the political elites of mature democracies a common concern for the decline of parliament, and for the consequences of this on the legitimacy of political institutions. In the United Kingdom, the Green Paper entitled 'The Governance of Britain', presented to Parliament by Prime Minister Brown in July 2007, aimed inter alia at 'limiting the powers of the executive', 'revitalising the House of Commons', and 'renewing the accountability of Parliament'. In the event, the legislation that emerged as a result of this initiative (the Constitutional Reform and Governance Act 2010) did not rise to this challenging rhetoric. It included changes affecting two areas of executive power, only one of which was expressly calculated to extend the functions of parliament;[44] and it seems unlikely that legislation alone will modify political attitudes that are based on long-seated practice rather than on law. However, a desire for change in the same direction of greater accountability appeared to drive both the ambitious constitutional reform in France in 2008 and the reform in 2006 of the German federal system (already mentioned). These various measures, arising in different political cultures and affecting different institutional mechanisms, may reflect a need to redress what has become an increasingly unbalanced relationship between parliament and government: but we cannot be confident that those who wield

[42] Von Beyme (n 36), 82.

[43] On this see among others Philipp Kiiver, 'The Composite Case for National Parliaments in the European Union: Who Profits from Enhanced Involvement?' (2006) 2(2) *European Constitutional Law Review* 227ff.

[44] The legal basis of the civil service and its management was removed from the royal prerogative but this was unlikely to affect ministers' control of the civil service. More significant was the conferment on Parliament of a role in approving approve treaties concluded by the executive.

executive power will willingly expose themselves to the prospect of more effective and transparent political challenge.

In discussing the main features of parliamentarism in this chapter, we have outlined the historical antecedents to forms of parliamentary government that exist today and we have explained that many differing forms of parliamentarism exist today. We have not examined the question whether, as a system of government, it is superior to or more stable than forms of presidentialism.[45] Nor have we sought to review empirical evidence on which an answer to this question might be based. In 1990, in a celebrated analysis of 'the perils of presidentialism', Juan J. Linz concluded that parliamentary democracies have had a superior historical performance and that parliamentarism is more conducive to stable democracy; among the difficulties posed by presidentialism is greater rigidity and the existence of dual legitimacies when executive and legislature are separately elected.[46] Criticism of this conclusion emphasized the possibilities for conflict that may exist in parliamentary systems, the variable stability of systems of political parties, the lack of legislative check on the executive when the government has a clear majority in the legislature, and the wide range of different versions of presidentialism and parliamentarism that exist.[47]

More recently, José A. Cheibub has argued that it is not the nature of presidential institutions as such that causes instability in presidential systems, since there are many other factors that determine how these systems operate: thus the instability of presidential regimes is seen most often in countries where in any event democracy of any type would be unstable.[48] This debate has often been based on the experience of countries in Latin America and to a lesser extent on that of new constitutional systems in Eastern Europe. In countries with a longer record of democratic government, as in Western Europe, the model of parliamentarism, with all its potential variants, is more commonly found than the model of presidentialism, despite the pressures in the modern world that work towards the personalization of political decision-making.

Bibliography

Bruce Ackerman, 'The New Separation of Powers' (2000) 113 *Harvard Law Review* 685

Walter Bagehot, *The English Constitution* ([1867] 1983)

Vernon Bogdanor (ed), *The British Constitution in the Twentieth Century* (2003)

Edmund Burke, *Speech to the Electors of Bristol* (1774), reported in Philip Kurland and Ralph Lerner (eds), *The Founders' Constitution* (vol I, 1987)

José Antonio Cheibub, *Presidentialism, Parliamentarism, and Democracy* (2007)

Durga Das Basu, *Introduction to the Constitution of India* (20th edn, 1989)

A.V. Dicey, *The Law and the Constitution* (10th edn, ECS Wade ed, 1959)

Robert Elgie and Sophia Moestrup, *Semi-Presidentialism Outside Europe* (2007)

Jeffrey Jowell and Dawn Oliver (eds), *The Changing Constitution* (2nd edn, 1989)

[45] See Chapter 29 on presidentialism in this volume.

[46] Juan J. Linz, 'The Perils of Presidentialism' in Larry Diamond and Marc Plattner (eds), *The Global Resurgence of Democracy* (1993), 108–26. And see Alfred Stepan and Cindy Skach, 'Presidentialism and Parliamentarism in Comparative Perspective' in Juan J. Linz and Arturo Valenzuela (eds), *The Failure of Presidential Democracy: Comparative perspectives* (1994), ch 4.

[47] Scott Mainwaring and Matthew Shugart, 'Juan Linz, Presidentialism, and Democracy: A Critical Appraisal' (1997) 29(4) *Comparative Politics* 449–71. See also Scott Mainwaring and Matthew Shugart (eds), *Presidentialism and Democracy in Latin America* (1997).

[48] José Antonio Cheibub, *Presidentialism, Parliamentarism, and Democracy* (2007), chs 1, 7.

Joseph LaPalombara and Myron Weiner (eds), *Political Parties and Political Development* (1966)
Juan J. Linz and Arturo Valenzuela (eds), *The Failure of Presidential Democracy: Comparative Perspectives* (1994)
John Stuart Mill, *Considerations on Representative Government* (1861), reprinted in John Stuart Mill, *On Liberty and Other Essays* (John Gray ed, 1991)
Boris Mirkine-Guetzévitch, *Les nouvelles tendances du droit constitutionnel* (1936)
Thomas Poguntke and Paul Webb, *The Presidentialization of Politics. A Comparative Study of Modern Democracies* (2005)
Kaare Strøm, Wolfgang C. Müller, and Torbjörn Bergman (eds), *Delegation and Accountability in Parliamentary Democracies* (2003)
M.J.C. Vile, *Constitutionalism and the Separation of Powers* (1967)
Klaus von Beyme, *Parliamentary Democracy. Democratization, Destabilization, Reconsolidation, 1789–1999* (2000)
Katja S. Ziegler, Denis Baranger, and A.W. Bradley (eds), *Constitutionalism and the Role of Parliaments* (2007)

CHAPTER 31

THE REGULATORY STATE

SUSAN ROSE-ACKERMAN

New Haven

I. Introduction

The modern regulatory state challenges settled constitutional doctrines. These challenges reflect the differing histories of the relation between the state and the market across modern democracies. Public law is the product of statutory, constitutional, and judicial choices over time; it blends constitutional and administrative concerns.[1] Contrast the United States with its long tradition of private ownership that includes public utilities with Europe where the state has traditionally operated public companies supplying those services. Recent trends to deregulate and privatize these services raise distinct constitutional challenges.

The regulation of complex economic and social phenomena forces all modern democracies to confront the constitutional and democratic legitimacy of delegated policymaking. A rigid separation of powers—where the legislature is the only source of legal norms, the government bureaucracy implements the law, and the judiciary oversees compliance with the law—cannot withstand the pressures of modern policymaking realities. In the United States the non-delegation doctrine has long provided only a weak background constraint on the writing of

[1] For a recent compilation of scholarship that illustrates these alternative models see Susan Rose-Ackerman and Peter Lindseth, *Comparative Administrative Law* (2010). Portions of this chapter are drawn from our introductory chapter.

statutes. Invoking the constitutional separation of powers, the federal courts accept statutory decisions to vest rule-making power in the executive branch and in independent agencies. In Germany with a very different constitutional structure, the Federal Constitutional Court has been similarly permissive, interpreting the language of the Grundgesetz to permit delegation and finding that it does not violate either the legislative primacy of the parliament or the protection of individual rights.[2] The French Constitution explicitly recognizes the legitimacy of delegation in specific areas, and the British courts, with no written document, similarly reject rigid ideas of parliamentary sovereignty.[3]

However, judicial acceptance of delegation does not end the matter. Acceptance leads the courts to assess the constitutional exercise of that power to assure that it comports with democratic values and does not violate rights. Very few constitutional texts, however, deal explicitly with the administrative process.[4] Most leave it to the courts to apply the constitution to the administrative process and to the legislature to enact procedures to guide the exercise of delegated power. Some constitutional courts, especially in parliamentary systems, have been very hands off. Most statutes that mandate policymaking procedures do not include provisions to make them judicially enforceable. This situation contrasts with the United States where the Administrative Procedure Act mandates certain rulemaking procedures and makes their use subject to judicial review.[5] This legal framework can be understood as a way to assure the democratic acceptability of policymaking delegation. In contrast, the administrative procedure acts in most other polities concentrate on administrative acts, usually defined to exclude broad rulemaking activity that determines general norms. Thus, from a constitutional point of view, there is an important practical gap in the operation of legitimate democratic government in many political systems. Delegation of policymaking is inevitable and desirable in the modern regulatory/welfare state, and for that very reason, it ought to be carried out consistent with democratic values. Ideally, this principle ought to have constitutional status, yet in most states it does not. Even in the United States, where the APA and other statutory provisions help to fill the gap, the principles expressed by the APA have a contested constitutional pedigree. Several scholars, however, do argue that the APA is a 'landmark' or a 'super statute' with constitutional or quasi-constitutional status.[6]

In other modern democracies, the claim that the policymaking process inside ministries or agencies should be legally constrained clashes with notions of the proper division between politics and law. Because it seems to risk politicizing the courts, the judiciary pulls back from review. One problem outside the United States is the lack of clear legal standards for judicial review of government or agency rulemaking. Of course, much of US administrative law concerns ambiguities in the judicial review provisions of the APA. However, the text does limit judicial review of the substance of regulations, and Supreme Court opinions have outlined the extent of judicial deference to agency interpretations of their own statutory mandates.

[2] Susan Rose-Ackerman, *Controlling Environmental Policy; The Limits of Public Law in Germany and the United States* (1995), 57–8.

[3] French Constitution of 1958 as amended, Art 37, available at <http://www.assemblee-nationale.fr/english/8ab.asp>. For a collection of articles discussing judicial review in the United Kingdom see Christopher Forsyth, *Judicial Review and the Constitution* (2000). Kaare Strøm, Wolfgang C. Müller, and Torbjörn Bergman (eds), *Delegation and Accountability in Parliamentary Democracies* (2003) provides a wide range of case studies.

[4] See Tom Ginsburg, 'Written Constitutions and the Administrative State: On the Constitutional Character of Administrative Law' in Rose-Ackerman and Lindseth (n 1), 117.

[5] APA, 5 USC §§ 551–559, 701–706.

[6] William N. Eskridge Jr and John Ferejohn, 'Super Statutes' (2001) 50 *Duke Law Journal* 1215; Bruce Ackerman, 'The Holmes Lectures: The Living Constitution' (2007) 120 *Harvard Law Review* 1727.

Elsewhere, the field is open, and it is not surprising that courts have resisted entering into the review of rules and norms absent any constitutional or statutory standards. Sometimes courts do review general rules if the plaintiffs claim that their rights have been violated, but review as a way to maintain democratic legitimacy occurs only indirectly or under cover of the review of rights.[7] Finding a proper place for judicial review is not the only problem that arises at the intersection between constitutional and administrative law. A second trend in the administrative process also highlights the tension between democratic values and delegated rulemaking. That is the push by social scientists and some public officials to import stronger commitments to cost–benefit analysis, risk assessment, and impact assessment that challenge traditional modes of policymaking. Debates over the proper role of technocratic analysis and public participation and accountability raise issues of constitutional moment.

The challenges to constitutional law raised by the modern administrative state take contrasting forms in presidential and parliamentary systems. I particularly focus on the differences between the US presidential system and the procedural requirements of its APA, on the one hand, and parliamentary democracies where the government must maintain the confidence of the legislature, on the other. The need to assure technical competence may clash with both public accountability under the APA and political accountability to parliament.

This chapter considers four key issues. Section II discusses delegation of policymaking authority outside the legislature. Section III concentrates on the creation of independent agencies and their connection to regulatory policy and government oversight. Section IV considers the role both of economic analysis in the policy process and of procedural requirements designed to further political and public accountability. Finally, Section V brings in the courts' role in reviewing and overseeing the regulatory process in the rest of government. The chapter concludes in Section VI with some reflections on the connection between administrative law, public policymaking, and democratic legitimacy.

II. The Political Economy of Delegation

Regulatory policy can be made through detailed statutes administered by agencies on a case-by-case basis. However, in practice, such a high degree of specificity would be extremely impractical. Most regulatory laws allocate considerable discretion to the executive or to specialized agencies not just to set enforcement priorities but also to make policy under delegated authority.

Why are legislators willing to delegate policymaking authority to agencies and executive departments? There are, of course, many functional reasons for delegation—agency technical expertise, the legislators' lack of time, the value of removing implementation decisions from overtly political fora. However, besides these prudential arguments for delegation, legislatures delegate for political reasons. Three seem most important.

First, delegation may reflect the legislators' self-interest.[8] Elected representatives satisfy their constituents, not only by taking positions on broad legislative initiatives, but also by doing individual favors for voters. Thus, they may design laws with opportunities for 'casework' that aids constituents or campaign contributors. After the law is on the books, legislators can earn points with constituents by intervening in agency processes. They may prefer

[7] For a discussion of the German case see Rose-Ackerman (n 2), 72–81, 125–31.

[8] Morris Fiorina and Roger G. Noll, 'Voters, Legislators and Bureaucracy: Institutional Design in the Public Sector' (1978) 68 *American Economic Review, Papers and Proceedings* 256, reprinted in Susan Rose-Ackerman (ed), *Economics of Administrative Law* (2007), 5.

agency administration to direct enforcement by the courts because there may be few opportunities for politicians to aid constituents when enforcement depends upon private lawsuits.[9] Secondly, delegation is a way to pass on difficult choices to bureaucrats while claiming credit for the broadly popular aspects of policy. Delegation represents a compromise when politicians want to enact a statue in a particular area but cannot agree on the details because of conflicting political constituencies. As a general rule, legislators will delegate the implementation of policies with concentrated costs and diffuse benefits so that agencies must make the hard choices. Conversely, when benefits are concentrated and costs are diffuse, the legislature will want to specify the beneficiaries itself and claim credit.[10]

Thirdly, the degree of delegation may depend upon whether or not the interests of the executive and legislature are aligned. In a presidential system, bureaucrats may be given more discretion under unified government.[11] The US Congress is willing to delegate more power the less it thinks the exercise of that power will diverge from its own preferences. If some agencies, such as the Federal Trade Commission, are independent of direct presidential control, the legislature may give such agencies more discretion compared to executive departments. In a parliamentary system, the cabinet can propose statutory texts that delegate power to itself confident that the supporting coalition in the legislature usually will enact the government's draft bills.

Operating against these reasons for delegation is the worry that agencies will either be captured by the industries they regulate or, conversely, will be overly subservient to other groups such as labor unions, consumer groups, or environmental organizations. Older research stressed the possibility of agency capture by regulated entities able to offer private inducements or to dominate agency deliberations.[12] These claims have been challenged by research that points to the legislators' ability to draft statutes that give them an ongoing ability to monitor regulatory agencies. Matthew D. McCubbins and Thomas Schwartz contrast two types of oversight: 'police patrols' and 'fire alarms'.[13] The former involves members of the legislature in direct oversight. The latter sets up a process, embedded in the original statutory scheme, under which private individuals and groups carry out the monitoring. McCubbins then collaborated with Roger Noll and Barry Weingast to argue that the APA is a prime example of such oversight where the legislature 'stacks the deck' in favor of the groups favored by the enacting coalition.[14] The APA's requirements for notice, hearings, and reason-giving help to assure third-party participation and to limit closed-door decision-making. Even though the constraints are nominally procedural, they have substantive effects.

The deck-stacking hypothesis is a bold and interesting thesis and has generated a range of critical responses.[15] Jeffrey S. Hill and James E. Brazier detail the restrictive conditions under

[9] Morris Fiorina, 'Legislative Choice of Regulatory Forms: Legal Process or Administrative Process?' (1982) 39 *Public Choice* 33, reprinted in Rose-Ackerman (n 8), 10.

[10] James Q. Wilson, *The Politics of Regulation* (1980).

[11] David Epstein and Sharyn O'Halloran, 'Administrative Procedures, Information, and Agency Discretion' (1994) 38 *American Journal of Political Science* 697, reprinted in Rose-Ackerman (n 8), 29.

[12] George Stigler, 'The Theory of Economic Regulation' (1971) 2 *Bell Journal of Economics and Management Science* 3; Richard Posner, 'Theories of Economic Regulation' (1974) 5 *Bell Journal of Econmics and Management Science* 335; Samuel Peltzman, 'Toward a More General Theory of Regulation' (1976) 19 *Journal of Law and Economics* 211.

[13] Mathew D. McCubbins and Thomas Schwartz, 'Congressional Oversight Overlooked: Police Patrols and Fire Alarms' (1984) 28 *American Journal of Political Science* 165, reprinted in Rose-Ackerman (n 8), 85.

[14] Mathew D. McCubbins et al, 'Administrative Procedures as Instruments of Political Control' (1987) 3 *Journal of Law, Economics and Organization* 243, reprinted in Rose-Ackerman (n 8), 100.

[15] See eg R. Douglas Arnold, 'Political Control of Administrative Officials' (1987) 3 *Journal of Law Economics and Organization* 279, reprinted in Rose-Ackerman (n 8), 135.

which deck stacking can operate effectively. According to them, *ex ante* controls only operate well when

> (1) the enacting coalition provides the agency with clear guidance...; (2) the enacting coalition has designed the structure and process requirements with the specific intention of maintaining agreements reached by the coalition; and (3) the courts provide a reliable mechanism for enforcing these... requirements....[16]

In a similar vein, David Spence questions the ability of elected politicians to constrain the policy choices of agencies over time through structural and procedural means.[17] His study of the US Federal Energy Regulatory Commission shows that such controls may not have the intended impacts. Steven Balla shows that the hypothesis has little explanatory power for reimbursement policies under Medicare, the US public health insurance system for the elderly.[18]

Of course, in the limit, if an agency makes choices that diverge too far from the preferences of lawmakers, it will invite the politicians to amend the law. In the US presidential system, an agency, operating under an existing statute, can strategically pick a policy between its own preferred choice and that of the legislative oversight committee so that the committee will take no action.[19] However, the possibility of a presidential veto constrains the legislature and may give the agency more leeway. The limits of *ex post* control then ought to affect the design of statutes in the first place. Legislators might balance political control against expertise as they look to the future.[20]

Delegation to the executive branch and to independent agencies may be a preferred strategy for legislators under the conditions outlined above, but what about the preferences of voters? In a presidential system, Jerry Mashaw argues that voters may favor delegation to executive agencies because of the President's accountability to a national constituency.[21] David Spence and Frank Cross point to other reasons why voters may favor delegation and argue that delegation is often a route to more effective policy.[22] According to them, agencies are not always more subject to capture than lawmakers. Delegation permits the use of expertise, favors specialization, encourages professional distance from politics, permits decisions to be tailored to diverse conditions throughout the country, and leads to procedures that are open to public participation.

In short, as a normative matter, delegation has many desirable features, and as a positive matter, it is an ongoing feature of modern government. Even if the legislature tries to control agencies by stacking the deck in various ways, discretion will persist as an important aspect of regulatory policy and implementation.

[16] Jeffrey S. Hill and James E. Brazier, 'Constraining Administrative Decisions: A Critical Examination of the Structure and Process Hypothesis' (1991) 7 *Journal of Law, Economics, and Organization* 373, reprinted in Rose-Ackerman (n 8), 143.

[17] David B. Spence, 'Managing Delegation Ex Ante: Using Law to Steer Administrative Agencies' (1999) 28 *Journal of Legal Studies* 413, reprinted in Rose-Ackerman (n 8), 171.

[18] Steven J. Balla, 'Administrative Procedures and Political Control of the Bureaucracy' (1998) 92 *American Political Science Review* 663.

[19] John Ferejohn and Charles Shipan, 'Congressional Influence on Bureaucracy' (1990) 6 *Special Issue Journal of Law, Economics, and Organization* 1, reprinted in Rose-Ackerman (n 8), 207.

[20] Kathleen Bawn, 'Political Control Versus Expertise: Congressional Choices About Administrative Procedures' (1995) 89 *American Political Science Review* 62, reprinted in Rose-Ackerman (n 8), 227.

[21] Jerry Mashaw, 'Prodelegation: Why Administrators Should Make Political Decisions' (1985) 1 *Journal of Law, Economics, and Organization* 81, reprinted in Rose-Ackerman (n 8), 335.

[22] David B. Spence and Frank Cross, 'A Public Choice Case for the Administrative State' (2000) 89 *Georgetown Law Journal* 97.

III. Independent Agencies[23]

The functional tasks facing the modern state, along with public demands for transparency and accountability, pose a challenge to conventional constitutional thinking that stresses the threefold division of the state into legislative, executive and judicial branches.[24] Substantive policy demands have led to institutional innovations, beginning with the creation of independent regulatory agencies, ranging from central banks to broadcasting commissions. Furthermore, the need for oversight and control of delegated authority has led to the creation of monitoring organizations, such as supreme audit agencies and ombudsmen, and to judicial review.

In designing a regulatory program the legislature must decide whether to assign its implementation to an agency under the political control of the president or the cabinet or whether to create a body that is somewhat independent. Independence generally means that a public entity falls outside the cabinet structure of government and has some degree of separation from day-to-day political pressures.[25] Independence is defended as a way to assure that decisions are made by neutral professionals with the time and technical knowledge to make competent, apolitical choices. The heart of the controversy over independence stems from the agencies' disconnect from traditional democratic accountability. Attempts to legitimate such agencies in democratic terms often stress the importance of processes that go beyond expertise to incorporate public opinion and social and economic interests. The ideal is an expert agency that is independent of partisan politics but sensitive to the concerns of ordinary citizens and civil society groups. In contrast, others defend independence as a way to avoid just such influences and to assure a stable, market-friendly business environment. Critics worry about capture by narrow interests.

The worldwide growth of independent regulatory and oversight agencies is a consequence both of the privatization of public utilities and of increasing calls for monitoring of core government activities. Whatever the agencies' functional merits, their constitutional status is often in question. Most so-called independent agencies are not in fact free-standing entities. Independence is a relative concept.

Even in the United States, with a history that goes back to the establishment of the Interstate Commerce Commission in 1887, independent agencies are not completely independent. The President appoints commissioners with Senate approval and selects the chair. Most agencies operate with appropriated budget funds and face congressional scrutiny. The legislature frequently builds oversight of some kind into the statutory scheme. However, even if the appointment process is highly political, staggered terms that exceed the terms of the President and members of Congress, political-party balance requirements, and removal only for cause limit executive control, compared with departments directly in the presidential chain of command.

In Europe, under pressure from the European Union, Member States have privatized many state-owned public utilities, although many states still retain a partial ownership share and a role in the selection of the board. These privatizations created the need for the ongoing regulation of firms to constrain monopoly power and to further other goals, such as universal service, energy conservation, and environmental protection. Especially if the state has an ownership stake, the regulatory body needs to be independent of the rest of government to avoid conflicts of interest. This raises a contested issue in constitutional design. Most member

[23] This section is derived from one part of the introduction to Rose-Ackerman and Lindseth (n 1).

[24] Bruce Ackerman, 'The New Separation of Powers' (2000) 113 *Harvard Law Review* 633.

[25] Martin Shapiro, 'A Comparison of US and European Independent Agencies' in Ackerman and Lindseth (n 1), 293.

states are parliamentary or quasi-parliamentary systems. Such constitutional structures tend to look askance at public institutions that operate independently of the rest of government, subject only to weak parliamentary control. Yet, the functional argument for independence is especially strong in these cases. As long as the state retains an ownership share, an independent regulator can help to avoid conflicts of interest. The challenge that independent agencies pose to unitary constitutional traditions varies across parliamentary systems. Thus, Germany and Britain have been more resistant to the creation of independent bodies than the French. France has a history of independent regulatory bodies that dates from at least the 1970s, and it has recently enhanced agency independence by borrowing extensively from American and EU models while retaining some distinctive features.[26] In contrast, in Germany faith in the capacity of the legislature and executive to define and pursue rational policy remains reasonably strong. Outside certain narrow, functionally specific domains, there are few calls for independent administrative agencies.[27] In common law parliamentary systems, such as the United Kingdom and other countries of the Commonwealth, notions of unitary government policymaking and agency independence are also often in serious tension.[28] As a consequence, the new German and English agencies that regulate privatized public utilities are formally under the authority of an individual cabinet minister or the cabinet as a whole. This strengthens their claims to be acting in politically accountable way.

At the level of the European Union, agencies have proliferated, but their lack of strong democratic legitimacy has meant the substitution of 'technocratic for democratic legitimacy'.[29] Agency boards include member state representatives, but this is a political compromise. In practice, it leads to the dominance of technical experts, who are appointed by member states and interact with specialized member state ministries.[30]

Elsewhere, transplanted institutional structures may operate quite differently than in their countries of origin. For example, in Brazil's presidential system 'independent' agencies, although borrowing from American models, are clearly subordinate to the executive whatever their nominal form. Hence, they struggle to provide credible commitments to investors both domestic and foreign.[31] Taiwan's independent regulatory agency for telecommunications ran up against a Supreme Court that struck down the appointments process for giving too large a role to the legislature.[32]

A growing number of independent agencies police the accountability of the government itself. Here the case for independence is particularly strong, but so is the need for oversight to prevent either their capture by regime opponents or their lapse into inaction. The political

[26] Dominique Custos, 'Independent Administrative Authorities in France: Structural and Procedural Change at the Intersection of Americanization, Europeanization and Gallicization' in Rose-Ackerman and Lindseth (n 1), 277.

[27] Daniel Halberstam, 'The Promise of Comparative Administrative Law: A Constitutional Perspective' in Rose-Ackerman and Lindseth (n 1), t 185.

[28] Lorne Sossin, 'The Puzzle of Administrative Independence and Parliamentary Democracy in the Common Law World: A Canadian Perpective' in Rose-Ackerman and Lindseth (n 1), 205.

[29] Shapiro (n 25); see also G. Majone, 'Two Logics of Delegation: Agency and Fiduciary Relations in EU Governance' (2001) 2 *European Union Politics* 103.

[30] Catherine Donnelly, 'Participation and Expertise: Judicial Attitudes in Comparative Perspective' in Rose-Ackerman and Lindseth (n 1), 357.

[31] Marianna Mota Prado, 'Presidential Dominance from a Comparative Perspective: The Relationship between the Executive Branch and Regulatory Agencies in Brazil' in Rose-Ackerman and Lindseth (n 1), 225.

[32] Jiunn-rong Yeh, 'Experimenting with Independent Commissions in a New Democracy with a Civil Law Tradition: The Case of Taiwan' in Rose-Ackerman and Lindseth (n 1), 246.

coalitions that created these bodies may not be able to maintain the bodies' efficacy over time.[33] Controversy surrounds the operation of independent electoral commissions, human rights ombudsmen, anti-corruption agencies, and supreme audit offices throughout the world. Yet, in spite of the controversy, they can serve as important checks on incumbent regimes if professionally run and if granted sufficient independence and authority.

IV. Administrative Procedures, Public Participation, and Technocratic Analysis

The constitutional challenges facing the modern regulatory state arise not only from structural issues involving political control and the separation of powers. In addition, even a regulatory body that is entirely within the cabinet structure of government can act in ways that raise questions of democratic and popular accountability. Public accountability goes beyond purely structural relations between government institutions.

Administrative law imposes constraints on agencies' delegated authority, and it gives the courts a tool to monitor the exercise of that authority. Constitutional constraints frequently take the form of protections for individual rights, as in the due process and equal protections clauses in the US Constitution or the protections for both substantive and procedural rights in the German Grundgesetz. Recently, the European Convention on Human Rights, as interpreted by the European Court of Human Rights and national courts, has been influencing judicial review and administrative practice throughout Europe. Without denying the importance of these rights-based constraints on government action, this chapter focuses attention on a different issue—assuring the democratic accountability and legitimacy of policymaking inside government departments and independent agencies. Public agencies promulgate regulations for many different purposes. They seek to correct market failures, protect rights, and distribute the benefits of state actions to particular groups—ranging from the poor or disadvantaged minorities to politically powerful industries such as agriculture or oil and gas. All representative democracies face the need to balance democratic accountability against the use of technical expertise to assure the competent implementation of complex statutes. I begin by discussing the role of cost–benefit analysis as an analytic tool that can serve political purposes. I then discuss the potential tensions between assuring competent technocratic policymaking in the executive and permitting public participation and accountability.

1. Cost–Benefit Analysis

In the regulation of the economy, a prominent form of expertise derives from economics. However, such expertise does not merely represent technocratic competence. Rather, it is bound up with normative commitments that may clash with popular sentiments. The normative position espoused by most public policy analysts trained in economics is the cost–benefit test, a criterion that recommends choosing policies to maximize net social benefits measured in monetary terms. The aim is to avoid waste and inefficiency and to maximize the size of the

[33] John M. Ackerman, 'Understanding Independent Accountbility Agencies' in Rose-Ackerman and Lindseth (n 1), 265. On the way presidents can subvert oversight agencies, see the cases of Argentina and the Philippines discussed in Susan Rose-Ackerman, Diane Desierto, and Natalia Volosin, 'Hyper-Presidentialism: Separation of Powers without Checks and Balances' (2011) 29 *Berkeley Journal of International Law* 246.

social pie.[34] A statement in favor of the use of cost–benefit analysis in health and safety regulation by a group of leading policy economists argues that it should be carried out for all major regulatory decisions. It 'has a potentially important role to play in policymaking, although it should not be the sole basis of such decisionmaking.'[35] If the costs of a policy are out of line with the benefits, an agency ought to be required to justify its choice.

In its pure form the cost–benefit test ignores the distribution of the benefits and only asks if it would be *possible* for the gainers to compensate the losers. This leaves open the question of the fairness of the distribution of benefits and costs—a question that cannot be answered by economics standing alone.[36] Public policy analysts argue for the use of cost–benefit analysis in the promulgation of regulations and government programs designed to improve efficiency and argue that distributive justice concerns should be reflected in taxes, subsidies, and spending levels. On this view, cost–benefit analysis is an input into the subsequent regulatory process that sets policy, not the decisive determinant of policy.[37] This is a fine response in principle, but, in reality, policy choices cannot be so neatly cabined.

In the United States economists have been active critics of existing regulatory programs that fail to pass cost–benefit tests. This work has spurred calls for reform that concentrate on the use of better analysis inside agencies and in the drafting of statutes. However, those urging greater reliance on economic criteria need to recognize that these approaches can themselves be used as tools to obtain political advantage. If cost–benefit criteria are applied by an office that reports to the President or the Prime Minister, the cost–benefit tool, which appears neutral on its face, can be manipulated for political ends. This is possible because many judgment calls must be made in any analysis. Seldom will there be a single 'right' answer that anyone trained in the technique will accept. For example, the choice of a discount rate and proper way to monetize morbidity and mortality are both fraught with controversy even among those committed to the method.[38]

Recent US presidents have instituted White House review of regulations in the Office of Information and Regulatory Affairs (OIRA) using cost–benefit criteria.[39] Although originally policy analysis was applied to spending programs, recently the emphasis has shifted to regulatory programs, where most of the costs and benefits are not included in the government budget. The Executive Order that requires executive branch agencies to carry out cost–benefit analyses for major rules has the effect of strengthening the President's hand in the regulatory area.

In response to concerns about the political uses of analysis, some commentators have suggested special science courts or other types of independent reviews. Justice (then Judge) Stephen Breyer, for example, urged the creation of a separate expert agency with the mission of rationalizing regulatory policy across programs that regulate risk.[40] Bruce Ackerman recommends the creation of an integrity branch—concerned with transparency and limiting

[34] E.J. Mishan and Euston Quah, *Cost Benefit Analysis* (2006); David L. Weimer and Aidan R. Vining, *Policy Analysis: Concepts and Practices* (5th edn, 2011).

[35] Kenneth J. Arrow et al, 'Is There a Role for Benefit-Cost Analysis in Environmental Health and Safety Regulation?' (1996) 272 *Science* 221, reprinted in Rose-Ackerman (n 8), 357.

[36] I.M.D. Little, *A Critique of Welfare Economics* ([1958] 2003).

[37] Cass R. Sunstein, *The Cost–Benefit State: The Future of Regulatory Protection* (2002); Matthew D. Adler and Eric A. Posner, *New Foundations of Cost-Benefit Analysis* (2006).

[38] Susan Rose-Ackerman, 'Putting Cost–Benefit Analysis in Its Place: Rethinking Regulatory Review' (2011) 65 *University of Miami Law Review* 335.

[39] Elena Kagan, 'Presidential Administration' (2001) 114 *Harvard Law Review* 2245; Richard H. Pildes and Cass R. Sunstein, 'Reinventing the Regulatory State' (1995) 62 *Univeristy of Chicago Law Review* 1.

[40] Stephen Breyer, *Breaking the Vicous Circle* (1993).

corruption—and a regulatory branch insulated from day-to-day political influences but required to justify its actions publicly.[41] I argue for a more limited reform that separates OIRA review of regulations from technical debates over the proper analytic methods. I argue for the creation of an independent office that I call ORPAT or the Office for the Review of Policy Analytic Techniques within the Government Accountability Office or perhaps the National Academy of Sciences.[42]

How does research on cost–benefit analysis contribute to our understanding of the constitutional legitimacy of regulatory policymaking? At one level, this work is a plea for the use of expertise in the drafting and implementation of statutes. Proponents of cost–benefit analysis favor more delegation to technocrats trained in these techniques. If, however, the use of cost–benefit analysis essentially serves to strengthen the hand of the president or the prime minister over cabinet departments and agencies, it may be resisted by legislative committees and interest groups that have more impact at the ministry or agency level than with the chief executive. Cost–benefit analysis and its sisters, risk assessment and cost–effectiveness analysis, are universalizing techniques that cut across substantive fields and provide a way to compare programs and allocate funds using uniform criteria. In the US Congress with its strong substantive committees, this is unlikely to be a favored outcome. Thus, the rational choice approach to legislative studies suggests that Congress will not support a generalized imposition of cost–benefit tests unless their own preferences are very far from those of the executive and close to the conclusions of the cost–benefit test. For example, during the Clinton Administration under divided government, members of Congress introduced several bills to mandate cost–benefit analysis and other related techniques. In a unitary parliamentary system such legislative initiatives are unlikely, but the underlying conflicts may still exist beneath the surface.

2. Public Participation in the Regulatory Process

Discussions of 'good' policy by social scientists, risk analysts, and other specialists sometimes clash with the democratic accountability of agency policymaking. In the United States the APA requires notice, consultation, and reason-giving for most federal rulemaking.[43] The final rule can then be subject to judicial review, which reaches beyond compliance with the procedural demands of the APA to consider the rational underpinnings of the rule and its consistency with the implementing statute. Moves in this direction are occurring elsewhere as regulatory agencies have begun to introduce consultation and transparency requirements. However, these reforms are seldom legally enforceable, essentially leaving their continued viability to the regulators themselves, who may or may not find them to be politically expedient.

The tension between technical competence and democratic legitimacy may be less evident in legal systems outside the United States where the law does little to constrain policymaking processes compared with the adjudication of individual administrative acts.[44] Judicial review, except where human rights or other constitutional prescriptions are at stake, does not usually take on the merits of broad policy choices. However, even if the tension is not so obvious elsewhere, it is still present, but the American model is not the only way to deal with the issue.

[41] Ackerman (n 24), 688–714.

[42] Rose-Ackerman (n 38).

[43] APA §§ 553 and 706.

[44] Rose-Ackerman (n 2); Susan Rose-Ackerman, *From Elections to Democracy: Building Accountable Government in Hungary and Poland* (2005).

In Europe there is a lively debate on the benefits of expanded public participation and transparency requirements in rulemaking. This debate is occurring at the same time as substantive policymaking principles are also being scrutinized under the rubric of Impact Assessment.[45] However, administrative law remains relatively untouched; it concentrates on decisions in individual cases as opposed to the policymaking process.

However one views the debate over policymaking as an administrative law matter, it is a key area of contestation over regulatory policy. Tensions between technical expertise and democratic accountability exist in many countries, and the courts have frequently tried to manage that tension. Courts uphold statutory public participation requirements but seldom impose them on their own initiative. According to one study, in the United States and the European Union, courts act as a counterweight to the prevailing ethos—upholding expertise in the United States, and treating claims of expertise with caution in the European Union. The UK courts view both public participation and expertise with skepticism and they legitimate administrative action based on a Weberian understanding of a hierarchical, professional, politically neutral civil service.[46]

The tension between public participation and competent policy implementation is frequently overstated by committed technocrats. Participation and transparency can serve not just as ways to protect rights but also as means to the end of better policy outcomes. Greater public involvement may both produce more effective policy and increase the acceptability of the regulatory process both in representative democracies and in entities, such as the European Union, that also seek public legitimacy.[47] As a practical matter, however, regulatory agencies may not move toward greater participation and stronger standards of transparency and reason-giving absent a concerted public outcry. In the United States the APA arguably arose from congressional effort to constrain delegated policymaking under a separation-of-powers system.[48] No such incentives exist in parliamentary systems.[49]

Paradoxically, however, many new regulatory agencies in Europe have introduced accountable procedures on their own initiative even though they are isolated from electoral politics.[50] Regulators in France, the United Kingdom, and Sweden supported greater public involvement because they needed outside support to survive and could imitate established models in the United States and elsewhere. More participatory and transparent processes were seen as a way of increasing their own legitimacy. However, these moves did not always have that effect. Sometimes they simply increased the power of the regulated industry. In some cases, however, the agencies reacted to the risk of capture by taking steps to facilitate consumer input.

For policies where a cost–benefit test seems appropriate, the regulator could combine cost–benefit analysis with transparency as a means of blocking agencies from adopting measures that benefit narrow interests. Cost–benefit criteria could be a default criterion for regulations designed to improve the efficiency of the economy, subject to override by statutory mandates

[45] Jonathan B. Wiener and Alberto Alemanno, 'Comparing Regulatory Oversight Bodies Across the Atlantic: The Office of Information and Regulatory Affairs in the US and the Impact Assessment Boad in the EU' in Rose-Ackerman and Lindseth (n 1), 309.

[46] Donnelly (n 30), 357.

[47] On the EU see Peter Lindseth, *Power and Legitimacy: Reconciling Europe and the Nation State* (2010).

[48] McCubbins et al (n 14).

[49] Rose-Ackerman (n 2); Terry Moe and Michael Caldwell, 'The Institutional Foundations of Democratic Government: A Comparison of Presidential and Parliamentary Systems' (1994) 150 *Journal of Institutional and Theoretical Economics* 116.

[50] Dorit Rubinstein Reiss, 'Administrative Agencies as Creators of Administrative Law Norms: Evidence from the UK, France, and Sweden' in Rose-Ackerman and Lindseth (n 1), 373.

and to constitutional limits.[51] In spite of the potential inconsistency between democratic choice and cost–benefit analysis, the courts could impose policy analytic techniques on agencies as a way to limit capture by narrow interests. The legislature would be able to override the norm with explicit statutory language, but non-transparent efforts to induce agencies to benefit narrow interests could not be implemented. This requirement could have legal force if applied by the courts. A judicial presumption in favor of net benefit maximization increases the political costs for narrow groups, which would have to obtain explicit statutory language in order to have their interests recognized by courts and agencies. This proposal is, of course, controversial even in the United States and would presumably be unworkable in legal regimes with little court review of rulemaking. Yet it raises an important question that is central to the following discussion of administrative litigation. What should be the judiciary's role in reviewing the policymaking activities of modern executive branch bodies and regulatory agencies? Going further, should the courts review the process of statutory drafting, particularly in unitary parliamentary regimes?

V. Judicial Review

The final piece of the administrative law and policy puzzle is the judiciary. Statutes often include provisions for judicial review of regulatory action. Why would the legislature write such provisions into statutes when they know that the courts either may not share their policy preferences or may be constrained by their judicial role? According to William Landes and Richard Posner, the US Congress includes judicial review so that courts will ratify the original statutory deal if agencies overreach.[52] There is obviously some tension between the view of courts as carrying out oversight functions for the legislature and courts as composed of judges with their own policy preferences which may differ from those of the enacting legislature.

To see how the US courts actually operate begin with *Chevron, USA, Inc v National Resources Defense Council*.[53] Consistent with the Landes and Posner view, the decision holds that courts should be sure that agencies have followed congressional intent. However, departing from that view, it goes on to hold that if the intent is unclear, courts should be deferential to reasonable agency interpretations of their statutory mandates. Writing soon after the decision, however, Justice (then Judge) Breyer argues against such a strict interpretation of the decision and at the same time urges that courts should show more deference to agency expertise on policy matters.[54] William N. Eskridge Jr and John Ferejohn, in contrast, argue that aggressive judicial review of both law and policy is desirable to rein in agencies that have become too independent of the legislature.[55] Thus, for them, *Chevron* is an unfortunate move in the wrong direction. Why would judges tie their own hands when it comes to statutory interpretation? One explanation comes from Linda R. Cohen and Matthew L. Spitzer who explain the puzzle with a self-interest explanation that is contingent on the political

[51] Susan Rose-Ackerman, *Rethinking the Progressive Agenda: The Reform of the American Regulatory State* (1992); Sunstein (n 37), 191–228.

[52] William M. Landes and Richard Posner, 'The Independent Judiciary in an Interest Group Perspective' (1975) 18 *Journal of Law and Economics* 875.

[53] 467 US 837 (1984).

[54] Stephen Breyer, 'Judicial Review of Questions of Law and Policy' (1986) 38 *Administrative Law Review* 363, reprinted in Rose-Ackerman (n 8), 455.

[55] Willam N. Eskridge Jr and John Ferejohn, 'Making the Deal Stick: Enforcing the Original Constitutional Structure of Lawmaking in the Modern Regulatory State' (1992) 8 *Journal of Law, Economics, and Organization* 165, reprinted in Rose-Ackerman (n 8), 491.

configurations of the time. They claim that by the mid-1980s both the Supreme Court and the agencies had become more conservative than the lower courts. *Chevron* was a way for the Supreme Court to rein in the lower courts and give more leeway to agencies.[56]

The strategic interactions between the courts and agencies cannot be measured by looking only at decided cases. Agencies seek to avoid the time and trouble of lawsuits and also seek to avoid the consequences of an unfavorable outcome. If they tailor their actions to avoid judicial challenges, one should be able to see a connection between the ideological composition of the courts and agency behavior even if no cases have been litigated. To test this proposition, Brandice Canes-Wrone collected data on the Army Corps of Engineers' decisions to grant or to withhold permits to develop wetlands. The Corps operates throughout the United States, and US district judges have jurisdiction over lawsuits filed against the Corps. Canes-Wrone found that 'officials were significantly less likely to issue a permit the more liberal the lower courts in which the decision could be litigated.'[57]

Finally, one needs to consider the regulated entities themselves and the organized beneficiaries of regulation, such as labor unions and environmental groups. Judicial review is not automatic and will not occur unless someone has an incentive to bring a case.[58] One benefit of court review may be a delay in the implementation of a final rule. As Mashaw argues, the current situation gives regulated entities too few incentives to comply promptly. He supports a reduction in the possibilities for pre-enforcement review so that the courts would only get involved after the rule has gone into effect. This would limit the strategic options for firms, but there are difficulties. Challenges to agency rulemaking processes, which are at the heart of the democratic justification for delegation, would then be very difficult to bring successfully if considerable time has elapsed between the promulgation of a rule and its review by a court.[59]

Comparative analysis takes account of the differences in constitutional structures and permits one to assess some of the general claims made by political economic research on the United States. Under the Landes and Posner view, judicial review is a result of the legislature's desire to check the executive, and its inability to do this effectively on its own. The legislature is the dominant actor that can assign tasks to the courts. Hence, parliamentary systems ought to provide for lower levels of judicial oversight of the administration than presidential systems. In a parliamentary system the same political coalition controls both branches, and so legislators from the majority coalition do not want the courts to intervene to oversee executive action. Court review of administrative action cannot lock in past political choices because statutes are quite easy to change when executive and legislature are under unified political control. In contrast to these expectations, Elizabeth Magill and Daniel Ortiz find that courts in the United Kingdom, France, and Germany are quite active in reviewing administrative actions.[60] Either the theory of legislative behavior has limited force, or other factors prevent the government from constraining the courts. The courts themselves seem to be independent actors at least insofar as they assert jurisdiction and oversee the executive. Tom Zwart argues

[56] Linda R. Cohen and Matthew L. Spitzer, 'Solving the Chevron Puzzle' (1994) 57 *Law and Contemporary Problems* 65.

[57] Brandice Canes-Wrone, 'Bureaucratic Decisions and the Composition of the Lower Courts' (2003) 47 *American Journal of Political Science* 205, reprinted in Rose-Ackerman (n 8), 554.

[58] Jerry Mashaw, 'Improving the Environment of Agency Rulemaking: An Essay on Management, Games, and Accountability Law and Contemporary Problems' (1994) 57 *Law and Contemporary Problems* 185.

[59] Rose-Ackerman (n 2); Susan Rose-Ackerman, 'Consensus versus Incentives: A Skeptical Look at Regulatory Negotiation' (1994) 43 *Duke Law Journal* 1206.

[60] M. Elizabeth Magill and Daniel R. Ortiz, 'Comparative Positive Political Theory' in Rose-Ackerman and Lindseth (n 1), 134.

that if the legislature does not provide aggressive oversight of the executive, the courts will be under pressure from the public and interest groups to take on this role. Under this dynamic view of checks and balance, if judges believe that executive discretion needs to be controlled and if the legislature is doing little, they may step in, grant standing to public interest plaintiffs, and limit executive power.[61]

VI. Conclusions

As the regulatory state emerged over the course of the twentieth century, administrative law helped to mediate the exercise of public power. It operates at the borders between the private and public sectors. Its constitutional role extends beyond the assurance of fair and transparent procedures and the protection of individual rights. It also concerns the democratic legitimacy of government policymaking. A fair and open policymaking process helps democratic citizens to hold modern government to account in the face of demands for delegation and regulation, both within and beyond the state. Thus, administrative law must be in dialogue with constitutional law as the modern state develops.

Recent research in economics and political economy can help one to understand why delegation accompanied by judicial review occurs and how the self-interest of political, bureaucratic, and judicial actors interacts with institutional structures to determine outcomes. It can also illuminate the normative role of economic analysis in helping politicians and policymakers design and implement policies. However, a number of limitations of existing scholarship suggest directions for future research. The political economy literature is often quite impoverished in dealing with normative issues. To the extent a normative position can be inferred, accountability is generally couched in terms of the compatibility between what the Congress wants and what the agency does. However, a full evaluation of the accountability of agencies needs to bring in the preferences of the public. If the representative character of the lawmaking and oversight processes in Congress is in doubt, then government accountability to citizens may be enhanced by delegation.

Proponents of deliberative democracy support a strong version of this view. For example, Mark Seidenfeld defends APA procedures on a civic republican theory under which ideal policy is made through a deliberative process that produces consensus.[62] However, the hope for consensus is a false promise as a general ideal for policymaking. At the heart of public choice problems are often deep disagreements over values that go beyond narrow self-interest. Nevertheless, in the United States informal rulemaking under the APA can increase the range of interests consulted and produce more transparent and defensible policies. The Act's rulemaking provisions, which require notice, open hearings, and reason-giving, not only permit Congress to find out about and influence what is happening, but also help to assure that those especially concerned with a particular issue have their say. The final decision is made by the agency, subject to the political oversight of the President and the legislature and to judicial review, but the process gives a role to those outside government with an interest in the matter. Far from being a subversion of constitutional, democratic principles, these procedures are a check on agency action and indirectly on congressional actions

[61] Tom Zwart, 'Overseeing the Executive: Is the Legislature Reclaiming Lost Territory from the Courts?' in Rose-Ackerman and Lindseth (n 1), 148.

[62] Mark Seidenfeld, 'A Civic Republican Justification for the Bureaucatic State' (1992) 105 *Harvard Law Review* 1511.

as well.[63] Parliamentary systems with quite different administrative law traditions face the same need to justify government and agency policymaking. Constitutional reformers thus need to consider expanding judicially enforceable rights of participations, transparency, and reason-giving even in such systems where the dynamics of ordinary politics will not produce statutes that require more accountable policymaking inside government.

Bibliography

Bruce Ackerman, 'The New Separation of Powers' (2000) 113 *Harvard Law Review* 633

Matthew D. Adler and Eric A. Posner, *New Foundations of Cost-Benefit Analysis* (2006)

Stephen Breyer, *Breaking the Vicous Circle* (1993)

Paul Craig and Adam Tomkins (eds), *The Executive and Public Law: Power and Accountability in Comparative Perspective* (2006)

Robert Kagan, *Adversarial Legalism: The American Way of Law* (2001)

R. Daniel Keleman, *The Rules of Federalism: Institutions and Regulatory Politics in the EU and Beyond* (2004)

Peter Lindseth, *Power and Legitimacy: Reconciling Europe and the Nation-State* (2010)

G. Majone, 'Two Logics of Delegation: Agency and Fiduciary Relations in EU Governance' (2001) 2 *European Union Politics* 103

Jerry Mashaw, 'Improving the Environment of Agency Rulemaking: An Essay on Management, Games, and Accountability' (1994) 57 *Law and Contemporary Problems* 185

Terry Moe and Michael Caldwell, 'The Institutional Foundations of Democratic Government: A Comparison of Presidential and Parliamentary Systems' (1994) 150 *Journal of Institutional and Theoretical Economics* 116

Richard Posner, 'Theories of Economic Regulation' (1974) 5 *Bell Journal of Econmics and Management Science* 335

Susan Rose-Ackerman, *Controlling Environmental Policy; The Limits of Public Law in Germany and the United States* (1995)

Susan Rose-Ackerman (ed), *Economics of Administrative Law* (2007)

Susan Rose-Ackerman, *From Elections to Democracy: Building Accountable Government in Hungary and Poland* (2005)

Susan Rose-Ackerman and Peter Lindseth (eds), *Comparative Administrative Law* (2010)

Martin Shapiro and Alec Stone Sweet (eds), *On Law, Politics and Judicialiation* (2002)

Kaare Strøm, Wolfgang C. Müller, and Torbjörn Bergman (eds), *Delegation and Accountability in Parliamentary Democracies* (2003)

Cass R. Sunstein, *The Cost–Benefit State: The Future of Regulatory Protection* (2002)

Luc Verhey, Hansko Broeksteeg, and Ilse Van Den Driessche (eds), *Political Accountability in Europe; Which Way Forward?* (2008)

James Q. Wilson, *The Politics of Regulation* (1980)

[63] Rose-Ackerman (n 2); Rose-Ackerman (n 43); Rose-Ackerman (n 57); Mashaw (n 21).

PART V

MEANINGS/ TEXTURES

CHAPTER 32

CONSTITUTIONAL INTERPRETATION

JEFFREY GOLDSWORTHY

Melbourne

I. Interpretive Methodologies and the Rule of Law

The provisions of national constitutions, like other laws, are often ambiguous, vague, contradictory, insufficiently explicit, or even silent as to constitutional disputes that judges must decide. In addition, they sometimes seem inadequate to deal appropriately with developments that threaten principles the constitution was intended to safeguard, developments that its founders either failed or were unable to anticipate.

How judges resolve these problems through 'interpretation' is problematic and controversial, mainly because legitimate interpretation is difficult to distinguish from illegitimate change.[1] Judges thought to have improperly changed the constitution while purporting to

[1] This chapter is confined to constitutional interpretation by courts. It is based on the introduction and final chapter of Jeffrey Goldsworthy (ed), *Interpreting Constitutions, a Comparative Study* (2006), referred to hereafter as '*Interpreting Constitutions*'.

interpret it are vulnerable to criticism for usurping the prescribed power of amendment, violating their duty of fidelity to law, retrospectively altering litigants' legal rights, flouting the principles of democracy and federalism (if the amending procedure requires special majorities to protect regional interests), and straying beyond their legal expertise into the realm of politics.

How judges interpret other laws can also be controversial, but the stakes are much higher where constitutions are concerned. As fundamental laws, they allocate and regulate the powers of government and the rights of citizens. Their interpretation can have profound effects on the institutional structure of society, and the exercise of political power within it. It can affect the distribution of powers or rights between organs of government (legislature, executive, and judiciary), levels of government (national and state), and government and citizen. Moreover, legislatures can readily change other laws if they disapprove of the way judges have interpreted them, but constitutions are usually much more difficult to amend, and erroneous or undesirable judicial interpretations therefore more difficult to correct (except by the judges themselves).

This is why political scientists rightly depict constitutional courts as political institutions that wield enormous power. Whenever judicial decisions change the law, judges exercise political power, and when that law is their nation's constitution, they exercise the highest political power that exists in the state. Yet judges, perhaps even more than other political actors, are supposed to be constrained by laws, including the very laws they are responsible for interpreting. Any study of the behaviour of political actors in a society that aspires to the rule of law must include some account of how effectively their exercise of power is ruled by law.[2] Crucial to such an account, in the case of a constitutional court, is the methodology that it uses to interpret the constitution: the considerations it takes into account, explicitly or implicitly, and their relative priority or weight. It is crucial partly because such a court is rarely subject to regular review by any other institution: its fidelity to law depends mainly on its judges' commitment to their own professional ethic, implemented by the procedures and methods of reasoning they follow. Their interpretive methodology constitutes their response to the tension between fidelity to the terms of the constitution, including its amending procedure, and the need to act creatively to resolve indeterminacies in its meaning or (perhaps) even to modify that meaning to deal with other pressing difficulties. That methodology also implicitly defines the boundary between interpretation aimed at revealing or clarifying the meaning that the constitution already possesses, and interpretation that is essentially creative, supplementing or modifying that meaning. This is implicit because judges rarely acknowledge the creative component of their interpretive function.

In drawing this boundary, some courts are more attracted to what can be called, solely for convenience, 'legalism'. This term is used here in a purely descriptive sense, neither to applaud nor to denigrate, but merely to denote interpretive philosophies motivated by distrust of discretionary judicial lawmaking: that is, decision-making guided by subjective values rather than objective legal norms, which changes the law by establishing authoritative precedent. As previously suggested, there are many reasons for this distrust, including equity among litigants, predictability, democracy, and the rule of law.[3]

[2] The concept of the 'rule of law' is notoriously contested, and itself the subject of political debate. Moreover, this Anglophone concept differs from its European counterparts, such as the German *Rechtstaat* and the French *État de droit*. It is assumed here that the latter incorporate the former. For a full discussion, see Michel Rosenfeld, 'Constitutional Adjudication in Europe and the United States: Paradoxes and Contrasts' (2004) 2 *International Journal of Constitutional Law* 633, 638–52. Also see Chapter 10.

[3] See the second paragraph above.

Legalists would prefer law to be objective, determinate, and comprehensive, so that it can provide answers to every dispute, which judges can reliably ascertain and apply. We have already noted that this ambition is impossible to realize in practice, because constitutions inevitably include ambiguities, vagueness, inconsistencies, and 'gaps'. Judges cannot wash their hands of a dispute and leave the parties to fight it out in the street. It follows that they must act creatively to resolve stubborn indeterminacies and gaps in the constitution, by using extra-constitutional principles of justice or public policy to ascribe to it meanings that it did not previously possess. In the real world, legalists must accept the inevitability of both legal indeterminacy and consequential judicial discretion.[4] They can, however, advocate maximal determinacy.

Legalism in constitutional law has been associated with various tendencies, including literalism, formalism, positivism, and originalism. For present purposes, it is useful to characterize legalism as a preference for positivism rather than normativism, and originalism rather than non-originalism. Neither distinction is a dichotomy: each pair of alternatives represents a spectrum of possibilities. Judges, courts, and legal cultures adopt positions somewhere between the two ends of each spectrum, sometimes closer to the legalist end, and sometimes closer to the opposite end. Particular interpretive philosophies could be plotted on a graph, with these distinctions forming the two axes. But they are somewhat opaque, and require further elaboration.

By 'positivism' I mean, in this context, a conception of a constitution as a set of discrete written provisions, whose authority derives from their having been formally adopted or enacted. By 'normativism', I mean a holistic conception of a constitution as more than the sum of its written provisions: as a normative structure whose provisions are, either explicitly or implicitly, based on deeper principles, and ultimately on abstract norms of political morality that are the deepest source of its authority. At one extremity of this spectrum, positivism degenerates into literalism: the meanings of the constitution's written provisions are taken to be fixed by conventional word meanings and rules of grammar, independent of the founders' purposes. Less extreme versions of positivism are purposive: they are prepared to interpret the words of express provisions in light of their purposes, without allowing those purposes to either supplement or override the words, or to have independent normative force. A stronger version of purposivism permits the recognition of implications, provided that they are necessary for express provisions to achieve their purposes. As one moves even further towards the normativist end of the spectrum, increasingly abstract formulations of purpose are preferred, and to implement them more effectively, the enacted words may be stretched or compressed, supplemented or overridden—in effect, rewritten. At the extreme end, the most abstract norms attributed to the constitution are directly enforced in their own right, independently of express provisions.

By 'originalism', I mean the thesis that the content of a constitution is determined partly by the intentions or purposes of its founders, or the understandings of the founding generation. 'Non-originalism' treats these considerations as either irrelevant or of little weight, and licenses judges to interpret the constitutional text according to the supposed meanings, values,

[4] This should be uncontroversial except, perhaps, in Germany where the Basic Law still 'tends to be regarded as a self-sufficient code of law' which 'contain[s] the right answer to almost any constitutional dispute': Donald P. Kommers, 'Germany: Balancing Rights and Duties' in *Interpreting Constitutions* 161, 207–8. The Basic Law is expressly based on abstract moral principles, but even if these are objective moral truths accessible to human reason, human choices are often necessary to apply such principles to specific circumstances: see eg John Finnis, *Natural Law and Natural Rights* (1980), 281–9.

or understandings of contemporary society. There are, again, more or less moderate versions of both alternatives. Each one is compatible with either positivism or normativism. An originalist may be a positivist, who maintains that the meanings of express provisions are determined by original intentions or understandings, or a normativist, who equates the constitution's deepest norms with the founders' deepest purposes. Similarly, a non-originalist may be either a positivist or a normativist, regarding either the meanings of express provisions, or the constitution's deepest norms, as determined by contemporary understandings or values.

Non-originalist normativism is a particularly potent agent of substantive constitutional change through judicial interpretation. If a constitution is regarded as based on unwritten, abstract norms of political morality, which can trump the specific terms of written provisions or even be independently enforced, and if those norms can change according to the judges' impressions of contemporary values or their personal values, then the judges possess a remarkable power to reshape the constitution. Indeed, extreme non-originalist normativism may be indistinguishable from natural law philosophies that regard law as a branch of political morality, to which positive law always remains subordinate. Both positions may also be practically indistinguishable from a strong form of pragmatism, which holds that judges should be guided by positive law only insofar as that is the best option, all things considered. Even originalist normativism can be difficult to distinguish from these positions, if the founders' deepest purposes are formulated as abstractly as 'to achieve justice'.

The relationship between these distinctions and the objectivity, determinacy, and comprehensiveness of law is debatable. Normativism makes law more comprehensive than positivism, because it offers much richer normative resources to guide decision-making. Discrete written provisions, even if they are interpreted purposively, provide less comprehensive guidance than abstract norms of political morality. But legalists believe that this greater comprehensiveness comes at the cost of objectivity and determinacy. They distrust the incorporation of moral and political norms into law, on the ground that the usual abstraction and vagueness of such norms compels judges to resort to discretionary value judgments. This is particularly the case if these norms can be used to trump, or be enforced independently of, the wording of enacted provisions.

Legalists fear that strong forms of non-originalism and normativism license judges to change constitutions in three ways: (1) by changing the meanings of their words; (2) by in effect rewriting their express provisions to better implement deeper values; and (3) by adding to them new, 'unwritten' principles. Legalists insist that judges should be bound not only by the founders' ultimate ends, but also by the means they chose to achieve those ends. To be guided only or mainly by their ultimate ends is not to be significantly bound at all.

But legalist critiques are not necessarily persuasive. For example, there can be no doubt that implications are sometimes justified: the content of a constitution, as of any law and indeed any communication, is never completely explicit. Full comprehension of its meaning inevitably depends partly on an understanding of purpose, illuminated by contextual information, and on background assumptions that are taken for granted.[5] Just as indeterminacy gives rise to a superstructure of judge-made law built on the constitutional text, inexplicitness requires a substructure of unwritten purposes to be excavated beneath the text. Furthermore, a strong case can be made for courts sometimes making adjustments for the inability of language in an old constitution, if strictly applied, to achieve its purposes in the modern world, because of

[5] Jeffrey Goldsworthy, 'Implications in Language, Law and the Constitution' in Geoffrey Lindell (ed), *Future Directions in Australian Constitutional Law* (1994), 150.

technological or social developments that its founders did not anticipate. Take the provision in the US Constitution that vests exclusive power in Congress to raise and maintain 'armies' and 'a navy' and to regulate 'the land and naval forces'.[6] When military aircraft were developed, it would have defeated the provision's obvious purpose if Congress had been denied the power to raise an air force. It is widely accepted that in such cases, the courts may adopt a purposive rather than a literal interpretation, by stretching the provision's literal meaning to give effect to what it originally meant, in a broad sense of 'meant' that is informed by its purpose. But if 'rewriting' to this small extent is justified, where should the line be drawn?

Consider also the extent to which courts should remedy failures on the part of the constitution's founders expressly to provide for problems, even if they should have foreseen them. When interpreting statutes, judges usually refuse to rectify failures of that kind, on the ground that the legislature should do so. But when dealing with a constitution, they should arguably be more willing to provide a solution. If a constitution fails to achieve one of its main purposes, the potential consequences are grave. They include the danger of constitutional powers being abused, of the democratic process or the federal system being subverted, and of human rights being violated. If the constitution is difficult to amend formally, or if amendment requires action by the very politicians who pose the threat needing to be checked, there may be good moral reasons for judges to intervene. True fidelity to the constitution may require some adjustment of its terms. On the other hand, legalists worry that such reasoning can be used to justify extensive judicial rewriting of the constitution, especially if the founders' purposes are pitched at a very abstract level ('they wanted to achieve a just society, and this is necessary to achieve justice'). Legalists deny that judges are 'statesmen', appointed to fill the shoes of the founders and continue the task of constitution-making as an ongoing enterprise.

One conclusion that should be drawn from this brief discussion is that constitutional interpretation is an extraordinarily difficult enterprise, which requires striking an appropriate balance between competing, weighty considerations. The distinction between legitimate and illegitimate change depends on a host of other difficult distinctions, such as between determinacy and indeterminacy, purpose used to clarify meaning and purpose used to change it, genuine implications and spurious ones, evidence of intentions or understandings that illuminates original meanings and that which does not, changes in the meaning of a provision and changes in its application, and so on. The sheer difficulty of drawing such distinctions, even for philosophers after prolonged reflection, let alone for busy judges, should make anyone pause before criticizing judges too forcefully. It is doubtful that the most appropriate balance is, even in principle, determined by wholly objective, 'strictly legal' considerations. Ultimately, it requires normative judgment. And how the balance should be struck no doubt varies, depending on the unique circumstances in which any constitutional court finds itself.

II. Comparing Interpretive Methodologies

Comparative studies of how constitutions have been interpreted in different legal systems have a variety of objectives. Sometimes the objective is wholly practical: to help to interpret a provision in one constitution by learning how similar provisions have been interpreted elsewhere. Courts around the world increasingly seek this kind of guidance.[7] Indeed, why, how,

[6] *The Constitution of the United States of America* (1787), Art I, s 8.

[7] The literature is already enormous: see eg Sujit Choudhry (ed), *The Migration of Constitutional Ideas* (2006).

and to what extent they do so has itself become a subject of comparative study.[8] But this can be part of a much broader inquiry into the interpretive methodologies that different courts employ, and their underlying philosophies, in negotiating the tension previously noted between fidelity to the terms of a constitution, including its amending procedure, and the necessity or desirability of some measure of judicial creativity.[9]

Such an inquiry can be of value to lawyers and political scientists, who are both concerned with practical implementation of the rule of law. Moreover, it can broaden lawyers' horizons by dispelling any sense of false necessity and expanding their sense of what is possible. Learning how foreign courts tackle interpretive problems might reveal that one's own courts 'simply fail adequately to address arguments that apparently sensible people in other nations have addressed'.[10] Of course, it does not follow that practices appropriate in one country are universally applicable: another potential benefit of comparative study is to help to explain or even to justify differences in terms of institutional, political, social, and cultural circumstances. For example, a recent study of constitutional interpretation in Australia, Canada, and the United States attempts to explain the rise of originalism in US academic, political, and judicial circles since the 1980s in terms of cultural circumstances unique to that country.[11] What is necessary or appropriate to the rule of law in one country might not be the same in another. On the other hand, if it turns out that some approaches to constitutional interpretation are almost universal, that might strengthen the case in their favour.

Such an inquiry must not be confined to the interpretation of constitutional provisions that protect human rights, although most of the comparative literature has that focus.[12] Constitutions are not mainly or even primarily about protecting rights from the powers of governmental institutions. Before doing that, they must establish and empower those institutions, and resolve numerous 'structural' issues concerning methods of appointment, decision-making procedures, demarcations of powers, checks and balances, and so on. Just as important as rights guarantees are provisions dividing powers between chambers in a bicameral legislature, between the legislative, executive, and judicial branches of government, and between the national and regional polities in a federation. An overemphasis on rights protection leads to exaggerated claims, such as that the principle of proportionality has made textual interpretation mostly redundant in constitutional cases, or that the main function of constitutional review is to articulate, promote, and enforce the political morality of the community.[13]

[8] See eg Sujit Choudhry, 'Globalization in Search of Justification: Toward a Theory of Comparative Constitutional Interpretation' (1999) 74 *Indiana Law Journal* 819; Tony Blackshield, 'National Constitutions in an International World' (2008) *Indian Journal of Constitutional Law* 104.

[9] See eg *Interpreting Constitutions*.

[10] Vicki C. Jackson and Mark Tushnet, *Comparative Constitutional Law* (1999), 145.

[11] Jamal Greene, 'On the Origins of Originalism' (2009) 88 *Texas Law Review* 1.

[12] See Vicki C. Jackson, 'Comparative Constitutional Federalism and Transnational Judicial Discourse' (2004) 2 *International Journal of Constitutional Law* 91, 93–4, 100. Two recent comparative studies of federalism are Gerald Baier, *Courts and Federalism: Judicial Doctrine in the United States, Australia and Canada* (2006) and Greg Taylor, *Characterisation in Federations: Six Countries Compared* (2006). However, Baier is concerned mainly with the role of judicial doctrine (judicially constructed principles, tests etc) in adjudicating federalism disputes, rather than with the interpretive methods used to construct those tests, while Taylor is concerned mainly with one kind of judicial doctrine—that which is used to decide whether legislation deals with subject matters allocated to the enacting legislature. See also Chapter 27.

[13] The first claim is made by David M. Beatty, *The Ultimate Rule of Law* (2004), ch 1, esp 5, and is criticized in Vicki C. Jackson, 'Being Proportionate About Proportionality' (2004) 21 *Constitutional Commentary* 803, esp 814–19 and 842–7 and 859. The second claim is made by David Robertson, *The Judge as Political Theorist* (2010), passim. See also Chapters 33 and 34.

A fixation with rights might also distort an analysis of interpretive methodologies, for reasons given below.[14]

In what follows, I attempt to summarize the interpretive methodologies of the courts of six federations that were the subject of a recent comparative study,[15] and then provide some explanations of the differences between them. They are Australia, Canada, Germany, India, South Africa, and the United States. A more comprehensive comparative study would be desirable. For example, it has been claimed that in Europe, 'recourse to originalism is virtually non-existent'.[16] But constitutional interpretation in Austria, at least in relation to the federal division of legislative powers, involves a combination of originalist and structuralist reasoning.[17]

Attempting an overall characterization of the interpretive philosophy of any court is hazardous. It may be distorted if undue emphasis is given to a small number of prominent but only partially representative decisions (eg decisions exclusively about rights guarantees rather than structural provisions). It involves generalizing about interpretive philosophies that are rarely well theorized by judges and never wholly coherent, using terminology such as 'originalist' that is often ambiguous, vague, and contested. Judges may disagree about these interpretive philosophies, and it may be unclear whose views predominate. Courts that have been in business for a long time may have changed their interpretive approach, possibly more than once.[18] Moreover, to some extent all courts are guided by a diversity of considerations, pursuing what Mark Tushnet calls 'eclecticism'.[19] Consequently, observers may reasonably disagree in characterizing the predominant interpretive methodology even in a single case, and a fortiori in a large number of cases. Nevertheless, there is often widespread agreement among comparativists about the general tendencies and patterns of reasoning of different national courts. It is universally agreed, for example, that the Australian High Court has traditionally been much more legalist (as previously defined) than its Canadian, German, Indian, and South African counterparts.[20]

Constitutional interpretation is guided by much the same set of considerations in all six countries studied. The main ones are: the words of the constitutional text, understood in the context of related provisions; other evidence of the intentions, understandings, or purposes of the founders; presumptions favouring broad, or purposive, interpretations; so-called 'structural' principles regarded as underlying particular provisions, groups of provisions or the constitution as a whole; precedent and judicial doctrine developed from it; and considerations of justice, practicality, and public policy.[21] Other considerations include additional

[14] See text between nn 138 and 143 below.

[15] *Interpreting Constitutions.*

[16] Rosenfeld (n 2), 656; see also 634.

[17] See Taylor (n 12), ch 6, esp 98–106 (Austrians use the term 'petrification theory' to describe this approach).

[18] There have been remarkable changes in the approaches of the Supreme Courts of Canada and India: see *Interpreting Constitutions*, chs 2 and 5.

[19] See Mark Tushnet, 'The United States: Eclecticism in the Service of Pragmatism' in *Interpreting Constitutions*, 7. On this point, see Vicki C. Jackson, 'Constitutions as "Living Trees"? Comparative Constitutional Law and Interpretive Metaphors' (2006) 75 *Fordham Law Review* 921, 925 and 927.

[20] Jeffrey Goldsworthy, 'Australia: Devotion to Legalism' in *Interpreting Constitutions*, 106; Greene (n 11); Baier (n 12); Taylor (n 12); Vicki C. Jackson and Jamal Greene, 'Constitutional Interpretation in Comparative Perspective: Comparing Judges or Courts?' in Rosalind Dixon and Tom Ginsburg (eds), *Handbook in Comparative Constitutional Law* (2011).

[21] These can all be sorted into Philip Bobbitt's well-known 'modalities' of constitutional interpretation, namely, textual, historical, structural, doctrinal, ethical, and prudential: see Philip Bobbitt *Constitutional Fate: Theory of the Constitution* (1982).

presumptions and maxims of interpretation, sometimes counselling deference to long-standing practice or the elected branches of government, international and comparative law, and academic opinion.

But it would be a mistake to overemphasize this similarity in judicial methodology. Careful discrimination is required. Judges rarely attempt rigorous theoretical analysis of interpretive problems or the methods they use to resolve them. In particular, they seldom acknowledge the difference between attempting to clarify a constitution's pre-existing meaning, and creatively supplementing or modifying it. Most of the considerations just listed can be used for either purpose: for example, considerations of justice and public policy can be used as evidence of the framers' intentions ('they could not have intended *that*') or as independent guides to creative gap-filling. Moreover, there are substantial differences in the relative priorities or weights given to these diverse considerations in the six countries studied. For example, precedents and established judicial doctrine naturally play a larger role in common law jurisdictions, and in the interpretation of older constitutions (partly because they have more precedents); academic opinion has far more influence in Germany than in common law jurisdictions; original intentions or understandings are relied on more in the United States and Australia than elsewhere; 'structural' principles play a more pervasive role in Canada, Germany, India, and South Africa than in Australia or the United States; justice and public policy seem more influential in India than anywhere else; and comparative law is given much less attention in the United States than in the other countries. These differences cannot be demonstrated in detail here; particulars are provided in the comparative study previously cited.[22]

Perhaps even more significant are substantial differences in the underlying philosophies of interpretation favoured by courts in the six countries. Australian and US judges have tended to be more attracted to legalist philosophies than their Indian and Canadian counterparts, who changed their approaches, in the 1970s and 1980s respectively; German and South African judges arguably sit somewhere in between; and US judges appear to have been more divided than others over these issues.

1. The United States

Professor Tushnet has depicted constitutional interpretation in the United States as, for the most part, straightforwardly legalist. When the Supreme Court interprets a constitutional provision without the assistance of precedent, either because the issue is novel or because the Court regards existing precedents as erroneous, it starts with the constitutional text, understood in the context of related provisions, and in light of original understandings and the political theory that the Court finds in the text.[23] But in most cases, relevant precedents do exist, and are the predominant consideration, followed by text-based and originalist considerations that 'often go hand in hand'.[24] Professor Tushnet asserts that 'some version of a jurisprudence of original understanding remains an essential element of nearly all practical resolutions of interpretive controversies.'[25] In the recent case of *Heller*, evidence of original meaning notoriously prevailed over a 69-year-old Supreme Court precedent and hundreds of

[22] *Interpreting Constitutions*. These observations are generally confirmed by Greene (n 11) and Jackson and Greene (n 20).

[23] Tushnet (n 19), 40 and 48–9.

[24] Ibid 42 and 47.

[25] Ibid 38.

federal court opinions based on it.[26] Resort to 'structural' principles is less frequent, except in separation of powers and individual rights cases, and is used mainly to support other arguments; and explicit reference to moral or political philosophy is rare except when the text expressly incorporates moral principles.[27] Where the text does so, the Court is entitled to ignore the founders' possibly mistaken expectations about the proper application of those principles; any accusation of 'activism' in such cases is therefore unfair.[28] Sometimes the Court is criticized for excessive formalism.[29]

Yet the Supreme Court has acquired a reputation for activism, because of perceived innovations such as substantive due process, the 'incorporation' of the Bill of Rights in the Fourteenth Amendment, broad interpretation of some provisions contrary to the apparent original understanding, and unenumerated rights, such as the right to privacy recognized in *Griswold v Connecticut* and extended to abortions in *Roe v Wade*.[30] Professor Tushnet acknowledges that the Warren Court had an 'aggressive agenda', which aroused considerable controversy over its alleged activism from the 1950s onwards.[31] But he maintains that its decisions fell well within the bounds set by standards of professional competence.[32] Some if not all of those decisions can be defended on orthodox legalist grounds: substantive due process, for example, reflected a technical meaning acquired by the words 'due process' before they were inserted into the Constitution, and the implied right to privacy is arguably as legitimate as implied intergovernmental immunities.[33]

Professor Tushnet argues that orthodox interpretive considerations—text, original understanding, precedent, and so on—have been unable to significantly constrain decision-making.[34] Precedent, for example, has not provided 'stability' partly because the judges have been unwilling to subordinate their views to those expressed in the precedents. Consequently, the precedents have come to provide an array of alternatives from which current judges can choose.[35] And original understandings have failed to constrain, partly because they often merely reveal disagreements among the founders themselves, and partly because they can be specified at different levels of generality, which point to different conclusions.[36] Consequently, judges can implement their own 'values and visions' by choosing appropriate interpretive methods, without exceeding the bounds set by standards of professional competence.[37]

But to the outside observer, the impression conveyed by the political battles that often attend the confirmation of Supreme Court nominees is that interpretive standards are deeply conflicted in the United States.[38] Decisions attacked as activist fall outside the standards

[26] *District of Columbia v Heller* 128 S Ct 2783 (2008) and *US v Miller* 307 US 174 (1939), discussed in Greene (n 11), 12.

[27] Tushnet (n 19), 32, 39–40 and 47.

[28] Ibid 39.

[29] Ibid 21–2.

[30] See eg Robert H. Bork, *The Tempting of America: the Political Seduction of the Law* (1990) Part I, for a critique along these lines. On abortion, see Chapter 51.

[31] Tushnet (n 19), 14, 52.

[32] Ibid 50–1 and 54.

[33] Ibid 28, citing John V. Orth, *Due Process of Law* (2003); see also Tushnet (n 19), 20 and 32 esp n 77. See also Chapter 44.

[34] Ibid 50.

[35] Ibid 17–20.

[36] Ibid 35–8 and 50–1.

[37] Ibid 50–1.

[38] See Christopher Eisgruber, *The Next Justice: Repairing the Supreme Court Appointments Process* (2009).

accepted by some sections of the profession, even though they are within the standards accepted by others. If so, US constitutional culture might best be characterized as a site of conflict over interpretive philosophies, within the profession as well as outside it.

Professor Tushnet's chapter includes some evidence that professional standards are conflicted, with many lawyers accepting normativist standards that others repudiate. First, he point outs that the early debate between Justices Iredell and Chase in *Calder v Bull*, about the legitimacy of 'unwritten principles' of reason and justice, was never resolved.[39] Consequently, a controversial strain of natural law thinking seems to have persisted in US constitutional jurisprudence. For example, Justice Chase's insistence that all governments in the United States are necessarily limited may have provided the crucial 'structural' pre-supposition behind the much-criticized right to privacy.[40]

Second, Professor Tushnet claims that the American people have come to accept that constitutional interpretation 'is the means by which the Constitution is recurrently revised to accommodate the general values embodied in the Constitution with the realities of governance in a changing world.'[41] This view can be traced back to Chief Justice Marshall's influential statement in *McCulloch v Maryland*, that the Constitution was 'intended to endure for ages to come, and, consequently, to be adapted to the various crises of human affairs'.[42] According to Professor Tushnet, this became 'the touchstone for everyone who defended the idea of a living Constitution'.[43] The notion of a 'living constitution' that the courts can 'adapt' to changing circumstances is ambiguous: it could mean either that broad but unchanging meanings must be applied to new and unexpected phenomena, or that the meanings themselves must sometimes be changed for that purpose. As Professor Tushnet explains, the principal method of adapting the Constitution to external change has been to identify the general purposes or principles underlying specific constitutional terms, and then to determine how those principles apply to contemporary problems.[44] It is notable that in *Heller*, the principal dissenting judgment involved just such reasoning.[45] This is what I have called 'originalist normativism'. If the underlying principles are couched at a sufficiently abstract level of generality, the specific terms may lose their grip. That, one suspects, has been a bone of contention.

2. Canada

The Privy Council almost took a literal approach to the Canadian Constitution, refusing to consult legislative history to ascertain the founders' intentions or purposes. The text itself had been drafted in a deliberately ambiguous fashion, and the ambiguities were resolved according to the judges' preconceptions of the nature of a genuine federation.[46] In other words, the judges' own ideology proved decisive.[47] It generally favoured broad interpretations of provincial powers and narrow interpretations of national ones, which may have suited Canadian society better than the founders' intentions, by mollifying separatist sentiment in Quebec.[48] This is a good example of how literalism, by excluding extra-textual evidence of legislative purpose and intention, can increase textual indeterminacy and the consequential need for discretionary judicial lawmaking.[49]

[39] Tushnet (n 19), 26–7, discussing *Calder v Bull* 3 US 386 (1798).
[40] Tushnet (n 19), 32. [41] Ibid 49; see also 7, 16–17 and 54.
[42] *McCulloch v Maryland* 17 US 316, 415 (1819).
[43] Tushnet (n 19), 24. [44] Ibid 37.
[45] *District of Columbia v Heller* (n 26), Stevens J dissenting.
[46] Peter Hogg, 'Canada: From Privy Council to Supreme Court' in *Interpreting Constitutions*, 66.
[47] Ibid 75–6. [48] Ibid 76, 104. [49] Ibid 104.

The Privy Council described the Constitution as a 'living tree capable of growth and expansion within its natural limits',[50] but probably did not have in mind changes in the meaning of the text resulting from judicial interpretation.[51] It probably intended merely to endorse 'generous', rather than 'dynamic', interpretation.[52] But the modern Supreme Court has enthusiastically employed the metaphor to justify dynamic interpretation: the notion that, without any need for formal amendment, the Constitution should be capable of 'growth, development and adjustment to changing societal needs'.[53] Professor Hogg states that originalism has 'never enjoyed any significant support in Canada', and 'indifference to the original understanding lingers on in the modern Supreme Court'.[54] Indeed, the lawyers and politicians who drafted and adopted the Charter apparently assumed that the Court would not be bound by their intentions.[55] Consequently, the Court has held that a provision embodied the US doctrine of substantive due process, even though it had been deliberately drafted so as not to do so.[56] The judicial choice of the opposite meaning to the one intended goes well beyond 'adaptation' of the provision to cope with developments unanticipated by its framers: it involves altering the provision's intended meaning in circumstances that they fully anticipated. Professor Hogg describes the principle of 'progressive (or dynamic) interpretation' as 'the dominant theory of interpretation in Canada'.[57] It should be noted, however, that originalist reasoning has played a large part in so-called 'confederation bargain' cases, concerning constitutional provisions thought to embody pragmatic compromises rather than high principles.[58]

Over the last quarter of a century, the Supreme Court seems to have shifted from a positivist to a normativist conception of the Constitution, giving to fundamental, unwritten principles a normative force that is independent of specific provisions.[59] Professor Hogg asserts that the Court has sometimes invented, rather than discovered, these principles, thereby amending the Constitution by judicial fiat in defiance of the prescribed procedures for amendment.[60] The supposed unwritten principle of judicial independence is a product of non-originalist normativism, since the principle runs counter to textual evidence of the founders' intentions.[61] While such principles could be found 'to accommodate virtually any grievance about government policy', Professor Hogg notes that lately, the Court has shown 'some sign of reigning in its creative impulses'.[62] An example is a recent unanimous statement that 'in a constitutional

[50] *Edwards v A-G Canada* [1930] AC 124, 136 (Lord Sankey).

[51] Bradley W. Miller, 'Origin Myth: The *Persons Case*, The Living Tree, and the New Originalism' in Grant Huscroft and Bradley W. Miller (eds), *The Challenge of Originalism; Essays in Constitutional Theory* (2011); Hogg (n 46), 84.

[52] Ibid 87.

[53] *Re British Columbia Motor Vehicle Act* [1985] 2 SCR 486, 509 (Lamer CJ).

[54] Hogg (n 46) 83; also 78–9.

[55] Ibid 87.

[56] *Re British Columbia Motor Vehicle Act* [1985] 2 SCR 486. Admittedly, the choice of the words 'fundamental justice' to avoid that result was a remarkably inept piece of drafting.

[57] Ibid 87. See also Greene (n 11), 18–40. Bradley W. Miller argues that Canadian legal theory has failed to grapple with these issues with any sophistication, and consequently overlooks many critical distinctions: 'Beguiled by Metaphors: The "Living Tree" and Originalist Interpretation in Canada' (2009) 22 *Canadian Journal of Law and Jurisprudence* 331.

[58] Miller (n 57), 345.

[59] Hogg (n 46), 90–1.

[60] Ibid 90 and 104.

[61] Ibid 91–2.

[62] Ibid 92.

democracy such as ours, protection from legislation that some might view as unjust or unfair properly lies not in the amorphous underlying principles of our Constitution, but in its text and the ballot box.'[63]

The Supreme Court has interpreted Charter rights more broadly than their US equivalents have been interpreted, and has enthusiastically adopted an activist approach.[64] Its judges seem much more united in embracing non-originalism and normativism than their US counterparts.

3. Australia

Of all six courts studied, the High Court of Australia has been the most legalist. Its judges have frequently expressed aversion to changing the Constitution through creative interpretation.[65] At least since 1920, the Court has devoted itself to a predominantly positivist methodology. Many of its judges have praised 'dry legal argument',[66] insisted on not straying too far from the text,[67] repudiated political and pragmatic considerations,[68] and spoken disparagingly of reasoning from such abstractions as the 'spirit' of the Constitution or 'vague and imprecise expressions of political philosophy'.[69] Indeed, much of the Court's jurisprudence before the late 1980s can fairly be described as literalist and formalist. The Court's commitment to positivism is epitomized by Chief Justice Latham's declaration that even if the Commonwealth used its financial supremacy to destroy the federal system, the Court might be powerless to stop it.[70]

The judges have often referred to 'underlying principles' such as federalism, representative and responsible government, the rule of law and the separation of powers, but have generally used them to aid the interpretation of express provisions. They have tended to be wary of implications, which are usually required to be 'necessary' for express provisions to achieve their purposes.[71] They have recognized a limited doctrine of implied intergovernmental immunities, and a much more robust doctrine of the separation of judicial power, but the latter has plausible support in the constitutional text.[72] Recent attempts to derive implications directly from the principle of representative government were scotched, on the ground that it must not be treated as a 'free-standing' principle.[73]

[63] *British Columbia v Imperial Tobacco Canada Ltd* [2005] 2 SCR 473, 2005 SCC 49, para 66. See also Kent Roach, 'Judicial Activism in the Supreme Court of Canada' in Brice Dickson, *Judicial Activism in Common Law Supreme Courts* (2007), 102–3.

[64] Robert Harvie and Hamar Foster, 'Ties that Bind: the Supreme Court of Canada and American Jurisprudence' (1990) 28 *Osgoode Hall Law Journal* 729. See also Hogg (n 46), who uses the term 'activist', 71, 81, 88 and 103–5, and Roach (n 63), 118.

[65] Many cases are cited by Jeffrey Goldsworthy (n 20), 119–20, 121–2, 133, 141–2, 146, 151, 153, and 154–5.

[66] Sir Garfield Barwick, *A Radical Tory* (1994), 66; *A-G (NSW) v Brewery Employees Union of NSW* (1908) 6 CLR 469, 559.

[67] *Henry v Boehm* (1973) 128 CLR 482 (Gibbs J).

[68] *SA v Commonwealth* (*First Uniform Tax* case) (1942) 65 CLR 373, 411–12.

[69] *Huddart, Parker and Co Pty Ltd v Moorehead* (1909) 8 CLR 330, 388 (Isaacs J); *A-G (Cth) (ex rel McKinley) v Commonwealth* (1975) 135 CLR 1, 17 (Barwick CJ).

[70] *South Australia v Commonwealth* (1942) 65 CLR 373, 429 (Latham CJ).

[71] Goldsworthy (n 20), 128 and 136. See eg *McGinty v Western Australia* (1996) 186 CLR 140, 427 (McHugh J).

[72] Goldsworthy (n 20), 128–9.

[73] *McGinty v Western Australia* (1996) 186 CLR 140; *Lange v Australian Broadcasting Corporation* (1987) 189 CLR 520.

The Court has usually endorsed a moderate version of originalism. It has maintained that the meaning of the text (its 'connotation') cannot be changed through interpretation, even though its application to external facts (its 'denotation') can change, and it has often relied on historical evidence of what a provision was originally understood to mean.[74] Its commitment to moderate originalism has been fortified in recent years by its willingness to consult the Convention Debates and other historical evidence of original understandings and purposes.[75] Only a handful of judges have expressly endorsed a 'living tree' theory of the Constitution.[76]

The Court's approach became less legalist after 1987, when Sir Anthony Mason became Chief Justice. The Court repudiated literalism and formalism, and adopted a more purposive and substantive approach.[77] It purported to find an implied freedom of political communication in the Constitution, which was criticized as an example of its increasing activism.[78] Commentators spoke of a 'Mason Court revolution', but this was an exaggeration.[79] After Mason's retirement, the Court's refusal to expand the recognition of implied rights, together with some decisions remarkable for their legalism, suggested that the movement away from legalism had stalled.[80] But the Court continued to be more willing than formerly to interpret and apply provisions purposively, and to acknowledge the need for judicial discretion on policy grounds to resolve stubborn indeterminacies. Recent judges have also been less certain as to whether the meaning, or connotation, of constitutional terms cannot change, but in most cases their reasoning has remained predominantly positivist and moderately originalist.[81] The main exceptions to this are cases dealing with judicial authority and independence, which the Court has always been eager to protect even when that has required an unacknowledged compromise of its usual legalist methodology.[82]

4. Germany

The interpretive philosophy of Germany's Federal Constitutional Court is extremely normativist, partly because the Basic Law virtually dictates a normativist approach. Like other postwar constitutions, it expressly enumerates many 'structural principles' that its detailed provisions are intended to implement.[83] Opinions have differed as to the nature and source of authority of these principles, with 'higher law' conceptions—especially popular after the

[74] Many cases are cited by Goldsworthy (n 20), 124–7 and 150–2.

[75] The trend started with *Cole v Whitfield* (1988) 165 CLR 360. See Goldsworthy (n 20), 126–7.

[76] Ibid 150.

[77] See Sir Anthony Mason, 'The Role of a Constitutional Court in a Federation: A Comparison of the Australian and the United States Experience' (1986) 16 *Federal Law Review* 1.

[78] H.P. Lee, 'The Implied Freedom of Communication' in H.P. Lee and George Winterton (eds), *Australian Constitutional Landmarks* (2003), 392; Goldsworthy (n 20), 146 and 157–8.

[79] Compare Jason Louis Pierce, *Inside the Mason Court Revolution: The High Court of Australia Transformed* (2006), with Fiona Wheeler and John Williams, 'Restrained Activism" in the High Court of Australia' in Dickson (n 63), 19.

[80] Exemplary legalist decisions include *Re Wakim; ex p McNally* (1999) 198 CLR 511, discussed in Goldsworthy (n 20), 132–3, and *Al-Kateb v Godwin* (2004) 219 CLR 562.

[81] For a brief discussion of recent trends, see Goldsworthy (n 20), 144–52; Wheeler and Williams (n 79); Greene (n 11), 50–61; Jeffrey Goldsworthy, 'Original Meanings and Contemporary Understandings in Constitutional Interpretation' in H.P. Lee and Peter Gerangelos (eds), *Constitutional Advancement in a Frozen Continent, Essays in Honour of George Winterton* (2009) 245, 262–8.

[82] See nn 230–2 below; Goldsworthy (n 20), 148–50 and 160; *Kirk v Industrial Relations Commission of NSW* (2010) 239 CLR 531.

[83] Although these have been supplemented by the FCC: Kommers (n 4), 191.

War—recently losing ground to originalist theories.[84] But the Court has not limited itself to the interpretation and application of enumerated principles. It has inferred other, unwritten or 'supra-positive', principles from 'the normative realities underlying the Basic Law'.[85] For example, it has inferred 'objective values' from constitutional rights, values that are taken to impose positive obligations on all organs of the state in addition to the negative obligation of not infringing the rights.[86] Moreover, the Court does not regard constitutional norms as separate from extra-legal political or social norms: the constitutional order and the broader community are regarded as interdependent, each helping to define and refine the other.[87]

Professor Kommers observes that 'Structural reasoning is deeply ingrained in Germany's culture of interpretation.'[88] In comparison with the United States, where it is resorted to only occasionally, when other interpretive considerations are indeterminate, in Germany it is 'as standard as doctrinal reasoning in the common law tradition'.[89] According to him, the Federal Constitutional Court has had to maintain a 'creative balance' between the many competing principles of the constitutional order, and also to creatively adjust the Basic Law to 'necessity'.[90]

Yet German lawyers are not attracted to the notion that substantive constitutional change may be brought about through interpretation. The Court frequently relies on evidence of the founders' intentions or purposes, including the Basic Law's legislative history, especially in cases involving federal–state conflicts.[91] Indeed, it has been said that 'the importance placed on historical considerations is the most distinctive feature of German scope [of legislative power] doctrine.'[92] When political or social realities begin to diverge from the founders' handiwork, Germans turn to formal amendment, which has been frequently utilized.[93] 'Any judicially imposed remodelling of the Basic Law—enduring and binding changes in particular—would diminish the clarity, precision, and predictability required of the constitutional *Rechtsstaat*.'[94]

Although many judges agree that there is no 'slide rule' to calculate how to weigh and balance the competing values set out in the Basic Law, so that some judicial discretion is inevitable, most 'are reluctant to admit publicly that they are doing anything other than engaging in objective constitutional interpretation.'[95] They generally insist that the process of interpretation is apolitical, even though most would concede that its effects are political.[96] The old civil law conception of written laws as self-sufficient codes lingers on: 'many judges regard the Basic Law, like the civil code, as a unified body of rules and principles that contain the right answer to almost any constitutional dispute.'[97] Despite the quasi-legislative nature of its role, it 'was expected to employ strictly judicial methods of interpretation, methods designed, in

[84] Ibid 180, 182–3, and 189.

[85] Ibid 189. The trend started with *Southwest State Case* 1 BVerfGE 14, 61 (1951), the landmark decision that has been compared to *Marbury v Madison* 1 Cranch 137 (1803).

[86] Kommers (n 4), 180–1.

[87] Ibid 178.

[88] Ibid 199.

[89] Ibid 178–9 and 213–14.

[90] Ibid.

[91] Ibid 191–2 and 197–8.

[92] Taylor (n 12), 84 (summarizing 77–84).

[93] Kommers (n 4), 179.

[94] Ibid 171; see also 179.

[95] Ibid 179 and 213; see also 207.

[96] Ibid 213, which seems to qualify the statement at 179. See also 211.

[97] Ibid 208.

the FCC's perception of its task, to determine rationally and objectively the true meaning of the Basic Law.'[98]

The theory that the Basic Law embodies an 'objective order of values', which are hierarchically ordered, in itself suggests that subjective judicial value judgments and discretion are unnecessary.[99] These values are considered to be specified by the constitutional text, as informed by history, rather than a product of judicial precedent.[100] Basic constitutional doctrines, according to the Federal Constitutional Court, 'reflect the normative realities underlying the Basic Law.'[101] Moreover, German jurisprudence continues to rely heavily on formal reasoning: 'the emphasis in legal education... on theory, conceptual clarification, deductive reasoning, and systematization... [is] reflected in general commentaries on the Basic Law.'[102] Definitional refinement and doctrinal elaboration, as well as normative theorizing, dominate the Court's opinions, which aim to prove the 'rightness, neutrality, and integrity of decisional outcomes'.[103]

Many observers will be sceptical about this aspiration to apolitical, objective legalism. But even if German constitutional reasoning is not objective, in a strong sense of the word, it may articulate a greater degree of inter-subjective agreement than exists in, say, the United States. The key to reconciling normativism and legalism in Germany seems to be professional consensus, which is converted into judicial doctrine and then steadfastly maintained. Leading journals are edited by practitioners, judges, and professors, and the Federal Constitutional Court pays as much if not more attention to leading academic commentaries as to judicial precedents. '[T]he "ruling opinion" in the literature takes pride of place in the interpretation of the Basic Law.'[104] The process by which the Court prepares its opinions is one of genuinely collegial decision-making aimed at achieving consensus within the Court, and general acceptance outside it,[105] especially within the legal academy, which the opinions are mainly aimed at convincing.[106] The Court's standard practice of handing down single, unsigned opinions also emphasizes the law's 'rationality, objectivity, and depersonalisation'.[107]

5. India

The Indian Supreme Court has radically changed its interpretive philosophy. For two decades, its philosophy was very similar to that of the Australian High Court. This is not surprising, since both courts initially adopted the rules of statutory interpretation that had been developed by British judges in the nineteenth century. The position adopted in *Gopalan* (1950), that courts can only enforce limits found in the Constitution by express provision or necessary implication, rather than 'a spirit supposed to pervade the Constitution but not expressed in words',[108] is identical to that adopted in the leading Australian case of *Engineers* (1920).[109] The

[98] Ibid 207.
[99] Ibid 179–80.
[100] Ibid 180 n 70.
[101] See n 85 above.
[102] Kommers (n 4), 209.
[103] Ibid 210.
[104] Ibid 193.
[105] Ibid 211–12.
[106] Ibid 210.
[107] Ibid 208.
[108] *Gopalan v India* AIR 1950 SC 27 (Kania J).
[109] *Amalgamated Society of Engineers v Adelaide Steamship Co Ltd* (1920) 28 CLR 129, discussed in Goldsworthy (n 20), 120.

Supreme Court did not always adhere to its early positivism: in a series of cases, it adopted strained interpretations of constitutional provisions in order to protect private property from expropriation without full compensation.[110]

The Court shifted to a more normativist approach when it circumscribed Parliament's power of constitutional amendment. In *Golaknath* (1967), it purported to adopt a literal, positivist interpretation of the relevant provisions, but constitutional experts regarded this as obviously erroneous, and concluded that the Court had really been guided by the anti-majoritarian sentiments expressed in the judgments.[111] The Court also, for the first time, adopted prospective overruling, which 'flew in the face of the theory that the judges did not make law, but merely interpreted it'.[112] In *Kesavanand* (1973), the Court read into the amending power a limitation nowhere expressed, nor contemplated by the founders.[113] Although the Court purported to rely partly on the words 'the Constitution shall stand amended', they were interpreted in light of the underlying structure or spirit of the document, comprised of enduring constitutional values.[114]

Since then, the Court has applied the 'basic structure' doctrine in other contexts,[115] overturned government action that violated broad, unwritten principles rather than specific provisions,[116] taken the non-justiciable Directive Principles into account in interpreting the Fundamental Rights,[117] interpreted an article that was deliberately drafted so as not to incorporate substantive due process as doing the opposite,[118] found many new, unenumerated, 'positive' rights to be implied by the right to life and personal liberty,[119] and interpreted several of the Fundamental Rights as incorporating international human rights that did not exist when the Constitution was adopted.[120]

In some of its most creative decisions, the Court relied on a 'basic structure' argument, as well as a Directive Principle, to interpret a provision requiring the government merely to 'consult' with the Chief Justice, before making judicial appointments, as requiring it to act on his recommendations. It then added a novel requirement that the Chief Justice must consult with four senior colleagues before tendering any recommendations.[121] Although this interpretation seems completely unsupported by the provision's express words, especially when understood in light of appointment practices at the time the Constitution was adopted ('consulted' never meant 'obeyed'), the Court did claim to be guided by the founders' purposes.[122] As recently as 2001, the Court stated that 'it is the function of the Court to find out the intention of the framers of the constitution'.[123] The judges' strategy therefore seems to be to appeal to

[110] S.P. Sathe, 'India: From Positivism to Structuralism' in *Interpreting Constitutions*, 239–42.

[111] Ibid 242–3.

[112] Ibid 224.

[113] *Kesavanand Bharati v Kerala* AIR 1973 SC 1473, discussed in Sathe (n 110), 244.

[114] Ibid 246.

[115] See eg *Indira Gandhi v Rajnarain* AIR 1975 SC 2299; *Minerva Mills v India* AIR 1980 SC 1789; *SR Bommai v India* AIR 1994 SC 1918; discussed in Sathe (n 110), 245–7.

[116] See eg the principle of secularism, in *Ismail Faruqui v India* (1994) 6 SCC 360; *Aruna Roy v India* (2002). See Sathe (n 110), 262.

[117] See eg *Hanif Quareshi v Bihar* AIR 1958 SC 731, cited by Sathe (n 110), 251.

[118] *Maneka Gandhi v India* AIR 1978 SC 597, cited by Sathe (n 110), 252.

[119] See many cases discussed in Sathe (n 110), 252–3.

[120] *Vishaka v Rajastha* (1997) 6 SCC 241, discussed by Sathe (n 110), 254.

[121] *SP Gupta v India* AIR 1982 SC 149; *Supreme Court Advocates on Record Association v India* (1993) 4 SCC 441; discussed by Sathe (n 110), 259–60.

[122] Ibid 260.

[123] *SR Chaudhuri v Punjab* AIR 2001 SC 2707 at 2717; (2001) SCC 126.

the founders' purposes at a very abstract level, and then to 'adapt' their words to give better effect to those purposes. That is very a strong form of normativism.

On several occasions, Professor Sathe comments that the Court interpreted the Constitution in ways that were clearly inconsistent with the founders' intentions.[124] It has said that the Fundamental Rights have 'no fixed contents', and acknowledged that it may be justified in finding 'new rights'.[125] It has openly embraced a creative role in interpreting the Constitution, which it has described as 'a vibrant document alive to the social situation [rather than] as an immutable cold letter of law unconcerned with the realities'—a 'living organ' that must change to meet the 'felt necessities of the time'.[126] In *Golaknath* (1967), Chief Justice Subba Rao stated that:

> Arts. 32, 141 and 142 are couched in such wide and elastic terms as to enable this court to formulate legal doctrines to meet the ends of justice. To deny this power to the Supreme Court on the basis of some outmoded theory that the Court only finds the law but does not make it is to make ineffective the powerful instrument of justice placed in the hands of the highest judiciary in this country.[127]

6. South Africa

It is difficult to characterize the jurisprudence of a Constitutional Court that has been in existence for such a short period. So far, it seems to have adopted a moderately normativist approach, which does not subordinate the language of the text to underlying values.

The South African Constitution expressly incorporates abstract values and principles. Section 1, for example, declares that the state is 'founded on certain basic values' including human dignity, equality, human rights, the rule of law, and democracy. Section 39(1) requires the Court to interpret constitutional rights so as 'to promote the values that underlie an open and democratic society based on human dignity, equality and freedom.' Governing principles also precede specific chapters, including those dealing with cooperative governance, public administration, and the security services. In a striking innovation, section 39 requires that international law be taken into account in interpreting the Bill of Rights. This could reasonably be construed as a sign that the founders intended constitutional rights to be interpreted dynamically, in response to global developments in the understanding of human rights.

Such provisions clearly encourage a normativist approach. Concerned that this might be taken too far, Justice Kentridge warned that if the language of the text were ignored in favour of a general resort to values, the result would be 'divination' rather than interpretation, allowing the judges to make the Constitution mean whatever they would like it to mean.[128] The Court subsequently declared that interpretation should be 'generous and purposive', giving expression to the Constitution's underlying values, 'whilst paying due regard to the language that has been used'.[129] Professor Klug provides several examples of cases in which rights were

[124] See eg Sathe (n 110), 252.

[125] *India v Association for Democratic Reforms* (2002) 5 SCC 294, and *Kapila Hingorani v Bihar* (2003) 6 SCC 1, cited by Sathe (n 110), 253.

[126] *Kapila Hingorani v Bihar* (2003) 6 SCC 1 and *Indra Sawney v India* (1992) ATC 385, respectively; quoted by Sathe (n 110), 253 and 262.

[127] *Golaknath v Punjab* AIR 1967 SC 1643 at 1669.

[128] *S v Zuma* 1995 (2) SA 642 (CC) para 17, quoted by Heinz Klug, 'South Africa: From Constitutional Promise to Social Transformation' in *Interpreting Constitutions*, 292.

[129] *Makwanyane* 1995 (3) SA 391 (CC) para 9, quoted by Klug (n 128), 292.

not interpreted as broadly as they might have been, because of textual, contextual, and purposive considerations.[130]

The Court takes into account the circumstances in which the Constitution was adopted, and even its legislative history, but only when this clearly illuminates the purpose of a provision. It does not examine the comments of individuals who participated in the constitution-making process in order to construct an 'original intent'.[131]

Some of the Court's decisions seem strongly normativist. In one case, a majority adopted a non-literal interpretation of section 241(8) of the 'interim' Constitution, which provided that 'pending cases shall be dealt with as if the Constitution had not been passed'. Although the case had commenced before the Constitution was adopted, they held that the petitioners were entitled to the benefit of new constitutional rights. They interpreted the section as including an implied qualification limiting its effect to the preservation of the jurisdiction of courts in which pending cases had been commenced.[132] Despite the apparent breadth of the enacted words, the Constitution's founding values and emphasis on rights was thought to constitute stronger evidence that a narrower meaning had been intended. Justice Mahomed expressly treated the Constitution as 'a holistic and integrated document with critical and important objectives'.[133] But the majority's reasoning exemplifies originalist rather than non-originalist normativism.[134] Justice Sachs insisted that:

> This is not a case of making the Constitution mean what we like, but of making it mean what the framers wanted it to mean; we gather their intention not from our subjective wishes, but from looking at the document as a whole.[135]

The Court has also inferred, from the reference to the rule of law in section 1, an implied requirement of legality that is independent of the administrative justice clause. Neither the Parliament nor the President may act capriciously or arbitrarily, and the President must exercise his powers in good faith.[136] This principle is treated as an additional requirement that underpins the express rights, including the right to administrative justice, which are treated as elaborations of it.[137]

III. Explaining the Differences

What explains these different interpretive philosophies? Judges are not, of course, automatons whose opinions are entirely 'caused' by external factors. They have reasons for their opinions, such as the principled reasons for preferring non-originalism to originalism, or vice versa. The simplest explanation might therefore be that judges in different countries just happened to find different sets of reasons persuasive. But a deeper explanation seems called for, given that these highly intelligent people did not find the same reasons compelling and converge on the same interpretive philosophy. It seems undeniable that social, cultural, political, and institutional circumstances help to explain the differences.

[130] Klug (n 128), 293–5.
[131] *S v Makwanyane* 1995 (3) SA 391, discussed by Klug (n 128), 286–7.
[132] *S v Mhlumgu* 1995 (3) SA 391 (CC), discussed by Klug (n 128), 292–3.
[133] *S v Mhlumgu*, para 15.
[134] Ibid paras 100, 102.
[135] Ibid para 112.
[136] *President of the Republic of South Africa v South African Rugby Football Union* 2000 (1) SA 1 (CC).
[137] Ibid; discussed by Klug (n 128), 278–9.

1. The Nature and Age of the Constitution

The nature of a constitution is surely an important factor in determining how it is interpreted. The Australian Constitution deals mainly with structural matters such as establishing governmental institutions and dividing powers among them. Its origins as a British statute, its relatively prosaic nature, and its lack of both a ringing appeal to national aspirations and a bill of rights, have surely contributed to the High Court's legalist approach to its interpretation.[138] Structural provisions, such as those dividing powers, are often interpreted by more legalistic methods—focusing on text, structure, and original intent—than rights guarantees. This may be because divisions of powers are often interdependent components of historically contingent 'package deals', reflecting deliberate and hard-won compromises between competing interests, which constitute 'original intentions' that courts are reluctant to disturb.[139] The meaning of provisions embodying such contingent and specific bargains seems less amenable to illumination by reference to abstract principles reflecting general human experience than is the meaning of rights guarantees commonly found throughout the world.[140] As a study of judicial doctrine in federalism cases concludes, 'The comparative evidence does not indicate that there is a core of universal federalism values or principles that motivates courts.'[141] This is no doubt a matter of degree rather than kind: indeterminacies in structural provisions are also resolved partly by appealing to their purposes, which usually involve political principles as well as pragmatic compromise. Moreover, some structural principles such as judicial independence are as ubiquitous as human rights.[142]

Constitutions that protect abstract rights require judges to make moral choices that arguably should not, and probably cannot, be governed by the framers' opinions or expectations.[143] Some modern constitutions explicitly require judgments of political morality rather than original intent. Section 39 of the South African Constitution requires that rights interpretations 'must promote the values that underlie an open and democratic society based on human dignity, equality and freedom', and section 1 of the Canadian Charter refers to 'such reasonable limits prescribed by law as can be demonstrably justified in a free and democratic society'. The adoption of the Charter of Rights in 1982 inspired a transformation in the interpretive philosophy of the Canadian Supreme Court, which adopted a strongly normativist approach and a pattern of enthusiastic activism throughout its jurisdiction, in non-Charter as well as Charter cases.[144]

But there may be significant differences between bills of rights. Professor Robertson argues that bills of rights in some older constitutions are treated as merely 'list[s] of highly individuated and specific things' that governments have a negative duty not to violate, whereas more modern ones appear more integrated, holistic, and purposive, intended to embody a coherent hierarchy of values that government has a positive duty to promote.[145]

138 Goldsworthy (n 20), 109, 113, 153, and 155.

139 Jackson (n 12), 102–8.

140 Ibid.

141 Baier (n 12), 159; see also ibid 18–19.

142 Robertson (n 13), 361–2 and 370.

143 See text accompanying n 28 above. The framers' intentions are arguably binding only insofar as they illuminate the meaning of the law they made: their opinions and expectations as to how judges should apply that law are not part of the law that the judges are bound to accept.

144 Hogg (n 46), 71, 88, and 103. The term 'activism' is used by Professor Hogg.

145 Robertson (n 13), 355; see also ibid 27.

Those of Germany and South Africa are examples of 'transformative' constitutions, designed to make a fresh start and repudiate discredited past values and practices by including founding values and structural principles whose interpretation requires a normativist approach.[146] As a result, the German Federal Constitutional Court is always able to invoke values internal to the Constitution, whereas the US Supreme Court, although it can appeal to structural principles embedded in the Constitution, often appeals to values external to the Constitution.[147]

The structure of a constitution can have many effects on interpretive methods. Constitutional rights appear to be interpreted more expansively in Canada and South Africa than in the United States, partly because their constitutions expressly mandate a two-stage inquiry, in which infringements of rights established at the first stage can be justified to the court at the second stage. The possibility of justification at the second stage relieves the courts of the need to adopt narrow interpretations of rights in order to accommodate legitimate competing interests.[148] Also, the presence in the Canadian Charter of the famous 'notwithstanding clause', which enables legislatures to insulate their statutes from judicial invalidation for violating the Charter, might have encouraged judges to be more expansive in construing Charter rights and less deferential to legislatures in enforcing them.[149] It has also been suggested that the relative terseness of the US Bill of Rights, and its impractical depiction of rights as absolutes, has made it necessary for the Supreme Court to be more creative, and more reliant on subjective judicial ideology.[150]

The degree of difficulty in formally amending a constitution may also be a factor. Professor Tushnet argues that because the US Constitution is inherently difficult to amend, and the political culture averse to formal amendments, the Supreme Court has felt compelled to make adaptations through creative interpretation, and the American people have accepted this as the appropriate method of updating the Constitution.[151] The Supreme Court of Canada has explicitly cited the difficulty of amending its Constitution as a justification for allowing 'growth and development over time'.[152] This is corroborated by the German experience where, Professor Kommers suggests, the comparative ease of formal amendment has reinforced judicial reluctance to bring about substantial changes through interpretation.[153] But this factor can also cut the other way: in India, the Constitution was so easy for the dominant Congress Party to amend, that the Supreme Court felt compelled to act creatively to restrict the amending power.[154]

Professor Tushnet suggests that the age of the US Constitution, as well as the difficulty of amending it, has encouraged adaptation through judicial interpretation.[155] It does seem inevitable that, as a constitution ages, its language will become less capable of fulfilling its underlying purposes, when applied to unanticipated technological and social changes. The development of an air force in the United States, mentioned previously, is an example.[156] On the other hand, the degree of difficulty of the constitution's amendment procedure is probably the more important factor. The pattern of legalism versus activism in the six countries studied does not correlate strongly with the relative ages of their constitutions. The two most activist

[146] Ibid, see also 256. [147] Rosenfeld (n 2), 661–2.

[148] Hogg (n 46), 70, 103; Klug (n 128), 293. [149] *Canada Constitution Act* 1982, s 33.

[150] Robertson (n 13), 27. [151] Tushnet (n 19), 7, 16–17, and 54.

[152] *Hunter v Southam* [1884] 2 SCR 145, 155, quoted by Hogg (n 46), 77.

[153] Kommers (n 4), 171–2. [154] Sathe (n 110), 242–5.

[155] Tushnet (n 19), 7. [156] See n 6 above.

courts, in India and Canada, deal with a Constitution, and a Charter of Rights, that are both relatively new.[157]

The greater age of the US Constitution is significant in two other respects. First, the fact that comparative jurisprudence is paid much less attention in the United States than elsewhere is surely due partly to that Constitution having been adopted before any of the others. To the extent that the meaning of a constitution (or a constitutional amendment) is determined by the intentions or understandings of its makers, the interpretation of constitutions adopted subsequently in other countries is of little relevance.[158] The constitutions of all the other countries studied here include provisions copied wholly or partly from other constitutions. It is often reasonable to assume that such a provision was intended to have a meaning similar to the meaning it had in the country of origin at the time it was copied. Even in the United States, British constitutional traditions up to 1789 have often been examined to shed light on concepts and principles derived from them.[159]

The second respect in which relative age is significant is that precedents naturally play a much larger role in the interpretation of older constitutions, simply because there are more of them. When constitutions are young, courts have a greater need to seek guidance elsewhere, which diminishes as they build up their own stock of indigenous precedents.

2. Legal Culture

An obviously important factor is the legal culture in which judges receive their legal education, and practise their profession before appointment to the bench. The judges responsible for interpreting the constitutions of Canada, Australia, and India—the Privy Council and the Canadian Supreme Court, the Australian High Court, and the Indian Supreme Court respectively—were all steeped in the British legal tradition, and initially set out to apply British principles of statutory interpretation.[160] By the end of the nineteenth century, if not before, the British legal tradition had become much more legalist than that of the United States.[161] Not that British principles of statutory interpretation were monolithic: they were themselves open to rival interpretations, which helps to explain early disagreements between the Privy Council in Westminster and courts in Australia and Canada.[162] But on any interpretation they were strongly positivist and moderately originalist. They did not permit judges to stray far from the text: any implications had to be 'necessary'. Although they did not permit recourse to legislative history to establish the lawmakers' intentions, they did allow reference to the legal and historical context in which a statute was enacted, in order to reveal the 'mischief' it was intended to remedy. And they did not permit the meanings of statutory terms to change over time, except through formal amendment or fidelity to erroneous judicial precedent.

157 This assessment is corroborated in a recent comparative study of judicial activism: Dickson (n 63), 12–13 and 15.

158 Tushnet (n 19), 45–6. But only 'to that extent', because the interpretation of constitutions elsewhere can be useful for other purposes.

159 Ibid 28–9 and 45.

160 Hogg (n 46), 104; Goldsworthy (n 20), 115–21; Sathe (n 110), 227.

161 Patrick Selim Atiyah and Robert Samuel Summers, *Form and Substance in Anglo-American Law* (1987), summarized at 408–15.

162 Hogg (n 46), 75; Goldsworthy (n 20), 115–19.

Legal education and scholarship in Australia, Canada, and India were less receptive to sociological jurisprudence and legal realism, which swept through US law schools in the early twentieth century, and to the scepticism about legal determinacy that they preached. It seems likely that the post-Charter shift in Canada, to an enthusiastic judicial activism, is partly due to its proximity to the United States, and consequential influence of US jurisprudence on the Canadian legal academy and profession.[163] In Australia, the controversial emergence of a limited and tentative form of judicial activism in the 1990s has been attributed partly to the introduction of more pragmatic, consequentialist theories at Sydney Law School in the 1950s.[164]

In South Africa, widespread condemnation of the legal positivism that dominated legal thinking in the apartheid era, and which some feared would stunt implementation of the new Constitution, has no doubt inspired judges to adopt a more normativist approach.[165]

The importance of legal culture is also evident in the section on Germany. The Federal Constitutional Court's legalist philosophy clearly owes much to what Professor Kommers calls the 'civilian-positivistic' tradition, which treats legal codes as 'unified bodies of law covering all possible contingencies arising out of human interaction'.[166] He depicts legal education in Germany as highly formalistic, its main objective being mastery of pre-existing legal rules and principles, with an emphasis on 'theory, conceptual clarification, deductive reasoning, and systematization'.[167] In Germany, too, ordinary principles of statutory interpretation were carried over to the field of constitutional law.[168]

On the other hand, inherited legal culture is clearly not determinative. Professor Sathe observes that in India, a tradition of narrow, technical, 'black letter' legal education continued until quite recently. This was well after legalism in constitutional jurisprudence came to an end in the 1970s, which must be attributed to other factors.[169]

3. Judicial Appointments and Homogeneity

In Australia, the social and intellectual homogeneity of the High Court bench—drawn almost exclusively from the conservative Melbourne and Sydney bars—has probably helped to preserve the tradition of legalism inherited from Britain, and broad judicial consensus as to the proper interpretive methodology.[170] Recent appointments to the bench have been deliberately designed by the government to preserve that consensus.[171] Another relevant factor is the function of a court charged with constitutional review. If it is a court of general jurisdiction, whose tasks also include the interpretation and application of ordinary law, then its judges are naturally inclined to apply the same professional techniques and habits of thought to all aspects of their work. That has certainly been the case in Australia and the United States, and initially, in Canada and India. On the other hand, judges in exclusively constitutional, or 'Kelsenian', courts are more likely to approach constitutional review in a different spirit.[172] In Germany, judges of the Federal Constitutional Court have until recently been recruited from a broader field than ordinary judges, including prominent politicians, civil servants, judges, and academics (they are now appointed mainly from the judiciary and academia).[173] It has been suggested that the Court would have been much less adventurous had its judges been appointed from the same career hierarchy as private law judges, many of whom strongly

[163] Hogg (n 46), 81. [164] Haig Patapan, *Judging Democracy* (2000), 20–2.
[165] Klug (n 128), 269 and 292. [166] Kommers (n 4), 208 and 207 respectively.
[167] Ibid 209. [168] Ibid 208. [169] Sathe (n 110), 263.
[170] Goldsworthy (n 20), 112–13 and 155. [171] Ibid 157–8.
[172] Robertson (n 13), 12. [173] Kommers (n 4), 174–5.

resented its intrusions into their field.[174] The same point has been made about the South African Supreme Court.[175] On the other hand, all German Federal Constitutional Court judges have had legal training of a kind that strongly encourages professional consensus.[176] It has also been suggested that, although Canadian judges seem less homogeneous in terms of regional and professional background than their Australian counterparts,[177] they have generally been of unquestioned professional standing and seem broadly to agree on the Court's non-originalist and relatively activist stance.

In the United States, there appears to have been even greater diversity in judicial appointments, which until recently were sometimes used to reward a President's friends and supporters, or appease powerful lobby groups.[178] One suspects that politicians such as Earl Warren, upon appointment to the bench, were less committed to professional craft norms than life-long practising lawyers or serving judges.[179] Indeed, a recent study purports to demonstrate a correlation between the more highly politicized appointments of US Supreme Court judges, and the greater influence of personal ideology in their decision-making, compared (in both respects) with their Australian and Canadian counterparts.[180] In addition, the legal profession in the United States seems, to an outsider, much more diverse—socially, culturally, politically, and intellectually—than in many other countries. Even today, when concerns about judicial activism have prompted a new emphasis on technical legal expertise and prior judicial experience as qualifications for appointment to the Supreme Court, intense political battles over confirmation reflect competition between rival interpretive philosophies.[181] The inference is not that the Supreme Court is more activist than other constitutional courts: on the contrary, the Indian Supreme Court seems to deserve that title.[182] Rather, the inference is a more sharply divided bench in the United States compared with other countries. Professor Tushnet points out that US judges have been socialized into a professional culture that frowns upon judicial wilfulness, making them unlikely to be wilful in any interesting sense.[183] Yet Supreme Court judges regularly attack one another for being wilful, which suggests that instead of a generally unified professional culture sharing interpretive norms, there are distinct sub-cultures—'liberal' and 'conservative'—that are almost deadlocked in a competition for influence.

It has yet to be seen how the express constitutional requirement in South Africa, that the judiciary should reflect the racial and gender composition of the nation, a requirement that the composition of the Constitutional Court already satisfies, will affect its interpretive methodology.[184]

There is some evidence that the method of judicial appointment affects the way federal distributions of powers are interpreted. The power of appointment enjoyed by national governments in Australia and the United States have probably contributed to the relatively generous

[174] Robertson (n 13), 380.

[175] Ibid 279.

[176] Kommers (n 4), 208–9.

[177] Hogg (n 46), 58–9.

[178] Tushnet (n 19), 14.

[179] Ibid 15.

[180] David L. Weiden, 'Judicial Politicization, Ideology, and Activism at the High Courts of the United States, Canada and Australia' (2010) 20 *Political Research Quarterly* 1, available online at <http://prq.sagepub.com/content/early/2010/03/23/1065912909352775.full.pdf+html>.

[181] Tushnet (n 19), 14–15.

[182] This assessment is corroborated in Dickson (n 63), 12–13, 15, and ch 4.

[183] Tushnet (n 19), 54.

[184] Klug (n 128), 284.

interpretation of national powers in those countries.[185] Professor Tushnet argues that this is part of a broader pattern of Supreme Court decisions reflecting the 'regime principles' of the national political elite to which its judges belong.[186] In both Canada and Germany, on the other hand, a jurisprudence much more sympathetic to regional governments was constructed by judges whose appointments were either completely independent of the national government (the Privy Council), or partially dependent on the regional governments (the Federal Constitutional Court).[187] In Canada, after appeals to the Privy Council were abolished in 1949, the main lines of its federal–state jurisprudence were not changed by the Supreme Court, perhaps partly because statutory requirements and constitutional convention require the Court's judges to be representative of different regions.[188] Australia and Canada are particularly strong contrasting examples, because in both cases the result of judicial interpretation was the opposite of what the founders intended (weak and strong central government respectively).[189] Evidence is lacking in India, where federal–state disputes have arisen less often, and have usually been resolved politically rather than legally.[190]

4. Political Culture

The judges charged with interpreting the Canadian, Australian, and Indian constitutions had imbibed the British constitutional tradition of parliamentary sovereignty. In these countries, the adoption of new national constitutions was not the consequence of armed struggle against perceived tyranny, but of pragmatic reform assisted by the imperial government (albeit, in India, only after much popular agitation). Although not strictly applicable to any legislature operating under a written, federal constitution, the principle of parliamentary sovereignty was nevertheless very influential. It encouraged broad interpretations of legislative power, trust in legislative rectitude, and deference to legislative will.[191] It was inhospitable both to broad interpretations of express rights, and to the imposition of new, supposedly implied, constraints on legislative power.

In the United States, on the other hand, the War of Independence was fought largely over Britain's resolve to impose the sovereignty of its Parliament over its American colonies, and in prosecuting the War, some of the new state legislatures adopted draconian measures.[192] One consequence was ingrained distrust of legislatures, which favoured narrow interpretations of their powers, broad interpretations of express rights, and the recognition of additional, implied constraints.

As for Germany, the Nazi experience profoundly disturbed the traditional European veneration of parliaments, and subordination of courts to 'apolitical civil service-like agencies entrusted with faithfully carrying out the will of legislative majorities.'[193] 'Profound distrust of politicians as a consequence of the disastrous policies of the Third Reich... made the soil particularly fertile for expansive rule by untainted constitutional judges.'[194] As the chief guardian of the Constitution, the Federal Constitutional Court was accorded a constitutional status and administrative autonomy that is unique among German courts.[195] Many Germans were

185 Goldsworthy (n 20), 156.
186 Tushnet (n 19), 53.
187 Hogg (n 46), 62–3, 75–6, 104 and Kommers (n 4), 187–8.
188 Hogg (n 46), 58, 62–3, and 95.
189 Ibid 75–6, 104, and Goldsworthy (n 20), 108.
190 Sathe (n 110), 232–4.
191 Hogg (n 46), 56; Goldsworthy (n 20), 109–10, 148, and 156; and Sathe (n 110), 227.
192 Jeffrey Goldsworthy *The Sovereignty of Parliament, History and Philosophy* (1999), 192–7 and 204–15.
193 Kommers (n 4), 206.
194 Rosenfeld (n 2), 641; see also ibid 665.
195 Kommers (n 4), 172–3.

attracted to notions of a 'higher law' that neither positive law nor the will of the people can alter or override,[196] and at least in its early years, the Court rejected the legal positivism of the Weimar period.[197] Similarly, in South Africa, the doctrine of parliamentary sovereignty that prevailed under the former apartheid regime was decisively rejected in favour of a form of constitutionalism emphasizing the protection of human rights.[198] The Constitutional Court often refers to the founders' deliberate decision to make a clean break with the values of the pre-existing legal order.[199] Professor Robertson argues that this is typical of constitutional review under 'transformative' constitutions, which are designed to inaugurate a new era based on new principles such as human dignity and equality.[200]

Political culture can change. In India, judicial attitudes of deference to the legislature were initially reinforced by the superior prestige of elected politicians compared with that of judges. But politicians' abuses of power during the 1975 emergency, and increasing corruption, diminished their superior prestige and the trust that had been reposed in them, not least by the judges. This provided judges with both the motivation, and the opportunity, to act creatively to impose new limits on the executive and legislature. Public esteem for the Supreme Court was enhanced by activist decisions designed to check abuses of power by the political branches of government. Indeed, Professor Sathe suggests that one reason the Court assumed an activist stance after 1977 was to restore its credibility, by demonstrating that it was prepared to stand up to the politicians.[201]

The influence of prevailing political culture is also evident in the impact of the recent global 'rights revolution' on judicial philosophies. In Canada, the adoption of the Charter coincided with this transformation of political attitudes, propelled by increasing distrust of majoritarian democracy. The result has been enthusiastic judicial activism in non-Charter as well as Charter cases.[202] It is as if the Canadian Supreme Court has adopted what Professor Tushnet calls 'holistic' interpretation, whereby the adoption of an amendment (in this case, in a non-technical sense, the Charter) is taken to change the overarching 'spirit' of the entire constitution, so as to justify new readings of older, unamended provisions. This is a technique not yet accepted by the US Supreme Court.[203] The 'rights revolution' has no doubt transformed public attitudes as well as judicial ones. Consequently, Canadian politicians are not well placed to resist perceived judicial activism. Their inability to use the 'notwithstanding clause' (s 33) to override judicial interpretations of the Charter, suggests that the general public is unlikely to condone any political attack on the judiciary.[204]

The rights revolution no doubt influenced Australian judges as well, contributing to the High Court's greater creativity in the 1990s, evident in the 'discovery' of an implied freedom of political speech. But the Court's perceived departure from its long-standing tradition of legalism did not, as in India, enhance its standing relative to the elected branches of government. Australian politicians reacted to nascent judicial activism in a way that was not open to their Indian counterparts. They were angered by it, and used their power of judicial appointment to turn the Court back to a more legalist approach.[205] This may corroborate an opinion that Australian judges have sometimes expressed, that 'strict legalism' is the best means of maintaining public confidence in the Court as a neutral umpire.[206] If that is so, the contrast with

[196] Ibid 167 and 180. [197] Ibid 182.
[198] Klug (n 128), 269. [199] eg ibid 315.
[200] Robertson (n 13), 29; ibid 265 on South Africa.
[201] Sathe (n 110), 251. [202] Hogg (n 46), 105.
[203] Tushnet (n 19), 29. [204] Hogg (n 46), 69 and 99 n 162.
[205] Goldsworthy (n 20), 157–8. [206] Ibid 157.

India and Canada is stark. Australia may have a more robust political culture than Canada, in terms of the willingness of politicians to denounce judicial decisions in strong language. It also differs from Canada in lacking what Charles Epp has called 'a support structure for legal mobilization': a body of well-funded human rights lobby groups that use litigation to advance their political objectives. In Canada, these groups form part of a 'court party' that vigorously defends the judiciary from political attack.[207]

Political backlash also seems to have affected judicial methodology in the United States, where the rise (or perhaps revival) of originalism since the 1980s has been the explicit goal of a populist political movement opposed to the perceived 'judicial activism' of the Supreme Court since the 1950s.[208] This movement has perhaps been assisted by the US tendency to venerate the Constitution and its Founding Fathers to an extent unknown in most other countries.[209] It has also been suggested that the Constitution's quasi-sacred status might be associated with its crucial role in forging the nation's identity, and with the higher levels of religiosity in that country compared with other Western democracies.[210]

Another example of how political culture influences interpretive methodology is the impact in the United States of the ideology of autonomous individualism, evident in the expansive interpretation of free expression, and hostility to social and economic rights,[211] compared with the greater openness of German jurisprudence to communitarianism, which led to a strikingly different treatment of abortion.[212] The Constitutional Court in South Africa has also struggled with tensions between individualist and communitarian conceptions of freedom, which may in the future be resolved through development of the indigenous concept of *ubuntu*.[213]

Regional heterogeneity has clearly been a factor in some countries, although it can cut in different ways. In Canada, the Quebeckers' concern to protect their language and culture led them to demand provincial rights, which other Canadians accommodated due to fear of Quebec separatism.[214] On the other hand, in the United States, regional heterogeneity may have had the opposite effect. According to Professor Tushnet, the activism of the Warren Court reflected the distrust held by national political elites for white majorities in the American South, as well as distaste for 'outlier' legislation in other states that had fallen behind progressive developments in the rest of the nation.[215] Fear of religious fundamentalism and intolerance that are more prominent in some regions than others may also have been a factor in decisions of the Indian Supreme Court.[216] And no doubt differences between the Kwazulu-Natal Province and other provinces in South Africa will have an impact on interpretive methods there.[217] Strong regional variations of this kind are absent in Australia, which is more culturally homogeneous.[218]

[207] Charles Epp, *The Rights Revolution* (1998); Brian Galligan and Frederick L. Morton, 'The Rights Revolution in Australia' in Tom Campbell, Jeffrey Goldsworthy, and Adrienne Stone (eds), *Protecting Rights Without a Bill of Rights: Institutional Performance and Reform in Australia* (2006); Rainer Knopff and Frederick L. Morton, *The Charter Revolution and the Court Party* (2000).

[208] See Greene (n 11), 6–7, 13–14, and 17. Possibly 'revival' because a version of originalism was the dominant interpretive methodology in nineteenth-century America: ibid, 14 and 85.

[209] Ibid 63–5.

[210] Ibid 66–9, 78–1; Rosenfeld (n 2), 657.

[211] Tushnet (n 19), 52. See also Chapters 49 and 50.

[212] Kommers (n 4), 178 n 60, 183, 190 and 213–14.

[213] Klug (n 128), 302–3 and 316–17.

[214] Hogg (n 46), 93–4.

[215] Tushnet (n 19), 52.

[216] Sathe (n 110), 262.

[217] Klug (n 128), 290–1.

[218] Goldsworthy (n 20), 156.

5. 'The Felt Necessities of the Time'

There is a popular perception that no matter what their stated interpretive philosophy, judges somehow manage to find ways of adjusting their constitutions to 'the felt necessities of the time.'[219] That might explain, to take just one example, why the Privy Council consistently interpreted national powers in Canada narrowly, while the Australian High Court interpreted national powers broadly, in both cases contrary to the founders' intentions, despite both courts purporting to apply British principles of statutory interpretation.

Are the interpretive philosophies described in this chapter mainly rhetoric, that conceal essentially result-oriented decision-making? Two issues must be distinguished. The first is the extent to which law remains stubbornly indeterminate, whatever interpretive methodology is employed, thereby requiring judges to exercise discretion on moral or policy grounds. The second is the extent to which judges are willing either to misapply, or to abandon, their orthodox methodology in order to reach strongly desired conclusions.

Professor Tushnet argues that in the United States, orthodox interpretive methods have proved sufficiently indeterminate that judges have been able to 'do the jobs [they] think need to be done at any specific time.'[220] Whether his argument holds universally is debatable. The judicial interpretation of national powers in Canada and Australia, contrary to the founders' intentions, might be examples of indeterminacy: British principles of statutory interpretation did not allow recourse to legislative history to resolve textual indeterminacy. On the other hand, many cases can be cited in which the Australian High Court's legalist methods led to very different conclusions than the US Supreme Court had previously reached. They include cases on interstate commerce, freedom of religion, and electoral equality. It is possible that such differences merely reflect the judges' different political ideologies. Alternatively, they might be the result of the larger number of abstract, and therefore less determinate, principles in the US Constitution, of a broader range of interpretive methods being accepted within the US judiciary as orthodox, or of the accumulation in the United States of a larger and more diverse body of precedents that can be used to rationalise result-oriented decisions.

As for the second issue, it is clear that judges sometimes feel they have no alternative but to act creatively in order to defuse a crisis, or to prevent or remedy what seems to them a particularly outrageous breach of some important constitutional value. When judges previously committed to legalist methods find them an obstacle in that regard, they sometimes either covertly misapply them, or abandon them (temporarily or permanently) in favour of normativism. From a legalist perspective, such cases involve a conflict, whether or not the judges perceive it, between their sense of moral responsibility, and their limited legal authority, to intervene. From a normativist perspective, especially a non-originalist one, there is less likely to be a conflict.[221]

Professor Hogg describes three examples of what he calls 'crisis management', where the Canadian Supreme Court exceeded the normal limits of its authority to craft an unorthodox solution to a looming political or legal crisis. In each case the Court adopted a normativist strategy, by resorting to 'unwritten principles'. Professor Hogg acknowledges that in one case, it is hard to see how the Court could responsibly have reached any other conclusion.[222] But he implies that in the other two cases, the Court's solution was neither necessary nor clearly

[219] A phrase famously used by Oliver Wendell Holmes Jr in *The Common Law* (1881), 1.

[220] Tushnet (n 19), 7. Tushnet acknowledges that they are not wholly indeterminate—eg the structural provisions of the Constitution are often clear-cut: ibid 27–8.

[221] See discussion of normativism in Section I above.

[222] Hogg (n 46), 98, referring to the *Manitoba Language Reference* case.

desirable.[223] In one of them, it adopted a novel idea that had never been publicly suggested before or even argued by counsel.[224]

In India, the shift from a predominantly positivist to a strongly normativist approach was initially motivated by fear that the power of constitutional amendment would be abused, a fear subsequently vindicated during the 1975 emergency.[225] The Supreme Court's post-emergency activism was aimed at curbing majoritarian threats to constitutional values, political corruption, and oppression of the most marginalized and deprived segments of Indian society.[226]

Professor Tushnet notes that the US Supreme Court has sometimes relied on moral concepts to surmount limitations inherent in other interpretive approaches.[227] The Warren Court's activism was motivated by strong disapproval, shared by national political elites, of the distinctive culture of the American South, and archaic laws in a few other states that were out of step with progressive developments in the rest of the nation.[228] The paradigm example is *Brown v Board of Education*, concerning racial segregation in schools, whose moral authority even originalists have found difficult to challenge, although it is hard to defend on originalist grounds.[229] *Griswold v Connecticut*, dealing with a state prohibition of contraception, is another example.[230]

One relevant factor, then, is the number of occasions that judges are confronted, or fear they may be confronted, by executive or legislative measures they regard either as contrary to a vital national interest or as morally outrageous. One is reminded of Oliver Wendell Holmes' famous 'puke' test—any law that made him want to puke must be invalid—which Felix Frankfurter converted into a 'shocks the conscience' test.[231]

Of all potential threats to constitutional values, encroachments upon their own exclusive authority or independence often cause the greatest shock to the judicial conscience. In Australia, the most legalist of the six countries, the High Court first began to construct a doctrine of strict separation of judicial power in a case where it was contrary both to the constitutional text and the founders' intentions.[232] More recently, the Court partially extended this doctrine to most state courts, although this was inconsistent both with previous authority and with strong disapproval of 'free standing' unwritten principles expressed in recent cases.[233] This was followed by an even more radically novel interpretation of provisions that mention state courts, based on a patently implausible appeal to original intent, in order to invalidate state legislation restricting judicial review of decisions of inferior courts and administrative agencies.[234] In Canada, even the Privy Council before 1949 and, later, the Supreme Court, struck down laws granting judicial power to administrative tribunals, although 'the basis for the decisions was unclear or implausible'.[235] In 1997, the Supreme Court invoked an 'unwritten principle' of judicial independence, and proceeded to construct 'an elaborate edifice of

[223] Ibid 99–100.

[224] Ibid 96–100, quotation at 100, referring to *Re Secession of Quebec* [1998] 2 SCR 217.

[225] Sathe (n 110), 243, 247.

[226] Ibid 262.

[227] Tushnet (n 19), 39.

[228] Ibid 52–3, discussing Lucas A. Powe Jr, *The Warren Court and American Politics* (2000).

[229] Tushnet (n 19), 40–1.

[230] Ibid 32.

[231] Letter from Justice Holmes to Harold Laski (23 October 1926), in Mark DeWolfe Howe (ed), *Holmes-Laski Letters* (1953), 888; *Rochin v California* 342 US 165, 172 (1952).

[232] *New South Wales v Commonwealth* ('the *Wheat* case') (1915) 20 CLR 54, discussed in Goldsworthy (n 20), 125–6 and 128–9.

[233] *Kable v DPP for NSW* (1996) 189 CLR 51, discussed in Goldsworthy (n 20), 148–9.

[234] *Kirk v Industrial Relations Commission of NSW* (2010) 239 CLR 531.

[235] Hogg (n 46), 73, referring to *Re Residential Tenancies Act* [1981] 1 SCR 714, and *MacMillan Bloedel v Simpson* [1995] 4 SCR 725.

doctrine with little or no basis in the text in order to protect the power, influence, salaries and perquisites of themselves and their colleagues.'[236] The Indian Supreme Court, arguably with stronger moral justification, implausibly interpreted a provision requiring the Chief Justice to be consulted before new puisne justices were appointed, as requiring his advice to be followed, and then added a requirement with no textual support whatsoever, that the Chief Justice must consult with his four most senior colleagues before tendering that advice.[237] In South Africa, many of the grounds on which the Court initially objected to the draft constitutional text related to its own jurisdiction and authority.[238]

Creative decisions that give principles highly valued by the judges greater protection than is warranted by the constitutional text, as originally understood, are not always 'progressive'. Judges share the values, including the prejudices, of the social class from which they are drawn.[239] In India, for example, the Supreme Court during its most legalist phase attempted to limit the legislature's efforts to enhance social justice by redistributing property.[240] In the United States, the doctrines of substantive due process and freedom of contract were notoriously applied before 1937 to invalidate labour laws and other legislative reforms designed to improve social welfare. In Canada, the 'unwritten principle' of judicial independence was invoked to protect judges' salaries from public sector budget cuts that posed no conceivable threat to their independence.[241] And in Australia, an implied freedom of political speech was 'discovered' and used to invalidate legislation aimed at reducing the dependence of political parties on the wealthy individual and organizations that donate the funds needed for expensive political advertising.[242]

The object of this chapter, however, has not been to criticize the interpretive methods and philosophies described in this book. It has merely been to compare and explain them.

Bibliography

Gerald Baier, *Courts and Federalism: Judicial Doctrine in the United States, Australia, and Canada* (2006)

Brice Dickson (ed), *Judicial Activism in Common Law Supreme Courts* (2007)

Jeffrey Goldsworthy (ed), *Interpreting Constitutions, A Comparative Study* (2006)

Jamal Greene, 'On the Origins of Originalism' (2009) 88 *Texas Law Review* 1

Vicki C. Jackson, 'Comparative Constitutional Federalism and Transnational Judicial Discourse' (2004) 2 *International Journal of Constitutional Law* 91

Vicki C. Jackson, 'Constitutions as "Living Trees"? Comparative Constitutional Law and Interpretive Metaphors' (2006) 75 *Fordham Law Review* 921

Vicki C. Jackson and Jamal Greene, 'Constitutional Interpretation in Comparative Perspective: Comparing Judges or Courts?' in Rosalind Dixon and Tom Ginsburg (eds), *Handbook in Comparative Constitutional Law* (2011)

David Robertson, *The Judge as Political Theorist* (2010)

Michel Rosenfeld, 'Constitutional Adjudication in Europe and the United States: Paradoxes and Contrasts' (1994) 2 *International Journal of Constitutional Law* 633

Greg Taylor, *Characterisation in Federations: Six Countries Compared* (2006)

[236] Hogg (n 46), 74, referring to *Re Remuneration of Judges* [1997] 3 SCR 3.

[237] Sathe (n 110), 259–61.

[238] Klug (n 128), 302.

[239] Sathe (n 110), 264.

[240] Ibid 239–41.

[241] *Re Remuneration of Judges* [1997] 3 SCR 3, discussed in Hogg (n 46), 73 and 92.

[242] *Australian Capital Television v Commonwealth* [1992] 177 CLR 106, discussed in Goldsworthy (n 20), 145.

CHAPTER 33

PROPORTIONALITY (1)

BERNHARD SCHLINK*

Berlin

* I would like to thank the Netherlands Institute for Advanced Study in the Humanities and Social Sciences for the fellowship in Fall 2010 during which much of this chapter was written.

I. A Triad of Justice

1. Proportionality and Justice

For Aristotle 'the just is the proportional, the unjust is what violates the proportion'.[1] When society distributes honour, money, or other goods to reward merits, Aristotle demands that the goods be in proportion to the merits; and when transactions occur he demands that what one side gives and gets is in proportion to what the other side gets and gives. When one person robs or hurts another person, Aristotle discusses involuntary transactions; here too, the damage and the compensation or punishment must be in proportion. 'Evil for evil...good for good'.[2]

Aristotle knows that proportionality is not a simple concept. Proportionality requires a measure for the distribution of goods and the reward of merits. It has to use money to make commensurable what both sides give and get in a transaction; it has to weigh and balance crime and compensation and crime and punishment. That a person suffers what he or she did is not enough. One must take into consideration the circumstances under which and the state of mind in which the person committed the crime. But as difficult as each of these requirements may be, Aristotle believes that the proportion can be determined and realized.

For Perelman, more than 2,000 years later, justice still concerns proportionality.[3] He summarizes the discussion since Aristotle as a fight over whether justice requires giving each according to his merits, or to his work, his needs, or his rank in society. Accounts of justice giving each the same or each according to his legal entitlement do not lead far enough. To give each the same can only mean to give each member of the same category the same, and shifts the problem to categorizing people justly. To give each according to his legal entitlement shifts the problem to determining which legal entitlements are just. The remaining accounts of justice differ as to the property with which the goods a person gets should correlate, but agree that the correlation should be proportional. Indeed, however socialist, liberal, or conservative notions of justice disagree, however ideas of meritocratic justice and affirmative justice, free market justice and social justice clash in the political arena, justice always requires that the share everyone gets be in proportion to something.

2. The Elements of Proportionality

Many lawyers and laypersons alike associate the principle of proportionality first and foremost with criminal law and with the proportionality of crime with punishment. That punishing a person justly means punishing in proportion to the crime seems obvious. This idea fosters an understanding of proportionality as a principle determining the proper correlation between two elements: between the punishment and the crime; between the goods that one deserves and one's merits, work, needs, or rank; between the goods that one party gives and gets and the goods that the other party gets and gives. According to this understanding a decision on proportionality requires a comparison between punishment and crime, goods and merits, goods and work, goods and needs, goods and rank, the results of a transaction for both parties.

[1] Aristotle, *Nicomachean Ethics*, Bk 5, 1131b (15) in J. Barnes (ed), *The Complete Works of Aristotle. The Revised Oxford Translation*, vol 2 (1995), 1786.

[2] Ibid 1132b (30), 1133a (1), 1788.

[3] Claim Perelmann, *The Idea of Justice and the Problem of Argument* (1963), 5ff. On justice and the constitution more generally, see Chapter 16.

But proportionality has a triadic rather than a dyadic structure. As any comparison needs a *tertium comparationis*, the comparison of proportionality analysis requires a reference point. The reference point is not just a tool for comparison; it is the pivotal point of the decision on proportionality.

Giving each according to his merits builds on the idea of a mission that people have that they may accomplish or fail to accomplish. Giving each according to his work builds on an idea of work, as opposed to other, unproductive activities, on what its purpose is and its results should be. Similarly the relevant needs cannot be determined without understanding whether the goal is mere survival or a fulfilled life and what mere survival and a fulfilled life require. Rank can be a criterion of justice only in a hierarchically ordered society where the hierarchy deserves to be upheld. To uphold the hierarchy, to grant mere survival or a fulfilled life, to foster productivity or to support people in accomplishing their mission are the ends for which proportional giving is crucial.

The same holds for infringement and penalty, crime and punishment. In 1979 the European Court of Justice found the penalty for failing to report the use of a license disproportionate, because the penalty for failing to use the license was the same.[4] The two infringements are serious in different degrees and therefore deserve different penalties, reflecting the regulation's goals. The goals are to make sure that the licenses are used as applied for, and that the administration knows about the use. To achieve these goals, the regulation must use the threat of a severe penalty to force licensees who do not use their licenses and want to hide their non-use to report it, while the threat of a mild penalty suffices to remind licensees who use their license and have nothing to hide merely of their duty to report.

In 2003 the US Supreme Court did not find disproportional a life sentence for defendants who committed a felony and had been convicted of two or more serious or violent felonies.[5] It found that the State of California had 'a reasonable basis for believing that dramatically enhanced sentences for habitual felons advance the goals of its criminal justice system in a substantive way.' The goals were 'to deter and to segregate habitual criminals'. The Court viewed the sentence as a sufficiently plausible deterrent and therefore sufficiently proportional to the crime.

One could argue that the US Supreme Court should explore the problem more deeply. That it should question whether the State of California defined the goals of its criminal justice system properly: Is it proper to exclude rehabilitation, reintegration, and appreciation of the defendant's guilt: That it should investigate whether the effects of California's sentencing practice are desirable: Is it desirable to drive parolees out of California into other states? The Court did not feel the need to raise these questions because it applied 'a narrow proportionality principle, which forbids only extreme sentences that are grossly disproportional to the crime'. But even when understood narrowly, proportionality requires more than just comparing two elements of a dyad. Proportionality operates as a triad, with a goal as the reference point to which both elements are related.

3. Approaches to Proportionality Analysis

That proportionality, though triadic in structure, can seem like a correlation between two elements, leads to two different approaches to proportionality analysis.

[4] *Buitoni v Fonds d'Orientation* [1979] ECR 677, 20 February.

[5] *Ewing v California* 35 US 11 (2003).

Under one approach, proportionality analysis starts with comparing, weighing, and balancing the two elements—on one hand the crime, on the other the punishment. Is the balance right or should there be a correction for a harsher or a milder punishment? Balancing requires weighing, and weighing in turn leads to identifying the goals of the criminal justice system. Crimes are assigned different weights in light of different goals; and punishments are more or less suited or necessary for achieving the different goals.

This balancing approach is not confined to issues of punishment. In 1985 the US Supreme Court reviewed the use of deadly force against fleeing felons and balanced the state's interest in preventing the escape of a criminal with the individual's interest in life.[6] To find the proper balance, the Court focused on the goal of using force against fleeing felons—as it often focuses on the goal.[7] The goal is to protect citizens; therefore the use of deadly force is constitutional only when necessary against a fleeing felon who poses a serious physical threat. Similarly in English human rights jurisprudence, courts have come to use a means–ends analysis as part of their balancing approach.[8] Accordingly, in the literature on proportionality balancing is often presented as the framework for proportionality analysis.[9]

Under the other approach proportionality analysis acknowledges the triadic structure from the outset. It starts with the search for the end—what is the end of the challenged measure?—and turns to an inquiry of the measure's quality as a means to this end. What are the goals of punishing? Does the punishment help to achieve the goals? How helpful, how necessary, is the punishment to this end? Here balancing comes into play as a controlling last step. Even though the punishment is a helpful and necessary means for the criminal justice system's goals, it may still feel wrong. Is there maybe an imbalance that must be corrected? How serious is the crime in light of the goals? Does the harshness or mildness of the punishment reflect the seriousness?

This approach, too, pertains to all conflicts concerning rights and interests, not just to issues of punishment. In 1963 the German Federal Constitutional Court reviewed whether the state could extract a defendant's cerebrospinal fluid in order to determine his mental capacity.[10] The Court decided that determining his mental capacity was a legitimate goal; the extraction was helpful and necessary. However, the Court recognized that since extraction is painful and dangerous, the state may require an extraction to resolve only a serious crime. As there is literature that presents balancing as the framework for proportionality analysis, so too there is literature that presents balancing as the last step of proportionality analysis.[11] One way or the other, the relation between balancing and proportionality analysis is close.

[6] *Tennessee v Garner* 471 US 1 (1985).

[7] See T. Alexander Aleinikoff, 'Constitutional Law in the Age of Balancing' (1987) 96 *Yale Law Journal* 943, 946, 963ff; Moshe Cohen-Eliya and Iddo Porat, 'The Hidden Foreign Law Debate in Heller: The Proportionality Approach in American Constitutional Law' (2009) 46 *San Diego Law Review* 367, 395ff; Jud Mathews and Alec Stone Sweet, 'All Things in Proportion? American Rights Review and the Problem of Balancing' (2011) 60 *Emory Law Journal* 797.

[8] See Jeffrey Jowell, 'Beyond the Rule of Law: Towards Constitutional Judicial Review' (2000) *Public Law* 671, 678ff.

[9] Aleinikoff (n 7), 986ff; Frank M. Coffin, 'Judicial Balancing: The Protean Scales of Justice' (1988) 163 *New York University Law Review* 16; Paul Gewirtz, 'Privacy and Speech' (2001) *Supreme Court Review* 139, 195ff.

[10] *Spinal Tap Case*, 16 BVerfGE 194 (10 June 1963).

[11] Robert Alexy, 'Balancing, Constitutional Review, and Representation' (2005) 3 *International Journal of Constitutional Law* 572; Aharon Barak, 'Proportional Effect: The Israeli Experience' (2007) 57 *University of Toronto Law Journal* 369; Dieter Grimm, 'Proportionality in Canadian and German Constitutional Jurisprudence' (2007) 57 *University of Toronto Law Journal* 383; Matthias Kumm, 'What Do You Have in Virtue of Having a Constitutional Right? On the Place and Limits of Proportionality Requirements' in George Pawlakos (ed), *Law, Rights and Discourse. The Legal Philosophy of Robert Alexy* (2007), 131ff; Cohen-Eliya and Porat (n 7), 385ff; Bernhard Schlink, 'Der Grundsatz der Verhaeltnismaessigkeit' in Peter Badura and Horst Dreier (eds), *Festschrift 50 Jahre Bundesverfassungsgericht*, vol 2 (2001), 445ff.

So whether there is a conflict between state and citizen or between two citizens or even between two state agencies, the attempt to solve these conflicts can—and does in the practice of the courts—start in two different ways: comparing, weighing, and balancing the conflicting interests or rights; or with an inquiry into the goal or end of the contested measure or action, whether that goal or end is legitimate, and whether the measure or action is a helpful and necessary means for achieving that goal or end. The first approach leads to the second: weighing and balancing gains substance in evaluating, for both sides, the contested measure or action's meaning or goal, in evaluating what one side gains from it and what the other loses, and whether there are alternatives more acceptable to one side or even both sides. Similarly the second approach easily yields the final comparison, whether the conflicting rights or interests are equally important or different, and deserve equal or different acknowledgement.

In practice, more crucial than the approach to the analysis is the diligence with which it is pursued. One can accept the weight that a legislature implicitly gives the interest of the state over a citizen's right in enacting a freedom-restricting statute, as long as it does not look completely unacceptable, or only after a rigorous analysis. One can accept the relevant reality on which the means–end correlation depends as the legislature sees it, or one can investigate that reality independently. One can reduce the whole analysis to whether the contested statute looks somewhat reasonable or completely unreasonable.

II. Steps of Proportionality Analysis

Regardless of the approach to proportionality analysis and the degree of diligence, proportionality analysis has different steps, each distinctive in its own right.

1. Categorically Prohibited Means

Proportionality analysis concerns the review of governmental, legislative, administrative, and judicial measures and even citizens' actions as means to an end. Once categorically prohibited, a measure or action may not be considered a means to an end. Once torture is understood as a violation of human dignity and prohibited under all circumstances, it is prohibited even if it seems to be the only means to an end of paramount importance. The prohibition precludes proportionality analysis. This does not mean that proportionality analysis cannot do justice to deontological constraints.[12] Deontological constraints have no place within proportionality analysis, but limit and define its terrain from the outside.

This makes clear from the outset that the use of proportionality analysis depends on the quality of the citizens' rights upon which the measure or action intrudes. When rights are protected categorically, intrusions are equally categorically prohibited and not subject to proportionality analysis. When a right does not permit at least some intrusion, the question whether a particular intrusion is a proportional means is meaningless.

2. Legitimacy of the End

Once one considers a measure or action as a means to an end, the proportionality analysis obviously requires considering whether the end is legitimate. The legitimacy of a governmental,

[12] For this critique of proportionality analysis see Kumm (n 11), 141ff; Richard H. Pildes, 'Avoiding Balancing: The Rule of Exclusionary Reasons in Constitutional Law' (1994) 45 *Hastings Law Journal* 711.

administrative, or judicial measure follows from the constitution and the relevant statutes. The legitimacy of a legislative measure, that is, a statute, follows from the constitution alone. A federal form of government distinguishes the ends that may be pursued into those of the federal and those of the state legislatures. Apart from that and given the democratic legitimation that the legislature enjoys, a legislative end is legitimate as long as the constitution does not clearly forbid the legislature to pursue it. A democracy in which citizens are free also presumes the legitimacy of a citizen's action, as long as a relevant law does not refute it.

There are illegitimate legislative ends. Freedom of speech and freedom of religion make it illegitimate for the legislature to proselytize. The legislature must not advocate good as opposed to bad ideas, beneficial as opposed to dangerous cults; the end that it pursues when it infringes speech or religion must be viewpoint-neutral. Nor is it legitimate in a democracy that grants freedom and equality for the legislature to pursue paternalistic or discriminatory ends. It is not for the legislature to enforce ideals of high as opposed to trash culture, of heterosexual as opposed to homosexual relationships, of nuclear as opposed to patchwork families. It is for society to consent or not to consent to such ideals.

Sometimes the constitution substantiates the legitimacy of an end by requiring particular ends for limiting and intruding upon particular rights. The German Constitution, for example, allows for limitations of the freedom of movement and for intrusions into the home only if they are necessary to protect and defend public safety and order and also life or health against specific dangers.

Sometimes when deciding the legitimacy of a particular end courts move into some kind of balancing. In a trend-setting 1986 decision, the Supreme Court of Canada required an end 'of sufficient importance to warrant overriding a constitutionally protected right of freedom'.[13] The Court left the balancing of the specific right and its specific intrusion or limitation with the legislative end for a later step, but required some balancing in advance of the specific determination. The European Court of Human Rights has a similar requirement, but a different approach; it requires that the end, in addition to being legitimate, be a 'pressing social need' justifying the breach of a fundamental right in the interests of democracy. But the court checks this additional quality of the end in the context of balancing only in a later step in the analysis.[14]

3. Fitness or Suitability

A measure or action that is a proportional means to a legitimate end participates in the end's legitimacy. The measure or action can be a proportional means only if it is truly a means, that is, if it is truly helpful and contributes to achieving the end. The contribution may be big or small, obvious and agreed upon, or in doubt and open to debate. But if the measure or action fails altogether to contribute to achieving the end, then it is not truly a means to the end. Then the measure immediately fails the test of proportionality.

This step in proportionality analysis is often called the fitness or suitability test. It requires an empirical check: whether extracting cerebrospinal fluid to determine a person's mental capacity or whether draconian sentences deter future crimes, are matters of fact, not norms. The facts may be hard or even impossible to determine. Then the analyst must decide who gets the benefit of the doubt, the intruder or the one intruded upon. Nevertheless the decision requires a review of actual facts.

[13] *R v Oakes* [1986]1 SCR 103, 28 February.

[14] See Jowell (n 8), 679ff for a summary of the jurisprudence of the European Court of Human Rights.

4. Necessity

That a measure or action is an appropriate fit or suitable means to an end does not mean that it is the only means. There may be other means and among them means that intrude less upon the citizen's right. Then, the state has no good reason to use the more rather than the less intrusive means; the less intrusive means serves the citizen's interest better and serves the state's interest just as well. The more intrusive means is unnecessarily intrusive or, stated more simply, unnecessary. The less intrusive means optimizes the potential to resolve the conflict. Sometimes this optimization is identified as a legal counterpart to Pareto-optimality in welfare economics: the resolution of a conflict is optimal only if making one party better off than he is in the resolution would make the other party worse off.[15]

This step in proportionality analysis is often called the necessity test. The alternative means actually has to work; this test is first of all once again an empirical test, creating the same problem of doubt and offering the same solution of allocating the benefit of the doubt to one or the other party to the conflict. Whether the alternative means is less intrusive is a value judgment. But it is an easy one: it reflects the perspective of the citizen who suffers the intrusion. What matters is the intensity of the intrusion to the citizen, not valuation of the intensity in light of the end.

5. Balancing

The attempt to evaluate the intrusion in light of the end is part of the next element or step of proportionality: balancing. The least intrusive means may yet be too intrusive. The only and therefore also least intrusive means to ensure that a determined woman does not have an abortion is to imprison her. Even fervent advocates for the unborn believe that imprisonment goes too far and that legislating imprisonment would be too intrusive. But others go that far and argue that the value of life and specifically unborn life takes priority over the value of autonomy and specifically the pregnant woman's autonomy. Both sides disagree about how to weigh and balance the value of unborn life against the value of the woman's autonomy. Since some regard this weighing and balancing as the core of proportionality analysis, this step is also called the test of proportionality in the narrow sense.

Since balancing involves not facts but values and value judgments, it is the most contested step of proportionality analysis. The question is how balancing can be saved from being a playground of subjectivity. Is it possible to verify or falsify a value judgment? How precise can weighing and balancing be? Can the result be objective?

Aharon Barak tries to answer.[16] He acknowledges that the different sides—interests, rights, principles, values—do not have weights that can be accurately measured. Talk of weighing and balancing is metaphorical. The task is to research the relevant case law; to determine the proper status of the conflicting rights and interests in the legal system, particularly their statutory and constitutional status; to examine their societal value in the totality of societal values; and, finally, to decide on the relative value of the conflicting rights and interests on the national scale of values. The result 'is not always dictated by the legal system, and it is related to the use of judicial discretion.'[17]

[15] Alexy (n 11), 573; Bernhard Schlink, *Abwägung im Verfassungsrecht* (1976), 178ff; Alec Stone Sweet and Jud Mathews, 'Proportionality Balancing and Global Constitutionalism' (2008) 47 *Columbia Journal of Transnational Law* 72, 95.

[16] Aharon Barak, 'Proportionality and Principled Balancing' (2010) 4 *Law and Ethics of Human Rights* 1; Aharon Barak, *The Judge in a Democracy* (2006), 166ff.

[17] Barak, *Judge* (n 16), 169.

Robert Alexy tries to suggest a more precise process.[18] His three-step approach to balancing requires first, determining the detriment to one side if the other side should win; secondly, determining the detriment to the other side if the first side should win; thirdly, determining whether the importance of one side winning justifies the detriment to the other. Alexy advises measuring detriment and importance with a scale that distinguishes between a low, a moderate, and a high degree of realization in order to compare, weigh, and balance the different sides ('Weight Formula'). Like Barak's solution, Alexy's relies on judicial discretion, though Alexy's three-step approach provides for a more appealing presentation of the results.

David M. Beatty seeks to transform balancing from a subjective to an objective process, from a matter of value judgments to a matter of fact finding.[19] He wants judges to respect and enforce the values that society as a whole and individual parties empirically accept, share, and cherish. But sometimes it is hard to find what a society actually values; sometimes a society is deeply torn as to how to value rights and interests; and sometimes not even a strong consensus of the majority helps, because the minority has a right to be protected against the majority. Sometimes Beatty himself recognizes that parties may become so caught up in the battle that they distort their values; it then becomes necessary for a court to make its own evaluation. Again, judicial discretion inevitably comes into play.

The process of balancing remains methodologically obscure. There seems to be a consensus among those who favor the process[20] that it requires an open eye for all relevant facts, interests, rights, principles, and values, as well as a careful analysis of how different outcomes of the conflict may inflict, burden, threaten, or enhance these factors. Assigning weights to the conflicting interests and rights, principles and values, and comparing the weights, entails an insurmountable element of subjectivity. In order to reduce the subjectivity somewhat, one may take into account, as far as is possible, the legal and moral values to which a society adheres, both by tradition and in actual fact, and also the relevant case law.

III. The Structure of Proportionality Analysis

1. A Right Order for Proportionality Analysis?

Since the different accounts of proportionality analysis differ in the order of using their elements, Dieter Grimm asks whether there is a right order. His answer is that order matters. He argues that going from an inquiry into the legitimacy of the end to the fitness test, then to the necessity test and finally to balancing has a 'disciplining and rationalizing effect...Each step requires a certain assessment. The next step can be taken only if the law that is challenged has not failed on the previous step.'[21]

There is a logic in starting with the inquiry into the legitimacy of the end. If there is no legitimate end, there can be no legitimate means. There is also a logic in testing the facts before balancing the values. First, it is often easier to agree on an assessment of facts than on a value judgment. Secondly, the value judgment often relies on factual knowledge. There is finally a logic in testing the fitness of a means before testing its necessity; it means taking the easier step

[18] Robert Alexy, 'The Construction of Constitutional Rights' (2010) 4 *Law and Ethics of Human Rights* 20; Alexy (n 11), 574ff.

[19] David M. Beatty, *The Ultimate Rule of Law* (2004), 169ff.

[20] See besides the authors mentioned in nn 16, 18, and 19, Aleinikoff (n 7), 962f; Coffin (n 9), 22ff; Grimm (n 11), 395ff.

[21] Grimm (n 11), 397.

before the more difficult one, the step that opens up the field of factual investigation before the step that has to go closely into factual alternatives and comparisons.

But the sequence of the inquiry and performance of the tests is of minor importance. If a court sees that the real issue in a case is the necessity of the means and therefore jumps right to the necessity test, there is no reason to criticize its neglect of the first and second steps. If it becomes clear immediately that a means is necessary but might exceed its end, the court's immediate turn to balancing makes sense. Following the order Grimm suggests may sometimes protect against balancing conflicting rights and interests that do not have to be balanced because, as the necessity test shows, one side can be helped without the other being harmed. But, as shown above,[22] the balancing step requires an in-depth examination of the relevant facts that inevitably involve issues of fitness and necessity.

The true problem is not the sequence of the steps, but their application. How thorough should the court be? What role should each step play? Is it right for a court to replace the legislature's balancing of conflicting rights and interests with its own? Balancing is unavoidably subjective and political. Why should the court's subjectivity and political assessment matter more than the legislature's? Should the court simply stick to determining, in an objective and empirical manner, issues of fitness and necessity? And with these issues other problems arise. The fitness and the necessity of a means may sometimes be hard or even impossible to determine. How much political discretion should the legislature enjoy in judging the fitness and necessity of a means to achieve a legitimate end? Who should bear the burden of proof? Who should get the benefit of the doubt? The state claims that it pursues a legitimate end. But, the citizen does not understand why he should sacrifice his freedom if the sacrifice does not reliably pursue the end. These questions involve constitutional issues, foremost the interplay between the supreme or constitutional courts and the other powers.

2. General or Particular Proportionality Analysis?

Similar questions arise in relation to another structural problem: the level of particularity or generality of proportionality analysis. Frank M. Coffin uses the term 'balancing', but means 'proportionality analysis':

> Balancing can degenerate into such a microscopic, particularistic, fact-specific decision that it offers no guidance for future cases.... The opposite danger, when a problem is addressed at a very high level of generality, is that a far-reaching rule will be announced, far beyond the needs of the case.[23]

Both dangers are serious. The structural problem cannot be resolved by encouraging courts to avoid one danger by turning to the side where the other danger lurks. Sometimes the case itself provides an orientation: It can be the case of a particular citizen defending his freedom against a particular intrusion or, where a constitutional court permits it, the case of a minority in parliament challenging the constitutionality of a statute passed by the majority. The first case must deal with particulars, the second with the statute's general effect. But courts can neglect the particulars and address the problems of the particular citizen and the particular intrusion on a high level of generality, when their aim is providing guidance for future cases. They can also focus on this or that particular effect of a statute, because they see the particular effect as the crux of the

[22] Section I.3.

[23] Coffin (n 9), 33; see also Aleinikoff (n 7), 979ff on the 'distinction between "definitional" and "ad hoc" balancing' and Barak, *Judge* (n 16), 171 on 'principled balancing and ad hoc balancing'.

constitutional problem. Again, the true issue is not the level of particularity or generality, but the questions mentioned above. If the state bears the burden of proving the necessity of its intrusions, the court must examine and develop the particular facts in order to determine whether the particular intrusion into the particular citizen's freedom is actually necessary. If, on the other hand, the legislature enjoys substantial political discretion in choosing the means, the court will focus less on particulars and more on general issues. Again, the interplay between the courts and the other powers—a constitutional determination—is what matters.

3. The Range of Proportionality Analysis

The last structural issue in proportionality analysis is its range. Proportionality certainly prohibits going too far, further than a legitimate end requires, further than what is suitable, further than what is necessary, so far that the balance tips. Does it sometimes also prescribe going further? Further than the legislature went in protecting someone's rights and interests?

The German Federal Constitutional Court views proportionality as a protection against the state, whether the state extends its reach too far or not far enough, whether the state has done too much or too little: too little to protect a right or interest.[24] This aspect of proportionality is supposed to come into play particularly in conflicts between individuals. The more the law of landlord and tenant protects the landlord's interests, the less it protects the tenant's interests, and vice versa; the greater the protection an abortion law provides to a pregnant woman, the less the protection for the fetus and, again, vice versa. The idea of the German Federal Constitutional Court is that proportionality not only keeps the state from intruding too far but also from not intruding far enough if protection of the conflicting right or interest should require. The Court rejected the legislature's abortion law twice for not adequately protecting the life of the fetus.[25]

Again what is at stake is a constitutional issue—the interplay between the court and the other powers. Proportionality as a protection against the state not doing enough is not a problem concerning the legitimacy of an end or the suitability or necessity of a means; it is pure balancing. If the court has the right to substitute its own balancing for the legislature's, there is no reason to limit the court's power to correct only for the legislature's over-extensive reach and not also for its insufficient reach. It is no surprise that the Supreme Court of Canada refrains from balancing and also argues that the legislature is not constitutionally obliged to furnish protection, 'only that it may do so if it wishes'.[26]

IV. Evolution, Constitutional Foundation, and Distribution of the Principle of Proportionality

How proportionality analysis should be performed, how thoroughly a court should inquire, who should get the benefit of the doubt when questions of suitability and necessity cannot be answered, what role balancing should play—resolution of these problems follows from the

[24] See on this new '*Untermassverbot*' as a sibling of the old '*Uebermassverbot*' Grimm (n 11), 392; on the similar jurisprudence of the Russian Constitutional Court see Alexander Blankenagel, 'Werden die Letzten die Ersten sein? Die Rechtsprechung des russischen Verfassungsgerichts zum Wirtschaftsverfassungsrecht' in Alexander Blankenagel, Ingolf Pernice, and Helmut Schulze-Fielitz (eds), *Verfassung im Diskurs der Welt* (2004), 605, 622ff.

[25] *Abortion Case 1*, 39 BVerfGE 1 (25 February 1974); *Abortion Case 2*, 88 BVerfGE 203 (28 May 1993).

[26] *R v Edwards Books and Art Ltd* [1986] 2 SCR 713, 18 December.

constitutional locus and impact of its founding principle, the principle of proportionality. Where is the principle found in the constitution? What is its impact on the interplay of the powers?

1. The Evolution of the Principle of Proportionality

The principle already had a long career before becoming a constitutional principle. As indicated above, it played and plays a crucial role in the philosophical quest for justice. It also played and plays a crucial role in moral discourse, whenever the discourse concerns resolving a conflict between different individuals, their freedoms and interests. Let us suppose that one family member wants his quiet, another wants to play the piano. Resolution requires asking obvious questions: Why does one want his quiet? Is he sick? Why does the other want to play the piano? Does she have to practice for an exam? Is it a sickness where one should lie down or maybe take a walk and get some fresh air? Can he lie down in a room that is not his, but quieter? Can she practice at her friend's house? If both should be able to do what they want only if they are right next door to each other, then how severe is his sickness, how unpleasant or threatening, how important is her exam, can it be repeated or is it a once in a lifetime chance to get into a master class? These questions are the access to a proportionality analysis.

In law the principle of proportionality is often traced back to German roots.[27] In Germany the principle came into its own in administrative law when the police acted to protect the public.[28] From the late eighteenth to the early twentieth century, the relevant norm provided little more than a definition of the task of the police: The police had to do what was necessary to fight dangers to public safety and order.[29] The norm was meant to give the police wide discretion in fighting dangerous behavior of all sorts: from offending the Prussian king at a socialist rally to building a house without proper structural engineering or to running a chemical plant without proper waste disposal. In the beginning, the norm was even meant to give the police uncontrolled discretion. But once the ideas of individual rights and the Rechtsstaat (the state under the rule of law) began to prevail, the courts started to institute controls over the police. The days of uncontrolled discretion were over. In the last decades of the nineteenth century the Prussian High Administrative Court developed this norm, a norm that did no more than define the task of the police into a jurisprudence of proportionality. The police were entitled to use only means that were fit, necessary, and proportional in the narrow sense. The means had to work, there was to be no other means that would be equally effective but less intrusive, and the end was to be important enough to justify the intrusion.

The court had two and only two normative premises. First, the police were entitled to do what is necessary to fight dangers to public safety and order. Secondly, citizens' life, liberty, and property were protected against police intrusion. Together the two premises create a dilemma. It is impossible to fight dangers without intruding into citizens' life, liberty, and property. So how can the police fight dangers and intrude and at the same time protect citizens

[27] Barak (n 11), 370; Moshe Cohen-Eliya and Iddo Porat, 'American Balancing and German Proportionality: The Historical Origins' (2010) 8 *International Journal of Constitutional Law* 263, 271ff; Christoph Knill and Florian Becker, 'Divergenz trotz Diffusion? Rechtsvergleichende Aspekte des Verhaeltnismaessigkeitsprinzips in Deutschland, Grossbritannien und der Europaeischen Union' (2003) 36 *Die Verwaltung* 447, 454ff; Stone Sweet and Mathews (n 15), 74, 97ff.

[28] See Bodo Pieroth, Bernhard Schlink, and Michael Kniesel, *Polizei- und Ordnungsrecht mit Versammlungsrecht* (6th edn, 2010), 4ff.

[29] Allgemeines Landrecht für die die Preussischen Staaten, Teil II, Titel 17, §10.

against intrusion? The court resolved the dilemma by allowing the police to intrude, but not in an arbitrary way, and by defining the non-arbitrary way as the proportional way.

In the second half of the twentieth century, the German Federal Constitutional Court found itself with two very similar premises and not much more. The German Constitution contains a bill of rights that grants individuals a variety of rights and freedoms. At the same time, the Constitution empowers the legislature to limit these rights and freedoms and intrude upon them. Again there is the dilemma of how to reconcile these provisions. The Constitution's grant of rights cannot mean that the rights trump the legislature's power. Nor can the Constitution's empowering the legislature mean that the citizens' rights are meaningless. The provisions have to coexist, and again, together they can mean only that the legislature is empowered to limit and intrude, but not in an arbitrary way. And again, the Court defined and defines this non-arbitrary or reasonable way as the way under the principle of proportionality: The laws that the legislature enacts in pursuing its ends must be proportional.

What other definition of the non-arbitrary way could the Court have devised? Once there is significant, but not total, empowerment to achieve an end, and to use means to achieve the end, the only way to curtail and control the empowerment is to require the means to be proportional. There is nothing inherently German about the roots of the principle of proportionality, nor is the introduction of the principle into other constitutional contexts a transfer of a German principle. It is a response to a universal legal problem.

2. The Constitutional Foundation of the Principle of Proportionality

Once it is understood that an authority's reach is extensive but also limited, without specifying the limits, the principle of proportionality serves as an instrument for reconciling both: the extensive reach with the unspecified limits.

The universal legal problem and the principle of proportionality as a response to that problem are not restricted to conflicts of state versus citizen and citizen versus citizen. When state agencies have conflicting powers, not clearly defined in their reach and limits, and the fiat of a higher authority cannot resolve the conflict, then a court must resolve the conflict and the principle of proportionality can again come into play.[30] The US Supreme Court relied on the principle of proportionality, perhaps for the first time, in its jurisprudence under the Dormant Commerce Clause on the relation between the federal government and the states that the clause establishes.[31]

But the principle comes into play primarily in conflicts over fundamental rights and freedoms. Fundamental rights and freedoms and the legislature's power to limit and intrude on them constitute the field of law in which the principle is most meaningfully employed. The principle's task is to protect the fundamental rights and freedoms against limitations and intrusions; the principle emanates from them and has its constitutional foundation in them. Sometimes the articles of the constitution that protect fundamental rights and freedoms state the principle of proportionality explicitly.[32]

[30] See Aleinikoff (n 7), 947 on US Supreme Court jurisprudence; Schlink (n 11), 449 on the jurisprudence of the German Federal Constitutional Court; Knill and Becker (n 27), 464 on the jurisprudence of the European Court of Justice.

[31] See Mathews and Stone Sweet (n 7); J.H. Mathis, 'Balancing and Proportionality in US Commerce Clause Cases' (2008) 35 *Legal Issues of Economic Integration* 273.

[32] European Charter of Fundamental Rights, Art 52; the Constitutions of Greece, Art 25; Poland, Art 31; Portugal, Art 18; Russia, Art 55; Switzerland, Art 36; Basic Law of Israel: Human Dignity and Freedom, s 8.

In Germany the constitutional foundation of the principle of proportionality is often traced to the principle of the Rechtsstaat, itself enshrined in the Constitution, under which all state action must respect individual rights and freedoms, be regulated by law, and operate under judicial control.[33] But however valid this may be for Germany historically, where, in the nineteenth century the Rechtsstaat was established before fundamental rights and freedoms were constitutionally granted, it is not systemically valid. The fact that the principle of proportionality plays the same role in Germany as it does in other countries, where the dominance of the law is guaranteed not by a constitutionally enshrined principle of the Rechtsstaat but in other ways, indicates that the constitutional foundation of the principle lies in the fundamental rights and freedoms. In Germany, argument exists even for a third foundation of the proportionality principle: the essence of law.[34] In this perspective the proportionality principle is one of the general principles of law, without which law does not work.

Robert Alexy has found something of a following for his interpretation of fundamental rights as principles and the proportionality principle as a consequence of the principled quality of fundamental rights. As principles, so goes his idea, fundamental rights express values and require optimization of the values they express, their realization to the greatest extent possible. Thus fundamental rights unavoidably conflict with other fundamental rights that require optimization of their own sets of values. Also fundamental rights may conflict with the principles that guide the state in pursuing its goals. The only resolution of these conflicts is to search for a Pareto-optimum that satisfies both sides in the conflict, and if that is not enough, to balance the two principles. So for Alexy fundamental rights are the constitutional foundation of the principle of proportionality—because they are principles.[35]

The interpretation of fundamental rights as principles expressing values is a problem in its own right. Once rights are interpreted as expressing values, it is a small and easy step to distinguish between a valuable and a valueless use that an individual makes of them—a step towards paternalism and discrimination. Since the constitution does not offer a hierarchy of principles, each conflict between a citizen's fundamental right and the state's interest in pursuing a goal is a conflict of equally strong principles. Fundamental rights are in danger of losing their prominence. The interpretation of fundamental rights as principles may seem to promise a particularly rich meaning and strong impact for fundamental rights, but it does not ensure that the exercise of fundamental rights may take priority over the state's interest.

It is not helpful to link the principle of proportionality to the controversial interpretation of rights as principles. Nor is it necessary. Fundamental rights that protect against limitations and intrusions but also allow them can protect only against some limitations and intrusions and must allow others. The principle of proportionality provides a plausible method for finding out which limitations and intrusions to allow. The method is open to variation: Proportionality analysis can be carried out with more or less rigor; it can emphasize the factual assessments of the suitability and necessity tests or the value judgments of the balancing step; it can put the burden of proof on or give the benefit of the doubt to the limiting and intruding state or to the affected citizen. It is open to various understandings of the relationship between citizen and state, and between the supreme or constitutional court and the legislature. This openness is an asset. It makes proportionality analysis the arena in which the different

[33] See Horst Dreier in Horst Dreier (ed), *Grundgesetz Kommentar*, vol 1 (2nd edn, 2004), 128ff; Donald Kommers, *The Constitutional Jurisprudence of the Federal Republic of Germany* (2nd edn, 1997), 46; see Jowell (n 8), 672ff on the relationship of the rule of law to the principle of proportionality.

[34] Dreier (n 33), 128ff.

[35] Alexy (n 11), 572f; see also Kumm (n 11), 136f; Stone Sweet and Mathews (n 15), 93ff.

understandings of the relationship between citizen and state and between the supreme or constitutional court and the legislature can rationally confront one another.

3. Distribution of the Principle of Proportionality

Wherever courts find themselves with two premises and not much more, the first that rights and freedoms are protected against limitations and intrusions, the second that these rights and freedoms can be limited and intruded upon, the answer must be that the limitations and intrusions must not be arbitrary, but proportional.

But rights can also be granted in a different way. The Bill of Rights of the US Constitution protects fewer rights than other constitutions, but protects the most prominent among them categorically. The free exercise of religion must not be prohibited; freedom of speech, freedom of the press, the right to assemble peaceably must not be abridged. The legislature is not empowered to limit these rights or to intrude upon them. This does not mean that the rights do not conflict with goals that the state pursues or with rights of other citizens. But without a caveat for legislative limitations and intrusions, demarcations and categorizations help to resolve the conflict. The jurisprudence draws lines: the exercise of religion must end where a religion-neutral law as opposed to a religion-specific law states its commands or prohibitions; speech must end when it turns into a fight or commercial action or, as obscenity or defamation, lacks the value of speech; and it must also end where restrictions are not content-specific, but content-neutral, and refer only to the time, place, and manner of what is said. That does not mean that proportionality analysis does not come into play. Whenever US courts review limitations and intrusions with strict scrutiny or a middle tier of scrutiny or with a requirement of mere rationality, theirs is a means–end analysis that is a more or less thorough proportionality analysis.[36] The often-mentioned, praised, or criticized US exceptionalism exists. What it means is that the word 'proportionality' appears only rarely; that the means–end analysis is somewhat haphazard and that balancing and means–end analysis come systematically later; the first approach is to fine-tune the realm of the right, to specify its inner limitations before allowing for outer limitations by the legislature.

Other than the US Constitution, most modern constitutions protect a plethora of rights and freedoms, with the effect that all behavior, all action, all expression is protected, but the state can limit and intrude upon these protections, as long as it does so proportionally. Sometimes the constitutions were the response to a previous totalitarian or dictatorial regime; lack of freedom in all areas of life leads to an emphasis on the protection of freedom in all areas of life as well. But even without the experience of totalitarianism or dictatorship, in a world ever more crowded and ever more narrow, freedom in all areas of life is ever more valuable. With the far-reaching constitutional protection of rights and freedoms, the principle of proportionality spread across Europe, into the Commonwealth, to Israel, Central and South America, and beyond.[37] In European countries lacking constitutionally protected rights and freedoms or constitutional review, implementation of the European Convention on Human Rights into the national legal system leads also to implementation of the principle of

[36] See Aleinikoff (n 7), 963ff; Vicky C. Jackson, 'Ambivalent Resistance and Comparitive Constitutionalism: Opening up the Conversation on "Proportionality", Rights and Federalism' (1999) *University of Pennsylvania Journal of Constitutional Law* 583, 602ff; Mathews and Stone Sweet (n 7); Davor Susnjar, *Proportionality, Fundamental Rights, and Balance of Powers* (2010), 146ff.

[37] See with detailed references Cohen-Eliya and Porat (n 7), 13ff; Stone Sweet and Mathews (n 15), 74, 112ff.

proportionality in the national jurisprudence.[38] The European Court of Justice, the European Court of Human Rights, and the Panels and the Appellate Body of the World Trade Organization all operate under the principle of proportionality.[39]

V. The Strength of Rights and Freedoms in Proportionality Analysis

A frequent criticism of the proportionality principle is that it dilutes and relativizes rights and freedoms: a right or freedom is protected only to the extent that a state does not have a legitimate interest that requires its intrusion or limitation; it is not stronger than the state's legitimate interest; in fact, it is weaker, because, once one position can be saved only at the cost of the other position, the collective interest of the people as represented by the state must trump the single right of the individual citizen.

1. Strength through the State's Interest in Rights and Freedoms

However, this criticism is based on an oversimplification. It is a mistake to view individual rights or freedoms as always in opposition to the state's interest.[40] A conflict about a newspaper's publication of military plans and projects is not just a conflict between the newspaper's freedom of speech and the state interest in national safety. That a marketplace of ideas exists—a marketplace in which the press follows, monitors, and criticizes the state's and also the military's actions—is also in the state's own interest; the state has an interest in its citizens' use and enjoyment of freedom of speech.

Still, proportionality analysis is basically the same whether the publishing newspaper's freedom of speech is viewed as an individual freedom only or also as a constituting element in the marketplace of ideas. The issues of suitability and necessity are the same, and if national security requires prohibiting a publication, acknowledging the importance of a free marketplace of ideas will be no more than rhetorical.

2. Strength through the Exclusion of Reasons

Rights and freedoms show their strength in other ways. They do so by excluding reasons. Proportionality analysis is a reasoning process in which, prima facie, everything can be argued for or against the suitability or necessity of a means and the balance of the means and the end.

Rights can reduce this universe of discourse. Underlying freedom of speech is the notion that the state is not entitled to judge viewpoints, that for the state one viewpoint must be as good as another. Therefore, as shown above,[41] the legislature cannot be allowed to proselytize; such ends are illegitimate. But viewpoint neutrality goes even further. The justifications for restricting

[38] See, with detailed references for the United Kingdom, Jowell (n 8), 678ff.

[39] See, again with detailed references, Knill and Becker (n 27), 463ff; Stone Sweet and Mathews (n 15), 138ff; on the use of the principle of proportionality by the tribunals of the International Centre for the Settlement of Investment Disputes see Alec Stone Sweet, 'Investor–State Arbitration: Proportionality's New Frontier' (2010) 4 *Law and Ethics of Human Rights* 47.

[40] Stephen Breyer's opinion in *Bartnicki v Vopper* US 1753 (2001); Aleinikoff (n 7), 981ff; Coffin (n 9), 28ff; Gewirtz (n 9), 157ff.

[41] Section II.2.

freedom of speech must be viewpoint neutral. To argue that a limitation on freedom of speech for the legitimate goal of public safety and order is proportional because it affects only false, wrong, and evil ideas is unacceptable. Similarly, a limitation on religious freedom cannot be justified on the ground that it affects only particularly superstitious and unenlightened religious beliefs. Since equality prohibits not only open discrimination based on gender, race, or age but also arguments based on gender, race, or age as justification, homosexuals can be excluded from the military neither because they are homosexuals nor because homophobic traditions, conventions, or sentiments in the military must be respected in order to keep the military efficient.[42]

3. Strength through Imposition of the Burden of Proof

In proportionality analysis placing the burden of proof on the intrusive or restrictive state agency strengthens or bolsters individual rights and freedoms. But to do so creates problems. The problems that arise when an administrative agency or a court intrudes or restricts are relatively minor; an agency or court must act in accordance with the law setting conditions for intrusions or restrictions. The agency or court bears the burden of showing that these conditions are satisfied. However, the problem is severe when a legislature intrudes or restricts. If there is doubt whether a statute is a necessary means to a legitimate end, is it not enough that the legislature, subject only to the constitution and legitimized by election, thinks so? Should the legislature not enjoy a substantial margin of appreciation or discretion? On the other hand, placing the burden of proof on the citizen means that the citizen must justify his exercise of the freedom. Does freedom not include the right not to account for its exercise?

It may seem as if the solution to the problem raised by burden of proof is to assign courts responsibility for the evidence, for finding and hearing experts, for collecting and assessing the relevant empirical data. While the US Supreme Court says that it does 'not sit to weigh evidence in order to determine whether the regulation is sound or appropriate',[43] even though it sometimes does, in the continental legal tradition courts are responsible for compiling and weighing the evidence. But assigning responsibility for compiling evidence to a court does not necessarily strengthen rights and freedoms; it can also weaken them. The court that is better trained and equipped than the parties before it may conclude that an intrusion is not necessary even though the legislature tried to prove that it is, but it can also conclude that the intrusion or restriction is necessary even though the legislature was unable to prove that it is. The court may even find that the intrusion or restriction is not necessary for the goal for which the legislature thought that it was necessary but rather for a different goal. In any case, the burden-of-proof problem cannot be solved that way: the court can still end up with an impasse when the information that it gathers does not provide a clear answer.

This arises frequently. Often experience, science, and scholarship do not provide the information necessary to determine whether a means works and whether it is necessary. Then all one has, may well be contradictory experiences and assumptions and as many expert opinions as there are interests. In the conflict over the route of the fence separating Israelis and Palestinians, the Israeli Supreme Court[44] received contradictory opinions from two groups

[42] *Lustig-Prean and Beckett v United Kingdom*, App nos 31417/96 and 32377/96, 27 September 1999, para 71; Kumm (n 11), 137ff, 146f; see also Pildes (n 12), 727ff.

[43] *Railway Express Agency, Inc v New York* 336 US 106 (1949).

[44] *Beit Sourik Village Council v Government of Israel*, HCJ 2056/04, 30 June 2004.

of military experts. The military commander argued that only the contested route provides safety; military experts from the Council for Peace and Security argued that this route intrudes on local Palestinians lives more harshly than necessary, and that it is also not safe. If the burden is on the government to prove the military necessity of the contested route, then local Palestinians would have the upper hand. If, on the other hand, it is the Palestinians who must prove that the route is militarily unnecessary, then it is the government that has the upper hand. The court placed the burden of proof on the local Palestinians and accepted the route as necessary. But in the last step of its proportionality analysis the court found the route's intrusion on local Palestinians too harsh and unbalanced, and required the government to design a different route.

No country's constitutional jurisprudence relies exclusively on either of the two burden-of-proof rules. Decision-makers find more flexible approaches in between. Often they shift the burden of proof according to what is at stake. The more the citizen's freedom relates to his autonomy and the less important the end that the legislature pursues is for the common good, the more constitutional courts tend to require that the legislature demonstrates a statute's effectiveness and necessity beyond reasonable doubt. On the other hand, the more important the legislature's end and the less crucial the curtailed freedom, the more generous courts are to the legislature and allow it to act, even if many questions about the effectiveness and necessity of the statute remain unanswered. Of course, there are many degrees of more and less on this flexible scale and correspondingly many ways in which the burden of proof can shift or even be shared by the court itself; there are also many different notions of what doubts are reasonable and what doubts are unreasonable, and many different ideas about what is crucial to or at least relevant for citizens' autonomy and what is important for the common good. So it comes as no surprise that different traditions exist and shift as to how to distribute the burden of proof between the legislature and the citizens.[45]

4. Strength through Balancing

A third way to regard rights and freedoms as gaining strength is through balancing. This last step of the proportionality analysis allows the right or freedom to trump even if the intrusion or limitation is necessary for a legitimate end. Dieter Grimm presents the hypothetical of a statute that allows the police to kill someone if necessary to prevent him from stealing property and praises balancing as the only way for a court to acknowledge that the value of a person's life is more important than another's property and to reject the statute as unconstitutional.[46]

But balancing comes with a high price. That life is more valuable than property is so obvious that the decision of the court has an objective aura. In fact it is so obvious that the hypothetical seems contrived, but for times of riot, commotion, and plundering when the result of the balancing and the decision of the court would not be obvious. In most cases the results of balancing are nothing less than obvious; they do not have an objective aura, but are unavoidably and plainly subjective. However, the question arises why justices should value their

[45] See Susnjar (n 36), 83ff on similarities and differences between the jurisprudence of the German Federal Constitutional Court, the US Supreme Court, the European Court of Human Rights, and the European Court of Justice; Grimm (n 11), 390ff on the different traditions of the German Federal Constitutional Court and the Supreme Court of Canada; Mathews and Stone Sweet (n 7), on shifts in the jurisprudence of the US Supreme Court; Julian Rivers, 'Proportionality and Variable Intensity of Review' (2006) 65 *Cambridge Law Review* 174 on the jurisprudence of British courts; Barak, *Judge* (n 16), 226ff on the Israeli experience.

[46] Grimm (n 11), 396.

own subjectivity over the legislature's. Subjective decisions about how to pursue the common good are intrinsically political, and the democratic process, the election of the parliament as legislature, is the first and foremost way of legitimizing political decisions. When decisions are made on objective grounds, experts are legitimized to make them, and normative decisions about the legitimacy of an end and empirical decisions about the fitness and necessity of a means are sufficiently objective to be made by judicial experts. But their legal expertise cannot legitimize their rendering political decisions—not any better at least than democracy legitimizes the legislature. Judicial balancing is unproblematic as long as courts correct the balancing of lower courts or administrative agencies; this balancing takes place within the space that the legislature has designated for the judiciary and administration. Judicial balancing that corrects the legislature is and remains a problem. There is, as Antonio Scalia says about determining the weight of a government's need that conflicts with a private interest, 'a world of difference between the people's representatives' determining the need... and this court's doing so'.[47]

Judicial balancing does not necessarily make rights and freedoms stronger. The balancing process can tilt in both directions; it can strengthen rights and freedoms and it can weaken them. In either case it is a problem for democracy.

VI. The Future of Proportionality Analysis

1. Proportionality Analysis and Judicial Activism

Tolerating judicial balancing means modifying the democratic standard. It means accepting indirect democratic legitimacy as tantamount to direct democratic legitimacy—the appointment of judges by the president or the parliament as tantamount to the parliament's popular election. It also means a certain distrust in parliamentary decision-making and trust in judicial deliberation—the belief that experts in the law on a supreme or constitutional court have the wisdom and time to balance the crucial conflicts of a society more calmly and carefully than a legislature acting in the turbulence of political struggle. The courts that claim the right to control the balancing of the legislature and replace it with their own balancing know that balancing is democratically sensitive and never miss an opportunity to emphasize their respect for the legislature and legislative decision-making. Courts do not always interfere in the legislature's balancing. They interfere only on those occasions when they wish to, some courts more and some less.

This activism of courts can be related to a country's past, a past that may have bred more or less distrust or trust in the parliament or the courts. Countries with glorious revolutionary pasts tend to trust their parliaments more; parliaments were the offspring of the revolution, while courts were the conservative inheritance. Countries in which the democratic process set in motion fascist or communist dictatorships tend to hope that a strong supreme or constitutional court will reign in the political and legislative process and tame its dangerous tendencies. Countries with ethnic and religious conflicts tend to shift some of the burden of integration from politics to law and from the legislature to the supreme or constitutional court. But these are no more than tendencies, and grouping England and France into the first category, Germany, Spain, and Hungary into the second, and India and South Africa into the third can be done only with caution. The United States forms a group of its own and has developed its own brand of activism. There also seems to be a tendency at work that is unrelated to

[47] *Hamdi v Rumsfeld* 542 US 507 (2004).

the past. If the court's powers are not rigidly curtailed but allow some leeway, then courts embark on a journey into activism. Like all agencies, they expand to their limits.

Democracy is not the only ground for criticizing the activism of supreme and constitutional courts. Again and again criticism turns the principle of proportionality against itself; again and again politicians find proportionality analysis of legislation out of proportion. A statute has been prepared, deliberated, and decided in ministries, in committees, and in parliament—why now more empirical research into the efficiency and necessity of the statute, more balancing of rights and interests? It costs time, expertise, and patience, and in the end the court's decision may be as subjective as the parliament's. Is a fast decision not more productive and liberating than a fully researched and finely balanced decision that takes years? Is a decision that resolutely decides for or against the legislature not more pacifying than one that delves into proportionality and disproportionality and only emphasizes the complexity and difficulty of the issue?

Courts know about these criticisms as they know about the other problems of proportionality analysis. The twists and turns in their jurisprudence reflect not only the evolution of legal insight and doctrine on the bench but also the criticism that the courts encounter. They can affront the legislature once in a while, but not all the time. They have to develop a sense of how far they can push and where they have to give in. They have to develop a sense of their weight in the balance of powers. This is not opportunism; it is what an institution must do when its only authority—its shield and sword—rests on the word.

2. The Standardizing Effect of the Principle of Proportionality

The principle of proportionality has had a fantastic career: from a philosophical to a legal principle, from a principle of administrative law to a principle of constitutional law or even law as such. It has been named the ultimate rule of law,[48] and even though there is no such thing as an ultimate rule of law, the principle of proportionality is definitely a rule, at which all courts ultimately arrive. Even the US Supreme Court, shy about using the term, follows the rule in substance again and again.

Application of the principle has had and will have a standardizing effect on different constitutional cultures. Constitutional cultures with a doctrinal tradition will progressively be transformed in the direction of a culture of a case law. The oft-praised asset of proportionality analysis is its flexibility; from case to case facts may be assessed differently and rights and interests weighed and balanced differently. The case-specific configuration of facts, interests, and rights becomes more important and more significant than the doctrine that surrounds the case. Judges become more interested in finding the proportional solution for the case than in a decision that fits into established doctrine or helps to modify and to refine it. On the other hand, the principle of proportionality has a certain structuring quality and potency that introduces a minimal doctrinal element into constitutional cultures with a case law tradition.

Another way of viewing this is that the principle of proportionality does not have a standardizing effect on different constitutional cultures, but rather that it is a standard that constitutional cultures share and that they become more and more aware of. That it is part of a deep structure of constitutional grammar that forms the basis of all different constitutional languages and cultures. It comes to the surface as constitutions grow in theoretical and practical meaning.

[48] Beatty (n 19).

Bibliography

T. Alexander Aleinikoff, 'Constitutional Law in the Age of Balancing' (1987) 96 *Yale Law Journal* 943

Robert Alexy, *A Theory of Constitutional Rights* (German edn 1986, 2002)

Aharon Barak, 'Proportional Effect: The Israeli Experience' (2007) 57 *University of Toronto Law Journal* 369

David M. Beatty, *The Ultimate Rule of Law* (2004)

Dieter Grimm, 'Proportionality in Canadian and German Constitutional Jurisprudence' (2007) 57 *University of Toronto Law Journal* 383

Bernhard Schlink, 'Der Grundsatz der Verhaeltnismaessigkeit' in Peter Badura and Horst Dreier (eds), *Festschrift 50 Jahre Bundesverfassungsgericht*, vol 2 (2001)

Alex Stone Sweet and Jud Mathews, 'Proportionality Balancing and Global Constitutionalism' (2008) 47 *Columbia Journal of Transnational Law* 73

CHAPTER 34

PROPORTIONALITY (2)*

AHARON BARAK

Herzliya, Israel

* Translated from the Hebrew by Joel Linsider.

PROFESSOR Schlink has surveyed the scope of proportionality in all respects. In this chapter, I want to focus on one area governed by proportionality, namely, that of a right grounded in the constitution that is limited by a sub-constitutional norm (such as an 'ordinary' statute or common law rule). Such a limitation is constitutional only if it is proportional. I will consider as well the application of proportionality in those legal systems (such as the United Kingdom, New Zealand, and the Australian state of Victoria) in which there is no constitutional bill of rights and rights are based on a statute that provides, in its limitation clause, that the rights may be limited by law. That limitation, too, is lawful only if it is proportional.[1] In all of these matters I will concentrate on aspects that are complementary to those considered by Professor Schlink or on areas in which I disagree with him.

The starting point for my inquiry is the methodological aspect of proportionality as the standard for determining the constitutionality of a sub-constitutional norm that limits a constitutional right. That starting point is, by its nature, analytical, meant to investigate the legal construct on which proportionality is based. It will probe the four elements of proportionality—proper purpose, rational connection, necessity, and proportionality *stricto sensu* (balancing)—and investigate the formal role of proportionality in limiting a constitutional right.

The analytical investigation will determine the questions posed by the elements of proportionality, but analytical investigation alone cannot provide the answers to those questions. The answers are to be found primarily in the society's understanding of democracy, separation of powers, and constitutional rights. It is these answers that give proportionality its moral depth.

I. The Distinction between a Constitutional Right's Scope and Limitations on It

1. Scope and Limitation

The modern doctrine of constitutional rights took shape after the Second World War.[2] It distinguishes between two fundamental concepts: the scope of a constitutional right and the limitations to which it is subject.[3] The scope of a constitutional right defines the area that it covers—its content and its boundaries—and it can be changed only by constitutional amendment. The limitations on a constitutional right set the constitutional conditions under which the right may be less than fully realized. These conditions are based on the limitation clause, whether explicit or implied, and allow for a constitutional right to be limited, in a proportional manner, by a sub-constitutional (statutory or common law) norm. A small number of constitutional rights are absolute, subject to no limitations whatsoever.[4] Most constitutional human rights, however, are relative, subject to limitation by sub-constitutional norms. In some legal systems, relative rights have a core that cannot be limited;[5] that core is absolute. That a constitutional right is relative does not mean, however, that it is a prima facie right. A relative right is still a definite right.[6]

[1] See Aileen Kavanagh, *Constitutional Review under the UK Human Rights Act* (2009).

[2] See Lorraine Weinrib, 'The Post War Paradigm and American Exceptionalism' in Sujit Choudhry (ed), *The Migration of Constitutional Ideas* (2006), 84.

[3] See Gerhard Van der Schyff, *Limitation of Rights: A Study of the European Convention and the South African Bill of Rights* (2005), 11.

[4] eg the right not to be tortured: see the United Nations Convention against Torture and Other Cruel, Inhuman or Degrading Treatment or Punishment; under the German Basic Law human dignity is an absolute right: Art 1(1).

[5] See the German Basic Law, Art 19(2); Polish Constitution, Art 31(3).

[6] But see Robert Alexy, *A Theory of Constitutional Rights* (2002), 60.

This distinction between scope and limitation establishes two stages of constitutional analysis. At the first stage, the inquiry pertains to whether a constitutional right is limited by a sub-constitutional norm. At this stage, the burden of proof is on the party asserting the limitation. At the second stage, the inquiry considers whether the limitation on the constitutional right is proportional. The burden of proof at this stage is on the party asserting proportionality.

2. Scope of the Constitutional Right and Clash of Competing Rights

The scope of a constitutional right is determined in accord with the principles of constitutional interpretation[7]—in my view, on the basis of the purpose or rationale that underlies the right. In determining scope, one should not take account of any opposing constitutional right or conflicting public interest.[8] It follows that there will be many instances in which one constitutional right will clash with another. How are such conflicts to be resolved?[9] I would answer that when one of the competing rights is formulated as a rule (or both are so formulated), the conflict is resolved on the constitutional plane by application of the usual maxims under which the later norm prevails over the earlier (*lex posterior derogat priori*) and the specific norm prevails over the general (*lex specialis derogat legi generali*). These maxims determine the validity of the competing rights and their scope. That is not the case, however, where the competing rights are formulated as principles. In that event, the two rights maintain their full validity on the constitutional plane, and the clash must be resolved on the sub-constitutional plane. The validity of a law that limits one right (formulated as a principle) in order to realize the other (also formulated as a principle) will be determined in accord with the limitation clause—and that determination will be reached pursuant to the rules of proportionality.

3. The Role of Proportionality

The elements of proportionality are part of the constitution, explicitly stated in the limitation clause.[10] There may be a general limitation clause, applicable to all constitutional rights[11] or a specific limitation clause for each of them;[12] sometimes, both will exist side by side.[13] On occasion, a constitution will simply state that a constitutional right may be limited by law, making no explicit reference to proportionality, but the conventional view is that the limiting law must be proportional. In some cases, a constitution may declare the substance of a right without saying anything explicit about its limitation. The conventional view is that constitutional silence does not make the right absolute and that the right may be limited by law, as long as the limitation is proportional. In that situation, the proportionality is implied by the constitution; it is sometimes referred to as a 'judicial limitation clause'.

The proportional limitation of a constitutional right must be grounded in law. In civil law jurisdictions, that means the limitation must be in a statute enacted by the legislator. In common law jurisdictions, the limitation may also be in common law norms.[13a] In the absence of a law limiting a constitutional right, the question of proportionality becomes irrelevant.

[7] On constitutional interpretation, see Chapter 32 of this volume.

[8] See Aharon Barak, *Proportionality: Constitutional Rights and Their Limitation* (2012), ch 3.

[9] See Alexy (n 6); Eva Brems (ed), *Conflicts Between Fundamental Rights* (2008).

[10] See Van der Schyff (n 3).

[11] Canadian Charter of Human Rights, s 1; South African Constitution, s 36; Universal Declaration of Human Rights, Art 29.

[12] European Convention for the Protection of Human Rights and Fundamental Freedoms, Arts 7–11.

[13] See South African Constitution, 1996, ss 25–36.

[13a] See Barak (n 8), 118.

The formal role of proportionality is to ensure that a sub-constitutional norm limiting a constitutional right fulfills its four elements. If those elements are not fulfilled, the sub-constitutional norm will lack the force to limit the constitutional right, for a higher norm trumps a lower norm. In effect, then, the formal role of proportionality is to overcome the results of the constitutional norm's superiority. It follows that where a constitutional right is limited by another constitutional norm, the four elements of proportionality do not apply. The clash will be resolved not on the constitutional level but on the sub-constitutional level.

We have seen that proportionality is a legal construct. It puts in place four elements whose fulfillment will allow a limitation placed on a constitutional right by a sub-constitutional norm to be found constitutional. Every legal system that adopts proportionality must determine for itself, however, how the elements of proportionality are to be satisfied. In reaching such a conclusion, the legal system will be expressing its society's understanding of democracy. The conclusion will be derived from its position on the importance of constitutional rights and their relationship to the public interest and will reflect its approach to separation of powers and the role of each branch of government. Proportionality, then, is a framework that must be filled with content. The framework sets the four elements that must be fulfilled, but the content of those elements will be determined by a set of considerations that are external to proportionality and that inform it. That content therefore may vary from one legal system to another. But note: proportionality is not neutral with respect to human rights, and it is not indifferent to their limitation. It is grounded in the need to realize human rights. The limitations that proportionality imposes on the realization of constitutional rights draw their substance from the same source as the rights themselves; they are grounded in the society's understanding of democracy.

In sum, the elements of proportionality reflect the idea that a sub-constitutional norm may impose limits on a constitutional right, but that those limits are themselves bounded. This is the concept of 'limits on the limitations'.[14]

4. The Legal Sources of Proportionality

What is the legal source of proportionality?[14a] It appears by that name in only a handful of constitutions[15] and, even there, questions of interpretation arise regarding its elements. That is all the more so when it is not explicitly mentioned and is only implied. Some trace the jurisprudential origin of proportionality to democracy itself. Insofar as democracy has constitutional standing, it implies a need to strike a balance between human rights and countervailing constitutional principles. That balance is expressed through proportionality. Similarly, the rule of law (Rechtsstaat, l'état droit) may be seen as a principle having constitutional standing, from which proportionality may be inferred. Some see the basis for proportionality in the formulation of constitutional rights as principles. On this view, maintained by Alexy, 'principles are norms which require that something be realized to the greatest extent possible, given the legal and factual possibilities.'[16] The factual possibilities that limit realization of the principle are those set by the elements of proportionality pertaining to rational connection and necessity; the legal possibilities that limit realization of the principle are set by proportionality in the narrow sense, that is, balancing. It follows, according to Alexy's approach, that there is a direct and firm linkage between rights formulated as principles and proportionality. Finally, the source for proportionality may lie in constitutional interpretation. On this view, even if

[14] See Alexy (n 6), 192. [14a] See Barak (n 8), 211.

[15] See Swiss Federal Constitution, Art 36(3); Turkish Constitution, Art 13.

[16] See Alexy (n 6), 47.

proportionality is not explicitly mentioned in the constitution, it is implied by the architecture of human rights and public interest within it. These four explanations are complementary.

II. The Elements of Proportionality

1. Preliminary Remarks

Proportionality has four elements: proper purpose, rational connection, necessity, and proportionality in the narrow sense, that is, balance. Not all concur in that taxonomy, however. Some do not consider a proper purpose to be part of proportionality; others link the consideration of proper purpose to that of rational connection. At times, a legal system may not recognize one of the elements. The South African Constitution requires these four elements to be met, but states that they are not exclusive and that there may be other relevant considerations.[17]

The four elements of proportionality pertain with respect both to negative rights and to positive rights. Negative rights define the limitations on a constitutional right that the state is precluded from imposing. Positive rights define the actions that the state is obligated to take in order to protect a constitutional right.[18] With regard to negative rights, proportionality examines whether the limitation imposed by a law on the full realization of a constitutional right is proportional. With regard to positive rights, proportionality examines whether the failure to protect the full scope of the constitutional right is proportional. In both cases, the four elements noted above apply.[19]

In some common law jurisdictions, a question has arisen regarding the relationship between proportionality (with its four components) and reasonableness.[20] The latter is recognized in the administrative law of common law jurisdictions as a basis for judicial review of administrative actions, and it is sometimes applied in constitutional law as well. Does proportionality supplant reasonableness? The answers to these questions are not at all simple, given the lack of clarity regarding the elements of reasonableness.[21] We may distinguish between reasonableness in the weak sense and reasonableness in the strong sense.[22] Reasonableness in the weak sense sees an action as unreasonable if it is '[so] absurd that no sensible person could ever dream that it may lay within the powers of the authority'.[23] Reasonableness in this weak sense is not constructed step by step. It does not differentiate among various elements and does not clearly recognize a need to balance competing considerations. This way of thinking is substantively different from that associated with proportionality,[24] and the transition from

[17] See South African Constitution, 1996, s 36(1).

[18] See Alastair R. Mowbray, *The Development of Positive Obligations Under the European Convention on Human Rights by the European Court of Human Rights* (2004).

[19] See Dieter Grimm, 'The Protective Function of the State' in Georg Nolte (ed), *European and US Constitutionalism* (2005), 138; Alexy (n 6), 289.

[20] See Kavanagh (n 1), 243; Barak (n 8), 371.

[21] See Paul Craig, 'Unreasonableness and Proportionality in UK Law' in Evelyn Ellis (ed), *The Principle of Proportionality in the Laws of Europe* (1999), 85; Gráinne de Búrca, 'Proportionality and *Wednesbury* Unreasonableness: The Influence of European Legal Concepts on UK Law' (1997) 3 *European Public Law* 561; Jeffrey Jowell, 'Administrative Justice and Standards of Substantive Judicial Review' in Anthony Arnull, Piet Eeckhout, and Takis Tridimas (eds), *Continuity and Change in EU Law: Essays in Honour of Sir Francis Jacobs* (2008), 172; Michael Taggart, 'Proportionality, Deference, *Wednesbury*' (2008) *New Zealand Law Review* 423.

[22] See Wojciech Sadurski, '"Reasonableness" and Value Pluralism in Law and Politics' in Giorgio Bongiovanni, Giovanni Sartor, and Chiara Valentini (eds), *Reasonableness and Law* (2009), 129.

[23] See *Associated Provincial Picture Houses v Wednesbury Corporation* [1948] 1 KB 223.

[24] See *R v Secretary of State for the Home Department, ex p Daly* [2001] 3 All ER 433.

reasonableness in the weak sense to proportionality may be difficult. Reasonableness in the strong sense, however, is based on a balancing of competing interests. A decision is reasonable in the strong sense, if it was reached after giving due consideration to the various factors that should be taken into account. Reasonableness in this sense strikes a proper balance among the relevant considerations,[25] and it does not differ substantively from proportionality. Proportionality can be seen as a further development of reasonableness,[26] and there need be no difficulty in principle in making the transition between them

Finally, a question arises regarding when the four elements of proportionality must be satisfied by a law limiting a constitutional right. Is it enough that they are satisfied when the law is enacted? Or is it necessary that they are met on an ongoing basis? In my view, the requirements of proportionality are ongoing. The law to which they apply remains subject to them for as long as it remains in force.

2. Proper Purpose

The *first* element of proportionality requires that a law limiting a constitutional right has a proper purpose.[26a] This is a threshold requirement that does not entail concrete balancing. It is generally acknowledged that a limitation on a constitutional right is constitutional if it is intended to protect other rights (constitutional or sub-constitutional).[27] One enters a gray area with respect to proper purpose, however, when the constitutional right is to be limited to promote the public interest. What public interest can justify limiting a constitutional right? At times, the constitution itself will specify the public interests whose realization will warrant limiting certain constitutional rights. But what does one do when the constitution says nothing in that regard? German constitutional law regards it as sufficient that the public interest is not contrary to the constitution.[28] Canadian constitutional law, in contrast, requires that the public interest be pressing and pressing and substantial.[29] In both systems, the requirement of proper purpose applies to all constitutional rights, without any effort to distinguish among rights on the basis of their importance.

3. Rational Connection

The *second* component of proportionality is that the means adopted by the law must be capable of advancing the realization of its proper purpose.[30] This does not require that the means be the only one that can attain the purpose, or that it realize the purpose in full, or that it do so efficiently. The requirement is that the means have the potential to advance the purpose to some extent that is not merely marginal, scant, or theoretical.

[25] See Neil MacCormick, 'On Reasonableness' in C. Perelman and R. van der Elst (eds), *Les Notions A Contenu Variable En Droit* (1984), 131, 136; Robert Alexy, 'The Reasonableness of Law' in Giorgio Bongiovanni, Giovanni Sartor, and Chiara Valentini (eds), *Reasonableness and Law* (2009), 5.

[26] See G.N. Barrie, 'Proportionality—Expanding the Bounds of Reasonableness' in Gretchen Carpenter, *Suprema Lex: Essays on the Constitution Presented to Marinus Wiechers* (1998), 25.

[26a] See Barak (n 8), 245.

[27] See Declaration of the Rights of Man and of the Citizen, 1789, Art 4.

[28] See Dieter Grimm, 'Proportionality in Canadian and German Constitutional Jurisprudence' (2007) 57 *University of Toronto Law Journal* 383, 388.

[29] See *R v Oakes* [1986] 1 SCR 103, para 69.

[30] See Nicholas Emiliou, *The Principle of Proportionality in European Law: A Comparative Study* (1996), 28; Alexy (n 6), 135; Carlos Bernal Pulido, *El principio de proporcionalidad y los derechos fundamentals* (2007), 726; Wojciech Sadurski, *Rights Before Courts: A Study of Constitutional Courts in Postcommunist States of Central and Eastern Europe* (1990), 268; Barak (n 8), 303.

4. Necessity

The *third* component of proportionality requires that the proper purpose is not attainable by some other means less restrictive of the constitutional right.[31] If there exists some equally effective alternative that would entail less of a limitation on the constitutional right, the law in question is not necessary.[32] If, however, the alternative would intrude less on the constitutional right but would be able to attain the law's proper purpose only in part, the law would be necessary. It would be necessary as well if the alternative, though able to attain the law's proper purpose in full, would limit some other right or impair some other public interest. Accordingly, the law is necessary if an alternative is less restrictive of the constitutional right but more costly. Of course, rejection of those alternatives may not pass muster under the balancing test required by the fourth element of proportionality (proportionality *stricto sensu*).

The necessity test requires that the means selected by the law be tailored to realizing the proper purpose. One 'cannot shoot a sparrow with a canon';[33] the means must be suited to the ends. When the purpose can be attained by a means less restrictive of constitutional rights that means should be selected, and there is no necessity for the law under review. But while over-inclusiveness should be avoided, it becomes necessary when it is impossible to separate the narrower measures needed to realize the law's purpose from those that are over-inclusive. In these circumstances, the over-inclusiveness is dealt with in the context of the fourth component, that of balancing. As an example, consider a law whose purpose is to protect the public interest and the rights of the individual against terrorists. Given the inability to distinguish a terrorist from a non-terrorist by individual examination, a general prohibition may be imposed that affects the rights of non-terrorists as well. That inability to rely on individual examination (which imposes less of a limitation on the constitutional right) transforms the general prohibition (which limits the constitutional right comprehensively) into something necessary.[34]

5. Proportionality *Stricto Sensu*—Balancing

(a) The Social Importance of the Purpose and of Avoiding the Limitation on the Constitutional Right

The *fourth* element of proportionality requires a proper relationship between the social benefit of realizing the proper purpose and the social benefit of avoiding the limitation of the constitutional right.[35] The element of rational connection and the element of necessity deal with the relationship between the law's purpose and the means it adopts for realizing that purpose. The means–ends analysis conducted at that stage does not consider whether attaining the purpose is worth the associated limitation on the constitutional right; it is not based on balancing. But things are quite different when we come to proportionality *stricto sensu*. At that stage, we examine the relationship between the law's purpose and the constitutional rights that are affected, and that examination entails balancing.[36]

[31] See Pulido (n 30), 737; Emiliou (n 30), 30; Barak (n 8), 317.

[32] See Julian Rivers, 'Proportionality and Variable Intensity of Review' (2006) 65 *Cambridge Law Journal* 174, 189.

[33] See Fritz Fleiner, *Institutionen des deutschen Verwaltungsrechts* (1928), 404; *R v Goldstein* [1983] 1 WLR 151, 155.

[34] See HCJ 7052/03 *Adalah—A Legal Center for the Rights of the Arab Minority v Minister of Interior* [2006] (1) IsrLR 442, para 88 (Barak P).

[35] See Grimm (n 28), 396; Barak (n 8), 340.

[36] See Rivers (n 32), 200; Moshe Cohen-Eliya and Gila Stopler, 'Prioritizing Rights in the Age of Balancing' (2010) 4(1) *Law and Ethics of Human Rights*.

To speak of 'balancing' is to speak metaphorically,[37] but the mode of thought is normative. It is based on legal rules that determine when a proper purpose may be realized despite the limitation on a constitutional right. There is no consensus, however, regarding the substance of those legal rules. In my view, they should be based on a balancing of the social importance of the benefit gained by realizing the purpose (protecting rights or promoting the public interest) on the one hand and, on the other, the social importance of avoiding the limitation on the constitutional right.[38]

The comparison does not consider the overall importance of the purpose or the overall importance of the constitutional right being limited. Rather, the comparison is between the status of the purpose and the status of the right before and after the limiting law. The social importance of the law's marginal effect on attainment of the purpose is balanced against the social importance of avoiding the law's marginal limitation of the right. The comparison, then, is made in terms of marginal social benefit.[39]

On occasion, the scope of the comparison is even narrower. That is so when the inquiry into necessity considers an alternative less restrictive of the constitutional right but unable to realize in full the purpose of the law. Because it cannot realize the purpose in full, the less restrictive alternative does not preclude a finding of necessity. Nevertheless, insofar as the alternative is proportional, it may strike the proper balance between the importance of the marginal benefit of realizing the purpose and the importance of the marginal benefit of avoiding limitation of the right.

The social importance of the marginal benefit in realizing the purpose depends on the nature of the purpose. Not all proper purposes are of equal social importance. When the purpose is protection of a constitutional right, the marginal social benefit depends on the importance of the protected right. When the purpose is protection of a public interest, the marginal social benefit depends on the importance of attaining the purpose. That importance—with respect both to the protection of constitutional rights and to the advancing of the public interest—will be a function of the social history of the state, its socio-political ideology, its political and governmental structure, and its commitment to democratic values. In dealing with these matters, it is necessary to see society and its normative structure as a whole.

In determining the social importance of the marginal benefit in realizing the purpose, we must take account—when the purpose is protection of human rights—the degree of protection these rights enjoyed before the law and the protection they will be afforded under the law. That is the case as well with social purposes related to promoting a public interest. In all of these, we should consider the likelihood that the purpose will be realized if the law is allowed to stand. That likelihood depends on the factual situation and on a prognosis regarding the possibility that the purpose will be realized.[40]

The social importance of avoiding the limitation of the constitutional right depends on the social importance of the right. The key question here is whether all constitutional rights are of equal social importance. That is an issue on which there is no consensus. I believe that all constitutional rights are not equal with respect to their social importance. The importance of a constitutional right is determined on the basis of both external and internal considerations.

[37] See William Winslade, 'Adjudication and the Balancing Metaphor' in H. Hubien (ed), *Legal Reasoning* (1971), 403.

[38] See Moshe Cohen-Eliya and Iddo Porat, 'American Balancing and German Proportionality: The Historical Origins' (2010) 8(2) *International Journal of Constitutional Law* 263.

[39] See Grimm (n 28), 396.

[40] See Alexy (n 6), 44; Julian Rivers, 'Proportionality, Discretion and the Second Law of Balancing' in George Pavlakos (ed), *Law, Rights, and Discourse: The Legal Philosophy of Robert Alexy* (2007).

External considerations include the society's basic concepts, its social and cultural history, and its particular character. That sort of external background allows us, for example, to understand the great importance assigned in post-Nazi Germany and post-apartheid South Africa to the values of human dignity and equality. Internal considerations take account of the relationships among the various rights. In that sense, a right that serves as a precondition to the existence and operation of another right is regarded as the more important of the two. Hence the high social importance of the rights to life, dignity, equality, and political expression.

The social importance of avoiding the limitation of a right is influenced by the scope of the limitation and its extent. The severity of the limitation also bears on the social importance of avoiding it. A limitation on one right, accordingly, is not the same as a limitation on several; a limitation that approaches the core of a right is not the same as one that affects it only on its margins; a permanent limitation is not the same as a temporary one; and a limitation very likely to eventuate is not the same as one whose probability of realization is more remote.

(b) The Rule of Balancing

The balance between the marginal social benefit in realizing the purpose and the marginal social benefit in avoiding the limitation on the constitutional right can be expressed as follows:[40a] as the importance of avoiding the marginal limitation on the constitutional right and the likelihood of the limitation coming to pass increase, so do the required importance of the marginal benefit to the public interest or the competing private right and the required likelihood of that benefit being realized. This approach is consistent with the substantive law balancing developed by Alexy, according to which[41] 'the greater the degree of non-satisfaction of, or detriment to one principle, the greater must be the importance of satisfying the other.' Note, though, the difference between Alexy's approach and mine. Alexy does not take account of the importance of the right being limited but only of the degree of limitation. My balancing rule, in contrast, considers not only degree but also the importance of the purpose and the importance of the constitutional right. It thereby gives voice to the society's perspective on the marginal importance of the social purpose that the law means to advance—its substance and likelihood of realization—and on the marginal social importance of avoiding a limitation on a constitutional right that the society wants to protect.

What happens if the balance is even, and the marginal social importance of achieving the purpose equals the marginal importance of avoiding the limitation on the constitutional right?[42] The solution flows from fundamental concepts of constitutional democracy, regarding which there are likely to be differing and even conflicting opinions. It seems to me that where one constitutional right is limited in order to protect another, there is no reason to impugn the constitutionality of the limiting legislation. Where, however, the constitutional right is limited in order to advance the public interest, the constitutional right should be afforded priority: *in dubio pro libertate.*

(c) Development of the Proportionality Stricto Sensu Element (Balancing)

The central element of proportionality is that of balancing, expressed in the rule of balancing. That rule exists at a very high level of abstraction. It does not relate to specific aspects of various rights; does not focus on the principles that underlie the various rights and

[40a] See Barak (n 8), 345.

[41] See Alexy (n 6), 102; Pulido (n 30), 767.

[42] See Alexy (n 6), 411; Carlos Bernal Pulido, 'On Alexy's Weight Formula' in Agustín José Menéndez and Erik Oddvar Eriksen (eds), *Arguing Fundamental Rights* (2006), 104.

justify their being protected or limited; and does not reflect the considerations characteristic of proper protection of constitutionality. Against that background, I propose recognition of an additional level of norms, intermediate between the (highly abstract) basic rule of balancing and its practical implementation in each case (ie, concrete balancing). It could be termed 'principle balancing', and it would translate the basic rule of balancing into rules of balancing in principle that would be formulated at a level of abstraction below that of the basic rule but above that of concrete balancing. That level of abstraction would express the considerations of principle that underlie a constitutional right and the justifications for limiting it.[43]

Consider, for example, a law that limits the freedom of political expression, a right of the highest importance. Assume that the purpose of the restriction is to protect the public order against political speech that incites violence. The principle balancing in the clash between freedom of political expression and protection of public order against violent, inciting speech may determine that a limitation on political expression is acceptable only if the purpose of protecting public order against this speech's incitement to violence is deemed vital to achieving some pressing social need, such as avoiding widespread, immediate harm to the public order. Principle balancing is marked by its operation at a level of abstraction below that of balancing's basic rule but higher than that of concrete balancing. It operates at a level of abstraction that expresses the reasons underlying the right and justifying either its impairment or its protection.

III. The Zone of Proportionality

1. Legislator and Judge

The rules of proportionality are directed toward all branches of government. They grant governmental authorities discretion; that is, the power to choose among a number of constitutional options. But that discretion is not absolute. All governmental authority is restrained by the rules of proportionality, and the same rules of proportionality apply to all governmental authorities. Within the context of those rules, however, each governmental authority has its own characteristic sort of discretion, determined in accord with its role within the framework of separation of powers.[44]

Under the separation of powers, the role of the judicial branch is to ensure that the legislative branch deploys its legislative authority within the constitutional framework. The legislative branch is independent within its area of discretion as long as it acts within its powers. Separation of powers does not grant the legislator license to violate the constitution. In the event of a dispute over the scope of the legislative branch's constitutional authority, there must exist a mechanism for deciding whether the legislative branch has exceeded its authority. The mechanism must be independent of the legislative branch. It should be in the hands of the judicial branch. What follows from this is recognition of the judiciary's power to exercise judicial review of the constitutionality of a statute, either by declaration of incompatibility or by decision that the law is void. Judicial review is not intended to replace the legislative structure with one enacted by the judiciary. The court does not step into the legislator's shoes and does not ask itself what purpose it would want to serve through legislation. It examines the constitutionality of the statute, not its wisdom.

[43] See Cohen-Eliya and Stopler (n 36); Barak (n 8), 340.

[44] See Rivers (n 40), 108.

There is a widespread view, especially within common law systems, that in deciding the constitutionality of a statute, the court must defer to the decision of the legislative branch.[45] That deference would cause no problem if it meant only that the judicial branch was required to respect the legislative branch and consider its positions with seriousness, care, and restraint. Separation of powers itself requires no less. But deference includes something more; not satisfied merely with respect, it calls for submission.[46] On that approach, the judge is required to accept the legal position of the legislative branch with regard to the elements of proportionality in circumstances where, but for the commitment to deference, it would not accept it.[47] In my view there is no place for deference as I have defined it. I reason as follows: if the position taken by the legislative branch with regard to the elements of proportionality is sound even in the absence of deference, the judge is obligated to follow it regardless of deference. If, on the other hand, the position taken by the legislative branch is unsound in the absence of deference, the judge is obligated to reject it regardless of deference. Either way, deference plays no role.

2. The Zone of Proportionality and the Margin of Appreciation

The rules of proportionality leave the legislator an area of discretion encompassing such matters as the need for legislation, its purposes, the means adopted for attaining those purposes, and the limitations that might be imposed on constitutional rights. The legislator may set the relationship among those items as long as the rules of proportionality are satisfied; within the zone of proportionality, the legislator has freedom to maneuver. The boundaries of the zone of proportionality are what separate legislator from judge, consistent with the separation of powers. The zone of proportionality is the domain of the legislator. Maintaining the boundaries of that zone is the domain of the judge.

We must distinguish between the zone of proportionality and the margin of appreciation.[48] The latter affords an area of discretion to national bodies, in contrast to the discretion of the international court; among other things, it recognizes that there is no international consensus regarding the relative social importance of public interests and individual rights. Accordingly, it is proper to take account of the importance assigned them in the state whose law is being challenged as disproportionately restricting a human right set in an international agreement. Against that background, one can see the difference between the zone of proportionality and the margin of appreciation. The former reflects the constitutionality of a limitation on a right from a national point of view, while the latter reflects the constitutionality from an international perspective. The zone of proportionality expresses the boundary dividing the national legislator's discretion from that of the national judge; it is derived from the principle of separation of powers. The margin of appreciation, in contrast, expresses the boundary that separates the discretion of the national body—whether legislative, executive, or judicial—from the discretion of the international judge. It is not tied to the principle of separation of powers. Accordingly, margin of appreciation should not be relevant in the context of national law or to relationships between legislator and judge in that context.[49] In those contexts, only the zone of proportionality is applicable.

[45] On deference, see Barak (n 8), 379.

[46] See David Dyzenhaus, 'The Politics of Deference: Judicial Review and Democracy' in M. Taggart (ed), *The Province of Administrative Law* (1997), 279.

[47] See Paul Horwitz, 'Three Faces of Deference' (2008) 83 *Notre Dame Law Review* 1061, 1072.

[48] See Yutaka Arai-Takahashi, *The Margin of Appreciation Doctrine and the Principle or Proportionality in the Jurisprudence of the ECHR* (2002), 2; Barak (n 8), 415.

[49] See Rivers (n 32), 175.

IV. Assessing Proportionality

1. The Importance of Proportionality

Since the Second World War, the idea of proportionality (with balance at its core) has developed and come to be increasingly recognized. The principal reason for its success[49a] has been its insistence that governmental bodies justify every sub-constitutional limitation on a constitutional right. That justification is always subject to review, and the result of the requirement has been the emergence of a 'culture of justification'.[50] Democracy is based on human rights, and the restriction of those rights cannot become routine. It requires continuing justification, grounded in public reason.[51] The mindset associated with proportionality looks toward ongoing inquiry into whether there exists a pertinent justification for limiting a right, taking account of the circumstances of each case.

Proportionality is based on structured discretion, a process offering numerous advantages.[52] It requires the agent exercising that discretion to think in an orderly manner, overlooking nothing that should be taken into account. It makes the process transparent,[53] allowing its stages to be traced. That transparency enhances faith in the constitutionality of the decisions reached by governmental bodies and makes it possible to understand their bases. Understanding, in turn, promotes respect, even on the part of one who does not agree with the result. Transparency is the basis for intelligent public discourse and for a dialogue between the legislative and judicial branches,[54] precluding ulterior considerations and guaranteeing a high degree of objectivity.[55] Moreover, structuring the exercise of discretion promotes consideration of the proper factors within the proper contexts. It ensures, for example, that considerations related to the public interest or to protection of a constitutional right are taken into account at the stage in which restriction of the right is justified and not at the stage when the scope of the right is being set.

2. Criticism of Proportionality and Responses to It

Proportionality is subject to persistent criticism, directed primarily at the element of proportionality *stricto sensu*, that is, balancing.[56] The criticism can be divided into internal and external aspects,[57] and I will attempt to respond to both. I hope my responses are adequately

[49a] See Barak (n 8), 457.

[50] See Etienne Mureinik, 'A Bridge to Where? Introduction to the interim Bill of Rights' (1994) 10 *South African Journal on Human Rights* 31, 32; Moshe Cohen-Eliya and Iddo Porat, 'Proportionality and the Culture of Justification' (2011) 59 *American Journal of Comparative Law* 463.

[51] See Mattias Kumm, 'The Idea of Socratic Contestation and the Right to Justification: The Point of Rights based Proportionality Review' (2010) 4(2) *Law and Ethics of Human Rights* 141.

[52] See David M. Beatty, *The Ultimate Rule of Law* (2004), 172.

[53] See Sadurski (n 22), 139.

[54] On dialogue between legislatures and courts see Peter W. Hogg and Allison A. Bushell, 'The Charter Dialogue between Courts and Legislatures (Or Perhaps the Charter of Rights Isn't Such a Bad Thing After All)' (1997) 35 *Osgoode Hall Law Journal* 75; Peter W. Hogg and Allison A. Bushell, 'Reply to Six Degrees of Dialogue' (1999) 37 *Osgoode Hall Law Journal* 529; Kent Roach, 'Dialogue or Defiance: Legislative Reversals of Supreme Court Decisions in Canada and the United States' (2006) 4 *International Journal of Constitutional Law* 347.

[55] See Beatty (n 52).

[56] See Louis Henkin, 'Infallibility Under Law: Constitutional Balancing' (1978) 78 *Columbia Law Review* 1022; Stavros Tsakyrakis, 'Proportionality: An Assault on Human Rights?' (2003) 7 *International Journal of Constitutional Law* 468; Iddo Porat, 'The Dual Model of Balancing: A Model for the Proper Scope of Balancing in Constitutional Law' (2006) 27 *Cardozo Law Review* 1393; Grégoire Webber, *The Negotiable Constitution: On The Limitation of Rights* (2009); Stavros Tsakyrakis, 'Proportionality: An Assault on Human Rights?: A Rejoinder to Madhav Khosla' (2010) 8(2) *International Journal of Constitutional Law* 307; Barak (n 8), 481.

[57] See Alexander Aleinikoff, 'Constitutional Law in the Age of Balancing' (1987) 96 *Yale Law Journal* 943, 972.

reassuring; in any case—and this is the basis for my entire response—the alternatives offered by the critics are no better. Their deficiencies exceed those of proportionality.

The internal criticism maintains that the common denominator required for genuine balancing does not exist; the sides of the balance are incommensurable.[58] In the absence of commensurability, the balancing is not rational; it is intuitive, improvised, subjective, and imprecise. Its use of the balancing metaphor conveys a false sense of being scientific.

My response to the internal criticism is that a common denominator allowing for rational balancing exists;[59] it is the social importance of realizing one principle and avoiding limitation of another principle. The question posed is whether the marginal social benefit of the first principle suffices to justify the marginal limitation of the second. This contextual posing of the balancing affords it a common, rational basis. True, the balancing is not syllogistic and sometimes affords the balancer (be it legislator, executive, or judge) discretion, but the presence of discretion does not mean the balancing lacks rationality.[60]

The external criticism takes several forms.[60a] It is urged, first, that the element of balancing affords the judge excessive discretion, thereby impairing both legal certainty and protection of human rights. It is argued as well that balancing is the role of the legislator. A judge who engages in balancing is acting without constitutional legitimacy, for he is trespassing on the legislator's turf, contravening the separation of powers, and behaving undemocratically. Moreover, it is claimed, the judge lacks the tools needed to conduct proper balancing. The characteristics of the judicial process make the judicial perspective too narrow, and the judge has only limited ability to deal with empirical data. Finally, judicial insight leads to a narrowing of the scope of discretion, to the point that proportionality will fail to include the element of balancing.

Certainly, the balancing component affords the judge discretion. But by what standard can that discretion be said to be too broad? If the standard is that of the alternatives to proportionality, they, too, afford the judge discretion, and it has not been shown that the discretion associated with proportionality is broader. Is the discretion of the German Federal Constitutional Court broader than that of the US Supreme Court? How could such an assertion be proven? But even if the discretion associated with proportionality is broader, what harm is there in that? It has not been shown, for example, that legal systems in which proportionality and its associated balancing are accepted manifest less legal certainty than do other systems. And if there is a flaw in the scope of discretion afforded the judge under proportionality, is that flaw outweighed by the associated benefit? The critics of the balancing element of proportionality have not responded adequately to those questions.

With respect to protecting human rights, two points should be made. *First*, there is no reason to assume a priori that judges will afford less protection to human rights under a system of proportionality (centered on balancing) than under its alternatives. Proportionality is a framework that needs to be filled with content, and it allows for varied degrees of protection. *Secondly*, no proof has been offered that, as a practical matter, protection of human

[58] On incommensurability see Ruth Chang (ed), *Incommensurability, Incomparability, and Practical Reason* (1997), and the symposium on law and incommensurability at (1998) 146 *University of Pennsylvania Law Review* 1168.

[59] See Pulido (n 30), 789; Virgílio Afonso da Silva, 'Comparing the Incommensurable: Constitutional Principles, Balancing, and Rational Decision' (2011) 31(2) *Oxford Journal of Legal Studies* 273.

[60] See Robert Alexy, 'Constitutional Rights, Balancing, and Rationality' (2003) 16 *Ratio Juris* 131; Alexy (n 6), 101; Frederick Schauer, 'Balancing, Subsumption and the Constraining Role of Legal Text' in Matthias Klatt (ed), *Rights, Law, and Morality: Themes from the Legal Philosophy of Robert Alexy* (2009) ; Barak (n 8), 487.

[60a] See Barak (n 8), 482.

rights is any less under legal systems applying proportionality and balancing than under other legal systems. Moreover, it is hard to see how such a claim could be proven. The picture tends to be complicated enough to preclude an unambiguous answer. A precise answer would require examination of each and every right, at both the theoretical and the practical levels.

The formal answer to the asserted illegitimacy of judicial balancing is that the authority to conduct judicial review in general, and the judge's authority to balance competing principles (in the context of ruling on the limitation of a right) in particular, are grounded (expressly or impliedly) in the constitution itself. Just as the constitution affords legislative authority to the legislator, it affords to the judge the authority to determine that a statute is not proportional.

The substantive response to the charge of being undemocratic is that judicial balancing in fact safeguards democracy and separation of powers, protecting the constitution and ensuring that any limitation of rights is proportional. That safeguarding is the role of the judiciary under the separation of powers.[61] Of course, the legislator also strikes a balance between the rights of the individual and the public interest. But under the separation of powers, the final decision on the constitutionality of the balance struck by the legislator is vested in the judiciary. Just as separation of powers as applied in administrative law grants the judicial branch and not the executive final say with regard to balancing in the context of proportionality, so does the principle as applied in constitutional law grant the judicial branch and not the legislative final say with regard to balancing in the context of proportionality. Vesting the court with final say over balancing ensures the constitutional protection of human rights and realizes substantive democracy, based on a delicate balance between majority rule and individual rights.[62] The institutional structure of the court, its independence, and its remove from political pressures make judicial balancing closer than any other to the balancing required by the constitution. What really underlies the criticism of proportionality and balancing is nothing more than the general argument made against judicial review of a law's constitutionality—an issue beyond the scope of this chapter.

It is argued that the court lacks the tools needed to conduct the balancing required by proportionality, I believe that this argument is insufficiently supported. The structure of the system allows the court to assess the facts presented to it and examine whether they have been deployed in a proportional manner. That is what a judge does when he decides, in a tort case, whether a physician, a pilot, or an engineer acted negligently, and he can do the same thing in a constitutional law context, deciding whether the balancing has been done in a way that satisfies the requirement of proportionality. But note: the goal of the inquiry is not to enable the judge to put in place a new legislative structure that will be constitutional; it is to determine the constitutionality of the structure put in place by the legislator. The purpose of the court's examination is not to set national priorities; it is to decide whether the legislation enacted in accord with the priorities set by the legislator is proportional.

As for judicial insight, I note only that judicial insight cannot replace constitutional obligation. The court is not out to protect its power and its authority; it means to protect democracy and the constitution. If the constitution intends to preclude the court from implementing proportionality in general and balancing in particular, it should say so explicitly.

[61] See Jörg P. Muller, 'Fundamental Rights in Democracy' (1983) 4 *Human Rights Law Journal* 131; Stephen Gardbaum, 'A Democratic Defense of Constitutional Balancing' (2010) 4(1) *Law and Ethics of Human Rights* 77.

[62] See Kumm (n 51).

3. Alternatives to Proportionality

(a) *Proportionality Determined by the Legislator*

Proportionality is a device used to resolve clashes among constitutional rights and between constitutional rights and the public interest. But it is not the only device available for that purpose; others exist as well.[63] Central to them is the alternative that might be termed categorization, commonly used in the United States. Other alternatives include that proposed by Webber,[64] who suggests that the scope of constitutional rights is set by interpretation and construction by the legislature. The limitations are themselves part of the constitutional right, neither impairing nor negating it; rather, they fix its substance in according with the society's understanding at any given time. These understandings are expressed through the legislator's ordinary legislative process, which expresses the popular will. The legislator acts subject to the direction of the limitation clause, which requires the legislator to give voice to the right's underlying justification within a free and democratic society. It is the legislator that determines the limits of the right itself. Once those limits are set, the right is absolute. Proportionality and the balance at its core play no role and do not constrain the legislator. The judicial role is limited to considering whether the legislator's exercise of discretion was arbitrary.

Underlying Webber's negative approach to proportionality and balance is his concept of constitutional rights, a concept that strikes me as erroneous. The conventional, and proper, approach regards constitutional rights as meant to protect the individual against the majority, whose will is expressed through the legislator. On Webber's approach, in contrast, it is the majority, again expressing itself through the legislator, that determines the scope of constitutional rights. The limitations on legislative power, according to Webber, are narrow. It seems to me that Webber's understanding allows no room for a constitutional bill of rights; no room for limitations on legislative power with respect to human rights; no room for substantive judicial review of a statute that impairs constitutional rights; and certainly no room for proportionality and balancing as ways to limit that impairment. Webber's approach, then, is not simply an alternative to proportionality; it is an alternative to the conventional idea of constitutional rights. By treating the constitution as an ongoing process of negotiation within society, resolved by the legislator, he effectively divests the constitutional bill of rights of its power to protect the individual against the majority. What is presented as a constitutional right is really nothing more than a right at the sub-constitutional level. Interpreting the right and setting its limits from time to time are entirely the province of the legislator.

(b) *US Categorization*

The accepted approach in US constitutional law distinguishes substantively but not exclusively[64a] among three categories of constitutional right, each subject to a different level of constitutional scrutiny. What the three categories have in common is a lack of concrete balancing between the benefit of realizing the goal and the impairment of the constitutional right.[65] True, each category is based on a definitional or principled balancing that determines the scope of the right.[66]

[63] See Porat (n 56).

[64] See Webber (n 56), 1087, 1088.

[64a] See Alec Stone Sweet and Jud Mathews, 'All Things in Proportion? American Rights Doctrine and the Problem of Balancing' (2011) 60 *Emory Law Journal* 797.

[65] See Frederick Schauer, 'Categories and the First Amendment: A Play in Three Acts' (1981) 34 *Vanderbilt Law Review* 265; Kathleen M. Sullivan, 'Post-Liberal Judging: The Roles of Categorization and Balancing' (1992) 62 *University of Colorado Law Review* 293; Stone Sweet and Mathews (n 64a).

[66] See Melville B. Nimmer, 'The Right To Speak from Times To Time: First Amendment Theory Applied to Libel and Misapplied to Privacy' (1968) 56 *California Law Review* 935, 944.

But once such balancing is done, no further concrete (ad hoc) balancing is applied. The scope of this chapter does not allow for a full examination of the US system, including the way in which it determines the scope of the various rights and the limitations it imposes on each. US jurisprudence is extremely rich, marked by a range of different and even opposing perspectives[67] on how the scope of a right is determined, how the limitations on it are set, and how the two processes interact. I will therefore confine myself to analyzing the three levels of scrutiny that are accepted in US constitutional law,[68] without claiming thereby to have surveyed the US system in its full complexity.

First is the category of rights that US constitutional law terms 'fundamental rights'. These include freedom of expression and assembly, freedom of religion, freedom of movement within the country, and the right to vote. Also within this category is the right to equality, that is, to be free of suspect forms of discrimination based on residence, race, or certain other categories. A law restricting any of the rights in this category will be subjected to strict scrutiny,[69] extending both to the purposes of the statute and to the means selected for attaining them. With respect to purpose, a statute limiting a right in this category will be held unconstitutional unless it is meant to serve a compelling state interest or is a matter of pressing public necessity or substantial state interest. The means selected must be necessary and narrowly tailored to attaining the purpose. This idea entails two corollaries: that there not be some other means that would be less restrictive of the right and that the means not be over-inclusive or under-inclusive.

The second category includes equality, when the distinctions that are applied are 'quasi-suspect',[70] such as those related to gender or age, among other things. It also includes restrictions on commercial expression and on expression in a public forum. Legislative action in this category will pass constitutional muster only if its purpose is to serve an important governmental objective. The means selected to carry out the purpose will be constitutional if there is a substantial relation between them and the purpose (intermediate scrutiny).

The third category encompasses all other constitutional rights.[71] It includes the avoidance of discrimination on the basis of categories that are neither suspect (residence, race) nor quasi-suspect (gender, age), as well as other rights such as freedom of movement outside the United States. Restrictions on rights in this category are constitutional if they serve a legitimate governmental purpose; further inquiry into the importance of that purpose is not required. The means for attaining the purpose will be constitutional if they have a rational basis. In assessing rational basis, account is taken of consequences and of possible alternatives (minimal scrutiny).

It appears that US law's intermediate and minimal levels of scrutiny allow for broader limitations on the rights to which they pertain than would proportionality.[71a] Comparing the effects of strict scrutiny and proportionality is more difficult, however. The difficulty is twofold: a theoretical difficulty flowing from US law's lack of clarity regarding the terms of strict scrutiny, and a practical one related to comparing the effects of the differing requirements in practice.

When it comes to proper purpose, the requirements imposed by strict scrutiny appear more stringent than those required by most legal systems that make use of proportionality. The

[67] See Richard H. Fallon, 'Individual Rights and the Powers of Government' (1993) 27 *Georgia Law Review* 343, 362; Stephen Gardbaum, 'Limiting Constitutional Rights' (2007) 54 *UCLA Law Review* 789, 807; Stephen Gardbaum, 'The Myth and the Reality of American Constitutional Exceptionalism' (2008) 107 *Michigan Law Review* 391.

[68] See Laurence H. Tribe, *American Constitutional Law* (2nd edn, 1998), 769; Erwin Chemerinsky, *Constitutional Law: Principles and Policies* (3rd edn, 2006), 539.

[69] See Richard H. Fallon, 'Strict Judicial Scrutiny' (2007) 54 *UCLA Law Review* 1267.

[70] See Chemerinsky (n 68), 540.

[71] Ibid.

[71a] See Barak (n 8), 515.

principal difficulty is centered on the US requirement that the means be 'narrowly tailored' to attaining the purpose, requiring, among other things, the avoidance of over-breadth. But what is the result if the excess breadth is inherent, incapable of being severed, and the statutory purposes cannot be attained without means that entail over-breadth?[71b] The answer in US jurisprudence is not without uncertainty. If US law holds that inseverable over-breadth means the statute is not narrowly tailored to its purpose, it affords greater protection to rights invoking strict scrutiny than they would enjoy under proportionality. If, however, US law treats an inseverably over-broad statute as narrowly tailored and hence constitutional, it would afford less protection to rights in this category than they enjoy under proportionality. It is also possible that in a case of inseverable over-breadth, US law might adopt concrete balancing.[72] In that event, the gap between the systems would be narrowed.

Up to this point, we have compared strict scrutiny to proportionality on a theoretical level only and have not considered the practical aspect. The conventional view in the United States is that most restrictions on constitutional rights that invoke strict scrutiny are unconstitutional. Gunther's observation in this regard is well known: strict scrutiny is 'strict in theory and fatal in fact'.[73] That is not the case under proportionality.

Proportionality is not beyond criticism, but categorization is not the answer. Every system has its pros and cons, and every system has developed against the background of the history and problems of the society in which it operates. It is fair to assume that the two systems will converge in the future,[74] and US law is already showing the first signs of adopting proportionality.[75] We cannot yet assess the outcome, and it is entirely possible that categorization will displace proportionality.[76] Proportionality and categorization are both part of the jurisprudential architecture, each reflecting the society in which it is rooted and each influenced by events beyond the borders of that society. It is difficult to identify the vectors of development and influence.

Bibliography

Robert Alexy, *A Theory of Constitutional Rights* (Julian Rivers trans, 2002)

Robert Alexy, 'Constitutional Rights, Balancing, and Rationality' (2003) 16 *Ratio Juris* 131

Yutaka Arai-Takahashi, *The Margin of Appreciation Doctrine and the Principle or Proportionality in the Jurisprudence of the ECHR* (2002)

Aharon Barak, 'Proportional Effect: The Israeli Experience' (2007) 57 *University of Toronto Law Journal* 369

Aharon Barak, *Proportionality: Constitutional Rights and Their Limitation* (2012)

David Beatty, *The Ultimate Rule of Law* (2004)

71b See Barak (n 8), 517.

72 See Fallon (n 69), 1330; Stone Sweet and Mathews (n 64a).

73 See Gerald Gunther, 'The Supreme Court, 1971 Term—Foreword: In Search of Evolving Doctrine on a Changing Court: A Model for a Newer Equal Protection' (1972) 86 *Harvard Law Review* 1, 8.

74 See Vicki C. Jackson, *Constitutional Engagement in a Transnational Era* (2010).

75 See Thomas E. Sullivan and Richard S. Frase, *Proportionality Principles in American Law: Controlling Excessive Government Actions* (2009); Vicki C. Jackson, 'Ambivalent Resistance and Comparative Constitutionalism: Opening Up the Conversation on "Proportionality", Rights and Federalism' (1998–99) 1 *University of Pennsylvania Journal of Constitutional Law* 583; Moshe Cohen-Eliya and Iddo Porat, 'The Hidden Foreign Law Debate in Heller: The Proportionality Approach in American Constitutional Law' (2009) 46(2) *San Diego Law Review* 367; Alec Stone Sweet and Jud Mathews, 'All Things in Proportion? American Rights Doctrine and the Problem of Balancing' (2010) 60 *Emory Law Journal* 797; Cohen-Eliya and Porat (n 38).

76 See Frederick Schauer, 'The Exceptional First Amendment' in Michael Ignatieff (ed), *American Exceptionalism and Human Rights* (1980), 32.

Carlos Bernal Pulido, *El Principio de Proporcionalidad y Los Derechos Fundamentals* (2007)

Miguel Carbonell, *El Principio de Proporcionalidad y Protección de Los Derechos Fundamentals* (2008)

Halton Cheadle, 'Limitation of Rights' in Halton Cheadle, Dennis Davis, and Nicholas Haysom (eds), *South African Constitutional Law: The Bill of Rights* (2002)

Sujit Choudhry, 'So What is the Real Legacy of *Oakes*? Two Decades of Proportionality Analysis under the Canadian Charter's Section 1' (2006) 34 *South Carolina Law Review* 501

Moshe Cohen-Eliya and Iddo Porat, 'American Balancing and German Proportionality: The Historical Origins' (2010) 8 *International Journal of Constitutional Law* 263

Moshe Cohen-Eliya and Iddo Porat, 'Proportionality and the Culture of Justification' (2011) 59 *American Journal of Comparative Law* 463

Armand De Mestral et al, *The Limitation of Human Rights in Comparative Constitutional Law* (1986)

Evelyn Ellis, *The Principle of Proportionality in the Laws of Europe* (1999)

Nicholas Emiliou, *The Principle of Proportionality in European Law: A Comparative Study* (1996)

Richard Fallon, 'Strict Judicial Scrutiny' (2007) 54 *UCLA Law Review* 1267

Stephen Gardbaum, 'Limiting Constitutional Rights' (2007) 54 *UCLA Law Review* 789

Dieter Grimm, 'Proportionality in Canadian and German Constitutional Jurisprudence' (2007) 57 *University of Toronto Law Journal* 383

Dieter Grimm, 'The Protective Function of the State' in Georg Nolte (ed), *European and US Constitutionalism* (2005)

Mattias Kumm, 'What Do You Have in Virtue of Having a Constitutional Right? On the Place and Limits of the Proportionality Requirement' in George Pavlakos (ed), *Law, Rights, Discourse: Themes of The Work of Robert Alexy* (2007)

Bradley Miller, 'Justification and Rights Limitations' in Grant Huscroft (ed), *Expounding the Constitution: Essays in Constitutional Theory* (2008)

Kai Möller, 'Balancing and the Structure of Constitutional Rights' (2007) 3 *International Journal of Constitutional Law* 453

Julian Rivers, 'Proportionality and Variable Intensity of Review' (2006) 65 *Cambridge Law Journal* 174

Julian Rivers, 'Proportionality, Discretion and the Second Law of Balancing' in George Pavlakos (ed), *Law, Rights, and Discourse: The Legal Philosophy of Robert Alexy* (2007)

Wojciech Sadurski, *Rights Before Courts: A Study of Constitutional Courts in Postcommunist States of Central and Eastern Europe* (1990)

Frederick Schauer, 'Balancing, Subsumption and the Constraining Role of Legal Text' in Matthias Klatt (ed), *Rights, Law, and Morality: Themes from the Legal Philosophy of Robert Alexy* (2007)

Alec Stone Sweet and Jud Mathews, 'All Things in Proportion? American Rights Doctrine and the Problem of Balancing' (2011) 60 *Emory Law Journal* 797

Alec Stone Sweet and Jud Mathews, 'Proportionality Balancing and Global Constitutionalism' (2008) 47 *Columbia Journal of Transnational Law* 72

Thomas E. Sullivan and Richard S. Frase, *Proportionality Principles in American Law: Controlling Excessive Government Actions* (2009)

Stavros Tsakyrakis, 'Proportionality: An Assault on Human Rights?' (2003) 7 *International Journal of Constitutional Law* 468

Gerhard Van der Schyff, *Limitation of Rights: A Study of the European Convention and the South African Bill of Rights* (2005)

Grégoire Webber, *The Negotiable Constitution: On The Limitation of Rights* (2009)

Lorraine Weinrib, 'The Supreme Court of Canada and Section One of the Charter' (1988) 10 *Supreme Court Law Review* 469

Stu Woolman and Henk Botha, 'Limitations' in Stu Woolman et al (eds), *Constitutional Law of South Africa* (2006)

CHAPTER 35

CONSTITUTIONAL IDENTITY

MICHEL ROSENFELD

New York

I. The Concept

'Constitutional identity' is an essentially contested concept as there is no agreement over what it means or refers to.[1] The roots of constitutional identity go back to Aristotle who insisted that the identity of a state did not depend on its physical characteristics, but on its constitution.[2] Placed in their contemporary setting, conceptions of constitutional identity range from focus

[1] Compare eg Gary Jacobsohn, *Constitutional Identity* (2010) to Michel Rosenfeld, *The Identity of the Constitutional Subject: Selfhood, Citizenship, Culture, and Community* (2010) and to Michel Troper, 'Behind the Constitution? The Principle of Constitutional Identity in France' in András Sajó and Renata Uitz (eds), *Constitutional Topography: Values and Constitutions* (2010).

[2] See Aristotle, *The Politics* (Ernest Baker trans and ed, 1962), 98–9.

on the actual features and provisions of a constitution—for example, does it establish a presidential or parliamentary system, a unitary or federal state—to the relation between the constitution and the culture in which it operates,[3] and to the relation between the identity of the constitution and other relevant identities, such as national, religious, or ideological identity.[4] To the extent that the ideal of constitutionalism requires constitutions to provide a definition and limitation of the powers of government, commitment to adherence to the rule of law and protection of fundamental rights, all constitutions that comply with those prescriptions can be said to share a common identity. That identity, however, cannot account for the fact that similar provisions found in a number of constitutions can lead to widely divergent interpretations and applications.[5]

Three distinct general meanings of constitutional identity emerge. First, there is an identity that derives from the *fact* of having a constitution—polities with a constitution differ from those that do not; secondly, the *content* of a constitution provides distinct elements of identity—a federal constitution sets up a different kind of polity than one establishing a centralized unitary state; and thirdly, the *context* in which a constitution operates seems bound to play a significant role in the shaping of its identity—different cultures envision fundamental rights in contrasting and even sometimes contradictory ways.

Constitutional identity like national identity can be conceived as belonging to a collective self. Self-identity, moreover, can either connote sameness or selfhood.[6] I can recognize myself either because I look the same as I did yesterday or because in spite of all the changes which I have experienced since childhood—I no longer look the same, think the same, feel the same, etc—I have endured as a single self that is distinct from all other selves. Or, in other words, I have remained myself as against all others. Analogously, constitutional identity can be constructed on the basis of sameness or of selfhood, or more precisely, based on dynamic interaction between projections of sameness and images of selfhood. Moreover, the interaction in question may at times evoke complementarity and at other times contradiction.

For example, for more than two hundred years, the text of the US Constitution has remained the same, except for the addition of 27 amendments. Interpretations of provisions contained within the original 1787 text have, however, evolved through the years. To the extent that these interpretations can be cast in organic terms as part of a process of adaptation and growth, they can be understood as constructing and preserving identity in the sense of selfhood. Furthermore, the combination of interpretive selfhood and textual sameness can be viewed as complementary for purposes of elaborating a distinct constitutional identity. Or, conversely, inasmuch as constitutional interpretations depart from textualism or valorize certain plausible meanings of the text at the expense of others, textual sameness may stand in contrast to, and seemingly contradict, the evolving sense of selfhood fashioned by shifting trends in constitutional interpretation.

This contrast regarding the relationship between sameness and selfhood can be illustrated by reference to the US Constitution's Commerce Clause.[7] That clause grants the national

[3] See Robert Post, 'The Supreme Court, 2002 Term-Forward: Fashioning the Legal Constitution: Culture, Courts and Law' (2003) 117 *Harvard Law Review* 8.

[4] See Rosenfeld (n 1), 27–33.

[5] See Frederic Schauer, 'Free Speech and the Cultural Contingency of Constitutional Categories' in Michel Rosenfeld (ed), *Constitutionalism, Identity, Difference and Legitimacy: Theoretical Perspectives* (1994), 353 (similarly phrased free speech provisions given different meanings depending on the culture in which they are embedded).

[6] See Paul Ricoeur, *Soi-même comme un autre* (1990).

[7] US Constitution, Art I, s 8, cl 3.

government the power to regulate commerce 'among the several states', and has been pivotal in the evolution of American federalism over the past two centuries.[8] Indeed, the relative powers of the federal government vis-à-vis those of the states has fluctuated over the years, and has to a large extent depended on judicial line-drawing between interstate and intrastate commerce. In the early nineteenth century, interstate commerce was limited to trade, bartering, and commercial navigation across state boundaries.[9] By the 1940s, in contrast, the cultivation of a small amount of wheat by an individual on his own farm was held to be subject to federal regulation on the ground that the cumulative effect of like activities by all those similarly situated in the several states would have a substantial effect on the national market for wheat.[10] Both the relevant constitutional text and the categorical distinction between interstate and intrastate commerce remained the same between the early nineteenth and the mid-twentieth century. The scope of the federal power, however, changed dramatically during that period, from limited and confined during the early nineteenth century to nearly all-pervasive by the middle of the twentieth. Concurrently, the United States had been transformed from an essentially agrarian economy to the most powerful industrialized economy in the world.

Modern constitutional identity is distinguished from national identity—one can easily conceive of the French or German nation without reference to a constitution—but both originate in the late eighteenth century and both are identities constructed and projected by what Benedict Anderson has labeled 'imagined communities'.[11] As Anderson emphasizes, unlike the family or the tribe which form concrete groupings, the nation links together strangers who are bound together into an imagined community that came to replace 'the divinely ordained, hierarchical dynastic realm' whose legitimacy was undermined by the Enlightenment and the French Revolution.[12] Modern constitutionalism and the constitutional identity associated with it are also products of the Enlightenment. They were launched by the eighteenth-century American and French Revolutions and by the respective constitutions to which these gave rise. The two imagined communities, the national and the constitutional, differ though they may overlap and though they may comprise the same exact membership or closely intertwined ones. As will be elaborated below, constitutional identity is constructed in part against national identity and in part consistent with it. More generally, constitutional identity must constantly remain in dynamic tension with other relevant identities.

Inasmuch as constitutional identity transcends the mere fact of constitutionalism or content of a particular constitution, it emerges in the context of a dynamic process that must constantly weave together self-identity's two facets, sameness and selfhood. There are several different conceptions on how the dynamic in question yields a distinct constitutional identity. Robert Post, for example, asserts that 'constitutional law and culture are locked in a dialectical relationship, so that constitutional law both arises from and in turn regulates culture.'[13] According to Gary Jacobsohn, in contrast, constitutional disharmony drives the dynamic in question,[14] and the process is dialogical rather than dialectical. In Jacobsohn's own words,

> a constitution acquires an identity through experience.... [T]his identity exists neither as a discrete object of invention nor as a heavily encrusted essence embedded in a society's culture,

[8] On federalism, see Chapter 27.

[9] See *Gibbons v Ogden* 22 US 1 (1824).

[10] See *Wickard v Filburn* 317 US 111 (1942).

[11] See Benedict Anderson, *Imagined Communities: Reflections on the Origin and Spread of Nationalism* (1991).

[12] Ibid 7.

[13] Post (n 3), 8.

[14] Jacobsohn (n 1), 13.

> requiring only to be discovered. Rather identity emerges *dialogically* and represents a mix of political aspirations and commitments that are expressive of a nation's past, as well as the determination of those within the society who seek...to transcend that past.[15]

For Michel Troper, constitutional identity results from a process of extraction of certain principles which can be posited as essential and as such distinguishable from other constitutional norms and which can be relied upon to protect the integrity of the constitution in cases in which it confronts threats that might erode its vital bond to the people or nation which it is meant to serve.[16] A similar process for discovering (at least a partial) constitutional identity emerges from the European Court of Justice's (ECJ) endeavor to extract meaning from 'the common constitutional traditions' of the European Union (EU) member states for purposes filling a perceived constitutional gap at the supranational level of the EU.[17]

Conceiving of constitutional identity as belonging to an imagined community that must carve out a distinct self-image, I have argued that constitutional identity first emerges as *a lack* that must be overcome through a discursive process that relies on three principal tools: negation, metaphor, and metonymy.[18] Thus, for example, the French and the American Revolutions overthrew working orders based on cohesive narratives and distinct self-images. The two revolutions that led respectively to the 1787 US Constitution and to the various constitutions elaborated in the course of the French Revolution yielded constitution-making that has been characterized as being akin to creation *ex nihilo*.[19] Consistent with this, the *ancien régime* and its self-image must be shattered, hence creating a need for unleashing a process of negation. But negation alone only leads to a lack, and the new constitutional polity needs to build a frame of reference and a narrative that will allow it to perceive itself as a constituted imagined community. Negation must therefore be supplemented by tools that will facilitate construction of a distinct positive self-image. These tools are metaphor which consolidates relations of identity and metonymy which lays out relations of difference and paths of contiguity. Because a self-image cannot be built up in a vacuum, negation, metaphor, and metonymy must combine to reprocess pre-constitutional materials and extra-constitutional ones into a serviceable, flexible, and adaptable constitutional identity. Moreover, that identity must cohere both at the level of the constitution as a whole and of particular constitutional provisions and most notably those most likely to provoke contestation. Typical of the latter are rights to equality, including gender-based equality.[20] Assuming that men and women are identical for some purposes and different for others in relation to constitutional equality, metaphorical reasoning seems best suited to buttress the former—for example, men and women are to be portrayed as identical for purposes of equality in employment—and metonymical reasoning most apt to lend support to the latter—for example, differences between the sexes relating to reproduction justify constitutionalization of abortion rights to give a woman the same control over her body as a man has over his.[21]

[15] Ibid 7 (original emphasis).

[16] See Troper (n 1), 202.

[17] See Case 4/73 *J Nold KG v EC Commission* [1974] ECR 491, 507 (ECJ).

[18] See Rosenfeld (n 1), 45–65.

[19] See Ulrich Preuss, 'Constitutional Powermaking for the New Polity: Some Deliberations on the Relations Between Constituent Power and the Constitution' in Rosenfeld (n 5), 143.

[20] On gender see Chapter 19.

[21] See Rosenfeld (n 1), 61–2. See also Chapter 51.

II. The Place and Function of Constitutional Identity

Constitutional identity necessarily has a place and function within the ambit of a constitution and of the ideal of constitutionalism. Moreover, depending on the particular constitutional identity involved, it may advance or hinder the relevant constitutional project to which it happens to be linked. For example, in a religiously pluralistic polity, a constitutional identity that promotes the majority religion and its values as against those of minority religions could well stand in the way of affording adequate constitutional protection to the latter. Conversely, within the context of the same polity, a constitutional identity that would counter rather than promote society's tendency to favor the majority religion might best serve the constitutional objective of affording the best possible protection to all religions.[22]

What place and function constitutional identity has or ought to have depends to an important extent on one's conception of such identity. Thus, for Troper who conceives of constitutional identity as being located *within* the constitution, its place is at the level of constitutional principles and its function is to make possible a cogent determination of what is and what is not essential in an EU member state constitution for purposes of distinguishing between permissible and impermissible delegation of state sovereign powers to supranational entities such as the EU.[23] For the ECJ as mentioned above, on the other hand, the relevant (partial) constitutional identity is located *among* constitutions,[24] and its function is to harmonize the EU as a supranational polity without an explicit constitution with what is common to the constitutions of its member states for purposes of acquiring a requisite minimum of constitutional legitimacy.[25]

Whereas Troper and the ECJ, in the context evoked above, ascribe a limited place and function to constitutional identity, Jacobsohn and I reserve a much more extensive place for it and envision its function in systemic terms. For both Jacobsohn and me, constitutional identity furnishes essential links between the constitution, its environment, and those who launched it as well as those for whom it was intended. Jacobsohn's focus, however, seems narrower than mine.

For Jacobsohn, the essential function of constitutional identity is to deal with constitutional disharmony.[26] Such disharmony, moreover, can arise within the text of the constitution or in the context of historical change or political contestation.[27] Constitutional disharmony creates a need for adaptation and coping with conflict and dissonance, and constitutional identity must be shaped dialogically with a view to overcoming the causes of such disharmony.[28] The range of adaptation and the precise nature and elasticity of the constitutional identity in play

[22] Cf Cass R. Sunstein, 'On Property and Constitutionalism' in Rosenfeld (n 5), 383, 398 (arguing that the 1990's constitutions of former communist states should pull back from extensive protection of social and economic rights to aid transition from state dependency to creation of a vibrant private sector and civil society). On freedom of religion, see Chapter 43.

[23] See Troper (n 1), 201–3.

[24] See n 17 and accompanying text.

[25] The above statement refers to the situation prevalent in the mid-1970s. Since then, the EU did attempt to adopt a formal written constitution. The Treaty establishing a Constitution for Europe (TCE) was signed on October 29, 2004 by all the (then) 25 member states, but failed due to rejection in 2005 referenda in France and the Netherlands. However, the substantive provisions of the TCE were subsequently incorporated almost intact in the Treaty of Lisbon which entered into force on December 1, 2009. See Norman Dorsen et al, *Comparative Constitutionalism: Cases and Materials* (2nd edn, 2010), 77.

[26] See Jacobsohn (n 1), 4.

[27] Ibid 13–20.

[28] Ibid.

under a particular set of circumstances depend on the actual prescriptions found in the relevant constitutional text and on the prevailing historical and socio-political conditions within the polity involved. Jacobsohn distinguishes between *militant constitutions* and *acquiescent constitutions*.[29] The former are characterized by a profound gap between the founding ideals and the entrenched reality making for a wide range of disharmony; the latter, by a tendency toward preservation of societal values rather than toward transformation, thus providing for a narrower range of disharmony.[30]

As I conceive it in its broadest terms, the place and function of constitutional identity is determined by the need for dialectical mediation of existing, evolving, and projected conflicts and tensions between identity and difference—or, more precisely, identities and differences—that shape the dealings between self and other within the relevant polity committed to constitutional rule and favorably disposed toward the aims of constitutionalism. At its most abstract, constitutional identity figures in relation to the threshold decision of whether to pursue constitutionalism or to reject it altogether as would be the case in the context of a pure theocracy.[31] Once one opts in within the ambit of constitutionalism, constitutional identity must be molded to guide answers to three principal questions: *To whom* shall the constitution be addressed? *What* should the constitution provide? And, *how* may the constitution be justified?

'To whom' depends both on the constitution's proponents or makers and on those who are addressed, and expected to become bound, by the constitution in question. The 1787 US Constitution was made in the name of 'We the People', yet African-American slaves were excluded. Moreover, to the extent that the US population is made up today principally of the descendants of waves of immigration spreading over two centuries, how can today's 'We the People' identify with its 1787 counterpart and accept the latter's constitution as its own? Much more recently, the 1982 Canadian Constitution was intended for all Canadians, yet it was rejected by Quebec.[32] In short, constitutional identity should be channeled into a cogent narrative that will guide the determination under a particular set of circumstances of whether a multi-ethnic or mono-ethnic or a national or multinational constitution would best bind together the diverse groups and/or ideologies or interests within a polity into a sufficiently unified and cohesive constitutional self.

'What' should be included in the constitution also depends on a narrative based on a constitutional identity apt to unify the various competing selves and others within a polity into a single polity-wide constitutional self. For example, a multi-ethnic, multi-religious polity such as India may cohere into a single constitutional self in spite of profound differences and divisions provided, inter alia, a suitable federal structure is erected. Thus, each principal contending group could be granted its own federated entity upon assenting to cooperation on those matters entrusted to the federal government. In this context, neither the federation nor the federated entities, but their particular interrelation would furnish the locus of identity for the operative constitutional self.[33] Moreover, the role of constitutional identity in shaping consti-

[29] Ibid 23.

[30] Ibid.

[31] A theocracy may be less than fully comprehensive on a political plane and thus combine with some attributes of constitutional democracy or it may adopt, for strategic reasons, a purely formal constitution meant to be exclusively nominal rather than substantive.

[32] See *Re Quebec Objection to a Resolution to Amend the Constitution* [1982] 2 SCR 793 (Supreme Court of Canada) (technically, the 1982 Constitution was the product of amendments rather than of constitution-making from scratch).

[33] See S.D. Muni, 'Ethnic Conflict, Federalism, and Democracy in India' in Kumar Rupesinghe and Valery Tishkov (eds), *Ethnicity and Power in the Contemporary World* (1996), 179.

tutional content extends from broad structural provisions to design of the rule of law to designation of the specific rights meant to count as fundamental and to specific interpretations of the latter.[34]

Finally, concerning 'how' constitutions may be justified to a diverse and pluralistic constituency, constitutional identity figures at various levels of abstraction ranging from the highly theoretical to the fairly concrete ones relying on actual history or living traditions. The relevant justifications that must become integrated in an appropriate constitutional narrative are of three principal kinds: those based on a common history or traditions; those based on a hypothetical or actual consent; and those emanating from normative precepts deemed to be universally valid or indisputably valid for those meant to be subjected to the constitutional regime sought to be justified. Often these justifications or some of them may be combined. Thus, originalism, which enjoys a significant following in the United States, combines a narrative on tradition with one on consent (based on the ratification of the 1787 Constitution in state ratifying conventions).[35]

To fully grasp the place and role of constitutional identity, one must realize that constitutions rest on a paradox as they must at once be alienated from, and congruent with, the very identities that make them workable and coherent. Thus, the 'we' that gives itself a constitution must commit to renounce part of its pre-constitutional self, must agree to certain levels of self-constraint and self-restraint to guard against some of its potentially constitutionally undermining tendencies—for example, an ethnically divided polity may only thrive as a constitutional unit by downplaying ethnicity in its constitutional and everyday politics. At the same time, however, a constitution should not veer too far off its constituent groups' identities for that would impair its viability and undermine its implementation—for example, a minority group that feels excluded from, and unjustly treated by, the constitution may become completely alienated from the polity's overall self and give in to separatist inclinations. Consistent with this, constitutional identity must operate constantly and at all levels ranging from that of the polity and the constitution as a whole to that of the interpretation of a single constitutional provision. Moreover, such constitutional identity must at once differentiate itself from all other relevant pre- and extra-constitutional identities while preserving or reincorporating enough of the latter to secure a minimum of acceptance among all those who are meant to come under its sweep.[36]

III. The Identity of Constitutional Models

Constitutional identity leaves a distinct imprint on every constitution and its broad contours allow for delimitation of diverse constitutional models that emerge as useful prototypes. One can distinguish at this writing seven distinct constitutional models. These are: the German, the French, the American, the British, the Spanish, the European, and the post-colonial models.[37] These models are constructed with reference to actual historical experiences. The first five refer to their country of origin. The sixth model, the European one, in contrast, refers to its transnational historical setting, the EU, and differs from the five preceding ones in that the

[34] See Michel Rosenfeld, 'Hate Speech in Constitutional Jurisprudence: A Comparative Analysis' (2006) 24 *Cardozo Law Review* 1523 (comparing US toleration of Nazi hate speech as against Germany criminalization of it on the basis of differences of self-perception relating to the Holocaust).

[35] For a discussion of originalism, see Dorsen et al (n 25), 219–24.

[36] See Rosenfeld (n 1), 10–11.

[37] The following discussion summarizes that provided in ch 5 of Rosenfeld (n 1).

actual constitutional experience to which it is linked is one that has arguably not yet borne fruit.[38] Finally, the seventh model, the post-colonial one, refers not to a single actual historical experience, but to a number of them that may differ significantly from one another but that nonetheless can be subsumed under the same overall model.

1. The German Constitutional Model

The central defining feature of the German constitutional model is the *ethnos* which stands in sharp contrast to the *demos*, its counterpart in the context of the French model. In essence, the German model is built upon the concept of self-governance by and for a single homogenous ethnic group. Based on its reliance on *ethnos*, the German model imagines the existence of indissoluble pre-political bonds cemented through a common language, culture, ethnicity, religion etc, which enjoy absolute primacy. Consistent with this, the ethnic-based nation is conceived as indivisible, homogenous, and fully formed prior to the adoption of any constitution or to the advent of the state. In the German model, therefore, the state figures as a mere vehicle at the disposal of an already well-defined nation rather than as an indispensable instrument for nation-building purposes.

2. The French Constitutional Model

In contrast to the German model, in the French model, the nation is built upon the *demos* with the *ethnos* receding to the point of becoming almost invisible. Like the German model, the French conceives the constitutional polity on the scale of the nation-state. But whereas the German model is difficult to imagine beyond the confines of the nation-state, given its inextricable grounding on *ethnos*, the French model's ties to the nation-state appear to be historically contingent. Indeed, the French model is grounded on democratic self-government for a polity of equal citizens bound together by a social contract. Consistent with this model, each citizen regardless of her ethnic origin, enjoys rights conceived as universal. The French model is thoroughly individualistic and leaves no room at the constitutional level for recognition or deployment of group or national identity. The French revolutionary Abbé Sieyès envisioned the nation as 'a body of associates living under common laws and *represented* by the same *legislative* assembly'.[39] Within this conception, the constitution is meant to enshrine a democratic nation united through equal citizenship with a political framework suited to give an effective voice to the people as a whole.[40]

3. The American Constitutional Model

The American constitutional model is closer to the French than to the German. But whereas the French model requires an existing nation, the American model does not. Indeed, the 'We the People' that stood behind the 1787 US Constitution were but an embryonic prefiguration of the United States which was to be assembled gradually through multiple waves of immigration. For these highly diverse successive waves of immigrants to be able to cohere into '*E Pluribus Unum*', the motto inscribed on the Great Seal of the United States, it would be first necessary for them to become immersed in a 'melting pot' fueled by the norms and values

[38] See n 25.

[39] Emmanuel Joseph Sieyès, *What is the Third Estate?* (1789), 58.

[40] On citizenship, see further Chapter 48.

enshrined in the US Constitution. Consistent with this, in the American model, the constitution frames and provides a launching pad to the state and it precedes and anticipates the nation. Accordingly, what is crucial and constitutes a key feature of the American constitutional model is the pivotal role that the Constitution and constitutional identity have had in transforming over time a diverse multi-ethnic and multicultural population into a veritable people and into a unified distinct nation that coheres into a dynamic polity.

4. The British Constitutional Model

One may think that Britain does not have a constitution for although it has had laws that are constitutional in nature going as far back as the Magna Carta, these have not been gathered into a single written document. From a functional standpoint, however, Britain does have a full-fledged constitutional system. Though formally unrestrained, pragmatically the British Parliament exercises significant self-restraint. Britain also has a long tradition of adherence to the rule of law and its governmental institutions have consistently afforded substantial protection to fundamental rights, even if these are not guaranteed by a higher law. The British constitutional model is one of immanent constitutionalism that emerges gradually by means of a process of accretion. This gradualism and organic growth is due to many factors peculiar to Britain and to its history. These include the existence of some form of representative government since the end of the thirteenth century, no conquest or domination by a foreign power since 1066, and a cautious common-sense-oriented pragmatism that primes adaptation and abhors radical change and rupture. It is peculiarly British that institutions that were traditionally incompatible with constitutionalism or democracy such as the monarchy or the hierarchical and hereditary House of Lords, were gradually adapted to serve the institutional and political needs of a contemporary constitutional democracy. What ultimately sets apart US constitutionalism from the British model is that in the United States the constitution made in 1787 *transcends* the legal order in which it is deployed whereas under the British model the constitution remains *immanent* within the corresponding order.

5. The Spanish Constitutional Model

The Spanish model is distinct in two principal ways. First, it sets a framework for a multi-ethnic polity. And, secondly, it imports transnational norms, which it incorporates within the ambit of the nation-state. One of the most daunting challenges confronting the making of the 1978 Spanish Constitution was finding a proper balance between national unity and according a meaningful measure of autonomy to ethnic communities, such as the Basques and the Catalans, who had been suppressed ruthlessly during the Franco regime. The Spanish constituents found an ingenious solution that sought to bridge over contentious disputes over national identity—or more precisely, between national and subnational identities—through masterful use of open-endness and ambiguity. The Spanish Constitution provides for 'autonomous communities' ('*communidades autonomas*') with significant, though by no means fully spelled out, regional self-government powers.[41] Although both Spain and the United States are multi-ethnic societies, the Spanish constitutional model is multi-ethnic whereas the American one is not. That is because through constitutional accommodation of subnational ethnic groups, the Spanish model is suitable for a multi-ethnic *polity*. In contrast, the US Constitution

[41] See 1978 Spanish Constitution, Arts 143–158.

and the American model are compatible with a multi-ethnic *society*, but not with a multi-ethnic *polity*. The second important respect in which the Spanish model differs from the previously examined ones is in its incorporation of transnational (then European Community now) EU norms as part of its recasting the relationship between the Spanish nation and the Spanish state. With a view to its incorporation into the larger European polity, Spain imported and internalized European democratic values. These values though originally 'external' thus became 'internalized'.

6. The European Transnational Constitutional Model

As mentioned above, the attempt to endow the EU with a formal constitution ended in failure.[42] Nevertheless the EU experience is instructive for purposes of exploration of a transnational constitutional model tailored to constitutionalism in the EU. The main difference between the models fitted to the nation-state concerns the relative importance that each gives to particular elements, such as *demos* or *ethnos*, and how each model combines or approaches the elements common to all. In contrast, the EU appears to lack a sufficient common *ethnos* or identity and its institutions may well hinder the development of a workable *demos*. The lack of a common *ethnos* is not by itself determinative as attested by the success of various constitutions that come within the ambit of the Spanish model. However, none of the working multi-ethnic constitutions on the scale of the nation-state involve as extended an area or anything approaching the number of languages or cultures as those found within the confines of the EU. Moreover, though not comparable to its equivalents in nation-states, the EU does share several characteristics that may converge toward a common identity.[43] With that in mind, and postponing exploration of further details till Section VI below, it is possible to imagine a transnational EU model. That model, like the American, would be future-oriented; like the Spanish, it would be multi-ethnic. Furthermore, for the EU model to foster a proper balance between unity and diversity, most likely it would not do for it to become a supranational version of a nation-state model. Instead, the EU model would have to promote novel vertical and horizontal apportionments of powers allowing supranational, national, and infranational governance to work in harmony without being constrained by traditional forms of federalism or confederalism. The European model would have to find its own balance between *demos* and *ethnos*, a balance that would not be like that of the French or the German. Whether a European constitutional identity and a European constitutional model will emerge depends on the EU's will and capacity to generate a genuine constitutional practice and culture—a matter that remains an open question.

7. The Post-Colonial Constitutional Model

Unlike all the previously discussed constitutional models, the post-colonial one is not anchored in any single historical experience. Furthermore, the post-colonial model by no means extends to all constitutions adopted by former colonies. Indeed, the United States, Canada, Australia, Mexico, and Brazil are all former colonies that enacted post-colonial constitutions yet none of them fits within the post-colonial model. The post-colonial model encompasses above all constitutions adopted by former colonies in Africa and Asia that

[42] See n 25.

[43] See Armin von Bogdandy, 'The European Constitution and European Identity: Text and Subtext of the Treaty Establishing a Constitution for Europe' (2005) 3 *International Journal of Constitutional Law* 295.

achieved independence after the Second World War, including India, Nigeria, and several former French colonies in Africa. Finally, it is important to stress that whereas it was routine for former colonies to adopt a constitution upon achieving independence in the post-Second World War period, many of these were purely nominal. The most salient feature of the post-colonial model is that both the constitutional order and identity of the newly independent former colony are elaborated in a dialectical process involving an ongoing struggle between absorption and rejection of the former colonizer's most salient relevant identities. At the most abstract level, the former colony adopts a constitutional order fashioned in the image of that of its former colonizer and then seeks to fine-tune it to serve its own institutional and identity-based needs. The latter, moreover, will require adjustments to, and departures from, the colonizer's constitutional framework, but the work needed to adapt the inherited constitutional legacy to the needs of the new polity will almost inevitably happen to be defined in terms of the colonizer's political and constitutional framework. The case of India generally fits within this overall paradigm. In devolving power and granting India's provinces limited self-rule during the colonial period, the United Kingdom paved the way for the establishment of federalism in India, thus allowing for transformation and adaptation of the colonial institutional legacy to suit the particular constitutional needs of the newly independent former colony. From the British perspective, the grant of limited provincial self-rule may have been for purposes of containment, co-optation, and of dividing opposition within India to colonial rule. In contrast, for India besides facilitating the path to independence, provincial self-rule pointed to, and opened the doors toward, federalism. In sum, the post-colonial constitutional model is characterized by the predominance of a process involving an ongoing struggle between identification with, and differentiation from, the colonizer's constitutional identity, through concurrent negation and affirmation of the latter.

IV. Identity and Constitution-Making

Constitutional identity depends not only on the constitutional model involved, but also on the type of constitution-making that led to its adoption. Indeed, it seems logical that if constitution-making is preceded by a violent revolution, the relationship of the new constitutional order to pre-constitutional identity would be different than if there had been a peaceful transition to a new constitution. With that in mind, one can generally distinguish six different models of constitution-making which taken together with the seven constitutional models discussed above substantially circumscribe the formation and evolution of the main different types of constitutional identity.[44] The six models of constitution-making are: (1) the revolution-based model; (2) the invisible British model; (3) the war-based model; (4) the pacted transition model;)5) the transnational model; and (6) the internationally grounded model.

1. The Revolution-Based Model

Both a break with the past and a selective and transformative partial repression and partial reincorporation of certain of its key elements are necessary preconditions to successful constitution-making and to the viability of the resulting constitution. The revolution-based model seems best suited to the tasks of breaking away from the past through negation and of providing for an interim period for settling accounts according to the revolutionaries' conception of

[44] The following discussion summarizes that provided in ch 6 of Rosenfeld (n 1).

political justice. On the other hand, the revolution-based model may seem inherently unsuited for successful reincorporation of the pre-constitutional and extra-constitutional materials originating in the *ancien régime*. Upon further inquiry, the key distinction may be less that between constitution-making as the result of a revolution as opposed to in the absence of any revolutionary break, and more that between a revolutionary break that does not go beyond the minimum necessary to allow for a new constitutional beginning and a more radical revolution that makes it difficult to rethread the indispensable links between past and future. This last point is well illustrated by the salient difference between the French Revolution and the American Revolution. As Hannah Arendt underscores, the French Revolution created such a radical break with the past that the revolutionaries could not muster sufficient legitimacy or continuity successfully to lay down the new law of the land. In sharp contrast, the American revolutionaries—who had just won a war of liberation rather than a revolution in the strict sense of the term—overthrew the colonizer, but not the basic political organization of the newly emancipated colonies. Indeed, the people of the colonies were already organized into self-governing bodies prior to the conflict with England. This, moreover, provided a significant measure of legitimacy and continuity creating propitious conditions for the making of state constitutions, which in turn provided a stepping-stone for the making of the 1787 US Constitution.[45] In the last analysis, the success of revolution-based constitution-making depends on striking a proper equilibrium between a sufficiently emancipated constituent power and an adequately legitimated constituted power. This depends, in part, on *how much* and *what* of the past is destroyed. It also depends, in part, on how convincing a narrative of the new constitution's creation and contents can be elaborated on the basis of reworked pre-constitutional and extra-constitutional materials weaved together into an emerging and evolving account of constitution-making that can be productively meshed into a vibrant and dynamic working constitutional identity.

2. The Invisible British Model

As stressed above, the British constitutional model is an immanent one that unfolds through a process of accretion. Accordingly, the British Constitution seems grown not made and British constitutionalism independent from any discrete instances of constitution-making. Unlike the eighteenth-century French Revolution, the English revolutions of the seventeenth century did not result in abolishing the monarchy. Nonetheless, the constitutional conflicts that played out in seventeenth-century England resulted in significant, even if not full-fledged, constitution-making and in concerted efforts at concealment. In the first place, the source of legitimacy of the king's power, which was traditionally conceived as being divinely grounded, became recast as originating in the people. This led to a second major development: the invention of the concept of constituent power and its location in the 'people'. The third major development, which originated at the time of the restoration of the monarchy in 1660, consisted in the systematic negation of the second above-mentioned development. Specifically, the sovereignty of the people as such and their role as actual holders of constituent power were discredited in favor of the view that parliament was the true representative of the people, thus emerging as the ultimate source of constitutional legitimacy. The concealment and displacement of constituent power from the people to the Parliament had two major effects that set a sharp contrast between British and French

[45] See Hannah Arendt, *On Revolution* (1965), 165–6.

revolution-based constitution-making. First, unlike French Revolution constitution-making, its British counterpart, though surrounded by severe traumatic breaks in continuity—the execution of the king, followed by Cromwell's rule, the subsequent restoration, and the 1688 Revolution—was nonetheless shrouded in an appearance of continuity. This fostered a partial and ill-defined newly made constitution. Secondly, by making the Parliament the locus of the people's sovereignty, the British model triggers the collapse of the constituent power into the constituted power, thus abolishing the formal division between constitution-making and merely legislating. Constitution-making can thus become disguised as ordinary legislating, with the inevitable consequence of dissipating constitutional identity. The collapse of the constituent power into the constituted power can thus have both advantages and drawbacks. Where the constitution can be plausibly depicted as grown rather than made, and as drawing on deep-seeded traditions that lend support to the pursuit of the ideals of constitutionalism, the collapse in question may, on the whole, play a positive role. In contrast, where the traditions involved are significantly at odds with constitutionalism, and the blurring between constitutional and ordinary legislation can be easily manipulated to cast expediency as principle, then the absence of an independent constituent power can easily turn into a major liability.

3. The War-Based Model

The two salient examples of war-based constitution-making are those of post-Second World War Germany and Japan. Both in the case of Nazi Germany and of Imperial Japan tyrannical belligerent regimes experienced total defeat and unconditional surrender followed by a transition to constitutional democracy imposed by the victors. The war-based model, just like the revolution-based one involves a radical rupture with the past. Unlike the latter, however, the war-based model can only result in successful constitution-making if the citizenry of the defeated polity eventually embraces as its own the resulting constitution launched by the victors. In the context of the war-based model, the negation of the pre-constitutional past is first imposed by the victors, and so is the nature of the new constitution, at least in its broad outline. For a constitution made pursuant to this model to succeed, the defeated polity must accept the repudiation of its own (recent) past and embark upon the reconstruction of a constitutional identity initially framed by former foreign enemies to whom it was forced to surrender. Although the opportunities for negation of the pre-constitutional past are similar under the two models, the war-based model confronts serious obstacles that are much less likely to challenge the revolution-based model. In the latter case, much of the citizenry is likely to identify with the revolutionaries as did most Frenchmen with those who spoke on behalf of the Third Estate and most Americans with those who led them to their newly gained independence. There was obviously no comparable identification between the defeated Germans and their British, French, and American occupiers, or between the vanquished Japanese and their American military rulers. Notwithstanding this serious obstacle, war-based constitution-making has succeeded both in Germany and in Japan, though, in many key respects, the war-based model has proven a greater success in Germany than in Japan. This is in large part due to major differences in the circumstances in each of the two countries after the foreign occupiers eliminated their respective pre-constitutional orders and imposed on them the task of crafting a new constitution. West Germany, under the stewardship of the Adenauer government, moved quickly to make the foreign-initiated constitution-making project its own. In contrast, the constitution crafted in Japan was much more an imposed one bearing General MacArthur's implacable imprint.

4. The Pacted Transition Model

The pacted transition model is best exemplified by the making of the 1978 Spanish Constitution. Pacted transition as it occurred in Spain is contrasted to constitution-making stemming from revolution or war in that it occurs in a context in which no clear-cut winners or losers emerge. Negotiation and an eventual pact leading to a new constitution depend on both the leadership of the *ancien régime* (or in Spain their heirs) and the proponents of a new constitutional order being too weak to impose their will or to overtake their opponents by force. Pacted negotiations, moreover, take place without break in legality, thus avoiding 'bootstrapping' problems that beset revolution or war-based constitution-making. In Spain preservation of legality became possible only because of the certain remarkable and unpredictable events, such as the Franco-empowered Cortes voting for free elections, thus knowingly assuring their own political demise. Furthermore, pacted constitution-making depends on a confluence of internal and external factors. In Spain, the painful memories of the civil war combined with the desire to obtain membership of what would become the EU. The former provided a powerful internal impetus to move away from the past; the latter, inspiration and guidance in relation to the future constitution which needed to be crafted. In other words, memories of the past suggested what had to be negated and visions of a European future contributed elements to be incorporated in Spain's constitution-making undertaking and in the constitutional identity designed to emerge from it. In the last analysis, the principal virtue of the pacted transition model, besides the avoidance of violence, is that it unfolds in an ambit of legal continuity and that it affords far greater opportunities for compromise among a plurality of constitutional interests. The principal drawback of this model, on the other hand, is that it may lead to failure of genuine constitution-making in cases where there is a break with the past, but no resulting constitutional order or in those where there is simply no break from the standpoint of constitutional tradition or identity.

5. The Transnational Model

The members of the EU straddled the distinction between constitution and treaty while making the eventually rejected 2004 European Constitution—which they characterized as a 'treaty-constitution'. Initially the EU Treaty-Constitution was made in the name of 'We the Peoples of Europe'. Later, the constituents listed in the preamble shifted, and became the heads of state of the EU members, rendering the Treaty-Constitution, formally at least, more akin to a treaty than to a constitution. Treaties are inherently distinguishable from constitutions as the former typically regulate external relations among two or more distinct sovereigns whereas the latter regulate internal relations within a unified whole. Beneath the surface of this basic distinction, however, matters are more complex. Some contemporary multilateral treaties, such as the European Convention on Human Rights (ECHR), involve an (external) interstate relationship in relation to a subject matter, fundamental rights, that are typically internal. From the standpoint of fundamental rights, the ECHR looms as a hybrid between a treaty and (part of) a constitution: a treaty in form; part of a constitution in substance. The fact that a constitution for the EU may originate in a treaty rather than a constituent act of the peoples of Europe proceeding as one, may not in the end be that significant. This would seem especially true if the eventual European Constitution establishes an altogether new constitutional model that is radically different form all the models tailored to the particularities of the nation-state. One can imagine, for example, relations among the peoples involved, among the member states, and among the multiple institutional features deployed by the constitutional treaty to be neither purely vertical nor purely horizontal, neither purely external nor purely internal. In that case, the distinction between contract and treaty would most likely lose much of its importance for the new European order. The difference between treaty and constitution seems more significant if the European Constitution were to promote a supranational version of any of the models tailored to nation-states, or some hybrid version of these models. Even in that case, however, the difference need not be that significant if, for example, the treaty-constitution were to be ratified by referendum in each of the member states. As the plurality of legal regimes—both national and transnational such as the ECHR—bearing on the relevant legal actors multiplies, and as most of these regimes tend to become internally constitutionalized, how constitution-making is crafted and brought forth seems less crucial and less determinative. Unlike in the case of all other constitution-making models, where overcoming a pre-constitutional order that is mostly, or at least to a large extent, constitutionally deficient is a necessary prerequisite, that is not the case in the context of a European Constitution. Indeed, all the EU member states which approved the now failed Treaty-Constitution have nation-state constitutions that stand in harmony with the fundamental tenets of modern constitutionalism. The challenge confronting the EU constitution-makers was not, therefore, to eliminate some objectionable pre-constitutional order, but to recast the entrenched constitutional way of life within each of the member states and to redeploy it at the interstate level carved out by the EU. Under these circumstances, the most important negation does not target unacceptable pre- or extra-constitutional norms, but the settled conviction that the horizon for constitutional ordering stops at the boundaries of the nation-state.

6. The Internationally Grounded Model

In the last few decades, the international community has initiated, guided, and supervised constitution-making in particularly troubled nation-states. These initiatives involve 'constitutional intervention' to launch constitution-making in countries mired in political conflict and not otherwise in a position to embark on a successful constitution-making journey. Many of these 'interventions' were launched by the UN, starting with UN Security Council Resolution 544 of August 17, 1984. That resolution declared South Africa's new 1983 apartheid constitution 'null and void'. Whereas in the latter case, the intervention was essentially a negative one, the many subsequent cases, such as Cambodia in 1992 (SC Res 745), East Timor in 2001 (SC Res 1338), and Afghanistan in 2005 (SC Res 1589), the UN undertook positive interventions. Furthermore, other international actors besides the UN have also intervened in various countries ranging from Bosnia to Sudan. Many of the countries in which constitution-making by international intervention was launched were in, or just coming out of, a foreign war, civil war, or a combination of both. Nevertheless, the internationally grounded model clearly differs from the war-based model and from the pacted transition model. In countries in which international intervention has played an important role, opposing political forces have either been at war with one another or unable on their own to convene and to undertake a genuine pacted constitutional transition. The nature and degree of international intervention has varied greatly from one country to another. Nevertheless, in terms of an emerging model of constitution-making, three principal factors stand out. First, no genuine constitution-making process could have occurred absent the international intervention. Secondly, the international intervention leads to incorporation of certain external constitutional norms and standards into the actual constitution to which it eventually leads. And, thirdly, substantial decision-making power over the substantive particulars of the constitution-in-the-making must be left in the hands of relevant political actors within the nation-state affected. Viewed in terms of constitutional identity, these three factors add up to a requirement that the input introduced through international intervention not be regarded as biased or as serving the selfish interests of the intervening countries or organizations; to the acceptance of the legitimacy of incorporating external constitutional norms and standards into one's country's new constitution; and to the need that local actors be in a position to internalize the process coming from abroad and to incorporate substantive norms compatible with plausible legitimate articulations of their country's national and constitutional identity.

V. Identity through Constitutional Interpretation

Constitutional identity plays an important and multifaceted role in constitutional interpretation. The precise nature of this role varies depending on the theory of constitutional identity involved. Thus, in the context of the ECJ, as discussed in Section I above, the EU adjudicator must set out to seek commonalities among the constitutions of member states, thus focusing on similarities and analogies across national constitutions. For Troper, on the other hand, the national constitutional adjudicator must seek out constitutional identity in the face of ever greater encroachment by the EU, through a distillation of constitutional principles for purposes of setting apart those that are essential from the rest. In Post's view, the US Supreme Court regards its constitutional interpretations as being independent from culture when 'the Court in fact commonly constructs constitutional law in the context of an ongoing dialogue with culture, so that culture is inevitably (and properly) incorporated into the warp and woof of constitutional law.'[46]

Viewed systematically and dialectically, constitutional interpretation produces constitutional identity and is at the same time shaped, filled, and molded by the latter. Moreover, in some cases the constitutional adjudicator deliberately appeals to constitutional identity to guide her interpretation; in other cases, the adjudicator may be unaware that her interpretation is influenced, or her decision triggered, by factors rooted in constitutional identity.

A prime example of constitutional interpretation shaping the course of constitutional identity is provided by the US Supreme Court decision in *Roe v Wade*.[47] *Roe* recognized for the first time a constitutional right to abortion in the face of a total textual and precedential silence on the question. Undoubtedly, the act of judicial construction that resulted in the holding in *Roe* had an unmistakable and significant impact on the constitutional identity of the United States. On the one hand, given the nature of the religious, moral, and political debate concerning abortion, recognition of a constitutional right to abortion projects a noticeably different image of American constitutional identity than that which would have emerged had the Supreme Court refused to recognize such a right. On the other hand, given the bitter controversy that followed the *Roe* decision and the vigorous efforts over the years to have the *Roe* decision overturned,[48] it is hardly an exaggeration to claim that it provoked a crisis regarding an important aspect of the constitutional identity of Americans.

Conversely, constitutional interpretation can be influenced by constitutional identity, and a good example of a deliberate reliance on the latter by the adjudicator is provided by the German *Holocaust Denial Case*.[49] Whereas Holocaust denial is protected speech in the United

[46] See Post (n 3), 8.
[47] 410 US 113 (1973).
[48] See eg Laurence Tribe, *Abortion: The Clash of Absolutes* (2nd edn, 1992).
[49] 90 BFVerfGE 241 (1994) (German Federal Constitutional Court).

States, it is criminalized in Germany despite fairly similar freedom of speech provisions in the two countries. The German Federal Constitutional Court held the criminal prohibition against Holocaust denial to be constitutional, emphasizing that to hold otherwise would deprive Jews living in Germany full integration in the larger community. To a large extent, the German Basic Law was intended as an unwavering repudiation of the country's Nazi past, thus fostering a constitutional identity that strongly encourages full integration of German Jews within the post-war German polity.

An example of unconscious influence by constitutional identity on constitutional interpretation is found in the US Supreme Court decision in *Lynch v Donnelly*.[50] In *Lynch*, the Court upheld a city's Christmas display that included a crèche, located at the heart of the shopping district, as not violative of the constitutional prohibition against state establishment of religion.[51] To reach this result, the Court had had to find that there was a secular purpose to the display of the crèche, and that its display did not amount to an official endorsement of religion by the city. Since the crèche depicts the nativity scene, which is of profound religious significance to Christians but not to those who profess other faiths, the hurdles confronting the Court's 5–4 majority seemed rather formidable. Nevertheless, the Court managed to decide that public display of the crèche was constitutional. As against non-believers, Justices in the majority argued that display of the crèche did not endorse any particular religion any more than generally accepted practices, such as printing 'In God We Trust' on coins. As against both non-Christians and Christians for whom the crèche evokes strong religious convictions, the Court's majority trivialized the crèche, by stressing its display in the context of commercial and other national secular traditions now associated with the Christmas holiday. By nurturing the antagonism between these two entrenched positions, the Court's majority in *Lynch* manages to promote mainstream religion, portraying itself as carving a predominantly neutral middle course between ardent secularists and profoundly committed adherents to religion. At bottom, however, *Lynch* promotes, by placing upon it the imprint of constitutional identity, a particular brand of religion which is ultimately neither neutral, nor religiously pluralistic.

Finally, constitutional identity can influence constitutional interpretation even where there is a heated and entrenched conflict of interpretation among adjudicators. This is well illustrated by the recent controversy over citation of foreign authorities in interpreting the US Constitution that has sharply split the Justices on the Supreme Court.[52] This split corresponds to an intensification of the divide among the respective proponents of two opposed visions of the United States. The first of these is the exclusivist vision.[53] Under this view, the United States is a country with a unique destiny, exemplary values and ideals, which serves as a model for the rest of the world. Under the universalist view, on the other hand, the United States is a diverse cosmopolitan nation which is as much influenced by trends and developments coming from abroad as the rest of the world is influenced by it. The exclusivist view fosters a national identity focused on divergences; the universalist view, one centered on convergences. In their current incarnation, the exclusivist view is mainly held by political conservatives; the universalist, by progressives. Moreover, for the exclusivists the US Constitution must remain purely American and free from foreign influence or contamination.[54] For the universalist, in

[50] 465 US 668 (1984).

[51] US Constitution, Amendment 1 (1791).

[52] See 'The Relevance of Foreign Legal Materials in US Constitutional Cases: A Conversation Between Justice Antonin Scalia and Justice Stephen Breyer' (2005) 3 *International Journal of Constitutional Law* 519.

[53] See Mark Tushnet, 'Referring to Foreign Law in Constitutional Interpretation: An Episode in the Culture Wars' (2006) 35 *University of Baltimore Law Review* 299, 310–11.

[54] See 'The Relevance of Foreign Legal Materials' (n 52), 525.

contrast, there is a convergence of norms and values, at least among advanced constitutional democracies, which makes constitutional cross-fertilization attractive and often useful.[55] The split between these two constitutional visions is sharp and seemingly irreconcilable and reveals how closely related a particular conception of national identity may be to its corresponding conception of constitutional identity.

Exclusivists and universalists appear to sketch out different conceptions of national identity and of constitutional identity, though in both cases the former is closely intertwined with the latter. This raises the question of whether it would be more accurate to speak in the plural of competing national and constitutional identities rather than in the singular. Moreover, if the answer were in the affirmative, then it would seem that at both the national level and the constitutional one a clash of identities would be more likely than the consolidation of a commonly shared identity.

When viewed more closely, however, the controversy between exclusivists and universalists reveals that both American national identity and constitutional identity are dynamic, conflictual, and multifaceted. Exclusivists and universalists, however, are ultimately dialectically linked as they represent two distinct competing facets of the United States' self-perception as a country of destiny called upon to set an example for the rest of the world.[56] For the exclusivists, the United States can only accomplish this by strictly adhering to what makes it different. For the universalist, on the other hand, overemphasis on such differences led the United States to lag behind the most advanced constitutional democracies in certain respects, thus requiring that it catch up to them before it can legitimately reassert its leadership role. Overall, exclusivists and universalists provide two different means to the same end, but in the course of aiming at that end, they each seem to reinvigorate the very obstacle that the other seeks to overcome. Hence, the vehemence among the two, and its strong impact on national and constitutional identity.

VI. The Problem of Identity in Supranational Constitutions

As attested by the ill-fated EU 2004 Treaty-Constitution, supranational constitutions seem intrinsically problematic both on account of *demos* and of *ethnos*. Nevertheless, it seems indisputable that there is a widespread movement toward supranational and even perhaps global *constitutionalization*. Some even claim that the UN Charter amounts to a world constitution.[57] Upon reflection, neither the UN Charter nor transnational documents such as the ECHR—though they may contain certain norms that are functionally equivalent to constitutional ones—can be properly deemed to approximate full-fledged constitutions. In contrast, the 2004 EU Treaty-Constitution has all the trappings of a full-fledged constitution, but it was never ratified. Was that primarily because of a lack of transnational constitutional identity? Can such identity be envisaged? Could supranational constitutions do without it? And, if so, what would replace it at the supranational level?

One tempting way to attempt to overcome the lack of transnational *ethnos* is by combining the formal and structural attributes that are common to all constitutions with constitutional

[55] Ibid 528–9.

[56] See Anders Stephanson, *Manifest Destiny: American Expansion and the Empire of Right* (1995).

[57] See Bardo Fassbender, 'The United Nation Charter as a Constitution of the International Community' (1998) 36 *Columbia Journal of Transnational Law* 529.

patriotism as advocated by Jürgen Habermas.[58] The first of these two tasks seems quite plausible as there is a clear trend toward adoption of formal constitutional structures in all types of transnational and extra-national legal regimes, both public—for example, the World Trade Organization—and private.[59] Constitutional patriotism, which essentially seeks to redirect patriotism—an affective bond usually directed toward one's own nation-state—toward the ideals of constitutionalism, on the other hand, seems highly problematic. Can one profoundly and affectively identify with a conceptual ideal? And even if one could, would that provide a thick enough layer of identity to glue together all those coming within the sweep of a global or transnational constitution?

Whereas any answer at the global level would be purely speculative, the EU's experience does afford a basis for useful reflection regarding the possibility of sketching a viable supranational constitutional identity. To begin with, one can identify several aspects of a common EU identity: common origins, common values, common destiny, and a common differentiation from American identity.[60] Can these, though seemingly insufficient standing alone, nevertheless serve to sustain a viable constitutional identity through projection into the future along the lines of the American model? This possibility cannot be ruled out, but the American future-looking model seems at best of limited relevance for Europe. This becomes apparent through a comparison of the American motto '*E Pluribus Unum*' with the EU motto 'united in diversity' adopted in connection with the now failed Treaty-Constitution. The American motto projects a dynamic and evolving image with the Constitution acting as catalyst for the integration over time of successive waves of immigration into a single nation. In contrast, the European motto aptly characterized as 'weak'[61] is static and flat. Indeed, nothing thus far suggests how this abstract aspiration may be transformed into a vibrant process of mutual adaptation.

There may be another plausible interpretation of 'unity in diversity' that could prove more productive. In this reading, the unity in question would be taken to symbolize a dynamic process against Balkanization within and, by extension, among nation-states. Seen in this light, unity at the European level may serve to defuse tensions within multi-ethnic states and between individual states and their own ethnic minorities. By transferring some powers from the member states to the Union, more room may be made for greater regional autonomy and diversity. In that case, moreover, the identities in question would seem more in keeping with the multi-ethnic Spanish model than with its American counterpart.

With this in mind, a narrative concerning origins looms as a crucial component of a viable constitutional identity, and the reference to Europe's 'bitter experiences', introduced into the failed Treaty-Constitution's preamble, provides a promising starting point. It is true that this reference is 'minimal', but that may be more a virtue than a vice.[62] The reference itself does not provide a sufficient narrative, but it opens the door to one. It is clear that Nazism and Soviet communism are both European phenomena and the main culprits behind most of the human-caused misery perpetrated in the twentieth century. Moreover, the European project arose from the ashes of Nazism and, recently, has been extended to incorporate within the EU many of the formerly communist countries of Eastern Europe. Accordingly, a European constitutional identity could easily ground its narrative of origins on a repudiation of Nazism and

[58] See Jürgen Habermas, *Between Facts and Norms; Contributions to a Discourse Theory of Law and Democracy* (1996), 118.

[59] See Rosenfeld (n 1), 267–8.

[60] See von Bogdandy (n 43).

[61] Ibid 360.

[62] Ibid 310.

Soviet communism and on the need to create a political order that would minimize the chances of any return to tyrannical totalitarian rule.

From the perspective of constitutional identity, origins depend, in part, on negation. Negation alone, however, is insufficient to create a distinct image of origins. In the European case, therefore, rejection of Nazism or Soviet communism does not of itself suggest why a transnational constitutional order would be needed rather than a series of sound national constitutional regimes. However, if Nazism is regarded as involving a pathological and highly disproportionate promotion of *ethnos*, and Soviet communism as fostering excessive suppression of it, a narrative of origins could link the repudiations, mentioned above, to the building of a transnational multi-ethnic order promoting a proper equilibrium among a multiplicity of diverse ethnicities. In other words, if transnational constitutionalism can create a space that is particularly well suited for the coexistence of a multiplicity of ethnicities while minimizing the potential excesses of *ethnos*, then rejection of the 'bitter experiences', when coupled with the need for a lasting commonly shared framework that neither unduly magnifies nor unduly represses *ethnos*, provides a seemingly viable narrative of origins susceptible of successful incorporation into an emerging European constitutional identity.

The other elements of collective identity referred to in the failed Treaty-Constitution, namely, Europe as 'a community of destiny', as 'a special area of human hope', and as a 'community of values', could well figure in a European constitutional identity at some point in the future. They sound hollow at this juncture, however, because they remain abstract and largely generic. But this does not mean that in time common threads, found in the history and culture of the various member states, could not be woven together into, for example, a distinct and sufficiently differentiated 'community of destiny'.

Constitutional identity like national identity can also be defined, to some degree, by who 'we' are not, as opposed to who we are. Accordingly, anti-Americanism could have a genuine role to perform in circumscribing and thus defining a European identity. American constitutional identity is adamantly fixed on the nation-state and wary of international and transnational norms that are constitutional in substance if not in form. In contrast, the starting point for a new European constitutional identity is the rejection of a constitutional order imprisoned within the nation-state combined with the search for harmonization between national, supranational, and international constitutional norms. To be sure, a similar harmonization is sought under the Spanish model, which is tailored to the nation-state. Nevertheless, if one adds to existing transnational institutional arrangements within the EU its transnational constitutional aspirations, the contours of a plausible European constitutional identity begin to emerge.

It is a quite possible that eventually the EU will create a European constitutional identity and lead to a new transnational European constitutional model. That model, like the American, would be future-oriented; like the Spanish, it would be multi-ethnic. Furthermore, for the European model to foster 'unity in diversity', most likely the European model would have to promote novel vertical and horizontal apportionments of powers allowing supranational, national, and infranational governance to work in harmony without being constrained by traditional forms of federalism or confederalism. Whether a genuine European constitutional identity and a European constitutional model will emerge depends on the EU's will and capacity to generate a genuine constitutional practice and culture—which is very much an open question. Be that as it may, constitutional identity may find new vessels of expression and transmission, but its relational dialectical engagement with concretely grounded pre- and extra-constitutional constructs seems unlikely to be transcended or replaced by disembodied ideals such as constitutional patriotism.

Bibliography

Benedict Anderson, *Imagined Communities: Reflections on the Origin and Spread of Nationalism* (1991)

Seyla Benhabib, Ian Shapiro, and Danilo Petranovich (eds), *Identities, Affiliations, and Allegiances* (2007)

Armin von Bogdandy, 'The European Constitution and European Identity: Text and Subtext of the Treaty Establishing a Constitution for Europe' (2005) 3 *International Journal of Constitutional Law* 295

Dieter Grimm, 'Does Europe Need a Constitution?' (1995) 1 *European Law Journal* 282

Amy Gutmann, *Identity in Democracy* (2004)

Gary Jacobsohn, *Constitutional Identity* (2010)

Robert Post, 'The Supreme Court, 2002 Term-Forward: Fashioning the Legal Constitution: Culture, Courts and Law' (2003) 117 *Harvard Law Review* 8

Michel Rosenfeld, *The Identity of the Constitutional Subject: Selfhood, Citizenship, Culture, and Community* (2010)

Michel Rosenfeld (ed), *Constitutionalism, Identity, Difference and Legitimacy: Theoretical Perspectives* (1994)

Robert A. Shapiro, 'Identity and Interpretation in State Constitutional Law' (1998) 84 *Virginia Law Review* 389

Rogers Smith, *Civic Ideals: Conflicting Visions of Citizenship in US History* (1997)

Michel Troper, 'Behind the Constitution? The Principle of Constitutional Identity in France' in András Sajó and Renata Uitz (eds), *Constitutional Topography: Values and Constitutions* (2010)

Mark Tushnet, 'Referring to Foreign Law in Constitutional Interpretation: An Episode in the Culture Wars' (2006) 35 *University of Baltimore Law Review* 299

CHAPTER 36

CONSTITUTIONAL VALUES AND PRINCIPLES

GARY JEFFREY JACOBSOHN

Austin

I. Introduction

Values and principles are a familiar part of the landscape of constitutional adjudication, yet their jurisprudential status is a subject of considerable contestation, and their meaning and significance for courts vary markedly across national boundaries. Much of the controversy surrounding these terms relates to concerns over their potential abuse by judges in the interpretive process and the resulting impact this experience could have on the legitimacy of the judicial function. Another point of contention is entwined in a specifically terminological quandary; thus in one account invoking values and principles is mainly redundant, whereas alternatively the two references might be seen as implicating quite different constitutional lines of inquiry. Moreover, the meaning and significance of values and principles to the constitutional enterprise display additional variation when viewed against the broad panorama of comparative possibilities.

However, contentious values and principles may be within the context of scholarly debate, they function in important ways to affect the shape and substance of constitutional outcomes. Constitutions incorporate them formally or informally, judges invoke them liberally or grudgingly, and political actors respond to their deployments negatively or positively. In India and Ireland, for example, principles are explicitly enumerated within the constitutional text to serve as a directive source for political and social development. In South Africa the elevated status of constitutional principles is traceable to that nation's unique constitution-making process, in which the adoption of a final document was contingent on the Supreme Court's certification that a set of mandated principled commitments had been scrupulously followed in establishing a code of governance. In Germany the operative assumption of post-war constitutional jurisprudence has been that there exists an 'objective ordering of values' according to which the Constitutional Court's adjudication of cases will culminate in rulings supportive of the country's constitutive obligations.

This chapter considers some of the ways in which values and principles have influenced contemporary constitutional law and discourse. Although the two terms are often used interchangeably, the discussion proceeds on the basis of a distinction in their meanings that highlights certain key areas of dispute surrounding the enterprise of constitutional adjudication. The distinction is one that may be gleaned from the numerous textual invocations of the words in constitutional documents. Indeed, inspection of such documents reveals a ubiquitous designation of values and principles in a great variety of provisions that are subject to judicial interpretation. While many of these references do not help much in providing definitional clarity, a number of them point to a criterion for distinguishing these terms that is concerned with the contrast between general and particular concerns. Thus, constitutionally inscribed mentions of principles are associated more often with matters that are less culture-bound than one usually finds in the citation of values.

For example, the Costa Rican Constitution refers to 'the history and the values of the country'.[1] A provision in the East Timor document speaks of 'the culture and traditional values' of that nation.[2] The Egyptian Constitution mentions the 'character of the Egyptian family—together with the values and traditions it embodies'.[3] Rwandan constitutional language requires the 'promo[tion of] positive values based on cultural traditions'.[4] Turkey's Constitution invokes 'Turkish historical and moral values'.[5] Uganda's recognizes 'cultural and customary values which are consistent with fundamental rights'.[6] And in Venezuela there is a constitutional provision that details 'the duty of assisting in the dissemination of the values of folk traditions and the work of artists'.[7]

Other constitutional references to values are focused on more universal themes. The Argentina Constitution, for example, calls for 'the fostering of democratic values',[8] a theme often found in passages in many constitutions where one finds specific allusions to principles. Similarly, Brazil's Constitution marks 'equality and justice as supreme values of a fraternal, pluralist and unprejudiced society'.[9] Such assertions are consistent with an aspirational human rights agenda whose substantive commitments are not mainly determined by the indigenous conditions of particular constitutional polities. This more universally framed commitment is observable in a great many of the constitutions' enunciations of principle. Typical of such references are: Algeria, 'The State is based on the principles of democratic organization and social justice';[10] Croatia, 'universally accepted principles of the modern world';[11] Iraq, 'No law may be enacted that contradicts the principles of democracy';[12] and Lithuania, 'Lithuania shall follow the universally recognized principles and norms of international law'.[13]

Then there are the invocations of principles that are not really universal in scope but are seemingly less culture- and tradition-bound than is generally the case for the textual articulations of values. In this category are appeals to state-specific principles, principles that give expression to commitments that manifest critical aspects of a nation's constitutional identity.[14]

[1] Tit II, Art 15. [2] Tit II, s 59.
[3] Ch II, Art 9. [4] Ch II, Art 51. [5] Preamble.
[6] National Objectives and Directive Principles of State Policy, s 24.
[7] Ch VI, Art 101. [8] Ch IV, s 75, para 19.
[9] Preamble. [10] Ch III, Art 14.
[11] Preamble. [12] Section 1, Art 2B.
[13] Ch 13, Art 135. [14] On constitutional identity, see Chapter 35.

The precise substance of these principles is not always obvious from the immediate textual context; the ambiguity surrounding meaning constitutes an implicit invitation to engage in constitutional interpretation. Indonesia's Constitution requires compliance with 'the principles of the Unitary State of the Republic of Indonesia.'[15] The Russian document voices similar dependence on 'the basic principles of the constitutional order of the Russian Federation.'[16] In Venezuela 'the principles of Bolivarian thought' are to provide criteria for observance of constitutional obligations.[17] In such instances, principles have been assigned constitutive prominence in order to underscore the importance constitutional framers attached to precepts of political morality that possess a certain sovereign distinctiveness. Presumably they could be identical with principles of justice that transcend sovereign borders, or they could overlap tradition-based sources more familiar to the discussion about values.[18] An example of the first might be the United States, whose Constitution (which does not explicitly mention principles) is often thought to embody the universally applicable self-evident principles of the Declaration of Independence that are the basis of 'US exceptionalism'. Examples of the latter are those constitutions—for instance, Afghanistan, Egypt, Ireland—that point to the existence of certain religious principles as privileged sources for the resolution of constitutional questions.

While the categorical boundaries separating these different types are anything but precise, the distinctions drawn are necessary to inform the analysis of values and principles in the following sections. The first discusses the vexed nature of principles as sources of constitutional interpretation. While the claim often made on their behalf, that they are the cornerstones of the very concept of constitutionalism, provides a powerful adjudicative resource for jurists, the ease with which such principles are amenable to interpretive manipulation offers a counter-rationale to those troubled by the discretionary excesses they afford these actors. The next section is similarly concerned with the uses and abuses of values, which are distinguishable from principles by their association with the local environment and the traditions and histories that give definition to the constitutional identity of a given polity. Sometimes these different associations produce jurisprudential tensions, but the resulting dissonance may as easily lead to creative and productive results as dysfunctional ones. The concluding section further elaborates on the distinction by situating the contrast within the debate over the appropriateness of foreign law as a source for resolving constitutional disputes.

II. Principles: Universal Aspirations and Practical Accommodations

The status of principles as legitimate legal sources for judicial interpretation in constitutional adjudication is a hotly and long-contested issue. Consider, for example, this strong statement by the former President of the Israel Supreme Court, Aharon Barak: 'The interpretation of legal texts is dictated by fundamental principles, since they constitute the objective purpose of every legal text.'[19] That there might be disagreement about the substance of these fundamental principles is not excluded in this account, but that their deployment by judges deciding cases is an inevitable and necessary component of the judicial task is taken here as a given. Not everyone, however, sees it that way, and so it has been with equally strong conviction affirmed

[15] Ch VI, Art 18B. [16] Ch III, Art 77. [17] Ch VI, Art 107.

[18] On the constitution and justice, see further Chapter 16.

[19] Aharon Barak, *The Judge in a Democracy* (2006), 57.

that, 'the invocation of legal principles is misguided'.[20] Again, it is not the application of the wrong principles that is per se problematic, rather it is that there is no justification for the judicial use of any such principles.[21]

The disagreement over the use and appropriateness of principles in constitutional law has figured prominently in the jurisprudential literature, inspired to a great extent by Ronald Dworkin's famous critique of legal positivism. Directed mainly at H.L.A. Hart's version of legal positivism, it provocatively laid out the case for broadening the fundamental test for law to include, in addition to the legal rules of a sovereign community, standards that function differently than rules and that generically can be subsumed under the rubric of principles.[22] As Dworkin explained, a principle is 'a standard that is to be observed, not because it will advance or secure an economic, political, or social situation deemed desirable, but because it is a requirement of justice or fairness or some other dimension of morality'.[23] Principles, according to his account, are necessary for the correct judicial resolution of legal questions, although their application does not require a particular result in a given case. A dimension not present in regard to rules sets them apart, namely the weight these principles carry in the legal order within which they function. Another way of expressing this phenomenon is to claim, as Lawrence Tribe does, that principles in constitutional law 'go beyond anything that could reasonably be said to follow simply from what the Constitution expressly *says*'.[24] Thus, in the case of the US, there are postulates—for example, the anti-secession principle—whose importance is unrelated to the absence of any explicit mention in the text of the Constitution. In deciding cases a judge must, therefore, give due weight—which may of course be deemed considerable—to such constitutive principles.

As we have seen, however, explicit textual references to principles are very common in constitutional documents; they need not, in other words, appear to the observer as the foundation of an 'invisible constitution'. Many of these specific inscriptions—for example, Ireland's 'principles of social policy' (Art 45)—suggest that another attribute of principles in the Dworkinian model—their special connection to individual rights rather than collective goals—is not a universal fixture in the constitutional domain.[25] This empirical reality—the nexus between principles and things other than rights—need not be fatal to Dworkin's argument as long as we hold to the idea that the pursuit of collective or policy goals can proceed along a justice- or morality-based line of approach, that they need not, as Dworkin's rights thesis contends, be grounded in purely utilitarian calculations. Indeed, the inclusion of sections on 'directive principles' in a number of constitutions is predicated on the idea that the governing institutions of these societies have a constitutional responsibility to create law and policies consistent with

[20] Larry Alexander and Ken Kress, 'Against Legal Principles' in Andrei Marmor (ed), *Law and Interpretation: Essays in Legal Philosophy* (1995), 279.

[21] A less categorical rejection of principles has been articulated by the philosopher Joseph Raz, who allows that there be a comparative dimension to such an assessment.

> Some of the reasons for preferring rules to principles in the direct regulation of human behavior have to do with the particular conditions of various countries.... But at least one general reason for this preference is fairly obvious. Principles, because they prescribe highly unspecific acts, tend to be more vague and less certain than rules.

Joseph Raz, 'Legal Principles and the Limits of Law' (1972) 81 *Yale Law Journal* 823, 841.

[22] Ronald Dworkin, *Taking Rights Seriously* (1977).

[23] Ibid 22.

[24] Lawrence H. Tribe, *The Invisible Constitution* (2008), 28.

[25] 'Arguments of principle are arguments intended to establish an individual right; arguments of policy are arguments intended to establish a collective goal', Dworkin (n 22), 90.

the animating principles of the regime. Inasmuch as the attainment of the goals established by these directive principles is necessarily an incremental, cumulative process, there are sure to be political and economic trade-offs along the way, which, if the strict distinction between principles and policies is adhered to, means that the achievement of such non-individuated goals would technically be lacking a principled basis. When a constitutional decision is taken expressly to improve the average welfare of members of the community it is not, in the strict sense of Dworkin's model, a principled act, even if it manages to succeed in securing its policy objectives. Perhaps that explains why Justice Barak, otherwise an admirer of Dworkin's jurisprudence, 'do[es] not insist on this distinction'.[26]

A clear distinction between principles and policies may, however, provide some useful cover against the charge of judicial activism. Policymaking is conventionally viewed as an activity done by politicians within the executive and legislative branches and subject to the constraints of electoral accountability. To the extent that the application of principles is recognized as a distinctly judicial task, it may enhance the legitimacy of an institution whose standing in the democratic community depends in part on its perceived commitment to dispassionate justice. Even so, this may prove a difficult sell; witness Richard Posner's critique of the Dworkinian distinction to the effect that in practice a principle is nothing more than a policy with which we are in agreement.[27] Yet more difficult is the challenge faced by nations transitioning from authoritarian rule to democratic constitutionalism. For example, Iraq's new Constitution mandates that 'No law may be enacted that contradicts the principles of democracy'. One measure of how well the new regime succeeds in convincing its people that fundamental change has indeed occurred will be popular acceptance of the idea that Iraqi courts are both committed to such principles and able to enforce them against the policies of entrenched interests. Given the extended dismal history that preceded the new constitutional arrangements in that country, achievement of this acceptance will doubtless not be easy.

Those for whom the invocation of principles is a misguided judicial exercise will not be persuaded that a principled approach to constitutional adjudication can immunize judges from the accusation that their use of non-rule-based interpretive methodologies necessarily furthers the prospect of a result-oriented judicial abuse of authority. Consider in this connection the so-called 'level of generality' problem. As Mark Tushnet has pointed out, 'different interpreters will specify the principles underlying particular constitutional terms differently, some at an abstract level of generality, some at a more concrete level.'[28] Far from being an objectively grounded decision detached from the social and political realities of a given time and place, particular specifications are, a critic might say, surely to involve calculations mainly focused on attaining the judicially desired policy or ideological outcome. 'The fact is that all adjudication requires making choices among the levels of generality on which to articulate principles, and all such choices are inherently non-neutral.'[29]

To see this process at work one need look no further than the aforementioned Justice Barak. The unresolved dilemma in Israel's constitutional predicament is highlighted in that nation's

[26] Barak (n 19), 58.

[27] Richard Posner, *The Problems of Jurisprudence* (1990), 22.

[28] Mark Tushnet, 'The United States: Eclecticism in the Service of Pragmatism' in Jeffrey Goldsworthy (ed), *Interpreting Constitutions: A Comparative Study* (2006), 37.

[29] Paul Brest, 'The Fundamental Rights Controversy: The Essential Contradictions of Normative Constitutional Scholarship' (1981) 90 *Yale Law Journal* 1063, 1092. Robert Bork, on the other hand, believes that a particular jurisprudential approach—originalism—solves this problem:

Proclamation of Independence, with its particularist commitment to a Jewish State coexisting with a universalist promise of liberal democratic politics. The resulting—and perhaps inevitable—constitutional project is one of bringing clarity and unity of purpose to this predicament by mitigating the inner tensions of these dual aspirations. For many Israelis this means moving into a constitutional future that resembles the experience of other liberal democracies. Accordingly, judicial interpretation, in Justice Barak's view, must be 'purposive', with the goal 'of achieving unity and constitutional harmony'.[30] Mirroring the Proclamation, the Basic Law on Human Dignity (adopted in 1992) requires upholding 'the values of the State of Israel as a Jewish and democratic State'.[31] How is this to be understood from an interpretive point of view?

> The content of the phrase 'Jewish State' will be determined by the level of abstraction which shall be given it. In my [Justice Barak's] opinion, one should give this phrase meaning on a high level of abstraction, which will unite all members of society and find the common ground among them. The level of abstraction should be so high, until it becomes identical to the democratic nature of the state.[32]

For obvious reasons, this approach has engendered controversy in Israel. The attempt to mute, if not eliminate, the discordant notes in the nation's revolutionary legacy has surely politicized the Court by leading many, rightly or wrongly, to conclude that the justices identify with one side of this divided legacy. But the example also reflects a dynamic that can occur when the two kinds of principles earlier cited in the texts of various constitutions clash within the adjudicative arena as part of a nation's broader struggle to instantiate a constitutional identity. Thus there are principles and values that embody precepts of political morality rooted in a nation's past, whose meaning derives from experience within a specific political and cultural context, and whose reach may not extend beyond that local context. Other principles make a claim of universality, such that the moral truths they are said to embody are precisely the ones whose recognition is required for a constitution to exist in more than name only. Sometimes the jurisprudential response to the tensions that result from the presence of these two types of principles—one of which is hard to distinguish from values—is to accept the tension as an enduring component of the constitutional predicament, a posture that incorporates the implicit understanding of a nation's constitutional identity as one that develops dialogically, thereby entailing interpretive and political activity reflective of the inevitable disharmonies endemic to the constitutional condition.[33]

> Original understanding avoids the problem of generality…by finding the level of generality that interpretation of the words, structure, and history of the Constitution fairly supports. This is a solution applicable to all constitutional provisions as to which historical evidence exists.

Robert Bork, *The Tempting of America* (1990), 150. There is an extensive literature that challenges such claims of neutrality that are used in support of the theory of originalism. See in particular, Mark Tushnet, 'Following the Rules Laid Down: A Critique of Interpretivism and Neutral Principles' (1983) 96 *Harvard Law Review* 781. Moreover, it is a theory that varies markedly from country to country in terms of its interpretive significance. As Jeffrey Goldsworthy points out, in places such as Canada and India, there is much less interest in the doctrine than one finds in the United States. Goldsworthy (n 28), 325.

[30] Aharon Barak, 'The Constitutionalization of the Israeli Legal System as a Result of the Basic Laws and Its Effect on Procedural and Substantive Criminal Law' (1997) 31 *Israel Law Review* 3, 5.

[31] Aharon Barak, 'The Constitutional Revolution: Protected Human Rights' (1992–93) 1 *Mishpat Umimshal* 9, 30.

[32] Basic Law: Human Dignity and Liberty, s 1, 1992, SH 150 (Isr).

[33] This point is explored at length in Gary Jeffrey Jacobsohn, *Constitutional Identity* (2010).

A seemingly less accommodationist view has come to be associated with German jurisprudence. In the early landmark *Southwest Case*, the Federal Constitutional Court proclaimed: 'Every constitutional principle must always be interpreted in such a way as to render it compatible with the fundamental principles of the Constitution as a whole.'[34] Known as the principle of 'practical concordance' (*praktische Konkordanz*), it requires a holistic understanding of the Constitution, in which the principled commitments of the document are to be harmonized so that none are enforced at the expense of others. As Donald Kommers has shown, 'The principle flows from the conception of the Basic Law as a structural unity'.[35] How distinguishable this approach really is from the effort in Israel to reconcile ostensibly antagonistic governing principles is debatable; an important difference, however, is the existence in the German case of a broad consensus regarding the 'objective order of values' that is to guide the interpretive process.[36] 'Taken as a unit, a constitution reflects certain overarching principles and fundamental decisions to which individual provisions are subordinate.'[37]

The practical implications of such an objective ordering extend to one of the more fascinating issues in constitutional theory: whether a constitutional court should have the authority to invalidate an unconstitutional amendment. The German Court has never issued such a ruling, but it has been in the forefront of establishing the jurisprudential rationale for doing so. In the *Southwest Case* it affirmed:

> That a constitutional provision itself may be null and void, is not conceptually impossible just because it is a part of the constitution. There are constitutional provisions that are so fundamental and to such an extent an expression of a law that precedes even the constitution that they also bind the framer of the constitution, and other constitutional provisions that do not rank so high may be null and void, because they contravene those principles.[38]

It could hardly have gone unnoticed that in the course of elaborating on the conceptual plausibility of nullifying a constitutional provision through an assertion of judicial review, the Court expressly invoked the nation's recent nightmarish past to affirm that never again would formal legal means be used to legalize a totalitarian regime.

Indeed, proximity to the abyss has a way of concentrating the mind on the essentials of constitutionalism, which is to say that there are experiences in the life of a nation that may incline one to accept substantive limits on certain kinds of formal constitutional change. If we posit

[34] *The Southwest Case*, 1 BVerfGE 14 (1951).

[35] Donald Kommers, 'Germany: Balancing Rights and Duties' in Goldsworthy (n 28), 203.

[36] In the absence of a consensus, however, the achievement of 'practical concordance' may still be an important jurisprudential goal. As Gustavo Zagrebelsky has argued,

> [Constitutional principles] do not produce a unity statically realized, but a unity to be achieved dynamically. The requisite principles come into play through their combinatory possibilities, and legal science is challenged to produce the 'practical concordance' of discordances.

Gustavo Zagrebelsky, 'Ronald Dworkin's Principle Based Constitutionalism: An Italian Point of View' (2003) 1 *International Journal of Constitutional Law* 635.

[37] *The Southwest Case* (n 34). Much the same has been said about South Africa's Constitution. Thus Justice Arthur Chaskelon has noted,

> The Constitution now contains an objective normative value system, which must permeate all aspects of the law.... The courts are obliged to develop the law to bring it in conformity with [the Constitution's value system].

Arthur Chaskelon, 'From Wickedness to Equality: The Moral Transformation of South African Law' (2003) 1 *International Journal of Constitutional Law* 608.

[38] Ibid 14.

that there are moral/political principles whose adoption and enforcement are the necessary condition for a regime to be recognized as genuinely constitutional, then the extraordinary exertion of judicial power to declare an amendment destructive of those principles invalid could understandably strike one as justifiable. Yet what if the principles under assault were not of the kind that threatened the existence of constitutional governance; instead involving a particular expression of that governance, perhaps a polity constitutionally committed to principles requiring a strict separation of church and state? Imagine, in other words, an amendment that had as its target a specific variant of constitutional identity, albeit without disturbing the fundamentals of constitutionalism. In such an instance would we not be less inclined to accept a judicial ruling nullifying an amendment than if the very identity of the constitutional project were thought to be in jeopardy?

Of course, in the face of a perceived danger to constitutional principles the distinction between state-specific principles and those possessing a more generic significance could very well pass unnoticed by political actors directly involved in an immediate controversy or crisis. Either through misapprehension or strategic calculation, people invested in the status quo are likely to exaggerate the scope and reach of a threat to the continuity of settled constitutional practice. They might, then, in their defense of principle, portray such a threat as one that placed at risk the future of constitutional government in the nation rather than what might be more plausibly the case, the maintenance of its particular expression.

For example, in the landmark Indian case, *Kesavananda Bharati v State of Kerala*, a justice on that country's Supreme Court declared: '[Our Constitution] is based on a social philosophy and every social philosophy like every religion has two main features, namely, basic and circumstantial. The former remains but the latter is subject to change.'[39] In this judgment the Court, fully conversant with the reasoning of its German counterpart, decided it could invalidate a constitutional amendment that was in defiance of the 'basic structure' of the Indian Constitution. Under the theory that constitutional change must not destroy what it modifies, the Court affirmed its institutional authority to annul any amendment whose adoption would, in its view, result in radical transformation of regime essentials. Left uncertain and unresolved, however, were the criteria that would enable one to distinguish basic features from circumstantial ones. When does a change portend the subversion of principles essential to constitutional government, at the core of which is the rule of law and the impartial administration of justice; and when does it undermine principles critical to the nation's self-understanding as manifested in a distinctive identity embedded in its constitution?

Thus it may have been obvious to the Court in a subsequent case involving the efforts of Prime Minister Indira Gandhi to entrench dictatorial rule in India that the nullification of her amendments to the Constitution was vital to the preservation of constitutional government. The government had argued that Parliament could do anything it wanted through the amendment power, no matter how revolutionary or destructive, a repudiation of the very fundamentals of constitutionalism that the Court felt compelled to resist. Said one of the justices, 'the Constitution is a precious heritage; therefore you cannot destroy its identity'.[40] But how should an amendatory challenge to, say, secularism be viewed? Surely it would have the potential of transforming Indian constitutional identity; however, are the principles underlying this featured constitutional commitment so vital to the generic identity of a constitution that their

[39] *Kesavananda Bharati v State of Kerala*, 1973 SC 1461, 1624 (1973).

[40] *Minerva Mills, Ltd v Union of India*, AIR SC 1789 (1980), 1798.

possible evisceration would justify a similar intervention by the Supreme Court? Indeed, secularism has been declared a 'basic structure' of the Constitution, but the accompanying disagreement over the substance of the principles that comprise this hallowed regime feature reminds us that even if we demur from the idea that 'the invocation of principles is misguided', we might still question how in the end they should be deployed.

III. Values: Finding Constitutional Meaning in 'Local Habits'

Disagreement over the substance of principles is ubiquitous, an inherent aspect of the constitutional condition. So too is dispute over the import of values in constitutional discourse, which, given the common conflation of the term with principles, can be taken as just another way of expressing the same thing. As suggested earlier, however, it will clarify matters if we maintain a distinction between the two concepts, even if this requires that the manner in which designations of this kind are officially conveyed not be taken at face value. For example, the German 'objective order of values' (*eine objektive Wertordnung*) in fact refers to fundamental constitutional principles in the sense that, as the German Court once affirmed, it functions in that nation's jurisprudence 'as a yardstick for measuring and assessing all actions in the area of legislation, public administration, and adjudication'.[41] In this account an objective value is, as Donald Kommers has suggested, 'one specified by the constitutional text as informed, inter alia, by history and which the state, apart from any individual claim, must foster and protect.'[42] This understanding may be contrasted with the notion of 'fundamental values', as it operates, for example, in the US context, where, as Kommers points out, it appears in a more subjective role as a feature of common law jurisprudence and precedential reasoning.[43] Or, as it has been more strongly asserted, 'Values and principles are, from many points of view, antithetical to each other'.[44]

Thus, while both principles and values are always contestable, the latter has a culturally determined meaning that provides it with a particularistic significance that effectively severs the idea of values from any universalistic claims. Recall in this context the textual constitutional references to values in constitutional documents and their emphasis on history and tradition. In these constitutional settings judges must be attentive to societal values that are embedded in a nation's long-standing traditions. To be sure, this focus is not unique to those judges whose constitutions are explicit in their evocation of such values—witness the prominence given to the subject in US substantive due process jurisprudence—but their predicament displays in a sharply defined way the problem that all judges must confront in constitutional interpretation.

For example, Turkey's Constitution invokes 'Turkish historical and moral values'. How is such language to be understood? The governing Justice and Development Party's (AK Party) determined efforts to open the public sphere to Islamic influences, under the theory that a

[41] *Luth Case*, 7 BVerfGE 198 (1958).

[42] Kommers (n 35), 180.

[43] Ibid. Kommers' example for the US contrast is the right of marital privacy.

[44] Zagrebelsky (n 36), 628. Zagrebelsky makes the distinction in order to denounce the deployment of values in constitutional jurisprudence: 'he who parades values is often a cheat. The rule of values is: judge and act as seems congruous with regard to the goal you wish to reach.... [V]alues cannot be traceable to reasons subject to rational controls.' Ibid.

dominant religious tradition must not be confined to the realm of the purely personal, would no doubt identify that tradition with the people's historical and moral values.[45] But a judge inclined to accept that identification would have to address the argument that the framers of the Turkish Republic, inspired by a vision of a radical transformation of state/religion relations, also believed that their fervently held goal of Western-style modernization would not be achieved unless the impediment of traditional Islam were effectively overcome. Hence they incorporated a principle that was in essence a Western import—radical secularism—in order to ensure the ultimate success of their constitutional project.

Still, the pervasiveness of Islamic traditions in Turkish society, and the values attached thereto, strongly suggests that the content and parameters of the Constitution's secular mandate possess a mutability that varies with the relative strength of these traditions and their more worldly competitors. These values have been mainly championed in the national legislature, as when in 2008 it adopted two constitutional amendments enabling Turkish women to wear headscarves in institutions of higher learning. This was followed by the Constitutional Court's decisive ruling striking down these amendments for violating secularism, 'the basic principle of the Republic'. Unlike the Indian Constitution, the Turkish counterpart includes a provision (Art 2) that specifically immunizes certain principles (including secularism) from the amendment process. Yet much like in India, disagreement about which policies are inconsistent with the fundamental principle is an ongoing feature of the country's constitutional politics. Do the values that support a greater visibility for religion in public life in fact threaten the secular principle?

While posing the question in this way suggests that principles and values are indeed antithetical to each other, the dialogical progression unfolding in Turkey, as it has elsewhere, reveals a much more complicated relationship, in which the boundary line that separates the two concepts is not as impermeable as the oppositional characterization of the terms might lead one to believe. Principles may be distinguished by their universalistic reach, but their success or failure in concrete application will depend on how they are adapted to the circumstances and contexts of a given time and place. Such adaptation entails absorbing and integrating values from the society's dominant traditions, culminating in some modification in the scope and depth of constitutional principles without leaving them transformed with respect to their underlying and most fundamental commitments.

This process received its classic formulation with Edmund Burke, who saw constitutions as embodiments of unique histories and cultural traditions. His emphasis on particularities and prescription, and on the constitution as something that evolves to conform to the circumstances and habits of a people, is upon first glance suggestive of a moral sensibility strongly deferential to entrenched cultural norms. But the deference was not unqualified, as illustrated in Burke's rejection of Warren Hastings' main argument for his morally questionable actions in India. Hastings had framed a defense of 'geographical morality', which held that whatever happened in India was compatible with local customs and therefore could not be judged by external standards. Burke was categorical in rejecting this moral perspective, arguing in response that the governance of Indians had to respect the same universal laws of right conduct that applied to Englishmen. Necessary, for Burke, was a prudential balancing of the universal and the particular. 'The foundations of government [are ... in the constitution] laid ... in

[45] As Bernard Lewis has observed, 'Westernization has posed grave problems of identity for a people who, after all, came from Asia, professed Islam, and belonged by old tradition to the Middle Eastern Islamic world, where, for many centuries, they had been unchallenged leaders.' Bernard Lewis, *The Emergence of Modern Turkey* (3rd edn, 2002), xi.

political convenience and in human nature; either as that nature is universal, or as it is modified by local habits.'[46]

Two centuries later the interactive dynamic involving principles and values in independent India echoes the earlier balancing of universal and local interests in the colonial precursor. This may be seen in the various and persistent political contests between the forces of inclusive secularism seeking a transformation of traditional Indian society and those of religious nationalists in pursuit of a more culturally homogenous and dominant Hindu value system. This contestation has manifested itself in landmark constitutional rulings in which the Supreme Court has been challenged to accommodate the demands of a principled commitment to a composite, more egalitarian identity with a deeply entrenched way of life premised on a contrary vision of social ordering.[47] Burke's idea of the prescriptive constitution includes a presumption in favor of settled practice, which in contemporary India extends a measure of legitimacy to the very values that support the structural foundations of a society targeted for deconstruction by the Constitution's underlying principles. Interestingly, the judicial response to this challenge has been attacked from both ends of the political spectrum, underscoring the Court's cautious juridical strategy of selective incorporation of traditional values into the basic structure of the Constitution, while retaining the essential principled thrust behind that framing vision.[48]

The practice of selective incorporation is a staple of US constitutional jurisprudence and further illuminates the principle/value distinction, as well as the interpretive problem associated with its application. It arises in the Fourteenth Amendment context, specifically in connection with the decision about which of the rights included in the first ten amendments as protections against the national government were incorporated in the Due Process Clause as applicable to the states. For many years it had been an issue of jurisprudential concern for prominent jurists, notably Justice Benjamin Cardozo. In his most influential book, Cardozo wrote: 'A *constitution* states or ought to state not rules for the passing hour, but principles for an expanding future'.[49] Later in his most famous Supreme Court opinion, he concluded that only those liberties that were 'of the very essence of a scheme of ordered liberty' were to be guaranteed against state infringement by the Fourteenth Amendment.[50] Thus a right such as trial by jury had 'value and importance', but its abolition would not, he believed, violate 'a principle of justice so rooted in the traditions of our people as to be ranked as fundamental'.[51] Unclear, however, from Cardozo's discussion is whether we recognize something as a principle

[46] Quoted in Francis Canavan, 'Prescription of Government' in Daniel Ritchie, *Edmund Burke: Appraisals & Applications* (1990), 259.

[47] See eg *Prabhoo v Kunte*, 1 SC 130 (1996), and *SR Bommai v Union of India*, 3 SC 1 (1994). For an extended discussion of these cases, see Gary Jeffrey Jacobsohn, *The Wheel of Law: India's Secularism in Comparative Constitutional Context* (2003).

[48] In an oft-quoted observation, Alexander Bickel claimed, 'No good society can be un-principled; and no viable society can be principle-ridden'. Alexander Bickel, *The Least Dangerous Branch: The Supreme Court at the Bar of Politics* (2nd edn, 1986), 64. The lesson from this for Bickel was that the Supreme Court should avoid principled decisions when confronted by strong public opposition. In this connection, the 'passive virtues' are to be recommended. But another lesson might be that the too rigid enforcement of principle is ill-advised; and that rather than avoiding principles in fraught circumstances, courts should endeavor to lessen the severity of their implementation through prudent co-optation.

[49] Benjamin Cardozo, *The Nature of the Judicial Process* (1921), 83.

[50] *Palko v Connecticut* 301 US 319, 325 (1937).

[51] Ibid. What leads to this judgment is not clear. Thus in 1774 the Continental Congress declared,

> the first grand right is that of the people having a share in their own government by their representatives chosen by themselves, and in congruence, of being ruled by *laws*, which they themselves approve, not by *edicts* of *man* over whom they have no control.... The next great right is that of trial by jury.

of justice because it has been so validated by tradition, or whether its independent standing as a fundamental component of a scheme of ordered liberty means that it must therefore have been entwined in the habits of the people.

'Due process traditionalism'—the idea that 'long-standing cultural understandings are both necessary and sufficient for the substantive protection of rights'[52]—bears directly on the principal concern of this chapter. Thus when courts affirm or reject the existence of rights on the basis of their appearance or absence as protected interests in the dominant tradition of a society, they are in effect declaring that constitutional recognition and legitimation are to be exclusively extended to claims whose normative standing is a function of their historic validation. Or as Justice John Marshall Harlan II wrote in the landmark case of *Griswold v Connecticut*, there should be a 'continual insistence upon respect for the teachings of history [and] solid recognition of the basic values that underlie our society'.[53] But again, the absence of any guarantee that these values will be consistent with the truth of the normative claims that a judicially enforceable regime of rights might be expected to display is at the core of the interpretive dilemma. As Christopher Eisgruber has asked, 'What should it matter whether a claimed constitutional right has solid foundations in traditions? Traditional practices may, after all, be exquisitely unjust.'[54]

The question may be more difficult to answer in places where the constitutional text is explicit in its invocation of value-laden traditional sources. In the United States, where a jurisprudence of 'traditionalism' is a purely judicial construction, the suggestion that 'judges question traditions by the light of reason'[55] is surely a sensible and quite defensible approach to the problem of morally deficient values. If, for example, a question arises as to whether a particular configuration of the family warrants constitutional protection, a judge might fashion a response by assessing the 'traditional family' according to standards traceable to sources less rooted in historic practices.[56] On the other hand, a judge in Egypt might be more constrained in adopting such a course of action in light of his constitution's specific reference to the family and 'the values and traditions it embodies'. The options he faces might be further limited by theological considerations, which doubtless would be required once those constitutionally preferred values were subjected to exacting judicial scrutiny. Unlike his US counterpart, the judge would have a hard time declaring, as Justice Felix Frankfurter once did, 'Local customs, however hardened by time, are not decreed in heaven...'[57]

Of course the political reality that these and all judges confront is that heavenly prescribed values are, whatever one's theological convictions (or lack thereof), ultimately rooted in the mores of a people.[58] It was William Graham Sumner, the nineteenth-century American

Continental Congress to the Inhabitants of Quebec, October 26, 1774 in Philip Kurland and Ralph Lerner (eds), *The Founders' Constitution* (1987), 442.

[52] The phrase comes from Cass R. Sunstein, *A Constitution of Many Minds: Why the Founding Document Doesn't Mean What It Meant Before* (2009), 93.

[53] *Griswold v Connecticut* 381 US 479, 501 (1965).

[54] Christopher L. Eisgruber, *Constitutional Self-Government* (2001), 140.

[55] Sunstein (n 52), 119.

[56] What is more likely to occur is a 'level of generality' debate over exactly which version of the family is deeply rooted in the traditions of the country. See eg *Moore v East Cleveland* 431 US 494 (1977), and *Michael H v Gerald D* 491 US 110 (1989).

[57] *Cooper v Aaron* 358 US 1, 25 (1958).

[58] As Joseph Raz has pointed out, 'In most countries one of the general principles restraining judicial discretion enjoins judges to act only on those values and opinions which have the support of some important segment of the population.' Raz (n 21), 849. With respect specifically to the religious question, it has not gone unnoticed that throughout the world there has been a 'tremendous increase of popular support for principles of theocratic governance'. Ran Hirschl, *Constitutional Theocracy* (2010), 2. The challenge this poses for judges beholden to both the values entrenched in popular mores and the principles of constitutional government is arguably one of the great challenges of the twenty-first century.

sociologist, whose classic analysis of societal mores was well known in legal circles, and whose depiction illuminates the key distinction drawn in this chapter. '[T]he standards of good and right are in the mores.... For the men of the time there are no "bad" mores. What is traditional and current is the standard of what ought to be.'[59] A more jurisprudential rendering can shape the judicial task to one of translating into law the prevailing standards of right conduct, irrespective of their agreement or disagreement with norms of right conduct derived from a more transcendent conception of justice. The latter may be understood to incorporate *principles* whose presence are necessary to certify the existence of constitutional government, while the former implicates those *values* that will either remain in persistent tension with these principles, or coexist with them in a reconciled state of constitutional equilibrium.

IV. Conclusion: Values, Principles, and the Debate Over Foreign Sources

Constitutional globalization is surely one of the most significant developments of recent decades. One of its many consequences has been the increased attention directed to the variety of ways in which the practice of constitutionalism can be realized. This development in turn has spawned an accelerated effort by judges to use the enlarged resources of foreign law and jurisprudence to assist in the adjudication of domestic constitutional cases. Such assistance may lead to emulation, wherein a court in one country follows the example of another in how it addresses a similar constitutional issue, or it may culminate in a heuristic exercise in which the differences between the two settings serve simply to enhance understanding of the local circumstance through comparative scrutiny of relevant alternatives.

As constitutional borders have become more permeable to the entry of foreign legal ideas and precedents, controversy has arisen over the use of these materials.[60] Although mainly a US phenomenon, the disagreement involves considerations that all judges must weigh as they calculate the costs and benefits of constitutional borrowing. Even in India, before the practice became fairly routine in that country's judicial experience, a justice warned:

> The craze for American precedents can soon become a snare. A blind and uncritical adherence to American precedents must be avoided or else there will soon be a perverted Constitution operating in this land under the delusive garb of the Indian Constitution. We are interpreting and expounding our own Constitution.[61]

All constitutional polities represent a blend of characteristics revealing what is particular to the constitutional culture as well as what are widely viewed as common attributes of a universal culture of constitutionalism. And so the Indian judge's concern was surely understandable, as is the question raised in connection with the judge most closely associated with the critique of transnational judicial activities: 'Scalia the judge roots himself in an America whose values

[59] William Graham Sumner, *Folkways* (1907), 58, 59.

[60] One close observer has noted, 'The migration of constitutional ideas across legal systems is rapidly emerging as one of the central features of contemporary constitutional practice.' Sujit Choudhry, 'Migration as a Metaphor in Comparative Constitutional Law' in Sujit Choudhry (ed), *The Migration of Constitutional Ideas* (2006), 13. See also Chapter 64.

[61] *Mahadeb Jiew v Dr Sen*, AIR 1951 Cal. 563 (1951). Decades later Justice Antonin Scalia echoed this sentiment without, we must surmise, having been influenced by it. 'We must never forget that it is a Constitution for the United States of America that we are expounding'. *Thompson v Oklahoma* 487 US 815, 868 n 4 (1988).

he purports to be able to identify. If the job of the judge is to identify and then apply these distinctive values, why would it be relevant to study how other cultures approach similar questions?'[62]

An answer to this question also connects with the main point of this chapter. That a presumption against the deployment of a comparative judicial methodology should resonate strongly in some places makes sense to the extent that the importation of foreign materials is also viewed as a threat to the integrity of the indigenous constitutional experiment.[63] If a judge believes that the correct answer to a constitutional problem is entwined in the values and traditions of her society, and that these sources are expressive of what is unique and exceptional about her political community, she might properly reject inputs from an alien culture predicated on a contrasting value system. Even if such inputs could be justified by the possible benefits of dialogical engagement with another legal culture, the risks associated with the effort might well be thought prohibitive. But suppose it were the case that much of what contributed to a nation's exceptionalism was a constitutional commitment to principles whose validity was not tethered to the cultural and historical particularities of that nation? Would it not be prudent, which is to say just plain sensible, for a judge to consider the practices of other constitutional settings, if only to confirm that the norms held to be of transcendent significance were indeed manifest in the experiences of very different societies? And would it not then be instructive to learn of any contrasting perspectives and arrangements whose purpose was to achieve the realization of commonly held principles?

Returning, then, to the written constitutional texts with which we began, we might conclude that very little advantage is to be had from looking abroad to illuminate such nation-specific language as 'positive values based on cultural traditions', or 'the duty of assisting in the dissemination of the values of folk traditions and the work of artists'. Where, contrariwise, courts attempt to interpret and apply 'the principles of democracy' or 'the universally recognized principles and norms of international law', they are likely to benefit from, or at least not be undermined by, consideration of how others have addressed these aspirations in the various structural and interpretive choices that define their unique constitutional identities. Although the distinction between values and principles is not etched in bright lines—indeed the terms, as we have seen, are sometimes used interchangeably—the linkage of the former with the local environment and the latter with a more cosmopolitan milieu both explains and determines a good bit of cross-national jurisprudential behavior.[64] If we imagine the grand antinomy between the universal and the particular as providing the backdrop against which the many narratives of constitutionalism have been and are being played out, values and principles, in conjunction with political interests and ambitions, are the instruments that have powered, and will continue to power, the corresponding constitutional storylines.

[62] Sanford Levinson, 'Looking Abroad when Interpreting the United States Constitution: Some Reflections' (2004) 39 *Texas Journal of International Law* 361.

[63] See eg Robert Bork, *Coercing Virtue: The Worldwide Rule of Judges* (2003), 22.

[64] As an example of the interchangeability of the terms, consider this observation by Justice Barak:

> In principle, judges should recognize only values that appear to be fundamental to the society in which they live and operate. The social consensus around fundamental values is usually what ought to guide judges with regard to both the introduction of new fundamental principles and the removal from the system of fundamental principles that have become discredited.

Barak (n 19), 61. The argument of this chapter is captured very well by Gustavo Zagrebelsky: 'Much of the criticism directed at a "jurisprudence of values" should not be leveled against a "jurisprudence of principles". But the fact that this happens can be explained by unwarranted confusion of the two.' Zagrebelsky (n 36), 629.

Bibliography

Larry Alexander and Ken Kress, 'Against Legal Principles' in Andrei Marmor (ed), *Law and Interpretation: Essays in Legal Philosophy* (1995)

Aharon Barak, *The Judge In a Democracy* (2006)

Alexander Bickel, *The Least Dangerous Branch: The Supreme Court at the Bar of Politics* (2nd edn, 1986)

Robert Bork, *The Tempting of America* (1990)

Benjamin Cardozo, *The Nature of the Judicial Process* (1921)

Sujit Choudhry (ed), *The Migration of Constitutional Ideas* (2006)

Ronald Dworkin, *Taking Rights Seriously* (1977)

Jeffrey Goldsworthy (ed), *Interpreting Constitutions: A Comparative Study* (2006)

Gary Jeffrey Jacobsohn, *Constitutional Identity* (2010)

Joseph Raz, 'Legal Principles and the Limits of Law' (1972) 81 *Yale Law Journal* 823

Cass R. Sunstein, *A Constitution of Many Minds: Why the Founding Document Doesn't Mean What It Meant Before* (2009)

Lawrence H. Tribe, *The Invisible Constitution* (2008)

Mark Tushnet, 'Following the Rules Laid Down: A Critique of Interpretivism and Neutral Principles' (1983) 96 *Harvard Law Review* 781

Gustavo Zagrebelsky, 'Ronald Dworkin's Principle Based Constitutionalism: An Italian Point of View' (2003) 1 *International Journal of Constitutional Law* 635

PART VI

INSTITUTIONS

CHAPTER 37

ENSURING CONSTITUTIONAL EFFICACY

JULIANE KOKOTT AND MARTIN KASPAR

Luxembourg

I. Introduction

A clear and general definition of 'constitutional efficacy's has not yet been established. On a general level the term can be understood to cover all the requirements for a constitution to work well once it has been set in place. More precisely, constitutional efficacy relates to the difference between the 'written' constitution and constitutional reality: the smaller this difference, the higher the degree of efficacy. Naturally, a constitution's effectiveness depends on its own writing and design. While a short and basic constitution might work for some countries, others might be in need of a much more detailed constitution; an interrelated factor is a constitution's rigidity or flexibility: a short constitution tends to leave more room for judicial adaptations, whereas cumbersome constitutional amendment procedures are needed to adapt the text of a detailed constitution to circumstances changing throughout a constitution's lifetime.

Generally, a constitution is designed to create a network of prevention and control mechanisms—checks and balances—throughout all levels of the exercise of state authority and thereby remove the application of constitutional principles, in particular civil liberties, from the arbitrary discretion of those in power. Constitutional *efficacy* describes and measures if these methods used to secure constitutional rights and rules are successful. In contrast constitutional *efficiency* usually describes how smoothly government is able to function.[1]

In order to analyse *how* constitutional efficacy is ensured, this chapter will concentrate on identifying the different methods used in constitutions to safeguard the rights and rules enshrined. In the end it remains to be seen whether 'the important roles of Congress and the courts to . . . safeguard individual liberty' are sufficient, or whether 'we must rely on . . . leadership and constitutional due diligence to ensure [that] the Constitution's promise is redeemed in a system of separated and shared powers.'[2]

II. Constitutional Courts versus Parliamentary Sovereignty

Installing a constitutional court as 'guardian of the constitution', with the principal task to watch over the adherence to the constitutional rules by all state authorities is a seemingly obvious mechanism to ensure the efficacy of a constitution.

1. Evolution Towards Judicial Review

However, what seems to be an obvious choice today was highly disputed during the last century's inter-war period in Germany.[3] Scholars of constitutional law such as Heinrich Triepel and Carl Schmitt held that there was a certain contradiction between the nature of a constitution and the nature of a constitutional judiciary.[4] Constitutional disputes, they argued, were political disputes and not to be confounded with legal disputes. The more political a dispute, the less it was considered adequate to be resolved in court. The most outspoken opponent of this theory was Hans Kelsen who, on the basis of his practical experience in aiding in the design of the Austrian constitutional court in 1920, argued in favour of a constitutional court and the introduction of strictly legal solutions to constitutional conflicts.[5]

[1] See eg Fritz Breuss and Markus Eller, *Efficiency and Federalism in the European Union: The Optimal Assignment of Policy Tasks to Different Levels of Government* (2003); Andreas Pottakis, 'Legitimacy v Efficiency: The Democracy Constitutional Future of the European Union' (2005) 17 *European Review of Public Law* 1109.

[2] Scott Matheson, *Presidential Constitutionalism in Perilous Times* (2009), 2.

[3] Arguing against judicial review in the United States and in favour of 'populist constitutional law' see the politicized contribution by Mark Tushnet, *Taking the Constitution Away from the Courts* (1999).

[4] Michael Stolleis, *A History of Public Law in Germany 1914–1945* (2004), 97.

[5] The debate is recounted in detail in ibid 187ff.

According to Kelsen's theory of the hierarchy of norms the constitution is the paramount norm providing a framework to determine the validity of all ordinary law inferior to it. Accordingly, there must be an institution to resolve whether the frame had been transgressed.[6] Schmitt retorted that the consequence of judicial review would mean a loss of both legislature and judiciary as it would end up in a 'juridification of politics' and a 'politization of the judiciary'. The debate can even be dated back as early as 380 BC, when Plato generally regarded 'democracy' as a bad form of government and opted for the rule of intellectuals/philosophers instead.[7] At the centre of Plato's thoughts was the general distrust in the democratic power of the uneducated masses. Rule should be given to 'wiser men'.

The set-up of the German Federal Constitutional Court, the Bundesverfassungsgericht, after the Second World War can be regarded as a late triumph of Kelsen over his opponents. The German Constitution endowed the Bundesverfassungsgericht with ample powers ranging from the control of laws, the resolution of conflicts between constitutional institutions, and especially the constitutional complaint (*Verfassungsbeschwerde*) by individuals claiming a violation of their constitutional rights by state authorities. Post-war Germany can therefore be regarded as an example of a political system with ample legal control of the constitutionality of political acts by a constitutional court acting as guardian of the constitution.[8]

In democratic societies where judicial review is centralized in a constitutional court, such centralization was often the consequence of an experience of totalitarianism, that is, the experience that the constitutional limits to political power were ineffective. This is true for the aforementioned case of Germany (the Bundesverfassungsgericht was established in 1951) and Italy (Corte costituzionale, 1956), but also for Spain (Tribunal Constitutional, 1980), Portugal (Tribunal Costitutional, 1983), and the Eastern European countries where constitutional courts were established in the 1990s.[9] In comparison, countries with comparably long democratic traditions and no totalitarian experience tend to opt for systems with either little (the United Kingdom, the Netherlands) or a decentralized (the United States, the Nordic countries) control of the legislator.[10]

2. The Alternative Model: Parliamentary Sovereignty

Whereas in many European countries and democracies around the world, a constitutional court was introduced into the judicial system—in many cases in the second half of the twentieth century—there are countries, like the United Kingdom and the Netherlands which opted for the sovereignty of parliament and do without a constitutional court as explicit guardian of the constitution instead.[11] They question the practice of judicial review and 'whether the judicial safeguarding of those [constitutional] rights does not imply a failure of democratic institutions'.[12]

[6] Dieter Grimm, 'Constitutional Adjudication and Democracy' in Mads Adenas (ed), *Judicial Review in International Perspective* (2000), 103–4.

[7] *Plato, The Republic. Plato in Twelve Volumes* (Paul Shorey trans, 1969), Bk V, 473c–e.

[8] Rupert Scholz, 'Fünfzig Jahre Bundesverfassungsgericht' (2001) *Aus Politik und Zeitgeschichte* 13.

[9] eg Hungary (1990), Bulgaria (1991), Russia (1991), Slovenia (1991), the Czech Republic (1993), Slovakia (1993), Lithuania (1993), Moldavia (1995), Latvia (1996), and the Ukraine (1997). Poland had already established a constitutional court in 1986.

[10] See also Veli-Pekka Hautamäki, 'Reasons for Saying: No Thanks!—Analysing the Discussion about the Necessity of a Constitutional Court in Sweden and Finland' (2006) 10 *Electronic Journal of Comparative Law* 2.

[11] On parliamentarism, see Chapter 30.

[12] Thomas Lundmark, *Power and Rights in US Constitutional Law* (2nd edn, 2008), 7; see also Grimm (n 6), 103–20.

The United Kingdom is a good example of a country that, because of traditionally strong social conventions and a stable political system, has fared well with the dogma of the sovereignty of parliament, the corresponding limited judicial control of legislative acts, and no written constitution. Until 1998, courts were (and often still are) only competent to examine whether legal executive acts are compatible with parliamentary law. However, in 1998, the British system experienced a significant change when the European Convention on Human Rights and Fundamental Freedoms (ECHR) was transformed into national law via the Human Rights Act.[13] Since then, courts can examine the conformity of primary legislation with the ECHR.[14] This examination may lead to a declaration of incompatibility. Such a declaration has no immediate effect on the pending proceedings, but may result in fast-track legislation to rectify the incompatibility, even with retroactive effect.[15]

As social conventions become more fragile and diversification is on the rise in modern society, it will be interesting to assess whether the Human Rights Act was a first step towards a stronger judicial control of the legislator or whether the Westminster model will remain largely unchanged in the future.[16] The newly created 'Supreme Court of the United Kingdom', as the direct successor to the judicial duties of the House of Lords, unifies several competencies under a single new roof.[17] Whether this new court will try to expand its competences with regard to judicial review by way of a British *Marbury v Madison*,[18] remains to be seen.[19]

In the Netherlands, the constitution itself explicitly states that judges shall not assess the constitutionality of laws (art 120 of the *Grondwet*).[20] Here, judicial review is a complex issue and can only be exercised—if at all—indirectly. Although 'judges have power to test all national laws against the supra-national standards of European Union Law', they are prohibited from testing national laws 'against the constitution, . . . or [even] general principles'.[21] The Netherlands therefore focuses on parliamentary sovereignty like no other written constitution in Europe. The provision was even upheld in all constitutional amendments, proving that the choice in favour of parliamentary sovereignty is still present today.[22]

A quite unique solution to the question of judicial review and parliamentary sovereignty can be found in the Canadian 'notwithstanding clause'.[23] This clause gives the elected

[13] 1998, c 42.

[14] For a detailed analysis see Aileen Kavanagh, *Constitutional Review under the UK Human Rights Act* (2009).

[15] Bernd Wieser, *Vergleichendes Verfassungsrecht* (2005), 120ff; for a detailed overview of policy changes in response to litigation see 'Review of the implementation of the Human Rights Act' of 25 July 2006, 22, available at <http://www.conorgearty.co.uk/pdfs/HRAfull_review.pdf>, and for an appreciation by the ECtHR, *Burden v United Kingdom*, App no 13378/05, 2008 (Grand Chamber), paras 21–4 and 40–4.

[16] Roland Sturm, 'Das politische System Großbritanniens' in Wolfgang Ismayr (ed), *Die politischen Systeme Westeuropas* (2009), 301.

[17] eg devolution issues (questions on the legal competences of the devolved legislative and executive authorities in Scotland, Wales, and Northern Ireland and, in some cases, the executive authorities in England, formerly exercised by the Privy Council).

[18] 5 US 137 (1803).

[19] On the Europeanization of national constitutions and English administrative law, see Chris Hilson, 'The Europeanization of English Administrative Law: Judicial Review and Convergence' (2003) 9 *European Public Law* 125.

[20] For criticism of this situation see Maurice Adams and Gerhard van der Schyff, 'Constitutional Review by the Judiciary in the Netherlands: A Matter of Politics, Democracy or Compensating Strategy' (2006) 66 *Zeitschrift für ausländisches öffentliches Recht und Völkerrecht* 399.

[21] John Sap, *The Netherlands Constitution: 1948–1998 Historical Reflections* (2000), 18.

[22] Adams and van der Schyff (n 20), 403.

[23] The Canadian Charter of Rights and Freedoms, s 33, reads:

> (1) Parliament or the legislature of a province may expressly declare in an Act of Parliament or of the legislature, as the case may be, that the Act or a provision thereof shall operate not withstanding a provision included in section 2 [fundamental freedoms] or sections 7 to 15 [legal rights and equality rights].

legislature the power to overturn and nullify judicial review—at least in certain selected policy fields.[24] These clauses are initially applicable for five years only, so that the people may have the possibility to then again overturn this decision through regular elections. By regarding judicial review as the ordinary procedure in securing the effective enforcement of constitutional rights, this solution tries to secure the constitution's fundamental rights, on the one hand, while on the other hand the notwithstanding clause allows for the protection of parliamentary sovereignty. By 2005 the provincial legislatures had invoked this provision 17 times, but it was never invoked on the federal level.[25]

III. Non-Judicial Methods and Constitutional Efficacy

Although judicial control has been established as a last resort in many countries to ensure the efficacy of those rules, there are also other procedures through which state actors either control themselves or others when exercising state powers.

1. Preparing Legislation

The legislative procedure itself provides for many opportunities and mechanisms contributing to the recognition of state powers or fundamental rights and freedoms. This helps to ensure constitutional efficacy in the early stages of the legislative procedure and allows for governmental self-control.

Self-control begins with consultations between ministries on governmental legislative proposals—there may even be specific divisions of government charged with ensuring compliance with the constitution. In Germany, for example, an advanced federal initiative to introduce a general ban on smoking in restaurants and bars came to a standstill because the federal ministry of the interior, responsible for constitutional questions, issued an opinion that the ban fell within the exclusive powers of the regional entities, the *Länder*.[26]

Some countries have a specialized, more independent body to assist in the preparation of legislation in the form of a 'Council of State'. These councils and their powers are often explicitly provided for in the respective constitution, as for example Article 160 of the Belgian Constitution provides for the Conseil d'État/Raad von State/Staatsrat, Article 76(2) and (3) of

(2) An Act or a provision of an Act in respect of which a declaration made under this section is in effect shall have such operation as it would have but for the provision of this Charter referred to in the declaration.

(3) A declaration made under subsection (1) shall cease to have effect five years after it comes into force or on such earlier date as may be specified in the declaration....

See also Fritz Scharpf, 'Der einzige Weg ist, dem EuGH nicht zu folgen' (2008) *Magazin Mitbestimmung*, available at <http://www.boeckler.de/cps/rde/xchg/hbs/hs.xsl/20493_20507.htm> opting for a similar clause for the EU.

[24] Ibid.

[25] Catherine Fraser, 'Constitutional Dialogue between Courts and Legislatures: Can we Talk?' (2005) 14(3) *Constitutional Forum Constitutionnel* 10.

[26] See Matthias Rossi and Sophie-Charlotte Lenski, 'Föderale Regelungsbefugnisse für öffentliche Rauchverbote' (2006) 59 *Neue Juristische Wochenschrift* 2657.

the Constitution of Luxembourg for the Conseil d'État, Articles 37 to 39 of the French Constitution provide for the Conseil d'État, Articles 100, 103, and 108 of the Italian Constitution for the Consiglio di Stato, Articles 73 and 75 of the Dutch Constitution for the Raad van State, or Article 107 of the Spanish Constitution for the Consejo de Estado.

While these bodies often exercise judicial functions, as in the case of the French Conseil d'État, their participation in legislation is not judicial in nature.[27] They issue opinions on proposed legislation and in this context can examine their constitutionality. However, opinions are not binding, but only advisory. For example, France recently passed legislation banning the burqa, even though an opinion of the Conseil d'État declared such a ban unconstitutional.[28] The example shows that such opinions contribute to public debate, but do not effectively sanction any possible infringement of constitutional rights. Nevertheless, they provide an extra system of checks with regard to ensuring constitutional rights.

2. Parliament as Guardian of the Constitution

A system of checks and balances is essential to a modern democracy. The theory of separation of powers assumes that parliament will make laws and supervise the executive. Both roles imply that parliament will aim to ensure the respect of the constitution and thereby contribute to constitutional efficacy. However, in parliamentary democracies, the executive branch is often intertwined with the legislative branch, since the executive is usually formed and elected by parliament's majority and dependent on its continued confidence. This affects both roles of parliament. However, this situation can be different in political systems with traditions of minority governments. Here, issues of constitutionality may become important political arguments during legislative debates. Parliamentary independence from the executive is also much stronger in presidential systems like the United States or South American states, where the executive is decoupled from parliamentary confidence due to popular elections or in the complex system of the European Union, where the Commission balances the interests between the European Parliament and the member states, represented in the Council.

(a) On Supervision

In parliamentary democracies, rights of parliament to check and supervise the executive have to be regarded as ineffective tools of constitutional efficacy if they are tied to a regular majority requirement. The first option to strengthen parliamentary control rights therefore lies in the introduction of minority rights and providing for super-minority requirements only to initiate such control rights: control rights, like the right to initiate a parliamentary hearing or investigation, the right of interpellation and questioning members of the executive or—where applicable—the right to bring a legal-review case before the constitutional court. Although the 'talking out' of a bill (United Kingdom) or filibuster (United States) may be seen as a classic parliamentary minority right,[29] it is usually not directed at ensuring the efficacy of constitutional provisions or rights, but to obstruct legislation and to pursue political objectives instead. It should therefore not be counted amongst parliamentary control rights.

[27] This dual function can call the impartiality of the judicial branch of the Council of State into question, see ECtHR, *Procola v Luxembourg*, 1995-A362, para 45.

[28] Law no 2010-1192, JORF No 237, 18344 and the opinion of the Conseil d'État, 'Etude relative aux possibilités juridiques d'interdiction du port du voile intégral' of 25 March 2010, available at <http://www.conseil-etat.fr/cde/media/document/avis/etude_vi_30032010.pdf>.

[29] Also used eg in France by means of excessively amending legislation.

The probably most frequently used minority right is the right of interpellation,[30] which may be used by each individual member of parliament. Other examples underline the importance of super minority requirements for minority rights to be effective. A parliamentary investigation by a special committee, for example, can be initiated by one-quarter of the German parliament[31] and is therefore being used regularly, although not extensively (between 1949 and 2009 a total of 38 parliamentary investigations were launched).[32]

In most other systems, however, a parliamentary investigation has to be set in motion by a regular majority,[33] which significantly limits its practical application. In Denmark, for example, this led to the replacement of parliamentary investigation committees by judicial investigation committees composed of independent judges rather than members of parliament. Although such judicial committees also require a regular majority to be implemented, their composition with independent judges makes it easier for the majority parties to agree to such a committee.

(b) On Lawmaking

The strong relationship between the parliamentary majority and the executive is particularly evident in the field of legislation. Here, the executive often starts serving as the legislative branch. In Germany, for example, 57 per cent of all legislative proposals are made by the executive (success rate: 89 per cent), whereas only 35 per cent are from within the first chamber, the Bundestag (success rate: 34 per cent) and only 8 per cent come from within the second chamber, the Bundesrat (success rate: 27 per cent). From this perspective, it is unlikely that the parliamentary majority will exercise very strict constitutional scrutiny of legislative proposals.

The parliamentary minority can only assume a very limited role in such systems. One of the stronger minority rights with regard to the constitutionality of legislation is the option to initiate judicial review in a constitutional court. But such a review removes the assessment of constitutionality from parliament.

A means to strengthen the assessment of constitutionality in parliament is the creation of a specific body for this task. The Finnish Constitution, for example, provides for a special Constitutional Law Committee that is to be established within parliament (Art 35). This committee shall issue statements on the constitutionality of legislative proposals and other matters brought for its consideration, as well as on their relation to international human rights treaties (Art 74). Because of this advanced monitoring system for the constitutionality of legislation, no separate constitutional court was established,[34] though this does not exclude judicial review by ordinary courts. It can be assumed that the specific constitutional mission of this committee can help to reduce the impact of party politics.

In parliamentary systems with two chambers it is possible that one of them is not dominated by the parliamentary majority of the chamber carrying the government. For example thexGerman Bundesrat represents regional governments, the members of the Austrian Bundesrat are elected by the regional parliaments, the first chamber of the Dutch parliament is composed of members elected by an assembly of all regional parliaments, and the

[30] See eg Ingo Beckedorf, *Das Untersuchungsrecht des Europäischen Parlaments* (1995), 126.

[31] German Basic Law, Art 44(1), Art 226 of the Treaty on the Functioning of the European Union (TFEU) provides a similar threshold to initiate an investigation by the European Parliament.

[32] See <http://www.bundestag.de/dokumente/analysen/2009/untersuchungsausschuesse.pdf>.

[33] Beckedorf (n 30), 177.

[34] See <http://ec.europa.eu/civiljustice/legal_order/legal_order_fin_en.htm>.

composition of the UK House of Lords is only indirectly determined by political positions. Such chambers can be expected to exercise a more critical constitutional review of government proposals. However, the greater distance of such chambers from the electorate usually also implies a reduction of their influence on the legislative process.

An interesting example in this regard is the Constitution Committee of the House of Lords in the United Kingdom which examines bills for constitutional implications. As the Lords enjoy a certain independence from the political parties, this examination promises to be more impartial than a procedure controlled by a parliamentary majority. However, constitutional doubts of this Committee can be overridden by a regular majority in the House of Commons. Therefore, the impact of this assessment could be comparable to the role that the Councils of States play in other systems.

(c) Multilevel Governance and Subsidiarity

Multilevel governance, in particular federalism and supranationalism, is not necessarily limited to the composition of parliamentary chambers but can result in specific mechanisms to ensure the efficacy of constitutional rules on the distribution of powers between the different levels of government. The political dynamics of such systems pose the risk that levels encroach on each other. Usually, one can observe a trend towards centralization, in which the federal level acquires powers which were once exercised by the regional level, but in recent times there have been notable instances where regionalization reduced the powers of the central government.[35]

The European Union is characterized by a trend towards centralization. To control this trend, the principle of subsidiarity[36] was introduced by the Treaty of Maastricht in 1992.[37] It states that 'the Union shall act only if and in so far as the objectives of the proposed action cannot be sufficiently achieved by the Member States, . . . but can rather, by reason of the scale or effects of the proposed action, be better achieved at Union level.' Consequently the subsidiarity test consists of two steps: while the first one is to check whether the objectives of the proposed Union action cannot be sufficiently achieved by the member states, the second step requires an assessment of whether by reason of the scale or effects of the proposed action, these objectives can be better achieved at Union level. Both stages leave great room for interpretation, insofar as the assessment of the sufficiency of national measures and possible better achievement at Union level require value judgments.

It is not surprising that the mere statement of this principle did not create a demonstrable limitation of the EU's activities. Therefore, the Treaty of Amsterdam of 1997 introduced a protocol with specific rules to ensure the principle's observation.[38] In particular, the Commission was required to analyse in detail, whether the principle of subsidiarity was respected and to document these findings transparently for every new bill proposed. The Commission should also hold wide consultations on legislative proposals. As such it is an interesting example of procedural requirements that aim to ensure the efficacy of a specific constitutional principle.

Nevertheless, member states and regions of the EU were still not satisfied with the efficacy of the principle of subsidiarity. The Treaty of Lisbon therefore strengthened once more the

[35] Belgium, Spain, the United Kingdom, and Italy come to mind though huge differences in the degree of decentralization can be observed.

[36] Article 5(3) of the Treaty on European Union (TEU) (ex Art 5 EC Treaty).

[37] Article 3b TEU in its version of the Treaty of Maastricht, OJ [1992] C 191.

[38] Protocol on the application of the principles of subsidiarity and proportionality attached to the Treaty of Amsterdam, OJ [1997] C 340.

procedural safeguards of this principle.[39] Now, the legislative proposals will be widely distributed and will be subject to consultation with the relevant stakeholders.[40] National parliaments in particular are called upon to examine whether proposals comply with the principle of subsidiarity and, if necessary, they are supposed to raise objections. If a sufficient number of national parliaments object, the proposal needs to be reviewed.[41] Additionally, the Lisbon Treaty also introduced the right of national parliaments to initiate judicial review of EU legislation with regard to the principle of subsidiarity.[42]

This way, national parliaments can influence the legislative process of the EU. It is to be expected that the institutions, in particular the Commission, will carefully monitor the discussion of legislative projects in the member states and take objections more seriously. Of course, national parliaments can only expect an increase of influence in EU politics if they themselves sufficiently engage in this task. Interestingly, initial practical experiences show that national parliaments use this procedure not only if they have doubts with regard to the principle of subsidiarity[43] but also if they consider that this principle is respected,[44] simply to express their position on a legislative draft.[45]

It remains to be seen whether this mechanism can alleviate the impression that the EU encroaches on national or regional powers.

3. Promulgation: The Head of State as Co-Guardian of the Constitution

Mechanisms of final examination and promulgation by the Head of State can also serve to promote constitutional efficacy. However, they can create tension with the principle of democracy and with the division of powers, especially in countries where the head of state is not elected, but hereditary instead.

Luxembourg and Belgium recently dealt with the latter issue. Article 34 of the Constitution of Luxembourg provided that the Grand Duke approves and enacts the laws adopted by Parliament. When a law on euthanasia[46] was being debated, the Grand Duke indicated that for reasons of conscience he would not be able to promulgate the law if it was to be adopted. As a consequence, and to guarantee the political neutrality ('*irresponsabilité politique*') of the monarch, the Constitution was amended and the role of the head of state was limited to the simple enactment of laws without any mention of approval.[47] Luxembourg is therefore now in line with other states, like Israel, Japan, or Spain.

A similar situation with a different solution occurred 1990 in Belgium, where a bill on abortion was passed against the objections of the Head of State, King Baldouin I. Article 93 of the Belgian Constitution[48] provides that Parliament can declare that the King is unfit to rule. It was in all likelihood intended to deal with questions of royal succession due to physical or mental inability to rule, and resembles rudimentarily the Twenty-Fifth Amendment of the US

[39] Protocol no 2 on the application of the principles of subsidiarity and proportionality attached to the Treaties, OJ [2008] C 115, p 206.

[40] Ibid Art 2; see also Art 11(1)–(3) TEU.

[41] Ibid Arts 6 and 7.

[42] Ibid Art 8.

[43] eg Council Doc 15526/10.

[44] eg Council Docs 15057/10 and 15665/10.

[45] eg Council Docs 15683/10 and 16340/10.

[46] Mémorial A—No 46 of 16 March 2009, 615.

[47] Mémorial A—No 43 of 12 March 2009, 586.

[48] 'Should the King find himself unable to reign, the ministers, having observed this inability, immediately summon the Chambers. Regency and guardianship are to be provided by the united Chambers.'

Constitution.[49] Parliament used this provision to declare the King unfit to rule for one day, on which the law was passed. The King was then reinstated.[50] In this case, constitutional efficacy is at risk, since the provision was misused to circumvent the ordinary promulgation procedure.

In parliamentary democracies, where the head of state is directly or indirectly elected, such concerns are less pronounced than in parliamentary or constitutional monarchies. In this case the office enjoys democratic legitimacy. Nevertheless, even in such cases the power to examine the constitutionality can be disputed. Article 82 of the German Basic Law, for example, provides that the German president shall certify and promulgate laws enacted in accordance with the provisions of the Basic Law. While there is broad agreement that the president has to examine whether the procedural requirements of the constitution have been respected,[51] there is some dispute with regard to a substantial examination. In 1960 the German President for the first time refused to sign a bill because of substantial reasons. In 1991 and 2006 bills on airline security respectively and in 2006 on consumer rights were not signed into law because of substantial constitutional concerns.[52] Some believe that the substantial examination of legislation is primarily the domain of the constitutional court; others consider the lesser democratic legitimacy of the indirectly elected president in comparison with parliament. However, the German Federal Constitutional Court assumes that it is part of the responsibility of the president to assess the constitutionality of legislation before it is certified and promulgated.[53]

Other systems are more reluctant with regard to the examination of constitutionality by the head of state. Though the Austrian President enjoys the same rights and power on promulgation as the German President,[54] but a much higher democratic legitimacy due to his popular election, he has only refused to sign a bill into law once, where he saw the principle of '*ex post facto* law' violated.[55] An even weaker form of promulgation and veto power is the one used in Italy or Latvia, where a president's veto leads to the law being sent back to parliament but without any special majority requirements to override the veto.[56] This solution is far more flexible, as it depends—even more so than in the German case—on the head of state's moral authority.

A variation of the presidential veto on constitutional grounds is the referral of a bill to the constitutional court. Here, the role as constitutional co-guardian is dependent on another state actor.[57] This is the case in Ireland, where the head of state can refuse to sign a bill into law, but has to consult with a specially designed Council of State (Comhairle Stáit) before doing so. A refusal to sign automatically leads to the case being brought before the Supreme Court.[58]

[49] Section 3 of Amendment 25 provides that when the President transmits a written declaration to the Heads of the Senate and the House, stating that he is unable to discharge the office of the Presidency, and until he sends another written declaration declaring himself able to resume his office, the Vice President serves as Acting President. Section 4, which has never yet been invoked, provides the modalities on how the Vice-President and Cabinet can declare the President unfit to discharge his duties. The latter provision resembles the Belgian solution much more than section 3.

[50] *New York Times*, 4 April 1990.

[51] eg in 1951 or 1976, when legislation was submitted to the President without the necessary consent of the second chamber, the Bundesrat, or in 1969 and 1970, where the President concluded that the federal level was not constitutionally competent for the policy issues at hand, but the *Länder* instead. For an overview, see *Sueddeutsche Zeitung*, 24 October 2006.

[52] Ibid; on the bill of consumer protection rights, see press release of the German Presidential Office of 8 December 2006, available at <http://www.bundespraesident.de>.

[53] BVerfGE 34, 9 (23).

[54] Austrian Constitution, Art 47(1).

[55] See <http://www.bundespraesident.at/en/functions/rights-and-responsibilities/position/>.

[56] Italian Constitution, Art 74 and Latvian Constitution, Arts 71 and 72.

[57] For other examples, see Chapter 0.

[58] Irish Constitution, Art 26.

In France,[59] Estonia,[60] or Portugal[61] the president can—but is not obliged to—request a ruling of the constitutional court on the constitutionality of a bill that is submitted for signature.

A presidential system in which the head of state is by definition also the head of government—as for example in the United States or almost every Central and South American country—usually has more politicized veto powers.[62] Here, a president's refusal to sign a bill into law is much more part of the system of checks and balances than that of a constitutional guard.[63] While such strong veto powers do not exclude an assessment of the constitutionality of legislation it may be that political considerations become more important if legislation concerns presidential policy. Still, even in a presidential system the president's veto is almost never absolute, but may be overridden by a qualified majority of Congress. This is another way of the constitution trying to establish equilibrium between parliamentary sovereignty and constitutional review.

IV. Judicial Review and Constitutional Efficacy

Judicial review is a strong instrument to ensure constitutional efficacy.[64] The separation of powers as such is already considered to promote respect for the constitution and in particular of fundamental liberties. Nevertheless, judicial intervention can help to protect human and minority rights from majoritarian zeal.[65] This judicial intervention—or judicial review to be more precise—can be exercised a priori (*ex ante*) or a posteriori (*ex post*). It can further be categorized as *concrete* and *abstract*.[66] Concrete judicial review will be applied with regard to actual legal cases that raise constitutional questions in the context of ordinary litigation. In contrast, abstract review typically entails specific procedures in a constitutional court. Usually, such litigation can only be initiated by privileged actors, for example parliamentary minorities or regions in federal systems.

Although judicial review, as a method to guard individual rights enshrined in the constitution, has without a doubt many advantages when it comes to effectively guaranteeing those rights, it also has certain disadvantages.[67] It may encourage parliamentary minorities to try to implement their political choices as 'constitutional rules' with the help of a dynamic constitutional court. The idea of a politization of the court was also the origin of Roosevelt's 'court packing plan'[68]—a proposal aiming to influence the US Supreme Court by the appointment of additional judges. Such appointments could have undermined the authority of the court and could have provoked a constitutional crisis.

Nevertheless, judicial review can surely be counted as being one of the most important, if not the most important, instruments in ensuring a constitution's efficacy. Aside from the

[59] French Constitution, Art 61(2).

[60] Estonian Constitution, Art 107.

[61] Portuguese Constitution, Art 278.

[62] Cf the Presidency of Andrew Johnson (1865–1869).

[63] See eg US Constitution, Art 1, s 7.

[64] Cf John Hart Ely, *Democracy and Distrust: A Theory of Judicial Review* (1980), 73ff.

[65] Lundmark (n 12), 1.

[66] For an overview of the constitutional courts of EU member states in German see CEP, *Die Verfassungsgerichte der Mitgliedstaaten der Europäischen Gemeinschaft—Überblick über die Zuständig keiten und Zugänge*, available at <http://www.cep.eu/fileadmin/user_upload/Die_Europaeische_Union/Verfassungsgerichte_der_Mitgliedstaaten.pdf>.

[67] On the risk of judicial review, in particular judicialization of the political process, see Grimm (n 6), 112ff.

[68] For details on the 'Judiciary Reorganization Bill of 1937', see eg Marian McKenna, *Franklin Roosevelt and the Great Constitutional War: The Court-packing Crisis of 1937* (2002).

actual exercise of judicial review, the mere existence of such an instrument also has an anticipatory effect, insofar as the actors in the political process try to anticipate the possible outcome of judicial review and take those findings into account when drafting (and applying) legislation.[69]

Of course, judicial review can only function effectively in a system with true separation of powers and, in particular, an independent judiciary. Interrelated are the procedures of selection and nomination of judges, which are of significant importance. Constitutional judges must unquestionably be excellent lawyers. But in addition to this requirement, constitutional judges must have a certain political sensitivity and sense of responsibility. After all, the efficacy of constitutional justice depends on its acceptance by the people as well as by the other branches of government. Such acceptance is a matter of the legal culture of a country, but also of the way in which constitutional justices exercise their responsibilities.[70]

1. Judicial Review *ex ante*

Ex ante judicial review (or 'preventive norm control') is abstract in nature. The legislation in question is not tested with regard to a specific case or situation but in a very general manner. The assessment is similar to the assessments undertaken during the preparation and adoption of legislation. However, the result is not a mere opinion but a binding judgment.

Where present, judicial review *ex ante* is typically reserved for a very narrow group of privileged applicants. It has already been mentioned that in some systems presidents can refer draft legislation to a constitutional court for assessment before promulgation. In some countries, this right is also given to other state powers such as the government, the president of a parliamentary chamber, or even a certain number of members of parliament.[71] The restricted access to this type of review indicates that it may have been created as a strengthened version of advisory opinions on legislation, as they are delivered by many councils of state.[72]

Ex ante review may also result in reduced scrutiny in comparison with *ex post* review. For practical reasons, such an examination is often dealt with in a fast-track procedure. Article 61(3) of the French Constitution, for example, requires a decision within one month; a time limit which can even be reduced to eight days. In such a short time, the assessment can only be superficial. Moreover, at the time of an *ex ante* review, the practical effects of the legislation at issue are still unknown. The review may be based on excessive fears or may ignore significant problems that only become visible when law meets reality.

On the level of legal theory, *ex ante* review—even if it is binding—can also be understood as respecting the supremacy of parliamentary law: review is not applied to already binding law but to a draft only. The authority of parliament does not suffer from a ruling of unconstitutionality. From this perspective it is logical to provide for *ex ante* review of legislative bills but not for *ex post* review, as was the case in France before the Constitution was substantially amended in 2008.

Ex ante judicial review can contribute significantly to constitutional efficacy, mainly because it is able to stop unconstitutional legislation before any infringement can occur. However, *ex ante* review can also be considered a problem for the democratic political process as it inter-

[69] Kavanagh (n 14), 357 with practical examples; see also Grimm (n 6), 111.

[70] See Grimm (n 6), 109.

[71] eg in the Constitutions of France (Art 61), Portugal (Art 278), or Romania (Art 146).

[72] Cf François Luchaire, *Le conseil consitutionnel* (2nd edn, 1997), para 27, who discusses why the French Conseil d'État could not be used as a constitutional court.

venes at a very early stage. Many countries do not opt for the method of preventive norm control, because the danger of the courts becoming too involved in the day-to-day political debate is too great. It raises concerns with regards to the constitutional separation of powers.[73]

Another, less controversial, case of *ex ante* review is applied when assessing the constitutionality of international agreements; before such an agreement is signed and/or ratified, certain specific state organs can request that a court assesses its conformity with the constitution. As such agreements can only be accepted or refused in their entirety in the course of ratification and since parliament usually has no direct influence on negotiations, this review is less problematic with regard to democratic legitimacy. But while this procedure is known in the European Union[74]—Austria, Bulgaria, the Czech Republic, Latvia, Lithuania, Poland, Romania, Slovakia, and Spain[75]—this form of *ex ante* review is exactly the one which the US Supreme Court refused to exercise in one of its early decisions when George Washington requested such an opinion of the Supreme Court.[76]

2. Judicial Review *ex post*

Ex post review is the more typical version of judicial review. It is the essential nature of courts to assess the legality of measures after they have been taken. Systematic difficulties arise, if they are called to assess the legality of the law itself. After all, according to the separation of powers, courts are still bound by law. Therefore, any review of legislation seems to be excluded. One solution to this conundrum is the creation of specific constitutional courts which are only bound by the constitution. Another option lies in the hierarchy of legal acts: if ordinary legislation is subordinate to the constitution and courts are to apply the constitution like any other law, it is logical that they assess the validity of ordinary legislation in light of the constitution. This approach results in a decentralized version of judicial review of constitutionality.

(a) Constitutional Courts

Many countries have now explicitly opted in favour of judicial review exercised by a constitutional court. It is safe to assume that the formal existence of a centralized constitutional court tends to at least increase the degree of judicial review. The more a constitutional court deals with legal review cases, the likelier it is for the legislature to try to anticipate any constitutional hurdles before a bill becomes law. Furthermore, judicial review can also lead to political deadlock or can be used as leverage by the opposition. This is why a high degree of judicial review tends to correlate with a consensus democracy, while a lesser degree or the absence of judicial review tends to correlate with a majority system.[77]

The typical form of judicial review in countries with centralized legal review in form of a constitutional court is the *ex post* control of compatibility of primary legislation with the constitution. The three main approaches to constitutional review are the abstract review, the concrete review, and, in some countries, the individual constitutional complaint. The extent of judicial review mainly depends on two dimensions: the institutions/persons able to initiate such judicial review procedure and the degree of judicial self-restraint.

[73] See Robert Dahl, 'Decision-Making in a Democracy: The Supreme Court as a National Policy-Maker' (1957) 6 *Journal of Public Law* 279.

[74] Article 218(11) TFEU.

[75] See CEP (n 66).

[76] Joan Gundersen 'Advisory Opinion' in Kermit Hall et al (eds), *The Oxford Companion to the Supreme Court of the United States* (2nd edn, 2005).

[77] Ibid 216.

i. Abstract Review

The procedure of judicial review is abstract in cases where political institutions question the constitutionality of a given law and ask the constitutional court to assess its conformity with the constitution without the need of any actual case or specific infringement being present. In abstract review cases, the condition that a plaintiff is directly and individually concerned, does not apply. Abstract review can be exercised both *ex ante* (see above) and *ex post*. Abstract review exercised *ex post* has an important political dimension.[78] In Germany it is common that the parliamentary opposition challenges important legislation before the Federal Constitutional Court and thus tries to stop political choices on legal (constitutional) grounds. Examples are abortion (1975 and 1993),[79] the budget (2007),[80] or genetically modified crops (2010).[81]

The more a constitution allows political actors (especially the opposition) to launch a judicial review procedure, or the easier the modalities, the more judicial review *can* be exercised by a constitutional court. This is where either political culture and/or the degree of judicial self-restraint come into play. On the one hand, if hurdles to launch a judicial review procedure are low (ie the number of members of parliament to launch such a procedure), political actors can make use of their right more often. For example, in Germany and Austria, the federal government, governments of the *Länder*, one-quarter (Germany) or one-third (Austria) of the members of the federal parliament—and in Austria additionally also one-third of the members of a regional parliament—can question the constitutionality of a law,[82] in Belgium this is determined by law and therefore open to amendment,[83] and in Spain the President of the Government, the 'Defender of the People', 50 members of parliament, 50 Senators, the executive body of a Self-governing Community and, where applicable, its Assembly can question a law's constitutionality.[84] It is then mainly dependent on political culture, whether these actors make use of their right.

But constitutional efficacy is not only dependent on the actors able to initiate the procedure. Another form of political (judicial) culture may be even more important: the degree of judicial self-restraint. The question of the constitutionality of abortion serves as an example, where the German Federal Constitutional Court twice annulled legislative attempts at liberalization, while the Austrian constitutional court allowed such a law.[85] In the United States, the situation was reversed when an active Supreme Court annulled legislation prohibiting abortion in *Roe v Wade*.[86] Although the extent of judicial self-restraint or activism can be difficult to determine,[87] the matter is highly topical in terms of effectively guaranteeing constitutional rights.

[78] On the political effects of this method, see Georg Vanberg, 'Abstract Judicial Review, Legislative Bargaining, and Policy Compromise' (1998) 10 *Journal of Theoretical Politics* 299.

[79] BVerfGE 39, 1 and BVerfGE 88, 203.

[80] BVerfG, 2 BvF 1/04 of 9 July 2007, in *Neue Zeitschrift für Verwaltungsrecht* (2007), 1405.

[81] BVerfG, 1 BvF 2/05 of 24 November 2010.

[82] Article 93(1) No 2 of the German Basic Law and Austrian Constitution, Art 140.

[83] The Belgian Constitution, Art 142, states: 'A matter may be referred to the Court by any authority designated by the law'; as of right now, these comprise the Council of Ministers, the Government of a Community or Region of Belgium, the Presidents of the Chamber of Representatives, Senate and the Community and Regional Parliaments, at the request of two-thirds of its members.

[84] Spanish Constitution, s 162, cl 1a.

[85] Anton Pelinka, 'Das politische System Österreichs' in Wolfgang Ismayr (ed), *Die politischen Systeme Westeuropas* (2009), 634.

[86] 410 US 113.

[87] On measuring judicial activism, see Stefanie Lindquist and Frank Cross, *Measuring Judicial Activism* (2009); Markus Freitag and Adrian Vatter, *Die Demokratien der deutschen Bundesländer* (2008), 237; Linda Keith, *The US Supreme Court and the Judicial Review of Congress* (2008); Arend Lijphart, *Patterns of Democracy* (1999), 223.

In the US model of decentralized judicial review, abstract review can also be exercised by means of a 'facial challenge' especially when dealing with First Amendment issues. In such cases, the plaintiff files a motion on the grounds that a law *would* injure him/her in some significant way.[88] Such motions are filed immediately after a law is adopted but before it is applied. Even more than abstract review, facial challenges are 'the most difficult challenge to mount successfully'.[89]

ii. Disputes between State Organs

The procedure on disputes between state organs differs from abstract review cases insofar as it is not primarily the content of legislation which is concerned, but questions of state powers. Often, principles of state organization are at stake, and sometimes the procedure is also being politically (mis)used to question the procedural legality of an unfavourable law.

In the European Union, these questions probably arise more often than elsewhere. Here, Article 263 TFEU provides that the European Court of Justice (ECJ) 'have jurisdiction in actions brought... on grounds of lack of competence, infringement of an essential procedural requirement,... or misuse of powers.' With regard to legislation, such actions can only be initiated by EU institutions or member states. In such cases, questions often concentrate on the specific type of legislative procedure which should be used (co-decision procedure, consultation procedure, consent procedure, or Council and Commission acting alone), but also on whether the Union was competent to act at all. Examples in the EU can be found in the cases on tobacco advertisement (2000 and 2006),[90] on the legal protection of biotechnological inventions (2001),[91] on the working time of road transport workers (2004),[92] or on data retention (2006).[93]

In Germany, the Federal Constitutional Court also deals with competence questions (*Organstreitverfahren*),[94] between different branches of government. This type of procedure can also be found in parliamentary systems as a minority right, since it is ordinarily used by the parliamentary opposition. Examples in Germany are the dissolution of the Bundestag in 1983[95] or 2005,[96] on participation rights of the Bundestag in military out-of-area deployment cases,[97] the stationing of nuclear weapons,[98] or on parliamentary budget control of the intelligence services.[99]

Though formally concerned with state powers in some of these cases, the actual question concerns the policy issue underneath.[100] Therefore, it could be argued that this type of procedure is in a narrow sense ineffective, because it is being used as an instrument to secure

88 481 US 739.

89 Ibid 745.

90 ECJ, Case C-376/98 *Germany v Parliament and Council* [2000] ECR I-8419 and Case C-380/03 *Germany v Parliament and Council* [2006] ECR I-11573.

91 ECJ, Case C-377/98 *Netherlands v European Parliament and Council* [2001] ECR I-7079.

92 ECJ, Joined Cases C-184/02 and C-223/02 *Spain and Finland v Parliament and Council* [2004] ECR I-7789.

93 ECJ, Case C-301/06 *Ireland v Parliament and Council* [2009] ECR I-593.

94 German Basic Law, Art 93(1) No 1.

95 BVerfGE 62,1.

96 BVerfGE 114, 121.

97 BVerfGE 90, 286.

98 BVerfGE 68, 1.

99 BVerfGE 70, 324.

100 The actual question behind the constitutional complaint on military out-of-area deployment actually was whether such deployment was constitutional, not whether parliamentary rights were being respected in this instance.

parliamentary opposition rights instead of issues of state powers. In a wider sense, this judicial method on issues of state powers is effective, when speaking of parliamentary opposition rights and legislative control rights. Other countries like Bulgaria, Italy, Spain, or Switzerland also have judicial control on questions of state powers, each with their own degree of politicized usage.[101]

Because this judicial procedure can lead to political abuse, some countries such as the United States, France, the United Kingdom or Malta explicitly opted against such a procedure. Here, constitutional competence conflicts are settled by other means—be it by public debate and/or by one or several of the non-judicial methods described above. That these measures may not always suffice can be witnessed in US security policy where, officially, war may only be declared by Congress.[102] However, in over 125 instances, military intervention was ordered by the President without such a formal declaration,[103] leading—after the undeclared Vietnam War ended—to the 'War Powers Resolution' of 1973.[104] Although this complex legal question on the constitutional powers of the President and Congress cannot be discussed in detail here, the example shows that some countries try—some more effectively than others—to insure constitutional efficacy in competence questions by non-judicial ways and means.

iii. Concrete Review and Preliminary Reference

Although there are different ways to conduct concrete constitutional review, it can only be exercised *ex post* since it results from the application of constitutional law to a specific case. In systems with a decentralized constitutional review, ordinary courts will apply constitutional law to their case and—if necessary—invalidate ordinary legislation that is in conflict with the constitution. If constitutional review is centralized, issues of constitutional law can be brought before the constitutional court by way of a concrete review procedure and preliminary references (and in some cases even directly by way of a constitutional complaint, which will be dealt with later on). Taken together, these are probably the most commonly applied forms of constitutional review.[105]

Decentralized review guarantees that all aspects of a case are dealt with by the same court: it will assess the issues of ordinary law and—if necessary—correct the results in view of constitutional law. This may require the interpretation of ordinary law in conformity with the constitution or even the annulment of specific norms of ordinary law. A system of appeals can then be used to ensure the coherence of the legal system.

Concrete review in systems of centralized review typically results in a division between issues of ordinary law and issues of constitutional law related to any given case. Ordinary courts will only apply ordinary law although they may be required to take constitutional law into account.[106] If irreconcilable conflicts with constitutional law become apparent, it should be possible to refer the issue to the constitutional court, which can clarify the interpretation of the constitution and invalidate ordinary law which does not comply with the constitution. However, to resolve the issue once and for all, the case usually needs to be sent back to the

[101] Bulgarian Constitution, Art 149(1) no 3, Italian Constitution, Art 134, Spanish Constitution, s 161, cl 1c, and Swiss Constitution, Art 189.

[102] US Constitution, Art 1, s 8.

[103] Memorandum Opinion for the deputy Counsel to the President of 25 September 2001, available at <http://www.justice.gov/olc/warpowers925.htm>.

[104] Pub L 93-148.

[105] For EU Member States see CEP (n 56); for the ECJ see <http://curia.europa.eu/>; for others, see Lijphart (n 87).

[106] For Germany, see BVerfGE 2, 266 (281).

referring court. Although the preliminary reference procedure of the ECJ[107] is not the same as the procedure of concrete review, it is somewhat comparable—especially when analysing it with regard to its contribution to constitutional efficacy. Preliminary references to the ECJ can be made about *ordinary legislation* (how to interpret regulations and directives), which should obviously not be encompassed when analysing *constitutional* efficacy. But the procedure can also be applied to the Treaties themselves and therefore to assess the European 'constitutionality' of European legislation,[108] or—in cooperation with the referring national courts—the 'constitutionality' of national legislation.

The practical effect of these types of concrete review depends on the attitudes of the courts involved. If ordinary courts accept the powers and position of the constitutional court (the ECJ) over their cases they will be inclined to refer cases. It may be particularly attractive for lower courts to refer a case to the constitutional court directly in order to circumvent the jurisprudence of other or higher courts. This has been noted in particular with regard to the preliminary references to the ECJ.[109] To avoid this questionable phenomenon of circumventing the ordinary court system, the latest French constitutional reform does not provide for a direct reference to the constitutional court but requires that lower courts first address the respective supreme court of their hierarchy, the Cour de Cassation or the Conseil d'État, which then decide whether the question will be referred to the constitutional court.[110]

Another determining factor is whether the constitutional court is open or restrictive in accepting references for concrete review. On the one hand, the German Federal Constitutional Court, for example, sets very high standards for the admissibility of such references. A court may only make a reference if it is convinced that the norm in question is unconstitutional. This position must be exhaustively reasoned on the basis of existing jurisprudence and doctrine, taking all possible interpretations into account. Moreover, it must be convincingly shown that the reference is necessary to decide the case.[111] The ECJ, on the other hand, is much more open to preliminary references. Here, the only requirements are that the question is comprehensible and not obviously hypothetical.[112] This position is based on the idea that individuals contribute to the enforcement of EU law in the member states if they seek judicial protection of their rights resulting from the Treaties.[113]

Another factor which is purely practical, but no less important, may be the actual workload of the constitutional court. A system of preliminary references has a higher chance of reaching acceptance, if a decision is handed down within a reasonable time frame.

iv. Constitutional Complaint

The constitutional complaint can be an alternative or an addition to the system of preliminary references. The EU and some countries, such as France, do not provide for such a procedure, but many other countries, like the Czech and Slovak Republics, Germany, Poland, Spain,

[107] Article 267 TFEU.

[108] On the constitutionality of the Treaties, see ECJ, Case 294/83 *Parti écologiste 'Les Verts' v European Parliament* [1986] ECR 1339, para 23 in which the ECJ classifies the Treaties as a 'basic constitutional charter'; see also Peter Schiffauer, 'Zum Verfassungszustand der Europäischen Union nach Unterzeichnung des Vertrags von Lissabon' (2008) 35 *Europäische Grundrechtezeitschrift* 1; Ingolf Pernice and Evgeni Tanchev (eds), *Ceci n'est pas une Constitution—Constitutionalisation without a Constitution?* (2009).

[109] Cf ECJ, Case C-173/09 *Elchinov* [not yet published in the ECR], para 32.

[110] See French Constitution, Art 61(1) and Arts 23(1) ff of the Law 2009-1523, JORF No 287, 21379.

[111] eg BVerfGE 105, 61 (67).

[112] eg ECJ, Cases C-415/93 *Bosman* [1995] ECR I-4921, paras 59–61 and C-344/04 IATA and ELFAA [2006] ECR I-403, para 24.

[113] ECJ, Case C-26/62 *van Gend en Loos* [1963] ECR 1, 26.

Mexico, or many other Latin American countries provide for the possibility for any natural or judicial person to bring a case directly before the constitutional court by means of a constitutional complaint or 'writ of amparo'. In Slovenia, this constitutional complaint can only be initiated via a specially designated ombudsman.[114] Moreover, all member states of the Council of Europe fall under the jurisdiction of the European Court of Human Rights in Strasbourg. Therefore, they are subject to complaints alleging the infringement of the ECHR.

A common characteristic of a constitutional complaint is the exhaustion of ordinary or—in the case of the Strasbourg Court—domestic remedies, meaning that all other judicial appeals need to be exhausted before a constitutional complaint is admissible. This guarantees the best possible assessment of the whole case by the ordinary courts, including appreciation of the necessity of a reference to the constitutional court where such a reference is possible. However, in contrast to the reference, the constitutional complaint avoids all external filters. Therefore, the constitutional complaint bears an even greater risk than the preliminary reference procedure that the constitutional court is flooded with cases.

An overloaded constitutional court is a problem with regard to constitutional efficacy, a problem best summarized by the maxim 'justice delayed is justice denied'. Only an efficient court is able to guarantee individual rights within a reasonable time (cf Article 6 of the ECHR): judicial efficiency therefore leads to constitutional efficacy. If a constitutional court is flooded with cases, constitutional rights cannot be guaranteed for all citizens in time, simply due to a lack of human resources and time available. The European Court of Human Rights, for example, has a backlog of over 151,600 cases.[115] To overcome this backlog, Protocol No 14 recently amended the ECHR, providing for judgments by a single judge and reducing in general the requirements for the number of judges necessary to decide a case.[116] The German Federal Constitutional Court tries to handle the massive number of applications by deciding most cases in chambers of only three judges, rejecting many complaints without providing any reasoning and sometimes issuing fees for an abuse of the procedure.[117]

In contrast, the US Supreme Court enjoys broad discretion which cases it chooses to hear. This 'writ of certiorari' was established in 1891 with the Evarts Act,[118] after the Court became clogged with pro forma appeals.[119] Such an approach can be justified in a system of decentralized constitutional review, where at least the lower courts can ensure that the constitution is respected. In centralized systems, discretionary review bears the risk that in some cases the infringement of constitutional rights is not subject to sufficient judicial review. Therefore, a very difficult balance has to be struck between judicial efficiency and judicial efficacy in order to guarantee constitutional efficacy in the end.

In spite of these practical problems, concrete judicial review is generally perceived as one of the most effective instruments in securing individual rights of the constitution. Countless rulings in many countries by constitutional courts have already struck down legislation or administrative acts because of their unconstitutionality.

A possible downside of ensuring constitutional rights in this way is the increased role which constitutional review plays in the political process—judicial activism.[120] As constitutions often

[114] Slovenian Constitution, Art 159.

[115] ECHR, The European Court of Human Rights in Facts and Figures, available at <http://www.echr.coe.int>.

[116] See <http://conventions.coe.int/Treaty/EN/Treaties/Html/194.htm>.

[117] German Constitutional Court, 2 BVR 1806/95.

[118] 26 Stat 826.

[119] See <http://www.fjc.gov/history/home.nsf/page/landmark_12.html>.

[120] Cf Grimm (n 6), 111ff.

cannot be amended easily, some argue that the judicialization of the political process reduces parliamentary and public debate which may very well lead to political deadlock.[121] If the constitutional court gets involved in cases where it 'should' exercise judicial self-restraint,[122] the ineffectiveness of constitutional provisions on state powers and the separation of powers may be the result and the judiciary might be perceived as a de facto legislative body.

(b) Decentralized Judicial Review

As already mentioned, some countries did not opt for centralized constitutional review of legislation by a constitutional court but have 'decentralized' this task. In such a decentralized system, there is no single institution charged with the task of controlling the constitutionality of legislation. Instead the task is conferred on all courts of the country's legal system.[123] This model is often referred to as the 'American' model, whilst the centralized model is referred to as the 'European' model.[124] Nevertheless, the 'American' model is certainly not limited to the United States, but is also in use in the Nordic countries[125], and to a certain extent also in Greece.[126] Further examples are Argentina, Australia, Canada, India, and Japan,[127] as well as Mexico. Even in continental Europe, the introduction of the 'American' model had been considered by some countries, in particular in France, Germany, and Italy during the inter-war period.

It is a specific characteristic of many decentralized systems that it was not the constitution but the judicial system itself that introduced judicial review of legislation. Following the famous US Supreme Court decision *Marbury v Madison* of 1803,[128] similar rulings of the respective supreme courts were issued in Norway and Denmark in the nineteenth and the beginning of the twentieth century. The Swedish Reichsgericht gave its blessing to the judicial review of legislation in 1964.[129] Whereas to this day there is no explicit constitutional backing for the judicial review of legislation in the United States, the Finnish (s 106) and Swedish (Ch 11, s 14) Constitutions explicitly state the right of courts to control the constitutionality of legislation—a competence which is in practice only rarely applied.[130]

Where the judicial system imposed itself as guardian of the constitution, a paradox regarding constitutional efficacy appears: on the one hand, the constitution did not explicitly opt for judicial review by the supreme court or any court at all. To declare oneself competent as guardian of the constitution in order to ensure its efficacy can undermine constitutional efficacy

[121] But see eg the vivid public and parliamentary debates or conflicts caused by certain judgments as eg the cases of the ECJ, C-438/05 *International Transport Workers' Federation und Finnish Seamen's Union—Viking Line* [2007] ECR I-10779, C-341/05 *Laval un Partneri* [2007] ECR I-11767, C-346/06 *Rüffert* [2008] ECR I-1989, and C-319/06 *Commission v Luxembourg* [2008] ECR I-4323; see in this regard also Juliane Kokott, 'Der EuGH—eine neoliberale Institution?' in Christine Hohmann-Dennhardt et al (eds), *Grundrechte und Solidarität—Durchsetzung und Verfahren, Festschrift für Renate Jaeger* (2011), 115. For the ECtHR, see eg *M v Germany*, App no 19359/04, on preventive detention, and for the US Supreme Court, see eg *Brown v Board of Education* 347 US 483 (1954).

[122] Sceptical towards the concept of judicial self-restraint, see Grimm (n 6), 116.

[123] Louis Favoreu, 'Constitutional Review in Europe' in Louis Henkin and Albert J. Rosenthal (eds), *Constitutionalism and Rights—The Influence of the United States Constitution Abroad* (1990), 38–62 at 40–1 referring to Cappelletti and Cohn, *Comparative Constitutional Law*, 14.

[124] Favoreu (n 123), 40.

[125] Ibid 46ff.

[126] Greek Constitution, Art 100 provides for a 'Supreme Special Court' which only serves as a constitutional court when the three supreme courts take contradictory decisions or judge differently the constitutionality of a legal provision.

[127] Vicky C. Jackson and Mark Tushnet, *Comparative Constitutional Law* (1999), 456.

[128] *Marbury v Madison* 5 US 137 (1803).

[129] Wieser (n 15), 122ff.

[130] Hautamäki (n 10), 5.

with regard to the distribution of powers. After all, the founding fathers might have had other methods, or no method at all (meaning parliamentary sovereignty), in mind to ensure the constitution's effectiveness. On the other hand, if the constitution is regarded as binding law, it is logical to turn to the courts for its protection. Moreover, other considerations, such as the degree of judicial activism or judicial self-restraint should also be taken into account.[131] If de jure self-created competencies are de facto not being used, the constitution's allocation of competencies is being abided by and constitutional efficacy therefore ensured from a competence perspective.

The differences between the two concepts of centralized and decentralized judicial review reflect different understandings of the separation of powers.[132] While legislative action can be assessed from a rather abstract point of view in a centralized system, decentralized judicial review takes a more direct approach because it can only start from specific disputes.[133] For example, Article III, section 2 of the US Constitution restricts jurisdiction of federal courts to 'cases or controversies'. Accordingly, it has been decided that there can be no abstract judicial review.[134] However, as long as there is a specific case, judges are called upon to control the constitutionality of legislation. In *Marbury v Madison*, the US Supreme Court held that 'a law repugnant to the Constitution is void' and that, in consequence, courts must disregard the specific law and decide the case only on the basis of the superior constitutional principles.[135]

Another major difference between centralized and decentralized review lies in the binding force of the respective decisions. While centralized judicial review conducted by a constitutional court anchored in the constitution has a universal (*erga omnes*) binding effect and can thus declare a law to be unconstitutional with respect to all possible cases,[136] the question whether a 'decentralized' decision has the same binding force, is not as evident. A priori, such a decision has a binding force upon the parties involved in the specific case.[137] However, the outcome of a decentralized review decision by one of many lower courts cannot automatically have the same binding effect as a decision of a constitutional court. Consequently, the *erga omnes* effect of decentralized constitutional review is a difficult question as is exemplified by the US system. The judgment of lower courts develops a binding force insofar as they create precedents which may be relied upon for the resolution of similar questions in other cases. Nevertheless, in general, only judgments by the US Supreme Court have been treated as authoritative and binding for everyone.

Furthermore, in cases in which constitutional rights are at stake, and are resolved without the supreme court, the question of differing rulings in similar cases arises. Greece, which also favours a decentralized model, solved this problem by allowing appeals to the highest court of each respective branch. If different constitutional interpretations arise, an ad hoc constitutional court is formed to resolve the dispute.[138]

[131] On the different degrees of judicial activism, see Lijphart (n 87), 225ff.

[132] Favoreu (n 123), 42.

[133] Above Section IV.2(a); Michel Rosenfeld, 'Constitutional Adjudication in Europe and the United States: Paradoxes and Contrasts' in Georg Nolte (ed), *European and US Constitutionalism* (2005), 197.

[134] *Muskrat v United States* 219 US 346 (1911); cf also *Raines v Byrd* 521 US 811 (1997) (challenge by members of Congress on the losing side of legislation granting the President a 'line item veto' held to be not justiciable) as cited by Rosenfeld (n 124), 198).

[135] *Marbury v Madison* 5 US 137 (1803).

[136] Favoreu (n 123), 41; see eg the German Act on the Constitutional Court, s 31(2).

[137] Favoreu (n 123), 41.

[138] Greek Constitution, Art XXX100.

As a consequence of these considerations, the decentralized judicial model can be regarded as somewhat of an in-between solution between parliamentary sovereignty and a centralized constitutional court. In general, the legislature is being trusted and only if and when constitutional rights of an individual are concerned, is the judiciary allowed to intervene.[139] This concept excludes, in particular, the abstract review of legislation and can also limit the scope for disputes between state organs.

V. Conclusion

This chapter has shown several key instruments on how to ensure that a constitution's rights and rules are being respected and guaranteed effectively. In guaranteeing the effectiveness of a constitution, important constitutional principles, such as the supremacy of parliament, may sometimes have to be limited. Furthermore, the effective application of constitutional norms can (or maybe even needs to) reduce the efficiency of political systems, especially in federal or supranational systems. All in all, there can be no general conclusion on which instruments are better suited to guard the constitution's efficacy. The result varies from country to country depending on many factors, such as political culture, the constitution's length and precision, or even contradictory rights and principles within a constitution, to name but a few.

However, if we believe that constitutions matter, at least some of the instruments to ensure the constitution's efficacy are necessary. They are safeguards of these fundamental rights, rules, and principles. In detracting their alteration from the usual legal process and imposing supermajorities on possible amendments, the constitution provides a solid rock of and for a society and country, fundamentals all citizens can rely on and immune from the opportunistic daily life of politics.

Bibliography

Aharon Barak, 'The Role of the Supreme Court in a Democracy' in Mads Andenas (ed), *Judicial Review in International Perspective—Liber Amicorum Lord Slynn of Hadley* (2000)

Robert Dahl, 'Decision-Making in a Democracy: The Supreme Court as a National Policy-Maker' (1957) 6 *Journal of Public Law* 279

Robert Dahl, *On Democracy* (2000), 119–29

Dan Diner and Michael Stolleis (eds), *Hans Kelsen and Carl Schmitt—A Juxtaposition* (1999)

John Hart Ely, *Democracy and Distrust: A Theory of Judicial Review* (1980)

Hans Kelsen, *General Theory of Law and State* (Anders Wedberg trans, 1949)

Michael Rosenfeld, 'Constitutional Adjudication in Europe and the United States: Paradoxes and Contrasts' in Georg Nolte (ed), *European and US Constitutionalism* (2005)

[139] Rosenfeld (n 133), 220.

CHAPTER 38

CONSTITUTIONAL COURTS

ALEC STONE SWEET

New York

I. Introduction

Prior to the Second World War, only a handful of high courts in the world had routinely exercised the power of constitutional judicial review: the authority to invalidate statutes and other acts of public authority found to be in conflict with a constitution. In the 1950s, Western Europe began to emerge as the epicenter of a 'new constitutionalism',[1] a model of democracy and state legitimacy that rejects the dogmas of legislative sovereignty, prioritizes fundamental rights, and requires a mode of constitutional review. With successive waves of democratization, this new constitutionalism spread across the continent. By the 1990s, the basic formula—(1) an entrenched, written constitution, (2) a charter of fundamental rights, and (3) a mode of constitutional judicial review to protect those rights—had diffused globally.[2] The

[1] Martin Shapiro and Alec Stone, 'The New Constitutional Politics of Europe' (1994) 26 *Comparative Political Studies* 397.

[2] David Law and Mila Versteeg, 'The Evolution and Ideology of Global Constitutionalism' (2011) 99 *California Law Review* 1163; Shannon Roesler, 'Permutations of Judicial Power: The New Constitutionalism and the Expansion of Judicial Authority' (2007) 32 *Law and Social Inquiry* 545. Of 106 national constitutions written since 1985, every one contained a charter of rights, and all but five established a mode of rights review, *Data Set on Written Constitutions, Rights, and Constitutional Review since 1789*, compiled by the author and Christine Andersen, 2007, on file with the author.

availability of the constitutional court (CC) has been crucial to this process. For reasons to be discussed, the framers of new constitutions have been more attracted to the 'centralized model' of constitutional review, with a specialized CC at its core, than to the 'decentralized (or *American*) model' of judicial review exercised by the judiciary as a whole.

This chapter provides an introduction to the basic institutional features of CCs, as well as an overview of the small but growing comparative literature on their design, function, impact, and legitimacy.[3] Every CC that operates with any effectiveness exhibits certain unique attributes that have been important to its success, however relative, in making a constitution effective as enforceable law. Although important monographs have been produced on specific courts,[4] this chapter is pitched at a higher level of abstraction. It presents the CC as an ideal type, with its own functional logics, and surveys the comparative scholarship seeking to explain commonalities and differences across systems. The chapter will emphasize inter-disciplinarity, in part, because political scientists have been at the forefront of empirical research[5] and, in part, because powerful CCs have shaped and reshaped their own political environments. Successful CCs routinely subvert separation of powers schemes, including elements on which their legitimacy was originally founded. In consequence, new legitimacy questions and discourses have emerged.

II. Origins, Models, Diffusion

A CC is a constitutionally established, independent organ of the state whose central purpose is to defend the normative superiority of the constitutional law within the juridical order.

Prior to the turn of the twentieth century, several specialized, constitutional 'jurisdictions' had appeared in Europe, notably in Austria and the Germanic states. The modern constitutional court, however, is largely the invention of Hans Kelsen. Kelsen developed what is now called the 'centralized' or 'European' model of review, first, in his role as a drafter of the constitution of the Austrian Second Republic (1920–34), and then as a theoretician.[6] The founders of

[3] The first book in this genre to appear in English was Christine Landfried, *Constitutional Review and Legislation: An International Comparison* (1989), followed by: Herman Schwartz, *The Struggle for Constitutional Justice in Post-Communist Europe* (2000); Alec Stone Sweet, *Governing with Judges: Constitutional Politics in Europe* (2000); Wojciech Sadurski (ed), *Constitutional Justice, East and West: Democratic Legitimacy and Constitutional Courts in Post-Communist Europe in a Comparative Perspective* (2002); Tom Ginsburg, *Judicial Review in New Democracies: Constitutional Courts in Asia* (2003); Wojciech Sadurski, *Rights Before Courts: A Study of Constitutional Courts in Postcommunist States of Central and Eastern Europe* (2005); Victor Perreres Comella, *Constitutional Courts and Democratic Values: A European Perspective* (2009); and Andrew Harding and Peter Leyland (eds), *Constitutional Courts: A Comparative Study* (2009).

[4] Including, in order of publication, Donald Kommers, *Judicial Politics in West Germany* (1976); Alec Stone, *The Birth of Judicial Politics in France* (1992); Heinz Klug, *Constituting Democracy: Law, Globalism, and South Africa's Political Reconstruction* (2000); Mary Volcansek, *Constitutional Politics in Italy: The Constitutional Court* (2000); László Sólyom and Georg Brunner, *A Constitutional Judiciary in a New Democracy* [Hungary] (2000); Robert Barros, *Constitutionalism and Dictatorship: Pinochet, the Junta, and the 1980 Constitution* (2002); Georg Vanberg, *The Politics of Constitutional Review in Germany* (2005); Tamir Moustafa, *The Struggle for Constitutional Power: Law, Politics, and Economic Development in Egypt* (2007); and Alexei Trochev, *Judging Russia: Constitutional Court in Russian Politics, 1990–2006* (2008).

[5] Martin Shapiro and Alec Stone (eds), 'Special Issue: The New Constitutional Politics of Europe' (1994) 26 *Comparative Political Studies* 397; and Mary Volcansek (ed), 'Special Issue: Judicial Politics in Western Europe' (1992) 15 *West European Politics*.

[6] Hans Kelsen, 'La garantie juridictionnelle de la constitution' (1928) 45 *Revue de Droit Public* 197. The other indispensable classic is Charles Eisenmann's thesis, written under Kelsen's supervision, *La justice constitutionnelle et la Haute cour constitutionnelle d'Autriche* (1928, reprint 1986).

the present German and Italian systems constructed new CCs from the template Kelsen laid down.[7] His legacy was secured when constitutional reformers in Southern, Central, and Eastern Europe later rejected American-style judicial review, while embracing the Kelsenian court.[8]

As an ideal type, the 'centralized', or 'European', model of constitutional review can be broken down into four constituent components. First, CCs possess a monopoly on the power to invalidate infra-constitutional legal norms, including statutes, as unconstitutional. Meanwhile, the 'ordinary' courts (the judiciary, including specialized jurisdictions) are prohibited from doing so. In the United States, review authority inheres in judicial power: all judges possess it. Secondly, CCs resolve disputes about the interpretation and application of the constitution. The US Supreme Court is the highest court of appeal for almost all legal disputes in the American legal order, of whatever type. In contrast, CCs do not preside over litigation, which remains the purview of the ordinary courts. Instead, specifically designated authorities or individuals ask questions of CCs, challenging the constitutionality of specific legal acts; constitutional judges are then required to answer these questions, and to justify their answers with reasons. The rulings of CCs are final. Thirdly, CCs have links with, but are formally detached from, the legislative, executive, and judicial branches of government. Constitutional judges occupy their own 'constitutional space', which is neither clearly 'judicial' (the enforcement of preexisting legal norms in the course of litigation) nor 'political' (the creation of new legal norms) in classic continental terms. Fourthly, unlike the US Supreme Court, whose jurisdiction is constrained by the 'case or controversy' requirement, most CCs may review statutes 'in the abstract', before they have been enforced. 'Abstract review' is typically justified as a means of eliminating unconstitutional legislation and practices *before* they can do harm.

The successful diffusion of the Kelsenian court within Western Europe after the Second World War depended heavily on three factors. First, framers of new constitutions believed that the concentrated system of review would 'fit' a parliamentary system of government better than the decentralized, American system. A CC can be attached to the existing architecture of the state with minimal disruption to established orders, notably the separation of powers notions associated with legislative sovereignty. Under the European model, it remains possible to defend the notion that the ordinary courts are bound by the supremacy of statute, while constitutional judges are charged with preserving the supremacy of the constitution. More generally, whenever groups that negotiate new constitutions are dominated by political parties who are hostile to sharing their power with the judiciary, centralizing review authority in a single organ will appear to be a less costly option, compared to adopting the American system. Moreover, framers can easily design CCs so that their composition will reflect outcomes of political processes: members of CCs are typically appointed by elected officials or after bargaining among political parties; and members serve fixed terms.

Secondly, the new constitutionalism, with its heavy emphasis on rights and review, emerged first in Germany, in reaction to the horrors of the Holocaust and the destruction of the Second World War.[9] As authoritarian regimes collapsed in Southern Europe in the 1970s, and then across Central and Eastern Europe and the Balkans in the 1990s, that situation was reproduced in key respects, and the Austro-German approach to constitutionalism was adopted

[7] See also Hans Kelsen, 'Judicial Review of Legislation: A Comparative Study of the Austrian and the American Constitution' (1942) 4 *Journal of Politics* 183.

[8] The major exception is Greece, which adopted a mixed American/European system.

[9] Americans occupied West Germany and Italy during the founding period, and insisted that new constitutions include rights and review.

and adapted. In each of these episodes, the framers of new constitutions saw no contradiction between democracy and rights protection (at a time when the prestige of political parties and legislative authority was relatively low). On the contrary, a robust system of rights protection was viewed as a pre-condition for democratic rule. The Kelsenian court offered a means of prioritizing rights protection, while maintaining the prohibition of judicial review.

This last point raises a contradiction for the original model that deserves attention. In his seminal paper of 1928,[10] Kelsen laid out a blueprint for CCs, and a defense of the political legitimacy of the centralized model of review. Although he recognized that a constitutional judge's authority to invalidate unconstitutional statutes comprised a type of legislative power, he labored to distinguish between legislating and constitutional adjudication. Members of parliaments, he argued, are 'positive legislators': they make law freely, subject only to constitutional constraints, such as the rules of legislative procedure or federalism. Constitutional judges are 'negative legislators': their lawmaking authority is restricted to the annulment of legal norms that conflict with the constitutional law. The distinction between the positive and the negative legislator rests on the absence, within the constitutional law, of enforceable rights. Kelsen equated rights with (open-ended) natural law, and thought that, through the process of discovering and enforcing rights, a CC would inevitably obliterate the distinction between the negative and the positive legislator. The judges would become, in effect, supreme legislators. He therefore argued against conferring rights jurisdiction on CCs. The passage to the new constitutionalism proved Kelsen correct: any CC that protects rights with any measure of effectiveness will, at the same time, act as a positive legislator. Today, Kelsen's warning is usually politely ignored.

A third factor concerns the recursive nature of the diffusion process. Each adoption and adaptation of the Kelsenian court increases the likelihood that the next generation of constitutional framers will follow suit. Constitution-makers tend to copy arrangements that are considered successful. The CC has proved its worth as an instrument for consolidating constitutional democracy. In the 1970s, the framers in post-Franco Spain quite consciously copied the German system, without seriously considering the American model;[11] in the 1990s, the drafters of new constitutions in Central and Eastern Europe,[12] as well as in Latin America, looked to Germany and Spain;[13] the South African Constitution too was heavily influence by Germany.[14] In Asia, where American political influence is pronounced, the Austro-German model also served as a prototype for constitutional reform, most notably in South Korea.[15] As the institution has diffused, so has epistemic support for the decentralized model. Today, regional and global networks of judges, law professors, and rights-based non-governmental organizations actively defend the legitimacy of the model, further facilitating its broader diffusion.

As noted, virtually no one writes a constitution today without providing for rights protection and a mode of review. In 2005, of the 138 national systems of constitutional review that an

[10] Kelsen (n 6).

[11] See Enrique Guillén López, 'Judicial Review in Spain: The Constitutional Court' (2008) 41 *Loyola of Los Angeles Law Review* 530.

[12] Lach and Sadurski, 'Constitutional Courts of Central and Eastern Europe: Between Adolescence and Maturity' in Harding and Leyland (n 3), 52.

[13] For a survey of review systems in the region, see Patricio Navia and Juilo Ríos-Figueroa, 'The Constitutional Adjudication Mosaic of Latin America' (2005) 38 *Comparative Political Studies* 189.

[14] Jörg Fedtke, *Die Rezeption von Verfassungsrecht—Südafrika 1993–1996* (2000).

[15] Tom Ginsburg, 'East Asia: Constitutional Courts in East Asia: Understanding Variation' in Harding and Leyland (n 3), 291.

analyst could clearly classify as conforming to either the American or the Kelsenian model, 85 (62 percent) were Kelsenian. CCs comprise the dominant organ of review in Europe, Africa, and the Middle East, and have made in-roads into Asia, South East Asia, and Latin America (where 'mixed' systems of various types are common[16]). The American model clearly dominates only in North America and the Caribbean.[17] Two of the world's most active and effective CCs are found outside Europe, in Colombia and South Africa. Finally, leaders of authoritarian regimes, who may have no intention of democratizing or weakening one-party rule, may nonetheless establish CCs. As Moustafa has shown, with respect to Egypt in the 1980s and 1990s, rulers may create a CC as a way of signaling to the international community that it is committed to reform, legal security, and property rights, not least to attract needed foreign investment and external support more generally.[18] Similar dynamics can be found in Latin America.[19]

III. Design and Functions

The establishment of a system of constitutional review raises a primordial question. Why, at the foundational moment, would the most powerful political actors in a state choose to constrain the future exercise of their own lawmaking authority? After all, in most places where new CCs have been adopted, the various dogmas of legislative sovereignty had previously reigned as embedded orthodoxy. In responding to this question, scholars have gradually developed what is, in effect, a functional theory of delegation to CCs. The Kelsenian court helps those who build new constitutional arrangements to resolve certain dilemmas, including problems of imperfect contracting and commitment. These problems are especially acute in the domains of federalism and rights. Although functional logics may help us to understand, in broad-brush terms, the turn to constitutional review, more fine-grained analyses are necessary to explain variation across cases, or the design and functioning of any specific CC.

1. Functional Logics and Commitment

A diverse group of scholars have developed variants of delegation theory[20] to explain why the founders of new constitutions would establish and confer authority on CCs. In this account, the availability of the CC gives drafters the confidence to strike constitutional bargains *ex ante*, as well as a means of guaranteeing the credibility of commitments made *ex post*.

Ginsburg has elaborated and tested an 'insurance model of judicial review' that explains variation in the design of systems of review with reference to the extent to which political authority (or the party system) is fragmented at the *ex ante* moment.[21] In a system dominated by one person or political party, rulers have little incentive to construct a review system that

[16] Navia and Ríos-Figueroa (n 13).

[17] See the website maintained by Arne Mavčič, at <http://www.concourts.net/>.

[18] Tamir Moustafa, 'Law and Resistance in Authoritarian States: the Judicialization of Politics in Egypt' in Tom Ginsburg and Tamir Moustafa (eds), *Rule by Law: The Politics of Courts in Authoritarian Regimes* (2008), 132.

[19] Eduardo Dargent, 'Determinants of Judicial Independence: Lessons from Three "Cases" of Constitutional Courts in Peru' (2009) 41 *Journal of Latin American Studies* 251.

[20] For an introduction to delegation theory as applied to a range of political institutions, including courts, see Mark Thatcher and Alec Stone Sweet, 'Theory and Practice of Delegation to Non-Majoritarian Institutions' (2002) 25 *West European Politics* 1.

[21] Ginsburg (n 3).

would constrain them. When they do establish a CC, it is often to consolidate a regime meant to benefit them while disadvantaging their opponents; examples include many authoritarian regimes, but also the Gaullist-dominated France of 1958. More interesting: to the extent that a competitive party system exists, or can be foreseen, each negotiating party will have an incentive in building a more robust mode of review, in order to protect its interests when it is out of power.[22] Ginsburg's work is exemplary in that he supplements deductive theorizing and quantitative analysis with detailed case studies of the creation and subsequent operation of CCs in Asia.[23]

More generally, CCs help framers resolve a bundle of contracting problems.[24] Modern constitutions are contracts that are typically negotiated by political elites—representatives of competing groups or political parties—seeking to establish the rules, procedures, and institutions that will permit them, under the cloak of constitutional legitimacy, to govern. In establishing a democracy, each contracting party knows that it must compete for office, through elections. As Ginsburg emphasizes, constitutional contracting allows each to constrain opponents when the latter are in power. The constitution thus produces two common goods for the new polity: a set of enabling institutions, and a set of constraints. If the system is to be federal or strongly regional, review will provide a means of settling boundary conflicts. It is an old truism that federalism needs an umpire, which helps to explain why all federal constitutions provide for review in some form. To be credible, contracting rights, too, necessitates delegation of review powers.

All contracts are 'incomplete' to the extent that meaningful uncertainty exists as to the precise nature of the contract's terms. Due to the impossibility of negotiating specific rules for all possible contingencies, and given that, as time passes, conditions will change and the interests of the parties to the agreement will evolve, most agreements of any complexity are generated by what organizational economists call 'relational contracting'. The parties to an agreement seek to broadly 'frame' their relationship, by agreeing on a set of basic 'goals and objectives', fixing outer limits on acceptable behavior, and establishing procedures for 'completing' the contract over time.[25] Constitutions negotiated by multiple parties, and modern rights provisions, in particular, are paradigmatic examples of relational contracting.[26]

Take the following scenario, which is a stylized version of what has recurred across the globe since 1945. Once the founders choose to include a charter of rights in their constitution, they face two fierce dilemmas. The first concerns disagreements about the nature and content of rights. The left-wing contingent favors positive, social rights, and limits on the rights to property. The right is hostile to positive rights, and they want stronger property rights. They compromise, producing an extensive charter of rights that (1) lists most of the rights that each side wants, (2) implies that no right is absolute or more important than another, and (3) is vague about how any future conflict between two rights, or a right and a legitimate governmental purpose, will be resolved. Secondly, they face a problem of credible commitment: How will rights be enforced? Delegating review powers to a CC helps them manage both problems, allowing them to move forward.

[22] See also Ran Hirschl, *Towards Juristocracy: The Origins and Consequences of the New Constitutionalism* (2004).

[23] Ibid; see also Tom Ginsburg, 'Constitutional Courts in East Asia: Understanding Variation' in Harding and Leyland (n 3).

[24] Alec Stone Sweet, 'Constitutional Courts and Parliamentary Democracy' (2002) 25 *West European Politics* 77; Law and Versteeg (n 2).

[25] Paul Milgrom and John Roberts, *Economics, Organization and Management* (1992), 127–33.

[26] Stone Sweet (n 3), ch 2.

Delegation theorists assume that the more acute are the problems of imperfect commitment and incomplete contracting, the more authority—or discretion—the framers must delegate to the review court if constitutional arrangements are to be successful. Relational contracting—the reliance on relatively imprecise legal provisions to express important objectives—can help divided framers to reach agreement in the first place. Yet, in the context of review, textual imprecision, if it is not to paralyze the review court *ex post*, must be understood to comprise a tacit, second-order form of delegation to the Agent. The decision rules that govern constitutional amendment are also built into the delegation of discretion to the CC: the harder it is to nullify the effects of the CC's rulings *ex post*, through constitutional amendment, the more the CC will determine how constitutional arrangements evolve.

These points can be formalized in terms of a theoretical *zone of discretion*—the strategic environment—in which any CC operates. This zone is determined by (1) the sum of powers delegated to a CC, or possessed as a result of a CC's own accreted rulemaking, minus (2) the sum of control instruments available for use by other constitutionally recognized authorities to reverse outcomes resulting from the court's performance of its delegated tasks. Most CCs operate in an unusually permissive strategic environment, to the extent that even their most important rulings are unlikely to be overturned. Entrenchment is a commitment device. Most contemporary constitutions are far more difficult to amend than statutes; and many constitutions declare off-limits to revision certain core constitutional elements (the most common of which are rights, parliamentary democracy, and federalism). Further, some CCs have the express authority to review the constitutionality of amendments to the constitution, or have asserted on their own that the constitution imposes substantive constraints on amendment.[27]

For these reasons, the analyst may conceptualize CCs as 'trustees' of the constitutional order, rather than mere 'agents' of the contract.[28] In a judicial system based on statutory supremacy, the courts are 'agents' of the legislature. If judges construct the codes in ways that are undesirable, legislators, as 'principals', may amend the law to put things right. The CC, however, has no permanently constituted 'principal' that supervises its work. Once a constitution has been ratified and enters into force, those who negotiated it possess no authority to change it, at least not as the founders. Instead, the CC typically exercises its powers in the name of a fictitious entity: the sovereign People. Meanwhile, political elites compete for and exercise state power under rules and procedures laid down by the constitution, of which the CC is the authoritative interpreter.

2. Jurisdiction

The functional logics just discussed will apply to any bargaining context in which the framers set out to build a system of constitutional review—of whatever type. Compared with the major alternative, however, the specialized CC has a powerful advantage, in that the framers can more easily tailor the details of jurisdiction to specific purposes. The standard design questions—What acts are to be subject to review, through what procedures?—will be supplemented by another: What important control functions should be withheld from the ordinary courts? Thus, in addition to providing for the constitutional review of legal norms and acts, the framers may charge the CC with resolving electoral disputes, banning undemocratic political parties, presiding over the impeachment cases of elected officials, and so on. Put bluntly,

[27] Kemal Gözler, *Judicial Review of Constitutional Amendments: A Comparative Study* (2008).

[28] Alec Stone Sweet and Jud Mathews, 'Proportionality Balancing and Global Constitutionalism' (2008) 47 *Columbia Journal of Transnational Law* 68.

CCs are given functions that would be viewed as too 'political', or constitutionally important, to confer on the ordinary courts. Partly for this reason, CCs are loath to develop formal deference doctrines, such as the 'political question' doctrine of the US Supreme Court, which would signal abdication of their duties.

The most important function of the modern CC is the protection of rights by constitutional review. As noted, once the protection of fundamental rights is prioritized, sharing lawmaking power with a CC will usually be viewed a less costly option than giving all judges review powers. The American and the European models differ with respect to the pathways through which cases arise. In the United States, rights review is activated once a litigating party properly pleads a right before a judge—any judge. In countries with constitutional courts, a range of different procedures organize rights review, although not all systems have established all of them, or in the same way.

The first is *abstract review*: the pre-enforcement review of statutes. As Sadurski puts it, in this mode of review, 'it is the textual dimension of the rule [*in abstracto*] rather than its operationalization in application to real people and... legal controversies that is assessed by judges.'[29] Some systems require the statute to be reviewed before entry into force, others after promulgation but before application. Abstract review is also called 'preventive review', since its purpose is to filter out unconstitutional laws before they can harm anyone. In its most common form, abstract review is politically initiated: executives, parliamentary minorities, the heads of regions or federated entities, and so on, are authorized to refer laws considered to be unconstitutional to the CC.

The second mode is called *concrete review*, which is initiated by the judiciary in the course of litigation in the courts. Ordinary judges send questions—Is a given legal norm, judicial decision, or administrative act constitutional?—to the CC. The general rule is that the presiding judge ought to go to the CC if two conditions are met: (1) the constitutional question is material to litigation at bar (who wins or loses will depend on the answer to the question); and (2) there is reasonable doubt in the judge's mind about the constitutionality of the controlling norm. Referrals suspend proceedings pending the CC's response. Once rendered, the CC's ruling is sent back to the referring judge, who then uses it to dispose of the case. Ordinary judges are not permitted to invalidate a statute on their own. Instead, aided by litigants, they are enlisted to help the CC detect unconstitutional laws and practices. Concrete review is 'concrete' because the CC's intervention constitutes a stage in ordinary litigation taking place in the courts.

The third procedure is called the 'constitutional complaint', which brings individuals into the mix. Individuals, firms, and groups may be authorized to petition the CC when they believe that their rights have been violated, after all other remedies have been exhausted. Because of this threshold requirement, most individual complaints are, in effect, appeals of final judicial rulings. Thus, when adjudicating individual complaints, the CC performs functions more closely associated with appellate review in the American system (see Section IV below).

These three modes of review are basic to the rights-protecting mission of the German Federal Constitutional Court, arguably the most powerful and influential CC in the world. As the centralized model diffused, they were routinely adopted. The drafters of subsequent European constitutions added new features, pathways to the CC that the German and Italian founders did not even consider. In Europe, the rights ombudsman first appeared in the

[29] Sadurski (n 3), 5.

Spanish Constitution of 1978; the institution then spread across Central and Eastern Europe. The ombudsman may refer cases to the CC on her own, including petitioning for abstract review. Post-Communist constitutions in Central and Eastern Europe have also expanded the right to initiate abstract review to a diverse range of other actors, including prosecutors, state auditors, courts, local government officials, and even trade unions.[30] Thus in many newer systems, there are few if any jurisdictional or standing obstacles to getting to the CC. Under the constitutions of Hungary and Colombia, for example, everyone possesses the right to petition directly the CC, through an *actio popularis*. The 'popular action' initiates abstract review of statutes, although the petitioner need not show that the law referred has actually harmed her personally.

As a formal matter, any constitutionally-based system of rights protection can be considered to be less robust, or 'complete', the more it permits or tolerates gaps in rights protection. Since the end of the Second World War, one important trend has been toward completeness: presumptively, no legal norm, no public act, no violation of a right should be beyond the control of the constitutional judge. The situation contrasts sharply with the American system, where the case or controversy requirement, inter-branch comity, and 'political question' and other deference doctrines are expected to constrain the exercise of review will routinely produce gaps in rights protection. It is important to recognize in this regard that, unlike the US Supreme Court, many CCs were created, explicitly and as a constitutional priority, to protect rights.

3. Appointment and Composition

In a recent volume on CCs, edited by Harding and Leyland, contributors report valuable information on appointment rules and politics across Africa, Asia, Latin America, and Europe.[31] Although procedures and recruitment patterns vary widely, several general points can be made (with the caveat that none covers all cases).

First, appointments to CCs are treated differently than recruitment to the ordinary courts. Elected politicians dominate these procedures, which may require bargaining and compromise among officials and/sor legislative majorities and oppositions. In Germany, for example, the lower house appoints its quota of members to the Court through a special committee, composed of representatives of the political parties and reflecting their respective strength in the Bundestag, pursuant to a two-thirds majority vote. In Spain, the Congress and the Senate appoint members on the basis of a three-fifths vote, which in practice gives the opposition a veto. In some countries in Central and Eastern Europe, two branches of government (eg the Senate and the President in the Czech Republic) must reach consensus to appoint. Requiring compromise among political elites is less likely to produce a polarized court. Secondly, members of CCs do not enjoy lifetime tenure, but are typically appointed for a fixed 9–12-year term (often non-renewable). Thirdly, although many constitutions require that a minority of seats be filled by career judges drawn from the high courts, many CCs are composed of a majority of law professors and former governmental officials and elected politicians. As Perreres Comella has argued,[32] diversity in the make-up of these courts counts as an important 'virtue'. All significant constitutional questions mix the abstract and theoretical with the practical and governmental, and thus law professors and former politicians nicely complement one another.

[30] Ibid 5–6.
[31] Harding and Leyland (n 3).
[32] Perreres Comella (n 3), 39–43.

Taken together, these three elements are likely to contribute to the political legitimacy of a CC, when it enforces the constitutional law in ways that the political majority find unwelcome.

IV. Effectiveness and Impact

Scholars would have little interest in these developments if CCs do not influence broader processes: the consolidation of new democracies, the development of the constitution, the protection of rights, the making of public policy, competition among political elites, and so on. To the extent that constitutional review is *effective*, CCs will have impact such processes in ways that can be described and measured empirically.

1. Effectiveness

Constitutional review can be said to be *effective* to the extent that the important constitutional disputes arising in the polity are brought to the CC on a regular basis, that the judges who resolve these disputes give reasons for their rulings, and that those who are governed by the constitutional law accept that the court's ruling have some precedential effect.[33] On this definition, effectiveness is a variable: it varies across cases and across time in the same country.

Most review systems throughout world history have been relatively ineffective, even irrelevant. Political actors may seek to settle their disputes by force, rather than through the courts, sometimes with fatal consequences for the constitutional regime. Rulers may care much more about staying in power at any cost, or enriching themselves, or rewarding their friends and punishing their foes, or achieving ethnic dominance, then they care about building constitutional democracy. Dictators of various stripes may also design and deploy review courts to administer and maintain their own rule, as an important research project organized Ginsburg and Moustafa details.[34] Despite the odds, some CCs have operated with measurable effectiveness in authoritarian settings, as in Egypt[35] and Pinochet's Chile.[36]

Where review systems are relatively effective, constitutional judges manage the evolution of the polity through their decisions. There are three necessary conditions for the emergence of effective review systems; each is conditioned by the court's 'zone of discretion'. First, constitutional judges must have a caseload. If actors, private and public, conspire not to activate review, judges will accrete no influence over the polity. Secondly, once activated, judges must resolve these disputes and *give defensible reasons* in justification of their decisions. If they do, one output of constitutional adjudication will be the production of a constitutional case law, or *jurisprudence*, which is a record of how the judges have interpreted the constitution. Thirdly, those who are governed by the constitutional law must accept that constitutional meaning is (at least partly) constructed through the judges' interpretation and rulemaking, and use or refer to relevant case law in future disputes.

Some might quibble with this account of 'effectiveness'. Harding, Leyland, and Groppi, for example, argue that effectiveness should be gauged against the following criteria: (1) 'whether the court's interventions are consistent with the norms set out in the constitution, and

[33] On ensuring constitutional efficacy, see further Chapter 37.

[34] Ginsburg and Moustafa (n 18).

[35] Moustafa (n 4); Clark Lombardi, 'Egypt's Supreme Constitutional Court: Managing Constitutional Conflict in an Authoritarian Aspirationally "Islamic" State' in Harding and Leyland (n 3), 217.

[36] Barros (n 3).

whether these norms themselves are consistent with principles of "good governance" as we understand this term in international law and development discourse', and (2) 'whether the court's pronouncements are then actually embedded in practice, that is, whether they are followed'.[37] Trustee courts, however, have the capacity to alter the 'norms set out in the constitution', not least in order to enhance the centrality and enforceability of the constitutional law as a framework of 'good governance'. To take just two examples of many to be found, in 1971 the French CC incorporated rights provisions into the Constitution of the Fifth Republic, against the express wishes of the framers; and in 1958 the German CC ordered the ordinary courts to enforce the rights contained in the Basic Law when they adjudicate private law disputes.[38]

Why only some countries are able to fulfill effectiveness criteria is a controversial question in the social sciences. The achievement of stable system of constitutional justice depends heavily on the same factors and processes related to the achievement of stable democracy, and we know that democracy is difficult to create and sustain. Among other factors, the new constitutionalism rests on a polity's commitment to: elections; a competitive party system; protecting rights, including those of minorities; practices associated with the 'rule of law'; a system of advanced legal education and advocacy. Each of these factors is also associated with other important socio-cultural phenomena, including attributes of political culture, which may be illiberal and fragmented. Constitutional judges can contribute to the building of practices related to higher law constitutionalism, but there are limits to what they can do if they find themselves continuously in opposition to powerful elites, institutions, and cultural biases in the citizenry.[39] In Russia, the new CC was curbed after it began to build effectiveness, by the same elites who claimed to be committed to building constitutional rule of law.[40] Not surprisingly, one finds relatively effective review mechanisms in areas where one finds relatively stable democracy. Ranked in terms of effectiveness, the author would place the systems of Colombia,[41] the Czech Republic, Germany, Hungary, Indonesia,[42] Poland, Slovenia, South Africa, and South Korea on top of the list.

2. Democratic Transition

Since the Second World War, rights and review have been crucial to nearly all successful transitions from authoritarian regimes to constitutional democracy (including the countries just listed).[43] Indeed, it appears that the more successful any transition has been, the more likely one is to find an effective constitutional or supreme court at the heart of it (Japan may be the most important exception). A CC performs several functions that facilitate the transition to

[37] Andrew Harding, Peter Leyland and Tania Groppi, 'Constitutional Courts: Forms, Functions and Practice in Comparative Perspective' in Harding and Leyland (n 3).

[38] Alec Stone Sweet, 'The Juridical Coup d'Etat and the Problem of Authority' (2007) 8 *German Law Journal* 915.

[39] Donald Horwitz, 'Constitutional Courts: A Primer for Decision-Makers' (2006) 17 *Journal of Democracy* 125.

[40] Kim Lane Scheppele, 'Guardians of the Constitution: Constitutional Court Presidents and the Struggle for Rule of Law in Post-Soviet Europe' (2006) 154 *University of Pennsylvania Law Review* 157.

[41] Manuel Jose Cepeda-Espinosa, 'Judicial Activism in a Violent Context: The Origin, Role, and Impact of the Colombian Constitutional Court' (2004) 3 *Washington University Global Studies Law Review* 529.

[42] Also see Marcus Mietzner, 'Political Conflict Resolution and Democratic Consolidation in Indonesia: The Role of the Constitutional Court' (2010) 10 *Journal of East Asian Studies* 397.

[43] On democracy, see Chapter 11.

democracy.[44] It provides a system of peaceful dispute resolution for those who have contracted a new beginning, in light of authoritarian and violent pasts. It provides a mechanism for purging the laws of authoritarian elements, given that the new legislature may be overloaded with work. And a CC can provide a focal point for a new rhetoric of state legitimacy, one based on respect for democratic values and rights, and on the rejection of former rhetoric (of fascism, military or one-party rule, legislative sovereignty, the cult of personality, and so on).

3. Constitutional Lawmaking

Constitutional judges make law through interpreting the constitution.[45] Constitutional lawmaking is typically registered on two levels, *simultaneously*. In resolving a specific policy dispute under the constitutional law, the CC will help to make that policy; at the same time, the CC will construct the constitutional law, clarifying, supplementing, or amending it outright. The polity cannot access the benefits of review without activating the court's prospective lawmaking capacity. In a system of constitutional trusteeship, the CC will usually have the last word on any dispute about meaning, thereby generating normative guidance for future lawmaking and judging. In this way, constitutional case law, as it unfolds, creates the conditions for the 'judicialization of policymaking' (the impact of a CC on the legislative process) and for the 'constitutionalization of the law' (the impact of a CC on the judiciary).

The present author has developed a theory of 'the judicialization of politics', a process conceptualized as a structured set of 'constitutional dialogues' between the CC and legislators.[46] The impact of CCs on legislative activity varies as a function of three factors: the existence of abstract review, the number of veto points in the policy process, and the accretion of a policy-relevant jurisprudence. The more centralized is the policy process—the greater the parliamentary majority, the more that majority is under the control of a unified executive, and the fewer veto points there are in legislative procedures—the more opponents of governmental initiatives will go to the CC to block important initiatives. In Western Europe, legislative politics have become highly 'judicialized', as the web of constitutional constraints facing legislators has grown and become denser, as registered in the jurisprudence of CCs. Sadurski has elaborated a related model to explain constitutional politics in Central and Eastern Europe.[47] The more effective the CC, the more law it will make. In Kelsenian terms, it is indisputable that CCs across Europe have developed into powerful 'positive legislators' when they protect rights.

With respect to impact on the judiciary, the development of constitutional review is gradually transforming the role and function of the law courts, at least in Europe. This complex process, called 'the constitutionalization of the legal order', has generated the following major outcomes: constitutional norms—especially rights provisions—become to constitute a source of law, capable of being invoked by litigators and applied by ordinary judges in private law case; the CC, through its jurisdiction over concrete review referrals and individual complaints, evolves into a kind of high court of appeal for the judiciary, involving itself in the latter's tasks of fact finding and rule application; and the techniques of constitutional decision-making become an important mode of advocacy and decision-making in the ordinary courts.[48]

[44] Tom Ginsburg, 'The Politics of Courts in Democratization' in James Heckman, Robert Nelson, and Lee Cabatingan (eds), *Global Perspectives on the Rule of Law* (2010), 175.

[45] See further Chapter 32 on constitutional interpretation.

[46] Stone Sweet (n 3), chs 2–3.

[47] Sadurski (n 3), chs 3–4.

[48] Stone Sweet (n 24), ch 4.

Constitutionalization is partly the normative consequence of the horizontal effect (between private parties) of constitutional rights,[49] and in part the product of complex dialogues between constitutional judges and the judiciary.

Cross-national differences in the pace and scope of constitutionalization is closely tied to the existence of particular modes of review. Where concrete review and the individual constitutional complaint procedures coexist, extensive constitutionalization has proceeded rapidly, the paradigmatic examples being Germany and Spain. For a CC to decide on the merits of such claims, it must delve deeply into the workings of the judiciary, and it has the power to impose its own preferred outcome on any recalcitrant judge (if need be, by invalidating the judicial ruling as unconstitutional). The absence of the individual complaint reduces the capacity of the CC to control judicial outcomes. The paradigmatic case in Europe is Italy, where the CC must negotiate terms of engagement with the Supreme Court (Cassazione) on a continuous basis.[50]

VI. Conclusion: Legitimacy Discourses

Most CCs enjoy extensive formal legitimacy. Typically, the constitution itself designates the CC as the authoritative interpreter of the higher law, establishes enforceable rights, and lays out a blueprint for how the CC will interact with the other branches of government and the citizenry. The legitimacy resources that flow from explicit constitutional arrangements are enormously important. The contrast with the American situation—where the constitution does not expressly provide for judicial review, and rights protection, haunted by the 'counter-majoritarian difficulty', needs special justification—is palpable. Nonetheless, in every system in which a CC has been successful at enhancing the effectiveness of rights and review, legitimacy questions have been raised. In response, judges and scholars have been led to develop a range of defenses.[51]

This chapter has already noted variants of several dominant discourses. Today, for example, one still finds scholars invoking Kelsen's classic arguments, though these appear to be increasingly impotent. The more rights review is effective, the more the CC will function as a positive legislator, the more the legislative process will be judicialized, and the more the boundaries that once separated the respective jurisdictions of the CC and the ordinary courts will be blurred. The functional logics of delegation provide one type of response. We—the framers, the People, the epistemic community—delegated to the CC in order to realize certain higher purposes, such as protecting rights. The erosion of traditional separation of powers notions is the tax we pay for these benefits. Under this rubric, new questions (mixing the normative and the empirical) are posed. Do governments and parliaments legislate better, do the courts perform their functions better, by being placed under the supervision of CCs? The concept of effectiveness (discussed above) endogenizes a process-based source of legitimacy (the third necessary condition). Political legitimacy is created through use: CC's can only build effectiveness with the active complicity of political elites. After all, the same politicians that

[49] Mattias Kumm, 'Who is Afraid of the Total Constitution? Constitutional Rights as Principles and the Constitutionalization of Private Law' (2006) 7 *German Law Journal* 341.

[50] Tania Groppi, 'Italy: The Italian Constitutional Court: Towards a "Multilevel System" of Constitutional Review' in Harding and Leyland (n 3), 125.

[51] The most comprehensive attempt to defend the legitimacy of CCs, as activist courts, is Perreres Comella (n 3). Also see Sadurski (n 3).

complain of the CC's influence on policymaking do not hesitate to activate it through abstract review referrals when in opposition. More generally, the political and social demand for rights review has steadily increased, and most effective CCs are now chronically overloaded.

In today's world, the ideology of rights has, arguably, achieved the status of a civic religion. A precept of the new constitutionalism is that regimes are not democratically legitimate if they do not constrain majority rule through rights and review. It should not shock that Scheppele[52] and others are able to claim that CCs can be more democratic than elected officials. At times, constitutional judges are more responsive to citizens' concerns than politicians, and they may cajole officials to be more democratic than they would otherwise be. Today, even after the consolidation of stable party systems, CCs typically score far higher than do executives and legislatures in opinion polls. The civic religion of rights also grounds a global discourse on the legitimacy of review. Many successful review courts do not conceive of constitutionalism in restricted national terms, but in terms of an emerging 'global constitutionalism' with human rights at its core. The CCs of Colombia, Hungary, Indonesia, Poland, Slovenia, and South Africa, for example, do not hesitate to cite international human rights treaties and the decisions of other CCs.

The ultimate measure of legitimacy for any CC may well be its success at helping the polity construct a new 'constitutional identity'[53]—a massive undertaking. Most CCs are expressly created as part of new orders established in opposition to prior, now thoroughly illegitimate, regimes. Party systems may be in disarray or flux; lawmaking institutions may be paralyzed by partisanship and overwhelmed with pent-up demand for reform; judiciaries may be tainted by association with past abuses; citizens may have unreasonable hopes for fundamental change, while the problems that beset the former regime persist. Yet, as Scheppele writes, a CC is often 'the primary mechanism' for organizing the transition away from the former 'regime of horror' to constitutional democracy.[54] Insofar as CCs are successful, the legitimacy of the constitution, as a basic framework for the exercise of public authority, will become indistinguishable from the regime's political legitimacy.

Bibliography

Robert Barros, *Constitutionalism and Dictatorship: Pinochet, the Junta, and the 1980 Constitution* (2002)

Tom Ginsburg, *Judicial Review in New Democracies: Constitutional Courts in Asia* (2003)

Andrew Harding and Peter Leyland (eds), *Constitutional Courts: A Comparative Study* (2009)

Hans Kelsen, 'La Garantie Juridictionnelle de la Constitution' (1928) 45 *Revue de Droit Public* 197

Heinz Klug, *Constituting Democracy: Law, Globalism, and South Africa's Political Reconstruction* (2000)

[52] Kim Lane Scheppele, 'Democracy by Judiciary (Or Why Courts Can Sometimes Be More Democratic than Parliaments)' in Wojciech Sadurski, Martin Krygier, and Adam Csarnota (eds), *Rethinking the Rule of Law in Post Communist Europe: Past Legacies, Institutional Innovations, and Constitutional Discourses* (2005), 25.

[53] On the concept of constitutional identity see Gary Jeffrey Jacobsohn, *Constitutional Identity* (2010); and Michel Rosenfeld, *The Identity of the Constitutional Subject* (2010).

[54] Kim Lane Scheppele, 'Constitutional Interpretation after Regimes of Horror' in Susanne Karstedt (ed), *Legal Institutions and Collective Memories* (2009), 233.

Christine Landfried, *Constitutional Review and Legislation: An International Comparison* (1989)
Tamir Moustafa, *The Struggle for Constitutional Power: Law, Politics, and Economic Development in Egypt* (2007)
Victor Perreres Comella, *Constitutional Courts and Democratic Values: A European Perspective* (2009)
Wojciech Sadurski, *Rights Before Courts: A Study of Constitutional Courts in Postcommunist States of Central and Eastern Europe* (2005)
Kim Lane Scheppele, 'Constitutional Interpretation after Regimes of Horror' in Susanne Karstedt (ed), *Legal Institutions and Collective Memories* (2009), 233ff
Alec Stone Sweet, *Governing with Judges: Constitutional Politics in Europe* (2000)

CHAPTER 39

JUDICIAL INDEPENDENCE AS A CONSTITUTIONAL VIRTUE*

RODERICK A. MACDONALD
AND HOI KONG

Montreal

I. Introduction

Contemporary constitutional theory gives pride of place to a small number of concepts, three of which—separation of powers, the rule of law, judicial independence—directly implicate the role of the judiciary in a state's governance regime. The precise meaning of these three concepts

* We gratefully acknowledge the research assistance of Allison Rhoades and Owen Ripley, both BCL/LLB 2011 graduates of the McGill Faculty of Law and the financial support of the SSHRC and the Ratpan Fund.

and the manner of their instantiation varies widely among the 192 states that are members of the United Nations. Our first goal, consequently, is to situate the present chapter by clarifying the inquiries that it will address.

The nouns and adjectives of the title serve as organizing themes for framing our portrait. The topic is *judicial* independence but the word judicial is not free from ambiguity. The standard case is easy: a judge is a third party decision-maker occupying an institutional office deciding disputes between parties in an adjudicative proceeding. Yet each of these qualifiers is of uncertain dimension. Analysis could focus on the institution, on the decision-maker, on the substance of the matter being decided, or on the specific function or tasks being performed.

In many states there is a plethora of *institutions* performing court-like functions. These include state-created bodies such as administrative tribunals, central agencies of government such as inspectorates and licensing bodies, and even low-level decision-makers such as justices of the peace, and small claims court referees. In addition, in fields like labor law, commercial law, private law, and international law there are a wide variety of consensual arbitrators performing state-recognized judicial functions. To these must also be added international tribunals such as the International Criminal Court, the International Court of Justice, and the European Court of Human Rights.

Alternatively, were we to focus on the *decision-maker*, regardless of the institution, we would examine the entire range of activities performed by anyone called a judge, regardless of the institutional setting in which the tasks were performed. For example, in some states in the parliamentary tradition judges are routinely called upon to lead commissions of inquiry or even to oversee the distribution of benefits under ad hoc compensation programs.

In some states, the key criterion for defining the judicial power relates to the *substance* of the decision being taken. The jurisdiction of courts is held to involve hearing and deciding cases and controversies. Advisory opinions, political decisions, and hypothetical reference cases are not governance functions of a judicial character, even though in many states they may be part of a judge's normal activity.[1]

Finally, the judicial function is delimited in some states by the *character of the tasks* performed. A judicial function involves adjudication—the determination of the rights and obligations of the parties to a dispute by the rendering of a decision following the presentation of proofs of facts and arguments of law. Even when performed by a judge, and even when performed in a courtroom setting, allocative decisions such as the awarding of a license among numerous applicants, legislative acts such as the promulgation of rules of practice, mediation of family disputes, or purely managerial decisions such as the design and ongoing administration of school districts are not properly considered as judicial decisions.

The notion of judicial *independence* is equally polysemic. The root idea is that the judicial function requires judges to decide matters brought before them strictly on the basis of the record as presented by parties to a dispute. They are to decide uninfluenced by considerations particular to the parties but not relevant to the case, and to do so free from considerations relating to their own self-interest or the interest of the person or body that named them to their office. One might summarize the point by affirming that judges are independent when they decide by taking into account all relevant considerations, by not considering irrelevant considerations, by not acting to achieve an improper purpose, and by not acting to achieve a purely personal objective.

[1] Compare *Muskrat v United States* 219 US 346 (1911) with *Reference re Secession of Quebec* [1998] 2 SCR 217.

Independence can be understood *ex ante* as a description of the structural, procedural, and personnel decisions that conduce to uncorrupted decision-making. A primary inquiry is, therefore, to answer the question, 'Independence from whom or from what'? Invariably the initial response is 'the state', and the goal is to shield judges from reward or retaliation for judgments they render. But there are other private actors who may equally corrupt the process through money, threats, blackmail, or the promise of favor. Even other judges acting in disciplinary matters through Judicial Councils, or a Chief Justice allocating workloads, can act in ways that compromise the independence of individual decision-makers. Considerations such as selection processes, guaranteed tenure, protected salaries and benefits, and independent collegial governance loom large when independence is presented in this light.[2]

The above considerations also point to the need to distinguish between independence and impartiality, for even where an institutional structure may promote independence in general, particular judges in particular cases may, for a variety of reasons, not be impartial. In such cases one must also account for whether judges do in fact respond to guarantees of independence by rendering impartial justice.

There are three distinct ways in which the idea of *constitutional* independence can be understood. The focus may be on the judge, the function, or a particular office. Most obviously, constitutional independence may refer to explicit provisions of a constitutional document (although in some countries with partially unwritten constitutions, there may also be common law constitutional norms)[3] by which the status of all judges is meant to be protected from political and other interference, whether from one or both parties, from powerful third party economic interests, or from criminal threats, blackmail, or extortion.

A second sense of the idea lies in the protection of the judicial function. Some constitutions explicitly define or implicitly point to tasks deemed by their nature to be judicial. Performance of these tasks cannot be assigned by the legislature to any body that is not a court (eg an administrative agency), or to any person (eg a public servant or a minister) who is not appointed according to the procedures applicable to judges and vested with a guarantee of independence.[4]

In most states that are committed to judicial independence, the institutional and procedural guarantees extend to all judges within the judicial hierarchy. In some countries, however, the idea of constitutional independence has a more limited sense. It means that there is a separate body—a constitutional court—that has exclusive jurisdiction, whether *ex ante* or *ex post*, to decide constitutional questions.[5] This body is independent not only of the political branches of government, but also is separate from the regular judicial branch. In some states, independent constitutional courts are not even adjudicative bodies in the conventional sense, but are rather specialized multi-member bodies with a protected jurisdiction and enhanced guarantees of independence for their members.

The last term of the title, *virtue*, points to a number of considerations relating to the actual performance of the role of judge. A first of these relates to judicial ideology. If a judge is working within a system that involves a professional magistracy, the manner in which virtue is manifest will be different from that in a system where judges are recruited from the legal profession either through appointment or election. Moreover, the explicit recognition or denial of a

[2] See Luc Heuschling, 'Why Should Judges Be Independent?' in Katja S. Zielger et al (eds), *Constitutionalism and the Role of Parliaments* (2007), 199.

[3] *Reference re Remuneration of Provincial Court Judges* [1997] 3 SCR 3.

[4] See eg *R v Kirby; Ex parte Boilermakers' Society of Australia* [1956] HCA 10, (1956) 94 CLR 254.

[5] On constitutional courts, see Chapter 38.

judge's personal responsibility in decision-making will shape the manner in which independent judging is assessed in a given system.

Secondly, judicial virtue cannot mean judicial license. Judges must be accountable, and the central question is what type of accountability (and to whom) independence is meant to foster. Here again there are different dimensions in play. Independence is compromised when accountability is to a political process rather than to the disinterested pursuit of the rule of law. The idea of integrity is most often deployed to capture a judge's commitment to craft: respect for precedent, fidelity to established principles of statutory interpretation, and strict adherence to the norm of impartiality.[6]

Integrity also signals a third aspect of judicial virtue—*phroenesis*: sobriety, wisdom, courage, modesty, and the capacity to resist the siren song of notoriety for righting all wrongs regardless of one's formal jurisdiction to do so.

In measuring the degree of judicial independence in any state, the importance of attending to judicial virtue cannot be understated. The whole panoply of formal constitutional guarantees will not lead to the outcomes that judicial independence is meant to ensure if those named to courts are comfortable soliciting and acting upon illegitimate factors when deciding cases. Conversely, the absence of all structural and procedural mechanisms to insulate judges from inappropriate pressure will not prevent courageous and virtuous judges from displaying true independence and impartiality in maintaining the rule of law.[7]

The above considerations illustrate only some of the difficulties of definition and scope in developing a concept of judicial independence that could be used to organize a worldwide evaluative survey. The potential complexity of such an inquiry may suggest that a comparative approach to judicial independence is best undertaken by setting out an exhaustive list of institutional structures, procedural mechanisms, and constitutional guarantees that are related to judicial independence (conceived in the broadest possible sense), and then examining the extent to which these features are present in any given jurisdiction.[8] So, for example, a comparative table may list the following factors: (1) sources of threats to independence (external; internal); (2) targets of these threats (the judiciary as an institution; individual judges); (3) nature of the threats (structural threats; conditions of office-holding such as appointment, tenure, removal, promotion, remuneration, training, and discipline; court administration; direct attacks and exposure to reprisals); and (4) political culture (independent bar; free press; NGOs supportive of the judiciary; free elections to political office with a strong opposition).[9] In pursuing such a descriptive taxonomic undertaking, one might, for instance, also provide a catalog of judicial pronouncements about what concepts such as budgetary independence or judicial self-governance require.[10]

[6] See generally the essays in András Sajó (ed), *Judicial Integrity* (2004).

[7] See R.A. Macdonald, 'Parametres of Politics in Judicial Appointments', Research paper prepared for *La Commission d'enquête sur le processus de nomination des juges du Québec*, September 1, 2010, available at <http://www.cepnj.gouv.qc.ca/etudes-des-experts.html>.

[8] For an example of the 'checklist inventory' of essential characteristics of a legal concept meant to enable a comparative assessment of the degree to which a given state respects that concept, see the World Justice Project, *Rule of Law Index 2010* (2010).

[9] This inventory is drawn from Peter Russell, 'A General Theory of Judicial Independence Revisited' in Adam Dodek et al (eds), *Judicial Independence in Context* (2010), 599. Rafael La Porta et al, 'Judicial Checks and Balances' (2004) 112 *Journal of Political Economy* 445 show how an inventory like Russell's can be applied to a comparative survey of judicial independence.

[10] For a survey of such judicial pronouncements, see Norman Dorsen et al, *Comparative Constitutionalism: Cases and Materials* (2003), 308–27.

We reject formalistic checklist approaches to a comparative survey of judicial independence and instead ground our inquiry in three interrelated claims: that judicial independence is a particular kind of normative concept that is best understood through a particular normative theory; that this concept is made effective through institutional design choices; and that the socio-political features of specific contexts will dictate which design choices are normatively appropriate or politically possible.

In Section II, we elaborate upon the first of these claims. We argue that judicial independence is both an *essentially contested concept* and a *solution concept*. The fact that judicial independence is an essentially contested concept means that the nature and scope of the concept's characteristics are persistently open to question. The fact that the idea of judicial independence is a solution concept means that it poses a specific set of normative questions which all reasonable participants in the debate about the concept's content attempt to answer. We conclude Section II with the claim that the concept of judicial independence is best captured by a virtue ethics account and that such an account is superior to the main consequentialist alternatives.

In Section III we develop the second and third of our central claims. We present frameworks for analyzing the design choices that polities make when implementing and sustaining institutions and procedures that are meant to support judicial independence. One framework posits the factors that influence whether a state will, in the first instance, choose to establish institutions that support judicial independence. A second framework sets out contextual factors which influence whether members of the judiciary will in fact decide cases independently. A third framework focuses on normative and evaluative, rather than causal or predictive claims and assesses the extent to which institutional structures and procedures support or frustrate judges in their exercise of judicial virtues. The first two frameworks illustrate the claim that judicial independence is an essentially contested concept which requires context-specific institutional supports to be made effective. The third framework illustrates the normative nature of inquiries into the nature of judicial independence.

In our view, the comparative approach to judicial independence advanced in this chapter is an advance over alternatives which deny that the idea of judicial independence has any normative content, or assume that a simple description of the concept and the factors that conduce to it is either possible or desirable, or claim that there is a uniform set of institutional structures which is necessary and sufficient for the concept of judicial independence to be given effect in any specific context. We begin with a discussion of our normative conception of the idea of judicial independence.

II. Preliminary Questions and Methodological Perspectives

In this section, we elaborate our understanding of what kind of a concept judicial independence is, and what consequences for comparative analysis flow from this understanding. Our basic claim is that judicial independence is an essentially contested solution concept. Hence, there are no generally accepted criteria by which the widely differing experiences of states that claim to adhere to the concept could be compared. Consequently, much of the comparative evaluation will depend on how one assesses the normative value of judicial independence. If, as we argue, judicial independence is an intrinsic good, the assessment one makes of its various instantiations will be much different from an evaluation based on consequentialist accounts such as judicial independence being important because it promotes liberal-democratic constitutionalism. Next, we argue that the judicial independence is best understood from the standpoint of virtue ethics. These considerations enable us, in Section III, to examine the utility of different comparative approaches for assessing the extent to which a polity actually shows a commitment to judicial independence.

1. Judicial Independence: An Essentially Contested Solution Concept

A number of foundational concepts of constitutional law have been characterized by scholars as essentially contested concepts. Among these are the rule of law and judicial independence.[11]

Jeremy Waldron has argued that an essentially contested concept is normative and complex: participants in a debate about such a concept may agree that the achievement of that concept is valuable and that it involves multiple constituent parts, but disagree about the identity and relevance of the parts.[12] In our view, judicial independence is just such a concept. Moreover, we see judicial independence as an example of Waldron's claim that some essentially contested concepts are 'solution concepts'. A solution concept:

> is the concept of a solution to a problem we're not sure how to solve, and rival conceptions are rival proposals for solving it or rival proposals for doing the best we can in this regard given that the problem is insoluble.[13]

This understanding of the idea of judicial independence is particularly salient for present purposes because it permits us to put aside two general critiques of the concept of judicial independence. First, we take those involved in debates about the nature of judicial independence to be engaged in serious and purposeful discussion about the meaning and importance of the concept in constitutional design. We therefore do not attend to arguments raised by those who invoke judicial independence for exclusively rhetorical and strategic reasons.[14]

Secondly, we exclude from our discussion those who argue that judicial independence is an idea devoid of content. Some scholars argue that the idea of judicial independence raises definitional controversies, and that invocations of it merely serve to obscure genuine disagreements about the nature of adjudication, and about the effects of institutions on judicial performance.[15] In response, it may be noted that definitional uncertainties, flowing from competing normative theories, necessarily inhere in essentially contested concepts. Nonetheless, if such concepts are valuable in orienting debate teleologically, then the fact that there is uncertainty about the precise content of judicial independence does not undercut this value.

We now consider in what respects judicial independence is a 'solution concept'. Generally speaking, scholars engaged in debates about the content of judicial independence understand that protections for judicial independence serve the salutary purpose of insulating those charged with adjudicating disputes from pressures that would lead them to decide cases on

[11] For a well-argued characterization of judicial independence as an essentially contested concept, see Sanford Levinson, 'Identifying "Independence"' (2006) 86 *Boston University Law Review* 1297, 1298.

[12] Jeremy Waldron, 'Is the Rule of Law an Essentially Contested Concept?' (2002) 21 *Law and Philosophy* 137, 150.

[13] Ibid 158.

[14] Levinson (n 11), 1298, observes that the concept is often strategically wielded in attempts to justify, without argument, institutional design choices that favor one set of values (ie, judicial autonomy) over others (ie, political accountability).

[15] See eg Lewis A. Kornhauser, 'Is Judicial Independence a Useful Concept?' in Stephen B. Burbank and Barry Friedman (eds), *Judicial Independence at the Crossroads: An Interdisciplinary Approach* (2002), 9, 53–4.

the basis of irrelevant or inappropriate considerations. These considerations may relate to the actions of parties to a dispute, or of third parties such as the state, or to their personal self-interest.[16] The relevant protections may be designed to safeguard the integrity of the process of adjudication, of the judiciary as a whole, or of individual judges.[17] Particular conceptions of judicial independence aim to clarify the nature of the objective of safeguarding the decision-making capacity of judges and to identify the institutional, political, and cultural conditions necessary to bring about that objective, in a particular context. Viewed in this light, contestation between rival conceptions not only enriches understanding of the legal-political problems that judicial independence marks out and is meant to solve, but also of the conditions propitious to its flourishing.[18]

Seeing judicial independence as a contested solution concept has implications for one other general objection sometimes advanced by critics. According to that objection, because empirical evidence demonstrates that judges do not make decisions based exclusively on existing formal legal considerations, the notion of judicial independence is a myth.[19] Yet one can accept the empirical claim and still have productive discussions about judicial independence. This is because the objective of limiting the influence of improper influences on judicial decision-making is not coextensive with the objective of eliminating from such decision-making considerations that go beyond the facts and law as presented by litigants.

Most contemporary legal theorists accept that courts cannot resolve difficult legal questions by appealing to existing legal materials alone.[20] There may be disagreement about the appropriate degree and extent to which other considerations bear on judicial decision-making, and indeed even on the scope of the considerations that may be invoked.[21] Nonetheless, all reasonable participants in the debate accept that some considerations and some influences are

[16] In this chapter we claim that the judicial function follows what Martin Shapiro has called the 'logic of triad in conflict resolution'. Martin Shapiro, *Courts: A Comparative and Political Analysis* (1981), 1. See further A. Kojève, *Esquisse d'une phénoménologie du droit: exposé provisoire* (1981). As it does for Shapiro and Kojève, this open-ended conception of the judicial function allows us to include in our analysis a wide range of institutions in which participants would recognizably be seen to be exercising judicial functions, even if they do not correspond to what Shapiro identifies as 'the ideal type' of courts. For individual and institutional aspects of judicial independence, see John Ferejohn, 'Explaining Judges, Dependent Judiciary: Explaining Judicial Independence' (1999) 72 *Southern California Law Review* 353, 354–6.

[17] Typically, authors argue that judicial independence involves insulation from the influence of the executive and legislative branches. See eg Irving R. Kaufman, 'The Essence of Judicial Independence' (1980) 80 *Columbia Law Review* 671 and William R. Lederman, 'The Independence of the Judiciary' (1956) 34 *Canadian Bar Review* 769. Authors have noted that judicial independence, in the sense of the independence of individual judges, can also be compromised by institutional features of the judicial branch. Eg, lower court judges may seek to advance to higher courts by drafting decisions that appeal to those in charge of selecting appellate court judges. See Levinson (n 11), 1302. Or they may seek to curry favor and choice assignments by deciding in ways that please the chief justice of their court. See Roderick A. Macdonald, 'Appoint Elect, Draw Straws or Sell to the Highest Bidder? On Judicial Selection Processes' in Pierre Noreau (ed), *Mélanges Andrée Lajoie* (2008), 731. Similarly, in Japan, judges are incentivized, for career reasons, to avoid negative assessments by senior peers. See J. Mark Ramseyer and Eric B. Rasmusen, 'Why Are Japanese Judges So Conservative in Politically Charged Cases?' (2001) 95 *American Political Science Review* 331.

[18] See Waldron (n 12), 152.

[19] See eg Terri Jennings Peretti, 'Does Judicial Independence Exist? The Lessons of Social Science Research' in Burbank and Friedman (n 15), 103.

[20] Consider the positions of positivists and anti-positivists on this point. Compare H.L.A. Hart, *The Concept of Law* (2nd edn, Penelope A. Bulloch and Joseph Raz (eds), 1994), 205 and Ronald Dworkin, 'In Praise of Theory' (1997) 29 *Arizona State Law Journal* 353, 356–7.

[21] Some appellate court judges themselves acknowledge that the extent of their discretion is relatively broad, and that their decisions can, as a consequence, be fairly described as 'legislative' in nature. See eg Richard A. Posner, *How Judges Think* (2008), 15.

inappropriate.[22] For instance, no one contends that the 'telephone justice' of Soviet courts, wherein political actors dictated to judges the results of cases before them, and judges followed those dictates because they wanted to receive perquisites in exchange for doing so, reflects an appropriate conception of judicial independence.[23]

This limit on what the idea of judicial independence can reasonably entail reinforces the claim that judicial independence is a solution concept whose aim is to delineate the influences that can be appropriately brought to bear on judicial decision-making and the considerations that can be appropriately considered by judges. Despite what various authors have claimed, judicial independence is not a mere rhetorical device, nor is it a concept devoid of content, nor is it a form of *ex post* justification for judicial preferences. It is, rather, an essentially contested concept that presents a particular normative question to which scholarly and professional participants in debates about judicial independence attempt to respond.

2. The Intrinsic Value of Judicial Independence and the Concept of Judicial Virtue

If one accepts that judicial independence is an essentially contested concept and that those engaged in debates about the idea's content are involved in a normative undertaking, one would want to know more about the nature of this concept. The previous section argued that preserving decisional independence for judges is a good in itself. In this section we consider what the nature of that good is. Some contemporary scholars claim that judicial independence is inherently instrumental.[24] Judicial independence is not an intrinsic good, they argue, because no one would advocate for judicial license, unlimited by any constraints. This argument rests on a non sequitur. It is possible to conceive of judicial independence as an intrinsic good without claiming that such a conception implies that judicial independence entails unfettered judicial discretion. Indeed, we shall argue that a virtue ethics approach to judicial independence, which conceives of judicial independence as an intrinsic good, is superior to instrumental approaches.[25]

In order to explain why judicial independence is an intrinsic good, we must consider two ideas that often arise in debates about judicial independence: impartiality and accountability. Scholars routinely argue that independence and impartiality are distinct concepts. The judiciary and individual judges may enjoy independence from improper external influence, scholars argue, yet judges may nonetheless fail to decide cases impartially if they fail to weigh relevant considerations when making their decisions.[26] Other scholars have argued that a central challenge for constitutional systems lies in designing institutions that ensure the

[22] Posner (n 21), chs 6–8. For a similar claim, which aims to identify conditions of judicial *dependence*, see Christopher M. Larkins, 'Judicial Independence and Democratization: A Theoretical and Conceptual Analysis' (1996) 44 *American Journal of Comparative Law* 605.

[23] On telephone justice, see Stephen Breyer, 'Judicial Independence: Remarks by Justice Breyer' (2007) 95 *Georgetown Law Journal* 903, 904.

[24] See eg Stephen B. Burbank, 'What Do We Mean by 'Judicial Independence'?' (2003) 64 *Ohio State Law Journal* 323, 325: '*judicial independence is a means to an end (or, more probably, to more than one end)*' (original emphasis). See also Peter H. Russell, 'Toward a General Theory of Judicial Independence' in Peter H. Russell and David O'Brien (eds), *Judicial Independence in the Age of Democracy* (2001), 1.

[25] R.A. Macdonald, 'Exercising Judgement' in M. Robert (ed), *Which Judge for Which Society? Proceedings of the 2008 Judges Conference* (2008), 53.

[26] Frank Cross, 'Thoughts on Goldilocks and Judicial Independence' (2003) 64 *Ohio State Law Journal* 195, 198–9. See also Paul D. Carrington, 'Judicial Independence in Excess: Reviving the Judicial Duty of the Supreme Court' (2008–09) 94 *Cornell Law Review* 587.

correct mix of judicial independence and judicial accountability.[27] Close consideration of the ideas of impartiality, independence, and accountability, leads us towards a non-consequentialist, virtue-centered justification for judicial independence.

Kim Scheppele has claimed that in order for judges to be truly independent they must be in a position to examine the rules of positive law in light of principles that 'are at some greater level of generality and at some temporal remove from the statutes that judges are called on to apply.'[28] Where judges are protected from improper external influences by institutional safeguards, this recourse to higher law acts as an additional guarantee that judges are properly restrained, and are not deciding cases in accordance with mere whims or personal predilections. We interpret Scheppele to be arguing that a judge makes appropriate use of her independence when she properly fulfils her role as a judge, and part of that role involves acting impartially, or in Scheppele's terms, in accordance with a reasoned understanding of norms that are not commands dictated to her by political actors or interested parties. Scholars claim that the requirement to give reasons grounded in *ex ante* principle distinguishes courts from the political branches.[29] It is primarily through this kind of reason-giving that judges are held accountable to citizens for their decisions, and this form of accountability is distinct from the political mechanisms that render political actors accountable. One might say that judges most fully occupy their institutional role when they engage in principled reasoning.[30]

This focus on the *role of the judge* characterizes virtue jurisprudence, which positions itself as an alternative to consequentialist approaches to jurisprudence.[31] Virtue jurisprudence focuses on the characteristics or virtues associated with the judicial role, rather than on the consequences of judicial decision-making. In this chapter, we claim that, in any given context, a particular admixture of procedural, institutional, and personal mechanisms for safeguarding independence and accountability can be designed to provide decisional contexts in which judges can be faithful to the role of the virtuous judge.[32] What distinguishes our approach from consequentialist ones is that we do not assess the value of judicial independence in terms of its potential extra-judicial consequences, such as the realization of liberal-democratic values, market efficiency, or socio-political stability. Rather, we understand the idea of judicial independence and the role of the judge that this idea implies, to be a good in itself.[33]

[27] See eg Charles G. Geyh, 'Judicial Independence, Judicial Accountability and the Role of Constitutional Norms in Congressional Regulation of the Courts' (2003) 78 *Indiana Law Journal* 153 n 26. See also John A. Ferejohn and Larry D. Kramer, 'Independent Judges, Dependent Judiciary: Institutionalizing Judicial Restraint' (2002) 77 *NYU Law Review* 962, 975.

[28] Kim Lane Scheppele, 'Declarations of Independence: Judicial Reactions to Political Pressure' in Burbank and Friedman (n 15), 227, 245.

[29] See eg Christopher L. Eisgruber, *Constitutional Self-Government* (2001), 59–62. Others have argued that judicial accountability is preserved by a variety of institutions which make courts responsive to public opinion. See eg Barry Friedman, 'The Politics of Judicial Review' (2005) 84 *Texas Law Review* 257. Still others note that institutional controls are necessary to ensure that judges are subject to restraints on institution-aggrandizing tendencies. See eg Carlos Santiso, 'Economic Reform and Judicial Governance in Brazil: Balancing Independence with Accountability' in Siri Gloppen et al (eds), *Democratization and the Judiciary* (2004), 161, 172.

[30] Paul J. Kelly, 'Impartiality: A Philosophical Perspective' in Sajó (n 6), 17.

[31] See Lawrence B. Solum, 'Virtue Jurisprudence: A Virtue-Centered Theory of Judging' (2003) 34 *Metaphilosophy* 178; Macdonald (n 25), 61–70.

[32] For a similar, virtue-centered approach to judicial independence and accountability, which also rejects instrumentalist arguments for judicial independence, see David Pimentel, 'Reframing the Independence v Accountability Debate: Defining Judicial Structure in Light of Judges' Courage and Integrity' (2009) 57 *Cleveland State Law Review* 2. See also Macdonald (n 17).

[33] For a similar, non-consequentialist approach to judicial independence, see Ammon Reichman, 'Judicial Non-Dependence' in Adam Dodek and Lorne Sossin (eds), *Judicial Independence in Context* (2010), 438, 441 n 7.

One problem with consequentialist approaches is that the ends to which judicial independence can be said to aim are various and in some instances conflicting. For example, some scholars argue that in established liberal democracies an independent judiciary secures particular ends, including: (1) the regulation of relations among citizens and between citizens and the government according to well-defined laws which clearly set out rights and duties and (2) the provision of a mutually acceptable third party adjudicator to settle disputes about the content of those rights and duties.[34] But established liberal democracies are not the only polities that value judicial independence. Authoritarian regimes may create either the patina or the substance of independent judiciaries not to safeguard liberal-democratic ends, but rather, among other reasons: (1) to secure social control, by providing an appearance of legitimacy and by monitoring administrative agencies, (2) to send credible signals of market stability to foreign investors, and (3) to offload controversial policy decisions.[35] Similarly, governing parties in emerging democracies may create independent judiciaries either as a form of 'political insurance' against subsequent electoral reversals or as 'commitment' mechanisms to safeguard their policies should they lose office.[36]

This variety of possible extra-judicial objectives which the concept of judicial independence can be said to advance makes it difficult to conceive of a coherent instrumentalist approach to the concept. By contrast, a virtue-centered approach to judicial independence focusing on the role of the judge can be broadly captured in a formulation that applies across contexts. It is, for this reason, superior to an instrumentalist approach which must respond to the existence of contestable and sometimes conflicting ends. It is to our understanding of the judicial role and its attendant virtues that we now turn.

3. Delimiting the Scope of *Judicial* Independence

In this chapter, we adopt Martin Shapiro's concept of judicial activity. He writes:

> Cutting quite across cultural lines, it appears that whenever two persons come into a conflict that they cannot themselves solve, one solution appealing to common sense is to call upon a third for assistance in achieving a resolution. So universal across both time and space is this simple social invention of triads that we can discover almost no society that fails to employ it. And from its overwhelming appeal to common sense stems the basic legitimacy of courts everywhere. In short, the triad for purposes of conflict resolution is the basic social logic of courts, a logic so compelling that courts have become a universal political phenomenon.[37]

The utility of a broadly cast concept of the judicial action is that it enables us to focus on important substantive features of the judicial role, and in so doing avoid two problems that arise from approaches that attend only to those entities of the modern state which are denominated as 'courts'.

[34] Russell (n 24), 9–10.

[35] This list is drawn from Tamir Moustafa and Tom Ginsburg, 'Introduction: The Function of Courts in Authoritarian Politics' in Tamir Moustafa and Tom Ginsburg (eds), *Rule by Law: the Politics of Courts in Authoritarian Regimes* (2008), 1, 4–10.

[36] For the classic statement of the idea of judicial independence as a mechanism for securing legislative bargains, see William M. Landes and Richard A. Posner, 'The Independent Judiciary in an Interest-Group Perspective' (1975) 18 *Journal of Law and Economics* 875. For an application of the insurance theory to developing democracies, see Jodi S. Finkel, *Judicial Reform as Political Insurance: Argentina, Peru and Mexico in the 1990s* (2008).

[37] Shapiro (n 16), 1. See also Kojève (n 16) and Macdonald (n 17).

First, in our view, such a formalist approach is under-inclusive and treats the peripheral case as central. By contrast, if the mechanisms of judicial independence are understood to safeguard a social institution that supports a particular role, then a functionalist, rather than a formalist, approach to the scope of the concept seems warranted. Such an approach enables one to see how and to what extent both state and non-state entities that fulfil this socio-political role should have their independence safeguarded.[38] A functional approach flows, moreover, from adopting a virtue-centered conception of judicial independence. Such a conception points to the personal characteristics of judges which enable them to fulfil this socio-political role. A virtue-centered approach looks to how institutional and cultural conditions that protect judicial independence both facilitate the exercise of judicial virtues including temperance, courage, intelligence, and wisdom, and discourage judges from falling prey to judicial vices such as corruption, cowardice, incompetence, and foolishness.[39] Since we are concerned with how the role of the judge and its attendant virtues and vices plays into the concept of judicial independence, we are not preoccupied with whether actors fulfilling that role occupy a particular office denominated in a particular way by the state.[40]

The second pitfall that we avoid in adopting this functional conception of judicial action is that of over-inclusiveness. Not all activities undertaken by those state entities denominated as 'courts' are judicial, and not all activities undertaken by those named as judges involve adjudication. As a consequence, not all protections of judicial independence need extend equally to all the activities of all courts and all the activities of all judges.[41] For instance, if courts are engaged fundamentally in lawmaking, rather than in the resolution of conflicts in accordance with preexisting rules, then it is foreseeable that a variety of institutional mechanisms will aim at curtailing the independence of courts and ensuring that they are responsive to public opinion.[42] In short, we adopt an open-ended and functionalist understanding of what constitutes *judicial* activity because such an understanding opens avenues of research and permits fine-grained analyses that a formalist approach forecloses.

[38] In this sense, we accept Professor Edward Rubin's criticism of the 'jurocentric character of American legal scholarship'. See Edward L. Rubin, 'Independence as a Governance Mechanism' in Burbank and Friedman (n 15), 56, 56. For a critical examination of the idea of judicial independence, in the context of US administrative law judges, see James E. Moliterno, 'The Administrative Judiciary's Independence Myth' (2003) 64 *Ohio State Law Journal* 332. See also R.A. Macdonald, 'The Acoustics of Accountability' in Sajó (n 6), 141. For a comparative analysis of independent disinterested bodies, other than courts, which review public law and public policy, see Bronwen Morgan, 'The Internationalization of Economic Review of Legislation: Non-Judicial Legalization?' in Tom Ginsburg and Robert A. Kagan (eds), *Institutions and Public Law: Comparative Approaches* (2005), 245.

[39] For this list of judicial virtues and vices and what they entail, see Solum (n 31), 185–200.

[40] Indeed, scholars have noted that in certain circumstances, state-controlled adjudication may yield perverse consequences. In other situations, non-state adjudication is simply more prevalent than state-controlled adjudication. For the former, see Javier A. Couso, 'The Politics of Judicial Review in Chile in the Era of Democratic Transition, 1990–2002' in Gloppen et al (n 29), 70 at 88. For the latter, see Siri Glopen, 'The Accountability Function of Courts in Tanzania and Zambia' in Gloppen et al (n 29), 112 at 131.

[41] For the classic analysis of how courts in public law cases embrace activities beyond simple adjudication, see Abram Chayes, 'The Role of the Judge in Public Law Litigation' (1976) 89 *Harvard Law Review* 1281.

[42] See on this point, Stephen B. Burbank, 'Judicial Independence, Judicial Accountability and Interbranch Relations' (2008) 137 *Daedalus* 16, Nuno Garoupa and Tom Ginsburg, 'Guarding the Guardians: Judicial Councils and Judicial Independence' (2009) 57 *American Journal of Comparative Law* 103, and Friedman (n 29). For a comparative analysis of institutional responses, see Shapiro (n 16), 32–5. For a catalog of powers that post-socialist courts exercise, including powers that are explicitly legislative in nature, see Tom Ginsburg, 'Beyond Judicial Review: Ancillary Powers of Constitutional Courts' in Ginsburg and Kagan (n 38), 225. Of course, some lawmaking, such as the promulgation of rules of practice, is intrinsic to the adjudicative function, and should be covered by the judicial independence norm.

A virtue-centered functional approach also enables us to take a broad view of the concept of constitutional independence. We consider courts that have a constitutional function. In addition, we examine the question of what structural and institutional features appear to have a constitutional foundation, whether that be elaborated in a text or in unwritten constitutional principle, and whether these features apply only to state institutions or whether they apply to non-state domestic and international institutions as well.[43] With this virtue-centered approach to judicial independence and this conception of the judicial role in view we can set out our comparative law methodology and illustrate its pertinence with specific examples.

III. The Comparative Law of Judicial Independence

Comparative private law scholars have long engaged in taxonomic exercises, often with reference to legal systems or legal families understood in formalistic terms.[44] Even those who use functional analysis to contrast particular legal doctrines, rely on traditional taxonomies—civil law, common law, socialist law, customary law—as analytic categories.[45] More recently, public law scholars have favored instead a comparative methodology that focuses on generating testable hypotheses about institutional design choices.[46] This type of approach is particularly useful for exploring a virtue-centered understanding of judicial independence. It is evident in several studies considered in this section where scholars advance hypotheses about which social, economic, and political factors influence political actors constitutionally to entrench judicial independence or judicial review. It is also reflected in studies of how various institutional and socio-cultural influences can determine how broad the scope of independent judicial decision-making is.

These comparative studies reveal that different institutional, cultural, and political contexts give rise to different understandings of the appropriate influences that can be brought to bear on judicial decision-making.[47] Those differences can be internal to a particular jurisdiction, or revealed in comparisons drawn across jurisdictions or across time.[48] As we shall soon see, the significance of judicial independence and the configuration of institutional arrangements that safeguard it may differ depending (inter alia) on whether the judiciary belongs to the common or civil law system, on whether courts have effective enforcement powers, and on whether there is broad societal support for an independent judiciary. These background conditions can influence the configuration of appointments procedures, modes of determining remuneration and of advancing through the hierarchy and securing tenure, as well as the

[43] In so framing how we understand the concept of 'constitutionalized judicial independence', we are characterizing the judicial role in light of our understanding of the normative question posed by the concept of judicial independence. Other analyses, undertaken for other purposes might highlight other aspects of the judicial role. For a brief statement of those aspects see the 'Introduction' and 'Conclusion' to this chapter.

[44] The leading proponent of this kind of comparative law over the past half century has been René David. See R. David and C. Jauffret-Spinosi, *Les grands systèmes de droit comparé* (11th edn, 2002). For an overview of the literature, and a proposal for a novel innovative taxonomic scheme, see H. Patrick Glenn, *Legal Traditions of the World* (4th edn, 2010).

[45] Rudolf Schlesinger, *Comparative Law: Cases, Text, Materials* (6th edn, 1998).

[46] See Martin Shapiro, 'Law, Courts and Politics' in Ginsburg and Kagan (n 38), 275, 275.

[47] See Ferejohn (n 16), 377.

[48] Some have noted that the overwhelming focus of US scholarship has been on the Supreme Court, and have speculated about the career incentives that motivate scholars to maintain such a focus. See Stephen B. Burbank, 'The Architecture of Judicial Independence' (1999) 723 *Southern California Law Review* 315.

degree of the judicial branch's administrative independence and the extent to which the legislative and executive branches respond to judicial pronouncements.

Each context-specific variation represents, in our view, a particular understanding of the concept of judicial independence. By examining this diversity of understandings, we advance our ability to assess the value of judicial independence, of its attributes, and of the institutional and cultural conditions necessary for its flourishing.

In the sections that follow, we present different comparative approaches to judicial independence. The first section considers the kinds of incentives that scholars believe lie behind political decisions to establish independent judiciaries and cites examples of states whose decisions appear to be responding to these incentives. The second section examines the influences that scholars have claimed affect the nature and scope of judicial accountability and judicial discretion in a given state. We close our discussion by making normative, rather than explanatory or predictive, claims about judicial independence. Ultimately, we claim that a comparative law methodology aimed at different elements of institutional design reveals the value of a virtue-focused conception of judicial independence and that this methodology is superior to alternatives that aim at pure description or purportedly exhaustive taxonomies.[49]

1. Judicial Independence and the Politics of Institutional Design

According to the first group of scholars that we examine, governments choose to create constitutionally independent judiciaries in response to political incentives. In this section, we examine three theories that purport to identify the incentives that motivate governmental decisions to establish constitutionally independent judiciaries: (1) insurance theory; (2) commitment theory; and (3) rule of law theory.

(a) Insurance Theory

Perhaps the most prominent proponent of the insurance theory is Tom Ginsburg. Ginsburg builds his argument on empirical evidence that strongly suggests that constitutional designers are motivated by their own short-term interests, rather than by the long-term interests of their societies.[50] He formulates his general prediction as follows: 'Explicit constitutional power of and access to judicial review will be greater where political forces are diffused than where a single dominant party exists at the time of constitutional design.'[51]

Where a majority party dominates at the moment of constitution-making and anticipates continued domination, argues Ginsburg, there are few incentives to create a neutral judiciary charged with enforcing the constitutional bargain. The majority party will instead seek to maximize its ability to exercise power flexibly and will resist any measures or institutional checks that would limit that flexibility. By contrast, where there is political competition at the moment of constitutional founding, the party in power will anticipate the possibility of political reversal and will introduce institutions that limit the powers of subsequent majorities. An independent judiciary vested with a power of judicial review is one such institution and is

[49] We do not dismiss the informational usefulness of collections comprising state-specific descriptions of institutions, procedures, and practices that conduce to judicial independence. See eg Sajó (n 6), Burbank and Friedman (n 15), Russell (n 24), Dodek and Sossin (n 33), Ginsburg (n 35). Our claim is simply that our approach will prove more useful in evaluating the 'on the ground' success of law reform projects aimed at promoting judicial independence in individual states.

[50] See Tom Ginsburg, *Judicial Review in New Democracies: Constitutional Courts in Asian Cases* (2003), 23.

[51] Ibid 25.

a low-cost means by which constitutional founders seek to protect themselves and their policies against reversal by subsequent majorities. An independent judiciary provides a forum, outside majoritarian institutions, for minority voices to exercise political influence.

Ginsburg and others have tested the insurance theory in a variety of contexts and have found that the data seems to confirm the theory.[52] For instance, scholars note that only after the Labor Party in Israel ceased to dominate the political scene, and there emerged a pattern of alternation between Likud and Labor were legislators sufficiently motivated to eventually pass two Basic Laws that enabled the Israeli Supreme Court to void legislation that contravened those laws.[53]

Jodi Finkel's examination of the judiciaries in Argentina, Peru, and Mexico in the 1990s offers a nuanced version of the insurance theory that distinguishes between the initiation and the implementation stages of judicial reform. In the initiation stage, ruling parties create independent judiciaries to hedge against potential political downturns, and typically need to seek the support of opposition parties to satisfy super-majority requirements for constitutional amendment.[54] However, once the initiation phase is completed, legislative reforms are necessary to implement the changes, and such implementation only requires the support of legislative majorities. At this point, the ruling party may aggressively assert executive control over the judiciary as the Fujimori regime did in Peru in the 1990s.[55] But once faced with the risk of losing power due to political scandals, the regime reversed its policies and introduced reforms that sharply lessened executive control over the judicial branch.

(b) Commitment Theory

A second theory meant to explain why states may constitutionalize judicial independence propounds that legislative bargains struck by political interest groups are best preserved both by legislative procedural rules that increase the cost of repealing legislation and by judicial review by an independent judiciary.[56] According to this version of commitment theory, which has been developed by William Landes and Richard Posner, an independent judiciary will interpret legislation in accordance with the original legislative bargain.

The hypothesis is that because the value to political actors of an independent judiciary is a function of the predictability of judicial decisions and of the judiciary's willingness to enforce original legislative bargains, judges themselves are incentivized by self-interest to enforce those bargains and not to interpret legislation in ways that reflect the preferences of shifting legislative majorities. In addition, standard measures of protecting judicial independence,

[52] Ginsburg applies the theory in passing to the early history of the United States, to post-independence India, to post-war Japan, to post-Communist Hungary and to Russia after Yeltsin, ibid ch 4. The remainder of his book focuses on Taiwan, Korea, and Mongolia.

[53] Ibid 57–8. For a detailed examination see Ran Hirschl, 'The Political Origins of Judicial Empowerment through Constitutionalization: Lessons from Israel's Constitutional Revolution' (2001) 33 *Comparative Politics* 315.

[54] Finkel (n 36), 31–3. In Peru, constitutional reform also required ratification by referendum, which had the similar effect of ensuring opposition input into the process: Finkel (n 36), 68–9.

[55] Finkel (n 36), 71–9. Measures to undermine the independence of the judiciary, included delaying appointments of tenured judges, imposing super-majority requirements on the constitutional court in cases of judicial review of government action, and the creation of an *executive* oversight commission with the power to disband courts, to transfer judges out of politically significant postings, and to investigate judicial corruption.

[56] Landes and Posner (n 36), 878. Landes and Posner provide a variation on general theories about constitutional pre-commitment. For a general treatment, examining the facilitative and constraining aspects of constitutional pre-commitment, see Cass Sunstein, 'Constitutionalism and Secession' (1991) 58 *University of Chicago Law Review* 633, 636–43.

such as lengthy tenures and rules against *ex parte* contact insulate judges from interest group pressure. Those who adopt this theory also predict that where courts are willing to nullify legislative bargains, legislative actors will create administrative adjudicative bodies, with fewer safeguards for independence, even though these bodies, because of lower degrees of independence from interest group and legislative pressure, will generate less consistent decisions over time than will the judiciary.

Commitment theorists hypothesize that the scope and extent of a polity's constitutional protections for judicial independence will depend on the expected duration of legislative bargains. Scholars claim that when legislators enjoy tenures long enough to credibly offer to interest-groups long-term commitments, the value of an independent judiciary to legislators is lower. Legislators under these conditions will limit the independence of the judiciary by shortening the tenure of judges, either through introducing judicial elections or by appointing older judges. In addition, commitment theorists predict an inverse relationship between legislative tenure and judicial tenure; they posit that the longer the tenure of the legislators, the greater will be judicial turnover. The United States has been the primary site for testing the commitment theory approach, although others such as Mark Ramseyer have extended the analysis to jurisdictions, including Japan in the period in which that country was dominated by the Liberal Democratic Party, and concluded that this dominance correlated with a less independent judiciary.[57]

(c) *Rule of Law Theory*

We label 'the rule of law theory' a third approach to explaining when states will create and support independent judiciaries. According to this theory, an independent judiciary is one element of a rule of law regime which secures property rights and guarantees the enforcement of contracts.[58] La Porta et al have undertaken a global survey of jurisdictions, using a variety of measures ranging from subjective perceptions of the security of property rights to the extent of state ownership of commercial banks to evaluate degrees of economic freedom.[59] Their multi-jurisdiction survey of de jure and de facto institutions and procedures concludes that, in a given state, there is a strong causal relationship between judicial independence and high degrees of economic freedom.

Gretchen Helmke and Frances Rosenbluth dispute this claim about the causal effects of judicial independence, arguing that judicial independence does not automatically lead to respect for rule of law values, or to economic progress.[60] They conclude that whether the rule of law thrives is dependent on a range of factors, including a culture of public commitment to the institutions that support the rule of law and a system of separation of powers, of which an independent judiciary may be, but need not be, a part.

However this debate about the causal effects is resolved, it bears notice that some regimes will create at least the appearance of an independent judiciary in order to offer assurances to

[57] See J. Mark Ramseyer, 'The Puzzling (In)dependence of Courts: A Comparative Approach' (1994) 23 *Journal of Legal Studies* 721. The theory has been applied to US state courts by F. Andrew Hanssen, 'Is There a Politically Optimal Level of Judicial Independence?' (2004) 94 *American Economic Review* 712 and to various other jurisdictions by John Ferejohn et al, 'Comparative Judicial Politics' in Charles Boix and Susan C. Stokes (eds), *The Oxford Handbook of Comparative Politics* (2007), 727.

[58] See Edward Glaeser and Andrei Shleifer, 'Legal Origins' (2002) 117 *Quarterly Journal of Economics* 1193. See further Chapter 10.

[59] See La Porta et al (n 9), 451–2.

[60] Gretchen Helmke and Frances Rosenbluth, 'Regimes and the Rule of Law: Judicial Independence in Comparative Perspective' (2009) 12 *Annual Review of Political Science* 345, 347–8.

foreign investors. China is often cited as a case in point, although the efforts of the Chinese Communist Party have drawn criticism on the basis that they do not satisfy minimum criteria for judicial independence.[61] Moreover, as Randall Peerenboom argues, to assess the extent to which Chinese judges enjoy independence, it is important to examine closely the institutional and socio-political facts, rather than simply cataloging de jure indicators, and weighing vaguely formulated de facto measures.[62] The point is that scholars should be sensitive to context, and to the internal complexity of the Chinese judicial and political system.[63]

Peerenboom notes that although the Communist Party exerts influence on the judicial system (as is inevitable in a one-party socialist state), such influence cannot simply be presumed to be pernicious. Sometimes Party policies will limit access to courts to *enhance* the authority of the courts. For example, the Party has instituted policies to direct socio-economic disputes away from the courts, which lack resources and are incompetent to deal with them, towards

> administrative reconsideration, mediation, arbitration, public hearings and the political process more generally.... Forcing the courts to handle such cases had undermined the authority of the judiciary and contributed to a sharp rise in petitions and mass protests.[64]

This sensitivity to the particularities of the political, economic, and social context in which judiciaries are situated suggests that general context-independent causal claims about judicial independence should be advanced with care. Not only does context influence whether a particular state will claim to be promoting the constitutional independence of the judiciary, it will affect whether a state promotes judicial independence in practice. Context will also affect which of the inventory of possible design outcomes are necessary to achieve, in a particular state, the desired outcome of insulating judges from improper influence. In the next section, we argue that a productive path for scholars of comparative judicial independence lies in assessing factors that shape the context in which judges make decisions.

2. Contexts for Judicial Independence

The literature examined so far focuses on the factors that influence initial decisions by governments to create the institutions of an independent judiciary. In this section we look at studies that examine the factors that shape the extent to which judges can, in fact, exercise independent judgment. These factors include (1) the presence of an authoritarian regime, (2) the existence of cultural norms that downplay adjudication as a settlement device, (3) a commitment in civil and political society to judicial independence, and (4) whether the legal system falls within the civil law or common law tradition.

[61] See eg Graig R. Avino, 'China's Judiciary: An Instrument of Democratic Change?' (2003–04) 22 *Penn State International Law Review* 369, 369. See also Jean Pierre Cabestan, 'The Political and Practical Obstacles to the Reform of the Judiciary and the Establishment of the Rule of Law in China' (2005) 10 *Journal of Chinese Political Science* 43, 44, 49–50. Cabestan notes that the demand for an independent judiciary is also driven by the domestic demands of an increasingly sophisticated and complex economic system which requires reliable dispute settlement institutions. Ibid 48–9.

[62] See Randall Peerenboom, 'Judicial Independence in China: Common Myths and Unfounded Assumptions' in Randall Peerenboom (ed), *Judicial Independence in China: Lessons for Global Rule of Law Promotion* (2010), 69, 88–9.

[63] Cabestan (n 61), 47 describes

> a growing gap and a gradual disconnection between the most repressive and political aspects of Chinese law, in other words the Soviet (and imperial) legacy, on the one hand and the more modern, outward looking and Western inspired areas of this legal system on the other.

[64] Peerenboom (n 62), 79.

(a) *Authoritarianism and Its Effects on Judicial Independence*

Scholars have shown that authoritarian regimes create independent judiciaries for a variety of reasons. In addition, they have sought to describe the socio-political conditions under which authoritarian regimes are most likely to do so.[65] In this section, we explore *how* these regimes create incentive-structures that influence judicial decision-making. Tamir Moustafa and Tom Ginsburg have catalogued several ways in which authoritarian regimes will set boundaries for the exercise of judicial independence. First, through the threat of retribution, these regimes can encourage courts to act with self-restraint. The authors note that courts under such circumstances may reason expansively in some areas of law, but not in areas that affect the core interests of the relevant regime. Egypt is a prime example of a state where the constitutional court offered rulings that expansively interpreted individual rights and limited the executive, but 'never ruled on constitutional challenges to the emergency laws or civilian transfers to military courts, which formed the bedrock of regime dominance.'[66]

A second way in which regimes can constrain courts is by fragmenting the judicial system. Regimes can funnel politically sensitive disputes away from ordinary courts and towards adjudicative bodies over which they exert substantial executive control. In so doing, regimes limit the power of courts, without directly undermining their independence. Moustafa and Ginsburg point to Franco's Spain as an authoritarian regime in which the courts enjoyed considerable formal and de facto independence, but had a limited sphere of decision-making authority, since the regime had established a parallel adjudicative system to deal with politically sensitive matters.[67]

Authoritarian regimes can further constrain the capacity of courts to display judicial independence by limiting access to them, either by imposing procedural and financial barriers to access or, more commonly, by tightly limiting the kinds of disputes that courts will hear.[68] For example, in Mexico the autocratic regime created a procedure (the *amparo* trial) that enabled citizens to challenge state action in the courts, but limited the scope of the courts' jurisdiction such that it precluded challenges based on 'expropriation of property, harsh economic regulation, and the violation of due process'.[69] The independence of these courts is limited because the reasons for which parties can access them are limited. The result, at least in the Mexican case, is that the regime can monitor low-level administrative actors, but insulates itself from rights-based challenges.[70]

Finally, authoritarian regimes can constrain the courts by appealing to extra-judicial factors. Sometimes this is achieved by appealing to (or inventing) traditional cultural norms that

[65] Moustafa and Ginsburg argue that entrenched authoritarian regimes are more likely to create and support an independent judiciary than are those with a less secure position. The authors claim that secure regimes have greater latitude (1) to experiment with institutions, such as courts, that create conditions for long-term economic growth and set the foundations for complex administrative structures, and (2) to shift from a legitimating discourse that focuses on substantive outcomes to one that focuses on the rule of law. See Moustafa and Ginsburg (n 35), 11–12. For a fascinating variation on this literature, which focuses on the protections afforded the judiciary in the Indian subcontinent during states of emergency, see Anil Kalhan, 'Constitution and "Extraconstitution": Colonial Emergency Regimes in Postcolonial India and Pakistan' in Victor V. Ramraj and Arun K. Thiruvengadam, *Emergency Powers in Asia: Exploring the Limits of Legality* (2010), 89.

[66] Moustafa and Ginsburg (n 35), 15.

[67] Ibid 17.

[68] Ibid 19–20.

[69] Beatriz Magaloni, 'Enforcing the Autocratic Political Order and the Role of Courts: The Case of Mexico' in Moustafa and Ginsburg (n 35), 180 at 181.

[70] Ibid.

promote dispute settlement by non-adjudicative means such as an appeal to elders or conciliation processes. Alternatively, some regimes seek to undermine supports for an independent the judiciary—a strong bar, a free press, active NGOs, a popular culture of legalism in the general population—within wider civil society. We discuss these informal methods of limiting judicial independence, whether arising in authoritarian or democratic regimes, in the next two sections.

(b) *The Influence of Cultural Norms Downplaying Adjudication*

Some have noted that judicial independence can be curtailed in jurisdictions where there is no tradition of adjudication as a mode of dispute resolution. Graig Avino has argued that throughout China's history, Confucianism has been considered the dominant ideology, and that Confucianism emphasizes persuasion, education, moral example, social hierarchy, and mediation as mechanisms for social control, and relegates traditional legal institutions, including courts, to a secondary status.[71] In contemporary China the idea of an independent judiciary is unfamiliar because of this general preference for Confucian modes of social regulation, and because of the Cultural Revolution, which decimated a nascent legal system. Avino lists various indicators that support his claim. These include: (1) political control over judicial decision-making at every level of the judiciary; (2) judges who are not trained in law and are often appointed precisely because they can be expected to answer directly to political officials; and (3) endemic corruption in the judiciary. He concludes that recent judicial reforms, which aim to create an independent judiciary, are as yet insufficient to overcome these impediments.[72]

As noted, some scholars consider such claims about judicial independence in China to be overdrawn.[73] Others have directly challenged the claim about the influence of cultural beliefs like Confucianism on judicial independence. According to Ginsburg, a close examination of the recent history of Thailand, Korea, Taiwan, and Mongolia reveals that cultural barriers did not preclude the emergence of courts that were willing to engage in aggressive constitutional review and to significantly constrain political actors. This analysis is particularly striking because authoritarian regimes in East Asia have routinely invoked Confucian ideas to justify their rule, and because the intellectual history and resources of the region provide little to support indigenous theories of judicial review by independent courts.[74]

Despite these cultural obstacles, countries in East Asia during the 1980s and 1990s joined in the global trend of instituting judicial review of legislative and executive action.[75] Moreover, in each state he examined, Ginsburg found constitutional courts to be assertive in their judicial review function and that their institutional contexts supported this assertiveness. He concludes that two variables best explain the emergence of assertive judicial review in the countries he surveys: the existence of a middle class, and the diffusion of political power amongst political parties.[76]

(c) *A Commitment in Civil and Political Society to Judicial Independence*

If the East Asian example provides mixed evidence about whether cultural variables influence a state's receptivity to judicial independence and openness to the related phenomenon of

[71] Avino (n 61), 370–5.

[72] Ibid 379–91.

[73] Peerenboom (n 62) and accompanying text.

[74] Tom Ginsburg, 'Constitutional Courts in New Democracies: Understanding Variation in East Asia' (2002) 2 *Global Jurist Advances* 1, 1–2, 19.

[75] Ibid 3.

[76] Ibid 24.

aggressive constitutional review, other analyses suggest that judicial independence is likely to thrive in contexts where the civic and political culture supports the idea of insulating the judiciary from inappropriate political interference. Daniel Beers argues, based on two Central European case studies, that informal political and judicial culture is a better predictor of whether courts will exercise their judgment independently from external influences than are formal institutional indicia of judicial independence.[77] Beers claims that in Romania, formal institutional structures supporting judicial independence were created in response to pressures from external actors, including the European Union, but without the support of domestic elites.[78] By contrast, he notes that although the formal safeguards of judicial independence in the Czech Republic are much less sophisticated than those in Romania, Czech political and legal elites have fostered a culture of commitment to judicial independence.

Judges in the two countries were surveyed regarding judicial autonomy (their perceived degree of freedom from undue influence of outside actors or superiors), judicial integrity (susceptibility of judges to corruption), and the morale of the judiciary (professional satisfaction and commitment of judges).[79] Czech judges perceived significantly higher degrees of autonomy and integrity in their judicial system than did Romanian judges in theirs. To the extent that such perceptions are accurate indicators of the degree of independence the judiciary in fact enjoys, Beers' analysis suggests that, in states having recently become democracies, the informal culture of political and legal elites plays a more significant role in fostering judicial independence than do formal legal protections.

The experience of states in Latin America provides additional support for this conclusion. Rachel Sieder notes that significant investments in institutional reform of the Guatemalan legal system have not yielded an independent and effective judiciary, in large part because 'historical processes, cultural understandings and material interests' have militated against it.[80] According to Sieder, despite wide-ranging legal reforms, some of which were instituted with the support of international organizations,[81] there is pervasive corruption in the judiciary. Because Guatemalan judges are poorly trained and poorly paid, and largely immune from effective oversight, they are susceptible to corruption. Moreover, powerful elite groups, including the military, exercise significant influence in the judicial system and engage in extensive interference with judicial processes. As a consequence, she concludes, the public distrusts the justice system and relies instead on private solutions, including vigilante activities and extra-judicial executions, thus further undermining the authority of the state judicial system.[82]

By contrast, Columbia's Constitutional Court has effectively and actively controlled government abuses of power, in significant part because of widespread support for the court

[77] Daniel J. Beers, 'A Tale of Two Transitions: Exploring the Origins of Post-Communist Judicial Culture in Romania and the Czech Republic' (2010) 18 *Demokratizatsiya: Journal of Post-Soviet Democratization* 28, 31.

[78] Ibid 35. Among the formal institutional safeguards were:

> an independent self-governing council of judges (the Superior Council of Magistracy), one of the most well-developed and well-funded judicial training institutes in the region (the National Institute of Magistracy), and a strict system of exam-based hiring and promotion.

[79] Ibid 31–4.

[80] Rachel Sieder, 'Renegotiating "Law and Order": Judicial Reform and Citizen Responses in Post-war Guatemala' in Gloppen et al (n 29), 137.

[81] Ibid 145:

> Multiple donors were involved in justice reform, including the World Bank, the IDP, USAID, the UNDP, MINUGA, the Organization of American States (OAS), the US Department of Justice, the European Union and numerous bilateral donors.

[82] Ibid 152.

within civil society. Rodrigo Uprimny claims that this effectiveness can be explained by: (1) an established history of judicial review; (2) widespread disenchantment with the political processes, which led the population to seek from the judiciary resolutions of political disputes; (3) alliances between justices on the court and social actors to advance progressive constitutional values; and (4) a broad social understanding that it is appropriate for courts to engage in assertive judicial review.[83] These social and cultural factors, combined with a range of institutional factors (ie, a low-cost, accessible system of constitutional review, centralized authority in the Constitutional Court, and substantial financial investment in the Court), to support the actions of an independent-minded judiciary.[84]

(d) Civil Law versus Common Law

Although the tendency of comparative public law scholars today is to shift attention away from legal families and towards particular legal institutions, legal family comparisons are sometimes adopted in order to examine ways in which institutional characteristics of common and civil law systems shape the extent to which judges can exercise independent judgment. This approach does not presume that legal traditions have distinct and incommensurable epistemologies; rather, scholars examine the institutional features of legal traditions in order to assess whether and, if so, how these features might affect the ways in which judges actually decide cases.[85]

Some have argued that the significant differences between common and civil law systems as to how judges are appointed and how they advance through the judicial hierarchy influence the extent to which they exercise independent judgment. For instance, Charles Koch has argued that because civilian judges are specifically trained to be judges, and self-select and self-regulate, they are more likely to exercise independent judgment than their common law counterparts.[86] He claims that unlike common law judges, who bring to their positions prior experiences as lawyers, the civilian system of training inculcates in judges 'an otherworldly objectivity'.[87] Moreover, he notes that because civil law judges self-regulate they are not subject to external pressures, as are, for instance administrative law judges in the United States who do not enjoy security of tenure and who carry out the vast majority of adjudications.[88] Finally, notes Koch, judges in the civilian tradition engage in peer monitoring, which occurs through mentorship and through training that leads to advancement. According to him, collective

[83] Rodrigo Uprimny, 'The Constitutional Court and Control of Presidential Extraordinary Powers in Colombia' in Gloppen et al (n 29), 46 at 61–3.

[84] Ibid 61. For a series of empirical studies concluding that informal factors (including the confidence of citizens in the legal system) are a more significant influence than formal institutions on the extent to which a judiciary enjoys independence in fact, see Erik Jensen and Thomas Heller (eds), *Beyond Common Knowledge* (2003).

[85] Compare Charles H. Koch Jr, 'The Advantages of the Civil Law Judicial Design as the Model for Emerging Legal Systems' (2004) 11 *Indiana Journal of Global Legal Studies* 139 with Helmke and Rosenbluth (n 60) (disputing that legal tradition is a significant factor in determining degrees of judicial independence).

[86] Koch (n 85), 142. Of course, in speaking of 'the civil law tradition', one necessarily generalizes. Eg although there are family resemblances, there are important differences between the German and the Latin West European judicial systems, and there are, moreover, differences among the various countries in the latter category. For overviews, see Donald P. Kommers, 'Autonomy versus Accountability: The German Judiciary' and Carlo Guarnieri, 'Judicial Independence in Latin Countries of Western Europe' in Russell and O'Brien (n 24), 131 and 111 respectively.

[87] Koch (n 85), 144.

[88] Ibid 145.

decision-making of this kind provides opportunities for judges to check corruption and to overcome cognitive biases.[89]

While Koch highlights these features of civilian courts to illustrate how they contribute to greater degrees of judicial independence, others have argued that some of these features can undermine judicial independence.[90] Consider the issue of control over advancement in civil law systems. In the Japanese system, there is a judicial administrative office, the Secretariat, which is staffed by judges, is controlled by justices of the Supreme Court (who are politically appointed), and is responsible for assigning judges to (more or less prestigious) geographic locations and for moving judges up and down the judicial hierarchy. According to Ramseyer and Rasmusen, judges 'who flout the ruling party in politically volatile cases pay a career penalty';[91] the Secretariat effectively punishes them through its assignment and promotion decisions.[92] Garoupa and Ginsburg argue that common law judges, by contrast, have fewer opportunities for career advancement and for changes in assignment, and are therefore less susceptible to being influenced by decisions relating to these matters than are civil law judges.[93]

In addition to distinguishing common and civil law systems on the basis of their appointment, management, and advancement practices, scholars have argued that differences in degrees of bureaucratization and forms of reasoning have implications for the extent of judicial independence in the two traditions.[94] Edward Glaeser and Andreis Shleifer claim that codification of law facilitates centralized state control over courts, whereas common law principles do not. The authors argue that civil codes are compilations of bright-line rules and that the underlying purpose of codification is for the legislature to control judges: these rules limit the scope of judicial discretion and allow the legislators to verify and monitor the decisions of judges.[95] By contrast, Glaeser and Shleifer argue that common law judges have greater interpretive autonomy as they, rather than the legislature, establish the precedents that guide common law reasoning. Even when interpreting statutes and codified bodies of law, they also assert, common law judges do so in light of common law principles and of the specific facts of the case.[96]

These claims have attracted a range of criticisms, including that the differences between common and civil law traditions are exaggerated. Gillian Hadfield notes that comprehensive codes exist in common law countries, and that statutory regimes in civil law countries dealing with, for instance, environmental regulation are indistinguishable from those found in common law countries.[97] Moreover, authors note that civil law judges do not necessarily ignore decisions by previous courts, nor do civil law judges deny that they sometimes exercise a policy-making function.[98] Finally, the claims about relative degrees of legislative control over

[89] Ibid 148–9.

[90] J. Mark Ramseyer and Eric B. Rasmusen, 'Judicial Independence in a Civil Law Regime' (1997) 13 *Journal of Law, Economics, and Organization* 259, 265.

[91] Ramseyer and Rasmusen (n 17), 341.

[92] See also David M. O'Brien and Yasuo Ohkoshi, 'The Japanese Judiciary' in Russell and O'Brien (n 24), 37, 48, noting the salary differentials between judges who are favored and disfavored by the Secretariat and the Chief Justice of the Supreme Court.

[93] Nuno Garoupa and Tom Ginsburg, 'The Comparative Law and Economics of Judicial Councils' (2009) 27 *Berkeley Journal of International Law* 53.

[94] See eg Glaeser and Shleifer (n 58).

[95] Ibid 1216.

[96] Ibid 1212.

[97] Gillian K. Hadfield, 'The Levers of Legal Design: Institutional Determinants of the Quality of Law' (2008) 36 *Journal of Comparative Economics* 43, 44.

[98] Ibid and citations therein.

judges do not account for the fact that in civil law jurisdictions, as elsewhere, courts have been engaged in aggressive judicial review of legislation.[99] Particularly relevant for the present discussion is the fact that constitutional courts in civil law jurisdictions have engaged in expansive modes of interpretation that do not conform to the image of a judiciary bound by legislative dictates. As Alec Stone Sweet has observed, in France, the Constitutional Council has generated novel constitutional principles and in Germany, the Federal Constitutional Court has engaged in broad interpretations of the constitutional text.[100]

This survey of the literature suggests that the correlation of degrees of judicial independence with membership in a particular legal family is not self-evident. Nonetheless, we suggest that the impetus underlying public law scholars' arguments about correlations—namely, identifying factors that influence judicial decision-making—is a useful one. It reflects, indeed, the contemporary focus in the judicial independence literature on those institutional design elements which are assumed to protect judicial independence.[101]

3. The Virtues of Judging

In the previous section we explored what Lydia Tiede has called the 'institutional approach' to judicial independence, in which 'certain institutional configurations, or rules of the game, affect the behavior of political actors'.[102] We close this section with some reflections on the relationship between, on the one hand, the institutional and cultural contexts in which judges exercise judgment and, on the other hand, the role of the virtuous judge.

We begin our discussion by discussing two virtues identified by Pimentel: judicial courage and judicial integrity. According to Pimentel, this form of courage 'enables the judge to withstand pressures and influences, even threats and exercise true independence in her decision-making.'[103] Judicial integrity, he argues, is a necessary supplement to judicial courage and entails 'a commitment to the highest principles of judicial decision-making'.[104] These judicial virtues are related, but not reducible to the institutional analyses surveyed above. Features of their institutional context may provide incentives for judges to exercise independent judgment, or may offer disincentives for doing so. Nonetheless, a conception of judicial independence that emphasizes judicial virtues requires judges in some circumstances to resist the incentive structure in which they operate. Judges acting in accordance with the virtues exercise *phronesis*, or practical wisdom, and features of the contexts in which judges are trained, appointed, and work can cultivate and support the judicial capacity for practical wisdom.[105]

[99] That review can be *ex ante*, *ex post*, or both. See Ginsburg (n 50), 38–9.

[100] Alec Stone Sweet, *The Birth of Judicial Politics in France: The Constitutional Council in Comparative Perspective* (1992), 240.

[101] The standard institutional features relate to the following four elements: neutral appointment, security of tenure, financial independence, and administrative autonomy (including court administration, training, discipline, promotion, and conditions of retirement). For a comprehensive discussion see Russell (n 24); see also *Reference re Remuneration of Provincial Court Judges* (n 3).

[102] Lydia Brashear Tiede, 'Judicial Independence: Often Cited, Rarely Understood' (2006) 15 *Journal of Contemporary Legal Issues* 129, 136.

[103] Pimentel (n 32), 20.

[104] Ibid 23. The idea of integrity is usually deployed to capture a judge's commitment to craft: respect for precedent, fidelity to established principles of statutory interpretation, and strict adherence to the norm of impartiality. For a multi-jurisdictional conspectus of integrity, see Sajó (n 6).

[105] See Solum (n 31) and Macdonald (n 25), 61–70, who identify sobriety, wisdom, courage, modesty, and resisting the temptation to right all wrongs regardless of formal jurisdiction to do so as central elements of judicial *phroenesis*.

But even (or perhaps especially) in the absence of such supporting features, judges can exercise independent judgment or judgment that does not respond to inappropriate influences.

In examining what such judgment entails, we fold what Tiede has called the 'strategic interaction approach' into our conception of the necessary connection between judicial independence and judicial virtue. According to this approach, judges are strategic actors who recognize that in order to attain their preferred outcomes on issues they need to understand and anticipate the preference of other institutional actors, including legislatures, the executive, and other judges or courts.[106] An approach animated by the judicial virtues introduces two insights into this discussion. First, rather than conceive of judges as being motivated by a desire to induce legislators, executive actors and lower courts to comply with their personal policy preferences, a virtue-focused conception of judging understands judges to be making normative judgments that are not motivated by self-interest. Under such an approach, judges who exemplify judicial courage will write decisions that reflect their best interpretations of the law and relevant public policy. Of course, the elected branches may try to exert influence over the judiciary by, for instance, strategic appointments, limiting its resources, increasing the number of administrative agencies, and thus lessening the courts' ability to supervise government decision-making or to enforce compliance with their judgments.[107] The point we make here, however, is that when exercising the virtue of judicial courage, judges resist pressures on them to make self-interested judgments, whatever the institutional context in which they operate.

Recent examples of the virtue of courage include the experience of Judge J. Skelly Wright, a district court judge in Louisiana during the 1950s and 1960s who was the object of intense public criticism and threats of violence because of his desegregation rulings, and of Italian prosecuting magistrates such as Giovanni Falcone, who were murdered for their decisions. These examples are particularly striking, but there are myriad ways in which to exhibit judicial courage. Judges in systems that tie career advancement to judgments favoring the government can exhibit courage by ignoring these inducements. Similarly, judges in cultural and societal contexts in which corruption is endemic and political reprisals for decisions contrary to the interests of government are common can exercise their judgment without regard to these pressures. Finally, judges can exhibit courage by not seeking the approval of the press, the academy, or interest groups. In all of these instances, judicial courage is evidenced by a willingness to make decisions based on one's best understanding of the relevant legal principles. Of course, one can characterize the belief that one should be bound by legal principle as reflecting a personal preference. Yet, as others have argued, it is this kind of belief that marks out legal from non-legal reasoning, and moreover, it is a commitment to this kind of reasoning that characterizes the role of the judge.[108]

Difficult questions about judicial independence arise in circumstances where judges are called upon to make pragmatic judgments about how the political branches will respond to judicial decisions. Some scholars measure judicial independence by referring to the number of times that a court rules against the government.[109] Sophisticated models have been

[106] Tiede (n 102), 150–1. See also, McNollgast, 'Conditions for Judicial Independence' (2006) 15 *Journal of Contemporary Legal Issues* 105, 109–10.

[107] Ibid 110. In one version of this strategic interaction literature, the US Supreme Court is understood to be a principal and lower courts and administrative actors its agents.

[108] See Michael Dorf, 'Whose Ox is Being Gored? When Attitudinalism Meets Federalism' (2007) 21 *St John's Journal of Legal Commentary* 497, 518–19.

[109] See the overview of this literature, as applied to the Latin American context, in Larkins (n 22), 616–18. A related literature set examines the extent to which judges rule against the party that appointed them. See eg Lee Epstein and Jeffrey A. Segal, *Advice and Consent: The Politics of Judicial Appointments* (2005), 121–41; James Stribopolous and Moin Yahya, 'Does A Judge's Party of Appointment or Gender Matter to Case Outcomes?: An Empirical Study of the Court of Appeal for Ontario' (2007) 45 *Osgoode Hall Law Journal* 315.

developed to identify when courts will act strategically in anticipation of government reprisals. Scholars examining US courts argue that in the face of likely reprisals a judge will 'forego his or her most preferred choice and instead choose the next best option that he or she believes the other relevant institutional actors will support.'[110] In her analysis of the Argentine judiciary in the period from 1976 to 1999, Gretchen Helmke has argued that where judges do not enjoy effective protections against government reprisals, judges will engage in 'strategic defection'. This form of defection occurs when judges who share the preferences of the incumbent regime rule against it in anticipation of imminent regime change. Under these conditions, judges fear reprisals from the next government and render decisions to send signals in order to lessen the likelihood of potential reprisals from that government.[111]

The challenge for a virtue-centered conception of judicial independence lies in distinguishing cases that represent a reasoned and pragmatic interpretation of the law from those that evidence judicial self-interest. Constitutional law scholars have argued that when courts construct constitutional doctrine, they make pragmatic judgments about their institutional competences and about the likely institutional effects of their decisions.[112] These scholars argue against perfectionist accounts of constitutional law, which imagine constitutional reasoning to be coextensive with political theory.[113] Yet if constitutional doctrine is not identical to political theory, neither are the pragmatic judgments embedded in doctrine simple calculations based on self-interest, although they may *overlap with* self-interested actions. For instance, judges may refrain from issuing certain kinds of judgments because they are concerned that such judgments will attract governmental reprisals or governmental indifference that will undermine the credibility of the judiciary.[114] In such circumstances, they may be making considered decisions about the importance of protecting the credibility of the judiciary as an institution, at the same time as they are advancing their self-interest. What is significant for our account is that judges are only acting virtuously to the extent that their judgment is grounded in the former kind of justification.

Theunis Roux finds an example of pragmatic constitutional reasoning that can be characterized as exemplifying constitutional integrity in the jurisprudence of the South African Constitutional Court concerning the manner in which the government allocates public resources.[115] The scholarly literature routinely expresses concern about whether courts enjoy a democratic mandate or the institutional capacity to undertake this kind of review. Nonetheless, in a case challenging the constitutionality of a municipality's failure to provide temporary shelter to a homeless community,[116] the Court arrived at a holding that enabled it to enforce a constitutional right, without substituting its judgment for the judgment of the political branches about how to manage budgets. According to Roux, the Court found, in a holding reminiscent of *Brown v Board of Education* that 'it was unreasonable for the state to

[110] Gretchen Helmke, *Courts Under Constraints: Judges, Generals and Presidents in Argentina* (2005), 12, summarizing the work of Ferejohn (n 47).

[111] Helmke (n 110), 155.

[112] Mitchell N. Berman, 'Constitutional Decision Rules' (2004) 90 *Virginia Law Review* 1, 3.

[113] The claim that legal reasoning is not coextensive with political or moral reasoning is standard in the decision rules literature: see Richard H. Fallon Jr, *Implementing the Constitution* (2001), 26–36; Kermit Roosevelt III, *The Myth of Judicial Activism* (2006), 22–36; Lawrence G. Sager, *Justice in Plainclothes: A Theory of American Constitutional Practice* (2004).

[114] For a consideration of credibility costs, see Jesse H. Choper, *Judicial Review and the National Political Process: A Functional Reconsideration of the Role of the Supreme Court* (1980), 201–2, 258.

[115] Theunis Roux, 'Legitimating Transformation: Political Resource Allocation in the South African Constitutional Court' in Gloppen et al (n 29), 92.

[116] *Governor of the Republic of South Africa v Grootboom* (CCT11/00) [2000] ZACC 19.

"exclude" a significant element of society from the national housing programme, especially where such a group was poor or otherwise vulnerable.'[117] While nonetheless insisting that the political branches undertake reasonable measures to fulfill their constitutional obligations, the Court left them discretion to decide the timing and the amount of funding to allocate. Roux points to a variety of factors which have permitted the Court successfully to build its legitimacy and safeguard its jurisdictional authority in a period of constitutional transformation, notably that the judges themselves are of high caliber and that the judges broadly share the political views of the governing elites.[118] For our purposes, the South African Court's jurisprudence illustrates how judges can display the virtue of integrity—making pragmatic decisions that benefit the judiciary, without acting exclusively in their self-interest.

IV. Conclusion

Citizens have a legitimate interest in the quality of justice that is delivered by the several governance institutions of the state. In many contemporary states, the assumption is that the difficult issues of interpersonal, social, and economic justice will be settled by legislatures and that legislative enactments will be fairly administered by the agents of an accountable executive. In these states citizens also assume that should there be a disagreement about the meaning of a statute or other legal rule—whether the conflict is between citizens (private law), between citizen and state (administrative law), between citizen and society (criminal law), between orders and institutions of government (constitutional law), or about the fundamental principles of the legal order (the rule of law, civil liberties, human rights)—an independent, impartial third party institution (invariably courts) will hear the dispute and render a just decision.

While citizen intuitions about judicial independence find confirmation in constitutional theory and in the institutional arrangements actually in place in many states, the meaning of the concept is typically not well understood by the general public. The above review of the theory and practice of judicial independence reveals the complexity of the inquiry. Nevertheless, when we turn away from current examples and even from current theories we see that, in a broader sociological framework, the formalistic inquiry into institutions and practices promoting judicial independence could better be cast as one related to the integrity of 'processes of social ordering'. What kind of research agenda would such an inquiry command?

An initial challenge is to understand the total social, economic, and political context within which the concept of judicial independence is invoked in a given state. However conventional it may be to consider the judiciary as a necessary branch of modern government, it bears remembering that the decision to establish a judiciary is a political choice. Hence the question why almost all contemporary states have an official agency to decide disputes and, in doing so, to articulate fundamental legal-political commitments. Moreover, however much it may be that mediation is an appropriate mechanism for dispute-resolution in many fields, there are some tasks (typically involving the constitution: separation of powers, division of powers, bills of rights) where an authoritative third party decision is required.[119]

[117] Roux (n 115).

[118] Ibid 94–5.

[119] Shapiro (n 16); Kojève (n 16).

Yet even after we have decided what we want courts to do and the qualities we want to see reflected in our judicial system, we are still a long way from knowing what institutional design to adopt. For we also need to decide whether achieving a close match between the outcomes produced by a given judicial process and the substantive outcomes we desire is the only goal that we would attribute to a process of system design. The point can be illustrated by posing the following hypothetical alternatives: Do we want a judicial process that will generate the best substantive outcomes, even if that process is secret, mysterious, anti-democratic, corrupt, costly, and slow? Or do we want a process that is open, accessible, democratic, honest, efficient, and cheap, even if it generates suboptimal outcomes? Much of the challenge in institutional design is to recognize, organize, and justify the inevitable trade-offs among the different goals—procedural and substantive—we seek to achieve. Understandably, these trade-offs may not be made in precisely the same way in all states.

To imagine the concept of judicial independence as a central feature of political governance is to conceive the judiciary as an institution that enables citizens to achieve an impartial resolution of inter-subjective conflict, and to conscript the resources of the state to the enforcement of judgments courts render. A meaningful concept of the judiciary as a governance institution speaks as much to issues of *inter*dependence as it does to issues of *in*dependence. That is, in order for a judiciary to function as a governance institution, other substantive and procedural features must be present in a constitutional system. A judiciary assumes that there exist *ex ante* legal rules upon which citizens in a conflict may base a claim of right; it also assumes a rational process for framing, presenting, and contesting rights claims—rules of civil procedure, rules of evidence, the existence of a legal profession, a reasonably cheap, expeditious, and uncomplicated process that effects accessible justice; the possibility of designing remedies that provide a reasonable proxy for the actual hurt or conflict between the parties; the need for an effective process of enforcement of judgments; and finally, that the whole process, beginning to end, not be tainted by any hint of partiality, prejudice, or special interest—that all be equal before the law and before the judge.

To see the judiciary as an *in*dependent governance institution means that it stands apart from other governance institutions in a state and that it has a mind and will of its own under a doctrine of separation of powers sufficient to provide an effective check on the abuse of power by the political branches of government. The judiciary must have a high degree of structural autonomy and immunity. Autonomy and immunity sustain both the independence and the related, but distinct, idea of impartiality in the judicial process. A judiciary may be in principle independent, but in a particular case, a judge may not be impartial—that is, may display favoritism towards one party. So, for example, in a law suit against the government, or in a criminal trial, or in a case of judicial supervision of administrative discretion it is important that the judiciary be independent of the apparatus of the state—notably of the executive that has selected it, or the judicial bureaucracy within which a judge operates. Where decisions favor the state, it may be that although the judiciary is independent, it is not impartial and its decisions are coloured by inappropriate considerations. But impartiality may flow in the other direction. A judiciary may be independent of the executive and legislature but partial in favor of interests other than the state. Corporations may well have the resources to influence judicial decisions improperly. Some judges may refuse to convict obviously guilty murderers because they disbelieve in a mandatory death sentence.

At its most general level, applicable to all human decision-making institutions and roles, whether official or unofficial, public or private, judicial or non-judicial, the fundamental objective is to ensure that persons who have been assigned such a responsibility perform their function with due regard to the internal integrity of the role. Do we get good judges because we have good judicial institutions, or do we get good judicial institutions because we have good judges? The evidence worldwide is equivocal. Yet this much is clear. Because there is no such thing as mechanical judicial decision-making, there will always be a moment of personal judgment in every judicial decision. This suggests that the most important criterion for judicial independence and impartiality is the quality and character of the judges appointed. Institutional structure and procedures help to ensure that those already inclined to perform their role faithfully will do so, but structure and procedure will not alone lead to integrity of character in a morally lax person.

Independence requires fidelity to role—the personal integrity of the person appointed. To achieve a virtuous judiciary, it is not enough simply to choose them wisely. It is also necessary to: (1) celebrate their selection; (2) provide them with the information necessary to understand the tasks they will be expected to perform; (3) generate a commitment to the mission and the importance of the institution they are joining; (4) train them well; (5) provide them with meaningful feedback about their performance; (6) pay them decent salaries; (7) publicly value the job they are doing; (8) praise them for their successes; (9) provide them with the necessary help to do their job better; (10) furnish them with ongoing opportunities to learn and reflect about their role and responsibilities; (11) treat them properly and with respect; (12) give them a mandate that is within the capacity of a normal human being to accomplish; (13) avoid overburdening them with a caseload that is soul-destroying; and (14) defend them against ill-tempered and ill-considered critiques from those who have no clue about the nature of their job, the pressures they face, the pathologies and inconsistencies of the law they are meant to administer, and the sometimes perverse behavior of those who appear before them.[120]

All of the above factors operate in tandem with each other. The absence of a rigorous vetting of the quality of judges at the time of appointment might be compensated by structures and processes of in-service *encadrement*. The absence of institutional protections like life tenure and guaranteed remuneration might be compensated by strong administrative autonomy vested in courts. The absence of formal guarantees of independence in a written constitution might be compensated by a strong political and social culture supporting judicial integrity. The absence of a professional magistracy backed with years of training and a collegial decision-making process might be compensated by a legal culture that lionizes judges. How each of these plays out in any particular state and any particular institution will vary. The challenges and optimal responses are embedded in the sets of pressures that actually exist in time and place.

The fact that judicial independence is both an essentially contested concept, and can be achieved with a wide variety of matches of formal and informal, institutional and customary, *ex ante* and *ex post*, substantive and procedural norms, depending on the legal, political, and socio-economic-religious culture in a state, has implications for future comparative research. In our view, the appropriate research agenda would aim at discerning the strength of the norm of integrity among judges and their actual decision-making practices. It would also examine the institutional and cultural factors that are central in particular context to the inculcation, promotion, and protection of judicial virtue. This empirical and normatively focused inquiry promises more significant insights than taxonomic inventories of 'standard institutional and procedural features' that are purportedly necessary components of an independent judiciary.

[120] This list is taken from Macdonald (n 25).

Bibliography

Stephen B. Burbank and Barry Friedman (eds), *Judicial Independence at the Crossroads: An Interdisciplinary Approach* (2002)

John Ferejohn, 'Explaining Judges, Dependent Judiciary: Explaining Judicial Independence' (1999) 72 *Southern California Law Review* 353

Siri Gloppen et al (eds), *Democratization and the Judiciary* (2004)

Gretchen Helmke and Frances Rosenbluth, 'Regimes and the Rule of Law: Judicial Independence in Comparative Perspective' (2009) 12 *Annual Review of Political Science* 345

Ran Hirschl, 'The Political Origins of Judicial Empowerment through Constitutionalization: Lessons from Israel's Constitutional Revolution' (2001) 33 *Comparative Politics* 315

Irving R. Kaufman, 'The Essence of Judicial Independence' (1980) 80 *Columbia Law Review* 671

Rafael La Porta et al, 'Judicial Checks and Balances' (2004) 112 *Journal of Political Economy* 445

William M. Landes and Richard A. Posner, 'The Independent Judiciary in an Interest-Group Perspective' (1975) 18 *Journal of Law and Economics* 875

Christopher M. Larkins, 'Judicial Independence and Democratization: A Theoretical and Conceptual Analysis' (1996) 44 *American Journal of Comparative Law* 605

William R. Lederman, 'The Independence of the Judiciary' (1956) 34 *Canadian Bar Review* 769

Sanford Levinson, 'Identifying "Independence"' (2006) 86 *Boston University Law Review* 1297

McNollgast, 'Conditions for Judicial Independence' (2006) 15 *Journal of Contemporary Legal Issues* 105

Roderick A. Macdonald, 'Appoint Elect, Draw Straws or Sell to the Highest Bidder? On Judicial Selection Processes' in Pierre Noreau (ed), *Mélanges Andrée Lajoie* (2008)

Tamir Moustafa and Tom Ginsburg (eds), *Rule by Law: the Politics of Courts in Authoritarian Regimes* (2008)

Randall Peerenboom (ed), *Judicial Independence in China: Lessons for Global Rule of Law Promotion* (2010)

J. Mark Ramseyer, 'The Puzzling (In)dependence of Courts: A Comparative Approach' (1994) 23 *Journal of Legal Studies* 721

Peter Russell, 'A General Theory of Judicial Independence Revisited' in Adam Dodek et al (eds), *Judicial Independence in Context* (2010)

Peter H. Russell and David O'Brien (eds), *Judicial Independence in the Age of Democracy* (2001)

András Sajó (ed), *Judicial Integrity* (2004)

Martin Shapiro, *Courts: A Comparative and Political Analysis* (1981)

Alec Stone Sweet, *The Birth of Judicial Politics in France: The Constitutional Council in Comparative Perspective* (1992)

CHAPTER 40

THE JUDICIARY: THE LEAST DANGEROUS BRANCH?

DANIEL SMILOV

Sofia

I. Introduction: The Judiciary in Comparative Perspective

The judiciary is an essential element of all contemporary constitutional regimes, and yet, there is no single best model of institutionalizing the role of the magistrates vis-à-vis other branches of power. Most contemporary models envisage complex systems of checks and balances, or mutual interdependence.[1] While it is clear the judiciary needs constitutional prerogatives and guarantees of independence in order to make sure that there is sufficient division of power, or that 'Ambition [is] made to counteract ambition',[2] only a tentative checklist of such prerogatives and guarantees can be provided:[3]

(1) Judges and public prosecutors are only subject to the law.

(2) Judges and public prosecutors should be appointed for life or for such other period and conditions, so that the judicial independence is not endangered. Any change to the judicial obligatory retirement age must not have retroactive effect.

[1] András Sajó, *Limiting Government* (1999), 94.

[2] James Madison, *The Federalist Papers*, No 51 (1961), 322.

[3] See eg the Universal Charter of the Judges of Taipei (1999). In the summary of the principles, I follow Giacomo Oberto, Deputy Secretary General of the International Association of Judges <http://giacomooberto.com/prague/1.htm>.

(3) Judges and public prosecutors should be selected through competitive examinations. The selection and each appointment of a judge or of a public prosecutor must be carried out according to objective and transparent criteria based on proper professional qualifications.

(4) No influence should be given to the executive or to the legislative power in the process of selection of judges and public prosecutors.

(5) A High Council for the Judiciary should be established. The High Council for the Judiciary should be entrusted with the appointment, assignment, transfer, promotion, and disciplinary measures concerning judges and public prosecutors. This body should be composed of judges and public prosecutors, or at least have a majority representation of judges and public prosecutors.

(6) Judges and public prosecutors cannot be transferred, suspended, or removed from office unless it is provided for by law and then only by decision in the proper disciplinary procedure.

(7) Disciplinary action should be carried out by independent bodies that include substantial judicial representation. Disciplinary action against judges and public prosecutors can only be taken when provided for by preexisting law and in compliance with predetermined rules of procedure.

(8) Each judge and each public prosecutor has the right to be provided with an efficient system of initial and continuing judicial training; attendance at these two forms of training should be, for a certain period, compulsory for each judge or public prosecutor, or at least it should represent an essential condition for moving to a higher post. Judicial training should be provided by an independent institution.

(9) Judges and public prosecutors must be granted proper working conditions.

(10) Salaries of judges and of public prosecutors must be fixed by statute (and not by an act of the executive power) and linked to the salaries of parliamentarians or ministers. They should not be reduced for any reason.

(11) Judges and public prosecutors must be granted full freedom of association, both on the national and international level. Activity in such association must be officially recognized as judicial work.

These principles, or some such similar set, form the normative skeleton of the judicial power, especially in modern liberal democracies, but possibly in all types of regimes committed to constitutionalism. Yet, when it comes to concrete interpretations and the institutional implementation of these principles, consensus no longer exists.[4] One focus of substantial disagreement in the interpretation of the status of the judiciary concerns principles (4) and (5) from the list above.[5] Different constitutional systems allow for different degrees of checks and balances between the major branches of power. In some legal systems, contrary to the suggested

[4] Probably the best comparative analysis of the prerogatives of the judges and the organizational aspects concerning the judiciary is Carlo Guarnieri and Patrizia Pederzoli, *The Power of Judges: A Comparative Study of Courts and Democracy* (C.A. Thomas ed, 2002).

[5] For a more detailed account of different interpretations of the principles in Eastern Europe see Daniel Smilov, 'EU Enlargement and the Constitutional Principle of Judicial Independence' in Wojciech Sadurski, Adam Czarnota, and Martin Krygier (eds), *Spreading Democracy and the Rule of Law? Implications of EU Enlargement for the Rule of Law, Democracy and Constitutionalism in Post-Communist Legal Orders* (2006).

checklist, the Minister of Justice, or its functional equivalent, is authorized to make judicial appointments upon the advice of or nomination from senior members of the judiciary and he may have certain powers related to the promotion and demotion of already appointed magistrates, as well as to the imposition of disciplinary sanctions.

The entitlement of the executive and the legislative branch to appoint members of the body governing the judicial system may be deemed necessary in order to preserve a degree of *accountability* of the judiciary vis-à-vis the political branches of power and—ultimately—the citizens as electors. The principle of judicial independence should always be balanced against the principle of accountability of the judicial branch.

Different legal systems of established democracies balance these competing values—accountability and independence—in different ways. For instance, some systems rely on highly unrepresentative judiciaries as a social group. Other systems attempt to achieve a greater degree of representativeness including through popular elections of magistrates. Further, different ideas of accountability of the judiciary are also in operation. Some systems rely on political accountability, and in them political bodies (like the minister of justice) have greater powers in determining personnel policies of the judicial branch. Other systems rely more on the professional ethics of the community of lawyers as a self-regulating body: in these systems, accountability is treated as accountability to peers on the basis of professional standards, rather than as accountability to other branches of power.

Another point of divergence among the legal systems of established democracies is the character of internal accountability within the judiciary. The legal systems of continental countries (especially these of Latin Europe) rely on strong internal accountability, which means that senior magistrates exercise significant control in terms of career promotion and demotion over junior magistrates. In contrast, in common law countries there is greater internal independence of the magistrates.

A further point of disagreement in the interpretation of the principles of judicial independence involves the position of public prosecutors in the constitutional model. In some systems, the prosecutors are part of the executive, and thus accountable to politically elected bodies. In other systems they are part of the judiciary and enjoy different degrees of autonomy both vis-à-vis the other branches, but also vis-à-vis the other parts of the judiciary.

Finally, a controversial issue worthy of mention is the elaboration and the adoption of the budget of the judiciary. Again, different systems allow for various degrees of judicial 'independence' in this sense. In some, the government and parliament have greater leeway in the appropriation of funds for the judicial branch, while in other systems the draft budget is closely coordinated with the independent body governing the judicial system. The formulation of principle (10) from the list above could hardly address the complexity of the problem with the funding of the judicial system. Since financial independence is one of the key components of judicial independence in general, the vagueness of principle (10) illustrates a general point: convergence on normative principles exists only at a very high level of generality.

The existence of different institutional implementations of the principles of judicial independence could be interpreted in two ways. The first is that, from a constitutional point of view, there is a wide variety of legitimate competing solutions to the problem of the concrete status of the judiciary. Democratic constitutional regimes resolve this question in different ways depending on their traditions, the character of their political process, etc. There is no overall best solution: all of them have advantages and disadvantages. On this view, call it the *pluralist view*, there is a minimal set of abstract requirements—close to the checklist presented above but possibly even smaller—which all exemplary constitutional regimes must meet: after these requirements are met, however, a wide variety of institutional models, reflecting different conceptions of underlying principles and values, are acceptable. One disadvantage of this view is that it is not very helpful in the assessment of concrete constitutional arrangements: it leaves a vast number of options open, without being able to compare them in any meaningful way. Further, the pluralist view becomes heavily dependent on the local context: it relegates most interesting questions to the idiosyncrasies of different legal systems.

A second perspective on the divergence of institutional arrangements concerning the organization of the judiciary could be called *interpretative*.[6] It would argue that all legal systems follow basically the same (or very similar) sets of normative principles or values. However, differences in the context lead to different balancing of the same values: in some countries one set of normative concerns takes priority over others, which leads to different institutional solutions. All models, however, try to satisfy as far as possible all *common* normative values, albeit subject to different prioritizations. If we have taken into account all the relevant social, political, and economic differences among the given countries, we would be able to explain how following similar normative principles leads to different institutional solutions.

In contrast with the pluralist, the interpretativist might still maintain that there is a common *normative* theory of the status of the judiciary in constitutional regimes. A difficulty of this position is that the theory in question must be very, very detailed and complex, so that it could explain away all institutional differences by simultaneously preserving normative unity and coherence.

In what follows, I will use a very modest and limited interpretative strategy. I will suppose that behind the jurisprudence of different courts there is a relatively small number of common values, which, set against a different context, produce an astonishingly rich institutional variety of models. All these models ultimately address similar, if not the same, normative concerns. One advantage of this strategy is that it allows for the simultaneous discussion of the jurisprudence of markedly different judicial bodies—indeed, it needs difference in order to demonstrate the universal validity of the normative principles. The interpretative strategy treats all models as equals, and this arguably makes it less parochial. Of course, in the absence of Herculean powers, the interpretivist is bound to end up with a parochial theory pretending to be universal. But hopefully this minor drawback could be excused on account of the good and theoretically ambitious intentions at the start of the exercise.

II. The Normative Foundations of Judicial Power

In contemporary constitutional regimes, courts and the judiciary draw their legitimacy and their normative power from at least four different sources. These four sources, I argue, form a universally valid (for constitutional regimes) set of values, which models—institutionally very different from each other—try to optimize, although they may balance the basic values in different ways. Societies have specific—sometimes unique—histories and experiences, which explain the stronger emphasis on one value or another. Yet, it will be odd and exceptional to find a model committed to constitutionalism which systematically denies the validity of some of the following four foundational values underlying the status of the judiciary: *separation of powers; the rule of law; adjudication as a mark of sovereignty*; and *the need for independent arbiters in disputes between two parties*. These four grounds of legitimacy presuppose different doctrinal principles, different institutional arrangements, and modes of accountability. Some of the four grounds could be optimized simultaneously, but it is virtually impossible to have a model which optimizes all of

[6] I borrow the term and the methodology from Ronald Dworkin, *Law's Empire* (1986).

Table 40.1 Grounds of Legitimacy of Judicial Power

Normative grounds	Doctrinal principles	Basic instruments	Marks of success	Mode of accountability
Separation of powers	Judicial independence	Non-political appointment procedures and tenure guarantees; separate budget; checks on the political branches (judicial review); independent decision-making; rigid constitution	Assertive, activist[7] judiciary, vetoing decisions of the political branches of power	Checks and balances—limited dependence on the other branches in order to provide a guarantee against deadlocks
Rule of law	The judiciary is only subject to the law	Strict professional requirements for appointment; presumption against judicial discretion, judicial rulemaking, advisory opinions; giving of reasons for decisions	Non-politicized, highly professionalized, rule-bound judiciary	Only internal accountability in cases of violation of standards of professionalism
Sovereignty as expressed in adjudication of conflicts	Courts should have ultimate jurisdiction in cases of legal disputes	Finality of court judgments; presumption against legal pluralism; appointment by the supreme bodies of state power—parliament, president, king, etc	Judiciary committed to protect the statehood and the authority of main state bodies and rules	Judiciary accountable to the supreme highest representatives of the state: parliament, head of state, president, king, prime minister, etc
Impartial arbiters in a dispute between two parties (the triad model)	Impartiality	Doctrinal limitations on programmatic, large-scale political action—case-by-case adjudication, limited grounds of reasoning, etc	Judiciary enjoying the trust of both the people and the main institutions	Judiciary responsive to the people and main institutions

[7] The issue of judicial activism deserves a detailed treatment of its own. For my understanding of the concept see Daniel Smilov, 'The Character and Legitimacy of Constitutional Review: Eastern European Perspectives' (2004) 2 *International Journal of Constitutional Law* 177.

them at the same time, since they have different (and sometimes incompatible) criteria of success and failure. In Table 40.1 and the sections below, I consider all four grounds of legitimacy of courts and the judiciary separately by drawing examples from a number of jurisdictions.

1. Separation of Powers and the Judiciary

Separation of powers is an instrumentally important guarantee of liberty: it prevents the concentration of powers in the hands of one holder, and ensures a minimum degree of pluralism at the highest level of government. Judicial independence is just one aspect of separation of powers—it guarantees that there is at least one other branch of power, different from the other (political) holders of power. Virtually all contemporary constitutional models consider the judiciary as a separate branch of power. A key to such institutionalization is the prerogatives effectively to check the political branches of power through some sort of judicial review—either constitutional or administrative. Equally important is the possibility of independent decision-making on specific cases: judges, courts, and magistrates more generally should be able to make their decisions in the absence of external influence from the other branches.[8]

The separation is complicated by the proximity of judicial decision-making to sovereignty and the sovereign. In the controversial *Refah Partisi v Turkey* case,[9] the European Court of Human Rights (ECtHR) held that 'legal pluralism'—a system where different religious communities are regulated separately and adjudicate conflicts separately—violates the requirements of the European Convention on Human Rights (ECHR). The fear of the judges was that if a pluralist system were introduced, the state would lose its capacity and prerogative ultimately to resolve legal disputes, and thus would lose its power to protect human rights. The ECHR in practice endorsed the view that sovereignty and adjudication are closely connected, and that the exclusivity of jurisdiction, which is a mark of the sovereign, should be a feature of the work of the judiciary as well.

That the judiciary constitutes a separate branch of state power was an idea vehemently rejected by totalitarian 'constitutional' ideologies. The communist doctrines, for instance, acknowledged the *functional* division of labor within the state, but rejected the idea of *division of power*. And indeed, communist constitutionalism—which is probably an oxymoron—was based on the idea of concentration of power and the primacy of the Communist Party in public life.[10] It is no surprise that, on the exit from totalitarianism, societies break with the past by endowing the judiciary with significant powers to check the political branches.

The other key element of independence—apart from the prerogatives to check the political branches—is the independence of judicial decision-making. The institutional variance on this issue is probably less pronounced, although there are certainly difficult cases, as for instance the powers of courts martial. *In Morris v United Kingdom*,[11] the ECtHR interpreted the

[8] On judicial independence, see Chapter 39.

[9] *Refah Partisi (The Welfare Party) and Others v Turkey*, App nos 41340/98, 41342/98, 41343/98, and 41344/98, Judgment of 13 February 2003.

[10] Article 126 of the Stalinist Constitution of 1936 stated that the Communist Party was 'vanguard of the working people in their struggle to strengthen and develop the socialist system and is the leading core of all organizations of the working people, both public and state.' For a discussion see J. Arch Getty, 'State and Society Under Stalin: Constitutions and Elections in the 1930s' (1991) 50(1) *Slavic Review* 19, 22.

[11] App no 38784/97, 26 February 2002.

independence and impartiality requirement for a military tribunal, noting that in the relevant procedures of the United Kingdom 'the presence of safeguards was insufficient to exclude the risk of outside pressure being brought to bear on the two relatively junior serving officers who sat on the applicant's court martial.' They had no legal training and remained subject to army discipline and reports. Further, the ECtHR found problematic the possibility for a non-judicial reviewing authority to overturn the sentence of the court, which undermined the binding character of the decisions of the tribunal. Other branches of power should not have the right to influence (to overturn, so to speak) decisions of judicial bodies.[12]

Once it is established that the judiciary is a separate branch of power, the issue of institutional guarantees of its independence comes to the fore. However, the practices here could hardly be systematized: the variance in terms of appointment, selection, promotion, and budgeting of the judiciary is great. Yet, a key explanatory factor of the variance seems to be the experience of previous abuse by political branches (in authoritarian or totalitarian models) and the professional reputation of the magistrates. The Italian constitutional model, for instance, has attempted to make the judiciary an almost self-sustaining body by granting it powers of appointment, tenure, and even influence in the budgeting of the judicial branch.[13] These powers are exercised through the Superior Council of the Magistracy—a body composed of four members elected by the judiciary, and two members by Parliament. Similar arrangements exist in France and the Mediterranean countries in general, and the model has been picked up by East European countries such as Bulgaria and Romania. For instance, in the Bulgarian Supreme Judicial Council, about half of the members are elected by the judiciary.[14] The Mediterranean model arguably provides the highest degree of institutional protection in terms of outside influence regarding personnel policy and budgeting, which reflects very high fears of possible intervention by political bodies and lack of a previous record of responsible behavior by the judiciary.

Even such rather extreme measures cannot always insulate the judiciary against political interference. For example, in Bulgaria political majorities have several times during the 1990s managed to dissolve the Supreme Judicial Council before the expiration of its constitutional term in office. Typically, this happened through an amendment to the law on the judiciary, introducing structural changes in the organization of courts, the prosecutorial office, and the investigators. The Bulgarian Constitutional Court invalidated most of these laws (with one exception) but because of the lack of retroactive effect of the decisions of the court, parliament had already managed to dissolve the old council and appoint a new one under the new law.[15]

The danger of political interference in the workings of the judiciary in countries with a history of such abuses justifies high levels of institutional insulation of the judicial system from the other branches. But this insulation creates serious problems in terms of loss of accountability. Therefore, in order for the judiciary not to become over-politicized, separation of powers requires a degree of checks and balances and horizontal accountability among the different branches. The US federal model attempts to balance prerogatives and powers allocated among the branches, although problems also exist there. The possibility of politicization of the US

[12] For a discussion of the case see Norman Dorsen, Michel Rosenfeld, András Sajó, and Susanne Baer, *Comparative Constitutionalism* (2003), 313–15.

[13] Ibid 325–6.

[14] Bulgarian Constitution (SG 56/13 JUL 1991), Arts 129 and 130.

[15] For a discussion of this jurisprudence see my chapter in Daniel Smilov, 'The Hybridity of Constitutional Courts: Arbiters in the Absence of Rules' in Alexander Kiossev and Petya Kabakchieva (eds), *'Rules' and 'Roles': Fluid Institutions and Hybrid Identities in East European Transformation Processes (1989–2005)* (2009).

Supreme Court is one example;[16] another is the politicization of independent prosecutors, as the impeachment procedure against President Clinton demonstrated.[17]

The question of prosecutors is generally a sensitive one. In a number of countries, again due to fears of improper interference of political actors in judicial proceedings, prosecutors enjoy the same level of institutional insulation as the judiciary per se: Italy and Bulgaria are examples. In Italy, the independence of prosecutors and investigative judges led to spectacular successes against the Mafia and its links with the political establishment. But one negative side effect of this arrangement is the continuous involvement of the judiciary in the political process and its direct impact on the restructuring of the party system and political competition. The appearance of populist politicians, who thrive on the negative publicity generated by endless judicial trials, is a cost of the model, which needs to be taken into account.[18] Generally, in order for the model to be successful, it must carefully balance independence with accountability: if the balance is wrong, the judiciary could grow progressively alienated from the problems of society at large, or could become over-politicized, pursuing partisan agendas.

2. The Rule of Law and the Judiciary

By focusing exclusively on separation of powers as a normative concern for the organization of the judiciary one question remains wide open: Why exactly *judicial* independence? Why not independence of the police, the postal services, or the medical profession? Why should judges enjoy a more privileged, constitutionally protected status than other authorities, professions, and businesses?

From a normative perspective the answer is that not only is it valuable to have divided powers, but it is also important to guarantee *law-governed and rule-bound behavior* in society. Judges' main function—as professional experts on rules and following the law—raises their importance in comparison with other guilds and professions. The endorsement of rule-bound behavior, as well as the idea that all conflicts should be resolved on the basis of rules and the law, are the cornerstones of the rule of law ideal. In this way, the rule of law lends additional normative weight and legitimacy to the judiciary, and explains why exactly judges should enjoy a privileged status.[19]

The main principle that follows from the rule of law ground of justification is that the judiciary should only be subject to the law. Of course, legal systems differ in their rigor in endorsing this principle doctrinally: for instance, in Germany judges are subject both to law and justice, although 'justice' has been invoked exceptionally rarely in the practice of the major German courts.[20] From an institutional point of view, the rule of law ground of legitimacy is backed by specific requirements for a *professional* judiciary. Generally, becoming a judge or a lawyer requires specific training and education, apprenticeships, practice etc. The lawyers and

[16] Ronald Dworkin, 'The Bork Nomination', *NY Review of Books* (1987).

[17] The impeachment trial caused a certain politicization of theoretical constitutional debate as well. For a sample of the heated exchanges see eg Richard Posner, 'Dworkin, Polemics, and the Clinton Impeachment Controversy' (1999) 94 *Northwestern University Law Review* 1023.

[18] For a discussion of the link between contemporary populism and the rule of law see Daniel Smilov, *Populism, Courts, and the Rule of Law: A Policy Brief* (2007), a publication of the Foundation for Law, Justice and Society in collaboration with the Centre for Socio-Legal Studies, University of Oxford, available at <http://www.fljs.org/uploads/documents/Smilov_Policy_Brief%231%23.pdf>.

[19] On the rule of law, see Chapter 10.

[20] Donald Kommers, *The Constitutional Jurisprudence of the Federal Republic of Germany* (2nd edn, 1997), 124–8.

the judicial profession more narrowly are strictly regulated. The selection of judges is normally based heavily on professional criteria. Everywhere, judges are treated as experts/professionals in procedures and rules—experts in 'process writ small', to allude to John Hart Ely's famous portrayal of the judicial profession.[21] Appointments, promotions, and demotions are supposed to reflect the expertise and the professional experience of judges.

The requirements of professionalism and specialized expertise have been central in many cases dealt with by high courts interpreting the status of the judiciary. Thus, in Ceylon in *United Engineering Workers Union v Devanayagam Privy Council*[22] the court considered the issue whether judges, as part of the 'judicature', should be appointed by a specialized judicial body (judicial service commission) and not by the Public Service Commission.[23] The issue was whether the acts of the labor tribunals, whose members were appointed by the Public Service Commission, were without jurisdiction and invalid because of the very fact of appointment. It was ultimately resolved that the office of president of a labor tribunal is not a judicial office, and may be appointed by a Public Service Commission: despite this, however, it was not disputed that the 'judicature' should be appointed on the basis of expertise and in highly specialized and professionalized procedures.

In Jamaica, *Hinds v The Queen Privy Council*,[24] the judges interpreted the special function and professional role of the judiciary in society. In essence, they dealt with the question what makes a court a court.[25] They started with the observation that it is not important whether a body is called a 'court' by the law, but:

> What is the nature of the jurisdiction to be exercised by the judges ... Does the method of appointment and the security of their tenure conform to the requirements of the constitution applicable to the judges ...

In conclusion, it was held that what Parliament cannot do, consistently with separation of powers, is to transfer from the judiciary to any executive body whose members are not appointed in the proper way as that for appointing judges, a discretion to determine the severity of punishment to be inflicted upon an individual member of a class of offenders. Rule application—especially concerning rights of people and punishments—is in the exclusive domain of the judiciary.

Another consequence of the rule of law being a ground for the legitimacy of the judiciary are the quite common presumptions against judicial rulemaking and judicial discretion. The idea behind these two presumptions is that courts and judges should *follow* the rules and *apply* them to specific disputes. They should not *make* rules.

The United States is famous for its rather rigorous endorsement of the ban on advisory opinions issued by courts to the other branches; a ban which is justified on the basis of the understanding that courts should not step into rulemaking areas. The issue of judicial rulemaking arose in the very first years of the application of the US Constitution, but still produces some interesting jurisprudence. Thus, in *Mistretta v United States* the US Supreme Court recognized the constitutionality of a 'twilight area in which the activities of the separate branches merge ... That judicial rulemaking ... falls within this twilight area is no longer an issue for dispute ...'[26]

[21] John Hart Ely, *Democracy and Distrust* (1980).
[22] [1967] 2 All ER 367.
[23] See Dorsen et al (n 12), 309–13.
[24] [1977] AC 195.
[25] Dorsen et al (n 12), 315–18.
[26] 488 US 361 (1989).

The Supreme Court here was answering the question whether a commission composed of judges could come up with binding rules for courts aiming to harmonize sentencing practices. The commission in question was part of the judicial power, but was not a court and was fully accountable to Congress. The Court ultimately recognized the legitimacy of such 'twilight' judicial rulemaking. Justice Scalia, dissenting, argued that 'the power to make law cannot be exercised by anyone other than Congress, except in conjunction with the lawful exercise of executive or judicial power ...' His dire prediction was that there might emerge 'all manner of "expert" bodies, insulated from the political process, to which Congress will delegate various portions of its law making responsibility'.

Twilight rulemaking by courts is rather common, however. In continental systems advisory and rulemaking prerogatives of the courts are deeply constitutionally entrenched. France is famous for its administrative law traditions, according to which the Conseil d'État is both a highest administrative court and an advisor to the government.[27] Constitutional courts in many states have the right to interpret the constitutional text *in abstracto*—that is, without a link to a specific case or controversy: this power of the courts leads to incremental rulemaking. Furthermore, it is quite common that high courts are given powers to issue interpretative decisions, aiming to harmonize the practices of law application by the lower courts.

The issue of judicial discretion further illustrates the point.[28] Here, there is a pronounced difference between continental and common law systems. In the common law world, the power of judges incrementally to make law is rather accepted, despite Ronald Dworkin's famous theoretical campaign against it.[29] In continental systems, however, doctrinally judicial discretion is very often ruled out: judges should only apply the law. Again, however, the most this amounts to is a significant presumption against judicial discretion. After all, universally courts are empowered to resolve disputes and cases on the basis of highly abstract and indeterminate rules. Courts normally cannot drop the case due to the lack of precise rules: they have to come up with a judgment. This naturally leads to discretionary decisions and to incremental rulemaking.

Thus, the rule of law justification of the legitimacy of courts and the judiciary leads to something of a paradox. On the one hand, it portrays the judiciary as a professional guild with expertise on existing rules and their application in specific cases. As such, the group—the argument goes—should be subject only to internal, professional forms of accountability. Judges should be appointed, promoted, demoted, dismissed etc only on the basis of professional criteria and internal judicial system procedures. Yet, however, it cannot be denied that certain twilight rulemaking activities do exist, for which forms of external accountability are appropriate. In the *Mistretta* case, the rulemaking judicial commission was subject to supervision by Congress, for instance. So, even the rule of law justification might allow for certain, although rather limited, forms of external accountability of judges. Yet, when it comes to their incremental rulemaking and implied discretionary powers, comparative analysis shows that such forms of external accountability are most commonly not in place.

The proximity of the judiciary to the sovereign determines special modes of accountability for judicial work. There should be some residual forms of accountability of the judiciary

[27] For a review of the French constitutional system and the role of the Conseil d'État see John Bell, *French Constitutional Law* (1992).

[28] On the concept of discretion see Denis Galligan, *Discretionary Powers: A Legal Study of Official Discretion* (1986) and David Robertson, *Discretion in the House of Lords* (1998).

[29] Ronald Dworkin, 'Judicial Discretion' (1963) 50 *Journal of Philosophy* 624.

vis-à-vis the highest bodies of power, expressive of sovereignty in the state. This accountability does not concern judgments in specific cases, of course, but may go beyond the appointment powers of the highest political bodies. Thus, senior magistrates may be called to inform parliament about systemic problems concerning the workings of the judiciary, as is the case in Bulgaria. Even forms of indirect accountability of individual judges to supreme bodies of sovereignty, like the parliament, could be envisaged. Staying with the Bulgarian example, an inspectorate dealing with the individual performance of the judges was established, appointed with a fixed term of office by the Parliament with a two-thirds majority: once appointed, the inspectors cannot be replaced.[30] Their monitoring of the record of individual judges is meant to be decisive for promotion and disciplinary decisions taken by the Supreme Judicial Council. Such curious institutional innovations result from the existence of competing pressures on legislators: on the one hand they are supposed to respect judicial independence but, on the other, accountability always remains an issue when it comes to the exercise of sovereign powers.

3. The Judiciary, Sovereignty, and Statehood

Historically, the claim of resolution of disputes through adjudication has been the mark of sovereignty.[31] This functional proximity to the sovereign has been another normative ground of the legitimacy of the judiciary, which produces a set of more specific normative principles and concrete constitutional doctrines defining the status of the magistrates. As one British senior judge argued:

> Judicial power is the power which sovereign authority must of necessity have to decide controversies between its subjects, or between itself and its subjects... The exercise of this power does not begin until some tribunal which has power to give binding and authoritative decision... is called upon to take action.[32]

On the basis of this understanding courts normally claim exclusive and final authority over the resolution of legal disputes. What is more, very often they themselves police the borderline between what is a legal dispute—falling in their jurisdiction—and a political one, which should be outside it. As the history of the US doctrine of 'political question' demonstrates, the courts may expand their reach into areas formerly considered 'political'.[33]

4. The Judiciary as an Impartial Arbiter

On the model presented in this chapter, the final normative ground legitimizing the status of the judiciary views courts and judges as adjudicators whose legitimacy depends on a relationship of a 'triadic' character, as famously pointed out by Martin Shapiro.[34] In a 'triadic' model, two persons decide to call upon a third neutral umpire in order to resolve the disagreement.

[30] Bulgarian Constitution (SG 56/13 JUL 1991), Art 132a.

[31] On sovereignty more generally, see Chapter 17.

[32] *Huddart Parker & Co Proprietary v Moorehead* (1909) 8 CLR 330, 357.

[33] In *Baker v Carr* 369 US 186 (1962) the US Supreme Court famously opened the door to judicial intervention in electoral law irregularities and mal-apportionment issues more specifically, which before that were considered a 'political thicket': Samuel Issacharov, Pamela Karlan, and Richard Pildes, *The Law of Democracy: Legal Structure of the Political Process* (2002), 147–62.

[34] Martin Shapiro, *Courts: A Comparative and Political Analysis* (1981).

The triadic model does not fit perfectly with the role of the judiciary. For a start, it does not fully appreciate the proximity of courts to the sovereign: normally, courts claim exclusive and binding jurisdiction, while the arbitrator is freely chosen by the disputing parties. Further, there are more elements of the triadic model in ordinary adjudication, in comparison to, say, constitutional review *in abstracto*. Yet, even in constitutional review one could possibly speculate that the outvoted parliamentary minority or the President, on the one hand, and the parliamentary majority on the other, could be seen as two parties going to a neutral umpire—the court.[35]

Yet, Shapiro's idea of courts as impartial arbiters in a triadic relationship does seem to capture a fundamental point. Courts generate trust when they become instrumental to broad sections of society in series of concrete disputes between two parties. There are numerous specific normative principles and institutional arrangements which follow from this ground of legitimation. First, all contemporary systems attempt to limit the exposure of the judiciary to partisanship and open politicization in order to make it attractive as a neutral arbiter—a topic, which has already been discussed. Courts normally do not stand to gain directly from the success or failure of a particular partisan governmental agenda in terms of re-election, for instance. Furthermore, they could hardly develop a complete and coherent agenda of their own, due to various well-known institutional and doctrinal constraints. To start with, courts *react* to petitions, and are generally constrained to ruling on issues involved in such petitions. Also, courts are prevented through a variety of instruments from endorsing coherent, comprehensive ideologies and programs in their jurisprudence: no matter how the constitutional 'text' is treated, judges can use only a limited set of doctrinal arguments, which are not sufficient for the creation of a truly comprehensive and coherent agenda. They are also not free in using generalizations and analogies but are governed by highly formalized rules of judicial reasoning. Courts are further prohibited from issuing 'programmatic' documents, and even if judges cannot resist the temptation of expressing their more general political views from time to time, these expressions are not systematic, coherent, or comprehensive as political programs claim to be. To sum up, courts seem to be intentionally handicapped as endorsers of comprehensive political programs and doctrines, which sets them quite radically apart from political bodies and legislatures.

Further, doctrines of access to the courts are of crucial importance for the generation of trust in the judiciary. If access is very difficult, if judicial proceedings are too expensive, courts will become detached from broad sections of society: they will be turned into a luxury instrument for the upper classes. If, however, access to the courts is too easy, then most probably there will be huge backlogs and inefficiencies, which will also lead to the loss of trust in the judicial system. Even extremely authoritative courts, such as the ECtHR in Strasbourg, for instance, may become vulnerable to efficiency problems due to unmanageable levels of petitions. Thus, a well-organized judiciary should correctly balance the competing values of accessible justice and manageable caseloads. Since judicial proceedings are in any event expensive and time-consuming, there should be alternative forms of extra-judicial settlement for specific groups of cases.

Finally, it does matter who the judges actually are. It is true that judges are to be selected primarily for their expertise, but if this criterion leads to very an unrepresentative character of the judiciary, trust in it may be undermined. In India, for instance, there have been efforts to include in the judiciary representatives of all social strata.[36] Similar concerns were faced in South Africa after the end of the regime of apartheid. All these efforts are designed to make the

[35] For a discussion see Woiciech Sadurski (ed), *Constitutional Justice, East and West: Democratic Legitimacy and Constitutional Courts in Post-Communist Europe in a Comparative Perspective* (2003), 167–71.

[36] Dorsen et al (n 12), 325–6.

judiciary more responsive and more accountable to the people in general, as the ultimate goal is to increase trust in the judiciary, trust, which is essential for its functions as a neutral arbiter.

III. Conclusions: The Least Dangerous Branch?

The judiciary is the least dangerous branch of power,[37] because it does not keep either the purse or the sword of the polity, as it is well known. From this perspective, the metaphor of juristocracy[38] is largely far-fetched: no matter how important in terms of decision-making, the judiciary is not on a par with the political branches of power in contemporary political regimes. Still, the judiciary is a branch of *power* in the constitutional regime, and very often it could play a crucial role in the determination of important state policies, as well as in the resolution of key controversies. In the course of such decisions, sometimes it might empty the purse of the polity,[39] while at others it could make the use of the sword inevitable, as the US Supreme Court did with its infamous *Dred Scott*[40] judgment.

In this chapter I have argued that the judiciary is normatively framed by four major grounds of legitimation: separation of powers, the rule of law, sovereignty, and impartiality of arbitration. All these four grounds entail more specific principles for the organization of the judiciary, and imply different modes of accountability. The four normative grounds may have different weight in different societies, depending on their objective circumstances and on the perceptions of people of these circumstances. The bottom line is that different societies *must* prioritize some of these grounds in given periods of their development. The result is a wide variety of institutional organizations of the judiciary, animated, however, by a limited number of common normative foundations.

Table 40.2 presents some of the most common prioritizations of the four normative grounds against different socio-political context:

Table 40.2 The Legitimacy of Judicial Power in Political Context

	Separation of powers	Rule of law	Sovereignty	Impartial arbiters
Transition from authoritarian/totalitarian regimes	High priority	High priority[41]	Low priority	Medium priority
Transition from apartheid or racism	Low priority	High priority	Low priority	High priority
Aggressively majoritarian democracy	High priority	Medium priority	Low priority	Low priority
Widespread corruption	Medium priority	High priority	Low priority	High priority
Social inequality and widespread poverty	Low priority	Low priority	Low priority	High priority
Nation-building	Low priority	Low priority	High priority	Low priority

[37] Alexander Bickel, *The Least Dangerous Branch* (1962).

[38] Ran Hirschl, *Towards Juristocracy: The Origins and Consequences of the New Constitutionalism* (2004).

[39] András Sajó, 'How the Rule of Law Killed the Welfare Reform' (1996) 5 *East European Constitutional Review* 31.

[40] *Dred Scott v Sandford* 60 US 393 (1857).

[41] On the complex dilemmas caused by the rule of law in transitional context see Venelin Ganev, 'The Rule of Law as an Institutionalized Wager: Constitutions, Courts and Transformative Social Dynamics in Eastern Europe' (2009) 1 *Hague Journal of the Rule of Law* 263.

Table 40.2 suggests that when societies exit from a totalitarian or authoritarian rule, normally a very high priority is placed on the separation of powers and rule of law values. Sometimes this leads to specific overkill in the opposite direction: in order for the judiciary to prove that it is non-political and independent, it might become self-absorbed and irresponsive to the public in general, it may also become too formalistic in its activity, which might lead to further alienation from the people.

If the society is on the exit of a racist regime, then it is of key importance to restore the trust of the people in its impartiality as arbiter. Efforts need to be made to create a proper racial balance in the judiciary, reflective of the society at large. However, of equal importance will be the preservation of the professionalism of the judiciary and upholding the rule of law, as a sign of breaking with the old regime.

When the question of widespread poverty is concerned, courts need to build the trust of all social strata, and especially of those at the bottom of the ladder. The composition of courts needs to reflect the existence of different strata, but also their jurisprudence must be responsive to the claims of all, which may lead to a more aggressive and activist interpretation of socio-economic rights, for instance.

In addition, in a democratic context of aggressive majoritarianism—a situation in which a given political majority tries to impose its will on the opposition and independent institutions—emphasis should be put on the preservation of the separation of powers, which may entail activist jurisprudence of courts defending their autonomy in terms of budgeting, appointment etc.

A most interesting case presents the role of the judiciary in a society which is affected by widespread corruption. On the one hand, the judiciary needs to be highly independent in order to tackle political corruption, but it also needs to be accountable in order to be able to address its own internal corruption. It is very often the case that the judiciary itself is suspected of corrupt practices, which indicates that its independence of other branches should not be turned into a constitutional fetish.

Societies do not pursue only one priority at a time: they might want simultaneously to tackle corruption and poverty on the exit of a totalitarian regime, while trying to create a nation-state. Some compromises will always be necessary, and the question is of the right balance of values. Also, societies are not static: they go through different stages of development, which implies that priorities may change.

It is probably somewhat paranoid to think of power in terms of the potential dangers it might pose: after all power and authority are necessary for the rational guidance of human affairs. The judiciary is a sophisticated instrument of authority, the proper functioning of which depends on a complex process of fine-tuning carried out not only by experts on law and court management, but also by people with an ear for broader social and political problems. Without such fine-tuning the instrument could produce a cacophony of sounds, and may ultimately create a Kafkaesque socio-political environment, in which the villain and the hero, the rule and the exception, justice and injustice become indistinguishable.

Bibliography

Alexander Bickel, *The Least Dangerous Branch* (1962)

Norman Dorsen, Michel Rosenfeld, András Sajó, and Susanne Baer, *Comparative Constitutionalism* (2003)

Ronald Dworkin, 'Judicial Discretion' (1963) 50(21) *Journal of Philosophy* 624

Ronald Dworkin, *Law's Empire* (1986)

John Hart Ely, *Democracy and Distrust* (1980)

Denis Galligan, *Discretionary Powers* (1986)

Venelin Ganev, 'The Rule of Law as an Institutionalized Wager: Constitutions, Courts and Transformative Social Dynamics in Eastern Europe' (2009) 1 *Hague Journal of the Rule of Law* 263

John Arch Getty, 'State and Society Under Stalin: Constitutions and Elections in the 1930s' (1991) 50(1) *Slavic Review* 18

Carlo Guarnieri and Patrizia Pederzoli, *The Power of Judges: A Comparative Study of Courts and Democracy* (C.A. Thomas ed, 2002)

Ran Hirschl, *Towards Juristocracy: The Origins and Consequences of the New Constitutionalism* (2004)

Samuel Issacharov, Pamela Karlan, and Richard Pildes, *The Law of Democracy: Legal Structure of the Political Process* (2002)

Donald Kommers, *The Constitutional Jurisprudence of the Federal Republic of Germany* (2nd edn, 1997)

James Madison, *The Federalist Papers*, No 51 (1961)

Richard Posner, 'Dworkin, Polemics, and the Clinton Impeachment Controversy' (1999) 94 *Northwestern University Law Review* 1023

David Robertson, *Discretion in the House of Lords* (1998)

Woiciech Sadurski (ed), *Constitutional Justice, East and West: Democratic Legitimacy and Constitutional Courts in Post-Communist Europe in a Comparative Perspective* (2003)

Wojciech Sadurski, Adam Czarnota, and Martin Krygier (eds), *Spreading Democracy and the Rule of Law? Implications of EU Enlargement for the Rule of Law, Democracy and Constitutionalism in Post-Communist Legal Orders* (2006)

András Sajó, 'How the Rule of Law Killed the Welfare Reform' (1996) 5 *East European Constitutional Review* 31

András Sajó, *Limiting Government* (1999)

Martin Shapiro, *Courts: A Comparative and Political Analysis* (1981)

Daniel Smilov, 'EU Enlargement and the Constitutional Principle of Judicial Independence' in Wojciech Sadurski, Adam Czarnota and Martin Krygier (eds), *Spreading Democracy and the Rule of Law? Implications of EU Enlargement for the Rule of Law, Democracy and Constitutionalism in Post-Communist Legal Orders* (2006)

Daniel Smilov, 'The Character and Legitimacy of Constitutional Review: Eastern European Perspectives' (2004) 2 *International Journal of Constitutional Law* 177

CHAPTER 41

POLITICAL PARTIES AND THE CONSTITUTION

CINDY SKACH

Oxford

I. Introduction

Shortly before his death, Max Weber published an op-ed in the *Berliner Börsenzeitung*, calling for the direct election of the Reichpräsident in the newly founded Weimar Republic. His colleague, Friedrich Ebert, a member of the German Social Democratic Party, had just been elected president, through an indirect method, by the members of the National Assembly. Weber cautioned that, were the next president not to be *directly* elected by the German people, the new constitutional order in Weimar and the unity of the republic would be gravely compromised—for Weber considered the proportionally elected parliament to be dominated by particularism and increasingly threatened by factious, regional political parties, vested economic interests, and as he put it, closed-minded, philistine MPs who cared little about national politics.[1] Weber died in 1920, and so never knew that the twin unraveling of the constitutional order and the instability of the party system in the mid to late-1920s were indeed responsible, to a good extent, for the Republic's inability to defend itself against the rise of fascism.

Political parties and party system dynamics are, as they were then, critical to understanding how constitutions work, and why they may not, in spite of well-intentioned designs. Unfortunately, much of the recent literature in comparative constitutional law has paid little attention to the multiple ways our basic constitutional structures are conditioned by political parties and party system dynamics. The US Constitution makes no direct mention of political parties, but a non-negligible part of the US Supreme Court docket has directly concerned the role political parties play, and should play, in American democracy. Around the globe, and in the post-war constitution-making frenzy, founding documents paid greater attention to political parties, from explicitly sanctioning their role in democratic politics and delineating the 'acceptable' ideological space for their competition (German Basic Law, Article 21), to requiring the representation of minority parties in government committees, and requiring that national legislation provide funding for all parties on an 'equitable and proportional basis' (eg Constitution of the Republic of South Africa, section 236).

With a plea for greater integration between studies of parties and constitutions, this chapter offers an overview of the interaction effects between political parties and party systems, and the three constitutional types found in the democratic world today—presidentialism, parliamentarism, and semi-presidentialism. The chapter concludes with an illustration of these effects from the case of Weimar Germany.

II. Political Parties and the Party Space

As Weber noted in 1919, albeit with some trepidation, political parties are situated crucially between society and government. They are, as such, intermediaries, and, positively understood, key actors in any democracy founded on the principle of representation.[2] Yet not every country with free and fair elections and political parties necessarily has a *party system*. According to one of the earliest comparativists to examine parties, Giovanni Sartori, political parties *only* 'make for a "system"... when they are parties (in the plural); and a party system is precisely the *system of interactions* resulting from inter-party competition.'[3] A party system is then said to be institutionalized when it exhibits the following characteristics:[4]

- regularity in the pattern of party competition (low volatility);
- stability of party roots in society and of citizens' strong and consistent attachment to parties;

[1] *Berliner Börsenzeitung*, February 25, 1919, reprinted in Max Weber, *Gesammelte Politische Schriften* (1988).

[2] Note the similarities between early and more recent comparative-historical work on the role of parties in representative democracy, in Carl Schmitt, *Verfassungslehre* (1928), and Juan J. Linz and Alfred Stepan, *Problems of Democratic Transition and Consolidation* (1996). Another line of inquiry regarding variations in representation and its usefulness in democracy includes Hanna Fenichel Pitkin, *The Concept of Representation* (1967), with an attempt to respond to the idea of representation as useful to democracy found in Carole Pateman, *Participation and Democratic Theory* (1970).

[3] Giovanni Sartori, *Parties and Party Systems: A Framework for Analysis* (1976), 44, original emphasis. The sections below draw from my *Borrowing Constitutional Designs* (2005).

[4] Giovanni Sartori, 'Political Development and Political Engineering' (1966) 17 *Public Policy* 261, 293; Scott Mainwaring and Timothy R. Scully (eds), *Building Democratic Institutions: Party Systems in Latin America* (1995), 20.

- citizens and other organized interests' perception that parties are 'the way to go', and acceptance of them as the legitimate intermediary and means of influence in the democratic process;
- stability of party organization, with party influence at both national and local levels, and party elites' loyalty to their parties.

Certainly no party system in the world meets all these characteristics in full. All party systems can be placed along a continuum running from non-institutionalized to institutionalized, and most democratic countries fall somewhere near the institutionalized pole. Institutionalization is a desirable quality if we care about the performance of a constitution, because

> where the party system is more institutionalized, parties are key actors that structure the political process; where it is less institutionalized, parties are not so dominant, they do not structure the political process as much, and politics tends to be less institutionalized and therefore more unpredictable.[5]

Non-institutionalized party systems have characteristics that are the reverse of institutionalized systems: low levels of predictability, high party fluidity, high volatility. These characteristics impede actors, such as candidates for office and party leaders, from having necessary information about their strengths and the strengths of their opponents. This lack of information makes bargaining difficult,[6] and unless a polity can produce single-party majorities to support individual pieces of legislation or government programs, coalitions are a necessity, and thus so is bargaining.

III. Shaping the Party Space

1. Designing Legislative Elections

The number of parties in a country's party system, and their relative ideological distance from one another, are usually first determined by social, economic, religious, and other cleavages in a society. Eventually, however, party systems are shaped and manipulated by other factors, including electoral systems.[7] There are many electoral system tools, but all can be loosely divided into two types, with competing objectives: (1) those aimed at reflecting in the legislature the various cleavages and interests in a country in proportion to their strength in society, and (2) those aimed at distorting the ratio of votes to seats in order to manufacture majorities in the legislature, at the expense of smaller parties and less popular interests. Variations of majority electoral systems include the absolute majority with a second round limited to the top two candidates (*ballotage*), the absolute majority with a plurality in the second round, the alternative vote, and the first-past-the-post (or plurality) systems. The non-majority electoral systems include a variety of proportional representation systems (PR), and semi-PR or intermediary systems. PR systems vary in their degree of proportionality, depending on the mathematical method used to distribute seats, which varies from the very proportional *Sainte-Laguë* method to the least proportional *d'Hondt* formula.[8]

[5] Mainwaring and Scully (n 4), 22.

[6] See William Riker, *The Theory of Political Coalitions* (1962), especially his discussion of bargaining through side-payments, 105–23.

[7] Sartori (n 3).

[8] See Vernon Bogdanor, *What is Proportional Representation? A Guide to the Issues* (1984).

A constitutional democracy's choice of electoral system is often a negotiated decision, one as critical and contested as the constitution itself; and some countries prefer to sacrifice any gains in efficiency that might come with fewer political parties in order to privilege the representativeness of the system through PR. In these cases where PR is chosen, PR's fragmentation-permitting effects, those of which Weber was so fearful, are in contemporary democracies often limited, either by (1) the *d'Hondt* method of seat allocation, (2) a high threshold requiring parties and party lists to meet a certain percentage of votes in order to be counted in the distribution of legislative seats, or (3) by reducing district magnitude.[9] The smaller the district magnitude, the smaller the number of seats available for distribution.[10] Thus, majority electoral systems can help to manufacture majorities or, in the case of corrected PR and semi-PR, at least encourage majorities by keeping smaller parties out of the legislature. This is not to say that majority electoral systems and corrected PR are, overall, a better choice for all constitutional democracies.[11] In fact, sometimes the exclusion of a party through barriers such as thresholds and majority electoral formulae can lead to frustration with the institutions and push excluded parties to adopt an anti-system attitude, which may in turn threaten democracy. The important point here, which will be taken up below, is simply that majority electoral formulae seem quite crucial for effective and efficient government under certain constitutions, and yet, these majority electoral formulae may be incompatible with the goals and norms of a particular polity and its people.

2. Designing Presidential Elections

In presidential and semi-presidential constitutions, electing a president bears some similarity to electing a legislative representative for a single seat in a single, nationwide district. However, the presidential seat, unlike a legislative seat, is worth much more in the overall political game. It is also a non-divisible prize and presidential elections can have considerable effects on the development of the party system.[12] Weber had argued that a directly elected president could

[9] See Douglas W. Rae, *The Political Consequences of Electoral Laws* (1967), esp 114–25; Arend Lijphart, *Electoral Systems and Party Systems: A Study of Twenty-Seven Democracies, 1945–1990* (1994), 21–46.

[10] See Arend Lijphart, *Patterns of Democracy: Government Forms and Performance in Thirty-Six Countries* (1999), 150–1. This is also discussed in detail in Matthew Soberg Shugart and John M. Carey, *Presidents and Assemblies: Constitutional Design and Electoral Dynamics* (1992), 226–9.

[11] Majority formation is only one possible goal of electoral system design. Accurate reflection of minority parties in the legislature is another—often opposite—goal. Majority electoral systems tend to satisfy the first goal, while PR systems tend to satisfy the second. A discussion of these goals and the respective electoral systems for achieving them is found in the classic handbook by Dieter Nohlen, *Wahlsysteme der Welt: Daten und Analysen, Ein Handbuch* (1978), 13–18 and 48–56, respectively. Also see Vernon Bogdanor and David Butler (eds), *Democracy and Elections: Electoral Systems and Their Consequences* (1983); Lani Guinier, *The Tyranny of the Majority: Fundamental Fairness in Representative Democracy* (1994); and Lijphart (n 9), 10–56.

[12] As Linz remarks,

> the control of the executive in presidential systems is in principle 'winner take all'. In addition it is 'loser loses all' for defeated presidential candidates, who might end without any public office after the election and, unless they have strong positions as leaders of their party, might have gambled away all their political resources.

See Juan J. Linz, 'Presidential or Parliamentary Democracy: Does it Make a Difference?' in Juan J. Linz and Arturo Valenzuela, *The Failure of Presidential Democracy* (1994), 14. On presidentialism more generally, see Chapter 29.

preserve the unity of a constitutional democracy, suggesting that the electoral dynamics set in place through popular election would act as a 'dam' to divisive interests, 'forcing' parties to cooperate throughout the federation.[13] There are two basic types of direct presidential electoral systems: the absolute majority system with two or more rounds, and the plurality system.[14] In the plurality system, the candidate with the greatest percentage of votes wins and there is only one round of voting. A special type of plurality system is known as the concurrent plurality, in which candidates must win a plurality at the national level while simultaneously winning a specified percentage in each of several different regions of the country. This system discourages presidents from relying on regionally concentrated support, and is therefore thought to be a useful consociational tool for ethnically divided societies.[15]

The absolute majority system requires a second (or sometimes even a third) round of voting if none of the candidates gets the required majority in the first round. The second round may be direct and limited to the top two candidates (*ballotage*), or top three candidates; the second round may also be thrown to the decision of the legislature. The absolute majority run-off is sometimes advocated as a tool for encouraging a majoritarian norm in the political system, and in order to moderate party system polarization.[16] However, the incentives in a two-round presidential electoral system do not have a single, simple logic. In fact the incentives are multiple, complicated, and even contradictory; and also depend on the context within which they function. Often this electoral system induces electoral campaigns that appear rather extreme in the first round, and then quite centripetal in the second. The first round serves in many ways like a presidential primary, drawing out the most popular candidate from within a party or party block; whereas the second round necessarily sees the losers within that party or party block offering support to the front-runner.[17] If these incentives operate together and as anticipated, two majority blocks are expected to form, and these blocks are expected to lean towards the center, thereby creating, over time, a two-party system. But these incentives can only be expected to work as such when the party system is institutionalized and where two main ideological or programmatic blocks already *exist* or have the *potential to form* (which is unfortunately not the case for many transitional democracies). In pure form this is the Downsian logic.[18] However, the Downsian logic only holds if the structure of competition is distributed such that the electorate is concentrated in the middle of the ideological (or other) spectrum, and if the two main party blocks compete for these middle voters. If the voter distribution is bi-modal with two concentrations on either far end of the spectrum, or if there is high voter

[13] Weber (n 1), 500.

[14] Empirically, variations on these two themes obviously exist. In Costa Rica, for example, the president is required to get 40 percent of the valid votes cast, which is, strictly speaking, neither a majority nor a plurality, but is known rather as a qualified plurality.

[15] This system was used to elect the president of Nigeria between 1979 and 1983. It requires candidates to have cross-regional support in order to avoid the majority's feeling of exclusion by regionally concentrated ethnic groups. See Donald L. Horowitz, *A Democratic South Africa? Constitutional Engineering in a Divided Society* (1991), esp 206–10.

[16] Sartori believes this is particularly the case for legislative elections. See Giovanni Sartori, *Comparative Constitutional Engineering* (1994), 61–9. Also see Domenico Fisichella, *Elezioni e democrazia: un'analisi comparata* (1982), ch IX, s 2, 'Partiti "anti-sistema" e doppio turno', 274–86.

[17] Jean-Luc Parodi, 'Le nouvel espace politique français' in Yves Mény (ed), *Idéologies, partis politiques, et groupes sociaux* (1991), 55.

[18] Downs' model suggests that electors vote for policies, and that parties are political entrepreneurs that alter the policies they are not particularly attached to in order to attract the greatest percentage of votes and win office. See Downs, *An Economic Theory of Democracy*; also see Ian Budge and Hans Keman, *Parties and Democracy: Coalition Formation and Government Functioning in Twenty States* (1990), esp 26–31.

abstention or indecision, then the two-round electoral competition may exacerbate existing voter divisions. Then, a two-round electoral system has little chance of bringing the party bloks closer together.[19] Moreover, if the party system is inchoate and volatile, or when parties are so divided that not even a minimal winning coalition can be put together, a majority run-off election can exacerbate the polarization and fragmentation within the polity. This is so because the first round under these circumstances seems to encourage a 'go for broke' attitude. Recalling the incentives in this system, the first round is designed as a primary in which candidates from the same block try to distinguish themselves from the other members of their block, and thus candidates are induced to push themselves (programmatically or ideologically) away from each other. When there are no blocks, when the system is so polarized and fragmented that minimal winning coalitions are impossible, the second round cannot be expected to pull anyone together or towards the center. Thus the majoritizing incentives of the second round are made obsolete, and the 'extremizing' effects of the first round become the *only* effects of this electoral system.

Another potential difficulty of the two-round, absolute majority presidential electoral system, one which has proven particularly challenging for democratic constitutionalism, is that it may inflate the perception of the president's legitimacy, especially when there are many candidates in the first round. To illustrate, assume that a first-round candidate having won 21 percent of the popular vote is admitted to the second round because he is one of the two front-runners. He then wins the second round with 53 percent of the vote. Is it accurate to count this 53 percent as a measure of his legitimacy, or is the 21 percent a more accurate reflection? His 21 percent in the first round seems to be the more accurate measure, given that the restriction in the second round to only two candidates manufactures and inflates his actual electoral popularity, which was demonstrated in the unrestricted first round. This is the actual percentage the French presidential candidate Jacques Chirac won in the first round of presidential elections on April 23, 1995. The second round, limited to the two front-runners, which included him and Socialist candidate Lionel Jospin, gave him 53 percent. This inflated legitimacy may, in some democracies, encourage anti-party presidential behavior, and turn problematic when a president finds himself faced with opposition in the legislature, and uses this inflated sense of legitimacy to push his powers beyond their constitutional limit, toward constitutional dictatorship.[20]

A special form of majority voting called the alternative vote has also been suggested as a presidential electoral system for encouraging majorities. Voters list several of their preferences for the presidential office on one ballot. In the absence of a clear majority in the first preferences, the second and third preferences are counted until arriving at a winner. This system combines the psychology of two-round voting in one actual round, and is therefore much like the ballotage system; the 'outsider effect' and the 'go for broke' attitude are just as likely to occur.[21] That is because an outsider candidate without party support has the same incentives to run as an individual under this system as he does under the *ballotage* system.

[19] In other words,

> a bipolar [party] system assumes a normal, bell-curve distribution (a Gauss-Laplace curve) of where the electors place themselves along a left-right (or other) continuum, whereas bipolarization assumes a double-peaked distribution of political opinion with an almost empty center.

See Sartori (n 16), 14 n 15.

[20] See my 'Constitutional Origins of Dictatorship and Democracy' (2005) 16(4) *Constitutional Political Economy* 347.

[21] The counter-argument is given by Horowitz, who claims that with this system,

A final factor that affects the party system and, in turn, the performance of the presidential and semi-presidential constitutions, is the relative timing of presidential and legislative elections. Evidence to date indicates that presidential and legislative elections held simultaneously are more likely to give a president a majority in the legislature, than are non-simultaneous elections, other things being equal.[22] The simultaneous holding of presidential and legislative elections is a possibility for presidential regimes in which the fixed terms of the president and the legislature coincide (eg four years each). In semi-presidentialism, constitutional prerogatives often allow presidents to call early legislative elections shortly after taking office (or during the term) to try to re-equilibrate the presidential and legislative majorities, as Mitterrand did after his election in 1981.

In a similar vein, the simultaneity of municipal and presidential elections is a possible tool for building concurrent majorities. While local elections do not directly affect the number of parties or the presence of majorities in the national assembly, the coincidence of elections may encourage the president's party (or majority) at the local level, weaving a multi-layer fabric of presidential support throughout the polity, particularly in federal or decentralized systems where substantial power over decisions might be delegated to subunits or local municipalities.[23] These incentives, however, all assume that the presidential candidates are in fact 'party men', integrated into the party system and both supported *by* and supportive *of* parties. Presidential candidates who act as independent, non-party personalities are certainly possible, but more likely to emerge in non-institutionalized or weakly institutionalized systems where political society is underdeveloped. Since parties do not play an important channeling role in non-institutionalized or weakly institutionalized systems, the presidential door is open for independent candidates who may even employ an anti-party rhetoric and campaign on an anti-party and even anti-system platform. In this case, the incentive is for non-cooperative behavior, and it works against majorities. Of course, anti-party presidents can, and do, logically exist even in institutionalized party systems, but the linking of the incentives with the party system makes it more probable that they will emerge in non-institutionalized systems. It is no accident, then, that Yeltsin in Russia, and Kuchma in Ukraine, never became 'party men' presidents.

> the only way to secure a victory is... through interparty agreements. The president, therefore, cannot escape his party membership—it is the key to the vote exchanges that will elect him... The presidential illusion of an independent mandate... is extremely unlikely under these circumstances.

See Horowitz (n 15), 211. He goes on to argue:

> This is particularly the case where the legislature is elected by the same method. Then the presidential election is likely to become part of a nation-wide interparty electoral arrangement that may also have the effect of building bridges between the separately elected branches of government.

Horowitz neglects the methodological point that presidential and legislative electoral systems need separate analysis. He transfers the effects of this system at the legislative level to the presidential level, which is analytically incorrect. Also see the critique in Shugart and Carey (n 10), 218–19.

[22] Sartori notes, 'Concurrent elections cannot fabricate undivided majorities that are not potentially in the works; but staggered elections do facilitate divided majority outcomes': Sartori (n 16), 179. This said, it does seem to be the case that the electorate is encouraged to vote 'usefully' in concurrent elections. Also see Shugart and Carey (n 10), 229–58 and Appendix B.

[23] On the critical role political parties and party systems play in holding federations together, see Jenna Bednar, *The Robust Federation* (2008).

There is almost no safeguard to ensure that independents do not run for presidential office, and independent presidential candidates do emerge in institutionalized systems as well (as did H. Ross Perot in the United States in 1992). Neither semi-presidentialism nor pure presidentialism has any institutional incentive for chief executives to be 'party men'.[24] Only parliamentarism has such incentives, via executive responsibility to the legislature. At the legislative level in presidential and semi-presidential systems, closed party lists give parties more control over candidates, reducing the personalization of campaigns, enhancing the value of the party label in local elections, and enabling the party to reward the most loyal rank-and-file members by placing them on the list. But the lack of party control at the presidential level may lead to the 'outsider' phenomenon, exemplified by Perot in the United States, Fujimori in Peru, and Tyminski in Poland's 1990 presidential race. Tyminski, described as an 'unknown Polish expatriate businessman', running on an anti-party campaign, was able to pass up the previous Solidarity Prime Minister Tadeusz Mazowiecki in the first round election by a 3.1 percent margin, and advance to the second round against Lech Walesa.[25] When an outsider or anti-party president is actually elected, he must then face a legislature in which he will predictably have no initial party support, and may find it difficult to build this necessary support if his presidential campaign relied on anti-party discourse, which is typical of independent candidates. Without party backing, such a president is immediately in a more conflictual constitutional configuration than he would have been, other things being equal, with a party majority behind him in the legislature. This was the case with Russia's Boris Yeltsin, who had no choice but to broker support for the government's agenda in piecemeal fashion, as he was unable to count on a stable, coherent majority at any point throughout his terms. For non-conflictual constitutionalism, then, a party-man president, one that is integrated into the party system and is both supported by and supportive of parties, seems necessary. This mutual dependence increases the constraints on the behavior and discipline of both the president and his party.

3. Fostering (Constitutionally) Party-Based Leadership

Presidential and semi-presidential constitutions can differ widely with respect to the incentives they offer to individual leaders and political parties, given that the powers *constitutionally* granted to any president vary from country to country, and this differently affects the executive's relationship to the legislature.[26] A president's constitutionally granted powers are usually specified in a country's constitutional text, and are also usually amenable to measurement and quantification.[27] Yet, any *specific* president's use of these powers is not easily quanti-

[24] See Shugart and Carey (n 10), 171.

[25] See Frances Millard, *The Anatomy of the New Poland: Postcommunist Politics in its First Phase* (1994), 128.

[26] Not all powers are equal. Eg, Jack Hayward, in his discussion of the presidents of the French Fifth Republic, distinguishes between constitutional *powers* and constitutional *prerogatives*, the latter not requiring countersignature but rather, 'made on [the president's] own nonaccountability': Jack S. Hayward, *Governing France: The One and Indivisible French Republic* (1973), 101.

[27] See Shugart and Carey (n 10), 148–58. Shugart and Carey devised a scale to measure and compare presidents' constitutional powers. While useful for demonstrating the variation in executive strength across countries, the scale fails to take into account the absolutely crucial idea of emergency powers. Moreover, this scale does not distinguish adequately between powers and prerogatives, nor does it measure the legislature's powers in the areas where the president also has power, which obfuscates the dynamic between president and the legislature. Since power must be conceived of in relational terms (ie, power over *whom*, resistance to power, etc) it would be important to include the legislature in this scale.

fiable, and usually necessitates careful analysis of a president's behavior over time.[28] Not all presidents are ideal leaders; efficient, democratic presidents are required to have a very acute sense of political judgment and distinguished leadership qualities, which are in fact quite rare.[29] As US President Lyndon B. Johnson noted:

> Every President has to establish with the various sectors of the country what I call 'the right to govern'. Just being elected to the office does not guarantee him that right... [e]very President has to become a leader, and to be a leader he must attract people who are willing to follow him. Every President has to develop a moral underpinning to his power, or he soon discovers that he has no power at all.[30]

Yet when presidents exhibit special leadership characteristics and establish a personal 'right to govern', throughout various sectors of the country, they may also be more likely to push their constitutional powers to the limits, establish new presidential prerogatives, and, in semi-presidential systems, dominate their prime ministers.[31] This is most likely to happen when political parties are weakly institutionalized. Charles de Gaulle, for example, at the beginning of the Fifth Republic, set a trend of using his constitutional powers widely and established presidential precedents, such as using unilateral presidential referenda for policy decisions, with successive presidents of the republic using the referendum in a similar way.[32] Problematically, in some cases, the president's use of powers can have far-reaching effects, especially if a particular president believes that 'he who has the right to set new laws therewith also has the power to change the goals of society'.[33]

In addition to varying the powers of the president in a constitution, some modern constitutional drafters, suspicious of the potential harm of factious political parties or non-institutionalized party systems, not unlike Weber, have crafted special designs to enhance the power of the executive vis-à-vis the legislature (eg the *vote bloqué* and the confidence vote procedure in France after 1958) offering the government greater control over the legislative process, and thereby insulating them from some of the divisiveness of party politics.[34] French governments have often used these procedures in order to avoid parliamentary obstruction and immobilism, and have passed several important pieces of legislation, including national budgets, through these procedures. These measures, to the extent that they limit parliamentary discussion on crucial aspects of national policy, may be democracy-constraining, especially

[28] Also see Maurice Duverger, *Échec au roi* (1978), 31–44, for a discussion of presidential constitutional powers versus actual presidential practice in France, Finland, Weimar Germany, Portugal, Austria, Ireland, and Iceland.

[29] See Arthur M. Schlesinger Jr, *The Imperial Presidency* (1973); and Henry Hardy and Roger Hauscheer, (eds), *Isaiah Berlin, The Proper Study of Mankind: An Anthology of Essays* (1997), esp 30–1, and the essays on Churchill and Roosevelt, 605–37.

[30] Lyndon B. Johnson quoted in Charles O. Jones, 'Separating to Govern: The American Way' in Byron Shafer (ed), *Present Discontents: American Politics in the Very Late Twentieth Century* (1997), 1.

[31] Werner Kaltefleiter contrasts the president with a majority, and what he considers the 'opposite extreme' of political reality, when there is no effective majority, as in the end of the Weimar Republic, 'when the complete immobilization of the party system had led to paralysis of political power and the *Reichspräsident* recovered a monopoly over decisions without any sort of effective controlling institutions': Kaltefleiter, *Die Funktionen des Staatsoberhauptes* (1970), 186–7.

[32] On the referendum as part of the presidential *prerogatives*, see Hayward (n 26), 101–2. Also see the discussion of the importance of informal presidential powers in Shugart and Carey (n 10), 58–61.

[33] Otto Kirchheimer, *Politik und Verfassung* (1964).

[34] See John D. Huber, *Rationalizing Parliament: Legislative Institutions and Party Politics in France* (1996); on France, also see Dominique Chagnollaud and Jean-Louis Quermonne, *Le gourvernement de la France sous la Ve République* (1996), esp 325–9; and Robert Elgie and Moshe Maor, 'Accounting for the Survival of Minority Governments: An Examination of the French Case, 1988–1991' (1991) 14(2) *West European Politics* 62.

when they are used excessively by the executive, as a substitute for party backing. Less problematic for democracy is the constructive vote of no confidence, a constitutional design that is aimed at disciplining parties in that it allows a legislative majority to turn an unpopular or ineffective government out of office through a vote of no confidence, *if and only if* that legislative majority is able to name a new prime minister to whom they guarantee immediate majority support. This procedure was first written into the 1949 German Basic Law and was 'meant as a safety-valve against the destruction of governments through negative majorities', and was later adopted in several countries, including post-Franco Spain and post-communist Hungary.[35]

III. Comparative Configurations: Parties and Constitutional Dynamics

These party system characteristics, electoral system designs, and constitutional rules concerning executive powers vis-à-vis the legislature combine in ways that affect constitutional performance, explaining why comparable constitutional designs with extremely similar structures nevertheless produce very divergent outcomes; and why, given the nature of political parties and party systems in some countries, certain constitutional types might be more problematic than others. The key to understanding this variation is found by analyzing how an executive can find itself in a situation in which it does not have a legislative majority. In presidentialism, this situation results only from the interaction of the constitution and the voters' choices. That is, the constitution stipulates the power structure among the branches of government and the fixed duration of executive and legislative terms. The voters, in turn, make their separate choices for the executive and legislative seats. In parliamentarism, the minority situation of the executive can result from the interaction of the constitution and the voters' choices, *plus* the government's decision, *and* the legislators' decision. That is, the constitution stipulates the division of powers, the voters choose their legislators, the government that forms decides whether or not to form a minority or majority coalition based on a variety of incentives and constraints, and the legislators decide whether or not to support that government. In semi-presidentialism, the situation can result from the interaction of: the constitution, the voters, the government, the legislators, and now also the president. The same interactions of parliamentarism occur, but the president often has dissolution and decree powers which also become part of the strategic interaction in the formation and duration of governments. Another way of stating this is that semi-presidentialism's strategic landscape is more complex than that of pure presidentialism, and more complex than that of parliamentarism; for as we move from a presidential country to a parliamentary country to a semi-presidential country, we also move toward more institutional players in the origins and demise of governments.

[35] Wolfgang Rudzio, *Das politische System der Bundesrepublik Deutschland: Eine Einführung* (1991), 245. A similar procedure, known as the *doble confianza*, was written into the constitution of the Second Spanish Republic (1931–36), but with a key difference. According to this procedure, the president could dissolve the legislature twice within his six-year term, but upon the second dissolution, the newly elected legislature would immediately investigate and determine the necessity of the president's dissolution. If it determined that there were no grounds for such dissolution, the president would himself be automatically removed from office (hence the name, *doble confianza*). Contrary to the positive vote of no confidence, then, the *doble confianza* vote exacerbated governmental instability by allowing for a double dissolution of both president and parliament. See Gabriel Jackson, *The Spanish Republic and the Civil War, 1931–1939* (1965), esp ch 3, 'The Creation of a Constitution'; and Juan Linz, 'Excursus: The President in the Spanish Republic, 1931–1936' in Linz and Valenzuela (n 12), 56–7.

Table 41.1 Constitutional Dynamics: Comparative Configurations

	Presidentialism	Parliamentarism	Semi-presidentialism
Subtypes where executive controls <50% of legislature	Divided government	Minority government (single party or coalition)	Divided majority government (cohabitation) or Divided minority government
This division a function of:	Constitution + voters' choice	Constitution + voters' choice + legislators' choice	Constitution + voters' choice + legislators' choice + president's choice

Simply put, this greater complexity comes from the presence of more strategic actors. See Table 41.1.

IV. An Empirical Illustration: Parties and the Weimar Constitution

Returning to Weimar Germany, where we began this chapter, it is interesting to reflect again on Weber's concerns, remembering how dynamics between the party system and the constitution played a key role in the breakdown of the Republic. The semi-presidential constitution in Weimar set up a particular kind of political 'neighborhood', which became vulnerable to the mechanisms of rapid segregation. Democratic parties initiated the Republic, drafted the constitution, and controlled almost all of the Weimar cabinets at the onset of the republic. Figure 4.1 shows the 29 cabinets in Weimar, from 1919–33. Each point in time reflects one cabinet, and shows the percentage of that cabinet whose members were from democratic parties, versus the percentage of cabinet members whose members were from non-democratic parties.[36]

Members of three of the four main democratic parties in 1919—the Social Democratic Party (Sozialdemokratische Partei Deutschlands, SPD), the Zentrum Party (Ztr), and the German Democratic Party (Deutsche Demokratische Partei, DDP)—embarked on the challenge of constructing a democratic order and crafting a liberal constitution.[37] Towards the center of the ideological spectrum one found the Zentrum Party. The Zentrum strongly advocated a political role for the Catholic Church, and this part of its mandate pushed it away from other democratic (but more secular) parties. The Bayerische Volkspartei (BVP) was an important regional splinter of the Zentrum Party, but with a slightly more conservative accent.[38] For their part,

[36] I have assumed these categories of 'democratic parties' and 'non-democratic' to be static in composition, dichotomous, mutually exclusive, and jointly exhaustive, which is fairly reasonable given the parties in Weimar.

[37] The classification of these three parties, the 'Weimar Coalition', as democratic can be found in Rainer Lepsius, 'From Fragmented Party Democracy to Government by Emergency Decree and National Socialist Takeover: Germany' in Juan J. Linz and Alfred Stepan (eds), *The Breakdown of Democratic Regimes* (1978).

[38] The BVP's conservatism made coalition formation problematic for its Catholic partner, the Zentrum, since the BVP refused most of the Zentrum's cooperative efforts with parties further to the left. See Ellen L. Evans, 'The Center Wages Kulturpolitik: Conflict in the Marx-Keudell Cabinet of 1927' (1969) 2 *Central European History* 139; Rudolf Morsey, 'The Centre Party Between the Fronts' in Theodor Eschenburg et al (eds), *The Road to Dictatorship: Germany, 1918–1933* (1962); and Fritz Schäffer, 'Die Bayerische Volkspartei (BVP)' (1974) 25 *Politische Studien* 616.

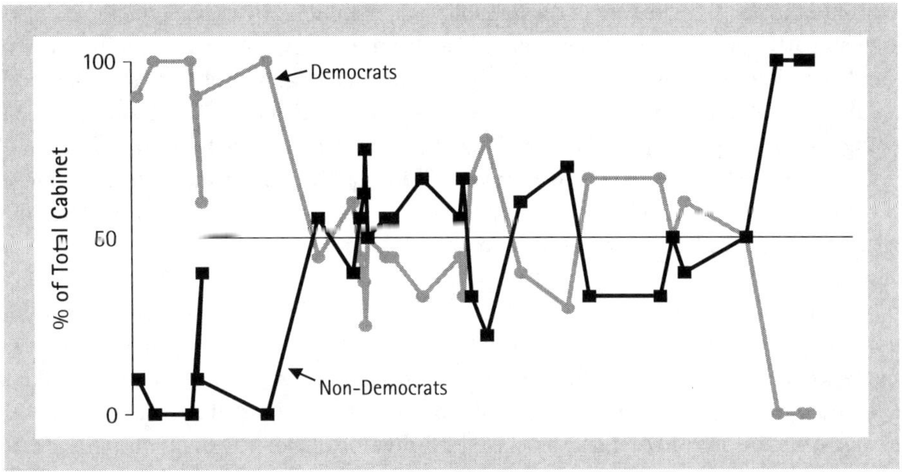

FIGURE 41.1 Cabinet Composition in Weimar 1919–33

the SPD were located ideologically toward the left and center-left, and provided the main party representation for German trade unions, which 'were committed to the Republic . . . [and] provided the backbone of the SPD's support electorally'.[39] On the ideologically conservative, but still democratic, end of the spectrum was the fourth democratic party, the DDP, which was strongly opposed to the increasing bureaucratization of the German economy, and the socialization of the forces of production.

In the non-democratic camp was the other liberal party, located further to the right on the ideological spectrum than the DDP, a supporter of democracy only in the very early Weimar years: the Deutsche Volkspartei (DVP). On the far right of the ideological spectrum was the nationalistic Deutschnational Volkspartei (DNVP), which advocated a strong state and compulsory military service and was generally skeptical of democracy and representative government.[40] On the undemocratic, but far left part of the ideological spectrum, was the Kommunistische Partei (KPD). The Communists, for their part, never accepted the Republic as truly democratic, and opposed it on such grounds. Capturing both the extreme left and extreme right was the National Socialists or the Nazi Party (Nationalsozialistische Deutsche Arbeiterpartei, NSDAP).[41]

Thus the division of the parties into the democratic camp (SPD, DDP, Zentrum, BVP) and non-democratic camp (DVP, KPD, DNVP, NSDAP). The SPD's center-left and pro-democratic placement in the complex party system of the Weimar Republic made it one of the most important, and most viable, coalition partners throughout the Republic. In terms of both votes in the national elections and seats in the Reichstag, the SPD also remained the strongest

[39] Anthony J. Nicholls, *Weimar and the Rise of Hitler* (1968), 49. The SPD also had among its members several distinguished German intellectuals, including Friedrich Naumann and Max Weber.

[40] Lepsius (n 37), 34–79.

[41] A compilation of documents and historical data concerning the KPD is found in Enzo Collotti, *Die Kommunistische Partei Deutschlands, 1918–1933: Ein bibliographischer Beitrag* (1961); for a study of how different internal factions weakened the KPD, see Siegfried Bahne, 'Zwischen "Luxemburgismus" und "Stalinismus": Die "ultralinke" Opposition in der KPD', *Vierteljahreshefte für Zeitgeschichte*, vol 9 (1961), 359–83.

party until the penultimate year of the Republic, 1932.[42] In the early years of the Republic, the SPD had participated in coalitions with the Zentrum, the DDP, and occasionally, the DVP. From November 1923 onward, however, the SPD remained in the opposition (with the exception of a last attempt to ward off fascism in 1928 with the formation of the Grand Coalition). Throughout the Republic, the SPD remained under intense pressure from the left. The SPD President Friedrich Ebert forged governing coalitions and alliances with moderate parties, but because of this, he risked losing the support of the SPD's working class base, and the more radical parties on the left and factions within the SPD were eager to capture this electoral support the moment the SPD lost it.

Over the course of the Republic, therefore, the SPD gradually began to remain in the opposition rather than form a government, in spite of the fact that it retained the plurality of legislative seats until 1932. Given that the SPD was still the largest party in the Reichstag for almost the entire duration of the Republic, and that it was centrally located in Weimar's multiple cleavage structure, the SPD actually blocked the formation of majority coalitions. Without the support of the SPD, most coalitions were often minority coalitions or, at best, held a slight, precarious majority. Thus the SPD's decision had far-reaching consequences for the entire party system, and this is what makes the segregation model of cabinet formation and dissolution extremely useful for understanding the processes that unfolded in Weimar.

The SPD's ambivalence toward forming and joining governing coalitions was found in the fact that the SPD, like many parties, was internally divided. The left wing of the SPD showed little interest in participating in broad government coalitions, particularly when these coalitions involved the center-right DDP, or the non-democratic parties of the right. Moreover, the SPD's earlier coalitions with the moderate right parties resulted in the loss of proletarian electoral support to the parties on the extreme and undemocratic left, especially the Independent Social Democrats (Unabhängige Sozialdemokratische Partei Deutschlands, USPD)—and the KPD.[43] And yet, analysis of the SPD party program in 1925 shows that a majority of the SPD believed that the party 'must try... with all of its energy, to go out from opposition into coalition with the bourgeoisie middle and left, in order to take part again in government power.'[44] Unfortunately, the party leadership was not able to convince its Reichstag delegates of this plan.

Because the SPD preferred to remain in the opposition rather than take part in government, the

> middle-of-the-road parties tended to bring the right wing into their governments... no parliamentary government could be formed without the acquiescence of the SPD, yet the logical consequence—Social Democratic participation in government—was not drawn.

The SPD's non-participation in government coalitions also pushed other parties away from the center, toward the extremes, exacerbating what was becoming a systemic polarization.

[42] See the data collected and published in *Informationen zur politischen Bildung: Die Weimarer Republik*, No 109/110 (1988).

[43] Hans Mommsen, *From Weimar to Auschwitz* (1991), 50. The SPD, therefore, eventually had to abandon the policy of reaching out to the growing middle classes. However, this was not a sound strategy, in the end, given that the blue-collar workforce was in substantial decline as a result of the social re-stratification during the Republic. As a result, the SPD lost substantial electoral support from the working classes, and also failed to tap the growing middle class. See ibid 2–4; also see Hans Mommsen, 'Die Sozialdemokratie in der Defensive: Der Immobilismus der SPD und der Aufstieg des Nationalsozialismus' in Hans Mommsen (ed), *Sozialdemokratie zwischen Klassenbewegung und Volkspartei* (1974).

[44] Ernst Rudolf Huber, *Deutsche Verfassungsgeschichte seit 1789: Band VI, Die Weimarer Reichsverfassung* (1981), 242.

As a consequence of the SPD's non-cooperative behavior, certain parties were forced to seek coalitions with parties located near the non-democratic extremes. For example, the anti-democratic prelate, Ludwig Kaas, was elected leader of the Zentrum Party in 1928. Kaas then moved the Zentrum, a democratic party and an important coalition partner for the SPD, toward the right in search of new coalition partners. The centrifugal trends in the system took control.[45] The DNVP, always a party of the right, was pushed further toward the extreme right in 1928, when the party elected an extreme nationalist, Alfred Hugenberg, as party chairman.[46] Hugenberg, upon taking control of the party, radicalized its program with the aim of enabling the DNVP to share in the 'social respectability, the political influence, and the financial resources of these [anti-system] circles and simultaneously to become part of a broad "National Opposition" to the Weimar Republic.'[47]

Thus the 'logical consequence' of the SPD being the largest party during most of Weimar was for it to participate in governing coalitions. As Bracher suggests, however, that this did not happen because

> The parties had only very limited talent for coalition and compromise, and the inhibitions on both sides were too great, due both to the traditional misgivings of the middle-class parties and to the immutable oppositional tendencies and feeble power drive of the SPD, which lacked full understanding of its role as the strongest party in a parliamentary democracy.[48]

V. Conclusion

One might conclude that Weber was indeed correct: constitutional drafters cannot help but pay attention to the nature of the political parties within the polity when thinking through various possible design models. For the complexity of interactions between parties, on the one hand, and constitutional rules and incentives, on the other hand—here illustrated with the case of Weimar—suggests that even democratic political parties can, when faced with the incentives of certain constitutions, contribute to democracy's collapse. Our efforts to understand comparative constitutional law need to pay heed to Weber's early warning, bringing political parties and party systems more systematically back to the study of constitutional law.

Bibliography

Jenna Bednar, *The Robust Federation: Principles of Design* (2009)
Gary W. Cox, *Making Votes Count: Strategic Coordination in the World's Electoral Systems* (1997)
Anthony Downs, *An Economic Theory of Democracy* (1957)
Maurice Duverger, *La monarchie républicaine* (1974)

[45] Lepsius (n 37), 45; for the argument that the Zentrum had already moved to the right even before Kaas took over the chairmanship of the party in 1928, see Josef Becker, 'Joseph Wirth und die Krise des Zentrums während des IV Kabinetts Marx (1927 bis 1928): Darstellung und Dokumente', *Zeitschrift für die Geschichte des Oberrheins*, vol 109 (1961), 361–482.

[46] Henry Ashby Turner Jr, *Stresemann and the Politics of the Weimar Republic* (1963), 245–6; also see John A. Leopold, 'The Election of Alfred Hugenberg as Chairman of the German National Peoples' Party' (1972) 7(2) *Canadian Journal of History* 149.

[47] Karl Dietrich Bracher, *The German Dictatorship: Origins, Structure and Consequences of National Socialism* (1991), 168.

[48] Ibid 77–8.

Maurice Duverger, *Les partis politiques* (1951)
Maurice Duverger, *Political Parties: Their Organization and Activity in the Modern State* (1954)
Lani Guinier, *The Tyranny of the Majority: Fundamental Fairness in Representative Democracy* (1994)
Werner Kaltefleiter, *Die Funktionen des Staatsoberhauptes in der Parlamentarischen Demokratie* (1970)
Michael Laver and Norman Schofield, *Multiparty Government: The Politics of Coalition in Europe* (1990)
Michael Laver and Kenneth A. Shepsle, *Making and Breaking Governments: Cabinets and Legislatures in Parliamentary Democracies* (1996)
Arend Lijphart, *Patterns of Democracy: Government Forms and Performance in Thirty-Six Countries* (1999)
Dieter Nohlen and Rainer-Olaf Schultze, *Wahlsysteme der Welt: Daten und Analysen, Ein Handbuch* (1978)
Carole Pateman, *Participation and Democratic Theory* (1970)
Hanna Fenichel Pitkin, *The Concept of Representation* (1967)
Douglas W. Rae, *The Political Consequences of Electoral Laws* (1967)
Giovanni Sartori, *Comparative Constitutional Engineering: An Inquiry into Structures, Incentives, and Outcomes* (1994)
Giovanni Sartori, *Parties and Party Systems: A Framework for Analysis* (1976)
Carl Schmitt, *Verfassungslehre* (1928)
Cindy Skach, *Borrowing Constitutional Designs: Constitutional Law in Weimar Germany and the French Fifth Republic* (2005)
Max Weber, *Gesammelte Politische Schrifte* (1921)

PART VII

RIGHTS

CHAPTER 42

FREEDOM OF EXPRESSION

ERIC BARENDT

London

I. The Constitutional Significance of Free Expression

Constitutional courts have frequently emphasized that freedom of expression is essential in a liberal democracy. In one of its earliest rulings on the guarantee of the freedom in the post-war German Basic Law, the Constitutional Court in Karlsruhe said:[1]

> To a free democratic constitutional order [freedom of expression] is absolutely basic, for it alone makes possible the continuing intellectual controversy, the contest of opinions that forms the lifeblood of such an order... [i]t is the basis of all freedom whatever, 'the matrix, the indispensable condition of nearly every other form of freedom'.

The quotation comes from the judgment of Justice Cardozo in *Palko v Connecticut*,[2] in which the US Supreme Court had recognized that freedom of speech has a special status in the constitutional order. Freedom of expression is basic, in that its exercise enables democratic government to claim legitimacy when it regulates the conduct of its citizens, perhaps even

[1] *Lüth* case, BVerfGE 7, 198, 208. The translation of this passage is taken from David P. Currie, *The Constitution of the Federal Republic of Germany* (1994), 175. On constitutional courts more generally, see Chapter 38.

[2] 302 US 319, 327 (1937).

when it restricts the exercise of other rights—for example, procedural or property rights—which are not basic in this sense. Only citizens who are free to challenge the wisdom of, say, economic or social legislation, can be expected to comply with its requirements.[3]

Another argument for the special position of freedom of expression is that its exercise is essential for social progress and for the intellectual and moral development of individuals.[4] There is also the argument from truth, which received its classic philosophical statement in the writings of John Stuart Mill.[5] Truth, as Justice Wendell Holmes put it in his famous judgment in *Abrams*,[6] should be determined in the marketplace of ideas, rather than by regulation. Even if we are sceptical of the claim that truth will triumph in the free market, we are probably less willing to allow governments to decide what is true and which expressions may be proscribed as false. Further, it is the role of constitutional courts to protect the people against the tyranny of 'governing majorities',[7] so freedom of expression must be protected, even when its exercise is limited in accordance with the wishes of a freely elected parliament or congress.

The significance of freedom of expression for liberal democratic government may be shown by reference to the constitutional position in Australia. The Constitution of Australia (1900) lacks a Bill of Rights, so there is no *explicit* guarantee of freedom of expression.[8] Yet its High Court has held in a number of decisions from the early 1990s that a freedom of political communication must be implied in the federal Constitution;[9] it would make no sense for it to provide for democratic elections to the Senate and House of Representatives, unless people were free to debate political issues. This development is of considerable theoretical and comparative interest. Freedom of expression is narrower in Australia than it is under the constitutions of other jurisdictions, for it does not cover commercial or literary speech;[10] on the other hand, the implied freedom shows that a constitutional state must recognize freedom of political expression, unless it is to forfeit its distinctive character.

Freedom of expression as a *constitutional* right must be distinguished from the freedom as a human right, guaranteed by international conventions such as the International Covenant on Civil and Political Rights, the European Convention on Human Rights (ECHR), or the Inter-American Convention on Human Rights (IACHR). Both the ECHR and the IACHR have exercised an enormous influence on the development of the right to freedom of expression (and other rights) in the legal systems of the states which are parties to these conventions. For example, contempt of court law in the United Kingdom, which had significantly curtailed the freedom of the media to publish material prejudicing legal proceedings, was made less restrictive following the seminal ruling of the Strasbourg Court in the *Sunday Times* case.[11] But national courts rarely treat the decisions of international courts as decisive. They must interpret and apply constitutional freedom of expression provisions in accordance with the text of

[3] For this argument, see Robert C. Post, 'Racist Speech, Democracy, and the First Amendment' (1991) 32 *William and Mary Law Review* 267, 279–90.

[4] *Handyside v UK* (1976) 1 EHRR 737, para 49 (European Court of Human Rights).

[5] 'Of the Liberty of Thought and Discussion' in *On Liberty and Other Essays* (1991).

[6] *Abrams v US* 250 US 616, 630–1 (1919).

[7] Brandeis J in *Whitney v California* 274 US 357, 375–8 (1927).

[8] Commonwealth of Australia Act 1900 (UK statute). For commentary on freedom of expression in Australia, see George Williams, *Human Rights under the Australian Constitution* (2002), ch 7.

[9] Among the leading decisions are *Australian Capital Television v Commonwealth* (1992) 177 CLR 106 (invalidating restrictions on election advertising) and *Coleman v Power* (2004) 220 CLR 1 (holding that law prohibiting insulting speech must be interpreted in conformity with freedom of political communication).

[10] For further discussion of the scope of freedom of expression, see Section III.2 below.

[11] *Sunday Times v UK* (1979) 2 EHRR 245.

the constitution as a whole, distinctive national principles of interpretation, and relevant precedents within their own jurisdiction, as well as the decisions of international courts and tribunals.

Constitutional freedom of expression guarantees must of course be distinguished from both statutory rights to freedom of speech and any speech and press freedoms recognized by ordinary civil law or by the common law in Anglo-American legal systems. The difference is that constitutional rights may trump limits imposed on the exercise of the freedoms by ordinary legislation or by competing civil or common law rights, say, to reputation or privacy;[12] statutory free speech rights in contrast have no more weight than these conflicting rights or interests. However, sometimes the freedoms conferred by legislation or other texts may be treated as constitutional, even if they are not set out formally in the constitution itself. This is the position in Sweden, where freedom of the press,[13] and freedom of expression by other means,[14] have been conferred by fundamental laws, which cannot be amended by the usual legislative process, and in France, where ordinary legislation must comply with the Declaration of the Rights of Man and of the Citizen (1789).[15]

The status of the right to the freedom of expression is less clear in the United Kingdom. It is now protected by the Human Rights Act 1998 (HRA), incorporating (most of) the rights in the ECHR; UK courts must interpret legislation as far as possible in conformity with the right to freedom of expression,[16] but they do not have authority to invalidate a statute, even if it plainly infringes the right.[17] Even before the enactment of the HRA, the House of Lords (now the Supreme Court) had sometimes characterized the right to freedom of expression as 'constitutional',[18] but it is doubtful whether it should really be accorded that status.

However, one final introductory point is very clear. There is no difference between 'freedom of expression' and 'freedom of speech'. Common law systems have tended to use the latter term, while civil law systems use the former. An argument can be made that 'freedom of expression' has a broader meaning, in that it includes not only verbal and written communications, but the arts, for example dramatic performances, painting, and sculpture. Courts in common law jurisdictions have, however, been prepared in appropriate cases to hold that 'freedom of speech' covers all forms of communication, not just the written and spoken word. Nevertheless, the scope of the freedom, whether of expression or of speech, remains a difficult issue for the courts.[19]

II. Constitutional Freedom of Expression Clauses

The best known free speech clause is the First Amendment to the US Constitution. It is also one of the shortest:

[12] But see Section IV.2 below for conflicts between freedom of expression and *constitutional* rights.

[13] The original Freedom of the Press Act was enacted in 1766 and is the oldest general freedom of expression clause in the world: see now Freedom of the Press Act 1949.

[14] Fundamental Law on Freedom of Expression 1991.

[15] This principle was established by the Constitutional Council in Decision 71–44 DC of 16 July 1971, and has frequently been applied to ensure that bills comply with the free communication of thought and opinion recognized by Art 11 of the Declaration.

[16] HRA 1998, s 3.

[17] They make a declaration that legislation is incompatible with the Convention (HRA 1998, s 4), but the government is not required by UK law to cure the incompatibility.

[18] See in particular, the speech of Lord Steyn in *Reynolds v Times Newspapers* [2001] 2 AC 127, 207.

[19] See Section III.1 below.

> Congress shall make no law... abridging the freedom of speech, or of the press, or of the right of the people peaceably to assemble, and to petition the Government for a redress of grievances.

But even this apparently simple provision bristles with difficulties. Among them are the following: Does the clause limit the competence of the executive and the states, as well as that of the federal Congress? What does 'abridging' mean, and how does the free press limb of the clause relate to 'the freedom of speech'? Many of these problems have been resolved by the Supreme Court, although it has not provided a conclusive answer to all of them. In particular, it remains unclear whether the media enjoys greater rights under the free press limb than those conferred on individuals by the First Amendment.

The freedom of expression provisions in modern post-war constitutions are typically much more detailed. The German Basic Law of 1949 is a good example. Article 5(1) confers on everyone 'the right freely to express and disseminate his opinion by speech, writing and pictures and freely to inform himself from generally accessible sources.' The provision specifically guarantees press, broadcasting, and cinema freedom, and it also stipulates: 'There shall be no censorship.' But these rights may be limited by general laws and by provisions to protect young people, and in order to protect the right to personal honour.[20] Only freedom of the arts and science is more or less absolutely protected.[21]

The German provisions illustrate a number of features of modern free expression provisions. By conferring a freedom to *receive* and impart information, as well as a general freedom of expression, they recognize that the audience, as well as the speaker, may claim constitutional free speech rights.[22] Usually press freedom and that of the other media are guaranteed by these provisions.[23] Sometimes freedom of assembly, academic freedom, and freedom of literary, artistic, or scientific creation are additionally covered by the freedom of expression clause,[24] though they are often covered by separate constitutional provisions. Freedom of expression is regarded in Hungary as a 'mother' right, from which these other freedoms are derived.[25] An explicit ban on censorship is very common: for instance, the Spanish Constitution provides that the exercise of the rights conferred by the freedom of expression clause 'cannot be restricted by any type of prior censorship'.[26] But the scope of this ban is rarely, if ever, spelt out, leaving the courts to decide whether it applies to court orders prohibiting a publication, as well as to administrative censorship.

While the First Amendment appears to provide an absolute right to freedom of speech, other constitutions, such as Article 5 of the German Basic Law, confer a qualified freedom: the exercise of the right to freedom of expression may be restricted by general laws or in order to safeguard other rights or interests. But a constitution may also limit the circumstances in which freedom of expression may be restricted. The Canadian Charter, for example, provides

[20] Basic Law, Art 5(2).

[21] Ibid Art 5(3) which also protects freedom of research and teaching. Teaching freedom does not however absolve professors and teachers from loyalty to the constitution.

[22] eg see Spanish Constitution, Art 20(1)(d); Hungarian Constitution, Art 61, para (1); South Africa Federal (SA) Constitution, s 16(1)(b).

[23] The German Basic Law is unusual in singling out 'freedom of reporting by means of broadcasts and films'. The Canadian Charter of Rights and Freedoms (1982) and the SA Constitution refer to the freedom of 'other media' in addition to press freedom.

[24] Spanish Constitution, Art 20(1)(b) and (c); SA Constitution, s 16(1)(c) and (d).

[25] See the decision of the Constitutional Court in Case 30/1992 (V 26) AB.

[26] Article 20(2). Also see Japanese Constitution, Art 21. The post-war Constitution of Italy (1948) provides that the press may not be subject to licensing or censorship: Art 21, para 2.

that rights, including the freedom of expression conferred by section 2(b), are 'subject only to such reasonable limits prescribed by law as can be demonstrably justified in a free and democratic society.'[27] The state may not, therefore, have unfettered discretion to restrict the exercise of freedom of expression whenever it thinks this course appropriate; there is a presumption in favour of freedom of expression.

The constitution may itself provide that the freedom does not cover certain types of expression. The South Africa Constitution,[28] following the International Covenant on Civil and Political Rights, provides that freedom of expression does not extend to war propaganda, incitement of imminent violence, or hate speech 'based on race, ethnicity, gender or religion', which amounts to incitement of harm. It cannot even be argued that these types of speech are covered by the right to freedom of expression. Other types of speech under this Constitution, for instance child pornography, are covered, though they are of little value and the state will find it easy to justify their proscription.[29]

III. Interpreting Freedom of Expression Clauses

1. The Scope of Freedom of Expression

Often the crucial question in a particular case is whether a communication is covered by the freedom of expression clause. If it is not, in the absence of other constitutional arguments, its dissemination can be restricted or banned; on the other hand, if it is covered, it is for the state to show that any restriction on its dissemination is compatible with freedom of expression. Courts generally take a broad view of the scope of the freedom. A particularly generous approach is taken by the Supreme Court of Canada which has held that section 2(b) of the Charter covers any form of activity attempting to convey a meaning. Only violent acts are excluded, even if, as perhaps in the case of terrorist atrocities, one of their objectives is to convey a political message. It is immaterial whether the speech is valuable or not; even tasteless and trivial discourse is covered.[30] But it is doubtful whether the Supreme Court would hold that the Canadian Charter covers expression such as perjury, bribes, and contractual promises. Although these types of expression amount to 'speech' or 'expression' in the dictionary meaning of these words, it is generally agreed that they are not covered by freedom of expression provisions. None of the reasons for recognizing a constitutional right to freedom of expression justifies their coverage; a bribe or false statement in court, for example, does not contribute to public discourse or the search for truth.[31]

Two questions in particular have presented real difficulties. The first is how the line should be drawn in this context between expression on the one hand, and conduct on the other. The question creates acute difficulties when, for example, a demonstrator engages in an unorthodox form of protest such as desecrating or burning an army registration card or the national flag in protest against government policy,[32] or when a nightclub presents nude dancing or live sexual activity. On one view these displays amount to conduct which can be regulated without

[27] Charter, s 1. For a similar provision see SA Constitution, s 36.

[28] Section 16(2).

[29] *De Reuck v Director of Public Prosecutions* 2004 (1) SA 406 (Constitutional Court SA).

[30] *Irwin Toy v A-G of Quebec* [1989] 1 SCR 927. For discussion of the Canadian approach, see Richard Moon, *The Constitutional Protection of Freedom of Expression* (2000) 33–5.

[31] The best discussion of these issues is in Kent Greenawalt, *Speech, Crime and the Uses of Language* (1989) ch 2.

[32] For US cases, see *United States v O'Brien* 391 US 367 (1968) and *Texas v Johnson* 491 US 397 (1989).

free expression arguments. But they can equally be understood as radical messages communicated by non-traditional means.[33] The most sensible approach to this issue is for the court to ask whether a public authority which, say, prohibits nude dancing intended to stop the dissemination of subversive ideas, rather than to prevent the concentration in a city centre of noisy night clubs. If the former was its aim, then the measure engages freedom of expression and should be subject to constitutional scrutiny.[34] This principle has been applied in the United States and Canada to subject limits on election expenditure to scrutiny to ensure that they do not interfere disproportionately with freedom of expression during election campaigns of political parties, candidates, and their supporters.[35]

The second issue is more general. It is whether the freedom of expression provision covers all types of speech, or is confined to communications on social and political issues, often described as 'political speech'. The question has arisen most frequently with regard to commercial advertising and sexually explicit literature and art. For a court which adopts the approach of the Supreme Court of Canada to the freedom, there is no difficulty; freedom of expression naturally covers commercial and sexually explicit speech, though it may be easy for the state to justify the imposition of restrictions on its availability or particular content limits, for example on tobacco or alcohol advertising. The US Supreme Court used to take the view that commercial advertising, and some other kinds of speech, notably libel, fell wholly outside the scope of the First Amendment.[36] That is no longer its position. The First Amendment now covers the publication of defamatory allegations,[37] whether they concern public officials and figures or ordinary people. Its scope has also been extended to cover non-fraudulent commercial speech and advertising.[38] Moreover, 'obscenity' has been defined restrictively; only a very narrow category of sexually explicit material, lacking any serious literary, artistic, or other value, may be proscribed without infringing the First Amendment.[39]

Similar developments have occurred in other jurisdictions.[40] In Germany, for example, the coverage of Article 5 has been extended to the publication of defamatory allegations, at least

[33] Courts often treat nude dancing as low value expression, so regulation can easily be justified: *Erie v Pap's AM* 527 US 277 (2000), and *Philips v DPP, Witwatersrand Local Division* 2003 (3) SA 345 (Constitutional Court SA).

[34] The Court of Appeal in England has taken this approach, holding that a ban on the entry into the UK of an extremist preacher engaged freedom of expression: *R (Farrakhan) v Secretary of State for the Home Department* [2002] 4 All ER 289.

[35] Among the leading cases in this controversial area of free speech law are *Buckley v Valeo* 424 US 1 (1976) and *A-G of Canada v Harper* (2004) 239 DLR (4th) 193. In the latter case, the Supreme Court of Canada upheld limits on advertising expenditure by individuals, as a proportionate measure to ensure electoral fairness. In contrast, in *Buckley* and many later cases the US Supreme Court has dismissed this justification for restrictions on election expenditure.

[36] See the statement of principle in *Chaplinsky v New Hampshire* 315 US 568 (1942) (some limited classes of speech such as libel, obscenity, and insulting or 'fighting' words do not raise constitutional problems) and *Valentine v Chrestensen* 316 US 52 (1942) (ban on distribution of commercial advertising did not raise freedom of speech issues).

[37] See the landmark decision of the Supreme Court in *New York Times v Sullivan* 376 US 254 (1964), more fully discussed in Section IV.2 below.

[38] Commercial speech was first fully brought within the First Amendment in *Virginia State Board of Pharmacy v Virginia Citizens Consumer Council* 425 US 748 (1976).

[39] The leading modern obscenity case is *Miller v California* 413 US 15 (1973).

[40] The European Court of Human Rights has reviewed the compatibility of state libel laws with the ECHR guarantee of freedom of expression in a number of cases, notably *Lingens v Austria* (1986) 8 EHRR 407, and has held that commercial speech is covered by the guarantee: *Markt Intern & Beerman v Germany* (1990) 12 EHRR 161.

when they raise matters of public concern;[41] the Federal Constitutional Court has also held that freedom of expression covers commercial advertisements, insofar as they contribute to the formation of public opinion, for example on environmental or health issues,[42] and pornography, unless it is addressed to children.[43] Unless the text of the freedom of expression provision, as in the case of South Africa, explicitly excludes particular categories of speech from its coverage, courts prefer to hold that it extends to all types of expression.

These developments are a little surprising. If the principal purpose of the freedom of expression guarantee is to protect uninhibited political discourse, it is unclear why its coverage should have been extended to types of speech, such as commercial advertising and pornography, which do not usually involve any discussion of political or social matters.[44] One explanation is that it may be difficult to draw a sharp line between political speech on the one hand, and commercial or sexually explicit speech on the other. The author or publisher of pornography may argue, moreover, that he could not communicate libertarian ideas about sexual relationships unless he is free to illustrate his ideas with explicit pictures. The difficulty is most acute with regard to defamatory allegations, often impossible to divorce from their context which may be a matter of clear public concern. The seminal US case, *New York Times v Sullivan*, for example, involved the publication of a newspaper advertisement protesting against the harsh treatment of civil rights demonstrators, for which, it was suggested, the commissioner of police was responsible.[45] Courts are rightly reluctant to trust the capacity of government to distinguish between speech which cannot lawfully be restricted and speech which can be regulated. This reluctance is particularly marked in the United States, where the Supreme Court will rarely uphold legislation which imposes 'content-based' restrictions on speech—that is, restrictions which allow the expression of some views, but not others, or which allow the discussion of only a restricted range of topics or confer privileges on particular speakers.

2. The Character of Freedom of Expression

Constitutional courts must sometimes determine whether the right to freedom of expression confers only a *liberty* to speak, free from interference by the state and public authorities, or whether in some contexts it also confers on individuals *positive claim-rights* to communicate their ideas or to disseminate, or acquire, information. Positive claims may be made in a variety of situations. It can be argued, for instance, that individuals should have rights to disseminate their views in the press or on television, or that the state should subsidize artistic expression.[46] There are powerful arguments for recognizing some positive rights; otherwise only a few people, in particular the wealthy and the articulate, will enjoy effective opportunities to express their views to the public. But courts are reluctant to uphold wide *constitutional* positive rights, for their recognition would compel government, or a regulatory authority, to frame appropriate rules to determine when the rights should be respected, for example when a political party

[41] See *Flugblatt* case, BVerfGE 43, 130 (1976), and the Strauss 'coerced democrat' case, BVerfGE 82, 272 (1990).

[42] BVerfGE 102, 347 (2001).

[43] BverfGE 30, 337 (1971) and *Mutzenbacher* case, BVerfGE 130 (1990).

[44] For a classic statement of this view, see Robert Bork, 'Neutral Principles and Some First Amendment Problems' (1971) 47 *Indiana Law Journal* 1.

[45] See n 37 above.

[46] For a discussion of the range of circumstances in which such claims may be made and the difficulties in upholding them, see Eric Barendt, *Freedom of Speech* (2007), 100–8.

or pressure group should have a right to broadcast.[47] That difficulty does not arise, of course, if a government chooses to enact legislation conferring access rights, say, to use public or private property for speech or to acquire information from public authorities.[48]

Courts most commonly recognize constitutional positive freedom of expression rights in two categories of case. Claims to demonstrate on the streets or in other public places are often upheld, particularly if there is evidence that the authority had discriminated against the applicant when it refused permission to hold the meeting.[49] As Chief Justice Lamer said in the *Committee for the Commonwealth of Canada* case, 'the freedom of expression cannot be exercised in a vacuum…and it necessarily implies the use of physical space in order to meet its underlying objectives.'[50] Moreover, freedom of expression arguments are often strengthened by a specific provision in the constitution for freedom of assembly or public meeting. Courts have also upheld constitutional freedom of expression rights for the media and for the general public to attend legal proceedings, even when the parties would prefer them to be held in private.[51] There seems no logical reason why the courts should be prepared to uphold positive rights in these cases, but not in others. The best explanation is probably that these rights have traditionally been respected in liberal democratic societies, so it is easy for courts to recognize them when their existence or scope is contested.[52]

There is less uniformity in another important context: the treatment of the right of reply to media attacks. There are powerful freedom of expression arguments for recognition of this right; it enables individuals to communicate their version of events, when they feel they have been misrepresented by the media, and it gives readers and listeners access to both sides of a story. But the US Supreme Court has firmly rejected a *statutory* right of reply as incompatible with press freedom, in particular with the freedom of editors to determine the composition of their newspaper.[53] So it is inconceivable that it would recognize a constitutional right to reply under the First Amendment, and it is unlikely that the UK Supreme Court or other Commonwealth courts would take that step. Rights of reply are generally provided in these jurisdictions by informal press codes, but are not legally enforceable.

On the other hand, an explicit constitutional right to reply and make corrections to inaccurate media stories is provided by some constitutions,[54] while in other jurisdictions courts have upheld statutory provisions for such rights as protecting personality rights of the individuals

[47] See the Supreme Court denial of a First Amendment right to compel a broadcaster to transmit a political advertisement in *Columbia Broadcasting System v Democratic National Committee* 412 US 94 (1973) and the German Administrative Court rejection of a claim by a social welfare recipient for state payment of his travel costs to take part in a demonstration: BVerwGE 72, 113 (1985).

[48] For UK legislation requiring universities to permit visiting speakers (and members of their staff and students) to speak freely within the law on their campuses, see Education (No 2) Act 1986, s 43, discussed by Barendt (n 46), 501.

[49] eg decisions of the US Supreme Court in *Hague v CIO* 307 US 496 (1939), *Cox v Louisiana* 379 US 536 (1965), and *Chicago Police Dept v Mosley* 408 US 92 (1972), and of the Supreme Court of Canada in *Committee for the Commonwealth of Canada v Canada* [1991] 1 SCR 139.

[50] See n 49 above, 155, quoted with approval by Lord Hutton in a leading case in England, *DPP v Jones* [1999] 2 AC 240, 288.

[51] *Edmonton Journal v A-G of Alberta* [1989] 2 SCR 1326 (Supreme Court of Canada); BVerfGE 50, 234 (1979) (German Federal Constitutional Court).

[52] See the judgments of Burger CJ and Blackmun J in *Richmond Newspapers v Virginia* 448 US 555 (1980).

[53] *Miami Herald Publishing Co v Tornillo* 418 US 241 (1974).

[54] See eg Constitution of Turkey, Art 32 and Constitution of Portugal, Art 37(4). For commentary on these and other provisions, see Kyu Ho Youm, 'The Right of Reply and Freedom of the Press: An International and Comparative Perspective' (2008) 76 *George Washington Law Review* 1017.

concerned and promoting the freedom of expression of readers to hear both sides of a story.[55] Indeed, a reply right may be considered necessary to safeguard personality rights which must be respected under the constitution.[56] (However, the French Law of the Press of 1881 provides a very wide right of reply to articles naming or referring to a particular individual, irrespective whether they amounted to an infringement of the individual's personality rights.) The 'right of reply' controversy, therefore, nicely brings out many difficulties in interpreting freedom of expression: whether the right is only a liberty or may also confer positive rights, and the relationship of freedom of expression for individuals to the freedom of the institutional press and editorial freedom. To these difficulties are added, at least in some constitutions, the balance between press freedom on the one hand, and on the other the rights of individuals to human dignity and the free development of their personality.

Freedom of expression may entail a positive right to acquire information from the state and public authorities. Without adequate information, citizens, it is argued, cannot properly exercise their freedom of expression to contribute to debate on political issues.[57] Moreover, the press and other media will be unable to discharge their role as 'watchdogs' on behalf of the public, unless they have access to information from government and other official sources. These are strong arguments, but they do not show that freedom of information should be treated as an aspect of freedom of expression. The arguments prove too much, for they would also show that the law should regard rights to a good education and to travel as aspects of freedom of expression. Moreover, it seems odd to recognize freedom of expression rights in the absence of a willing speaker. Freedom of information involves rights to acquire information from authorities reluctant to supply it.

As has already been pointed out,[58] freedom of expression clauses frequently provide a right to *receive* information, as well as a right to disseminate it. But recipient rights have ample content without bringing freedom of information within their protection. A recipient may be in a better position than the disseminator of the information to assert freedom of expression, for example when the latter is physically outside the jurisdiction and cannot easily claim the constitutional right.[59] In these circumstances, the recipient right is a freedom to receive information from a willing speaker, or as the German Basic Law puts it, from 'generally available sources'. It would be another step to hold that recipients have constitutional rights to acquire information from sources which do not want to provide it. US courts have declined to uphold First Amendment rights to acquire information; they draw a distinction between the freedom to communicate information which the media or other publisher has already acquired, and the freedom to gather information.[60] Freedom of speech covers the former, but not the latter.

These points are not made to establish that freedom of information is misconceived. The argument is only that the freedom should be conferred by statute, as has been done in many

[55] See the decisions of the German Federal Constitutional Court, BVerfGE 97, 125 (1998), and the Hungarian Constitutional Court, 57/2001 (XII.5) AB. For commentary on the latter, see András Koltay, 'The Development of Freedom of the Media in a Newborn Democracy: The Hungarian Perspective' (2010) 2(1) *Journal of Media Law* 25, 37–41.

[56] Stephen Gardbaum, 'A Reply to "The Right of Reply"' (2008) 76 *George Washington Law Review* 1065, 1065–6.

[57] Wouter Hins and Dirk Voorhoof, 'Access to State-Held Information as a Fundamental Right under the European Convention on Human Rights' (2007) 3 *European Constitutional Law Review* 114.

[58] Section II above.

[59] See the German cases, BVerfGE 27, 71 (1969), where the recipient challenged the confiscation of literature he had imported from the former German Democratic Republic, and BVerfGE 90, 27 (1994), when Turkish immigrants asserted a right to receive satellite television programmes from Turkey.

[60] *Houchins v KQED* 438 US 1 (1978).

countries,[61] rather than treated as an aspect of freedom of expression. However, whatever the merits of these points, parties to the ECHR and to the IACHR may now be impelled to recognize freedom of information as implicit in the Convention rights to freedom of expression. For the Inter-American Court of Human Rights,[62] and more recently the European Court of Human Rights,[63] have recognized a right of access to state-held information as falling under the freedom of expression provisions in the Conventions. The Inter-American Court made plain that states have a positive obligation to provide the information or justify the refusal by reference to one of the exceptions allowed by Article 13 of the IACHR.[64]

3. The Censorship Ban

Some freedom of expression provisions explicitly ban censorship and press licensing.[65] That is because authoritarian regimes generally institute strict systems for the prior scrutiny of books, newspapers, and other printed matter to ensure that they do not contain subversive material or other disapproved content. The censorship ban is intended to outlaw this practice. It is unclear, however, whether it should be interpreted to cover all types of censorship, for example the censorship of exceptionally violent or sexually explicit films and videos, and whether it applies to injunctions and other court orders restraining the publication, say, of official or commercial secrets and confidential information.

The best answer to both these questions depends perhaps on the reasons for the special hostility to censorship or systems of 'prior restraint', the term often used in Anglo-American legal systems. On one view the vice of prior restraints is that they prevent a publication from seeing the light of day, so the public never has an opportunity to comment on it. As a prominent American constitutional scholar put it, '[A] criminal statute chills, prior restraint freezes.'[66] But that is too simple. The threat or fear of subsequent criminal prosecutions or civil actions may have as great an impact on the willingness of publishers to distribute radical and challenging ideas as any censorship system. Indeed, film distributors may prefer the security of a prior restraint system with which they are familiar; they know that if their film passes scrutiny by a censorship board, there is little chance it will face prosecution. The real drawback of censorship systems is that they are operated by administrative boards, generally applying unclear standards and without adequate procedural safeguards for the publisher or film distributor to explain his work. Moreover, censorship authorities are probably predisposed to refuse a permit from time to time, for otherwise there would be no point to their existence.[67]

On this perspective, systems of film censorship may be unobjectionable, at least if they provide adequate procedural safeguards for film distributors. This is the position in the United

[61] eg Freedom of Information Act 1966 (USA); Freedom of information Act 2000 (UK).

[62] *Marcel Claude Reyes v Chile*, judgment of 19 September 2006, on which see Eduardo Andrés Bertoni, 'The Inter-American Court of Human Rights and the European Court of Human Rights: A Dialogue on Freedom of Expression Standards [2009] EHRLR 332, 347–8.

[63] *Társaság a Szabadságjogokért v Hungary*, Decision of 14 April 2009; *Kenedi v Hungary* (2009) 27 BHRC 335. It is unclear whether these rulings will be followed in later cases, since the state conceded it had infringed freedom of expression by denying access to official documents, and the European Court departed from earlier decisions in which it had refused to hold that access to information was an aspect of freedom of expression: *Leander v Sweden* (1987) 9 EHRR 433 and *Guerra v Italy* (1998) 26 EHRR 357.

[64] See n 62 above, para 77.

[65] See text accompanying n 26 above.

[66] Alexander Bickel, *The Morality of Consent* (1975), 61.

[67] All these arguments are deployed more fully in Barendt (n 46), 118–24.

States, where the Supreme Court has declined to hold them unconstitutional as such,[68] but has imposed strict procedural safeguards: it is for the censor to show that a film did not meet clear standards spelt out in legislation, and a final order banning distribution should only be made by a court after a prompt adversary hearing at which the distributor could oppose its grant.[69] Other courts have gone further. An Ontario court held that the system of censorship in that province was incompatible with the right to freedom of expression in the Charter, as the standards with which a film must comply for its release were stricter than the grounds on which a criminal prosecution could be brought. A comprehensive system of film censorship could not be sustained, although a more limited scheme to safeguard children would be compatible with freedom of expression.[70] It is hard to see why a comprehensive film censorship system should be regarded as compatible with freedom of expression, when comparable controls over theatre have been abandoned in liberal democracies. On the other hand, it has been common for broadcasting programmes to be subject to some degree of prior scrutiny by a special regulatory authority, while governments may retain legal authority to stop particular material being broadcast.[71]

The US Supreme Court and European courts have taken different positions on court injunctions. The Supreme Court will rarely uphold a judicial prior restraint, even in cases involving the publication of material likely to prejudice the outcome of pending or contemporaneous legal proceedings, where the defendant's constitutional right to a fair trial might be endangered.[72] In the famous *Pentagon Papers* case,[73] it declined to continue a temporary order stopping the publication in two newspapers of confidential State Department documents relating to the involvement of the United States in the Vietnam War. Justices Black and Douglas would have declined to uphold a prior restraint in any circumstances, but other members of the 6:3 majority would have been prepared to uphold one if the government could show that publication would almost certainly result in 'direct, immediate and irreparable damage to our Nation or its people'.[74] A US court will grant an injunction to stop a publication only in very exceptional circumstances.[75]

The general understanding of the censorship ban in European jurisdictions is that it applies only to administrative censorship systems, and not to court orders preventing a publication. That is certainly the position in Germany, where the issue has been considered by the Federal Constitutional Court on a number of occasions; it has explained that the *Zensurverbot* applied only to systems requiring the submission of material to authorities for scrutiny prior to publication.[76] It did not cover orders by a court for which an application must be made. In England

[68] *Times Film v Chicago* 365 US 43 (1965).

[69] *Freedman v Maryland* 380 US 51 (1965).

[70] *R v Glad Day Bookshops Inc* (2004) 239 DLR (4th) 119. The Inter-American Court of Human Rights has held the Chile censorship system under which all films had to be submitted for scrutiny before release incompatible with IACHR, Art 13(4), under which 'public entertainments may be subject by law to prior censorship for the sole purpose of regulating access to them for the moral protection of childhood and adolescence': *The Last Temptation of Christ*, judgment of 5 February 2001, Series C, no 73.

[71] See the UK Communications Act 2003, s 336. An earlier provision was upheld by the House of Lords as compatible with freedom of expression in *R v Home Secretary, ex p Brind* [1991] AC 696. The ECHR, Art 10(1) in its third sentence provides: 'This Article shall not prevent States from requiring the licensing of broadcasting, television, or cinema enterprises.'

[72] *Nebraska Press Association v Stuart* 427 US 539 (1976).

[73] *New York Times v US* 403 US 713 (1971).

[74] Ibid, 730 per Stewart J, with whom White J concurred.

[75] In *US v Progressive Inc* 467 F Supp 990 (1979) a District Court granted a temporary injunction to stop publication of an article describing the manufacture of the H-bomb.

[76] BVerfGE 33, 52 (1972).

and other countries injunctions are frequently granted to stop the publication of material likely to imperil commercial confidentiality, personal privacy, or state secrecy, or to endanger the fairness of legal proceedings. There is nothing objectionable in this practice, provided the media or other defendant has an opportunity to argue that it would be wrong to grant an injunction. It is imperative to ensure that these procedural rights are safeguarded.[77] The European Court of Human Rights has rejected the argument that prior restraints are as such incompatible with the right to freedom of expression, though it has emphasized that they should be carefully scrutinized,[78] and further that administrative orders must be liable to prompt judicial review.[79] Court injunctions do not carry the same dangers for freedom of expression as systems of administrative scrutiny, for courts do, or should, not suffer from any prejudice in favour of censorship, they apply the law, rather than exercise administrative discretion, and they should provide both parties with adequate opportunities to argue their case.

IV. Balancing Freedom of Expression and Other Interests

In practice the most important issue for courts in free expression cases is how the right should be balanced against other interests. Their approach may depend on the character of the competing interest. If it is national security, public order, or some other general interest, they may require the state to show that the interest cannot be safeguarded without a constraint, or even a ban, on exercise of the right to freedom of expression and that this restraint is not excessive or disproportionate in the circumstances. In these cases there is a presumption in favour of the right. Courts sometimes defer to the government's assessment that, say, national security would be imperilled if the speaker were allowed to disseminate his ideas.[80] Such deference legitimates, perhaps even encourages, the suppression of free expression and associated freedoms, particularly at times of tension, so it is much better for courts to insist there is evidence of a link between the spread of the (extreme) political speech and the insurrection or disorder thought likely to occur as a result. The latter approach is evidenced by the important decision of the US Supreme Court in *Brandenburg v Ohio*,[81] when it required the state to show that incitement was *likely* to lead to *imminent* violence or other lawless action before it could penalize its dissemination.

Courts must adopt a different approach when they balance freedom of expression against another right, particularly if that other right is also guaranteed by the constitution. They cannot rely on a presumption in favour of freedom of expression, for the other right, for example to privacy or to a fair trial, may equally be entitled to constitutional protection. So courts must then consider the weight of the rival claims, to freedom of expression on the one hand, and to privacy, reputation, or intellectual property rights on the other, if they are to strike a fair balance between them. This entails asking questions about the value, say, of the particular communication or the degree of intrusion on the claimant's privacy. But detailed weighing of all

[77] See the UK HRA 1998, s 12(2) requiring that defendants should be notified of the application for an interlocutory order, unless there are compelling reasons why this should not be done.

[78] *Observer and Guardian v UK* (1992) 14 EHRR 153, 191.

[79] *Association Ekin v France* (2002) 35 EHRR 1207.

[80] See the much criticized decision of the US Supreme Court in *US v Dennis* 341 US 494 (1951), reached during the McCarthy period when there was much nervousness at the possibility of a Communist insurrection.

[81] 395 US 444 (1969).

the factors complicates the judicial process and makes the end result unpredictable, so some courts prefer to formulate clear rules, or guidelines, on the basis of which these conflicting claims can be resolved relatively easily.[82]

It is impossible here to do justice to all areas of law in which courts balance freedom of expression (and associated rights such as freedom of assembly or academic freedom) against conflicting public interests or private rights. Some remarks should be made about three topics where balancing is particularly difficult and where national legislatures and courts have adopted radically different solutions: hate speech, libel and the invasion of privacy, and pornography.

1. Hate Speech

Many liberal democracies proscribe the dissemination of hate speech: communications inciting hatred against social groups defined by reference to their race, religion, or ethnic or national origins.[83] Some hate speech laws also protect sexual minorities and the physically disabled.[84] In many European states and in Israel, Holocaust denial is explicitly proscribed, while in others, notably Canada, deniers have been prosecuted under general criminal laws.[85] Sharply different views have been taken about the compatibility of these laws with freedom of expression. At one extreme is the position in South Africa, where the Constitution excludes hate speech altogether from the guarantee.[86] European constitutional courts and the Supreme Court of Canada have generally upheld the application of hate speech laws. In contrast, courts in the United States have almost always ruled them incompatible with the First Amendment guarantee of freedom of speech. Notably, the Supreme Court in *RAV v City of St Paul*[87] held that the city infringed the guarantee by enacting an ordinance singling out for proscription the expression of hatred 'on the basis of race, color, creed, religion, or gender'. Either all forms of hate speech must be banned, or none. Racist hate speech must be permitted, as much as speech targeting Democrats or Republicans, or other types of extremist speech.[88]

The usual perspective in the United States is that hate speech forms part of public discourse; only if racialists and extremists are allowed to express their ideas, can the state justify to them the application of anti-discrimination and other criminal laws regulating their conduct.[89] Racists cannot then argue that they have not even been allowed to express their opinions. Another important argument is that of the 'slippery slope': once racist and other forms of hate speech are proscribed, it will be difficult to resist the extension of the criminal law to ban the dissemination of, say, radical anarchist or socialist ideas. Defenders of hate speech laws argue

[82] See Section IV.2 below for further consideration of the merits of factual and rule-based balancing in the context of libel and privacy claims.

[83] For comparative treatment of hate speech laws, see Michel Rosenfeld, 'Hate Speech in Constitutional Jurisprudence: A Comparative Analysis' (2003) 24 *Cardozo Law Review* 1523 and Ivan Hare and James Weinstein (ed), *Extreme Speech and Democracy* (2009).

[84] See the essays by Eric Heinze and Pascal Mbongo in Hare and Weinstein (n 83), 182 and 221 respectively. On issues of gender, see Chapter 19.

[85] In *R v Zundel* [1992] 2 SCR 731 a bare majority of the Supreme Court of Canada held the application of a law penalizing the dissemination of false news to a Holocaust denier a disproportionate restriction on freedom of expression.

[86] See n 28 above.

[87] 505 US 377 (1992).

[88] See James Weinstein, 'An Overview of American Free Speech Doctrine and its Application to Extreme Speech' in Hare and Weinstein (n 83), 81, 85–8.

[89] See Post (n 3) and Ronald Dworkin, Foreword to Hare and Weinstein (n 83), vii.

that they are needed to preserve community relations and in the long term to prevent a breakdown in law and order. But arguments of this kind are difficult to accept. They are incompatible with general perspectives underlying arguments for free expression, that it is better for a society to debate its underlying tensions and that the state infringes the freedom if it outlaws the dissemination of ideas which the majority dislikes or which are offensive, even insulting, to particular communities.

The proponents of hate speech laws may be on stronger ground when they argue that they protect the constitutional rights of the targeted groups, particularly their equality rights.[90] For then the courts must balance the constitutional right to freedom of expression against another constitutional right, which presumptively is of equal weight. In assessing their importance, it can be argued, as Chief Justice Dickson said for the majority of the Canadian Supreme Court in its leading hate speech decision, that racist speech has 'low value'.[91] However, it is unclear how hate speech, unlike the discriminatory denial of, say, housing or education, directly infringes the equality rights of the targeted group. Equality arguments carry little more conviction than the contention that hate speech 'silences' members of the targeted community, so infringing their own freedom of expression.

Another dimension of this discussion is, of course, that each country has a distinct historical experience of the dangers of hate speech. On that basis it is understandable that after the apartheid regime the framers of the South African Constitution decided wholly to exclude hate speech from the free expression guarantee. Equally, Holocaust denial laws make sense in countries which have recently experienced Nazi and other anti-Semitic regimes,[92] or in which there is good reason to believe that, left unchecked, the fabrications of revisionist historians will be widely accepted. But with the passage of time, it would surely be wrong for the state to determine historical truth; a law banning the publication of 'revisionist' histories of the atrocities committed by religious communities, say, during the Crusades or the Thirty Years War, would infringe freedom of expression, however insulting these accounts are to their members now.

2. Libel and the Infringement of Privacy

In *New York Times v Sullivan*,[93] the Supreme Court held for the first time that libel actions were not immune from scrutiny under the First Amendment. Like prosecutions for seditious libel, a civil action for libel damages could limit freedom of political expression, not only for the defendant in the particular action, but for other writers deterred from publishing out of fear of legal proceedings. The Court fashioned a broad rule under which libel actions brought by a public official could succeed only if he proved that the allegations were published with the knowledge of their falsity or with reckless indifference to their truth. The principle was extended to cover actions brought by any 'public figure', for example an army commander or sports personality, while private individuals must show fault if they are to succeed in libel proceedings.[94] More controversially, it has applied the same principles to privacy cases, where the

[90] Kathleen Mahoney, 'Hate Speech, Equality, and the State of Canadian Law' (2009) 44 *Wake Forest Law Review* 321.

[91] *R v Keegstra* [1990] 3 SCR 697, 760.

[92] In the famous Auschwitz lie case, the German ban on Holocaust denial was upheld against a freedom of expression challenge: BVerfGE 90, 241 (1994), discussed by Dieter Grimm, 'The Holocaust Denial Decision of the Federal Constitutional Court of Germany' in Hare and Weinstein (n 83), 557.

[93] 376 US 254 (1964).

[94] The leading cases are *Curtis Publishing Co v Butts* 388 US 130 (1967) (public figures) and *Gertz v Robert Welch* 418 US 323 (1974) (private individuals).

public interest in publishing the intimate details of a politician's or celebrity's personal life is much weaker than it usually is in defamation actions.[95]

The advantage of this approach is that it provides some certainty for the press and other media; they know that they can safely publish defamatory allegations about public officials and figures, which they believe to be true, even though it turns out that the stories are inaccurate. The *New York Times* rule removes the 'chilling effect' of libel laws, which deter the press from publishing defamatory allegations it considers to be of public interest about political and other public figures when it is unsure it could prove their truth to the satisfaction of the libel jury. Under the rule an editor does not have to assess the weight of all the facts before deciding it is safe to publish the story; he has only to determine whether the claimant is a public official or figure. The same argument may apply in privacy cases, though in these circumstances the case for application of the *New York Times* rule is much less persuasive; it is unclear that there is a real public interest in exposing details of even a politician's private life, unless their conduct interfered with discharge of their public duties.[96]

On the other hand, the difficulty with *New York Times* and later Supreme Court decisions is that they give too strong protection to freedom of expression, in particular of the media, at the cost to the individual's reputation or privacy. After all, a mistaken article might destroy the standing of a minor figure in, say, local government. For this reason, courts in England and other Commonwealth countries, in applying their own constitutional provisions, have rejected the US approach, while giving much more weight than they had under common law to freedom of expression in libel actions. Similarly, the German approach is to weigh all relevant factors before determining whether freedom of expression should trump the individual's interest in protecting his reputation.[97] It adopts the same approach in privacy cases.[98] The then House of Lords in England also examined all the facts carefully in these cases, most notably when it awarded Naomi Campbell damages after a tabloid newspaper published a photograph of her leaving a meeting of Narcotics Anonymous where she had been receiving treatment.[99]

It is certainly right to apply freedom of expression principles to libel and privacy actions. But courts must take equal account of reputation and privacy rights, particularly when they enjoy constitutional protection. (One explanation of the approach in the United States is that reputation and privacy against media disclosures are not constitutional rights, so do not enjoy the same status as freedom of speech and of the press.) There is no good reason to privilege freedom of expression over human dignity, so individuals should be able to secure redress for egregious attacks on their privacy or constant harassment by the media. In this context it is worth emphasizing that most infringements of personal privacy are committed by the media, in particular the tabloid press, which is often ready to claim freedom of expression rights to defend their commercial interests in satisfying the public demand for celebrity gossip.

[95] Among the leading decisions are *Time v Hill* 385 US 374 (1967) and *Bartnicki v Vopper* 532 US 514 (2001). On privacy more generally, see Chapter 46.

[96] See the argument in Melville Nimmer's classic article, 'The Right to Speak from *Times* to *Time:* First Amendment Theory Applied to Libel and Misapplied to Privacy' (1968) 56 *California Law Review* 935.

[97] The approach of the courts in England, Commonwealth jurisdictions, and Germany to balancing in libel cases is discussed in Barendt (n 46), 211–22. A similar approach has now been adopted by the Supreme Court of Canada: *Grant v Torstar Corporation* 2009 SCC 61.

[98] See the *Lebach* case, BVerfGE 35, 202 (1973), discussed in Barendt (n 46), 236.

[99] *Campbell v MGN* [2004] 2 AC 457.

3. Pornography

Courts adopt a number of approaches to pornography—sexually explicit literature, film, and other material. Extreme hard-core pornography may be excluded altogether from the coverage of freedom of expression, on the ground that it is indistinguishable from the provision of sex toys and does not communicate any ideas so as to constitute 'expression'. This perspective is reflected in the constitutional definition of 'obscenity' in the United States; matter which appeals to a prurient interest in sex, is patently offensive, and lacks any serious artistic, political, or other value may be proscribed without the risk of First Amendment challenge.[100] There is also no serious freedom of expression argument against bans on the circulation of child pornography when its production involved the participation of young children.

Attempts to control the spread of other types of pornography may, however, run into constitutional difficulties. A government may not justify tight regulation of sexually explicit literature simply on the argument that its consumption is morally wrong or lowers the tone of society; members of the public have a freedom of expression right to determine what they read and look at. The state must point to some specific harm. This might be the increased incidence of rape and other sexual offences, or the psychological damage to children from premature exposure to sexually explicit material. The weakness of these arguments is that it is unclear that the consumption of such material does cause, or even contribute to, these harms. Also controversial is the feminist case that pornography demeans women, and perhaps silences them, so denying them freedom of expression. The Supreme Court of Canada has decided that hard-core material can be proscribed if it degrades women,[101] or gays and lesbians.[102] The feelings of diminished self-esteem resulting from the dissemination of this material is a harm the state is entitled to prevent without infringing free expression. But US courts have rejected this justification for pornography regulation; it is not the business of the state to determine which views of women are acceptable.[103]

Even US courts have been sympathetic to regulations concerning the *location* of sex cinemas and shops, on the ground that their siting in proximity to each other would lead to the development of a red-light district, or if permitted close to a residential area would damage the quality of life and reduce property values.[104] It is striking that this type of regulation is regarded as compatible with freedom of expression, even though it plainly discriminates against the provision of one type of material—sexually explicit speech, regarded as expression of low value when balanced against the public interest in the general quality of life in a city or residential area. The same perspective was taken by the House of Lords when it upheld a Belfast City ban on the siting of sex shops in a city centre area.[105] This approach is acceptable, given the availability of pornographic material by mail order and now over the internet: such regulation does not have the same impact on freedom of expression as a total ban on the dissemination of sexually explicit material.

[100] See text accompanying n 39.

[101] *R v Butler* [1992] 1 SCR 452.

[102] *Little Sisters Book and Art Emporium v Minister of Justice* [2000] 2 SCR 1120.

[103] *American Booksellers Ass'n v Hudnut* 771 F2d 323 (7th Cir 1985).

[104] See *Young v American Mini Theatres* 427 US 50 (1976) and *Renton v Playtime Theatres* 475 US 41 (1986).

[105] See Lord Hoffmann and Lady Hale in *Miss Behavin' Ltd v Belfast City Council* [2007] 1 WLR 1420, paras 16 and 38 respectively.

V. Freedom of Expression and the Media

It goes without saying that the mass media—the press and broadcasters—may claim freedom of expression, whether or not they enjoy the protection of a specific right to press or media freedom, often conferred by the same constitutional provision.[106] Indeed, in some contexts, notably libel and privacy proceedings, freedom of expression is almost invariably asserted by the media, rather than by individual writers. But the relationship between freedom of expression and media claims is far from straightforward. The media themselves inevitably limit the dissemination of information and ideas when they refuse, say, to publish an individual's reply to a personal attack they have printed or broadcast, or deny a pressure group the opportunity to communicate its views in an article or television documentary. In these circumstances, the media and the individual may both assert freedom of expression, and courts must decide who has the stronger constitutional claim. It has been pointed out that the approaches of the US and European courts differ with regard to the constitutionality of reply rights.[107] The former take the view that press freedom prevails over individual claims, even though that may be to the cost of readers' understanding of events.

Of course, unregulated press and broadcasters are infinitely preferable to a mass media subservient to government. But sometimes the values underlying freedom of expression—the dissemination of a range of views on political and social issues—justifies media regulation, for example to ensure that they are not controlled by one or two press barons or media corporations. That is the reason why in European countries, and even sometimes in the United States,[108] there have been limits on, say, the share of a newspaper or broadcasting market which can be controlled by a single media company. The French Constitutional Council, the Italian Constitutional Court, and the German Federal Constitutional Court have all ruled that media regulation to ensure pluralism is not only permissible, but required by constitutional freedom of expression provisions.[109] The freedom does not give the mass media immunity from regulation to prevent oligopolies or to ensure that they transmit news and other serious programmes; moreover, it should never be forgotten that media corporations often claim to defend the freedom and press freedom, when they are really protecting their commercial interests.

Finally, it is important to consider whether the internet affects this perspective. Its advent certainly increases the effective opportunities for all individuals to communicate their views—often anonymously—to other members of the public. Further, some traditional arguments for broadcasting regulation—the scarcity of frequencies and the unique power of television—hardly apply to the new electronic media.[110] But it does not follow that the internet undermines the case for mass media regulation. For the internet has not yet replaced, and may never replace, the print and broadcasting media altogether, though it may have contributed to the significant recent decline in newspaper readership. The point is that the internet is used most frequently by individuals to communicate their views to other individuals, rather than to a mass audience; its role is for the most part supplementary to that of the traditional press and broadcasting media. If there are good free expression arguments for regulation of the mass media, in order to ensure that they provide a forum for lively political debate, they are unaffected by the arrival of the new electronic media.

[106] Section II above.

[107] See text accompanying nn 53–6 above.

[108] See the judgment of Black J in *Associated Press v US* 326 US 1, 20 (1945).

[109] Barendt (n 46), 67–71 and 429–33.

[110] See *Reno v American Civil Liberties Union* 521 US 844 (1997).

Bibliography

Eric Barendt, *Freedom of Speech* (2007)

David Currie, *The Constitution of the Federal Republic of Germany* (1994)

Edward Eberle, *Dignity and Liberty: Constitutional Visions in Germany and the United States* (2002)

Kent Greenawalt, *Speech, Crime and the Uses of Language* (1989)

Ivan Hare and James Weinstein (eds), *Extreme Speech and Democracy* (2009)

Wolfgang Hoffman-Riem, *Kommunikationsfreiheiten* (2002)

Richard Moon, *The Constitutional Protection of Freedom of Expression* (2000)

Jean Morange, *La liberté d'expression* (2009)

Alessandro Pace and Michela Manetti, *La Libertà di manifestazione del proprio pensiero* (2006)

Robert Post, 'Racist Speech, Democracy, and the First Amendment' (1991) 32 *William and Mary Law Review* 267

Robert Post, 'The Constitutional Concept of Public Discourse: Outrageous Opinion, Democratic Deliberation, and *Hustler Magazine v Falwell*' (1990) 103 *Harvard Law Review* 601

Michel Rosenfeld, 'Hate Speech in Constitutional Jurisprudence: A Comparative Analysis' (2003) 24 *Cardozo Law Review* 1523

Fred Schauer, 'Categories and the First Amendment: A Play in Three Acts' (1981) 34 *Vanderbilt Law Review* 265

Roger Shiner, *Freedom of Commercial Expression* (2003)

Geoffrey Stone, 'Restrictions of Speech Because of its Content: The Peculiar Case of Subject-Matter Restrictions' (1978) 46 *University of Chicago Law Review* 81

George Williams, *Human Rights under the Australian Constitution* (2002)

CHAPTER 43

FREEDOM OF RELIGION

ANDRÁS SAJÓ AND RENÁTA UITZ

Budapest

HISTORICALLY, freedom of religion evolved through the competition of state sovereign power and religious communities. The development of the applicable legal regime also depends of the nature and intensity of religious beliefs and the social functions of religion. Religions have different and changing theological positions regarding the scope of individual religious freedom, while religious organizations are known to have denied the religious freedom of believers of other religions. Nevertheless, from ancient times in a few historical instances people were allowed to worship their own God, due to a tolerant theological position prevailing at the moment or the pragmatic benevolence of the emperor in a multi-confessional state.

The formulation of freedom of religion and conscience as an individual right stems partly from placing religious choices in individual conscience, and partly from the fact that strong, privileged claims against the state are formulated most successfully in the language of rights. While concerns of free exercise of religion may prevail in the regulation of religion, considerations related to the collective aspects of religious exercise and historical traditions in matters of church–state relations continue to play a role in the regulatory area.

I. The Changing Meaning of Freedom of Religion

In Europe at the time of the Reformation (1517–1648), the competition of Catholic and Protestant churches resulted in persecution and extended civil and interstate wars. In the international regime that emerged the absolute supremacy of the state prevailed. As summarized in the adage of *cuius regio, eius religio* (whose realm, his religion) of the Peace Treaty of Augsburg (1555): subjects had to follow the faith of the ruling sovereign. As the history of the

English Acts of Uniformity indicates, the centralizing state power was inclined to enforce uniformity in public worship.[1] The result of such religious homogenization was discrimination and persecution of all dissenters with lasting effects.[2] At this point, freedom of religion was primarily a matter of non-persecution and the permissibility of private worship for Christians.

With the emergence of competing religions and their fratricidal wars, the individual right of freedom of religion became an issue of the 'liberty of moderns'.[3] The earliest laws against religious persecution were concerned with the freedom of communities to choose their faith (priests), while the sovereign ruler was prohibited from imposing his own confession.[4]

A similar logic dictated by the needs of multi-ethnic and multi-religious societies prevailed slowly in the American colonies, which were settled by various persecuted religious minorities. Beginning in 1636, Rhode Island passed laws against persecution of non-Trinitarians and providing for the separation of church and state. Undeniably, the theological views of Roger Williams, who based universal religious freedom on the 'right of their error', did play an important role here.[5] Other colonies enacted regimes of toleration to people of all or most faiths. Nevertheless, religious minorities were often persecuted and most colonies had their state church.[6]

At the turn of the seventeenth century a demand for toleration, partly based on philosophical considerations, emerged.[7] John Locke in particular emphasized that it is not for the state to enforce religion: the duty of the civil government to take care of 'civil interests' does not and cannot include 'care of the soul'.[8]

For rather peculiar historical reasons, some eighteenth-century societies became pluri-religious and the state could not easily take sides with one religion without running the risk of destabilization. As Voltaire stated, idealizing the situation in England: 'If there were only one religion in England there would be danger of despotism, if there were two they would cut each other's throats, but there are thirty, and they live in peace and happiness.'[9]

During the American Revolution, free exercise was increasingly seen as an individual right pertaining to all believers. This extension is understandable in a struggle that is carried out in the name of freedom and in need of broad popular support. In the typical formulation of the Delaware Declaration of Rights of 1776:

> all men have a natural and unalienable right to worship Almighty God according to the dictates of their own consciences and understandings; and that no man ought or of right can be compelled to attend any religious worship or maintain any ministry contrary to or against his own free will and consent, and that no authority can or ought to be vested in, or assumed by

[1] The Acts of Uniformity of 1549, 1552, and 1662 all determined the Book of Common Prayer.

[2] eg in England the Catholic Relief Act restored the political and certain civil rights of Catholics only in 1829.

[3] See Benjamin Constant, 'The Liberty of the Ancients Compared With That of the Moderns' in *Political Writings* (Biancamaria Fontana ed, 1988).

[4] See the Transylvanian Diet's (parliament) 1568 law; the Warsaw Confederation of 1573; and to some extent the Union of Utrecht of 1579 that served as the foundation of the modern Dutch state against Catholic Spain and referred to individual freedom of religion.

[5] See Roger Williams, *The Bloody Tenent of Persecution for Cause of Conscience* (1644).

[6] On the complexity of the colonial development see Michael W. McConnell, 'The Origins and Historical Understanding of Free Exercise of Religion' (1990) 103 *Harvard Law Review* 1409ff.

[7] Pierre Bayle, *Philosophical Commentary* (1708), 229–31.

[8] John Locke, *Letter Concerning Toleration* (James Tully ed, 1983).

[9] Voltaire, *Letters on England* (1980), 41.

> any power whatever that shall in any case interfere with, or in any manner control the right of conscience in the free exercise of religious worship.

Beginning with the American Revolution, respect for individual conscience, in a *personal* moral sense, increasingly became the source of freedom of religion. It is understood as a matter of non-coercion. The 1776 Virginia Declaration of Rights (following George Mason's reinterpretation of Locke) proclaimed as fundamental and undeniable truth, 'that religion or the duty which we owe to our Creator and the manner of discharging it, can be directed only by reason and conviction, not by force or violence.' Nevertheless, while the First Amendment of the Federal Constitution prohibited the establishment of a state church at the federal level, the state of Massachusetts ended its multiple establishment system (public support to specific denominations) only in 1833.

Under the influence of Enlightenment Emperor Joseph II of Austria, his Patent of Toleration of 1781 granted protestants and some other denominations the right to have their churches, albeit without direct entrance from the street, and protestants became eligible for civil service.[10] But only the revolutionary Declaration of the Rights of Man and of the Citizen of 1789 granted an individual right of free exercise and only in the form of a guarantee on non-persecution, subject to public order considerations.[11] During the French Revolution, the full equalization of believers and beliefs was provided at the expense of the monarchy's loss of authority, and it was more a matter of citizens' equality than of freedom of religion. The sovereignty of state (people) was recognized at the price of subordinating churches: an oath on the Constitution was demanded from the clergy.[12]

The emerging liberal constitutionalism resisted such radical anticlericalism. In fact, early liberal constitutions like that of Spain in 1812 recognize state religion; in this case the Apostolic Roman Catholic religion was the only true religion. While in the United States a 'wall of separation between Church & State' envisioned by Thomas Jefferson has gradually emerged, elsewhere a number of constitutions consolidated the privileged status of one or another, or of a few religious organizations. This caused unequal civil status among believers and the ease of manifesting a religion or belief was also affected. Notwithstanding such early institutional arrangements, thanks partly to the conflicts between state and church, the principle of free exercise of one's religion as an individual right became gradually accepted in liberal constitutional systems in the nineteenth century. However, practical social and political discrimination of believers of non-privileged and new faiths and the faithless continue to exist well into our era.

Outside liberal constitutionalism, freedom of religion remained a matter of group protection in the form of group rights. The international law of the nineteenth century, partly reflecting increasing Western political interventionism, emphasized that religious minorities deserve international protection, favoring Christian communities in the form of international treaty guarantees. This principle was imposed in particular on the Ottoman Empire.[13] The international protection of minorities continued to prevail in the League of Nations system, and various peace treaties treated freedom of religion as a matter of minority rights protection, which

[10] See also the 1787 Edict of toleration in France.

[11] Article 10: 'No one may be disturbed on account of his opinions, even religious ones, as long as the manifestation of such opinions does not interfere with the established Law and Order.'

[12] See the law entitled Civil Constitution of the Clergy (Constitution civile du clergé) passed on July 12, 1790 during the French Revolution.

[13] To grant rights to religious minority groups was not completely alien to the political organization of the Islamic state, which traditionally recognized a level of autonomy to non-Muslim religious communities in the form of the *millet* system.

implied an understanding of free exercise as a collective right. After the Second World War, the individual right to free exercise had been recognized in the Universal Declaration as a distinct matter within the freedom of thought or conscience. The collective nature of religion remains reflected in the individual right to worship in community.

II. Reasons for and Justifications of Freedom of Religion

In the history of mankind, religion has proved itself a fundamental component of human existence. The centrality and power of religious beliefs for the individual and for the state (that intends to maximize control over the individual by controlling its belief system) explains why religious practices are endorsed by the state.

Religion satisfies basic psychological needs of the individual. For many people it serves to reduce existential uncertainty, it provides meaning to events as well as personal and collective (social) goals and identity. It has implications for people's mental and social life, including its contribution to prejudice and discrimination.

As to the social functions of religion, Émile Durkheim in particular considered religion to be a source of stability and cohesion: a shared set of religious beliefs creates a cohesive moral community and a collective conscience.[14] Ceremonies and rituals are important tools of such processes. Religious homogeneity is believed to foster homogeneity in the state and without such homogeneity (that translates today into cultural community) the solidarity and loyalty that are the preconditions of a functioning state and provide a constitutional identity to the people behind the state become shaky.

E.W. Böckenförde, a former German constitutional judge, argues that religious and cultural coherence (homogeneity) is a prerequisite for a constitutional state. Until the nineteenth century, the (unitary) Christian religion was the fundamental power that provided coherence in public life inside the state. With the emancipation of the individual, first it was the nation-state to grant such coherence, while after 1945 only common moral values would provide such coherence. Subjectivity and positivism inherent in the private value system undermine coherence and freedom. In a system of open neutrality between state and religion (a system exemplified in the German constitutional system), the secular state recognizes the religion-ordered life of its citizens, and is based on and bound by a lived common culture (*gelebte Kultur*). This cultural-religious basis of coherence is undermined by increasing heterogeneity. Both Böckenförde and Cardinal Ratzinger (now Pope Benedict XIV) were of the view that when granting religious freedoms the state must preserve its cultural roots.[15]

Contemporary behavioral sciences[16] and evolutionary psychology indicate that religious beliefs and practices affect a wide range of behavioral outcomes. They not only contribute to

[14] Émile Durkheim, *The Elementary Forms of the Religious Life* (Joseph Ward Swain trans, 1915), 47; 'they mutually show one another that they are all members of the same moral community and they become conscious of the kinship uniting them': ibid 358.

[15] Ernst-Wolfgang Böckenförde, *Recht, Staat, Freiheit. Studien zur Rechtsphilosophie und Verfassungsgeschichte* (2006); Ernst-Wolfgang Böckenförde, 'Wie können die Religionen friedlich und frei beisammen leben? Über den säkularen Staat, seine Neutralität und die Probleme, mit denen er im 21. Jahrhundert konfrontiert ist' (23 June 2007) *Neue Züricher Zeitung* 143. See further Jürgen Habermas and Joseph Ratzinger, *The Dialectics of Secularization* (2005).

[16] Laurence R. Iannaccone, 'Economics of Religion Introduction to the Economics of Religion' (1998) 36 *Journal of Economic Literature* 1465ff.

the maintenance of hierarchical relations but they have the potential to disrupt the political order as they might lead one to disobedience, resistance, and martyrdom, which fuel destructive religious conflict. Religious fundamentalism is inclined to authoritarianism with important consequences for contemporary democracy.

The religious foundation of freedom of religion offers a controversial justification for a universal right to freedom of religion. Where religion is the way to truth and salvation it commands that its rules be strictly followed. Many religions (at least at certain stages of their development) have commands *not* to allow other forms of worship and force all people to the only salvation that they happen to offer. Such an approach lacks *mutual respect* for all the other religions and non-religious or non-collective beliefs, and cannot justify a universal right to religious freedom.

Where freedom of religion originates from religious considerations, further complications will result from the uncertain relation between religion (religious organization) and the state. Sometimes, at least some churches (the Catholic in particular), claim sovereignty and organizational autonomy, and individual freedom exists within this autonomous organization. From the perspective of constitutional theory, such relation is a matter of sovereignty: the modern state (as a constitutional democracy) claims that the source of all political power be the sovereign state (and behind it the people). To the extent that religion is the source of religious freedom, state sovereignty might be challenged. Vice versa, sovereignty might be and is a limit to such freedom, among others in the form of public order.

The argument of toleration often refers to mutual respect for religions, although this approach should not be conflated with an equality-based approach.[17] To being with, from a religious/moral perspective it is hard to respect what is considered wrong, especially where religious doctrine claims that the wrong religion endangers the salvation of its believers. The religious ground for toleration was not equality of beliefs, but that one cannot reach salvation through coercion. Hobbes and Locke turned this idea into a primarily secular argument, detaching it from its religious foundation. Locke related toleration (as a source of freedom of religious practice and even civic equality) to the functions of the civil government: given that the magistrate is concerned with life, liberty, health, and property and it is only for the preservation of those interests where coercion can be used, it follows that government has no mandate to use coercion in order to promote salvation. Locke accepted that many 'other' religions are objectionable; tolerance is a (public) attitude in front of error.[18]

This position on tolerance is to be contrasted to the one that recognizes all beliefs and believers as equal (though not necessarily 'right' in their belief). Toleration in this way cannot be a source of rights, but it is reasonable permissiveness towards socially non-harmful error. Tolerance can be argued on epistemological grounds. Locke himself talked about 'true religion' with some skepticism (as magistrates often believe in the wrong religion). According to the agnostic argument of James Madison,[19] the majority has no power to legislate on matters of religion, while on the other hand the freedom to observe religion, which is of divine origin, has to be a right equal to all, as others may have a different view on religious matters. As equals, they cannot be coerced to support a specific view.

Pragmatic toleration based on concern of socially disruptive intolerance runs into objections. Jeremy Waldron has recently argued that religious persecution may serve the preservation

[17] For an overview of arguments for tolerance from a constitutional perspective see Matthias Mahlmann, 'Freedom and Faith: Foundations of Freedom of Religion' (2009) 30 *Cardozo Law Review* 2473, 2481–93.

[18] For primarily political reasons, he did not extend toleration to Papists, as their religion prescribed allegiance to a foreign power. Faulty religions are tolerated, political betrayal is not.

[19] Memorial and Remonstrance Against Religious Assessments, 1785.

of peace, and force may be effective in changing religious beliefs (an argument that is also used against the right to proselytize).[20] Thus, it would not stop a person who used religious persecution for some end other than religious conversion, such as preserving the peace.

In the Enlightenment project that stood against religious persecution in the name of human reason, *freedom of conscience* did emerge as a background assumption demanding toleration, although the principal argument for religious tolerance referred to the human tragedy resulting from religious persecution. Because religion was considered a source of intolerant prejudice, Voltaire insisted on leaving religious prejudice at home. As religion is not accepted as a source of legitimate consideration in public, the equality of beliefs or at least believers became a possibility.

Equality-based toleration rests on the following personal assumption: 'Even though we disagree, they are as fully members of society as I am ... [N]either their way of living nor mine is uniquely *the* way of our society.'[21] This is certainly sufficient to deny the right to persecute and it enables religious manifestations as a matter of liberty, but this approach does not set a moral foundation for a right that would limit the state.

Toleration may need normative justifications to ground freedom of religion as an individual right. It can be argued that religious toleration is a specific application of tolerance, which is essential for democracy, where 'proper social life is naturally based on reciprocal concessions and mutual tolerance'.[22] It often relies on the limited or non-existent power of the state (as an entity that derives its powers from citizens) in matters of conscience. Respect for freedom of conscience serves as an independent justification for freedom of religion as a right, where freedom of religion *follows* from a fundamental personal choice. Here, religion or other core beliefs are central for the individual, and respect of the individual entails respect of his personal choices. In *Planned Parenthood of Southeastern Pennsylvania v Casey*, the US Supreme Court relied on such respect:

> These matters, involving the most intimate and personal choices a person may make in a lifetime, choices central to personal dignity and autonomy, are central to the liberty protected by the Fourteenth Amendment. At the heart of liberty is the right to define one's own concept of existence, of meaning, of the universe, and of the mystery of human life.[23]

The individual, with her choices, is the constituent of society and the state. Therefore, society and its government shall respect personal autonomy and ensuing core decisions, including religion. The state's position shall reflect the respect its constituent citizens have to hold for each other: individuals have to respect each other 'because they seek truth in their own way, and because [man] respects in them human nature and human dignity ...'.[24] If individual autonomy is the intrinsic value that justifies freedom of religion as a right, then religious freedom will fit into the fundamental rights structure. This would enable its coexistence with other fundamental rights, and freedom of speech in particular.[25]

[20] Jeremy Waldron, 'Locke, Toleration, and the Rationality of Persecution' in Jeremy Waldron, *Liberal Rights: Collected Papers 1981–1991* (1993), 88–114.

[21] Thomas Scanlon, 'The Difficulty of Tolerance' in David Heyd (ed), *Toleration: An Elusive Virtue* (1992), 231.

[22] *Ch J Barak in CA 105/92, Re'em Eng'g Contractors Ltd v Municipality of Upper Nazareth* 47(5) PD 189, 211. See Aharon Barak, *The Judge in a Democracy* (2006), 64.

[23] *Planned Parenthood of Southeastern Pennsylvania v Casey* 505 US 833, 851 (1992).

[24] Jacques Maritain, 'Truth and Human Fellowship' in Jacques Maritain, *On the Use of Philosophy: Three Essays* (1961), quoted in Martha Nussbaum, *Liberty of Conscience* (2008), 23.

[25] eg religious statements are protected as ('offensive') speech, without the need for a special right to proselytize.

III. What is Religion?

Reflecting a tradition of respect for individual conscience as fundamental moral autonomy,[26] in international human rights law and constitutional jurisprudence the protection of individual freedom of religion or belief extends to religious as well as non-religious convictions, including pacifism and atheism.[27] Article 18 of the Universal Declaration of Human Rights opens with the statement that 'Everyone has the right to freedom of thought, conscience and religion', a formulation which is also mirrored in Article 18 of the International Covenant on Civil and Political Rights (ICCPR).

A legal definition of 'freedom of religion' indicates the scope of protection a legal system is willing to provide to individuals and groups claiming that their religious liberty has been restricted. For instance, a definition of religion which is premised on the worship of 'God' or the 'Creator'—and which ultimately seems adequate from a Judeo-Christian or a Muslim perspective—leaves Buddhism or Taoism outside constitutional protection.[28] While an under-inclusive definition runs the risk of exposing followers of 'foreign', lesser known, or unpopular creeds to harm, or even persecution, an over-inclusive definition may open opportunities for misplacing or abusing benefits which may stem from constitutional protection.

Although religious liberty retains important collective (organizational) dimensions, these—though often complementary and reinforcing—in practice may collide with the individual dimension of the right. Prior recognition of a religious community (church) cannot become a precondition of individual free exercise of religion.[29] Courts have afforded constitutional protection to such individual manifestations of religious freedom that clearly departed from the doctrine of the religious association to which the petitioners belonged.[30] Churches do not get to determine what amounts to the proper exercise of a religion for the purposes of constitutional protection.[31]

Courts appear rather reluctant to craft general, abstract definitions of what amounts to religion, for fear of reaching an under-inclusive decision that leaves individual liberty without constitutional protection, and also because of genuine deference. As Chief Justice Latham for the High Court of Australia stated in *Adelaide Company of Jehovah's Witnesses, Inc v The Commonwealth*: 'It is not for a court, upon some *a priori* basis, to disqualify certain beliefs as incapable of being religious in character.'[32]

[26] For the contrary position that religious freedom is a collective right which is meant to secure the liberty of a community of believers see eg Julian Rivers, 'Religious Liberty as a Collective Right' in Richard O'Dair and Andrew Lewis (eds), *Law and Religion* (2001), 227.

[27] While noting the importance of the constitutional protection to non-religious convictions, this chapter will concentrate on protection afforded to religious beliefs.

[28] *Torcaso v Watkins* 367 US 488 (1961).

[29] See ECtHR, *Masaev v Moldova*, App no 6303/05; Judgment of 12 May 2009, para 26:

> The State may set requirements for... but cannot sanction through such requirements the individual members of an unregistered religious denomination for praying or otherwise manifesting their religious beliefs.

[30] eg Germany: *Blood transfusion case*, 32 BVerfGE 98, 106 (1971) and the *Decision on halal slaughter*, 1 BvR 1783/99 (January 15, 2002); Canada: *Syndicat Northcrest v Amselem* [2004] 2 SCR 551; also note ECtHR: *Cha'are Chalom ve Tsedek v France*, App no 27417/95, Judgment of 30 March 1999.

[31] See eg *Syndicat Northcrest v Anselem*, para 46.

[32] *Adelaide Company of Jehovah's Witnesses, Inc v The Commonwealth* (1943) 67 CLR 116, para 6. See further the ECtHR requiring that protected convictions 'attain a certain level of cogency, seriousness, cohesion and importance' (*Campbell and Cosans v United Kingdom*, App nos 7511/76 and 7743/76, Judgment of 25 February 1982, para 36).

Courts cannot become arbiters of religious teachings and truth in this process, nor can they pass judgment on the legitimacy, value, or utility of religious teachings for the state or society. Thus, courts tend not to assess the contents of religious doctrine and teachings, but appear to focus on the *function* that a particular belief has in the individual's self-perception. As the US Supreme Court found, the judicial task is 'to decide whether the beliefs professed by (an applicant) are sincerely held and whether they are, in his own scheme of things, religious.'[33] While this approach respects individual autonomy, its application admittedly might become problematic when courts are requested to assess the extent to which a religiously neutral law burdens an individual's religious beliefs or sentiments, especially in contexts (like prisons) where special treatment or benefits are sought in the name of religious liberty.

Freedom of religion is typically defined in constitutional provisions as an *individual right* and not as an entitlement of churches or members of the clergy. While not all communities of believers aspire to formal legal recognition, lack of legal status, or the formal refusal thereof, however, is likely to undermine the success of individual claims in the future, especially where a state grants special legal status to (some) religious organizations.[34] As the European Court of Human Rights (ECtHR) reiterated in *Metropolitan Church of Bessarabia v Moldova*,[35] the Court cannot accept tolerance towards religious organizations 'as a substitute for recognition, since recognition alone is capable of conferring rights on those concerned'.[36]

There is no international or constitutional obligation on any state to provide recognition to those religious communities which are seen as legitimate churches elsewhere.[37] Religious or cultural tension, and ensuing threats, might prompt states to maintain 'sect observatories' or even to disband religious groups which are seen as a threat to public security or public order. It becomes a matter of special concern, though, when such governmental vigilance appears to single out particular religious communities, and when religious teachings themselves become the ground for government disapproval irrespective of the conduct of believers,[38] or when governmental communication creates a climate of suspicion or intolerance towards certain religious communities.[39]

IV. What is Protected as Religious Freedom?

Classic constitutions did not contain details on the scope of constitutional protection. Being one of the briefest among them, the First Amendment of the US Constitution prohibits Congress to pass a law 'respecting an establishment of religion, or prohibiting the free exercise thereof'. Such short clauses leave the task of defining the scope of religious freedom to future

[33] *United States v Seeger* 380 US 163, 185, as reaffirmed in *Welsh v United States* 398 US 333, 339 (1970).

[34] Despite similarities in constitutional language, which use the non-specific term 'religion', national legal systems differ greatly as far as on what ground, how, and for what purposes (eg tax exemption) they provide legal recognition to religious practices and beliefs, and even more so when it comes to the recognition of religious groups as organizations (churches).

[35] ECtHR, *Bessarabia v Moldova*, App no 45701/99, Judgment of 13 December 2001, para 129.

[36] The Pakistani Supreme Court denied the Ahmedi being Muslims, notwithstanding the fact that they do follow practices mandated by Islam. Such qualification resulted in their persecution as apostates. *Zaheerudin v State* 26 SCMR 1718 (SCt 1993) (Pakistan).

[37] The example of Scientology (which is accepted as a religious organization in the United States, but not in Germany) stands as an illustration.

[38] See the ECtHR in *Förderkreis v Germany*, App no 58911/00, Judgment of 6 November 2008.

[39] UN Commission on Human Rights, 'Civil and Political Rights, including the Question of Religious Intolerance', Report of the Special Rapporteur on freedom of religion or belief, Asma Jahangir, 9 January 2006, E/CN.4/2006/5.

legislation and court decisions. Modern liberal constitutions generally follow the more detailed formulation of the Universal Declaration.

Although there is no universally accepted formulation on freedom of religion, nor on its acceptable limitations, the prohibition of coercion in matters of conscience has remained a paramount concern.[40] Freedom of religion (as a form of freedom of conscience) includes freedom *from* religion, which includes the right not to practice any religion and not to live according to the precepts of a given religion. This problem emerges, for example, in countries where one can marry, divorce, or be buried only according to specific religious laws administered by religious authorities. Freedom from religion is also at the heart of claims seeking exemptions from religious oaths for public office, and mandatory religious education in public schools.

While being mindful of grave national differences, Arcot Krishnaswami explained in 1960 that 'Freedom to maintain or to change religion or belief falls primarily within the domain of the inner faith and conscience of an individual. Viewed from this angle, one would assume that any intervention from outside is not only illegitimate but impossible.'[41] In contrast, whenever the external display (manifestation) of such deeply held beliefs falls outside the absolute of the internal core, religious freedom may well be subjected to limitations as prescribed by international instruments and national constitutions. This divide is best traceable in the language of Article 9(2) of the ECHR providing expressly that

> Freedom to manifest one's religion or beliefs shall be subject only to such limitations as are prescribed by law and are necessary in a democratic society in the interests of public safety, for the protection of public order, health or morals, or the protection of the rights and freedoms of others.

As the ECtHR reiterates: 'Article 9 . . . does not protect every act motivated or influenced by a religion or belief'.[42] It remains the duty of courts to determine permissible interference with manifestations of religious liberty. However, the core of free exercise remains the unhindered worship, non-persecution, and non-discrimination of believers in public life on grounds of their religion or belief.

Manifestations of religious freedom include not only such commonly recognizable acts of worship as individual or group prayer, religious services at designated places of worship, burial rituals, or pilgrimages to holy places.[43] Problems typically arise when a religious minority seeks to exercise practices in its own way that is distinct from the majority culture (like Hindus and Sikhs scattering ashes in rivers in Canada, or using open-air pyres to burn the dead instead of crematoriums in the United Kingdom[44]). Other minority religious practices are not immune

[40] Article 18(2) of the ICCPR: 'No one shall be subject to coercion which would impair his freedom to have or to adopt a religion or belief of his choice'.

[41] Study of discrimination in the matter of religious rights and practices, by Arcot Krishnaswami, Special Rapporteur of the Sub-Commission on Prevention of Discrimination and Protection of Minorities, 'Study of Discrimination in the Matter of Religious Rights and Practices', 1960, available at <http://www2.ohchr.org/english/issues/religion/docs/Krishnaswami_1960.pdf>.

[42] ECtHR, *Refah Partisi (The Welfare Party) and Others v Turkey*, App nos 41340/98, 41342/98, 41343/98 and 41344/98, Judgment of 13 February 2003, para 92.

[43] The right of parents to have their children educated in line with the dictates of their conscience or religious belief is usually formulated as a separate right. See Art 13(3) of the International Covenant on Economic, Social and Cultural Rights (ICESCR) on religious education complementing Art 18 of the ICCPR, also Art 2 of Protocol No 1 to the European Convention complementing Art 9 on freedom of religion.

[44] *R (Ghai) v Newcastle upon Tyne City Council (Ramgharia Gurdwara, Hitchin and others intervening)* [2010] EWCA Civ 59; [2010] WLR (D) 36.

to limitations when the majority understands them as being without any spiritual significance and thus falling under the scope of general secular rules. While Sunday may be a secular day of rest in many parts of the world, believers of certain religions may be required to refrain from work on other days of the week. Many religions retain dietary strictures ranging from designated periods of fasting to requirements of slaughter, preparation, or eating extending to all meals. Religious requirements on clothing and general appearance which are applicable not only for members of a clergy but also for ordinary believers are also a source of manifestation of religious beliefs.

Minority, new, or unknown religions are always at risk of being denied protection for what laws and courts are not prepared or not able to recognize as religious practice. Such bans often reflect majority prejudice and border on persecution. As the US Supreme Court per Justice Kennedy explained in *Church of Lukumi Babalu Aye v City of Hialeah*,[45] in the context of an animal cruelty rule which—in reality—targeted a specific religious animal sacrifice: 'The neutrality of a law is suspect if First Amendment freedoms are curtailed to prevent isolated collateral harms not themselves prohibited by direct regulation.'[46] The lack of neutrality indicates discrimination.

Freedom to change one's religion (apostasy), an inherent core aspect of freedom of conscience which is mentioned expressly in Article 18 of the Universal Declaration as well as in Article 9 of the European Convention is curiously missing from the ICCPR,[47] perhaps because apostasy remains a most serious crime in parts of the world. Articles 26 and 27 of the Arab Charter on Human Rights (not yet in force) do not mention the right to change one's religion.

Change of religion is closely related to proselytism. The term, while it is often used in a pejorative sense, refers to an invitation to convert to a belief, often by confessing one's own religious convictions, which includes the duty to teach others about one's religion.[48] It is argued that certain 'local' religions are vulnerable, and therefore proselytism by financially strong missionary groups is a form of cultural imperialism or unfairness in the competition of ideas.[49] Hostility towards proselytizing is best explained once the significance of the state or dominant religion in (re)shaping national identity is acknowledged.[50] In *Kokkinakis v Greece*, the ECtHR accepted that 'improper proselytism' may be prohibited in national law to the extent it is incompatible with respect of individual religious freedom.[51] However, the Court held that

> freedom to manifest one's religion... includes in principle the right to try to convince one's neighbour, for example through 'teaching', failing which, moreover, 'freedom to change [one's] religion or belief'... would be likely to remain a dead letter.[52]

[45] *Church of Lukumi Babalu Aye v City of Hialeah* 508 US 520 (1993).

[46] Ibid 539.

[47] For the drafting history see Bahiyyah Tahzib, *Freedom of Religion of Belief, Ensuring Effective International Legal Protection* (1995), 84ff.

[48] A prohibition on proselytism was inserted into several constitutions, among which the Greek Constitution (Art 13(2)), dating back to 1844, is probably the best known in Europe. Free speech clauses prohibiting compulsion to express or denounce a conviction (eg Russian Constitution, Art 29(3); Romanian Constitution, Art 29(1)) may also be seen as indirect prohibitions on proselytism.

[49] Abdullahi Ahmed An-Na'im, *Islam and the Secular State. Negotiating the Future of Shari'a* (2008), 237.

[50] Paul M. Taylor, *Freedom of Religion. UN and European Human Rights Law and Practice* (2005), 65.

[51] ECtHR, *Kokkinakis v Greece*, App no 14307/88, Judgment of 25 May 1993, paras 48–9.

[52] Ibid para 31.

V. Accommodation

The classic right of freedom of religion meant that no *specific* prohibitions be imposed on particular religious practices and no restrictions be applicable to believers of a specific faith; that is, religion was understood as a freedom. Note, however, that manifestations of religious beliefs may easily run counter to the prescriptions of generally applicable legal rules even when not targeted by mal-intentioned statutory prohibitions. When freedom of religion is understood as a principle in constitutional regimes, it commands a principled position that does not prevent the emergence of restrictive practices especially when it comes to minority and non-traditional religions and beliefs.

Contemporary constitutional debate in liberal democracies concerns mostly the level to which religion-dictated behavior must be exempted (accommodated) from generally applicable rules in everyday life. In this logic, individual manifestations do not call for invalidating an otherwise legitimate regulatory measure altogether, but may be respected by allowing an individualized exception for the believers adversely affected by the measure.[53] Claims for accommodation arise in many aspects of everyday life including food, dress, alcohol, bodily integrity (see genital interventions), days of rest, workplace safety, and even in a broader context, in claims to organize the religious community's life separate from the rest of society.[54] The counter-argument is that such recognition would provide special benefits on grounds of religious beliefs. But for the person who is forced to disregard her fundamental belief, the disadvantage might be a greater burden and hence a more serious injustice than the unfairness that the 'less privileged' have to endure because of her privileged treatment.

The extent to which legislation is constitutionally required to afford accommodation to religiously-dictated personal life choices, especially to grant (some kind of) religiously motivated regulatory and jurisdictional autonomy to religious communities,[55] is highly debated. The state interest in preserving the uniform application and enforcement of legal rules across the land is closely associated with the more fundamental claim to sovereignty, thus, accommodation of religiously motivated behavior comes at a potentially high price, endangering the cohesion of a political community under a single constitution.

The clash between sovereignty, concerns of equality, and generality (neutrality) of laws, on the one hand, and individual rights, on the other hand, is well illustrated in the US Supreme Court's decision in *Employment Division v Smith*[56] concerning the constitutionality of a state unemployment law which deprived known drug offenders (among them religiously inspired users of a hallucinogenic substance, peyote, used in Native American ceremonies) from social welfare benefits. Justice Scalia writing for the majority—and departing in a way from previously established precedent—expressed the view that

> To make an individual's obligation to obey such a law contingent upon the law's coincidence with his religious beliefs, except where the State's interest is 'compelling'—permitting him, by virtue of his beliefs, 'to become a law unto himself',—contradicts both constitutional tradition and common sense.[57]

[53] Where the lack of accommodation amounts to a 'substantive burden' on the religious liberty to follow one's religion, the matter is generally framed as one of free exercise. *Sherbert v Verner* 374 US 98 (1963).

[54] Should a secular practice that is offensive to a religion in a community (outside the living quarters of believers) be permitted or banned? Should the same offensive practice be permitted in the neighborhood of the believers? See *MK Marina Solodkin v Beit Shemesh Municipality* Supreme Court of Israel HCJ 953/01 (2003).

[55] See András Sajó, 'Preliminaries to the Concept of Constitional Secularism' (2008) 6 *International Journal of Constitutional Law* 494ff.

[56] *Employment Division, Department of Human Resources of Oregon v Smith* 494 US 872 (1990).

[57] Ibid 885.

This, of course, does not preclude the constitutionality of legislative exceptions that allow the individual to follow his beliefs in public life. Exempting facially neutral general laws from demanding judicial scrutiny is problematic as legislative sentiment against particular religious groups can easily be masked in general, seemingly neutral, statutory language.

When in response Congress restored the compelling interest test in the Religious Freedom Restoration Act,[58] a unanimous US Supreme Court applied the compelling interest standard and accepted a faith-based exemption from federal drug laws to another hallucinogenic substance (hoasca) used by a small religious group.[59] On this occasion, the Court noted that the governmental interest in the uniform application of federal drug laws does not justify the limitation of religious freedom, partly because the government itself had already agreed to grant similar exemptions for otherwise banned hallucinogenic substances used for Native American religious ceremonies.

Among the most dramatic exemptions granted by governments to religious believers are various exemptions offered to conscientious objectors to military service. Here, individual religious freedom is balanced against national security considerations, translated into constitutional obligations of the citizen to defend the country.[60] Although several national constitutions (eg the German Basic Law) provide some protection to conscientious objectors, conscientious objection is typically not mentioned expressly as a protected manifestation in the religion clauses in international instruments. Lacking a clear international obligation to this effect, the emerging international trend nonetheless provides access to alternative service for conscientious objectors.[61]

In first decade of the twenty-first century, the debate on the scope of accommodation has been dominated by controversies on the display of religious symbols and clothing, especially but not solely of the Islamic veil.[62] The intensity of the conflict between majority values and a religious minority has more to do with the extent of apparent divergence from a wide range of majority values than with the religious nature of the requirement per se, and courts are not in agreement on the factors which are decisive in such cases.

In 2001, the ECtHR found that in a neutral state it was acceptable to ban the Islamic headscarf of a primary school teacher.[63] In the *Dahlab* decision, the ECtHR noted that in the context of primary school education

[58] In *City of Boerne v Flores* 521 US 507 (1997), the Supreme Court held that the powers of Congress to 'promote' freedom of religion by demanding a compelling state interest test is limited to federal legislation.

[59] *Gonzales v O Centro Espirita Beneficente União do Vegetal* 544 US 973 (2005).

[60] See further in Renáta Uitz, *Freedom of Religion in European Constitutional and International Case-Law* (2007), 66–84.

[61] Human Rights Committee, Communications Nos 1321/2004 and 1322/2004: Republic of Korea, January 23, 2007, CCPR/C/88/D/1321-1322/2004:

> As the Human Rights Committee stressed recently 'it is in principle possible, and in practice common, to conceive alternatives to compulsory military service that do not erode the basis of the principle of universal conscription but render equivalent social good and make equivalent demands on the individual, eliminating unfair disparities between those engaged in compulsory military service and those in alternative service.

See also ECtHR, *Bayatyan v Armenia*, App no 23459/03, Judgment of 7 July 2011 (Grand Chamber), para 109, finding that conscientious objection to military service comes solely within the protection of freedom of religion under Art 9.

[62] For decisons involving the display of the crucifix in the classroom, see eg Germany, *Classroom Crucifix case* BVerfGE 93, 1, see also ECtHR, *Lautsi v Italy*, App no 30814/06, Judgment of 18 March 2011 (Grand Chamber). See also Chapter 62 on Islam and the constitutional order.

[63] ECtHR, *Dahlab v Switzerland*, App no 42393/98, Decision of 15 February 2001, inadmissible.

> it cannot be denied outright that the wearing of a headscarf might have some kind of proselytising effect, seeing that it appears to be imposed on women by a precept which is laid down in the Koran and which, as the [Swiss] Federal Court noted, is hard to square with the principle of gender equality.[64]

Subsequently, in 2005, the ECtHR agreed with the Turkish Constitutional Court on how a Turkish law banning headscarves from university premises was acceptable in a religiously diverse, secular state, as 'it may be necessary to place restrictions on freedom to manifest one's religion or belief in order to reconcile the interests of the various groups and ensure that everyone's beliefs are respected.'[65] Since then, the ECtHR has found several times that public safety and national security justifications permit the enforcement of legal rules demanding the temporary removal of religious garb, for example for airport security checks or ID photos. In all the above cases, the courts accepted the choice of the legislature. This seems to imply that accommodation remains a matter of sovereign choice, unless it becomes discriminatory, although in the judicial balancing process the extent of the impact of central religious beliefs[66] plays a role in the context of third party impacts (eg indoctrination, competing interpretations on the meaning and messages transmitted by these symbols etc).[67]

Discrimination, and even the feeling of being discriminated against, may push courts to enforce accommodation against the will of legislation, as illustrated by the Canadian Supreme Court when it paid more attention to a symbol's religious nature in a case involving a ban on sharp objects in public schools which also applied to the Sikh ritual dagger (kirpan).[68] The justices found that a 'total prohibition against wearing a kirpan to school undermines the value of this religious symbol and sends students the message that some religious practices do not merit the same protection as others.'[69] In addition, the Court also noted that as a result of the ban the petitioner decided to leave the public school system, thus the ban interfered not only with his religious freedom but also impaired his right to attend public school.[70]

It remains to be seen whether the arguments made by courts in the education setting, and premised on constitutional requirements of secularity or neutrality, will need to be reassessed in light of legislative attempts to ban religious clothing in public in general. The ECtHR itself was seen to apply a different approach to the criminal prohibition of religious garments in public.[71] Yet, in its decision on the law prohibiting the concealment of faces in public (known more popularly as the burqa ban), the French Constitutional Council accepted Parliament's argument that women wearing a burqa in public 'are placed in a situation of exclusion and inferiority patently incompatible with constitutional principles of liberty and equality', and approved the law as a proportionate restriction on individual rights in the name of public order.[72]

[64] Ibid para 1.

[65] ECtHR, *Leyla Sahin v Turkey*, App no 44774/98, Judgment of 10 November 2005, para 106.

[66] In the *Eweida* case a stewardess was not allowed to wear a cross. The High Court found it important that, contrary to other situations (eg Sikhs in armed forces), the religion did not require the wearing of the symbol. (After Ms Eweida left British Airways, the airline changed its policy.) *Eweida v British Airways plc* [2010] EWCA Civ 80; [2010] WLR (D) 37 currently pending before the ECtHR as *Eweida and Chaplin*, App nos 48420/10 and 59842/10.

[67] A similar approach is traceable in the headscarf decision of the German Federal Constitutional Court (the *Ludin* case, BVerfGE 108, 282 (2003)).

[68] *Multani v Commission scolaire Marguerite-Bourgeoys* [2006] 1 SCR 256.

[69] Ibid para 79.

[70] Ibid para 40.

[71] ECtHR, *Ahmet Arslan and others v Turkey*, App no 41135/98, Judgment of 23 February 2010.

[72] Decision no 2010-613 DC of October 7, 2010.

While accommodation reflects a positive enforcement of freedom of religion, it may remain a matter of concern for religious minorities, especially where only majority practices are accommodated or where the neutral law enforces majority practices and beliefs. Blasphemy laws are a particularly potent instrument,[73] as they operate in a selective fashion and only protect a preferred God or creed, but do not work across religions.[74] In particularly severe cases, blasphemy prohibitions may be used to persecute minority religious groups openly as happened with a minority Muslim sect, the Ahmadis, in Pakistan. Thus, in addition to being a curious instrument for limiting freedom of expression, blasphemy rules also highlight a profound equality problem associated with the protection of religious freedom. Repeated—and largely failed—attempts on the international scene to reinvigorate protection against 'defamation of religion' in order to protect the dignity of religions and to combat intolerance towards certain religions[75] call on us to reinforce the precept that religious freedom protects the believer and not a particular church or belief.

Admittedly, many instances of denial of accommodation and of simple manifestation of religion could also have been addressed as matters of direct or indirect discrimination.[76] The choice between an equality-based or a rights-based approach is often strategic, and does not always follow from deeper, theoretical considerations concerning the essence of religious freedom. A jewelry ban applicable in schools (which also applied to the wearing a Hindu nose stud) was challenged as a matter of indirect discrimination.[77] In this context, Justice Langa of the South African Constitutional Court said that 'religious and cultural practices are protected because they are central to human identity and hence to human dignity which is in turn central to equality.'[78]

VI. Models of Church–State Relations

The actual relations between the state and religious organizations (hereinafter Church–State relations) are of direct relevance for freedom of religion and for the constitutional organization of the state itself, with far-reaching consequences for public life. The progression of Church–State relations is best understood in terms of secularization, meaning the churches' loss of public power and secular resources (eg nationalization of church property, demise of educational monopolies etc).[79] It would be wrong to assume that modernization necessarily

[73] Although the concept of blasphemy is elusive, prohibitions of blasphemy are meant to foreclose any expression of disrespect, hostility, or irreverence towards God or sacred, religious organizations, ceremonies, or personnel. Such prohibitions were originally meant to protect not only God but also the established religion; today these laws protect religious sensitivities (see Robert Post, 'Cultural Heterogeneity and the Law: Pornography, Blasphemy and the First Amendment' (1988) 76 *California Law Review* 297).

[74] In the United Kingdom, the prohibition of Salman Rushdie's novel, *The Satanic Verses*, for blasphemous libel was sought unsuccessfully because the book affected the Prophet who is not covered by the blasphemous libel rule. *R v Chief Metropolitan Stipendiary Magistrate, ex p Chaudhry* [1991] 1 All ER 306. The blasphemy law was repealed in 2008 by the Criminal Justice and Immigration Act.

[75] For one of the successes see the non-binding Resolution 7/19 of the UN Human Rights Council on combating defamation of religions, passed on the proposal of Pakistan, on March 27, 2008.

[76] See *Multani v Commission scolaire Marguerite-Bourgeoys* (n 68).

[77] The challenge was brought under the Promotion of Equality and Prevention of Unfair Discrimination Act 4 of 2000. *MEC for Education: Kwazulu-Natal and Others v Pillay* (CCT 51/06) [2007] ZACC 21.

[78] Ibid para 62.

[79] In terms of ideological power, secularization implies disenchantment of the world (*die Entzauberung der Welt*) and the diminishing intensity of religious beliefs. Max Weber, *The Protestant Ethic and the Spirit of Capitalism* (Talcott Parsons trans, 1958), 104. The above also entails lesser participation in religious services and the growing number of non-believers, where people increasingly follow their own choices in everyday life, including in matters of morals.

leads to the permanent decline of religion: 'religious traditions throughout the world are refusing to accept the marginal and privatized role which theories of modernity as well as theories of secularization had reserved for them.'[80]

Historically and logically, models of Church–State relations range from the total control of the state by the Church (theocracy) to the total prohibition of religion and, therefore, of churches (militant atheist communism). The state may dominate the state church, or it may establish public law relations of cooperation (concordats), or consider churches private actors. Indeed, many models of Church–State relations remain compatible with constitutionalism because in a secularized world churches have lost public power and therefore the conflicts with the state diminish. The current intensification of religious beliefs contributes to renewed public aspirations of religious organizations and increases demand of autonomy for religious communities organized within the church.

The principles governing Church–State relations are often spelled out in constitutions. The text of the constitution, however, is not decisive when it comes to provisions concerning the (former) state religion or state church(es).[81] The specific 'national' religion and its church may receive special constitutional recognition in view of the role the Church played to sustain national identity in the absence of a nation-state (see eg Poland). In other instances, the constitution consolidates the status quo, which often amounts to the recognition of historical privileges.[82]

The actual relations depend on—among others—the intensity of faith, the capacity of religious organizations to control the faith, and the power of the state to provide social services and control social organizations, as well as actual political needs of the political powers to be. Throughout its history, the Catholic (universal) Church was in competition with the state (royal power) and claimed supremacy.[83] Islam, as state religion, was mostly subordinated to the state in the sense that the emperor as Caliph, at least in principle, was the supreme religious authority. A privileged constitutional position might be related to specific theological positions, as in the case of Eastern Orthodoxy which holds that 'symphony' shall prevail in the relation of the Orthodox Church to the state (see further the doctrine of the Church of England). Moreover, specific religious traditions of the majority church get characterized as cultural traditions and customs and thus become part of the legal system.[84]

Notwithstanding secularization, some constitutional democracies have reserved the privileged public law status of a state religion in their historical constitution. For example, in England the monarch is the head of the state church and Norway has a state church. The

[80] José Casanova, *Public Religions in the Modern World* (1994), 5.

[81] The Greek Constitution allows for the exercise of 'all known religions' in Art 13(2) which shall be read in light of its Art 3(1) providing that the 'prevailing religion in Greece is that of the Eastern Orthodox Church of Christ'. The Italian Constitution also singled out the Catholic faith, but gradually the Constitutional Court and legislation extended the treatment granted to the Catholic Church to other religious communities.

eg in addition to safeguarding individual religious freedom in its Art 28, the Russian Constitution proclaims in its Art 14(1) that 'The Russian Federation is a secular state. No religion may be established as a state or obligatory one'. The Constitution is silent about the Russian Orthodox Church, which however retains special relations with the government that have an impact on other religious communities.

[82] eg in Germany the collection of church taxes is enforced through state tax agencies.

[83] With the emergence of the modern state, even where Catholicism remained the state religion the state claimed sovereign power and legitimacy for itself irrespective of the power of Rome (see Gallicism in France.)

[84] Sunday observance laws are perhaps the best known example, causing difficulties and a sense of inequality for Jews, Muslims, and other Sabbatarians, in countries where they are in the minority.

special constitutional status of a church/national religion may remain symbolic and countered by practical measures of state neutrality and equality of religions and believers, but where a church or denomination is constitutionally recognized as the nation's faith this may have potential discriminatory consequences in holding public office or in civil equality.[85]

The formal legal status of the religious organization does not rule out a relation based on mutual respect. In this concept, exemplified by German constitutional doctrine, the state's constitutional duty is benevolent non-interference in church affairs which goes beyond neutral respect of autonomy. It enables, and even requires, a positive attitude of the state to promote freedom of religion in a dialogue with churches. However, positive cooperation does not entail that the state has to endorse religion in public administrative activities.

The French-type laïcité and the US idea of non-endorsement and non-entanglement are often described as the alternative of the cooperation model. In the model of laïcité, as envisioned in the 1905 French law on separation of Church and state,[86] religious organizations operate as entities recognized by private law, without the financial support of the state, and without public functions. In reality, buildings of the religious associations may be state-sponsored, and the state provides financial support to denominational (private) schools. A victim of stereotypes, French laïcité was and is sometimes labeled as anti-religious because it favors non-religious solutions in public life. But it was the Mexican Constitution of 1917 (as amended in 1934 and 1946) that showed how far-reaching separationism may go towards anti-clericalism.[87]

What should the attitude of the state be to religious organizations if it intends to sustain its own sovereignty that is based on equal citizenship and democratic decision-making? Freedom of religion flourishes where life spheres are emancipated from the control of churches and religions (typically of the hegemonic religion). The Turkish Constitutional Court offers the justification of separationism in public life: 'Within a secular state religious feelings simply cannot be associated with politics, public affairs and legislative provisions. Those are not matters to which religious requirements and thought apply.'[88] Other democracies are more permissive as to the presence of religion in the public sphere, but even here it remains contested to what extent religious grounds are acceptable in legislation. It is argued that without proper separation the state will divert the church and its tenets for its own purposes, it will not respect freedom of opinion, and state power will become factional and divisive. Thus, separation from the state 'unburdens' religion.[89]

To the extent state interference in the internal affairs of religious organizations allows the state to influence the way the dictates to the religion are followed, the state may have political interests in shaping these very dictates. It is in this regard that the state's position is subject to constitutional limits expressed in the concept of (internal) church *autonomy*. The German legal concept of autonomy entails that it is up to the churches to determine the scope of their religious mission and it entails regulatory autonomy within religious organizations.[90]

[85] On the impact of Church–State relations on individual religions freedom see Cole W. Durham, 'Perspectives on Religious Liberty: A Comparative Framework' in Johan van de Vyver and John Witte (eds), *Religious Human Rights in Global Perspective: Legal Perspectives* (1996), 1.

[86] Loi du 9 décembre 1905 concernant la séparation des Églises et de l'État.

[87] The separationist doctrine that prevailed in nineteenth-century America served as the basis for anti-Catholic (and anti-immigrant and anti-minority) bias; it served state interference in denominational education.

[88] *Refah Partisi (The Welfare Party) and Others v Turkey* (n 42), para 40.

[89] See the Virginia Statute for Religious Freedom, 1786, drafted by Jefferson in 1777, which prohibited governmental compulsion to religious worship.

[90] Article 137 (3) of the 1919 Weimar Constitution (in force) provides that 'every religious community independently regulates and administers its own affairs'.

The concept of autonomy sets limits to the applicability of general non-discrimination laws.[91] However, when the state supervises legal relations within religious organizations, this cannot be regarded per se contrary to church autonomy, *as far as these matters affect the public order*. Even where church autonomy is respected, the state may claim the right to determine the legal status of religious organizations, setting sometimes quantitative and qualitative thresholds (see also definition of religion, above) which, however, may not be so excessive as to make registration of religious organizations impracticable or impossible.[92]

While the organizational differences among states are remarkable, in principle the democratic state is supposed to keep equal distance from all religions by not taking a stand on religious matters, favoring or disfavoring a position, or a group or organization standing for such position (*neutrality*). For example, it shall not identify in its functions with religions, their symbols and practices. As the Turkish Constitutional Court has stated, the neutral state is prevented

> from manifesting a preference for a particular religion or belief and constituted the foundation of freedom of conscience and equality between citizens before the law. Intervention by the State to preserve the secular nature of the political regime had to be considered necessary in a democratic society.[93]

Does it follow from the principle of neutrality that religious organizations cannot undertake governmental functions? In such a case the public function would be identified with a religion or with religions. In practice, however, the differences are blurred because of the prevailing understanding of what constitutes public function (and the exercise of public power), a confusion that reflects historical developments. While in secular France and in cooperationist Germany marriage and civil registry are part of the state power monopoly, the strongly separationist Americans allow churches to carry out public functions in regard to marriages, probably because marriage and registration are considered private acts. Americans are keen on denying public funding to denominational schools, while this is well-established practice in France and it is constitutionalized in Germany to the extent that the absence of non-confessional schools is permissible in public education as long as the interdenominational public schools respect individual freedom of conscience.

The principle of state neutrality does not provide consistent guidance as to the proper role of religious organizations in public life and politics. Political and practical (public order) considerations may prevail here: in religiously divided societies political movements based on religion are viewed as dangerous and are sometimes constitutionally prohibited (see Bulgaria), or such restrictions are held constitutional (India). What matters for the emerging normative frames in contemporary secularized democracies is how strong the impact of religion on the mentalities

[91] See eg Council Directive 2000/78/EC of 27 November 2000 establishing a general framework for equal treatment in employment and occupation, OJ L 303, 02/12/2000, pp 0016–0022, Art 4(2):

> Member States may maintain national legislation in force... in the case of occupational activities within churches and other public or private organisations the ethos of which is based on religion or belief, a difference of treatment based on a person's religion or belief shall not constitute discrimination where, by reason of the nature of these activities or of the context in which they are carried out, a person's religion or belief constitute a genuine, legitimate and justified occupational requirement....

[92] See eg ECtHR, *Moscow Branch of the Salvation Army v Russia*, App no 72881/01, Judgment of 5 October 2006, paras 58–61; *Religionsgemeinschaft der Zeugen Jehovas and others v Austria*, App no 40825/98, Judgment of 31 July 2008.

[93] On the ban on the Welfare Party that advocated the introduction of sharia law, quoted in *Refah Partisi (The Welfare Party) and Others v Turkey* (n 42), para 25.

('soul') of individuals and their forms of social organization is, and what kind of division of labor in the provision of social services has been arranged (mostly outside public law).

It is argued that, in a democratic state, reasons justifying the law have to be accessible to all, without the privilege of religious revelation.[94] According to the religious critics, this requirement of public reason-giving disadvantages the religious citizen who cannot formulate his arguments according to his genuine beliefs. However, the requirement of public reason does not preclude the use of religious arguments in the debate leading to legislation but the law itself will remain impermissibly biased as long as it is justified by non-secular arguments only. For example, a pro-life (anti-abortion) law may satisfy the requirement of neutrality as long as it reasonably serves the protection of the health of the mother or even a population policy (as long as it does not violate rights) without reliance on divine revelation, a source of knowledge not accessible to all.

Relying on demands of free exercise and reinforced by concepts of multiculturalism and the individual's right to live a life according to the tenets of one's religion, it is argued that a plurality of religiously-inspired legal systems should be allowed to function in a multi-religious state. Many religions have a set of elaborate 'legal' rules or legal systems (see, eg the Catholic Church, Judaism, and Islam). In secular states, the religious legal regime operates as a parallel universe with its own lawmaking and enforcement mechanisms, and—as far as laymen go—it is based on voluntary compliance. The recent demands for legalizing family law arbitration based on sharia expose the fragility of the status quo and impose clear demands on the state to recognize the consequences of religious legal rules. It is possible to see such state intervention as an opportunity to assist in freeing individuals from ties which are unacceptable in a constitutional regime due to being denigrating and utterly discriminatory.[95]

At the same time, it is important to notice that in its purest form such a system would categorize everyone according to his religious beliefs and would allow him rights and freedoms not as an individual but according to his allegiance to a religious movement, perhaps with an opt-out (or opt-in) possibility. Such a system 'would oblige individuals to obey, not rules laid down by the state in the exercise of its above-mentioned functions, but static rules of law imposed by the religion concerned.'[96] The European Court of Human Rights ruled that such a system would violate human rights, 'as the State has a positive obligation to ensure that everyone within its jurisdiction enjoys in full' fundamental rights, 'and without being able to waive them'[97] and that such system is discriminatory. In broader terms:

> the secular state cannot tolerate a religiously required behavior... if the behavior contradicts the very essentials of the constitutional order. There is no obligation to sacrifice the identity of civil society to religious demands. The question of what belongs to these essentials will be answered for every society by itself.[98]

[94] Richard Rorty, 'Religion As Conversation-Stopper in Contingency, Irony, and Solidarity' in Richard Rorty, *Philosophy and Social Hope* (1999), 172ff. For the opposite position see Michael J. Perry, 'Why Political Reliance on Religiously Grounded Morality Is Not Illegitimate in a Liberal Democracy' (2001) 36 *Wake Forest Law Review* 217.

[95] From a historical perspective it is ironic that many claims are made in family law, as in Europe it was a major achievement of the Reformation successfully to challenge Church authority over marriage and replace it with the jurisdiction of the secular sovereign (state). John Witte, *Law and Protestantism* (2002), 199–232.

[96] *Refah Partisi (The Welfare Party) and Others v Turkey* (n 42), para 119.

[97] Ibid.

[98] Dieter Grimm, 'Conflicts Between General Laws and Religious Norms' (2009) 30 *Cardozo Law Review* 2369, 2380.

BIBLIOGRAPHY

Abdullahi Ahmed An-Na'im, *Islam and the Secular State. Negotiating the Future of Shari'a* (2008)

Aharon Barak, *The Judge in a Democracy* (2006)

Jean Bauberot, *La laïcité à l'épreuve. Religions et libertés dans le monde* (collective work under the direction of Jean Baubérot), *Encyclopædia Universalis* (2004)

Pierre Bayle, *Philosophical Commentary* (1708)

Ernst-Wolfgang Böckenförde, *Recht, Staat, Freiheit. Studien zur Rechtsphilosophie und Verfassungsgeschichte* (2006)

Ernst-Wolfgang Böckenförde, 'Wie können die Religionen friedlich und frei beisammen leben? Über den säkularen Staat, seine Neutralität und die Probleme, mit denen er im 21. Jahrhundert konfrontiert ist' (23 June 2007) *Neue Züricher Zeitung* 143

José Casanova, *Public Religions in the Modern World* (1994)

Cole W. Durham, 'Perspectives on Religious Liberty: A Comparative Framework' in Johan van de Vyver and John Witte (eds), *Religious Human Rights in Global Perspective: Legal Perspectives* (1996)

Émile Durkheim, *The Elementary Forms of the Religious Life* (Joseph Ward Swain trans, 1915)

Kent Greenawalt, *Religion and the Constitution* (2008)

Dieter Grimm, 'Conflicts Between General Laws and Religious Norms' (2009) 30 *Cardozo Law Review* 2369

Jürgen Habermas and Joseph Ratzinger, *The Dialectics of Secularization* (2005)

Laurence R. Iannaccone, 'Economics of Religion Introduction to the Economics of Religion' (1998) 36 *Journal of Economic Literature* 1465

Arcot Krishnaswami, Special Rapporteur of the Sub-Commission on Prevention of Discrimination and Protection of Minorities, 'Study of Discrimination in the Matter of Religious Rights and Practices', 1960, available at <http://www2.ohchr.org/english/issues/religion/docs/Krishnaswami_1960.pdf>

John Locke, *Letter Concerning Toleration* (James Tully ed, 1983)

Matthias Mahlmann, 'Freedom and Faith: Foundations of Freedom of Religion' (2009) 30 *Cardozo Law Review* 2473

Jacques Maritain, 'Truth and Human Fellowship' in Jacques Maritain, *On the Use of Philosophy: Three Essays* (1961)

Michael W. McConnell, 'The Origins and Historical Understanding of Free Exercise of Religion' (1990) 103 *Harvard Law Review* 1409

Martha Nussbaum, *Liberty of Conscience* (2008)

Michael J. Perry, 'Why Political Reliance on Religiously Grounded Morality Is Not Illegitimate in a Liberal Democracy' (2001) 36 *Wake Forest Law Review* 217

Robert Post, 'Cultural Heterogeneity and the Law: Pornography, Blasphemy and the First Amendment' (1988) 76 *California Law Review* 297

Julian Rivers, 'Religious Liberty as a Collective Right' in Richard O'Dair and Andrew Lewis (eds), *Law and Religion* (2001)

Richard Rorty, 'Religion As Conversation-Stopper in Contingency, Irony, and Solidarity' in Richard Rorty, *Philosophy and Social Hope* (1999)

András Sajó, 'Preliminaries to the Concept of Constitional Secularism' (2008) 6 *International Journal of Constitutional Law* 494

Thomas Scanlon, 'The Difficulty of Tolerance' in David Heyd (ed), *Toleration: An Elusive Virtue* (1992)

Bahiyyah Tahzib, *Freedom of Religion of Belief, Ensuring Effective International Legal Protection* (1995)
Paul M. Taylor, *Freedom of Religion. UN and European Human Rights Law and Practice* (2005)
Renáta Uitz, *Freedom of Religion in European Constitutional and International Case-Law* (2007)
UN Commission on Human Rights, 'Civil and Political Rights, including the Question of Religious Intolerance', Report of the Special Rapporteur on freedom of religion or belief, Asma Jahangir, January 9, 2006, E/CN.4/2006/5
Voltaire, Letters on England (1980)
Jeremy Waldron, 'Locke, Toleration, and the Rationality of Persecution' in Jeremy Waldron, *Liberal Rights: Collected Papers 1981–1991* (1993), 88ff
Max Weber, *The Protestant Ethic and the Spirit of Capitalism* (Talcott Parsons trans, 1958)
Roger Williams, *The Bloody Tenent of Persecution for Cause of Conscience* (1644)
John Witte, *Law and Protestantism* (2002)

CHAPTER 44

DUE PROCESS

RICHARD VOGLER

Sussex

THE apparent simplicity of the idea of due process, with its 'precise technical import',[1] conceals a much-contested reality. Although the phrase conveys a powerful ideological message of commitment to the rule of law, its exact meaning tends to disintegrate under cross-examination. For example, can a mere procedure—any procedure—be protective of human rights in all contexts? And where is the unexplained theory of procedure which lies behind the assertion that certain forms may be considered 'due' and others not? To many, the phrase 'due process' carries with it coded suggestions about the superiority of Western or specifically Anglo-American jurisprudence, and indeed the North American reading of due process is very different and very much more complex, than that which it is given in the rest of the world.

A major part of the difficulty of assessing due process is the chameleon-like nature of the concept; its so-called 'blessed versatility'.[2] Williams suggests no less than eight completely different understandings of due process in the US context alone.[3] Perhaps the best way of considering this diversity is to imagine the idea as multi-layered, not only in philosophical and jurisprudential terms but also in its historical and geographical dimensions. A detailed exposition of the highly nuanced range of meanings within US jurisprudence is clearly beyond the scope of this review. However, it will be helpful to begin this account with a brief examination

[1] Alexander Hamilton, 'Remarks on an Act for Regulating Elections, New York Assembly, 6 February 1787' in Harold Syrett (ed), *The Papers of Alexander Hamilton*, vol 4 (1961), 35.

[2] Felix Frankfurter, *The New Republic*, 27 April 1932.

[3] Ryan Williams, 'The (One and Only) Substantive Due Process Clause' (2010) 120 *Yale Law Journal* 408, 419 ff.

of the constitutional origins of due process and some of the ways in which it has been understood, interpreted, and mobilized as a concept in its common law homelands. This is particularly important given the Anglo-American role in shaping contemporary understandings of the concept around the world and, above all, in developing its association with adversarial justice. The main discussion will address the issue of procedural due process as it is understood globally in light of instruments such as the International Covenant on Civil and Political Rights (ICCPR) and the European Convention for the Protection of Human Rights and Fundamental Freedoms (ECHR). Finally, the contribution of the international courts and agencies in promoting adversarial due process around the world will be evaluated. The focus throughout will be on due process in criminal proceedings.

I. The Troubled History of the Constitutional Due Process Clause

The constitutional history of due process is one of successive reinventions. The main point of departure, for common lawyers at least, is the celebrated Clause 39 of Magna Carta of 1215, to the effect that

> No freeman shall be arrested or imprisoned or disseised or outlawed or exiled or in any other way harmed. Nor will we [the king] proceed against him, or send others to do so, except according to the lawful sentence of his peers and according to the Common Law [*per legem terrae*].

The specific early medieval reading of this text, which actually concerned immunities for feudal magnates, fails signally as McIlwain put it, to 'guarantee anything to all Englishmen'.[4] It bears almost no relation to the first incarnation of the wording 'due process of law' in a 1354 Statute of Edward III,[5] which was nevertheless creatively bracketed with Magna Carta in paragraphs (iii) and (iv) of the Petition of Right in 1628. Sir Edward Coke perpetuated this reading by claiming that the concept of due process was the 'true sense and exposition' of the original 1215 wording '*per legem terrae*'.[6] The reinvention of Magna Carta in the seventeenth century and its use in the revolutionary struggles of the English Civil War is well known. However, 'due process of law' appears in no English statute other than the above and only incidentally in the work of Hawkins and Blackstone.[7] Its historical importance is largely retrospective and an invention of nineteenth- and twentieth-century myth-makers[8] such as the distinguished American jurists Kent, Story, and Cooley and the legal historian Mott, who claimed that 'In the great constitutional crises involving life, liberty, and property, it was the concept of "due process of law" which took hold of men's minds most mightily.'[9] On the contrary, its might is predominantly modern and predominantly North American.

[4] C.H. McIlwain, 'Due Process of Law in Magna Carta' (1914) 14 *Columbia Law Review* 27, 51.

[5] 28 Edw III, c 3.

[6] Edward Coke, *Institutes of the Laws of England (Part Two)* (1671), 50.

[7] See Keith Jurow, 'Untimely Thoughts: A Reconsideration of the Origins of Due Process of Law' (1975) 19 *American Journal of Legal History* 265.

[8] Jane Rutherford, 'The Myth of Due Process' (1992) 72 *Boston University Law Review* 1.

[9] Rodney Mott, *Due Process of Law: A Historical and Analytical Treatise of the Principles and Methods Followed by the Courts in the Application of the Concept of the 'Law of the Land'* (1926), 71.

None of the pre-revolutionary American states enacted 'due process' clauses in their charters, preferring the 'law of the land' formulation derived directly from Magna Carta.[10] The decisive change came with the decision by James Madison to import the terminology of due process into the Fifth Amendment to the US Constitution, which was adopted in 1791. Although the implications of the wording were not debated at the time—it being assumed that the right which was enacted related uncontroversially to criminal process[11]—nevertheless the consequences for US, and subsequently global, jurisprudence are hard to overestimate. One of the major complications with the interpretation of due process in the US context is that, by the second half of the nineteenth century, the doctrine seems to have been broadened, for purely domestic reasons, to include what is referred to as 'substantive due process'. In other words, a clause which was intended to require a legitimate procedural basis for actions involving the deprivation of life, liberty, and property, could be construed as a wider statement of substantive right against government. Successive waves of reformers, particularly Temperance and Abolitionist activists, therefore saw the 'due process' clause in the Bill of Rights, interpreted in this light, as a convenient weapon. At the time of the American Civil War, slave-owners argued that the 'substantive' interpretation of the due process clause protected their ownership of slaves, whereas abolitionists responded with the Lockean argument that slaves should not be deprived of the fruits of their labour without 'due process of law'.[12] These arguments were resolved to some extent by the outcome of the Civil War and the enactment of the Fourteenth Amendment, containing a due process clause identical to that of the Fifth Amendment. Since then, argument has continued, both in academic writing and in the courts, as to whether the two clauses represented two different concepts of due process, one procedural and one substantive.[13]

Not surprisingly, in view of these complications, the constitutional career of the 'due process clause' appears to have begun and ended with the United States. It does not, for example, appear—possibly because it is untranslatable into French—in the 1789 Declaration of the Rights of Man, which requires merely that arrest and imprisonment should be 'according to the forms prescribed by law'.[14] Only countries which expressly modelled their constitutions on US precedents, such as Liberia[15] or Puerto Rico,[16] were prepared to insert the words 'due process of law'. Even Japan, which developed its constitutional provisions in 1946 under the direct tutelage of the US occupying forces, deliberately diluted the wording and omitted the word 'property' in Article 31, leaving only a requirement that 'No person shall be deprived of life or liberty…except according to procedure established by law'. Scepticism towards due process clauses was also demonstrated by constitutional drafting bodies throughout the common law area. Attempts in the UK Parliament to insert such a clause within the Government of Ireland Bill in 1893 soon foundered on the grounds that 'Nobody seemed to understand what…[the words "due process of law"] really meant' and the view that the provision operated badly in the United States.[17] Similar proposals for the Australian Federal Constitution of

[10] Williams (n 3), 435ff. [11] Ibid 445ff.

[12] Charles Miller, 'The Forest of Due Process Law' in Roland Pennock and John Chapman (eds), *Due Process* (1977), 14ff; Williams (n 3), 470ff.

[13] Williams (n 3), 500ff.

[14] Article 7.

[15] Article 20.

[16] Section 7.

[17] Wallace Mendelson, 'Foreign Reactions to American Experience with Due Process of Law' (1955) 41 *Virginia Law Review* 493, 494.

1898,[18] the Government of India Act 1935,[19] and the Indian Constitution of 1946,[20] were rejected for the same reasons. Canada and Israel dispensed with the idea entirely whereas Pakistan, in common with many Commonwealth countries, merely referred to 'in accordance with law'.[21]

Difficulties with due process clauses were also encountered during the drafting of international human rights conventions. Article 3 of the 1948 Universal Declaration of Human Rights (UDHR), for example, enacts only the right to 'life liberty and security of Person'. The original draft of this extraordinarily influential document, known familiarly as the 'global Magna Carta', had contained the reservation 'except in cases prescribed by law and after due process'. However, Dr F.R. Bienenfeld, speaking for the World Jewish Congress, objected that many of the Nazi crimes against the Jewish people had been carried out in accordance with the so-called 'law' of the Third Reich and after a process which was apparently lawful at the time within that jurisdiction. The due process clause was consequently deleted from the final text.[22] The clauses which deal with the practicalities of due process in criminal procedure are also somewhat limited and are confined to the freedom from 'arbitrary arrest, detention or exile' (Art 9), the entitlement 'in full equality to a fair and public hearing by an independent and impartial tribunal' (Art 10), the presumption of innocence and rights of defence (Art 11(1)).

In just the same way, the ECHR, enacted two years later and drafted largely by English common lawyers, has no due process clause but nevertheless set out for the first time some extensive procedural due process provisions in relation to arrest and detention (Art 5) and criminal procedure (Art 6). Article 5(1) of the ECHR repeats verbatim the UDHR right to liberty and security of the person and sets out six circumstances, including 'the lawful arrest or detention of a person . . . on reasonable suspicion of having committed an offence' in which the right may be defeated in accordance with 'a procedure prescribed by law'. The process provisions here include notification of rights and the reason for arrest (Art 5(2)), prompt production before a judge (Art 5(3)), the right to test the lawfulness of the detention in court (Art 5(4)), and the right to compensation for wrongful arrest or detention (Art 5(5)). Fair trial provisions under Article 6 are even more extensive and add to the UDHR provisions the right to full notification of the accusation (Art 6(3)(1)), time and opportunity for the preparation of defence (Art 6(3)(2)), defence in person or through counsel (Art 6(3)(3)), to examine witnesses (Art 6(3)(4)), and interpretation rights (Art 6(3)(5)).

The ICCPR, which finally entered into force in March 1976, was even more explicit regarding due process rights. However, it similarly omits any specific reference to 'due process' itself, preferring to prohibit 'arbitrary arrest and detention' in Article 9(1) and insisting that 'No one shall be deprived of his liberty except on such grounds and in accordance with such procedure as are established by law'. As before, 'due process' wording was rejected in the drafting process, this time on the basis of a proposal by the United States.[23] The ICCPR reproduces in its Article 9, almost verbatim, the arrest and detention provisions which are set out at Article 5 of the ECHR, without specifying the exceptions. Article 14 of the ICCPR, which deals with due process in criminal procedure, again uses substantially the same wording as the ECHR but adds rights to a speedy trial (Art 14(3)(c)) and presence at trial and free legal assistance (Art 14(3)(d)), the right not to self-incriminate (Art 14(3)(g)), special provisions for juveniles (Art 14(4)), appeal (Art 14(5)), compensation for wrongful conviction (Art 14(6), and a restriction on double jeopardy (Art 14(7)).

[18] Ibid 493ff. [19] Ibid 500. [20] Ibid 497.

[21] Constitution of the Islamic Republic of Pakistan, Art 4(2)(a).

[22] Johannes Morsink, *The Universal Declaration of Human Rights: Origins, Drafting, and Intent* (2000), 39, 50.

[23] Mendelson (n 17), 499.

There are no due process clauses in the American Convention on Human Rights which was adopted in 1969 and which repeats, largely verbatim, the procedural provisions outlined above[24] nor in the Banjul African Charter on Human and Peoples' Rights which was approved in 1981, with rather more concise procedural requirements in Articles 6 and 7. The 1998 Rome Statute of the International Criminal Court makes no mention of due process nor does the 2000 Charter of Fundamental Rights of the European Union which sets out a range of criminal justice due process provisions in Articles 47 to 51. In continental Europe the wording 'due process of law' simply does not bear the same cultural significance which it does in the common law world. The terminology is only rarely used by the European Court of Human Rights (ECtHR), except in reference to discussions of US case law,[25] and the leading account of human rights in criminal proceedings by Stefan Trechsel[26] does not refer at any length to the idea of due process.

However, constitutional abstention with regard to the terminology of 'due process of law' does not mean that the concept itself has not been influential in many regions, particularly in the post-war period and particularly under the influence of US-led 'rule of law' initiatives such as the Western-hemisphere focused, 'Due Process of Law Foundation'.[27] For example, the availability of a workable Spanish translation (*debido processo*) and US influence in Latin America has helped to ensure that the due process is widely debated and endorsed in Hispanic literature.[28] Before looking at this wider international approach however, it may be helpful to consider the way in which the concept has been interpreted as a mode of analysis in the Anglo-American tradition.

II. Concepts of Due Process

Debates over procedural methodology have used a wide variety of terminologies, many of which overlap with due process. The literature in this area is immense and ranges from socio-legal concepts such as Weber's 'formal legal rationality', to positivist accounts of law's 'rules of adjudication', which in Hart's view, enable authoritative determinations to be made as to whether a primary rule has been broken.[29] However, a number of authors, particularly those writing in the United States have developed due process itself as a theoretical construct.

The most well-known understanding of the concept of due process is that it represents a sense of 'justice' in its broadest terms. According to Justice Frankfurter, speaking at the height of the Cold War:

> 'due process,' unlike some legal rules, is not a technical conception with a fixed content unrelated to time, place and circumstances. Expressing as it does in its ultimate analysis respect enforced by law for that feeling of just treatment which has been evolved through centuries of Anglo-American constitutional history and civilization, 'due process' cannot be imprisoned within the treacherous limits of any formula. Representing a profound attitude of fairness

[24] Article 7 (right to freedom), Art 8 (right to a fair trial).

[25] See eg ECtHR, *Jalloh v Germany*, App no 54810/00, 11 July 2006, para 49.

[26] Stefan Trechsel, *Human Rights in Criminal Proceedings* (2005). Nor is there mention in Jeremy McBride, *Human Rights and Criminal Procedure. The Case Law of the European Court of Human Rights* (2009). On the European Court of Human Rights more generally, see Chapter 59.

[27] See <http://www.dplf.org/index.php?lID=12>. See further Chapter 10 on rule of law.

[28] See eg Alvarado Velloso and Oscar Zorzoli, *El Debido Proceso* (2006).

[29] Herbert Hart, *The Concept of Law* (1994), 96.

> between man and man, and more particularly between the individual and government, 'due process' is compounded of history, reason, the past course of decisions, and stout confidence in the strength of the democratic faith which we profess.[30]

This approach elides some of the most intractable contradictions within the concept, as if notions of formal legal rationality and popular 'fairness' could be compounded together by the alchemy of due process.

Other authors have been more circumspect. John Rawls characterized due process as an essential element in his theory of Justice. If the rule of law is necessary for liberty, then a legal system must contain rules of evidence that guarantee rational procedures of inquiry. Therefore 'the rule of law requires some form of due process: that is, a process reasonably designed to ascertain the truth, in ways consistent with the other ends of the legal system, as to whether a violation has taken place and under what circumstances.'[31] Rawls distinguishes between perfect procedural justice, which always produces the right factual outcome (eg guilt or innocence) and imperfect procedural justice, which does not. As he points out: 'Even though the law is carefully followed, and the proceedings fairly and properly conducted, it may reach the wrong outcome'.[32] This represents one of the most perplexing aspects of due process theory and one which has been long debated by Legal Realists such as Frank, who was troubled by the 'constitutionally correct' procedure but 'egregiously unfair' outcome of the Sacco-Vanzetti trial.[33] It has also caused great difficulties for tribunals, such as the ECtHR which have tried to enforce Convention due process standards without acting as a 'court of fourth instance'. In a bold dissenting judgment in the case of *Göktan v France*,[34] Judge Loucaides dared to challenge the long-standing principle that the ECtHR was concerned only with process rights and not outcomes:

> I believe that the right to a fair hearing/trial is not confined to procedural safeguards but extends also to the judicial determination itself of the case. Indeed, it would have been absurd for the Convention to secure proper procedures for the determination of a right or a criminal charge and at the same time leave the litigant or the accused unprotected as far as the result of such a determination is concerned. Such approach would allow a fair procedure to end up in an arbitrary or evidently unjustified result.[35]

In short, as with all methodologies concerned with due process alone, a legitimate procedure may nevertheless produce an illegitimate outcome.

By far the most influential account of due process in criminal procedure over the past few decades has been that provided by Herbert Packer in his 1968 *Limits of the Penal Sanction*.[36] More cited than actually read,[37] Packer's work appears as an orthodoxy in most Anglo-American criminal justice textbooks and even the most radical and progressive of commentators seem to have found his approach indispensible. His influence pervades, for example, the 1999 United Nations Global Report on Crime and Justice[38] and a succession of influential government reports in both the United States and England.[39] Contemporary analyses of

[30] *Joint Anti-Fascist Refugee Committee v McGrath* 341 US 123 (1951).
[31] John Rawls, *A Theory of Justice* (2003), 210.
[32] Ibid 75.
[33] Jerome Frank, *Courts on Trial: Myth and Reality in American Justice* (1973), 88.
[34] ECtHR, App no 33402/96, 2 July 2002.
[35] Ibid, Partly Dissenting Opinion of Judge Loucaides.
[36] Herbert Packer, *The Limits of the Criminal Sanction* (1968).
[37] Paul Rock, 'Chronocentrism and British Criminology' (2005) 56 *British Journal of Sociology* 473ff n 17.
[38] Graeme Newman, *Global Report on Crime and Justice*. (1999), 71ff.
[39] See eg 1981 Royal Commission on Criminal Procedure in England.

international criminal law[40] and mutual legal assistance treaties,[41] as well as sentencing practices,[42] government attempts to inspire confidence in criminal justice,[43] and 'populist leniency'[44] have all been based upon Packer's theoretical approach to due process.

Briefly, Packer presents two ideal types of criminal justice process; two normative models[45] which he hopes will help to explain the choices which underlie the details of criminal justice practice. The two alternative models are the 'crime control model' (CCM) and the 'due process model' (DPM). According to Packer, the CCM 'requires that primary attention be paid to the managerial efficiency with which the criminal process operates to screen suspects, determine guilt and secure appropriate dispositions of persons convicted of crimes.'[46] The complete freedom of action of the investigators, enabling them to establish an accurate prediction of guilt or innocence, is essential. Indeed, the model requires a rigorous initial screening process so that subsequent stages can be significantly abbreviated. Above all, the process must not be 'cluttered up with ceremonial rituals which do not advance the progress of a case'.[47] Although he does not mention it—and indeed has been repeatedly criticized for his failure to look beyond US procedure[48]—the model which he describes is remarkably close to Napoleonic criminal procedure.

If the crime control model resembles an 'assembly line' continues Packer, 'the due process model looks very much like an obstacle course'.[49] This model erects procedural barriers and is based upon a presumption of fallibility and error and a distrust of informal fact-finding methods. It is a system of quality control in which the reliability of the product takes precedence over the efficiency with which it is produced.[50]

Although Packer does not say as much, these models have generally been interpreted as constituent elements of a zero-sum game in which advances in due process will entail retreats in crime control and vice versa in 'almost infinite modulation and compromise'.[51] As Dubber puts it:

> In 1968, when Packer set up the contrast between these two models—ostensibly for analytic purposes—the Crime Control Model was seen as gaining ground on the Due Process Model. Packer's book reads like a last stand against a creeping erosion of the time-honored principles of the Due Process Model, which he apparently regarded as preceding the Crime Control Model, though he never set out a detailed historical sequence of principles gained and lost.[52]

[40] Colin Warbrick, 'International Criminal Courts and Fair Trial' (1998) 3 *Journal of Conflict and Security Law* 45.

[41] L. Song Richardson, 'Due Process for the Global Crime Age: A Proposal' (2008) 41 *Cornell International Law Journal* 347.

[42] Ralph Henham, 'Human Rights, Due Process and Sentencing' (1998) 38 *British Journal of Criminology* 592.

[43] Daniel Gilling, 'Crime Control and Due Process in Confidence-Building Strategies: A Governmentality Perspective' (2010) 50 *British Journal of Criminology* 1136.

[44] Richard Jones, 'Populist Leniency, Crime Control and Due Process' (2010) 14 *Theoretical Criminology* 331.

[45] Packer (n 36), 153.

[46] Ibid 158.

[47] Ibid 159.

[48] John Griffith, 'Ideology in Criminal Procedure or a Third "Model" of the Criminal Process' (1970) 79 *Yale Law Journal* 359, 360.

[49] Packer (n 36), 163.

[50] Ibid 165.

[51] Ibid 153.

[52] Markus Dubber, 'The Possession Paradigm: The Special Part and the Police Model of the Criminal Process' in R.A. Duff and S. Green (ed), *Defining Crimes: Essays on the Special Part of the Criminal Law* (2005), 91.

Dubber may be wrong in suggesting that Packer's intentions were purely analytical since he suggests firmly that his aim was normative.[53] Indeed, the enduring appeal of his formulation indicates how successfully he has been able to give expression to the aspirations of those involved in criminal justice and to the fundamental conflicts between the professional interests of the police and the prosecution and those of the lawyers and judges.

There are three well-known problems with Packer's formulation. The first is that, put simply, crime control is patently an *objective* whereas due process is a *method*. In no sense can they be considered as polar opposites or 'antinomies' and to do so is to give unwarranted priority to the model which promises results over the model which merely describes a procedure. So, far from being value-neutral, the terms of the argument are loaded from the outset. There is also an unexplored assumption in Packer's terminology that 'efficiency' in apprehension and conviction will necessarily result in crime control. It may well be, on the contrary, that the ruthless efficiency of the CCM may alienate sufficient sections of the population to make crime control more difficult. A consensual DPM approach to justice might actually be more effective in restricting levels of offending and, as Roach has pointed out, 'due process is for crime control'.[54] Roach, further attacks Packer for his failure to perceive the 'empirical irrelevancy' of his models, to the extent that 'the due process model begins to look like a thin, shiny veneer that dresses up the ugly reality of crime control.'[55] Finally, the whole idea that due process rights can be sacrificed in the interests of 'balance' with another objective, has long been regarded with scepticism.[56]

Subsequent scholarship has sought to address the somewhat restricted scope of Packer's vision by adding further models. Griffith was the first and most notable 'remodeller', objecting that 'the essential nature of [the] problem is such as to permit only two polar responses'.[57] Rehabilitation and, more importantly for Griffith, conciliation, are left entirely out of account in this conflict model of criminal justice. Griffith is therefore moved to offer a third model which he describes as a non-conflictual 'family model'.[58] Griffith's intervention opened the floodgates to a succession of remodellers amongst whom the prize for sustained invention must be given to Davis, Croall, and Taylor who consider a grand total of seven models to be absolutely indispensible to a full understanding of criminal justice process.[59]

Strangely enough, considering the pervasive international extent of his influence over many years, his work is determinedly ahistorical, strictly confined to the United States and is unsupported by much in the way of empirical evidence. Nevertheless, as I have indicated above, determined attempts have been made by scholars to analyse international and comparative criminal justice through the lens of Packer's formulation and these accounts to some extent reveal its limitations. Using data from the United Nations Surveys on Crime Trends and the Operations of Criminal Justice Systems, Sung attempted in 2006 to identify the eight dependent variables (incarceration rate, police contact rate etc) which in his view define the difference between due process and crime control approaches. 'Authoritarianism' in criminal justice

[53] Packer (n 36), 153.

[54] Kent Roach, 'Four Models of the Criminal Process' (1999) 89 *Journal of Criminal Law and Criminology* 671, 688.

[55] Ibid 688ff.

[56] Andrew Ashworth, 'Crime, Community and Creeping Consequentialism' (1996) *Criminal Law Review* 220; Henham (n 42), 593ff.

[57] Griffith (n 48), 369.

[58] Ibid 373.

[59] Malcolm Davies, Hazel Croall, and Jane Tyrer, *Criminal Justice: An Introduction to the Criminal Justice System in England and Wales* (1998), 25.

could thus be compared with levels of democracy as defined by the Freedom House register.[60] Due process, on the other hand, is strongly associated with liberal democracy and is characterized by a personnel structure involving a small police force, prosecutorial staff, and prison service combined with low arrest rates, prosecution rates, conviction rates, and incarceration rates.[61] Despite the rather questionable nature of these attributions, the methodology, and the very short time frame (a maximum of six years for some countries), Sung purports to find that an 'evolution from an authoritarian criminal justice system to a democratic [eg due process] one is cumulative but not inevitable'.[62]

Packer's main achievement was to popularize the view that due process cannot be seen in isolation from other factors in criminal justice. His due process model is based upon the supposition that efficiency is dispensable when it conflicts with reliability or, as he puts it: 'If efficiency demands short cuts around reliability, then absolute efficiency must be rejected'.[63] But can such a process be considered 'fair' or 'due' where the protection of the accused's interests take such a clear priority over those of the state in a rapid, accurate, and efficient factual determination? Surely a more comprehensive idea of due process, while rejecting the zero-sum game approach referred to above, demands an equitable balance between these interests and those of the community as a whole? This is not at all apparent from the various constitutional 'due process' provisions described above, which are concerned exclusively with the rights of accused persons. The rights of the victims of crime,[64] the rights of the community, and the rights of the state are conspicuous by their absence from such legislation. A broader concept of due process would extend well beyond this narrow assertion of defence rights and instead encapsulate a procedure which sought a fair balance between legitimate conflicting interests in criminal justice. Of course it can be objected that the defendant alone faces threats to life and liberty in criminal procedure and the systematic abuse of the rights of accused individuals is so much more extensive and dangerous than threats to the community and state, that the lopsided character of due process provisions is entirely justified. Nevertheless, as a means of analysis and as a basis for progressive reform, this exclusive focus on due process as understood in the Packer sense, has its limitations.

I have suggested elsewhere that, based on the three Weberian paradigms of *Gemeinschaft* (or the organic-familial), *Gesellschaft* (or the contractual commercial-individualistic), and the bureaucratic-administrative responsibilities of the state, criminal process can be best understood as a forum in which inevitable conflicts between these fundamental interests may be debated and resolved.[65] In practice, these three social interests (community, individual, and state) are represented by the three great historical methodologies of, respectively, popular, adversarial, and inquisitorial justice, all of which have left significant residues in every contemporary system of criminal justice. In describing the long historical evolution of each of these methodologies and their complex interaction, I have argued that each has a crucial role to play in a legitimate system of criminal justice. Indeed, in principle, 'due process' might just as well refer to popular, jury-determined justice and inquisitorial, judge-determined justice as to party-driven adversariality. However, the global dominance of totalitarian and colonial

[60] Hung-En Sung, 'Democracy and Criminal Justice in Cross-National Perspective: From Crime Control to Due Process' (2006) 605 *The Annals of the American Academy of Political and Social Science* 311.

[61] Ibid 316.

[62] Ibid 329.

[63] Packer (n 36), 165.

[64] Mykola Sorochinsky, 'Reconciling Due Process and Victims' Rights: Towards a Power Balance Model of Criminal Process in International Human Rights Law' (2009) 31 *Michigan Journal of International Law* 1.

[65] See Richard Vogler, *A World View of Criminal Justice* (2005).

forms of government for much of the twentieth century has bequeathed to us a considerable 'adversarial deficit', which I have suggested has distorted criminal justice in most regions. The traditional Anglo-American association of due process with adversarial process has coincided with this deficit to ensure that most contemporary debates are centred on the restoration of due process adversariality rather than otherwise. Demands for more 'inquisitorial' efficiency and rationality in criminal justice, for example, are not currently conducted using the terminology of due process. For this reason it is necessary to consider recent global developments in due process, not in its broader sense outlined above but, as conceived by Packer and others, in association with adversarial justice.

III. The Rise and Fall of Adversarial Due Process in England and the United States

The connection between the concepts of due process and adversariality has always been close. Both were eighteenth-century reinventions of ancient doctrines—in the case of due process, the feudal obligations of Magna Carta and in the case of adversariality, the medieval notion of trial by accusatorial contest. Both were founded in Enlightenment ideas of individual autonomy, described by John Locke as:

> a state of perfect freedom to order their actions, and dispose of their possessions and persons as they think fit, within the bounds of the law of nature, without asking leave, or depending upon the will of any other man.

Disposition by the 'arbitrary will of another'[66] was therefore unacceptable. Two fundamental aspects of adversarial due process emerged from this approach. The first was the publicity of the criminal trial. Beccaria had attacked secrecy in Book XV of his 1764 *Dei Delitti et della Pene* as an 'impenetrable shield of tyranny' and demanded that 'All trials should be public'. At a more profound level, theorists of the English Enlightenment contributed to the disconnection of the criminal trial from its existing dependence upon the rational investigation of a single, testable reality. Both Newton and Locke were deeply hostile to the Cartesian emphasis on the search for absolute truth through logic and mathematics, which had proved so influential in the development of continental *Inquistionsprozess*.[67] Instead of proceeding on the basis of a priori reasoning, they insisted on the use of empirical methods for establishing various degrees of probability. Shapiro and others have shown how John Locke's concept of proof 'to the highest degree of probability' became imbedded in notions of 'beyond reasonable doubt' and the deeply contingent epistemology of adversariality.[68] Galileoan and Cartesian postulates were also specifically rejected by Hale and Gilbert, the authors of the new English concept of evidence law, which has been described as a common law 'science of probabilities'.[69]

This probabilistic world of empirical proof provided the intellectual environment in which adversarial due process, based on competing empirical projects and the protection of individual rights, could flourish. But it was not the great juridical authors of the period who first created the adversarial due process revolution. It was the Lockean common lawyers, working in the Old Bailey and the Courts of Assize in England during a relatively short period between

[66] John Locke, *Two Treatises of Government*, vol 2 (1963), 17.

[67] See Vogler (n 65), 45ff.

[68] Barbara Shapiro, *'Beyond Reasonable Doubt' and 'Probable Cause': Historical Perspectives on the Anglo-American Law of Evidence* (1991), 196.

[69] Lynn Hunt, *Inventing Human Rights. A History* (2007), 81.

1730 and 1770. On the basis of the painstaking research carried out by (amongst others) Cockburn, Langbein, Landsman, Beattie, May, and Hostettler, it is possible to observe with some focus, the arrival of lawyers for the first time in these criminal courts and the impact which they had upon practice. I have pointed out elsewhere[70] that it is no coincidence that the first sightings of due process adversariality and a rights-based trial process occurred in England at this period. The doctrine, in many ways, was inspired by the market, was pioneered by the men who represented the new capitalists, and was imbued with the ideologies of the Industrial Revolution.[71] Earlier developments, such as Habeas Corpus, the Bill of Rights of 1688, or the Treason Trials Act 1696, although prefiguring the birth of criminal process rights, were largely concerned with the interests of the Whig elites. The new adversarial criminal trial, by contrast, extended such rights to all. Indeed, the proposition that the Crown in a criminal prosecution was an adversary on equal terms with the humblest subject was startling and far-reaching in its application. What is more, the same common lawyers who achieved this practical transformation from deference to active debate, went on to elevate the doctrine to a full-blown political ideology in the revolutionary creeds of the late eighteenth century. It was to provide the empirical basis for the great universal codes of the US Constitution and Bill of Rights and the French Declaration of the Rights of Man referred to above and to transform the relations between the individual and the state in a way which would lead eventually to a political and legal culture based primarily on rights.

What was created in this period, by the patient and repeated arguments of the trial lawyers, was the concept of a criminal defendant who was not the passive object of an official inquiry but an active subject and participant in the process. The criminal trial was for the first time divided into two phases, the first dominated by the prosecution, the second by the defence. Moreover, the whole procedure was now ordered by an array of process rights and presumptions which were all aimed at protecting the defendant from the disproportionate power of the state. The rights, developed at this period, included the right to a fair trial in public, the presumption of innocence,[72] the right of silence, the evidential protections against hearsay and bad character testimony, and the burden of proof on the prosecution. All such protections were guaranteed by the presence of a highly partisan defence counsel.

This empowerment of the defence had two closely linked aspects. The first was the protection of the defendant from torture or physical abuse practised by an aggressive, fact-finding state authority[73] and the second was the provision of procedural weapons which could be used for an active defence. All these advances were obtained through the medium of law and it is this notion of legality, protecting the active, rights-bearing defendant, which is at the heart of the adversarial concept. However, the darker side of adversarial due process, its amorality and its rejection of the Cartesian commitment to scientific truth, has soured its legacy. As an ideology it is confined to the interests of the individual, and suffers from all the vices of the market economy which gave it birth. The outcomes of criminal justice are determined largely by the ability of an individual defendant to afford counsel and to construct an energetic defence. A trial therefore becomes a beauty contest between lawyers and the plea bargain, a morally neutral accommodation in which there is little difference between buyer and seller. Unchecked

[70] Vogler (n 65), 131ff.

[71] The reasons for the transition have been widely debated. See Vogler (n 65), 140ff.

[72] François Quintard-Morenas, 'The Presumption of Innocence in the French and Anglo-American Legal Traditions' (2010) 58 *American Journal of Comparative Law* 107.

[73] Of course, such protection can never in practice be absolute as some commentators have endeavoured to suggest. See Paul Roberts, 'Comparative Criminal Justice Goes Global' (2008) 28 *Oxford Journal of Legal Studies* 369, 380.

adversariality provides the spectacle of the well-resourced defendant, such as O.J. Simpson or Slobodan Milošević, manipulating their due process rights protections to drive the criminal process into the sand.

Adversariality, like all forms of justice, is historically conditioned and since its first appearance in the Georgian courtroom, it has passed through at least three stages of development. The first, described above, was the early period in which the English model of the trial spread rapidly throughout Europe, the British Empire, and beyond. Its adoption was amongst the first priorities of the French Revolutionary Constituent Assembly in 1789–91, largely because it was the abuses perpetrated by *ancien régime* inquisitorial justice which had provided the most potent motivation for the uprising. As Nicolas Bergasse, one of the architects of the revolutionary reform of justice put it:

> It is easy to see that no methods are talked about here except those furnished by the system of jurisprudence adopted in England and free America for the prosecution and punishment of offences...we cannot do better than adopt it without delay, ameliorating it, however, in certain details.[74]

Some years later, Napoleon's well-known antipathy towards due process protections led him to embark on a radical revision of the English model, effectively resurrecting the *ancien régime* pre-trial procedures of the 1670 *Code Louis*, stripped of their recourse to torture but preserving their secrecy, scientificity, and absolute denial of rights to the accused. The outcome was the 1808 *Code d'Instruction Criminelle*, which retained just enough due process adversariality (notably the trial in open court with the participation of counsel) to satisfy the liberal elites of post-revolutionary France, while ensuring absolute state control of the investigation process, unhindered by any exercise of adversarial rights. As Esmein eloquently puts it, as the procedure progressed:

> We pass from obscurity into the full light of day. There the procedure was secret, written and always favourable to the prosecution, not leaving to the defense even the right of confrontation; here everything is publicity, oral trial, free defense, and full discussion. In the one case, there are the traditions of the Ordinance of 1670, in the other, the principles announced by the Constituant Assembly and put into operation in the Laws of the Intermediate Period.[75]

The Napoleonic compromise remains the most enduring and popular form of criminal process in the world, not only as a result of its imposition in countries of the French Empire but also since it provided a model for newly emerging regimes in Europe, Africa, Asia, and Latin America. The code satisfied the need to demonstrate a nominal liberal commitment to rights-driven due process without abandoning authoritarian control of the pre-trial.

The progressive destruction of the adversarial model entered a yet more dark and dangerous phase following its encounter with European Positivism in the late nineteenth century when even those remnants of adversarial due process which had been preserved by Napoleon, were subjected to vigorous attack. By this period, the probabilistic Lockean justifications for adversariality were looking increasingly shaky, ensuring that it became one of the main targets for the Positivist movement, championed by the leaders of the Italian School, Enrico Ferri and Raffaele Garofalo. According to the latter in 1885, adversarial conflict reduced the position of the judge to 'the state of a dancing puppet with the two adversaries alternately pulling the strings'. Short-sighted progressives, he argued, had undermined the great scientific inquisitor-

[74] Adhémar Esmein, *A History of Continental Criminal Procedure with Special Reference to France* (1914), 408.

[75] Ibid 510.

ial tradition established by Louis XII which was based on the 'critical and impartial search for truth'.[76] This criminological orthodoxy, proclaimed by the leading international conferences of the period, led directly to the stripping away of the remaining elements of adversarial due process and the descent of criminal justice into the tyranny of the Soviet show trials or the Nazi Volksgerichthof.[77]

The impact of Positivist critiques of due process adversariality were also felt in the Western democracies. Up to the late nineteenth century, the main protection in England for an unrepresented defendant (as most were) was his or her incapacity as a witness. There was little point in torturing or abusing a defendant whose testimony was worthless as evidence. As the French observer Cottu so scornfully noted,[78] a hat on a pole would serve for the defendant in an English trial process. Police codes down to 1912 prohibited officers from questioning the defendant at all—a highly effective defence against abuse[79] and, as Fisher points out, 'Not until the second half of the nineteenth century could accused criminals anywhere in the common law world testify under oath at their own trials.'[80] Needless to say, this protective rule appeared a monstrous absurdity to the Positivist School, committed to the idea of the criminal process as a scientific method for the establishment of absolute truth. Despite a spirited defence of the incapacity provision, it was finally abolished by the Criminal Evidence Act 1898, England being one of the last common law nations to abandon the rule.

The abolition of the protective incapacity rule for defendants ushered in a second stage of adversariality. Eliminated from almost all criminal justice systems outside the countries of the former or contemporary British Empire, adversariality survived in its heartland only in an attenuated form. Miscarriages of justice against unrepresented and unprotected defendants became frequent in both the United Kingdom and the United States[81] whilst European and Soviet criminal justice stripped out the remaining elements of adversarial due process. Such provisions were seen as unscientific or, in the Soviet case, 'bourgeois' residues. The way was now clear for the descent into the nightmare of rights-free, mass-processing of defendants by totalitarian states in the interests of 'social-defence'.[82]

This was to change with end of the Second World War, when many countries outside the Soviet bloc, reverted to their former practices by reintroducing due process protections. In the United States and the United Kingdom a new form of adversariality was adopted through the mass 'lawyerization' of the pre-trial in both countries from the 1960s. The credit for this 'due process revolution' must be attributed first to the liberal activism of the US Supreme Court of the period. Although the legacy of the Warren Court is contested[83] nevertheless, a series of landmark decisions establishing basic process rights in the pre-trial, reinvigorated adversariality in the United States. These reforms were echoed in England by the Police and Criminal Evidence Act 1984 which set out a robust network of pre-trial adversarial rights

[76] Raffaele Garofalo, *Criminology* (1968), 344ff.

[77] Vogler (n 65), 61ff.

[78] Charles Cottu, *On the Administration of Criminal Justice in England and the Spirit of the English Government* (1922), 105.

[79] Vogler (n 65), 147ff.

[80] George Fisher, 'The Jury's Rise as Lie Detector' (1997) 107 *Yale Law Journal* 575, 579.

[81] Carolyn Ramsey, 'Was the Bill of Rights Irrelevant to Nineteenth-Century State Criminal Procedure?' (2009) 18 *Journal of Contemporary Legal Issues* 501.

[82] Vogler (n 65), 61ff.

[83] Yale Kamisar, 'The Warren Court and Criminal Justice: A Quarter-Century Retrospective' (1995) 31 *Tulsa Law Journal* 1; Eric Miller, 'The Warren Court's Regulatory Revolution in Criminal Procedure' (2010) 43 *Connecticut Law Review* 1.

enforced by detailed codes of practice.[84] Both of these new regimes were underpinned by the creation of a new market for legal services in each country which attracted large numbers of lawyers into criminal practice. The new found sense of confidence in adversarial due process encouraged the United States to embark on an international programme of promoting reform in criminal justice practices which has prompted the extraordinary international shift towards adversarial due process procedures discussed below. However, just as the pace of adversarial reform has gathered momentum around the world, there have been distinct signs in the adversarial heartlands that all is not well.

Deep cuts in the funding of counsel for the indigent in both the United Kingdom and the United States have combined with an expansion of plea bargaining, managerial case management,[85] and an increasingly punitive turn in charging and sentencing,[86] to inflict serious damage on the adversarial methodology. In England, recent legislation attacking defence rights, particularly for terrorist defendants looked at in conjunction with the increasing empowerment of prosecutors, has been seen as a move:

> away from adversarialism because it is costly in terms of time and of money, at a time when government wants to be tough on crime and when the trend is towards greater criminalization as a response to social problems.[87]

Following a high-profile campaign of criticism against the supposed irrationality of the adversarial method in the United States, waged by scholars such as Langbein[88] and Pizzi[89] and Thomas,[90] amongst others, there has been a perceptible loss of confidence in traditional safeguards. Reduced funding for public defender offices has encouraged plea bargaining from a position of weakness and, in the views of some participants, a progressive 'dismantling' of adversariality.[91] Others have argued that the decline in the participation of defence counsel can be compensated for by a more professional and scientifically rigorous investigation by police and prosecution, capitalizing on the supposed benefits of new technologies. Findlay describes this as the 'reliability model', a joint enterprise between prosecution and defence involving enhanced technical and professional standards.[92] According to him, adversarial adjudication is imbalanced and inadequately funded and simply 'not up to the task', whereas his 'new due process' shifts the emphasis back to an improved investigation phase.[93] Although Findlay envisages the continuing importance of defence counsel in these new procedures, others are more radical. In Brown's view:

[84] Vogler (n 65), 152ff.

[85] John Raine and Michael Willson, 'Managerialism and Beyond: the Case of Criminal Justice' (1996) 9 *International Journal of Public Sector Management* 20; John Raine and Michael Willson, 'Beyond Managerialism in Criminal Justice' (1997) 36 *Howard Journal of Criminal Justice* 80.

[86] Loïc Wacquant, *Punishing the Poor. The Neoliberal Government of Social Insecurity* (2009).

[87] Jacqueline Hodgson, 'The Future of Adversarial Criminal Justice in 21st Century Britain' (2010) 35 *North Carolina Journal of International Law and Commercial Regulation* 320, 360.

[88] John Langbein, *The Origins of Adversary Criminal Trial* (2003).

[89] William Pizzi, *Trials Without Truth: Why our System of Criminal Trials has Become an Expensive Failure and What We Need to Do to Rebuild It* (2000).

[90] George Thomas, *The Supreme Court on Trial: How the American Justice System Sacrifices Innocent Defendants* (2008).

[91] Richard Goemann, 'First You Cripple Public Defense: Musings on How Policymakers Dismantle the Adversarial System in Criminal Cases' (2008) 9 *Loyola Journal of Public Interest Law* 239.

[92] K.A. Findley, 'Toward a New Paradigm of Criminal Justice: How the Innocence Movement Merges Crime Control and Due Process' (2008) 41 *Texas Technical Law Review* 133.

[93] Ibid 174.

crime labs can replace part of the function of diminished defense counsel, and can do so in a way likely to garner more sustained political support.[94]

In exactly the same way that Jackson has recommended an 'epistemic shift' for the International Criminal Court,[95] Brown proposes a refocusing of decision-making away from the public trial to a judicialized pre-trial inquiry, with 'broad discovery' for all parties. Like Jackson, he contends that such a move inevitably results from the failures of adversariality 'to detect factual error'.[96] Neither scholar seems to be aware that these are exactly the same arguments which so fatally damaged adversariality at the beginning of the twentieth century and prepared the way for 'social defence' and the horrors of totalitarian justice. We should not make these mistakes twice within a century. To condemn adversarial due process on the basis of its failure to deliver factually accurate outcomes is profoundly to misunderstand its ideology and purpose. Of course it cannot promise the same scientific outcomes as the inquisitorial method but that is not its function, nor does it mean that its place in criminal justice is redundant.

IV. The Global Revolution in Due Process

Ironically, while adversarial due process is coming under increasing attack in the Anglo-American context, it is enjoying a contemporary renaissance elsewhere. As indicated above, attempts to insert due process clauses at a constitutional level have failed comprehensively. However, adversarial due process reforms at the level of criminal procedure codes have achieved spectacular results. Never at any period in the history of the world has the pace of due-process-driven reform across the world been so rapid or so sustained. The global campaign for due process has been waged since the Second World War by an extraordinary variety of international and regional agencies[97] backed by the hegemonic authority of the Western powers and has gathered pace significantly in recent years. First in the field and still exerting considerable influence in the promotion of due process rights, is the United Nations. States parties to the ICCPR who have also opted to ratify the First Optional Protocol[98] voluntarily accept the competence of the Human Rights Council (HRC),[99] which can hear individual petitions from persons who claim to be victims of state violation of Covenant rights. Although lacking an enforcement mechanism, the HRC has developed a considerable body of case law principles, protective of the rights of suspected and accused persons.[100]

Some regional institutions have considerably more teeth. The ECtHR has been aggressive in the development of the fair trial provisions in Article 6 of the ECHR, which represent by far

[94] Darryl Brown, 'The Decline of Defense Counsel and the Rise of Accuracy in Criminal Adjudication' (2005) 93 *California Law Review* 1585, 1643.

[95] John Jackson, 'Finding the Best Epistemic Fit for International Criminal Tribunals: Beyond the Adversarial-Inquisitorial Dichotomy' (2009) 7 *Journal of International Criminal Justice* 17.

[96] Brown (n 94), 1644.

[97] See eg the list provided by Kirsti Samuels, *Rule of Law Reform in Post-Conflict Countries: Operational Initiatives and Lessons Learnt* (2006), 25ff.

[98] First Optional Protocol to the International Covenant on Civil and Political Rights, GA Res 2200A (XXI), 21 UN GAOR Supp (No 16) at 59, UN Doc A/6316 (1966), 999 UNTS 302, entered into force 23 March 1976.

[99] Until 2006, the Human Rights Committee. See Françoise Hampson, 'An Overview of the Reform of the UN Human Rights Machinery' (2007) 7 *Human Rights Law Review* 7.

[100] Jakob Möller and Alfred de Zayas, *United Nations Human Rights Committee Caselaw 1977–2008: A Handbook* (2008).

the largest category of cases.[101] After the influx of new accession states which followed the collapse of the Soviet Union, the Court saw its caseload mushroom from under 8,400 cases in 1999 to 61,300 in 2010 and it is no exaggeration to suggest that the activities of the ECtHR have revolutionized European attitudes towards due process in criminal procedure and provided a constant and powerful emphasis on adversariality[102] and rights protection for suspected and accused persons which extends far beyond its regional mandate. The influence of the ECtHR is now truly global, its jurisprudence being cited with approval around the world[103] and even 'mirrored' by the practices of the International Criminal Court[104] and other international tribunals.

Since the 1980s, the European Union itself has also played a very significant role in promoting due process protections. The focus was intensified yet further following the Treaty of Lisbon in 2009, after which the Swedish Presidency of the European Union launched its 'Stockholm Roadmap',[105] aimed at protecting suspected and accused persons and ensuring them fair trial rights throughout the European Area of Freedom Security and Justice.[106] As a starting point, amendments were introduced to a draft law in the European Parliament[107] establishing a Europe-wide 'letter of rights' for suspected persons[108] and in July 2011 a Green Paper on the Application of EU Criminal Justice Legislation in the Field of Detention was published.

Also active in promoting due process reform in the European/Eurasian area is the Organization for Security and Co-operation in Europe, which works with the Office for Democratic Institutions and Human Rights (OSCE/ODIHR).[109] These organizations are able to apply considerable pressure on post-Soviet governments in particular, to incorporate due process provisions into their criminal procedure codes, as well as organizing regular summer schools, trial monitoring and regional Criminal Justice Forums for senior officials.[110] National governments have also taken a lead in the international promotion of due process in criminal justice. UK government agencies such as the Department for International Development and the British Council[111] and German agencies such as Deutsche Gesellschaft für Technische Zusammenarbeit (GTZ) GmbH[112] have all played important funding roles although their contributions have been dwarfed by those of the United States.

Since the end of the Cold War, rule of law initiatives undertaken by the United States have promoted a strong due process agenda[113] a change signalled by the growing ascendency of new

[101] Council of Europe, *Annual Report 2010* (2011), Rüdiger Wolfrum and Ulrike Deutsch, *The European Court of Human Rights Overwhelmed by Applications: Problems and Possible Solutions* (2009).

[102] Trechsel (n 26), 89ff.

[103] Alec Sweet and Helen Keller, *Assessing the Impact of the ECHR on National Legal Systems* (2008).

[104] Nicolas Croquet, 'The International Criminal Court and the Treatment of Defence Rights: A Mirror of the European Court of Human Rights' Jurisprudence?' (2011) 11 *Human Rights Law Review* 91.

[105] Elspeth Guild and Sergio Carrera, 'Towards the Next Phase of the EU's Area of Freedom, Security and Justice: The European Commission's Proposals for the Stockholm Programme. CEPS Policy Brief No 196' (2009) *Centre for European Policy Studies* 1.

[106] Brussels, 31 July 2009, Doc 12531/09, DROIPEN 78, COPEN 150.

[107] See <http://www.europarl.europa.eu/en/pressroom/content/20110314IPR15481/html/A-Letter-of-Rights-to-help-ensure-fair-trials-in-all-EU-countries>.

[108] Taru Spronken, *EU-Wide Letter of Rights in Criminal Proceedings: Towards Best Practice* (2010).

[109] OSCE, *Criminal-Justice Systems in the OSCE Area.Reform Challenges and ODIHR Activities* (2006).

[110] See <http://www.osce.org/odihr/69446>.

[111] See <http://www.britishcouncil.org/development-expertise-governance-human-rights-justice.htm>.

[112] See <http://www.gtz.de/en/unternehmen/1718.htm>.

[113] Allegra McLeod, 'Exporting US Criminal Justice' (2010) 29 *Yale Law and Policy Review* 83, 102.

Department of Justice agencies such as the Office of Overseas Prosecutorial Development, Assistance and Training (OPDAT), the International Law Enforcement Academies (ILEAs), and the International Criminal Investigative Training Assistance Program (ICITAP), over the traditional aid providers such as USAID. Some commentators have seen this shift as a strategic change in US foreign policy goals towards the prosecution of an international 'war on crime' aimed in part at the establishment of 'global governance' through criminal justice reform.[114]

These agencies deploy staff, usually former US Prosecutors, around the world in support of criminal procedural reform.[115] Macleod asserts that recipient states are encouraged to devote energies to US-style criminal procedure reforms above other unsubsidized development priorities by the conditionality of wider funding on the achievement of certain benchmarks.[116] Other critics have suggested that US agencies have favoured plea bargaining and adopted a 'cookie cutter' approach to reform where 'aid providers... treat each nation as unformed dough, onto which the Cookie Cutter of a Western legal system is applied.'[117] However, there is no doubt that, in collaboration with the American Bar Association (ABA) and US regional organizations such as the Central and Eastern European Law Initiative (ABA/CEELI)[118] these agencies have made a significant contribution to due process protection around the world.

All these developments have been everywhere promoted and supported by the activism of the international non-governmental organizations (NGO) community whose impact on the due process agenda in criminal justice has been considerable.[119] Despite questions about their legitimacy,[120] NGOs such as Amnesty International and Human Rights Watch clearly provide a vital mechanism for providing 'essential expertise, enhance public support for intergovernmental organizations, assistance in translating norms developed in these organizations into realities on the ground.'[121]

The outcome of this sustained pressure for due process reform over the past few decades has been dramatic. Adversarial due process reform of criminal justice has swept across Western Europe, enacting profound transformations in Spain in the 1980s, Italy in 1989, France in 2001 and 2004, before moving on to regions as diverse as China,[122] Japan,[123] South Korea,[124] and Taiwan.[125] In Latin America 80 per cent of all countries, including Guatemala,[126]

[114] Ibid 102ff. [115] Ibid 124. [116] Ibid 116.

[117] Cynthia Alkon, 'The Cookie Cutter Syndrome: Legal Reform Assistance under Post-Communist Democratization Programs' (2002) 2002 *Journal of Dispute Resolution* 327, 328.

[118] Stephen Ryan, 'Out from Under Soviet Rule-With the Help of CEELI Former Satellites Rebuild a Legal System' (1996) 11 *Criminal Justice* 11.

[119] Gerd Oberleitner, *Global Human Rights Institutions. Between Remedy and Ritual* (2007), 164ff.

[120] Steve Charnovitz, 'Nongovernmental Organizations and International Law' (2006) 100 *The American Journal of International Law* 348, 364ff.

[121] Oberleitner (n 119), 169.

[122] Peter Liu and Yingye Situ, 'Mixing Inquisitorial and Adversarial Models: Changes in Criminal Procedure in a Changing China' (2001) 53 *Contributions in Criminology and Penology* 133.

[123] Malcolm Feeley and Setsuo Miyazawa, *The Japanese Adversary System in Context: Controversies and Comparisons* (2002).

[124] Kuk Cho, 'The Unfinished "Criminal Procedure Revolution" of Post-Democratization South Korea' (2002) 30 *Denver Journal of International Law and Policy* 377.

[125] Margaret Lewis, 'Taiwan's New Adversarial System and the Overlooked Challenge of Efficiency-Driven Reforms' (2009) 49 *Virginia Journal of International Law* 651.

[126] Andrés Torres, 'From Inquisitorial to Accusatory: Colombia and Guatemala's Legal Transition', Law and Justice in the Americas Working Paper Series (2007).

Nicaragua,[127] Mexico,[128] Chile,[129] and Argentina[130] have abandoned inquisitorial for more adversarial procedures within a decade.[131] Langer has described recent changes in which 14 countries and numerous provinces produced entirely new criminal procedural codes within 15 years as 'the deepest transformation that Latin American criminal procedure has undergone in two centuries'.[132]

The fall of the Soviet Union and its East European satellite regimes after 1991 has also had a dramatic impact. In 2001 Russia enacted what has been described as the 'most progressive Criminal Procedure Code in the Newly Independent States'[133] which emphasized adversariality as a central guiding principle.[134] Lithuania in 2003,[135] Estonia in 2004,[136] Bulgaria in 2005,[137] and Georgia in 2009, for example, all attempted similar adversarial due process reform and this pattern has been repeated in most of the states of the former Soviet bloc. The international tribunals which have been developed around the world since 1993 were also deeply influenced by adversarial principles.[138] In brief, this shift towards adversarial due process in criminal procedure, which has been likened by some scholars to the reception of Roman law in the European *ius commune* period,[139] has become one of the most important and ubiquitous cultural developments of our generation.

V. Conclusion

These changes are a vivid reminder of the continuing power and importance of the idea of due process. As a constitutional precept, as an analytical concept, and finally as a principle of adversarial rights-based reform, it still exercises a powerful gravitational pull. Perhaps it is the sheer versatility of the due process idea which is an essential element of its enduring appeal. The argument here, however, has been that whilst the concept of due process has not succeeded in lodging itself internationally at the level of constitutional law, it has nevertheless achieved a remarkable global proliferation in procedural law from the late eighteenth century

[127] Richard Wilson, 'Criminal Justice in Revolutionary Nicaragua: Intimations of the Adversarial in Socialist and Civil Law Traditions' (1991) 23 *University of Miami Inter-American Law Review* 269.

[128] Carlos Rios Espinoza, 'Abandoning the Inquisitor: Latin America's Criminal Procedure Revolution: Redesigning Mexico's Criminal Procedure: The States' Turning Point' (2008) 15 *Southwestern Journal of Law and Trade in the Americas* 53.

[129] Carlos Rodrigo de la Barra Cousino, 'Adversarial vs Inquisitorial Systems: The Rule of Law and Prospects for Criminal Procedure Reform in Chile' (1998) 5 *Southwestern Journal of Law and Trade in the Americas* 323.

[130] Andrés D'Alessio, 'Argentina's Sluggish Journey Toward a Constitutional Criminal Procedure' (2008) 15 *Southwestern Journal of Law and Trade in the Americas* 31.

[131] Jonathon Hafetz, 'Views on Contemporary Issues in the Region: Pretrial Detention, Human Rights, and Judicial Reform in Latin America' (2003) 26 *Fordham International Law Journal* 1754.

[132] Máximo Langer, 'Revolution in Latin American Criminal Procedure: Diffusion of Legal Ideas from the Periphery' (2007) 55 *American Journal of Comparative Law* 617.

[133] Matthew Spence, *The Complexity of Success: The US Role in Russian Rule of Law Reform* (2006).

[134] John Diehm, 'The Introduction of Jury Trials and Adversarial Elements into the Former Soviet Union and Other Inquisitorial Countries' (2001) 11 *Journal of Transnational Law and Policy* 1.

[135] See <http://www.euro-justice.com/member_states/lithuania/country_report>.

[136] Estonian Code of Criminal Procedure 2004, Art 14(1).

[137] Gergana Marinova, 'Bulgarian Criminal Procedure: The New Philosophy and Issues of Approximation' (2006) 31 *Review of Central and East European Law* 45.

[138] Kai Ambos, 'International Criminal Procedure: "Adversarial", "Inquisitorial" or Mixed?' (2003) 31 *International Criminal Law Review* 1.

[139] Wolfgang Weigand, 'The Reception of American Law in Europe' (1991) 39 *American Journal of Comparative Law* 229.

and again, after the collapse of the earlier movement, in the period since the Second World War. Although these events have been to a large extent determined by political change, the inherently unstable history of due process suggests that the doctrine, viewed in isolation, is particularly vulnerable to attack. Analysis of due process as a separate and semi-detachable element of justice—as dictated by the priority given to it as a constitutional principle—has left it very vulnerable to critiques based on rationality and efficiency and has contributed to its catastrophic decline in the early years of the twentieth century. Exactly the same arguments have been levelled against it in recent decades, when due process adversariality has again been accused of undermining the scientific rationality of the trial process and impeding crime control. It has been proposed here that one solution may lie in a wider approach to the idea of due process. In this view, rights-based (adversarial) procedure could be seen to contribute only one element—albeit an urgent and crucial one—to an acceptable understanding of criminal justice. A broader concept might engage productively with wider debates about the tripartite relationship between adversarial rights, rational efficiency, and democratic participation in criminal justice, thereby suggesting an outline for the missing theory of 'due' process referred to above.

Bibliography

Adhémar Esmein, *A History of Continental Criminal Procedure with Special Reference to France* (1914)

John Langbein, *The Origins of Adversary Criminal Trial* (2003)

Jeremy McBride, *Human Rights and Criminal Procedure: The Case Law of the European Court of Human Rights* (2009)

C.H. McIlwain, 'Due Process of Law in Magna Carta' (1914) 14 *Columbia Law Review* 27

Allegra McLeod, 'Exporting US Criminal Justice' (2010) 29 *Yale Law and Policy Review* 83

Wallace Mendelson, 'Foreign Reactions to American Experience with Due Process of Law' (1955) 41 *Virginia Law Review* 493

Charles Miller, 'The Forest of Due Process Law' in Roland Pennock and John Chapman (eds), *Due Process* (1977)

Jakob Möller, and Alfred de Zayas, *United Nations Human Rights Committee Caselaw 1977–2008: A Handbook* (2008)

Herbert Packer, *The Limits of the Criminal Sanction* (1968)

Jane Rutherford, 'The Myth of Due Process' (1992) 72 *Boston University Law Review* 1

Stefan Trechsel, *Human Rights in Criminal Proceedings* (2005)

Richard Vogler, *A World View of Criminal Justice* (2005)

Ryan Williams, 'The (One and Only) Substantive Due Process Clause' (2010) 120 *Yale Law Journal* 408

CHAPTER 45

ASSOCIATIVE RIGHTS (THE RIGHTS TO THE FREEDOMS OF PETITION, ASSEMBLY, AND ASSOCIATION)

ULRICH K. PREUβ

Berlin

I. Introduction: Historical and Socio-Political Context

'The most natural privilege of man, next to the right of acting for himself, is that of combining his exertions with those of his fellow creatures and of acting in common with them. The right of association therefore appears to me almost as inalienable in its nature as the right of personal liberty'—arguably this statement by Alexis de Tocqueville in 'Democracy in America'[1] is the most concise depiction of the subject of this chapter. Associative rights cover those constitutional guarantees which deal with joint actions of individuals. The focus is on the constitutional implications of the fact that the coordinated action of individuals entails a new type of social activity which is qualitatively different from individual actions, even individual mass action. It is the source of power which inheres in the association of individuals as such. As Hannah Arendt observed, 'power is never the property of an individual; it belongs to a group and remains in existence only so long as the group keeps together.'[2] Hence the promise of associative rights to individuals is the most effective means of their empowerment in the polity. At the same time, this guarantee gives rise to a decentralized power structure in society which has a major bearing on the modes of how collective decisions are made in the polity.[3]

Three constitutional rights are pertinent in this respect, ranging here in the order of increasing empowerment and, consequently, structural effects on the polity: the right to petition for the redress of grievances, the right to the freedom of assembly, and the right to the freedom of association. Needless to say, in the subsequent comparative overview only those constitutions are considered which effectively shape the character of the polity, where, in other words, collective actions of citizens are an inherent element of an entrenched sphere of socio-political autonomy.

II. The Right to Petition for the Redress of Grievances

Among the fundamental rights codified in national constitutions and international covenants the right to petition generally receives minor attention. Although it has been codified in most EU member state constitutions and in the EU Charter of Fundamental Rights[4] as a distinct right, its political and associative dimension has been marginal so far. It is lacking in virtually all international human rights covenants. In the United States it has been absorbed by the freedom of expression, although it is expressly mentioned in the First Amendment alongside the freedoms of speech, the press, and assembly.[5] The obviously inferior significance of the right to petition is understandable in the light of the manifold judicial and political vehicles of which citizens dispose who live in constitutional states and want to voice individual and collective concerns, ranging from recourse to the courts through their right to democratic representation to the guarantees of free speech and of free media.

Yet there are tendencies towards a renaissance of the political and associative character of the right to petition which has a venerable history as a vehicle of political demands before the rise of the constitutional state. In its pre-modern version, it can be traced back to the Roman

[1] Alexis de Tocqueville, *Democracy in America* ([1840] 1990), vol 1, ch XII, 196.

[2] Hannah Arendt, 'On Violence' in Hannah Arendt, *Crises of the Republic* (1972), 143.

[3] Mark E. Warren, *Democracy and Association* (2001), 82ff.

[4] Articles 43, 44, distinguishing between petitions to the Ombudsman and to the European Parliament.

[5] Cf S.A. Higginson, 'A Short History of the Right to Petition Government for the Redress of Grievances' (1986) 96(1) *Yale Law Journal* 142.

Empire and, in the Anglo-Saxon constitutional history, to the eleventh century from where it advanced into a human right codified in the first modern bills of rights.[6] Originally, the right to petition served as an individual legal redress which in England since the fourteenth century evolved into a common law right of appeal. Its political dimension as a right to legislative hearing unfolded in the seventeenth century in the struggles between the Parliament and the Stuarts and became part of the Bill of Rights of 1689.[7] In the United States, the First Amendment clause stemmed from the right to petition local assemblies in colonial America, and thus had, next to a judicial function, a political dimension from the outset. In both dimensions, the right to petition implied the right to a fair hearing and consideration.[8] This revealed that 'the interests served by petitioning go to the very heart of the principle of popular sovereignty'.[9] The lack of procedural statutory rules about the enforcement of the right entailed its institutional fragility, which turned into outright collapse when petitions became an instrument of the expression of collective dissent, especially in the political struggles about the abolition of slavery in the first half of the nineteenth century.[10] The right to petition gradually developed into a version of the freedom of expression, shaking off the right to fair hearing, consideration and response.[11]

In the European context, the right to petition has preserved its original content, namely the right of a petitioner not only to voice requests, but to obtain a fair hearing and handling of her concern and an official notice.[12] The memory of its historical relationship to the principle of popular sovereignty may be indicated in those constitutions which stipulate the right not only as an individual, but expressly as a collective right as well,[13] or which designate the parliament as the main addressee of petitions.[14] Still, there are few signs, if any, that petitions to parliaments have affected their agenda in any considerable manner.[15]

On the other hand, in countries where practices of direct democracy are constitutionally prevented (like in the United States or in Germany, on the federal level respectively) the use of mass petitions may evolve as a surrogate for deficient plebiscites. Such a tendency is now facilitated by the internet which allows the collection of huge numbers of supporters for a petition within extremely short periods of time.[16] Thus, in 2005 the German Bundestag established an e-petition platform on which public petitions are published and can be co-signed by supporters.[17] Submitters of such petitions which reach more than 50,000 signatures within the first

[6] See the English Bill of Rights, 1689; First Amendment of the US Constitution, 1789; French Constitution, 1791, Title I No 3 (no mention, however, in the Declaration of the Rights of Man and of the Citizen, 1789, nor in the Constitution of 1793).

[7] Norman B. Smith, 'Shall Make No Law Abridging…: An Analysis of the Neglected, but Nearly Absolute, Right of Petition' (1986) 54 *University of Cincinnati Law Review* 1153, esp 1154ff.

[8] Higginson (n 5), 155.

[9] Smith (n 7), 196.

[10] Higginson (n 5), 158ff; Smith (n 7), 1175ff, esp 1179 n 164.

[11] *Minnesota Board for Community Colleges v Knight*, 465 US 271 (1984), 283ff; see also James E. Pfander, 'Sovereign Immunity and the Right to Petition: Toward a First Amendment Right to Pursue Judicial Claims Against the Government' (1997) 91(1) *Northwestern University Law Review* 899.

[12] F. Sebastian, M. Heselhaus, and Carsten Nowak, *Handbuch der europäischen Grundrechte* (2006), s 49, margin no 35.

[13] Germany, Art 17; Spain, Art 29.

[14] European Charter of Fundamental Rights, Art 44; Germany, Art 17; Italy, Art 50; Spain, Art 77.

[15] See eg Annual Report of the Committee on Petitions of the German Bundestag. Available, in German for 2009, at <http://www.bundestag.de/bundestag/ausschuesse17/a02/Docs/PetJahresbericht2010.pdf>.

[16] Lorenzo Mosca and Daria Santucci, 'Petitioning Online. The Role of E-Petitions in Web Campaigning' in Sigrid Baringhorst, Veronika Kneip, and Johanna Niesyto (eds), *Political Campaigning on the Web* (2009), 121ff.

[17] See <https://epetitionen.bundestag.de>.

three weeks of publication on the e-petition platform are heard in person by the Committee on Petitions. The most successful e-petition in Germany reached a total of 134,015 co-signatures within four days. The parliaments in Great Britain, Scotland, South Korea, and of Queensland Australia use this instrument as well.[18]

III. The Right to the Freedom of Assembly

1. Historical Background and Present-Day Constitutional Foundations

The historical origins of the freedom of assembly date back to eighteenth-century England and North America where the first meetings were held for the public deliberation and debate of petitions to the parliaments. Article XVI of the Constitution of Pennsylvania of 1776, the first constitutional codification of the freedom of assembly, exhibits this inherently political character of this right and its relationship to the principle of popular sovereignty: 'That the people have a right to assemble together, to consult for their common good, to instruct their representatives, and to apply to the legislature for redress of grievances, by address, petition, or remonstrance.' The wording of the First Amendment of the US Constitution resonates this context by connecting the freedoms of expression, of assembly, and of petition.[19] However, in the current legal and political discourse of the United States the freedom of assembly has experienced the same fate as the right to petition, namely to be ignored as a distinct right and to be absorbed by the freedom of expression.[20]

The first constitutional codification of the freedom of peaceful assembly on the European continent occurred in the French Constitution of 1791. It was subject to extensive police regulations,[21] a condition which moulded the restrictive French tradition of the freedom of assembly throughout the nineteenth century.[22] The other constitutional states of the European continent largely followed the model of the Belgian Constitution of 1831, which in its Article 19 introduced the distinction between outdoor and other assemblies, whereby only the former were subject to restrictions in cases of endangerment of the public order.

Today, the freedom of association is codified as a fundamental right in the constitutions of all EU member states, in the United Kingdom in the Human Rights Act.[23]

2. The Physical Dimension of Assemblies and its Constitutional Implications

The freedom of assembly has mainly—but not exclusively—the function to provide minorities with an instrument to convey their opinions and concerns to the public and to participate in the process of democratic will-formation.[24] The inherently political character of this freedom

[18] Cf references in Andreas Jungherr and Pascal Jürgens, 'The Political Click: Political Participation through E-petitions in Germany', Conference Paper presented at the Oxford Internet Institute (2010), available at <http://microsites.oii.ox.ac.uk/ipp2010/system/files/IPP2010_Jungherr_Jurgens_Paper.pdf>.

[19] John D. Inazu, 'The Forgotten Freedom of Assembly' (2010) 84 *Tulane Law Review* 565, 571ff.

[20] Tabatha Abu El-Haj, 'The Neglected Right of Assembly' (2009) 56(3) *UCLA Law Review* 543, 589.

[21] Title I, para 6 (author's numbering).

[22] Martin Quilisch, *Die demokratische Versammlung* (1970), 43; Claude-Albert Colliard, *Libertés publiques* (Roseline Letteron ed, 8th edn, 2005).

[23] 1998, c 42.

[24] Wolfgang Hoffmann-Riem, art 8 (commentary), margin no 7, in Denninger et al (eds), *Alternativkommentar zum Grundgesetz für die Bundesrepublik Deutschland* (2001), band I (art 1-17a), 3.

finds expression in the fact that many constitutions guarantee it only for their citizens.[25] The freedom of assembly is an expressive right in a particular sense. An assembly is characterized by the physical presence of a multitude of individuals who are aligned by the common purpose to collectively communicate a cause to the general public.[26] While the expression of their views is protected by the freedom of speech and can be performed more and more through the immaterial medium of the internet, it is the mere bodily togetherness of a group of people in a particular place at a particular time which creates a public sphere and political debate. This suggests a plebiscitarian, perhaps even plebeian, overtone to this right. Thus, due to its inherently physically expressive character, an assembly may degenerate into collective violence and actuate dangers to public security or public order.[27] Borderline cases are sit-down blockades (eg in front of military installations) as means of public protest. The German Federal Constitutional Court has recognized them as constitutionally protected assemblies as long as they are peaceful.[28]

The freedom of assembly means first and foremost the right to assemble without prior notification, requirement of permission, or any other condition which hampers the peaceful gathering of individuals. However, the authorities need prior knowledge of place, time, and expected number of participants in a demonstration in order to protect the rights and interests of uninvolved persons and of the public in general. Hence content-neutral[29] regulations including the obligation of prior notification of an assembly are consistent with the constitutional right to the freedom of assembly as long as they do not impede the communicative dimension of an assembly.[30] Nor must they inhibit spontaneous demonstrations. The European Court of Human Rights (ECtHR) seems to represent the prevailing opinion of constitutional courts in its statement 'that the right to hold spontaneous demonstrations may override the obligation to give prior notification to public assemblies only in special circumstances, namely if an immediate response to a current event is warranted in the form of a demonstration.'[31]

Freedom of association involves the freedom from fear of actual or potential participants to be sanctioned or to suffer other disadvantages for making use of that fundamental right. One new instrument to create diffuse anxiety in this respect (and thus to restrict the freedom of assembly) is the taking of overall images (camera-monitor transmission) of the participants of assemblies and the non-incident-related recording and stockpiling of these data. In a recent case concerning the police law of a German state, the Federal Constitutional Court issued a temporary injunction which limited the relevant powers of the police.[32] The final decision in this case is still pending.

A further issue which is closely related to the physical dimension of the freedom of assembly is the question of the right place for an assembly. Public streets, places, and parks are the private property of the municipalities or the state; however, their property rights are restricted by their function as a public forum. In the public forum in which communicative activities

[25] eg France 1791; Belgium 1831; Italy 1946; Germany 1949.

[26] Cf German Federal Constitutional Court, 69 BVerfGE 315 (1985), 342ff.

[27] Ulrich K. Preuß, 'Nötigung durch Demonstration: zur Dogmatik des Art 8 GG' in Hans-Ernst Bötcher (ed), *Recht—Justiz—Kritik. Festschrift für Richard Schmidt* (1985), 419–45.

[28] German Federal Constitutional Court, 73 BVerfGE 206 (1986) 248/9 chamber decision of 7 March, 2011, Ref No 1 BvR 388/05, available at <http://www.bundesverfassungsgericht.de/entscheidungen/rk20110307_1bvr038805.html>, margin nos 32, 33.

[29] Of course, the meaning of 'content-neutral' is ambiguous. For clarification see Geoffrey R. Stone et al, *Constitutional Law* (5th edn, 2005), 1300–3.

[30] 69 BVerfGE 315 (1985), at 350–1 (Germany); Supreme Court of Zambia, *Christine Mulundika v The People*, 1995/SCZ Judgment No 25, quoted in Norman Dorsen et al, *Comparative Constitutionalism. Cases and Materials* (2003), 1309ff; *Thomas et al v Chicago Park District* 534 US 316, 322ff (2002).

[31] ECtHR, *Éva Molnár v Hungary*, App no 10346/05, 7 October 2008, para 38.

[32] 122 BVerfGE 342 (2009), 368ff. Reference No 1 BvR 2492/08 (for the English version see n 33).

typically unfold, restrictions on their use for assemblies are only constitutional if they are 'are narrowly drawn to achieve a compelling state interest'[33] and content-neutral (eg noise near a school, near a clinic, and the like). Less obvious is the degree of constitutional protection with respect to privately owned spaces which are open to the public for functional use (eg shopping malls) or which have a formally private status but are owned by the state or other public authorities (eg airports, railway stations). As to the first constellation, in 1976 the US Supreme Court denied that the prohibition of a picketing line in a shopping centre by the owner implicated the First Amendment.[34] It overruled a decision of 1968 which had argued the reverse.[35] In a similar constellation relating to a dispute in the United Kingdom, the ECtHR did not rule out the possibility that the government had a positive obligation to protect European Convention rights by restricting property rights, but found no violation of Article 11 of the Convention in the concrete case.[36] As to the second constellation, the US Supreme Court denied that airports owned and regulated by a public authority are a public forum and accepted the prohibition of the sale or distribution of merchandise including the sale of literature within those locations.[37] In a similar case, the German Federal Constitutional Court determined that a protest rally in the terminal of Frankfurt Airport was protected by the constitutional freedom of assembly because corporations in which public authorities hold a majority stake are directly bound by the fundamental rights of the Constitution.[38]

IV. The Right to the Freedom of Association

1. Historical Conditions

(a) *Constitutional Origins*

Among the fundamental rights guaranteed by the constitutions of modern states, the freedom of association is a laggard. It is an offspring of the nineteenth century. Neither the Bill of Rights of the US Constitution nor the French Declaration of the Rights of Man and of the Citizen—two pioneering documents of eighteenth-century constitutionalism—mention the freedom of association.

Obviously, the French revolutionaries were deeply inspired by Rousseau's individualistic construction of democracy and its incompatibility with any kind of intermediate groups which were suspected to endanger the purity of the general will.[39] This ideological thrust amalgamated into two aligned tendencies: the revolution's irreconcilable opposition to the *ancien régime* in which intermediary forces had been the pillars of its feudo-absolutist rule,[40] and the rise of economic individualism which recognized only contracts as the appropriate social form of liberty dictated by reason itself.[41] Unsurprisingly, particular groups, especially collective actions of workers for the improvement of their working conditions, were regarded as a

33 Cf *International Society for Krishna Consciousness v Lee* 505 US at 678 and the cases in Stone (n 29), 1307ff.

34 *Hudgens v NLRB* 424 US 507, 521 (1975).

35 *Food Employees Local 590 v Logan Valley Plaza* 391 US 308, 313ff (1968).

36 ECtHR, *Appleby and others v United Kingdom*, App no 44306/98, 6 May 2003.

37 *International Society for Krishna Consciousness v Lee* 505 US 672, 680ff (1992).

38 German Federal Constitutional Court, Judgment of 22 February, 2011, 1 BvR 699/06, margin nos 45ff, available at <http://www.bundesverfassungsgericht.de/entscheidungen/rs20110222_1bvr069906.html?Suchbegriff=Versammlungsfreiheit+Flughafen>.

39 Jean-Jacques Rousseau, *The Social Contract* (Maurice Cranston trans, [1762] 1968), Bk II, ch 3, 72ff.

40 Cf R.C. van Caenegem, *An Historical Introduction to Western Constitutional Law* (1995), 185–6.

41 Cf Alain Supiot, *Homo Juridicus. On the Anthropological Functions of the Law* (2007), 78ff.

threat to the new individualistic order; the *Loi le Chapelier* of 14 June 1791 unequivocally attests to that apprehension. Throughout the whole nineteenth century the creation of voluntary associations was subject to severe restrictions which were not abolished until 1901.[42] It took another 70 years before the French Constitutional Council recognized the freedom of association as one of the 'fundamental principles acknowledged in the laws of the Republic'.[43]

The US case is more complex. Its perception is strongly shaped by Tocqueville's interpretation of nineteenth-century US history according to which in the United States an associational infrastructure formed a counterbalance against the centralized power of the sovereign state. The US constitutional approach to associations is at antipodes to the French in that they 'have distrusted collective organizations as embodied in government while insisting upon their own untrammelled right to form voluntary associations.'[44] While in Europe—here, of course, France is Tocqueville's primary example—the powers taken from the feudal corporations and intermediary forces of the Old Regime had been transferred to the state, in the United States, he claimed, they had been dispersed among a great number of groups composed of private citizens. In his view, this socio-political reality was a bare necessity of any democratic state in which 'all the citizens are independent and feeble; they can do hardly do anything by themselves, and none of them can oblige his fellow men to lend him their assistance.' Even more, he regarded the citizens' habit of forming associations as a mark of civilization.[45] Although he realized that under certain conditions the right of association could turn destructive, he valued it so highly that it appeared to him 'almost as inalienable in its nature as the right of personal liberty'.[46]

However, it is doubtful whether the Founding Fathers of the United States shared this view. After all, they, too, were inspired by the accentuated individualism of the political and social philosophy predominant at the end of the eighteenth century. It is hardly by accident that the US Constitution was silent about an explicit right to the freedom of association. Madison famously argued in the Federalist Papers against the 'mischiefs of faction'.[47] He was not the only sceptic of associations among the members of the founding generation, many of whom regarded political criticism from private groups as tending to be disloyal and seditious,[48] although his view was not shared by all.[49] However, on balance one may summarize that the 'framers of the Constitution sought to protect the "natural" and "inalienable" rights of individual men from official tyranny but were not concerned with assuring private associations the fulfilment of their objectives.'[50] Consequently, until the twentieth century the freedom of association 'had been protected..., if at all, only as an aspect of the less well pedigreed rights of privacy and personhood.'[51]

In Germany, obviously a constitutional latecomer, the nineteenth century was no auspicious age for constitutionalism in general and the guarantee of fundamental rights including

[42] Cf *Loi du 1er juillet 1901 relative au contrat d'association.*

[43] Decision of 16 July 1971; cf Vicky C. Jackson and Mark Tushnet, *Comparative Constitutional Law* (2nd edn, 2006), 595ff.

[44] Arthur Meier Schlesinger, *Paths to the Present* (1949), 23.

[45] Tocqueville (n 1), vol 2, ch V, 107, 110.

[46] Ibid vol 1, ch XII, 196.

[47] Clinton Rossiter (ed), *The Federalist Papers*, No 10 (1961), 78.

[48] Robert M. Chesney, 'Democratic-Republican Societies, Subversion, and the Limits of Legitimate Political Dissent in the Early Republic' (2004) 82 *North Carolina Law Review* 1525ff.

[49] See Robert J. Bresler, *Freedom of Association: Rights and Liberties under the Law* (2004), 22ff.

[50] Mark DeWolfe Howe, 'The Supreme Court, 1952 Term. Foreword: Political Theory and the Nature of Liberty' (1953) 67(1) *Harvard Law Review* 91, 91.

[51] Laurence H. Tribe, *American Constitutional Law* (2nd edn, 1988), 1010–11 (s 12–26).

the freedom of association in particular.[52] Although, in the second half of the nineteenth century, an era of rapid industrialization and urbanization, associations became a structural element of the evolving capitalist-industrial society and its system of interest aggregation, the dominant type of association was not the small voluntary fellowship of free and equal local dignitaries who promoted specific shared ideas but the highly organized syndicate of mostly economic stakeholders who pooled their interests in order to increase their political influence through collective action.[53] The 'pseudo-constitutional system' (Holborn) of Bismarck's authoritarian Reich[54] fostered the development of power-related interest aggregation while it was suspicious of all kinds of civic activism. Associations were perceived as potential threats to the stability of the social and political order, and 'political associations' were subject to constant police control. The Germans had to wait until 1919 when for the first time the Weimar Constitution guaranteed the freedom of association without the requirement of prior state permission,[55] complemented by the separately codified right of every individual and every occupation or profession to form associations to safeguard and improve working and economic conditions.[56]

(b) The Twentieth Century: Modern Mass Democracy: the 'Society of Organizations'

In fact, it was no earlier than in the twentieth century when the liberal 'society of individuals'[57] turned into a society of organizations that the freedom of association became a pivotal issue in almost all constitutional states. As an effect of the accomplishment of universal male and female suffrage which was largely concluded after the First World War in Europe and the United States 'the entry of the lower classes into the arena of national politics'[58] required new institutional patterns of social and political organization. Moreover, after a war the popular masses typically demand major improvements both of their socio-economic situation and of their status in the polity as a compensation for their war-time sufferings and sacrifices; this is what happened in Europe after the two world wars in 1919 and 1945. Two kinds of organization became the cornerstones of mass democracy: labour unions and political parties. The former are means of functional, that is, collective representation of the economic interests of dependent workers, the latter are institutions of civic integration.[59] In the twentieth century both types of organization were crucial for the status of citizenship in modern mass democracy.

Hence it comes as no surprise that most constitutions of the twentieth century focus on these mass organizations when they stipulate the freedom of association, albeit with different intensity. Germany's Weimar Constitution of 1919, the first attempt to reconcile the principles

[52] Cf Wolfgang Hardtwig, 'Verein. Gesellschaft, Geheimgesellschaft, Assoziation, Genossenschaft, Gewerkschaft' in Otto Brunner, Werner Conze, and Reinhart Koselleck (eds), *Geschichtliche Grundbegriffe. Historisches Lexikon zur politisch-sozialen Sprache in Deutschland*, Bd 6 (1990), 789, 809ff; Friedrich Müller, *Korporation und Assoziation. Eine Problemgeschichte der Vereinigungsfreiheit im deutschen Vormärz* (1965).

[53] Cf Alfred Rinken, 'Artikel 9 Absatz 1 (Vereinigungsfreiheit)' in Erhard Denninger et al (eds), *Kommentar zum Grundgesetz für die Bundesrepublik Deutschland (Reihe Alternativkommentare)* Bd I (Art 1-17a) (3rd edn, 2001), 1, 1–52, margin nos 3ff; excellent analysis of the structural differences between these two kinds of association in Gunther Teubner, *Organisationsdemokratie und Verbandsverfassung: Rechtsmodelle für politisch relevante Verbände* (1978), 21ff, 30ff.

[54] Cf Hajo Holborn, *A History of Modern Germany: 1840–1945* (1982), 251ff, quote 297.

[55] Article 124.

[56] Article 159.

[57] The concept is borrowed from Norbert Elias, *The Society of Individuals* (1991).

[58] Reinhard Bendix, *Nation-building and Citizenship: Studies of our Changing Social Order* (1977), 89ff, 96.

[59] Ibid 104, 121.

of liberal constitutionalism with the requirements of class-divided mass democracy,[60] guaranteed the freedom of association of German citizens in its Article 124 and added in Article 159 the specific 'right to form associations to safeguard and improve working and economic conditions guaranteed to every individual and to every occupation or profession'—largely viewed as *the* fundamental right of trade unions. Although the political system of the Weimar Republic was based upon the principle of party competition, an analogous special guarantee for political parties was missing. After the Second World War, a general tendency towards the constitutionalization of unions (and like professional interest groups) and political parties took hold. The French Constitution of 1946 incorporated in its Preamble the rights and freedoms of man and the citizen of the anti-associational Declaration of Rights of 1789, but added a list of political, economic, and social principles 'as being especially necessary to our times'. Whereas political parties were ignored, everyone's rights to form unions, to belong to the union of one's choice, to defend one's rights and interests through union action, and the right to strike was guaranteed. Obviously this constitutional pledge foreshadowed the right of everyone 'to form and to join trade unions for the protection of his interests', stipulated in Article 23(4) of the UN Universal Declaration of Human Rights which was mainly drafted by the French jurist, diplomat, and politician René Cassin and proclaimed by General Assembly on 10 December 1948.

2. Constitutional Guarantees on National Levels

The first document which in Europe after the Second World War guaranteed the freedom of association and, separately, the rights to form unions and to strike plus to 'freely associate in political parties in order to contribute by democratic methods to determine national policy' was the constitution of Italy of 27 December 1947.[61] West Germany's Basic Law of 23 May 1949 followed suit.[62] The French Constitution of the Fifth Republic of 1958 incorporated the above Preamble to the Constitution of 1946 and added in its Article 4 the guarantee of the freedom to form political parties. Remarkably, this guarantee is codified in its section 'On Sovereignty', while an individual right to the freedom of association is still absent.

The constitutions drafted after the 'third wave of democratization' in the twentieth century[63] in the now post-communist countries of Eastern and Central Europe are particularly focused on protection against any kind of compulsory association in state-controlled monopolistic mass organizations. Thus, the very first sentence of the Constitution of Hungary[64]—a series of patchwork amendments of the Constitution of 1949 that added up to a new document[65]—begins with the words: 'In order to facilitate a peaceful political transition to a constitutional state, *establish a multi-party system*...'[66] and envisages a pluralistic system of interest

[60] See the overview of the jurisprudential doctrines which mirrored the novelty of this constitution in Arthur J. Jacobson and Bernhard Schlink (eds), *Weimar. A Jurisprudence of Crisis: Philosophy, Social Theory, and the Rule of Law* (2000); see also Ulrich K. Preuß, 'Die Weimarer Republik—ein Laboratorium für neues verfassungsrechtliches Denken' in Andreas Göbel, Dirk van Laak, and Ingeborg Villinger (eds), *Metamorphosen des Politischen. Grundfragen politischer Einheitsbildung seit den 20er Jahren* (1995), ss 177–87.

[61] Articles 18, 39, 40, 49; see Fulco Lanchester, 'Die Institution der politischen Partei in Italien' in Dimiris Th. Tsatsos, Dian Schefold, and Hans-Peter Schneider (eds), *Parteienrecht im europäischen Vergleich* (1990), 367, 381.

[62] Article 9(1): freedom of association, like in Weimar, restricted to Germans; Art 9(3): the right guaranteed to every individual and to every occupation or profession 'to form associations to safeguard and improve working and economic conditions'; Art 21: the freedom to associate in political parties.

[63] Samuel P. Huntington, *The Third Wave: Democratization in the Late Twentieth Century* (1991).

[64] Expiring 31 December 2011.

[65] Jon Elster et al, *Institutional Design in Post-communist Societies. Rebuilding the Ship at Sea* (1998), ch III.

[66] Emphasis added.

representation (Art 4). The Polish Constitution of 1997 guarantees the freedom for the creation and functioning of political parties, trade unions, socio-occupational organizations of farmers, societies, citizens' movements, and foundations (Art 12), laying emphasis on their strictly voluntary character and banning 'political parties and other organizations whose programmes are based upon totalitarian methods' (Art 13). Similarly, the Bulgarian Constitution of 1991 proclaims in its very first article that 'No part of the people, no political party nor any other organization, state institution or individual shall usurp the expression of the popular sovereignty.' This is corroborated by the stipulation in Article 11 which establishes the 'fundamental' principle that political activity in the Republic of Bulgaria shall be founded on the principle of political pluralism and that 'No political party or ideology shall be proclaimed or affirmed as a party or ideology of the State'. Within this framework, the bill of rights guarantees the citizens' freedom to associate (Art 44). Articles 49 and 50 take a corporatist view in that they, conscious of the different socio-economic statuses of employees and employers, distinguish between the freedom of the former 'to form trade union organizations and alliances in defence of their interests related to work and social security' including the right to strike and the freedom of the latter 'to associate in defence of their economic interests'. Incidentally, the same distinction is made by the Constitution of South Africa, another country of transition from authoritarian to democratic governance: in its bill of rights it distinguishes the freedom of association (Art 18)—set in close neighbourhood to the freedoms of expression, petition, and assembly—from rights concerning trade, occupation, profession, and labour relations. It guarantees separately the corporatist freedoms of workers to form and join labour unions, to participate in their activities, and to strike, and of employers to form interest organizations and to participate in their activities. Moreover, those organizations enjoy a high degree of autonomy due to the constitutional right to determine their administration, programmes, and activities (Art 23).

In the United Kingdom, the freedom of association is guaranteed in the Civil Rights Act of 1998[67] which was enacted in order to give effect to rights and freedoms guaranteed under the European Convention on Human Rights; it merely repeats the Convention's guarantee of the freedom of association (Art 11). Much more detailed regulations of the corporatist dimension of associative freedom, namely the industrial relations between employers and trade unions, are stipulated in the Employment Relations Act 1999.[68] By contrast, political parties are largely regarded as factual phenomena of political life as there is no legal regime except the mere obligation to register according to the Registration of Political Parties Act of 1998.[69]

3. International Guarantees of the Freedom of Association

Most international human rights documents include the guarantee of the freedom of association, if with different emphasis. The UN Declaration of 10 December 1948 proclaims the freedom of association in close relationship to the liberal freedoms of expression and assembly and includes the negative right not to be compelled to belong to an association (Art 20). Separately, in Article 23 which deals with individual rights in the area of labour relations everyone's 'right to form and to join trade unions for the protection of his interests' is codified in paragraph 4.

[67] 1998, c 42.

[68] 1999, c 26; cf T. Novitz, 'International Promises and Domestic Pragmatism: To What Extent will the Employment Relations Act 1999 Implement International Labour Standards Relating to Freedom of Association' (2000) 63(3) *Modern Law Review* 379.

[69] 1998, c 48.

In the two UN Human Rights Covenants of 16 December 1966—the International Covenant on Civil and Political Rights (ICCPR) and the International Covenant on Economic, Social and Cultural Rights (ICESCR)—the individualistic-associative and the collective-corporatist dimensions of the freedom of association are carefully differentiated. While the former codifies comprehensively everyone's 'right to freedom of association with others, including the right to form and join trade unions for the protection of his interests' (Art 22(1)), the latter specifies, unsurprisingly, the socio-economic and collective significance of this right. Thus, in Article 8, everyone's right to form and to join unions, the unions' rights to 'function freely' and to organize nationally and internationally, and the right (of unionized workers) to strike is codified in Article 8(1). These rights have been concretized by the institutions and procedures of the International Labour Organization (ILO) which have been established for the purpose of promoting respect for trade union rights in law and in fact.[70] Among its numerous rules and principles, the Freedom of Association and Protection of the Right to Organise Convention of 17 June 1948[71] (No 87), ratified by 145 states, and the Right to Organise and Collective Bargaining Convention of 8 June 1949[72] (No 98), ratified by 154 states (both as of 1 January 2006) are the most relevant ones.

Among the regional International Human Rights charters, the European Convention for the Protection of Human Rights and Fundamental Freedoms (ECHR) of 4 November 1950[73] is the only one which is enforced by an international court, the ECtHR. Individuals, non-governmental organizations, or groups of individuals can sue any contracting party for having violated one of their rights stipulated in the Convention (Art 34). As a counterweight to this rather bold move, the Convention includes only a relatively small number of the well-established fundamental rights of liberal constitutionalism. Thus, Article 11(1) of the Convention pools the 'rights to freedom of peaceful assembly and to freedom of association with others, including the right to form and to join trade unions for the protection of his interests.' In its jurisprudence, the ECtHR had to deal quite frequently with the ban on political parties in member states, the judgments about the prohibitions of the Turkish Communist Party (1998) and of the Turkish Welfare Party (2003) arguably being the major cases in this field[74] which, however, is not the subject of this chapter. Among the cases not related to political parties, the scope of the rights of trade unions play a prominent role. In a recent landmark decision the Court has revised its former stance 'that the right to bargain collectively and to enter into collective agreements does not constitute an inherent element of Article 11' and, 'having regard to the developments in labour law, both international and national, and to the practice of Contracting States in such matters', recognized that 'the right to bargain collectively with the employer has, in principle, become one of the essential elements of the 'right to form and to join trade unions for the protection of [one's] interests' set forth in Article 11 of the Convention . . . '.[75]

[70] Cf ILO (ed), *Freedom of Association Digest of Decisions and Principles of the Freedom of Association Committee of the Governing Body of the ILO* (5th edn, 2006), 1ff.

[71] See <http://www.ilo.org/ilolex/english/convdisp1.htm>.

[72] See ibid.

[73] As amended by Protocol No 14, entry into force 1 June 2010, available at <http://conventions.coe.int/Treaty/Commun/ChercheSig.asp?NT=194&CM=2&DF=19/02/2010&CL=ENG>.

[74] ECtHR, *United Communist Party of Turkey and others v Republic of Turkey*, App no 19392/92, 30 January 1998, 1998-I; *Refah Partisi (the Welfare Party) and Others v Turkey*, App nos 41340/98, 41342/98, 41343/98, and 41344/98, 13 February 2003 (Grand Chamber), 2003-II.

[75] ECtHR, *Demir and Baykara v Turkey*, App no 34503/97, 12 November 2008, paras 153–4; the significance of this judgment is discussed by K.D. Ewing and John Hendy, 'The Dramatic Implications of *Demir* and *Baykara*' (2010) 39(1) *Industrial Law Journal* 1.

4. The Scope of the Freedom of Association

The concept of association encompasses an extremely broad spectrum of social relationships in which individuals act in concert on the basis of some at least minimal institutional consolidation. The social areas and the social functions of associations diverge considerably. In a rough classification, one can distinguish (1) associations in the field of economic and labour relations (associations of employers, employees, professions, producers, consumers, economic lobbying groups); (2) associations in the field of charities and analogous non-profit welfare institutions; (3) associations in the field of sports, leisure, and entertainment; (4) associations in the field of religion, culture, art, and science; (5) non-partisan political associations and advocacy groups; and (6) private social clubs.[76]

This functional variety translates into a differentiation of structural features which affect both the character of conflicts concerning associative activities and the need for constitutional protection. For purely self-sufficient social associations with a small and select membership, the freedom of association has another meaning than for anonymous mass organizations which mainly provide services to their membership, and it is once more different for mass organizations which strive for a public cause or for political power. A rough distinction may be drawn between 'expressive' and 'instrumental' associations which Stuart White has suggested. Expressive associations are communities 'whose members are united by sharing a distinctive set of religious or ideological beliefs.' In contrast, instrumental associations are organizations 'whose primary purpose is to secure for its members improved access to strategic goods, such as income and wealth.'[77] Economic and professional interest groups and trade unions are the obvious examples. A similar, but somewhat narrower distinction was introduced by Justice Brennan in *Roberts v United States Jaycees*. He distinguished between the intrinsic and the instrumental element of the freedom of association, the former (intimate relationships like marriage, family, and friendship) having intrinsic value for personal liberty, the latter being instrumental for the promotion or defence of First Amendment rights.[78] Whether purely economic aggregates like joint-stock companies qualify for the freedom of association is debatable. In a landmark case concerning the German Co-Determination Act of 1976,[79] the Federal Constitutional Court expressed doubts in this respect arguing that fundamental freedoms including the freedom of association protect primarily the freedom of persons, not economic functions like the collection and use of capital.[80]

The right to the freedom of association protects the *positive freedom of association*, that is, the individuals' right to create, to enter, and to remain in an association. Moreover, it contains the association's right to exist and its right to self-determination (autonomy), that is, the right to decide about the admission and exclusion of members, to establish rules about its internal order including the rights and obligations of its members, and to decide autonomously about the change of its purpose, its dissolution, or its integration into a federation of like associations. The external activity of an association—for example the operation of a publishing house or of sporting activities—is not protected by the freedom of association but by the pertinent guarantee (eg right to freedom of the press, or to the free development of the personality, respectively). Consequently, the limits of those freedoms, not of the freedom of association apply. Only where the external activity of an association is part of the

[76] Cf the similar typologies of George Kateb, 'The Value of Association' in Amy Gutmann (ed), *Freedom of Association* (1998), 35, 36 and Rinken (n 53), margin nos 12ff.

[77] Stuart White, 'Trade Unionism in a Liberal State' in Gutmann (n 76), 334–5.

[78] 50 BVerfGE 290 (1979).

[79] 50 BVerfGE 290 (1979).

[80] Ibid 355ff.

constitutional guarantee—for example in the Article 11 ECHR guarantee of everyone's 'right to form and to join trade unions for the protection of his interests'—these activities, arguably including strikes, lie within the scope of the freedom of association.[81]

The constitutional guarantee includes the *negative freedom of association*, that is, the individual's freedom to abstain from and to leave an association and not to be deprived of opportunities and benefits by reason of non-membership in a particular association (eg political party, trade union, scientific society). One issue which plays a major role in countries with a strong corporatist tradition (like Germany or Austria) is the question of whether the freedom of association protects against compulsory membership in legally established public corporations such as chambers of commerce, crafts, lawyers, or medical doctors. The German Federal Constitutional Court has consistently, although not unchallenged, held that the freedom of association protects only against compulsory membership in associations of private law; protection against compulsory membership in public corporations is guaranteed by the (much weaker) right to free development of one's personality.[82]

Also so-called 'closed shop' or 'union shop'[83] regimes raise the question of their compatibility with the negative freedom of association. Under such regimes, employment in a particular firm is conditional upon union membership. As the preparatory notes on Article 11 of the ECHR attest, in 1950 there were several founding European countries in which this system existed, whilst at the beginning of the twenty-first century, according to the account of the ECtHR, it subsists only in Denmark and Iceland.[84]

Judging the compatibility of the closed shop system with the Convention's guarantee of the freedom of association (Art 11), the ECtHR has taken a somewhat ambiguous stance. In a judgment of 1981 it evaded an answer to that question and satisfied itself with the assumption that Article 11 does not guarantee the negative aspect of that freedom on the same footing as the positive aspect, and that therefore 'compulsion to join a particular trade union may not always be contrary to the Convention'.[85] In a more recent case, it slightly changed the said assumption and stated that it 'does not in principle exclude that the negative and the positive aspects of the Article 11 right should be afforded the same level of protection in the area under consideration.'[86] While according to the Court this assessment does not exclude closed-shop agreements between unions and employers 'which run counter to the freedom of choice of the individual inherent in Article 11', the Contracting State's margin of appreciation 'must be considered reduced'.[87] In the Danish cases at hand, the Court considered it to be a violation of a person's freedom of association to be compelled to become a member of a specific trade union in order to be employed.[88] Note that in these cases the Court did not assert a horizontal effect

[81] See end of Section I(3)(c) above.

[82] Cf 38 BVerfGE 281, 297ff with further references.

[83] Closed shop means that the employer hires only union members and has to fire those who quit the union; union shop means that also non-members can be hired, but must join the union within a certain period of time.

[84] Cf ECtHR cases of *Sørensen* and *Rasmussen v Denmark*, App nos 52562/99 and 52620/99, 11 January 2006, paras 33, 34; see also case of *Sigurdur A. Sigurjónsson v Iceland*, App no 16130/90, 30 June 1993.

[85] ECtHR, *Young, James and Webster v United Kingdom*, App nos 7601/76 and 7806/77, 13 August 1981, para 55.

[86] *Sørensen* and *Rasmussen v Denmark* (n 84), para 56.

[87] Ibid para 58.

[88] For an elaborate analysis of this issue see V. Mantouvalou, 'Is There a Right Not to Be a Union Member? Labour Rights under the European Convention on Human Rights' in C. Fenwick and T. Novitz (eds), *Human Rights at Work: Perspectives on Law and Regulation* (2010), ch 16; see also the comprehensive study of Tonia Novitz, *International and European Protection of the Right to Strike: A Comparative Study of Standards Set by the International Labour Organization, the Council of Europe and the European Union* (2003).

of Article 11 of the Convention; rather, it judged whether the Contracting State had violated its obligation under the Convention to secure to the applicants under domestic law their right to freedom of association.[89]

In the United States, the Taft–Hartley Act of 1947 bans closed shops but does not outlaw union shops, although states can prohibit them through so-called right-to-work laws. It seems that the free-rider problem is now largely solved by diverse union security agreements according to which employers collect dues from the employees for the union without committing them to union membership. Obviously this kind of burden-sharing of non-members is not a matter of freedom of association and hence irrelevant for this chapter.

Both the positive and the negative freedoms of association are directed against encroachment by public authorities; they have no horizontal effect. Although especially mass organizations with a monopoly over resources (eg trade unions or professional associations) are in a position to neglect the interests of outsiders and of internal minorities, the freedom of association does not confer protection against the power of an association; notably it does not require that their internal organization must conform to democratic principles. However, this does not mean that the freedom of association grants associations unlimited powers over their members or outsiders. The now widely recognized protective dimension of fundamental rights and the general duty of the state to pursue the public interest includes its obligation to regulate the conduct of private power-holders, especially of monopolistic associations (eg imposing rules against arbitrary exclusion of members, or against discrimination).

5. Legal Design, Legal and Factual Restrictions of the Freedom of Association

The freedom of association is neither self-executive nor unlimited. Just as most other freedom rights it requires legal design and limits which compatibilize it with conflicting freedoms of others and with the public interest. Statutes which establish rules about the formation of associations, their internal organization, and their financial affairs are enabling, not restricting, devices. However, the borderline between enabling and constraining devices is equivocal. It is a matter of debate whether, for instance, section 46 of the British Trade Union Act 1992[90] which establishes the duty of the union to hold elections for certain positions is enabling or restricting the members' freedom of association by restricting the association's autonomy. Legal restrictions of the freedom of association have to conform to the principle of proportionality, that is, they have to be appropriate and necessary and must not encroach exceedingly upon the protected freedom.

(a) Legally Imposed Membership

As mentioned in the previous section, the freedom of association includes the association's right to decide autonomously about the admission and exclusion of its members; the legal duty to accept the membership of an unwanted person interferes with this right.[91] The US Supreme Court dealt with different variants of this question.[92] Based upon the above-mentioned distinction between intimate and expressive associations, the Court stated that the degree of constitutional protection varies for these two types of association. For the former,

[89] Ibid para 57; see also Stuart White, 'Trade Unionism in a Liberal State' in Gutmann (n 76), 344ff; Stone (n 29), s VII E 5, 1437ff.

[90] 1992, c 52.

[91] Cf Tribe (n 51), ss 15–17, 1400ff.

[92] *Roberts v United States Jaycees* 468 US 609 (1984); *Board of Directors of Rotary International v Rotary Club of Duarte* 481 US 537 (1987); *New York State Club Association v City of New York* 487 US 1 (1988); *Boy Scouts of America v Dale* 530 US 640 (2000).

the Bill of Rights must 'afford a substantial measure of sanctuary from unjustified interference by the State'; the freedom of the latter can be restricted by state regulations for the sake of compelling state interests. In the *Roberts* case, the Court held that the state's interest in eradicating discrimination against its female citizens was compelling and justified the restriction of the association's autonomy.[93] Four years later, the Court qualified this regulation-friendly stance with respect to expressive associations and admitted that the freedom of expressive associations may also require the confinement of its membership to those 'who share the same sex, for example, or the same religion'.[94] Finally, in *Boy Scouts of America* of 2000, the Court, upholding the distinction between intimate and expressive associations, specified the scope of the latter's protection in situations where the forced inclusion of an unwanted person—in this case, an openly self-declared homosexual—affected the expression of the association's values and mission.[95] This line of argument was extended to political parties in *California Democratic Party v Jones* in which the Court denied the constitutionality of so-called 'blanket' primaries in which each voter's ballot lists every candidate regardless of party affiliation and allows the voter to choose freely among them.[96] Blanket primaries violate the parties' freedom of association in its expressive dimension because they force them 'to associate with—to have their nominees, and hence their positions, determined by—those who, at best, have refused to affiliate with the party, and, at worst, have expressly affiliated with a rival.'[97]

The issue of legally imposed unwanted companionship also came up in the above-mentioned case of the German Co-Determination Act of 1976, according to which the board of governors of companies above a certain size must consist of employee and shareholder representatives in equal measure, whereby about one-third of the employee representatives may include union representatives not affiliated to the company. The Federal Constitutional Court reasoned that the personal element in the constitution of joint-stock companies had only marginal significance. Hence, recognizing the legislator's broad discretion to find a proper balance between the affected companies' freedom and the public interest, it held that the Co-Determination Act did not violate the companies' freedom of association.[98]

(b) *Restrictions for the Public Service*

An issue which pertains to the right to form and to join trade unions is the question of whether certain groups of the population may be excluded from the enjoyment of this right due to their special responsibilities and the functional necessities of their work: the military and police personnel, and possibly all employees of the civil service. This question not only includes the permissibility of strikes and similar collective action in a labour dispute, but the

[93] 468 US 609, 623 (1984); affirmed by *Board of Directors of Rotary International v Rotary Club of Duarte* 481 US 537, 544–5 (1987); cf the critical view of Douglas O. Linder, 'Freedom of Association After *Roberts v United States Jaycees*' (1984) 82 *Michigan Law Review* 1878; Nancy L. Rosenblum, 'Compelled Association: Public Standing, Self-respect, and the Dynamic of Exclusion' in Gutmann (n 76), 75; see also Stuart White, 'Freedom of Association and the Right to Exclude' (1997) 5(4) *Journal of Political Philosophy* 373; Evelyn Brody, 'Entrance, Voice, and Exit: The Constitutional Bounds of the Right of Association' (2002) 35(4) *University of California at Davis Law Review* 821.

[94] *New York State Club Association v City of New York* 487 US 1, 13 (1988).

[95] This argument was prefigured in *Hurley et al v Irish-American Gay, Lesbian, and Bisexual Group of Boston* 515 US 557, 574ff (1995), concerning the admission of an unwanted group to a parade.

[96] 530 US 567 (2000).

[97] Ibid 577.

[98] 50 BVerfGE 290 (1979).

appropriate methods of regulating labour relations in those spheres. Constitutions are largely equivocal because the relevant stipulations, if there are any at all, embody compromises which leave much room for interpretation. Ultimately it is the business of the courts to find an answer which is acceptable for the involved collective actors, the affected outsiders, and society at large.

The South African Defence Act, 44 of 1957 had denied the permanent members of the military force to join trade unions and to participate in their activities. The Constitutional Court of South Africa declared these restrictions unconstitutional and invalid, with the exception of the prohibition of their participation in strikes.[99] This jurisprudence is largely in accordance with the guidelines of the ILO which establish that the

> right to strike may be restricted or prohibited: (1) in the public service only for public servants exercising authority in the name of the State; or (2) in essential services in the strict sense of the term (that is, services the interruption of which would endanger the life, personal safety or health of the whole or part of the population).[100]

Similarly, in a recent decision the ECtHR accepted that certain categories of civil servants could be prohibited from taking strike action, but stated that the ban did not extend to all public servants or to employees of state-run commercial or industrial companies.[101]

(c) *The Faint Borderline Between Freedom of Association and Conspiracy*

Generally, solitary conduct which is not prohibited by law may not be defined as unlawful if it is performed in an associative mode.[102] But exceptions may exist. An individual's intention to commit a crime, even the mere preparation of a criminal act which has not yet reached the stage of an attempt, is usually exempt from punishment, but it may become a punishable act if performed in association—here the associative mode of an otherwise harmless conduct generates a threat to society and turns into punishable conspiracy.[103]

Sometimes the law which imposes limits on the freedom of association is so vaguely worded that the boundary between conduct within the scope of associational freedom and illicit conspiracy is not easily drawn. Thus, in the heyday of the Cold War, the US Supreme Court affirmed the conviction of leading members of the US Communist Party based on the Smith Act of 1940 which, among other things, made unlawful and punishable any attempt 'to organize or help to organize any society, group, or assembly of persons who teach, advocate, or encourage the overthrow or destruction of any government in the United States by force or violence.'[104] In *Dennis v United States*, the Court, despite recognizing that the Communist Party's attempt to overthrow the government of the United States was 'doomed from the outset because of inadequate numbers or power of the revolutionists', held that the law met the 'clear-and-present-danger' test because

[99] *South African National Defence Union v Minister of Defence*, CCT 27/98 (1999); see also CCT 65/06 (2007).

[100] ILO (n 70), para 576.

[101] ECtHR, *Enerji Yapi-Yol Sen v Turkey*, App no. 68959/01, 21 April 2009.

[102] Cf Tribe (n 51), 1014, ss 12–26.

[103] Cf German Criminal Code, s 129a.

[104] Smith Act of 1940 18 USC §2385, ss 2 and 3.

> the damage which such attempts create both physically and politically to a nation makes it impossible to measure the validity in terms of the probability of success, or the immediacy of a successful attempt.... It is the existence of the conspiracy which creates the danger.[105]

(d) Factual State Interferences

Apart from restrictions of the freedom of association through legal and administrative acts, factual restrictions caused by public authorities also occur. The German Federal Constitutional Court has judged that the undercover observation and infiltration of a political party through state agents is a serious mode of state interference which requires not only a distinct authorization by law but, in addition, a special justification which meets the standards of the principle of proportionality.[106] Other cases involve the denial of governmental benefits, be it employment in the civil service, the allotment of contracts, or other opportunities. Although these factual restrictions are rarely overt, they are often an indirect, albeit effective, instrument of government to dissuade people from joining associations suspected by the government. As long as such associations are not legally prohibited, these factual restrictions violate the freedom of association.[107] A different view was taken by the German Federal Constitutional Court and other German courts which argued that the loyalty of public employees had to be assured beyond any reasonable doubt and justified the ban of the access to the civil service of applicants who were or had been members or sympathizers of radical, if not prohibited, associations.[108]

Bibliography

Tabatha Abu El-Haj, 'The Neglected Right of Assembly' (2009) 56(3) *UCLA Law Review* 543

Robert J. Bresler, *Freedom of Association: Rights and Liberties under the Law* (2004)

Evelyn Brody, 'Entrance, Voice, and Exit: The Constitutional Bounds of the Right of Association' (2002) 35(4) *University of California at Davis Law Review* 821

Thomas I. Emerson, 'Freedom of Association and Freedom of Expression' (1964) 74(1) *Yale Law Journal* 1

K.D. Ewing and John Hendy, 'The Dramatic Implications of Demir and Baykara' (2010) 39(1) *Industrial Law Journal* 1

Amy Gutmann (ed), *Freedom of Association* (1998)

Wolfgang Hardtwig, 'Verein. Gesellschaft, Geheimgesellschaft, Assoziation, Genossenschaft, Gewerkschaft' in Otto Brunner, Werner Conze, and Reinhart Koselleck (eds), *Geschichtliche Grundbegriffe. Historisches Lexikon zur politisch-sozialen Sprache in Deutschland*, Bd 6 (1990)

S.A. Higginson, 'A Short History of the Right to Petition Government for the Redress of Grievances' (1986) 96(1) *Yale Law Journal* 142

P. Hirst, 'Renewing Democracy through Associations' (2002) 73(4) *Political Quarterly* 409

[105] *Dennis v United States* 341 US 494, 511 (1951); the question whether the US Communist Party was a legitimate party or a conspiracy is extensively discussed by Bresler (n 49), 38ff; see also Inazu (n 19), 606ff.

[106] Decision of 18 March 2003, 107 BVerfGE 339, 365ff, margin nos 77ff, available at <http://www.bundesverfassungsgericht.de/entscheidungen/bs20030318_2bvb000101.html>.

[107] Cf Tribe (n 51), 1016ff, ss 12–26.

[108] 39 BVerfGE 334 (1975).

ILO (ed), *Freedom of Association Digest of Decisions and Principles of the Freedom of Association Committee of the Governing Body of the ILO* (5th edn, 2006)

John D. Inazu, 'The Forgotten Freedom of Assembly' (2010) 84 *Tulane Law Review* 565

V. Mantouvalou, 'Is There a Right Not to Be a Union Member? Labour Rights under the European Convention on Human Rights' in C. Fenwick and T. Novitz (eds), *Human Rights at Work: Perspectives on Law and Regulation* (2010)

Jason Mazzone, 'Freedom's Association' (2002) 77 *Washington Law Review* 639

Lorenzo Mosca and Daria Santucci, 'Petitioning Online. The Role of E-Petitions in Web Campaigning' in Sigrid Baringhorst, Veronika Kneip, and Johanna Niesyto (eds), *Political Campaigning on the Web* (2009)

F. Müller, *Korporation und Assoziation. Eine Problemgeschichte der Vereinigungsfreiheit im deutschen Vormärz* (1965)

William J. Novak, 'The American Law of Association: The Legal-Political Construction of Civil Society' (2002) 15(2) *Studies in American Political Development* 163

James E. Pfander, 'Sovereign Immunity and the Right to Petition: Toward a First Amendment Right to Pursue Judicial Claims Against the Government' (1997) 91(1) *Northwestern University Law Review* 899

Martin Quilisch, *Die demokratische Versammlung* (1970)

Reena Raggi, 'An Independent Right to Freedom of Association' (1977) 12(1) *Harvard Civil Rights-Civil Liberties Law Review* 1

Alfred Rinken, 'Artikel 9 Absatz 1 (Vereinigungsfreiheit)' in Erhard Denninger et al (eds), *Kommentar zum Grundgesetz für die Bundesrepublik Deutschland (Reihe Alternativkommentare) Band I (Art 1-17a)* (3rd edn, 2001)

Norman B. Smith, 'Shall Make No Law Abridging...: An Analysis of the Neglected, but Nearly Absolute, Right of Petition' (1986) 54 *University of Cincinnati Law Review* 1153

K.J. Strandburg, 'Freedom of Association in a Networked World: First Amendment Regulation of Relational Surveillance' (2008) 49 *Boston College Law Review* 741

Mark E. Warren, *Democracy and Association* (2001)

Stuart White, 'Freedom of Association and the Right to Exclude' (1997) 5(4) *Journal of Political Philosophy* 373

Roy Whitehead Jr and Walter Block, 'Boy Scouts, Freedom of Association, and the Right to Discriminate: A Legal, Philosophical, and Economic Analysis' (2004) 29 *Oklahoma City University Law Review* 851

Erik Olin Wright (ed), *Associations and Democracy* (1995)

CHAPTER 46

PRIVACY

MANUEL JOSÉ CEPEDA ESPINOSA

Bogotá

I. Introduction

Is there indeed a 'right to privacy' in comparative constitutional law? The question has been asked in constitutional legal scholarship whether the bundle of interests protected by 'privacy' are manifestations of the same underlying notion, or whether they are, rather, a set of disparate and unrelated rights.[1] Thus, it has been described as a polymorph, protean, and heteroclite right whose content is unpredictable[2] and 'not susceptible of exhaustive definition'.[3]

[1] Laurence Tribe, *American Constitutional Law* (2nd edn, 1988), 1303 ('a name for a grab-bag of unrelated goodies').

[2] Marie-Therese Meulders-Klein, 'L'irrésistible ascension de la "vie privée" au sein des droits de l'homme' in Frédéric Sudre, *Le droit au respect de la vie privée au sens de la convention européenne des droits de l'homme* (2005), 307.

[3] ECtHR, *Pretty v United Kingdom*, App no 2346/02, 2002-III.

Privacy is not mentioned in the constitutions of countries such as the United States and Germany, where high courts have rendered landmark decisions on privacy. Most post-1990 constitutions refer to it, as do international[4] and regional[5] human rights treaties.

Indeed, the protection of private spheres was a matter foreign to constitutional law until the second half of the twentieth century. Different instruments helped to impede or repair intrusions into the realm of the individual, such as trespass in property law, civil torts,[6] criminal procedure with respect to search and seizure,[7] and the so called 'rights of personality' in some countries of the civil law tradition.[8] These instruments protected the private sphere of an individual not only against police authorities but also against actions of private individuals. It can be argued that the conception and the scope of the right to privacy in each country depend on the pre-constitutional legal protections granted, but with the passage of time this umbilical cord has been cut. Thus, in the United States there are intense debates about the physical spaces protected by the constitutional right to privacy (not a telephone line, in *Olmstead*, then corrected in *Katz*),[9] whilst in Europe the expansion of the right beyond the individual home has been relatively less controversial.[10] Thus, even within Western culture, there are differences in approaches to basic elements of privacy. Beyond, the differences are greater since the idea of privacy is context-bound and linked to culture.[11]

The rise of privacy as a constitutional right means that the legislature, not only the police or administrative authorities, is bound to respect and protect it. The judiciary must also ensure that in the course of ordinary procedures—civil, criminal, administrative etc—privacy is not violated. This has led to an infusion of constitutional law into other branches of law. In regions where an international human rights convention is judicially enforced, privacy transforms classic legal rules under a human rights flag, as was noticed in Europe after *Marckx v Belgium*, a 1979 European Court of Human Rights (ECtHR) decision holding that a legal rule that did not recognize a maternal bond for 'illegitimate' children breached the obligation to respect family life.[12]

Privacy as an autonomous constitutional right was first judicially protected in the 1960s. In 1965, in the leading case *Griswold v Connecticut*, the US Supreme Court derived a right to

[4] International Covenant on Civil and Political Rights (1966), Art 17(1).

[5] Convention for the Protection of Human Rights and Fundamental Freedoms (1950), Art 8; American Convention on Human Rights (1969), Art 11(2).

[6] William L. Prosser, 'Privacy' (1960) 48 *California Law Review* 383, 389.

[7] *Hester v United States* 265 US 57 (1924).

[8] James Q. Whitman, 'The Two Western Cultures of Privacy: Dignity Versus Liberty' (2004) 113 *Yale Law Journal* 1151, 1189–201.

[9] In *Olmstead v United States* 277 US 438 (1928), the Court said that a telephone line could be subject to surveillance since there was no physical intrusion in the home, but in *Katz v United States* 389 US 347 (1967), concerning a telephone cabin, it corrected this approach. Other cases related to places protected by the Fourth Amendment are the bag of a taxi client (*Arkansas v Sanders* 442 US 753 (1979)) and the office of the chief executive of a corporation investigated for fiscal fraud (*GM Leasing Corp v United States* 429 US 338 (1977)). But the trunk of a car belonging to another person (*United States v Ross* 456 US 798 (1982)) and trash-cans left to be picked up on a public road (*California v Greenwood* 486 US 35 (1988)) are not protected.

[10] Places not owned but clearly destined for private activities, even temporary ones, are protected. Thus a temporary hotel room is protected in Spain (STC, 17 January 2002, no 10-2002), and occasional offices for business activities are protected in France (CCD, 29 December 1983, no 83-164 DC). In Germany the protection includes tents and hotel rooms as well as bureaux see Constance Grewe, 'Allemagne' (2000) *Annuaire International de Justice Constitutionnelle (AIJC)* 139.

[11] In Japan, where web personal open diaries are popular, what is regarded as 'most intimate' in Western culture is often made public.

[12] *Marckx v Belgium* 13 June 1979, Ser A no 31.

privacy from the various 'zones of privacy' emanating from several constitutional guarantees, and prohibiting government intrusion into the intimate matters of married couples.[13] In 1968, the ECtHR in the *Belgian Linguistic Case* held that Article 8 of the European Convention on Human Rights regarding private and family life had the object 'of protecting the individual against arbitrary interference by the public authorities in his private family life'.[14] In 1969, the German Federal Constitutional Court in the *Microcensus Case* held that

> The State has no right to pierce the [protected] sphere of privacy by thoroughly checking into the personal matters of its citizens. [It] must leave the individual with an inner space for the purpose of the free and responsible development of his personality. Within this space the individual is his own master.[15]

Nonetheless, the vision of privacy in each landmark decision is different. *Griswold* saw privacy as an absolute bar against governmental intrusion into the intimate aspects of a couple's life. The *Belgian Linguistic Case* dealt with decisions made by families on the education of their children, and privacy was used as a check against arbitrary governmental decisions bearing on family life. The *Microcensus Case*, in turn, was about safeguarding an absolute realm of dignity for the individual, by protecting her personal life from scrutiny. Informational privacy was directly linked to an autonomy right, since a person would not be able to develop her personality freely under constant public gaze.

Other jurisdictions protected the right to privacy much later. For example, in France, the first step was given by the legislature, amending the Civil Code in 1970 in broad terms, but only in 1995 did the Constitutional Council recognize such a constitutional right in its *Videosurveillance Case*.[16]

Privacy in comparative constitutional law is associated in some countries with specific legal ideas, such as inviolability of domicile and the secrecy of correspondence,[17] whereas in others it is related to broad concepts such as freedom, dignity, and autonomy. Some jurisdictions provide an all-encompassing idea of 'privacy', whereas others provide different sets of compartmentalized rights. The US conception sees privacy as a 'right of the individual to decide for himself',[18] found in the 'penumbras' of several provisions of the Bill of Rights.[19] In contrast, the French Constitutional Council sees it as a form of 'liberty', as does the Indian Supreme Court.[20] Other jurisdictions, such as Germany, Colombia,[21] and South Africa,[22] in turn, derive the right to privacy from a basic conception of human dignity, notwithstanding the fact that their constitutions already provide specific protections for informational privacy.

However, most jurisdictions share several key trends. The basic one is accelerated expansion, not only in terms of protected interests but most significantly in terms of the transfor-

[13] *Griswold v Connecticut* 381 US 479 (1965).

[14] *Belgian Linguistic Case* 23 July 1968, Ser A no 6.

[15] *Microcensus* 27 BVerfGE 1 (1969).

[16] *Videosurveillance* Decision no 94-352 DC, 18 January 1995.

[17] France is a case in point. The *Videosurveillance* decision (ibid) links privacy to 'anonymity', 'secret', and 'inviolability of domicile'. Another example is the Constitution of the Republic of Hungary (1995), Art 59(1): 'everyone shall have the right to a good reputation, to inviolability of one's home as well as to the protection of private secrets and personal data.'

[18] Alan F. Westin, *Privacy and Freedom* (1970), 42.

[19] *Griswold* (n 13).

[20] *Kharak Singh v State of UP* (1964) 1 SCR 332; *Naz Foundation v Government of NCT of Delhi and Others*, WP(C)7455/2001, High Court of Delhi.

[21] Colombian Constitutional Court, Decision T-413/1993.

[22] South African Constitutional Court, *S v Jordan*, 2002 (6) SA 642 (CC), para 81.

mation of the very core of the right, which goes beyond the idea of privacy as seclusion and as a shield from intrusion and unwanted gaze. It protects a decisional aspect of the individual, seeking to safeguard a realm of autonomous development of the person situated in social life and in relation to others. Thus, privacy is rarely defined in fixed terms; rather, it is seen as a fluid concept constantly extending its frontiers to face new demands and the challenges of changing contexts. This fluidity has even led privacy into the realms of environmental law, since a strident sound or a hideous smell can affect the life of individuals within their homes.[23]

Albeit difficult to define, there are unavoidable issues concerning the basic elements of privacy (Section II), its protection and its limits (Section III).

II. Basic Issues

1. What Is It?

Privacy was initially seen as the 'right to be let alone', a simple yet powerful concept.[24] This negative view of privacy, however, has been surpassed by several developments in comparative constitutional law. Privacy is nowadays understood not only as a right to be free from outside interference or observation in one's own private sphere, but also as a right to define and construct one's own identity, not only in isolation but in social relations.[25] A conceptual dichotomy derived by the ECtHR illustrates these two dimensions of privacy: individual privacy and social privacy.[26]

Privacy is a flexible idea whose uses have shifted over time and its frontiers moved in reaction to the challenges of social life in post-war societies, from the emergence of mass tabloid media to the rise of computer processing power capable of cross-referencing data on a massive scale and carrying out complete profiles.[27] The gaze of the media in the private life of certain individuals has motivated protest against their 'effrontery',[28] and some of the seminal cases regarding privacy in a range of jurisdictions have been concerned with this 'informational' aspect of privacy.[29] At its core is the idea of preserving a reserved sphere from the view or knowledge of others and the restriction of access to and circulation of personal information pertaining to an individual, even though there are diverse approaches towards what types of information are covered by privacy.[30] But other jurisdictions have built extensively upon

[23] *Lopez Ostra v Spain*, 9 December 1994, Ser A no 303-C.

[24] Samuel D. Warren and Louis D. Brandeis, 'The Right to Privacy' (1890) 4 *Harvard Law Review* 195.

[25] The German Federal Constitutional Court very early said that 'the image of man behind the Basic Law is not one of an individual isolated and sovereign' (BVerfG, 20 July 1954, 4, 7, 15–16). It is not 'Robinsonian liberty' according to the classic commentary to the Basic Law. Maunz et al, *Grundgesetz Kommentar* (1991), under Art 2.

[26] *Niemietz v Germany*, 16 December 1992, Ser A no 251-B.

[27] *Census Act Case* 65 BVerfGE 1 (1983). Moreover, 'anonymization' of personal information is insufficient, since it can be re-identified and profiles may be built by cross-referencing common information contained in different databases.

[28] Warren and Brandeis (n 24).

[29] *Campbell v MGN Ltd* [2004] UKHL 22; Hungarian Constitutional Court, Decision 60/1994 (XXII.22), AB; Indian Supreme Court, *Kharak Singh v State of UP* (n 20); *Olmstead* (n 9) Brandeis J dissenting.

[30] Thus, in general, in the United States financial information is not considered private while in Europe it is protected by the right to privacy, Whitman (n 8), 1191. In Colombia, financial information was considered by the Constitutional Court as semi-private data, which means that it receives a lesser degree of protection. Colombian Constitutional Court, Decision SU-082/1995.

another facet of privacy, which we may denominate the 'decisional' aspect. The German Federal Constitutional Court recognizes a 'right to self-determination',[31] and the ECtHR already expressly recognized a 'right to personal development'.[32] The right to privacy also protects the autonomy of individuals to make choices with regard to the construction of their own identities and ways of life,[33] such as decisions on sexual orientation,[34] sexual identity,[35] and pregnancy.[36] Thus, as shown by the US Supreme Court,

> The cases sometimes characterized as protecting 'privacy' have in fact involved at least two different kinds of interests. One is the individual interest in avoiding disclosure of personal matters, and another is the interest in independence in making certain kinds of important decisions.[37]

This decisional aspect of privacy has also been protected by the ECtHR, for example not only against the criminalization of certain sexual relations[38] but moreover to further the right of a transsexual to marry.[39]

These two aspects are not wholly unrelated. The first is a mostly negative right, which treads upon protection of a person's information about features which define their identity from external intrusion or unwanted observation, both by the state and private powers. The second aspect is a mostly positive right that espouses an individual's continuous construction of their own identity and way of life which obliges the state to create proper conditions and remove obstacles for this autonomous shaping of individual identity even against unjustified interferences by private powers.[40]

The definition of the 'private realm' which is to be free from outside interference is not exempt from difficulties. Sir Edward Coke held that 'The house of everyone is to him as his castle and fortress'.[41] It would thus seem that most of what goes on inside a person's home would be a private matter, free from public interference.[42] But this is not necessarily true in all cases. There is a trend among liberal democracies to allow the state to interfere in homes where physical abuse may be taking place, such as marital rape in the United Kingdom.[43] On the other hand, until fairly recently, several jurisdictions criminalized sodomy even in private spaces.[44] Sodomy has now been decriminalized in many jurisdictions on the basis of privacy,

[31] *Census Act Case* (n 27).

[32] This right was evoked in ECtHR, *Botta v Italy*, App no 21439/93, 1998-I, and fully recognized in *Bensaid v United Kingdom*, App no 44599/98, 2001-I.

[33] Jethro K. Lieberman, *The Evolving Constitution* (1992), 407ff.

[34] Indian Supreme Court, *Gobind v State of MP* (1975) 2 SCC 148; South African Constitutional Court, *National Coalition for Gay and Lesbian Equality v Minister of Justice* 1999 (1) SA 6 (CC); Colombian Constitutional Court, Decision C-481/1998.

[35] Colombian Constitutional Court, Decision SU-337/1999. This case dealt with a hermaphrodite child whose decision on which sexual identity to adopt was protected by the Court.

[36] *Roe v Wade* 410 US 113 (1973).

[37] *Whalen v Roe* 429 US 589 (1977).

[38] *Dudgeon v United Kindgom*, 22 October 1981, Ser A no 45.

[39] ECtHR, *Christine Goodwin v United Kindgom* App no 28957/95 (Grand Chamber), 2002-VI.

[40] The Colombian Constitutional Court prohibited the expulsion of pregnant female students from Catholic schools, Decision T-393/1997, and the imposition of haircuts on students, Decision SU-642/1998.

[41] *Semayne's Case*, 77 Eng Rep 194, 195; 5 Co Rep 91, 195 (KB, 1604).

[42] South African Constitutional Court, *Case v Minister of Safety and Security*, 1996 (3) SA 617 (CC), para 91.

[43] This goes beyond constitutional law. Eg since 1990, British courts have started to convict husbands of rape, overturning the centuries-old proposition to the effect that marital rape was not a criminal offence, *SW v United Kingdom*, 22 November 1995, Ser A no 335-B.

[44] *Bowers v Hardwick* 478 US 186 (1986).

not merely because it occurs behind closed doors, but because sexual choice is an area of life where the state should not, at least in principle, interfere.[45] The line establishing a public/private divide thus moves according to subject matter in some contexts, regardless of the variable of physical space.

Similarly, privacy may protect individuals even outside their own homes. The *Von Hannover* case before the ECtHR serves to illustrate that even the outdoor leisure activities of a public figure may be protected by the right to privacy.[46] This trend echoes the famous dictum by the US Supreme Court that 'the Fourth Amendment protects people, not places'.[47] The reach of the protective aegis of the right to privacy depends not simply on specific locations but on what some courts have termed a 'reasonable expectation of privacy'.[48]

Who should reasonably expect privacy? The definition of privacy depends on several factors—ranging from cultural beliefs to technological instruments—but they usually revolve around three basic variables: space, relations, and subject matter.

(a) Space

The first variable is physical space. The right to be let alone operates principally in the secluded physical area in which the individual expects not to be observed. This is the notion underlying the prohibitions of unreasonable searches and seizures which exist in most constitutions. Whereas a person may be physically observed by a policeman whilst strolling down the street, this is not so for activity inside their home unless, usually before a judge, certain argumentative and evidentiary burdens are met.[49]

Nevertheless, space continues to be a significant variable to define the scope of privacy. The viewing of obscene material by a person in his home[50] is different from showing it to the public.[51] Seizing an item inside a person's house is different from seizing an item in plain view.[52] New developments pose new difficulties, some of which have been resolved through an expansive interpretation of 'space'. In US constitutional law, the front lawn is an extension of a person's home,[53] but a person's trash in the street is not.[54]

On the other hand, privacy does not disappear in public places and, hence, the growing controversy over the proliferation of street cameras.[55] Debates continue on how to draw the line between private and non-private affairs in the workplace[56] and privacy in public places.

However, the prohibition of intrusion into a certain physical space does not fully explain the complex structure of the right to privacy, since privacy is not only about physical activity

[45] *Naz Foundation* (n 20); *Lawrence v Texas* 539 US 558 (2003); *Dudgeon* (n 38); *National Coalition* (n 34).

[46] ECtHR, *Von Hannover v Germany*, App no 59320/00, 2004-VI.

[47] *Katz* (n 9).

[48] *HRH Prince of Wales v Associated Newspapers Ltd* [2006] EWHC Civ 1776; ECtHR, *Halford v United Kingdom*, App no 20605/92, 1997-III.

[49] *Kyllo v United States* 533 US 27 (2001).

[50] *Stanley v Georgia* 394 US 557 (1969).

[51] *Miller v California* 413 US 15 (1973).

[52] *Horton v California* 496 US 128 (1990).

[53] *Oliver v United States* 466 US 170 (1984).

[54] *Greenwood* (n 9).

[55] See Chapter 45.

[56] *City of Ontario v Quon* 560 US ___ (2010) (a police department can inspect personal text messages sent and received on a government pager but obtained from a private provider to check excessive use); Colombian Constitutional Court, Decision T-768/2008 (a bank can place hidden security cameras in its offices and employees cannot obstruct them to kiss unseen).

or information held within the confines of a living area. The issue of data retention illustrates this point. The right to privacy may comprise a right to 'informational self-determination'[57] or *habeas data*.[58] This right does not turn on the location where the data originated, or the location where it is held,[59] but on the content of the data and the purpose for which it is registered in a database or handed by one holder to another.[60]

(b) Relations

The second relevant variable is the subject to whom the decisional conduct and/or communication is directed. Unless covered by a form of secrecy,[61] communication directed towards the state or the public would usually not be protected by the right to privacy. Conversely, conduct and communication towards a life-partner would enjoy such protection.[62] This protection may exist regardless of the physical space where it occurs.[63] The fact that a famous public figure was photographed in the company of her family, spending leisure time with her children, instead of, say, addressing a conference, seems to have been a dispositive fact in the *Von Hannover* case which overturned the holding of the German Federal Constitutional Court.[64] The importance of maintaining an inner sanctum within the family is stressed by the phrasing of provisions which protect both 'private life' and 'family life'.

But the relational variable goes beyond close members of the already existing family. In the decisional aspect it covers the way an individual chooses to establish and sustain social relations that define her way of life and are essential to the construction of personal identity. This is why privacy in the United States has been held to protect decisions on sexuality of both married[65] and unmarried couples.[66] The main thrust of this concept of privacy is, according to the South African Constitutional Court, 'a sphere of private intimacy and autonomy which allows us to establish and nurture human relationships without interference from the outside community.'[67] Thus, it struck down the criminal law ban on sodomy. Other courts have protected the formalization of same-sex couples.[68] Decisional privacy covers both existing relations and relations in the making.[69]

On the other hand, certain relations with close family members in domestic physical spaces are not inevitably excluded from external intervention. Incest, irrespective of age, is the obvious example in most cultures. Moreover, if vulnerable human beings are exposed to harm,

[57] *Census Act Case* (n 27).

[58] Colombian Constitutional Court, Decision T-414/1992.

[59] But in the United States the financial information held by a bank was considered as not protected: *United States v Miller* 425 US 435 (1976). Congress then adopted the Right to Financial Privacy Act, 12 USC §§3401–22.

[60] In *District Registrar and Collector, Hyderabad and another v Canara Bank and another* (2005) 1 SCC 496, the Indian Supreme Court struck down a provision allowing authorities to inspect banking records that could lead to proof of an offense, holding that the right to privacy protected documents handed over by customers on a confidential basis.

[61] Most jurisdictions provide that criminal evidence is secret until a certain stage of the trial.

[62] 27 BVerfGE 344 (1970); *Jordan* (n 22), para 80.

[63] Thus, *Katz* (n 9).

[64] *Von Hannover* (n 46).

[65] *Griswold* (n 13).

[66] *Eisenstadt v Baird* 405 US 438 (1972).

[67] *National Coalition* (n 34).

[68] Statutes have been upheld 105 BVerfGE 313, Constitutional Council Decision n 94-352 DC, 18 January 1995; or judicially extended from heterosexual to homosexual couples, Colombian Constitutional Court, Decision C-075/2007.

[69] *Loving v Virginia* 388 US 1 (1967).

neither the space variable nor the relational variable is sufficient to justify excluding the intervention of the state. Thus, the state can impede the battering of a woman by her husband in the home and the mistreatment of children by their parents. The state also has a duty to create effective criminal protection against rape[70] and threats and harassment by family members.[71] These conducts at home are arbitrary abuses of physical force not protected by decisional or informational privacy.

(c) Subject Matter

Finally, the third variable concerns the subject matter of the conduct or communication being protected. Privacy comprises, first and foremost, information, conduct, and situations which are typically classified as intimate, such as entries in a private diary, confidential communication between spouses, sexuality, abnormal social behavior, and illnesses.[72] The US Supreme Court has allowed the government to regulate cannabis in order to make it more difficult to acquire,[73] but has struck down as a breach of privacy a provision doing so for the acquisition of contraceptives by unmarried couples.[74] The underlying notion is that certain acts, such as consensual sex, are so personal and so fundamental for the construction of identity that they cannot in principle be interfered with by the state.[75] Controversial areas exist in other subject matter. In Colombia, Congress cannot criminalize the personal consumption of narcotics[76] or punish pietistic homicide if the will of a terminally ill patient is clear.[77] Other jurisdictions regard euthanasia as not protected by the realm of intimate decision-making.[78]

The same is true for data protection. Medical records and personal health information, even of public figures,[79] enjoy a higher degree of protection than data on commercial activity, even of ordinary citizens. The German Federal Constitutional Court devised a three-tier constitutional protection of privacy (the so-called 'theory of spheres'), depending on the subject matter of the information at issue. At the core of privacy are the intimate details of a person's life which enjoy absolute protection, not subject to public interest limitations or balancing considerations (the 'intimate sphere').[80] In the outer circle are conduct and behavior that should not be disclosed if occurring in a secluded space (the 'private sphere'). Information such as recorded conversations, not necessarily including personal data, but carried out on a confidential basis, would be prima facie protected by the right to privacy but subject to disclosure in accordance with public interest concerns.[81] Finally, there is information which is not of a personal nature, and has not been generated on a confidential basis. This includes information regarding 'the relation of the person to the world around him', which would not be protected by the right to privacy at all (the 'public sphere').[82]

[70] *X and Y v The Netherlands*, 26 March 1985, Ser A no 91.

[71] ECtHR, *Osman v United Kingdom*, App no 23452/94, 1998-VIII.

[72] BVerfGE 80, 367; 27, 344; 47, 46; 49, 286; 44, 353; 32, 373.

[73] *Gonzales v Raich* 545 US 1 (2005).

[74] *Griswold* (n 13).

[75] *National Coalition* (n 34); *Naz Foundation* (n 20).

[76] Colombian Constitutional Court, Decision C-221/1994.

[77] Colombian Constitutional Court, Decision C-239/1997.

[78] *Washington v Glucksberg* 521 US 702 (1997); BVerfGE 90, 145.

[79] ECtHR, *Editions Plon v France*, App no 58148/00, 2004-IV (case related to the revelation of the secret cancer of President Mitterrand).

[80] *Microcensus Case* (n 15). See also 34 BVerfGE 238 (1973) and 1 BvR 2378/98 (2004).

[81] *Secret Recordings Case* (n 80).

[82] *Microcensus Case* (n 15).

The Colombian Constitutional Court has extended habeas data as an autonomous right to the protection of non-private information,[83] but it fixed more strict conditions on the gathering and processing of private data. 'Sensitive data' dealing with aspects such as sexual orientation or religious or political affiliation may not be gathered in some jurisdictions without appropriate safeguards,[84] and in others may not be gathered if its recollection could lead directly or indirectly to a discriminatory policy.[85]

The Australian, British, and French debates about the risk to privacy of citizen ID cards illustrate that subject matter can be very specific, as are concerns with customer loyalty cards, sensitive consumer data, and security in business databases.

The nature of the information or decision cannot be established without considering the will of the individual concerned. When the informational and decisional aspects of privacy concur, the decisional aspect has more importance. The obvious case is intimate information that the individual chooses to make public. Thus, subject matter can move from the intimate sphere to the public sphere by the autonomous decision of the interested individual. On the other side, the question arises whether information which was once public may become private because the interested individual so decides at a later point in time. This issue can be narrowly tailored to the idea of an individual's control over her past personal information[86] or broadly framed, in the case of sanctions, as a right to be forgotten.[87]

Privacy thus projects itself at different levels and in diverse forms. The three variables of space, relations, and subject matter are useful to define and distinguish these different levels and forms. A private act, in a secluded space, in the context of an intimate relationship, will most likely be at the core of the protection of the right to privacy. A change in one of these variables may weaken this protection; but the presence of one of these variables may extend the reach of privacy to unsuspected domains.

The 'right to be let alone' seems nowadays under-inclusive. Privacy is a right which protects an inner sphere of the individual from outside interference from the state and private powers, both on informational and decisional aspects, and allows the individual to make autonomous life choices regarding the construction of her identity, not only secluded from others but also situated in personal, family, and social contexts. Privacy expands or contracts depending on the way the three basic variables of subject matter, relations, and space are present in a concrete case. As the external frontiers of privacy expand, internal frontiers are established to protect other important constitutional rights and interests.

2. What Does it Cover?

(a) *The Sources of the Right*

The matters, relations, and spaces covered by privacy are dependent on the text from which the right to privacy has sprung in different jurisdictions. Most judges protect privacy based on

[83] Colombian Constitutional Court, Decision T-729/2002.

[84] Convention for the Protection of Individuals with regard to Automatic Processing of Personal Data (1981); Directive 95/46/EC of the European Parliament and of the Council of 24 October 1995 on the protection of individuals with regard to the processing of personal data and on the free movement of such data (1995), Art 8(1) of which prohibits 'the processing of personal data revealing racial or ethnic origin, political opinions, religious or philosophical beliefs, trade-union membership, and the processing of data concerning health or sex life.'

[85] Colombian Constitutional Court, Decision T-307/1999.

[86] ECtHR, *Rotaru v Romania*, App no 28341/95, 2000-V.

[87] David H. Flaherty, *Protecting Privacy in Surveillance Societies* (1989), 210; *Habeas Data Case* (n 58).

general or specific clauses provided in the constitution, but treaties may impact the protection of privacy in certain jurisdictions. In France, important privacy judgments are rendered by courts other than the Constitutional Council. The ordinary and administrative jurisdictions control whether French law is in conformity to Article 8 of the European Convention[88]—it is a review of conventionality, not of constitutionality. In the United Kingdom, since the incorporation of the Convention through the Human Rights Act 1998, judges protect privacy not only as a common law matter but also as a human rights issue.[89] In other countries, as in Colombia, even if there is a constitutional source, the right to privacy like any other constitutional right must be interpreted in harmony with the relevant treaty source.[90] The impact of the treaty source on the domestic protection of privacy is part of the broader subject of the interrelation between legal orders and the so-called internationalization of constitutional law.[91]

(b) The Scope of the Right

The scope of the right of privacy varies according to the corresponding textual source, but depends even more on the conceptions prevailing in each country. The distinction between procedural and substantive guarantees is useful in this respect.

The basic protection of privacy in most constitutional texts is the protection against search and seizure without a judicial warrant, a procedural guarantee. The corresponding provisions do not establish an all-encompassing right to privacy, but only a protection against unjustified police interference in a private realm, usually physically defined as the home (domicile) and the body (person). This, however, is a starting point for the right to privacy. In times when the most immediately perceived threat against liberty and dignity was government intrusion, constitutions established specific procedures against such interference; mainly the previous authorization by a judge based on grounds previously determined by the legislature and after the burden of proof was met.

But the greatest safeguard is the establishment of a substantive, not only procedural, guarantee of privacy. This means that even with judicial authorization based on a previous statute, the state cannot interfere with the inner sphere of the individual. The cases concerning former criminal offenses, such as abortion or sodomy, illustrate this transformation across countries and continents. In each country nuances apply once privacy became a substantial limit to the state. For example, in the United States where the *Lochner* era[92] still lingers and the right to abortion grounded on decisional privacy is still extremely controversial, in 2003 the protection of sexual relations between same-sex couples was grounded on liberty and freedom,[93] not privacy. In countries such as South Africa and India, whose constitutions also do not contain express autonomy clauses, privacy played an important role in such cases. Thus, the cases striking down prohibitions on sodomy which affirmed broad autonomy rights were based on the right to privacy in both instances,[94] notwithstanding the fact that in the South African case, the right to privacy is classed as a protection of data and information and protection against search and seizure, not protection of personal choice.[95]

[88] Stavros Tsiklitiras, *La protection effective des libertés publiques par le juge judiciarie en droit français* (1991); Anne Debet, *L'influence de la Convention européenne des droits de l'homme sur le droit civil* (2002).

[89] *Campbell* (n 29).

[90] Colombian Constitutional Court, Decision T-1319/2001.

[91] See Chapter 56.

[92] Substantive due process is linked to the *Lochner* case which delayed President Roosevelt's New Deal, *Lochner v New York* 198 US 45 (1905).

[93] *Lawrence* (n 45).

[94] *Naz Foundation* (n 45); *National Coalition* (n 34).

[95] Constitution of the Republic of South Africa (1996), s 14.

Another useful distinction is between a unified and a compartmentalized view of privacy. Even where the right of privacy has been conceptualized in an all-encompassing way, the detailed rules for its protection vary widely depending on the zone in which it is threatened. For example, there are very detailed rules concerning search and seizure of domiciles that cannot be transposed to personal data protection, and vice versa. Thus, within a country there is a coexistence of diverse regimes for the protection of privacy, separate from each other and with their own specificities. Some are judicially created; others are established by the legislature.

Some countries contemplate distinct rights for inviolability of domicile, secrecy of correspondence, image,[96] intimacy, habeas data, and free development of personality. Thus, habeas data is a distinct right to privacy and both may concur, or not, depending on the content of the data.[97] In Europe, personal data are covered by the right to privacy, and 'The mere storing of data relating to the private life of an individual amounts to an interference' with the right to private and family life.[98]

A surprising example of compartmentalization is the protection against search and seizure, which in several countries is not treated under the general heading of a violation of the right to privacy, but under the violation of more specific procedure-oriented rules, such as the requirement to show 'probable cause' before a search.[99] Hence, the rules for excluding evidence may be conceived as an expression of due process.[100]

(c) *Negative and Positive Obligations*

The right to privacy generally implies negative obligations on behalf of the state, which is therefore bound not to interfere in the personal realm of the individual. Such is the case with the prohibition of retrieving personal data on sensitive matters.[101] Private parties are also bound by this negative dimension of privacy, notably the media. As noted, this is not a recent phenomenon but an originating factor in the emergence of a right to privacy.

There are some situations, however, in which privacy does imply positive obligations. Privacy entails not only a right to exclude others, but also a right to be protected from others by the positive actions of the state. The German Federal Constitutional Court underscored the positive aspect of privacy in the *Sex Change Case*, in which authorities were obliged to register a change of sex in the identity documents of the petitioner, pursuant to the right to free development of personality.[102] The UK Supreme Court also recognized an obligation on the state 'to protect one individual from an unjustified invasion of private life by another individual and... to interpret legislation in a way which will achieve that result.'[103]

Positive obligations derived from the right to privacy have prompted interesting innovations by the ECtHR, thus redefining the obligations of state parties. The positive obligations are very diverse: states must enact comprehensive criminal legislation against rape in order to safeguard the right to private life even where the victim has not opposed physical violence;[104]

[96] In Spain, this right is violated by the commercialization of a video of a dying torero (TC 231/1988, 2 December). For Canada see *AIJC*, 181.

[97] Colombian Constitutional Court, Decision T-729/2002.

[98] ECtHR, *S and Marper v United Kingdom*, App no 30562/04, 4 December 2008 (Grand Chamber).

[99] *Ornelas v United States* 517 US 690, 696 (1996).

[100] ECtHR, *Khan v United Kingdom*, App no 35394/97, 2000-V; *Mapp v Ohio* 367 US 643 (1961); but Colombian Constitutional Court, Decision SU-159/2002.

[101] 34 BVerfGE 238 (1973); 1 BvR 2378/98 (2004); Colombian Constitutional Court, Decision T-307/1999.

[102] 49 BVerfGE 286 (1979). The Colombian Constitutional Court also recognized a right to sexual self-determination for a hermaphrodite child to decide on his/her sex (n 35).

[103] *Douglas v Hello* [2005] EWCA Civ 595.

[104] ECtHR, *MC v Bulgaria*, App no 39272/98, 2003-XII.

the state must allow a child to discover her biological origins by an expedient procedure;[105] the state must provide prison inmates with the materials needed to establish correspondence;[106] a judicial decision of eviction must be executed to allow an owner to regain possession of his apartment.[107] There are even positive obligations to provide information in order for families to take decisions concerning their health[108] and to enact measures allowing effective and timely access to legal therapeutic abortion.[109] The Strasbourg Court has refused, however, to recognize a positive obligation of the state to extend to the father the right of financed maternal leave granted by the state to the mother.[110] More surprisingly, since it had previously recognized the positive obligation of the state to facilitate the identification of the natural father,[111] it has refused to recognize this same obligation concerning the mother, when she expressly wished to give birth anonymously.[112]

III. The Protection of the Right to Privacy

1. How is it Protected?

The right to privacy is protected by the legislature, the administration, and the executive. But the institutional arrangements vary. A comparison of the procedural protections in place may be drawn from four different areas.

First, most jurisdictions generally establish *ex post* remedies, but some also include *ex ante* protections. This explains the proliferation of independent administrative agencies in the field. Also, the French *referée*, is a fast and urgent judicial procedure that prevents violation of certain rights by non-constitutional judges. Since the 1950s civil judges have developed this preventive writ and applied it in newsworthy cases—such as the diaries of a famous actress[113]—and some publications were halted or even seized by this method.[114] It became regulated by legislation in 1970.

Secondly, most jurisdictions generally provide both constitutional and civil remedies for breaches of privacy. In the United States, tort law provides four specific civil torts for private breaches of privacy: intrusion upon seclusion or solitude; public disclosure of embarrassing private facts; publicity which places the plaintiff in a false light; and appropriation of name or likeness.[115] German law provides a general civil tort action to protect privacy as part of a 'general right of personality'.[116]

[105] *Mikulic v Croatia*, App no 53176/99, 2002-I.
[106] *Cotlet v Romania*, App no 38565/97, 3 June 2003.
[107] *Cvijetic v Croatia*, App no 71549/01, 2004.
[108] *MacGinley and Egan v United Kingdom*, App no 21825/93, 1998-III.
[109] *Tysiąc v Poland*, App no 5410/03, 2007-IV.
[110] *Petrovic v Austria*, App no 20458/92, 1998-II.
[111] *Mikulic* (n 105).
[112] *Odièvre v France*, App no 42326/98 (Grand Chamber), 2003-III.
[113] The Case of the Diaries of Marlene Dietrich, Cour d'appel de Paris, 16 March 1955. The first case is one century older. A tribunal ordered the destruction of any publication with photographs of an actress lying dead on her bed; Tribunal Civil de la Seine, 16 June 1858.
[114] The first case of seizure of a magazine was in 1965 concerning photographs of a minor receiving medical attention in hospital. The highest civil court, the Cour de Cassation, upheld the seizure (*France Editions et Publications v Veuve Gerard Philippe*, 12 July 1965).
[115] Prosser (n 6), 389.
[116] Section 823(1) of the BGB; Federal Court of Justice, NJW 1954, 1404 (Leserbrief).

Thirdly, some constitutional remedies provide an action for concrete breaches of privacy, but some jurisdictions also include the possibility of abstract constitutional review. Thus, jurisdictions such as Austria, France, Germany, Spain, Colombia, and Hungary, where abstract review is generally exercised by the constitutional courts, provide an all-embracing remedy against possible legislative breaches of privacy, mainly the invalidation of the legislative act.

Fourthly, while most concrete constitutional remedies require state action, other remedies encompass possible breaches of privacy by private action. The state action requirement has been somewhat circumvented in some cases—as in the United States[117] and Germany[118]—through the review of lower court judgments on private litigation under the lens of constitutional principles.[119] In Colombia, the writ of protection of fundamental rights (*acción de tutela*) may be brought against private powers with whom the petitioner is in a relation of subordination or defenselessness.[120]

2. What Limits Can it Have?

The possible limits to the right to privacy may be grouped in three basic categories. In the first, privacy is restricted when a decision implicates the rights of others. Tension commonly occurs between privacy and freedom of the press. The relative weight of each right varies according to the character of the information at issue and the person involved. In the case of public figures the right to privacy is diluted to a varying extent,[121] since persons who have voluntarily 'assumed roles of especial prominence in the affairs of society'[122] put their personal privacy at risk by choice. However, this is only true of 'newsworthy' events, which the public has an interest in knowing.[123] In the United States, freedom of the press has greater weight and thus even the name of a rape victim can be published.[124]

Secondly, there are public interest justifications. This is generally the underlying notion behind limitations in the context of criminal procedures, espionage, or prevention of terrorism. Virtually all jurisdictions accept state intervention in private spheres when a certain evidentiary threshold is met and certain procedural safeguards are followed. These safeguards have undergone serious restrictions with antiterrorist legislation passed in several countries in recent years.[125] The reason behind this is that states want to enjoy some power to obtain evidence not only for criminal investigations but for the prevention of crime.

Thirdly, self-regarding duties have given a basis for upholding prohibitions on drugs and assisted suicide in Germany and the United States.[126] The Colombian Constitutional Court has

[117] *Shelley v Kraemer* 334 US 1 (1948).

[118] 7 BVerfGE 198 (1958).

[119] Mark Tushnet, 'The Issue of State Action/Horizontal Effect in Comparative Constitutional Law' (2003) 1 *International Journal of Constitutional Law* 79ff.

[120] Political Constitution of Colombia (1991), Art 86.

[121] *Rosenbloom v Metromedia, Inc* 403 US 29 (1971). A more restrictive standard is taken by the ECtHR in *Von Hannover* (n 46). Also, in the *Soraya* case, where the German Federal Constitutional Court held: 'An imaginary interview adds nothing to the formation of real public opinion. As a against press utterances of this sort, the protection of privacy takes unconditional priority', 34 BVerfGE 269 (1973). British courts take a similar stance: *Campbell* (n 29).

[122] *Gertz v Robert Welch, Inc* 418 US 323 (1974).

[123] *Time, Inc v Hill* 385 US 374 (1967).

[124] *Cox Broadcasting Corp v Cohn* 420 US 469 (1975).

[125] eg the USA PATRIOT Act (2001) relaxed some of the rules which constrained US federal authorities in conducting surveillance through wiretaps. The UK Terrorism Act 2000, ss 41–3, allows police officials to search a person reasonably suspected of being a terrorist without a warrant.

[126] 90 BVerfGE 145 (1994); *Glucksberg* (n 78).

adopted a restrictive reading of self-regarding duties by distinguishing between 'perfectionist' and 'self-protecting' measures.[127] The latter seek reasonably to protect an individual from imminent harm, the former seek to unacceptably impose a model of morality and virtue on the individual.

The limits themselves are generally limited by judges through several devices. First, a legal ground is generally demanded (principle of legality).[128] The limitation must somehow be established by law, and not be the result of a particular decision made on a discretionary basis. Moreover, the legal basis must be clear and detailed.[129] Secondly, there must be a legitimate interest in restricting privacy, and some relation between the means used and the ends sought (principle of rationality).[130] Thirdly, some courts have engaged in a balancing of rights, to determine whether a limitation is excessive (principle of proportionality).[131] Fourthly, the burden of argumentation and proof is distributed in some way, according to the relative weight accorded to privacy with respect to other rights.[132] But some specific forms of restriction on privacy are bound by specific rules, not open balancing, as is the case with search and seizure and the exclusionary rule.

IV. Conclusion

Some new challenges to privacy have prompted deep concern, such as the ever-gazing eye of permanent surveillance.[133] The issues are almost infinite: Can there be DNA databases, retention, and profiling?[134] How should personal information sent and deactivated on the internet be regulated?[135] Can telecommunications data be retained, for how long, and for what purposes?[136] Are Google street-view cars violating privacy standards?[137] Is airport whole-body scanning an arbitrary strip search?[138]

Some wonder if the increasing power to see what any individual is or does, will lead to the end of privacy. Others argue that the expansion of the decisional aspect of privacy will lead to the end of basic social arrangements and institutions. Both apocalyptic concerns are

[127] Colombian Constitutional Court, Decision C-309/1997.

[128] Elisabeth Zoller, 'Le droit au respect de la vie privée aux Etats Unis' in Sudre (n 2), 67. See also BVerfGE 33, 1.

[129] *Kruslin v France*, 24 April 1990, Ser A no 176-A.

[130] Décision no 2005-532 DC, 19 January 2006; Décision no 2007-557 DC, 15 November 2007; *Planned Parenthood v Casey* 505 US 833 (1992).

[131] ECtHR, *Chapman v United Kingdom*, App no 27238/95 (Grand Chamber), 2001-I.

[132] eg the German Federal Constitutional Court has gone through at least three fluctuating stages in the protection of privacy against the protection of other constitutional rights: David P. Currie, *The Constitution of the Federal Republic of Germany* (1994), 181.

[133] See Chapter 45.

[134] No, according to *S and Marper* (n 98); yes, according to *R v Rodgers* [2006] 1 SCR 554.

[135] 'Report of Findings' into Facebook Inc under the Personal Information Protection and Electronic Documents Act, Assistant Privacy Commissioner of Canada.

[136] Yes, according to Directive 2006/24/EC of the European Parliament and of the Council of 15 March 2006 on the retention of data generated or processed in connection with the provision of publicly available electronic communications services or of public communications networks and amending Directive 2002/58/EC (2006); no, according to a recent decision by the German Federal Constitutional Court, 1 BvR 256/08 (2010).

[137] No, according to the US Federal Trade Commission, in 2010; yes, according to the Privacy Commissioner of Canada, in 2010, but due to a 'careless error'.

[138] Legislatures are calling hearings and lawsuits are beginning on this issue.

exaggerated. The evolution of privacy indicates that each new challenge prompts an expansion of the right, and that as the right expands new internal frontiers are established to protect the rights of others. But as fluidity and complexity increase, the protection of privacy depends increasingly on safeguards derived from privacy-enhancing techniques, independent agencies, and specific legislative remedies and designs. The enduring challenge is for the capacity of courts to preserve the right to privacy.

Bibliography

Annuaire International de Justice Constitutionnelle, Economica et Presses Universitaires d'Aix-Marseilles (2001)

Colin Bennett and Rebecca Grant, *Visions of Privacy. Policy Choices for the Digital Age* (1999)

David Flaherty, *Protecting Privacy in Surveillance Societies* (1992)

Francoise Gilbert, *Global Privacy and Security Law* (2010)

William L. Prosser, 'Privacy' (1960) 48 *California Law Review* 383

Francois Rigaux, *La protection de la vie privée et des autres biens de la personnalité* (1990)

Jed Rubenfeld, 'The Right of Privacy' (1988) 102 *Harvard Law Review* 737

Daniel Solove, *Understanding Privacy* (2008)

Frédéric Sudre, *Le droit au respect de la vie privée au sens de la convention européenne des droits de l'homme* (2005)

Samuel Warren and Louis Brandeis, 'The Right to Privacy' (1890) 4 *Harvard Law Review* 195

Raymond Wacks, *Privacy: A Very Short Introduction* (2010)

Alan Westin, *Privacy and Freedom* (1967)

John Whitman, 'The Two Western Cultures of Privacy: Dignity versus Liberty' (2004) 113 *Yale Law Journal* 1151

Web Resources

Independent Agencies for Data Protection

Australia, Office of the Privacy Commissioner (http://www.privacy.gov.au/)

Canada, Office of the Privacy Commissioner (http://www.priv.gc.ca/index_e.cfm)

France, CNIL (http://www.cnil.fr/english/)

Germany, Federal Commissioner for Data Protection (http://www.bfdi.bund.de/cln_134/EN/Home/homepage_node.html)

Spain, Spanish Agency for Data Protection (http://www.agpd.es/portalwebAGPD/index-ides-idphp.php)

United Kingdom, Information Commissioner's Office (http://www.ico.gov.uk/)

United States, Federal Communications Commission (http://www.fcc.gov/)

United States, Federal Trade Commission (http://www.ftc.gov/)

Privacy Statutes and Guidelines

National Omnibus Privacy Laws (http://www.privacyexchange.org/legal/nat/omni/nol.html)

National Sectoral Privacy Laws (http://www.privacyexchange.org/legal/nat/sect/natsector.html)

OECD Guidelines on the Protection of Privacy and Transborder Flows of Personal Data (http://www.oecd.org/document/18/0,3343,en_2649_34255_1815186_1_1_1_1,00.html)

Other Web Resources

Article 29 Data Protection Working Party (http://ec.europa.eu/justice/policies/privacy/workinggroup/index_en.htm)
Electronic Privacy Information Center (http://epic.org/)
Privacy International (http://www.privacyinternational.org/)

CHAPTER 47

EQUALITY

SUSANNE BAER

Berlin and Ann Arbor

In law, equality is everywhere. But equality (Greek, *isotes*; Latin, *aequitas*, *aequalitas*; French, *égalité*; German, *Gleichheit*) is not just a legal issue, as an idea of justice, a principle, or a right. Not least since the French Revolution, equality has also been a political claim, and one of the most controversial ones, oscillating between egalitarianism (associated with Marxism or socialism, but also with the welfare state) and anti-egalitarianism (associated with capitalism, (neo) liberalism, but also with a liberal state). In philosophy, equality is a canonical topic with controversies around the meaning of equality, the relation between justice and equality, the material requirements and measure of the ideal of equality (equality of what?), the scope of equality (equality among whom?), and its status within a theory of justice (the value of equality).[1]

In law, several notions of equality inform constitutionalism around the globe. Equality is foundational to *the idea of justice*, to law as a form or a mode of regulation, in that the very idea of legal norms implies that they apply to all legal subjects alike. In a sense, equality forms the bedrock of the rule of law and a key component of constitutionalism. This is based on a notion of substantive universal moral equality of all human beings, an embrace of individuality. It was not endorsed by Aristotle or Plato, but has been widely held since the Stoics who emphasized the natural equality of all rational beings. Similar positions can be found in early New Testament Christianity, in the Talmud, and in Islam, as well as in Hobbes,[2] Locke,[3] and

[1] Stefan Gosepath, 'Equality' in Edward N. Zalta (ed), *Stanford Encyclopedia of Philosophy* (2007), available at <http://plato.stanford.edu/entries/equality/>.

[2] Thomas Hobbes, *Leviathan* (1651).

[3] John Locke, *The Second Treatise of Government* (1690).

Rousseau,[4] culminating in Kant's moral philosophy.[5] In Kant's categorical imperative, a recognition of equal freedom for all rational human beings forms the sole principle of fundamental human rights.[6] This is the idea that many a constitutional preamble alludes to (examples include the United States, India, Egypt, Kenya, etc 'We the people'). It is also the idea of fundamental equality which informs most liberty rights ('everyone has the right').

More recent constitutions not only emphasize *individual*, but also address *collective* notions of belonging which undergrid diversity. This is often the case in postcolonial settings,[7] as well as in transnational constitutionalism, as in the EU[8] which rests upon non-discrimination among member state nationals.[9]

In addition, notions of equality also oscillate between *recognition* and *redistribution*, a right to be among equals and a right to an equal share. Constitutional law in fact merges both. Political rights are not only about recognition, but in fact distribute political power, or agency. Similarly, economic rights may appear to redistribute resources, but also regulate recognition in that they not only prevent poverty, but also marginalization (thus, precarization) and social exclusion.

Finally, a constitutional right to equality may address specific *inequalities*, such as privilege or disadvantage, in clauses that prohibit discrimination regarding race, sex, disability, age, etc. It may also target different *spheres of application*, as political equality, equal taxation, equality in education, equal access to employment etc.

To grasp the multiplicity of relevant rules and meanings, I first discuss key equality guarantees in law today. I then focus on different understandings of the right to equality: as either a principle or an individually enforceable claim (the status); as an 'empty idea', a rationality test, or a 'substantive' right (the content); as a right of individuals or for groups (who bears the right?). I next examine equality as categorically distinctly structured as opposed to or as similar to other liberty interests (the test); as a general entitlement or as a specific guarantee to address particular inequalities, either separate or intersecting (the inequalities); and as general or specific regarding the application in distinct areas of life (the reach). Finally, I address the often crucial question of whether equality as a fundamental right is directed exclusively against the state, or whether it may also have binding effects on other actors.

I. Key Equality Guarantees

Equality clauses are found at all levels of law, ranging from the Universal Declaration of Human Rights (which promises equality in Articles 1, 2, 7, 10, 16, 21, 23, and 26), numerous provisions in the human rights treaties of the United Nations and of regional systems,[10]

[4] Jean-Jacques Rousseau, *Discours sur l'origine et les fondements de l'inégalité parmi les hommes* [*A Discourse on Inequality*] (1755).

[5] Imanuel Kant, *Metaphysik der Sitten* (1797) in Preußische Akademie der Wissenschaften (ed), *Kants Gesammelte Schriften* (1902).

[6] Ibid vol V, 230.

[7] See Constitution of the Republic of South Africa: 'united in our diversity' as well as 'every citizen is equally protected by law'.

[8] See Charter of Fundamental Rights of the European Union, Preamble: 'The Union contributes to the preservation and to the development of these common values while respecting the diversity of the cultures and traditions of the peoples of Europe as well as the national identities of the Member States.'

[9] See Ch 2 of the Lisbon Treaty on European Citizenship.

[10] See Art 1 of the American Convention on Human Rights, as interpreted in Proposed Amendments to the Naturalisation Provisions of the Constitution of Costa Rica, Advisory Opinion OC4-84, 1984, Inter-American Court of Human Rights, Ser A No 4 (1984); African Charter on Human and Peoples' Rights, Arts 2 and 3.

to national, subnational, or local and communal constitutions. Equality provisions are also found in statutes and in by-laws of non-state entities, like a private club, a university, or a corporation. As in all multilevel law, equality law does not always amount to a coherent body of norms, but as an instance of legal pluralism, equality law is more or less consistent, sometimes inherently ambivalent and even at times contradictory.

In global human rights law, equality features prominently in all key documents, from the non-binding Universal Declaration to the binding International Covenant on Civil and Political Rights (ICCPR) and the International Covenant on Economic, Social and Cultural Rights (ICESCR), as well as several treaties that address specific inequalities (discussed below). In international customary law, equality is not explicitly guaranteed, although the prohibitions against genocide and against slavery can be understood as targeting the most murderous aspects of a systematic inequality that fly in the face of equal dignity for all human beings. Regional human rights systems guarantee the right to equality.[11] The EU Treaty references international human rights law and emphasizes sex equality,[12] while the Charter of Fundamental Rights also addresses distributive aspects of equality.[13] Also, under the ICCPR, even measures taken in states of emergency may not discriminate, since 'there are elements or dimensions of the right to non-discrimination that cannot be derogated from in any circumstances'.[14] Moreover, seemingly all national constitutions feature an equality clause.

While equality is ubiquitous in treaties and constitutions, language differs significantly, as do levels of specificity in defining the meaning and scope of equality. Often, constitutions and treaties guarantee a *general right* to equality. This is phrased as a right to equal treatment, equality before the law or of the law, a principle of non-distinction, and, in more recent texts, non-discrimination, or a combination of these terms and concepts. As an example, in the 2010 Constitution of Kenya, Article 27 ('equality and freedom from discrimination') guarantees equality before the law, equal protection and equal benefit of the law, the equal enjoyment of all rights and fundamental freedoms, equal treatment of and equal opportunities for women and men, and prohibits direct and indirect discrimination. Much more succinctly, the Fourteenth Amendment to the US Constitution, adopted in 1868, proclaims that no state shall 'deny to any person within its jurisdiction the equal protection of the laws'.[15]

However, even such general clauses *often also institute inequalities*. In section 2, the Fourteenth Amendment to the US Constitution specifies that 'Indians not taxed' will not be represented, and that the right to vote is limited to 'any of the male inhabitants of such State, being twenty-one years of age and citizens of the United States' who has not participated 'in rebellion, or other crime'. Similarly, the French Declaration of the Rights of Man in 1789 did not extend its equality guarantee[16] to women, inspiring an alternative draft by Olympe de Gouges in 1791; also, in spite of lobbying efforts, it did not prohibit slavery. At present, the ICCPR guarantees equality (Art 26), but only prohibits the death penalty regarding persons below age 18 and pregnant women (Art 6(5)) and reserves the right to vote for nationals (Art 25). Also, the non-binding Cairo Declaration on Human Rights in Islam (1990) proclaims a right to equality but, based on a notion of essential difference, also endorses several

[11] Cf Inter-American Convention on Human Rights, Art 1(1); African Charter on Human and Peoples' Rights, Art 2; ECHR, Art 14 and Protocol 12.

[12] See Arts 2, 3, 15, and 157.

[13] See Ch III on equality, Ch IV on solidarity.

[14] Gen Comment No 29, CCPR/C/21/Rev.1/Add.11.

[15] Section 1.

[16] See Art I: 'Men are born and remain free and equal in rights. Social distinctions can be founded only on the common utility.'

inequalities otherwise not accepted in human rights law, particularly regarding religion and gender.[17] Similar inequalities are enshrined in the Arab Charter of Human Rights, revised in 2005.[18] Thus, equality may be simultaneously guaranteed *and* limited in constitutional and human rights law; the supreme law of the land may thus promise equality but also entrench inequality and institutionalize discrimination. Some constitutions expressly address this internal tension, as Malaysia in Article 2(2).[19] While equality as a fundamental right is thus ubiquitous, it differs enormously in status, binding force, content, rigor of enforcement or structure, inequalities targeted, and reach.

II. The Status of a Right to Equality

Equality may be guaranteed and interpreted in both constitutional law and human rights law, as either a principle or as a right. This may be explicit in the legal text, but it may also be implied by reference to different procedural options. Whether or not one is able to lodge an individual complaint before a constitutional court or human rights body and to present claims subject to enforcement, can distinguish a right from a principle.

As a *principle*, equality informs the very idea of law as a general norm. Some constitutions command the state to pursue equality, as in the German Basic Law.[20] And often, equality informs all other human rights as is expressly stated in clauses that read 'Everyone has the right to. . . .' Equality is, then, the 'starting point of all liberties';[21] it informs all human rights.[22] As an example, under Article 14 of the European Convention on Human Rights (ECHR), discrimination is expressly prohibited in relation to one of the substantive rights set forth in the Convention.[23]

More specifically, some constitutions feature *distributive notions* of equality. As such, equality is closely linked to social rights (see Chapters 49 and 50), but it is technically guaranteed as a principle that informs the interpretation of liberties. Then, a liberty may turn into a right to participate, or a right of equal access, which in fact amounts to a specific equality test (below).

Much more often, equality is guaranteed as a *free-standing human right against discrimination*. In the European human rights system, this move to an independent right was achieved by way of an amendment[24] and in court decisions.[25] In many constitutions, equality is expressly

[17] See Art 7, which states that

> (a) Woman is equal to man in human dignity, and has her own rights to enjoy as well as duties to perform, and has her own civil entity and financial independence, and the right to retain her name and lineage. (b) The husband is responsible for the maintenance and welfare of the family.

[18] See Art 3(3):

> Men and women are equal in respect of human dignity, rights and obligations within the framework of the positive discrimination established in favor of women by the Islamic Shariah, other divine laws and by applicable laws and legal instruments. Accordingly, each State party pledges to take all the requisite measures to guarantee equal opportunities and effective equality between men and women in the enjoyment of all the rights set out in this Charter.

[19] 'Except as expressly authorized by this Constitution, there shall be no discrimination. . . .'

[20] See Art 3(2)(2): 'The state shall promote the actual implementation of equal rights for women and men and take steps to eliminate disadvantages that now exist.'

[21] Justice Tanaka, *South West Africa Cases* [1966] ICJ Reports 304.

[22] UN Charter (1945), Art 1(3).

[23] But note *Burden v United Kingdom*, App no 13378/05, 29 April 2008 (Grand Chamber), para 58.

[24] Protocol 12 (n 11).

[25] *Broeks v Netherlands*, Comm 172/1984 and *Zwaan-de Vries v Netherlands*, Comm 182/1984 (sex discrimination in social security law).

guaranteed as such. It is an individual right directed against unequal treatment, and more specifically recently, against discrimination. Some constitutions refer to historical disadvantage, like section 15 of the Canadian Charter. Article 1 of the Convention on the Elimination of All Forms of Discrimination against Women (CEDAW) lists

> any distinction, exclusion or restriction . . . which has the effect or purpose of impairing or nullifying the recognition, enjoyment or exercise . . . of human rights and fundamental freedoms in the political, economic, social, cultural, civil or any other field.

Legal language thus already points to a variety of concepts that inform the content of a right to equality.

III. The Content of a Right to Equality

Equality has been described as many things, among them an empty idea, a guarantee of rationality, a formal right, a substantive right, and there are discussions contrasting equality of opportunity and equality of results. There is thus no single concept that defines equality as a right, but rather several controversial interpretations of it.

The starting point of all understandings of equality is that equality is not identity or sameness, but that equality implies, based on the moral equality of all human beings, being different but fundamentally similar. However, the focuses of equality theories do shift. Some focus on the claim that all individuals *are* equal, others on the claim that all should be *treated* alike, some ground their arguments in metaphysics, some in politics. In the present context, equality means to not differentiate between individuals in irrational ways, because we are essentially equal. This is a right to equal treatment, derived from a concept of humanity, featured most prominently in Kantian rationality. This symmetrical and formal approach goes back to Aristotle and has been discussed in law as a similarly situated test.[26]

As such, equality amounts to the *prohibition against arbitrariness*, and thus to an obligation to act rationally. Some philosophers conceptualize equality in that tradition, that is, as a right to rationality,[27] a right to justification,[28] a right to treatment of persons as equals, with equal concern and respect,[29] an 'egalitarian plateau',[30] a promise of a deliberative reasoning before something is done. The more we consider a social distinction irrational, the more a right to equality prohibits making that distinction. In the history of equality jurisprudence, the focus on rationality has however served to weaken claims for equal treatment. The weakness of this equality concept derives from the similarity test: the more we understand people or situations to be different, the less we demand equality for them. To name an infamous example, German Nazis relied on this concept to argue that since Jews are not similar to 'Aryans', they could be progressively excluded from the community of Germans, up to the point of mass murder. The

[26] 'Treat like cases as like' according to Aristotle, in Sarah Broadie and Christopher Rowe, *Aristotle Nicomachean Ethics: Translation, Introduction, and Commentary* (2002), vol 3, 1131a10–sb15; '*Politics Book III*' in Jonathan Barnes (ed), *The Complete Works of Aristotle: The Revised Oxford Translation* (1984), III.9.1280 a8–15, III. 12. 1282b18–23; 'persons similarly situated must be treated similarly'; *Trimble v Gordon* 430 US 762 (1977).

[27] Isaiah Berlin, 'Equality' in LVI *Proceedings of the Aristotelian Society* (1955–56).

[28] Rainer Forst, 'The Justification of Human Rights and the Basic Right to Justification: A Reflexive Approach' (2010) 120(4) *Ethics* 711.

[29] Ronald Dworkin, *Sovereign Virtue. The Theory and Practice of Equality* (2000), 370.

[30] Will Kymlicka, *Contemporary Political Philosophy: An Introduction* (1990), 5.

US Supreme Court based its endorsement of segregation between 'Blacks' and 'Whites' on a 'separate but equal' doctrine in *Plessy v Ferguson*,[31] claiming that a separation was not unequal treatment. In the 1954 decision of *Brown v Board of Education*,[32] the Supreme Court eventually found that such a differentiation bears the seed of discrimination, such that 'separate educational facilities are inherently unequal'.[33]

Even if we would argue that segregation violates human dignity and the right to life, a similarity test generally allows for the exclusion and marginalization of some for being 'different', rather than strive for equality for all. Today, widespread examples are law on pregnancy, and law on abortion. The more one defines these to be unique, dissimilar, or 'different', the more one can justify 'different' treatment, which, in contexts of gender inequality, has the effect of discriminating against women.

At the other end of the interpretive spectrum, a right to equality may be understood as a prohibition of any distinction, because to distinguish between humans who are essentially the same is irrational. Constitutions may therefore feature a general equal treatment clause, directed against arbitrariness, and specific equality clauses, as rights against discrimination. Examples are Article 3 of the German Basic Law, section 15 of the Canadian Charter of Rights and Freedoms, Article 32 of the Polish Constitution, or Articles 14 to 18 of the Constitution of India. Such specific clauses may then be understood to strictly prohibit any distinction which takes into account a difference that 'doesn't make a difference'. For example, a right to sex equality may then be understood as a right against ever using sex to make a difference (which is discussed as 'degendering' in gender studies). Such an approach would indeed solve many problems of people who do not conform to a rigid sex-gender system, that is, intersexuals or people with a transgender identity. If we do not allow for sex to ever justify a difference, to make a distinction, it would not matter who we are sexually. On the other hand, an overly radical degendering may hinder an adequate understanding of diversity and pluralism, and of sex based inequality as well, that is, if one renders sex-differentiated data on inequality to be problematic. As another example, a concept of equality as a right against distinctions may inform radical secularism or laicity, which prohibits any reference to religion or belief as discriminatory. This may indeed solve problems of marginalized beliefs and non-believers, but it would also produce complicated clashes between a desire to pursue one's spiritual life and a state that does not allow for that to matter (see Chapter 43). Thus, a rule that will not allow for any religiously inspired clothing will affect mainstream Christians much differently than devout Muslim women or orthodox Jewish men. As another example, an understanding of citizenship as radically 'national' and not diverse or pluralistic regarding ethnicity may inform consistent politics of equal treatment, but it may, as in France, also serve to refuse any collection of data that would bring to light discriminatory social structures. Therefore, a symmetrical or a radically 'blind' approach with a focus on distinctions does not allow us to address the complicated cases relating to equality in a pluralist world. Rather, an asymmetrical approach to equality seems fit to address the power relations involved, which lead to injustice in the form of discrimination.

A starting point of constitutionalism is that people are fundamentally equal in that they are human beings (based on metaphysics, or on politics), but the whole point about being human is the ability to differ, by choosing to lead one's own life, in situations that differ tremendously, around the globe, but also within a region, a city, a social entity. This is why a constitutional right to equality is often interpreted as a right to recognition of such diversity. Historically, the

[31] 163 US 537 (1896). [32] 347 US 483 (1954). [33] Ibid 495.

focus has shifted from an emphasis on similarity to a recognition of difference, and eventually, dominance.

Then, equality is a claim to diversity *and* a call for equal treatment. This tension has been called by authors like Minow 'a dilemma of difference' in equality law;[34] it is a central challenge to politics of multiculturalism and pluralism, to minority rights and other group based privileges (see Chapter 53). Philosophers such as Gosepath have argued that in light of this, equality is not one concept, but a bundle of principles to ensure social justice.[35] In defining the content of a right to equality, we need to grapple with the fact that a right *against* a distinction does indeed target something a person may *want* to be positively identified with (eg a right to sex equality for people who identify as male or female, a right against disability discrimination for people who want to be recognized as facing specific barriers, a right against ageism for people who identify as old or young). Formal equality may not help us in certain situations where we may need an accommodation of difference.

Equality law may therefore be seen as directed against a difference we care for. Again, this is why it is so important to distinguish between an understanding of equality as a right *of* or *to* differences and equality as a right *against* discrimination. The challenge is particularly evident in the case of rights against discrimination relating to a disability. Disability is, in a world shaped according to specific standards, a status of non-conformity with that standard, a way of being different. Equality law cannot fight that difference, but needs to accommodate that feature of human diversity, in light of the power relations in play. Thus, human rights law like the UN Convention on the Rights of Persons with Disabilities from 2006 obligates states to respect and accommodate disabled people as equals (Arts 3 and 4). It calls upon us, indeed an obligation, to change the world into a barrier-free environment for all (Arts 5(3), (4) and 9). Equality then means to modify the standards we live with, rather than modify a person who does not 'fit'. Here, equality law becomes a right to transformation, to change the structures and to redistribute power, rather than a right to change oneself to fit in.

In other instances, equality law may have to accept a difference we care for but may be directed at those aspects of that difference which amount to dominance, resulting in disadvantage. Feminist lawyer and theorist MacKinnon has famously rejected the difference approach, and conceptualized the dominance approach to equality. As a substantive right, in this view, equality is a claim to equal treatment in recognition of one's differences: it is the prohibition of a difference amounting to an inequality. Thus, it is not difference but dominance that matters.[36] It is called asymmetrical, substantive, or material accommodation of those who are disadvantaged, with a focus on dominance, subordination, discrimination. Here, equality is a right against being hurt, against violating the harm principle of liberal constitutionalism according to which your liberty ends when others suffer.

The substantive approach is dominant in much human rights law.[37] Several constitutions explicitly prohibit 'discrimination', and courts are very clear that authorities that engage in or tolerate violence against historically disadvantaged groups or minorities violate a right to equality. The European Court of Human Rights (ECtHR), in *Alekseyev v Russia*,[38] stated that lack of police

[34] Martha Minow, *Making All the Difference: Inclusion, Exclusion, and American Law* (1991), 20.

[35] Gosepath (n 1).

[36] Catharine MacKinnon, 'Difference and Dominance: On Sex Discrimination' in *Feminism Unmodified* (1988), 32–45.

[37] Christian Tomuschat, *Human Rights* (2008), 205. Committees emphasize that human right to equality 'mandate both de facto and de jure equality'; Committee on Economic, Social and Cultural Rights, General Comment No 16, 2005, para 7.

[38] ECtHR Appl nos 4916/07, 25924/08 and 14599/09, 23 October 2010.

protection for gay rights activists in Russia is a violation of human rights.[39] It is, according to the Court, discrimination prohibited by equality law.[40]

In addition, constitutional law may explicitly name the harm it is meant to stop. For example, the South African Constitution names racism and sexism as inequalities a constitution shall not tolerate.[41] Also, the Canadian Charter of Fundamental Rights and Freedoms, states that

> (1) Every individual is equal before and under the law and has the right to the equal protection and equal benefit of the law without discrimination and, in particular, without discrimination based on race, national or ethnic origin, colour, religion, sex, age or mental or physical disability.
>
> (2) Subsection (1) does not preclude any law, program or activity that has as its object the amelioration of conditions of disadvantaged individuals or groups including those that are disadvantaged because of race, national or ethnic origin, colour, religion, sex, age or mental or physical disability.[42]

In jurisprudence, it is the Canadian Court which articulated this approach in *Andrews v Law Society of British Columbia*.[43] Justice McIntyre explained that the similarly situated

> test as stated...is seriously deficient in that it excludes any consideration of the nature of the law. If it were to be applied literally, it could be used to justify the Nuremberg laws of Adolf Hitler. Similar treatment was contemplated for all Jews....Thus, mere equality of application to similarly situated groups or individuals does not afford a realistic test for a violation of equality rights.

Rather, 'consideration must be given to the content of the law, to its purpose, and its impact upon those to whom it applies, and also upon those whom it excludes from its application.' Finally, the Justice added, the rights to equality 'are granted with the direction contained in s. 15 itself that they be without discrimination. Discrimination is unacceptable in a democratic society because it epitomizes the worst effects of the denial of equality, and discrimination reinforced by law is particularly repugnant.' The Justice went on to define discrimination:

> [it] may be described as a distinction, whether intentional or not but based on grounds relating to personal characteristics of the individual or group, which has the effect of imposing burdens, obligations, or disadvantages on such individual or group not imposed upon others, or which withholds or limits access to opportunities, benefits, and advantages available to other members of society. Distinctions based on personal characteristics attributed to an individual solely on the basis of association with a group will rarely escape the charge of discrimination, while those based on an individual's merits and capacities will rarely be so classed.

[39] Ibid:

> 77. ...The Court concludes that the Government failed to carry out an adequate assessment of the risk to the safety of the participants in the events and to public order ...
>
> 81. The Court further reiterates that it would be incompatible with the underlying values of the Convention if the exercise of Convention rights by a minority group were made conditional on its being accepted by the majority. Were this so, a minority group's rights to freedom of religion, expression and assembly would become merely theoretical rather than practical and effective as required by the Convention.

[40] Ibid para 109.

[41] South African Constitution, s 1(b).

[42] Secion 15, 'Equality Rights'.

[43] [1989] 1 SCR 143.

If equality means more than rationality, but rather addresses substantive issues, there are additional questions to answer. A famous controversy addresses the tension between *equality of opportunity* and *equality of results*. In what is closely related to this tension, the Preamble to the Constitution of India promises equality of status and of opportunity. In liberal constitutionalism, it is rather obvious that a right to equality cannot mean a right to resources others may aspire to as well, since their liberty interests would be violated, in a discriminatory fashion, if the state were to define who gets what or belongs where. Rather, liberal constitutionalism ensures that opportunities are equal, fairly distributed to all. Based on this, it all depends upon one's understanding of social reality: When do opportunities end and results begin?

Affirmative action or *positive measures* or *quota* are a case in point. Do laws that promote certain individuals who have been discriminated against in the past or who are underrepresented in a particular context violate or implement the right to equality? Does it violate the right to equality if women or members of linguistic minorities or African-Americans or disabled people are given a job instead of an equally qualified man, member of an ethnically defined majority, or a person not physically challenged? Most cases arise in the area of employment, but affirmative measures are also controversial in politics as I discuss below.

Generally, many courts have stated that affirmative action promotes equality, rather than violating it. More specifically, the German Federal Constitutional Court stated in 1992 that 'the provision that men and women shall have equal rights is designed not only to do away with legal norms that base advantages or disadvantages on sex but also to bring about equal opportunity for men and women in the future. Its aim is the equalization of living conditions.'[44] Also, the South African Constitutional Court stated in *Hugo*,[45] a complex case brought by fathers that were excluded from being pardoned from a prison term like mothers:

> The prohibition on unfair discrimination in the interim Constitution seeks not only to avoid discrimination against people who are members of disadvantaged groups. It seeks more than that. At the heart of the prohibition of unfair discrimination lies a recognition that the purpose of our new constitutional and democratic order is the establishment of a society in which all human beings will be accorded equal dignity and respect regardless of their membership of particular groups. The achievement of such a society in the context of our deeply inegalitarian past will not be easy, but that that is the goal of the Constitution should not be forgotten or overlooked.

However, it all depends on the legal scheme chosen in a given context. The European Court of Justice has developed a sophisticated jurisprudence in the area of employment. The Court stated in *Kalanke*[46] that laws designed to promote women over equally qualified men in male-dominated employment sectors are meant to 'counteract the prejudicial effects on women in employment which arise from social attitudes, behaviour and structures'.[47] But not every law will do. The Court stated that

> a national rule which provides that, where equally qualified men and women are candidates for the same promotion in fields where there are fewer women than men at the level of the relevant post, women are automatically to be given priority, involves discrimination on grounds of sex.

[44] *Nocturnal Employment Case*, 85 BVerfGE 191 (1992).
[45] 1997 (4) SA 1 (CC).
[46] Case C-450/93 [1995] ECR I-3051.
[47] Ibid para 20.

In fact, there may be good reasons to prefer an individual man. Affirmative action then needs to guarantee an opportunity, but not an 'automatic' result. Similarly, the Supreme Court of India, in *Uttar Pradesh v Pradip Tandon*,[48] struck down a rule which reserved places in medical school for candidates from rural areas because it was overbroad. It emphasized, however, that the government may very well design better schemes to promote 'socially and educationally backward classes of citizens'.

In *Marschall*,[49] the European Court of Justice explained that

> it appears that even where male and female candidates are equally qualified, male candidates tend to be promoted in preference to female candidates particularly because of prejudices and stereotypes concerning the role and capacities of women in working life and the fear, for example, that women will interrupt their careers more frequently, that owing to household and family duties they will be less flexible in their working hours, or that they will be absent from work more frequently because of pregnancy, childbirth and breastfeeding. For these reasons, the mere fact that a male candidate and a female candidate are equally qualified does not mean that they have the same chances. It follows that a national rule in terms of which, subject to the application of the saving clause, female candidates for promotion who are equally as qualified as the male candidates are to be treated preferentially in sectors where they are under-represented may [be consistent with the right to equality] if such a rule may counteract the prejudicial effects on female candidates of the attitudes and behaviour described above and thus reduce actual instances of inequality which may exist in the real world. However, ... such a national measure specifically favouring female candidates cannot guarantee absolute and unconditional priority for women ... [But if the rule] contains a saving clause does not exceed those limits if, in each individual case, it provides for male candidates who are equally as qualified as the female candidates a guarantee that the candidatures will be the subject of an objective assessment which will take account of all criteria specific to the individual candidates and will override the priority accorded to female candidates where one or more of those criteria tilts the balance in favour of the male candidate. In this respect, however, it should be remembered that those criteria must not be such as to discriminate against female candidates.

Put differently, affirmative action rules promote equality if they themselves do not reinforce stereotypes and perpetuate discrimination, not even through the back door of a savings clause.

This is also a key issue in US jurisprudence on affirmative action in education. The end of formal segregation, *Brown v Board of Education*, did not end substantive inequality. In particular, US universities have sought to promote minorities and diversify student bodies with a variety of rules which have repeatedly been attacked in the courts. There is a long line of cases decided by the US Supreme Court, the last to date being *Grutter v Bollinger*,[50] where the Court stated that:

> We have held that all racial classifications imposed by government must be analyzed by a reviewing court under strict scrutiny.... This means that such classifications are constitutional only if they are narrowly tailored to further compelling governmental interests.... When race-based action is necessary to further a compelling governmental interest, such action does not violate the constitutional guarantee of equal protection so long as the narrow-tailoring requirement is also satisfied.

[48] (1975) 1 SCC 267.

[49] Case C-409/95 [1997].

[50] 539 US 306 (2003).

And then, the Court says: 'context matters'. In the case, Michigan Law School, as part of its goal of 'assembling a class that is both exceptionally academically qualified and broadly diverse', seeks to 'enrol a "critical mass" of minority students'. The Law School's interest, the Court stated,

> is not simply to assure within its student body some specified percentage of a particular group merely because of its race or ethnic origin. That would amount to outright racial balancing, which is patently unconstitutional.... Rather, the Law School's concept of critical mass is defined by reference to the educational benefits that diversity is designed to produce.

And, the Court continued, 'These benefits are substantial'. In addition, the Court noted, the Law School did not perpetuate stereotyping:

> The Law School does not premise its need for critical mass on 'any belief that minority students always (or even consistently) express some characteristic minority viewpoint on any issue.'... To the contrary, diminishing the force of such stereotypes is both a crucial part of the Law School's mission, and one that it cannot accomplish with only token numbers of minority students.

To achieve this, a system must be narrowly tailored, it cannot use a quota system—it cannot 'insulat[e] each category of applicants with certain desired qualifications from competition with all other applicants'. Instead, a university may consider race or ethnicity only as a '"plus" in a particular applicant's file', without 'insulat[ing] the individual from comparison with all other candidates for the available seats'. In other words, an admissions program must be 'flexible enough to consider all pertinent elements of diversity in light of the particular qualifications of each applicant, and to place them on the same footing for consideration, although not necessarily according them the same weight.'

More generally, equality also touches on the limits of democracy. Who shall be allowed to be treated like a citizen? Who loses the right to be treated as a citizen? Not only postnational and multilevel democracies have to grapple with political equality, global migration has resulted in multinational populations, which also form transnational networks. The German Federal Constitutional Court decided that 'there can be no democratic state without a body politic,... the people, from whom all state authority emanates', but held that this body must that be a 'cohesive, unified group'.[51] Later, the German Basic Law, as many other EU member state laws, was amended to extend local voting rights to EU citizens. However, 'third country nationals' have no vote. In addition, many states do deny voting rights to citizens living permanently abroad, such as Korea.[52] Today, in light of a post-Westphalian global order, discussions of cosmopolitanism revive calls for a right to political equality. Basically, equality then means to have a resident voice in local matters, independent of nationality. This is not a new notion, since it has been known to the Stoics as well as Erasmus von Rotterdam, to Grotius as well as Kant, and more recently, to philosophers like Rawls, Tilly, Benhabib, Pogge, or Held. But it is, generally, not the law.[53]

Finally, many conflicts arise when states strive to ensure representation of all factions of society in politics, including minorities. In France, the Constitutional Council rejected

[51] German Federal Constitutional Court, *Foreign Voters Case*, 83 BVerfGE 37 (1990).

[52] Korean Constitutional Court, *Overseas Citizens Voting Rights Ban*, 11-1 KCCR 54, 97Hun-Ma253.

[53] See Gillian Brock and Harry Brighouse (eds), *The Political Philosophy of Cosmopolitanism* (2005).

minority rules in *Elections in New Caledonia*.[54] India is known to employ several mechanisms in that realm. In *Murthy et al v India*,[55] the Supreme Court upheld reserved seats for members of backward classes in local self-government, the panchayats. It used a strict proportionality test, which results in ordering a maximum level of reserved seats, but also leaves room for minority quotas. The Court made a distinction between election and selection:

> The nature and purpose of reservations in the context of local self-government is considerably different from that of higher education and public employment.... [T]he principles that have been evolved in relation to the reservation policies [there] cannot be readily applied in the context of local self-government. Even when made, they...can be much shorter.

Socio-economic deprivation, it stated, may result in disadvantages when people are selected for a job, but may not necessarily have such effects when people are elected for a seat. According to this jurisprudence, the right to equality is not a formal claim, but needs to be applied in context. Similarly, the Hong Kong court struck a balance between a strict right to equality in elections, and an equally valid claim to ensure participation of minorities, by referring to international law, the ICCPR. In *Tse Kwan Sang v Pat Heung Rural Cttee*[56] it stated that even rules that ensure representation of indigenous people need to be non-discriminatory in nature, that is, may not exclude women. In the US case *Santa Clara Pueblo v Martinez*,[57] that balance however tilted against a woman who sought equal rights in a minority context in the United States and inspired a lasting controversy on the tension between group equality rights and individual ones.[58] Overall, equality law confronts complicated questions which arise from our multiplicity of belongings today.

IV. The Scope: Who Bears the Right to Equality?

Equality is a right to address the fundamental similarity of human beings as well as the differences among them, to eventually target discrimination. As a fundamental human right, it is a claim for individuals, but equality also invites collective claims, as in the case of Martinez against her Pueblo kinship.[59] As another example, equality may motivate a state to impose an official language on its territory, but equality will also invite claims by people who identify with another language, as a right to differ. Often, courts then seek a rather pragmatic compromise among competing goals. In Latvia, the Constitutional Court upheld a law which empowered the state to transcribe German last names into Latvian spelling, yet required the state to add a 'special note' with the original name in documents.[60] But does this solve the tension between a collective entity and the individual?

Famously, Article 27 of the ICCPR addresses rights of minorities, yet is interpreted as an individual right.[61] Also, some national constitutions protect minorities, and constitutional law

[54] 85-196 DC, 8 August 1985.
[55] 356 OF 1994, May 10, 2010.
[56] [1999] 3 HKLRD 267.
[57] 436 US 49 (1978).
[58] Joshua Cohen and Matthew Howard (eds), *Is Multiculturalism Bad for Women?* (1999).
[59] See n 57.
[60] *Mentzen Case* no 2001-04-0103.
[61] General Comment No 23.

may also grant rights of recognition and redistribution to corporations or other legal entities. Most prominently, much constitutional law grants rights of self-determination to churches and religious communities, often based on the notion of equal treatment of all religious beliefs. However, such rights, similar to rights of linguistic or cultural minorities, not only serve to protect their existence, but can also be used to curtail the rights of their members in relation to such organizations or groups. A tension arises around 'Minorities within Minorities'[62] or more precisely: of diverse individuals in seemingly homogenous groups. Such a concept of equal rights for groups assumes that such collectives may be clearly distinguished from one another, and that people always belong to any one group, rather than many. Empirically, this is highly problematic because most groups have boundaries which are both blurred and shifting, and because individuals live different group identities or share multiple group characteristics. Thus, the construction of groups in law, as 'legal groupism',[63] collides with a notion of individual rights. In light of this, some argue that there are two aspects of the right to equality: to prevent discrimination and to support minorities.[64] Others conceptualize equality as an individual right for respect of a socially situated identity, which eventually protects a group as well. In *Santa Clara Pueblo v Martinez*, Justice White argued in his dissent that equality strives to protect individuals from arbitrary and unjust actions, including those of their tribal governments.

V. The Test

We have seen that a concept of equality as a guarantee of rationality and a right to justification informs a similarly situated test, most famously known as the test applied by the US Supreme Court, but explicitly rejected by Canadian jurisprudence and not applied by the European Court of Justice and others. The more equality is understood as a right against discrimination, the more a test moves away from a comparative exercise and resembles a liberty test, directed against a violation of a fundamental interest or need. In addition, equality allows for an interpretation of liberties as social rights. Thus, there are, in the world of constitutional law, three different tests for equality: a similarity assessment, a discrimination test (a negative 'freedom from' state intervention), or an egalitarian test (a positive 'claim to' access, distribution, resources).

Regarding the *egalitarian test* of equality as a positive claim to something, there are two versions of equality guarantees: as a minimum guarantee of basic resources or as access to resources without discrimination. Many European constitutions contain social or welfare state clauses.[65] The Hungarian Constitutional Court has interpreted the right to social security—that is, basic economic equality—as a principle only (in Article 70E). Conversely, the German Federal Constitutional Court has famously interpreted the principle of the welfare state in Article 20 of the Basic Law, in conjunction with the right to dignity, Article 1, as an individual right to a minimum guarantee of existence,[66] an obligation to care for 'those in

[62] This is the title of a book edited by Avigail Eisenberg and Jeff Spinner-Halev, *Equality, Rights and Diversity* (2005).

[63] On social groupism, see Rogers Brubaker, *Ethnicity without Groups* (2004).

[64] Francesco Capotorti, *Study on the rights of persons belonging to ethnic, religious and linguistic minorities* (1978), reprinted in 1991, UN Centre for HR E.91.XIV.2, 26 para 585.

[65] See Finnish Constitution, s 15: 'Public authorities shall...secure for everyone adequate social welfare and health services....'

[66] BVerfGE 1, 97 (104f) 1951.

need', like people with physical or mental handicaps, to secure 'the basic conditions for a dignified existence'.[67] This may also be understood as a right to basic economic equality: the state must 'provid[e] the basic conditions for a humane existence of its citizens.... As long as these basic conditions are not at stake, it lies in the discretion of the legislator to what extent social assistance can and is to be granted.'[68] In contrast, the *discrimination test* serves to protect individuals from the state discriminating against them either explicitly (direct discrimination) or by way of seemingly neutral measures (indirect or disparate impact discrimination). Here, the decisive step is not to compare someone to others, but to understand whether someone has been harmed.

However, equality as a right to *equal access* to liberties may also amount to a constitutional obligation of state action. This is explicit in derivative equality clauses that guarantee equal enjoyment of liberties.[69] The ECtHR as well as the UN Human Rights Committee have used what could be called the equal access test in cases on sex, sexual orientation, or marital status discrimination in social security.[70] Another example is the EU law on equal pay for equal work with an elaborate jurisprudence on sex equality regarding renumeration. If the state offers or enforces or protects something, it has to do this for all citizens or even residents alike. Courts do not determine *what* is distributed, but courts ensure that there must be no discrimination in distribution. This has been stated by the ECtHR. In a case of a woman who sought divorce from an abusive husband, but had no money to pay for legal advice, the ECtHR argued:

> fulfillment of a duty under the Convention on occasion necessitates some positive action on the part of the State; in such circumstances, the State cannot simply remain passive and there is...no room to distinguish between acts and omissions. The obligation to secure an effective right of access to the courts falls into this category of duty.[71]

However, comparative studies indicate that such positive rights claims are less successful than negative ones.[72] It should be noted however, that several fundamental rights catalogues of the late twentieth and twenty-first centuries do explicitly set forth rights to social security, to work and to protection against unemployment, to rest and leisure, including periodic holidays with pay, to an adequate standard of living, to education, and to the protection of one's scientific, literary, and artistic production.[73] This is often labeled as the rise of a new 'generation' of human rights.

However, the jurisprudence of rights to equal access may be understood as an application of the right to equality to liberties, which eventually informs enforceable social rights. This shatters the categorization of human rights as 'generations', a conceptual frame that follows the history of dominant ideas.[74] Rather, one may understand both as components of constitutionalism.[75]

[67] BVerfGE 40, 121 (133) 1975.

[68] BVerfGE 82, 60 (1990); also in BVerfG, 1 BvL 1/09 (2010) Hartz IV.

[69] As in ECHR, Art 14, now expanded in Protocol 12 (n 11).

[70] See ECtHR, *Carson and Others*, App no 42184/05, 2010 (Grand Chamber), para 63; General Comment No 18 (37th session, 1989, UN Doc HRI/GEN/1 Rev.3).

[71] *Airey v Ireland*, 32 ECtHR (Ser A), para 25 (1979).

[72] See Ran Hirschl, *Towards Juristocracy* (2004/2007), on Canada, New Zealand, South Africa, and Israel.

[73] Universal Declaration of Human Rights, Arts 22–27; European Charter of Fundamental Rights; Banjul Charter.

[74] See Henry J. Steiner, Philip Alston, and Ryan Goodman (eds), *International Human Rights in Context: Law, Politics, Morals* (3rd edn, 2008), Pt A.

[75] Susanne Baer, 'Dignity, Liberty, Equality: A Fundamental Rights Triangle of Constitutionalism' (2009) 4 *University of Toronto Law Journal* 417.

The first generation, according to the common narrative, consists of civil and political rights, while the second generation features economic, social, and cultural rights, with a third generation for collective rights to development, sustainability, etc. Yet as a cross-cutting right, equality is a principle that informs the liberties of the first generation, and the defining feature of the second generation, originating in notions of distributive justice, the socialist traditions of the Saint-Simonians of early nineteenth-century France and various emancipatory movements in different regions, at different times, and with different inequalities to struggle against. These movements in fact, just like the current efforts to fight poverty, sought to break free of the chains of inequality, and thus demanded liberties to further that claim. In some ways, a call for equal rights is thus a reaction to a limited concept of liberty, which tolerates or even legitimizes the exploitation of people for profit, be it in colonies or factories. Different from that, one may also understand equality to inform all rights to liberty. Some courts do thus employ equality to safeguard fair contracts, or emphasize that no person can have his or her dignity or enjoy a liberty if economically or socially backward, for example the Indian Supreme Court in *Kesavananda v Kerala*.[76] The same court stated that 'socio-economic democracy' is built into the Indian constitution, in *Ahmedabad Municipal Co v Nawab Khan et al*.[77]

Overall, equality and the notion of social rights are thus closely related, exemplified in Article 2 of the ICESCR, in Article 26 of the American Convention on Human Rights, and in the African Charter on Human and Peoples' Rights 1981, while granted separately in the European Social Charter (revised in 1996). The close relation is evident in cases on equal access to water, which are currently rather prominent. The South African Court held that not every citizen has a right to the same type of access, but that it must nonetheless install a proportionate scheme which delivers water, in light of limited resources, to all.[78] Also, equality informs much jurisprudence on health care, since unequal access to medical treatment may easily be read to constitute discrimination rather than just a decision on how to distribute social goods. Examples include the *DiBella Treatment* case in India,[79] in which the International Criminal Court held that there must be equal access to treatment. In Latvia, the Constitutional Court held in 2005 that childcare cannot be limited to parents not working. In Egypt, an Administrative Court stopped a new drug-pricing system, because it would violate the right to equal access to drugs of all Egyptians if prices were not kept low.[80]

VI. The Inequalities

Philosophers tend to ask: Equality 'in what respect'? This is also a key question in law. Constitutions and human rights treaties mostly contain a general equality clause, but very often also name specific inequalities, either separate from each other or intersecting, and either in exhaustive lists or in non-exhaustive lists. Such lists may be seen as naming paradigmatic examples of structural or systemic discrimination, which, if non-exhaustive, do promise equal rights in analogous cases as well.

Historically, the call for equality was a rejection of specific inequalities, and at least a call for justification, and as such a truly modern right. Neither nobility nor place of birth nor religion nor sex nor certain physical features (still termed 'race') shall make a difference, which is what

[76] (1973) Supp SCR 1, 280.
[77] (1996) Supp 7 SCR 548.
[78] *Lindiwe Mazibuko & Others v City of Johannesburg & Others*, Case CCT 39/09, [2009] ZACC 28.
[79] 1998.
[80] Case No 2457/64 (2010).

older equality clauses promise. Gradually, sexual orientation, disability and age and genetic features are added to such lists. Furthermore, some constitutions feature the prohibition of discrimination of people from particular regions, like the mountains, which indicates that social deprivation and exclusion may be related to geographic location. However, equality law does usually not prohibit economic inequalities. The US Supreme Court, in *San Antonio Independent School District v Rodriguez*,[81] expressly declined to recognize the poor as a suspect class for equal protection analysis. Also, *DeShaney v Winnebago County Department of Social Services*,[82] may be understood to hand distributive questions regarding state protection via welfare programs over to 'democratic political processes'.[83] However, even in the United States, some state constitutions oblige the legislature to care for the poor.[84] And again, much law addresses economic discrimination in combining liberty claims with equality to inform rights of access, as social rights (discussed above).

As one prominent example, the South African Constitution from 1996 names racism and sexism as key targets,[85] and also lists 'race, gender, sex, pregnancy, marital status, ethnic or social origin, colour, sexual orientation, age, disability, religion, conscience, belief, culture, language and birth' as specific inequalities the Constitution shall strive to erase. The constitution of Kenya, in 2010, prohibits discrimination 'on any ground, including race, sex, pregnancy, marital status, health status, ethnic or social origin, colour, age, disability, religion, conscience, belief, culture, dress, language or birth.'[86] The European Charter of Fundamental Rights, drafted in 2000, prohibits discrimination on 'any ground such as sex, race, colour, ethnic or social origin, genetic features, language, religion or belief, political or any other opinion, membership of a national minority, property, birth, disability, age or sexual orientation.' The African Charter on Human and Peoples' Rights names 'race, ethnic group, color, sex, language, religion, political or any other opinion, national and social origin, fortune, birth or other status',[87] and protects women and children in additional charters.[88] In the global human rights system, general equality clauses with basic lists have been supplemented with specific conventions that target one inequality at a time, namely racism,[89] sexism discriminating against women,[90] ageism regarding children,[91] racism and xenophobia regarding migrant laborers,[92] and ableism/disability.[93]

Although such lists—either exhaustive or not—seem similar, and imply an analogy of inequalities, there is a tendency to treat inequalities unequally. The German Basic Law emphasizes sex equality in Article 3(2), lists specific aspects which should not amount to privilege or disadvantage in Article 3(3)(1), and provides an affirmative guarantee regarding disability in Article 3(3)(2). Similarly, the UN human rights treaties differ in scope and structure, and often do address sex inequality separately (ie Article 3 of the ICESCR and the ICCPR), but also

[81] 411 US 1 (1973).

[82] 489 US 189 (1989).

[83] Ibid 195.

[84] eg Alabama, Kansas, New York, and Oklahoma.

[85] Section 1(b).

[86] Article 27(4).

[87] Article 2.

[88] The Maputo Protocol 2000 and the Charter on Rights of the Child 1990.

[89] International Convention on the Elimination of All Forms of Racial Discrimination (ICERD) (1966).

[90] CEDAW (1976).

[91] Convention on the Rights of the Child (CRC) (1989).

[92] International Convention on the Protection of the Rights of All Migrant Workers and Members of Their Families (ICRMW) (1990).

[93] Convention on the Rights of Persons with Disabilities (CRPD) (2006).

emphasize that several inequalities often intersect. Discrimination does not focus on one characteristic or ground only, but subordinates individuals in a multidimensional way, where the specific interdependency of sex/ual orientation, ethnicity, ability, age etc matter.[94]

In addition, even 'classic' items on the list are controversial. The paradigmatic example is 'race', prominent in many constitutions to target racism, yet in itself an expression of a racist theory, a theory which claims that people belong to different races. This has been addressed by the UN World Conference against Racism, Racial Discrimination, Xenophobia and Related Intolerance in Durban in 2001, which strongly rejected 'any doctrine of racial superiority, along with theories which attempt to determine the existence of so-called distinct human races.'

As another example, the meaning of dis/ability is often unclear. Also, the meaning of sex became controversial. While some constitutional jurisprudence treats a right to sex equality to also protect people who love people of the same sex against discrimination,[95] others treat this as a different topic, either analogous to other listed grounds,[96] or accepted as a 'rational' distinction. The controversy is displayed in a US decision, *Romer v Evans*,[97] where the majority struck down a state referendum that banned laws that prohibit discrimination against homosexual or bisexual practices or relationships, thus limiting the reach of equal rights, while the dissenters would have upheld such laws which they interpreted as only prohibiting 'special treatment' of sexual minorities. Based on a constitution that names sexual orientation as a ground in need of equal rights protection, the South African Court has consistently held that there is no reason whatsoever to disadvantage people because of the sex of the person they love.[98] But even when such express protection is absent, fundamental rights jurisprudence around the globe gradually extends equality protection to sexual minorities. In *Salgueiro da Silva Mouta v Portugal*,[99] a gay father was protected against the denial of parenthood because of his sexual orientation. The argument that a child should grow up in a 'traditional Portuguese family' was rejected as discriminatory. In 2011, the Brazilian Supreme Court held that all rights granted to 'stable unions' must be granted to homosexual and heterosexual relationships alike.[100]

Also, some see 'sex' as relating to men and women only, while others have used sex equality guarantees to protect transsexuals as well as transgender and intersexuals against discrimination. However, cross-dressing or transvestism has not been accepted as such an inequality.[101] This is based on an understanding of listed inequalities as characteristics which people cannot choose to live or not live, but that form a component of one's identity. Therefore, many legislators state very clearly that equality regarding sex or sexual orientation does not protect sexual practices that harm others, like sexual abuse of children or pedophilia. Rather, non-harmful sexual practices are protected as part of private life.[102] In light of this, same-sex couples may

[94] Dagmar Schiek and Victoria Chege (eds), *European Union Non-Discrimination Law: Comparative Perspectives on Multidimensional Equality Law* (2008).

[95] Most famously *Toonen v Australia*, Communication No 488/1992, UN Doc CCPR/C/50/D/488/1992 (1994), and ECtHR, *Kozak v Poland*, App no 13102/02, 2 March 2010.

[96] See the Canadian Supreme Court, *Egan v Canada* [1995] 2 SCR 513: 'The historic disadvantage suffered by homosexuals has been widely recognized and documented'.

[97] 517 US 620 (1996).

[98] See *Minister of Home Affairs v Fourie*, 2006 (1) SA 524 (CC).

[99] ECtHR, App no 33290/96, 1999.

[100] ADI 4277 and ADPF 132.

[101] NL Equal Treatment Commission (Commissie Gelijke Behandeling), Opinion 1996-108.

[102] Under the ECHR, see ECtHR, *Smith and Grady v United Kingdom*, App nos 33985/96 and 33986/96, 1999-VI; *L and V v Austria*, App nos 39392/98 and 39829/98, 9 January 2003.

enjoy family life, *Schalk and Kopf v Austria*,[103] yet were not granted a human right to be treated like heterosexuals regarding marriage.[104]

VII. The Reach

Similar to the differences it underscores in listing specific inequalities, constitutional law like human rights law targets inequalities in different areas of life, thus varying in its reach.

As a starting point of constitutionalism, the basic notion of universal moral equality informs *political equality*, thus democracy, by requiring that a political system equally recognize all those who are governed by it.[105] Here, equality guarantees voice in categorical contrast to regimes which formally distinguish classes of citizens, as in apartheid, colonialism, or caste systems. This is why courts have generally subjected elections to a strict equality standard. Some states strip citizens of voting rights for being imprisoned,[106] while the South African Court extended the right to vote to prisoners, in *August v Electoral Commission*,[107] similar to the Canadian Federal Court of Appeal, in *Sauvé v Canada*.[108] The Canadian Supreme Court, however, also upheld an exclusion from membership in parliament for people convicted of an illegal practice related to voting.[109] The South African Court, although strict regarding prisoners, however upheld an ID requirement to ensure equality in that one person has not more than one vote, even if such requirement imposes an additional burden on people. Although 'the importance of the right to vote is self-evident and can never be overstated', the South African Constitutional Court stated that

> the mere existence of the right to vote without proper arrangements for its effective exercise does nothing for a democracy; it is both empty and useless, which is why the state may require special IDs because and when the old IDs were issued by the apartheid government on a racial basis and thus 'constitute a powerful symbol and reminder of a shameful past.[110]

However, Justice O'Regan dissented: since a large number of voters carried the older ID, one should not disenfranchise them by asking for another form, 'in a country where such a right is only in its infancy'. Formal requirements are different form economic expectations. The US Supreme Court stated that the right to equality in elections is violated by a state 'whenever it makes the affluence of the voter or payment of any fee an electoral standard'.[111] Nor may local voting rights be tied to property.[112] But it remains highly controversial whether less direct property-related opportunities to influence elections, like party or campaign funding by corporations, violate the right to political equality. The US Supreme Court upheld such financial power,[113] while many constitutional systems at least require full transparency and often mandate absolute caps or tax deduction caps on such donations.

[103] App no 30141/04, 24 June 2010.

[104] Ibid 62: 'In that connection the Court observes that marriage has deep-rooted social and cultural connotations which may differ largely from one society to another'.

[105] See *Reynolds v Sims* 377 US 533, 561–2 (1964): 'The right of suffrage is a fundamental matter in a free and democratic society'.

[106] See eg US Constitution, Amendment 14.

[107] 1999 (3) SALR 1 (CC).

[108] [1999] 180 DLR (4th) 385.

[109] *Harvey v New Brunswick* [1996] 2 SCR 876.

[110] *New National Party v RSA*, 1999 (3) SALR 191 (CC).

[111] *Harper v Virginia Bd Of Elections* 383 US 663, 666 (1966).

[112] *Kramer v Union School District* 395 US 621 (1969).

[113] *Citizens United v Federal Election Commission* 558 US 50 (2010).

Closely related to political equality is equality before the law, as equal access to law enforcement and equal treatment in the legal system. This is why many constitutions feature rights to fair trial, rights to public hearings in court, and rights to access to justice. Again, some courts interpret equality as a right to equal access in fact, that is, a mandate to support poor people who want to bring a case, a public defender system, and similar safeguarding measures.

Another constitutional dimension of equality focuses on distribution, as a right to *socio-economic equality*. As discussed above, this is often constructed as equal access to a liberty, a social dimension of fundamental rights. More specifically, tax law is also very often subjected to rigid yet formal equality standards, in that everyone shall be taxed based on individual economic status. In fact, however, many constitutional courts are regularly confronted with tax measures that disparately burden people in a given society. In addition, several constitutions and all social rights catalogues expressly address equality in employment. As one example, EU law prohibits sex discrimination in pay.

Finally, equality rights may also extend to cultural recognition, a right to *cultural equality*. More recent constitutional and human rights law addresses equal respect in the sense of pluralism in that they guarantee both for equal treatment and non-discrimination but simultaneously affirm diversity, heritage, tradition, and culture. Examples include the Constitutive Act of the African Union, Article 2, as well as Articles 8 and 10 of the Treaty on the Functioning of the European Union (TFEU). Often, such equality law is guaranteed in the context of education and rights to schools, where constitutional courts may protect minority curricula or institutions. More specifically, many constitutions and human rights treaties take particular care regarding equality of families, in that they guarantee equal rights for children born in or outside marriage, or guarantee a right to equal access to marriage and against forced marriage, often using age as a proxy to indicate that children shall not marry since one cannot know whether it is based on free will, absent coercion. Again, the meaning of fundamental rights has changed significantly. Historically, this has been understood as a right against sex discrimination consisting in not to have daughters married off. While today this remains a key issue, it also needs to be regarded as a right to protect men from forcibly being married to women they do not know.

VIII. The Binding Force of a Right to Equality

Generally, constitutions limit state power, as do human rights. However, inequalities are often deeply embedded in our societies, which is why a right against discrimination may be rendered ineffective if it is limited to address state action only. Regarding political equality, it may suffice to have a constitutional right to vote and to stand for elections, as in Article 39 of the European Charter of Fundamental Rights, as the relevant domain is exclusively within the purview of the state. But regarding economic, social, and cultural equality, private actors also engage in discrimination, whether intentionally or not. Therefore, although the binding force of fundamental rights to equality is particularly controversial, it is more likely than liberty interests to be expanded to cover private actors. According to the German doctrine of third party effect, constitutional law does at least address public enforcement of private acts. According to EU equality law, private actors, both in employment as in markets of goods and services, are bound by strong equality directives. Also, UN human rights law expressly addresses some inequalities in private spheres, as does CEDAW to protect women in all walks of life. Thus, equality may be more than a negative right against the state, and it may inform a positive obligation of states to act against discrimination.

In the area of human rights, committees have argued for a state obligation to prevent discrimination by public and by private actors.[114] Similarly, some constitutions explicitly extend the binding force of a right to equality to all actors.[115] But in most constitutions, equality is simply stated as a right, with no further specification. Then, general standards of constitutional law apply: courts that enforce private law are bound by the constitution, and may thus interpret private action, protected as liberty—that is, of contracting—to be limited when it amounts to discrimination. As an example, the German Federal Constitutional Court has developed a doctrine of 'disturbed contractual parity', to stop banks from exploiting naive customers based on rigid credit contracts, or to stop companies from harming former employees in contracts which oblige those to not take up employment close to their former job.[116] Here, the general right to equality, in the sense of equal standing and recognition based on equal knowledge and competence is applied to limit an overly libertarian understanding of liberty. Rather, a fundamental right to equality seems to inform a notion of individual rights of socially situated individuals.

Bibliography

Elizabeth Anderson, 'What Is the Point of Equality? (1999) 109 *Ethics* 287

Aristotle, '*Nicomachean Ethics*' in Sarah Broadie and Christopher Rowe, *Aristotle Nicomachean Ethics: Translation, Introduction, and Commentary* (2002)

Aristotle, '*Politics Book III*' in Jonathan Barnes (ed), *The Complete Works of Aristotle: The Revised Oxford Translation* (1984)

Isaiah Berlin, 'Equality' in LVI *Proceedings of the Aristotelian Society* (1955–56)

Eva Brems, *Human Rights: Universality and Diversity* (2001)

Gillian Brock and Harry Brighouse (eds), *The Political Philosophy of Cosmopolitanism* (2005)

Ronald Dworkin, *Sovereign Virtue. The Theory and Practice of Equality* (2000)

Fay Faraday, Margaret Denike, and M. Kate Stephenson (eds), *Making Equality Rights Real: Securing Substantive Equality Under The Charter* (2006)

Rainer Forst, 'The Justification of Human Rights and the Basic Right to Justification: A Reflexive Approach' (2010) 120(4) *Ethics* 711

Stefan Gosepath, 'Equality' in Edward N. Zalta (ed), *Stanford Encyclopedia of Philosophy* (2007), available at <http://plato.stanford.edu/entries/equality/>

Catharine MacKinnon, *Towards a Feminist Theory of the State* (1989)

Christopher McCrudden (ed), *Anti-Discrimination Law* (2004)

Martha Minow, *Making All the Difference: Inclusion, Exclusion, and American Law* (1991)

Thomas Nagel, 'Equality' in Thomas Nagel, *Mortal Questions* (1979)

Martha Nussbaum, *Women and Human Development: The Capabilities Approach* (2000)

John Rawls, *A Theory of Justice* ([1971] 1999)

Dagmar Schiek and Victoria Chege (eds), *European Union Non-Discrimination Law: Comparative Perspectives on Multidimensional Equality Law* (2008)

Amartya Sen, *Inequality Reexamined* (1992)

Henry J. Steiner, Philip Alston, and Ryan Goodman (eds), *International Human Rights in Context: Law, Politics, Morals* (3rd edn, 2008)

Stuart White, *Equality* (2006)

Iris Marion Young, *Justice and the Politics of Difference* (1990)

114 ICCPR, ie *Nahlik v Austria* (608/95).

115 Kenya, Art 27(5): 'A person shall not discriminate directly or indirectly against another person . . .'.

116 Another example is BVerfG, 1 BvR 12/92 (2001) marriage contract.

CHAPTER 48

CITIZENSHIP

AYELET SHACHAR

Toronto

DESPITE all the fashionable predictions regarding the demise of citizenship, it is back with a vengeance.[1] Politicians worldwide stress its importance; public policymakers debate how best to make citizenship meaningful in an age of globalized economic and communication flows, as well as growing migration pressures. Legislatures have also taken an interest, introducing new citizenship tests and crafting more restrictive admission criteria for various migrant categories. Constitutional and high courts around the globe have become embroiled in citizenship matters, too. They have found themselves called upon to address not only perennial dilemmas (such as defining the boundaries of membership as they intersect, for example, with changing definitions of marriage and the family),[2] but also foundational questions concerning the constitutional limits of state power in determining whether to give legal sanction to indefinite detention of non-citizens, or the rationality of using immigration law as anti-terrorism law.[3]

Scholars, too, have turned their gaze to citizenship once again after many years of neglect. This renaissance of sorts has given birth to the multidisciplinary field of citizenship studies which has drawn insightful contributions from law to cultural studies, philosophy to international relations. This new scholarship frequently gives ample attention to emerging

[1] Catherine Dauvergne, 'Citizenship with a Vengeance' (2007) 8 *Theoretical Inquiries in Law* 489.

[2] The growing recognition of same-sex marriage, eg, has led to expanded access to membership for gay and lesbian partners and spouses in many jurisdictions, removing inequalities that were based on sexual orientation. These changes have occurred through legislation, court decree, or executive order. The latter route was followed in the United States whereas Canada embarked on the legislative path. In South Africa, the Constitutional Court played a key role. See *National Coalition for Gay and Lesbian Equality v Minister of Home Affairs* 2000 (2) SA 1 (CC).

[3] See also Chapter 21 on states of emergency and Chapter 22 on war powers in this volume.

postnational, supranational, or transnational conceptions of membership more than to the core legal and constitutional aspects of citizenship. This chapter aims to address this imbalance by bringing back into the heart of our discussion the role of law, institutions, and the state, highlighting from a comparative perspective the trials and tribulations of citizenship in a world of increased mobility and diversity.

The discussion is divided into three parts. Section I provides a concise overview of citizenship's multiple meanings and interpretations. Section II constitutes the bulk of the discussion. It begins by exploring questions of membership acquisition and transfer, which legally determine 'who belongs' within the boundaries of a given political community, either by birth or naturalization. It then assesses three recent developments: the growing recognition of dual nationality; the revival of debates about involuntary citizenship revocation; and the 'cultural turn' in citizenship discourse, which often makes inclusion in the body politic more difficult for those deemed 'too different' from the majority community. Section III charts the major challenges and opportunities facing citizenship in the twenty-first century.

I. Citizenship Matters

While citizenship has been variously defined and gone through many transformations, the basic facts are simple enough. As Rogers Smith observes, the 'oldest, most basic, and most prevalent meaning [of citizenship] is a certain sort of membership in a political community'.[4] Although the scale and scope of the political community has ranged from city-state to empire, citizenship has always been associated (at least since Aristotle) with political relations. From the Athenians we draw the tradition of associating citizenship with collective self-governance. From the Roman tradition we carry forward the idea of citizen as possessing a formal legal status with certain associated privileges and responsibilities.[5]

Today, citizenship laws also serve to determine who is entitled, as a recent Canadian federal court put it, to 'full, legally sanctioned membership in a state... All free and democratic states at all times have established a unique status of this kind and all such states have always accorded some special rights and privileges to their citizens.'[6] This definition represents what we might call the *static* view of the relationship between the individual and the state, emphasizing the rights and obligations that accompany membership. Several aspects of this static view are being challenged today by a more dynamic reality of cross-border mobility, recognition of dual nationality and multiple affiliations, as well as the growing role played by regional and international human rights mechanisms and adjudicatory bodies that may grant protection to *persons* rather than just citizens. But before discussing these new frontiers, it is imperative that we step back and take into view the broader picture.

Most courts and commentators agree that 'Citizenship has entailed membership, membership of the community in which one lives one's life'.[7] Already under Roman jurispru-

[4] Rogers Smith, 'Citizenship: Political' in Neil J. Smelser and Paul B. Baltes (eds), *International Encyclopedia of the Social & Behavioral Studies* (2001), 1857.

[5] The emphasis on citizenship as political relations is perhaps best captured by Aristotle's famous phrase that in democracies the citizen is both ruler and ruled in turn. For a now-classic account of the ancient Athenian and Roman conceptions of citizenship, and their impact on contemporary understandings of citizenship, see J.G.A. Pocock, 'The Ideal of Citizenship since Classical Times' in Ronald Beiner (ed), *Theorizing Citizenship* (1995), 29, 35–6.

[6] *Lavoie v Canada* [1995] 2 FC 623 (Federal Court, Trial Division); [2000] 1 FC 3 (Federal Court of Appeals); [2002] 1 SCR 769 (Supreme Court of Canada).

[7] David Held, 'Between State and Civil Society: Citizenship' in Geoff Andrews (ed), *Citizenship* (1991), 19, 20; Richard Bellamy, *Citizenship: A Very Short Introduction* (2008), 52.

dence, '"citizen" came to mean someone free to act by law, free to ask and expect the law's protection'.[8] This status entitled the citizen to 'whatever prerogatives and ... whatever responsibilities are attached to membership'.[9] From the French Revolution onward, the modern state began to administer and assign citizenship, which has since come to signify equality of rights and duties among members of the same political community.[10] This government-designated entitlement also tells us 'who the state considers a full member, how that membership is transmitted inter-generationally, and how it can be lost, gained, and reclaimed.'[11]

Even in today's age of increased globalization and privatization, the power to provide access to, and formal membership in, the political community remains the prerogative of sovereign states.[12] Securing full membership in the political community remains one of the few goods that even the mightiest economic conglomerate cannot offer to an international migrant; only governments can bestow the legal status of citizen upon the individual.[13] International law still provides significant room for autonomy and discretion by states in defining their membership boundaries: that 'It is for each [s]tate to determine under its own law who are its nationals'.[14]

By labeling certain individuals as members, citizenship offers, however, more than just a juridical, legal status and the promise of equality before the law. It also opens up a host of rights, opportunities, and privileges for those who count as full members. Citizenship also has the potential to play a significant role in societal struggles for recognition and inclusion by those once excluded because it bears the moral and legal force to make 'a claim to be accepted as full members of the society' hold firm.[15] As a multidimensional concept and institution, citizenship's varied interpretations and dimensions are neither fixed nor closed, and potentially cut across each other. The most familiar elements in the citizenship bundle include: equal legal status, rights and obligations, political voice and participation, the freedom to enter and exit one's home country, and the less tangible notions of identity, belonging, and a

[8] Pocock (n 5).

[9] Michael Walzer, 'Citizenship' in Terence Ball, James Farr, and Russell L. Hanson (eds), *Political Innovation and Conceptual Change* (1989), 211.

[10] Rogers Brubaker, *Citizenship and Nationhood in France and Germany* (1992); Patrick Weil, *How To Be French: Nationality in the Making Since 1789* (Catherine Porter trans, 2008).

[11] Kim Barry, 'Home and Away: The Construction of Citizenship in an Emigration Context' (2006) 81 *NYU Law Review* 11, 20.

[12] Even in the European Union, which has developed the most advanced form of regional citizenship in today's world, the grant of Union citizenship remains derivative. One must first acquire the nationality of a member state:

> Citizenship of the Union is hereby established. Every person holding the nationality of a Member State shall be a citizen of the Union. Citizenship of the Union shall be additional to and not replace national citizenship.

See Art 20, Consolidated Version of the Treaty on the Functioning of the European Union, OJ C115/56, 9.5.2008.

[13] Ayelet Shachar, *The Birthright Lottery: Citizenship and Global Inequality* (2009), 54–66.

[14] The terms nationality and citizenship are here used interchangeably. See Art 1 of the 1930 Hague Convention (Convention on Certain Questions Relating to the Conflict of Nationality Laws), April 12, 1930, 179 LNTS 89. The same principle is reasserted in Art 3(1) of the 1997 European Convention on Nationality, although Art 3(2) sets certain limitations for the acceptance of a given country's nationality law by other states. The case law of the European Court of Justice has also clarified that

> whenever a Member State, having due regard to Community law, has granted its nationality to a person, another Member State may not, by imposing an additional condition for its recognition, restrict the effects of the grant of that nationality.

See C-369/90 *Micheletti* [1992] ECR I-4239.

[15] T.H. Marshall, *Citizenship and Social Class* (1950), 8.

sense of home.[16] This multiplicity of meanings gives rise to the ever-possible reinterpretation and renegotiation of the content of citizenship, its boundaries, and its values.[17] In order to set the stage for these current debates, it is important to elaborate how, as a legal matter, we are assigned membership in 'this or that political community'.[18] This is often referred by legal experts as the variety of ways, or the modes of acquisition, in which people can obtain the legal status of citizenship in a given country.

Reading the great books of liberal and democratic theory one might expect choice and consent of the governed to play a decisive role in the core legal principles defining who is assigned citizenship in the state and according to what criteria. Many are surprised to learn that the reality is quite different from the theory. The vast majority of the world's population acquires citizenship not on the basis of individual volition, choice, and consent (as the theory predicts) but according to fortuitous circumstances that none of us control: where and to whom we are born. Although birthright entitlement has been discredited in virtually all other fields of public life, it remains the primary legal route through which citizenship is assigned in today's world. This is a striking exception to the modern trend *away* from ascribed status.[19] The latest global statistics show that only a miniscule percentage (approximately 3 percent) of the world's population have managed to gain a new membership affiliation *post*-birth, that is, through international migration and naturalization. Everyone else is largely 'trapped' by the lottery of their birth, at least in terms of the formal membership status they hold, typically, from cradle to grave. A recent report solemnly captures this last point: 'Even in today's mobile and globalized world, most people die in the same country in which not only they are born, but their parents as well.'[20]

II. On Becoming a Citizen: The Legal Dimension

As the US Supreme Court memorably pronounced in *Wong Kim Ark* (1898), there are 'two sources of citizenship, and only two: birth and naturalization'.[21] I will elaborate the former before exploring the latter. The attribution of membership at birth is governed in virtually all countries by two dominant legal principles: *jus soli* (the territoriality principle) and *jus sanguinis* (the descent principle). I discuss each in turn.

1. *Jus Soli*: The Territoriality Principle

The most crucial factor here is whether the child was born *within* the territory over which the state maintains (or in certain cases has maintained or wishes to extend) its sovereignty.[22] The

[16] For excellent discussions of citizenship's multiple dimensions and interpretations, see Irene Bloemraad et al, 'Citizenship and Immigration: Multiculturalism, Assimilations and Challenges to the Nation-State' (2008) 32 *Annual Review of Sociology* 153; Linda Bosniak, 'Citizenship Denationalized' (2000) 7 *Indiana Journal of Global Legal Studies* 447; Joseph H. Carens, *Culture, Citizenship, and Community: A Contextual Exploration of Justice as Evenhandedness* (2000); Christian Joppke, 'Transformation of Citizenship: Status, Rights, Identity' (2007) 11 *Citizenship Studies* 37; Will Kymlicka and Wayne Norman, 'Return of the Citizen: A Survey of Recent Work on Citizenship Theory' (1994) 104 *Ethics* 352.

[17] Recent years have also seen the proliferation of arguments in favor of defining citizenship beyond the state. I describe these developments below.

[18] Seyla Benhabib, *The Rights of Others: Aliens, Residents and Citizens* (2004), 141.

[19] I discuss this birthright-citizenship puzzle in detail in Shachar (n 13).

[20] See Maarten P. Vink and Gerard-Rent de Groot, *EUDO Citizenship Observatory—Birthright Citizenship: Trends and Regulations in Europe* (2010), 3.

[21] *United States v Wong Kim Ark* 169 US 649 (1898).

[22] Patrick Weil, 'Access to Citizenship: A Comparison on Twenty-Five Nationality Laws' in T. Alexander Aleinikoff and Douglas Klusmeyer (eds), *Citizenship Today: Global Perspectives and Practices* (2001).

jus soli principle, which is part of the common law tradition, implies a territorial understanding of citizenship. It recognizes the right of each person born within the physical jurisdiction of a given state to acquire full and equal membership of that polity. The *jus soli* principle finds its historical roots in the feudal system of medieval England, in which 'ligeance' and 'true and faithful obedience' to the sovereign were owed by a subject from birth: 'for as soon as he is born he oweth by birth-right ligeance and obedience to his Sovereign'.[23] In the landmark *Calvin's Case*, decided in 1608, Lord Coke employed the concept of ligeance to explain the unmediated relationship that is created for life between the monarch and all subjects born within the monarch's dominion. In its modern guise, *jus soli* no longer refers to the connection between a monarch and his or her subjects. Instead, it refers to the *political* relationship between elected governments and their citizens, offering full membership in the political community to each new generation born on the territory—irrespective of the legal status of the parents.

A main advantage of the *jus soli* principle in a world of growing international mobility is that it provides an attributive mechanism that prospectively incorporates the children of newly arrived immigrants who were born in the territory into full legal membership of the respective political community, thus avoiding the familiar second-generation phenomenon of inherited non-citizenship status that has long plagued European countries that relied primarily on the *jus sanguinis* principle. In its modern variant, *jus soli* is therefore seen as democratic and inclusive: children born to non-citizen parents (even if the latter are themselves barred from legalization and naturalization) are given a fresh start, with all the rights, protections, and opportunities that attach to full and equal membership.

Brazil, Canada, and the United States exemplify this generous model of conferral of automatic citizenship to everyone born within their borders. Brazil's Constitution grants citizenship to 'those born in the Federative Republic of Brazil, even if of foreign parents'.[24] In Canada, a statutory provision of the Citizenship Act establishes that a person 'born in Canada' is a citizen.[25] Perhaps the most famous articulation of the *jus soli* principle is found in the opening sentence of the Fourteenth Amendment of the US Constitution (the Citizenship Clause): 'All persons born ... in the United States, and subject to the jurisdiction thereof, are citizens of the United States and of the state wherein they reside.'[26]

In other parts of the common law world the unqualified application of the territoriality principle has witnessed a retreat, however. In 1981, the British Nationality Act, section 1, changed the previous common law rule (where the place of birth was the sole determination

[23] *Calvin's Case*, 77 Eng Rep 377 (KB, 1608), 382.

[24] Constitution of Brazil, Ch 3, Art 12.1.

[25] Citizenship Act, RSC, 1985, c C-29, para 3(1) (Canada).

[26] The Fourteenth Amendment's Citizenship Clause overturned the infamous US Supreme Court *Dred Scott* (1857) decision. The Citizenship Clause has long been interpreted as providing a constitutional guarantee of birthright citizenship to all persons born within the territorial limits of the United States (with the very limited exception of children born in the United States of foreign diplomats). However, acrimonious debates in recent years have given rise to legislative attempts to restrict and narrow the application of the *jus soli* principle by defining the phrase 'subject to the jurisdiction thereof' to include only children born to US citizens or permanent resident aliens. To date, all such attempts have failed. Legal opinion strongly advises against such a change, which would break away with over a century of consistent application of the *Wong Kim Ark* decision that applies to all persons born in the United States. As the Office of Legal Council noted in a 1995 statement submitted to the Congressional Subcommittee on Immigration:

> in 1862 President Lincoln's Attorney General wrote an opinion for the Secretary of the Treasury asserting '[a]s far as I know ... you and I have no better title to citizenship which we enjoy than the "accident of birth"—the fact that we happened to be born in the United States.'

in citizenship) to a modified birthplace principle that now takes into account the parents' status and residence considerations. Children born on the territory to unauthorized migrants can still acquire full citizenship status, if they fulfill the habitual residency requirement. Related changes have taken root elsewhere, including Australia (1986), Ireland (2004; through a constitutional referendum that is widely interpreted as an attempt to curtail the legal implications of the European Court of Justice's *Chen* decision[27]), and New Zealand (2006), to mention but a few prime examples.[28] Importantly, these legal changes do not amount to a retreat from the principle. Instead, they reveal a modification: the introduction of a *jus-sanguinis*-like component of descent into otherwise territorially centered membership rules.[29]

Another element to consider is the residual effect of gender and marital status on citizenship attribution, raising constitutional equality concerns when the legal capacity to transmit membership depends on the gender of the parent. While most countries have now repealed gender-discriminatory laws that only permitted fathers (and not mothers) to transmit citizenship to their children, some constitutions still do not regard mothers and fathers as holding equal standing in their ability to transmit citizenship to their offspring born outside the country.[30] For instance, the Malaysian Constitution defines who qualifies as a citizen, following the principle of gender equality in the transmission of citizenship when a child in born within the borders of that country. Alas, only a Malaysian father can transmit citizenship to a child born abroad. A similar provision, which held that a child born outside Kenya could only become a citizen at birth if the father was a Kenyan citizen, was recently overturned by the new Kenyan Constitution adopted in 2010. The new Constitution reinstates status to children born outside Kenya before its effective date, if either the mother or the father were Kenyan citizens.

The Canadian Supreme Court, too, had to weigh in on the intersection of citizenship and gender in the *Benner* (1997) case.[31] In that decision, a provision of the Canadian Citizenship Act, according to which a child born abroad to a Canadian father was automatically entitled to Canadian citizenship upon registration of his or her birth whereas a child born under similar circumstances to a Canadian mother was not automatically entitled to citizenship (such a child had to prove the absence of a criminal record and his or her willingness to swear an oath of allegiance), was challenged as violating the equality principle enshrined in the Canadian Charter of Rights and Freedoms. The Court struck down the provision, holding that it violated the Charter's equality guarantees (s 15) and was unjustifiable in a free and democratic

[27] Case C-200/02 [2004] ECR I-9925.

[28] There are additional variations. Eg the Constitution of Costa Rica recognizes the citizenship of a child born on Costa Rican soil to non-citizen parents, but requires that the parent register the minor child or that the child herself register by the age of 21. See Constitution of Costa Rica, Title 2, Art 13(3). Or consider another tactic for narrowing the application of the territorial-centered membership rules. The Dominican Republic follows the *jus soli* principle, providing automatic citizenship to children born on its territory, expect for those born to persons in transit or to persons residing illegally in the Dominican Republic. This 'in transit' provision has been interpreted to mean that 'parents of Haitian heritage are perpetually in transit', thus barring automatic citizenship to their children born in the Dominican Republic part of the Hispaniola island.

[29] Randall Hansen and Patrick Weil (eds), *Towards a European Nationality: Citizenship, Immigration, and Nationality Law in the EU* (2001).

[30] Historically, under the common law doctrine of coverture a woman lost her citizenship when she married and acquired the citizenship of her husband, based on the theory that the husband and wife were one and the 'one' this union created was male—'subsuming' or covering the female. This also meant that the transmission of citizenship to children occurred through the father. An unmarried woman could, however, pass citizenship to her child born out of wedlock. These distinctions and categories have now by and large been erased from the law books of most countries, but their lingering effect is still found in the margins.

[31] *Benner v Canada (Secretary of State)* [1997] 1 SCR 358 (Canada).

society (s 1) because it restricted access to citizenship 'on the basis of something so intimately connected to and so completely beyond the control of the [child] as the gender or his or her Canadian parent.'[32]

The United States has recently seen a string of constitutional challenges to the provisions of the Immigration and Nationality Act that distinguish between unwed mothers and fathers in their legal capacity to transmit citizenship abroad. In a trilogy of cases, *Miller* (1988), *Nguyen* (2001), and *Flores-Villar* (2011), the US Supreme Court had to decide whether mothers and fathers may be treated differently in determining whether their children may claim American citizenship, and whether such sex-based classifications violated equal protection principles.[33] The Supreme Court affirmed the statutory provisions, holding that they did not amount to constitutionally impermissible unequal treatment given the important governmental interests at stake. In *Nguyen*, the key issue was whether the provisions of the statute holding that a child born outside the country to an unwed mother will automatically receive citizenship whereas a child born outside the United States to an unmarried father will receive citizenship only if 'a blood relationship between the person and the father is established by clear and convincing evidence' violated the Equal Protection Clause. In a slim majority, the Court upheld the law, despite a sharply diverged minority opinion stating that the legislation at issue upheld

> a historic regime that left women with responsibility, and freed men from responsibility, for nonmarital children.... [R]ather than confronting the stereotypical notion that mothers must care for these children and fathers may ignore them, [the majority] quietly condones the very stereotype the law condemns.

In addition to the argument that such regulation of the transmission of citizenship reinforces the gender-norm that fathers bear little responsibility to their non-marital children, the more general point at issue (resembling the approach of the Canadian Supreme Court) is this: in a society committed to equality between the sexes, the gender of the parent bears no relationship on the individual's ability to transmit citizenship. The most recent equality challenge in this trilogy, *Flores-Villar*, focused on the constitutionality of imposing longer residency periods on unwed fathers than on unwed mothers whose children were born abroad, a provision that, unlike the *Nguyen* case, does not turn on biological factors concerning the establishment of paternity. This challenge ultimately proved futile, ending with a Supreme Court deadlock (4:4 split, with the recusal of one judge). This leaves in place, for now, an affirmation by an equally divided court of the gendered differential imposed by the statute.

2. *Jus Sanguinis*: The Parentage Principle

Whereas *jus soli* elevates the fact of birthplace into a guiding constitutional principle, the *jus sanguinis* principle confers political membership on the basis of *parentage* and *descent*. The children of present members of the polity, irrespective of place of birth, are automatically defined as citizens of their parents' political community. Whereas *jus soli* is traditionally followed in common law countries, *jus sanguinis* is the main principle associated with civil law jurisdictions in Europe and well beyond the continent, making it the leading membership transmission principle globally in terms of the sheer number of countries that follow it and of the individuals and families that are affected by its parameters.

[32] Ibid 401.

[33] *Miller v Albright* 523 US 420 (1998); *Tuan Anh Nguyen v INS* 533 US 53 (2001); *Flores-Villar v United States* 564 US __ (2011).

The modern inception of *jus sanguinis* came with the post-French Revolution Civil Code of 1804, which broke away from the territoriality principle. The French Civil Code held that *as citizens*, parents (specifically, fathers) had the right to transfer their status of political membership to their offspring at birth, regardless of whether the child was born in France or abroad.[34] During the Napoleonic period, the concept of attributing membership on the basis of descent was considered fresh and radically egalitarian. As Patrick Weil explains, the *jus sanguinis* principle broke away from the feudal tradition of *jus soli*, which linked subjects to a particular land (and to the lord who held the land).[35] In contrast, *jus sanguinis* linked citizens to each other (and to their joined political enterprise) through membership in the state. Together, they constituted 'a class of persons enjoying common rights, bounded by common obligations, formally equal before the law'.[36] Through codification and imitation, the nineteenth century saw the adoption of the *jus sanguinis* principle by many other European countries, including Austria, Belgium, Spain, Prussia, Italy, Russia, the Netherlands, Norway, and Sweden.[37] European colonial expansion, as well as legal 'transplanting', further spread the *jus sanguinis* principle to the four corners of the world.

For countries facing the combined pressures of immigration and emigration, *jus sanguinis* has the benefit of sustaining ties with citizens living abroad and their progeny.[38] Several constitutions explicitly provide easier access to citizenship to descendents, up to the third generation, of those who left the home country. This approach can be found in the Polish, Hungarian, and other Central and East European citizenship regimes. Armenia provides a simplified procedure for citizenship to individual of 'Armenian origin',[39] whereas the Irish Constitution highlights the significance of a cultural identity and heritage, declaring that the 'Irish nation cherishes its special affinity with people of Irish ancestry living abroad who share its cultural identity and heritage'.[40] Israel establishes an entitlement to citizenship to those with a Jewish ancestry (as defined by the Law of Return), treating them as *in potentia* members of the state, thus creating a legal and symbolic link between existing members of the polity and a large diaspora community. This 'right to return' is extended to family members, up to a third generation, regardless of their own religious affiliation or place of birth, as long as they can claim a lineage to a person who would have been entitled to make *aliyah* (Hebrew: 'to ascend') to Israel, even if that person is already deceased or never actually settled there. These variations on a theme of heritage, lineage, and ancestry illustrate the family affinity of the *jus sanguinis* principle with what has been termed the cultural or ethno-national conception of citizenship.[41] The main concern with this conception of identity and belonging is that it bears exclusionary tendencies, turning members of the political community—who, despite holding the status of formal, legal citizenship, are not part of the dominant 'we' majority—into potential outsiders. I return to address this metamorphosis of protected and often vulnerable minorities into feared 'outsiders' from within, in discussing citizenship's 'cultural turn', which is raising its head again across Europe.

[34] Weil (n 22), 19. [35] Ibid 19. [36] Brubaker (n 10), 39. [37] Weil (n 22), 21.

[38] Christian Joppke, 'Citizenship in between De- and Re-Ethnicization' (2003) 44 *Archives européennes de sociologie* 429.

[39] Constitution of Armenia, Ch 1, Art 11.3.

[40] Constitution of Ireland, Art 2.

[41] Gershon Shafir and Yoav Peled, 'Citizenship and Stratification in an Ethnic Democracy' (1998) 21 *Ethnic and Racial Studies* 408; Ayelet Shachar, 'Religion, State and the Problem of Gender: Reimaging Citizenship in Diverse Societies' (2005) 50 *McGill Law Journal* 3, 35–8.

Importantly, there is nothing intrinsic or inevitable in this cultural turn. It certainly is not a built-in feature of the parentage-based membership principle. Under any version of the *jus sanguinis* principle, the crucial question to determine is who gains the right to transmit membership to the as-yet-unborn generations. Most countries have resolved this constitutive dilemma by adopting what has been termed the 'zero option', whereby *all* persons residing in the territory of the newly established country on a particular day (usually declared soon after independence) are automatically granted citizenship. In theory, this permits the creation of a heterogeneous and inclusive community to be 'reproduced': when citizens procreate, this diversity of composition is transmitted to future generations through the parentage-based birthright principle, especially if coupled with naturalization provisions that make it relatively easy for immigrants from different parts of the world to acquire full membership status within the adoptive country.[42]

In practice, however, the reliance on descent in the transmission of citizenship may lead to exclusionary overtones associated with privileging the majority community, especially where there are few (if any) mechanisms for newcomers who do not already 'belong to the fold' on the basis of national, linguistic, religious, or cultural heritage, to gain access to citizenship. Reliance on 'bloodline' as the sole connecting factor for allotting automatic citizenship may, under such conditions, prohibit children of immigrants from becoming full members of the country in which they were born and raised due to a criterion that is firmly beyond their control—their ancestry.

Perhaps the most familiar, and now discredited, example of perpetual intergenerational exclusion (through *jus sanguinis*) of long-term permanent residents from full membership in the polity can be seen in German citizenship law, prior to its reform in 2000. In the past, German citizenship law attributed membership based exclusively on descent. Naturalization was exceptional. Thus, even lawful permanent residents born and bred on German soil had no legal right to become full members of the body politic. This non-citizen status would be propagated from generation to generation: once the parents were excluded from membership, neither they nor their children could alter this designation through residency, consent, or voluntary action. This policy created a class of second- and third-generation children of immigrants whose ancestry prevented them from obtaining citizenship—and the added layer of protection and opportunity that it grants—no matter their level of self-identification with the country, or the fact that they had resided there for their entire lives.

When this hard-won change in German citizenship law finally took effect, children born to *Gastarbeiter* and other settled immigrants gained the right to acquire German citizenship based on their birth in the territory, rather than on their ancestry. As with recent changes in *jus soli* countries that have added a component of *jus sanguinis* into their citizenship attribution regimes, there is no prohibition against modifying the *jus sanguinis* model, as in this example, by the addition of a *jus soli* component.

3. Emergent Trends: Borrowing, Dual Nationality, and the Loss of Citizenship

In the maze of constitutional provisions and citizenship laws defining formal access to membership we clearly need to keep track of each country's distinct rules and procedures. But it is

[42] William Rogers Brubaker, 'Introduction' in William Rogers Brubaker (ed), *Immigration and the Politics of Citizenship in Europe and North America* (1989).

also possible to identify emergent common themes. Most notable is the pattern of mutual 'borrowing' from one system to another, which is of course familiar to us from the broader field of comparative constitutional law. In the study of citizenship this is referred to as the convergence thesis.[43] Another significant trend is the growing recognition of dual nationality.[44] Whereas the Preamble to the 1930 Hague Convention on Conflict of Nationality Laws declared that 'it is in the general interest of the international community to secure that all its members should recognize that every person should have a nationality and should have *one nationality only*', today, approximately half the world's countries permit their citizens to hold dual nationality, either by birth or naturalization.[45] This transformation has led some commentators to claim that we are witnessing the 'inevitable lightening of citizenship'.[46] There is some truth to this description, especially for those residing in well-off countries in Europe and North America. But even in these regions of the world, the picture is more complex. Arguably, it simultaneously reveals *both* the relaxation ('lightening') and the tightening (or 're-bordering') of citizenship.

To provide one illustration of the latter pattern, consider the rekindling of the old debate about the revocation of citizenship: the involuntary stripping of an individual's legal status as a member of the political community. The United Kingdom offers a telling example. The British Nationality Act was amended in 2002 and then again in 2006 with the adoption of the Immigration, Asylum and Nationality Act that broadened the power of the Home Secretary to revoke British citizenship in circumstances where 'that deprivation is conducive to the public good'.[47] Heated debates surrounding categories such as 'breach of allegiance' or 'disloyalty toward the state' are of course anything but new.[48] The distinctiveness of this new provision, however, lies in the criteria for revoking citizenship that 'is content with a vague determination (by the state) that the very holding of citizenship [rather than specific conduct] has become harmful to the public interest'.[49]

This broad authorization for the British government to deprive an individual from citizenship, what Hannah Arendt famously called, 'the basic right to have rights', stretches beyond what is currently permitted in other major countries that follow the common law tradition. Canada, for example, only permits the revocation of citizenship for reasons of fraud, false representation, or concealment of material circumstances.[50] In the United States, birthright citizens cannot have their citizenship involuntarily stripped, whereas naturalized citizens can have their citizenship revoked at any time, if that naturalization was illegally procured or procured by concealment of a material fact or by willful misrepresentation.[51] As a result of several constitutional challenges, including the landmark decision in *Afroyim v Rusk* (1967), the US Supreme Court ruled that Congress cannot revoke citizenship involuntarily, concluding that:

[43] This trend was identified by Hansen and Weil in their trailblazing work in the field. See Hansen and Weil (n 29).

[44] Peter J. Spiro, 'Dual Citizenship as Human Right' (2010) 8 *International Journal of Constitutional Law* 111.

[45] Preamble (emphasis added). Sejersen T. Brondsted '"I Vow Thee My Countries"—The Expansion of Dual Citizenship in the 21st Century' (2008) 42 *International. Migration Review* 523.

[46] Christian Joppke, 'The Inevitable Lightening of Citizenship' (2010) 1 *Archives européennes de sociologie* 9.

[47] Immigration, Asylum and Nationality Act 2006, s 56(1). For a thorough analysis, see Shai Lavi, 'Punishment and the Revocation of Citizenship in the United Kingdom, United States and Israel' (2010) 13 *New Criminal Law Review* 404.

[48] In the common law tradition, they have deep feudal roots. But civil law countries have also struggled with such categories. Eg French law permits the revocation of citizenship if one commits certain crimes, such as terrorism, that are held to be incompatible with the status of being French.

[49] Lavi (n 47), 410.

[50] Citizenship Act, §10 (Canada).

[51] Immigration and Nationality Act, §340, codified as 8 USC §1451. For further discussion, see Leti Volpp in 'Citizenship Undone' (2007) 77 *Fordham Law Review* 2579.

> We hold that the Fourteenth Amendment was designed to, and does, protect every citizen of this Nation against a congressional forcible destruction of his [or her] citizenship, whatever his [or her] creed, color, or race. Our holding does no more than to give to this citizen that which is his [or her] own, a constitutional right to remain a citizen in a free country unless he [or she] voluntarily relinquishes that citizenship.[52]

This core notion of giving to a member of the political community that which is *already* hers—a constitutional right to remain a citizen—is at risk with the revival of the practice of the involuntary revocation of citizenship. One of history's little ironies is that the formal or legalistic aspect of citizenship, which postnational and other scholars have come to treat as irrelevant and anachronistic at best, may in fact prove of tremendous importance to protecting the individual in today's more turbulent world. It is this 'bare legal status' which grants, as it were, a basic shield or security of membership, operating like 'a thin but unbreakable guard rail'.[53]

4. Naturalization: The Return of Culture

The *only* legal method for acquiring citizenship other than through birthright is by naturalization. When we speak of naturalization, we refer to the final step in the process of acquiring citizenship *after* birth. The word derives from *nasci* (Latin), which means 'to be born'; the term *natur*alization therefore suggests that the post-birth admission to citizenship is a symbolic and political 're-birth' into the new membership community. This usually requires agency, action, and expressed consent by the individual, as well as acceptance by the political community into which she emigrates.

To gain a shot at acquiring post-birth membership in a desired destination country, one must first reach its territory and establish lawful permanent residence. In a world of regulated borders, this may prove harder than is commonly thought: each polity is obliged to allow entrance to its territory only to its *own* citizens. A non-citizen has no similar right.[54] Global inequality patterns also make their mark here: citizens of countries perceived to be poorer or less stable are often subjected to more stringent requirements when they seek admission to more affluent countries. These inequalities are felt even when applicants are seeking short-term entrance visas only, let alone permits for permanent residence.[55]

While the precise requirements of naturalization may vary from one country to another, the basic premise is that 'the power to admit or exclude aliens is a sovereign prerogative'.[56]

[52] *Afroyim v Rusk* 387 US 253 (1967). The principle stated in *Afroyim* was unanimously reaffirmed by the US Supreme Court in *Vance v Terrazas* 444 US 252 (1980). See T. Alexander Alienikoff, 'Theories of Loss of Citizenship' (1986) 84 *Michigan Law Review* 1471.

[53] Audrey Macklin, 'Exile on Main Street: Popular Discourse and Legal Manoeuvres around Citizenship' in *Law and Citizenship* (2006), 24.

[54] The major exception here is the obligation that nations that signed the 1951 Refugee Convention have taken upon themselves to provide a safe haven to persons who qualify as refugees. Even then, the receiving country is obliged to provide temporary shelter only, not necessarily long-term residency.

[55] Most countries are committed to granting access on the basis of marriage or family ties to a person who is already a citizen or permanent resident of the destination country, where individuals have a right to bring certain categories of family members. In Europe, this commitment is enshrined in Art 8 of the European Convention on Human Rights. Here, too, there has been a good amount of legal gymnastics, as in the distinction between family reunification (permitted) and establishment of marriage life where one partner is not settled in the admitting country (limited). The new pre-entry integration tests that take place abroad apply to spouses in such applications.

[56] *Landon v Plascencia* 459 US 21, 32 (1982) is a classic example of the static view of citizenship.

Here, too, we can identify a double transition: certain naturalization requirements have been procedurally 'lightened', as exemplified by the reduction of the number of years of residence that a state can require of the individual before he becomes eligible to apply for citizenship.[57] At the same time, the substantive requirements have been tightened up and revamped, exemplified by the rise of citizenship tests from The Hague at the heart of Europe to Canberra in the far edges of the New World, contributing to the 'wider agenda of reinforcing shared values' (as a British government document recently put it). Another example of the renewed emphasis on integration as a condition for inclusion in the body politic hails from France, where immigrants are now required to sign the Contract d'accueil et d'intégration, which articulates the centrality of the principle of laïcité to the Republic. These developments, which I now turn to explore, can be labeled as the 'cultural turn' in citizenship discourse and practice, and they reflect a majoritarian tilt.

Typically, the most basic requirement for naturalization is that the applicant must have resided continuously in the admitting country for several consecutive years as defined in statutory or regulatory legal residency requirements. The applicant must demonstrate basic knowledge of their new home country's language, political system, and forms of government. Another key requirement present across the spectrum of admitting countries is that the would-be citizen must not have a criminal record; an applicant who is deemed to pose a security risk to the state will also be disqualified. In the United States, even minor brushes with the criminal code are likely to bar a person from gaining citizenship, often leading to the deportation of the immigrant back to the country of origin. For those permitted to complete the transition process towards post-birth citizenship, the naturalization process culminates in a symbolic public ceremony, in which applicants pledge allegiance to their new home country (or its constitution), sing the national anthem, and salute its flag.[58] Taken together, these acts represent symbolically the culmination of a unidirectional and graduated transformation, or 're-birth': from alien to citizen.

The description of the path to naturalization that I have just recounted is the classic narrative that is told from the viewpoint of the admitting society. Yet in a more dynamic global reality, the script may have to undergo a modification. Note the almost complete absence of the sending country from the narrative, or what Rainer Baubock calls the 'external citizenship' dimension of transnational migration, whereby certain individuals continue to hold and nourish meaningful ties to the new home country and the old. The growing recognition of dual nationality begins to capture this changed reality on the ground, but there are many challenges ahead. Indeed, some are suggesting that the pressures of globalization and the perception of a 'loss of control' over borders and membership boundaries are in part motivating a new zealous turn toward regulating who gets in and who of those not born as citizens can be defined as eligible for inclusion in the innermost circle of members through *natur*alization. The introduction of civic integration exams abroad—with the Netherlands taking the lead—and citizenship tests and ceremonies at home provide insights into the present 'cultural turn'. These new developments have come to the forefront of the debate in Germany, Denmark, Australia, and the United Kingdom, to mention a few key examples.[59]

[57] Joppke (n 46).

[58] The symbolic meaning of such acts is discussed by Sanford Levinson, 'Constituting Communities through Words that Bind: Reflections on Loyalty Oath' 84 *Michigan Law Review* 1440 (1986).

[59] Amitai Etzioni, 'Citizenship Tests: A Comparative, Communitarian Perspective' (2007) 78 *Political Quarterly* 353; Liav Orgad, 'Illiberal Liberalism: Cultural Restrictions on Migration and Access to Citizenship in Europe' (2010) 58 *American Journal of Comparative Law* 53.

These citizenship tests feature civics questions about the adoptive country's system of government, the political process, and the values of a constitutional state. The more controversial aspects relate to matters of culture, identity, and ethics. As Liav Orgad observes, some of these new tests are designed to examine the applicant's personal beliefs and moral judgments, and are 'unusual in the intrusiveness of [the] questions... about gender equality, religion, conversion, politics, marital relations, promiscuity, and culture.'[60] In the German *Land* of Baden-Wurttemberg, a questionnaire that was later retracted and replaced by a federal citizenship test, originally included questions such as the following: 'Your adult daughter or your spouse would like to dress like other German girls and women. Would you try to prevent it? If yes, by which means?'[61] The Dutch, unlike the Americans, do not provide applicants with copies of prospective questions that may appear on their actual citizenship tests on the theory that 'the proper attitude... cannot be learnt by heart.'[62] As part of the effort to make citizenship meaningful, the centrality of the concept of integration has risen, and multiculturalism (a term that has come to serve as a scapegoat for any public policy that has granted some degree of recognition to cultural and religious diversity or explored whether legal accommodation is merited and justified) explicitly disavowed. Germany's Chancellor, Angela Merkel, perhaps best expressed this sentiment in stating that 'multikulti' had 'failed, and failed utterly'.

In the United Kingdom, this new commitment to integration has translated into heightened language requirements and the introduction of citizenship tests and ceremonies. This was soon followed by Australia, the only new-world society that did not previously adopt a formal citizenship test. These fast-paced changes reflect a commitment to actively promoting and 'strengthen[ing] the things—the values, the habits, the qualities—that we have in common', as *The Path to Citizenship* government document puts it.[63] Christian Joppke has caught the spirit of the moment in describing such tests as instances of 'repressive liberalism'. Others have used related labels, such as illiberal liberalism, cautioning that such measures 'violate the same values they seek to promote'.[64]

In addition to citizenship tests that apply to immigrants who already reside in the destination country, naturalization processes have also become more closely intertwined with immigration control.[65] This is evident, for example, in the Dutch policy of demanding visa applicants abroad to demonstrate knowledge and linguistic abilities *before* the person reached Dutch soil, effectively turning linguistic and cultural knowledge into a precondition for gaining an entry visa to the country, rather than the more traditional view of seeing it as a result of a process of integration that occurs only *after* settlement in the new home country.

Another manifestation of the cultural turn in citizenship discourse and practice can be found in the fierce controversies surrounding the legislation to ban head-to-toe veiling in public, especially the more extensive forms of face covering (the niqab and burqa). France was the first country in Europe to implement such a ban through legislation that prohibits

[60] Orgad (n 59), 67. [61] Ibid.

[62] Dimitri Kochenov, 'Mevrouw de Jong Gaat Eten: EU Citizenship and the Culture of Prejudice', EUI Working Paper, RSCAS 2011/06 (EUDO Citizenship Observatory, 2011), 8.

[63] Government Green Paper, *The Path to Citizenship: Next Steps in Reforming the Immigration System* (2008), para 42.

[64] Orgad (n 59), 92. The term 'repressive liberalism' is drawn from Christian Joppke, 'Beyond National Models: Civic Integration Policies for Immigrants in Western Europe' (2007) 30 *West European Politics* 1.

[65] In addition to this cultural turn, we are also witnessing the invention and implementation of what I have elsewhere called the 'shifting [territorial] border of immigration regulation'. See Ayelet Shachar, 'The Shifting Border of Immigration Regulation' (2007) 3 *Stanford Journal of Civil Rights-Civil Liberties* 165.

clothing concealing the face in public places. A woman wearing a face veil in defiance of the law risks a fine that can be accompanied or replaced by compulsory citizenship classes. Such state action purports to advance the goals of gender equality, secularism, and public order, but it may stand in tension with constitutionally protected principles of religious freedom, as well as the values of individual choice and autonomy. Such generalized bans and their compatibility with constitutional principles and human rights protections will surely occupy domestic and regional courts in years to come. At present, it remains undisputed that the relentless attention paid to veiling by Muslim women has only further politicized the matter. In this charged environment, every act of veiling (or its rejection) is interpreted by multiple actors as a statement about one's 'loyalty' and 'belonging'. What is often lost in the discussion is the recognition that immigrant women who belong to minority or marginalized religious communities are constantly negotiating their *multiple* affiliations (to their gender, their faith, their families, their new and old home countries, and so on) while operating within a tight space for action. Nevertheless, they—and their (covered) bodies—have become the visual markers of far broader struggles over power and identity, secularism and expression of 'difference', the blurring of once fixed lines distinguishing the metropolitan from the rest of the (once-colonized) world, the struggle to 'speak' for oneself as opposed to artificially being placed in predefined boxes and categories, in addition to reinforcing the majority culture as the norm and by default delineating certain communities as implicitly 'foreign'.

Many of these themes came to a head in the *Faiza M* ruling, in which the Conseil d'État upheld a decision to decline a naturalization request submitted by a Muslim female immigrant who was legally admitted to France, spoke fluent French, was married to a citizen, and had three French children, because 'she had adopted a radical practice of her religion, incompatible with the essential values of the French communaté, especially the principle of equality between the sexes.' This decision was based on Article 21–4 of the Civil Code as it applied in 2005, stating that, 'By decree in the Conseil d'État, the Government may, on grounds of indignity or lack of assimilation other than linguistic, oppose the acquisition of French nationality by the foreign spouse.' The formal legal basis for the denial was not the religious attire per se as much as the governmental assessment of Silmi's 'insufficient assimilation' into the French Republic. In practice, however, as one astute legal observer noted, 'it remains uncertain whether Silmi was denied citizenship due to her beliefs, or her conduct, or both'.[66] The practical result of the denial of Silmi's request for securing citizenship, the direct bond between the individual and the state—a status that is *independent* of her husband (once bestowed upon her), is that in the name of gender equality she was left in a dependent position vis-à-vis both her partner, who already had a secure legal status, and the political community at large. The turn to collective identity claims by the majority, then, has a sharp edge, making it potentially harder for non-dominant members of minority religions to gain full inclusion or even mere legal admission (if they are not yet citizens).

Beyond the growing significance of the claims of culture in determining who shall gain (or be denied) the 'final prize' of full, legal membership in the state, another kind of re-bordering of citizenship is occurring on a different plane; namely, the rising impact of economic and human-capital accretion considerations to shaping targeted immigration policies in countries that seek to gain or sustain a relative advantage. In this vein, governments are now willing to proactively use their control over allocating membership resources as part of their economic

[66] Orgad (n 59), 64.

or global competitive strategy to attract highly skilled migrants and wealthy individuals whose admission is seen as a net gain for the polity. At the same time, these very same destination countries are trying to do whatever they can within the bounds of legality to fend off 'unwanted' immigrants that they see as falling into the net-burden category. This selective migration policy is reflected, for example, in the tailoring of 'incentive packages' that contain the promise of putting certain migrants on the fast track toward acquisition of full membership.[67] This pattern of change touches upon the most delicate and contentious issues of citizenship: defining who may gain access to membership in the political community, and on what basis.

Just as admission is becoming harder and harder to secure for those trying to gain entry visas based on family ties or arriving from destinations that are perceived as culturally 'too different' from the majority society, the golden gates of immigration are being opened ever more widely to those regarded as the world's 'brightest minds' based on an assessment of their skills, innovation, and adaptability.[68] Related reconfigurations of citizenship are simultaneously occurring in emigrant-sending countries. Whereas in the past skilled migrants were regarded as lost causes who had 'betrayed' the home national community, these individuals are now courted as long-lost sons and daughters of the home nation, whose 'literal "worth" to the state is invoked, conjuring a vision of citizenship-by-economic contribution'.[69] This new interpretation allows successful migrants to maintain legal ties with their original home countries as well as the political communities in which they have settled.[70]

III. Piercing into the Future: Citizenship's New Frontiers

The discussion thus far has proceeded on the assumption that citizenship is distinguished by the 'rules of access to citizenship status and the scope and quality of the rights this status entails within a given territory'.[71] This captures well the standard or static vision of citizenship, according to which 'all the members of the political community [are] bounded by the borders of the state—and only they—were to have equal rights and duties and an equal stake in decisions regarding matters of the state.'[72] This unified and state-centered understanding of citizenship has always been more of a myth than a reality, but it is arguably harder to sustain in an increasingly interconnected world that has given rise to new and more dynamic forms of multilevel governance and attachment that are proliferating, both above and below the nation state level. The classic example here is the creation of European citizenship at the supranational level. Although the grant of Union citizenship is still derivative on acquiring citizenship in the member states, according to their own nationality laws, the European Court of Justice

[67] For further discussion of these transformations, see Ayelet Shachar, 'The Race for Talent: Highly Skilled Migrants and Competitive Immigration Regimes' (2006) 81 *NYU Law Review* 148.

[68] Ayelet Shachar, 'Picking Winners: Olympic Citizenship and the Global Race for Talent' (2011) 120 *Yale Law Journal* 2088.

[69] Barry (n 11), 124.

[70] Rainer Bauböck, 'Toward a Political Theory of Migrant Transnationalism' (2003) 37 *International Migration Review* 700; Devesh Kapur, 'The Janus Face of Diasporas' in Barbara J. Merz et al (eds), *Diasporas and Development* (2007).

[71] Eniko Horvath and Ruth Rubio-Marin, '"Alles Oder Nichts"? The Outer Boundaries of the German Citizenship Debate' (2010) 8 *International Journal of Constitutional Law* 72.

[72] Ibid 72–3.

has famously and repeatedly declared that each individual EU citizen enjoys rights and owes duties that together make up this new status—EU citizenship—which is 'destined to become the fundamental status of nationals of the Member States'.[73] Over time, the European Court of Justice has begun giving this declaration some teeth. Most recently, in the much anticipated *Zambrano* (2011) decision, the Court ruled that the non-EU parents of an EU citizen child must be allowed to live and work in the state in which their children were born, even if the parent(s) otherwise had no right to remain in that country.[74] This is the reversal of the classic *jus sanguinis* narrative: instead of parents passing down citizenship to their offspring, here, the EU-born children, as citizens of the Union—acquired by virtue of the *jus soli* principle or specialized provisions to avert statelessness—secure the residency status of their parents within the territory of the Union. As several commentators have noted, the unintended consequences of this expansive judgment might well be to create further incentives for member states, the gatekeepers of Union citizenship, to make it 'all the more difficult for individuals to gain access to European citizenship in the first place'.[75] Such restrictions, motivated by 'loss of control' fears, would only further accentuate the re-bordering trends identified earlier in our discussion of the cultural turn. At the subnational level, greater attention is paid to the core role played by cities and localities in shaping the integration experience of immigrants. New York, London, and Amsterdam come to mind as prime examples. Regional and provincial distinctions also play a role in shaping the experience of citizenship. For instance, the cultural turn just discussed has been more pronounced in Quebec (which, like France, introduced legislation to prohibit face-covering in public spaces) than the rest of Canada; its effects more strongly manifested in the Flemish regions of Belgium than its Walloon parts.

Another important development on the ground is found in the pattern of circular migration and the emergent transnational understandings of membership. Here, the focus is less on legal status and more on the lived experience of individuals and families who have successfully managed to maintain active and meaningful connections, ventures, and opportunities in both their new home countries and the old. Of particular interest are attempts to extend and facilitate the rights of political participation (including voting rights) to emigrant citizens living abroad, allowing individuals to enjoy a wide range of associative and political relations across borders. A mirror-image development is found in campaigns to extend the franchise to noncitizens who are long-term residents of a given polity by granting them the right to vote in local, and possibly national, elections as well.[76]

Philosophers, ancient and contemporary, have idealistically envisioned cosmopolitan conceptions of citizenship, while others now speak of a borderless world, although this often takes the form of an ethical or aspirational plea to recognize and respect each person's equal worth and dignity, irrespective of formal membership status, rather than an attempt to provide a legal and institutional blueprint for a new world order. Activists have called attention to 'citizenship on the ground' or 'globalization from below', whereby individuals assert rights and demand recognition through democratic politics, sometimes in total disregard of the fact that

[73] C-184/99 *Grzelczyk* [2001] ECR I-6193, para 31.

[74] C-34/09 *Zambrano* [2011]; the Court removed the requirement of sufficient funds that was present in *Chen*, invoking Art 20 TFEU rather than the Citizen Directive 2004/38/EC.

[75] See Anja Wiesbrock, 'The Zambrano Case: Relying on Union Citizenship Rights in "Internal Situations"', EUDO Citizenship Observatory, March 2011.

[76] The right to vote in local elections is guaranteed to citizens of the EU, whichever member state they reside in. For detailed analysis, see Jo Shaw, *The Transformation of Citizenship in the European Union: Electoral Rights and Restructuring of Political Space* (2007). See also Cristina M. Rodriguez, 'Non-Citizen Voting and the Extra-Constitutional Construction of the Polity' (2010) 8 *International Journal of Constitutional Law* 30.

formally they lack legal status in the eyes of the respective community or its established law and jurisprudence.[77]

Being political does not by itself suffice to shield one from the full force of existing categories, including those of removal and expulsion from the country in which one lives and 'acts' as a citizen, but it may help transform these very categories. A telling example of the deployment of citizenship as democratic action and participation is found in the recent campaign for the legalization of undocumented students in the United States, which saw these students mobilize politically by telling their own compelling life stories, including self-identification as lacking legal status, under the slogan of 'unlawful and unafraid'. Like so many other once-excluded groups and constituencies who were barred from formal citizenship (on the basis of race, gender, sexual orientation, and so on), the appeal here is to change the law so that the promise of equal membership is extended to new subjects and new domains. For these young men and women, many of whom were brought into the United States as babies or toddlers, the United States has become the center of their life. Yet under traditional principles of citizenship acquisition they are deprived of membership. Instead, they face the hanging sword of deportation from the only country they know as home. The urgency of reform is undisputed. It may include regularization programs or the addition of a new root of title to citizenship for those who already 'practice' it. This I have elsewhere labelled the *jus nexi* principle, which can operate alongside the *jus soli* and *jus sanguinis* principles, offering a more fitting interpretation of membership for a world of increasing mobility and interdependence.[78]

The constitutive elements of citizenship's simultaneous 'lightening' and 're-bordering' are now fully in view. This paradoxically fits in line with the historical record of citizenship, which rather than offering a linear story of progression is full of competing narratives.[79] Because it is an emancipatory promise, it is too early to bid citizenship farewell; it may be changing its scale and scope, but it still offers a baseline of security and protection to the individual that no other human rights instruments have to date achieved. Being relevant, and back with a vengeance, it turns out, is a measure of the great gaps that we still need to fill before we can give up on the ideal of equal membership in the political community, which, despite its many shortfalls, changing scales and ever-evolving interpretations, remains one of the finest institutions, to date, that we have created to justly govern our collective affairs and individual freedoms.

Bibliography

T. Alexander Alienikoff, 'Theories of Loss of Citizenship' (1986) 84 *Michigan Law Review*. 1471

Rainer Bauböck, 'Toward a Political Theory of Migrant Transnationalism' (2003) 37 *International Migration Review* 700

Seyla Benhabib, *The Rights of Others: Aliens, Residents and Citizens* (2004)

Linda Bosniak, 'Citizenship Denationalized' (2000) 7 *Indiana Journal of Global Legal Studies* 447

Rogers Brubaker, *Citizenship and Nationhood in France and Germany* (1992)

Joseph H. Carens, *Culture, Citizenship, and Community: A Contextual Exploration of Justice as Evenhandedness* (2000)

Thomas Faist and Peter Kivisto (eds), *Dual Citizenship in Global Perspective: From Unitary to Multiple Citizenship* (2007)

[77] Luis Cabrera, *The Practice of Global Citizenship* (2010).

[78] Ayelet Shachar, 'Earned Citizenship: Property Lessons for Immigration Reform' (2011) 23 *Yale Journal of Law & the Humanities* 110.

[79] Rogers M. Smith, *Civic Ideals: Conflicting Visions of Citizenship in US History* (1997).

Owen Fiss, *A Community of Equals: The Constitutional Protection of New Americans* (1999)

Randall Hansen, 'The Free Economy and the Jacobin State, or How Europe Can Cope with the Coming Immigration Wave' in Carol M. Swain (ed), *Debating Immigration* (2008)

Engin F. Isin, Peter Nyers and Bryan S. Turner (eds), *Citizenship between Past and Future* (2008)

Christian Joppke, *Citizenship and Immigration* (2010)

Will Kymlicka, *Multicultural Citizenship: A Liberal Theory of Minority Rights* (1995)

T. H. Marshall, *Citizenship and Social Class* (1950)

Liav Orgad, 'Illiberal Liberalism: Cultural Restrictions on Migration and Access to Citizenship in Europe' (2010) 58 *American Journal of Comparative Law* 53

J.G.A. Pocock, 'The Ideal of Citizenship since Classical Times' in Ronald Beiner (ed), *Theorizing Citizenship* (1995)

Saskia Sassen, *Losing Control? Sovereignty in an Age of Globalization* (1996)

Peter H. Schuck, 'Three Models of Citizenship' in Michael S. Greve and Michael Zoller (eds), *Citizenship in America and Europe: Beyond the Nation-State?* (2009)

Ayelet Shachar, *The Birthright Lottery: Citizenship and Global Inequality* (2009)

Jo Shaw, *The Transformation of Citizenship in the European Union: Electoral Rights and Restructuring of Political Space* (2007)

Rogers M. Smith, *Civic Ideals: Conflicting Visions of Citizenship in US History* (1997)

Peter J. Spiro, 'Dual Citizenship as Human Right' (2010) 8 *International Journal of Constitutional Law* 111

Leti Volpp, 'The Culture of Citizenship' (2007) 8 *Theoretical Inquiries in Law* 571

Patrick Weil, 'Access to Citizenship: A Comparison on Twenty-Five Nationality Laws' in T. Alexander Aleinikoff and Douglas Klusmeyer (eds), *Citizenship Today: Global Perspectives and Practices* (2001)

CHAPTER 49

SOCIO-ECONOMIC RIGHTS

D. M. DAVIS

Cape Town

I. Introduction

Social and economic rights cannot be examined in isolation from other forms of rights claims. They form an integral part of the vocabulary of rights. The fact that they are sometimes termed 'second generation' rights affords luminous support for this argument and, at the same time, it points to differences to first-generation rights. While these differences will be canvassed, it will be argued that their existence and justification are inextricably linked to the first generation of human rights, being civil and political rights.

Briefly stated, the nature of first-generation rights was heavily influenced by the French and the American Revolutions which left an indelible imprint upon their nature and scope. Revolutionaries in both countries proclaimed that human rights, which they proclaimed, were sourced in the values of civilization. These rights were claimed in the name of all free men (and later women) and were not to be limited by geographical considerations. The first generation of rights were conceived negatively, being 'freedoms from' as opposed to imposing positive 'entitlements upon'.[1] This generation of rights included freedom of opinion, conscience and religion, freedom of expression, of the press, of movement, the right to due process of law and hence protection against arbitrary detention or arrest, and the right to property.

It is apparent from a careful examination of this generation of rights that not all of these rights can be simply reduced to the exercise of state power and so fall neatly into the category

[1] Isaiah Berlin, 'Two Concepts of Liberty' in Henry Hardy (ed), *Liberty* (2002).

of negative rights. As an illustration, the right of every citizen to participate in a free election or the right to a fair trial imposes positive obligations upon the state to devote sufficient resources to guarantee a free election or to ensure the establishment of independent courts in which the free trial can be conducted. The attempt to divide the negative from the positive must wait until later in the chapter.

Let us turn to the second generation of rights. Briefly stated, the conventional wisdom is that they were sourced in the development of twentieth-century struggles and institutions. Their historical pedigree goes back much further. In the eighteenth century in Bavaria and Prussia, the state was viewed as an 'agent of social happiness' responsible for caring for the needy and for the provision of work for those who lacked the means and opportunities to support themselves. Similarly, the French Constitution of 1793 included the obligation on the state to provide public assistance for the needy.[2]

In the nineteenth century, Bismarck introduced social legislation which covered income-related insurance in cases of unemployment, accident, and illness, as well as pension and compensation schemes and a residual category of welfare. Not surprisingly, the Weimar Constitution of 1919 recognized the importance of these rights, including labour rights. In 1919, the establishment of the International Labour Organization triggered an attempt to establish certain international labour standards, and a second generation of human rights was introduced into the legal discourse, characterized by an express obligation upon a state to intervene rather than merely abstain from encroaching onto the private domain of the citizen. Rights to decent working conditions, to social security could not be attained without positive obligations being imposed upon the state. These second-generation rights constituted claims upon the state to fulfil obligations rather than to refrain from acting which lay at the heart of the prevailing wisdom about negative freedoms. Apart from Germany, the Mexican Constitution of 1917 included social rights in the text as did the Soviet Constitution of 1936, Part 7 of which contained a comprehensive list of socio-economic rights including the right to work, the right to health care, education, and housing. The Irish Constitution of 1937 also recognized these rights but in a far weaker form, being contained in directive principles of state policy designed to guide the government in its choice of policy and the judiciary in its interpretation of all rights.

But it was after the Second World War that a number of countries adopted or amended their constitutions to include social and economic rights.[3] The development of a human rights jurisprudence which was initially powered by the United Nations gave great impetus to the expansion of these rights in national and international texts.[4] The wider recognition of social and economic rights was coupled to the idea that these rights were part of the concept of citizenship. T.H. Marshall in an influential book suggested that social rights included.

> the whole range from the right to a modicum of economic welfare and security to the right to share to the full in the social heritage and to live the life of a civilized being according to the standards prevailing in the society. The institutions most closely connected with it are the educational system and the social services.[5]

[2] Gunter Frankenberg, 'Why Care? The Trouble with Social Rights' (1996) 17 Cardozo Law Review 1365, 1373.

[3] Lorraine Weinrib, 'The Post War Paradigm and American Exceptionalism' in Sujit Choudhry (ed), *The Migration of Constitutional Ideas* (2006). On economic rights, see further Chapter 50.

[4] Mary Glendon, *A World Made New: Eleanor Roosevelt and the Universal Declaration of Humand Rights* (2000).

[5] T.H. Marshall, *Citizenship and Social Class* (1964), 72.

As much writers such as Marshall saw these rights as critical in tempering the social consequences of unbridled capitalism and further that these rights had appeared in pre-war constitutions, a conceptual divide between these rights and traditional civil and political rights appeared always to be present.

Quincy Wright sought already in 1947 to distinguish between the two generations of rights when he wrote:

> Individual rights are in the main correlative to negative duties of the State and social rights are in the main correlative to positive duties of the State. Individual rights require that the State abstain from interference with the free exercise of the individual of his capacities, while social rights require that the State interfere with many things the individual would like to do....[6]

In summary, the initial drive for negative human rights can be sourced in the revolutions of France and America, whereas the initial drive for social and economic rights in the socialist struggles of the first two decades of the twentieth century, and later the period after the Second World War which saw a further development of second-generation and the emergence of third-generation rights. In 1948, the Universal Declaration of Human Rights recognized both civil and political rights as well as economic and social rights.[7]

By 1966, the Commission on Human Rights, itself spawned from the 1948 Universal Declaration of Human Rights, had developed two covenants, the International Covenant on Civil and Political Rights and the International Covenant on Economic Social and Cultural Rights (ICESCR), the latter of which came into force on 3 January 1976. Initially, the ICESCR lacked a complaints mechanism but by 1987 the UN Committee on Economic, Social and Cultural Rights had begun to develop a jurisprudence through its general comments and state specific reports.

Further, important developments took place within national constitutional law. In 1954 in *Brown v Board of Education*,[8] the US Supreme Court, in one of its most publicized and controversial decisions when delivered struck down the concept of separate but equal and thus paved the way for non-discriminatory access to education. In 1972, the German Federal Constitutional Court held that the right to a free choice of occupation obliged universities to demonstrate that they had effectively deployed all available resources to maximize the number of university places available to students.[9] During the 1970s, the Indian Supreme Court began to develop a range of social rights, from the right to life read together with a directive principles of state policy which were contained in the Indian Constitution,[10] its judgment in *Sunil Batra v Delhi Administration*.[11]

A third generation of human rights emerged during this period. Karel Vasak stated in his inaugural lecture to the tenth study session of the International Institute of Human Rights in July 1979 that this third generation of human rights:

> are new in the aspirations they express, are new from the point of view of human rights in that they seek to infuse the human dimension into areas where it is all too often being missing, having been left to the State or States... [t]hey are new in that they may both be invoked

[6] Wright, cited in Stephen Marks, 'Emerging Human Rights: A New Generation for the 1980s' (1981) 33 *Rutgers Law Review* 435, 439.

[7] GA Res 217A (III) UN DOC A/810 at 71 (1948).

[8] 347 US 483 (1954).

[9] *Numerus Clausus I* case (1972) 33 BVerfGE 303.

[10] See eg *Sunil Batra v Delhi Administration* 1978 SC 1675.

[11] 1978 SC 1675.

> against the State and demanded of it; but above all (herein lies their essential characteristic) they can be realised only through the concerted efforts of all the actors on the social scene: the individual, the State, public and private bodies and the international community.[12]

For Vasak, the first generation of human rights corresponded to the principle of 'liberty', the second generation to equality and the third to some form of humanity or fraternity.

In summary, most national constitutions, which were drafted after the Second World War, guaranteed a range of social rights, the key provisions being a right to housing, medical care, education, employment, and nutrition, all of which were in addition to the protection of first-generation rights, traditionally considered to be negative rights.[13]

Unlike first-generation rights, social rights were considered to be controversial and, even more so when courts were granted the power to render them enforceable. It is here that the key argument against the legal nature and hence the recognition of social rights are to be found. Two key arguments are raised against the enforceability of second generation rights: it is argued that courts lack the capacity to translate a general claim to social welfare rights into the equivalent of an enforceable first-generation right. Secondly, judicial enforcement of social rights is considered to constitute a major intrusion into the function and scope of a democratically elected legislature. In particular, the enforcement of social and economic rights holds significant implications for the government budget. Therefore, in adjudicating upon disputes based on these rights, the judiciary plays an extensive and indeed undemocratic role in major distributional questions which on should be left to democratically elected arms of state. To express it differently, because independent courts are not required to respond to transient democratic pressures, their judgments can interfere with the citizens' ability to employ a democratic election to achieve particular goals.[14]

This chapter has two primary objectives: to interrogate these objections to social and economic rights and, secondly, to examine the extent to which these objections have given rise to different forms of judicial and constitutional responses to social and economic rights in comparative national jurisdictions.

II. The Essential Objections to Socio and Economic Rights

The essence of the main objection is that a reliance on positive constitutional rights is ultimately misguided. Social rights cannot be adequately enforced by the judiciary because of the indeterminacy of their guarantees.[15] Take, for example, a litigant who claims that she has not received adequate government support. It is contended that a court would not be able to determine a sufficiently clear standard in order to decide whether the individual was sufficiently impoverished to qualify to so invoke this right.[16] But, even if the litigant was considered to qualify under a judicially conceived standard, the court would confront a further difficulty of crafting an order, namely whether to direct that the litigant be paid a certain sum of money or that specific services should be provided, and further, whether the remedy should be enforced nationally or be restricted geographically. Cross continues his critique thus:

12 Marks (n 6), 441.

13 Thomas Grey, 'Traditional Review, Legal Pragmatism' (2003) 38 *Wake Forest Law Review* 473.

14 Alexander Bickel, *The Least Dangerous Branch: Supreme Court at the Bar of Politics* (1962).

15 Frank Cross, 'The Error of Positive Rights' (2001) 48 *UCLA Law Review* 857.

16 Ibid.

> What if the federal budgets were strapped and a court order would necessitate higher taxes or that money be taken from other programmes such as defence and environmental protection? Would alternative uses of the money be relevant? Could the court consider the possibility that the plaintiff bore some responsibility for his impoverished status? What if he had gambled away a considerable sum of money? What if he had lost his job due to misfeasance?[17]

Once a court has determined that the government's priorities are unconstitutional, for example because it should implement a social welfare right before embarking upon further additions to national defence or national infrastructure, such as roads or telecommunications, a court would have displaced the legislature's judgment about how social policy should be ranked and accordingly would supplant the role of this democratically elected arm of the state.

In a more pragmatically based attack on social rights, Cass Sunstein contends that in transitional countries, which have moved from a planned to a market economy, social and economic rights would conflict with the objective of creating a relatively unregulated free market in which the market produces the key distributional outcomes rather than state regulation or indeed court adjudication.[18] In other words, the inclusion of social and economic rights in the constitution would interfere with a flexibility which the transitional country would require to develop an economy which best meets the expectations of that country's citizens.

Expressed differently, these criticisms constitute what Amartya Sen has described as comprising both an institutionalization and feasibility critique.[19] The institutionalization critique suggests that if social and economic rights are to be considered rights they must be institutionalized; if not they cannot be described as rights. If they are institutionalized, then courts are given powers which they are not capable of implementing, given the nature of the competing distributional demands posed by such claims. The feasibility critique suggests it may not be feasible to arrange for the realization of economic and social rights, whereas traditional, political, and civil rights are not difficult to implement, in that, at core, they require governments essentially to leave citizens alone. Social and economic rights impose significant economic burdens on countries, many of which cannot be reasonably called upon to fund a meaningful application of these rights.

A variation of the criticism of the inclusion of socio and economic rights in any constitutional instrument turns on an argument of under-enforcement. The core of the argument can be described as follows: if X has a right to A, then a court must be able to enforce the right, upon the demand of X to her entitlement to A. If a court is unable to enforce this right on demand, as it would a right to assembly or freedom of speech, then a social or economic right cannot be considered to be a legal right. In other words, a court may not be able to act as a primary enforcer of such a right but, at best, may engage in secondary enforcement, by insisting that a rational procedure be adopted in the allocation of material benefits to prevent an arbitrary denial thereof. On its own, therefore, it is argued that this cannot be considered to be an enforcement of a right on demand from the claimant. Accordingly, so the argument runs, social and economic rights should not be considered to fall within the scope of legal rights.[20]

[17] Ibid 913.

[18] Cass Sunstein, *Free Markets and Social Justice* (1997).

[19] Amartya Sen, 'Elements of the Theory of Human Rights' (2004) 32 *Philosophy and Public Affairs* 315.

[20] This argument has recently been developed by Ronald Dworkin in *Justice for Hedgehogs* (2010). See in this connection Lawrence Sager, 'On Material Rights, Underenforcement and the Adjudication Thesis' (2010) *Boston University Law Review* 579.

III. A Response to the Critics

Critical to the distinction between civil and political rights which are described as negative rights and social and economic rights which are said to be positive rights, is the argument that a positive right is a claim to something such as a share of material goods or for as positive programmes as encapsulated in the right to a clean environment. A negative right is a right for something not to be done to a person or some particular form of conduct to be withheld.[21] But as has been observed already, it is not that easy to distinguish between negative and positive rights on this basis alone. Some negative rights involve material consequences. The right to be tried in an independent court, with the assistance of legal counsel, may not be considered to be a positive right but it imposes clear material obligations upon the state to set up a judicial system whereby judges are paid and courts are adequately equipped with juries and court officials and in significant cases, defence counsel are paid by the state. A similar argument could be made with regard to political rights such as the right to vote and the right to participate in elections which have to be organized and consequently paid for by the state.

The argument that A only has a right if she can enforce it on demand and, if not, that the under-enforcement of the right must lead to the conclusion that there is no legal right, cannot simply be confined to so-called positive rights. If A has a right to free speech and B has an obligation to respect that right, it may well lead to the conclusion that B has to limit her exercise of the same right. Alternatively, the right to free speech may well conflict with another's right to privacy. Take the concept of the public disclosure tort which applies where a disclosure would be highly offensive to a reasonable person and could not be considered to be of legitimate public concern. The Secondary Statement of Torts suggests the following:

> In determining what is a matter of a legitimate public interest, account must be taken of the customs and conventions of the community.... The line is to be drawn when the publicity ceases to be the giving of information to which the public is entitled, and becomes a morbid and sensational prying into private lives for its own sake.[22]

It appears that, even with a negative right, it may be that an inquiry has to engage in the importance of the interest from which the right is sourced.[23] This discovery of the interest becomes the basis of the test in order to decide whether A possesses a right. It assumes that if A's right was recognized, as a result of which some interest of B could be seriously harmed, it may then be that we can conclude that A's right is insufficiently important to justify an erosion of B's interest or cannot justify holding a third party under a duty to perform in order for A's right to be recognized.

But that still leaves alive the most popular objection, that social and economic rights give rise to claims to scarce goods which can never be respected in every case on the grounds of the scarcity of public resources which are required to recognize these rights in substance. The question which arises is whether in order to be classified as a legal right, a social or economic right invariably will require a defined amount of money to be provided by the state in order for the right to be vindicated. The response to this difficulty is that social and economic rights do not invariably impose so stringent a demand on the state to fulfil the obligation to fund each socio and economic right in an unqualified fashion.[24]

[21] Charles Fried, *Right and Wrong* (1978).

[22] American Law Institute (2nd), *Torts* (1977), para 652o.

[23] Joseph Raz, *The Morality of Freedom* (1986).

[24] Cecile Fabre, 'Constituting Social Rights' (1998) 6 *Journal of Political Philosophy* 263, 279.

Lawrence Sager provides a good example of the more limited scope of a socio and economic right which still stands to be classified as a right. Take the right to adequate medical care as being a constitutional entrenched right. The court in dealing with the implementation of this right would have to engage in serious questions regarding strategy, responsibility, social coordination, and prioritization.[25] A court would have to answer a strategic question namely; should it ensure that the medicine be given to any person who is in need thereof or should it ensure that certain of the scarce resources go to prevention of disease. How should the government ensure the implementation of the right? Should it ensure that every claimant is provided with money or should it implement a national health scheme? The court would have to consider who would be responsible for the implementation of the right. Would it impose the obligation on national or local government? What role would have to be played by employers and by insurance whether public or private? An even more difficult question would turn on the prioritization to be given to the right to health care as opposed, for example, to other constitutionally entrenched rights, such as those to housing or to education. How would a court, without a full grasp of the budgetary implications, engage in trade-offs between these various rights?

In seeking to answer these difficult questions without jettisoning the promise of the implementation of social and economic rights as envisaged in a constitutional text, a judiciary may eschew the role of a primary enforcer of these rights and develop a role as the secondary enforcer by ensuring that fair procedures are adapted both in the allocation and the withholding of any benefits envisaged as a result of the inclusion of these rights in a constitutional text. It accomplishes this role by ensuring that a plausible justification is provided in the event that the state allocates or withholds benefits selectively.[26]

In this way the judiciary enforces social and economic rights in a manner which is compatible with the choices made by a democratically elected legislature and executive. It can ensure that government is not only reminded of its duties, pursuant to express constitutional guarantees, but that it implements policies which give as much respect as possible to those social and economic rights which are constitutionality enshrined. The court's role, instead of directly implementing the rights, is rather to inform the government on how the latter must fulfil its duty by assuming the role of a partner in a dialogic relationship with the legislature and the executive.

To the argument that judges do not have the necessary skills to examine the national budget or the distributional implications of social and welfare policies, the answer is that judges can examine the evidence placed before their court by independent experts and then, on the basis of a forensic evaluation thereof, develop a jurisprudence of justification as opposed to policy conceptualization. There is now a growing body of national and international jurisprudence which is illustrative of legal choices that courts have made in order to give content to social and economic rights, thereby supporting a rebuttal of the critics. It is to these various approaches to social and economic rights that I now turn.

IV. Enforcement: The Scope for Relief

Throughout the previous examination of the justification for social and economic rights, there is either an express or implied view that social and economic rights are not susceptible to a strong form of review.[27] A traditional conception of a strong form of review is exemplified in

[25] Sager (n 20), 583. [26] Ibid 580.

[27] Mark Tushnet, *Weak Courts, Strong Rights. Judicial Review and Social Welfare Rights in Comparative Constitutional Law* (2008).

the approach of the US Supreme Court in *Cooper v Erin* that the federal courts are 'supreme in the exposition of the law of the Constitution' and that accordingly the duties imposed by the legislature and indeed the executive must be followed in the interpretation to the provision as given by the court.[28] With strong forms review, the decision of a court is final. Accordingly, the tension between this form of judicial review of a constitutional text and the decisions of a democratically elected government are exacerbated. As Tushnet has written:

> The people have little recourse when the courts interpret the Constitution reasonably but, in the reasonable alternative view of the majority mistakenly. We can amend the Constitution or wait for judges to retire or die and replace them with judges who hold the better view of what the Constitution means.[29]

By contrast, weak forms of judicial review seek to engage constructively with the tension between rights and democracy or, expressed differently, with the counter-majoritarian dilemma. Underpinning the concept of weak review is the idea that rights, which are contained in a constitution, are best conceived as a means to facilitate dialogue between the three arms of the state. Within the context of socio-economic rights, this model envisages a constitutional dialogue between the judiciary, legislature, and executive as well, arguably, as powerful private actors, which requires all of the latter to give serious and reasoned consideration to the claims of those litigants who lack access to basic economic and social resources. In addition, engagement should ensure a transparent justification for the implementation of a particular right or the failure to achieve its realization.

V. Weak Rights/Weak Review

In turn, there are different forms of weak review which can give rise to different and not always predictable results. The experiences of South Africa and Germany are illustrative. The inclusion of socio-economic rights into the Constitution of the Republic of South Africa 1996 represented one of the boldest moves taken by a young democracy towards the transformation of its legal system. As President Mandela said, in reflecting upon the societal structure inherited by his government:

> A simple vote without food, shelter and health care is to use first generation rights as a smoke screen to obscure the deep underlying forces which deem human rights people. It has created an appearance of equality and justice, while by implication socio-economic inequality is entrenched. We do not want freedom without bread, nor do we want bread without freedom.[30]

Early in the development of its socio-economic rights jurisprudence, the Constitutional Court in *Government of the Republic to South Africa v Grootboom and others*[31] developed a reasonableness model of review which was sourced in administrative law. The Court refused to define social and economic rights in terms of its content and scope. Instead, it insisted that any programme developed by government to implement a constitutional obligation imposed upon the state in respect of a particular socio-economic right was required to commence with

[28] 358 US 1, 18 (1958).

[29] Tushnet (n 27), 22.

[30] Cited by Sandra Liebenberg, *Socio-economic Rights: Adjudication under a Transformative Constitution* (2010), 9.

[31] 2001 (1) SA 46 (CC).

addressing the conditions of the poorest of the poor. A programme that did not so commence was unconstitutional. In this way, the Court looked at the reasonableness of the programme but eschewed the development of a substantive interpretation of the right in question. In other words, the rights was not to be given a minimum core, by which standard each rights claim would be assessed.

This approach has recently been developed by the Constitutional Court in *Mazibuko and others v City of Johannesburg*.[32] In this case the Court was required to examine the constitutionality of the City of Johannesburg's free basic water policy of 25 litres per person per day and to determine whether this was sufficient to meet the basic needs of the residents who had brought the application.

In refusing to make a determination as to the amount of water which would meet the right enshrined in the Constitution, that everyone has the right to have access to sufficient food and water, the Court set out its approach thus:

> it is institutionally inappropriate for a court to determine precisely what the achievement of any particular socio and economic right entails and what steps government should take to ensure the progressive realisation of the right. This is a matter, in the first place, for the legislature and the executive, the institutions of government best place to investigate social conditions in the light of available budgets and to determine what targets are achievable in relation to socio-economic rights. Indeed, it is desirable as a matter of democratic accountability that they should do so for it is their programmes and promises that are subjected to democratic and popular choice.[33]

The Court noted that national government had introduced regulations which stipulated that the basic water supply constituted 25 litres per person per day or six kilolitres per household monthly. The City's free basic water policy was based on this regulation and it could not be said that it was unreasonable for the City not to have supplied more water to the applicants. The Court also noted that the free water policy which had been attacked by the applicants' expert witnesses, as being insufficient to sustain a dignified existence, had continually been reconsidered by the City which investigated ways to ensure that the poorest inhabitants gained access not only to more water but to other services such electricity, sanitation, and refuse removal. The Court noted that the City:

> has continued to review its policy regularly and undertaken sophisticated research to seek to ensure that it meets the needs of the poor within the City. It cannot therefore be said that the policy adopted by the City where inflexible. . . .[34]

In this case, a weak version of constitutional review failed the applicants who left the courtroom empty handed. Contrast this judgment to a decision of the German Federal Constitutional Court. This case was concerned with social assistance benefits and particularly unemployment benefits. The question which vexed the Court was whether the amount of a standard unemployment benefit in securing the livelihood of adults and children under the age of 14 in the period between 21 January 2005 and 30 June 2005 was compatible with the provisions of the German Basic Law. The Federal Constitutional Court did not have the benefit of an express socio-economic right which covered the question, such was the case with the South African Constitution. Instead, it worked with the fundamental right to human dignity as set

[32] [2007] BCLR 239 (CC). On the dynamic between constitutionalism and impoverishment, see Chapter 6.

[33] Ibid para 61.

[34] Ibid para 97.

out in Article 1 of the Basic Law, read together with the principle of a social state as enshrined in Article 20 thereof.

The Court found that these two provisions, read together, ensured that every needy person was entitled to the material conditions which were indispensable for his or her physical existence and for a minimum participation in social and cultural political life. The Court engaged in a careful analysis of the statistical model which the legislature had applied and found that the computational benefits which were produced by the model were incompatible with the right to dignity which the Basic Law enjoined was the right to be enjoyed by each citizen. Accordingly, the Court ordered that the legislature was required to initiate a fresh procedure to ascertain the benefits necessary for securing a subsistence minimum that was congruent with the enshrined right to dignity and which was realistic and took account of actual need.[35]

In the South African case, an expressly formulated socio-economic right was subjected to a weak form of review which meant that the Court was not prepared to determine the exact amount of water which was required to be provided by the state in order that the applicants constitutional right could be vindicated. In the German case, the Court worked with implied rights and like its South African counterpart did not determine the exact amount of social assistance benefits which flowed from such implied rights but insisted that the mechanism employed by the legislature did not pass constitutional muster. Accordingly a fresh procedure was needed to ascertain the constitutional benefits which were to be enjoined by the citizens.

In *Mazibuko*, the Court adopted an approach which can be classified as an interpretation of a socio-economic right which results in the creation of a weak right and, in this case, coupled it to a weak remedy. By contrast, the German Federal Constitutional Court may not have introduced a strong right by way of its working with the fundamental right to human dignity, which it read together with a principle of a social state. However, it granted the applicants a strong remedy, in that the legislature was required to initiate new procedures which in turn would give rise to the benefits fresh computation of; the clear implication being that an improved system of benefits had to be produced by government.

But courts, even within the national state, are not always consistent. A further example of a weak right/strong remedy approach is to be found in the judgment of the same South African Constitutional Court in *Occupiers of 51 Olivia Road v City of Johannesburg*.[36] In this case, the City of Johannesburg sought to evict some 300 people from six properties which were located in the inner city. The City justified these evictions in terms of a so-called 'regeneration strategy' for the inner city of Johannesburg, one important characteristic of which was the identification, clearance, and redevelopment of 'bad buildings' which had been occupied by approximately 70,000 people within the inner city.

The question for decision turned on whether the City by evicting the residents, had violated their right to access to adequate housing in terms of section 26 of the South African Constitution in that it had sought these evictions without any programme which was designed to rehouse those who had been evicted. When the matter reached the Constitutional Court, it noted that the City would have been aware not only of the possibility but the probability that those evicted would have become homeless as a result of the decision of the City to so evict them. Accordingly, those involved in the management of the City ought, at the very least, to have engaged meaningfully with the residents before a process of eviction was implemented. The Court developed a concept of engagement; that is 'a two-way process' in which the City

35 German Federal Constitutional Court, 9 February 2010: 1 BvL 1/09.

36 2008 (5) BCLR 475 (CC).

and those who were about to become homeless would talk to each other meaningfully in order to achieve certain objectives. These objectives included a determination of the consequences of the eviction, whether the City could assist in alleviating these consequences, whether it was possible to render the buildings concerned relatively safe and conducive to the health of the residents for an interim period, and ultimately whether the City had any obligation to the occupiers within the context of the facts of the case. Although the Court agreed that the right to housing, in terms of section 26, did not constitute a complete obstacle to the removal of residents from unhealthy and unsafe buildings, it found that there was, within the scope of the provision, an obligation placed upon the City to engage with the affected people, who would be rendered homeless after the eviction.

The order of the Court was designed not only to ensure engagement between the City and the applicants but also to retain jurisdiction over the dispute, in that both the City and the applicants were ordered to file further affidavits reporting on the result of their engagement. In this case, the engagement appeared to have been successful because the Court was later informed that an agreement of settlement had been entered into between the City and the applicant occupiers. In this case, while the Court worked with a weak right given its interpretation of section 26, it provided a relatively strong remedy which contained significant opportunity for legal relief between impoverished applicants.

VI. Stronger Forms of Right and Relief

Columbia provides a rich source of research for the implications of a stronger form of review. For example, in 2008, the Constitutional Court of Columbia handed down a decision that ordered the state to dramatically restructure the countries health system.[37]

The background to this case is illustrative of the Court's jurisprudence. In 1993 the Columbia health-care system was reformed. Law 100 altered the government subsidies from a supply to demand system and used public and private insurers as surrogates to purchase health care for insured patients, the object being directed toward the improvement of efficiency. A two-tier system of medical benefits was established: one for those formally employed or earning more than twice the minimum wage and a second being a subsidized regime which included approximately one half of the benefits which were available in the contributory regime. Literally tens of thousands of petitions (tutelas) were presented to the courts relating to the constitutional right to health and the concomitant breach of that right by Law 100.

In its 2008 decision, the Court collected 22 tutelas which were selected to illustrate the problems endemic to the health system. The Court reiterated that the constitutional right to health is enforceable in favour of plaintiffs who are unable to afford health care when the right to health, if not protected immediately, would result in the violation of fundamental rights, being the right to life. Further, in a case which involves people in particularly vulnerable circumstances, such as children, pregnant women, or the elderly, and where the provision of the particular health service in question fell within, what the court considered to be, the minimum core content of the right to health, the right would be enforced in favour of the plaintiffs.

In terms of this interpretation of the right to health, the Court has ordered the provision of a wide range of goods and services, including antiretrovirals, cancer medication, and even the

[37] Corte Constitutional de Columbia (2008) Sala Segunda de Revisión, Sentencia T-760, 31 July 2008, Magistrado Ponente: Manuel José Capeda.

financing of treatment of patients abroad, when the appropriate medical treatment was unavailable in Colombia.

In 2008, the Constitutional Court was confronted with a number of cases where there were restrictions on access to medical care that flowed from an inappropriate transfer of administrative costs on to patients and a failure to provide effective access to medical care, for example, not catering for the transportation needs of patients.

The Court went even further and examined the nature of the benefit plans which were inherent in the applicable legislation. The Court directed the National Commission for Health Regulation immediately and, thereafter on an annual basis, to update the benefits which were to be provided, pursuant to a subsidized scheme. It also ordered the appropriate executive agencies to unify the multiplicity of plans which had been introduced throughout the country, pursuant to the adoption of the relevant legislation, initially for children, later for adults and in a latter case, taking into account of financial sustainability as well as the epidemiological profile of the population.

In a further development, the Court ordered the government to adopt deliberate measures progressively to realize universal medical coverage by 2010, together with various compliance deadlines which have taken place between 2008 and 2009.

As Yamin and Parra-Vera note, the approach of the Colombian Court has been to implement the right to health within a framework set out by the United Nations Committee on Economic Social and Cultural Rights.[38] However, the Court has gone on to specify the multiple obligations which have to be carried by the state, pursuant to the constitutional right to health, further declaring that the state was responsible for adopting the deliberate measures to achieve the progressive realization of the right to health and further that the state is required to adopt a transparent approach and provide access to information in respect of its health coverage.

The Court heard another case in October 2009 in which it set out definitive guidelines for the provision of an abortion service.[39] In this case, the Court held that a women, who sought a legal therapeutic abortion from a health-care provider as a result of serious fetal malformation that made it unviable, had a right to choose freely whether she would have an abortion or continue the pregnancy without coercion, duress, or any type of manipulation. It confirmed that abortion services should be available throughout the country and called upon the Ministries of Education and Social Protection to implement a plan within three months of the decision, to promote the sexual and reproductive rights of women, which must include information about the grounds of which abortion was legal in the country. The Court also listed the services that are prohibited with regard to provision of abortion.

The effect of a strong remedy is illustrated by the far-reaching nature of this decision. For this reason, it is useful to look at the detail of the order which included the following obligations imposed by the court upon a range of state authorities.

- To hold medical meetings, or auditors' meetings to review or approve the request, which result in unjustified waiting periods to perform the abortion.
- To establish additional requirements, such as demanding forensic medical reports, judicial orders, health examination not practised timely, authorization by family members, legal consultants, auditors, or a multiple number of doctors.

[38] Alicia Ely Yamin and Oscar Para Vera, 'How Do Courts Set Health Policy? The Case of the Colombian Constitutional Court' (2009) 6 *PLoS Medicino* 147.

[39] The decision of the Columbian Constitutional Court T-388/2009.

- To submit collective conscientious objections, which result in institutional and unfounded claims of conscientious objection.
- To subscribe to agreements—individuals or collective—to deny abortion services.
- To use forms or template disclaimers which results in hospitals not having among their personnel, doctors willing to perform abortions.
- To discredit patient evaluations drafted by psychologists, whose status as health professionals has been recognized by legislation.
- To be reluctant in complying with all the rules in the cases in which abortion services are not available at the health centre where the patient requested the abortion.
- Not to have any available abortion services within the network of public health-care providers at the departmental, district, and municipal level.

The relatively strong right/strong remedy approach adopted by the Columbian Constitutional Court may arguably be explained in terms of a more interventionist civil law culture. But while legal culture manifestly influences jurisprudence, it is an argument that need not detain us because there are illustrations of a similar approach adopted by courts which function in common law jurisdictions.

Take, for example, the Indian Supreme Court, whose jurisprudence has briefly been mentioned and which court system was inherited from the British colonial power. India has a written constitution which provides for fundamental rights for its citizens. However, it did not include, as justiciable rights, any of the social and economic rights with which we have been engaged in this chapter. In Part IV of the Indian Constitution there is provision for directive principles of state policy which are required to be followed by the state when it develops its social and economic policies. Thus, Article 38 requires the state to secure a social order for the promotion of the welfare of the people, in which justice—social, economic, and political—shall inform all institutions of national life. Similarly, Article 39 provides that the state shall direct its policy towards securing that 'the citizens—men and women equally—have the right to adequate means of livelihood'.

These provisions are not couched as rights but rather as principles which should guide the state in the formulation and implementation of its policy but without giving a litigant the ability to demand that any of these principles be enforced as of right by way of a judicial order. The courts, however, have made creative use of these directive principles of state policy, reading them together with some fundamental rights. Thus, in *Olga Tellis and others v Bombay Municipal Corporation and other*,[40] the applicants were living on Bombay pavements or slums in the vicinity of their workplace. They were then forcibly evicted and their dwellings demolished by the municipality. They challenged their eviction on the basis that it violated their constitutional rights; in particular the right to life which was enshrined in Article 21. The Court held that the right to livelihood was to treated as being part of the constitutional right to life and hence, by depriving a person of his or her means of livelihood, this action would effectively deprive the person of his right to life. On this basis, therefore, the Court thus placed an obligation upon the Bombay Municipality to provide shelter for the applicants.

More recently, in *Peoples Union for Civil Liberties v Union of India and others*[41] the Supreme Court was faced with various interim orders which had been passed, from time to time, directing governmental authorities to see that food was provided to aged, infirmed, disabled,

[40] 1985 (3) SCC 545.
[41] 2004 (12) SCC 108.

destitute men who were in danger of starvation, pregnant and lactating women, and destitute children. This class had insufficient funds to live free of malnutrition.

The Court framed the dispute by way of the following question:

> Article 21 of the Constitution of India protects for every citizen a right to live with human dignity. Would the very existence of life of those families which are below poverty line not come under danger for want of appropriate schemes and implementation thereof, to provide requisite aid to such families?

The Court then ordered that nutritious food had to be provided for those undernourished or malnourished applicants and further directed that an integrated child development scheme be implemented through various government centres, first to supply nutritious food and supplements to children, adolescent girls, and pregnant and lactating women under a scheme which so provided for 300 days in a year.

In this case the Court, operating broadly within a common law tradition inherited from the United Kingdom, and adjudicating within the context of a Constitution which had no express judiciable social and economic rights, interpreted various provisions of its Constitution to create amongst other rights, a basic right to housing and the right to food. A strong right/strong remedy was developed from reading the implications of the constitutional text.

VII. Conclusion

Conceptually, it is possible that social and economic rights can be considered to be strong rights whenever a court enforces these rights without deferring to a legislative process and whenever there is a conclusion that government has failed its constitutional obligations imposed by the specific social or economic right. Colombia and India, on occasion, have performed in this manner. But as the South African experience illustrates, courts may be reluctant to interpret social and economic right in order to bring about the result in which no substantial deference to a legislative judgment can be offered by the court; hence the reasonableness test adopted by the South African Constitution Court. But even in this kind of case, the court may offer a plausible reason for developing a weak right:

> Moreover, what the right requires will vary over time and context. Fixing a quantified content might, in a rigid and counter-productive manner, prevent an analysis of context. The concept of reasonableness places context at the centre of the enquiry and permits an assessment of context to determine whether a government programme is indeed reasonable.[42]

The Court suggests in this dictum that adherence to a weak right may afford greater possibility for progressive development in the longer term than might be the case with a strong right that is interpreted, for example, so as to impose a fixed obligation upon the state to provide 50 litres of water a day to each applicant. In all of these cases, courts have recognized that, while civil and political rights are valuable in that they are predicated on the premise that individual citizens should have control over their lives as autonomous, sentient beings possessed of a protected sphere of dignity, the absence of substantive conditions to permit the vindication of these rights, renders these rights somewhat illusory. Where social and economic right are included in a constitution, either by way of express rights or by way of directive principles of state policy, courts have sought, by means of differing approaches, to recognize that these rights are morally valuable in providing a basis

[42] *Mazibuko* (n 32), para 60.

for individuals to have some form of acceptable control over their lives, as Mr Mandela understood, when he reflected upon the social and economic structure inherited from apartheid. If the residents of a country are hungry, ill, thirsty, or cold and living under a constant threat of poverty, it is extremely difficult to see how they could decide on any meaningful conception of a good life for themselves and further, to what extent the first generation of rights would have significant meaning for them, living as they do in parlous conditions. Arguably, the existence of these rights justifies a move away from a narrow conception of individual right-holders so central to first-generation rights. Ultimately socio-economic rights promote a sense of community, and thus are claimed by groups of impoverished and marginalized people who seek to preserve a sense of dignified community. In turn, this compels a different vision of rights, one which is not based exclusively upon an individual rights bearer.

It does, however, appear that the conceptual obstacles posed in the way of social and economic rights have far less intellectual traction than does the enforceability question, which it cannot be denied means that, generally speaking, adjudicating upon a dispute based on a negative right involves a process of adjudication which is different from that involving a dispute predicated on a social and economic right. But, this must be qualified. Decisions based on negative rights are not necessarily immunized from considerations relating to the public allocation of resources. Further, judges may not be able—given their technical competence, the limitations created by a lack of evidence, and their inability to deal with the polycentric implications of a decision based upon the interpretation of social or economic rights—to enforce the latter as they may the right to fair trial or the right to assembly.

However, when courts have compelled the legislature or the executive to justify a policy choice in terms of an articulated conception the meaning of a social and economic right, a process of deliberation flows therefrom which cannot be discounted. It leads to more accountable government, it provides a voice for litigants who would otherwise be silenced, and, in a number of cases, as described in this chapter, this results in the provision of a basic minimum of goods and services to those who otherwise would have been left out in the proverbial cold.

Bibliography

American Law Institute (2nd), *Torts* (1977)

Isaiah Berlin, 'Two Concepts of Liberty' in Henry Hardy (ed), *Liberty* (2002)

Alexander Bickel, *The Least Dangerous Branch: Supreme Court at the Bar of Politics* (1962)

Frank Cross, 'The Error of Positive Rights' (2001) 48 *UCLA Law Review* 857

Cecile Fabre, 'Constituting Social Rights' (1998) 6 *Journal of Political Philosophy* 263

Gunter Frankenberg, 'Why Care? The Trouble with Social Rights' (1996) 17 *Cardozo Law Review* 1365

Thomas Grey, 'Traditional Review, Legal Pragmatism' (2003) 38 *Wake Forest Law Review* 473

Sandra Liebenberg, *Socio-economic Rights: Adjudication under a Transformative Constitution* (2010)

Stephen Marks, 'Emerging Human Rights: A New Generation for the 1980s' (1981) 33 *Rutgers Law Review* 435

T.H. Marshall, *Citizenship and Social Class* (1964)

Joseph Raz, *The Morality of Freedom* (1986)

Lawrence Sager, 'Material Rights, Underenforcement and the Adjudication Thesis' (2010) 90 Boston University Law Review 579

Amartya Sen, 'Elements of the Theory of Human Rights' (2004) 32 *Philosophy and Public Affairs* 315

Cass Sunstein, *Free Markets and Social Justice* (1997)

Mark Tushnet, *Weak Courts, Strong Rights. Judicial Review and Social Welfare Rights in Comparative Constitutional Law* (2008)

Lorraine Weinrib, 'The Post War Paradigm and American Exceptionalism' in Sujit Choudhry (ed), *The Migration of Constitutional Ideas* (2006)

Alicia Ely Yamin and Oscar Para Vera, 'How Do Courts Set Health Policy? The Case of the Colombian Constitutional Court' (2009) 6 *PLoS Medicino* 147

CHAPTER 50

ECONOMIC RIGHTS

K. D. EWING

London

I. Introduction

Constitutions are ideological texts.[1] Like any other document, they reflect the moment when they were drafted, the values of their authors, and the purposes they are to serve. To this last end, they thus reflect the type of society for which they are designed, and the anticipated role of the state in that society. Liberal democracies of various stripes require different kinds of constitutional texts than do social democracies of various stripes, though clearly there will be many common features in constitutional texts of whatever stripe. Liberal constitutions such as those of the United States, however, are designed principally to limit the power of government, and to regulate public rather than private power. In doing so, they elevate principles

[1] For a nice—if now implausible—expression of this, see *Gujarat Steel Tubes v Its Mazdoor Sabha* 1980 AIR 1980 SC 1896:

> The Constitution of India is not a non—saligned parochial parchment but a partisan of social justice with a direction and destination which it set out in the Preamble and Art 38 ... ours is a mixed economy with capitalist mores, only slowly mobilizing towards a socialist mores. (Krishna Iyer J at 1908–9)

developed initially by the common law, principles said by the historian Christopher Hill as having been designed to 'meet the needs of commercial society', so that 'men of property could do what they would with their own'.[2]

There is, however, a very different constitutional tradition often overlooked by common lawyers. This is the social democratic tradition, which prevails in mainly European jurisdictions, a tradition characterized by a more active state with duties underpinned by the constitution. It is also a tradition characterized by a desire to regulate the imbalance of power in private law relationships, notably the relationship between property and labour. To this end, social democratic constitutions may seek to underpin what has been referred to as the 'economic constitution', said to be 'the very key to the achievement of social democracy' itself.[3] Constitutions in this latter tradition will typically include two species of economic rights, the first being the rights of property traditionally to be found in liberal constitutions, and the second being the rights of labour which traditionally are *not* to be found in liberal constitutions.

In addressing these matters in this chapter, the main concern is with rights of labour rather than with rights of property. It is the idea of labour rights as constitutionally protected economic rights that gives rise to most difficulty and incredulity in the common law world, a response which is surprising in view of the widespread embrace of such rights outside English-speaking jurisdictions, of which many common lawyers appear to be profoundly ignorant. It is also the case that at the present time in our global economic development, it is the rights of labour rather than the rights of property that are especially vulnerable, and especially in need of constitutional and any other form of protection that may be available. Moreover, it is the economic rights of labour rather than the economic rights of property that are currently flying on the magic carpet of the international human rights movement, following important decisions of the European Court of Human Rights (ECtHR) in particular.

In a neoliberal global economy, however, there may be an air of unreality about any suggestion that labour rights can be fully and effectively protected by national constitutions. Apart from the legacy of ideology and the growing influence of human rights, the third voice in this conversation is the voice of economic orthodoxy in an open and competitive global economy where social, economic, and political power is moving in the direction of transnational corporations and global financial institutions, beyond the capacity of national governments to confront. Constitutional commitments to labour rights were a reflection of a public policy and an economic orthodoxy that emphasized the need for secure employment rights, high labour standards, and a powerful voice for organized workers. Then, economics, politics, and law ran with the same grain. Now, employment rights, labour standards, and organized workers are not so much an instrument of economic policy, as its victim.

II. Economic Liberalism

Principles of economic liberalism are embedded in the US Constitution, which protects economic freedom and private property in a number of ways. In the first place, Article 10(1) prohibits the states from making any law 'impairing the obligation of contracts', though it has been said that in practice this so-called 'contracts clause' is a 'specialised and limited restriction on state government regulation', violated

[2] Christopher Hill, *Intellectual Origins of the English Revolution* (1972), 256.

[3] See Ruth Dukes, 'Constitutionalising Employment Relations: Sinzheimer, Kahn-Freund and the Role of Labour Law' (2008) 35 *Journal of Law and Society* 341.

> only when the state acts unilaterally to avoid its own contractual obligations, or to retroactively modify the contractual arrangements between particular private entities, and there is not a sufficient public interest justification for the state's doing so.[4]

More significant then is the Fifth Amendment which provides that no one is to be 'deprived of life, liberty, or property, without due process of law; nor shall private property be taken for public use, without just compensation.' This is an altogether more important provision, though it does not appear to impose a serious brake on government power.[5]

The Fifth Amendment has been said to preserve the right of eminent domain, the courts accepting that property may be taken in the public interest provided that compensation is paid. In some cases, government regulation that affects the use of private property may also constitute a taking for these purposes, with compensation to be paid as a result.[6] In addition, the Fifth Amendment's limits on the federal government are to be found in the Fourteenth Amendment's limits on the states. This latter prohibition on depriving 'any person of life, liberty, or property, without due process of law' has been said to have come into being 'primarily' to protect African-Americans from 'discrimination'.[7] Mr Justice Black continued by saying that 'while some of its language can and does protect others, all know that the chief purpose behind it was to protect ex-slaves.'[8]

But despite its origins, judicial developments have taken the due process clause well beyond what could conceivably have been contemplated when it was drafted. Perhaps the most famous indication of this is *Goldberg v Kelly*[9] where the Supreme Court held that welfare benefits could be withdrawn from recipients by state authorities only if the latter first gave a full hearing to the individuals in question. It was not enough that there was an informal pre-termination review or a right of appeal after the event. This, however, was not a view universally supported, with Mr Justice Black writing for the minority that it 'somewhat strains credulity to say that the government's promise of charity to an individual is property belonging to that individual when the government denies that the individual is honestly entitled to receive such a payment.'[10]

But notwithstanding developments such as *Goldberg v Kelly*, the US Constitution is a one-sided bargain. There is no provision for the economic rights of workers or labour unions,[11] for whom constitutional law is as much a threat as a protection. It will be recalled that in the *Lochner* line of cases the starting point for the Court was that 'the general right to make a contract in relation to his business' was 'part of the liberty of the individual protected by the Fourteenth Amendment'.[12] Problems of inequality of bargaining power were later brushed aside on the ground that

> it is from the nature of things impossible to uphold freedom of contract and the right of private property without at the same time recognizing as legitimate those inequalities of fortune that are the necessary result of the exercise of those rights.[13]

[4] See Robert A. Sedler, 'United States', *International Encyclopaedia of Laws, Constitutional Law*, vol 8 (2005), para 401, and the cases cited at paras 497–500.

[5] Ibid para 396.

[6] Ibid paras 391–6.

[7] *Goldberg v Kelly* 397 US 254, 276 (1970).

[8] Ibid.

[9] 397 US 254 (1970).

[10] Ibid 276.

[11] See *National Federation of Postal Clerks v Blount* 325 F Supp 879 (1971) (no constitutionally protected right to strike).

[12] *Lochner v New York* 198 US 45, 57 (1905).

[13] *Coppage v Kansas* 236 US 1, 22 (1914).

So in the interests of freedom of contract and infused with principles of economic liberalism, the Court struck down a New York statute setting maximum hours for bakery and other workers.[14]

The Court also struck down a Kansas statute prohibiting employers from offering employment on the condition that the applicant agreed not to join a trade union, the Supreme Court citing with approval a passage from the Supreme Court of Kansas:

> In this respect the rights of the employer and employee are equal. Any act of the legislature that would undertake to impose on the employer the obligation of keeping in his service one whom, for any reason, he should not desire, would be a denial of his constitutional right to make and terminate contracts and to acquire and hold property. Equally so would an act the provisions of which should be intended to require one to remain in service of one whom he should desire not to serve.[15]

True, the progeny of *Lochner* was eventually overturned by the Supreme Court just in time to protect a number of New Deal initiatives—including the National Labor Relations Act—from suffering a similar fate.[16] Nevertheless, the threat of constitutional law to workers' economic rights did not disappear completely, with the statutory rights of workers now having to coexist alongside—and be applied consistently with—other constitutional norms.

In the hands of powerful and determined employers, the latter could be used gravely to weaken the economic rights of workers in individual cases. So although the National Labor Relations Act survived constitutional challenge, it must nevertheless yield to unspecified property rights of the employer. In *NLRB v Babcock & Wilcox Co*,[17] it was held by the US Supreme Court that

> an employer may validly post his property against non-employee distribution of union literature if reasonable efforts by the union through other available channels of communication will enable it to reach the employees with its message …[18]

According to the Supreme Court, 'Organization rights are granted to workers by the same authority, the National Government, that preserves property rights', and 'Accommodation between the two must be obtained with as little destruction of one as is consistent with the maintenance of the other.'[19]

III. The Weimar Legacy

As already suggested, there is another legacy. Constitutions may exist not only to restrain the state, but also to require the state to extend defined values or principles into what in some systems might be regarded as the private realm. Such measures serve two related ends. The first is to enrich political democracy in the belief that there can be no democracy without equality; and the second is to extend democratic principles from the political to the social and economic spheres. In the second generation of modern constitutions, a socialist or social democratic or social market function often informs and is sometimes clearly expressed in the text of

[14] *Lochner v New York* (n 12). Also *Adkins v Children's Hospital* 261 US 525 (1923): District of Columbia statute setting minimum wage rates for women.

[15] *Coppage* (n 13), 23.

[16] See *West Coast Hotel Co v Parrish* 300 US 379 (1937) (reversing *Adkins* (n 14), to uphold Washington State minimum wage law), and *NLRB v Jones and Laughlin Steel Corp* 301 US 1 (1937) (upholding National Labor Relations Act).

[17] 351 US 105 (1956). [18] Ibid 112–13. [19] Ibid 113.

the document itself. Historically, the best known example of such an arrangement is the Weimar Constitution,[20] with its constitutional-ization of social and economic rights; its constitutional ambition to create an 'economic constitution', and its formal engagement of economic actors in the political process.[21]

In making detailed provision for economic rights, the Weimar Constitution provided that 'the economy has to be organized based on the principles of justice, with the goal of achieving life in dignity for everyone', and that 'within these limits the economic liberty of the individual is to be secured' (Art 151). The same article recognized the freedom of trade and industry. Like the US Constitution, the Weimar Constitution also made provision for economic rights, relating to both contract and property. Freedom of contract was said to be the foundation of economic transactions (Art 152), while property was said to be 'guaranteed by the constitution' (Art 153). A takings clause allowed for expropriation, but only in accordance with law, in the public interest, and on the payment of compensation (Art 153), though alternative provision could be made by law. Guarantees were also made for the right of inheritance, with the state's right to any property of the deceased to be determined by law (Art 154).

As might be expected, the Weimar Constitution expressly anticipated the possibility of expropriation of private property. This was first to ensure adequate housing and, secondly, for reasons of economic management. Thus, real estate was to be supervised to prevent abuse and to secure housing for German families (especially for those with large numbers of children), while land could be expropriated for this and other purposes (including food production) (Art 155). Similarly, provision was made for the nationalization of enterprises, though the power could be used only 'if the rules relating to expropriation were followed, and the principles relating to compensation were not violated'. The Constitution also provided that the Reich could 'join in the administration of economic enterprises or syndicates or may order the states or communities to do so'. The Reich could otherwise assume a decisive influence in the running of such enterprises (Art 156).

But as well as contract, property, and inheritance, the Weimar Constitution also famously recognized the rights of labour. Article 157 provided that 'Labour enjoys the special protection of the Reich', which would 'provide uniform labour legislation'. Specific provision was made for 'the right to form unions and to improve conditions at work as well as in the economy', rights 'guaranteed to every individual and to all occupations' (Art 159). All agreements and measures limiting or obstructing this right were declared 'illegal' (Art 159). Provision was made in the Constitution for a comprehensive system of social insurance 'in order to protect motherhood and to prevent economic consequences of age, weakness and to protect against the vicissitudes of life' (Art 161), and support was declared for 'an international regulation of the rights of the workers, which strives to safeguard a minimum of social rights for humanity's working class' (Art 162).

So far as the 'economic constitution' is concerned, Article 165 provided that 'Workers and employees are called upon to participate, on an equal footing and in cooperation with the employers, in the regulation of wages and working conditions as well as in the economic development of productive forces.' There then followed a great deal of detail about enterprise works councils, district work councils, and the Reich works council, 'in order to fulfil the economic tasks and to execute the socialization laws in cooperation with the employers'. This is in addition to District economic councils and a Reich Economic Council, 'to be organized in such a way, that all important professions are represented according to their economic

[20] See <http://www.zum.de/psm/weimar/weimar_vve.php>.

[21] See Dukes (n 3).

and social importance.' The Reich Economic Council would have the right to consider all proposed legislation before being presented to the Reichstag, and a right to initiate legislation even against the wishes of the government. Article 165 was intended to create 'a pyramid structure' of economic councils and works councils, which would serve in their operation to democratize the economic sphere. With its authority to consider and propose legislation, the Reich Economic Council would straddle both the economic and the political spheres.[22] That said, Kahn Freund records that bodies such as the Reich Economic Council were never intended to be 'ultimate decision-making bodies'. He continued:

> They were to be subordinate to the political sphere, only consultative and therefore innocuous. They would be consulted on all matters concerning the economy, but not on questions of foreign policy and other non-economic matters. There, the state would be autonomous.[23]

For Kahn Freund and others, it was thus essential that

> there was an autonomous political sphere in which decisions would have to be made by political organs, that is to say, by a democratically elected parliament, and by a government, supposed to depend on Parliament and giving orders to a civil service.[24]

But although famous for its attempt by constitutional law to cover the economic sphere, the Weimar Constitution was just as famously the subject of excoriating criticism, not least by those who had been most disappointed by its failure to resist capture by the national socialists. Notable among the critics was Kahn Freund who argued that many of these 'beautifully-worded Articles were nothing but sententious platitudes, binding no one, least of all the legislator, and soon to be characterized by the courts as "merely programmatic announcements" without any legal value.'[25] Some of the provisions relating to the 'economic life' were said to 'bear the imprint of unreality',[26] while such 'real' achievements of the Weimar Republic as there were 'might have been attained without such deceptive pronouncements'.[27] Kahn Freund made an exception for the provisions relating to the rights to organize and collective bargaining as set out in Article 165(1).[28] As for the rest, it remained a 'dead letter'.[29]

IV. Social Democracy Renewed

According to Kahn Freund, the Weimar Constitution was 'inspired by an almost fetishistic belief in the efficacy of constitutional arrangements', reflecting 'a pathetic faith in the effectiveness of institutions and formulated codes'.[30] But whatever the limitations of the Weimar system, the end of the Second World War was a period in which intellectual opinion and political orthodoxy was strongly in favour of (social and) economic rights. This is seen in the powerful restatement of principle in the International Labour Organization's (ILO) Declaration of

[22] I am grateful to Dr Ruth Dukes for this point, and for additional points in the text.

[23] Dukes (n 3), 202.

[24] Ibid.

[25] Otto Kahn-Freund, 'The Weimar Constitution' (1944) 15 *Political Quarterly* 229, 230.

[26] Ibid, referring here specifically to Art 151.

[27] Ibid 231.

[28] Ibid. These were destined 'to play a decisive role in the history of the German republic, and to form the basis of its noteworthy system of labour law.' He was later to refer to the 'Alice in Wonderland' nature of Art 165(2)–(5): Otto Kahn-Freund, *Labour Law and Politics in the Weimar Republic* (Roy Lewis and Jon Clark eds, 1981), 201.

[29] Ibid.

[30] Ibid 230.

Philadelphia of 1944, in the proposal from Roosevelt for a 'second bill of rights' for the United States, and in the work of intellectuals like Georges Gurvitch in France (advocating a Bill of Social Rights to secure the 'jural negation of all exploitation and domination, of all arbitrary power, of all inequality, of all unjustified limitation of liberty of groups, collectivities, and individuals'),[31] and T.H. Marshall in England (charting a great historical progression from civil to political to social rights).[32]

These forces helped to shape national constitutions, many of which in the post-war era were to bear the heavy imprint of ideology, and in some cases heavily pregnant with social democratic or socialist rhetoric. Italy, for example, is 'a democratic republic based on labor' (Art 1) (sic). Not only that, but it is 'the duty of the republic to remove all economic and social obstacles that, by limiting the freedom and equality of citizens, prevent full individual development and the participation of all workers in the political, economic, and social organization of the country' (Art 3), while according 'to capability and choice', every citizen has 'the duty to undertake an activity or a function that will contribute to the material and moral progress of society' (Art 4). This in turn led to a full chapter of economic rights in the constitution, which at the time was probably the most comprehensive in West European states.

But if these social democratic constitutions were to bear the heavy imprint of ideology, they were also to bear the imprint of liberal pragmatism that informs at least one strand of social democratic thinking.[33] And like the Weimar Constitution, they too reflect the fact that in a democracy, constitutions must be an instrument of government for all the people, and instruments for progressive rather than revolutionary change. So in Italy the right to free enterprise is recognized, provided that it is not conducted contrary to the public interest, or in a way that 'harms public security, liberty, or human dignity'. It is also recognized, however, that Italy may be a mixed economy in the sense that 'economic goods may belong to the state, to public bodies, or to private persons'. So while private ownership is recognized and guaranteed by law, private property may be expropriated in accordance with law provided that compensation is paid (Art 42).

It has been emphasized by Cartabia in a valuable exposition of the Italian 'economic constitution' that the property rights protected therein are 'conditioned by social rights and interests', which it is said helped to establish what were 'precise and peculiar features' in relation to other mixed economies. Thus, Article 41 also provides that 'public and private economic activities may be directed and coordinated towards social ends', while Article 42 also provides that private property may be regulated by law 'to ensure its social function and to make it accessible to all'. Cartabia further points out, however, that these arrangements have not prevented the adaptation of 'economic and social relations to political transformation', including most recently an 'extensive programme of privatisation'. The main instrument of state intervention appears to have been through the medium of state-owned private companies, a form of intervention being said to have reached 'extremely high levels'.[34]

What emerges here is the presence of some fairly liberal principles in a social democratic wrapping: the right to private property, and the right to compensation if the property is appropriated. Although there is a formal recognition of free enterprise, there is also a notable formal

[31] Georges Gurvitch, *The Bill of Social Rights* (1945), 71.

[32] Thomas H. Marshall, *Citizenship and Social Class* (1950).

[33] See Eduard Bernstein, *Preconditions of Socialism* (Henry Tudor ed and trans, 1993): social democracy the 'legitimate heir' to liberalism (147).

[34] See Valerio Onida et al, 'Italy', *International Encyclopaedia of Laws, Constitutional Law*, vol 5 (2005), paras 467–71.

recognition of the social function of private property. Similar themes emerge in the three European constitutions that were created in the 1970s, with even the most conspicuously ideologically committed text nevertheless making what is by now the standard commitment to 'the right to private property and to its transfer during lifetime or by death'. The Portuguese Constitution also swims with the conventional tide by providing that while private property may be expropriated, this may only be done in accordance with law and on the payment of fair compensation (Art 62). Indeed, Portugal also now provides for the privatization of property that had been taken into public ownership under earlier regimes.[35]

If we turn finally to the Nordic countries, here too there is full recognition of property rights, in some cases going beyond the corresponding recognition of labour rights. Although property may not be forfeited in Norway (Art 104), this is subject to an exception where expropriation (of movable or immovable property) is necessary in the interests of the state, in which case compensation is payable. In Finland, the constitutional protection of property has been widely interpreted to cover intellectual property as well as unemployment and welfare benefits (s 15).[36] Apart from the wide scope of the property protected, the constitutional guarantee is violated by regulation that makes private property useless or valueless to the owner. In terms of special protections of private property, the Danish Constitution makes the usual provision about expropriation, but provides remarkably that

> Where a Bill relating to the expropriation of property has been passed, one-third of the Members of the Parliament may within three week-days from the final passing of such Bill demand that it shall not be presented for the Royal Assent until new elections to the Parliament have been held and the Bill has again been passed by the Parliament assembling thereupon.

V. Workers' Rights

So far as economic rights are concerned, it is in relation to the economic rights of labour that social democratic constitutions make what is their most distinctive contribution. Two types of labour rights are to be found in constitutional texts, notably individual and collective rights (or in the latter case individual rights that in practice may only be exercised collectively). The former deal with the rights of workers, the latter with the rights of trade unions. So far as workers' rights are concerned, these have a number of distinguishing features, one of which is that they are *contingent and promotional*, and now probably beyond the capacity of any single state to deliver. They are *contingent* in the sense that the French Constitution proclaims that 'every individual has the duty to work and the right to employment', while the Portuguese Constitution recognizes that 'all have the right to work' and imposes a duty on the state to implement policies of full employment (Art 58).[37]

An alternative way of expressing the responsibility of the state for securing work for all is to be found in the *promotional* provisions in countries like Spain where 'special emphasis will be placed on the realization of a policy aimed at full employment' (Art 40), or in Denmark where 'efforts should be made to afford work to every able-bodied citizen on terms that will secure

[35] On privatization generally see Terence Daintith and Monica Sah, 'Privatisation and the Economic Neutrality of the Constitution' [1993] *Public Law* 465.

[36] Ilkka Saraviita, 'Finland' in *International Encyclopaedia of Laws, Constitutional Law*, vol 3 (2009), para 534.

[37] According to the US Department of Labor, in June 2011 unemployment in France stood at 9.3 per cent, and in Portugal at 12.2 per cent: see <http://www.bls.gov/ilc/intl_unemployment_rates_monthly.htm#Rchart2>.

his existence' (s 75). Similarly in Italy, where the Republic 'recognizes the right of all citizens to work', and 'promotes such conditions as will make this right effective' (Art 4); and Greece. where the Constitution recognizes that 'work is a right', but then provides that the state must seek 'to create conditions of employment for all citizens' (Art 22). Less urgent is Finland where public authorities are required to 'promote employment' and 'strive to secure the right to work for everyone' (s 15), and the Netherlands where it is the 'concern' of the authorities to 'promote the provision of sufficient employment' (Art 19).[38]

Apart from being contingent on factors beyond the control of any nation state, economic rights of workers are characterized also by being inevitably *opaque and open-textured*. This is true of those provisions that deal with wages. In Norway, for example, 'it is the responsibility of the authorities of the State to create conditions enabling every person capable of work *to earn a living* by his work' (Art 110). In Italy in contrast, 'workers are entitled to remuneration commensurate with the quantity and quality of their work, and in any case *sufficient to ensure* to them and their families a free and honorable existence' (Art 36). All Spaniards have a right 'to a *sufficient remuneration to satisfy their needs* and those of their family' (Art 35). In Belgium, there is another variation on the theme, with the right to dignity embracing 'the right to just working conditions and *equitable remuneration*' (Art 23), while in Portugal, there is a guarantee of remuneration that will ensure a '*respectable livelihood*' (Art 59(1)(a)).

What is striking about these provisions is that constitutions typically prescribe a right not to a *minimum* wage, but to a *living* wage (Norway), a *sufficient* wage (Italy and Spain), or a *fair* wage (Belgium). But in doing so they do not determine the principles by which wage levels are to be set, and generally leave the matter to be fixed by Parliament or others. It is also striking that not all the foregoing countries have a statutory minimum wage. Indeed this is true not only of Norway and Italy of the countries mentioned, but of other countries in the social democratic tradition, including Sweden and Denmark. In the case of Italy, however, the constitutional obligation is met in part by a requirement that workers should be paid in accordance with the most relevant collective agreement,[39] while in Sweden there is a very strongly established principle that wages should be determined by autonomous collective bargaining between employers and trade unions.

The fact that not all social democracies make constitutional provision for wages highlights a third aspect of economic rights of workers. This is the rather *incomplete* treatment of these rights in the constitutions of social democratic regimes, the treatment thus sometimes appearing rather random. A full catalogue of such rights is to be found in international treaties, notably the European Social Charter of 1961 which addresses the right to work, the right to just conditions of work, the right to safe and healthy working conditions, the right to a fair remuneration, the right to organize, and the right to bargain collectively (including the right to strike). But no social democracy covers anything like the same ground, with the possible exception of Portugal where the constitution covered the right to work, the rights of workers (covering pay, working conditions, rest, and recreation), and job security (Arts 53, 58, and 59).

[38] In none of these countries has the state been able to secure full employment on a consistent basis, with the US Department of Labor reporting unemployment levels in June 2011 running at 21 per cent (Spain), and 7.2 per cent (Denmark): ibid. The country with the least urgent duty coincidentally has the lowest level of unemployment, with the Netherlands being said to have unemployment levels of 4.2 per cent: ibid.

[39] See Tiziano Treu, 'Italy' in Roger Blanpain (ed), *International Encyclopaedia of Labour Law and Industrial Relations*, vol 7 (2010), 90.

Indeed, Germany makes little provision for the employment relationship,[40] while Denmark, Norway, and Sweden make no contribution to substantive rights beyond that already referred to.[41] The Netherlands provides that rules for the protection of workers and co-determination 'shall be laid down in an Act of Parliament' (Art 19), while Greece similarly provides that 'general working conditions are determined by law and are supplemented by collective agreements' (Art 22). Although France recognizes a right to work, the bulk of the Constitution's economic rights relate to freedom of association. Otherwise, a full catalogue of social rights can be constructed, but only by asking for contributions from each jurisdiction, including a right to paid holidays (with working time to be regulated by law) (Italy); a right to 'just working conditions' (Belgium); the promotion of workplace safety (Spain); and a right not to be unfairly dismissed (Finland).

VI. Trade Union Rights

In contrast to the individual rights discussed above, collective rights are those rights which relate to the arrangements for participating in economic decisions, that is to say in the enterprise, or in the branch or sector of the economy in which the individual is engaged, or otherwise in relation to workplace issues. Institutional arrangements of this kind are normally built around the practice of collective bargaining whereby trade unions acting on behalf of workers negotiate terms and conditions of employment. In social democracies this does not mean enterprise-based bargaining that affects only the workers in the enterprise in question, the trade union acting as an agent or as a representative of the workers concerned. Rather, as already suggested it means branch or sector-wide bargaining in which the trade union acts in a regulatory or de facto legislative capacity, negotiating terms and conditions of employment for workers across an entire sector.

In some countries, these agreements may be extended by legislation—or by other means—to employers who are not members of the associations which conclude the agreements. Where regulatory collective bargaining of this kind takes place, collective bargaining density may be as high as 98 per cent (as in Austria), compared to liberal democracies such as Canada (33 per cent) and the United States (11 per cent) where a different form of collective bargaining takes place.[42] Although social democratic constitutions do not typically set out in great detail the machinery of the 'economic constitution', they do nevertheless underpin it with strong trade union rights of a kind unfamiliar in the liberal democracies of the common law world. These include the right to organize in a trade union (there can be no bargaining unless there is organization on both sides), a right to bargain collectively, and a right to strike (there can be no bargaining without a sanction in the event of impasse).

This role of *collective bargaining* is recognized in a number of constitutions, notably in France where the preamble to the 1946 text not only provides that individuals have the right to defend their interests by trade union action, but that 'every worker shall participate through his delegates in the collective arrangement of work conditions, as well as in the running of the firm.' Drafted at about the same time, the Italian Constitution recognizes not only that trade

[40] Though see Manfred Weiss, 'The Interface Between Constitution and Labour Law in Germany' (2005) 26 *Comparative Labor Law and Policy Journal* 181.

[41] Sweden does deal with the right to strike, dealt with below, and Norway makes provision for co-determination.

[42] See ETUI, 'Collective Bargaining', available at <http://www.worker-participation.eu/National-Industrial-Relations/Across-Europe/Collective-Bargaining2>.

unions have a legal status, but that they may 'negotiate collective agreements having compulsory value for all persons belonging to the categories to which said agreements refer' (Art 39). There is no comparable provision in the German Basic Law drafted also at that time, but such arrangements are embedded in the foundations of the state in the post-war era, and there is a suggestion that the right to bargain collectively is implied by the constitutional guarantee of freedom of association.[43]

The pivotal role of collective bargaining in social democratic constitutions is reflected by its recognition in more recent texts, including those of Greece, Spain, and Portugal. The first provides that the 'general conditions of work shall be determined by law and supplemented by collective agreements arrived at by free collective bargaining' (Art 22), the second that the 'law shall guarantee the right to collective labor negotiations between the representatives of workers and employers, as well as the binding force of agreements' (Art 37), and the third that 'trade unions have the power to conclude collective agreements, though it is also provided that the rules governing the power to make collective agreements as well as the scope of these agreements is to be determined by law' (Art 56).[44] The right to bargain collectively is recognized in Belgium (Art 23) (along with the right to information and consultation), though not in the revised Swedish Instrument of Government.[45]

Perhaps curiously, the *right to strike* appears to be more widely recognized in European social democracies than the process of collective bargaining of which it is an essential feature. In many cases it is expressly recognized (France, Italy, Sweden, Portugal, Spain, Greece), but in others it has been created by the courts as being a consequence of the right to freedom of association (Germany and Finland).[46] Beyond that, there are differences in terms of 'ownership' of the right: in some cases (Germany, Greece) it is expressed as the right of the union, whereas in other cases (Portugal, Spain) it is expressed as the right of the individual worker. There are also differences as to the substance of the right, though most of the constitutional texts (Italy, Spain, Greece, Sweden) allow limits to be imposed by law.[47] In the case of France, the courts have imposed limits on an otherwise unqualified right,[48] while in Portugal the right is stated to be unlimited.

The right to strike is thus widely but not universally recognized by the constitutions of social democratic societies, the Netherlands being a notable exception. In an important deci-

[43] Manfred Weiss, 'The Interface Between Constitution and Labour Law in Germany' (2005) 26 *Comparative Labor Law and Policy Journal* 181.

[44] The Portuguese Constitution also guarantees trade unions the right to participate in the preparation of labour legislation, the management of social security institutions, the monitoring of the implementation of economic and social plans, and to be represented on bodies engaged in the harmonization of social questions (Art 56).

[45] Despite the great importance of collective bargaining as a regulatory procedure in the Nordic social democracies, there is no recognition of it in any of the national constitutions.

[46] In the case of Germany, by a decision of the Federal Labour Court in 1955 (on which see Manfred Weiss and Marlene Schmidt in Roger Blanpain (ed), *International Encyclopaedia of Labour Law and Industrial Relations*, vol 7 (2010), 203); in the case of Finland also by judicial decision (see *Viking Line v ITF* [2005] EWCA Civ 1299, [2006] IRLR 58, at para 26).

[47] In the case of Italy, there is no 'law', the scope of the right being left to the courts to determine: see Michele Ainis and Temistocle Martines, *Codice Costituzionale* (2001), 295–304. In the case of Spain, there is no law made since the Constitution took effect, the position being governed in part by a royal decree made shortly after the end of the Franco era, much of which was ruled unconstitutional by the Constitutional Court on 8 April 1981.

[48] See M. Forde, 'Bills of Rights and Trade Union Immunities—Some French Lessons' (1984) 13 *Industrial Law Journal* 40.

sion of the Hoge Raad,[49] however, domestic effect was given to the right to strike as expressed in the European Social Charter of 1961. By Article 6(4) this provides that the High Contracting Parties undertake to recognize 'the right of workers and employers to collective action in cases of conflicts of interest, including the right to strike . . . '. The Dutch Constitution recognizes the binding effect of treaties that have been approved by Parliament (Art 93), with the result that domestic law is not applicable if it conflicts with such a treaty (Art 94). In giving domestic effect to Article 6(4) of the Social Charter, the Court was incorporating into domestic law the provisions of a treaty that was a highpoint of the social democratic consensus in post-war Western Europe.

VII. Economic Rights and the 'New Democracies'

Although the economic rights provisions of the Weimar Constitution were not adopted by the German Federal Republic, it is said that the Weimar legacy continued more clearly in the Constitution of the former DDR in 1949. The latter, however, was revised in 1968 and again in 1974, the 1974 Constitution proclaiming a 'socialist state of workers and farmers', 'under the leadership of the working class and its Marxist-Leninist party'. Revised in the same era, the Constitution of the USSR (1977) marked the 'epoch-making turn from capitalist to socialism'. It was based on the principle of 'democratic centralism' (Art 3), in which the Communist Party of the Soviet Union (CPSU) operated as the 'leading and guiding force of the Soviet society and the nucleus of its political system, of all state organisations and public organisations' (Art 6). Special provision was made for trade unions and others to participate 'in managing state and public affairs, and in deciding political, economic, and social and cultural matters' (Art 7).

This is not the place to engage with arguments that the Soviet Constitutions 'have existed to maximize the legal authority of a revolutionary government and the unbounded exercise thereof', or with claims that the constitution was otherwise 'machinery or decoration'.[50] For present purposes, it is enough to note that when these constitutional arrangements were transformed in the USSR and a number of other countries after 1989, there was little evident desire in most of these countries to adopt an unequivocal liberal constitutionalism of the kind encountered in the United States or elsewhere, however much free enterprise and liberal democracy may have been admired. Not only is Russia said to be 'a social state' (Art 7), but the same is true of Bulgaria (Preamble) and Romania (Preamble), while Hungary (Preamble), Poland (Art 20), and Slovakia (Art 55) are declared to be social market economies, and yet other 'new democracies' demonstrate some commitment to social justice.

Given their recent history, it is unsurprising that these counter-revolutionary states should embrace economic rights of various kinds, including rights of entrepreneurship and rights relating to private property. As to the former, the Republic of Bulgaria is based on 'free economic initiative', in which the state 'shall establish and guarantee equal legal conditions for economic activity to all citizens and corporate entities by preventing any abuse of a monopoly status and unfair competition and by protecting the consumer' (Art 19). Similarly, 'Hungary recognizes and supports the right to enterprise and the freedom of competition in the economy' (Art 9),[51] while in Slovakia everyone has 'the right to engage in entrepreneurial or

[49] *NV Dutch Railways v Transport Unions FNV, FSV and CNV* [1988] 6 Int Lab Reps 57.

[50] Samuel Edward Finer, *Five Constitutions* (1979), 29.

[51] For a critical account of some of the problems this has created in adapting to a new political order, see András Sajó, 'How the Rule of Law Killed Welfare Reform' (1996) 5 *East European Constitutional Review* 31.

other gainful activity' (Art 35). While the foregoing are hymns to the virtues of free enterprise, Poland at least has a the measure of its vices: 'Public authorities shall protect consumers, customers, hirers or lessees against activities threatening their health, privacy and safety, as well as against dishonest market practices' (Art 76).

So far as property rights are concerned, the new constitutions typically seek to offer what is by now the conventional guarantee: recognition of the right to private property, with compensation to be paid in the event of expropriation in the public interest. There is a sense in which these guarantees are drafted with a greater sense of purpose than in earlier constitutions and with a stronger sense of protection. In the case of Poland, forfeiture may take place only with judicial approval (Art 46), while in Hungary the Constitution emphasizes that 'expropriation shall only be permitted in exceptional cases, when such action is in the public interest, and only in such cases and in the manner stipulated by law, with provision of full, unconditional and immediate compensation' (Art 13). There continues to be recognition that some property may be owned by the state, as in Slovakia, 'to meet the needs of society, the development of the national economy, and public interest' (Art 20).

In all of these cases detailed provision is made for labour rights, in some cases in much greater detail than in any of the social democracies already referred to. The most ambitious is perhaps Slovakia, which provides that 'employees have the right to equitable and adequate working conditions', and that the law guarantees, 'the right to remuneration for work done, sufficient to ensure the employee's dignified standard of living', 'protection against arbitrary dismissal and discrimination at the place of work', the protection of health and safety at work, the longest admissible working time, the regulation of working time (including rest periods and holidays), and the right to collective bargaining (Art 36). But with few exceptions, all of these countries make express provision for trade union freedom (including the right to strike), albeit that it is the freedom of a different kind of trade unionism than the one previously encountered.

But although mimicking social democratic constitutionalism, it is to be noted that in most of the so-called 'new democracies', the institutional infrastructure of social democracy is not as fully developed as in the countries of Western Europe. Trade union membership tends to be lower (and in some case much lower),[52] while collective bargaining is more likely to take place at enterprise rather than sectoral level. Collective bargaining density thus tends to be low, especially when compared to most of the EU15 (with the exception of the United Kingdom).[53] It is also the case that constitutional guarantees of trade union rights (including the right to strike) have not prevented successful complaints being made from some of the 'new democracies' to the ECtHR (Russia),[54] the Social Rights Committee of the Council of Europe (Bulgaria),[55] and the ILO (Bulgaria, Hungary, Poland, Romania, Russia, Slovenia, in 2011 alone).[56]

[52] ETUI, 'Trade Unions', available at <http://www.worker-participation.eu/National-Industrial-Relations/Across-Europe/Trade-Unions2>.

[53] ETUI, 'Collective Bargaining' (n 42).

[54] *Danilenkov v Russia*, ECtHR App no 67336/01, 30 July 2009.

[55] Case No 32/2005, *European Trade Union Confederation (ETUC), Confederation of Independent Trade Unions in Bulgaria (CITUB), Confederation of Labour 'Podkrepa' (CL 'Podkrepa') v Bulgaria*: available at <http://www.coe.int/t/dghl/monitoring/socialcharter/Complaints/CC32Merits_en.pdf>.

[56] ILO, 98th Session, Report of the Committee of Experts on the Application of Conventions and Recommendations, Report III (Part 4A) (2011).

VIII. Economic Rights and Liberal Democracies

These difficulties in reaching and maintaining international minimum standards on economic rights is by no means a problem unique to the constitutional law of 'new democracies'. Nevertheless, we can only marvel at the optimism of at least some in the 'new democracies' to establish countervailing sources of power to the power of the state, and the awareness of the need to establish balanced sources of private power, features also on display in the new South African Constitution (though here too with a contestable impact). So what about the long-established liberal democracies in the predominantly English-speaking world? These are the constitutions built expressly (or impliedly in the case of Canada) on property rights. Could they be persuaded to embrace the economic rights of labour? If so how could this be done? And why?

It is true of course that at subnational level in some of these countries we encounter some commitment to economic rights. A good example of this in the United States is the state constitution of New York, with its glorious embrace of the principle that 'labor is not a commodity' (s 17), while Canada offers a good example in the form of the Quebec Charter of Human Rights and Freedoms, with its right of every worker to 'fair and reasonable conditions of employment' (s 46). There have also been political moves in some liberal democracies to expand human rights protection to include economic rights, most notably in Canada where the ill-fated federal and provincial intergovernmental Charlottetown Accord in 1992 proposed amending the constitution to include provisions for a social and economic union. These—non-justiciable policy objectives—would include protection for the right of workers to organize and bargain collectively.[57]

Attention in Canada has long since switched from the political arena to the courts, though at first blush the courts seem to be mining a shallow seam. As we have seen, liberal constitutions in the common law tradition were initially hostile to the economic rights of workers and their organizations, though some (but not all) have since been persuaded to occupy a position of tolerance. But it is a long way from tolerance to protection, especially when that protection would require a creative and expansive interpretation of civil and political rights relating to freedom of association. Could such a right be strong enough to include the freedom not only *to be* in association with others, but also the freedom *to act* in association with others? And if so, could such a guarantee be read to include the right to organize in a trade union, the right to bargain collectively, and the right to strike? And by what standard would the substance of any such right be determined?

In an appeal from Trinidad and Tobago in 1970, the Privy Council famously provided one answer: the right to freedom of association for a trade union member means no more than the right to be a member of a trade union.[58] Although taking an approach not quite this narrow, in its equally famous 'labour trilogy' in the 1980s, the Supreme Court of Canada likewise held that the right to freedom of association did not include a right to bargain collectively or a right to strike; but that even if it did, the restrictions in these cases would be permitted by section 1 of the Charter, which allows reasonable restrictions to be imposed on Charter rights.[59] In a

[57] Consensus Report on the Constitution, Final Text, 28 August 1992. We can only speculate on whether the Canadian courts would have developed such non-justiciable principles as courageously as their Indian counterparts, on which see this volume, Chapter 49.

[58] *Collymore v Attorney General of Trinidad and Tobago* [1970] AC 538.

[59] For an account of these cases, see T.J. Christian and K.D. Ewing, 'Labouring under the Canadian Constitution' (1988) 17 *Industrial Law Journal* 73.

more recent 'labour trilogy', however, the Supreme Court of Canada has changed its mind, and held in the first of these cases that the denial of collective bargaining rights to agricultural workers was a violation of the Charter right to freedom of association, emphasizing the potentially collective dimension to the Charter.[60]

This is a development that requires some explanation, and cannot be understood as a sudden embrace of strong social democratic values. What does stand out, however, is an example of the growing influence of international human treaties in the work of regional and national courts. In a decision reflecting closely the approach of the ECtHR a year later,[61] the Canadian Supreme Court said in the second decision of the recent trilogy that 'the *Charter* should be presumed to provide at least as great a level of protection as is found in the international human rights documents that Canada has ratified.'[62] For this purpose, the Court referred specifically to three treaties, namely the International Covenant on Civil and Political Rights, the International Covenant on Economic, Social and Cultural Rights, and ILO Convention 87, the last dealing with freedom of association and protection of the right to organize. To say the least, these were controversial benchmarks, none of which referred expressly to the right to bargain collectively, a matter dealt with separately by ILO Convention 98, which Canada has not ratified.

But although significant, this development should not be exaggerated. It is one thing to acknowledge international human rights treaties, but another matter to give effect to international human rights principles and norms, leading to doubts about whether the sow's ear of liberal constitutional liberty can ever produce the means necessary to produce the silk purse of social democratic equality. So although re-affirming its commitment to ILO principles in the third decision in the recent trilogy, the Canadian Supreme Court has settled on a definition of collective bargaining for the purposes of the principle of freedom of association that is unique to the SCC, and which falls some way short of the ILO principles to which it referred. According to the Court, 'the bottom line' is simply that workers 'are entitled to meaningful processes by which they can pursue workplace goals'.[63] As a result, the Court upheld legislation authorizing a diluted form of workplace representation that had already been condemned by the ILO supervisory bodies.[64]

IX. Back to *Lochner*?

The narrative so far leads tentatively in two directions. The first is the 'normality' of including both species of economic rights in national constitutions, despite the apparent retreat of social democracy in the global economy. Apart from the countries already discussed, this a feature of the major constitutional texts of South America (notably Brazil) and Asia (notably India). Moreover, new constitutions are more likely to embrace than reject economic rights of both species. The second (and more tentative) is that economic rights are beginning to be sustained

[60] *Dunmore v Ontario* 2001 SCC 94, [2001] 3 SCR 1016.

[61] *Demir and Baykara v Turkey* [2008] ECHR 1345 (K.D. Ewing and John Hendy QC, 'The Dramatic Implications of *Demir and Baykara*' (2010) 39 *Industrial Law Journal* 2). See also the *Viking* and *Laval cases* below.

[62] *Health Services and Support—Facilities Subsector Bargaining Association v BC* 2007 SCC 27, [2007] 2 SCR 391, para 70.

[63] *Ontario (AG) v Fraser* 2011 SCC 20, para 117.

[64] For the CFA, see Complaint against the Government of Canada presented by the United Food and Commercial Workers Union Canada (UFCW Canada), supported by the Canadian Labour Congress and UNI Global Union, Report No 358, Case No 2704, para 355.

by civil and political rights in systems where they are not otherwise fully included. Apart from the evolving developments to this effect in Canada, there are signs that even the British courts may be stirring.[65] To some extent this latter development can also be attributed to the enduring impact of social democratic values, to the extent that the developments in question are inspired by international treaties themselves monuments to the legacy of social democracy.

The traffic is not, however, all one way, with the spirit of *Lochner* worryingly surviving in a number of jurisdictions.[66] By some way the most serious of these threats is that presented by the European Court of Justice/Court of Justice of the European Union, particularly in relation to the social democracies of Western Europe. In the first of several recent cases, a Finnish shipping company (Viking Line) proposed to re-flag a vessel in Estonia, where it could take advantage of lower wages. Concerned about the impact that this might have on jobs and terms and conditions of employment, the Finnish Seamen's Union (FSU) objected and enlisted the support of the International Transport Workers' Federation (ITF), which in turn gave instructions to national affiliated trade unions not to deal with the Viking Line. The company brought proceedings in the English courts (London being the base of the ITF), alleging that the conduct of the ITF violated the EC Treaty, on the ground that it interfered with the company's right to freedom of establishment (Art 43).[67]

On a reference by the English Court of Appeal seeking guidance on a number of questions, the European Court of Justice (ECJ) responded in a quite unpredictable way, elevating the rights of business over the rights of trade unions.[68] Although accepting that the right to strike was a fundamental principle of EU law, the ECJ imposed a number of qualifications on the exercise of the right, which were consistent with neither the Finnish constitution, nor the principles of the ILO. A week later, the same court held in the parallel *Laval* case that a trade union could not take collective action against a Latvian building firm in order to compel it to observe Swedish collective agreements for workers it had posted to Sweden from Latvia.[69] Again, the right of businesses to freedom to provide services (EC Treaty, Article 49) took priority over the right to strike accepted as a fundamental principle of EU law and protected by the Swedish Constitution.

It is important to emphasize that because of the principle of the overriding supremacy of EU law, these decisions have direct effect in national legal systems, and take priority over even national constitutional arrangements. Indeed, it is already the case that both the FSU and the ITF settled an undisclosed sum in favour of the Viking Line, and that the Swedish unions were held liable by the Swedish Labour Court to pay damages to Laval,[70] in both cases for taking action that was apparently constitutionally protected and permissible under national law. It is true that the decisions impose qualifications (*Viking*) and restrictions (*Laval*) on constitutional (and other) rights only where the rights in question are being exercised in a transnational EU context, such as the relocation of a business or the posting of workers from one member state to another. But as the ILO Committee of Experts has pointed out:

[65] *RMT v Serco Ltd; ASLEF v London and Birmingham Railway Ltd* [2011] EWCA Civ 226 [2011] ICR 848.

[66] The best example of this recently in national law is *Ryanair v Labour Court* [2007] IESC 6, where the Irish Supreme Court held that legislation was to be 'given a proportionate and constitutional interpretation so as not unreasonably to encroach on Ryanair's right to operate a non-unionised company'. This is widely thought to have given corporations a constitutional right *not* to deal with trade unions, Ireland thereby elevating by means of constitutional law the rights of businesses above the rights of its citizens.

[67] *Viking Line v ITF* [2005] EWCA Civ 1299 and [2005] EWHC 1222 (Comm), [2006] IRLR 58.

[68] Case C-438/05 *Viking Line v ITF*, 11 December 2007.

[69] Case C-341/05 *Laval v Svenska Byggnadsarbetareforbundet*, 18 December 2007.

[70] Mia Ronnmar, '*Laval* returns to Sweden: The Final Judgment of the Swedish Labour Court and Swedish Legislative Reforms' (2010) 39 *Industrial Law Journal* 210.

> in the current context of globalization, such cases are likely to be ever more common, particularly with respect to certain sectors of employment, like the airline sector, and thus the impact upon the possibility of the workers in these sectors of being able to meaningfully negotiate with their employers on matters affecting the terms and conditions of employment may indeed be devastating.[71]

Well might Danny Nicol refer to *Viking* and *Laval* as the EU's '*Lochner* moment',[72] the ECJ having elevated an old ideology from the trenches of the common law, to the high plains of treaty interpretation, trampling on constitutional achievements along the way.[73] For although the EU proclaims to be a 'social market economy' which 'confirms its attachment to the fundamental social rights of workers',[74] and although it has impressively embedded a process of social dialogue in its lawmaking machinery,[75] social democratic ambitions nevertheless appear to have been contained. It is true that the EU Charter of Fundamental Rights recognizes the right to collective bargaining and action (Art 28). But it is also true that this is subject to the qualification that the right may be exercised 'in accordance with Union law and national laws and practices', a provision which post-Lisbon effectively entrenches the *Viking* and *Laval* doctrines in the constitutional DNA of the EU.[76]

Quite apart from the fact that the ECJ/CJEU has so conspicuously used a 'constitutional' text (the EU Treaty) to subordinate the rights of labour to the needs of property, *Viking* and *Laval* are all the more striking for the fact that they are so far out of step with the line of travel being pursued by the other European court, namely the ECtHR. In a number of cases decided after *Viking* and *Laval*, the ECtHR has held that the right to freedom of association in the European Convention on Human Rights (Art 11) includes the right to bargain collectively and the right to take collective action, in the former case at the standard set by ILO Convention 98.[77] In taking these steps, the ECtHR did so by having regard to developments both international and national, 'and to the practice of Contracting States in such matters'.[78] The developments in question included not only ILO Convention 98, but also the Council of Europe's Social Charter, and (ironically) the EU Charter of Fundamental Rights.

X. Conclusion

Historically, there has been a constitutional evolution in the treatment of economic rights in national constitutions, and from a comparative point of view the emergence of two different political traditions. The recognition of property rights transcends both liberal and social democratic constitutions, but in both property rights tend to be read widely. The inclusion of welfare benefits as a form of property, however, appears to vary in its implications, giving rise to procedural obligations in the United States, but in some cases to substantive expectations in

[71] ILO, 98th Session, Report of the Committee of Experts on the Application of Conventions and Recommendations, Report III (Part 4A) (2011).

[72] Danny Nicol, 'Europe's *Lochner* Moment' [2011] *Public Law* 308.

[73] It is notable also that although the ECJ in both *Viking* and *Laval* took into account ILO Conventions, it did do in a way that distorted their meaning.

[74] TEU, Art 3(3) and Preamble respectively.

[75] TFEU, Arts 154, 155.

[76] The TEU, Art 6 now provides that the Charter 'shall have the same legal value as the treaties'.

[77] See esp *Demir and Baykara v Turkey* [2008] ECHR 1345. An account of the other cases is to be found in Ewing and Hendy (n 61).

[78] *Demir and Baycara* (n 61), para 154.

the Council of Europe, even though in the latter case the jurisprudence may flatter to deceive.[79]

The economic rights of labour in contrast to the economic rights of property are associated with social democratic principles and the socialization of the private sphere. They represent a statement about how a society is to be governed in all of its aspects, rather than a statement about what a government may or may not do. Crucially, the constitutional rights of labour suited the prevailing economic orthodoxy at the time they were developed, one which emphasized the need to increase the spending power of workers, to stimulate demand for goods, to reduce unemployment and welfare dependency, and to alleviate distress and reduce the risk of social unrest.

These economic rights of labour sit uncomfortably in a new economic orthodoxy of open markets, transnational corporations, and free trade in an intensely competitive global economy. Now, wages and other terms and conditions are being squeezed to reduce prices, and jobs are being moved to reduce costs for the behemoths that now dominate economic and political life. In that context the constitutional protection of labour rights takes on a new role and a new responsibility, these entrenched rights running against the grain of an orthodoxy they seem so spectacularly ill-equipped to confront.[80]

Recent developments suggest that one challenge for the evolving purpose of labour rights as constitutional rights will be to ensure that such rights in national constitutions both meet and are permitted to operate at the minimum level set by international human rights instruments, and in particular at the level set by the ILO. Developments in places as diverse as the Canadian Supreme Court and the ECJ suggest that that while judges are willing to acknowledge these principles, there is not the same willingness on the part of all judges to engage with their substance. In the current climate, lip-service is hardly good enough.

Bibliography

Harry W. Arthurs, 'Labour and the 'Real' Constitution' (2007) 48 Les *Cahiers de Droit* 43

Terence Daintith and Monica Sah, 'Privatisation and the Economic Neutrality of the Constitution' [1993] *Public Law* 465

Ruth Dukes, 'Constitutionalising Employment Relations: Sinzheimer, Kahn-Freund and the Role of Labour Law' (2008) 35 *Journal of Law and Society* 341

K.D. Ewing and John Hendy QC, 'The Dramatic Implications of *Demir and Baycara*' (2010) 39 *Industrial Law Journal* 2

M. Forde, 'Bills of Rights and Trade Union Immunities—Some French Lessons' (1984) 13 *Industrial Law Journal* 40

Georges Gurvitch, *A Bill of Social Rights* (1945)

Otto Kahn-Freund, *Labour Law and Politics in the Weimar Republic* (Roy Lewis and Jon Clark eds, 1981)

Otto Kahn-Freund, 'The Weimar Constitution' (1944) 15 *Political Quarterly* 229

Danny Nicol, 'Europe's *Lochner* Moment' [2011] *Public Law* 308

Manfred Weiss, 'The Interface Between Constitution and Labour Law in Germany' (2005) 26 *Comparative Labor Law and Policy Journal* 181

[79] *Stec v United Kingdom* [2006] ECHR 293; *R (RJM) v SSWP* [2008] UKHL 63, [2009] 1 AC 311.

[80] On which, see Harry W. Arthurs, 'Labour and the "Real" Constitution' (2007) 48 *Les Cahiers de Droit* 43.

PART VIII

OVERLAPPING RIGHTS

CHAPTER 51

THE CONSTITUTIONALIZATION OF ABORTION

REVA B. SIEGEL*

New Haven

COMPARATIVE constitutional study of abortion has generally focused on the decisions of a few influential jurisdictions, particularly Germany and the United States, where constitutional frameworks begin from dramatically divergent premises—protecting, respectively, unborn life and decisional autonomy.[1] Some comparative studies are dynamic, observing that

* For comments on the manuscript, I am grateful to Rebecca Cook, Tom Ginsburg, Vicki Jackson, Julieta LeMaitre, Miguel Maduro, Susanna Mancini, Robert Post, Judith Resnik, Ruth Rubio-Marin, and Hunter Smith. I was fortunate to explore the cases in this chapter with the research assistance of Joanna Erdman and in conversation with her. I look forward to continuing to learn together. Thanks also to Alyssa King, Jena McGill, and Danieli Evans.

[1] See eg Mary Ann Glendon, *Abortion and Divorce in Western Law* (1987); Donald P. Kommers, 'Autonomy, Dignity and Abortion' in Tom Ginsburg and Rosalind Dixon (eds), *Comparative Constitutional Law* (2011), 441–58 (discussing Ireland, Germany, and the United States). See also Norman Dorsen, Michel Rosenfeld, András Sajó, and Susanne Baer, *Comparative Constitutionalism: Cases and Materials* (2nd edn, 2010), 539–64 (discussing the United States, Canada, Germany, Poland, and Mexico); Vicki C. Jackson and Mark V. Tushnet, *Comparative Constitutional Law* (2nd edn, 2006), 2–139, 196–210 (discussing Canada, Germany, Ireland, and the United States). Comparative studies of abortion legislation are more comprehensive. See eg Albin Eser and Hans-Georg Koch, *Abortion and the Law: From International Comparison to Legal Policy* (2005); Reed Boland and Laura Katzive, 'Developments in Laws on Induced Abortion: 1998–2007' (2008) 34 *International Family Planning Perspectives* 110; see also Anika Rahman, Laura Katzive, and Stanley K. Henshaw, 'A Global Review of Laws on Induced Abortion, 1985–1997' (1998) 24 *International Family Planning Perspectives* 56.

constitutional doctrine in Germany and the United States has evolved to allow forms of abortion regulation that share more in common than the divergent constitutional frameworks authorizing them would suggest.[2]

This chapter analyzes constitutional decisions concerning abortion in the United States and Germany, their evolution over time, and their influence across jurisdictions. But rather than assume the existence of constitutional law on abortion—as so much of the literature does—the chapter asks how abortion was constitutionalized.[3] Examining the conflicts, within and across borders, that led to the first judicial decisions addressing the constitutionality of abortion laws in the 1970s sheds light on questions that prompted the birth of this body of law, and continue to shape its growth. The first constitutional decisions on abortion grew out of debates over women's citizenship, engendering doctrine that to this day is haunted by 'the woman question', conflicted about whether government may or must control women's decisions about motherhood. Attention to this question in turn sheds light on the relationship of constitutional politics and constitutional law: it demonstrates how political conflict shapes constitutional law and constitutional law endeavors to shape political conflict.[4]

Constitutional decisions on abortion began in an era when a transnational women's movement was beginning to contest the terms of women's citizenship, eliciting diverse forms of reaction, both supportive and resisting. As I show, the woman question haunts the abortion decisions, where it is initially addressed by indirection, and over time comes to occupy a more visible role, whether as an express concern of doctrine, *or* as a problematic nested inside of the growing body of law articulating a constitutional obligation to protect unborn life.

The body of constitutional law on abortion that has grown up since the 1970s is concerned with the propriety, necessity, and feasibility of controlling women's agency in decisions concerning motherhood. Some courts have insisted that government should respect women's decisions about motherhood, while many others have insisted that protecting unborn life requires government to control women's decisions about motherhood. Over the decades a growing number of courts have allowed government to protect life by persuading (rather than coercing) women to assume the role of motherhood. Across Europe, a growing number of jurisdictions are now giving women the final word in decisions about abortion—on the constitutional ground that it is the best way to protect unborn life. These remarkable developments suggest deep conflict about whether law should and can control women's agency in

[2] See eg Richard E. Levy and Alexander Somek, 'Paradoxical Parallels in the American and German Abortion Decisions' (2001) 9 *Tulane Journal of International and Comparative Law* 109; Udo Werner, 'The Convergence of Abortion Regulation in Germany and the United States: A Critique of Glendon's Rights Talk Thesis' (1996) 18 *Loyola of Los Angeles International and Comparative Law Review* 571. For dynamic accounts attentive to transnational influence, see Federico Fabbrini, 'The European Court of Human Rights, the EU Charter of Fundamental Rights and the Right to Abortion: *Roe v Wade* on the Other Side of the Atlantic?' (2011) 18 *Columbia Journal of European Law* 1; Sjef Gevers, 'Abortion Legislation and the Future of the "Counseling Model"' (2006) 13 *European Journal of Health Law* 27.

[3] One comparative study that begins by investigating the political origins of the first constitutional decisions on abortion is Machteld Nijsten, *Abortion and Constitutional Law: A Comparative European-American Study* (1990).

[4] On the relationship of law and politics in the abortion cases, see Reva B. Siegel, 'Dignity and Sexuality: Claims on Dignity in Transnational Debates over Abortion and Same Sex Marriage' (2011) 9 *International Journal of Constitutional Law* (forthcoming). See also Linda Greenhouse and Reva B. Siegel, 'Before (and After) *Roe v Wade*: New Questions About Backlash' (2011) 120 *Yale Law Journal* 2028; Robert Post and Reva B. Siegel, 'Roe Rage: Democratic Constitutionalism and Backlash' (2007) 42 *Harvard Civil Rights-Civil Liberties Law Review* 373; and Reva B. Siegel, 'Dignity and the Politics of Protection: Abortion Restrictions Under Casey/Carhart' (2008) 117 *Yale Law Journal* 1694.

decisions about motherhood. Reading the cases with attention to this conflict identifies questions that courts are grappling with in the latest generation of abortion decisions, illuminating ambiguities in the normative basis of constitutional frameworks and in their practical architecture.

At the same time, this approach to the abortion cases offers a fascinating vantage point on constitutional decision-making in the face of persistent social conflict. On one familiar view, constitutional adjudication raises the stakes of the abortion debate because it requires courts to choose between competing principles, and so inhibits compromise and incites polarization. But this chapter offers a more complicated story in which escalating political conflict precipitates constitutional adjudication, and, over time, constitutional adjudication endeavors to mediate political conflict. Recent judicial decisions on abortion seem to appreciate the tenacity of the abortion conflict, and in varying ways have come to internalize its implications for constitutional adjudication. Judgments frequently integrate opposing normative perspectives into one constitutional framework, in order to channel conflict that courts lack power to settle. Rather than endeavoring to impose values, courts often employ techniques that inform politics with constitutional value, just as recent abortion legislation aspires to shape judicial reasoning about constitutional matters. These judicial and legislative frameworks endeavor to vindicate contested constitutional values by means that preserve social cohesion.

This chapter's interest in the conflicts that engendered the constitutionalization of abortion shapes its focus. The chapter does not systematically compare abortion legislation worldwide[5] or investigate social practices concerning its enforcement. The chapter considers legislation for the purpose of exploring the roots and dynamic logic of constitutional law. These same interests shape its coverage of constitutional doctrine. The chapter's focus is on the development in national constitutions of broad normative frameworks concerning abortion.

The chapter proceeds in three sections. Section I briefly considers developments in the 1960s and 1970s, a time when reformers of many kinds persuaded legislatures around the world to liberalize access to abortion; when a mobilizing feminist movement first claimed that repeal of abortion restrictions was required as a matter of justice for women; when those who sought to preserve abortion's criminalization began to mobilize against change in the name of a 'right to life'; and when courts in five nations first issued judgments explaining what forms of abortion regulation their respective constitutions required or allowed.

Section II examines key constitutional decisions in the United States and Germany which together illustrate differences and similarities in the logic of constitutionalization. In the 1970s, courts in both jurisdictions struck down abortion laws and provided guidelines for future legislation, reasoning from very different constitutional norms. In 1973, the US Supreme Court interpreted its Constitution to require legislatures to respect the decision of a woman and her physician whether to terminate a pregnancy, as long as the fetus was not viable;[6] in 1975, the West German Federal Constitutional Court interpreted its Basic Law to require legislatures to protect unborn life, by prohibiting abortion in all cases except those that would impose extraordinary burdens on the pregnant woman.[7] In the 1990s, commentators observe, in the midst of domestic political conflict, each court significantly modified its judgment, to allow access to abortion after abortion-dissuasive counseling. Less remarked upon is the way that

[5] For comparative literature on abortion legislation, see n 1.

[6] *Roe v Wade* 410 US 113 (1973).

[7] BVerfGE 1 (1975), translated in John D. Gorby and Robert E. Jonas, 'West German Abortion Decision: A Contrast to *Roe v Wade*' (1976) 9 *John Marshall Journal of Practice & Procedure* 605 (the *Abortion I* case).

the reasoning of the courts in the 1990s was shaped by constitutional struggles of the preceding decades. I consider in particular how the view of women as citizens expressed in the US and German abortion opinions of the 1970s and 1990s evolved.

Section III looks to the logic of constitutional law today, considering how several dominant frameworks address the woman question. Some jurisdictions now require constitutional protections for women's dignity and welfare in government regulation of abortion of a kind unheard of before the modern women's movement. Many jurisdictions require constitutional protection for unborn life, providing for these purposes detailed judgments about what legislatures may or must do in regulating women's conduct. Perhaps the most remarkable aspect of this story is how understanding of this recently articulated duty to protect unborn life has evolved: over time and across jurisdictions, the constitutional duty to protect unborn life has been articulated in terms that increasingly acknowledge, accommodate, and even respect women citizens as autonomous agents—even in matters concerning motherhood. A growing number of jurisdictions now invoke the constitutional duty to protect unborn life as reason for giving women the final word in decisions concerning abortion.

I. From Constitutional Politics to Constitutional Law

In the mid-twentieth century, abortion laws around the world varied greatly. Some countries allowed abortion on request; others criminalized abortion except to save the life of the pregnant woman. Between these extremes, countries permitted abortion on various 'indications' (therapeutic, eugenic, juridical (rape), and socio-economic), subject to different procedures and requirements.[8] From 1967 to 1977, at least 42 jurisdictions changed their abortion laws, with the vast majority expanding the legal indications for abortion.[9] It was during this same period that courts in the United States, Canada, and Europe began to review laws regulating abortion for conformity with their constitutions.[10]

Comparativists who have addressed the constitutionalization of the abortion debate as an historically specific development have tended to equate constitutionalization with adjudication or judicialization.[11] Some commentary in this vein views judicialization of abortion as accelerating polarization or backlash.[12] But at least one constitutional comparativist has located the dynamics of polarization and constitutionalization of the abortion debate in politics[13]—an approach that my own work on the history of abortion conflict in the United States

[8] Ruth Roemer, 'Abortion Law: The Approaches of Different Nations' (1967) 57 *American Journal of Public Health* 1906, 1908–18.

[9] Rebecca J. Cook and Bernard M. Dickens, 'A Decade of International Change in Abortion Law: 1967–1977' (1978) 68 *American Journal of Public Health* 637, 643–4. See also Ruth Roemer, 'Abortion Law Reform and Repeal: Legislative and Judicial Developments' (1971) 61 *American Journal of Public Health* 500, 504–5.

[10] Nijsten (n 3).

[11] See Glendon (n 1), 45; Kim Lane Scheppele, 'Constitutionalizing Abortion' in Marianne Githens and Dorothy McBride Stetson (eds), *Abortion Politics: Public Policy in Cross-Cultural Perspective* (1996), 29–54.

[12] This theme recurs but it is not clearly developed in the literature, see Glendon (n 1), 45; Scheppele (n 11), 29–30; Donald P. Kommers, 'The Constitutional Law of Abortion in Germany: Should Americans Pay Attention?' (1994) 10 *Contemporary Journal of Health Law and Policy* 1, 31 (limiting claim to US judicialization).

[13] Nijsten (n 3), 1, 228, 232.

inclines me to adopt.[14] Although the matter plainly deserves further investigation, the record suggests that shifts in the form of political debate about abortion prompted and shaped subsequent constitutional litigation over the practice

In the 1960s, abortion was not generally understood as presenting constitutional questions. Arguments for liberalizing access to abortion were couched in practical and policy-based terms. In Western Europe and North America, where abortion was criminally banned but available when authorized by doctors for particular indications, poor women often relied on illegal and unsafe providers; critics argued that criminalization imposed health harms on women that were unequally distributed by class.[15] A different kind of public health concern arose in the 1960s as pregnant women who sought to become mothers discovered that they had been exposed to drugs or illness known to cause developmental harms to the unborn (eg thalidomide, measles).[16] Doctors endeavoring to care for their women patients worried about erratically enforced criminal abortion laws, and sought freedom in which to practice their profession.[17] In some jurisdictions, advocates for liberalization raised concerns about overpopulation—a concern that could take eugenic or environmental forms.[18]

These arguments for liberalizing abortion laws on public health, professional, and populationist grounds were not initially expressed or understood in constitutional terms. But youth movements challenging traditional sexual mores and a newly mobilizing women's movement advanced very different kinds of arguments for liberalizing access to abortion.[19]

By 1971, feminists on both sides of the Atlantic were calling for complete repeal of laws criminalizing abortion. They used 'speak-out' strategies to publicize their claims, conducting 'self-incrimination' campaigns in which women 'outed' themselves as having had abortions, and so exposed themselves to criminal prosecution—asserting, through these acts of civil disobedience, a claim to dignity, in defiance of custom and criminal law. In France, 343 women drew international attention by declaring that they had had abortions in a public manifesto that appeared in *Le Nouvel Observateur* in April 1971.[20] The text of the manifesto, written by Simone de Beauvoir and signed by many prominent French women, called for an end to secrecy and silence and demanded access to free birth control and to abortion services.[21] Two months after the release of the French manifesto, Aktion 218, a women's organization in West Germany named after the Penal Code Section criminalizing abortion, followed the French example, publishing abortion stories and the names of 374 German women in *Der Stern* in a

[14] On the relationship of constitutional politics and constitutional law, see n 4.

[15] See Dagmar Herzog, *Sexuality in Europe: A Twentieth-Century History* (2011), 156, 159; Greenhouse and Siegel (n 4), 2036.

[16] See Herzog (n 15), 156; Greenhouse and Siegel (n 4), 2037; Christopher Tietze, 'Abortion in Europe' (1967) 57 *American Journal of Public Health* 1923, 1926.

[17] Nijsten (n 3), 29–33.

[18] Greenhouse and Siegel (n 4), 2038–9; Nijsten (n 3), 33.

[19] Greenhouse and Siegel (n 4), 3029–46; Herzog (n 15), 156–60; Nijsten (n 3), 30; Reva B. Siegel, '*Roe*'s Roots: The Women's Rights Claims that Engendered *Roe*' (2010) 90 *Boston University Law Review* 1875. See also Myra Marx Ferree, William Anthony Gamson, Jürgen Gerhards, and Dieter Rucht, *Shaping Abortion Discourse: Democracy and the Public Sphere in Germany and the United States* (2002), 131–53; Dorothy McBride Stetson (ed), *Abortion Politics, Women's Movements, and the Democratic State: A Comparative Study of State Feminism* (2003); Joni Lovenduski and Joyce Outshoorn (eds), *The New Politics of Abortion* (1986).

[20] 'La liste des 343 françaises qui ont le courage de signer le manifest "je me suis fait avorter"' ['The list of 343 French women who have the courage to sign the manifesto "I have had an abortion"'] *Le Nouvel Observateur*, April 5, 1971, at 5 (author's translation).

[21] See Herzog (n 15), 156.

statement asserting that the law criminalizing abortion subjected women to 'degrading and life-threatening circumstances', coerced women, and 'branded them as criminals'.[22] Within months, women in Italy undertook their own self-incrimination campaign, releasing on August 4, 1971 a statement that women signed, acknowledging that they had had an abortion, and calling for abolition of the crime, on the ground that abortion should be 'available for each class' and that motherhood should be a 'free, conscious choice'.[23] Women in the United States also joined in, with a petition, on the model of the French campaign, published in the spring 1972 edition of *Ms Magazine*.[24]

Feminists changed the shape of the debate about abortion. Public health advocates and others who sought to liberalize access to abortion in the 1960s argued for incremental reform on the indications model, which they defended by appeal to shared values (health, class equity). By contrast, feminists sought categorical change—repeal of laws criminalizing abortion—which they justified on symbolic as well as practical grounds.

Feminists protested the criminalization of abortion as a symptom of a social order that devalued and disempowered women, and asserted that repeal of laws criminalizing abortion was a necessary first step in women's emancipation. In 1969, Betty Friedan, president of the National Organization for Women, mobilized these arguments in a call for the repeal of laws criminalizing abortion:[25]

> Women are denigrated in this country, because women are not deciding the conditions of their own society and their own lives. Women are not taken seriously as people. Women are not seen seriously as people. So this is the new name of the game on the question of abortion: that women's voices are heard.
>
> ... [W]omen are the ones who therefore must decide, and what we are in the process of doing, it seems to me, is realizing that there are certain rights that have never been defined as rights, that are essential to equality for women, and they were not defined in the Constitution of this, or any country, when that Constitution was written only by men. The right of woman to control her reproductive process must be established as a basic and valuable human civil right not to be denied or abridged by the state.[26]

Friedan insisted:

> there is no freedom, no equality, no full human dignity and personhood possible for women until we assert and demand the control over our own bodies, over our own reproductive process.... The real sexual revolution is the emergence of women from passivity, from *thingness*, to full self-determination, to full dignity...[27]

[22] Wir haben abgetrieben! [We Aborted] *Stern* (Hamburg), June 6, 1971 at 16 (author's translation). See also Alice Schwarzer (ed), *Frauen gegen den §218. 18 Protokolle, aufgezeichnet von Alice Schwarzer* [*Women Against §218: Eighteen Interviews, Recorded by Alice Schwarzer*] (1971), 146 (author's translation).

[23] 'Anche in Italia "autodenunce" per l'aborto', *Liberazione Notizie*, August 4, 1971, reprinted at *Even in Italy 'autoenunce' for abortion*, available at <http://old.radicali.it/search_view.php?id=44852&lang=&cms=>. See Herzog (n 15), 159 n 24; Marina Calloni, 'Debates and Controversies on Abortion in Italy' in Stetson (n 19), 181.

[24] Barbaralee D. Diamonstein, 'We Have Had Abortions', *Ms Magazine*, Spring 1972, 34; cf Siegel, '*Roe*'s Roots' (n 19), 1880, 1885. For the language of some of the manifestos, see Siegel, 'Dignity and Sexuality' (n 4), ms at 7 (on file with author).

[25] Betty Friedan, President, National Organization for Women, Address at the First National Conference on Abortion Laws: Abortion: A Woman's Civil Right (February 1969), reprinted in Linda Greenhouse and Reva B. Siegel (eds), *Before* Roe v Wade: *Voices that Shaped the Abortion Debate Before the Supreme Court's Ruling* (2010), 38.

[26] Greenhouse and Siegel (n 25), 39.

[27] Ibid 39–40.

Long shrouded in silence, the practice of abortion was now the object of political struggle, and increasingly a site of fundamental rights claims premised on the understanding that the regulation of abortion defined the standing of citizens and the nature and values of the polity. French feminists challenging the criminalization of abortion appealed to the ideals and traditions of the French revolutionary founding.[28] A leaflet spread in Vienna, Austria announced: 'The fight against the law prohibiting abortions is part of the fight for the women's right of self-determination, for their equal rights, in the law, in the public, at the places of work and within the families!'[29]

Growing calls for liberalization of abortion law provoked countermobilization in defense of the status quo. Opponents of abortion reform, often led by lay and clerical leaders of the Catholic Church who mobilized before feminists even entered the debate,[30] tended also to employ a categorical and symbolic style of politics. In the United States, for example, the Catholic Church created a national organization in 1967 designed to block any relaxation of criminal restrictions on abortion;[31] that same year, Church leaders mobilized parishioners against passage of an indications law in New York by invoking a God-given 'right of innocent human beings to life' and equating incremental reform of the law criminalizing abortion with murder and genocide.[32]

In West Germany, conservative Catholic opponents of abortion reform invoked Nazism.[33] As in the United States, conservative Catholics argued that incremental reform of abortion law would put in jeopardy the moral fabric of the nation. In 1970, the Central Committee of German Catholics, an association of Catholic lay persons, objected that 'the respect of human life is not subject to compromise', and warned that 'A state that denies to becoming life the protection of law puts life in general in danger. It thereby puts its own inner legitimacy at stake...'[34] Catholic opponents of decriminalization, like feminist proponents, tied abortion to fundamental questions of human dignity.[35] The Central Committee of German Catholics argued that decriminalizing abortion would violate West German constitutional guarantees of dignity: 'If becoming life is not protected, including with the means of the criminal law, unconditional fundamental principles of a society founded on human dignity are not assured for long.'[36] As the West German Parliament considered liberalizing access, the conference of German Catholic Bishops called for a suit challenging the constitutionality of the abortion reform legislation if enacted,[37] and Robert Spaemann, a Catholic philosopher and public intellectual, observed in 1974 that the proposed abortion liberalization 'would, in the eyes of many

[28] Jean C. Robinson, 'Gendering the Abortion Debate: The French Case' in Stetson (n 19), 86, 88.

[29] Maria Mesner, 'Political Culture and the Abortion Conflict: A Comparison of Austria and the United States' in David F. Good and Ruth Wodak (eds), *From World War to Waldheim: Culture and Politics in Austria and the United States* (1999), 187–209, 196 (citing Maria Mesner, *Frauensache? Zur Auseinandersetzung um den Schwangerschaftsabbruch in Österreich nach 1945* (1994), 207).

[30] Greenhouse and Siegel (n 4), 2048–52 (United States); Anne Egger and Bill Rolston (eds), *Abortion in the New Europe: A Comparative Handbook* (1994), 33, 40 (Britain and Austria).

[31] Greenhouse and Siegel (n 4), 2046–51, 2077–9.

[32] Ibid 2049. See generally Greenhouse and Siegel (n 25), 69–115 (surveying religious and secular arguments against abortion reform in the United States in the decade before *Roe*).

[33] Dagmar Herzog, *Sex After Fascism: Memory and Morality in Twentieth Century Germany* (2005), 225; Lewis Joachim Edinger, *West German Politics* (1986), 281.

[34] Manfried Spieker, *Kirche und Abtreibung in Deutschland: Ursachen und Verlauf eines Konflikts* (2nd edn, 2008), 22 (author's translation).

[35] Siegel, 'Dignity and Sexuality' (n 4), ms at 9, 16, 19–20; Spieker (n 34), 23.

[36] Spieker (n 34), 22–3.

[37] Edinger (n 33), 282.

citizens of our country, violate the legitimacy of the State at its very foundations for the first time since 1949.... With the periodic model our State would, to them, cease to be a Rechtsstaat.'[38]

During the 1970s, these national and transnational debates led to the enactment of legislation in a number of countries that liberalized access to abortion, either on the indications model (doctors given authority to perform abortion upon verification of conditions satisfying a therapeutic, juridical, or social indication) or periodic model (women allowed to obtain abortion during a specified period, often in the first 10 to 12 weeks of pregnancy). But conflict over the new laws spilled out of the legislative arena, and those frustrated in politics increasingly brought their claims to court,[39] where conflict was readily intelligible as a *constitutional* conflict because it had *already* been expressed as an argument about justice and the fundamental character of the polity.

In the 1970s, courts in the United States, France, the Federal Republic of Germany, Austria, and Italy reviewed for the first time the constitutionality of abortion laws.[40] As Machteld Nijsten has observed, 'The European courts had no discretionary power in deciding the issue: In Germany, France and Austria, the courts were seized under the power of abstract review, and as such they served as a political instrument for the defeated opposition in Parliament.'[41] In the United States and Italy courts struck down laws criminalizing abortion, in France and Austria courts upheld laws liberalizing access to abortion, while in the Federal Republic of Germany, the Federal Constitutional Court declared unconstitutional legislation allowing abortion in the early weeks of pregnancy.

II. Foundational Frameworks and their Evolution: United States and Germany

Much attention has been devoted to the 1970s decisions of the US and West German courts because there is such a dramatic difference in their normative frameworks: the US case struck down legislation criminalizing abortion in order to protect decisional autonomy, while the West German case struck down legislation legalizing access to abortion in order to protect

[38] Robert Spaemann, *Kein Recht Auf Leben?: Argumente zur Grundsatzdiskussion um die Reform des §218* (1974), 10 (author's translation). For a history of Catholic Church opposition to reform in the years leading up to the Court's ruling, see Hermann Tallen, *Die Auseinandersetzung über §218 StGB* (1977).

[39] Nijsten (n 3), 232.

[40] In the United States, movements seeking repeal of abortion legislation began litigation in a number of states in a quest to move federal courts to address the constitutionality of restrictions on abortion, ultimately prevailing in January of 1973 in the Supreme Court. *Roe* (n 6). See Siegel (n 19), 1884–94. Over two years (1974–75), four courts in Western Europe issued judgments on the constitutionality of the legal regulation of abortion: *Abortion I* (n 7), Judgment of October 11, 1974, Verfassungsgerichtshof [1974] Erklärungen des Verfassungsgerichtshof 221, translated and reprinted in Mauro Cappelletti and William Cohen, *Comparative Constitutional Law: Cases and Materials* (1979), 615 (Austria); Judgment of January 15, 1975, Conseil constitutionnel, 1975 DS Jur 529, translated and reprinted in Cappelletti and Cohen, ibid 577 (France); Judgment of February 18, 1975, Corte costituzionale [Rac uff corte cost] 201, 98 Foro It I 515, translated and reprinted in Cappelletti and Cohen, ibid 612 (Italy). See Nijsten (n 3), 232. See also Donald P. Kommers, 'Liberty and Community in Constitutional Law: The Abortion Cases in Comparative Perspective' (1985) 3 *Brigham Young University Law Review* 371, 371–2.

[41] Nijsten (n 3), 232. See also n 34 and accompanying text.

unborn life.[42] Each judgment provided a framework to ensure that future abortion legislation would respect constitutional values. Decisions in the 1990s reaffirmed these constitutional frameworks, in the course of moderating them.

Commentators have attributed the difference in constitutional concern animating the 1970s judgments to differences in constitutional or political culture.[43] For example, Gerald Neuman contrasts the US and German legal systems in their willingness to recognize a constitutional duty of protection and to impose affirmative obligations on the state.[44] Donald Kommers points to differences in political culture, asserting that US constitutional law expresses a

> vision of personhood [that] is partial to the city perceived as private realm in which the individual is alone, isolated, and in competition with his fellows, while the [German] vision is partial to the city perceived as a public realm where individual and community are bound together in reciprocity.

Given these differences in political culture, Kommers reasons, the 'authority of the community, as represented by the state, to define the liberty interest of mothers and unborn life finds a more congenial abode in the German than in American constitutional law.'[45]

Practices of comparison may exaggerate intergroup differences and occlude intragroup conflicts. Differences in political culture could well have made the West German judgment more acceptable in West Germany than it would have been in the United States; but polls showed widespread disagreement with the West German Court's decision to strike down the new abortion legislation.[46] Comparative constitutional inquiry can consider how judicial decisions respond to political conflict, and not simply to political culture.[47] In the United States and the Federal Republic of Germany, courts issued constitutional judgments on abortion after protracted debate over whether to liberalize access to abortion—a debate joined in the years immediately preceding the judgments by a mobilizing feminist movement calling for repeal of the criminal law.[48] Close comparative analysis of how this conflict shaped the judgments, or how the judgments aspired to shape this conflict is beyond the scope of this chapter. But a few observations about the relation of the judgments and the conflict suggest that further comparative inquiry of this kind would be fruitful.

[42] See n 1. For an early example, Donald P. Kommers, 'Abortion and the Constitution: United States and West Germany' (1977) 25 *American Journal of Comparative Law* 255, 276–85.

[43] Commentators do not generally look to constitutional text to explain the divergent approaches of the US and German courts; constitutions do not begin expressly to address abortion until after the decisions of the 1970s. See eg Republic of Ireland, Eighth Amendment of the Constitution Act, 1983, 1983 Acts of the Oireachtas, October 7, 1983 (amending Irish Constitution, Art 40.3.3:

> The State acknowledges the right to life of the unborn and, with due regard to the equal right to life of the mother, guarantees in its laws to respect, and, as far as practicable, by its laws to defend and vindicate that right.

[44] See Gerald L. Neuman, 'Casey in the Mirror: Abortion, Abuse, and the Right to Protection in the United States and Germany' (1995) 43 *American Journal of Comparative Law* 273, 274.

[45] Kommers (n 1), 452—3 (describing the United States as a liberal democracy and Germany as a social democracy).

[46] Simone Mantei, *Nein und Ja zur Abtreibung: Die Evangelische Kirche in der Reformdebatte um §218 StGB (1970–1976)* (2004), 448 (author's translation); Edinger (n 33), 283; Siegel, 'Dignity and Sexuality' (n 4), [TAN 56–58].

[47] See eg Levy and Somek (n 2); Nijsten (n 3); Siegel, 'Dignity and Sexuality' (n 4); see also Ferree, Gamson, Gerhards, and Rucht (n 19).

[48] See sources in n 19 (feminist advocates of liberalization); nn 30–38 (opponents of liberalization).

In what follows, I show that in the first round of decisions constitutionalizing abortion, each court responded to feminist claims. And the response of each court changed over time. By the 1990s, the autonomy claims of women came to play a more significant role in the abortion cases of *each* nation. The inquiry illustrates how constitutional judgments about the agency of women citizens are nested within constitutional protections for life, and how these judgments evolved in the late twentieth century.

1. The 1970s

In 1973, the US Supreme Court struck down a nineteenth-century criminal law that banned abortion except to save a woman's life, as well as a twentieth-century law that permitted abortion on the basis of more expansive indications. *Roe v Wade*[49] held that the constitutional right to privacy (a liberty right protected by the Fourteenth Amendment) encompassed a woman's decision in consultation with her physician whether to terminate a pregnancy. At the same time, the Court recognized that the privacy right 'is not absolute...at some point the state interests as to protection of health, medical standards, and prenatal life, become dominant.'[50] To coordinate the right and its regulation, the Court set forth a 'trimester framework' that allowed increasing regulation of women's abortion decision over the course of a pregnancy, permitting restrictions on abortion to protect unborn life only at the point of viability (when a fetus is deemed capable of surviving outside a woman's womb).[51]

Roe responded both to public health and feminist claims. The decision offered an account, unprecedented in constitutional law, of the physical and emotional harms to women that criminal abortion laws inflict, and declared that the law's imposition of these harms on women a matter of constitutional concern: 'The detriment that the State would impose upon the pregnant woman by denying this choice altogether is apparent.'[52] The Court declared these harms constitutionally significant after years of public health reporting and feminist testimony, on the street and in court, about the ways that criminalization of abortion harms women.[53]

Even so, the Court's opinion in *Roe* seems mainly responsive to public health arguments, and at best only indirectly responsive to feminist claims. While the appellant's brief in *Roe* argued that the Texas law banning abortion 'severely impinges [a woman's] dignity, her life plan and often her marital relationship',[54] the *Roe* decision focused much more clearly on the *doctor's* autonomy than on his patients', repeating statements of this kind:

> The decision vindicates the right of the physician to administer medical treatment according to his professional judgment up to the points where important state interests provide compelling justifications for intervention. Up to those points, the abortion decision in all its aspects is inherently, and primarily, a medical decision, and basic responsibility for it must rest with the physician.[55]

As importantly, the Court's account of the harms to women that criminal abortion laws inflict focused on the physical and psychological difficulties of pregnancy that 'a woman and her responsible physician necessarily will consider in consultation'.[56] The Court's account of harms did not speak in the register of citizenship or status about the injury to a woman's dignity in

[49] Greenhouse and Siegel (n 25), 256–8. [50] Ibid 155. [51] Ibid 164–5.

[52] See *Roe* (n 6), 153.

[53] See Section I; Siegel (n 19), 1885–94.

[54] Brief for Appellants, *Roe v Wade* 410 US 113 (1973), (No 70-18) 1971 WL 128054, reprinted in Greenhouse and Siegel (n 25), 230, 234.

[55] *Roe* (n 6), 153. Siegel (n 19), 1897. [56] *Roe* (n 6), 153.

being coerced by government to bear a child and to become a mother.[57] The opinion's discussion of the state's interest in restricting abortion to protect potential life makes no mention of these concerns.[58]

By contrast, the 1975 decision of the German Federal Constitutional Court was much more explicit in its engagement with feminist claims. The West German Court held that a 1974 law, which decriminalized abortion during the first 12 weeks of pregnancy for women provided abortion-dissuasive counseling, violated the Basic Law: 'The life which is developing in the womb of the mother is an independent legal value which enjoys the protection of the Constitution.'[59] The Court reasoned that the duty of the state to protect unborn life was derived from the Basic Law's protection for life and for dignity: 'Where human life exists, human dignity is present to it'.[60]

The Federal Constitutional Court warned the legislature not to 'acquiesce' in popular beliefs about abortion that might have developed in response to 'passionate discussion of the abortion problematic'.[61] The Court expressly and rather brusquely dismissed the Parliament's efforts to devise a framework that respected the dignity of women *and* of the unborn:

> The opinion expressed in the Federal Parliament during the third deliberation on the Statute to Reform the Penal Law, the effect of which is to propose the precedence for a particular time 'of the right to self-determination of the woman which flows from human dignity vis-à-vis all others, including the child's right to life'... is not reconcilable with the value ordering of the Basic Law.[62]

Given the overriding importance of the dignity of human life, the Court concluded, 'the legal order may not make the woman's right to self-determination the sole guideline of its rule-making. The state must proceed, as a matter of principle, from a duty to carry the pregnancy to term.'[63]

Thus, the Federal Constitutional Court engaged with feminist dignity and autonomy arguments for decriminalizing abortion by striking down legislation enacted in response to them as unconstitutional in principle, and, further, by recognizing a constitutional duty to protect life that requires law to enforce the maternal role and responsibilities of women.

Judgments about the maternal role and responsibilities of women are nested throughout the opinion's account of the constitutional duty to protect life. The duty to protect life was 'entrusted by nature in the first place to the protection of the mother. To reawaken and, if required to strengthen the maternal duty to protect, where it is lost, should be the principal goal of the endeavors of the state by the protection of life'; the duty to protect life obliged government to 'strengthen the readiness of the expectant mother to accept the pregnancy as her own responsibility'.[64] Having established that government had a duty to protect life enforceable against pregnant women, the Court distinguished between the 'normal' burdens of motherhood, which the duty to protect life obliged government to exact by law, and extraordinary burdens of motherhood, such as those posing a threat to a woman's life or health, which are non-exactable by law.[65] The Court reasoned that when a pregnant woman faced difficulties

[57] See Siegel (n 19), 1899.

[58] Reva B. Siegel, 'Reasoning From the Body: An Historical Perspective on Abortion Regulation and Questions of Equal Protection' (1992) 44 *Stanford Law Review* 261, 275–7.

[59] *Abortion I* (n 7), 605.

[60] Ibid 641 (citing Arts 2(2)(1) and 1(1)(2)).

[61] Ibid 661. See also ibid 662.

[62] Ibid 643 (citing German Federal Parliament, Seventh Election Period, 96th Sess, Stenographic Reports, 6492).

[63] Ibid 644. [64] Ibid 644. [65] Ibid 647.

other than the 'normal' burdens of motherhood, her 'decision for an interruption of pregnancy can attain the rank of a decision of conscience worthy of consideration', and in these circumstances it would be inappropriate to use criminal law or 'external compulsion where respect for the sphere of personality of the human being demands fuller inner freedom of decision'.[66] By contrast, women who 'decline pregnancy because they are not willing to take on the renunciation and the natural motherly duties bound up with it' may decide 'upon an interruption of pregnancy without having a reason which is worthy of esteem within the value order of the constitution.'[67] The Court recognized a woman's concern about continuing a pregnancy that posed a threat to her life or grave risk to her health as respect-worthy, hence warranting an exemption from legal compulsion. The Court authorized the legislature to permit abortion on the basis of other analogously non-exactable indications.[68]

> Even in these cases the state may not be content merely to examine, and if the occasion arises, to certify that the statutory prerequisites for an abortion free of punishment are present. Rather, the state will also be expected to offer counseling and assistance with the goal of reminding pregnant women of the fundamental duty to respect the right to life of the unborn, to encourage her to continue the pregnancy....[69]

2. The 1990s

In the 1990s, acting under different forms of political pressure, the US and German courts each revisited their judgments of the 1970s, reaffirming and modifying them.[70] Each court continued to reason from its original premises, yet did so in ways that gave far greater recognition to women's autonomy in making decisions about motherhood.

The Supreme Court's 1992 decision in *Planned Parenthood of Southeastern Pennsylvania v Casey*[71] analyzed the constitutionality of a Pennsylvania statute that imposed a 24-hour waiting period before abortions could be performed, required a woman seeking an abortion to receive certain information designed to persuade her to choose childbirth over abortion, required a minor to obtain parental consent, and required a woman seeking an abortion to provide notice to her spouse.[72] The Court reaffirmed what it termed the central principle of *Roe*: 'the woman's right to terminate her pregnancy before viability'.[73] But the *Casey* Court rejected *Roe*'s trimester framework and announced that it would allow government regulation for the purpose of protecting potential life *throughout* the term of a pregnancy, *as long as* the

66 Ibid. 67 Ibid 653.

68 Ibid 624, 647–8. The Court gave the legislature discretion whether to allow abortion on eugenic, rape, and social emergency indications. Ibid.

69 Ibid 649.

70 East Germany allowed abortion during the first 12 weeks of pregnancy as West Germany did not, and so, in the 1990s, the abortion issue became entangled in negotiations over reunification, leading to the enactment of more liberal abortion legislation. See Peter H. Merkl, *German Unification in the European Context* (1993), 176–80.

In the United States, abortion became entangled in the competition of the national political parties for voters. Even before *Roe*, leaders of the Republican Party changed position on abortion to attract Catholics who had historically voted with the Democratic Party, as well as Americans opposed to feminist understandings of the family. By the late 1980s, a majority of Republican voters opposed abortion, and the party had reshaped the composition of the Supreme Court in ways that threatened *Roe*. Greenhouse and Siegel (n 4); Post and Siegel (n 4).

For an account of the changing political context of the 1990s and renewed feminist and Catholic mobilization in Germany and the United States, see Ferree, Gamson, Gerhards, and Rucht (n 19), 39–43.

71 505 US 833 (1992). 72 Ibid 844. 73 Ibid 871.

law did not impose an 'undue burden' on the pregnant woman's decision whether to bear a child. To determine whether regulation imposed an undue burden the Court announced it would ask whether the statute has 'the purpose or effect of placing a substantial obstacle in the path of a woman seeking an abortion of a nonviable fetus.'[74]

Even as the Court revised the *Roe* trimester framework to allow restrictions on abortion throughout pregnancy, it restated the constitutional basis of the abortion right in terms that gave far more recognition to women's decisional autonomy. *Casey*'s 'undue burden' framework allowed government to deter abortion, but only by means that inform, rather than block, a woman's choice about whether to end a pregnancy: 'What is at stake is the woman's right to make the ultimate decision.'[75]

At the same time, *Casey* emphasized, in ways *Roe* did not, that constitutional protections for decisions about abortion vindicate women's dignity, their liberty, and their equality as citizens.[76] The portion of the plurality opinion attributed to Justice Kennedy invoked dignity to explain why the Constitution protects decisions regarding family life: 'These matters, involving the most intimate and personal choices a person may make in a lifetime, choices central to personal dignity and autonomy, are central to the liberty protected by the Fourteenth Amendment.'[77] Protecting women's authority to make their own decisions about motherhood simultaneously vindicates constitutional values of equality as well as liberty. Reaffirming the abortion right, *Casey* locates its constitutional basis in evolving views of women's citizenship that give to women, rather than the state, primary authority in making decisions about their roles:

> Her suffering is too intimate and personal for the State to insist, without more, upon its own vision of the woman's role, however dominant that vision has been in the course of our history and our culture. The destiny of the woman must be shaped to a large extent on her own conception of her spiritual imperatives and her place in society.[78]

In *Casey*, the Court applied the undue burden standard and upheld all of Pennsylvania's regulations, except for the provision requiring a woman to inform her spouse before she could end a pregnancy—which the Court characterized as inconsistent with modern understandings of women as equal citizens.[79]

In striking down the spousal notice provision, the Court again invoked liberty and equality values, explaining how women's standing as citizens had evolved with changing understandings of women's roles:

[74] Ibid 877. [75] Ibid 877.

[76] See Siegel, 'Dignity and the Politics of Protection' (n 4), 1735–66, 1773–80. For an account tracing these arguments from the 1970s to the US Supreme Court's most recent abortion decision, see Siegel (n 19). See also Siegel, 'Dignity and Sexuality' (n 4) (analyzing competing claims about dignity and abortion historically and transnationally). Since *Casey*, scholars in the United States have increasingly discussed the abortion right as grounded in equality as well as liberty. See Reva B. Siegel, 'Sex Equality Arguments for Reproductive Rights: Their Critical Basis and Evolving Constitutional Expression' (2007) 56 *Emory Law Journal* 815.

[77] Ibid 851 (O'Connor, Kennedy, Souter JJ, Joint Opinion).

[78] Ibid 852 (O'Connor, Kennedy, Souter JJ, Joint Opinion); ibid 856 (O'Connor, Kennedy, Souter JJ, Joint Opinion):

> for two decades of economic and social developments, people have organized intimate relationships and made choices that define their views of themselves and their places in society, in reliance on the availability of abortion in the event that contraception should fail. The ability of women to participate equally in the economic and social life of the Nation has been facilitated by their ability to control their reproductive lives.

The opinion ties constitutional protection for women's abortion decision to the understanding, forged in the Court's sex discrimination cases, that government cannot use law to enforce traditional sex roles on women.

[79] *Casey* (n 71), 893–8.

> Only one generation has passed since this Court observed that 'woman is still regarded as the center of home and family life', with attendant 'special responsibilities' that precluded full and independent legal status under the Constitution. These views, of course, are no longer consistent with our understanding of the family, the individual, or the Constitution. . . . A State may not give to a man the kind of dominion over his wife that parents exercise over their children.[80]

Casey protected women's dignity in making the very decisions about motherhood that the Federal Constitutional Court held were governed by natural duty—as, for example when the German Court reasoned that women who 'decline pregnancy because they are not willing to take on the renunciation and the natural motherly duties bound up with it' may decide 'upon an interruption of pregnancy without having a reason which is worthy of esteem within the value order of the constitution.'[81]

In 1990s, the Federal Constitutional Court would reaffirm this understanding, but in a framework that indirectly afforded far greater recognition to women's autonomy in making decisions about motherhood. The reunification of Germany required reconciling the law of East Germany, which allowed women to make their own decisions about abortion in early pregnancy with the law of West Germany, which did not.[82] The German Parliament enacted legislation that allowed women to make their own decisions about abortion in the first 12 weeks of pregnancy after participating in a counseling process designed to persuade them to carry the pregnancy to term—a form of regulation presented as more effective in deterring abortion than a criminal ban and respecting both 'the high value of unborn life and the self-determination of the woman'.[83] The Federal Constitutional Court invalidated the legislation, but shifted ground as it did so.

The Court reaffirmed that protection for the unborn vis-à-vis its mother is only possible if the legislature forbids a woman to terminate her pregnancy.[84] The legislature was obliged to use the criminal law to demarcate obligations exactable of the woman, in order clearly to communicate the scope of the duty to protect—an obligation bearing not only on the pregnant woman herself, but also on others in a position to support her in carrying the pregnancy to term.[85] But the legislature was not obliged to protect unborn life through the threat of criminal sanction itself. The legislature could devise a scheme of counseling to persuade pregnant women to carry to term, and as long as the counseling was effective to that end, could even decide to dispense with the threat of criminal punishment 'in view of the openness necessary for counseling to be effective'.[86] The legislature could base its protection concept

> on the assumption—at least in the early phase of pregnancy—that effective protection of unborn human life is only possible *with* the support of the mother. . . . The secrecy pertaining to the unborn, its helplessness and dependence and its unique link to its mother would appear to justify the view that the state's chances of protecting it are better if it works together with the mother.[87]

The Court presented this new account of the state's duty of protection as in 'conformity with the respect owed to a woman and future mother',[88] observing that the counseling concept endeavors to exact what the pregnant woman owes 'without degrading her to a mere object of protection' and 'respects her as an autonomous person by trying to win her over as an ally in the protection of the unborn'.[89] While the Court presented the decision as requiring legislative

[80] Ibid 896–8 (citation omitted). [81] *Abortion I* (n 7) at 653; see nn 63–8. [82] See n 70.

[83] See 88 BVerfGE 203 (1993), [36]–[37] available at <http://www.bverfg.de/entscheidungen/fs19930528_2bvf000290en.html> (the *Abortion II* case) (official court translation).

[84] Ibid [149]. [85] Ibid [173]–[174]; see also ibid [170]–[172]. [86] Ibid [178].

[87] Ibid [183]. [88] Ibid [185]. [89] Ibid [214].

adherence to its 1975 judgment, the Court's willingness to accept the substitution of counseling for threat of criminal prosecution augured a new view of the citizen-subject that abortion regulation addresses, and a transformed understanding of the constitutional duty to protect unborn life. In this emergent view, women citizens are persons who exercise autonomy even as to the ways they inhabit family roles; that exercise of autonomy is sufficiently respect-worthy that women would be degraded were abortion law to treat them as a mere object or instrument for protecting unborn life.

In the wake of the 1993 decision, abortion remains criminally prohibited except under restricted indications, but a woman who completes counseling can receive a certificate granting her immunity from prosecution for an abortion during the first 12 weeks of pregnancy.[90] In this new framework, Catholic lay groups are involved in counseling, and where necessary, issuing abortion certificates and providing the sex education required by law, although this has been the subject of much and extended controversy.[91]

III. Contemporary Constitutional Frameworks

As we have seen, courts in the United States and Germany imposed different frameworks on the regulation of abortion designed to vindicate competing constitutional values; but within two decades, courts in each nation had reaffirmed and modified those frameworks to give greater recognition to women's agency in the abortion decision, while simultaneously emphasizing the importance of protecting unborn life. The 1990s cases reject the view that constitutionalization of abortion is a 'zero-sum game', and present frameworks that vindicate competing constitutional values, endeavoring to mediate conflicts among them.

Today, we can see constitutionalization of abortion taking several forms. Some jurisdictions require government to respect women's dignity in making decisions about abortion, and consequently require legislators to provide women control, for all or some period of pregnancy, over the decision whether to become a mother. Many jurisdictions require constitutional protection for unborn life, criminalizing abortion while permitting exceptions on an indications basis to protect women's physical or emotional welfare, but not their autonomy. Yet other jurisdictions protect unborn life through counseling regimes that are result-open; these jurisdictions begin by recognizing women's autonomy for the putatively instrumental reason that it is the best method of managing the modern female citizen, and then come to embrace protecting women's dignity as a concurrent constitutional aim of depenalizing abortion.

In what follows, I explore these three forms of constitutionalization, in order of their historical emergence, and briefly illustrate with contemporary examples. The forms are distinguishable along several dimensions. As will become apparent, the frameworks of review that jurisdictions have adopted vary in the *constitutional values* that courts expect abortion legislation to vindicate (eg respecting women's dignity, protecting unborn life, protecting women's welfare), and the *legislative regimes* associated historically and symbolically with the vindication of these constitutional values (eg 'periodic' regimes which allow abortion at a woman's

[90] See German Penal Code (StGB), para 218a; in English available at <http://www.gesetze-im-internet.de/englisch_stgb/englisch_stgb.html#StGB_000P218>.

[91] Mary Anne Case, 'Perfectionism and Fundamentalism in the Application of the German Abortion Laws' in Susan H. Williams (ed), *Constituting Equality: Gender Equality and Comparative Constitutional Law* (2009) 93, 96; Nanette Funk, 'Abortion Counselling and the 1995 German Abortion Law' (1996–97) 12 *Connecticut Journal of International Law* 33.

request for a period of pregnancy; 'indications' regimes which prohibit abortion except on indications determined by a third party; and 'result-open' dissuasive counseling regimes which allow a woman to make the ultimate decision after she is counseled against abortion). Historical and symbolic ties between constitutional values and particular legislative abortion regimes have endowed those regimes with powerful social meaning, even as enforcement of abortion legislation may provide women access in striking variance. Finally, there is variance within these forms in the *judicial constraints* courts impose on representative government (do courts allow, require, or prohibit legislation vindicating particular constitutional values?). In some cases, these differences in judicial constraint seem connected to the values the case law vindicates; but in others they suggest an interesting story about the interaction of courts and representative government in the articulation of constitutional law.

There are other expressions of this evolving relationship between courts and legislatures. Over the decades, constitutions have been amended to address abortion more or less directly, and statutes have been enacted that include constitutionalized preambles, either in response to antecedent constitutional law or in an effort to call into being new bodies of constitutional law. With the growth of legislative constitutionalism in abortion regulation, the boundaries between constitutional law and politics grow ever blurrier.

1. Respecting Women's Dignity: Periodic Legislation

This approach, originating in the United States, constitutionalizes the regulation of abortion with attention to women's autonomy and welfare. It is associated with periodic legislation which coordinates values of decisional autonomy and protecting life by giving women control over the abortion decision, often for an initial period of the pregnancy, thereafter allowing restrictions on abortion except on limited indications (eg for life or health).

This approach begins in court decisions but now also finds expression in constitutionalized preambles. In South Africa, for example, the preamble to a statute allowing abortion on request in the first 12 weeks of pregnancy announces that it vindicates 'the values of human dignity, the achievement of equality, security of the person, non-racialism and non-sexism, and the advancement of human rights and freedoms which underlie a democratic South Africa.'[92] The High Court upheld the legislation's constitutionality in a 2004 decision: 'the Constitution not only permits the Choice on Termination of Pregnancy Act to make a pregnant woman's informed consent the cornerstone of its regulation of the termination of her pregnancy, but indeed requires the Choice Act to do so.'[93]

Legislation recently enacted in Mexico City providing for abortion on request during the first 12 weeks of pregnancy appeals to a constitutional provision that guarantees Mexican citizens the freedom to decide the number and spacing of children;[94] the preamble to the Mexico

[92] South Africa. *The Choice on Termination of Pregnancy Act, 1996* (Act No 92 of 1996).

[93] *Christian Lawyers Association v Minister of Health* [2004] 4 All SA 31 (T), 39. See also ibid 39:

> The South African Constitution recognises and protects the right to termination of pregnancy or abortion in two ways, firstly under section 12(2)(a), that is, the right to bodily and psychological integrity which includes the right to make decisions concerning reproduction, and secondly, under section 12(2)(b), that is, the right to control over one's body.

In an earlier judgment, the law was upheld as constitutional against claims of violation of the right to life on the view that legal personhood commences only at live birth. *Christian Lawyers Association of South Africa & others v Minister of Health & others* 1998 (4) SA 113 (T).

[94] Constitución Política de los Estados Unidos Mexicanos, as amended, Art 4, Diario Oficial de la Federación, February 5, 1917 (Mexico) (Right to Choose Clause) (author's translation).

City statute provides: 'Sexual and reproductive health care is a priority. Services provided in this matter *constitute a means for the exercise of the right of all persons to decide freely, responsibly and in an informed manner on the number and spacing of children*.'[95] The Supreme Court of Mexico recently confirmed the constitutionality of the legislation.[96] The state was constitutionally permitted to decriminalize abortion.

Protecting Life/Protecting Women: Indications Legislation

Other jurisdictions follow the German tradition in constitutionalizing a duty to protect life; these jurisdictions require action in furtherance of the duty to protect, and typically require or authorize legislatures to criminalize abortion with certain exceptions or indications determined by a committee of doctors or some decision-maker other than the pregnant woman. As we have seen, constitutional judgments about women are inevitably nested within the constitutional duty to protect life, and emerge in any effort to specify the terms on which abortion is to be banned (and thus also permitted). Constitutionalization in this form has tended to incorporate gender-conventional, role-based views of women's citizenship—for example that the burdens of pregnancy are naturally assumed by women, or by women who have consented to sex, except when such burdens exceed what is normally to be expected of women, at which point women may be exempt from penal sanction for aborting a pregnancy.[97]

Constitutionalization in this form is paternalist, in its conception of women as well as the unborn, reasoning about women as dependants who may deserve protection, and protecting them against injuries to their physical and emotional welfare, rather than to their autonomy. (Jurisdictions that protect unborn life by banning abortion except on third party indication typically excuse women from the duty to bear a child to protect women's physical survival and to protect women's physical and emotional welfare; only recently have some considered protecting women's dignity.) Courts' reasoning in this tradition typically permit, but do not require, abortion legislation to protect the welfare and autonomy of women citizens who are pregnant; courts may, however, hold that a constitution requires the state to allow abortion to save a woman's life.

The Republic of Ireland, which first amended its Constitution to address abortion, expressly relates the protections it accords the life of the unborn and the life of the mother: 'The State acknowledges the right to life of the unborn and, *with due regard to the equal right to life of the mother*, guarantees in its laws to respect, and, as far as practicable, by its laws to defend and vindicate that right.'[98] Ireland seems to construe a woman's 'equal right to life' as including protection for a woman's physical survival but not her dignity. When an adolescent woman who was pregnant by rape was enjoined from traveling abroad for an abortion, the Irish Supreme Court overturned the injunction, reasoning that the young woman's risk of suicide satisfied the standard of a 'real and substantial risk' to the pregnant woman's life.[99] In other words, in order to fit the case within the right to life that Ireland guarantees equally to women and the

[95] Mexico, Federal District, Decree Reforming the Federal District Penal Code and Amending the Federal District Health Law, Official Gazette of the Federal District No 70, April 26, 2007 (author's translation) (emphasis added).

[96] Acción de inconstitucionalidad 146/2007 y su acumulada 147/2007, Pleno de la Suprema Corte de Justicia de la Nación, Novena Época, August 28, 2008, available at <http://www.informa.scjn.gob.mx/sentencia.html>.

[97] On gender, see further Chapter 19.

[98] Republic of Ireland, Eighth Amendment of the Constitution Act, 1983 (n 43) (emphasis added).

[99] *Attorney General v X and others* [1992] 1 IR 1, para [44].

unborn, the Court had to efface the young women's agency—her refusal to have sex with her rapist and the consequent risk she might harm herself if compelled to bear her rapist's child; instead the Court approached the young woman's case as if it concerned a physiological risk from pregnancy. The Court explained that its Constitution's abortion clause should be interpreted in terms informed by the virtue of charity: 'not the charity which consists of giving to the deserving, for that is justice, but the charity which is also called mercy.'[100]

In 1985 the Spanish Constitutional Court declared that its Constitution protected the life of the unborn, in the tradition of the first West German judgment, yet declared that it was constitutional for the legislature to allow abortion on several indications, including rape. In discussing the justification for the indication for rape, the Spanish Court emphasized that in such a case 'gestation was caused by an act...harming to a maximum degree her [a woman's] personal dignity and the free development of her personality', emphasizing that 'the woman's dignity requires that she cannot be considered as a mere instrument'.[101] Even so, the Court reasoned that the exceptions to Spain's abortion law were constitutionally *permitted*, not required, and emphasized that the legislation was enacted for the purpose of protecting unborn life.[102]

A more recent decision of the Colombian Supreme Court interpreting a constitution understood to protect unborn life offers a striking contrast. The Colombian Court held that a statute banning abortion was constitutionally *required* to contain exceptions for certain indications in light of 'the constitutional importance of the bearer of the rights...the pregnant woman'.[103] '[W]hen the legislature enacts criminal laws, it cannot ignore that a woman is a human being entitled to dignity and that she must be treated as such, as opposed to being treated as a reproductive instrument for the human race.'[104] '[A] criminal law that prohibits abortion in all circumstances *extinguishes the woman's fundamental rights*, and thereby *violates her dignity* by reducing her to a mere receptacle for the fetus, *without rights or interests of constitutional relevance worthy of protection*.'[105]

Thus, the Colombian Court held that the legislature was constitutionally obliged, and not merely permitted, to include indications in its abortion law. The Court explained that failure to allow for abortion in cases of rape would be in 'complete disregard for human dignity and the right to the free development of the pregnant woman *whose pregnancy is not the result of a free and conscious decision*, but the result of arbitrary, criminal acts against her in violation of her autonomy.'[106] 'A woman's right to dignity prohibits her treatment as a mere instrument for reproduction, and her consent is therefore essential to the fundamental, life-changing decision to give birth to another person.'[107] By this same reasoning, however, the legislature *was*

[100] Ibid para 32 (citing *McGee v Attorney General* [1974] IR 284, 318–19).

[101] Tribunal Constitucional, STC 53/1985, Pt 11(b), April 11, 1985, 1985-49 Boletin de Jurisprudencia Constitucional 515 (Spain), available at <http://www.boe.es/aeboe/consultas/bases_datos/doc.php?coleccion=tc&id=SENTENCIA-1985-0053>. Official court translation available at <http://www.tribunalconstitucional.es/es/jurisprudencia/restrad/Paginas/JCC531985en.aspx>.

[102] See eg ibid, Pt 9: 'We are required to consider whether legislation [sic] is *constitutionally permitted* to use a different technique [to protect unborn life], by means of which punishability is specifically excluded for certain offences.' A dissenting judgment objects that the majority employs rights rhetoric without conferring rights 'despite the rhetorical claims to the contrary, it totally ignores the fundamental rights of physical and moral integrity and that of privacy enshrined in the Constitution, and to which pregnant women are indeed entitled.' Ibid, dissenting opinion of Senior Judge Francisco Rubio Llorente (no paragraph numbering in the judgment).

[103] Corte Constitucional (Constitutional Court), May 10, 2006, Sentencia C-355/2006, 25, Gaceta de la Corte Constitucional (Colombia) (partial translation is available in *Women's Link Worldwide, C-355/2006: Excerpts of the Constitutional Court's Ruling that Liberalized Abortion in Colombia* (2007).

[104] Ibid 36. [105] Ibid 50 (emphasis added). [106] Ibid 51 (emphasis added). [107] Ibid 53.

allowed to criminalize abortion in cases of consensual sex, aso long as the legislature provided exceptions for women's life, health, and cases of fetal anomaly.[108] This approach presumes that, for women, consent to sex *is* consent to procreation.

3. Protecting Life/Respecting Women: Result-Open Counseling

Yet other jurisdictions begin from a constitutional duty to protect life, and, like Germany, have begun to explore approaches for vindicating the duty to protect life that do not involve the threat of criminal prosecution. These jurisdictions constitutionally justify depenalization of abortion, coupled with abortion-dissuasive, result-open counseling, as more effective in protecting the unborn than the threat of criminal punishment. The justifications for life-protective counseling, as well as its form, are evolving over time, in ways that progressively incorporate values of women's autonomy. At a minimum, these jurisdictions recognize women as the type of modern citizens who possess autonomy of a kind that law must take into consideration if it hopes to affect their conduct; some go further and are beginning to embrace protecting women's dignity as a concurrent constitutional aim.[109]

Constitutional review of counseling regimes originates in the German cases. In 1975, the German Court endorsed abortion-dissuasive counseling as a mode of protecting life in cases where the legislature deemed abortion non-exactable;[110] in 1993, the German Court expanded that approach, reasoning that a legislature might find counseling coupled with depenalization of abortion generally more effective than the threat of criminal punishment in meeting its duty to protect life, observing that depenalization was *also* consistent with women's autonomy.[111]

The Hungarian Court has amplified the woman-respecting aspects of this approach. In 1998, the Hungarian Court held that it was unconstitutional for the state to make verification of a 'situation of serious crisis' indication depend *solely* on woman's signature: 'Such provisions themselves cannot secure for the foetus the level of minimum protection required by the [Constitution]... and in fact, they do not secure any protection, as the regulation is concerned with the mother's right to self-determination, only.'[112] The Court explicitly rejected this legislative scheme as a concealed version of periodic regulation,[113] while holding that the state could remedy the legislation through directed counseling measures or third party verification. The Court then discussed abortion-dissuasive counseling as a method of protecting unborn life that was *also* respectful of women's rights. 'In principle, such a consulting service would not... violate her freedom of conscience.'[114] While 'The state may not compel anyone to accept a situation which sows discord within, or is irreconcilable with the fundamental convictions which mould that person's identity' obligatory participation in counseling violates neither principle 'having particular regard to the fact that she [the pregnant woman] is only obligated

[108] Ibid 54–7.

[109] For discussion of counseling and its normative bases as a 'third model' in abortion regulation (supplemental to periodic/indication models), see Eser and Koch (n 1); for analysis of the counseling framework attentive to its gendered premises, see Ruth Rubio-Marin, 'Constitutional Framing: Abortion and Symbolism in Constitutional Law' (2009 draft). For discussion of counseling in the United States see Siegel, 'Dignity and the Politics of Protection' (n 4).

[110] See text accompanying n 69.

[111] See text accompanying nn 83, 89.

[112] Alkotmánybíróság (Constitutional Court), Decision 48/1998 (XI.23), Official Gazette (Magyar Közlöny) MK 1998/105 (Hungary), Section III, Pt (3)(d) (p 26), official court translation available at <http://www.mkab.hu/admin/data/file/710_48_1998.pdf>

[113] Ibid Section III, Pt (3)(c) (p 24).

[114] Ibid Section IV, Pt (2)(a) (p 34).

to participate without any [further] obligation . . . [A]s far as *its outcome is concerned, the consultation*—while clearly focusing on the protection of the fetus—*must be open*.'[115]

Portugal has taken further steps in this direction.[116] In upholding legislation that allowed abortion during the first ten weeks of pregnancy after a waiting period and result-open counseling, the Portuguese Constitutional Court emphasized that the new law was an effective means of protecting life. However, a counseling regime the Court upheld was not expressly dissuasive.[117] Strikingly, the recent Portuguese decision employed the reasoning of the 1993 German decision to dispense with the need for expressly dissuasive counseling of the kind mandated by the 1993 German decision. As it did so, the Portuguese decision invoked women's dignity as a justification for result-open counseling.[118] The Portuguese case thus features emergent elements of women's rights, both as to justification and as to legislative form. But the constitutional framework yet remains at some distance from the women's dignity-periodic access cases of jurisdictions such as the United States and South Africa. The Portuguese Court ruled that a result-open counseling framework in the early period of pregnancy is constitutionally *permitted*, not required, as it would be in a traditional woman's rights framework.

The abortion legislation Spain enacted in 2010 presses result-open counseling in ways that even more robustly associate it with protecting women's rights. The legislation allows abortion on request in the first 14 weeks, subject to counseling. Its preamble reasons in constitutional-

[115] Ibid Section IV, Pt 2(a) (p 35) (emphasis added).

[116] For rich discussion, see Rubio-Marin (n 109).

[117] Tribunal Constitucional, Acórdão no 75/2010, Processos nos 733/07 and 1186/07, March 26, 2010, Diário da República vol 60, at 15566 (Portugal), available at <http://w3.tribunalconstitucional.pt/acordaos/acordaos10/1-100/7510.htm> (author's translation).
The Court observed at 11.4.15:

> Our legislature has made clear the goal of the counseling by stating that such counseling is aimed at providing the pregnant woman access to all relevant information necessary to make a free, genuine ('*consciente*'), and responsible decision.

The Court further observed that the legislation directed that the pregnant woman would receive information concerning government assistance should she carry the pregnancy to term, and stated at 11.4.15 that:

> the body of information to be provided to the pregnant woman in a mandatory counseling process . . . has the objective effect of promoting in her the consciousness of the value of the life that she carries in her (or, at least, it will clearly be perceived by her as an attempt to do so) . . . The fact that the counseling process is not, expressly and ostensively, orientational does not impose, ipso facto, its qualification as merely informative and deprived of any intention to favor a decision to carry on with the pregnancy.

[118] See ibid 11.4.16:

> By abstaining, even at a communicational level, from any indication that might be felt by the woman as an external judgment imposing a particular decision, the legislator acted in line with the underlying reasoning supporting the decision not to punish abortion.
>
> This is based on the belief that only the free adhesion of the woman to carry on with the pregnancy guarantees, at this stage, the protection of the unborn life.
>
> . . .
>
> It is objectively founded for a legislator that has decided, also for reasons of efficiency, to trust in the sense of responsibility of the pregnant woman by calling her to cooperate in the duty of protection that belongs to the State, not to create a context of decision that may run counter that purpose.
>
> The trust in the sense of responsibility of the woman and in her predisposition to be open to the reasons contrary to abortion would not be compatible with a tutelage and paternalistic approach. The protection of the woman's dignity is also affirmed by the way in which the counseling process imposed on her takes place.

ized terms about the values the legislation is designed to vindicate, including both 'the rights and interests of women and prenatal life'. The preamble asserts that 'protecting prenatal life is more effective through active policies to support pregnant women and maternity', and therefore that 'protection of the legal right at the very beginning of pregnancy is articulated through the will of the woman, and not against it', and directing public officials to 'establish the conditions for adopting a free and responsible decision'.[119]

In the decades since the German Court's 1993 decision, this hybrid framework has spread, legitimating result-open counseling early in pregnancy as a method of protecting unborn life,[120] while increasingly acknowledging, accommodating, and sometimes even explicitly respecting women's autonomy in making decisions about motherhood.[121] Whether or not the fetal-protective justification for results-open counseling is accompanied by a women's dignity-respecting justification, women are accorded the final word in decisions about whether they become mothers. Drawing elements from two disparate forms of constitutionalization, this hybrid form has transformative potential: one day it might combine community obligation to support those who nurture life with community obligation to respect their judgments. Realization of this potential depends on both expressive and practical aspects of implementation.

The emergence in the last two decades of fetal-protective justifications for providing women control over decisions concerning abortion is especially striking in light of the concurrent spread of woman-protective justifications for denying women access to abortion (eg banning or restricting abortion for the asserted purpose of protecting women from harm or coercion).[122] In both cases, a particular legislative regime is justified by appeal to constitutional values historically associated with an opposing form of abortion regulation: legislation that allows abortion is associated with the constitutional protection of unborn life, and legislation that restricts abortion is associated with the constitutional protection of women. Rhetorical inversions of this kind may be produced through social movement struggle, or they may emerge as movements employ the discourse of a reigning constitutional order in order to challenge it.[123]

After decades of conflict, a constitutional framework is emerging in Europe that allows legislators to vindicate the duty to protect unborn life by providing women dissuasive counseling and the ability to make their own decisions about abortion. Constitutionalization in this form values women as mothers first, yet addresses women as the kind of citizens who are autonomous in making decisions about motherhood, and may even warrant respect as such. The spread of constitutionalization in this form attests to passionate conflict over abortion and women's family roles; it also suggests increasing acceptance of claims the women's movement has advanced in the last 40 years, however controverted they remain. Jurisdictions that permit result-open counseling in satisfaction of the duty to protect unborn life express evolving understandings of women as citizens, in terms that reflect community ambivalence and assuage community division, while continuing to engender change.

[119] Ley Orgánica 2/2010, de 3 de marzo, de salud sexual y reproductiva y de la interrupción voluntaria del embarazo (Spain) (author's translation).

[120] See Eser and Koch (n 1); Gevers (n 2).

[121] See Rubio-Marin (n 109).

[122] See Siegel, 'Dignity and the Politics of Protection' (n 4).

[123] See eg Myra Max Ferree, 'Resonance and Radicalism: Feminist Framing in the Abortion Debates of the United States and Germany' (2003) 109 *American Journal of Sociology* 304; Siegel, 'Dignity and the Politics of Protection' (n 4). For similar reasons, appeals to dignity now play a significant role on both sides of the abortion debate, transnationally. See Siegel, 'Dignity and Sexuality' (n 4).

Bibliography

Albin Eser and Hans-Georg Koch, *Abortion and the Law: From International Comparison to Legal Policy* (2005)

Myra Marx Ferree, William Anthony Gamson, Jürgen Gerhards, and Dieter Rucht, *Shaping Abortion Discourse: Democracy and the Public Sphere in Germany and the United States* (2002)

Mary Ann Glendon, *Abortion and Divorce in Western Law* (1987)

Linda Greenhouse and Reva B. Siegel, 'Before (and After) *Roe v Wade*: New Questions About Backlash' (2011) 120 Yale Law Journal 2028

Linda Greenhouse and Reva B. Siegel (eds), *Before Roe v Wade: Voices that Shaped the Abortion Debate Before the Supreme Court's Ruling* (2010)

Donald P. Kommers, 'Autonomy, Dignity and Abortion' in Tom Ginsburg and Rosalind Dixon (eds), *Comparative Constitutional Law* (2011)

Richard E. Levy and Alexander Somek, 'Paradoxical Parallels in the American and German Abortion Decisions' (2001) 9 *Tulane Journal of International and Comparative Law* 109

Gerald L. Neuman, 'Casey in the Mirror: Abortion, Abuse, and the Right to Protection in the United States and Germany' (1995) 43 *American Journal of Comparative Law* 273

Machteld Nijsten, *Abortion and Constitutional Law: A Comparative European-American Study* (1990)

Kim Lane Scheppele, 'Constitutionalizing Abortion' in Marianne Githens and Dorothy McBride Stetson (eds), *Abortion Politics: Public Policy in Cross-Cultural Perspective* (1996)

Reva B. Siegel, 'Dignity and Sexuality: Claims on Dignity in Transnational Debates over Abortion and Same-Sex Marriage' (2011) 9 *International Journal of Constitutional Law* (forthcoming)

Dorothy McBride Stetson (ed), *Abortion Politics, Women's Movements, and the Democratic State: A Comparative Study of State Feminism* (2003)

CHAPTER 52

IMMODEST CLAIMS AND MODEST CONTRIBUTIONS: SEXUAL ORIENTATION IN COMPARATIVE CONSTITUTIONAL LAW

KENJI YOSHINO
AND MICHAEL KAVEY

New York

I. Introduction

In a foundational 1999 essay, Professor Mark Tushnet outlined three frameworks through which to consider the contributions of comparative constitutional law: functionalism, expressivism, and bricolage.[1] According to Tushnet, 'Functionalism claims that particular constitutional provisions create arrangements that serve particular functions in a system of governance.'[2] Expressivism, in contrast, looks more to the symbolic, rather than to the instrumental, aspects of constitutions: 'According to the expressivist view, constitutions help constitute the nation, to varying degrees in different nations, offering to each nation's people a way of understanding themselves as political beings.'[3] Finally, bricolage, a term borrowed from Claude Lévi-Strauss, takes up constitutional analogs from other nations without much

[1] Mark Tushnet, 'The Possibilities of Comparative Constitutional Law' (1999) 108 *Yale Law Journal* 1225ff.

[2] Ibid 1228. [3] Ibid.

concern about justifying their selection or deployment.[4] Tushnet does not claim that these perspectives are exhaustive. His taxonomy nonetheless provides a useful starting point to consider how comparative constitutionalism might illuminate rights relating to sexual orientation.

Tushnet does not indulge in hyperbole about the contributions of comparative constitutional law. As he acknowledges, his 'claim is, in the end, rather modest: U.S. courts can sometimes gain insights into the appropriate interpretation of the U.S. Constitution by a cautious and careful analysis of constitutional experience elsewhere.'[5] We share this assessment. Nevertheless, we contend that the modest contributions of comparative law acquire enhanced force when the claims made by constitutional interpreters are themselves immodest. In the context of sexual orientation, constitutional arguments often assume a categorical, 'always/everywhere' tenor that exposes them to contestation on comparative grounds. We develop this claim by focusing on three issues: bans on lesbian, gay, and bisexual (LGB) individuals[6] from military service, the criminalization of same-sex sexual conduct, and relationship recognition for same-sex couples. We follow Tushnet in using US constitutional law as our primary point of departure, solely because we are most familiar with it.

We diverge from Tushnet's taxonomy in some respects. Tushnet describes functionalism as a means to examine how different constitutional provisions and arrangements serve similar functions in different legal systems. Through this inquiry, he suggests, it may be 'possible to consider whether the U.S. constitutional system could use a mechanism developed elsewhere to perform a specific function, to improve the way in which that function is performed here.'[7] Expanding the perspective slightly, we examine here how particular rules within legal and constitutional institutions (such as bans on open service by LGB people in the military or bans on same-sex marriage) have been justified in constitutional law by reference to the functions that those norms purportedly serve (such as national security or procreation). Put differently, we examine not only constitutional institutions, but also constitutional justifications.

We also depart from Tushnet's taxonomy in taking bricolage out of the conversation. Bricolage accurately describes how comparative constitutional law often works. However, we are not persuaded, as yet, that this framework has an independent normative justification. As Tushnet acknowledges, it has a random, ad hoc quality. We therefore focus on the functionalist and expressivist modalities of comparative constitutional interpretation. We believe that bans on gays from military service provide a particularly sharp instance of the functionalist modality, while bans on sodomy provide an equally sharp instance of the expressivist modality. In contrast, we believe that the relationship recognition cases demonstrate a confluence of functionalism and expressivism.

II. Military Service: Functionalism Ascendant

In the military context, a common legal problem across jurisdictions is how to balance the rights of gay servicemembers against the governmental interest in national security. Several courts have filtered this perceived conflict through constitutional or quasi-constitutional

[4] Ibid 1229 (citing Claude Lévi-Strauss, *The Savage Mind* ([1962] 1966), 16–17).

[5] Ibid 1228.

[6] We confine our analysis to lesbians, gay men, and bisexuals, rather than extending it to include transgender individuals. The challenges facing transgender individuals, while crucial, are too complex and distinct to be covered in an intervention of this length. For the sake of simplicity, moreover, we use the word 'gay', in addition to the term LGB, to refer to lesbians, gay men, and bisexuals. On gender in the Constitution, see Chapter 19.

[7] Tushnet (n 1), 1228.

frameworks; in doing so, they have made or met two interlocking 'immodest' claims. The first insists that courts should grant so much deference to decisions by the political branches regarding military affairs as to render those decisions effectively non-justiciable. The second asserts that courts should defer to the specific legislative or executive assessment that openly gay servicemembers significantly disrupt unit cohesion. Comparative analysis suggests both claims are unjustified.

The United States only recently lifted its so-called 'don't ask, don't tell' policy, which had barred openly LGB individuals from service in the US military.[8] In late 2010, Congress enacted a bill permitting the executive branch to end the policy; in July 2011, the executive branch completed a Congressionally mandated certification process, which triggered the policy's repeal on September 20, 2011.[9] While the US policy's demise thus came about principally through legislative and executive action,[10] we feel our (admittedly juriscentric) intervention on comparative constitutional law should focus on how *courts* responded to the multiple lawsuits challenging the policy's constitutionality during the nearly two decades in which it was enforced.[11] We contrast how federal appellate courts in the United States rejected constitutional challenges to 'don't, ask, don't tell' with how the European Court of Human Rights ruled in favor of military personnel challenging a similar ban in the United Kingdom.

[8] Don't Ask, Don't Tell Repeal Act of 2010, Pub L 111-321, December 22, 2010, authorizing repeal of 10 USC §654.

[9] US Department of Defense, 'Repeal of "Don't Ask, Don't Tell" (DADT): Quick Reference Guide', October 28, 2011, available at <http://www.defense.gov/home/features/2010/0610_dadt/Quick_Reference_Guide_Repeal_of_DADT_APPROVED.pdf>; see also n 10 (discussing events leading to repeal).

[10] This is not to say that litigation was irrelevant to the repeal process. While the impact of judicial rulings is difficult to assess, recent rulings may have increased pressure on the political branches to jettison the ban. In early October 2010, for instance—less than three months before Congress enacted the repeal bill—a federal district court held that 'don't ask, don't tell' was unconstitutional. See *Log Cabin Republicans v United States* 716 F Supp 2d 884, 888 (CD Cal 2010). The Ninth Circuit Court of Appeals issued a stay of the lower court's ruling on October 20, 2010. *See Log Cabin Republicans v United States* 2010 WL 4136210 (9th Cir October 20, 2010) (No 10-56634). Much of the debate over repeal took place in the shadow of this litigation; indeed, the Secretary of Defense alluded to the litigation in late November when he urged Congress to move forward with its repeal legislation. See Liz Halloran, 'Gates To Senate: End "Don't Ask" Before Courts Do', *NPR*, November 30, 2010, available at <www.npr.org/2010/11/30/131697322/pentagon-study-dismisses-risk-of-openly-gay-troops>. In July 2011, many months after Congress approved the repeal bill—but before the executive's certification process was complete—the Ninth Circuit lifted its earlier stay, and then, a week later, re-issued the stay in part. See *Log Cabin Republicans v United States* 2011 WL 2982102 (9th Cir July 15, 2011) (No 10-56634). One week after this confusing set of orders, the executive branch certified the repeal. See also International Commission of Jurists, *Sexual Orientation, Gender Identity and Justice: A Comparative Law Casebook* (2011), 123, available at <http://www.icj.org/dwn/database/Sexual%20Orientation,%20Gender%20Identity%20and%20Justice-%20A%20Comparative%20Law%20Casebook[1].pdf> (observing, with references to Australia, Canada, and the United States, that 'The impetus for legislative reform [of anti-gay military policies] has often originated in judicial or quasi-judicial processes'); US Department of Defense, 'Report of the Comprehensive Review of the Issues Associated with a Repeal of "Don't Ask, Don't Tell"', 2010, 90 (noting that 'In Germany and Australia, national defense leaders changed their [anti-gay military] policies to head off adverse outcome[s] in pending court challenges' (footnote omitted)).

[11] Prior to Congress's 1993 enactment of the 'don't ask, don't tell' statute, openly LGB individuals were barred from military service under a Department of Defense directive declaring homosexuality to be 'incompatible with military service'. See US Department of Defense, 'Report of the Comprehensive Review' (n 10), 20–1 (summarizing legal prohibitions on military service by openly LGB individuals prior to the enactment of 'don't ask, don't tell'). Courts rejected challenges to these earlier prohibitions as well. See eg *Steffan v Perry* 41 F3d 677 (DC Cir 1994).

Federal appellate courts in the United States that directly addressed the constitutionality of 'don't ask, don't tell' all upheld the policy.[12] In doing so, they adhered to both extreme claims described above. First, they relied heavily on the Supreme Court's statement in the 1981 *Rostker v Goldberg* case that 'judicial deference... is at its apogee when legislative action under the Congressional authority to raise and support armies and make rules and regulations for their governance is challenged.'[13] Courts also urged deference to the specific Congressional finding embodied in the legislation:

> The presence in the armed forces of persons who demonstrate a propensity or intent to engage in homosexual acts would create an unacceptable risk to the high standards of morale, good order and discipline, and unit cohesion that are the essence of military capability.[14]

The first claim is 'immodest' because it effectively forecloses judicial review over core military functions. While the *Rostker* Court stated that 'deference' did not mean 'abdication',[15] courts' extreme degree of deference makes the distinction elusive.[16] Civil rights claims that would almost certainly have succeeded outside the military context have received comparatively short shrift within it, as *Rostker*, which upheld a facial sex-based distinction, itself demonstrates.[17]

One danger of such extreme deference is that it leads courts to credit immodest claims made by the government to defend the policy. The Second Circuit Court of Appeals, for instance, relied heavily on a deference rationale in refusing even to consider a trial court's conclusion that the government's defense of 'don't ask, don't tell'—and the Congressional findings supporting that defense—were irrationally and impermissibly rooted in anti-gay animus.[18] The trial court had found 'overwhelming evidence' in the record that the government's 'unit cohesion' argument, for example, was merely a 'euphemism for catering to the prejudices of heterosexuals'.[19] The trial court had also observed that even assuming this prejudice could form a legitimate basis for public policy, no concrete or credible evidence supported the government's assertion that 'don't ask, don't tell' would protect or enhance the government's asserted interests.[20]

Reversing the trial court's judgment, the Second Circuit declined to engage in these inquiries. After expounding at length on the need for judicial deference to military-related Congressional findings, the court credited the government's defense of 'don't ask, don't tell'

[12] See eg *Able v United States* 155 F3d 628 (2d Cir 1998); *Thomasson v Perry* 80 F3d 915 (4th Cir 1996). Servicemembers challenging anti-gay discrimination in the military won at least two victories before the Ninth Circuit Court of Appeals, but those decisions did not invalidate the military's anti-gay policies as a general matter. See eg *Witt v Dep't of Air Force* 527 F3d 806 (9th Cir 2008); *Watkins v United States Army* 875 F2d 699 (9th Cir 1989).

[13] 453 US 57, 70 (1981).

[14] 10 USC §654.

[15] *Rostker* 453 US at 70.

[16] See eg *Cook v Gates* 528 F3d 42, 60 (1st Cir 2008) (rejecting a constitutional challenge to 'don't ask, don't tell', and explaining that 'where Congress has articulated a substantial government interest for a law, and where the challenges in question implicate that interest, judicial intrusion is simply not warranted').

[17] See 453 US at 83; see also *Goldman v Weinberger* 475 US 503 (1986) (upholding Air Force regulation that prohibited a rabbi from wearing his yarmulke). The Supreme Court's deference to the military is not categorical. *See Frontiero v Richardson* 411 US 677 (1973) (striking down a facial sex-based distinction in a military benefits scheme). However, the Court did not raise the issue of 'military deference' in *Frontiero*, perhaps because the benefits scheme at issue did not relate to a core military function.

[18] See *Able* 155 F3d 628.

[19] *Able v United States* 968 F Supp 850, 858 (EDNY 1997).

[20] See eg ibid 859.

without addressing the merits of the lower court's analysis. While the appellate court repeatedly noted the existence of Congressional testimony in support of the military's policy—and briefly quoted the statements of two witnesses—it failed to evaluate the testimony's content or quality.[21]

A closer look would have revealed that the testimony in support of the policy was vague and unsupported. For instance, the court cited General H. Norman Schwarzkopf, who testified: 'I have experienced the fact that the introduction of an open homosexual into a small unit immediately polarizes that unit and destroys the very bonding that is so important for the unit's survival in time of war.'[22] He further asserted that 'in every case I am familiar with, and there are many, whenever it became known in a unit that someone was openly homosexual, polarization occurred, violence sometimes followed, morale broke down, and unit effectiveness suffered.'[23] General Schwarzkopf provided no specifics that would have permitted verification of his claims that 'immediate' polarization occurred upon the introduction of an open homosexual or that effectiveness suffered in 'every case with which [he was] familiar'—sometimes with 'violence'. Given that he emphasized the existence of 'many' such cases, it should not have been difficult to name at least one. Despite these shortcomings, the Second Circuit and two other federal courts quoted and relied on his statements in upholding the ban on openly gay servicemembers.[24]

To see how a comparative perspective might chasten extreme claims regarding military deference and the purported harms of allowing openly LGB people to serve, consider the 1999 case of *Lustig-Prean and Beckett v United Kingdom*.[25] In this case, the European Court of Human Rights held that the United Kingdom had violated servicemembers' 'right to respect for ... private ... life'[26] under the European Convention on Human Rights by discharging them pursuant to a blanket ban on gays in the military.[27] Several servicemembers with exemplary records brought suit. The government responded with versions of the two 'immodest' claims. According to the Court, the government first contended that 'given the national security dimension to the present case a wide margin of appreciation was properly open to the State'.[28] The government's proposed standard diverged substantially from the Court's normal practice in cases involving significant intrusions into private life, where states were typically afforded only a 'narrow margin of appreciation'.[29] The government then claimed

> that the presence of known or strongly suspected homosexuals in the armed forces would produce certain behavioural and emotional responses and problems which would affect morale and, in turn, significantly and negatively affect the fighting power of the armed forces.[30]

The Court rejected both claims. Regarding military deference, the Court acknowledged that 'When the core of the national security aim pursued is the operational effectiveness of the

[21] See *Able* 155 F3d at 635–6. [22] S Rep No 103-112, at 280. [23] Ibid.

[24] See eg *Able* 155 F3d at 635; *Thomasson* 80 F3d at 929; *Cook v Rumsfeld* 429 F Supp 2d 385, 402 n 25 (D Mass 2006), affirmed sub nom *Cook v Gates* 528 F3d 42 (1st Cir 2008).

[25] *Lustig-Prean and Beckett v United Kingdom* (1999) 29 EHRR 548.

[26] Convention for the Protection of Human Rights and Fundamental Freedoms, ETS No 5, entered into force September 3, 1953, Art 8.

[27] See also *Smith and Grady v United Kingdom* (1999) 29 EHRR 548. The *Smith* judgment, which similarly addressed the United Kingdom's ban on gays in the military, was issued on the same day as *Lustig-Prean*. The Court reached the same conclusion in both *Lustig-Prean* and *Smith* regarding gay servicemembers' right to respect for their private lives.

[28] *Lustig-Prean*, para 70. [29] Ibid. [30] Ibid para 47.

armed forces, it is accepted that each State is competent to organise its own system of military discipline and enjoys a certain margin of appreciation in this respect.'[31] However, it did not translate this deference into the extreme claim that the military was effectively immune from judicial review. To the contrary, the Court observed that 'the national authorities cannot rely on such rules to frustrate the exercise by individual members of the armed forces of their right to respect for their private lives, which right applies to service personnel as it does to others within the jurisdiction of the State.'[32] For the European Court of Human Rights, deference required actual rather than theoretical review.

Moreover, the Court rejected the claim that allowing openly gay servicemembers would lead to the decline of unit cohesion. At first glance, the government's position appeared to be well supported. The UK Ministry of Defence had established a Homosexuality Policy Assessment Team (HPAT), which published a report in 1996 that ran to approximately 240 pages. The report focused 'upon the anticipated effects [open service by gays would have] on fighting power'.[33] However, despite its length, the report provided no concrete evidence that open service by gay servicemembers would cause disruption. To the contrary, the HPAT report seemed to locate the problem not in the openly gay servicemembers but in their anti-gay colleagues. As the Court observed, the attitudes of servicemembers documented by the HPAT report 'ranged from stereotypical expressions of hostility ... to vague expressions of unease about the presence of homosexual colleagues.'[34] The Court held that such 'negative attitudes, cannot, of themselves, be considered by the Court to [justify] interferences with the applicants' rights ... any more than similar negative attitudes towards those of a different race, origin or colour.'[35] So while the government claimed its policy rested on evidence rather than animus, its evidence was an anthology of animus. The Court noted that the HPAT report 'did not, whatever its value, provide evidence of such damage in the event of the policy changing'.[36] After this ruling, the UK military permitted gay individuals to serve openly. By the government's own account, the changes were implemented without disruption.[37] By 2004, the Royal Air Force was actively recruiting gays and lesbians.[38]

Functionalism invites comparisons that undermine extreme instrumental claims, which tend to be empirical. Broadly, the US appellate cases on 'military deference' suggested that the sky would fall if courts meddled with decisions by the political branches pertaining to the military. This was, and remains, a testable claim—either military deference will undermine military readiness or it will not. The European Court of Human Rights decision in *Lustig-Prean*, and the United Kingdom's compliance with it, have shown that at least the British portion of the sky has not fallen. The decision and its aftermath have demonstrated that individual

[31] Ibid para 82.
[32] Ibid.
[33] Ibid para 47.
[34] Ibid para 90.
[35] Ibid.
[36] Ibid para 92.
[37] A Ministry of Defence Review, leaked to the press in 2000, reported 'widespread acceptance of the new policy', noting that 'The change in policy has been hailed as a solid achievement'. Ben Summerskill, 'It's Official: Gays Do Not Harm Forces', *The Observer*, November 19, 2000, 5; cf Suzanne B. Goldberg, 'Open Service and Our Allies: A Report on the Inclusion of Openly Gay and Lesbian Servicemembers in US Allies' Armed Forces' (2011) 17 *William and Mary Journal of Women and Law* 547, 556–7, 564–5, 568, 572–3, 579–82, 584–5.
[38] See Matthew Hickey, 'RAF in drive to recruit more gays', *Daily Mail*, August 27, 2004, 27.

rights relating to sexual orientation can be protected in the military in a manner that differs only in degree from how such rights are protected in civilian life. More specifically, the US appellate court cases on 'don't ask, don't tell' rested on the predicate that openly gay servicemembers would lead to the destruction of unit cohesion. Again, *Lustig-Prean* and the United Kingdom's resulting policy change have suggested that this position lacks support. While it is still too early to draw definitive conclusions on the effect of allowing openly LGB people to serve in the US military, preliminary reports indicate that unit cohesion has not suffered, much less been 'destroyed', in the months since the repeal of 'don't ask, don't tell'; on the contrary, senior military officers have increasingly expressed confidence that the repeal has not and will not cause any meaningful disruption.[39]

Some supporters of 'don't ask, don't tell' have insisted, both before and after the policy's repeal, that the US experience is somehow so exceptional that the experience of other jurisdictions is irrelevant. Yet this, too, is an extreme claim. Many other military forces had already integrated on the basis of sexual orientation by the time the US repealed its ban. More to the point, US forces had already worked alongside those other integrated forces—including British forces—in joint missions.[40] The British government in *Lustig-Prean* strove mightily to contend that the smooth integration that had occurred in other military forces was irrelevant, in part because that integration had been 'relatively recent'. The Court rejected that claim, observing that 'European countries operating a blanket legal ban on homosexuals in their armed forces are now in small minority', and further noting that 'even if relatively recent, the Court cannot overlook the widespread and consistently developing views and associated legal

[39] Recent statements from the top officer of the US Marine Corps, Commandant General James Amos, provide a striking example of how views on this issue are changing now that the repeal has taken place. General Amos, previously a staunch supporter of 'don't, ask, don't tell', made headlines in December 2010 when he suggested that the presence of openly gay troops on the battlefield would create a 'distraction' that could 'cost Marines lives'. Gordon Lubold, 'Marine chief: Repeal could cost lives', Politico, December 14, 2010, available at <http://www.politico.com/news/stories/1210/46390.html>. By late November 2011, two months after the repeal took effect, Amos was offering a different assessment: in an interview with the Associated Press, he called the repeal 'a non-event', stated that he was 'very pleased with how it has gone', and noted that he had seen no signs of disruption. Robert Burns, 'Gay ban's repeal was a "a non-event," Amos says', Associated Press, November 28, 2011; see also ibid (describing a statement by a Defense Department spokeswoman that 'implementation of the repeal of the gay ban is proceeding smoothly across the military'); Carol Ross Joynt, 'Looking Back: The Anniversary of the Repeal of "Don't Ask, Don't Tell"', December 21, 2011, available at <http://www.washingtonian.com/blogarticles/22002.html> (quoting a statement from the chairman of the Senate's Armed Services Committee that 'We routinely ask military leaders whether they are experiencing any problems with the repeal, and so far they have not identified any incidents related to the repeal').

[40] The US Department of Defense reported in 2010 that its Working Group found that 35 of the United States' partner nations in the North Atlantic Treaty Organization (NATO) and the International Security Assistance Force (ISAF) allow gays and lesbians to serve openly in the military. US Department of Defense, 'Report of the Comprehensive Review' (n 10), 89. At the time of the Report, only six nations in NATO and ISAF prohibited gays from serving openly (Bulgaria, Jordan, Poland, Turkey, United Arab Emirates, and the United States); the policies of two other nations (Republic of Macedonia, Singapore) were undetermined. Ibid. The Report accepted that a comparison between the US and foreign militaries, while 'far from perfect', was nevertheless 'relevant to [the] assessment' of how openly LGB servicemembers would affect the US military. Ibid. The research supporting the Report had focused in particular on Canada, the United Kingdom, and Australia, because those three countries, the Report explained, 'are in many ways culturally similar to the United States, and their militaries are, like the U.S. military, all-volunteer forces and of similar size proportionate to their national populations. These nations also work closely with U.S. forces in international operations'. Ibid 90.

changes to the domestic laws of Contracting States.'[41] Now that more than a decade has passed, the 'relatively recent' defense has become even less tenable. It also bears note that the British government observed that countries which had 'no legal ban on homosexuals were more tolerant, had written constitutions and therefore a greater tradition of respect for civil rights'.[42] From a US perspective, this is a rather ironic distinction, as it suggests that countries like the United States with written constitutions should be more, not less, likely to integrate successfully.

III. Sodomy Cases: Expressivism Ascendant

The sodomy context appears more conducive to analysis through an expressivist lens rather than through a functionalist one. In the cases we examined, the governmental rationale for criminalizing consensual sodomy tended not to rest on some instrumental purpose, such as encouraging procreative sexual conduct. Rather, the state's justification was some version of 'morality'. These constitutional claims about morality can be viewed as 'expressivist' because, in Tushnet's terms, they 'offer to each nation's people a way of understanding themselves as a polity'.[43]

The expressivist claims can be immodest in two different directions, which we call universal-expressivist and parochial-expressivist. Universal-expressivist claims contend that the polity's constitutional norms conform to values which, if not ubiquitous, are at least transnational. Parochial-expressivist claims, in contrast, contend that only a nation's own mores should count in its constitutional jurisprudence.

Prominent examples of universal-expressivist claims in US constitutional law can be seen in Justice White's majority opinion and Chief Justice Warren Burger's concurring opinion in *Bowers v Hardwick*. *Bowers* was the 1986 Supreme Court case that rejected a constitutional privacy challenge to a sodomy statute.[44] Elaborating on historical claims made by Justice White's majority opinion, Chief Justice Burger claimed that private homosexual conduct had been subjected to state intervention 'throughout the history of Western civilization', and that the 'condemnation of those practices is firmly rooted in Judeo-Christian moral and ethical standards'.[45] His opinion quoted, with apparent approval, Blackstone's characterization of homosexual sex as an offense of 'deeper malignity' than rape.[46] To protect this conduct within the ambit of fundamental rights jurisprudence, he argued, 'would be to cast aside millennia of moral teaching'.[47]

In overruling *Bowers* 17 years later, the landmark case of *Lawrence v Texas* challenged many of Justice White's and Chief Justice Burger's unqualified claims.[48] Writing for the Court, Justice Kennedy observed that 'The sweeping references by Chief Justice Burger to the history of Western civilization and to Judeo-Christian moral and ethical standards did not take account of other authorities pointing in an opposite direction.'[49] The *Lawrence*

[41] *Lustig-Prean* (n 25), para 97.
[42] Ibid para 51.
[43] Tushnet (n 1), 1228.
[44] *Bowers v Hardwick* 478 US 186, 194 (1986), overruled by *Lawrence v Texas* 539 US 558 (2003).
[45] *Bowers* 478 US at 196 (Burger CJ concurring).
[46] Ibid 197 (quoting 4 W. Blackstone, *Commentaries* *215).
[47] Ibid.
[48] *Lawrence v Texas* 539 US 558 (2003).
[49] Ibid 572.

Court made special note of the ruling by the European Court of Human Rights in *Dudgeon v United Kingdom*,[50] which held that a Northern Ireland law criminalizing homosexual sodomy violated the European Convention's 'private...life' provision. Justice Kennedy noted that this ruling, rendered 'almost five years before *Bowers* was decided', contradicted 'the premise in *Bowers* that the claim put forward was insubstantial in our Western civilization'.[51]

Justice Kennedy's use of comparative law drew intense criticism. Yet Kennedy's opinion was simply responding to a comparative claim made in the opposite direction. Justice White's majority opinion and Chief Justice Burger's concurrence in *Bowers* 'opened the door' to such analysis by making reckless claims about the uniformity with which homosexuality had been condemned in the Western tradition.

Justice Scalia's impassioned dissent in *Lawrence* avoided the force of this argument by maintaining that the use of comparative law by either side was illegitimate. He claimed that the *Bowers* majority did not in fact rely on international and comparative sources. To the contrary, Justice Scalia stated that *Bowers* had 'rejected the claimed right to sodomy on the ground that such a right was not "deeply rooted in *this Nation's* history and tradition"'.[52] Justice Scalia characterized the *Lawrence* majority's 'discussion of these foreign views' as 'meaningless dicta'.[53] At the same time, he found it to be 'Dangerous dicta...since "this Court...should not impose foreign moods, fads or fashions on Americans".'[54]

Justice Scalia misapprehended the *Bowers* majority. Justice White's opinion clearly included foreign and international sources in his allusion to 'this Nation's history and tradition'. White's historical discussion began with the claim that prohibitions on homosexual sodomy 'have ancient roots', citing a law review article.[55] The cited page of the law review article reads as follows:

> Current state laws prohibiting homosexual intercourse are ancient in origin. The earliest legal argument for outlawing homosexuality can be found in Plato's *Laws*. Plato believed that homosexuality had to be forbidden because it undermined the important Greek values of masculinity and procreation. While accepting Plato's reasoning, Judeo-Christian opposition to homosexuality derives from the legendary account in Genesis of the fire and brimstone destruction of Sodom and Gomorrah. The word sodomy is derived from Sodom. The Mosaic Law sets forth an absolute prohibition against homosexuality: 'Thou shalt not lie with mankind as with woman kind; it is abomination.'[56]

Thus while Justice White's reliance on the 'Judeo-Christian tradition' and 'millennia of moral teaching' was less obvious than Chief Justice Burger's, it was nonetheless present in his conception of 'the Nation's history and traditions'.

However utopian it may be, it is worth exploring Justice Scalia's parochial-expressivist claim, which rests not on a universal conception of morality, but on an isolationist one. It describes a fantasy in which the US Constitution both can and should be entirely divorced

[50] ECtHR, Ser A no 45, 1981.

[51] *Lawrence* 539 US at 573.

[52] Ibid 598 (quoting *Bowers* 478 US at 193–4). Justice Scalia supplied the emphasis in this passage.

[53] Ibid.

[54] Ibid (quoting *Foster v Florida* 537 US 990 (2002) (Thomas J concurring in denial of certiorari)).

[55] Ibid 192 (citing 'Survey on the Constitutional Right to Privacy in the Context of Homosexual Activity' (1986) 40 *University of Miami Law Review* 521, 525).

[56] Ibid 'Survey', 525.

from the rest of the world. It is important to take this view seriously, as other jurisdictions have embraced the parochial-expressivist view.

The Indian government put forward such a claim in the 2009 *Naz Foundation v Union of India* case.[57] In *Naz Foundation*, the High Court of New Delhi in India struck down the nation's sodomy statute. It quickly dispensed with any 'functionalist' rationale for the statute, observing that although the government had 'referred to the issue of public health and healthy environment, the affidavit has not set out elaborately the said defence.'[58] The Court concluded that 'resistance to the claim in the petition is founded on the argument of public morality'.[59] In expounding on that 'public morality', the government did not rely on universal or Western moral values. To the contrary, the government lawyer asserted that 'Social and sexual mores in foreign countries cannot justify de-criminalisation of homosexuality in India'.[60] Indeed, the lawyer maintained 'in the western societies the morality standards are not as high as in India'.[61]

As Professor Sujit Choudhry has pointed out, this nationalistic argument was rejected by using both a universalist and culturally specific conception of Indian law.[62] Choudhry observes that comparative constitutional law was used to show that India would suffer if it clung to such a parochial conception of its position in the global order. At the same time, Choudhry observes that the arguments about Indian culture were also met with counter-arguments that relied solely on Indian constitutional culture, specifically the contention that one of the underlying themes in the Indian Constitution is 'inclusiveness'.[63] Choudhry long ago identified this dynamic as 'dialogic constitutionalism'.[64]

We see the same rejection of the parochialism of *Bowers* in *Lawrence*. On the one hand, Justice Kennedy repudiated the parochialism of the *Bowers* formulation by noting that we shared values with 'a wider civilization'.[65] On the other hand, he also observed that developments within US constitutional law itself had undermined *Bowers*'s holding. In a pincers movement, Justice Kennedy precluded the United States from either isolating itself from a broader global community or asserting that, even if it could, it possessed a uniform national heritage.[66]

[57] (2009) 160 DLT 277.

[58] Ibid para 14.

[59] Ibid.

[60] Ibid para 24.

[61] Ibid.

[62] Sujit Choudhry, 'How To Do Comparative Constitutional Law in India: *Naz Foundation*, Same Sex Rights, and Dialogical Interpretation' in Sunil Khilnani, Vikram Raghavan, and Arun Thiruvengadam (eds), *Comparative Constitutionalism in South Asia* (2010).

[63] Ibid 29.

[64] Sujit Choudhry, 'Globalization in Search of Justification: Toward a Theory of Comparative Constitutional Interpretation' (1999) 74 *Indiana Law Journal* 819ff.

[65] Ibid 560.

[66] Our examples from the United States, Europe, and India are not meant to suggest that the invalidation of sodomy laws is a universal phenomenon. While such laws have been repealed or declared invalid throughout Europe and in most countries in the Americas, 76 nations around the world still criminalize private, consensual same-sex sexual conduct. See UN High Commissioner for Human Rights, 'Discriminatory laws and practices and acts of violence against individuals based on their sexual orientation and gender identity', UN Doc A/HRC/19/41, November 17, 2011, paras 40–4.

IV. Marriage and Relationship Recognition: Functionalism and Expressivism

With its 1989 *Lov om registreret partnerskab* (Registered Partnership Act), Denmark became the first country in the world to grant nationwide legal recognition to same-sex couples with nearly all of the benefits of marriage.[67] Several of its northern European neighbors and other scattered jurisdictions followed suit in the 1990s, though the scope of these laws varied.[68] In 2001, the Netherlands broke new ground, becoming the first country to legalize same-sex marriage.[69] The global movement toward recognition of same-sex unions has since accelerated: At the time of writing, ten countries on four continents have enacted national legislation authorizing civil marriage for same-sex couples,[70] with approximately 20 other countries granting nationwide legal recognition to same-sex couples in other forms.[71]

[67] Law no 372 (June 7, 1989) (Denmark); see William N. Eskridge Jr and Darren R. Spedale, *Gay Marriage: For Better or for Worse? What We've Learned from the Evidence* (2006), 58 and n 43, 259; Ingrid Lund-Andersen, 'The Danish Registered Partnership Act' in Katharina Boele-Woelki and Angelika Fuchs (eds), *Legal Recognition of Same-Sex Couples in Europe* (2003), 13ff, 215. More limited forms of same-sex partnership recognition had been approved in the Netherlands in 1979, Denmark in 1986, and Sweden in 1987. See Robert Wintemute, 'Conclusion' in Robert Wintemute and Mads Andenæs (eds), *Legal Recognition of Same-Sex Partnerships: A Study of National, European and International Law* (2001), 759–61.

[68] See Eskridge and Spedale (n 67), 43–89; Wintemute (n 67), 761–2; Boele-Woelki and Fuchs (n 67), (Appendix) 215–310.

[69] Wintemute (n 67), 761; Boele-Woelki and Fuchs (n 67), (Appendix) 231.

[70] These countries are Argentina, Belgium, Canada, Iceland, the Netherlands, Norway, Portugal, South Africa, Spain, and Sweden. See Law no 26.618 (July 21, 2010) (Argentina); Loi ouvrant le mariage à des personnes de même sexe et modifiant certaines dispositions du Code civil (February 13, 2003) (Belgium); Civil Marriage Act (July 20, 2005) (Canada); Law no 65 (June 22, 2010) (Iceland); Law of 21 December 2000 amending Book 1 of the Civil Code in connection with the opening of marriage for same-sex couples (Netherlands); Law no 53 (June 27, 2008) (Norway); Law no 9/2010 (May 31, 2010) (Portugal); Law 13/2005 (July 1, 2005) (Spain); Act No 17 (November 29, 2006) (South Africa); Law 2009:260 (April 1, 2009) (Sweden); see also Macarena Sáez, 'Same-sex Marriage, Same-sex Cohabitation, and Same-sex Families Around the World: Why "Same" is so Different' (2011) 19 *Journal of Gender, Social Policy and the Law* 1 ff; Paul Axel-Lute, 'Same-Sex Marriage: A Selective Bibliography of the Legal Literature', February 17, 2011, available at <http://law-library.rutgers.edu/SSM.html>; Esteban Restrepo-Saldarriaga, 'Advancing Sexual Health through Human Rights in Latin America and the Caribbean', Draft manuscript, 2011 (on file with authors); 'El décimo país del mundo, el primero de Latinoamérica', *El País*, July 15, 2010 (Spain).

[71] These countries now include Andorra, Australia, Austria, Brazil, Colombia, Croatia, the Czech Republic, Denmark and Greenland, Ecuador, Finland, France, Germany, Hungary, Ireland, Liechtenstein, Luxembourg, New Zealand, Slovenia, Switzerland, the United Kingdom, and Uruguay. See National Supreme Court of Justice, Decision AI 2/2010 (2010) (Mexico) (Ministro Valls Hernández concurring), 3–51 (summarizing and analyzing foreign laws and judicial decisions on same-sex marriage and partnership recognition); *Schalk v Austria*, ECtHR App no 30141/04, 2010, paras 27–34 (summarizing national laws regarding same-sex marriage and partnership recognition within the 47 member states of the Council of Europe); Sáez (n 70), 15–31; International Commission of Jurists (n 10), 309–80; American Bar Association Section of Family Law, 'A White Paper: An Analysis of the Law Regarding Same-sex Marriage, Civil Unions and Domestic Partnerships' (2004) 38 *Family Law Quarterly* 339; Boele-Woelki and Fuchs (n 67) (Appendix), 213–31; Maureen Cosgrove, 'Liechtenstein voters approve civil partnership law', *Jurist*, June 20, 2011, available at <http://jurist.org/paperchase/2011/06/liechtenstein-voters-approve-civil-partnership-law.php>; see also Restrepo-Saldarriaga (n 70), 57–8, 74–88 (discussing legislative and judicial developments regarding same-sex marriage and partnership recognition, as well as sexual-orientation discrimination, in Latin America).

In other countries, advances have occurred primarily at the regional and local level. Mexico City, for example, legalized marriage and adoption by same-sex couples in 2009,[72] and in the United States, over one-third of the population now lives in a state or district that recognizes either same-sex marriages or a close equivalent, such as civil unions[73]—though the federal government continues not to recognize these relationships.[74]

While the increasing number of jurisdictions recognizing same-sex relationships invites comparative legal analysis, the diversity of legal processes, decisions, and provisions

[72] Código Civil para el Distrito Federal, Arts 146, 391 (Mexico); see also National Supreme Court of Justice, Decision AI 2/2010 (2010) (Mexico), paras 205–7.

[73] At the time of writing, Connecticut, the District of Columbia, Iowa, Massachusetts, New Hampshire, New York, and Vermont authorize same-sex marriage. See *Gill v Office of Pers Mgmt* 699 F Supp 2d 374, 377 n 9 (D Mass 2010) (listing state-level marriage developments); see also NH Rev Stat §457:1-a; NY Dom Rel Law §10-a; 15 Vt Stat Ann §8; *Jackson v Dist of Columb Bd of Elections & Ethics* 999 A2d 89 (DC 2010); *Kerrigan v Comm'r of Pub Health* 957 A2d 407 (Conn 2008); *Varnum v Brien* 763 NW 2d 862 (Iowa 2009); *Goodridge v Dep't of Pub Health* 798 NE 2d 941 (Mass 2003). California recognizes same-sex marriages if they were performed in that state between June 16, 2008 and November 5, 2008, or if they were validly performed in a different jurisdiction at any time before November 5, 2008. For any same-sex marriage performed on or after November 5, 2008, the state recognizes the unions for all purposes except the designation 'marriage'. See California Family Code §§297, 297.5, 308. Maryland recognizes same-sex marriages lawfully performed in other jurisdictions, see 'Marriage—Whether Out-of-State Same-Sex Marriage That is Valid in the State of Celebration May be Recognized in Maryland', 95 Op Att'y Gen Md 3 (February 23, 2010) (Maryland), and may soon also authorize recognition of same-sex marriages performed within the state, see John Wagner, 'Same-sex marriage bill passes house of delegates', *Washington Post*, February 17, 2012, available at <http://www.washingtonpost.com/local/dc-politics/same-sex-marriage-bill-passes-maryland-house-of-delegates/2012/02/17/gIQARk7XKR_story.html>. Delaware, Illinois, Hawaii, Nevada, New Jersey, Oregon, Rhode Island, and Washington State have enacted legislation authorizing same-sex partnerships without the designation 'marriage'. Other states, including Colorado, Maine, and Wisconsin, afford more limited recognition to same-sex couples. See generally Human Rights Campaign, 'Marriage Equality & Other Relationship Recognition Laws', July 6, 2011, available at <http://www.hrc.org/files/assets/resources/Relationship_Recognition_Laws_Map%281%29.pdf>; Axel-Lute (n 70); International Commission of Jurists (n 10), 312–13, 322–6. Population statistics for each state are available through the US Census Bureau, 'State & County QuickFacts', at <http://quickfacts.census.gov/qfd/index.html>.

State laws affecting same-sex relationships have changed rapidly over the last decade. No state, for example, recognized same-sex marriage or any equivalent status prior to 2000. This rapid progress, however, has triggered fierce backlash: a majority of states have enacted state constitutional amendments restricting marriage to one man and one woman; many of these provisions also bar recognition of civil unions or domestic partnerships. See Human Rights Campaign, 'Statewide Marriage Prohibitions', January 13, 2010, available at <http://www.hrc.org/about_us/state_laws.asp>. Change is likely to remain fast-paced. At the time of writing, for example, same-sex marriage advocates in Maine are working to gather enough signatures to place a marriage equality proposal on the 2012 ballot, while in neighboring New Hampshire, the legislature is widely expected to approve a bill repealing a marriage equality law that took effect only in 2010. See Rebekah Metzler, 'Gathering of signatures can begin in effort to legalize gay marriage', *Portland Press Herald*, August 18, 2011, available at <http://www.pressherald.com/news/gathering-of-signatures-can-begin-in-effort-to-legalize-gay-marriage_2011-08-18.html>; Norma Love, 'Gay marriage repeal a top issue in New Hampshire', Associated Press, December 25, 2011, available at <http://articles.boston.com/2011-12-25/news/30557074_1_marriage-law-gay-marriage-civil-unions>. The New Hampshire proposal would replace same-sex marriage with civil unions.

[74] The current Administration has taken some minor steps toward very limited recognition of same-sex partners, and while it continues to enforce the federal statute defining marriage as exclusively heterosexual, it has taken the position that the statute is unconstitutional. See Charlie Savage and Sheryl Gay Stolberg, 'In Shift, US Says Marriage Act Blocks Gay Rights', *NY Times*, February 23, 2011, available at <http://www.nytimes.com/2011/02/24/ us/24marriage.html>; see also Defense of Marriage Act (DOMA) §3, 1 USC §7. Various pending lawsuits are challenging DOMA's constitutionality. See eg *Massachusetts v US Dep't of Health & Human Servs* 698 F Supp 2d 234, 235–6 (D Mass 2010), notice of appeal filed October 12, 2010.

surrounding same-sex relationship rights—not to mention underlying cultural and political differences[75]—mandates caution. Many readers—particularly in North America—may be quick to associate controversies over same-sex relationships with high-stakes court battles and bold judicial opinions on constitutional rights. Yet much of the worldwide progress for same-sex relationship recognition has occurred at the legislative level, often without overt prompting from courts.[76] Moreover, in the numerous countries where constitutional litigation has helped to shape the development of same-sex relationship-recognition laws, the litigation and its political repercussions have not fit a uniform mold. Only in South Africa has a national court expressly ruled that the exclusion of same-sex couples from marriage violated the national constitution.[77] In Canada, and to some extent Argentina, court rulings involving same-sex couples helped to produce momentum for national legislative action to legalize same-sex marriage, but no national court ruling ever held that the country's constitution mandated marriage equality.[78] In Belgium and Mexico, national courts considered (and rejected) constitutional challenges to legislatively enacted laws that opened the door to same-sex marriage; a similar challenge to Spain's 2005 law permitting same-sex marriages has been pending for over six years in the country's Constitutional Court.[79] Numerous other courts at the regional, national, and international level have mandated recognition of same-sex relationships for some purposes but have stopped short of requiring same-sex marriage. These include national constitutional courts of Brazil, Colombia, Hungary, Germany, and Slovenia, the European Court of Human Rights, , and the states of Vermont and New Jersey in the United States.[80] In several countries, such as Italy, Venezuela, and Costa Rica, efforts to secure recognition of same-sex relationships have so far failed in both the national legislatures and the national courts.[81]

There is also broad variation among constitutional *texts* with respect to, among other things, equality, dignity, family, and marriage. In some countries, including Bolivia, Ecuador, Portugal, South Africa, and Sweden, national constitutions expressly prohibit discrimination based on 'sexual orientation'[82]—though this is not necessarily a guarantee of equality for same-sex couples. In Ecuador, for example, the Constitution proscribes sexual-orientation

[75] In many countries, broad legal recognition of same-sex couples does not necessarily reflect broad cultural acceptance of LGB people. See eg Robyn Dixon, 'In South Africa's black townships, being gay can be fatal', *Los Angeles Times*, May 27, 2011, available at <http://articles.latimes.com/2011/may/27/world/la-fg-south-africa-gay-killings-20110528>.

[76] See eg Boele-Woelki and Fuchs (n 67), (Appendix) 215–310.

[77] See *Minister of Home Affairs v Fourie*, 2006 (1) SA 524 (CC), 587.

[78] See eg *Re Same Sex Marriage* [2004] 3 SCR 698 (Canada); *Halpern v Canada* (Attorney General) [2003] 65 OR3d 161 (Ont CA), *EGALE Canada Inc v Canada* (Attorney General) [2003] 225 DLR (4th) 472 (BCCA); see also *Sentencia Freyre Alejandro v GCBA Sobre Amparo* (Art 14 CCABA), Juzgada 1ra Inst en lo Contencioso Adm y Trib No 15, Expediente 34292/0 (October 11, 2009) (Argentina); International Commission of Jurists (n 10), 344, 365–9.

[79] See Sáez (n 70), National Supreme Court of Justice, Decision AI 2/2010 (2010) (Mexico); Cour D'Arbitrage, Decision no 159/2004, October 20, 2004, Moniteur Belge, October 29, 2004, 74.279-91 (Belgium); see also E. Martín, 'Bolo-Bolo pide al PP que retire el recurso contra los matrimonios homosexuales', *La Tribuna de Toledo*, March 8, 2011, available at <http://www.latribunadetoledo.es/noticia.cfm/Local/20110308/bolobolo/pide/pp/retire/recurso/ matrimonios/homosexuales/B0247ED5-FCAE-6949-BB7B24C0BDB07BDC>.

[80] See sources cited at nn 70–71.

[81] See generally Sáez (n 70), 4–6, 12–13; Axel-Lute (n 70); see also National Supreme Court of Justice, Decision AI 2/2010 (2010) (Mexico) (Ministro Valls Hernández concurring), 3–51 (summarizing and analyzing foreign laws and judicial decisions on same-sex marriage and partnership recognition); *Schalk v Austria*, ECtHR App no 30141/04, 2010), paras 27–34 (summarizing national laws regarding same-sex marriage and partnership recognition within the 47 member states of the Council of Europe).

[82] UN High Commissioner for Human Rights (n 66), para 49.

discrimination and guarantees rights for 'stable, monogamous' domestic partnerships, whether same-sex or heterosexual, while other provisions in the Constitution define 'marriage' as a heterosexual union and prohibit adoption by same-sex couples.[83] Constitutions also differ in their definition and protection of the terms 'marriage' and 'family'. Some texts, for instance, expressly ban recognition of same-sex marriage, while others guarantee marriage for heterosexual couples without an express ban on same-sex marriage; still others protect 'marriage' or the 'family' without defining the terms.[84]

Although the diversity among constitutional texts, courts, and cultures limits the possibilities of comparative constitutionalism, it does not foreclose meaningful comparative analysis. As in the military and sodomy contexts, the context of partnership rights is rife with incautiously broad arguments.[85] However modest the contributions of comparative analysis may be, they can at least check such immodest claims. These immodest arguments are both functionalist and expressive.

1. Functionalism

The primary functionalist argument against same-sex marriage is that the purpose of marriage is procreation. Though the argument takes many guises, one of its most 'immodest' iterations rests on the notion that denying legal protections to same-sex couples (and their children) will somehow encourage procreative sex among heterosexuals, prevent a decline in a jurisdiction's birth rate, and help to 'perpetuate the species'.[86] We find these arguments implausible. In the words of former New York Chief Judge Judith Kaye, 'no one rationally decides to have children because gays and lesbians are excluded from marriage'.[87]

Yet the arguments show no sign of disappearing. In upholding Washington State's ban on same-sex marriage, a plurality of the state Supreme Court concluded in 2006 that 'the legislature was entitled to believe that limiting marriage to opposite-sex couples furthers procreation, essential to survival of the human race'.[88] A Justice on the Connecticut Supreme Court argued in a 2008 dissenting opinion that the state legislature—which had already legalized civil unions for same-sex couples—could rationally conclude that opening marriage to gay couples 'could have a significant effect on the number of opposite sex couples who choose to

[83] Constitución de Ecuador, Arts 11(2), 66(9), 67, 68, 83(14).

[84] See ibid; Axel-Lute (n 70); Restrepo-Saldarriaga (n 70).

[85] For purposes of this chapter, we use the terms 'partnership rights' and 'partnership laws' to refer to a variety of forms of legal recognition for same-sex couples that stop short of full marriage equality, such as civil unions and civil partnerships.

[86] An increasingly common variation of the procreation argument posits that marriage exists primarily or solely to mitigate the effects of 'accidental' or 'reckless' procreation among heterosexuals. See Edward Stein, 'The "Accidental Procreation" Argument for Withholding Legal Recognition for Same-Sex Relationships' (2009) 84 *Chicago-Kent Law Review* 403. Even assuming that encouraging marriage among heterosexuals helps to mitigate the effects of accidental procreation, however, it is fanciful to suggest that withholding marriage licenses from same-sex couples serves any similar purpose.

Comparative analysis becomes relevant to 'reckless procreation' claims when opponents of LGB rights argue that legal recognition of same-sex relationships has contributed to an increase in non-marital birth rates in European countries. Various scholars have discredited these claims. See eg Eskridge and Spedale (n 67), M.V. Lee Badgett, *When Gay People Get Married: What Happens When Societies Legalize Same-Sex Marriage* (2009), 64–85.

[87] *Hernandez v Robles* 855 NE2d 1, 31 (NY 2006) (Kaye CJ dissenting).

[88] *Andersen v King County* 138 P3d 963, 969 (Wa 2006).

procreate and raise children together'.[89] In state and federal constitutional litigation in other states, including California, Maryland, and New York, opponents of same-sex marriage have filed briefs stressing that 'society needs babies'.[90] Two of these briefs—filed by a group of prominent family and legal scholars—point to low birth rates in Europe, warning that the 'decline in the extent to which marriage is seen as a childbearing institution[] play[s] a clear role' in the low fertility.[91]

When opponents of same-sex marriage make such specific causal claims about the experience of other countries, courts should examine that experience. Consider the frequent suggestion that same-sex relationship recognition has caused a crisis in European countries (particularly in the Netherlands and Scandinavia) by contributing to lower marriage rates and lower birthrates.[92] We know of no reliable study demonstrating such a causal link. To the contrary, scholars have systematically debunked such claims.[93] Perhaps more to the point, while US opponents of LGB rights point to a supposed depopulation crisis fueled by same-sex

[89] *Kerrigan v Comm'r of Pub Health* 957 A2d 407, 531 (Conn 2008) (Zarella J dissenting). The same year, the state of Iowa cited its 'declining birth rate' and asserted an interest in 'encouraging procreative marriage' in its unsuccessful attempt to defend its ban on same-sex marriage before the state's Supreme Court. Final Brief of Defendant-Appellant at 43, 53, *Varnum v Brien* 763 NW2d 862 (Iowa 2009) (No 07-1499); see also *Smelt v County of Orange* 374 F Supp 2d 861, 880 (CD Cal 2005):

> Because procreation is necessary to perpetuate humankind, encouraging the optimal union for procreation is a legitimate government interest.... By excluding same-sex couples from... marriage,... the government is communicating to citizens that opposite-sex relationships have special significance. Congress could plausibly have believed sending this message makes it more likely people will enter into opposite-sex unions, and encourages those relationships.

Vacated in part on other grounds, 447 F3d 673 (9th Cir 2006). For a recent example of a similar argument, see Reply Brief for Intervenor-Appellant the Bipartisan Legal Advisory Group of the United States House of Representatives, *Commonwealth of Massachusetts v US Dep't of Health and Human Servs*, No 10-2204 (1st Cir December 1, 2011), 2011 WL 6147004, at *23 (arguing that 'Congress reasonably could have concluded' that 'changing the definition of marriage' to allow same-sex marriage 'might affect [heterosexuals'] decisions whether to marry or have children in marriage').

[90] Brief of Amici Curiae of James Q. Wilson et al, Legal and Family Scholars, in Support of Defendants-Appellants at 15, *Conaway v Deane* 932 A2d 571 (Md 2007) (No 44); Brief of Amici Curiae James Q. Wilson et al, Legal and Family Scholars in Support of Defendants-Respondents at 20, *Hernandez v Robles* 855 NE2d 1 (NY 2006); Brief of Appellee Campaign for California Families at 37, 50, *Smelt v County of Orange* 447 F3d 673 (9th Cir 2006) (No 05-56040).

[91] Brief of Amici Curiae of James Q. Wilson et al, Legal and Family Scholars, in Support of Defendants-Appellants at 16, *Conaway v Deane* (n 90); Brief of Amici Curiae James Q. Wilson et al, Legal and Family Scholars in Support of Defendants-Respondents at 21, *Hernandez v Robles* (n 90).

[92] See eg Brief Amici Curiae of James Q. Wilson et al, Legal and Family Scholars, in Support of Defendants-Appellants at 15–17, *Conaway v Deane* (n 90) (arguing against same-sex marriage by warning that 'A growing number of countries view their low birth rates with the resulting population decline and ageing to be a serious crisis, jeopardizing the basic foundations of the nation and threatening its survival', and pointing specifically to Western Europe); see also Brief of Amici Curiae National Organization for Marriage, National Organization for Marriage Rhode Island, and Family Leader in Support of the Intervening Defendants-Appellants 28–29, *Perry v Schwarzenegger*, No 10-16696 (9th Cir September 24, 2010); Brief Amicus Curiae of The American Center for Law & Justice In Support of Respondent Proposition 22 Legal Defense And Education Fund at 4–6, *In re Marriage Cases* 183 P3d 384 (Ca 2008) (No S147999).

[93] See Badgett (n 86), 64–85; Eskridge and Spedale (n 67), 131–202, 271–9; Brief of Amici Curiae Legislators from United States Jurisdictions that Have Legalized Same-Sex Marriage in Support of Plaintiffs-Appellees and Affirmance at 19–27, *Perry v Schwarzenegger*, No 10-16696 (9th Cir October 5, 2010) (reviewing, and providing citations and weblinks to, evidence that debunks myths about the supposed negative effects of same-sex marriage and relationship recognition in foreign jurisdictions); see also Ohlsson-Wijka, 'Sweden's Marriage Revival: An Analysis of the New-millennium Switch from Long-term Decline to Increasing Popularity' (2011) *Population Studies* 1–18.

marriage and partnership recognition in Western Europe, the countries themselves do not seem to share their alarm. In 2009 and 2010, Iceland, Norway, and Sweden *expanded* their protection of same-sex couples by replacing partnership laws with full marriage equality.[94]

With the passage of time and the growth in the number of jurisdictions recognizing same-sex couples, the field from which to gather evidence grows larger and more diverse. Courts and other decision-makers, moreover, should more carefully scrutinize the evidence on which opponents of same-sex relationship recognition tend to rely for their claims, particularly claims that on their face appear counterintuitive or far-fetched. The family and legal scholars noted above supported their claim that same-sex marriage would lead to a decline in heterosexual procreation with scholarly articles that did not actually discuss—or even mention—the legal recognition of same-sex relationships.[95] Unfortunately, they are not the only litigants to misread, misinterpret, or misrepresent their sources in debates over same-sex relationship rights.

2. Expressivism

Defenders of bans on same-sex marriage or other forms of relationship recognition for same-sex couples also often rely on extreme expressivist claims. Those who defend differential treatment of same-sex unions, for example, frequently claim that the law's heterosexual definition of marriage simply reflects and expresses marriage's 'biological' foundation, or its otherwise 'inherent', 'pre-legal' nature. Insofar as these arguments rest on a conception of marriage as antecedent to law, comparative constitutional law may not appear capable, in the abstract, of offering much of a response. In practice, however, opponents of same-sex marriage typically defend characterizations of marriage's 'inherently' heterosexual nature by pointing to a 'universal' consensus among the world's legal traditions; to refuse to recognize same-sex marriage, they argue, is merely to adhere to globally shared values. Comparative constitutional analysis may play a modest but meaningful role in responding to these universal-expressivist justifications by unsettling the supposed empirical foundations for the anti-same-sex-marriage view.

Litigants and judges invoking theories of marriage's true 'essence' could more comfortably rely on empirical arguments in the years before any jurisdiction had authorized same-sex marriages. When the Attorney General of Canada argued in the early 1990s, for example, that the heterosexual definition of marriage was 'fundamental to the very nature of the social institution', she could bolster that claim with the observation that 'no jurisdiction in the world' had recognized same-sex marriage, and that 'Even societies in which homosexuality has been accepted make a clear distinction between heterosexual marriage and the society's recognition and acceptance of homosexual relationships.'[96] Likewise, when New Zealand defended its refusal to recognize same-sex marriage in proceedings before the United Nations Human

[94] See sources cited at n 70.

[95] See John C. Caldwell and Thomas Schindlmayr, 'Explanation of the Fertility Crisis in Modern Societies: A Search for Commonalities' (2003) 57(3) *Population Studies* 241–63; Patrick Festy, 'Looking for European Demography, Desperately?', Paper presented at the Expert Group Meeting on Policy Responses to Population Ageing and Population Decline in New York, October 16–18, Population Division, Department of Economic and Social Affairs, United Nations, 2000; Population Division, Department of Economic and Social Affairs, United Nations Secretariat, 'Partnership and Reproductive Behavior in Low-Fertility Countries', *Population Newsletter* 74–6 (December 2002).

[96] Factum of the Attorney General of Canada, paras 17, 37, 38, *Layland v Ontario* (Minister of Consumer and Commercial Relations), 14 OR (3d) 658, 104 DLR (4th) 214 (Div Ct) (1993).

Rights Committee several years later, it could support its position that marriage was 'inherent[ly]' heterosexual by noting that 'all other States parties' to the International Covenant on Civil and Political Rights had defined the institution as 'open only to individuals of opposite sexes.'[97]

With the advent of legal same-sex marriage and the spread of partnership laws, such categorical claims must be retired. Nonetheless, those who oppose legal recognition of same-sex unions have not significantly adjusted their sweeping rhetoric. In the ongoing federal constitutional challenge to California's prohibition of same-sex marriages, for example, the defendants have argued that the heterosexual definition of marriage reflects not prejudice, but an 'undeniable biological reality', and that 'the existential purpose of marriage in every society is, and has always been, to regulate sexual relationships between men and women.'[98] At a January 2011 hearing before a federal appeals court, the attorney defending the same-sex marriage ban repeatedly claimed that marriage was universally understood to include only cross-sex couples; for example, he argued (in a universal-expressivist register that also sounded in a functionalist one) that 'The key reason that marriage has existed at all in any society and at any time is that sexual relationships between men and women naturally produce children.'[99]

In Mexico, where the National Supreme Court of Justice recently upheld Mexico City's 2009 marriage equality law, one of two dissenting Justices insisted that 'the concept and structural elements' of marriage 'respond to a defined reality with concrete biological and above all anthropological foundations'.[100] There is an 'international consensus', the Justice argued, 'that only a man and a woman can form a marriage'; to hold otherwise, he insisted, would be 'to alter the essence of things' and 'to distort' marriage's 'nature'.[101] Similarly categorical claims appeared in a decision from the Supreme Court of Costa Rica in 2006. Rejecting a constitutional challenge to the country's ban on same-sex marriage, the Court's majority emphasized the 'biological' roots of the family, and claimed that an 'anthropological' analysis of marriage as it had existed 'throughout human history' and 'through the present' reveals that 'marriage and the family have always had a heterosexual composition in all human civilizations'.[102]

As in the context of sodomy laws, comparative constitutional analysis can discipline carelessly broad statements about ostensibly universal values that societies express through bans on same-sex relationship recognition. This is not merely a question of counting up the

[97] *Joslin v New Zealand*, Human Rights Comm, Comm No 902/1999, P 8.3, UN Doc CCPR/C/75/D/902/1999 (2002), para 4.11 (paraphrasing New Zealand's position). The Committee found in favor of New Zealand on other grounds. Ibid paras 8.1–9. By the time of the Committee's decision, Netherlands had legalized same-sex marriage. See ibid para 5.5.

[98] Defendant-Intervenors-Appellants' Opening Brief, *Perry v Schwarzenegger*, No 10-16696 (9th Cir September 17, 2010), 2010 WL 3762119, at *54.

[99] Oral argument, *Perry v Schwarzenegger*, No 10-16696 (9th Cir December 6, 2010), available at <http://www.c-spanvideo.org/program/296911-1>.

[100] Versión taquigráfica de la sesión pública ordinaria del pleno de la Suprema Corte de Justicia de la Nación, 9 (August 3, 2010) (Señor Ministro Aguirre Anguiano), Expediente 00002/2010-00 (Mexico) (August 16, 2010).

[101] Ibid 37.

[102] See Exp: 03-008127-0007-CO, Res No 2006007262 (2006) (Sala Constitucional de la Corte Suprema de Justicia) (Costa Rica). In Spain, members of a center-right party have argued before the country's Constitutional Court that the government's 2005 legalization of same-sex marriage 'distorts the very nature and essence' of the institution as it has been understood under the legal tradition of both Spain and the 'Western world'. Recurso de inconstitucionalidad contra la Ley 13/2005 de 1 de julio, at 17 (September 28, 2005) (Spain).

jurisdictions that have opened the door to same-sex relationship recognition (though that sort of 'nose counting' may also serve a useful, albeit limited, purpose), but also of engaging with the reasoning of foreign constitutional courts. Courts across the globe, including in Argentina, Belgium, Colombia, Costa Rica, Germany, Hungary, Italy, Mexico, New Zealand, Portugal, Slovenia, South Africa, and the United Kingdom, and over a dozen jurisdictions within the United States and Canada, have grappled with the definition and meaning of marriage and the possibility of legal recognition for same-sex couples. A growing number of these courts have offered compelling reasons to reject the claim that marriage or other legal protections can or must be limited to heterosexual couples.[103]

Courts and advocates cannot be faulted for turning to these decisions for information and guidance when confronted with claims that marriage must, always and everywhere, mean one thing. Nor is this a question of cherry-picking: we do not dispute that decisions hostile to same-sex relationship rights may also form part of the global conversation. Indeed, what we urge in response to many of the 'immodest' claims of same-sex marriage opponents is a greater recognition that the meaning, definition, and scope of relationship rights and marriage are contestable and increasingly contested.

As in the sodomy context, objections to legal recognition of same-sex couples have relied not only on purportedly 'universal' values, but also national and local values. And like universal-expressivist arguments, parochial-expressivist arguments are often couched in inflexibly categorical terms.

In one variation of the parochial-expressivist opposition to same-sex marriage, litigants and judges have appealed to national religious culture, arguing that legal recognition of same-sex couples would necessarily infringe on the religious convictions held by the majority of a country's people. In a 2008 Spanish case, a local judge who objected to a same-sex couple's marriage application brought an unsuccessful challenge before the country's Constitutional Court. The judge argued that the 2005 legalization of same-sex marriage 'contravened not only the Catholic Church's heterosexual conceptualization of marriage and the definition of marriage provided in the Dictionary of the Royal Academy of the Spanish Language', but also various provisions of the Spanish Constitution. More specifically, the judge claimed that the law unconstitutionally disregarded the religious beliefs of the Spanish people in violation of constitutional guarantees of equality and religious freedom.[104] Opponents of Belgium's same-sex marriage law made similar claims in court, unsuccessfully.[105]

We see nothing extreme in asking a court to take account of a national or state culture; in fact, such an accounting is often a proper component of constitutional analysis. To argue, however, that affording legal recognition to same-sex couples will *necessarily* infringe on the religious freedom of those who oppose such recognition—such that the rights of same-sex couples must categorically be denied—does strike us as overbroad. It is also a testable claim, given the increasing number of jurisdictions that recognize both religious freedom and same-sex partnerships or marriage. It therefore invites a careful comparative analysis.

[103] See Axel-Lute (n 70); see also National Supreme Court of Justice, Decision AI 2/2010 (2010) (Mexico) (Ministro Valls Hernández concurring), 3–51 (summarizing and analyzing foreign laws and judicial decisions on same-sex marriage and partnership recognition).

[104] Auto 12/2008, Tribunal Constitucional de España (January 16, 2008). The claim failed on procedural grounds.

[105] See Cour D'Arbitrage, Decision no 159/2004, October 20, 2004, Moniteur Belge, October 29, 2004, 74.279-91 (Belgium).

Indeed, the invitation to engage in comparative inquiries is often explicit, as those who appeal to national or local value (religious or otherwise) to oppose the rights of same-sex couples do not necessarily refrain from their own reliance on foreign experience and judgment. In Mexico, where the Supreme Court recently upheld a Mexico City law allowing same-sex couples to marry and adopt children, dissenting Justice Aguirre Anguiano struggled to find a balance between a limited comparative inquiry and a proper respect for national values. Although he cited a Danish study of adopted children to support his position that the Mexican Constitution prohibited adoption by same-sex couples, he also commented that 'obviously the Danish do not resemble us Mexicans much', adding that 'they are a peculiar people' and that 'those Scandinavian countries are markedly different from us'.[106] Justice Aguirre Anguiano's trouble in articulating a coherent position with respect to Denmark is telling. The widespread nature of the developments and controversies surrounding the rights of same-sex couples makes it increasingly difficult—if not impossible—for constitutional interpreters to pretend that they can close their eyes completely to foreign law and experience.

V. Conclusion

Interpreters who use comparative law are sometimes criticized for permitting judges too much discretion. Chief Justice Roberts framed the critique well in his confirmation hearings:

> In foreign law you can find anything you want. If you don't find it in the decisions of France or Italy, it's in the decisions of Somalia or Japan or Indonesia or wherever. As somebody said in another context, looking at foreign law for support is like looking out over a crowd and picking out your friends. You can find them, they're there. And that actually expands the discretion of the judge. It allows the judge to incorporate his or her own personal preferences, cloak them with the authority of precedent because they're finding precedent in foreign law, and use that to determine the meaning of the Constitution. I think that's a misuse of precedent, not a correct use of precedent.[107]

The 'other context' Justice Roberts was speaking of was that of legislative history, in which it is often said that jurists can 'look out over a crowd and pick out their friends'.[108] Yet the analogy breaks down here, as it is seldom stated (to our knowledge) that 'no legislative history supports the position' when a great deal of legislative history does. In the comparative context, however, there is a tendency to make 'always/everywhere' claims that implicitly contend that no other jurisdiction has gone the other way. Put differently, to 'look out over a crowd and pick out your friends' is a perfectly legitimate exercise when raised to counter the immodest argument that one has no friends at all.

[106] Versión taquigráfica de la sesión pública ordinaria del pleno de la Suprema Corte de Justicia de la Nación, 41–2 (August 12, 2010) (Señor Ministro Aguirre Anguiano), Expediente 00002/2010-00 (Mexico) (August 16, 2010).

[107] Confirmation Hearing on the Nomination of John G. Roberts Jr to be Chief Justice of the United States Before the S Comm on the Judiciary, 109th Cong 200, 200-01 (2005).

[108] See eg Patricia Wald, 'Some Observations on the Use of Legislative History in the 1981 Supreme Court Term' (1983) 68 *Iowa Law Review* 195, 215:

> consistent and uniform rules for statutory construction and use of legislative materials are not being followed today. It sometimes seems that citing legislative history is still, as my late colleague Harold Leventhal once observed, akin to 'looking over a crowd and picking out your friends'.

Bibliography

American Bar Association Section of Family Law, 'A White Paper: An Analysis of the Law Regarding Same-sex Marriage, Civil Unions and Domestic Partnerships' (2004) 38 *Family Law Quarterly* 339

M.V. Lee Badgett, *When Gay People Get Married: What Happens When Societies Legalize Same-Sex Marriage* (2009)

Katharina Boele-Woelki and Angelika Fuchs (eds), *Legal Recognition of Same-Sex Couples in Europe* (2003)

John C. Caldwell and Thomas Schindlmayr, 'Explanation of the Fertility Crisis in Modern Societies: A Search for Commonalities' (2003) 57(3) *Population Studies* 241

Sujit Choudhry, 'Globalization in Search of Justification: Toward a Theory of Comparative Constitutional Interpretation' (1999) 74 *Indiana Law Journal* 819

William N. Eskridge Jr and Darren R. Spedale, *Gay Marriage: For Better or for Worse? What We've Learned from the Evidence* (2006)

Patrick Festy, 'Looking for European Demography, Desperately?', Paper presented at the Expert Group Meeting on Policy Responses to Population Ageing and Population Decline in New York, October 16–18, Population Division, Department of Economic and Social Affairs, United Nations, 2000

Suzanne B. Goldberg, 'Open Service and Our Allies: A Report on the Inclusion of Openly Gay and Lesbian Servicemembers in US Allies' Armed Forces' (2011) 17 *William and Mary Journal of Women and Law* 547

International Commission of Jurists, *Sexual Orientation, Gender Identity and Justice: A Comparative Law Casebook* (2011)

Sunil Khilnani, Vikram Raghavan, and Arun Thiruvengadam (eds), *Comparative Constitutionalism in South Asia* (2010)

Claude Lévi-Strauss, *The Savage Mind* ([1962] 1966)

Esteban Restrepo-Saldarriaga, 'Advancing Sexual Health through Human Rights in Latin America and the Caribbean', Draft manuscript, 2011 (on file with authors)

Macarena Sáez, 'Same-sex Marriage, Same-sex Cohabitation, and Same-sex Families Around the World: Why "Same" is so Different' (2011) 19 *Journal of Gender, Social Policy and the Law* 1

Edward Stein, 'The "Accidental Procreation" Argument for Withholding Legal Recognition for Same-Sex Relationships' (2009) 84 *Chicago-Kent Law Review* 403

'Survey on the Constitutional Right to Privacy in the Context of Homosexual Activity' (1986) 40 *University of Miami Law Review* 521

Mark Tushnet, 'The Possibilities of Comparative Constitutional Law' (1999) 108 *Yale Law Journal* 1225

United Nations High Commissioner for Human Rights, 'Discriminatory laws and practices and acts of violence against individuals based on their sexual orientation and gender identity', UN Doc A/HRC/19/41, November 17, 2011

United States Department of Defense, 'Report of the Comprehensive Review of the Issues Associated with a Repeal of "Don't Ask, Don't Tell"', 2010

Patricia Wald, 'Some Observations on the Use of Legislative History in the 1981 Supreme Court Term' (1983) 68 *Iowa Law Review* 195

Ohlsson-Wijka, 'Sweden's Marriage Revival: An Analysis of the New-millennium Switch from Long-term Decline to Increasing Popularity' (2011) *Population Studies* 1

Robert Wintemute and Mads Andenæs (eds), *Legal Recognition of Same-Sex Partnerships: A Study of National, European and International Law* (2001)

CHAPTER 53

GROUP RIGHTS IN COMPARATIVE CONSTITUTIONAL LAW: CULTURE, ECONOMICS, OR POLITICAL POWER?

SUJIT CHOUDHRY

*New York**

* I would like to thank Michael Sabet and David Vitale, for excellent research assistance.

I. Introduction

Group rights are part of the grammar of contemporary constitutional politics. In divided societies, in which ethnicity serves as the principal basis of political mobilization, ethnic groups—especially ethnic minorities—assert a range of group rights directly, or as the underlying root of a range of public policies. It is claimed that there are group rights to separate educational and social institutions, to federal subunits in which ethnic groups exclusively wield or dominate the exercise of political power, and to land and resources. Group rights are the basis for rules on internal migration and land ownership, for distinct systems of religious personal law, for official multilingualism, for executive power-sharing, and for a share of natural resource revenues. Moreover, the assertion of group rights is not just a political claim; it is also a legal claim directed at the very design of the constitutional order and its subsequent interpretation. Group rights serve two constitutional functions. They are shields and swords against majority rule, which protect ethnic minorities from being outvoted on policies that affect the interests that those rights protect. But equally importantly, the entrenchment of group rights reflects and projects a conception of the very nature of the constitutional order itself, in which the group which holds rights is constitutionally identified as a constituent element. Citizenship in the broader political community is mediated through membership in the group. Thus, group rights have both *regulative* and *constitutive* functions.

In contemporary constitutional practice, group rights exist alongside the standard schedule of individual rights that are found in constitutional bills of rights—the liberal freedoms (expression, assembly, association, and religion), and the rights to bodily integrity and due process, to participation in the democratic process, and to equality. However, these two varieties of rights embody competing constitutional logics. Group rights institutionalize ethnic identity in the very design of the constitutional order, whereas individual rights are guaranteed irrespective of ethnic identity and are hostile to the institutionalization of ethnic difference. Rights to equality and non-discrimination presumptively prohibit the distribution of rights and opportunities on the basis of ethnic identity—for example, through rules governing preferential treatment in public sector employment, the receipt of public services, or in land ownership. The guarantee of rights on equal terms—for example, the right to vote and hold public office, the right to property—presumptively forbids the unequal enjoyment of the interests protected by those rights, including on the basis of ethnicity. More fundamentally, individual rights call upon citizens to abstract away from race, religion, ethnicity, and language, which have previously served as the grounds of political identity and political division. They encode a vision of political community built around citizens who are equal bearers of constitutional rights—a constitutional patriotism or civic nationalism—a transcendent form of political membership unmediated by group identity.[1]

Individual rights clearly have regulative and constitutive functions as well, and these functions not only differ, but also conflict with the parallel functions served by group rights. So one of the most pressing issues of contemporary constitutional law is to understand the precise interrelationship between group and individual rights. Yet the most serious work on this question

[1] See Sujit Choudhry, 'After the Rights Revolution: Bills of Rights in the Post-Conflict State' (2010) 6 *Annual Review of Law and Social Science* 301; Sujit Choudhry, 'Bills of Rights as Instruments of Nation Building in Multinational States: The Canadian *Charter* and Quebec Nationalism' in James B. Kelly and Christopher P. Manfredi (eds), *Contested Constitutionalism: Reflections on the Canadian Charter of Rights and Freedoms* (2009), ch 12.

is found not in the literature on comparative constitutional law, but in the cognate discipline of political theory, which often presupposes the constitutional practice of group rights, in order to better understand the political sociology of claims for those rights, and to assess them normatively. Constitutional scholarship, in turn, is parasitic on political theory. Indeed, because of its orientation around real-world examples, the political theory literature informs contemporary debates over group rights in constitutional politics, especially during moments of constitutional transition.

Political theorists presuppose that group rights entail the right to self-government over matters integral to cultural identity. But on careful examination, there is a gap between the constitutional image of group rights relied on by many political theorists and the actual constitutional provisions that can lay claim to constituting group rights. Group rights often arise out of conflicts over economic and political power that may bear little connection to questions of cultural difference, or whose relationship to culture is more complex than political theorists would suggest. Normative theorizing and constitutional analyses about group rights are therefore premised on inaccurate foundations. Moreover, the inaccurate image of extant constitutional orders may distort practical debates over constitutional design and interpretation. The goal of this contribution is to sketch an alternative picture of group rights and the political sociology that underlies them. This kind of descriptive and analytical work yields not only a different picture of group rights, but reframes the precise character of the conflict between individual and group rights, which is the precursor to normative analysis.

II. Group Rights in Political Theory

An analytic and descriptive account of constitutionally entrenched group rights should have the following components: (1) the interests the group right seeks to protect; (2) which groups claim and hold such rights; (3) the juridical structure of these rights, including what is the subject matter and scope of such rights, who are the rights-holders, who owes corresponding duties, how those rights are exercised, and the relationship of group rights to territory; and (4) the nature of the relationship between group rights and individual rights.

The political theory literature on group rights is vast, is riven by internal debates, and resists easy generalization. However, we can distill a shared set of answers to these questions from political theorists: (1) group rights protect the interest of members of ethnic groups in cultural survival or integrity; (2) group rights are primarily held by three kinds of minorities—national minorities, indigenous minorities, and religious minorities; (3) group rights consist of rights to decision-making authority over matters integral to cultural survival, are held by groups collectively, are exercised by the group through its governing institutions or on the group's behalf by an unelected leadership, often but do not necessarily entail territorial jurisdiction, and can bind both members and non-members of the group; and (4) group rights come into conflict with the individual rights of group members, but do not raise serious issues regarding the rights of non-members. I address each point in turn.

1. Group Rights Protect Culture

For political theorists, what defines ethnic groups, and distinguishes them from each other, is a distinct cultural identity. As we shall see, different kinds of groups vary in terms of what defines their cultural distinctiveness (eg national minorities versus religious minorities), which in turn shapes the subject matter of their group rights (eg official language policy versus family law). But notwithstanding these differences, group rights have the common goal of protecting the integrity and survival of distinct cultures. As Jürgen Habermas writes, group rights are aimed at 'protection of cultural lifeforms'.[2] The leading normative justification for group rights is the liberal culturalist account, offered by Joseph Raz,[3] Will Kymlicka,[4] David Miller,[5] and Yael Tamir.[6] From within the liberal tradition, liberal defenders of groups conceptualize culture as a primary social good in the Rawlsian sense. A stable culture provides a context of choice for individuals within which they formulate their life-plans. Cultures furnish individuals with options for how to pursue their lives, and assign values to those options. The future viability of a culture is determined by myriad public decisions (eg regarding official language policy across the public and private sectors, religious establishment or disestablishment, land ownership, internal migration etc) and private decisions within that publicly enacted legal framework. Minority cultures are vulnerable to the economic and political decisions of the majority. In some cases, this will be a product of deliberate hostility, with the goal of eradicating or denigrating the minority culture because it is inferior or primitive (eg traditional religions), fueling demands for recognition or respect. But in other cases, it will be considered to be the unavoidable by-product of policies designed to promote a common national identity necessary to underwrite liberal democratic policies or distributive justice (eg official language policies). In yet other cases, minority cultures may be vulnerable to indifference or inadvertence by political decision-makers who lack first-hand experience or knowledge of the minority culture. By contrast, majority cultures do not face these dangers. It is the unequal risks faced by minority and majority cultures that give rise to claims for group rights.

2. Group Rights are Held by Specific Groups

The definition of culture is broad enough to encompass a broad range of social groups and, indeed, political theorists often tie treatments of group rights to the larger phenomenon of identity politics, which encompasses claims to recognition by racial minorities, gays and lesbians, and women. However, when political theorists discuss group rights, they have narrowly focused on three sets of ethnic groups: national minorities, indigenous peoples, and religious minorities.

National minorities constitute a majority in a traditional homeland over which they previously exercised self-government, but were incorporated into a larger state involuntarily, for example through conquest (Quebec, Catalonia, Russia) or royal marriage (Scotland). Even apparently voluntary unions may have been entered into under the direction or pressure of large international powers (eg Belgium, Czechoslovakia). In many cases, they possessed a complete set of economic and political institutions prior to their incorporation into the larger state, which may have survived and are regarded as the institutionalization of group identity. A further distinction can be drawn between national minorities who constitute a majority in a neighboring or kin state (eg the Hungarian and Russian minorities in many Central and East

[2] Jürgen Habermas, 'Struggles for Recognition in Constitutional States' (1993) 1(2) *European Journal of Philosophy* 128, 129.

[3] Avishai Margalit and Joseph Raz, 'National Self-Determination' (1990) 87(9) *Journal of Philosophy* 439.

[4] Will Kymlicka, *Liberalism, Community and Culture* (1989); Will Kymlicka, *Multicultural Citizenship: A Liberal Theory of Minority Rights* (1995).

[5] David Miller, *On Nationality* (1995).

[6] Yael Tamir, *Liberal Nationalism* (1993).

European states) and those that do not (the Quebecois, Catalans, Kurds). The latter subset of national minorities are sometimes referred to as losers in the process of state formation and consolidation, who could easily have ended up with a state of their own, whereas the former subset appear to have ended up on the wrong side of an international border.[7]

Indigenous peoples are difficult to define, and indeed, which groups can lay claim to indigenous status is a matter of considerable controversy under international law. But the paradigmatic examples are the original inhabitants of the settler societies of North and South America and Australasia. Because of their status as prior occupants and sovereigns, they are similar to national minorities. But there are many important differences: indigenous peoples are usually far less numerous, occupy relatively smaller territories, are not integrated into modern economic and political life, and suffer from extreme socio-economic deprivation. Moreover, their pre-colonial institutions are rarely intact, and even if restored, could not operate across the whole range of spheres of modern life. As we shall see, although the political language surrounding the justification for indigenous rights and the rights of national minorities is often the same (ie, the right to self-determination), these differences shape the scope of their respective rights.[8]

Finally, political theorists often analyze the group rights of religious minorities, and have almost exclusively focused on the insular minorities who lead traditional lifestyles, and severely limit their participation in shared economic and political institutions by choice (eg Amish, Mennonites, Hutterites, and Orthodox Jews). In principle, religious identities are not necessarily ethnic (because of the possibility of conversion) or territorial (because the claims of religious groups often concern in-group relations without a territorial component, for example marriage and divorce). But in practice membership in these religious communities is inherited, and members often live in self-contained rural communities or segregated neighborhoods. This renders religious minorities analogous to national and indigenous minorities, and connotes parallel constitutional strategies for group rights.[9]

3. Group Rights as Collective Rights

Avishai Margalit and Moshe Halbertal describe a group right in terms of the right to culture:

> Human beings have a right to culture—not just any culture, but their own.... A culture essentially requires a group and the right to culture may involve giving groups a status that contradicts the status of the individual in the liberal state. The right to culture may involve a group whose norms cannot be reconciled with the conception of the individual in a liberal society. For example, the group may recognize only arranged marriages and not those resulting from the free choice of the partners.[10]

Margalit and Halbertal's description sets out the essential, juridical features of a constitutional group right, as conceptualized by political theorists.

First, group rights are held collectively—that is, they are held by the group as a whole. Yael Tamir likewise holds that group rights 'are bestowed on a collective *as a whole* rather

[7] See Will Kymlicka, *Politics in the Vernacular: Nationalism, Multiculturalism, and Citizenship* (2001); Stephen Tierney, *Constitutional Law and National Pluralism* (2004).

[8] See S. James Anaya, *Indigenous Peoples in International Law* (2nd edn, 2004).

[9] See Ayelet Shachar, *Multicultural Jurisdictions: Cultural Differences and Women's Rights* (2001); Jacob T. Levy, *The Multiculturalism of Fear* (2000).

[10] Avishai Margalit and Moshe Halbertal, 'Liberalism and the Right to Culture' (Fall 1994) 61(3) *Social Research* 491, 491.

than on individual members of the collective'.[11] Even Will Kymlicka, who distinguishes between 'the rights of communities (as opposed to individuals)' and 'community-specific rights' supposes that both rights are held collectively, and differ only in their scope, with the former encompassing the power to violate individual rights, while the latter not.[12] Moreover, as Allen Buchanan explains, group rights are still held collectively even when individuals have standing to enforce them.[13] For example, the right of individuals to minority language education is legally enforceable by individuals, but (1) only operates when there is a critical mass of minority students to make such institutions viable (and so cannot be enforced by an individual without the existence of a minority community), and (2) also entails a collective right by a minority linguistic community to manage and control those facilities. The bare legal form of a group right may conceal its collective character.

This leads to the second point—that group rights necessitate a procedure for the collective exercise of a right. As James Nickel has argued, inherent in the very idea of group rights is the problem of agency.[14] Broadly speaking, procedures for group agency can be categorized along two dimensions: (1) the degree of institutionalization, and (2) the extent of democracy. Political theorists do not set out a specific concept of agency that applies across all group rights. But they appear to assume that decision-making within indigenous peoples and religious minorities is undemocratic (eg led by unelected religious and/or traditional leaders), although it can vary in its degree of institutionalization. By contrast, there is a tendency to assume that decision-making among minority nations is democratic and highly institutionalized, often in the form of federal subunits or, in the event of secession, an independent state. As we see below, there is a link between the agency issue and the precise character of the internal minority problem.

The third point is the nature of the right. For political theorists, the core group right is decision-making power or jurisdiction over matters that are integral to cultural survival. This translates into a different set of competences by group, depending on the scope of its culture. For minority nations, a culture is built around a common national identity, a shared set of economic and political institutions, and a common language. Accordingly, the group right is a right to autonomy or self-government over policy areas necessary to engage in nation-building, and is very broad, encompassing education at all levels (including the language of instruction), the official language of the public and private sector, and both international and internal immigration.[15] The vehicle for self-government is either a federal subunit with extensive jurisdiction in which the minority nation constitutes a significant majority, or an independent state. Accordingly, some scholars link group rights for minority nations with the right to secession.[16] The link is clearest in national self-determination theories of secession, such as the one set out by Joseph Raz and Avishai Margalit, who argue for the right of a group to statehood in

[11] Yael (Yuli) Tamir, 'Against Collective Rights' in Lukas H. Meyer, Stanley L. Paulson, and Thomas W. Pogge (eds), *Rights, Culture, and the Law: Themes from the Legal and Political Philosophy of Joseph Raz* (2003), ch 11, at 183 n 1.

[12] Will Kymlicka, 'Individual and Community Rights' in Judith Baker (ed), *Group Rights* (1994), ch 1.

[13] Allen Buchanan, 'Liberalism and Group Rights' in Jules Coleman and Allen Buchanan (eds), *In Harm's Way* (1994), ch 1.

[14] James W. Nickel, 'Group Agency and Group Rights' in Ian Shapiro and Will Kymlicka (eds), *Ethnicity and Group Rights: Nomos XXXIX* (1997), ch 9.

[15] See Margaret Moore, *The Ethics of Nationalism* (2001); Levy (n 9).

[16] See Allen Buchanan, 'Democracy and Secession' in Margaret Moore (ed), *National Self-Determination and Secession* (1998), ch 2; Margaret Moore, 'Introduction: The Self-Determination Principle and the Ethics of Secession' in Margaret Moore (ed), *National Self-Determination and Secession* (1998), ch 1.

cases where it is necessary for the viability of that group's culture.[17] But remedial theories of secession (eg Allen Buchanan's) in which the right to secede flows from the serious violation of basic human rights (eg genocide) or systematic and enduring discrimination in the distribution of economic and political power can also support a group right for minority nations to statehood, because minority nations are disproportionately likely to be the victims of those wrongs.[18]

In contrast to minority nations, indigenous peoples lack the institutional capacity to exercise extensive rights of self-government over issues integral to cultural survival. As Jacob Levy points out: 'Their languages have frequently fallen into near or total disuse; the land they occupy is often not their traditional homeland (because of forced population transfers); and sometimes they do not have any discrete territory or homeland at all.'[19] Accordingly, while indigenous peoples might possess the same interest in cultural integrity as minority nations, political theorists argue for a group right that is far more limited in scope than for minority nations. The territorial base is smaller, and may be too small to constitute a federal subunit. But the substantive focus is the same—cultural integrity—and therefore would encompass the right to live under institutions operating according to traditional modes of governance and decision-making, and with a particular focus on membership, land use, and family law, in order to preserve traditional indigenous lifestyles and communities.

Political theorists also argue that religious communities have constitutional rights to self-government. Unlike for national minorities and indigenous peoples, there is no assumption of territorial jurisdiction (eg religious federalism). The focus has been on non-territorial modes of self-governance over matters that are integral to the survival of distinct religious identities. Principal among these has been personal law, a broad category that encompasses marriage, divorce, child custody and support, and inheritance. Another important area of jurisdiction is education. In addition, since insular religious communities are territorially concentrated, political theorists have sometimes posited that their group rights include control over the character of social and economic rules in their communities—for example, days of rest, public dress codes, and commercial life (eg liquor licensing etc).[20]

Finally, group rights carry with them the power to impose legal duties in exercise of the jurisdiction over cultural autonomy, although they vary with respect to who is subject to the legal duties imposed by groups. On the political theorists' account of group rights, this varies on the basis of whether jurisdiction is territorial or non-territorial. Territorial jurisdiction—possessed by national minorities and indigenous peoples—extends to anyone within the group's territory, which in principle includes both members of the group as well as non-members. By contrast, non-territorial jurisdiction—held by religious minorities—extends only to members of the religious community. As I explain below, this difference creates an ambiguity over who constitutes an internal minority that has standing to challenge exercises of group rights for violating individual rights.

[17] Margalit and Raz (n 3).

[18] Buchanan (n 16).

[19] Jacob T. Levy, 'Indigenous Self-Government' in Stephen Macedo and Allen E. Buchanan (eds), *Secession and self-determination* (2003), ch 5, at 120.

[20] See Shachar (n 9); Carl Knight, 'Liberal Multiculturalism Reconsidered' (2004) 24(3) *Politics* 189; Jeff Spinner-Halev, 'Extending Diversity: Religion in Public and Private Education' in Will Kymlicka and Wayne Norman (eds), *Citizenship in Diverse Societies* (2000), ch 3.

4. Group Rights and Internal Minorities

It is often argued that there is an irreconcilable tension at a conceptual level between group and individual rights, because of their conflicting logics. The political theorists' constitutional model of group rights supplements this abstract claim with an account of how these rights generate legal conflicts in practice. If a constitutional order grants an ethnic group the legal power to preserve its cultural integrity, that group may impose legally binding obligations that may conflict with individual rights protected by a bill of rights. It is this problem which lies at the heart of the political theory literature, which relies on a stock set of recurrent examples to illustrate this point:

(a) National Minorities

Nation-building policies designed to promote the language and cultural identity of a national minority that constitutes a majority, either in a federal subunit or a newly independent state, may conflict with individual rights to freedom of expression and assembly, the right to non-discrimination, and/or rights to participate in the democratic process. Quebec's language legislation, which seeks to establish French as the common medium of social, political, and economic life, and attempted to do so by establishing French as the sole language of the legislature, the executive, and the courts, by restricting the use of English in advertising and private sector employment, and restricting access to English language education, was attacked on these grounds.

(b) Indigenous Peoples

For indigenous peoples, the two leading examples come from the Pueblo Indians. One concerned the impact of marriage outside the indigenous community on membership. Women who married non-Pueblo lost their membership, whereas men who married non-Pueblo did not, a practice that constitutes discrimination on the basis of sex. The Pueblo also presented an instance of theocracy, with indigenous beliefs constituting an established faith. Pueblo who converted to Christianity and refused to participate in communal activities centered on the celebration of indigenous spiritual traditions were deemed by the group's leadership to be apostates, and were denied access to public resources, challenged these policies on the grounds of freedom of religion and the right to non-discrimination.[21]

(c) Religious Minorities

The most frequently discussed issue concerns religious personal law, especially the rules governing divorce, property division, and spousal support. Under most systems of religious personal law, women face discrimination on some or all of these issues. The most celebrated example is the *Shah Bano* case, concerning the inadequate levels of maintenance upon divorce under India's Muslim personal law, which was attacked for constituting discrimination on the basis of sex.[22] Another issue that has attracted attention is the problem of religious education, in which religious groups assert the right to withdraw their children from state schools and/or to exempt them from a secular curriculum, and instead provide them with a curriculum that reflects religious beliefs in schools under the control of the religious community. The question

[21] See Chandran Kukathas, 'Are There Any Cultural Rights?' in Will Kymlicka (ed), *The Rights of Minority Cultures* (1995), ch 10; Shachar (n 9), ch 2.

[22] *Mohd Ahmed Kham v Shah Bano Begum & Ors* [1985] RD-SC 99 (April 23, 1985).

is whether this infringes the right of children to develop the capacity to exercise free religious choice as adults.[23]

On the political theorists' account of constitutional order, the conflict between group and individual rights raises two issues. The first issue is whether exercises of group rights are even subject to individual rights entrenched in bills of rights. Some theorists (eg Will Kymlicka) argue that if group rights allow the creation of binding legal obligations irrespective of individual consent, groups wield a power analogous to that wielded by the state.[24] Since the corollary of coercive state power is the obligation to comply with individual rights, exercises of group rights must also comply with bills of rights. This is a point of dispute among political theorists. Chandran Kukathas, for example, argues that groups should be free to violate individual rights, and that the appropriate remedy for individuals to protect their rights is the right to exit from the group, which falls within the scope of the right to liberty.[25] The argument from exit has been attacked along two lines. One response has been to suggest the implausibility of exit, either for children (who lack legal capacity), or for community members for whom the economic, social, and cultural costs of exit from a religious community that is core to their identity are too high. But the main difficulty with this argument is that exit is a corollary of a model of group rights built around private associations, with groups acting in their private capacity and creating binding obligations among individuals who voluntarily associate with a group. While private associations must operate within the general law (eg the criminal law), they are not subject to bills of rights, which bind coercive public power. The question of whether the application of bills of rights should be extended to private associations is a genuinely hard question, because it pits those rights against the right of freedom of association. But if groups wield coercive public power, the idea that they must presumptively comply with the constraints on public power, including bills of rights, is not a difficult one. The more challenging issue is how to structure the relevant constitutional inquiry, a point that political theorists are silent on, and to which I return toward the end of this chapter.

The second issue is who constitutes an internal minority whose individual rights are at risk through exercises of group rights. This label implies that: (1) groups exercise their rights to create legal obligations that reflect the preferences (as expressed through a democratic process) and/or the norms of the majority of a group (either through a democratic process, or through unelected traditional or religious leaders), and (2) a minority of group members is bound by these obligations and opposes them. However, upon closer examination, who is an internal minority varies depending on whether the group right is non-territorial or territorial. For religious minorities, jurisdiction is structured on a non-territorial basis, and is only applicable to members of the religious group, but not to non-believers. Internal minorities are group members (eg women, apostates, religious reformers). By contrast, since national minorities possess territorial jurisdiction, there are two kinds of internal minorities—members of the group *and* non-members who live within the territory. Indeed, the leading examples of internal minorities opposed to nation-building policies are non-members (eg English speakers in Quebec). A parallel situation holds for indigenous peoples, who also possess territorial jurisdiction. While the leading examples of rights-based objections to policies to promote

[23] See Susan Moller Okin, 'Multiculturalism and Feminism: No Simple Question, No Simple Answers' in Avigail Eisenberg and Jeff Spinner-Halev (eds), *Minorities within Minorities: Equality, Rights and Diversity* (2005), ch 3; Martha Nussbaum, 'Personal Laws and Equality: The Case of India' in Tom Ginsburg (ed), *Comparative Constitutional Design* (forthcoming 2012).

[24] Kymlicka, *Multicultural Citizenship: A Liberal Theory of Minority Rights* (n 4).

[25] Kukathas (n 21); Chandran Kukathas, *The Liberal Archipelago: A Theory of Diversity and Freedom* (2003).

indigenous identity come from within indigenous communities (eg within the Pueblo), this simply reflects the fact that indigenous communities tend to be ethnically homogenous. But in principle, internal minorities vulnerable to exercises of indigenous rights can consist of both group and non-group members.

The impact on the nature of a group's jurisdiction on the definition of an internal minority has important implications for how to understand the clash between group and individual rights. Political theorists disagree over whether and the extent to which internal minorities can constrain exercises of group rights that violate individual rights, and have devoted considerable attention to this issue. By contrast, they are in apparent agreement that group rights do not pose any such threat to the rights of individuals in the *majority*, an issue on which there is surprisingly little commentary. Kymlicka, for example, sets out the distinction between 'external protections' and 'internal restrictions' as a principle of constitutional design.[26] External protections are group rights that protect a minority group from the economic and political decisions of 'the larger society' or 'other groups', supplement but do not restrict individual rights, and are accordingly permitted. Internal restrictions are directed at 'a group against its own members', entail 'restricting individual rights', and are prohibited. These definitions bundle together (1) the target of the exercise of a group right (external restrictions apply to non-members, internal restrictions apply to members) and (2) the effect of that exercise on individual rights (external restrictions do not infringe individual rights, whereas internal restrictions do). But the relationship between the targets of the exercise of a group right and its effect on individual rights will depend on the nature of a group's jurisdiction. If a group's jurisdiction is non-territorial, and hence limited to its own members, the exercise of a group right cannot violate the rights of non-members. But if its jurisdiction is territorial, it clearly can. Language laws (eg those in Quebec and Catalonia) are a well-known example. Another example would be rules governing land alienation in areas governed by indigenous peoples. Under the Malaysian and Indian Constitutions, federal subunits or areas within subunits dominated by indigenous peoples have the constitutional power to restrict the alienation of land, in order to stem in-migration by non-indigenous persons and to preserve the indigenous character of the region.[27] These restrictions on land ownership collide with the right to mobility and right to non-discrimination of members of the majority. So as a descriptive matter, political theorists cannot argue that non-members do not face the risk of having their individual rights violated by the exercise of group rights. Moreover, as we shall see, expanding the range of persons whose rights are at stake to encompass non-members is part of a broader strategy to pierce behind the veil of the claim that exercises of group rights are always genuinely rooted in the protection of cultural difference.

III. Group Rights in Comparative Constitutional Law

So this is the constitutional image of group rights that is presupposed by political theorists, and which shapes contemporary constitutional debates over group rights. But if we turn to the actual comparative constitutional law of group rights, a picture emerges which is at odds with this picture along every dimension. According to this counter-narrative: (1) group rights are a response to political mobilization not only on issues of cultural survival, but around the unequal distribution of economic resources and opportunities, the unequal enjoyment of public services, and unequal access to political power; (2) group rights are claimed by a broad

[26] Will Kymlicka, *Contemporary Political Philosophy* (2nd edn, 2001), 340–1.

[27] Fifth Schedule to the Constitution of India, ss 5–6; Federal Constitution of Malaysia, Art 161A.

variety of groups, including territorially dispersed minorities and groups that may constitute a majority in the state; (3) in addition to rights to self-government or autonomy, group rights relate to political power, and are designed to ensure representation and participation in common institutions, take a broad variety of forms (exemptions, accommodations, guaranteed representation, difference-conscious but facially neutral rules), arise in a variety of institutional contexts (electoral system design, political party regulation, legislative voting rules, the structure of political executive, courts), are usually not held and exercised by groups acting as a corporate entity, and are sometimes best understood as mechanisms to incorporate a group perspective into collective decision-making; and (4) these group rights produce a variety of conflicts with the individual rights of group members *and* non-members that are materially different from the kinds of rights violations that the political theorists' constitutional image of group rights would suggest.

1. Demands for Group Rights are Rooted Not Just in Claims to Protect Culture

Political theorists assume that demands for group rights flow from political mobilization to protect and promote distinct cultural identities, which in turns shapes the content of those rights. However, in contemporary constitutional politics, conflict among ethnic groups, even where culture is both a subjective and objective marker of group difference, is not necessarily *about* culture. Indeed, the comparative politics literature on politics in deeply divided societies has long understood ethnic conflict to arise out of: (1) competition over economic opportunities, (2) the equal enjoyment of public services, and (3) the distribution of political power, which underpins points (1) and (2). The relationship of these conflicts to cultural conflict is complex and highly variable.

First, consider the material roots of group conflict, which have suffered from comparative neglect in normative political theory. To be sure, nation-building by national minorities concerns questions of identity, and involves the promotion of an official history and culture to create a subnational identity. But the centerpiece of minority nationalism is official language policy. The designation of a language as official certainly has an important bearing on cultural survival. If a language is the official language of the state and therefore attracts the state's support for its use as the medium of cultural life, it thereby privileges the cultural identities that are associated with that language, and disadvantages those that are not. But official language status also operates to distribute economic opportunities. The designation of a language as the official internal working language of the public sector distributes employment opportunities in favor of those fluent in the language, and disadvantages native speakers of other languages. Moreover, the internal working language of government has a network externality effect on the language of the private sector. The same holds true for the language of higher education. And so political competition among language groups over official language policy, framed in the language of group rights, is often fuelled by economic competition, not claims for cultural respect and recognition. In comparative constitutional law, perhaps the leading example of economically-driven constitutional change rooted in group conflict is the redrawing of state boundaries on a linguistic basis in post-independence India. This was largely driven by disputes over official language policy and its impact over public sector employment within multilingual states among speakers of different languages.[28]

[28] Sujit Choudhry, 'Managing Linguistic Nationalism Through Constitutional Design: Lessons from South Asia' (2009) 7(4) *International Journal of Constitutional Law* 577.

Cultural difference may also serve to demarcate economic hierarchies and divisions of labor, apart from and outside the public sector. In many countries, national governments have undertaken projects of internal settlement, to encourage the migration of members of the ethnic majority into less populated areas occupied by minority groups. Contemporary China furnishes many examples of this kind of policy, with the vast internal migration of Han Chinese into Xinjiang and Tibet.[29] On a culturalist interpretation, the primary motivation behind internal settlement is cultural nationalism, and its objective cultural assimilation. But the goal underlying the promotion of Han migration is economic modernization through the integration of the periphery into the national economy through the development of natural resources and/or industrialization in urban areas. What Han migrants encounter is not just a different culture, but also different, traditional modes of economic production. The conflicts that have arisen from this mass migration are not just about cultural difference, but also competing economic models which distribute opportunities unequally. An urban, market, industrial economy values literacy and formal education much more than an agricultural or pastoral economy, and these employment attributes are distributed unequally across different ethnic groups. There may be cultural consequences to economic competition. Cultural practices which may be centered in rural communities and underpinned by agricultural and pastoral lifestyles may be threatened by economic modernization. But the ethnic conflict given rise to by economic transitions is primarily about distribution, not about culture. While the case of contemporary China presents a situation where Han migrants may eventually outnumber the local majority, the same dynamic may come into play with the migration of small, literate elite minorities. A leading example would be the migration of Bengalis into Assam in the nineteenth and twentieth centuries.[30]

Ethnic conflict is often rooted in controversies over unequal access to public services. A core complaint of minority groups is that the state discriminates in the distribution of primary social goods in the Rawlsian sense, particularly liberty, opportunity, income, and wealth. The focus is not educational policy or family law—the principal arenas of group conflict identified by political theorists—but public programs that are far removed from questions of cultural identity and survival, such as the criminal justice system, the provision of infrastructure, and the welfare state. There are two kinds of situations here. First, public services or expenditure may be administered in a discriminatory fashion. While cultural antipathy may fuel discrimination, the dispute between minority and majority groups over public services is not an instance of cultural conflict. The claim is not that cultural difference must be taken into account in the delivery of these programs, but rather that those programs be administered without distinction on the basis of cultural difference—a traditional but powerful claim of formal equality. A leading example of this kind of political dynamic is Northern Ireland, where the Roman Catholic (Nationalist) minority long suffered systemic discrimination in public housing and employment at the hand of institutions dominated by the Protestant (Unionist) majority.[31] The demand was for not cultural rights (eg on questions of religion), but in the first instance, for non-discriminatory treatment. Secondly, cultural difference may serve as a barrier to the equal enjoyment of public services, which leads to demands for modifications in the design of public services. The main cultural difference that

[29] See Andrew Martin Fischer, 'Urban Fault Lines in Shangri-La: Population and Economic Foundations of Inter-Ethnic Conflict in the Tibetan Areas of Western China', June 2004, Crisis States Programme Working Papers Series No 1, Working Paper no 42.

[30] Myron Weiner, *Sons of the Soil: Migration and Ethnic Conflict in India* (1978).

[31] Brendan O'Leary and John McGarry, *Understanding Northern Ireland: Colonialism, Control and Consociation* (3rd edn, 2011).

impedes equal enjoyment of public services is language. An example of this is in Belgium where in 2007, the Flemish Minister of the Interior Government refused to appoint three French-speaking mayors in Flemish municipalities, despite their being democratically elected. The municipalities in which they were elected had a large number of French-speaking inhabitants as well as special language arrangements ('linguistic facilities') entitling those inhabitants to request that French be used in their dealings with public authorities (even though the official language of these municipalities is Dutch). The Minister refused to appoint the three mayors on the basis that they had communicated with French-speaking electors in French and had allowed members of their municipal council to use French during their meetings.[32] The goods whose unequal distribution fuels conflict in this case is not primarily respect or recognition, but the ability to enjoy equal and effective access to public services, such as health care.

Finally, ethnic conflict among culturally distinct groups may concern the distribution of political power. As a large body of research in comparative politics has demonstrated, in a divided society, where ethnic identity is the principal basis of political mobilization, ethnic diversity translates into political division, and fosters the rise of ethnic political parties. Whereas in a polity in which cultural differences have not become the principal axis of political cleavage, minorities form part of shifting majority coalitions who compete for their support, in a divided polity, political competition occurs across, not within groups. The result is a process of ethnic outbidding that produces a flight to the political extremes, and dampens the incentives for moderation and cross-ethnic political cooperation. Ethnic groups may be systematically excluded from public power in one of two kinds of situations. The clearest case is where there is a dominant majority group, and an ethnic minority that is frozen out of power in perpetuity—for example, as is the case in most of the countries of Eastern and Central Europe. This problem also arises in an ethnically fractured polity with no clear majority, which may offer greater opportunities for groups to wield power as members of a governing coalition, but which nonetheless face the prospect of exclusion for a lengthy period. Groups that are perpetual losers in the political process may demand group rights that guarantee them access to political power.

There is a fundamental link between the systematic exclusion of groups from political power and the various non-cultural roots of group conflict. Ultimately, conflicts arising from economic competition and unequal access to public services are rooted in public policy decisions. And so not surprisingly, alongside questions of cultural integrity and survival, it is these issues that are at the heart of the platforms of ethnic political parties, which compete on the basis of their ability to ensure that their members secure public sector employment, profit from the economic opportunities made possible by decisions regarding economic development, and have their needs met in the design and delivery of public services. The ability of a political party to protect its group's interests in these spheres will be a direct function of its political power. So political power in institutions that make these decisions is perhaps the most basic constitutional demand of ethnic groups.

[32] Robert Mnookin and Alain Verbeke, 'Persistent Nonviolent Conflict with no Reconciliation: The Flemish and Walloons in Belgium' (2009) 72 *Law and Contemporary Problems* 151; Council of Europe, Congress of Local and Regional Authorities, Chamber of Local Authorities, 'Local democracy in Belgium: non-appointment by the Flemish authorities of three mayors', October 31, 2008, CPL(15)8REP.

2. Group Rights are Demanded by a Diverse Set of Groups

In addition to broadening our understanding of the sources of ethnic conflict, we also need to broaden the range of groups who claim constitutional rights as groups. The political theorists' constitutional model of group rights focuses on the claims of two kinds of territorially concentrated groups, national minorities and indigenous groups, as well as insular religious groups that are not territorially dispersed. However, contemporary constitutional politics reveals a broader range of cultural groups that voice constitutional claims for group rights.

First, there are ethnic minorities that are territorially dispersed, who live among members of the ethnic majority or other groups from which they are culturally distinct, but where the principal point of cleavage is *not* religion.[33] Consider a few examples. In some cases, the point of cleavage is on the question of national identity, and the ethnic minority makes claims to self-determination, but it is not territorially concentrated and is therefore incapable of asserting claims to federalism and self-government. Northern Ireland again provides an example.[34] Although the communities use the labels Protestant and Roman Catholic to name themselves, the principal point of dispute is over national identification, not religion. In another set of cases, the members of a territorially concentrated ethnic minority do not dispute a shared national identity with their fellow citizens, but nonetheless frame their political claims in the language of group rights. For example, Croatia contains a dizzying area of ethnic minorities which have all demanded and been accorded group rights (see below): Serbs, Hungarians, Italians, Czechs, Slovaks, Austrians, Bulgarians, Germans, Poles, Roma, Rumanians, Ruthenians, Russian Turks, Ukrainians, Vlachs, Jews, Albanians, Bosniaks, Montenegrins, Macedonians, and Slovenes. While it is true that many of these minorities belong to groups with states of their own, their demands are not for secession or federalism. In contemporary constitutional practice, there is a distinction between 'minorities'—communities with a long-standing presence in the state that often predates the state's creation—and more recently arrived immigrants.[35] In yet other cases, the group is a subgroup within a larger community, such as the Scheduled Castes (also known as 'untouchables') in India, who occupy a subordinate position both outside and below the Hindu caste system that reinforces their social and economic deprivation, but who claim equal status within Hinduism.

Secondly, group rights are asserted not only by national minorities, but also by national majorities, even though they are not vulnerable to being outvoted on decisions as a minority would be. The majority may have lacked political power historically because power lay in the hands of an ethnic minority within the same state. Consider Belgium, where for most of the nineteenth century, a French-speaking minority that established French as the common language of economic and political life dominated Belgium. The story of twentieth century Belgium has been the demand by the Flemish majority for the reconfiguration of the Belgian state, which is now a highly decentralized and layered federation of three linguistic regions and three linguistic communities, each of which privileges a sole official language in political institutions and public administration. While the Flemish constitute a majority, they nonetheless view these policies as exercises of a group right to create economic and political

[33] See Marc Weller (ed), *Political Participation of Minorities: A Commentary on International Standards and Practice* (2010).

[34] O'Leary and McGarry (n 31).

[35] See Tove H. Malloy, *National Minority Rights in Europe* (2005), 21; Weller (n 33), 532.

institutions that operate in Flemish. They invoke the language of group rights to justify a range of nation-building policies regarding the privileging of the group's identity in national symbols, place names, official history, and the choice of official language in a manner identical to how a minority group would—that is, as a defensive response to majority nation-building, even though the creation of statehood has eliminated that risk. They are sometimes described as 'minoritized majorities'. Indeed, in Brussels and the French-speaking parts of Belgium, they do constitute a minority, and assert rights that flow from that status.[36]

3. Group Rights and Representation

At their core, many if not most group rights in contemporary constitutional law are designed to redress inequalities in those groups' access to political power. Group rights can be further divided into arrangements for self-rule and shared rule. The political theorists' image of constitutional law has been doubly narrow—in emphasizing shared rule over self-rule, and in emphasizing the protection of cultural integrity as the principal driver for self-rule arrangements. Constitutional practice illustrates how it needs to be expanded along both dimensions.

Arrangements for both territorial and non-territorial forms of self-rule protect members of a group from being outvoted on questions on important public policy, or from the discriminatory application and enforcement of government policies. Of these two, federal arrangements have commanded the greatest attention, because they have been offered as a mechanism for dampening or diffusing secessionist conflict, where the very existence of the state is at issue. Many states in the developing world have adopted federal arrangements to manage group conflict, such as India, Ethiopia, Iraq, and Nigeria. Moreover, the advocacy of federalism as a tool for managing group conflict continues to gather momentum around the globe. In South Asia, federalism has been advocated as a solution for group conflict in Nepal, Pakistan, and Sri Lanka. Federalism has also been proposed as a remedy to the frozen conflicts of the former Soviet Union: Armenia, Azerbaijan, Georgia, Abkhazia, South Ossetia, and Nagorno Karabach. In these cases, countries where federalism has been used to manage group conflict, such as Canada, Belgium, and Spain, are used as positive models of comparative constitutional experience, whereas the failed federations of Eastern and Central Europe—the Soviet Union, the Czech Republic, and Yugoslavia—have been held up as examples of how federalism can fuel, not dampen secession. As I have argued elsewhere, ultimately federalism dampens the secession in democratic states whereas it seems to not have done so in non-democratic states.[37]

Halberstam, in Chapter 27 of this volume, addresses the full geographic range and diversity of existing federal arrangements, including in countries where federalism has been used to manage group conflict, so I will not dwell on those institutional details in this chapter. For present purposes, what bears emphasis is that the root of demands for federal arrangements are often not cultural, but material, and turn on disputes over public sector employment, the uneven impact of economic modernization, and discrimination in public expenditure and public

[36] See Kris Deschouwer and Philippe Van Parijs, 'A Country-wide Electoral District for Belgium's Federal Parliament' in *Electoral Engineering for a Stalled Federation: A Country-wide Electoral District for Belgium's Federal Parliament* (2009).

[37] Sujit Choudhry and Nathan Hume, 'Federalism, Devolution and Secession: From Classical to Post-conflict Federalism' in Tom Ginsburg and Rosalind Dixon (eds), *Comparative Constitutional Law* (2011), ch 20.

services. For example, in India, three new states were created in 2000—Uttarakhand, Jharkhand, and Chattisargh—out of the existing states of Uttar Pradesh, Bihar, and Madhya Pradesh, respectively.[38] An official ideology has built up around each state which emphasizes its distinct history and cultural identity, which supports an argument that the political movements for these states were framed around demands for respect and recognition. But at the root of the demands was not cultural difference or threats to cultural integrity, but rather, the allegation that these regions suffered from neglect in public expenditure and in public sector employment at the hands of a state government controlled by political elites whose electoral base and clientilistic networks were based in another part of the state. In parallel fashion, once new federal subunits have been created, we should be skeptical about the invocation of culture as the justification for particular exercises of a group right to self-government.

While self-rule in general, and federalism in particular, has dominated the constitutional image of group rights, there is a dense constitutional practice on the question of redressing inequalities in access to shared rule. These inequalities arise from the unequal impact of facially neutral rules that either (1) do not evince an intention to disadvantage political participation by a group, or (2) may be designed with this intent in mind. These concerns arise in a variety of institutional contexts, including electoral system design, political party regulation, legislative voting rules, the structure of political executive, and the courts. Although the institutional settings in which this concern arises vary, group rights for political power tend to take one of a standard set of forms: exemptions, accommodations, or new facially neutral rules that are group-conscious—that is, that are chosen because their effect is to promote the interests of minority groups.[39]

Consider electoral systems, which translate votes into the allocation of legislative seats. Many features of electoral system design can operate to the political disadvantage of minority groups. For example, under systems of proportional representation, high thresholds disadvantage parties that appeal to a relatively narrow electoral base. In Turkey, for example, the 10 percent threshold has operated to the disadvantage of political parties that represent the Kurdish minority, which cannot meet that threshold because of their size.[40] Comparative constitutional law provides a variety of models of 'group right' that could promote legislative representation by Kurdish parties. It could be a group-specific exemption, such as those that exist in Germany for elections to the Bundestag, and the legislatures of Brandenburg and Schleswig-Holstein, which waive the 5 percent threshold for parties representing national minorities.[41] It may consist of an accommodation, such as the creation of reserved seats for the Kurdish minority, modeled along the lines for reserved seats for the Italian and Hungarian minorities in Slovenia.[42] Alternatively, the legislative representation of Kurdish parties could be promoted through a facially neutral rule that does not distinguish on the basis of group identity. For example, the numerical threshold could be lowered to 5 percent, or it could even be eliminated entirely (as was done in South Africa in order to promote the inclusion of minority parties).[43]

Constituency systems subject to plurality voting can be analyzed in a parallel manner, and are amenable to a parallel set of responses. Constituency systems produce disproportionality

[38] See Emma Mawdsley, 'Redrawing the Body Politic: Federalism, Regionalism and the Creation of New States in India' (2002) 40(3) *Commonwealth & Comparative Politics* 34.

[39] See Weller (n 33).

[40] Law no 2839 (Turkey), s 33.

[41] Federal Electoral Law (Germany), art 6(6).

[42] National Assembly Elections Act (Slovenia), art 2.

[43] Schedule 3 to the Constitution of the Republic of South Africa, 1996.

between votes cast and seat count, which in a divided polity can disadvantage parties representing minority groups in securing legislative seats. In part, this may be a function of the delineation of electoral boundaries, which can impede the election of representatives from minority parties if they do not constitute a sufficiently large group in an electoral district. There are a number of constitutional strategies available to remedy this disadvantage. Within the constituency system, an accommodation would entail the redrawing of constituency boundaries in order to enhance the minority group's voting power, as has been done in favor of African Americans in the United States. Alternatively, legislative districts could be reserved for candidates from a minority group, as has been done in India, where 120 of the 543 seats in Parliament can only be contested by members of the Scheduled Castes or Scheduled Tribes, although elections are held on the basis of a universal voters' roll.[44] A facially neutral mechanism to enhance the representation of minority groups that attacks the issue of disproportionality directly would be to move away from a pure constituency system, to a mixed electoral system (eg mixed-member proportional or MMP) or a system of proportional representation, as occurred in Northern Ireland in order to overcome the persistent election of Protestant majorities.[45]

These examples raise a number of important points. In contemporary constitutional politics, groups may refer to the whole range of these policies as 'group rights'. However, they vary greatly in their juridical structure. Thus, an exemption leaves a facially neutral rule in place, but holds it inapplicable to groups. Accommodations, by contrast, require positive measures that exist alongside a facially neutral rule. Both exemptions and accommodations, however, incorporate group identity into their very structure, because only group members and the parties that represent them, not voters or political parties at large, can invoke them. By contrast, a group right may entail the adoption of new facially neutral rules that are group-conscious—that is, that are chosen because their effect is to promote the interests of minority groups. To be sure, changes such as lowering thresholds, or moving to a proportional representation system, would benefit all small political parties, not merely those that represent groups. However, these constitutional practices may be primarily identified as measures to enhance group representation, and may give rise to a defensive constitutional politics that resists amendments to those practices because of their deleterious effects on groups. This is even true for electoral rules not initially adopted to protect groups, but which come to take on this function. For example, the tendency of constituency-based electoral systems toward disproportionality hurts parties representing minority groups except for regional minorities. In Canada, this has benefited the Quebec nationalist party, the Bloc Quebecois, and has fuelled resistance to proposals toward MMP.

Political party regulations provide another illustration of how facially neutral rules may be nonetheless viewed as a form of group right, against the backdrop of a divided political community and in comparison to another facially neutral rule that disadvantages political parties that represent minority groups. There are three kinds of regulations that are relevant: substantive policy bans, national scope requirements, and ethnic party bans. Substantive policy bans flow from the idea of militant democracy, which prohibits anti-democratic parties (eg in Germany,[46] Poland,[47] and Spain[48]). In divided societies, constitutions may prohibit political

[44] Constitution of India, Art 330.

[45] Northern Ireland Act 1998, s 40.

[46] Basic Law for the Federal Republic of Germany, Art 21.

[47] Constitution of the Republic of Poland, Arts 11 and 13.

[48] Ley Orgánica 6/2002, de 27 de junio, de Partidos Políticos (Spain), Art 9.

parties from advocating issues that may lie at the very heart of a group's political agenda. In Turkey, for example, the Constitution bans political parties that challenge the state's territorial integrity, the idea of a single nation, equality, and national sovereignty.[49] This has been a barrier to the formation of political parties that seek to represent the interests of the Kurdish minority by campaigning on a platform that promotes the idea of Turkey as a partnership between two nations, Turkish and Kurdish, that Turkey should be restructured as a federation and be officially bilingual, and that the Kurdish-majority portions of the country should have the right to secede. A national scope requirement is designed to encourage the formation of state-wide parties, and has a comparable effect on parties that represent small territorially dispersed groups or large groups that are territorially dispersed. For example, Russia requires political parties to have regional offices in at least 50 percent of Russia's regions, and that each regional chapter have 500 members.[50] Finally, many jurisdictions ban ethnic parties—indeed, on paper, at least 40 of 48 countries in Sub-Saharan Africa do so.[51] Given that minority groups create political parties when they feel they cannot advance their interests through existing parties, this is the most direct form of regulatory constraint.

These policies can be attacked on two grounds. The first sounds in liberty, and argues that these restraints interfere with the liberal freedoms of speech and association. The second sounds in equality, and highlights that these restrictions are unequal in their impact on majority and minority groups. In divided polities, substantive policy bans protect constitutional provisions that entrench the policy positions of the majority from democratic contestation, national scope requirements do not affect majorities who are able to politically organize across the state, and ethnic party bans do not prevent majority groups from dominating parties that are formally not ethnic in character. The constitutional claim for a 'group right' is for a facially neutral rule that provides the space for minority groups to form their own parties, to advance positions on any issue, and to be able to operate in only part of the state. Indeed, this claim combines the arguments from equality and liberty, and can be understood as the demand for a rule that allows for the equal enjoyment of basic liberal freedoms across groups. The model would be the constitutional practice in Spain, Belgium, and Canada, where such legal restrictions on political parties do not exist. As for the case of electoral rules, these rules do not take the legal form of a group right, and the potential beneficiaries of these changes would not be limited to minority groups. Nonetheless, in constitutional politics these permissions are perceived as rights in those polities where they exist, and are framed in such terms in response to proposals to eliminate them.

Claims of group rights for minorities are often made with respect to legislatures and political executives. Indeed, for Arend Lijphart and those writing in the consociational tradition, this is the primary locus of power-sharing among ethnic groups.[52] The goal is to ensure that electoral success and legislative representation translates into genuine political power. It is often assumed that the only constitutional mechanisms are accommodations that expressly empower groups through the design of: (1) legislative voting rules and (2) the constitution and decision-making of political executives. An example of the former is found in Belgium, where legislators must self-identify as French or Flemish, and many laws related to Belgium's linguistic divide can only be passed when half of each linguistic group is present, by a double major-

[49] Constitution of the Republic of Turkey, Art 68.

[50] Federal Law 'On Political Parties' (Russian Federation), Art 3.

[51] Matthias Basedau, 'Parties in Chains: Do Ethnic Party Bans in Africa Promote Peace?' 17(2) *Party Politics* 205.

[52] Arend Lijphart, *Democracy in Plural Societies: A Comparative Exploration* (1977).

ity of each linguistic group, and by an overall 2:3 majority.[53] Belgium's double-majority rules have inspired similar provisions in the Constitutions of Bosnia-Herzegovina,[54] Kosovo,[55] and Macedonia.[56] There are many examples of the latter. Belgium's Constitution mandates equal representation of French and Flemish speakers, although the French are a demographic minority.[57] In Switzerland, the federal executive is headed by a seven-member Federal Council, which is selected on the basis of a simple majority vote of the two federal legislative chambers. On its own, this would ensure the dominance of the German majority, but according to the 'magic formula'—a long-standing political tradition, now underpinned by a constitutional provision—non-Germans receive two seats on the Federal Council.[58] In Bosnia-Herzegovina and Northern Ireland, by contrast, the mandated group representation is limited to the head of the executive branch. In the former, there is a three-person collective presidency consisting of a Serb, a Croat, and a Bosniak, each directly elected.[59] In the latter, the First Minister and Deputy First Minister are elected as a pair by an overall majority of the legislative assembly, and a double majority of Roman Catholic and Protestant members, which in effect requires a Protestant First Minister and a Roman Catholic Deputy First Minister.[60]

But with respect to legislatures and executives, there is a role for facially neutral rules that are adopted with the express intent of protecting group interests, which are understood in constitutional politics to be a form of group right. Thus, in the place of the family of double-majority rules that proceeds from the labeling of legislators as belonging to different ethnic groups, one can substitute super-majority requirements to achieve the same end. In a parallel fashion, party standing in the legislature, as opposed to ethnic representation, can determine cabinet membership. For example, in Northern Ireland, cabinet seats are allocated through the d'Hondt formula, which was expressly adopted with the purpose of ensuring minority group representation.[61] The possibility of facially neutral, yet difference-conscious alternatives to accommodations that incorporate group identity into their very structure raises questions about the trade-offs between these options. Arend Lijphart usefully contrasted these two families of constitutional strategies as pre-determination versus self-determination, which has been helpfully recast by McGarry, O'Leary, and Simeon as a difference between liberal and corporate approaches to protecting group rights.[62] On the corporate conception, constitutional rules predetermine which groups are to be the beneficiaries of group rights, and carry with them assumptions about the political sociology of group membership—that is, assuming that the boundaries between groups are clear, that groups are internally homogeneous, and that group membership is immutable. Moreover, privileging ascriptive identities may not simply reflect preexisting patterns of political mobilization, but will create political incentives to mobilize on that basis, and disincentives to mobilize on other grounds, such as class. For the

[53] Constitution of Belgium, Art 4.

[54] Constitution of the Federation of Bosnia and Herzegovina, Part IV, Section a, 5–6, Arts 17a–18a.

[55] Constitution of the Republic of Kosovo, Art 81.

[56] Constitution of the Republic of Macedonia, Amendment X (replacing Art 69).

[57] Constitution of Belgium, Art 99.

[58] Federal Constitution of the Swiss Federation, Art 175.

[59] Constitution of the Federation of Bosnia and Herzegovina, Part IV, Section b, 1, Arts 1–2.

[60] Northern Ireland Act 1998, s 16A.

[61] Ibid s 18.

[62] Arend Lijphart, 'Self-Determination versus Pre-Determination of Ethnic Minorities in Power-Sharing Systems' in Kymlicka (n 21), ch 12; John McGarry, Brendan O'Leary, and Richard Simeon, 'Integration or Accommodation? The Enduring Debate in Conflict Regulation' in Sujit Choudhry (ed), *Constitutional Design for Divided Societies: Integration or Accommodation?* (2008), ch 1.

same reason, these rules will empower existing group leaders. By contrast, the liberal conception permits, but does not require, group identity to serve as the basis of political identity. It allows for a different understanding of group identity, where boundaries between groups are not clear, where groups are internally diverse, and membership is mutable or even unimportant. Moreover, it allows for shifting patterns of political mobilization over time, and creates the institutional space for non-group-based modes of politics to arise.

As we shall see, the distinction between liberal and corporate forms of group rights is at the heart of the various objections leveled at group rights to political participation in the name of individual rights, and holds open the door to resolving or diffusing them. But if we put that distinction to one side for the moment, on either the liberal or corporate account, the structure of these rights does not square with the claim that group rights are usually not held and exercised by groups acting as a collective entity. The key point is the role of political parties as the intermediating institution between groups and legislatures. Within each group, parties compete for electoral support, which tends to produce intra-group cleavages. There is no singular entity that speaks for the group as a whole, but rather, a set of parties who vie for that role. A useful contrast can be drawn between the recognition of a single, official group institution, such as its religious leadership. Moreover, these questions of group agency become even more complex when one factors in how political executives are composed. McGarry, O'Leary, and Simeon contrast complete consociations consisting of a grand coalition representing all major groups, a concurrent consociation with representatives of the majority of each group, and plurality consociations in which at least a plurality of each group is represented in the political executive.[63] Whereas the leaders of different groups could lay claim to speaking on behalf of the group as a whole in complete consociations, they cannot do so in either concurrent or pluralist consociations.

In sum, the premise behind group rights regarding political participation is that it enables minority groups to shape political decisions that affect a variety of interests, takes a variety of forms, and applies across a broad variety of institutional contexts. However, it does not necessarily entail in every situation that group representatives who hold public office will necessarily partake in the direct exercise of political power. This will often be the case for minority legislators from smaller communities, whose numbers are too small to give them sufficient leverage to wield decisive legislative power or secure representation in the political executive. The interesting question is whether there is nonetheless a way of understanding minority representation to be of value. We can come at this from another direction—the notion of a group right to minority representation on a constitutional court.[64] Minority groups may demand this right because the various forms of group right to political participation may require judicial enforcement, and/or are open to competing interpretations. However, there are two kinds of group right at play. The first is to reserve to groups the power of appointment. For example, in Kosovo, the appointment of two of the nine members of the Constitutional Court requires the approval of a double majority of all members and those holding seats guaranteed to minority groups.[65] In Bosnia-Herzegovina, the power of appointment rests with ethnically controlled constituent units, so that the Serb Republic appoints two judges, the Federation of Bosnia and Herzegovina (which is dominated by Croats and Bosniaks) appoints four, with the

[63] McGarry, O'Leary, and Simeon (n 62).

[64] Sujit Choudhry and Richard Stacey, 'Independent or Dependent? Constitutional Courts in Divided Societies' in Colin Harvey and Alex Schwartz (eds), *Bills of Rights in Divided Societies* (2012).

[65] Constitution of the Republic of Kosovo, Art 114, cl 3.

remaining three appointed by the President of the European Court of Human Rights.[66] This is an indirect method of ensuring a court that includes judges from minority groups. The second is to mandate group composition directly. In Belgium, for example, it is required that the 12-person Constitutional Court consist of an equal number of French and Flemish-speaking judges.[67] In Canada, there is a requirement that three of the nine judges be from Quebec, which has been understood to require at least two of those judges to be from the French-speaking minority.[68]

What is interesting is that in all of these cases, courts make their judgments through simple majority vote—as opposed to a decision-rule that empowers judges from minority groups, such as a super-majority or double-majority requirement. But this type of representation is valuable, for reasons offered by Anne Philips.[69] Anne Phillips has argued in favor of these policies under the rubric of a politics of presence. For Phillips, the value of guaranteeing representation of historically excluded groups is the increased likelihood that they will be particularly alert to the interests of their communities, and how they are affected by public policies, and will advance arguments and adduce evidence that the majority is less likely to do. The claim is that in the process of legislative deliberation, these arguments may resonate with members of the majority, who will be persuaded by the strength of the reasons and evidence offered. Phillips's institutional focus is the legislature, but can be extended to the judiciary. On constitutional questions which go to the very nature of citizenship and identity in a multi-ethnic state, judges from excluded groups bring to bear arguments and evidence that draw upon their experience, in order to persuade their fellow judges from outside the community.

4. Group Rights versus Individual Rights

Recasting the nature of group rights forces us to reframe the conflict between individual and group rights. Although these conflicts still exist, their character is different. I approach this issue by setting out the standard method for rights-based adjudication that has taken root in most constitutional systems. Most individual rights are not absolute, and can give way to competing considerations, and most constitutional systems use the doctrine of proportionality as the juridical framework for the limitation of individual rights. Exercises of group rights count as a form of public power, and are assessed in the same way. The conflict between individual and exercises of group rights can play out at two different stages of a proportionality analysis: (1) the permissibility of limiting an individual right through the exercise of a group right in order to protect or promote a distinct cultural identity, and (2) the proportionality of the means for doing so.

If we examine contemporary constitutional politics, we can set a preliminary (and no doubt incomplete) taxonomy of the kinds of conflicts that arise between particular exercises of group rights and individual rights. As we shall see, these conflicts are quite different from the kinds of examples that preoccupy political theorists. For each, I will identify the stage of the proportionality analysis at which they would appear to play out (ie, legitimate purposes and/or proportionate means).

[66] Constitution of the Federation of Bosnia and Herzegovina, Part IV, Section c, 3, Art 9.

[67] Special Act of 6 January 1989 On the Constitutional Court (Belgium), art 31.

[68] Supreme Court Act, RSCH 1985, ch S-26 (Canada), s 6.

[69] Anne Phillips, *The Politics of Presence* (1995).

(a) Group Rights Discriminate Against Non-Members

As we saw earlier, for political theorists, group rights are external protections that do not violate the rights of non-members. But the notion of an internal minority is misleading in cases where groups possess territorial jurisdiction, because there are non-members who are subject to particular exercises of group rights. Consider the following examples. In Nigeria, states have come to be identified with specific ethnic groups, and many states only hire individuals of that state who are 'indigenes' of that state for the civil service. Individuals are considered indigenes if they are members of an ethnic group indigenous to the state, and have an official certificate that authenticates their status.[70] The effect is that long-term residents, whose families may have lived in the state for many generations, may not qualify as indigenes, and are effectively barred from public sector employment. These hiring policies violate the right to equality. The main question under proportionality is what the actual motive underlying these policies is. They are defended as instruments to protect the distinct cultural character of states, often coupled with a claim of redressing historic disadvantage. However, the material motivations underlying demands for group rights in general, counsels a degree of skepticism about this stated objective. This skepticism is reinforced by the broad nature of these preferences, which are not targeted at disadvantaged individuals. Taken together, they suggest that the policy may be a form of economic self-dealing by political insiders. A second example concerns restrictions on land alienation. The Malaysian Constitution has exempted the states of Sabah and Sarawak from the right to equality, to allow them to restrict sales of private and public lands to native inhabitants, and to reserve lands to native inhabitants.[71] The exercise of this group right would be a form of internal restriction, because it fetters the right of members to alienate property to outsiders. But (contra political theorists) it also limits the rights of non-members to equality and mobility, because they are barred from entering into transactions with insiders and taking up residence in that territory. Non-members lack the political power to check those rules because of their non-resident status, which those very rules perpetuate. The question is what the objective of this policy is. The economic roots of many conflicts over migration, settlement, and economic development argue for circumspection regarding the claim that these policies are strictly designed to preserve the cultural character of a district.

(b) Under-Inclusiveness of Group Rights

Another set of conflicts between group rights to political representation and individual representation arises if those policies are under-inclusive. For example, Poland's electoral law exempts parties representing 'national minorities' from its 5 percent threshold.[72] This exemption from a facially neutral rule is a group right, and is understood in constitutional politics in these terms. Under Polish law, there are nine officially recognized national minorities who can legally claim the benefit of this exemption: Belorussians, Czechs, Lithuanians, Germans, Armenians, Russians, Slovaks, Ukrainians, and Jews. Omitted from this list are Silesians, who assert their status as a national minority. Arguably, the exclusion of Silesians is a violation of the right to equality. The question is what the rationale is for denying official recognition to the Silesian minority. Polish authorities accept the existence of a Silesian ethnic

[70] Human Rights Watch, '"They Do Not Own This Place": Government Discrimination Against "Non-Indigenes" in Nigeria', April 2006, Vol 18, No 3(A), available at <http://www.hrw.org/sites/default/files/reports/nigeria0406webwcover.pdf>.

[71] Federal Constitution of Malaysia, Arts 153 and 161A.

[72] *Case of Gorzelik and Others v Poland*, ECtHR App no 44158/98, Judgment of 17 February 2004.

minority, but argue that it lacks national consciousness. Indeed, to grant it national minority status when it does not warrant it would constitute discrimination against other groups, and create the perverse incentive for them to claim national minority status, which could fragment Polish democratic politics. However, there is another possible explanation—the existence of a Silesian autonomy movement, which seeks an autonomous or independent Silesia. The unstated, yet barely, reasons for the government's stance is that Silesians do in fact possess national consciousness, and the fear that permitting a Silesian party to contest elections would facilitate political mobilization toward federalism and eventually secession, a threat not posed by any officially recognized minority. Let us consider both objectives under a proportionality analysis. For the first objective, there is a mismatch between the system of granting exemptions for national minorities, and the fear that such a system might encourage the proliferation of ethnic political parties. A mismatch between means and ends is indicative of a colorable motive. But taking the motive at face value, a proportionate alternative to this corporate consociational arrangement would be a facially neutral regime with a lower threshold or none at all. If the purpose is to stem secessionist mobilization per se, that is an impermissible purpose. A legitimate objective would be to prevent violent secessionist mobilization, which can be targeted directly by prohibiting political parties that advocate violence (as in Spain).

Another form of under-inclusion is to create distinctions among groups that hold group rights. Consider the long-standing constitutional dispute in Belgium over the BHV electoral district. Belgium's House of Representatives is elected on the basis of regional proportional representation, with separate lists for each constituency. There are 11 constituencies in total—five in (French-speaking) Wallonia, five in (Flemish-speaking) Flanders, and Brussels (which is in Flanders, but is a separate electoral district because of its large French-speaking population). The political party system is fractured along linguistic lines, with parties only fielding lists in their linguistic region. Moreover, parties do not attempt to collect votes outside of their linguistic zones, because the numbers of voters (eg French in Flanders, Flemish in Wallonia) would be too small to elect a representative. So linguistic minorities in practice must vote for a party operating in the majority language of the region. The one exception is BHV, an electoral district that combines Brussels with surrounding areas (HV) with a significant French-speaking population that are in Flanders and which would otherwise be in a Flemish constituency. Since French parties field candidates in Brussels, this allows French-speakers to cast votes for French parties, and for French parties to collect votes in Flanders. However, the converse is not true. Flemish nationalists object to this arrangement as discriminatory. Under a proportionality analysis, the questions would be the purpose served by the BHV constituency, and the proportionate alternatives to meeting this objective. If the objective is a legitimate one—to enable linguistic minorities to cast votes for parties from their language group—then the question would be whether comparable arrangements can be made for the Flemish minority in the border regions of Wallonia. This would be a corporate consociational alternative; a liberal one would be to have a single, Belgium-wide electoral district in which all parties could compete.[73]

[73] See Office for Democratic Institutions and Human Rights, 'Belgium Federal Elections 10 June 2007—OSCE/ODIHR Election Assessment Mission Report', October 19, 2007, available at <http://www.osce.org/odihr/elections/belgium/28213>; Patrick Peeters and Jens Mosselmans, 'The Brussels-Halle-Vilvoorde Question: A Linguistic Trap' (2009) 15(1) *European Public Law* 5.

(c) Compelled Identification and Association

Under some systems of group rights to political participation, the right of individuals to participate in elections requires that they self-identify as members of an ethnic group. Consider two examples.

Under the Cypriot electoral system, there are separate communal electoral rolls for the Greek and Turkish communities. This creates two parallel elections, each contested by two sets of parties which do not attempt to collect votes across the ethnic divide. In addition, there are three smaller Christian communities in Cyprus, the Armenians, the Maronites, and the Latins, who are not members of either community, and which are constitutionally recognized as religious groups. Article 2(3) of the Cyprus Constitution required those groups, within three months of Cypriot independence in 1960 to collectively join either the Greek or Turkish communities, the consequence of which is inclusion in its electoral roll.[74] Individuals have a right of opt-out, but are then deemed to belong to the other community in its electoral roll. Turks and Greeks do not have any choice of the electoral roll to which they belong. The province of Bolzano in Italy has a similar electoral system. Bolzano is home to three linguistic communities—Italian, German, and Ladin-speakers. Political offices are allocated across the three linguistic communities. In order to hold elected office, individuals must self-identify with a linguistic community and stand for election as a member of that group. Unlike in Cyprus, individuals can choose to be unaffiliated. But if they do so, they are ineligible to stand for office (although they may still vote).[75]

Both electoral systems require individuals to declare an ethnic identity, and condition their political rights (the right to vote, and/or the right to run for office) on that basis. Individuals who wish to exercise these rights unmediated by group membership have no ability to do so. Through the lens of individual rights, these arrangements can be objected to on three grounds—compelled identification, freedom of association, and discrimination. In Cyprus, individuals must identify themselves as members of a political community in order to exercise their rights to vote and stand for office; in Italy, group identification is a precondition to running for election. Compelled identification can be understood as a form of compelled expression, or as a violation of the right to privacy. The argument from freedom of association for members for the Greek and Turkish communities in Cyprus, and for all linguistic communities in Bolzano, would be this: the structure of the electoral systems compels political associations (ie, political parties) among co-ethnics and, conversely, prohibits or erects severe barriers to inter-ethnic or non-ethnic political parties. In addition, for the religious minorities in Cyprus, the argument would be the opposite—that it prohibits political associations among co-ethnics, and compels them to associate across inter-ethnic lines. The argument from discrimination builds on both of these lines of analysis: persons who do not wish to identify with an ethnic group enjoy unequal political rights relative to those that do (and for religious minorities in Cyprus, those who wish to identify with group members for political purposes cannot). These systems of group rights are designed to protect the political representation of minorities—Turks in Cyprus, and German and Ladin-speakers in Bolzano—a legitimate objective.[76] The question is whether the means are proportional. Again, the possibility of

[74] Constitution of the Republic of Cyprus, Art 2(3).

[75] Special Statute for Trentino Alto-Adige.

[76] Council of Europe: Secretariat of the Framework Convention for the Protection of National Minorities, *Advisory Committee on the Framework Convention for the Protection of National Minorities: Second Opinion on Cyprus, Adopted on 7 June 2007*, July 9, 2008, ACFC/OP/II(2007)004, available at <http://www.coe.int/t/dghl/monitoring/minorities/3_fcnmdocs/PDF_2nd_OP_Cyprus_en.pdf>.

achieving the same ends through liberal consociational means that permit political mobilization on the basis of ethnicity, but do not require it, is the issue.

IV. Conclusion

Political theorists rely on an image of group rights in which: (1) group rights protect the interest of members of ethnic groups in cultural survival or integrity; (2) group rights are primarily held by three kinds of minorities—national minorities, indigenous minorities, and religious minorities; (3) group rights consist of rights to decision-making authority over matters integral to cultural survival, are held by groups collectively, are exercised by the group through its governing institutions or on the group's behalf by an unelected leadership, often but do not necessarily entail territorial jurisdiction, and can bind both members and non-members of the group; and (4) group rights come into conflict with the individual rights of group members, but do not raise serious issues regarding the rights of non-members.

A careful examination of constitutional practice reveals that: (1) group rights are a response to political mobilization not only on issues of cultural survival, but around the unequal distribution of economic resources and opportunities, the unequal enjoyment of public services, and unequal access to political power; (2) group rights are claimed by a broad variety of groups, including territorially dispersed minorities and groups that may constitute a majority in the state; (3) in addition to rights to self-government or autonomy, group rights relate to political power, and are designed to ensure representation and participation in common institutions, take a broad variety of forms (exemptions, accommodations, guaranteed representation, difference-conscious but facially neutral rules), arise in a variety of institutional contexts (electoral system design, political party regulation, legislative voting rules, the structure of political executive, courts), are usually not held and exercised by groups acting as a corporate entity, and are best understood as mechanisms to incorporating a group perspective into collective decision-making; and (4) these group rights produce a variety of conflicts with the individual rights of group members *and* non-members that are materially different from the kinds of rights violations that the political theorists' constitutional image of group rights would suggest.

The principal goal of this contribution has been analytical—to lay the groundwork for future normative analysis by ensuring it proceeds on an accurate foundation. I defer that normative analysis to another occasion.

Bibliography

Sujit Choudhry (ed), *Constitutional Design for Divided Societies: Integration or Accommodation?* (2008)
Will Kymlicka, *Multicultural Citizenship: A Liberal Theory of Minority Rights* (1995)
Arend Lijphart, *Democracy in Plural Societies: A Comparative Exploration* (1977)
Ayelet Shachar, *Multicultural Jurisdictions: Cultural Differences and Women's Rights* (2001)
Stephen Tierney, *Constitutional Law and National Pluralism* (2004)
Marc Weller (ed), *Political Participation of Minorities: A Commentary on International Standards and Practice* (2010)

CHAPTER 54

AFFIRMATIVE ACTION

DANIEL SABBAGH

*Paris**

BROADLY defined, 'affirmative action' encompasses any measure that allocates goods—such as admission into selective universities or professional schools, jobs, promotions, public contracts, business loans, and rights to buy, sell, or use land and other natural resources—through a process that takes into account individual membership in designated groups, for the purpose of increasing the proportion of members of those groups in the relevant labor force, entrepreneurial class, or student population, where they are currently underrepresented as a result of past oppression by state authorities and/or present societal discrimination. 'Unlike traditional welfare policies grounded in distributional equity, affirmative action takes its moral force from a corrective justice ideal':[1-2] it targets a specific type of disadvantage arising from the illegitimate use of a morally irrelevant characteristic of individuals in the allocation of scarce resources. However, these measures, which may result from constitutional mandates, statutes, administrative regulations, court orders, or voluntary initiatives, go beyond antidiscrimination policy strictly conceived, insofar as they do not require evidence of discrimination on an individual basis. Their ultimate goal is to counter deeply entrenched social practices that

* Previous versions of this chapter were presented at the meeting of the American Political Science Association, Seattle, September 1–4, 2011, and at the 'Protective Discrimination: Comparative Inquiries' conference, University of Delhi, October 14–15, 2011. For helpful comments and suggestions on these earlier drafts, I thank Gwénaële Calvès, Ashok Acharya, Sofia A. Perez, Graziella Moaes Dias Da Silva, and Sarah Wallace Goodman.

[1-2] Sean Pager, 'Antisubordination of Whom? What India's Answer Tells Us about the Meaning of Equality in Affirmative Action' (2007) 41 *University of California at Davis Law Review* 336.

reproduce group inequality even in the absence of intentional discrimination, by producing positive externalities beyond their individual recipients. As a general matter, they benefit groups 'with whose position and esteem in society the affiliated individual may be inextricably involved'.[3]

Beyond this most general definition, affirmative action policies vary substantially across (and within) jurisdictions, regarding their *intended beneficiaries* (ethnic, racial, or religious groups (or castes) held to be economically and/or socially disadvantaged, aboriginal peoples, women, and the disabled), the *form* of the programs involved, the *legal norms* from which they derive, the measures' *domain of implementation*,[4] and the *justification(s)* adduced to support them. They also vary in the *explicitness* with which and the *extent* to which group membership operates in the decision-making process. In this respect, at least three different types of affirmative action may be identified:

Indirect affirmative action refers to measures that are apparently neutral yet actually designed to benefit disadvantaged groups and might be construed as indirect discrimination (in European terms) or discrimination of the 'disparate impact' variety (in US terms) if the distribution of their costs among groups affected by them were just the opposite. In the case of race and ethnicity, an example is the 1997 Texas law[5] instructing state universities to admit the top 10 percent of every high school's graduates (regardless of test scores) in order to increase the proportion of black and Hispanic students, given the large number of high schools in that state from which virtually all graduates belong to either one of these two minority groups.[6] Another

[3] US Supreme Court decision *Beauharnais v Illinois* 343 US 250, 263 (1952) (a free speech case preceding and not directly related to the affirmative action debate). See also Owen Fiss, 'Groups and the Equal Protection Clause' (1976) 5 *Philosophy and Public Affairs* 148 (making the point that blacks—the group for which US affirmative action programs were originally designed—'are viewed as a group; they view themselves as a group; their identity is in large part determined by membership in the group; their social status is linked to the status of the group; and much of our action, institutional and personal, is based on these perspectives'); Melissa Williams, 'In Defence of Affirmative Action: North American Discourses for the European Context?' in Erna Appelt and Monika Jarosch (eds), *Combating Racial Discrimination: Affirmative Action as a Model for Europe* (2000), 67 (suggesting that affirmative action targets 'marginalized ascriptive groups' that have four characteristic features:

> (1) patterns of social and political inequality are structured along the lines of group membership; (2) generally, membership in them is not experienced as voluntary; (3) generally, membership in them is not experienced as mutable; and (4) generally, there are negative meanings assigned to group identity by the broader society or the dominant culture.)

[4] While in most cases—including those of the United States, Canada, South Africa, and Malaysia—affirmative action programs cover both the public and the private sectors, in India 'reservations' do not apply to private institutions. Yet even in countries where no such restriction is to be found affirmative action regimes are often more exacting in the public sector. Eg in the United Kingdom—except for Northern Ireland—the obligation imposed on public employers to monitor the ethnic distribution of their workforce (Race Relations Act 1976 (Statutory Duties) Order 2001 (SI 2001/3458), Art 5) and to revise their hiring procedures and set up a Race Equality Scheme in case of unexplainable discrepancies (Race Relations Act 1976 (Statutory Duties) Order 2001 (SI 2001/3458), Art 2) contrasts with the theoretically non-compulsory nature of positive action measures for private employers (see generally Christopher McCrudden, 'Equality and Non-Discrimination' in David Feldman (ed), *English Public Law* (2004) 581ff). Only in the United States does affirmative action stand on more shaky ground in the public than in the private sector, as the popular initiative referenda leading to the elimination of the policy in states such as California and Michigan since the mid-1990s have only targeted the former.

[5] Texas House Bill 588, an Act relating to uniform admission and reporting procedures for institutions of higher education.

[6] On the broadly similar district quota system set up in Sri Lanka in 1974 with a view to increasing the proportion of Cinhalese university students at the expense of the better-performing Tamils, see Michael M. Burns, 'Lessons of the Third World: Spirituality as the Source of Commitment to Affirmative Action' (1990) 14 *Vermont Law Review* 401ff.

illustration is the French set of formally color-blind yet arguably 'race-oriented' policies under which residents of educationally and/or economically disadvantaged areas benefit from the additional input of state resources targeting those areas, since some of the criteria used for delineating the latter (the rate of failure in high school, the unemployment rate, and the percentage of residents under 25 years old) are correlated with ethnic (African) origin.[7] Those are (more or less conspicuous) instances of a 'substitution strategy' under which what looks like the secondary effect of a formally neutral principle of allocation is at least in part the reason why that principle has been adopted in the first place, given the perceived illegitimacy and/or unlawfulness of pursuing the decision-maker's true objective in a more straightforward manner.[8]

Outreach encompasses measures designed only to bring a more diverse range of candidates into a recruitment (or promotion) pool. In this case, group membership is explicitly taken into account, but in a limited way: it is allowed to enter the picture only within the preliminary process of enlarging the set from which individuals will be selected eventually, not at the selection level itself. An example in British law would be the provisions of the Race Relations Act 1976 allowing employers to 'specially encourage racial minorities to apply when they are underrepresented in the workforce' and to grant 'persons of a particular racial group access to facilities or services to meet the special needs of persons of that group in regard to their... training...'[9]

Often conceived as a last-resort conflict management device designed to deal with or prevent the occurrence of mass violence potentially disruptive of the existing political order in 'deeply divided societi[es]',[10] *positive discrimination*—or *preferential treatment*—consists in measures that grant an advantage to the members of designated groups in the final decision over the allocation of scarce goods, through more or less flexible policy instruments (compulsory quotas, tie-break rules, aspirational 'goals' or 'targets'). In this case, an applicant from one of the designated groups (DGA1) will be selected for a position (for which he or she is minimally qualified)[11] in spite of there being at least one applicant from a non-designated group whose qualifications were deemed to be higher. This means that if another applicant from a designated group (DGA2) had come up with exactly the same qualifications as the applicant who was not selected, the person in charge of making the selection would have selected him or her instead of DGA1.[12] In other words, group membership is the key factor triggering the outcome: DGA1 succeeds in obtaining the position that he or she applied for and would have

[7] In this case indirect affirmative action is the only option available, since Art 1 of the 1958 Constitution provides that 'France... ensures the equality of all citizens before the law, *without any distinction of origin, race, or religion*' (emphasis added). See generally Gwénaële Calvès, 'Affirmative Action in French Law' (1998) 19 *Revue Tocqueville/The Tocqueville Review* 167ff.

[8] See generally Jon Elster, *Local Justice: How Institutions Allocate Goods and Necessary Burdens* (1992), 116–20.

[9] Race Relations Act 1976, Part VI, ss 38 and 35. This is about the only kind of affirmative action allowed under British law (again, with the exception of Northern Ireland). While the Race Relations Act 1976—in contrast to the US Civil Rights Act of 1964—exceptionally permits the use of race when it can be shown to be a genuine occupational qualification (eg 'when the holder of the job provides persons of that racial group with personal services promoting their welfare, and those services can most effectively be provided by a person of that racial group' (s 5)), the courts have interpreted this provision narrowly, and it did not pave the way for the introduction of preferential treatment policies.

[10] Postamble to the Constitution of the Republic of South Africa Act 200 of 1993 ('National Unity and Reconciliation' section).

[11] Of course, this 'minimal' degree of qualification needed to be considered eligible may well be set at a very high level, depending on the nature of the position.

[12] See Thomas Nagel, 'Equal Treatment and Compensatory Discrimination' (1976) 2 *Philosophy and Public Affairs* 348.

failed but for his or her being identified as a member of a designated group. As a general matter, positive discrimination can thus be criticized for conflicting with two distinct principles more or less widely embraced in the different societies under consideration: the meritocratic principle, according to which the most qualified applicant for a position should always be selected; and the principle of 'color (gender/caste...)-blindness', under which it would always be intrinsically wrong to draw distinctions on the basis of such characteristics—for state authorities at least. Because, as a matter of fact, this third type of affirmative action is the main subject of current legal controversies, most of the following developments will focus on it specifically.

Setting aside the case of indirect affirmative action programs—the legal status of which is arguably distinctive and less clearly defined—both outreach and positive discrimination policies display at least two generally observable traits whose coexistence seems paradoxical: on the one hand, since in theory the goal of special treatment for members of disadvantaged groups is to make the need for it disappear as quickly as possible, the temporary nature of such policies is often described as being both one of their defining features and a key condition of their legal validity;[13] on the other hand, in democratic societies where benefits, once given, cannot easily be withdrawn, as a practical matter affirmative action tends to become permanent,[14] irrespective of the changing circumstances that may seem to warrant the termination of the policy.[15] Still,

[13] Illustrations include Art 1(4) of the UN International Convention on the Elimination of All Forms of Racial Discrimination adopted in 1966, allowing for

> special measures taken for the sole purpose of securing adequate advancement of certain racial or ethnic groups...requiring such protection as may be necessary in order to ensure such groups...equal enjoyment or exercise of human rights and fundamental freedoms..., provided...that such measures do not, as a consequence, lead to the maintenance of separate rights for different racial groups and that they shall not be continued after the objectives for which they were taken have been achieved.

The US Supreme Court decision *Grutter v Bollinger* (539 US 306, 342–3 (2003)):

> race-conscious admissions policies must be limited in time...all governmental use of race must have a logical end point...We expect that 25 years from now, the use of racial preferences will no longer be necessary to further the interest approved today.

And section 44(7) of the Constitution of the Republic of the Fiji Islands (1997):

> an Act establishing a program under this section [entitled 'Social Justice and Affirmative Action'] expires on the tenth anniversary of its commencement, but the program may be re-established, unless the benefited...groups have demonstrably ceased to be in need of it.

[14] In India, while the original reservations specified in the Constitution of 1950 were set to expire ten years later, they have since been extended by amendment several times for additional ten-year periods (see Marianne Bertrand, Rema Hanna, and Sendhil Mullainathan, 'Affirmative Action in Education: Evidence from Engineering College Admissions in India' (2010) 94 *Journal of Public Economics* 18). In Malaysia, preferences for Malays enshrined in the 1957 Constitution were supposed to remain in place for a period of 15 years only and be repealed in 1972; as a matter of fact, they were not (see Christopher McCrudden, *Buying Social Justice: Equality, Government Procurement, and Legal Change* (2007), 74). An exception is the case of the Netherlands, where the 1998 'SAMEN' law requiring all firms with over 35 employees to monitor the ethnic distribution of their workforce and enact positive action measures in order to reach predefined 'targets' if need be was discontinued in 2004: see Virginie Guiraudon, Karen Phalet, and Jessica ter Wal, 'Monitoring Ethnic Minorities in the Netherlands' (2005) 57 *International Social Science Journal* 75ff.

[15] Pakistan is a case in point: while originally the main rationale for affirmative action there was to mitigate socioeconomic inequalities between its eastern and western regions and reduce the underrepresentation of East Pakistan's Bengalis in the civil service, the military, business, and the professions, the policy has persisted and developed long after East Pakistan broke away in 1971 to form the independent nation of Bangladesh; see generally Mohammad Waseem, 'Affirmative Action Policies in Pakistan' (1997) XV *Ethnic Studies Report* 223ff.

beyond those two common features—and regardless of whether some collective entities are also legally acknowledged as the bearers of *cultural rights*[16]—a preliminary distinction may be drawn among affirmative action regimes according to the permissibility of focusing on the relative status of groups as a matter of constitutional law. This criterion arguably leads to a representation of the existing variety of empirical cases as a series of 'concentric circles',[17] the largest of which would include—as we shall see—the most transparently group-oriented legal orders of Malaysia, South Africa, and India,[18] but also Canada[19] and the Fiji Islands,[20] while the United States would stand as the most restrictive inner circle, given its strictly individual-centered conception of equality,[21] and the European Union, in view of its apparent endorsement of group-regarding equality for groups defined on the basis of gender,[22] would fall somewhere in between (although much closer to the US side). Moreover, aside from this last, somewhat ambiguous case, the above-mentioned distinction overlaps another one based on the existence (Section I) or absence (Section II) of a 'constitutional precommitment'[23] in favor of affirmative action that leads to two sharply distinct patterns: on the one hand, in the context of a regime change materialized by the creation of a new constitutional order, the expansion in scope—in terms of the number of groups targeted for benefits and/or policy areas covered—

[16] See generally Jacob Levy, 'Classifying Cultural Rights' in Will Kymlicka and Ian Shapiro (eds), *NOMOS XXXIX: Ethnicity and Group Rights* (1997), 22ff.

[17] Jason Morgan-Foster, 'From Hutchins Hall to Hyderabad and Beyond: A Comparative Look at Affirmative Action in Three Jurisdictions' (2003) 9 *Washington and Lee Race and Ethnic Ancestry Law Journal* 74.

[18] As noted by Priya Sridharan, even the individualization involved in the exclusion of the better-off members of the 'Other Backward Classes'—defined on the basis of caste membership—from the benefits of reservations (see Section I.2 below) is meant to preserve the adequacy of the group status as a proxy for disadvantage: individual characteristics are used in order to 'maintain the salience of the group as the primary organizing variable' (Priya Sridharan, 'Comment: Representations of Disadvantage: Evolving Definitions of Disadvantage in India's Reservation Policy and the United States' Affirmative Action Policy' (1999) 6 *Asian Law Journal* 146).

[19] Section 15(2) of the 1982 Canadian Charter of Rights and Freedoms states that the antidiscrimination principle incorporated in s 15(1)

> does not preclude any law, program or activity that has as its object the amelioration of conditions of disadvantaged individuals or groups including those that are disadvantaged because of race, national or ethnic origin, colour, religion, sex, age or mental or physical disability.

[20] According to s 44(1) of the Constitution of the Fiji Islands, 'the Parliament must make provision for programs designed to achieve for all groups or categories of persons who are disadvantaged effective equality of access' to a range of enumerated goods, while the 'effective equality of access to a level or branch of service of the State' for an ethnic community is defined in s 44(9) as being 'represented there in a number broadly proportionate to its number in the adult population as a whole, unless its under-representation is due solely to its particular occupational preferences.'

[21] 'The rights created by the first section of the Fourteenth Amendment are, by its terms, guaranteed to the individual. The rights established are personal rights' (*Shelley v Kraemer* 334 US 1, 22 (1948)); 'the...Fourteenth Amendment[s] to the Constitution protect[s] persons, not groups' (*Adarand v Pena* 515 US 200, 227 (1995)).

[22] Article 157(4) of the Treaty on the Functioning of the European Union (2010):

> With a view to ensuring full equality in practice between men and women in working life, the principle of equal treatment shall not prevent any Member State from maintaining or adopting measures providing for specific advantages in order to make it easier for the under-represented sex to pursue a vocational activity or to prevent or compensate for disadvantages in professional careers.

On gender, see Chapter 19.

[23] Cass Sunstein, 'Constitutionalism and Secession' (1991) 58 *University of Chicago Law Review* 637–43.

of affirmative action programs of the positive discrimination variety explicitly acknowledged as such and designed to reach a prevalent, relatively stable and generally agreed-upon goal (Section I); on the other hand, the predominance in the case law of a highly formalist approach committed to 'a... largely fictional system of "individualized consideration"'[24] of each applicant's merits in the decision-making process paving the way for either the rejection of preferential treatment or an implicit—and paradoxical—injunction to conceal or at least euphemize it in a way that obscures the policy's actual purpose (Section II). We shall consider these two patterns in turn.

I. The Constitutionalization of Affirmative Action and its Side Effects

As far as it seems, when the disadvantaged groups that receive the benefits of affirmative action are numerical majorities from the start, because there is no seriously threatening challenge to the legitimacy of positive discrimination as a matter of principle, programs that qualify as such are comparatively extensive, subject to few formal constraints, and overtly designed to help bring about a structural transformation of society in a more egalitarian direction, within the frame of a large-scale social engineering project explicitly embraced by state authorities. At least as much can be gathered from a condensed examination of the legal underpinnings of affirmative action in two relatively well-endowed developing countries and former British colonies—Malaysia and South Africa.[25]

1. Affirmative Action for Politically Dominant Yet Economically Disadvantaged Groups: Malaysia and South Africa

In Malaysia, because the marginalization of the bumiputeras through their relegation in the rural component of the economy was then widely understood as resulting from the large-scale immigration of the Chinese and Indians encouraged by the British as part of their standard 'divide and rule' policy, special rights for Malays were entrenched in the 1957 Federal Constitution as a necessary step toward the eradication of the old colonial order.

[24] Robert Post and Neil Siegel, 'Theorizing the Law/Politics Distinction: Neutral Principles, Affirmative Action, and the Enduring Legacy of Paul Mishkin' (2007) 95 *California Law Review* 1493. On the US case, in addition to what follows, see generally Paul J. Mishkin, 'The Uses of Ambivalence: Reflections on the Supreme Court and the Constitutionality of Affirmative Action' (1983) 131 *University of Pennsylvania Law Review* 907ff.

[25] As a result of the shift that saw the Malay population expanding and Chinese numbers contracting following the expulsion of Singapore from the Federation of Malaya in 1965, in Malaysia those who benefit from affirmative action—the ethnic Malays, also called bumiputeras ('sons of the soil'), and other indigenous groups—now comprise about 65 percent of the estimated 28.3 million population, while the Chinese are 26 percent and the Indians 7.7 percent. See 'Background Note: Malaysia', available at <http://www.state.gov/r/pa/ei/bgn/2777.htm>. Similarly, in post-apartheid South Africa, in 2011 'blacks' (including 'Africans', 'Coloureds', and 'Indians') made up 91 percent of the estimated 47.9 million population, and whites 9 percent. See <http://www.southafrica.info/about/people/population.htm>. Other countries in which affirmative action benefits politically dominant groups include Nigeria (see Frank de Zwart, 'The Dilemma of Recognition: Administrative Categories and Cultural Diversity' (2005) 34 *Theory and Society* 137ff), Sri Lanka (see Thomas Sowell, *Affirmative Action around the World: An Empirical Study* (2004), 78–94), and the Fiji Islands (see Jill Cottrell and Yash Ghai, 'Constitutionalizing Affirmative Action in the Fiji Islands' (2007) 11 *International Journal of Human Rights* 227ff).

Under this new social compact, the non-Malay minorities, in return for being granted citizenship based on the principle of *jus soli*, agreed to having privileges conferred on the Malays in order to uplift their economic position.[26] As a result, while Article 8(2) of the Constitution prohibits 'discrimination against citizens on the ground...of religion, race, descent, gender, or place of birth in any law or in the appointment to any office or employment under a public authority', Article 8(5) makes clear that this general non-discrimination principle does not ban provisions for the advancement of Malays, and Article 153(2) specifies that those provisions will consist in 'reservation[s] for Malays...of such proportion as...may [be] deem[ed] reasonable of positions in the public service ..., scholarships...and other similar educational or training privileges or special facilities given...by the Federal Government', but also 'of such permits and licences...required by federal law...for the operation of any trade or business.' Moreover, in yet another unusual extension of the reach of affirmative action, Article 89 empowers state authorities to reserve areas of land for exclusive bumiputera ownership. Last but not least, in the aftermath of the May 1969 riots between Chinese and Malay residents of Kuala Lumpur which resulted in a death toll of several hundred persons, additional steps were taken to help to prevent further unrest. First, the 1948 Sedition Act was revised so as to make it illegal to question, inter alia, 'any matter, right, status, position, privilege, sovereignty or prerogative established or protected by the provisions of...Article...153...of the Federal Constitution.'[27] In Malaysia, criticizing affirmative action thus constitutes a criminal offence punishable by up to three years in jail,[28] a provision with no equivalent in any other country. Secondly, in 1971 the government launched the New Economic Policy (NEP), which basically extended the principle of reservations for bumiputeras from the public to the private sector, as part of a 'restructuring of society' designed to 'eliminate the identification of race with economic function' and make the distribution of the workforce in each segment of the economy reflect the racial composition of the population by 1990.[29] The project of achieving a radical social transformation was thus made strikingly explicit.

In South Africa the 1996 Constitution was also intended to forestall any argument as to the permissibility of positive discrimination for members of disadvantaged groups, with a view to avoiding legal controversies of the kind that were then unfolding in the United States. To begin with, instead of framing affirmative action and other remedial initiatives as an exception or a limitation to equality, section 9(2) states that '*to promote the achievement of equality*, legislative and other measures designed to protect or advance persons, or categories of persons, disadvantaged by unfair discrimination may be taken.'[30] More unusually, while section 9(3) indicates that 'the state may not *unfairly* discriminate directly or indirectly against anyone on one or more grounds, including race, gender, sex, pregnancy, marital status, ethnic or social origin, colour, sexual orientation, age, disability, religion, conscience, belief, culture, language

[26] On the dynamic between constitutionalism and impoverishment, see Chapter 6.

[27] Sedition Act 1948 (Act 15), s 3(1)(f).

[28] Section 4(1)(d).

[29] K.S. Jomo, 'The New Economic Policy and Interethnic Relations in Malaysia', Identities, Conflict and Cohesion Programme, Paper no 7, United Nations Research Institute for Social Development (2004).

[30] Constitution of the Republic of South Africa, Act No 108 of 1996, Ch 2, s 9(2) (emphasis added). See also *Harmse v City of Cape Town* (2003) 24 ILJ 1130, 1145 (LAC) (Waglay J), holding that 'The protection and advancement of persons or categories of persons disadvantaged by unfair discrimination...is part of the fabric and woven into the texture of the fundamental right to equality.'

and birth',[31] section 9(5) makes clear that, in some cases, 'discrimination' may be considered 'fair', and the 1998 Employment Equity Act confirms both that affirmative action measures designed 'to ensure the[ir] equitable representation [of members of designated groups] in all occupational categories and levels of the workforce' fall under this rubric[32] and that those measures 'include preferential treatment'.[33] Finally—and most distinctively—under section 20(5) of the Act a designated group member's lack of the necessary qualifications is not a sufficient reason for hiring a non-designated group member instead: the employer 'may not unfairly discriminate against a person solely on the grounds of that person's lack of relevant experience',[34] the only legitimate matter of concern being the applicant's 'capacity to acquire, within a reasonable time, the ability to do the job'.[35] By squarely rejecting the very criterion of merit as conventionally defined by the current level of qualification, the South African legislation thus embraces an expansive conception of affirmative action that responds most directly to historical circumstances in which the majority of the population, defined by race, was systematically deprived of opportunities to earn the qualifications needed for managerial positions.[36] Furthermore, the obviousness of the causal link between current group inequality and the recently dismantled and morally discredited apartheid regime is such that this reconceptualization of merit is not broadly challenged. In this case, like in Malaysia, the legitimacy of the general concept of affirmative action is relatively well established, and the policy most visibly partakes of a simultaneously corrective and prospective strategy geared towards the dismantlement of historically embedded structures of subordination through the state-led deracialization of economic power, in line with the reference in the Preamble to the 1993 Interim Constitution to the 'crea[tion] of a new order'[37] and the Postamble's definition of this document's ultimate purpose as being no less than the '*reconstruction of society*'.[38]

2. Identifying the Disadvantaged: The Indian Dilemma

When the disadvantaged groups targeted for affirmative action initially are numerical minorities, the constitutionalization of the policy may have the effect of restricting the ambit of political and legal controversies to the issue of who else might have a valid claim to be included among the beneficiaries. In India, this led both to an increase in the number of targeted groups over time and to the emergence of an unusually complex, internally differentiated affirmative action regime.

[31] Constitution of the Republic of South Africa, Ch 2, s 9(3) (emphasis added).

[32] Employment Equity Act, No 55 of 1998, ss 1 and 6(2).

[33] Section 15(3). Under this same section, 'quotas' are excluded, however. In this respect, the South African case stands as an exception to the otherwise observable pattern connecting the constitutionally sanctioned nature of affirmative action with the use of this most rigid instrument (as in India and Malaysia) and the absence of an explicit constitutional authorization for the policy with the prevalence of supposedly more flexible procedures (as in the EU and the United States).

[34] Section 20(5).

[35] Section 20(3)(d).

[36] In the same vein, see also the unadorned acknowledgment of the double standard entailed by the positive discrimination variety of affirmative action in *Motala and Another v University of Natal Supreme Court* (Durban and Coast Local Division 1995 (3) BCLR 374 (D), 1995 SACLR LEXIS 256, February 24, 1995): 'the procedure adopted by the respondent in order to compensate for the defect in the education available to African matriculants... involves assessing African applicants on a different basis'; 'matriculation results of accepted African applicants will in almost all cases be lower... than those of other applicants who are not accepted' (9, 17).

[37] Constitution of the Republic of South Africa Act 200 of 1993.

[38] 'National Unity and Reconciliation' (emphasis added).

When push comes to shove, Indian authorities do acknowledge the conflict between the local instantiation of affirmative action and the meritocratic principle.[39] They also do not object to the use of quotas as a policy instrument: the Supreme Court only limited their extent by capping at 50 percent the proportion of positions to be allocated in this way by any single decisional unit.[40] Much more divisive has been the extension of 'reservations' in government employment and university admissions from the Scheduled Castes (SCs)[41] and Scheduled Tribes (STs)[42] to a set of more numerous and somewhat better-off lower castes now estimated to be about 41 percent of the Indian population.[43] As a matter of fact, while the introduction of reservations for the SCs and STs had been nearly consensual, this transformation of the national affirmative action regime into one benefiting a majoritarian conglomerate of ascriptive (non-gender-based) groups eventually came about after some protracted, large-scale resistance from different quarters over a period of several decades.

After independence, the 1950 Indian Constitution retained the principle of affirmative action for the most disadvantaged groups (the SCs and STs) that the British had set up originally by mandating the reservation of a proportional number of seats for them in the federal[44] and state[45] legislative assemblies and enabling states to set aside a population-linked share of government jobs for their benefit. As a result of the 1951 First Amendment designed to overrule a Supreme Court decision striking down a quota system for lower-caste applicants at a state-run medical school as invalid under the equality clause in Article 15(1) of the Constitution,[46] Parliament also decided to permit the extension of reservations to groups other than the SCs and STs and to goods other than government jobs and legislative seats by inserting Article 15(4).[47] Yet, while the principle of affirmative action was constitutionally sanctioned, the ratios to be used, and even the delineation of the relevant groups—in the case of these 'Other Backward Classes' (OBCs), as they came to be called—were left for the executive to determine, and by no means was it pre-ordained that ritual status in the caste system should be their main defining feature. Aside from the case of the SCs and STs, both

[39] 'It cannot...be ignored that the very idea of reservation implies selection of a less meritorious person...we recognise that this much cost has to be paid, if the constitutional promise of social justice is to be redeemed...the small difference, that may be allowed at the stage of initial recruitment is bound to disappear in course of time' (Indian Supreme Court, *Indra Sawhney v Union of India* (1992) Supp (3) SCC 217, 1992 SCC (L&S) Supp 1, JT (1992) 6SC 273, SCC 751, para 836).

[40] *Balaji v State of Mysore*, AIR 1963 SC 649.

[41] Since 1935 'Scheduled Castes' has been the official, euphemized phrase for referring to the Untouchables—the group standing at the very bottom of the Indian status hierarchy. According to the 2001 Census, SCs now comprise 16.2 percent of the Indian population (Economic Survey of Delhi, 2007–2008, 'Scheduled Castes and Scheduled Tribes Population 2001 Census India', available at <http://delhiplanning.nic.in/Economic%20percent20Survey/ES2007-08/T18.pdf>).

[42] The 'Scheduled Tribes' are other groups defined by their supposedly aboriginal status, religious, linguistic, and cultural specificities, and geographic isolation. They now comprise 8.1 percent of the Indian population (ibid).

[43] See Satish Deshpande, 'Social Justice and Higher Education in India Today: Markets, States, Ideologies, and Inequalities in a Fluid Context' in Zoya Hasan and Martha Nussbaum (eds), *Equalizing Access. Affirmative Action in Higher Education: India, US, and South Africa* (2012).

[44] 1950 Constitution, Art 330.

[45] Ibid Art 332.

[46] 'The State shall not discriminate against any citizen on grounds only of religion, race, caste, sex, place of birth or any of them'. The Supreme Court decision is *State of Madras v Champakam Dorairajan*, AIR 1951 SC 226.

[47] 'Nothing in this article...shall prevent the State from making any special provision for the advancement *of any socially and educationally backward classes of citizens* or for the Scheduled Castes and the Scheduled Tribes' (emphasis added).

the Constituent Assembly and successive parliaments after independence expected criteria of 'backwardness' to be defined in economic terms and dismissed the recommendations of the first 'Backward Classes Commission'—appointed in 1953 under Article 340 of the Constitution—that caste be relied on for that purpose for about 40 years. Only in 1990 did the executive accept the proposal included in the 1980 Report of the second Backward Classes Commission—chaired by B.P. Mandal—to add a national 27 percent quota in government jobs for the OBCs to the existing 22.5 percent quota for the SCs (15 percent) and STs (7.5 percent).[48] The Central Educational Institutions (Reservation in Admission) Act of 2006 then extended the 27 percent reservation for the OBCs to all government-funded institutions of higher education, a law whose constitutionality the Indian Supreme Court indirectly upheld in April 2008.[49] Finally, most Supreme Court decisions limiting the reach of affirmative action spawned constitutional amendments with cross-party support designed to nullify or circumvent them.[50] Judicial review thus proved unable to counter the political dynamic triggered by reservations and allowing for the policy's self-sustaining expansion.

As noted by several American scholars, all in all, one of the most remarkable features of the Indian case is the extent to which it illustrates the 'path not taken' in the United States, partly as a result of distinct patterns of institutional decision-making.[51]

First, it is generally agreed upon that the key rationale for affirmative action is to remedy the effects of past and present societal discrimination on the basis of caste, and this agreement on the main purpose of the policy has obvious implications for the identification of its beneficiaries. In contrast with the US relative neglect of this question and casual reliance on 'a mixture of... interest group politics... and... inadequately examined [racial] folk categories'[52] presumed to be socially and economically disadvantaged, Indian authorities have developed a sophisticated methodology to systematically measure the disadvantage ascribed to the systemic discrimination faced by various caste-defined groups in order to select the beneficiaries of reservations on that empirical basis. As a general matter, 'backwardness' is thus determined by considering a broad range of standardized criteria such as literacy rates, land-ownership, income and education level, occupation, housing quality, and access to the civil service and elective offices. It is in reference to this variety of mostly socio-economic indicators that the Mandal commission, after conducting a national survey, ended up listing no less than 3,743 castes as forming the 'Other Backward Classes' eligible for affirmative action (irrespective of whether the disadvantage that they faced could be

[48] See generally Christophe Jaffrelot, *India's Silent Revolution: The Rise of the Lower Castes in North India* (2003).

[49] *Ashoka Kumar Thakur v Union of India and Others*, 6 SCC 1 (April 10, 2008).

[50] The 76th Amendment (1994) eliminated the 50 percent limit on reservations (see n 40) in the state of Tamil Nadu. The 77th Amendment (1995) and 85th Amendment (2001) essentially undid the Court's decision in *Indra Sawhney v Union of India* (1992) to confine reservations for the SCs and STs to initial appointment and forbid them in promotions. The 93rd Amendment (2005) enabled the state to introduce reservations for the SCs, STs, and OBCs in private as well as public educational institutions, thus overruling the Court's decision in *PA Inamdar and Others v State of Maharashtra and others*, AIR 2005 SC 3226.

[51] The following paragraph mostly synthetizes elements derived from the following sources Pager (n 1-2); Clark D. Cunningham and N.R. Madhava Menon, 'Race, Class, Caste ...? Rethinking Affirmative Action' (1999) 97 *Michigan Law Review* 1297ff; and Laura Dudley Jenkins, *Identity and Identification: Defining the Disadvantaged* (2003).

[52] Clark D. Cunningham, Glenn Loury, and John David Skrentny, 'Passing Strict Scrutiny: Using Social Science to Design Affirmative Action Programs' (2002) 90 *Georgetown Law Journal* 879.

traced to some judicially identifiable discrimination for which the institution seeking to grant the remedy would have been responsible). In short, India has attempted to identify the legitimate beneficiaries of reservations using precisely the 'sociological and political analysis' dismissed by the US Supreme Court as 'not ly[ing] within judicial competence'.[53] This was made possible by the reliance on an 'administrative process model'[54] under which the judiciary both articulates the principles constraining the exercise of discretion so as to ensure that the selection proceeds in a transparent way, according to objective criteria, *and* prescribes that this task be delegated to an institution endowed with greater fact-finding abilities.[55]

Secondly, in the 1992 decision *Indra Sawhney v Union of India*, not only did the Supreme Court support the recommendations of the Mandal commission and confirm that low-caste status was a constitutive, *necessary* component of 'backwardness', thus striking down the 10 percent quota for 'other economically backward sections of people' not covered by existing schemes of reservations that the government had introduced as an attempt to accommodate the underprivileged amongst the upper castes;[56] it also made a decisive contribution to the legal construction of an heterogeneous affirmative action regime predicated upon the acknowledgment of the existence of different degrees of disadvantage among the policy's beneficiaries and of the irreducibly distinctive nature of the SCs and STs' condition. In fact, this heterogeneity was already apparent in that even after the turning point of the early 1990s only those two groups—and not the OBCs—were granted reservations of legislative spots. Still, in *Sawhney* two momentous decisions were made. On the one hand, the Court upheld a quota for the OBCs (27 percent) almost twice as small as their proportion in the Indian population (52 percent according to the Mandal Report), even though the SCs and STs—who then represented 15 percent and 7.5 percent of the population respectively—had been granted a proportional quota of 22.5 percent of government jobs and university places. That 27 percent figure was almost exactly what was left of the 50 percent available for reservation after the SC and ST quotas had been taken into account.[57] The SCs and STs had their own separate reservations; they did not need to compete for reserved seats against the more numerous and frequently more affluent and influential OBCs. On the other hand, in order to address the concern that the benefits of reservations were not distributed evenly throughout each 'backward' group but instead were monopolized by persons at the socio-economic top of the group, the Supreme Court made it compulsory to *combine* caste and class for ascertaining whether a given individual ought to be eligible for such benefits (in contrast with the predominant mention of class as a potential *substitute* for race in the US affirmative action debate).[58] It held that OBC membership only created a rebuttable presumption that a member needed affirmative action and so directed the government to adopt

[53] *Regents of the University of California v Bakke* 438 US 265, 297 (1978). See also the short development in Section II below.

[54] Pager (n 1-2), 298.

[55] See *Indra Sawhney v Union of India*, 81, directing the central government to set up at the state and national levels 'a permanent body, in the nature of a Commission..., to which complaints of wrong inclusion or non-inclusion of groups... in the lists of OBCs can be made.'

[56] Symmetrically, in the 1963 *Balaji v State of Mysore* decision, the Supreme Court had already held that, just like economic disadvantage after *Sawhney*, caste could not be the only criterion considered for establishing OBC status.

[57] See n 40.

[58] See generally Deborah Malamud, 'Class-Based Affirmative Action: Lessons and Caveats' (1996) 74 *Texas Law Review* 1847ff.

an economic means test in order to screen out those privileged members of a 'backward class'—the so-called 'creamy layer'—who should not receive government assistance.[59] Yet this disaggregation of the collection of potential recipients according to a class criterion and the individualized determination of economic disadvantage as a condition for affirmative action eligibility apply only to the OBCs—not to the SCs and STs. In this respect, too, members of the groups generally considered as the most disadvantaged are treated differently than the other beneficiaries of the programs involved. At the end of the day, quite unlike in the United States, the broadening of the set of targeted groups did prove compatible with a quasi-official and deeply consequential acknowledgment of the qualitative differences between its various components.

II. The Non-Constitutionalization of Affirmative Action and its Side Effects

In countries where affirmative action has not been constitutionalized and where the beneficiaries (women excepted) are minority groups, the legal validity of a program of this kind will depend upon whether it meets a set of formal requirements. The most important of those is arguably that the outcome of the decisional process by which scarce goods are being allocated should not be exclusively determined by group membership. Thus, the European Court of Justice has rebuked schemes under which equally qualified women were to be automatically preferred to men in employment sectors where women were underrepresented[60] yet approved of a tie-break rule giving priority to women in civil service promotions as long as an equally qualified individual male candidate had the opportunity to establish that 'reasons specific to [his situation]' should 'tilt the balance in his favour'.[61] While arguably more restrictive than the US case law in that they rule out positive discrimination altogether, these holdings are broadly similar to Justice Powell's controlling opinion in the *Bakke* decision striking down inflexible racial quotas in university admissions as unconstitutional[62] yet allowing race to be considered as a functionally equivalent 'plus' factor, as long as it stands as just one among many potentially 'diversity'-enhancing features, to be weighed competitively against others within an individualized assessment of each applicant's distinct contribution.[63] Still, a brief examination of some of the most salient EU and US developments uncovers distinctive features definitely worth highlighting. We shall consider them in turn.

[59] *Indra Sawhney v Union of India*, 558–60.

[60] ECJ, Case C-450/93 *Kalanke v Freie Hansestadt Bremen* [1995] ECR I-3051.

[61] ECJ, Case C-409/95 *Marschall v Land Nordrhein-Westfalen* [1997] ECR I-6363, 566.

[62] Those were later upheld under strict scrutiny, but only as a court-ordered remedy for an egregious pattern of persistent discrimination by a state actor (conditions unmet in the *Bakke* case); see *United States v Paradise* 480 US 149 (1987).

[63] *Regents of the University of California v Bakke*, 315–18. Since then the Supreme Court has also prescribed that the extent of the boost provided by affirmative action should not be *fixed ex ante, quantified, and substantial enough to be decisive* (without specifying whether a judgment of unconstitutionality would be triggered by any of these factors considered in isolation); see *Gratz v Bollinger* 539 US 244 (2003) striking down the affirmative action program of the University of Michigan's undergraduate school, which automatically distributed 20 points out of the 100 needed to guarantee admission to all members of underrepresented racial or ethnic minorities.

1. The Soft, Gender-Focused, 'Discrimination-Blocking'[64] EU Affirmative Action Model

Aside from a general resistance to the use of any kind of *positive discrimination* as defined above—and to quotas and set-asides in particular[65]—at least two broad cross-European trends stand out.

First, there are considerable differences in the development of positive action across the different equality grounds. Because gender equality in the employment field has been within the competence of the European Community from the start,[66] in contrast with all the other major affirmative action regimes, gender-based schemes are the most widespread by far and therefore have always been at the center of legal debates. While Article 5 of the Racial Equality Directive provides that 'the principle of equal treatment shall not prevent any Member State from maintaining or adopting specific measures to prevent or compensate for disadvantages linked to racial or ethnic origin',[67-68] in that case leaving it to the states to decide whether or not to adopt such measures—a choice applying to all kinds of affirmative action—almost always resulted in their abstaining to do so.

Secondly, like in India, the European Court of Justice mainly conceives affirmative action as a mechanism for counterbalancing—and remedying the effects of—societal (direct and indirect) discrimination—in that case, discrimination on the basis of sex. As explained in the *Marschall* decision, 'even where male and female candidates are equally qualified, male candidates tend to be promoted in preference to female candidates.'[69] This is so either 'because... [employers] apply traditional promotion criteria which in practice put women at a disadvantage, such as... seniority', or

> because of prejudices and stereotypes concerning the role and capacities of women in working life and the fear, for example, that women will interrupt their careers more frequently, that owing to household and family duties they will be less flexible in their working hours, or that they will be absent from work more frequently because of pregnancy.[70]

This judicially approved justification for affirmative action offers a stark contrast with the currently prevailing 'diversity' rationale peculiar to the US case law.

[64] See Elizabeth Anderson, *The Imperative of Integration* (2010), 144–8.

[65] There are a small number of narrowly circumscribed exceptions. One is when the program applies in areas ancillary to the hiring decision itself, such as the allocation of training positions (see ECJ, Case C-158/97 *George Badeck and others* [2000] ECR I-1875). Another is when the measure benefits disabled persons (see Lisa Waddington and Anna Lawson, *Disability and Non-Discrimination Law in the European Union: Thematic Report of the European Network of Legal Experts in the Non-Discrimination Field* (2009)). A third one is the requirement in s 46 of the Police (Northern Ireland) Act 2000 that equal numbers of Catholics and non-Catholics be appointed to the Police Service from a pool of qualified applicants, a provision upheld by the Northern Irish High Court in *In the Matter of an Application by Mark Parsons for Judicial Review* [2002] NIQB 46.

[66] Article 119 of the Treaty of Rome (1957).

[67-68] Council Directive (EC) 2000/43 implementing the principle of equal treatment between persons irrespective of racial or ethnic origin [2000] OJ L180/22.

[69] *Marschall v Land Nordrhein-Westfalen*, para 29.

[70] Ibid paras 4 and 29.

2. A Pattern of Diversion: The (Exceptional) US Affirmative Action Regime

Because the Equal Protection Clause of the Constitution's Fourteenth Amendment (1868), according to which 'no state shall deny to any person within its jurisdiction the equal protection of the laws', was deliberately drafted so as to let courts rule on the constitutionality of racial classifications by state authorities on a case-by-case basis,[71] the legal status of affirmative action has been an uncertain, shifting, and paradoxical judicial construct. From a comparative perspective, at least three distinctive features bear special emphasis.

One is the increasingly restrictive nature of the policy's conditions of validity as defined in the Supreme Court's case law, at least as far as race-based affirmative action is concerned. Thus, while in *Fullilove v Klutznick*[72] the Court had confirmed the constitutionality of minority set-asides in public contracting introduced by Congress, in *City of Richmond v JA Croson Co*[73] it struck down a similar program set up in Richmond, Virginia, arguing that this program failed the 'strict scrutiny' test that any race-based classification by state or local—as opposed to federal—authorities had to pass, because it was not 'narrowly tailored' to the 'compelling governmental interest'[74] of remedying the effects of some specific, judicially established instance of intentional past discrimination. Finally, in *Adarand Constructors, Inc v Pena*[75] the Court discarded the federal versus non-federal-level-of-authority distinction and held that all race-based classifications had to meet the requirements of strict scrutiny, regardless both of which racial group was to benefit and of which government unit the program was an emanation. In contrast, presumably less 'suspect' gender-based classifications—including affirmative action programs—are subject to the less exacting standard of 'intermediate scrutiny', under which they must only be 'substantially related' to the achievement of an 'important governmental objective[s]'.[76] Moreover, the Supreme Court has found that some of those gender-based classifications designed 'to remedy discrimination against women in the job market' understood as a diffuse phenomenon did meet that test,[77] in contradistinction to its rejection of the 'societal discrimination' rationale as 'too amorphous a basis for imposing a racially classified remedy'[78] while properly constraining its scope.

This rejection and its most momentous side effect—the emergence in the case law of an alternative, ultimately dominant, justification for broad affirmative action programs focused on their alleged contribution to viewpoint diversity, a retrospective rationalization with little or no relationship to the policy's original *raison d'être*—is another distinctively American development, arising in part from implications of the separation of powers as understood by some members of the Supreme Court. The main reason why Justice Powell in *Bakke* ended up recasting race-based affirmative action as an instrument for bringing into selective universities and professional schools students with different 'experiences, outlooks, and

[71] See Andrew Kull, *The Color-Blind Constitution* (1992).

[72] *Fullilove v Klutznick* 448 US 448 (1980).

[73] *City of Richmond v JA Croson Co* 488 US 469 (1989).

[74] *Wygant v Jackson Board of Education* 476 US 267, 274 (1986).

[75] *Adarand Constructors, Inc v Pena* 515 US 220 (1995).

[76] *Craig v Boren* 429 US 190, 197 (1976).

[77] *Califano v Webster* 430 US 313, 319 (1977).

[78] *Wygant v Jackson Board of Education*, 276.

ideas'[79] whose interactions would give rise to an 'atmosphere [of] speculation, experiment and creation',[80] in accordance with the traditional, knowledge-oriented mission of academic institutions, is that this did not require the Court itself to draw lines between competing claimants. In contrast, the societal discrimination argument inevitably relies on a comparative assessment of the unequal victimization experienced by all groups likely to think of themselves as deserving of compensation, an assessment in need of judicial oversight yet involving a 'kind of variable sociological and political analysis... [that] does not lie within judicial competence'.[81] While 'the legislative authority' is 'free to recognize degrees of harm...and...may confine its restrictions to those classes of cases where the need is deemed to be clearest',[82] the courts cannot legitimately 'evaluate the extent of the prejudice...suffered by various minority groups'—and decide that 'those whose...injury is thought to exceed some arbitrary level of tolerability then would be entitled to preferential classifications.'[83] From this boundary-policing, integrity-preserving perspective, deferring to the value of 'academic freedom' and pretending not to interfere in the selection of the means best suited to achieve an end presumably internal to the academic sphere apparently seemed like the safer course.[84] To a certain extent, 'substantive constitutional doctrine' may thus be understood as a by-product of 'institutional arrangements',[85] namely of the *incomplete and largely unavowed* 'juridicalization'[86] of political decision-making characteristic of the American public culture.

Aside from the many theoretical shortcomings of the diversity rationale[87]—including its unacknowledged lack of fit with the maintained requirement that affirmative action programs should be temporary[88]—one of the most striking legal developments since *Bakke*, however, has been the semantic extension of 'diversity' far beyond Powell's original emphasis on its heuristic dimension as an educational tool. As reconceptualized—and validated anew—in the 2003 *Grutter v Bollinger* decision, this construct is now held to be a 'compelling state interest' both on epistemic and on political grounds, as it is expected to promote 'cross-racial understanding',[89] 'break down racial stereotypes',[90] and legitimize elite institutions.[91] In short, as

[79] *Regents of the University of California v Bakke*, 314.

[80] Ibid 312 (quotation omitted).

[81] Ibid 297.

[82] *West Coast Hotel Company v Parrish* 300 US 379, 400 (1937) (quotation omitted).

[83] *Regents of the University of California v Bakke*, 296–7.

[84] Ibid 312–14.

[85] Mark Tushnet, 'Interpreting Constitutions Comparatively: Some Cautionary Notes with Reference to Affirmative Action' (2004) 36 *Connecticut Law Review* 655.

[86] Martin Shapiro, 'Juridicalization of Politics in the United States' (1994) 15 *International Political Science Review* 101ff.

[87] See Daniel Sabbagh, *Equality and Transparency: A Strategic Perspective on Affirmative Action in American Law* (2007), ch 2.

[88] See n 13. As emphasized by the legal scholar Robert Post, 'the justification of diversity, unlike remedy, has no built-in time horizon' (Robert Post, 'The Supreme Court 2002 Term: Fashioning the Legal Constitution: Culture, Courts, and Law' (2003) 117 *Harvard Law Review* 67 n 306). See also Tushnet (n 85), 662:

> The different experiences members of racial minorities bring to their classes are rooted in culture, and whatever improvements in material conditions there might be seem unlikely to do much—at least within twenty-five years, the Court's purported 'end point'—to alter culture-based experiences.

[89] *Grutter v Bollinger*, 330.

[90] Ibid.

[91] 'In order to cultivate a set of leaders with legitimacy in the eyes of the citizenry, it is necessary that the path to leadership be visibly open to talented and qualified individuals of every race and ethnicity' (ibid 332).

argued by philosopher and legal scholar Elizabeth Anderson, the umbrella term that 'diversity' has become is just 'another way of talking about integration'[92] and the eradication of the remnants of racial hierarchy. That such a circuitous—and ideologically consequential—path has been taken before coming full circle—without this detour being explicitly acknowledged for what it is by the Supreme Court—nonetheless remains a distinctive trait of the US legal affirmative action regime.

Finally—and most paradoxically—the pattern of obfuscation perceptible in US case law concerns both the *actual end purpose of affirmative action* and the *race-conscious dimension of the policy itself*; as a general matter, in order for an affirmative action plan to be deemed constitutionally permissible, the extent to which—or even the fact that—group membership has been taken into account should simply be left in the background. As much was suggested initially by Justice Powell in *Bakke*, in that nothing prevented the bonus informally given to minority applicants that he endorsed from being implicitly calibrated so as to ensure the attainment of a previously defined minimal level of (racial) 'diversity'. At the end of the day, the difference between quotas and supposedly flexible affirmative action programs was thus 'administrative and symbolic':[93] it lay not in the size of the advantage granted to blacks and Hispanics but in the fact that flexible programs do not 'make public the extent of the preference and the precise workings of the system'.[94] Similarly, in *Croson* Justice O'Connor argued that Richmond should have attempted to 'use alternative, race-neutral means' such as 'simplification of bidding procedures, relaxation of bonding requirements, and training or financial aid for [all] disadvantaged entrepreneurs' *in order 'to increase minority participation in city contracting'*.[95] The same point was made in the concurring opinion of Justice Scalia: because

> blacks have been disproportionately disadvantaged by racial discrimination, any race-neutral remedial program aimed at the disadvantaged as such will have a disproportionately beneficial impact on [them]. Only such a program, and not one that *operates on the basis of race*, is in accord with... our Constitution.[96]

It follows that as long as the decision-making authority proceeds discreetly enough, it will be left free to enact measures that are superficially color-blind yet deliberately favorable to minority members. Affirmative action for racial groups previously discriminated against is authorized, provided it remains indirect.[97] Lastly, that a measure of opacity regarding its modus operandi is the key condition an affirmative action plan must meet in order to be considered legal has been confirmed by the Supreme Court in 2003, as it validated the program of the University of Michigan Law School that sought to enroll an unspecified 'critical mass' of underrepresented minority students in *Grutter v Bollinger* while striking down the more detailed plan of the University of Michigan's undergraduate school in the companion case of *Gratz v Bollinger*.[98] Only in the dissents did some of the Justices voice their misgivings as to the Court's approbation of precisely those schemes that 'get their racially diverse results without

[92] Elizabeth Anderson, 'Racial Integration as a Compelling Interest' (2004) 21 *Constitutional Commentary* 24.

[93] Ronald Dworkin, *A Matter of Principle* (1985), 309.

[94] *Regents of the University of California v Bakke*, 379 (opinion of Justices Brennan, Marshall, White, and Blackmun).

[95] *City of Richmond v Croson*, 471, 509–10 (emphasis added).

[96] Ibid 528 (emphasis added).

[97] In the same vein, see also *Parents Involved in Community Schools v Seattle School District No 1* 551 US 701, 787–9 (2007) (concurring opinion of Justice Kennedy).

[98] See n 63.

saying directly what they are doing or why they are doing it',[99] 'through winks, nods and disguises'.[100] It would seem, then, that the constitutional validity of US affirmative action policies depends in practical terms upon whether the degree to which they take race into account remains properly concealed.

III. Conclusion

In all the countries included in this brief comparative overview, affirmative action is an instrument designed to achieve a more or less explicitly acknowledged goal of structural transformation. In all—with the possible exception of Malaysia—that transformation is geared towards an ideal of *societal integration*, to be realized by equalizing the distribution of a set of status-conferring goods among ascriptive groups so as to reduce the salience of the boundaries between them. As a practical matter, the constitutionalization of the policy makes it possible to pursue this quintessentially political objective in a relatively transparent way. In the absence of such a constitutional precommitment, however, the awareness of 'the divisive power of visible race-conscious interventions'[101]—that is, the fear of perpetuating stigmatizing stereotypes and of fostering perceptions of unfairness and resentment among the non-beneficiaries—may well lead the courts toward prescribing that affirmative action become (or remain) *implicit, indirect—or both*. Given the strong likelihood of triggering such perceptions,[102] if 'Justice must satisfy the appearance of justice'[103] and if the 'double-consciousness' involved in 'mak[ing] the public's view a factor within [the judge's] own' is 'a necessary aspect of constitutional adjudication',[104] a doctrinal requirement of obscurity is the unsettling yet nearly inevitable result.

Bibliography

Elizabeth Anderson, *The Imperative of Integration* (2010)
Gwénaële Calvès, *La Discrimination positive* ([2004] 2010)
Christopher McCrudden, *Buying Social Justice: Equality, Government Procurement, and Legal Change* (2007)
Paul J. Mishkin, 'The Uses of Ambivalence: Reflections on the Supreme Court and the Constitutionality of Affirmative Action' (1983) 131 *University of Pennsylvania Law Review* 907
Marshall Cohen, Nagel Thomas, and Scanlon Thomas (eds), *Equality and Preferential Treatment* (1977)
European Commission, *International Perspectives on Positive Action Measures: A Comparative Analysis in the European Union, Canada, the United States and South Africa* (2009)
Marc Galanter, *Competing Equalities: Law and the Backward Classes in India* (1984)
Devanesan Nesiah, *Discrimination with Reason? The Policy of Reservations in the United States, India, and Malaysia* (1997)

[99] *Gratz v Bollinger*, 298 (dissenting opinion of Justice Souter).
[100] Ibid 305 (dissenting opinion of Justice Ginsburg).
[101] Richard Primus, 'The Future of Disparate Impact' (2010) 108 *Michigan Law Review* 1374.
[102] On the US case, see Paul Sniderman and Thomas Piazza, *The Scar of Race* (1993), 103–4.
[103] *Regents of the University of California v Bakke*, 319 (quotation omitted).
[104] Richard Primus, 'Double-Consciousness in Constitutional Adjudication' (2007) 13 *Review of Constitutional Studies* 20.

Richard Primus, 'Equal Protection and Disparate Impact: Round Three' (2003) 117 *Harvard Law Review* 493

Michel Rosenfeld, *Affirmative Action and Justice: A Philosophical and Constitutional Inquiry* (1991)

Jed Rubenfeld, 'Affirmative Action' (1997) 107 *Yale Law Journal* 427

Daniel Sabbagh, *Equality and Transparency: A Strategic Perspective on Affirmative Action in American Law* (2007)

Olivier De Schutter, 'Positive Action' in Dagmar Schiek, Lisa Waddington, and Mark Bell (eds), *Anti-discrimination Law: Ius Commune Casebooks for the Common Law of Europe* (2007)

John David Skrentny (ed), *Color Lines: Affirmative Action, Immigration, and Civil Rights Options for America* (2001)

Mark Tushnet, 'Interpreting Constitutions Comparatively: Some Cautionary Notes with Reference to Affirmative Action' (2004) 36 *Connecticut Law Review* 649

CHAPTER 55

BIOETHICS AND BASIC RIGHTS: PERSONS, HUMANS, AND BOUNDARIES OF LIFE

JUDIT SÁNDOR

Budapest

The basic concept of human rights is that people have certain moral rights by virtue of being human. But it does not follow from this concept that international instruments of human rights and the national constitutions protect all rights agreed or shared within international or national communities. The recent incorporation of certain bioethical norms into constitutional amendments and, more typically, into new interpretations of general constitutional rights in the domain of health care, therefore, is a result of a long history. Moreover, bioethics and human rights have, for many decades, developed separately. The two disciplines have different historical roots; they each have distinct scopes, perspectives, and methods of interpretation. Except for the right to be informed before a 'medical experimentation', which appeared soon after the Second World War,[1] many of the bioethical norms have been formulated as basic human rights only in the last decades of the twentieth century. Furthermore, it should be emphasized that rights and values within bioethics are not regarded as automatically transferable to constitutional rights, nor even to statutory rights.

The main point of departure from the previous, paternalistic model[2] was the possibility to treat many chronic diseases, and the availability of several non-therapeutic interventions, biomedical research, genetic screening, and reproductive services. These medical interventions presuppose entirely different doctor–patient relationships than, for instance, in emergency care. The patients' autonomy, their views on life, are material in the decisions on making choices between different alternatives. Furthermore, by the beginning of the twenty-first century, several new technologies, such as genetic testing, assisted reproduction, stem cell research and therapy, nanotechnology, synthetic biology, and neuroscience have provided insights into basic processes of life, human behavior, and human heredity. The splendid isolation of science has been seriously questioned by social scientists, bioethicists, and by the public; science is no longer regarded as a value-free pure domain of research. Its ambition to unlock the basic elements of our human existence required a common thinking on the implications.

In this chapter, the connections between bioethics and basic rights will be explored partly by analyzing the basic legal norms of bioethics, and partly by comparing thematic cases from the jurisdictions of the European Court of Human Rights (ECtHR) and the US Supreme Court, as well as some cases from other jurisdictions. I will primarily focus on two major lines of thought in contemporary bioethics: the first is concerned with the boundaries of life (eg issues of embryo research, assisted reproduction, and end of life decisions) and the second is related to the contemporary exploration of the frontiers of the human body (issues such as the use of human tissues and human DNA for research and other purposes). In what follows, I will examine questions that are eminently bioethical but I will not tackle problems that arise in the context of general moral concerns, such as the permissibility of abortion—which will only be considered when *sui generis* bioethical issues, such as access to prenatal genetic tests or the institutionalization of informed consent before the termination of pregnancy or sterilization, emerge at the intersection of basic rights and bioethics.

I. Bioethics and Human Rights

Bioethics traditionally focuses on establishing moral limits between different types of acts in the field of life sciences and their medical application. There is no established method to recognize the moment when some universal norms have crystallized from the literature of bioethics and when they become basic rights in fields of bioethics.

Since its first use, the term 'bioethics' has had at least two different meanings, one broader than the other. The broader concept was coined by Van Rensselaer Potter in 1970[3]

[1] In 1949, the Nuremberg Code adopted the rules of medical experimentation as a response the basic violations of human rights during the Second World War; the International Covenant on Civil and Political Rights, 1966. Art 7 states that 'No one shall be subjected to torture or to cruel, inhuman or degrading treatment or punishment. In particular, no one shall be subjected without his free consent to medical or scientific experimentation.'

[2] Exceptionally, some early judicial decisions had already recognized the doctrine of consent, such as the famous decision of Cardozo in *Schloendord v Society of New York Hospital* 211 NY 125, 105 NE (1914).

[3] He first used the term in a 1970 article and then in his book: Van Rensselaer Potter, *Bioethics: A Bridge to the Future* (1971).

and it advocates a comprehensive and global view of bioethics that integrates even environmental ethics. A different type of interpretation was advocated by André E. Hellegers[4] who used the term 'bioethics' for the first time in an academic field of learning and in the context of public policy and the human life sciences. Bioethics in this view is a way of approaching and resolving moral conflicts generated by a new concept of medicine. This more restricted view has become dominant in much of the theory and practice of bioethics.

Recently, bioethics has also been regarded as a discipline that provides a critical perspective not only on the practice of medicine and biotechnology, but also on the traditional framework of human rights. Therefore, authors such as Brooke A. Ackerly consider grouping bioethics together with queer theory, cultural studies, critical race theory, and multiculturalism as a critical approach to the universal human rights.[5] Indeed, bioethics shapes the contours of basic rights in two different ways. First, it broadens the catalog of basic rights or at least aims to stretch the interpretation of rights to the domain of bioethics. Secondly, the bioethics movement extends to the subjects of protection, for example to 'future generations'. In other words, bioethics encompasses not just biological but also legal and philosophical conceptions of the person.

1. The Influence of Normative Bioethics

Human rights instruments after the Second World War paid little attention to issues related today to bioethics except for the problem of 'medical experimentation without consent'. The turn occurred around 1997 when the Human Genome Project[6] and the possibility of cloning mammals put bioethics at the forefront of human rights debates. And even though all attempts at human cloning have failed thus far, it is still considered to be one of the most controversial problems in bioethics, both from political and legal perspectives. This fear even motivated the United Nations to draft an international declaration specifically on human cloning which prohibits all forms of cloning if they contradict the protection of human dignity.[7]

The fundamental principles of bioethics are recognized in international declarations developed under the aegis of the UN network. The General Conference of UNESCO has adopted three significant, though not binding, international declarations.[8] The first, and most important, is the 1997 Universal Declaration on the Human Genome and Human Rights, and the title itself is a telling reference to the Universal Declaration of Human Rights (UDHR). This declaration has led to the development of universally accepted bioethical principles, such as respect for human dignity, non-commercialization, benefit sharing, and scientific progress, which have attained high recognition in international law, at a level equivalent to that of the UDHR. This Declaration repeatedly evokes the concept of 'human dignity': in referring in Article 2 to

[4] Warren Thomas Reich, 'The "Wider View": André Hellegers's Passionate, Integrating Intellect and the Creation of Bioethics' (1999) 9 *Kennedy Institute of Ethics Journal* 25–51.

[5] Brooke A. Ackerly, *Universal Human Rights in a World of Difference* (2008), 57.

[6] In various societies, and also in science, several different kinds of meanings and uses can be attached to human genes. Genes can be conceived as sources and information for research, for forensic identification, tools for therapy, information for actuarial calculus, and for many other uses.

[7] The 59th General Assembly adopted the United Nations Declaration on Human Cloning on March 8, 2005 by a vote of 84:34:37.

[8] The chronologically second to be adopted International Declaration on Human Genetic Data, which will not be discussed here, laid out norms for conducting research on human tissues and DNA and has served as a model for several laws on the protection of human DNA.

the uniqueness of the human genome and in Article 11 as a reason for prohibiting reproductive cloning.[9]

Additionally, Beauchamp and Childress have developed four major principles of bioethics[10] which have since been used worldwide in analyzing cases, as well as in ethics education. These four principles are: *respect for autonomy*, which means respecting the decision-making capacities of autonomous persons that enable individuals to make informed choices; *beneficence*, which considers the balancing of benefits of treatment against the risks and costs; *non-maleficence*, which dictates avoiding harm; and finally *justice*, which is applicable in deciding both the allocation and costs, and the benefits and risks within health-care systems.

2. Is There a Common European Approach?

The recognition of the above principles and the emergence of the constitutional and human rights aspects in bioethics are reflected at the regional supranational level. The Charter of Fundamental Rights of the European Union, now legally binding within the scope of EU law, offers a catalog of common bioethical principles, such as human dignity and integrity and the right to life. Regarding human integrity, the Charter refers to free and informed consent, non-commercialization, and the prohibition of eugenic practices and human reproductive cloning. Human embryonic research and the boundaries of human embryonic stem cell (hESC) research, issues central to the European debate, are not addressed directly.

Bioethics and ethical aspects of new technologies are viewed within the European Union as subjects that fall within the competence of the member states, as part of EU commitments to ethical pluralism and the principle of subsidiary. Nevertheless, over the years an increasing number of European norms have been adopted that are to be considered with regard to biomedical research. One part of these norms contains safety requirements, but an increasing number of legal requirements that are similar to ethical standards have been formulated.

A further interesting feature of the European approach is that—even though several international ethical norms, such as the Helsinki Declaration, are not legally binding—for international research projects to be financed by the Commission, they must comply with a number of ethical norms that are otherwise not included in legally binding European norms. In general, though, the European framework indicates that diversity among European states is the prevailing characteristic of regulating the ethical boundaries of biomedical research.

3. The European Convention of Human Rights and Biomedicine

Though the European Convention on Human Rights (ECHR) was adopted in 1950, bioethics was not included in it until the 1997 Oviedo Convention of the Council of Europe. However, the lack of universal endorsement indicates the ongoing constitutional differences and differences in national interests among the European states.[11] The European nature of the document

[9] The latest of the three, the 2005 Universal Declaration on Bioethics and Human Rights, deals with this subject more generally, as a further indication that bioethical norms have attained high recognition in international law.

[10] Tom L. Beauchamp and James F. Childress, *Principles Biomedical Ethics Oxford* (6th edn, 2008).

[11] eg Germany has not signed the Oviedo Convention because of the ambiguity on certain terms, such as 'health purposes' and 'genetic counseling in case of predictive genetic test' (in Art 12). Jürgen Robienski and Jürgen Simon, 'Recent Development in the Legal Discourse on Genetic Testing in Germany' in Andre den Exter (ed), *Human Rights and Biomedicine* (2010). The Oviedo Convention is a living instrument in the sense that it provides a gradually expanding field for biomedical law and bioethics, due to the (exercised) ability to amend it with additional protocols.

is expressed by the emphasis laid on human dignity as the fundamental value in biomedicine. Its scope is both broad and ambiguous: instead of the term 'everyone', 'all human beings' is used, which indicates a more biologically oriented notion of legal subjects[12] as well as the ambition to cover a broader field of subject.[13]

4. Bioethics and the European Convention on Human Rights

While the legal regulation of bioethics is principally covered by the national systems of the member states, the jurisprudence of the ECtHR reveals the contradictions and dilemmas of the prevailing European constitutional approach. The ECtHR follows the logic and limits of the ECHR, but within the frame of the rights protected under the Convention the ECtHR has had to reflect on bioethical dilemmas. It follows from the 'living instrument' approach that the ECHR reflects on moral or/and technical progress in various fields. However, general moral concerns and bioethical concerns should be differentiated. For instance, general religious and other moral concerns often appear in the legal debates on the permissibility of abortion.[14] However, when the content of informed consent before abortion or the accessibility of less invasive methods of abortion, or access to prenatal genetic tests appear before the Court, then rules and principles of bioethics can be taken into consideration, such as the principles of autonomy or non-maleficence.

5. Bioethical Considerations in National Constitutions

Recent advances in biomedicine and biomedical research have raised ethical concerns that have forced international and supranational organizations to take a stand and incorporate bioethical norms into various conventions, declarations, and recommendations. On the national level, however, this process has resulted mainly in specific statutory provisions in health-care law, civil law, family law, and data protection law. In other words, constitutions, with some minor exceptions, have remained untouched by this normative process.[15]

Despite the overall lack of specific constitutional provisions on bioethical issues, the application of the concepts of dignity, liberty, privacy, freedom of expression, and freedom of scientific research can offer some help in interpreting and analyzing the legal contours of contested new technologies. But as Sheila Jasanoff has stated, the 'Constitution provides no guidance on the questions of how social change in general, and scientific change particular, should bear on the interpretation of constitutional prohibitions or guarantees.'[16]

Human dignity plays a central role in basic rights and values in several constitutions, and also in the basic international norms of bioethics: for instance, in the Oviedo Convention[17]

[12] Article 1; similar concerns are raised by Umberto Vincenti, *Diritto senza identitá: La crisi delle categorie giuridiche tradizionali* (2007).

[13] One of the most debated parts of this Convention among the member states is Art 18 on research on embryos *in vitro*, which will be discussed later.

[14] On the constitutionalization of abortion, see Chapter 51.

[15] Among the exception provisions of recently adopted constitutions or constitutions of new states are, eg, Art 17 of the Constitution of the Slovak Republic which declares 'the law will specify in which cases a person can be admitted to, or kept in, institutional health care without his or her consent.'

[16] Sheila Jasanoff, 'Biology and the Bill of Rights: Can Science Reframe the Constitution?' (1987–88) 13 *American Journal of Law and Medicine* 249–89.

[17] Oviedo Convention (emphasis added):

> Article 1—Parties to this Convention shall protect the *dignity* and identity of all human beings and guarantee everyone, without discrimination, respect for their integrity and other rights and fundamental freedoms with regard to the application of biology and medicine. Each Party shall take in its internal law the necessary measures to give effect to the provisions of this Convention.

and in the Universal Declaration of Bioethics and Human Rights. Dignity can serve as a basis for several rights such as self-determination, right to refuse medical treatment, and equal respect; all relevant in the field of treating vulnerable patients. (See Chapter 18.)

A further fundamental constitutional pillar is the freedom of science. This is expressed in numerous constitutions (see eg Art 5 of the German Basic Law; Art 33 of the Italian Constitution; Art 59 of the Slovenian Constitution).[18] Protecting the freedom of science has been interpreted as safeguarding scientific research and the dissemination of research results from undue influence, such as censorship or state control for the purposes of using science as a biopolitical goal. However, commercial interests may distort scientific results and their application, and this is also an emerging challenge for constitutionality.

The constitutional principle of scientific freedom, however, does not presuppose that science is a value-free and objective enterprise. Judicial interpretation runs into difficulty when it has to analyze scientific activity in a complex way: to separate scientific advances from commercial interests, to peel off the legacy of an older, paternalistic professional tradition, and to deflect eugenic and reductionist thinking.

In the constitutions that do offer explicit provisions relevant for bioethical questions—similarly to international conventions and declarations—the most recent issues (even theoretical possibilities, such as reproductive human cloning) have attracted more attention than the classical issues (such as informed consent, death, and dying).

Article 24 of the Serbian Constitution[19] declares that 'Human life is inviolable. There shall be no death penalty in the Republic of Serbia. Cloning of human beings shall be prohibited.' It is interesting to note that while international bioethical norms prohibit human cloning based on the principle that it violates human dignity, the Serbian approach derives this prohibition from the right to life. One can assume that while the dignity-based approach focuses on the moral aspects of cloning human beings, the right-to-life-based prohibition places the emphasis on safety, as human cloning (in its currently developing state) threatens life.

One of the most detailed constitutional frameworks of bioethics is provided by the Swiss Constitution, which details conditions for research conducted in the fields of assisted reproduction and gene technology. Donation of the human embryo and human ova are prohibited and even the number of harvested human oocytes is maximized in the Constitution. Organ and oocyte trade, as well as surrogacy, are also *expressis verbis* forbidden in the Swiss Constitution.

The rich constitutional dimension of bioethics can be further demonstrated by the lively debate on anonymity in assisted reproduction. As a result of public debate initiated by a referendum, the Swiss Constitution has recognized the right to genetic identity.[20]

In the US context, a unique example is the California Stem Cell Research and Cures Act that resulted in adding Article XXXV on Medical Research to the California Constitution. Section 5 of this article establishes a constitutional right to conduct stem cell research. Section 3, however, prohibits funding for reproductive cloning.

Peru, Paraguay, and Chile express in their constitutions a strong pro-life position, where a major issue is even whether the use of contraception contradicts the right to life as enshrined in the Peruvian Constitution.

[18] Freedom of science, although it may seem to support a liberal position for a new technology, does not however help to predict legal attitude. Eg both Italy and Germany adopted a conservative law on assisted reproduction.

[19] The Serbian Constitution was adopted in 2006.

[20] Dominique Manaï, 'La procréation médicalement assistée en droit suisse: Verité sur la conception et l'identité du donneur de gamètes' in Brigitte Feuillet-Liger (ed), *Procréation médicalement assistée et anononymat* (2008), 264–5.

The Inter-American Commission on Human Rights held that the Costa Rican Constitutional Court decision prohibiting *in vitro* fertilization (IVF)[21] itself violated the right to be free from arbitrary interference with one's private life, the right to found a family, and women's right to equality.[22]

II. The Jurisprudence of Core Bioethical Questions

1. Beginning of Life and Reproductive Rights in Light of New Technologies

The edges of life constitute the fields where most bioethics problems arise. Moral limits and legal frontiers of euthanasia and end of life decisions, as well as termination of pregnancy, have resulted in many constitutional and human rights cases. In cases of assisted reproduction, with the advent of new technology courts have had to face numerous bio-cultural issues and differences that they had never faced in the context of non-medicalized reproduction.[23] In the domain of reproductive rights, the right to privacy (in the United States) and the right to private and family life (in Europe) provide the main pillars of the constitutional framework.

One of the most rapidly developing fields is the interpretation of procreative liberties vis-à-vis new reproductive technologies. At the European level, there is no consensus on the nature and status of the embryo and/or fetus, although they are beginning to receive some protection in light of scientific progress and the potential consequences of research into genetic engineering, medically assisted procreation, and embryo experimentation. The ECtHR is convinced that it is neither desirable, nor even possible as matters stand, to answer in the abstract the question whether the unborn child is a person for the purposes of the right to life provision in the Convention (*Vo v France*).[24]

Recent cases concern access to IVF, wrongful life and birth, and custodial rights over embryos. In these instances, the potentiality of life has to be assessed but the applicability of abortion case law is disputable. For instance, the very same legal regimes that allow termination of pregnancy during the first trimester based on the request of the pregnant woman may come to an entirely different conclusion when a woman expresses her wish alone to have an *in vitro* embryo implanted in her.

The complexity of the legal questions of assisted procreation has urged many countries to establish a specialized board of ethics with the aim of mapping both the ethical and legal issues before legislation, incorporating ethical concerns into recommendation for legislation.[25] Perhaps it is this focus on ethics that has led to the very different legal solutions even within

[21] No 2306 of 2000.

[22] Report No 85/10, Case 12.361.

[23] On the related conceptual uncertainties see Marcia C. Inhorn (ed), *Reproductive Disruptions* (2007).

[24] *Vo v France*, App no 53924/00, 8 July 2004. See further *Brueggemann and Scheuten v Germany* (1981) 3 EHRR 244; *Paton v United Kingdom* (1981) 3 EHRR 408; *Open Door Counselling v Ireland* (1993) 15 EHRR 244; *Evans v United Kingdom*, App no 6339/05, 10 April 2007, nyr; *SH and Others v Austria*, App no 57813/00, 1 April 2010.

[25] See eg Warnock Committee in the United Kingdom (1982); Benda Commission (1984) in Germany. The report submitted by Noëlle Lenoir, entitled 'Aux Frontières de la vie: Pour une éthique biomedicale à la française', provided the foundation and adoption of French bioethics law in 1994. This '*ethics committee*' method was subsequently followed in the elaboration of several statutory laws, including the German law on stem cells.

Europe. For example, the United Kingdom and Spain have developed a liberal approach, while Germany, despite its strong embryo protection law, has allowed the import and use of already existing embryonic stem cell lines.

Assisted reproduction was one of the first widespread technologies that raised both ethical and legal questions. The ECtHR was faced with these questions in the *Evans v United Kingdom* case,[26] where the applicant claimed that her privacy rights were infringed by granting a legal possibility to destroy her embryos based on her partner's request. While access to many forms of IVF is accepted as a rule,[27] the issue here was the conflict between the rights of the prospective mother and the male producer of the embryo. It is the *in vitro* procedure and *ex utero* storage that create disruption between the phases of human reproduction. The legal contradiction here is that while assisted reproduction was developed with the aim of helping to ensure rights of the infertile and to grant them privacy and a health service that would eliminate the pain of being childless, the disruption of the procedure then created an opportunity to invade the privacy and right to family life in regular cases of reproduction. As the *Evans* case shows, procreative liberties are often recognized as negative liberties (women should not be prevented from carrying on their pregnancy), but this liberty is not applicable in cases of *in vitro* treatment when the Court recognized that here the father's right not to become a parent should prevail over the woman's interest in becoming a mother.[28]

This case may have many different interpretations. The Court took into account the assessment of the new reproductive technologies when it recognized the disruption of procreation and pregnancy in the case of *in vitro* treatment. However, the ethical theory it used is not clear, thereby showing that the logic of bioethics is not directly transferable into law which relies on traditional forms of rights and interests. If, in this instance, bioethics was of any influence then it was manifested only in reference to the main sources of bioethics.[29] A competing view, that would follow from bioethics, would take into account and assess the difference in the burden of physical involvement in the procedure. Lengthy hormonal treatment and invasive extraction of the human eggs pose significantly more of a burden on women than is the case with sperm donation.

The main ethical dilemma of the *Evans* case, therefore, was whether biological differences in gamete donation could be taken into account in assessing the rights of male and female donors. Furthermore, the Court missed the opportunity to recognize the difference between preventing someone from becoming a parent and the denial of the right to change opinion on biological parenthood.[30]

[26] *Evans v United Kingdom* (n 24).

[27] In *Dickson v United Kingdom* the ECtHR had to examine Art 8 and the refusal of facilities for artificial insemination to the applicants, a prisoner and his wife. The Court found that Art 8 was applicable as the article encompasses respect for the individual's decision to become genetic parents. In the case of *SH and Others v Austria* (n 24) on the prohibition of ova donation for *in vitro* fertilization adopted by the Austrian legislature, the Court took into consideration medical/scientific certainty as a condition for reproductive rights. Since IVF treatment gives rise to sensitive moral issues in the context of a fast-moving medical and scientific field, and since there is no common ground amongst the member states, the Court was of the view that a wide margin of appreciation should be afforded to member states.

[28] *Evans v UK* (n 24), para 71.

[29] In deciding, the Court provided a detailed comparison of the applicable legal solutions in the member states of the Council of Europe, referring to the Oviedo Convention, and to the principles set by the Steering Committee on Bioethics (CDBI) in 1989, and the 2005 UNESCO Declaration.

[30] On the other hand, Hungarian law permits the continuation of the procedure, by giving preference to the woman's wish, with information granted to the male. He may exclude the possibility of continuation for such cases, but may not decide so later when the treatment is already being performed.

2. Informed Consent Rules and Reproductive Rights

In the recent ECtHR case of *RR v Poland*,[31] the applicant was prevented from undergoing prenatal genetic testing within the statutory time limit within which abortion was still legal, despite her repeated requests to have access to a genetic test that could have confirmed whether her fetus was healthy. After several doctors in Poland refused to offer her the test, and when the genetic test was finally performed after significant delay, she had already missed the deadline for requesting an abortion. Eventually, the baby was born with Turner syndrome. According to the ECtHR, the right to access to this type of genetic information falls within 'the ambit of the notion of private life'.[32] In the absence of access to genetic test rights, protection would have remained 'theoretical or illusory'.[33]

3. Concept of Procreative Liberties and Bioethics in US Jurisprudence

US jurisprudence on procreative liberties developed parallel to the recognition of rights to privacy.[34] In addition, freedom of research in the United States in general has led to a favorable environment for various technologies in the field of assisted reproduction and procreative liberties.[35] It should be noted, however, that judicial views that support the concept of negative liberties in procreation do not automatically generate access rights to services to assisted procreation, at least in the US constitutional tradition. However, cases in the field of eugenic practices do often serve as a basis for critical reflections on genetics. Ever since the early eugenic episodes in science were reaffirmed by judicial acknowledgment, eugenic thinking and eugenic jurisprudence have served as a learning experience for the contemporary conception of how and what to regulate in science.[36]

Buck v Bell[37] is the seminal eugenic decision of the US Supreme Court, and is still one of the most frequently cited cases in the fields of disability, gender, and bioethics. The *Buck* Court upheld the constitutionality of non-voluntary sterilization in cases of preventing inherited 'degeneration', with Justice Holmes asserting that the 'principle that sustains compulsory vaccination is broad enough to cover cutting the Fallopian tubes'.[38] The Supreme Court has never overruled the decision in the *Buck v Bell*, although society's perception of disability and on the value of life has entirely changed since the decision. In *Skinner v Oklahoma*,[39] the US Supreme Court, however, held unconstitutional an Oklahoma statute that provided for the involuntary sterilization of the poor and of certain categories of recidivists that were characterized by 'moral turpitude'. The Supreme Court determined that the Equal Protection Clause prohibited the enforcement of the Oklahoma statute which required sterilization of persons who had been convicted of certain specified crimes. The distinction between categories of crimes, nevertheless, indicated a hidden eugenic pattern of thought.

[31] ECtHR, *RR v Poland*, App no 27617/04, 26 May 2011.

[32] Ibid para 197.

[33] Ibid para 191.

[34] Elyse Whitney Grant, 'Assessing the Constitutionality of Reproductive Technologies Regulation: A Bioethical Approach' (2010) 61 *Hastings Law Journal* 997–1034.

[35] John A. Robertson, 'Procreative Liberty and Harm to Offspring in Assisted Reproduction' (2004) 30 *American Journal of Law and Medicine* 24–39.

[36] eg the Human Genome Project has been scrutinized since its inception by introducing Ethical, Legal and Social Implications (ELSI), a parallel project.

[37] *Buck v Bell* 274 US 200, 207 (1927).

[38] Ibid.

[39] *Skinner v Oklahoma* 316 US 535 (1942).

In *Griswold v Connecticut*,[40] the Court invalidated a statute that penalized the distribution of contraceptives. A further step was made in constructing reproductive rights in *Eisenstadt v Baird*,[41] when Justice Brennan held that 'if the right to privacy means anything, it is the right of the individual, married or single, to be free of unwarranted governmental intrusion into matters so fundamentally affecting a person as the decisions whether to bear or beget a child.'[42]

Roe v Wade[43] provided a trimester framework that guided states on whether they may regulate some elements of abortion. Furthermore, the *Roe v Wade* Court recognized the privacy rights of the pregnant woman and her attending physician in deciding about termination of pregnancy during the first trimester. Later, the *Casey* case[44] offered new possibilities for regulation provided that they do not pose an undue burden on women. However, although abortion cases are often cited in the context of new reproductive technologies, significant moral and practical differences between *in vivo* and *in vitro embryo* question or at least reduce the applicability of these norms. The possibility of *extra corporal* reproduction has resulted in numerous legal problems, such as postmortem reproduction, custodial rights over the embryo, right to identity, and medical confidentiality. In *Hecht v Superior Court*,[45] the Court did not find any public policy that would prohibit or deny postmortem insemination and, as a consequence, they granted access as the late partner had clearly expressed his wish before his death.

In the context of new reproductive technologies, access to IVF treatment seems to pose different kinds of legal problems in the United States than in Europe.[46] The validity of surrogacy agreements served as the basis of several Court decisions, such as the *Baby M* case.[47] In *Johnson v Calvert*,[48] the California Supreme Court rejected a claim by the gestational (surrogate) mother that she be recognized as the mother of the IVF child. Although birth may establish maternity, the Court developed a different standard by referring to genetic consanguinity and intention expressed by the genetic parents to raise the child. The recognition of family based on genetic ties rather than on marriage has also influenced paternity rights, which is demonstrated in numerous cases, such as the dissent in *Michael H v Gerald D*,[49] in which Justice Scalia in the majority opinion defended the marital/'unitary family' idea.

4. Research on Human Embryos and on Embryonic Stem Cells

One of the most sensitive issues in current bioethics is the research conducted on the (surplus, *in vitro*) human embryo. The Oviedo Convention[50] leaves the question of the status of the human embryo and research on the human embryo partially open by the provision of Article 18(1) which states that 'where the law allows research on embryos in vitro, it shall ensure adequate protection of the embryo'. Arguably, this could encompass the destruction of human embryos in an adequately safeguarded process for the purpose of hESC derivation. The more

[40] 381 US 479 (1965).

[41] 405 US 438 (1972).

[42] 405 US 438, 453 (1972).

[43] *Roe v Wade* 410 US 113 (1973).

[44] *Planned Parenthood of Southeastern Pennsylvania v Casey* 505 US 833 (1992).

[45] *Hecht v Superior Court* 20 Cal Rptr 2d 275, 287 (Ct App 1993).

[46] Richard F. Storrow, 'The Bioethics of Prospective Parenthood: In Pursuit of the Proper Standard for Gatekeeping in Infertility Clinics' (2007) 28 *Cardozo Law Review* 2291.

[47] *In re Baby M* 109 NJ 396, 447–9, 537 A2d 1227, 1253–4 (1988).

[48] *Johnson v Calvert* 851 P2d 776 (Cal 1993).

[49] *Michael H v Gerald D* 491 US 110, 115 (1989).

[50] See n 11.

contentious provision in Article 18(2)—which has prevented ratification of the Convention by all Council of Europe states as it has been considered alternately either too liberal or too conservative—prohibits the creation of embryos for research purposes.

The Constitution of Ecuador in Article 49(1) explicitly prohibits research on human embryos. Germany and Switzerland prohibit all forms of human cloning whereas others, among them the United Kingdom, China, and Israel, allow the creation of cloned human embryos for research.[51]

A distinction should be made between cases where research on the human embryo is allowed for the purposes of improving reproductive technologies and cases where the embryo is harvested in order to produce embryonic stem cell lines.

When human biological materials are used as building blocks for stem cells, usually the act of harvesting biological materials poses other types of legal issues as it might involve an instrumentalization of the human body. In these new types of research, bodily substances are used in two different ways: they are used not only as sources and objects of scientific observation but also as materials for creating cell lines.

The influence of bioethics can also be seen in the latest development of the patentability of biotechnological inventions in the field of regenerative medicine. In order to provide the effective and harmonized legal protection of biotechnological inventions, the embryo needs to be given an autonomous definition in EU law.

The *WARF*[52] decision of the European Patent Office Enlarged Board of Appeal[53] confirmed in 2008 that the 'industrial or commercial use' clause, which was introduced to prohibit the commodification of the human embryo, excludes the patentability of hES cells or cell lines due to the fact that the production of hES cells requires the destruction of the human embryos used as their source. The decision did not, however, make a distinction between embryos according to their origin, developmental phase, and acceptable uses, a distinction key to national regulations on embryonic research. A landmark decision was made at the end of 2011 in the *Brüstle* case[54] when the European Court of Justice ruled that a process which involves the removal of a stem cell from a human embryo at the blastocyst stage, entailing the destruction of that embryo, cannot be patented.

The need of the biotechnology industry for human embryos and their use for embryonic stem cell research and for therapy often results in incoherent legal solutions. In 2008, the Brazilian Supreme Court[55] upheld the Biosecurity Law that allowed the destruction of human embryos for the purposes of creating embryonic stem cell lines, while abortion has remained restricted in the country.[56] A double inconsistency can be observed in the German position on research on the human embryo: research on the human embryo is not authorized, although

[51] See <http://www.who.int/ethics/topics/cloning/en/>.

[52] Wisconsin Alumni Research Foundation is an entity at the University of Wisconsin which owned the rights of the invention.

[53] See <http://archive.epo.org/epo/pubs/oj009/05_09/05_3069.pdf>.

[54] C-34/10 *Oliver Brüstle v. Greenpeace eV*.

[55] Brazilian Biosecurity Law (11.105/2005), see <http://www.loc.gov/lawweb/servlet/lloc_news?disp3_l20540518_text>.

[56] In the *Alyne da Silva Pimentel v Brazil* case, access to reproductive health care was confirmed by the UN Committee on the Elimination of Discrimination against Women (CEDAW). Governments have a human rights obligation to guarantee that all women in their countries have access to timely, non-discriminatory, and appropriate maternal health services. Even when governments outsource health services to private institutions, they remain directly responsible for their actions and have a duty to regulate and monitor said institutions.

the German Basic Law guarantees the freedom of research and science in broad terms; however, embryonic stem cell lines can be imported and used for research.[57]

In the United States, political ideological conflicts govern the issues of embryo research. The federal ethics committee created under the Clinton administration, the National Bioethics Advisory Commission (NBAC), in its 1999 report[58] accepted that ethical positions regarding the moral status of the human embryo differ in society and different sources of human embryos may attract different moral positions.[59]

The liberal ethical position on the federal level changed when in 2005 a report from the President's Council on Bioethics,[60] appointed by the Bush administration, suggested that in the United States the protection of human life from the earliest stages of development, including the human embryo, is an ethical norm widely accepted in society.[61] It held that seeking therapies by means of destroying human embryos is ethically unacceptable and in order to reconcile scientific progress with the requirements of bioethics, biomedicine must find ethically acceptable sources for hES cells. However, a state constitutional amendment granted a right to conduct stem cell research in California.

A 2007 Executive Order[62] gave priority to ethically responsible ways of conducting hESC research. It emphasized that ethically acceptable sources of hESC lines exclude cell lines which necessitate the creation of embryos for research purposes or destroying, discarding, or subjecting to harm a human embryo. It also held that the destruction of embryos violates the principle of non-commodification and that human embryos are 'members of the human species'. The Executive Order envisioned the United States progressing in biomedical research while maintaining the clearly established ethical boundaries and standards of medical research and respecting human life and dignity.

The debate reached another turning point in 2009 when the Obama administration reviewed the federal funding moratorium imposed in 2001. The 2009 Executive Order[63] emphasized the necessity of hESC research for the purposes of enhancing human biomedical knowledge and creating new therapies.

Biotechnological inventions enjoy broad protection in the US Constitution and jurisprudence. The US Constitution in Article I, section 8 authorizes the Congress 'to promote the Progress of Science and Useful Arts' by granting authors and inventors the exclusive rights to their works for a limited time. The breakthrough in the history of biotechnological patents

[57] Stammzellgesetz, Bundesgesetzblatt (Federal Law Gazette) June 29, 2002.

[58] National Bioethics Advisory Commission, *Ethical Issues in Human Stem Cell Research* (1999), available at <http://bioethics.georgetown.edu/pcbe/reports/past_commissions/nbac_stemcell1.pdf>.

[59] In the encyclical letter *Humanae Vitae* (1968), Pope Paul VI condemned any form of direct interruption of pregnancy. Two exceptions were made: ectopic pregnancy and cancerous uterus. In these cases, death of the fetus was considered a secondary effect of removing the uterus in order to save the life of the woman.

[60] The President's Council on Bioethics, *Alternative Sources of Human Pluripotent Stem Cells. A White Paper* (2005).

[61] This view reflects mainly the official Roman Catholic position in which

> obtaining stem cells from embryos that remain after in vitro fertilization involves the intentional destruction of a genetically unique living member of the human species that deserves full protection from the beginning of its existence.... This judgement of the Church, however, is not directed against stem cell research as such, but is concerned only with the use of certain kind of sources for obtaining stem cells, and with the methods of collecting them.

Béla Somfai, 'Religious Traditions and Stem cell Research' in Judit Sándor (ed), *Society and Genetic Information: Codes and Laws in the Genetic Era* (2003), 88.

[62] Executive Order (13435 of 20 June 2007).

[63] Executive Order (13505 of March 2009).

occurred in the US case of *Diamond v Chakrabarty*,[64] which has since been labeled as granting patents on life.

In 2010, a preliminary injunction created uncertainty in the field of financing research on embryonic stem cells.[65] Since the Obama administration has developed a more favorable environment for embryonic stem cell research, the issue was whether the increasing number of new projects should consequently receive financial support. The main issue was whether the National Institutes of Health should fund additional research projects on stem cells that involve the destruction of the human embryo. One year later, the District Court ruled in favor of the National Institute of Health and removed this injunction.

5. End of Life Decisions in Europe

As methods of intensive therapies have significantly increased the possibilities for artificial prolongation of human life, several issues have been raised. Who should decide on the health care of the terminally ill? Who can substitute the decision of a patient in a persistent vegetative stage? The principle of *autonomy* can serve as an ethical basis in cases where the terminally ill are still capable of expressing their wish. However, the principle of *non-maleficence* would prevent doctors from complying with requests for refusal of medical treatment unless the law recognizes that this refusal is self-determination within the concept of human dignity or/and encompassed by the concept of interests of liberty. As suffering and death take many forms, diverse solutions have emerged to face this medico-legal problem in different cultures and legal systems. In such concrete cases, legal terms, such as 'euthanasia', have become confusing, because we tend to define it to include many different types of actions and inactions.

The simultaneous existence of individual autonomous action and the assistance of a physician or a relative usually lead to legal proceedings. As Derrick Beyleveld and Roger Brownsword point out, human dignity 'can encourage a paternalism that is incompatible with the spirit of self-determination that informs the mainstream of human rights thinking.'[66]

In all euthanasia debates, an accurate legal delineation between different forms of ending life is very difficult to achieve. Voluntary active euthanasia is legalized only in the Benelux countries while assisted suicide is not regarded as a crime in Switzerland. But what constitutes passive euthanasia is still debated in several jurisdictions.[67] The question is still dominated by two independently developed fields of law. While public health law focuses on the duties of physicians and requires professional integrity and the saving of life, the more recent legal developments based on patients' rights respect the right to self-determination even in cases where the patient refuses medical intervention.

Alternately, these decisions may be treated as outside the realms of the courts and may be left in the hands of physicians. The Dutch position was the first directly to target the issue of this confidentiality in end of life decisions and Dutch statutory law gradually developed based on the analysis of the publication of confidential decisions on ending life based on, and even without, the patient's request.[68] Less radical steps have been taken in other European countries,

[64] 447 US 303 (1980).

[65] *Sherley v Sebelius* 2010 US Dist LEXIS 86441.

[66] Deryck Beyleveld and Roger Brownsword, 'Human Dignity, Human Rights, and Human Genetics' (1998) 61 *Modern Law Review* 662.

[67] For more detailed analysis of the constitutional aspects of euthanasia see Violeta Beširević, *Euthanasia: Legal Principles and Policy Choices* (2006).

[68] Remmelink Report, September 10, 1991, the first, official government study of the practice of Dutch euthanasia.

and after a long debate the French Parliament recognized the right of the terminally ill to refuse medical treatment although it did not legalize active forms of euthanasia.

The most significant case on the legal dilemmas of assisted suicide appeared in *Pretty v United Kingdom*.[69] The applicant was suffering from a serious degenerative disease due to which she was paralyzed from the neck downwards. She requested the ECtHR to give her authorization for her to end her life in dignity and to guarantee her husband freedom from prosecution if he assisted her in committing suicide, an exemption that was denied in the United Kingdom. She claimed that the right to life also includes the right to self-determination in life-related issues. Consequently, life is a right and not an obligation. She submitted that this included the right to choose when and how to die, and that nothing could be more intimately connected to the manner in which a person conducted her life than the manner and timing of her death. The judges in Strasbourg concluded that the individual had no right to death, or life, in the sense that the legal system should accept the right to assist any suicide as a general principle. However, the Court acknowledged that

> under Article 8 that notions of the quality of life take on significance. In an era of growing medical sophistication combined with longer life expectancies, many people are concerned that they should not be forced to linger on in old age or in states of advanced physical or mental decrepitude which conflict with strongly held ideas of self and personal identity.[70]

The *Pretty* case generated significant debate on autonomy and terminal illness. Since then, several European countries, including Austria and Finland, have enacted laws on the recognition of continuing power of attorney which provide stronger guarantees of the self determination of the terminally ill.[71]

6. End of Life Cases in the United States and Other Jurisdictions

One of the main dilemmas in bioethics occurs when the principle of autonomy clashes with the principles of non-maleficence. In the language of constitutional law, similar hard cases appear when individual liberty and state interest in protecting life demand different solutions in cases of end of life decisions.

In the United States, there has been a piecemeal development of the recognition of liberty rights in the field of terminal illness. Thus, the lower court cases of *Karen Quinlan*,[72] *Bouvia*,[73] and *Re Conroy*,[74] and the Supreme Court *Cruzan*[75] case provided the main pillars of the recognition of some forms of euthanasia in cases of terminal illness or of persistent vegetative state. In *Cruzan*, although the US Supreme Court affirmed that the legal requirement of Missouri on *clear and convincing* evidence of the will of the patient who is no longer capable of expressing her wish does not violate the Constitution, it still provided a constitutional basis embedded in the liberty interest to encompass the wish to

[69] ECtHR, *Pretty v United Kingdom*, App no 2346/02, 29 April 2002.

[70] Ibid para 65.

[71] See further Recommendation CM/Rec(2009)11 adopted on 9 December 2009 at the 107th meeting of the Ministers's Deputies. The Recommendation promotes dignity and self-determination in the cases of terminal illness.

[72] *In the Matter of Karen Quinlan* 355 A2d 647 (NJ 1976).

[73] *Bouvia v Superior Court of the State of California* 2d 179 Ca App 3d 1127 (1986).

[74] 486 A2d 1209 (NJ 1985).

[75] *Cruzan v Director, Missouri Department of Health* 497 US 261 (1990).

terminate life-saving nutrition and hydration. However, this development towards extending liberty interests in end of life decisions was interrupted when the issue of whether medical assistance in suicide can be granted reached the Supreme Court in the *Washington v Glucksberg* case.[76]

In *Washington v Glucksberg*,[77] the US Supreme Court failed to recognize a fundamental right to access medically assisted suicide, based on the request of the dying patient. Instead, the Supreme Court held that Washington's prohibition against 'causing' or 'aiding' a suicide does not violate the Due Process Clause. The Court's reasoning was based on a historical argument, rather than acknowledgment of the conditions of liberty rights.

Different layers of statutory law may further shrink liberty interests: as exemplified by the issue in *Gonzales v Oregon*[78] in 2006, when the US Supreme Court ruled that State Attorneys General could not enforce the Federal Controlled Substances Act against physicians who prescribed drugs for assisted suicide in compliance with Oregon state law.

Outside the United States and Europe, a law legalizing euthanasia was adopted in the Northern Territory of Australia in 1995,[79] but was nullified by the federal parliament two years after it went into effect. In Canada, the *Rodriquez*[80] case tackled the issues of assisted suicide, requested by a patient suffering from a serious illness. The patient based her argument on the Canadian Charter of Rights and Freedoms, which provides in section 7 that 'everyone has the right to life, liberty and security of the person and the rights not to be deprived thereof except in accordance with the principles of fundamental justice.' Justice Sopinka, writing for a narrow majority, rejected the claim of the petitioner that she just wanted to determine the time and manner of her death, and therefore denied her request.

A very different logic was followed in the leading UK case, *Airedale NHS Trust v Bland*.[81] There, the House of Lords ruled in favor of those representing Tony Bland, a patient in a persistent vegetative state with no hope of recovery, allowing his artificial feeding, and therefore his life, to be ended. The court's decision was based on the reasoning that it was in the patient's 'best interests' for treatment to be withdrawn and that its discontinuance was in accordance with good medical practice.

7. Extending Basic Rights to Human Tissues and Cells

The legal concept of the right to privacy provides a theoretical foundation for guaranteeing various forms of self-determination over the human body. However, when the issue of disconnected body parts, human tissue,[82] and DNA is raised, the concept of privacy seems to be an insufficient legal category to describe the complex relationship between the donor and the stored human tissue samples that are used for research purposes. On the one hand, the human DNA sample symbolizes and represents the person but, on the other hand, it is also regarded as a gift or personal contribution to research of public interest, as a symbol of public participation. When we deal with the legal implications of genetic data or storing human tissue samples in biobanks, a preliminary legal question has to be addressed, namely whether we are facing a

[76] Ronald Dworkin, 'Assisted Suicide: the Philosopher's Brief', *New York Review of Books* (February 27, 1997).

[77] *Washington v Glucksberg* 117 S Ct 2258 (1997).

[78] 546 US 243 (2006).

[79] Rights of the Terminally Ill Act (1995).

[80] *Rodriguez* [1993] 3 SCR 519.

[81] *Airedale NHS Trust v Bland* [1993] 1 All ER 821.

[82] Christian Lenk, Judit Sándor, and Bert Gordijn (ed), *Biobanks and Tissue Research* (2011).

human rights problem or are we in a field which requires regulation of the safety and logistics of research on human DNA.[83]

Defining the boundaries of the human body is especially relevant and justifies legal scrutiny when we look at research conducted on human beings, because of the potential abuses and possibilities of psychological or physical harm.[84] However, most research carried out today is not conducted on human beings but on human tissue, blood samples, and human DNA. Humans as research subjects are not actually present in the laboratories when research 'on them' is carried out. In other words, more and more human research is done not on the human body but on human bodily substances.

Research rules therefore have to be developed in order to respond to these different kinds of uses. For instance, legally, it still matters how human biological materials are being collected, and consent for collection and for specific use should be a precondition for research. Legal policy should then differentiate whether the research material still carries personal information.

In the field of the application of genetic research, legal issues are mostly concentrated around the problem of how new genetic information affects our basic human relations, family ties, decisions over the reproduction, insurance, employment, and intellectual property. To be more precise, how genetic information should be qualified, what kinds of rights can be established based on this knowledge, who should hold this knowledge, and who is to control this intrinsically individual, wide-ranging information that can easily be obtained by others are all major legal issues. Is it the genetic sample itself that should be protected, or rather the data that can be revealed during an examination of the sample? Or is it both of them in an identical manner, the sample as a set of data or separately as human tissue, or that the DNA information should be regarded as a special type of personal data?

These concerns often manifest when considering *biobanks*,[85] where there are two main methods of considering related legal issues. One is the concept of privacy; the other is the question of ownership.[86] While privacy aims to restrict access to samples and data, current tendencies in interpreting ownership point towards increased demand for the public use of biobanks. A right to privacy in biobank regulations refers mainly to the protection of personal data in collecting, storing, and processing samples and data, as well as the techniques for

[83] Directive 2004/23/EC of the European Parliament and of the Council of 31 March 2004 on setting standards of quality and safety for the donation, procurement, testing, processing, preservation, storage and distribution of human tissues and cells; Commission Directive 2006/17/EC of 8 February 2006 implementing Directive 2004/23/EC of the European Parliament and of the Council as regards certain technical requirements for the donation, procurement and testing of human tissues and cells; Commission Directive 2006/86/EC of 24 October 2006 implementing Directive 2004/23/EC of the European Parliament and of the Council as regards traceability requirements, notification of serious adverse reactions and events and certain technical requirements for the coding, processing, preservation, storage and distribution of human tissues and cells.

[84] Judit Sándor, 'Body Immortal' in Jennifer Gunning and Søren Holm (eds), *Ethics, Law and Society III* (2007), 123–35.

[85] Human biobanks and genetic research databases (HBGRDs) are

> structured resources that can be used for the purpose of genetic research, which include: a) human biological materials and/or information generated from the analysis of the same; and b) extensive associated information.
>
> Source: OECD Draft Guidelines for Human Biobanks and Genetic Research Databases, 2008.

[86] Judit Sándor, 'Legal Concepts of the Right to Privacy and Ownership in the Regulation of Biobanks' in Kris Dierickx and Pascal Borry (eds), *New Challenges for Biobanks: Ethics, Law and Governance* (2009), 123.

shielding data from the curious eyes of third parties. Most international norms and national laws focus on protecting the data subject while claiming enhanced guarantees for securing privacy and confidentiality in the domain of biobanks. Some authors, such as Graeme Laurie, have already elaborated a notion of *genetic privacy*.[87] Based on privacy concerns, the Dutch National Steering Committee decided in 2001 that samples in the national repository of dried blood spots of newborns have to be destroyed five years after the blood is taken.[88]

In the ECtHR, the most important ruling so far is *Marper v United Kingdom*,[89] which has had far-reaching repercussions: while it primarily dealt with human rights guarantees in criminal procedures in the context of storing DNA samples taken from criminal suspects, it also touched on the legal classification of genetic samples and data, ruling that 'the retention at issue constitutes disproportionate interference with the applicants' right to respect for private life and cannot be regarded as necessary in a democratic society'.[90] In the Court's view, all the unlawfully retained information—the fingerprints, the DNA profiles, and the sample itself—*qualify as personal data* under the data protection convention, since each one can be directly linked to the individual suspect.[91] *Obiter dicta* the Court also mentioned that both genetic samples and derived genetic data fall under the protection of private life,[92] which supports those who consider genetic material and data a special case because of the possibility of personal identification.

Moore v Regents of the University of California[93] is a US state case that deals with the use of human cells for research and for commercial purposes. While the Court ruled that individuals do not have an ownership interest in their cells after the cells have been removed from their bodies, it nevertheless recognized an important bioethical principle based on informed consent and on *fiduciary duties* by claiming that physicians need to disclose their research interests to their patients. Justice Mosk, in his dissenting opinion, was in favor of considering the patients' contribution to biological invention more significantly.

Not only individual patients but patients' groups may also actively participate in biomedical research. In 2003, in *Greenberg v Miami Children's Hospital Research Institute*,[94] a group of individuals provided samples and medical data for researchers to explore the Canavan disease. However, when a patent was developed, the patients were not notified and could not benefit from the new tests or its profits. The federal district court ruled that individuals do not own their tissue samples.

One of the most well-known debates over the ownership of biological samples was elaborated in *Washington University v Catalona*.[95] In this case, Dr William Catalona set up a biobank at Washington University and, over the course of 25 years, collected 3,500 samples from

[87] Graeme Laurie, *Genetic Privacy* (2002). Genetic data is seen as a special case as it is shared by relatives, and requires the re-interpretation of anonymity as even in the lack of personal identifier it may lead to a concrete natural person by a simple match.

[88] Jasper A. Bovenberg, *Property Rights in Blood, Genes and Data* (2006), 7.

[89] ECtHR, *S and Marper v United Kingdom*, App nos 30562/04 and 30566/04, 4 December 2008.

[90] Ibid.

[91] Judit Sándor, Petra Bárd et al, 'The Case of Biobank with the Law: Between a Legal and a Scientific Fiction' (2011) *Journal of Medical Ethics* (forthcoming).

[92] *S and Marper v United Kingdom* (n 89), 68.

[93] *Moore v Regents of the University of California* 51 Cal 3d 120 (Supreme Court of California 1990).

[94] *Greenberg v Miami Children's Hospital Research Institute* 264 F Supp 2d 1064 (SD Fla 2003).

[95] *Washington University v William J Catalona, MD* United States Discrict Court Eastern District of Missouri Eastern Division, No 4:03CV1065, E Dist Mo April 14, 2006, *William J Catalona, MD v Washington University*, 8th US Circuit Court of Appeal, Nos 06-2286 and 06-2301, (2007). In 2008, the US Supreme Court declined to review this biological specimen ownership case.

patients diagnosed with prostate cancer. In this case, agreements between the researcher and the donors were overridden by the fact that the biobank had been used by the university for public purposes. The Court regarded the biological sample collection differently from a biobank, and considered it as a public entity belonging to the university and not to the scientist. The Court held that individual donors who provide biological specimens for research do not 'retain an ownership interest allowing [them] to direct or authorize the transfer of such materials to a third party'.

These disputes have also reached the field of intellectual property law. In 2010, a US district court invalidated Myriad Genetics' BRCA gene patent claims,[96] finding that human intervention and isolation did not produce markedly different characteristics than those possessed by genes in the human body. A federal court of appeals further held that isolated DNA may be unpatentable, as in order to state that a product of nature is patentable it must be qualitatively different from the product occurring in nature with markedly different characteristics from characteristics found in nature. In July 2011, the Court of Appeals for the Federal Circuit[97] partially reversed the lower court's decision and held that 'isolated' DNA, including genes and sequence-specific probes for detecting breast and ovarian cancer, are patent-eligible subject matter, since these molecules are 'markedly different' new chemical entities that do not exist in nature. Even after this judicial compromise that gives some gesture to the biotechnological industry, the debate on the patentability of human genes has not been settled.

Cases on property and privacy rights in relation to human tissues and cells point to a general theoretical problem, namely what are the frontiers of individual self-determination in respect of human tissue samples. Is my DNA and tissue is still *me*? Even if it is not identical with the individual, would it increase or, on contrary, decrease the protection of the individual if the law is becoming more permeable at the frontiers of the self? Here it seems that the 'bioethical mission' has influenced the previous legal notions and a more complex bio-social concept of the human being has been extended protection.

III. Conclusions

The perspective of bioethics increasingly serves as a tool for framing and interpreting various emerging biomedical technologies and helps to assess their moral and legal implications. Bioethics as a discipline, however, is relatively new and therefore its theoretical positions, legal interpretations, and policy consequences are not yet well known among the judiciary or at least not sufficiently elaborated to be widely used in court cases. As a result, courts often limit their references to bioethics discourse to a mere listing of various binding and non-binding instruments, even disregarding their scope and context.

However, if one examines closely the discourse on the legal subjects of rights in biomedicine, a significant extension of the field can be observed. Respect for human dignity, and the right to privacy, is used to interpret the decisions on human biological materials, DNA samples, decisions over the custodial rights of the *in vitro* embryo, and is even applicable in shaping the right to decide what types of research are to be conducted on previously collected biological samples.

[96] *ACLU v Myriad Genetics* 09 Civ 4515.

[97] See <http://www.genomicslawreport.com/wp-content/uploads/2011/07/Decision-in-USPTO-vs-MYGN.pdf>.

Judiciaries worldwide are facing these complex issues of the developing bio-social identities of humans and, in this field, bioethics seems to do significant preparatory work by exploring fundamental ethical issues and implications of new biotechnologies. Not all of these concerns should be recognized as basic rights but bioethics serves as an important laboratory in crystallizing basic norms and methods for interpreting new technologies in the field of life sciences.

Law should avoid two extreme positions in respect of these new technologies. One is to avoid over and premature regulation, which happens when the law jumps too quickly to the latest scientific advances without leaving sufficient time for reflection on the ethical and social implications of a new technology. The other extreme position, which is more common and has its roots in several constitutional traditions, is the clear separation thesis in which judges refrain from touching 'science'.

Here, the conceptual problem is how to define the core of science and related social professional norms. The delineation between science and its application in the latest fields of biotechnology is often hard to make. Furthermore, interpretation of scientific results in a broader scope of society is often problematic. If law simply codifies or acknowledges the science of today, it often contributes to enlarging the fallacies of current scientific paradigms. As a result, scientific determinism and inevitable reductionism may end up extending biologism and shrinking persons to a simple mass of cells and tissues.

Interpretation of scientific discoveries has many traps. Bioethical analyses are not necessarily based on an accurate assessment of scientific developments, and these interpretations sometimes misread the effects of applying new biotechnologies. Moreover, normative interpretations may also be distorted due to factors that are entirely independent from scientific research. Judicial interpretations, then, must analyze scientific activities in a complex way and separate scientific advances from commercial interests, to peel off the legacy of an older, paternalistic professional tradition, and to deflect eugenic and reductionist thinking. In this complex work, bioethics may offer some help.

As we have seen, reproductive and regenerative medicine is an especially contested field for constitutional interpretation. The vast quantity of data and the ever-growing body of knowledge produced by the Human Genome Project and the various biobank programs provide important resources for scientific analysis and have led to the development of a wide range of therapies. Stem cell research opens up new vistas not only for prolonging the human life-span but also for offering new types of reproductive services to those who need them.

These new biotechnologies represent serious challenges to constitutional concepts and often require new interpretations of human dignity, bodily self-determination, identity and parenthood, notions of person and reproductive rights, principles of data protection and consent, and the boundaries of the body and personhood. Existing constitutional frameworks and accepted bioethical principles seem to provide answers in classical frontiers of life cases but remain insufficient and inconsistent when boundaries of personhood and the human body are concerned.

Bibliography

Brooke A. Ackerly, *Universal Human Rights in a World of Difference* (2008)

Margaret P. Battin, Rosamond Rhodes and Anita Silvers (eds), *Physician Assisted Suicide* (1998)

Tom L. Beauchamp and James F. Childress, *Principles Biomedical Ethics* (6th edn, 2008)

Violeta Beširević, *Euthanasia: Legal Principles and Policy Choices* (2006)

Deryck Beyleveld and Roger Brownsword, 'Human Dignity, Human Rights, and Human Genetics' (1998) 61 *Modern Law Review* 661

Jasper A. Bovenberg, *Property Rights in Blood, Genes and Data* (2006)
Marcia C. Inhorn (ed), *Reproductive Disruptions* (2007)
Sheila Jasanoff, 'Biology and the Bill of Rights: Can Science Reframe the Constitution?' (1987–88) 13 *American Journal of Law and Medicine* 249
Graeme Laurie, *Genetic Privacy* (2002)
Christian Lenk, Judit Sándor, and Bert Gordijn (eds), *Biobanks and Tissue Research* (2011)
Dominique Manaï, 'La procréation médicalement assistée en droit suisse: Verité sur la conception et l'identité; du donneur de gamètes' in Brigitte Feuillet-Liger (ed), *Procréation médicalement assistée et anononymat* (2008)
Warren Thomas Reich, 'The "Wider View": André Hellegers's Passionate, Integrating Intellect and the Creation of Bioethics' (1999) 9 *Kennedy Institute of Ethics Journal* 25
John A. Robertson, 'Procreative Liberty and Harm to Offspring in Assisted Reproduction' (2004) 30 *American Journal of Law and Medicine* 2
Jürgen Robienski and Jürgen Simon, 'Recent Development in the Legal Discourse on Genetic Testing in Germany' in Andre den Exter (ed), *Human Rights and Biomedicine* (2010)
Nicolas Rose, *The Politics of Life Itself* (2007)
Barry R. Schaller, *Understanding Bioethics and the Law* (2008)
Richard F. Storrow, 'The Bioethics of Prospective Parenthood: In Pursuit of the Proper Standard for Gatekeeping in Infertility Clinics' (2007) 28 *Cardozo Law Review* 2283

PART IX

TRENDS

CHAPTER 56

INTERNATIONALIZATION OF CONSTITUTIONAL LAW

WEN-CHEN CHANG AND JIUNN-RONG YEH

Taipei

I. Introduction

When 'internationalization of constitutional law' and 'constitutionalization of international law' were initially phrased at the beginning of the twenty-first century, most constitutional and international lawyers were not certain about what the two phrases really meant or were intended to mean.[1] In less than a decade, law review articles and edited works addressing these two and related topics have burgeoned at unprecedented speed. Now, comparative constitutional lawyers typically include some international courts and their case laws such as the European Court of Human Rights (ECtHR) and its jurisprudence as part of their scholarly canons. Likewise, international lawyers began embracing concepts and mechanisms in domestic constitutions such as judicial review, democratic accountability, or federalism into their analytical terrains.[2] Many scholars have treated these two and related developments in both constitutional and international law as the emergence of 'world constitutionalism',[3] 'global constitutionalism',[4] or 'transnational constitutionalism'.[5]

Indeed, 'constitutionalization of international law' and 'internationalization of constitutional law' are inseparable and interrelated. Once international laws are 'constitutionalized' in that they enjoy direct and primary effects upon the domestic laws of member states, such as in the case of EU law, domestic laws, and to a certain extent even constitutions, these are then inevitably penetrated by these international laws. In a similar vein, when some domestic constitutions extend their influences to transnational or international levels, they become part of the inspirations, persuasions, or in some cases even binding sources of international law[6] or other national laws. This facilitates a reciprocal relationship between international and domestic laws having the possibility of influencing each other. As a result, our understandings of both international and domestic laws, their natures, and boundaries are fundamentally altered.[7]

This chapter focuses on only one aspect of these interrelated phenomena: internationalization of constitutional law.[8] The introduction is followed by the discussion of major trends in internationalization of constitutional law, including incorporation of international human rights treaties into constitutions, convergence and comparativism of national constitutions, and constitutional devolution or treaty-becoming constitutions. Next we make inquiries into the driving forces that push the development of constitutions across and beyond their borders. We argue that the current internationalization of constitutional law results primarily from the expansion of a global market, the triumph of rights-based discourse, and, most importantly, the emergence of transnational networks by governments, non-governmental organizations (NGOs), and technocrats or professionals.

[1] The two phrases were first discussed together in Herman Schwartz, 'The Internationalization of Constitutional Law' (2003) 10 *Human Rights Brief* 10, 10ff.

[2] See Deborah Z. Cass, 'The Constitutionalization of International Trade Law' (2001) 12 *European Journal of International Law* 39, 49ff.

[3] Bruce Ackerman, 'The Rise of World Constitutionalism' (1997) 83 *Virginia Law Review* 771, 771ff.

[4] Ernest A. Young, 'The Trouble with Global Constitutionalism' (2003) 38 *Texas International Law Journal* 527, 527ff.

[5] Jiunn-Rong Yeh and Wen-Chen Chang, 'The Emergence of Transnational Constitutionalism: Its Features, Challenges and Solutions' (2008) 27 *Penn State International Law Review* 89.

[6] Statute of the International Court of Justice, Art 38(b), (c).

[7] Yeh and Chang (n 5), 98ff.

[8] 'The Constitutionalization of Public International Law' (Chapter 58) and other related issues such as constitutional comparisons are addressed in other chapters of this volume.

Despite the trend in internationalization, we nevertheless find that disparity abounds in practice. Instead of internationalization, regionalization is a better catchword for what has been happening regarding the association of domestic constitutions. Moreover, the selection of what becomes international and what does not is partial, contested, and even cherry-picking. Choices are usually made on colonial legacy, affinity in the legal system, language or culture, and most importantly, power politics by competing actors, governments, and courts alike. The fact that the two most popularly referenced courts, the US Supreme Court and the German Federal Constitutional Court seldom engage in comparative analysis speaks to the power disparity of courts in this round of constitutional dialogues. And we should be alert to the resulting bipolar extremes of internationalism versus nationalism that not only calls into question current internationalization but also politicizes and even delegitimizes the recent triumph of liberal constitutionalism over the last quarter of the twentieth century.

The last two sections of this chapter are devoted to the debates on and prospects for internationalization of constitutional law. We address three main concerns typically expressed in the debate: democratic accountability, rule of law, and checks and balances. We argue that along the line of internationalization of constitutional law, multiple actors grounded on multifaceted sources of international and domestic laws will demand with much rigor transparency, information, and free and fair competition and function as checks and balances on one another. We conclude by forecasting that the current internationalization of constitutional law is likely to continue as a rivalry between convergence and divergence. There is no need to contain or suppress either. What is really important is—by exacting scrutiny of comparative and international law and politics—to unveil power politics or even power manipulations behind convergence or divergence in such a way that fairer and healthier engagements, dialogues, or competitions can proceed.

II. Trends

International laws and constitutional laws are usually regarded as different sets of laws that rarely cross paths. It thus becomes quite intriguing to even consider ways that domestic constitutions are becoming international or internationalized. In the following, we discuss three recurring themes in the development of the internationalization of constitutional law.

1. Incorporation of International Human Rights into Domestic Constitutions

The first—and perhaps most important—way that constitutions may become international or internationalized is by the incorporation of international human rights treaties and norms into domestic constitutions.[9] As the rights guaranteed by domestic constitutions are convergent—or even identical—with those enshrined in international documents, constitutions are indeed becoming international.

The most apparent example is the Constitution of Bosnia and Herzegovina that annexes 15 international human rights documents to the Constitution[10] and mandates a state duty for

[9] Wen-Chen Chang, 'An Isolated Nation with Global-minded Citizens: Bottom-up Transnational Constitutionalism in Taiwan' (2009) 4(3) *National Taiwan University Law Review* 203, 206ff.

[10] See Constitution of Bosnia and Herzegovina, Annex I: Additional Human Rights Agreements to be Applied in Bosnia and Herzegovina.

implementation and compliance.[11] The same Constitution also imposes a state duty to ensure 'the highest level of internationally recognized human rights and fundamental freedoms'[12] and give rights and freedoms protected in the European Convention on Human Rights (ECHR)[13] and its Protocols direct applicability and superior status in the domestic legal system.[14] Another noticeable example is the Canadian Charter of Rights and Freedoms that incorporates both the International Covenant on Civil and Political Rights (ICCPR) and the International Covenant on Economic, Social and Cultural Rights (ICESCR).[15]

Many recently enacted or revised constitutions of new democracies such as South Africa or those in Central and Eastern Europe typically include a chapter on rights reflective of international human rights. These new constitutions may also add one or two clauses to give international human rights laws direct applicability and superior normative status in the domestic legal system and instruct governments and courts to take into consideration these international human rights laws.[16] Additionally, domestic incorporation of international human rights can be made through legislation. In states without written constitutions, legislative incorporation indicates no less effect than constitutional incorporation. The Human Rights Act of the United Kingdom that authorizes courts to review whether domestic legislation is compatible with the rights protected in the ECHR evidences this.[17]

Incorporation of international human rights into domestic legal systems may also be carried out effectively through judicial interpretation. Courts may reference international human rights on their own assertion with or without any clear constitutional or legislative mandate. Those referenced rights are not necessarily contained in treaties to which those states have acceded.[18] Judges may ground their incorporation of those rights on legal concepts such as the law of nations, generally accepted norms, or principles recognized by civilized nations.[19] Judicial incorporation becomes particularly justifiable if those international human rights have been developed the status of *jus cogens* or customary international law.[20] In the process of judicial incorporation, not only international human rights or documents ensuring those rights are discussed or referenced, but also decisions or interpretations by international courts regarding those rights and documents. The process of internationalization hence becomes self-reinforcing and ever expanding.

2. Convergence and Comparativism of National Constitutions

The second trend in internationalization of constitutional law involves convergence and comparativism across constitutional jurisdictions. The last quarter of the twentieth century witnessed the triumph of liberal constitutionalism. A record number of nations now have written or unwritten constitutions which meet modern constitutional standards. As a result, the

[11] See Constitution of Bosnia and Herzegovina, Art II, paras 4, 7, 8.

[12] See ibid Art II, para 1.

[13] European Convention for the Protection of Human Rights and Fundamental Freedoms (Rome, 1950).

[14] See Constitution of Bosnia and Herzegovina, Art II, para 2.

[15] William W. Black, 'Canada's Human Rights System and the International Covenant' (2011) 6(1) *National Taiwan University Law Review* 207, 211ff.

[16] eg, Constitution of South Africa, s 39(1), Constitution of Republic of Hungary, Art 9(1), and also the Constitution of South Korea, Art 6(1).

[17] Douglas W. Vick, 'The Human Rights Act and the British Constitution' (2002) 37 *Texas International Law Journal* 329, 351ff.

[18] Yeh and Chang (n 5), 96ff.

[19] eg *The Paquete Habana* 175 US 677 (1900); *Knight v Florida* 528 US 990 (1999); *Atkins v Virginia* 536 US 304 (2002). See also the Alien Torts Claims Act, 28 USC §1350.

[20] eg *Hamdan v Rumsfeld* 548 US 557 (2006).

majority of nations in all parts of the globe share similar constitutions, which typically include a list of fundamental rights and freedoms and institutional mechanisms like constitutional courts or human rights commissions to ensure the realization of those rights.

The convergence or assimilation of constitutions has created an unprecedented opportunity for courts of different states to learn from one another. The domestic lists of fundamental rights and freedoms in national constitutions are reflective of one another as well as of post-war international human rights documents. The similar—if not identical—concept of rights and freedoms has given rise to a common constitutional language across jurisdictions, permitting judges to look elsewhere for consultation or inspiration even in interpreting their own constitutional clauses. After all, free speech, due process, equality, right to life, or principle of proportionality is guaranteed in the majority—if not all—constitutions. Accordingly, an increasing number of courts have cited foreign constitutions or foreign cases in their own decisions.[21] A celebrated trio of decisions referencing foreign law across jurisdictions involved the death penalty in the South African Constitutional Court, the Canadian Supreme Court, and the US Supreme Court.[22] In addition, this common language also fares easier for judges across jurisdictions to gather and converse on the important constitutional questions they face.

In the eyes of many, a new era of judicial dialogue, or engagement, has arrived.[23] This not only subjects comparative constitutionalism to yet another unexplored terrain, but also establishes a closer link between constitutional law and international law as consensus on the latter is more easily reached by convergent practices in the former everywhere around the globe.

3. Constitutional Devolution or Treaty-Becoming Constitutions: Federalism, Autonomous Regions, and Indigenous Rights

The third—and perhaps less studied—trend is that a constitution may become a treaty or provide treaty-like functions between subunits of a state or between different ethnic groups within a state. That a constitution is a treaty or provides treaty-like functions is not new.[24] The Articles of Confederation by 13 states of America upon the Declaration of Independence in 1776 were indisputably seen as a treaty between sovereign states. The 1787 US Constitution maintained this treaty spirit and adopted a federal-state arrangement that recognized the dual sovereignty of the states and the federal union. This practice is far from an exception.

Recent years have witnessed an increasing number of constitutions that began to provide—in varying degrees—treaty or treaty-like functions in dealing with autonomous assertions of sub-regions or ethnic minorities. The much-discussed case of constitutional devolution is the Spanish Constitution of 1978.[25] In order to resolve persistent conflicts between various ethnic and regional groups, the Spanish Constitution grants them the right to autonomy. Specifically, it allows bordering provinces with common ethnic, historical, cultural, and economic

[21] Antonin Scalia, 'Outsourcing American Law: Foreign Law in Constitutional Interpretation', American Enterprise Institute, Working Paper No 152, 2009.

[22] They include the South African Constitutional Court's decision in *State v Makwanyane*; the Canadian Supreme Court's decision in *United States v Burns*, [2001] 1 SCR 283; and the US Supreme Court's decision in *Roper v Simmons* 543 US 551 (2005).

[23] Anne-Marie Slaughter, *A New World Order* (2004); Vicki C. Jackson, *Constitutional Engagement in a Transnational Era* (2010), 71ff.

[24] Ackerman (n 3), 771ff; Wen-Chen Chang, 'Constructing Federalism: The EU and US Models in Comparison' (2005) 35 *EurAmerica* 733.

[25] Michel Rosenfeld, 'Constitution-Making, Identity Building, and Peaceful Transition to Democracy: Theoretical Reflections Inspired by the Spanish Example' (1998) 19 *Cardozo Law Review* 1891.

characteristics to accede to self-governing autonomous communities. These autonomous communities are provided with a wide array of legislative and executive powers with their own parliaments and governments. Given this high degree of autonomy left to sub-regions and national groups, the Spanish Constitution is widely seen as a pact to keep together a nation of subnations.[26] Paradoxically, by making a constitution like a treaty, and granting sovereign-like powers to subunits, a constitution eventually sustains its status as a domestic constitution and prevents the dissolution of the state.

The same paradox occurred in the Peace Accord between the republics of Bosnia and Herzegovina, which subsequently became part of their Constitution.[27] The reason that this Constitution annexes so many international human rights treaties as part of its content is to underscore the sovereign—or sovereign-like—status of each republic and at the same time to keep them together under a single constitutional umbrella. Similar arrangements or claims have been made elsewhere. For example, section 33 of the Canadian Charter of Rights and Freedoms permits the legislature of a province to declare certain Acts operative notwithstanding any inconsistency with the Charter. Canadian provinces are thus given a constitutional privilege to have provincial laws in defiance of the national constitution. This section was negotiated primarily out of a concern for Quebec separatism.[28] It evidences, again, the strength of a treaty-becoming constitution in being self-sustaining and keeping a state together.

More and more advocates for indigenous rights seek to model this treaty-like constitutional arrangement on the relationship between aboriginal groups and their states. The United Nations Declaration on the Rights of Indigenous Peoples[29] asserts the right to self-determination by indigenous peoples and, more importantly, their right to greater autonomy within the state: strengthening their distinct political, legal, economic, social, and cultural institutions, while retaining their right fully to participate, if they so choose, in the political, economic, social, and cultural life of the state.[30] To realize the promise made in such a declaration, a domestic constitution can adopt the strategy of either establishing a sovereign-like relation with the indigenous groups or allow them direct applicability of international human rights without any fear of losing its own integrity.

III. Driving Forces

Internationalization of constitutional law is a recent development. The forces behind it are generated by the latest progress in technology and renovations in economic and social cooperation. On top of these forces standsthe global market, rights-based discourse, and transnational networks.

1. The Expansion of the Global Market

It is undeniable that the recent internationalization of constitutional law largely concerns economic globalization. The attempt of both advanced economies and fast developing economies to expand the scale of the global market at an accelerating speed is the key driving force. To

[26] Juan J. Linz, 'State Building and Nation Building' (1993) 1(4) *European Review* 355.

[27] Section II.1 above.

[28] Peter W. Hogg and Allison A. Bushell, 'Charter Dialogue between Courts and Legislatures, (Or Perhaps the Charter of Rights Isn't Such a Bad Thing after All)' (1997) 35 *Osgoode Hall Law Journal* 75, 75ff.

[29] Adopted by GA Res 61/295 on 13 September 2007.

[30] UN Declaration on the Rights of Indigenous Peoples, Arts 4 and 5.

ensure that such a broadened market across all constitutional jurisdictions can function, basic rules such as free exchange, market stability, contractual certainty and enforcement, and even a high degree of respect for private property and other market-oriented rights, must be harmonized if not equated.[31]

To do so, one strategy is to develop a strong global legal framework that infiltrates all domestic legal regimes, or is at least voluntarily complied with or referenced by domestic courts. The European Union provides the best example in this strategy that leads to internationalization of constitutional law. Beginning merely as a coal and steel free trade area between France and Germany, the EU gradually expanded its mission to free trade across the entire European continent. To ensure legal harmony across jurisdictions, the European Court of Justice (ECJ) had already in 1963 decided that the Community (as it then was) constituted a new legal order for the benefit of all states as well as their nationals, and thus Community law and regulations needed to produce direct effect and create individual rights, which national courts had to protect.[32] This led inevitably to internationalization—even if only Europeanization—of domestic constitutions and laws in EU member states. While domestic courts such as the German Federal Constitutional Court may find this process problematic, they eventually surrendered to the need for harmonization for free trade.[33] Similar strategies have also been employed in other economic cooperations between states, such as the largest one, the World Trade Organization (WTO).[34]

The other strategy is similar to the first but not necessarily with a corresponding global or transnational legal framework. To illustrate, a broadened market naturally provides an incentive for states to establish similar—if not identical—domestic legal frameworks that are conducive to trade. These domestic constitutional systems eventually become receptive to market-oriented liberal rights and freedoms. For instance, as China opened up to global trade, it took action to amend its Constitution to show due respect for private property and ensure abidance to the rule of law.[35] The constitutional convergence—albeit to a limited degree—by the Chinese is illustrative of the function of a global market to the current convergence of domestic constitutions.

2. The Global Triumph of Rights-Based Discourse

Another primary force driving internationalization of constitutional law is the rights-based discourse that had begun with the United Nations Charter and Universal Declaration of Human Rights (UDHR) and reached its climax in the Velvet Revolution of third-wave democracies.[36] Both the UN Charter and UDHR recognize that the existence of fundamental

[31] See Maxwell O. Chibundu, 'Globalizing the Rule of Law' (1999) 7 *Indiana Journal of Global Legal Studies* 79, 84ff.

[32] Case 26/62 *NV Algemene Transport-en Expeditie Onderneming van Gend & Loos v Nederlandse Administratie der Belastingen* [1963] ECR 1, 12, 16.

[33] The German Federal Constitutional Court had challenged the direct applicability of EU rules if they are in conflict with the German Basic Law. For a brief introduction of the struggle between the two courts and efforts towards harmonization, see Andreas Voßkuhle, 'Multilevel Cooperation of the European Constitutional Courts' (2010) 6 *European Constitutional Law Review* 175; W.T. Eijsbouts, 'Wir Sind Das Volk: Notes about the Notion of "The People" as Occasioned by the Lissabon-Urteil' (2010) 6 *European Constitutional Law Review* 199.

[34] See Cass (n 2), 49ff.

[35] See Marc Rosenberg, 'The Chinese Legal System Made Easy: A Survey of the Structure of Government, Creation of Legislation, and the Justice System under the Constitution and Major Statues of the People's Republic of China' (2000) 9 *University of Miami International and Comparative Law Review* 225, 226ff.

[36] Jackson (n 23), 45ff.

human rights is independent of states, and that these rights are vested directly in each and every human person.[37] This universal nature of human rights accordingly leads to two things. First is an international normative legal order that guarantees these rights and compels states—as well as all other public and private actors—to respect, protect, and fulfill these rights in their respective domestic legal regimes.[38] Secondly, is the recognition that all fundamental rights and freedoms guaranteed in domestic constitutions are manifestations of universal human rights, and thus a convergent understanding and realization of these rights is inevitable.[39]

The political imagination underlying this rights-based discourse is an unmitigated tension between local forces and a global rights-based regime that transcends those forces. The local typically nation-states were perceived as imposing, manipulative, and unjust. The global rights-based discourse led by moral activists was developed to rescue unfair and fractioned domestic constitutional orders that had been hijacked by self-interested nation-states.[40] In this view, the internationalization of constitutional law must be seen as a moral and legal development: one that transcends citizenship to prevent any human person from being exploited by state and non-state actors in any given locality. The convergence of constitutional orders is part of this paramount rights-based moral process.

3. The Emergence of Transnational Networks

Due to technological innovation and global travel, the emergence of transnational networks between governments, NGOs, technocrats, or professionals has significantly facilitated this recent internationalization of domestic constitutions.[41] In the past, sovereign nations dominated the international arena, and local opinions would have to be screened and selected by a series of (mis)representations. Now, with the advance of technology, access to all kinds of international gatherings and networking is made direct and available not only to governments but also to NGOs and professionals such as lawyers and judges. Scholars have demonstrated that international judicial gatherings have contributed to a recent significant increase in foreign law references and comparative analysis by various domestic courts. The networking of domestic and international NGOs has allowed these NGOs to be better informed and capable of participating directly even in the advocacy of international lawmaking.

For domestic NGOs involved in these international activities, their advocacies are dual: one in creating a global legal order of their concerns, and the other is making their domestic legal order convergent with that global legal order. In other words, they are the agency in intermediating international and constitutional regimes where international and domestic human rights laws meet. The best example is provided by the advocacies of NGOs in Taiwan, the most-isolated democracy today due to its complicated relationship with China. Through networking with international human rights NGOs, the Taiwanese NGOs pushed forward domestic incorporation of international human rights treaties—to which the government of

[37] See Charter of the United Nations (San Francisco, 1945), Preamble and Universal Declaration of Human Rights, Preamble.

[38] Henry J. Steiner, Philip Alston, and Ryan Goodman, *International Human Rights in Context: Law, Politics and Morals* (3rd edn, 2008), 187ff.

[39] Jackson (n 23), 46.

[40] See Harold Koh, 'Transnational Public Law Litigation' (1991) 100 *Yale Law Journal* 2347, 2398ff.

[41] Chang (n 9), 203ff, 228ff.

Taiwan could not accede—and in some cases even facilitated international lawmaking.[42] Noticeably, in response to the rise of transnational networks, many international regimes have also opened up to participation by those NGOs and professionals. This in turn creates a nuanced opportunity for further reconfiguration of international law and domestic constitutions.

IV. Divergent Practices

Admittedly, the internationalization of constitutional law has divergent practices around the globe. Domestic entrenchment of international human rights and the convergence of constitutional rights and institutions seem stronger and more revealing in some parts of the world than in others. While the EU presents a clear case for internationalization of constitutional law and even for constitutionalization of international law, the United States as well as many Association of Southeast Asian Nations (ASEAN) countries continue to stress their distinctiveness in the course of constitutional development.[43] Singaporean and Malaysian courts are instructed to interpret the constitution and laws only within 'their four walls'.[44] East Asian courts are criticized for rarely referring directly to international human rights or engaging explicitly in comparative legal analysis.[45] Dependent upon where and how one looks, one can make a claim for either a strong appearance of internationalization of constitutional law or its nonexistence.

1. Regionalization Rather Than Internationalization

The internationalization of constitutional law tends to concentrate on particular places, and judicial dialogues take place only among certain courts. Instead of internationalization, regionalization may be a better expression for the present constitutional convergence. Most evident is the European Union. Within the EU, the constitutional laws of its member states have a greater degree of resemblance with regard to constitutional rights, principles, and institutions. Outside the EU, however, the picture of internationalization looks very different. It is true that the prevailing majority of states have ratified both the ICCPR and the ICESCR—the two UN human rights covenants—and that the list of constitutional rights in most constitutions presents a strong resemblance with the two covenants. Yet what is written is not always reflective of what is happening in practice. A great many states that ratified both covenants have had a poor human rights record and have shown no sign of significant improvement even after ratification. Ratification of human rights treaties has not yet imposed a direct obligation on states for domestic constitutional or legal incorporation, let alone direct judicial enforcement.[46]

Constitutional entrenchment of international human rights has typically been undertaken in the new democracies of Central and Eastern Europe. The list of constitutional rights was

[42] Such as participating in the drafting and passage of the WHO Framework Convention on Tobacco Control (FCTC).

[43] See eg *Sei Fujii v California* 38 Cal 2d 718, 242 P 2d 617 (1952).

[44] *Government of the State of Kelantan v Government of the Federation of Malaya & Anor* [1963] 1 MLJ 355, 358.

[45] See Tom Ginsburg, 'Eastphalia as the Perfection of Westphalia' (2010) 17 *Indiana Journal Global Legal Studies* 27.

[46] Oona Hathaway, 'Do Human Rights Treaties Make a Difference?' (2002) 111 *Yale Law Journal* 1935.

heavily influenced by the ECHR and the constitutions of their Western neighbors. As a result of such constitutional resemblance, it was not unusual for courts in these new European democracies to refer to the precedents of the ECtHR even if only for 'decorative' or practical purposes. But new democracies outside Europe do not necessarily opt for the constitutional entrenchment of the international bill of rights. New democracies in North and East Asia, for example Mongolia, South Korea, and Taiwan, despite all having a list of constitutional rights more or less liberal in nature, have not directly incorporated any human rights covenants into their domestic constitutions. Nor have they adopted a constitutional provision like South Africa that requires courts to consider international law, or like Argentina that reminds the legislature of issues of international human rights in the course of lawmaking.[47] The common constitutional provision adopted by these new democracies is one that merely advises their governments to respect treaty obligations and to give duly ratified treaties the status of domestic law.[48] The constitutional courts of South Korea and Taiwan, along with Supreme Court of Japan, whose decisions are evidence of strong foreign law influences—typically German and American—are nevertheless strongly criticized for seldom applying international human rights treaties including those ratified in their domestic cases.[49]

Perhaps some may contend that, partly due to the high threshold of constitution-making or amending, domestic constitutional entrenchment of international human rights should be allowed more time, and thus the situation centered in Europe at present should not be deemed as mere regionalization. They may further point to constitutional assimilation or comparativism as a stronger indication of internationalization of domestic constitutions. To their dismay, however, constitutional assimilation or comparativism occurs only in a cluster of states that share particular—including but not limited to regional—affiliations. Take, for example, that much discussed phenomenon in constitutional convergence, establishment of a constitutional court. The majority of states that have created a constitutional court since the late 1980s are the newly democratized states of Central and Eastern Europe primarily based upon the model of the German Federal Constitutional Court.[50] Constitutional courts created outside Europe have resulted mainly from those countries' association with the civil law system, which gives these states easy access to the European model of a constitutional court. Constitutional courts recently established in Asia, such as in Indonesia, Mongolia, South Korea, Thailand, and Taiwan, all claimed their inspiration from the German Federal Constitutional Court.[51] In contrast, most common law countries have not adopted a constitutional court. The Constitutional Court of South Africa, a common law country, is a rare exception. A contrasting civil law exception is Japan. Despite its scholarly culture that tends to closely follow the German legal system, Japan has not adopted a constitutional court due to strong US influence over its post-war constitutional design. By and large, the issue that distinguishes adoption or non-adoption of a constitutional court is a state's association with Europe or a shared history with a legal system, civil law or common law. Constitutional assimilation is clearly not an international phenomenon.

[47] Constitution of the Republic of South Africa, s 39; Constitution of the Argentine Nation, Art 75, ss 22 and 24.

[48] Constitution of Mongolia, Art 10.

[49] See eg Keun-Gwan Lee, 'From Monadic Sovereignty to Civitas Maxima: A Critical Perspective on the (Lack of) Interfaces between International Human Rights Law and National Constitutions in East Asia' (2010) 5(1) *National Taiwan University Law Review* 155.

[50] Tom Ginsburg, *Judicial Review in New Democracies* (2003), 6ff.

[51] *JY Interpretation No 371*, 7 Shizi 26 (Const Ct, January 20, 1995); Ginsburg (n 50), 165ff, 217ff.

Nor is judicial engagement of comparative constitutional analysis a complete global phenomenon. Despite scholarly excitement in declaring that the days of one-way transmission in legal reception had passed with the arrival of an active dialogue in a wider range of constitutional courts,[52] the reality proves to be the opposite. Most constitutional courts in Europe have not exhibited a strong tendency to cite foreign laws or engage in constitutional comparison. For example, the German Federal Constitutional Court, whose decisions are often referred to by other courts in Europe or even in Asia, has seldom referred to the decisions of other courts: it has done so in only seven decisions between 1998 and 2009, referring mostly to its European counterparts such as the French, Swiss, and UK courts.[53] A similar tendency exists in other European courts. The Italian Constitutional Court referred to less than a dozen foreign cases between 1980 and 2009, mostly from other European jurisdictions.[54] The Austrian Constitutional Court, the oldest of the kind in Europe, has relied on only about 50 judicial precedents since the 1980s, most of which were also in other European jurisdictions.[55] The new constitutional courts in Europe, such as those in Portugal, Hungry, and Romania, are no exception. Compared to the more established courts in Europe, these new courts make a greater number of references to foreign decisions the sources of which are mainly the ECtHR and other older courts in Europe.[56] On rare occasions, the decisions of the US Supreme Court might appear in the case law of its European counterparts; but such rarity hardly suffices as meaningful dialog across the Atlantic.

And this does not render any injustice to the other side of the Atlantic. The US Supreme Court, whose decisions are widely referred to in the United States and even in Asia, has seldom referred to foreign cases in its decisions. Even if such a rarity does occur, the references point mostly to English precedent.[57] The most celebrated court that has shown great willingness in the engagement of comparative analysis is the Canadian Supreme Court. But this Court refers mainly to English and US cases and in a few instances has cited precedents from South Africa or Israel.[58] Other courts in the Americas, for example the Supreme Court of Argentina, exhibit a similar attitude.[59]

Evidently, judicial dialogues conducted thus far are confined within regional boundaries. Trans-regional discourse is rare, and even if it does occur, it usually takes place between courts of the same legal family, civil law or common law. The usual example of transnational judicial engagement is the trio of references made between the South African Constitutional Court,

[52] Claire L'Heureux-Dubé, 'The Importance of Dialogue: Globalization and the International Impact of the Rehnquist Court' (1998) 34 *Tulsa Law Journal* 12, 21ff; Slaughter (n 23), 99ff.

[53] See Jörg Fedtke, 'Report on Germany', Interest Group on the Use of Foreign Precedents by Constitutional Judges, unpublished manuscript, 2010.

[54] Anna Bruno, 'The Sidelining of Foreign Precedents and the Italian Hesitation on "Alieni Juris"', Interest Group on the Use of Foreign Precedents by Constitutional Judges, unpublished manuscript, 2010.

[55] Anna Gamper, 'Report on Austria', Interest Group on the Use of Foreign Precedents by Constitutional Judges, unpublished manuscript, 2010.

[56] Elena Simina Tanasescu, 'Report on Romania', Interest Group on the Use of Foreign Precedents by Constitutional Judges, unpublished manuscript, 2010; T. Violante, 'The Portuguese Constitutional Court and the "Dialogue of Judges"—A Verifiable Truth?', Interest Group on the Use of Foreign Precedents by Constitutional Judges, unpublished manuscript, 2010.

[57] It did occasionally refer to case law of the ECtHR and extremely rarely it referred to cases decided by Supreme Court of Canada and other courts in the Americas such as the Colombian Constitutional Court and the Brazilian Court. See Angioletta Sperti, 'The Use of Foreign Law by the Supreme Court of the United States', Interest Group on the Use of Foreign Precedents by Constitutional Judges, unpublished manuscript, 2010.

[58] L'Heureux-Dubé (n 52), 15, 22.

[59] Walter F. Carnota, 'Report on Argentina', Interest Group on the Use of Foreign Precedents by Constitutional Judges, unpublished manuscript, 2010.

the Canadian Supreme Court, and the US Supreme Court. All three being from the same common law tradition.

Asian courts are no exception. There is little judicial dialogue in the region. Most Asian courts of civil law tradition, such as Japan's Supreme Court, Korea's Constitutional Court, and Taiwan's Constitutional Court, exhibit a similar attitude to their counterparts in Europe: having scarce engagement in explicit comparative analysis.[60] Other common law courts in Asia, such as courts in Hong Kong, the Philippines, India, and to a less extent Singapore and Malaysia, have a much more open attitude. Yet they mostly reference old English cases or cases from other common law jurisdictions.[61]

2. Partial Internationalization: Power, Politics, or Cherry-Picking

Disparity in the internationalization of constitutional law is certainly not limited to regionalization or groupings of legal families. What becomes international and what does not is usually the result of competing powers, politics, preferences, or even mere cherry-picking.

As previously discussed, the US Supreme Court and the German Federal Constitutional Court whose decisions are popularly referred to in their respective regions and legal families rarely engaged in any comparative analyses. In some other courts that are more inclined to reference others, the dialogues have huge disparity. For example, while the Canadian Supreme Court and the South African Constitutional Court cross-reference each other, the latter cites the former almost *three hundred times more often* than vice versa.[62] Between 1995 and 2009, the latter cited the former on a total of 850 occasions,[63] but it happened in reverse only in three cases.[64] In the common law jurisdictions of Asia, courts usually reference English case law as part of their common law heritage, but when they occasionally reference each other, a disparity also exists in some referencing the Supreme Court of India that does not always act reciprocally.[65]

Power undoubtedly speaks for influence. But where does this judicial discursive power come from? Colonial power seems to play a very tiny part as English case law continues to command referencing authority even in decolonized states. Yet, the discursive power of the US Supreme Court bears scant connection to colonialism. The referencing popularity of the

[60] Akiko Ejima, 'The Enigmatic Attitude of the Supreme Court of Japan towards Foreign Precedents—Refusal at the Front Door and Admissions at the Back Door' (2009) 16 *Meiji Law Journal* 19; Wen-Chen Chang and Jiunn-Rong Yeh, 'Judges as Discursive Agent: The Use of Foreign Law and Its Relationship with Judges' Learning Backgrounds', Interest Group on the Use of Foreign Precedents by Constitutional Judges, unpublished manuscript, 2010.

[61] See Li-ann Thio, 'Beyond the "Four Walls" in An Age of Transnational Judicial Conversations: Civil Liberties, Rights Theories, and Constitutional Adjudication in Malaysia and Singapore' (2006) 19 *Columbia Journal of Asian Law* 428.

[62] David S. Law and Wen-Chen Chang, 'The Limits of Transnational Judicial Dialogue' (2011) 86 *Washington Law Review* 532.

[63] See Christa Rautenbach, 'Use of Foreign Precedents by South African Constitutional Court Judges: Making Sense of Statistics', Interest Group on the Use of Foreign Precedents by Constitutional Judges, unpublished manuscript, 2010.

[64] A search of the CANSCC-CS database on Westlaw conducted on February 4, 2011 for any and all appearances of the words 'South Africa' between 1995 and 2009 yielded a total of 15 results; of these, only three involved actual citations of a decision of the South African Constitutional Court. See *Marcovitz v Bruker* [2007] 3 SCR 607; *R v Hall* [2002] 3 SCR 309; *United States v Burns*, [2001] 1 SCR 283.

[65] See Arun K. Thiruvengadam, 'The Use of Foreign Law in Constitutional Cases in India and Singapore: Empirical Trends and Theoretical Concerns', Interest Group on the Use of Foreign Precedents by Constitutional Judges, unpublished manuscript, 2010.

German Federal Constitutional Court by other European courts is astonishing if the horrors the Nazi regime for its neighbors are taken into consideration. Neither do the age or history of the court bear significant weight. The Austrian Constitutional Court, the oldest of the kind, has received scant, if any, attention in transnational judicial dialogue.[66] The decisions of the High Court of Austria, the second to the US Supreme Court in the history of judicial review, are far less referenced in common law jurisdictions than some younger courts such as the Canadian or Indian Supreme Court.[67] Language and cultural proximity provide no better explanation. While German, Swiss, or Austrian courts tend to reference one another in a very limited number of comparative analyses, they nonetheless extend a great deal of consideration to English or US law.[68] Many judges and lawyers of the civil law tradition both in and outside Europe do not speak German as their native language, but that does not seem to undermine their enthusiasm in overcoming the high linguistic barrier to reference German law. Spanish is spoken throughout most of Latin America, but it is the US Supreme Court rather than the Spanish Constitutional Court that become most often referenced. If not colonial legacy, age, or history of the courts or constitutions, language, or culture proximity, then is it after all mere cherry-picking?

Scholars have contended that judicial networking or conferences were a prime attribute to the recent wave of transnational judicial references and comparative analyses.[69] Notwithstanding the lack in empirical evidence of such a claim, these scholars fail to notice that those meetings and workshops were attended by prominent judges mostly from Europe or North America with only very few from Africa, South America, or Asia. And the selective few judges from minority jurisdictions usually have some individual associations with distinguished academic or professional institutions in Europe or North America. Elsewhere we have argued that the background of a judge has a direct impact on his or her preference for comparative analyses.[70] Judges from scholarly backgrounds engage to a far greater degree than those practitioners in foreign law citations. And even more importantly, judicial references tend to be made to the jurisdictions with which judges become acquainted by substantive training for their master or doctoral degree.[71] It is evident that individual affiliations with dominant institutions in Europe or North America do matter and contribute to this partial internationalization of constitutional law.

The choice of institutional affiliation by judges or scholars is anything but mere personal preference. Aside from region, legal tradition, language, or culture, a number of much less noticed but nonetheless important factors also include academic politics at both domestic and international levels and even economic soft powers such as scholarships or grants. Most illustrative is the competition with legal influences between the United States, Germany, and more recently the Council of Europe (the treaty body of the ECHR). The international dominance of the United States has extended its legal influence to civil law countries even on the opposite side of the world. A good many prominent judges and constitutional law scholars in Japan, Korea, and Taiwan—three major civil law jurisdictions of East Asia—obtained a master or doctoral degree in distinguished US law schools. After a rapid economic revival following defeat in

[66] Perhaps the most interesting appearance is in the decision of Taiwan's Constitutional Court as a result of one Taiwanese Justice having a PhD in law in Austria. Law and Chang (n 62), 567.

[67] The High Court of Australia was established in 1901 and has exercised judicial powers of review since 1903.

[68] Fedtke (n 53); Sergio Gerotto, 'The Use of Foreign Precedent by the Swiss Federal Tribunal', Interest Group on the Use of Foreign Precedents by Constitutional Judges, unpublished manuscript, 2010; Gamper (n 55).

[69] Slaughter (n 23), 70.

[70] Chang and Yeh (n 60).

[71] Law and Chang (n 62), 544f.

the Second World War, Germany sought to reclaim its lead position in political and legal developments in Europe and beyond. For example, its government-affiliated foundations such as the Deutscher Akademischer Austausch Dienst (DAAD) and the Konrad-Adenauer-Stiftung have since the 1960s provided generous scholarships to foreign scholars for study and research in Germany and hosted many glamorous conferences on the spreading influence of the German legal system—particularly of the German Federal Constitutional Court—over other jurisdictions and courts. Established in 1999, an advisory body to the Council of Europe, the European Commission for Democracy through Law (better known as the Venice Commission) has significantly increased European visibility in constitutional developments in other parts of the world. Thus there should be little wonder about the sharp increase of referencing ECtHR case law in constitutional jurisdictions even beyond Europe.

3. Persistent National Reticence towards Internationalization

The decades-long development of globalization has created bipolar extremes rather than one global village. After the 9/11 attacks and the ensuing war on terror, our world seemed to be divided into one majority camp of liberal constitutional democracies against the other minority camp of illiberal states. A similar—but not necessarily corresponding—division also became existent in the attitude towards the internationalization of constitutional law: a growing majority of constitutional jurisdictions that are open to international and comparative laws versus a persistent minority that remains reticent towards such internationalization.

The United States stands out as a paramount example in such a persistent minority. After the US Supreme Court sent a very small sign of having engaged in international or comparative analyses,[72] Congress wasted no time in introducing bans of such practice to the floor.[73] At the present, the US constitutional law scholarship is divided on this issue: some wholeheartedly advocating constitutional comparativism while others strongly opposing it. Other jurisdictions with a strong reticence towards internationalization include Malaysia and Singapore. An earlier precedent instructing that 'the Constitution is primarily to be interpreted within its own four walls and not in the light of analogies drawn from other countries' was followed in both Malaysian and Singaporean courts.[74] In a great many cases, both courts rejected foreign laws on the ground that they were made in other legal systems different from their own or that they were inappropriate in the local context. Most striking was the Singaporean court's recent rejection of English law—which had been closely followed as part of its colonial legacy—on the ground that English laws have been changed and been greatly influenced by the ECtHR as a result of the domestic incorporation of the ECHR.[75] Interestingly, however, on rare occasions, the Singaporean court still chose to rely on English or US cases that directly support its conservative position.[76]

It should be clear by now that reticence towards internationalization of constitutional law does not necessarily entail wholesale rejection of foreign or international law. What usually matter are conclusions derived from such comparative analyses: compatible/incompatible

[72] eg *Roper v Simmons* 543 US 551 (2005); *Hamdan v Rumsfeld* (n 20).

[73] Constitutional Restoration Act of 2004: Hearing on HR 3799, 108th Congress (2004); Appropriate Role of Foreign Judgments in the Interpretation of American Law: Hearing on H Res 568, 108th Congress (2004).

[74] *Government of the State of Kelantan v Government of the Federation of Malaya & Anor* [1963] MLJ 355.

[75] eg *Attorney General v Wain and Others* [1991] SLR 383; *Chee Siok Chin v Minister for Home Affairs* [2006] 1 SLR 582; *Attorney-General v Chee Soon Juan* [2006] 2 SLR 650.

[76] eg *Nguyen Tuong Van v PP* [2005] 1 SLR 103 and *Jabar v Public Prosecutor* [1995] 1 SLR 617.

with liberal/conservative positions taken by the majority/minority of courts or the general public. Time and again, we have seen many courts directly referencing foreign or international law not to extend but to limit the protection of rights explicitly or impliedly guaranteed in domestic constitutions.[77] As discussed earlier, what gets cited and what does not is primarily the result of politics at both domestic and international levels. Despite their different attitudes towards comparative analysis, one reticent and the other open, the US Supreme Court and the German Federal Constitutional Court, the decisions of which are mostly referenced by others, rarely engage in any foreign law analysis. In contrast, as open as it has been towards foreign or international law, the Supreme Court of India does not always rely on these laws to enlarge domestic constitutional protections. In some cases, while finding that the Indian Constitution incorporated women's rights contained in the Convention on the Elimination of All Forms of Discrimination against Women (CEDAW), the Court nevertheless found that it was not desirable to declare local customs as unconstitutional as such a declaration might result in chaos.[78] And as resistant as it has been to foreign and international law, the Japanese Supreme Court may implicitly rely on foreign law and has at times recognized the value of international human rights law if not for the courts at least for reasons of public discussion or social education.[79]

To the extent that power politics on comparative analysis at both domestic and international levels continues, the bipolar extremes of openness on the one side and reticence on the other is likely to continue. Neither side necessarily represents moral victory. Politics of referencing or not referencing external norms is much more complex than a line drawn to reflect convergence versus resistance.

V. Debates

Given the enormous disparity in practice, it is little wonder that the debate about internationalization of constitutional law has been strong and has shown no sign of compromise. However, both proponents and opponents have focused their debates on three major issues: democratic accountability, rule of law, and checks and balances. In the following we address them directly in the hope of pointing out future directions.

1. Democratic Accountability

To the extent that incorporation of international human rights, constitutional convergence, or devolution is made through domestic constitutional or legislative enactments, they do not necessarily suffer from a democratic deficit. Even if such incorporation, convergence, or devolution cedes considerably government decision-making powers to international authority, such decisions are nonetheless taken through domestic political processes by which decisions are legitimized and under which decision-makers are made accountable.

Opponents may argue that notwithstanding the political process, blank checks like section 39 of the South African Constitution or Article 9(1) of the Hungarian Constitution may be

[77] Wen-Chen Chang, 'The Convergence of Constitutions and International Human Rights: Taiwan and South Korea in Comparison' (2011) 36 *North Carolina Journal of International Law and Commercial Regulation* 593ff.

[78] *Chairman, Railway Board and Appellants v Mrs Chandrima Das and Others* (2000) AIR 988; *Vishaka v State of Rajasthan* (1997) 6 SCCC 241; *Apparel Export Promotion Council v AK Chopra* (1999) AIR 625.

[79] Ejima (n 60), 19ff.

cashed a great more than expected. And democratic legitimacy and accountability suffer to the greatest extent when affected citizens have no access to influence the norm-generating process and to make norm-generators accountable. In the case of treaty-like constitutions, democratic decision-making mechanisms such as separation of powers or federalism are also likely to be undermined and accountability collapsed.[80] In addition, opponents are mostly concerned with judicial incorporation of or references to international and foreign laws under the banner of universal rights or better answers found in comparative analysis. For opponents, neither judges nor those international or foreign laws relied upon are democratically chosen and made accountable in domestic legal regimes.

For proponents of internationalization, deficit in democratic legitimacy or accountability is not a sound rejection as this problem exists in almost all forms of political organization even including functioning democracies. The deficiency is a matter of degree but not of kind. Proponents argue that international legal regimes can enhance their democratic legitimacy and accountability by making them easily accessible, transparent, and participatory for governments and NGOs.[81] With those improvements, domestic incorporation of international law suffers a much smaller democratic deficit. And this was precisely what happened to the EU which has undergone the process for some time. While judicial reference to foreign law does raise democratic concerns, those who make these references can easily be made accountable in any of the domestic constitutional regimes. And a more rigorous development in comparative constitutional laws can address these concerns and ameliorate—if not correct—judicial mistakes.[82]

2. Rule of Law

The concept of rule of law, while not entirely uncontested, entails at least legal certainty and legal clarity.[83] However, both are inevitably undermined in internationalization of constitutional law. Domestic incorporation of international human rights law—often as a blank check—leads to a certain degree of normative instability, as the contents of domestic laws depend on and change with the international legal regime. Certainty and clarity become seriously obstructed—if not totally collapsed—when courts rely on international and foreign laws at will in the course of their decision-making. It will be difficult, if not impossible, for any affected citizens to know *ex ante* the exact rules that may apply to their cases.[84]

Interestingly, however, proponents of internationalization defend the above criticism by arguing that the advancement in internationalization of domestic constitutions may facilitate the establishment of an 'international rule of law'. As recent cases in international courts demonstrate, a hierarchy of international laws with preemptory human rights norms sitting at the top is emerging.[85] The openness—or so-called blank checks—of domestic constitutions to international human rights accepted in major treaties or regarded as *jus cogens* or customary international law is merely to recognize the superior status of these human rights that must supersede conflicting domestic norms from the perspective of the international rule of law. Judicial incorporation of or referencing of these rights with or without explicit domestic

[80] See Young (n 4), 533ff.

[81] Yeh and Chang (n 5), 115ff.

[82] Cheryl Saunders, 'The Use and Misuse of Comparative Constitutional Law' (2006) 13 *Indiana Journal of Global Legal Studies* 37, 67.

[83] See Barry M. Hager, *The Rule of Law: A Lexicon for Policy Makers* (1999), 19ff.

[84] See Young (n 4), 533ff.

[85] eg a case decided by the ECJ: Joined Cases C-402/05 P and C-415/05 P *Yassin Abdullah Kadi and Al Barakaat International Foundation*, 3 September 2008.

mandates is not arbitrary action but proper implementation of these rights at the local level. In this view, incomplete incorporation or sporadic references are what should be blamed for the current chaos in the domestic rule of law. But these problems are only temporary in the process of internationalization.

That said, however, the international rule of law is still in its infancy if not entirely illusory. After all, international law has yet to impose a state duty for implementation through constitutional incorporation.[86] For moderates, the rule of law deficiency in the internationalization of domestic constitutions is to be rescued not by illusory concepts like the international rule of law but by strengthening articulations of domestic constitutions.[87] This may be seen in the recent decisions of the US Supreme Court in referencing international norms.[88] Having recognized the weakness in rule of law, the Court gave lengthy and thoughtful opinions articulating comparable constitutional principles with those international norms.

3. Checks and Balances

The last focus of the debate is on checks and balances. Given that decision-making powers are delegated to international authorities in the process of internationalization, many important decisions with grave impacts for domestic constitutional rights and institutions are made outside the domestic arena. The domestic applicability of these decisions becomes a serious concern. One worry among the many is on failing checks and balances in domestic regimes.[89] Opponents of internationalization are very skeptical of the extent to which states may participate in the process of decision-making to provide any effective checks and balances on those international authorities, let alone make them accountable.

Proponents, however, are not pessimistic about this.[90] They remind opponents that accession to international mechanisms always requires state consent, the process of which gives domestic actors opportunities to bargain with international authorities. And as international mechanisms are opened up for various forms of participation and transparency, these international decision-making authorities cannot be said to have no effective checks and balances. More importantly, domestic courts may provide effective judicial checks and balances with transnational decision-making authorities in the course of their adjudication. For example, the German Federal Constitutional Court empowered itself to review whether EU laws were consistent with the purpose and basic principles of the EU, and if such inconsistency were found, whether those laws were binding on German territory.[91]

In addition, checks and balances may be provided at the international level. Recent decisions by international courts are indicative of nuanced ways for international actors including courts to provide checks and balances with one another.[92] The legality of UN policies may be examined at the ECJ, WTO policies may be challenged at the ECtHR and vice versa. This is

[86] Yuval Shany, 'How Supreme is the Supreme Law of the Land?' (2006) 31 *Brooklyn Journal of International Law* 341ff.

[87] Yeh and Chang (n 5), 115.

[88] eg *Hamdan v Rumsfeld* (n 20); *Roper v Simmons* (n 22); *Lawrence v Texas* 539 US 558 (2003).

[89] Young (n 4), 533ff. For some opponents such as Justice Scalia of the US Supreme Court, this might even generate illegitimacy concerns, which is another issue that is dealt with in elsewhere in this volume.

[90] Yeh and Chang (n 5), 115ff.

[91] See 89 BVerfGE 155 (FRG); see also 33 ILM 388 (1994). Later, they also reviewed decisions of the ECJ and ECtHR, but this remains somewhat contested. The efforts of harmonization between the two have continued. See Voßkuhle (n 33), 175ff.

[92] Yeh and Chang (n 5), 120ff.

best demonstrated by a very interesting case involving a UN security policy that traveled from the UN Security Council to the EU, then from the Irish Supreme Court to the ECJ, and finally to the ECtHR.[93] All courts involved claimed the power to review relevant laws and regulations made in other international regimes. It is without doubt that cases involving international decision-making may now move from court to court, thereby creating a complex set of checks and balances. This possibility of judicial checks and balances at both international and constitutional levels, and the sophisticated judicial dialogue or engagement that may take place in these processes have made some moderates in this debate lean towards—if not yet fully endorse—the current internationalization trend.

VI. Prospects

Despite a few solutions proposed, reasoned debates or power politics on internationalization of constitutional law at both domestic and international levels is likely to continue.

On the one hand, international human rights treaties are likely to expand their membership, and an ever increasing number of constitutions may give privileged normative status of some sort to international human rights laws. Engagement in comparative analysis or referencing foreign or international law in the course of constitutional adjudication is likely to grow. Empowering local or ethnic authorities by granting them a certain degree of autonomy under a domestic constitution or allowing the operation of a separate legal system is likely to continue. And these local or ethnic groups—along with other less privileged groups in a domestic polity—are likely to be aided by the mounting body of international or comparative law in their respective power struggles against the central authority. Although not always effective, the emergent use of international or comparative law as legal or political strategy taken in domestic or international sites is irreversible. The demand for internationalization of constitutional law remains strong, and the resulting impact of such a demand is as controversial as it has always been.

On the other hand, the dissenters are likely to rise in significant strength. The growing number of ratifications of international human rights treaties does not yield any corresponding degree of compliance, let alone domestic constitutional incorporation. Judicial referencing of foreign or international law continues to be partial, selective, and cherry-picking. Those few powerful courts like the German Federal Constitutional Court, the US Supreme Court, and the French Constitutional Counsel which rarely engage in comparative analysis but are constantly referenced by other courts are likely to sustain their dominance in this global game of judicial 'dialogue'. Occasionally their dominance may be challenged by other equally powerful judicial organs at the transnational level like the International Court of Justice, ECtHR, or even WTO Appellate Body,[94] or at least put into doubt in comparative analyses by other less privileged courts. There will also be a few courts that continue to be reticent towards foreign or international law, and in being so they might even attempt to gain the upper hand in this ensuing judicial discursive war.

These seemingly conflicting trends should not be seen as a surprise to constitutional lawyers. They are inevitable given the contested nature of convergence vis-à-vis divergence and the power struggles in them. What constitutional lawyers should be really concerned with in the

[93] See *Bosphorus Hava Yollari Turizm ve Ticaret Anonim Sirketi v Ireland*, 2005-VI ECtHR 440, paras 1, 14, 40, 43.

[94] See Section V.3 above.

present internationalization of constitutional law are free and transparent competition, open and sincere dialogue, and thorough and exacting scrutiny of what becomes international and what does not. Comparative constitutional lawyers must work hard to lift the veil of ignorance on politics behind the internationalization of constitutional law. No state or court may hide behind convergence or divergence. Instead, motives and power struggles must be fully exposed. It is important to know who are like others and why. And it is equally important to know who are unlike others and why. That is a really daunting task for comparative law and politics.

Bibliography

Bruce Ackerman, 'The Rise of World Constitutionalism' (1997) 83 *Virginia Law Review* 771

Alexander Aleinikoff, 'Thinking Outside the Sovereignty Box: Transnational Law and the US Constitution' (2004) 82 *Texas Law Review* 1989

Wen-Chen Chang, 'An Isolated Nation with Global-minded Citizens: Bottom-up Transnational Constitutionalism in Taiwan' (2009) 4(3) *National Taiwan University Law Review* 203

Simon Chesterman, 'An International Rule of Law?' (2008) 56 *American Journal of Comparative Law* 331

Monica Claes, *The National Courts' Mandate in the European Constitution* (2006)

W.T. Eijsbouts, 'Wir Sind Das Volk: Notes about the Notion of "The People" as Occasioned by the Lissabon-Urteil' (2010) 6 *European Constitutional Law Review* 199

Akiko Ejima, 'The Enigmatic Attitude of the Supreme Court of Japan towards Foreign Precedents—Refusal at the Front Door and Admissions at the Back Door' (2009) 16 *Meiji Law Journal* 19

Bardo Fassbender, 'The United Nations Charter as Constitution of the International Community' (1997) 36 *Columbia Journal of Transnational Law* 529

Tom Ginsburg, 'Eastphalia as the Perfection of Westphalia' (2010) 17 *Indiana Journal Global Legal Studies* 27

Claire L'Heureux-Dubé, 'The Importance of Dialogue: Globalization and the International Impact of the Rehnquist Court' (1998) 34 *Tulsa Law Journal* 15

Vicki C. Jackson, 'Paradigms of Public Law: Transnational Constitutional Values and Democratic Challenges' (2010) 8 *International Journal of Constitutional Law* 517

Vicki C. Jackson, *Constitutional Engagement in a Transnational Era* (2010)

Harold Koh, 'The Ninth Annual John W. Hager Lecture, The 2004 Term: The Supreme Court Meets International Law' (2004) 12 *Tulsa Journal of Comparative and International Law* 1

Mattias Kumm, 'Democratic Constitutionalism Encounters Institutional Law: Terms of Engagement' in Sujit Choudhry (ed), *The Migration of Constitutional Ideas* (2006)

David Law and Wen-Chen Chang, 'The Limits of Transnational Judicial Dialogue' (2011) 86 *Washington Law Review* 532

Frank Michelman, 'W(h)ither the Constitution?' (2000) 21 *Cardozo Law Review* 1063

Ernst-Ulrich Petersmann, 'The WTO Constitution and Human Rights' (2000) 3 *Journal of International Economic Law* 19

Cheryl Saunders, 'The Use and Misuse of Comparative Constitutional Law' (2006) 13 *Indiana Journal of Global Legal Studies* 37

Herman Schwartz, 'The Internationalization of Constitutional Law' (2003) 10 *Human Rights Brief* 10

Dinah Shelton, 'Normative Hierarchy in International Law' (2006) 100 *American Journal of International Law* 291

Anne-Marie Slaughter, *A New World Order* (2004)

Li-ann Thio, 'Beyond the "Four Walls" in An Age of Transnational Judicial Conversations: Civil Liberties, Rights Theories, and Constitutional Adjudication in Malaysia and Singapore' (2006) 19 *Columbia Journal of Asian Law* 428

Nicholas Tsagourias (ed), *Transnational Constitutionalism: International and European Models* (2007)

Mark Tushnet, 'The Possibilities of Comparative Constitutional Law' (1999) 108 *Yale Law Journal* 1225

Jiunn-Rong Yeh and Wen-Chen Chang, 'The Emergence of Transnational Constitutionalism: Its Features, Challenges and Solutions' (2008) 27 *Penn State International Law Review* 89

Ernest A. Young, 'The Trouble with Global Constitutionalism' (2003) 38 *Texas International Law Journal* 527

CHAPTER 57

THE EUROPEAN UNION'S UNRESOLVED CONSTITUTION

NEIL WALKER

Edinburgh

I. Introduction: Imagining the Non-State Polity in Constitutional Terms

In the summer of 2007 the European Council announced its decision to 'abandon' the 'constitutional concept' it had endorsed so optimistically only four years previously on receiving a draft of a first Constitutional Treaty for the European Union from the Convention on the

Future of Europe.[1] After the 'no' votes to the 2005 French and Dutch referenda on the (duly promulgated) Constitutional Treaty, and in recognition of the document's dubious popularity and unratified status in various other member states, Europe's leaders eventually opted to jettison the brave new world of a supranational constitution and return to the more familiar international law vehicle of a 'Reform Treaty'.[2] The move appeared to pay a political dividend. Agreement was reached as early as the Lisbon Summit of December 2007 and, despite further delay occasioned by a fresh referendum defeat in Ireland, the new 'postconstitutional Treaty'[3] was successfully implemented before the end of 2009.[4]

It is a striking irony that the ultimately fatal difficulties encountered by the Convention coincided with the growing acceptance of some kind of constitutional status for the EU—even if understood in 'small "c"' rather than documentary 'big "C"' terms.[5] Yet this is more than coincidence. A written constitution would not have appeared on the European political agenda without a growing readiness to think in constitutional terms about a process begun half a century earlier as an interwoven attempt at continental market-building and political rapprochement after the ravages of the Second World War.[6] And the extensive debate over the Constitutional Treaty that ensued reinforced that trend, encouraging many interested in the EU—practitioners and commentators—to cast their appreciation of the EU in constitutional language where previously they would have been indifferent or hostile to such a characterization.

The gradual adoption of a common terminology and a shared or overlapping narrative of constitutional origins do not, however, imply an emerging consensus about the contemporary constitutional quality or constitutional potential of the EU. Rather, the constitutional turn encompassed different and frequently opposing perspectives. That opposition was most apparent over the key strategic question itself—for or against an explicit constitutional settlement. But the big 'C' constitutional debate engaged a deeper and wider diversity of perspectives between, within, and, indeed, cutting across the immediate strategic alternatives.[7]

For the big 'C' constitutional enthusiast, the (re)conceptualization of the new order as already amounting to an unwritten constitution supported a written constitution on quite different grounds and to sharply divergent ends. The emergence of an unwritten constitution could be cited as a threshold of accomplishment deserving formal recognition. On this view, a written constitutional settlement becomes appropriate as a way of charting the progress or even according 'finality'[8] to the distinctive constitutional achievement of the evolved supranational form or, more ambitiously, as a platform from which to build on the undocumented *acquis* towards fuller constitutional maturity.[9] In marked contrast, the development of a

[1] German Presidency Conclusions: European Council, Brussels, 21–22 June 2007.

[2] Treaty of Lisbon amending the Treaty on European Union and the Treaty establishing the European Community, 13 December 2007, 2007 OJ (C 306) 01.

[3] Alexander Somek, 'Postconstitutional Treaty' (2007) 8 *German Law Journal* 1121.

[4] See eg Paul Craig, *The Lisbon Treaty: Law, Politics and Treaty Reform* (2010).

[5] Neil Walker, 'Big "C" or Small "c"?' (2006) 12 *European Law Journal* 12.

[6] See eg Joseph Weiler, *The Constitution of Europe* (1999), esp ch 7.

[7] For a fuller discussion of the approaches brought to the Convention, see Neil Walker, 'Europe's Constitutional Momentum and the Search for Polity Legitimacy' (2005) 3 *International Journal of Constitutional Law* 211, 225–31.

[8] In the well-known formulation of Joschka Fischer, Foreign Minister of the Federal Republic of Germany, 'From Confederacy to Federation—Thoughts on the Finality of European Integration', Speech at the Humboldt University, Berlin, 12 May 2000. This speech is widely credited as a key moment in the mobilization of political opinion behind a big 'C' constitutional process.

[9] See eg Jürgen Habermas, 'Why Europe needs a Constitution' (2001) 11 *New Left Review* 5.

supranational entity to a point where its powers could be claimed to be of constitutional weight might, from a position wary of expansion and stressing the continuing subordination of the EU to its member states, call for more formal constitutional recognition as a way of reining in and containing these powers.[10]

For the big 'C' constitutional sceptic, too, endorsement of the unwritten constitutional credentials of the EU supported various narratives of development. To highlight the peculiar achievement of the informal constitutional *acquis* might suggest that a self-styled written constitutional text, far from being timely, was actually redundant. More specifically, to stress the organic development and complex richness of an unprecedented supranational accommodation of legal and political forces might indicate the intrinsic difficulty, even inappropriateness, of attempts to reduce that accommodation to a single documentary constitution.[11] Or, in a more uncompromising variation of the sceptical theme, resort to constitutional language might serve to dramatize the gap between those modest aspects of constitutionalism suited to the supranational domain and grander aspirations and accomplishments familiar from the state tradition, so accentuating the deep incongruence—or 'category error'[12]—of a fully-fledged written constitution in this new domain.

The relationship between endorsement of the unwritten constitutional credentials of the EU and position-taking in the strategic context of the documentary constitutional debate, then, is complex, much dependent on the overall approach to the EU polity espoused or assumed. We may usefully re-plot this complexity, therefore, in terms of a spectrum of ambition encompassing three main polity visions. At the modest end of the spectrum, the EU polity assumes a truncated form, in constitutional terms measurable against but emphatically less than statehood. The EU as polity-lite possessing only the more elementary features of statehood is seen either as attracting a constitutionalism-lite which does not merit the imprimatur of a written expression, or, if a written form is contemplated, as it was by Eurosceptic opinion at the height of debate over the documentary constitution, it is only to curb the state-like tendencies of the supranational polity. In a complex middle ground, the EU is seen as a *sui generis* work-in-progress or achievement, whose development and constitutional narrative clearly diverges from the state model. Again, this model may or may not be viewed as appropriately served by a written constitution, in this case depending upon whether one stresses its expressive value as a vindication of supranational distinctiveness or the excessive rigidity or irrelevance of its fixed form before the moving picture of European integration. Finally, at the ambitious end of the spectrum, the state again become the direct point of comparison, but no longer viewed as a necessarily higher constitutional form than the EU. Rather, constitutionalization is seen as a point of departure for a fuller realization of the EU polity, if not *as* a state, at least as a meaningfully state-analogous entity in terms of key indices of polity formation and maturation; an ambition which, at least in the dominant modern constitutional tradition, has been seen to require a documentary expression.

We will return to these different polity visions—truncated and derivative polity, polity *sui generis*, and mature polity—and how they inform ongoing or renewed debate on Europe's constitutional future in the concluding section. The immediate point of these initial

[10] See eg *The Economist*, 4 November 2000. The conversion of the notoriously Eurosceptic magazine to the case for a written constitution was contingent upon such a limiting approach.

[11] See eg Joseph Weiler, 'In Defence of the Status Quo: Europe's Constitutional *Sonderweg*' in Joseph Weiler and Marlene Wind (eds), *European Constitutionalism Beyond the State* (2003); Stephen Weatherill, 'Is Constitutional Finality Feasible or Desirable? On the Case for European Constitutionalism and a European Constitution' (2002) 7 *Conweb: Webpapers on Constitutionalism & Governance beyond the State* 1.

[12] See eg Andrew Moravcsik, 'A Category Error', *Prospect*, July 2005, 22.

observations is to show how widespread and, simultaneously, how volatile the language of constitutionalism has become in today's EU. Our main focus in what follows is upon the 'raw material' from which the various contemporary readings of Europe's constitutional achievement and potential are drawn. We pose the baseline question of the very possibility of a constitutional law for the EU—a question that *all* positions in favour of a constitution, written or unwritten, are bound to answer affirmatively. Given the types of things that the idea of constitutional law tends to signify and, given where constitutional law is situated and how distributed across our global maps of legal meaning and authority, to what extent and in what ways can we conceive of the EU as a suitable constitutional site? This inquiry requires us, first, to consider the EU against a general background of constitutional imagination and definition. In so doing, we explain why our understanding of the EU is influenced by the historic centrality of the modern state to constitutional theory and practice, but also why, in these inescapable but incomplete terms, the EU is an *unresolved* constitutional entity. We then consider how the EU's putatively constitutional features have emerged and unfolded, in so doing focusing on the centrality of law. And as this centrality has come under pressure in the mature EU, we consider, finally, the changing constitutional challenges and opportunities of this new post-state polity.

II. The Possibility of European Union Constitutional Law

1. In the Shadow of the State: The Specific, the Relational, and the General

Within our contemporary conceptual maps of legal authority and meaning there are three different modes in which we recognize and according to which we situate constitutional law. Each mode figures in at least some understandings of the EU's constitutional credentials. First, and still emphatically foremost, as indicated by the tenor of debate over a big 'C' Constitution, we typically view constitutional law as polity-specific. We comprehend constitutional law as rooted in, peculiar to, concentrated upon, and, most fundamentally, as in significant ways 'constitutive' and configurative of a particular polity or political community—providing a unique regulatory frame that embraces and contains the whole. Today, however, the polity-specific perspective far from exhausts understandings of constitutionalism.[13] Where in the high modern age constitutional law was the primary law internal to states and international law the dominant law between such mutually exclusive constitutional polities, that neat demarcation no longer holds. With the rise of non-state polities, including the EU itself, which overlap and intersect other polities, including state polities, as an outgrowth of the first polity-specific mode we increasingly also understand constitutional law in relational terms, as a nexus connecting different polities and their polity-specific systems of constitutional law. This altered landscape is part and parcel of the intensified wave of globalization or transnationalization of the key circuits of social, economic, and political power we have witnessed since the second half of the twentieth century.[14] Thirdly, there is a way of viewing constitutional law as polity-indifferent; neither dedicated to a particular polity, nor even located at the interface between particular polities, but mobile between or otherwise recurrent across a wide range of

[13] On constitutionalism, see further Chapter 8.

[14] See eg A. Jones, *Globalization: Key Thinkers* (2010).

polities. In this mode, which in a further feature of the globalizing trend has also become more prominent in recent years, constitutional law, most emphatically in the area of individual rights, is perceived as a floating category of discrete or only loosely aggregated legal phenomena possessing a universal or at least more general moral or practical resonance regardless of polity location.[15]

Common to all three modes of constitutional law is the heavy imprint of the modern state. This is especially so of the first mode. The paradigm case of polity-specific constitutional law is the constitutional law of the state polity. The very *form* in which we view constitutional law in this mode, as discrete and delimited, follows the model of the modern state. Equally, how we understand constitutional rules in this polity-specific form as typically co-designed or co-evolved in a holistic fashion—the 'joined-up' normative patterning of political life—is exemplified and largely sustained by the modern state tradition. Further, the detailed *content* of constitutional rules appropriate to the form of the discrete and joined-up polity are also much influenced by the long state tradition of usage and development. Constitutional law in relational mode, too, remains under the influence of the state tradition, since the leading players remain the states themselves, and the constitutional pedigree and character of these state players inevitably affect closely the terms of inter-polity relations. Finally, even where we consider constitutional law as non-polity-specific and non-holistic, but as so many discrete and mobile rules, their meaning and migratory course remains conditioned by the polity setting where they are received and adapted, and the still most prominent such settings remain states.

2. The Ambivalent Legacy of State Constitutionalism

The powerful legacy of state constitutionalism has decidedly mixed implications for the EU. Through the power of example the state tradition has encouraged and shaped the constitutional credentials of the EU more than it has any other non-state polity. The state tradition provides a cue for recognizing and a template for developing the EU as a discrete and joined-up polity. In addition, as we shall see, much of the content of the structures and doctrines of EU constitutional law is adapted from state constitutional law.

Yet the prominent statist heritage also challenges our constitutional understanding of the EU. It does so both conceptually and practically. Conceptually, despite a strong family resemblance in some features, the EU is not a state. Although it may seek to develop functional equivalents, it lacks the crucial aspects of exclusivity of final authority, originality of collective agency and primacy of political identity associated with the mature constitutional state, especially in the high modern phase of the system of states. Exclusivity of authority refers to the classical notion of state sovereignty.[16] It holds that the state exhibits the one supreme ordering authority for a territorial polity—an authority that defers to no other internal or external authority and to which all other authorities must defer. Originality of collective agency refers to the idea of state sovereignty as the product of an irreducible *pouvoir constituant* or constituent power—a power residing in 'the people' conceived of as a non-derivative and unencumbered source. Primacy of political identity refers to a deep aspect of political culture—the idea that the governing political persona of the subject is citizenship of the state polity, and that such citizenship announces the general associative bond through which particular political

[15] See eg Lorraine Weinrib, 'The Postwar Paradigm and American Exceptionalism' in Sujit Choudhry (ed), *The Migration of Constitutional Ideas* (2006).

[16] On sovereignty, see Chapter 17.

interests and beliefs are articulated and negotiated and other commitments and loyalties circumscribed.

Practically, the key reason why the EU does not and cannot possess these statist features of authority, agency, and identity, or at least cannot in the fullest sense associated with modern statehood, is precisely because it must exist alongside and in relation to states. While states themselves are undoubtedly challenged, altered, and somewhat diluted in their constitutional character by the rise of non-state polities such as the EU in the late modern phase of globalization, they still in some measure claim these scarce and competitive attributes for themselves.

To appreciate the EU in constitutional terms, therefore, we must look *to* and *beyond* the template of the state. We look *to* the state for what the EU can adopt or adapt. As seen in the big 'C' constitutional debate, this is a sharply divisive move. It can be made more or less modestly, depending on the underlying polity vision held, and whether functional equivalents to the state's mature constitutional aspects are considered feasible or desirable. We must also look *beyond* the state for those 'constitutional' features that are not based upon the state model and cannot be considered their functional equivalent. In so doing, let us concentrate on the first and, by extension, the second mode for thinking about the constitutional credentials of the EU, both premised on the idea of constitutional law as polity-specific, while remaining mindful of the third, polity-indifferent, way of thinking about constitutionalism.

3. Framing the Modern Constitutional Polity

The still dominant idea of constitutional law as polity-specific predates the modern state, although the modern state has provided its (re)defining vehicle in recent centuries. Originating in the Latin verb *constituere* (to establish) and its associated noun *constitutio*, and in a cluster of predecessor notions in Ancient Greece, the constitutional concept was gradually extended from the natural world to the world of the 'body politic',[17] first of the classical republics and then through various fuller incarnations of the state. As already intimated, the term constitution implies a discrete and holistic entity as the framed object of 'constitutional' reference. There are two distinct steps within this framing logic, and the movement from one to the other describes the emergence of modern constitutionalism. First, the mediaeval and early modern idea of constitution as an embracing descriptor of the inherited polity reflects a deepening assumption and spreading recognition that political society is appropriately concentrated within certain stable and territorially-coded containers of social space. Secondly, and crucially, in the age of the modern state this idea gradually assumes a more constructive and a more progressive hue. The constitution is no longer simply an acknowledgement and expression of the established order of things within the 'imagined'[18] setting of the bounded polity. It is now also a constructive achievement, an active project of collective self-organization—pursued in the interests, and eventually the name of that collective—of a polity conceived as a community of free and equal persons. As such, it contains enabling and constraining elements, concerned both with the effective pursuit of the collective interests and with the

[17] See eg Dieter Grimm, 'The Constitution in the Process of Denationalization' (2005) 12 *Constellations* 447.

[18] See eg Benedict Anderson, *Imagined Communities: Reflections on the Origins and Spread of Nationalism* (2006).

protection of certain basic rights and freedoms of the free and equal individuals and groups who make up that community.[19]

The mechanics are complex. The new constructive constitution, through various interlocking framing registers, establishes the wherewithal to shape and sustain the imagined political community. What does the pattern of interlocking framing registers consist of? Basically, constitutional thought in the modern state develops a set of distinctions but also a dense web of connections between a legal or *normative* framing register and other registers, which we may categorize as *political* and *socio-cultural*. The concentrated treatment of collective action problems and possibilities within any polity requires an appropriate normative blueprint. The normative register, in turn, divides into various sub-registers. There is a *formal* sub-register, consisting of the building blocks through which an autonomous and integrated legal system forms and equips itself with a normative capacity fit for modern constitutional purpose. There is also a *jurisdictional* sub-register, referring to the substantive scope of the legal order—the positive and negative means by which it specifies its boundaries of competence. There is, finally, an *integrative* sub-register, referring to how the formally connected bones of an expansively scoped legal system flesh out and cohere as an organic whole.

The state constitutional order also requires an authoritative assemblage of dedicated political institutions, itself generated or recognized by that normative order, as the complex of public power which acts upon, secures, and further develops that normative order.[20] We can again identify sub-registers within the *political* register. There is an *institutional* sub-register, referring to the architecture of government itself—the combination and organization of legislative, executive, judicial, and administrative branches through which the normative order is activated and renewed. There is, in addition, an *authorizing* sub-register, referring to the expression and operationalization of the distinctively modern idea of the normative and institutional constitution as an artefact—shaped through collective human agency. It denotes the constituency by which and the way in which, in that constituency's own terms, the constitutional order is initiated and constructed, or at least appropriated *as* an active constitutional order. This authorization may be a process or an event, informal or formal, elite or popular, but in the mature modern model of 'foundational constitutionalism'[21] the constitutional order is typically understood to be instituted through a formal episode of inclusive self-legislation—a popularly authorized project of documentary constitution-making. Finally, there is a *socio-cultural* register. This requires an associative field—variously called a society, a people, a community, and a *demos*—as the cultural resource that energizes and sustains and is in turn fertilized by the mutually supportive legal and political orders.[22]

Because our sense of a modern constitutional order requires the interlocking of these framing registers, our threshold definition demands a minimum level of 'activity' within each field. There must be some evidence of expansive and integrating legal order and of a self-authorized rather than merely inherited or imposed institutional apparatus, and there must be some level of broad cultural recognition and endorsement of the constitutional artefact. Beyond that threshold, we can distinguish between more or less intense achievements of constitutionalism as an active project of collective self-legislation. An autonomous legal order and dedicated

[19] See eg Mattias Kumm, 'The Cosmopolitan Turn in Constitutionalism: On the Relationship between Constitutionalism in and beyond the State' in Jeffrey L. Dunoff and Joel P. Trachtman (eds), *Ruling the World? Constitutionalism, International Law, and Global Governance* (2009).

[20] See eg Niklas Luhmann, *Das Recht Der Gesellschaft* (1993).

[21] Nico Krisch, *Beyond Constitutionalism: The Pluralist Structure of Postnational Law* (2010), ch 2.

[22] See eg Dieter Grimm, 'Integration by Constitution' (2005) 3 *International Journal of Constitutional Law* 193.

architecture of political institutions provide the 'thin' essentials of any constitutional construction, including candidates for constitutionalism beyond the state. A fuller set of links, involving a more significant investment in the expansive jurisdictional and integrative dimensions of the normative register, in the authorizing dimension of the political register and in the associative bonds available under the socio-cultural register, becomes necessary for a 'thicker' constitutional settlement.[23]

It is through this fuller set of links that we comprehend the mature anatomy of state constitutionalism. The combination of fully developed legal, political, and socio-cultural framing registers maps onto the three 'peaks' of exclusive final authority, original collective agency, and primary political identity. In constitutional terms, exclusive final authority is a function of the interlocking of a formally autonomous legal order, a jurisdictional range unchallenged and unfettered by other authorities and a dedicated set of authoritative political institutions. Original collective agency is a function of an acknowledged act or process of self-authorization by which the constituent power generates these institutions or assumes ownership of them. Primacy of political identity depends upon a symbiosis of culture and legal and political structure. It requires a sufficient sense of common political bond at the socio-cultural level to provide support for and sustained recognition of these sovereign legal and political institutions as duly self-authorized, including the act or process of self-authorization itself, which institutional accomplishment and event history in turn reinforces the common bond of citizenship.[24]

4. Distinguishing EU Constitutionalism: The Unresolved Constitution

Much analysis of the constitutional quality of the EU follows this conventional approach. Such is the relative novelty of the subject at supranational level, indeed, that its literature often pays more attention to the rudiments of constitutional framing than is typical of the more taken-for-granted world of state constitutionalism on which that conceptual structure is closely modelled. Before examining the trajectory of EU constitutional development in these terms, however, we should indicate the broad underlying differences between the EU and the state context. As already remarked, for all the discrete and holistic properties of the EU polity, it lacks those traditionally state-defining features of exclusive final authority, original collective agency, and primary political identity that provide the fullest constitutional model of interlocking legal, political, and socio-cultural frames available to us. In terms dictated by the statist template, the EU has operated at the 'thinner' end of the spectrum of constitutional development. Yet the absence of certain statist features is also a space of constitutional possibility. The EU increasingly utilizes many tools and much of the vocabulary of constitutionalism in ways that explore new and often contested horizons of political meaning and authority and which employ or imply alternative polity visions. There is, in short, something open-ended and fundamentally *unresolved* about the EU's constitutional formation, and this is demonstrated in various more specific elements of absence, openness, or special development.

First, there is the basic matter of the more restricted depth and breadth of the polity horizon. The intensity achievable through the high modern state in terms of its three peaks of sovereignty, constituent power, and citizenship implies a claim to be source and container of

[23] See eg Miguel Maduro, 'The Importance of Being Called a Constitution; Constitutional Authority and the Authority of Constitutionalism' (2005) 3 *International Journal of Constitutional Law* 332.

[24] See eg Dieter Grimm, 'The Achievement of Constitutionalism and its Prospects in a Changed World' in Petra Dobner and Martin Loughlin (eds), *The Twilight of Constitutionalism?* (2010).

collective action for a political community which is only *self*-limiting in jurisdictional reach, asserts comprehensive normative capacity to deliver within that range, and provides the primary frame of reference for members. This is reflected in the self-referential character of the state's constitutional posture—its self-orientation as a comprehensively self-sufficient and culturally prior form of political organization. In comparison, the EU possesses both a narrower competence and a less comprehensive normative capacity within that narrower competence, as well as a supplementary status in terms of political identity. In short, it invokes a jurisdiction only *partial* in scope and effective capacity and it involves a way of political being that is culturally secondary and *accessory* to state citizenship.

This more restricted and crowded horizon also has implications for how the EU relates to other polities. Whereas the only *self*-limiting state polity treats other polities as mere delegates or as its (mutually exclusive) fully sovereign counterparts, the partial EU polity is perforce a polity whose jurisdiction and capacity may, from one perspective, overlap the boundaries of other polities, and, from a more fluid perspective, represent the 'crowded space' or intersection of various different polities. These two perspectives upon the situation and spatialization of the EU polity—'inside-out' boundary overlap and 'outside-in' interlocking or commingling—indicate three further features of the EU as an unresolved constitutional polity. The first perspective supplies two contrasting features of the EU's open and overlapping boundaries. On the one hand, as a limited polity in terms of scope and capacity, the EU's orientation towards states and other polities is often as a collaborative and *complementary* polity, seeking through a complex of inter-systemic normative 'bridging mechanisms'[25] to coordinate its means and ends with these other polities. On the other hand, the shift from self-reference to external reference also has a negative connotation, and again the contrast with states is marked. The exclusively empowered and self-sufficient state treats its authority, and that of other exclusively empowered and self-sufficient states, in monopolistic terms. For its part, given its extensive overlap with other (primarily state) polities, alongside and in tension with its collaborative approach to these other polities, the EU stands in a *competitive* relationship with these polities over their respective domains of authority.

The situation is further complicated by the third relational dimension of the EU polity, where the logic of polity interpenetration is extended and the environment of polity diversity is understood not just to affect the EU polity margins but to shape its internal composition. Whereas the comprehensively and exclusively authorized state polity possesses structural integrity or singularity, in which not just all normative elements but also all institutional elements and relations contribute to and are resolved in terms of the one polity whole (even if their initial reference points are different territorial, ethnic, or functional parts), the EU may instead be viewed as a *composite* entity. It is a hybrid—a 'mixed'[26] or 'compound'[27] structure—which in its different institutions (Council, European Council, Commission, Parliament, Court) and normative emphases reflects and interlocks its differently polity-sourced parts.

Alongside these spatial features there are two temporal features of the EU's constitutional particularity. Although their resilience is highly variable[28] and their causal sequence of

[25] Stephen Weatherill, *Law and Integration in the European Union* (1995), chs 4–5.

[26] See eg Giandomenico Majone, 'Delegation of Regulatory Powers in a Mixed Polity' (2002) 8 *European Law Journal* 319; Neil MacCormick, *Questioning Sovereignty* (1999), ch 9.

[27] Sergio Fabbrini, *Compound Democracies: Why the United States and Europe Are Becoming Similar* (2007).

[28] See eg Zachary Elkins, Tom Ginsburg, and James Melton, *The Endurance of National Constitutions* (2009).

development can vary dramatically—from the US model where the self-authorizing constitutional instrument predates the cultural construction of 'national' community and the political architecture of the state to various European models where either or both 'state' and 'nation' predate the explicitly constitutional project[29]—we encounter most enduring state constitutions as achieved states of affairs. We typically contemplate them as always/already 'thickly' accomplished projects whose dynamic is of consolidation or adaptation. This is not so for the EU. Whether or not its future development is envisaged in state-analogous terms, the EU remains a constitutional work in progress—an *incipient* structure still self-consciously under construction rather than a fully realized form. Moreover, and closely related, the EU's unresolved condition is conceptual as well as empirical. Whereas the completeness of the state constitutional model presupposes a recognizable template for its mature form, and so determinacy and finality of conception, the incompleteness of the EU in state-centred terms and its irreducibility to state-centred terms suggests the absence of any model of its mature form—an *indeterminacy* and open-endedness of conception.

A final distinctive characteristic of EU constitutionalism flows from the previous features. The state constitutional polity is a settled political form. Such is its embeddedness, self-sufficiency, self-containment, and structural unity, its typical manifestation as an already accomplished state and conformity to a familiar template, that neither its basic eligibility as a constitutional polity nor the general terms on which that eligibility depends are the subject of serious contestation. That does not mean that the basic status qua constitutional state claimed for a polity will not be challenged. Either the identity of the state or, more commonly, its satisfaction of basic constitutional standards may be contested, externally or internally. But however sharply engaged, the contest remains one about specific cases rather than the general type. The constitutional polity of the EU, in contrast, is a constitutionally *disputed* polity. In light of its limited jurisdiction, its secondary form of political identity and agency, its open and unsettled relationship with states and other polities, its hybrid structure, its still emergent status and provisional conception, both its basic eligibility as a constitutional polity and the terms on which that eligibility rest are subject to serious and continuing contestation.

In a nutshell, whereas the state has generally been considered as a culturally prior, comprehensive, exclusive, monopolistic, singular, accomplished, determinate, and settled political form and constitutional polity, the EU remains an accessory, partial, complementary, competitive, composite, incipient, indeterminate, and disputed political form and constitutional polity.

III. The Trajectory of EU Constitutionalism

Let us cash out this preliminary conceptual analysis through an examination of the evolving terms of the EU's unresolved constitutionalism. In so doing, we focus on these predominantly legal sub-registers within which emerged—largely unheralded in these terms at the time—what was subsequently consecrated as the 'thin' version of EU constitutionalism. Having described that achievement, we will consider its strengths and limitation, and why it came under increased pressure in the lead-up to the big 'C' project.

[29] See Michel Rosenfeld, *The Identity of the Constitutional Subject: Selfhood, Citizenship, Culture and Community* (2010), chs 5–7.

1. The Elements of 'Thin' Constitutionalism

(a) The Formal Sub-Register

The birth of small 'c' constitutionalism in the EU context is closely associated with the elaboration of the *formal* sub-register of legal order. As noted earlier, this involves a cluster of interconnected features that supply the basic structure of a self-standing legal system. Self-ordering refers to the capacity of a legal system to reach and regulate all matters within its domain, typically through its successful embedding of certain lawmaking 'secondary' norms as a means to generate and validate a comprehensive body of 'primary' norms of conduct,[30] which norms may be further distinguished as higher or lower, more or less binding and entrenched. Self-interpretation refers to the capacity of some organ(s) internal to the legal order, typically located in the adjudicative branch, to have the final word as regards the meaning of its own norms. Self-extension refers to the capacity of a legal system to determine the extent of its own jurisdiction—sometimes known as *Kompetenz-Kompetenz*. Self-amendment refers to the existence of a mechanism for changing the content of the legal order provided for in terms of that order and empowering organs internal to that order as the agents of the amendment process. Self-enforcement refers to the capacity of the legal order, through the development of a body of procedural law and associated sanctions, to secure the application and implementation of its own norms.

Finally, the quality of self-discipline depends on the platform established by these features. When the legal order reaches a threshold of coverage and constancy in its production of primary norms (self-ordering), when it attains a level of effectiveness in its rules of standing, justiciability, and liability (self-enforcement), when it acquires some capacity to adjust its own normative structure, and provided it can guard against external influences undermining these system-building endeavours (self-amendment, self-interpretation, and self-extension), it is in a formal position (though far from guaranteed) to satisfy two aspects of self-discipline. First, it can offer a level of generality and predictability of treatment of those subject to its norms, so helping to promote and vindicate a system-constraining cultural presumption against arbitrary rule. Secondly, a legal order with mature claims to autonomy, comprehensive coverage, and effectiveness provides the opportunity and cultivates the expectation that even the institutional or governmental actors internal to the legal order should be subject to restraint in accordance with that mature order. These two core ideas—the 'rule of law, not man' and a 'government limited by law'[31]—provide a key element of all Western legal traditions, whether couched in the language of 'rule of law', *état de droit*, or *Rechtsstaat*, supplying a cornerstone of constitutionalism understood as a discourse not just of legal authority but also of legal virtue.[32]

From its inception in the three founding Treaties of the 1950s,[33] the EU legal order, through a mix of legislation and judicial assertion, boasted many formal features of a self-standing legal order. Its development, however, has also been conditioned by its 'spatial' situation as an overlapping polity in a relationship of mutual dependence and competition with state polities. The EU both invites and depends upon the cooperation and is vulnerable to the self-assertion

[30] H.L.A. Hart, *The Concept of Law* (2nd edn, 1997), ch 5.

[31] See eg Brian Tamanaha, *On The Rule of Law* (2004), ch 9.

[32] See eg Neil Walker, 'Opening or Closure? The Constitutional Intimations of the ECJ' in Miguel Maduro and Loic Azoulai (eds), *The Past and Future of EU Law* (2010).

[33] The European Coal and Steel Community of 1951, the Euratom Treaty of 1957, and most importantly, the European Economic Community Treaty of the same year.

of other legal orders within a broader 'pluralist' configuration,[34] and so its formal autonomy is coloured both by collaborative openness and boundary rivalry.

In terms of self-ordering and self-interpretation the EU legal order comes closest to a fully self-contained system. Its founding Treaties provides the EU's own internal hierarchy of instruments—Treaty provisions, directives, regulations, and decisions,[35] and this framework has been rationalized over subsequent Treaties.[36] For its part, from its pivotal early assertion of the 'supremacy' or 'primacy' of its norms over the norms of other legal systems,[37] the European Court of Justice (ECJ) has ensured that, at least from the internal perspective of the EU legal order, that hierarchy prevails over the ordering claims of competing legal systems. This and other early acts act of self-assertion in its formative jurisprudence helped the ECJ to consolidate its position, suggested but not determined by the framework provisions of the Treaties, as a 'Supreme Court' for the EU, and so its final interpretive authority.[38] But even in these areas of greatest strength, supranational authority is qualified at the margins. Dependence upon national instruments for implementation of EU measures other than regulations curtails the self-ordering chain of validity. Additionally, as the ECJ's main jurisdiction is one of preliminary reference to obtain authoritative resolution of questions as to the interpretation or validity of EU law,[39] and so within the referring gift and subject to the disposal of the domestic referring court, it is not a final appellate court. It lacks the capacity to have the last word, including the very means to 'decide what to decide'.

While still well developed compared to other transnational regimes, other aspects of the formal autonomy of the EU are more significantly qualified. As regards self-extension, through the doctrine of implied powers and an expansive reading of its own 'necessary and proper' clause,[40] the ECJ lays serious claim to determine the range of its competence. In the final analysis, however, this is limited by the EU's dependence upon (textually) conferred powers.[41] It is also counterbalanced by the preparedness of the domestic courts of Germany, Spain, Denmark, Poland, and the Czech Republic and elsewhere[42] to (re)assert national constitutional authority from time to time against what they see as the actual or potential overreach of the EU law. This overreach may involve Treaty powers encroaching too far on traditional areas of state sovereignty,[43] or supranational legislative acts or executive powers deemed to interfere with fundamental rights[44] or with other national constitutional protections.[45] In any event, the

[34] The literature on so-called constitutional pluralism in the EU is now extensive. For an excellent overview, see Monica Claes, *The National Courts' Mandate in the European Constitution* (2006).

[35] Article 189 EEC.

[36] See now, Art 249 Treaty on the Functioning of the European Union (TFEU).

[37] *Costa v ENEL* [1964] ECR 585.

[38] See eg Alec Stone Sweet, *The Judicial Construction of Europe* (2004).

[39] Article 267 TFEU.

[40] Article 352 TFEU.

[41] Article 5 TEU.

[42] See eg Julio Baquero Cruz, 'The Legacy of the Maastricht-Urteil and the Pluralist Movement' (2008) 14 *European Law Journal* 389; Wojciech Sadurski, 'Solange, Chapter 3: Constitutional Courts in Central Europe—Democracy—European Union' (2008) 14 *European Law Journal* 1.

[43] Often in the context of Treaty reform, as in the German Federal Constitutional Court's famous judgments on the legality of the Maastricht and Lisbon Treaties; see eg *Brunner v European Union Treaty* [1994] 1 CMLR 57; Judgment of 30 June 2009 (2 BvE 2 / 08, 5 / 08; 2 BvR 1010 / 08, 1022 / 08, 1259 / 08, 182 / 09).

[44] See eg *Internationale Handelsgesellschaft mbH v Einfuhr- und Vorratstelle fur Getreide und Futtermittel* [1974] 2 CMLR 540.

[45] See eg the recent cases challenging the constitutionality of the European Arrest Warrant, discussed in Cruz (n 42).

fact or prospect of such reactions may invite a more prudent approach by the judicial and other branches of the EU when contemplating the range of their jurisdictional ambition.[46]

Outside the generous limits of self-interpretation, the power of constitutional self-amendment, strictly construed, remains lacking. Instead, the EU relies upon a mechanism external to its institutional edifice—namely the Intergovernmental Conference—for formal Treaty amendment. In a significant concession, however, recent Treaties have introduced simplified and less onerous non-Treaty-based procedures for the revision of some of their own terms.[47] In the area of self-enforceability, a key element has been the doctrine of the 'direct effect' of EU norms in national legal orders, which developed and operates in close tandem with the primacy doctrine.[48] Yet even within the limited set of those supranational rules considered sufficiently clear, precise and unconditional to be domestically justiciable, the cooperation of national judges is patently necessary for enforcement. And beyond this, the EU legal order depends upon national authorities both for the legislative transposition and for the executive and (again) judicial application of non-directly effective norms, although the gradual expansion by the ECJ of the doctrine of state liability[49] as a way of plugging the gaps has become a selectively effective sanction against non-compliance.

Self-discipline provides a final tableau of significant yet incomplete authority. The idea of the 'rule of law' applying comprehensively to the institutions of the EU itself was elevated to *the* litmus test of constitutionality by the ECJ when it coined the small 'c' word in *Les Verts*[50] to justify the non-Treaty addition of the Parliament to the list of bodies subject to judicial review. However, the ambition of comprehensive internal legal oversight remains vulnerable to the non-justiciability or limited justiciability of certain areas of EU law, notably, despite recent improvements, in the newer, non-core domains of the Area of Freedom, Security and Justice and the Common Foreign and Security Policy.[51]

(b) *The Jurisdictional Sub-Register*

The other normative sub-registers have gradually built on the platform of formal autonomy. Jurisdiction has assumed a highly distinctive shape in the EU. In the state constitutional context the jurisdictional sub-register closely tracks the defining modern constitutional idea of a broad division between a collectively-enabling public sphere of comprehensive policy capacity and a collectively-constraining protected sphere of private autonomy. Typically, we find a combination of positive and negative norms—of prescription and proscription. On the one hand, there is a functionally unlimited legislative and executive jurisdiction in pursuit of the common good, while on the other, that jurisdiction is circumscribed by a set of individual-centred 'forbearance' rights or basic freedoms.

In the EU, both collective competence and individual freedoms have been treated differently, as has the relationship between them. Collective competence is not functionally unlimited. What is more, collective competence is defined not *against* but *in terms of* the 'functional' pursuit of a particular subset of individual freedoms, namely the so-called 'four freedoms' of movement of goods, services, capital, and persons necessary to secure a common transnational market. The common good and individual freedom, therefore, are treated not as

[46] See Weiler (n 6), 320 (discussing the relevance of the logic of Mutually Assured Destruction).

[47] Article 48(6)–(7) TEU.

[48] *Van Gend en Loos v Nederlandse Administratie der Belastingen* [1963] ECR 1.

[49] See eg Case C-224/01 *Kobler v Austria* [2003] ECR I-10239.

[50] Case 294/83 *Parti Ecologiste ('Les Verts') v European Parliament* [1986] ECR 1339, [1987] 2 CMLR 343; for discussion see Walker (n 32).

[51] Articles 275–6 TFEU.

distinct, sometimes divergent, and mutually restraining ends, but as indistinct and convergent, if self-limiting objectives. And reflecting the new relational openness of the EU polity context, the constraining edge of this jurisdiction is mostly externally directed, towards the member states through prohibitions upon the maintenance or introduction of national measures constituting barriers to trade, creating other obstacles to free and undistorted competition,[52] or impeding the free movement of persons, services, and capital.[53] Thus the 'market-making' pursuit of the four freedoms is largely by the technique of 'negative integration',[54] with the ECJ and the Commission enabling *through* constraining—specifying and policing the permissive boundaries of the market against state encroachment.

If this paints a jurisdictional picture sharply at odds with the state constitutional model, other developments suggest a more familiar pattern. First, the functional jurisdiction of the EU has also gradually come to be pursued through 'positive integration', namely the elaboration by legislative and other measures of a regulatory system at the level of the larger supranational unit.[55] To some extent, this has remained concerned with market-making—for example, the harmonization of divergent national product standards. Additionally, however, and accelerating from the time of the Single European Act (1987) and the Treaty of Maastricht (1992), the increase in positive integration tracks the expansion of EU jurisdiction beyond the four freedoms into various 'market-correcting' provisions of social and environmental regulation as well as other flanking measures, primarily in internal and external security, owing little to the economic rationale of integration and more to other kinds of collective policy capacity associated with the state.[56] The reasons for this and its implications for the stability of the 'thin' constitutional settlement are considered below.[57]

A second, more recent state-like jurisdictional development addresses the other side of the coin. It concerns the informal adoption in 2000 and eventual Treaty recognition of the wide-ranging Charter of Fundamental Rights.[58] Applicable against both member states and the EU's own institutions and other bodies, this initiative, in pursuing the idea of a general constitutional protection of private autonomy, means that, on the proscriptive as well as the prescriptive side, EU jurisdiction more closely approximates the domestic model.

(c) *The Integrative Sub-Register*

The integrative sub-register provides the most explicit example within the supranational constitutional register of direct borrowing from the domestic heritage. At issue here is how the mix of European law gradually thickened to fill the gaps left by the purely mechanical coherence of the formal model. Through the idea of general principles which, initially in the case law, and now the Treaties, are deemed to derive from 'common constitutional traditions' of the member states, the ECJ has equipped itself with a number of non-textual lodestars—fundamental rights, equality, proportionality, legal certainty, effectiveness etc.[59] In a 'synthetic'[60] process, these ideas, while their national origins are never disowned, are gradually refined so as to acquire distinct

[52] Articles 26, 34–7 TFEU.

[53] Articles 45, 49, and 56 TFEU.

[54] Fritz Scharpf, *Governing in Europe: Effective and Democratic?* (1999), 45.

[55] Ibid.

[56] See eg Weiler (n 6), ch 2.

[57] See Section III.2.

[58] Article 6(1) TEU, as amended by the Treaty of Lisbon.

[59] See eg Takis Tridimas, *The General Principles of EU Law* (2nd edn, 2006).

[60] John Erik Fossum and Agustin Jose Menendez, *The Constitution's Gift: A Constitutional Theory for a Democratic European Union* (2011), esp ch 2.

significance as doctrines of supranational law. In this way, the EU legal order seeks to garner the normative resources necessary to address hard questions raised by its expanding jurisdiction; both the need to construe new areas of law for which there are no existing thick interpretive practices and the imperative to do so in a manner that seeks consistency and coherence across an increasingly wide range of functional objectives and core values.[61] As with the jurisdictional sub-register, the dynamic of constitutionalism in this sub-register is incremental, mapping a gradual movement away from the 'thin' end of the constitutional spectrum

(d) The Institutional Register

Patently, the EU from the outset has boasted its own specialized and closely defined institutional structure as both product and mobilizing force of its legal order. Through a dedicated court (ECJ), administrative college (Commission), and legislator (Council), the founding scheme supplied a more elaborately differentiated and strongly empowered institutional complex than possessed by other international Treaty organizations.[62] What is more, in terms of the range and depth of institutions and the density of their relations, today the EU's political system has evolved far beyond that baseline. Yet we should be wary of overstating similarities between supranational and state architecture. To recall our earlier discussion, it is in this institutional sub-register that the distinctiveness of the EU as a mixed or composite polity becomes evident. Whereas the primary axis of institutional division within the state polity is the governmental branch and function—legislative, executive, or judicial—regarding one and the same polity object, the EU system has no single centre of gravity. Its key axis of institutional division, instead, is the representation, in functionally overlapping form, of separate 'estates'[63] and interests, which constituencies refer back to diverse polity sources, or at least, diverse conceptions of the Euro-polity. Traditionally, the European Commission and the ECJ reflect the supranational interest, the 'intergovernmental' Council and the European Council (of Heads of States) engage the distinct interests of the states, while the European Parliament refers, ambiguously, to the representation of the European 'peoples' (national) or 'people' (supranational). Rather than the separation of (types of governmental) powers, therefore, the key structural imperative of the mixed constitutional polity is closer to a dispersed, pre-state conception of institutional balance.[64]

Just because of the background diversity of interests, however, that balance has tended to contested, and also increasingly complex. The initial technocratic disposition in pursuit of the common market—'the Commission proposes, the Council disposes'—lasted only until the shift under the transitional provisions of the initial Treaty from unanimity to qualified majority voting in the Council threatened ultimate national control over the legislative process. This generated the so-called 'empty chair' crisis in the Council—provoked by French President de Gaulle and only resolved by the 1966 Luxembourg Compromise—which provided that decisional unanimity would continue where important national interests were at stake. A long consolidation of national executive hegemony over new macro-policy initiatives followed, reflected in the increasing prominence of the European Council[65] and in an extended period

[61] See eg Koen Laenerts and Jose Gutierrez-Fonz, 'The Constitutional Allocation of Powers and General Principles of EU Law' (2010) 47 *Common Market Law Review* 1629.

[62] See eg Paul Craig, 'Institutions, Powers and Institutional Balance' in Paul Craig and Gráinne de Búrca (eds), *The Evolution of EU Law* (2nd edn, 2011).

[63] See Majone (n 26).

[64] See Craig (n 62).

[65] Having been informally established at the Paris Summit of 1974, it was not accorded Treaty recognition until the Single European Act of 1987.

of legislative immobility not overcome until a series of Treaty initiatives beginning with the Single European Act (1987) and continuing with the Treaties of Maastricht (1992) and Amsterdam (1997). These measures relaxed the national veto by introducing qualified majority voting in the Council, first in the area of internal market law and then more broadly. At the same time, direct national executive influence was further diluted by the increasing recognition of the European Parliament as a third proactive player in the legislative process, first through the cooperation procedure and then the stronger co-decision procedure.

The easing of legislative gridlock and the emerging policy-making tripartitism, however, far from resolves all questions of institutional balance. One regular battleground of the last two decades has been the compositional and internal decision-making rules of the key institutional players. Another has been the division of 'sub-legislative' executive and regulatory authority between Commission and Council in more detailed policy areas. In both arenas, the tensions of a composite polity remain vivid.[66]

2. The Strengths and Limitation of Thin Constitutionalism

(a) The Centrality of Law

Understandings vary as to how the ingredients of thin constitutionalism—formal, jurisdictional, integrative, and political-institutional—combine, but all versions of the 'grand narrative'[67] have in common the idea of law performing a vital and well-tailored role in the construction and sustenance of the EU polity. The centrality of law to the emergent constitutional settlement rests on a number of considerations—instrumental, structural, ideological, anthropological, and, most fundamentally, philosophical. Let us look briefly at each.

The instrumental dimension concerns the indispensability of law as the basic motor of supranationalism—the key means to the end of European integration. Writing in the early 1980s, before the development of qualified majority voting and the pronounced expansion of jurisdiction beyond the market-making core, Joseph Weiler noted the 'the dual character of supranationalism'[68] as the defining frame of Europe's early evolution. At that stage, the developed character of legal or normative supranationalism in the area of the internal market, particularly the ECJ's assertive development of the EU's formal properties as an autonomous legal system, stood in stark contrast to a modestly conceived decisional or political supranationalism. Yet the two were strategically related. The early prominence of legal supranationalism occurred not in spite of political underdevelopment but precisely *because* political supranationalism remained so modest, with the member states retaining a de jure or de facto veto in most areas of European policymaking. The basic key to the attractiveness of law as the vehicle of supranational agency, therefore, lay with its regulatory capacity to steer, to consolidate, and, typically through judicial recognition of the claims of private litigants, to guarantee positive-sum intergovernmental bargains across wide-ranging aspects of economic integration and some more limited aspects of market-correcting regulation, and to do so without threatening key national political prerogatives. The law's instrumental value was twofold. It provided a

[66] See Craig (n 62); see also Gráinne de Búrca and Joanne Scott (eds), *Law and New Governance in the European Union and the United States* (2006); Christian Joerges and Jurgen Neyer, 'From Intergovernmental Bargaining to Deliberative Political Processes: The Constitutionalisation of Comitology' (1997) 3 *European Law Journal* 273.

[67] Alec Stone Sweet, 'The European Court of Justice' in Craig and de Búrca (n 62), 132.

[68] Joseph Weiler, 'The Community System: The Dual Character of Supranationalism' (1981) *Yearbook of European Law* 267.

legible and stable method of charting and co-coordinating the supranational settlement. Additionally, in a context of market-making where the temptation for each national member of the continental trade-liberalizing cartel to engage in protectionism and other forms of discrimination while exploiting the general opening of the markets of the other national members posed a significant collective action problem, the consistent application and enforcement of the rules of the game by independent legal institutions was crucial in forestalling free-riding and rendering common commitments more credible.[69]

Structural factors reinforce the instrumental attractiveness of law. The ECJ's empowerment as the apex court responded to a conception of the constitutional settlement understood, in the language of organizational economics, as an incomplete contract. Framework texts, even the relatively detailed codes of successive European Treaties, always possess open texture. Textual leeway both lowers the bar of prerequisite consensus and allows judicial adaptation to changing conditions without new resort to the legislative drawing board. The resulting margin of judicial manoeuvre is key to reconciling stability and flexibility in any constitutional context; emphatically so in the EU, where the political conditions for regular textual reform, certainly over the first quarter of a century, were highly unfavourable. The ECJ, then, became a vital mechanism to avoid blockages and conflicts associated with the divergence and opposition of national interests. As a 'trustee court',[70] delegated significant power to bind its national principals and able through development of its formal constitutional attributes to fortify and expand its zone of discretion, it could address 'completing' the supranational contract both by advancing the material agenda of integration case by case and by adjusting the balance, so sensitive in the mixed polity, in boundary conflicts over the powers of the diversely-sourced institutions.[71]

The fiduciary role of a trustee court, however, is not legitimated solely by system functionality. Ideological factors also matter. The tradition of legal formalism, assiduously cultivated in the context of an ECJ composed of senior jurists from all member states and conducting its business in a typically laconic and scrupulously non-partisan 'legalese', has lent cumulative authority to the court's decision-making.[72] The fact that much of the constitutional jurisdiction of the EU and its judicial organs could be articulated in terms of rights—both its positive jurisdiction, and, with increasing emphasis, its negative jurisdiction—has reinforced this ideological advantage. The ECJ has been able to engage in a constitutional vein in terms closely associated with its own authority as a court—in the language of individual rights and remedies so familiar from the historical lexicon of constitutional law.[73]

Underpinning these instrumental, structural, and ideological considerations, there is a strong cultural dimension. Recent anthropological research has underlined how important the original network of elite supranational actors in and around the ECJ was in developing the theme of 'Europeanization through case-law'.[74] Not only did the key formative decisions on supremacy and direct effect emerge in acknowledgement of and response to the difficulties associated with political integration, but they involved a conscious and self-reinforcing mobilization of the very notion of the supranational community as a community of *law*. Rather than

[69] See eg Martin Shapiro, 'The European Court of Justice' in Craig and de Búrca (n 62), 321.

[70] See Stone Sweet (n 38).

[71] See eg Shapiro (n 69), 321–2.

[72] See eg Weiler (n 6), ch 5.

[73] See eg Stone Sweet (n 67); Fritz Scharpf, 'Legitimacy in the Multilevel European Polity' in Dobner and Loughlin (n 24).

[74] See eg Antoine Vauchez, 'The Transnational Politics of Judicialization *Van Gend en Loos* and the Making of EU Polity' (2010) 16 *European Law Journal* 1, 2.

comprehending law-centred theories of integration as purely external and retrospective accounts of a secular process, therefore, we should also understand them as active structuring devices by which judges, civil servants, academics, MEPs, national diplomats, and Commissioners became engaged 'in real time' in a 'circular circulation of ideas'[75] which contributed cumulatively to the ascent of legal constitutionalism.

If the assertion of such a robust legal persona has been the key to the capacity of the EU operating from its narrow stronghold of institutional power to exercise continental regulatory authority, its success at root depends upon its resonance with the early philosophical justifications of the EU. In different ways, two of the most influential founding theories, the German ordoliberal tradition[76] and Hans Ipsen's idea of the EU as a special purpose association,[77] encouraged a law-centred perspective. For the ordoliberals, the Treaty of Rome supplied Europe with its own economic constitution, a supranational market-enhancing system of rights whose legitimacy *required* the absence of democratically responsive will formation and consequential pressure towards market-interfering socio-economic legislation at the supranational level, a matter best left to the member states—and even there only insofar as compatible with the bedrock economic constitution. Ordoliberal theory, then, provides a classic model of how an autonomous legal order, through ring-fencing economic exchange centred on the four freedoms, provides a platform for the efficient operation of a capitalist economic logic. Ipsen's theory, to which Giandomenico Majone's contemporary work on the idea of a European 'regulatory state'[78] is a notable successor, shares with ordoliberalism the idea that supranationalism should transcend partisan politics. Here, however, the ambit of law is extended so that the invisible hand of the market is supplemented by the expert hand of the technocrat. In Majone's elaborately developed conception—one that has continued to capture the sensibility of a significant part of the Brussels elite—these additional regulatory measures are concerned not with macro-politically sensitive questions of distribution, but with risk-regulation in matters such as product and environmental standards where expert knowledge is deemed paramount, and where accountability is arguably best served by administrative law measures aimed at transparency and enhanced participation in decision-making by interested and knowledgeable parties rather than the volatile preferences of broad representative institutions.

(b) The Exhaustion of the Legal Paradigm

The delicate balance achieved by locking the EU's collective agency within a law-centred discourse and a narrow market-based justification could not hold indefinitely. The pursuit and perfection of the narrow economic objectives of the Union has progressively impinged upon a wide range of social issues, making 'spillover'[79] into politically contentious areas of

[75] Ibid 22.

[76] See eg Ernst-Joachim Mestmacker, 'On the Legitimacy of European Law' (1994) 58 *Rabels Zeitschrift* 615; see also Damian Chalmers, 'The Single Market: From Prima Donna to Journeyman' in Jo Shaw and Gillian More (eds), *New Legal Dynamics of European Union*. On the continuities between the political thought of the Weimar Republic and post-war thinking about supranationalism more generally, see Christian Joerges and Navraj Singh Ghaleigh (eds), *Darker Legacies of Law in Europe* (2003).

[77] Hans-Peter Ipsen, 'Europaische Verfassung—Nationale Verfassung' (1987) 22 *Europarecht* 195.

[78] Giandomenico Majone, 'The Rise of the Regulatory State in Europe' (1994) 17 *West European Politics* 77; Giandomenico Majone, *Europe as the Would-be World Power: The EU at Fifty* (2009); on the connections between Ipsen and Majone, see Christian Joerges, '"Good Governance" in the European Internal Market: An Essay in Honour of Claus-Dieter Ehlermann', EUI Working Papers, RSC No 2001/29.

[79] See eg Leon Lindberg, 'Political Integration: Definitions and Hypotheses' in Brent Nelsen and Alexander Stubb (eds), *The European Union: Readings on the Theory and Practice of European Integration* (2nd edn, 1998).

traditionally national jurisdiction inevitable. Both ordoliberal and regulatory state approaches, in consequence, have become increasingly vulnerable to the charge of drawing artificial distinctions between technical questions of market-making and standard-setting and deeply contested questions of value preference and transnational resource and risk allocation.[80]

Such a tension was in truth present from the birth of supranationalism. Economic policies always carried significant implications, whether supportive or restrictive, for wider political projects and ambitions at the national or supranational level. Importantly, indeed, it was a powerfully supportive nexus between the economic and political which from the beginning allowed the common market to be elevated to the defining supranational priority not just on wealth-maximizing grounds. Just as important was the wider political prize of lasting peace for a continent long blighted by war that a culture of economic cooperation and shared affluence could help to secure.[81] Less felicitous connections between the narrow economic and wider political poles of integration, however, became evident as the EU increasingly sought market-making or market-correcting interventions involving politically salient choices, in so doing reducing the capacity of states to act independently in these policy areas. The robust juridical elaboration and protection of the single market at the heart of legal constitutionalism had flourished in a formative context where market-making measures impinged only lightly on other social policy objectives, or at least where states retained the procedural means to veto politically controversial collective commitments in pursuit of these other objectives—and so were slow to make such commitments where there were obvious winners and losers. But the gradual expansion of the scope of negative integration from the narrow market-making sphere and the concomitant growth of positive integration, with its shift towards a qualified majoritarian logic, decisively altered the dynamic of collective action.

The gathering danger was that the very strength of the law in supplying 'both the object and agent of integration'[82]—in supplying the fruit of the 'thin' constitutional settlement as well as the channel for arriving at that settlement—would become a liability. On the one hand, as the *agent* of integration, the law would become a medium whose prudent husbanding of the integration *acquis* would instead translate as excessive political unresponsiveness. The threat was that legal proofing of particular agreements against political reappraisal and the prevention of new supranational initiatives except through still highly consensual and only moderately democratically inclusive procedures, or through the recondite increments of the ECJ, would become more a way of avoiding or excluding the legitimate expression of political choice and contestation and less a means of protection against free-riding or ideologically inspired resistance or fickleness towards positive-sum collective commitments. On the other hand, as and when the pressure towards positive integration *has* led to legal change, and as more controversial value choices have begun to reflect onto the legal domain—this has also affected the ideological potency of law as the *object* of integration, stripping some of the detached, efficiency-maximizing veneer from legal supranationalism.[83]

[80] See eg Andreas Follesdal and Simon Hix, 'Why There is a Democratic Deficit in the EU: A Response to Majone and Moravcsik' (2006) 44 *Journal of Common Market Studies* 533; Simon Hix, *What's Wrong with the European Union and How to Fix it* (2008).

[81] See eg Weiler (n 6), ch 7.

[82] Renaud Dehousse and Joseph Weiler, 'The Legal Dimension' in William Wallace (ed), *The Dynamics of European Integration* (1990), 243.

[83] See eg Weiler (n 6), ch 2.

IV. The Future of the Unresolved Constitution

The gradual fraying of the 'permissive consensus'[84] around legal supranationalism provides the deep background for the emergence of the big 'C' constitutional debate emerged. Other factors contributed, notably the wave of eastward Enlargement after the fall of the Berlin Wall. The increase in the EU from 15 members in 1997 to 27 in 2007 raised acute questions about the adequacy of an institutional structure built for a homogenous West European club of six states to a sprawling pan-European expanse of 500 million persons. Indeed, Enlargement and its unmet institutional needs provided an important rhetorical framework for the EU's reform decade. It was the thread connecting the busy sequence of Treaty amendments from Maastricht to Nice in 2001, whose unfinished business in turn prompted the historic decision at the Laeken Summit to establish a Convention on the Future of Europe.[85] Yet the focus on Enlargement merely channelled and accelerated a process of reflection and contestation over the kind of polity the EU was and could become that was unavoidable in light of the increasing inadequacy of the received model.

In the introduction it was suggested that three polity visions accompanied the big 'C' constitutional debate. Each can be seen as a response to the gradual extension of supranational capacity beyond what could comfortably be accommodated in the earlier model. The truncated vision, first, was one of retrenchment, concerned to draw a line in the sand through mechanisms such as a competence catalogue, the entrenchment of the Charter of Rights, and the empowerment of national Parliaments. Here constitutionalism was invoked. both materially and symbolically, as a barrier against the further evacuation of state power to the supranational level.[86] The *sui generis* vision, secondly, was concerned with pursuing or consolidating Europe's *Sonderweg*.[87] Its defining priority was not the protection of state prerogatives, but ensuring against the political blockage and institutional stasis which would prevent Europe making the regulatory adjustments necessary for its distinctive 'post-national' accommodations between market and state, intergovernmental and supranational, legal fixity and political openness, to be maintained and updated. In its pragmatic attention to the demands of a novel problem-solving context and in its non-alignment with 'old' state-sovereigntist coded oppositions, this view was the quiet motor of much of the pro-Convention movement. Choosing the big 'C' option here assumed importance less for any (state-regarding) inferences as to constitutional content and more as way of re-energizing and re-validating a macro-political reform process which, given the progressive disappointments and deferrals of the Amsterdam and Nice Treaties, was falling foul of the law of diminishing returns.[88]

The mature polity vision, thirdly, hoped to bring the benefits of thick constitutionalism to bear on the Europolity. Its ambition was for the EU constitution, through a combination of inclusive process, integrative content, and culturally unifying symbolic product, to deliver

[84] See eg Lisbet Hooghe and Gary Marks, 'A Postfunctionalist Theory of European Integration: From Permissive Consensus to Constraining Dissensus' (2008) 39 *British Journal of Political Science* 1.

[85] See eg Neil Walker, 'Constitutionalising Enlargement, Enlarging Constitutionalism' (2003) 9 *European Law Journal* 365.

[86] Tellingly, each of these measures was central to the original post-Nice 'leftovers' agenda which triggered the Laeken Summit and the Convention on the Future of Europe, see Walker (n 7).

[87] Weiler (n 11).

[88] See eg Joseph Weiler, 'One the Power of the Word: Europe's Constitutional Iconography' (2005) 3 *International Journal of Constitutional Law* 173; Bruno de Witte, 'The Closest Thing to a Constitutional Conversation in Europe: The Semi-Permanent Treaty Revision Process' in Paul Beaumont, Carole Lyons, and Neil Walker (eds), *Convergence and Divergence in European Public Law* (2002).

some kind of functional equivalent to the peaks of comprehensive jurisdiction, self-authorization, and deeper political identity. By this route might be overcome the 'asymmetry'[89] of a settlement where the EU lacked the political resources to deliver legitimate and effective collective solutions to politically and intergovernmentally contentious issues of economic and social policy increasingly falling beyond the independent capability of national governments. This third vision was not the most commonly endorsed approach feeding the Convention momentum, but it was undoubtedly the most heavily invested in the big 'C' solution. For the most part[90] it did not envisage the EU *as* a federal state, so acknowledging the concerns of the state-centred constitutionalists. It did not, therefore, seek to replace the states as the single focus of final authority, original collective agency, and deep political identity. Rather, it sought to develop or recognize these state-familiar constitutional assets of political community on an independent footing for the EU, and in a manner envisaging neither superiority nor subordination to the states but engagement in a non-hierarchical relationship with them. So the EU would have an authority that was autonomous without being exclusive or exhaustive. It would have a foundation and reference point of collective agency (ie, the European people) that was distinctive and self-standing without being the only distinctive and self-standing collective reference point for the various constituencies (ie, European states, European 'peoples') which made up the new collective agency. Finally, building on the supranational citizenship provisions in place since Maastricht,[91] it would also possess a form of framing or organizing political identity, complete with rights, obligations, and membership status, which again was distinctive but not unique in function, instead operating in tandem with the other (predominantly state-centred) organizing political identities of its subjects.[92]

The Constitutional Treaty which eventually emerged from the deliberations of the Convention and the Intergovernmental Conference reflected something of each vision. For the retrenchers there was a skeletal competence catalogue, a Charter of Rights, and a greater involvement of national Parliaments in the legislative process as a way of adding meat to the bare bones of the neglected Maastricht standard of 'subsidiarity'. For the pragmatic post-Enlargement reformers there was an increase in the areas of competence subject to qualified majority voting and Parliamentary co-decision, and so ripe for positive integration, together with institutional reform to streamline the Commission and increase the power and profile of the European Council. For the proponents of a mature state-like polity there was the fully fledged constitution-making process itself, a first textual affirmation of the primacy of European law and many of the symbolic incidents of constitutionalism, including the constitutional label, a single constituent document, and the introduction of a constitutionally resonant vocabulary of laws, foreign ministers etc.

For all that the text itself showed evidence of hybridity, given the disparity of visions brought to the table it is no surprise that the big 'C' constitutional initiative eventually failed. Once the solidarity of the Convention process had faded and the debate was reframed within the national arenas of the ratifying member states, the differences in principle between different polity visions which the posing of the constitutional question exposed served to overshadow the detailed compromises and accommodations that had been worked out. Here, then, we saw the unresolved quality of the EU polity in bold relief. The very conditions of competitiveness,

[89] Scharpf (n 73).

[90] On Europe as a federal state, see G. Federico Mancini, 'Europe: The Case for Statehood' (1998) 4 *European Law Journal* 29.

[91] See now Arts 20–5 TFEU.

[92] See eg Weiler (n 6), ch 10.

mixity, and indeterminacy feeding the constitutional initiative also generated the open horizon of alternatives and the intensity of disputation which invited its failure.

Should this, then, lead us to conclude, especially in the light of the successful implementation of the subsequent Reform Treaty which, tellingly, retained nearly all of the substance but little of the symbolism of the Constitutional Treaty, that the idea of big 'C' constitutionalism in the EU is a dead letter? Is its resurrection neither feasible nor desirable? Whatever the future trajectory of supranational constitutionalism, ought not it now revert to the informal, small 'c' course around whose historical credentials and continuing contribution there has recently emerged such a clamorous overlapping consensus?

We need not draw such a hasty conclusion. The wider constitutional debate may be in abeyance, but it is not resolved and cannot be while its animating polity visions remain so deeply at odds with one another, and where the symptoms of that deep fracture in the dearth of common terms of engagement over key choices and strategic directions in both European domestic and foreign policy in the early decades of the new century remain so pertinent and pressing.[93] In these circumstances, however unlikely its immediate prospects, a revival of the big 'C' constitutional project cannot and should not be discounted.

But even if this were to happen, the sceptic might dismiss it as a futile gesture, trapped in a self-defeating logic of contestation. There is no guarantee that the process, whatever its initial momentum, would be any more successful next time round. And even if it were, this would provide no magic solution to the problems of the mutual frustration and overall dilution of collective capability in a multilevel political space which, quite differently conceived and articulated, exercise the exponents of all three visions. In particular, a successful constitutional episode would supply no compelling case in favour of the third and most optimistically positive-sum vision to those who would rather promote supranational capability in other ways (second vision) or concentrate on protecting or resurrecting national capability (first vision). For, as has been forcefully pointed out, a successful constitutional process offers no guarantee of more inclusive ongoing participation, no deliberative panacea, and no promise of increased support by its citizens or effective policymaking and implementation capacity to the extent that such participatory and deliberative dividends are forthcoming.[94]

Yet the specification of a distinctive collective authorship and political identity that the constitutional self-attribution of title announces could serve another more limited, but prior purpose. This concerns the realization of the very sense of collective pre-engagement in whose absence it is difficult to see how *any* attempt to reconcile polity visions in the European legal and political space, *regardless* of where and how these attempts strike the balance, can be securely grounded. For the constitutional arena—and perhaps *only* the constitutional arena, offers this possibility: that, as we close the curtain on an era that allowed first-order economic decision-making to proceed and its benefits to accrue substantially unaffected by second-order considerations of what and who the EU stood for other than a legally demarcated set of interests delegated by the constituent states, we might at least be able to begin the process of overcoming increasingly disabling second-order differences over the basic character of the

[93] The sovereign debt crisis of 2011, and the failures of supranational policymaking in the context of the economic problems of Greece, Portugal, and Ireland, is but the latest such symptom.

[94] Perhaps most effectively, and most trenchantly, by Andrew Moravcsik; see eg his 'What Can We Learn from the Collapse of the European Constitutional Project?' (2006) 47 *Politische Vierteljahresschrift* 2; Karl-Heinz Ladeur, "We, the European People..."—Relâche?' (2008) 14 *European Law Journal* 147; Peter L. Lindseth, *Power and Legitimacy: Reconciling Europe and the Nation-State* (2010).

EU polity in and through the act of recognizing and addressing such differences as *our* common predicament. More specifically, a documentary constitutional commitment may, in boot-strapping fashion, supply the platform for the generation of a reflexive awareness of a common sense of authorship and for the gradual accumulation of a common constitutional experience and memory to deepen and consolidate that common sense.[95]

While it would be wrong to imagine this as any more than one modest element in the remaking of the European polity along lines which command broader acceptance, we should avoid the opposite error of underestimating its importance. A written constitution is always both trace and catalyst. It is a trace because its very promulgation is already a sign, however modest, of the commitment and common understanding it seeks to encode. And the constitution is a catalyst insofar as it provides a means by which and a context in which to stimulate the deepening of that commitment and common understanding. Indeed, it is precisely this Janus-faced quality—the backward-looking recollection of common resources and gathering of existing potential just in order to solve forward-looking collective action problems amongst those of different interests, preferences, and identities—that has given documentary constitutionalism its uniquely modern hue. For in its assumption that nothing is more basic or more apt than our own joint commitment to shape our common world, constitutionalism invokes a social technology unknown to pre-modern cultures. Perseverance with the techniques of documentary constitutionalism, then, may be unavoidable for all who maintain that the EU is best understood as a continuation by other and as yet 'unresolved' means of political modernity's defining project of the collective reconciliation of freedom and equality, rather than a venture into a wholly uncharted political imaginary.

Bibliography

Paul Craig, *The Lisbon Treaty: Law, Politics and Treaty Reform* (2010)

Paul Craig and Gráinne de Búrca (eds), *The Evolution of EU Law* (2nd edn, 2011)

John Erik Fossum and Agustin Jose Menendez, *The Constitution's Gift: A Constitutional Theory for a Democratic European Union* (2011)

Dieter Grimm, 'Integration by Constitution', (2005) 3 *International Journal of Constitutional Law* (I.CON) 193 ff

Jürgen Habermas, 'Why Europe Needs a Constitution' (2001) 11 *New Left Review* 5

Christian Joerges and Jurgen Neyer, 'From Intergovernmental Bargaining to Deliberative Political Processes: The Constitutionalisation of Comitology' (1997) 3 *European Law Journal* 273

Peter L. Lindseth, *Power and Legitimacy: Reconciling Europe and the Nation-State* (2010)

Neil MacCormick, *Questioning Sovereignty* (1999)

Miguel Maduro, 'The Importance of Being Called a Constitution: Constitutional Authority and the Authority of Constitutionalism' (2005) 3 *International Journal of Constitutional Law* 332

Miguel Maduro and Loic Azoulai (eds), *The Past and Future of EU Law* (2010)

Giandomenico Majone, *Europe as the Would-be World Power: The EU at Fifty* (2009)

Andrew Moravcsik, 'What Can We Learn from the Collapse of the European Constitutional Project?' (2006) 47 *Politische Vierteljahresschrift* 2

Fritz Scharpf, *Governing in Europe: Effective and Democratic?* (1999)

Alec Stone Sweet, *The Judicial Construction of Europe* (2004)

[95] See eg Jürgen Habermas, 'On Law and Disagreement: Some Comments on "Interpretative Pluralism"' (2003) 16 *Ratio Juris* 187.

Neil Walker, 'Europe's Constitutional Momentum and the Search for Polity Legitimacy' (2005) 3 *International Journal of Constitutional Law* 211
Joseph Weiler, 'The Community System: The Dual Character of Supranationalism' (1981) *Yearbook of European Law* 267
Joseph Weiler, *The Constitution of Europe* (1999)
Joseph Weiler and Marlene Wind (eds), *European Constitutionalism Beyond the State* (2003)

CHAPTER 58

THE CONSTITUTIONALIZATION OF PUBLIC INTERNATIONAL LAW

ERIKA DE WET*

Pretoria and Amsterdam

I. Mapping the Territory

In the well-known *Kadi* decision of 2008, the European Court of Justice (ECJ) was confronted with the legality of the absence of due process for individuals residing in European Union member states whose assets were frozen, due to their being blacklisted by the UN Security

* This chapter forms part of a project financed by the Netherlands Organization for Scientific Research (NWO): 'The emerging international constitutional order: the implications of hierarchy in international law for the coherence and legitimacy of international decision-making'.

Council (UNSC) as 'international terrorists'.[1] The dispute was rooted in UNSC Resolutions 1267 of 15 October 1999,[2] 1333 of 19 December 2000,[3] and the measures subsequently adopted within the EU in order to implement those resolutions uniformly in all member states.[4]

The UNSC adopted these resolutions, which were binding on UN member states under Chapter VII of the UN Charter,[5] following the attacks on the American embassies in Kenya and Tanzania and the suspected involvement of Osama bin Laden with those acts. These resolutions, geared towards pressuring the (then) de facto Taliban regime in Afghanistan into extraditing Osama bin Laden to the United States, authorized the Al-Qaeda and Taliban Sanctions Committee—a sub-organ of the UNSC—to identify and blacklist individuals and entities associated with the Taliban, Osama bin Laden, and Al-Qaeda. The assets of blacklisted individuals and entities were to be frozen by the state of residence of those individuals and entities until such time as the Al-Qaeda and Taliban Sanctions Committee might remove them from the list. This de-listing procedure was political in nature and the UNSC resolutions did not provide for an independent judicial procedure for reviewing the listing of the affected individuals.

The EU implemented Resolution 1267 (1999) and subsequent resolutions through Common Positions and Council Regulations in order to ensure uniform application in all member states.[6] The respective Council Regulations had direct effect in member states and the issue of the right to a fair trial was bound to arise before courts within the EU. After all, it is a right guaranteed by the constitutional orders of EU member states and the EU legal order itself. In addition, this right is guaranteed by international human rights treaties to which all the EU member states are a party, notably Article 6(1) of the European Convention on Human Rights and Fundamental Freedoms of 1950 (ECHR).[7]

A right guaranteed within the domestic, regional, and international legal orders of the member states was now seemingly suspended in the interest of international peace and security by a UNSC resolution. This development exemplified the intensification of the shift of public decision-making away from the nation-state, towards international actors such as international organizations. It further highlighted the increasing direct relevance of decision-making by such organizations for individuals, as opposed to them merely affecting interstate relations. It illustrated the progression of international law from a law of coordination between

[1] Joined Cases C-402/05 P and C-415/05 P *Yassin Abdullah Kadi and Al Barakaat International Foundation v Council of the European Union and Commission of the EC* [2008] ECR I-6351 (*Kadi* ECJ case); Case T-306/01 *Ahmed Ali Yusuf and Al Barakaat International Foundation v Council of the European Union and Commission of the EC* [2005] ECR II-3533.

[2] SC Res 1267 (15 October 1999) UN Doc S/RES/1267.

[3] SC Res 1333 (19 December 2000) UN Doc S/RES/1333.

[4] See inter alia Council Common Position 2002/402/CFSP of 27 May 2002 Concerning Restrictive Measures against Usama bin Laden, members of the Al-Qaida Organisation [2002] OJ L139/4; see also Council Regulation (EC) 881/2002 of 27 May 2002 Imposing Certain Specific Restrictive Measures Directed against Certain Persons and Entities Associated with Usama bin Laden, the Al-Qaida Network and the Taliban [2002] OJ L139/9. Both measures implemented the targeted sanctions of SC Res 1267 (1999) (n 2), SC Res 1333 (2000) (n 3) and SC Res 1390 (28 January 2002) UN Doc S/RES/1390.

[5] Charter of the United Nations (adopted 26 June 1945, entered into force 24 October 1945) 1 UNTS XVI.

[6] Council Common Position 2002/402/CFSP (n 4), and Council Regulation (EC) 881/2002 (n 4).

[7] Convention for the Protection of Human Rights and Fundamental Freedoms (European Convention on Human Rights, as amended); for a discussion see Erika de Wet, 'Human Rights Considerations in the Enforcement of Security Council Sanctions in the EU Legal Order' in Bardo Fassbender (ed), *The United Nations Security Council and Human Rights* (forthcoming).

loosely affiliated states to a law of close cooperation in some areas and which reaches far into the realm of traditionally domestic concerns.[8] This progressive development of international law, both in terms of the subject matters it covers and its increased normative density, has been described as a process of constitutionalization.[9]

For most authors in the field of public international law, however, the notion of constitutionalization entails more than an increased process of legalization of the international legal order. It also concerns the need to place legal restrictions on the exercise of public power on the international level, refers to concrete manifestations of such limitations, or a combination of both. A case such as *Kadi* is illustrative on this point: it exposes the difficulty experienced by domestic legal orders to provide meaningful legal protection to individuals in situations where international obligations have eroded such protection. The case also serves as a useful illustration of the eroding impact of the continuous shift of public decision-making away from the nation-state to the international plain on the relevance of the two doctrines that traditionally explained the relationship between domestic (constitutional) law and international law: namely dualism and monism.[10]

According to the dualist doctrine, international law and domestic law are viewed as separate, self-contained (autonomous) legal systems that govern different types of subjects and legal relations. Whereas international law regulates the conduct of states and interstate relations, domestic law regulates the relations between state organs and individuals, as well as between individuals themselves.[11] Rules that are not created within the domestic system may nevertheless enter the system through its rules of reference.[12] The rules and references of the domestic system, frequently found in the Constitution, determine the status of international law in the domestic legal order. For example, the Constitution may determine that international law ranks below the Constitution but above ordinary legislation, or that international law is on a par with ordinary legislation. The classic dualist perspective does not accept the argument in public international law according to which international law necessarily takes precedence over all domestic law, including state constitutions.[13] Similarly, that perspective

[8] Christian Tomuschat, 'International Law: Ensuring the Survival of Mankind on the Eve of a New Century' (1999) 281 *Recueil des Cours de L'Académie de Droit International* 9, 63; Wouter G. Werner, 'The Never-ending Closure: Constitutionalism and International Law' in Nicholas Tsagourias (ed), *Transitional Constitutionalism: International and European Models* (2008), 329, 332; Andrea Hamann and Hélène Ruiz Fabri, 'Transnational Networks and Constitutionalism' (2008) 6 *International Journal of Constitutional Law* 481, 482; Oliver Diggelmann and Tilmann Altwicker, 'Is there Something Like a Constitution of international Law?—A Critical Analysis of the Debate on World Constitutionalism' (2008) 68 *Zeitschrift für Ausländisches Öffentliches Recht und Völkerrecht* 623, 626.

[9] Anne Peters, 'Compensatory Constitutionalism: The Function and Potential Fundamental International Norms and Structures' (2006) 1 *Leiden Journal of Internatiional Law* 579, 597; Brun-Otto Bryde, 'Das Völkerrecht zwischen Konstitutionalisierung, Hegemonie und Renationalisierung' in Heinrich-Böll-Stiftung (ed), *Die Zukunft des Völkerrechts in einer Globalisierten Welt* (2006), 88, 91; Stefan Kadelbach and Thomas Kleinlein, 'Überstaatliches Verfassungsrecht. Zur Konstitutionalisierung im Völkerrecht' (2006) 44 *Archiv des Völkerrechts* 235, 240.

[10] See also Christian Walter, 'International Law in a Process of Constitutionalization' in Janne Elisabeth Nijman and André Nollkaemper (eds), *New Perspectives on the Divide Between National and International Law* (2007), 191, 192.

[11] Giorgio Gaja, 'Dualism—A Review' in Nijman and Nollkaemper (n 10), 52, 54.

[12] Ibid 52–3.

[13] eg *Treatment of Polish Nationals and Other Persons of Polish Origin in the Danzig Territory* (Advisory Opinion) PCIJ Rep Ser A/B No 44.

does not accept that international law can reach individuals directly, without having first been incorporated by means of a statute.[14]

Dualism can be contrasted with monism, according to which international law and domestic law are part of a single legal order. Within this unified legal order international law is supreme and can be invoked before domestic courts without prior incorporation through a statutory instrument. The monist perspective is motivated by the desire to ensure the binding character of international law and to prevent norm conflicts between legal systems.[15] However, in reality, the difference between monist and dualist systems has always been one of degree. Countries with a dualist tradition to treaties such as Germany and South Africa (to name but two examples) have a monist approach to customary international law. In addition, some dualist constitutions allow for the direct invocation of so-called self-executing treaties before domestic courts, acknowledging that these treaties address individuals in a manner that bestow rights upon them.

For their part, monist states such as the Netherlands and Switzerland rarely apply customary international law directly, and frequently incorporate international treaties through statutes in order to give those instruments effect in the domestic legal system. Monist systems withhold direct effect from treaties if the latter are regarded as too vague to be invoked directly by individuals before courts. Alternately, monist systems tend to be restrictive in determining whether the purpose of the treaty is to bestow rights on individuals. Domestic provisions that conflict with international law are not necessarily declared invalid or inapplicable within monist systems.[16]

In essence, throughout the twentieth century most domestic constitutional orders (whether dualist or monist) developed legal tools with which to give effect to international obligations applicable in those orders, while simultaneously protecting principles of fundamental domestic importance against excessive international influence. In practice, therefore, most systems functioned as a hybrid, incorporating both monist and dualist elements. However, these mechanisms are progressively eroding in an era where both the quantity of international decisions that directly affect individuals and the intensity with which such decisions affect the relationship between individuals vis-à-vis the state (and other individuals) are increasing.

Once again, the *Kadi* case is illuminating. The Court of First Instance of the European Communities (CFI) initially determined that the UNSC obligations would prevail over all other conflicting obligations including those of a human rights nature.[17] Subsequently on appeal, the ECJ overturned the CFI decision and gave preference to the protection of the right to a fair trial as a fundamental right under EU law.[18] The ECJ decision was based exclusively on EU law and did not address the norm conflict between EU law (and domestic constitutional law) and UNSC resolutions. Although the ECJ decision had the appearance of a dualist

[14] Gaja (n 11), 54.

[15] Hans Kelsen, 'Les rapports de système entre le droit Interne et le droit international public' (1926) 14 *Recueil de Cours* 227, 273; Gaja (n 11), 53, 62; Andreas L. Paulus, 'The Emergence of the International Community and the Divide Between International and Domestic Law' in Nijman and Nollkaemper (n 10), 216, 228.

[16] Paulus (n 15), 228–9; further, see extensively the various country studies in Hellen Keller and Alec Stone Sweet, *A Europe of Rights: the Impact of the ECHR on National Legal Systems* (2007).

[17] Case T-315/01 *Yassin Abdullah Kadi v Council of the European Union and Commission of the EC* [2005] ECR II-3649 (*Kadi* CFI case); see also the Swiss Federal Tribunal in *Youssef Nada v State Secretariat for Economic Affairs and Federal Department of Economic Affairs, Administrative appeal judgment* Case No 1A 45/2007, BGE 133 II 450, 14 November 2007, ILDC 461 (CH 2007) (*Nada* case).

[18] *Kadi* ECJ case (n 17).

approach intended to protect the EU legal order as an autonomous legal order, it remains to be seen whether it will have lasting effect. Some EU member states, for example the United Kingdom, are effectively circumventing the impact of the decision by adopting domestic legislation that gives de facto preference to the UNSC resolutions.[19]

Against this background the constitutionalization of international law could be summarized as an attempt to exercise legal control over politics within the international legal order itself, in order to compensate for the erosion of such control within domestic constitutional orders.[20] In doing so, it attempts to translate to the international plane concepts that were traditionally reserved for domestic constitutions.[21] Prominent domestic elements featuring in the debate concerning the constitutionalization of public international law include a hierarchy of norms, enforceable individual rights, and judicial review. The (limited) presence of these concepts in the international legal order plays a central role in the debate as to whether the constitutionalization process in the international legal order has thus far been limited to partial constitutionalization (either within particular international organizations or in the form of transgovernmental networks), or whether one can indeed speak of the constitutionalization of the international order as a whole.

II. The Emergence of a Hierarchy of Norms within International Law

On the domestic plain the term 'constitutionalism' usually implies a hierarchical relationship with the remaining elements of the respective domestic legal order.[22] Although international law was traditionally characterized by the absence of a hierarchy between the different sources or types of international obligations, certain hierarchical elements have been developing within international law itself since the second half of the twentieth century. The most important manifestations thereof are the concepts of *jus cogens*, the (sometimes overlapping) concept of *erga omnes* and the supremacy clause contained in Article 103 of the UN Charter.[23]

[19] See eg the UK Terrorist Asset-Freezing (Temporary Provisions) Act 2010, ch 2, available at <http://www.opsi.gov.uk/acts/acts2010/ukpga_20100002_en_1>; for a discussion, see also de Wet forthcoming (n 7), s C1.

[20] Werner (n 8), 330; Bardo Fassbender, 'The Meaning of International Constitutional Law' in Nicholas Tsagourias (ed), *Transitional Constitutionalism: International and European Models* (2008), 307, 308; Geir Ulfstein, 'Institutions and Competences' in Jan Klabbers, Anne Peters, and Geir Ulfstein (eds), *The Constitutionalization of International Law* (2009), 45, 80; Christain Tomuschat, 'Obligations Arising for States Without or Against their Will' (1993) 241 *Recueil des Cours de L'Académie de Droit International* 195, 235; Hamann and Ruiz Fabri (n 8).

[21] The debate pertaining to European constitutionalization has illustrated the utility of the transposition of abstract notions of constitutionalism, for the purpose of acquiring control over decision-making taking place beyond national borders, see J.H.H. Weiler and Marlene Wind, 'Introduction: European Constitutionalism Beyond the State' in J.H.H. Weiler and Marlene Wind (eds), *European Constitutionalism Beyond the State* (2003), 1, 3; Miguel Poiares Maduro, 'Europe and the Constitution: What if this is as Good as it Gets?' in Weiler and Wind, ibid 74, 82, 85; Neil Walker, 'Post-national Constitutionalism and the Problem of Translation' in Weiler and Wind, ibid 27, 34; Hamann and Ruiz Fabri (n 8), 503; Jan Klabbers, 'Setting the Scene' in Klabbers, Peters, and Ulfstein (n 20), 1, 21.

[22] Kadelbach and Kleinlein (n 9), 236, 248.

[23] UN Charter (n 5); Kadelbach and Kleinlein (n 9), 238.

1. *Jus Cogens* Obligations

The concept of *jus cogens* (peremptory norms of international law) was formally introduced in positive international law through Article 53 of the Vienna Convention on the Law of Treaties of 1969 (VCLT).[24] This article determines that:

> a treaty is void if, at the time of its conclusion, it conflicts with a peremptory norm of general international law. For the purposes of the present Convention, a peremptory norm of general international law is a norm accepted and recognized by the international community of States as a whole as a norm from which no derogation is permitted and which can be modified only by a subsequent norm of general international law having the same character.

The question whether a particular norm has reached peremptory status depends on whether it is accepted as such by a majority of states. States constitute the main subjects of the international legal order and, together with other entities that have international legal personality (notably international organizations), the international community. That a norm has been accepted as peremptory can be reflected inter alia in diplomatic correspondence of states, statements of the Ministry of Foreign Affairs, resolutions of international organizations, and judicial decisions of international and domestic courts applying international law.[25]

Within the international legal order, states were traditionally only bound to those obligations to which they had consented, for example by ratifying a treaty or joining an international organization and thereby accepting to be bound by its decisions. Similarly, states can be so-called persistent objectors to customary (general) international law, which is formed when a large number of states engage in a consistent practice (state practice) under the belief that they are legally bound to do so (*opinio juris* necessitates).[26] In principle, all states are bound by norms that have acquired customary international law status and it is possible that a norm that is codified in a treaty has also acquired customary status under international law. In such an instance, states that have not ratified the treaty will nonetheless be bound by those norms in that treaty that also qualify as customary international law. However, there is a caveat to the extent that those states that persistently object to a particular customary norm will not be bound by that norm.

[24] Vienna Convention on the Law of Treaties (adopted 23 May 1969, entered into force 27 January 1980) 1155 UNTS 331.

[25] Vienna Convention on the Law of Treaties (n 24), Art 53.

[26] As in the case of peremptory norms, the extent to which states accept a norm has having acquired customary status can be reflected in statements by the executive, in resolutions from international organizations and decisions by courts and tribunals applying international law. An example of a norm that is widely considered to be one of customary international law is the prohibition of the execution of minors/juveniles. For an extensive overview of documents in support of the 'virtually unanimous international consensus against the execution of persons who were under 18 years of age at the time of their offense', see the *Amicus Curiae* brief submitted to the US Supreme Court in light of *Roper v Simmons* 543 US 551 (2005) by the EU and various other members of the international community, available at <http://www.internationaljusticeproject.org/juvSimmonsEUamicus.pdf>. See in particular the UN Human Rights Committee's General Comment No 24, (52) in which it determined that treaty reservations by states to inter alia this norm are contrary to customary international law, UN Doc CCPR/C/21/Rev.1/Add.6 (1994), [8]; See also the affirmation of this norm as customary in Resolution 2000/17 of the UN Sub-Commission on the Promotion and Protection of Human Rights on the Death Penalty in Relation to Juvenile Offenders which was adopted by consensus, UN Doc E/CN.4/Sub.2/RES/2000/17 (2000); the Inter-American Commission on Human Rights upped the ante in 2002 by determining that even the persistent objection to the creation of this customary norm by the US in international fora did not exempt that state from the binding nature of the prohibition as the norm had since become one of *jus cogens*, see IACHR *Domingues v United States* (Merits) (Case no 12.285) 22 October 2002, Report no 62/02, [84]–[85].

However, the persistent-objector rule does not apply to *jus cogens* norms. The latter constitute an exception to the consensual character of international law.[27] The nature (substance) of the norm in question is of such importance that it justifies an exception to the notion that states cannot be bound to obligations under international law to which they have not consented. The VCLT does not give any indication of norms that would qualify as such, and the number of generally accepted *jus cogens* norms that have developed through state practice remains limited. According to the UN International Law Commission (ILC), an authoritative body created by the UN General Assembly (UNGA) for the promotion of the progressive development of international law and its codification,[28] peremptory norms include the prohibition of aggression, slavery, slave trade, genocide, racial discrimination, apartheid, and torture as well as basic rules of the law of armed conflict and the right to self-determination.[29]

Although the concept of *jus cogens* was initially designed to invalidate interstate treaties that violated peremptory norms of international law,[30] current legal doctrine tends to accept that the concept also applies to customary international law and decisions of international organizations.[31] As a result, any other international norm conflicting with a *jus cogens* norm would be *ipso facto* invalid.[32] For example, in the unlikely event that the UNSC, acting under Chapter VII of the UN Charter, authorized states to engage in torture practices when interrogating suspected terrorists, such an authorization would be invalid and is not to be enforced or relied on by states. However, as the analysis in subsequent paragraphs illustrates, the main challenge in relation to *jus cogens* obligations remains their enforcement by states. In a decentralized international legal order, which does not (yet) possess a centralized international judiciary with mandatory jurisdiction over states, this remains an ongoing challenge.

2. *Erga Omnes* Obligations

The concept of *erga omnes* obligations gained recognition through the jurisprudence of the International Court of Justice (ICJ), when it distinguished between the obligations of a state towards the international community as a whole, and those borne towards other (individual) states. In the *Barcelona Traction* case,[33] the ICJ determined that the former obligations are the concern of all states. All states can be held to have a legal interest in the protection of such rights in view of the importance of the rights involved: they are obligations *erga omnes*. This

[27] Tomuschat (n 20), 211; Werner (n 8), 335; Fassbender (n 20), 317.

[28] GA Res 174 (II) (21 November 1947).

[29] ILC, 'Report of International Law Commission on the Work of its the 58th Session' (1 May–9 June and 3 July–11 August 2006) UN Doc A/61/10 (ch 12 'The Fragmentation of International Law: Difficulties Arising from the Diversification and Expansion of International Law'), [233]–[251], 400; *Armed Activities on the Territory of the Congo (DRC v Rwanda)* (Judgment) [2006] ICJ Rep 6 [64] (*DRC v Rwanda* case).

[30] See in particular Alexander Orakhelashvili, *Peremptory Norms in International Law* (2006).

[31] The CFI assumed that this was the case in the *Kadi* CFI case (n 17), [226]; Erika de Wet, 'The Prohibition of Torture as an International Norm of *Jus Cogens* and its Implications for National and Customary Law' (2004) 15 *European Journal of International Law* 97, 97ff; Sandesh Sivakumaran, 'Impact on the Structure of International Obligations' in Menno T. Kamminga and Martin Scheinin (eds), *The Impact of Human Rights Law on General International Law* (2009), 133, 147.

[32] Pierre-Marie Dupuy, 'Some Reflections on Contemporary International Law and the Appeal to Universal Values: A Response to Martii Koskenniemi' (2005) 16 *European Journal of International Law* 131, 133.

[33] *Barcelona Traction, Light and Power Company Ltd (Belgium v Spain)* (Second Phase, Judgment) [1970] ICJ Rep 3 (*Barcelona Traction* case); *Legal Consequences of the Construction of a Wall in the Occupied Palestinian Territory* (Advisory Opinion) [2004] ICJ Rep 136; ILC Report 58th Session (n 29), [419]; Sivakumaran (n 31), 148.

concept of community-oriented obligations further finds recognition in the law of state responsibility, which has created a system of responsibility for serious violations of international obligations towards the international community as a whole. The principles of the system are contained in the ILC's Articles on State Responsibility of 2001.[34] Though not formally binding, those Articles constitute the most authoritative source on state responsibility at this time.

The Articles on State Responsibility draw a distinction between breaches of bilateral obligations and obligations of a collective interest nature.[35] Breaches of a bilateral nature involve situations where the performance of an obligation involves two individual states, even though the treaty framework or customary rule in question establishes obligations applicable to all states (parties).[36] In such an instance the nature of the obligations stemming from the multilateral treaty or customary rule can be described as 'bundles of bilateral obligations'.[37] An example in point would be Article 22 of the Vienna Convention on Diplomatic Relations,[38] where the obligation to protect the premises of a diplomatic mission is owed by the individual receiving state to the individual sending state.[39] The fact that many states are party to this treaty does not alter the fact that in relation to any particular situation resulting from the Convention, the obligations owed only concern two particular states.

Breaches of a collective interest nature concern obligations that have been established for the protection of the collective interest of a group of states (*erga omnes partes*) by means of a treaty, or indeed of the international community as a whole (*erga omnes*).[40] Concrete examples of *erga omnes* (*partes*) obligations can be found in particular in human rights law and international criminal law treaties. Obligations stemming from regional or universal human rights treaties would first of all have *erga omnes partes* effect towards other states party to the treaty. In addition, they will have *erga omnes* proper effect (towards the international community as a whole), to the extent that the obligations in the treaty have been recognized as customary international law and are therefore binding on all states.[41]

The same would apply to those obligations articulated in the Statute of the International Criminal Court (ICC)[42] and which grant the ICC jurisdiction over the most serious crimes of concern to the 'international community as a whole', namely genocide, crimes against humanity, and war crimes. Whilst treaty obligations aimed at environmental protection would also be strong contenders for *erga omnes* (*partes*) status, it remains controversial whether obligations pertaining to trade liberalization constitute 'bundles of bilateral obligations' rather than

[34] ILC Draft Articles on Responsibility of States for Internationally Wrongful Acts (Articles on State Responsibility) available in James Crawford (ed), *The International Law Commission's Articles on State Responsibility: Introduction, Text and Commentaries* (2002).

[35] Crawford (n 34), Arts 42, 48.

[36] Ibid 257.

[37] Ibid 258.

[38] Vienna Convention on Diplomatic Relations (adopted 18 April 1961, entered into force 24 April 1964) 500 UNTS 95.

[39] *US Diplomatic and Consular Staff in Tehran (USA v Iran)* (Judgment) [1980] ICJ Rep 1980 3, [257]–[258] (*Teheran Hostages* case).

[40] Crawford (n 34), 277.

[41] Pierre-Marie Dupuy, 'L'Unité Formelle de l'Ordre Juridique International. Cours Général de Droit International Public' (2002) 297 *Recueil des Cours de L'Académie de Droit International* 93, 382, 384; Crawford (n 34), 277–8; UN Human Rights Committee, General Comment No 31, (80) on the Nature of the General Legal Obligation Imposed on States Parties to the Covenant CCPR/C/21/Rev.1/Add.13, [2].

[42] Rome Statute of the International Criminal Court (adopted 17 July 1998, entered into force 1 July 2002) 2187 UNTS 90 (Rome Statute).

erga omnes (*partes*) obligations.[43] Some authors regard free trade to be a pre-condition for the realization of human rights, and in that sense consider it inherently connected to *erga omnes* obligations. This point is taken up again below in relation to the constitutionalization of the World Trade Organization (WTO) as a manifestation of a sectoral constitution within international law.[44]

As far as the relationship between the *jus cogens* and *erga omnes* obligations is concerned, the *Barcelona Traction* decision of the ICJ provides authority for the conclusion that *jus cogens* norms would have *erga omnes* effect.[45] Without expressly referring to *jus cogens*, the ICJ implied as much by the types of norms it mentioned as examples of *erga omnes* norms.[46] These norms included the outlawing of the unilateral use of force, and the prohibition of genocide, slavery, and racial discrimination. Given the fact that these same obligations are widely regarded in doctrine as being of a peremptory nature, one can conclude that fundamental obligations from which no derogation is permitted will normally be applicable to all members of the international community.[47]

However, although it is accurate to assume that all *jus cogens* norms are simultaneously of an *erga omnes* character, it would not be accurate to assume that the opposite necessarily applies as well: namely that *erga omnes* norms would constitute peremptory norms of international law. To begin with, not all norms with a collective interest have acquired customary international law (and thus *erga omnes* proper) status. In order to acquire peremptory status, an *erga omnes* norm first has to be accepted by a large number of states as belonging to the body of customary international law. Additionally, the majority of states have to regard that norm as being a customary norm of a very special nature, namely one from which no derogation is possible.[48] This double threshold is both high and difficult to cross, which explains the small number of generally recognized peremptory norms to date.

This in turn raises the question regarding the added value of those *erga omnes* norms that do not qualify as peremptory norms of international law. First, there is uncertainty surrounding the scope of this layer of obligations.[49] Secondly, the interstate mechanisms designed to enforce *erga omnes* obligations in the Articles on State Responsibility are modest. According to Article 48, states other than injured states are entitled to invoke responsibility where the obligation breached is owed to the international community as a whole. When invoking responsibility in this fashion, the invoking state may claim cessation of the internationally wrongful act as well as performance of the obligation or reparation in the interest of the beneficiaries from the responsible state.

[43] See in particular Joost Pauwelyn, 'A Typology of Multilateral Treaty Obligations: Are WTO Obligations Bilateral or Collective in Nature?' (2003) 14 *European Journal of International Law* 907.

[44] Ernst-Ulrich Petersmann, 'Time for a United Nations "Global Compact" for Integrating Human Rights into the Law of Worldwide Organizations: Lessons from European Integration' (2002) 13 *European Journal of International Law* 621, 636ff; Ernst-Ulrich Petersmann, 'The WTO Constitution and Human Rights' (2000) 3 *Journal of International Economic Law* 19, 19; cf Armin von Bogdandy, 'Law and Politics in the WTO—Strategies to Cope with a Deficient Relationship' (2001) 5 *Max Planck Yearbook of UN Law* 609, 653–6; Eric Stein, 'International Integration and Democracy: No Love at First Sight' (2001) 95 *American Journal of International Law* 489, 502; Thomas Cottier and Maya Hertig, 'The Prospects of 21st Century Constitutionalism' (2003) 7 *Max Planck Yearbook of UN Law* 261, 273–4.

[45] *Barcelona Traction* case (n 33).

[46] Jochen A. Frowein, 'Collective Enforcement of International Obligations' (1987) 47 *Zeitschrift für Ausländisches Öffentliches Recht und Völkerrecht* 67, 71; ILC Report 58th Session (n 29), [421].

[47] ILC Report 58th Session (n 29), [421].

[48] Ibid [38]; Dupuy (n 41), 385.

[49] This issue is also linked to the debate on whether state practice and *opinio juris* are still decisive for determining the formation of customary international law; G. Thalinger, 'Sense and Sensibility of the Human Rights Obligations of the United Nations Security Council' (2007) 67 *Zeitschrift für Ausländisches Öffentliches Recht und Völkerrecht* 1015, 1022ff.

For the time being, there are no other generally accepted mechanisms for the enforcement of *erga omnes* obligations. In this context it is worth keeping in mind that the jurisdiction of the ICJ is limited to those states that have voluntarily accepted that jurisdiction. This is either done through compromissary clauses in treaties that recognize the ICJ's jurisdiction for disputes pertaining to the treaty in question,[50] or through a unilateral declaration by a state that recognizes the ICJ's jurisdiction in relation to all disputes arising between itself and other states which similarly accepted the ICJ's jurisdiction.[51] However the ICJ has declined to recognize the existence of an *actio popularis* that would allow any state(s) as member(s) of the international community to initiate proceedings for vindicating the violation of community interests.

In its controversial *South West Africa* decision of 1966, the ICJ inter alia motivated its position with the argument that the ICJ statute did not explicitly provide for such an *actio popularis*.[52] Furthermore, the ICJ gave a very restricted interpretation of the notion of 'legal interest'.[53] Although the inclusion of Article 48 in the Articles on State Responsibility does not provide a solution for the fact that the ICJ statute fails to provide for an *actio popularis*, it may in future encourage the ICJ to adopt a broader notion of 'legal interest' in instances where the violation of an *erga omnes* obligation is disputed between two or more states that have accepted the ICJ's jurisdiction in accordance with Article 36(1) or (2) of its statute.[54] All in all, however, the opportunity for the ICJ to enforce *erga omnes* obligations remains limited and this is unlikely to change in the near future.

3. Obligations Under (Article 103 of) the UN Charter[55]

The third manifestation of hierarchy in international law concerns Article 103 of the UN Charter, which determines that UN Charter obligations prevail over other obligations that member states may have under any other international agreement. This supremacy of obligations not only extends to the articles of the UN Charter itself, it also applies to binding decisions of the UNSC, which this organ can take in the interest of international peace and security under Chapter VII of the UN Charter. It is by now well-established practice that such UN Charter obligations may also prevail over inconsistent customary international law.[56]

It is further generally accepted that the UN, as a subject of international law (and by extension also its organs), is bound by *jus cogens* norms. Therefore, in the perhaps unlikely event of a conflict occurring between a binding UNSC obligation and a *jus cogens* norm, the latter would prevail.[57] However, the relationship between UN Charter obligations (in particular UNSC obligations) and those *erga omnes* obligations that do not constitute peremptory norms

[50] See Statute of the International Court of Justice (adopted 26 June 1945, entered into force 24 October 1945) 1 UNTS XVI, Art 36(1).

[51] See ICJ Statute (n 50), Art 36(2).

[52] ICJ Statute (n 50); see Joined Cases *Ethiopia v South Africa* and *Liberia v South Africa* (Second Phase, Judgment) [1966] ICJ Rep 6 [88] (*South West Africa* case); *DRC v Rwanda* case (n 29), [64], [125]; Sivakumaran (n 31), 149.

[53] *South West Africa* case (n 52), [44]. The ICJ was unwilling to assume that a state may have a legal interest in vindicating a principle of international law, even though it has not suffered material damages—unless this was explicitly provided for in an international text or instrument.

[54] Crawford (n 34), 279; Sivakumaran (n 31), 149.

[55] UN Charter (n 5).

[56] ILC Report 58th Session (n 29), [35].

[57] Ibid [40].

of international law are highly controversial. In the *Kadi* case the CFI took the controversial position that *jus cogens* obligations would constitute the only constraint to the UNSC. UNSC obligations would prevail over all other conflicting obligations and could limit human rights obligations extensively.[58] While the ECJ avoided dealing with this point on appeal (and decided the matter exclusively on the basis of EU law) this remains hotly disputed in legal doctrine. Those disagreeing with the position of the CFI underscore the fact that, in accordance with Article 24(2) of the UN Charter, the UNSC shall act in accordance with the purposes and principles of the UN Charter; this includes in particular the promotion of human rights in Article 1(3).[59] However, the absence of a detailed 'Bill of Rights' in the UN Charter has led others to claim that the reference to human rights in Article 1(3) is too vague to be of any help.[60]

In essence, therefore, the three layers of hierarchy which are currently identifiable within international law raise questions pertaining to the scope and the (lack of) enforcement of such norms, the relationship between the different layers, as well as how such norms relate to other norms of international law. These questions have significantly influenced the debate on the extent of the constitutionalization of public international law.

III. Partial Constitutionalization of the International Legal Order

1. The Constitutionalization of International Organizations

The constitutionalization of international organizations concerns attempts to limit or control the exercise of public power by such organizations. Within this context, such organizations are regarded as autonomous units that function within a particular legal framework on the basis of a particular mandate. A constitutional approach to international organizations thus implies that the constitutive treaties of organizations such as the WTO, the World Health Organization, or the UN are regarded as a veritable Constitution. That Constitution defines the outer limits within which the organization, as a subject of international law, may exercise those powers conferred on it by states.[61] Stated differently, the constitution of an international organization embodies the legal framework within which an autonomous community made up by states realizes the goals as articulated in the constitutive treaty such as trade liberalization or the maintenance of international peace and security.[62]

The rhetoric of constitutionalization in relation to international organizations is particularly strong where the legal norms embodied in the constitutive document can be enforced by judicial review, that is, the reviewing of the legality of actions of the member states or the executive or legislative organs of the organization (or any combination of these) by an independent judicial body.[63] As mentioned, the ICJ has no centralized jurisdiction and only exer-

[58] *Kadi* CFI case (n 17).

[59] Erika de Wet, *The Chapter VII Powers of the United Nations Security Council* (2004), 133ff.

[60] eg Anthony Aust, 'The Role of Human Rights in Limiting the Enforcement Powers of the Security Council: A Practitioner's View' in Erika de Wet and André Nollkaemper (eds), *Review of the Security Council by Member States* (2003), 31ff.

[61] *Legality of the Threat or Use by a State of Nuclear Weapons* (Advisory Opinion) [1996] ICJ Rep 226, [19]; Werner (n 8), 349.

[62] See also Diggelmann and Altwicker (n 8), 627.

[63] Werner (n 8), 349; Klabbers (n 21), 20.

cises jurisdiction to the extent that states have voluntarily accepted its authority. Yet, some organizations have adopted judicial or quasi-judicial mechanisms that provide for centralized judicial review in relation to the particular area of law that falls within the mandate designed by the organization's constitutive document.[64] The most prominent example in this regard concerns the centralized dispute settlement system within the WTO, which consists of quasi-judicial panels and an Appellate Body.[65]

Although this dispute resolution mechanism plays a significant role in clarifying the boundaries of the economic freedoms provided to member states by the General Agreement on Tariffs and Trade (GATT),[66] the impact of the mechanism within the domestic jurisdictions of member states is reduced by the refusal of most of those member states to grant the GATT rules (or the decisions of the dispute settlement bodies) direct effect within the domestic legal order.[67] Supporters of direct effect point out that by enabling individuals to rely directly on subjective rights that are distilled from the GATT rules before domestic courts, one would further strengthen the judicial control over executive decision-making.[68] This in turn would strengthen the constitutional impact of the WTO's Appellate Body as the apex of a centralized dispute settlement system. It would succeed in safeguarding the autonomy of the individual against the executive—which is one of the core elements of traditional (domestic) constitutionalism. Thus far member states have been reluctant to accept such an extensive 'constitutionalization through judicialization' of GATT norms.[69]

This reluctance of states also reveals the sustained influence these entities have on the actions of the organs of an international organization, despite the fact that organizations such as the WTO constitute separate legal entities (subjects) under international law. The objectives of the (powerful) member states cannot be completely separated from the actions of the organization. Organs within the organization, including dispute settlement bodies, would not be allowed to stray too far from the will of the member states. The controlling impact of judicial review exercised within international organizations would therefore only be effective to the extent that this review is accepted by the member states. Stated differently, the efficacy of the constitutionalization of the organization through the introduction of judicial review would, in the final instance, depend on the cooperation of precisely those subjects that the review process is supposed to control.[70]

However, even though judicial review would not be a panacea for ensuring that member states and/or organs of international organizations act within the limits of the respective

[64] Jan Klabbers, 'Constitutionalism Lite' (2004) 1 *International Organizations Law Review* 31, 33; Kadelbach and Kleinlein (n 9), 240.

[65] Peters (n 9), 596; Matthias Knauff, 'Konstitutionalisierung im inner- und Überstaatlichen Recht—Konvergenz oder Divergenz?' (2008) 68 *Zeitschrift für Ausländisches Öffentliches Recht und Völkerrecht* 453, 460.

[66] General Agreement on Tariffs and Trade 1994 (GATT 1994) (15 April 1994) LT/UR/A-1A/1/GATT/2.

[67] Peter Behrens, 'Towards Constitutionalization of International Investment Protection' (2007) 45 *Archiv des Völkerrechts* 153, 154.

[68] A strong proponent of the notion of a right to trade is Petersmann in the contributions cited in n 44; see also Behrens who asserts that international investment law is undergoing a process of constitutionalization as investment treaties increasingly provide private investors with subjective rights that can be enforced before an international arbitration panel, Behrens (n 67), 177.

[69] Behrens (n 67), 153; Peters (n 9), 597; Kadelbach and Kleinlein (n 9), 239; Sol Picciotto 'Constitutionalizing Multilevel Governance?' (2008) 6 *Journal of International Constitutional Law* 457, 458.

[70] Peters (n 9), 594; Klabbers (n 64), 44–5.

competencies of such member states and/or organs, the absence of judicial review would significantly reduce such control. The most poignant example remains the UN, where the ability of the ICJ to review the legality of UNSC decisions remains extremely limited and controversial. The limited power of the ICJ in exercising judicial review does not only apply vis-à-vis states, but also towards the actions of the other principal organs of the UN itself (the ICJ being its principal judicial organ).

The only explicit textual link in the UN Charter to judicial review of the other principle organs of the UN is contained in Article 96(1). It provides the UNGA and the UNSC with the power to request an advisory opinion from the ICJ on any legal question. This clause is phrased in wide language and would arguably also permit the UNGA to request the ICJ for an advisory opinion on the legality of binding UNSC resolutions, where the latter is unwilling to submit such a request itself.[71] Even though advisory opinions are not legally binding, the opinions do carry significant weight within the membership of the UN as instruments that clarify the law as presented by the UN Charter. In the wake of such an opinion, the UNSC might therefore be persuaded to withdraw or amend certain binding decisions.[72] In practice, however, the UNGA has not attempted to request an advisory opinion for this purpose thus far. This relates inter alia to the fact that such a request needs to be supported by a two-thirds majority within the UNGA, which is a high threshold. The only advisory opinion to date that resulted in review of the legality of a UNSC resolution resulted from the latter's own (and thus far only) request for an advisory opinion, which concerned South Africa's illegal occupation of (what is now known as) Namibia.[73]

Member states of the UN cannot individually request advisory opinions from the ICJ. Article 96(1) limits this competence to organs of the organization, namely the UNSC and the UNGA. However, the issue of judicial review of UNSC resolutions can become incidentally relevant in contentious proceedings between states before the ICJ. This would be the case where a particular UNSC resolution directly affects a legal dispute between two or more state parties in relation to an issue over which the ICJ indeed does have jurisdiction. Such was the case in the Lockerbie proceedings that concerned the interpretation of the Convention for the Suppression of Unlawful Acts Against the Safety of Civil Aviation of 1971 (the Montreal Convention),[74] which contained a compromissory clause in Article 14.[75] As the UNSC had adopted binding resolutions that went to the heart of the interpretation of this Convention, the ICJ would not have been able to decide the dispute without reviewing these resolutions, including their potential illegality.

It is well known that the UN Charter does not provide the ICJ with any explicit power to exercise judicial review in such an incidental manner. The question that remains unclear is whether such a competence exists implicitly. Since the parties to the Lockerbie proceedings

[71] See in particular *Legal Consequences of the Construction of a Wall in the Occupied Palestinian Territory* (n 33), [36]ff; for a comprehensive analysis of the powers of the UNGA in terms of Art 96(1) of the UN Charter (n 5) see de Wet (n 59), 42ff.

[72] See de Wet (n 59), 58ff. Similarly, though contentious proceedings are only binding *inter partes*, such proceedings also have considerable weight with states and the UN itself.

[73] *Legal Consequences for States of the Continued Presence of South Africa in Namibia (South West Africa) Notwithstanding Security Council Resolution 276* [1971] ICJ Rep 16, [12]ff (*Namibia* case).

[74] Montreal Convention for the Suppression of Unlawful Acts against the Safety of Civil Aviation (signed 23 September 1971, entered into force 26 January 1973) 974 UNTS 177.

[75] *Case Concerning Questions of Interpretation and Application of the 1971 Montreal Convention Arising from the Aerial Incident at Lockerbie (Libyan Arab Jamahiriya v USA)* (Preliminary Objections) [1998] ICJ Rep 9, [115]ff (*Lockerbie* case).

requested the withdrawal of the merits phase of the dispute from the role of the ICJ in September 2003, the matter remains unresolved. Equally disputed is the implicit competence of any other court (whether international, regional, or domestic) to engage in incidental review of the legality of UNSC resolutions. This issue will be taken up again in Section III.3(b) below. Here it suffices to say that the reason why courts such as the ECJ in *Kadi* were confronted with reviewing the legality of UNSC resolutions—incidental to enforcing the law of the legal system for which they were created—is closely linked to the absence of an extensive judicial review mechanism within the UN itself.

In essence therefore the constitutional features of the UN—insofar as it relates to judicial review—remain very weak. The mechanisms for ensuring that a powerful organ like the UNSC remains within the 'constitutional boundaries' provided by the UN Charter are essentially political in nature, and take the form of the (threat of the) veto power that can be exercised by any of the five permanent members during UNSC decision-making. This, in turn, has provoked some authors to question the utility of constitutional language for the purpose of curbing the power of the UN claiming that, in the end, it may prove as powerless as the doctrine of functionality.[76]

2. Constitutionalization through Transgovernmental Networks

A related but nonetheless separate strand of constitutionalization concerns the development of transgovernmental networks. Although the networks also have a functional focus, the structural features of those networks are more fluid than those of international organizations. The networks can consist of various international organizations and disaggregated components of the state, which interact and cooperate in relation to a particular functional (sectoral) area.[77] According to this line of argument, different organizations and state entities concerned with trade liberalization would form a trade network, whereas those involved in human rights protection would constitute a human rights network. Yet others may constitute a security network or an investment network.[78] Such networks generally do not possess international legal personality and therefore cannot incur rights or obligations under international law.

Within a particular network there would be a criss-cross interaction of norms. The interaction would be horizontal in nature (eg between different international organizations with a functional overlap), as well as vertical (eg between international organizations and particular state entities).[79] In addition, there would be a norm hierarchy within the network itself to the extent that a dense layer of international norms relating to the purpose and function of the network would override conflicting domestic regulations. Stated differently, the functional paradigm (or bias) of the network in question would make it increasingly difficult for domestic actors within that network to safeguard domestic legal principles (whether of a domestic

[76] Klabbers (n 64), 594.

[77] Anne-Marie Slaughter, 'The Real New World Order' (1997) 76 *Foreign Affairs* 183, 186; Picciotto (n 69), 458; Walter (n 10), 173, 194–5, 198.

[78] While public international law is concerned with networks consisting of different components of the state, transnational networks composed of private actors involved in self-regulation also exist. To some extent, this type of regulation and interaction is synonymous with *lex mercatoria*. See Hamann and Ruiz Fabri (n 8), 486; Knauff (n 65), 472; Andreas Fischer-Lescano and Gunther Teubner, 'Regime-Collision: The Vain Search for Legal Unity in the Fragmentation of Global Law' (2004) 25 *Michigan Journal of International Law* 999, 999ff.

[79] Peters (n 9), 601; Diggelmann and Altwicker (n 8), 635.

constitutional nature or otherwise) from the overriding influence of the international norms.[80]

As transgovernmental networks do not operate in neatly separated areas but often have complementary or competing powers, the question of how to resolve inter-network (one might also say inter-regime) conflicts arise. The *Kadi* case is a pertinent example of how a regional court was confronted with competing norms originating from different networks or regimes. Whereas the CFI gave preference to the norms resulting from a 'security network' with Article 103 of the UN Charter at its apex, the ECJ on appeal gave preference to what could be described as a 'European human rights network'.[81]

This example already illustrates that, in the absence of a generally accepted hierarchy between the different functional networks, different judicial bodies operating within different functional paradigms may resolve a particular norm conflict in very different ways.[82] Other examples that illustrate this point would include potential norm conflicts between international trade or investment networks and human rights networks. Thus far there has been a marked reluctance on the part of the Appellate Body as well as WTO officials to assert that the trade obligations of member states had to be interpreted in harmony with the human rights obligations of those member states.[83] In addition, states have been reluctant to invoke human rights obligations before a WTO body as a justification for not complying with trade obligations. This could be interpreted as acceptance that any human rights obligations of member states have a very limited place in determining the scope of the member states' trade obligations within the WTO.[84] Similarly, it remains disputed if and to what extent investment arbitration panels concerned with disputes between an investor and a host state should take into account the human rights of the investors and/or third parties affected by the dispute.[85] An international human rights body, on the other hand, might be prone to give preference to human rights obligations when faced with similar disputes, given that it is embedded in a different functional paradigm.

Such conflicting results would enhance the fragmentation of international law, as it entrenches the notion of interwoven but yet separate networks of legal regimes.[86] This seems to run counter to the approach suggested by the Study Group of the ILC on the Fragmentation of International Law, which regarded international law as a unified system within which potentially conflicting norms should be resolved through interpretation and accommodation.[87] In addition, it would entrench the possibility that individual human rights protection could be abolished within functional transgovernmental networks pertaining to, for example, international security or trade liberalization. This, in turn, would run counter to the aims of those who see the constitutionalization of internal law as a means for limiting the exercise of public power on the international level, notably in order to protect the rights of individuals.

[80] Peters (n 9), 591.

[81] For other examples of inter-regime conflict, also in relation to jurisdictional issues, see Ulfstein (n 20), 136ff.

[82] Walter (n 10), 194–5, 198; Fischer-Lescano and Teubner (n 78), 999ff; Anne-Marie Slaughter, *A New World Order* (2004), 131.

[83] Picciotto (n 69), 473.

[84] Ibid 473.

[85] See generally Pierre-Marie Dupuy, Ernst-Ulrich Petersmann, and Francesco Francioni (eds), *Human Rights in International Investment Law and Arbitration* (2009).

[86] Peters (n 9), 601; Diggelmann and Altwicker (n 8), 635; Werner (n 8), 350.

[87] ILC Report 58th Session (n 29), [35]ff; Picciotto (n 69), 474.

This type of fragmentation could be countered only if one were to accept that the different functional networks were embedded into a larger constitutional whole, which contains hierarchically superior norms that underpin the international order in its entirety and which serve as guidelines for interpretation in instances of inter-regime conflicts.[88] Authors who support this line of argument tend to attribute a unifying role to *jus cogens* and *erga omnes* obligations within a constitutional matrix that applies to the international legal order as a whole. It is to these perspectives that the analysis will now turn.

3. Constitutionalization of the International Legal Order as a Whole

(a) *The Special Status of the UN Charter*

Those authors who describe current developments in international law as a manifestation of the constitutionalization of the international legal order as a whole all in some way or another link their arguments to the UN Charter. Whereas some see the UN Charter as 'the international constitution', others regard it more as a building block or connecting factor within an international constitutional order that demarcates the outer limits for the exercise of public power.[89]

Those who regard the UN Charter as the Constitution of the international legal order, refer to the nature of the UN Charter as a 'world-order treaty'. The UN has universal membership and promotes the goals of safeguarding international peace and security, as well as human rights in the interest of the international community as a whole. In addition, the UN provides for a binding system for enforcement through Chapter VII of the UN Charter in combination with the supremacy clause contained in Article 103 of the UN Charter.[90] One very idealistic vision of the UN Charter describes it as a (potential) mechanism through which member states and the citizens thereof can be perceived as the constituent parts of world society.[91] Skeptics do not hesitate to point out that the lack of a proper separation of powers within the UN, the lack of direct effect of UNSC decisions in the domestic order, as well as the absence of a full-fledged human rights catalog and a centralized judiciary within the UN severely weaken the impact of the UN Charter as a constitutional blueprint for the behavior of member states.[92]

However, for those who see the UN as a connecting factor within a larger constitutional whole—rather than deeming its Charter as the international Constitution itself—these deficits do not necessarily defy the existence of an international constitutional order. From their perspective the UN serves the dual role of a functional regime ('network') for international peace and security and key connecting factor, as its universal membership links the different states into the international community. Although the international community would also

[88] Kadelbach and Kleinlein (n 9), 243; Knauff (n 65), 472; M. Rosenfeld 'Rethinking Constitutional Ordering in an Era of Legal and Ideological Pluralism' (2008) 6 *Journal of International Constitutional Law* 415, 421.

[89] Tomuschat (n 20), 219.

[90] Fassbender (n 20), 324; Ronald St John Macdonald, 'The International Community as a Legal Community' in Ronald St John Macdonald and Douglas M. Johnston (eds), *Towards World Constitutionalism, Issues in the Legal Ordering of the World Community* (2005), 853, 853ff.

[91] Jürgen Habermas, 'Hat die Konstitutionalisierung des Völkerrechts noch eine Chance?' in Jürgen Habermas, *Der Gespaltene Westen* (2004), 159.

[92] Kadelbach and Kleinlein suggested that Art 103 of the UN Charter (n 5) would constitute a rule to regulate a conflict of norms, without elevating the UN Charter itself to a constitution, Kadelbach and Kleinlein (n 9), 250.

include other subjects of international law such as international organizations with separate legal personality,[93] states still form the primary subjects of international law. Therefore, through its linking function, the UN has an important impact on the composition of the international community.[94]

Moreover, the UN Charter serves as a catalyst for the emerging human rights hierarchy in the form of *jus cogens* and *erga omnes* obligations as outlined above in Section II.1(b). It therefore serves as a catalyst for the evolution of an international value system, which is to be understood as those norms of positive law with a strong ethical underpinning and which have acquired a special hierarchical status through state practice.[95] Due to the inspirational role of in particular Article 1(3) of the UN Charter in combination with Articles 55, 56, 62, and 68, human rights norms were promoted in such a fashion as to be elevated to the core elements of the international value system. These articles significantly contributed to a climate in which an elaborate system for human rights protection was created both within the UN Charter system and within regional and/or (other) functional regimes. In turn, these mechanisms of protection coupled with the concretization of the norms derived from such mechanisms significantly contributed to the recognition of the *erga omnes* (*partes*) character and in some instances even peremptory status of human rights norms such as the prohibition of torture and genocide.[96]

In this manner the normative framework of the UN Charter has been instrumental in bringing about a verticalization in the relations of member states *inter se*. It has been the catalyst for the development of an international legal order based on hierarchically superior values, as opposed to one exclusively based on the 'equilibrium or value of sovereigns'.[97] It inspired the development of a human rights regime that can inform decision-making within functional regimes or networks by serving as guidelines or principles of interpretation.

In accordance with this line of argument, decision-making within a particular network would have to give due consideration to international human rights standards in cases where such standards conflict with other international obligations. Judicial or quasi-judicial bodies such as international arbitration panels, the WTO Appellate Body or executive bodies such as the UNSC should pay deference to international human rights standards relevant to the dispute or situation at hand and motivate explicitly in instances where such standards are limited

[93] For a progressive view of the composition of the international community, emphasizing the role of non-governmental organizations and individuals, see Anne Peters, 'Membership in the Global Constitutional Community' in Klabbers, Peters, and Ulfstein (n 20), 154ff.

[94] Erika de Wet, 'The International Constitutional Order' (2006) 55 *International Comparative Law Quarterly* 51, 54ff; Dino Kritsiotis, 'Imagining the International Community' (2002) 13 *European Journal of International Law* 961, 967ff.

[95] De Wet (n 94), 57; Dupuy (n 32) 133; Bryde (n 9), 97; Sabine von Schorlemer, 'Konstitutionalisiering der Universellen Völkerrechtsordnung die Menschenrechte' in Eckart Klein and Christoph Menke (eds), *Universialität—Schutzmechanismen—Diskriminierungsverbote: 15 Jahre Wiener Weltmenschenrechtskonferenz Berlin* (2008), 609ff.

[96] Pierre-Marie Dupuy, 'The Constitutional Dimension of the Charter of the United Nations Revisited' (1997) 1 *Max Planck Yearbook of International Law* 1, 10–11, 31; Ian Johnstone, 'The US-UN Relations after Iraq: The End of the World (Order) as We Know It?' (2004) 15 *European Journal of International Law* 813, 824.

[97] Daniel Thürer, 'Internationales "Rule of Law"—Innerstaatliche Demokratie' (1995) 5 *Schweizerische Zeitschrift für Internationales und Europäisches Recht* 455, 457; Fassbender (n 20), 548, 554, 574; Tomuschat (n 20), 216; Michael Byers, 'Conceptualizing the Relationship between *Jus Cogens* and *Erga Omnes* Rules' (1997) 66 *Nordic Journal of International Law* 211, 212.

or not followed.[98] In this manner the human-rights-based value system common to all regimes connects these different regimes into a larger international community and shapes the outer limits for the exercise of public power.[99]

This vision of a human-rights-based international value system that serves as a connecting factor within the international constitutional order has been criticized (amongst other things) for lack of legitimacy. In the current context, legitimacy should be understood as the extent to which the international value system is accepted as being representative of the values of those who are affected by it.[100] For many authors such legitimacy is closely connected to the process by means of which the respective value system came into being and, in particular, the democratic quality of that process.[101] Critics regard the value system developing under the influence of international institutions including international courts and tribunals as an unrepresentative, superimposed normative system that takes place beyond any form of democratic control or accountability.[102]

These arguments have in turn been criticized for mythologizing national democratic governance as a model for international governance and assuming that there is one specific national model of democratic governance that can set threshold conditions for the legitimacy of international governance.[103] In addition, one can question whether democratic governance is the only form of legitimate decision-making and whether legitimacy could instead also be achieved through the quality (expertise) of the decision-making process, transparency, and accessibility through public participation. These questions become particularly pertinent in a context where the structural differences between the composition of the international community and national communities make it questionable whether democracy could ever have the same meaning internationally as it does domestically.[104]

In this context, it is noteworthy that there is a formal overlap in content between the international and domestic human rights systems. Most modern constitutions in various parts of the world—and notably those drafted by democratically elected constitutional assemblies—contain human rights standards closely resembling those of international and regional human rights instruments. The fact that this overlap exists despite the democratic deficit on the international level may be an indication that the development of a representative value system within the international legal order is not necessarily excluded by the existence of a democratic deficit. Skeptics would nonetheless insist that the existing overlap between domestic and international value systems is shallow and exclusively formal in nature.[105] In essence therefore, the legitimacy of the international value systems remains controversial and faces constant

[98] Kadelbach and Kleinlein (n 9), 263ff; Behrens (n 67), 175; Niels Petersen, 'Der Wandel des Ungeschriebenen Völkerrechts im Zuge der Konstitutionalisierung' (2008) 46 *Archiv des Völkerrechts* 502, 507; Diggelmann and Altwicker (n 8), 635; Knauff (n 65), 467, 522.

[99] De Wet (n 94), 53.

[100] Ibid 71.

[101] Stein (n 44), 491; Mattias Kumm, 'The Legitimacy of International Law: A Constitutionalist Framework Analysis' (2004) 15 *European Journal of International Law* 907, 915.

[102] Stein (n 44), 491; Jed Rubenfeld, 'The Two World Orders' (2003) 27 *Wilson Quarterly* 22, 28.

[103] José E. Alvarez, 'Multilateralism and Its Discontents' (2000) 11 *European Journal of International Law* 393, 399, 410; see extensively de Wet (n 94), 72ff.

[104] Daniel Bodansky, 'The Legitimacy of International Governance: A Coming Challenge for International Environmental Law?' (1999) 93 *American Journal of International Law* 596, 613; for an elaboration of the democratic deficit in international law, see Anne Peters, 'Dual Democracy' in Klabbers, Peters, and Ulfstein (n 20), 263ff.

[105] See Klabbers (n 21), 26.

challenges from those who regard it as manifestation of Western (notably European) hegemony.[106]

(b) *Decentralized Enforcement of the International Constitutional Order*

The enforcement of the fundamental elements (notably the value system) of the international constitutional order, whether through political or judicial means, remains essentially decentralized in nature.[107] As indicated above in Section II.2, at this stage of the development of international law there are hardly any centralized mechanisms through which 'the international community'—whether represented by a single state, a group of states, or non-state actors—can enforce violations of obligations *erga omnes*. The efficacy of the most powerful political organ for the enforcement of *erga omnes* obligations, namely the UNSC, would remain notoriously dependable on the unpredictable presence of the political will of its permanent members.

Judicial enforcement will depend on the extent to which regional, functional and even domestic judicial bodies are incidentally confronted with inter-regime norm conflicts as were at issue in the *Kadi* case. In addition, the domestic judicial bodies will have to reflect a willingness to attribute the implicit competence to enforce the international value system on behalf of the international community to themselves. At this point in time the practice of such courts and tribunals is too limited to determine whether they have asserted a secondary role as enforcers of the fundamental values of the international constitutional order in addition to their primary function of enforcing the law of a particular domestic, regional, or functional regime.[108]

The only functional regime that has, in the course of time, frequently reviewed other treaty obligations against human rights obligations has been the European Court of Human Rights (ECtHR).[109] The range of cases in which the ECtHR has reviewed the application of public international law obligations against the obligations in the ECHR[110] range from absolute rights that may not be restricted or derogated from, even in times of war or public emergency, for example the prohibitions on torture and cruel, inhuman or degrading treatment, and punishment;[111] to rights that may be restricted for narrow purposes such as in times of emergency, for example the right to a fair trial;[112] and rights that may be restricted for broad purposes, such as

[106] Martti Koskenniemi, 'International Law in Europe: Between Tradition and Renewal' (2005) 16 *European Journal of International Law* 113, 115, 117; but see also Dupuy (n 32), 135–6.

[107] De Wet (n 94), 64ff; see also Ulfstein who noted that any redesign of the decentralized international judicial architecture by states is unlikely, Ulfstein (n 20), 141.

[108] This is reflected notably in the *Kadi* CFI case (n 17) where the CFI was very reluctant to accept such a competence; see also the *Nada* case (n 17); the ad hoc criminal tribunals for Yugoslavia and Rwanda respectively have claimed such a competence for themselves, see *Prosecutor v Tadić* (Decision on the Defense Motion for the Interlocutory Appeal on Jurisdiction) IT-94-1-AR72 (2 October 1995), [27]ff (*Tadić: Jurisdiction* case) and *Prosecutor v Kanyabashi* (Decision on Jurisdiction) ICTR-96-15-T (18 June 1997).

[109] See Chapter 59 on the jurisprudence of the European Court of Human Rights.

[110] ECHR (n 7).

[111] *Soering v UK*, App no 14038/88 (1989) Ser A no 161, 11 EHRR 439; *Iorgov v Bulgaria* (2005) 40 EHRR 7; *Mamatkulov and Askarov v Turkey* (2005) 41 EHRR 25; *Öcalan v Turkey* (2005) 41 EHRR 45; see also J. Dugard and C. van den Wyngaert, 'Reconciling Extradition with Human Rights' (1998) 92 *American Journal of International Law* 187, 210ff.

[112] *Waite and Kennedy v Germany*, App no 26083/94 (1999) Ser A 1999-I, 30 EHRR 261; *Al Adsani v United Kingdom* (2002) 34 EHRR 11; *Fogarty v United Kingdom* (2002) 34 EHRR 12; *McElhinney v Ireland* (2002) 34 EHRR 13; *Bosphorus Hava Yollari Turzim ve Ticaret Anonim Sirketi v Ireland* (2006) 42 EHRR 1 (*Bosphorus* case).

public safety, the protection of public order, the prevention of crime, and the protection of the rights and freedoms of others, for example the right to privacy and family life; the right to vote, and the right to property.[113]

Although the ECtHR has on occasion given preference to the obligations under the ECHR above other conflicting treaty obligations, it first attempts to reconcile the different international obligations at stake.[114] Also, the ECtHR has shown itself reticent to engage in incidental review of UNSC resolutions. This was notably the case in the *Behrami* and *Saramati* decisions, where the ECtHR declared a case that could have resulted in a potential conflict between the right to life in Articles 2(1) and 5(1) of the ECHR and obligations resulting from UNSC Resolution 1244 (1999) inadmissible.[115] Given the extraterritorial nature of these cases it is uncertain whether they can serve as precedents for conflicts between UNSC obligations and human rights obligations, which concern events that occurred within the territory of a member state.[116]

A main challenge confronting an international constitutional order that has to rely on decentralized judicial bodies for the enforcement of its core values is that of divergent results. Such divergence is a real risk where the different judicial bodies are confronted with similar norm conflicts involving core values of the international community and other international obligations implies. The different paradigms (institutional biases) between human rights courts on one hand and other functional tribunals or domestic courts on the other may enhance the divergences. Whereas one may expect that a human rights court which was set up to enforce a particular set of human rights obligations would accord a higher status to human rights obligations vis-à-vis other international obligations, the same could not necessarily be expected of (other) functional judicial bodies or national courts that operate within a different paradigm.[117]

Moreover, even in situations where a regional court (other than a regional human rights court) or domestic court gives preference to human rights norms, this would not necessarily be motivated by respect for or deference to the international value system. This is illustrated by the decision of the ECJ in the *Kadi* case, which focused exclusively on (certain aspects of) the EU value system in coming to its decision to grant extensive judicial protection. By refusing to examine if and to what extent this value system overlapped with an international value system and how the latter relates to UNSC resolutions, the ECJ enhanced the perception that an inter-regime normative conflict between the European legal regime and UN security regime indeed existed; a conflict which could only be resolved by protecting either one of the regimes. Stated differently, the Court seemed to have assumed that an international value system applicable to and connecting both the EU and the UN could not be, as a result of which fragmentation would be an unavoidable reality.[118]

[113] *Matthews v United Kingdom*, App no 24833/94 (1999) Ser A 1999-I, 28 EHRR 361; *Slivenko v Latvia* (2004) 39 EHRR 24; *Bosphorus* case (n 112).

[114] Erika de Wet, 'The Emergence of International and Regional Value Systems as a Manifestation of the Emerging International Constitutional Order' (2006) 19 *Leiden Journal of International Law* 611, 618ff.

[115] SC Res 1244 (10 June 1999) UN Doc S/RES/1244; *Behrami v France* (Decision on Admissibility) (2007) 45 EHRR SE10 and *Saramati v France Germany and Norway* (2007) 45 EHRR SE10.

[116] Case C-402/05 *Opinion of Mr AG Poiares Maduro delivered on 16 January 2008. Yassin Abdullah Kadi and Al Barakaat International Foundation v Council of the European Union and Commission of the EC* [2008] ECR I-6351, n 42.

[117] De Wet (n 114), 629.

[118] On a practical level it is also worth mentioning that decentralized judicial enforcement of the international value system can only provide limited relief. The regional or domestic determination that an international human rights obligation would trump any other treaty obligation could not result in an annulment of the international obligation as such. The obligation remains in force on the international level—even if it is not applied on the domestic or regional level—until such a time as it is revoked or by the procedure provided for in the treaty in question.

However, it is possible to take a more positive outlook on these challenges, by arguing that divergent decisions of this kind may be a mere transient phenomenon. Due to the increased dialogue in recent years between domestic, regional, and international courts, decisions on inter-regime conflicts in one judicial body are likely to inform and sharpen the debate regarding similar conflicts in other judicial and also political bodies.[119] The fact that decisions stemming from one regime are not legally binding outside the regime in question (or perhaps even only binding on the parties to the dispute), does not necessarily prevent such decisions from influencing decisions taken within other regimes. Judicial organs are often keen to take note of developments in other jurisdictions, regardless of whether this stems from a concrete legal obligation. As this dialogue is likely to intensify in an era where infringements of human rights increasingly originate from within international organizations, it may in time result in more underlying consensus between the different actors, fewer differences in interpretation, and better acknowledgment of an international value system with human rights protection at its core. Seen from this perspective the current diffuse and potentially fragmentary practice would be of a passing nature and international and domestic courts and tribunals may, in practice, function increasingly as an integrated system.[120]

IV. Conclusion

In the final analysis it is fair to say that the constitutionalization of international law is an incremental process that is occurring in practice in the absence of a formal act of constitution-making.[121] Traditional characteristics of domestic constitutionalism such a normative hierarchy, enforceable individual rights, and judicial review tend to be well developed or developing only within certain functional areas of international law or international organizations, rather than the international legal order as a whole. In particular, the decentralized character of international law poses a challenge for the effective enforcement of even the most fundamental norms of the international constitutional order.[122]

As a result, critics regard attempts to use concepts of domestic constitutionalism as a mechanism for controlling the international exercise of public power as over-ambitious. This argument is also fuelled by the lack of conceptual clarity in the debate pertaining to international constitutionalism and the controversies pertaining to the legitimacy of the value-laden hierarchy of norms in international law. However, supporters of the constitutional paradigm would point out that an imperfect international constitutional order backed by selective and decentralized judicial review would constitute progress and not a problem.[123] It contributes significantly to highlighting the limited ability of the international legal order, at its current stage of development, to control the exercise of public power in a globalized environment. In addition, it encourages and facilitates mechanisms for overcoming such deficits, even if only in an incremental fashion.

[119] Ulfstein (n 20), 141. [120] Ibid 146. [121] Peters (n 9), 599; Klabbers (n 21), 23.
[122] Werner (n 8), 341. [123] Peters (n 93), 350.

Bibliography

Armin von Bogdandy, 'Law and Politics in the WTO—Strategies to Cope with a Deficient Relationship' (2001) 5 *Max Planck Yearbook of United Nations Law* 609

Erika de Wet, 'The International Constitutional Order' (2006) 55 *International and Comparative Law Quarterly* 51

Pierre-Marie Dupuy, 'Some Reflections on Contemporary International Law and the Appeal to Universal Values: A Response to Martii Koskenniemi' (2005) 16 *European Journal of International Law* 131

Jürgen Habermas, 'Hat die Konstitutionalisierung des Völkerrechts noch eine Chance?' in Jürgen Habermas, *Der Gespaltene Westen* (2004)

Andrea Hamann and Helene Ruiz Fabri, 'Transnational Networks and Constitutionalism' (2008) 6 *International Journal of Constitutional Law* 481

Stefan Kadelbach and Thomas Kleinlein, 'Überstaatliches Verfassungsrecht. Zur Konstitutionalisierung im Völkerrecht' (2006) 44 *Archiv des Völkerrechts* 235

Menno T. Kamminga and Martin Scheinin, *The Impact of Human Rights Law on General International Law* (2009)

Hans Kelsen, 'Les rapports de système entre le droit interne et le droit international public' (1926) 14 *Recueil de Cours* 227

Jan Klabbers, Anne Peters, and Geir Ulfstein (eds), *The Constitutionalization of International Law* (2009)

Mattias Knauff, 'Konstitutionalisierung im inner- und Überstaatlichen Recht—Konvergenz oder Divergenz?' (2008) 68 *Zeitschrift für Ausländisches Öffentliches Recht und Völkerrecht* 453

Martti Koskenniemi, 'International Law in Europe: Between Tradition and Renewal' (2005) 16 *European Journal of International Law* 113

Andreas L. Paulus, 'The Emergence of the International Community and the Divide Between International and Domestic Law' in Janne Elisabeth Nijman and André Nollkaemper (eds), *New Perspectives on the Divide between National and International Law* (2007)

Anne-Marie Slaughter, 'The Real New World Order' (1997) 76 *Foreign Affairs* 183

Nicholas Tsagourias (ed), *Transitional Constitutionalism: International and European Models* (2008)

Neil Walker, 'Post-national Constitutionalism and the Problem of Translation' in Joseph H.H. Weiler and Marlene Wind (eds), *European Constitutionalism Beyond the State* (2003)

Christian Walter, 'International Law in a Process of Constitutionalization' in Janne Elisabeth Nijman and André Nollkaemper (eds), *New Perspectives on the Divide Between National and International Law* (2007)

CHAPTER 59

JURISPRUDENCE OF THE EUROPEAN COURT OF HUMAN RIGHTS AND THE CONSTITUTIONAL SYSTEMS OF EUROPE

DEAN SPIELMANN*

Strasbourg

* I am deeply indebted to Nathalie Vaneenoo, for helpful research accomplished during her study visit at the Court. I extend my thanks also to Gabrielle Guillemin and Catherine Brisson of the Research Division of the Court as well as James Brannan of the English Language Division of the Court. I am also grateful to Dr Patrick Kinsch, *Avocat à la Cour* (Luxembourg) and Visiting Professor, University of Luxembourg for helpful feedback on an earlier draft. Any views expressed are personal.

I. Introduction

In the landmark case of *Loizidou v Turkey*, the European Court of Human Rights (ECtHR) referred to 'the Convention as a constitutional instrument of European public order (ordre public)'.[1] Indeed, the European Convention on Human Rights (ECHR), being a treaty of a specific nature, embodies elements of European public order.[2] Admittedly, the purpose of human rights is the same at domestic and international levels. But the possibilities for individuals to rely on human rights in domestic courts are not identical in all states.[3] As Judge Lech Garlicki has observed,

> In all the countries that have adopted the idea of a written constitution, there is a set of constitutional provisions on rights and liberties, and there are mechanisms for the protection and enforcement of those liberties by an independent judiciary [and] the last word in constitutional interpretation is reserved to a separate constitutional court.[4]

But he adds that

> What makes a fundamental difference, however, is the phenomenon of the multidimensionality of constitutional protection. Particularly in the area of human rights, there is a constant process of internationalization: more and more rules, principles, and standards are incorporated in international law instruments and become universally binding all over the world.[5]

Domestic treatment of fundamental rights differs. There are a great variety of constitutional provisions regarding the Convention contained in national texts. Referring to major publications,[6] Giuseppe Martinico points out that there are constitutions that acknowledge the special status of the international human rights treaties or some of those treaties, whereas others are characterized by the acknowledgement of a super-legislative or simply a legislative ranking in the domestic legal order. In any event, constitutional courts have undoubtedly made a fundamental contribution in clarifying the domestic binding force of the Convention, in spite of the divergences as to its status in domestic law.[7]

In this chapter, two main aspects of this multidimensionality in connection with the ECHR will be examined. First, the status of the Convention in domestic legal systems, which remains a question of constitutional law, is scrutinized. Secondly, the status and implementation of the judgments of the Court deserve particular attention. We deliberately leave aside the complex dimension of fundamental rights in the European Union. Suffice it to mention that with the entry into force of the Lisbon Treaty, the EU Charter of Fundamental Rights has become a

[1] *Loizidou v Turkey* (Preliminary Objections), 23 March 1995, para 75, Ser A no 310.

[2] Alexander Orakhelashvili, 'The European Convention of Human Rights and International Public Order' (2002–03) 5 *Cambridge Yearbook of European Legal Studies* 237.

[3] Piet Hein Van Kempen, 'The Protection of Human Rights under National Constitutions and the European Convention: An Incomplete System?' (1996) 3 *Journal of Constitutional Law in Eastern and Central Europe* 225, 226, 227.

[4] Lech Garlicki, 'Cooperation of Courts: The Role of Supranational Jurisdictions in Europe' (2008) 6 *International Journal of Constitutional Law* 509, 509.

[5] Ibid 510. On the internationalization of constitutional law, see further Chapter 56.

[6] Helen Keller and Alec Stone Sweet, 'Assessing the Impact of the ECHR on National Legal Systems' in Helen Keller and Alec Stone Sweet (eds), *A Europe of Rights, The Impact of the ECHR on National Legal Systems* (2009) and Laura Montanari, *I diritti dell'uomo nell'araa europea tra fonti internazionali e fonti interne* (2002).

[7] Giuseppe Martinico, 'National Judges and Supranational Laws: Goals and Structure of the Research' in Giuseppe Martinico and Oreste Pollicino (eds), *The National Judicial Treatment of the ECHR and EU Laws. A Comparative Constitutional Perspective* (2010), 7, 12, 13.

binding instrument, which is to be interpreted, in relation to the corresponding rights of the Convention, in the same way as the Convention rights concerned (Art 52(3)). Moreover, Article 6(2) of the consolidated version of the Treaty on European Union (TEU) now provides that the Union, which succeeded the European Community and has been given legal personality (Arts 1 and 47 TEU), 'shall accede' to the Convention and that consequently fundamental rights will be protected, insofar as most EU member states are concerned, through a triangular set of norms, namely, domestic constitutions, the Charter of Fundamental Rights, and the Convention.

To illustrate the argument in this chapter, four domestic systems, selected for their particular relevance, are highlighted. Three of them have a written constitution (Germany, France, and Belgium) and the fourth, the United Kingdom, has a human rights 'catalogue' (the Human Rights Act 1998) comparable to a constitution. There are many similarities between adjudication under the Convention[8] and adjudication under domestic constitutions.[9] Constitutional adjudication is normally entrusted to the highest courts, be they named constitutional or supreme. Some courts apply the Convention directly, others only apply domestic legal instruments of a constitutional nature. The issue of the Convention's status in the domestic forum is therefore one of great importance and is closely linked to the effect of the Strasbourg judgments.

II. The Status of the European Convention of Human Rights in Domestic Constitutional Systems

1. Introduction

The above-mentioned important characterization by the Court of the Convention 'as a constitutional instrument of European public order' did not imply a radical change of perspective, replacing domestic constitutions by a European catalogue of fundamental rights. It did not even impose any obligation on member states to consider the Convention as a superior legal instrument taking precedence in cases of conflict with domestic norms. As already indicated, the question of the status of the Convention has always been, and undoubtedly remains, a question of constitutional law, specific to each member state, and the Court has always refrained from establishing any stringent principle in this respect. Quite the contrary: In *James and Others v United Kingdom*,[10] the Court made it clear that the Convention did not require its domestic incorporation:

> 84. . . . neither Article 13 nor the Convention in general lays down for the Contracting States any given manner for ensuring within their internal law the effective implementation of any of the provisions of the Convention (see the *Swedish Engine Drivers' Union* judgment of 6 February 1967, Series A no. 20, p. 18, para. 50). Although there is thus no obligation to incorporate the Convention into domestic law, by virtue of Article 1 of the Convention the substance of the rights and freedoms set forth must be secured under the domestic legal order, in some form or another, to everyone within the jurisdiction of the Contracting

[8] On this topic see Steven Greer, 'Constitutionalizing Adjudication under the European Convention on Human Rights' (2003) 23 *Oxford Journal of Legal Studies* 405.

[9] András Sajó, *Limiting Government: An Introduction to Constitutionalism* (1999).

[10] *James and Others v United Kingdom*, 21 February 1986, Ser A no 98.

> States (see the *Ireland v. the United Kingdom* judgment of 18 January 1978, Series A no. 25, p. 91, para. 239)....[11]

However, as Rudolf Bernhardt has emphasized, even if the Convention does not lay down any given manner for ensuring its effective implementation, no state can refer to its domestic law in order to escape obligations derived from the Convention. The Convention, like any other rules of international law, requires that the parties guarantee a certain result—the conformity of their domestic law and practice with conventional duties—but leaves the manner in which the result is achieved to the discretion of all states concerned. International law may have the rank of domestic constitutional law (or an even higher rank), it may have an intermediate position between constitutional and statute law, or it may lack legal validity in domestic law. All the different solutions are, according to the still-prevailing opinion, compatible with the principles of the international order, as long as the conformity of the domestic legal order with the international obligations is the result achieved.[12] The examples of the United Kingdom, Germany, France, and Belgium are particularly eloquent as they illustrate the panoply of solutions. It is submitted that whatever solution is chosen, the overall result is a satisfactory one.

2. The United Kingdom

The United Kingdom has no written constitution and the Convention is not formally incorporated as such. A strict dualist approach in connection with international treaties prevails. But since the Human Rights Act 1998,[13] described as the 'perfect device to allow judicial review of legislation, while retaining the final word for the Parliament itself',[14] which came into force on 2 October 2000, the rights drawn from the Convention are implemented, by virtue of Schedule 1 to the Act, by domestic courts. Significant case law has been developed under the Act since its enactment.[15] Indeed, its purpose is 'to give further effect to the rights and freedoms guaranteed by the Convention'. The Act does not simply give statutory recognition to an international treaty, it creates positive actionable rights based on human rights grounds.[16]

An interesting procedure entrusted to the courts is the declaration of incompatibility pursuant to section 3 of the Human Rights Act.[17] Connor Gearty eloquently describes the said declarations as 'courteous requests for a conversation, not pronouncements of truth from on high'.[18] Section 3(1) requires primary and subordinate legislation to be interpreted in a way which is compatible with Convention rights 'as far as possible'.[19] Indeed, legislation must be read and given effect, insofar as it is possible to do so, in a way which is compatible with the

[11] See Jörg Polakiewicz, 'The Status of the Convention in National Law' in Robert Blackburn and Jörg Polakiewicz (eds), *Fundamental Rights in Europe. The European Convention on Human Rights and its Member States, 1950–2000* (2001), 31–53.

[12] Rudolf Bernhardt, 'The Convention and Domestic Law' in Ronald St J. Macdonald et al (eds), *The European System for the Protection of Human Rights* (1999), 26.

[13] See Francis Geoffrey Jacobs, Robin C.A. White, and Clare Ovey, *The European Convention on Human Rights* (5th edn, 2010), 102–5, with further references.

[14] Conor A. Gearty, *Principles of Human Rights Adjudication* (2004) and *Can Human Rights Survive? The Hamlyn Lectures 2005* (2006) quoted by Cian C. Murphy, 'Report on UK and Ireland' in Martinico and Pollicino (n 7), 489.

[15] For an appraisal see Richard Clayton, 'The Human Rights Act Six Years On: Where Are We Now?' (2007) *European Human Rights Law Review* 11.

[16] Robert Blackburn, 'The United Kingdom' in Blackburn and Polakiewicz (n 11), 960–1.

[17] 'So far as it is possible to do so, primary legislation and subordinate legislation must be read and given effect in a way which is compatible with the Convention rights.'

[18] Gearty (n 14), 96. [19] Murphy (n 14), 488.

Convention rights. If a higher court at or above the level of the High Court or equivalent, as listed in section 4(5) of the Act, finds itself unable to do so in respect of primary legislation, or secondary legislation in respect of which primary legislation prevents the removal of any incompatibility with the Convention rights other than by revocation, it may make a declaration of incompatibility under section 4 of the Act. Such declarations constitute a notification to Parliament that an Act of Parliament is incompatible with the Convention rights. However, essential to this mechanism is that it is a declaration of a non-legal character: it does not affect the 'validity, continuing operation, or enforcement' of the provision in respect of which it is made (s 4(6)(a)).[20] Neither does it bind the parties before the Court (s 4(6)(b)). According to a report of July 2010,[21] since the Human Rights Act came into force, 26 declarations of incompatibility have been made,[22] of which 18 have become final (in whole or in part) and none of which are subject to further appeal. Eight have been overturned on appeal. Of the 18 declarations of incompatibility that have become final, ten have been remedied by later primary legislation, one has been remedied by a remedial order under section 10 of the Human Rights Act, four relate to provisions that had already been remedied by primary legislation at the time of the declaration, and three are under consideration as to how to remedy the incompatibility. As a prominent example,[23] the declaration in *A and Others v Secretary of State for the Home Department* may be mentioned.[24] The case concerned the detention under the Anti-terrorism, Crime and Security Act 2001 of foreign nationals who had been certified by the Secretary of State as suspected international terrorists, and who could not be deported without breaching Article 3. They were detained without charge or trial in accordance with a derogation from Article 5(1) provided by the Human Rights Act 1998 (Designated Derogation) Order 2001. The Human Rights Act 1998 (Designated Derogation) Order 2001 was quashed because it was not a proportionate means of achieving the aim pursued and could not therefore fall within Article 15. Section 23 of the Anti-terrorism, Crime and Security Act 2001 was declared incompatible with Articles 5 and 14 as it was disproportionate and permitted the detention of suspected international terrorists in a way that discriminated on grounds of nationality or immigration

[20] Blackburn (n 16), 963.

[21] Ministry of Justice, *Responding to Human Rights Judgments. Government Response to the Joint Committee on Human Rights' Fifteenth Report of Session 2009–10* (Cm 7892, 2010).

[22] This information was last updated on 13 July 2010. As notable examples the following declarations, amongst them those 'that have survived scrutiny in appeal proceedings', ((sic) Gearty (n 14), 96) should be mentioned in this non-exhaustive list:

R (H) v Mental Health Review Tribunal for the North and East London Region and Secretary of State for Health [2001] EWCA Civ 415; *McR's Application for Judicial Review* [2002] NIQB 58; *International Transport Roth GmbH v Secretary of State for the Home Department* [2002] EWCA Civ 158; *R (Anderson) v Secretary of State for the Home Department* [2002] UKHL 46; *R (D) v Secretary of State for the Home Department* [2002] EWHC 2805 (Admin); *Blood and Tarbuck v Secretary of State for Health*, unreported, 28 February 2003; *Bellinger v Bellinger* [2003] UKHL 21; *R (M) v Secretary of State for Health* [2003] EWHC 1094 (Admin); *A and others v Secretary of State for the Home Department* [2004] UKHL 56; *R (Sylviane Pierrette Morris) v Westminster City Council & First Secretary of State (No 3)* [2005] EWCA Civ 1184; *R (Gabaj) v First Secretary of State*, Administrative Court, unreported, 28 March 2006; *R (Balai and others) v Secretary of State for the Home Department and another* [2006] EWHC 823 (Admin); *R ((1) June Wright (2) Khemraj Jummun (3) Mary Quinn (4) Barbara Gambier) v (1) Secretary of State for Health (2) Secretary of State for Education & Skills* [2006] EWHC 2886 (Admin); *Smith v Scott* [2007] CSIH 9, Registration Appeal Court (Scotland); *Nasseri v Secretary of State for the Home Department* [2007] EWHC 1548 (Admin); *R ((1) F (2) Angus Aubrey Thompson) v Secretary of State for the Home Department* [2008] EWHC 3170 (Admin).

[23] Information about each of the 26 declarations of incompatibility is set out in an annex to the above-mentioned report. See Ministry of Justice (n 21).

[24] [2004] UKHL 56.

status; the provisions were repealed by the Prevention of Terrorism Act 2005, which put in place a new regime of control orders; it came into force on 11 March 2005.[25]

3. Germany

Germany, in conformity with its tradition of a moderately dualist understanding of international law, made the Convention applicable in the national legal order in the form of a non-constitutional federal law.[26] The Convention was incorporated into German law in accordance with Article 59(2) of the Basic Law, which provides that 'Treaties which regulate the political relations of the Federation or relate to matters of federal legislation shall require the consent or participation, in the form of a federal law, of the bodies competent in any specific case for such federal legislation.' The Convention has been assigned the status of federal law, thus overriding all laws enacted by the *Länder*.[27] It has therefore a lower rank than the Constitution, the Basic Law, but has nevertheless binding effect, as applicable statute law, for all organs of the executive and for all courts.[28] As mandatorily applicable statute law, the Convention has a direct effect in this respect. Every German judge and administrative official is bound by it. In the event that national provisions collide with the Convention, they must be interpreted, in accordance with the principle of the German legal system's openness towards international law, in a manner that is compatible with the Convention so that conflicts are avoided.[29] However, the Basic Law's fundamental *reservation of sovereignty* implies the following principle: that the Convention is a federal law that is subordinate to the Constitution and that the Basic Law, in the unlikely event of its provisions conflicting with the Convention, has the final say.[30]

The Federal Constitutional Court decides as to the interpretation and application of the Basic Law. The review of constitutionality of laws (enacted after the entry into force of the Basic Law in 1949) is entrusted, by virtue of Articles 93 and 100 of the Basic Law, to the sole jurisdiction of the Federal Constitutional Court, which enjoys the monopoly of judicial review in this respect.[31] As Jutta Limbach explains, anyone who feels that their fundamental rights have been infringed by the public authorities may lodge a constitutional complaint. It may be directed against a measure of an administrative body, against a decision of a court, or against a statute. Such a complaint requires acceptance for adjudication, which means that, if the alleged infringement of fundamental rights is of special severity or the applicant would suffer a particularly severe detriment from failure to determine the issue, it must be accepted that the complaint is of fundamental constitutional importance. The Federal Constitutional Court itself decides on the prerequisites for acceptance before examining the constitutional complaint. As a further condition, the applicant must have brought his complaint unsuccessfully

[25] Ministry of Justice (n 21). For an appraisal of declarations of incompatibility, see *A and Others v United Kingdom*, App no 3455/05, 19 February 2009 (Grand Chamber), para 158.

[26] Hans-Jürgen Papier, 'Execution and Effects of the Judgments of the European Court of Human Rights from the Perspective of German National Courts' (2006) 27 *Human Rights Law Journal* 1, 1; R. Herzog, 'The Hierarchy of Constitutional Norms and Its Function in the Protection of Basic Rights' (1992) 13 *Human Rights Law Journal* 93.

[27] Andreas Zimmermann, 'Germany' in Blackburn and Polakiewicz (n 11), 337–8 with further references.

[28] Basic Law, Art 20(3).

[29] Papier (n 26), 1.

[30] Ibid 3.

[31] Philipp Cede, 'Report on Austria and Germany' in Martinico and Pollicino (n 7), 65.

before the competent courts, as they are themselves bound to respect the supremacy of the Constitution.[32] But only the Federal Constitutional Court decides on the interpretation and application of the Constitution with final binding force.[33] Although Convention law does not constitute an independent parameter of review for the assessment of constitutionality,[34] it plays an important role for the interpretation of the fundamental rights and intervenes as a tool to support the review in light of the standards guaranteed by the Basic Law.[35] The Federal Constitutional Court has made the Convention a standard of its review where state organs have not taken the Convention into account in a way that is relevant to fundamental rights in spite of their being bound to applicable statute law.[36] Indeed, the Federal Constitutional Court's case law has established a practice according to which the fundamental rights guaranteed by the Basic Law are complemented by an interpretation in conformity with the corresponding (or otherwise relevant) right afforded by the Convention.[37] In its *Görgülü* decision,[38] the Federal Constitutional Court stated in this respect that 'in this [manner, it] is indirectly [acting] in the service of enforcing international law'.[39]

4. France

The status of the Convention, like any other international treaty, is defined by Article 55 of the Constitution, pursuant to which:

> Treaties or agreements duly ratified or approved shall, upon publication, have an authority superior to statutes, provided that the relevant agreement or treaty is applied by the other party.

French courts have, however, been reluctant to apply this principle,[40] as Catherine Dupré points out, in particular concerning the Convention. A notable example is the famous case of 1975 leading to a decision of the Conseil constitutionnel. The applicants claimed that the new and much debated abortion bill was a breach of Article 2 of the Convention. In that case the constitutional judges referred to the reciprocity requirement of Article 55 of the Constitution and set out a distinction between the *contrôle de constitutionnalité*, 'review of constitutionality' (compatibility with the Constitution) and the *contrôle de conventionnalité*, 'review of conventionality' (compatibility with international treaties).[41]

The Conseil stated that whilst review of constitutionality was clearly its express function, reviews of conventionality went beyond its jurisdiction. Consequently, the constitutional

[32] Basic Law, Art 1.

[33] Jutta Limbach, 'The Protection of Human Rights in Germany' in Basil S. Markesinis (ed), *The Coming Together of the Common Law and the Civil Law* (2000), 153. See also Jutta Limbach, 'Inter-jurisdictional Cooperation within the Future Scheme of Protection of Fundamental Rights in Europe' (2000) 21 *Human Rights Law Journal* 333.

[34] BVerfGE 41, 88, at 105.

[35] Cede (n 31), 65.

[36] Papier, (n 26), 2.

[37] Cede (n 31), 62, mentioning BVerfG, 6 May 1997, I BvR 711/96, *Neue Juristische Wochenschrift*, 1997, 2811–2812 or BVerfG, 2 September 2009, I BvR 3171/08. The Federal Constitutional Court also regularly cites the judgments of the ECtHR.

[38] BVerfGE 11, 307 at 328 (2005) 25 *Human Rights Law Journal* 99.

[39] On this important decision see Section III.3 below.

[40] Catherine Dupré, 'France' in Blackburn and Polakiewicz (n 11), 313ff.

[41] Ibid 316.

judges refused to review the 'conventionality' of the abortion bill with reference to the Convention, on the basis that this operation was of a different nature from its usual role of providing constitutional adjudication. Treaties, wrote the constitutional judges, are 'relative and contingent' because they depend on reciprocal application by the parties: they cannot therefore be used as a comparative standard in the same way as the Constitution. It should be noted, however, that three years later the ECtHR rejected any idea of reciprocity in its landmark judgment of *Ireland v United Kingdom*.[42] In this judgment, the ECtHR held for the first time that,

> Unlike international treaties of the classic kind, the Convention comprises more than mere reciprocal engagements between contracting States. It creates, over and above a network of mutual, bilateral undertakings, objective obligations which, in the words of the Preamble, benefit from a 'collective enforcement'.[43]

In any event, the Conseil constitutionnel did not even mention the Convention in its ruling and found the bill to be constitutional on the sole basis of the French Déclaration des Droits de l'Homme et du Citoyen of 1789.[44] Be that as it may, the Convention can nevertheless be considered as a shadow constitution,[45] the French Constitution being an open document featuring the so-called *bloc de constitutionnalité*, permitting integration of the Convention's principles. The Conseil takes into account the provisions of the Convention even if it does not refer to the Convention in its judicial review when monitoring the conformity of national laws to the Convention.[46] As a notable exception, the Conseil's capacity as judge of the procedural propriety of elections should be mentioned. Here the Conseil constitutionnel regularly verifies the compatibility of domestic provisions with the Convention.[47]

As to the superiority principle enshrined in Article 55, French courts have gradually accepted that international treaties prevail over domestic legislation. Indeed, the national courts supervise the conformity of the national laws to the Convention under the *contrôle de conventionnalité*, as opposed to the *contrôle de constitutionnalité*.[48] Comparing the approach of the Conseil constitutionnel to that of the ordinary courts, Noëlle Lenoir explains that, in the very famous judgment *Administration des Douanes v Société Jacques Vabre*,[49] the French Cour de cassation held that Article 95 of the EEC Treaty, prohibiting barriers to competition, prevailed over statutory provisions regulating the taxation of imported coffee even though they had been enacted after the Treaty. Since then the ordinary courts have consistently followed the decision and upheld the primacy of international law over statutes, even where they have been enacted subsequently.[50] The Cour de cassation has regularly mentioned the Convention in its rulings since 1975 and has even examined ex officio the compatibility of French provisions with it. The Conseil d'État, since 1989,[51] has also accepted the direct effect of many Convention provisions.[52] Both Courts are less reluctant to disapply national legislation

[42] *Ireland v United Kingdom*, 18 January 1978, Ser A no 25.
[43] Ibid para 239.
[44] Dupré (n 40), 316.
[45] Martinico (n 7).
[46] Maria Fartunova, 'Report on France' in Martinico and Pollicino (n 7), 207.
[47] Dupré (n 40), 318, 319.
[48] Fartunova (n 46).
[49] *Cour de cassation* (ch mixte), 24 May 1975, *Dalloz*, 1975, 497; [1975] 2 CLMR 336.
[50] Noëlle Lenoir, 'The Response of the French Constitutional Court to the Growing Importance of International Law' in Markesinis (n 33), 164.
[51] *Conseil d'Etat* (ass), 20 October 1989, *Nicolo*, *Recueil*, 190, concl Frydman.
[52] Dupré (n 40), 318.

in order to ensure the primacy and direct effect of European instruments, and in particular, the Convention.

For example, the Cour de cassation, in three judgments delivered on 19 October 2010,[53] stated that the present system of *garde à vue* (police custody) did not meet the requirements of Article 6 as interpreted by the ECtHR, and that to conform with those requirements, the following principles had to be respected:

- the right to a lawyer should be restricted only where there are compelling reasons for doing so, based on the circumstances of the case and not merely on the nature of the offence;
- detainees have to be informed of their right to remain silent;
- detainees have to be given the assistance of a lawyer in conditions which enable them to organize their defence and prepare, with the lawyer, for any questioning. The lawyer should be able to attend the police interview.[54]

Concerning the applicability of the provisions of the ECHR, the case law of the Conseil d'État is equally relevant. As Maria Fartunova[55] explains, the Conseil d'État takes into account in judicial review proceedings Articles 8 and 6 of the Convention.[56] Any conflict between the Convention and the Constitution is, however, resolved in favour of the latter.[57]

An interesting procedure was introduced in 2008. With the constitutional revision of 23 July 2008,[58] Article 61-1 of the French Constitution now entrusts the Conseil constitutionnel with the competence of delivering preliminary rulings:

> If, during proceedings before a court of law, it is claimed that a statutory provision infringes the rights and freedoms guaranteed by the Constitution, the matter may be referred by the Conseil d'État or by the Cour de cassation, within a determined period, to the Conseil constitutionnel.[59]

Maria Fartunova explains that this important procedure provides that an application for a priority preliminary ruling on the issue of constitutionality (*question prioritaire de constitutionnalité*) entails the right of any person who is involved in legal proceedings before a court to argue that a statutory provision infringes rights and freedoms guaranteed by the Constitution.

[53] No 5699 (12-82.902), no 5700 (10-82.306), and no 5701 (10-82.051).

[54] I am grateful to Paul Harvey, lawyer at the Registry of the Court for valuable information and the translation into the English language of the principles decided by the Cour de cassation.

[55] Fartunova (n 46).

[56] Conseil d'État (ass), 30 November 2001, M. Diop and Conseil d'État, 9 February 2007, M. Gardedieu. See, however, for a refusal of the Conseil d'État to take into account the case law of the ECtHR concerning the position of the *commissaire du gouvernement*, see Conseil d'État, 29 July 1998, M. Esclatine, and compare with *Reinhardt and Slimane-Kaïd v France*, 31 March 1998, Reports of Judgments and Decisions 1998-II.

[57] Conseil d'État (ass), 30 October 1998, MM. Sarran, Levacher, and ors, and Cour de cassation (ass plén), 2 June 2000, Mlle Fraisse. Both decisions are mentioned by Fartunova (n 46).

[58] Loi constitutionnelle no 2008-724 du 23 juillet 2008 de modernisation des institutions de la Ve République, Official Journal, 24 July 2008. On that law, see among many articles, Paul Tavernier, 'Le Conseil constitutionnel français et la Convention européenne des droits de l'homme', *Droits fondamentaux*, January 2008–December 2009.

[59] 'Lorsque à l'occasion d'une instance en cours devant une juridiction, il est soutenu qu'une disposition législative porte atteinte aux droits et libertés que la Constitution garantit, le Conseil constitutionnel peut être saisi de cette question sur renvoi du Conseil d'État ou de la Cour de cassation qui se prononce dans un délai déterminé.'

The Constitutional Act no 2009-1523 of 10 December 2009 concerning the application of Article 61-1 of the Constitution has given priority status to the issue of constitutionality. According to this author, this means first that, when it is raised before a court of first instance or a court of appeal, the issue must be addressed without delay. The time devoted to dealing with the preliminary ruling should not delay the overall proceedings. Secondly, when the Court is asked to rule on arguments challenging both the constitutionality of a statute (preliminary ruling on the issue of constitutionality) and the failure of the said statute to comply with international treaties and agreements (plea of failure to comply with international obligations) the Court is required to address the issue of constitutionality as a priority. The new procedure came into force on 1 March 2010.[60]

Lodging an action before a judicial or an administrative court to assert constitutional rights by means of the priority constitutional reference is not a *direct action* as only supreme courts like the Cour de cassation or the Conseil d'État may put this type of question to the Conseil constitutionnel. It is nonetheless submitted that this modification reinforces the harmonization between constitutional norms and European conventional norms, as is shown by the recent decision of the Conseil constitutionnel of 30 July 2010,[61] concerning the rules of criminal procedure in the context of *garde à vue* (police custody). The Conseil constitutionnel held as follows:

> 25.... Police custody remains a measure of constraint necessary for certain operations of the criminal investigation police. The above-mentioned evolutions [in the use of police custody] must, however, be accompanied by suitable guarantees as regards recourse to this measure and the manner in which it is conducted, such as to ensure the protection of the rights of the defence.
>
> ...
>
> 28.... [the relevant provision of the Code of Criminal Procedure] does not allow the person undergoing questioning, and held against his will, to have the benefit of effective assistance from a lawyer. Such a restriction on the rights of the defence is imposed in a general manner without any consideration of particular circumstances likely to justify the measure, in order to collect or conserve evidence or ensure the protection of persons. The person taken into police custody is, moreover, not informed of his right to remain silent.
>
> 29. In such conditions, [the relevant provisions of the Code of Criminal Procedure] do not offer suitable guarantees as to the use made of police custody, taking into account the above-mentioned evolutions. The reconciling on the one hand of the need to prevent breaches of the peace and seek out offenders with, on the other hand, the need to ensure the exercise of constitutionally guaranteed freedoms, can no longer be considered to be balanced. Thus these provisions fail to comply with Articles 9 and 16 of the Declaration of 1789 and must therefore be held to be unconstitutional.

The Conseil constitutionnel also held that the finding of unconstitutionality would take effect on 1 July 2011. Even though the implementation of those principles was postponed until 1 July 2011, to give the legislature time to pass a new law, the example of effective assistance by a lawyer during *garde à vue*—examined by the Conseil constitutionnel under the principles of fundamental constitutional rights and by the Cour de cassation under the principles governed by the ECHR and its interpretation by the ECtHR[62]—shows that provisions of the Convention as

[60] Fartunova (n 46), 217.

[61] Conseil constitutionnel, Dec no 2010-14/22 QPC (*Daniel W et al*).

[62] See eg *Salduz v Turkey*, App no 36391/02, 27 November 2008 (Grand Chamber); *Panovits v Cyprus*, App no 4268/04, 11 December 2008.

well as constitutional principles override domestic legislation, albeit subject to legislative change, and may lead to an identical result.

5. Belgium

Unlike France, the Belgian Constitution does not contain a provision regarding the relationship between international and national law.[63] In Belgium, the status of the Convention as superior law has had a long tradition since the ruling of the Cour de cassation in *Fromagerie Franco-Suisse 'Le Ski'* of 27 May 1971 deciding that international law prevails over domestic law.[64] Indeed, as Andrew Drzemczewski notes, it may be assumed that directly applicable provisions of *all* international agreements will be given primacy over conflicting national legislation irrespective of the date of enactment of the statute in question. He sums up the principles as follows. The conflict which exists between a rule of law established by an international treaty and a rule of law established by a subsequent statute is not a conflict between two statutes. The rule, according to which a law repeals the earlier law insofar as the two conflict, is not applicable in the case of a treaty conflicting with a law. When the conflict is one between a rule of domestic law and a rule of international law having direct effects within the domestic legal order, the rule established by the treaty must prevail; its pre-eminence follows from the very nature of international treaty law. It follows from the preceding considerations that the Court has the duty to reject the application of the provisions of domestic law that are contrary to this provision of the treaty. The courts are competent to review the compatibility of any statute with those provisions of a treaty considered to have direct effect in Belgian law if the law is compatible with the treaty provisions.[65]

The ordinary courts, including the highest administrative court, the Conseil d'État, have applied those principles in their constant case law.[66] According to recent case law, the Convention even prevails over the Belgian Constitution.[67]

But conflicts between the Constitution and the Convention are very rare. The Belgian legislature even attempts to streamline both sets of guarantees, as shown by the example of privacy, governed by Article 22 of the Belgian Constitution and Article 8 of the Convention. When introducing the right to privacy, the constitutional lawmaker tried to ensure concordance with Article 8 of the Convention in order to avoid disputes regarding the content of the respective provisions.[68]

The Belgian Constitutional Court, formerly the Cour d'Arbitrage, has since its creation in 1984 insisted on strict observance of the provisions of the Convention and of the interpretations given by the ECtHR. Basically, the Constitutional Court delivers a posteriori rulings, after having been seized directly by public authorities or individuals, as to the compatibility of legislative acts with the Constitution. If an incompatibility is found the relevant Act is annulled. However, a case may also be referred to the Constitutional Court by ordinary courts which request a preliminary ruling. If the Court finds an incompatibility with the Constitution, the relevant norm is set aside in this particular case, but not annulled. It should be noted that a

[63] Patricia Popelier, 'Report on Belgium' in Martinico and Pollicino (n 7), 83.

[64] Pasicrisie belge, 1971, I, 886-920; Journal des Tribunaux, 1971, 471–4; (1972) CMLR 330–76.

[65] Andrew Drzemczewski, *European Human Rights Convention in Domestic Law* (1983), 65–6.

[66] Numerous examples are provided by Olivier de Schutter and Sébastien van Drooghenbroek, *Droit international des droits de l'homme devant le juge national* (1999).

[67] Cour de cassation (2nd ch), 9 November 2004, Journal des Tribunaux, 2004, 856–8. See, however, for a contrary view Francis Delpérée, *Le droit constitutionnel de la Belgique* (2000), 686, no 802.

[68] Popelier (n 63).

specific filtering procedure allows the Court to declare inadmissible applications that are manifestly ill-founded or not compatible with other admissibility requirements.

The Constitutional Court has pronounced many judgments concerning the rights guaranteed by the Convention, and its jurisprudence has always been in accordance with that of the ECtHR.[69] Through a creative interpretation method, the Court has linked the rights of the Convention to Articles 10 and 11 of the Constitution governing the principles of equality and non-discrimination.[70] Applying the principles of equality and proportionality, the Court has incorporated through its case law the substantive provisions of the Convention in its reasoning. Since 2003, the Court's competence has been formally extended to include direct review of legislative acts as to their compatibility with the rights laid down in Title II of the Belgian Constitution.[71] A recent amendment to the Special Law on the Constitutional Court introduced (in 2009) the obligation for the courts to lodge a preliminary reference before the Constitutional Court if a party to the proceedings alleges a violation of a fundamental right, protected both under the Constitution and the Convention or any other international or supranational norm (Art 26 of the Special Law of 6 January 1989 on the Constitutional Court amended by the Special Law of 12 July 2009). However, a court is exempted from this if an international court has already decided upon the issue. If the Constitutional Court upholds the law in the light of the Constitution, the referring court is still free to examine the law in the light of the international norm.[72]

III. The Status and Implementation of the Judgments of the European Court of Human Rights

1. Introduction

Pursuant to Article 46(1) of the Convention, 'The High Contracting Parties undertake to abide by the final judgment of the Court in any case to which they are parties'. In the judgment of *Verein gegen Tierfabriken Schweiz (VgT) v Switzerland (No 2)*,[73] the ECtHR held as follows:

> 85. As regards the requirements of Article 46, it should first be noted that a respondent State found to have breached the Convention or its Protocols is under an obligation to abide by the Court's decisions in any case to which it is a party. In other words, a total or partial failure to execute a judgment of the Court can engage the State Party's international responsibility. The State Party in question will be under an obligation not just to pay those concerned the sums awarded by way of just satisfaction, but also to take individual and/or, if appropriate, general measures in its domestic legal order to put an end to the violation found by the Court and to redress the effects, the aim being to put the applicant, as far as possible, in the position he would have been in had the requirements of the Convention not been disregarded (see, among many other authorities, *Scozzari and Giunta v. Italy* [GC], nos. 39221/98 and 41963/98, § 249, ECHR 2000-VIII, and *Assanidze v. Georgia* [GC], no. 71503/01, § 198, ECHR 2004-II).

[69] Silvio and Phillipe Marcus-Helmons, 'Belgium' in Blackburn and Polakiewicz (n 11), 179.

[70] Popelier (n 63) mentioning judgment nos 16/91 of 13 June 1991, 20/94 of 10 February 1994, and 60/2007 of 18 April 2007.

[71] See for details Marc Uyttendaele, *Précis de droit constitutionnel belge. Regards sur un système institutionnel paradoxal* (2005), 587.

[72] Popelier (n 63), 93.

[73] App no 32772/02, 30 June 2009 (Grand Chamber).

> 86. These obligations reflect the principles of international law whereby a State responsible for a wrongful act is under an obligation to make restitution, consisting in restoring the situation which existed before the wrongful act was committed, provided that restitution is not 'materially impossible' and 'does not involve a burden out of all proportion to the benefit deriving from restitution instead of compensation' (Article 35 of the Draft Articles of the International Law Commission on Responsibility of States for Internationally Wrongful Acts—see paragraph 36 above). In other words, while restitution is the rule, there may be circumstances in which the State responsible is exempted fully or in part from this obligation, provided that it can show that such circumstances obtain.

The Court also observed:

> 88. . . . subject to monitoring by the Committee of Ministers, the respondent State in principle remains free to choose the means by which it will discharge its obligations under Article 46 § 1 of the Convention, provided that such means are compatible with the conclusions set out in the Court's judgment (see *Scozzari and Giunta*, cited above, § 249, and *Lyons and Others*, cited above). However, in certain special circumstances the Court has found it useful to indicate to a respondent State the type of measures that might be taken to put an end to the situation—often a systemic one—which has given rise to the finding of a violation (see, for example, *Öcalan v. Turkey*, no. 46221/99, § 210 *in fine*, ECHR 2005-IV; *Broniowski*, cited above, § 194; and *Popov v. Russia*, no. 26853/04, § 263, 13 July 2006). Sometimes, the nature of the violation does not even leave any choice as to the measures to be taken (see *Assanidze*, cited above, § 202).

Supervision of judgments is entrusted to the Committee of Ministers of the Council of Europe, a political body. There are three parts to the implementation of a judgment of the Court, the payment of *just satisfaction* and other *individual measures* required to put the applicant as far as possible in the position he would have been in had the breach not occurred, and *general measures* required to prevent the breach happening again, or to put to an end breaches that still continue.

The question as to the effect beyond the particular case raises a different issue. Already in 1993, Georg Ress had insisted on a clear-cut trend—less strictly from the 'legal' than from the practical side—for national courts to adapt their decisions to the interpretations furnished by the Court.[74] Admittedly, even though he acknowledged that a commitment along the lines of a *stare decisis* principle to the interpretation recommended by the Court cannot be demonstrated, he rightly stressed the importance of complying with the rulings in order to pre-empt any future finding of a violation by the Court.[75] Indeed, a European Court judgment contains clarification of the obligations of the Convention over and above the individual case, and thus also significantly indicates to member states how they can guarantee the effective application of the Convention in their domestic law.[76] President Jean-Paul Costa has referred in this respect to the notion of *de facto erga omnes* effect of Strasbourg judgments[77] and the Court in *Opuz v Turkey*[78] clearly stated that,

[74] Georg Ress, 'The Effects of Judgments and Decisions of Domestic Law' in Macdonald (n 12), 810.

[75] Ibid.

[76] Ibid.

[77] See President Costa's Foreword to the 2008 Annual Report of the European Court of Human Rights; see also Elisabet Fura-Sandström, 'Amplifying the Effect of the Court's Case-law in the States Parties', in Council of Europe Steering Committee for Human Rights (CDDH), *Reforming the European Convention on Human Rights: A Work in Progress* (2009), 511.

[78] *Opuz v Turkey*, App no 33401/02, 9 June 2009.

> In carrying out this scrutiny, and bearing in mind that the Court provides final authoritative interpretation of the rights and freedoms defined in Section I of the Convention, the Court will consider whether the national authorities have sufficiently taken into account the principles flowing from its judgments on similar issues, even when they concern other States.[79]

Moreover, it is submitted that the so-called pilot judgment procedure is a major development as to the broader effect of judgments[80] as it represents a reaction to 'systemic violations', that is, situations in which repetitive violations of individual rights result from a general, legislative, and/or administrative environment and affect a significant number of persons.[81] Pilot judgments undoubtedly

> contain, by definition, a 'constitutional' component, addressing a problem and not only a singular violation. That coexistence of individual and systemic components demonstrates the dual nature of pilot judgments and, perhaps, illustrates a more general evolution of the European Court of Human Rights towards a constitutional court.[82]

Indeed, as Judge Lech Garlicki has emphasized, 'the very idea of the system is that the Convention should be applied by the national authorities (domestic courts) in a way which assures an effective protection of human rights.'[83] In connection with this goal, he identifies three scenarios of interaction between the ECtHR and domestic courts. According to him, two scenarios can be described as scenarios of cooperation, in which the positions of the ECtHR and of the domestic courts become identical or—at least—similar, the 'first move' or inspiration originating either in Strasbourg or in a member state. The rule is not without exceptions and consequently a scenario of conflict may surface.[84] Scrutiny of the practice in the four domestic systems identified shows the accuracy of the said scenarios.

2. The United Kingdom

In its 2009–10 report the Joint Committee on Human Rights deplored some very lengthy delays in the implementation of certain judgments. Individual measures, like the payment of just satisfaction, are sometimes delayed, as has been acknowledged in the government's response to this report.[85] Of greater interest is the attitude of UK judges towards the principles decided in Strasbourg. Section 2(1) of the Human Rights Act 1998 requires courts 'to take into account' any judgment of the ECtHR in determining any question to which such judgment is relevant.

In a nutshell, the status of the judgments of the ECtHR can best be described, as Eric Metcalff has eloquently done in a recent article, by the 'mirror principle'.[86] In *Ullah*,[87] Lord Bingham

[79] Ibid para 163.

[80] The first pilot judgment goes back to 2004. *Broniowski v Poland*, App no 31443/96, ECHR 2004-V (Grand Chamber).

[81] Lech Garlicki, 'Broniowski and After: On the Dual Nature of "Pilot Judgments"' in Lucius Caflisch et al (eds), *Liber Amicorum Luzius Wildhaber, Human Rights—Strasbourg Views* (2007), 191.

[82] Ibid 192.

[83] Lech Garlicki, 'Some Observations on Relations between the ECtHR and the Domestic Jurisdictions' in Julia Iliopoulos-Strangas (ed), *Cours suprêmes nationales et cours européennes: Concurrence ou collaboration?: In Memoriam Louis Favoreu* (2007), 305.

[84] Ibid 307.

[85] Ministry of Justice (n 21).

[86] Eric Metcalff, '"Free to Lead as Well as to be Led": Section 2 of the HRA and Relationship between the UK Courts and Strasbourg' (2010) 1 *Justice Journal* 22, quoting Jonathan Lewis, 'The European Ceiling on Human Rights' (2007) *Public Law* 720.

[87] *Ullah v Special Adjudicator* [2004] UKHL 26.

expressed the view that, absent good reasons to the contrary, a claimant in a British court can expect to obtain the same result as he or she would in Strasbourg: 'no more, but certainly no less'.[88] In general, courts follow the Strasbourg rulings, especially Grand Chamber judgments involving the United Kingdom where the ruling is clear on its terms, but in a small number of cases, UK courts have judged Strasbourg rulings too unclear to implement, the most notable example being the case of *Horncastle*[89] concerning a departure from the ECtHR's case law as to anonymous witnesses.[90] Yet, as Lord Hope has put it recently, determining in the affirmative the question whether the Supreme Court should follow the ECtHR's judgment in *Salduz*:[91]

> 45. The starting point is section 2(1) of the Human Rights Act 1998, which provides that a court which is determining a question which has arisen in connection with a Convention right must 'take into account' any decision of the Strasbourg court. The United Kingdom was not a party to the decision in *Salduz* nor did it seek to intervene in the proceedings. As the Lord Justice General observed in *McLean*, para 29, the implications for the Scottish system cannot be said to have been carefully considered. But in *R (Alconbury Developments Ltd) v Secretary of State for the Environment, Transport and the Regions* [2001] UKHL 23, [2003] 2 AC 295, para 26, Lord Slynn of Hadley said that the court should follow any clear and constant jurisprudence of the Strasbourg court. And in *R (Anderson) v Secretary of State for the Home Department* [2002] UKHL 46, [2003] 1 AC 837, para 18, Lord Bingham of Cornhill said the court will not without good reason depart from the principles laid down in a carefully considered judgment of the court sitting as a Grand Chamber. In *R v Spear* [2002] UKHL 31, [2003] 1 AC 734, on the other hand, the House refused to apply a decision of the Third Section because, as Lord Bingham explained in para 12, they concluded that the Strasbourg court had materially misunderstood the domestic legal context in which courts martial were held under United Kingdom law. And in *R v Horncastle* [2009] UKSC 14, [2010] 2 WLR 47 this court declined to follow a line of cases in the Strasbourg court culminating in a decision of the Fourth Section because, as Lord Phillips explained in para 107, its case law appeared to have been developed largely in cases relating to the civil law without full consideration of the safeguards against an unfair trial that exist under the common law procedure.[92]

UK courts are cautious in extending Strasbourg jurisprudence too far in marginal cases, but sometimes they anticipate the developments in circumstances where the ECtHR has yet to rule.[93] It should be added that section 2 of the Human Rights Act does not displace the normal

[88] Ibid para 20:

> [Lord Slynn's statement in *Alconbury*] reflects the fact that the Convention is an international instrument, the correct interpretation of which can be authoritatively expounded only by the Strasbourg court. From this it follows that a national court subject to a duty such as that imposed by section 2 should not without strong reason dilute or weaken the effect of the Strasbourg case law. It is indeed unlawful under section 6 of the 1998 Act for a public authority, including a court, to act in a way which is incompatible with a Convention right. It is of course open to member states to provide for rights more generous than those guaranteed by the Convention, but such provision should not be the product of interpretation of the Convention by national courts, since the meaning of the Convention should be uniform throughout the states party to it. The duty of national courts is to keep pace with the Strasbourg jurisprudence as it evolves over time: no more, but certainly no less.

[89] [2009] UKSC 14.

[90] *Al-Khawaja and Tahery v United Kingdom*, App nos 26766/05 and 22228/06, 20 January 2009. This case is pending before the Grand Chamber pursuant to a referral.

[91] *Salduz v Turkey*, App no 36391/02, 27 November 2008 (Grand Chamber).

[92] *Cadder v Her Majesty's Advocate (Scotland)* [2010] UKSC 43, per Lord Hope (with whom Lord Mance agreed).

[93] See eg concerning destitution of asylum seekers contrary to Art 3 of the Convention, *R v Secretary of State for the Home Department, ex p Limbuela* [2005] UKHL 66; concerning the margin of appreciation to be afforded to in respect of discrimination between married and unmarried couples (arrogation by the

operation of *stare decisis*. Indeed, lower courts remain bound to follow the decisions of higher courts, even where they are inconsistent with subsequent Strasbourg authority.[94]

3. Germany

It is admitted that, even though the judgments of the ECtHR do not, legally speaking, have *erga omnes* effect, the interpretation chosen by the ECtHR in a particular case has a de facto relevance for the subsequent application of the domestic law in all similar pending or parallel cases.[95] If such an interpretation 'in conformity' with the domestic statutes is possible, the ECtHR's interpretation is considered relevant. The limitation to this principled openness occurs if the domestic law does not allow an interpretation 'in conformity' (ie, the case has already become final or the wording of the statute is inconsistent with Strasbourg interpretation).[96] It should be noted also that, since 1998, reopening of criminal proceedings has been possible after delivery of a judgment of the ECtHR, under Article 359 of the Code of Criminal Procedure. Since 2006 a similar provision has been enacted concerning civil proceedings.[97]

Concerning the status and implementation of the judgments of the ECtHR, the well-known *Görgülü* saga is of particular interest. The case concerned a denial of custody and access rights for the biological father in respect of a child born out of wedlock. The applicant in this case was a father whose son was living with foster parents and who had been denied the right to see his child on a regular basis by the competent Regional Court of Appeal. The ECtHR decided that the decision of the German court was contrary to the provisions of the Convention. In particular, it held that the denial of custody and access rights infringed the right to respect for family life guaranteed under Article 8 of the Convention.[98] However, the Regional Court of Appeal upheld its decision and argued that the judgment of the ECtHR had no effect in the domestic legal order and was thus not binding for the individual courts.[99] This refusal to implement the Strasbourg judgment was subsequently challenged before the Federal Constitutional Court which held[100] that decisions of the ECtHR were binding on domestic courts, but that this binding effect was not unconditional. The Federal Constitutional Court first ruled that being bound by statute and law (Art 20(3) of the Basic Law; *Grundgesetz*—GG) includes taking into account the guarantees of the ECHR and the decisions of the ECtHR according to the canons of justifiable interpretation of the law. Both a failure to consider a decision of the ECtHR and the 'enforcement' of such a decision in an automatic way, in violation with superior law, may violate fundamental rights in conjunction with the principle of the rule of law. Secondly, the Federal

courts of this margin to themselves rather than to Parliament, *Re G (Adoption: Unmarried Couple)* [2008] UKHL 38; and regarding expulsion of individuals (a mother and a daughter) to a country where there would be a breach of the Art 8 rights, *EM (Lebanon)* [2008] UKHL 64. See also Lady Hale's speech of 4 June 2010 to the Salford Human Rights Conference, available at <http://www.supremecourt.gov.uk/docs/speech_100604.pdf>.

94 Metcalff (n 86), 10. See eg *R (C) v Commissioner of the Police of the Metropolis* [2010] WLR (D) 193. When faced with conflicting authorities from the ECtHR and the House of Lords (now the Supreme Court) on the indefinite retention of DNA profiles and fingerprints by the police, the Divisional Court held that they were bound to follow the House of Lords.

95 Cede (n 31), 69.

96 Ibid 70.

97 Ibid 71.

98 *Görgülü v Germany*, App no 74969/01, 26 February 2004.

99 Niels Petersen, *The Reception of International Law by Constitutional Courts through the Prism of Legitimacy*, Reprint of the Max Planck Institute for Research on Collective Goods (2009), 21.

100 BVerfGE 11, 307 at 328; (2005) 25 *Human Rights Law Journal* 99.

Constitutional Court held that, in taking into account the decisions of the ECtHR, the state bodies must include the effects on the national legal system in their application of the law. This applies in particular when the relevant national law is a balanced partial system of domestic law that is intended to achieve an equilibrium between competing fundamental rights.[101]

This decision of the Federal Constitutional Court[102] contains an important caveat, the so-called all-effects caveat (*Auswirkungsvorbehalt*). As Dagmar Richter has rightly explained,

> According to this caveat, German courts must consider all effects that a decision of an international court might possibly entail within the German legal order, particularly with respect to those subsystems of the German legal system which are thoughtfully designed to balance conflicting basic rights. German courts and authorities should thus defend German sovereignty…against international judgments particularly in cases in which not all of the parties to the court procedure have also been parties to the international court procedure or in which extending the individual rights of one person necessarily reduces the rights of others (mehrpolige Grundrechtsverhältnisse).[103]

According to Judge Lech Garlicki, the Federal Constitutional Court confirmed, in principle, the authority of the ECtHR's judgments. But he correctly adds that the position of the Federal Constitutional Court seems to be clear: while the domestic courts are under an obligation to give full effect to the judgments of the ECtHR, they should also avoid situations in which implementation of a Strasbourg judgment would result in violation of constitutionally protected rights of the other parties to the original dispute.[104] A more critical comment has been made by Jens Meyer-Ladewig,[105] for whom the reasoning of the Federal Constitutional Court in this respect is 'misleading and superfluous' and difficult to reconcile with Article 46(1) of the Convention.[106]

[101] Unofficial translation by the Secretariat General of the German Federal Constitutional Court, revised by the editors of the *Human Rights Law Journal.*

[102] For comments, see among many articles: Rainer Hofmann, 'The German Federal Constitutional Court and Public International Law: New Decisions, New Approaches?' (2004) 47 *German Yearbook of International Law* 9; Dagmar Richter, 'Does International Jurisprudence Matter in Germany?—The Federal Constitutional Court's New Doctrine of 'Factual Precedent' (2006) 49 *German Yearbook of International Law* 51; Papier (n 26); Frank Hoffmeister, 'Germany: Status of European Convention on Human Rights in Domestic Law' (2006) 4 *International Journal of Constitutional Law* 722; Jens Meyer-Ladewig, 'The German Federal Constitutional Court and the Binding Force of Judgments of the European Court of Human Rights under Art 46 ECHR' in Hanno Hartig (ed), *Trente ans de droit européen des droits de l'homme: Etudes à la mémoire de Wolfgang Strasser* (2007), 215; Jörg Gerkrath, 'L'effet contraignant des arrêts de la Cour européenne des droits de l'homme vu à travers le prisme de la Cour constitutionnelle allemande' (2006) *Revue trimestrielle des droits de l'homme* 712.

[103] Richter (n 102), 65. Another example of multipolar fundamental rights relations occurred in the case of *Von Hannover v Germany*, App no 59320/00, ECHR 2004-VI. Hofmann (n 102) argues that

> the criteria developed in the jurisprudence of the First Senate of the FCC to balance conflicting fundamental rights in cases involving the right to privacy, on the one hand, and the freedom of the press, on the other hand, are finely tuned and indeed result in such equilibrium; but it must also be stressed that these criteria are not the only ones which achieve such equilibrium, which is also obtained by the criteria developed by the ECtHR in its judgment in the *Caroline of Monaco* Case. So, in a situation where the judgment of the ECtHR results in equilibrium, to leave it to the courts whether and to what extent they are prepared to accept a binding effect of an ECtHR judgment, and to open the risk of a clear violation of Germany's treaty obligations, is not acceptable.

[104] Garlicki (n 4), 521 and in a similar vein concerning the difficulty of implementing Strasbourg judgments in 'multipolar legal relations in connection with the fundamental rights issues', Papier (n 26), 3.

[105] Meyer-Ladewig (n 102), 224.

[106] Ibid 222–5, and compare with Hofmann (n 102), who, as mentioned in n 103, finds it unacceptable that, in a situation where the judgment of the ECtHR results in equilibrium, to leave it to the courts to decide whether and to what extent they are prepared to accept the binding effect of an ECtHR judgment.

4. France

In principle, French ordinary courts tend to comply 'spontaneously' with the ECtHR by following its case law[107] and generally the judgments of the ECtHR lead to amendment of legislation if need be.[108] As Maria Fartunova explains, since the first judgment of the Court delivered in a case concerning France,[109] French legislation has been amended as a result of the condemnation of France by the ECtHR.[110] Examples include cases concerning the duration of detention on remand,[111] restrictive inheritance rights of adulterine children,[112] length of proceedings before administrative courts,[113] and the structure of administrative jurisdictions.[114] The position of the Conseil constitutionnel is more nuanced. It should first be noted that, as Maria Fartunova observed,[115] the Conseil has never been asked to look into any conflict between the Convention and the Constitution. Its position, adopted in 1975, namely that it has no jurisdiction to ensure the precedence of international norms over national laws on the basis of Article 55, has not changed. The Conseil nevertheless takes European instruments into account in its judicial review when there is a concomitance between the rights guaranteed by the Constitution and the rights guaranteed under the Convention. As examples, the guarantees in the field of criminal procedure,[116] rights of defence,[117] freedom of expression,[118] and the principle of non-discrimination[119] are mentioned. The Conseil has also made a significant contribution in the field of positive obligations and as Maria Fartunova stresses, the Conseil constitutionnel takes into account the provisions of the Convention in its decisions even if it does not refer to the Convention in its judicial review when monitoring the conformity of national laws to the Constitution.[120] As Noëlle Lenoir points out, the Conseil's case law on the relationship with international law is evolving. The Conseil has gradually clarified the scope and legal force of Article 55 of the Constitution[121] and in terms of substance, it is increasingly inclined to follow the reasoning techniques of international courts such as that of Strasbourg, in particular as regards fundamental rights. The decisions of the ECtHR have had a spectacular impact on the decisions of the Conseil, even though this may sometimes be imperceptible. But, according to Noëlle Lenoir, the originality of the French situation lies in the fact that the Conseil constitutionnel does not indicate where it has been inspired by international law in general and the decisions of the international courts in particular. More and more frequently, it defines and interprets the rights and freedoms secured by the Constitution by

[107] See Martine Fabre and Annie Gouron-Mazel, *Convention européenne des droits de l'homme. Application par le juge français* (1998).

[108] See Section II.4 above, the three judgments of the Cour de cassation of 19 October 2010 (no 5699 (12-82.902), no 5700 (10-82.306), and no 5701 (10-82.051)).

[109] *Bozano v France*, 18 December 1986, Ser A no 111.

[110] Fartunova (n 46), 207.

[111] Following the judgment in *Muller v France*, 17 March 1997, Reports of Judgments and Decisions 1997-II.

[112] Following the judgment in *Mazurek v France*, App no 34406/97, ECHR 2000-II.

[113] Following the judgment in *Beaumartin v France*, 24 November 1994, Ser A no 296-B.

[114] Following the judgment in *Kress v France*, App no 39594/98, ECHR 2001-VI (Grand Chamber).

[115] Fartunova (n 46), 207.

[116] Conseil constitutionnel, Dec no 88-248 DC, 17 January 1989 (*CSA*).

[117] Conseil constitutionnel, Dec no 80-127 DC, 19 and 20 January 1981 (*Sécurité et liberté*); Conseil constitutionnel, Dec no 89-260 DC, 28 July 1989 (*COB*). In this latter decision, the Conseil referred to the interpretation given by the ECtHR in *Delcourt v Belgium* (17 January 1970, Ser A no 11). *Adde*, Conseil constitutionnel, Dec no 2010-14/22 QPC, 30 July 2010 (*Daniel W et al*). See Section II.4 above.

[118] Conseil constitutionnel, Dec no 84-181 DC, 10 and 11 October 1984 (*Entreprise de presse*). The Conseil referred to *Handyside v United Kingdom*, 7 December 1976, Ser A no 24.

[119] According to Fartunova (n 46), the Conseil has adopted a different approach to that of the ECtHR.

[120] Ibid 212.

[121] See Section II.4 above.

reference—implicitly—to the ECHR and the case law of the ECtHR. As already mentioned, the Conseil has accordingly incorporated into the set of constitutional rules it applies (the '*bloc de constitutionnalité*'), principles that are not expressly stated there but which seem to flow from it.[122]

5. Belgium

In general, Belgian authorities tend to follow the Strasbourg case law, even if the famous *Marckx* judgment,[123] concerning discrimination between legitimate and illegitimate children, was only fully implemented in 1987 through amendment of the relevant legislation. It should be mentioned that the openness is followed by all courts, including the Cour de cassation and the Constitutional Court. The Constitutional Court does not hesitate to reverse its case law in order to insert the Strasbourg jurisprudence into the Constitution.[124] It thus uses the Strasbourg case law to modernize the constitutional human rights catalogue without the intervention of the constitutional legislator.

Judgments of the ECtHR are faithfully implemented[125] according to the long-standing doctrine of the *autorité de la chose interprétée*,[126] equivalent to the *de facto erga omnes* effect, even in relation to the case law concerning other High Contracting Parties. Its case law does not deviate from that of Strasbourg.[127] A very interesting and recent example concerns the effects of the Chamber judgment of the ECtHR delivered on 13 January 2009 in the case of *Taxquet*.[128] The Court found a violation of Article 6 of the Convention holding that the procedure of trial by jury did not comply with that provision. The Chamber judgment was followed by the Cour de cassation, which felt compelled to reject the relevant provisions of the Code of Criminal Procedure:

> On account of the binding effect of interpretation now attaching to [the Chamber judgment] and the prevalence over domestic law of the international legal rule deriving from a treaty ratified by Belgium, the court [of cassation] is compelled to reject the application of Articles 342 and 348 of the Code of Criminal Procedure in so far as they lay down the rule, now criticised by the European Court, that the jury's verdict does not contain reasons.[129]

[122] Lenoir (n 50), 186–8.

[123] *Marckx v Belgium*, 13 June 1979, Ser A no 31.

[124] Popelier (n 63), 89, mentioning the Constitutional Court, no 81/2007, 7 June 2007.

[125] It should be noted that the Cour de cassation in early 1982 applied the Strasbourg jurisprudence not without difficulty. The judgment in *Le Compte, Van Leuven and De Meyere v Belgium* (23 June 1981, Ser A no 43) was not followed in two judgments of the Cour de cassation of 21 January 1982 (Pasicrisie belge, 1982, I, 623 and Journal des Tribunaux, 1982, 446). It was only after the judgment delivered in *Albert and Le Compte v Belgium* (10 February 1983, Ser A no 58) that the Belgian Supreme Court followed the principle established by the ECtHR as to the applicability of Art 6 in disciplinary matters. See two judgments of the Cour de cassation, 14 April 1983, no 6789, Pasicrisie belge, 1983, I, no 441 and Journal des Tribunaux, 1983, 607 and no 6785, Pasicrisie belge, 1983, I, no 442.

[126] Walter Ganshof van der Meersch, 'La garantie des droits de l'homme et la Cour européenne de Strasbourg' (1982) *Journal des Tribunaux* 102, 107; Jacques Velu and Rusen Ergec, *La Convention européenne des droits de l'homme* (1990), 1076, no 1234.

[127] Michel Melchior and Claude Courtoy, 'General Report on the Relations between the Constitutional Courts and the Other National Courts Including the Interference in this Area of the Action of the European Courts. XIIth Conference of European Constitutional Courts, Brussels, 14–16 May 2002' (2002) 23 *Human Rights Law Journal* 327.

[128] *Taxquet v Belgium*, App no 926/05, 13 January 2009 (extracts). This case is currently pending before the Grand Chamber of the Court.

[129] Judgment no 2505 (P.09.0547.F) of 10 June 2009, *Jurisprudence de Liège, Mons et Bruxelles*, 2009, 1392. The Assize Court Reform Act of 21 December 2009 has introduced a requirement for the Assize Court to state the main reasons for its verdict.

The binding effect of interpretation is thus a robust tool to allow courts to take into account the Strasbourg jurisprudence, which is, in general, faithfully followed and applied.

IV. Conclusion

In this chapter we have focused on four domestic systems with very different constitutional traditions. Notwithstanding the discrepancies as to its application, the ECHR enjoys a special status in the sense that the principles enshrined are of fundamental importance for national authorities. Fundamental rights are protected by constitutional (Germany, France, and Belgium) or quasi-constitutional (like the Human Rights Act 1998) provisions. The rights and freedoms guaranteed by the Convention are either directly applicable (France and Belgium) or introduced into the domestic system by means of a separate legislative Act (United Kingdom and Germany). In any event, the multidimensionality of fundamental rights protection has been increased with the entry into force of the Lisbon Treaty and the European Union Charter of Fundamental Rights.

The case law of the highest constitutional and supreme courts in the four countries examined shows that on the whole the Strasbourg jurisprudence is faithfully implemented and not departed from without good reason. 'Taking into account' the Strasbourg case law has proven to be much more than 'just considering' it and indicates a clear willingness on the part of the highest domestic judges to protect fundamental rights through a logic of dialogue with the ECtHR.

Bibliography

Robert Blackburn and Jörg Polakiewicz (eds), *Fundamental Rights in Europe. The European Convention on Human Rights and its Member States, 1950–2000* (2001)

Richard Clayton, 'The Human Rights Act Six Years On: Where Are We Now?' (2007) *European Human Rights Law Review* 11

Jean-Paul Costa, 'Foreword' in *2008 Annual Report of the European Court of Human Rights* (2009)

Francis Delpérée, *Le droit constitutionnel de la Belgique* (2000)

Olivier de Schutter and Sébastien van Drooghenbroek, *Droit international des droits de l'homme devant le juge national* (1999)

Andrew Drzemczewski, *European Human Rights Convention in Domestic Law* (1983)

Martine Fabre and Annie Gouron-Mazel, *Convention européenne des droits de l'homme. Application par le juge français* (1998)

Elisabet Fura-Sandström, 'Amplifying the Effect of the Court's Case-law in the States Parties' in Council of Europe Steering Committee for Human Rights (CDDH), *Reforming the European Convention on Human Rights: A Work in Progress* (2009)

Walter Ganshof van der Meersch, 'La garantie des droits de l'homme et la Cour européenne de Strasbourg' (1982) *Journal des Tribunaux* 102

Lech Garlicki, 'Broniowski and After: On the Dual Nature of "Pilot Judgments"' in Lucius Caflisch et al (eds), *Liber Amicorum Luzius Wildhaber, Human Rights—Strasbourg Views* (2007)

Lech Garlicki, 'Some Observations on Relations between the ECtHR and the Domestic Jurisdictions' in Julia Iliopoulos-Strangas (ed), *Cours suprêmes nationales et cours européennes: Concurrence ou collaboration?: In Memoriam Louis Favoreu* (2007)

Lech Garlicki, 'Cooperation of courts: The role of supranational jurisdictions in Europe' (2008) 6 *International Journal of Constitutional Law* 509

Conor A. Gearty, *Can Human Rights Survive? The Hamlyn Lectures 2005* (2006)

Conor A. Gearty, *Principles of Human Rights Adjudication* (2004)

Jörg Gerkrath, 'L'effet contraignant des arrêts de la Cour européenne des droits de l'homme vu à travers le prisme de la Cour constitutionnelle allemande' (2006) *Revue trimestrielle des droits de l'homme* 712

Steven Greer, 'Constitutionalizing Adjudication under the European Convention on Human Rights' (2003) 23 *Oxford Journal of Legal Studies* 405

R. Herzog, 'The Hierarchy of Constitutional Norms and Its Function in the Protection of Basic Rights' (1992) 13 *Human Rights Law Journal* 93

Frank Hoffmeister, 'Germany: Status of European Convention on Human Rights in Domestic Law' (2006) 4 *International Journal of Constitutional Law* 722

Rainer Hofmann, 'The German Federal Constitutional Court and Public International Law: New Decisions, New Approaches?' (2004) 47 *German Yearbook of International Law* 9

Francis Geoffrey Jacobs, Robin C.A. White, and Clare Ovey, *The European Convention on Human Rights* (5th edn, 2010)

Helen Keller and Alec Stone Sweet, 'Assessing the Impact of the ECHR on National Legal Systems' in Helen Keller and Alec Stone Sweet (eds), *A Europe of Rights, The Impact of the ECHR on National Legal Systems* (2009)

Jutta Limbach, 'Inter-jurisdictional Cooperation within the Future Scheme of Protection of Fundamental Rights in Europe' (2000) 21 *Human Rights Law Journal* 333

Ronald St J Macdonald et al (eds), *The European System for the Protection of Human Rights* (1999)

Basil S. Markesinis (ed), *The Coming Together of the Common Law and the Civil Law* (2000)

Giuseppe Martinico and Oreste Pollicino (eds), *The National Judicial Treatment of the ECHR and EU Laws. A Comparative Constitutional Perspective* (2010)

Michel Melchior and Claude Courtoy, 'General Report on The Relations between the Constitutional Courts and the Other National Courts Including the Interference in this Area of the Action of the European Courts. XIIth Conference of European Constitutional Courts, Brussels, 14–16 May 2002' (2002) 23 *Human Rights Law Journal* 327

Eric Metcalff, '"Free to Lead as Well as to be Led": Section 2 of the HRA and Relationship between the UK Courts and Strasbourg' (2010) 1 *Justice Journal* 22

Jens Meyer-Ladewig, 'The German Federal Constitutional Court and the binding force of judgments of the European Court of Human Rights under Art 46 ECHR' in Hanno Hartig (ed), *Trente ans de droit européen des droits de l'homme: Etudes à la mémoire de Wolfgang Strasser* (2007)

Ministry of Justice (United Kingdom), *Responding to Human Rights Judgments. Government Response to the Joint Committee on Human Rights' Fifteenth Report of Session 2009–10* (Cm 7892, 2010)

Laura Montanari, *I diritti dell'uomo nell'araa europea tra fonti internazionali e fonti interne* (2002)

Alexander Orakhelashvili, 'The European Convention of Human Rights and International Public Order' (2002–03) 5 *Cambridge Yearbook of European Legal Studies* 237

Hans-Jürgen Papier, 'Execution and Effects of the Judgments of the European Court of Human Rights from the Perspective of German National Courts' (2006) 27 *Human Rights Law Journal* 1

Niels Petersen, *The Reception of International Law by Constitutional Courts through the Prism of Legitimacy*, Reprint of the Max Planck Institute for Research on Collective Goods (2009)

Dagmar Richter, 'Does International Jurisprudence Matter in Germany?—The Federal Constitutional Court's New Doctrine of "Factual Precedent"' (2006) 49 *German Yearbook of International Law* 51

András Sajó, *Limiting Government: An Introduction to Constitutionalism* (1999)

Paul Tavernier, 'Le Conseil constitutionnel français et la Convention européenne des droits de l'homme', *Droits fondamentaux* (January 2008–December 2009)

Marc Uyttendaele, *Précis de droit constitutionnel belge. Regards sur un système institutionnel paradoxal* (2005)

Piet Hein Van Kempen, 'The Protection of Human Rights under National Constitutions and the European Convention: An Incomplete System?' (1996) 3 *Journal of Constitutional Law in Eastern and Central Europe* 225

Jacques Velu and Rusen Ergec, *La Convention européenne des droits de l'homme* (1990)

CHAPTER 60

MILITANT DEMOCRACY

JAN-WERNER MÜLLER[*]

Princeton

... if my fellow citizens want to go to Hell I will help them. It's my job.

(Oliver Wendell Holmes, 1920)

One has to remain faithful to one's flag, even when the ship is sinking.

(Hans Kelsen, 1932)

A constitution is not a prescription for suicide, and civil rights are not an altar for national destruction.

(Aharon Barak, 2002)

I. Introduction

'Militant democracy'—sometimes also called 'defensive democracy' or 'fighting democracy'—refers to the idea of a democratic regime which is willing to adopt pre-emptive, prima facie illiberal measures to prevent those aiming at subverting democracy with democratic means from destroying the democratic regime.[1] The intuition behind militant democracy is at least as old as St Just's famous principle of 'no liberty for the enemies of liberty'. However, the specific expression 'militant democracy' was first used in the mid-1930s by the German exile political scientist Karl Loewenstein, at a time when one European country after another had been taken over by authoritarian movements contesting elections in order to abolish or at least decisively

* For comments and suggestions I am indebted to Giovanni Capoccia, Peter Niesen, and Kim Lane Scheppele.

[1] On constitutionalism in illiberal polities, see further Chapter 5. On democracy more generally, see Chapter 11.

weaken liberal democracy once they had gained power. The paradigmatic example was Germany, where Joseph Goebbels infamously gloated after the Nazis' legal 'seizure of power': 'it will always remain one of the best jokes of democracy that it provided its mortal enemies itself with the means through which it was annihilated.'[2]

It was also in (West) Germany that a doctrine of militant democracy was not just comprehensively developed by legal scholars, but also officially adopted by the Federal Constitutional Court in the early 1950s. The Court held that the Constitution had made a 'basic decision' in favour of a substantive (as opposed to formal) understanding of democracy, a set of values that had to be defended against its declared enemies.[3] In other words, enemies of the constitutional order should be repressed before they had a chance to enter public office—as opposed to finding that a party's ideas are unconstitutional *ex post facto*, as with judicial review. However, there are many other countries—in particular those which regained democracy after more or less protracted authoritarian episodes—where at least some instruments of militant democracy (if not the expression itself) can be found in the constitution or at least in ordinary law: the 1958 French Constitution, for instance, empowers the President to defend the institutions of the Republic, while the 1978 Spanish Constitution requires that political parties are democratically organized (the assumption being that parties not democratically organized will be hostile to liberal democracy in general).

It might seem somewhat surprising, then, that there exists no general legal or, for that matter, proper normative theory of militant democracy—a theory, that is, which could solve, or even just address, what is often referred to as the 'democratic paradox' or the 'democratic dilemma', namely the possibility of a democracy destroying itself in the process of defending itself. To be sure, there are many related discussions, of tolerance and state neutrality for instance, or of legitimate limits on free speech and of the abuse of rights—but there is no 'model' of militant democracy that might straightforwardly be adopted by a newly consolidated democracy, and there exist no clear general normative guidelines as to how liberals should take their own side in an argument without ceasing to be liberals.[4]

This absence is arguably best explained by deep differences among the historical experiences of different countries—and, even more so, deep differences in what lessons were drawn from a history of authoritarianism, and, furthermore, which particular policies such lessons implied. For instance, an experience with authoritarianism could give rise to a heightened willingness to engage in party bans—but it could also have the opposite effect, that is to say, a demand to be exceptionally tolerant even vis-à-vis potentially extremist parties, as banning parties is itself seen as a typically authoritarian measure: an example of the first is Germany; Spain by and large constitutes an instance of the second.[5] In fact, even in the abstract, many political philosophies

[2] In the original: Das wird immer einer der besten Witze der Demokratie bleiben, daß sie ihren Todfeinden die Mittel selbst stellte, durch die sie vernichtet wurde.

[3] For the distinction between formal and substantive definitions of democracy and the implications for militant democracy, see in particular Gregory H. Fox and Georg Nolte, 'Intolerant Democracies' (1995) 36 *Harvard International Law Journal* 1. Fox and Nolte further distinguish between militant and tolerant democracies, thus leaving us with a matrix of four types—though the distinction militant/tolerant has rightly been criticized as insufficiently clear-cut. See Markus Thiel, 'Comparative Aspects' in Markus Thiel (ed), *The 'Militant Democracy' Principle in Modern Democracies* (2009), 379–424.

[4] Taking up Robert Frost's supposed claim that a liberal is 'a man who cannot take his own side in an argument'.

[5] Austria is also exceptionally *non*-militant—though the picture is complicated here by the fact that after 1945 Nazism was often presented as an invasion from without, and not a 'properly Austrian past' that might return if not properly guarded against.

might well mandate militant democracy *and* its exact opposite: anti-communism, for instance, could justify militant democracy ('We have to fight the enemies of liberal democracy!') and non-militant democracy ('We do not want to be like them and destroy pluralism!'). John Rawls essentially threw up his hands when confronted with a 'practical dilemma which philosophy alone cannot resolve'.[6] I will argue further below that partly for philosophical, but above all, for historical, reasons a convergence on a shared understanding of militant democracy even within at least partially shared political spaces such as the European Union is unlikely.

Apart from this absence of a general theory of militant democracy, the justifications for militant democracy even within individual countries have often remained unclear or, for that matter, highly contested. Nearly all participants in the debates on the meaning of (and appropriate measures associated with) militant democracy are aware of the democratic dilemma, but of course not everyone agrees *how* democracies trying to defend themselves can avoid eroding their own foundations. In one sense, this danger was a clear and present one during the twentieth century's intense ideological competition—what the historian Eric Hobsbawm has famously called 'the Age of Extremes' (and the Cold War in particular). From the 1920s to the early 1990s, enemies of democracy, or so it seemed, could easily be recognized by their relationship to totalitarianism, whether fascism or Soviet Communism (and, after 1945 specifically, their relationship to the fascist past and the Soviet Union in the present). But this seeming clarity could also give rise to McCarthyism and other illiberal excesses.

Less obviously, during the Age of Ideologies even totalitarian movements often invoked the language (and values) of democracy, thereby contesting and directly competing with liberal democracies: many Communists promised to realize full, participatory 'people's democracy', as opposed to the merely 'formal' democracies of the capitalist West; but even fascists sometimes claimed that their version of the national or racial community constituted 'real democracy': for instance, Giovanni Gentile, the foremost philosopher of Italian Fascism, held that 'the Fascist State... is a people's state, and, as such, the democratic state *par excellence*'.[7] In other words, parties and movements subject to militant democratic measures were not just openly competing within democracies—they also often quite openly contested liberal democracies in the name of allegedly 'real democracy'.

With the end of the Cold War, definitions of the supposed enemies of democracy have become much more diffuse and difficult to establish: 'populism' remains a notoriously vague concept; while attempts to link present-day parties to the totalitarian past—as with the German National Democratic Party (NPD) or post-communist parties in Central and Eastern Europe—often feel forced (and have in fact often fallen foul of the courts). For a while at least, it seemed that the paradigm of militant democracy was being replaced with that of the preventive, security-oriented state which mainly searches for effective measures against terrorists.[8] In other words, the new, post-Cold War enemies of liberal democracies were said not to be competing for power *within* democracy, but to try to subvert it through spectacular and shocking acts of violence from without.[9] The preventive state might also restrict rights and ban associations—

[6] John Rawls, *A Theory of Justice* (1971), 219.

[7] Giovanni Gentile, 'The Philosophic Basis of Fascism' (1927–28) 6 *Foreign Affairs* 290, 302.

[8] András Sajó, 'From Militant Democracy to the Preventive State?' (2006) 27 *Cardozo Law Review* 2255.

[9] Of course, this is not an entirely hard-and-fast distinction: after all, terrorists could also be said to abuse civil liberties and the normative guarantees of the rule of law in order to subvert liberal democracy. And sometimes terrorists have electoral wings, so to speak. Still, there is a good argument to be made that what Giovanni Capoccia has called '"peaceful" extremism' requires a particular repertoire of measures and responses, even if there is overlap with an anti-terror strategy. Loewenstein himself insisted that fascism's success was 'based on its perfect adjustment to democracy'; it would be rather hard to argue that terrorism is 'perfectly adjusted to democracy'. See Giovanni Capoccia, *Defending Democracy: Reactions to Extremism in Interwar Europe* (2005), 232.

but unlike militant democracy proper, which openly confronts what it deems to be antidemocratic *parties* and *associations*—much of its work is likely to be clandestine.

Terrorism is clearly a different tactic than subverting democratic values through contesting elections. It is not, I would argue, an object of militant democracy as traditionally understood. But there is one other area of highly contentious contemporary politics where militant democracy has again been invoked more frequently in recent years: challenges to secularism. Countries with a strict separation of church and state, such as France and Turkey, have construed certain types of religiosity—whether practised individually or organized collectively—as threats to democracy as such. The European Court of Human Rights has often followed them in this assumption, without ever going quite so far as to claim that secularism is an indispensable part of liberal democracy. Conflicts with religious actors—who do not necessarily organize in parties, but who might publicly invoke individual rights (again, in a manner that terrorists generally do not)—is a new and complex terrain for militant democracy, so much so that it remains contested whether democratic self-defence should really be practised against religious actors at all (who often have no intention of wielding the levers of government power). It is arguably the area where today democratic dilemmas—and the temptations of illiberalism—are most acute.

Given these general dilemmas, past lack of clarity and present-day uncertainties, this chapter proceeds in three steps: I first briefly reconstruct the intellectual history of militant democracy, starting with Loewenstein's work and moving on to the ways in which the doctrine of militant democracy was developed in post-war West German constitutional law in particular. Subsequently, I compare varieties of militant democracy, mostly, but not only in different post-authoritarian countries, before briefly touching on the jurisprudence of the European Court of Human Rights, which has developed its own perspective on militant democracy.[10] In the last, briefer section, I return to the normative core questions surrounding militant democracy and ask whether one might conclude that some strategies for defending democracy are clearly superior to others—and what their implications are for constitutional law.

II. A Very Brief Intellectual and Constitutional History

Militant democracy was first been defined by Karl Loewenstein in 1937.[11] Loewenstein was a lawyer by training, but had wide-ranging interests in political science and sociology: he studied with Max Weber in Munich just before the latter's death.[12] He left Germany in December 1933 and re-trained himself as an American political scientist. Loewenstein published extensively on political and legal developments in Europe. In two articles in the *American Political Science Review* in 1937 he argued that democracies were incapable of defending themselves against fascist movements if they continued to subscribe to 'democratic fundamentalism', 'legalistic blindness', and an 'exaggerated formalism of the rule of law'.[13] They should not, he insisted, tolerate 'Trojan horses' using elections to destroy the very core of democracy.[14]

[10] On the European Court of Human Rights more generally, see Chapter 59.

[11] Karl Loewenstein, 'Militant Democracy and Fundamental Rights I' (1937) 31 *American Political Science Review* 417.

[12] See the biography by Markus Lang, *Karl Loewenstein: Transatlantischer Denker der Politik* (2007).

[13] Loewenstein (n 11), 424.

[14] Loewenstein had posited the state's 'duty of self-preservation' as early as 1931 and called for the exclusion of parties determined to destroy parliamentarism. See Hans-Jürgen Papier and Wolfgang Durner, 'Streitbare Demokratie' (2003) 128 *Archiv des öffentlichen Rechts* 340, 345–6.

Loewenstein was not arguing with straw men. The constitution of the Weimar Republic, which Loewenstein had witnessed going down to defeat, had set no limits to political and legal changes enacted by the legislature. Leading constitutional lawyers claimed that Article 76 allowed transformations of the structure of the state (eg from federalism to a unitary state), and even a shift from democracy to dictatorship. Even the foremost democratic theorists among constitutionalists tended to assume that democracy was necessarily associated with relativism. Gustav Radbruch held that in a democracy power would have to be ceded to a majority, no matter what, since 'no political view could be proven or disproven'; and Hans Kelsen explicitly argued that democracy, to remain faithful to its own principles, should allow all forces to develop, even those bent on the 'annihilation' of democracy.[15]

To be sure, there had been some legislation during Weimar designed to protect the Republic from violent political movements: the Republikschutzgesetz envisaged the prosecution of those preparing the assassination of political figures, as well as those supporting associations which had as their goal the subversion of democracy. On a more symbolic level, disparaging the republican flag was criminalized. Still, none of these democratic self-defence measures were constitutionally entrenched and virtually all of them were only applied in a very half-hearted way. For instance, from 1923 onwards the Nazi Party was banned in the Reich, but it was allowed to be re-founded in 1925; the political police in Prussia kept an eye on the Nationalsozialistische Deutsche Arbeiterpartei (NSDAP) until 1932, but never decisively weakened the party.

Partly as a reaction to these failures, a number of constitutionalists began to move away from a relativistic conception of democracy—though it was in general too little too late. Carl Schmitt was one of the first to argue that Article 76 did not allow for a transformation of Weimar's political form (eg into a monarchy or a soviet republic) through super-majorities in the legislature; only the *pouvoir constituant* could do so. In his 1932 *Legality and Legitimacy* Schmitt warned that a 'value-neutral' interpretation of the Constitution could turn into 'neutrality until suicide' (*Neutralität bis zum Selbstmord*). In other words, a fundamental change in political principles enacted by the legislature might appear legal—but it would be not be legitimate.

Other European countries in the 1920s and 1930s were implementing measures consistent with Loewenstein's conception of militant democracy more successfully, in particular banning parties and associations.[16] However, many of these anti-extremist measures were ad hoc (and often only legitimized through *ex post facto* legislation), and no constitution contained anything resembling a real doctrine of democratic self-defence.

Part of the new challenge posed by interwar anti-democratic forces was that, according to Loewenstein, fascism had no proper intellectual content, relying on a kind of 'emotionalism' with which democracies could never compete. Implicit in Loewenstein's argument about the 'suppression of constitutional government by emotional government' were many of the assumptions of 'crowd psychology', according to which 'the masses' who had entered European political life for good with the end of the First World War, were incapable of thinking; all they could do was feel or be guided by instinct. Hence they were easily swayed by demagogues and charismatic leaders appealing to their emotions and instincts.

Argument in favour of liberalism, then, would lead nowhere. Consequently, according to Loewenstein, democracies—which was really to say, elites who still believed in democracy—had to find repressive answers to anti-democratic forces, such as banning parties and militias.

[15] Hans Kelsen, *Vom Wesen und Wert der Demokratie* (1929).

[16] See Capoccia (n 9) for examples drawn from a number of European countries.

They should also restrict the rights to assembly and free speech, deny individuals access to public office and even threaten the loss of citizenship.[17] As Loewenstein put it, 'fire should be fought with fire'; and that fire, in his view, could only be lit by a new, 'disciplined' or even 'authoritarian' democracy.[18] Loewenstein made it absolutely explicit that, rather than practising unlimited tolerance and therefore potentially end with their 'self-abnegation', democracies should defend themselves 'even at the risk and cost of violating fundamental principles'. He also thought they should establish a special institution—a kind of political police—for that very purpose.

Loewenstein's idea of militant democracy subsequently became highly influential in the Federal Republic of Germany.[19] The country's Constitution itself (the so-called Basic Law, or Grundgesetz) contained a number of articles meant to guarantee liberal democracy in perpetuity. First of all, the so-called 'eternity clause' of Article 79(3) stipulated that the federal and democratic nature of the German state cannot be changed *at all*, and neither can the protection of human dignity and human rights laid out in Article 1 of the Basic Law. As Martin Klamt has pointed out, the Basic Law cannot prevent a revolution—but it renders a *legal* revolution impossible.[20]

Secondly, the Basic Law—unlike the Weimar Constitution—constitutionalized the role of political parties in 'forming the will of the people'—but it also allowed for the banning of parties deemed unconstitutional. An application for a party ban can only be brought by a political organ (the parliament, the upper house, or the executive); a decision on banning a party can only be made by the Federal Constitutional Court—a provision to ensure that government parties would not simply start outlawing their competitors. As a further safeguard against abusing party bans, no political disadvantage must be created for a party on which a decision is pending, but which has not been declared unconstitutional. Other associations deemed unconstitutional can be dissolved by the interior ministries, according to Article 9(2) of the Basic Law. In other words, parties are distinctly privileged, in the sense of being especially protected from bans (what in Germany is known as the *Parteienprivileg*).

The Grundgesetz also made explicit provisions for restricting the rights to free speech and assembly for those deemed to pose a danger to democracy. In other words, the Basic Law envisaged militant measures against *institutions*, but also against *individuals*, who could forfeit their rights. Conversely, Article 20(4) also gave any citizen the right to resist those trying to abolish the liberal democratic order. In practice, neither of these articles has played any significant role in German politics: there have been only four applications to the Court concerning forfeiture of rights. All of them were unsuccessful. Both articles concerning what one might call individualist militant democracy are now generally interpreted as fulfilling a mere symbolic function: they are a prominent political *warning* more than anything else.

However, the Federal Constitutional Court did draw on the principles of militant democracy for two far-reaching decisions restricting political activity, namely the banning of the

[17] Karl Loewenstein, 'Militant Democracy and Fundamental Rights II' (1937) 31 *American Political Science Review* 638, 647.

[18] Ibid 656–7.

[19] Another influence was the sociologist Karl Mannheim, who called for a militant democracy in his 1943 *Diagnosis of Our Time*; the 1951 German edition contained the expression 'streitbare Demokratie' which was adopted by the German Federal Constitutional Court. Part of the Mannheim's 'diagnosis' was also the rise of 'mass society', which posed radically new challenges to democratic politics—and democratic self-defence.

[20] Martin Klamt, 'Militant Democracy and the Democratic Dilemma: Different Ways of Protecting Democratic Constitutions' in Fred Bruinsma and David Nelken (eds), *Explorations in Legal Cultures* (2004), 133–58.

quasi-Nazi Socialist Reich Party (SRP) in 1952 and the German Communist Party (Kommunistische Partei Deutschlands, KPD) in 1956.[21] In both cases, the Court appealed to the need to protect the *freiheitlich-demokratische Grundordnung* (liberal democratic basic order), a phrase that appears no less than six times in the Basic Law.[22] In 1952 the Court famously defined this order as one

> which excludes any form of tyranny or arbitrariness and represents a governmental system under the rule of law, based upon self-determination of the people as expressed by the will of the existing majority and upon freedom and equality. The fundamental principles of this order include at least: respect for human rights given concrete form in the Basic Law, in particular for the right of a person to life and free development; separation of powers; responsibility of government; lawfulness of administration; independence of the judiciary; the multi-party principle; and equality of opportunities for all political parties.[23]

The Court also affirmed that the Constitution entailed a 'basic decision in favour of militant democracy' (*streitbare Demokratie*). There is considerable controversy as to whether this basic order is identical with the principles explicitly protected in Article 79—in other words, whether strident opposition to the specific federalist and parliamentary conception of democracy in the Federal Republic of Germany ought to be subject to the measures of militant democracy, or whether what is at stake is hostility to basic democratic values as such. Legal opinion nowadays tends towards the latter interpretation: the democratic order in general, not the specific institutional set-up of the German polity, is to be protected.[24]

In addition to opposition to the liberal democratic basic order parties have to exhibit what the Court, in the decision on the KPD, called an 'actively fighting, aggressive attitude'. This vague formulation has been subject to much controversy. In particular, it has often been pointed out that the Court explicitly denied that the likelihood of a party actually toppling the political system is relevant, thereby putting the emphasis almost entirely on what appear as ultimately subjective mentalities of party members and, in particular, a party leadership. The importance of investigating subjective attitudes also increased the role of institutions that are mandated to 'observe political parties', including through undercover work, wiretapping telephones etc, in particular the Verfassungsschutz (Office for the Protection of the Constitution), which is completely separate from ordinary German police and also from secret services dealing with threats emanating from outside the country (in a sense, the Verfassungsschutz is the political police for which Loewenstein had been calling).

Five applications to have parties banned have been filed so far. Only two of them were successful. An application by the Hamburg Senate to have the constitutionality of the Nationale Liste verified in 1994 failed, as did an application by the Federal Government and the Upper House with regard to the Freiheitliche Deutsche Arbeiterpartei. Both were rejected by the Federal Constitutional Court, because they were deemed not to be real parties trying to gain political power. The last application—to ban the NPD—was filed in 2001 and failed in 2002—on which more below. However, these small figures are somewhat misleading in that many

[21] BVerfGE 2:1 and BVerfGE 5:139.

[22] This is usually translated as 'free democratic basic order'. But *freiheitlich* is not just free—it implies a more extensive commitment to freedom and values associated with it (such as self-development). It is the equivalent for 'liberal' chosen at a time—the 1950s—when party-political liberalism was often seen as discredited, or even as having paved the way to totalitarianism.

[23] BVerfGE 2, 1, 12–13, in Walter F. Murphy and Joseph Tannenhaus (eds), *Comparative Constitutional Law* (1977), 603; with the translation amended.

[24] Papier and Durner (n 14), 356–8.

more associations (*Vereine*) have been banned: up until the 1964 law on associations 328 extremist *Vereine* had been banned; more than 80 have been outlawed since. As said above, while only the Federal Constitutional Court can ban parties, the Interior Ministry can outlaw simple associations. The criterion is the same, however: associations have to exhibit an 'actively fighting, aggressive attitude' vis-à-vis the basic liberal-democratic order.

As Peter Niesen has pointed out, the approach of the Federal Constitutional Court in the 1950s and beyond was *anti-extremist*: the dangers to democracy were not associated exclusively with the anti-democratic movement and the regime against which the political identity of the Federal Republic defined itself—that is to say, National Socialism; rather, threats were deemed to emanate from the extreme right *and* the extreme left.[25] In other words, the Court's approach to democratic self-defence mirrored the theory of totalitarianism (with its implied 'equidistance' to extremist movements); and the SRP decision in fact explicitly identified the threat of the 'total state'.

Critics charged from the very beginning that anti-extremism could easily be instrumentalized against legitimate opposition (especially left-wing opposition); as Ulrich Preuß has claimed, its justification was 'an obscure combination of civil religion and "constitutional patriotism" which has been operating as a substitute for the traumatized national self-esteem of West Germans, and which at times has entailed a reduced capacity... to endure dissent.'[26] At the same time, critics have argued, anti-extremism did little to help to deal with the Nazi past. If anything, its implicit equation of Soviet Communism (and its alleged foreign agents) and Nazism seemed to *relativize* the specific evil of Nazism. Such criticisms became even louder in the 1970s, when individuals associated with radical left-wing causes were barred from holding public office—including rather innocuous ones like working in the Post Office (which, like posts for school teachers, comes with the status of *Beamter*, that is to say, tenured civil servant).

The prohibition of extremists holding certain state positions actually went back to the early 1950s, when it had been directed mainly at former Nazis. In the 1970s, then Chancellor Willy Brandt and the heads of the federal states underlined in a declaration of principles concerning the employment of 'enemies of the constitution' by the state that membership in a party or organization deemed hostile to the Basic Law was sufficient reason to exclude individuals from the civil service (the so-called *Radikalenerlass*). The principles were above all aimed at members of the Deutsche Kommunistische Partei (DKP), the re-founded German Communist Party.

In a highly controversial 1975 decision the Federal Constitutional Court clarified that lack of loyalty to the liberal democratic basic order justified exclusion from the civil service. But it did not endorse the notion that membership in a certain type of organization was sufficient proof for such a lack of loyalty. Within Germany, the issue died down by the 1980s, though exactly 20 years after the Federal Constitutional Court's decision, the European Court of Human Rights ruled that the dismissal of a DKP member from the civil service (as opposed to the refusal to employ a DKP member in the first place) had indeed violated the rights of the plaintiff.

Germany developed the most explicit—and the most far-reaching—theory of militant democracy. But developments in Germany fit into a larger West European trend: the idea of

[25] Peter Niesen, 'Anti-Extremism, Negative Republicanism, Civic Society: Three Paradigms for Banning Political Parties' in Shlomo Avineri and Zeev Sternhell (eds), *Europe's Century of Discontent: The Legacies of Fascism, Nazism and Communism* (2003), 249–68.

[26] Ulrich K. Preuß, 'Political Order and Democracy: Carl Schmitt and His Influence' in Chantal Mouffe (ed), *The Challenge of Carl Schmitt* (1999), 168.

constraining democracies—and in particular parliaments—through unelected bodies such as constitutional courts. In a sense, Europeans used a Kelsenian instrument (the constitutional court) to pursue a Schmittian strategy (of denying all political contestants an equal chance of gaining power). Militant democracy—the thing, not the word—was not limited to Germany and was one expression of what Peter Lindseth has called a new post-war 'constitutionalist ethos', which reflected a deep distrust of popular sovereignty (akin to Loewenstein's contempt for 'the masses').[27] By contrast, the United States, even at the height of anti-communism remained exceptional, as political prohibitions were largely enforced trough the criminal code against individuals (with no provisions to relax a robust presumption in favour of free speech in the electoral arena, and no special constitutional provisions for democratic self-defence).[28]

In Italy, the Christian Democrats, Alcide de Gasperi in particular, sought to establish a form of 'protected democracy'—*una democrazia protetta*.[29] The Transitory and Final Provisions of the Italian Constitution had already explicitly prohibited the re-establishment of the Fascist Party and placed restrictions on the political activity of former fascist leaders; Article XII stated:

> It shall be forbidden to reorganize, under any form whatsoever, the dissolved Fascist Party. Notwithstanding Article 48, the law has established, for not more than five years from the implementation of the Constitution, temporary limitations to the right to vote and eligibility for the leaders responsible for the Fascist regime.[30]

In 1952 the Italian Parliament enacted the 'Scelba Law', which reinforced these goals: associates of the Fascist Party would be removed from the active and passive electorate for five years. The law applied in particular to the group Ordine Nuovo (which, however, never gained any parliamentary representation with or without militant measures). In 1956 the Italian Constitutional Court upheld the principles of the Scelba Law, when it deemed the promotion of fascism as violating the legal and constitutional order.[31] Later on, the parties of the so-called 'constitutional arch' collaborated effectively to exclude the MSI from government (although the party—rebranded as Alleanza Nazionale—did form part of Silvio Berlusconi's first administration in 1994 and has since been absorbed into his party Il Popolo della Libertà).

Italy thus exhibited what Niesen has termed 'negative republicanism'—the self-definition of a militant democracy in contrast to a particular authoritarian past, in a way that differs markedly from the abstract and quasi-universal German approach of anti-extremism. Negative republicanism is a specific instance of what Kim Lane Scheppele has called 'aversive'—as opposed to 'aspirational'—constitutionalism: an attempt to craft a constitution against the background of a negative past, not in terms of positive projects for the future.[32] It is noteworthy that in Italy negative republicanism came into effect *after* the process of dealing with the fascist past had been officially (and, many critics would say, prematurely) concluded—that is to say, after the Act of Amnesty of 22 June 1946; unlike in the German case, democratic self-defence and the process of dealing with the legacies of dictatorship were not to be mixed.

[27] Peter Lindseth, 'The Paradox of Parliamentary Supremacy: Delegation, Democracy, and Dictatorship in Germany and France, 1920–1950s' (2004) 113 *Yale Law Journal* 1341.

[28] Samuel Issacharoff, 'Fragile Democracies' (2007) 120 *Harvard Law Review* 1405, 1417.

[29] Paul Ginsborg, *A History of Contemporary Italy* (1990), 142.

[30] Quoted by Stefano Ceccanti and Francesco Clementi, 'Italy' in Markus Thiel (ed), *The 'Militant Democracy Principle'* (2009), 210.

[31] Ibid 212.

[32] Kim Lane Scheppele, 'Aspirational and Aversive Constitutionalism: The Case for Studying Cross-Constitutional Influence through Negative Models' (2003) 1 *International Journal of Constitutional Law* 296.

Interest in militant democracy waned after the 1970s. However, some of the new liberal democracies in Central and Eastern Europe adopted militant democracy and, in particular, militant democracy on an anti-extremist basis: the new orders were defined against communism as much as against fascism, and parties—or sometimes just symbols—associated with the great totalitarian movements were subject to bans.

Meanwhile, in Germany interest in militant democracy surged again around the turn of the millennium. In 2001, both houses of the German Parliament and the Interior Ministry applied to the Federal Constitutional Court to have the NDP banned. The applications followed a series of racially motivated acts of violence, which politicians connected to the rise of right-wing extremist movements and parties (not only the NPD), and which was to be countered with both the traditional instruments of militant democracy and a comprehensive mobilization of democratic civil society (the so-called *Aufstand der Anständigen*, or 'uprising of decent citizens').[33] In 2003, the case was discontinued, because an insufficient number of judges thought it possible to proceed, once it had been revealed that a significant group of politicians and activists in the leadership of the party were in fact acting as informers for the Office for the Protection of the Constitution (Bundesverfassungsschutz).[34]

Meanwhile, scholars both in law and political science—not just in Germany—began to advocate a shift from militant democracy, with its emphasis on repression, to a new paradigm of 'defending democracy'—a more comprehensive approach which included more positive efforts to protect democracy through civic education and an engagement with (and even mobilization of) civil society, as well as strategies to take seriously the grievances of supporters of extremist parties and split off potential moderates who might be included in democratic deliberation.[35] The emphasis here was less on constitutional provisions, and more on a kind of public pedagogy and deliberative engagement. Outright party bans were now often dismissed as relics of the Cold War and the Age of Ideologies. Some scholars advocated abandoning the term 'militant democracy' altogether.

Thus the arsenal of democratic self-defence became enlarged—but so, in fact, did the potential targets of militant or defensive democracy. From the mid-1990s onwards, courts across Europe began reviewing more and more decisions to ban or restrict the actions of actors broadly speaking inspired by religion. Decisions at the nation-state level were frequently upheld by the European Court of Human Rights—always with reference to proportionality, but also sometimes with reference to the doctrine of 'margin of appreciation', and sometimes, much more controversially, with arguments that seemed to suggest that secularism is necessarily a part of democracy.

III. Varieties of Militancy

How can one meaningfully compare and classify different types of militant democracies? As should have become clear, very few countries explicitly employ the language of militant or defensive or self-protective democracy. But many do have provisions to deal with threats other than crime, foreign aggression, or terrorism. I suggest that these can best be understood along

[33] A shortened version of the Bundestag's application can be found at <http://www.extremismus.com/dox/antrag-bt.htm>.

[34] Thilo Rensmann, 'Procedural Fairness in a Militant Democracy: The "Uprising of the Decent" Fails Before the Federal Constitutional Court' (2003) 4 *German Law Journal* 1117.

[35] See eg Stefan Rummens and Koen Abts, 'Defending Democracy: The Concentric Containment of Political Extremism' (2010) 58 *Political Studies* 649, where banning parties is only 'the measure of last resort'.

two axes of analysis: on the one hand, one can chart to what extent, if at all, such provisions are constitutionally entrenched, or merely a matter of ordinary law. On the other hand, one can distinguish different kinds of militant democracy according to the underlying conceptions of what constitutes a threat triggering repressive measures. Here Frankenberg's and Niesen's dichotomy of anti-extremism and negative republicanism is helpful: Does a democracy work with a relatively open or even universal understanding of 'extremism', where threats can emanate from different parts of the political spectrum, or is militancy more particularist, so to speak, and thus essentially aimed at preventing the return of a specific, highly problematic historical past?

In such a matrix, Germany, the paradigmatic case of militant democracy, occupies a unique position: militancy is clearly enshrined in the constitution, and anti-extremism has been most clearly developed as the underlying doctrine justifying militant measures. This particular constellation owes a great deal to historical context: on the one hand, it was a useful fiction that Weimar had foundered because of the deficiencies of the Constitution (as opposed to a rueful lack of citizens prepared to defend democracy), and that, by contrast, a militant constitution could 'guarantee' democracy (even when it was doubtful how many genuine democrats could be found in 1950s and 1960s West Germany). On the other hand, anti-extremism fit the Cold War and the age of totalitarianism theory. Not surprisingly, anti-extremist justifications of militant democracy have become attenuated after the end of the Soviet Union: the German Parliament's application to ban the NPD in 2001 was framed in the language of negative republicanism. It sought to demonstrate 'essential affinities' between the party and the NSDAP, that is to say, the main party-political institution of the negative past against which the liberal-democratic basic order defines itself in the present. In the language of Günter Frankenberg (one of the authors of the Bundestag's application to ban the NPD), the 'learning sovereign' had adapted to different times and based its perceptions of threats and potential pre-emptive measures on new foundations.[36] A less high-minded way of putting the point would be to say that militant democracy can never be divorced from political (though not necessarily party-political) considerations—which is not to say that it is political through and through and that all arguments and reasons marshalled in debates on militant measures are mere smokescreens to hide power.

Many other countries have been militant in the sense of banning parties and associations—but most have not done so with the help of constitutional provisions or, even if they have constitutional provisions, anything like an overarching *constitutional principle* of militant democracy (as with the Grundgesetz). The reasons for banning organizations and the restriction of individual liberties have generally centred, in the helpful schema developed by Nancy Rosenblum, on actual violence, on incitement to hate, on foreign support or even control (or, more generally put: the insufficiently democratic and self-determining nature of a party), and, lastly and most controversially, on existential threats to national or, in many cases more accurately, *constitutional* identity.[37] The first of these seems straightforward, but has often been hard to handle in practice: very few party leaders engage in violence themselves, and often parties could only be banned, because the state enlarged the definition of what counted as 'violent behaviour': a failure to condemn violence can be interpreted as preparedness for violence and hence justifiable grounds for banning. This is essentially the basis for the early calls to ban the Batasuna party in Spain. To be sure, things are easier when parties mimic military

[36] Günter Frankenberg, 'The Learning Sovereign' in András Sajó (ed), *Militant Democracy* (2004).

[37] Nancy L. Rosenblum, *On the Side of the Angels: An Appreciation of Parties and Partisanship* (2008), 415.

organizations or in fact have paramilitary units. In Germany and Spain the inner life of parties must be structured along democratic principles; and France, Spain, and Italy ban organizations of a military character outright.

Incitement to hatred is arguably even harder to define. Some countries prohibit any political mobilization for elections in terms of race or ethnic identities; others are prepared to ban parties whose leaders advocate the removal of certain parts of the population: India and its banning of 'corrupt practices' is an example of the former, the prohibition of the Israeli Kach Party an instance of the latter. In Israel Amendment 9 (to s 7A) of the Basic Law of the Knesset names three criteria for disqualifying party lists, inciting racism among them (denying the character of Israel as a state of the Jewish people and denying the character of Israel as a democracy are the others).[38]

Foreign control was a particular concern during the Cold War, when fear of Moscow-sponsored 'fifth columns' gripped publics in the West. The charge that the American Communist Party was not really a party at all (and thus de facto unresponsive to its own members), but an instrument of world communism as directed from the Soviet Union, was central to calls for banning it altogether. To be sure, concerns about remote-controlled parties and associations have resurged in recent years, as groups like the Muslim Brotherhood and its various offshoots have grown in Western states—though the worry here is less that they could contest (or even win) elections than that they serve as incubators for extremism and, ultimately, political violence.

Both the criteria of violence and of incitement fall clearly within an anti-extremist framework. Threats to national or constitutional identity might do so as well, but they can also be viewed through the lens of negative republicanism. Arguably, the latter is more plausible when it comes to understanding (though not necessarily justifying) recent bans of parties and restrictions on the liberties of individuals who are deemed to have violated principles of secularism. Even the most ardent defenders of secularism will not claim that a complete separation of church and state is a prerequisite for liberal democracy. But secularism is clearly an integral part of some democracies' particular constitutional identity—Turkey and France being the prime examples. The preamble of the current Turkish Constitution announces that 'as required by the principles of secularism, there shall be no interference whatsoever by sacred religious feelings in state affairs and politics'. In France, the 1905 law comprehensively separated church and state (with the exception of Alsace-Lorraine, which remains a special case). Both countries have banned religious symbols in the public realm, with Turkey enforcing a ban on headscarves in schools and universities, and France, since 2004, banning headscarves in schools. The Turkish Constitutional Court has also outlawed parties and associations—most prominently the Refah (Welfare) party in 1997, when Refah was actually the main governing party. The Court justified the ban with the argument that the party sought to introduce shariah. It could be argued that the Court was not employing a general anti-extremist framework, but a negative republican reasoning: while all religions were potentially a threat to Turkish secularism, the specific concern was the *return* of a pre-republican, pre-Kemalist past, in which religious leaders exercised state power. Militant democracy here was about protecting a particular constitutional identity against a particular threat which had to be understood against the background of the country's history.[39]

[38] See <http://www.knesset.gov.il/laws/special/eng/basic2_eng.htm>.

[39] For the idea that constitutional identity is always formed through historical experience—fairly obvious in general, but difficult to specify in detail—see Gary Jeffrey Jacobsohn, *Constitutional Identity* (2010).

The European Court of Human Rights reviewed the decision and held that the ban was justified (though only in the face of an 'imminent threat'). The judges argued that Refah was attempting to introduce a form of legal pluralism on the basis of different religious and secular beliefs, thereby, in the words of the Court, doing 'away with the State's role as the guarantor of individual rights and freedoms and the impartial organizer of the practice of various beliefs and religions in a democratic society.' At the same time, the European Court did *not* commit to the notion that secularism is necessarily part of democracy: it merely affirmed that secularism was 'in harmony' with democracy. In *Şahin v Turkey*, the Court, with similar reasons and stressing the particularity of Turkish historical experience, upheld the banning of headscarves in universities—thereby allowing not just restricting parties with particular agendas and individuals abusing political rights, but the civil freedoms of citizens held to be in disagreement with substantive values of the constitutional order.[40] The Court explicitly affirmed that 'upholding the principle of secularism... may be considered necessary to protect the democratic system in Turkey'.

From a supranational European perspective, then, militancy in the name of secularism can be subject to the margin of appreciation and proportionality testing; precisely because it is a form of negative republicanism and hence more particularist, it can be condoned, even if the measures justified in its name would appear as outright intolerance in other contexts (which is to say: against the background of other constitutional identities).[41] The same is not true of separatist movements, where the European Court has made it clear that parties and movements that do *not* advocate violence or are linked to organizations perpetrating violence should be part of legitimate political debate. In other words—and perhaps paradoxically—there can be legitimate particularism among nation-states about (universalist) secularism, but not about defending territorial integrity (and, by implication, national identity). Or, put more simply: militant secularism is generally acceptable, militant anti-separatism is only so if the advocates of separatism can be linked to political violence.

It is harder to argue that French militant secularism is really a form of militant democracy based on negative republicanism. To be sure, French political culture was for centuries split between clerical and anti-clerical forces; and the Republic (or, more accurately, the five republics) defined themselves against the return of a particular past—that of the *ancien régime*, with its prominent political role for the Catholic Church. But the actual justifications for banning religious symbols associated with Islam in recent years have little to do with traditional republican anti-clericalism: the Stasi Commission, whose work led to the 2004 ban on headscarves, stressed the need to combat threats of violence from family (especially older brothers) against girls who refuse to wear the headscarf; while French constitutional identity played an important role in the background, a highly specific policy consideration based on an empirical investigation was said to be decisive.[42] In the eyes of critics, however, there has been a worrying drift towards intolerance in the name of democracy (or perhaps more accurately: liberalism), a situation where democracy becomes opposed to religion in the abstract, but—in the particular case—*always* to aspects of Islam. More disconcertingly still, it is a particular form of democracy or even explicitly national identity that is turned into the basis for militant

[40] I am indebted here to Patrick Macklem, 'Guarding the Perimeter: Militant Democracy and Religious Freedom in Europe' (unpublished paper on file with author).

[41] To be sure, the European Court has not always accepted negative republican justifications: in *Vajnai v Hungary* the Court did not uphold the arrest and conviction of the vice-president of the Workers' Party for wearing a 'totalitarian symbol'—the red star.

[42] Patrick Weil, 'Why the French Laïcité is Liberal' (2009) 30 *Cardozo Law Review* 2699.

measures. Here the particularism of negative republicanism is retained—but the more universalist aspects are gone; the final outcome could be not a variety of militant democracy, but a form of militant *culture*.[43]

It is thus important to remember that national identity and constitutional identity are not the same (the term 'political identity' often runs them together in a profoundly unhelpful way).[44] Threats to the latter can legitimately be subject to militant democratic measures, although constitutional identity can be interpreted more or less narrowly and therefore give rise to more or less tolerance vis-à-vis parties and movements. As we saw above, the narrow definition of the liberal democratic basic order to be protected by German militant democracy would imply that advocates of a unitary state or of constitutional monarchy might automatically be classified as 'extreme'—whereas on the more capacious (and more plausible) reading of the basic order as one of general democratic values (and not the specific institutional arrangements and interpretations of human rights codified in the Basic Law) their views would be perfectly reasonable (if unlikely to be realized in practice).

IV. Contesting and Constraining Militant Democracy

Only a few basic points in the debate about militant democracy are beyond contention. It makes little sense categorically to distinguish militant and non-militant democracies: under certain circumstances any democracy might engage in vigorous acts of self-defence; it is a question of political will, rather than pre-existing provisions for self-defence. Secondly, such provisions—no matter how deeply entrenched constitutionally—cannot save a democracy which lacks a sufficient number of citizens with firmly democratic convictions. Thus, thirdly, virtually all legal and political theorists nowadays tend to advocate complementing legal measures with educational ones, as well as engaging the legitimate concerns of voters turning to populist or extremist parties. They do so not least because, fourthly, all measures of militant democracy are at risk of being abused for political purposes (or for purely symbolic, which is to say ineffective, politics along the lines of 'something has to be done!'). It does not follow from this that militant democracy is always merely politics by other (legal) means; but extremely careful attention has to be paid to safeguarding against such abuse.

And which vision of militant democracy is least likely to be subject to abuse? Clearly, it helps if the decisions about militancy are removed from day-to-day decision-making by executives and legislatures. Giving the monopoly of banning to an institution relatively isolated from political pressures (the paradigmatic example being the German Federal Constitutional Court) still seems the most justifiable arrangement—even if, as many studies have shown, in times of genuine (or just genuinely felt) threat and emergency courts tend to defer to the executive.

Does the framing of militant democracy as, broadly speaking, anti-extremist or negative republican make much difference? Many German writers have been wary of 'anti-extremism'—partly because they associate it with an outdated Cold War mindset, partly because they

[43] For an example of sliding from constitutional to national identity, see John Finnis, 'Endorsing Discrimination Between Faiths: A Case of Extreme Speech?' in Ivan Hare and James Weinstein (eds), *Speech and Democracy* (2009).

[44] Michel Rosenfeld, *The Identity of the Constitutional Subject: Selfhood, Citizenship, Culture, and Community* (2009).

hold that anti-extremism is systematically biased against the Left.[45] By contrast, negative republicanism has been credited with 'particularist self-restraint', because its militant measures will be directed against the recurrence of very specific political phenomena, as opposed to a potentially scattershot approach associated with anti-extremism.

There is, however, also a peculiar danger associated with negative republicanism: it may give rise to militant measures as a form of symbolic self-affirmation of the political community vis-à-vis a discredited past, by focusing on supposed manifestations of that past in the present which are not really any substantial threats to liberal democracy. This is one way of reading the application to ban the NPD in 2001; the fact that the party has continued to operate ever since seems to have done no serious damage to German democracy, nor has it led to a steady rise in racism (the particular concern of some proponents of a ban) or other pollutions of the political culture (and the public sphere in particular). More generally, negative republicanism is subject to all the problems associated with thinking in historical analogies: its parameters might lead to distortions of political judgment in the present, because in order to do something about a threat to democracy, that threat always has to be framed as somehow a replay of the past.

Does it follow, then, that anti-extremism is preferable as a normative basis for militant democracy? The problem is of course that determining thresholds for extremism will depend on answering the question: Extreme in relation to what? A narrow definition of a set of democratic core principles (as proposed, for instance, by an identification of liberal democracy with Article 79(3) of the Basic Law) could lead to highly illiberal outcomes; but a wide one would leave the door open to supposed extremists claiming that their understanding of democracy is just radically different—but still recognizably democratic or even liberal.

Still, even short of anything like clear and present danger, attacks on core democratic principles are recognizable as such, if one or more of the following apply:

- the proponents of extremist views seek permanently to exclude or dis-empower parts of the democratic people (this is a different agenda than separatism, whose advocacy—without violence—should not be subject to militant measures);
- the proponents of extremist views systematically assault the dignity of parts of the democratic people. Such a notion will be fanciful in legal systems with very robust free speech traditions, but not in those that find it legitimate to erect restrictions on free speech because of specific historical experiences (an obvious example of such a 'dignitarian'—as opposed to the primarily American libertarian—approach is legislation on Holocaust denial);
- the proponents of extremist views clearly clothe themselves in the mantle of former perpetrators of ethnic cleansing or genocide;[46]
- and, finally, and probably most controversially: the proponents of extremist views seek to speak in the name of the people as a whole, systematically denying the fractures and divisions of society (in particular those associated with the contest of political parties) and systematically seek to do away with the checks and balances which have come to be associated with *all* European democracies created after 1945 (as the clearest result of the

[45] See eg Claus Leggewie and Horst Meier, *Republikschutz: Maßstäbe für die Verteidigung der Demokratie* (1995).

[46] I owe this modified version of negative republicanism—one less vulnerable to abuse—to Peter Niesen.

particular post-war constitutionalist ethos). This taking of a part for the whole, the attempt to have and speak for a people in plenitude fully identical and reconciled with itself (and, for that matter, transparent to itself), is often associated with the concept of populism—though it actually conforms more closely to Claude Lefort's conceptualization of totalitarianism as the inevitable shadow of modern democracy.[47]

These criteria are intended to be context-sensitive; they concede the basic insight of negative republicanism that militant democracy's legitimacy will depend on specific historical background conditions. This also means, however, that they risk the kind of illiberalism associated with a narrower, more particular understanding of democracy. Yet that risk is containable, I would submit, because the criteria outlined above emphasize that whatever the supposed enemies of liberal democracy are doing—they have to do it *systematically* (with the exception of adopting the symbols of a former regime—which is empirically verifiable in a fairly straightforward way and explicit calls to strip certain people of the basic rights of citizenship, which also can be observed directly). In other words, this approach looks for *arguments* (or, more precisely, the structure in which arguments hang together), and not so much *attitudes*, as in the German Federal Constitutional Court's potentially highly subjective test for 'fighting attitudes'.

These are of course contestable criteria, but in conjunction with giving the monopoly over banning and other militant measures to a politically insulated institution they might stand a good chance of guarding against abuses of militant democracy. As argued throughout this essay, however, it is highly unlikely that Western democracies will converge on such an approach in constitutional law anytime soon.

Bibliography

Giovanni Capoccia, *Defending Democracy: Reactions to Extremism in Interwar Europe* (2005)

Gregory H. Fox and Georg Nolte, 'Intolerant Democracies' (1995) 36 *Harvard International Law Journal* 1

Samuel Issacharoff, 'Fragile Democracies' (2007) 120 *Harvard Law Review* 1405

Martin Klamt, 'Militant Democracy and the Democratic Dilemma: Different Ways of Protecting Democratic Constitutions' in Fred Bruinsma and David Nelken (eds), *Explorations in Legal Cultures* (2004)

Karl Loewenstein, 'Militant Democracy and Fundamental Rights I' (1937) 31 *American Political Science Review* 417

Karl Loewenstein, 'Militant Democracy and Fundamental Rights II' (1937) 31 *American Political Science Review* 638

Peter Niesen, 'Anti-Extremism, Negative Republicanism, Civic Society: Three Paradigms for Banning Political Parties' in Shlomo Avineri and Zeev Sternhell (eds), *Europe's Century of Discontent: The Legacies of Fascism, Nazism and Communism* (2003)

Nancy L. Rosenblum, *On the Side of the Angels: An Appreciation of Parties and Partisanship* (2008)

[47] I am reluctant to attribute redemptive potential, or at least the power to politicize a supposedly post-political settlement (allegedly based on a rationalist liberal—Habermasian or Rawlsian—consensus) to populism in the way it has been suggested—with due caution and hedging—by theorists as different as Margaret Canovan and Ernesto Laclau. See Margaret Canovan, 'Trust the People! Populism and the Two Faces of Democracy' (1999) 47 *Political Studies* 2 and Ernesto Laclau, *La razón populista* (2005).

Stefan Rummens and Koen Abts, 'Defending Democracy: The Concentric Containment of Political Extremism' (2010) 58 *Political Studies* 649
András Sajó (ed), *Militant Democracy* (2004)
Kim Lane Scheppele, 'Aspirational and Aversive Constitutionalism: The Case for Studying Cross-Constitutional Influence through Negative Models' (2003) 1 *International Journal of Constitutional Law* 296
Markus Thiel (ed), *The 'Militant Democracy' Principle in Modern Democracies* (2009)

CHAPTER 61

CONSTITUTIONALISM AND TRANSITIONAL JUSTICE

JUAN E. MÉNDEZ*

Washington DC

I. Introduction

In 2001, the international community was forcibly awoken to the ways in which local and global security issues were threatened by the socio-political situation in Afghanistan. As foreign states and international organizations began in earnest to consider how to alleviate these tensions, it quickly became apparent that the Afghan system of law and governance had seemingly collapsed under the weight of centuries of conflict.[1] A robust drug trade, along with Soviet occupation, buffeted by decades of tribal conflict, and the harshness of Taliban rule had left generations of Afghans with the belief that the only law that existed came in the form of Kalashnikovs and blood money.[2] In December 2001, a UN-facilitated meeting resulted in the

* I gratefully acknowledge comments on an earlier draft by Prof Hermann Schwartz of the Washington College of Law, and an opportunity to present ongoing research on the matter afforded by the faculty of the same law school. I am also grateful for the research assistance of Kavita Kapur (JD Candidate, 2011) and Nayna Malayang (JD 2009, LLM, 2010) of the Washington College of Law.

[1] International Crisis Group, 'Afghanistan: Judicial Reform and Transitional Justice' (2003), 3.

[2] Amy Senier, 'Rebuilding the Judicial Sector in Afghanistan: the Role of Customary Law' (2006) *Al Naklah*.

Bonn Agreement on Provisional Arrangements in Afghanistan Pending the Re-establishment of Permanent Government.[3] Part of this agreement called for the establishment of a commission mandated to work towards a new constitution,[4] as well as giving the UN the mandate to investigate human rights violations during the interim period.[5] Since early 2002, the Afghan Independent Human Rights Commission has, among its other activities, collaborated with other organizations to conduct surveys and develop policies in order to pursue a transitional justice process.[6] However, after millions of dollars and the well-intentioned efforts of thousands of legal practitioners and scholars from many standing democracies, the impact of efforts at reform, and in particular at transitional justice, have been slow, and unclear at best.[7]

As the country undergoes the delicate process of rebuilding a judicial backbone from the dust of violent conflict,[8] Afghanistan provides a provoking example of the question this chapter attempts to explore: How do communities emerge from the rubble and make for themselves a new legal space? Transitional justice, offering as it does a basket of international tools and approaches through which to view this endeavor, confronts—directly and powerfully—the traditionally domestic enterprise of constitution-building. And while this confluence has been dissected in detail with respect to specific situations, there has not been much analysis on broader terms that may support a theory of cooperation, or at least harmony between the two processes. This chapter seeks to bring to the foreground the factors that surround the meeting of transitional justice and constitutionalism within the wider perspective of viewing each as a means towards a common end.

Transitional justice is a set of methods through which communities that have suffered gross and systemic violations of fundamental human rights seek to distance themselves from that past and move forward in a manner consistent with the need for justice for those who have suffered.[9] A 2004 Report of the UN Secretary-General to the Security Council uses the term 'transitional justice' as encompassing 'the full range of processes and mechanisms associated with a society's attempts to come to terms with a legacy of large-scale past abuses in order to ensure accountability, serve justice and achieve conciliation.'[10] The objective, then, is to repair and rebuild, within the confines of the rule of law. This is usually broken down into four obligations: (1) to tell the truth and distill an authoritative account of the history of the conflict;

[3] Agreement on Provisional Arrangements in Afghanistan in Pending the Re-establishment of Permanent Government Institutions (Bonn Agreement) (2001).

[4] Ibid IV.

[5] Ibid Annex II.

[6] See International Center for Transitional Justice, 'Afghanistan' (2008).

[7] See United States Institute of Peace, 'Special Report 117: Establishing the Rule of Law in Afghanistan' (2004).

[8] The categorization of Afghanistan as a fully post-conflict state remains questionable as violence continues even at the time of writing. Nonetheless, the types of nationally and internationally facilitated processes of state-building under way in the region are the focus of this analysis. While continued instability complicates the success of these efforts at constructing a fresh legal framework, Afghanistan still provides an important example of how seeking justice for past abuses is integrally related to establishing constitutional rule of law.

[9] See International Center for Transitional Justice, 'What is Transitional Justice?' (2010):

> Transitional justice is a response to systematic or widespread violations of human rights. It seeks recognition for victims and to promote possibilities for peace, reconciliation and democracy. Transitional justice is not a special form of justice but justice adapted to societies transforming themselves after a period of pervasive human rights abuse.

[10] UN Secretary-General, 'Report of the Secretary-General on the Rule of Law and Transitional Justice in Conflict and Post-Conflict Societies' (2004), UN Doc S/2004/616, para 8.

(2) to prosecute those responsible for the violations; (3) to offer reparations to the victims; and (4) to conduct institutional reform to dismantle extant systems which promote the perpetration of abuse.[11] These four actions are state-driven and 'official', but their impetus is to affirm memory and reject denial or oblivion, and in that sense they nurture and reinforce other efforts by civil society and by the national culture to emphasize remembrance of human rights crimes as a means of ensuring non-repetition. Reconciliation is not a specific mechanism to be applied separately from the previous four (except for the need for inter-communal conversations when the crimes have had a very specific ethnic or religious dimension), but reconciliation is definitely the ultimate objective of all policies and practices of transitional justice.[12] Recent years have seen the expansion of the scope of activities associated with transitional justice, and many in the fields of development, conflict prevention, and post-conflict reconstruction have seen significant overlaps between their own areas of focus and issues located within the 'transitional' framework.[13]

Constitutionalism, as it will be used here, refers specifically to the processes undertaken by a community to set forth a fundamental law upon which all other laws will stand.[14] The Secretary-General's Report referenced above emphasizes that the processes circumscribed by transitional justice, whether judicial or non-judicial, must be integrated, to the furthest extent possible, with existing national capacities, and that this is 'best served by the definition of a national process, guided by a national justice plan and shepherded by specially appointed independent national institutions.'[15] While many of the actual means for fulfilling transitional justice obligations will fall under more specific laws or administrative decisions, constitutions born in the aftermath of conflict nevertheless bear the first steps towards building the institutions necessary to address the need to afford remedies for past abuse. These constitutions—whether of an interim or more permanent character[16]—also contain a framework for the administration of transitional justice specific to that community's context and become the mandate against which the legitimacy of transitional justice mechanisms and initiatives will be measured. Indeed, the initiation of proceedings aimed at justice is often the first assertion of a newly constituted legal system and, as such, an important foundation for further legal and social development.

Constitutional processes and norms thus weave themselves intricately into the matrices of transitional justice, which are heavily influenced by evolving norms in international law, even though they are to be implemented domestically. This interaction between two normative frameworks and spheres of influence—one domestic, the other international—has become increasingly evident, highlighting the need for further examination.

[11] Juan E. Méndez, 'Accountability for Past Abuses' (1997) 19 *Human Rights Quarterly* 255. On the rule of law more generally, see Chapter 10.

[12] José Zalaquett, 'Confronting Human Rights Violations Committed by Former Governments: Principles Applicable and Political Constraints' (1990) 13 *Hamline Law Review* 623.

[13] Pablo de Greiff and Alexander Mayer-Rieckh, *Justice as Prevention* (2006).

[14] For a general overview on the history and key concepts of constitutionalism and constitutional theory, see generally Francis D. Wormuth, *The Origins of Modern Constitutionalism* (1949); cf Laurence H. Tribe, *The Invisible Constitution* (2008).

[15] UN Secretary-General (n 10), para 37.

[16] Ruti G. Teitel, *Transitional Justice* (2000), 196:

> Constitution making…often begins with a provisional constitution, predicated on the understanding of subsequent, more permanent constitutions. Despite prevailing notions of constitutional law as the most forward-looking and enduring of legal forms, transitional constitution making is frequently impermanent and involves gradual change.

II. Transitional Justice Obligations and Constitutional Norms

Measures of transitional justice (prosecution, truth-telling, reparations, and institutional reform) on occasion depend for their legality on the interpretation of constitutional principles. If they are considered mandatory, it is generally not because of a constitutional imposition, but rather as an obligation established by international law. Contemporary developments in international law have seen the emergence of affirmative State obligations with respect to legacies of mass atrocities, particularly if under the circumstances those atrocities are deemed to constitute torture, war crimes, or crimes against humanity. In the sense that many constitutions establish some status for treaties (and in some cases also for customary international law norms) the transitional justice measures may be seen as constitutionally mandated.[17]

By and large, however, prosecutions for human rights violations, truth-telling exercises, reparations schemes, and institutional reform initiatives are a matter of policy. Their implementation often requires some legislation or statutory or administrative authority. If so, their legality will depend on constitutional norms of separation of powers. In transitional periods, their very legitimacy and credibility with the citizenry will also hinge on the degree to which such orders are well within the functions and powers attributed by the constitution to the branch of government from which they emanate. For example, under some legal frameworks, it is a constitutional infringement for the President to order the prosecution of certain individuals. In other countries, in contrast, such orders are not unconstitutional as long as prosecutors retain a measure of professional autonomy and their actions are reviewable by an independent and impartial judiciary. In the last quarter of a century there have been many occasions when the highest courts of various countries have had to decide on the legality of transitional justice measures as they may be affected by constitutional provisions.[18]

The intersection of transitional justice with constitutional norms, therefore, varies greatly with each country's legal order and the historical moment in which the legacies of past abuses are attempted to be reckoned with. Nevertheless, some classification may be possible. First, even if the transitional justice measures are seen largely as policy choices, the constitution may impose significant constraints on the *manner* in which those measures will be carried out. Secondly, the constitution may in fact include a *mandate* to conduct transitional justice initiatives, or at least contain some explicit enabling norms to that effect; such is the case of interim or transitional constitutions like the one South Africa enacted as part of the negotiations to put an end to apartheid. Another example of a *transformative* constitution that specifically addresses what must be done about past abuses is the Rwandan Constitution enacted after the 1994 genocide. Thirdly, constitutions may be silent on transitional justice but the state understands that international law obliges the state to avoid impunity for major international crimes. In this case, the manner in which the constitution incorporates international law into the domestic jurisdiction is crucial to understand both the imperatives the constitution may impose to deal with the past, and the restrictions on how to do so. The existence of potential conflicts between the mandate and the restrictions will be resolved by an analysis of how the constitution integrates treaties into the domestic legal order.

[17] See Constitution of Argentina, Art 75(22).

[18] See eg *Azapo and Others v President of the Republic of South Africa* 1996 (4) SA 672 (CC).

1. Truth-Telling

The creation of Truth Commissions and similar bodies does not generally affect a constitutional norm, since investigatory bodies of various kinds are frequently used either by the legislative or the executive branch and their powers are delegated by Congress or the President. Much care needs to be exercised in devising the mandate and attributes of the Commission so that it does not infringe on powers of a separate branch of government. For example, human rights organizations have demanded that such Commissions be able to compel testimony from public officials and other witnesses that can be expected to be hostile (especially if they are suspected perpetrators of abuse). This applies equally to the legal ability of the Truth Commission to obtain documents from official sources and archives that are not generally made available. Unarguably, the success of an investigatory commission would be greatly enhanced if it were bestowed with such powers. Nevertheless, in most examples of Truth Commissions—and after some debate—the authorities have chosen not to grant them subpoena powers for fear that they could be seen as invading the sphere of judicial functions. For the most part, Truth Commissions are instructed to convey their materials to the appropriate courts or prosecutors' offices as soon as they encounter evidence that a crime has been committed or of the likely criminal liability of a person named.[19] In some cases, there have been attempts to incorporate prosecutors or legislators in the composition of the Commission, with the express purpose of allowing them to exercise subpoena or search-and-seizure powers inherent to their offices or that can be delegated to them. Such solutions, however, still present separation-of-powers problems as they suggest that institutions with subpoena powers would share them with individuals who do not have them. In addition, they could distort the real function of a truth commission.

Another challenge to the practice of Truth Commissions that could have constitutional repercussions is the issue of whether they should 'name names' in their final report. Even if they mention the names of presumed perpetrators while expressly refusing to pass judgment on their guilt or innocence, the naming carries a very public stigma and could be interpreted as an official or semi-official condemnation. On the other hand, if the Commission comes across evidence pointing to certain individuals and yet suppresses that part of what it has learned, it could be accused of telling only part of the truth. If there are ongoing criminal investigations or they will start soon after the Truth Commission finishes its work, it is best for it to withhold names in the final report and simply pass on the relevant leads or information to courts or prosecutors.[20] However, if under the circumstances there is no likelihood of prosecutions for serious crimes, revealing names in the final report will be a condition of credibility for the whole exercise. In those cases, the Truth Commission will have to follow some rules to ensure impartiality and thoroughness. In the first place, a serious effort should be made to ensure that all potential culprits are investigated for this purpose, and not only those belonging to one party to the conflict or to some specific branch of government while others are spared. The South African Truth and Reconciliation Commission (TRC) was the only one of its kind empowered to offer amnesty (indemnity from prosecution) to perpetrators who came forward and revealed

[19] Such were the powers conferred on Argentina's National Commission on Disappearance of Persons in 1983, and on the Chilean Truth and Reconciliation Commission in 1989.

[20] In Sierra Leone, the Truth Commission was prevented by the Special Court (both organs created under the UN-brokered peace process) from obtaining testimony from individuals facing prosecution. In a more extreme case, the Supreme Court of El Salvador refused to cooperate in any manner with the UN-sponsored Truth Commission, despite the commitment made to it by the state in signing the peace accords with the insurgents.

the truth of what they knew.[21] Precisely because of the delicate constitutional issues that such powers raise, the Truth and Reconciliation Statute made it clear that a special panel of the TRC consisting only of judges would hear individual petitions for amnesty.[22] In addition, the truth investigators must show that they have made efforts to corroborate the evidence they have received and to evaluate it for relevance, probative value, and credibility. Thirdly, the persons to be named have to be afforded an opportunity to rebut or to give their own version. These rules are derived from generally accepted principles of due process that, in most cases, would have constitutional underpinnings. And even if the process that is due before inclusion in a truth commission report is not as strict as would be required for a criminal conviction, it nevertheless is a condition of fairness that has bearing both on the legality and the legitimacy of the truth-telling exercise. Similar constitutional concerns govern the question of powers assigned to truth commissions beyond those related to investigating and disclosing information that is hidden. If they are going to be asked to disburse reparations to victims, they must be given appropriate budgets and, more importantly, statutory authority to make such determinations.

In general, however, Truth Commission reports generally focus on a description of the circumstances surrounding abhorrent practices resulting in severe human rights violations, often including an assessment of 'root causes' found in the recent history of the country. They also formulate recommendations addressed to the appropriate authorities in the areas that are logical follow-up to their findings: prosecutions, reparations to victims, protection of witnesses, educational programs, social and economic policies. It is clear that those recommendations are not mandates, so they do not present constitutional problems, even if there is a reasonable expectation that their implementation will be taken seriously by those in position to execute them.[23]

2. Prosecutions

Fulfillment of the obligation to investigate, prosecute, and punish mass atrocities is a central part of any program of transitional justice. In this view, truth-seeking, reparations, and institutional reform are never to be conceived of as 'alternatives' to prosecution, but rather as non-judicial measures to complete and supplement the inevitably limited reach of prosecutions. Whether accompanied by non-judicial measures or not, criminal prosecution of violations of human

[21] The Truth and Reconciliation Commission created in Indonesia had similar powers, and in that case amnesty was not discretionary but automatic. The Supreme Court of Indonesia struck it down as unconstitutional because of the state's obligation to investigate, prosecute, and punish international crimes.

[22] Promotion of National Unity and Reconciliation Act 34 of 1995. In addition, the statute contained objective criteria on how the indemnity panel was to exercise its discretion. The question whether those criteria complied with international standards has been debated. See John Dugard, 'Reconciliation and Justice: The South African Experience' (1998) 8 *Transnational Law and Contemporary Problems* 277; Juan E. Mendez and Garth Meintjes, 'Reconciling Amnesties with Universal Jurisdiction' (2000) 2 *International Law Forum* 2 (agreeing in principle with Dugard but arguing that, 'as applied', some decisions to grant amnesty violated South Africa's international obligations). It may well be that in 1994 the TRC Statute complied with international standards; today it may not, since international law has developed rapidly in this area, especially after the promulgation in 1998 of the Rome Statute for an International Criminal Court (UN Doc A/Conf.183/9, 1998).

[23] Despite this clear difference between truth-seeking and prosecution, the issue of constitutionality of non-prosecutorial inquiries has also been raised in the context of a hearing at the US Congress on the need for a commission of inquiry about allegations of arbitrary detention and torture in the so-called 'global war on terror'. David Rivkind, a former official in the George W. Bush Administration, argued that a commission of inquiry would violate the due process rights of officials who could potentially be defendants in criminal prosecution under the same set of facts. He did not, however, call for prosecutions.

rights committed on a widespread or systematic basis is always the hardest task to accomplish. In most cases, the potential targets of such prosecutions retain an important measure of political power and influence, and their comrades-in-arms and political allies can exercise considerable pressure over political leaders, prosecutors, judges, and members of civil society to assure the suspects of impunity. Such political pressures notwithstanding, there are times in the life of a country emerging from repression in which the impulse to break the cycle of impunity does succeed in opening space for some criminal proceedings against persons suspected of human rights crimes. At that time, potential defendants will exercise their right to a fair trial (ironically, the right they denied their victims of prolonged arbitrary detention, extra-judicial execution, torture, or disappearance) and constitutional issues will come to the fore.

It is a condition of legitimacy of all programs of transitional justice that every measure adopted must respect human rights standards.[24] In the matter of prosecutions, such standards include all of the guarantees of fair trial and due process of law. These are principles that are well established in the international law of human rights and they are also enshrined in most modern constitutions All guarantees that form the nucleus of due process of law are frequently brought up in the course of prosecutions or at the indictment stage.

If they are members of the military (and in some countries also of the police) defendants will raise the argument that they should be tried by courts of military jurisdiction and not by ordinary criminal courts. They invoke the principle that has been called of *juge naturel*, consisting of the right to be tried by a regularly constituted court established before the prosecution. This challenge to the jurisdiction of ordinary criminal courts has been resolved as a constitutional issue at the highest courts in many countries undergoing transitional justice prosecutions. Military court jurisdiction has been found not to be applicable to these cases because military jurisdiction is not a privilege to be enjoyed by military men because of their status, and because criminal jurisdiction of these courts is limited to offenses of a specifically military nature. The 'functional crimes' that they can hear are those that cannot be committed by civilians, like disobedience to orders, breach of discipline, cowardice in front of the enemy, and the like. In times of war these courts can also try more serious breaches of the laws of war, but only if committed in combat situations. Major human rights crimes like murder, torture, and abduction are not 'functional crimes' and, because of that, the 'natural judges' to try military officers for human rights crimes are the same courts that would try ordinary citizens for similar acts. To be sure, military courts are valid instruments of justice if they are surrounded by guarantees of independence and impartiality; in reality, in most countries they are not. In fact, especially in Latin America, military courts have been a pretext for impunity. If they have claimed jurisdictional primacy at all it has not been to prosecute human rights crimes in good faith but as an effort to wrest jurisdiction away from ordinary courts. Their efforts have resulted in prolonged delays in processing these cases, even though in the end the higher courts have almost always ruled in favor of ordinary courts. In some egregious cases, military courts have operated almost in secret to process a case without participation of the victims or access by public opinion in order to create a 'fraudulent *res judicata*' that a military officer can then invoke if he is investigated by a regular court.[25] This principle nullifying bad faith

[24] Zalaquett (n 12).

[25] An example of this is the dismissal, in the waning days of the dictatorship, of charges by an Argentine military court to benefit Navy Lt Alfredo Astiz for the death of Swedish teenager Dagmar Hagelin. The Supreme Court eventually declared that dismissal void and therefore not an obstacle to Astiz's prosecution in ordinary courts.

pseudo-prosecutions has been incorporated in the 1998 Statute of Rome for an International Criminal Court.[26]

Prosecution of past human rights crimes also faces challenges emanating from de jure obstacles to prosecution. The most common are amnesty laws (or pseudo-amnesty laws that are not called amnesties) that have the purported effect of preventing investigation or prosecution of these crimes. These laws are sometimes called *blanket amnesties* because they cover whole categories of crimes and potential defendants and are absolutely unconditional. In contrast, some amnesty laws exclude the most serious crimes that are also considered international crimes, or—like in South Africa—are made conditional on some affirmative act of confession and atonement from its beneficiary. 'Self-amnesty' laws are those passed by the dictatorships themselves in order to shield their operators from prosecution. Military dictators in Latin America have enacted them before leaving office; the most recent examples are the twin laws passed by the Fujimori-dominated Congress in Peru in the 1990s, after the revelation of the existence of a clandestine unit in the Armed Forces that committed the notorious massacre of Barrios Altos and the disappearance of students and a professor in the La Cantuta University.[27] Supreme courts have voided these self-amnesty laws, generally following decisions by international human rights courts.

A more complicated picture is that of amnesties promulgated by democratically elected governments after the end of dictatorships, like the Ley de Caducidad in Uruguay and the laws of Punto Final and Due Obedience in Argentina. Politically, those laws were almost literally extorted from the legislatures at the point of a gun when the military establishment flexed its muscle in the early days of a fledgling democracy. Yet formally they were unimpeachable. In both those countries, the legal effect of those laws was to prevent prosecution of major crimes for very long periods. Lately, however, courts have found ways around them at first and then have declared them inapplicable. In October 2009, the Supreme Court of Uruguay declared the Caducidad law unconstitutional as contrary to treaty obligations.[28] The Argentine Supreme Court had ruled the same way in 2005.[29] The constitutional argument in these decisions is based on the fact that treaties occupy a special place in the constitutional hierarchy of the juridical order, either as incorporated into the constitution or occupying a position below the constitution but above statutes and decrees, as in the so-called 'Kelsen pyramid'.[30] Human rights treaties have been found to establish the obligation to investigate, prosecute, and punish human rights violations that amount to crimes against humanity.[31] In that sense, if those laws were enacted at the time those treaties were in force for the country, or if they are deemed to violate a *jus cogens* obligation, they are—according to the Supreme Courts of Argentina and Uruguay—unconstitutional *ab initio*.

The Argentine Supreme Court later used similar reasoning to declare pardons (promulgated by President Carlos Menem in 1989 and 1990 to favor the highest ranking leaders of the military dictatorship) also unconstitutional and therefore not an obstacle to renewed criminal

[26] Rome Statute, Art 17(2)(a).

[27] 'The Judgment Against Fujimori for Human Rights Violations' (2010) 25 *American University International Law Review* 657, 697 (partial transcript translated by Aimee Sullivan). The second law simply said that the previous one was unreviewable by courts and had been prompted by the decision of a judge to go on investigating the La Cantuta disappearances.

[28] *In re Nibia Sabalsagaray* (2009). In October 2010 the Supreme Court ratified this decision.

[29] *Simón, Julio Héctor y otros s/ privación ilegítima de la libertad*, Case S 1767.XXXVIII (14 June 2005).

[30] See Hans Kelsen, 'What is the Pure Theory of Law?' (1960), 34 *Tulane Law Review* 269.

[31] Antonio Cassese, 'Reflections on International Criminal Justice' (1998) 61 *Modern Law Review* 1, 3–6 excerpted in Louis Henkin et al, *Human Rights* (2nd edn, 2009); Diane Orentlicher, 'Report of the Independent Expert to Update the Set of Principles to Combat Impunity' (2005), E/CN.4/2005/102.

prosecutions.[32] Other forms of clemency may not be contrary to international law and therefore not unconstitutional. Pardons decreed after trial and conviction and based on humanitarian reasons (because the convicted felon is infirm or in seriously ill health) and commutations and reductions of sentences do not infringe the affirmative obligation to investigate, prosecute, and punish, as long as they come after the judicial process has run its course and the end result is not a bad faith effort to make a mockery of justice. International law may require that punishment be proportionate to the seriousness of the crimes committed, but neither international law nor judicial practice has yet determined with any certainty what quantum of penalty is proportionate.[33]

In some cases, the legislative branch of newly democratic governments has attempted to repeal or nullify amnesty laws. The gesture is eminently political and therefore symbolic; the legal effect is dubious at best. A repeal will not erase the legal effect of the amnesty because, under the rule of lenity, criminal defendants and even convicted offenders enjoy the benefit of the 'most benign criminal law' that can be applicable to their acts from the moment of commission on. In that sense, an amnesty that erases the criminality of the act is precisely that kind of 'most benign criminal law' and must be applied even after repeal. The declaration by Congress or Parliament that an amnesty is 'null and void' is meaningless: Congress can repeal but not nullify prior enactments and, in any event, the nullifying statute may not be enough to overcome the rule of lenity. In Argentina, Congress has attempted both courses of legislative action at different times and under different administrations (and different parliamentary majorities). It is significant that in the judicial decision mentioned above, the Supreme Court did not rely on those pieces of legislation but rather, as stated, on the unconstitutional nature of laws that, at enactment, violated international obligations of the state. In this regard, those decisions found ample support in the several pronouncements of the Inter-American Commission and Inter-American Court of Human Rights since 1988.[34] In Chile, without a formal declaration of unconstitutionality, the highest court has for many years refused to apply Pinochet's self-amnesty law using the same arguments (under Chilean law, judicial pronouncements have no *stare decisis* and are valid only for the case under study). The Inter-American Court has recognized this line of judicial decisions but has insisted that Chile must take the self-amnesty law off the books.[35]

Other obstacles to prosecution are presented by the application of statutes of limitation, especially if political circumstances have allowed a long time to elapse since the commission of the crimes. Defendants and their lawyers insist that the accused has a due process right to have time computed in his favor. This may be true and perhaps this right is of constitutional rank; but the notion of crimes against humanity establishes a clear exception: murder, torture, enslavement, and other acts, when committed on a widespread or systematic basis, are not

[32] *Riveros* (2006). President Menem's pardon of General Santiago Omar Riveros was issued pre-trial, while General Jorge R. Videla and other Junta members were pardoned for crimes for which they had been convicted in 1986. They are again facing prosecution, Videla for crimes other than those for which he was originally convicted.

[33] In *La Rochela v Colombia*, the Inter-American Court of Human Rights hinted, in dicta, to this requirement of proportionality but left open the question of whether, as applied, a law offering reduced sentences to paramilitary groups in exchange for demobilization and confessions was consistent with the American Convention on Human Rights. On proportionality, see further Chapters 33 and 34.

[34] Reports 28 (Argentina) and 29 (Uruguay) of the Inter-American Commission on Human Rights, 1992; and Inter-American Court decisions in *Velasquez-Rodriguez v Honduras*, 1988 (on the affirmative duty to investigate, prosecute, and punish crimes against humanity); *Barrios Altos v Peru*, 2000 (on the invalidity of amnesties with this effect).

[35] *Almonacid-Arellano*, 2006

subject to statutes of limitation.[36] The role of the courts, therefore, is to examine the evidence and see whether the specific acts are part and parcel of a pattern of widespread or systematic violations; if they are, the statute of limitations does not apply.

The European Court of Human Rights has repeatedly interpreted Article 7 of the European Convention ('No punishment without law') as not constituting a bar to prosecution of human rights crimes even though sanctioned by the state at the time of commission, beginning with the 'German Border Guards' case, a Grand Chamber decision approved unanimously.[37] More recently, the European Court has held that the evaluation of whether a Hungarian captain was guilty of crimes against humanity had to be assessed on the basis of the prevailing understanding of that category of crime at the time of the acts committed.[38] During the same year, a similar judgment was reached against Latvia, finding that the war crimes conviction of a former Soviet soldier violated his right to *ne bis in idem*. However, in 2010, a subsequent Grand Chamber decision on the case at the request of the Latvian government reversed this holding, reasoning that it had been sufficiently clear at the time of commission that the acts of the applicant had amounted to war crimes. This jurisprudence indicates that the issue of *ne bis in idem* is the central focal point of analysis in the validity of these prosecutions.[39]

Much has been said about whether similar principles should apply to the actions of insurgent forces that, contemporaneously with the human rights violations, also committed murders and other violent acts. In several countries (South Africa, Argentina, Uruguay, El Salvador, Guatemala) potential defendants who were members of rebel forces benefitted at times from different amnesties enacted to encourage them to lay down their arms and join the peaceful political process. In fact, crimes against humanity can be committed by members of an organized group of non-state actors, as long as the crimes are also widespread or systematic and they are part of a general attack on the civilian population.[40] There would be no obstacle, therefore, for a court to prosecute a member of the insurgent forces for such crimes even overriding an amnesty or a statute of limitations. But this is conditioned on the existence of a factual pattern that does indeed elevate the specific crimes charged to the category of crimes against humanity. It must be noted that international law does not prohibit every kind of amnesty; on the contrary, amnesties that are truly meant to put an end to armed conflict are actually encouraged by international law.[41] This norm, however, applies to the domestic offenses of sedition, rebellion, or treason; not to actions that constitute grave breaches of the laws of war, whether committed by state or non-state actors.

Prosecution of past crimes can be vulnerable to constitutional challenge in one significant area: the right to a speedy trial. The complexity of the crimes investigated, the large number of defendants, victims and witnesses, and the fact that the judicial infrastructure is almost always inadequate to handle these cases have resulted in long delays in bringing them to trial or to a final resolution. If the accused is actually in custody during those lengthy proceedings, his constitutional rights are certainly violated. It must be noted that, in general, courts are sensitive to this issue and frequently release defendants on bail or transfer them to house arrest after a certain time has elapsed without a determination.

[36] See eg 'Set of Principles for the Protection and Promotion of Human Rights through Action to Combat Impunity' (the 'Joinet Principles') (1997), principle 24.

[37] *Streletz, Kessler and Krenz v Germany* ECtHR App nos 34044/96, 35532/97 and 44801/98, 22 March 2001.

[38] *Korbely v Hungary*, ECtHR App no 9174/02, 19 September 2008.

[39] *Kononov v Latvia*, ECtHR App no 36376/04, 17 May 2010.

[40] Rome Statute, Art 7.

[41] Protocol Additional to the Geneva Conventions of 12 August 1949, and relating to the Protection of Victims of Non-International Armed Conflicts (Protocol II) (1977), Art 6(5).

3. Reparations and DDR Mechanisms

Under international law, the concept of reparations is inextricably linked to the concept of state responsibility for violations of obligations owed either to individuals, collectives, or other states. This forms the bedrock for the mandate governing the inclusion of an effective and prompt reparations process in the transitional justice paradigm. In 2005, the United Nations General Assembly adopted Resolution 60/147,[42] which laid out basic principles on reparations to victims of gross human rights violations. While this resolution is not binding and does not reflect customary international law, it nevertheless outlines key aspects of the nature of reparations that transitional justice tools have sought to implement. Under the resolution, 'effective and prompt' reparations include the equal and effective access to justice, and access to information concerning reparation mechanisms.[43] Unlike the concept of reparations under ordinary domestic procedures, transitional justice reparations are not often truly compensatory. While many of them involve the transfer of something material to account for a loss, the material—whether money, property, or some other similar token—is more a symbolic act of atonement rather than an attempt at restoring the *status quo ante*. Thus reparations can, among others, take the form of monetary restitution such as that usually awarded by the Inter-American Court of Human Rights; apologies or other such public acknowledgment of responsibility such as those given by Japan and Germany after the Second World War; collective reparations for gross violations, including those paid by Germany to Israel, that paralleled individual reparations to Jews, slaves, and the Roma; or the granting of preferred treatment, as in the government aid programs and education benefits awarded to descendants of the direct victims.

Reparations usually come at the end of a long-drawn-out process of assigning blame and establishing lines of accountability. Moreover, reparations are not paid by one individual to another, but rather by the state held accountable for the past abuse to the community as a whole, even in instances where the beneficiaries may in fact be certain identifiable persons. In many cases, the question arises as to who takes the place of the original victim and is thus entitled to claims for reparation, and who precisely is responsible for paying and distributing the award. Transitional justice adopts the 'political persecution' principle, which allows those involved to differentiate between claims connected with past conflict for reparatory purposes, and those that are not. However, this is not always easily done. In the Philippines, for example, the monetary award granted to the victims of the Marcos regime has yet to be distributed because the identity of many of the claimants is under dispute.[44] There is also a larger question as to whether the present administration, heavily backed by political and financial support from the Marcos heirs, has the political will to pursue the distribution of compensation awarded to nearly 10,000 identified recipients and prosecution of the graft cases that are pending to this day before Philippine courts.[45]

In addition to reparations, successor regimes often implement measures that are reparative in nature, although not exactly compensatory, as a way of returning stability to the state. These include DDR (demobilization, disarmament, and reintegration) mechanisms, often utilized

[42] Basic Principles and Guidelines on the Right to a Remedy and Reparation for Victims of Gross Violations of International Human Rights Law and Serious Violations of International Humanitarian Law (2005), GA Res 60/147.

[43] Ibid 12–15.

[44] Jefferson Plantilla, 'Elusive Promise: Transitional Justice in the Philippines' (1997) *Carnegie Council Human Rights Dialogue* Ser 1 No 8.

[45] Al Labita, 'Marcos Family Re-stakes its Claims', *Asia Times Online*, March 26, 2009.

in areas where large parts of the population had become militarized. The Democratic Republic of Congo, Sierra Leone, and Liberia are just three instances where DDR was a critical part of the transition process and re-establishment of the rule of law.

In both reparations and DDR, constitutional questions of due process can be implicated, specifically with respect to groups that have previously been divided. Strong due process and equal protection guarantees would go far in the effort to accord these groups with similar rights and privileges as citizens of a common state and stakeholders in the common democratic enterprise. The identification and processing of claims, as well as the corresponding recognition of complicity in past abuse, calls for constitutional norms that protect the individual from pre-judgment, summary punishment and further alienation and that ensure the protections of a fair trial.

4. Institutional Reform and Non-Judicial Sanctions

Efforts to reform the state institutions that in the past have served as the instruments of repression do not generally present constitutional problems, as long as the reform complies with separation of powers arrangements. There is one area of reform that does raise constitutional problems in execution: the 'vetting' or disqualification of officials of state institutions known to have abused their powers in them to violate human rights. The constitutional problem is not so much in the decision itself of purging institutions of wrongdoers; in fact, it may be argued that international human rights law actually requires it among the measures to ensure non-repetition of atrocities.[46] But the manner in which disqualification processes are conducted can indeed raise constitutional problems. Vetting or disqualification is in itself a sanction and therefore it cannot be applied without due process guarantees. It is not a criminal sanction and therefore it may not require the full-blown guarantees of fair trial associated with criminal punishment; but it is a serious action against employment and reputation of the targeted person. In that sense, vetting processes must incorporate some elements of due process before the decisions are arrived at. Persons to be separated from their official jobs must be given notice, an opportunity to be heard and to rebut accusations against them, and the ability to seek judicial review of the administrative decision.[47]

At the end of the Cold War, many East European countries enacted 'lustration' laws that allowed the authorities to disqualify persons found to have collaborated with the Communist regimes of the recent past from serving in a variety of capacities.[48] These laws went beyond institutional reform in that they were not only applied to former officials who had abused their authority in institutions, but also to citizens whose names appeared in records of intelligence services as having rendered some form of covert support to illegal surveillance and spying. It is not possible to generalize because the statutes in each country were different in some material aspects, but some of them would certainly have raised constitutional issues.[49] In the first place, the activities that triggered the sanctions may well have been legal at the time when they were performed, so the sanction could offend the norm against *ex post facto* imposition of penalties,

[46] Joinet Principles (n 36), 40–2.

[47] De Greiff and Mayer-Riekh (n 13).

[48] See Herman Schwartz, 'Lustration in Eastern Europe' (1994) 1(2) *Parker School Journal of Eastern European Law* 141.

[49] For different approaches in Germany, Bulgaria, and the Czech Republic, see the essays by Joachim Gauck, Dimitrina Petrova, and Karel Schwarzenberg respectively in Alex Boraine, Janet Levy, and Ronel Scheffer (eds), *Dealing with the Past* (1994). For a more extreme form of lustration in latter-day Poland, see Adam Michnik, 'The Polish Witch-Hunt' in (2007) *New York Review of Books*.

also known as the 'principle of legality' or *nullum crimen sine lege*. In addition, these sanctions were imposed by an administrative authority and not a judicial one, which raises an obvious separation-of-powers issue. In those cases where the law did not contemplate any form of notice, hearing, petition for review, or appeal to the courts, the process affects constitutional rights to due process of law. Indeed, the European Court of Human Rights has issued a number of judgments on lustration laws in post-Communist states. In multiple cases against Lithuania, the European Court found that the application of the KGB Act to former members of the KGB many years after they left that group should not be allowed to prevent them from accessing private sector employment because this would constitute a violation of their right to private life.[50] This jurisprudence, along with a subsequent case against Latvia,[51] underscores that lustration laws must be finely tuned in their scope and cannot endure indefinitely. Responsibilities for oppressive behavior may well be widely shared, but sanctions cannot be collective nor applied to categories of persons (such as all officials of a certain level, as done in Iraq post-Saddam Hussein). Punishment of any sort should only be personal and linked to specific behavior.

In contrast, laws that regulate access to files of the previous regime in an orderly and transparent manner are not only constitutional but actually necessary to fulfill the state's obligation to investigate and disclose the truth. They are also an embodiment of the right of citizens—enshrined in human rights treaties and also in several modern constitutions—to have access to information contained in government files, especially if they affect them personally, but also as a general state obligation towards transparency and publicity of the acts of government. Some East European laws have actually established procedures by which individuals can correct wrong, false, or misleading information about themselves included in such files. In these cases, such measures are not only permissible on constitutional grounds but may actually be responsive to constitutional mandates to preserve honor and reputation of citizens, to guarantee their presumption of innocence, and to protect them from being the subject of sanctions without due process.

III. The Relation of International Standards Embodied in Transitional Justice to Constitutional Norms and Processes

What can be seen from much of the foregoing discussion is that international standards are the foundation for transitional justice. As they interact with the domestic processes of reparation, prosecution, institutional reform, and truth-telling, these international standards begin to inform the propriety of the efforts by the state in transition as against the yardstick of international law. Thus constitutions that embody such standards as a means of dealing with the aftermath of conflict are not only formative, but *trans*formative as well.[52] Transformative constitutions are founded upon a need to break with the past, and form a thick line between what was, and what will be. This stands in contrast to constitutions that, as Sunstein emphasizes, are more preservative of tradition; for transformative constitutions, the point is disassociation with rather than continuation of norms.[53]

[50] *Sidabras and Džiautas v Lithuania*, ECtHR, App nos 55480/00 and 59330/00, 27 July 2004; *Rainys and Gasparavičius v Lithuania*, ECtHR App nos 70665/01 and 74345/01, 7 April 2005.

[51] *Ždanoka v Latvia*, ECtHR App no 58278/00, 16 March 2006 (Grand Chamber).

[52] Karl Klare, 'Legal Culture and Transformative Constitutionalism' (1998) 14 *South African Journal on Human Rights* 146.

[53] Cass R. Sunstein, *Designing Democracy: What Constitutions Do* (2001), 67.

In fact, the impact of transitional justice initiatives on constitutional processes in countries that have made the transition from dictatorship to democracy is both 'backward-looking and forward-looking, retrospective and prospective, continuous and discontinuous'.[54] In Latin America, the process can be seen, at least in general, as an effort to restore constitutional precepts that were always part of the countries' legal traditions, after a period in which they were trampled upon by military dictatorships or by autocratic leadership. In South Africa, the effort was more self-consciously transformative, because it was meant not only to redress past wrongs but also as 'an enterprise of inducing large-scale social change through non-violent political processes grounded in law'.[55] In spite of this initial difference, however, the constitutional processes influenced by transitional justice in both continents tend generally to adopt transformative features.

A constitution may be considered transformative both in process and in product. Engaging in a process of participatory constitutionalism involves 'a conversation, conducted by all concerned, open to new entrants and issues, seeking a workable formula that will be sustainable rather than assuredly stable'.[56] This type of constitutional process serves to bring in marginalized populations and to empower healing and reconciliation through dialogue aimed at forging a new consensus for the future.[57]

The constitution produced through a participatory process may have two particularly transformative consequences. First, interpretation of constitutional norms will favor ones that uphold this dissociative intent. Judicial review will be exercised not against a backdrop of precedent, but against the desire to create new norms antithetical to what past practice may have been. Take, for example, section 39(1) of the new South African Constitution, which explicitly states that when considering interpretations of fundamental rights, courts 'must consider international law'.[58] This has resulted in several decisions by the Constitutional Court that have largely repudiated long-standing traditional practice.[59] Many recent amendments to Latin American constitutions assign a special place to the international law of human rights, and that trend is directly related to the experiments with transitional justice, because most obstacles to justice, truth, reparations, and reform were removed with support from international standards embodied in human rights treaties and in decisions of international courts.

A second consequence of the dissociative character of transformative constitutions is found in the source of their legitimacy.[60] Unlike preservative constitutions that anchor their legal legitimacy in the weight of previous practice and acceptance, transformative constitutions are founded in the socio-political wake of gross violations of human rights; for that reason, they affirm norms established during the period of reconstruction that immediately preceded their creation. If, during the transformative process, these norms have included affirmations of international law and standards on freedom, democracy, and the rule of law, the constitutions

[54] Teitel (n 16).

[55] Klare (n 52).

[56] Eileen F. Babbit, *The New Constitutionalism: An Approach to Human Rights from a Conflict Transformation Perspective* (2010).

[57] Ibid.

[58] Constitution of the Republic of South Africa (1996), s 39(1)(b).

[59] The outstanding example would be the case of *State v Makwanyane*, 1995 (3) *SALR* 391 (CC), the Constitutional Court struck down the use of the death penalty as a viable punishment, despite the use of it prior to the assumption of the ANC and the still overwhelming evidence of public support for it under the circumstances.

[60] See eg Theunis Roux, 'Principle and Pragmatism on the Constitutional Court of South Africa' (2009) 7 *International Journal of Constitutional Law* 106.

subsequently formed will incorporate international human rights treaties, to the extent that they were critical to the transformation process.

Three general points can thus be made with respect to the manner through which international norms can mesh with the domestic processes of constitutional law. One is that the constitution becomes a codification of the standard itself, which contributes to the crystallization of norms at the international level. The development of customary norms of international law requires this evidence of state practice, and states that are willing to embrace international standards and 'domesticate' them within their constitutions because of the need for transitional justice end up—albeit often unconsciously—adding to the strength of human rights norms.

Another point is that international standards operate as a factor in subsequent judicial review of laws enacted pursuant to the constitution's mandates. Constitutions that contain formulations of international standards easily lend themselves to constructions that incorporate the corpus of international law. Corollary to this is that even in constitutions that may not expressly provide for its incorporation, international law can nevertheless be utilized through statutory constructions informed by it. In Bosnia-Herzegovina, the Constitution commits the government to ensuring the 'highest level of internationally recognized human rights and fundamental freedoms'.[61] Beyond this general reference to international human rights principles, the Constitution goes further and states that the European Convention for the Protection of Human Rights and Fundamental Freedoms, as well as its protocols, applies in Bosnia-Herzegovina and has priority over all other law.[62] Argentina's new Constitution, enacted in 1994, provides that treaties have an elevated relationship to legislated provisions in the country's legal hierarchy.[63] The Constitution references a number of regional and international legal instruments including, inter alia, the International Covenant on Civil and Political Rights as well as the International Covenant on Economic, Social and Cultural Rights that explicitly acquire this constitutional hierarchy.

Lastly, the inclusion of international standards informs the state's 'constitutional journey', thus becoming an integral part of how that legal regime builds itself in relation to its past and the standards it wishes to set for its agents in the future. South African jurists and commentators stress the deliberative and participatory nature of the approach to the dialogue and contestation through which new norms emerge in a democratic society.[64] Trials and Truth Commissions in every country have been characterized by active, organized, and concerned participation by victims and independent organizations of civil society, and that attitude towards adjudication spill over into similar processes of intense public interest that are not necessarily legacies of a repressive past but important to the agenda of the newly democratic arrangements. States with constitutions that have strongly incorporated international standards based on transitional justices paradigms will find it harder to justify to both their citizens and the international community at large any future action departing from these norms and, especially, any attempt to ignore or cover up egregious abuses committed in the recent past.

Even if the ideal of social change was not explicitly contemplated in Latin American transitions, it is possible to state that where transitional justice has gone the farthest, the

[61] Constitution of Bosnia-Herzegovina, Art II(1), General Framework for Agreement for Peace in Bosnia and Herzegovina (Dayton Peace Accords) (1995), annex 4.

[62] Ibid Art II(2).

[63] Constitucion de la Nacion Argentina, Art 75(22).

[64] Albie Sachs, Justice of the Constitutional Court, in his vote in *Minister of Health NO v New Clicks South Africa (Pty) Ltd (Treatment Action Campaign as amicus curiae)*.

impetus towards a more open, tolerant, egalitarian society has also been the strongest. In the wake of trials and truth-telling, the young democracies have also produced impressive change in matters like privacy rights, institutions to protect citizens against discrimination, removal of censorship and broader freedoms of expression and association, greater transparency in government processes, and even same-sex marriage. Though perhaps without a deliberate plan—and perhaps in a non-linear, messy way—Latin Americans are engaging in the type of transformation described by Chief Justice Pius Langa, of the South African Constitutional Court:

> Transformation is a permanent ideal, a way of looking at the world that creates a space in which dialogue and contestation are truly possible…and in which change is unpredictable but the idea of change is constant.[65]

As defined in the South African context, constitutional transformation is a long-term project of enactment, interpretation, and enforcement directed at achieving large-scale social change.[66] A transformative constitution, then, is not concerned simply with the document itself and how it facilitates healing in the aftermath of atrocities, but also with how the provisions can be applied in a way that is responsive to emerging injustices. Thus, the constitution facilitates more than mere 'transition' in the sense that may be most intuitive to scholars of transitional justice. Instead it serves as the framework for the construction of 'a new political, social, and economic order based on democratic values, social justice, and fundamental human rights.'[67]

This understanding of the transformative capacity of constitutions may do much to further reconciliation between parties, perhaps more than transitional processes that lean more towards healing through truth-telling than towards judicial redress. In Latin America, there may have been more emphasis on criminal prosecutions, although truth-telling and reparations have also been central to the transitional justice agendas. Providing redress for those who have been victimized by violations is a necessary component of true reconciliation. It is certainly true that redress should come in comprehensive, integrated forms; but the absence of justice for egregious human rights violations will leave the job only half done. In this respect, a constitution should provide a structure that enables the victims, or the state acting on behalf of victims, to pursue justice. While the constitution need not explicitly spell out an obligation to prosecute, it should be sure not to pose barriers that obstruct the state from fulfilling its international obligations to bring perpetrators to justice.

IV. Conclusion

In the point of rupture between the old regime and the new, the embarkation upon constitutional and transitional justice processes provides an important milestone in a community's history. A redrawing of norms is taking place, and the idea is to engage in transforming the legal landscape in order to make it inhospitable to violations by the state and agents of fundamental human rights, both past and future. At the same time, the post-conflict constitutional process provides the perfect opportunity for a direct injection of international standards into the machineries of domestic law, and thus can contribute to the development and crystalliza-

[65] Pius Langa, 'Transformative Constitutionalism' (2006) 17(3) *Stellenbosch Law Review* 351–60.

[66] Sandra Liebenberg, *Socio-Economic Rights: Adjudication under a Transformative Constitution* (2010), 24.

[67] Ibid 27.

tion of important norms. While constitutional processes and norms will not provide the nuts and bolts for the fulfillment of obligations to punish, record, repair, and reform, they are nevertheless important components of it. This coincides with the commentary of Ruti Teitel, who suggests that transitional justice, as it solidifies into an important building block for democratic institution-building in the twenty-first century, will necessarily move towards a more nationalistically textualized approach.[68]

The circumscription of judicial power, the delineation of due process, the provision of balancing tests between the rights of the accused and the accuser, and the inclusion of affected groups in the deliberative enterprise can provide touchstones for the transitional justice effort in a given state. On the flip side, transitional justice measures such as commissions and international bodies established to prosecute perpetrators of abuse are important paving stones for the constitutional process itself. Without these mechanisms, it would be difficult, if not impossible, for a community devastated by generations of conflict to build the capacities to take the complex steps towards nation-rebuilding and reconciliation.

Bibliography

Eileen F. Babbit, *The New Constitutionalism: An Approach to Human Rights from a Conflict Transformation Perspective* (2010)

Pablo de Greiff and Alexander Mayer-Rieckh, *Justice as Prevention* (2006)

Sandra Liebenberg, *Socio-Economic Rights: Adjudication under a Transformative Constitution* (2010)

Naomi Roht-Arriaza and Javier Mariezcurrena, *Transitional Justice in the Twenty-First Century: Beyond Truth versus Justice* (2006)

Theunis Roux, 'Principle and Pragmatism on the Constitutional Court of South Africa' (2009) 7 *International Journal of Constitutional Law* 106

Herman Schwartz, 'Lustration in Eastern Europe' (1994) 1(2) *Parker School Journal of Eastern European Law* 141

Ruti Teitel, *Transitional Justice* (2000)

Laurence H. Tribe, *The Invisible Constitution* (2008)

[68] Ruti G. Teitel, 'Transitional Justice Genealogy' (2004) 16 *Harvard Human Rights Journal* 69, 77:

> Given tensions present in the administration of transitional justice in its second phase, the principles of justice associated with [the previous phase] were increasingly questioned.... Accordingly, the move away from judgment associated with international justice reflected a shift in the understanding of transitional justice, which became associated with the more complex and diverse political conditions of nation-building.

CHAPTER 62

ISLAM AND THE CONSTITUTIONAL ORDER

CHIBLI MALLAT*

Salt Lake City and Beirut

I. The Setting: Three Arcs of Crisis

With nominal Muslims second in the world in number to nominal Christians,[1] Islam matters as a constant mirroring image of the West in recorded history, originally across the Mediterranean, and now increasingly worldwide.

In the words of French historian Lucien Febvre, Islam 'created' Europe by splitting what was until then a united Mediterranean world. Building on a remark by his colleague Marc Bloch about 'the birth of Europe when the Roman Empire died', Febvre showed how the rise of Europe could not be understood without the irremediable 'loss' of half of the Mediterranean to the

* I completed this work at Harvard Law School as Custodian of the Two Holy Places Visiting Professor of Islamic Legal Studies in 2011, and am grateful to Bill Alford, Martha Minow, and Frank Michelman and to the colleagues in the Faculty Workshop at HLS for their comments, to Judge Andrew Allen in London, and to Tanner Strickland Lenart SJ Quinney College of Law 2011, for their thorough review of the chapter. I am particularly grateful to Michel Rosenfeld for his comments. All mistakes and shortcomings are exclusively mine.

[1] '2.039 billion Christians, 32% of the world (dropping), 1.57 billion Muslims (22% (growing))', table at <http://www.religioustolerance.org/worldrel.htm>.

Muslim conquests starting in the seventh century CE.[2] The success of Arab-Muslim conquests in the eighth century established a southern European frontier that did not previously exist, with lasting inroads in Spain, Sicily, and the Balkans and counter-offensives illustrated in the ebb and flow of crusades over the following centuries.[3] From this perspective, the crime against humanity committed in September 2001 in New York, similar massacres in London and Madrid,[4] and the subsequent Western wars in Iraq and Afghanistan, are the latest epiphenomena of a '*longue durée*' perspective in a millennium-long antagonism in which 'Islam and Europe', then 'Islam and the West', have been the two main poles.[5]

While less well recorded, the conflict also operated on the farther Eastern side of Muslim conquests, where the contemporary prolongations of an equally millennial unrest loom large: from the main socio-political fracture of India, to long-standing rebellions in southern Thailand, to a Malay-Indonesian Muslim archipelago in which Indonesia stands as the most populous country in the Muslim world, to the Uighur rebellion in China, the constitutional order of key Asian countries is challenged by the rise of political Islam. While the battle has not disrupted the established post-colonial order in these countries in the dramatic way that shook up Iran in 1978–79, the challenge is structural and long-standing. *Mutatis mutandis*, this is true at the southern frontier of the Muslim world in Africa, where, from the Sudan to Senegal, a battle of religions seems to be developing chiefly between the Muslim and Christian *Gebiet*.[6] Other fracture lines are taking place around Muslim immigrant communities in Europe and the Christian West at large.[7] A zeitgeist has been steadily developing over the past four decades, displacing the world division from socialism versus capitalism, poverty versus wealth, and classic nationalistic disputes in favor of religiously defined dichotomies. The late

[2] Lucien Febvre, *L'Europe. Genèse d'une civilisation* (1999), 87, citing Bloch, 'L'Europe a surgi très exactement quand l'Empire romain a croulé' and at 107:

> Or un tel monde, ainsi axé, centré sur la Méditerranée, un tel monde est devenu impensable aux temps carolingiens, pour beaucoup de raisons, mais d'abord pour celle-ci: la fermeture de la Méditerranée par les Arabes.

[3] Alphonse Dupront, *Le mythe de croisade* (4 vols, 1997) (monumental work on the European perception of the crusades across the ages).

[4] On September 11 as a crime against humanity, see my short 'The Original Sin: "Terrorism" or "Crime against Humanity"?' (2002) 34 *Case Western Journal of International Law* 245, and the more elaborate policy argument in 'The Need for a Paradigm Shift in American Thinking: Middle Eastern Responses to "What we are Fighting for"' in John Borneman (ed), *The Case of Ariel Sharon and the Fate of Universal Jurisdiction* (2004), 150, and in David Blankenhorn et al (eds), *The Islam/West Debate* (2005), 215 (also published in French as 'Pour un changement de paradigme dans la pensée américaine: Réponse à "la Lettre des intellectuels américains"' (2004) 73 *Travaux et Jours* 115, and in Arabic in *Nahar*, Part 1, 20 January 2003; Part 2, 27 January 2003).

[5] Albert Hourani, *Islam in European Thought* (1991), and *Europe and the Middle East* (1980), are solid introductory works.

[6] The scholarly literature seemed to be running behind events as I was completing the present study, with South Sudan formally voting the division of Sudan into two independent states along the Christian–Muslim fault line between South and North. For a good choice of books in English on the Sudan, see the interview of Richard Cockett on the FiveBooks site at <http://fivebooks.com/interviews/richard-cockett-on-sudan>.

[7] In a large literature on growing Muslim minorities in Europe and the United States, and the concomitant rise of distrust, in which vituperative sound vibes dominate the debate, see the thoughtful book by Sumbul 'Ali-Karamali, *The Muslim Next Door: the Qur'an, the Media, and that Veil Thing* (2008). For Muslim minorities vying for recognition in various parts of the globe, in particular their family/personal status laws, see an early comprehensive collection in Chibli Mallat and Jane Connors (eds), *Islamic Family Law* (1993) (esp chapters on Muslim minorities in China by A.R. Dicks; in Europe by Riva Kastoryano, Sebastian Poulter, and Dima Abdulrahim; on 'Khaek, Moro, Rohinga' in Thailand, the Philippines and Burma, by Andrew Huxley; and in India by Werner Menski and Tahir Mahmood). The literature has grown significantly since, including case law on female dress code, state constitutional amendments banning Islamic law in the United States, and an expansive political and legal scholarship.

Samuel Huntington put it in the most eloquent terms as a clash between world civilizations.[8] In fact, rather than Confucianism or any of the five or six other religions/civilizations he identified, the concern has since been almost exclusively fixated upon Islam: in China, the United States, Russia, the Middle East, Central Asia, India, and Africa, the clash has Islam as a religion/civilization at its center.

Considering the immense span of time and space, an order of priorities is needed for analytical purposes. Between the Eastern and Western frontiers of Islam, the constitutional order is under assault over an almost continuous territorial stretch of the planet from Morocco to Indonesia. In addition to the various challenges on a national level, three largely unsettled arcs of crises emerge, one of which is now over half a century old, the second over one-third of a century old, with the last arc of crisis having persisted now for over a century. The first arc runs from Iran to India, from the brutal partition of Pakistan from India in 1947–48, to the secession of Bangladesh from Pakistan in 1971, through Afghanistan's occupations and wars, where the violent crises have gone uninterrupted since 1978–79.[9] The Central Asian republics, and the Russian Muslim-majority areas of the Caucasus are intermittently but durably affected, but the heart of the crisis consists of the so-called AfPak complex,[10] with inevitable extensions to India and Iran.[11]

Iran, which is also part of that AfPak constellation, is at the center of the second arc of crisis. Since 1979, political Islam's *aggiornamento* has been carried first and foremost by the Islamic Republic of Iran. The Iranian Constitution bears some of this hallmark, by considering the country to be responsible for the cause of Muslims worldwide.[12] In practice, the matter is more nuanced, and a cyclical ebb and flow of militant Islam shows decade-long shifts between

[8] Samuel Huntington, 'The Clash of Civilizations?' (1993) 72 *Foreign Affairs* 22, later developed into a book, *The Clash of Civilizations and the Remaking of World Order* (1996).

[9] Former Carter administration National Security Council Head Zbigniew Brzezinski coined the word in 1979, see 'The Crescent of Crisis', *Time Magazine*, January 15, 1979, available at <http://www.time.com/time/magazine/article/0,9171,919995-1,00.html>. Also George Lenczowski, 'The Arc of Crisis: Its Central Sector' (1979) 57 *Foreign Affairs* 796. For an adjusted contemporary mapping of the crises, see Saad Salloum, 'Gilles Kepel and the Middle East's triangular crises', interview in *Niqash* (Baghdad), February 3, 2010, available at <http://www.niqash.org/content.php?contentTypeID=75&id=2600&lang=0>.

[10] Then presidential candidate Barack Obama emphasized the word during his campaign, which underlies the importance of Pakistan for the future of Afghanistan, and the resulting complexity in dealing with two large countries with significant Muslim populations, some 30 million people in Afghanistan and 170 million in Pakistan.

[11] With the political and military flux on the AfPak theater, it is hard to distinguish the contours of the constitutional order being shaped against the continuous Afghani wars since the Soviet invasion of 1979, and the increasing violence in Pakistan and the surrounding countries. For Pakistan, a useful introduction is Ahmad Rashid, *Descent into Chaos* (2008). For Afghanistan, a classic book from before the Soviet invasion is by Louis Dupree, *Afghanistan* ([1973] 2002). The literature since the 1990s is understandably large, and Barnett Rubin and Olivier Roy have written extensively on Afghanistan in crisis. See also Bruce Riedel, *The Search for al Qa'eda—Its Leadership, Ideology, and Future* (2008). For a comparative constitutional view on Afghanistan, see Chibli Mallat, 'Constitutions for the Twenty-First Century. Emerging Patterns—The EU, Iraq, Afghanistan' in Peri Berman, Wolfhart Heinrichs, and Bernie Weiss (eds), *The Law Applied: Contextualizing the Islamic Shari'a* (2008), 194 (also published as 'Constitutions for the 21st Century: Emerging Patterns—the EU, Iraq, Afghanistan…' (2009) 1 *Duke Law CICLOPs* 41.

[12] Iranian Constitution, Art 3:

> The government of the Islamic Republic of Iran has the duty of directing all its resources to the following goals:… (p) the formulation of the foreign policy of the country on the basis of Islamic criteria, brotherly commitment to all Muslims, and the unstinting support of all oppressed and deprived people throughout the world.

See ch 5, 'Iran, Shi'ism and the Arab Middle East' in Chibli Mallat, *The Middle East into the 21st Century* (1996), 127–72.

aggressive, strident militancy, and the longing for a less exuberant and revolutionary foreign policy. Between 1979, when the Revolution toppled the Shah, and 1989, when Khumaini died, Iran lay at the heart of a turmoil characterized by an eight-year-long devastating war with Iraq. In the next decade, until 2005, the Islamic Republic turned far more moderate in its international activities, and the presidency of Muhammad Khatami succeeded in keeping the country shielded from the surrounding violence and international isolation. Since the accession to the presidency of Mahmud Ahmadi-Nejad in 2005, the cycle is back to militant, outreaching politics, including immense repression at home after the rigged presidential elections of summer 2009. With revolutionary Islam in Iran seeking regional leadership by way of a foothold in the Mediterranean, and finding it in the Palestinian (Hamas) and Lebanese (Hizbullah) similarly motivated Islamic constituencies, the 1979 Islamic Revolution meshed with the third and most enduring arc of crisis, the one represented by the Israeli–Palestinian conflict.

It is in Israel–Palestine that the deepest running violent conflict in modern history continues to threaten world order. In the Middle East, the Israel–Palestine arc of crisis is over a hundred years old. There, colonization has left its heaviest mark since Zionist settlers adopted the European-style constitutional yearning in the late nineteenth century, and created in 1948 a Jewish nation-state in a Palestine where the large majority of the inhabitants were Muslim.[13] Several narratives compete for the depiction of the Israel-centered crisis: in Zionist lore, it is a return home for the Jewish diaspora after two millennia of forced exile, and an ingathering for the Jews of the world under *aliyah* (lit: elevation, ascent). For the Palestinians, it is a *nakba*, a catastrophe of massive displacement from their homes by an alien colonizer. Beyond the hard to reconcile narratives, the enduring Israel–Palestine crisis varies from its depiction as a hundred-year-long civil war to the continuation of the Western crusades in a Jewish form. For the purposes of this chapter, this arc of crisis elicits a sectarian logic that essentially pits two communities, Jewish and Muslim, against each other, both claiming a territory which each considers its own exclusively as a matter of right.

To sum up: Amidst a planet-wide array of crises, three are central: the AfPak arc, which includes Pakistan, Afghanistan, India (and the surrounding countries in Central Asia as well as Iran); the Iranian Revolution (which, in addition to Pakistan and Afghanistan, impacts directly on Saudi Arabia and the Gulf States, and the so-called Shiʿi crescent, comprising Iraq, Syria under the ʿAlawis, a small Shiʿi sect, and Lebanon); and Israel, with its own crisis radiating across the Middle East and beyond. In all these arcs of crisis, Islam as religion-civilization is vying to define an alternative constitutional order.

In this complex framework of three persistent arcs of crisis, the fracture occasioned in the constitutional ordering of the world can be approached through a dual prism. One is *international*: depending on where the analyst positions herself, the matter is of an Islamic universal call for domination, or one of self-defense. The other is *internal*, and challenges the constitutional order within the nation-state in its Westphalian characteristics as best summarized by Max Weber: the state's exclusive right to use force over a given territory.[14]

[13] In 1948, approximately one-third of the population of historic Palestine was Jewish (600,000), against two-thirds non-Jewish, Christians, and Muslims (1.2 million). About 850,000 non-Jewish Palestinians fled or were driven from their homes in what became Israel. The most important book on the period is Benny Morris, *The Birth of the Palestinian Refugee Problem Revisited* ([1988] 2nd edn, 2004). In 2010, there is almost population parity in historic Palestine between Jews and non-Jews.

[14] Weber's famous statement on 'the monopoly of legitimate physical violence' by the state appears in his lecture on 'Politics as vocation (*Politik als Beruf*)' in 1918.

Both international and national perspectives dovetail significantly in the modern world of constitutionalism. Section II provides international perspectives on Islam and the constitutional order. Section III offers an appreciation of Islam within a primarily domestic constitutional set-up.

II. International Perspectives

1. The Personal Logic of Islamic/Middle Eastern Law

Classical Islamic law had far less to say about the constitutional order than about war as a collective aspect of mobilization when society or religion are endangered. One testimony among many is Ahmad 'Isa 'Ashur's, a middle-of-the-road proselytizer in Egypt from the Muslim Brotherhood, who describes *jihad* (just war) as 'the fight against unbelievers for the victory of Islam and the defense of the nation'.[15] In this popular primer on Islamic law, originally published *c*. 1972, he repeats the basics of *jihad* in classical law: just war is considered a necessary duty incumbent on all Muslims when in defense of their territory, and an individual duty for all free male Muslims at least once a year.[16]

The issue of war underlines a paradox. On the one hand, Islam is an eminently personal law. A Muslim is bound by Islamic law wherever he or she finds him or herself. Yet Islam does not cover the entire planet, and classical jurists divided the world into 'war' or '*jihad* territory' (*dar al-jihad*), and 'Muslim' or 'peace' territory (*dar al-islam*, or *dar al-silm*). Personal rules could not therefore always prevail, and a mixed set of legal rules developed around the concept of religious communities/sects, together with regulations affecting Muslims who found themselves in alien/enemy territory, as well as non-Muslims in Islamic territory. The latter rules were easier to implement, naturally, and a fully sectarian system ensued: Christians, Jews, and other tolerated minorities could live and work under Islamic rule, but they were not considered equals in rights or duties to their Muslim compatriots. A whole array of discriminatory practices was developed to ensure that their subaltern role would be consecrated, especially in peace time through the payment of a special poll tax called *jizya*. In a thorough examination of *jizya* practices in the Geniza archives, Samuel Goitein persuasively undermined the received notion that the tax was benign.[17]

On the other side of the accommodation to the reality that Islam had to contend with land it did not control, jurists had far less to say. Muslims were expected to carry on their normal duties, to the extent possible, in the so-called 'territory of compromise' (*dar al-sulh*).[18]

[15] '*qital al-kuffar li-nasrat al-islam wal-difa' 'an al-watan*', in Ahmad 'Isa 'Ashur, *al-fiqh al-muyassar fil-'ibadat wal-mu'amalat* ('the law of rituals and transactions simplified') ([*c*. 1972] 1984), 299. 'Ashur died in the late 1980s and was a companion to historic figures in the Muslim Brotherhood, Hasan al-Banna and Sayyed Qutb. Banna was assassinated in 1949, probably by agents of the Egyptian monarchy. Qutb was hanged by the Naser regime in 1966.

[16] Ibid ch on *jihad*, 299–305.

[17] S.D. Goitein, *A Mediterranean Society: The Jewish Communities of the Arab World as Portrayed in the Documents of the Cairo Geniza* (5 vols, 1967–88). Study of *jizya* in *The Community* (vol 2), 380–95.

[18] See eg Chibli Mallat, entry on 'International Law: Islamic Public Law' in Stanley Katz (ed), *The Oxford International Encyclopedia of Legal History* (6 vols, 2009), 3: 280–2, and bibliography. Entries on *jihad*, war and peace in Islam, *dar al-sulh*, and related concepts in leading specialized encyclopedias provide competent departing points to the literature. See in particular the three editions of the *Encyclopedia of Islam* since 1913, as well as John L. Esposito (ed), *The Oxford Encyclopedia of the Modern Islamic World* (1995) and Stanley N. Katz (ed), *The Oxford International Encyclopedia of Legal History* (2009). For a good overview on the contemporary scene, see Gilles Kepel, *Jihad; The Trail of Political Islam* ([French 2000] 2002); Noah Feldman, *After Jihad: America and the Struggle for Islamic Democracy* (2003).

'Compromise' was needed in enemy territory when it was not at war with Islam, and forms of reciprocity were engineered by the jurists. A complicated picture remains in a long and complex history. Capitulations (treaties originally meant to secure the religious integrity of Muslims in foreign land against a reciprocal rule for non-Muslim foreigners in Muslim land) developed over time as leonine extraterritorial arrangements that worked only in one direction—namely to protect Westerners from the reach of local law. Regardless, capitulations provide a strong illustration of the logic of personal versus territorial law. As definers of the peace in between wars, a more careful examination of their operation over the centuries shows the powerful and elusive logic of the personal versus territorial dimension of international relations in a world chiefly defined through the prism of religion. Religion as the political marker of a group or a community is not circumscribed to a region or a country in human history. In the contemporary world, however, it is chiefly Middle Eastern.

This characteristic of a dominant religious definition of individuality, known also as sectarian, confessional, communal, or communitarian, may be as old as the Middle East.[19] The scheme operates internationally and domestically. The domestic dimension, the more disturbing one in terms of the constitutional order, is addressed more fully below. The international dimension is more elusive, but its importance has increased in recent years with the planet-wide violence associated with the late twentieth century rise of Islamic militancy.

Nor are communities straddling several states a novelty to constitutionalism. The actions and perceptions of say, German communities in mid-twentieth century Mitteleuropa, were a major factor in the instability that led to the Second World War, and the Basque community straddling France and Spain remains a lingering issue of concern, as does the Protestant–Catholic divide in Ireland or the Balkan mosaic. In the Middle East, injustice towards the Kurds in the division of their land in between five countries is probably the most conspicuous example of the disjunction between community and nation-state.

Within the world of Islam, the logic of sectarianism is also pervasive. The large divide between Sunnism and Shi'ism partakes of the same border-related unease, but operates *sui generis* for the constitutional order. Shi'is are the second largest Muslim community, with estimates at 10 to 15 percent of the Muslim population, against over 80 percent Sunnis. This divide is probably the most important within the logic of religious sectarianism which has slowly engulfed the Muslim world since the Iranian Revolution in 1979. Sunnism is associated with orthodoxy, and Shi'ism represents the main religious schism in the history of Islam, akin to Catholicism and Protestantism in the Christian Church, with the followers of Shi'ism giving a special status to 'Ali, the Prophet's cousin and son-in-law, and to the descendants of 'Ali and Fatima, the Prophet's daughter. The divide did not stop there, and subdivisions in various countries became sharper with the presence of smaller sects. The majority of Shi'is follow 12 descendants of the Prophet starting with 'Ali, and are therefore known as 'Twelvers, *ithna 'asharis*'. Smaller Shi'i sects are the Zaydis in the Yemen, who acknowledge seven such descendants, while Isma'ilis, known in India as Bohras, stop at five. Smaller Muslim sects include the Druzes in the Levant, and of more recent divide, Babis and Baha'is, whose eponyms date from nineteenth-century Persia. Amongst the Sunnis, the most internationally active sect is constituted by the Wahhabis, whose eponym promoted a purist version of Islam in eighteenth-century Arabia, and whose followers are closely associated with modern Saudi rule.

Unlike national/ethnic groups, the response of the respective Sunni and Shi'i communities and their numerous offshoots to nation-state boundaries is specific in two ways. In the first

[19] J.N. Postgate, *Early Mesopotamia: Society and Economy at the Dawn of History* (1992), and my discussion in Chibli Mallat, *Introduction to Middle Eastern Law* (2007), 141–80.

place, there has been by and large no attempt to redraw the boundaries of nation-states along a Sunni–Shi'i configuration. This means that Sunnis or Shi'i leaders or communities at large, even when they assert their identities as Sunni or Shi'i, have never requested the division of their countries along such lines. This does not mean that ethnic cleansing has not taken place where the fault lines have operated historically; indeed, the formation of modern Iran is premised on large-scale ethnic cleansing of non-Shi'is by the dominant Shi'i power since the Safavid dynasty took over Persia at the beginning of the sixteenth century and established Shi'ism as the official, and therefore exclusive, state religion/sect.[20] In that perspective, ethnic cleansing was a de facto, as opposed to a de jure, response to the uneasy coexistence between Muslim communities.

A different phenomenon developed de jure, which is more easily identifiable for Shi'is than for Sunnis on the constitutional plane. The transnational legal structure of the two communities is a distinctive aspect of the Sunni–Shi'i divide. Let us consider the allure of their respective internationalism in turn.

2. 'The Shi'i International'

Shi'i projections beyond the nation-state I have called 'the Shi'i International'.[21] Although occasionally displaced by Qum in Iran, the Shi'i international's epicenter was Najaf, in Iraq, the oldest place of learning in the Shi'i world. Its characteristic trait is the educational dimension in which it has developed, and the transnational legal structure under which it operates.

At the origins of the Shi'i international is a complex historical development. Shi'i law saw in the early modern period a battle between two schools of thought. One was literalist, the Akhbari school, the other, the Usuli school, was contextualist. Usulis prevailed in the late eighteenth century, and this meant that the jurists became a necessary intermediary between God and people. Shi'is as people are divided in two categories, that of the normal, individual Shi'i, and the scholar. Individuals are *muqallids*, imitators or followers, of the learned class of ayatollahs who are *mujtahids*, the Shi'i scholars who are legal experts and exponents of the law.

The divide bears significant consequences in the modern world: traditionally, the individual as 'follower' had a personal relation to the scholar he chose to imitate, and the system was fluid. Followers would support a particular scholar, but the relationship was not codified, nor was it coercive. A follower may choose whomever he or she wished to emulate, and much of the shape and intensity that emulation could take. Most important was the personal devotion in the form of questions and answers to the scholar on points of law, more often than not of a ritual nature—for example, how does one perform the fast when traveling? How are ablutions to be carried out before prayer when water is scarce?

Of importance also was the financial support contributed by the follower directly to the scholar, or to an institution or a charity that the scholar preferred, which included or augmented the tax owed as 'the share of the Imam' (*sahm al-imam*) whom the scholar represented on earth.[22] The top scholars, who reach the summit of the learned pyramid by a combination of peer recognition and the importance of their pool of followers across the world for the quality

[20] See on the Ottoman-Safavid formation of the 'Shi'i–Sunni' frontier in the eighteenth-century wars, Robert Olson, *The Siege of Mosul and Ottoman–Persian Relations, 1718–1743* (1975).

[21] Chibli Mallat, *The Renewal of Islamic Law: Muhamad Baqer as-Sadr, Najaf, and the Shi'i International* (1993).

[22] *Imam* is generally the leader of the prayer. Although there are no capital letters in Arabic, *Imam* rendered with a capital I represents the 12 Imams of the Shi'i tradition, the *ahl al-bayt* (people of the house [of the Prophet]). With a small i, an *imam* is a religious leader generally.

of their legal standing, tend to be preoccupied with arcane fields of Islamic legal theory.[23] They do not have the means to enforce decisions or legal choices they make, and they cannot use the state to coerce tax out of the public. The system has one main characteristic, which prevails to date: it is completely voluntary. This phenomenon attests to the special type of civil society where the public creates, outside the realm of the state, autonomous spaces for a whole array of meaningful social relations.[24] The main characteristic of that operation appears in the lack of coercive violence, constituting forms of democratic participation at work in the Shi'i community.

Also characteristic is the international dimension of the system. As a Shi'i from Lebanon, or Pakistan, or India, the follower is part of a personal law-based community that does not know state boundaries, and it was and remains common for him or her to follow a scholar from Qum or Najaf. The individual Shi'i, male or female, can choose the scholar they prefer, and they generally do not limit themselves to their local religious leader. Many Lebanese and Iranian Shi'is follow Sayyed 'Ali al-Sistani, the top scholar in Najaf, Iraq. With the ease of communication and the rise of religious fervor, the international phenomenon has become important in the modern world.

With that prevalence come a number of tensions. The most obvious is the disjunction between the nation-state and the Shi'i international. The choice of the most important scholars by their followers operates across the borders, with Najaf and Qum scholars at the heart of the international system. The more renowned scholars stand out by sheer reputation within a given college where they congregated in both cities. Since their direct involvement in the political world in the Iranian Revolution of 1978–79, and their recognition as 'leaders' by the Iranian Constitution, no less,[25] the picture has become more complicated. Two poles have emerged since 2003, when Iraq was freed from single-party sectarian dictatorship. In Iran, the top scholars, and since a constitutional amendment of 1989, one top scholar, are chosen by an assembly of peers (called the Assembly of Experts):[26] Ruhullah al-Khumaini between 1980 and 1989, 'Ali Khamene'i since. In Iraq, the prominence of Najaf is not constitutionally noted, save for a passing reference on the need to preserve the autonomy of the religious places from state encroachment.[27] The top scholars keep their traditional appellation of *marja'*, plural *maraje'*, literally 'reference'. In Najaf, there were four recognized *maraje'* in 2011: 'Ali al-Sistani, who is generally considered *primus inter pares*, Muhammad Sa'id al-Hakim, Bashir al-Najafi, and the Afghani-born Ishaq al-Fayyad.

Shi'i scholars, in turn, act through a large number of channels, least obvious amongst them the unique network of intermarriage amongst the most famous scholars' families and the prominent families of merchants and landowners.[28] Other channels consist of 'representatives',

[23] Arabic *usul al-fiqh*, roots or principles of jurisprudence. See Mallat (n 19), ch 1 and literature cited.

[24] Argument developed in chs 1–3 of Mallat (n 21).

[25] *rahbar*, leader, Arts 5 (historic and religious leadership transformed into constitutional leadership) and Arts 107–12 (election, powers and duties).

[26] Persian *majlis-e khubregan*, Iranian Constitution, Arts 107 and 108 (modality of Leader's election by the Assembly of Experts).

[27] Iraqi Constitution, Preamble (historic leadership role of scholars), Art 10 (Protection of Holy Places), Art 41 (freedom in choice of personal status), Art 44 (freedom to practise collective rituals).

[28] An early presentation of these interlocking channels between the merchants and the scholars on the eve of the Iranian Revolution can be found in Michael Fischer, *Iran: From Religious Dispute to Revolution* (1980), 80–95. A current illustration is found in the Sadr family, where marriage, education/scholarship, and to some extent business relations are key to understanding the family leadership in Iraq (the late Muhammad Baqer al-Sadr and Muhammad Sadeq al-Sadr, assassinated by Saddam Hussein in 1980 and 1999 respectively); Lebanon (Lebanese Shi'i historic leader and Iranian-born Musa al-Sadr, 'disappeared' in Libya by military

wakils, who speak in the name of the important *maraje'*. Since the 1990s, offices of leading *maraje'* are openly transnational, and the Khu'i Foundation, for instance, has retained beyond the death of Abul Qasem al-Khu'i in 1992 an educational operation ranging far and wide, including London and New York. With the politicization of Islam since the Iranian Revolution, the channels dovetail with the foreign policy of Shi'i Iran, less so in the case of Iraq after the fall of Saddam Hussein because of the particular set of circumstances in which the Shi'i majority overhauled the domination of the former sectarian Sunni government. While the weight of transnational Shi'ism radiating from Iraq has steadily grown in 2003, it never had the assurance or the stridency of its Iranian counterpart.

The case of the Shi'i international is peculiar in terms of the working of the law. It is not that transnational channels were adopted in a codified shape, for there is no recognition by international law of this specific format of civil society articulated around the scholars. Unlike other aspects of the internationalization of civil society like the human rights movement, the Shi'i International is reflected de jure merely in the domestic sphere, and so far exclusively in Iran. The most famous instance of this reflection was made by Ruhollah al-Khumaini in his pamphlet, written during his long Najaf exile, as a treatise on 'Islamic government', also known as 'the rule of the jurist'.[29] While constitutions continue to be coextensive with domestic law, albeit religious law, legal developments within countries that have a sizeable Shi'i population can hardly be understood outside the reality of the Shi'i International.[30] The power and appeal of the top scholar is never limited to the nation-state in which he lives.

3. Sunni Internationalism

Altogether different is Sunni internationalism. The differences with Shi'ism are structural, and can be summed up in a number of characteristics. Sunnis constitute a massively majoritarian community in the Muslim world, and the international dimension of Sunnism has tended to function in a very different way from that of the Shi'i minority. In countries with a Sunni majority, Muslim constituencies tend to adhere to the nation-state as such, and conduct their policies within their boundaries. When 'exported', Sunnism has been closely associated with Egypt and Saudi Arabia, respectively the largest in population and the richest in oil amongst the Arab states. The scholars in Egypt or Saudi Arabia have always been very much part of the fabric of government in their countries, and they rarely act without the blessing or tolerance of their respective governments in Cairo and Riyadh. The international expression of violence carried out by mostly Saudi nationals in September 2001 was shorn of any scholarly blessing. Although it set a worldwide trend that has turned into a self-fulfilling Sunni International

dictator Mu'ammar al-Qaddafi in 1978); and Iran (former president Muhammad Khatami, married to Musa al-Sadr's niece). See Raffaele Mauriello, *Descendants of the family of the Prophet in contemporary history: a case study, the Shi'i religious establishment of Al-Nagaf (Iraq)*, Supplementi alla Revista degli Studi Orientali, Pisa 2011, and extensive biographies of some prominent family members in 'Abd al-Hussein Sharafeddin, *Bughiyat al-raghibin* (2 vols, 1991).

[29] Khumaini's influential lectures in Najaf were published in Arabic and Persian alternatively as *Al-hukuma al-islamiyya* (Islamic government) and *wilayat al-faqih* (*velayat-e faqih* in Persian, the rule of the jurist). Translated in English and annotated by Hamid Algar, *Islam and Revolution* (1981), 27. In a large scholarly library on Iran, the works of Said Amir Arjomand provide an excellent departing point for comparative constitutionalism. See eg his *After Khomeini* (2009).

[30] This is the case in Syria, Saudi Arabia, Afghanistan, Pakistan, India, Kuwait, and Lebanon, where important Shi'i communities can be found without constituting an absolute numerical majority. In Iran and Iraq, Shi'is form a clear majority, constituting over 80 percent and 60 percent of the population in conservative estimates. Small Bahrain has also a large Shi'i majority ruled by a quasi-absolute Sunni dynasty.

called al-Qa'eda, the legal parameters in which it takes place are profoundly different from the tight structure of the scholar-led Shi'i International.[31]

Sunni internationalism took various forms initially, none particularly violent or over-militant. In the same way as clusters of countries came together under forms of regional organizations, countries with a sizeable number of Muslim inhabitants formed the Organization of Islamic Conference (OIC), which had grown since inception in Morocco in 1969 to 57 member states in 2010. Few tangible effects resulted, and the OIC remains a parleying forum with even less influence than other similarly ineffective institutions like the League of Arab States.[32] More effective forms of internationalism were mass political movements like the Muslim Brotherhood and its Pakistani correspondents, most prominently the Jama'at-i Islami.[33] By and large, these movements were non-violent on the international scene, and shared nonviolence with wide membership organizations where the political dimension of Islam was significantly muted, like the various Sufi orders.[34] Unlike Sufism, the Muslim Brotherhood contributed an important set of leaders who shared a committed political world-view and developed transnational networks of various importance in the formation of governments and in mass predication. Abu 'Ala' al-Mawdudi in Pakistan, Hasan Banna and Sayyed Qutb in Egypt, later Yusuf al-Qaradawi, turned into household names with large followings and occasional success in government.[35]

Before the spectacular espousal of violence by al-Qa'eda, forms of Sunni internationalism challenging the domestic constitutional order in various countries were muted by the closeness between national Sunni scholars and the government, which invariably pays scholars' salaries as civil servants and supports their institutions. In Rabat, Tunis, Cairo, Damascus, Riyadh, Islamabad, Jakarta, and other major capitals, Sunni scholars have long been enmeshed with the governing elites. Armed rebellion which developed in all these countries was generally the expression of disenfranchised Muslims in the poorer strata of society, and scholars who spoke for them belonged to the lower rungs of the Islamic legal establishment. When the process of internationalism was afoot, it only rarely operated outside the purview of the ruling government. Saudi Arabia is a case in point, where petrodollars were used massively to build

[31] Note that the term al-Qa'eda (which has several meanings in Arabic including rule, as in legal rule, and basis, as in the basis of the pyramid) is not the original term which ben Laden and his colleagues chose publically for their movement. The word was reportedly chosen by ben Laden in the late 1980s to mean the register of names (*sijill al-qa'eda*) or roster of those who had joined the fight against the Soviets in Afghanistan, in order to facilitate queries made by their families to him as one of the prominent leaders of the anti-Soviet 'Arab *mujahidin*' in Afghanistan. This was in 1988, see Kamil al-Tawil, *Al-Qa'eda wa akhawatuha* (Al-Qa'eda and its sisters) (2007), 31. When ben Laden formally launched the movement as an international organization, he chose the more telling '*al-jabha al-islamiyya al-'alamiyya li-qital al-yahud wal-salibiyyin*' (the Islamic international front to fight the Jews and the Crusaders), which was announced in a press conference in Khost, Afghanistan, on February 23, 1998. English annotated translation of the Front's manifesto in Gilles Kepel and Jean-Pierre Milelli, *Al Qa'eda in its Own Words* (2008), 53 (original French *Al-Qaida dans le texte* (2005)).

[32] See Mallat (n 19), 151–4 and references cited.

[33] On Egypt's Muslim Brotherhood, the works of Robert Mitchell and Olivier Carré stand out; on the more recent scene of political Islam in Egypt, see Gilles Kepel, *Muslim Extremism in Egypt: The Prophet and Pharaoh* ([French 1984] 2003). On Pakistan's Jama'at-i Islami, see eg entry by Seyyed Vali Reza Nasr in Esposito (n 18), vol 2, 356–60 and bibliography.

[34] See the various entries on Sufism in Esposito (n 18) vol 4, 102–33. Over the immense stretch of movements, schools, and practices across history, association of non-violence with the mystical trends in Sufism and in the traditional Sunni political movements needs to be of course qualified.

[35] All these figures are prolific writers, and numerous studies have also been devoted to each. For a selection of modern political writings, see John Donohue and John Esposito (eds), *Islam in Transition: Muslim Perspectives* (new edn 2006).

mosques and support networks of Wahhabis—a small schism in eighteenth-century Islam which would have remained insignificant without the staggering flow of money to the Saudi state coffers since the 1950s. Such networks could occasionally slip into unruly challenges to local governments. On the whole, conservative governments avoided supporting firebrand Muslim leadership in the rest of the world, in large part for fear of boomerang effects.

But boomerang effect there was, and we have in the Jordanian-born Abu Mus'ab al-Zarqawi an important illustration of the new scope of the Sunni International when it turned violent, and a theory that supports its legal and political mode of thinking.

The Zarqawi phenomenon is illustrative of Sunni internationalism in two ways. First is the significance of Zarqawi's representativeness in the elusive network building around al-Qa'eda. The second is the legal underpinnings as articulated in a message from Zarqawi to ben Laden.[36]

Until his violent death on 7 June 2006 in Baghdad, Jordanian-born Zarqawi, who had been arrested and jailed for a long period in Amman, was the most prominent leader of Sunni international militancy in Iraq. He embodies ruthless forms of violence, culminating in civil war and ethnic cleansing on an unprecedented scale in a modern Iraqi history where the amount of brutality is considerable already. Fanned by an increasingly violent US occupation, including torture in the jails of Abu Ghreib by members of the US military, Zarqawi's vindictiveness against the new order was immense. Much violence was predictable, considering the ways Sunni militants hiding on the northern side of the Iran–Iraq border at the outset of the war were pulverized in the first days of the war by a relentless bombing that went by and large unnoticed. Anti-Americanism, therefore, was well established in Zarqawi's circles, and had been fuelled in his own case by a long period in jail in Jordan, America's ally in the region. Those two traits—deep antagonism towards the West that considers all its behavior as a mere extension of the crusades, and hatred and violence against local governments—fuse in the persona of Zarqawi the basics of the challenge to the prevailing order in the Middle East and beyond.

The legal justifications that this internationalism adopts are the more intriguing aspects of the world-view of Zarqawi and his group. By 2003, he had developed close links with Osama ben Laden, and was the anointed leader of al-Qa'eda in Iraq, in Arabic *al-qa'ida fi bilad al-rafidayn* (the land of the two rivers). The carrier of a message allegedly sent to ben Laden from Zarqawi was arrested in Iraq in January 2004. The long missive he was transmitting reads as a textbook for militant Sunni internationalism world-view. It carried a strong anti-Shi'i sectarian message, and it called for a policy of extreme ethnic cleansing and the burning to the ground of any opposition to the establishment of an Islamic state ill-defined, except for being strictly 'ruled by Islamic law'.

Even in the case of the Afghanistan and the 'Afghans Arab *mujahidin*', an important expression of the Sunni International, it may be useful to keep in mind that the master executioner of the US–Saudi combined anti-Soviet armed policy was none other than the much decried Osama ben Laden. Sometime in the mid-1990s, when his usefulness was spent, all US and Saudi government contacts with him were severed, resulting in a suddenly disenfranchised leader who turned his anger against both governments with a vengeance. In his major biographies,[37] the contrast surfaces occasionally between a once-adulated anti-Soviet freedom fighter

[36] Full text of the letter, with comments, in Chibli Mallat, *Iraq: Guide to Law and Policy* (2009), 365–77, 390–2. In contrast to the Ben Laden manifesto of 1998 (n 31), the focus of the fight was for Zarqawi the Shi'i community and the government of Iraq, rather than the US forces.

[37] eg Jonathan Randal, *Osama: The Making of a Terrorist* (2004); Peter Bergen, *The Osama bin Laden I Know* (2006).

who was organizing Saudi recruits in a register (*qa'eda*), and his overnight abandonment by those who had raised him to the pinnacle. One question deserves a more thorough answer than the current overview allows: would there have been a ben Laden or a Zarqawi in the first place if their respective Saudi and Jordanian governments had been even minimally democratic, and allowed them a political voice in their respective societies?

Sunni internationalism should therefore be studied from the viewpoint of domestic actors who 'go international', without losing sight of the domestic legitimacy of their nemesis, the rulers of the countries to which they belonged. This is equally true of the Shi'i International. In Khumaini's founding book of 1970, the transnational perspective is all but absent. Even in the later iterations of the Islamic Republic, the attempt to seize power, mostly in Iraq and Lebanon where the largest relative presence of Shi'is is found, was never premised on the Shi'i International as such. The domestic-international dialectic is complex, but the prevailing term in the constitutional order is domestic.

III. Domestic Perspectives

1. Constitution and Symbols

Domestically, the patterns of challenge to, and interaction with, the constitutional order are less elusive than their international counterparts. One way to approach the constitutional order within is to apply a modified Kelsenian pyramid.

At the top of the pyramid stands the official name of the country concerned, the flag adopted, and the explicit reference to Islam or Islamic law in the constitution. There are a large variety of appellations (eg Republic of Indonesia, State of Qatar, Kingdom of Morocco). Most Muslim countries do not refer to Islam in their title. Jordan and Saudi Arabia's names refer to their ruling families. Only Pakistan, Iran, Mauritania, and Afghanistan are officially 'Islamic republics'. The green color, which is considered in the modern world as the color of Islam, has been adopted by a number of Muslim states on their flags, and both Saudi Arabia and Iraq have adorned it with founding Islamic phrases—'There is no God but God, and Muhammad is his Prophet', in the case of Saudi Arabia, and 'God is Great', in Iraq, while Iran includes the name of God, in Arabic, in an elaborate calligraphy.

However powerful socially, symbols and titles remain of limited institutional importance. What matters is the logic they force on the constitutional system. In a country like Afghanistan under the Taliban, or Saudi Arabia under the house of Saud, foreigners are equated with non-Muslims, and Shi'is equally unwelcome. The logic of religion morphs quickly into a logic of sectarianism, which is by nature exclusive of citizens who happen to belong to the wrong sect—Christians and Jews in many Middle Eastern countries, Christians and Muslims in Israel, Shi'is in the Sunni-dominated system under Saddam Hussein, and Sunnis in the 'Alawi (a small branch of Shi'ism)/Asad-dominated Syria. The sectarian logic can be excessive—such as the destruction of other symbols like the Buddha statues of Afghanistan, the systematic wasting of non-Hanbali symbols in Saudi Arabia; and in the full course of 60 years since the emergence of the State of Israel, the literal bulldozing of Arab qua non-Jewish villages and orchards in Palestine.

2. Islam in Constitutional Courts

The picture is not invariably that excessive, and the roads to the incorporation of religious tenets within the system can take more felicitous, more circuitous, and less exclusive shape.

Within the constitutional texts emphasizing Islam, important points of contention pit a now familiar controversy which initially jelled in Egypt's amendment of its 1971 Constitution. To assuage activist Muslims at a time when such associations were perceived to bolster his position against challenges from the more secular left, then president Anwar Sadat introduced in 1980 an amendment to Article 2 of the Constitution to read: 'The principal source of legislation is Islamic law.' Previously, Islamic law was mentioned as 'a', and not 'the' principal source of legislation. This coincided with the rise of the Egyptian Supreme Constitutional Court, which was tasked with interpreting legislation in accordance with the Constitution. Inevitably, the Supreme Constitutional Court would have to consider whether legislation stood in conformity with Islamic law. Its subtlety and hard work in this regard were impressive.

First, Egypt, like Pakistan when it came to its financial legislative edifice, parsed the Islamic supremacy clause in a way that did not eventually blow the received system asunder.[38] When the argument that Islamic law did not comport with the Islamic prohibition of interest risked destroying key provisions for debtors in the Egyptian Civil Code, the Court decided that Article 2 would not apply retrospectively to every single piece of legislation that Egypt passed in the twentieth century.[39] The article would apply merely prospectively, said the Court. And when the Court saw it appropriate to apply the clause, it made sure that it would not be done vindictively and without due process, namely without paying attention and deference to the legislative process as the presumed expression of the people's general will. There was no reason to presume that the legislator would antagonize the Islamic tradition.[40] Mostly, the Court showed that an elaborate, scholarly, and sound reading of the tradition did not mean that it was perforce 'backward and medieval'. Contrary to the excessive description of the whole of Islamic law as 'incompatible with the fundamental principles of democracy' by the European Court of Human Rights,[41] the Supreme Constitutional Court succeeded in reading the Islamic legal tradition in a progressive, humanist manner that salvaged in the process Islamic law's better import and philosophy, one that associates interpreting divine rule with a legal process that facilitates

[38] This 'supremacy clause' is called the 'non-repugnancy clause' in Pakistan. Pakistani Constitution, Art 227(1):

> All existing laws shall be brought in conformity with the Injunctions of Islam as laid down in the Holy Quran and Sunnah, in this Part referred to as the Injunctions of Islam, and no law shall be enacted which is repugnant to such Injunctions.

See generally Martin Lau, *The Role of Islam in the Legal System of Pakistan* (2006).

[39] SCC, Year 1, Case 20, decided 4 May 1985, SCC 3, 209–28, translated in English as 'Supreme Constitutional Court (Egypt)—Shari'a and Riba' (1985) 1 *Arab Law Quarterly* 100. Confirmed in several other decisions, starting with SCC, Year 4, Case 47, decided 21 December 1985, SCC 3, 274–86. Supreme Constitutional Court decisions were published in ten volumes carefully edited by the presidents of the Court until 1998. In Pakistan, two significant decisions on the legality of interest, in late 1991 absolutely prohibiting it from the financial system, *Mahmood-ur-Rahman Faisal v Secretary, Ministry of Law*, PLD 1992 FSC 1 (Federal Shariat Court) and in 2002 by the Supreme Court reversing the decision in *Bank Limited v Farooq Brothers and Others*, PLD 2002 SC 800. See discussion in Mallat (n 19), 338–45.

[40] See cases and discussion in Mallat (n 19), 196–207.

[41] ECtHR, *Refah Partisi (The Welfare Party) and others v Turkey*, App nos 41340/98, 41342/98, 41343/98 and 41344/98, 13 February 2003, available at <http://www.unhcr.org/refworld/country,,ECHR,,TUR,,3fe7097e4,0.html> (prohibition of party advocating Islamic law by the Turkish Constitutional Court valid as in conformity with the need to protect democracy under the European Convention on Human Rights, see especially para 123 of the Grand Chamber decision).

people's lives.[42] The Qur'an repeatedly mentions ease, facilitation, the Arabic root word *yusr*.[43]

The reading could also go in a different, intolerant way. 'Readings of the Qur'an,... as of any Bible, can support the most diverse glosses.'[44] Disturbing practices are mostly encountered in repressive countries that claim their ideology in an allegedly literalist interpretation of Islamic law. In countries like Iran, Saudi Arabia, Somalia, Sudan, the Indonesian province of Aceh, and some Northern Nigeria states, criminal law is codified and applied by courts in ways incompatible with universal human rights standards.[45] Women in particular are victimized by an inegalitarian and coercive reading of the tradition.

The battle over interpretation has long been joined. In my preferred reading of the legal tradition, Islamic law (and the Middle Eastern legal tradition at large, Jewish, Christian, Babylonian, Zoroastrian) provides a formidable wealth of documents, especially in Arabic, that deserves to be given its rightful place in modern society. The debate whether Islam, Islamic law, or Islamic principles is or are 'a' or 'the' main reference in the legal order appears increasingly stale if such a larger humanist prism is adopted. The better question is how to fuse in scholarship Islamic and other Middle Eastern legal traditions with the most advanced principles of law elsewhere on the planet. For that, only scholarship of the highest order is needed, and there is no shortcut.[46] Here also, the Murr Supreme Constitutional Court has forged ahead, as have the less known UAE Federal Supreme Court and to some extent Pakistan's high courts.[47]

3. The Personal Logic of Middle Eastern Law, Again

We have discovered in the personal dimension of Islamic/Middle Eastern law an essential basis for various forms of Islamic internationalism. The personal logic of Middle Eastern law is equally central to the understanding of the central conundrum of Middle Eastern constitutionalism.

In the Middle East, the Christian, Jewish, or Muslim individual is defined by law as primarily such: Christian, Jewish, or Muslim. He is only secondarily a citizen in a given country. This trait continues to be at odds with the secular logic of individual equality at the basis of modern Western constitutionalism.

The two mutually exclusive logics—citizens as strictly equal, and citizens as part of unevenly rights-endowed communities—survive to date, most apparently in the problems of conflicts of law and jurisdiction when it comes to such central family transactions like marriage,

[42] On the humanist reading see the late President of the Supreme Constitutional Court, 'Awad al-Murr (d. 2004), 'The Supreme Constitutional Court of Egypt and the Protection of Human and Political Rights' in Chibli Mallat (ed), *Islam and Public Law* (1993), 229.

[43] '*fa nazratun ila maysara*' ('give attention to ease' Q.2: 280); '*yassir li amri*' ('make it easier on me' Q. 20:26); '*nuyassiruka lil-yusra*' ('we make it easy on you to be at ease' Q. 87:8). I have counted over thirty explicit references to *yusr* as facilitation of people's lives in the Qur'an. For standard concordances to the Qur'an see in Arabic Fu'ad 'Abd al-Baqi, *Al-mu'jam al-mufahras li-alfaz al-qur'an al-karim* ('Lexicon of the Qur'an') ([1935–39] 1987); in English Hanna Kassis, *A Concordance to the Qur'an* (1983) under tripartite Arabic root /y s r/.

[44] 'la lecture d'un Koran..., comme toute Bible, peut supporter les gloses les plus diverses', Robert Fossaert, *Le Monde au 21ème siècle* (1991), 501.

[45] For a competent scholarly survey, see Rudolph Peters, *Crime and Punishment in Islamic Law: Theory and Practice from the Sixteenth to the Twenty-First Century* (2005), 142–85.

[46] An example of such needed scholarship is the recent study of federalism by Najaf scholar Hasan Bahr al-'Ulum, *al-Islam wal-fidiraliyya* ('Islam and federalism') (2010).

[47] Developments in Mallat (n 19), 191–207 (Yemen, UAE, Egypt) and 338–45 (Pakistan).

divorce, custody, and inheritance. A person who gets married is bound, irrespective of her beliefs, by the rules of her religion. As the application of Islamic law receded under colonial occupation, that area of personal law escaped the logic of a constitutional order defined by the equality of the citizens. Instead, religious tribunals belonging to a person's sect apply the specific traditional family laws in case of dispute, as in Lebanon or Israel. Often, as in Egypt or Iraq, the national tribunals have taken over, but they apply sect-based laws sometimes couched in national terms.

The individual is therefore subjected to several competing legal logics: as a religiously defined person, he is bound by the laws of his religious community. The sectarian logic is so pervasive that the 'community' does not stop at the overall distinction of Muslim/non-Muslim. The Muslim community itself gets sharply divided into sub-components, of which the most significant are Sunnism and Shi'ism, but the offshoots are many: Druze, 'Alawis, Zaydis, Isma'ilis, Babis, and Baha'is, ... Similarly, Christians and Jewish communities were subdivided following historically formed clusters: Greek Orthodox, Greek Catholic, Maronite, Protestant, Nestorians, Copts, etc for Christian, conservative, or reformist and other subdivisions for Jews.[48] For the constitutional order, these divisions mean far more than the set of conflicts developing around the main areas of family law. The picture that emerges is that of a constitutional order where religiously defined communities act as *constitutional agents* for their members.

Here lies the main problem of Middle Eastern constitutionalism, which projects also beyond in Indian 'communalism', in several countries of East Asia and sub-Saharan Africa, and in the Muslim minorities in the West. In the Middle East and elsewhere, accommodation of sects as constitutional agents is particularly difficult. Mere occultation of the problem in dictatorial systems like Syria and Iraq under the Ba'th party leads to privileging the dominance of a minority sect over the system: this is the case of the Sunnis under Saddam Hussein and 'Alawis under the Asads. At the opposite pole is the Lebanese 'confessional' system, which openly acknowledges the communities as bearers of collective rights that trump the individual citizen's rights. Seventeen or eighteen religious sects are therefore acknowledged in law, with Christian Maronites, Muslim Sunnis, and Muslim Shi'is apportioned a set of government positions in an inevitably complex conundrum that renders governance almost impossible. As soon as one of the three major sects considers a matter to be essential to its well-being, the constitutional system grinds to a halt. Majoritarianism is powerless in such a context.

Between the two poles (total ignorance and dominance of one minority sect under dictatorial systems, and impossibility of governance when a sect is given veto power) appear a number of variations specific to each country depending on the size of its communities and changing historical conditions. Jewish communities have been decimated across the Middle East and in much of the Muslim world. In Egypt and Iraq, where a once thriving Jewish community has all but disappeared, Christians and Muslims coexist in difficult mode, as the logic of sectarianism similarly undermines the Christian minorities. Iraqi Christians are a small minority, and their power in government is practically nonexistent. Their struggle, in the face of immense adversity carried on by a long string of regional and domestic wars, is one of survival. Yet the main fracture takes place between Sunnis and Shi'is, the latter constituting a much larger community. Shi'i dominance, in turn, is checked by the national division in Iraq between Arabs and Kurds. In Egypt, the national movement that prevailed between the two world wars carried a strong message of equality, and the Christian nationalist leaders refused quotas by arguing their total 'Egyptianhood' as equals in rights and duties with all other

[48] Elaboration of the argument and references in Mallat (n 19), 171–80.

Egyptians. Since the dictatorship took hold in the wake of the military coup of 1952, the scene has receded dramatically for Egyptian Christians. Within the narrowed participation in government dictated by military takeover, their representation in government has been at best symbolic, while sectarian issues repeatedly come to the fore. The case of Israel bears its own peculiarity, but its constitutional conundrum is similar to other countries in the region, except that the Jewish community plays the dominant, if not exclusive, role in the country's governing leadership.

IV. Epilogue: Emerging Hopes

With the deadlock occasioned by constitutional structures that fit uneasily with the sectarian logic, domestically and internationally, the Middle East and the Islamic world generally appear as an exception on the planet. Violence on a large international scale, adding to the domestic and regional strife, has become the hallmark of the region. If one were to reduce it to a single structural factor, the personal as opposed to territorial character of the law may provide the most useful clue to the dominant clash of two legal logics: the nation-state and its protection of the individual citizen, and the religious-sectarian state of communities that operate as constitutional agents irrespective of the individual.

In a less bleak vision, conviviality actively seeks novel modes for the constitutional order. Federal arrangements, notably in the Iraqi Constitution, try to accommodate sectarian and national divisions by a less crude mode than in a tripartite Kurd/Shi'i/Sunni constitutionally regulated division of spoils. More generally, the discourse of human rights, both for individuals as such and individuals as part of a group, together with the demand for increased political participation in government, appear as more promising routes for the constitutional order, domestically in the first place, and in its international projections. Universal rights can operate both to transcend the limitation of the logic of territorial law and that of personal law.[49] Considering the weight of historic atavisms, however, any such constitutional project will require the full span of the twenty-first century to take root. It may have started in Tunisia in January 2011.[50]

Bibliography

Islamic and Middle Eastern Law, general

Norman Anderson, *Law Reform in the Muslim World* (1976). Precise legal information on Islamic legislative reforms before the *aggiornamento* of Islamic law in 1979 Iran

Eugene Cotran and Chibli Mallat (and other subsequent co-eds), *Yearbook of Islamic and Middle Eastern Law* (1994). Includes an annual survey of legislative and judicial developments in several Middle Eastern jurisdictions

49 I am grateful to Professor Frank Michelman for drawing my attention to this perspective.

50 For an early appreciation of the Middle East Revolution in its 'constitutional moment', see my 'Comparing the Middle East in 2011 and Europe in 1989: Nonviolence and Democratic Strategy', Lecture at the Harvard Middle East Center, March 4, 2011, available at at <http://www.righttononviolence.org/?p=365>. For Egypt and for Bahrain, see the work completed with students on constitutional reform, respectively as 'Revising Egypt's Constitution: A Contribution to the Constitutional Amendment Debate', *Harvard International Law Journal*, published online February 22, 2011, and 'Constitutional Options in Bahrain', published April 12, 2011 in the *Virginia Journal of International Law* online.

Noel Coulson, *A History of Islamic Law* (1964). Despite scholarly shortcomings, the most readable introduction to date in the field

Wael Hallaq, *Shari'a: Theory, Practice, Transformations* (2009). Competent, but belabored and uneven treatise by a non-lawyer

Chibli Mallat, 'Comparative Law and the Islamic (Middle Eastern) Legal Culture' in Mathias Reimann and Reinhard Zimmermann (eds), *Oxford Handbook of Comparative Law* (2006, paperback 2008), 609ff. Summary of previous entry

Chibli Mallat, *Introduction to Middle Eastern Law* (2007, paperback edn with new preface 2009). Provides a mapping of the field with attention to historical and comparative law, and an emphasis on court decisions

Joseph Schacht, *An Introduction to Islamic Law* (1964). Arid but competent treatise on Islamic law by noted Western scholar of Islamic law in the twentieth century

Encyclopaedias

Encyclopaedia of Islam (1st edn 1916–36, 2nd edn 1954–2005, 3rd edn 2007), multiple editors. Main reference work in the field of Islamic studies

The Oxford Encyclopedia of the Modern Islamic World (4 vols, 1995). General editor John Esposito, provides good choice of entries on key concepts, individuals, and countries

The Oxford International Encyclopedia of Legal History (6 vols, 2009). General editor Stanley Katz, Islamic law editor Baber Johansen, puts Islamic and Middle Eastern law on the map of international legal scholarship

CHAPTER 63

CONSTITUTIONAL TRANSPLANTS, BORROWING, AND MIGRATIONS

VLAD PERJU*

Boston

I. Introduction

All fields of knowledge are shaped by ideas that travel in time and space. From history to economics to the natural sciences, the circulation of ideas is both 'a fact of life and a usefully enabling condition of intellectual activity'.[1] Law is no exception. As Roscoe Pound remarked in *The Formative Era of American Law* (1938), the 'history of a system of law is largely a history of borrowings of legal materials from other legal systems and of assimilation of materials from outside of the law.'[2] The development of the English common law, the Roman-Canonic *jus commune*, and the advent of constitutionalism in the second half of the twentieth century are

* I am grateful to the Clough Center for the Study of Constitutional Democracy at Boston College for a grant that supported research for this project.

[1] Edward Said, *The World, the Text, and the Critic* (1983), 226.

[2] Roscoe Pound, *The Formative Era of American Law* (1938), 94.

examples of phenomena in which the circulation of legal norms and ideas changed not only legal systems but also the course of history.

The study of legal transplants in comparative law aims to understand how the complex dynamic of cross-jurisdictional legal transfers brings legal systems into contact and eventually causes them to change.[3] For most of the twentieth century, comparative legal studies focused almost exclusively on rules of private law. Constitutional norms, and public law generally,[4] were perceived as too enmeshed with politics to allow for the same rigorous and systematic treatment that could be applied to the study of contract or property law.

And yet, instances of constitutional borrowing are now everywhere. Not only has the idea of a (written) constitution spread to virtually every corner of the world but constitutions are gaining recognition as enforceable legal documents, rather than mere declarations. The institution of judicial review, the principle of the separation of powers, and the enactment of a bill of rights have become fixtures on the world constitutional map. As one scholar noted, 'Reading across any large set of constitutional texts, it is striking how similar their language is; reading the history of any nation's constitution making, it is striking how much self-conscious borrowing goes on.'[5] Much the same can be said about borrowing at the subsequent stages of constitutional application and interpretation. Courts around the world, from Israel to Brazil and from South Korea to Canada and Hungary often consult the work of their foreign peers in interpreting similarly worded constitutional provisions. Faster means of communication, the ease of travel, and the globalization of legal education contribute to the intensification of constitutional borrowing. As Sujit Choudhry has recently noted, 'the migration of constitutional ideas across legal systems is rapidly emerging as one of the central features of contemporary constitutional practice.'[6]

These developments make it all the more surprising that constitutional borrowing as a standalone topic has been rather marginal in comparative constitutional law. While scholars in the field study various aspects of how constitutional systems interact, the mechanics of cross-constitutional interaction rarely receive comprehensive treatment. As late as 1990, a bibliographical study concluded that the literature on cross-border influence was 'virtually inexistent'.[7] More recently, Ran Hirschl noted that 'from a methodological standpoint, we have yet to encounter a coherent theory of inter-court constitutional borrowing.'[8] Nothing resembling the transplants debate in comparative private law can yet be found in the field of comparative constitutional law.

At one level, this should not necessarily cause concern. The transplants debate in comparative private law became deadlocked in a polarized contest between scholars arguing that

[3] See Alan Watson, *Legal Transplants* (1974).

[4] This chapter discusses exclusively comparative constitutional law; it does not integrate other forms of comparative public law, such as comparative administrative law. For a recent overview of that field, see Susan Rose-Ackerman and Peter L. Lindseth, *Comparative Administrative Law* (2010). For a discussion of cross-jurisdictional influence, see Tim Koopmans, 'Globalization of Administrative Law—The European Experience' in Gordon Anthony et al, *Values in Global Administrative Law* (2011), 400ff.

[5] Robert Goodwin, 'Designing Constitutions: The Political Constitution of a Mixed Commonwealth' in Richard Bellamy and Dario Castiglione (eds), *Constitutionalism in Transformation: European and Theoretical Perspectives* (1996), 223.

[6] Sujit Choudhry, 'Migration as a New Metaphor in Comparative Constitutional Law' in Sujit Choudhry (ed), *The Migration of Constitutional Ideas* (2006), 16.

[7] Andrzej Rapaczynski, 'Bibliographical Essay: The Influence of US Constitutionalism Abroad' in Louis Henkin and Albert Rosenthal (eds), *Constitutionalism and Rights* (1990), 406.

[8] Ran Hirschl, 'On the Blurred Methodological Matrix of Comparative Constitutional Law' in Choudhry (n 6), 43.

transplants can be found everywhere and other scholars who proclaimed legal transplants impossible because law is embedded in culture and cultures cannot be transplanted. That debate obscured as much as it illuminated the relationship between law and its broader environment. Moreover, as we will see, the field of comparative constitutional law is already developing on its own rich ways of conceptualizing the interplay between (constitutional) law and (constitutional) culture.

Nevertheless, comparative constitutional law is comparative law. And comparative legal studies have much to offer, at both conceptual and normative levels, for thinking about legal borrowing in general. Understanding the many dangers associated with borrowing in the constitutional context—dangers involving misunderstanding, exclusion, or limitations of self-government and democratic experimentalism—is enhanced by recourse to the traditions and formative debates of comparative law. Perhaps more than anything else, such recourse can help to infuse the field of comparative constitutional law with a much-tested comparative sensibility—that 'usefully enabling condition of intellectual activity'.

This chapter is structured as follows. Section II discusses terminology. The choice of metaphors is central to comparative private and constitutional law and should be the starting point for an overview of the topic. Section III introduces the transplants debate in comparative private law and discusses the distinction between private and public, specifically constitutional, law. Section IV is a prolegomena to an anatomy of constitutional transplants that draws, whenever possible, on the resources of comparative private law. It includes an analysis of the object of constitutional transplants, their timing, motivations, and patterns. The justification of constitutional patterns is discussed in Section V, in the context of the use of foreign law in constitutional adjudication as a specific form of constitutional borrowing. The chapter concludes with a brief meditation on the topic of constitutional convergence.

II. Terminology: The Battle of Metaphors

A survey of the literature reveals great concern about the choice of metaphors to capture cross-constitutional interactions.[9] Available options include 'transplants', 'diffusion', 'borrowing', 'circulation', 'cross-fertilization', 'migration', 'engagement', 'influence', 'transmission', 'transfer', and 'reception'. Four of these metaphors have had greater staying power: 'transplants' and its 'borrowing' equivalent in comparative constitutional law; 'circulation' and its 'migration' equivalent in comparative constitutional law.

Alan Watson's *Legal Transplants* (1974) brought this concept to the centre of comparative legal studies.[10] A scholar of legal history, Watson's study of the English common law and of the reception of Roman law in continental Europe led him to conclude that foreign transplants are the main mechanism by which private law evolves. Because legal rules are largely autonomous from the larger social and cultural surroundings, their transplant across jurisdictions is 'socially easy'.[11] Comparative law properly so called should therefore study the interaction between legal systems through the mechanism of legal transplants.

[9] See also Michele Graziadei, 'Comparative Law and the Study of Transplants and Receptions' in Mathias Reimann and Reinhard Zimmermann (eds), *The Oxford Handbook of Comparative Law* (2006), 443ff.

[10] It took comparative law as an academic discipline a little over seven decades, counting from the 1900 Congress of Paris, to turn to the question of transplants. See Graziadei (n 9), 442ff.

[11] Watson (n 3), 95.

As we will see in the next section, the mechanistic overtones of 'transplants' have not travelled well to comparative constitutional law. 'Borrowing' is the analogous metaphor used to capture the phenomena of constitutional transplants. The inaugural symposium of the premier peer-review journal in the field, *the International Journal of Constitutional Law*, was dedicated to constitutional borrowing.[12] However, critics have argued that 'borrowing' is a deceiving metaphor. Leading the charge, Kim Lane Scheppele has pointed out that borrowing signifies a voluntary exchange among equals whereby the borrowed good will be returned unmodified, after a determined period, to the lender who remains its owner. That description does not apply to constitutional transfers. Unlike consumer goods, constitutional norms are not owned by particular legal system. They can be modified in the process of transfer and are not to be 'returned' at term. Finally, borrowing implies consent when in fact not all instances of constitutional transfer are voluntary.[13]

The proposed alternative to constitutional borrowing is constitutional 'migration'.[14] The fluidity of this new metaphor is said to capture more accurately the complex dynamic of cross-constitutional exchanges. By contrast to the misleading linearity of borrowing, migrations describe

> all movements across systems, overt or covert, episodic or incremental, planned or evolved, initiated by the giver or receiver, accepted or rejected, adopted or adapted, concerned with substantive doctrine or with institutional design or some more abstract or intangible constitutional sensibility or ethos.[15]

Interestingly, the shift from borrowing to migration mirrors a similar shift in comparative law from transplant to 'circulation'.[16]

The battle of metaphors is not 'transcendental nonsense'. Only a sufficiently transparent and capacious lens can capture the complexity of cross-constitutional interactions.[17] Consider, for example, the *rejection* of foreign models. If comparative law aims to understand the interaction between constitutional systems, then instances of rejection of foreign norms are presumably just as relevant as when such norms are incorporated.[18] One learns as much about Poland from its rejection of an American-style structure of government model in 1919

[12] 'Symposium on Constitutional Borrowing' (2003) 1 *International Journal of Constitutional Law* 177.

[13] Kim Lane Scheppele, 'Aspirational and Adversative Constitutionalism: The Case for Studying Cross-constitutional Influence through Negative Models' (2003) 1 *International Journal of Constitutional Law* 296, 296ff; Kim Lane Scheppele, 'The Migration of Anti-constitutional Ideas: The Post-9/11 Globalization of Public Law and the International State of Emergency' in Choudhry (n 6), 347ff.

[14] See generally Choudhry (n 6).

[15] Neil Walker, 'The Migration of Constitutional Ideas and the Migration of the Constitutional Idea: The Case of the EU' in Choudhry (n 6), 320–1.

[16] Edward M. Wise, 'The Transplant of Legal Patterns' (1990) 38 *American Journal of Comparative Law Supplement* 1.

[17] See also Günter Frankenberg, 'Constitutional Transfer: The IKEA Theory Revisited' (2010) 8 *International Journal of Constitutional Law* 563, 566:

> These [metaphors]...are not 'only words' but signifiers of rather different theoretical approaches and interpretations, at times deployed casually, at others defended with religious zeal.

[18] It has been argued that type and intensity of rejection is also relevant. Kim Lane Scheppele has distinguished situations when foreign options are considered and rejected in favour of alternatives must be differentiated from cases where the foreign models are perceived as so abhorrent as to endanger the very identity of the receiving system. See Scheppele (n 13), 303ff. See also Heinz Klug, 'Model and Anti-Model: The United States Constitution and the "Rise of World Constitutionalism"' (2000) *Wisconsin Law Review* 597.

as one does from its adoption of a French-inspired constitution two years later.[19] Proponents of the migration metaphor worry that these sorts of constitutional interactions are less visible when one looks for instances of borrowing: 'the traditional focus of cross-constitutional influence only on 'constitutional borrowings' tends to highlight the positive models and hide negative ones.'[20]

At one level, this is an odd claim since nothing prevents scholars from examining, as some have,[21] instances of non-borrowing. But it is true that such projects are few and far between. So a deeper shift is at work here, and it has to do with the comparative agenda itself. The exclusive focus on borrowing, just like a focus on transplants, is primarily concerned with the mechanics of constitutional transfer and the interaction among constitutional systems. By contrast, non-borrowing reveals as much about a given constitutional order as it does about the dynamic between systems. The shift from borrowing to migration, or circulation, takes some of the emphasis away from the interaction itself and toward the deeper causes that lead systems to interact or to refuse interaction. As one author put it, interaction becomes an 'interpretative foil'[22] for exposing a constitutional system's deeper normative structures.

Nevertheless, the significance of the choice of metaphors should not be exaggerated. First, constitutional phenomena are so diverse that no single metaphor can aptly capture them all. For all its advantages, migration is too amorphous a metaphor for the political scientist who sees cross-jurisdictional borrowing as choices of institutional design.[23] Secondly, the shaping role of metaphors is limited. It is true that using the wrong lens can mislead the comparativist's audience and maybe confuse the comparativist himself. But that danger is limited. Metaphors are important, as all words and images are, but they are just metaphors. Moreover, their meanings often overlap. Far from describing constitutional borrowing in mechanistic terms, its proponents see it as a 'complex and somewhat open-ended phenomenon that, at its greatest reach, embraces influences of various kinds that cross constitutional borders.'[24] This definition is strikingly similar to that of constitutional migrations. The same is true for legal transplants. Alan Watson defined the object of transplants as legal rules, but by rules he meant ideas.[25] 'What is borrowed'—or, what migrates, we may add—'is very often the idea.'[26] This is hardly a linear or mechanistic process.

Since disagreement about words does not suspend the need to use them, in the rest of this chapter I use the metaphors of borrowing and transplants, interchangeably. When that lens is too limiting, as it will be at times, I switch to the migration lens. The section headings refer to transplants, for consistency purposes. I do not use the migration metaphor as the default in order to emphasize the continuity between the study of interactions in private and public law. The next section turns to this topic.

[19] Wiktor Osiatynski, 'Paradoxes of Constitutional Borrowing' (2003) 1 *International Journal of Constitutional Law* 244, 250.

[20] Scheppele (n 13).

[21] Lee Epstein and Jack Knight, 'Constitutional Borrowing and Nonborrowing' (2003) 1 *International Journal of Constitutional Law* 196.

[22] Choudhry, 'Migration as a New Metaphor' (n 6), 22.

[23] Epstein and Knight (n 21).

[24] Berry Friedman and Cheryl Saunders, 'Editors' Introduction to the Symposium on Constitutional Borrowing' (2003) 1 *International Journal of Constitutional Law* 177.

[25] Alan Watson, 'Legal Transplants and Legal Reform' (1976) 92 *Law Quarterly Review* 79.

[26] Alan Watson, 'Comparative Law and Legal Change' (1978) 37 *Cambridge Law Journal* 313, 315.

III. The Missing Legacy of Comparative Law

1. The Transplants Debate in Comparative Law

Alan Watson argued that, in Western private law, jurist-initiated legal transplants have been 'the most fertile source of development'.[27] Their success is partly explained by the fact that the transplant of legal rules is 'socially easy' so that 'the recipient system does not require any real knowledge of the social, economic, geographical and political context of the origin and growth of the original rule.'[28] Longevity is a salient feature of legal rules, which is understandable since rules remain largely unaffected by changes in their surroundings.[29] Jurists transplant foreign rules whenever the(ir) need for coherence and consistency demands it.[30] In Watson's view, comparative law is the study of the interaction of legal systems through the voluntary transplant of private law rules.

The transplant approach to comparative legal studies clashes with the 'mirror theory of law'[31] which, from Montesquieu to Hegel and Savigny, understood the legal system to reflect in its letter the spirit of the community—'each society reveals though its law the innermost secrets of the manner in which it holds men together'.[32] Drawing on the hermeneutics of legal meaning, Watson's most outspoken critic, Pierre Legrand, linked the existence of a rule to its intersubjective meaning in the community of interpreters: 'the meaning of a rule is . . . a function of the interpreter's epistemological assumptions which are themselves historically and culturally conditioned.'[33] Since meaning is an essential part of a legal rule and because meaning cannot travel, it follows in Legrand's view that rules—and legal norms more generally—do not travel. Meaning changes between the points of origin and destination on a scale of magnitude that radically transforms the so-called transplant. While Watson acknowledged that rules are altered in the process of transmission,[34] Legrand argued that Watson's formalistic, rule-centred approach led him to downplay the scale of transformation. Law's rich 'nomos'[35] makes convergence impossible.[36]

[27] Watson (n 3), 95.

[28] Watson (n 25), 81.

[29] As Watson later put it (ibid), upon reflection on

> the main point [he] was trying to make in Legal Transplants', his point is that 'however historically conditioned in their origins might be, rules of private law in their continuing lifetime have no inherent close relationship with a particular people, time or place.

[30] There are different ways of understanding the nature of that need. It can be understood as the jurists' own need for authority, see Watson (n 3), 57ff, 88ff, and Wise (n 16), 5. Alternatively, the need can be understood as having deeper roots in the 'normative self-reference and recursivity [that] creates a preference for the internal transfer within the global legal system', in Gunther Teubner, 'Legal Irritants: Good Faith in British Law or How Unifying Law Ends Up in New Divergencies' (1998) 61 *Modern Law Review* 11, 18.

[31] William Ewald, 'Comparative Jurisprudence (II): The Logic of Legal Transplants' (1995) 43 *American Journal of Comparative Law* 489.

[32] Roberto Unger, *Law in Modern Society* (1976), 47.

[33] Pierre Legrand, 'The Impossibility of Legal Transplants' (1997) 4 *Maastricht Journal of European and Comparative Law* 111, 114. See also Pierre Legrand, *Le Droit comparé* (3rd edn, 2009).

[34] Watson acknowledged that 'with transmission or the passing of time modifications may well occur, but frequently the alternations in the rules have only limited significance', Watson (n 26). But by drawing attention to the direction of change, Legrand makes clear the political stakes of comparative method. See generally David Kennedy, 'The Method and Politics' in Pierre Legrand and Roderick Munday (eds), *Comparative Legal Studies: Traditions and Transitions* (2003), 312ff.

[35] See Robert Cover, 'Nomos and Narrative' (1983) 97 *Harvard Law Review* 4. See also, in this context, William P. Alford, 'On the Limits of "Grand Theory" in Comparative Law' (1986) 61 *Washington Law Review* 945.

[36] Pierre Legrand, 'European Legal Systems are Not Converging' (1996) 45 *International and Comparative Law Quarterly* 52.

So this spectrum has at one end Watson's account of convergence based on the ubiquity of legal transplants and, at the opposite end, Legrand claim that transplants are flat-out 'impossible'.[37] But framing the choice as between convergence through transplants or divergence through fidelity to culture is, to use Rodolfo Sacco's measured but stern warning, 'too simple'.[38] Much of the value of the transplants debate and its relevance to comparative constitutional law derives from subsequent qualifications that present a more nuanced and multilayered relationship between law and the broader culture. For instance, scholars have (re)interpreted Watson to argue for a 'weak isolation thesis'[39] that the relationship between law and society is complex, not inexistent. Understanding legal transplants requires case-by-case approach.[40] Similarly, the binary choice between general culture and legal rules can be enriched by intermediary terms such as 'legal formants'[41] that capture some of law's institutional dimension. At the other end of the spectrum, James Whitman has praised Legrand's emphasis on law's larger cultural context while also calling for a dynamic approach to legal culture.[42] Cultures change and law's role in those processes of change must be on the comparativist's agenda.[43]

The relationship between law and its outside environment or culture is central to the transplants debate in comparative law. One of its most interesting aspects has been how homogeneity—cultural or otherwise—breaks down under the pressures of social differentiation. The same year as Watson's publication of *Legal Transplants*, Otto Kahn-Freund noted the differential impact of developments such as industrialization, urbanization, and the development of communication on political as compared to non-political factors (environmental, cultural, or social). Departing from an approach that clusters together all these factors, he argued that rules organizing political power are 'organic' and resistant to transplantation, whereas other rules are 'mechanical' and can be transplanted. Would-be reformers must thus ask, 'How far does this rule or institution owe its continued existence to a distribution of power in the foreign country which we do not share?'[44]

[37] This debate replicated in substance an earlier debate between diffusionists and evolutionists in anthropology. See Wise (n 16), 16.

[38] Rodolfo Sacco, 'Diversity and Uniformity in the Law' (2011) 49 *American Journal of Comparative Law* 171, 172.

[39] Ewald (n 31), 500ff.

[40] Similarly, Edward Wise shares the 'weak' reading of Watson's claim. In Wise (n 16), 3:

> To deny that law merely reflects its social context is not to say that exogenous factors are entirely irrelevant. But social and economic factors have a much more limited and attenuated effect than is indicated by the a priori assertion that law mirrors society.

[41] Rodolfo Sacco, 'Legal Formants: A Dynamic Approach to Comparative Law' (1991) 39 *American Journal of Comparative Law* 1.

[42] James Q. Whitman, 'The Neo-Romantic Turn' in Legrand and Munday (n 34), 312ff. See also John H. Langbein, 'Cultural Chauvinism in Comparative Law' (1997) 5 *Cardozo Journal of International and Comparative Law* 41, 46ff. On the same topic, see the essays in the collection by David Nelken and Johannes Feest (eds), *Adapting Legal Cultures* (2001).

[43] See also Choudhry, 'Migration as a New Metaphor' (n 6), 21: 'given the centrality of migration to the contemporary practice of constitutionalism, the truly interesting question is why and how such changes take place'.

[44] Otto Kahn-Freund, 'On Uses and Misuses of Comparative Law' (1974) 34 *Modern Law Review* 1. This assumes that it possible to tell how entrenched a given rule is in the power structure. In his answer to Kahn-Freund, Watson voices doubt on that score. See Watson (n 25), 82. Constitutional rules are closest to the most 'organic', non-transplantable end of the spectrum, but even areas closer to 'private law' might be too. For such an argument in the context of company law, see Eric Stein, 'Uses, Misuses—And Nonuses of Comparative Law' (1978) 72 *Northwestern University Law Review* 198, 204ff. On the idea of transferability of political institutions, specifically in the East European context, by reference to Kahn-Freund, see also Eric Stein, 'Post-Communist Constitution-Making: Confessions of a Comparativist' (1993) 1 *New European Law Review* 421, 438ff.

Kahn-Freund's framework can be helpful for thinking about constitutional borrowing and perhaps also about the related but distinct issue of convergence. Factors such as globalization have arguably brought about political assimilation and have facilitated constitutional borrowing.[45] Finally, the transplants debate offers a further twist on Kahn-Freund's framework. Gunther Teubner has argued that a study of legal transplants must go beyond political differentiation to consider a greater 'fragmented multiplicity of discourses' in areas such as health, science, or technology. Legal transplants are 'irritants'[46] that trigger reactions from within each social subsystem, not only from within legal culture. The norm transplanted changes in that process just as it changes the culture(s) of the host system. Mutual irritation is the name for 'assimilatory modification' of travelling legal norms in advanced industrialized societies.[47]

2. Transplants in Private and Public Law

Since the transplants debate is limited to Western private law, its relevance to comparative constitutional law is uncertain.[48] Even authors sympathetic to Watson's approach have found his claims about private law not defensible in a public law context. William Ewald has contrasted the American Revolution's dramatic impact on public law with its 'very little direct effect'[49] on the system of courts and on private law generally, concluding that 'the private law...displays the inertness and stability predicted by Watson's theory—a stability that persisted even in the face of volatile changes elsewhere in the legal order.'[50] A similar conclusion could be reached about the survival in Eastern Europe of nineteenth-century civil law codes in altered but recognizable form throughout the Communist regimes which had profoundly changed the constitutional and administrative structure of the state.

However, this distinction between private and public norms is not universally embraced.[51] Montesquieu himself did not distinguish, at least not in this context, between *'les lois civiles'* and *'les lois politiques'*. In his view, rules of contract and property are just as embedded in the spirit and soil of a place—and therefore unmovable across space—as rules about political power.[52]

[45] See eg David Law, 'Globalization and the Future of Constitutional Rights' (2008) 102 *Northwestern University Law Review* 1277. For a study of globalization on constitutional law, see Horatia Muir Watt, 'Globalization and Comparative Law' in Reimann and Zimmermann (n 9), 579ff.

[46] Teubner (n 30).

[47] Wise (n 16), 17: 'modifications are so common in cultural borrowing that authorities like Malinovski have regarded the process as scarcely less creative than other forms of innovation'. See also Horacio Spector, 'Constitutional Transplants and the Mutation Effect' (2008) 83 *Chicago-Kent Law Review* 129; Stephen Holmes and Cass Sunstein, 'The Politics of Constitutional Revision in Eastern Europe' in Sanford Levinson (ed), *Responding to Imperfection: The Theory and Practice of Constitutional Amendment* (1995), 275ff.

[48] It has been argued that the transplants debate can no more apply to public law than it can apply beyond the ambit of European legal systems. See Ewald (n 31), 503.

[49] William B. Ewald, 'The American Revolution and the Evolution of Law' (1994) 42 *American Journal of Comparative Law Supplement* 1, 9 (1994).

[50] Ibid 13.

[51] The question of the transplantability of private versus public law rules is related but not identical to the question whether there is a substantive difference between private and public law. Whatever the answer to the latter question, it remains possible that the rules of contracts or property are different—in a way that affects their transplantability—from norms of administrative or constitutional law.

[52] The equal treatment of all laws was, as Kahn-Freund put it, 'decisive for Montesquieu's entire political and jurisprudential thinking and determining his place in the history of ideas', Kahn-Freund (n 44), 7. Unsurprisingly, Alan Watson argued that 'Montesquieu badly—very badly—underestimated the amount of successful borrowing which had been going on, and was going on, in his day', in Watson (n 25), 80.

Contemporary scholars sometimes make no distinction between private and public and public norms.[53] On what grounds can such a distinction rest?

There is, first, a widespread perception that rules of private law are more technical than constitutional rules. The latter structure and channel political power, whereas private law rules are politically neutral and regulate the interaction among individuals in their private capacity. As Watson argued, the 'indifference'[54] of political rulers gives jurists leeway to transplant rules of private law that do not affect their office. In this view, constitutional transplants remain possible but they depend on the alignment of the rulers' interests. Their study is highly contextual and varies case by case. It follows that transplanting private law rules is 'socially easy' whereas the transplant of public law rules is less common, albeit not impossible, and, in any event, not easy.

Now, it is true that some property and contract rules are more technical than, for instance, notoriously open-ended bill of rights provisions. But their technical nature should not obscure their political stakes.[55] Conversely, even open-ended constitutional provisions are not self-evidently at the mercy of political factors, lest they should not be recognized as 'law'.[56] Secondly, the above explanation ignores the existence of periods of intensive constitutional borrowing when the ideological and/or reputational interests of political elites are sufficiently stable to make the transplant of public rules predictable and 'socially easy'.

Another interpretation of the distinction between private and public rules underscores their different radiating ranges. In this view, 'contract and tort law, for instance, only determine the way in which we should behave in some sort of bracketed interactions. But constitutional law has a deeper impact.'[57] This 'deeper impact' can be interpreted as a reference to the expressive function of constitutional norms. Constitutional norms are more complex signifiers than private norms, which regulate the transactional or non-transactional relations among individuals.[58] Constitutional norms represent the will of the ultimate sovereign: the people. In some historical circumstances, 'the people' may want to borrow from a foreign system precisely for expressive reasons. But self-determination and the expressive nature of constitutional norms do explain why constitutional transplants can be more onerous than the transplant of more technical rules, such as, for example, legal rules regarding bankruptcy.[59] The problem with this interpretation lies elsewhere. In many legal systems, the expressive dimension of constitutional norms is much less poignant than in the United States, for instance because their constitutions are easily amendable and/or their endurance is nowhere near that of the US Constitution. Furthermore, in some legal systems rules of private law can have as much if not greater expressive value. It is a well-known saying that the Code civil is France's 'real' Constitution.

[53] See Jonathan Miller, 'A Typology of Legal Transplants Using Sociology, Legal History and Argentine Examples to Explain the Transplant Process' (2003) 51 *American Journal of Comparative Law* 839.

[54] Alan Watson, cited in Ewald (n 31), 501.

[55] See eg Duncan Kennedy, 'The Political Stakes in "Merely Technical" Issues of Contract Law' (2001) 1 *European Review of Private Law* 7.

[56] The classic is Herbert Wechsler, 'Toward Neutral Principles in Constitutional Law' (1959) 73 *Harvard Law Review* 1.

[57] Carlos F. Rosenkrantz, 'Against Borrowing and Other Nonauthoritative Uses of Foreign Law' (2003) 1 *International Journal of Constitutional Law* 269, 295.

[58] For instance, Brenda Crossman has studied how cultural representations travel in the in the context of constitutional interpretations of equality striking down the ban on same-sex marriage. Brenda Crossman, 'Migrating Marriages and Comparative Constitutionalism' in Choudhry (n 6), 209ff.

[59] See Frederick Schauer, 'The Politics and Incentives of Legal Transplantation' in Joseph Nye Jr and John Donahue (eds), *Governance in a Globalizing World* (2000), 259.

Finally, private and public law norms can be distinguished as to their transplantability by reference to legal history of the kind on which Watson relies. But such arguments will likely leave unexplained the post-Second World War worldwide spread of constitutionalism. Another ground for distinction refers to disparities in the ease of implementation. The literature on the 'transplant effect'[60] emphasizes the need for institutional structures to ensure the interpretation of a norm. Since institutional structures themselves do not migrate, the effects of the transplanted rule in the receiving system will be different from those in the system of origin. While such a conclusion requires empirical support, it might be the case that the support system that constitutions require is more extensive than that of private law rules.[61]

My aim in questioning the distinction between private and public law norms in this context is not to imply that claims about the transplantability of private rules apply equally in the context of public, and specifically constitutional, norms. Rather, it is to suggest that the transplants debate in comparative law could be of use, heuristically and beyond, in the context of comparative constitutional law.

IV. The Anatomy of Constitutional Transplants

1. Object

The study of the object of constitutional transplants begins with constitutional text. The smallest unit of transplant can be a rule of constitutional structure—for instance the 'constructive no confidence' procedure borrowed from the German Basic Law into the 1992 amendments to the post-Communist Polish constitutional arrangement[62]—or an institution, such as the Ombudsman.[63] Fundamental rights provisions can also be the result of borrowing—or non-borrowing. Sujit Choudhry has documented the decision not to include in the Canadian Charter of Rights a US-style due process clause for fear that the judiciary might use it to usher in Lochner-like laissez-faire constitutional doctrines.[64]

But an exclusive textual focus on discrete and insular constitutional provisions is problematic. Like legal formants in comparative law, discreet constitutional norms are often interrelated—in obvious or less than obvious ways—with other provisions, doctrines, or larger institutional structures. Mark Tushnet refers to this characteristic as 'modularity'.[65] He gives as example how legislative standing in the United States is related to provisions which authorize judicial review, and generally to the overall structure of the separation of powers.[66] The overall

[60] Daniel Berkowitz, Katharina Pistor, and Jean-Francois Richard, 'The Transplant Effect' (2003) 51 *American Journal of Comparative Law* 163.

[61] See Frederick Schauer, 'On the Migration of Constitutional Ideas' (2005) 37 *Connecticut Law Review* 907, 912.

[62] Andrzej Rapaczynski, 'Constitutional Politics in Poland: A Report on the Constitutional Committee of the Polish Parliament' (1991) 58 *University of Chicago Law Review* 595, 629.

[63] Gabriele Kucsko-Stadlmayer, *European Ombudsman-Institutions* (2008).

[64] Sujit Choudhry, 'The Lochner Era and Comparative Constitutionalism' (2004) 2 *International Journal of Constitutional Law* 1, 16ff.

[65] Mark Tushnet, 'Returning with Interest: Observations on Some Putative Benefits of Studying Comparative Constitutional Law' (1998) 1 *University of Pennsylvania Journal of Constitutional Law* 325, 330. See also Mark Tushnet, 'Interpreting Constitutions Comparatively: Some Cautionary Notes, with Reference to Affirmative Action' (2004) 36 *Connecticut Law Review* 649.

[66] Tushnet, 'Returning with Interest' (n 65), 330ff.

structure of implementation can also be part of modularity, broadly understood. In the case of hate speech, the choice between a US-style protection and a system that does not extend such protection is at least partly correlated with the degree to which the enforcement of criminal law is centralized. Centralization affects the possibility of abusive restrictions on speech and thus the level of constitutional protection for speech.[67]

An even larger unit of migration can be the regime itself. Examples include the borrowing of US presidentialism in Latin America and the borrowing of mixed, or semi-presidential, systems in Eastern Europe from the French Fifth Republic.[68] Large structure borrowing is almost always subject to assimilatory modifications such that the final results are often a pastiche. For instance, the 1991 Romanian Constitution borrowed the French mixed regime of the Fifth Republic but, for historical reasons having to do with its recent period of dictatorship, it limited the powers of the president by not borrowing the powers of the French president to dissolve the legislature.[69]

In addition to overlooking modularity, an exclusive focus on constitutional text glosses over the difference between constitutional text and constitutional practice. The necessity of looking behind text is perhaps greater with constitutional norms than with rules of private law.[70] The phenomenon of 'constitutions without constitutionalism'[71]—constitutional text that lacks political and cultural traction—is known beyond the ambit of African post-colonial constitutions for which it was coined. Since the standard reference to the phantasmagoric generosity of the text of the 1936 Soviet Constitution is no longer available, we will have to settle for the 'rights' provision of the North Korean Constitution.[72] Now, of course, structural discrepancy between text and practice is also known, *mutatis mutandis*, to constitutional democracies,

[67] See Mark Tushnet, 'Some Reflections on Method in Comparative Constitutional Law' in Choudhry (n 6), 76ff. For another discussion of the importance of institutional structure, specifically the centralized versus decentralized judicial review, see Michel Rosenfeld and András Sajó, 'Spreading Liberal Constitutionalism: An Inquiry into the Fate of Free Speech in New Democracies' in Choudhry (n 6), 174ff. On the migration of centralized judicial review, see Victor Ferreres Comella, *Constitutional Courts and Democratic Values* (2009), 3ff. On the question of free speech, see Michel Rosenfeld, 'Constitutional Migration and the Bounds of Comparative Analysis' (2001) 58 *NYU Annual Survey of American Law* 67, 76ff.

[68] For a study showing the complexity of the East European constitutions, see generally Rett R. Ludwikowski, '"Mixed" Constitutions—Product of an East-Central European Constitutional Melting Pot' (1998) 16 *Boston University International Law Journal* 1. For a study of the similarities between the French model and the constitutional structure of the Weimar regime, see Cindy Skach, *Borrowing Constitutional Designs: Constitutional Law in Weimar Germany and the French Fifth Republic* (2005).

[69] The substance of the assimilatory modification depends also on borrowing within a jurisdiction, so to speak. These are cases of borrowing over time. Eg many post-Communist constitutions in Eastern Europe borrowed from their own pre-war constitutions. See Jon Elster, 'Constitutionalism in Eastern Europe: An Introduction' (1991) 58 *University of Chicago Law Review* 447, 476.

[70] For a discussion of the difference between 'law in the books' and 'law in action' in the constitutional context and its implications for constitutional transplants, see Morton Horwitz, 'Constitutional Transplants' (2009) 10 *Theoretical Inquiries in Law* 353, 547ff. This is a topic much discussed in the context of African constitutionalism. For a study of the gap between Kenya's postcolonial constitutional text and constitutional practice, see J.B. Ojwang, *Constitutional Development in Kenya: Institutional Adaptation and Social Change* (1990), mentioned in Heinz Klug, 'Participating in the Design: Constitution-Making in South Africa' (1996) 3 *Review of Constitutional Studies* 18, 30. In the same context, see also Charles Manga Fombad, 'The Separation of Powers and Constitutionalism in Africa: The Case of Botswana' (2005) 25 *Boston College Third World Law Journal* 301.

[71] H.W.O. Okoth-Ogendo, 'Constitutions without Constitutionalism: Reflections on an African Political Paradox' in Douglas Greenberg et al (eds), *Constitutionalism and Democracy: Transitions in the Contemporary World* (1993).

[72] To pick randomly, Art 65 of the North Korean Constitution provides that 'citizens shall have equal rights in all spheres of the state and social life'.

especially when there is a hierarchy within constitutional provisions whereby some norms—for instance, social and economic guarantees—are 'under-enforced'.[73]

Constitutional method too can be the object of migration. The most notable contemporary example is the proportionality method which migrated from its origins in nineteenth-century Prussian administrative law to many national and supranational courts around the world. As Alec Stone Sweet and Jud Mathews have argued,

> By the end of the 1990s, virtually every effective system of constitutional justice in the world, with the partial exception of the United States, had embraced the main tenets of proportionality analysis... [It has become] a foundational element of global constitutionalism.[74]

So fast and far has proportionality spread that one scholar has called it the 'most successful legal transplant of the twentieth century'.[75]

Two final points are in order. First, connecting the dots of the smaller-scale units (rules, methods, regimes, institutions, doctrines, discourses), entire legal paradigms can be the object of constitutional migration. Lorraine Weinrib has described the post-war juridical/human rights paradigm that characterizes liberal democracies as including elements such as the proportionality method, fundamental rights, judicial review, and a certain understanding of constitutional values.[76] Secondly, the object of migration can also be a constitutional insight or a contrasting image that shows foreign peer courts adopting solutions that the host legal system rejects as unfathomable. The South African constitutional equality jurisprudence has been invoked to such effect in US constitutional law.[77]

2. Timing

'No one begins writing a constitution from scratch'[78]—at least, not anymore. But tracing the origins of the first draft, so to speak, is more important for a constitution than for rules of private law. Writing about the latter, Alan Watson noted that 'however historically conditioned in

[73] On the idea of under-enforced norms, see Lawrence Sager, 'Fair Measure: The Legal Status of Underenforced Constitutional Norms' (1978) 91 *Harvard Law Review* 1212. For a discussion in the context of social and economic rights, see Katharine G. Young, 'The Minimum Core of Economic and Social Rights: A Concept in Search of Content' (2008) 33 *Yale Journal of International Law* 113.

[74] Alec Stone Sweet and Jud Mathews, 'Proportionality Balancing and Global Constitutionalism' (2008) 47 *Columbia Journal of Transnational Law* 72, 74, 160. See also David Beatty, *The Ultimate Rule of Law* (2004). For a study of proportionality in the context of US law generally, see E. Thomas Sullivan and Richard S. Frase, *Proportionality Principles in American Law* (2008); Jed Matthews and Alec Stone Sweet, 'All Things in Proportion? American Rights Review and the Problem of Balancing' (2011) 60 *Emory Law Journal* 797; Moshe Cohen-Eliya and Iddo Porat, 'The Hidden Foreign Law Debate in Heller: The Proportionality Approach in American Constitutional Law' (2009) 46 *San Diego Law Review* 367; Moshe Cohen-Eliya and Iddo Porat, 'American Balancing and German Proportionality: The Historical Origins' (2010) 8 *International Journal of Constitutional Law* 263.

[75] Mattias Kumm, 'Constitutional Rights as Principles: On the Structure and Domain of Constitutional Justice' (2003) 2 *International Journal of Constitutional Law* 574, 595.

[76] See Lorraine E. Weinrib, 'The Postwar Paradigm and American Exceptionalism' in Choudhry (n 6). Weinrib argues that US law does not partake in this paradigm, even though its origins go back to the Warren Court era. For a mention of the role of the Canadian legal elite in bringing the Warren Court model to Canada, see Horwitz (n 70), 547ff.

[77] See Frank Michelman, 'Reasonable Umbrage: Race and Constitutional. Antidiscrimination Law in the United States and South Africa' (2004) 111 *Harvard Law Review* 1378; Frank Michelman, 'Reflection' (2004) 82 *Texas Law Review* 1739.

[78] Osiatynski (n 19). One can go even further back and identify the global migration of the American Declaration of Independence of 1776. For a study, see David Armitage, *The Declaration of Independence: A Global History* (2007).

their origins might be, rules of private law in their continuing lifetime have no inherent close relationship with a particular people, time or place.'[79] Not so with (written[80]) constitutions. The distinction between voluntary and involuntary transplants is especially important in this context. At one end of the spectrum, we find examples such as foreign inspiration of the American Founders or the borrowing between the states in the pre-revolutionary period in America.[81] At the other end are the post-war Japanese Constitution,[82] the German Basic Law, and the post-colonial constitutions of African nations.[83] External influence on the 1995 Bosnian Constitution, the 2005 Iraqi Constitution, and the 2004 Constitution of Afghanistan places them closer to the same end of the spectrum.[84] There are other situations wherein voluntariness is harder to ascertain. For instance, East European countries, which were in principle free to disregard, in the constitution-making process after the fall of Communism, the myriad recommendations of the Council of Europe and the European Community regarding the borrowing of specific constitutional institutions, but at the unpalatable price of being denied membership in these organizations.[85]

Constitutional borrowing can also occur at the interpretative stage in the life cycle of a constitution. Judges around the world are reading, citing, and generally 'engaging', as Vicki Jackson put it,[86] the decisions of their foreign peers. Over the past few decades, the dialogue of constitutional courts has become a major venue for the migration of constitutional ideas.[87]

It would be interesting to compare judges' roles in this context with the roles that Watson argues jurists played in the legal transplants of private law rules. Among the factors contributing to the creation in the constitutional context of a 'global community of courts'[88] are, in addi-

[79] Watson (n 25).

[80] For a discussion of the idea of a written constitution as a constitutional transplant, Horwitz (n 70), 540ff.

[81] G. Alan Tarr, 'Models and Fashions in State Constitutionalism' (1998) *Wisconsin Law Review* 729. For a wonderful example of foreign inspiration in the context of the American Founding, see Thomas Jefferson's letter to James Madison dated August 28, 1789 (available at <http://www.gutenberg.org/files/16783/16783-h/16783-h.htm#2H_4_0010>). I am grateful to Mary Bilder for bringing this letter to my attention.

[82] See Sylvia Brown Hamano, 'Incomplete Revolutions and Not-So-Alien Transplants: The Japanese Constitution and Human Rights' (1999) 1 *University of Pennsylvania Journal of Constitutional Law* 415; Dale M. Hellegers, *We the Japanese People: World War II and the Origins of the Japanese Constitution* (2002).

[83] Ruth Gordon, 'Growing Constitutions' (1999) 1 *University of Pennsylvania Journal of Constitutional Law* 528, 530–1 (footnotes omitted):

> Constitutions can flourish and succeed only if they are firmly planted in the cultural soil from which they gain legitimacy. Thus, growing constitutions embodies the not so novel idea that constitutions and laws should reflect and be derived from the cultural norms in which they must endure. Constitutions that are not firmly grounded in the cultural mores of the society in which they operate are destined to fail, become irrelevant, or be shaped and adapted to meet the needs of the culture and society in which they are situated. Indeed, most postcolonial constitutions in the Sub-Saharan Africa have largely succumbed to irrelevance and debacle.

[84] Zaid Al-Ali, 'Constitutional Drafting and External Influence' in Tom Ginsburg and Rosalind Dixon (eds), *Research Handbook in Comparative Constitutional Law* (2011), 77ff. See also Noah Feldman and Roman Martinez, 'Constitutional Politics and Text in the New Iraqi Constitution: An Experiment in Islamic Democracy' (2006) 75 *Fordham Law Review* 883.

[85] Osiatynski (n 19), 249.

[86] Vicki Jackson, *Constitutional Engagement in a Transnational Era* (2010); Vicki Jackson, 'Federalism and the Uses and Limits of Law: Printz and Principle' (1998) 111 *Harvard Law Review* 2180.

[87] See generally Gary Jeffrey Jacobson, 'The Permeability of Constitutional Borders' (2004) 82 *Texas Law Review* 1763; Basil Markesinis and Jorg Fedtke, *Engaging with Foreign Law* (2009); Basil Markesinis, 'Judicial Mentality: Mental Disposition or Outlook as a Factor Impeding Recourse to Foreign Law' (2006) 80 *Tulane Law Review* 1325.

[88] Anne-Marie Slaughter, 'A Global Community of Courts' (2003) 44 *Harvard International Law Journal* 191.

tion to domestic legal developments, external developments including the increased availability online of foreign materials, the globalization of legal education, and the ease of travel and communication which have set the conditions for an epistemic community of constitutional decision-makers.[89]

The frequency of foreign citations varies across space and even in time within the same jurisdiction. For instance, D.M. Davis has argued that, after an early period when the South African Constitutional Court drew heavily on foreign law, over time the number of references decreased.[90] This is noteworthy considering that section 39(c) of the South African Constitution provides that courts interpreting the Bill of Rights 'may consider foreign law'.

The lack of similar authorization has made the legitimacy of judicial borrowing the subject of intense debate in US constitutional law and politics. Even though the number of cases wherein the Supreme Court has cited foreign law is small by comparison to other jurisdictions,[91] controversy has engulfed courts, the academy, and even Congress.[92] Critics such as Justice Antonin Scalia have acknowledged the legitimacy of drawing inspiration from foreign models at the constitutional drafting stage, but have argued that the migration of foreign constitutional ideas at the interpretative stage erodes democratic self-government.[93] To some extent, this is a surprising position. The authority of foreign law in constitutional domestic interpretation is not content-independent. Rather, it depends on how persuasive a judge finds a particular legal idea.[94] Contrast this to the precedential authority of the US Supreme Court decisions in Argentina under the 1853 constitutional regime, which had largely copied the US Constitution. Judicial decisions interpreting the US Constitution received precedential authority as if they were the decisions of an Argentinean court.[95] But, as the next section shows in the broader context of the justification of transplants, no such argument has been advanced in the contemporary debate.[96]

3. Motivations

Voluntary constitutional borrowing has no single or simple motivation or set of motivations. One possible classification of the different motivations discussed in the literature mentions functionalist, reputational, normative, sociological, and, finally, 'chance' borrowing.

[89] Anne-Marie Slaughter, *A New World Order* (2004), 65ff.

[90] D.M. Davis, 'Constitutional Borrowing: The Influence of Legal Culture and Local History in the Reconstruction of Comparative Influence: The South African Experience' (2003) 1 *International Journal of Constitutional Law* 181, 194.

[91] See eg *Atkins v Virginia* 536 US 304, 316 n 21 (2002) (Stevens J) (referring to the opinion of the world community that executing the mentally retarded is wrong), *Lawrence v Texas* 539 US 558, 571–3 (2003) (discussing the values of Western civilization regarding homosexual conduct), *Roper v Simmons* 543 US 551 (2004) (Kennedy J) (mentioning the 'stark reality' that the United States is the only country in the world that gives official sanction to juvenile death penalty).

[92] The latest legislative proposal introduced in the 112th Congress (2011–12) is HR 973 IH– Proposal To amend title 28, USC, to prevent the misuse of foreign law in federal courts, and for other purposes, available at <http://www.gpo.gov/fdsys/pkg/BILLS-112hr973ih/pdf/BILLS-112hr973ih.pdf>.

[93] *Printz v US* 521 US 989, 921 n 11 (1995).

[94] See generally Patrick Glenn, 'Persuasive Authority' (1987) 32 *McGill Law Journal* 261. See also Vlad Perju, 'The Puzzling Parameters of the Foreign Law Debate' (2007) *Utah Law Review* 167.

[95] On the 'borrowed statute doctrine' in this context, see Rosenkrantz (n 57), 275.

[96] See Stanford Levinson, 'Looking Abroad When Interpreting the US Constitution: Some Reflections' (2004) 39 *Texas Journal of International Law* 353, 353 (arguing that it would be foolish to claim that foreign decisions have precedential authority).

The first motivation is that the proposed 'cost-saving'[97] transplant 'works' in the host system. Rather than reinventing the wheel, a particular system should, in this view, borrow solutions that have already been tested in other systems. Similar functionalist motivations have been advanced in private law where the motivation for legal transplant has been 'the quality of a given foreign solution'.[98] One difficulty with these accounts is how to define what 'works'. Given the importance of constitutional modularity at institutional, doctrinal, and perhaps even professional levels, understanding constitutional function requires tools that functionalism itself cannot provide.[99]

A second motivation is reputational; borrowing has 'legitimacy generating'[100] effects. For example, it can signal to the world community the breaking with an undemocratic past.[101] When courts are the agents of borrowing, they can import traditions that are lacking in their own systems and on which judges can then build 'local' doctrines over time.[102] Moreover, judicial borrowing helps courts to deliver decisions that appear objective and impartial, which is particularly valuable to newly establish constitution courts. Engagement with foreign peers can also boost the external prestige of courts even when it leads to the rejection of foreign approaches.[103]

Reputational effects also accrue on political actors and motivate borrowing at the constitutional drafting stage. Lee Epstein and Jack Knight have studied borrowing in the context of the choices of institutional design that constitutional drafters must make. They have argued that political actors seek to maximize their own preferences and reputation when exercising those choices. The authors

> analyze borrowing—institutional choices, really—as a bargaining process among relevant political actors, with their decisions reflecting their relative influences, preferences, and beliefs at the moment when the new institution is introduced, along with (and critically so) their level of uncertainty about future political circumstances.[104]

Similarly, Ran Hirschl has explained the worldwide migration of the idea of judicial review of legislation as a mechanism by which disadvantaged elites promote their political self-interest. Hirschl writes that

> the current global trend toward judicial empowerment through constitutionalization is part of a broader process whereby self-interested political and economic elites, while they profess

[97] Miller (n 53), 854ff.

[98] Jorg Fedtke, 'Legal Transplants' in J.M. Smits (ed), *Elgar Encyclopedia of Comparative Law* (2006), 434: 'The decision to draw on the ideas found in other legal systems is... often justified by the quality of a given foreign solution'.

[99] See Matthew D. Adler, 'Can Constitutional Borrowing be Justified: A Comment on Tushnet' (1998) 1 *University of Pennsylvania Journal of Constitutional Law* 230.

[100] Miller (n 53).

[101] Frederick Schauer invokes this reputational dimension to explain the prominence of Canadian and German constitutional systems, in Schauer (n 59), 260ff. For an interesting study of the German influence in Eastern Europe, see Luis Lopez Guerra, 'The Application of the Spanish Model in the Constitutional Transitions in Central and Eastern Europe' (1998) 19 *Cardozo Law Review* 1937. See also Gianmaria Ajani, 'By Chance and Prestige: Legal Transplants in Russia and Eastern Europe' (1995) 43 *American Journal of Comparative Law* 93; Victoria Schwartz, 'The Influences of the West on the 1993 Russian Constitution', (2009) 32 *Hastings International Comparative Law Review* 101.

[102] See Herman Schwartz, 'The New Courts: An Overview' (1993) *East European Constitutional Review* 28. See also Herman Schwartz, *The Struggle for Constitutional Justice in Post-Communist Europe* (2000).

[103] eg Hungarian and South African constitutional courts engaged—and rejected—the US Eighth Amendment doctrine in cases of the constitutionality of capital punishment. See *State v Makwanyane* SA 391 1195 (4) BCCR 605 (CC) (1995) (South Africa); 107 1990 MK, UT, 1, 1 (Hungary, 1990).

[104] Epstein and Knight (n 21), 200.

> support for democracy and sustained development, attempt to insulate policy-making from the vagaries of democratic politics.[105]

Other authors interpret the interests of elites somewhat more broadly. For instance, David Law has identified among the forces of conversion toward what Hirschl calls 'new constitutionalism' the state's competition for investment capital. Because capital is free to move wherever it sees fit, attracting it—and thus securing the basis for economic development—requires that constitutional systems offer investors property rights protected by an independent judiciary.[106]

At least two more kinds of motivations deserve mention at this stage. Normative universalist motivations see the spread of liberal constitutionalism—both constitutional structure (separation of powers, checks and balances, independent judiciary) and bill of rights—as the recognition of a universal set of principles for organizing political power in a way that protects individual freedom in the modern state. Writing in the context of the constitution-making in post-Communist Eastern Europe, Richard Epstein has argued that it is little surprising that virtually all new modern constitutions are slight variations on a common theme.[107] There are also sociological motivations, of the kind discussed above in the context of judicial dialogue.

Finally, it is an interesting question what role 'chance' borrowings, that is, borrowings that lack any motivation, play. The process of constitutional borrowing seems fraught with dangers of misunderstanding.[108] Consider the possibility of mistaken interpretation of foreign law. Watson intriguingly claimed that 'foreign law can be influential even when it is totally misunderstood'.[109] How accidental are such mistakes? That answer turns on whether the comparativist's approach to legal culture has any room for the possibility of accidents.[110]

4. Patterns

Patterns of migration require an assessment of constitutional proximity. Rarely is such proximity a function of physical distance. More commonly, culture, history, reputation, politics, and ideology shape perceptions of constitutional space and determine the direction of constitutional migrations.

Let us first begin by distinguishing on the y-axis between vertical and horizontal constitutional migrations. Vertical migrations occur between different jurisdictional levels, for instance between national and subnational levels, such as the units comprising a federation. For example, the drafters of the Russian Constitution were reportedly inspired by state constitutions in the

[105] Ran Hirschl, *Towards Juristocracy: The Origins and Consequences of the New Constitutionalism* (2004), 217. But see David Erdos, 'Aversive Constitutionalism in the Westminster World: The Genesis of the New Zealand Bill of Rights Act (1990)' (2007) 5 *International Journal of Constitutional Law* 343.

[106] Law (n 45).

[107] See Richard Epstein, 'All Quiet on the Eastern Front' (1991) 58 *University of Chicago Law Review* 555.

[108] One reason why avoiding mistakes can be difficult is that they it requires knowledge of how a particular constitutional mechanism functions in the host country. For a discussion of the transplant of constitutional complain guarantee in the German Basic Law, Art 93(1), as an (in)effective protection of fundamental rights, see Frankenberg (n 17), 572.

[109] Watson (n 3), 99.

[110] As Lawrence Friedman describes his approach in *A History of American Law*, the book presents the American system

> not as a kingdom unto itself, not as a set of rules and concepts, not as a province of lawyers alone, but as a mirror of society. It takes nothing as historical accident, nothing as autonomous, everything as modelled by economy and society.

Lawrence Friedman, *A History of American Law* (2nd edn, 1985), 12, cited in Wise (n 16).

United States.[111] The most common vertical migrations originate from the supranational toward the national level, as when the state must implement at the constitutional level human rights obligations assumed under an international treaty.[112] But these can also be *complex migrations*. One example is the spread of the proportionality method from national to supranational jurisdictions such as the European Court of Justice, from which it travels to a national system that had not been on the receiving end of horizontal migrations from the initial source.[113]

Horizontal migrations occur between similarly situated jurisdictions. The United States, Germany, the United Kingdom, and France are models of constitutional structure and the source of most worldwide borrowing. An interesting phenomenon, related to the reputation of constitutional models, occurs in situations of repeated borrowing which create 'transplant biases'. As Alan Watson explains it, transplant bias refers to situations when

> a system's receptivity to a particular outside law, which is distinct from acceptance based on a thorough examination of possible alternatives. Thus, it means for instance a system's readiness to accept Roman law rules *because* they are Roman law rules, or French rules *because* they are French rules.[114]

At first glance, it seems that constitutional borrowings are somewhat insulated from the dangers of transplant biases. To the extent such biases rely on 'habits',[115] their relevance is mitigated by the low frequency of opportunities for constitution-drafting. There are, however, opportunities for repeated borrowing at the interpretative stage.

The formation of transplant bias assumes accessibility, hence a process of socialization in which legal education and legal culture make particular foreign sources intelligible.[116]

Language plays an essential role, although the spread of English tends to obscure its importance. As we will see, the use of a lingua franca heightens the dangers of nominalism and creates an appearance of constitutional convergence that can be misleading. The contrast between comparative constitutional law and comparative law is particularly stark in this respect, in the sense that language and translation are among the grand topics of comparative law but are virtually inexistent in the constitutional field. A second aspect of intelligibility and accessibility involves the question whether 'legal families'[117] have an impact on constitutional borrowing. Stephen Gardbaum's work on the Commonwealth model of constitutionalism shows the shaping effect

[111] Robert Sharlet, 'Legal Transplants and Political Mutations: the Reception of Constitutional Law in Russia and the Newly Independent States' (1998) 7 *East European Constitutional Review* 59.

[112] See generally Mattias Kumm, 'Democratic Constitutionalism Encounters International Law: Terms of Engagement' in Choudhry (n 6), 256 ff.

[113] ECJ, C11/70 *Internationale Handelsgesellschaft*. See generally Evelyn Ellis, *The Principle of Proportionality in the Laws of Europe* (1999).

[114] Watson (n 26), 327.

[115] Wise (n 16), 7:

> borrowing from a particular foreign system tends to become a habit: a bias develops in favor of treating that system as the primary quarry for legal rules whenever local law is silent.

[116] For a discussion of the shaping role of legal education on constitutional culture, see Pnina Lahav, 'American Moment(s): When, How and Why Did Israeli Law Faculties Come to Resemble Elite US Law Schools?' (2009) 10 *Theoretical Inquiries in Law* 653.

[117] On the concept of 'legal families', see René David, *Les grands systemes de droit contemporains* (1964). See also Konrad Zweigert and Hein Kotz, *Introduction to Comparative Law* (2nd edn, 1987), 63ff. For a discussion in the East European context, see Zoltan Peteri, 'The Reception of Soviet Law in Eastern Europe: Similarities and Differences between Soviet and East European Law' (1987) 61 *Tulane Law Review* 1397. For a discussion about the possibilities of borrowing between Islamic and US law, see Azizah Y. al-Hibri, 'Islamic and American Constitutional Law: Borrowing Possibilities or a History of Borrowing?' (1999) 1 *University of Pennsylvania Journal of Constitutional Law* 492.

of legal traditions.[118] Similarly, Tom Ginsburg has shown that the 1992 Constitution of Mongolia rejected the American and Japanese-style systems to decentralized constitutional review partly because of Mongolia's civil law origins in a Soviet-inspired legal system.[119] A comprehensive study of the impact of the civil law/common law legal traditions on constitutional borrowing remains to be conducted.

History is of course a central factor that shapes perceptions of constitutional proximity. Scholars have studied how English-speaking Africa used the Westminster model and bicameral legislatures, separation of powers, judicial review, and bill of rights; French-speaking Africa adapted a French model.[120] As far as geographical proximity is concerned, this factor plays a limited role in phenomena of voluntary constitutional migration. To take only one example, there are relatively few African influences in the South African Constitution.[121] By contrast, the post-Communist constitutional arrangement in Albania was influenced by neighbouring Greece and Italy.[122]

V. The Justification of Constitutional Transplants: The Case of Foreign Law

Comparative law is law.[123] As law, it must address the normative justification for constitutional borrowing, and more broadly the conditions for its success. This section maps normative approaches to constitutional borrowing in the context of a particularly controversial type of borrowing, already described in the previous section, namely the use of foreign law by US courts in the process of constitutional interpretation. I use this debate not because it is representative of global trends—in fact, the opposite is true—but rather in order to exhibit the richness of the normative debate about constitutional borrowing, especially with regard to the relationship between law and its outside cultural, social, and political environment.[124] The comparative law transplants debate has had little impact on the constitutional realm.

[118] Stephen Gardbaum, 'The Commonwealth Model of Constitutionalism' (2001) 49 *American Journal of Comparative Law* 707. See also Stephen Gardbaum, 'Reassessing the New Commonwealth Model of Constitutionalism' (2010) 8 *International Journal of Constitutional Law* 167.

[119] Tom Ginsburg, *Judicial Review in New Democracies: Constitutional Courts in Asian Cases* (2003), 165ff.

[120] Isaac I. Dore, 'Constitutionalism and the Post-Colonial State in Africa: A Rawlsian Approach' (1997) 41 *St Louis University Law Journal* 1301, 1304ff:

> Having been designed abroad, there was a fundamental mismatch between the values of the people of Africa and the western values which inspired the drafters of the new constitutions.

[121] Davis (n 90), 194. See also Jeremy Sarkin, 'The Effect of Constitutional Borrowings on the Drafting of South Africa's Bill of Rights and Interpretation of Human Rights Provisions' (1999) 1 *University of Pennsylvania Journal of Constitutional Law* 176.

[122] Elster (n 69), 477.

[123] Whitman (n 42), 343:

> legal systems are normative systems. 'Law' is not best thought of as a rooted set of cultural facts that can be 'understood' only in cultural context. 'Law' is best thought of as an activity that aims at normative justification of certain human acts and of the exercise of the authority of some humans over others.

[124] The central lesson is that the dynamic between constitutional text and constitutional culture is essential for understanding the success of constitutional borrowing. Rosenfeld and Sajó (n 67), 174ff. See further Chapter 64 on the use of foreign law in constitutional interpretation.

Judicial references to foreign law in the constitutional context have been roundly criticized in the United States as haphazard, lacking in method, and for being an unprincipled tool available for use whenever and however judges wish. Critics worry that fundamental methodological questions remain unanswered. For instance, to which jurisdictions should courts refer? How can judges be prevented from picking and choosing the jurisdictions that support their own choices? How does foreign law affect the integrity of the judicial process and how should the accuracy and relevance of foreign citations be checked? etc.[125] These are undoubtedly important questions. They are also questions which reflect the fact that constitutional borrowings are not perceived to occur within what comparativists call a 'legal family', that is, within a community of legal systems that share fundamental methods and assumptions.[126] But perhaps even belonging to a legal family would be insufficient given the special role of the constitution as a charter of self-government. In the context of constitutional borrowing, unprincipled means 'undemocratic'.[127]

To understand what makes borrowing undemocratic, recall that in comparative private law transplants are considered the most fertile source of change. A similar claim in the constitutional context would be an overstatement (revolutions are more 'fertile' than legal transplants…), but at least it identifies the normative pedigree of opposition to change. Thus, changes must be resisted as undemocratic unless they originate organically from within the body politic and, according to the self-referential logic of the constitution, they follow the mechanisms provided for in the constitutional text.

This position allows for a number of variations. One variation, call it a normative universalist claim, is that change via judicial constitutional borrowing is undemocratic under any version of constitutional self-government, save when the sovereign people have authorized it. A different, more culturally specific, position singles out factors such as history, politics, and the environment which make constitutional self-government incompatible with the practice of judicial borrowing. For instance, Jed Rubenfeld has contrasted American democratic constitutionalism, which sees the constitution as 'the product of a national participatory political process, though which people commit to writing the fundamental values or principles that will govern their society',[128] with European self-government where national participatory processes are less important than the protection of human rights, including the rights of minorities and the establishment of the rule of law.

On its face, this is a descriptive approach. It does not take a position on whether cultures can change, whether these particular constitutional cultures can change, or whether they should

[125] See Joan L. Larsen, 'Importing Constitutional Norms from a "Wider Civilization": Lawrence and the Rehnquist Court's Use of Foreign and International Law in Domestic Constitutional Interpretation' (2004) 65 *Ohio State Law Journal* 1283, 1327:

> This 'everyone's doing it' approach to constitutional interpretation requires explanation and justification. Yet, to date, neither the Court nor the academy has offered a justification that satisfies. Until they do, it seems we are better off to abandon this particular use of foreign and international law.

See also Diane Marie Amann, '"Raise the Flag and Let It Talk": On the Use of External Norms in Constitutional Decision Making' (2004) 2 *International Journal of Constitutional Law* 597.

[126] The reason is perhaps not the lack of a family as such (eg liberal constitutional democracies could be such a family) but rather the perception that US law belongs to a family of one—the old saga of US exceptionalism. See generally Michael Ignatieff (ed), *American Exceptionalism and Human Rights* (2005).

[127] See generally John O. McGinnis, 'Foreign to Our Constitution' (2006) 100 *Northwestern University Law Review* 303; Eric Posner, *The Perils of Global Legalism* (2009).

[128] Jed Rubenfeld, 'Unilateralism and Constitutionalism' (2004) 79 *NYU Law Review* 1971, 1993.

change.[129] Now, presumably change is possible. After all, these cultures have been shaped by history and history has not yet come to an end. So the critical question is how cultures change.

A strong culturalist approach to constitutional law argues that cultures cannot change *intentionally*. Paul Kahn has forcefully argued that 'the rule of law is a cultural practice', and thus 'a cultural approach begins by bracketing off the study of law from the practice of reforming the law'.[130] To try to change legal culture is to misunderstand legal culture. Hence, comparative constitutionalism, when aiming at reform, including through but not limited to constitutional borrowing, misunderstands—or worse, it instrumentalizes[131]—constitutional culture. The point of comparative law is to understand, not to reform.[132] A particularly illuminating analogy comes from Alan Watson who compared the purported comprehensiveness of constitutional law with that of a religious faith. Just as one need not—indeed, may not—reach out for answers to other faiths, so here one should not reach beyond the ambit of the US Constitution, as the foundation of America's civic religion.[133]

Culturalism's emphasis on constitutional self-government coupled with its anti-functionalist methodology explain its appeal and relevance. In a different context, scholars of African constitutionalism have made the argument that constitutions must 'grow' organically. Invoked in this context is the survival of the 'presidentialist character of Africa's constitutional politics'[134] despite the textual provisions of many postcolonial constitutions in many Sub-Saharan

[129] For Rubenfeld's answers to these questions, in the analogous context of the US approach to international law, see ibid 2020:

> Democracy is not the only value in the world. International law could be worth supporting even if it is undemocratic. The point is a matter of candor. To support international law is to support fundamental constraints on democracy.

[130] Paul Kahn, 'Comparative Constitutionalism in a New Key' (2003) 101 *Michigan Law Review* 2677, 2678. On the definition of 'constitutional culture', see Robert Post, 'Foreword: Fashioning the Legal Constitution: Culture, Courts, and Law' (2003) 117 *Harvard Law Review* 4, 6ff (defining constitutional culture as the beliefs and values of non-judicial actors, and discussing the dialectical relationship between it and constitutional law). For an earlier approach along similar lines with particular application to legal rights, see Martha Minow, 'Interpreting Rights' (1987) 96 *Yale Law Journal* 1860, 1861ff:

> efforts to create and give meaning to norms, through a language of rights, often and importantly occur outside formal legal institutions such as courts. 'Legal interpretation', in this sense, is an activity engaged in by nonlawyers as well as by lawyers and judges.

[131] This is what Günter Frankenberg calls the 'IKEA' theory of constitutional (and legal) transfer. According to this theory,

> global constitutionalism is created by or rather emanates from processes of transfer and functions as a reservoir or, for that matter, a supermarket, where standardized constitutional items—grand design as well as elementary particles of information—are stored and available, prêt-à-porter, for purchase and reassemblage by constitution makers around the world.

Frankenberg (n 17), 565. See also Günter Frankenberg, 'Comparing Constitutions: Ideas, Ideals, and Ideology—Towards a Layered Narrative' (2006) 4 *International Journal of Constitutional Law* 439.

[132] See also Sacco (n 41), 2: 'the effort to justify comparative law by its practical uses sometimes verges on the ridiculous'.

[133] Alan Watson, 'From Legal Transplants to Legal Formants' (1995) 43 *American Journal of Comparative Law* 469, 472.

[134] H. Kwasi Prempeh, 'Africa's Constitutionalism Revival: False Start or New Dawn?' (2007) 5 *International Journal of Constitutional Law* 469, 497, at 498:

> The long absence in postcolonial Africa of a tradition of parliamentary autonomy has severely handicapped Africa's legislature in defining or protecting their institutional interests and prerogatives. Despite new openings and opportunities to assert a meaningful role for parliaments in Africa's post-authoritarian constitutional politics, contemporary legislature-executive relationships continue to be defined by conventions established under the executive-dominated ancient regime.

constitutions.[135] The justification of transplants depends on how one conceptualizes that relationship between law and culture. How, then, is judicial borrowing defended?

In the context of foreign law, functionalism in comparative constitutional law can take the form of crude instrumentalism or more sophisticated pragmatism.[136] While crude instrumentalism has no defenders, as long as the use of foreign law lacks a methodology, judicial borrowing will be criticized as an inherently unprincipled tool that can be used strategically.[137] The pragmatist justification reverts to the 'it works' rationale.[138] Foreign law can shed an 'empirical light',[139] in Justice Breyer's words, on issues of constitutional structure such as federalism as well as fundamental rights.[140]

Among other defences of foreign law, Anne-Marie Slaughter has proposed a broader explanation of inter-court borrowing as the outcome of the disintegration of states into networks of judges, legislators, and executives that reach across to their foreign peers.[141] Both professional and sociological factors contribute to the creation of 'a global community of courts'. Slaughter's account is compatible with a dialogical model.[142] According to this model, the use of foreign law is a means by which a constitutional system or culture engages with the outside world.[143] The outcome of such engagement is to better understand the presuppositions of one's own constitutional culture and legal system and, presumably, to change whatever aspects one does not like and has a mandate to change. Since the national judge is always a filter, foreign law as having persuasive authority and its usage is therefore not undemocratic.

Stronger views of the authority of foreign law are also possible.[144] Jeremy Waldron has argued that foreign law is new *jus gentium* (the law of nations).[145] Referring specifically to situations of emerging world consensus, such as the ban on the death penalty for juvenile offenders, Waldron argues that, just like in science, consensus provides 'an established body of legal

[135] See generally Ruth Gordon, 'Growing Constitutions' (1999) 1 *University of Pennsylvania Journal of Constitutional Law* 528.

[136] For a discussion of functionalist explanations of constitutional transformation, see Hirschl (n 105), 34ff (discussing functionalist, evolutionary, and institutional economic theories of constitutional transformation); Tushnet (n 67), 76ff (discussing functionalism in the context of constitutional structure).

[137] See eg Ernest Young, 'The Trouble with Global Constitutionalism' (2003) 38 *Texas International Law Review* 527.

[138] Of course, the question is, 'it works' for what? Eg in the context of the Argentine 1853 Constitution, borrowing from US law was done for the purpose of replicating the US success at attracting foreign investment and immigration. See generally Jonathan Miller, 'The Authority of a Foreign Talisman: A Study of the US Constitutional Practice as Authority in Nineteenth Century Argentina and the Argentine Elite's Leap of Faith' (1997) 46 *American University Law Review* 1483. See also Mitchell Gordon, 'Don't Copy Me, Argentina: Constitutional Borrowing and Rhetorical Type' (2009) 8 *Washington University Global Studies Law Review* 487. More generally on the question of the success of legal transplants, see David Nelken, 'Comparativists and Transferability' in Legrand and Munday (n 34), 452ff.

[139] *Printz v US* 521 US 898, 977 (1997) (Breyer J dissenting).

[140] *Washington v Glucksberg* 521 US 702, 770 (Rehnquist CJ) (discussing the experience with the legalization of physician-assisted suicide in the Netherlands in the context of a possibility of abuse).

[141] Slaughter (n 89).

[142] Vlad Perju, 'Comparative Constitutionalism and the Making of A New World Order' (2005) 12 *Constellations* 464.

[143] See generally Sujit Choudhry, 'Globalization in Search of Justification: Toward a Theory of Comparative Constitutional Interpretation' (1999) 74 *Indiana Law Journal* 819, 855ff; Jackson, *Constitutional Engagement* (n 86).

[144] Perhaps the strongest view, grounding the authority of foreign law in natural law has not yet found supporters in the literature. For a discussion of what such an argument might look like, see Roger P. Alford, 'In Search of a Theory for Comparative Constitutionalism' (2005) 52 *UCLA Law Review* 639, 659–73.

[145] See Jeremy Waldron, 'Foreign Law and the Modern *Ius Gentium*' (2005) 119 *Harvard Law Review* 129.

insight, reminding [one] that the particular problem had been confronted before and that they…should think it through in the company of those who have already dealt with it.'[146] Common answers form an area of 'overlap, duplication, mutual elaboration, and the checking and rechecking of results that is characteristic to true science.'[147] This theory provides a strong justification for the use of foreign law, but one that is limited to situations of emerging world consensus. More recently, it has been argued that the cosmopolitan ideal in constitutional law can justify constitutional borrowing by judges without regard to the existence of consensus.[148]

VI. Conclusion: The Problem of Convergence

Reflecting on the history of comparative law, Rudolf Schlesinger noted that periods of 'contractive comparisons', when the emphasis is on differences between legal systems, alternate with periods of 'integrative comparison', when the focus is on similarities.[149] It is perhaps too soon to tell if the same evolution will shape the field of comparative constitutional law. It is clear, however, that a debate is under way on whether and on what scale constitutional migrations are leading or can lead to constitutional convergence.[150] At one level, at least some degree of convergence seems unquestionable. The world constitutional map looks drastically different today than it did half a century ago. The complex phenomenon of globalization makes further convergence all but inevitable.[151] At the same time, recent empirical studies cast doubt on whether constitutional systems are converging.[152] Moreover, convergence might not be desirable if it stifles democratic experimentation and shuns local expertise and traditions.[153]

In this context, the pervasiveness of the English language in the comparative constitutional materials shapes the comparative landscape and somewhat artificially enhances the perception of congruence. Unlike comparative private lawyers, who are trained to reflect on the problem of translation, the comparative constitutional lawyer has few such concerns. The trap of nominalism becomes particularly worrisome.[154] This is the trap that similar-sounding concepts share an identical meaning. Even when these legal concepts are the outcome of constitutional borrowing,

[146] Ibid 133.

[147] Ibid 139.

[148] Vlad Perju, 'Cosmopolitanism and Constitutional Self-Government' (2010) 8 *International Journal of Constitutional Law* 326.

[149] Rudolf B. Schlesinger, 'The Past and Future of Comparative Law' (1995) 43 *American Journal of Comparative Law* 477.

[150] Rosalind Dixon and Eric Posner, 'The Limits of Constitutional Convergence' (2011) 11 *Chicago Journal of International Law* 399 (identifying four paths to convergence: superstructure theories; learning theories; coercion theories; competition theories). It helps to keep in mind that, even when transplants/borrowing results in convergence, that remains only one strategy of convergence. See generally John Henry Merryman, 'On the Convergence (and Divergence) of the Civil Law and the Common Law' (1981) 17 *Stanford Journal of International Law* 358, 365ff.

[151] See also Mark Tushnet, 'The Inevitable Globalization of Constitutional Law' (2009) 49 *Virginia Journal of International Law* 985, 987 (pointing out that convergence is not tantamount to uniformity). See also Sacco (n 41), 2 (discussing the difference between uniformization and unification).

[152] David Law and Mila Versteeg, 'The Evolution and Ideology of Global Constitutionalism' (2011) 99 *California Law Review* 1163.

[153] See Walker (n 15), 317.

[154] See Bruce Ackerman, 'The Rise of World Constitutionalism' (1997) 83 *Virginia Law Review* 771; Mark Tushnet, 'The Possibilities of Comparative Constitutional Law' (1995) 108 *Yale Law Journal* 1225. See also See Watson (n 3), 10ff.

we have seen that their meaning changes in the course of borrowing. A healthy dose of comparative sensibility helps at this stage.

Comparative constitutional law as a field can benefit from engaging with the transplants debate in comparative law, in particular with respect to topics such as convergence and divergence, the relationship between law and culture, and the importance of language and professional culture. Conversely, that debate, and comparative law more generally, can benefit from a study of constitutional borrowings and from the normative finesse that define comparative constitutionalism. This mutually beneficial dialogue also lays the ground for an integrative account of legal transplants, borrowings, and migrations.

Bibliography

Matthew D. Adler, 'Can Constitutional Borrowing be Justified: A Comment on Tushnet' (1998) 1 *University of Pennsylvania Journal of Constitutional Law* 230

Sujit Choudhry, 'Globalization in Search of Justification: Toward a Theory of Comparative Constitutional Interpretation' (1999) 74 *Indiana Law Journal* 819

Sujit Choudhry (ed), *The Migration of Constitutional Ideas* (2006)

D.M. Davis, 'Constitutional Borrowing: The Influence of Legal Culture and Local History in the Reconstruction of Comparative Influence: The South African Experience' (2003) 1 *International Journal of Constitutional Law* 181

Rosalind Dixon and Eric Posner, 'The Limits of Constitutional Convergence' (2011) 11 *Chicago Journal of International Law* 399

Lee Epstein and Jack Knight, 'Constitutional Borrowing and Nonborrowing' (2003) 1 *International Journal of Constitutional Law* 196

William B. Ewald, 'The American Revolution and the Evolution of Law' (1994) 42 *American Journal of Comparative Law Supplement* 1

Günter Frankenberg, 'Constitutional Transfer: The IKEA Theory Revisited' (2010) 8 *International Journal of Constitutional Law* 563

Ruth Gordon, 'Growing Constitutions' (1999) 1 *University of Pennsylvania Journal of Constitutional Law* 528

Louis Henkin and Albert Rosenthal (eds), *Constitutionalism and Rights* (1990)

Ran Hirschl, 'On the Blurred Methodological Matrix of Comparative Constitutional Law' in Sujit Choudhry (ed), *The Migration of Constitutional Ideas* (2006)

Morton Horwitz, 'Constitutional Transplants' (2009) 10 *Theoretical Inquiries* 353

Vicki Jackson, *Constitutional Engagement in a Transnational Era* (2010)

David Law, 'Globalization and the Future of Constitutional Rights' (2008) 102 *Northwestern University Law Review* 1277

Pierre Legrand, 'The Impossibility of Legal Transplants' (1997) 4 *Maastricht Journal of European & Comparative Law* 111

Pierre Legrand and Roderick Munday (eds), *Comparative Legal Studies: Traditions and Transitions* (2003)

Wiktor Osiatynski, 'Paradoxes of Constitutional Borrowing' (2003) *International Journal of Constitutional Law* 244

Michel Rosenfeld and András Sajó, 'Spreading Liberal Constitutionalism: An Inquiry into the Fate of Free Speech in New Democracies' in Sujit Choudhry (ed), *The Migration of Constitutional Ideas* (2006)

Carlos F. Rosenkrantz, 'Against Borrowing and Other Nonauthoritative Uses of Foreign Law' (2003) 1 *International Journal of Constitutional Law* 269

Frederick Schauer, 'The Politics and Incentives of Legal Transplantation' in Joseph Nye Jr and John Donahue (eds), *Governance in a Globalizing World* (2000)

Kim Lane Scheppele, 'Aspirational and Adversative Constitutionalism: The Case for Studying Cross-constitutional Influence through Negative Models' (2003) 1 *International Journal of Constitutional Law* 296

Kim Lane Scheppele, 'The Migration of Anti-constitutional Ideas: The Post-9/11 Globalization of Public Law and the International State of Emergency' in Sujit Choudhry (ed), *The Migration of Constitutional Ideas* (2006)

Anne-Marie Slaughter, 'A Global Community of Courts' (2003) 44 *Harvard International Law Journal* 191

Horacio Spector, 'Constitutional Transplants and the Mutation Effect' (2008) 83 *Chicago-Kent Law Review* 129

Symposium on Constitutional Borrowing (2003) 1(2) *International Journal of Constitutional Law*

Symposium on Contextuality & Universality: Constitutional Borrowings on the Global Stage (1998) 1(2) *University of Pennsylvania Journal of Constitutional Law Symposium*

Mark Tushnet, 'Returning with Interest: Observations on Some Putative Benefits of Studying Comparative Constitutional Law' (1998) 1 *University* of *Pennsylvania Journal of Constitutional Law* 325

Mark Tushnet, 'Some Reflections on Method in Comparative Constitutional Law' in Sujit Choudhry (ed), *The Migration of Constitutional Ideas* (2006)

Alan Watson, *Legal Transplants* (1974)

Edward M. Wise, 'The Transplant of Legal Patterns' (1990) 38 *American Journal of Comparative Law Supplement* 1

CHAPTER 64

THE USE OF FOREIGN LAW IN CONSTITUTIONAL INTERPRETATION

GÁBOR HALMAI

Budapest

I. Introduction: The Migration of Constitutional Ideas

Judicial use of foreign law is a product of globalization of the practice of modern constitutionalism: it has been made possible by a dialogue among high court judges with constitutional jurisdiction around the world, conducted through mutual citation and increasingly direct interactions. This growing 'constitutional cross-fertilization' can prove to be not only a tool for better judicial judgments, but eventually also for the construction of a 'global legal system'.[1] The globalization of constitutional law means that constitutionalism is no longer the privilege of the nation-state, but it has instead become a worldwide concept and standard.[2] Globalization is especially encouraged by

[1] See Anne-Marie Slaughter, *A New World Order* (2004), 65–103.

[2] Bruce Ackerman, 'The Rise of World Constitutionalism' (1997) 87 *Virginia Law Review* 771.

advances in transportation and communications, and by the deepening of political, economic, cultural, and legal ties.[3] Since economic globalization includes competition among nations for investment and human capital, these globalization processes are limited to countries that compete internationally for investment and human capital.[4] At least for those among them which use foreign law. As discussed below, constitutional jurisdictions tend to fall into one of three categories: those which do not use foreign law (as we will see, the US Supreme Court seldom cites foreign court decisions), those which do use foreign law but do not do so explicitly (eg Hungary), and those which do so explicitly (eg South Africa).[5] According to some scholars, the explicit and non-explicit reference to judicial decisions in other jurisdictions can lead to a convergence among them and their exporters' constitutional systems, even if this globalization does not entail uniformity.

Before going further, we should clarify that 'using' foreign law in this chapter will typically mean the use of national law in another national jurisdiction. (In some cases we will also deal with the use of international law in national jurisdictions, and national law in international jurisdictions.) The use to which this foreign law is put is in the context of the interpretation of a domestic legal provision, and not of a direct application of the foreign law in the domestic court's jurisprudence. Thus the focus is here on foreign law used transnationally.[6] As we will see, cited foreign cases can have different degrees of influence. The less influential is when judges merely mention foreign law, the next step is when they actually 'follow' such cases as some form of authority, and also 'distinguish' them.[7] With the exception here of some rarely discussed uses of binding international law, the authority of cited foreign law is only persuasive in the process of judicial interpretation.[8]

There are different types of use of comparative materials, which can be characterized through metaphors. One is 'legal transplant', which consists of transferring rules between legal systems.[9] Another is its counterpart, 'constitutional borrowing'.[10] The users of the third metaphor, the 'migration' of constitutional ideas argue that only this approach encompasses a broader range of relationships between the recipient jurisdiction and constitutional ideas, and takes both constitutional difference and comparative engagement seriously; the latter not necessarily directing courts towards constitutional convergence.[11]

[3] See David S. Law, 'Globalization and the Future of Constitutional Rights' (2008) 102 *Northwestern University Law Review* 1277, 1280.

[4] Mark Tushnet, 'The Inevitable Globalization of Constitutional Law' (2009) 49 *Virginia Journal of International Law* 985.

[5] On the use of human rights law see this categorization in Christopher McCrudden, 'A Common Law of Human Rights?: Transnational Judicial Conversations on Constitutional Rights' (2000) 20 *Oxford Journal of Legal Studies* 499, 511.

[6] This is also the approach of McCrudden's study. See ibid 510.

[7] Ibid 512.

[8] The rise of persuasive authority is the most important factor of 'constitutional cross-fertilization'. See Slaughter (n 1), 75–8.

[9] In his early work, Alan Watson claimed that the discipline of comparative law should be oriented toward the study of transplants. See *Legal Transplants: An Approach to Comparative Law* (1974). In his critique of Watson, Pierre Legrand states that legal transplants are impossible, and he calls for difference in response to the urge for convergence. See 'What "Legal Transplants"' in D. Nelken and J. Feest (eds), *Adapting Legal Cultures* (2001).

[10] See the contributions of the symposium on constitutional borrowing published in (2003) 1 *International Journal of Constitutional Law* 177–324.

[11] Sujit Choudhry, 'Migration As a New Metaphor in Comparative Constitutional Law' in Sujit Choudhry (ed), *Migration of Constitutional Ideas* (2006). Elsewhere, Choudhry termed this use of comparative materials as 'dialogical interpretation', which falls outside the framework of constitutional borrowing but within the scope of the migration of constitutional ideas: 'Globalization in Search of Justification: Toward a Theory of Comparative Constitutional Interpretation' (1999) 74 *Indiana Law Journal* 819, 835. This model of comparative constitutional interpretation is similar to the 'engagement model' of Vicki C. Jackson, *Constitutional Engagement in a Transnational Era* (2010) and the 'dialogic model' used by Sarah K. Harding, 'Comparative Reasoning and Judicial Review' (2003) 28 *Yale Journal of International Law* 409.

The subject of this chapter, the use of foreign law in constitutional interpretation, is only one example of the migration of constitutional ideas across legal systems, which also includes the use of foreign constitutions as models in the process of constitution-making.[12] After looking at the normative basis of the use of citations I will investigate the questions why and where these uses takes place.

II. Normative Underpinning: Is It Legitimate?

It is generally agreed that the notion that foreign materials should be used for constitutional interpretation is gaining currency, and that the migration of constitutional ideas has been identified at a descriptive level. But many scholars complain that the basic conceptual issues, the methodology of migration, as well as the normative underpinning are lacking, and yet proponents of this practice cannot offer a theoretical justification for it. While some scholars argue that constitutional theory is just a vehicle for making sense of a constitutional practice,[13] others raise the even more general question about the legitimacy of constitutional comparativism, and whether comparativism is simply a methodology employed for a judge's particular theory, or alternatively whether a special comparative constitutional theory is possible. This theory is profoundly procedural in seeking a particular comparativist methodology, but also substantive in that it maintains the existence of universal norms.[14] One, less convincing, methodological reason for a comparative theory is that a parochial methodology places the countries that follow it (eg the United States) at odds with international norms and creates diplomatic tensions with foreign allies.[15] Another explanation is to enhance transnational dialogue and the global rule of law through a 'global jurisprudence'.[16] Among the substantive reasons are the maintenance of the existence of universal norms, advocacy of the internalization of international norms into the constitutional jurisprudence, together with the ability to promote political democracy and substantive justice by respecting a morally defensible set of individual rights.[17]

In the scholarly controversy over the uses of comparative constitutionalism, especially judicial recourse to foreign law, there are three broadly defined positions:[18]

(1) Scholars supporting the idea of the use of foreign law legitimate this practice with the sameness of both the problems and solutions of constitutional law for all constitutional democracies. One of the representatives of this position is David Beatty, who claims that the ultimate goal of all constitutional adjudication is to subject constitutional controversies to resolutions according to the dictates of the principle of proportionality, which Beatty describes

[12] In this respect, Frederick Schauer differentiates between imposed, transplanted, indigenous, and transnational constitutions: 'On the Migration of Constitutional Ideas' (2005) 37 *Connecticut Law Review* 907.

[13] 'Cases get decided, and behind them is a theory of constitutional law': Lawrence Lessig, 'The Puzzling Persistence of Bellbottom Theory' (1997) 87 *California Law Review* 535, 1838.

[14] Roger P. Alford, 'In Search of a Theory for Constitutional Comparativism' (2005) 52 *UCLA Law Review* 639.

[15] See Harold Hongju Koh, 'Paying "Decent Respect" to World Opinion on the Death Penalty' (2002) 35 *University of California at Davis Law Review* 1123.

[16] Slaughter (n 1), 78.

[17] See Richard H. Fallon Jr, 'How to Choose a Constitutional Theory' (1999) 87 *California Law Review* 539.

[18] See this categorization in Michel Rosenfeld, 'Principle or Ideology? A Comparativist Perspective on the US Controversy Over Supreme Court Citations to Foreign Authorities' in Zsuzsa Gaspár and András Hanák (eds), *Sajó 2009* (2009). Vicki C. Jackson very similarly talks about three postures toward the transnational. See 'Constitutional Comparisons: Convergence, Resistance, Engagement' (2005) 119 *Harvard Law Review* 109.

as the 'ultimate rule of law'.[19] This test for justification of rights' limitations articulated by many constitutional systems is a component of 'generic constitutional law', which offers a formula for limiting rights.[20] This position tends towards national identification with transnational and international legal norms, towards constitutional universalism. This means that the representatives of this model claim a process of transnational norm convergence.

(2) The second position's starting point is that although the problems of constitutional law are the same for all democratic countries, the solutions to should differ from one constitutional system to another. This position, which is advocated by Mary Ann Glendon,[21] highlights differences and tries to explain how different one constitutional system is from another, and why they differ. This is also the idea behind Vicki Jackson's engagement approach, considering foreign or international law without a presumption that it necessarily be followed.[22] In other words, the engagement model does not treat foreign and international law as a binding source. Jackson argues that the appropriate posture for the US Supreme Court to take would be one of engagement.

(3) The followers of the third position claim that neither the constitutional problems nor their solutions are likely to be the same for different constitutional democracies. This is called a resistance posture by Vicki Jackson. This position goes back to Montesquieu's observation that 'the political and civil laws of each nation... should be so appropriate to the people for whom they are made that it is very unlikely that the laws of one nation can suit another.'[23] This other extreme position concludes that comparisons are likely to be arbitrary, and that comparativists' choices are driven mostly by ideology. For instance, Günther Frankenberg criticized comparativists for imposing Western hegemonic approaches, not being able to avoid acting as colonialists, and characterized constitutional comparativism as 'a postmodern form of conquest executed through legal transplants and harmonization strategies'.[24] Another objection, raised by Otto Kahn-Freund, is that constitutional law is much less amenable to legal transplant from one country to another than is private law.[25]

Richard A. Posner claims that the citations of foreign decisions by US Supreme Court Justices, such as Antony Kennedy, is related to moral vanguardism. Posner labels Justice Kennedy as a kind of 'judicial Ronald Dworkin' and (as he does Professor Dworkin) as a natural lawyer, arguing that the basic idea of natural law is that there are universal principles of law that inform and constrain positive law.[26] Indeed, some proponents also argue that the citation of foreign law is best understood as an application of natural law[27] or postmodern natural law[28]; while according to others only a theory articulated in terms of *ius gentium*, that is, 'the

[19] See David M. Beatty, *The Ultimate Rule of Law* (2004), 159–88.

[20] See Mark Tushnet, 'Comparative Constitutional Law' in Mathias Reimann and Reinhard Zimmermann (eds), *The Oxford Handbook of Comparative Law* (2008).

[21] See Mary Ann Glandon, 'Rights in Twentieth-Century Constitutions' (1992) 59 *University of Chicago Law Review* 519, 532 and *Comparative Legal Traditions* (2nd edn, 1994), 10.

[22] See Jackson (n 11).

[23] Charles de Secondat, Baron de Montesquieu, *The Spirit of Laws* (Anne M. Cohler et al ed and trans, 1989), 8.

[24] Günther Frankenberg, 'Stranger than Paradise: Identity and Politics in Comparative Law' (1997) *Utah Law Review* 259, 262–3.

[25] O. Kahn-Freund, 'On Uses and Misuses of Comparative Law' (1974) 37 *Modern Law Review* 1, 17–18.

[26] See Richard A. Posner, 'Forward: A Political Court' (2005) 110 *Harvard Law Review* 31, 84–9.

[27] See eg Alford (n 14).

[28] Catherine Dupré, 'Globalisation and Judicial Reasoning: Building Blocks for a Method of Interpretation' in Andrew Halpin and Volker Roeben (eds), *Theorising the Global Legal Order* (2009).

accumulated wisdom of the world on rights and justice from the decisions of judges and lawmakers', in other words, a consensus among 'civilized,' or 'freedom-loving' countries, justify the citations.[29]

The different normative arguments concerning the relevance of foreign materials in constitutional cases, especially in US Supreme Court practice, can be followed in a conversation between Justice Antonin Scalia and Justice Stephen Breyer.[30] They both agreed that the use of comparative law is not 'authoritative', that is, that it is not binding as a precedent. But, as Scalia noted, such citations are neither legitimate nor useful, while for Justice Breyer, they are useful and legitimate as long as they are considered for their insight and not regarded as authoritative. Breyer offered a pragmatic rationale, suggesting that foreign courts

> have problems that often, more and more, are similar to our own.... If here I have a human being called a judge in a different country dealing with a similar problem, why don't I read what he says if it's similar enough? Maybe I'll learn something....[31]

In Scalia's originalist view, foreign law 'is irrelevant with one exception: old English law, which served as the backdrop for the framing of the constitutional text.'[32] Scalia also stated that judges using foreign materials cite comparative law selectively, such that 'when it agrees with what the justices would like the case to say, we use the foreign law, and when it doesn't agree we don't use it.'[33] This means that the citation of comparative case law 'lends itself to manipulation'.[34] For Justice Breyer, one of the justifications for citing the case law of other national courts was to consolidate judicial review in transitional democracies.[35] As Justice Breyer emphasized in the discussion, even where there are no apparent firm convergences, human beings across cultures and national borders confront many of the same problems. What is at stake in these situations is a 'dialogue' (à la Choudhry) or 'engagement' (à la Jackson) with foreign decisions, which does not necessarily mean any disposition towards endorsement or adoption of particular foreign approaches.

Scalia's and Breyer's positions can also be seen as the dichotomy of American exceptionalism, that is, the refusal by many US courts and Justices—including those of the Supreme Court—to engage in comparative interpretation, and the 'postwar juridical paradigm' of rights protection, a common constitutional model found in a variety of liberal democracies.[36] As

[29] See Jeremy Waldron, 'Foreign Law and the Modern *Ius Gentium*' (2005) 119 *Harvard Law Review* 129.

[30] The hour-long face-to-face conversation was sponsored by the US Association of Constitutional Law, January 13, 2005, Washington College of Law at American University in Washington, DC moderated by Norman Dorsen, New York University School of Law. The transcript was published in (2005) 3 *International Journal of Constitutional Law* 519–41.

[31] Ibid 522.

[32] Ibid 525.

[33] Ibid 521. Also McCrudden mentions as one possible explanation that the use of foreign judgments is simply result-drive: that advocates and judges simply use the foreign decision that supports the result they want in the particular case before the court. He even raises the suspicion that the selective use of foreign judgments is inevitably associated with a rights-expanding agenda. But then he rejects this by referring to Justice Frankfurter, who was consistently the US Supreme Court Justice most favourably disposed towards citing foreign cases, and was certainly not pursuing a rights-expanding agenda. See McCrudden (n 5), 527.

[34] Ibid 531.

[35] Sujit Choudhry criticizes this justification as crude, overblown, and real politik, as well as his failures to respond Scalia's challenges and explain why courts should cite comparative case law. See 'Migration As a New Metaphor' (n 11), 4–10.

[36] See this contrast of models in Lorraine Weinrib, 'The Postwar Paradigm and American Exceptionalism' in Choudhry, *Migration of Constitutional Ideas* (n 11).

Scalia's arguments demonstrate, the starting points of American exceptionalism are that constitutional judicial review is undemocratic and illegitimate, and consequently views the use of foreign law as a form of judicial activism, which further undermines the legitimacy of judicial review. The post-war juridical paradigm model views judicially enforced constitutional rights as subjects of comparative constitutional interpretation.

III. Jurisprudential Aspects: Why It Happens?

In this section, I try to identify some criteria that can explain why particular judges and courts decide to use or, conversely, not to use foreign materials. Christopher McCrudden lists the following factors that seem to lead judges to engage with foreign materials: (1) the type of political regime in which the foreign court is situated, (2) a pedagogical impulse to look at more established democracies, or warning not to use certain laws, (3) their audience, (4) the existence of common alliances, (5) filling the vacuum of a temporary absence of (preferred) indigenous jurisprudence, (6) the perceived nature of the constitution as transformative or conservative, (7) theories of law and legal interpretation, (8) foreign law empirical fact, (9) perceived judicial competence in the area of foreign law in issue, and (10) differences in constitutional structure.[37] But the most important criterion common in all these factors, is to look for good persuasive ideas in other national jurisprudence, which would help to solve similar constitutional problems through interpretation. As the number of liberal democratic countries is constantly increasing, the migration of constitutional ideas within this community cannot be a one-way process: some courts always being 'givers' of law while others always 'receivers'. Of course the courts in the countries of the 'postwar juridical paradigm' (Weinrib) of rights protection use more case law from the courts of older and more established democracies, like that of the US Supreme Court. As Justice Albie Sachs of the South African Constitutional Court writes:

> If I draw on statements by certain United States Supreme Court Justices, I do so not because I treat their decisions as precedents to be applied in our Courts, but because their dicta articulate in an elegant and helpful manner problems which face any modern court dealing with what was loosely been called state/church relations. Thus, though drawn from another legal culture, they express values and dilemmas in a way which I find most helpful in elucidating the meaning of our own constitutional text.[38]

But the growing interdependency also means that courts with long records of constitutional interpretation, like the US Supreme Court, should also 'learn something' as Justice Breyer said in the discussion with Justice Scalia. Before we discuss in the next section the practice of some national courts, which after their transition to liberal democracy have the most frequently cited foreign law in constitutional interpretation, let us observe the slowly changing development of the US Supreme Court from the exceptionalist approach of the majority of the Justices to some recent decisions in which the majority did refer to foreign and international case law.

Justice Frankfurter, from the 1940s onwards, drew on the opinions of other countries in the Anglo-Saxon tradition 'not less civilized than our own' as reflected in their statutes, decisions, and practices. In *Adamson v California*,[39] for instance, he based his interpretation on 'those

[37] See McCrudden (n 5), 516–27.

[38] *S v Lawrence, S v Negal, S v Solberg* (4) SA 1176, 1223 (South Africa 1997). Quoted by Slaughter (n 1), 77.

[39] 332 US 46 (1947).

canons of decency and fairness which express the notions of justice of English-speaking peoples', a view he repeated in *Rochin v California*,[40] and for which he became increasingly marginalized by his fellow Justices—for instance by Justice Black who not without irony asked 'Why we should consider only the notions of English-speaking peoples to determine what are immutable and fundamental principles of justice?'[41] In the *Furman v Georgia* case,[42] which was a major decision of the Supreme Court on the death penalty, Justice Thurgood Marshall argued that the abolition of capital punishment would enable the United States to 'join the approximately 70 other jurisdictions in the world which celebrate their regard for civilization and humanity by shunning capital punishment.' For Justice Powell, in dissent, the comparative experience pointed to the opposite conclusion. But despite the different outcomes of the opinions, both those in favour and those against used comparative arguments. In *Thompson v Oklahoma*,[43] Justice Brennan argued in the majority judgment that to allow the execution of a criminal who was less than 16 years old at the time of the offence would offend civilized standards of decency, and this 'is consistent with the views that have been expressed…by other nations that share our Anglo-American heritage, and by the leading members of the Western European community.' Justice Brennan also cited as evidence the brief of Amnesty International. In his dissent, Justice Scalia not only disagreed with the ruling, but also with the use of the comparative approach itself: 'we must not forget that it is the Constitution for the United States that we are expounding.'[44] In *Stanford v Kentucky*,[45] this dissenting view became the majority. Despite the dissent's reliance on comparative arguments, Justice Scalia, writing this time for the majority, said that it is 'American conceptions of decency that are dispositive, rejecting the conception of petitioners…that the sentencing practices of other countries are relevant.'[46] In *Knight v Florida*,[47] where the question was whether 20 years on death row was cruel and unusual punishment under the Eighth Amendment, Justice Thomas for the majority observed that 'Were there any support in our own jurisprudence, it would be unnecessary for proponents of the claim to rely on the European Court of Human Rights, the Supreme Court of Zimbabwe, the Supreme Court of India, or the Privy Council.'[48] Justice Breyer in his dissent emphasized that the US Supreme Court has a history of looking at 'the way in which foreign courts have applied standards roughly comparable to our constitutional standards in roughly comparable circumstances.'[49] In another dissenting opinion, Justice Breyer also cited *The Federalist Paper*, no 63, in support of the idea that 'attention to judgement of other nations' is useful.[50] Not only in cases of rights, but in those concerning the relevance of foreign constitutional experiences in the context of federalism was Justice Scalia rejective. In *Printz v United States*,[51] he said that 'comparative analysis [is] inappropriate to the task of interpreting a constitution though it [is,] of course, quite relevant to the task of writing one.'[52] Justice Breyer's dissent admitted that 'we are interpreting our own constitution, not that of other nations and there may be relevant political and structural differences', but nonetheless 'their experience may…cast an empirical light on the consequences of different solutions to a common legal problem.'[53]

[40] 342 US 165, 169 (1952). [41] Ibid 176. [42] 408 US 238 (1972).
[43] 487 US 815 (1987). [44] Ibid 869. [45] 492 US 361 (1989).
[46] Ibid 370. [47] 528 US 990 (1999). [48] Ibid 990.
[49] Ibid 997. [50] *Foster v Florida* 537 US 990 (2002).
[51] 521 US 898 (1997). [52] Ibid 921 n 11. [53] Ibid 977.

However, around the beginning of the new millennium, many observers noted that 'the Court's manifest awareness of other constitutional systems is on the rise'.[54] One early sign was *Washington v Glucksberg*,[55] where the Court referred to experience in foreign jurisdictions in its first decision on the constitutionality of assisted suicide. In *Atkins v Virginia*, Justice Stevens referred in a footnote to the opinion of the 'world community' in support of what he called a 'national consensus' against the execution of the mentally retarded.[56] The reference was sharply criticized in dissents by both Chief Justice Rehnquist and Justice Scalia, who stated that

> the Prize for the Court's Most Feeble Effort to fabricate 'national consensus' must go to its appeal . . . to views of assorted professionals and religious organizations, members of the so-called 'world community', and respondents to opinion polls.[57]

But the decisive steps were the *Lawrence* and the *Roper* cases. In *Lawrence v Texas*,[58] the Court struck down the criminal prohibition of sodomy, departing from its earlier decision in *Bowers v Hardwick*.[59] In the majority judgment, Justice Kennedy cited the decision of the European Court of Human Rights in *Dudgeon v United Kingdom*[60] to illustrate 'that the reasoning in *Bowers* has been rejected elsewhere'.[61] One commentator went so far as to state that the citation 'suggests that constitutional courts are all engaged in a common interpretative enterprise'.[62] But Justice Scalia's dissent shows that there is no agreement on this within the Court. He first made it clear that the '*Bowers* majority opinion never relied on values we share with other civilization', and secondly emphasized that

> The Court's discussion of . . . foreign views [ignoring of course, the many countries that have retained criminal prohibitions on sodomy] is therefore meaningless dicta. Dangerous dicta, however, since this Court . . . should not impose foreign moods, fads or fashions on Americans.[63]

In *Roper*, both the debate on the juvenile death penalty and on the migration of constitutional ideas continued. Justice Kennedy, arguing for the majority about the unconstitutionality of capital punishment for juveniles, reviewed a range of foreign sources and stated that they 'while not controlling our outcome . . . provide respected and significant confirmation for our own conclusions', and went on to say that in this general praise for the use of foreign law:

> These doctrines and guarantees are central to the American experience and remain essential to our present-day self-definition and national identity. Not the least of reasons we honor the Constitution, then is, because we know it to be our own. It does not lessen our fidelity to the Constitution or our pride in its origins to acknowledge that the express affirmation of certain fundamental rights by other nations and peoples simply underscores the centrality of those same rights within our own heritage of freedom.[64]

[54] See Vicki C. Jackson, 'Narratives of Federalism: Of Continuities and Comparative Constitutional Experience' (2001) 51 *Duke Law Journal* 223, 252. Jackson notes the citing of foreign constitutional law by even its most vocal opponent—Justice Scalia in a dissent—in *McIntyre v Ohio Elections Commission* 514 US 334, 381–8 (1995). Justice Scalia invoked Australian, Canadian, and English jurisprudence in the mid-1990s when dealing with the question whether the source of an election campaign leaflet opposing a school tax levy proposed in Ohio should be revealed to the public.

[55] 521 US 702 (1997).

[56] 536 US 304, 316 n 21 (2002).

[57] Ibid 337.

[58] 539 US 558 (2003).

[59] 478 US 186 (1986).

[60] 45 ECtHR (1981).

[61] 539 US 558, 2483 (2003).

[62] See Michael Ramsey, 'International Materials and Domestic Rights: Reflections on Atkins and Lawrence' (2004) 98 *American Journal of International Law* 69.

[63] 539 US 558, 598 (2003).

[64] *Roper v Simmons* 543 US 551, 1200 (2005).

Justice Scalia's dissent again attacks the Court's comparative approach by accusing the majority of holding the view 'that American law should conform to the laws of the rest of the world'—a view which 'ought to be rejected out of hand'.[65]

IV. Case Studies: How Far and Where It Happens?

This section discusses the more empirical questions of the use of foreign materials, namely to what extent does it happen, and where? For this purpose, I have selected four case studies, which all fall under Lorain Weinrib's 'postwar juridical paradigm': Germany, Hungary, Israel, and South Africa. The explanation for this selection is that American exceptionalism, discussed in the previous section, is partly based on the fact that, until the end of the Second World War, the US Supreme Court was the only constitutional court that did enough to warrant studying by the emerging new democracies,[66] such as Germany or Israel. But from the beginning of the 1950s onwards, when the German Federal Constitutional Court was established, it also became an important source of migrating constitutional ideas for other new constitutional states, such as Hungary. At the beginning of the 1990s, other states governed by the rule of law emerged, such as South Africa, whose Constitutional Court's decision on the unconstitutionality of the death penalty used US, German, and also Hungarian case law; needless to say, the decisive one was not that of the US Supreme Court.

1. Germany

The constitutional law of the Federal Republic of Germany after the Second World War was definitely influenced by American constitutionalism, but the Basic Law of 1949 cannot be labelled as an imposed constitution. Although the constitution-making process was set in motion by the occupying Allied powers, and the final product was subject to Allied approval, the actual drafting was essentially a German process drawing on German models and traditions.[67] References to American constitutional ideas and principles in the Parliamentary Council covered a variety of subjects, for instance issues of federalism and a bill of rights, and scholars of German constitutional theory and practice also paid close attention to American constitutionalism.[68] The same can be said concerning the jurisprudence of the German Federal Constitutional Court: there were some important decisions at the very beginning which were influenced by US Supreme Court rulings, but the number of directly cited decisions decreased after the Federal Constitutional Court established its own jurisdiction.[69]

[65] Ibid 1226.

[66] On this important influence see Louis Henkin and Albert J. Rosenthal (eds), *The Influence of the US Constitution Abroad* (1990).

[67] See Schauer (n 12), 908–9. Schauer states that although the drafting in the shadow of the necessary approval by an occupying power undoubtedly had an effect on the process, it was less than the Allied powers had hoped for, and certainly much less than existed in Japan.

[68] See Helmut Steinberger, 'American Constitutionalism and German Constitutional Development' in Henkin and Rosenthal (n 66), 212–16.

[69] There is no comprehensive analysis of comparative constitutional law used by the German courts. Of the sparse statistical data, one study in 1974 counted 24 decisions of the Federal Constitutional Court which had recourse to comparative law. See Jörg Martin Mössner, 'Rechtsvergleichung und Verfassungsrechtsprechung' (1974) *Archiv des öffentlichen Rechts* 193. Another analysis can be found in Ulrich Drobnig, 'Rechtsvergleichung in der deutschen Rechtsprechung' (1987) *Rabels Zeitschrift für ausländisches und internationales Privatrecht* 610–30. The latest survey refers mainly to the court practice of the Federal High Courts, including the Federal Constitutional Court in the years 1950 to

However, the influence of American constitutional thinking was always present among the various constitutional court Justices, such as Gerhard Leibholz, Konrad Hesse, Dieter Grimm, Wolfgang Hoffmann-Riem, and Brun-Otto Bryde.[70] This explains why there are no fundamental objections against referring to international and foreign sources in the German Federal Constitutional Court. For discussions such as the one taking place in the United States to form the background of their argument would be plainly unthinkable in Germany.[71] One German constitutional scholar even advocates making comparative law 'the fifth method of interpretation' in constitutional law, alongside text, context, history, and policy.[72]

There is an important difference between the German and the American attitude towards international law which, at least, makes the use of rules of international law much easier in Germany. According to Article 25 of the German Basic Law (Grundgesetz), the generally recognized rules of public international law are part of federal law, and they have priority over national law. In disputed cases, the Federal Constitutional Court is entitled to interpret these rules. In 1982, for instance, the Court added a further criterion for the examination of cases, in which an accused is sentenced in his absence, that is, the minimum procedural requirement of public international law. The Court referred to the decisions of three European countries to show that the application of such standards is justified.[73] In other cases, where the Court interprets procedural guarantees which are not spelled out in the Basic Law, for example the presumption of innocence, they deduce this right from the rule of law; but since it had no textual basis in the Basic Law, it cited the words of the European Court of Human Rights and drew heavily on the case law of the Strasbourg organs in its jurisprudence.[74]

One of the first rulings of the Court to cite foreign materials was the dissolution of the Kommunistische Partei Deutschlands (KPD) case of 1956, when the Court banned the West German Communist Party, by partly distinguishing the Federal Republic of Germany from its Western neighbours:

> The constitutional logic of these [Western] democracies... lies in the fact that citizens are free or, as under the Italian Constitution of 1947, even encouraged to form political parties without limitation.... Recent developments, have however, shown that free democracies can equally not ignore the practical and political problems of excluding parties from public life which are hostile to the constitutional order if the threat to the State reaches a certain level of intensity.... The Communist Party was thus prohibited in France and Switzerland in 1939 and 1940 by government regulations. In the United States the party was required to register in order to allow public authorities to effectively monitor its activity as a subversive organization.[75]

1990. Approximately 70 of the reported cases were handed down by the Federal Supreme Court (Bundesgerichtshof), another 25 cases originate from the Federal Constitutional Court. In contrast, the other Federal High Courts have used comparative law in only a few instances. See Ulrich Drobnig, 'The Use of Foreign Law by the German Courts' in Sir Basil Markesinis and Jörg Fedtke (eds), *Judicial Recourse to Foreign Law* (2006).

[70] On the influence of US thinking in the development of the German equality doctrine see Alexander Somek, 'The Deadweight of Formulae: What Might Have Been the Second Germanization of American Equal Protection Review' (1998) 1 *University of Pennsylvania Journal of Constitutional Law* 284, 296.

[71] See Brun-Otto Bryde, 'The Constitutional Judge and the International Constitutionalist Dialogue' in Markesinis and Fedtke (n 69), 298–301.

[72] See Peter Häberle, 'Grundrechtsgeltung und Grundrechtsinterpretation im Verfassungsstaat' (1989) *Juristenzeitung* 913.

[73] BVerfGE 59, 280, at 283 and 286.

[74] BVerfGE 35, 311, at 320, BVerfGE 74, 102, at 121, BVerfGE 74, 358, at 370, BVerfGE 82, 106, at 114.

[75] BVerfGE 5, 85, at 135–6.

One of the leading cases on freedom of expression, and one of the Court's most important decisions overall, is the *Lüth* case of 1958,[76] in which the Court cites both the French Declaration of Human Rights, in French, and Justice Cardozo of the US Supreme Court, in English, on 'the matrix of indispensable condition of nearly every other form of freedom'.

In the famous *Spiegel* decision of 1966, four judges out of the eight members of the Senate referred to papers presented at an international conference on the legal position of the press in criminal proceedings concerning the question whether members of the press can refuse to give evidence in criminal proceedings involving treason and opted against such a right.[77] This argument was rejected by the other four judges, but on substantial reasons, and not because of the use of comparative law.

As Justice Bryde states, despite the mentioned hidden background influence, there are relatively few open references to foreign law.[78] He mentions the following examples. When the Court decided, against popular opinion (both on the matters of animal rights and of xenophobia), for a Muslim halal butcher, it found it helpful to point out that the Austrian Constitutional Court had reached the same result.[79] In establishing the constitutionality of same-sex unions, it also put on record in how many countries such unions have become accepted practice.[80] In another case, the Court also referred to international human rights jurisprudence for the difficult task of reconciling the rule of law regarding retroactive punishment with the avoidance of impunity for crimes committed under a non-democratic regime.[81] Ulrich Drobnig refers to some other concrete decisions, such as the one regarding interpretation of Article 4(3) of the Basic Law, which deals with the right of conscientious objection to military service. In this case, the Court was looking for help from foreign legal systems, but found no common ground either on the international level or in the Western democracies.[82] Another case concerned the interpretation of the notion of 'political treaty' in Article 59(2). The Court found in the laws of several Central European countries a uniform understanding of that concept and used this as a basis for its decision.[83] A similar result was reached by the Court concerning the interpretation of the term 'home', which Article 13(1) of the Basic Law declares as inviolable. The Court finding decisions in four countries which interpreted 'home' relatively broadly also used this approach.[84]

Without concrete citations and even despite different arguments used, but seemingly considering decisions of the US Supreme Court, one can find decisions where the German Federal Constitutional Court has reached similar results to its US counterpart. One example is abortion rights, which were carved out by both Courts using different approaches.[85] In the first case in each country, ruled in the 1970s, *Roe v Wade* by the US Supreme Court[86] and the *Abortion I* case by the German Federal Constitutional Court,[87] the two Courts struck almost the same balance between the pregnant woman's right to obtain an abortion and the state's

[76] BVerfGE 7, 198. [77] BVerfGE 20, 162, at 229–31.

[78] According to Drobnig, important as some of the decisions citing foreign law are, their share of all the published decisions amounts to no more than 1 per cent. See Drobnig (n 69), 141.

[79] BVerfGE 104, 337, at 349.

[80] BVerfGE 105, 313, at 315.

[81] BVerfGE 95, 96, at 133.

[82] BVerfGE 28, 243 at 258.

[83] BVerfGE 1, 372, at 382.

[84] BVerfGE 32, 54, at 70.

[85] See for this example Rosenfeld (n 18), 190–1, but also in Richard E. Levy and Alexander Somek, 'Paradoxical Parallels in the American and German Abortion Decisions' (2001) 9 *Tulane Journal of International and Comparative Law* 109.

[86] 410 US 113 (1973). [87] BVerfGE 39, 1.

interest in the protection of the fetus's right to life—although the doctrinal analyses are in sharp contrast.[88]

The same is also true in respect of communication rights: US law is more free in its individualism and more zealous in the protection of expression. For example, in *RAV v St Paul* the Supreme Court protected the right of white individuals to express hatred by placing a burning cross late at night in the fenced-in yard of a black neighbour who lived across the street.[89] In the *Auschwitz Lie* case, the Federal Constitutional Court banned a demonstration intending to assert that the Holocaust never occurred, by arguing that 'freedom of opinion by no means always takes precedents over protection of personality'.[90] (This is why some US scholars call the German Basic Law a 'constitution of dignity' whereas the US Constitution is labelled a 'constitution of liberty'.[91]) It seems that the German Court here formulates its approach of the limitation of hate speech against the US one. This is called by Andrzej Rapaczynski a 'negative influence', a process in which a model (eg the American model) is known, considered, and rejected, or in which an experience perceived as undesirable is used as an argument for not following that example.[92] But despite these different approaches based on different historical backgrounds and legal cultures, the right to communication is an equally essential aspect of both constitutional systems.[93]

2. Israel

The uniqueness of the case of Israel concerning the use of foreign law in constitutional interpretation is the very fact that the state has no formal written constitution.[94] This means that Israeli judges are engaged in an ongoing process of constitutionalization. In the *United Mizrahi Bank* case,[95] Chief Justice Aharon Barak,[96] arguing for judicial review of constitutionality by the Israeli Supreme Court, besides referring to Hamilton (*The Federalist Papers*, no 78), H.L.A. Hart (*The Concept of Law*), John Rawls (*Political Liberalism*), and John Hart Ely (*Democracy and Distrust: A Theory of Judicial Review*), also evokes *Marbury v Madison* of the US Supreme Court. Legitimizing the test of the constitutionality of constitutional amendments, he mentions the opinion of the Supreme Court of India in the case of *Kesavananda v State of Kerala*,[97] and quotes the following words of the German Federal Constitution Court:

> Laws are not constitutional merely because they have been passed, in conformity with procedural provisions.... They must be substantively compatible with the highest values, and must

[88] See Chapter 51 in this volume. [89] 505 US 377 (1989). [90] BVerfGE 90, 241, 148.

[91] Donald P. Kommers argues that 'in the American view [as contrasted with the German], the community has no valid claim upon the individual person, particularly in the domain of mind and morals': 'The Jurisprudence of Free Speech in the United States and the Federal Republic of Germany' (1980) 53 *Southern California Law Review* 678, 694.

[92] See Andrzej Rapaczynski, 'Bibliographical Essay: Influence of the US Constitution' in Henkin and Rosenthal (n 66). Similarly, Kim Lane Scheppele also investigates constitutional influence through the use of negative models. See Kim Lane Scheppele, 'Aspirational and Aversive Constitutionalism. The Case for Studying Cross-Constitutional Influence Through Negative Models' (2003) 1(2) *International Journal of Constitutional Law* 296.

[93] See Edward J. Eberle, *Dignity and Liberty. Constitutional Visions in Germany and the United States* (2002), 231–6.

[94] See Gary Jeffrey Jacobsohn, *Apple of Gold. Constitutionalism in Israel and the United States* (1993), 98.

[95] *United Mizrahi Bank Ltd v Migdal Village*, Supreme Court (Israel), CA 6821/93, 49(4)P.D.221 (1995).

[96] For Aharon Barak's commitment to the use of comparative law see ch 10 of his book, *The Judge in a Democracy* (2006).

[97] AIR 1973 SC 146.

also conform to unwritten fundamental constitutional principles as well as the fundamental decisions of the Basic Law.[98]

Freedom of expression is probably the area of constitutional law where doctrinal developments in the United States have had the most influence in Israel.[99] The first important decision was the *Kol-Ha'am Co Ltd v Minister of Interior* case.[100] In 1953, the daily newspaper *Ha'aretz* reported that the Israeli Ambassador to the United States had stated that in the eventuality of a war between the United States and the Soviet Union, Israel would supply the United States with a military force of 200,000 troops. The newspaper of Israel's Communist Party, *Kol-Ha'am* (*The People's Voice*) published an editorial denouncing the 'anti-nationalist policy of the Ben-Gurion government which profiteers in the blood of Israeli youth'. Four days later, the Minister of Interior suspended publication of the newspapers for periods of ten and 15 days. A unanimous panel of three Justices[101] overruled the order. Justice Agnarat, writing for the Court, declared freedom of expression and freedom of the press to be basic principles of Israel's unwritten constitutional law by virtue of Israel's commitment to democracy, concluding that given the components of the probable danger test, the suspension order could not stand. According to a commentator of the decision, the 'probability' test breaks 'from the notion of "acceptable speech" and focuses on concrete harms to society', which is very similar to the American test of 'clear and present danger'.[102]

Another landmark case was *Ha'aretz v Electronic Company*, in which during a recession one of Israel's largest government enterprises purchased a luxury car for its director general. *Ha'aretz* published an article asserting that the company against its former promise had no interest in selling the car. The company brought a libel suit. First, the Supreme Court's ordinary panel of three Justices overruled the district court decision against *Ha'aretz* by a 2:1 (*Ha'aretz I*).[103] Justice Shamgar, one of the majority, used the arguments of the US Supreme Court in *New York Times v Sullivan* favouring the free criticism of public officials.[104] Four years later, the Israeli Supreme Court reversed its decision and reinstated the libel verdict (*Ha'aretz II*),[105] rejecting the *Sullivan* test, and protecting the reputation of the public official.

The third major case is *Kahane v Broadcasting Authority*,[106] in which Justice Barak used the 'near certainty of a real injury' test, when deciding the constitutionality of banning the broadcast of the radical Rabbi Kahane's hatred speech towards Israeli Arabs, which was again similar to the American 'clear and present danger' test, used in the case of the prohibition of the march of the Nazis in the streets of Skokie, Illinois.[107] Justice Barak argued that the Broadcasting Authority could not prevent Kahane's broadcasts on the ground that this constituted an improper exercise of prior restraint. According to Justice Barak, however, not only was this blanket exclusion of Kahane (not including news coverage of his activities) unconstitutional, but he also maintained that the Broadcasting Authority could not impose a policy of excluding

[98] BVerfGE 6, 32.

[99] This is the very reason that Gray Jeffrey Jacobsohn, in his book on the comparison of constitutionalism in Israel and the United States discusses the Israeli Supreme Court's embrace of the American free speech doctrine. See (n 96), 177–227.

[100] 7 PD 871 (1953).

[101] Israel's highest court typically sits in a panel of three. In this case Justice Agranat was joined by Justices Sussman and Landau.

[102] Pnina Lahav, 'American Influence on Israel's Jurisprudence of Free Speech' (1981) 9 *Hastings Constitutional Law Quarterly* 27.

[103] 31 (2) PD 281 (1974).

[104] 376 US 254 (1964).

[105] 32 (3) PD 337 (1978).

[106] 41 (3) PD 255 (1986).

[107] US District Court decision in *Collin v Smith* 447 F Supp 676 (1978).

the broadcasting of racist views and sentiments on the basis of content alone. This position was criticized by Justice Gabriel Bach, who argued that the type of racist speech for which Kahane was known should be categorized as unprotected.[108] Justice Barak cited 18 US cases (and 14 scholarly works), some of which provoked Justice Bach to say that 'one should not apply these decisions to the case at bar, which deals with the right of public authorities to prevent broadcast of specific programs banned by an explicit law.'[109] This debate was not about the use of foreign law, but over its limits. As we can see, US free speech jurisprudence—sometimes embraced, sometimes rejected—has been an important source in forming the praxis of the Supreme Court. As in the case of Germany, where historical circumstances very much influenced the use of the US Supreme Court's free speech jurisprudence, the same has also happened in Israel, where communal integrity was a decisive factor in the implementation of US doctrine.

3. Hungary

During its transition to democracy, Hungary has chosen its own unique method of constitution-making, retaining—in name, if not in form—the Constitution from the beginning of the country's Communist period, but radically changing its content in a process of comprehensive amendment in 1989. Like the High Court of Justice in Israel, the Constitutional Court of Hungary has also developed an activist practice of judicial review of parliamentary legislation.

The first nine-year cycle of the Hungarian Constitutional Court's proceedings came to an end in 1999. Those nine years will enter not only into Hungarian political and public law history as the era of the Sólyom Court, but—and what is at least as important to a genuine constitutional judge/court—into the legal textbooks as well. Judge László Sólyom was the president of the court during this time, and the Court's jurisprudence and style very much reflected his leadership. Especially in this period, the use of foreign law in the interpretation of the Constitution was a deliberate strategy by the Hungarian Constitutional Court, which merely designates the law of a foreign legal system without being bound by it in the same way as when a foreign law is incorporated, or international law ratified.

As Catherine Dupré's book[110] on the import of the concept of human dignity shows, the judges first carefully chose the German model as a suitable model, and then instrumentalized it through a very activist interpretation of the Hungarian Constitution.[111] On that basis, the Court developed its own autonomous concept of human dignity. The first sign of this active instrumentalization was in Decision 8/1990. This decision judged unconstitutional the pre-transition regulation of the Labour Code, which empowers labour unions to represent workers—even if they are not union members and perhaps even against their expressed will—

[108] *Kahane*, 41 (3) PD at 312. [109] Ibid 316.

[110] Catherine Dupré, *Importing the Law in Post-Communist Transitions. The Hungarian Constitutional Court and the Right to Human Dignity* (2003).

[111] As one German scholar observed, the influence of the German Federal Constitutional Court was decisive on the jurisprudence of political and civil rights. See Andreas Zimmermann, 'Bürgerliche und politische Rechte in der Verfassungsrechtsprechung mittel- und osteuropäischer Staaten unter besonderer Berücksichtigung der Einflüsse der deutschen Verfassungsgerichtsbarkeit' in Jochen Abr Frowein (ed), *Grundfragen der Verfassungsgerichtsbarkeit in Mittel- und Osteuropa* (1998), 89–124. In the same volume, the then President of the Hungarian Constitutional Court and his advisor acknowledge this use of German law in constitutional interpretation. See László Sólyom, 'Anmerkiungen zur Rezeption auf dem Gebiet der wirtschaftlichen und sozialen rechte aus ungarischer Sicht', 213–27 and Gábor Halmai, 'Bürgerliche und politische Rechte in der Verfassungsrechtsprechung Ungarns', 125–9.

without their separate power of attorney. The basis for nullifying this regulation was the principle of human dignity in the Constitution, which the Constitutional Justices (on the recommendation of Sólyom as the presenting Justice in the case) declared to be an expression of 'the general rights of individuals'. This right, which does not appear in the Constitution, is, according to Sólyom's view, 'carved out' from the right to human dignity, a 'birthright'; namely, it is a subsidiary of such a fundamental right that the Constitutional Court as well as all other courts in every instance can cite it in defence of individual autonomy if none of the specifically named fundamental laws apply to the case in question. Next, the Justices determined in Decision 57/1991 that 'the right to self-identity and self-determination is part of the "general rights of individuals" '. Further, this right includes everyone's most personal right to discover their parentage. The following year, Decision 22/1992 declared unconstitutional the requirement that enlisted officers request permission from their superiors to marry, on the basis that the right to marry, as part of the right to self-determination, is such a fundamental right that it stands under constitutional guardianship. As Dupré also indicates,[112] the Hungarian Constitutional Court elaborated another conception of human dignity, reading it in conjunction with the right to life as an absolute, and not allowing any limitations on it. The first and most prominent example of this concept is the Court's decision on the death penalty (23/1990). The next major examples of the Hungarian Constitutional Court's liberal understanding of human dignity are the decisions on abortion (48/1991 and 64/1998), which centre on individual and human autonomy, and are divested of human dignity's implication and impact on the community and society. Describing the genesis of a new legal system in Hungary, Dupré states that relying on law importation to develop its case law in the transitional period, the Hungarian Constitutional Court discovered new rights in the wake of human dignity and general personality rights.

The other main area of the use of foreign law as also in the case of both Germany and Israel, is freedom of expression, and especially hate speech. As we already have seen, US free speech doctrine was clearly more liberal than its German and Israeli counterparts. However, as Michel Rosenfeld and András Sajó observe, 'paradoxically, it may be that anti-liberalism towards authoritarianism may be a better weapon in the fight of liberalism against illiberalism in formerly authoritarian polities such as Germany and Hungary.'[113] But assessing the free speech jurisprudence of the latter, they conclude that the Hungarian Constitutional Court in many regards adopted an absolutist theory of speech going beyond the US Supreme Court's position.[114] The free speech practice of the Court can, rather, be characterized with the divide in the standards applied in US jurisprudence, which rejects all limitations, and those of a (Western) Europe inclined more towards resolute limitation based on the 'concept of militant democracy'. The Hungarian Constitutional Court first encountered the problem in examining the constitutionality of the provision in the nation's Criminal Code concerning public incitement. In Decision 30/1992, the Constitutional Court found the facts of the crime of incitement of hatred to be constitutional and annulled that form of defamation. Its reasoning was based on the notion that freedom of expression has a distinguished role among other fundamental rights guaranteed by the Constitution; that in fact it is a type of a 'mother right' of the so-called right to 'communication'.

According to the Justices, the right to free expression of opinion protects opinion without regard to its content in terms of value and truth, for this condition alone lives up to the

[112] See Dupré (n 110), 70ff.

[113] Michel Rosenfeld and András Sajó, 'Spreading Liberal Constitutionalism: An Inquiry into the Fate of Free Speech Rights in New Democracies' in Choudhry, *Migration of Constitutional Ideas* (n 11), 149.

[114] Ibid 159.

ideological neutrality of the Constitution. In confirming the constitutionality of the facts of the crime of incitement, the Justices apparently reasoned on grounds similar to US Supreme Court Justice Oliver Wendell Holmes's famous test of 'clear and present danger'. At the same time, it must be said that the 'danger' attached by the Hungarian Constitutional Court Justices as a condition of constitutionality is more distant and contingent than the type their erstwhile American peers had in mind. Presumably, this is why the Constitutional Court elaborated on its decision by explaining that the 'unavoidable social tensions of system-change' (ie the post-1989 political-economic transition) notably increase the danger of incitement, before large public audiences, to hatred against certain groups. In contrast to US jurisprudence, the Hungarian Constitutional Court did not address the problem of the 'scope' of the facts, that is, whether the incitement provision can be applied even in the absence of a real possibility that hatred will develop. In other words, the Hungarian Justices did not set a constitutional standard that requires incitement to hatred actually to *cause* 'clear and present danger'. This approach, along with citing the historical circumstances of the change of system, recalls not so much the US concept of justice in this respect, but that of Germany's Federal Constitutional Court, which likewise cites historical reasons in reacting to militant threats to democracy by limiting freedom of expression—namely, Germany's interest in avoiding a repeat of the scenario that followed the collapse of the Weimar Republic. The main reason for declaring defamation unconstitutional was, however, that in this case the Hungarian Parliament had in fact made its qualification on the basis of the value content of the opinion expressed, in other words, with the violation of public peace attached to this only on the basis of presumption and statistical probability. Moreover, the Constitutional Court pointed out, not even the public peace is independent of the degree of freedom of expression that prevails in society. Indeed, in countries where people can encounter numerous different opinions, public opinion becomes more tolerant, whereas in closed societies particular instances in which people express opinions outside the norm have far more potential to disturb the public peace. Further, the needless and disproportionate limitation of freedom of expression has a detrimental effect on an open society. Indeed, in such a society those who use abusive language only mark themselves as 'slanderers' in the arena of public opinion. Criticism is the appropriate response to slander, not criminal prosecution, argued the Constitutional Court Justices. At the same time, they added that the need to protect the 'dignity of communities' may constitute a valid constitutional limitation on the freedom of expression. Thus the Court decision does not rule out the possibility that Hungary's lawmakers might establish such protection under criminal law even beyond the scope of incitement to hatred. In the assessment of the Justices, however, the expansion of other legal instruments, for example non-pecuniary compensation, is also suitable for the effective protection of the 'dignity of communities'. In other words, in deciding on the constitutionality of this particular element of fact in the statutory provision on incitement, the Justices looked to an American standard still being applied in the present day.

One of the key conditions of the new open society occasioned by Hungary's change of system was the dismantling of the earlier inviolability of state authority and public officials and representatives—that is to say, the ban on criticizing them. With Decision 36/1994, the Constitutional Court annulled, with immediate effect, the provision of the Criminal Code referring to 'the defamation of state authority or a person in public office'. This was the statutory provision based on which courts had condemned politicians and social scientists who had criticized heads of government ministries. As for the patterns that served as the basis for this decision, one is certainly the 1964 US Supreme Court decision of *New York Times v Sullivan*. The other pattern followed by Hungary's

Constitutional Court Justices was the consistent jurisprudence of the European Court of Human Rights, whose most important decisions are indeed cited in the reasoning of the Hungarian decision—the best known among these being *Lingens v Austria* (1986). The Hungarian Constitutional Court's 1994 decision thus follows not only the jurisprudence of the US Supreme Court but especially that of Strasbourg in setting a lower threshold for criticism of politicians than is the case for criticism of private individuals, arguing that the reputation of such public figures must be balanced with society's interest in ensuring the free and open debate of public affairs.

4. South Africa

The country's transition from apartheid to a constitutional democracy was very much influenced by constitutional borrowings. Both the interim constitution under which the country was governed until the general election was held, and the final one, negotiated by the democratically elected representatives drew heavily upon comparative constitutional law, particularly the law of the United States, Canada, Germany, and the European Convention on Human Rights.[115] One of the obvious reasons for this was the simple fact that South African lawyers had had no real experience of constitutional law or bills of rights prior to the Interim Constitution.[116] The Constitutional Court established by the Interim Constitution was required to certify that the text of the final Constitution complied with the 34 principles of the Convention for the Democratic South Africa agreed by the negotiating partners. This new text for the first time in constitutional history enabled the Court to import international and foreign law: section 39 of the 1996 Constitution (indexed as Interpretation of the Bill of Rights) states that

> (1) When interpreting the Bill of Rights,
> a) a court, tribunal or forum *must* promote the values that underlie an open and democratic society based on human dignity, equality and freedom;
> b) *must* consider international law; and
> c) *may* consider foreign law.
>
> (2) When interpreting any legislation, and when developing the common law or customary law, every court, tribunal or forum *must* promote the spirit, purport and objects of the Bill of Rights.
>
> (3) The Bill of Rights does not deny the existence of any other rights or freedoms that are recognized or conferred by common law, customary law or legislation, to the extent that they are consistent with the Bill.[117]

[115] See D.M. Davis, 'Constitutional Borrowing: The Influence of Legal Culture and Local History in the Reconstruction of Comparative Influence: The South African Experience' (2003) 1 *International Journal of Constitutional Law* 181, 186.

[116] When drafting of the Interim Bill of Rights, it had been difficult to find five South African experts for the Technical Committee who had the knowledge and expertise to draft a Bill of Rights. See Richard Spitz and Matthew Chaskalson, *The Politics of Transition: A Hidden History of South Africa's Negotiated Settlement* (2000), 252–67, 255.

[117] Emphasis added. Section 35 of the Interim Constitution of 1993 contained a similar provision, but with the phrase removed from the final text that the use of international and foreign law is an obligation only 'where applicable'.

From the very first decisions delivered shortly after its establishment in 1995, the Constitutional Court made extensive use of international and foreign law.[118] In *Zuma and others v State*,[119] the Court declared the provision of the criminal procedure code in force during apartheid, according to which a confession of guilt could be gathered even by police force members without it having to be repeated during the trial. The Court lists how the same issue was dealt with by the US and the Canadian Supreme Courts, analysing three US (*Tot v US, Leary v United States*, and *Country Court of Ulster Country, New York et al v Allen et al*) and two Canadian cases (*Regina v Big M Drug Mart Lt* and *Regina v Oakes*).

In its landmark decision in *Makwanyane v State*,[120] the Court investigated the constitutionality of the provision of the Criminal Procedure Act on capital punishment in relation to sections 8 (equality before law), 9 (right to life), 10 (protection of human dignity), and 11 (unlawfulness of cruel, inhuman, or degrading treatment and punishment) of the Interim Constitution. The Court engaged in a critical assessment of various countries' constitutional jurisprudence on the death penalty. First the Court examined the US Supreme Court's rulings that confirmed the constitutionality of the death penalty not being cruel and unusual punishment. The next subject for comparison was the 1949 Constitution of India and the jurisprudence of the Indian Supreme Court, which was also not considered to be compatible or useful for resolving the problem of the death penalty's unconstitutionality under the South African constitutional system. On the contrary, reference was made to both the Canadian Supreme Court in *Kindler v Canada* of 1992 which defines the death penalty as cruel and inhuman treatment that damages human dignity, and also Decision 23/1990 of the Hungarian Constitutional Court declaring capital punishment as a violation of both right to life and human dignity.

In the *De Klerk v Du Plessis* case,[121] the question was whether the constitutional guarantee of freedom of expression could serve as a defence to a defamation action, but the case also raised questions about the retroactivity of constitutional guarantees as well as the horizontal effect of constitutional rights to private actions. All the opinions in the decision devote considerable attention to analysing how other jurisdictions have approached the question of the relationship between private law and constitutional rights, as well as the question of retrospectivity. For instance, Justice Kentridge discusses in detail the US Supreme Court's ruling in *Shelley v Kraemer*, as well as Canadian, Irish, and German case law, while Justice Ackermann analysed 'Drittwirkung', the German approach to horizontality. With the substantial influence of this German legal thinking, the Court finally opted for an indirect application of fundamental rights in the private sphere.

But the use of comparative law was not uncontroversial in *Klerk v Du Plessis*. In his dissent, Justice Kriegler emphasized the unique character of the South African constitutional arrangements and warned against too much reliance on foreign law, sometimes without an understanding of the legal system of the cited jurisdiction. He later repeated these concerns in *Bernstein and Others v Bester NO and Others*[122] and in *State v Mamabolo*.[123] In some cases, other Justices also joined his concerns.[124] There were other decisions in which the majority

[118] Scrutinizing Supreme Court and Constitutional Court judgments between July 1994 and August 1998, there were no less than 1,258 references to the decisions of US, Canadian, British, German, European, and Indian courts. See Jörg Fedtke, *Die Rezeption von Verfassungsrecht. Südafrica 1993–96* (2000), 446.

[119] CCT 5/94.

[120] CCT 3/94.

[121] CCT 3/96.

[122] CCT 4/96.

[123] CCT 5/2000.

[124] See eg Sir Sydney Kentridge, 'Comparative Law in Constitutional Adjudication', in Markesinis and Fedtke (n 69), 334.

rejected the recourse to foreign law, one of which is *Ferreira v Levine NO and Others*,[125] which dealt with the statutory duty of company employees to disclose confidential business information under specific circumstances. Justice Ackermann, after referring to the writings of Sir Isaiah Berlin and the opinion of Dickson CJC in the Canadian case *R Big M Drug Mart*, proposed to expand the protective scope of the Interim Constitution's provision on human dignity to include a general right to freedom. Finally, the majority of the judges rejected Justice Ackermann's approach, but not simply because it was strongly influenced by foreign law, rather, because it would have amounted to a full legal transplant, not just an expansion or development of the law on the basis of constitutional principles already enumerated in the 1993 text of the Interim Constitution.[126] The other case, *Sate v Solberg*,[127] was a decision that upheld a ban on the sale of certain alcoholic beverages on Sundays, Good Friday, and Christmas as not violating the freedom of religion provision of the Interim Constitution. In a concurring opinion, Justice Sachs relying on the US First Amendment's Establishment Clause and its jurisprudence, for instance in *Lynch v Donelly*, argued that the law did violate freedom of religion.[128]

But despite these debates within the Court, the very extensive use of comparative judgments means that the Court insists that the migration of constitutional values throughout the legal systems is absolutely vital, and it also draws heavily on comparative and international law in reaching this conclusion.[129]

V. Conclusions: Transnationalization of Constitutional Interpretation?

We can conclude that despite the different postures towards use of foreign law, constitutionalism and judicial review have 'gone global', and there is definitely a growing horizontal communication between constitutional systems; and given this dramatic development, the traditional neglect of the study of comparative law is becoming harder to justify.[130] This means that there are more and more countries engaging with foreign and international—that is, transnational—norms. The expanding universe of law through the internet also makes it much harder nowadays to avoid taking a position on the role of international or foreign law.[131] Whether a consequence of this development will be the emergence of a 'transnational constitutionalism' or the international community becoming a constitutional community, is yet to be seen. It is even more difficult to foresee whether this movement will lead to a convergence towards a liberal democratic constitutional model as universalist followers of the convergence posture predict or even claim for the current situation. For instance, T.R.S. Allan sets out a constitutional theory framed around 'the basic principles of liberal constitutionalism' which is 'broadly applicable to every liberal democracy of the familiar Western Type'.[132] Also, Lorraine Weinrib states that the migration of constitutional

[125] CCT 1/96. [126] See Markesinis and Fedtke (n 69), 95. [127] CCT 10/97.

[128] See Michel Rosenfeld, 'Constitutional Migration and the Bounds of Comparative Analysis' (2001) 58 *NYU Annual Survey of American Law* 67. Rosenfeld focuses on Justice Sachs's opinion rather on that of the Court's majority.

[129] See Mayo Moran, 'Inimical to Constitutional Values: Complex Migration of Constitutional Rights' in Choudhry, *Migration of Constitutional Ideas* (n 11), 254.

[130] Cf Ran Hirschl, *Towards Juristocracy* (2004), 222.

[131] See this argument in Jackson (n 11), 5–6.

[132] See T.R.S. Allan, *Constitutional Justice: A Liberal Theory of the Rule of Law* (2001), Preface.

ideas has already led to the emergence of a constitutional model and a convergence of constitutional analysis across different jurisdictions.[133] In contrast with this assessment, other scholars argue against the existence of convergence,[134] or even raise doubts whether convergence would be a good thing at all, since significant variations necessarily continue to distinguish different liberal constitutions.[135]

Another interesting, but also still open, question of the use of comparative constitutional law, is how far can international law be the source of migration of ideas. The real question behind this is whether current international law is really able to serve the aims of transnational constitutionalism. In some fields it definitely does not. As Kim Lane Scheppele proved in the case of the post-9/11 war on terror, international law can be a source of anti-constitutional ideas.[136] Therefore the even more challenging perspective of the extensive use of comparative constitutional law is when and how this conceptual lens of constitutionalism will migrate to international law.

Bibliography

Bruce Ackerman, 'The Rise of World Constitutionalism' (1997) 87 *Virginia Law Review* 771

Roger P. Alford, 'In Search of a Theory for Constitutional Comparativism' (2005) 52 *UCLA Law Review* 639

Sujit Choudhry, 'Globalization in Search of Justification: Toward a Theory of Comparative Constitutional Interpretation' (1999) 74 *Indiana Law Journal* 819

Sujit Choudhry, 'Migration As a New Metaphor in Comparative Constitutional Law' in Sujit Choudhry (ed), *Migration of Constitutional Ideas* (2006)

Moshe Cohen-Eliya and Gila Stopler, 'Probability Threshold as Deontological Constraints in Global Constitutionalism' (2010) 49 *Columbia Journal of Transnational Law* 75

D.M. Davis, 'Constitutional Borrowing: The Influence of Legal Culture and Local History in the Reconstruction of Comparative Influence: The South African Experience' (2003) 1 *International Journal of Constitutional Law* 181

Rosalind Dixon and Eric A. Posner, 'The Limits of Constitutional Convergence' (2011) 11(2) *Chicago Journal of International Law* 399

Brian Flanagan and Sinéad Ahern, 'Judicial Decision-Making and Transnational Law: A Survey of Common Law Supreme Court Judges' (2011) 60 *International and Comparative Law Quarterly* 1

David Fontana, 'The Rise and Fall of Comparative Constitutional Law in the Postwar Era' (2011) 36(1) *The Yale Journal of International Law* 1

Rex. D. Glensy, 'Constitutional Interpretation Through a Global Lens' (2010) 75(4) *Missouri Law Review* 1171

Jeffrey Goldsworthy, 'Questioning the Migration of Constitutional Ideas. Rights, Constitutionalism and the Limits of Convergence' in Sujit Choudhry (ed), *Migration of Constitutional Ideas* (2006)

Sarah K. Harding, 'Comparative Reasoning and Judicial Review' (2003) 28 *Yale Journal of International Law* 409

133 See Weinrib (n 36).

134 Cf Rosenfeld and Sajó (n 113).

135 See Jeffrey Goldsworthy, 'Questioning the Migration of Constitutional Ideas. Rights, Constitutionalism and the Limits of Convergence' in Choudhry, *Migration of Constitutional Ideas* (n 11).

136 See Kim Lane Scheppele, 'The Migration of Anti-Constitutional Ideas: The Post-9/11 Globalization of Public Law and the International State of Emergency' in Choudhry, *Migration of Constitutional Ideas* (n 11).

Vicki C. Jackson, 'Constitutional Comparisons: Convergence, Resistance, Engagement' (2005) 119 *Harvard Law Review* 109

Vicki C. Jackson, *Constitutional Engagement in a Transnational Era* (2010)

David S. Law, 'Globalization and the Future of Constitutional Rights' (2008) 102 *Northwestern University Law Review* 1277

Sir Basil Markesinis and Jörg Fedtke, *Judicial Recourse to Foreign Law* (2006)

Christopher McCrudden, 'A Common Law of Human Rights?: Transnational Judicial Conversations on Constitutional Rights' (2000) 20 *Oxford Journal of Legal Studies* 499

Michel Rosenfeld, 'Constitutional Migration and the Bounds of Comparative Analysis' (2001) 58 *NYU Annual Survey of American Law* 67

Michel Rosenfeld, 'Principle or Ideology? A Comparativist Perspective on the US Controversy Over Supreme Court Citations to Foreign Authorities' in Zsuzsa Gaspár and András Hanák (eds), *Sajó 2009* (2009)

Anne-Marie Slaughter, *A New World Order* (2004)

Mark Tushnet, 'The Inevitable Globalization of Constitutional Law' (2009) 49 *Virginia Journal of International Law* 985

Eric Voeten, 'Borrowing and Nonborrowing among International Courts' (2010) 39 *Journal of Legal Studies* 547

Jeremy Waldron, 'Foreign Law and the Modern *Ius Gentium*' (2005) 119 *Harvard Law Review* 129

Alan Watson, *Legal Transplants: An Approach to Comparative Law* (1974)

Lorraine Weinrib, 'The Postwar Paradigm and American Exceptionalism' in Sujit Choudhry (ed), *Migration of Constitutional Ideas* (2006)

Index

Printed and bound by CPI Group (UK) Ltd, Croydon, CR0 4YY